# Spain

Gregor Clark, Duncan Garwood, Anthony Ham, Damian Harper, Catherine Le Nevez, Isabella Noble, John Noble, Josephine Quintero, Regis St Louis, Andy Symington

## PLAN YOUR TRIP

PAWEL KAZMIERCZAK/SHUTTERSTOCK ©

BOLONIA P675

MARQUES/SHUTTERSTOCK ©

PICOS DE EUROPA P526

## ON THE ROAD

# Contents



**COVID-19**

We have re-checked every business in this book before publication to ensure that it is still open after the COVID-19 outbreak. However, the economic and social impacts of COVID-19 will continue to be felt long after the outbreak has been contained, and many businesses, services and events referenced in this guide may experience ongoing restrictions. Some businesses may be temporarily closed, have changed their opening hours and services, or require bookings; some unfortunately could have closed permanently. We suggest you check with venues before visiting for the latest information.

## ON THE ROAD



RONDA P744

SEANPAVONEPHOTO/GETTY IMAGES ©

# Contents

Right: Performer in the Tablao Los Gallos flamenco show (p637), Seville

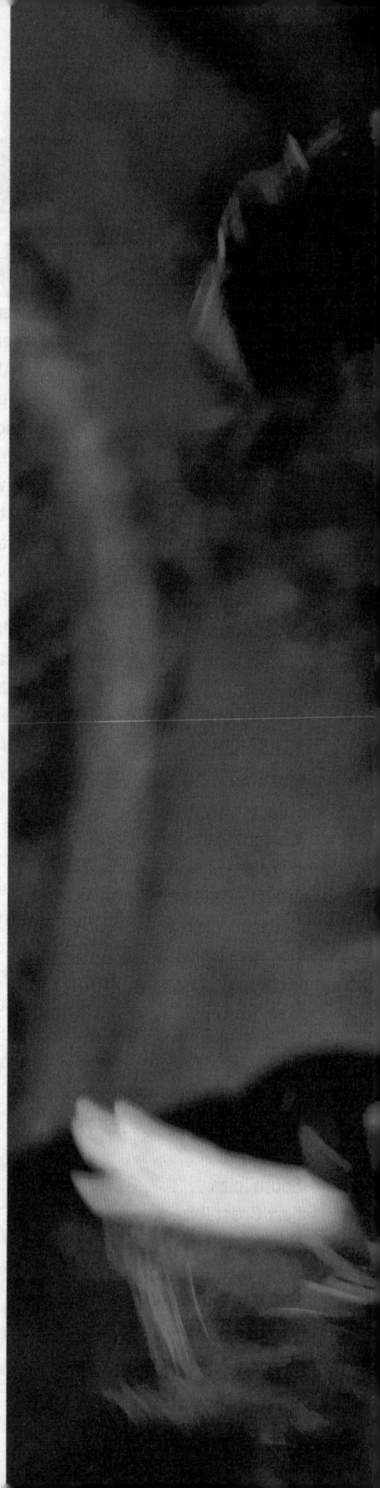

ANDREA PISTOLESI/GETTY IMAGES ©

WELCOME TO

# Spain

*My Spanish love affair began in Madrid, but I long ago fell in love with the rest of the country. The passions of Spain's people are the fabric of daily life here: this is a country with music in its soul, a love of fine food, wonderfully wild landscapes, and a unique talent for celebrating all that's good in life. Spain is home to me now, and it's something I feel just as keenly in the silence of a remote Castilian village as I do when immersed in the irresistible joy of a Madrid street.*

**By Anthony Ham, Writer**
@AnthonyHamWrite anthonyham2002
For more about our writers, see p927

# Spain

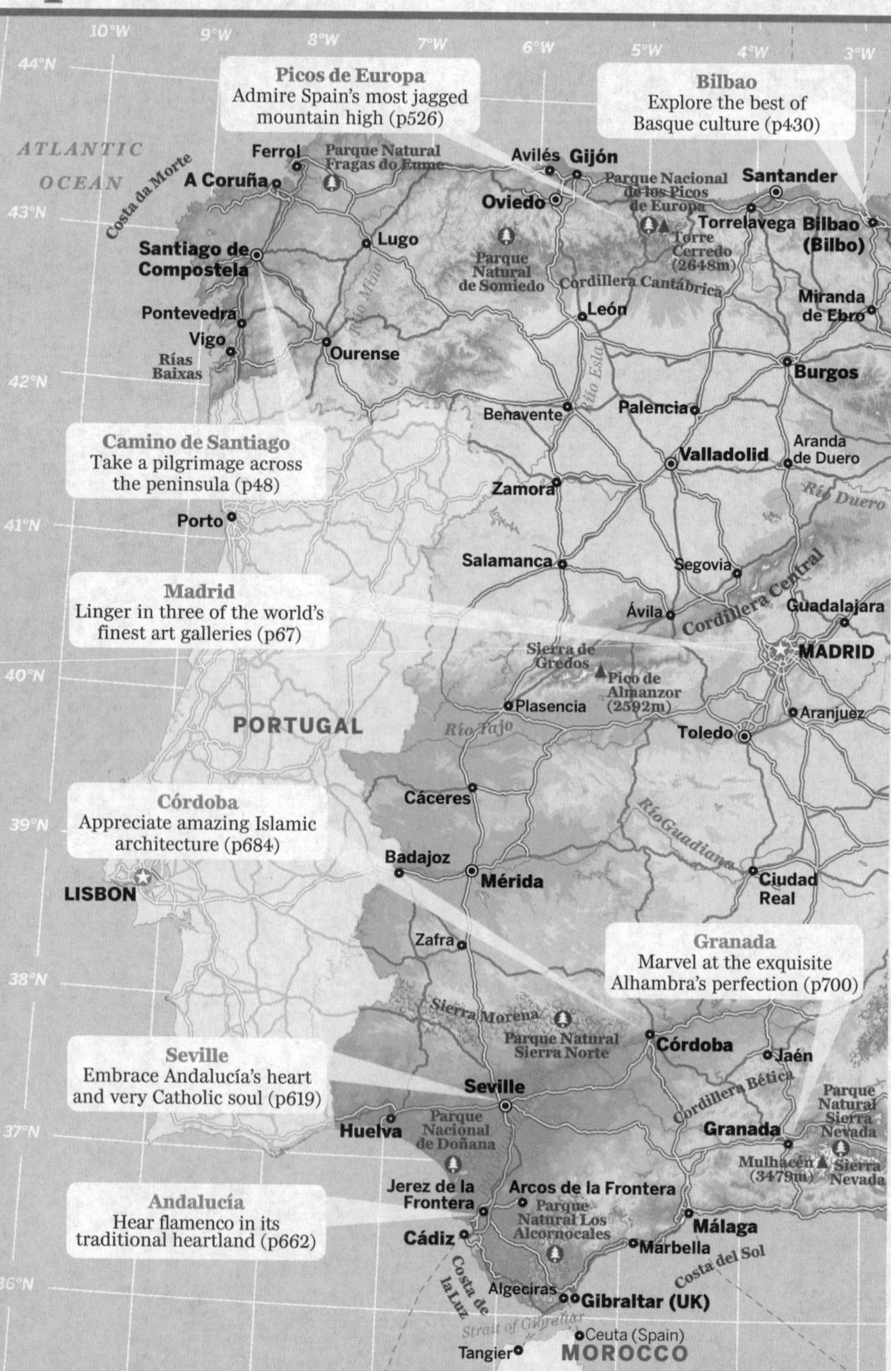
Picos de Europa
Admire Spain's most jagged mountain high (p526)
Bilbao
Explore the best of Basque culture (p430)
Camino de Santiago
Take a pilgrimage across the peninsula (p48)
Madrid
Linger in three of the world's finest art galleries (p67)
Córdoba
Appreciate amazing Islamic architecture (p684)
Granada
Marvel at the exquisite Alhambra's perfection (p700)
Seville
Embrace Andalucía's heart and very Catholic soul (p619)
Andalucía
Hear flamenco in its traditional heartland (p662)
ATLANTIC OCEAN
Costa da Morte
A Coruña
Ferrol
Parque Natural Fragas do Eume
Avilés
Gijón
Oviedo
Parque Nacional de los Picos de Europa
Torre Cerredo (2648m)
Santander
Torrelavega
Bilbao (Bilbo)
Santiago de Compostela
Lugo
Parque Natural de Somiedo
Cordillera Cantábrica
Miranda de Ebro
León
Pontevedra
Vigo
Rías Baixas
Ourense
Río Miño
Río Esla
Burgos
Benavente
Palencia
Valladolid
Aranda de Duero
Zamora
Río Duero
Porto
Salamanca
Segovia
Ávila
Cordillera Central
Guadalajara
MADRID
Sierra de Gredos
Pico de Almanzor (2592m)
Plasencia
Aranjuez
PORTUGAL
Río Tajo
Toledo
Cáceres
Río Guadiana
Badajoz
Mérida
Ciudad Real
LISBON
Zafra
Sierra Morena
Parque Natural Sierra Norte
Córdoba
Jaén
Seville
Cordillera Bética
Huelva
Parque Nacional de Doñana
Granada
Parque Natural Sierra Nevada
Mulhacén (3479m)
Sierra Nevada
Jerez de la Frontera
Arcos de la Frontera
Parque Natural Los Alcornocales
Cádiz
Málaga
Marbella
Costa del Sol
Costa de la Luz
Algeciras
Gibraltar (UK)
Strait of Gibraltar
Ceuta (Spain)
Tangier
MOROCCO
10°W
9°W
8°W
7°W
6°W
5°W
4°W
3°W
44°N
43°N
42°N
41°N
40°N
39°N
38°N
37°N
36°N

0 200 km
0 100 miles
FRANCE
San Sebastián
Discover Spain's best tapas experience (p448)
Bay of Biscay
Bayonne
Irún
San Sebastián (Donostia)
Toulouse
Montpellier
The Pyrenees
Hike the dramatic Pyrenean high country (p364)
Golfe du Lion
Pyrenees
Vitoria-Gasteiz
Pamplona (Iruña)
Logroño
Mt Perdido (3355m)
Pico de Aneto (3404m)
Perpignan
ANDORRA
Parque Nacional de Ordesa y Monte Perdido
Parc Nacional d'Aigüestortes i Estany de Sant Maurici
ANDORRA LA VELLA
Figueres
Girona
Costa Brava
Huesca
Soria
Zaragoza
Lleida
Blanes
Barcelona
Tarragona
Costa Daurada
Costa Brava
Enjoy beautiful beaches and Dalí's masterworks (p325)
Barcelona
Immerse yourself in Spain's style city (p237)
Costa del Azahar
Teruel
Menorca
Maó
Cuenca
Castellón de la Plana (Castelló de la Plana)
Palma de Mallorca
Valencia
Golfo de Valencia
Mallorca
Balearic Islands (Islas Baleares)
Ibiza
Albacete
Ibiza Town
Formentera
Menorca
Relax on stunning, remote Mediterranean beaches (p786)
Parque Natural Sierras de Cazorla, Segura y las Villas
Alicante (Alicant)
Costa Blanca
Elche (Elx)
Murcia
Torrevieja
MEDITERRANEAN SEA
Cartagena
Costa Cálida
1°E
2°E
3°E
4°E
2°W
ELEVATION
2000m
1500m
1250m
1000m
800m
600m
400m
200m
100m
0
ALGIERS
Parque Natural de Cabo de Gata-Níjar
Almería
0° (Greenwich)
ALGERIA
1°W
Oran

# Spain's Top Experiences

ALEX SEGRE/SHUTTERSTOCK ©

## 1 CITY HIGHS

The buzz of Spanish street life grows to a peak around midday, quietens down in the afternoon, and rises again as the sun sinks. There's nothing quite like a day spent seeing the sights and shops of a Spanish city, punctuated by cafe and restaurant visits (and maybe a short siesta), followed by drinks, dinner or tapas, and then some live music or a club deep into the night...

Above: Plaza de Santa Ana (p86), Madrid

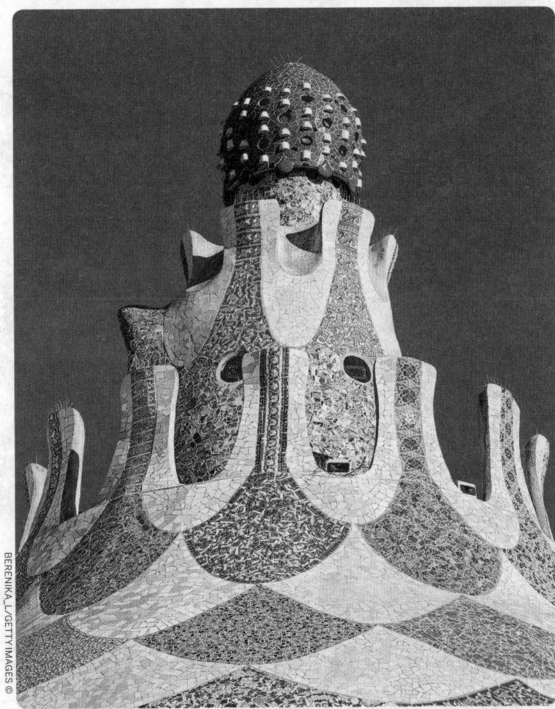
BERENIKA_L/GETTY IMAGES ©

## Madrid

In Spain's life-loving capital you can dine on food from every Spanish region (and beyond), explore great art museums, imbibe in the world's greatest concentration of bars, stroll in delightfully large parks – and carouse till dawn if you have enough energy left. p67

NITO/SHUTTERSTOCK ©

MARQUES/SHUTTERSTOCK ©

## Barcelona

Stylish Barcelona exudes its distinct Catalan identity with a huge set of cultural attractions – starting with the fabled architecture of Antoni Gaudí – and a superlative dining scene. What's more, it's a seaside city, with sandy beaches strung along the sparkling Mediterranean. p237

Above: Platja de la Barceloneta (p257), Barcelona

Top: Park Güell (p267), Barcelona

## Granada

If you *had* to choose just one of Spain's many fascinating cities after the big two, there's nowhere quite like Granada, a magical city on a refreshingly manageable scale. After the exquisite Alhambra Moorish palace, wander the medieval lanes of the Albayzín and sip teas in Arabic-style teahouses. p700

Above: Palacio de Carlos V (p706), Alhambra, Granada

GOSKOVA TATIANA/SHUTTERSTOCK ©

# 2 A CULINARY FEAST

Spain is a gastronomic destination of the first order, with immense regional food variety. The traditional essence of Spanish cooking is to take the best ingredients and interfere with them as little as possible. And the best ingredients are often local, whether ham from the western hills, seafood from Galicia's rocky coast, tangy cheeses and grilled meats from green northern valleys or olive oil from the plains of Andalucía.

JACKMALIPAN/GETTY IMAGES ©

STARCEVIC/GETTY IMAGES ©

## Market Meals

Some of Spain's most enthralling food scenes are city markets with their own eateries serving truly 'market-fresh' dishes. Don't miss Madrid's Mercado de San Miguel (p116; above right) or Santiago de Compostela's Mercado de Abastos (p547).

## Lunch by the Beach

The long lunch is a sacred Spanish delight, and there are few better venues for it than the shade of a beach-side restaurant in summer. Barcelona's bustling Xiringuito Escribà (p297) and Tarifa's Tangana are perfect examples (p678).

## Tapas Treats

After a big lunch, a few tapas may be all you need to satisfy evening hunger. Every city has zones where tapas bars congregate. In cities such as Granada, Almería, Ávila, León and Segovia, you'll generally get a free tapa with each drink.

# 3 SAND, SURF & PRECIPICES

From sun-kissed Mediterranean sands to the wild northwestern cliffs, Spain's 5000km coastline, while overdeveloped in parts, packs enough beauty for years of exploring. For traditional sunbathing and sea-bathing, head to the warm Mediterranean beaches and Andalucía's Costa de la Luz. Northern coasts too harbour many beautiful strands (and Spain's best surf) – but with chillier Atlantic waters – strung between soaring cliffs, jagged rocks and colourful ports and fishing villages.

## Cabo de Gata

This southeastern peninsula is like a chunk of North Africa transplanted to Europe – a desert-like, volcanic landscape fringed by cliffs and capes of surreal grandeur interspersed with unspoiled beaches and lazy little villages. p767

Below: Playa de Mónsul (p770)

PAWEL KAZMIERCZAK/SHUTTERSTOCK ©

## Costa Brava

Much of Catalonia's 'Rugged Coast' still retains its old magic of white villages, pine-topped cliffs and sandy coves. The 30km between Palamós and Sa Tuna are a particular delight. p325

Above: Calella de Palafrugell (p326)

## Costa da Morte

Named for its many shipwrecks, Galicia's remote 'Coast of Death' is a hauntingly beautiful 200km string of rocky capes, roaring seas, ocean beaches, lighthouses and stone villages. p553

Right: Cabo Vilán lighthouse (p556)

# 4 PARTY, PARTY, PARTY

There's a reason why the Spanish word 'fiesta' is understood worldwide. Spaniards love to party – on the streets, in bars, restaurants and clubs, in their homes – and especially at the innumerable annual celebrations held in every town, city and village. Choose any day in the year and there'll be fiestas happening in several places in Spain.

## Las Fallas

In mid-March Valencia lets rip with days of round-the-clock partying, fireworks, music and processions. Festivities culminate in the ritual burning of over 300 enormous, colourful, satirical effigies (the *fallas*) in the streets. p813

## Semana Santa

Easter week sees parades of hooded Catholic penitents bearing large holy statues for hours on end through many cities, towns and villages. Most spectacularly celebrated in Seville, it's an important expression of community spirit. p632

## Romería del Rocío

Focused on Pentecost weekend (the seventh after Easter), up to a million people sing, drink, dance and romance their way from across southern Spain in festive pilgrimage to remote El Rocío village among the Doñana wetlands. p647

Above: Romería del Rocío festivities

# 5 INTO THE WILD

From the snowy Pyrenees to Almería's arid desertscapes, the variety and beauty of Spain's landscape are endless. The hiking is superb and opportunities abound to get close to nature by descending canyons, climbing cliffs, cycling or riding horses. On many mountain walks you'll sight large mammals such as ibex, chamois or deer. You can spot wild bears in Asturias and lynx in Andalucía. Huge raptors scour the skies nationwide.

MARQUESPHOTOGRAPHY/GETTY IMAGES ©

ESCOCIA/SHUTTERSTOCK ©

PEDROSALA/SHUTTERSTOCK ©

## Picos de Europa

Few European ranges concentrate as much mountain drama in a compact area as Spain's Picos de Europa. It's a walker's wonderland, from the Cares gorge to the Naranjo de Bulnes. p526

Top left: Lagos de Covadonga (p529)

## Monfragüe

Extremadura's Monfragüe National Park is Spain's single best location for observing large raptor colonies, including some 300 pairs of black vultures, Europe's biggest bird of prey. p603

Above: Black vulture

## Canyoning

Fancy a few hours jumping, sliding and abseiling your way down a sheer-walled canyon? The picturesque Aragón village of Alquézar is a top European centre for the sport of canyoning. p419

# 6 AN ARTISTIC TREASURE CHEST

FABIOSEDA/GETTY IMAGES ©

MANUEL ASCANIO/SHUTTERSTOCK ©

Spaniards are an artistic people, and in the country that gave birth to Goya, Picasso and Velázquez, every city worth its salt boasts at least one classy art museum. Madrid's trio of the Prado, Reina Sofía and Thyssen-Bornemisza is world-famous for both international and Spanish art. Barcelona houses major museums devoted to Picasso, Miró and Tápies; Goya is feted in Zaragoza; down south, Málaga is an emerging hub with several exciting collections.

## Picasso

Arguably the major artistic personage of the 20th century, Pablo Picasso has large museums devoted to him in Málaga and Barcelona. His masterpiece *Guernica* hangs in Madrid's Centro de Arte Reina Sofía. p90

## Surrealist Supreme

Immerse yourself in the weird world of Salvador Dalí in his native Catalonia at Figueres' Teatre-Museu Dalí (his final resting place; pictured top) and the equally wacky Casa Museu Dalí, his seaside home near Cadaqués. p342

## The Guggenheim

The shimmering titanium shapes of the riverside Museo Guggenheim Bilbao, by architect Frank Gehry, are an extraordinary work of contemporary art themselves and did much to spark Bilbao's 21st-century revival. p430

Top: Teatre-Museu Dalí (p347), Figueres

Bottom: Museo Guggenheim Bilbao (p430)

# 7 WHERE TIME SLOWS DOWN

Away from the buzz of the cities and towns, you enter a different Spain where the pace of life slows to an amble. The countryside has suffered a population drain since the mid-20th century but many delightful old villages still thrive. These places of twisting streets, crooked stone houses, a plaza with a couple of bars, a church and a half-ruined castle may be among the fondest memories you'll take home.

## Santillana del Mar

This centuries-old Cantabrian jewel is so perfectly preserved it could almost be a film set. And the great prehistoric cave art of Altamira is just a few minutes away. p499

Below: Stone window facade in Santillana del Mar

JOSE MIGUEL SANCHEZ/SHUTTERSTOCK ©

## Albarracín

The fortified capital of a medieval mini-state, picturesquely pink-hued Albarracín (pictured above), in a remote Aragonese canyon, was almost abandoned by the mid-20th century. It has since been resurrected as a living monument of great authenticity and charm. p425

## Capileira

The hillside villages of the Alpujarras valleys near Granada still bear the imprint of their original medieval Moorish settlers. Pretty Capileira (pictured right), high in the dramatic Poqueira gorge, makes a great base for Sierra Nevada mountain hikes. p725

# 8 THE BOUNTIFUL VINE

Spain has over 12,000 sq km of vineyards, more than any other country. Wines here have improved in recent decades as vintners invest in up-to-date technology and experiment with different grape varieties (today increasingly organic). A big pleasure of travelling round Spain is sampling the widely varied regional wines – usually the perfect accompaniment to local food.

## Rioja

Spain's premier wine region, Rioja boasts two good wine museums and some extravagant architect-designed wine establishments as well as humbler wineries for tours and tastings. The medieval fortress town Laguardia is an appealing base. p487

## Catalonia

Home of sparkling, Champagne-like *cava*, Catalonia's Penedès wine region also produces fine light whites and tasty reds. Famous names like Freixenet, Codorníu and Torres all offer winery tours. p377

Above: Penedès vineyards

## Galicia

Best known for fruity albariño whites from the Rías Baixas around Cambados, Galicia has other rising wine zones too – notably Ribeira Sacra, yielding rich mencía reds from some staggeringly steep hillside vineyards. Many wineries welcome visitors. p567

# Need to Know

For more information, see Survival Guide (p879)

### Currency
Euro (€)

### Language
Spanish (Castilian). Also Catalan, Basque and Galician.

### Visas
Generally not required for stays of up to 90 days per 180 days; not required at all for members of EU or Schengen countries. Some nationalities need a Schengen visa.

### Money
ATMs widely available. Credit cards accepted in most hotels and restaurants.

### Mobile Phones
Local SIM cards are widely available and can be used in European and Australian mobile phones. Not compatible with many North American or Japanese systems.

### Time
Central European Time (GMT/UTC plus one hour).

## When to Go

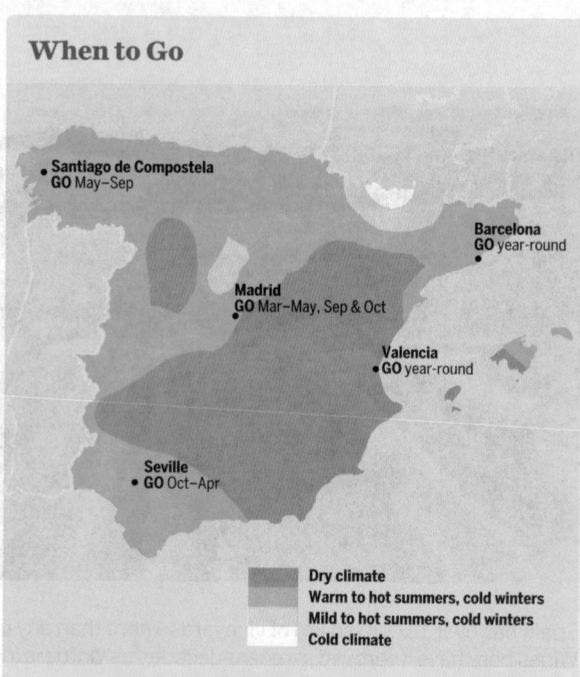


### High Season
(Jun–Aug, public holidays)

- Accommodation books out and prices increase by up to 50%.
- Low season in parts of inland Spain.
- Expect warm, dry and sunny weather; more humid in coastal areas.

### Shoulder
(Mar–May, Sep & Oct)

- A good time to travel: mild, clear weather and fewer crowds.
- Local festivals can send prices soaring.
- Fewer hikers on trails but weather unpredictable.

### Low Season
(Nov–Feb)

- Cold in central Spain; rain in the north and northwest.
- Mild temperatures in Andalucía and the Mediterranean coast.
- This is high season in ski resorts.
- Many hotels are closed in beach areas, but elsewhere along the coast prices plummet.

## Useful Websites

**Lonely Planet** (www.lonelyplanet.com/spain) Destination information, hotel bookings, traveller forums and more.

**Fiestas.net** (www.fiestas.net) Festivals around the country.

**Turespaña** (www.spain.info) Spanish tourist office's site.

**Paradores** (www.parador.es) Spain's finest hotel experiences with plenty to get you dreaming.

**Renfe** (Red Nacional de los Ferrocarriles Españoles; www.renfe.com) Spain's rail network.

**All You Can Read** (www.allyoucanread.com/spanish-newspapers) Links to Spain's top 30 news sites, mostly in Spanish.

## Important Numbers

There are no area codes in Spain.

| | |
|---|---|
| **Spain's country code** | ☎34 |
| **International access code** | ☎00 |
| **International directory enquiries** | ☎11825 |
| **National directory enquiries** | ☎11818 |
| **Emergencies** | ☎112 |

## Exchange Rates

| | | |
|---|---|---|
| **Australia** | A$1 | €0.65 |
| **Canada** | C$1 | €0.67 |
| **Japan** | ¥100 | €0.77 |
| **New Zealand** | NZ$1 | €0.60 |
| **UK** | UK£1 | €1.16 |
| **US** | US$1 | €0.83 |

For current exchange rates, see www.xe.com.

## Daily Costs

### Budget: Less than €80

- Dorm bed: €20–30
- Double room in *hostal* (budget hotel): €50–65 (€60–75 in Madrid, Barcelona and Balearics)
- Self-catering and lunch *menú del día* (set menu): €20–30

### Midrange: €80–175

- Double room in midrange hotel: €65–140 (€75–200 in Madrid, Barcelona and Balearics)
- Lunch and/or dinner in local restaurant: €20–40
- Car rental: per day from €25

### Top end: More than €175

- Double room in top-end hotel: €140 and up (over €200 in Madrid, Barcelona and Balearics)
- Fine dining for lunch and dinner: €150–250
- Admission to Madrid's Museo del Prado: €15

## Opening Hours

**Banks** 8.30am–2pm Monday to Friday; some also open 4–7pm Thursday and 9am–1pm Saturday

**Central post offices** 8.30am–9.30pm Monday to Friday, 8.30am–2pm Saturday; most other branches 8.30am–2.30pm Monday to Friday, 9.30am–1pm Saturday

**Nightclubs** Midnight or 1am to 5am or 6am Friday and Saturday

**Restaurants** Lunch 1–4pm; dinner 8.30pm to 11pm or midnight

**Shops** 10am–2pm and 4.30–7.30pm or 5–8pm Monday to Friday or Saturday; big supermarkets and department stores generally open 10am–10pm Monday to Saturday

## Arriving in Spain

**Adolfo Suárez Madrid-Barajas Airport** (Madrid) The metro (€4.50, 30 minutes to the centre) runs from 6.05am to 1.30am; the Exprés Aeropuerto bus (€5; 30 to 40 minutes) runs 24 hours between the airport and Puerta de Atocha train station/Plaza de Cibeles. Taxis cost €30.

**El Prat Airport** (Barcelona) Buses cost €5.90 and run every five to 10 minutes from 5.35am to 1.05am; it's 30 to 40 minutes to the centre. Trains (€4.60, 25 to 30 minutes to the centre) run half-hourly from 5.42am to 11.38pm. Taxis cost €25 to €35.

## Getting Around

Spain's public transport system is one of the best in Europe, with a fast and supermodern train system, extensive domestic air network, an impressive and well-maintained road network, and buses that connect villages in the country's remotest corners.

**Train** Extremely efficient rail network, from slow intercity regional trains to some of the fastest trains on the planet. More routes are added to the network every year.

**Car** Vast network of motorways radiating out from Madrid to all corners of the country, shadowed by smaller but often more picturesque minor roads.

**Bus** The workhorses of the Spanish roads, from slick express services to stop-everywhere village-to-village buses.

For much more on **getting around**, see p895

# What's New

While Spain struggles with its image of itself – one nation or many? politically stable or deeply divided? – the country just keeps on showing its sunniest face to travellers. Even in the COVID-ravaged summer of 2020 the high-end, state-run Paradores chain launched a brand-new, architecturally innovative hotel at Muxía in Galicia, and enjoyed a highly successful opening season. Innovation lies at the heart of everything here, as does fidelity to tradition. Holding these two together is a rare Spanish gift.

## Best in Travel

Cádiz province was awarded seventh place in Lonely Planet's list of top 10 regions in 2020. With a string of gastronomic triumphs, the province in the west of Andalucía is wandering into the spotlight. Michelin stars are appearing in the region's restaurants, including in Jerez de la Frontera (aka Queen of the Sherry Triangle), El Puerto de Santa María and Novo Sancti Petri. Vejer de la Frontera has recast itself as a foodie and boutique-hotel hub, and up-to-the-minute cafes, restaurants and accommodation have breathed fresh energy into Phoenician-origin Cádiz.
Even sherry is fashionable again! Throw in flights to Jerez and this region is ripe for discovery.

## Cooking Classes

Food has always been, and remains, an experiential highlight of travelling in Spain. Cooking classes across the country are increasingly adding a whole new dimension to that experience. From Galicia (near Cambados) to Las Alpujarras in Andalucía, it's now possible to learn all about Spanish cooking and the culture that lies behind it. Madrid has the greatest number of choices, but Barcelona also has options. It's a fun, immersive way to understand what all the fuss is about, and a wonderful way to take a little bit of that home with you.

## Village Life

If you believe the news, Spanish rural life is in crisis. While it may be true in some

LOCAL KNOWLEDGE

### WHAT'S HAPPENING IN SPAIN

*Anthony Ham, Lonely Planet writer*

For years, all that anyone in Spain seemed to talk about was the economic crisis. Then it was Catalonia. Then the rise of Vox and the far right. And then COVID-19. Take it to heart and it can seem as if the country is living through a never-ending series of crises.

But in all likelihood, this is all being discussed over craft beers or innovative tapas while everyone seems to be having a terribly good time. Spain's speciality is to do everything with great passion, talk about it at full volume, and embrace and come to terms with whatever's new, so that all that's good about living and travelling in Spain remains as little touched as possible by the problems.

What does change is the details – the sudden transformation of a previously quiet street into the Next Big Thing, or a quiet revolution in how the world can experience mainstays such as Spanish village life, the Camino de Santiago and the extraordinary richness of Spanish cuisine. Just like the kind of artful conversion of a medieval palace into a warm and contemporary architectural showpiece at which Spain so clearly excels, the country just keeps on changing without selling its soul.

areas where villages are struggling to stay afloat, many more are riding a wave of popularity among Spanish and international tourists. Nowhere is this more the case than in the Spanish heartland of Castilla y León, where travellers are 'discovering' the quiet back roads and the *pueblos* (villages) that bring such charm to travelling in Spain. In places such as the Sierra de Francia, Burgos province and elsewhere, local tourist authorities are joining the dots and creating itineraries designed to tap into the growing passion for the Spain that lies a world away from the lure of sun, sand and sangría.

## Calle de Ponzano

It's unusual that one street becomes so popular so quickly that its name becomes a verb. Very often when *madrileños* go out in the evening now, they *ponzanear* (to go out on Calle de Ponzano). Madrid's most dynamic night-time street, Calle de Ponzano is massively popular for its bars serving the capital's best tapas and long lists of Spanish wines, as well as craft beer and cocktails. The street is also a touchstone for a wider phenomenon – the *barrio* (district) of Chamberí, where Calle de Ponzano is found, has ignited the local passion for *castizo* (authentic) experiences and is *the* neighbourhood to watch over the coming years.

## The Camino

The Camino de Santiago has been a *cause célèbre* for as long as we can imagine. But the whole idea of the Camino is evolving, maturing if you like. The proportion of walkers and pilgrims who choose the main Camino Francés, once synonymous with the Camino in the popular mind, has fallen from 85% to under 55% in the past decade or so, as walkers repopulate more and more of the other routes to Santiago de Compostela. Travellers are also returning to Spain to do the Camino for a second or third time, and looking for a slightly different experience each time. With all of this comes better infrastructure along the trails, as well as a broadening of the whole concept of the Camino de Santiago.

## Political Games

It would be difficult to find a more intriguing political backdrop to travelling in Spain than the current situation. Political deadlock at a national level; the push in some quarters for Catalonia's independence and the resulting constitutional crisis; the rise of the Vox party and the far right; and the national effort to lift the economy out of the COVID doldrums... Spain is a country at a crossroads, and while politics are unlikely to seriously affect most travellers' experiences, the news sure does provide one fascinating soundtrack to your visit.

### LISTEN, WATCH & FOLLOW

For inspiration and up-to-date news, visit www.lonelyplanet.com/spain/articles.

**Spanish Sabores** (http://spanishsabores.com) Spanish food with a focus on Madrid, Barcelona and Seville.

**El País** (www.elpais.com) Major print and digital newspaper with English-language section.

**Trepidatious Traveller** (http://magwood.me) Excellent blog on the Camino de Santiago.

**News in Slow Spanish** (www.newsinslowspanish.com) Spanish news told at a not-so-Spanish pace.

### FAST FACTS

**Food trend** Take-away

**Olive oil** Produces 44% of the world's olive oil

**Foreign tourists** 83.5 million/year (2019)

**Pop** 47.4 million

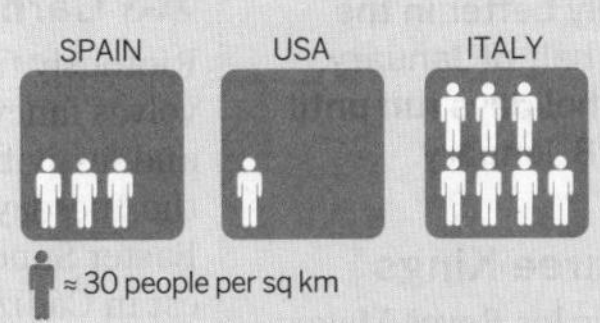

# Month by Month

**TOP EVENTS**

**Semana Santa (Holy Week)**, usually March or April

**Las Fallas de San José**, March

**Bienal de Flamenco**, September

**Carnaval**, February or March

**Feria de Abril**, April

## January

**In January, ski resorts in the Pyrenees and the Sierra Nevada are in full swing. Snow in Catalonia is usually better in the second half of January. School holidays run until around 8 January.**

### Three Kings

El Día de los Reyes Magos, or simply Reyes, on 6 January, is the highlight of a Spanish kid's calendar. The evening before, three local politicians dress up as the three wise men and lead a sweet-distributing frenzy (Cabalgata de Reyes) through most towns.

## February

**Often the coldest month, with temperatures close to freezing, especially in the north and inland regions. If you're heading to Carnaval, accommodation is at a premium wherever the celebration occurs.**

### Barcelona's Winter Bash

Around 12 February, the Festes de Santa Eulàlia celebrates Barcelona's first patron saint with a week of cultural events, from parades of giants to *castells* (human castles). (p283)

### Carnaval

Riotously fun, Carnaval involves fancy-dress parades and festivities, ending on the Tuesday 47 days before Easter Sunday. It's wildest in Cádiz (p655), Sitges, (p375) Badajoz (p611) and Ciudad Rodrigo (p158). Other curious celebrations are held at Vilanova i la Geltrú and Solsona.

### Fiesta Medieval

In one of Spain's coldest corners, Teruel's inhabitants don their medieval finery and step back to the Middle Ages with markets, food stalls and a re-enactment of a local lovers' legend during Las Bodas de Isabel de Segura. (p424)

## March

**With the arrival of spring, Spain shakes off its winter blues (such as they are), the weather starts to warm up ever so slightly and Spaniards start dreaming of a summer by the beach.**

### Flamenco in Jerez

One of Spain's most important flamenco festivals takes place in the genre's heartland in late February or early March. (p662)

### Las Fallas de San José

The extraordinary festival of Las Fallas consists of several days of all-night dancing and drinking, first-class fireworks and processions from 15 to 19 March. Its principal stage is Valencia City, and the festivities culminate in the ritual burning of effigies in the streets. (p813)

## April

**Spain has a real spring in its step, with wildflowers in full bloom, Easter celebrations and school holidays. It requires some advance planning (book ahead), but it's a great time to be here.**

### Semana Santa (Holy Week)

Easter (the dates change each year) entails parades of *pasos* (holy figures), hooded penitents and huge crowds. It's extravagantly celebrated in Seville (p632), as well as Málaga (p734), Ávila (p151), Cuenca (p227), Lorca (p847) and Zamora (p174).

### Dance of Death

The Dansa de la Mort on Holy Thursday in the Catalan village of Verges is a chilling experience. This nocturnal dance of skeleton figures is the centrepiece of Holy Week celebrations.

### Los Empalaos

On Holy Thursday, Valverde de la Vera, in northeast Extremadura, plays out an extraordinary act of Easter self-abnegation. The devotion and self-inflicted suffering of the barefoot penitents leaves most onlookers in awe. (p601)

### Catalan Food

The central Catalan town of Vic (p369) puts food at the centre of Easter celebrations with the Mercat de Ram, a food and agriculture fair that's quite the spectacle.

### Feria de Abril

This week-long party, held in Seville in the second half of April, is the biggest of Andalucía's fairs. *Sevillanos* dress up in their traditional finery, ride around on horseback and in elaborate horse-drawn carriages, and dance late into the night. (p632)

### Moros y Cristianos (Moors & Christians)

Colourful parades and mock battles between Christian and Muslim 'armies' in Alcoy, near Alicante, make Moros y Cristianos one of the most spectacular of many such festivities staged in Valencia and Alicante provinces in late April. Other versions are held elsewhere at other times. (p838)

### Romería de la Virgen

On the last Sunday in April, hundreds of thousands of people make a mass pilgrimage to the Santuario de la Virgen de la Cabeza near Andújar, in Jaén province. A small statue of the Virgin is paraded about, exciting great passion. (p758)

## May

**A glorious time to be in Spain, May sees the countryside carpeted with spring wildflowers and it feels like summer is just around the corner.**

### Feria del Caballo (Horse Fair)

A colourful equestrian fair in Andalucía's horse capital, Jerez de la Frontera, the Feria del Caballo is one of Andalucía's most festive and extravagant fiestas. It features parades, horse shows, bullfights and plenty of music and dance. (659)

### Córdoba's Courtyards Open Up

Scores of beautiful private courtyards in Córdoba are opened to the public for the Fiesta de los Patios de Córdoba. It's a rare chance to see an otherwise-hidden side of Córdoba, strewn with flowers and freshly painted. (p690)

### Fiesta de San Isidro

Madrid's major fiesta celebrates the city's patron saint with parades, concerts and more. Locals dress up in traditional costumes, and some of the events, such as the bullfighting season, last for a month. (p111)

### Muslim Pirates

Sóller, in northern Mallorca, is invaded by Muslim pirates in early May. The resulting 'battle' between townsfolk and invaders, known as Es Firó, recreates an infamous (and unsuccessful) 16th-century assault on the town.

### World Music in Cáceres

Cáceres hosts the annual Womad, a fabulous festival dedicated to world music and drawing top-notch musicians from across the globe to perform in the city's medieval squares. (p591)

## June

**By June, the north is shaking off its winter chill and the Camino de Santiago's trails are becoming crowded. In the south, it's warming**

**up as the coastal resorts ready themselves for the summer onslaught.**

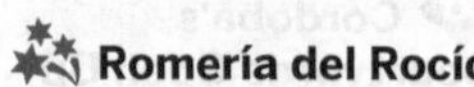

### Romería del Rocío

Focused on Pentecost weekend (the seventh after Easter), this festive pilgrimage is made by up to one million people to the shrine of the Virgin in El Rocío. This is Andalucía's Catholic tradition at its most curious and compelling. (p647)

### Primavera Sound

One of Spain's biggest music festivals, Primavera Sound lures a host of international DJs and musicians to Barcelona for three days in late May or early June. (p283)

### Corpus Christi

On the Thursday in the ninth week after Easter (sometimes May, sometimes June), religious processions and celebrations take place in Toledo and other cities. The strangest is the baby-jumping tradition of Castrillo de Murcia. (p193)

### Electronica Festival

Performers and spectators come from all over the world for Sónar, Barcelona's two-day celebration of electronic music, which is said to be Europe's biggest festival of its kind. Dates vary each year. (p283)

### Noche Blanca del Flamenco

An all-night fest of top-notch flamenco by leading song, guitar and dance artists of the genre, in picturesque venues around Córdoba. All performances are free. It all happens on a Saturday night around 20 June. (p690)

### Bonfires & Fireworks

Midsummer bonfires, fireworks and roaming giants feature on Nit de Sant Joan (23 June; p357), the eve of Fiesta de San Juan, notably along the Mediterranean coast – especially Barcelona and Ciutadella, Menorca, where you can see splendid equestrian skills in parades.

### Wine Battle

Haro, one of the premier wine towns of La Rioja, enjoys the Batalla del Vino on 29 June. Participants squirt wine all over the place in one of Spain's messiest play fights, pausing only to drink the good stuff. (p485)

### Flamenco in Madrid

The soul-filled Suma Flamenca festival draws some of the biggest names in the genre to Teatros del Canal and some of the better-known *tablaos* (flamenco venues) around town. (p111)

## July

**Temperatures in Andalucía and much of the interior can be fiercely hot, but July is a great time to be at the beach and is one of the best months for hiking in the Pyrenees.**

### Mad Cool

Madrid's largest music festival draws 60,000 people to the IFEMA convention centre out near the airport. Headline acts for the four-day extravaganza in 2020 included Billy Eilish, Kings of Leon, Faith No More and the Pixies. Genres range widely from rock and indie to pop and electronica. (p111)

### Córdoba Guitar Festival

Córdoba's contribution to Spain's impressive calendar of musical events, this fine international guitar festival ranges from flamenco and classical to rock, blues and beyond. Headline performances take place in the city's theatres. (p690)

### Running of the Bulls

The **Fiesta de San Fermín** is the week-long nonstop festival and party in Pamplona with the daily *encierro* (running of the bulls) as its centrepiece. PETA (www.peta.org.uk) organises eye-catching protests a couple of days before.

### Celtic Pride

Groups from as far off as Nova Scotia come to celebrate their Celtic roots with the *gallegos* (Galicians) at Festival Ortigueira, a bagpipe- and fiddler-filled music fest held in Galicia. (p549)

### Día de la Virgen del Carmen

Around 16 July in most coastal towns, particularly in El Puerto de Santa María and Nerja, the image of the patron of fisherfolk is carried into the sea or paraded on a flotilla of small boats.

### Benicàssim Music Fest

Spain is awash with outdoor concert festivals attracting big-name acts from around the country and abroad, especially in summer. This one, in the Valencian town of Benicàssim, remains one of the original and best. (p822)

### Fiestas del Apóstol Santiago

The Día de Santiago on 25 July marks the day of Spain's national saint (St James) and is spectacularly celebrated in Santiago de Compostela. With so many pilgrims around, it's the city's most festive two weeks of the year. (p546)

## August

**Spaniards from all over the country join Europeans in converging on the coastal resorts of the Mediterranean. Although the weather can be unpredictable, Spain's northwestern Atlantic coast offers a more nuanced summer experience.**

### Classical Drama in Mérida

The peerless Roman theatre and amphitheatre in Mérida, Extremadura, become the stage for the classics of ancient Greece and Rome, and the occasional newbie such as Will Shakespeare. Performances are held most nights during July and August. (p607)

### Galician Wines

The fabulous wines of Galicia are the reason for the Festa do Albariño in Cambados on the first weekend of August. Expect five days of music, fireworks and intensive consumption of Galicia's favourite fruity white wine. (p568)

### Galician Octopus

Galicia's passion for octopus boils over at the Festa do Pulpo de O Carballiño on the second Sunday in August. Tens of thousands of people converge on the small town of O Carballiño to eat as much of the stuff as they can. (p580)

### Barcelona Street Festival

Locals compete for the most elaborately decorated street in the popular week-long Festa Major de Gràcia, held around 15 August. People pour in to listen to bands in the streets and squares, fuel up on snacks, and drink at countless street stands. (p283)

### Cipotegato

In the otherwise quiet Aragonese town of Tarazona, every 27 August during Cipotegato the townsfolk re-create a local tradition whereby a prisoner could win their freedom by trying to outrun a stone- (or a tomato-) throwing mob. (p398)

### Natural Cider Festival

Gijón's Fiesta de la Sidra Natural gives expression to the Asturian obsession with cider and includes an annual world-record attempt for the number of people simultaneously pouring cider in one place. It also involves musical concerts. (p514)

### La Tomatina

Buñol's massive tomato-throwing festival (p820), held in late August, must be one of the messiest get-togethers in the country. Thousands of people launch about 100 tonnes of tomatoes at one another.

## September

**This is the month when Spain returns to work after a seemingly endless summer. Numerous festivals take advantage of the fact that weather generally remains warm until late September at least.**

### Fiesta de la Virgen de Guadalupe

Pretty Guadalupe in Extremadura celebrates its very own Virgin Mary during the Fiesta de la Virgen de Guadalupe. A statue is paraded about on the evening of 6 September and again on 8 September, which also happens to be Extremadura's regional feast day. (p598)

### Bienal de Flamenco

There are flamenco festivals all over Spain throughout the year, but this is the most prestigious of them all. Held in Seville in even-numbered years (and Málaga every other year), it draws the biggest names in the genre. (p632)

### Romans & Carthaginians

In the second half of the month, locals dress up to re-enact ancient battles during the festival of Carthagineses y Romanos in Cartagena. It's among the more original mock battles staged around Spain to honour the distant past. (p844)

### Human Castles in Tarragona

Tarragona's Festival de Santa Tecla is a wonderful chance to see Catalonia's *castells* (human castles) in all their glory. Teams of *castellers* stand on each other's shoulders to build towers up to nine levels high. (p382)

### San Sebastián Film Festival

It may not be Cannes, but San Sebastián's annual two-week celebration of film is one of the most prestigious dates on Europe's film-festival circuit. It's held in the second half of the month and has been gathering plaudits since 1957. (p452)

### La Rioja's Grape Harvest

Logroño celebrates the feast day of St Matthew (Fiesta de San Mateo) and the year's grape harvest. There are grape-crushing ceremonies and endless opportunities to sample the fruit of the vine in liquid form. (p482)

### Barcelona's Big Party

Barcelona's co-patron saint, the Virgin of Mercy, is celebrated with fervour in the massive four-day Festes de la Mercè around 24 September. The city stages special exhibitions, free concerts and street performers galore. (p283)

## October

**Autumn can be a lovely time to be in Spain, with generally mild temperatures throughout the country, although the winter chill can start to bite in central and northern areas.**

### Sitges International Film Festival

Early October brings the world's top festival of fantasy and horror films to the Catalan coast (www.sitgesfilmfestival.com). Latest release sci-fi and scary cinema is shown in venues across town.

### Fiesta de Santa Teresa

The patron saint of Ávila is honoured with 10 days of processions, concerts and fireworks around her feast day. Huddled behind medieval walls, the festival brings to life the powerful cult of personality surrounding Ávila's most famous daughter. (p151)

### Fiestas del Pilar

In Zaragoza on 12 October, the faithful mix with hedonists to celebrate this festival dedicated to Our Lady of the Pillar. Festivities peak with the Ofrenda de Flores (Offering of Flowers) around the Virgin's image, brought out on to Plaza del Pilar from the basilica. (p394)

## November

**A quiet time on the festival calendar, November is cool throughout the country. Depending on the year, the ski season usually begins in the Pyrenees and Sierra Nevada.**

### Jazz Madrid

Madrid's annual jazz festival draws a prestigious cast of performers from across the globe and is an increasingly important stop on the European jazz circuit. Venues vary, from the city's intimate jazz clubs to grander theatrical stages across town. (p111)

## December

**The weather turns cold, but Navidad (Christmas) is on its way. There are Christmas markets, *turrón* (nougat), a long weekend at the beginning of the month and a festive period that lasts until early January.**

### Navidad

The main Christmas family get-together is on the night of 24 December (Noche Buena) with much feasting. Although Spanish families now celebrate both Christmas Day (when Papa Noel brings presents) and Three Kings on 6 January, the latter was traditionally the main present-giving occasion.

### Noche Vieja

At midnight on New Year's Eve, all eyes turn to the television as the 12 chimes are broadcast live from Madrid's Puerta del Sol and Spaniards young and old try to eat a grape for every chime of the clock as they ring out

# Itineraries

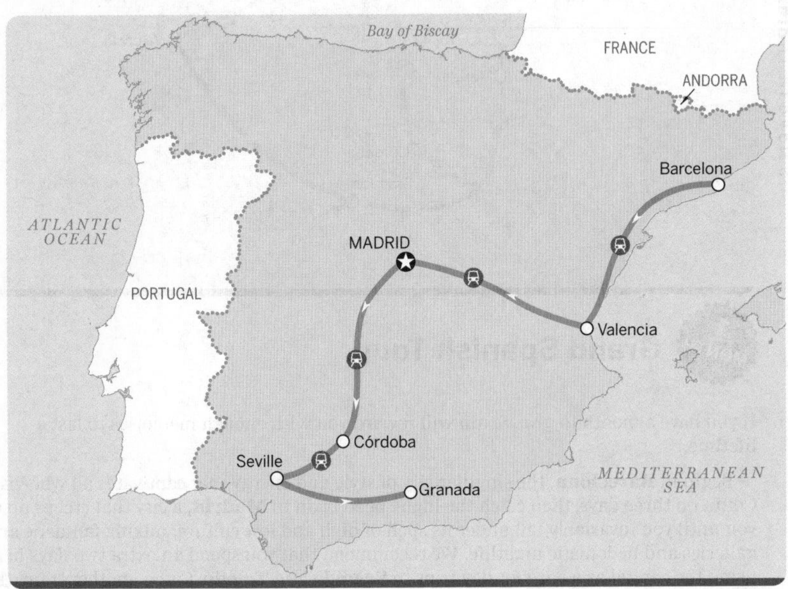

## Essential Spain

**If you want to understand why many visitors fall in love with Spain and never want to leave, look no further than its vibrant, passionate, beautiful cities. This itinerary takes you through the best Spain has to offer.**

So many Spanish trails begin in **Barcelona**, Spain's second-biggest city and one of the coolest places on earth. Explore the architecture and sample the food, before catching the train down the coast to **Valencia** for a dose of paella, nightlife and the 21st-century wonders of the Ciudad de las Artes y las Ciencias. A fast train whisks you inland to the capital, mighty **Madrid**, for the irresistible street energy, the pretty plazas and one of the richest concentrations of art museums on the planet. Yet another fast train takes you deep into Andalucía, with **Córdoba** your entry point into this wonderful corner of Spain; the most obvious highlight is the city's 8th-century Mezquita. From Córdoba it's a short hop to fabulous **Seville**. But we've saved the best until last: **Granada** boasts the extraordinary Alhambra, its soulful alter ego the Albayzín, and an eating and drinking scene that embraces Spanish culinary culture in all its glorious variety.

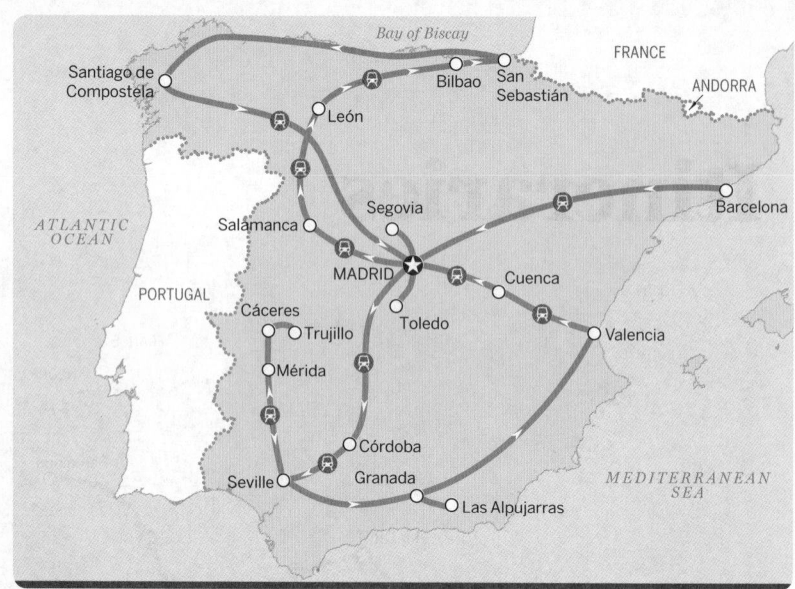

## Grand Spanish Tour

If you have a month to give, Spain will reward you with enough memories to last a lifetime.

Begin in **Barcelona**, the singular city of style and energy that captivates all who visit. Count on three days, then catch the high-speed train to **Madrid**, a city that creeps up on you until you invariably fall under its spell of high and low culture, mixing fantastic art galleries and hedonistic nightlife. We recommend that you spend an extra two days here, using the capital as a base for day trips to **Segovia** and **Toledo**. Catch another train, this time heading for **Salamanca**, that plateresque jewel of Castilla y León. After a night in Salamanca, travel north by train to stay overnight in **León** and see the extraordinary stained-glass windows of its cathedral, before continuing to **Bilbao**, home of the Museo Guggenheim Bilbao and so much that is good about Basque culture. Spend a night here, followed by another couple in splendid **San Sebastián**. A couple of days' drive around the Cantabrian, Asturian and Galician coasts will take you along Spain's most dramatic shoreline en route to **Santiago de Compostela**, where you need two nights minimum to soak up this sacred city. Wherever you travel in the north, from San Sebastián to Santiago, make food a centrepiece of your visit.

Catch the train back to Madrid, then take a high-speed train to **Córdoba** for two nights and **Seville** for two nights. While you're in the area, detour north by bus or train to the Roman ruins of **Mérida** for a night, the fabulous old city of **Cáceres** for another night and medieval **Trujillo** for a third night. Return to Seville and make immediately for **Granada**; plan on two nights. Add an extra couple of nights and a rental car and you can visit the lovely villages of **Las Alpujarras**. Keep the car (or catch the train) and travel from Granada to **Valencia** to spend a couple of days enjoying its architecture, paella and irresistible energy. You've just enough time to catch the high-speed train to cliff-top **Cuenca** for a night on your way back to Madrid at journey's end.

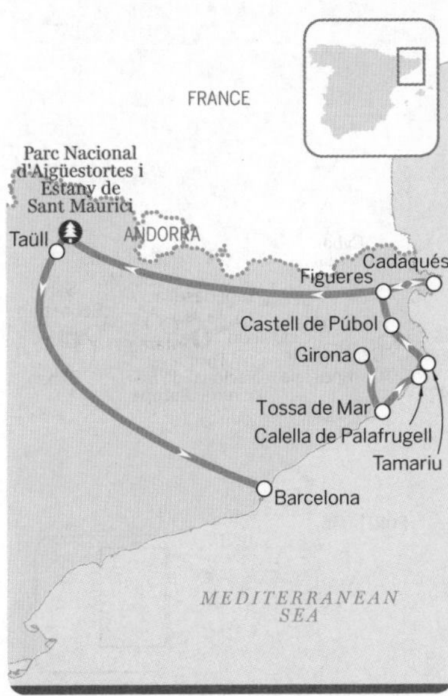

## Catalan Coast & Pyrenees

Yes, Barcelona gets all the headlines, but there's so much more to Catalonia than Spain's coolest city.

**Girona** is one of those timeless Spanish cities where the whispers of the past seem to echo through the medieval streets. Glorious, intimate streetscapes steeped in history, fabulous restaurants, and fine museums combine to make Girona worth at least two days of your time.

Head for the coast north of Barcelona, starting with **Tossa de Mar** and its castle-backed bay, then **Calella de Palafrugell** and **Tamariu**, two beautifully sited coastal villages. The next day is all about Salvador Dalí, from his fantasy castle **Castell de Púbol** to his extraordinary theatre-museum in **Figueres**, and then his one-time home, the lovely seaside village of **Cadaqués**. The next morning, leave the Mediterranean behind and drive west in the shadow of the Pyrenees. Your reward for the long drive is a couple of nights in **Taüll**, gateway to the magnificent **Parc Nacional d'Aigüestortes i Estany de Sant Maurici**. A loop south via Lleida then east has you back in Barcelona by mid-afternoon on your final day.

10 DAYS

## Andalucian Adventure

This route takes you through iconic cities and some of the region's most beautiful villages.

Begin in **Málaga**, whose airport receives flights from almost every conceivable corner of Europe. It has enough attractions to keep you occupied for one very full day. No Andalucian itinerary is complete without at least a couple of nights in peerless **Granada**. Rent a car and make for the otherworldly valleys of **Las Alpujarras** with their mountain scenery and North African–style villages. Still with the car, head west for three days along quiet back roads to some of Andalucía's most spectacular villages and towns: Mudéjar **Antequera**, spectacular **Ronda**, whitewashed **Tarifa**, beguiling **Vejer de la Frontera**, and **Arcos de la Frontera**, one of Andalucía's most glorious *pueblos blancos* (white villages). With three days left, leave the car and spend a night in fun-filled **Cádiz**, one of Europe's oldest cities, then catch a train to **Jerez de la Frontera**, allowing time to visit its sherry bodegas. Finally, continue north to flamenco-rich **Seville**, which is, for many, the essence of Andalucía.

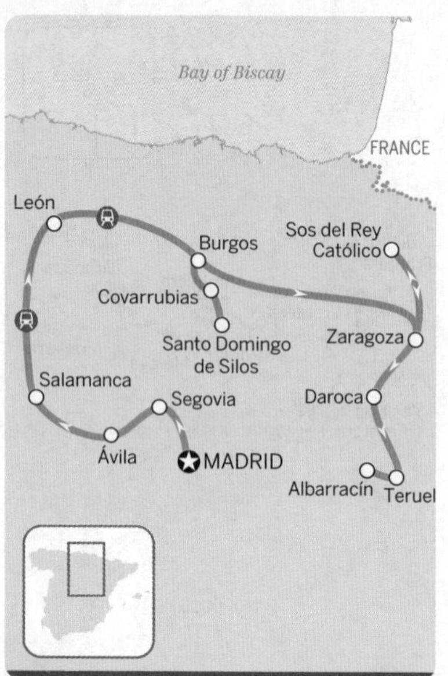

## 2 WEEKS Castilla & Aragón

The Spanish interior may not fit the stereotype of sun, sand and sangría, but we love it all the more for that. This route takes in a stirring mix of lesser-known cities and stunning villages.

From **Madrid**, head to some of the loveliest towns of the Spanish heartland: **Segovia**, with its Disney-esque castle and Roman aqueduct, walled **Ávila** and vibrant **Salamanca** will occupy around four days of your time, with short train rides connecting the three. Trains also connect you to **León** and **Burgos**, home to two of Spain's most extraordinary churches. Spend at least a day in each. An extra night in Burgos will allow you to take a day trip to the medieval villages of **Covarrubias** and **Santo Domingo de Silos**. Make for **Zaragoza**, one of Spain's most vibrant cities, with a wealth of monuments and great tapas – two days is a must. Next, rent a car and head for the hills, where **Sos del Rey Católico** looks for all the world like a Tuscan hill town. Drive south for an overnight stop in dramatic **Daroca**, then on to **Teruel**, filled with Mudéjar architectural gems. Finish your journey in **Albarracín**, one of Spain's most spectacular villages.

## 10 DAYS Northern Spain

Spain's Mediterranean Coast may get the crowds, but the northern coastline from San Sebastián to Santiago is one of the most spectacular in Europe.

There is no finer introduction to the north of the country than **San Sebastián**, with its dramatic setting and fabulous food. Two nights is a minimum here. West of San Sebastián by train, **Bilbao** is best known as the home of the showpiece Museo Guggenheim and warrants at least a night, preferably two. To make the most of the coast, you'll need a car. Cantabria's cobblestone **Santillana del Mar**, the rock art at **Altamira** and the village of **Ribadesella** will fill one day, with another taken up by the steep valleys of the **Picos de Europa**. After a third night in irresistible **Oviedo**, tackle Galicia's coastline, one of Spain's great natural wonders, punctuated with secluded fishing villages and stunning cliffs. Don't miss **Cabo Ortegal**, dynamic **A Coruña** and the **Costa da Morte**. For the last two nights, linger in the thoroughly Galician city of **Santiago de Compostela**, a place of pilgrim footfalls, fine regional cuisine and a cathedral of power.

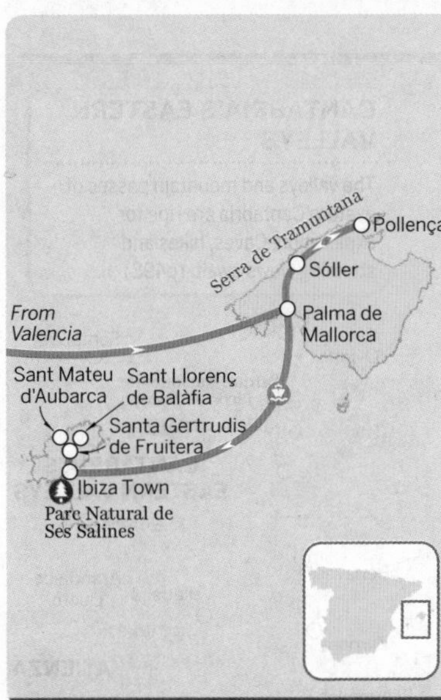

## 2 WEEKS Valencia & the Balearics

This journey takes you from the shores of the Mediterranean to Mallorca and Ibiza, two of the most beautiful islands in the Med. You'll need a car to explore each.

Begin in **Valencia**, that most appealing of Mediterranean cities, which is worth a couple of nights. Fly or catch a boat to **Palma de Mallorca**, a dynamic city with stirring architecture and world-class food. After a couple of nights, take two days to drive Mallorca's west coast and **Serra de Tramuntana**. Pretty **Sóller** makes a terrific place to rest along the way. Base yourself in **Pollença** to explore the island's north for a couple more days, before returning to Palma for the ferry to Ibiza. On arrival, take a couple of days to soak up the considerable charms of Ibiza Town's **Dalt Vila** and wonderful nightlife. Then leave it all behind for Ibiza's quiet north coast, stopping in **Sant Llorenç de Balàfia**, with its great restaurants, remote little **Sant Mateu d'Aubarca**, and artsy **Santa Gertrudis de Fruitera**. When you can tear yourself away, head for the **Parc Natural de Ses Salines**, some of the wildest and most beautiful country in Mediterranean Spain.

## 10 DAYS Extreme West

Extremadura is one of Spain's least known corners - a good reason to visit.

Begin with a night in Extremadura's north, in **Plasencia**, which is jammed with notable buildings, churches and convents. Catch the train to **Cáceres**, whose Ciudad Monumental is one of the finest surviving medieval cores in any Spanish city. After two nights here, including a half-day excursion to charming **Garrovillas**, regular buses take an hour to nearby **Trujillo**, a smaller but equally enchanting relic of the Middle Ages. Spend two nights here, including one for a day trip by rental car to the charming hill town and pilgrims' destination of **Guadalupe**. From Trujillo it's around an hour by bus to **Mérida**, but the journey spans the centuries: Mérida boasts some of Spain's most impressive Roman ruins. While there (two nights), rent a car for a half-day trip to **Medellín** with its Roman echoes. Further south again by bus lies whitewashed **Zafra**, a precursor to Andalucía in spirit, architecture and geography. Detour via the *jamón* (ham) town of **Monesterio**, before all roads lead to magical **Seville**, one of Andalucía's most captivating cities.

# Off the Beaten Track: Spain

### CAMINO TO ATIENZA

Walk to Atienza on a little-trekked southern branch of the Camino de Santiago through a quintessential Castilian landscape of arid hills punctuated by half-forgotten, semi-abandoned villages. (p234)

### CANTABRIA'S EASTERN VALLEYS

The valleys and mountain passes of eastern Cantabria are ripe for exploration. Caves, hikes and stunning views await. (p498)

### LAS HURDES

Las Hurdes sits in one of Extremadura's most remote corners. Ladrillar is picturesque, while Riomalo de Arriba is home to the region's best collection of original stone-and-slate homes. (p601)

### GARROVILLAS DE ALCONÉTAR

Little Garrovillas de Alconétar has a truly remarkable Plaza Mayor, surrounded by arched porticoes and two-storey buildings dating back as far as the 15th century – it's one of the most beautiful in Extremadura. (p594)

### EASTERN ALPUJARRAS

This is tough, isolated mountain country, with the long-distance GR7 path traversing the area. The small villages here – Bérchules, Cádiar, Mecina Bombarón, Yegen, Válor, Mairena – provide oases of greenery. (p728)

## JÁNOVAS

Jánovas is a village with a story. Expropriated in the 1960s for a hydro-electric scheme that never came to fruition, former Jánovas villagers are now restoring the village piece by piece. (p417)

## CONGOST DE MONT-REBEI

The spectacular river gorge of Mont-rebei offers a dazzling vision of Catalan wilderness. It's one of Catalonia's only gorges left in a near pristine state – with no roads or electric lines marring its beauty. (p375)

## CORDERA DE EBRE

The hilltop settlement of Cordera de Ebre stands as one of the most vivid reminders of the horrors of the Spanish Civil War. (p386)

## LA GEODA DE PULPÍ

This rare geological marvel – the world's second-largest geode – opened to the public in northeastern Almería's Sierra del Aguilón in 2019. (p764)

## THE MAESTRAZGO

Seek out the smaller villages like spectacular Ares, which overhangs a cliff, or Vilafranca with its excellent museum covering the dry-stone-wall tradition. (p825)

Paella

## Plan Your Trip

# Eat & Drink Like a Local

For most Spaniards, eating is among life's more pleasurable obsessions. In this chapter, we'll initiate you into the wonderful world of Spanish food, demystifying the art of ordering tapas, taking you on a journey through regional Spanish specialities, and generally immersing you in this fabulous culinary culture.

CL-MEDIEN/SHUTTERSTOCK ©

# The Year in Food

Spain's relatively balmy climate ensures that, unusually for Europe, fruit and vegetables can be grown year-round.

### Winter (Dec–Feb)

Across inland Spain, winter is the time for fortifying stews (such as *cocido* or *fabada*) and roasted meats, especially *cochinillo* (suckling pig) and *cordero* (spring lamb).

### Winter to Spring (Nov–Apr)

Catalans salivate over *calçots*, those large spring onions that are eaten with your hands and a bib, and *romesco* (a rich sauce of red peppers and ground almond). This is also *pulpo* (boiled octopus) season in Galicia.

### Summer (Jun–Aug)

The cold soups gazpacho and *salmorejo*, both specialities of Andalucía, only appear in summer. Rice dishes by the Mediterranean are another key ingredient of the Spanish summer.

### Autumn (Sep–Nov)

La Rioja's grape harvest gets underway in September. Logroño's Fiesta de San Mateo (mid-September) gets it all happening.

# Food Experiences

## Meals of a Lifetime

**Arzak** (p454) This San Sebastián restaurant is the home kitchen of Spain's most revered father-daughter team.

**Martín Berasategui Restaurant** (p454) One of Spain's most respected celebrity chefs. Also in San Sebastián.

**El Celler de Can Roca** (p337) This Girona eatery represents everything that's good about innovative Catalan cuisine.

**DiverXo** (p123) Avant-garde Madrid temple to experimentation, with surprising twists to the whole dining experience.

**Lasarte** (p299) Seriously inspired cooking from two of Spain's best chefs, in Barcelona.

**Paco Roncero Restaurante** (p119) Located in Madrid, this is one of the country's temples to laboratory-led innovations.

**Disfrutar** (p299) The playfulness and sophistication of Catalan cooking at its best in Barcelona.

**Quique Dacosta** (p832) Molecular gastronomy brought to the Mediterranean. In Dénia.

## Food & Wine Festivals

**Feria del Queso** (p596) Trujillo's orgy of cheese tasting and serious competition in late April or early May.

**Feira do Viño do Ribeiro** (p580) Ribadavia in Galicia's south hosts one of the region's biggest wine festivals on the first weekend of May.

**Batalla del Vino** (p485) A really messy wine fight, held on 29 June in Haro, La Rioja.

**Festa do Pulpo de O Carballiño** (p580) On the second Sunday of August, 70,000 people cram into the Galician town of O Carballiño for a mass octopus-eating binge.

**Fiesta de la Sidra Natural** (p514) Gijón's August fiesta includes an annual world-record attempt on the number of people simultaneously pouring cider.

**Fiesta de San Mateo** (p482) Logroño celebrates La Rioja's September grape harvest with grape-crushing ceremonies and tastings.

## Cheap Treats

**Tapas or pintxos** Possibly the world's most ingenious form of snacking. Madrid's La Latina and Chamberí *barrios* (districts), Zaragoza's El Tubo and most Andalucian cities offer rich pickings, but a *pintxo* (Basque tapas) crawl in San Sebastián's Parte Vieja is one of life's most memorable gastronomic experiences.

**Tortilla de patatas** Great for vegetarians and carnivores alike, the Spanish egg-and-potato omelette is especially good when the egg's runny. It's served as an in-between-meals snack, although it can be a meal in itself.

**Chocolate con churros** These deep-fried doughnut strips dipped in thick hot chocolate are a Spanish favourite for breakfast, afternoon tea or at dawn on your way home from a night out. Madrid's Chocolatería de San Ginés (p126) is the most famous purveyor.

**Bocadillos** Rolls filled with *jamón* (ham) or other cured meats, cheese or (in Madrid) deep-fried calamari.

**Pa amb tomàquet** Bread rubbed with tomato, olive oil and garlic – a staple in Catalonia and elsewhere.

## Cooking Courses

**Alambique** (p109) Cooking classes in Madrid covering Spanish and international themes.

**De Olla y Sartén** (p109) Madrid classes that span most local and world cuisines.

**Apunto** (p109) Excellent range of cooking styles in Madrid.

**Kitchen Club** (p109) Another excellent Madrid cooking school.

**Barcelona Cooking** (p282) Hands-on Barcelona classes with a market visit thrown in.

**Quinta de San Amaro** (p568) Galician and international cuisines taught near Cambados.

**L'Atelier** (p727) Award-winning vegetarian chef Jean-Claude Juston runs vegetarian cooking courses in Andalucía's Las Alpujarras.

## Dare to Try

**Oreja** Pig's ear, cooked on the grill. It's a little like eating gristly bacon.

**Callos** Tripe cooked in a sauce of tomato, paprika, garlic and herbs. It's a speciality in Madrid.

**Rabo de toro** Bull's-tail or oxtail stew. It's a particular delicacy during bullfighting season in Madrid and Andalucía, when the tail comes straight from the bullring...

**Percebes** Goose barnacles from Galicia. The first person to try them sure was one adventurous individual, but we're glad they did.

**Garrotxa** Formidable Catalan cheese that almost lives up to its name.

**Morcilla** Blood sausage. It's blended with rice in Burgos, with onion in Asturias.

**Criadillas** Bull's testicles. Eaten in Andalucía.

**Botillo** Spanish version of haggis from Castilla y León's Bierzo region.

**Pestorejo** Fleshy part of a pig's neck; much loved in Mérida.

# Local Specialities

## Food

Spaniards love to travel in their own country, and given the riches on offer, they especially love to do so with some culinary purpose in mind. Tell a Spaniard that you're on your way to a particular place and they'll likely start salivating at the mere thought of the local speciality, and they'll surely have a favourite restaurant at which to enjoy it.

### Basque Country & Catalonia

The confluence of sea and mountains has bequeathed to the Basque Country an extraordinary culinary richness – seafood and steaks are the pillars upon which Basque cuisine has been traditionally built. San Sebastián, in particular, showcases the region's diversity of culinary experiences and it was from the city's kitchens that *nueva cocina vasca* (Basque nouvelle cuisine) emerged, announcing Spain's arrival as a culinary superpower. San Sebastián is also Spain's undisputed king of tapas (or *pintxos,* as the Basques call them).

Catalonia blends traditional Catalan flavours and expansive geographical diversity with an openness to influences from the rest of Europe. All manner of seafood, paella, rice and pasta dishes, as well as Pyrenean game dishes, are regulars on Catalan menus. Sauces are more prevalent here than elsewhere in Spain.

### Inland Spain

The best *jamón ibérico* comes from Extremadura, Salamanca and Teruel, while *cordero asado lechal* (roast spring lamb) and *cochinillo asado* (roast suckling pig) are winter mainstays. Of the hearty stews, the king is *cocido,* a hotpot or stew with a noodle broth, carrots, cabbage, chickpeas, chicken, *morcilla* (blood sausage), beef and lard. *Migas* (breadcrumbs, often cooked with chorizo and served with grapes) are also regulars.

Cheeses, too, are specialities here, from Extremadura's creamy, spreadable Torta del Casar to Castilla-La Mancha's *queso manchego* (a hard sheep's-milk cheese).

### Galicia & the Northwest

Galicia is known for its bewildering array of seafood, and the star is *pulpo á feira* (spicy boiled octopus, called *pulpo a la gallega* or *pulpo gallego* in other parts of Spain), a dish whose constituent elements (octopus, oil, paprika and garlic) are so simple yet whose execution is devilishly difficult. Neighbouring Asturias and Cantabria produce Spain's best *anchoas* (anchovies).

In the high mountains of Asturias and Cantabria, the cuisine is as driven by mountain pasture as it is by the daily comings and goings of fishing fleets. Cheeses are particularly sought after, with special fame reserved for the untreated cow's-milk cheese *queso de Cabrales. Asturianos* (Asturians) are also passionate about their *fabada asturiana* (a stew made with pork, blood sausage and white beans) and *sidra* (cider) straight from the barrel.

### Valencia, Murcia & the Balearic Islands

There's so much more to the cuisine of this region than oranges and paella, but these signature products capture the essence of the Mediterranean table. You can get a paella just about anywhere in Spain, but to enjoy one cooked as it should be cooked, look no further than the restaurants in Valencia's waterfront Las Arenas district or La Albufera. In the Balearics, paella, rice dishes and lashings of seafood are similarly recurring themes.

Murcia's culinary fame brings us back to the oranges. The littoral is known simply as 'La Huerta' ('the garden'). Since Moorish times, this has been one of Spain's most prolific areas for growing fruit and vegetables.

### Andalucía

Seafood is a consistent presence the length of the Andalucian coast. Andalucians are famous above all for their *pescaito frito* (fried fish). A particular speciality of Cádiz, fried fish Andalucian-style means that just about anything that emerges from the sea is rolled in chickpea and wheat flour, shaken to remove the surplus, then deep-fried ever so briefly in olive oil, just long enough to form a light, golden crust that seals the essential goodness of the fish or seafood within.

In a region where summers can be fierce, there's no better way to keep cool than with a *gazpacho andaluz* (Andalucian gazpacho), a cold soup with many manifestations. The base is almost always tomato, cucumber, vinegar and olive oil.

## Wine

All of Spain's autonomous communities, with the exceptions of Asturias and Cantabria, are home to officially recognised wine-growing areas.

La Rioja, in the north, is Spain's best-known wine-producing region. The principal grape of Rioja is the tempranillo, widely believed to be a mutant form of the pinot noir. Its wine is smooth and fruity, seldom as dry as its supposed French counterpart. Look for the 'DOC Rioja' classification on the label and you'll find a good wine. Not far behind are the wine-producing regions of Ribera del Duero (in Castilla y León), Navarra, Somontano (Aragón), and Valdepeñas in southern Castilla-La Mancha. The last is famous for

### JAMÓN

Spanish *jamón* is, unlike Italian prosciutto, a bold, deep red and well marbled with buttery fat. At its best, it smells like meat, the forest and the field.

Like wines and olive oil, Spanish *jamón* is subject to a strict series of classifications. *Jamón serrano* refers to *jamón* made from white-coated pigs introduced to Spain in the 1950s. Once salted and semi-dried by the cold, dry winds of the Spanish sierra, most now go through a similar process of curing and drying in a climate-controlled shed for around a year. *Jamón serrano* accounts for about 90% of cured ham in Spain.

*Jamón ibérico* – more expensive and generally regarded as the elite of Spanish hams – comes from a black-coated pig indigenous to the Iberian Peninsula and a descendant of the wild boar. Gastronomically, its star appeal is its ability to infiltrate fat into the muscle tissue, thus producing an especially well-marbled meat. If the pig gains at least 50% of its body weight during the acorn-eating season, it can be classified as *jamón ibérico de bellota,* the most sought-after designation for *jamón.*

# Spanish Food & Wine

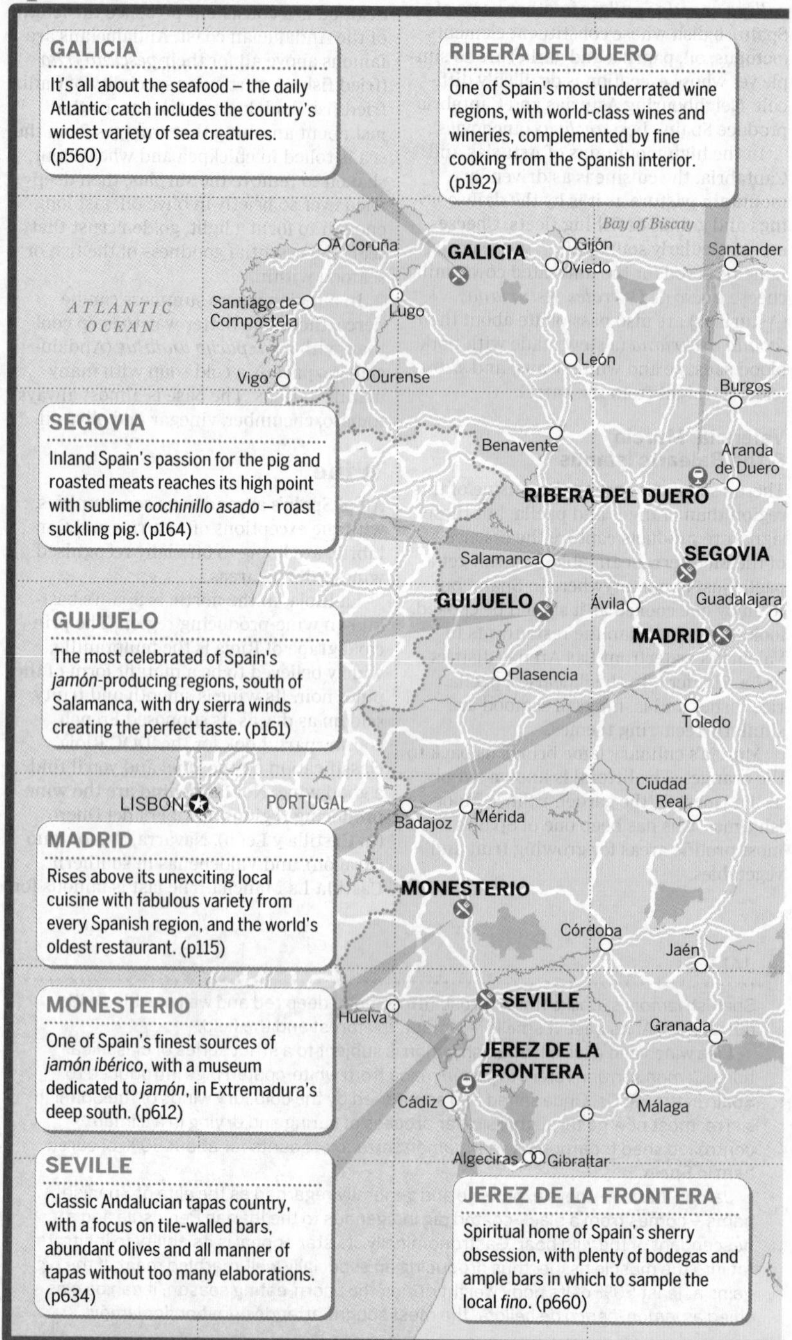

## GALICIA

It's all about the seafood – the daily Atlantic catch includes the country's widest variety of sea creatures. (p560)

## RIBERA DEL DUERO

One of Spain's most underrated wine regions, with world-class wines and wineries, complemented by fine cooking from the Spanish interior. (p192)

## SEGOVIA

Inland Spain's passion for the pig and roasted meats reaches its high point with sublime *cochinillo asado* – roast suckling pig. (p164)

## GUIJUELO

The most celebrated of Spain's *jamón*-producing regions, south of Salamanca, with dry sierra winds creating the perfect taste. (p161)

## MADRID

Rises above its unexciting local cuisine with fabulous variety from every Spanish region, and the world's oldest restaurant. (p115)

## MONESTERIO

One of Spain's finest sources of *jamón ibérico*, with a museum dedicated to *jamón*, in Extremadura's deep south. (p612)

## SEVILLE

Classic Andalucian tapas country, with a focus on tile-walled bars, abundant olives and all manner of tapas without too many elaborations. (p634)

## JEREZ DE LA FRONTERA

Spiritual home of Spain's sherry obsession, with plenty of bodegas and ample bars in which to sample the local *fino*. (p660)

0 200 km
0 100 miles
SAN SEBASTIÁN
Has more Michelin stars per capita than any city on earth, and a peerless *pintxo* (Basque tapas) smorgasbord in the old town. (p454)
LA RIOJA
Spain's most celebrated wine region lies in the country's northeast, with an emphasis on quality reds. (p481)
BARCELONA
Extraordinarily rich gastronomic city and the showpiece for the superb concoctions of Catalan cooking. (p290)
SAN SEBASTIÁN
FRANCE
Bilbao
Vitoria-Gasteiz
Pamplona
ANDORRA
ANDORRA LA VELLA
Logroño
LA RIOJA
Huesca
Girona
Soria
Zaragoza
Lleida
BARCELONA
Tarragona
Golfo de Valencia
Teruel
Menorca
Cuenca
Maó
MALLORCA
Palma de Mallorca
VALENCIA
Balearic Islands (Islas Baleares)
Ibiza
Albacete
Ibiza Town
Formentera
Alicante
Murcia
Cartagena
MEDITERRANEAN SEA
Almería
ALGIERS
ALGERIA
MALLORCA
Rice dishes, suckling pig, fresh Mediterranean seafood and nouvelle Balearic innovations, and that's just in Palma de Mallorca. (p775)
VALENCIA
Paella's homeland is still the place to go for the country's best paella, whether the traditional one served with beans, rabbit and chicken, or one with seafood. (p812)

DEBORAH LEE ROSSITER/SHUTTERSTOCK ©

quantity rather than quality, but is generally well priced and remains popular.

For white wines, the Ribeiro wines of Galicia are well regarded. Also from the area is one of Spain's most charming whites – albariño. This crisp, dry and refreshing drop is unusual, designated as it is by grape rather than region.

The Penedès region in Catalonia produces whites and sparkling wine such as *cava,* the traditional champagne-like toasting drink of choice for Spaniards at Christmas.

### Wine Classifications

Spanish wine is subject to a complicated system of classification. If an area meets certain strict standards for a given period, covering all aspects of planting, cultivating and ageing, it receives Denominación de Origen (DO; Denomination of Origin) status. There are currently over 60 DO-recognised wine-producing areas in Spain.

An outstanding wine region gets the much-coveted Denominación de Origen Calificada (DOC), a controversial classification that some in the industry argue should apply only to specific wines, rather than every wine from within a particular region. At present, the only DOC wines come from La Rioja in northern Spain and Catalonia's small Priorat area.

The best wines are often marked with the designation *crianza* (aged for one year in oak barrels), *reserva* (aged for two years, at least one of which is in oak barrels) or *gran reserva* (two years in oak and three in the bottle).

### Sherry

Sherry, the unique wine of Andalucía, is Spain's national dram and is found in almost every bar, *tasca* (tapas bar) and restaurant in the land. Dry sherry, called *fino,* begins as a fairly ordinary white wine of the palomino grape, but it's 'fortified' with grape brandy. This stops fermentation and gives the wine taste and smell constituents that enable it to age into something sublime. It's taken as an *aperitivo* (aperitif) or as a table wine with seafood. *Amontillado* and *oloroso* are sweeter sherries, good for after dinner. *Manzanilla* is produced only in Sanlúcar de Barrameda near the coast in southwestern Andalucía and develops a slightly salty taste that's very appetising. It's possible to visit bodegas (wineries) in Sanlúcar, as well as in Jerez de la Frontera and El Puerto de Santa María.

## Cider

Very few grape harvests come from Cantabria, Asturias and parts of the Basque Country. Up there, it's all about the apples. *Sidra* (cider) is something of an obsession in these parts, and *sidrerías* (cider bars) are found in cities and towns across these regions, as well as in Madrid, Barcelona and elsewhere. In *sidrerías* they'll also serve food, but it's very much secondary to the tangy, light and mildly effervescent *sidra.* Poured expertly straight from the barrel or vat – in many *sidrerías,* each barrel may be named after a different saint – and usually from a height of around 1.5m, *sidra* is either served *gasificada* (mass produced, sweet or dry) or *natural* (homemade, cloudier and fruitier). You should never fill your glass too full: the drink can go off rapidly once out of the barrel and needs to be drunk quickly before you go back for more. *Sidra* goes especially well with seafood.

# How to Eat & Drink

Having joined Spaniards around the table for years, we've come to understand what eating Spanish-style is all about. If we could distil the essence of how to make food a highlight of your trip into a few simple rules, they would be these: always ask for the local speciality; never be shy about looking around to see what others have ordered before choosing; always ask the waiter for his or her recommendations; and, wherever possible, make your meal a centrepiece of your day.

## When to Eat

### Breakfast

*Desayuno* (breakfast) Spanish-style is generally a no-nonsense affair taken at a bar mid-morning or on the way to work. A *café con leche* (half coffee and half milk) with a *bollo* (pastry) or croissant is the typical breakfast. Other common breakfast orders are a *tostada,* which is simply buttered toast, or a *sandwich mixto* (toasted ham-and-cheese sandwich).

In hotels, breakfast can begin as early as 6.30am and may continue until 10am (usually later on weekends).

### Lunch

*Comida* or *almuerzo* (lunch) is the main meal of the day – not for most Spaniards a sandwich on the run. During the working week, few Spaniards have time to go home for lunch, so many end up eating in restaurants, and *menús del día* (all-inclusive three-course meals) are as close as they can come to eating home-style food without breaking the bank. On weekends or in summer, Spaniards are not averse to lingering for hours over a meal with friends and family.

Lunch rarely begins before 2pm (restaurant kitchens usually open from 1.30pm until around 4pm).

### Dinner

*Cena* (dinner) is usually a lighter meal, although that may differ on weekends. Going out for a drink and some tapas is a popular way of eating dinner in many cities.

It does vary from region to region, but most restaurants open from 8.30pm to 11pm, later on weekends.

## Vegetarians & Vegans

Pure vegetarianism was traditionally an alien concept in most Spanish kitchens; cooked vegetable dishes, for example, often contain ham. Such is their love for meat, fish and seafood, many Spaniards, especially the older generation, don't really understand vegetarianism. As a result, dedicated vegetarian restaurants are still pretty thin on the ground outside the major cities.

That said, a recent study found that nearly 10% of Spaniards now consider themselves to be vegetarian or vegan, and an ever-growing selection of vegetarian restaurants is springing up around the country. Barcelona and Madrid, in particular, have plenty of vegetarian restaurants

### ORDERING TAPAS

Unless you speak Spanish, ordering tapas can seem one of the dark arts of Spanish etiquette. Fear not – it's not as difficult as it first appears.

In the Basque Country, Zaragoza and many bars in Madrid, Barcelona and elsewhere, it couldn't be easier. With tapas varieties lined up along the bar, you either take a small plate and help yourself or point to the morsel you want. If you do this, it's customary to keep track of what you eat (by holding on to the toothpicks, for example) and then tell the bar staff how many you've had when it's time to pay. Otherwise, many places have a list of tapas, either on a menu or posted up behind the bar. If you can't choose, ask for *la especialidad de la casa* (the house speciality) and it's hard to go wrong.

Another way of eating tapas is to order *raciones* (literally 'rations'; large tapas servings) or *medias raciones* (half-rations; smaller tapas servings). Remember, however, that after a couple of *raciones* you'll be full. In some bars you'll also get a small (free) tapa when you buy a drink.

### THE TRAVELLER'S FRIEND: MENÚ DEL DÍA

One great way to cap prices at lunchtime on weekdays is to order the *menú del día,* a full three-course set menu, water, bread and wine. These meals are priced from around €10, although €12 and up is increasingly the norm. You'll be given a menu with a choice of five or six starters, the same number of mains and a handful of desserts – you choose one from each category; it's possible to order two starters, but not two mains.

to choose from, and most other cities have a few choices.

Salads are a Spanish staple and often are a meal in themselves. You'll also come across the odd vegetarian paella, as well as dishes such as *verduras a la plancha* (grilled vegetables); *garbanzos con espinacas* (chickpeas and spinach); and potato dishes, such as *patatas bravas* (potato chunks bathed in a slightly spicy tomato sauce) and *tortilla de patatas* (egg, potato and onion omelette). The prevalence of legumes ensures that *lentejas* (lentils) and *judías* (beans) are also easy to track down, while *pan* (bread), *quesos* (cheeses), *alcachofas* (artichokes) and *aceitunas* (olives) are always easy to find. *Tascas* (tapas bars) usually offer more vegetarian choices than sit-down restaurants.

If vegetarians can feel like a rarity among Spaniards, vegans may feel as if they've come from another planet, although labelling on menus and an awareness of such issues has improved greatly in recent years. To make sure that you're not misunderstood, ask if dishes contain *huevos* (eggs) or *productos lácteos* (dairy).

## Drinking Etiquette

Wherever you are in Spain, there'll be a bar close by. More than just places to drink, bars are centres of community life. Spaniards drink often and seem up for a drink almost any time of the day or night, but they rarely do so to excess; drinking is rarely an end in itself, but rather an accompaniment to good conversation, food or music. Perhaps they've learned that pacing themselves is the key to lasting until dawn – it's a key strategy to make the most of your Spanish night.

## Where to Eat & Drink

**asador** Restaurant specialising in roasted meats.

**bar de copas** Gets going around midnight and serves hard drinks.

**casa de comidas** Basic restaurant serving well-priced home cooking.

**cervecería** The focus is on *cerveza* (beer) on tap.

**horno de asador** Restaurant with a wood-burning roasting oven.

**marisquería** Bar or restaurant specialising in seafood.

**restaurante** Restaurant.

**taberna** Usually a rustic place serving tapas and *raciones* (large tapas).

**tasca** Tapas bar.

**terraza** Open-air bar, for warm-weather tippling, tapas and *raciones*.

**vinoteca** Wine bars where you can order by the glass.

## Menu Decoder

**a la parrilla** grilled

**asado** roasted or baked

**bebidas** drinks

**carne** meat

**carta** menu

**casera** homemade

**ensalada** salad

**entrada** entrée or starter

**entremeses** hors d'oeuvres

**frito** fried

**menú** usually refers to a set menu

**menú de degustación** tasting menu

**pescado** fish

**plato combinado** main-and-three-veg dish

**postre** dessert

**raciones** large-/full-plate-size serving of tapas

**sopa** soup

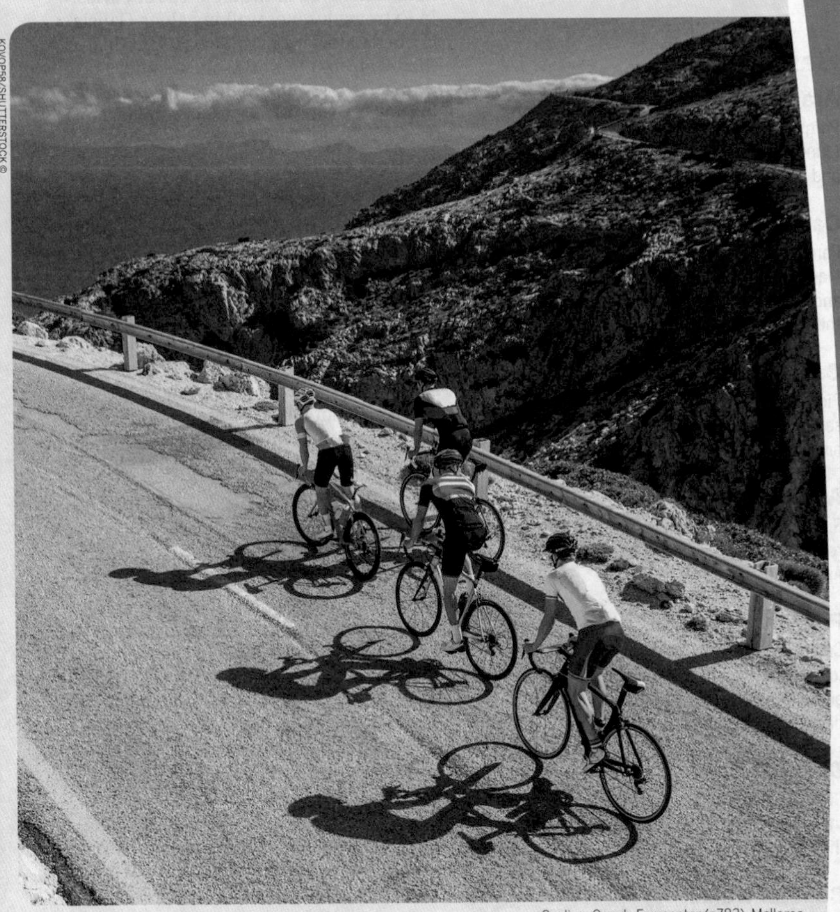


Cycling, Cap de Formentor (p783), Mallorca

## Plan Your Trip

# Outdoor Activities

Spain's landscapes are almost continental in their scale and variety, and they provide the backdrop to some of Europe's best hiking, most famously the Camino de Santiago. Skiing is another big draw, as are cycling, water sports, river-rafting and wildlife-watching, among other stirring outdoor pursuits.

## Best Hiking

### Aragón

Parque Nacional de Ordesa y Monte Perdido (June to August): the best of the Pyrenees and Spain's finest hiking.

### Catalonia

Parc Nacional d'Aigüestortes i Estany de Sant Maurici (July to September): glacial lakes and mountains make a stunning backdrop to this wilderness.

### Cantabria & Asturias

Picos de Europa (June to August): a close second to the Pyrenees for Spain's best hiking.

### Andalucía

Sierra Nevada (July to mid-September): remote peaks and snow-white villages in the Alpujarras valleys.

### Pilgrimage

Camino de Santiago (Camino Francés; May to September): one of the world's favourite pilgrimages, across northern Spain to Santiago de Compostela.

### Coast to Coast

GR11 (Senda Pirenáica; July and August): traverses the Pyrenees from the Atlantic to the Med.

### Coastal Walks

Camiño dos Faros (May to September): an adventurous 200km trail along Galicia's spectacular Costa da Morte (Death Coast) from Malpica de Bergantiños to Cabo Fisterra.

## Hiking

Spain is famous for superb walking trails that explore mountains and hills in every corner of the country, from the alpine meadows of the Pyrenees to Andalucía's sultry Cabo de Gata coastal trail. Other possibilities include conquering Spain's highest mainland peak, Mulhacén (3479m), in the Sierra Nevada above Granada; following in the footsteps of Carlos V in Extremadura; or walking along Galicia's Costa da Morte (Death Coast). And then there's one of the world's most famous pilgrimage trails – the route to the cathedral in Galicia's Santiago de Compostela.

### When to Go

Spain takes in a number of different climatic zones, ensuring that it's possible to hike year-round. As a general rule, winter hiking is best in the south, summer hiking in the north.

In Andalucía conditions are at their best from March to June and in September and October; July and August are unbearable in most parts of the region (though they're the ideal months for the high Sierra Nevada). From December to February most trails remain open, except in the high mountains.

If you prefer to walk in summer, do what Spaniards have traditionally done and escape to the north. The Basque Country, Asturias, Cantabria and Galicia are best from June to September. Pyrenean passes are usually only accessible from around mid-June until some time in October. August is the busiest month on the northern trails, so if you plan to head to popular national parks and stay in *refugios* (wilderness hostels), book ahead.

Hiking in the north can be splendid in September and early October – the summer crowds have gone, there's (usually) still enough sunshine to go with the lovely autumn colours and there's plenty of room in the *refugios*.

## Hiking Destinations

### Pyrenees

For good reason, the Pyrenees, separating Spain from France, are Spain's premier walking destination. The range is prim and chocolate-box pretty on the lower slopes, wild and bleak at higher elevations, and relatively unspoiled compared to many European mountain ranges. The Pyrenees contain two outstanding national parks: Aigüestortes i Estany de Sant Maurici (p361) and Ordesa y Monte Perdido (p411). The former is home to the magnificent Carros de Foc (p367), a loop route linking nine major *refugios*.

The spectacular GR11 (Senda Pirenáica) traverses the range, connecting the Atlantic (at Hondarribia in the Basque Country) with the Mediterranean (at Cap de Creus in Catalonia). Walking the whole 35- to 50-day route is an unforgettable challenge, but there are also magnificent day hikes in the national parks and elsewhere.

### Picos de Europa

Breathtaking, accessible limestone ranges with distinctive craggy peaks (usually hot rock-climbing destinations too) dominate Spain's first national park, the Picos de Europa (p526), which straddles Cantabria, Asturias and León provinces. It's one of Spain's best hiking areas.

El Anillo de Picos (www.elanillodepicos.com) hiking itinerary links the Picos' most important *refugios* in several neat loops.

### Elsewhere in Spain

To walk in mountain villages, the classic spot is Las Alpujarras (p723), near the Parque Nacional Sierra Nevada in Andalucía. The Sierras de Cazorla (p761) and Sierra de Grazalema (p668) are also outstanding. The long-distance GR7 trail traverses the first two of these regions – you can walk all or part of the route, depending on your time and inclination.

Great coastal walking abounds, even in heavily visited areas such as the south coast. Camiño dos Faros (p555) is an adventurous 200km trail along Galicia's magnificent Costa da Morte from Malpica de Bergantiños to Cabo Fisterra (practicable in one direction only at the time of writing). Other excellent Galician routes include the Ruta Cañón do Río Mao (p581), a beautiful day hike in the inland Ribeira Sacra region, and the Camino Natural de la Ruta del Cantábrico, a walking and biking trail running 154km along the northern coast from Ribadeo to the Ría de Ortigueira. The Camino Natural passes the famous Praia As Catedrais, among other places.

Along Andalucía's wildest stretch of coast, Almería's Parque Natural de Cabo de Gata-Níjar (p767) includes around 50km of coastal trails between San Miguel de Cabo de Gata and Agua Amarga. It's a fabulous three-day hike, although shorter day hikes are also possible. Some sections take you past beaches with no road access.

Catalonia's Parc Natural de la Zona Volcànica de la Garrotxa (p352) is another popular walking area with unique volcanic landscapes.

Mulhacén, Sierra Nevada (p726)

Another fine coastal path is the Camí de Ronda (p346), which runs all the way up the Costa Brava and is really rather special in places.

## Information

For detailed info on walking routes in Spain's national parks, check out www.mapama.gob.es/es/red-parques-nacionales/nuestros-parques.

Region-specific walking (and climbing) guides are published by Cicerone Press (www.cicerone.co.uk).

Bookshops around Spain sell guides and maps. In Madrid, try **Librería Desnivel** (Map p84; ☎91 429 12 81; www.libreriadesnivel.com; Plaza de Matute 6; ⏲10am-8.30pm Mon-Fri, 11am-8pm Sat; Ⓜ Antón Martín) or **La Tienda Verde** (☎91 534 33 13; www.facebook.com/latiendaverde; Calle de Maudes 23; ⏲10am-2pm Mon-Fri; Ⓜ Cuatro Caminos), while Altaïr (p318) is best in Barcelona. The best Spanish guides are *Prames* and *Adrados*, while Editorial Alpina publishes an excellent map series.

## The Camino

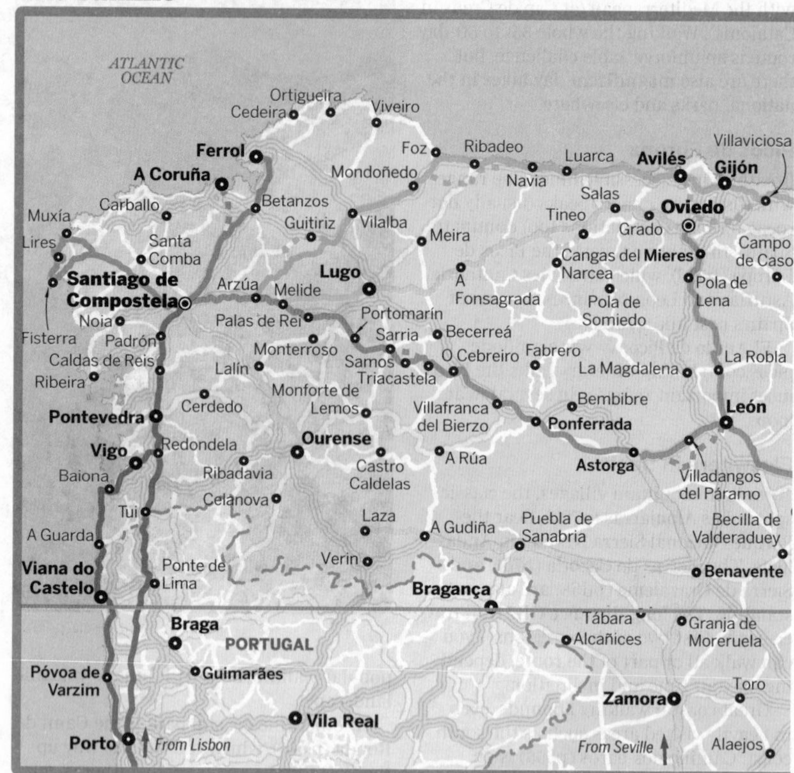


## Camino de Santiago

"The door is open to all, to sick and healthy, not only to Catholics but also to pagans, Jews, heretics and vagabonds."

So goes a 13th-century poem describing the Camino – words that still ring true 800 years later. The Camino de Santiago (Way of St James) originated as a medieval pilgrimage and, for more than 1000 years, people have taken up the Camino's age-old symbols – the scallop shell and staff – and set off on the adventure of a lifetime to the tomb of St James the Apostle in Santiago de Compostela (p540), in the Iberian Peninsula's far northwest.

There are several *caminos* (paths) to Santiago de Compostela in Galicia, passing through a number of Spanish regions, including Navarra (p469), Cantabria & Asturias (p489), Castilla y León (p147) and Galicia (p582). The most popular is the Camino Francés, which spans 770km of Spain's north, starting on the French side of the Pyrenees and attracting walkers of all backgrounds and ages from across the world. Its list of assets (cultural, historical and natural) is impressive, as are its accolades. Not only is it the Council of Europe's first Cultural Itinerary and the centrepiece of the Camino's Unesco World Heritage listing but, for believers, it's a pilgrimage equal to visiting Jerusalem, and by finishing it you're guaranteed a healthy chunk of time off purgatory.

To feel, absorb, smell and taste northern Spain's diversity, for a great physical challenge, for a unique perspective on rural and urban communities, and to meet intriguing travel companions, this is an incomparable walk. 'The door is open to all'...so step on in.

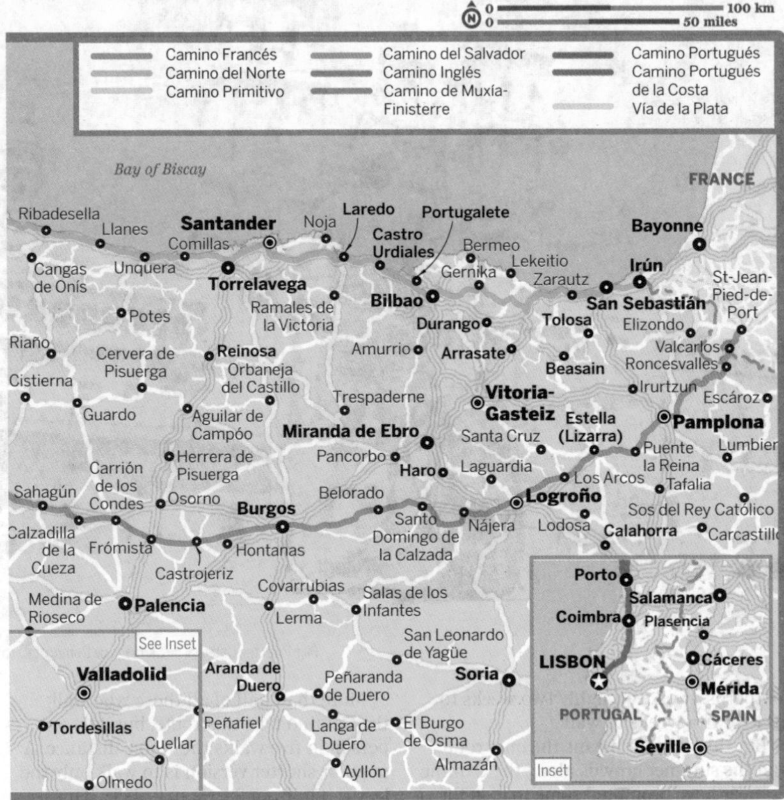


## History

In the 9th century a remarkable event occurred in the poor Iberian hinterlands: following a shining star, Pelayo, a religious hermit, unearthed the tomb of the apostle James the Greater (or, in Spanish, Santiago). The news was confirmed by the local bishop, the Asturian king and later the pope. Its impact is hard to truly imagine today, but it was instant and indelible: first a trickle, then a flood of Christian Europeans began to journey towards the setting sun in search of salvation.

Compostela became the most important destination for Christians after Rome and Jerusalem. Its popularity increased with an 11th-century papal decree granting it Holy Year status: pilgrims could receive a plenary indulgence – a full remission of your lifetime's sins – during a Holy Year. These occur when Santiago's feast day (25 July) falls on a Sunday: the next one is in 2021.

The 11th and 12th centuries marked the heyday of the pilgrimage. The Reformation was devastating for Catholic pilgrimages, and by the 19th century, the Camino had nearly died out. In its startling late 20th-century reanimation, which continues today, it's most popular as a personal and spiritual journey of discovery, rather than one necessarily motivated by religion.

## Routes

Of the many paths to Santiago, by far the most popular is, and was, the 770km-long Camino Francés, which crosses the Pyrenees from France and heads west. Waymarked with cheerful yellow arrows and scallop shells, the 'trail' is a mishmash of rural lanes, paved secondary roads and

Pilgrim at the Catedral de Santiago de Compostela (p542)

footpaths. It takes roughly two weeks to cycle or five weeks to walk.

But this is by no means the only route, and the summer crowds along the Camino Francés have prompted some to look for alternatives: in 2005, nearly 85% of walkers took the Camino Francés; by 2019 this had fallen to 55% and four additional routes or variations were added to the Camino de Santiago's Unesco World Heritage listing in 2015.

## Camino Francés

*5 weeks*

The ever-popular Camino Francés (French Way) runs from St-Jean Pied de Port in France, across Navarra, La Rioja, Castilla y León and Galicia to Santiago; many consider this to be the 'true' Camino. Along the way it traverses beautiful Pyrenean valleys, passes within sight of vineyards and crosses the *meseta,* the high-altitude plateau of Spain's interior, before crossing into Galicia. Highlights include cities such as Pamplona, Burgos and León, as well as quiet Castilian villages with fine sandstone churches, including Frómista, Villalcázar de Sirga and Sahagún.

More than half of all those who walk the Camino take this route, but only one person in five walks the whole distance. A popular shorter version is to walk only the last 114km from Sarria in Galicia. This is the last starting point that meets the minimum 100km requirement for receiving the official Compostela certificate of completion given out by the Catedral de Santiago de Compostela.

## Camino Portugués

*Around 3½ weeks*

From Lisbon (600km) or Porto (240km, 10 days) to Santiago, the Camino Portugués crosses the border into Spain at Tui, 115km before Santiago. The route is generally considered easier than most of the Spanish routes in terms of hills, but the amount of time spent walking on paved roads, hard pavements and cobblestones can be hard on feet and knees. Where the main Camino Portugués often heads inland, from Porto the alternative Camino Portugués de la Costa (Portuguese Coastal Way) more closely follows the Atlantic coast.

### Camino del Norte

*5 weeks*

From Irún, the Camino del Norte shadows the coasts of the Basque Country, Cantabria and Asturias to Ribadeo, then heads inland across Galicia to Santiago. Taken by around 20,000 people every year, the route was only lightly trammelled by pilgrims even in medieval times, and appeals to those seeking a quieter experience. The trail passes some spectacular coastal stretches and lovely hill country, especially early on in the Basque Country, but spends far more time crossing the interior. Highlights include San Sebastián, Bilbao, Santander, Comillas, Ribadesella, Luarca and Gijón.

### Camino Primitivo

*2 weeks*

The Camino Primitivo (Original Way) connects the Camino del Norte (from Oviedo) with the main Camino Francés. It's a lovely, if demanding walk through the green hills of Spain's north. Its name derives from the fact that this 320km route follows the footsteps of the first recorded pilgrimage to St James' tomb – made by king Alfonso II of Asturias from Oviedo in the 820s. Not many walkers take this route, which passes through Lugo, encircled by over 2km of Roman walls, then joins the Camino Francés at Melide for the final 55km to Santiago.

### Camino de Muxía-Finisterre

*4 to 6 days*

After finishing the Camino proper, some walkers and pilgrims continue beyond Santiago to the small fishing villages of Fisterra (Finisterre; Land's End) and Muxía, both 86km from Santiago and linked by a 28km trail. Wild, wind-battered cliffs and the Cabo Fisterra (Cape Finisterre) lighthouse make for dramatic scenery, but Muxía carries the strongest spiritual resonance: its 18th-century church marks the site where the Virgin Mary is believed to have appeared to Santiago (St James) in a stone boat.

### Camino Inglés

*5 days*

This short, relatively easy route within Galicia, known as the 'English Way', covers just 115km from Ferrol, north of Santiago. Its name derives from British and Irish pilgrims who would sail to Ferrol and other nearby ports in medieval times, then complete the pilgrimage from there. It's a good choice if time is tight and is growing in popularity, with around 15,000 yearly walkers. Among the highlights are the pretty coastal inlets and beautiful towns such as Pontedeume and Betanzos. You can also start in A Coruña, a two- to three-day walk into Santiago.

### Vía de la Plata

*5 to 6 weeks*

The longest of the main routes, the Vía de la Plata runs nearly 1000km from Seville, capital of Andalucía, to Santiago. Unlike most paths, distances between towns and villages (and therefore lodgings and

### PILGRIM HOSTELS

There are over 300 *albergues* or, as they're sometimes called, *refugios* (simple hostels) along the Camino Francés, and numerous *albergues* on the other routes. These are owned by parishes, 'friends of the Camino' associations, private individuals, town halls and regional governments. While in the early days these places were run on donations and provided little more than hot water and a bed, today's pilgrims are charged €6 to €12 for a bed in a multi-bed dorm. You can expect showers, kitchens and washing machines; some also have more expensive private rooms, some with private bathrooms. Most *albergues* are run by local or regional governments and operate, as they always have, on a first-come, first-served basis, intended for those doing the Camino solely under their own steam. However, an increasing number of *albergues* now accept advance reservations. For an idea of what's available on the various routes, www.alberguescaminosantiago.com is an excellent resource. In addition to the *albergues*, most towns along the Camino also have all the usual, privately run Spanish accommodation, including *hostales*, hotels and *casas rurales*.

sources of food) can be very long, some stages are monotonous, and the extreme heat from June to September on the southern half of the route can be positively dangerous. March, April, May and October are the best months to walk the Vía de la Plata. Despite its drawbacks, it's a great choice if you want to avoid crowds: only just over 2000 people a year make the full trip from Seville. The route's attractions include olive groves and vineyards, oak forests and historic cities such as Roman Mérida, medieval Cáceres, Renaissance Salamanca and Romanesque Zamora. The trail takes its name from the Roman road linking the important Roman cities of Mérida and Astorga.

### Other Camino Routes

In addition to the routes covered here, there are dozens of other established routes from all over Spain, from Portugal, France and even beyond.

Two that are often mentioned in relation to the Camino de Santiago are the **Camino Lebaniego** and the **Camino Vasco-Riojano**. The former runs from either Santander or San Vicente de la Barquera to the important Monasterio de Santo Toribio de Liébana in Cantabria; it's not actually a Camino de Santiago but is part of the Unesco listing nonetheless. The Camino Vasco-Riojano is an alternative start to the Camino Francés, beginning in Irún, but is really just a little-used way of reaching the Camino Francés from the Basque Country.

### ROCK CLIMBING

Spain offers plenty of opportunities to see the mountains and gorges from a more vertical perspective. Vie ferrate are growing fast in number and in popularity around the country. A good source of info is the excellent (but Spanish-only) site http://deandar.com.

For an overview of Spanish rock climbing, check out Rockfax (www.rockfax.com) and Climb Europe (www.climb-europe.com). Both include details on the country's best climbs. Rockfax also publishes various climbing guidebooks covering Spain.

## Information

For more information about the Credencial (like a passport for the Camino, in which pilgrims accumulate stamps at various points along the route) and the Compostella certificate, visit the website of the cathedral's Centro Internacional de Acogida al Peregrino (p552). Almost alongside the cathedral in Santiago, the Museo das Peregrinacións e de Santiago (p544) provides fascinating insights into the phenomenon of Santiago (man and city) down the centuries.

There are a number of excellent Camino websites:

**Camino de Santiago** (http://santiago-compostela.net) Extensive info on routes as well as maps.

**Camino de Santiago – Galicia** (www.caminodesantiago.gal) Useful resource for the Galicia sections of the Camino.

**Mundicamino** (www.mundicamino.com) Excellent, thorough descriptions and maps.

**Camino de Santiago** (www.caminodesantiago.me) Has a huge selection of news groups, where you can get all of your questions answered.

**Camino Forum** (http://caminodesantiago.me) Forum and an excellent resource.

**Trepidatious Traveller** (http://magwood.me) Terrific Camino blog by Maggie Woodward.

## When to Walk

People walk and cycle the Camino year-round. In May and June the wild flowers are glorious and the endless fields of cereals turn from green to toasty gold, making the landscapes a huge draw. July and August bring crowds of summer holidaymakers and scorching heat, especially through Castilla y León. September is less crowded and the weather is generally pleasant. From November to May there are fewer people on the road, as the weather can bring snow, rain and bitter winds. Santiago's feast day, 25 July, is a popular time to converge on the city.

Parque Natural de Somiedo (p524)



## National & Natural Parks

Much of Spain's most spectacular and ecologically important terrain – about 40,000 sq km or 8% of the entire country, if you include national hunting reserves – is under some kind of official protection. Most of these areas are at least partly open to walkers, naturalists and other outdoor enthusiasts, but degrees of conservation and access vary.

The *parques nacionales* (national parks) are areas of exceptional importance and are the country's most strictly controlled protected areas. Spain has 15 national parks: 10 on the mainland, four in the Canary Islands and one in the Balearic Islands. The hundreds of other protected areas fall into at least 16 classifications and range in size from 100-sq-metre rocks off the Balearics to Andalucía's 2099-sq-km Parque Natural Sierras de Cazorla. For more information, see p53 and visit www.mapama.gob.es/es/red-parques-nacionales/nuestros-parques.

## Cycling

Spain has a splendid variety of cycling possibilities, from gentle family rides to challenging two-week expeditions. If you avoid the cities (where cycling can be nerve-racking), Spain is also a cycle-friendly country, with drivers accustomed to sharing the roads with platoons of Lycra-clad cyclists. The excellent network of secondary roads is ideal for road touring.

### Cycling Destinations

Every Spanish region has both off-road (called BTT in Spanish, from *bici todo terreno,* meaning 'mountain bike') and touring trails and routes. Mountain bikers can head to just about any sierra (mountain range) and use the extensive *pistas forestales* (forestry tracks).

In Aragón, the valleys, hills and canyons of the Sobrarbe district around Aínsa in the Pyrenees foothills are a mountain-biking paradise, with nearly 1000km of off-road tracks, many of them waymarked for riders. Here, the Zona Zero (p416) project provides masses of information and brings

## SPAIN'S BEST PARKS

| PARK | FEATURES | ACTIVITIES | BEST TIME TO VISIT |
|---|---|---|---|
| **Parc Nacional d'Aigüestortes i Estany de Sant Maurici** (p361) | beautiful Pyrenees lake region | walking, wildlife-watching | Jun-Sep |
| **Parque Nacional de Doñana** (p644) | bird and mammal haven in Guadalquivir delta | 4WD tours, walking, wildlife-watching, horse riding | year-round |
| **Parque Nacional de Ordesa y Monte Perdido** (p411) | spectacular section of the Pyrenees, with chamois, raptors and varied vegetation | walking, rock climbing | mid-Jun–Jul & mid-Aug–Sep |
| **Parque Nacional de los Picos de Europa** (p526) | beautiful mountain refuge for chamois, and a few wolves and bears | walking, rock climbing | May-Jul & Sep |
| **Parques Nacional & Natural Sierra Nevada** (p721) | mainland Spain's highest mountain range, with ibexes, 60 types of endemic plants and the beautiful Alpujarras valleys on its southern slopes | walking, rock climbing, mountain biking, skiing, horse riding | year-round, depending on activity |
| **Parque Natural Sierras de Cazorla, Segura y Las Villas** (p761) | abundant wildlife, 2300 plant species and beautiful mountain scenery | walking, driving, mountain biking, wildlife-watching, 4WD tours | Apr-Oct |
| **Parque Natural Sierra de Aracena y Picos de Aroche** | rolling, lightly wooded hill country, stone villages | hiking | year-round |
| **Áreas Naturales Serra de Tramuntana** | spectacular mountain range on Mallorca | walking, birdwatching | late Feb-early Oct |
| **Parque Nacional de Monfragüe** (p603) | spectacular birds of prey | birdwatching | Mar-Oct |
| **Parque Natural Sierra de Grazalema** (p668) | lovely, green, mountainous area with rich birdlife | walking, caving, canyoning, birdwatching, paragliding, rock climbing | Sep-Jun |
| **Parc Natural Cadí-Moixeró** (p358) | steep pre-Pyrenees range | rock climbing, walking | Jun-Sep |
| **Parc Natural de la Zona Volcànica de la Garrotxa** (p352) | beautiful wooded region with 30 volcanic cones | walking | Apr-Oct |
| **Parque Natural Sierra de Gredos** | beautiful mountain region, home to Spain's biggest ibex population | walking, rock climbing, mountain biking | Mar-May & Sep-Nov |
| **Parque Natural de Somiedo** (p524) | dramatic section of Cordillera Cantábrica | walking | Jul-Sep |
| **Parque Natural de Cabo de Gata-Níjar** (p768) | sandy beaches, volcanic cliffs, flamingo colony and semi-desert vegetation | swimming, birdwatching, walking, horse riding, diving, snorkelling | year-round |
| **Parque Natural de los Valles Occidentales** | superb Pyrenean valley and mountain scenery | walking, climbing, canyoning | Jun-Sep |
| **Parque Natural Posets-Maladeta** (p418) | spectacular mountain and valley scenery including the Pyrenees' two highest peaks | walking, climbing | Jun-Sep |
| **Valles de Hecho & Ansó** (p403) | superb Pyrenean valley and mountain scenery | walking, climbing, canyoning | Jun-Sep |

together service providers such as bike-friendly accommodation, repair shops, guides and bike-transport services. Most riders bring their own bikes, but there are a couple of rental outlets in Aínsa. Another increasingly popular BTT in Aragón is Benasque-Castejón de Sos.

Galicia has set up several Centros BTT in rural areas, with bikes and helmets for rent and signposted routes in the local areas, including one in the very scenic Ribeira Sacra region. For more information, check www.turismo.gal/que-facer/centros-btt.

One highly recommended and challenging off-road excursion takes you across Andalucía's snowy Sierra Nevada. Classic long-haul touring routes include the Camino de Santiago, the Ruta de la Plata and the 600km Camino del Cid, which follows in the footsteps of Spain's epic hero, El Cid, from Burgos to Valencia. Guides in Spanish exist for all of these, available at bookshops and online.

For something a little less challenging, head to the Senda del Oso, a popular, easy cycling route in Asturias. Mallorca is another popular destination, with cyclists ranging from ordinary travellers to Bradley Wiggins, 2012 Tour de France winner, who trained on the mountain roads of the Serra de Tramuntana.

## Information

Bike Spain (p111) in Madrid is one of the better cycling tour operators.

For hotels providing bike storage, workshop and bike-washing areas, as well as cycling routes, visit http://bikefriendly.es.

Events called Marchas Cicloturistas (known as Gran Fondos or sportives in English-speaking countries) are hugely popular. These are organised mass-participation road-cycling events. There are loads of them around the country; check http://laguiadelciclismo.com/marchas-cicloturistas or http://triatletasenred.sport.es/actualidad/mejores-cicloturistas.

Most cycling guidebooks are in Spanish:

- *España en bici* (Paco Tortosa & María del Mar Fornés) A good overview, but quite hard to find.
- *Cycle Touring in Spain: Eight Detailed Routes* (Harry Dowdell) A helpful planning tool; also practical once you're in Spain.
- *The Trailrider Guide – Spain: Single Track Mountain Biking in Spain* (Nathan James & Linsey Stroud) Another good resource.

### VÍAS VERDES

Spain has a growing network of Vías Verdes (literally 'Green Ways', equivalent to the 'rail trail' system in other countries), an outstanding system of decommissioned railway tracks converted into bicycle (or hiking) trails. They're terrific cycling routes with gentle gradients, many pass through scenic countryside and there are bikes for rent along the routes. There are over 2400km of trail spread across 111 routes throughout Spain, ranging from 1.2km to 128km. Check out www.viasverdes.com.

# Skiing & Snowboarding

For winter powder, Spain's skiers (including the royal family) head to the Pyrenees of Aragón and Catalonia. Outside the peak periods (the beginning of December, 20 December to 6 January, Carnaval and Semana Santa), Spain's top resorts are relatively quiet, cheap and warm in comparison with their counterparts in the Alps.

The season runs from December to April, though January and February are generally the best, most reliable times for snow. However, in recent years snowfall has been a bit unpredictable.

## Skiing & Snowboarding Destinations

In Aragón, two popular resorts are Formigal (p410) and Candanchú (p412). Just above the town of Jaca, Candanchú has some 60km of runs with various pistes (as well as 35km of cross-country track) and 25 lifts. In Catalonia, Spain's first resort, La Molina (p358), is still going strong and is ideal for families and beginners. Considered by many to have the Pyrenees' best snow, the 72-piste resort of Baqueira-Beret-Bonaigua (p366) boasts 30 modern lifts and 104km of downhill runs for all levels. Nearby Masella (p358) is another fine resort, linked to La Molina by a lift. **Espot** (☎973 62 40 58; www.espotesqui.cat; day pass adult/child €32/26; ⊙Dec-Mar) and Núria (p355) are two smaller Catalan resorts.

WESTEND61/GETTY IMAGES ©

Skiing, Sierra Nevada (p721)

Spain's other major resort is Europe's southernmost: the Sierra Nevada (p721), outside Granada. The 106km of runs here are at their prime in March, and the slopes are particularly suited for families and novice-to-intermediate skiers.

## Surfing

Spain has good surfing for beginners and experienced surfers alike. The north coast has what many claim to be the best surf in mainland Europe, but Atlantic Andalucía also gets decent winter swells. Despite the flow of vans loaded with surfboards along the north coast in the summer, it's actually autumn through to spring that's the prime time for a decent swell, with October probably the best month overall. The variety of waves along the north coast is impressive: there are numerous open, swell-exposed beach breaks for the summer months, and some seriously heavy reefs and points that only come to life during the colder, stormier months.

### Surfing Destinations

The most famous wave in Spain is the legendary river-mouth left at Mundaka (p445). On a good day, there's no doubt that it's one of the best waves in Europe. However, it's not very consistent, and when it's on, it's always very busy and very ugly.

Heading east, good waves can be found throughout the Basque Country. Going west, into neighbouring regions of Cantabria and Asturias, you'll also find a superb range of well-charted surf beaches, such as Rodiles (p516) in Asturias and Liencres in Cantabria; Playa de Somo (p493) in Santander is another good spot.

Galicia's beaches are an increasingly popular surfing destination. Even so, if you're looking for solitude, some isolated beaches along Galicia's beautiful Costa da Morte (p553) remain empty even in summer. In the Rías Altas, Praia de Pantín (p563), close to Cedeira, has a popular right-hander and in late August or early September it hosts the Pantín Classic, a qualifying event in the World Surf League. There are also some summer surf schools in the area.

Southwest Andalucía has a number of powerful winter beach breaks, particularly between Tarifa and Cádiz. El Palmar (674), just northwest of Cabo de Trafalgar, is the pick of the bunch, while weekdays off Conil de la Frontera, a little further up the coast, can be sublimely lonely.

### Information

In summer a short wetsuit (or, in the Basque Country, board shorts) is sufficient except in Galicia, which picks up the icy Canaries current; you'll need a light full suit here.

Surf shops abound in the popular surfing areas and usually offer board and wetsuit hire. If you're a beginner joining a surf school, ask the instructor to explain the rules and to keep you away from the more experienced surfers.

There are a number of excellent surf guidebooks to Spain.

➡ Lonely Planet author Stuart Butler's English-language *Big Blue Surf Guide: Spain*.

➡ José Pellón's Spanish-language *Guía del Surf en España*.

➡ Low Pressure's superb *Stormrider Guide: Europe – the Continent*.

## Plan Your Trip

# Family Travel

Spain is a family-friendly destination with excellent transport and accommodation infrastructure, food to satisfy even the fussiest of eaters, and an extraordinary range of attractions that appeal to both adults and children. Visiting as a family does require careful planning, but no more than for visiting any other European country.

## Children Will Love...

Spain has a surfeit of castles, horse shows, ferias, interactive museums and even the Semana Santa (Holy Week) processions, to name just a few highlights for kids. Many of Spain's beaches, especially on the Mediterranean coast, are custom-made for children, sheltered from the open ocean by protective coves. Elsewhere, some of Spain's signature buildings look as if they emerged from some childhood fantasy, there are theme parks aplenty, and then there's live flamenco, something that every child should see once.

### Beaches

**Playa de la Concha, San Sebastián** (p448) Spain's most easily accessible city beach.

**Aiguablava & Fornells** (p330) Sheltered, beautiful Costa Brava coves.

**Cala Sant Vicenç** Four of Mallorca's loveliest cove beaches.

**Menorca** (p786) Quiet north-coast beaches, even in summer.

**Zahara de los Atunes** (p6745) Cádiz-province beach with pristine sand.

### Architecture

**Alcázar, Segovia** (p161) The inspiration for Sleeping Beauty's castle.

**Park Güell** (p267) Gaudí's weird and wonderful Barcelona creation.

**Castillo de Loarre, Aragón** (p4051) Classic turreted castle.

## Keeping Costs Down

### Public Transport

Discounts are available for children (usually under 12) on public transport. Those under four generally go free.

### Sights

Child concessions (and family rates) often apply to tours, admission fees, accommodation and transport, with some discounts as high as 50% off the adult rate. However, the definition of 'child' varies between under five years, 12 years or 18 years, so always check. Even those that don't offer discounted entry usually have a day, or time of the day, when entry is free for everyone, which is especially good value for families.

### Car Safety Seats

Ideally bring your own child safety seats rather than pay hire fees.

### Eating Out

A small but growing number of restaurants offer a *menú infantil* (children's menu), which usually includes a main course (hamburger, chicken nuggets, pasta and the like), a drink and an ice cream or milkshake for dessert.

**Camp Nou, Barcelona** (p314) Football, football, football...

**Museo Guggenheim Bilbao** (p430) Watch them gaze in wonder.

### Theme Parks & Horse Shows

**Terra Mítica, Benidorm** (p834) The spirit of spangly American theme parks comes to the Med.

**Oasys Mini Hollywood, Almería** (p767) Wild West movie sets in the deserts.

**Parc d'Atraccions Tibidabo, Barcelona** (p280) Great rides and a puppet museum.

### Live Shows

**Real Escuela Andaluza del Arte Ecuestre** (p661) Andalucian horse shows in all their finery.

**Caballerizas Reales** (p689) Another excellent horse show, this time in Córdoba.

**Casa de la Memoria** (p637) Live flamenco at its spine-tingling best in Seville.

**Estadio Santiago Bernabéu** (p107) Soak up the atmosphere at a Real Madrid game.

**Casa Patas** (p133) Watch live flamenco in Madrid, with flamenco classes a possibility.

## Region by Region

### Madrid & Around

A big city, but playgrounds lie scattered across town, the Parque del Buen Retiro (p91) is a wonderful, expansive city park and there's everything from live flamenco to football, with terrific, interactive museums.

### Castilla y León

Attractions include evocative hilltop castles – such as Segovia's Alcázar (p161), which inspired Disneyland's Sleeping Beauty castle – Astorga's chocolate museum, and even the chance to see wolves.

### Toledo & Castilla-La Mancha

Castles and echoes of *Don Quijote* (there are children's versions of Cervantes' novel) lie at the heart of this region's appeal (p203).

### Barcelona

Theme parks, a wax museum, a chocolate museum, all manner of other museums with interactive exhibits, beaches, gardens... Barcelona (p237) is one of Spain's most child-friendly cities – even its architecture seems to have been imagined by a child.

### Catalonia

Sheltered beaches all along the Costa Brava (p325), Roman ruins at Tarragona and hiking trails to suit all ages in the Pyrenees make this an excellent region to explore.

### Aragón

Compact region with good hiking in the Pyrenean mountains and gentler foothills. Zaragoza (p390) has good museums, child-friendly food and is easy to cover on foot.

### Basque Country, Navarra & La Rioja

Great food (kids should try *pintxos* in San Sebastián), excellent museums such as Bilbao's Museo Guggenheim (p430) and plenty of beaches should keep everyone happy.

### Cantabria & Asturias

Beaches are the main attraction here, as they're generally quite sheltered and don't suffer the Mediterranean crowds. The cave paintings at Altamira (p501) and family-friendly cities and food are also features.

### Santiago de Compostela & Galicia

Galician food can be particularly child-friendly, there are Roman ruins in Lugo (p584), and beaches here are far less busy than elsewhere in Spain; the flip side is that Atlantic waves hit many with full force.

### Extremadura

Extremadura has few child-centric attractions, but does have its share of castles and Roman ruins, the Parque Nacional de Monfragüe (p605) with wildlife and manageable walking trails, and deserted Granadilla.

### Seville & Andalucía's Hill Towns

Seville has numerous child-friendly attractions and playgrounds and is manageable on foot. There are beaches along the south coast, and Parque Nacional de Doñana (p644) is good for animals. Avoid July and August for the heat.

### Granada & South Coast Andalucía

Ski in the Sierra Nevada (p721), swim in the Mediterranean. Although you could manage this all in one day, there's no rush. Most cities have plenty to entertain the kids.

## Balearic Islands

With so many resorts and a history of catering to families from across Europe, the islands of Ibiza, Menorca and especially Mallorca (p775) are child-friendly in every sense, from calm beaches to family resorts.

## Valencia & Murcia

Valencia is a lovely city for families, with great food, plenty of parks and a world-class aquarium (p808). Both here and in Murcia, expect busy but beautiful beaches.

# Good to Know

Look out for the 👪 icon for family-friendly suggestions throughout this guide.

**Hotel cots** Most hotels (but rarely budget places) have cots, although most only have a handful, so reserve one when booking your room. If requesting a *cuna* (cot), ask for a larger room. Cots sometimes cost extra; other hotels offer them for free.

**Babysitting** In top-end hotels you can sometimes arrange childcare, and in some places child-minding agencies cater to temporary visitors.

**Playgrounds** Most towns and some top-end hotels have children's play areas and/or swimming pools.

**Emergency supplies** Spain is likely to have everything you need, but bring a small supply of items you're used to having back home in case (eg for Sundays, when most pharmacies are closed).

**High chairs** You cannot rely on restaurants having *tronas* (high chairs), although many do.

**Nappy-changing facilities** Very few restaurants or other public places have nappy-changing facilities.

**Eating hours** One challenge can be adapting to Spanish eating hours – when kids get hungry between meals, zip into the nearest tapas bar or supermarket; carry emergency snack supplies for those times when there's simply nothing open.

# Useful Resources

**Lonely Planet Kids** (www.lonelyplanetkids.com) Loads of activities and family travel blog content.

**Book: First Words Spanish** (shop.lonelyplanet.com) A beautifully illustrated introduction to the Spanish language for ages five to eight.

**Spain Family Travel Guide** (https://tsatraveltips.us/spain-family-travel-guide) High-level overview for families visiting Spain

**National Geographic Kids** (https://kids.nationalgeographic.com/geography/countries/article/spain) Fun facts about Spain and its environment.

# Kids' Corner

## Say What?

| | |
|---|---|
| **Hello.** | Hola. o·la |
| **Goodbye.** | Adiós. a·*dyos*. |
| **Thank you.** | Gracias. *gra*·thyas |
| **My name is...** | Me llamo... me *lya*·mo... |

## Did You Know?

- It's not the Tooth Fairy who visits when you lose a tooth here. It's a mouse called Ratoncito Pérez.

## Have You Tried?

**Caracoles**
Snails

# Regions at a Glance

## Madrid & Around

Art
Nightlife
Food

### Art's Golden Mile

Madrid is among the world's premier cities for public art, with the Museo del Prado, the Centro de Arte Reina Sofía and the Museo Thyssen-Bornemisza all within easy walking distance of each other. And they're just the beginning.

### Killing the Night

Nightclubs that don't really get going until 3am. Sophisticated cocktail bars where you mingle with A-list celebrities while sipping your mojito. A dynamic live-music scene that starts with flamenco, moves on to jazz and showcases every genre imaginable. Welcome to one of Europe's nightlife capitals.

### Tapas & Traditional Food

The world's oldest restaurant and the best in regional Spanish cooking make for memorable eating experiences, even if traditional Madrid food is nothing to get excited about. La Latina has one of the country's finest concentrations of tapas bars, but Chamberí is fast catching up.

p67

## Castilla y León

Medieval Towns
Villages
Food

### City as Art

Rich in history, cathedrals and other grand public monuments, the splendid towns of old Castilla can be difficult to choose between. But if we must, it would be plateresque Salamanca, fairy-tale Segovia and gorgeous León.

### Quiet Pueblos

The *pueblos* (villages) of Castilla y León feel like Spain before mass tourism and the modern world arrived on Iberian shores: from the Sierra de Francia in the far southwest to medieval hamlets such as Pedraza de la Sierra, Covarrubias, Puebla de Sanabria and Calatañazor.

### Hearty Inland Fare

Roasted and grilled meats are specialities in the Spanish interior; Spaniards travel here from all over the country for a winter meal. *Jamón* (cured ham) and other cured meats from Guijuelo are another regional passion.

p147

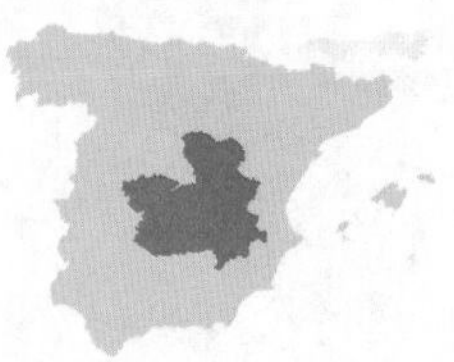

## Toledo & Castilla-La Mancha

History
Literature
Villages & Castles

### City of Three Faiths

In the Middle Ages, Toledo was one of the most cosmopolitan cities in Spain, as shown by its evocative mosque, fine Jewish sites and a cathedral of real power adorned with works by El Greco, Zurbarán and Velázquez.

### Tilting at Windmills

The Don Quijote trail through Castilla-La Mancha offers the rare opportunity to follow the terrain trod by one of literature's most eccentric figures. Windmills and sweeping plains evoke Cervantes' novel to such an extent that you can almost hear Sancho Panza's patter.

### Beautiful Villages

Amid the often-empty horizons of La Mancha, pretty villages can seem like oases. Almagro and Sigüenza are our favourites, while the castles close to Toledo – this was a long-time frontier between Moorish and Christian Spain – are simply magnificent.

p203

## Barcelona

Architecture
Food
Art & History

### Modernista Masterpieces

From Gaudí's unfinished masterpiece – the wondrous Sagrada Família – to Domènech i Montaner's celestial Palau de la Música Catalana, Catalan visionaries have made Barcelona one of Europe's great Modernista centres, a showcase for the imaginative, surreal and captivating.

### Culinary Gems

Barcelona's artistry doesn't end at the drawing board. Feasting on seafood overlooking the Mediterranean, enjoying tapas at the magnificent Boqueria market, indulging in celebrated Michelin-starred restaurants – it's all essential to the Barcelona experience.

### Artistry of the Past

A once-vibrant settlement of ancient Rome, Barcelona has over 2000 years of history hidden in its old lanes. The old Gothic centre has 14th-century churches and medieval mansions that hold more recent treasures, from a sprawling Picasso collection to pre-Columbian masterpieces.

p237

## Catalonia & the Costa Brava

Food
Beaches
Hiking

### The Catalan Kitchen

Vying with the Basque Country for Spain's highest per-capita ratio of celebrity chefs, Catalonia is something of a pilgrimage for gastronomes. Here, even in the smallest family establishments, cooks fuse ingredients from land and sea, always keeping faith with rich culinary traditions even as they head off in exciting new directions.

### The Catalan Coast

The picturesque coastlines known as the Costa Brava and Costa Daurada are studded with postcard-pretty villages and beaches that are generally less crowded than those further south. And not far away, signposts to Salvador Dalí and the Romans make for fine day trips.

### Spain's High Country

Northern Catalonia means the Pyrenees, where shapely peaks and quiet valleys offer some of the best hiking anywhere in the country.

p323

## Aragón

**Mountains**
**Villages**
**History**

### Head for the Hills

Perhaps the prettiest corner of the Pyrenees, northern Aragón combines the drama of steepling summits with the quiet pleasures of deep valleys and endless hiking trails. The Parque Nacional de Ordesa y Monte Perdido ranks among Spain's most picturesque national parks.

### Stone Villages

Aragón has numerous finalists in the competition for Spain's most beautiful village, among them Aínsa, Sos del Rey Católico and Albarracín. Many sit in the Pyrenean foothills against a backdrop of snowcapped mountains.

### Romans, Moors & Christians

Centred on one of Spain's most important historical kingdoms, Aragón is strewn with landmarks from the great civilisations of ancient and medieval times. Zaragoza in particular spans the millennia with grace and fervour, and Teruel is an often-missed Mudéjar jewel.

p389

## Basque Country, Navarra & La Rioja

**Food**
**Wine**
**Villages**

### Spain's Culinary Capital

To understand the buzz surrounding Spanish food, head for San Sebastián, which is at once *pintxos* (Basque tapas) heaven and home to outrageously talented chefs. Not far behind are Bilbao, Logroño, Vitoria and Pamplona.

### The Finest Drop

La Rioja is to wine what the Basque Country is to food. Wine museums, wine tastings and vineyards stretching to the horizon make this Spain's most accessible wine region. And, of course, *vino* accompanies every meal here.

### Pretty Pueblos

There are stunning villages to be found throughout the Basque Country and La Rioja, but those in the Pyrenean foothills and high valleys of Navarra are a match for anything the rest of Spain has to offer.

p429

## Cantabria & Asturias

**Coastal Scenery**
**Mountains**
**Food & Drink**

### The Scenic Coast

Wild, rocky walls encircle a beautiful sandy cove at Playa del Silencio, just one of hundreds of beaches tucked away along the rugged, emerald-green Asturian coastline, behind which rise gorgeous villages and marvellous mountainscapes.

### Picos de Europa

The jagged Picos de Europa have some of the most stunning hiking country in Spain. Vertiginous precipices stretch down into the dramatic Garganta del Cares gorge, while the Naranjo de Bulnes peak beckons from beyond high mountain passes.

### Cheese & Cider

Knocking back cider is Asturias' favourite pastime, particularly along Oviedo's *el bulevar de la sidra,* while the tangy Cabrales cheese from the foothills of the Picos de Europa is one of Spain's best.

p489

## Santiago de Compostela & Galicia

**Coastal Scenery**
**Food**
**History**

### The Wildest Coast

Galicia's stunningly beautiful, windswept coast is one of Europe's most dramatic. On the Rías Altas, cliffs plunge from enormous heights into roiling Atlantic waters, interspersed with picturesque fishing villages and isolated sandy beaches.

### Fruits of the Sea

Galicia has some of the world's best seafood. Head to Santiago de Compostela's bustling market, the Mercado de Abastos, for some of the freshest seafood in Spain – and the chance to enjoy it at restaurants on the spot.

### A Sacred Past

In few places are long-gone centuries as alive as they are in Santiago de Compostela. Its magnificent cathedral, churches, streets and plazas represent 1300 uninterrupted years as the goal of that great pilgrimage route, the Camino de Santiago.

p539

## Extremadura

**Medieval Towns**
**Roman Ruins**
**Food**

### Medieval Film Sets

Spain may be replete with wonderfully preserved old towns that date back to the Middle Ages, but Cáceres and Trujillo are up there with the best. Meandering their cobblestoned lanes is a journey back into an epic past.

### Roman Mérida

Spain's most beautiful Roman theatre, its longest Roman-era bridge, a breathtaking museum and a slew of other ruined glories – welcome to Emerita Augusta, now known as Mérida and Spain's finest Roman site. Nearby, little-known Medellín, and the fabulous bridge at Alcántara, also merit a visit.

### Ham & Cheese

Some of Spain's finest *jamón* comes from Extremadura, most notably from around Monesterio, which has Spain's best *jamón* museum. The Torta del Casar cheese from just north of Cáceres is another culinary star.

p587

## Seville & Andalucía's Hill Towns

**Music**
**History & Architecture**
**Food & Wine**

### Cradle of Flamenco

The towns and cities of western Andalucía pretty much invented modern flamenco. Look no further than the *bulerías* of Jerez, Cádiz' *alegrías* and Seville's *soleares* – songs performed with passion in local *tablaos* (choreographed flamenco shows) and *peñas* (flamenco clubs).

### White Towns

They're all here, Spain's famous *pueblos blancos,* with their ruined hilltop castles, geranium-filled flower boxes and small somnolent churches. Arcos, Jimena, Grazalema, Vejer...the ancient sentinels on a once-volatile frontier that divided two great civilisations.

### Fish & Sherry

Where the Atlantic meets the Mediterranean you're bound to find good fish, which the Andalucians traditionally (but lightly) deep-fry in olive oil to create *pescaíto frito.* Then there's the sherry made from grapes that grow near the coast – a perfect pairing.

p615

## Granada & South Coast Andalucía

Architecture
Beaches
Walks

### Hybrid Granada

La Alhambra, the celebrated Nasrid palace-fortress, a hilltop Moorish quarter, opulent *cármenes* (large mansions with walled gardens), and a baroque-Renaissance cathedral – the city of Granada is a magnificent collection of just about every architectural style known to European building.

### Southern Beaches

The south coast's beaches are an industry, bagging more tourist euros than the rest of the region put together. Choose according to your budget and hipster rating between Estepona, Marbella, Torremolinos, Málaga, Nerja and Almuñécar.

### Wild Areas

Walk the dry, craggy coastline of Cabo de Gata, hook onto the GR7 long-distance footpath in Las Alpujarras or get lost looking for wildlife on the trails in the highlands east of Cazorla. Andalucía has its untamed side, if you know where to look.

p697

## Balearic Islands

Beaches
Walking & Water Sports
Nightlife

### Coastal Bliss

White sand, black sand, pebbles or rocky inlets: each of the islands offers variety with (in general) fine sand on their southern shores and rougher stuff to the north.

### Outdoor Adventure

Watery fun – sailing, windsurfing, diving or simply splashing about in all the major coastal resorts – is the most popular activity, but the Balearics are also fine trekking and cycling destinations, particularly along the Serra de Tramuntana, Mallorca's wild, craggy north.

### Through the Night

It's not only the mega-venues of Ibiza that pound until dawn. In season, Ciutadella, on Menorca, draws in clubbers from all over the island; Palma de Mallorca is the big draw for locals on Mallorca; and the smaller music bars of diminutive Formentera hold their own.

p773

## Valencia & Murcia

Fiestas
Food
Beaches

### Bulls, Fire & Knights in Armour

The biggest and noisiest party is Valencia's Las Fallas in March. But almost every *pueblo* has its fiesta, usually with fireworks and often with bulls. Lorca's Semana Santa (Holy Week) festivities rival those of Andalucía.

### Simmering Rice

Paella first simmered over an open fire in Valencia. Rice dishes are everywhere, supplemented by fish and seafood from the Mediterranean and the freshest of vegetables grown along the fertile coastal strip down into Murcia.

### Strands & Rocky Coves

From small bays to vast beaches stretching over kilometres, from tiny rocky coves to the sandy sweeps of Denia, Benidorm and Murcia's Costa Cálida (Hot Coast), there's always room to stretch out your towel.

p803

# On the Road

Cantabria & Asturias
p489
Santiago de Compostela & Galicia
p539
Basque Country, Navarra & La Rioja
p429
Catalonia & the Costa Brava
p323
Castilla y León
p147
Aragón
p389
Barcelona
p237
Madrid & Around
p67
Balearic Islands
p773
Toledo & Castilla-La Mancha
p203
Extremadura
p587
Valencia & Murcia
p803
Seville & Andalucía's Hill Towns
p615
Granada & South Coast Andalucía
p697

## AT A GLANCE

**POPULATION**
3.27 million

**OLDEST TREE**
Mexican conifer (p98) in the Parque del Buen Retiro, planted in 1633

**BEST ROOFTOP BAR**
La Terraza del Urban (p128)

**BEST FLAMENCO**
Corral de la Morería (p132)

**BEST ROOMS WITH A VIEW**
ApartoSuites Jardines de Sabatini (p112)

**WHEN TO GO**

**Jan–Feb** Winter can be cold but glorious in Madrid when the weather's fine.

**Apr–May** Warmer spring weather brings *madrileños* (residents of Madrid) out into the city's *terrazas*.

**Sep–Oct** Madrid shakes off its summer torpor with (usually) lovely autumn weather.

Gran Vía (p105)
SEANPAVONEPHOTO/GETTY IMAGES

# Madrid & Around

Madrid is a miracle of human energy and peculiarly Spanish passions, an irresistible place with a simple message: this city knows how to live. It's true Madrid doesn't have the immediate cachet of Paris, the monumental history of Rome or the reputation for cool of that other city just up the road. But it's a place whose contradictory impulses are legion, the perfect expression of Europe's most passionate country writ large. This city has transformed itself into one of Spain's premier style centres and its calling cards are many: astonishing art galleries, relentless nightlife, an exceptional live-music scene, a feast of fine restaurants and tapas bars, and a population that's mastered the art of the good life. It's not that other cities don't have these things: it's just that Madrid has all of them, and in bucketloads.

**INCLUDES**

# Madrid & Around Highlights

**1 Museo del Prado** (p92) Watching the masterpieces of Velázquez and Goya leap off the canvas at the world-famous gallery.

**2 El Rastro** (p82) Searching for treasure in this massive Sunday flea market, then joining the crowds in Parque del Buen Retiro.

**3 Plaza de Santa Ana** (p86) Soaking up the buzz with a *caña* (small beer) or glass of Spanish wine on this gorgeous square.

**4 Calle de Ponzano** (p120) Going on a tapas, wine and craft-beer crawl along Madrid's most happening street, in Chamberí.

**5 Chocolatería de San Ginés** (p126) Ordering *chocolate con churros* (deep-fried doughnut strips dipped in hot chocolate) close to dawn.

**6 Estadio Santiago Bernabéu** (p134) Making a sporting pilgrimage to see the stars of Real Madrid play.

**7 Mercado de San Miguel** (p116) Immersing yourself in the buzz of bars and tapas in the heart of town.

**8 Café de la Iberia** (p144) Feasting on roast lamb in utterly charming Chinchón.

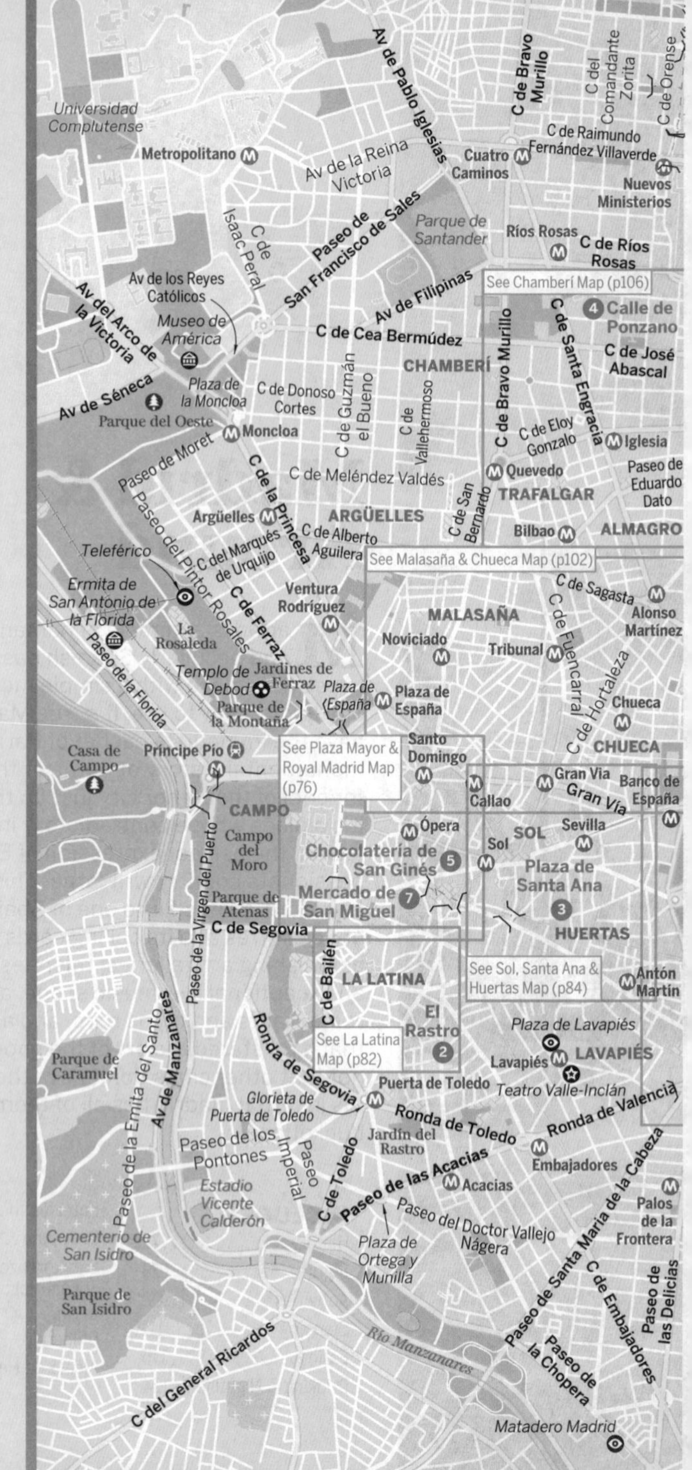

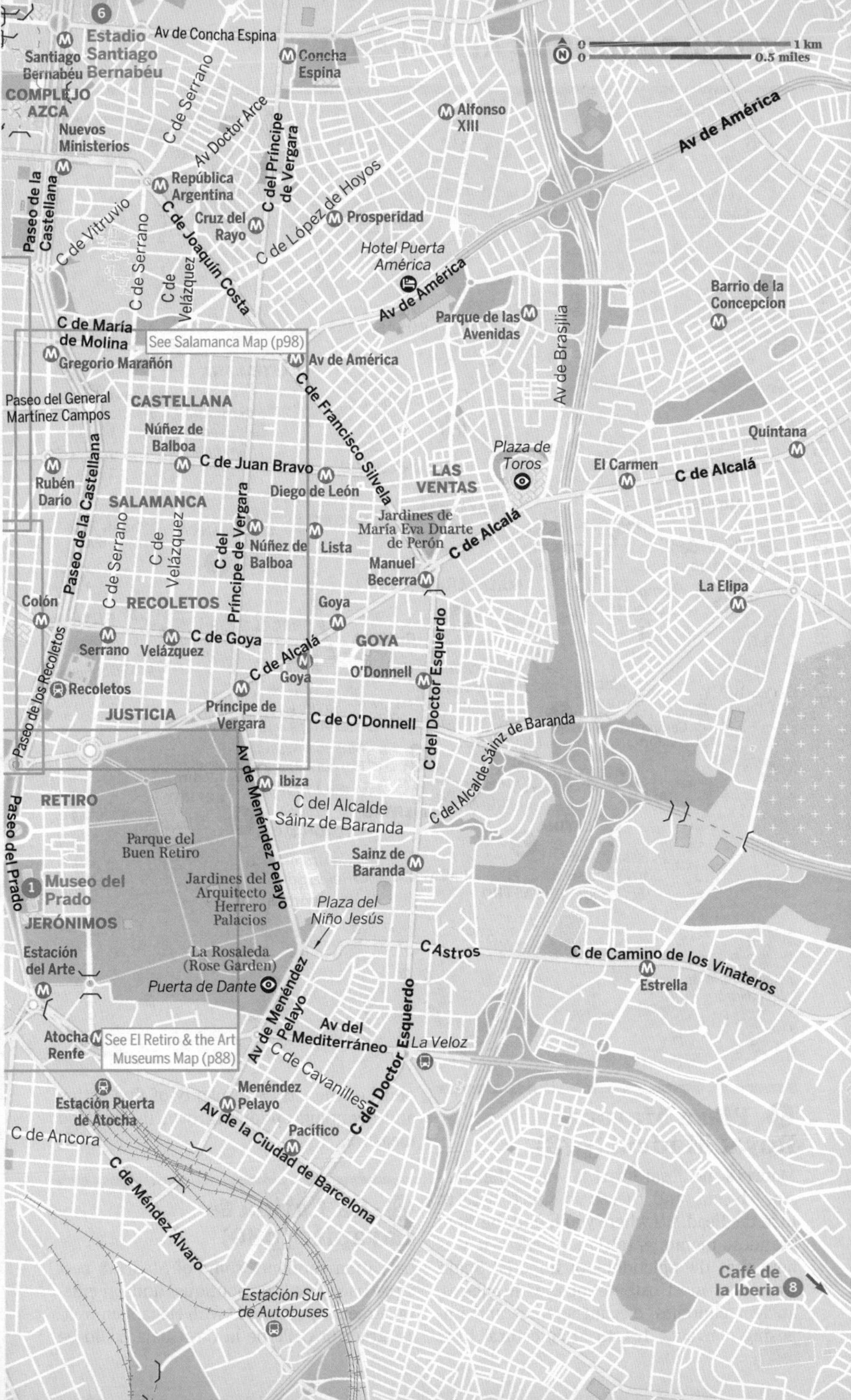

6
Estadio Santiago Bernabéu
Av de Concha Espina
Santiago Bernabéu
Concha Espina
COMPLEJO AZCA
Nuevos Ministerios
Alfonso XIII
Av de América
República Argentina
Cruz del Rayo
Prosperidad
Hotel Puerta América
Paseo de la Castellana
C de Serrano
Av Doctor Arce
C del Príncipe de Vergara
C de López de Hoyos
C de Vitruvio
C de Joaquín Costa
C de Velázquez
Barrio de la Concepcion
Parque de las Avenidas
Av de Brasilia
C de María de Molina
See Salamanca Map (p98)
Gregorio Marañón
Av de América
Paseo del General Martínez Campos
CASTELLANA
C de Francisco Silvela
Núñez de Balboa
C de Juan Bravo
Plaza de Toros
Quintana
LAS VENTAS
El Carmen
C de Alcalá
Rubén Darío
Diego de León
SALAMANCA
Jardines de María Eva Duarte de Perón
Núñez de Balboa
Lista
Manuel Becerra
La Elipa
Colón
RECOLETOS
Goya
C de Goya
Serrano
Velázquez
GOYA
Goya
O'Donnell
Paseo de los Recoletos
Recoletos
JUSTICIA
Príncipe de Vergara
C de O'Donnell
C del Doctor Esquerdo
C del Alcalde Sáinz de Baranda
Ibiza
RETIRO
Av de Menéndez Pelayo
Paseo del Prado
Parque del Buen Retiro
Sainz de Baranda
1
Museo del Prado
Jardines del Arquitecto Herrero Palacios
Plaza del Niño Jesús
JERÓNIMOS
C Astros
C de Camino de los Vinateros
Estación del Arte
La Rosaleda (Rose Garden)
Estrella
Puerta de Dante
Av del Mediterráneo
Atocha Renfe
See El Retiro & the Art Museums Map (p88)
La Veloz
C de Cavanilles
Estación Puerta de Atocha
Menéndez Pelayo
C de Ancora
Av de la Ciudad de Barcelona
Pacífico
C de Méndez Álvaro
Café de la Iberia
8
Estación Sur de Autobuses
0
1 km
0
0.5 miles

# NEIGHBOURHOODS AT A GLANCE

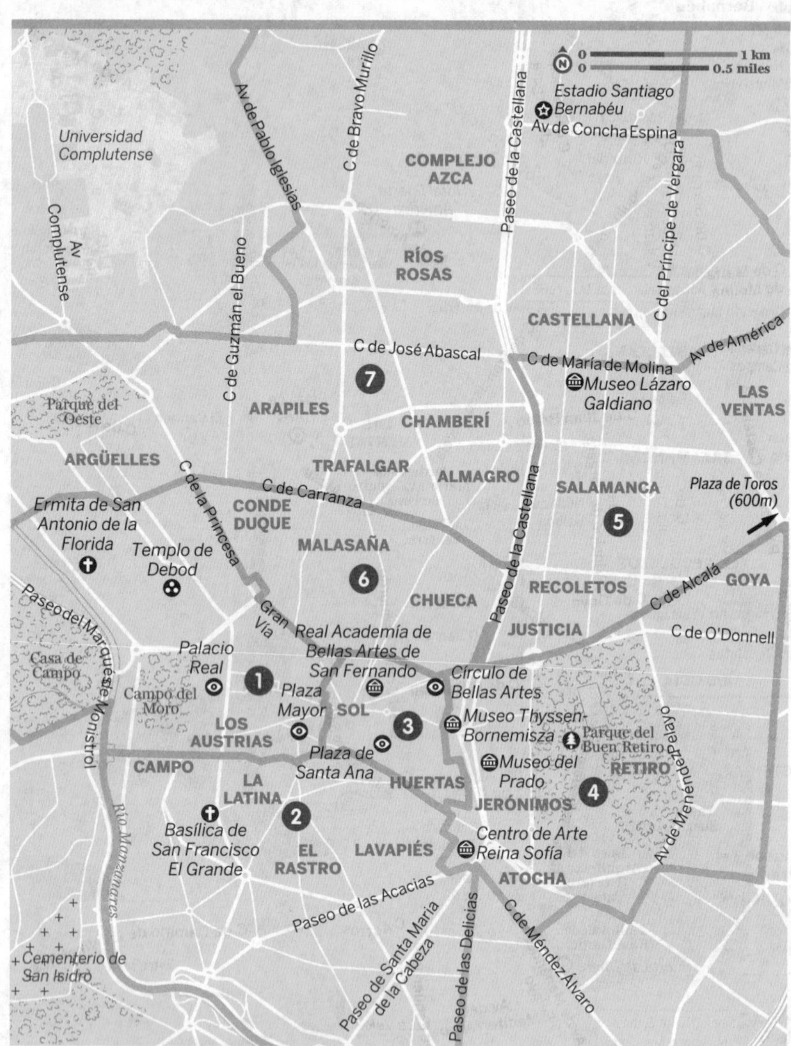


## ❶ Plaza Mayor & Royal Madrid (p73)

Madrid's medieval heart is where the city's story began, and there's so much here to turn the head. It's where you'll find the city's grandest monumental landmarks – it was here that the splendour of imperial Spain was at its most ostentatious, with palaces, ancient churches, elegant squares and imposing convents. It's an architectural high point of the city, with plenty of fine eating and shopping options thrown in for good measure.

## ❷ La Latina & Lavapiés (p80)

La Latina combines some of Madrid's best tapas bars, fine little boutiques and a medieval streetscape studded with elegant churches; graceful Calle de la Cava Baja could be our favourite street in town. Down the hill, Lavapiés is one of the city's oldest *barrios* (districts) and the heart of multicultural Madrid. Spanning the two neighbourhoods is the Sunday flea market of El Rastro.

## ❸ Sol, Santa Ana & Huertas (p86)

These tightly packed streets are best known for nightlife that crescendoes once the sun goes down, but there's also the pretty Plaza de Santa Ana and a stirring literary heritage in the Barrio de las Letras. At the Sol end of things, Madrid's beating heart, you'll find the sum total of all Madrid's personalities, with fabulous shopping, eating and entertainment options.

## ❹ El Retiro & the Art Museums (p88)

From Plaza de la Cibeles in the north, the buildings arrayed along Paseo del Prado read like a roll call of Madrid's most popular attractions. Temples to fine arts include the Museo del Prado, Museo Thyssen-Bornemisza and Centro de Arte Reina Sofía, which rank among the world's most prestigious art galleries. Up the hill to the east, the marvellous Parque del Buen Retiro helps to make this one of the most attractive areas of Madrid in which to spend your time.

## ❺ Salamanca (p100)

The *barrio* of Salamanca is Madrid's most exclusive quarter. Like nowhere else in the capital, this is where stately old-money mansions set back from the street share space with big local and international designer boutiques. Salamanca's sprinkling of fine restaurants, designer tapas bars and niche museums are also very much at home here.

## ❻ Malasaña & Chueca (p105)

The two inner-city *barrios* of Malasaña and Chueca are where Madrid gets up close and personal. Here, it's more an experience of life as it's lived by *madrileños* (people from Madrid) than the traditional traveller experience of ticking off from a list of wonderful, if more static, attractions. These are *barrios* with attitude and personality, where Madrid's famed nightlife, shopping and eating choices live and breathe and take you under the skin of the city.

## ❼ Chamberí & Northern Madrid (p107)

Madrid's north contains some of the city's most attractive *barrios,* including Chamberí, which is a wonderful escape from the downtown area and offers unique insights into how locals enjoy their city – Calle de Ponzano is one of Madrid's coolest streets for bars and tapas. Up north, Estadio Santiago Bernabéu is a major highlight for sports fans, while some of Madrid's top restaurants also inhabit the city's inner north.

## History

When Iberia's Christians began the Reconquista (c 722) – the centuries-long campaign by Christian forces to reclaim the peninsula – the Muslims of Al-Andalus constructed a chain of fortified positions through the heart of Iberia. One of these was built by Muhammad I, emir of Córdoba, in 854, on the site of what would become Madrid. The name they gave to the new settlement was Mayrit (or Magerit), which comes from the Arabic word *majira*, meaning 'water channel'.

### A Worthy Capital?

Madrid's strategic location in the centre of the peninsula saw the city change hands repeatedly, but it was not until 1309 that the travelling Cortes (royal court and parliament) sat in Madrid for the first time. Despite the growing royal attention, medieval Madrid remained dirt-poor and small-scale: 'In Madrid there is nothing except what you bring with you', observed one 15th-century writer. It simply bore no comparison with other major Spanish – let alone European – cities.

By the time Felipe II ascended the Spanish throne in 1556, Madrid was surrounded by walls that boasted 130 towers and six stone gates, but these fortifications were largely built of mud and designed more to impress than provide any meaningful defence of the city. Madrid was nonetheless chosen by Felipe II as the capital of Spain in 1561.

Madrid took centuries to grow into its new role and despite a handful of elegant churches, the imposing Alcázar and a smattering of noble residences, the city consisted of, for the most part, precarious whitewashed houses. The monumental Paseo del Prado, which now provides Madrid with so much of its grandeur, was a small creek.

During the 17th century, Spain's Golden Age, Madrid began to take on the aspect of a capital and was home to 175,000 people, making it the fifth-largest city in Europe (after London, Paris, Constantinople and Naples).

Carlos III (r 1759–88) gave Madrid and Spain a period of comparatively common-sense government. After he cleaned up the city, completed the Palacio Real, inaugurated the Real Jardín Botánico and carried out numerous other public works, he became known as the best 'mayor' Madrid had ever had.

*Madrileños* (residents of Madrid) didn't take kindly to Napoleon's invasion and subsequent occupation of Spain in 1805 and, on 2 May 1808, they attacked French troops around the Palacio Real and what is now Plaza del Dos de Mayo. The ill-fated rebellion was quickly put down by Murat, Napoleon's brother-in-law and the most powerful of his military leaders.

### Wars, Franco & Terrorism

Turmoil continued to stalk the Spanish capital. The upheaval of the 19th-century Carlist Wars was followed by a two-and-a-half-year siege of Madrid by Franco's Nationalist forces from 1936 to 1939, during which the city was shelled regularly from Casa de Campo and Gran Vía became known as 'Howitzer Alley'.

After Franco's death in 1975 and the country's subsequent transition to democracy, Madrid became an icon for the new Spain as the city's young people unleashed a flood of pent-up energy. This took its most colourful form in the years of *la movida madrileña*, the endless party that swept up the city in a frenzy of creativity and open-minded freedom that has in some ways yet to abate.

On 11 March 2004, just three days before the country was due to vote in national elections, Madrid was rocked by 10 bombs on four rush-hour commuter trains heading into the capital's Atocha station. The bombs had been planted by terrorists with links to al-Qaeda, reportedly because of Spain's then support for the American-led war in Iraq. When the dust cleared, 191 people had died and 1755 were wounded, many seriously. Madrid was in shock and, for 24 hours at least, this most clamorous of cities fell silent.

### MADRID CATS

Madrid's ruined wall, the Muralla Árabe, may be modest now, but it plays an important historical role in the way *madrileños* (people from Madrid) see themselves. When a Christian soldier scaled the walls of the besieged city just before it passed from Muslim hands in the 11th century, one of his comrades cried out, 'Look, he moves like a cat!' The name stuck and ever since a true *madrileño* is known as a *gato* (cat). Traditionally, the honour of being a *gato* is restricted to those whose four grandparents were born in Madrid.

Then, 36 hours after the attacks, more than three million *madrileños* streamed onto the streets to protest against the bombings, making it the largest demonstration in the city's history. Although deeply traumatised, Madrid's mass act of defiance and pride began the process of healing. Visit Madrid today and you'll find a city that has resolutely returned to normal.

### Madrid's New Politics

When the left lost control of Madrid's town hall in 1989, they could scarcely have imagined that such a free-wheeling city would remain the preserve of the conservative right for the next 26 years.

Madrid had done it tough during the long years of the economic crisis, but by 2015 the city was very much on the road to recovery. Retail revenues were up, property sales were gathering pace and unemployment was falling, all adding to a sense that Madrid's worst days were behind it. With the economy improving, the growing optimism coincided with a seismic shift in the capital's politics.

In 2015, a local leftist coalition Ahora Madrid, backed by the nationwide Podemos, won municipal elections, and retired judge Manuela Carmena became Madrid's first female mayor. Carmena, widely and affectionately known as *'La abuela'* (the Grandmother), was unlike any mayor Madrid had seen. She rode the metro to work, eschewed many of the trappings of office, and quickly earned herself a reputation for getting things done. Common-sense policies (such as the upgrading of the city's transport ticketing system) and a more compassionate approach to those hit hardest by the crisis won her plaudits.

It would only last four years. In 2019, Mayor Carmena performed well in local elections, emerging with the largest single party vote (30.9%). But the Popular Party (24.22% – its worst-ever result in Madrid) was able to form a coalition with Ciudadanos (19.12%) and the far-right Vox (7.63%). At the regional level, the Comunidad de Madrid's government has been ruled by the Popular Party since 1995.

Madrid's new mayor, the PP's José Luis Martínez-Almeida, had promised during the campaign to undo many of Carmena's reforms, and part of the Vox party's platform included anti-immigration measures and moving Madrid's Gay Pride Festival from Chueca to the Casa de Campo. At the time of writing, it was too early to gauge both the extent of the new government's willingness to change direction or the level of influence exercised by Vox.

### MADRID CENTRAL

One of the main (and most controversial) pillars of Mayor Manuela Carmena's platform was Madrid Central. Designed to dramatically improve Madrid's air quality and generally improve the city's rather unimpressive green credentials, Madrid Central had as its centrepiece a very simple idea: by making central Madrid largely off limits to non-residential vehicles, the government hoped to reduce air pollution. Similar to successful schemes in London, Berlin and elsewhere, Madrid Central was a spectacular success – pollution fell by 20% in its first year.

When the conservative coalition took over city hall in 2019, they did so on a promise of overturning Madrid Central. In early 2020, the national, Socialist-led government announced that all towns throughout Spain with more than 50,000 inhabitants must implement a Madrid Central–style plan to cut traffic and emissions.

## Sights

Madrid's attractions are numerous and varied, but many of the standout highlights revolve around art – the city's art galleries are world-class and you could easily spend a week exploring them. A handful of excellent museums, beautiful parks, a stunning royal palace and some of Europe's most agreeable squares provide considerable depth to the Madrid experience.

## Plaza Mayor & Royal Madrid

As you'd expect from the former centrepiece of old Madrid, there are numerous highlights in this corner of the city: the royal palace, ornamental gardens (Jardines de Sabatini and the Campo del Moro), lavish convents, and storied plazas (Plaza Mayor and Plaza de la Villa) where the architecture is as captivating as the street life that animates it. And in the absence of a cathedral worthy of the name, it's the smaller churches, including two of Madrid's oldest, that provide the focal point for the city's religious past.

TOP SIGHT
# PLAZA MAYOR

**It's easy to fall in love with Madrid in the Plaza Mayor. This is the beating heart of the city and the grand stage for so many of its most important historical events. Here, Madrid's relentless energy courses across its cobblestones beneath ochre-hued apartments, wrought-iron balconies, frescoes and stately spires.**

### DON'T MISS

- Spires and slate roofs
- Real Casa de la Panadería
- Markets

### PRACTICALITIES

- Map p76
- Ⓜ Sol

## A Grand History

Ah, the history the plaza has seen! Inaugurated in 1619, its first public ceremony was suitably auspicious – the beatification of San Isidro Labrador (St Isidore the Farm Labourer), Madrid's patron saint. Thereafter, it was as if all that was controversial about Spain took place in this square. Bullfights, often in celebration of royal weddings or births, with royalty watching on from the balconies and up to 50,000 people crammed into the plaza, were a recurring theme until 1878. Far more notorious were the *autos-da-fé* (the ritual condemnations of heretics during the Spanish Inquisition from the 15th to 19th centuries), followed by executions – burnings at the stake and deaths by garrotte on the north side of the square, hangings to the south.

## A Less Grand History

Not all the plaza's activities were grand events and, just as it is now surrounded by shops, it was once filled with food vendors. In 1673, King Carlos II issued an edict allowing the

vendors to raise tarpaulins above their stalls to protect their wares and themselves from the refuse and raw sewage that people habitually tossed out of the windows above. Well into the 20th century, trams ran through Plaza Mayor.

## Real Casa de la Panadería

The exquisite frescoes of the 17th-century **Real Casa de la Panadería** (Royal Bakery; Map p76; Plaza Mayor 27) rank among Madrid's more eye-catching sights. The present frescoes date to just 1992 and are the work of artist Carlos Franco, who chose images from the signs of the zodiac and gods (eg Cybele) to provide a stunning backdrop for the plaza. The frescoes were inaugurated to coincide with Madrid's 1992 spell as the European Capital of Culture. The building now houses the city's main tourist office.

## Spires & Slate Roofs

The plaza was designed in the 17th century by Juan Gómez de Mora who, following the dominant style of the day, adopted a Herrerian style (named after Spanish Renaissance architect Juan de Herrera). The slate spires and roofs are the most obvious expression of this pleasing and distinctively Madrid style, and their sombre hues are nicely offset by the warm colours of the uniformly ochre apartments and their 237 wrought-iron balconies.

# Plaza Mayor & Royal Madrid

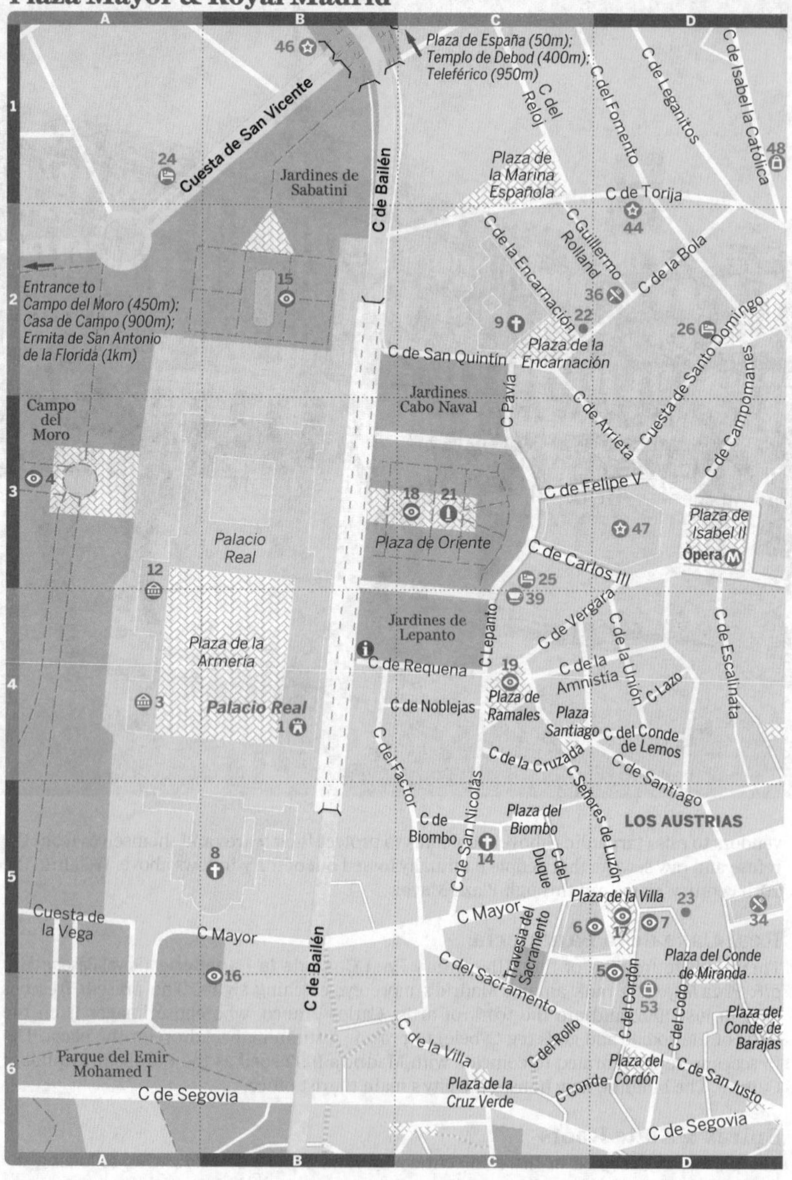


**★ Palacio Real** PALACE

(Map p76; ☎91 454 87 00; www.patrimonionacional.es; Calle de Bailén; adult/concession €10/5, guide/audio guide €4, EU citizens free last 2hr Mon-Thu; ⊙10am-8pm Apr-Sep, to 6pm Oct-Mar; Ⓜ Ópera) Spain's jewel-box Palacio Real is used only occasionally for royal ceremonies; the royal family moved to the modest Palacio de la Zarzuela years ago.

When the *alcázar* (Muslim fortress) burned down in 1734, Felipe V, the first of the Bourbon kings, decided to build a palace that would dwarf all its European counterparts. Felipe died before the palace was fin-

ished, which is perhaps why the Italianate baroque colossus has a mere 2800 rooms, just one-quarter of the original plan.

The official tour (self-guided tours are also possible and follow the same route) leads through 50 of the palace rooms, which hold a good selection of Goyas, 215 absurdly ornate clocks, and five Stradivarius violins still used for concerts and balls. The main stairway is a grand statement of imperial power, leading to the Halberdiers' rooms and to the sumptuous **Salón del Trono** (Throne Room), with its crimson-velvet wall coverings and Tiepolo ceiling. Shortly after, you reach the **Salón de Gasparini**, with its exquisite stucco ceiling and walls resplendent with embroidered silks.

Outside the main palace, visit the **Farmacia Real** (Real Botica; Map p76; Plaza de la Armería, Palacio Real; admission incl with Palacio Real entry; ⏲10am-8pm Apr-Sep, to 6pm Oct-Mar) at the southern end of the patio known as the **Plaza de la Armería** (Plaza de Armas). Westwards across the plaza is the **Armería Real** (Royal Armoury; Map p76; Plaza de la Armería, Palacio Real; admission incl with Palacio Real entry; ⏲10am-8pm Apr-Sep, to 6pm Oct-Mar), a shiny collection of weapons and armour, mostly dating from the 16th and 17th centuries.

### ★Ermita de San Antonio de la Florida — GALLERY

(Panteón de Goya; ☎91 542 07 22; www.sanantoniodelaflorida.es; Glorieta de San Antonio de la Florida 5; ⏲9.30am-8pm Tue-Sun mid-Sep–mid-Jun, 9.30am-2pm Tue-Fri, to 7pm Sat & Sun mid-Jun–mid-Sep; Ⓜ Príncipe Pío) FREE The frescoed ceilings of the restored Ermita de San Antonio de la Florida are one of Madrid's most surprising secrets. The southern of the two small chapels is one of the few places to see Goya's work in its original setting, as painted by the master in 1798 on the request of Carlos IV. It's simply breathtaking.

The frescoes on the dome depict the miracle of St Anthony, who is calling on a young man to rise from the grave and absolve his father, unjustly accused of his murder. Around them swarms a typical Madrid crowd.

The painter is buried in front of the altar. His remains (minus the mysteriously missing head) were transferred in 1919 from Bordeaux (France), where he died in self-imposed exile in 1828.

Guided visits run from 9.30am to 1pm Tuesday to Friday when there are enough people.

### ★Templo de Debod — RUINS

(Paseo del Pintor Rosales; ⏲10am-8pm Tue-Sun; Ⓜ Ventura Rodríguez) FREE Yes, that *is* an Egyptian temple in downtown Madrid. The temple was saved from the rising waters of

## Plaza Mayor & Royal Madrid

**Top Sights**
1 Palacio Real ........ B4
2 Plaza Mayor ........ E5

**Sights**
3 Armería Real ........ A4
4 Campo del Moro ........ A3
5 Casa de Cisneros ........ D5
6 Casa de la Villa ........ D5
7 Casa de los Lujanes ........ D5
8 Catedral de Nuestra Señora de la Almudena ........ B5
9 Convento de la Encarnación ........ C2
10 Convento de las Descalzas Reales ........ F3
11 Edificio Carrión ........ F2
12 Farmacia Real ........ A4
13 Iglesia de San Ginés ........ E4
14 Iglesia de San Nicolás de los Servitas ........ C5
15 Jardines de Sabatini ........ B2
16 Muralla Árabe ........ B6
17 Plaza de la Villa ........ D5
18 Plaza de Oriente ........ C3
19 Plaza de Ramales ........ C4
20 Real Casa de la Panadería ........ E5
21 Statue of Felipe IV ........ C3

**Activities, Courses & Tours**
22 Alambique ........ C2
23 Bike Spain ........ D5

**Sleeping**
24 ApartoSuites Jardines de Sabatini ........ A1
25 Central Palace Madrid ........ C3
26 Gran Melia Palacio de Los Duques ........ D2
27 Hostal Madrid ........ F5
28 Hotel JC Rooms Puerta del Sol ........ E3
29 Pestana Plaza Mayor ........ E6

**Eating**
30 Casa Revuelta ........ E6
31 El Pato Mudo ........ E3
32 Gourmet Experience ........ F2
33 La Campana ........ E5
La Ideal ........ (see 33)
34 Mercado de San Miguel ........ D5
35 Restaurante Sobrino de Botín ........ E6
36 Taberna La Bola ........ D2
37 Taberna La Daniela ........ E6

**Drinking & Nightlife**
38 Bodegas Ricla ........ E6
39 Café de Oriente ........ C4
40 Chocolatería de San Ginés ........ F4
41 Plaza Menor ........ E6
42 Teatro Joy Eslava ........ F4

**Entertainment**
43 Café Berlín ........ E2
44 Café de Chinitas ........ D2
45 La Coquette Blues ........ E4
46 Las Tablas ........ B1
47 Teatro Real ........ D3

**Shopping**
48 Antigua Casa Talavera ........ D1
49 Así ........ E4
50 Atlético de Madrid Store ........ E1
51 Casa Hernanz ........ E6
52 El Arco Artesanía ........ E5
53 El Jardín del Convento ........ D6
54 Maty ........ F4
55 Sombrerería Medrano ........ E6
56 Torrons Vicens ........ E4

Lake Nasser in southern Egypt when Egyptian president Gamal Abdel Nasser built the Aswan High Dam. After 1968 it was sent block by block to Spain as a gesture of thanks to Spanish archaeologists in the Unesco team that worked to save the monuments that would otherwise have disappeared forever.

**Plaza de la Villa** SQUARE
(Map p76; Ⓜ Ópera) The intimate Plaza de la Villa is one of Madrid's prettiest. Enclosed on three sides by wonderfully preserved examples of 17th-century *barroco madrileño* (Madrid-style baroque architecture – a pleasing amalgam of brick, exposed stone and wrought iron), it was the permanent seat of Madrid's city government from the Middle Ages until recent years, when Madrid's city council relocated to the grand Palacio de Cibeles on Plaza de la Cibeles (p99).

On the western side of the square is the 17th-century **former town hall** (Map p76; Ⓜ Ópera), in Habsburg-style baroque with Herrerian slate-tile spires. On the opposite side of the square is the Gothic **Casa de los Lujanes** (Map p76; Ⓜ Ópera), whose brickwork tower is said to have been 'home' to the imprisoned French monarch François I after his capture in the Battle of Pavia (1525). Legend has it that as the star prisoner was paraded down Calle Mayor, locals were more impressed by the splendidly attired Frenchman than they were by his more drab captor, the Spanish Habsburg emperor Carlos I, much to the chagrin of the latter. The plateresque (15th- and 16th-century Spanish baroque) **Casa de Cisneros** (Map p76;

Ⓜ Ópera), built in 1537 with later Renaissance alterations, also catches the eye.

**Plaza de Oriente** SQUARE

(Map p76; Ⓜ Ópera) This graceful square is one of central Madrid's most beautiful, home as it is to a royal palace that once had aspirations to be the Spanish Versailles, sophisticated cafes watched over by apartments that cost the equivalent of a royal salary, and the Teatro Real (p132), Madrid's opera house and one of Spain's temples to high culture.

At the centre of the plaza, which the palace overlooks, is an equestrian **statue of Felipe IV** (Map p76;; Ⓜ Ópera). Designed by Velázquez, it's the perfect place to take it all in, with marvellous views wherever you look. If you're wondering how a heavy bronze statue of a rider and his horse rearing up can actually maintain that stance, the answer is simple: the hind legs are solid, while the front ones are hollow. That idea was Galileo Galilei's. Nearby are some 20 marble statues, mostly of ancient monarchs. Local legend has it that these ageing royals get down off their pedestals at night to stretch their legs when no one is looking.

The adjacent **Jardines Cabo Naval** are a great place to watch the sunset.

**Jardines de Sabatini** GARDENS

(Map p76; ⏲9am-10pm May-Sep, to 9pm Oct-Apr; Ⓜ Ópera) FREE The formal French-style Jardines de Sabatini are to the north of the Palacio Real, a palace with lush gardens.

**Campo del Moro** GARDENS

(Map p76; ☎91 454 88 00; Paseo de la Virgen del Puerto; ⏲10am-8pm Apr-Sep, to 6pm Oct-Mar; Ⓜ Príncipe Pío) FREE These gardens beneath the Palacio Real were designed to mimic the gardens surrounding the palace at Versailles; nowhere is this more in evidence than along the east–west **Pradera**, a lush lawn with the Palacio Real as its backdrop. The gardens' centrepiece, which stands halfway along the Pradera, is the elegant **Fuente de las Conchas** (Fountain of the Shells), designed by Ventura Rodríguez, the Goya of Madrid's 18th-century architecture scene. The only entrance is from Paseo de la Virgen del Puerto.

**Convento de las Descalzas Reales** CONVENT

(Convent of the Barefoot Royals; Map p76; www.patrimonionacional.es; Plaza de las Descalzas 3; €6, incl Convento de la Encarnación €8, free for EU citizens 4-6.30pm Wed & Thu; ⏲10am-2pm & 4-6.30pm Tue-Sat, 10am-3pm Sun; Ⓜ Ópera, Sol) The grim plateresque walls of the Convento de las Descalzas Reales offer no hint that behind the facade lies a sumptuous stronghold of the faith. The compulsory guided tour (in Spanish) leads you up a gaudily frescoed Renaissance stairway to the upper level of the cloister. The vault was painted by Claudio Coello, one of the most important artists of the Madrid School of the 17th century whose works adorn San Lorenzo de El Escorial.

**Iglesia de San Ginés** CHURCH

(Map p76; Calle del Arenal 13; ⏲8.45am-1pm & 6-9pm Mon-Sat, 9.45am-2pm & 5.45-9pm Sun; Ⓜ Sol, Ópera) FREE Due north of Plaza Mayor, San Ginés is one of Madrid's oldest churches: it has been here in one form or another since at least the 14th century. What you see today was built in 1645 but largely reconstructed after a fire in 1824. The church houses some fine paintings, including El Greco's *Expulsion of the Moneychangers from the Temple* (1614), which is beautifully displayed; the glass is just 6mm from the canvas to avoid reflections.

The church has stood at the centre of Madrid life for centuries. It is speculated that, prior to the arrival of the Christians in 1085, a Mozarabic community (Christians in Muslim territory) lived around the stream that later became Calle del Arenal and that their parish church stood on this site.

Spain's premier playwright Lope de Vega was married here and novelist Francisco de Quevedo was baptised in its font.

**Convento de la Encarnación** CONVENT

(Map p76; www.patrimonionacional.es; Plaza de la Encarnación 1; €6, incl Convento de las Descalzas Reales €8, free for EU citizens 4-6.30pm Wed & Thu; ⏲10am-2pm & 4-6.30pm Tue-Sat, 10am-3pm Sun; Ⓜ Ópera) Founded by Empress Margarita de Austria, this 17th-century mansion built in the Madrid baroque style (a pleasing amalgam of brick, exposed stone and wrought iron) is still inhabited by nuns of

### MUSEUM DISCOUNTS & CLOSING TIMES

Many museums (including the Museo del Prado and Centro de Arte Reina Sofía) offer free entry at selected times – check the opening hours throughout this chapter.

### MUSEO DE LAS COLECCIONES REALES

There have been plans since the 1930s for a museum dedicated to royal artworks and other paraphernalia, from horse-drawn carriages to decorative pieces. Finally, construction began on the museum in 2017 with an originally projected (pre-COVID) completion date of 2020, now expected to be 2022. It's centred on Cuesta de la Vega, west of the Muralla Árabe and down below the cathedral and Palacio Real.

the Augustine order. The large art collection dates mostly from the 17th century, and among the many gold and silver reliquaries is one that contains the blood of San Pantaleón, which purportedly liquefies each year on 27 July. The convent sits on a pretty plaza close to the Palacio Real.

**Catedral de Nuestra Señora de la Almudena** CATHEDRAL
(Map p76; ☎91 542 22 00; www.catedraldelaalmudena.es; Calle de Bailén; cathedral & crypt by donation, museum adult/child €6/4; ⏲9am-8.30pm Mon-Sat, museum 10am-2.30pm Mon-Sat; Ⓜ Ópera) Paris has Notre Dame and Rome has St Peter's Basilica. In fact, almost every European city of stature has its signature cathedral, a standout monument to a glorious Christian past. Not Madrid. Although the exterior of the Catedral de Nuestra Señora de la Almudena sits in harmony with the adjacent Palacio Real, Madrid's cathedral is cavernous and largely charmless within; its colourful, modern ceilings do little to make up for the lack of old-world gravitas that so distinguishes great cathedrals.

**Muralla Árabe** LANDMARK
(Map p76; Cuesta de la Vega; Ⓜ Ópera) Behind the cathedral apse and down Cuesta de la Vega is a short stretch of the original 'Arab Wall', the city wall built by Madrid's early-medieval Muslim rulers. Some of it dates as far back as the 9th century, when the initial Muslim fort was raised. Other sections date from the 12th and 13th centuries, by which time the city had been taken by the Christians.

**Palacio Gaviria** MUSEUM
(Map p84; ☎91 060 08 00; https://palaciodegaviriamadrid.com; Calle del Arenal 9; adult/child €14/free; ⏲10am-8pm Sun-Thu, to 9pm Fri & Sat; Ⓜ Sol) Until recently this 19th-century Italianate palace was a nightclub. It has since been artfully converted to a dynamic artistic space, with major temporary art exhibitions that have included an Escher retrospective and Flemish masters. Coupled with high-quality exhibitions is a soaring Renaissance palace with extraordinary ceiling frescoes. It's one of Madrid's least known yet most rewarding artistic spaces outside the major galleries.

**Iglesia de San Nicolás de los Servitas** CHURCH
(Map p76; ☎91 559 40 64; Plaza de San Nicolás 6; ⏲8am-1.30pm & 5.30-8.30pm Mon, 8-9.30am & 6.30-8.30pm Tue-Sat, 9.30am-2pm & 6.30-9pm Sun & holidays; Ⓜ Ópera) FREE Tucked away up the hill from Calle Mayor, this intimate little church is Madrid's oldest surviving building of worship; it may have been built on the site of Muslim Mayrit's second mosque. The most striking feature is the restored 12th-century Mudéjar (a Moorish architectural style) bell tower; much of the remainder dates in part from the 15th century. The vaulting is late Gothic while the fine timber ceiling, which survived a 1936 fire, dates from about the same period. Opening hours can be unreliable.

**Plaza de España** SQUARE
(Map p102; Ⓜ Plaza de España) This central Madrid square was being given a major overhaul when we last visited. They'll no doubt find room for the 1927 statue of Cervantes, alongside a bronze statue of his immortal characters Don Quijote and Sancho Panza. The 1953 **Edificio de España** (Spain Building) on the northeast side clearly sprang from the totalitarian recesses of Franco's imagination, such is its resemblance to austere Soviet monumentalism. To the north stands the 35-storey **Torre de Madrid** (Madrid Tower).

## La Latina & Lavapiés

Although there are exceptions, these two *barrios* are more about experiences than traditional sights. That said, a handful of fine churches rise above La Latina, Plaza de la Paja is one of Madrid's loveliest squares, and the tangled streets of La Morería are a return to the city's distant past. And then, of course, there's El Rastro, Madrid's flea mar-

## MADRID IN...

### One Day

So many Madrid days begin in the **Plaza Mayor** (p74) or nearby with a breakfast of *chocolate con churros* (chocolate with deep-fried doughnuts) at **Chocolatería de San Ginés** (p126). Drop by the **Plaza de la Villa** (p78) and **Plaza de Oriente** (p79), then stop for a coffee or wine at **Café de Oriente** (p126) and visit the **Palacio Real** (p76). Have lunch at **Mercado de San Miguel** (p116), one of Madrid's most innovative gastronomic spaces. Spend as much of the afternoon as you can at the **Museo del Prado** (p92). When this priceless collection of Spanish and European masterpieces gets too much, visit the **Iglesia de San Jerónimo El Real** (p100) and **Caixa Forum** (p99). To kick off the night, take in a flamenco show at **Teatro Flamenco Madrid** (p133), followed by dinner at the world's oldest restaurant, **Restaurante Sobrino de Botín** (p116), then a leisurely drink at **Plaza Menor** (p126). If you're up for a long night, **Teatro Joy Eslava** (p126) is an icon of the Madrid night.

### Two Days

Get to the **Centro de Arte Reina Sofía** (p90) early to beat the crowds, then climb up through sedate streets to spend a couple of hours soaking up the calm of the **Parque del Buen Retiro** (p91). Wander down to admire the **Plaza de la Cibeles** (p99). After lunch at **Estado Puro** (p119), one of Madrid's most creative tapas bars, catch the metro across town to admire the Goya frescoes in the **Ermita de San Antonio de la Florida** (p77). Afterwards, **Templo de Debod** (p77) and **Parque del Oeste** are fine places for a stroll. Begin the night at **Plaza de Santa Ana** (p86) for a drink or three at an outdoor table if the weather's fine, followed by dinner at **Casa Alberto** (p119). After another tipple at **La Venencia** (p127), check out if there's live jazz on offer at wonderful **Café Central** (p133). Have an after-show drink at **El Imperfecto** (p127). The night is still young – **Costello Café & Niteclub** (p133) is good if you're in the mood to dance, **La Terraza del Urban** (p128) or **Radio** (p128) if you're in need of more sybaritic pleasures.

### Three Days

Begin the morning at the third of Madrid's world-class art galleries, the **Museo Thyssen-Bornemisza** (p88). It's such a rich collection that you could easily spend the whole morning here. If you have time to spare, consider dipping back into the Prado or Reina Sofía. Have lunch at **Platea** (p120), one of Madrid's most exciting culinary experiences. Head out east to take a tour of the **Plaza de Toros** (p100) bullring, before dipping into the **Museo Lázaro Galdiano** (p104). Spend the rest of the afternoon shopping along Calle de Serrano, Calle de José Ortega y Gasset and surrounding streets. As dusk approaches, make for La Latina and spend as long as you can picking your way among the tapas bars of **Calle de la Cava Baja** (p118) – even if you're not hungry, stop by for a beer or wine to soak up the atmosphere. Dinner at **Juana La Loca** (p118), a wine at **Taberna El Tempranillo** (p126) and a mojito out on **Plaza de la Paja at Delic** (p126) should set you up for the night ahead.

ket par excellence, and the gateway to some of Madrid's most enjoyable traditions.

### ★Basílica de San Francisco El Grande — CHURCH

(Map p82; Plaza de San Francisco 1; adult/concession €5/3; ⏰Mass 8-10.30am Mon-Sat, museum 10.30am-12.30pm & 4-6pm Tue-Sun Sep-Jun, 10.30am-12.30pm & 5-7pm Tue-Sun Jul & Aug; Ⓜ La Latina, Puerta de Toledo) Lording it over the southwestern corner of La Latina, this imposing baroque basilica is one of Madrid's grandest old churches. Its extravagantly frescoed dome is, by some estimates, the largest in Spain and the fourth largest in the world, with a height of 56m and diameter of 33m.

Legend has it that St Francis of Assisi built a chapel on this site in 1217. The current version was designed by Francesco Sabatini, who also designed the Puerta de Alcalá (p99) and finished off the Palacio Real. He designed the church with an unusual floor plan: the nave is circular and

## La Latina

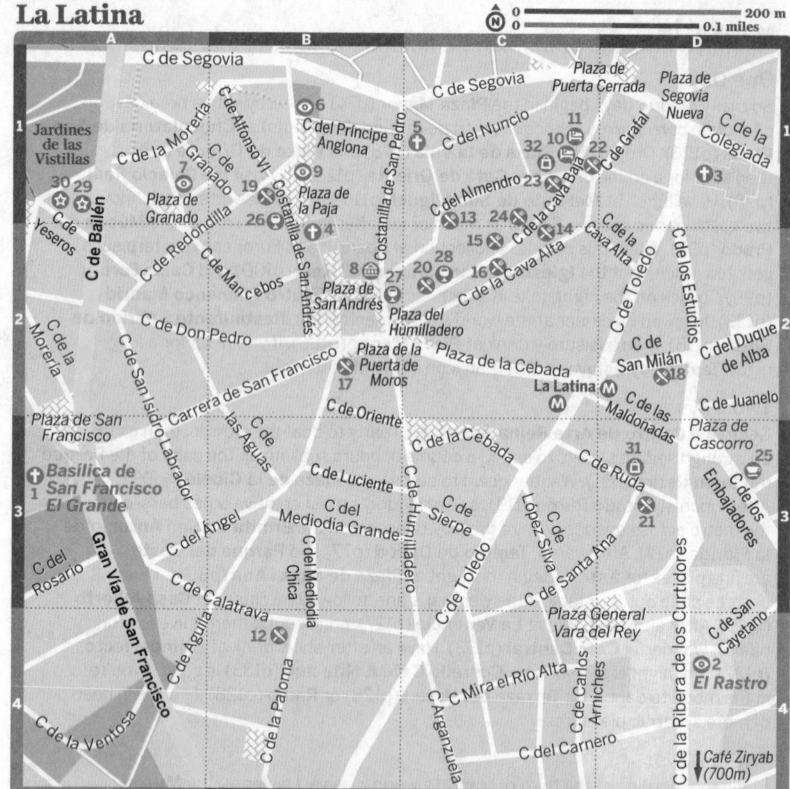


surrounded by chapels guarded by imposing marble statues of the 12 apostles; 12 prophets, rendered in wood, sit above them at the base of the dome. Each of the chapels is adorned with frescoes and decorated according to a different historical style, but most people rush to the neo-plateresque Capilla de San Bernardino, where the central fresco was painted by Goya in the early stages of his career. Unusually, Goya has painted himself into the scene (he's the one in the yellow shirt on the right).

A series of corridors behind the high altar (accessible only as part of the guided visit) is lined with works of art from the 17th to 19th centuries; highlights include a painting by Francisco Zurbarán, and another by Francisco Pacheco, the father-in-law and teacher of Velázquez. In the sacristy, watch out for the fine Renaissance *sillería* (the sculpted walnut seats where the church's superiors would meet).

A word about the opening hours: although entry is free during morning Mass times, there is no access to the museum and the lights in the Capilla de San Bernardino won't be on to illuminate the Goya. At all other times, visit is by Spanish-language guided tour (included in the admission price). Just to confuse matters, you may face a similar problem if you're here on a Friday afternoon or any time Saturday if there's a wedding taking place.

**★El Rastro** MARKET

(Map p82; Calle de la Ribera de los Curtidores; 8am-3pm Sun; La Latina) A Sunday morning at El Rastro flea market, Europe's largest, is a Madrid institution. You could easily spend the entire morning inching your way down the hill and the maze of streets. Cheap clothes, luggage, old flamenco records, even older photos of Madrid, faux-designer purses, grungy T-shirts, household goods and electronics are the main fare. For every 10

## La Latina



pieces of junk, there's a real gem (a lost masterpiece, an Underwood typewriter) waiting to be found.

The crowded Sunday flea market was, back in the 17th and 18th centuries, largely a meat market (*rastro* means 'stain', in reference to the trail of blood left behind by animals dragged down the hill). The road leading through the market, Calle de la Ribera de los Curtidores, translates as 'Tanners' Alley' and further evokes this sense of a slaughterhouse past. On Sunday mornings it's the place to be, with all of Madrid here in search of a bargain.

Antiques are also a major drawcard, with a concentration of stores at Nuevas Galerías and Galerías Piquer; most shops open 10am to 2pm and 5pm to 8pm Monday to Saturday and not all open during El Rastro.

A word of warning: pickpockets love El Rastro as much as everyone else, so keep a tight hold on your belongings and don't keep valuables in easy-to-reach pockets.

**Plaza de la Paja** SQUARE

(Straw Square; Map p82; M La Latina) Around the back of the Iglesia de San Andrés, the delightful Plaza de la Paja slopes down into the tangle of lanes that once made up Madrid's Muslim quarter. In the 12th and 13th centuries, the city's main market occupied the square. At the top of the square is the **Capilla del Obispo** (Map p82; ☎91 559 28 74; reservascapilladelobispo@archimadrid.es; €2; ⏱6-8.30pm Mon-Wed, noon-1.30pm & 6-8.30pm Thu & Fri, noon-1.30pm & 8-10pm Sat, noon-2pm & 6.15-8pm Sun), while down the bottom (north side) is the walled **Jardín del Príncipe Anglona** (Map p82; ⏱10am-10pm Apr-Oct, to 6.30pm Nov-Mar), a peaceful 18th-century garden.

**Matadero Madrid** ARTS CENTRE

(☎91 252 52 53; www.mataderomadrid.org; Paseo de la Chopera 14; M Legazpi) FREE This contemporary-arts centre is a stunning multipurpose space south of the centre. Occupying the converted buildings of the old Arganzuela livestock market and slaughterhouse, Matadero Madrid covers 148,300 sq metres and hosts cutting-edge drama, musical and dance performances and exhibitions on architecture, fashion, literature and cinema. It's a dynamic space and its proximity to the riverbank makes for a non-touristy alternative to sightseeing in Madrid, not to mention a brilliant opportunity to see the latest avant-garde theatre or exhibitions.

**Museo de San Isidro** MUSEUM

(Museo de los Origenes; Map p82; ☎91 366 74 15; www.madrid.es/museosanisidro; Plaza de San Andrés 2; ⏱10am-7pm Tue-Sun mid-Jun–mid-Sep,

## Sol, Santa Ana & Huertas

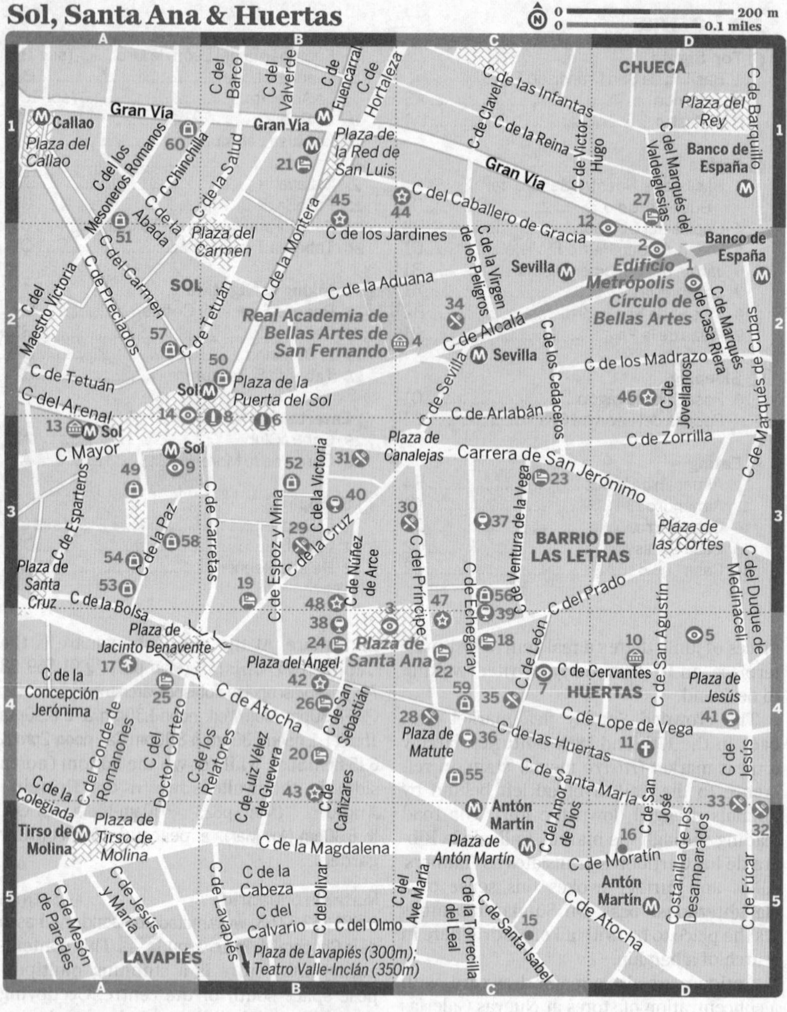


to 8pm Tue-Sun rest of year; Ⓜ La Latina) FREE This engaging museum occupies the spot where San Isidro Labrador, patron saint of Madrid, ended his days around 1172. A particular highlight is the large model based on Pedro Teixeira's famous 1656 map of Madrid. Of great historical interest (though not much to look at) is the 'miraculous well', where the saint called forth water to slake his master's thirst. In another miracle, the son of the saint's master fell into a well, whereupon Isidro prayed until the water rose and lifted his master's son to safety.

**Basílica de Nuestra Señora del Buen Consejo** CHURCH

(Catedral de San Isidro; Map p82; ☎91 369 20 37; Calle de Toledo 37; ⏲7.30am-1pm & 6-9pm; Ⓜ Tirso de Molina, La Latina) FREE Towering above the northern end of bustling Calle de Toledo, and visible through the arches from Plaza Mayor, this imposing church long served as the city's de facto cathedral until the Catedral de Nuestra Señora de la Almudena (p80) was completed in 1992. Still known to locals as the Catedral de San Isidro, the austere baroque basilica was found-

## Sol, Santa Ana & Huertas

**Top Sights**
1 Círculo de Bellas Artes....D2
2 Edificio Metrópolis....D2
3 Plaza de Santa Ana....B4
4 Real Academia de Bellas Artes de San Fernando....C2

**Sights**
5 Barrio de las Letras....D4
6 Bear Statue....B3
7 Calle de Cervantes 2....C4
8 Carlos III Equestrian Statue....B3
9 Casa de Correos....A3
10 Casa de Lope de Vega....D4
11 Convento de las Trinitarias....D4
12 Edificio Grassy....D2
13 Palacio Gaviria....A3
14 Plaza de la Puerta del Sol....A2

**Activities, Courses & Tours**
15 Academia Amor de Dios....C5
16 Cooking Point....D5
Fundación Conservatorio Casa Patas....(see 43)
17 Hammam al-Andalus....A4

**Sleeping**
18 Catalonia Las Cortes....C4
Hostal Adria Santa Ana....(see 19)
19 Hostal Adriano....B3
20 Hostal Fonda Horizonte....B4
21 Hostal Luis XV....B1
22 Hotel Alicia....C4
23 Hotel Urban....C3
24 Me Madrid Reina Victoria....B4
25 Mola! Hostel....A4
26 NH Collection Palacio de Tepa....B4
27 Principal Madrid....D1

**Eating**
28 Casa Alberto....C4
29 Casa Toni....B3
30 La Finca de Susana....C3
31 Lhardy....B3
32 Maceiras....D4
33 Maceiras....D5
34 Paco Roncero Restaurante....C2
35 Vinos González....C4

**Drinking & Nightlife**
Café del Círculo de Bellas Artes....(see 1)
36 El Imperfecto....C4
Glass Bar....(see 23)
La Azotea....(see 1)
La Terraza del Urban....(see 23)
37 La Venencia....C3
38 Radio....B4
39 Salmón Gurú....C4
40 Taberna Alhambra....B3
41 Taberna La Dolores....D4

**Entertainment**
42 Café Central....B4
43 Casa Patas....B4
44 Costello Café & Niteclub....C1
45 Sala El Sol....B1
46 Teatro de la Zarzuela....D2
47 Teatro Español....C4
48 Villa Rosa....B3

**Shopping**
49 Almacén de Pontejos....A3
50 Casa de Diego....A1
51 Casa de Diego....B2
52 Guantes Luque....B3
53 José Ramírez....A3
54 Justo Algaba....A3
55 Librería Desnivel....C4
56 Licores Cabello....C3
57 Real Madrid Store....A2
58 Santarrufina....A3
59 The Corner Shop....C4
60 Tienda Real Madrid....A1

ed in the 17th century as the headquarters for the Jesuits.

The basilica is today home to the remains of the city's main patron saint, San Isidro (in the third chapel on your left after you walk in). His body, apparently remarkably well preserved, is only removed from here on rare occasions, such as in 1896 and 1947 when he was paraded about town in the hope he would bring rain (he did, at least in 1947).

**Plaza de Lavapiés** SQUARE
(M Lavapiés) The triangular Plaza de Lavapiés is one of the few open spaces in Lavapiés and is a magnet for all that's good (a thriving cultural life) and bad (drugs and a high police presence) about the *barrio*. It's been cleaned up a little in recent years and the **Teatro Valle-Inclán** (☎91 505 88 01; https://cdn.mcu.es/valle-inclan; tickets from €15; M Lavapiés), on the southern edge of the plaza, is a striking addition to the eclectic Lavapiés streetscape.

**Iglesia de San Pedro El Viejo** CHURCH
(Map p82; ☎91 365 12 84; Costanilla de San Pedro; 9am-12.30pm & 5-8pm Mon-Thu & Sat, 7am-9pm Fri, 9am-12.30pm Sun; M La Latina) FREE This fine old church is one of the few remaining windows on post-Muslim Madrid, most notably its clearly Mudéjar brick bell tower, which dates from the 14th century.

The church is generally closed to the public, but it's arguably more impressive from the outside; the Renaissance doorway has stood since 1525. If you can peek inside, the nave dates from the 15th century, although the interior largely owes its appearance to 17th-century renovations.

## Sol, Santa Ana & Huertas

The Real Academia de Bellas Artes de San Fernando and the Plaza de Santa Ana capture two of Madrid's most enduring sources of appeal – the exceptional museums dedicated to fine art and the irresistible energy that dominates the city's streets, a high-culture-life-on-the-streets combination that's very Madrid. The charm and sense of history that define the intimate Barrio de las Letras is another completely different perspective on life, just as appealing and just as much a part of the Madrid experience.

### ★Real Academia de Bellas Artes de San Fernando — MUSEUM

(Map p84; ☎91 524 08 64; www.realacademiabellasartessanfernando.com; Calle de Alcalá 13; adult/child €8/free, Wed free; ⏰10am-3pm Tue-Sun Sep-Jul; Ⓜ Sol, Sevilla) The Real Academia de Bellas Artes, Madrid's 'other' art gallery, has for centuries played a pivotal role in the artistic life of the city. As the royal fine arts academy, it has nurtured local talent, thereby complementing the royal penchant for drawing the great international artists of the day into their realm. The pantheon of former alumni reads like a who's who of Spanish art, and the collection that now hangs on the academy's walls is a suitably rich one.

### ★Plaza de Santa Ana — SQUARE

(Map p84; Ⓜ Sevilla, Sol, Antón Martín) Plaza de Santa Ana is a delightful confluence of elegant architecture and irresistible energy. It presides over the upper reaches of the Barrio de las Letras (p87) and this literary personality makes its presence felt with the statues of the 17th-century writer Calderón de la Barca and Federíco García Lorca, and in the **Teatro Español** (Map p84; ☎91 360 14 84; www.teatroespanol.es; Calle del Príncipe 25; Ⓜ Sevilla, Sol, Antón Martín) at the plaza's eastern end. Apart from anything else, the plaza is the starting point for many a long Huertas night. The square was laid out in 1810 during the controversial reign of Joseph Bonaparte (elder brother of Napoleon), giving breathing space to what had hitherto been one of Madrid's most claustrophobic *barrios*. The plaza quickly became a focal point for intellectual life, and the cafes surrounding it thronged with writers, poets and artists engaging in endless *tertulias* (literary and philosophical discussions).

### ★Círculo de Bellas Artes — ARTS CENTRE, VIEWPOINT

(La Azotea; Map p84; ☎91 360 54 00; www.circulobellasartes.com; Calle de Alcalá 42; admission to roof terrace €5; ⏰roof terrace 9am-2am Sun-Thu, to 2.30am Fri & Sat; Ⓜ Banco de España, Sevilla) For some of Madrid's best views, take the lift to the 7th floor of the 'Fine Arts Circle'. You can almost reach out and touch the glorious dome of the Edificio Metrópolis and otherwise take in Madrid in all its finery, including the distant mountains. Two bars, lounge music and places to recline add to the experience. Downstairs, the centre has exhibitions, concerts, short films and book readings. There's also a fine belle-époque

### MUSLIM MAYRIT

During the almost 230 years of Muslim rule (from 854 to 1083), the great landmarks of modern Madrid such as the Plaza Mayor were not even a glint in an architect's eye and the Paseo del Prado was a small and rather unappealing creek. Only Muslims could live within the walls of the small Islamic bastion, which was reinforced with almost 200 turrets. When Madrid passed into Christian hands, the new owners moved in, the Muslims moved outside the walls and the tangle of lanes clinging to the hillside at the western end of what is now the *barrio* of La Latina has been known as **La Morería** (Moorish Quarter; Map p82; Ⓜ La Latina) ever since. Strain the imagination a little and the maze of winding and hilly lanes even now retains a whiff of a North African medina. La Morería is crowned to the east by the Plaza de la Puerta de Moros (the Plaza of the Gate of the Moors), which in the 11th century and subsequent centuries marked the divide between Christian and Muslim Madrid.

### WHERE ARE THEY BURIED?

While other countries have turned cemeteries and the graves of famous locals into tourist attractions, Spain has been slow to do the same. That may be because mystery surrounds the final resting places of some of Spain's most towering historical figures.

**Diego Velázquez** (1599–1660) According to historical records, Spain's master painter was buried in the Iglesia de San Juanito, but the church was destroyed in the early 19th century by Joseph Bonaparte to make way for what would later become the **Plaza de Ramales** (Map p76; Ⓜ Ópera). Excavations in 2000 revealed the crypt of the former church, but Velázquez was nowhere to be found.

**Francisco Goya** (1746–1828) In 1919, 91 years after Goya's death in Bordeaux, France, his remains (minus the head) were entombed in the Ermita de San Antonio de la Florida (p77), the small chapel still adorned by some of Goya's most celebrated frescoes. But his head was never found. Goya lived in a house on Calle del Espejo from 1777 until 1779; a plaque marks the building.

**Miguel de Cervantes Saavedra** (1547–1616) Cervantes, the author of *Don Quijote,* lived much of his life in Madrid and upon his death his body was buried at the Convento de las Trinitarias, in the Barrio de las Letras. In the centuries that followed, his body was somehow misplaced until, in early 2015, forensic archaeologists announced that they had discovered the bones of Cervantes in a crypt in the convent. Still home to cloistered nuns, the convent is closed to the public except for Mass.

**cafe** (Map p84; ☎91 521 69 42; ⌚9am-1am Sun-Thu, to 3am Fri & Sat) on the ground floor.

**Barrio de las Letras** AREA

(District of Letters; Map p84; Ⓜ Antón Martín) The area that unfurls down the hill east of Plaza de Santa Ana is referred to as the Barrio de las Letras because of the writers who lived here during Spain's Golden Age of the 16th and 17th centuries. Miguel de Cervantes Saavedra (1547–1616), the author of *Don Quijote,* spent much of his adult life in Madrid and lived and died at **Calle de Cervantes 2** (Map p84; Ⓜ Antón Martín); a plaque (dating from 1834) sits above the door.

Sadly, the original building was torn down in the early 19th century. When Cervantes died his body was interred around the corner at the **Convento de las Trinitarias** (Map p84; Calle de Lope de Vega 16; Ⓜ Antón Martín), which is marked by another plaque. Still home to cloistered nuns, the convent is closed to the public; forensic archaeologists finally found Cervantes' remains in 2015. A commemorative Mass is held for him here every year on the anniversary of his death, 23 April. Another literary landmark is the **Casa de Lope de Vega** (Map p84; ☎91 429 92 16; www.casamuseolopedevega.org; Calle de Cervantes 11; ⌚guided tours every 30min 10am-6pm Tue-Sun; Ⓜ Antón Martín) FREE, the former home of Lope de Vega (1562–1635), Spain's premier playwright. It's now a museum containing memorabilia from Lope de Vega's life and work.

**Plaza de la Puerta del Sol** SQUARE

(Map p84; Ⓜ Sol) The official centre point of Spain is a gracious, crowded hemisphere of elegant facades. It is, above all, a crossroads: people here are forever heading somewhere else, on foot, by metro (three lines cross here) or by bus (many lines terminate and start nearby). Hard as it is to believe now, in Madrid's earliest days, the Puerta del Sol (Gate of the Sun) was the eastern gate of the city.

The **Casa de Correos** (Map p84; Ⓜ Sol) houses the regional government of the Comunidad de Madrid and was built as the city's main post office in 1768. The clock was added in 1856 and on New Year's Eve people throng the square to wait impatiently for the clock to strike midnight, and at each gong swallow a grape – not as easy as it sounds! On the footpath outside the Casa de Correos is a plaque marking Spain's **Kilometre Zero**, the point from which Spain's network of roads is measured. Facing the Casa de Correos from the rooftops opposite is the towering **Tío Pepe sign**, long a city landmark.

The semicircular junction owes its present appearance in part to the Bourbon king Carlos III (r 1759–88), whose **equestrian statue** (Map p84), complete with his unmistakable nose, stands in the middle. Look

## El Retiro & the Art Museums

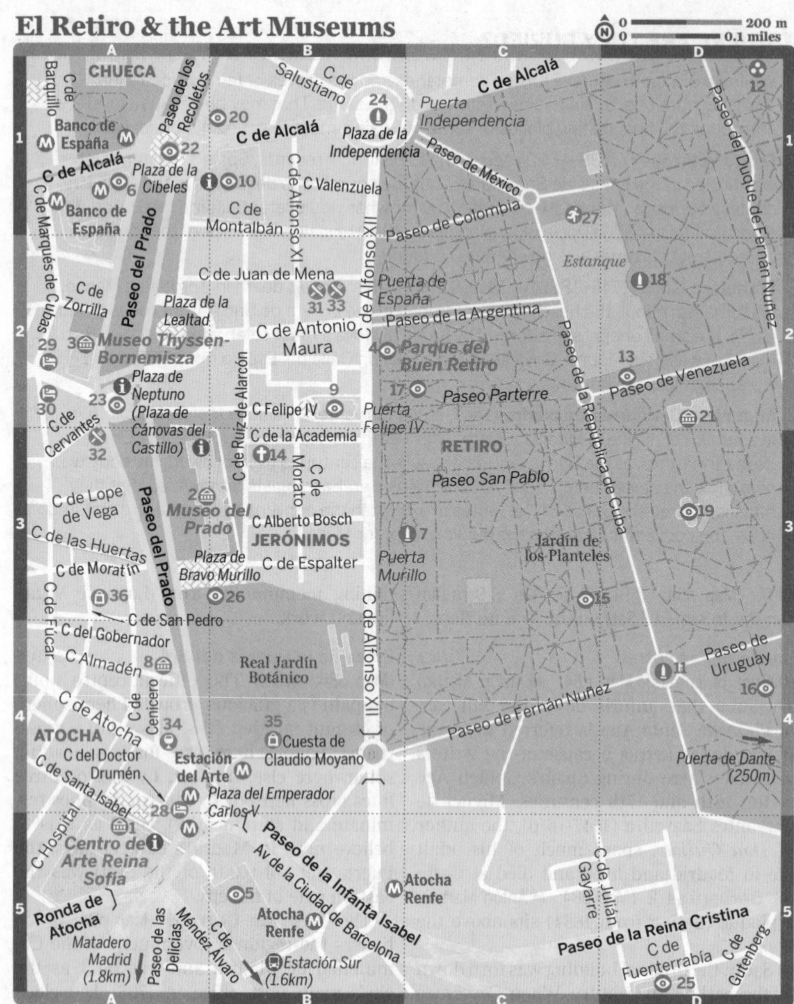


out for the **statue of a bear** (Map p84; Plaza de la Puerta del Sol; Ⓜ Sol) nuzzling a *madroño* (strawberry tree) at the plaza's eastern end; this is the official symbol of the city.

## El Retiro & the Art Museums

Some of Madrid's most memorable sights inhabit this *barrio*, with most of them on or within short walking distance of the Paseo del Prado. The three world-class art museums (Prado, Thyssen-Bornemisza and Reina Sofía) get most of the attention, and rightly so. But the Parque del Buen Retiro is a stunning oasis in the heart of the city, at once expansively green and studded with stirring monuments. Throw in more museums and a daring exhibition space (Caixa Forum), and you have reason enough to spend two or three days in this neighbourhood alone.

**★Museo Thyssen-Bornemisza** MUSEUM
(Map p88; ☎902 760511; www.museothyssen.org; Paseo del Prado 8; adult/child €13/free, Mon free; ⏲10am-7pm Tue-Sun, noon-4pm Mon; Ⓜ Banco de España) The Thyssen is one of the most extraordinary private collections of predominantly European art in the world. Where the Prado or Reina Sofía enable you to study the body of work of a particular

## El Retiro & the Art Museums



artist in depth, the Thyssen is the place to immerse yourself in an incredible breadth of artistic styles. Most of the big names are here, sometimes with just a single painting, but the Thyssen's gift to Madrid and the art-loving public is to have them all under one roof. Begin on the top floor and work your way down.

### ➡ Second Floor

The 2nd floor, which is home to medieval art, includes some real gems hidden among the mostly 13th- and 14th-century and predominantly Italian, German and Flemish religious paintings and triptychs. Unless you've got a specialist's eye, pause in Room 5, where you'll find one work by Italy's Piero della Francesca (1410–92) and the instantly recognisable *Portrait of King Henry VIII* by Holbein the Younger (1497–1543), before continuing on to Room 10 for the evocative 1586 *Massacre of the Innocents* by Lucas Van Valckenborch. Room 11 is dedicated to El Greco (with three pieces) and his Venetian contemporaries Tintoretto and Titian, while Caravaggio and the Spaniard José de Ribera dominate Room 12. Two paintings by Zurbarán (Room 14) and a single painting by Murillo (Room 15) add further Spanish flavour in the two rooms that follow, while the exceptionally rendered views of Venice by Canaletto (1697–1768) should on no account be missed.

Best of all on this floor is the extension (Rooms A to H) built to house the collection of Carmen Thyssen-Bornemisza. Room C houses paintings by Canaletto and Van Gogh, while the stunning Room H includes works by Monet, Sisley, Renoir and Pissarro.

Before heading downstairs, a detour to Rooms 19 through 21 will satisfy those devoted to 17th-century Dutch and Flemish masters, such as Anton van Dyck, Jan Brueghel the Elder, Rubens and Rembrandt (one painting).

### ➡ First Floor

If all that sounds impressive, the 1st floor is where the Thyssen really shines. There's a Gainsborough in Room 28 and three paintings by Goya in Room 31, but if you've been skimming the surface of this overwhelming collection, Room 32 is the place to linger over each and every painting. The astonishing texture of Van Gogh's *Les Vessenots* is a masterpiece, but the same could be said for paintings by Gauguin and Cézanne. Room 33 is also something special, with Toulouse-Lautrec and Degas.

In the 1st floor's extension (Rooms I to P), the names speak for themselves. Room K has works by Pissaro and Sisley, while Room

LOCAL KNOWLEDGE

### PEDRO ALMODÓVAR'S MADRID LOCATIONS

➡ Plaza Mayor – *La flor de mi secreto* (The Flower of My Secret; 1995)

➡ El Rastro – *Laberinto de pasiones* (Labyrinth of Passion; 1982)

➡ Villa Rosa – *Tacones lejanos* (High Heels; 1991)

➡ Café del Círculo de Bellas Artes – *Kika* (1993)

➡ Viaducto de Segovia – *Matador* (1986)

➡ Museo del Jamón (Calle Mayor) – *Carne trémula* (Live Flesh; 1997)

L is the domain of Gauguin (including his iconic *Mata Mua*) and Toulouse-Lautrec. Rooms N (Kandinsky and Munch), O (Matisse) and P (Matisse, Edward Hopper and Juan Gris) round out an outrageously rich journey through the masters. On your way to the stairs there's Edward Hopper's *Hotel Room.*

#### ➡ Ground Floor

On the ground floor, the foray into the 20th century that you began in the 1st-floor extension takes over with a fine spread of paintings from cubism through to pop art.

In Room 41 you'll see a nice mix of the big three of cubism – Picasso, Georges Braque and Madrid's own Juan Gris – along with several other contemporaries. Kandinsky is the main drawcard in Room 43, while there's an early Salvador Dalí alongside Max Ernst and Paul Klee in Room 44. Picasso appears again in Room 45, another one of the gallery's standout rooms; its treasures include works by Marc Chagall and Dalí's hallucinatory *Dream Caused by the Flight of a Bee Around a Pomegranate, One Second Before Waking Up.*

Room 46 is similarly rich, with Joan Miró's *Catalan Peasant with a Guitar,* the splattered craziness of Jackson Pollock's *Brown and Silver I,* and the deceptively simple but strangely pleasing *Green on Maroon* by Mark Rothko taking centre stage. In Rooms 47 and 48 the Thyssen builds to a stirring climax, with Roy Lichtenstein, and Lucian Freud, Sigmund's Berlin-born grandson, all represented.

### ★Centro de Arte Reina Sofía — MUSEUM

(Map p88; ☎91 774 10 00; www.museoreinasofia.es; Calle de Santa Isabel 52; adult/concession €10/free, 1.30-7pm Sun, 7-9pm Mon & Wed-Sat free; ⏲10am-9pm Mon & Wed-Sat, to 7pm Sun; Ⓜ Estación del Arte) Home to Picasso's *Guernica,* arguably Spain's most famous artwork, the Centro de Arte Reina Sofía is Madrid's premier collection of contemporary art. In addition to plenty of paintings by Picasso, other major drawcards are works by Salvador Dalí and Joan Miró. The collection principally spans the 20th century up to the 1980s. The occasional non-Spanish artist makes an appearance (including Francis Bacon's *Lying Figure;* 1966), but most of the collection is strictly peninsular. Tickets are cheaper if purchased online.

The permanent collection is displayed on the 2nd and 4th floors of the main wing of the museum, the Edificio Sabatini. *Guernica's* location never changes – you'll find it in Room 206 on the 2nd floor. Beyond that, the location of specific paintings can be a little confusing. The museum follows a theme-based approach, which ensures that you'll find works by Picasso or Miró, for example, spread across the two floors. The only solution if you're looking for something specific is to pick up the latest copy of the *Planos de Museo* (Museum Floorplans) from the information desk just outside the main entrance; it lists the rooms in which each artist appears (although not individual paintings).

In addition to Picasso's *Guernica,* which is worth the admission fee on its own, don't neglect the artist's preparatory sketches in the rooms surrounding Room 206; they offer an intriguing insight into the development of this seminal work. If Picasso's cubist style has captured your imagination, the work of the Madrid-born Juan Gris (1887–1927) or Georges Braque (1882–1963) may appeal.

The work of Joan Miró (1893–1983) is defined by often delightfully bright primary colours, but watch out also for a handful of his equally odd sculptures. Since his paintings became a symbol of the Barcelona Olympics in 1992, his work has begun to receive the international acclaim it so richly deserves – the museum is a fine place to see a representative sample of his innovative work.

The Reina Sofía is also home to 20 or so canvases by Salvador Dalí (1904–89), of which the most famous is perhaps the surrealist extravaganza that is *El gran masturbador* (1929). Among his other works is a strange bust of a certain *Joelle,* which Dalí created with his friend Man Ray (1890–1976). Another well-known surrealist painter, Max Ernst (1891–1976), is also worth tracking down.

If you can tear yourself away from the big names, the Reina Sofía offers a terrific opportunity to learn more about sometimes lesser-known 20th-century Spanish artists. Among these are Miquel Barceló (b 1957); *madrileño* artist José Gutiérrez Solana (1886–1945); the renowned Basque painter Ignazio Zuloaga (1870–1945); Benjamín Palencia (1894–1980), whose paintings capture the turbulence of Spain in the 1930s; Barcelona painter Antoni Tàpies (1923–2012); pop artist Eduardo Arroyo (1937–2018); and abstract painters such as Eusebio Sempere (1923–85) and members of the Equipo 57 group (founded in 1957 by a group of Spanish artists in exile in Paris), such as Pablo Palazuelo (1916–2007). Better known as a poet and playwright, Federico García Lorca (1898–1936) is represented by a number of his sketches.

Of the sculptors, watch for Pablo Gargallo (1881–1934), whose work in bronze includes a bust of Picasso, and the renowned Basque sculptors Jorge Oteiza (1908–2003) and Eduardo Chillida (1924–2002).

**★Parque del Buen Retiro** GARDENS
(Map p88; Plaza de la Independencia; ⏲6am-midnight Apr-Sep, to 10pm Oct-Mar; Ⓜ Retiro, Príncipe de Vergara, Ibiza, Atocha) **FREE** The glorious gardens of El Retiro are as beautiful as any you'll find in a European city. Strewn with marble monuments, landscaped lawns, the occasional elegant building (the Palacio de Cristal is especially worth seeking out) and abundant greenery, it's quiet and contemplative during the week but comes to life on weekends. Put simply, this is one of our favourite places in Madrid.

Laid out in the 17th century by Felipe IV as the preserve of kings, queens and their intimates, the park was opened to the public in 1868, and ever since, when the weather's fine and on weekends in particular, *madrileños* from all across the city gather here to stroll, read the Sunday papers in the shade, take a boat ride or nurse a cool drink at the numerous outdoor *terrazas* (open-air cafes).

The focal point for so much of El Retiro's life is the artificial *estanque* (lake), which is watched over by the massive ornamental structure of the **Monument to Alfonso XII** on the east side, complete with marble lions. As sunset approaches on a Sunday afternoon in summer, the crowd grows, bongos sound out across the park and people start to dance. **Row boats** (Map p88; per 45min weekdays/weekends €6/8; ⏲10am-8.30pm Apr-Sep, to 5.45pm Oct-Mar; Ⓜ Retiro) can be rented from the lake's northern shore – an iconic Madrid experience. On the southern end of the lake, the odd structure decorated with sphinxes is the **Fuente Egipcia** (Egyptian Fountain; Map p88;); legend has it that an enormous fortune buried in the park by Felipe IV in the mid-18th century rests here. Hidden among the trees south of the lake is the **Palacio de Cristal** (Map p88; ☎91 574 66 14; www.museoreinasofia.es; ⏲10am-10pm Apr-Sep, to 7pm Oct, to 6pm Nov-Mar; Ⓜ Retiro), a magnificent metal-and-glass structure that is arguably El Retiro's most beautiful architectural monument. It was built in 1887 as a winter garden for exotic flowers and is now used for temporary exhibitions organised by the Centro de Arte Reina Sofía. Just north of here, the 1883 **Palacio de Velázquez** (Map p88; www.museoreinasofia.es; admission varies; ⏲10am-10pm May-Sep, to 7pm Oct, to 6pm Nov-Apr) is also used for temporary exhibitions.

At the southern end of the park, near **La Rosaleda** (Rose Garden; Map p88) with its more than 4000 roses, is a statue of **El Ángel Caído** (Map p88). Strangely, it sits 666m above sea level... The **Puerta de Dante**, in the extreme southeastern corner of the park, is watched over by a carved mural of Dante's *Inferno*. Occupying much of the southwestern corner of the park is the **Jardín de los Planteles**, one of the least visited sections of El Retiro, where quiet pathways lead beneath an overarching canopy of trees.

*continued on p98*

## GOYA IN MADRID

Madrid has the best collection of Goyas on earth. Here's where to find them:

- **Museo del Prado** (p92)
- **Real Academia de Bellas Artes de San Fernando (**p86)
- **Ermita de San Antonio de la Florida** (p77)
- **Museo Lázaro Galdiano** (p104)
- **Basílica de San Francisco El Grande** (p81)
- **Museo Thyssen-Bornemisza** (p88)

ANIBAL TREJO/SHUTTERSTOCK ©

TOP SIGHT
# MUSEO DEL PRADO

**Welcome to one of the world's premier art galleries. The Museo del Prado's collection is like a window onto the historical vagaries of the Spanish soul, at once grand and imperious in the royal paintings of Velázquez, darkly tumultuous in Goya's *Pinturas negras* (Black Paintings) and outward looking with sophisticated works of art from all across Europe.**

## Casón del Buen Retiro

One of few vestiges of the 17th-century Palacio del Buen Retiro, this austere **building** (Map p88; ☎902 107077; Calle de Alfonso XII 28; ⏲9am-2.30pm Mon-Fri mid-Jun–mid-Sep, hours vary rest of year; Ⓜ Retiro) overlooking the Parque del Buen Retiro has been restored and now hosts an academic library by the Museo del Prado. There are occasional guided visits to the stunning Hall of the Ambassadors, crowned by Luca Giordano's astonishing 1697 ceiling fresco *The Apotheosis of the Spanish Monarchy*. Visits can be arranged at the 'Educación' desk just inside the Puerta de los Jerónimos in the Museo del Prado.

## Edificio Jerónimos

The Prado's eastern wing (Edificio Jerónimos) is part of the museum's stunning modern extension. Dedicated to temporary exhibitions (usually to display Prado masterpieces held in storage for decades for lack of wall space), its main attraction is the 2nd-floor cloisters. Built in 1672 with local granite, the cloisters were until recently attached to the adjacent Iglesia de San Jerónimo El Real (p100).

### DON'T MISS

- Velázquez
- Goya
- Flemish Collection
- *The Garden of Earthly Delights*
- El Greco
- *Emperor Carlos V on Horseback*
- Edificio Villanueva
- Edificio Jerónimos

### PRACTICALITIES

- Map p88
- www.museodelprado.es
- Paseo del Prado
- adult/concession/child €15/7.50/free, 6-8pm Mon-Sat & 5-7pm Sun free, audio guide €3.50, admission plus official guidebook €24
- ⏲10am-8pm Mon-Sat, to 7pm Sun
- Ⓜ Banco de España

## Edificio Villanueva

The Prado's western wing (Edificio Villanueva) was completed in 1785 as the neoclassical Palacio de Villanueva. It served as a cavalry barracks for Napoleon's troops between 1808 and 1813. In 1814 King Fernando VII decided to use the palace as a museum. Five years later the Museo del Prado opened with 311 Spanish paintings on display. This is the heart of the collection.

## El Greco

This Greek-born artist (hence the name) is considered the finest of the Prado's Spanish Renaissance painters. The vivid, almost surreal works by this 16th-century master and adopted Spaniard, whose figures are characteristically slender and tortured, are perfectly executed. Two of his more than 30 paintings in the collection – *The Annunciation* and *The Flight into Egypt* – were painted in Italy before the artist arrived in Spain, while *The Trinity* and *Knight with His Hand on His Breast* are considered his most important works.

## Emperor Carlos V on Horseback (Titian)

Considered one of the finest equestrian and royal portraits in art history, this 16th-century work is said to be the forerunner to similar paintings by Diego Rodríguez de Silva Velázquez a century later. One of the great masters of the Renaissance, Titian (1488–1576) was entering his most celebrated period as a painter when he created this, and it is widely recognised as one of his masterpieces.

## Goya

Francisco Goya is sometimes described as the first of the great Spanish masters and his work is found on all three floors of the Prado. Begin at the southern end of the ground or lower level where, in Rooms 64 and 65, Goya's *El dos de mayo* and *El tres de mayo* rank among Madrid's most emblematic paintings. In the adjacent rooms (66 and 67), his disturbing *Pinturas negras* (Black Paintings) are so named for the distorted animalesque appearance of their characters. The *Saturno devorando a su hijo* (Saturn Devouring His Son) is utterly unsettling, while *La romería de San Isidro* and *Aquelarre* or *El gran cabrón* (The Great He-Goat) are dominated by the compelling individual faces of the condemned souls. An interesting footnote to *Pinturas negras* is *El coloso,* a Goya-esque work hanging next to the *Pinturas negras* that was long considered part of the master's portfolio until the Prado's experts decided otherwise in 2008.

### PRADO FLOOR PLAN

The free plan to the Prado (available at or just inside the entrance) lists the location of 50 Prado masterpieces and gives room numbers for all major artists. It's also available online.

**Although entry for the last two hours of every day is free, the Prado can be extremely crowded at these times. If you can afford to, it's better to arrive first thing in the morning before the crowds gather.**

### TICKETS

Entrance to the Prado is via the eastern Puerta de los Jerónimos; tickets must first be purchased from the **ticket office** (Puerta de Goya; Map p88; www.museodelprado.es; Calle de Felipe IV; ⌚9.45am-7.30pm Mon-Sat, to 6.30pm Sun; Ⓜ Banco de España) at the northern end of the building, opposite the Hotel Ritz and beneath the Puerta de Goya.

# Museo del Prado

## PLAN OF ATTACK

Begin on the 1st floor with ① **Las meninas** by Velázquez. Although it alone is worth the entry price, it's a fine introduction to the 17th-century Golden Age of Spanish art; nearby are more of Velázquez' royal paintings and works by Zurbarán and Murillo. While on the 1st floor, seek out Goya's ② **La maja vestida and La maja desnuda**, with more of Goya's early works in neighbouring rooms. Downstairs at the southern end of the Prado, Goya's anger is evident in the searing ③ **El dos de mayo and El tres de mayo**, and the torment of Goya's later years finds expression in the adjacent rooms with ④ **pinturas negras** (Black Paintings). Also on the lower floor, Hieronymus Bosch's weird and wonderful ⑤ **The Garden of Earthly Delights** is one of the Prado's signature masterpieces. Returning to the 1st floor, El Greco's ⑥ **Adoration of the Shepherds** is an extraordinary work, as is Peter Paul Rubens' ⑦ **Las tres gracias**, which forms the centrepiece of the Prado's gathering of Flemish masters. A detour to the 2nd floor takes in some lesser-known Goyas, but finish in the ⑧ **Edificio Jerónimos**, with a visit to the cloisters and the outstanding bookshop.

## TOP TIPS

➡ Purchase your ticket online (www.museodelprado.es) and avoid the queues.

➡ Best time to visit is as soon as possible after opening time.

➡ The website (www.museodelprado.es/coleccion/que-ver) has self-guided tours for one- to three-hour visits.

➡ Nearby are Museo Thyssen-Bornemisza and Centro de Arte Reina Sofía. Together they form an extraordinary trio of galleries.

IMAGNO / GETTY IMAGES ©

**Las meninas (Velázquez)**

This masterpiece depicts Velázquez and the Infanta Margarita. According to some experts, the images of the king and queen appear in mirrors behind Velázquez.

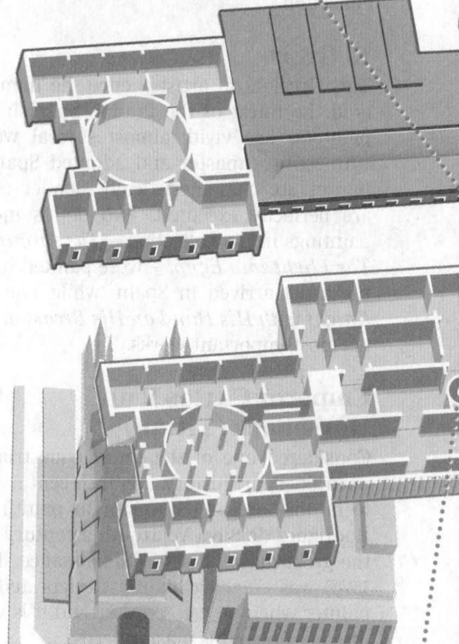


**Adoration of the Shepherds (El Greco)**

There's an ecstatic quality to this intense painting. El Greco's distorted rendering of bodily forms came to characterise much of his later work.

**Edificio Jerónimos**

Opened in 2007, this state-of-the-art extension has rotating exhibitions of Prado masterpieces held in storage for decades for lack of wall space, and stunning 2nd-floor granite cloisters that date back to 1672.

**Las tres gracias (Rubens)**
A late Rubens masterpiece, *The Three Graces* is a classical and masterly expression of Rubens' preoccupation with sensuality, here portraying Aglaia, Euphrosyne and Thalia, the daughters of Zeus.

**La maja vestida & La maja desnuda (Goya)**
These enigmatic works scandalised early-19th-century Madrid society, fuelling the rumour mill as to the woman's identity and drawing the ire of the Spanish Inquisition.

DEAGOSTINI / GETTY IMAGES ©

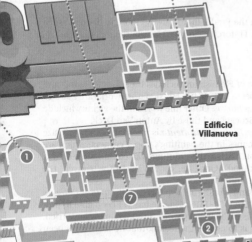

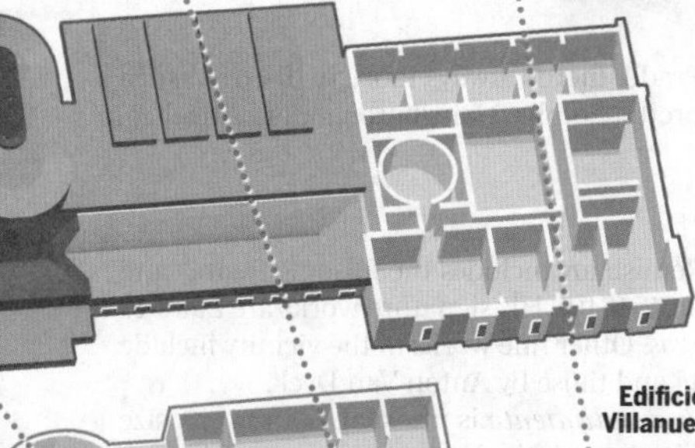


DEAGOSTINI / GETTY IMAGES ©

**El dos de mayo & El tres de mayo (Goya)**
Few paintings evoke a city's sense of self quite like Goya's portrayal of Madrid's valiant but ultimately unsuccessful uprising against French rule in 1808.

**Las pinturas negras (Goya)**
*Las pinturas negras* are Goya's darkest works. *Saturno devorando a su hijo* evokes a writhing mass of tortured humanity, while *La romería de San Isidro* and *El aquelarre* are profoundly unsettling.

**The Garden of Earthly Delights (Bosch)**
A fantastical painting in triptych form, this overwhelming work depicts the Garden of Eden and what the Prado describes as 'the lugubrious precincts of Hell' in exquisitely bizarre detail.

PABLO BLAZQUEZ DOMINGUEZ / GETTY IMAGES ©

Up on the 1st floor, other masterful works include the intriguing *La família de Carlos IV,* which portrays the Spanish royal family in 1800; Goya portrayed himself in the background just as Velázquez did in *Las meninas*. Also present are *La maja vestida* (The Young Lady Dressed) and *La maja desnuda* (The Young Lady Undressed). These portraits of an unknown woman, commonly believed to be the Duquesa de Alba (the rumour at the time was that she was Goya's lover), are identical save for the lack of clothing in the latter.

## The Best of the Rest

No matter how long you spend in the Prado, there's always more to discover, such as the paintings by Dürer, Rafael, Tintoretto, Sorolla, Gainsborough, Fra Angelico, Tiepolo...

## The Flemish Collection

The Prado's outstanding collection of Flemish art includes the fulsome figures and bulbous cherubs of Peter Paul Rubens (1577–1640). His signature works are *Las tres gracias* and *Adoración de los reyes magos*. Other fine works in the vicinity include *The Triumph of Death* by Pieter Bruegel and those by Anton Van Dyck.

Van Der Weyden's 1435 painting *El descendimiento* is unusual, both for its size and for the recurring crossbow shapes in the painting's upper corners, which are echoed in the bodies of Mary and Christ (the painting was commissioned by a Crossbow Manufacturers Brotherhood). Once the central part of a triptych, the painting is filled with drama and luminous colours.

On no account miss the weird and wonderful *The Garden of Earthly Delights* (Room 56A) by Hieronymus Bosch (c 1450–1516). No one has yet been able to provide a definitive explanation for this hallucinatory work, although many have tried. The closer you look, the harder it is to escape the feeling that he must have been doing some extraordinary drugs.

*Judith at the Banquet of Holofernes,* the only painting by Rembrandt in the Prado, was completed in 1634; note the signature and date on the arm of the chair. It shows a master at the peak of his powers, with an expert use of the chiaroscuro style, and the astonishing detail in the subject's clothing and face.

### ONLY IN MADRID

Madrid must be the only city in the world where a near riot was caused by an art exhibition. John Hooper in his book *The New Spaniards* tells the story of how in 1990 the Prado brought an unprecedented number of works by Velázquez out of storage and opened its doors to the public. The exhibition was so popular that more than half a million visitors came to see the rare showing. Just before the exhibition was scheduled to end, the Prado announced that they would keep the doors open for as long as there were people wanting to enter. When the doors finally shut at 9pm, several hundred people were still outside waiting in the rain. They chanted, they shouted and they banged on the doors of this august institution with their umbrellas. The gallery was reopened, but queues kept forming and when the doors shut on the exhibition for good at 10.30pm, furious art lovers clashed with police. At midnight, there were still almost 50 people outside chanting 'We want to come in'.

Statue of Diego Velázquez

## Velázquez

Velázquez' role as court painter means that his works provide a fascinating insight into 17th-century royal life and the Prado holds the richest collection of his works. Of all the works by Velázquez, *Las meninas* (The Maids of Honour; Room 12) is what most people come to see. Completed in 1656, it is more properly known as *La família de Felipe IV* (The Family of Felipe IV). It depicts Velázquez himself on the left and, in the centre, the infant Margarita. There's more to it than that: the artist in fact portrays himself painting the king and queen, whose images appear, according to some experts, in mirrors behind Velázquez. His mastery of light and colour is never more apparent than here. An interesting detail of the painting, aside from the extraordinary cheek of painting himself in royal company, is the presence of the cross of the Order of Santiago on his vest. The artist was apparently obsessed with being given a noble title. He received it shortly before his death, but in this oil painting he awarded himself the order years earlier!

The rooms surrounding *Las meninas* (Rooms 14 and 15) contain more fine paintings of various members of royalty who seem to spring off the canvas, many of them on horseback. Also nearby is his *La rendición de Breda* (The Surrender of Breda), while other Spanish painters worth tracking down in the neighbouring rooms include Bartolomé Esteban Murillo, José de Ribera and the stark figures of Francisco de Zurbarán.

### PASEO DEL ARTE

If you plan to visit the Museo del Prado, Museo Thyssen-Bornemisza and Centro de Arte Reina Sofía while in Madrid, the Paseo del Arte combined ticket covers them all for €31 and is valid for one visit to each gallery during a 12-month period; buying separate tickets would cost €38.

**To get to the Prado, you have a bit of a walk along the Paseo del Prado from the nearest metro stations, which are Banco de España (line 2; on Plaza de la Cibeles to the north) or Atocha (line 1; on Plaza del Emperador Carlos V to the south).**

### TOP TIPS

➡ Plan to make a couple of visits; the Prado can be overwhelming if you try to absorb it all at once.

➡ A single-day ticket costs €15. A two-day pass (valid for any two days in a year) costs €22.

➡ Buy your tickets online in advance to avoid the queues.

## Salamanca

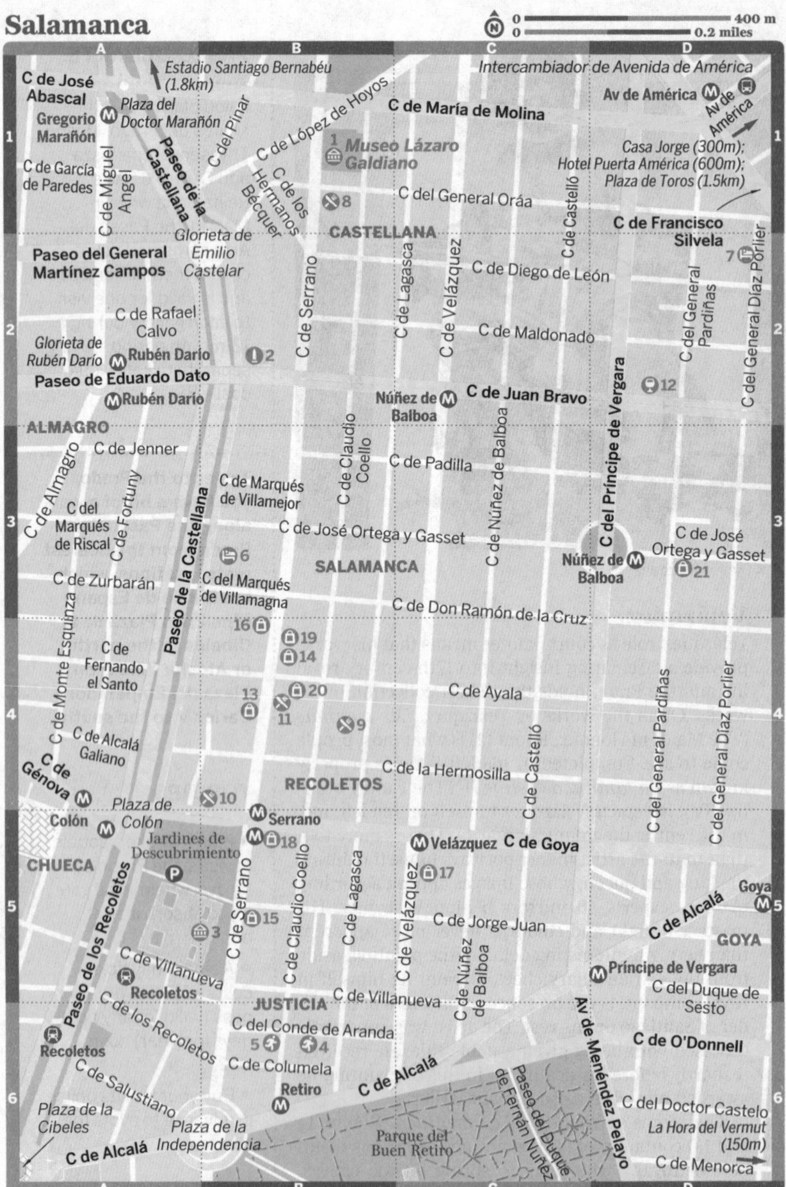


West of here is the moving **Bosque del Recuerdo** (Memorial Garden; Map p88; Calle de Alfonso XII; 6am-10pm; Retiro), an understated memorial to the 191 victims of the 11 March 2004 train bombings. For each victim stands an olive or cypress tree. To the north, just inside the Puerta de Felipe IV, stands what is thought to be **Madrid's oldest tree** (Map p88; Plaza de la Indepencia; Retiro), a Mexican conifer *(ahuehuete)* planted in 1633.

In the northeastern corner of the park is the **Ermita de San Isidro** (Map p88; Paseo del Quince de Mayo 62; Retiro), a small country chapel noteworthy as one of the few, albeit

## Salamanca

**Top Sights**
1 Museo Lázaro Galdiano........................B1

**Sights**
2 Museo al Aire Libre..............................B2
3 Museo Arqueológico Nacional.............A5

**Activities, Courses & Tours**
4 Chi Spa................................................B6
5 Lab Room Spa......................................B6

**Sleeping**
6 Villa Magna..........................................B3
7 VP El Madroño......................................D2

**Eating**
8 Astrolabius...........................................B1
9 Casa Dani.............................................B4
10 Platea.................................................B4
11 Street XO............................................B4

**Drinking & Nightlife**
12 Almonte..............................................D2

**Shopping**
13 Agatha Ruiz de la Prada......................B4
14 Bomboneriás Santa.............................B4
15 Camper...............................................B5
16 De Viaje..............................................B4
17 Ekseption............................................C5
18 Loewe.................................................B5
19 Manolo Blahnik...................................B4
20 Mantequería Bravo..............................B4
21 Oriol Balaguer.....................................D3

modest, examples of Romanesque architecture in Madrid. When it was built, Madrid was a small village more than 2km away.

**Plaza de la Cibeles** SQUARE
(Map p88; Ⓜ Banco de España) Of all the grand roundab7outs that punctuate the Paseo del Prado, Plaza de la Cibeles most evokes the splendour of imperial Madrid. The jewel in the crown is the astonishing Palacio de Comunicaciones (p99). Other landmark buildings around the plaza's perimeter include the **Palacio de Linares and Casa de América** (Map p88; ☎91 595 48 00, ticket reservations 902 221424; www.casamerica.es; Plaza de la Cibeles 2; adult/student & senior/child €8/5/free; ⏰guided tours 11am, noon & 1pm Sat & Sun Sep-Jul, shorter hours Aug, ticket office 10am-3pm & 4-8pm Mon-Fri; Ⓜ Banco de España), the **Palacio Buenavista** (Map p102; Plaza de la Cibeles; Ⓜ Banco de España) and the national **Banco de España** (Map p88; Calle de Alcalá 48). The spectacular fountain of the goddess Cybele at the centre of the plaza is one of Madrid's most beautiful.

Ever since it was erected by Ventura Rodríguez in 1780, the fountain has been a Madrid favourite. Carlos III liked it so much he tried to have it moved to the royal gardens of the Granja de San Ildefonso, on the road to Segovia, but *madrileños* kicked up such a fuss that he let it be.

There are fine views east from Plaza de la Cibeles towards the Puerta de Alcalá or, even better, west towards the Edificio Metrópolis (p105).

**CentroCentro** ARTS CENTRE
(Map p88; ☎91 480 00 08; www.centrocentro.org; Plaza de la Cibeles 1; ⏰10am-8pm Tue-Sun; Ⓜ Plaza de España) FREE One of Madrid's more surprising and diverse cultural spaces, CentroCentro is housed in the grand Palacio de Comunicaciones. It has cutting-edge exhibitions covering 5000 sq metres over four floors (floors 1, 3, 4 and 5), as well as quiet reading rooms and some stunning architecture, especially in the soaring Antiguo Patio de Operaciones on the 2nd floor. On the 8th floor is the Mirador de Madrid (p99).

**Mirador de Madrid** VIEWPOINT
(Map p88; www.centrocentro.org; Plaza de la Cibeles, Palacio de Comunicaciones, 8th fl; adult/child €3/1.50; ⏰10.30am-2pm & 4-7.30pm Tue-Sun; Ⓜ Banco de España) The views from the summit of the Palacio de Comunicaciones are among Madrid's best, sweeping out over Plaza de la Cibeles, up the hill towards the sublime Edificio Metrópolis and out to the mountains. Buy your ticket up the stairs then take the lift to the 6th floor, from where the gates are opened every half-hour. You can either take another lift or climb the stairs up to the 8th floor.

**Puerta de Alcalá** MONUMENT
(Map p88; Plaza de la Independencia; Ⓜ Retiro) This imposing triumphal gate was once the main entrance to the city (its name derives from the fact that the road that passed under it led to Alcalá de Henares) and was surrounded by the city's walls. It was here that the city authorities controlled access to the capital and levied customs duties.

**Caixa Forum** MUSEUM, ARCHITECTURE
(Map p88; ☎91 330 73 00; https://obrasociallacaixa.org/en/cultura/caixaforum-madrid; Paseo del Prado 36; adult/child €4/free; ⏰10am-8pm;

Ⓜ Estación del Arte) This extraordinary structure is one of Madrid's most eye-catching landmarks. Seeming to hover above the ground, the brick edifice is topped by an intriguing summit of rusted iron. On an adjacent wall is the *jardín colgante* (hanging garden), a lush (if thinning) vertical wall of greenery almost four storeys high. Inside there are four floors of exhibition space awash in stainless steel and with soaring ceilings. The exhibitions here are worth checking out and include photography, contemporary painting and multimedia shows.

Caixa Forum's shop (mostly books) is outstanding. You can visit the shop without paying the entrance fee.

**Real Jardín Botánico** GARDENS

(Royal Botanical Garden; Map p88; ☎91 420 04 38; www.rjb.csic.es; Plaza de Bravo Murillo 2; adult/child €6/free; ⏲10am-9pm May-Aug, to 8pm Apr & Sep, to 7pm Mar & Oct, to 6pm Nov-Feb; Ⓜ Estación del Arte) Madrid's botanical gardens are a leafy oasis in the centre of town, though they're not as expansive or as popular as the Parque del Buen Retiro. With some 30,000 species crammed into a relatively small 8-hectare area, it's more a place to wander at leisure than laze under a tree, although there are benches dotted throughout the gardens where you can sit.

**Iglesia de San Jerónimo El Real** CHURCH

(Map p88; ☎91 420 35 78; www.parroquiasanjeronimoelreal.es; Calle de Ruiz de Alarcón; ⏲10am-1pm & 5-8pm mid-Sep–Jun, 10am-1pm & 6-8.30pm Jul–mid-Sep; Ⓜ Atocha, Banco de España) FREE Tucked away behind Museo del Prado, this chapel was traditionally favoured by the Spanish royal family, and King Juan Carlos I was crowned here in 1975 upon the death of Franco. The sometimes-sober, sometimes-splendid mock-Isabelline interior is actually a 19th-century reconstruction that took its cues from Iglesia de San Juan de los Reyes in Toledo; the original was largely destroyed during the Peninsular War. What remained of the former cloisters has been incorporated into the Museo del Prado.

**Real Fábrica de Tapices** LANDMARK

(Royal Tapestry Workshop; Map p88; ☎91 434 05 50; http://realfabricadetapices.com; Calle de Fuenterrabía 2; adult/child €5/4; ⏲10am-2pm Mon-Fri Sep-Jul, guided tours hourly; Ⓜ Atocha Renfe, Menéndez Pelayo) If a wealthy Madrid nobleman ever wanted to impress, he went to the Real Fábrica de Tapices, where royalty commissioned the pieces that adorned their palaces and private residences. The Spanish government, Spanish royal family and the Vatican were the biggest patrons of the tapestry business: Spain alone is said to have collected four million tapestries. With such an exclusive clientele, it was a lucrative business and remains so, 300 years after the factory was founded.

**Antigua Estación de Atocha** NOTABLE BUILDING

(Old Atocha Train Station; Map p88; Plaza del Emperador Carlos V; Ⓜ Atocha Renfe) In 1992 the northwestern wing of the Antigua Estación de Atocha was given a stunning overhaul. The structure of this grand iron-and-glass relic from the 19th century was preserved, while its interior was artfully converted into a light-filled tropical garden with more than 500 plant species. The project was the work of architect Rafael Moneo, and his landmark achievement was to create a thoroughly modern space that resonates with the stately European train stations of another age.

## Salamanca

In the *barrio* of Salamanca, the unmistakeable whiff of old money settles comfortably upon the aspirations of Spain's nouveau riche. It's the place to put on your finest clothes, regardless of your errand, and be seen. Sights are thinly spread but worth tracking down, with a focus on the arts, architecture and the very Spanish passion of bullfighting.

**★ Plaza de Toros** STADIUM

(☎91 356 22 00; www.las-ventas.com; Calle de Alcalá 237; ⏲10am-5.30pm; Ⓜ Ventas) FREE East of central Madrid, the Plaza de Toros Monumental de Las Ventas (Las Ventas) is the most important and prestigious bullring in the world, and a visit here is a good way to gain an insight into this very Spanish tradition. The fine **Museo Taurino** (☎91 725 18 57; https://lasventastour.com/en/the-bullfighting-museum; Calle de Alcalá 237; ⏲10am-7pm May-Oct, to 6pm Nov-Apr; Ⓜ Ventas) FREE is also here, and the architecture will be of interest even to those with no interest in *las corridas* (bullfights). Bullfights are still held regularly here during the season, which runs roughly mid-May to September.

One of the largest rings in the bullfighting world, Las Ventas has a grand Mudéjar exterior and a suitably coliseum-like arena surrounding the broad sandy ring. It was

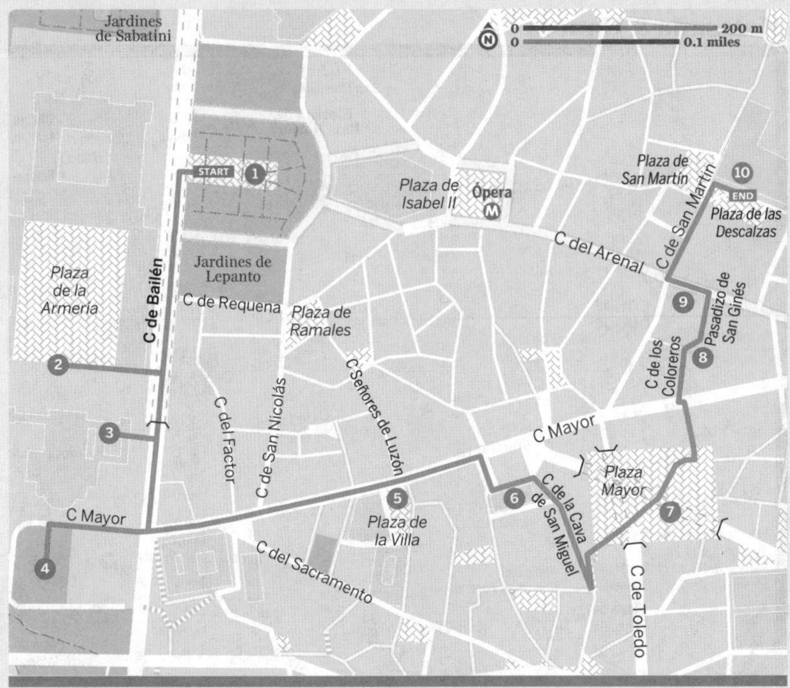




# City Walk
# Old Madrid

**START** PLAZA DE ORIENTE
**END** CONVENTO DE LAS DESCALZAS REALES
**LENGTH** 2KM; TWO HOURS

This walk takes you past the iconic architecture of imperial Madrid and into the heart of the modern city – two very different cities that often overlap.

Begin in 1 **Plaza de Oriente** (p79), a splendid arc of greenery and graceful architecture that could be Madrid's most agreeable plaza. You'll be surrounded by gardens, the Palacio Real and the Teatro Real, with an ever-changing cast of *madrileños* at play. Overlooking the plaza, 2 **Palacio Real** (p76) was Spain's seat of royal power for centuries. Almost next door is 3 **Catedral de Nuestra Señora de la Almudena** (p80); it may lack the solemnity of other Spanish cathedrals, but it's a beautiful part of the skyline. Drop down to the 4 **Muralla Árabe** (p80), a short stretch of the original 'Arab Wall', then climb gently up Calle Mayor, pausing to admire the ruins of Madrid's first cathedral, Santa María de la Almudena, then on to 5 **Plaza de la Villa** (p78), a cosy square surrounded by some of the best examples of Madrid baroque architecture. A little further up the hill and just off Calle Mayor, 6 **Mercado de San Miguel** (p116), one of Madrid's oldest markets, has become one of the coolest places to eat and mingle with locals in downtown Madrid.

Head down the hill along Cava de San Miguel, then climb up through the Arco de Cuchilleros to 7 **Plaza Mayor** (p74), one of Spain's grandest plazas. Down a narrow lane north of the plaza, 8 **Chocolatería de San Ginés** (p126) is justifiably famous for its *chocolate con churros*, the ideal Madrid indulgence at any hour of the day. Almost next door, along pedestrianised Calle del Arenal, is the pleasing brick-and-stone 9 **Iglesia de San Ginés** (p79), one of the longest-standing relics of Christian Madrid.

A short climb to the north, the 10 **Convento de las Descalzas Reales** (p79) is an austere convent with an extraordinarily rich interior. In the heart of the city, it's a great place to finish up.

# Malasaña & Chueca

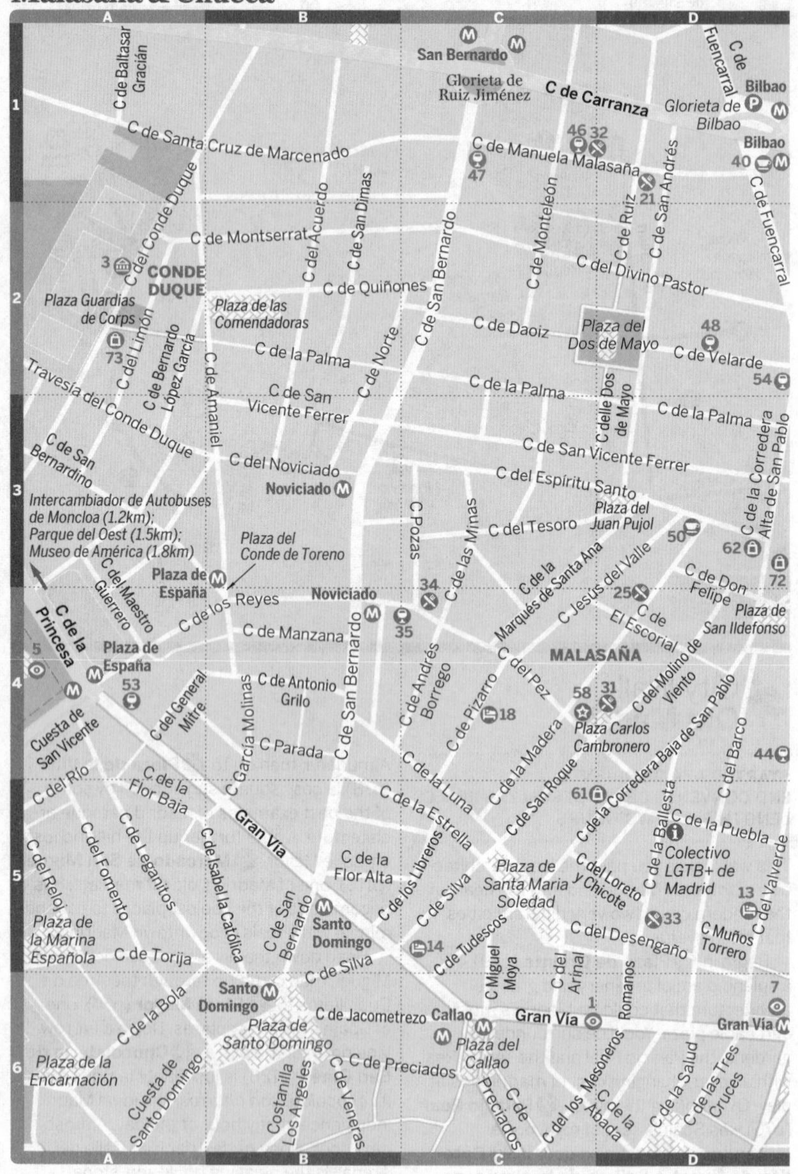


opened in 1931 and hosted its first fight three years later; its four storeys can seat 25,000 spectators. Like all bullrings, it evokes more a sense of a theatre than a sports stadium. It also hosts concerts.

To be carried high on the shoulders of aficionados out through the grand and decidedly Moorish Puerta de Madrid is the ultimate dream of any *torero* (bullfighter) – if you've made it at Las Ventas, you've reached the pinnacle of the bullfighting world. The gate is suitably known more colloquially as the 'Gate of Glory'. Guided visits (in English and Spanish) take you out onto the sand and

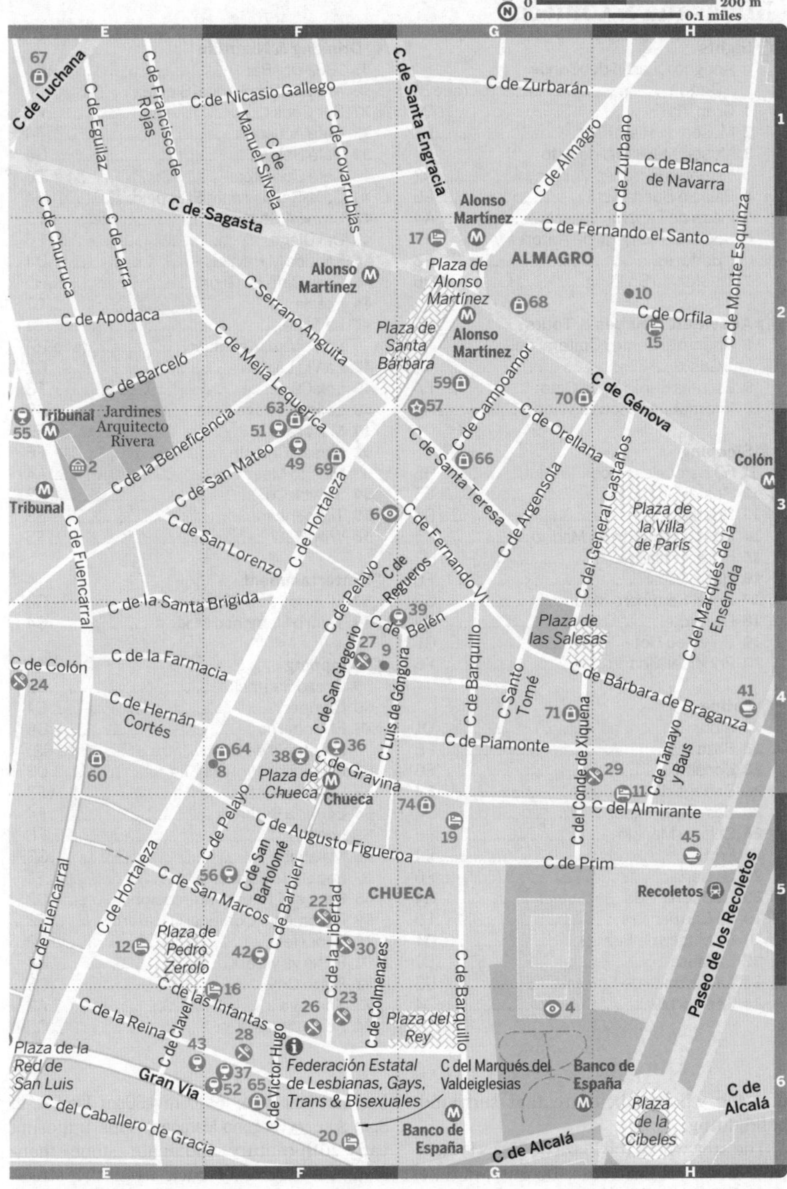




into the royal box; tours must be booked in advance through **Las Ventas Tour** (☎687 739032; https://lasventastour.com; adult/child €15/6; ⊙10am-5.30pm, days of bullfight 10am-1.30pm; Ⓜ Ventas).

The recently renovated Museo Taurino contains a new space dedicated to bullfighting legend Manolete, as well as a curious collection of paraphernalia, costumes (the *traje de luces,* or suit of lights, is one of bullfighting's most recognisable props), photos and other bullfighting memorabilia up on the top floor above one of the two courtyards by the ring. It's a fascinating insight

## Malasaña & Chueca

**Sights**

Antiguo Cuartel del Conde Duque........................(see 3)
1 Gran Vía........................C6
2 Museo de Historia........................E3
3 Museo Municipal de Arte Contemporáneo........................A2
4 Palacio Buenavista........................G6
5 Plaza de España........................A4
6 Sociedad General de Autores y Editores........................F3
7 Telefónica Building........................D6

**Activities, Courses & Tours**

8 Apunto – Centro Cultural del Gusto........................F4
9 Escuela Europea de Cata........................F4
10 International House Madrid........................H2

**Sleeping**

11 60 Balconies Recoletos........................H5
12 Hostal Don Juan........................E5
13 Hostal La Zona........................D5
14 Hostal Main Street Madrid........................C5
15 Hotel Orfila........................H2
16 Hotel Óscar........................F6
17 Hotel Sardinero Madrid........................G2
18 Life Hotel........................C4
19 Only You Hotel........................G5
20 Principal Madrid........................F6

**Eating**

21 Albur........................D1
22 Bazaar........................F5
23 Bocaito........................F6
24 Bodega de la Ardosa........................E4
25 Casa Julio........................D4
26 Celso y Manolo........................F6
27 Frida........................F4
28 La Barraca........................F6
29 La Buena Vida........................H4
30 La Carmencita........................F5
31 La Mucca de Pez........................D4
32 La Musa........................D1
33 La Tasquita de Enfrente........................D5
34 Pez Tortilla........................C4

**Drinking & Nightlife**

35 1862 Dry Bar........................C4
36 Antigua Casa Ángel Sierra........................F4
37 Bar Cock........................F6
38 Café Acuarela........................F4
39 Café Belén........................G4
40 Café Comercial........................D1
41 Café-Restaurante El Espejo........................H4
42 Club 54 Studio........................F5
43 Del Diego........................E6
44 Fábrica Maravillas........................D4
45 Gran Café de Gijón........................H5
46 Irreale........................C1
47 La Tape........................C1
La Terraza de Óscar........................(see 16)
48 La Vía Láctea........................D2
49 Lola09........................F3
50 Lolina Vintage Café........................D3
51 Macera........................F3
52 Museo Chicote........................F6
53 Nice to Meet You........................A4
54 Stuyck Co........................D2
55 Tupperware........................E3
56 Why Not?........................F5

**Entertainment**

57 El Junco Jazz Club........................G2
58 Teatro Flamenco Madrid........................C4

**Shopping**

59 Cacao Sampaka........................G2
60 Camper........................E4
61 El Moderno........................D5
El Templo de Susu........................(see 62)
62 Flamingos Vintage Kilo........................D3
63 La Cervecista........................F3
64 Librería Berkana........................F4
65 Loewe........................F6
66 Malababa........................G3
67 Papelería Salazar........................E1
68 Pasajes Librería Internacional........................G2
69 Patrimonio Comunal Olivarero........................F3
70 Poncelet........................G2
71 Reserva y Cata........................G4
72 Retro City........................D3
73 Sportivo........................A2
74 Xoan Viqueira........................G5

into the whole subculture that surrounds bullfighting.

The area where the Plaza de Toros is located is known as Las Ventas because, in times gone by, several wayside taverns *(ventas)*, along with houses of ill repute, were to be found here.

★**Museo Lázaro Galdiano** MUSEUM
(Map p98; ☎91 561 60 84; www.flg.es; Calle de Serrano 122; adult/concession/child €7/4/free, last hour free; ⏰10am-4.30pm Tue-Sat, to 3pm Sun; Ⓜ Gregorio Marañón) This imposing early-20th-century Italianate stone mansion, set discreetly back from the street, belonged to Don José Lázaro Galdiano (1862–1947), a successful businessman and passionate patron of the arts. His astonishing private collection, which he bequeathed to the city upon his death, includes 13,000 works of art and objets d'art, a quarter of which are on show at any time.

**Museo al Aire Libre** SCULPTURE
(Map p98; Paseo de la Castellana; 24hr; M Rubén Darío) FREE This fascinating open-air collection of 17 abstract sculptures includes works by renowned Basque artist Eduardo Chillida, Catalan master Joan Miró, as well as Eusebio Sempere and Alberto Sánchez, among Spain's foremost sculptors of the 20th century. The sculptures are beneath the overpass where Paseo de Eduardo Dato crosses Paseo de la Castellana, but somehow the hint of traffic grime and pigeon shit only adds to the appeal. All but one are on the eastern side of Paseo de la Castellana.

**Museo Arqueológico Nacional** MUSEUM
(Map p98; 91 577 79 12; www.man.es; Calle de Serrano 13; admission €3, 2-8pm Sat & 9.30am-noon Sun free; 9.30am-8pm Tue-Sat, to 3pm Sun; M Serrano) The showpiece National Archaeology Museum contains a sweeping accumulation of artefacts behind its towering facade. Daringly redesigned within, the museum ranges across Spain's ancient history and the large collection includes stunning mosaics taken from Roman villas across Spain, intricate Muslim-era and Mudéjar handiwork, sculpted figures such as the *Dama de Ibiza* and *Dama de Elche,* examples of Romanesque and Gothic architectural styles and a partial copy of the prehistoric cave paintings of Altamira (Cantabria).

## Malasaña & Chueca

Malasaña and Chueca are more for doing than seeing. But with a handful of architectural stars (the Antiguo Cuartel de Conde Duque, the Museo de Historia, the Sociedad General de Autores y Editores, and Gran Vía's marvellous facades), there's plenty to turn your head as you skip from bar to shop and back to the bar again. The neighbourhoods' squares – Plaza Dos de Mayo in particular – also provide much-needed breathing space as you wander the tightly packed streets.

**Gran Vía** STREET
(Map p102; M Gran Vía, Callao) It's difficult to imagine Madrid without Gran Vía, the grand boulevard lined with towering belle-époque facades that climbs up through the centre of Madrid from Plaza de España then down to Calle de Alcalá. But it has only existed since 1910, when it was bulldozed through a labyrinth of old streets. Fourteen streets disappeared off the map, as did 311 houses, including one where Goya had once lived.

Plans for the boulevard were first announced in 1862 and so interminable were the delays that a famous *zarzuela* (Spanish mix of theatre, music and dance), *La Gran Vía,* first performed in 1886, was penned to mock the city authorities. It may have destroyed whole *barrios,* but Gran Vía is still considered one of the most successful examples of urban planning in central Madrid since the late 19th century.

One eye-catching building, the **Edificio Carrión** (Map p76; cnr Gran Vía & Calle de Jacometrezo; M Callao), was Madrid's first pre-WWI tower-block apartment hotel. Also dominating the skyline about one-third of the way along Gran Vía is the 1920s-era **Telefónica building** (Map p102; 91 580 87 00; https://espacio.fundaciontelefonica.com; Calle de Fuencarral 3; 10am-8pm Tue-Sun; M Gran Vía) FREE, which was for years the highest building in the city. During the civil war, when Madrid was besieged by Franco's forces and the boulevard became known as 'Howitzer Alley' due to the artillery shells that rained down upon it, the Telefónica building was a favoured target.

Among the more interesting buildings is the stunning, French-designed **Edificio Metrópolis** (Map p84; Gran Vía; M Banco de España, Sevilla), built in 1907, which marks the southern end of Gran Vía. The winged victory statue atop its dome was added in 1975 and is best seen from Calle de Alcalá or Plaza de la Cibeles. A little up the boulevard is the **Edificio Grassy** (Map p84; Gran Vía 1; M Banco de España, Sevilla), with the Rolex sign and built in 1916. With its circular 'temple' as a crown, and profusion of arcs and slender columns, it's one of the most elegant buildings along Gran Vía.

Otherwise Gran Vía is home to around twice as many businesses (over 1050 at last count) as homes (nearly 600); over 13,000 people work along the street; and up to 60,000 vehicles pass through every day (including almost 185 buses an hour during peak periods). There are over 40 hotels on Gran Vía, but, sadly, just three of the 15 cinemas for which the boulevard was famous remain.

**Museo de Historia** MUSEUM
(Map p102; 91 701 16 86; www.madrid.es/museodehistoria; Calle de Fuencarral 78; 10am-8pm Tue-Sun; M Tribunal) FREE The fine Museo de Historia (formerly the Museo Municipal) has an elaborate and restored baroque entrance, raised in 1721 by Pedro de Ribera.

## Chamberí

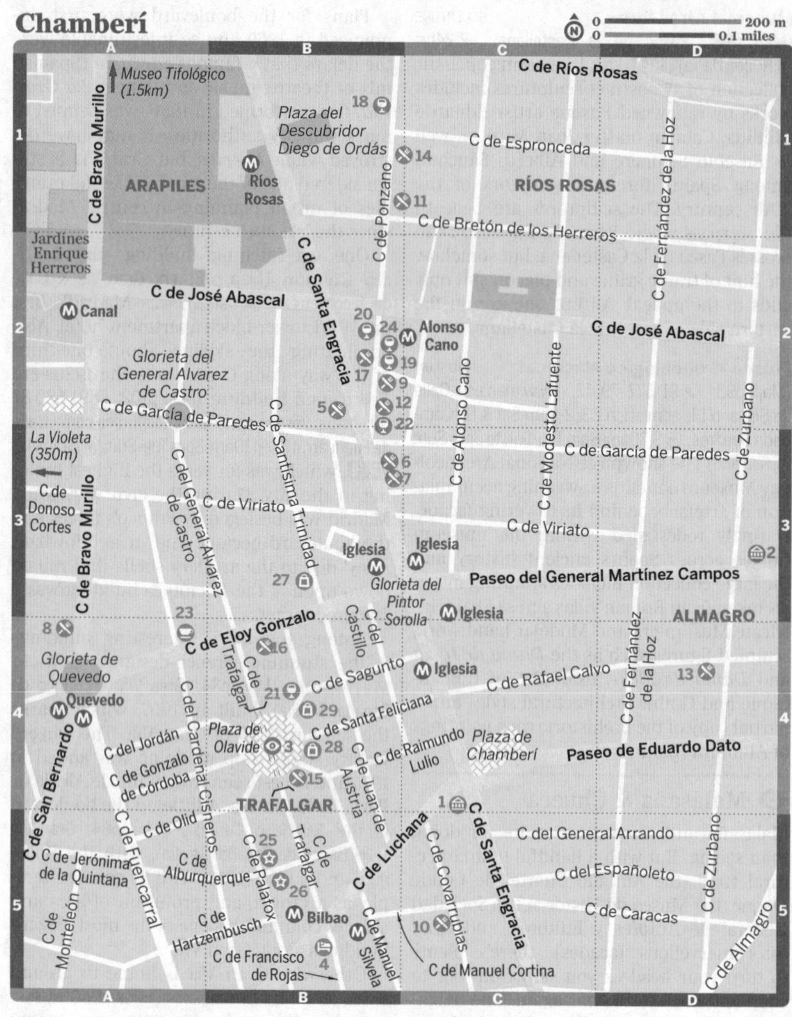


Behind this facade, the collection is dominated by paintings and other memorabilia charting the historical evolution of Madrid. The highlights are Goya's *Allegory of the City of Madrid* (on the 1st floor); the caricatures lampooning Napoleon and the early 19th-century French occupation of Madrid (1st floor); and the expansive model of Madrid as it was in 1830 (basement).

**Sociedad General de Autores y Editores** ARCHITECTURE
(General Society of Authors & Editors; Map p102; Calle de Fernando VI 4; Ⓜ Alonso Martínez) This swirling, melting wedding cake of a building is as close as Madrid comes to the work of Antoni Gaudí, which so illuminates Barcelona. It's a joyously self-indulgent (if slightly grimy) ode to Modernisme (an architectural and artistic style, influenced by art nouveau and sometimes known as Catalan modernism) and is virtually one of a kind in Madrid. Casual visitors are actively discouraged, but what you see from the street is impressive enough.

The only exception is on the first Monday of October, International Architecture Day, when its interior staircase alone is reason enough to come and look inside.

## Chamberí

**Sights**
1 Estación de Chamberí ... C4
2 Museo Sorolla ... D3
3 Plaza de Olavide ... B4

**Sleeping**
4 Hotel One Shot Luchana 22 ... B5

**Eating**
5 Alma Cheli ... B2
6 Bienmesabe ... B3
7 Bodega de la Ardosa ... B3
8 Costa Blanca Arrocería ... A4
9 Fide ... B2
10 La Favorita ... C5
11 La Malcriada ... B1
12 Lambuzo ... B2
13 Las Tortillas de Gabino ... D4
14 Le Qualité Tasca ... B1
15 Mama Campo ... B4
16 Sagaretxe ... B4
17 Sala de Despiece ... B2

**Drinking & Nightlife**
18 Arima ... B1
19 Catarsis ... B2
20 Cervecería El Doble ... B2
21 Dash ... B4
22 El Sainete ... B2
23 Saint Georges Cafe ... A4
24 Taberna Averías ... B2

**Entertainment**
25 Fun House ... B5
26 Sala Clamores ... B5

**Shopping**
27 Bazar Matey ... B3
28 Calzados Cantero ... B4
29 Relojería Santolaya ... B4

**Museo Municipal de Arte Contemporáneo** MUSEUM
(Map p102; ☎91 588 59 28; www.madrid.es/museoartecontemporaneo; Calle del Conde Duque 9-11; ⏲10am-2pm & 3-9pm Tue-Fri, 10am-2pm & 5.30-9pm Sat, 10.30am-2.30pm Sun; Ⓜ Ventura Rodríguez) FREE This rich collection of modern Spanish art includes mostly paintings and graphic art with a smattering of photography, sculpture and drawings. Highlights include Eduardo Arroyo and Basque sculptor Jorge Oteiza. Running throughout the collection are creative interpretations of Madrid's cityscape – avant-garde splodges and almost old-fashioned visions of modern Madrid side by side, among them a typically fantastical representation of the Cibeles fountain by one-time icon of *la movida madrileña* (the Madrid scene), Ouka Leele.

The museum is inside the **Antiguo Cuartel del Conde Duque** (Map p102; Calle del Conde Duque 9; Ⓜ Plaza de España, Ventura Rodríguez, San Bernardo). This grand former barracks dominates Conde Duque on Malasaña's western fringe with its imposing facade stretching 228m down the hill. Built in 1717 under the auspices of architect Pedro de Ribera, its highlight is the extravagant 18th-century doorway, a masterpiece of the baroque Churrigueresque style.

## Chamberí & Northern Madrid

Madrid's north has some remarkable sights. The Estadio Santiago Bernabéu is an icon in the world of sport, while Moncloa has a handful of attractions. Many sights are pretty far-flung, so be prepared to spend some time on the metro hopping from one to the other.

★ **Estadio Santiago Bernabéu** STADIUM
(☎tickets 902 324324, tours 91 398 43 70; www.realmadrid.com; Avenida de Concha Espina 1; tours adult/child €25/18; ⏲tours 10am-7pm Mon-Sat, 10.30am-6.30pm Sun, except match days; Ⓜ Santiago Bernabéu) Football fans and budding Madridistas (Real Madrid supporters) will want to make a pilgrimage to the Estadio Santiago Bernabéu, a temple to all that's extravagant and successful in football. Self-guided tours take you up into the stands for a panoramic view of the stadium, then through the presidential box, press room, dressing rooms, players' tunnel and even onto the pitch. The tour ends in the extraordinary Exposición de Trofeos (trophy exhibit). Better still, attend a game alongside 80,000 delirious fans.

For tours of the stadium, buy your ticket at window 10 (next to gate 7).

**Plaza de Olavide** SQUARE
(Map p106; Ⓜ Bilbao) Plaza de Olavide is one of Madrid's most agreeable public spaces, a real *barrio* special. There are park benches, two children's playgrounds, and bars with outdoor tables all around the perimeter.

The plaza hasn't always had its current form. From 1934 the entire plaza was occupied by a covered, octagonal market. In November 1974, the market was demolished in a spectacular controlled explosion, opening

WORTH A TRIP

## CASA DE CAMPO

Sometimes called the 'lungs of Madrid', **Casa de Campo** (Ⓜ Batán) is a 17-sq-km stand of greenery stretching west of the Río Manzanares. There are prettier and more central parks in Madrid but its scope is such that there are plenty of reasons to visit. And visit the *madrileños* do, nearly half a million of them every weekend, celebrating the fact that the short-lived Republican government of the 1930s opened the park to the public (it was previously the exclusive domain of royalty).

For city-bound *madrileños* with neither the time nor the inclination to go further afield, it has become the closest they get to nature, despite the fact that cyclists, walkers and picnickers overwhelm the byways and trails that criss-cross the park. There are tennis courts and a swimming pool, as well as the **Zoo Aquarium de Madrid** (☎902 345014; www.zoomadrid.com; Casa de Campo; adult/child €24/19; ⏲11am-10pm Sun-Thu, to midnight Fri & Sat Jul & Aug, shorter hours Sep-Jun; 🚌37 from Intercambiador de Príncipe Pío, Ⓜ Casa de Campo) and the **Parque de Atracciones** (☎91 463 29 00; www.parquedeatracciones.es; Casa de Campo; adult/child €33/26; ⏲noon-midnight Jul & Aug, hours vary Sep-Jun; 🚌37 from Intercambiador de Príncipe Pío). The **Teleférico** (☎91 406 88 10; https://teleferico.emtmadrid.es; cnr Paseo del Pintor Rosales & Calle de Marqués de Urquijo; one-way/return adult €4.50/6, child €4/5; ⏲noon-9pm May-Aug, reduced hours Sep-Apr; Ⓜ Argüelles) also takes you here with good views en route. At Casa de Campo's southern end, restaurants specialise in wedding receptions, ensuring plenty of bridal parties roaming the grounds in search of an unoccupied patch of greenery where they can take photos. Also in the park, the Andalucian-style ranch known as Batán is used to house the bulls destined to do bloody battle in the Fiestas de San Isidro Labrador.

up the square. To see the plaza's history told in pictures, step into Bar Méntrida at No 3 to have a drink and admire the photos on the wall.

**Museo Sorolla** GALLERY
(Map p106; ☎91 310 15 84; www.culturaydeporte.gob.es/msorolla/inicio.html; Paseo del General Martínez Campos 37; adult/child €3/free, 2.30-8pm Sat & all day Sun free; ⏲9.30am-8pm Tue-Sat, 10am-3pm Sun; Ⓜ Iglesia, Gregorio Marañón) The Valencian artist Joaquín Sorolla immortalised the clear Mediterranean light of the Valencian coast. His Madrid house, a quiet mansion surrounded by lush gardens that he designed himself, was inspired by what he had seen in Andalucía and now contains the most complete collection of the artist's works.

**Estación de Chamberí** MUSEUM
(Andén 0; Map p106; https://museomadrid.com/anden-cero; cnr Calles de Santa Engracia & de Luchana; ⏲11am-1pm & 5-7pm Fri, 10am-2pm Sat & Sun; Ⓜ Iglesia, Bilbao) FREE Estación de Chamberí, the long-lost ghost station of Madrid's metro, is now a museum piece that recreates the era of the station's inauguration in 1919 with advertisements from that time (including Madrid's then-four-digit phone numbers), ticket offices and other memorabilia up to a century old. It's an engaging journey down memory lane.

**Museo de América** MUSEUM
(☎91 549 26 41; www.culturaydeporte.gob.es/museodeamerica/el-museo.html; Avenida de los Reyes Católicos 6; adult/concession €3/1.50, free 2-8pm Thu & all day Sun; ⏲9.30am-3pm Tue, Wed, Fri & Sat, to 7pm Thu, 10am-3pm Sun; Ⓜ Moncloa) Empire may have become a dirty word but it defined how Spain saw itself for centuries. Spanish vessels crossed the Atlantic to the Spanish colonies in Latin America, carrying adventurers one way and gold and other looted artefacts from indigenous cultures on the return journey. These latter pieces – at once the heritage of another continent and a fascinating insight into imperial Spain – are the subject of this excellent museum.

## Activities

**Lab Room Spa** SPA
(Map p98; ☎91 431 21 98; www.thelabroom.com; Calle de Claudio Coello 13; massages €35-100, other treatments €35-270; ⏲11am-8pm Mon-Fri, to 7pm Sat; Ⓜ Retiro) An exclusive spa and beauty parlour whose past clients include Penélope Cruz, Jennifer Lopez, Gwyneth Paltrow and Gael García Bernal, the Lab Room is close to the ultimate in pampering

for both men and women. It offers a range of make-up sessions, massages and facial and body treatments; prices can be surprisingly reasonable.

**Chi Spa** SPA

(Map p98; ☎91 578 13 40; www.thechispa.com; Calle del Conde de Aranda 14; massages €40-95, other treatments from €25; ⏰9am-9pm Mon-Fri, 10am-6pm Sat; Ⓜ Retiro) Wrap up in a robe and slippers and prepare to be pampered in one of Spain's best day spas. There are separate areas for men and women, and services include a wide range of massages, facials, manicures and pedicures. Now, what was it you were stressed about?

**Hammam al-Andalus** SPA

(Map p84; ☎91 429 90 20; http://madrid.hammamalandalus.com; Calle de Atocha 14; treatments €35-120; ⏰10am-midnight; Ⓜ Sol) Housed in the excavated cellars of old Madrid, this imitation of a traditional Arab bath offers massages and aromatherapy beneath graceful arches, accompanied by the sound of trickling water. Prices are cheapest from 10am to 4pm Monday to Friday; reservations required.

## Courses

### Cooking

There are plenty of places in Madrid to learn Spanish cooking. In most cases, you'll need at least passable Spanish, but some run special classes for English speakers.

**Alambique** COOKING

(Map p76; ☎91 547 42 20; www.alambique.com; Plaza de la Encarnación 2; per person from €50; Ⓜ Ópera, Santo Domingo) Most classes here last from 2½ to 3½ hours and cover a range of cuisines. Most are conducted in Spanish, but some are in English and French.

**Cooking Point** COOKING

(Map p84; ☎91 011 51 54; https://cookingpoint.es; Calle de Moratín 11; adult/child €70/35; ⏰9.30am-9.30pm Mon-Sat; Ⓜ Antón Martín) This excellent cooking school includes a trip to the local market and English-language classes on how to cook paella or prepare traditional tapas.

**Escuela Europea de Cata** COOKING

(Map p102; ☎666 300039; www.escuelaeuropeadecata.com; Calle de San Lucas 3; per person from €49) Learn everything you ever wanted to know and more about the wonders of Spanish olive oil, from the complex system of official classifications as to quality to tastings of the final product. It's a wonderful introduction into this quintessentially Spanish world. Most classes are in Spanish.

**De Olla y Sartén** COOKING

(☎639 835299; www.deollaysarten.com; Calle de Béjar 13; per person from €45; ⏰office 10am-7pm Mon-Fri; Ⓜ Avenida de América) There aren't many cuisines they don't teach here, from sweets to seafood, rice to Thai, Japanese and Arab cooking. There are even classes for kids. Most classes are in Spanish.

**Apunto – Centro Cultural del Gusto** COOKING

(Map p102; ☎91 702 10 41; www.apuntolibreria.com; Calle de Hortaleza 64; per person from €50; Ⓜ Chueca) This engaging little bookstore runs fun yet professional cooking classes. It also has a stellar range of nearly 5000 cookbooks for sale.

**Kitchen Club** COOKING

(☎91 522 62 63; www.kitchenclub.es; Calle de Orense 12; per person from €70; Ⓜ Santiago Bernabéu, Neuvos Ministerios) Kitchen Club spans the globe with a range of courses north of the centre. The Spanish cooking classes (such as the four-hour Grand Spanish Classics), conducted in Spanish, are especially popular. After each course there's time to eat what you've cooked.

### Flamenco

Madrid can be an excellent place to learn flamenco in all its various forms, including dance, guitar, singing, piano, and even percussion. The two places listed here focus primarily on serious students dedicated to learning over a long time period, but there are also classes for newcomers just passing through town.

**Fundación Conservatorio Casa Patas** DANCING

(Map p84; ☎91 429 84 71; www.fundacioncasapatas.com; Calle de Cañizares 10; 1hr class from €45; Ⓜ Antón Martín, Tirso de Molina) There's every conceivable type of flamenco instruction here, including dance, guitar, singing and much more. It's upstairs from the Casa Patas flamenco venue.

**Academia Amor de Dios** DANCING

(Centro de Arte Flamenco y Danza Española; Map p84; ☎91 360 04 34; www.amordedios.com; Calle de Santa Isabel 5, 1st fl; Ⓜ Antón Martín)

DON'T MISS

## MADRID FOOTBALL EXPERIENCES

The Estadio Santiago Bernabéu (p107) is one of the world's great football arenas; watching a game (tickets can be bought online, or the week before a game at gate 42 of the stadium on Avenida de Concha Espina) alongside 80,000 passionate Madridistas (Real Madrid supporters) will send chills down your spine. Even if there's no game when you're in town, take the self-guided stadium tour, or shop for merchandise at the stadium (p136) and two more stores – one on Gran Vía (p136), another close to Sol (p136). And if you're lucky enough to be in town when Real Madrid wins a major trophy, head to Plaza de la Cibeles (p99) and wait for the all-night party to begin.

Madrid's other team, **Atlético de Madrid** (www.atleticodemadrid.com) has a cult following, attracts passionate support and fans of the *rojiblancos* (red-and-whites) declare theirs to be the real Madrid team. The state-of-the-art home of Atlético de Madrid – they moved there in late 2017 – is the **Wanda Metropolitano** (☎902 260403, 91 365 09 31; www.atleticodemadrid.com; Avenida de Luís Aragonés 4; tours adult/child from €19/12; ⏱guided tours 11am, 12.30pm, 3.30pm & 5pm Mon-Thu, 11am & 12.30pm Fri, self-guided tours 3-7pm Fri, 11am-7pm Sat & Sun; Ⓜ Estadio Metropolitano), which seats 67,703 people and has already become a firm favourite among fans, even those who miss the cauldron-like Estadio Vicente Calderón. Tickets to matches can be purchased online – click on 'Entradas' then 'Aforo General'. Stadium tours, both guided and self-guided, start at gate 10, and are possible when there are no matches. They also have a club shop in the city centre (p135) and when they win something, they celebrate in the **Plaza de Neptuno** (Plaza de Cánovas del Castillo; Map p88; Ⓜ Banco de España).

This is the best-known course for flamenco dancing (and probably the hardest to get into). Although it's more for budding professionals (as the list of past graduates attests to) than casual visitors, it does have the odd Spanish-language *'cursillo'* (little course) that runs for a day or more. It's on the top floor of the Mercado de Antón Martín.

Even if you're not keen to immerse yourself in the flamenco world, it may be worth stopping by just for a look.

### Language

**Universidad Complutense Madrid** LANGUAGE
(☎91 394 53 25; www.ucm.es/ccee/informacion; Secretaria de los Cursos para Extranjeros, Facultad de Filologia, Universidad Complutense Madrid; Ⓜ Cuidad Universitaria) A range of language and cultural courses throughout the year. Courses range from 120 contact hours (12 hours per week; €1349) to 200-hour courses (20 hours per week; €2126).

**International House Madrid** LANGUAGE
(Map p102; ☎91 310 13 14; www.ihmadrid.es; Calle de Zurbano 8; Ⓜ Alonso Martínez) Intensive courses lasting two/four weeks cost €420/800 (20 hours per week) to €770/1500 (30 hours per week). Staff can organise accommodation with local families.

## Tours

**Devour Madrid Food Tour** FOOD & DRINK
(☎695 111832; www.madridfoodtour.com; tours €50-130) With five tours for different tastes and budgets, Devour Madrid shows you the best of Spanish food and wine in the centre of Madrid. Tours are themed: wine and tapas, flamenco, authentic local markets, history or (for the most serious foodies) the Ultimate Spanish Cuisine tour, which takes you to eight tasting stops in four hours.

**Wanderbeak Tours** FOOD & DRINK
(☎932 20 61 01; www.wanderbeak.com) This excellent company has been running tours in Barcelona for years and has expanded into Madrid. Expect an excellent insight into the city's culinary scene.

**Spanish Tapas Madrid** FOOD & DRINK
(☎672 301231; www.spanishtapasmadrid.com; tours from €70) Local boy Luis Ortega takes you through some iconic Madrid tapas bars, as well as offering tours that take in old Madrid, flamenco and the Prado.

**Adventurous Appetites** FOOD & DRINK
(☎639 331073; www.adventurousappetites.com; 4hr tours €50; ⏱8pm-midnight Mon-Sat) English-language tapas tours through central Madrid. Prices include the first drink but exclude food.

**Insider's Madrid** TOURS
(☎699 493193; www.insiderstravel.io; tours from €70) An impressive range of tailor-made tours, including walking, shopping, fashion, fine arts, tapas, flamenco and bullfighting tours.

**Wellington Society** HISTORY
(☎609 143203; www.wellsoc.org; tours from €95) A handful of quirky historical tours laced with anecdotes, led by the inimitable Stephen Drake-Jones.

**Bike Spain** CYCLING
(Map p76; ☎91 559 06 53; www.bikespain.com; Calle del Codo; bike hire half-/full day from €12/18, tours from €30; ⏲10am-2pm & 4-7pm Mon-Fri Mar-Oct, 10am-2pm & 3-6pm Mon-Fri Nov-Feb; MÓpera) Bicycle hire plus English-language guided city tours by bicycle, by day or (Friday) night, as well as longer expeditions.

## Festivals & Events

**Festival Flamenco** FLAMENCO
(www.facebook.com/flamencomadridfest; ⏲May) Five days of fine flamenco music in one of the city's theatres. Big names in recent years have included Enrique Morente, Carmen Linares and Diego El Cigala. Dates are movable. In 2019 it was held in the Teatro Fernán Gómez, but that may change in subsequent years.

**Fiestas de San Isidro Labrador** CULTURAL
(www.esmadrid.com; ⏲May) The Fiestas de San Isidro Labrador, the city's big holiday on 15 May, marks the feast day of its patron saint, San Isidro. Crowds gather in central Madrid to watch the colourful procession, which kicks off a week of cultural events across the city. The night of the 14th is a big night out in town.

This week marks the start of the city's bullfighting season.

**Suma Flamenca** FLAMENCO
(www.madrid.org/sumaflamenca; ⏲Jun) A soul-filled flamenco festival that draws some of the biggest names in the genre to Teatros del Canal and some of the better-known *tablaos* (flamenco venues) around town.

**Día del Orgullo LGTBI** LGBT
(http://orgullolgtb.org; ⏲Jun) The colourful gay pride parade, on the last Saturday in June, sets out from the Puerta de Alcalá in the early evening, and winds its way around the city in an explosion of music and energy, ending up at the Puerta del Sol.

**Mad Cool** MUSIC
(www.madcoolfestival.es; Avenida del Partenón, IFEMA; 3-/4-day ticket per person €169/179; ⏲Jul; MFeria de Madrid) Madrid's largest music festival draws 60,000 people to the IFEMA convention centre out near the airport. Genres range widely from rock and indie to pop and electronica.

**Veranos de la Villa** CULTURAL
(https://veranosdelavilla.madrid.es; ⏲Jul & Aug) Madrid's town hall stages a series of cultural events, shows and exhibitions throughout July and August, known as Summers in the City.

**DCode** MUSIC
(www.dcodefest.com; ⏲Sep) Held in September at Madrid's Complutense University, this terrific music festival gets better with each passing year. Franz Ferdinand, Liam Gallagher, Amaral, Kaiser Chiefs, Beck and Kings of Convenience have all been headline acts on a programme that includes local and international groups.

**Jazz Madrid** MUSIC
(https://festivaldejazz.madrid.es; ⏲Nov) Madrid's annual jazz festival draws a prestigious cast of performers from across the globe and is an increasingly important stop on the European jazz circuit. Venues vary, from the city's intimate jazz clubs to grander theatrical stages across town.

## Sleeping

Madrid has high-quality accommodation at prices that haven't been seen in the centre of other Western European capitals in decades. Five-star temples to good taste and a handful of buzzing hostels bookend a fabulous collection of midrange hotels; most of the midrangers are creative originals, blending high levels of comfort with an often-quirky sense of style.

### Plaza Mayor & Royal Madrid

**Hostal Madrid** HOSTAL, APARTMENT €
(Map p76; ☎91 522 00 60; www.hostal-madrid.info; Calle de Esparteros 6; s €40-75, d €55-115, apt €45-150; ❄📶; MSol) The 24 rooms at this well-run *hostal* have exposed brickwork, updated bathrooms and a look that puts many three-star hotels to shame. It also has

terrific apartments (ageing in varying stages of gracefulness and ranging in size from 33 sq metres to 200 sq metres) with fully equipped kitchens, their own sitting area and bathroom – check online at www.apartamentosmadrid.info.

**Hotel JC Rooms Puerta del Sol** HOTEL €
(Map p76; ☎91 559 40 14; www.jchoteles-puertadelsol.com; Calle de la Flora; r €48-145; ❄@📶; Ⓜ Ópera) Colourful rooms adorned with large photos of Madrid's attractions are reason enough to stay here, with the central location and outrageously reasonable prices added bonuses. Some of the rooms are a bit small, but otherwise it's an excellent choice.

★**Central Palace Madrid** HOTEL €€
(Map p76; ☎91 548 20 18; www.centralpalacemadrid.com; Plaza de Oriente 2; d without/with view €130/161; ❄📶; Ⓜ Ópera) Now here's something special. The views alone would be reason enough to come to this hotel and definitely worth paying extra for – rooms with balconies look out over the Palacio Real and Plaza de Oriente. The rooms themselves are lovely and light-filled, with tasteful, subtle faux-antique furnishings, comfortable beds, lightwood floors and plenty of space.

★**Pestana Plaza Mayor** HOTEL €€
(Map p76; ☎91 005 28 22; www.pestanacollection.com; Calle Imperial 8; d/f from €127/170, r with plaza view from €174; ❄@📶; Ⓜ Sol) Taking advantage of one of the most sought-after addresses in downtown Madrid, this fine hotel has been stunningly renovated with exposed brick and blue-velvet feature walls dominating a stylish look that's contemporary yet faithful to its surrounds. The rooms with Plaza Mayor views are simply wonderful.

**ApartoSuites Jardines de Sabatini** APARTMENT €€
(Map p76; ☎91 542 59 00; www.jardinesdesabatini.com; Cuesta de San Vicente 16; studio without/with view from €77/127, ste without/with view from €129/165; ❄📶; Ⓜ Plaza de España, Príncipe Pío) Modern, spacious studios and suites are only half the story at this terrific property just down the hill from Plaza de España. Definitely pay extra for a room with a view and the studios with a balcony and uninterrupted views over the lovely Jardines de Sabatini to the Palacio Real – simply brilliant. The Campo del Moro is just across the road.

**Gran Melia Palacio de Los Duques** HOTEL €€€
(Map p76; ☎91 541 67 00; www.melia.com; Cuesta de Santo Domingo 5; d from €250; Ⓜ Santo Domingo) With a marvellous sense of light and space that you rarely find in Madrid's downtown hotels, the Gran Melia Palacio de Los Duques is a five-star belle. Rooms have a white-and-gold colour scheme that won't be to everyone's tastes, but with supreme levels of comfort, a Thai wellness centre and gorgeous public areas, not to mention faultless service, it's difficult to complain.

## La Latina & Lavapiés

**Mola! Hostel** HOSTEL €
(Map p84; ☎91 590 05 09; www.molahostel.com; Calle de Atocha 16; dm €15-23, d from €55; ❄@📶; Ⓜ Sol, Tirso de Molina) This sparkling hostel overlooking the Plaza de Jacinto Benavente in the heart of town is a terrific deal. Rooms are colourful, warmly decorated and well sized, and dorms (with four to 10 beds) are rather stylish. It's a friendly place where the staff are eager to connect you with other travellers and help you make the most of your time in Madrid.

**Hostal Fonda Horizonte** HOSTAL €
(Map p84; ☎91 369 09 96; www.hostalhorizonte.com; Calle de Atocha 28, 2nd fl; s/d €48/67, with shared bathroom €35/54; 📶; Ⓜ Antón Martín) Billing itself as a *hostal* run by travellers for travellers, Fonda Horizonte is a well-run place. Rooms have far more character than your average *hostal*, with high ceilings, deliberately old-world furnishings and modern bathrooms. The King Alfonso XII room is especially well presented.

★**Posada del León de Oro** BOUTIQUE HOTEL €€
(Map p82; ☎91 119 14 94; www.posadadelleondeoro.com; Calle de la Cava Baja 12; d/ste from €75/95; ❄📶; Ⓜ La Latina) This rehabilitated inn has muted colour schemes and generally large rooms. There's a *corrala* (traditional internal or communal patio) at its core and thoroughly modern rooms along one of Madrid's best-loved streets. The downstairs bar is terrific.

★**Posada del Dragón** BOUTIQUE HOTEL €€
(Map p82; ☎91 119 14 24; www.posadadeldragon.com; Calle de la Cava Baja 14; s/d from €75/89; ❄📶; Ⓜ La Latina) At last a boutique hotel in the heart of La Latina. This restored 19th-century *posada* sits on one of our fa-

vourite Madrid streets, and rooms either look out over it or the pretty internal patio. Most of the rooms are small but have extremely comfortable beds and bold, brassy colour schemes and designer everything. There's a terrific bar-restaurant.

## Sol, Santa Ana & Huertas

**Hostal Adriano** HOSTAL €

(Map p84; ☎91 521 13 39; www.hostaladriano.com; Calle de la Cruz 26, 4th fl; s/d from €50/59; ❄📶; Ⓜ Sol) They don't come any better than this bright and friendly hostel wedged in the streets that mark the boundary between Sol and Huertas. Most rooms are well sized and each has its own colour scheme. Indeed, more thought has gone into the decoration than at your average *hostal,* from the bed covers to the pictures on the walls.

On the same floor, the owners run the **Hostal Adria Santa Ana** (r €125; ❄📶), which is a step up in price, style and comfort. Both *hostales* drop their prices in summer.

★ **Hotel Alicia** BOUTIQUE HOTEL €€

(Map p84; ☎91 389 60 95; www.room-matehoteles.com; Calle del Prado 2; d €122-146, ste from €178; ❄📶; Ⓜ Sol, Sevilla, Antón Martín) One of the landmark properties of the designer Room Mate chain of hotels, Hotel Alicia overlooks Plaza de Santa Ana with beautiful, spacious rooms. The style (the work of designer Pascua Ortega) is a touch more muted than in other Room Mate hotels, but the supermodern look remains intact, the downstairs bar is oh-so-cool, and the service is young and switched on.

**Catalonia Las Cortes** HOTEL €€

(Map p84; ☎91 389 60 51; www.hoteles-catalonia.es; Calle del Prado 6; s/d from €150/168; ❄📶; Ⓜ Antón Martín) Occupying an 18th-century palace and renovated in a style faithful to the era, this elegant hotel is a terrific choice right in the heart of Huertas. It's something of an oasis surrounded by the nonstop energy of the streets in this *barrio.* Service is discreet and attentive and the hotel gets plenty of return visitors, which is just about the best recommendation we can give.

**NH Collection Palacio de Tepa** HOTEL €€

(Map p84; ☎91 389 64 90; www.nh-collection.com; Calle de San Sebastián 2; d from €165; ❄📶; Ⓜ Antón Martín) Inhabiting a 19th-century palace a stone's throw from Plaza de Santa Ana, this flagship property of the respected NH chain has modern designer rooms with hardwood floors and soothing colours. Service is professional and the location is outstanding. The premium rooms and junior suites in particular have real class.

**Me Madrid Reina Victoria** LUXURY HOTEL €€

(Map p84; ☎91 701 60 00; www.melia.com; Plaza de Santa Ana 14; r from €175; ❄📶; Ⓜ Sol, Antón Martín) Once the landmark Gran Victoria Hotel, the Madrid home of many a famous bullfighter, this audacious hotel is a landmark of a different kind. Overlooking the western end of Plaza de Santa Ana, the luxury hotel is decked out in minimalist white with curves and comfort in all the right places.

**Hostal Luis XV** HOSTAL €€

(Map p84; ☎91 522 10 21; www.hrluisxv.net; Calle de la Montera 47, 8th fl; s/d/tr €60/77/94; ❄📶; Ⓜ Gran Vía) The spacious rooms, attention to detail and pretty much everything else make this family-run *hostal* feel pricier than it is. You'll find it hard to tear yourself away from the balconies outside every exterior room, from where the views are superb (especially from the triple in room 820). You're so high up that noise is rarely a problem.

**Hotel Urban** LUXURY HOTEL €€€

(Map p84; ☎91 787 77 70; www.derbyhotels.com; Carrera de San Jerónimo 34; r from €215; ❄📶🏊; Ⓜ Sevilla) This towering glass edifice is the epitome of art-inspired designer cool. It boasts original artworks from Africa and Asia; dark-wood floors and dark walls are offset by plenty of light; and the dazzling bathrooms have wonderful designer fittings – the washbasins are sublime. The rooftop swimming pool is one of Madrid's best and the gorgeous terrace is heaven on a candlelit summer's evening.

## El Retiro & the Art Museums

★ **Lapepa Chic B&B** B&B €

(Map p88; ☎91 369 27 14; www.lapepa-bnb.com; Plaza de las Cortes 4, 7th fl; s/d from €60/67; ❄📶; Ⓜ Banco de España) A short step off Paseo del Prado and on a floor with an art nouveau interior, this fine little B&B has lovely rooms with a contemporary, clean-line look so different from the dour *hostal* furnishings you'll find elsewhere. Modern art or even a bedhead lined with flamenco shoes give the place personality in bucketloads. It's worth paying extra for a room with a view.

★ **60 Balconies Atocha** APARTMENT €€

(Map p88; ☎91 755 39 26; www.60balconies.com; Plaza del Emperador Carlos V 11; apt €115-260; ❄📶; Ⓜ Estación del Arte) As convenient for Atocha train station as for the city's major art galleries, and well connected to the rest of the city on foot or by metro, 60 Balconies is an exciting new project by a dynamic young architectural team. The apartments range from 31-sq-metre studios up to 103-sq-metre, three-bedroom apartments, all stylish, spacious and a wonderful alternative to hotels. Another similarly excellent property is over in Chueca.

**Westin Palace** LUXURY HOTEL €€€

(Map p88; ☎91 360 80 00; www.marriott.com; Plaza de las Cortes 7; d/ste from €247/541; ❄📶; Ⓜ Banco de España, Antón Martín) An old Madrid classic, this former palace of the Duque de Lerma opened as a hotel in 1911 and was Spain's second luxury hotel. Ever since it has looked out across Plaza de Neptuno at its rival, the Ritz, like a lover unjustly scorned. It may not have the world-famous cachet of the Ritz, but it's not called the Palace for nothing.

## Salamanca

**VP El Madroño** BOUTIQUE HOTEL €€

(Map p98; ☎91 198 30 92; www.madrono-hotel.com; Calle del General Díaz Porlier 101; d/tr from €115/140; ❄📶; Ⓜ Diego de León) You're a long way from touristy Madrid out here, not far from the bullring, and therein lies part of this swish place's appeal. All of the rooms have been renovated, either in a vaguely classic style or with more contemporary designer flair. It also has family rooms and there's a lovely garden out back.

★ **Villa Magna** HOTEL €€€

(Map p98; ☎91 587 12 34; www.hotelvillamagna.es; Paseo de la Castellana 22; d €345-450, ste from €475; P❄📶; Ⓜ Rubén Dario) This is a very Salamanca address, infused as it is with elegance and impeccable service. The look is brighter than you might imagine with the use of Empire chairs, Bauhaus ideas and even Chinese screens. Rooms are studiously classic in look with supremely comfortable furnishings and plenty of space. No expense has been spared in the rooftop suites.

## Malasaña & Chueca

★ **Hostal Main Street Madrid** HOSTAL €

(Map p102; ☎91 548 18 78; Gran Vía 50, 5th fl; r from €72; ❄📶; Ⓜ Callao, Santo Domingo) Excellent service is what travellers rave about here, but the rooms – modern and cool in soothing greys – are also some of the best *hostal* rooms you'll find anywhere in central Madrid. It's an excellent package, and not surprisingly it's often full, so book well in advance.

**Hostal La Zona** HOSTAL €

(Map p102; ☎91 521 99 04; www.hostallazona.com; Calle de Valverde 7, 1st fl; s €42-65, d €55-75, all incl breakfast; ❄📶; Ⓜ Gran Vía) Catering primarily to a gay clientele, the stylish Hostal La Zona has exposed brickwork, subtle colour shades and wooden pillars. We like a place where a sleep-in is encouraged – breakfast is served from 9am to noon, which is exactly the understanding Madrid's nightlife merits. Arnaldo and Vincent are friendly hosts.

**Life Hotel** HOTEL €

(Map p102; ☎91 531 47 44; www.hotellifemadrid.es; Calle de Pizarro 16; s/d from €45/60; ❄📶; Ⓜ Noviciado) If only all places to stay were this good. This hotel inhabits the shell of a historic Malasaña building, but the rooms are slick and contemporary with designer bathrooms. You're also just a few steps up the hill from Calle del Pez, one of Malasaña's most happening streets. It's an exceptionally good deal, even when prices head upwards.

**Hostal Don Juan** HOSTAL €

(Map p102; ☎91 522 31 01; www.hostaldonjuan.net; Plaza de Pedro Zerolo, 2nd fl; s/d/tr €44/60/84; ❄📶; Ⓜ Gran Vía) Paying cheap rates for your room doesn't mean you can't be treated like a king. This elegant two-storey *hostal* is filled with original artworks and antique furniture that could grace a royal palace, although mostly it resides in the public areas. Rooms are large and simple but luminous; most have a street-facing balcony. The location is good, close to where Chueca meets Gran Vía.

★ **60 Balconies Recoletos** APARTMENT €€

(Map p102; ☎91 755 39 26; www.60balconies.com; Calle del Almirante 17; apt €125-210; ❄📶; Ⓜ Chueca) In a classy corner of Chueca, these architect-designed apartments, ranging from 45 sq metre up to 130 sq metre, are stylish and make you feel like you've found your own Madrid pad. They're a similar deal to their Atocha property and rank among the best apartment choices in town.

**Hotel Óscar** BOUTIQUE HOTEL €€
(Map p102; ☎91 701 11 73; www.room-matehoteles.com; Plaza de Vázquez de Mella 12; d €85-195, ste from €140; ; Gran Vía) Hotel Óscar belongs to the highly original Room Mate chain of hotels. Designer rooms are stylish and sophisticated, some with floor-to-ceiling murals. The lighting is always cool, and the colour scheme has splashes of pinks, lime greens, oranges or more minimalist black and white.

**Only You Hotel** BOUTIQUE HOTEL €€€
(Map p102; ☎91 005 27 46; www.onlyyouhotels.com; Calle de Barquillo 21; d €195-290; @; Chueca) This stunning boutique hotel makes perfect use of a 19th-century Chueca mansion. The look is classy and contemporary thanks to respected interior designer Lázaro Rosa-Violán. Nice touches include all-day à la carte breakfasts and a portable router that you can carry out into the city to stay connected.

**Principal Madrid** HOTEL €€€
(Map p84; ☎91 521 87 43; www.theprincipalmadridhotel.com; Calle del Marqués de Valdeiglesias 1; r €200-375, ste from €450; @; Sevilla) Just off the pretty end of Gran Vía and within sight of one of its more charming landmarks, the Edificio Metrópolis, the Principal is a fine, central choice. Some of the standard rooms are on the small side for a five-star hotel, but those with views towards Gran Vía are splendid. The pocket-wi-fi device is a nice touch.

## Chamberí & Northern Madrid

★**Hotel One Shot Luchana 22** HOTEL €
(Map p106; ☎91 292 29 40; www.hoteloneshotluchana22.com; Calle de Luchana 22; r from €72; ; Bilbao) Classy, contemporary rooms in an early 20th-century, neoclassical palace close to Plaza de Olavide in Chamberí make for a pleasant alternative to staying downtown. The wrap-around loft has abundant light and a modern four-poster bed.

★**Hotel Puerta América** LUXURY HOTEL €€
(☎91 744 54 00; www.hotelpuertamerica.com; Avenida de América 41; d/ste from €140/275; P; Cartagena) Given the location of their hotel (halfway between the city and the airport), the owners knew they had to do something special – to build a self-contained world so innovative and luxurious that you'd never want to leave. Their idea? Give 22 of architecture's most creative names (eg Zaha Hadid, Norman Foster, Ron Arad, David Chipperfield, Jean Nouvel) a floor each to design. The result is an extravagant pastiche of styles, from zany montages of 1980s chic to bright-red bathrooms that feel like a movie star's dressing room. Even the bar ('a temple to the liturgy of pleasure'), restaurant, facade, gardens, public lighting and car park had their own architects. It's an extraordinary, astonishing place.

**Hotel Sardinero Madrid** HOTEL €€
(Map p102; ☎91 206 21 60; www.hotelsardineromadrid.com; Plaza de Alonso Martínez 3; r/ste from €96/276; @; Alonso Martínez) There's lots to like at this charming hotel, from the location that's as handy for untouristy Chamberí as it is for everything else in Madrid to the large and stylish rooms with muted colours and supremely comfortable everything. The 24-hour gym is ideal for those with jet lag, although we found the Library Cocktail Bar to be just as effective. Travellers love the personal service, too.

★**Hotel Orfila** HOTEL €€€
(Map p102; ☎91 702 77 70; www.hotelorfila.com; Calle de Orfila 6; r from €242; P; Alonso Martínez) One of Madrid's best hotels, Orfila has all the luxuries of any five-star hotel – supremely comfortable rooms, for a start – but it's the personal service that elevates it into the upper echelon; regular guests get bathrobes embroidered with their own initials. An old-world elegance dominates the decor, and the quiet location and sheltered garden make it the perfect retreat.

# Eating

Madrid has transformed itself into one of Europe's culinary capitals, not least because the city has long been a magnet for people (and cuisines) from all over Spain. Travel from one Spanish village to the next and you'll quickly learn that each has its own speciality; travel to Madrid and you'll find them all.

## Plaza Mayor & Royal Madrid

**★Mercado de San Miguel** TAPAS €
(Map p76; ☎91 542 49 36; www.mercadodesanmiguel.es; Plaza de San Miguel; tapas from €1; ⏰10am-midnight Sun-Thu, to 1am Fri & Sat; Ⓜ Sol) This is one of Madrid's oldest and most beautiful markets, within early 20th-century glass walls and an inviting space strewn with tables. You can order tapas and sometimes more substantial plates at most of the counter bars, and everything here (from caviar to chocolate) is as tempting as the market is alive. Put simply, it's one of our favourite experiences in Madrid.

All the stalls are outstanding, but you could begin with the fine fishy *pintxos* (Basque tapas) atop mini toasts at **La Casa de Bacalao** (Stalls 16–17), follow it up with some *jamón* or other cured meats at **Carrasco Guijuelo** (Stall 18), cheeses at Stalls 20–21, all manner of pickled goodies at Stall 22, or the gourmet tapas of **Lhardy** (Stalls 61–62). There are also plenty of places to buy wine, Asturian cider and the like.

**★Casa Revuelta** TAPAS €
(Map p76; ☎91 366 33 32; Calle de Latoneros 3; tapas from €3; ⏰10.30am-4pm & 7-11pm Tue-Sat, 10.30am-4pm Sun, closed Aug; Ⓜ Sol, La Latina) Casa Revuelta puts out some of Madrid's finest tapas of *bacalao* (cod) bar none – unlike elsewhere, *tajadas de bacalao* don't have bones in them and slide down the throat with the greatest of ease. Early on a Sunday afternoon, as the Rastro crowd gathers here, it's filled to the rafters. Other specialities include *torreznos* (bacon bits), *callos* (tripe) and *albóndigas* (meatballs).

**LOCAL KNOWLEDGE**

### WHAT'S COOKING IN MADRID?

**Cocido a la madrileña** (Madrid meat-and-chickpea hotpot) – Taberna La Bola, Lhardy (p119) or Malacatín

**Cordero o cochinillo asado** (roast lamb or suckling pig) – Restaurante Sobrino de Botín

**Sopa de ajo** (garlic soup) – Posada de la Villa

**Callos a la madrileña** (Madrid-style tripe) – Taberna La Bola

**Huevos rotos** (potatoes cooked with eggs and ham) – Casa Lucio or Almendro 13 (p118)

**★Gourmet Experience** FOOD HALL €€
(Map p76; www.elcorteingles.es/aptc/gourmet-experience; Plaza del Callao 2, 9th fl; mains €8-20; ⏰10am-10pm; Ⓜ Callao) Ride the elevator up to the 9th floor of the El Corte Inglés department store for one of downtown Madrid's best eating experiences. The food is excellent, with everything from top-notch tapas or Mexican to gourmet hamburgers, and the view is fabulous, especially over Plaza del Callao and down Gran Vía.

**El Pato Mudo** SPANISH €€
(Map p76; ☎91 559 48 40; elpatomudo@hotmail.es; Calle Costanilla de los Ángeles 8; mains €13-24; ⏰1-4pm & 8-11.30pm Wed-Sun; Ⓜ Ópera) El Pato Mudo isn't the most famous paella restaurant in Madrid, but it's known to locals for its variety of outstanding rice dishes at reasonable prices. Specialities include black rice with squid ink, soupy rice, authentic *paella valenciana* and shellfish paella. Served directly from the pan for two or more people, they go well with the local wines.

**Taberna La Bola** SPANISH €€
(Map p76; ☎91 547 69 30; www.labola.es; Calle de la Bola 5; mains €16-25; ⏰1.30-4.30pm & 8.30-11pm Mon-Sat, 1.30-4.30pm Sun, closed Aug; Ⓜ Santo Domingo) Going strong since 1870 and run by the sixth generation of the Verdasco family, Taberna La Bola is a much-loved bastion of traditional Madrid cuisine. If you're going to try *cocido a la madrileña* (meat-and-chickpea stew; €21) while in Madrid, this is a good place to do so. It's busy and noisy and very Madrid.

**★Restaurante Sobrino de Botín** CASTILIAN €€€
(Map p76; ☎91 366 42 17; www.botin.es; Calle de los Cuchilleros 17; mains €18-28, set menus €46.50; ⏰1-4pm & 8pm-midnight; Ⓜ La Latina, Sol) It's not every day that you can eat in the oldest restaurant in the world (as recognised by the *Guinness Book of Records* – established in 1725). The secret of its staying power is fine *cochinillo asado* (roast suckling pig) and *cordero asado* (roast lamb) cooked in wood-fired ovens. Eating in the vaulted cellar is a treat.

**Taberna La Daniela** SPANISH €€€
(Map p76; ☎91 366 20 18; www.tabernadeladaniela.com; Calle de los Cuchilleros 9; mains €19-25; ⏰1-5pm & 8pm-midnight Mon-Thu, 1-5pm

& 8pm-12.30am Fri, 1-5.30pm & 8.30pm-12.30am Sat, 1-5.30pm & 8.30pm-midnight Sun; M Sol) Great tapas and a range of other local staples should be reason enough to come here. But for us, it's all about their *cocido a la madrileña* (€25) which, according to many devotees down through the decades, is the best in town.

## La Latina & Lavapiés

La Latina is Madrid's best *barrio* for tapas, complemented by plenty of fine sit-down restaurants. Calle de la Cava Baja and its surrounding streets is where it all happens. Lavapiés is more eclectic and multicultural and, generally speaking, the further down the hill you go, the better it gets, especially along Calle de Argumosa.

**La Musa Latina** SPANISH €

(Map p82; 91 354 02 55; https://grupolamusa.com/en/restaurante-lamusalatina; Costanilla de San Andrés 1; tapas €5-8, mains from €9.75; 10am-1am Sun-Wed, to 1.30am Thu, to 2am Fri & Sat; M La Latina) Laid-back La Musa Latina has an ever-popular dining area and food that's designed to bring a smile to your face. The outdoor tables are lovely when the weather is warm, while the downstairs bar in the former wine cellar, complete with table tennis and table football, is also charming. Like its sister restaurant in Malasaña, it serves creative tapas, including international adaptations.

**Almacén de Vinos** TAPAS €€

(Casa Gerardo; Map p82; 91 221 96 60; Calle de la Calatrava 21; tapas/raciones from €4/9; 1-4pm & 8.30pm-midnight Sun-Thu, 1-5pm & 8.30pm-12.30am Fri & Sat; M La Latina) It doesn't come much more traditional in La Latina than this tiled space with a marble bar and *tostas* (toasts; with *bacalao,* for example), *raciones* (such as *jamón ibérico* with wild mushrooms) and vermouth on tap. When busy, it has that unmistakable buzz of a place beloved by locals whose attitude seems to be, 'Why change something this good?'.

**Malacatín** SPANISH €€

(Map p82; 91 365 52 41; www.malacatin.com; Calle de Ruda 5; mains €11-17; 11am-5.30pm Mon-Wed & Sat, 11am-5.30pm & 8.15-11pm Thu & Fri, closed Aug; M La Latina) If you want to see *madrileños* enjoying their favourite local food, this is one of the best places to do so. The clamour of conversation bounces off the tiled walls of the cramped dining area adorned with bullfighting memorabilia. The speciality is as much *cocido* (meat-and-chickpea stew) as you can eat (€21).

**LOCAL KNOWLEDGE**

### BOCADILLO DE CALAMARES

One of the lesser-known culinary specialities of Madrid is the *bocadillo de calamares* (a small baguette-style roll filled to bursting with deep-fried calamari). You'll find them in many bars in the streets surrounding Plaza Mayor and neighbouring bars along Calle de Botoneras off Plaza Mayor's southeastern corner. At around €3, they're the perfect street snack. **La Ideal** (Map p76; 91 365 72 78; Calle de Botoneras 4; bocadillos from €3; 9am-11pm Sun-Thu, to midnight Fri & Sat; M Sol) and **La Campana** (Map p76; 91 364 29 84; Calle de Botoneras 6; bocadillos from €3; 9am-11pm Sun-Thu, to midnight Fri & Sat; M Sol) are two spots to try them.

**La Bobia** ASTURIAN €€

(Map p82; 91 737 60 30; www.facebook.com/labobiamadrid; Calle de San Millán 3; tapas from €4.50, mains €12-22; 1-11pm Sun-Thu, to midnight Fri & Sat; M La Latina) An icon of 1980s Madrid, La Bobia has been updated for the 21st century, but is still the authentic Asturian cider house that lies at the secret of its longevity. Pungent blue cheeses, fine *croquetas, fabada asturiana* (an Asturian stew) and high-quality steaks dominate an extensive menu, but when it comes to drinks, it's cider straight from the barrel.

**★Casa Lucio** SPANISH €€€

(Map p82; 91 365 82 17; www.casalucio.es; Calle de la Cava Baja 35; mains €15-30; 1-4pm & 8.30pm-midnight, closed Aug; M La Latina) Casa Lucio is a Madrid classic and has been wowing *madrileños* since 1974 with its light touch, quality ingredients and home-style local cooking such as eggs (a Lucio speciality) and roasted meats in abundance. There's also *rabo de toro* (bull's tail) during the Fiestas de San Isidro Labrador and plenty of *rioja* (red wine) to wash away the mere thought of it.

**Posada de la Villa** SPANISH €€€

(Map p82; 91 366 18 80; www.posadadelavilla.com; Calle de la Cava Baja 9; mains €19-33; 1-

### TAPAS STREET: CALLE DE LA CAVA BAJA

Any of the bars along Calle de la Cava Baja should serve good tapas – they don't survive long here if they don't.

Our favourite places to start include **Casa Lucas** (Map p82; ☎91 365 08 04; www.casalucas.es; Calle de la Cava Baja 30; tapas/raciones from €5/7; ⊙1-3.30pm & 8pm-midnight Thu-Tue, 1-3.30pm Wed; Ⓜ La Latina), **Taberna Txakolina** (Map p82; ☎91 366 48 77; Calle de la Cava Baja 26; tapas from €4.50; ⊙8pm-midnight Tue, 1-4pm & 8pm-midnight Wed-Sat, 1-4pm Sun; Ⓜ La Latina) or **Enotaberna del León de Oro** (Map p82; ☎91 119 14 94; www.posadadelleondeoro.com; Calle de la Cava Baja 12; mains €13-23; ⊙1-4pm & 8pm-midnight; Ⓜ La Latina). Other decent choices are **Lamiak** (Map p82; ☎91 365 52 12; Calle de la Cava Baja 42; tapas €3, raciones €8.50-16; ⊙1pm-midnight Tue-Sat, to 4pm Sun; Ⓜ La Latina) and **La Antoñita** (Map p82; ☎91 119 14 24; www.posadadeldragon.com; Calle de la Cava Baja 14; raciones from €7, mains €12-17; ⊙1.30pm-12.30am; Ⓜ La Latina), both of which push tapas into new directions, or a more traditional Andalucian tavern, **Casa Curro** (Map p82; ☎91 364 22 59; www.tabernacasacurro.com; Calle de la Cava Baja 23; raciones €7-16; ⊙7pm-1.30am Tue, noon-4.30pm & 7pm-1.30am Wed & Thu, noon-1.30am Fri-Sun; Ⓜ La Latina).

Nearby, **Almendro 13** (Map p82; ☎91 365 42 52; Calle del Almendro 13; mains €8-17; ⊙1-4pm & 7.30pm-midnight Sun-Thu, 1-5pm & 8pm-1am Fri & Sat; Ⓜ La Latina), for *huevos rotos con jamón* (broken eggs with ham) and **Juana La Loca** (Map p82; ☎91 366 55 00; www.juanalalocamadrid.com; Plaza de la Puerta de Moros 4; tapas from €4.50, mains €10-30; ⊙1.30-5.30pm Tue-Sun, 7pm-midnight Sat-Wed, to 1am Thu-Fri; Ⓜ La Latina), for one of Madrid's best *tortilla de patatas* (Spanish potato omelette), are worth the very short detour.

For bars where the choice of wines is even better than the tapas, we love Taberna El Tempranillo (p126) and El Bonanno (p127).

For formal sit-down dining back along Calle de la Cava Baja, Casa Lucio (p117), Posada de la Villa (p117) and **Restaurante Julián de Tolosa** (Map p82; ☎91 365 82 10; https://juliandetolosa.com; Calle de la Cava Baja 18; mains €26-38; ⊙1.30-4pm & 8.30-11.30pm Mon-Sat, 1.30-4pm Sun; Ⓜ La Latina) are all Madrid legends.

4pm & 8pm-midnight Mon-Sat, 1-4pm Sun, closed Aug; Ⓜ La Latina) This wonderfully restored 17th-century *posada* (inn) is something of a local landmark. The atmosphere is formal, the decoration sombre and traditional (heavy timber and brickwork), and the cuisine decidedly local – roast meats, *cocido* (which usually needs to be pre-ordered), *callos* (tripe) and *sopa de ajo* (garlic soup).

## Sol, Santa Ana & Huertas

**Casa Toni** SPANISH €

(Map p84; ☎91 532 25 80; Calle de la Cruz 14; mains €8-15; ⊙noon-4.30pm & 7pm-midnight; Ⓜ Sol) Locals flock to Casa Toni, one of Madrid's best old-school Spanish bars, for simple, honest cuisine fresh off the griddle. Specialities include cuttlefish, gazpacho and offal – the crispy (some would say gristly) pork ear is out of this world. While you're here, you can try one of the local Madrid wines. The prices are great and the old Madrid charm can't be beat.

**La Finca de Susana** SPANISH €

(Map p84; ☎91 369 35 57; www.facebook.com/lafincadesusana; Calle del Príncipe 10; mains €8-17; ⊙1-11.30pm Sun-Wed, to midnight Thu-Sat; 📶; Ⓜ Sevilla) It's difficult to find a better combination of price, quality cooking and classy atmosphere anywhere in Huertas. The softly lit dining area has a sophisticated vibe and the sometimes-innovative, traditional food draws a hip young crowd. No reservations.

**Maceiras** GALICIAN €

(Map p84; ☎91 429 58 18; www.tabernamaceira.com; Calle de las Huertas 66; mains €7-16; ⊙1.15-4.15pm & 8pm-12.15am Mon-Thu, 1.30-4.45pm & 8.30pm-1am Fri & Sat, 1.30-4.45pm & 8pm-midnight Sun; Ⓜ Antón Martín) Galician tapas (octopus, green peppers etc) never tasted so good as in this agreeably rustic bar down the bottom of the Huertas hill, especially when washed down with a crisp white Ribeiro. The simple wooden tables, loyal customers, Galician music playing in the background and handy location make it a fine place before or after visiting museums along the Paseo del Prado.

There's another **branch** (Map p84; Calle de Jesús 7; mains €6-14; ⊙1.15-4.15pm & 8.30pm-12.15am Mon-Fri, 1.30-4.30pm & 8.30pm-1am Sat, 1.30-4.30pm & 8.30pm-midnight Sun; Ⓜ Antón Martín) around the corner.

**★Casa Alberto** TAPAS €€
(Map p84; ☎91 429 93 56; www.casaalberto.es; Calle de las Huertas 18; tapas €3.50-12, raciones €7-17, mains €16-23; ⊙restaurant 1.30-4pm & 8pm-midnight Tue-Sat, 1.30-4pm Sun, bar noon-1.30am Tue-Sat, 12.30-4pm Sun, closed Sun Jul & Aug; Ⓜ Antón Martín) One of the most atmospheric old *tabernas* (taverns) of Madrid, Casa Alberto has been around since 1827 and occupies a building where Cervantes is said to have written one of his books. The secret to its staying power is vermouth on tap, excellent tapas at the bar and fine sit-down meals.

**Vinos González** TAPAS €€
(Map p84; ☎91 429 56 18; www.casagonzalez.es; Calle de León 12; tapas from €5, raciones €9-18; ⊙9.30am-midnight Mon-Thu, to 1am Fri & Sat, 11.30am-5pm Sun; Ⓜ Antón Martín) This is our sort of deli, one that combines the full benefits of a deli with the sit-down comforts of a tapas bar. On offer is a tempting array of local and international cheeses, cured meats and other typically Spanish delicacies. The tables are informal, cafe style and we recommend lingering.

**★Paco Roncero Restaurante** SPANISH €€€
(Map p84; ☎91 532 12 75; www.casinodemadrid.es; Calle de Alcalá 15; mains €44-56, set menus €80-195; ⊙1-4pm & 9pm-midnight Mon-Sat; Ⓜ Sevilla) Perched atop the lavish Casino de Madrid building, this temple of haute cuisine is the proud bearer of two Michelin stars and is presided over by celebrity chef Paco Roncero. It's all about culinary experimentation, with a menu that changes as each new idea emerges from the laboratory and moves into the kitchen. The *menú de degustación* (€155) is a fabulous avalanche of tastes.

**Lhardy** SPANISH €€€
(Map p84; ☎91 521 33 85; www.lhardy.com; Carrera de San Jerónimo 8; mains €26-40, set menus €59-78; ⊙1-3.30pm & 8.30-11pm Mon-Sat, 1-3.30pm Sun, closed Aug; Ⓜ Sol, Sevilla) This Madrid landmark (since 1839) is an elegant treasure trove of takeaway gourmet tapas downstairs and six dining areas upstairs that are the upmarket preserve of traditional Madrid dishes with an occasional hint of French influence. House specialities include *cocido a la madrileña* (€37), pheasant and wild duck in an orange perfume. The quality and service are unimpeachable.

## El Retiro & the Art Museums

**Condumios** TAPAS €
(Map p88; ☎91 805 74 04; www.condumios.es; Calle de Juan de Mena 12; mains €8-17; ⊙8am-5pm Mon, 10am-midnight Tue-Sat; Ⓜ Banco de España) One of our favourite bars anywhere in the area, this terrific place does all manner of Spanish staples – try the *croquetas de jamón y gambas al ajillo* (ham and garlic-prawn croquettes). The wine list is excellent.

**★Estado Puro** TAPAS €€
(Map p88; ☎91 330 24 00; www.tapasenestadopuro.com; Plaza de Neptuno (Plaza de Cánovas del Castillo) 4; tapas €4-14; ⊙noon-midnight; Ⓜ Banco de España, Estación del Arte) A slick but casual tapas bar, Estado Puro serves up fantastic tapas that push the boundaries of traditional recipes. It's known for many things, among them splendid *croquetas* (with *jamón*, bull's tail or wild mushrooms). The kitchen is overseen by Paco Roncero, head chef at La Terraza del Casino, who learned his trade with master chef Ferran Adrià.

**★Viridiana** FUSION €€€
(Map p88; ☎91 531 10 39; www.restauranteviridiana.com; Calle de Juan de Mena 14; mains €20-35, set menus €60-85; ⊙1.30-3.30pm & 8.30-11.30pm Tue-Sat, 1.30-4pm Sun; Ⓜ Banco de España) Chef Abraham García is a much-celebrated Madrid figure and his larger-than-life personality is reflected in Viridiana's menu. Many influences are brought to bear on the cooking here, among them international innovations and ingredients and well-considered seasonal variations.

This place was doing fusion cooking long before it became fashionable and has developed a fiercely loyal clientele as a result. In short, it's one of Madrid's best restaurants.

## Salamanca

**★Casa Dani** SPANISH €
(Map p98; ☎91 575 59 25; Calle de Ayala 28, Mercado de la Paz; tapas/mains from €3/8; ⊙7am-8pm Mon-Fri, to 5pm Sat; Ⓜ Serrano) Deep in Salamanca's Mercado de la Paz, Casa Dani is a wildly popular spot for lunch and it gets going earlier than most: most weekdays, there's a queue at 1pm. But any

## TAPAS STREET: CALLE DE PONZANO

Whether you're up for a few drinks or looking for some of Madrid's best tapas, there is no more happening street in Madrid right now than Chamberí's Calle de Ponzano. It's so popular, the street has even had a brand-new verb named after it, at least unofficially – to go out along this street is known locally as *ponzanear*. If you want to feel the buzz of the Madrid night, Calle de Ponzano is a pretty sure bet.

In Madrid the dividing line for going for a drink or a meal may often be a false dichotomy, but if drinking is your main reason for being here, then **El Sainete** (Map p106; ☎91 445 63 62; https://elsainete.com; Calle de Ponzano 6; ⏰1pm-1am Tue-Thu, to 2am Fri & Sat, to 5pm Sun; Ⓜ Alonso Cano) with its craft beers, **Taberna Averías** (Map p106; ☎91 603 34 50; www.tabernaaverias.com; Calle de Ponzano 16; ⏰7pm-12.30am Mon-Wed, noon-4pm & 7pm-12.30am Thu, noon-1am Fri-Sun; Ⓜ Alonso Cano) for an extraordinary wine list, or **Arima** (Map p106; ☎91 109 15 99; www.arimabasquegastronomy.com; Calle de Ponzano 51; ⏰1-4.30pm & 8-11.30pm Mon-Sat, 1-4.30pm Sun; Ⓜ Ríos Rosas) with its vermouths are all good choices for first drinks. Later on in the night, **Catarsis** (Map p106; ☎663 725124; Calle de Ponzano 14; ⏰5pm-2am Tue-Sun; Ⓜ Alonso Cano) is one of Madrid's more creative cocktail bars. At any time, **Cervecería El Doble** (Map p106; ☎91 591 94 62; Calle de Ponzano 17; ⏰noon-4.15pm & 7pm-2am; Ⓜ Alonso Cano) is good for a *caña* (beer).

Of course, you should never drink on an empty stomach, and the choices for tapas (or, sometimes, a sit-down meal) can seem endless, all of them packed to the rafters on most nights. Start with the old-timers, those bars that have been here since long before Ponzano acquired its recent fame. Bodega de la Ardosa (p122), **Fide** (Map p106; ☎91 442 20 89; www.facebook.com/CerveceriaFIDE; Calle de Ponzano 8; tapas from €5; ⏰11am-4.30pm & 7pm-midnight Mon-Thu, 11am-4.30pm & 7pm-1am Fri, 11am-5.30pm & 7pm-1am Sat, 11am-5.30pm & 7pm-midnight Sun; Ⓜ Alonso Cano) and **Alma Cheli** (Map p106; ☎91 517 28 27; www.almacheli.com; Calle de Santa Engracia 103; mains €8-20; ⏰noon-midnight Sun-Thu, to 1.30am Fri & Sat; Ⓜ Alonso Cano) are all fine choices. If you can defy the crowds and carve out a space for yourself, **Sala de Despiece** (Map p106; ☎91 752 61 06; www.saladedespiece.com; Calle de Ponzano 11; mains €7.50-25; ⏰1-5pm & 7.30pm-midnight Sun-Thu, 1-5.30pm & 7.30pm-1am Fri & Sat; Ⓜ Alonso Cano) and **Le Qualité Tasca** (Map p106; ☎683 510538; www.lequalitetasca.com; Calle de Ponzano 48; raciones €15-25; ⏰8.30-11.30pm Tue & Wed, 1pm-midnight Thu, 1pm-1.30am Fri & Sat, 1-11pm Sun; Ⓜ Ríos Rosas) are among the street's best. For a slice of urban Andalucía in Madrid, there's **Bienmesabe** (Map p106; ☎91 827 52 42; https://tabernasbienmesabe.com/en; Calle de Santa Engracia 72; mains €11-23; ⏰1pm-1am Sun-Wed, to 2am Thu-Sat; Ⓜ Iglesia, Alonso Cano) or **Lambuzo** (Map p106; ☎91 513 80 59, 637 303818; www.barlambuzo.com; Calle de Ponzano 8; tapas from €3.50, shared dishes from €10; ⏰1-4.30pm & 8pm-12.30am Tue-Sat, 1-4.30pm Sun; Ⓜ Alonso Cano). **La Malcriada** (Map p106; ☎685 869699; www.facebook.com/lamalcriadaponzano; Calle de Ponzano 38; tapas & raciones €2.50-14; ⏰12.30pm-1.30am Mon-Thu, to 2.30am Fri & Sat, to 1.30am Sun; Ⓜ Alonso Cano, Ríos Rosas) is another good choice.

time is good for the homemade *tortilla de patatas* (potato-and-onion omelette), which is among Madrid's best. Pull up a bar stool if you don't fancy waiting for a table.

### ★Astrolabius FUSION €€

(Map p98; ☎91 562 06 11; www.astrolabius-madrid.com; Calle de Serrano 118; mains €7-22; ⏰1-4pm & 8.30pm-midnight Tue-Sat, closed Aug; Ⓜ Núñez de Balboa) This terrific family-run place in Salamanca's north has a simple philosophy – take grandmother's recipes and filter them through the imagination of the grandchildren. The result is a fabulous mix of flavours that changes regularly. The atmosphere is edgy and modern, but casual in the best Madrid sense.

### ★Platea SPANISH €€

(Map p98; ☎91 577 00 25; www.plateamadrid.com; Calle de Goya 5-7; ⏰noon-12.30am Sun-Wed, to 2.30am Thu-Sat; Ⓜ Serrano, Colón) The ornate Carlos III cinema opposite the Plaza de Colón has been artfully transformed into a dynamic culinary scene with more than a hint of burlesque. There are 12 restaurants, three gourmet food stores and cocktail bars.

**Street XO** TAPAS €€

(Map p98; ☎91 531 98 84; www.streetxo.com; Calle de Serrano 52, El Corte Inglés; mains €8-30; ⏱1.30-4pm & 8.30-11pm Mon-Wed, 1.30-4pm & 8-11.30pm Thu, 1.30-4.30pm & 8-11.30pm Fri & Sat, 1.30-4.30pm & 8.30-11pm Sun; Ⓜ Serrano) After the success of his Michelin-starred DiverXO, Dabiz Muñoz has opened a more accessible but equally creative street-food version. There's always a queue (cocktail orders are taken while you wait), and the dishes are an endless cast of surprises, as you'd expect from one of Spain's most restless and talented chefs.

## Malasaña & Chueca

**★ Pez Tortilla** TAPAS €

(Map p102; ☎653 919984; www.peztortilla.com; Calle del Pez 36; tapas from €4; ⏱6pm-1am Mon-Wed, noon-1.30am Thu, to 2.30am Fri & Sat, to 1am Sun; Ⓜ Noviciado) Every time we come here, this place is full to bursting, which is not surprising given its philosophy of great tortilla (15 kinds!), splendid *croquetas* (croquettes) and craft beers (more than 70 varieties, with nine on tap). The *croquetas* with black squid ink or the tortilla with truffle brie and *jamón* (ham) are two stars among many.

**★ Casa Julio** SPANISH €

(Map p102; ☎91 522 72 74; Calle de la Madera 37; 6/12 croquetas €6/12; ⏱1.30-3.30pm & 6.30-11pm Mon-Sat Sep-Jul; Ⓜ Tribunal) A citywide poll for the best *croquetas* in Madrid would see half of those polled voting for Casa Julio and the remainder not doing so only because they haven't been yet. They're that good that celebrities and mere mortals from all over Madrid come here to sample the traditional *jamón* variety or more creative versions such as spinach with gorgonzola.

The place acquired a certain celebrity when U2 chose the bar for a photo shoot some years back.

**Bazaar** SPANISH €

(Map p102; ☎91 523 39 05; Calle de la Libertad 21; mains €8.30-14; ⏱1-11.30pm Sun-Wed, to midnight Thu-Sat; 📶; Ⓜ Chueca) Bazaar's popularity among the well-heeled Chueca set shows no sign of abating. Its pristine white interior design, with theatre-style lighting and wall-length windows, may draw a crowd that looks like it stepped out of the pages of *¡Hola!* magazine, but the food is extremely well priced and innovative, and the atmosphere is casual. Reservations are available only for dinner Sunday to Thursday. At all other times, get there early or be prepared to wait, regardless of whether you're famous or not. The cocktail list is long and prices start at just €5.

**Bodega de la Ardosa** TAPAS €

(Map p102; ☎91 521 49 79; www.laardosa.es; Calle de Colón 13; tapas & raciones €4-12; ⏱8.30am-2am Mon-Fri, 12.45pm-2.30am Sat & Sun; Ⓜ Tribunal) Going strong since 1892, the wood-panelled bar of Bodega de la Ardosa is brimful with charm. To come here and not try the *salmorejo* (cold tomato soup made with bread, oil, garlic and vinegar), *croquetas* or *tortilla de patatas* (potato and onion omelette) would be a crime. On weekend nights there's scarcely room to move.

**La Musa** FUSION €

(Map p102; ☎91 448 75 58; https://grupolamusa.com/restaurante-lamusa; Calle de Manuela Malasaña 18; tapas €5-7, mains from €10; ⏱9am-1am Mon-Thu, to 2am Fri, 1pm-2am Sat, to 1am Sun; Ⓜ San Bernardo) Snug, loud and unpretentious, La Musa is all about designer decor, lounge music and memorably fun food. The menu is divided into three types of tapas – Spanish, international and those from a wood-fired oven. Try the *degustación de tapas* (€32) for two.

**★ La Carmencita** SPANISH €€

(Map p102; ☎91 531 09 11; www.tabernalacarmencita.es; Calle de la Libertad 16; mains €14-25; ⏱9am-2am; Ⓜ Chueca) Around since 1854, La Carmencita is the bar where legendary poet Pablo Neruda was once a regular. The folk of La Carmencita have taken 75 of their favourite traditional Spanish recipes and brought them to the table, sometimes with a little updating but more often safe in the knowledge that nothing needs changing.

**★ Albur** TAPAS €€

(Map p102; ☎91 594 27 33; www.restaurantealbur.com; Calle de Manuela Malasaña 15; mains €13-26; ⏱12.30-5pm & 7.30pm-midnight Mon-Thu, 12.30-5pm & 7.30pm-1.30am Fri, 1pm-1.30am Sat, to midnight Sun; 📶; Ⓜ Bilbao) One of Malasaña's best deals, this place has a wildly popular tapas bar and a classy but casual restaurant out the back. The restaurant waiters never seem to lose their cool, and the well-priced rice dishes are the stars of the show, although in truth you could order anything here and leave satisfied.

★**La Barraca** VALENCIAN €€

(Map p102; ☎91 532 71 54; www.labarraca.es; Calle de la Reina 29; mains €15-22; ⏲1.30-4pm & 8-11.30pm; Ⓜ Gran Vía) The place to come for a real paella, not the tourist version too often found in Madrid, La Barraca has been serving down-home Valencian cooking in the capital since 1935. Try *el esgarrat con aceite de oliva* (roasted red peppers with cod) and, of course, what many believe to be the best paella in Madrid.

It does all paella varieties, but the true Valencian version – with beans, chicken and/or rabbit – is the speciality. It takes two to make a paella order.

★**Frida** INTERNATIONAL €€

(Map p102; ☎91 704 82 86; http://fridamadrid.com; Calle de San Gregorio 8; mains €10-17; ⏲9am-1am Mon-Fri, 10am-2am Sat & Sun; Ⓜ Chueca) What a lovely little spot this is. Set on a tiny square, its wooden tables flooded with natural light through the big windows, Frida is ideal for a casual meal, a quietly intimate encounter or simply an afternoon spent reading the papers. Food is simple but tasty – designer pizzas, tagine, kebab…

**Bocaito** TAPAS €€

(Map p102; ☎91 532 12 19; www.bocaito.com; Calle de la Libertad 4-6; tapas €2.50-8, mains €12-29; ⏲1-4pm & 8.30pm-midnight Mon-Sat; Ⓜ Chueca, Sevilla) Film-maker Pedro Almodóvar once described this traditional bar and restaurant as 'the best antidepressant'. Forget about the sit-down restaurant (though well regarded) and jam into the bar, shoulder-to-shoulder with the casual crowd, order a few Andalucian *raciones* off the menu and slosh them down with some gritty red or a *caña* (small glass of beer). Enjoy the theatre in which the busy bartenders excel. Specialities include the *tostas* (toasts), *bocaitos* (small filled rolls) and the mussels with béchamel, canapés and fried fish.

**Celso y Manolo** TAPAS €€

(Map p102; ☎91 531 80 79; www.celsoymanolo.es; Calle de la Libertad 1; mains €12-15; ⏲1-4.30pm & 8pm-2am; Ⓜ Banco de España) One of Chueca's best bars, Celso y Manolo serves up *tostadas* for those in need of a snack, oxtail for those looking for a touch of the traditional, and a host of dishes from Spain's north and northwest. There are also good wines, good coffee, even better cocktails and an artfully restored interior.

**La Mucca de Pez** TAPAS €€

(Map p102; ☎91 521 00 00; www.lamucca.es; Plaza Carlos Cambronero 4; mains €9-21; ⏲12.30pm-1.30am Sun-Wed, to 2am Thu, to 2.30am Fri & Sat; Ⓜ Callao) The only problem with this place is that it's such an agreeable spot to spend an afternoon it can be impossible to snaffle a table. An ample wine list complements the great salads, creative pizzas and a good mix of meat and seafood mains, and the atmosphere simply adds to the overall appeal.

★**La Buena Vida** SPANISH €€€

(Map p102; ☎91 531 31 49; www.restaurantelabuenavida.com; Calle del Conde de Xiquena 8; mains €25-29; ⏲1.30-4pm & 9-11.30pm Tue-Thu, 1.30-4pm & 9pm-12.30am Fri & Sat; Ⓜ Chueca, Colón) A cross between a Parisian bistro and old-school upmarket Madrid restaurant, this prestigious Chueca place is popular with a well-heeled, knowledgeable crowd. The seasonal menu ieans towards classic Spanish tastes, although dishes like the red tuna sirloin with guacamole and sesame seeds suggest that the chefs are not averse to the odd playful interpretation. It's consistently among Madrid's best.

★**La Tasquita de Enfrente** SPANISH €€€

(Map p102; ☎91 532 54 49; Calle de la Ballesta 6; mains €24-38, set menus €79; ⏲1.30-4.30pm & 8.30pm-midnight Mon-Sat; Ⓜ Gran Vía) It's difficult to overstate how popular this place is among people in the know in Madrid's food scene. The seasonal menu prepared by chef Juanjo López never ceases to surprise while also combining simple Spanish staples to stunning effect. The *menú de degustación* (tasting menu; €79) would be our choice for first-timers. Reservations are essential.

## Chamberí & Northern Madrid

★**Bodega de la Ardosa** TAPAS €

(Map p106; ☎91 446 58 94; Calle de Santa Engracia 70; raciones from €7; ⏲9am-3pm & 6-11.30pm Thu-Tue; Ⓜ Iglesia) Tucked away on the cusp of Calle de Ponzano, Madrid's (and Chamberí's) most happening bar and tapas street, this fine relic and local institution serves some of the best *patatas bravas* (fried potatoes with spicy tomato sauce) in town. There's also vermouth on tap, and an extravagantly tiled facade complete with shrapnel holes dating back to the Spanish Civil War.

**★Mama Campo** SPANISH €

(Map p106; ☎91 447 41 38; www.mamacampo.es; Plaza de Olavide; mains €9-14; ⊙1.30-4pm & 8.30pm-midnight Mon-Sat, 1.30-4pm Sun; Ⓜ Bilbao, Iglesia, Quevedo) Mama Campo breaks the mould of sameness that unites the bars surrounding Plaza de Olavide. Positioning itself as an ecofriendly take on the Spanish *taberna* (tavern), it's gone for a winning white decor within and a fresh approach to Spanish staples, always with an emphasis on fresh, organic ingredients. It also has tables on one of our favourite squares.

**La Favorita** SPANISH €€

(Map p106; ☎91 448 38 10; www.restaurantelafavorita.com; Calle de Covarrubias 25; mains €12-26, set menus €50-70; ⊙1.30-4pm & 9pm-midnight Mon-Fri, 9pm-midnight Sat; Ⓜ Alonso Martínez) Set in a delightful old mansion, La Favorita is famous for its opera arias throughout the night, sung by professional opera singers masquerading as waiters – they break into song from 9pm to midnight Monday to Friday, and 1.30pm to 4pm Saturday. The music and food (which leans towards the cuisine of the northeastern Spanish region of Navarra) are top drawer.

The outdoor garden courtyard is delightful on a summer's evening.

**Costa Blanca Arrocería** SPANISH €€

(Map p106; ☎91 448 58 32; Calle de Bravo Murillo 3; mains €11-25; ⊙1.30-4pm Mon, 1.30-4pm & 8.30-11.30pm Tue-Fri, 2-4pm & 8.30-11.30pm Sat & Sun; Ⓜ Quevedo) Even if you don't have plans to be in Chamberí, it's worth a trip across town to this bar-restaurant that offers outstanding rice dishes, including paella. The quality is high and prices are among the cheapest in town. Start with *almejas a la marinera* (baby clams) and follow it up with *paella de marisco* (seafood paella) for the full experience.

**Sagaretxe** TAPAS €€

(Map p106; ☎91 446 25 88; www.sagaretxe.com; Calle de Eloy Gonzalo 26; tapas €2.50, set menus €16-35, mains €20-28; ⊙noon-5pm & 7pm-12.30am Sun-Thu, noon-5pm & 7pm-1am Fri & Sat; Ⓜ Iglesia) One of the best *pintxos* bars in Madrid, Sagaretxe takes the stress out of eating tapas, with around 20 varieties lined up along the bar (and more than 100 that can be prepared in the kitchen upon request). Simply point and any of the wonderful selection will be plated up for you.

**WORTH A TRIP**

## CASA JORGE

Arguably Madrid's best Catalan restaurant, classy **Casa Jorge** (☎91 416 92 44; www.casajorge.com; Calle de Cartagena 104; mains €13-22, set menus €39; ⊙1.30-4.30pm & 8.45pm-midnight Mon-Thu, 8.45pm-1am Fri & Sat, 1.30-4pm Sun, closed Aug; Ⓜ Cartagena) serves up exquisite specialities from Spain's northwest, including *caracoles* (snails), perfectly executed rice dishes and, in season (roughly December to March or April), *calçots con salsa romescu* (big spring onions served with a tomato and red-pepper sauce); you eat the last of these with a bib, and they're delicious.

**Las Tortillas de Gabino** SPANISH €€

(Map p106; ☎91 319 75 05; www.lastortillasdegabino.com; Calle de Rafael Calvo 20; tortillas €11-16, mains €14-22; ⊙1.30-4pm & 9-11.30pm Mon-Sat; Ⓜ Iglesia) It's a brave Spanish chef that fiddles with the iconic *tortilla de patatas*, but the results here are delicious. All manner of surprising combinations are available including tortilla with octopus. This place also gets rave reviews for its *croquetas*. The service is excellent and the bright yet classy dining area adds to the sense of a most agreeable eating experience.

**★DiverXo** FUSION €€€

(☎91 570 07 66; www.diverxo.com; Calle del Padre Damián 23; set menu €250; ⊙2-3.30pm & 9-10.30pm Tue-Fri, closed 3 weeks in Aug; Ⓜ Cuzco) Madrid's only three-Michelin-starred restaurant, DiverXo in northern Madrid is one of Spain's most unusual culinary experiences. Chef David Muñoz is something of the *enfant terrible* of Spain's cooking scene, almost Dalí-esque in his refusal to be bound by culinary conventions. It's all about surprises – his team of chefs appear as you're mid-bite to add surprising new ingredients.

The carefully choreographed experience centres on the short (2½-hour, seven-course) or long (four-hour, 11-course) menus, and is utterly unlike the more formal upmarket dining options elsewhere. The nondescript suburban setting and small premises (chefs sometimes end up putting the finishing touches to dishes in the hallway) only add to the whole street-smart atmosphere.

**1.** Plaza de Olavide (p107) **2.** El Rastro flea market (p82)
**3.** Parque del Buen Retiro (p91) **4.** Mercado de San Miguel (p116)

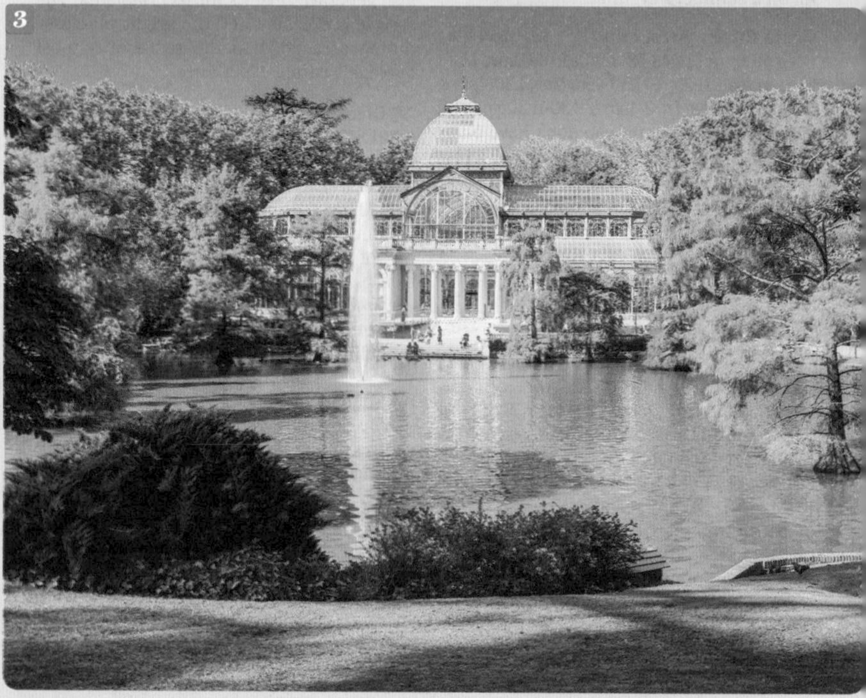

3

# Locals' Madrid

**Madrid can take time to get under your skin, but once it does it rewards your patience a thousand times over. A little local knowledge is key.**

## A Very Madrid Sunday

*Madrileños* (residents of Madrid) like nothing better than Sunday morning at El Rastro flea market (p82), followed by tapas and vermouth around 1pm along Calle de la Cava Baja (p118) in La Latina. Then it's across town to the Parque del Buen Retiro (p91) where, east of the lake, crowds gather, drums start to beat and people begin to dance as the sun nears the horizon.

## Food Icons

In this food-obsessed city you'll find countless treasures that capture the city's culinary essence. The Mercado de San Miguel (p116) epitomises the irresistible buzz that goes with eating here. Nearby Casa Revuelta (p116) is not much to look at but it's similarly adored by locals.

## Calle de Ponzano

If you want to understand why people fall in love with Madrid, head for Calle de Ponzano (p120) in Chamberí in Madrid's inner north. Fabulous tapas, great wines, craft beer, and the captivating atmosphere of wall-to-wall people with nary a tourist in sight. It's the essence of Madrid, and a brilliant night out.

## Barrio Life

North of the centre, the locals reclaim their city. Plaza de Olavide (p107) is the heart and soul of Chamberí and offers an authentic slice of local life. It's not that there's much to see here: instead, the agreeable hum of *madrileños* going about their day, watched from the outdoor tables that encircle the plaza, provides a fascinating window on how locals experience Madrid.

The reservation system (https://diverxo.com/en/reservations) is itself unlike anywhere else – only possible a month in advance, you buy 'tickets' for €250 etc.

## Drinking & Nightlife

Nights in the Spanish capital are the stuff of legend. They're invariably long and loud most days of the week, rising to a deafening crescendo as the weekend nears.

### Plaza Mayor & Royal Madrid

**★Teatro Joy Eslava** CLUB
(Joy Madrid; Map p76; ☎91 366 37 33; www.joy-eslava.com; Calle del Arenal 11; €10-18; ⏲11.30pm-6am; Ⓜ Sol) The only things guaranteed at this grand old Madrid dance club (housed in a 19th-century theatre) are a crowd and the fact that it'll be open (it claims to have operated every single day since 1981). The music and the crowd are a mixed bag, but queues are long and invariably include locals, tourists and the occasional *famoso* (celebrity).

**★Chocolatería de San Ginés** CAFE
(Map p76; ☎91 365 65 46; www.chocolateriasangines.com; Pasadizo de San Ginés 5; ⏲24hr; Ⓜ Sol) One of the grand icons of the Madrid night, this *chocolate con churros* (Spanish doughnuts with chocolate) cafe sees a sprinkling of tourists throughout the day, but locals pack it out in their search for sustenance on their way home from a nightclub somewhere close to dawn. Only in Madrid...

**Plaza Menor** COCKTAIL BAR
(Map p76; ☎665 813821; Calle de Gómez de Mora 3; ⏲6pm-1am Mon-Fri, 4pm-2.30am Sat & Sun; Ⓜ La Latina, Sol) Killer cakes backed by killer cocktails served in a subterranean cavern frequented by in-the-know locals – Plaza Menor is a fab place for an intimate drink; good tapas as well.

**Vermutería Chipén** BAR
(☎91 541 98 80; https://vermuteriachipen.es; Calle del Tutor 1; ⏲11am-11pm; Ⓜ Ventura Rodríguez) In a lovely bar flooded with natural light, Chipén serves up more types of vermouth than you knew existed, as well as *cavas*, champagne and spirits. It's a fine spot to see what all the fuss is about when it comes to the city's love affair with vermouth.

**Bodegas Ricla** BAR
(Map p76; ☎91 365 20 69; Calle de los Cuchilleros 6; ⏲1-4pm & 7pm-midnight Wed-Sat & Mon, 1-4pm Sun; Ⓜ Tirso de Molina) Bodegas Ricla is so tiny you might be rubbing haunches with other customers as you sip your wine. For more than 100 years, it's been serving tasty authentic tapas and local vintages: red, white and pink wines, *cavas* and vermouth. Inside, little has changed in decades, with old-style terracotta barrels and pictures of bullfighters lining the walls.

**Café de Oriente** CAFE
(Map p76; ☎91 541 39 74; Plaza de Oriente 2; ⏲8.30am-1.30am Mon-Thu, 9am-2.30am Fri & Sat, 9am-1.30am Sun; Ⓜ Ópera) The outdoor tables of this distinguished old cafe are among the most sought-after in central Madrid, providing as they do a front-row seat for the beautiful Plaza de Oriente, with the Palacio Real as a backdrop. The building itself was once part of a long-gone, 17th-century convent and the interior feels a little like a set out of Mitteleuropa.

### La Latina & Lavapiés

**★Taberna El Tempranillo** WINE BAR
(Map p82; ☎91 364 15 32; Calle de la Cava Baja 38; ⏲1-4pm Mon, 1-4pm & 8pm-midnight Tue-Sun; Ⓜ La Latina) You could come here for the tapas, but we recommend Taberna El Tempranillo especially for its wines, of which it has a selection that puts numerous Spanish bars to shame. It's not a late-night place, but it's always packed in the early evening and on Sunday after El Rastro. Many wines are sold by the glass.

**★Delic** BAR
(Map p82; ☎91 364 54 50; www.delic.es; Costanilla de San Andrés 14; ⏲11am-2am Sun & Tue-Thu, to 2.30am Fri & Sat; Ⓜ La Latina) We could go on for hours about this long-standing cafe-bar, but we'll reduce it to its most basic elements: nursing an exceptionally good mojito or three on a warm summer's evening at Delic's outdoor tables on one of Madrid's prettiest plazas is one of life's great pleasures. Bliss.

**Boconó Specialty Coffee** CAFE
(Map p82; ☎91 040 20 19; www.facebook.com/bocono.coffee; Calle de los Embajadores 3; ⏲8.30am-8.30pm Mon-Thu, from 9.30am Fri-Sun; 📶; Ⓜ La Latina, Tirso de Molina) Close attention to every detail makes Boconó special – coffee is roasted on-site and fanatics have a choice of styles: espresso, AeroPress and Chemex, among others. Coffee is weighed before brewing and water is dosed out by the millilitre. The decor is minimal, with reclaimed

wood and rough brick, the wi-fi is fast and the service is friendly.

**El Eucalipto** COCKTAIL BAR
(☎91 527 27 63; www.facebook.com/eeucalipto; Calle de Argumosa 4; ⏲5pm-2am Sun-Thu, to 3am Fri & Sat; Ⓜ Lavapiés) This fine little bar is devoted to all things Cuban – from the music to the clientele and the Caribbean cocktails (including nonalcoholic), it's a sexy, laid-back place. Not surprisingly, the mojitos are a cut above average, but the juices and daiquiris also have a loyal following.

**El Bonanno** WINE BAR
(Map p82; ☎91 366 68 86; https://elbonanno.com; Plaza del Humilladero 4; ⏲noon-2am; Ⓜ La Latina) If much of Madrid's nightlife starts too late for your liking, Bonanno could be for you. It made its name as a cocktail bar, but many people also come here for the great wines. It's usually full of young professionals from early evening onwards. Be prepared to snuggle up close to those around you if you want a spot at the bar.

## Sol, Santa Ana & Huertas

**★ La Venencia** BAR
(Map p84; ☎91 429 73 13; Calle de Echegaray 7; ⏲12.30-3.30pm & 7.30pm-1.30am; Ⓜ Sol, Sevilla) La Venencia is a *barrio* classic, with *manzanilla* (chamomile-coloured sherry) from Sanlúcar and sherry from Jeréz poured straight from the dusty wooden barrels, accompanied by a small selection of tapas with an Andalucian bent. There's no music, no flashy decorations; here it's all about you, your *fino* (sherry) and your friends.

**Salmón Gurú** COCKTAIL BAR
(Map p84; ☎91 000 61 85; www.salmonguru.es; Calle de Echegaray 21; ⏲5pm-2.30am Wed-Sun; Ⓜ Antón Martín) When Sergi Arola's empire collapsed and the celebrated Le Cabrera cocktail bar went with it, Madrid lost one of its best cocktail maestros, Diego Cabrera. Thankfully, he's back with a wonderful multifaceted space where he serves up a masterful collection of drinks – work your way through his menu of 25 Cabrera *clásicos* to get started.

**La Azotea** LOUNGE
(Map p84; ☎91 530 17 61; www.azoteadelcirculo.com; Calle Marqués de Casa Riera 2, 7th fl; €4; ⏲9am-2am Mon-Thu, to 2.30am Fri, 11am-2.30am Sat & Sun; Ⓜ Banco de España, Sevilla) Order a cocktail, then lie down on the cushions and admire the vista from this fabulous rooftop terrace. It's a brilliant place to chill out, with the views at their best close to sunset.

> **LOCAL KNOWLEDGE**
>
> ### LA HORA DEL VERMUT
>
> Sunday, one o'clock in the afternoon, a dark bar off Calle de la Cava Baja. In any civilised city the bar would be shut tight, but in Madrid the place is packed because it's *la hora del vermut* (vermouth hour), a long-standing tradition whereby friends and families head out for a quick aperitif before Sunday lunch. Sometimes referred to as *ir de Rastro* (going to the Rastro) because so many of the traditional vermouth bars are in and around El Rastro market, this Sunday tradition is deeply ingrained in *madrileño* culture. Some of the best bars for vermouth are along La Latina's Calle de la Cava Baja, while Casa Alberto (p119) is another legendary part of this fine tradition.

**El Imperfecto** COCKTAIL BAR
(Map p84; ☎680 904436; www.facebook.com/elimperfectobar; Plaza de Matute 2; ⏲3pm-2am; Ⓜ Antón Martín) Its name notwithstanding, the 'Imperfect One' is our ideal Huertas bar, with occasional live jazz and a drinks menu as long as a saxophone, ranging from cocktails and spirits to milkshakes, teas and creative coffees. Its pina colada is one of the best we've tasted and the atmosphere is agreeably buzzy yet chilled.

**Taberna La Dolores** BAR
(Map p84; ☎91 429 22 43; Plaza de Jesús 4; ⏲11am-1am; Ⓜ Antón Martín) Old bottles and beer mugs line the shelves behind the bar at this Madrid institution (1908), known for its blue-and-white-tiled exterior and a thirty-something crowd that often includes the odd *famoso* or two. It claims to be 'the most famous bar in Madrid' – that's pushing it, but it's invariably full most nights of the week, so who are we to argue?

**Taberna Alhambra** BAR
(Map p84; ☎91 521 07 08; Calle de la Victoria 9; ⏲11am-1am Sun-Wed, to 2am Thu, to 2.30am Fri & Sat; Ⓜ Sol) There can be a certain sameness about the bars between Sol and Huertas, which is why this fine old *taberna* stands out. The striking facade and exquisite tile-work of the interior are quite beautiful;

### MADRID'S BEST VERMOUTH

**La Violeta** (p131) Vermouth on tap and in great variety.

**Casa Alberto** (p119) The essence of Madrid's love affair with *vermut*.

**La Hora del Vermut** Outstanding vermouth east of El Retiro.

**Vermutería Chipén** (p126) Beloved by Madrid's aficionados for its dedicated *vermut* menu.

**Arima** (p120) Wide selection in Madrid's inner north.

however, this place is anything but stuffy and the feel is cool, casual and busy. It serves tapas and, later at night, there are some fine flamenco tunes.

**La Terraza del Urban** COCKTAIL BAR

(Map p84; ☎91 787 77 70; Carrera de San Jerónimo 34, Urban Hotel; ⊙noon-8pm Sun & Mon, to 3am Tue-Sat mid-May–Sep, 1-9pm Wed-Sun rest of year; Ⓜ Sevilla) A strong contender for best rooftop bar in Madrid, this indulgent terrace sits atop the five-star Urban Hotel and has five-star views with five-star prices – worth every euro.

In case you get vertigo, head downstairs to the similarly high-class **Glass Bar** (Map p84; Carrera de San Jerónimo 34, Hotel Urban; ⊙noon-3am; Ⓜ Sevilla).

**Radio** COCKTAIL BAR

(Map p84; ☎91 701 60 00; http://radiomemadrid.com; Plaza de Santa Ana 14, 7th fl; ⊙5pm-2am Mon, 1.30pm-2am Tue-Thu, to 3am Fri & Sat, to 1am Sun; Ⓜ Antón Martín, Sol) High above the Plaza de Santa Ana, this sybaritic open-air cocktail bar has terrific views over Madrid's rooftops. It's a place for sophisticates, with chill-out areas strewn with cushions, DJs and a dress and door policy designed to sort out the classy from the wannabes.

## El Retiro & the Art Museums

**La Hora del Vermut** BAR

(☎681007700; https://lahoradelvermut.wordpress.com; Calle de Fernán Gonzalez 48; ⊙noon-4pm & 7-10.30pm Mon-Thu, noon-11pm Fri & Sat, to 10.30pm Sun; Ⓜ Goya, O'Donnell) Out in the otherwise sedate streets east of El Retiro, this fine neighbourhood bar is one of the best places in Madrid to try *vermut* (vermouth), from the top-shelf stuff to the basics on tap for €2 a glass. Great tapas, from pickled olives and the like to empanadas (filled pastries), too. There's an outpost downtown in the Mercado de San Miguel (p116).

**Teatro Kapital** CLUB

(Map p88; ☎91 420 29 06; www.teatrokapital.com; Calle de Atocha 125; admission from €20; ⊙midnight-6am Thu-Sat; Ⓜ Estación del Arte) One of the most famous megaclubs in Madrid, this seven-storey venue has something for everyone, from cocktail bars and dance music to karaoke, salsa, hip-hop, chilled spaces and an open-air rooftop. There's even a 'Kissing Room'. Door staff have their share of attitude and don't mind refusing entrance if you give them any lip (and even if you don't).

It's such a big place that a cross-section of Madrid society hangs out here (VIPs and the Real Madrid set love this place) without ever getting in each other's way.

## Salamanca

**Almonte** CLUB

(Map p98; ☎91 563 25 04; www.almontesalarociera.com; Calle de Juan Bravo 35; ⊙9pm-5am Sun-Fri, 10pm-6am Sat; Ⓜ Núñez de Balboa, Diego de León) If flamenco has captured your soul but you're keen to do more than watch, head to Almonte. Live acts kick off the night, paying homage to the flamenco roots of Almonte in Andalucía's deep south. The young and the beautiful who come here have *sevillanas* (a flamenco dance style) in their soul and in their feet.

## Malasaña & Chueca

★**Museo Chicote** COCKTAIL BAR

(Map p102; ☎91 532 67 37; www.museochicote.com; Gran Vía 12; ⊙1pm-3am Mon-Sat, to 1am Sun; Ⓜ Gran Vía) This place is a Madrid landmark, complete with its 1930s-era interior, and its founder is said to have invented more than 100 cocktails, which the likes of Ernest Hemingway, Ava Gardner, Grace Kelly, Sophia Loren and Frank Sinatra all enjoyed at one time or another.

★**Café Belén** BAR

(Map p102; ☎91 308 27 47; www.elcafebelen.com; Calle de Belén 5; ⊙3.30pm-3am Tue-Thu, to 3.30am Fri & Sat, to 10pm Sun; 📶; Ⓜ Chueca) Café Belén is cool in all the right places – lounge and chill-out music, dim lighting, a great range of drinks (the mojitos are especially good) and a low-key crowd that's casual but classy. It's one of our preferred Chueca watering holes.

**★Café Comercial** CAFE

(Map p102; ☎91 088 25 25; www.cafecomercialmadrid.com; Glorieta de Bilbao 7; ⊙noon-midnight; 📶; ⓂBilbao) The city's oldest cafe has a special place in the hearts of many *madrileños*. Open for more than a century, it's still pulsing with life. Any day of the week you can enjoy a coffee or some food at one of the old marble-topped tables and feel like you're part of Madrid's literary and cultural scene.

**★1862 Dry Bar** COCKTAIL BAR

(Map p102; ☎609 531151; www.facebook.com/1862drybar; Calle del Pez 27; ⊙3.30pm-2am Sun-Thu, to 2.30am Fri & Sat; ⓂNoviciado) Great cocktails, muted early 20th-century decor and a refined air make this one of our favourite bars down Malasaña's southern end. Prices are reasonable, the cocktail list extensive and new cocktails appear every month.

**Nice to Meet You** BAR

(Map p102; ☎638 908559; www.dearhotelmadrid.com/en/nice-to-meet-you; Gran Vía 80, Dear Hotel, 14th fl; ⊙noon-1.30am Sun-Thu, to 2.30am Fri & Sat; ⓂPlaza de España) This rooftop bar occupying the top floor of Dear Hotel has a spectacular view of Plaza España and Malasaña. Come any time of day to sit down with a cocktail and enjoy the view, or try something to eat – food specialities include Mediterranean staples like cod and ox steak. The ultra-cool lounge opens from 9pm.

**Café-Restaurante El Espejo** CAFE

(Map p102; ☎91 308 23 47; Paseo de los Recoletos 31; ⊙8am-midnight Mon-Fri, from 9am Sat & Sun; ⓂColón) Once a haunt of writers and intellectuals, this architectural gem blends Modernista and art deco styles, and its interior could well overwhelm you with all the mirrors, chandeliers and bow-tied service of another era. The atmosphere is suitably quiet and refined, although our favourite corner is the elegant glass pavilion out on Paseo de los Recoletos.

**Gran Café de Gijón** CAFE

(Map p102; ☎91 521 54 25; www.cafegijon.com; Paseo de los Recoletos 21; ⊙7am-1.30am; ⓂChueca, Banco de España) This graceful old cafe has been serving coffee and meals since 1888 and has long been favoured by Madrid's literati for a drink or a meal – *all* of Spain's great 20th-century literary figures came here for coffee and *tertulias* (literary and philosophical discussions). You'll find yourself among intellectuals, conservative Franco diehards and young *madrileños* looking for a quiet drink.

**Macera** COCKTAIL BAR

(Map p102; ☎91 011 58 10; www.maceradrinks.com; Calle de San Mateo 21; ⊙1pm-1am Tue & Wed, to 2am Thu, to 3.30am Fri & Sat, 4-11pm Sun; ⓂAlonso Martínez) This bar defies labels – literally. Macera's crew distils all of their own spirits, which makes for both an impressive



## CRAFT BEER IN MALASAÑA

Madrid has taken longer than you might imagine to embrace the wonderful world of *cervezas artesanales* (craft beers), but Malasaña has more bars where you can find them than any other *barrio*.

**Fábrica Maravillas** (Map p102; ☎91 521 87 53; www.fmaravillas.com; Calle de Valverde 29; ⊙6pm-midnight Mon-Wed, to 1am Thu, to 2am Fri, 12.30pm-2am Sat, to midnight Sun; ⓂTribunal, Gran Vía) is one of Madrid's craft breweries of longest standing, and its 'Malasaña Ale' is a classic and, for devotees, the taste of the *barrio*. **La Tape** (Map p102; ☎91 593 04 22; www.latape.com; Calle de San Bernardo 88; ⊙9am-12.30am Sun-Thu, 10am-1.30am Fri & Sat; ⓂBilbao, San Bernardo) has arguably the greatest selection, while **Irreale** (Map p102; ☎91 172 28 02; www.facebook.com/irrealemadrid; Calle de Manuela Malasaña 20; ⊙6pm-1am Sun-Wed, to 2am Thu, 1pm-2.30am Fri & Sat; ⓂBilbao) not far away is also good. For variety and a tap list that changes regularly, try **Stuyck Co** (Map p102; ☎91 466 92 98; www.thestuyckco.com; Calle Corredera Alta de San Pablo 33; ⊙6.30pm-midnight Mon-Fri, from 1pm Sat & Sun; ⓂTribunal). If you don't mind a bit of a walk and you're looking for take-home Spanish and international craft beers, head for **La Cervecista** (Map p102; ☎91 593 04 99; www.loscervecistas.es; Calle de Mejía Lequerica 3; ⊙11am-9pm Mon-Sat; ⓂAlonso Martínez) in neighbouring Chueca.

## GAY & LESBIAN MADRID

Madrid is one of Europe's most gay-friendly cities. The heartbeat of gay Madrid is the inner-city *barrio* of Chueca, where Madrid didn't just come out of the closet, but ripped the doors off in the process. But even here the crowd is almost always mixed gay/straight. The best time of all to be in town if you're gay or lesbian is around the last Saturday in June, for Madrid's gay and lesbian pride march, Día del Orgullo LGTBI (p111). Madrid also hosts the annual **Les Gai Cine Mad festival** (☎91 593 05 40; www.lesgaicinemad.com; ⌚late Oct/early Nov), a celebration of lesbian, gay and transsexual films. An excellent place to stay is Hostal La Zona (p114).

**Café Acuarela** (Map p102; ☎91 522 21 43; Calle de Gravina 10; ⌚11am-2am Sun-Thu, to 3am Fri & Sat; Ⓜ Chueca) A few steps up the hill from Plaza de Chueca, this longtime centrepiece of gay Madrid – a huge statue of a nude male angel guards the doorway – is an agreeable, dimly lit salon decorated with, among other things, religious icons. It's ideal for quiet conversation and catching the weekend buzz as people plan their forays into the more clamorous clubs in the vicinity.

**Club 54 Studio** (Map p102; ☎615 126807; www.studio54madrid.com; Calle de Barbieri 7; ⌚8pm-3.30am Wed-Sun; Ⓜ Chueca) Modelled on the famous New York club Studio 54, this nightclub draws a predominantly gay crowd, but its target market is more upmarket than many in the *barrio*. Unlike other Madrid clubs where paid dancers up on stage try to get things moving, here they let the punters set the pace.

**Why Not?** (Map p102; ☎91 521 80 34; Calle de San Bartolomé 7; €10; ⌚10.30pm-6am; Ⓜ Chueca) Underground, narrow and packed with bodies, gay-friendly Why Not? is the sort of place where nothing's left to the imagination (the gay and straight crowd who come here are pretty amorous) and it's full nearly every night of the week. Pop and Top 40 music are the standard, and the dancing crowd is mixed but all serious about having a good time.

**Librería Berkana** (Map p102; ☎91 522 55 99; www.libreriaberkana.com; Calle de Hortaleza 62; ⌚10.30am-9pm Mon-Fri, from 11.30am Sat, noon-2pm & 5-9pm Sun; Ⓜ Chueca) One of the most important gay and lesbian bookshops in Madrid, Librería Berkana stocks gay books, movies, magazines, music, clothing, and a host of free magazines for nightlife and other gay-focused activities in Madrid and around Spain.

cocktail list and a striking ambience. The drinks are kept behind the bar in clear, backlit glass jars; the effect falls somewhere between psychedelic and old-world apothecary. Craft your own concoction or consult the ample list of original cocktails (from €7).

**Lola09** COCKTAIL BAR

(Map p102; ☎91 310 66 95; www.lola09.com; Calle de San Mateo 28; ⌚5.30pm-1am Mon, to 1.30am Tue & Wed, to 2am Thu, 4.30pm-2.30am Fri & Sat, 5pm-1am Sun; Ⓜ Alonso Martínez) A happy Madrid crowd packs this place out on weekends. The food's good, but it's the designer cocktails that make the bar stand out. If you get here any later than midnight on Friday or Saturday nights, there might not be room.

**Tupperware** CLUB

(Map p102; ☎91 446 42 04; www.tupperwareclub.com; Calle de la Corredera Alta de San Pablo 26; ⌚9pm-3am Mon-Wed, 8pm-3.30am Thu-Sat, to 3am Sun; Ⓜ Tribunal) A Malasaña stalwart and prime candidate for the bar that best catches the enduring *rockero* (rocker) spirit of the neighbourhood, Tupperware draws a thirty-something crowd, spins indie rock with a bit of soul and classics from the '60s and '70s, and generally revels in its kitsch (eyeballs stuck to the ceiling, and plastic TVs with action-figure dioramas lined up behind the bar). By the way, locals pronounce it 'Tupper-warry'.

**Antigua Casa Ángel Sierra** TAVERNA

(Map p102; ☎91 531 01 26; http://tabernadeangelsierra.es; Calle de Gravina 11; ⌚noon-1am; Ⓜ Chueca) This historic old *taberna* is the antithesis of modern Chueca chic – it has hardly changed since it opened in 1917. As Spaniards like to say, the beer on tap is very 'well poured' here and it also has vermouth on tap. It can get pretty lively on weekend evenings when it spills over onto the vibrant Plaza de Chueca and takes it over.

**Lolina Vintage Café** CAFE
(Map p102; ☎91 523 58 59; www.lolinacafe.com; Calle del Espíritu Santo 9; ⊙9.30am-1am Mon-Thu, to 2.30am Fri, 10.15am-2.30am Sat, to 1am Sun; Ⓜ Tribunal) Lolina Vintage Café seems to have captured the essence of the *barrio* in one small space, with its studied retro look (comfy old-style chairs and sofas, gilded mirrors and 1970s-era wallpaper). It's low-key, full from the first breakfast to closing, and it caters to every taste with salads and cocktails.

**La Terraza de Óscar** LOUNGE
(Map p102; Plaza de Vázquez de Mella 12; ⊙5pm-1am Mon-Wed, to 2am Thu & Fri, 4pm-2am Sat, to midnight Sun; Ⓜ Gran Vía) One of Madrid's stunning rooftop terraces, this chilled space atop Hotel Óscar (p115), with gorgeous skyline views and a small swimming pool, has become something of a retreat among A-list celebrities.

**La Vía Láctea** BAR
(Map p102; ☎91 446 75 81; www.facebook.com/lavialacteabar; Calle de Velarde 18; ⊙8pm-3am Sun-Thu, to 3.30am Fri & Sat; Ⓜ Tribunal) A living, breathing and delightfully grungy relic of *la movida madrileña*, La Vía Láctea remains a Malasaña favourite for a mixed, informal crowd who seems to live for the 1980s. The music ranges across rock, pop, garage, rockabilly and indie. There are plenty of drinks to choose from and by late Saturday night anything goes. Expect long queues to get in on weekends.

**Bar Cock** COCKTAIL BAR
(Map p102; ☎91 532 28 26; www.barcock.com; Calle de la Reina 16; ⊙7pm-3am Mon-Thu, to 3.30am Fri & Sat; Ⓜ Gran Vía) With a name like this, Bar Cock could go either way, but it's definitely cock as in 'rooster'. The decor evokes an old gentlemen's club and the feeling is more elegant and classic than risqué. It's beloved by A-list celebrities and wannabes, and a refined thirty-something crowd who come here for the lively atmosphere and great cocktails.

On weekends all the tables seem to be reserved, so be prepared to hover on the fringes of fame.

**Del Diego** COCKTAIL BAR
(Map p102; ☎91 523 31 06; www.deldiego.com; Calle de la Reina 12; ⊙7pm-3am Mon-Thu, to 3.30am Fri & Sat; Ⓜ Gran Vía) Del Diego is one of the city's most celebrated cocktail bars. The decor blends old-world cafe with New York style, and it's the sort of place where the music rarely drowns out the conversation. Even with around 75 cocktails to choose from, we'd still order the signature 'El Diego' (vodka, advocaat, apricot brandy and lime).

## Chamberí & Northern Madrid

★**La Violeta** BAR
(☎667 058644; www.lavioletavermut.com; Calle de Vallehermoso 62; ⊙7pm-1am Tue-Thu, 1-4.30pm & 7pm-2am Fri, 1pm-2am Sat, 1-5pm Sun; Ⓜ Canal) This breezy little Chamberí bar has many calling cards – among them, great music and a sense of being a real old-style Madrid neighbourhood bar. But we like it for its *vermut*, one of the city's favourite drinks. Unusually, there are more than 20 different versions to try and staff are adept at pairing the perfect tapa with each variety.

**Saint Georges Cafe** CAFE
(Map p106; www.instagram.com/saintgeorgescafe; Calle del Cardenal Cisneros 62; ⊙8am-5pm Mon-Fri; Ⓜ Quevedo) Javier and Zoë, a Spanish-Australian couple, named their cafe after St Georges Rd in Zoë's native Melbourne, and the Aussie legacy doesn't end there. They brought with them single-origin coffee (flat-white or *cortado?*), avocado on toast served with feta and pomegranate, baked goodies and a commitment to healthy takeaway meals. It's a tiny brick-walled space, and a gorgeous, friendly spot.

**Dash** COCKTAIL BAR
(Map p106; ☎687 949064; www.facebook.com/thedashmadrid; Calle de Murillo 5; ⊙5pm-2am Tue-Thu, to 2.30am Fri & Sat, to midnight Sun; Ⓜ Iglesia) This neighbourhood spot with its big marble bar top evokes the classic cocktail bars of Madrid's past, but it's a casual place with few pretensions. There's a terrific mix of cocktails, all expertly mixed.

**Real Café Bernabéu** BAR
(☎91 458 36 67; www.realcafebernabeu.es; Avenida de Concha Espina, Estadio Santiago Bernabéu, Gate 30; ⊙10am-2am; Ⓜ Santiago Bernabéu) Overlooking one of the most famous football fields on earth, this trendy cocktail bar will appeal to those who live and breathe football or those who simply enjoy mixing with the beautiful people. Views of the stadium are exceptional, although it closes two hours before a game and doesn't open until an hour after. There's also a good restaurant.

# Entertainment

Madrid is the cultural capital of the Spanish-speaking world, and it shows. There's a world-class live-music scene, its role on the Europe-wide touring circuit augmented by top-notch flamenco, jazz and a host of performers you may never have heard of but who may just be Spain's next big thing. For a dose of high culture, there's opera and *zarzuela* (Spanish mix of theatre, music and dance).

## Plaza Mayor & Royal Madrid

**Las Tablas** FLAMENCO

(Map p76; ☎91 542 05 20; www.lastablasmadrid.com; Plaza de España 9; admission incl drink/meal from €29/66; ⏱shows 7pm & 9pm; Ⓜ Plaza de España) Las Tablas has a reputation for quality flamenco and reasonable prices; it's among the best choices in town. Most nights you'll see a classic flamenco show, with plenty of throaty singing and soul-baring dancing. Antonia Moya and Marisol Navarro, leading lights in the flamenco world, are regular performers here.

**La Coquette Blues** LIVE MUSIC

(Map p76; ☎91 530 80 95; Calle de las Hileras 14; ⏱9pm-2.30am Tue-Sat, to midnight Sun; Ⓜ Ópera) Madrid's best blues bar in a cosy, subterranean brick cavern has been around since the 1980s and its Sunday jam session is legendary. Live acts perform most nights.

**Café Berlín** JAZZ

(Map p76; ☎91 559 74 29; www.berlincafe.es; Costanilla de los Ángeles 20; €5-20; ⏱9pm-3am Tue-Thu, to 5am Fri & Sat; Ⓜ Santo Domingo) Café Berlín has been something of a Madrid jazz stalwart since the 1950s, although a makeover has brought flamenco, R&B, soul, funk and fusion into the mix. Headline acts play at 11pm, but check the website as some can begin as 'early' as 9pm. It's one of downtown Madrid's more dynamic live-music programmes.

**Café de Chinitas** FLAMENCO

(Map p76; ☎91 547 15 02; www.chinitas.com; Calle de Torija 7; admission incl drink/meal €40/72; ⏱shows 8.15pm & 10.30pm Mon-Sat; Ⓜ Santo Domingo) One of the most distinguished *tablaos* in Madrid, drawing in everyone from the Spanish royal family to Bill Clinton, Café de Chinitas has an elegant setting and top-notch performers. It may attract loads of tourists, but its authentic flamenco also gives it top marks. Reservations are highly recommended.

**Teatro Real** OPERA

(Map p76; ☎902 244848; www.teatro-real.com; Plaza de Oriente; Ⓜ Ópera) After spending over €100 million on a long rebuilding project, the Teatro Real is as technologically advanced as any venue in Europe, and is the city's grandest stage for elaborate operas, ballets and classical music. The cheapest seats are so far away you'll need a telescope, although the sound quality is consistent throughout.

> **WORTH A TRIP**
>
> **CAFÉ ZIRYAB**
>
> For a fine, well-priced flamenco show that draws as many locals as tourists, **Café Ziryab** (☎91 219 29 02; www.cafeziryab.com; Paseo de la Esperanza 17; adult/child €25/8; ⏱shows 9.30pm Mon-Thu, 7.30pm & 9.30pm Fri-Sun; Ⓜ Acacias) is a bit out of the city centre but worth the excursion. At 11pm on some Fridays, the *peña flamenca* is a jam session for those who feel the urge and, when it works, it's authentic flamenco at its improvised, soul-stirring best.

## La Latina & Lavapiés

**★ Casa Patas** FLAMENCO

(Map p84; ☎91 369 04 96; www.casapatas.com; Calle de Cañizares 10; admission incl drink €40; ⏱shows 10.30pm Mon-Thu, 8pm & 10.30pm Fri & Sat; Ⓜ Antón Martín, Tirso de Molina) One of the top flamenco stages in Madrid, this *tablao* always offers flawless quality that serves as a good introduction to the art. It's not the friendliest place in town, especially if you're only here for the show, and you're likely to be crammed in a little, but no one complains about the standard of the performances.

**★ Corral de la Morería** FLAMENCO

(Map p82; ☎91 365 84 46; www.corraldelamoreria.com; Calle de la Morería 17; admission incl drink from €50; ⏱shows 7.30pm & 9.30pm Sun-Thu, 8pm & 10.45pm Fri & Sat; Ⓜ Ópera) This is one of the most prestigious flamenco stages in Madrid, with 50 years of experience as a leading venue and top performers most nights. The stage area has a rustic feel, and tables are pushed up close. Unusually for Madrid's *tablaos*, the Michelin-starred restaurant is excellent. Set menus from €44 (additional to the admission fee).

**ContraClub** LIVE MUSIC
(Map p82; ☎699 741885; www.contraclub.es; Calle de Bailén 16; €3-15; ⏰10pm-6am Thu-Sat; Ⓜ La Latina) ContraClub is a crossover live-music venue and nightclub, with an eclectic mix of live music (pop, rock, indie, singer-songwriter, blues etc). After the live acts (from 10pm), resident DJs serve up equally diverse beats (indie, pop, funk and soul) to make sure you don't move elsewhere.

## ☆ Sol, Santa Ana & Huertas

**★Sala El Sol** LIVE MUSIC
(Map p84; ☎91 532 64 90; www.salaelsol.com; Calle de los Jardines 3; admission incl drink €10, concert tickets €6-30; ⏰midnight-5.30am Tue-Sat Jul-Sep; Ⓜ Gran Vía) Madrid institutions don't come any more beloved than the terrific Sala El Sol. It opened in 1979, just in time for *la movida madrileña* and quickly established itself as a leading stage for all the icons of the era, such as Nacha Pop and Alaska y los Pegamoides.

**★Villa Rosa** FLAMENCO
(Map p84; ☎91 521 36 89; www.tablaoflamencovillarosa.com; Plaza de Santa Ana 15; admission incl drink €39; ⏰11pm-6am Mon-Sat, shows 8.30pm & 10.45pm; Ⓜ Sol) Villa Rosa has been going strong since 1914, and in that time it has seen many manifestations. It established itself as a flamenco venue and has recently returned to its roots with well-regarded shows.

The extraordinary tiled facade (1928) is the work of Alfonso Romero, who was also responsible for the tile work in the Plaza de Toros – the facade is a tourist attraction in itself. This long-standing nightclub even appeared in the Pedro Almodóvar film *Tacones lejanos* (High Heels; 1991).

**★Café Central** JAZZ
(Map p84; ☎91 369 41 43; www.cafecentralmadrid.com; Plaza del Ángel 10; €15-20; ⏰11.30pm-2.30am Sun-Thu, to 3.30am Fri & Sat, shows 9pm; Ⓜ Antón Martín, Sol) In 2011, the respected jazz magazine *Down Beat* included this art deco bar on the list of the world's best jazz clubs, the only place in Spain to earn the prestigious accolade (said by some to be the jazz equivalent of earning a Michelin star). With well over 1000 gigs under its belt, it rarely misses a beat.

Big international names like Chano Domínguez, Tal Farlow and Wynton Marsalis have all played here and you'll hear everything from Latin jazz and fusion to tango and classical jazz. Performers usually play here for a week and then move on, so getting tickets shouldn't be a problem, except on weekends. Shows start at 9pm and tickets go on sale from 6pm before the set starts. You can also reserve by phone.

> **ⓘ WHAT'S ON IN MADRID?**
>
> **EsMadrid Magazine** (www.esmadrid.com) Monthly tourist-office listings.
>
> **Guía del Ocio** (www.guiadelocio.com) Weekly magazine available for €1 at news kiosks.
>
> **Metrópoli** (www.elmundo.es/metropoli) *El Mundo* newspaper's Friday supplement magazine.
>
> **La Noche en Vivo** (www.lanocheenvivo.com) Live-music listings.

**★Teatro de la Zarzuela** THEATRE
(Map p84; ☎91 524 54 00; http://teatrodelazarzuela.mcu.es; Calle de Jovellanos 4; tickets €5-60; ⏰box office noon-6pm Mon-Fri, from 3pm Sat & Sun; Ⓜ Banco de España, Sevilla) This theatre, built in 1856, is the premier place to see *zarzuela*. It also hosts a smattering of classical music and opera, as well as the cutting-edge Compañía Nacional de Danza.

**Costello Café & Niteclub** LIVE MUSIC
(Map p84; ☎91 522 18 15; www.costelloclub.com; Calle del Caballero de Gracia 10; €8-20; ⏰8pm-2.30am Tue, to 3am Wed & Thu, to 3.30am Fri & Sat; Ⓜ Gran Vía) The very cool Costello Café & Niteclub weds smooth-as-silk ambience to an innovative mix of pop, rock and fusion in Warhol-esque surrounds. There's live music (pop and rock, often of the indie variety) at 9.30pm every night except Sunday and Monday, with resident and visiting DJs keeping you on your feet until closing time the rest of the week.

## ☆ Malasaña & Chueca

**★Teatro Flamenco Madrid** FLAMENCO
(Map p102; ☎91 159 20 05; www.teatroflamencomadrid.com; Calle del Pez 10; adult/student & senior/child €27/18/14; ⏰6.30pm & 8.15pm Sun-Fri,

6.30pm, 8.15pm & 10pm Sat; Ⓜ Noviciado) This excellent new flamenco venue is a terrific deal. With a focus on quality flamenco (dance, song and guitar) rather than the more formal meal-and-floor-show package of the *tablaos*, and with a mixed crowd of locals and tourists, it generates a terrific atmosphere most nights for the hour-long show. Prices are also a notch below what you'll pay elsewhere. It also has flamenco-themed theatre productions.

**El Junco Jazz Club** JAZZ
(Map p102; ☎91 319 20 81; www.eljunco.com; Plaza de Santa Bárbara 10; €6-15; ⏰11pm-5.30am Tue-Thu, to 6am Fri & Sat; Ⓜ Alonso Martínez) El Junco has established itself on the Madrid nightlife scene by appealing as much to jazz aficionados as to clubbers. Its secret is high-quality live jazz gigs from Spain and around the world, followed by DJs spinning funk, soul, nu jazz, blues and innovative groove beats. There are also jam sessions at 11pm in jazz (Tuesday) and blues (Sunday).

The emphasis is on music from the American South and the crowd is classy and casual.

## ☆ Chamberí & Northern Madrid

**★ Estadio Santiago Bernabéu** FOOTBALL
(☎902 324324; www.realmadrid.com; Avenida de Concha Espina 1; tickets from €40; Ⓜ Santiago Bernabéu) Watching Real Madrid play is one of football's greatest experiences, but tickets are difficult to find. They can be purchased online, by phone or in person from the ticket office at gate 42 on Avenida de Concha Espina; turn up early in the week before a scheduled game. Numerous online ticketing agencies also sell tickets. Otherwise, you'll need to take a risk with scalpers.

The football season runs from September (or the last weekend in August) until May, with a two-week break just before Christmas until early in the New Year.

**Fun House** LIVE MUSIC
(Map p106; ☎638 057601, 91 017 66 19; www.funhousemusicbar.com; Calle de Palafox 8; from €4; ⏰10pm-5am Tue-Thu, to 5.30pm Fri & Sat; Ⓜ Bilbao) This tiny, intimate venue is quite the surprise – this is where a consistent programme of well-known, middle-tier groups and musicians come to play at the end of their European tours, having earlier passed through Madrid and played at a larger venue. You never quite know who might turn up here, and performers love it as much as their fans.

**Sala Clamores** LIVE MUSIC
(Map p106; ☎91 445 79 38; www.clamores.es; Calle de Alburquerque 14; €6-20; ⏰6.30pm-2am Sun-Thu, to 5.30am Fri & Sat; Ⓜ Bilbao) Clamores is a one-time classic jazz cafe that has morphed into one of the most diverse live-music stages in Madrid. Jazz is still a staple, but flamenco, blues, world music, singer-songwriters, pop and rock all make regular appearances. Live shows can begin as early as 7pm on weekends but sometimes really only get going after 1am.

# Shopping

Madrid is a fantastic place to shop. Often run by the same families for generations, the city's small boutiques and quirky shops counter the commercialisation of mass-produced Spanish culture with everything from fashions to old-style ceramics, rope-soled espadrilles or gourmet Spanish food and wine.

## Plaza Mayor & Royal Madrid

**★ Antigua Casa Talavera** CERAMICS
(Map p76; ☎91 547 34 17; www.antiguacasatalavera.com; Calle de Isabel la Católica 2; ⏰10am-1.30pm & 5-8pm Mon-Fri; Ⓜ Santo Domingo) The extraordinary tiled facade of this wonderful old shop conceals an Aladdin's cave of ceramics from all over Spain. This is not the mass-produced stuff aimed at a tourist market, but instead comes from the small family potters of Andalucía and Toledo, ranging from the decorative (tiles) to the useful (plates, jugs and other kitchen items).

**★ El Arco Artesanía** ARTS & CRAFTS
(Map p76; ☎91 365 26 80; www.artesaniaelarco.com; Plaza Mayor 9; ⏰11am-9pm Mon-Sat, noon-8pm Sun; Ⓜ Sol, La Latina) This original shop in the southwestern corner of Plaza Mayor sells an outstanding array of homemade designer souvenirs, from stone, ceramic and glass work to jewellery and home fittings. The papier-mâché figures are gorgeous, but there's so much else here to turn your head. It sometimes closes earlier in the depths of winter.

**Maty** FLAMENCO
(Map p76; ☎91 531 32 91; www.maty.es; Calle del Maestro Victoria 2; ⏰10am-1.45pm & 4.30-8pm Mon-Fri, 10am-2pm & 4.30-8pm Sat, 11am-2.30pm

## SHOPS OF OLD MADRID

It's increasingly true of modern travel that the kinds of shops you find in one city are often not that different from those in any other city, even on the other side of the world. Thankfully, downtown Madrid has numerous bastions against the sameness of globalisation, and each offers an opportunity to take home an authentic piece that you could only buy in Madrid. And it's just as much about the atmosphere – of old-style civility and service, of decor untouched by the passing of time – as it is about what's for sale.

For a start, there's Casa de Diego (p136), purveyor of genuine *abanícos* (Spanish fans) and *paraguas* (umbrellas). When it comes to artisan accessories, there are the gloves of **Guantes Luque** (Map p84; Calle de Espoz y Mina 3; ⊙10am-1.30pm & 5-8pm Mon-Fri; MSevilla, Sol), the hats of **Sombrerería Medrano** (Map p76; ☎91 366 42 34; www.sombrereriamedrano.com; Calle Imperial 12; ⊙10am-2.30pm & 4.30-8pm Mon-Fri, 10am-2pm Sat; MSol), and the DIY Aladdin's cave for those who love to sew and knit at **Almacén de Pontejos** (Map p84; ☎91 521 55 94; www.almacendepontejos.com; Plaza de Pontejos 2; ⊙9.30am-2pm & 4.30-8.15pm Mon-Fri, 9.30am-2pm Sat; MSol). If religious iconography is your thing, **Santarrufina** (Map p84; ☎91 522 23 83; www.santarrufina.com; Calle de la Paz 4; ⊙10am-2pm & 4.30-8pm Mon-Fri, 10am-2pm Sat; MSol) turns its attention to Spain's devout Catholic past on bended knee, while just across the road, **Justo Algaba** (Map p84; ☎91 523 37 17; www.justoalgaba.com; Calle de la Paz 4; ⊙10am-2pm & 5-8pm Mon-Fri, 10am-2pm Sat; MSol) is where the bullfighters go for their *traje de luces* (suit of lights). And sometimes it's all about a workshop unchanged by the passing of time, just like the guitar-makers of **José Ramírez** (Map p84; ☎91 531 42 29; www.guitarrasramirez.com; Calle de la Paz 8; ⊙10am-2pm & 4.30-8pm Mon-Fri, 10am-2pm Sat; MSol) and **Juan Alvarez** (Map p88; ☎91 429 20 33; www.guitarrasjuanalvarez.com; Calle de San Pedro 7; ⊙5-8pm Mon, 10am-1.30pm & 5-8pm Tue-Fri, 10am-1.30pm Sat; MAntón Martín).

& 4.30-8pm 1st Sun of month; MSol) Wandering around central Madrid, it's easy to imagine that flamenco outfits have been reduced to imitation dresses sold as souvenirs to tourists. That's why places like Maty matter. Here you'll find dresses, shoes and all the accessories that go with the genre, with sizes for children and adults. These are the real deal, with prices to match, but they make brilliant gifts.

**Casa Hernanz** SHOES

(Map p76; ☎91 366 54 50; Calle de Toledo 18; ⊙9am-1.30pm & 4.30-8pm Mon-Fri, 10am-2pm Sat; MLa Latina, Sol) Comfy, rope-soled *alpargatas* (espadrilles), Spain's traditional summer footwear, are worn by everyone from the king of Spain down. You can buy your own pair at this humble workshop, which has been hand-making the shoes for five generations; you can even get them made to order. Prices range from €6 to €40 and queues form whenever the weather starts to warm up.

**Atlético de Madrid Store** SPORTS & OUTDOORS

(Map p76; ☎902 260403; Gran Vía 47; ⊙10am-9.30pm Mon-Thu, to 10pm Fri & Sat, 11am-8pm Sun; MSanto Domingo) Atlético de Madrid has something of a cult following in the city and has enjoyed considerable footballing success in recent years. Its downtown store has all the club's merchandise. In theory you can also buy tickets to games here, but most matches are sold out before you'll get a chance.

**Así** TOYS

(Map p76; ☎91 521 97 55; www.tiendas-asi.com; Calle del Arenal 20; ⊙10am-8.30pm Mon-Sat, noon-3.30pm & 4.30-8pm Sun; MÓpera) Beautifully crafted baby dolls make a lovely gift or souvenir of your little one's visit to the city. These are the real deal, not mass-produced, and there are some fine baby's outfits to go with them.

**Torrons Vicens** FOOD

(Map p76; ☎91 548 94 02; www.vicens.com; Calle del Arenal 21; ⊙10am-10pm; MÓpera, Sol) One of Spain's finest purveyors of *turrón* (nougat) has finally set up shop in Madrid. One of a number of outlets across town, this central option overflows with countless varieties of a sweet that's especially popular at Christmas.

**El Jardín del Convento** FOOD

(Map p76; ☎91 541 22 99; www.eljardindelconvento.net; Calle del Cordón 1; ⊙11am-2.30pm & 5.30-8.30pm Tue-Sun; MÓpera) In a quiet lane just south of Plaza de la Villa, this appealing little shop sells homemade sweets baked by nuns in abbeys, convents and monasteries all across Spain.

## La Latina & Lavapiés

★**Helena Rohner** JEWELLERY
(Map p82; ☎91 365 79 06; www.helenarohner.com; Calle del Almendro 4; ⏲9am-8.30pm Mon-Fri, noon-2.30pm & 3.30-8pm Sat, noon-3pm Sun; Ⓜ La Latina, Tirso de Molina) One of Europe's most creative jewellery designers, Helena Rohner has a spacious boutique in La Latina. Working with silver, stone, porcelain, wood and Murano glass, she makes inventive pieces that are a regular feature at Paris fashion shows. In her own words, she seeks to recreate 'the magic of Florence, the vitality of London and the luminosity of Madrid'.

**El Rastro** MARKET
(Map p82; Calle de la Ribera de los Curtidores; ⏲8am-3pm Sun; Ⓜ La Latina, Puerta de Toledo, Tirso de Molina) Welcome to what is claimed to be Europe's largest flea market (p82). Antiques are also a major drawcard with a concentration of stores at Nuevas Galerías and Galerías Piquer; unlike the flea market's stalls, most shops in the area open 10am to 2pm and 5pm to 8pm Monday to Saturday and not all open during the Sunday flea market.

**Eturel** HOMEWARES
(Map p82; ☎91 240 49 12; www.eturel.com; Calle de Ruda 8; ⏲10.30am-2pm & 5-8.30pm Mon-Fri, 10.30am-2.30pm Sat & Sun; Ⓜ La Latina) Fabrics, patterns and designs from rural Castilla-La Mancha, updated with the merest style twists, lie behind this lovely store that sells cushions, throws and all manner of wantables for your home. Faithful to old patterns and never flashy, Eturel is the perfect case of a rural aesthetic brought to the city and looking immediately as if it's right at home.

## Sol, Santa Ana & Huertas

**Casa de Diego** FASHION & ACCESSORIES
(Map p84; ☎91 522 66 43; www.casadediego.com; Plaza de la Puerta del Sol 12; ⏲9.30am-8pm Mon-Sat; Ⓜ Sol) This classic shop has been around since 1858, making, selling and repairing Spanish fans, shawls, umbrellas and canes. Service is old-style and occasionally grumpy, but the fans are works of antique art. There's another **branch** (Map p84; ☎91 531 02 23; Calle de los Mesoneros Romanos 4; ⏲9.30am-1.30pm & 4.45-8pm Mon-Sat; Ⓜ Callao, Sol) nearby.

**Licores Cabello** WINE
(Map p84; ☎91 429 60 88; www.facebook.com/licorescabello; Calle de Echegaray 19; ⏲9am-3pm & 5.30-10pm Mon-Sat; Ⓜ Sevilla, Antón Martín) All wine shops should be like this. This family-run corner shop really knows its wines and the interior has scarcely changed since 1913, with wooden shelves and even a faded ceiling fresco. There are fine wines in abundance (mostly Spanish, and a few foreign bottles), with some 500 labels on show or tucked away out the back.

**The Corner Shop** CLOTHING
(Map p84; ☎91 737 58 02; https://thecornershop.es; Calle de las Huertas 17; ⏲10.30am-9.30pm Mon-Sat, from noon Sun; Ⓜ Antón Martín) This fine Huertas shop does a carefully curated collection of men's and women's fashions, with brand names like Scotch Soda, Blue Hole, Andy and Lucy and many others. Regardless of brands, it's always worth stopping by to check its casual streetwear with a touch of style and a hint of the offbeat.

**Tienda Real Madrid** SPORTS & OUTDOORS
(Map p84; ☎91 755 45 38; www.realmadrid.com; Gran Vía 31; ⏲10am-9pm Mon-Sat, from 11am Sun; Ⓜ Gran Vía, Callao) The Real Madrid club shop sells replica shirts, posters, caps and just about everything else under the sun to which it could attach a club logo. In the centre of town there's a smaller **branch** (Map p84; ☎91 521 79 50; Calle del Carmen 3; ⏲10am-9pm Mon-Sat, 11am-8pm Sun; Ⓜ Sol) and, in the city's north, the **stadium branch** (☎91 458 72 59; Avenida de Concha Espina 1, Estadio Santiago Bernabéu, Gate 55; ⏲10am-9pm Mon-Sat, 11am-7.30pm Sun; Ⓜ Santiago Bernabéu).

## El Retiro & the Art Museums

**Cuesta de Claudio Moyano Bookstalls** BOOKS
(Map p88; Cuesta de Claudio Moyano; ⏲hours vary; Ⓜ Atocha) Madrid's answer to the booksellers that line the Seine in Paris, these secondhand bookstalls are an enduring city landmark. Most titles are in Spanish, but there's a handful of offerings in other

languages. Opening hours vary from stall to stall, and some of the stalls close at lunchtime.

## Salamanca

**★Agatha Ruiz de la Prada** FASHION & ACCESSORIES
(Map p98; ☎91 319 05 01; www.agatharuizdelaprada.com; Calle de Serrano 27; ⏲10am-8.30pm Mon-Sat; Ⓜ Serrano) This boutique has to be seen to be believed, with pinks, yellows and oranges everywhere you turn. It's fun and exuberant, but not just for kids. It also has serious and highly original fashion. Agatha Ruiz de la Prada is one of the enduring icons of *la movida madrileña*, Madrid's 1980s outpouring of creativity.

**Bombonerías Santa** FOOD & DRINKS
(Map p98; ☎91 576 76 25; www.bomboneriassanta.com; Calle de Serrano 56; ⏲10am-2pm & 5-8.30pm Mon-Fri, 10.30am-2pm & 5-8pm Sat; Ⓜ Serrano) If your style is as refined as your palate, the exquisite chocolates in this tiny shop will satisfy. The packaging is every bit as pretty as the *bombones* (chocolates) within, but they're not cheap – count on paying around €60 per kilo of chocolate.

**Oriol Balaguer** CHOCOLATE
(Map p98; ☎91 401 64 63; www.oriolbalaguer.com; Calle de José Ortega y Gasset 44; ⏲9am-8.30pm Mon-Fri, from 8.30pm Sat, 10am-2.30pm Sun, closed Aug; Ⓜ Núñez de Balboa) Catalan pastry chef Oriol Balaguer has a formidable CV – he's worked in the kitchens of Ferran Adrià in Catalonia, won the prize for the World's Best Dessert (the 'Seven Textures of Chocolate') and his croissants once won the title of Spain's best. His chocolate boutique is presented like a small art gallery dedicated to exquisite chocolate collections and cakes.

**Mantequería Bravo** FOOD & DRINKS
(Map p98; ☎91 575 80 72; www.bravo1931.com; Calle de Ayala 24; ⏲10am-2.30pm & 5.30-8.30pm Mon-Fri, 10am-2.30pm Sat; Ⓜ Serrano) Behind the attractive old facade lies a connoisseur's paradise, filled with local cheeses, sausages, wines and coffees. The products here are great for a gift, but everything is so good that you won't want to share. Not that long ago, Mantequería Bravo won the prize for Madrid's best gourmet food shop or delicatessen.

**Manolo Blahnik** SHOES
(Map p98; ☎91 575 96 48; www.manoloblahnik.com; Calle de Serrano 58; ⏲10am-2pm & 4-8pm Mon-Sat; Ⓜ Serrano) Nothing to wear to the Oscars? Do what many Hollywood celebrities do and head for Manolo Blahnik. The showroom is exclusive and each shoe is displayed like a work of art.

**Ekseption** FASHION & ACCESSORIES
(Map p98; ☎91 577 43 53; www.ekseption.es; Calle de Velázquez 28; ⏲10.30am-8.30pm Mon-Sat; Ⓜ Velázquez) This elegant showroom store consistently leads the way with the latest trends, spanning catwalk designs alongside a look that is more informal, though always sophisticated. The unifying theme is urban chic and its list of designer brands includes Balenciaga, Givenchy, Gucci and Dries van Noten.

Victoria Beckham was a regular customer here in her Madrid days; make of that what you will.

**Camper** SHOES
(Map p98; ☎91 578 25 60; www.camper.com; Calle de Serrano 24; ⏲10am-9pm Mon-Sat, noon-8pm Sun; Ⓜ Serrano) Spanish fashion is not all haute couture, and this world-famous cool and quirky shoe brand from Mallorca offers bowling-shoe chic with colourful, fun designs that are all about quality coupled with comfort. There are other outlets throughout the city, including a **Malasaña shop** (Map p102; ☎91 531 23 47; Calle de Fuencarral 42; ⏲10am-8pm Mon-Sat; Ⓜ Gran Vía, Tribunal); check the website for locations.

## Malasaña & Chueca

**★El Moderno** CONCEPT STORE
(Map p102; ☎91 348 39 94; https://elmoderno.es; Calle de la Corredera Baja de San Pablo 19; ⏲11am-9pm Sun-Thu, to 9.30pm Fri & Sat; Ⓜ Callao, Gran Vía) This concept store down the Gran Vía end of Malasaña is the epitome of style, although it's less Malasaña retro than a slick new-Madrid look. Designer homewares, jewellery, stationery, quirky gifts and shapely furnishings, all laid out in an open gallery space, allow you to indulge your inner interior designer.

**Loewe** FASHION & ACCESSORIES
(Map p102; ☎91 522 68 15; www.loewe.com; Gran Vía 8; ⏲10am-8.30pm Mon-Sat, 11am-8pm Sun; Ⓜ Gran Vía) Born in 1846 in Madrid, Loewe is arguably Spain's signature line in

## VINTAGE MALASAÑA

Malasaña is the perfect home for Madrid's love affair with all things vintage. As befits Malasaña's edgy attitude, styles range from inoffensive retro to downright in-your-face – down through the years, we've seen everything from a mocked-up cover of 'National Pornographic' to Pope John Paul II with fist raised and 'Vatican 666' emblazoned across the front.

Up near the Plaza de San Ildefonso, the southern end of Calle de la Corredera Alta de San Pablo is rich in vintage shops – Retro City (p139) has long been a *barrio* icon, but there are plenty of other shops nearby. Just around the corner in Calle del Espíritu Santo, Flamingos Vintage Kilo (p139) and **El Templo de Susu** (Map p102; 91 523 31 22; Calle del Espíritu Santo 1; 10am-2.30pm & 5.30-9pm Mon-Sat; M Tribunal) lead the way, but the whole street has numerous options; Lolina Vintage Café (p131) is the perfect place for a pitstop. A block to the north, the eastern end of Calle de Velarde has become a real hub for vintage clothing, with nearly a dozen stores.

high-end fashion and its landmark store on Gran Vía is one of the most famous and elegant stores in the capital. Classy handbags and accessories are the mainstays. Prices can be jaw-droppingly high, but it's worth stopping by, even if you don't plan to buy. There's another branch in **Salamanca** (Map p98; 91 426 35 88; Calle de Serrano 26 & 34; 10am-8.30pm Mon-Sat; M Serrano).

**Patrimonio Comunal Olivarero** FOOD
(Map p102; 91 308 05 05; Calle de Mejía Lequerica 1; 10am-2pm & 5-8pm Mon-Fri, 10am-2pm Sat Sep-Jun, 9am-3pm Mon-Sat Jul; M Alonso Martínez) For picking up some of the country's olive-oil varieties (Spain is the world's largest producer), this place is perfect. With examples of the extra-virgin variety (and nothing else) from all over Spain, you could spend ages agonising over the choices. Staff know their oil and are happy to help out if you speak a little Spanish.

**Malababa** FASHION & ACCESSORIES
(Map p102; 91 203 59 51; www.malababa.com/es; Calle de Santa Teresa 5; 10.30am-8.30pm Mon-Thu, to 9pm Fri & Sat; M Alonso Martínez) This corner of Chueca is one of Madrid's happiest hunting grounds for the style-conscious shopper who favours individual boutiques with personality above larger stores. One such place, light-filled Malababa features classy Spanish-made accessories, including jewellery, handbags, shoes, purses and belts, all beautifully displayed.

**Xoan Viqueira** FASHION & ACCESSORIES
(Map p102; 91 173 70 29; www.xoanviqueira.com; Calle de Gravina 22; 11am-2pm & 5-8.30pm Mon-Fri, 11am-2pm Sat; M Chueca) We love the playfulness of this designer Chueca store where screen-printing artist Xoan Viqueira throws his creativity at everything from *alpargatas* o clothing and homewares. Bearded gay men are recurring motifs, but it's fun and mischievous rather than in-your-face.

**Sportivo** CLOTHING
(Map p102; 91 542 56 61; www.sportivostore.com; Calle del Conde Duque 20; 10am-9pm Mon-Sat, noon-8pm Sun; M Plaza de España) It's rare to find a Madrid store that focuses solely on men's fashions, but this place bucks the trend. Brands like Carven, YMC and Commune of Paris draw an appreciative crowd of metrosexuals, lumbersexuals and any fellow who appreciates style.

**Cacao Sampaka** CHOCOLATE
(Map p102; 91 319 58 40; www.cacaosampaka.com; Calle de Orellana 4; 10.15am-8.30pm Mon-Sat; M Alonso Martínez) If you thought chocolate was about fruit 'n' nut, think again. This gourmet chocolate shop is a chocoholic's dream, with more combinations to go with humble cocoa than you ever imagined possible. The emphasis is on dark chocolate, with surprising mixes, including balsamic vinegar or chilli.

**Poncelet** FOOD
(Map p102; 91 308 02 21; https://poncelet.es; Calle de Argensola 27; 10.30am-9pm Mon-Sat; M Alonso Martínez) With 80 Spanish and 240 European cheese varieties, this fine cheese shop is the best of its kind in Madrid. The range is outstanding and the staff really know their cheese.

**Reserva y Cata** WINE
(Map p102; 91 319 04 01; www.reservaycata.com; Calle del Conde de Xiquena 13; 11am-2pm & 5.30-8.30pm Mon-Fri, 11am-2pm Sat; M Colón, Chueca) This old-style shop stocks an excel-

lent range of local wines, and the knowledgeable staff can help you pick out a great one for your next dinner party or a gift for a friend back home. It specialises in quality Spanish wines that you just don't find in El Corte Inglés department store. There's often a bottle open so you can try before you buy.

**Flamingos Vintage Kilo** VINTAGE
(Map p102; ☎91 504 83 13; www.vintagekilo.com; Calle del Espíritu Santo 1; ⊙11am-9pm Mon-Sat; M Tribunal) Flamingos sells vintage clothing for men and women, including a selection of old denim, cowboy boots, leather jackets, Hawaiian shirts and more. Some articles have a set price, while others are sold by the kilo. It's a great place to browse for the cool and unexpected from the '70s, '80s and '90s.

**Retro City** CLOTHING
(Map p102; Calle de Corredera Alta de San Pablo 4; ⊙noon-2.30pm & 5.30-9pm Mon-Sat; M Tribunal) Malasaña down to its Dr Martens, Retro City lives for the colourful '70s and '80s and proclaims its philosophy to be all about 'vintage for the masses'. Whereas other such stores in the *barrio* have gone for an angry, thumb-your-nose-at-society aesthetic, Retro City just looks back with nostalgia.

## Chamberí & Northern Madrid

★ **Papelería Salazar** STATIONERY
(Map p102; ☎91 446 18 48; www.papeleriasalazar.es; Calle de Luchana 7-9; ⊙9.30am-1.30pm & 4.30-8pm Mon-Fri, 10am-1.30pm Sat; M Bilbao) Opened in 1905, Papelería Salazar is a priceless relic, Madrid's oldest stationery store and is now run by the fourth generation of the Salazar family. It's a treasure trove that defies description and combines items of interest only to locals (old-style Spanish bookplates, First Communion invitations) with useful items like Faber-Castell pens and pencils, maps, notebooks and drawing supplies.

**Bazar Matey** GIFTS & SOUVENIRS
(Map p106; ☎91 446 93 11; www.matey.com; Calle de la Santísima Trinidad 1; ⊙9.30am-1.30pm & 4.30-8pm Mon-Sat, closed Sat afternoon Jul & Aug; M Iglesia, Quevedo) Bazar Matey is a wonderful store catering to collectors of model trains, aeroplanes and cars, and all sorts of accessories. The items here are the real deal, with near-perfect models of everything from old Renfe trains to obscure international airlines. Prices can be sky-high, but that doesn't deter the legions of collectors who stream in from all over Madrid on Saturday.

**Relojería Santolaya** ANTIQUES
(Map p106; ☎91 447 25 64; www.relojeriasantolaya.com; Calle Murillo 8; ⊙10am-1pm & 5-8pm Mon-Fri; M Quevedo, Iglesia, Bilbao) Founded in 1867, this timeless old-clock repairer just off Plaza de Olavide is the official watch repairer to Spain's royalty and heritage properties. There's not much for sale here, but stop by the tiny shopfront and workshop to admire the dying art of timepiece repairs, with not a digital watch in sight.

**Calzados Cantero** SHOES
(Map p106; ☎91 447 07 35; Plaza de Olavide 12; ⊙9.45am-2pm & 4.45-8.30pm Mon-Fri, 9.45am-2pm Sat; M Iglesia) A charming old-time shoe store, Calzados Cantero sells a range of shoes at rock-bottom prices. It's most famous for its rope-soled *alpargatas* which start from €8. This is a *barrio* classic, the sort of place where parents bring their children as their own parents did a generation before.

**Pasajes Librería Internacional** BOOKS
(Map p102; ☎91 310 12 45; www.pasajeslibros.com; Calle de Génova 3; ⊙10am-9.30pm Mon-Fri, to 8.30pm Sat; M Alonso Martínez) One of the best bookshops in Madrid, Pasajes has an extensive English section (downstairs at the back), which includes high-quality fiction (if it's a new release, it'll be the first bookshop in town to have it), as well as history, Spanish subject matter and travel, and a few literary magazines. There are also French, German, Italian and Portuguese books, children's books and DVDs, and a useful noticeboard.

## ℹ Information

### DANGERS & ANNOYANCES

Madrid is generally safe, but as in any large European city, keep an eye on your belongings and exercise common sense.

➡ El Rastro, around the Museo del Prado and the metro are favourite pickpocketing haunts, as are any areas where tourists congregate in large numbers.

➡ Avoid park areas (such as the Parque del Buen Retiro) after dark.

➡ Keep a close eye on your taxi's meter and try to keep track of the route to make sure you're not being taken for a ride.

### EMERGENCY

To report thefts or other crime-related matters, your best bet is the **Servicio de Atención al**

**Turista Extranjero** (Foreign Tourist Assistance Service; 91 548 80 08, 902 102112; www.esmadrid.com/informacion-turistica/sate; Calle de Leganitos 19; 9am-midnight; Plaza de España, Santo Domingo), which is housed in the central *comisaría* (police station) of the National Police. Here you'll find specially trained officers working alongside representatives from the Tourism Ministry. They can also assist in cancelling credit cards, as well as contacting your embassy or your family.

There's also a general number (902 102112; 24-hour English and Spanish, 8am to midnight other languages) for reporting crimes.

There's a **comisaría** (91 322 10 21; Calle de las Huertas 76; Antón Martín) down the bottom end of Huertas, near the Paseo del Prado.

| | |
|---|---|
| **Country code** | 34 |
| **International access code** | 00 |
| **EU standard emergency number** | 112 |
| **Ambulance** | 061 |
| **Fire Brigade (Bomberos)** | 080 |
| **Local Police (Policía Municipal)** | 092 |
| **Military Police (Guardia Civil)** For traffic accidents. | 062 |
| **National Police (Policía Nacional)** | 091 |
| **Teléfono de la Víctima** Hotline for victims of racial or sexual violence. | 902 180995 |

### INTERNET ACCESS

Most *hostales*, hostels and hotels, as well as many cafes and restaurants, have wi-fi.

Most of Madrid's internet cafes have fallen by the wayside. You'll still find some small *locutorios* (small shops selling phonecards and cheap phone calls) all over the city, and many have a few computers out the back.

### MEDICAL SERVICES

All foreigners have the same right as Spaniards to emergency medical treatment in a public hospital. EU citizens are entitled to the full range of health-care services in public hospitals free of charge, but you'll need to present your European Health Insurance Card (EHIC); enquire at your national health service before leaving home. Even if you have no insurance, you'll be treated in an emergency, with costs in the public system ranging from free to €150 for a basic consultation. Non-EU citizens have to pay for anything other than emergency treatment – one good reason among many to have a travel-insurance policy. If you have a specific health complaint, obtain the necessary information and referrals for treatment before leaving home.

**Hospital General Gregorio Marañón** (91 586 80 00; Calle del Doctor Esquerdo 46; Sáinz de Baranda, O'Donnell, Ibiza) One of the city's main (and more central) hospitals.

**Unidad Médica** (Anglo American; 91 435 18 23, 24hr 649 870068; www.unidadmedica.com; Calle del Conde de Aranda 1; 9am-8pm Mon-Fri, 10am-1pm Sat Sep-Jul, 10am-5pm Mon-Fri, to 1pm Sat Aug; Retiro) A private clinic with a wide range of specialisations and where all doctors speak Spanish and English, with some also speaking French and German. Each consultation costs around €125.

### TOURIST INFORMATION

**Centro de Turismo de Madrid** (Map p76; 91 578 78 10; www.esmadrid.com; Plaza Mayor 27; 9.30am-9.30pm; Sol) The Madrid government's Centro de Turismo is terrific. Housed in the Real Casa de la Panadería on the north side of the Plaza Mayor, it offers free downloads of the metro map to your mobile; staff are helpful.

**Punto de Información Turística Adolfo Suárez Madrid-Barajas T2** (www.esmadrid.com; between Salas 5 & 6; 9am-8pm; Aeropuerto T1, T2 & T3)

**Punto de Información Turística Adolfo Suárez Madrid-Barajas T4** (www.esmadrid.com; Salas 10 & 11; 9am-8pm; Aeropuerto T4)

**Punto de Información Turística Centro-Centro** (Map p88; 91 454 44 10; www.esmadrid.com; Plaza de la Cibeles 1; 10am-8pm Tue-Sun; Banco de España)

**Punto de Información Turística Estadio Santiago Bernabéu** (www.esmadrid.com; Paseo de la Castellana 138; 9.30am-8.30pm; Santiago Bernabéu)

**Punto de Información Turística Palacio Real** (Map p76; www.esmadrid.com; Calle de Bailén; 9.30am-8.30pm; Ópera, Plaza de España)

**Punto de Información Turística Plaza del Callao** (Map p76; www.esmadrid.com; Plaza del Callao; 9.30am-8.30pm; Callao)

**Punto de Información Turística Paseo del Prado** (Map p88; 91 578 78 10; www.esmadrid.com; Plaza de Neptuno; 9.30am-9.30pm; Atocha)

**Punto de Información Turística Reina Sofía** (Map p88; www.esmadrid.com; Calle de Santa Isabel 52; 9.30am-8.30pm; Estación del Arte)

## Getting There & Away

### AIR

Madrid's **Aeropuerto Adolfo Suárez Madrid-Barajas** (902 404704; www.aena.es; Aeropuerto T1, T2 & T3, Aeropuerto T4) is 15km northeast of the city. It's Europe's sixth-busiest hub, with more than 53 million passengers passing through here every year.

Barajas has four terminals. Terminal 4 (T4) deals mainly with flights of Iberia and its partners, while the remainder leave from the conjoined T1, T2 and (rarely) T3. To match your airline with a terminal, visit the Adolfo Suárez Madrid-Barajas section of www.aena.es and click on 'Airlines'.

Although all airlines conduct check-in *(facturación)* at the airport's departure areas, some also allow check-in at the Nuevos Ministerios metro stop and transport interchange in Madrid itself – ask your airline.

There are car-rental services, ATMs, money-exchange bureaux, pharmacies, tourist offices, left-luggage offices and parking services at T1, T2 and T4.

### BUS

**Estación Sur de Autobuses** (91 468 42 00; Calle de Méndez Álvaro 83; Méndez Álvaro), just south of the M30 ring road, is the city's principal bus station. It serves most destinations to the south and many in other parts of the country. Most bus companies have a ticket office here, even if their buses depart from elsewhere.

**Intercambiador de Avenida de América** (Map p98; Avenida de América; Av de América) has bus departures within Madrid but also to some towns in Spain's north.

Northwest of the centre and connected to lines 1 and 3 of the metro, the subterranean **Intercambiador de Autobuses de Moncloa** (Plaza de la Moncloa; Moncloa) sends buses out to the surrounding villages and satellite suburbs that lie north and west of the city. Major bus companies include:

**ALSA** (902 422242; www.alsa.es) One of the largest Spanish companies with many services throughout Spain. Most depart from Estación Sur with occasional services from T4 of Madrid's airport and other stations around town.

**Avanzabus** (902 020052; www.avanzabus.com; Calle de Méndez Álvaro 83, Estación Sur de Autobuses) Services to Extremadura (eg Cáceres), Castilla y León (eg Salamanca and Zamora) and Valencia via Cuenca, as well as Lisbon, Portugal. All leave from the Estación Sur.

### CAR & MOTORCYCLE

Madrid is surrounded by two main ring roads, the outermost M40 and the inner M30; there are also two partial ring roads, the M45 and the more distant M50. The R5 and R3 are part of a series of toll roads built to ease traffic jams.

The big-name car-rental agencies have offices all over Madrid and at the airport, and some have branches at Atocha and Chamartín train stations.

### TRAIN

Madrid is served by two main train stations. The bigger of the two is **Estación Puerta de Atocha** (www.renfe.es; Avenida de la Ciudad de Barcelona; Atocha Renfe), at the southern end of the city centre, while **Chamartín** (91 243 23 43; www.renfe.es; Paseo de la Castellana; Chamartín) lies in the north of the city. The bulk of trains for Spanish destinations depart from Atocha, especially those going south. International services arrive at and leave from Chamartín. For bookings, contact **Renfe** (91 232 03 20; www.renfe.com).

High-speed Tren de Alta Velocidad Española (AVE) services connect Madrid with Albacete, Barcelona, Burgos, Cádiz, Córdoba, Cuenca, Huesca, León, Lerida, Málaga, Palencia, Salamanca, Santiago de Compostela, Seville, Valencia, Valladolid, Zamora and Zaragoza. In coming years, more destinations should come on line.

## Getting Around

Madrid has an excellent public transport network. The most convenient way of getting around is via the metro, whose 11 lines crisscross the city, with a couple more serving satellite towns; no matter where you find yourself, you're never far from a metro station. The bus network is equally extensive and operates under the same ticketing system, although the sheer number of routes (around 200) makes it more difficult for first-time visitors to master. Taxis in Madrid are plentiful and relatively cheap by European standards.

### TO/FROM THE AIRPORT

#### Bus

The **Exprés Aeropuerto** (Airport Express; www.emtmadrid.es; per person €5; 24hr; ) runs between Atocha train station and the airport. From 11.30pm until 6am, departures are from the Plaza de la Cibeles, not the train station. Departures take place every 15 to 20 minutes from the station or at night-time every 35 minutes from Plaza de la Cibeles.

A free bus service connects all four airport terminals.

#### Metro

One of the easiest ways into town from the airport is line 8 of the metro to the Nuevos Ministerios transport interchange, which connects with lines 10 and 6 and the local overground *cercanías*

### METRO & BUS TICKETS

**Tarjeta Multi**

Visitors travelling on the city's public transport system require a Tarjeta Multi, a rechargeable card that can be purchased for a one-off €2.50 at machines in all metro stations, *estancos* (tobacconists) and other authorised sales points. As with London's Oyster Card, you top up your account at machines in all metro stations and *estancos*, and touch-on and touch-off every time you travel. Options include 10 rides (bus and metro) for €12.20 or a single-journey ticket for €1.50.

**Tarjeta Turística**

The handy Tarjeta Turística (Tourist Pass) allows for unlimited travel on public transport across the Comunidad de Madrid (Community of Madrid) for tourists. You'll need to present your passport or national identity card and tickets can be purchased at all metro stations. Passes are available for one/two/three/five/seven days for €8.40/14.20/18.40/26.80/35.40.

(local trains serving suburbs and nearby towns). It operates from 6.05am to 1.30am. A single ticket costs €4.50 including the €3 airport supplement. If you're charging your public transport card with a 10-ride Metrobús ticket (€12.20), you'll need to top it up with the €3 supplement if you're travelling to/from the airport. The journey to Nuevos Ministerios takes around 15 minutes, around 25 minutes from T4.

**Taxi**

A taxi to the centre (around 30 minutes, depending on traffic; 35 to 40 minutes from T4) costs a fixed €30 for anywhere inside the M30 motorway (which includes all of downtown Madrid). There's a minimum €20, even if you're only going to an airport hotel.

### BICYCLE

Bike lanes are increasingly a part of the inner city's thoroughfares. Be aware, however, that the latter are relatively new and few drivers are accustomed to keeping an eye out for cyclists.

You can transport your bicycle on the metro all day on Saturday and Sunday, and at any time from Monday to Friday except 7.30am to 9.30am, 2pm to 4pm and 6pm to 8pm. You can also take your bike aboard *cercanías* at any time.

### BUS

Buses operated by **Empresa Municipal de Transportes de Madrid** (EMT; ☎902 507850; www.emtmadrid.es) travel along most city routes regularly between about 6.30am and 11.30pm. Twenty-six night-bus *búhos* (owls) routes operate from 11.45pm to 5.30am, with all routes originating in the Plaza de la Cibeles.

### METRO

Madrid's modern metro (www.metromadrid.es), Europe's second largest, is a fast, efficient and safe way to navigate the city, and generally easier than getting to grips with bus routes. There are 11 colour-coded lines in central Madrid, in addition to the modern southern suburban MetroSur system, as well as lines heading east to the population centres of Pozuelo and Boadilla del Monte. Colour maps showing the metro system are available from any metro station or online. The metro operates from 6.05am to 1.30am.

### TAXI

Daytime flagfall is, for example, €2.40 in Madrid, and up to €2.90 between 9pm and 7am, and on weekends and holidays. You then pay €1.05 to €1.20 per kilometre depending on the time of day. Several supplementary charges, usually posted inside the taxi, apply. These include: €5.50 to/from the airport (if you're not paying the fixed rate); €3 from taxi ranks at train and bus stations; €3 to/from the Parque Ferial Juan Carlos I; and €6.70 on New Year's Eve and Christmas Eve from 10pm to 6am. There's no charge for luggage.

Among the 24-hour taxi services is **Tele-Taxi** (☎91 371 2131; www.tele-taxi.es; ⏲24hr).

A green light on the roof means the taxi is *libre* (available). Usually a sign to this effect is also placed in the lower passenger side of the windscreen. Tipping taxi drivers is not common practice, though rounding fares up to the nearest euro or two doesn't hurt.

# AROUND MADRID

It may be one of Spain's smallest *comunidades* by area, but there's still plenty to see in Madrid's hinterland. Both San Lorenzo de El Escorial and Aranjuez combine royal grandeur with great food, while Alcalá de Henares is a surprise packet with stirring monuments, a real sense of history and night-time buzz. Chinchón also has one of Spain's loveliest *plazas mayores*.

# San Lorenzo de El Escorial

POP 18,088

In the otherwise quiet town of El Escorial in the foothills of the Sierra de Guadarrama northwest of Madrid, the palace-monastery of San Lorenzo de El Escorial is one of the grandest monuments anywhere in the Spanish interior. It makes for a memorable day trip from the capital.

## History

After Felipe II's decisive victory in the Battle of St Quentin against the French on St Lawrence's Day, 10 August 1557, he ordered the construction of the complex in the saint's name above the hamlet of El Escorial. Several villages were razed to make way for the huge monastery, royal palace and mausoleum for Felipe's parents, Carlos I and Isabel. It all flourished under the watchful eye of the architect Juan de Herrera, a towering figure of the Spanish Renaissance.

The palace-monastery became an important intellectual centre, with a burgeoning library and art collection, and even a laboratory where scientists could dabble in alchemy. Felipe II died here on 13 September 1598.

In 1854 the monks belonging to the Hieronymite order, who had occupied the monastery from the beginning, were obliged to leave during one of the 19th-century waves of confiscation of religious property by the Spanish state, only to be replaced 30 years later by Augustinians.

## Sights

**★Real Monasterio de San Lorenzo** MONASTERY, PALACE

(☎902 044 454; www.patrimonionacional.es; adult/child, senior & student €12/6, EU & Latin American citizens & residents free Wed & last 3hr Sun; ⏲10am-8pm Tue-Sun, to 6pm Oct-Mar) Home to the majestic monastery and palace complex of Real Monasterio de San Lorenzo, the one-time royal getaway of San Lorenzo de El Escorial rises up from the foothills of the mountains that shelter Madrid from the north and west. Although it attracts its fair share of foreign tourists, this prim little town and its fresh, cool air has been drawing city dwellers here since the complex was built on the orders of King Felipe II in the 16th century.

The monastery's main entrance is on its west side. Above the gateway a **statue of St Lawrence** stands watch, holding a symbolic gridiron, the instrument of his martyrdom (he was roasted alive on one). From here you'll first enter the **Patio de los Reyes** (Patio of the Kings), which houses the statues of the six kings of Judah.

Directly ahead stands the sombre **basilica**. As you enter, look up at the unusual flat vaulting by the choir stalls. Once inside the church proper, turn left to view Benvenuto Cellini's white Carrara marble **statue of Christ crucified** (1576). The remainder of the ground floor contains various treasures, including some tapestries and an **El Greco painting** – impressive as it is, it's a far cry from El Greco's dream of decorating the whole complex. Then head downstairs to the northeastern corner of the complex.

You pass through the **Museo de Arquitectura** and the **Museo de Pintura**. The former tells (in Spanish) the story of how the complex was built, the latter contains a range of 16th- and 17th-century Italian, Spanish and Flemish art.

Head upstairs into a **gallery** around the eastern part of the complex known as the Palacio de Felipe II or Palacio de los Austrias. You'll then descend to the 17th-century **Panteón de los Reyes** (Crypt of the Kings), where almost all Spain's monarchs since Carlos I are interred. Backtracking a little, you'll find yourself in the **Panteón de los Infantes** (Crypt of the Princesses).

Stairs lead up from the **Patio de los Evangelistas** (Patio of the Gospels) to the **Salas Capitulares** (Chapter Houses) in the southeastern corner of the monastery. These bright, airy rooms, with richly frescoed ceilings, contain a minor treasure chest of works by El Greco, Titian, Tintoretto, José de Ribera and Hieronymus Bosch (known as El Bosco to Spaniards).

Just south of the monastery is the **Huerta de los Frailes** (Friars Garden; ⏲10am-8pm Apr-Sep, to 6pm Oct-Mar, closed Mon) garden. To the east is the **Jardín del Príncipe** (Prince's Garden; ⏲10am-8pm Apr-Sep, to 6pm Oct-Mar, closed Mon) FREE, a lovely monumental garden which leads down to the town of El Escorial (and the train station), and contains the **Casita del Príncipe** (€5; ⏲10am-8pm Apr-Sep, to 6pm Oct-Mar, closed Mon), a little neoclassical gem built in 1772 by Juan de Villanueva under Carlos III for his heir, Carlos IV.

## Eating

**La Cueva** SPANISH €€
(☎91 890 15 16; www.mesonlacueva.com; Calle de San Antón 4; mains €14-23, set menus €23-30; ⊙1-4pm & 9-11pm Tue-Sat, 1-4pm Sun) Just a block back from the monastery complex, La Cueva has been around since 1768 and it shows in the heavy wooden beams and hearty, traditional Castilian cooking – roasted meats and steaks are the mainstays, with a few fish dishes.

**Restaurante Charolés** SPANISH €€€
(☎91 890 59 75; www.charolesrestaurante.com; Calle Floridablanca 24; mains €17-26, cocido per person €30; ⊙1-4pm & 9pm-midnight) One of the most popular destinations for *madrileños* heading for the hills, Charolés does grilled or roasted meats to perfection, and it's much loved for its *cocido* for lunch on Monday, Wednesday and Friday – perfect on a cold winter's day.

## Information

**Tourist Office** (☎91 890 53 13; www.sanlorenzoturismo.org; Calle de Grimaldi 4; ⊙10am-2pm & 3-6pm Tue-Sat, 10am-2pm Sun) Right opposite the monastery complex.

## Getting There & Away

San Lorenzo de El Escorial is 59km northwest of Madrid and it takes 40 minutes to drive there. Take the A6 highway to the M600, then follow the signs to El Escorial.

Every 15 minutes (every 30 minutes on weekends) buses 661 and 664 run to El Escorial (€3.50, one hour) from platform 30 at Madrid's Intercambiador de Autobuses de Moncloa.

**Renfe** (☎91 232 03 20; www.renfe.es) C8 *cercanías* make the trip daily from Madrid's Atocha or Chamartín train stations to El Escorial (€1.50, one hour, frequent).

# Aranjuez & Chinchón

Aranjuez was founded as a royal pleasure retreat, away from the riff-raff of Madrid, and it remains a place to escape the rigours of city life. The **Palacio Real** (☎91 891 07 40; www.patrimonionacional.es; palace adult/concession €9/4, guide/audio guide €4/3, EU citizens & residents last 3 hours Wed & Thu free, gardens free; ⊙palace 10am-8pm Apr-Sep, to 6pm Oct-Mar, gardens 8am-9.30pm mid-Jun–mid-Aug, shorter hours rest of year) started as one of Felipe II's modest summer palaces, but took on a life of its own as a succession of royals lavished money upon it. The obligatory guided tour (in Spanish) provides insight into the palace's art and history. In the lush gardens, you'll find the **Casa de Marinos**, which contains the **Museo de Falúas** (⊙10am-6pm Oct-Mar, to 8pm Apr-Sep) FREE, a museum of royal pleasure boats from days gone by. The 18th-century neoclassical **Casa del Labrador** (☎91 891 03 05; €5; ⊙10am-8pm Apr-Sep, to 6pm Oct-Mar) is also worth a visit. If you're here for lunch, try the Michelin-starred **Casa José** (☎91 891 14 88; www.casajose.es; Calle de Abastos 32; mains €15-30, set menus €55-75; ⊙1.45-3.30pm & 9-11.30pm Tue-Sat, 1.45-3.30pm Sun Sep-Jul) or the more informal **Casa Pablete** (☎91 891 03 81; Calle de Stuart 108; tapas from €3, mains €13-24; ⊙1.30-4pm & 8.30-11pm Wed-Mon). Aranjuez is accessible from Madrid aboard C3 *cercanías* that leave every 15 or 20 minutes from Madrid's Atocha train station (€3.40). For more information, visit the **tourist office** (☎91 891 04 27; www.turismoenaranjuez.com; Plaza de San Antonio 9; ⊙10am-2pm & 4-6pm Tue-Sun).

Another fine day trip is to Chinchón, just 45km from Madrid yet worlds away. Visiting here is like stepping back into a charming, ramshackle past, with most of the appeal concentrated around the glorious **Plaza Mayor**. **Café de la Iberia** (☎91 894 08 47; www.cafedelaiberia.com; Plaza Mayor 17; mains €13-28; ⊙12.30-4.30pm & 8-10.30pm) is the pick of the restaurants serving roasted meats surrounding the square. To get here, the **La Veloz bus 337** (☎91 409 76 02; www.samar.es/empresa/samar/laveloz; Avenida del Mediterráneo 49; ⓂConde de Casal) leaves half-hourly for Chinchón from Avenida del Mediterráneo in Madrid, 100m west of Plaza del Conde de Casal. The 50-minute ride costs €3.60.

# Alcalá de Henares

POP 195,649

East of Madrid, Alcalá de Henares is full of surprises with historical sandstone buildings seemingly around every corner. Throw in some sunny squares and a legendary university, and it's a terrific place to escape the capital for a few hours.

## Sights

**Museo Casa Natal de Miguel de Cervantes** MUSEUM
(☎91 889 96 54; www.museocasanataldecervantes.org; Calle Mayor 48; ⊙10am-6pm Tue-

Fri, to 7pm Sat & Sun) FREE The town is dear to Spaniards because it's the birthplace of Miguel de Cervantes Saavedra. The site believed by many to be Cervantes' birthplace is recreated in this illuminating museum, which lies along the beautiful colonnaded Calle Mayor.

**Universidad de Alcalá** UNIVERSITY
(☎91 883 43 84; www.uah.es; guided tours €5; 9am-9pm) FREE Founded in 1486 by Cardinal Cisneros, this is one of the country's principal seats of learning. A guided tour gives a peek into the Mudéjar chapel and the magnificent Paraninfo auditorium, where the King and Queen of Spain give out the prestigious Premio Cervantes literary award every year.

## Eating

★**Hostería del Estudiante** CASTILIAN €€
(Santo Tomás; ☎91 888 03 30; www.parador.es; Calle de los Colegios 3; mains €12-29, set menus from €36; 1.30-4pm & 8.30-11pm) Across the road from the *parador*, this charming restaurant has wonderful Castilian cooking and a classy ambience in a dining room decorated with artefacts from the city's illustrious history.

**Barataría** TAPAS €€
(☎91 888 59 25; www.facebook.com/baratarialainsula; Calle de los Cerrajeros 18; mains €14-27; noon-4pm & 8pm-midnight Mon, Tue & Thu-Sat, noon-4pm Sun) A wine bar, tapas bar and restaurant all rolled into one, Barataría is a fine place to eat whatever your mood. Grilled meats are the star of the show, with the ribs with honey in particular a local favourite.

## Information

**Tourist office** (☎91 881 06 34; www.turismoalcala.es; Callejón de Santa María 1; 10am-2pm & 5-8pm Tue-Fri, 10am-8pm Sat, to 3pm Sun) Free guided tours of the Alcalá of Cervantes at 5.30pm Saturday and Sunday, as well as information on the town.

## Getting There & Away

Alcalá de Henares is just 35km east of Madrid, heading towards Zaragoza along the A2.

There are regular bus departures (€3.25, about one hour, every five to 15 minutes) from Madrid's Intercambiador de Avenida de América.

**Renfe** (☎91 232 03 20; www.renfe.es) C2 and C7 *cercanías* trains (€2.65, 50 minutes) make the trip to Alcalá de Henares daily.

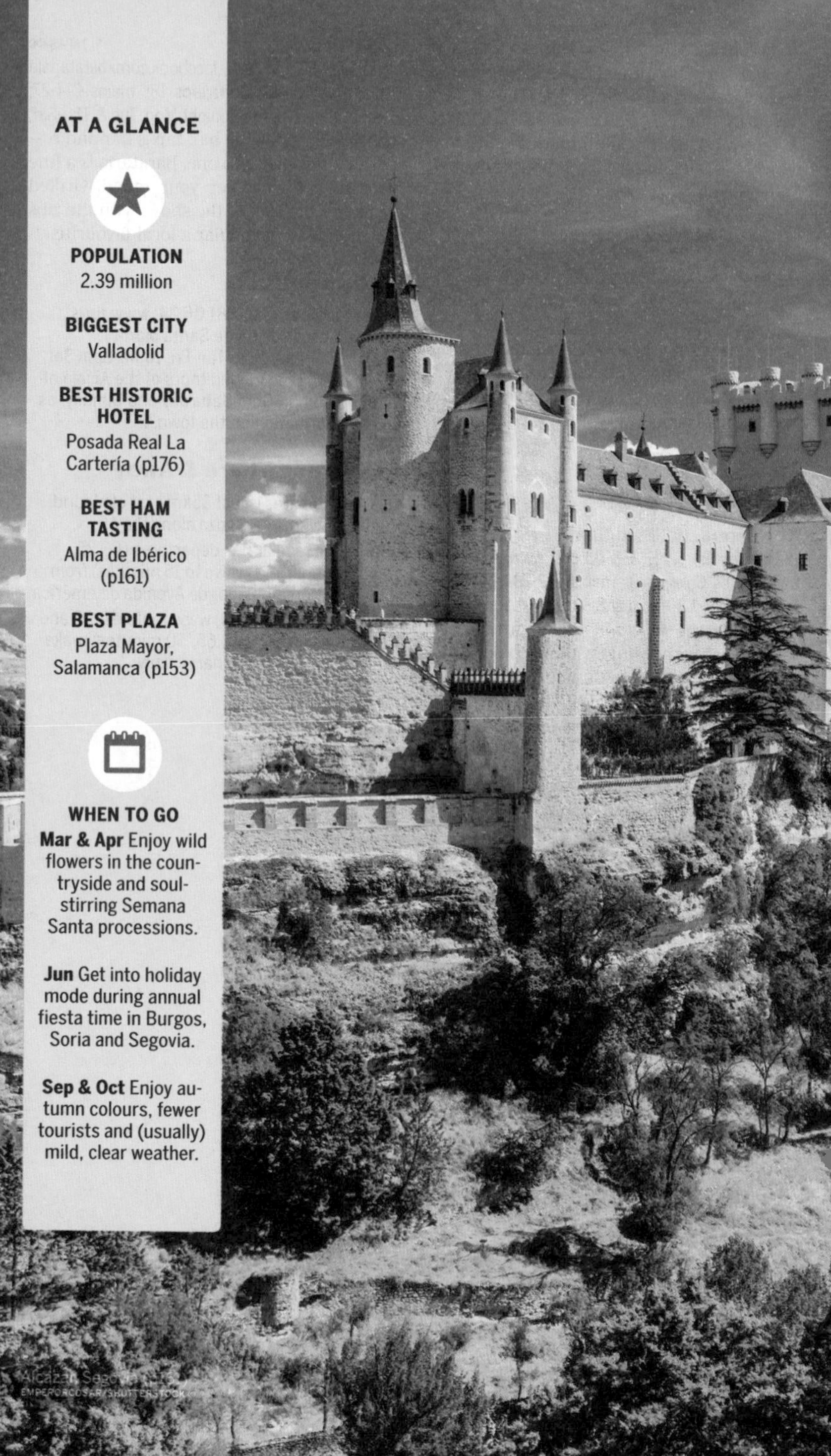

## AT A GLANCE

**POPULATION**
2.39 million

**BIGGEST CITY**
Valladolid

**BEST HISTORIC HOTEL**
Posada Real La Cartería (p176)

**BEST HAM TASTING**
Alma de Ibérico (p161)

**BEST PLAZA**
Plaza Mayor, Salamanca (p153)

**WHEN TO GO**

**Mar & Apr** Enjoy wild flowers in the countryside and soul-stirring Semana Santa processions.

**Jun** Get into holiday mode during annual fiesta time in Burgos, Soria and Segovia.

**Sep & Oct** Enjoy autumn colours, fewer tourists and (usually) mild, clear weather.

Alcázar, Segovia
EMPERORCOSAR/SHUTTERSTOCK

# Castilla y León

If you're looking for a window into the Spanish soul, head to Castilla y León. This is Spain without the stereotypes: vast plains, spectacular mountain peaks and evocative medieval towns and villages. Experience fabled cities like Salamanca, with its lively student population, and Segovia, famed for a fairy-tale fortress that inspired Disneyland's *Sleeping Beauty* castle. The multiturreted walls of Ávila have similar magical appeal, while the lofty cathedrals of León and Burgos are among Europe's most impressive. As with most of Spain, food here is an agreeable obsession, promising the country's best *jamón* (cured ham), roast lamb and suckling pig.

The region's story is equally told through its quiet back roads, half-timbered hamlets and isolated castles. From the scenic Sierra de Francia in the southwest to Covarrubias, Calatañazor and Medinaceli in the east, this is the hidden Spain most travellers don't know still exists.

**INCLUDES**

## Castilla y León Highlights

1 **Salamanca** (p153) Being charmed by architectural elegance and energy.

2 **León** (p178) Savouring the ethereal light in León's breathtaking cathedral.

3 **Santo Domingo de Silos** (p191) Being transported to medieval times listening to Gregorian chants.

4 **Pedraza de la Sierra** (p166) Dining on *cordero asado* in this hilltop village.

5 **Medinaceli** (p199) Escaping city life in a historic village.

6 **Segovia** (p161) Imagining yourself somewhere between ancient Rome and Disneyland.

7 **Sierra de la Culebra** (p174) Wolf-spotting near medieval Puebla de Sanabria.

8 **Sierra de Francia** (p159) Exploring beautiful villages that time forgot.

9 **Guijuelo** (p161) Finding the source of Spain's best *jamón*.

## SOUTHWEST CASTILLA Y LEÓN

You could easily spend a week or more in southwestern Castilla y León, one of the region's most engaging corners. Salamanca, Ciudad Rodrigo and Ávila are three of the most appealing towns in central Spain, but the time-worn villages of the Sierra de Francia promise fascinating breaks from city life.

# Ávila

POP 57,655 / ELEV 1130M

Ávila's old city, surrounded by imposing city walls comprising eight monumental gates, 88 watchtowers and more than 2500 turrets, is one of the best-preserved medieval bastions in Spain. In winter, when an icy wind whistles in off the plains, the old city huddles behind the high stone walls as if seeking protection from the harsh Castilian climate. At night, when the walls are illuminated to magical effect, you'll wonder if you've stumbled into a fairy tale. It's a deeply religious city that for centuries has drawn pilgrims to the cult of Santa Teresa de Ávila, with its many churches, convents and high-walled palaces. As such, Ávila is the essence of Castilla and the epitome of old Spain.

## Sights

**★Murallas** WALLS

(☎920 35 00 00; www.muralladeavila.com; incl multilingual audio guide adult/child €5/3.50, 2-4pm Tue free; ⌚10am-8pm Apr-Jun & Sep-Oct, to 9pm Jul & Aug, to 6pm Tue-Sun Nov-Mar; 👪) Ávila's splendid 12th-century walls stretch for 2.5km atop the remains of earlier Roman and Muslim battlements and rank among the world's best-preserved medieval defensive perimeters. Two sections of the walls can be climbed – a 300m stretch that can be accessed from just inside the **Puerta del Alcázar**, and a longer (1300m) stretch from **Puerta de los Leales** that runs the length of the old city's northern perimeter. At dusk they attract swirls of swooping swallows – and they're magical when floodlit at night.

**★Catedral del Salvador** CATHEDRAL

(☎920 21 16 41; www.catedralavila.es; Plaza de la Catedral; incl audio guide €6, bell tower €2; ⌚10am-8pm Mon-Fri, to 9pm Sat, 11.45am-7.30pm Sun Apr-Jun, Sep & Oct, 10am-9pm Mon-Sat, 11.45am-9pm Sun Jul & Aug, 10am-6pm Mon-Fri, to 7pm Sat, to 5.30pm Sun Nov-Mar) Ávila's 12th-century cathedral is both a house of worship and an ingenious fortress: its stout granite apse forms the central bulwark in the historic city walls. The sombre, Gothic-style facade conceals a magnificent interior with an exquisite early 16th-century **altar frieze** showing the life of Jesus, plus Renaissance-era carved choir stalls. There is also a **museum** with an El Greco painting and a splendid silver monstrance by Juan de Arfe. (Push the buttons to illuminate the altar and the choir stalls.)

**★Los Cuatro Postes** VIEWPOINT

(Calle de los Cuatro Postes, off N110) Northwest of the city, on the road to Salamanca, Los Cuatro Postes provides the best views of Ávila's walls. It also marks the place where Santa Teresa and her brother were caught by their uncle as they tried to run away from home (they were hoping to achieve martyrdom at the hands of the Muslims).

**Convento de Santa Teresa** CHURCH, MUSEUM

(☎920 21 10 30; www.teresadejesus.com; Plaza de la Santa; church & relic room free, museum €2; ⌚10am-2pm & 4-7pm Tue-Sun) Built in 1636 around the room where Santa Teresa was born in 1515, this is the epicentre of the cult surrounding the saint. There are three attractions in one here: the church, a relic room and a museum. Highlights include the gold-adorned **chapel** (built over the room where she was born), the baroque **altar** and the (macabre) **relic** of the saint's ring finger, complete with ring. Apparently Franco kept it at his bedside throughout his rule.

**Monasterio de Santo Tomás** MONASTERY, MUSEUM

(☎920 22 04 00; www.monasteriosantotomas.com; Plaza de Granada 1; €4; ⌚10.30am-9pm Jul & Aug, 10.30am-2pm & 3.30-7.30pm Sep-Jun) Commissioned by the Reyes Católicos (Catholic Monarchs), Fernando and Isabel, and completed in 1492, this monastery is an exquisite example of Isabelline architecture,

### VISITÁVILA CARD

If you plan on seeing all of Ávila's major sights, it may be worth buying the **Visitávila Card** (www.avilaturismo.com/en/organize-your-visit/visitavila-tourist-card; per person/family €13/25), which is valid for 48 hours and covers entrance fees to the main sights around town.

## Ávila

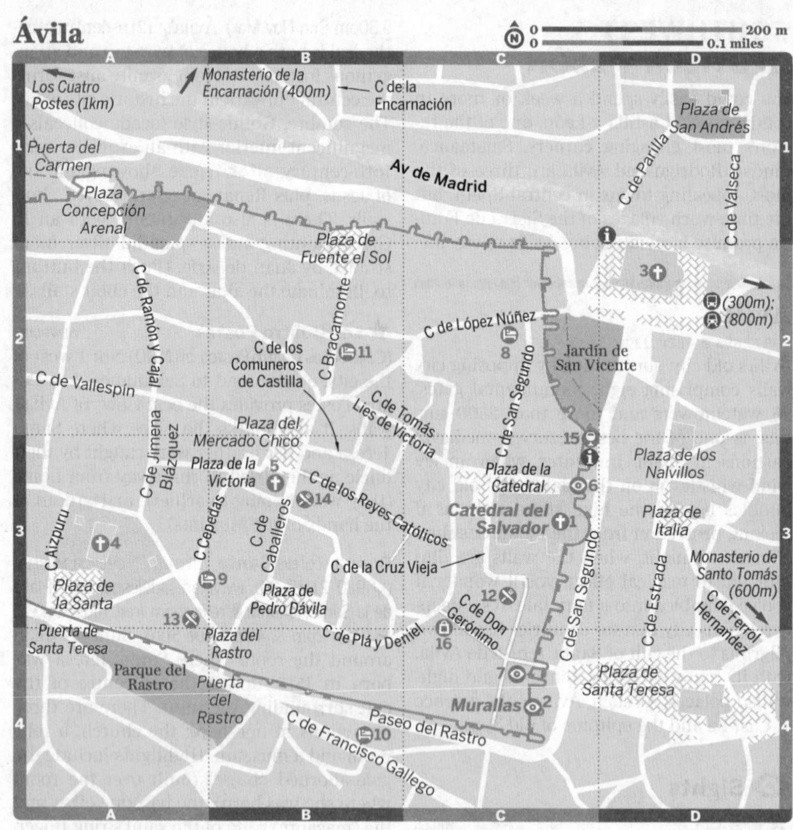


## Ávila

**Top Sights**
1 Catedral del Salvador......C3
2 Murallas......C4

**Sights**
3 Basílica de San Vicente......D2
4 Convento de Santa Teresa......A3
5 Iglesia de San Juan Bautista......B3
6 Puerta de Los Leales......C3
7 Puerta del Alcázar......C4

**Sleeping**
8 Hostal Arco San Vicente......C2
9 Hotel El Rastro......A3
10 Hotel Las Leyendas......B4
11 Hotel Palacio de Monjaraz......B2

**Eating**
12 Hostería Las Cancelas......C3
13 Mesón del Rastro......A3
14 Soul Kitchen......B3

**Drinking & Nightlife**
15 La Bodeguita de San Segundo......C3

**Shopping**
16 La Flor de Castilla......C3

rich in historical resonance. Three interconnected cloisters lead to the church that contains the alabaster **tomb of Don Juan**, the monarchs' only son.

**Basílica de San Vicente** CHURCH
(☎920 25 52 30; www.basilicasanvicente.es; Plaza de San Vicente; incl audio guide €2.30; ⏰10am-6.30pm Mon-Sat, 4-6pm Sun Apr-Oct, 10am-1.30pm & 4-6.30pm Mon-Sat, 4-6pm Sun Nov-Mar) This graceful church is a masterpiece of Romanesque simplicity: a series of largely Gothic modifications in sober granite contrasted with the warm sandstone of the Romanesque original. Work started in the 11th century, supposedly on the site where three

### WHO WAS SANTA TERESA?

Teresa de Cepeda y Ahumada, probably the most important woman in the history of the Spanish Catholic Church (after the Virgin Mary, of course...), was born in Ávila on 28 March 1515, one of 10 children of a merchant family. Raised by Augustinian nuns after her mother's death, she joined the Carmelite order at age 20. After early, undistinguished years as a nun, she was shaken by a vision of hell in 1560, which crystallised her true vocation: she would reform the Carmelites.

In stark contrast to the opulence of the church in 16th-century Spain, her reforms called for the church to return to its roots, taking on the suffering and simple lifestyle of Jesus Christ. The Carmelites demanded the strictest of piety and even employed flagellation to atone for their sins. Not surprisingly, all this proved extremely unpopular with the mainstream Catholic Church. With the help of many supporters, Teresa founded convents all over Spain and her writings proved enormously popular. She died in 1582 and was canonised by Pope Gregory XV in 1622.

martyrs – Vicente and his sisters, Sabina and Cristeta – were slaughtered by the Romans in the early 4th century. Their canopied **cenotaph** is an outstanding piece of Romanesque style, with nods to the Gothic.

**Monasterio de la Encarnación** MONASTERY
(☎920 21 12 12; Calle de la Encarnación; church free, museum €2; ⏲9.30am-1pm & 4-7pm Mon-Fri, 10am-1pm & 4-7pm Sat & Sun May-Sep, 9.30am-1.30pm & 3.30-6pm Mon-Fri, 10am-1pm & 4-6pm Sat & Sun Oct-Apr) North of the city walls, this unadorned Renaissance monastery is where Santa Teresa fully took on the monastic life and lived for 27 years. One of the three main rooms open to the public is where the saint is said to have had a vision of the baby Jesus. Also on display are relics, such as the piece of wood used by Teresa as a pillow (ouch!) and the chair upon which St John of the Cross made his confessions.

**Iglesia de San Juan Bautista** CHURCH
(Plaza de la Victoria; ⏲Mass 10am & 7.30pm Mon-Sat, noon Sun) FREE This quiet parish church dates from the 16th century and contains the font in which Santa Teresa was baptised on 4 April 1515.

## Festivals & Events

**Semana Santa** RELIGIOUS
(Holy Week; ⏲Mar/Apr) Ávila is one of the best places in Castilla y León to watch the solemn processions of Easter. It all begins on Holy Thursday, though the most evocative event is the early morning (around 5am) Good Friday procession, which circles the city wall.

**Fiesta de Santa Teresa** CULTURAL
(⏲Oct; 👪) This annual festival, held during the second week of October, honours the city's patron saint with processions, concerts and fireworks.

## Sleeping

★**Hotel El Rastro** HISTORIC HOTEL €
(☎920 35 22 25; www.elrastroavila.com; Calle Cepedas; s €30-45, d €45-90; ❄📶) This atmospheric hotel occupies a former 16th-century palace with original stone, exposed brickwork and a natural, earth-toned colour scheme exuding a calm, understated elegance. Each room has a different form, but most have high ceilings and plenty of space. Note that the owners also run a marginally cheaper *hostal* (budget hotel) of the same name around the corner.

**Hostal Arco San Vicente** HOSTAL €
(☎920 22 24 98; www.arcosanvicente.com; Calle de López Núñez 6; r incl breakfast from €37; ❄📶) This gleaming *hostal* has small, carpeted rooms with pale paintwork and wrought-iron bedheads. Rooms on the 2nd floor have attic windows and air-con; some on the 1st floor look out at the Puerta de San Vicente.

★**Hotel Palacio de Monjaraz** HOTEL €€
(☎920 33 20 70; www.palaciodemonjaraz.com; Calle Bracamonte 6; s €55-110, d €65-137; ❄📶) Stunning rooms in a wonderfully converted 16th-century Ávila town house make this one of our favourite places in town. The rooms are large, have airy high ceilings and there's a quiet extravagance to the decor that changes from one room to the next. Some have Persian carpets and four-poster beds.

**Hotel Las Leyendas** HISTORIC HOTEL €€
(☎920 35 20 42; www.lasleyendas.es; Calle de Francisco Gallego 3; s €35-55, d €49-85; ❄📶) Occupying the house of 16th-century Ávila

nobility, this intimate hotel overflows with period touches wedded to modern amenities. Some rooms have views out across the plains, others look onto an internal garden. The decor varies between original wooden beams, exposed brick and stonework, and more modern rooms in muted earth tones. Breakfast is a little sparse.

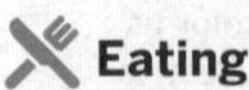

## Eating

You don't have to walk far within the upper end of the old town and surrounding streets to find an excellent restaurant. Ávila is famous for its *chuleton de Ávila* (T-bone steak) and *judías del barco de Ávila* (white beans, often with chorizo, in a thick sauce).

**★Soul Kitchen** CASTILIAN €€
(☎920 21 34 83; www.soulkitchen.es; Calle de Caballeros 13; mains €9-19; ⏰10am-midnight Mon-Fri, 11am-2am Sat, to midnight Sun) This place has the kind of energy that can seem lacking elsewhere. The eclectic menu changes regularly and ranges from salads with dressings like chestnut and fig to hamburgers with cream of *setas* (oyster mushrooms). Lighter dishes include bruschetta.

**Mesón del Rastro** CASTILIAN €€
(☎920 35 22 25; www.elrastroavila.com; Plaza del Rastro 1; mains €13-25; ⏰1-4pm & 9-11pm) The dark-wood-beamed interior announces immediately that this is a bastion of robust Castilian cooking, which it has been since 1881. Expect delicious mainstays such as *judías del barco de Ávila* (white beans, often with chorizo, in a thick sauce) and *cordero asado* (roast lamb), mercifully light salads and, regrettably, the occasional coach tour.

The *menú de degustación,* priced for two people (€42), comes warmly recommended, but only if you're really hungry.

**Hostería Las Cancelas** CASTILIAN €€
(☎920 21 22 49; www.lascancelas.com; Calle de la Cruz Vieja 6; mains €14-26; ⏰1-4pm & 7.30-11pm) This courtyard restaurant occupies a delightful interior patio dating back to the 15th century. Renowned for being a mainstay of Ávila cuisine (steaks, roast lamb or suckling pig), traditional meals are prepared with a salutary attention to detail.

DON'T MISS

### CASTILLA Y LEÓN'S PRETTIEST VILLAGES


- Covarrubias (p190)
- Pedraza de la Sierra (p166)
- Medinaceli (p199)
- San Martín del Castañar (p159)
- Orbaneja del Castillo (p188)
- Frías (p188)
- Mogarraz (p159)
- Puebla de Sanabria (p175)
- La Alberca (p160)
- Calatañazor (p197)
- Yanguas (p198)
- Santo Domingo de Silos (p191)

## Drinking & Nightlife

**★La Bodeguita de San Segundo** WINE BAR
(☎920 25 73 09; Calle de San Segundo 19; ⏰11am-midnight Wed-Mon) Situated in the 16th-century Casa de la Misericordia, this superb wine bar is standing-room only most nights, though more tranquil in the quieter afternoon hours. Its wine list is renowned throughout Spain, with over a thousand wines to choose from and tapas-sized creative servings of cheeses and cured meats as the perfect accompaniment.

## Shopping

**La Flor de Castilla** FOOD
(☎920 21 11 58; Calle de Don Gerónimo; ⏰8.30am-11pm Mon-Thu, to midnight Fri, 9am-midnight Sat & Sun) This patisserie-cafe is a fine place to buy a *yema de Santa Teresa,* a sticky, ultrasweet treat made of egg yolk and sugar that's said to have been invented by the saint herself.

## Information

**Centro de Recepción de Visitantes** (☎920 35 40 00, ext 370; www.avilaturismo.com; Avenida de Madrid 39; ⏰9am-8pm Apr-Sep, to 6pm Oct-Mar) Municipal tourist office.

**Oficina de Turismo de Castilla y León** (☎920 21 13 87; www.turismocastillayleon.com; Casa de las Carnicerías, Calle de San Segundo 17; ⏰9.30am-2pm & 5-8pm Mon-Sat, 9.30am-5pm Sun Jul–mid-Sep, 9.30am-2pm & 4-7pm Mon-Sat, 9.30am-5pm Sun mid-Sep–Jul) Regional tourist office.

## Getting There & Around

Frequent bus services run from the **bus station** (☎920 25 65 05; Avenida de Madrid 2) to Segovia (€7.50, one hour), Salamanca (€9, 1½ hours, five daily) and Madrid (€12, 1½ hours).

There are **Renfe** (☎902 240202; www.renfe.es) trains to Madrid (from €13, 1¼ to two hours, up to 17 daily), Salamanca (from €13, 1¼ hours, eight daily) and León (from €22, three to four hours, five daily).

Local bus 1 runs past the train station to Plaza de la Catedral.

## Salamanca

POP 143,980

Whether floodlit by night or bathed in late-afternoon light, there's something magical about Salamanca. This is a city of rare beauty, awash with golden sandstone overlaid with ochre-tinted Latin inscriptions – an extraordinary virtuosity of plateresque and Renaissance styles. The monumental highlights are many and the exceptional Plaza Mayor (illuminated to stunning effect at night) is unforgettable. This is also Castilla's liveliest city, home to a massive Spanish and international student population that throngs the streets at night and provides the city with so much vitality.

**DON'T MISS**

**TOP TOWN SQUARES**

- Salamanca
- Segovia (p162)
- La Alberca (p160)
- Pedraza de la Sierra (p166)
- Peñafiel (p193)
- Medinaceli (p199)

### Sights

**★Plaza Mayor** SQUARE

Built between 1729 and 1755, Salamanca's exceptional grand square is widely considered to be Spain's most beautiful central plaza. It's particularly memorable at night when illuminated (until midnight). Designed by Alberto Churriguera, it's a remarkably harmonious and controlled baroque display. The medallions placed around the square bear the busts of famous figures. Bullfights were held here well into the 19th century; the last ceremonial *corrida* (bullfight) took place in 1992.

**★Catedral Nueva** CATHEDRAL

(☎923 21 74 76; www.catedralsalamanca.org; Plaza de Anaya; adult/child incl audio guide & Catedral Vieja €6/4; ⏲10am-8pm Apr-Sep, to 6pm Oct-Mar) The tower of this late-Gothic cathedral lords over the city centre, its compelling Churrigueresque (an ornate style of baroque architecture) dome visible from almost every angle. The interior is similarly impressive, with elaborate choir stalls, main chapel and retrochoir, much of it courtesy of the prolific José Churriguera. The ceilings are also exceptional, along with the Renaissance doorways – particularly the **Puerta del Nacimiento** on the western face, which stands out as one of several miracles worked in the city's native sandstone.

**★Catedral Vieja** CATHEDRAL

(☎923 21 74 76; www.catedralsalamanca.org; Plaza de Anaya; adult/child incl audio guide & Catedral Nueva €6/4; ⏲10am-8pm Apr-Sep, to 6pm Oct-Mar) The Catedral Nueva's largely Romanesque predecessor, the Catedral Vieja is adorned with an exquisite 15th-century **altarpiece**, one of the finest outside Italy. Its 53 panels depict scenes from the lives of Christ and Mary and are topped by a haunting representation of the Final Judgement. The cloister was largely ruined in an earthquake in 1755, but the **Capilla de Anaya** houses an extravagant alabaster sepulchre and one of Europe's oldest organs, a Mudéjar work of art from the 16th century.

**Universidad Civil** HISTORIC BUILDING

(☎923 29 44 00, ext 1150; www.salamanca.es; Calle de los Libreros; adult/concession €10/5, audio guide €2; ⏲10am-7pm Mon-Sat, to 2pm Sun mid-Sep–Mar, 10am-8pm Mon-Sat, to 2pm Sun Apr–mid-Sep) Founded initially as the Estudio General in 1218, the university reached the peak of its renown in the 15th and 16th centuries. The visual feast of the entrance facade is a tapestry in sandstone, bursting with images of mythical heroes, religious scenes and coats of arms. It's dominated by busts of Fernando and Isabel. Behind the facade, the highlight of an otherwise-modest collection of rooms lies upstairs: the extraordinary **university library**, the oldest in Europe.

**Convento de San Esteban** CONVENT

(☎923 21 50 00; www.conventosanesteban.es; Plaza del Concilio de Trento; adult/child €4/free; ⏲10am-1.15pm & 4-7.15pm Apr-Oct, 10am-1.15pm & 4-5.15pm Nov-Mar) Just down the hill from the cathedral, the lordly Dominican Convento de San Esteban's church has an extraordinary altar-like facade, with the stoning of San Esteban (St Stephen) as its central motif. Inside is a well-presented museum dedicated to the Dominicans, a splendid

## Salamanca

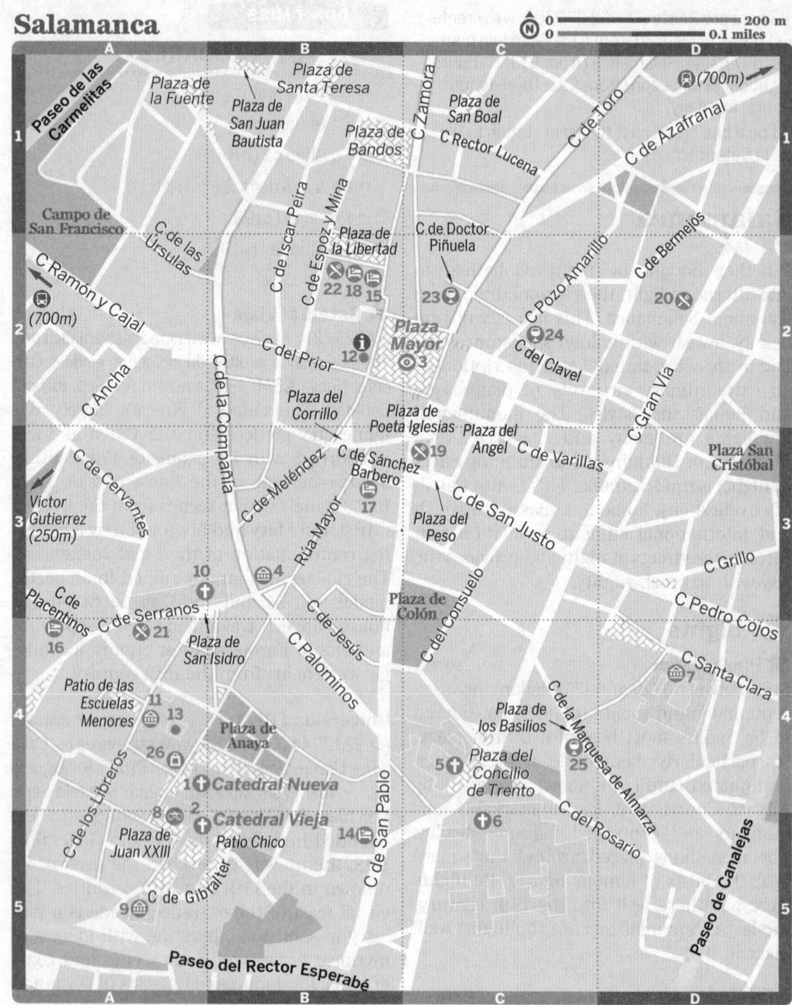


Gothic-Renaissance cloister and an elaborate church built in the form of a Latin cross and adorned by an overwhelming 17th-century **altar** by José Churriguera.

You can now also climb to the terrace directly above the facade, worth doing for the fine Salamanca views. The climb is open at 11.30am, noon, 12.30pm, 7pm and 7.30pm Tuesday to Saturday, 10.30am, 11am and 11.30am on Sundays from April to October, with shorter hours the rest of the year.

**Museo de Art Nouveau y Art Decó** MUSEUM
(Casa Lis; ☎923 12 14 25; www.museocasalis.org; Calle de Gibraltar; adult/child €4/free, 11am-2pm Thu free; ⏲11am-8pm; 👪) Utterly unlike any other Salamanca museum, this stunning collection of sculpture, paintings and art deco and art nouveau pieces inhabits a beautiful, light-filled Modernista (Catalan art nouveau) house. There's abundant stained glass and exhibits that include Lalique glass, toys by Steiff (inventor of the teddy bear), Limoges porcelain, Fabergé watches, fabulous bronze and marble figurines, and a vast collection of 19th-century children's dolls (some strangely macabre), which kids will love. There's also a cafe and an excellent gift shop.

## Salamanca

**Top Sights**
1 Catedral Nueva A4
2 Catedral Vieja A5
3 Plaza Mayor C2

**Sights**
4 Casa de las Conchas B3
5 Convento de las Dueñas C4
6 Convento de San Esteban C5
7 Convento de Santa Clara D4
8 Ieronimus A5
9 Museo de Art Nouveau y Art Decó A5
10 Real Clerecía de San Marcos A3
11 Universidad Civil A4

**Activities, Courses & Tours**
12 Guided Tours B2
13 University of Salamanca A4

**Sleeping**
14 Don Gregorio B5
15 Hostal Concejo B2
16 Microtel Placentinos A4
17 Rúa Hotel B3
18 Salamanca Suite Studios B2

**Eating**
19 El Pecado C3
20 La Cocina de Toño D2
21 Mandala Café A4
22 Zazu Bistro B2

**Drinking & Nightlife**
23 Doctor Cocktail C2
24 Tío Vivo C2
25 Vinodiario C4

**Shopping**
26 Mercatus A4

**Real Clerecía de San Marcos** CHURCH
(San Marcos; 923 27 71 00; www.torresdelaclerecia.com; Calle de la Compañia; San Marcos €3, Scala Coeli €3.75, combined ticket €6; San Marcos 10.30am-12.45pm & 4-5.30pm Tue-Fri, 10.30am-1.30pm & 4-5.30pm Sat, 10.30am-1.30pm Sun, Scala Coeli 10am-7.15pm) Visits to this colossal baroque church and the attached Catholic university are via obligatory **guided tours** (in Spanish), which run every 45 minutes. You can also climb the **Scala Coeli** (tower) – some 166 steps, including the bell tower – to enjoy superb panoramic views.

**Ieronimus** VIEWPOINT
(Puerta de la Torre; 923 26 67 01; www.ieronimus.es; Plaza de Juan XXIII; €3.75; 10am-7pm) For fine views over Salamanca, head to the tower at the southwestern corner of the Catedral Nueva's facade. From here, stairs lead up through the tower, past labyrinthine but well-presented exhibitions of cathedral memorabilia, then – a real bonus – along the interior balconies of the sanctuaries of the Catedral Nueva and Catedral Vieja and out onto the exterior balconies. Guided night tours take place at 8.15pm and 10pm (per person €6).

**Casa de las Conchas** HISTORIC BUILDING
(House of Shells; 923 26 93 17; Calle de la Compañia 2; 9am-9pm Mon-Fri, 9am-2pm & 4-7pm Sat, 10am-2pm & 4-7pm Sun) FREE One of the city's most endearing buildings, Casa de las Conchas is named after the 300 scallop shells clinging to its facade. The house's original owner, Dr Rodrigo Maldonado de Talavera, was a doctor at the court of Isabel and a member of the Order of Santiago, whose symbol is the shell. It now houses the public **library**, entered via a charming colonnaded courtyard with a central fountain.

**Convento de Santa Clara** MUSEUM
(660 108314; Calle Santa Clara 2; adult/child €3/free; 9.30am-12.45pm & 4.25-6.10pm Mon-Fri, 9.30am-2.10pm Sat & Sun) This much-modified convent started life as a Romanesque structure and now houses a small museum. You can admire the beautiful frescoes and climb up some stairs to inspect the 14th- and 15th-century wooden Mudéjar ceiling at close quarters. You can visit only as part of a (Spanish-language) **guided tour**.

**Convento de las Dueñas** CONVENT
(923 21 54 42; Plaza Concilio de Trento; €2; 10.30am-12.45pm & 4.30-7.15pm Mon-Sat) This Dominican convent is home to the city's most beautiful cloister, with some decidedly ghoulish carvings on the capitals.

## Courses

In addition to the language courses offered by the University of Salamanca, the tourist office has a list of accredited private colleges.

**University of Salamanca** LANGUAGE
(Cursos Internacionales, Universidad Civil; 923 29 44 18; https://cursosinternacionales.usal.es/en; Patio de las Escuelas Menores) Salamanca is one of the most popular places in Spain to study Spanish and the University of Salamanca is the most respected language school.

## Tours

Two-hour **guided tours** (☎622 524690; visitasplaza@hotmail.es; tour per person €15) are run from the tourist office on Plaza Mayor. Although there are variations, daytime tours take in the main monumental highlights of Salamanca, while the 8pm Friday and Saturday tour is all about local legends and curiosities. Check departure times and buy your ticket in advance from the tourist office.

## Sleeping

**Hostal Concejo** HOSTAL €
(☎920 87 521; www.hostalconcejo.com; Plaza de la Libertad 1; s/d from €28/36; P❄📶) A cut above the average *hostal,* the stylish Concejo has polished-wood floors, tasteful furnishings, light-filled rooms and a superb central location. Try to snag one of the corner rooms, such as No 104, which has a traditional, glassed-in balcony, complete with a table, chairs and people-watching views.

★**Microtel Placentinos** BOUTIQUE HOTEL €€
(☎923 28 15 31; www.microtelplacentinos.com; Calle de Placentinos 9; r incl breakfast €38-110; ❄📶) One of Salamanca's most charming boutique hotels, Microtel Placentinos is tucked away on a quiet street and has rooms with exposed stone walls and wooden beams. The service is faultless, and the overall atmosphere is one of intimacy and discretion. All rooms have a hydromassage shower or tub and there's an outside whirlpool spa (summer only).

**Salamanca Suite Studios** APARTMENT €€
(☎923 27 24 65; www.salamancasuitestudios.com; Plaza de la Libertad 4; r €55-120; ❄📶) This excellent place has smart and contemporary modern studios and apartments with kitchens; some have Nespresso coffee machines and all are sleek and stylish. The location is lovely and central and the service is discreet but attentive. Ask for a plaza-facing room.

**Rúa Hotel** HOTEL €€
(☎923 27 22 72; www.hotelrua.com; Calle de Sánchez Barbero 11; s/d from €52/69; ❄@📶) The former apartments here have been converted to seriously spacious rooms with sofas and fridges. Light-wood floors, rag-rolled walls and arty prints set the tone. You can't get more central than this.

★**Don Gregorio** BOUTIQUE HOTEL €€€
(☎923 21 70 15; www.hoteldongregorio.com; Calle de San Pablo 80; r/ste incl breakfast from €200/310; P❄📶) A palatial hotel with part of the city's Roman wall flanking the garden. Rooms are decorated in soothing café-con-leche shades with crisp white linens and extravagant extras, including private saunas, espresso machines, complimentary minibar, king-size beds and vast hydromassage tubs. Sumptuous antiques and medieval tapestries adorn the public areas.

## Eating

**Mandala Café** MEDITERRANEAN €
(☎923 12 33 42; Calle de Serranos 9-11; set menu €13.50; ⏰8am-11pm; 👪) Come here with an appetite, as cool and casual Mandala offers a three-course set menu (unusually available for lunch *and* dinner) with dishes like black rice with seafood, and vegetable lasagne. There are also 18 flavours of hot chocolate, 52 types of milkshake, 56 juice combinations and more teas than we could count.

★**La Cocina de Toño** TAPAS €€
(☎923 26 39 77; www.lacocinadetoño.es; Calle Gran Via 20; tapas from €1.60, mains €11-23, set menus from €17; ⏰11am-4.30pm & 8-11.30pm Tue-Sat,

**DON'T MISS**

### FROG-SPOTTING

Arguably a lot more interesting than trainspotting, a compulsory task facing all visitors to Salamanca is to search out the frog sculpted into the facade of the Universidad Civil (p153). Once pointed out, it's easily enough seen, but the uninitiated can spend considerable time searching. Why bother? Well, they say that those who detect it without help can be assured of good luck and even marriage within a year; some hopeful students believe they'll be guaranteed to ace their examinations. If you believe all this, stop reading now – spoilers ahead.

If you need help, look at the busts of Fernando and Isabel. From there, turn your gaze to the largest column on the extreme right. Slightly above the level of the busts is a series of skulls, atop the leftmost of which sits our little amphibious friend (or what's left of his eroded self).

11am-4.30pm Sun; 📶) This place owes its loyal following to its creative *pinchos* (tapas) and half-servings of dishes such as escalope of foie gras with roast apple and passion fruit jelly. The restaurant serves more traditional fare as befits the decor, but the bar is one of Salamanca's gastronomic stars.

**Zazu Bistro** ITALIAN €€

(☎923 26 16 90; www.restaurantezazu.com; Plaza de la Libertad 8; mains €11-17; ⏰2-4pm & 8.30pm-midnight) Enjoy a romantic intimate ambience and Italian-inspired dishes like asparagus, mint and cheese risotto or farfalle with tomato, bacon, vodka and parmesan. The culinary surprises extend to desserts, like that delectable British standard, sticky toffee pudding. Every dish is executed to perfection. Snag a table by the window overlooking this tranquil square.

**El Pecado** CONTEMPORARY SPANISH €€

(☎923 26 65 58; www.elpecadorestaurante.es; Plaza del Poeta Iglesias 12; mains €15-19, menú de degustación €25-35; ⏰1.30-4pm & 8.30-11.30pm; 🌶) A trendy place that regularly attracts Spanish celebrities and well-to-do locals, El Pecado (The Sin) has an intimate dining room and a quirky, creative menu. The hallmarks are fresh tastes, a lovely lack of pretension, intriguing combinations and dishes that regularly change according to what is fresh in the market that day. The *menú de degustación* is outstanding.

**★Victor Gutiérrez** CONTEMPORARY SPANISH €€€

(☎923 26 29 73; www.restaurantevictorgutierrez.com; Calle de Empedrada 4; set menus €72-120; ⏰1.30-4pm & 8.30-11pm Tue-Fri, 1.30-4pm & 9-11pm Sat, 1.30-4pm Sun; 📶) This is still the best table in town. Chef Victor Gutiérrez has a Michelin star and his place has a justifiably exclusive vibe, with an emphasis on innovative dishes with plenty of colourful drizzle. The choice of what to order is largely made for you with some excellent set menus that change regularly. Reservations essential.

## Drinking & Nightlife

**★Tío Vivo** BAR

(☎923 215 768; www.tiovivosalamanca.com; Calle del Clavel 3-5; ⏰3.30pm-late) Sip drinks by flickering candlelight to a background of '80s music, enjoying the whimsical decor of carousel horses and oddball antiquities. There's live music Tuesday to Thursday from midnight, sometimes with a €5 cover.

WORTH A TRIP

### LEDESMA

Around 35km northwest of Salamanca along the SA300, Ledesma is a quiet medieval gem. It clings to the hilltop high above the Río Tormes, which is itself spanned by two pretty bridges; the **Puente Mocho** dates back to Roman times. The town's summit has an attractive town square, watched over by the towering Gothic **Iglesia de Santa María la Mayor**. Down the hill south of the church are the crenellated walls of the town's 15th-century **castle**. Ledesma is also famous for its *rosquillas de Ledesma*, a doughnut-shaped sweet pastry; watch for small shops selling them around town. For more information, visit www.turismoledesma.com.

**Doctor Cocktail** COCKTAIL BAR

(☎923 26 31 51; www.facebook.com/thedoctorsalamanca; Calle del Doctor Piñuela 5; ⏰4pm-late) Excellent cocktails, friendly bar staff and a cool crowd make for a fine mix just north of the Plaza Mayor. Apart from the creative list of cocktails, it has over 30 different kinds of gin to choose from and above-average tonic to go with it.

**Vinodiario** WINE BAR

(☎923 61 49 25; www.vinodiario.com; Plaza de los Basilios 1; ⏰noon-5pm & 8pm-12.30am) Away from the crowds of the old-city centre, this quiet but classy neighbourhood wine bar is run by knowledgeable bar staff and loved by locals who, in summer, fill the outdoor tables for evening drinks.

## Shopping

**★Mercatus** GIFTS & SOUVENIRS

(☎923 29 46 48; www.mercatus.usal.es; Calle de Cardenal Pla y Deniel; ⏰10am-8.15pm Mon-Sat, 10.15am-2pm Sun) The official shop of the University of Salamanca has a stunning range of stationery items, leather-bound books and other carefully selected reminders of your Salamanca visit.

## Information

**Oficina de Turismo** (☎923 21 83 42; www.salamanca.es; Plaza Mayor 32; ⏰9am-7pm Mon-Fri, 10am-7pm Sat, to 2pm Sun) An audio guide to city sights can be accessed on your smartphone via www.audioguiasalamanca.es.

## Getting There & Away

The **bus station** (☎923 236 717; www.estacionautobusessalamanca.es; Avenida de Filiberto Villalobos 71) is a 10-minute walk northwest of the Plaza Mayor. Buses include the following destinations: Madrid (regular/express €18/26, 2½ to three hours, hourly), Ávila (€9, 1½ hours, five daily), Segovia (€17, 2½ hours, four daily) and Valladolid (€11, 1½ hours, eight daily). There is a limited service to smaller towns with just one daily bus – except on Sunday – to La Alberca (€6.50, around 1½ hours), with stops in the villages of the Sierra de Francia, such as Mogarraz and San Martín del Castañar.

Regular trains depart to Madrid's Chamartín station (from €18.50, 1½ to four hours), Ávila (€13, 1¼ hours) and Valladolid (from €9, 1½ hours). The train station is a 15-minute walk northeast of the centre, along Paseo de la Estación.

# Ciudad Rodrigo

POP 12,515

Close to the Portuguese border and away from well-travelled tourist routes, sleepy Ciudad Rodrigo is one of the prettier towns in western Castilla y León. It's an easy day trip from Salamanca, 80km away, but staying overnight within its walls enables you to better appreciate the town's medieval charm.

## Sights

**★Murallas** WALLS

FREE There are numerous stairs leading up onto the crumbling ramparts of the city walls that encircle the old town and which were built between the 12th and 15th centuries. You can follow their length for about 2.2km around the town for fabulous views.

**★Catedral de Santa María** CATHEDRAL

(www.catedralciudadrodrigo.com; Plaza de San Salvador 1; adult/concession €3/2.50, 4-6pm Sun free, tower €2; ⌚church & museum 11.30am-2pm Mon, 11.30am-2pm & 4-7pm Tue-Sat, noon-2pm & 4-6pm Sun) This elegant, weathered sandstone cathedral, begun in 1165, towers over the historic centre. Of particular interest are the **Puerta de las Cadenas**, with splendid Gothic reliefs of Old Testament figures; the elegant **Pórtico del Perdón**; and inside, the exquisite, carved-oak choir stalls. You can also climb the 142-step **tower** at 1.15pm on Saturday and Sunday.

**Plaza Mayor** SQUARE

The long, sloping Plaza Mayor is a fine centrepiece for this beautiful town. At the top of the hill, the double-storey arches of the **Casa Consistorial** are stunning, but the plaza's prettiest building is the **Casa del Marqués de Cerralbo**, an early 16th-century town house with a wonderful facade.

**Palacio de los Ávila y Tiedra** HISTORIC BUILDING

(Plaza del Conde 3; ⌚9am-7pm Mon-Sat)  The 16th-century Palacio de los Ávila y Tiedra boasts one of the town's most engaging plateresque facades – it's the pick of a handful of fine examples that surround the Plaza del Conde. While most of the building is off limits, you can wander in to admire the pretty, compact courtyard surrounded by columns.

## Festivals & Events

**Carnaval** CARNIVAL

(www.carnavaldeltoro.es; ⌚Feb) Celebrated with great enthusiasm in February. In addition to the outlandish fancy dress, you can witness (or join in) a colourful *encierro* (running of the bulls) and *capeas* (amateur bullfights).

## Sleeping & Eating

Head for Plaza Mayor, Rúa del Sol and the surrounding pedestrian streets for the best choice of restaurants.

**Hospedería Audiencia Real** HISTORIC HOTEL €€

(☎923 49 84 98; Plaza Mayor 17; d €45-85; ❄📶) Right on Plaza Mayor, this fine 16th-century inn has been beautifully reformed and retains a tangible historic feel with lovely exposed stone walls. Some rooms have wrought-iron furniture and several sport narrow balconies overlooking the square.

**★Parador Enrique II** HISTORIC HOTEL €€€

(☎923 46 01 50; www.parador.es; Plaza del Castillo 1; r €120-185; P❄@📶) Ciudad Rodrigo's premier address is a plushly renovated castle built into the town's western wall. Converted in 1931, it's the third-oldest *parador* in Spain. The views are good, the rooms brim with character and the delightful terraced gardens out back overlook the Río Agueda. The restaurant (mains €18 to €25, set menus from €28) is Ciudad Rodrigo's best.

**El Sanatorio** TAPAS €€

(☎923 46 10 54; Plaza Mayor 14; raciones & mains €5-16; ⌚11am-late) Dating from 1937, the interior here doubles as a fascinating social history of the town. The walls are papered floor to ceiling with B&W photos, mainly of the annual Carnaval and bullfights. The tapas and *raciones* are good: ask about the *farinato* (a rich, local pork sausage made with all manner of spices) – this version has a quail's egg inside.

### Information

**Oficina de Turismo de Ciudad Rodrigo** (☎923 49 84 00; www.turismociudadrodrigo.com; Plaza Mayor 27; ⏰10am-1.30pm & 4-7pm Sat & Sun Apr-Sep, hours vary Oct-Mar)

### Getting There & Away

From the **bus station** (☎923 46 10 36; Calle del Campo de Toledo) there are up to 13 daily services (fewer on weekends) to Salamanca (€7.45, one hour). For the Sierra de Francia, you'll need to go via Salamanca.

> **DON'T MISS**
>
> **A TOILET MUSEUM**
>
> Chamber pots, commodes, bed pans… Ciudad Rodrigo's **Museo del Orinal** (Chamber Pot Museum; ☎952 38 20 87; www.museodelorinal.es; Plaza Herrasti; adult/child under 10yr €2/free; ⏰11am-2pm Fri-Wed; 👪) may be located opposite the cathedral, but its theme is definitely more down to earth than sacred. This city is home to Spain's (possibly the world's) only museum dedicated to the not-so-humble chamber pot (or potty, as it is known in the UK). The private collection of former local resident José María del Arco comprises a staggering 1300 exhibits. Hailing from 27 countries, there are some truly historic pieces.

## Sierra de Francia

Hidden away in a remote corner of southwestern Castilla y León and until recently secluded for centuries, this mountainous region with wooded hillsides and stone-and-timber villages was once one of Spain's most godforsaken regions. Today it's among Castilla y León's best-kept secrets. Quiet mountain roads connect pretty villages that you could easily spend days exploring. Here, the pace of life remains relatively untouched by the modern world.

### Sights

The main tourist centre of the Sierra de Francia is La Alberca (p160). Having your own car enables you to immerse yourself in quiet villages such as **Mogarraz**, east of La Alberca, which has some of the most evocative old houses in the region. It's also famous for its *embutidos* (cured meats), as well as the more recent novelty of over 300 portraits of past and present residents, painted by local artist Florencio Maíllo and on display outside the family homes. The history of this extraordinary project dates from the 1960s, when poverty was rife and many locals were seeking work, mainly in South America – they needed identity cards and it is this that inspired the portraits.

**Miranda del Castañar**, further east, is similarly intriguing, strung out along a narrow ridge. But **San Martín del Castañar** is the most enchanting. It's a medieval world of half-timbered stone houses, flowers cascading from balconies, a bubbling stream and a small village bullring at the top of the town, next to the renovated castle with its historic cemetery. **Villanueva del Conde** is another pretty hamlet.

The main natural attraction of the region is the highest peak in the area, **Peña de Francia** (1732m). Topped by a monastery and reached by a sinuous 12km climb from close to La Alberca, it's a stunning place with views that extend east to the Sierra de Gredos, south into Extremadura and west towards Portugal. Watch for extravagantly horned Spanish ibex by the roadside.

### Sleeping & Eating

★**Abadía de San Martín** HOTEL €€
(☎923 43 73 50; www.hotelruralabadiadesanmartin.es; Calle Paipérez 24, San Martín del Castañar; d/ste from €60/85; 📶) Lovely, contemporary rooms in a converted old home in one of the Sierra de Francia's loveliest villages – what more could you ask for?

**Hotel Spa Villa de Mogarraz** HOTEL €€
(☎923 41 81 80; www.hotelspamogarraz.com; Calle Miguel Ángel Maíllo 54, Mogarraz; r €80-180; ❄📶) At the pedestrian entrance to gorgeous Mogarraz, this artfully converted spa-hotel has amply sized rooms, some with wooden beams, others with exposed stone walls. We especially like the views down the cobblestone main street from room 125.

### Getting There & Around

Roads lead into the Sierra de Francia from Ciudad Rodrigo (SA220), Salamanca (CL512 and SA210) and Béjar (SA220). The drive south into Extremadura through the dreamy Valle de

## WHAT'S COOKING IN CASTILLA Y LEÓN?

Castilla y León's cuisine owes everything to climate. There's no better way to fortify yourself against the bitterly cold winters of the high plateau than with *cordero asado* (roast lamb), a speciality all over the province; or *cochinillo* (roast suckling pig), a particular speciality of Segovia that you can try at Casa Duque (p165). Other regional delights include *chuleton de Ávila* (T-bone steak, from Ávila) available in the city's traditional restaurants, such as Méson del Rastro (p152). Still on the meaty route, it's a fact that an estimated 60% of Spain's famous *jamón ibérico* (cured ham) comes from the Salamanca region, with the best coming from Guijuelo. Other local specialties include *morcilla de Burgos* (Burgos blood sausage), which you can try at Cervecería Morito (p189), or *cocido maragato* (meat-and-chickpea stew, eaten in the reverse order to everywhere else in Spain; try the latter at Astorga's Restaurante Las Termas (p184).

las Batuecas is spectacular. Just beyond La Alberca, a sweeping panorama of cascading lower mountain ranges opens up before you. The road corkscrews down into the valley. Time your visit for spring when purple heather and brilliant yellow rapeseed blanket the hillsides.

The only public transport here is with Autoacres Cosme (www.autocarescosme.com), which runs twice-daily services between the towns of the Sierra de Francia and Salamanca (€6.50) on weekdays, with just one service each on Saturday and Sunday.

## La Alberca

POP 1105 / ELEV 1048M

La Alberca is one of the largest and most beautifully preserved of Sierra de Francia's villages; a historic huddle of narrow alleys flanked by gloriously ramshackle houses built of stone, wood beams and plaster. Look for the date they were built (typically the late 18th century) carved into the door lintels. It's also the Sierra de Francia's most popular village – can get busy on weekends.

The **Plaza Mayor**, sloping and ramshackle, is a gorgeous spot with a stone cross and fountain as a centrepiece; there's a market here on Saturday mornings. Just south of the Plaza Mayor, the 15th-century Gothic **Iglesia de Nuestra Señora de la Asunción** has an elaborately carved pulpit.

### Sleeping & Eating

**★Hotel Doña Teresa** HOTEL €€
(☎923 41 53 08; www.hoteldeteresa.com; Carretera de Mogarraz; r €63-99; P❄📶) Lovely Doña Teresa is a perfect modern fit for the village's old-world charm. The large rooms combine character (wooden beams and exposed stone) with all the necessary mod cons; some open onto a garden. The owners also run a spa 1.5km away, with treatments available at reduced rates for guests.

**Restaurante El Encuentro** SPANISH €€
(☎923 41 53 10; www.restauranteelencuentro.es; Calle de Tablado 8; mains €9-18, set menus €15-18; ⏲1-4pm & 8.30-11pm Thu-Tue) The consistently good reports from travellers made us sit up and take notice of this place. The decor is pretty average but the food is excellent, from the *albóndigas de ternera* meatballs to the oxtail, pigs trotters and pheasant. Spaniards love this place for the authenticity of the cooking and no-nonsense service.

### Information

**Oficina de Turismo** (☎923 41 52 91; www.laalberca.com; Plaza Mayor 11; ⏲10am-2pm & 4.30-6.30pm Tue-Sat, 10.30am-2pm Sun) Useful advice on walking routes through town.

### Getting There & Away

Buses travel between La Alberca and Salamanca (€6.50, one to 1½ hours) twice daily on weekdays and once a day on weekends.

# THE CENTRAL PLATEAU

There's something soul-stirring about the high *meseta* (plateau) with its seemingly endless horizon. But from the plains spring the delightful towns of the Castilian heartland – magical Segovia, energetic Valladolid, the Romanesque glories of Zamora and the exceptional cathedral of Palencia. Throw in some lovely mountain scenery in the Montaña Palentina, the chance to see wolves in the Sierra de la Culebra, and the beguiling village of Puebla de Sanabria, and you'll want to spend as much time in this region as you can.

# Segovia

POP 51,685 / ELEV 1002M

Unesco World Heritage–listed Segovia has always had a whiff of legend about it, not least in the myths that the city was founded by Hercules or by the son of Noah. It may also have something to do with the fact that nowhere else in Spain is such a stunning Roman-era monument (the soaring aqueduct) surviving in the heart of a vibrant modern city. Or maybe it's because art really has imitated life Segovia-style – Walt Disney is said to have modelled the *Sleeping Beauty* castle in California's Disneyland on Segovia's Alcázar. Whatever it is, the effect is stunning: a magical city of warm terracotta and sandstone hues set amid the rolling hills of Castilla, against the backdrop of the Sierra de Guadarrama.

## Sights

**★Acueducto** LANDMARK

Segovia's most recognisable symbol is El Acueducto (Roman Aqueduct), an 894m-long engineering wonder that looks like an enormous comb plunged into Segovia. First raised here by the Romans in the 1st century CE, the aqueduct was built with not a drop of mortar to hold together more than 20,000 uneven granite blocks. It's made up of 163 arches and, at its highest point in Plaza del Azoguejo, rises to 28m.

It was originally part of a complex system of aqueducts and underground canals that brought water from the mountains more than 15km away. Its pristine condition is attributable to a major restoration project in the 1990s. For a different perspective, climb the stairs next to the aqueduct that begin behind the tourist office.

**★Catedral** CATHEDRAL

(921 46 22 05; www.turismodesegovia.com; Plaza Mayor; adult/child €3/free, Sun morning free, tower tour €4; 9am-9.30pm Apr-Oct, 9.30am-6.30pm Nov-Mar, tower tours 10.30pm, noon, 1.30pm & 4pm year-round, plus 6pm & 7.30pm Apr-Oct) Started in 1525 on the site of a former chapel, Segovia's cathedral is a powerful expression of Gothic architecture that took almost 200 years to complete. The austere three-nave interior is anchored by an imposing choir stall and enlivened by 20-odd chapels, including the **Capilla del Cristo del Consuelo**, with its magnificent Romanesque doorway, and the **Capilla de la Piedad**, containing an important altarpiece by Juan de Juni. Join an hour-long guided tour to climb the tower for fabulous views.

**★Alcázar** CASTLE

(921 46 07 59; www.alcazardesegovia.com; Plaza de la Reina Victoria Eugenia; adult/concession/child €5.50/3.50/free, tower €2.50, audio guide €3; 10am-8pm Apr-Oct, to 6pm Nov-Mar; ) Rapunzel towers, turrets topped with slate witches' hats and a deep moat at its base make the Alcázar a prototypical fairy-tale castle – so much so that its design inspired Walt Disney's vision of *Sleeping Beauty's*

WORTH A TRIP

### GUIJUELO & JAMÓN

Many experts agree that Spain's best *jamón* comes from Guijuelo and the surrounding area. Fittingly, the town's interactive **Museo de la Industria Chacinera** (Museo Guijuelo; 923 59 19 01; Calle Nueva 1; adult/child €2/1; 10.30am-2pm Mon-Sat) is dedicated to *jamón* with videos demonstrating its production, exhibits on the special *cerdos ibéricos* (Iberian pigs) that form the centrepiece of this industry, and, not for the squeamish, the ritual of *matanza* (the slaughter). Displays and videos are in Spanish only.

A handful of Guijuelo *jamón* producers offer guided visits of their factories. There are no fixed times, so you'll need to ring or email ahead to find out when they have groups leaving. Guijuelo's **oficina de turismo** (923 58 04 72; www.guijuelo.es; Plaza Mayor 11-12; 9am-3pm & 4-7pm Mon-Fri, 9am-3pm Sat) also has a list of those offering tours, including respected producer **Simón Martín** (923 58 01 29; www.simonmartin.es; Calle de Sierra de Herrero; tour per person €20-30; by appointment). Part shop, part *jamón*-tasting centre, **Alma de Ibérico** (923 58 09 44; www.almadeiberico.com; Calle de Alfonso XIII 18; tapas from €3; 10am-7pm Mon-Fri, 10am-3.30pm Sat & Sun) is where you can try local *jamón*. To buy some take-home *jamón ibérico de bellota en lonchas* (ham made from acorn-fed pigs), try **Sabor Guijuelo** (923 58 12 87; Calle Fragua 2; 10am-6.30pm).

Guijuelo lies just off the A66/E803, 50km south of Salamanca, or 20km north of Béjar.

## Segovia

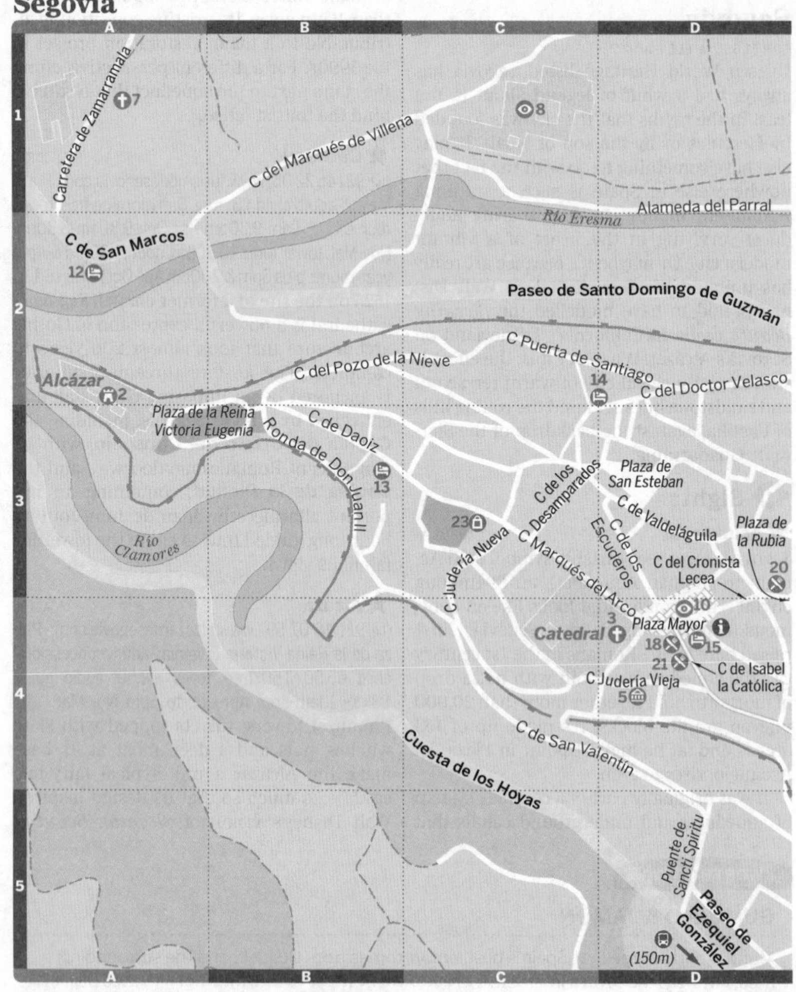


castle. Fortified since Roman days, the site takes its name from the Arabic *al-qasr* (fortress). It was rebuilt in the 13th and 14th centuries, but the whole lot burned down in 1862. What you see today is an evocative, over-the-top reconstruction of the original.

Highlights include the **Sala de las Piñas**, with its ceiling of 392 pineapple-shaped 'stalactites', and the **Sala de Reyes**, featuring a three-dimensional frieze of 52 sculptures of kings who fought during the Reconquista. The views from the summit of the Torre de Juan II, which was restored in 2016, are truly exceptional.

**Plaza Mayor** SQUARE

Watched over by the cathedral, shady Plaza Mayor is the nerve centre of old Segovia, lined by an eclectic assortment of buildings, arcades and cafes and with an open pavilion in its centre.

**Plaza de San Martín** SQUARE

This is one of the most captivating small plazas in Segovia. The square is presided over by a statue of Juan Bravo; the 14th-century **Torreón de Lozoya** (921 46 24 61; 6-9pm Tue-Fri, noon-2pm & 6-9pm Sat & Sun) FREE, a tower that now houses exhibitions; and the **Iglesia de San Martín** (10am-6pm Mon-Sat)

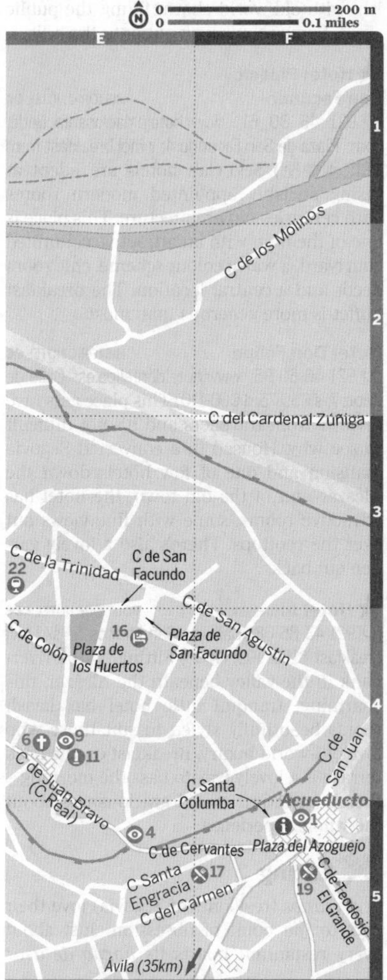


## Segovia

**Top Sights**

1 Acueducto ... F5
2 Alcázar ... A2
3 Catedral ... D4

**Sights**

4 Casa de los Picos ... E5
5 Centro Didáctico de la Judería ... D4
6 Iglesia de San Martín ... E4
7 Iglesia de Vera Cruz ... A1
8 Monasterio de Santa María del Parral ... C1
9 Plaza de San Martín ... E4
10 Plaza Mayor ... D4
11 Torreón de Lozoya ... E4

**Sleeping**

12 Hotel Alcázar ... A2
13 Hotel Don Felipe ... B3
14 Hotel Exe Casa de Los Linajes ... D2
15 Hotel Infanta Isabel ... D4
16 Hotel Palacio San Facundo ... E4

**Eating**

17 Casa Duque ... F5
18 Limón y Menta ... D4
19 Mesón de Cándido ... F5
20 Mesón José María ... D3
21 Restaurante El Fogón Sefardí ... D4

**Drinking & Nightlife**

22 Canavan's Theatre ... E3

**Shopping**

23 Montón de Trigo Montón de Paja ... C3

FREE, a Romanesque jewel with a Mudéjar tower and arched gallery. Just down the hill is the **Casa de los Picos** (www.easdsegovia.com; Calle de Juan Bravo), a grand Renaissance mansion with a diamond-patterned facade.

**Centro Didáctico de la Judería** MUSEUM
(921 46 23 96; www.juderia.turismodesegovia.com; Calle de la Judería Vieja 12; €1, free Wed; 10am-2pm Mon & Tue, 10am-2pm & 4-6pm Wed & Fri, 10am-1pm & 4-6pm Thu & Sat, 10am-1pm Sun, guided tours 1pm Thu, Sat & Sun) This interpretation centre and museum in Segovia's old Jewish quarter provides a fascinating history of the Jewish community in Segovia. It occupies the former 15th-century home of one of the community's most important members, Abraham Seneor. The adjacent **Iglesia de Corpus Cristi** occupies the site of Segovia's ancient synagogue.

**Iglesia de Vera Cruz** CHURCH
(921 43 14 75; Carretera de Zamarramala; adult/child €2/free, Tue free; 4-7pm Tue, 10.30am-1.30pm & 4-7pm Wed-Sun Apr–mid-Oct, 4-6pm Tue, 10.30am-1.30pm & 4-6pm Wed-Sun mid-Oct–Mar) This 12-sided church is one of the best preserved of its kind in Europe. Built in the early 13th century by the Knights Templar and based on Jerusalem's Church of the Holy Sepulchre, it once housed a piece of the Vera Cruz (True Cross), which now rests in the nearby village church of Zamarramala (on view only at Easter). The two-storey chamber in the circular nave (the inner temple) is where the knights' secret rites took place.

**Monasterio de Santa María del Parral** MONASTERY
(☎921 43 12 98; Calle del Marqués de Villena; by donation; ⊙guided tours 11am & 5pm Wed-Sun) Ring the bell to see part of the cloister and church; the latter is a proud, flamboyant Gothic structure. The monks chant a Gregorian Mass at noon on Sundays, and at 1pm daily in summer.

## Festivals & Events

**Titirimundi International Puppet Festival** THEATRE
(www.titirimundi.es/festival; ⊙mid-May; ) A week-long festival that celebrates puppetry and puppet theatre with shows and street events throughout the city.

**Fiestas de San Juan y San Pedro** RELIGIOUS
(⊙24-29 Jun; ) On San Juan's day (29 June), a pilgrimage takes place to a hermitage outside town. Throughout the six days of festivities, there are parades, concerts and bullfights.

## Sleeping

**Hotel Infanta Isabel** HOTEL €
(☎921 46 13 00; www.hotelinfantaisabel.com; Plaza Mayor 12; r from €45; ) The colonnaded building fits well with the hotel's interior of period furnishings in most of the spacious rooms. The style may be classic in orientation, but there's a lovely sense of light and space here and most bathrooms have been recently updated. Some rooms overlook Plaza Mayor.

**Hotel Exe Casa de Los Linajes** HOTEL €
(☎921 41 48 10; www.exehotels.com; Calle del Doctor Valesco 9; r without/with views €57/65; ) The rooms here are large and stylish, with old-world charm filling the public areas. Some rooms look out onto the hills.

★**Hotel Palacio San Facundo** HISTORIC HOTEL €€
(☎921 46 30 61; www.hotelpalaciosanfacundo.com; Plaza de San Facundo 4; r incl breakfast from €81; ) Segovia's hotels are adept at fusing stylishly appointed modern rooms with centuries-old architecture. This place is one of the best, with an attractive columned courtyard, a warm colour scheme, chic room decor and a central location. The breakfast buffet is more generous than most.

**Hotel Don Felipe** HISTORIC HOTEL €€
(☎921 46 60 95; www.hoteldonfelipe.es; Calle de Daoiz 7; s €55-75, d €60-110) This place gets rave reviews from travellers and it's not difficult to see why. Housed in a converted Segovia mansion and one of few hotels down the Alcázar end of the old town, the hotel has attractive rooms, some with fine views out over the rooftops. There's also a lovely garden out back.

★**Hotel Alcázar** BOUTIQUE HOTEL €€€
(☎921 43 85 68; Calle de San Marcos 5; s/d incl breakfast €150/195; ) Sitting by the riverbank in the valley beneath the Alcázar, this charming, tranquil little hotel has lavish rooms beautifully styled to suit those who love old-world luxury. Breakfast on the back terrace is a lovely way to pass the morning – there's an intimacy and graciousness about the whole experience.

## Eating

*Segovianos* (residents of Segovia) love their pigs to the point of obsession. Just about every restaurant boasts its *horno de asar*

DON'T MISS

### A SPANISH VERSAILLES

Originally built for the Bourbon King Felipe V, **La Granja de San Ildefonso** (www.patrimonionacional.es; Sierra de Guadarrama; gardens free, Palacio Real adult/child €9/4, fountains €4, free for EU citizens 3-6pm Wed & Thu Oct-Mar & 5-8pm Wed & Thu Apr-Sep; ⊙10am-8pm Tue-Sun Apr-Sep, to 6pm Tue-Sun Oct-Mar; ) in the foothills of the Sierra de Guadarrama, this palace was intended to recreate his own miniature Versailles, the palace of his French grandfather, Louis XIV. The 300-room **Palacio Real**, once a favoured summer residence for Spanish royalty, is impressive and includes the colourful **Museo de Tapices** (Tapestry Museum). The magnificent, elaborate baroque gardens – famous for their 28 extravagant fountains depicting ancient myths – date from 1720.

If you time your visit for Wednesday, Saturday or Sunday at 5.30pm you can see the fountains in action. There's also a maze. Up to a dozen daily buses to La Granja depart regularly from Segovia's bus station (€2.40, 20 minutes).

DON'T MISS

## CASTILLA Y LEÓN'S BEST CASTLES

While Segovia's Disneyesque Alcázar and the wonderful fortified walls of Ávila may get all the attention, lonely hilltop castles are something of a regional speciality. Top choices include the following:

**Coca** (☎617 573 554; www.castillodecoca.com; Coca; guided tours €2.70; ⌚tours 10.30am-1pm & 4.30-6pm Mon-Fri, 11am-1pm & 4-6pm Sat & Sun) An all-brick, virtuoso piece of Gothic-Mudéjar architecture 50km northwest of Segovia.

**Peñafiel** (p193) One of the longest in Spain; now a wine museum.

**Castillo de Gormaz** (p200) A 10th-century, Muslim-era fortress with 21 towers; 14km south of El Burgo de Osma.

**Castillo de Pedraza** (p166) An unusually intact outer wall northeast of Segovia.

**Turégano** (☎634 460215; €2; ⌚11am-2pm & 5-8pm Jul & Aug, hours vary rest of year) A unique 15th-century castle-church complex; 30km north of Segovia.

**Peñaranda de Duero** (☎947 552 063; Calle del Castillo; adult/child €2/1; ⌚4.30-6.30pm Tue & Wed, noon-2pm & 4.30-6pm Thu-Sat, noon-2pm Sun Jun-Sep, 3.30-5.30pm Fri, 11am-2pm & 3.30-5.30pm Sat & Sun Oct-May) This elongated 10th-century fortress is a forest of turrets and crenellations.

(roast ovens). The main speciality is *cochinillo asado* (roast suckling pig), but *judiones de la granja* (butter beans with pork chunks) also loom large.

**Limón y Menta** BAKERY €
(☎921 46 21 41; www.pastelerialimonymenta.com; Calle de Isabel la Católica 2; cakes from €2.50; ⌚9am-9.30pm Mon-Fri, to 8.30pm Sat & Sun) This patisserie just off Plaza Mayor is a good place to indulge in your passion for *ponche segoviano*, a rich, lemon-infused sponge cake coated with marzipan and topped in icing sugar with a distinctive crisscross pattern.

**★Restaurante El Fogón Sefardí** JEWISH €€
(☎921 46 62 50; www.lacasamudejar.com; Calle de Isabel La Católica 8; tapas from €3.75, mains €13-22, set menus €20-35; ⌚1.30-4.30pm & 8.30-11.30pm) Located within the Hospedería La Gran Casa Mudéjar, this is one of the most original places in town. Sephardic Jewish cuisine is served either on the intimate patio or in the splendid dining hall with original 15th-century Mudéjar flourishes. The theme in the bar is equally diverse. Stop here for a taste of the award-winning tapas. Reservations recommended.

**★Mesón José María** CASTILIAN €€
(☎921 46 11 11; www.restaurantejosemaria.com; Calle del Cronista Lecea 11; mains €15-27, set menu €53; ⌚restaurant 1-4pm & 8-11.30pm, bar 9am-1am Sun-Thu, 10am-2am Fri & Sat; 👪) Offers fine bar tapas and five dining rooms serving exquisite *cochinillo asado* and other local specialities – most of which, including the suckling pig, are displayed in the window. The bar is standing-room only at lunchtime.

**Mesón de Cándido** GRILL €€
(☎921 42 81 03; www.mesondecandido.es; Plaza del Azoguejo 5; mains €12-26) Set in a delightful 18th-century building in the shadow of the aqueduct, Mesón de Cándido is famous for its *cochinillo asado* and game dishes such as pheasant.

**★Casa Duque** SPANISH €€€
(☎921 46 24 87; www.restauranteduque.es; Calle de Cervantes 12; mains €22-33, set menu €40; ⌚12.30-4.30pm & 8.30-11.30pm) *Cochinillo asado* has been served at this atmospheric *mesón* (tavern) since the 1890s. For the uninitiated, try the *menú de degustación*, which includes *cochinillo*. Downstairs is the informal *cueva* (cave), where you can get tapas and full-bodied *cazuelas* (stews).

## Drinking & Nightlife

**Canavan's Theatre** CLUB
(☎921 46 02 52; www.facebook.com/canavanstheatre; Plaza de la Rubia; ⌚midnight-6.30am Thu-Sat) This is no cheesy disco – the decor is sumptuous, with exquisite friezes, flocked wallpaper, chandeliers and an overall extravagant theatrical feel.

## Shopping

**Montón de Trigo Montón de Paja** GIFTS & SOUVENIRS
(☎921 46 07 69; www.montondetrigomontondepaja.com; Plaza de la Merced 1; ⊙11.30am-2pm & 3.30-7pm Mon-Fri, 11.30am-3pm & 4-7.30pm Sat & Sun, longer hours in summer) With handcrafted handbags, jewellery, block-prints of Segovia and a host of other artsy, locally made items, this shop is ideal for creative gifts.

## Information

**Centro de Recepción de Visitantes** (☎921 46 67 20; www.turismodesegovia.com; Plaza del Azoguejo 1; tour per person €10-17; ⊙10am-8pm Mon-Sat, to 7pm Sun Apr-Sep, 10am-6.30pm Mon-Sat, to 5pm Sun Oct-Mar) Segovia's main tourist office runs at least two guided tours of the city's monumental core daily. Reserve ahead.

**Oficina de Turismo** (☎921 46 03 34; www.segoviaturismo.es; Plaza Mayor 10; ⊙9.30am-2pm & 5-8pm Mon-Sat, 9.30am-5pm Sun Jul–mid-Sep, 9.30am-2pm & 4-7pm Mon-Sat, to 5pm Sun mid-Sep–Jun) Information on the wider region.

## Getting There & Away

The bus station is just off Paseo de Ezequiel González. Buses depart to Madrid (€9, 1½ hours, hourly), Ávila (€7.50, one hour, eight daily) and Salamanca (€17, 2½ hours, four daily), among other destinations.

The high-speed Avant train from Madrid (from €14, 28 minutes) deposits you at the Segovia-Guiomar station, 5km from the aqueduct.

## Getting Around

Bus 9 does a circuit through the historic centre, bus 8 goes to Segovia train station and bus 11 goes to Segovia-Guiomar station. All services cost €1.30 and leave from outside the aqueduct.

# Around Segovia

## Pedraza de la Sierra

POP 360

The captivating walled village of Pedraza de la Sierra, about 37km northeast of Segovia, is eerily quiet during the week; its considerable number of restaurants, bars and eclectic shops spring to life with the swarms of weekend visitors. It's a gorgeous place – one of the prettiest villages in this part of the country.

On the first and second Sunday in July, Pedraza hosts the atmospheric **Concierto de las Velas** (☎921 50 99 60; www.pedraza.net/concierto-de-las-velas; admission free, concerts from €50; ⊙Jul) when the electricity shuts down and live classical music is performed by candlelight. It's free to come here to see the town lit with candles; concerts cost extra.

## Sights

The evocative 14th-century **Plaza Mayor** is noteworthy for its ancient columned arcades, best admired just before sunset. At the far (northwestern) end of town – go any further and you'll fall into the valley – the lonely **Castillo de Pedraza** (Castillo de Ignazio Zuluaga; ☎653 602277; www.elcastillodepedraza.com; Plaza del Castillo; adult/concession €6/4; ⊙11am-2pm & 5-8pm Wed-Sun Jun-Sep, 11am-2pm & 4-7pm Wed-Sun Oct-May) dates to the 13th century.

## Sleeping & Eating

★**Hospedería de Santo Domingo** INN €€
(☎921 50 99 71; www.hospederiadesantodomingo.com; Calle Matadero 3; s €85-110, d €95-130, ste €110-155; ❄📶) This excellent *hospedería* (inn) has terrific rooms decked out in warm ochre and earth colours. Most have large terraces overlooking the low hills nearby, criss-crossed with drystone walls.

**El Hotel de la Villa** HOTEL €€
(☎921 50 86 51; www.elhoteldelavilla.com; Calle de Calzada 5; s/d from €80/110; 📶) An astonishing breadth of rooms at this excellent place range from tiled floors, wooden beams and wrought-iron furnishings to frilly four-poster beds, floorboards and bright colours.

**El Yantar de Pedraza** SPANISH €€
(☎921 50 98 42; www.facebook.com/yantar.dedraza; Plaza Mayor; mains €12-25; ⊙1-4.30pm Thu-Sun) With a lovely setting overlooking Plaza Mayor from its upstairs balcony, El Yantar does near-perfect *cordero asado* and *cochinillo* and the many repeat customers tell us all we need to know about the quality. Its set menus are excellent value, but other menu highlights include the light salads, the homemade *croquetas* (croquettes) and local sheep's cheese.

**La Olma de Pedraza** SPANISH €€
(☎921 50 99 81; www.laolma.com; Plaza del Álamo 1; mains €12-24; ⊙1.30-4pm Sun-Thu, 1.30-4pm & 9-11pm Fri & Sat) On a small square just west

of Plaza Mayor, this lovely place feels every bit like the rural bastion of traditional cooking that it is, with warm service to match. Besides the usual, perfectly cooked roasted meats, try its *croquetas de setas* (wild mushroom croquettes); otherwise just let staff choose the dishes that play to its strengths.

## Information

**Oficina de Turismo** (☎921 50 86 66; www.pedraza.info; Calle Real 3; ⊙11am-2.30pm & 3-7.30pm Wed-Sun)

## Getting There & Away

Pedraza is just north of the N110 and best reached by car. Bus services are sporadic with just a couple of weekly services from Segovia.

### VALLADOLID CARD

A terrific way to save your euros, the Valladolid Card (www.vallodolid.com/vallodolid-card; adult/child €8/6) allows free access to a number of museums – including the Museo Nacional de Escultura, Casa-Museo de Colón, Museo Patio Herreriano and the Catedral and its museum – plus free travel on the **Bus Turístico de Valladolid** (☎983 33 03 59; www.auvasa.es/auv_busturistico.asp; Acera de Recoletos; adult/child €8/6; ⊙hourly 5-7pm Fri, noon-1pm & 5-7pm Sat & Sun Apr-Sep, hourly 5-6pm Fri, noon-1pm & 5-6pm Sat & Sun Oct-Mar) over a 24-hour period. The card can be purchased at either of the two tourist offices.

# Valladolid

POP 298,865

Valladolid is a lively provincial Spanish city and a convenient gateway to northern Spain. The city has a rich history – it was Spain's capital for a time, and its story is peopled by kings and queens, Cervantes and Christopher Columbus (Cristobal Colón in Spanish). These days, it's an attractive place with a very Spanish character, striking monuments, some excellent museums, and a buzzing culinary scene.

## Sights

**★Museo Nacional de Escultura** MUSEUM
(☎983 25 03 75; www.culturaydeporte.gob.es/mnescultura/inicio.html; Calle de San Gregorio 2; adult/concession €3/1.50, Sun & 4-7.30pm Fri & Sat free; ⊙10am-2pm & 4-7.30pm Tue-Sat, 10am-2pm Sun) Spain's premier showcase of polychrome wood sculpture is housed in the former **Colegio de San Gregorio** (1496), a flamboyant Isabelline Gothic–style building where exhibition rooms line an exquisite, two-storey galleried courtyard. Works by Alonso de Berruguete, Juan de Juní and Gregorio Fernández are the star attractions. Don't miss Fernández' painfully realistic sculpture of the dead Christ in Room 15 or the choir stalls in Room 8. And don't forget to look up – some of the ceilings are extraordinary.

**★Casa-Museo de Colón** MUSEUM
(☎983 29 13 53; Calle de Colón; adult/child €2/free, Wed adult €1; ⊙10am-2pm & 5-8.30pm Tue-Sun; 🚻) The Casa-Museo de Colón is a superb museum spread over four floors. It has interactive exhibits, as well as wonderful old maps that take you on a journey through Christopher Columbus' trips to the Americas. The top floor describes Valladolid in the days of the great explorer (who died here in 1506).

**Plaza de San Pablo** SQUARE
This open square is dominated by the exquisite **Iglesia de San Pablo** (☎983 351 748; ⊙7.30am-1.30pm & 7-9.30pm Mon-Sat, 8am-2pm & 6-9.30pm Sun), which hesas one of northern Spain's most extraordinary church facades. Excepting some side chapels, the church's interior is elegant and simple by comparison. Also here is the **Palacio de Pimentel** (⊙10am-2pm & 5-7pm Tue-Sat) FREE, the birthplace of Felipe II.

**Catedral** CATHEDRAL
(☎983 30 43 62; Calle Arribas 1; adult/concession €3/1.50; ⊙10am-1.30pm & 4.30-7pm Tue-Fri, 10am-2pm Sat, 11.45am-1.30pm Sun, tours every 45min) Valladolid's 16th-century cathedral is not Castilla's finest, but it does have an extravagant altarpiece by Juan de Juní and a processional monstrance by Juan de Arfe in the attached **Museo Diocesano y Catedralicio** (Calle Arribas 1; adult/concession €3/1.50; ⊙10am-1.30pm & 4.30-7pm Tue-Fri, 10am-2pm Sat, 11.45am-1.30pm Sun). Guided tours (adult/concession €5/4) of the cathedral and bell tower last 45 minutes and the views are fabulous; combined with a guided visit to the museum (adult/concession €8/6) it takes two hours. (You can visit the cathedral and museum on your own, but not the tower.)

# Valladolid

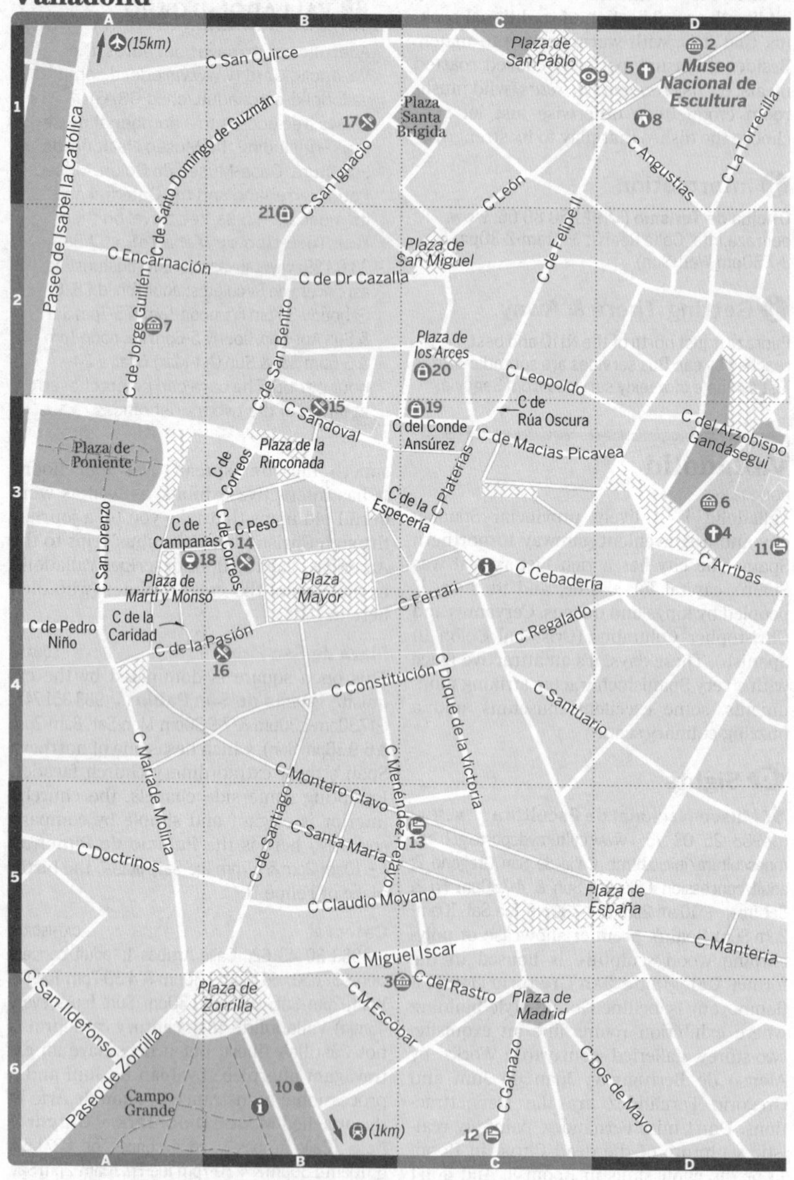


## Casa de Cervantes

MUSEUM

(☎983 30 88 10; www.mecd.gob.es/museocasacervantes; Calle del Rastro; adult/child under 12yr €3/free, Sun free; ⏰9.30am-3pm Tue-Sat, 10am-3pm Sun) Cervantes was briefly imprisoned in Valladolid; his house is happily preserved behind a quiet little garden. The museum is a mix of period furnishings that date back to Cervantes' day as well as many of his personal effects and examples of his writings.

## Museo Patio Herreriano

GALLERY

(☎983 36 29 08; www.museoph.org; Calle de Jorge Guillén 6; ⏰11am-2pm & 5-8pm Tue-Fri, 11am-8pm

Sat, to 3pm Sun) FREE Dedicated to post-WWI Spanish art, this surprising museum contains works by Salvador Dalí, Joan Miró, Basque sculptor Eduardo Chillida, Jorge Oteiza, Antoni Tàpies and Esteban Vicente, all arrayed around the cloisters of a former monastery.

## Valladolid

**Top Sights**

1 Casa-Museo de Colón ........ F3
2 Museo Nacional de Escultura ........ D1

**Sights**

3 Casa de Cervantes ........ C6
4 Catedral ........ D3
5 Iglesia de San Pablo ........ D1
6 Museo Diocesano y Catedralicio ........ D3
7 Museo Patio Herreriano ........ A2
8 Palacio de Pimentel ........ D1
9 Plaza de San Pablo ........ C1

**Activities, Courses & Tours**

10 Bus Turístico de Valladolid ........ B6

**Sleeping**

11 Hotel El Coloquio ........ D3
12 Hotel Gareus ........ C6
13 Hotel Mozart ........ C5

**Eating**

14 El Corcho ........ B3
15 Hermanos Hoyos ........ B3
16 Los Zagales de Abadía ........ B4
17 Martín Quiroga ........ B1

**Drinking & Nightlife**

18 Café de la Comedia ........ A3

**Shopping**

19 Alimentación Panta ........ C3
20 El Gato Que Bebia Cerveza ........ C2
21 Majuelos Singulares ........ B2

## Sleeping

**★Hotel Mozart** HOTEL €

(983 29 77 77; www.hotelmozart.net; Calle Menéndez Pelayo 7; s/d €60/72; ) This is an extremely well-priced hotel, given the quality of its refurbished rooms and the location. Here you'll find king-size beds, plush, earth-colour furnishings and fabrics, polished parquet floors, dazzling marble bathrooms and space enough for a comfortable armchair. The entrance has a whiff of grandeur about it as well – which contributes to the surprise of the budget-bracket price.

**Hotel Gareus** BOUTIQUE HOTEL €€

(983 21 43 33; www.hotelgareus.com; Calle de Colmenares 2; r from €74; ) Polished floorboards, warm colours and creative lighting make these rooms some of the best in Valladolid. The service is similarly warm and welcoming and the place has a quiet sophistication. The location, just a 10-minute walk from the Plaza Mayor, is also excellent.

**Hotel El Coloquio** HOTEL €€
(☎983 04 40 35; https://elcoloquio.zenithoteles.com/es; Plaza de la Universidad 11; s/d from €59/75; P❄📶) Attractive rooms with all manner of interesting angles dominate this four-star place that inhabits a reconstructed 19th-century building overlooking one of the quieter and prettier squares in downtown Valladolid. It's right next to the cathedral, the rooms have double glazing and service is excellent. Helpfully, the website lists the rooms that have views of the square.

## Eating

Valladolid's liveliest eat streets are west of the Plaza Mayor, especially Calle de la Pasión, Calle de la Caridad and Calle de Correos.

**El Corcho** TAPAS €
(Calle de Correos 2; tostas from €2, set menu €18; ⏰1-4pm & 8-11.30pm) This bar, on the city's top street for tapas bars, wins the prize of public opinion for its excellent selection of *tostas* (toasts) with tasty toppings.

**Hermanos Hoyos** TAPAS €
(☎670 721908; www.hermanoshoyos.es; Mercado del Val, Puesto 7, Calle Sandoval; tapas from €3.30, mains €6.50-13; ⏰9am-11pm Mon-Wed, 8.30am-12.30am Thu-Sat, 10am-4pm Sun) Inside Valladolid's main produce market, this respected producer of fine *jamón* from the Salamanca region has set up a casual bar with a range of *tostas* and other tapas with a *jamón* theme. The mains are all about pork, from meatballs or ribs to steaks and salads.

★**Martín Quiroga** CASTILIAN €€
(☎605 787117; Calle San Ignacio 17; mains €15-21; ⏰noon-4pm & 8pm-midnight Mon & Wed-Sat, noon-4pm Tue) With just four tables and a typical waiting list of a month, you might imagine that this extraordinarily high-quality gastrobar would have prices to match. It doesn't. There is no menu – dishes depend on what's seasonally fresh and available from the market that day – but there's plenty of choice. Special diets are catered to with advance notice. Reservations essential.

**Los Zagales de Abadía** CASTILIAN €€
(☎983 38 08 92; www.loszagales.com; Calle de la Pasión 13; mains €6-20, set menus €20-37; ⏰1-4pm & 7-11pm Mon-Sat, 1-4pm Sun) This bar is much-awarded for its creative tapas – they've done well not just at local competitions but nationwide. To see what all the fuss is about, try the Menú Maridaje: nine of the prize-winning tapas for €38. Restaurant servings are generous and the food excellent.

## Drinking & Nightlife

Central Valladolid brims with welcoming bars and cafes. The richest pickings are in the blocks west of the Plaza Mayor, especially Plaza de Martí y Monsó, which really gets going after midnight.

**Café de la Comedia** COCKTAIL BAR
(☎983 34 00 80; Plaza de Martí y Monsó 4; ⏰3.30pm-late) Decor here is suitably comedic, with Laurel and Hardy on the screen and Chaplin pics (and similar) decorating the walls. It's a reliable, popular choice that goes beyond fads and serves good cocktails and wines by the glass.

## Information

**Oficina de Turismo** (☎983 21 93 10; www.info.valladolid.es; Acera de Recoletos; ⏰9.30am-2pm & 5-8pm Mon-Sat, 9.30am-3pm Sun Jul–mid-Sep, 9.30am-2pm & 4-7pm Mon-Sat, 9.30am-3pm Sun mid-Sep–Jun)

DON'T MISS

### SHOPPING FOR A PICNIC

With the famed wines of Ribera del Duero being produced just down the road, Valladolid is a good place to pick up some local *vino*, whether for a picnic or a gift back home. **Majuelos Singulares** (☎983 37 09 74; www.majuelossingulares.com; Calle de San Ignacio 9; ⏰noon-1.45pm & 6-8.15pm Mon-Fri, 10am-2pm Sat) has carefully chosen wines from the Ribera del Duero and beyond. Not far away, **Alimentación Panta** (☎983 35 82 51; Calle del Conde Ansúrez 1; ⏰9am-3pm & 5-9pm Mon-Fri, 9am-3pm Sat, 10am-2pm Sun) sells regional wines, cured meats and cheeses, and an enticing range of packaged goodies. And for something a little different, **El Gato Que Bebia Cerveza** (☎983 08 01 74; www.gatocerveza.com; Calle Zapico 12; ⏰11am-2pm & 5.30-8.30pm Mon-Fri, 11.30am-2.30pm Sat) is one of few places in Valladolid where you can pick up craft beers, both Spanish and international. For a picnic, Campo Grande, just south of the town centre, is a good choice.

**Oficina de Turismo** (☎983 33 08 93; www.info.valladolid.es; Plaza de Fuente Dorada; ⏰11am-1.30pm & 5-7pm Tue-Sat, 11am-1.30pm Sun)

### Getting There & Around

More than a dozen daily high-speed AVE train services connect Valladolid with Madrid (from €31, one hour); there are also slower services (three hours) for €25. Other regular trains run to León (from €11, 1¼ to two hours), Burgos (from €6, about 1½ hours) and Salamanca (from €8, 1½ hours).

Local buses 2 and 10 pass the train and bus stations on their way to Plaza de España.

# Around Valladolid

## Medina de Rioseco

POP 4715

Medina de Rioseco is something of a faded jewel. This once-wealthy trading centre has a tangible medieval feel whose time has passed. Head for Calle Mayor, with its colonnaded arcades held up by ancient wooden columns; market stalls set up here on Wednesday mornings.

### Sights

**Iglesia de Santa María de Mediavilla** CHURCH
(Calle de Santa María; guided tours €2.50; ⏰11am-2pm & 4-7pm Tue-Sun mid-Mar–Oct, shorter hours rest of year) This grandiose Isabelline Gothic work has three star-vaulted naves and the rightfully famous **Capilla de los Benavente** chapel. Anchored by an extravagant altarpiece by Juan de Juní and carved over eight years from 1543, it's sometimes referred to as the 'Sistine Chapel of Castilla'.

**Museo de San Francisco** CHURCH, MUSEUM
(☎983 70 00 20; www.museosanfrancisco.es; Paseo de San Francisco 1; adult/child €3/free, last tour Sun free; ⏰guided tours hourly 11am-2pm & 5-8pm Tue-Sun May-Aug, shorter hours rest of year) This 16th-century former convent has an extravagant *retablo* (altarpiece) by Fray Jacinto de Sierra, as well as a wide-ranging collection of sacred art. Tours in Spanish.

**Museo de Semana Santa** MUSEUM
(Calle de Lázaro Alonso; adult/concession/child €3.50/2.50/1; ⏰11am-2pm & 5-8pm Tue-Sun mid-Jun–mid-Sep, shorter hours rest of year) Medina de Rioseco is famous for its Easter processions, but if you can't be here during Holy Week, this museum provides an insight into the ceremonial passion of Easter here. Like its sister museum in Zamora (p173), it's dedicated to *pasos* (floats carried in Semana Santa processions) and an extensive range of other Easter artefacts.

> **COMBINED TICKETS**
>
> If you plan on visiting all four of Medina de Rioseco's main sights, consider buying the combined ticket for €7/5 for adults/seniors. It can be purchased at any of the four sights and will save you €3.50. Note that between April and September this combined ticket can be purchased only at weekends.

### Sleeping & Eating

**Vittoria Colonna** HOTEL €
(☎983 72 50 87; www.hotelvittoriacolonna.es; Calle de San Juan 2B; s/d/ste €45/60/84; ❄📶) This modern three-star hotel, with its raspberry-pink frontage, offers well-sized and brightly coloured rooms a short walk from all of Medina de Rioseco's sights. Some rooms are nicer than others, but all have smart grey-and-white bathrooms.

**Casa Manolo** CASTILIAN €€
(☎676 289845; Calle de Las Armas 4; mains €9-16; ⏰8am-midnight Fri-Wed) The best of a clutch of restaurants on this side street in the historic centre. The courtyard provides a pleasant setting for enjoying reliably good, hearty Castilian dishes.

### Information

**Oficina de Turismo** (☎983 72 03 19; www.medinaderioseco.com; Paseo de San Francisco 1; ⏰10am-2pm & 4-6pm Tue-Sat, 10am-2pm Sun) Alongside the Museo de San Francisco.

### Getting There & Away

Up to eight daily buses run to León (€8.80, 1¼ hours); up to 10 go to Valladolid (€4.45, 30 minutes).

## Tordesillas

POP 8825

Commanding a rise on the northern flank of Río Duero, this pretty little town has a historical significance that belies its size. Originally a Roman settlement, it later played a major role in world history in 1494, when Isabel and Fernando sat down here with Portugal to hammer out a treaty determining who got what in Latin America. Portugal got Brazil and much of the rest went to Spain. The museum dedicated to the moment and a stunning convent are the main reasons to come here.

## Sights

**Museo del Tratado de Tordesillas** MUSEUM
(983 77 10 67; Calle de Casas del Tratado; 10am-1.30pm & 5-7.30pm Tue-Sat, 10am-2pm Sun Jun-Sep, 10am-1.30pm & 4-6.30pm Tue-Sat, 10am-2pm Sun Oct-May) FREE Dedicated to the 1494 Treaty of Tordesillas, which divided the New World into Spanish and Portuguese spheres of influence, the informative displays in this museum look at the world as it was before and after the treaty, with some fabulous old maps taking centre stage. There's also a video presentation.

**Real Convento de Santa Clara** CONVENT
(983 77 00 71; www.patrimonionacional.es; Calle de Alonso Castillo Solorzano 21; adult/child €6/free, EU citizens & residents 4-6.30pm Wed & Thu free; 10am-2pm & 4-6.30pm Tue-Sat, 10.30am-3pm Sun) Still home to a few Franciscan nuns living in near-total isolation, this Mudéjar-style convent dates from 1340, when it was begun as a palace for Alfonso XI. In 1494, the Treaty of Tordesillas was signed here. A 50-minute guided tour (in Spanish) takes in a wonderful Mudéjar patio left over from the palace, and the church with its stunning *techumbre* (roof). Other highlights include the Mudéjar door, Gothic arches, superb Arabic inscriptions and the Arab baths.

## Sleeping & Eating

**Hostal San Antolín** HOSTAL €
(983 79 67 71; www.hostalsanantolin.com; Calle San Antolín 8; s/d/tr €25/40/50; ) Near Plaza Mayor, this *hostal*'s overall aesthetic is modern, with rooms painted in bright pastel tones. Its main focus is the attached restaurant (mains €11 to €21), with *raciones* downstairs in the bar and a pretty flower-decked inner patio.

★ **Parador de Tordesillas** LUXURY HOTEL €€
(983 77 00 51; www.parador.es; Carretera de Salamanca 5; r from €75; ) Tordesillas' most sophisticated hotel is the low-rise, ochre-toned *parador,* surrounded by pine trees and just outside town. Some rooms have four-poster beds, all are large and many look out onto the tranquil gardens. There's also a cafe and an excellent restaurant that showcases local specialities.

**Don Pancho** SPANISH €€
(983 77 01 74; www.restaurantedonpancho.com; Plaza Mayor 10; mains €8-19; 1-4pm & 8.30pm-midnight) Don Pancho, with its tiled bar and home cooking – including meats roasted in a wood-fired oven – is the best sit-down restaurant in the old-town centre.

## Information

**Oficina de Turismo** (983 77 10 67; www.tordesillas.net; Calle de Casas del Tratado; 10am-1.30pm & 5-7.30pm Tue-Sat, 10am-2pm Sun Jun-Sep, 10am-1.30pm & 4-6.30pm Tue-Sat, 10am-2pm Sun Oct-Apr) Next to the Casas del Tratado.

## Getting There & Away

From the **bus station** (983 77 00 72; Avenida de Valladolid), regular buses depart for Valladolid (€2.95, 30 minutes) and Zamora (€6.50, one hour).

# Zamora

POP 61,825

First appearances can be deceiving: as with so many Spanish towns, your introduction to provincial Zamora is likely to be nondescript apartment blocks. But persevere, because the *casco historico* (old town) is hauntingly beautiful, with sumptuous medieval monuments that have earned Zamora the sobriquet the 'Romanesque Museum'. It's a subdued encore to the monumental splendour of Salamanca and one of the best places to be during Semana Santa.

## Sights

**Catedral** CATHEDRAL
(980 53 19 33; Plaza de la Catedral; adult/child €5/free; 10am-7pm Apr-Sep, 10am-2pm & 5-8pm Oct-Mar) Zamora's largely Romanesque cathedral features a square tower, an unusual, Byzantine-style dome surrounded by turrets, and the ornate **Puerta del Obispo**. The star attraction is the **Museo Catedralicio**, which features a collection of Flemish tapestries dating from the 15th century. Inside the 12th-century cathedral itself, the magnificent early-Renaissance choir stalls depict clerics, animals and a naughty encounter between a monk and a nun. Another major highlight is the **Capilla de San Ildefonso**, with its lovely Gothic frescoes.

**Castillo** CASTLE
(Parque del Castillo; 10am-2pm & 7-10pm Tue-Sun Apr-Sep, 10am-2pm & 4-6.30pm Tue-Sun Oct-Mar; ) FREE This fine, aesthetically restored castle of 11th-century origin is filled with local sculptures; you can also climb the tower and walk the ramparts.

**Museo Etnográfico** MUSEUM
(980 53 17 08; www.museo-etnografico.com; Calle del Sacramento 3; adult/child €3/free, plus 5-8pm Sun & 7-8pm Tue-Thu free; 10am-2pm & 5-8pm Tue-Sun) This excellent museum is a window onto the cultural history of Castilla y León, with everything from artefacts from everyday life down through the ages to sections on local legends and fiestas. It also has a dynamic calendar of temporary exhibitions, workshops and performances.

**Museo de Semana Santa** MUSEUM
(980 53 60 72; www.semanasantadezamora.com; Plaza de Santa María La Nueva; adult/child €4/2; 10am-2pm & 5-8pm Tue-Sat, 10am-2pm Sun) This museum will initiate you into the weird and wonderful rites of Easter, Spanish-style. It showcases the carved and painted *pasos* that are paraded around town during the colourful processions.

**Iglesia de la Magdalena** CHURCH
(Rúa de los Francos; 10am-2pm & 5.30-8pm Tue-Sat, 10am-2pm Sun Apr-Sep, 10am-2pm & 4.30-7pm Tue-Sat, 10am-2pm Sun Oct-Mar) FREE The southern doorway of this church is considered the city's finest for its preponderance of floral motifs. The interior has the austere simplicity so typical of the Romanesque.

**Iglesia de San Juan de Puerta Nueva** CHURCH
(Plaza Mayor; 10am-2pm & 5.30-8pm Tue-Sat, 10am-2pm Sun Apr-Sep, 10am-2pm & 4.30-7pm Tue-Sat, 10am-2pm Sun Oct-Mar) FREE Iglesia de San Juan de Puerta Nueva provides a lovely Romanesque centrepiece for the central Plaza Mayor. Right outside, there's a fine statue of hooded Semana Santa penitents.

WORTH A TRIP

## TORO

With a name that couldn't be more Spanish and a stirring history that overshadows its present, Toro, just south of the A11 between Zamora and Tordesillas, is your archetypal Castilian town. It was here that Fernando and Isabel cemented their primacy in Christian Spain at the Battle of Toro in 1476. The town sits on a rise high above the north bank of the Río Duero and has a charming historic centre with half-timbered houses and Romanesque churches, where there's also a **tourist office** (980 69 47 47; www.turismotoro.com; Plaza Mayor 6; 10am-2pm & 4-7pm Tue-Sat, 10am-2pm Sun).

The 12th-century **Colegiata Santa María La Mayor** (Plaza de la Colegiata; church free, sacristy €4; 10.30am-2pm & 5-7.30pm Tue-Sun Apr-Oct, 10am-2pm & 4.30-6.30pm Tue-Sun Nov-Mar) rises above the town and boasts the magnificent Romanesque-Gothic Pórtico de la Majestad. Treasures inside include the famous 15th-century painting *Virgen de la mosca* (Virgin of the Fly) in the sacristy; see if you can spot the fly on the virgin's robe. Southwest of the town centre, the **Monasterio Sancti Spiritus** (Calle del Canto 27; €4.50; guided visits 10.30am, 11.30am, 12.30pm, 4.30pm & 5.30pm Tue-Sun mid-Apr–mid-Dec) features a fine Renaissance cloister and the striking alabaster tomb of Beatriz de Portugal, wife of Juan I.

If you decide to stay overnight, **Hotel Juan II** (980 69 03 00; www.hotelesentoro.es; Paseo del Espolón 1; s €55-70, d €60-95; P) has charming rooms with warm terracotta-tiled floors, dark-wood furniture and large terraces; request room 201 for its fabulous double-whammy vista of the Río Duero to one side and the Colegiata Santa María La Mayor to the other. The restaurant (mains €14 to €23), specialising in hearty meat dishes, is one of Toro's best. **Asador Castilla** (980 69 02 11; Plaza Bollos de Hito; mains €12-23; 1-4pm & 8.30pm-midnight Tue-Sun) is also recommended for its *cabrito* (roasted goat kid).

In Morales de Toro, 8km east of Toro, **Pagos del Rey** (980 69 67 63; www.pagosdelreymuseodelvino.com; Avenida de los Comuneros 90; guided/unguided incl wine tasting €8/5; 10.30am-6.30pm Tue-Sat, to 3pm Sun) is a state-of-the-art wine museum that covers the respected Toro wine-producing area, known for its full-bodied reds.

## Festivals & Events

**Semana Santa** RELIGIOUS

(Holy Week; Mar or Apr) If you're in Spain during Holy Week (the week before Easter), make your way to Zamora, a town made famous for its elaborate celebrations. It's one of the most evocative places in the country to view the hooded processions. Watching the penitents weave their way through the historic streets, sometimes in near-total silence, is an experience you'll never forget.

## Sleeping

**Hostal Chiqui** HOSTAL €

(980 53 14 80; www.hostalchiqui.es; 2nd fl, Calle de Benavente 2; s/d from €38/50) One of the best urban *hostales* in this part of Castilla y León, this fine place gets rave reviews and plenty of repeat visitors. Every room is different, but all are stylish and colourful, and the owners are switched on to what travellers need. It's outrageously good value.

**NH Palacio del Duero** HOTEL €€

(980 50 82 62; www.nh-hotels.com; Plaza de la Horta 1; r from €80; P ❄ @ ) In a superb position next to a lovely Romanesque church, the seemingly modern building has cleverly encompassed part of the former convent, as well as – somewhat bizarrely – a 1940s power station (the lofty brick chimney remains). As you'd expect from this excellent chain, the rooms here are stylishly furnished and the service is attentive.

★ **Parador Condes de Alba y Aliste** HISTORIC HOTEL €€€

(980 51 44 97; www.parador.es; Plaza Viriato 5; r €90-175; ❄ @ ) Set in a sumptuous 15th-century palace, this is modern luxury with myriad period touches (mostly in the public areas). There's a swimming pool and – unlike many *paradores* – it's right in the heart of town. On the downside, there is very limited parking available (just eight places). The restaurant (set menu €38) is, like most *parador* restaurants, high quality.

## Eating

Just west of Plaza Mayor, you'll find a half dozen gourmet food shops and delis selling cheeses, cured meats, wine and local pastries – great for a local-accented picnic.

**La Rua** CASTILIAN €€

(980 53 40 24; Rúa de los Francos 21; mains €9-21; 1-4pm Sun-Fri, 1-4pm & 8.30-11.30pm Sat) Devoted to down-home Zamora cooking, this central place is a good place to try *arroz a la zamorana* (rice with pork and ham or chorizo), although you'll usually need two people ordering for staff to make it.

## Information

**Municipal Tourist Office** (980 53 36 94; www.zamora-turismo.com; Plaza de Arias Gonzalo 6; 10am-2pm & 5-8pm daily Jun-Sep, 10am-2pm & 4-7.30pm Mon-Sat, 10am-2pm Sun Oct-May)

**Regional Tourist Office** (980 53 18 45; www.turismocastillayleon.com; Avenida Príncipe de Asturias 1; 10am-2pm & 4.30-8.30pm Mar-Oct, 10am-2pm & 4-7pm Nov-Feb)

## Getting There & Away

Bus services operate almost hourly to/from Salamanca (from €6 one hour, five to 13 daily), with less frequent departures on weekends. Other regular services include those to León (€11, 1½ hours), Valladolid (€8.50, 1½ hours) and Burgos (€22, 4½ hours).

The fast-train line cuts travel times to Madrid (from €20.50, 1½ hours, seven daily) considerably. Trains also head to Valladolid (€13, 1½ hours, one daily) and Puebla de Sanabria (from €9, 1¼ hours, five daily).

# Around Zamora

## Sierra de la Culebra

The Sierra de la Culebra, running along the Spanish–Portuguese border between Puebla de Sanabria and Zamora, consists of some lovely rolling hill country and pretty stone villages that rarely see foreign visitors. Best of all, this is one of the top places in Europe to see wolves in the wild.

### Sights

**Centro de Lobo Ibérico de Castilla y León** MUSEUM, ZOO

(980 56 76 38, 608 373 962; www.centrodellobo.es; Robledo; with/without guided tour €8/6; 10am-2pm & 3.30-7.30pm, guided tours 10.30am & 4pm Fri-Sun, Tue-Thu by appointment) This excellent interpretation centre devoted to the Iberian wolf is built in the form of a traditional, circular corral used by local farmers to protect their livestock from wolves. It presents displays on legends surrounding wolves, their position in local culture and scientific studies of them. On the hill behind the main building, seven wolves in-

habit three large enclosures, offering a good chance to take a photo if you missed seeing them in the wild.

## Activities

**★Wild Wolf Experience** WILDLIFE
(☎636 031472; www.facebook.com/wildwolf experience) Englishman John Hallowell runs excellent wolf-watching (and birdwatching) excursions in the Sierra de la Culebra; he's a knowledegable guide and puts together packages that begin and end at Madrid or Oviedo airports. He can also combine them with bear-watching in Asturias.

**★Zamora Natural** WILDLIFE
(☎655 821899; www.zamoranatural.com) If you're keen to catch a glimpse of a wolf or two in the Sierra de la Culebra, contact Zamora Natural, which runs year-round excursions, including a dawn and sunset spent at a lookout overlooking areas commonly frequented by wolves. Sightings are not guaranteed, though; chances range between 20% and 40%, with the best months from October through to May or June.

## Festivals & Events

**Festival Territorio Lobo** CULTURAL
(Villardeciervos; ⏲early Aug) This fun festival features live music, great local food, presentations about the Iberian wolf and excursions into the sierra.

## Sleeping & Eating

**★Santa Cruz** GUESTHOUSE €
(☎619 850010; www.loscuerragos.com; Santa Cruz de los Cuérragos; per person full board €30; P wi-fi) Now here's something a little bit special. Fernando and Carmen have been largely responsible for bringing this charming stone village back to life. Their lovely rural home is beautifully restored and decorated with exposed stone walls, polished floorboards, comfortable beds and a general warmth.

**Hotel Remesal** HOTEL €
(☎980 65 49 11; www.hotelruralremesal.com; Calle de Mediodía 25, Villardeciervos; s/d €40/60; P wi-fi) This excellent three-star hotel in Villadeciervos has 10 pretty rooms, all with exposed stone walls and excellent heating. It's on the main road through town and makes a convenient base for exploring the sierra, with numerous wolf-watching locales relatively nearby. There's a good restaurant.

### ONE OF SPAIN'S OLDEST CHURCHES

The lonely 7th-century **San Pedro de la Nave** (☎660 233995, 696 292400; Calle Larga, Campillo; ⏲10.30am-1.30pm & 5-8pm Tue-Sun Apr-Sep, 10am-1.30pm & 4.30-6.30pm Fri & Sat, 10am-1.30pm Sun Oct-Mar), about 24km northwest of Zamora, is a rare and outstanding example of Visigoth church architecture, with blended Celtic, Germanic and Byzantine elements. Of special note are the intricately sculpted capitals. The church was moved to its present site in Campillo in 1930, during the construction of the Esla reservoir, northwest of Zamora. To get there from Zamora, take the N122, then follow the signs to Campillo.

**La Enredadera** SPANISH €€
(☎980 59 31 21; Calle de Arriba 26, Ferreras de Arriba; mains €9-16, set lunch menu €14; ⏲1.30-4pm & 8.30-11.30pm Thu-Tue) What a find! In the otherwise-nondescript village of Ferreras de Arriba, close to some of the best wolf-watching spots, La Enredadera looks for all the world like a cool urban cafe. The food is thoughtfully presented, the service is friendly and its specialities include *bacalao* (cod) or *carnes a la brasa* (grilled meats).

## Getting There & Away

The N631, which connects Zamora with Puebla de Sanabria, runs parallel to the Sierra de la Culebra, with numerous side roads climbing up into the hills. Villardeciervos is the largest village in the region. Robledo, home to the Centro de Lobo interpretation centre, lies at the northwestern end of the range and is accessible from Puebla de Sanabria.

# Puebla de Sanabria

POP 1410

Close to the Portuguese border, this captivating village is a tangle of medieval alleyways that unfold around a 15th-century castle and trickle down the hill, giving the impression you've stepped back centuries. This is one of Spain's loveliest hamlets and it's well worth stopping overnight.

## Sights

Apart from the pleasure of wandering Puebla de Sanabria's rough-hewn streets, most of the attractions are at the top of the village.

From the top, a path runs down the eastern edge of the old town, with fine views out over the river and beyond, all the way down.

**Castillo** CASTLE

(adult/child under 12yr €3/free; ⏲11am-2pm & 4-8pm; P 👪) Crowning the village's high point and dominating its skyline for kilometres around, the castle has some interesting displays on local history, flora and fauna; a slide show about the village; and a camera obscura. Kids will love the chance to try on the pieces of armour. The views from the ramparts are also superb.

## Sleeping & Eating

★**Posada Real La Cartería** HISTORIC HOTEL €€

(☎980 62 03 12; www.lacarteria.com; Calle de Rúa 16; r from €90-150; ❄@📶) This stunning old inn is one of the best hotels in this part of the country. It blends modern comforts with all the old-world atmosphere of the village itself, featuring large, delightful rooms with exposed stone walls and wooden beams. The bathrooms have Jacuzzi tubs and there is even a small gym (as if walking around this hilly village wasn't exercise enough!).

The restaurant reflects the local obsession with wild mushrooms (*setas* and *boletus*) and *trucha* (trout), caught in the river below the village. Mains start at €13.

**La Hoja de Roble** HISTORIC HOTEL €€

(☎980 62 01 90; www.lahojaderoble.com; Calle Constanilla 13; s/d from €47/78; ❄📶) Close to the bottom of the hill where you begin the climb up into the old town, this hotel is an outstanding choice. The building dates to the 17th century and the rooms have a real sense of history (exposed stone walls, wooden beams) without ever being oppressive. There's also a wine bar and restaurant.

**La Posada de Puebla de Sanabria** CASTILIAN €€

(☎980 62 03 47; Plaza Mayor 3; mains €11-18; ⏲1.30-4pm & 8.30-11pm Thu-Tue) This excellent restaurant on Plaza Mayor has a white-tableclothed elegance and serves up local steaks and the wild mushrooms for which this region is famed. When the two are mixed, such as in the *tenera estofada con boletus*, a kind of hotpot of beef with wild mushrooms, the results are outstanding.

WORTH A TRIP

### PALENCIA'S NORTHERN PLAINS

The open plains north of Palencia are classic Camino de Santiago country, with quiet trails, big horizons and small villages crowned with surprising Romanesque churches. Whether you're walking or driving, the P980 between Frómista and Carrión de los Condes is a wonderful stretch of road. Starting (or ending) in Frómista, the **Iglesia de San Martín** (☎979 81 01 44; Plaza de San Martín; adult/child €2/free; ⏲9.30am-2pm & 4.30-8pm Apr-Sep, 10am-2pm & 3.30-6.30pm Oct-Mar) dates from 1066 and is one of rural Spain's loveliest Romanesque churches. Restored in the early 20th century, this beautifully proportioned church is adorned with a veritable menagerie of human and zoomorphic figures just below the eaves. A couple of kilometres west of Frómista, at the entrance to the small hamlet of **Población de Campos**, the simplicity of the 13th-century **Ermita de San Miguel**, beneath its honour guard of trees, is a quietly beautiful Romanesque gem.

Around 6km northwest of Frómista, quiet **Revenga de Campos** is home to the **Iglesia de San Lorenzo**, built between the 12th and 16th centuries. A couple of kilometres further on, in **Villalcázar de Sirga**, the **Iglesia de Santa María La Blanca** (☎979 88 08 54; €2; ⏲11am-2pm & 5-8pm daily Jun–mid-Sep, 10.30am-2pm & 4-6pm Sat & Sun mid-Sep–Apr), an extraordinary fortress-church and important landmark along the Camino de Santiago, rises up from the Castilian plains. Begun in the 12th century and finished in the 14th, it spans both Romanesque and Gothic styles.

Some 19km northwest of Frómista, in **Carrión de los Condes**, it's worth stopping by the **Hotel Monasterio Real San Zoilo** (☎979 880 049; www.sanzoilo.com; Calle San Zoilo; s/d from €45/65; P❄📶). It has a lovely riverside setting and inhabits part of an 11th-century monastery. If you do decide to stay, this fine place has charming rooms with wooden beams, exposed brickwork and ochre-painted walls, and there's a good restaurant as well.

## Information

**Oficina de Turismo** (980 62 07 34; www.turismosanabria.es; Castillo; 11am-2pm & 4-8pm) Inside the castle.

## Getting There & Away

There are sporadic bus services to Puebla de Sanabria from Zamora (from €8.90, 1¼ hours).

# Palencia

POP 79,865

Palencia boasts an immense Gothic cathedral, some pretty squares and a colonnaded main pedestrian street (Calle Mayor) flanked by shops and several other churches. It's an attractive town and one of the quieter provincial capitals. Most travellers come here on a day trip from Valladolid.

## Sights

Palencia is embellished with some real architectural gems, including the 19th-century Modernista **Mercado de Abastos** (Fresh Food Market) on Calle Colón, the eye-catching **Collegio Vallandrando** on Calle Mayor and the ornate neo-plateresque **Palacio Provincial** on Calle Burgos.

**★Catedral** CATHEDRAL
(979 70 13 47; www.catedraldepalencia.org; Calle Mayor Antigua 29; adult/child €5/2; 10am-1.30pm & 4-7.30pm Mon-Fri, 10am-2pm & 4-7.30pm Sat, 4.30-8pm Sun May-Oct, 10am-1.30pm & 4-6pm Mon-Fri, 10am-2pm, 4-5.30pm & 6.45-7.30pm Sat, 4-7pm Sun Nov-Apr) The sober exterior of this vast house of worship (one of the largest in Castilla) belies the extraordinary riches within – it's widely known as 'La Bella Desconocida' (Unknown Beauty). The **Puerta del Obispo** (Bishop's Door) is the highlight of the facade. Once inside, head for the **Capilla El Sagrario**: its ceiling-high altarpiece tells the story of Christ in dozens of exquisite panels. The stone screen behind the choir stalls is a masterpiece of bas-relief, attributed to Gil de Siloé.

**Iglesia de San Miguel** CHURCH
(979 74 07 69; Calle de Mayor Antigua; 9.30am-1.30pm & 6.30-7.30pm Mon-Sat, 9.30am-1.30pm & 6.30-8pm Sun) FREE This church stands out for its tall Gothic tower with a castle-like turret. San Miguel's interior is unadorned and austerely beautiful. According to legend, El Cid, an 11th-century Castilian knight, was betrothed to his Doña Jimena here.

WORTH A TRIP

### MONASTERIO DE SAN MIGUEL DE ESCALADA

Rising from Castilla's northern plains, **Monasterio de San Miguel de Escalada** (€3, Thu Nov-Apr free; 10.30am-2pm & 4.30-7.30pm Tue-Sun May-Oct, 10am-2.30pm Thu-Sun Nov-Apr) is a beautifully simple treasure built in the 9th century by refugee monks from Córdoba atop the remains of a Visigoth church dedicated to the Archangel Michael. Although little trace of the latter remains, the church is notable for its Islamic-inspired horseshoe arches, rarely seen so far north in Spain. The graceful exterior and its portico are balanced by the impressive marble columns within. The entrance dates from the 11th century.

To get here, take the N601 southeast of León. After about 14km, take the small LE213 to the east; the church is 16km after the turn off.

## Sleeping & Eating

**Eurostars Diana Palace** BUSINESS HOTEL €€
(979 01 80 50; www.eurostarsdianapalace.com; Avenida de Santander 12; s/d incl breakfast from €63/78; P) A comfortable, modern block of a hotel within walking distance of the town centre. The look is contemporary with a predominantly business clientele.

**Gloria Bendita** CASTILIAN €€
(979 10 65 04; Calle de la Puebla 8; mains €13-25; 1.30-4pm & 9pm-midnight Mon-Sat, 1.30-4pm Sun; ) Ignore the drab surroundings of modern apartment blocks and seek out this, one of Palencia's new breed of elegant restaurants serving sophisticated Castilian cuisine with a modern twist. Meat and fish dishes are the emphasis here, with classics such as braised beef served with oyster mushrooms. Reservations are essential.

**★Lucio Asador Gastrobar** CASTILIAN €€€
(979 74 81 90; www.lucioasadorgastrobar.com; Calle de Don Sancho 2; mains €9-25; 10am-midnight Mon-Sat, to 4pm Sun) This Palencia institution combines *asador* (restaurant specialising in roasted meats) with slick gastrobar. The Castilian speciality of *cordero asado* (€45 for two) is exceptionally good, but it would be a shame to dine here and not try the creative tapas.

## Information

**Patronato de Turismo** (979 70 65 23; www.turismocastillayleon.com; Calle Mayor 31; 9.30am-2pm & 5-8pm Mon-Sat, 9.30am-5pm Sun Jul–mid-Sep, 9.30am-2pm & 4-7pm Mon-Sat, 9.30am-5pm Sun mid-Sep–Jun) Information about Palencia province and city, encompassing both the municipal and regional tourist offices.

## Getting There & Away

From the **bus station** (979 74 32 22; Carerra del Cementerio) there are regular services to Valladolid (€5, 45 minutes), Madrid (from €13, 3½ hours) and Aguilar de Campóo (€9, 1½ hours).

The AVE fast train connects Palencia to Madrid (from €25.50, 1½ to three hours) and León (from €12, 45 minutes). Other services include Burgos (from €8, 45 minutes) and Valladolid (from €6, 30 minutes).

# THE NORTHWEST

## León

POP 124,770 / ELEV 837M

León is a wonderful city, combining stunning historical architecture with an irresistible energy. Its standout attraction is the cathedral, one of the most beautiful in Spain, but there's so much more to see and do here. By day you'll encounter a city with its roots firmly planted in the soil of northern Castilla, with its grand monuments, loyal Catholic heritage and a role as an important staging post along the Camino de Santiago. By night León is taken over by a deep-into-the-night soundtrack of revelry that floods the narrow streets and plazas of the picturesque old quarter, the Barrio Húmedo. It's a fabulous mix.

### Sights

Set aside the best part of a day to make sure that you see all of León's attractions. Stop by the Municipal Tourist Office to pick up *Horarios de Museos y Monumentos de León* for a list of current opening hours.

The main pedestrian shopping street is Calle Ancha. Don't miss the fabulous **Farmacia Alonso Nuñez** (Calle Ancha 3; 9.30am-2pm & 4.30-8pm Mon-Fri, 9.30am-1.30pm Sat) at number 3. It dates from 1827 and, aside from the displays of anti-wrinkle creams and condoms, the sumptuous interior and ornate ceiling haven't changed a bit.

★**Catedral** CATHEDRAL

(987 87 57 70; www.catedraldeleon.org; Plaza Regla; adult/concession/child €6/5/free, combined ticket with Claustro & Museo Catedralicio-Diocesano €9/8/free; 9.30am-1.30pm & 4-8pm Mon-Fri, 9.30am-noon & 2-6pm Sat, 9.30-11am & 2-8pm Sun May-Sep, 9.30am-1.30pm & 4-7pm Mon-Sat, 9.30am-2pm Sun Oct-Apr) León's 13th-century cathedral, with its soaring towers, flying buttresses and breathtaking interior, is the city's spiritual heart. Whether spotlit by night or bathed in glorious northern sunshine, the cathedral, arguably Spain's premier Gothic masterpiece, exudes a glorious, almost luminous quality. The show-stopping facade has a radiant rose window, three richly sculpted doorways and two muscular towers. The entrance is lorded over by a scene of the Last Judgement, while an extraordinary gallery of *vidrieras* (stained-glass windows) awaits inside.

French in inspiration and mainly executed from the 13th to the 16th centuries, the windows' kaleidoscope of coloured light is breathtaking. There seems to be more glass than brick here – 128 windows with a surface of 1800 sq metres in all – but mere numbers cannot convey the ethereal quality of light permeating this cathedral.

Other treasures include a silver urn by Enrique de Arfe on the altar, containing the remains of San Froilán, León's patron saint. Also note the magnificent **choir stalls**.

Combine the cathedral with a visit to the **Claustro & Museo Catedralicio-Diocesano** (www.catedraldeleon.org; Plaza Regla; adult/concession/child under 12yr €5/4/free, combined ticket with Catedral €9/8/free; 9.30am-1.30pm & 4-8pm Mon-Fri, 9.30am-noon & 2-6pm Sat, 9.30-11am & 2-8pm Sun Jun-Sep, 9.30am-1.30pm & 4-7pm Mon-Sat, 9.30am-2pm Sun Oct-May), just around the corner. In the peaceful, light-filled *claustro* (cloisters), 15th-century frescoes provide a perfect complement to the main sanctuary, while the museum has an impressive collection encompassing works by Juní and Gaspar Becerra, alongside a precious assemblage of early Romanesque carved statues of the Virgin Mary.

★**Museo de Arte Contemporáneo** GALLERY

(Musac; 987 09 00 0e0; www.musac.es; Avenida de los Reyes Leóneses 24; adult/concession/child €3/2/1, 5-9pm Sun & 7-8pm Tue-Thu free; 11am-2pm & 5-8pm Tue-Fri, 11am-3pm & 5-9pm Sat & Sun, guided tours 1pm & 6pm) León's showpiece

DON'T MISS

### IBERIA'S FINEST ROMAN VILLA

OK, it's not Pompeii, but it is the most exciting and best preserved Roman villa on the Iberian Peninsula. Located seemingly in the middle of nowhere, the **Villa Romana La Olmeda** (979 14 20 03; www.villaromanalaolmeda.com; off CL615; adult/child under 12yr €5/free; 10.30am-6.30pm Tue-Sun; P) is surrounded by fertile plains and hidden behind an incongruous, futuristic-looking building. Step inside, however, to be transported back to the 4th century CE – once the villa of a wealthy aristocrat and landowner, the property spans some 1000 sq metres and contains some of the finest mosaics to be discovered in a private Roman villa anywhere in Europe.

On the fertile plains south of the Montaña Palentina (hills in the far north of Castilla y León), the turn-off to the site is 3km south of Saldaña, along the CL615. If you want to delve further, ask at the ticket office here about details on the monographic museum in Saldaña where many of the excavated artefacts are on display.

Museo de Arte Contemporáneo has been acclaimed for the 37 shades of coloured glass that adorn the facade; they were gleaned from the pixelisation of a fragment of one of the stained-glass windows in León's cathedral. Within the museum is one of Spain's most dynamic artistic spaces. The airy galleries mostly display temporary exhibitions of cutting-edge Spanish and international photography, video installations and other similar forms; it also has a growing permanent collection. Concerts are held here.

**★ Real Colegiata de San Isidoro** HISTORIC BUILDING

(Panteón Real; 987 876 161; www.museosanisidorodeleon.com; Plaza de San Isidoro; adult/child €5/free; 10am-2pm & 4-7pm Mon-Sat, 10am-2pm Sun) Attached to the Real Basílica de San Isidoro, the stunning Panteón Real houses royal sarcophagi, which rest with quiet dignity beneath a canopy of some of the finest Romanesque frescoes in Spain. Colourful motifs of biblical scenes drench the vaults and arches of this extraordinary hall, held aloft by marble columns with intricately carved capitals. The museum, where you can admire the shrine of San Isidoro and a mummified finger(!) of the saint, was undergoing a major expansion when we visited.

Abutting the southwestern corner of the basilica is a fragment of the former **muralla** (old city wall).

**Real Basílica de San Isidoro** CHURCH

(987 87 61 61; Plaza de San Isidoro; 7.30am-11pm) FREE Even older than León's cathedral, the Real Basílica de San Isidoro provides a stunning Romanesque counterpoint to the former's Gothic strains. Fernando I and Doña Sancha founded the church in 1063 to house the remains of the saint, as well as the remains of themselves and 21 other early Leónese and Castilian monarchs. Sadly, Napoleon's troops sacked San Isidoro in the early 19th century, but there's still plenty to catch the eye.

**Convento de San Marcos** CONVENT

FREE You'll have to check into the **Hostal de San Marcos parador** (987 23 73 00; www.parador.es; Plaza de San Marcos 7; P) to appreciate most of this palatial former monastery, although the historic chapter house and magnificent cloister can be viewed by nonguests. The plateresque exterior is also superb, sectioned off by slender columns and decorated with delicate medallions and friezes that date from 1513. It's particularly lovely when floodlit at night. It was undergoing renovation at the time of research.

**Museo Gaudí** HISTORIC BUILDING

(Casa Botines; 987 35 32 47; www.casabotines.es; Plaza de San Marcelo 5; adult/child €8/free, guided visit €12; 11am-2pm & 4-8pm Mon, Tue & Thu-Sat, 4-8pm Wed, 11am-2pm Sun) Antoni Gaudí's contribution to León's skyline is the castle-like, neo-Gothic Casa Botines (1893), though the zany architect of Barcelona fame seems to have been subdued by more sober León. The interior includes displays on the great man, some interactive exhibits, a recreated 19th-century apartment and, on the top floor, some wonderful artworks, including a room devoted to watercolour interpretations of Dante's *Inferno* by Salvador Dalí (Room 7) and another with drawings by Goya (Room 2) from his *Los Caprichos* series. A statue of Gaudí sits outside.

## León

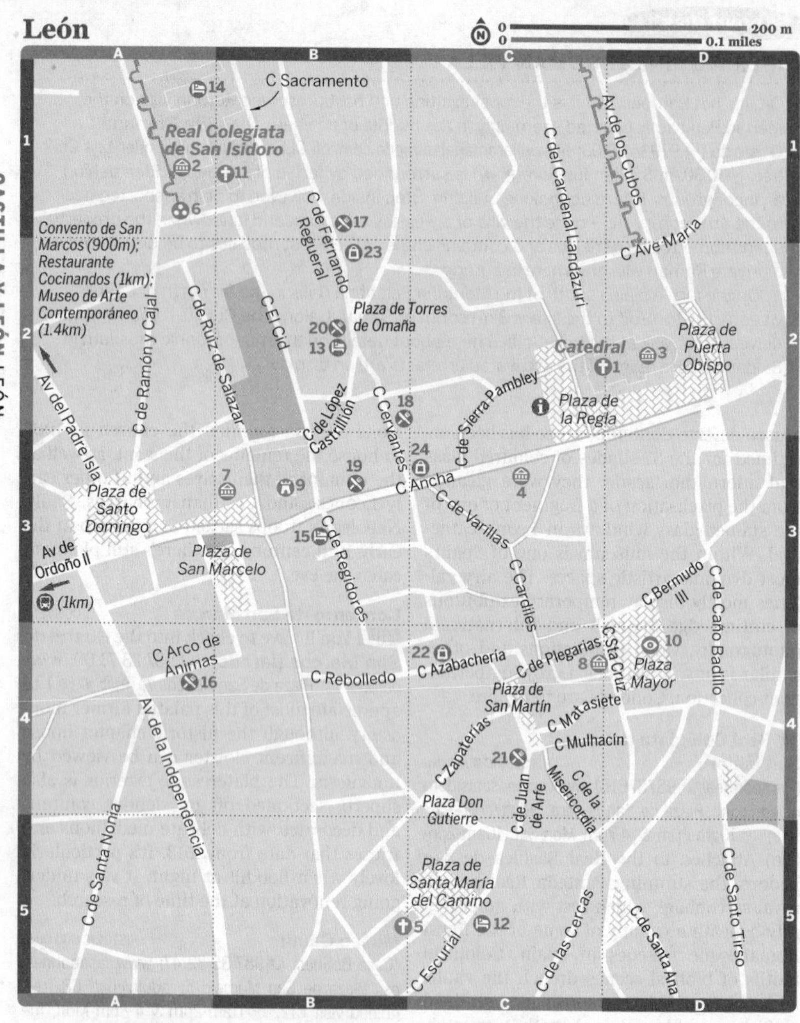


**Palacio de los Guzmanes** PALACE

(☎987 292 204; Plaza de San Marcelo 6; adult/child €2/1; ⊙11.30am-5pm Wed-Sun) León's recurring Renaissance theme finds expression in the splendid Palacio de los Guzmanes (1560), where the facade and patio stand out. The latter is accessible only by a free **guided tour** that leaves regularly from 11.30am to 4.30pm.

**Plaza Mayor** SQUARE

At the eastern end of the old town is the beautiful and time-worn 17th-century Plaza Mayor. Sealed off on three sides by porticoes, this sleepy plaza is home to a bustling **produce market** on Wednesday and Saturday. On the west side of the square is the late 17th-century, baroque **old town hall**.

**Iglesia de Santa María del Mercado** CHURCH

(Plaza de Santa María del Camino; ⊙for Mass) Down the hill, the careworn, stone Romanesque Iglesia de Santa María del Mercado looks out over a delightful square that feels like a cobblestone Castilian village plaza. Opening hours can vary but it's the exterior and the setting that most appeal.

## León



## Festivals & Events

**Semana Santa** RELIGIOUS

(Holy Week; Mar/Apr) León is an excellent place to see solemn Holy Week processions of hooded penitents, with the city's monuments as a stirring backdrop.

**Fiestas de San Juan y San Pedro** FIESTA

(Jun) The city lets its hair down on the cusp of summer – from 21 to 30 June – with concerts, street stalls and general merriment.

## Sleeping

**Hostal San Martín** HOSTAL €

(987 87 51 87; www.sanmartinhostales.es; Plaza de Torres de Omaña 1; s/d €30/43, s with shared bathroom €18-23; ) In a splendid central position occupying an 18th-century building, this is good old-fashioned budget value in the heart of town. The candy-coloured rooms are light and airy; all have small terraces. The spotless bathrooms have excellent water pressure and tubs, as well as showers, and there's a comfortable sitting area.

★ **Hotel Real Colegiata San Isidoro** HISTORIC HOTEL €€

(987 87 50 88; www.hotelrealcolegiata.com; Plaza de Santo Martino 5; r incl breakfast €85; P) Now here's something special. Arrayed around a medieval courtyard and an annexe to the Real Colegiata de San Isidoro, this gorgeous place has contemporary rooms with soothing linen tones and stone walls. Some of the small windows overlook the cloister, and the use of motifs from the neighbouring museum's frescoes is understated but nicely done.

**La Posada Regia** HISTORIC HOTEL €€

(987 21 31 73; www.regialeon.com; Calle de Regidores 9-11; s €54-70, d €59-130; ) This place has the feel of a *casa rural* (village or farmstead accommodation) despite being in the city centre. The secret is a 14th-century building, magnificently restored (with wooden beams, exposed brick and understated antique furniture), with individually styled rooms and supremely comfortable beds and bathrooms. As with anywhere in the Barrio Húmedo, weekend nights can be noisy.

**Hospedería Monástica Pax** HOSTAL €€

(987 34 44 93; www.hospederiapax.com; Plaza de Santa María del Camino; s/d incl breakfast €64/73; ) Overlooking one of the loveliest squares in León, this excellent place inhabits a restored former monastery; the rooms are mostly spacious and stylishly appointed. Unless you're a really light sleeper, ask for a room overlooking the square.

## Eating

**Ezequiel** TAPAS €€

(987 00 19 61; Calle Ancha 20; raciones €15-22; noon-midnight) It can be difficult to fight your way to the bar upstairs but it's worth doing so for the generous-sized *raciones*, including all kinds of cured meats straight from its own pig farm up in the far north of Castilla y León. In the downstairs restaurant, some of the best dishes give a nod to Asturias, with the appearance of *cabrales* (a strong goat's cheese) to fire things up.

DON'T MISS

## A TAPAS TOUR OF LEÓN

León is one of Castilla y León's culinary stars, and its tapas scene is outstanding. And as is the Spanish way, many of these tapas bars are also terrific places to drink.

A good place to start is Plaza de San Martín, where the pick of a mixed bunch is easily **Racimo de Oro** (☎987 21 47 67; www.racimodeoro.com; Plaza de San Martín 8; raciones from €8.50, mains €12-19; ⏲1-5pm & 8pm-12.30am), its lovely brick-lined interior an appealing backdrop for *raciones* predominantly from Castilla y León's north, such as cured meats, strong cheeses and roasted red peppers.

Not far away, **Camarote Madrid** (www.camarotemadrid.com; Calle de Cervantes 8; tapas from €3.50, raciones €12-23; ⏲10am-4pm & 8pm-12.30am), with legs of ham displayed like some meaty Broadway chorus line, is famed for its tapas – the little ceramic cup of *salmorejo* (a cold, tomato-based soup) is rightly famous. A few doors away, **La Trébede** (☎637 259197; Plaza de Torres de Omaña; tapas from €3, raciones from €8; ⏲8pm-midnight Mon, 1-5pm & 8pm-midnight Tue-Sat) is as good for tapas (try the croquettes) as for first drinks (wines by the glass start at €1.50). The decor is eclectic – deer antlers, historic wirelesses and the scales of justice – and the sign outside declaring 350km to Santiago may just prompt you to abandon the Camino and stay a little longer. And just up the road, **Bar La Ribera** (☎987 27 04 08; Calle de Fernando G Regueral 8; raciones €5-15; ⏲11am-4.30pm & 8pm-midnight Mon & Wed-Fri, 1-4.30pm & 8pm-midnight Sat, 1-4.30pm Sun) is the kind of Spanish bar that doesn't look up to much, but has a loyal neighbourhood following for its *raciones*. They keep it simple: *croquetas* (croquettes), *albóndigas* (meatballs), *calamares* (calamari), *morcilla* (blood sausage), *mejillones* (mussels) and the like, but it's all very, very good.

**Alfonso Valderas** SEAFOOD €€
(☎987 20 05 05; www.restaurantevalderas.com; Calle Arco de Ánimas 1; mains €13-22, set menus €30-56; ⏲1.30-4pm & 9-11.15pm Mon-Sat, 1.30-4pm Sun) Alfonso Valderas is León's most famous restaurant for *bacalao* (salt cod), prepared around 25 different ways. If this is your first encounter with this versatile fish, order it *al pil-pil* (with a mild chilli sauce) – this preparation is devilishly difficult to get right, but they always do here..

★**Restaurante Cocinandos** MODERN SPANISH €€€
(☎987 07 13 78; www.cocinandos.com; Calle de las Campanillas 1; set menus €50-90; ⏲1.45-3.15pm & 9.30-10.30pm Tue-Sat) The proud owner of León's first Michelin star, Cocinandos brings creative flair to the table with a menu that changes weekly with the seasons and market availability. The atmosphere is slightly formal so dress nicely and book in advance, but the young team puts diners at ease and the food is exceptional (in that zany new-Spanish-cuisine kind of way).

## Shopping

**La Despensa de Fer** FOOD & DRINKS
(☎987 04 46 46; www.embutidodeleon.net; cnr Calles Ancha & de Cervantes; ⏲10am-2pm & 5.30-8.30pm Mon, Tue, Thu & Fri, 10.30am-2.30pm Sat & Sun) One of the better delicatessens around town, selling much-praised cured meats (including *cecina,* one that's typical of the region), cheeses and, unusually, some local craft beers. They also sell *nicanores*, a local pastry from the León region.

**Don Queso** CHEESE
(☎987 20 99 43; Calle Azabachería 20; ⏲10am-2pm & 5.30-8pm Mon-Fri, 10am-2.30pm Sat) This marvellous little cheese shop has been around forever. The selection is outstanding and they usually let you try before you buy.

**El Escribano** ARTS & CRAFTS
(☎987 07 32 22; www.elescribano.com; Calle de Fernando Regueral 6; ⏲11.30am-1.30pm & 6-8pm Mon-Sat, 11.30am-1.30pm Sun) Some lovely etchings and reproductions of medieval art are among the many attractions of this classy shop.

## Information

**Oficina de Turismo de Castilla y León** (☎987 23 70 82; www.turismocastillayleon.com; Plaza de la Regla 2; ⏲9.30am-2pm & 5-8pm Mon-Sat, 9.30am-5pm Sun Jul–mid-Sep, 9.30am-2pm & 4-7pm Mon-Sat, 9.30am-5pm Sun mid-Sep–Jun) Opposite the cathedral. Also has info on Castilla y León in general.

## Getting There & Away

The train and bus stations lie on the western bank of Río Bernesga, off the western end of Avenida de Ordoño II.

Bus services depart from the **bus station** (☎987 21 10 00; Paseo del Ingeniero Sáez de Miera) to Madrid (from €15, 3½ hours, eight daily), Astorga (€4, one hour, 17 daily), Burgos (from €8.50, two hours, three daily) and Valladolid (€12, two hours, nine daily).

The AVE fast-train network has services to/from Valladolid (from €13, 1¼ to two hours) and Madrid (from €27.50, 2¼ to five hours). Other non-AVE destinations include Burgos (from €7.50, two hours).

## Getting Around

León's central city underground car parks are privately owned and costlier than most (per hour €1.50) with, unusually, no reduction for overnight stays. You may want to consider a hotel with private parking instead. Parking bays (€12 to €16 for 12 hours) can be found in the streets surrounding Plaza de Santo Domingo. Alternatively, look for free parking in the large open-air car park outside the Junta de Castilla y León; it's west of the centre, close to the Hostal San Marcos.

# Astorga

POP 11,030 / ELEV 870M

Perched upon a hilltop on the frontier between the bleak plains of northern Castilla and the mountains that rise west towards Galicia, Astorga is a fascinating small town with a wealth of attractions out of proportion to its size. In addition to its fine cathedral, the city boasts a Gaudí-designed palace, a smattering of Roman ruins and a personality dominated by the Camino de Santiago. Most enjoyable of all, perhaps, is the museum dedicated to chocolate.

## Sights

**Palacio de Gaudí** MUSEUM, ARCHITECTURE

(Museo de los Caminos; ☎987 61 68 82; www.palaciodegaudi.es; Plaza Eduardo de Castro 15; adult/child €5/free, adult with tablet/guided tour €6/8; ⏲10am-2pm & 4-8pm May-Oct, 10.30am-2pm & 4-6.30pm Nov-Apr) Catalan architect Antoni Gaudí left his mark on Astorga in the fairy-tale turrets and frilly facade of this *palacio*. Built in the 19th century, it now houses the **Museo de los Caminos** (in the basement), an eclectic collection with Roman artefacts and coins; contemporary paintings (on the top floor); and medieval sculpture, Gothic tombs and silver crosses (on the ground and 1st floors). The highlight is the **chapel**, with its stunning murals and stained glass.

**Museo del Chocolate** MUSEUM

(☎987 61 62 20; Avenida de la Estación 16; adult/child €2.50/free, incl Museo Romano adult/child €4/free; ⏲10.30am-2pm & 4.30-7pm Tue-Sat, 10.30am-2pm Sun; 👪) Proof that Astorga does not exist solely for the virtuous souls of the Camino comes in the form of this quirky private museum. Chocolate ruled Astorga's local economy in the 18th and 19th centuries; this eclectic collection of old machinery, colourful advertising and lithographs inhabits a lovely old mansion within walking distance of the centre. Best of all, you get a free chocolate sample at the end.

### ROMAN ASTORGA

The Romans built the first settlement here, Astúrica Augusta, at the head of the Ruta del Oro. Housed in the Roman *ergástula* (slave prison), the **Museo Romano** (☎987 61 68 38; Plaza de San Bartolomé 2; adult/child €3/free, incl Museo del Chocolate adult/child €4/free; ⏲10am-2pm & 4.30-7pm Tue-Sat, 10am-2pm Sun Jul-Sep, 10am-2pm & 4-6pm Tue-Sat, 10am-2pm Sun Oct-May; 👪) has a modest selection of artefacts and an enjoyable big-screen slide show on Roman Astorga. Just down the hill to the south is the **Casa Romana** (Calle de Padres Redentoristas), the ruins of a mosaic-rich villa that once belonged to a wealthy Roman family. A block away are the low-slung ruins of the **Foro Romano** (Calle de Matias Rodríguez). To get an overview of it all, take the **Ruta Romana** (☎987 61 69 37; https://turismoastorga.es; per person incl Museo Romano €5; ⏲11am & 5pm Tue-Sat, 11am Sun), a 1¾-hour guided tour of Astorga's Roman remains (some of which are accessible only as part of this tour). The tours are conducted in Spanish only but most of the sites have English information panels.

For more in-depth coverage of the town's history, ask for the brochure *The History Begins in Astorga* at the tourist office, or visit www.asturica.com.

**Catedral** CATHEDRAL
(Plaza de la Catedral; incl museum & cloister €5; ⏲10am-8.30pm Mon-Sat, 10-11.15am & 1-8.30pm Sun Apr-Oct, 10.30am-6pm Nov-Mar) The cathedral's striking plateresque southern facade was created from caramel-coloured sandstone with elaborate sculptural detail. Work began in 1471 and continued over three centuries, resulting in a mix of styles. The mainly Gothic interior has soaring ceilings and a superb 16th-century altarpiece by Gaspar Becerra. The attached **Museo Catedralicio** features the usual religious art, documents and artefacts.

## Festivals & Events

**Festividad de Santa Marta** RELIGIOUS
(⏲late Aug; 👪) The sacred and the profane mix seamlessly as Astorga celebrates its patron saint with fireworks and bullfights in the last week of August.

## Sleeping

**Hotel Vía de la Plata** HOTEL €€
(☎987 61 90 00; www.hotelviadelaplata.es; Calle Padres Redentoristas 5; s/d/ste incl breakfast €55/70/100; ❄@📶) This spa hotel occupies a handsome former monastery just off Plaza de España. Guests receive a considerable discount for the spa treatments, which include the deliciously decadent-sounding *chocoterapia* (chocolate therapy). The rooms are slick and modern, with fashionable brown and cream decor, tubular lights and full-size tubs, as well as showers.

**Hotel Astur Plaza** HOTEL €€
(☎987 61 89 00; www.hotelasturplaza.es; Plaza de España 2; s/d/ste incl breakfast from €50/65/95; ❄@📶) Opt for one of the supremely comfortable rooms that face pretty Plaza de España – at weekends, however, you may want to forsake the view for a quieter room out the back. The suites have hydromassage tubs and there are three VIP rooms with 'super king-size' beds, but even the standard rooms here are good.

## Eating

There are tapas bars in the streets around Plaza de España.

★**Restaurante Las Termas** CASTILIAN €€
(☎987 60 22 12; www.restaurantelastermas.com; Calle de Santiago Postas 1; mains €10-23; ⏲1-4pm Tue-Sun; 👪) This lunchtime restaurant is run by Santiago (a popular name in these parts), who, apart from being a charming host, oversees a menu renowned for the quality of its *cocido maragato* (€22; meat-and-chickpea stew) and *ensalada maragata* (salad of chickpeas and cod). It's one of those places where you're made to feel welcome from the minute you enter, and the food is unimpeachable.

**Restaurante Serrano** CONTEMPORARY SPANISH €€
(☎987 61 78 66; www.restauranteserrano.es; Calle de la Portería 2; mains €13-23; ⏲1-4pm & 8.30-11.30pm Tue-Sun) The menu at upmarket Restaurante Serrano has a subtle gour-

### COCIDO MARAGATO

The local speciality in Astorga and surrounding villages (although you also find it in León) is *cocido maragato*. Its constituent elements are indistinguishable from a normal *cocido*, beloved in Madrid and across the Castilian heartland – it's a stew or hotpot made of various meats (some say seven meats), potatoes, chickpeas and a noodle soup. What makes it different to *cocido* elsewhere is that in a *cocido maragato* the various elements are served in reverse: first the meats, then the vegetables, then the soup.

The origins behind the tradition are much disputed. Some say that it dates back to a time when those transporting goods to and from Las Médulas by donkey chose to eat the most solid foods first as they were easiest to eat when on the move. Another story claims that bandits were common in the area and if a meal had to be interrupted, at least those eating had their fill of meat. More prosaically, local farmworkers are said to have eaten their *cocido* in this way because out in the open air, the meat would be cold by the time they got to it if eaten like a normal *cocido*.

Whatever the reason, portions are huge, so one order usually feeds two. It's also really only considered a lunchtime dish (which is why most Astorga restaurants don't even bother opening in the evening). Two of the best places to try it are Restaurante Las Termas (p184) and **Casa Maragata** (☎987 61 88 80; www.casamaragata.com; Calle de Húsar Tiburcio 2; cocido per person €22; ⏲1.30-4pm Wed-Mon)..

WORTH A TRIP

## LAS MÉDULAS

The ancient Roman **gold mines** at Las Médulas, about 20km southwest of Ponferrada, once served as the main source of gold for the entire Roman Empire – the final tally came to a remarkable 3 million kilograms. It's stunningly beautiful, especially at sunset – and one of the more bizarre landscapes you'll see in Spain. The best views are from the **Mirador de Orellán**, while there are some terrific **walks** from the village of Las Médulas.

Las Médulas' otherworldly aspect is not a natural phenomenon: an army of slaves honeycombed the area with canals and tunnels (some over 40km long), through which they pumped water to break up the rock and free it from the precious metal.

To get here, take the N536 southwest of Ponferrada, then take the signed turn off in the village of Carucedo. On the outskirts of Carucedo, the road forks. The left fork leads to the pretty stone village of **Orellán** (2.8km on), which tumbles down into a valley, and then on to the car park for the Mirador de Orellán. From the car park it's a steep 750m climb up to the lookout, from where the views are breathtaking.

Returning to the fork, the right branch leads on to Las Médulas village (3km on). Park at the entrance to the village, then stop at the **Aula Arqueológica** (987 42 28 48; www.ieb.org.es; adult/child €2/free; 10am-1.30pm & 4-8pm Apr-Sep, 10am-2pm Sun-Fri, 10am-1.30pm & 3.30-7pm Sat Oct-Mar), an interpretation centre with interesting displays on the history of the mines. If you're feeling fit, a 5.1km trail climbs to the Mirador de Orellán (one way/return three/4½ hours) from here.

Las Médulas can get overwhelmed with visitors on weekends. Las Médulas village has a handful of restaurants and *casas rurales* in case you're tempted to linger.

met flourish, with fresh summery starters, innovative meat and fish mains and plenty of tempting desserts with chocolate. It also serves *cocido maragato* and other local dishes. Reservations recommended.

### Shopping

**Confitería Mantecadas Velasco** FOOD
(987 61 62 80; www.mantecadasvelasco.com; Plaza Eduardo de Castro 1; 10.30am-2pm & 4.30-7.30pm) The word among locals in the know is that Confitería Mantecadas Velasco serves some of the best *mantecadas* (a cake-like sweet) and other pastries in Astorga. We've tried them and who are we to argue? It's an obligatory part of the Castilla y León foodie experience.

### Information

**Oficina de Turismo** (987 61 82 22; www.turismocastillayleon.com; Glorieta Eduardo de Castro 5; 10am-2pm & 4-8pm daily Apr-Sep, 10am-2pm & 4-6.30pm Tue-Sat, 10am-2pm Sun Oct-Mar) Opposite the Palacio de Gaudí.

### Getting There & Away

Regular bus services connect Astorga with León (€3.95, one hour, 17 daily) and Madrid (from €20, 4½ hours, three daily). The train station is inconveniently a couple of kilometres north of town.

## Sahagún

POP 2515 / ELEV 807M

A modest, picturesque town today, Sahagún was once home to one of Spain's more powerful abbeys; it remains an important way station for pilgrims en route to Santiago.

### Sights

**Santuario de La Peregrina** CONVENT
(987 78 10 15; off Avenida Fernando de Castro; €3; 10.30am-2pm & 4.30-8pm Tue-Sun Jul–mid-Sep, 11am-2pm & 4-6.30pm Wed-Sun, 4-6.30pm Tue mid-Sep–Jun) This 13th-century former convent has been stunningly restored, with glimpses of elaborate 13th-century frescoes and 17th-century Mudéjar plasterwork (the latter is in the chapel to the right of the main nave). Contemporary artworks fill the spaces in between and a modern addition to the convent houses some excellent scale models of Sahagún's major monuments.

**Iglesia de San Tirso** CHURCH
(Plaza de San Tirso; 10am-2pm & 3-5.50pm Wed-Sat, 10am-2pm Sun) FREE The early 12th-century Iglesia de San Tirso, at the western entrance to town, is an important stop on the Camino de Santiago. It's known for its pure Romanesque design and Mudéjar bell tower laced with rounded arches.

## Sleeping & Eating

**La Bastide du Chemin** HOSTAL €
(☎987 78 11 83; Calle del Arco 66; s/d €30/45; ) This small, cosy *hostal*, opposite the Albergue de Peregrinos (Hostel for Pilgrims), has pleasant rustic rooms with beamed ceilings.

**San Facundo** CASTILIAN €€
(☎987 78 02 76; Avenida de la Constitución 97-99; mains €13-27; 1-4pm & 8-11pm; ) Part of the **Hostal La Codorniz** (s/d €40/50; ), this traditional restaurant, which has an impressive carved Mudéjar ceiling, specialises in succulent roasted meats.

## Information

**Oficina de Turismo** (☎987 78 21 17; www.sahagun.org; Calle del Arco 87; noon-2pm & 6-9pm Mon-Thu, 11am-2pm & 4-9pm Fri-Sun) Located within the Albergue de Peregrinos.

## Getting There & Away

Trains run regularly throughout the day from León (from €5.95, 40 minutes) and Palencia (from €5.95, 35 minutes).

# THE EAST

## Burgos

POP 166,185 / ELEV 861M

The extraordinary Gothic cathedral of Burgos is one of Spain's glittering jewels of religious architecture – it looms large over the city and skyline. On the surface, conservative Burgos seems to embody all the stereotypes of a north-central Spanish town, with sombre grey-stone architecture, the fortifying cuisine of the high *meseta* (plateau) and a climate of extremes. But this is a city that rewards deeper exploration: below the surface lie good restaurants and, when the sun's shining, pretty streetscapes that extend beyond the landmark cathedral. There's even a whiff of legend about the place: beneath the majestic spires of the cathedral lies the tomb of Burgos' most roguish son, El Cid.

## Sights

Burgos' historic centre is austerely elegant, guarded by monumental gates and with the cathedral as its centrepiece. This quarter can be accessed from the south via two main bridges: the **Puente de San Pablo**, beyond which looms a romanticised **statue of El Cid** and, about 300m to the west, the **Puente de Santa María**, leading to the splendid Arco de Santa María, once the main gate to the old city and part of the 14th-century walls.

Running along the riverbank between the two bridges is the **Paseo del Espolón**, an attractive, tree-lined pedestrian area. Just back from the *paseo* (promenade) is the **Plaza Mayor**, with some striking facades.

**★Catedral** CATHEDRAL
(☎947 20 47 12; www.catedraldeburgos.es; Plaza del Rey Fernando; adult/child under 14yr incl audio guide €7/2, from 4.30pm Tue free; 9.30am-7.30pm mid-Mar–Oct, 10am-7pm Nov–mid-Mar) This Unesco World Heritage–listed cathedral, once a former modest Romanesque church, is a masterpiece. Work began on a grander scale in 1221; remarkably, within 40 years most of the French Gothic structure had been completed. You can enter from Plaza de Santa María for free access to the **Capilla del Santísimo**, with its much-revered 13th-century crucifix, and the **Capilla de Santa Tecla**, with its extraordinary ceiling. However, we recommend that you visit the cathedral in its entirety.

The cathedral's twin towers went up in the 15th century; each is 84m of richly decorated Gothic fantasy surrounded by a sea of similarly intricate spires. Probably the most impressive of the portals is the **Puerta del Sarmental**, the main entrance for visitors – although the honour could also go to the **Puerta de la Coronería**, on the northwestern side, which shows Christ surrounded by the evangelists.

Inside the main sanctuary, a host of other chapels showcase the diversity of the interior, from the light and airy **Capilla de la Presentación** to the **Capilla de la Concepción**, with its gilded, 15th-century altar, and the **Capilla de Santa Ana**, with its gorgeous *retablo*. The **Capilla del Condestable**, behind the main altar, bridges Gothic and plateresque styles; highlights here include three altars watched over by unusual star-shaped vaulting in the dome. The sculptures facing the entrance to the chapel are 15th- and 16th-century masterpieces of stone carving, portraying the Passion, death, resurrection and ascension of Christ.

The main altar is a typically overwhelming piece of gold-encrusted extravagance, while directly beneath the star-vaulted central dome lies the **tomb of El Cid**. With so much else to catch the eye, it's easy to miss the sublime main **dome**, high above the

## Burgos

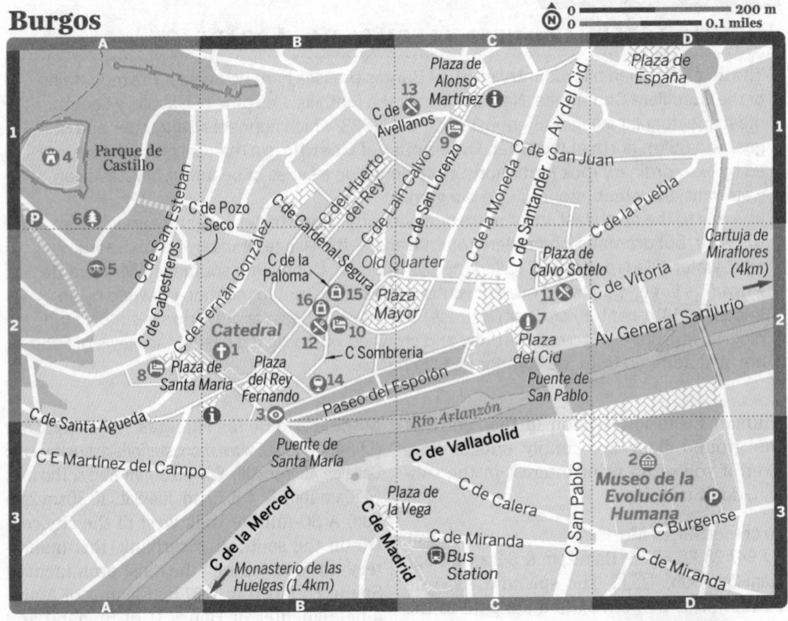


### Burgos

**Top Sights**
1 Catedral ... B2
2 Museo de la Evolución Humana ... D3

**Sights**
3 Arco de Santa María ... B2
4 Castillo de Burgos ... A1
5 Mirador ... A2
6 Parque de Castillo ... A1
7 Statue of El Cid ... C2

**Sleeping**
8 Hotel Mesón del Cid ... A2
9 Hotel Norte y Londres ... C1
10 Rimbombín ... B2

**Eating**
11 Casa Ojeda ... C2
12 Cervecería Morito ... B2
13 La Favorita ... C1

**Drinking & Nightlife**
14 Vermutería Victoria ... B2

**Shopping**
15 Casa Quintanilla ... B2
16 Jorge Revilla ... B2

main sanctuary – it's a masterpiece of the plateresque, with a few Gothic flourishes. Another highlight is Diego de Siloé's magnificent **Escalera Dorada** (Gilded Stairway) on the cathedral's northwestern flank.

Also worth a look is the peaceful cloister, with its sculpted medieval tombs. Off the cloister is the **Capilla de Corpus Cristi**, where, high on the northwestern wall, hangs what legend calls the coffin of El Cid, although doubts remain as to its origins. The adjoining **Museo Catedralicio** has a wealth of oil paintings, tapestries and ornate chalices, while the lower cloister covers the history of the cathedral's development.

**★ Museo de la Evolución Humana** MUSEUM

(MEH; ☎902 02 42 46; www.museoevolucionhumana.com; Paseo Sierra de Atapuerca; adult/concession/child €6/4/free, 4.30-8pm Wed, 7-8pm Tue & Thu free; ⏲10am-2.30pm & 4.30-8pm Tue-Fri, 10am-8pm Sat & Sun) This exceptional museum just across the river from the old quarter is a marvellously told story of human evolution. The basement exhibitions on Atapuerca (www.atapuerca.org), an archaeological site north of Burgos where a 2007 discovery of Europe's oldest human fossil remains was made, are stunning; the displays on Charles Darwin and the extraordinary

OFF THE BEATEN TRACK

## NORTHEASTERN CASTILLA Y LEÓN BY BACK ROADS

The quiet Castilian backcountry north of Burgos presses hard up against the mountains of the Cordillera Cantábrica. Nestled among the foothills are some of Castilla y León's most spectacular villages. Signposted off the N623, which connects Santander and Burgos, and 66km north of the latter, **Orbaneja del Castillo** is a magical place. Surrounded by extraordinary rock formations, built alongside a series of beautiful, crystal-clear waterfalls, this steep, stone village is a gem.

Away to the northeast, in far more open country, **Puentedey** is pretty enough from the west, but dramatic when seen from the east – the village sits above an extraordinary, water-filled rock tunnel called the Ojo Guareña. Continuing southeast, **Medina de Pomar** is larger, but its old quarter is utterly charming, not to mention crowned by an imposing, 14th-century *alcázar* (fortress). Further southeast again, **Frías** is simply stunning, strung out along a narrow ridge and crowned with a ruined castle; the views of Frías are best admired from the Mirador de El Peñasco.

'Human Evolution' section in the centre of the ground floor are simply outstanding. Even if you've no prior interest in the subject, don't miss it.

**Arco de Santa María** GATE
(947 28 88 68; 11am-2pm & 5-9pm Tue-Sat, 11am-2pm Sun) FREE The splendid Arco de Santa María was once the main gate to the old city and part of the 14th-century walls. It now hosts temporary exhibitions, but its real charm lies as a backdrop to the Puente de Santa María or Paseo del Espolón.

**Castillo de Burgos** CASTLE
(947 20 38 57; Parque de Castillo; adult/child under 14yr €3.70/2.60; hours vary; ) FREE Crowning the leafy hilltop **Parque de Castillo** are the fortifications of the rebuilt Castillo de Burgos. Dating from the 9th century, the castle has witnessed a turbulent history, suffering a fire in 1736 and being blown up by Napoleon's troops in 1813. There's a small **museum** covering the town's history; some of the original castle foundations are on view. Just south of the car park is a **mirador** with great views of the cathedral and city.

**Cartuja de Miraflores** MONASTERY
(947 25 25 86; www.cartuja.org; 10.15am-3pm & 4-6pm Mon-Sat, 11am-3pm & 4-6pm Sun) FREE Located in peaceful woodlands 4km east of the city centre, this monastery contains a trio of 15th-century masterworks by Gil de Siloé, the man responsible for so many of the more beautiful features in the Burgos cathedral. The walk to the monastery along Río Arlanzón takes about one hour. To get here, head north along Paseo de la Quinta (flanking the river), from where the monastery is clearly signposted.

**Monasterio de las Huelgas** MONASTERY
(947 20 16 30; www.monasteriodelashuelgas.org; Calle de Alfonso XIII; €6, 4-5.30pm Wed & Thu free; 10am-1pm & 4-5.30pm Tue-Sat, 10.30am-2pm Sun) A 30-minute walk west of the city centre on the southern riverbank, this monastery was once among the most prominent in Spain. Founded in 1187 by Eleanor of Aquitaine, daughter of Henry II of England and wife of Alfonso VIII of Castilla, it's still home to 35 Cistercian nuns. Entry is via one-hour guided tour only – unhelpfully, the timing of the tours is decided only at the beginning of each session, so it's worth ringing ahead.

## Sleeping

★**Rimbombín** HOSTAL €
(947 26 12 00; www.rimbombin.com; Calle Sombrería 6; d/tr/apt from €39/54/69; ) This *hostal* has an upbeat, contemporary feel – its slick white furnishings and decor are matched with light-pine beams and modular furniture. Three rooms have balconies overlooking the pedestrian street. Conveniently, it's in the heart of Burgos' compact tapas district.

**Hotel Norte y Londres** HISTORIC HOTEL €
(947 26 41 25; www.hotelnorteylondres.com; Plaza de Alonso Martínez 10; s/d from €40/45; P@) Set in a former 16th-century palace and decorated with understated period charm, this fine, family-run hotel promises spacious rooms with antique furnishings and polished wooden floors. All rooms have pretty balconies and double-glazed windows; those on the 4th floor are more modern. The bathrooms are exceptionally large and the service friendly and efficient.

**Hotel Mesón del Cid** HISTORIC HOTEL €€
(☎947 20 87 15; www.mesondelcid.es; Plaza de Santa María 8; d/ste from €60/115; P 📶) Facing the cathedral, this hotel occupies a centuries-old building. Rooms have Regency-style burgundy-and-cream fabrics, aptly combined with dark-wood furnishings and terracotta tiles. Several have stunning front-row seats of the cathedral.

## Eating

Burgos is famous for its *queso* (cheese), *morcilla* (blood sausage) and *cordero asado.* There's a buzzing tapas scene close to the cathedral; other excellent choices can be found across the old quarter.

★**Cervecería Morito** TAPAS €
(☎947 26 75 55; Calle de Diego Porcelos 1; tapas/raciones from €4/6; ⌚12.30-3.30pm & 7-11.30pm) Cervecería Morito is the undisputed king of Burgos tapas bars and as such it's always crowded. A typical order is *alpargata* (lashings of cured ham with bread, tomato and olive oil) or the *revueltos Capricho de Burgos* (scrambled eggs served with potatoes, blood sausage, red peppers, baby eels and mushrooms) – the latter is a meal in itself.

**La Favorita** TAPAS €€
(☎947 20 59 49; www.lafavoritaburgos.com; Calle de Avellanos 8; tapas from €4; ⌚10am-midnight Mon-Fri, noon-12.30am Sat & Sun) Away from the main Burgos tapas hub but still close to the cathedral, La Favorita has an appealing, barn-like interior of exposed brick and wooden beams. The emphasis is on local cured meats and cheeses (try the cheese platter for €15); wine by the glass starts at €2.

**Casa Ojeda** CASTILIAN €€€
(☎947 20 90 52; www.grupojeda.com; Calle de Vitoria 5; mains €18-27, set menu €36; ⌚1-3.30pm & 8-11pm Mon-Sat, 1-4pm Sun) Dating from 1912, this Burgos institution, all sheathed in dark wood with stunning mullioned windows, is one of the best places in town to try *cordero asado* or *morcilla de Burgos,* but there are some surprising twists, such as the *solomillo* (sirloin) medallions with foie gras and essence of raspberry. The upstairs dining room has outstanding food and faultless service.

## Drinking & Nightlife

There are two main hubs of nightlife. The first is along Calle de San Juan and Calle de la Puebla. For later nights on weekends, Calle del Huerto del Rey, northeast of the cathedral, has dozens of bars.

★**Vermutería Victoria** BAR
(☎947 11 58 75; Plaza del Rey San Fernando 4; ⌚noon-4pm & 7.30-11pm) This wildly popular bar is a Burgos classic perfect for first drinks. That time-honoured Spanish tradition of a pre-meal *vermut* (vermouth, or martini) comes with a twist here – at 10pm nightly the entire crowd launches into song with Burgos' unofficial anthem. The vermouth is award-winning, smooth and, as Spaniards like to say, perfectly poured.

### EL CID: HERO OR MERCENARY?

Few names resonate through Spanish history quite like El Cid, the 11th-century soldier of fortune and adventurer whose story tells in microcosm of the tumultuous years when Spain was divided into Muslim and Christian zones. That El Cid became a romantic, idealised figure of history, known for his unswerving loyalty and superhuman strength, owes much to the 1961 film starring Charlton Heston and Sophia Loren. Reality, though, presents a different picture.

El Cid (from the Arabic *sidi* for 'chief' or 'lord') was born Rodrigo Díaz in Vivar, a hamlet about 10km north of Burgos, in 1043. After the death of Ferdinand I, he dabbled in the murky world of royal succession, which led to his banishment from Castilla in 1076. With few scruples, El Cid offered his services to a host of rulers, both Christian and Muslim. With each battle, he became ever more powerful and wealthy.

It's not known whether he suddenly developed a loyalty to the Christian kings or smelled the wind and saw that Spain's future would be Christian. Either way, when he heard that the Muslim armies had taken Valencia and expelled all the Christians, El Cid marched on the city, recaptured it and became its ruler in 1094 after a devastating siege. At the height of his power and reputation, the man also known as El Campeador (Champion) retired to spend the remainder of his days in Valencia, where he died in 1099. His remains were returned to Burgos, where he lies buried in the town's cathedral (p186).

## Shopping

**Casa Quintanilla** FOOD
(☎947 20 25 35; www.casaquintanilla.es; Calle de la Paloma 17; ⏲10am-2pm & 5-8.30pm Mon-Sat, 10am-2pm Sun) This is the pick of many stores around the town centre offering local produce that's ideal for a picnic or a gift.

**Jorge Revilla** JEWELLERY
(☎947 274 040; www.jorgerevilla.com; Calle de la Paloma 29; ⏲10am-2pm & 5-8pm Mon-Fri, 10am-2pm Sat) Local Burgos jewellery designer Jorge Revilla is becoming a global name for his exquisite and sophisticated silver pieces.

## Information

**Oficina de Turismo de Burgos** (☎947 28 88 74; http://turismo.aytoburgos.es; Plaza de Santa María; ⏲9am-8pm daily Jun-Sep, 9.30am-2pm & 4-7pm Mon-Sat, 9.30am-5pm Sun Oct-May) Pick up its 24-hour, 48-hour and 72-hour guides to Burgos. (These helpful itinerary suggestions can also be downloaded as PDFs from the website.)

**Oficina de Turismo de Castilla y León** (☎902 20 30 30; www.turismocastillayleon.com; Plaza de Alonso Martínez 7; ⏲9.30am-2pm & 4-7pm Mon-Sat, 9am-5pm Sun) For information on Castilla y León.

## Getting There & Away

The **bus station** (☎947 26 55 65; Calle de Miranda 4) is south of the river, in the newer part of town. Regular buses run to Madrid (from €17, three hours, up to 20 daily), Bilbao (from €10, two hours, eight daily) and León (from €5.50, two hours, three daily).

The train station is a considerable hike northeast of the town centre; bus 2 (€1.50) connects the train station with Plaza de España. Renfe, the national rail network, has a convenient **sales office** (☎947 20 91 31; www.renfe.com; Calle de la Moneda 21; ⏲9.30am-1.30pm & 5-8pm Mon-Fri, 9.30am-1.30pm Sat) in the centre of town. Destinations include Madrid (from €22.50, 2½ to 4½ hours, six daily), Bilbao (from €11.50, 2¾ hours, four daily), León (from €15, two hours, four daily) and Salamanca (from €16.50, three hours, seven daily).

# Around Burgos

The hinterland of Burgos is one of the loveliest areas for exploring quiet Castilian villages. Two stand out – Covarrubias and Santo Domingo de Silos – but this region's quiet back roads have plenty of hidden treasures and churches in the most unexpected places.

# Covarrubias

POP 545 / ELEV 975M

A breath away from the Middle Ages, picturesque Covarrubias is one of Castilla y León's highlights. Spread out along the shady banks of the Río Arlanza, its distinctive, arcaded half-timbered houses overlook intimate cobblestone squares. A good time to be here is for the **Mercado de la Cereza** (www.covarrubias.es; ⏲Jul), a medieval market and cherry festival second weekend of July.

**★Colegiata de San Cosme y Damián** CHURCH
(€2.50; ⏲guided tours 11am, noon, 1pm, 4.30pm & 5.30pm Mon & Wed-Sat, 1pm & 4.30pm Sun) This evocative 15th-century Gothic church is home to Spain's oldest still-functioning church organ, and has a gloriously ostentatious altar, fronted by several Roman stone tombs, plus that of Fernán González, the 10th-century founder of Castilla. Don't miss the graceful cloisters and the *sacristía* (sacristy) with its vibrant 15th-century paintings by Van Eyck and triptych *Adoración de los Magos*. Entry is by guided visit only – check at the tourist office for tour times.

## Sleeping & Eating

Bar food dominates the Covarrubias scene, although there are some sit-down restaurants scattered around the old town, especially close to Plaza de Doña Urraca.

**Hotel Rural Princesa Kristina** HOTEL €
(☎947 40 65 43; www.hotelprincesakristina.com; Calle de Fernán González 5; s/d from €36/47; ❄📶) Tucked away up a quiet side street that doesn't see much foot traffic, but right in the heart of the village, the Princesa Kristina has appealing rooms with wooden beams and window frames, splashes of colour and fresh flowers. It's outstanding value.

**Hotel Rey Chindasvinto** HOTEL €
(☎947 40 65 60; www.hotelreychindasvinto.com; Plaza del Rey Chindasvinto 5; s/d incl breakfast €38/50; ❄📶) The Rey Chindasvinto has lovely, spacious rooms with wooden beams, exposed brickwork and a good restaurant.

**Restaurante de Galo** CASTILIAN €€
(☎947 40 63 93; www.degalo.com; Calle Monseñor Vargas 10; mains €10-21, set menu €22; ⏲1.30-4pm Thu & Sun-Tue, 9-11pm Fri & Sat) This fine restaurant in the heart of Covarrubias is recommended for its robust traditional dishes, cooked in a wood-fired oven. You can sample

# Camino Francés in Castilla y León

the regional speciality of *cordero asado*. It also does a fine *olla podrida* (rotten pot), a medieval Castilian stew that includes red beans, ribs and blood sausage.

## Information

**Oficina de Turismo** (947 40 64 61; www.covarrubias.es; Calle de Monseñor Vargas; 10am-3pm Sun & Tue, 10am-3pm & 4-6pm Wed-Sat) Under the arches of the imposing northern gate, the tourist office runs guided tours at noon most weekends.

## Getting There & Away

Two buses travel between Burgos and Covarrubias on weekdays, and one runs on Saturday (€4.50, one hour). There's free parking in the area along the northwest edge of the old town.

# Santo Domingo de Silos

POP 280

Nestled in the rolling hills south of Burgos, this tranquil, pretty stone village has an unusual claim to fame: monks from its monastery made the British pop charts in the mid-1990s with recordings of Gregorian chants. The monastery is one of the most famous in central Spain, known for its stunning cloister. The surroundings and general sense of calm make this a fine place to spend a day or two.

## Sights

For sweeping views over the town, pass under the **Arco de San Juan** and climb the hill to the south to the **Ermita del Camino y Via Crucis**. Best early to mid-morning.

### CAMINO FRANCÉS IN CASTILLA Y LEÓN

The Camino de Santiago cuts through the heart of northern Castilla y León, from east to west. The Camino Francés, the main *camino* trail, passes through Burgos, Sahagún, León and Astorga, and is one of the most appealing sections of the entire route.

**Abadía de Santo Domingo de Silos** MONASTERY
(947 39 00 49; www.abadiadesilos.es; Calle de Santo Domingo 2; adult/child €3.50/free; 10am-1pm & 4.30-6pm Tue-Sat, noon-1pm & 4-6pm Sun) The cloister and museum of this revered monastery is a two-storey treasure chest of some of Spain's most imaginative Romanesque art. The overall effect is spectacular, but the sculpted capitals are especially exquisite, with lions intermingled with floral and geometrical motifs. The guided tour covers the 17th-century **botica** (pharmacy) and a small **museum** containing religious artworks, Flemish tapestries and the odd medieval sarcophagus. Guided tours are in Spanish only.

**Basílica de San Sebastián** CHURCH
(Calle de Santo Domingo; 6am-2pm & 4.30-10pm, vespers 6am, 7.30am, 9am, 1.45pm, 7pm & 9.30pm) FREE Notable for its pleasingly unadorned Romanesque sanctuary dominated by a multidomed ceiling, this is where you can hear the monks chant vespers six times a day. The church was granted the coveted status of basilica by papal decree in 2000.

WORTH A TRIP

### MONASTERIO DE SAN PEDRO DE ARLANZA

The haunting ruins of **Monasterio de San Pedro de Arlanza** (BU-905; adult/child €2/free; ⌚11am-1.55pm & 4-7.50pm Wed-Sun Apr-Sep, 10.30am-5pm Wed-Sun Oct-Mar), on a rise above the Río Arlanza, show traces of both Gothic and Romanesque elements but the sense of elegant abandonment is what remains with you after a visit. Begun as a hermitage in the 10th century, it grew over the following centuries to become one of the most important monasteries in Castilla. It was abandoned in 1835, when the state decommissioned many churches and monasteries across the country. It's along the quiet BU-905 between Covarrubias and Hortigüela.

### Sleeping & Eating

**Hotel Santo Domingo de Silos** HOTEL, HOSTAL €
(☎947 39 00 53; www.hotelsantodomingodesilos.com; Calle Santo Domingo 14; s €38-54, d €45-72, apt €75-125; P❄☎☒) This place combines a simple *hostal* with a three-star hotel with large, comfortable rooms (some with spa bathtubs) right opposite the monastery. It also has several nearby apartments.

★**Hotel Tres Coronas** HISTORIC HOTEL €€
(☎947 39 00 47; www.hoteltrescoronasdesilos.com; Plaza Mayor 6; incl breakfast s €58-80, d €75-105; P❄☎) Set in a former 17th-century palace, this terrific hotel is brimming with character, with rooms of thick stone walls and old-world charm – including suits of armour and antique furnishings in the public spaces. The front rooms have lovely views over the square. The atmospheric restaurant (mains €12 to €23) specialises in meats roasted in a wood-fired oven.

### Information

**Oficina de Turismo** (☎947 39 00 70; www.turismocastillayleon.com; Plaza Mayor 1; ⌚10am-1.30pm & 4-6pm Tue-Sun)

### Getting There & Away

There is one daily bus (Monday to Saturday) from Burgos to Santo Domingo de Silos (€7.25, 1½ hours).

# Ribera del Duero

The banks of the Río Duero are lined with poignant ruined castles amid pretty old towns such as El Burgo de Osma and Lerma. The river cuts through two dramatic networks of canyons, the Cañón del Río Lobos and the Hoz del Duratón. Add to this the Ribera del Duero wine-producing region, one of Spain's most respected, and you could easily spend a week exploring the area.

## Lerma

POP 2560 / ELEV 827M

If you're travelling between Burgos and Madrid and finding the passing scenery none too eye-catching, Lerma rises from the roadside as a welcome diversion. An ancient settlement, Lerma hit the big time in the early 17th century, when Grand Duke Don Francisco de Rojas y Sandoval, a minister under Felipe II, launched an ambitious project to create another El Escorial. He failed, but the cobbled streets and delightful plazas of the historic quarter are an impressive legacy.

Pass through the **Arco de la Cárcel** (Prison Gate), off the main road to Burgos, climbing up the long Calle Mayor to the massive **Plaza Mayor**, which is fronted by the oversized **Palacio Ducal**, now a *parador* notable for its courtyards and 210 balconies. To the right of the square is the Dominican nuns' **Convento de San Blas**. A short distance northwest of Plaza Mayor, a pretty passageway and viewpoint, **Mirador de los Arcos**, opens up over Río Arlanza. Its arches connect with the 17th-century **Convento de Santa Teresa**.

### Sleeping & Eating

You're in the heart of Castilian wood-fired-oven territory here. Plaza Mayor is encircled by high-quality restaurants with *cordero asado* on the menu (around €40 for two).

**Posada La Hacienda de Mi Señor** HISTORIC HOTEL €€
(☎947 17 70 52; www.lahaciendademisenor.com; Calle del Barco 6; s/d incl breakfast €49/72; ❄@☎) This charming, quirky place near the top of the town (it's a couple of blocks down the hill from the square) is your best midrange bet, with enormous rooms in a renovated, historic building. The candy-floss colour scheme may start to grate if you stay too long; request room 205 for a more muted paint palette.

★**Parador de Lerma** HISTORIC HOTEL €€€
(Palacio Ducal; ☎947 17 71 10; www.parador.es; Plaza Mayor 1; r €78-190; P❄@☜) Undoubtedly Lerma's most elegant place to stay, this *parador* occupies the renovated splendour of the old Palacio Ducal, but is devoid of the ostentatious decor (suits of armour etc) you find in some *paradores*. Even if you're not staying here, take a look at the graceful, cloistered inner patio.

**Asador Casa Brigante** CASTILIAN €€
(☎947 17 05 94; www.casabrigante.com; Plaza Mayor 5; mains €13-23, roast lamb for two €45; ⊙1.30-4pm) Our favourite *asador* in town is the outstanding Asador Casa Brigante – you won't taste better roast lamb anywhere.

## Information

**Oficina de Turismo** (☎947 17 70 02; www.citlerma.com; Casa Consistorial, Calle de la Audiencia 6; ⊙10am-1.45pm & 4-8pm daily Apr-Sep, 10am-1.45pm & 4-7pm Tue-Sun Oct-Mar) Offers 1¼-hour guided tours (€5) of the town and most of its monuments up to three times daily from Wednesday to Saturday (and twice on Sunday) April to September.

## Getting There & Away

There are eight daily buses from Burgos (€5, 30 minutes), with only four on Saturday or Sunday. Some buses coming from Aranda de Duero or Madrid also pass through – but most will leave you down the hill with a long climb to the top.

# Peñafiel

POP 5090

Peñafiel is the gateway to the Ribera del Duero wine region, which makes it a wonderful base for getting to know the area's celebrated wines. Watched over by a fabulous castle and wine museum, and with one of the region's celebrated town squares, it also has a few charms of its own.

## Sights

★**Plaza del Coso** SQUARE
Get your camera lens poised for one of Spain's most unusual town squares. This rectangular, sandy-floored 15th-century 'square' was one of the first to be laid out for this purpose and is considered one of the most important forerunners to the *plazas mayores* across Spain. It's still used for bullfights on ceremonial occasions, and is watched over by distinctive, half-timbered facades.

★**Castillo de Peñafiel** CASTLE
(Museo Provincial del Vino; ☎983 88 11 99; castle adult/child €3.30/free, incl museum €6.60/free; ⊙10.30am-2pm & 4-8pm Tue-Sun Apr-Sep, 10.30am-2pm & 4-6pm Tue-Sun Oct-Mar) Perched dramatically over Peñafiel, this castle houses the state-of-the-art **Museo Provincial del Vino**. A comprehensive story of the region's wines, this wonderful museum has interactive displays, dioramas and wine tasting (book ahead). The rest of the castle, one of Spain's narrowest, is visited on a 40-minute **guided tour** which explores the castle's crenellated walls and towers (stretching over 200m, they're little more than 20m across). They were built and modified over 400 years, from the 10th century onwards.

## Sleeping & Eating

**Hotel Convento Las Claras** HISTORIC HOTEL €€
(☎983 87 81 68; www.hotelconventolasclaras.com; Plaza Adolfo Muñoz Alonso; r/ste from €85/199; P❄☜≋) This cool, classy hotel – a former convent – is an unexpected find in little Peñafiel, with quietly elegant rooms, as well as a full spa with thermal baths and treatments. On-site is an excellent restaurant with, as you'd expect, a carefully chosen wine list.

**Hotel Castillo de Curiel** HISTORIC HOTEL €€
(☎983 88 04 01; www.castillodecuriel.com; Curiel de Duero; s/d/ste from €81/90/132; P☜) Just north of Peñafiel in Curiel de Duero, this should be the hotel of choice for castle romantics. Occupying the oldest castle in the region (dating from the 9th century), the renovated hotel has lovely, antique-filled rooms, all with sweeping views.

### ONLY IN SPAIN

Every year since 1620, the tiny village of Castrillo de Murcia (25km west of Burgos) has marked the feast of Corpus Cristi with the **Baby-Jumping Festival** (El Salto del Colacho; ⊙May/Jun), lining up the village's babies on mattresses, while grown men leap over up to six supine (and somewhat bewildered) babies at a time. The ritual is thought to ward off the devil – but why jumping over babies? The villagers aren't telling. They do, however, assure us that no baby has been injured in the fiesta's recorded history.

## WINE TASTING IN THE RIBERA DEL DUERO

The Ribero del Duero vintage has the much-coveted Denominación de Origen Protegida (DOP) classification and its wines are possibly the oldest in Spain. Discerning Spanish wine lovers frequently claim that the wines of this region are the equal of the better-known Rioja wines. This is the largest wine-growing region in Castilla y León and it's famous for its reds, made primarily from the *tempranillo* grape variety; one of Spain's most celebrated wines, Vega Sicilia, comes from here.

Not all the 200-plus wineries here are open for tours and/or tasting (including, unfortunately, Vega Sicilia), but around 50 of them are. For a full list, including details about tours and tastings, pick up the excellent *Wine Tourism Guide* for the Ribera del Duero Wine Route, which has contact details and opening hours, and the *Mapa Enoturistico de la Denominación de Origin Ribera del Duero* from the tourist office (p194) in Peñafiel. The tourist office also has the latest list (including on its website). Another good resource is the website www.rutadelvinoriberadelduero.es.

Most of the wineries are located in the countryside surrounding Peñafiel; those that run tours and tastings include the following (advance bookings are *always* required):

**Matarromera** (☎983 10 71 00; www.bodegamatarromera.es; Valbuena de Duero; tasting & tour from €8; ⏲by appointment)

**Legaris** (☎983 87 80 88; www.legaris.es; Curiel de Duero; tasting & tour €14-19; ⏲by appointment)

**Protos** (☎983 87 80 11; www.bodegasprotos.com; Calle Bodegas Protos 24-28, Peñafiel; tour €11; ⏲by appointment)

**Convento de Las Claras** (☎983 88 01 50; www.bodegasconventodelasclaras.com; Carretera Pesquera de Duero, Km 1.5, Peñafiel; tour & tasting €12; ⏲by appointment)

Peñafiel has numerous wine sellers dotted around the village. Some of the better ones include **Vinos Ojosnegros** (☎983 88 00 68; www.vinosojosnegros.com; Plaza de San Miguel de Reoyo 1; ⏲9am-2pm & 5-8.30pm Mon-Fri, 9am-2.30pm & 4-8.30pm Sat) and **Ánagora** (☎983 88 18 57; Calle Derecha al Coso 31; ⏲10.30am-2pm & 5-8pm Mon, Tue, Thu & Fri, 11am-2pm & 5-8pm Sat, 11am-2pm Sun). Many of the shops have handy cards that rate the years in terms of the quality of the Ribera del Duero wines. The best years, according to experts, are 1995, 1996, 1999, 2001, 2004, 2009 to 2011 and 2014.

**Asados Alonso** SPANISH €€
(☎983 88 08 34; www.facebook.com/restauranteasadosalonso; Calle de Derecha al Coso 14; mains €14-23; ⏲1-4.30pm Sun & Tue-Thu, 1-4.30pm & 8.30-11.30pm Fri & Sat) Staff keep it simple at this long-standing *asador,* with roasted spring lamb cooked in a wood-fired oven.

### ℹ Information

**Oficina de Turismo** (☎983 88 15 26; www.turismopenafiel.com; Plaza del Coso 31-32; ⏲10.30am-2.30pm & 5-8pm Tue-Sun Apr-Sep, 10.30am-2pm & 4.30-7pm Tue-Sun Oct-Mar) Has a list of wineries that you can visit and rents out bicycles (half-/full day €3/5).

### ℹ Getting There & Away

Four or five buses a day run to Valladolid (€6, 45 minutes), 60km west of Peñafiel.

## Parque Natural del Cañón del Río Lobos

Some 15km north of El Burgo de Osma, this park promises forbidding rockscapes, some good hiking and a magnificent, deep-river canyon (visible from the lookout alongside the road through the park), as well as abundant vultures and other birds of prey. Set in a wooded area overlooking the river, the fine, early 13th-century **Ermita de San Bartolomé** has a wonderfully lonely aspect and showcases a fusion of styles between late Romanesque and early Gothic, but it's the church in its setting that really makes visiting worthwhile. It's about 4km in off the SO920; take the signposted turn-off at the foot of the switchback road, drive to the car park then walk the final 1km. **Posada Los Templarios** (☎649 656313; www.posadalostemplarios.com; Plaza de la Iglesia; s €48-55, d €62-80, ste €92-102; ❄📶) in Ucero, south of the park, is an excellent place to stay.

There is no public transport to the park so you'll need your own wheels to get here. Access is via the SO920, which runs between El Burgo de Osma and San Leonardo de Yagüe.

## El Burgo de Osma

POP 4925 / ELEV 943M

Beautiful El Burgo de Osma is one of Castilla y León's most underrated towns. Once important enough to host its own university, the town is still partially walled, has some elegant, colonnaded streetscapes and is dominated by a remarkable cathedral.

### Sights

Your initiation into the old town is likely to be along the broad **Calle Mayor**, its portico borne by an uneven phalanx of stone and wooden pillars. Not far along, it leads into **Plaza Mayor**, fronted by the 18th-century **ayuntamiento** (town hall) and the sumptuous **Hospital de San Agustín**, which is where you'll find the tourist office.

If you exit El Burgo de Osma from near the cathedral on Plaza de San Pedro de Osma, take a left for the village of Osma, high above which stand the ruins of the 10th-century **Castillo de Osma**.

**Catedral** CATHEDRAL
(☎975 34 03 19; Plaza de San Pedro de Osma; adult/child €2.50/free; ⏰10.30am-1pm & 4-7.30pm Jul-Sep, 10.30am-1pm & 4-6pm Tue-Fri, 10.30am-1.30pm & 4-7pm Sat Oct-Jun) Dating back to the 12th century, the cathedral's architecture evolved as a combination of the Gothic and, subsequently, baroque (notable in the weighty tower). The sanctuary is filled with art treasures, including the 16th-century main **altarpiece** and the **Beato de Osma**, a precious 11th-century codex (manuscript) displayed in the **Capilla Mayor**. Also of note are the circular **Capilla de Palafox**, a rare example of the neoclassical style in this region, and the beautiful **cloister** with original Romanesque traces.

### Sleeping & Eating

★**Hotel II Virrey** HOTEL €
(☎975 34 13 11; www.virreypalafox.com; Calle Mayor 2; r €50-65, ste €95-115; ❄📶) This place is a curious mix of old Spanish charm and contemporary flair; public areas remain dominated by heavily gilded furniture, porcelain cherubs, dripping chandeliers and a sweeping staircase. Rates soar on weekends in February and March, when people flock here for the ritual slaughter *(matanza)* of pigs and all-you-can-eat feasts.

**Mesón Marcelino** SPANISH €€
(☎975 34 12 49; Calle Mayor 71; mains €13-32, set menu €35; ⏰1-4.30pm & 8.30-11.30pm) A reliable choice along the main street, Mesón Marcelino feeds the passions of this unashamedly meat-loving town. It's all about *cordero* or *cochinillo asado* with steaks and game meats being what passes for variety in El Burgo de Osma. Salads are an essential side order. It has a good tapas bar next door.

### Information

**Oficina de Turismo** (☎975 36 01 16; www.sorianitelaimaginas.com; Plaza Mayor 9; ⏰9.30am-2pm & 4-7pm Wed-Sun) Pick up a copy of the excellent *Tierra del Burgo* brochure to guide your steps around town.

### Getting There & Away

Buses link El Burgo with Soria (€4.50, 50 minutes, two daily, one on Sunday) and Valladolid (€12, two hours, three daily).

## Soria

POP 39,110 / ELEV 1055M

Small-town Soria is one of Spain's smaller provincial capitals. Set on the Río Duero in the heart of backwoods Castilian

WORTH A TRIP

**UXAMA**

Just outside El Burgo de Osma lie the ruins of **Uxama** (N122; ⏰24hr) FREE, with layers of history sprinkled lightly across the hills. Originally a Celto-Iberian settlement, it became an important Roman town after falling under Roman control in 99 BCE; it eventually fell to the Muslims in the 8th century. Low-lying remains of a former home and other fragments will make you wonder what else lies beneath the earth waiting to be excavated. Further into the site, the 9th-century Atalaya (watchtower) affords fabulous views over the surrounding countryside, especially northeast towards El Burgo de Osma and the Castillo de Osma.

countryside, it's a great place to escape 'tourist Spain', with an appealing and compact old centre and a sprinkling of stunning monuments across the town and down by the river. Plan on at least one full day to see all there is to see.

## Sights

**★Monasterio de San Juan de Duero** RUINS
(☎975 22 13 97; Camino Monte de las Ánimas; €1, Sat & Sun free; ⏰10am-2pm Sun year-round, 10am-2pm & 4-8pm Tue-Sat Jul-Sep, 10am-2pm & 4-7pm Tue-Sat Feb-Jun & Oct, 10am-2pm & 4-6pm Tue-Sat Nov-Jan) The most striking of Soria's sights, this wonderfully evocative and partially ruined cloister boasts exposed and gracefully interlaced arches, which artfully blend Mudéjar and Romanesque influences; no two capitals are the same. Inside the church, the carvings are worth a closer look for their intense iconography. It's on the riverbank, down the hill from the historic centre.

**★Ermita de San Saturio** HISTORIC BUILDING
(☎975 18 07 03; Paseo de San Saturio; ⏰10.30am-2pm & 4.30-8.30pm Tue-Sat, 10.30am-2pm Sun Jul & Aug, shorter hours rest of year) FREE A lovely 2.3km riverside walk south from the Monasterio de San Juan de Duero will take you past the 13th-century church of the former Knights Templar, the **Monasterio de San Polo** (not open to the public) and on to the fascinating, baroque Ermita de San Saturio. This hermitage is one of Castilla y León's most beautifully sited structures, an octagonal building that perches high on the riverbank and over the cave where Soria's patron saint spent much of his life.

**Iglesia de Santo Domingo** CHURCH
(☎975 21 12 39; Calle de Santo Tomé Hospicio; ⏰7am-9pm) FREE Soria's most beautiful church is the Romanesque Iglesia de Santo Domingo. Its small but exquisitely sculpted portal is something special, particularly at sunset when its reddish stone glows.

**Palacio de Los Condes Gomara** HISTORIC BUILDING
(Calle de Aguirre) A block north of the Plaza Mayor is the majestic, sandstone, 16th-century Palacio de los Condes Gomara. It can only be admired from the outside.

**Museo Numantino** MUSEUM
(☎975 22 13 97; Paseo del Espolón 8; €1, Sat & Sun free; ⏰10am-2pm & 5-8pm Tue-Sat, 10am-2pm Sun Jul-Sep, 10am-2pm & 4-7pm Tue-Sat, 10am-2pm Sun Oct-Jun) Archaeology buffs with a passable knowledge of Spanish should enjoy this well-organised museum dedicated to finds from ancient sites across the province of Soria, especially the Roman ruins of Numancia. It has everything from mammoth bones to ceramics and jewellery, accompanied by detailed explanations of the historical developments in various major Celtiberian and Roman settlements.

## Festivals & Events

**Fiestas de San Juan y de la Madre de Dios** FIESTA
(www.sanjuaneando.com; ⏰Jun) Since the 13th century, the 12 *barrios* (districts) of Soria have celebrated this annual festival with

### ROMAN SORIA

**Numancia's Roman Ruins** (☎650 709671; www.numanciasoria.es; adult/concession/child under 8yr €5/3/free; ⏰10am-2pm & 4-8pm Tue-Sat, 10am-2pm Sun Jun-Sep, hours vary Oct-May) The mainly Roman ruins of Numancia, just outside the village of Garray (8km north of Soria), are all that remain of a city that proved one of the most resistant to Roman rule. Finally Scipio, who had crushed Carthage, starved the city into submission in 134 BCE. Under Roman rule, Numancia was an important stop on the road from Caesaraugustu (Zaragoza) to Astúrica Augusta (Astorga).

**Villa Romana La Dehesa** (Magna Mater; ☎626 992549; www.villaromanaladehesa.es; off SO100, Las Cuevas de Soria; €2, audio guide €2; ⏰11am-8pm Tue-Sat, to 2.30pm Sun Jul-Sep, hours vary Oct-Jun) This interpretation centre sits atop the site of an ancient Roman villa where stunning **floor mosaics** were found. The visit begins with a video presentation (in Spanish) of the villa's history, followed by a small **museum** of artefacts discovered at the site, before concluding with a walk along elevated walkways that overlook the remaining mosaics; the most spectacular mosaic now resides in Madrid's Museo Arqueológico (p105). The house, first unearthed in the 1930s, once covered 4000 sq metres.

considerable fervour. Held during the second half of June, and sometimes spilling over into July, the main festivities take place on Jueves (Thursday) La Saca, when each of the districts presents a bull to be fought the next day.

## Sleeping

**Hostería Solar de Tejada** BOUTIQUE HOTEL €

(975 23 00 54; www.hosteriasolardetejada.es; Calle de Claustrilla 1; s/d €38/56; ) This handsome boutique hotel right along the historic quarter's pedestrianised zone has individually designed (albeit small) rooms with homey, brightly coloured decor.

★**Apolonia** BOUTIQUE HOTEL €€

(975 23 90 56; www.hotelapoloniasoria.com; Puertas de Pro 5; s/d from €60/68; ) This smart hotel has a contemporary urban feel with its charcoal, brown and cream colour scheme, abundance of glass, abstract artwork and, in four of the rooms, an interesting, if revealing, colour-lighting effect between the main room and the large walk-in shower – best for romancing couples.

**Parador de Soria** HOTEL €€

(975 24 08 00; www.parador.es; Calle de Fortún López, Parque del Castillo; r from €85; ) This modern *parador* occupies a fantastic perch high above the town – the rooms don't have a whole lot of character but they're supremely comfortable, service is exemplary and the views are splendid.

## Eating

**Crepería Lilot Du Ble Noir** FRENCH €

(651 495317; www.facebook.com/creperialilot; Calle Fueros de Soria 12; crêpes €7-12; 1-4.30pm & 9pm-midnight) This appealing little French crêperie adds some much-needed variety to Soria's culinary scene. Savoury versions include minced meat with Camembert and mushrooms, or Asian-spiced pork with rice noodles. It also has sweet crêpes and salads, and an English menu.

**Fogón del Salvador** CASTILIAN €€

(975 23 01 94; www.fogonsalvador.com; Plaza de El Salvador 1; mains €16-24; 1.30-4pm & 9pm-midnight Mon, Tue & Thu-Sat, 1.30-4pm Sun) A Soria culinary stalwart and fronted by a popular bar, Fogón del Salvador has a wine list as long as your arm – literally – and a fabulous wood-fired oven churning out perfectly prepared meat-based dishes such as *cabrito al ajillo* (goat with garlic), as well steaks in all their red-blooded glory.

★**Baluarte** CASTILIAN €€€

(975 21 36 58; www.baluarte.info; Calle de los Caballeros 14; set menus €57-70; 1.30-4pm & 8.45-10.45pm Tue-Sat, 1.30-4pm Sun) Óscar García Marina is one of Spain's most exciting chefs and this Michelin-starred venture in Soria appropriately showcases his culinary talents. Dishes are based on classic Castilian ingredients but treated with just enough foam and drizzle to ensure that they're both exciting and satisfying without being too pretentious. Reservations essential.

## Information

**Oficina de Turismo** (975 22 27 64; www.soria.es; Plaza Mariano Granados; 10am-2pm & 4-7pm Tue-Sat, 10am-2pm Sun) Offers two-hour guided tours (€5) of the historic centre or the sights along the Río Duero on weekends, and more often in summer. Reserve in advance.

**Oficina de Turismo** (975 21 20 52; www.turismocastillayleon.com; Calle de Medinaceli 2; 9.30am-2pm & 4-7pm Mon-Sat, 9.30am-5pm Sun) Information on both the town and the wider Castilla y León region.

## Getting There & Away

From the **bus station** (975 22 51 60; Avenida de Valladolid), a 15-minute walk west of the city centre, there are regular services to Burgos (from €8, 2½ hours), Madrid (from €10, 2½ hours), Valladolid (€13, three hours) and Medinceli (€6, 45 minutes).

The **train station** (912 320 320; www.renfe.com; Carretera de Madrid) is 2.5km southwest of the city centre. Trains connect Soria with Madrid (€23, three hours, two daily), but there are few other direct services.

## Getting Around

In what must be the cheapest parking anywhere in any Spanish city, the underground **Aparcamiento Plaza del Olivo** (Plaza del Olivo; 24hr) in the city centre charges just €3 per 24 hours!

# Around Soria

## Calatañazor

POP 50 / ELEV 1071M

One of Castilla y León's most romantic hilltop villages, Calatañazor is a charming detour. Not visible from the highway (just 1km away), it has a crumbling medieval feel to it. Pass through the town gate and climb

DON'T MISS

**CASTILLA Y LEÓN'S BEST PARADORS**


- Zamora (p174)
- Tordesillas (p172)
- Lerma (p193)
- Ciudad Rodrigo (p158)
- Soria (p197)


the cobbled lanes, wandering through narrow streets lined by ochre stone-and-adobe houses topped with red-tiled roofs and distinctive conical chimneys. Scenes from the movie *Doctor Zhivago* were shot here.

**Castillo de Calatañazor** RUINS
(24hr) Towering above the village is the one-time Muslim fortress that gave Calatañazor its name (which comes from the Arabic Qala'at an-Nassur, literally 'the Vulture's Citadel'). Now in ruins, it has exceptional views from the walls and watchtowers, both down over the rooftops and north over a vast field called Valle de la Sangre (Valley of Blood). The name comes from an epic 1002 battle that saw the Muslim ruler Almanzor defeated.

## Sleeping & Eating

**El Mirador de Almanzor** GUESTHOUSE €
(975 18 36 42; www.elmiradordealmanzor.com; Calle Puerta Vieja 4; r €55-65; ) This place at the upper end of the village, in a 15th-century, half-timbered home beneath the castle, is a fine Calatañazor choice. Rooms have exposed stone walls, wrought-iron furnishings and soft lighting.

★**Casa del Cura de Calatañazor** GUESTHOUSE €€
(975 18 36 42; www.posadarealcasadelcura.com; Calle Real 25; r €65-75; ) The most stylish rooms in Calatañazor are to be found here, around halfway up the hill on the main cobblestone thoroughfare through the village. Rooms have polished floorboards, chairs with zebra-print upholstery and exposed wooden beams.

## Getting There & Away

There's no regular public transport to Calatañazor. If you're driving, the village lies around 1km north of the N122 – the well-signposted turn off is about 29km southwest of Soria and about 27km northeast of El Burgo de Osma.

# Sierra de Urbión & Laguna Negra

The Sierra de Urbión, northwest of Soria, is home to the beautiful Laguna Negra (Black Lake), a small glacial lake resembling a black mirror at the base of brooding rock walls amid partially wooded hills.

Located 18km north of the village of **Vinuesa**, the lake is reached by a scenic, winding and sometimes bumpy road. It ends at a car park, where there's a small **information office** (10am-2pm & 4-6.30pm Jun-Oct). It's a further 2km uphill to the lake, either on foot or via shuttle bus (return €1.50, departing half-hourly from 10am to 2pm and 4pm to 6.30pm June to October), which leaves you 300m short of the lake.

A steep trail leads from the lake up to the **Laguna de Urbión** in La Rioja or to the summit of the **Pico de Urbión**, above the village of Duruelo de la Sierra, and on to a series of other tiny glacial lakes.

If you continue north of Vinuesa along the SO-830 for 28km, you'll reach tiny **Montenegro de Cameros**, one of the prettiest mountain villages in this part of the country.

There's no public transport to this area; you'll need your own vehicle to get here.

# Yanguas

POP 90

The tiny village of Yanguas, close to where Castilla y León climbs into La Rioja, is one of the loveliest villages of Soria's beautiful Tierras Altas (High Country). Yanguas is hemmed in by canyons and hills on all sides and its beautiful, stone-built architecture and cobblestone lanes, accessed beneath a medieval stone arch, are utterly charming.

At the northern end of the village, the imposing 16th-century **Iglesia de Santa María** sits just across the road from a small medieval **stone bridge**. A free-standing **tower**, all that remains of the 12th-century Iglesia de San Miguel, is visible further up the valley and accessible via a trail that leads behind the church. In the town itself, the **Plaza de la Constitución** provides a rustic centrepiece to this quiet village.

## Sleeping & Eating

**Los Cerezos de Yanguas** GUESTHOUSE €
(975 39 15 36; www.loscerezosdeyanguas.com; Paseo San Sebastián 6; s/d €48/65, 2-bedroom apt €120; ) Close to the entrance of town, this family-run *casa rural* occupies a typical

stone-built Yanguas building. Rooms have an oldish style, with wooden bedheads and tiled or parquetry floors, but they're comfy enough. The home-cooked food is reason enough to stay here.

**El Rimero de la Quintina** GUESTHOUSE €
(☎625 485874; www.elrimerodelaquintina.net; Calle de la Iglesia 4; d/tr €55/77; ❄📶) At the top of the village just off Plaza de la Constitución, this fine *casa rural* has attractive rooms with wooden beams, tiled floors and pastel colours, not to mention a lovely garden out back.

## Getting There & Away

There is no regular public transport to Yanguas, which lies 47km northwest of Soria along the SO615.

# Medinaceli

POP 720 / ELEV 1210M

One of Castilla y León's most beautiful *pueblos* (villages), Medinaceli lies draped along a high, windswept ridge just off the A2 motorway. Its mix of Roman ruins, cobblestone laneways and terrific places to stay and eat make it an excellent base for exploring this beautiful corner of Castilla y León. Far down the hill below the old town, modern Medinaceli, along a slip road just north of the A2 motorway, is the contemporary equivalent of a one-horse town.

## History

Although a small settlement may have predated the arrival of the Romans in the 1st century BCE, it was under the Romans that Medinaceli thrived, as the town lay along the main road between two of the most important Roman cities in Iberia: Caesaraugusta (Zaragoza) and Emerita Augusta (Mérida).

Centuries later, thanks to its hilltop perch, the town occupied a site of great strategic importance along the frontier between Catholic and Muslim Spain. It was here in 1002 that the famed Muslim ruler Almanzor died after the Battle of Calatañazor; the town finally fell into Christian hands in 1129.

## Sights

Medinaceli's charm consists of rambling through silent cobblestone lanes and being surrounded by delightful stone houses redolent of the noble families who lived here after the town fell to the Reconquista in 1124. Roman ruins also lie dotted around the village. The tourist office has a brochure and map for a self-guided walk through Medinaceli's sights.

**★Plaza Mayor** SQUARE
The partly colonnaded Plaza Mayor is a lovely centrepiece to the village and one of Castilla y León's prettiest village squares. The oldest remaining building is the 16th-century **Alhónidga**, the only building on the square with two-storey colonnades.

**Arco Romano** RUINS
Watching over the entrance to the town and visible on the approach, Medinaceli's 1st-century-CE Arco Romano (Roman triumphal arch) is one of the best preserved in Spain. It's also the only one in the country to boast three intact arches.

**Santa María de la Huerta** MONASTERY
(☎975 327 002; www.monasteriohuerta.org; €3; ⏲10am-1pm & 4-6pm Mon-Sat, 10-11.15am & 4-6pm Sun) This wonderful Cistercian monastery 27km northeast of Medinaceli was founded in 1162, expropriated in 1835, then restored to the order in 1930; 20 Cistercians are now in residence. Before entering the monastery, note the church's impressive 12th-century facade, with its magnificent rose window. Inside the monastery, the **Claustro de los Caballeros** is the more beautiful of the two cloisters. Off it is the spare yet gorgeous *refectorio* (dining hall); built in the 13th century, it's notable for the absence of columns to support its vault.

OFF THE BEATEN TRACK

### CHAORNA

In a corner of Castilla y León's far east, almost entirely surrounded by Castilla-La Mancha, little Chaorna is one of the region's best-kept secrets. Inhabiting the clefts and twists of a narrow canyon, the village is unlike any other in Castilla y León. Its largely well-preserved stone buildings are crowned by the **Iglesia de San Miguel** and a **tower** that dates back to Islamic times. For the most dramatic views, get out and walk up to the top of the canyon for a vantage point looking down upon the village. Chaorna is 9km south off the A2 – the turn off is 15km northeast of Medinaceli.

OFF THE BEATEN TRACK

## SOUTHEASTERN CASTILLA Y LEÓN BY BACK ROADS

The area southwest of Soria and south of El Burgo de Osma includes some of Castilla y León's more appealing back roads, with dozens of fabulous attractions to explore.

Begin in Medinaceli (p199) and head north along the A15 to **Almazán**, one of those timeworn Castilian towns where the past overshadows the present. It frequently changed hands between the Muslims and Christians; improbably, for three short months it was chosen by Fernando and Isabel as their residence, which probably saved the town from everlasting obscurity and left behind a sprinkling of impressive historical landmarks. It's a worth an hour or two exploring if you're in the area.

Away to the east, Berlanga de Duero is lorded over by an extraordinary ruined **castle** (Berlanga de Duero; ⏲10am-2pm & 4-8pm) FREE made larger by the continuous ramparts at the base of its hill. The castle's oldest section dates from the 15th century, but most of the exterior was erected in the 16th century. About 8km southeast of Berlanga de Duero stands the **Ermita de San Baudelio** (off SO152; €0.60, Sat & Sun free; ⏲10am-2pm & 4-8pm Wed-Sat, 10am-2pm Sun Apr-Sep, 10am-2pm & 4-6pm Wed-Sat, 10am-2pm Sun Oct-Mar) FREE, the simple exterior of which conceals a remarkable 11th-century Mozarabic interior. A great pillar in the centre of the only nave opens up at the top like a palm tree to create delicate horseshoe arches. It's one of rural Castilla's most surprising finds. Just a little further southeast on the SO132, the hilltop stone village of **Rello** retains much of its medieval defensive wall and feels like the place time forgot. The views from the village's southern ledge are superb. There's at least one *casa rural* to stay in if you love peace and quiet.

Back to the northeast, and travelling via Berlanga del Duero, the remarkable **Castillo de Gormaz** (Fortaleza Califal de Gormaz; Gormaz; ⏲24hr) FREE rises above the virtual ghost town of Gormaz (population 21). Built by the Muslims in the 10th century and reportedly the largest Muslim fortress in Europe, the castle was for centuries an important bastion along the frontier between Islamic armies and the Christian forces of the Reconquista. Most of its 21 towers remain and the walls stretch for over a kilometre. When Fernando seized the castle from its Islamic defenders in 1059, one of his first acts in the following year was to construct the **Ermita de San Miguel de Gormaz** (☎975 34 09 02; Gormaz; €1.50; ⏲11am-2pm & 5-8pm Sat, 11am-2pm Sun Jun–mid-Jul, hours vary mid-Jul–May) on the slopes below the castle. While it's not much to look at from the outside, the frescoes inside the main sanctuary are stunning.

At the end of the quiet SO 4123 southwest of Gormaz, the tiny village of **Caracena** (population 15) climbs the slopes at the end of a long river valley in a beautiful collection of stone-and-terracotta houses. The town has two 12th-century Romanesque churches. On a summit above the village, the **Castillo de Caracena** seems to merge with the surrounding crags and is wonderfully atmospheric in the late afternoon.

**Palacio Ducal** PALACE

(Palacio del Duque de Medinaceli; ☎975 32 64 98; Plaza Mayor; €2, Wed free; ⏲10am-3pm & 4-7pm Wed-Mon) This largely 17th-century palace overlooks the Plaza Mayor, and hosts regular high-quality exhibitions of contemporary art in rooms arrayed around the stunning two-storey Renaissance courtyard. One room displays a 2nd-century **Roman mosaic** and information panels on the mosaics that have been found around Medinaceli. The building's facade is the work of Juan Gómez de Mora, who designed Madrid's Plaza Mayor. There's another 2nd-century **mosaic** (Plaza de San Pedro) under glass.

**Colegiata de Santa María** CHURCH

(Plaza de la Iglesia; €1, Mon free; ⏲11am-2pm & 4-7pm Sat & Sun, 11am-2pm Mon) This pretty Gothic church was built in 1561 on the site of what may have been a synagogue or mosque. The 17th-century late-Gothic tower is visible from across the town, while the highlights of the interior are the 18th-century Cristo de Medinaceli (Christ of Medinaceli) and Romanesque crypt.

**Puerta Árabe** GATE

Although modified down through the centuries, this gate on the west side of the village first served as one of four entrances to the settlement in Roman times and was an important gate during the era of Muslim occupation. It's a lovely corner, where narrow Medinaceli byways open out onto sweeping views of the rolling Castilian countryside.

## Festivals & Events

**Festival Lírico Medinaceli** MUSIC
(☎975 32 64 98; www.festivalliricomedinaceli.com; ⏱Aug) In August, Medinaceli's Palacio Ducal (p200) hosts fine operatic performances – the cloistered courtyard is a wonderful venue. Recent performances have included Verdi's *Aida*.

**Festival Internacional de Música** MUSIC
(www.facebook.com/festivalmusicamedinaceli; ⏱Jul) On a handful of dates in July, the Colegiata de Santa María hosts mostly classical concerts by international performers.

## Sleeping

**Hostal Rural Bavieca** BOUTIQUE HOTEL €
(☎975 32 61 06; www.bavieca.net; Calle del Campo de San Nicolás 6; s/d from €44/57; P❄📶) The bold colours and style of the rooms here may not be to everyone's taste, but this is unmistakably a boutique hotel offering high-quality rooms and ambience to match..

★ **Medina Salim** BOUTIQUE HOTEL €€
(☎975 32 61 72; www.hotelmedinasalim.com; Calle Barranco 15; s/d incl breakfast from €80/85; P❄📶) This welcoming boutique hotel sports large, airy rooms with fridges and terraces that overlook either the sweeping valley or medieval cobblestones out front. Decor is contemporary and light, with pale woodwork and excellent bathrooms. Perks include a small spa and a delightful breakfast room that overlooks part of the original Roman wall.

**La Ceramica** HOTEL €€
(☎975 32 63 81; Calle de Santa Isabel 2; s/d/tr incl breakfast €48/69/95; ⏱Feb–mid-Dec; 📶) Deep in the historic quarter, the rooms here are intimate and comfortable, with a strong dose of rustic charm. The attic room 22 is lovely, and the CR2 apartment, which sleeps four, feels just like home.

## Eating

Medinaceli has three good restaurants. From October onwards, opening hours for dinner can be unreliable – we stayed on a Tuesday in October and not a single restaurant opened for dinner in the old town.

**Asador de la Villa El Granero** CASTILIAN €€
(☎975 32 61 89; www.asadorelgranero.es; Calle de Yedra 10; mains €15-23; ⏱1.30-4pm & 9-11pm May-Sep, hours vary Oct-Apr) This well-signposted place, with a shop selling local food products at the front, is thought by many to be Medinaceli's best restaurant. The *setas de campo* (wild mushrooms) are something of a local speciality, though unsurprisingly, grilled and roasted meats dominate this bastion of hearty Castilian cooking.

**La Bavieca** SPANISH €€
(☎975 32 61 06; www.bavieca.net; Calle del Campo de San Nicolás 6; mains €9-25; ⏱1-4pm & 9-11pm Thu-Tue May-Sep, hours vary Oct-Apr) One of Medinaceli's more creative kitchens, La Bavieca does traditional specialities like lamb chops, but also a lovely pork-sirloin hamburger. For starters, why not try the quail eggs with truffles and wild mushrooms in a brandy and duck sauce? Service is attentive and the dining area classy.

**La Ceramica** SPANISH €€
(☎975 32 63 81; Calle de Santa Isabel 2; mains €8-21, set menus from €17; ⏱1-3.30pm & 9-11pm, closed mid-Dec–Jan) An intimate yet informal dining experience, La Ceramica serves excellent local specialities such as *migas del pastor* (shepherd's breadcrumbs) or *ensalada de codorniz* (quail salad).

## Shopping

**Iglesia Convento Santa Isabel** FOOD
(Calle Marimedrano 19; cookies from €7.50; ⏱10am-2pm & 4-7pm Mon-Sat) The cloistered nuns at this pretty convent bake up tasty cookies and other sweets; ring the bell and then make your selection through the revolving window.

## Information

**Oficina de Turismo** (☎975 32 63 47; www.medinaceli.es; Calle del Campo de San Nicolás; ⏱10am-2pm & 4-7pm Sat-Tue, 11am-3pm & 4-7pm Wed-Fri) At the entrance to town, just around the corner from the arch.

## Getting There & Away

**ALSA** (www.alsa.es; Plaza del Ayuntamiento) runs up to four daily buses to/from Soria (€5.70, 45 minutes) or three daily to/from Madrid (€11, 1¾ hours) from outside the *ayuntamiento* in the new town. There's no transport between the old and new towns, and it's a long, steep hike.

## AT A GLANCE

**POPULATION**
2.05 million

**BIGGEST CITY**
Albacete

**BEST MANCHEGO CHEESE EXPERIENCE**
Villadiego (p217)

**BEST MEDIEVAL VILLAGE**
Pastrana (p231)

**BEST MARZIPAN**
Santo Tomé (p213)

**WHEN TO GO**

**Mar & Apr** See Cuenca's spine-tingling and atmospheric Semana Santa parades.

**Apr & May** Enjoy the countryside's colourful dazzle of wildflowers against a lush green landscape.

**Sep & Oct** Hike amid Castilla-La Mancha's natural parks and picturesque villages.

Alley view of Catedral de Toledo (p204)

# Toledo & Castilla-La Mancha

Castilla-La Mancha is best known for its windswept fertile plains, stippled with olive groves and grape vines, stretching to a horizon you never seem to reach. Yet Spain's third-largest region also harbours a dramatic lake district, biologically rich wetlands, river gorges and captivating medieval villages. The ghosts of the past seem ever-present. This is, after all, where Cervantes set the fictional journeys of Don Quijote, and quixotic reminders loom near and far; from white-washed windmills to lofty hilltop castles fringed by early-morning mists.

The area's biggest draw is glorious Toledo, Spain's spiritual capital, while Cuenca is another wondrous place, seemingly about to topple off its eagle's-eyrie perch high above a gorge. On a more sensory level, this is where saffron is grown and also the capital of Spain's unrivalled Manchego cheese. The latter makes the perfect accompaniment to the local wines – Castilla-La Mancha grows more vines than any other region worldwide.

**INCLUDES**

# TOLEDO

POP 84,900 / ELEV 655M

Toledo is simply one of Spain's most magnificent cities. Dramatically sited atop a gorge overlooking the Río Tajo, it was known as the 'city of three cultures' in the Middle Ages, a place where – legend has it – Christian, Muslim and Jewish communities peacefully coexisted. Unsurprisingly, rediscovering the vestiges of this unique cultural synthesis remains modern Toledo's most compelling attraction. Horseshoe-arched mosques, Sephardic synagogues and one of Spain's finest Gothic cathedrals cram into its dense historical core. But the layers go much deeper. Further sleuthing will reveal Visigothic and Roman roots. Toledo's other forte is art, in particular the haunting canvases of El Greco, the influential, impossible-to-classify painter with whom the city is synonymous. Though the city is justifiably popular with day trippers, try to stay overnight to really appreciate Toledo in all its haunting glory.

## Sights

### ★Catedral de Toledo — CATHEDRAL

(☎925 22 22 41; www.catedralprimada.es; Plaza del Ayuntamiento; €10, incl Torre de las Campanas €12.50; ⏲10am-6.30pm Mon-Sat, 2-6.30pm Sun) Toledo's illustrious main church ranks among the top 10 cathedrals in Spain. An impressive example of medieval Gothic architecture, its enormous interior is full of the classic characteristics of the style, rose windows, flying buttresses, ribbed vaults and pointed arches among them. The cathedral's sacristy is a veritable art gallery of old masters, with works by Velázquez, Goya and – of course – El Greco. Admission also gives access to the nearby Museo de Tapices y Textiles de la Catedral (p209).

> **PULSERA TURÍSTICA**
>
> The **Pulsera Turística** (www.toledomonumental.com) is a bracelet (€10) that gets you into seven key Toledo sights (no time limit), each of which costs about €3 individually. Buy the bracelet at any of the sights covered, which are Monasterio San Juan de los Reyes, Sinagoga de Santa María la Blanca, Iglesia de Santo Tomé, Iglesia del Salvador, Iglesia de los Jesuitas (aka Iglesia San Ildefonso), Mezquita del Cristo de la Luz and Real Colegio de Doncellas Nobles.

From the earliest days of the Visigothic occupation, the current site of the cathedral has been a centre of worship. During Muslim rule, it contained Toledo's central mosque, converted into a church in 1085, but ultimately destroyed 140 years later. Dating from the 1220s and essentially a Gothic structure, the cathedral was rebuilt from scratch in a melting pot of styles, including Mudéjar and Renaissance. The Visigothic influence continues today in the unique celebration of the Mozarabic Rite, a 6th-century liturgy that was allowed to endure after Cardinal Cisneros put its legitimacy to the test by burning missals in a fire of faith; they survived more or less intact. The rite is celebrated in the Capilla Mozarabe at 9am Monday to Saturday, and at 9.45am on Sunday.

The high altar sits in the extravagant **Capilla Mayor**, the masterpiece of which is the *retablo* (altarpiece), with painted wooden sculptures depicting scenes from the lives of Christ and the Virgin Mary; it's flanked by royal tombs. The oldest of the cathedral's magnificent stained-glass pieces is the rose window above the Puerta del Reloj. Behind the main altar lies a mesmerising piece of 18th-century Churrigueresque (lavish baroque ornamentation), the **Transparente**, which is illuminated by a light well carved into the dome above.

In the centre of things, the *coro* (choir stall) is a feast of sculpture and carved wooden stalls. The 15th-century lower tier depicts the various stages of the conquest of Granada.

The *tesoro,* however, deals in treasure of the glittery kind. It's dominated by the extraordinary **Custodia de Arfe**: with 18kg of pure gold and 183kg of silver, this 16th-century processional monstrance bristles with some 260 statuettes. Its big day out is the Feast of Corpus Christi, when it is paraded around Toledo's streets.

Other noteworthy features include the sober cloister, off which is the 14th-century **Capilla de San Blas**, with Gothic tombs and stunning frescoes; the gilded **Capilla de Reyes Nuevos**; and the *sala capitular* (chapter house), with its remarkable 500-year-old *artesonado* (wooden Mudéjar ceiling) and portraits of all the archbishops of Toledo.

The highlight of all, however, is the *sacristía* (sacristy), which contains a gallery

# Toledo & Castilla-La Mancha Highlights

1 **Toledo** Peeling back the many layers of history while exploring the hilly cobblestone lanes.

2 **Atienza** (p234) Hiking into this hilltop medieval town on a southern branch of the Camino de Santiago.

3 **Consuegra** (p216) Taking *the* Don Quijote shot of the windmills stretching toward the horizon.

4 **Alcalá del Júcar** (p222) Visiting its cave houses, 15th-century castle and pretty riverfront.

5 **Cuenca** (p225) Admiring the extraordinary hanging houses and rambling medieval core of Cuenca.

6 **Almagro** (p217) Marvelling at the plaza and 17th-century theatre.

7 **Parque Natural de las Lagunas de Ruidera** (p223) Kayaking, hiking or relaxing in this pristine lakes district.

8 **Sigüenza** (p232) Exploring the town's evocative medieval centre.

# Toledo

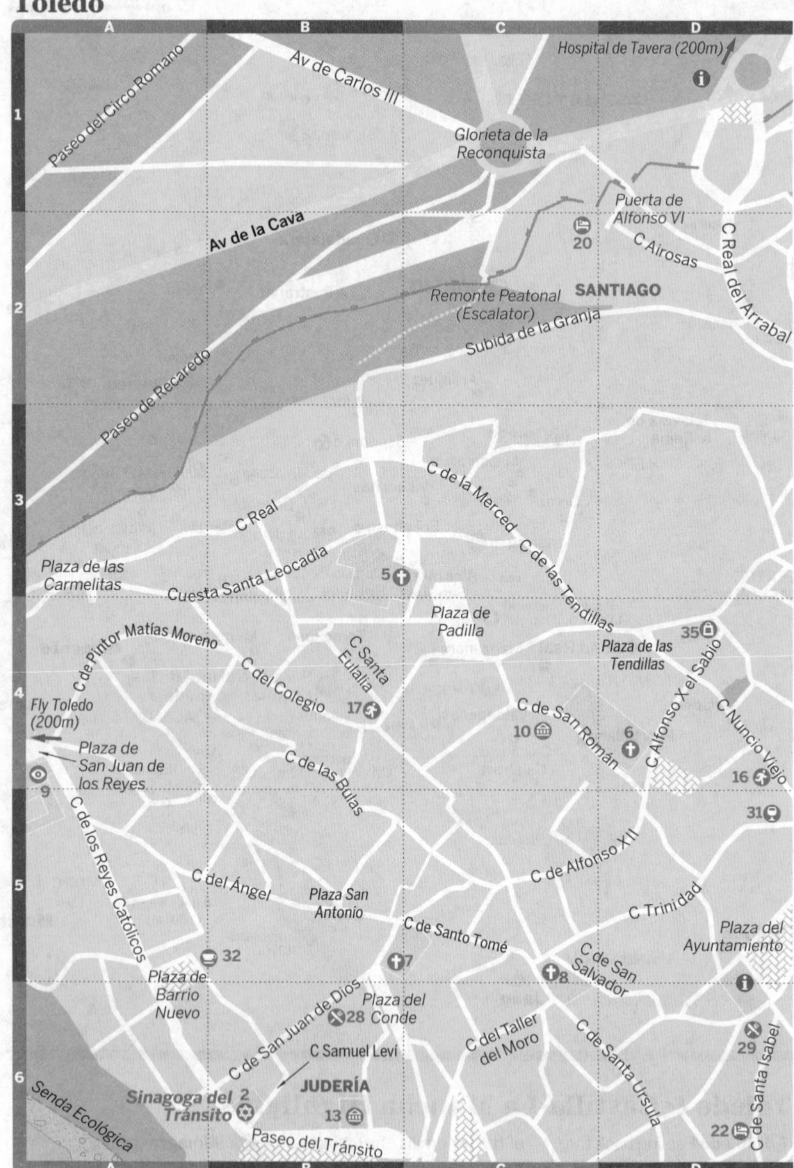


with paintings by masters such as El Greco, Zurbarán, Caravaggio, Titian, Raphael and Velázquez. It can be difficult to appreciate the packed-together, poorly lit artworks, but it's a stunning assemblage in a small space. In an adjacent chamber, don't miss the spectacular Moorish standard captured in the Battle of Salado in 1340. An extra €2.50 gets you entrance to the upper level of the cloister and the bell tower, which offers wonderful views over the centre of historic Toledo.

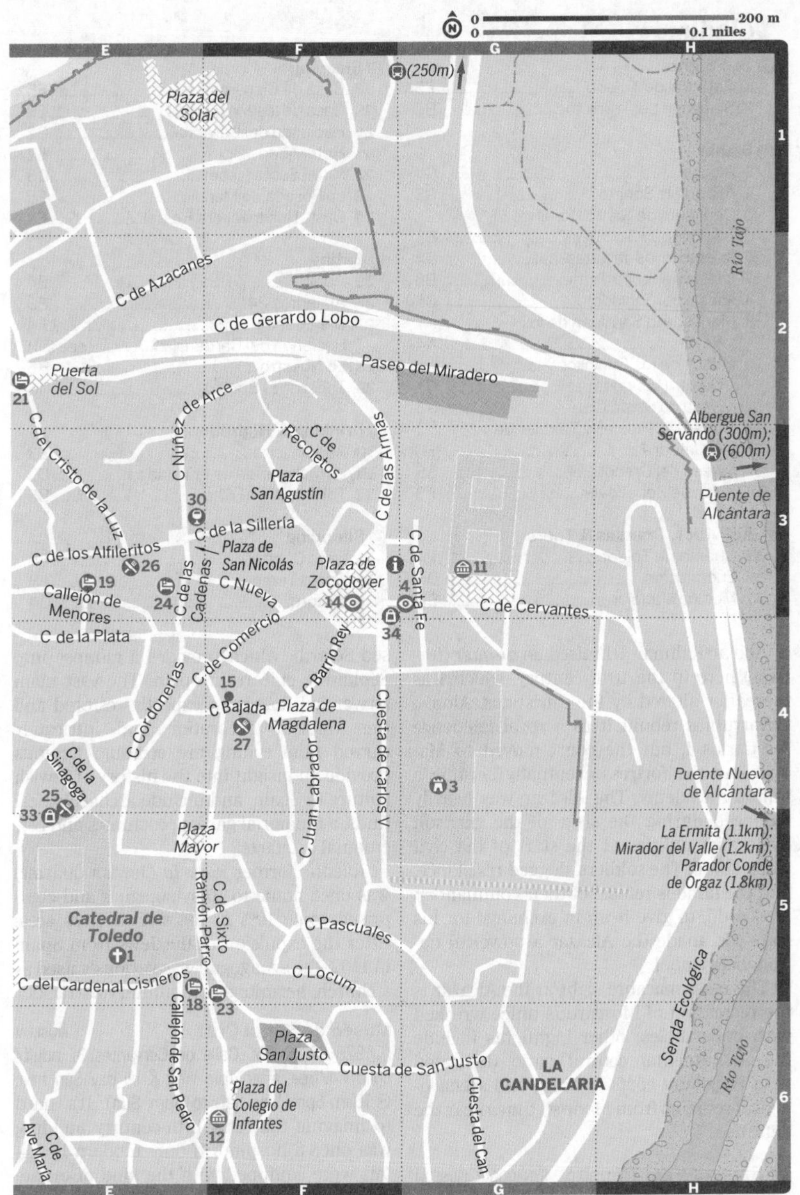




**Alcázar** FORTRESS, MUSEUM

(Museo del Ejército; ☎925 23 88 00; www.museo.ejercito.es; Calle de la Paz; adult/child €5/free, Sun free; ⏲10am-5pm Tue-Sun) At the highest point in the city looms the foreboding Alcázar. Rebuilt under Franco, it has been reopened as a vast military museum. The usual displays of uniforms and medals are here, but the best part is the exhaustive historical section, with an in-depth examination of the nation's history – albeit in terms of wars and long-simmering conflicts – in Spanish and English.

## Toledo

**Top Sights**
1 Catedral de Toledo ........ E5
2 Sinagoga del Tránsito ........ B6

**Sights**
3 Alcázar ........ G4
4 Arco de la Sangre ........ G3
5 Convento de Santo Domingo El Antiguo ........ B3
6 Iglesia de los Jesuitas ........ D4
7 Iglesia de Santo Tomé ........ B5
8 Iglesia del Salvador ........ C5
9 Monasterio San Juan de los Reyes ........ A4
10 Museo de los Concilios y la Cultura Visigoda ........ C4
11 Museo de Santa Cruz ........ G3
12 Museo de Tapices y Textiles de la Catedral ........ F6
13 Museo del Greco ........ B6
14 Plaza de Zocodover ........ F3

**Activities, Courses & Tours**
15 Cuéntame Toledo ........ F4
16 Enodifusion ........ D4
17 Medina Mudéjar ........ B4

**Sleeping**
18 Casa de Cisneros ........ E5
19 Casa de los Mozárabes ........ E3
20 Hacienda del Cardenal ........ C2
21 Hotel Abad ........ E2
22 Hotel Santa Isabel ........ D6
23 La Posada de Manolo ........ F5
24 Oasis Backpackers Hostel ........ E3

**Eating**
25 Adolfo ........ E4
26 Alfileritos 24 ........ E3
27 Bar Ludeña ........ F4
Hacienda del Cardenal ........ (see 20)
28 Lo Nuestro ........ B6
29 Taberna El Botero ........ D6

**Drinking & Nightlife**
30 Abadía ........ E3
31 La Malquerida de la Trinidad ........ D5
32 Teteria Dar Al-Chai ........ B5

**Shopping**
33 Casa Cuartero ........ E5
34 Santo Tomé ........ F3
35 Simón ........ D4

Abd ar-Rahman III raised an *al-qasr* (fortress) here in the 10th century, which was thereafter altered by the Christians. Alonso Covarrubias rebuilt it as a royal residence for Carlos I, but the court moved to Madrid and the fortress eventually became a military academy. The Alcázar was heavily damaged during the siege of the garrison by loyalist militias at the start of the civil war in 1936. The soldiers' dogged resistance, and the famous refusal of their commander, Moscardó, to give it up in exchange for his son's life, made the Alcázar a powerful nationalist symbol.

The most macabre sight at the Alcazár is the recreation of Moscardó's office wrecked with bullet holes; other highlights include the monumental central patio decorated with Habsburg coats of arms, and archaeological remains from Moorish times near the entrance.

**★Sinagoga del Tránsito** SYNAGOGUE, MUSEUM
(☎925 22 36 65; www.culturaydeporte.gob.es/msefardi; Calle Samuel Leví; adult/child €3/1.50, after 2pm Sat & all day Sun free; ⏰9.30am-7.30pm Tue-Sat Mar-Oct, to 6pm Nov-Feb, 10am-3pm Sun year-round) This magnificent synagogue was built in 1355 by special permission from Pedro I. The synagogue now houses the Museo Sefardí, which provides a glimpse into Sephardic culture in Spain. The vast main prayer hall has been expertly restored and the Mudéjar decoration and intricately carved pine ceiling are striking. Exhibits provide an insight into the history of Jewish culture in Spain, and include archaeological finds, a memorial garden, costumes and ceremonial artefacts.

Toledo's former *judería* (Jewish quarter) was once home to 10 synagogues and comprised some 10% of the walled city's area. After the expulsion of the Jews from Spain in 1492, the synagogue was variously used as a church, hermitage and military barracks.

**Museo de Santa Cruz** MUSEUM
(☎925 22 10 36; Calle de Cervantes 3; adult/child €4/free, after 4pm Wed & all day Sun free; ⏰10am-6pm Mon-Sat, to 3pm Sun) It's hard to imagine that this 16th-century building was once a hospital. If only modern hospitals were equipped with the kind of ornate plateresque portico that welcomes you to this beautiful arts and ceramics museum. The pièce de résistance is the huge ground-floor gallery laid out in the shape of a cross. The various art and sculpture exhibits are backed up by interesting explanatory boards that place all the pieces into their historical context.

**Museo del Greco** MUSEUM, GALLERY
(☎925 22 44 05; www.mecd.gob.es/mgreco; Paseo del Tránsito; adult/child €3/1.50, from 2pm Sat & all day Sun free; ⏰9.30am-7.30pm Tue-Sat Mar-Oct, to 6pm Nov-Feb, 10am-3pm Sun year-round) In the early 20th century, an aristocrat bought what he thought was El Greco's house and did a meritorious job of returning it to period style. He was wrong – El Greco never lived here – but the museum remains. As well as the house itself, there are pretty terraced gardens, fascinating excavated cellars from a Jewish-quarter palace and a good selection of paintings, including a Zurbarán, a set of the apostles by El Greco and works by his son and followers.

**Museo de Tapices y Textiles de la Catedral** MUSEUM
(☎925 22 22 41; Plaza del Colegio de Infantes; €2, with cathedral admission free; ⏰10am-6.30pm) Set in the former 17th-century school for choirboys (the Antiguo Collegio Infantes), this associated cathedral museum houses magnificent tapestries, some dating as far back as the 15th century. The tapestries have an annual airing on Corpus Christi when they hang outside the cathedral (despite the obvious ill effects from the elements).

**Mirador del Valle** VIEWPOINT
(Carretera Circunvalación) To get the ultimate photo of Toledo you need to cross the Río Tajo and climb the road on the other side to this strategic viewpoint. You can either walk up from the Puente Nuevo de Alcántara or catch the Trainvision (p215) from Plaza de Zocodover which makes a stop here during its 45-minute scenic journey. The view is not dissimilar to the one depicted by El Greco in his famous landscape, *Vista de Toledo* (1596–1600).

**Museo de los Concilios y la Cultura Visigoda** MUSEUM
(☎925 22 78 72; Calle de San Román; adult/child €2/free, Sun & Wed afternoon free; ⏰10am-2pm & 4-6pm Tue-Sat, 9am-3pm Sun) Sometimes

## EL GRECO IN TOLEDO

Of all Spain's old masters, El Greco is the most instantly recognisable. You don't need a degree in art history to be able to identify the talented Greek's distinctive religious canvases characterised by gaunt figures dressed in stark, vivid colours. Spread liberally around the museums and churches of Toledo, they practically jump out at you.

Born Doménikos Theotokópoulos on Crete in 1541, El Greco will always be intrinsically linked with Toledo, where he arrived as a bolshie 36-year-old in 1577. Never one to court popularity, the artist had already sparked controversy during a tempestuous apprenticeship in Italy where he had criticised the work of Michelangelo. His arrival in Spain proved to be equally thorny. Hindered by a thinly veiled arrogance and adhering to what were unconventional painting methods for the time (though 'revolutionary' by modern yardsticks), El Greco failed in his early attempts to ingratiate himself to the court of King Philip II. Gravitating instead to Toledo, he found an improbable artistic refuge where he worked to refine his style and establish his reputation.

Despite earning a degree of respectability during his lifetime, El Greco was largely ignored in the years following his death. Indeed, his prophetic work wasn't seriously reappraised until the early 20th century, when he was embraced by artists such as Picasso whose murky 'blue period' echoed the melancholy of some of El Greco's early compositions.

Outside Madrid's Museo del Prado, Toledo protects El Greco's greatest work. The Iglesia de Santo Tomé (p210) contains his magnum opus *El entierro del conde de Orgaz* (The Burial of the Count of Orgaz), depicting the count's burial in 1322. Look out for El Greco himself and Cervantes among the guests. The nearby Museo del Greco also has a solid collection of El Greco's works.

One of the oldest convents in Toledo, the 11th-century Convento de Santo Domingo El Antiguo (p213) includes some of El Greco's early commissions, other copies and signed contracts of the artist. Visible through a hole in the floor is the crypt and wooden coffin of the painter himself.

Other spots in Toledo where you can contemplate El Greco's works include the Museo de Santa Cruz), the *sacristía* (sacristy) in the cathedral (p204) and the **Hospital de Tavera** (☎925 22 04 51; www.fundacionmedinaceli.org; Calle Duque de Lerma 2; courtyard & chapel €4, full ticket €6; ⏰10am-2.30pm & 3-6.30pm Mon-Sat, 10am-2.30pm Sun).

### TOP TOLEDO VIEWS

For superb city views, head over the Puente de Alcántara to the other side of Río Tajo and follow the road that rises to your right (there's a pavement!), where the vista becomes more marvellous with every step. If you're staying overnight, along this road is the Parador Conde de Orgaz (p213), which has superlative views, as does the restaurant La Ermita (p214), which has a short, quality menu of elaborate Spanish cuisine.

In the town centre, you can also climb the towers at the **Iglesia de los Jesuitas** (Iglesia San Ildefonso; ☎925 25 15 07; Plaza Juan de Mariana 1; adult/child €3/free; ⏰10am-6.45pm Apr-Sep, to 5.45pm Oct-Mar) for up-close views of the cathedral and Alcázar.

dismissively called the 'Invisigoths' due to the scant record of their presence, the Visigoths inhabit a little-known chapter of Spanish history sandwiched in between the Romans and Moors. Information about them is often difficult to procure until you come to Toledo, their de-facto capital in the 6th and 7th centuries. The era's history can be partially relived at this modest museum set in the 13th-century San Román church – complete with Mudéjar-style architecture and eye-catching frescoes. Signage in Spanish only.

**Iglesia del Salvador** CHURCH
(☎925 04 09 05; Plaza del Salvador; adult/child €3/free; ⏰10am-6.45pm Mar–mid-Oct, to 5.45pm mid-Oct–Feb) This little-visited but intriguing church exposes multiple historical layers in true Toledan fashion. Until 1159, it was a mosque; before that, a Visigothic church. One of its most fascinating artefacts is a richly engraved Visigothic pillar scavenged by later builders to hold up the roof.

**Iglesia de Santo Tomé** CHURCH
(☎925 25 60 98; www.santotome.org; Plaza del Conde; adult/child €3/free; ⏰10am-6.45pm Mar–mid-Oct, to 5.45pm mid-Oct–Feb) Iglesia de Santo Tomé contains El Greco's most famous masterpiece *El entierro del conde de Orgaz* (The Burial of the Count of Orgaz), which is accessed by a separate entrance on Plaza del Conde. When the count was buried in 1322, Sts Augustine and Stephen supposedly descended from heaven to attend the funeral. El Greco's work depicts the event, complete with miracle guests including himself, his son and Cervantes.

## Activities

**★ Senda Ecológica** WALKING
This remarkably varied walking path tracks the Río Tajo through a steep-sided gorge where you'll feel as if you've left the city far behind (although urban life reverberates only metres above you). It stretches between the Alcántara and San Martín bridges and includes some relatively wild stretches where a wooden walkway has been hammered to the rock face.

**Fly Toledo** ADVENTURE SPORTS
(☎693 464845; www.flytoledo.com; Puente de San Martin 2; €10; ⏰11am-6.30pm) Heavy museum legs sometimes need to relieve themselves and this bracing high-wire act that catapults vertigo-shunners across the Río Tajo gorge via the longest urban *tirolina* (zip line) in Europe might just do the trick. The ride begins and ends close to the San Martín bridge on the western side of town.

**Medina Mudéjar** HAMMAM
(☎925 22 93 14; www.medinamudejar.com; Calle Santa Eulalia 1; bath circuit €30-33, incl massage €46-62; ⏰10am-10pm Mon-Fri, to 11pm Sat, to 8pm Sun) Luxuriate in the self-pampering surrounds of this peaceful hammam with its warm ochre walls, arches, exposed stone, and brick vaulted ceilings. Hot, warm and cold baths, steam baths and options for various massages make for a rejuvenating respite from sightseeing. Moroccan tea is served as an ideal finale.

**Enodifusion** WINE
(☎664 322292; www.enodifusion.com; Calle Nuncio Viejo 13; wine tasting €12-25; ⏰11.30am-4pm Sun-Wed, to 9pm Thu-Sat) Run by the vine-minded sommelier Ana Morales, this small wine shop offers regular tastings throughout the day, and it's a good place to learn about some of the great produce of La Mancha. Three-glass tastings (€12) also include regional cheese and olive oil.

## Tours

Various companies offer guided walking tours around the town. Themes include Three Cultures (Muslim, Christian and Jewish) and El Greco. There are also night tours based around local legends.

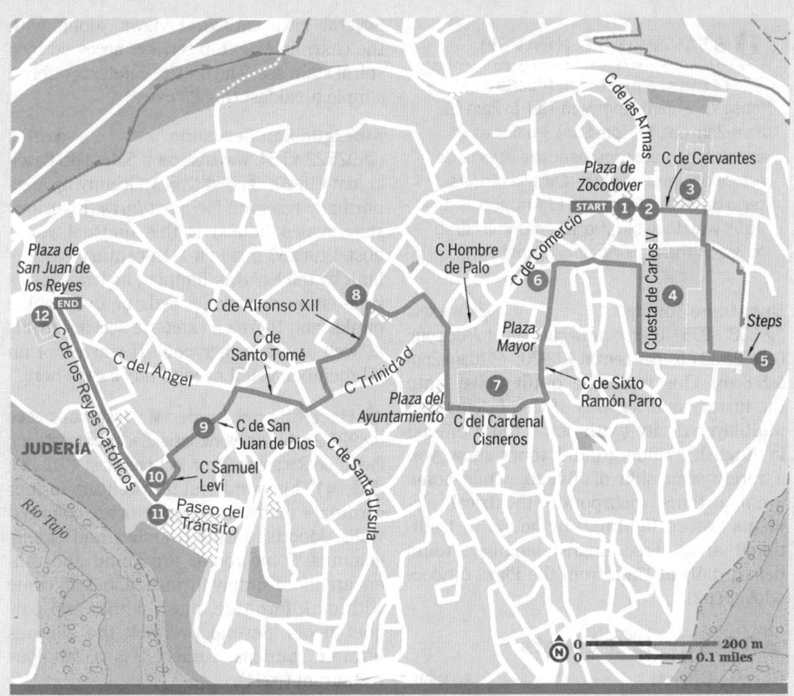


# Walking Tour
# A Stroll through History

**START** PLAZA DE ZOCODOVER
**END** MONASTERIO SAN JUAN DE LOS REYES
**LENGTH** 2KM, 1½–2½ HOURS

Start off in central 1 **Plaza de Zocodover**, for centuries the city's marketplace and scene for bullfights and Inquisition-led burnings at the stake, then pass through the 2 **Arco de la Sangre** (Calle de Cervantes) on the eastern side of the square to admire the facade of the 3 **Museo de Santa Cruz** (p208). Up the hill to the south is Toledo's signature 4 **Alcázar** (p207); continue around the building to the 5 **Mirador del Azor** for sweeping views over the Río Tajo. As the Alcázar's commanding position and sweeping views attest, Toledo was perfectly sited for medieval defences.

Wander back around the other side of the Alcázar and head west, passing the remnants of the 11th-century 6 **Mezquita de las Tornerías** before heading south to reach the 7 **Catedral de Toledo** (p204), the spiritual home of Catholic Spain. Twist your way northwest to the 8 **Iglesia de los Jesuitas** (p210). Note the carving above the entrance of St Ildefonso (Toledo's patron saint) receiving a cloak from the Virgin Mary, as allegedly occurred in the 7th century. Head up the bell tower for views over Toledo.

Down the hill you enter the heart of Toledo's old Jewish quarter. Admire the swords in the shops along 9 **Calle de San Juan de Dios** and head past the 10 **Sinagoga del Tránsito** (p208), a 14th-century synagogue with an exquisite prayer hall featuring Mudejar-style decoration. From there, stroll over to the 11 **Mirador del Paseo del Tránsito** to admire clifftop views over the river. Continue along Calle de los Reyes Católicos to the magnificent 12 **Monasterio San Juan de los Reyes** (925 22 38 02; www.sanjuandelosreyes.org; Plaza de San Juan de los Reyes 2; €3; 10am-6.45pm Mar-Oct, to 5.45pm Nov-Feb), which is best known for its two-storey cloister. This is a fine spot to end your walk, but you could drop down from here to the riverside pathway that will take you on a half-circuit of the old town back to near your starting point (an additional 2km).

### STAIRWAY TO HEAVEN

The **remonte peatonal** (Puerta de Alfonso VI; ⌚7am-11pm Mon-Thu, to 2am Fri, 8am-2am Sat, to 11pm Sun) – a series of escalators – starting near the Puerta de Alfonso VI and ending near the Monasterio de Santo Domingo El Antiguo, is a good way to avoid the steep uphill climb to reach the historic quarter of town.

**Cuéntame Toledo** WALKING
(☎608 935 856; www.cuentametoledo.com; Calle Bajada 5; per person €12-20; ⌚10am-2pm & 5-8pm) This reputable outfit delves into the history and legends of this fascinating, multilayered city (with some tours offered in English). Underground tours show you a rarely seen side of Toledo, while some evening tours incorporate theatrical elements (sword fighting!) by actors in traditional dress. Free English-language tours depart daily at 11am from the Plaza de Zocodover (p211).

## Festivals & Events

**Corpus Christi** RELIGIOUS
This is one of the finest Corpus Christi celebrations in Spain, taking place on the Thursday 60 days after Easter Sunday. Several days of festivities reach a crescendo with a procession featuring the Custodia de Arfe, a massive golden monstrance created in the 1500s.

## Sleeping

**Oasis Backpackers Hostel** HOSTEL €
(☎925 22 76 50; www.hostelsoasis.com; Calle de las Cadenas 5; dm €19, d €65-80, f €85; ❄@📶) One of five Oasis hostels in Spain, this hostel sparkles with what have become the chain's glowing hallmarks: laid-back but refreshingly well-organised service and an atmosphere that is fun without ever being loud or obnoxious. There are private rooms if you're not up for a dorm-share, and there's a small rooftop terrace and guest kitchen, plus an appealing cafe-restaurant next door.

**Hotel Santa Isabel** HOTEL €
(☎925 25 31 20; www.hotelsantaisabeltoledo.es; Calle de Santa Isabel 24; r €46-75; P📶) Providing a safe, economical base to stay in Toledo, the Santa Isabel is clean, central and friendly. It's encased in an old noble house with simple rooms set around two courtyards. Several have cathedral views, along with the charming rooftop terrace, accessed by a spiral staircase. The on-site cafeteria offers a simple breakfast (for €5 extra).

**Albergue San Servando** HOSTEL €
(☎925 22 45 54; www.reaj.com; Subida del Castillo; dm €16-20; P❄@📶🏊) Occupying digs normally reserved for *paradores* (luxurious state-owned hotels) is this unusual youth hostel tucked inside a 14th-century castle – built by the Knights Templar, no less. Dorms have either two single beds or two double bunks, and there's a cafeteria serving meals as well as a summer pool. If you're not an HI member, you'll need to buy a card here.

★**Hacienda del Cardenal** HISTORIC HOTEL €€
(☎925 22 49 00; www.haciendadelcardenal.com; Paseo de Recaredo 24; r incl breakfast €112-183; ❄📶🏊) This wonderful 18th-century former cardinal's mansion has pale ochre-coloured walls, Moorish-inspired arches and stately columns. Some rooms are grand and others are more simply furnished, but all come with dark furniture, plush fabrics and parquet floors. Several overlook the glorious terraced gardens. Attached is a fabulous restaurant (p214).

★**Casa de Cisneros** BOUTIQUE HOTEL €€
(☎925 22 88 28; www.hospederiacasadecisneros.com; 12 Calle del Cardenal Cisneros; r €65-191; ❄📶) Across from the cathedral, this seductive hotel is built on the site of an 11th-century Islamic palace, which can be best appreciated by visiting the basement restaurant. In comparison, this building is a 16th-century youngster, with pretty stone-and-wood beamed rooms and exceptionally voguish bathrooms. A rooftop terrace offers stunning views of the cathedral and beyond.

**La Posada de Manolo** BOUTIQUE HOTEL €€
(☎925 28 22 50; www.laposadademanolo.com; Calle de Sixto Ramón Parro 8; r €70-95; ❄📶) This memorable hotel has themed each floor with furnishings and decor reflecting one of the three cultures of Toledo: Christian, Islamic and Jewish. Rooms vary in size and cost, depending on whether they are interior or exterior, and some have balconies. There are stunning views of the old town and cathedral from the terrace, where breakfast is served, weather permitting.

**Hotel Abad** HOTEL €€
(☎925 28 35 00; www.hotelabad.com; Calle Real del Arrabal 1; r/ste/apt from €75/120/90; P❄📶)

Compact, pretty and pleasing, this hotel sits on the lower slopes of the old town and offers good value. Rooms very successfully blend modern comfort with exposed old brick; some have small balconies, but those at the back are notably quieter. There are also two- to four-bedroom apartments available in an adjacent building, and a ground-floor cafe.

**Parador Conde de Orgaz** HOTEL €€€
(925 22 18 50; www.parador.es; Cerro del Emperador; r €140-225; P❄📶🏊) High above the southern bank of Río Tajo, Toledo's low-rise *parador* as a classy interior and sublime views (ask for a room with a balcony!). Rooms are relatively spacious and not as heritage-heavy as other *paradores*. You'll need a car or a taxi ride (around €8) to get here from the old town. Be prepared: it's popular with tour groups.

**Casa de los Mozárabes** APARTMENT €€€
(689 766605; www.casadelosmozarabes.com; Callejón de Menores 10; apt €110-280; ❄📶) Occupying a historical Toledo house on a quiet central lane, these excellent apartments have modern furnishings that combine well with the exposed stone and brick and original features of the building. There's no reception desk, so checking in (via computer screen) can sometimes be a slow affair.

## Eating

**Bar Ludeña** SPANISH €
(925 22 33 84; Plaza de Magdalena 10; mains €9-14; noon-4.30pm & 8-11.30pm) Despite its central location close to Toledo's main tourist thoroughfare, Ludeña retains a wholesome local image courtesy of the flock of regulars who – despite the tourist infiltration – still frequent it. Join them as they prop up the bar with a *caña* (beer) and a plate of the Toledano speciality, *carcamusa* (pork and vegetable stew). Alternatively, grab a seat on the delightful shady terrace.

**★Alfileritos 24** SPANISH €€
(925 23 96 25; www.alfileritos24.com; Calle de los Alfileritos 24; mains €19-22, bar food €6-12; 1.30-4pm & 8-11.30pm) The 14th-century surroundings of columns, beams and barrel-vault ceilings are cleverly coupled with modern artwork and bright dining rooms in an atrium space spread over four floors. The menu demonstrates an innovative flourish in the kitchen, with dishes such as cannelloni stuffed with Iberian pulled pork, partridge with mushroom marinade, and trout with beets and fennel. The low-key tavern downstairs is a great spot for multicourse lunch specials (€12).

**★Taberna El Botero** SPANISH €€
(925 28 09 67; www.tabernabotero.com; Calle de la Ciudad 5; raciones €10-22; noon-5pm Mon, to 1.30am Wed-Sun) Handy for the cathedral, this atmospheric bar and restaurant offers up elaborately presented dishes based on traditional Spanish ingredients such as octopus, cod and game. It also does expertly prepared cocktails and mixed drinks – though you'll have to go early as the intimate space always packs a crowd.

**Lo Nuestro** SPANISH €€
(925 25 17 80; Calle San Juan de Dios 7; mains €10-15, two-course menu €18; noon-8pm) Tucked in the former Jewish quarter, Lo Nuestro has a devoted following for its outstanding multi-course menus that showcase Toledan cooking. In a covered 16th-century courtyard that exudes history, you can linger over saffron-scented soups, hearty game and Iberian pork, and traditional Manchegan sweets. Also an enticing tapas selection.

DON'T MISS

### MARZIPAN

Not a marzipan fan? Think again. You probably won't have tasted it so good anywhere else. Toledo is famed for this wonderful almond-based confectionery, which every shop seems to sell. The Santo Tomé marzipan brand is highly regarded and there are several outlets in town, including one on **Plaza de Zocodover** (925 22 11 68; www.mazapan.com; Plaza de Zocodover 7; 9am-10pm). Even the local nuns get in on the marzipan act; most of the convents sell the sweets. Behind the **Convento de Santo Domingo El Antiguo** (925 22 29 30; Plaza de Santo Domingo el Antiguo; adult/child €2.50/free; 11am-1.30pm & 4-7pm Mon-Sat, 4-7pm Sun), cloistered nuns sell their confections through a rotating compartment. Just ring the buzzer, let them know what you want (a handy product list with prices is nearby), place your money, and they'll deliver the heavenly goods through the antiquated contraption.

**Hacienda del Cardenal** SPANISH €€€
(☎925 22 08 62; www.haciendadelcardenal.com; Paseo de Recaredo 24; mains €21-26; ⊙1-4pm & 8.30-11pm Tue-Sat, 1-4pm Sun) This hotel restaurant enjoys one of Toledo's most magical locations for dining alfresco: it's tucked into a private garden entered via its own gate in the city walls. The food is classic Spanish, with roast meats to the fore – suckling pig and lamb are the prime dishes here. It's a bit touristy, but the location is unforgettable on a balmy summer's night.

**Adolfo** MODERN EUROPEAN €€€
(☎925 22 73 21; www.adolforestaurante.com; Callejón Hombre de Palo 7; mains €28-45, tasting menu €79; ⊙1-4pm & 8pm-midnight Tue-Sun) Toledo doffs its hat to fine dining at this temple of good food and market freshness. Run by notable La Mancha–born chef Adolfo Muñoz, the restaurant has been around for over 30 years, and in that time has morphed into one of Spain's best gourmet establishments. Partridge is the speciality.

**La Ermita** SPANISH €€€
(☎925 25 31 93; www.laermitarestaurante.es; Carretera de Circunvalación; mains €20-25; ⊙1.30-4pm & 8.45-11pm Tue-Sat, 1.30-4pm Sun) Fabulously located La Ermita sits across the Río Tajo gorge from the city, meaning you'll have the tangled medieval core of Toledo spread before you while perusing its small menu of beautifully presented Spanish cuisine. The dishes change regularly but you can expect to see wild boar, salmon and suckling pig prepared with innovative skill.

## Drinking & Nightlife

**Abadía** CRAFT BEER
(☎925 25 11 40; www.abadiatoledo.com; Plaza de San Nicolás 3; ⊙11am-midnight) In a former 16th-century palace, this atmospheric bar and restaurant has historical artefacts on display in the glassed niches of the brick-and-stone-clad rooms. The menu includes lightweight dishes and tapas, which pair nicely with the bar's own craft beers. For something heartier, opt for the three-course 'Montes de Toledo' menu (€22), showcasing regional delicacies like paté, pheasant and Manchego cheese.

**La Malquerida de la Trinidad** BAR
(☎925 67 20 54; Calle Trinidad 2; ⊙11am-midnight Sun-Thu, to 2am Fri & Sat) A few steps from the cathedral, this neighbourhood drinking den has a creative soul, with eclectic furnishings (cheese grater lamps, a drip-painted bar), a fine soundtrack (Caribbean salsa, Afro-Cuban jazz) and easy-going staff. Stop in for a vermouth or a local wine (the food can be hit or miss).

**Teteria Dar Al-Chai** TEAHOUSE
(☎925 22 56 25; Plaza de Barrio Nuevo 5; ⊙9.30am-9.30pm Mon, Tue, Thu & Fri, to 1.30pm Wed, 4-10.30pm Sat & Sun) Peel back the centuries at this atmospheric teahouse hidden on the west side of the old centre. Moroccan-style lamps, tile-covered walls and Mudéjar-style archways set the scene for a perfectly brewed pick-me-up. You can linger over creative blends like *Amanecer en Granada* (cinnamon, cardamom, rose, and ginger with black tea) or further unwind over hookahs from low pillows in the corner.

## Shopping

**Simón** ARTS & CRAFTS
(☎925 22 21 32; Plaza de San Vicente 1; ⊙10am-8.30pm) Since 1963, this small slightly shabby shop has specialised in *damasquinados* (damascene), the art of decorating steel with threads of gold and silver. It is one of just a handful of places that sells the genuine handmade pieces; the majority of what you see in Toledo these days is machine made. You'll find one-of-a-kind pendants, necklaces and decorative art pieces.

**Casa Cuartero** FOOD & DRINKS
(☎925 22 26 14; www.casacuartero.com; Calle Hombre de Palo 5; ⊙10am-2.30pm & 5-8pm) Just north of the cathedral, this fabulous food shop (here since 1920) sells marzipan, cured meats, wines, cheeses, olive oils and all manner of local delicacies from around Castilla-La Mancha. It's ideal for gifts to take home or to stock up for a picnic.

## Information

**Main Tourist Office** (☎925 25 40 30; www.toledo-turismo.com; Plaza Consistorio 1; ⊙10am-6pm) Within sight of the cathedral. There are also offices in Plaza de Zocodover (☎925 26 76 66; www.toledo-turismo.com; Plaza de Zocodover 8; ⊙9am-5pm Mon-Sat, 10am-3pm Sun) and the train station (☎925 23 91 21; www.toledo-turismo.com; Estación de Renfe, Paseo de la Rosa; ⊙9.30am-3pm).

**Regional Tourist Office** (☎925 25 10 05; www.turismocastillalamancha.es; Paseo de Merchán; ⊙10am-6pm Mon-Sat, to 2pm Sun) Has a wealth of information about the region. Located north of the old town.

## Getting There & Away

To get to most major destinations, you'll need to backtrack to Madrid.

From the striking neo-Mudéjar **train station** (☎912 32 03 20; www.renfe.es; Paseo de la Rosa), high-speed Alta Velocidad Española (AVE) trains run every hour or so to Madrid's Puerta de Atocha station (€14, 33 minutes).

From Toledo's **bus station** (Bajada Castilla La Mancha), buses depart for Madrid's Plaza Elíptica (from €5.60, one hour to 1¾ hours) roughly every half-hour with ALSA (www.alsa.es); some are direct, some via villages. There are also daily services to Cuenca (€14, two hours) with AISA (www.aisa-grupo.com).

## Getting Around

Buses (€1.50) run between Plaza de Zocodover and the bus station (bus 5) and train station (buses 61 and 62).

The **Trainvision** (☎625 301890; www.toledotrainvision.com; Plaza de Zocodover; adult/child €7/4.50; ⏰10am-6.30pm Sun-Thu, to 10pm Fri & Sat) trolley bus runs around the main monuments and up to the Mirador del Valle. It leaves from Plaza Zocodover every 30 minutes.

Driving in the old town is a nightmare. There are several paid underground car parks throughout the area, as well as the vast free Aparcamiento Safont near the bus station.

# WEST OF TOLEDO

# Talavera de la Reina

POP 83,400

Talavera de la Reina, long famous worldwide for its eponymous ceramics, has a laid-back appeal. Despite its size (the city has a larger population than the provincial capital, Toledo), it is little-visited by tourists. Talavera is strikingly located, surrounded by mountains, and divided by the Río Tajo. Three bridges connect the two sides of the city, one of which, Puente Romano, dates from Roman times and has been aesthetically restored. Historically the city is famed for being the site of the Battle of Talavera against Napoleon's army in 1809 when the Duke of Wellington successfully expelled the French troops from the city.

## Sights

**Museo Ruiz de Luna** MUSEUM

(☎925 80 01 49; museoruizdeluna@jccm.es; Plaza de San Agustín; adult/child €3/1.50; ⏰8.30am-3pm Tue-Fri, 10am-2pm Sat, 9.30am-2.30pm Sun mid-Jun–mid-Sep; 10am-2pm & 4-6pm Tue-Sat, 9.30am-2.30pm Sun mid-Sep–mid-Jun) Set in a former convent within the old city walls, this atmospheric museum displays classic Talavera ceramics from the distinctive blue-and-white 16th-century designs to more sophisticated and polychromatic 20th-century renditions, including the exquisitely crafted *Retablo Santiago*, a giant altarpiece from 1917.

**Basílica de Nuestra Señora del Prado** BASILICA

(www.basilicavirgendelprado.es; Jardines del Prado; ⏰hours vary) Talavera's main church is sometimes dubbed the 'Sistine Chapel of ceramics' for its intricate tilework, which showcases the city's finest *azulejos* (tiles), many of them painted with religious themes. It sits amid elegant gardens right next to Talavera's bullring, where an infamous *corrida* (bullfight) saw Spain's most famous bullfighter, 'Joselito El Gallo' fatally gored in May 1920. A statue of the fallen idol decorates the gardens outside.

## Shopping

**San Ginés** CERAMICS

(www.ceramicasangines.com; Calle de Matadero 7; ⏰9.30am-1.30pm & 5-8.30pm Mon-Fri, 10am-2pm Sat) The most famous ceramics store in town offers beautifully crafted pieces embellished with classic Talavera designs, including vases, tableware, candelabrum and jewellery, as well as a few pieces that might not fit in your luggage (urns, lamps). The quality is sky high (San Ginés has led major ceramic tiling projects in Spain).

## Information

**Tourist office** (☎925 82 63 22; www.turismotalavera.com; Ronda del Cañillo 22; ⏰10am-2pm & 5-7pm Mon-Fri, 10am-2pm Sat & Sun) Doubles as a gallery displaying – you guessed it – ceramics. It's located next to the old Roman bridge.

## Getting There & Away

The bus station is in the town centre. Regular buses between Madrid and Badajoz stop in Talavera de la Reina. Autocares Toletum (www.autocarestoletum.es; Avenida de Toledo) runs buses to Toledo (from €7.35, 1½ hours) every one to two hours. There is also a regular train service to Madrid (from €12, 1½ hours, seven daily) from the main train station on Paseo de la Estación to the north of the centre.

## Oropesa

POP 2700

The village of Oropesa, 34km west of Talavera de la Reina and enticingly visible south from the N5 motorway, is dominated by – and famous for – its turreted 14th-century castle that looks north across the plains towards the Sierra de Gredos. Parts of the old town walls survive and the village has a handful of noble mansions and a couple of Renaissance churches that are worth checking out, as well a small main square flanked by bars and restaurants.

### Sights

**Castillo de Oropesa** CASTLE

(☎925 45 00 06; Calle Castillo; adult/child €3/1.50; ⏲10am-2pm & 4-6pm Tue-Sat, 11am-2pm & 4-6pm Sun) This sturdy 14th-century castle built on older roots looks north across the plains to the mighty Sierra de Gredos. There are five towers, four of which can be climbed to access the ramparts and really appreciate the stunning views; not suitable for anyone with mobility issues, however. Part of the castle is now a *parador* hotel, but it can be visited separately.

### Sleeping

**Parador de Oropesa** HISTORIC HOTEL €€

(☎925 43 00 00; www.parador.es; Plaza Palacio 1; r €80-160; P ❄ ☎) Attached to Oropesa's hilltop castle is a 14th-century palace housing Spain's second-oldest *parador*, which has managed to retain a heady historical feel without the 'overheritaging' that typifies many Spanish *paradores*. Rooms are large and luxurious and decorated with antiques.

**Hotel Rural La Botica** GUESTHOUSE €€

(☎676 398381; www.labotica.net; Calle de Hospital 19; r €60-100; ❄ ☎) A short stroll downhill from the castle, this easy-going guesthouse has three spacious, modern rooms set around a small courtyard. Each is kitted out with comfortable mattresses, high ceilings, and heavy wooden furniture. The hosts aren't always on hand, so call ahead.

### Getting There & Away

Buses operated by Avanza (www.avanzabus.com) travel from Talavera de la Reina to Oropesa (€4, 40 minutes) three or four times daily. There are also trains connecting the two towns (from €4.15, 20 minutes), with onward service to Madrid (from €16, two hours).

# SOUTH CASTILLA-LA MANCHA

This is the terrain that typifies La Mancha for many people: the flat, often featureless plains of Spain's high inland *meseta* (plateau) stretching to the horizon, punctuated by the occasional farmhouse or emblematic windmill. The southeast, however, is surprisingly verdant and lush with rivers, natural parks and some of the prettiest villages in the province.

## Consuegra

POP 10,100

If you choose one place to go windmill-spotting in Castilla-La Mancha, make it Consuegra, home to an imposing castle and a medley of white-washed *molinos de vientos* (windmills) – all perched on a hillside just above a sleepy historical centre.

### Sights

**Castillo de Consuegra** CASTLE

(☎925 47 57 31; www.castillodeconsuegra.es; Cerro Calderico; adult/child incl Bolero windmill €4.50/2; ⏲10am-2pm & 3.30-6pm Mon-Fri, 10am-6pm Sat & Sun; P) Consuegra's atmospheric castle was once the stomping ground for the Order of St John of Jerusalem, sometimes known as the Knights Hospitaller, a famous medieval military order headquartered in Rhodes and, later on, Malta. In 1183 Castillan King Alfonso VIII invited the Knights to take on the Moorish Almohads, hence their presence here on what was once the porous frontier between battling Christian and Moorish dynasties. Information boards give historical insight and details about the rooms in English and French.

**Molino Rucio** WINDMILL

(☎925 09 53 39; www.elmolinoquefunciona.es; Carretera del Castillo; €2; ⏲9am-6.30pm) Of the 12 windmills that line a grassy ridge either side of Consuegra's castle, Molino Rucio is the only one in full working order. Inside there are displays on local saffron-farming, details of the mill's internal machinery, and samples of some of the flour it grinds.

### Sleeping

**La Vida de Antes** HOTEL €€

(☎925 48 21 33; www.lavidadeantes.com; Calle de Colón 2; s €55, d €75-90, apt €118; P ❄ ☎ 🏊 🐾) The best digs in Consuegra are encased in a noble old house with tiled floors, antique furnishings and a pretty patio that evokes a bygone era. The duplex rooms are particularly cosy and there's interesting art exhibited throughout the building.

## Eating

**★ Gastromolino** SPANISH €€
(☎925 09 51 44; www.gastromolino.com; Carretera del Castillo; raciones €10-16, tasting menu €27; ⏰11am-5pm Thu-Mon) In 2017 one of Consuegra's disused windmills was transformed into one of Castilla-La Mancha's most unusual restaurants, with a handful of tables tucked onto an upper floor of the 16th-century mill (plus terrace seating out front when weather permits). Gastromolino serves up beautifully prepared dishes featuring regional produce from a menu that changes monthly. Space is limited, so reserve ahead.

**El Alfar** SPANISH €€
(☎925 48 18 07; www.restaurantealfar.com; Calle Rosa del Azafrán 8; mains €16-25; ⏰1-5pm & 8pm-late Fri-Sun, 1-5pm Mon, 8pm-late Thu; 📶) Concentrating on exquisitely prepared La Mancha specialities, Consuegra's most ambitious restaurant is also something of a museum, inhabiting an old ceramics workshop that was built over the ruins of the town's ancient Roman circus. The three-course tasting menu includes dishes like partridge salad, *migas* (breadcrumbs, often cooked with chorizo and served with grapes) and a plethora of local wines. Reservations are recommended.

## ℹ Information

**Tourist office** (☎925 47 57 31; www.consuegra.es; Carretera del Castillo; ⏰9am-6pm, to 7pm Jun-Sep) Located in the Bolero windmill (they all have names), the first you come to as the road winds up from the town. You can climb the steps here and see the original windmill machinery (admission €4.50, including access to the Castillo de Consuegra). There's another tourist office next to the bus station.

## ℹ Getting There & Away

There are regular weekday buses (three on weekends) run by Samar (www.samar.es) between Consuegra and Toledo (€5.50, 1½ hours) and up to seven buses daily to Madrid's Estación Sur (€11, 2½ hours).

WORTH A TRIP

### VILLADIEGO

Visiting **Villadiego** (☎926 21 07 14; www.quesosvilladiego.com; Carretera Poblete-Alarcos Km 2, Poblete; €5; ⏰9am-3pm Mon-Fri), 11km southwest of Ciudad Real, is the cheese equivalent of visiting a winery. During the one-hour farm tour, you learn the fascinating art of producing *queso manchego*, arguably Spain's most famous cheese, with tasting an essential part of the visit. Tours don't run to a fixed timetable, so it's advisable to phone ahead during opening hours.

# Almagro

POP 8900

Almagro is to the theatre what Seville is to flamenco, the spiritual home of the art – at least in Spain – courtesy of its 'golden age' playhouse (Spain's oldest) and all-encompassing theatre museum. Not that you have to be a thespian to appreciate the place. The diminutive town, which gained importance during the Reconquista, might have been designed with 21st-century tourists in mind. Everything of note is a short, traffic-free stroll from its cobbled nexus, Plaza Mayor. Its warped, green-trimmed edifices might have you asking: is this the handsomest square in Spain?

## Sights

**Corral de Comedias** HISTORIC BUILDING
(☎926 88 24 58; www.corraldecomedias.com; Plaza Mayor 18; adult/child incl English audio guide €4/free; ⏰10am-2pm & 4-7pm) Opening onto the plaza is the oldest theatre in Spain. The 17th-century Corral de Comedias is an evocative tribute to the golden age of Spanish theatre, with rows of wooden balconies facing the original stage, complete with dressing rooms. Once daily (twice on Saturday) visits become 'theatrised' with costumed actors replacing the audio guide: this costs €3 more. It's still used for performances on Saturday evenings from the end of March to mid-December (though not in July); buy tickets via the website.

The history of the theatre is intriguing. It was founded in 1628 by a wealthy priest, but, after a century of performances, was closed during the cultural clampdowns of King

Felipe V. After that, the theatre was pretty much forgotten until a local inn-owner found a deck of old playing cards in the 1950s. Subsequent excavations on the site in Plaza Mayor led to the rediscovery of the theatre, which reopened for performances in 1954.

**Museo Nacional de Teatro** MUSEUM
(926 26 10 14; http://museoteatro.mcu.es; Calle Gran Maestre 2; adult/child €3/free; 10am-2pm & 4-6.30pm Tue-Fri, from 10.30am Sat, 10.30am-2pm Sun) Thespian or not, you could spend hours in Almagro's illustrious museum just sifting through the highlights. Theatrical musings include a deftly sculpted model of Mérida's Roman theatre, costumes and props relating to *zarzuela* (Spanish mix of theatre, music and dance) and – anchoring it all – a handsome 13th-century courtyard.

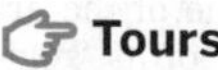

## Tours

**Visitas Guiadas a Almagro** WALKING
(609 793654; www.almagrovisitasguiadas.com; Plaza Mayor 41; per person €12) Aside from the standard two-hour Almagro walking tour, it also offers out-of-town tours to Calatrava la Nueva, Parque Nacional Tablas de Daimiel and Lagunas de Ruidera.

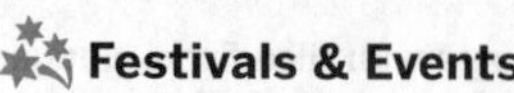

## Festivals & Events

**Festival Internacional de Teatro Clásico** THEATRE
(www.festivaldealmagro.com; Corral de Comedias; Jul) In July the Corral de Comedias holds a month-long international theatre festival, attracting world-class theatre companies performing, primarily, classical plays.

## Sleeping

★**Casa Rural Tía Pilar** GUESTHOUSE €€
(650 860475; www.tiapilar.com; Calle de los Carrascos 1; r €65-110; P) This beautiful 18th-century house is a delight with four patios, a lovely common room and a small but elegant swimming pool. Rooms are decorated with antiques and are well heated and/or air-conditioned for an old house. The owners live on-site to provide warm but discreet service. Excellent value.

**La Casa del Rector** HOTEL €€
(926 26 12 59; www.lacasadelrector.com; Calle Pedro de Oviedo 8; r €80-180; @) A three-way marriage between modern rooms, 'design' rooms and traditional historical rooms, the Rector is, in a word, magnificent. It's difficult to imagine what taste isn't being catered for in its lush interior set around three courtyards with elegant fountains, retro antiques (sewing machines!) and a streamlined cafe.

DON'T MISS

### CASTILLO DE CALATRAVA

The magnificent **Castillo de Calatrava la Nueva** (926 850 371; www.castillodecalatrava.com; Ctra de Calzada de Calatrava Km 2.3, Calzada de Calatrava; adult/child €4/2.50; 11am-2pm & 5.30-8.30pm Tue-Fri, 10am-2pm & 5.30-8.30pm Sat, 10am-2pm & 5-9pm Sun Apr-Sep, 11am-2pm & 4-6pm Tue-Fri, 10am-2pm & 4-6pm Sat, 10am-6pm Sun Oct-Mar; P) castle-monastery looms high in the sky some 35km south of Almagro, from where it once controlled the path into the Sierra Morena and Andalucía. A steep cobbled road takes you to the top, where you can alternate gazing at expansive views with exploring this extraordinary castle-cum-monastery in closer detail. Highlights include the vast basilica, a lofty watchtower and the grinding mill, which was turned by horses (the original drinking troughs are also present).

The chapter hall has fragments of 13th-century murals (two horsemen jousting) but remains closed for long-term restoration.

The complex was once headquarters for the Calatrava Knights, Spain's oldest military order, founded in 1158 to challenge Moorish power in Iberia. Their original base was Calatrava La Vieja, located 60km to the north, a castle twice snatched audaciously from the Moors. As the Christians pushed further into Moorish territory following Alfonso VIII's victory in the Battle of Las Navas de Tolosa in 1212, the Calatrava Knights commissioned this newer citadel in 1217 built using the labour of prisoners caught in the battle.

On weekends, a guided tour in Spanish (included in the price) is offered at 11.30am on Saturday and 6pm on Sunday (4.15pm from October to March).

Design rooms have wood-floor showers, coffee machines and electric window blinds. Modern rooms are a little more beige and mainstream. Traditional rooms retain many of the building's original features such as wood beams and heavy tiled floors. To top it all off, there's an on-site spa.

**Retiro del Maestre** HOTEL €€
(926 26 11 85; www.retirodelmaestre.com; Calle de San Bartolomé 5; s €60-95, d €85-110; P ❄ 📶) Enjoy cosseted treatment and style without the hurly-burly of a big hotel. Rooms here are spacious and washed in warm yellow and blue; go for one on the upper floor with a private balcony. The location, a five-minute walk from the Plaza Mayor, couldn't be better. The junior suite features a king-size bed and a Jacuzzi.

## Eating & Drinking

There are several cafes and bars spilling out onto Plaza Mayor, serving traditional Spanish fare including tangy pickled aubergines which are a specialty of Almagro.

★ **Restaurante Abrasador** CASTILIAN €€
(652 332410; www.abrasador.com; Calle San Agustín 18; mains €12-25; 11.30am-4pm & 8.30-11.30pm Mon-Wed, Fri & Sat, 11.30am-4pm Sun) Thoughtfully prepared cooking including perfectly grilled meats dominates the restaurant out the back. Snaffle the table next to the open fire in winter if you can. Out the front, you'll find some of the most creative tapas in Almagro – the famed local aubergine features prominently and it's our pick.

**El Patio de Ezequiel** SPANISH €€
(926 09 72 03; Calle de San Agustín 4; mains €11-18; 1pm-midnight; 📶) The most inviting setting in town with tables set in a softly lit patio, complete with trickling fountain. The place is famous for its extravagant gin and tonics (featuring smoked herbs, homemade gin with botanicals and other flourishes), though the food is also quite good: salads with smoked fish, partridge or sardines, plus egg-based dishes, grilled meats and fish.

## Information

**Tourist office** (926 86 07 17; www.ciudad-almagro.com; Calle Ejido de Calatrava; 10am-2pm & 5-8pm Tue-Fri, 10am-2pm & 5-7pm Sat, 10am-2pm Sun) This well-stocked tourist office next to the small bus station has helpful English-speaking staff. Opening and closing is one hour earlier from November to March.

## Getting There & Away

Interbus and AISA buses run several times daily to Ciudad Real (€4, 30 minutes).

# Parque Nacional Tablas de Daimiel

Some 35km north of Almagro, this small wetland national park is great for birdwatching. From the visitor centre, which has an exhibition on the fragile local ecosystem, three trails lead out along the lake shore and over boardwalks. From these, and the various observation hides – bring binoculars – you can see an astonishing variety of wildlife, including ducks, geese, kingfishers, flamingos, herons and other waders, tortoises and otters. Early morning and late afternoon are the best times to visit.

## Information

**National Park Visitor Centre** (Centro de Visitantes Parque Nacional de Daimiel; 926 85 03 71; www.lastablasdedaimiel.com; Carretera a las Tablas de Daimiel; 9am-9pm Jun-Sep, to 7pm Oct-May; 📶) Learn about the wetland and what to look for on the nearby walking paths at this small visitor hub in the centre of the park.

## Getting There & Away

The park is 10km northwest of the town of Daimiel, which is linked by regular buses to Ciudad Real. From Daimiel you'll need your own wheels.

# Campo de Criptana

POP 13,400

One of the most popular stops on the Don Quijote route, Campo de Criptana is crowned by 10 windmills visible from kilometres around. Revered contemporary film-maker Pedro Almodóvar was born here, but left for Madrid in his teens. The town is pleasant, if unexceptional.

## Sights

**Museo Eloy Teno** MUSEUM
(926 56 39 31; www.tierradegigantes.es; Calle Rocinante 39; adult/child €2/free; 10am-2pm & 4-6.30pm Tue-Sun; 👪) This small family-friendly museum in the tourist office displays local artisan products, models of windmills and clever art – often Don Quijote themed – made out of recycled metal. This is also the place to buy tickets to visit the windmills.

WORTH A TRIP

### PALACIO DE LA SERNA

Just a 20-minute drive south of bustling Ciudad Real in the sleepy village of Ballesteros de Calatrava, **Palacio de la Serna** (☎926 84 22 08; www.hotelpalaciodelaserna.com; Calle Cervantes 18, Ballesteros de Calatrava; r €115-170, ste €200-270; P ❄ 📶 ≋ 🐾) is a superb hotel that feels a world away. Set around a courtyard, it combines rural comfort with appealing design; the owner's evocative modern sculptures feature heavily. The modern rooms are bursting with character, with lots of mirrors, spot lighting, bright colours and edgy contemporary paintings. There's also a good on-site restaurant.

## Sleeping & Eating

**Casa los Tres Cielos** GUESTHOUSE €€
(☎926 56 37 90; www.casalos3cielos.com; Calle Libertad 11; r €60-70; ❄ 📶 ≋) On a winding lane in the village, this nine-room guesthouse makes a great base for taking in the windmill-studded scenery of the rolling countryside nearby. The wi-fi is weak, but the welcome is warm, and the pleasantly furnished rooms don't lack for comfort (the best have small terraces with pretty views). Bonuses include the breakfast and the pool.

**★Las Musas** SPANISH €€
(☎926 58 91 91; www.facebook.com/RestauranteLasMusas; Calle Barbero 3; mains €18-22, weekday lunch menu €15; ⊙1.30-4pm & 8.30-11pm) Across from the windmills, Las Musas is hands-down the best restaurant in town, and one of the top dining spots in the region. Painstakingly prepared dishes of high-quality Manchegan ingredients, a first-rate wine list and exceptional service make for a surprising find in small-town Campo de Criptana.

## Information

**Tourist office** (Calle Rocinante 39; ⊙10am-2pm & 4-6.30pm Tue-Sun) Located in a low-rise building opposite the Inca Garcilaso windmill.

## Getting There & Away

There are trains to Madrid's main Atocha station (€17, 1¾ hours, four daily) from the town's Estación de Tren located on Calle Agustín de la Fuente, about 1.5km south of the centre.



# El Toboso

POP 1770

If you're on the trail of Don Quijote, it's practically obligatory to stop in the small village of El Toboso, home of the Knight Errant's fictional sweetheart and one of the few places mentioned definitively by name in the book. So strong is the Quijote legend here that it is said that Bonaparte's troops refused to torch the place during the Peninsula War in the early 19th century.

El Toboso has several Quijote-themed museums and a wonderful statue of the Don kneeling gallantly before La Dulcinea in the pretty main square. Surrounded by vineyards it also sports some good bodegas, a couple of homey restaurants and an atmospheric Quijote-themed guesthouse.

## Sights

**Museo Cervantino** MUSEUM
(☎925 19 74 56; Calle de Daoíz y Velarde 3; adult/child €2/1; ⊙10am-2pm & 4-8pm Tue-Sun) This museum of over 700 books all with the same title (you've guessed it – *Don Quijote*) is more interesting than it sounds. Included among its well laid-out exhibits is the largest version in existence (a 120kg tome, which truth be told is only volume one), as well as copies of the Cervantes classic in numerous languages, including Basque, Hindi and Spanglish. There are also signed copies by notable personalities; look out for Nelson Mandela and – more chillingly – Adolf Hitler.

In an upstairs room, two short films (with English subtitles) relate key elements of the story of Don Quijote, with many locals recruited for the dramatisation.

**Casa-Museo de Dulcinea** MUSEUM
(☎925 19 72 88; Calle Don Quijote 1; adult/child €3/1.50; ⊙10am-2pm & 3-6.30pm Tue-Sat, 10am-2pm Sun) Since she was a fictional heroine and largely a figment of Don Quijote's imagination, this museum is obviously not the *real* house of the famous Dulcinea del Toboso. Rather it once belonged to Ana Martínez Zarco de Morales, a woman known to Cervantes who may have acted as a model for Dulcinea. Its aim is to evoke the spirit of Don Quijote and the book by displaying artefacts typical of the era.

**Bodega Campos de Dulcinea** WINERY
(☎925 56 81 63; www.camposdedulcinea.es; Calle Garay 1; tours €6; ⊙10am-7pm Mon-Fri, to 2pm Sat;

(P) One of the longest-standing wineries in town, the appropriately named Campos de Dulcinea has won numerous awards over the years; the *tempranillo* is a good constant bet if you want to make a purchase. Note, however, that tours of the bodega, along with wine tasting (with cheese), must be made in advance by phone or online.

## Sleeping

**★Casa de la Torre** GUESTHOUSE €€
(925 56 80 06; www.casadelatorre.com; Calle Antonio Machado 16; r €80-100; ) In a 16th-century manor house in the centre, the Casa de la Torre makes a memorable base for delving into the world of Quijote. The handsomely designed rooms are set with antique furnishings, artwork, poems and original architectural details.

The rest of the house is practically a museum dedicated to the anachronistic cavalier, including a study where a quill-wielding 16th-century bard would feel right at home. Warm-hearted host Isabel Fernández has a wealth of knowledge, and can happily guide you to the best restaurants, craftmakers and wineries in the region.

## Shopping

**La Aldaba** FOOD & DRINKS
(Calle Don Quijote 4; noon-2pm & 3.30-6pm Tue-Sat, 11am-2pm Sun) A great place to browse for gourmet gift ideas, La Aldaba stocks handsomely packaged tins of olive oils, local wines, cheeses and sweets, as well as the ever-popular canned partridge. You'll also find sun hats, T-shirts, tea towels and even a few antiques.

## Information

**Tourist office** (925 56 82 26; www.eltoboso.es; Calle de Daoíz y Velarde; 10am-2pm & 4-6.30pm Tue-Sat, 10am-2pm Sun) Has a handy town map with listed sights. Located inside the Museo Cervantino in the town centre.

## Getting There & Away

There's one daily bus to Toledo (€10, 2¼ hours) from Monday to Saturday run by Samar (www.samar.es).

# Belmonte

POP 1900

Partially enclosed by fortified walls, tranquil Belmonte is most notable for its storybook castle, the Castillo de Belmonte. The small town is enclosed by 15th-century walls with three original gateways still standing. It is well worth a stroll with other sights including a handsome Gothic church and a 17th-century former Jesuit monastery, now housing law courts and the post office.

## Sights

**Castillo de Belmonte** CASTLE
(678 646486; www.castillodebelmonte.com; Calle Eugenia de Montijo; adult/child incl audio guide €9/5; 10am-2pm & 4.30-8.30pm Tue-Sun May–mid-Sep, 10am-2pm & 4.30-6.30pm Tue-Sun mid-Sep–Apr; (P)) This is how castles *should* look, with turrets, largely intact walls and a commanding position over the plains of La Mancha from the ramparts. Visitors are well catered for with an elevator between the ground and 1st floor and a small cafe. The castle was once home to France's Empress Eugénie after her husband, Napoleon III, lost the French throne in 1871 and rooms have been grandly furnished in 19th-century style. The former dungeons are now home to a small armory.

## Sleeping & Eating

**Palacio Buenavista Hospedería** BOUTIQUE HOTEL €€
(967 18 75 80; www.palaciobuenavista.es; Calle Párroco Luis Andújar 2; s/d/ste incl breakfast €50/80/115; (P)) Palacio Buenavista Hospedería is a classy boutique hotel set in a 16th-century palace next to the town's iconic Iglesia Colegial de San Bartolomé. Stylish rooms are positioned around a balconied central patio with historic columns; request a room with a castle view, if possible. There's an excellent restaurant and a pretty outside terrace where the buffet breakfast is served (weather permitting).

**La Alacena de Belmonte** SPANISH €€
(617 584568; www.alacenadebelmonte.com; Calle San Juan del Castillo 35; mains €12-16, lunch menu €10.50; 9.30am-4pm Tue-Thu, 11am-4pm & 6.30-11pm Fri & Sat, 11am-4pm Sun) This sunny gastro-bar is a fine place to explore the cuisine of La Mancha's countryside, with cheese and charcuterie boards, classic *bocadillos* (sandwiches) and a small but well-curated selection of wines and craft beers. Heartier dishes include deer with mushroom sauce, lamb stew, and quail stuffed with Iberian ham.

WORTH A TRIP

### VILLANUEVA DE LOS INFANTES

Villanueva de los Infantes is an attractive and busy provincial town notable for its baroque and Renaissance architecture. It's also the starting point of Don Quijote's La Mancha wanderings, according to a group of scholars who published an exhaustively researched work *(El Lugar de la Mancha es...)* in 2005.

A highlight is its **Plaza Mayor**, with ochre-coloured buildings, wood-and-stone balconies, and several bars and restaurants. On the square stands the 15th-century **Iglesia de San Andrés**, where 16th-century poet Francisco de Quevedo is buried.

Exceptionally welcoming and thoughtful hosts combined with a prime location in the historic centre, just off the main square, make **La Morada de Juan de Vargas** (926 36 17 69; www.lamoradadevargas.com; Calle Cervantes 3; d €65-85; ) the best of the town's appealing rural hotel options. The rooms and common areas are full of lovely antiques and artful flourishes, and the hosts happily advise on activities in the area. Note that at weekends there is a minimum stay of two nights.

Interbus goes once daily to Ciudad Real (€9.40, 1¾ hours) from Sunday to Friday.

## Information

**Tourist office** (967 17 08 94; www.belmonte.es; Plaza Mayor; 9.30am-2.30pm Tue-Fri, 10am-1.30pm Sat & Sun) Can provide information on the village and surrounds and also assist with accommodation.

## Getting There & Away

There are two daily buses to Belmonte from Madrid's Estación Sur (€13, 2½ hours) operated by Samar (www.samar.es).

# Alcalá del Júcar

POP 1180

Northeast of Albacete, the deep, tree-filled gorge of Río Júcar makes for a stunning detour. About halfway along the CM3201, the crag-clinging town of Alcalá del Júcar comes into view as you descend via hairpin turns. Its landmark castle, dating mostly from the 15th century, towers over the houses (many in caves) that spill down the steep bank of the river gorge. At the foot of the town there's a medieval bridge with Roman origins and a leafy meeting-and-greeting plaza. It's a good destination for young kids, with a large, traffic-free area, and safe paddling in a bend of the river.

## Sights

**Cuevas del Diablo** CAVE
(657 986441; www.cuevasdeldiablo.com; Calle San Lorenzo 7; €3; 10.10am-6.30pm) Cuevas del Diablo is a vast cave complex with tunnels, a terrace overlooking the river, and a private collection of eccentric and historical artefacts and farming tools (there's also a dance floor with disco ball). A complimentary drink is included in the price. Owner Juan José Martínez is easy to spot around town thanks to his flamboyant Dalí-style moustache.

**Castillo de Alcalá del Júcar** CASTLE
(967 47 30 90; Calle Laberinto 10; €2.50; 11am-2pm & 5-8pm May-Sep, 11am-2pm & 3.30-6pm Oct-Apr) Alcalá del Júcar's landmark castle with its pentagonal main tower is of Almohad origin, but what you see today dates mostly from the 15th century. Aside from taking in the great views from the ramparts, you can also visit the *casa-cueva*, just below the fortified walls. This cavelike dwelling, full of period furnishings, shows how residents lived a century or so ago.

## Tours

**Avenjúcar** ADVENTURE
(639 305731; www.avenjucar.com; Avenida Constitución; half-day excursions €35-50; 9.30am-2pm & 4.30-8pm Mon-Sat, 11am-2pm Sun; ) This reputable outfitter a few paces from the Puente Romano offers a range of adventure activities, including rafting or canoeing trips, climbing and abseiling, canyoning, caving, as well as guided hikes amid some incredible scenery.

## Sleeping & Eating

**Hostal Rambla** HOSTAL €
(967 47 40 64; www.hostalrambla.es; Paseo de los Robles 2; s/d €48/60; ) One of several well-priced hotels in Alcalá, Hostal Rambla is by the Roman bridge. Rooms are compact

and fairly simple, though unique artwork on the walls adds a dash of character. It's also friendly and well located, and there's a pleasant restaurant with a large terrace.

**Fogones el Chato** SPANISH €€
(☎622 035696; Calle Canal 16; mains €12-19, set lunch menu €15; ⏰1-4pm & 8-11pm Fri-Mon) The sun-dappled terrace here is a place to linger, flanked by vegetable allotments (yes, expect organic fresh produce in the dishes), near the river. The uncomplicated menu concentrates on traditional dishes prepared with panache. The lunchtime menu of the day is excellent value. Reserve ahead.

## Information

**Tourist office** (☎967 47 30 90; Paseo de los Robles 1; ⏰10am-1.30pm & 4.30-7pm Sat, 10am-1.30pm Sun) The small tourist office has information about *casas rurales* (farmstead accommodation), cave accommodation and activities, including maps showing local walking trails. If it's closed the ticket office at the castle can also provide information and a town map.

## Getting There & Away

Public transport is virtually nonexistent here.

There's a large carpark (€2 for 24 hours) on the east side of the Río Júcar, a short walk north of the Puente Romano.

# Parque Natural de las Lagunas de Ruidera

This ribbon of 15 small lakes is surrounded by lush parkland, campgrounds, picnic areas, and discreetly situated restaurants and hotels. Turn off along the lakeshore in the town of Ruidera; along this road there are several places hiring pedalos, canoes and bikes, or offering horseriding to explore the area. **Lagunas de Ruidera Activa** (☎655 966794; www.lagunasderuideraactiva.com; Ave Castilla la Mancha 17, Ruidera; tours €20-30) is a good place to arrange adventures.

## Sleeping

**Camping Los Batanes** CAMPGROUND €
(☎926 69 90 20; www.losbatanes.com; Laguna Redondilla; sites incl 2 people, tent & car €22-36, bungalows €60-140; ⏰mid-Mar–Oct; P 🛜 🏊) This leafy campsite overlooks Laguna Redondilla, one of the larger lakes here, and has excellent facilities with a small supermarket, restaurant, cafe and children's playground, as well as two pools set amid pretty landscaped gardens. During the summer months there's an entertainment program for children. Rates vary considerably according to the season.

**Venta del Celemín** GUESTHOUSE €€
(☎967 09 05 66; www.ventadelcelemin.com; Camino Extramuros de San Pedro; r €80-110; P 🏊) This delightful country house makes a memorable setting to recharge and reconnect with Mother Nature. Whitewashed walls with traditional indigo trim, juniper wood-beamed ceilings, delightfully furnished rooms and a pleasant garden (with summertime pool) are all part of the charm. The welcoming hosts have a wealth of info on the area, and also offer tours with a literary, gastronomic or nature focus.

★ **Hotel Albamanjón** HOTEL €€€
(☎926 69 90 48; www.albamanjon.net; Camino Extramuros de San Pedro 16, Laguna de San Pedro; d €125-200; P ❄ 🛜) A great place to stay right on the shores of Laguna de San Pedro, 10km southeast of Ruidera. Running up the hill behind the main building, these attractive suites are all separate from each other and have a private terrace with lake views, wood fires for winter, and most have a Jacuzzi.

## Getting There & Away

Unfortunately, public transport is nonexistent here. You really need your own set of wheels to explore the park.

# Sierra de Alcaraz

Stretching across the southern strip of Albacete province, the cool, green peaks of the Sierra de Alcaraz offer a great escape from the dusty plains further north. The gateway to the region, sleepy hilltop Alcaraz, has a lovely renaissance Plaza Mayor and a lattice of narrow cobbled streets. The most scenic countryside is to be found along the east-west CM412, particularly between Puerto de las Crucetas (elevation 1300m) and Elche de la Sierra. And then there's the spectacular Nacimiento del Río Mundo.

## Sights

**Nacimiento del Río Mundo** WATERFALL
(Source of the River Mundo; CM3204; ⏰10am-dusk; P) Take a photo of yourself standing in front of the Nacimiento del Río Mundo, send it to the folks back home and they will think that you have sidestepped to Niagara

OFF THE BEATEN TRACK

## ROMAN SITES

Amid the rolling countryside of Castilla-La Mancha, several archaeological sites offer a fascinating glimpse into the past. You can visit one or both on a day trip from Cuenca.

**Segóbriga** (Roman ruins; ☎629 752257; www.segobriga.org; Saelices; adult/child €6/3, 4-6pm Tue & Fri free; ⏲10am-3pm & 4-7.30pm Tue-Sun Apr-Sep, 10am-6pm Tue-Sun Oct-Mar; P) Castilla-La Mancha's best-preserved Roman ruins may date as far back as the 5th century BCE. The highlights are a Roman theatre and amphitheatre on the fringes of the ancient city, looking out over a valley. Other remains include the outlines of a Visigothic basilica, various bathhouses, an Augustinian forum, and a necropolis that was partially destroyed to make way for chariot racing in the 2nd-century circus. A small museum has some striking exhibits.

The site is near Saelices, 2km south of the A3 motorway between Madrid and Albacete. From Cuenca, drive west 55km on the N400, then turn south on the CM202.

**Ruinas Romanas de Valeria** (Roman ruins; ☎969 20 89 19; www.valeriaromana.es; Calle Gran Valeria 2, Valeria; adult/child €4/2; ⏲10.30am-1.30pm & 5.30-9pm Jul & Aug, 10.30am-2pm & 4-6pm Sep-Jun, closed Wed & Sun afternoons Oct–mid-Mar; P) The fascinating archaeological site of Ruinas Romanas de Valeria is located just outside the village of Valeria, 34km south of Cuenca. Though not as extensive as the nearby ruins of Segóbriga, Valeria is less known to tourists meaning you'll have the rare, evocative pleasure of wandering around the site of a former sizeable Roman town without the distraction of coach tours and school groups. The location is fittingly sublime, set amid meadows and flanked by dramatic gorges.

Falls for the day. To get to these amazing waterfalls, follow the signs just before Riópar for around 8km on the CM3204 – past the amusing pictorial 'beware of the *anfibios* (amphibians)' signs – until you reach the entrance and car park.

It's a short walk through the forest of mainly coniferous trees to the bottom of the falls, where the water splashes and courses via several rock pools. There are two miradors: the first is at the base of the falls with neck-craning views of the dramatic waterfall above; it's a steep climb to the second mirador, but worth the effort. At some 800m above sea level, the water emerges from the rocks just above the platform, almost close enough to touch, in a dramatic drop of some 24m (spraying you liberally en route). The falls are surrounded by dense forest stretching to a rocky horizon – all those sceptics who say La Mancha is flat and boring should definitely visit these falls.

## Sleeping & Eating

**Mirador Sierra de Alcaraz** HOTEL €
(☎967 38 00 17; www.alcarazmirador.com; Calle Granada 1, Alcaraz; d €50-85; ❄📶) In the centre of Alcaraz, this handsome, mainly 16th-century building houses the Mirador Sierra de Alcaraz, with its central Moorish courtyard dating, incredibly, from the 9th century. The rooms have beamed ceilings, carved wooden bedheads and heavy period-style curtains and furnishings. All have good views and there is easy parking on the street outside.

**Las Salegas del Maguillo** HOTEL €€
(☎660 249692; www.lassalegasdelmaguillo.es; Carretera Riópar-Siles Km 11; d €90-112, 4-/6-person apt €150/210; P 🏊) High up in the hills above the road 11km southwest of Riópar, beyond the Nacimiento del Río Mundo carpark, this place consists of a collection of handsome stone buildings set amid the woods. Some of the villas have fireplaces and there is an outdoor swimming pool. It's rustic, tranquil and comfortable. Prices are lower from Sunday to Thursday nights.

The on-site restaurant serves excellent Manchegan cooking (menu of the day €18).

**Restaurante Alfonso VIII** GRILL €€
(☎067 380414; Calle Padre Pareja 1, Alcaraz; mains €12-22; ⏲9am-midnight Tue-Sun) Just off the town's stunning Plaza Mayor, this time-tested favourite serves traditional cooking with an emphasis on grilled meats, though you'll also find swordfish, salmon, squid and Cordoban-style *salmorejo* (a rich tomato soup) – a small reminder that Anda-

lucía is quite near. The three-course *menú del día* (€15) is good value. Reserve ahead on weekends.

Outside meal times, you can stop in for a coffee or something stronger at the attached cafe-bar.

### Getting There & Away

There are a couple of daily buses from Alcaraz to Albacete (€7, 1½ hours), but to fully explore the Sierra de Alcaraz you'll need your own set of wheels.

## NORTHEAST CASTILLA-LA MANCHA

This region has a rich hinterland of craggy mountains and lush green valleys studded by unspoiled, pretty villages. It is also home to some of the country's most enchanting *pueblos* and towns, including the provincial capital of Cuenca with its splendid medieval old town and refreshing lack of tourists.

## Cuenca

POP 54,700

A World Heritage site, Cuenca is one of Spain's most memorable cities, its old centre a stage set of evocative medieval buildings, many painted in bright colours, stacked on a steep promontory at the meeting of two deep river gorges. Narrow meandering streets separate tall houses with wooden balconies that literally jut out over the sheer cliffs. Yet, despite its age and Unesco listing, Cuenca has somewhat ironically established itself as a vortex of abstract modern art. Two of its most iconic buildings – including one of the famed *casas colgadas* (hanging houses) – have transformed their interiors into modern galleries. It's a theme continued in many of the town's hotels, museums and restaurants.

Like many Spanish cities, the surrounding new town is bland and modern, so keep the blinkers on during the approach – up the hill lies another world.

### Sights

**★Casas Colgadas** HISTORIC BUILDING

(Calle Canónigos) The most striking element of medieval Cuenca, the *casas colgadas* jut out precariously over the steep defile of Río Huécar. Dating from the 14th century, the houses, with their layers of wooden balconies, seem to emerge from the rock as if an extension of the cliffs. The best views of the *casas colgadas* is from the Puente de San Pablo footbridge. Today the houses host – somewhat improbably – an abstract art museum founded in the 1960s.

**★Museo de Arte Abstracto Español** MUSEUM

(Museum of Abstract Art; ☎969 21 29 83; www.march.es/arte/cuenca; Calle Canónigos; ⊙11am-2pm & 4-6pm Tue-Fri, 11am-2pm & 4-8pm Sat, 11am-2.30pm Sun) FREE From the outside, they look as if they've been sawn off from some high-altitude Tibetan temple, but, from the inside, Cuenca's famous *casas colgadas* have been transformed into a suite of airy, clean-lined galleries displaying some of central Spain's finest abstract art. Highlights here include the ethereal canvases of Fernando Zóbel (the museum's founder), meditative works by a trio of Basque luminaries (Jorge Oteiza, Eduardo Chillida and Néstor Basterretxea) and the radically stripped down creations of Catalan heavyweight Antoni Tàpies.

**Catedral de Cuenca** CATHEDRAL

(☎969 22 46 26, 649 693600; www.catedralcuenca.es; Plaza Mayor; €5; ⊙10am-7.30pm Jul-Oct, to 6.30pm Apr-Jun, to 5.30pm Nov-Mar) Luring visitors in with its impressive old-looking facade (it was actually cleverly rebuilt in neo-Gothic style in 1902), Cuneca's cathedral is well worth a visit. It was built on the site of the main mosque after the city's reconquest by Alfonso VIII in 1177. Highlights include the magnificent Renaissance doorway leading to the cloisters and the chapter house *artesonado* (wooden) ceiling painted in pastel colours. The striking abstract stained-glass windows were added in the 20th century. An excellent audio guide delves into the details.

For the complete experience, purchase a combination ticket (€8.50), which gives free access to the triforium (overlooking the nave), the treasury museum, the church of St Pedro (with its lofty bell tower affording fine views) and the Museo de la Semana Santa (p227).

**★Museo Paleontológico de Castilla-La Mancha** MUSEUM

(MUPA; ☎969 27 17 00; https://mupaclm.es; Calle de Río Gritos 5; adult/child €5/free, Wed free; ⊙10am-2pm & 4-7pm Tue-Sat, 10am-2pm Sun; ) Cuenca's cutting-edge palaeontology

## Cuenca

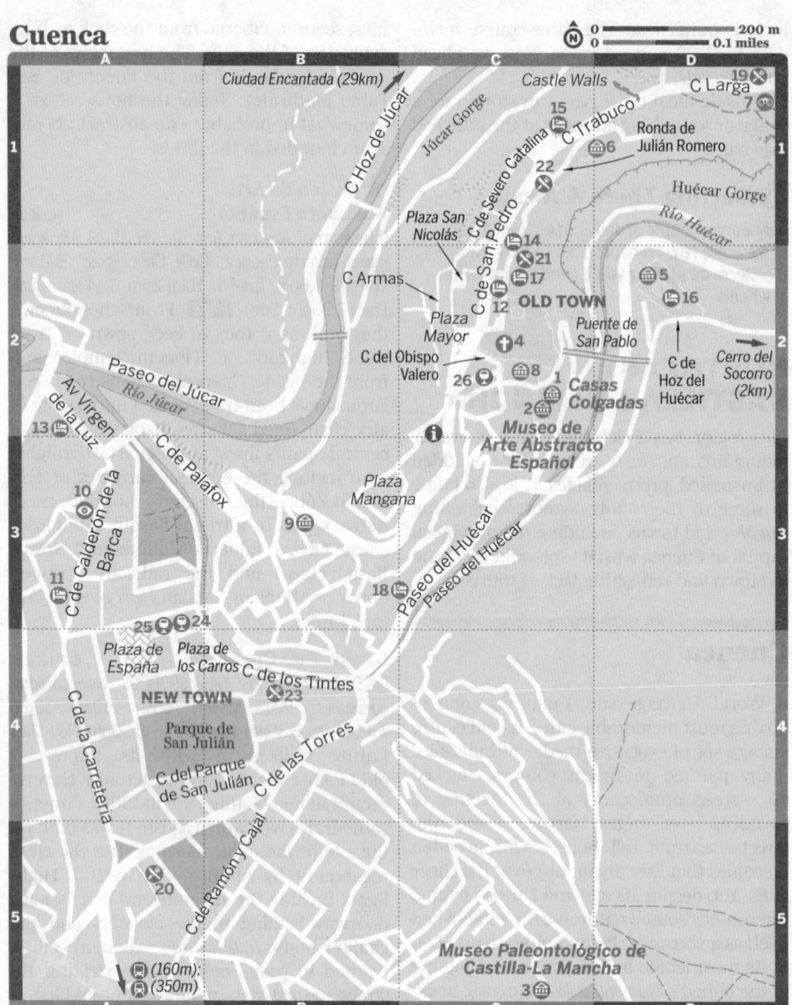




museum is a must for anyone interested in Spain's fascinating prehistorical record. Though anchored by its appropriately kid-friendly dinosaur exhibition (Tierra de Dinosaurios), this is a serious paleontology museum, with key specimens on display that have been instrumental in scientific breakthroughs, and signage in Spanish and English. Spacious modern galleries are decorated with locally found fossils, skeletons and skulls, plus mock-ups of enormous Cretaceous-era reptiles like the *Titanosaur*, among the largest land creatures to ever walk the earth.

Highlights include fossils of the *Iberomesornis* (a key species linking dinosaurs and modern birds), *Spinolestes* (a tiny prehistoric creature that upended notions of the simplicity of early mammals) and the remarkably intact skeleton of *Concavenator*, the unusual hump-backed dinosaur.

There are some fun audiovisual exhibits and the landscaped grounds are home to more prehistoric giants that kids can pose beside for that ultimate photo op for show-and-tell back home. It's about a 15-minute (uphill) walk south of the centre.

## Cuenca



**Museo de la Semana Santa** MUSEUM
(969 22 19 56; www.msscuenca.org; Calle Andrés de Cabrera 13; adult/child €3/free; 11am-2pm & 4.30-7.30pm Thu-Sat, 11am-2pm Sun, closed Aug) This museum is the next best thing to experiencing one of Spain's most spine-tingling Semana Santa parades first-hand. Spread over two floors, the accomplished audiovisual show moves from room to room showing the processions by local brotherhoods against a background of sombre music. Other rooms contain costumes, crosses and religious iconography.

**Túnel Calderón de la Barca** TUNNEL
(www.turismo.cuenca.es; Calle Calderón de la Barca; guided tour €3.50; hours vary) A molehill of tunnels lies under Cuenca's old town. Over time they have served multiple purposes as aqueducts, crypts and, most recently, air-raid shelters during the civil war. The tunnels have been restored and fitted with walkways, lighting and explanatory boards. Tours are guided only (in Spanish) and must be booked through the main tourist office (p230).

**Cerro del Socorro** HILL
This hill across the Río Huécar gorge from Cuenca's old town is crowned by a giant statue of Christ, which is illuminated at night. A 2km trail marked by the 14 Stations of the Cross follows a zigzag route to the top. It starts just behind the Parador de Cuenca.

**Fundación Antonio Pérez** GALLERY
(969 23 06 19; www.fundacionantonioperez.es; Ronda de Julián Romero 20; adult/child €2/free; 11am-2pm & 5-8pm) This huge modern-art gallery in the labyrinthine ex–Convento de las Carmelitas is a typical Cuenca synthesis of old and new. Stuffed with exhibits that may perplex, inspire and amuse, it is large, but crammed. Antonio Saura, Manolo Millares and Lucebert are well represented, as are plenty of other 1950s and '60s-era artists. Included in the collection are two minor works by the American pop artist Andy Warhol.

**Mirador Barrio del Castillo** VIEWPOINT
(Calle Larga) Climb to the top of the old town for this fine viewpoint over Cuenca and its plunging gorges. Catch bus number 2 from the new town which stops close by.

**Museo de Cuenca** MUSEUM
(969 21 30 69; Calle Obispo Valero 12; adult/child €3/free, Wed afternoon, Sat & Sun free; 10am-2pm & 4-7pm Tue-Sat, 10am-2pm Sun) The city's history museum is comprehensive, but heavily weighted towards the pre-medieval age. The story kicks off in the Bronze Age, but the real scoop is Sala 7, stuffed with original Roman statues (including of Emperor Augustus), plus columns and pediments plucked from the nearby archaeological sites at Segóbriga (p224) and Valeria (p224). Post-Renaissance history gets only a light dusting.

### Festivals & Events

**Semana Santa** RELIGIOUS
(www.juntacofradiascuenca.es; Easter) Cuenca's Holy Week celebrations are renowned throughout Spain for the eerie, silent processions through the streets of the old town.

There's even a town museum (p227) dedicated to the annual event.

## Sleeping

**Posada Huécar** HOSTAL €

(☎969 21 42 01; www.posadahuecar.com; Paseo del Huécar 3; s/d €35/48; ❄📶) Located squarely between the old and new towns, this good-value *hostal* (budget hotel) has spacious rooms with river views, rustic furnishings, ceramic tile floors and brightly painted walls. Packaged breakfast pastries and coffee are included in the price.

There is generally free parking available across the street

**Hostal Tabanqueta** HOSTAL €

(☎969 21 40 76; www.hostaltabanqueta.com; Calle Trabuco 13; d €55, apt €60-110; P❄📶) Up the hill from Plaza Mayor, this friendly spot has top-of-the-town views. The accommodation is excellent, with heating, stylish tiled bathrooms, attractive artwork and hotel-standard amenities such as toiletries, an espresso machine and hospitality tray with pastries. The owners also rent out a number of apartments nearby. You can generally find free parking just up the hill.

**Green River Hostel** HOSTEL €

(☎681 051779; www.greenriverhostel.com; Av Virgen de la Luz 15; dm €18-20, q €82-115; 📶) Near the banks of the Río Júcar, this handsomely converted 19th-century building has thoughtfully designed dorms and rooms with a neat, contemporary aesthetic. The main-floor lounge (and bar) is a fine place to relax after exploring, and there's also a small outdoor space.

**Posada de San José** HISTORIC HOTEL €€

(☎969 21 13 00; www.posadasanjose.com; Ronda de Julián Romero 4; s/d €65/90, with shared bathroom €37/52, d with view €97-162; ❄@📶) This 17th-century former choir school retains an extraordinary monastic charm with its labyrinth of rooms, eclectic artwork, uneven floors and original tiles. All rooms are different; cheaper ones are in former priests' cells and share bathrooms, while more costly doubles combine homey comfort with old-world charm. Several have balconies with dramatic views of the gorge.

There's a reputable restaurant on the ground floor.

LOCAL KNOWLEDGE

### ABSTRACT CUENCA

When Unesco listed Cuenca as a World Heritage site in 1996, it refrained from pushing the merits of its abstract art. But one of the latent joys of this historical city that hangs surreally above two dramatic gorges, is the way it has managed to incorporate modern avant-gardism into its crusty historic core.

Cuenca's penchant for abstract art can be traced back to the 1950s, when a loose collection of locally based artists formed what became known as the 'Cuenca School'. Notable in the group was Fernando Zóbel, a Spanish-Filipino painter and art collector who got together with Cuenca-born engineer-turned-artist Gustavo Torner in 1966 to open the Museo de Arte Abstracto Español (p225) inside the town's famous hanging houses. It was an inspired choice. Encased in a historical medieval residence, beautifully laid-out exhibits made use of reconfigured minimalist rooms. The museum prospered and others followed. In 1998 Sigüenza-born artist and poet Antonio Pérez opened up an eponymous foundation (p227) in an old Carmelite monastery and stuffed it with works from Warhol to Antoni Tàpies. Seven years later, Torner initiated his own museum, **Espacio Torner** (☎969 23 83 73; www.espaciotorner.es; Calle de Hoz del Huécar; adult/child €3/free), in Cuenca's San Pedro convent: it features a vibrant collection of his works including several site-specific installations.

But the abstractness extends beyond traditional museums. The brilliant yellow-and-orange stained glass in Cuenca's 12th-century cathedral (p225) was fashioned by Torner in the early 1990s to create a whimsical hybrid, while, further down the hill in the new town, the concrete-and-glass Museo Paleontológico de Castilla-La Mancha (p225), with its cube-like display halls, pays more than a passing nod to avant-gardism. You'll even spot abstract influences in the decor of some of Cuenca's hotels and restaurants, the arty interiors of which often belie their medieval outer shells.

**Convento del Giraldo** HISTORIC HOTEL €€

(☎969 23 27 00; www.hotelconventodelgiraldo.com; Calle de San Pedro 12; d/ste from €66/125; ❄@📶) Just above the cathedral, this conversion of a 17th-century convent wins points for location and style, though there aren't too many original features left. Nevertheless, the attractive rooms feature dark wooden furniture and big bathrooms, and many sport great views. You can find good discounts online.

**CH Victoria Alojamientos** HOTEL €€

(☎670 700090; www.chvictorialojamientoscuenca.es; Calle Mateo Miguel Ayllón 2; s €25-50, d €55-110; P❄📶) In a central location in the new town, the individually designed rooms at this well-maintained place offer stylish decoration, modern bathrooms, balconies throughout, and plenty of thoughtful extras. There's no reception, so you'll need to book in advance and arrange to pick up the key.

**Hostal San Pedro** HOSTAL €€

(☎969 23 45 43, 628 407601; www.hostalsanpedro.es; Calle de San Pedro 34; s/d €45/70; 📶) In this excellently priced family-run *hostal,* rooms have butter-coloured paintwork, traditional tiles, wrought-iron bedheads and rustic wood furniture and shutters; the bathrooms are large and modern. Great location in the old town.

**Parador de Cuenca** HISTORIC HOTEL €€€

(☎969 23 23 20; www.parador.es; Calle de Hoz del Huécar; r €120-190; P❄📶🏊) This majestic former convent commands possibly the best views in town of the *casas colgadas* (hanging houses) that are suspended on the opposite side of the gorge. The revamped rooms have a luxury corporate feel, while the public areas, including an old cloister, are headily historic with giant tapestries and antiques.

## Eating

**★El Bodegón** SPANISH €

(☎969 21 40 29; Cerrillo de San Roque A1; mains €7-12, set menu €10; ⏰10am-3.30pm & 7.30-11pm Tue-Sun; 📶) This no-frills place is much loved by locals for its great value, speedy service and warm atmosphere. Up a narrow lane in the new town, this sociable bar could turn out to be the Castilla-La Mancha eating experience that lingers longest in your memory. Try the excellent-value *menú del día*. Go early to beat the crowds.

**Romera Bistrót** INTERNATIONAL €€

(☎626 087832; www.romerabistrot.com; Calle de los Tintes 19; mains €16-24; ⏰noon-3pm & 8-11pm Mon-Sat) 🌿 Romero is one of Cuenca's new breed of contemporary restaurants with a well-executed menu with a dash of creativity: salmon ceviche, foie gras with mushroom crumble, a risotto of the day, and market-fresh fish. Everything happens in a 10-table, light-filled space that carries the air of a Parisian bistro. Vintage black-and-white cycling photos add to the allure.

**Asador María Morena** SPANISH €€

(☎969 23 88 25; www.asadormariamorena.com; Calle Larga 31; mains €16-19; ⏰11am-11pm) A good all-round restaurant located at the top of the old town with panoramic views over the river gorge, this place will satisfy both romantic diners and those seeking a more casual evening meal. Everything from the black paella (with squid ink) to homey *patatas a lo pobre* (potatoes with onions, garlic and peppers) are enhanced with a deft artistic touch.

**★Figón del Huécar** SPANISH €€€

(☎969 24 00 62; www.figondelhuecar.es; Ronda de Julián Romero 6; mains €18-25, set menus €26-36; ⏰1.30-3.30pm & 9-10.30pm Tue-Sat, 1.30-3.30pm Sun; 📶) With a romantic terrace offering spectacular views, Figón del Huécar is a highlight of old-town eating. Roast suckling pig, lamb stuffed with pine nuts and foie gras, and a host of Castilian specialities are presented and served with panache. The house used to be the home of Spanish singer José Luis Perales.

**Raff San Pedro** MODERN SPANISH €€€

(☎969 69 08 55; www.raffsanpedro.es; Ronda de Julián Romero; mains €16-25, set menus €24-40; ⏰1.30-3.30pm & 8.30-10.30pm Tue-Sat, 1.30-3.30pm Sun; 📶) Tucked down a narrow pedestrian street near the cathedral, Raff's innovative culinary convictions run deep with lively fresh flavours and combinations like roasted octopus with yams, purple potatoes and aioli. The set menus are an excellent way to taste a variety of contemporary-style dishes, although there is nothing nouvelle about the generous portion size.

## Drinking & Nightlife

**Pícaro** BAR

(☎679 693634; www.picarocuenca.com; Travesía Clavel 5; ⏰10am-5pm Mon, to 1am Tue-Sun; 📶)

WORTH A TRIP

### SERRANÍA DE CUENCA

Head out from Cuenca 27km via the CM2105 then CM2104 to the extraordinary **Ciudad Encantada** (www.ciudadencantada.es/en; Carretera CM2104, Km 19; adult/child €5/free; ⊙10am-sunset; P), where limestone rocks have been eroded into fantastical shapes by nature. Rejoining the CM2105 to the north, the road continues via the picturesque village of **Uña**, the crystal-clear waters of **Embalse del Tobar** and past the **Reserva Natural de El Hosquillo**, a protected park where reintroduced brown bears roam wild.

You can return to Cuenca via the CM210, a quiet rural route that passes several traditional villages like **Priego**, a lovely valley town that dates from Roman times. If you're heading on to Sigüenza, track northeast from Beteta to **Molina de Aragón**, a pretty town utterly dominated by one of Spain's most spectacular castles.

Near the cathedral, this Vespa-loving tapas bar and drinking den has a strong local following for its welcoming vibe, not to mention the tasty sharing plates, local wines and decent beers on draft served up by its easy-going bartenders. On warm days, grab a table on the terrace in front.

**La Bodeguilla de Basilio** BAR

(☎969 23 52 74; Calle Fray Luis de León 3; ⊙noon-4pm & 8-11pm Tue-Sat, 1-4pm Sun) Arrive here with an appetite, as you're presented with a complimentary plate of tapas when you order a drink, and not just a slice of dried-up cheese – typical freebies are a combo of quail eggs and fried potatoes or a bowl of *caldo* (meat-based broth). This is one of the most popular tapas bars in the new town, so get here early for a spot.

**La Tasca del Arte** BAR

(☎969 16 01 95; www.la-tasca-del-arte.es; Calle Fray Luis de León 9; ⊙1pm-2am Wed-Sun) Head to the *tasca* here to enjoy live flamenco in an intimate atmosphere where tapas and drinks are also served, including an impressive number of imported and craft beers. Performances take place from 9pm Thursday to Saturday but space is limited, so get here early to grab a table.

## Information

**Main Tourist Office** (☎969 24 10 51; http://turismo.cuenca.es; Calle de Alfonso VIII 2; ⊙10am-2pm & 4-7pm Mon-Fri, 10am-8pm Sat, 10am-2pm & 4-6pm Sun) Head here for good local info and to book tours of the Túnel Calderón de la Barca.

## Getting There & Away

Avanza (www.avanzabus.com) runs up to nine buses daily to Madrid (€13, 2½ hours). There are also daily services to Toledo (€14, two hours) with AISA (www.aisa-grupo.com).

Cuenca has two train stations. Fast AVE trains (serving Valencia and Madrid) use the modern **Estación de Cuenca-Fernando Zóbel** (☎912 43 23 43; www.renfe.com; Avenida Cerro de la Estrella; ⊙6.45am-10.30pm), 6km southwest of town. Bus 1 (€2.15) runs every 30 minutes (every 60 minutes on Saturday and Sunday) to the town centre, including Plaza Mayor.

The regional train station **Estación de Cuenca** (☎912 32 03 20; www.renfe.com; Calle Mariano Catalina 10; ⊙ticket office 8.30am-9.15pm) is located in the new part of town, southwest of Calle de Fermín Caballero and across from the bus station.

Numerous daily trains run to Madrid, ranging from slow *regionales* (trains operating within one region, usually stopping all stations; €15, three hours) to swift AVEs (€35, 55 minutes). The other way, to Valencia, is a similar deal (€16 to €38).

## Getting Around

Local buses 1 and 2 do the circuit from the new town to Plaza Mayor (€1.20) every 30 minutes (60 minutes on weekends), stopping outside the Estación de Cuenca-Fernando Zóbel. There's a large free car park on Calle Larga above the arch at the top of the old town.

# Alarcón

POP 150

One hundred kilometres or so south of Cuenca is the seductive medieval village of Alarcón. Flanked on three sides by the Río Júcar forming a natural moat, the approach is via a narrow road winding through three medieval defensive arches. The most famous sight here is the triangular-based Islamic castle, dating from the 8th century and captured by the Moors in 1184 after a nine-month siege. It is now a *parador* – one of Spain's smallest. The surrounding countryside is stunning and popular for hiking.

## Sleeping & Eating

**★ Parador de Alarcón** HISTORIC HOTEL €€€

(Marqués de Villena; ☎969 33 03 15; www.parador.es; Avenida Amigos de los Castillos 3; d €182-280; P❄📶) Parador de Alarcón is one of the grand castle *paradores* (luxurious state-owned hotels) found throughout the country, so you might as well go the whole hog and reserve a room with a four-poster bed and a chaise longue. Regal it might be, but this is actually one of Spain's smallest *paradores* with just 14 rooms. Historic, but intimate.

**La Cabaña de Alarcón** SPANISH €€

(☎969 33 03 73; www.restaurantelacabanadealarcon.es; Calle Álvaro de Lara 21; mains €12-16, set menu €18-26; ⏲1.30-4.30pm & 8.30-11pm Mon-Sat, 1-4pm Sun; 📶) The best restaurant in town is La Cabaña de Alarcón, with its picture windows, dark-pink paintwork, contemporary artwork and well-executed local dishes with an emphasis on game and grilled meats.

## Information

**Tourist office** (☎969 33 03 01; Calle Posadas 6; ⏲10am-2pm Tue-Sat, to 1pm Sun) Stop here for a map of walks around the village and beyond. If it's closed, there are signboards with maps two blocks south of there.

## Getting There & Away

On Monday, Wednesday and Friday, one bus connects Alarcón with Cuenca (€7, 1¼ hours) run by Rubiocar (www.rubiocar.com).

There's a large free car park at the foot of the village.

# Pastrana

POP 860

Pastrana should not be missed. It's an unspoiled place with twisting cobbled streets flanked by honey-coloured stone buildings, with small family-owned shops, good restaurants and atmospheric bars with tables on the cobblestones. It is famous for a notorious 16th-century court scandal as well as being home to some magnificent Flemish tapestries.

## Sights

The heart and soul of the town is the **Plaza de la Hora**, a large square framed by acacias and fronted by the sturdy **Palacio Ducal**. It's in Pastrana that the one-eyed princess of Éboli, Ana Mendoza de la Cerda, was confined in 1581 for having a love affair with the Spanish King Felipe II's secretary. You can see the caged window of her 'cell', where she died 10 years later, and join a tour on Saturday at 11.30am (Spanish only €5) run from the tourist office (p232).

**Iglesia de Nuestra Señora de la Asunción & Museo Parroquial** MUSEUM

(Colegiata; ☎949 37 00 27; www.museoparroquialdetapicesdepastrana.com; Calle Mayor; adult/child €5/free; ⏲11.30am-2pm & 4.30-7pm Tue-Fri, 1-2pm & 4.30-7pm Sun) Walk from the Plaza de la Hora along Calle Mayor and you'll soon reach the massive Iglesia de Nuestra Señora de la Asunción. Inside, the interesting little Museo Parroquial contains the jewels of the princess of Éboli, some exquisite 15th-century Flemish tapestries and even an El Greco. Access to the museum is by guided small group visit only (in Spanish) at scheduled times: 10.30am, 11.30am, 1.15pm, 4pm and 5.30pm. A five-group minimum is required except for the 1.15pm tour.

**Parque Arqueológico de Recópolis** ARCHAEOLOGICAL SITE

(Roman ruins; ☎949 37 68 98; www.cultura.castillalamancha.es; Carretera de Almoguera, Zorita de los Canes; adult/child €5/3; ⏲10am-6pm Fri & Sat, to 2pm Sun; P) Recópolis, a fascinating archaeological site, is a rarity. It was one of possibly only four cities that were built during the Visigothic era in Western Europe. Founded by King Leovigildo in 578 CE, it was originally conceived as a rival to Constantinople (the dream soon faded). The site is equipped with an interpretive centre that offers guided tours around the ruins, which lie 13km south of Pastrana, signposted off the Tarancón road (turn right just after passing the nuclear power plant).

## Sleeping & Eating

**Hotel Palaterna** HOTEL €

(☎949 37 01 27; www.hotelpalaterna.es; Plaza de los Cuatro Caños 4; d €65, ste €95-110; ❄📶) Hotel Palaterna is a pleasant, modern hotel overlooking a small square complete with bubbling fountain. Rooms are painted in cool colours with pretty fabrics and lightwood furniture, and the best (rooms 301, 302 and 303) have panoramic views over the countryside. Book Sunday to Thursday for the best rates.

**★Cenador de las Monjas** SPANISH €€
(☎949 37 01 01; www.cenadordelasmonjas.es; Travesía de Inés 1; mains €19-24, set menus €35-40; ⏰2-4pm & 9-11pm Fri & Sat, 2-4pm Sun; P) The dining room in the old 16th-century San José monastery offers beautifully prepared Spanish food that is anything but austere. Sit under a wood-beamed ceiling, overlooked by oil paintings of severe-looking nobility and indulge in venison meatballs or sardines with roast peppers and eggplant. Abiding by monastic tradition, most of the vegetables are grown here. Reservations are essential.

## Information

**Tourist Office** (☎949 37 06 72; www.pastrana.org; Plaza de la Hora 5; ⏰10am-2pm & 4-7pm Mon-Fri, 10am-2pm & 4-8pm Sat, 10am-2pm Sun) Has general info on the region. It also runs a two-hour historical tour (in Spanish) on Saturday morning at 11.30am (€5).

## Getting There & Away

Pastrana is 42km south of the regional capital of Guadalajara along the CM200. If travelling by public transport from either Madrid or Cuenca, you'll need to take a bus or train to Guadalajara, from where there's a daily bus run by Guadalbus (www.guadalbus.com) to/from Pastrana (€6.50, 1¼ hours).

# Sigüenza

POP 4300

Sleepy, historical and filled with the ghosts of a turbulent past, Sigüenza is well worth a detour. The town is built on a low hill cradled by Río Henares and boasts a castle, a cathedral and several excellent restaurants set among twisting lanes of medieval buildings. Start your ambling at the beautiful 16th-century Plaza Mayor. It's a popular day trip from Madrid

## Sights

**★Catedral de Santa María de Sigüenza** CATHEDRAL
(☎949 39 10 23; www.lacatedraldesiguenza.com; Plaza del Obispo Don Bernardo; adult/child €6/4.50; ⏰10.30am-7pm) Rising up from the heart of the old town is the city's centuries-in-the-making masterpiece – the Cathedral of Santa María. Begun as a Romanesque structure in 1130, work continued for four centuries as the church was expanded and adorned. The largely Gothic result is laced with elements of other styles, from plateresque through to Renaissance to Mudéjar. The church was heavily damaged during the civil war (note the pockmarks from bullets and shells in the bell tower), but was subsequently rebuilt.

The dark interior has a broodingly ancient feel and some fine stained glass, plus

WORTH A TRIP

### IMÓN

This tiny gem of a hamlet, located 16km northwest of Sigüenza, makes for an intriguing detour when passing through the area. There is some fine walking and birdwatching in the area, and a photogenic hotel that draws weekending *madrileños* looking for a countryside escape.

Don't miss the **salt-extraction pans** a short stroll away along the Sigüenza road; with the crumbling buildings around them as a backdrop, there are some great photo opportunities here. The pans were abandoned in 1996.

For an easy walk, follow the **Ruta Don Quijote** at the end of the main street (Calle Cervantes), heading north. The 4.5km pleasant stroll through fields leads to a 15th-century castle, **La Riba de Santiuste**, perched high on a rock above the semi-abandoned village of the same name. The castle is partly in ruins and is fascinating to explore.

Imón is also at the heart of the migratory destination for a large number of bird species, including the black stork, golden eagle and black-winged kite. A good area for spotting is the Atance Reservoir, about 8km southwest of Imón.

You can overnight in the **Salinas de Imón** (☎949 39 73 11; www.salinasdeimon.com; Calle Cervantes 49; d €75-150, ste €140-210; P ❄ 📶 🏊), an appealing 13-room inn set in a mid-17th-century stone building.

an impressive 15th-century altarpiece. Nearby, the **Capilla Mayor** is home of the reclining marble statue of Don Martín Vázquez de Arce (the statue is named *El Doncel*), who died fighting the Muslims in the final stages of the Reconquista.

Particularly beautiful is the jaw-dropping Rennaisance **Sacristía de las Cabezas**, with a ceiling adorned with hundreds of heads sculpted by Covarrubias. The **Capilla del Espíritu Santo's doorway** combines plateresque, Mudéjar and Gothic styles; inside is a remarkable dome and an *Anunciación*, one of the last works of El Greco.

An audio guide (English available) gives insightful commentary on the cathedral. Admission also gives access to the **Museo Diocesano** across from the cathedral's entrance.

**Castillo de Sigüenza** CASTLE

(www.parador.es; Plaza del Castillo; P) Calle Mayor heads south up the hill from the cathedral to a magnificent-looking castle, which was originally built by the Romans and was, in turn, a Moorish *alcázar* (fortress), royal palace, asylum and army barracks. Virtually destroyed during the Spanish Civil War, it was subsequently rebuilt under Franco as a *parador*.

Non-guests are welcome to wander in and dine in the restaurant, order a coffee in the cafe and take in the courtyard.

## Sleeping

**★ El Doncel** HOTEL €€

(949 39 00 01; www.eldoncel.com; Paseo de la Alameda 3; d €60-80; ) With earthy colours, exposed stone, spot lighting, fridges (for the *cava*), and marshmallow-soft duvets and pillows, this place is aimed squarely at couples on a romantic weekend away from Madrid. It's comfortable and attractive, and the on-site restaurant is one of the best in town.

**Parador de Sigüenza** HISTORIC HOTEL €€€

(949 39 01 00; www.parador.es; Plaza del Castillo; d €110-205; P) Sigüenza's luxurious *parador* is set in the castle, which dates back to the 12th century and overlooks the town. The magnificent courtyard is a wonderful place to pass the time. The rooms have period furnishings and castle-style windows, so they can be on the dark side; ask for one with a balcony to make the most of the natural light and views.

## Sigüenza

**Top Sights**
1 Catedral de Santa María de Sigüenza ........ B1

**Sights**
2 Castillo de Sigüenza ........ B4

**Sleeping**
3 El Doncel ........ A1
Parador de Sigüenza ........ (see 2)

**Eating**
4 Calle Mayor ........ B3
5 Nöla ........ B3
6 Restaurante Sánchez ........ A1

## Eating

**Calle Mayor** SPANISH €€

(949 39 17 48; www.restaurantecallemayor.com; Calle Mayor 21; mains €13-20; 1-3.30pm & 8.30-11pm Tue-Sun) Calle Mayor is a standout meal

OFF THE BEATEN TRACK

### CAMINO TO ATIENZA

Buses serving the hilltop-hugging town of Atienza are a little thin on the ground; but, for those with strong legs, there's a viable alternative. You can walk to the town on a little-trekked southern branch of the Camino de Santiago through a quintessential Castillan landscape of arid hills punctuated by half-forgotten, semi-abandoned villages.

While the hallowed Camino's well-trodden northern route now attracts over a quarter of a million walkers annually, this little-known southern branch – once a highway for pilgrims coming from destinations on Spain's Mediterranean coast – remains largely deserted. A signposted 32km section of the route connects the two historic towns of Sigüenza and Atienza, passing through the pinprick but atmospheric villages of Palazuelos, Olmeda de Jadraque and Riofrío del Llano.

To get started, head west out of Sigüenza via Calle Santa Bárbara. You'll pass a concrete-walled football field and cross a railway line, then head uphill along a paved unsigned road. At the top, take the unpaved road steeply downhill, just beside the CM110, and follow the purple and yellow 'Camino' signs decorated with the famous scallop symbol (sometimes, there's just a yellow arrow pointing the way). The path is good year-round (weather permitting), but, whichever season you hike, take plenty of food and water. The villages along the way offer little in the way of refreshment.

stop between the cathedral and castle. Be sure to order the simple starter of tomatoes, which are grown in the owner's backyard. Mains here tend to be traditional with local roasted meats, such as goat and lamb, as well as more elaborate creations like artichokes stuffed with prawns.

**Restaurante Sánchez** SPANISH €€
(☎949 39 05 45; www.restaurante-sanchez.com; Calle del Humilladero 11; mains €10-14; ⏲1-3.30pm & 8-11pm) Opened in 1916, this local icon has a loyal following for its unfussy home-style cooking, reasonable prices and surprisingly polished service. The dining room, strung with vintage photos and oil paintings of famous Sánchez *camareros* (waitstaff) lies hidden behind the bar: a fine setting for lamb meatballs, roast goat, eggs with blood sausage and pine nuts, and other meaty classics.

**Nöla** MODERN SPANISH €€€
(☎949 39 32 46; www.nolarestaurante.es; Calle Arcedianos 20; mains €16-26, set menu €28-44; ⏲1.30-3.30pm & 8.30-10.30pm Thu-Sat, 1.30-3.30pm Sun & Mon; 📶) Nöla is located in a grand Gothic Mudéjar mansion that also houses the Casa del Doncel, so is a place to linger. The seasonal menu stirs up traditional cuisine in creative ways with dishes like black rice with cuttlefish and aioli, and chargrilled venison with eggplants or roasted lamb with hazelnuts.

### ℹ Information

**Tourist office** (☎949 34 70 07; www.turismocastillalamancha.es; Calle de Serrano Sanz 9; ⏲10am-2pm & 4-6pm Mon-Thu & Sat, 10am-2pm & 4-8pm Fri, 10am-2pm Sun) Just down the hill from the cathedral. Opens and closes an hour later in the afternoon in summer.

### ℹ Getting There & Away

Regional trains go to Madrid's Chamartín station (€13 to €14, 1½ to 2 hours, four to seven daily) via Guadalajara; some go on to Soria in the other direction.

The **Tren Medieval** (☎912 32 03 20; www.renfe.com; Carretera de Atienza; adult/child €35/16) runs between Madrid's Charmartín station and Sigüenza on select Saturdays in April, May, June, September and October. During the 1½-hour journey passengers are treated to medieval music, costumed staff and traditional pastries. The fare includes a tour of the main Sigüenza sights.

## Atienza

POP 410

Standing amid the ruins of Atienza's blustery castle and looking out at the arid plains and low hills that couldn't be anywhere but Spain is one of Castilla-La Mancha's most vivid images. The diminutive but romantically atmospheric town doesn't get a lot of foreign visitors, but is a great place to come at weekends (when its museums actually open!) for some aimless wandering centred on the main half-timbered square. Atienza is situated 30km northwest of Sigüenza and its hilltop castle is visible for miles around.

## Sights

The main half-timbered square and former 16th-century market place, **Plaza del Trigo**, is overlooked by the Renaissance **Iglesia San Juan Bautista**, which has an impressive organ and lavish gilt *retablo* (altarpiece). It is a stunning square, although would be even more picture-perfect without the cars parked here. Three of the diminutive but muscular Romanesque churches hold small museums (open weekends only).

**Museo de San Gil** MUSEUM
(949 39 99 04; Iglesia de San Gil, Plaza de Don Agustín González Martínez Sacerdote; €3; 11am-2pm & 4-7pm Sat & Sun mid-Sep–mid-Jul, open daily mid-Jul–mid-Sep) This beautifully laid out museum is in the Romanesque Iglesia de San Gil. The church itself is perhaps the main 'exhibit' with its Mudéjar ceiling and plateresque door. Lined up in its naves you'll find religious art along with small sections on archaeology (arrowheads mainly) and palaeontology (fossils).

**Castillo Roquero** CASTLE
(Camino de San Salvador; sunrise-sunset; ) FREE Now that's what you call a castle! Looking like a natural extension of the crag upon which it stands, Atienza's romantically dishevelled *castillo* has Roman, Visigothic and Moorish antecedents. It was finally wrested from the Moors by Christian King Alfonso VI in 1085 and is now a windswept ruin overlooking the surrounding *meseta* (plains).

## Sleeping & Eating

**Hostal El Mirador** HOSTAL €
(949 39 90 38; www.elmiradordeatienza.com; Calle Barruelo; s/d €32/55; ) El Mirador, with spotless rooms that are a steal at this price, is a budget option in a modern whitewashed building offering great panoramic views over the fields below. The excellent restaurant shares the vistas and serves creative dishes, as well as the standard *cordero* (lamb) and *cabrito* (kid).

★ **Antiguo Palacio de Atienza** HISTORIC HOTEL €€
(949 39 91 80; www.palaciodeatienza.com; Plaza de Agustín González 1; d €60-90; ) Want to stay in a palace skilfully updated with well-chosen artworks, comfortable beds and exposed beams, fine enough to satisfy the expectations of modern-day princes and princesses (and tourists)? The variation in price relates to the size of the room and whether there's a hot tub in the stylish little bathrooms. Balconies overlook the lawns and pool, and there's a good restaurant.

**La Casa de San Gil** CASA RURAL €€
(626 165544; www.lacasadesangil.com; Calle Real 61; r €70-80; ) This traditional 18th-century stone cottage is located in the shadow of the Iglesia de San Gil and has been aesthetically restored by its *madrileño* owners. Each of the five rooms is different but all are soothingly decorated with earth colours and rustic charm. There's a sitting room with fireplace and pretty small garden.

## Information

**Tourist Office** (949 39 90 01; www.turismoatienza.es; Calle Héctor Vázquez 2; 11am-2pm & 4-6pm Mon-Sat, 11am-2pm Sun mid-Sep–mid-Jul, Sat & Sun only mid-Jul–mid-Sep) Contains a small museum displaying local costumes and paraphernalia relating to the town's customs and festivals.

## Getting There & Away

Buses are scant. An ALSA (www.alsa.es) bus leaves once daily in the morning, bound for Madrid (€12, 2¾ hours).

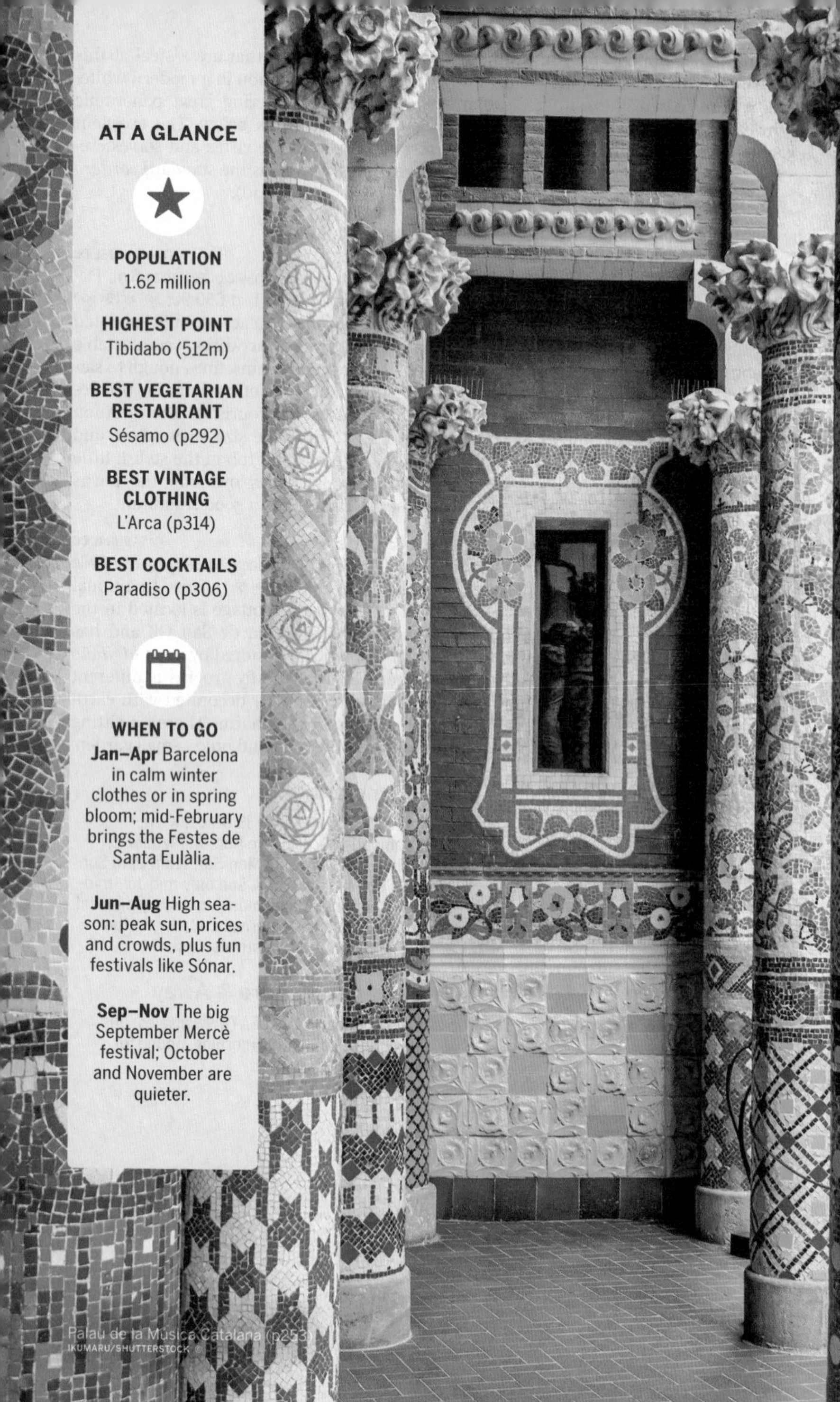

## AT A GLANCE

**POPULATION**
1.62 million

**HIGHEST POINT**
Tibidabo (512m)

**BEST VEGETARIAN RESTAURANT**
Sésamo (p292)

**BEST VINTAGE CLOTHING**
L'Arca (p314)

**BEST COCKTAILS**
Paradiso (p306)

**WHEN TO GO**

**Jan–Apr** Barcelona in calm winter clothes or in spring bloom; mid-February brings the Festes de Santa Eulàlia.

**Jun–Aug** High season: peak sun, prices and crowds, plus fun festivals like Sónar.

**Sep–Nov** The big September Mercè festival; October and November are quieter.

Palau de la Música Catalana (p253)
IKUMARU/SHUTTERSTOCK ©

# Barcelona

Catalonia's capital is a dazzling Mediterranean-hugging city of boundless culture, fabled architecture and museums, and an unrivalled drinking and dining scene. Barcelona's architectural treasures span more than 2000 years, from Roman-era Barcino to soaring Gothic cathedrals and whimsical masterpieces of Modernisme by Antoni Gaudí and his contemporaries. Since the late 19th century, the city has been breaking ground in art and style, as well as architecture, and its famed masters of molecular gastronomy are the latest part of a long, celebrated tradition of Catalan cooking.

Barcelona's sun-drenched white-gold beaches and deep-blue Mediterranean sea entice from the moment you spot them, while the pine-forested Collserola hills make a wonderfully scenic escape and hilltop Montjuïc offers endless explorations amid tangles of gardens. And as darkness falls, the city transforms with buzzing squares, heaving bars and live music.

**INCLUDES**

## Barcelona Highlights

❶ **La Sagrada Família** (p268) Marvelling at Antoni Gaudí's still-unfolding Modernista masterpiece.

❷ **Catalan cuisine** (p290) Feasting on fresh seafood in Barceloneta, and cutting-edge gastronomy everywhere.

❸ **Modernista achitecture** (p260) Uncovering L'Eixample jewels such as La Pedrera and wandering wondrous Park Güell.

❹ **Food markets** (p317) Sampling super-fresh Catalan produce at historic markets like La Boqueria or Santa Caterina.

❺ **Museu Picasso** (p254) Discovering early masterpieces.

❻ **El Poblenou & Sant Antoni** (p259) Soaking up the creative scene in these two recently reinvigorated neighbourhoods.

❼ **El Raval** (p240) Taking in the nightlife and food scene of this diverse bohemian neighbourhood.

❽ **La Catedral** (p243) Admiring a gem of Catalan Gothic architecture in the Barri Gòtic.

❾ **Montjuïc** (p272) Exploring this hilltop bastion of fine art and beautiful gardens.

❿ **Camp Nou** (p314) Joining the riotous carnival at an FC Barça match.

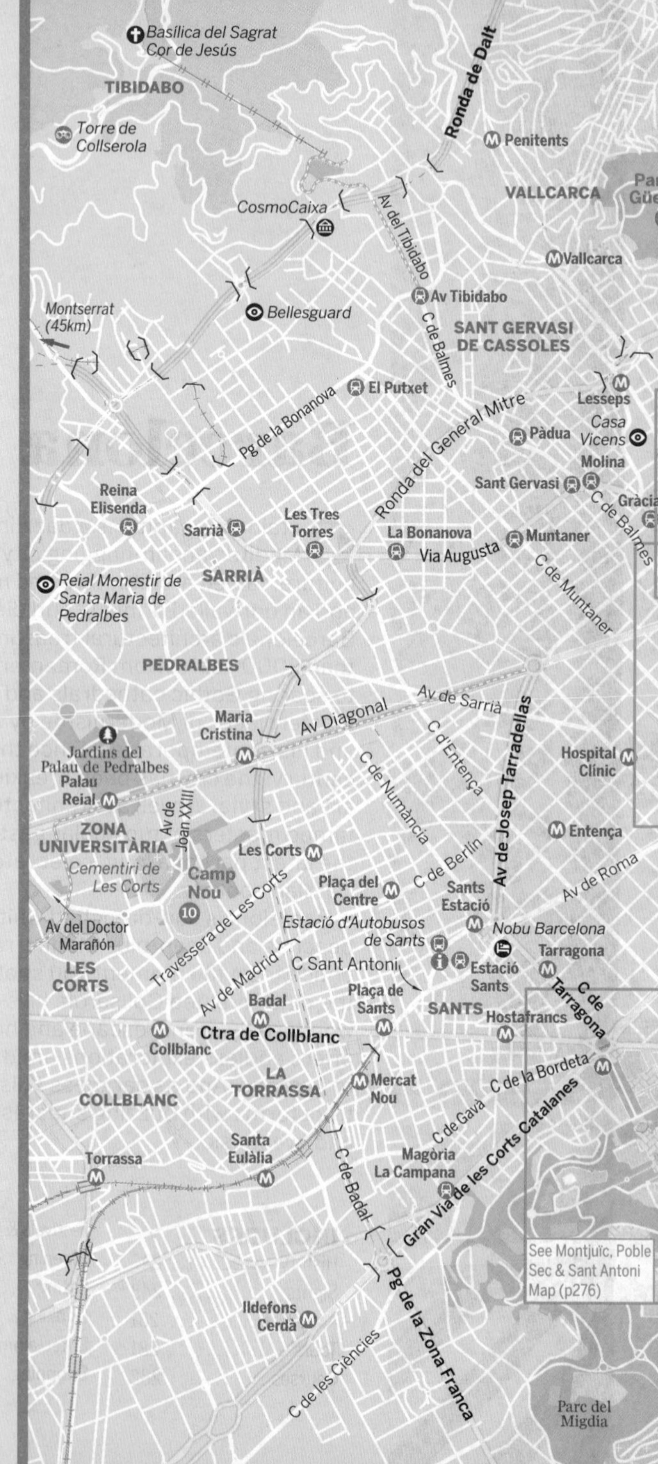

EL GUINARDÓ
Bunkers del Carmel
Túnel de la Rovira
EL CARMEL
Alfons X
Travessera de Dalt
Recinte Modernista de Sant Pau
Guinardó
Camp de l'Arpa
CAMP DE L'ARPA
Sant Pau/ Dos de Maig
Sagrera
Navas
Sant Martí
Bac de Roda
Clot
EL CLOT
SANT MARTÍ
LA VERNEDA
Encants
Joanic
See Gràcia Map (p272)
Sagrada Família
La Sagrada Família
Palau Macaya
Verdaguer
GRÀCIA
Monumental
See L'Eixample Map (p264)
El Poblenou
Cementiri del Poblenou
Platja de Bogatell
L'EIXAMPLE
Arc de Triomf
EL FORT PIENC
VILA OLÍMPICA
Platja de la Nova Icària
Port Olímpic
See La Ribera & El Born Map (p252)
Museu Picasso
Estació de França
See Barri Gòtic, La Rambla & El Raval Map (p244)
Urgell
Mercat de la Boqueria
La Catedral
El Raval
CIUTAT VELLA
Barceloneta
Platja de la Barceloneta
Platja de Sant Sebastià
Marina
Rocafort
Sant Antoni
Av del Paral·lel
POBLE SEC
PORTVELL
Platja de Sant Miquel
See Barceloneta, the Waterfront & El Poblenou Map (p258)
W Barcelona
Montjuïc
Port de Barcelona
MEDITERRANEAN SEA
Mirador del Migdia
Cementiri de Montjuïc
Sitges (38km)
Ronda del Litoral
Av Meridiana
C de Felip II
C de las Navas Tolosa
C de Sant Antoni Maria Claret
C d'Aragó
Gran Via de les Corts Catalanes
C de Pere IV
C de Bac de Roda
Av Diagonal
Rambla de Prim
Travessera de Gràcia
C de Pi i Margall
C de Còrsega
C de Padilla
C de Sardenya
Pg de Sant Joan
C dels Almogàvers
C de Pallars
Pg de Calvell
Pg de Gràcia
Ronda de Sant Pere
Pg de Pujades
Pg de Picasso
C de la Marina
Av del Litoral
Via Laietana
C del Comte d'Urgell
Ronda de Sant Antoni
La Rambla
Pg de Colom
0 1 km
0 0.5 mile

# NEIGHBOURHOODS AT A GLANCE

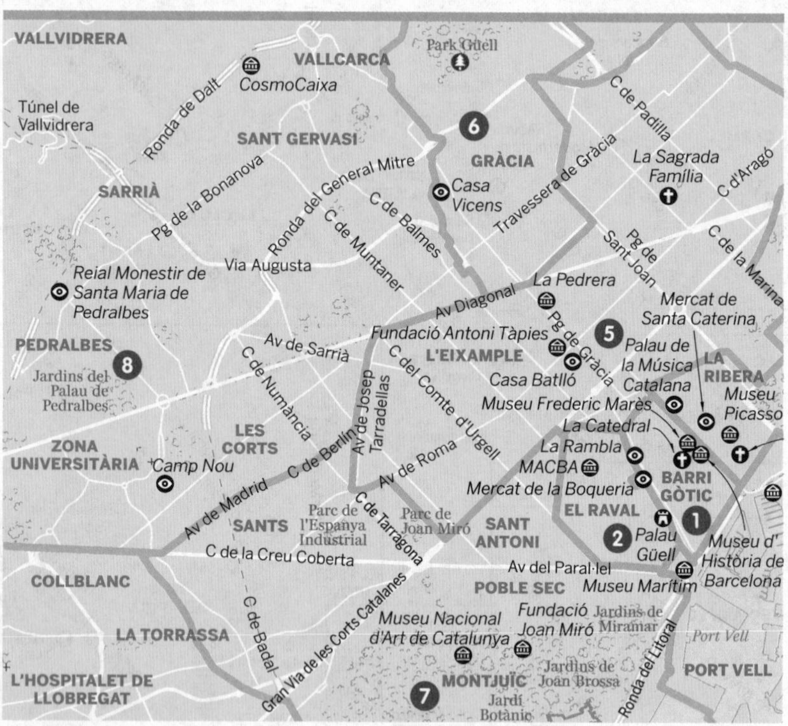


## ❶ La Rambla & Barri Gòtic (p243)

La Rambla, Barcelona's most famous pedestrian boulevard, is always a hive of activity, busy with tourists, locals and con artists (watch out!). The adjoining Barri Gòtic is packed with historical treasures – relics of ancient Rome, 14th-century Gothic churches and atmospheric cobblestone lanes lined with shops, bars and restaurants.

## ❷ El Raval (p250)

The once down-and-out district of El Raval is still seedy in parts, though it has seen remarkable rejuvenation in recent years, with the addition of cutting-edge museums and cultural centres. Other highlights include bohemian nightlife, one-of-a-kind shops and multicultural buzz.

## ❸ La Ribera & El Born (p252)

This charming, busy medieval quarter hosts some of the city's liveliest tapas bars and most original boutiques, along with key sights such as the Museu Picasso, the awe-inspiring Basílica de Santa Maria del Mar, the artfully sculpted Palau de la Música Catalana, and the leafy Parc de la Ciutadella.

## ❹ Barceloneta, the Waterfront & El Poblenou (p257)

Dramatically transformed since the 20th century, Barcelona's formerly industrial waterfront now boasts sparkling beaches, ultramodern high-rises and yacht-filled marinas. The gateway to the Mediterranean is the old-fashioned fishing quarter of Barce-

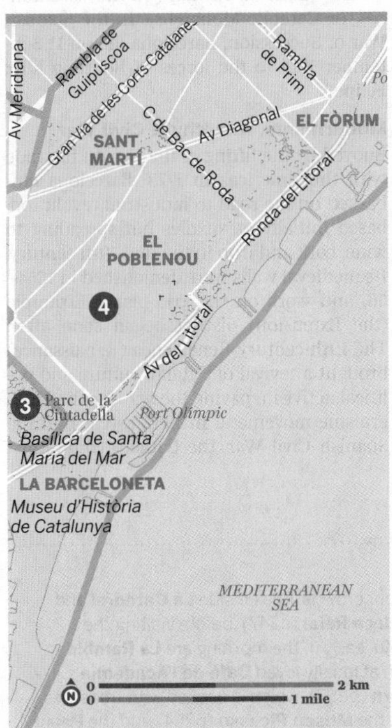


loneta, filled with seafood restaurants. To the northeast, post-industrial El Poblenou is a neighbourhood on the up, with a raft of creative design spaces.

## ❺ La Sagrada Família & L'Eixample (p260)

The elegant (traffic-filled) district of L'Eixample ('lay-sham-pluh') is a showcase for Barcelona's great Modernista architecture (including Gaudí's unfinished masterpiece, La Sagrada Família) spread along broad boulevards. L'Eixample also has a celebrated dining scene, along with high-end boutiques and wildly diverse nightlife, including the buzzing LGBTIQ+ clubs of the 'Gaixample'.

## ❻ Gràcia & Park Güell (p267)

Gràcia was an independent town until the 1890s, and its narrow lanes and picturesque plazas still have a village-like feel. Well-worn cafes and bars, vintage shops and a smattering of multicultural restaurants make it a magnet for a young, largely international crowd. To its north lies Gaudí's outdoor Modernista storybook of Park Güell. Recently opened Casa Vicens is another Gaudí highlight.

## ❼ Montjuïc, Poble Sec & Sant Antoni (p272)

Best reached by soaring cable car, the hillside overlooking the port hosts some of the city's finest art collections, plus gardens, an imposing castle and fabulous views. Just below Montjuïc lie the lively tapas bars and sloping streets of Poble Sec, while the newly fashionable neighbourhood of Sant Antoni draws a stylish young crowd.

## ❽ Camp Nou, Pedralbes & La Zona Alta (p277)

Some of Barcelona's most sacred sights are situated within the huge expanse stretching northwest beyond L'Eixample: the medieval monastery of Pedralbes and the great shrine to Catalan football, Camp Nou. Other reasons to venture here are Tibidabo hill, the wooded trails of the Parc Natural de Collserola, and the untouristed former towns of Sarrià and Sant Gervasi.

## History

Barcelona's recorded history really begins with the Romans when Barcino (much later Barcelona) was founded in the reign of Caesar Augustus, though it was overshadowed by Tarraco (Tarragona), 90km southwest. In the wake of Moorish occupation and then Frankish domination, Guifré el Pelós (Wilfred the Hairy) founded the house of the Comtes de Barcelona (Counts of Barcelona) in 878 CE. In 1137 Ramon Berenguer IV, the Count of Barcelona, became engaged to Petronila, heir to the throne of neighbouring Aragón, thus creating a joint state that set the scene for Barcelona's golden age. Jaume I wrenched the Balearic Islands and Valencia from the Moors in the 1230s to '40s. After the last of Guifré el Pelós' dynasty, Martí I, died heirless in 1410, Barcelona saw its star diminish when Catalonia effectively became part of the Castilian state, under the rule of Fernando from the Aragonese throne and Isabel, queen of Castilla (the Reyes Católicos, or Catholic Monarchs). In the Spanish War of Succession, Barcelona fell on 11 September 1714 to the forces of Bourbon king Felipe V.

### Modernisme, Anarchy & Civil War

Buoyed by the lifting of the ban on its trade with the Americas in 1778, Barcelona embarked on the road to industrial revolution, based initially on textiles but spreading to wine, cork and iron in the mid-19th century. Its medieval walls were demolished in 1854–56, and work on the grid-plan L'Eixample (the Extension) district began soon after. The 19th-century Renaixença (Renaissance) brought a revival of Catalan culture and political activism, paving the way for the Modernisme movement. In 1937, a year into the Spanish Civil War, the Catalan communist



### BARCELONA IN...

#### One Day

Head out early to explore the Barri Gòtic without crowds. Peek inside **La Catedral** and stroll through Plaça de Sant Josep Oriol and **Plaça Reial** (p247), before visiting the **Museu d'Història de Barcelona**. Most peaceful early in the morning are **La Rambla** (p248) and the **Mercat de la Boqueria**. Lunch at locally loved **Cafè de l'Acadèmia** (p291). In the afternoon, wander over to **El Born** (p252), which is packed with treasures: the **Basílica de Santa Maria del Mar** (p252), the **Museu Picasso** (p254) and the **Palau de la Música Catalana** (p253). Then tapas at **Bar del Pla** (p295) and **El Xampanyet** (p307).

#### Two Days

Start with a morning visit to **La Sagrada Família** (p268), Gaudí's wondrous work in progress, where you've (hopefully) prebooked. While here, also visit the **Recinte Modernista de Sant Pau** (p261) and buzzy Passeig de Sant Joan. Head to **Tapas 24** (p298) for delectable tapas. After lunch, explore more great Modernista buildings along Passeig de Gràcia, including Gaudí's **Casa Batlló** (p261) and **La Pedrera** (p260; again, prebooking helps!) Head up to village-like Gràcia for Catalan cooking at **La Pubilla** (p300) or **Extra Bar** (p300).

#### Three Days

Kick things off with a scenic **cable-car** (p281) ride up to Montjuïc, followed by a wander through the **Museu Nacional d'Art de Catalunya** (p272). Hop downhill to Poble Sec for lunch at **Palo Cortao** (p302) or **Quimet i Quimet** (p301), then knock around recently trendy-fied Sant Antoni, checking out the wonderful market and lively Carrer del Parlament. Spend the evening in boho El Raval, visiting the **MACBA** (p250), dining at **Elisabets** (p292) and bar-hopping along Carrer de Joaquín Costa.

#### Four Days

Time to take in the lovely Mediterranean along the Passeig Marítim. Wander through Barceloneta, then cram into tapas-tastic favourite **La Cova Fumada** (p296). Afterwards, relax at the nearby beaches (the sands northeast of the Port Olímpic are less touristed). Make your way over to the up-and-coming neighbourhood of El Poblenou and meander along Rambla del Poblenou, before grabbing dinner at magical **Can Recasens** (p296).

party (PSUC; Partit Socialista Unificat de Catalunya) took control of the city after fratricidal street battles against anarchists and Trotskyists. Barcelona became the Republicans' national capital in autumn 1937 – but the city fell to Franco in 1939.

### From Franco to the Present

Franco took a particularly hard line against Barcelona, most notably in banning public use of Catalan. Under Franco, 1.5 million immigrants from poorer parts of Spain poured into Catalonia (750,000 of them to Barcelona) in the 1950s and '60s looking for work. After the death of Franco in 1975, democracy gradually returned; in 1978 a new Spanish constitution created the autonomous community of Catalonia (Catalunya in Catalan; Cataluña in Castilian), with Barcelona as its capital. The 1992 Olympic Games put Barcelona on the map, with formerly run-down neighbourhoods revitalised.

### Separatism on the Rise

Over the last decade or so, the idea that Catalonia could break away from Spain as a sovereign republic has gained so much traction that it dominates the political landscape both regionally and nationally. Fuelled in no small part by soaring unemployment and painful austerity measures in the wake of the 2008 financial crisis – not to mention Catalonia's heavy tax burden – the fervour to secede has only grown in the last few years, spurred on by Catalonia's failed 2017 attempt to declare independence and the subsequent charges brought against Catalan separatist political leaders (p332).

## Sights

### La Rambla & Barri Gòtic

The Barri Gòtic is flanked by mile-long La Rambla to the southwest and the Via Laietana to the northeast.

**★La Catedral** CATHEDRAL
(Map p244; 93 342 82 62; www.catedralbcn.org; Plaça de la Seu; €7, roof or choir €3, chapter house €2; worship 8.30am-12.30pm & 5.45-7.30pm Mon-Fri, 8.30am-12.30pm & 5.15-8pm Sat, 8.30am-1.45pm & 5.15-8pm Sun, tourist visits 12.30-7.45pm Mon-Fri, 12.30-5.30pm Sat, 2-5.30pm Sun; M Jaume I) Barcelona's central place of worship presents a magnificent image. The richly decorated main facade, dotted with gargoyles and the kinds of stone intricacies you would expect of northern European Gothic, sets it quite apart from other Barcelona churches. The facade was actually added from 1887 to 1890. The rest of the building dates to between 1298 and 1460. Its other facades are sparse in decoration, and the octagonal, flat-roofed towers are a clear reminder that, even here, Catalan Gothic architectural principles prevailed.

Highlights include the exquisitely sculpted late-14th-century timber **choir stalls**; the **crypt**, which contains the 14th-century tomb of Santa Eulàlia, one of Barcelona's two patron saints; and the leafy **cloister**, with its fountains and flock of 13 geese.

#### DISCOUNT CARDS

**Articket BCN** (www.articketbcn.org) Six major art galleries for €35.

**Arqueoticket** (www.barcelonaturisme.com) Four major archaeology/history museums for €14.50.

**Barcelona Card** (www.barcelonacard.com) Costs €20/46/56 for two/three/four days; free transport and discounted or free admission to many sights.

**Ruta del Modernisme** (www.rutadelmodernisme.com) Modernista sights at discounted rates; costs €12.

**★Mercat de la Boqueria** MARKET
(Map p244; 93 318 20 17; www.boqueria.barcelona; La Rambla 91; 8am-8.30pm Mon-Sat; M Liceu) Barcelona's most central fresh-produce market is one of the greatest sound, smell and colour sensations in Europe. It's housed in a packed-out Modernista-influenced building every bit as impressive, built from 1840 to 1914 under architect Josep Mas i Vila on the site of the former Sant Josep monastery. La Boqueria may have taken a tourist-oriented turn in recent years, but towards the back you'll discover what it's really about: bountiful fruit and vegetables, and seemingly limitless sea critters, cheeses and meats.

**★Museu d'Història de Barcelona** MUSEUM
(MUHBA; Map p244; 93 256 21 00; http://ajuntament.barcelona.cat/museuhistoria; Plaça del Rei; adult/concession/child €7/5/free, 3-8pm Sun & 1st Sun of month free; 10am-7pm Tue-Sat, to 8pm Sun; M Jaume I) One of Barcelona's most fascinating museums travels back through the centuries to the very foundations of

# Barri Gòtic, La Rambla & El Raval

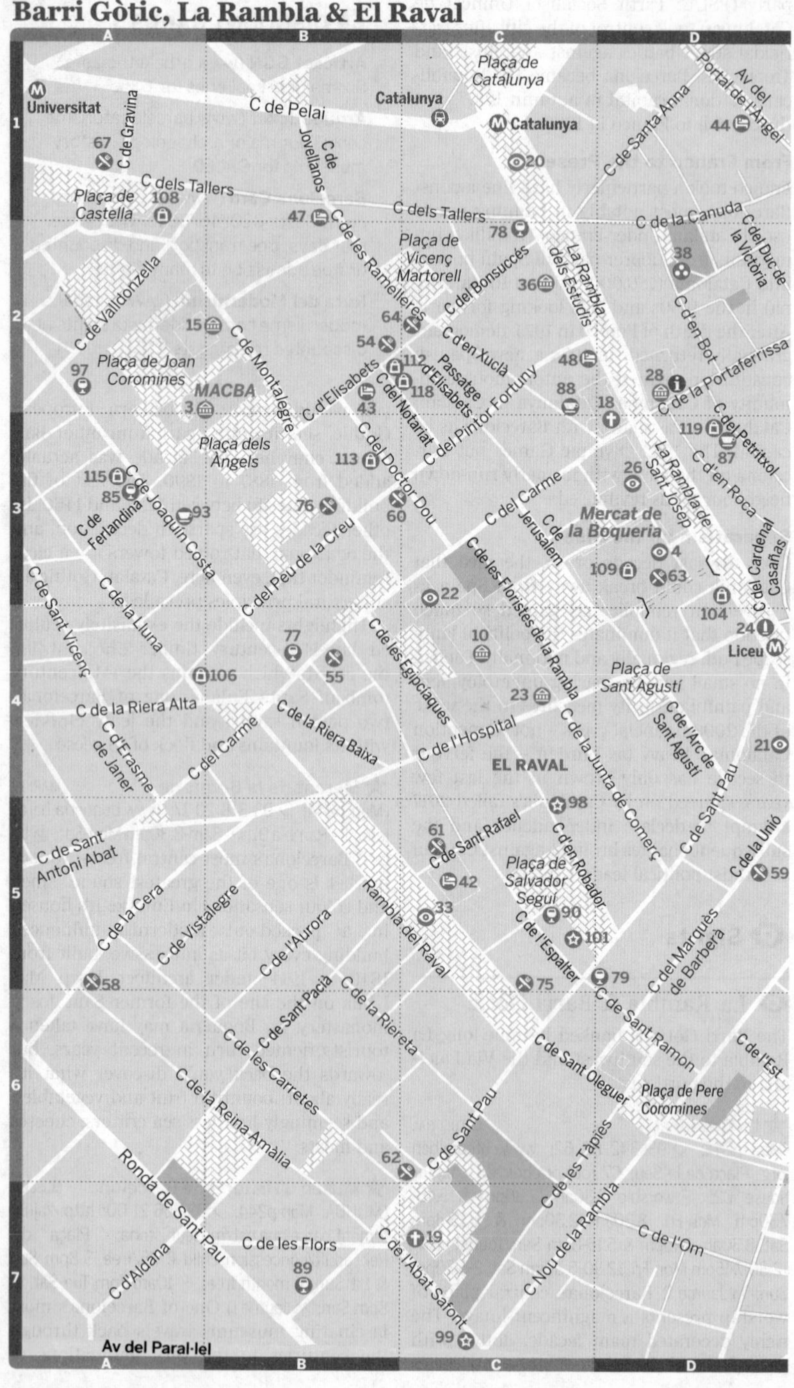


BARCELONA

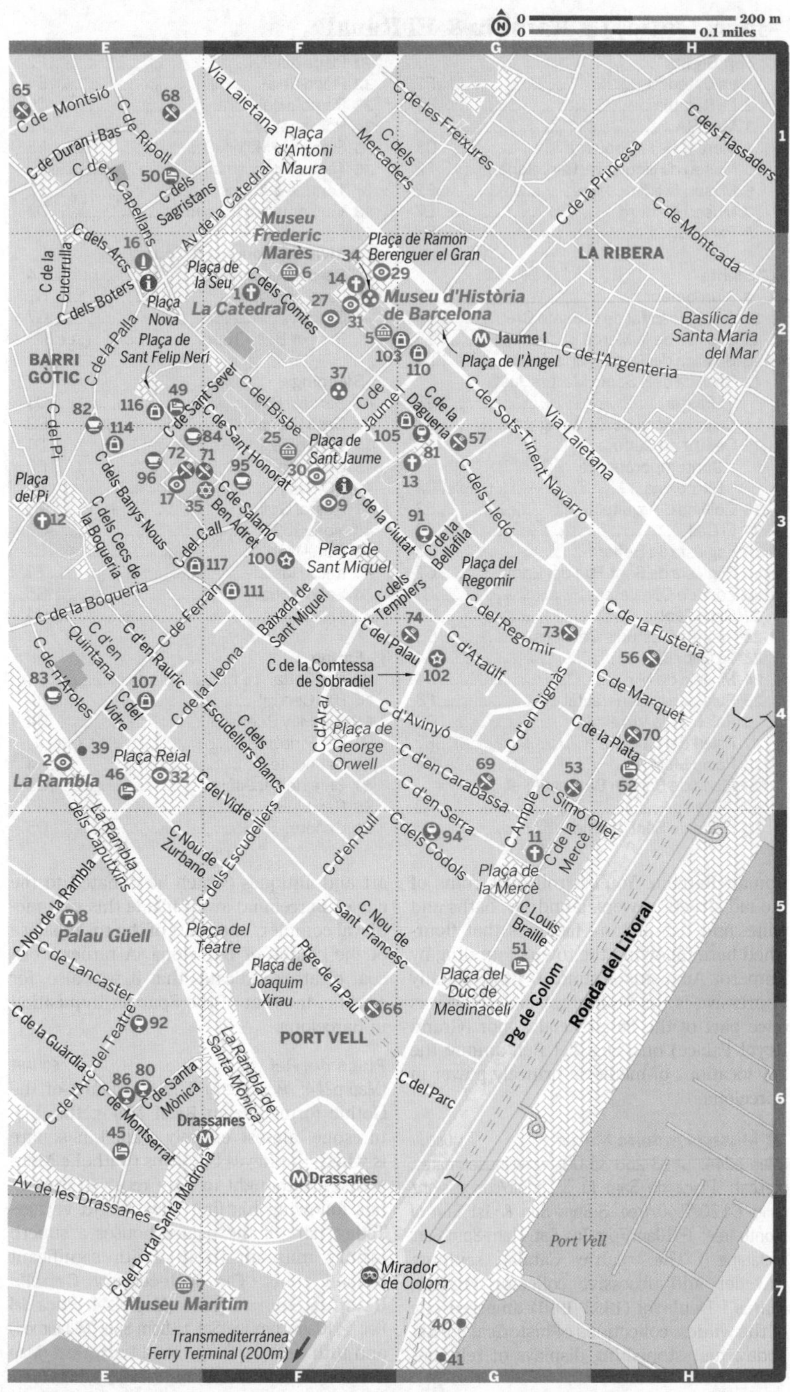

0 200 m
0 0.1 miles
Via Laietana
Plaça d'Antoni Maura
C de les Freixures
C dels Mercaders
C dels Flassaders
C de la Princesa
C de Montcada
C de Montsió
C de Duran i Bas
C de Ripoll
C dels Capellans
C dels Sagristans
Av de la Catedral
Museu Frederic Marès
Plaça de Ramon Berenguer el Gran
Museu d'Història de Barcelona
LA RIBERA
Basílica de Santa Maria del Mar
C de la Cucurulla
C dels Arcs
C dels Boters
Plaça de la Seu
C dels Comtes
La Catedral
Plaça Nova
Plaça de Sant Felip Neri
C de la Palla
BARRI GÒTIC
Jaume I
Plaça de l'Àngel
C de l'Argenteria
C del Sots-Tinent Navarro
C del Bisbe
C de Sant Sever
C de Sant Honorat
C de Jaume I
C de la Dagueria
C del Pi
C dels Banys Nous
Plaça de Sant Jaume
C dels Lledó
Plaça del Pi
C de Salamó Ben Adret
C de la Ciutat
C de la Bellafila
C dels Cecs de la Boqueria
C del Call
Plaça de Sant Miquel
Plaça del Regomir
C de la Boqueria
C de Ferran
Baixada de Sant Miquel
C dels Templers
C del Regomir
C de la Fusteria
C d'en Quintana
C d'en Rauric
C del Palau
C d'Ataülf
C de n'Aroles
C de la Comtessa de Sobradiel
C del Vidre
C de la Lleona
C dels Escudellers Blancs
C d'Avinyó
C d'en Gignàs
C de Marquet
C de la Plata
C d'Arai
Plaça de George Orwell
Plaça Reial
La Rambla
C d'en Carabassa
C Ample
C Simó Oller
C d'en Serra
C dels Escudellers
C Nou de Zurbano
C d'en Rull
C dels Còdols
C de la Mercè
Plaça de la Mercè
La Rambla dels Caputxins
C Nou de la Rambla
Palau Güell
Plaça del Teatre
C Nou de Sant Francesc
C Louis Braille
C de Lancaster
Plaça de Joaquim Xirau
Ptge de la Pau
Plaça del Duc de Medinaceli
Pg de Colom
Ronda del Litoral
PORT VELL
C de la Guàrdia
C de l'Arc del Teatre
La Rambla de Santa Mònica
C de Santa Mònica
C de Montserrat
C del Parc
Drassanes
Av de les Drassanes
C del Portal Santa Madrona
Port Vell
Mirador de Colom
Museu Marítim
Transmediterránea Ferry Terminal (200m)
BARCELONA

## Barri Gòtic, La Rambla & El Raval

**Top Sights**
1 La Catedral ... F2
2 La Rambla ... E4
3 MACBA ... A2
4 Mercat de la Boqueria ... D3
5 Museu d'Història de Barcelona ... F2
6 Museu Frederic Marès ... F2
7 Museu Marítim ... E7
8 Palau Güell ... E5

**Sights**
9 Ajuntament ... F3
10 Antic Hospital de la Santa Creu ... C4
11 Basilica de la Mercè ... G5
12 Basílica de Santa Maria del Pi ... E3
13 Basílica dels Sants Màrtirs Just i Pastor ... G3
14 Capella Reial de Santa Àgata ... F2
15 Centre de Cultura Contemporània de Barcelona ... B2
16 Col·legi d'Arquitectes ... E2
17 El Call ... E3
18 Església de Betlem ... D3
19 Església de Sant Pau del Camp ... C7
20 Font de Canaletes ... C1
21 Gran Teatre del Liceu ... D4
22 Institut d'Estudis Catalans ... C3
23 La Capella ... C4
24 Mosaïc de Miró ... D4
25 Palau de la Generalitat ... F3
26 Palau de la Virreina ... D3
27 Palau del Lloctinent ... F2
28 Palau Moja ... D2
29 Plaça de Ramon Berenguer el Gran ... F2
30 Plaça de Sant Jaume ... F3
31 Plaça del Rei ... F2
32 Plaça Reial ... E4
33 Rambla del Raval ... C5
34 Roman Walls ... F2
35 Sinagoga Major ... F3
36 Teatre Poliorama ... C2
37 Temple d'August ... F2
38 Via Sepulcral Romana ... D2

**Activities, Courses & Tours**
39 Barcelona Cooking ... E4
40 Las Golondrinas ... G7
41 Orsom ... G7
Runner Bean Tours ... (see 32)

**Sleeping**
42 Barceló Raval ... C5
43 Casa Camper ... B2
44 Catalonia Portal de l'Ángel ... D1
45 Chic&Basic Ramblas ... E6
46 DO Reial ... E4
47 Hostal Grau ... B1
48 Hotel 1898 ... C2
49 Hotel Neri ... E2
50 Itaca Hostel ... E1
51 Soho House ... G5
52 The Serras ... H4

**Eating**
53 Bar Celta ... G4
54 Bar Central ... B2
55 Bar Muy Buenas ... B4
Bar Pinotxo ... (see 4)
56 Belmonte ... H4
57 Cafè de l'Acadèmia ... G3
58 Can Lluís ... A5
59 Cañete ... D5

Roman Barcino. You'll stroll over ruins of the old streets, sewers, laundries, baths and wine- and fish-making factories that flourished here following the town's founding by Emperor Augustus around 10 BCE. Equally impressive is the building itself, which was once part of the Palau Reial Major (Grand Royal Palace) on Plaça del Rei, among the key locations of medieval princely power in Barcelona.

**★ Museu Frederic Marès** MUSEUM

(Map p244; ☎93 256 35 00; www.museumares.bcn.cat; Plaça de Sant Iu 5; adult/concession/child €4.20/2.40/free, 3-8pm Sun & 1st Sun of month free; ⏰10am-7pm Tue-Sat, 11am-8pm Sun; Ⓜ Jaume I) The wealthy Catalan sculptor, traveller and obsessive collector Frederic Marès i Deulovol (1893–1991) amassed one of the wildest collections of historical curios. Today, his astonishing displays of religious art and antiques (which he donated to the city of Barcelona) await inside this vast medieval complex, once part of the royal palace of the counts of Barcelona. A rather worn coat of arms indicates that it was also, for a while, the seat of the Spanish Inquisition in Barcelona.

**Plaça del Rei** SQUARE

(Map p244; Ⓜ Jaume I) The courtyard of the Gothic former Palau Reial Major, this picturesque, almost entirely walled-in square is where the Reyes Católicos (Catholic Monarchs) are thought to have received Columbus following his first New World voyage. Today, part of the palace houses a superb history museum (p243), with significant Roman ruins. The 14th-century **Capella Reial de Santa Àgata** (Map p244; Plaça del Rei; ⏰10am-7pm Tue-Sat, to 8pm Sun; Ⓜ Jaume I) and 16th-century **Palau del Lloctinent** (Map

60 Caravelle B3
61 Casa Leopoldo C5
Cecconi's (see 51)
Chichalimoná (see 3)
62 El Pachuco C6
63 El Quim D3
64 Elisabets C2
65 Els Quatre Gats E1
66 Federal F6
67 Flax & Kale A1
68 Koy Shunka E1
69 La Pachuca G4
70 La Plata H4
71 La Vinateria del Call F3
72 Levante E3
73 Milk G4
74 Rasoterra G4
75 Suculent C5
76 Veggie Garden B3

**Drinking & Nightlife**

77 33 | 45 B4
360° (see 42)
78 Bar Boadas C2
79 Bar Marsella D5
80 Bar Pastís E6
81 Bar Zim G3
82 Caelum E2
83 Cafè de l'Òpera E4
84 Čaj Chai E3
85 Casa Almirall A3
86 El Cangrejo E6
87 Granja La Pallaresa D3
88 Granja M Viader C2
89 La Confiteria B7
La Isabela (see 48)
90 La Monroe C5
91 L'Ascensor G3
92 Moog E6
93 Nømad Every Day A3
94 Polaroid G5
95 Salterio F3
96 Satan's Coffee Corner E3
97 Two Schmucks A2

**Entertainment**

98 23 Robadors C5
99 BARTS C7
100 El Paraigua F3
101 Filmoteca de Catalunya C5
Gran Teatre del Liceu (see 21)
102 Harlem Jazz Club G4

**Shopping**

103 Cereria Subirà G2
104 Escribà D3
105 Formatgeria La Seu G2
106 Grey Street A4
107 Herboristeria del Rei E4
108 Holala! Plaza A1
109 Joan La Llar del Pernil D3
La Central (see 54)
110 La Colmena G2
111 La Manual Alpargatera F3
112 La Variété B2
113 Lantoki B3
114 L'Arca E3
115 Les Topettes A3
116 Sabater Hermanos E2
117 Sombrerería Obach E3
118 Teranyina C2
119 Torrons Vicens D3

p244; Carrer dels Comtes; ⌚10am-7pm; Ⓜ Jaume I) FREE overlook the square, as does the 1555 (off-limits) **Mirador del Rei Martí** lookout tower, now part of the Arxiu de la Corona d'Aragón.

**Gran Teatre del Liceu** ARCHITECTURE

(Map p244; ☎93 485 99 00; www.liceubarcelona.cat; La Rambla 51-59; 45min tour adult/child €9/free; Ⓜ Liceu) If you can't catch a night at the opera (p312), you can still take in the awe-inspiring architectural riches of one of Europe's greatest opera houses. Opened in 1847, the Liceu launched Catalan stars such as Josep (José) Carreras and Montserrat Caballé, and seats up to 2300 people in its grand auditorium. Standard 45-minute tours of classic spaces (the foyer, Saló dels Miralls and auditorium) run in Catalan, Spanish and English; check updated schedules online.

**Plaça Reial** SQUARE

(Map p244; Ⓜ Liceu) One of the most photogenic squares in Barcelona, and certainly its liveliest. Numerous restaurants, bars and nightspots lie beneath the arcades of 19th-century neoclassical buildings, with a buzz of activity at all hours. The lamp posts by the central fountain are Antoni Gaudí's first known works in the city.

**Basílica de Santa Maria del Pi** CHURCH

(Map p244; ☎93 318 47 43; www.basilicadelpi.cat; Plaça del Pi; adult/concession/child under 8yr €4.50/3.50/free; ⌚10am-6pm; Ⓜ Liceu) Begun in 1320, on the site of a 10th-century Romanesque church, this striking 14th-century basilica is a classic of Catalan Gothic, with an imposing facade, a wide interior and a single nave. The simple decor in the main sanctuary contrasts with the gilded chapels and exquisite stained-glass windows that bathe the

EHSTOCK/GETTY IMAGES ©

TOP SIGHT
# LA RAMBLA

**Barcelona's most famous street is both a tourist magnet (beware the pickpockets and con artists) and a window into Catalan culture. Flanked by plane trees, the middle of La Rambla is a broad pedestrian boulevard, always crowded with a wide cross-section of society. Though the busy tourist-centric scene won't appeal to everyone, a stroll here is pure sensory overload: churches, theatres and intriguing architecture mingle with souvenir hawkers and pavement artists.**

### DON'T MISS

- Església de Betlem
- Mercat de la Boqueria
- Mosaïc de Miró
- Flower market
- Gran Teatre del Liceu

### PRACTICALITIES

- Map p244
- Ⓜ Catalunya, Liceu, Drassanes

## History

La Rambla takes its name from a seasonal stream (*ramal* in Arabic) that once ran here. From the early Middle Ages, it was better known as the Cagalell (Stream of Shit) and lay outside the city walls until the 14th century. Monastic buildings were then built (many were later destroyed) and, subsequently, mansions of the well-to-do from the 16th to the early 19th centuries. Unofficially, La Rambla is divided into five sections, which explains why many know it as Las Ramblas (Les Rambles in Catalan).

Horrific terrorist attacks in 2017, which killed 14 people, did little to diminish La Rambla's popularity with visitors or with the many hawkers, performers and living statues.

## La Rambla de Canaletes

The initial stretch south from Plaça de Catalunya is named after the **Font de Canaletes** (Map p244; La Rambla; Ⓜ Catalunya), an inconspicuous turn-of-the-20th-century drinking fountain and lamp post, the water of which supposedly emerges from what were once known as the springs of Canaletes. Delirious football fans gather here to celebrate whenever the main home side, FC Barcelona, wins a cup or the league championship.

### La Rambla dels Estudis

Running south from Carrer de la Canuda to Carrer de la Portaferrissa, La Rambla dels Estudis is named for the 15th-century university that once stood here.

Where La Rambla meets Carrer del Carme, the **Església de Betlem** (Map p244; ☎93 318 38 23; www.mdbetlem.net; Carrer d'en Xuclà 2; ⏲8.30am-1.30pm & 6-9pm; Ⓜ Liceu) was constructed in baroque style for the Jesuits in the late 17th and early 18th centuries to replace a 15th-century church destroyed by fire in 1671. The church was once considered the most splendid of Barcelona's few baroque offerings, but anarchists torched it in 1936.

Looming over La Rambla's eastern side, the neoclassical 18th-century **Palau Moja** (Map p244; https://palaumoja.com; Carrer de Portaferrissa 1; ⏲10am-9pm; Ⓜ Liceu) FREE houses a centre for Catalan heritage and tourist office (p320).

### La Rambla de Sant Josep

From Carrer de la Portaferrissa to Plaça de la Boqueria, what is officially called La Rambla de Sant Josep (named after a now nonexistent monastery) is lined with **flower stalls**, which give it the popular alternative name La Rambla de les Flors. It's flanked on the west side by the buzzing **Mercat de la Boqueria** (p243).

A rare example of post-baroque architecture in Barcelona, the **Palau de la Virreina** (Map p244; ☎93 316 10 00; https://ajuntament.barcelona.cat; La Rambla 99; ⏲11am-8pm Tue-Sun; Ⓜ Liceu) FREE is a grand 18th-century rococo mansion (with some neoclassical elements) that now hosts rotating photography exhibitions.

At Plaça de la Boqueria, just north of Liceu metro station, you can walk all over a colourful 1976 pavement **mosaic**, with one tile signed by the artist, Miró. Right next to the Mosaïc de Miró, a 12m-long engraved **memorial** commemorates the 14 victims of the 2017 terrorist van attack on La Rambla, with an anti-violence message inscribed in multiple languages.

### La Rambla dels Caputxins

La Rambla dels Caputxins, named after a former monastery, runs from Plaça de la Boqueria to Carrer dels Escudellers. On the western side of La Rambla is the **Gran Teatre del Liceu** (p312); to the southeast is the palm-shaded **Plaça Reial** (p247). Below this point La Rambla gets seedier.

### La Rambla de Santa Mònica

Named for the former Convent de Santa Mònica, the final stretch of La Rambla widens out to approach the Mirador de Colom overlooking the Port Vell.

### SPANISH CIVIL WAR

Many writers and journalists headed to Barcelona during the Spanish Civil War, including British author George Orwell, who vividly described La Rambla gripped by revolutionary fervour in the early days of the war in his book *Homage to Catalonia*. Orwell spent three days holed up in the 1894 **Teatre Poliorama** (Map p244; ☎93 317 75 99; www.teatrepoliorama.com; La Rambla 115; Ⓜ Catalunya, Liceu) during street battles.

**As one of the most touristed spots in Barcelona, there's no denying that La Rambla can feel a bit like a packed-out circus. Swing by first thing, around 8am, to enjoy this historic leafy boulevard with far fewer crowds. Alternatively, you could seek out some of the city's quieter rambles instead, such as Rambla del Raval (p251) or Rambla del Poblenou (p259).**

### TAKE A BREAK

Grab a coffee at **Café de l'Òpera** (Map p244; ☎93 317 75 85; www.cafeoperabcn.com; La Rambla 74; ⏲8.30am-2.30am; 📶; Ⓜ Liceu) or dip into El Raval for a more cutting-edge caffeine scene at Bar Central (p292).

### ROMAN REMAINS

**Temple d'August** (Map p244; 93 256 21 22; www.muhba.cat; Carrer del Paradís 10; 10am-2pm Mon, to 7pm Tue-Sat, to 8pm Sun; Jaume I) FREE Just southeast of La Catedral hide four columns and the architrave of Barcelona's 1st-century Roman temple.

**Roman Walls** (Map p244; Jaume I) One of the best-preserved sections is on the southern side of Plaça de Ramon Berenguer el Gran.

**Via Sepulcral Romana** (Map p244; 93 256 21 22; www.muhba.cat; Plaça de la Vila de Madrid; adult/concession/child €2/1.50/free; 11am-2pm Tue, to 7pm Sun; Catalunya) A block east of the top end of La Rambla is a sunken garden where Roman tombs from the 1st to 3rd century BCE were uncovered in the 1940s, after a 1588 Carmelite convent was demolished.

interior in ethereal light. The beautiful rose window – a brilliant 20th-century replica of the original – above the entrance is one of the world's largest.

**Plaça de Sant Jaume** SQUARE

(Map p244; Liceu, Jaume I) In the 2000 or so years since the Romans settled here, the area around this often-remodelled square, which started life as the forum, has been the focus of Barcelona's civic life – and it's still the central staging area for Barcelona's traditional festivals. Facing each other across the square are the **Palau de la Generalitat** (Map p244; http://presidencia.gencat.cat; Plaça de Sant Jaume; 2nd & 4th weekends of month Sep-Jul; Jaume I) FREE, seat of Catalonia's regional government, on the north side and Barcelona's **Ajuntament** (Casa de la Ciutat; Map p244; 93 402 70 00; www.bcn.cat; Plaça de Sant Jaume; 10am-2pm Sun; Jaume I) FREE on the south.

**Basilica de la Mercè** CHURCH

(Map p244; 93 315 27 56; www.basilicadelamerce.cat; Plaça de la Mercè 1; 9am-8pm; Drassanes) Raised in the 1760s on the site of its Gothic predecessor, following designs by architect José Mas Dordal, this baroque church is home to Barcelona's most celebrated patron saint. Though it was badly damaged during the civil war, what remains is quite a curiosity. The baroque facade facing the square contrasts with the Renaissance flank along Carrer Ample. Climb the steps behind the 1361 altar for a close-up view of the Virgin Mary statue for whom the church is named.

**Basílica dels Sants Màrtirs Just i Pastor** CHURCH

(Map p244; 93 301 74 33; www.basilicasantjust.cat; Plaça de Sant Just; 11am-2pm & 5-9pm Mon-Sat, 10am-1pm Sun; Jaume I) This slightly neglected single-nave church, with chapels on either side of the buttressing, was built in 1342 in Catalan Gothic style on what is reputedly the site of the oldest parish church in Barcelona. Inside, you can admire some fine stained-glass windows, then climb the bell tower (closed Sunday) for knockout views across central Barcelona. In front of it, in a pretty little square that was used as a film set (a smelly Parisian marketplace) in 2006 for *Perfume: The Story of a Murderer*, is what's claimed to be the city's oldest Gothic fountain.

## El Raval

★**MACBA** GALLERY

(Museu d'Art Contemporani de Barcelona; Map p244; 93 412 08 10; www.macba.cat; Plaça dels Àngels 1; adult/concession/child under 14yr €11/8.80/free, 4-8pm Sat free; 11am-7.30pm Mon & Wed-Fri, 10am-8pm Sat, 10am-3pm Sun & public holidays; Universitat) An extraordinary all-white, glass-fronted creation by American architect Richard Meier, opened in 1995, the MACBA has become the city's foremost contemporary art centre, with captivating exhibitions for the serious art lover. The permanent collection is dedicated to Spanish and Catalan art from the second half of the 20th century, with works by Antoni Tàpies, Joan Brossa, Miquel Barceló and Joan Rabascall. International artists, such as Paul Klee, Bruce Nauman, Alexander Calder, John Cage and Jean-Michel Basquiat, are also represented.

★**Palau Güell** PALACE

(Map p244; 93 472 57 75; www.palauguell.cat; Carrer Nou de la Rambla 3-5; adult/concession/child under 10yr incl audio guide €12/9/free, 1st Sun of month free; 10am-8pm Tue-Sun Apr-Oct, to 5.30pm Nov-Mar; Drassanes) Built off La

Rambla in the late 1880s for Gaudí's wealthy patron the industrialist Eusebi Güell, the Palau Güell is a magnificent example of the early days of the architect's fevered architectural imagination. This extraordinary neo-Gothic mansion (one of few major buildings of that era raised in Ciutat Vella) gives an insight into its maker's prodigious genius, and, though a little sombre compared with some of his later whims, it's a characteristic riot of styles (Gothic, Islamic, art nouveau) and materials.

**Antic Hospital de la Santa Creu** HISTORIC BUILDING

(Former Hospital of the Holy Cross; Map p244; Carrer de l'Hospital 56; 9am-10pm; M Liceu) FREE Behind the Mercat de La Boqueria stands the Gothic Antic Hospital de la Santa Creu, which was once the city's main hospital. Founded in 1401, it functioned until the 1930s, and was considered one of the best in Europe in its medieval heyday – it is famously the place where Antoni Gaudí died in 1926. Today it houses the **Biblioteca de Catalunya**, with its distinctive Gothic arches, and the **Institut d'Estudis Catalans** (Map p244; 93 270 16 20; www.iec.cat; Carrer del Carme 47; tours 10.30am, 11.30am & 12.30pm Tue & Thu; M Liceu). The hospital's 15th-century former chapel, **La Capella** (Map p244; 93 256 20 44; http://lacapella.barcelona; Carrer de l'Hospital 56; noon-8pm Tue-Sat, 11am-2pm Sun & public holidays; M Liceu) FREE, shows temporary exhibitions.

**Centre de Cultura Contemporània de Barcelona** GALLERY

(CCCB; Map p244; 93 306 41 00; www.cccb.org; Carrer de Montalegre 5; adult/concession/child under 12yr €6/4/free, 3-8pm Sun free; 11am-8pm Tue-Sun; M Universitat) A complex of auditoriums, exhibition spaces and conference halls, the CCCB opened in 1994 in what was formerly an 18th-century hospice, the Casa de la Caritat. Its courtyard, with a vast glass wall on one side, is spectacular. With 4500 sq metres of galleries in four separate areas, the centre hosts a constantly changing programme of exhibitions, film cycles and other events.

**Església de Sant Pau del Camp** CHURCH

(Map p244; 93 441 00 01; www.santpaudelcamp.org; Carrer de Sant Pau 101; adult/concession/child under 14yr €5/4/free; 10am-2pm & 3-6pm Mon-Sat, 10am-1pm Sun; M Paral·lel) The best example of Romanesque architecture in Barcelona is the dainty little cloister of this small 11th- or 12th-century church, which was founded in the 9th or 10th century but later rebuilt. The cloister's 13th-century polylobulated arches, sitting atop intricately carved capitals, are unique in Europe. The church itself contains the tombstone of Guifré II, son of Guifré el Pelós, a 9th-century count considered the founding father of Catalonia.

**Rambla del Raval** STREET

(Map p244; M Liceu) This broad boulevard was laid out in 2000 as part of the city's plan to open up this formerly sleazy neighbourhood, with some success. Now lined with palm trees and terrace cafes, it hosts a craft market every weekend and is presided over by the glossy Barceló Raval (p285) hotel. Fernando Botero's 7m-long, 2m-tall bronze sculpture of a plump cat, **El Gat de Botero**, which stands near the bottom of the Rambla, is something of a Barcelona icon.

DON'T MISS

## EL CALL

One of the most atmospheric and interesting parts of the Ciutat Vella is El Call (pronounced 'kye'), the medieval Jewish quarter that flourished here until a tragic 14th-century pogrom. Today its narrow lanes conceal what some historians consider to be the city's main medieval **synagogue** (Map p244; 93 317 07 90; www.sinagogamayor.com; Carrer de Marlet 5; adult/child €3.50/free; 10.30am-2.30pm & 3.45-6.30pm Mon-Fri, to 3pm Sun approx Nov-Mar, 10.30am-6.30pm Mon-Fri, to 3pm Sun approx Apr-Oct; M Liceu) and the remains of an old Jewish weaver's **house** (Map p244; 93 256 21 22; http://ajuntament.barcelona.cat/museuhistoria; Placeta de Manuel Ribé; adult/concession/child €2/1.50/free, 3-7pm Sun & 1st Sun of month free; 11am-2pm Wed, to 7pm Sat & Sun; M Jaume I). The boundaries of the original **Call Major** are roughly Carrer del Call, Carrer dels Banys Nous, Baixada de Santa Eulàlia and Carrer de Sant Honorat; another pocket, the **Call Menor**, extended across the modern Carrer de Ferran as far as Baixada de Sant Miquel and Carrer d'en Rauric.

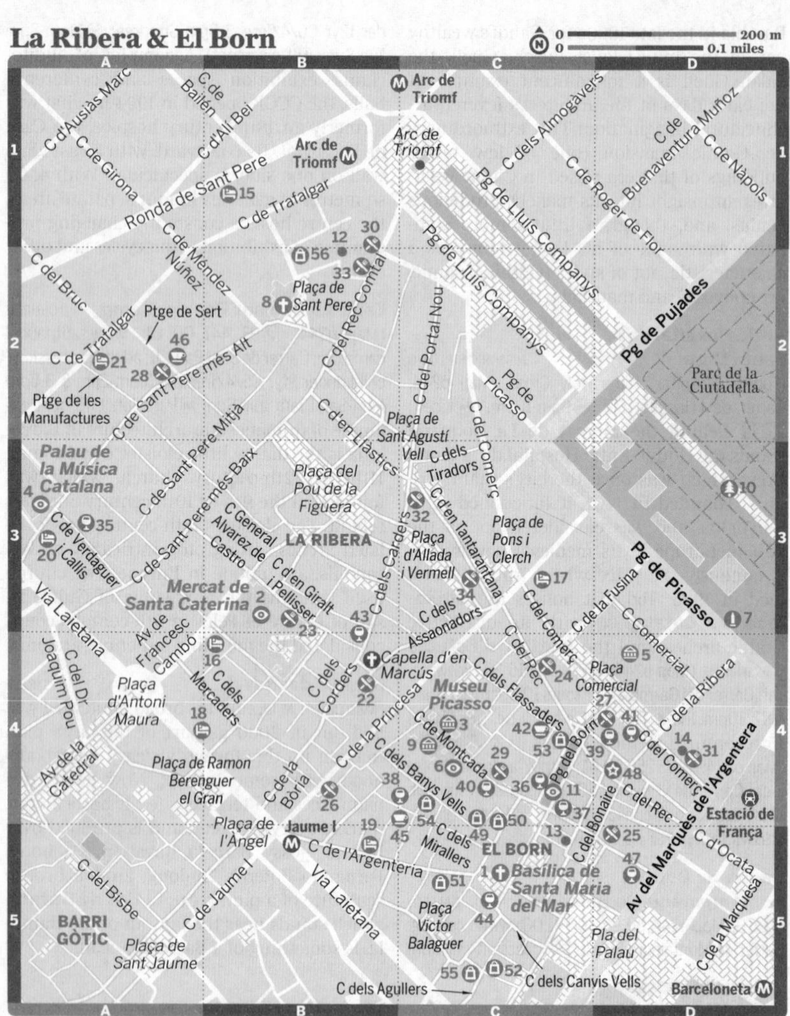


## La Ribera & El Born

The western half of La Ribera is known as 'Sant Pere' or 'Santa Caterina', after its colourful market (p253). The other half, around the Basílica de Santa Maria del Mar (p252), is known as 'El Born' and flanked to the east by the Parc de la Ciutadella (p256).

### ★ Basílica de Santa Maria del Mar — CHURCH

(Map p252; 93 310 23 90; www.santamariadelmarbarcelona.org; Plaça de Santa Maria del Mar; guided tour €8.50-10; 9am-8.30pm Mon-Sat, 10am-8pm Sun, M Jaume I) At the southwestern end of Passeig del Born stands Barcelona's finest Catalan Gothic church, Santa Maria del Mar (Our Lady of the Sea). Begun in 1329, under the watch of architects Berenguer de Montagut and Ramon Despuig, the church is remarkable for its architectural harmony and simplicity. Famously the parishioners themselves gave up their time to help construct the church, particularly the stevedores from the nearby port.

From 1pm to 5pm (2pm to 5pm on Sundays), visitors must join a guided tour (€10); a separate tour visits the roof (€8.50).

## La Ribera & El Born

**Top Sights**
1 Basílica de Santa Maria del Mar ........... C5
2 Mercat de Santa Caterina .................... B3
3 Museu Picasso ..................................... C4
4 Palau de la Música Catalana ................ A3

**Sights**
5 Born Centre de Cultura i Memòria ......... D4
6 Carrer de Montcada ............................ C4
7 Homenatge a Picasso ......................... D3
8 Monestir de Sant Pere de les Puelles ...... B2
9 Museu de Cultures del Món ................ C4
10 Parc de la Ciutadella .......................... D3
11 Passeig del Born ................................. C4

**Activities, Courses & Tours**
12 Barcelona Architecture Walks ............. B2
13 Bike Tours Barcelona .......................... C5
14 Wanderbeak ......................................... D4

**Sleeping**
15 360 Hostel Arts & Culture .................... B1
16 Barcelona Edition ................................ B4
17 Chic&Basic Born .................................. C3
18 Grand Hotel Central ............................ A4
19 Hotel Banys Orientals ......................... B5
20 Pensió 2000 ........................................ A3
21 Yurbban Passage ................................. A2

**Eating**
22 Bar del Pla ............................................ B4
23 Bar Joan ............................................... B3
24 Bormuth ............................................... C4
25 Cal Pep ................................................ D5
26 Can Cisa/Bar Brutal ............................. B4
27 Casa Delfín .......................................... D4
28 Casa Lolea ........................................... A2
29 Euskal Etxea ........................................ C4
30 Fismuler ................................................ B1
31 Koku Kitchen Buns .............................. D4
32 Mosquito .............................................. C3
33 Nakashita ............................................. B2
34 Tantarantana ........................................ C3

**Drinking & Nightlife**
35 Bar de l'Antic Teatre ............................ A3
36 Bar Sauvage ......................................... C4
37 Creps al Born ....................................... C4
38 Dr Stravinsky ....................................... C4
39 El Diset ................................................ D4
40 El Xampanyet ....................................... C4
41 Guzzo ................................................... D4
42 Hofmann a la Seca ................................ C4
43 La Catalista .......................................... B4
44 La Vinya del Senyor .............................. C5
45 Mag by El Magnífico ............................. C4
46 Nømad Cøffee Lab & Shop ................... A2
47 Paradiso/Pastrami Bar ......................... D5
The Roof ................................................ (see 16)

**Entertainment**
48 Farola ................................................... D4
Palau de la Música Catalana ................. (see 4)

**Shopping**
49 Capsule ................................................ C4
50 Casa Gispert ......................................... C4
51 El Magnífico ......................................... C5
52 Grey Street ........................................... C5
53 Hofmann Pastisseria ............................. C4
54 Ozz Barcelona ...................................... C4
55 Vila Viniteca ......................................... C5
56 Working in the Redwoods ..................... B2

### ★Palau de la Música Catalana — ARCHITECTURE

(Map p252; ☎93 295 72 00; www.palaumusica.cat; Carrer Palau de la Música 4-6; adult/concession/under 10yr €20/16/free; ⏱guided tours 10am-3.30pm Sep-Jun, to 6pm Easter & Jul, 9am-6pm Aug; Ⓜ Urquinaona) A fantastical symphony in tile, brick, sculpted stone and stained glass, this Unesco-listed, 2146-seat concert hall is a high point of Barcelona's Modernista architecture. Built by Domènech i Montaner, with the help of some of the best Catalan artisans of the time, between 1905 and 1908, for the Orfeo Català musical society, it was conceived as a temple for the Catalan Renaixença (Renaissance).

The *palau* shows off much of its splendour on the outside. The showstopper, however, is the richly colourful auditorium, with its ceiling of blue-and-gold stained glass and a shimmering 1000kg skylight. Unless you're here for a (recommended) show (p313), admission is by 55-minute guided tour.

### ★Mercat de Santa Caterina — MARKET

(Map p252; ☎93 319 57 40; www.mercatsantacaterina.com; Avinguda de Francesc Cambó 16; ⏱7.30am-3.30pm Mon, Wed & Sat, to 8.30pm Tue, Thu & Fri, closed afternoons except Fri Aug; Ⓜ Jaume I) FREE Come shopping for your tomatoes or pop in for lunch at this extraordinary produce market, designed by forward-thinking architects Enric Miralles and Benedetta Tagliabue to replace its 19th-century predecessor. Completed in 2005 (sadly after Miralles' death in 2000), it's distinguished by its undulating, kaleidoscopic roof, suspended above bustling produce stands, restaurants, cafes and bars by twisting slender branches of what look like grey steel trees.

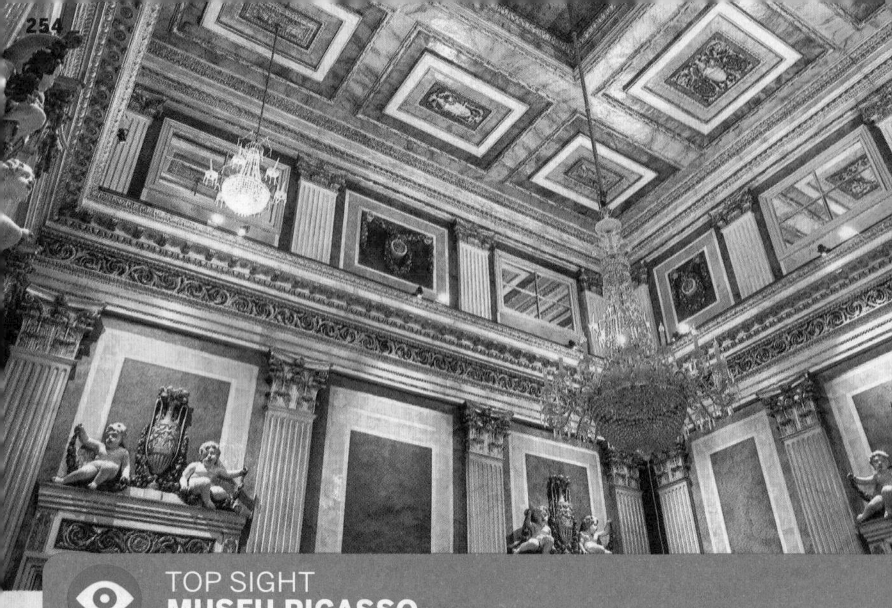



TOP SIGHT
# MUSEU PICASSO

**The setting alone, in five contiguous medieval stone mansions, makes Barcelona's Museu Picasso unique (and worth the queues). While the collection concentrates on Pablo Picasso's formative years – potentially disappointing lovers of his better-known later works – there is enough material from subsequent periods to showcase the artist's versatility and genius. Above all, you come away feeling that Picasso was the true original, always one step ahead of himself (let alone anyone else), in his search for new forms of expression.**

## History of the Museum

Allegedly it was Picasso himself who proposed the museum's creation in 1960, to his friend and personal secretary Jaume Sabartés, a Barcelona native. Three years later, the 'Sabartés Collection' was opened, since a museum bearing Picasso's name would have been met with censorship – Picasso's opposition to the Franco regime was well known. The Museu Picasso we see today opened in 1963. It originally held only Sabartés' personal collection of Picasso's art and a handful of other works, but the collection gradually expanded with donations from Salvador Dalí and Sebastià Junyer Vidal, among others. In 1968 Picasso himself donated the complete series of Las Meninas and in 1970 donated more early works including 236 oil painting 1149 drawings and 17 sketchbooks. His widow, Jacqueline Roque, also donated 41 ceramic pieces and the *Woman with Bonnet* painting after Picasso's death.

## DON'T MISS

- *Las Meninas* (The Ladies-in-Waiting)
- *Retrato de la tía Pepa* (Portrait of Aunt Pepa)
- *Ciència i Caritat* (Science and Charity)
- *Terrats de Barcelona* (Roofs of Barcelona)

## PRACTICALITIES

- Map p252
- 93 256 30 00
- www.museupicasso.bcn.cat
- Carrer de Montcada 15-23
- adult/concession/under 18yr permanent collection & temporary exhibit €14/7.50/free, 6-9.30pm Thu & 1st Sun of month free
- 10am-5pm Mon, 9am-8.30pm Tue, Wed & Fri-Sun, to 9.30pm Thu
- M Jaume I

Sabartés' contribution is honoured with Picasso's famous Blue Period portrait of him wearing a ruff (room B1).

### The Collection

The collection, which includes more than 3500 artworks, is strongest on Picasso's earliest years, up until 1904, which is apt considering that the artist spent his formative creative years in Barcelona.

A visit starts with sketches and oils from his earliest years in Málaga and A Coruña (1893–5). What makes this collection truly impressive – one-of-a-kind among the world's many Picasso museums – is the way in which it displays Picasso's extraordinary talent at such a young age. Faced with the technical virtuosity of a painting such as the enormous *Ciència i Caritat* (Science and Charity; room 3) or *Retrato de la tía Pepa* (Portrait of Aunt Pepa; room 2), it seems almost inconceivable that they could have been created by the hands of a 15-year-old. Some of his self-portraits and the portraits of his parents, which date from 1896, are further evidence of his precocious talent.

In rooms 5 to 7 hang paintings from his first Paris sojourn, while room 8 is dedicated to the first significant new stage in his development, the Blue Period. *Woman with Bonnet* is an important work from this period, as are the nocturnal blue-tinted views of *Terrats de Barcelona* (Roofs of Barcelona; room 8) and *El foll* (The Madman; often on loan).

### Las Meninas Through the Prism of Picasso

From 1954 to 1962, Picasso was obsessed with the idea of researching and 'rediscovering' the greats, in particular Velázquez. In 1957 he made a series of renditions of Velázquez' masterpiece *Las meninas* (The Ladies-in-Waiting), now displayed in rooms 12 to 14. It is as though Picasso has looked at the original Velázquez painting through a prism reflecting all the styles he had worked through until then, creating his own masterpiece in the process. This is a wonderful opportunity to see *Las meninas* in its entirety, in a beautiful space.

### Ceramics

What is also special about the Museu Picasso is its showcasing of his work in lesser-known media. The last rooms contain Picasso's engravings and, in the Neoclassic room, 41 ceramic pieces completed throughout the latter years of his unceasingly creative life. You'll see plates and bowls decorated with simple, single-line drawings of fish, owls and other animal shapes, typical for Picasso's daubing on clay..

### GETTING AROUND THE COLLECTION

The permanent collection is housed in the Palau Aguilar, Palau del Baró de Castellet and Palau Meca, all dating to the 14th century. The 18th-century Casa Mauri, built over medieval remains (even some Roman leftovers have been identified), and the adjacent 14th-century Palau Finestres, accommodate temporary exhibitions.

**At €15, the Carnet del Museu Picasso annual pass is barely more expensive than a day pass, and allows multiple entries. There is a special desk for this at Carrer de Montcada 23. Avoid queues by booking tickets online or arrive first thing.**

### TAKE A BREAK

Wander north along Carrer de Montcada for traditional-with-a-twist tapas at Bar del Pla (p295). Euskal Etxea (p294), along the same street, is one of the best *pintxos* (Basque tapas) bars in town.

**Carrer de Montcada** STREET

(Map p252; Ⓜ Jaume I) Today running between the Romanesque Capella d'en Marcús and Passeig del Born, this medieval high street (an early example of town planning) was driven towards the sea from the road that in the 12th century led northeast from the city walls. It became Barcelona's most coveted address for the merchant classes; the great mansions that remain today mostly date from the 14th and 15th centuries (several of them housing the Museu Picasso; p254).

**Parc de la Ciutadella** PARK

(Map p252; Passeig de Picasso; ⏲10am-10.30pm; 🚸; Ⓜ Arc de Triomf) Come for a stroll, a picnic, a lake boat ride, a tour of Catalonia's parliament or to marvel at the swirling waterfall-fountain in which Gaudí had a hand. This is the city's most central green lung, born in the mid-19th century on the former site of the much-hated huge fortress (La Ciutadella) on the eastern side of La Ribera.

**Passeig del Born** STREET

(Map p252; Ⓜ Barceloneta, Jaume I) Framed by the majestic Basílica de Santa Maria del Mar and the former Mercat del Born, leafy Passeig del Born was Barcelona's main playground from the 13th to 18th centuries. It's a place in which to sit as much as to promenade, and it's here in this graceful setting beneath the trees that El Born's essential appeal is obvious – thronging people, brilliant bars and architecture from a medieval film set.

**Born Centre de Cultura i Memòria** HISTORIC BUILDING

(Map p252; ☎93 256 68 51; http://elbornculturaimemoria.barcelona.cat; Plaça Comercial 12; centre free, exhibition adult/concession/child under 16yr €4.50/3.15/free; ⏲10am-8pm Tue-Sun; Ⓜ Jaume I) Launched in 2013 as part of the events held for the tercentenary of the Catalan defeat in the War of the Spanish Succession, this cultural space is housed in the former Mercat del Born, a handsome 19th-century structure of slatted iron and brick designed by Josep Fontserè. Excavations in 2001 unearthed remains of whole streets (now exposed on the subterranean level) flattened to make way for the much-hated Ciutadella (citadel), with some sections dating back to Roman and Islamic times.

OFF THE BEATEN TRACK

## ESCAPING BARCELONA'S CROWDS

Barcelona's popularity as a tourist destination has sky-rocketed in recent years – but explore beyond the busy city centre and you'll get to know *barris* (neighbourhoods) and *barcelonins* that few other visitors cross paths with.

**Sarrià-Sant Gervasi** (p282) This cluster of well-heeled former villages in northwest Barcelona is home to Gaudí's little-known Bellesguard (p280).

**Parc Natural de Collserola** (p280) Go hiking and biking amid bottle-green pines.

Pedralbes (p277) A 14th-century convent and little-visited Gaudí works, in the northwest.

**Horta** This tranquil northern *barri* appeals with its pretty squares and labyrinthine 18th-century **garden** (www.barcelona.cat; Passeig del Castanyers 1; labyrinth adult/child €2.25/1.50, Wed & Sun free; ⏲10am-8pm Apr-Oct, to 6pm Nov-Mar; Ⓜ Mundet); combine a visit with a lunch at **Can Cortada** (☎93 427 23 15; www.cancortada.com; Avinguda de l'Estatut de Catalunya; mains €13-29; ⏲1-4pm & 8-11pm; 🚸; Ⓜ Mundet, Valldaura), an atmospheric 11th-century estate.

**El Poblenou** Though this post-industrial *barri* is on the up, it remains a breath of fresh air away from the city-centre masses, with several beaches.

**Sants and Les Corts** Between the centre and Camp Nou, Sants has a restored 1913 market, an elevated garden promenade along the Rambla de Sants, and the 2019-opened top-end hotel and restaurant **Nobu** (☎93 493 60 26; https://barcelona.nobuhotels.com; Avinguda de Roma 2-4; r incl breakfast from €250; ❄📶; Ⓜ Sants Estació, Tarragona). Les Corts offers enticing bars around Plaça de la Concòrdia.

### BARCELONA'S BEST BEACHES

While some of the best local beaches lie just outside the city (p267), there's plenty of sunny sandy space in central Barcelona.

**El Poblenou Platges** (Map p258; Ⓜ Ciutadella Vila Olímpica, Llacuna, Poblenou, Selva de Mar) A series of beautiful, sandy, slightly quieter golden beaches dotted with *xiringuitos* (seasonal beach bars) stretches northeast from the Port Olímpic marina.

**Platja de la Barceloneta** (Map p258; Ⓜ Barceloneta) Barceloneta's main golden-brown strip of sand is an iconic and convenient Barcelona spot, but can feel like a bit of a circus.

**Platja de Sant Miquel** (Map p258; Ⓜ Barceloneta) Taking its name from Barceloneta's 18th-century church, this central honey-gold stretch fills with beachgoers on warm days.

**Platja de Sant Sebastià** (Map p287; Ⓜ Barceloneta) At the far southern end of the beach fronting La Barceloneta, this is a handy patch of white-gold sand in front of the W Barcelona (p287).

**Monestir de Sant Pere de les Puelles** CHURCH

(Map p252; ☎93 26 80 742; www.benedictinessantperepuelles.cat; Carrer de Lluís el Piadós 1; ⌚9am-1pm & 5-7.45pm Mon-Fri, 9am-1pm & 4.30-6.45pm Sat, 11am-1.15pm Sun; Ⓜ Arc de Triomf) It was around this much-remodelled Romanesque church, founded in 945, that settlement began in La Ribera. In 985 a Muslim force under Al-Mansur largely destroyed what was then a Benedictine convent, killing or capturing the nuns. Now overlooking a leafy square, the church was rebuilt in early medieval times and in the 20th century. The pre-Romanesque Greek-cross floor plan survives, as do some Corinthian columns (beneath the 12th-century dome) and a much-damaged Renaissance vault leading into a side chapel.

**Museu de Cultures del Món** MUSEUM

(Map p252; ☎93 256 23 00; http://museuculturesmon.bcn.cat; Carrer de Montcada 12; adult/concession/under 16yr €5/3.50/free, 3-8pm Sun & 1st Sun of month free; ⌚10am-7pm Tue-Sat, to 8pm Sun; Ⓜ Jaume I) Opening through a grand courtyard overlooked by an 18th-century staircase, the medieval Palau Nadal and the Palau Marquès de Lió host Barcelona's world cultures museum. Exhibits from private and public collections, including many from Montjuïc's Museu Etnològic (p274), travel through the ancient cultures of Africa, Asia, the Americas and Oceania. There are some fascinating finds, with displays spinning from Andean weaving, Ethiopian religious art and Papua New Guinean skull hooks to 17th-century Chola bronzes from Tamil Nadu in southern India.

## Barceloneta, the Waterfront & El Poblenou

Heading northeast from the fishing quarter of Barceloneta, you'll reach the touristy **Port Olímpic** (Map p258; Moll de Mestral; Ⓜ Ciutadella Vila Olímpica), built for the 1992 Olympics, and Frank Gehry's shimmering *Peix* (Fish) sculpture (p260). A string of popular beaches stretches northeast past gentrifying El Poblenou to modern El Fòrum.

**★Museu Marítim** MUSEUM

(Map p244; ☎93 342 99 20; www.mmb.cat; Avinguda de les Drassanes; adult/child €10/5, from 3pm Sun free; ⌚10am-8pm; Ⓜ Drassanes) The city's maritime museum occupies the mighty Gothic Reials Drassanes (Royal Shipyards) – a remarkable relic from Barcelona's days as the seat of a seafaring empire. Highlights include a full-scale 1970s replica of Don Juan de Austria's 16th-century flagship, fishing vessels, antique navigation charts and dioramas of the Barcelona waterfront.

**★Museu d'Història de Catalunya** MUSEUM

(Map p258; ☎93 225 47 00; www.mhcat.cat; Plaça de Pau Vila 3; adult/child €6/free, 1st Sun of month 10am-2.30pm free; ⌚10am-7pm Tue & Thu-Sat, to 8pm Wed, to 2.30pm Sun; Ⓜ Barceloneta) Within the revitalised 1880s Palau de Mar, this excellent museum travels from the Stone Age through to the arrival of Modernisme in Catalonia and the Spanish Civil War (touching heavily on the cultural and political repression felt across Catalonia postwar) and into the 21st century. It's a busy multimedia hotchpotch of dioramas, artefacts, videos, models, documents and interactive bits: all

## Barceloneta, the Waterfront & El Poblenou

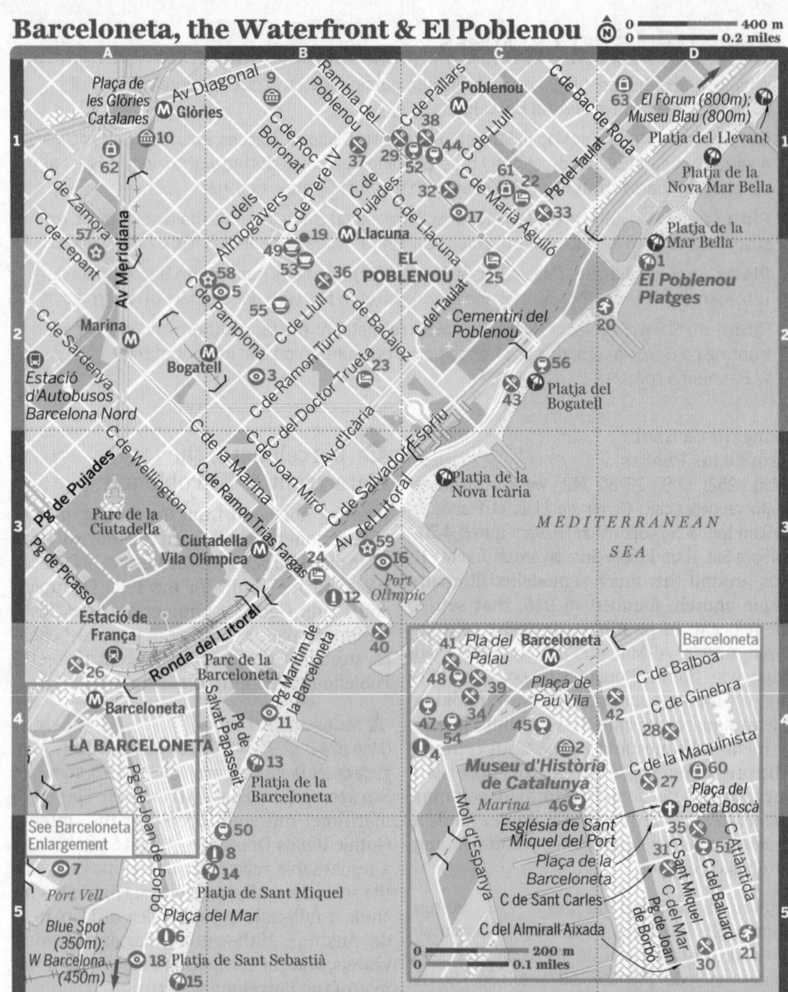


up, a thoroughly entertaining exploration of 2000 years of Catalan history. Signage is in Catalan, Spanish and English.

Afterwards, head upstairs to first-rate rooftop bar-restaurant **1881** (Map p258; ☎93 221 00 50; www.gruposagardi.com; mains €18-35; ⏲10am-midnight; ✎; Ⓜ Barceloneta).

**L'Aquàrium** AQUARIUM

(Map p258; ☎93 221 74 74; www.aquariumbcn.com; Moll d'Espanya; adult/child €21/16; ⏲10am-9pm Easter & Jun-Sep, reduced hours Oct-May; 👪; Ⓜ Drassanes) It's hard not to shudder at the sight of a shark gliding above you, displaying its toothy, wide-mouthed grin – but this 80m shark tunnel is the highlight of one of Europe's largest aquariums. Jutting out into the port, Barcelona's aquarium is home to the world's best Mediterranean collection, as well as plenty of colourful fish from as far off as the Red Sea, the Caribbean and the Great Barrier Reef. A staggering 11,000 creatures of 450 species reside here.

**Museu del Disseny de Barcelona** MUSEUM

(Map p258; ☎93 256 68 00; www.museudeldisseny.cat; Plaça de les Glòries Catalanes 37; adult/child €6/4, free from 3pm Sun & 1st Sun of the month; ⏲10am-8pm Tue-Sun; Ⓜ Glòries)

## Barceloneta, the Waterfront & El Poblenou

**Top Sights**
1 El Poblenou Platges ... D2
2 Museu d'Història de Catalunya ... C4

**Sights**
3 Edge Brewing ... B2
4 El Cap de Barcelona ... C4
5 Espacio 88 ... B2
6 Homenatge a la Natació ... A5
7 L'Aquàrium ... A5
8 L'Estel Ferit ... B5
9 Museu Can Framis ... B1
Museu de la Música ... (see 57)
10 Museu del Disseny de Barcelona ... A1
Palau de Mar ... (see 2)
11 Passeig Marítim de la Barceloneta ... B4
12 Peix ... B3
13 Platja de la Barceloneta ... B4
14 Platja de Sant Miquel ... B5
15 Platja de Sant Sebastià ... A5
16 Port Olímpic ... B3
17 Rambla del Poblenou ... C1
18 Telefèric del Port ... A5

**Activities, Courses & Tours**
43 The Spa ... (see 24)
19 Alblanc Atelier ... B1
20 Base Náutica Municipal ... D2
21 Molokai SUP Center ... D5

**Sleeping**
22 Amistat Beach Hostel ... C1
23 Bed & Beach ... B2
24 Hotel Arts Barcelona ... B3
25 Poblenou Bed & Breakfast ... C2

**Eating**
1881 ... (see 2)
26 Bar Ángel ... A4
27 Bodega La Peninsular ... D4
28 Can Maño ... D4
29 Can Recasens ... B1
30 Can Ros ... D5
31 Can Solé ... D5
32 El 58 ... C1
33 Els Pescadors ... C1
34 Green Spot ... C4
35 La Cova Fumada ... D5
36 Leka ... B2
37 Little Fern Café ... B1
38 Minyam ... C1
39 Oaxaca ... C4
40 Red Fish ... B4
41 Restaurant 7 Portes ... C4
42 Vaso de Oro ... D4
43 Xiringuito Escribà ... C2

**Drinking & Nightlife**
44 Balius ... C1
45 BlackLab ... C4
46 Blue Wave ... C4
47 Bodega Vidrios y Cristales ... C4
48 Can Paixano ... C4
49 Espai Joliu ... B2
50 La Deliciosa ... B5
51 La Violeta ... D5
52 Madame George ... C1
53 Nømad Roaster's Home ... B2
54 Perikete ... C4
SKYE Coffee ... (see 5)
55 Syra Coffee ... B2
56 Vai Moana ... C2

**Entertainment**
57 L'Auditori ... A2
58 Razzmatazz ... B2
59 Sala Monasterio ... B3

**Shopping**
60 Mercat de la Barceloneta ... D4
61 Mercat del Poblenou ... C1
62 Mercat dels Encants ... A1
63 Palo Market Fest ... D1

Nicknamed *la grapadora* (the stapler), Barcelona's fascinating design museum lies inside a monolithic contemporary building with geometric facades and a rather brutalist appearance. Inside, it houses a dazzling collection of ceramics, fashion, decorative arts and textiles, and is a must for anyone interested in the design world, with plenty of temporary exhibitions, too.

**Passeig Marítim de la Barceloneta** WATERFRONT
(Map p258; M Barceloneta, Ciutadella Vila Olímpica) On Barceloneta's seaward side are the first of Barcelona's beaches, which get packed in summer. The broad 1.25km promenade from Barceloneta to the Port Olímpic is a favourite with strollers, runners and sun-seekers. Cyclists zip by on a separate path nearby.

**Rambla del Poblenou** STREET
(Map p258) With its origins in the mid-19th century (when Poblenou's industrial boom kicked off), this leafy boulevard has long been the neighbourhood hub, sprinkled with tapas bars and restaurants, and flanked by a few Modernista buildings.

**Espacio 88** ARTS CENTRE
(Map p258; 93 356 88 18; www.espacio88.com; Carrer de Pamplona 88; 9am-5pm Mon-Fri; M Bogatell) Hosting everything from yoga classes, pop-up boutiques and brunches to

DON'T MISS

## ART ON THE STREETS

Barcelona hosts an array of intriguing street sculpture, such as Miró's 1983 **Dona i Ocell** (Woman and Bird; Map p276; Carrer de Tarragona, Parc de Joan Miró; Ⓜ Tarragona) in the park dedicated to the artist, and **Peix** (Map p258; Carrer de Ramon Trias Fargas 2; Ⓜ Ciutadella Villa Olímpica), Frank Gehry's shimmering, bronze-coloured headless fish facing the Port Olímpic. Halfway along La Rambla, at Plaça de la Boqueria, is Miró's **mosaic** (Map p244; Plaça de la Boqueria; Ⓜ Liceu). Picasso left an open-air mark with his design on the facade of the **Col·legi d'Arquitectes de Catalunya** (Map p244; https://arquitectes.cat; Plaça Nova; Ⓟ; Ⓜ Jaume I) opposite La Catedral in the Barri Gòtic. Other works include **El Cap de Barcelona** (The Barcelona Head; Map p258; Passeig de Colom; Ⓜ Barceloneta) by Roy Lichtenstein at the Port Vell and Fernando Botero's *El Gat* on the Rambla del Raval (p251).

Wander down to Barceloneta for Rebecca Horn's 1992 tribute to the old shacks that used to line the waterfront, **L'Estel Ferit** (The Wounded Shooting Star; Map p258; Passeig Marítim de la Barceloneta; Ⓜ Barceloneta). A little further south is the 2003 **Homenatge a la Natació** (Homage to Swimming; Map p258; Plaça del Mar; Ⓜ Barceloneta), by Alfredo Lanz. In 1983 Antoni Tàpies constructed **Homenatge a Picasso** (Tribute to Picasso; Map p252; Passeig de Picasso; Ⓜ Arc de Triomf, Jaume I) on Passeig de Picasso – essentially a glass cube set in a pond and filled with, well, junk.



the (permanent) uberpopular **SKYE** (Map p258; ☎699 542148; www.skye-coffee.com; Carrer de Pamplona 88; ⏰9am-1.30pm Mon-Wed, to 5pm Thu & Fri; 📶; Ⓜ Bogatell) coffee truck, this white-walled, concrete-floored warehouse-like space embodies all that's wonderful about El Poblenou's post-industrial resurgence. The arts take centre stage, with dynamic events and exhibitions typically focusing on fashion, design, photography, architecture, food and film.

**Edge Brewing** BREWERY

(Map p258; www.edgebrewing.com; Carrer de Llull 62; tours incl tastings €20; ⏰tours by appointment; Ⓜ Bogatell) Founded by two Americans in 2013, Edge Brewing has racked up some impressive awards for its craft beers (among other accolades, RateBeer.com named it the top new brewer in the world the year after it opened). Two-hour brewery tours take you behind the scenes and offer the chance to taste classic brews and seasonal varieties, like the Hoptimista, an award-winning 6.6% American IPA, and the passionfruit sour ale Apassionada.

**Museu Can Framis** MUSEUM

(Map p258; ☎93 320 87 36; www.fundaciovilacasas.com; Carrer de Roc Boronat 116-126; adult/child €5/2; ⏰11am-6pm Tue-Sat, to 2pm Sun, closed Aug & Sep; Ⓜ Glòries, Llacuna) Set in an 18th-century former textile factory surrounded by greenery, this contemporary gallery is a showcase for Catalan painting from the 1960s onwards. The galleries display around 300 works, arranged in thought-provoking ways – with evocative paintings by different artists (sometimes working in different time periods) creating fascinating intersections and collisions.

**Museu Blau** MUSEUM

(Museu de Ciències Naturals de Barcelona; ☎93 256 60 02; www.museuciencies.cat; Parc del Fòrum, Edifici Fòrum; adult/child €7/free, from 3pm Sun & 1st Sun of the month free; ⏰10am-7pm Tue-Sat, to 8pm Sun; Ⓜ El Maresme Fòrum) Set inside the futuristic Edifici Fòrum, the angular facades of which look like sheer cliff faces (with grand strips of mirror creating fragmented reflections of the sky), the sprawling Museu Blau takes visitors on a journey back in time and across the natural world. Multimedia and interactive exhibits explore topics such as the history of evolution, the earth's formation and the great scientists who have helped shaped human knowledge. There are also specimens from the animal, plant and mineral kingdoms, plus dinosaur skeletons.

## La Sagrada Família & L'Eixample

★**La Pedrera** ARCHITECTURE

(Casa Milà; Map p264; ☎93 214 25 76; www.lapedrera.com; Passeig de Gràcia 92; adult/child 7-12 yr from €25/14; ⏰9am-8.30pm & 9-11pm Mar-Oct, 9am-6.30pm & 7-9pm Nov-Feb; Ⓜ Diagonal) In the top tier of Gaudí's achievements, this madcap Unesco-listed masterpiece, with 33 balconies, was built in 1905–10 as a combined apartment and office block. Formally called Casa Milà, after the businessman who commissioned it, it is better known as La Pedrera (the Quarry) because of its uneven grey stone facade, which ripples around the corner of Carrer de Provença. Gaudí's approach to space and light as well as the blurring of the dividing line between decoration and functionality are astounding.

The roof is the most extraordinary element, where Gaudí's blend of mischievous form with ingenious functionality erupts into chimney pots looking like multicoloured medieval knights. Short concerts are often staged up here in summer. Buy tickets online (saving €3 on most ticket types) for opening time to avoid the crowds.

**★Casa Batlló** ARCHITECTURE

(Map p264; ☎93 216 03 06; www.casabatllo.es; Passeig de Gràcia 43; adult/child over 6 yr €29/26; ⏲9am-8pm, last admission 7pm; Ⓜ Passeig de Gràcia) One of Europe's strangest residential buildings, Casa Batlló (built 1904–6) is Gaudí at his fantastical best. From its playful facade and marine-world inspiration to its revolutionary experiments in light and architectural form (straight lines are few and far between), this apartment block is one of the most beautiful buildings in a city where the architectural stakes soar sky-high.

Gaudí eschewed the straight line, and so the staircase wafts you up to the 1st (main) floor, where the main salon looks on to Passeig de Gràcia. Everything swirls: the ceiling is twisted into a vortex around its sunlike chandelier; the doors, window and skylights are dreamy waves of wood and coloured glass. Twisting, tiled chimney pots add a surreal touch to the spine-like roof, while the back terrace feels like a kaleidoscopic fantasy garden in miniature, with flowerpots taking on strange shapes and over 300 pieces of *trencadís*.

**★Fundació Antoni Tàpies** GALLERY

(Map p264; ☎93 487 03 15; www.fundaciotapies.org; Carrer d'Aragó 255; adult/child €8/free; ⏲10am-7pm Tue-Thu & Sat, to 9pm Fri, to 3pm Sun; Ⓜ Passeig de Gràcia) The Fundació Antoni Tàpies is both a pioneering Modernista building (completed in the early 1880s) and the major collection of leading 20th-century Catalan artist Antoni Tàpies. Tàpies died in February 2012, aged 88. Known for his esoteric work, he left behind a powerful range of paintings and a foundation intended to promote contemporary artists.

**Recinte Modernista de Sant Pau** ARCHITECTURE

(☎93 553 78 01; www.santpaubarcelona.org; Carrer de Sant Antoni Maria Claret 167; adult/child €15/free, audio guide €4; ⏲9.30am-6.30pm Mon-Sat, to 2.30pm Sun Apr-Oct, 9.30am-4.30pm Mon-Sat, to 2.30pm Sun Nov-Mar; Ⓜ Sant Pau/Dos de Maig) Domènech i Montaner outdid himself as architect and philanthropist with the Modernista Hospital de la Santa Creu i de Sant Pau, renamed the 'Recinte Modernista' in 2014. Built between 1902 and 1930, it was long considered one of Barcelona's most important hospitals, but was repurposed into cultural centres, offices and a monument in 2009. A joint Unesco World Heritage Site together with the Palau de la Música Catalana (p253), the 27-building complex is lavishly decorated and each of its 16 pavilions unique.

**Casa Amatller** ARCHITECTURE

(Map p264; ☎93 216 01 75; www.amatller.org; Passeig de Gràcia 41; adult/child 7-12 yrs 1hr guided tour €24/12, 40min multimedia tour €19/9.50; ⏲10am-6pm; Ⓜ Passeig de Gràcia) One of Puig i Cadafalch's most striking flights of Modernista fantasy, Casa Amatller combines Gothic window frames and Romanesque flourishes with a stepped gable borrowed from Dutch urban architecture. But the busts and reliefs of dragons, knights and other characters dripping off the main facade are pure ca-

### LESSER-KNOWN MODERNISME

**Palau Macaya** (☎93 457 95 31; www.obrasociallacaixa.org; Passeig de Sant Joan 108; ⏲9am-8pm Mon-Fri; Ⓜ Verdaguer) FREE A little-known Modernisme gem by Josep Puig i Cadafalch, who also designed L'Eixample's Casa Serra and Palau Baró de Quadras.

**Palau Montaner** (Map p264; ☎93 317 76 52; www.fundaciotapies.org; Carrer de Mallorca 278; adult/child €7/free; ⏲by reservation; Ⓜ Passeig de Gràcia) A spectacular, sculpture-filled Domènech i Montaner mansion (1893).

**Casa Calvet** (Map p264; Carrer de Casp 48; Ⓜ Urquinaona, Tetuan) Gaudí's most conventional, baroque-inspired contribution (1901) to L'Eixample.

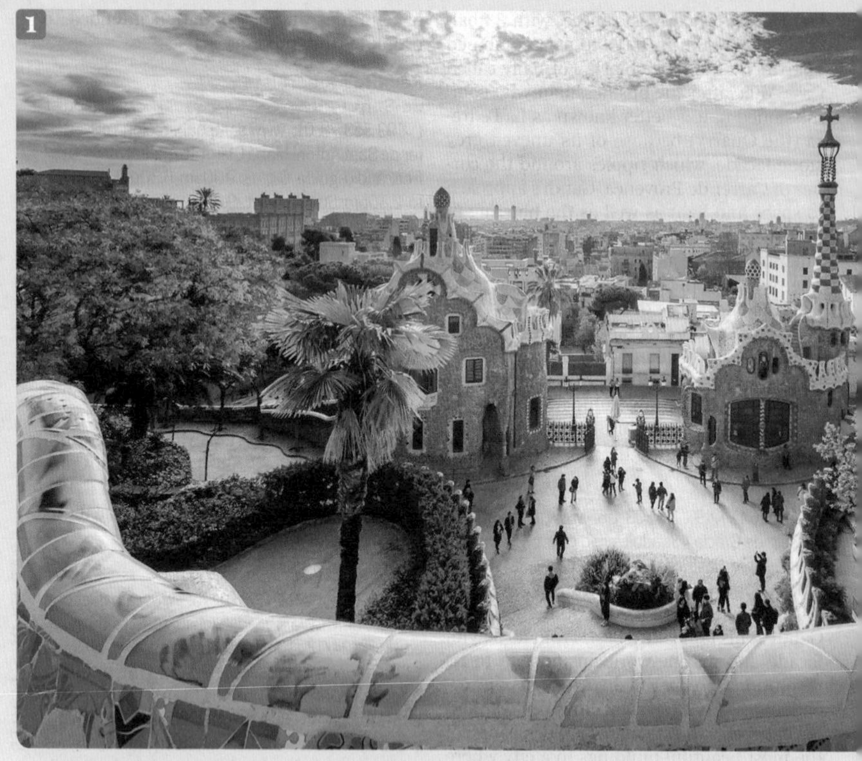

# The Genius of Gaudí

The name Gaudí has become a byword for Barcelona and the architect's unique creations remain one of the principal magnets for visitors to the city.

## A Catholic & a Catalan

Born in Reus and initially trained in metalwork, Antoni Gaudí i Cornet (1852–1926) personifies, and largely transcends, the Modernisme movement, which brought a thunderclap of innovative greatness to turn-of-the-century Barcelona. Gaudí was a devout Catholic and Catalan nationalist, and his architectural visions were a conscious expression of Catalan identity and, in some cases, of great piety.

## The Masterworks

Gaudí devoted much of the latter part of his life to what remains Barcelona's call sign: the (still) unfinished Sagrada Família (p268). His inspiration in the first instance was Gothic, but he also sought to emulate the harmony he observed in nature, eschewing the straight line and favouring curvaceous forms.

Gaudí used complex string models weighted with plumb lines to make his calculations. You can see examples in the upstairs minimuseum in La Pedrera (p260).

The architect's work is an earthy appeal to sinewy movement, but often with a dreamlike or surreal quality. The private apartment house Casa Batlló (p261) is a fine example in which all appears a riot of the unnaturally natural – or the naturally unnatural. Not only are straight lines eliminated, but the lines between real and unreal, sober and dream-drunk, good sense and play are all blurred. Depending on how you look at the facade,

1. Park Güell (p267)
2. La Pedrera (p260)
3. Capricho de Gaudí (p504)

you might see St George defeating a dragon, or a series of fleshless sea monsters straining out of the wall.

Gaudí seems to have particularly enjoyed himself with rooftops. At La Pedrera and Palau Güell (p250), in particular, he created all sorts of fantastical, multicoloured tile figures as chimney pots, those at the former looking like *Star Wars* imperial troopers and those at the latter like *Alice in Wonderland* mushrooms.

## Saint Antoni?

Much like La Sagrada Família, Gaudí's story is far from over. In March 2000 the Vatican decided to proceed with the examination of the case for canonising him, and pilgrims already stop by the crypt at La Sagrada Família to pay him homage. One of the key sculptors at work on the church, the Japanese Etsuro Sotoo, converted to Catholicism because of his passion for Gaudí.

### GAUDÍ'S BEST

➡ La Sagrada Família (p268), a symphony of religious devotion.

➡ La Pedrera (p260), officially Casa Milà but dubbed La Pedrera (the Quarry) for its rugged stone facade.

➡ Casa Batlló (p261), a residence resembling a fairy-tale dragon.

➡ Park Güell (p267), full of Modernista twists and turns.

➡ Palau Güell (p250), one of Gaudí's earliest commissions.

➡ Capricho de Gaudí (p504), in the Cantabrian town of Comillas.

## L'Eixample

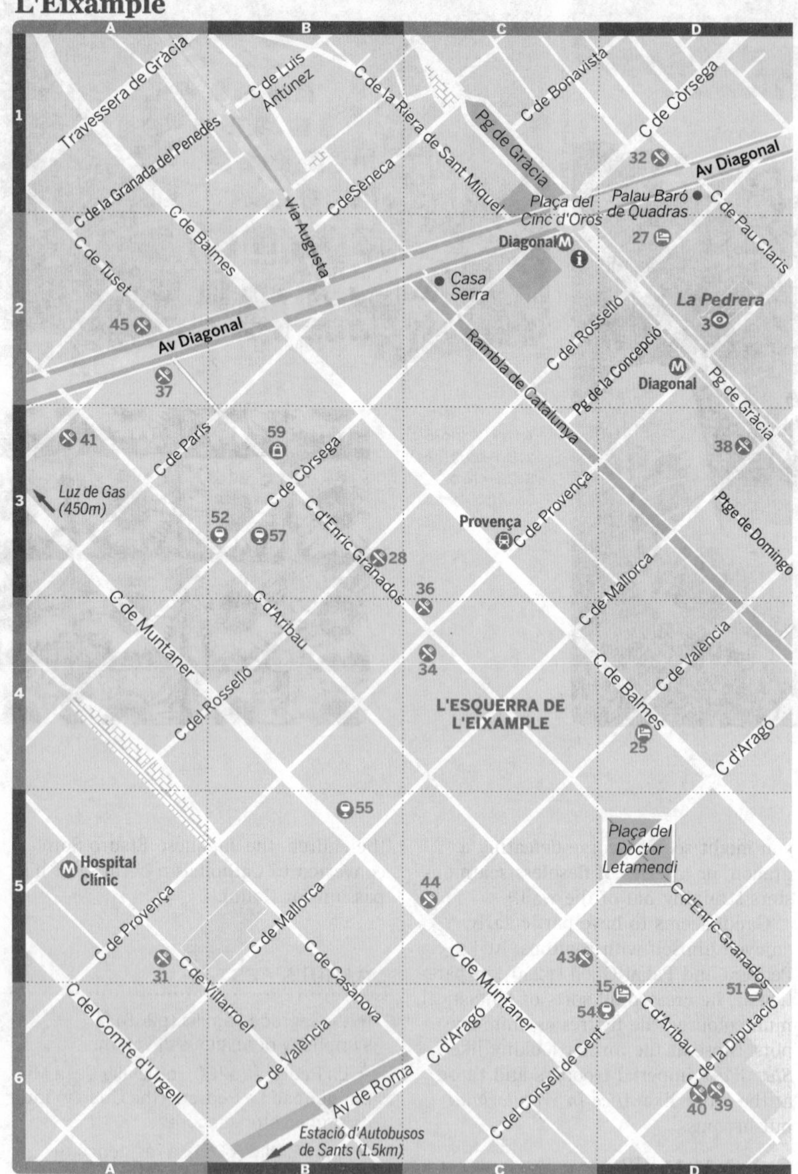


price. The beautifully tiled pillared foyer and staircase lit by stained glass feel like the interior of a romantic castle. The building was renovated in 1900 for chocolate baron and philanthropist Antoni Amatller (1851–1910).

**Casa de les Punxes** ARCHITECTURE

(Casa Terrades; Map p264; ☎93 018 52 42; www.casadelespunxes.com; Avinguda Diagonal 420; adult/child €13.50/10, tour €20/16; ⏰10am-7pm; Ⓜ Diagonal) Puig i Cadafalch's 1905 Casa Terrades is known as the Casa de les Punxes (House of Spikes) because of its pointed

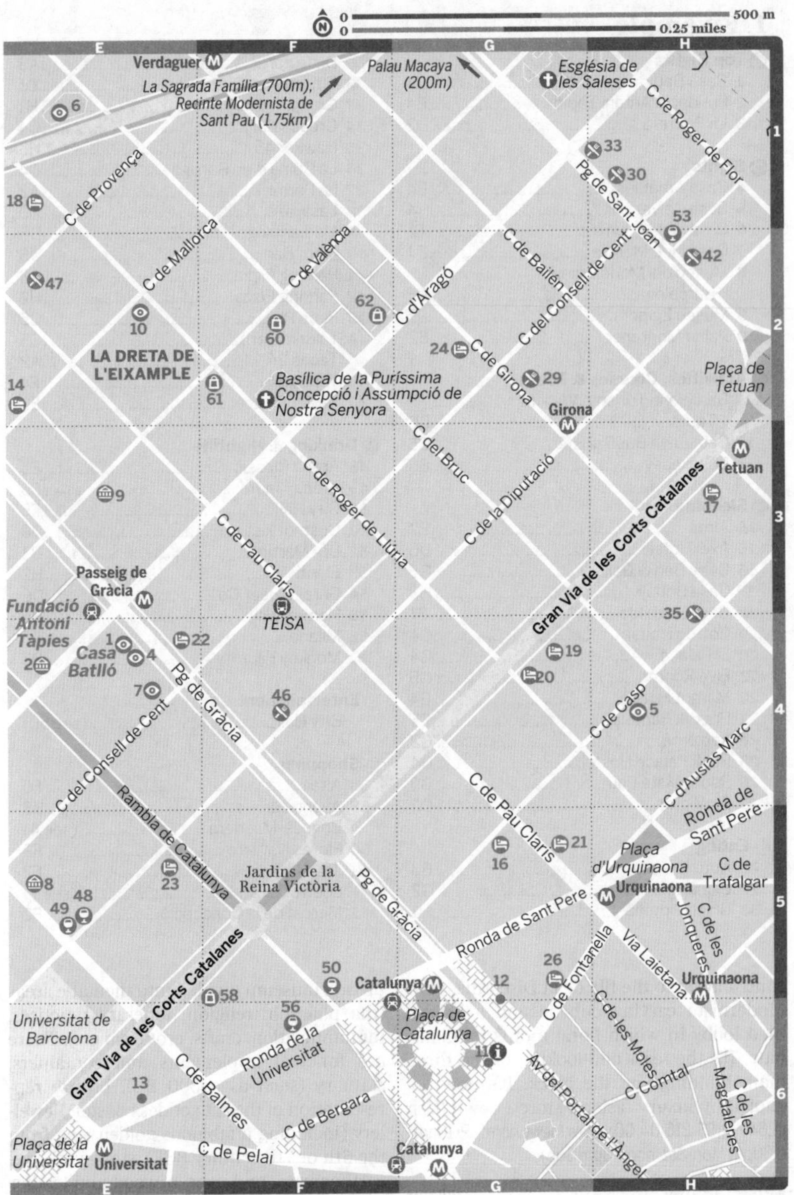


tile-adorned turrets. Resembling a medieval castle, this former apartment block is the only fully detached building in L'Eixample, and opened to the public only in 2017. Visits (with multilanguage audio guide) take in its stained-glass bay windows, handsome iron staircase, hydraulic floors, pillars and arches with floral motifs, and rooftop. Guided midday tours run in Spanish (Saturday) and Catalan (Sunday).

**Casa Lleó Morera** ARCHITECTURE

(Map p264; Passeig de Gràcia 35; M Passeig de Gràcia) This Domènech i Montaner's 1905

## L'Eixample

**Top Sights**
1 Casa Batlló ... E4
2 Fundació Antoni Tàpies ... E4
3 La Pedrera ... D2

**Sights**
4 Casa Amatller ... E4
5 Casa Calvet ... H4
6 Casa de les Punxes ... E1
7 Casa Lleó Morera ... E4
8 Museu del Modernisme Barcelona ... E5
9 Museu Egipci ... E3
10 Palau Montaner ... E2

**Activities, Courses & Tours**
11 Barcelona Turisme Walking Tours ... G6
12 Catalunya Bus Turístic ... G5
13 Speakeasy ... E6

**Sleeping**
14 Alma ... E2
15 Axel Hotel ... D6
16 Cami Bed & Gallery ... G5
17 Casa Bonay ... H3
18 Casa Mathilda ... E1
19 Cotton House ... G4
20 El Palace ... G4
21 Five Rooms ... G5
22 Margot House ... E4
23 Praktik Rambla ... E5
24 Retrome ... G2
25 Rock Palace Hostel ... D4
26 Room Mate Pau ... G5
27 Sir Victor ... D2

**Eating**
28 Auto Rosellon ... B3
29 Bicnic ... G2
30 Chichalimoná ... H1
31 Disfrutar ... A5
32 Entrepanes Díaz ... D1
33 Granja Petitbo ... H1
34 Gresca Bar ... C4
35 Hawker 45 ... H3
36 La Cuina d'en Garriga ... C4
37 La Dama ... A2
38 Lasarte ... D3
39 Mediamanga ... D6
40 Mont Bar ... D6
41 Parking Pizza ... A3
42 Parking Pizza ... H2
43 Pepa Pla ... C5
44 Taktika Berri ... C5
45 Tapas 24 ... A2
46 Tapas 24 ... F4
47 Xavier Pellicer ... E2

**Drinking & Nightlife**
48 Arena Classic ... E5
49 Arena Madre ... E5
50 City Hall ... F5
51 Cosmo ... D6
52 Dry Martini ... B3
53 El Viti ... H2
54 Garage Beer Co ... D6
55 Hemingway ... B5
56 Milano ... F6
57 Monkey Factory ... B3

**Entertainment**
City Hall ... (see 50)

**Shopping**
58 Altaïr ... F5
59 Avant ... B3
Bagués-Masriera ... (see 4)
60 Flores Navarro ... F2
61 Joan Múrria ... F2
Loewe ... (see 7)
62 Mercat de la Concepció ... F2

contribution to the Illa de la Discòrdia, with Modernista carving outside and a bright, tiled lobby in which floral motifs predominate. It's the least odd-looking of the three main buildings on the block. It's now occupied by luxury fashion store **Loewe** (Map p264; ☎93 216 04 00; www.loewe.com; ⏰10am-8.30pm Mon-Sat, noon-8pm Sun).

**Museu Egipci** MUSEUM
(Map p264; ☎93 488 01 88; www.museuegipci.com; Carrer de València 284; adult/child €12/5; ⏰10am-8pm Mon-Sat, to 2pm Sun Easter, Jun–mid-Sep & Dec, reduced hours rest of year; Ⓜ Passeig de Gràcia) Hotel magnate Jordi Clos has spent much of his life collecting ancient Egyptian artefacts, brought together in this private museum divided into thematic areas (the pharaoh, religion, funerary practices, mummification, crafts, eroticism etc). There are funereal implements and containers, statuary (such as a 300 BCE bronze representation of the cat goddess Bastet), jewellery (including a fabulous golden ring from the 6th or 7th century BCE), stonework and earthenware, and even a wood-and-leather bed dating to around 2800 BCE.

**Museu del Modernisme Barcelona** MUSEUM
(Map p264; ☎93 272 28 96; www.mmbcn.cat; Carrer de Balmes 48; adult/child €10/5; ⏰10.30am-2pm & 4-7pm Mon-Fri, 10.30am-2pm Sat; Ⓜ Passeig de Gràcia) Housed in a stuccoed, red-washed

1902 Modernista building by Enric Sagnier, this museum seems like a big Modernista-furniture showroom. Several pieces by Gaudí, including chairs from Casa Batlló and a mirror and chair from Casa Calvet, appear alongside a host of creations by his lesser-known contemporaries. The basement, which has mosaic-coated pillars, bare-brick Catalan vaults and metal columns, is lined with Modernista art, including paintings by Ramon Casas and Santiago Rusiñol, and statues by Josep Llimona and Eusebi Arnau.

## Gràcia & Park Güell

**★Park Güell** PARK, ARCHITECTURE

(☎93 409 18 31; www.parkguell.barcelona; Carrer d'Olot 7; adult/child €10/7; ⌚8am-9.30pm May-Aug, to 8.30pm Apr, Sep & Oct, to 6.15pm Nov–mid-Feb, to 7pm mid-Feb–Mar; 🚌H6, D40, V19, Bus Güell, Ⓜ Lesseps, Vallcarca, Alfons X) Around 1km north of Gràcia, the Unesco-listed Park Güell is where Antoni Gaudí turned his hand and imagination to landscape gardening. It's a surreal, enchanting place where the great Modernista's passion for natural forms really took flight and the artificial almost seems more natural than the natural.

The park is extremely popular, and access to the central area is limited to 400 people every half-hour – book ahead online. The rest of the park is free and can be visited without booking.

Park Güell was created in 1900, when Count Eusebi Güell hired Gaudí to create a miniature city of houses for the wealthy in landscaped grounds, based on the English 'garden cities'. The project was abandoned in 1914 – but not before Gaudí had created 3km of roads and walks, steps, a plaza and two gatehouses in his inimitable manner.

Arriving via the park's main eastern entrance, you'll reach the broad **Plaça de la Natura**, the centrepiece of which is the multicoloured tiled bench, **Banc de Trencadís**, completed in 1914 by Gaudí's close colleague Josep Maria Jujol (1879–1949). To the west of the square extends the **Pòrtic de la Bugadera** (Laundry Room Portico), a gallery where the twisted stonework columns and roof give the effect of a cloister beneath tree roots. Beneath the square, steps lead to the **Sala Hipóstila** (the Doric Temple); this forest of 86 stone columns was originally intended as a market, with its tiled ceilings and Catalan vaults. Just inside the park's (southern) Carrer d'Olot entrance, which sits below the Sala Hipóstila, stands the typically curvaceous **Casa del Guarda**. The spired rosy-pink 1904 house by the eastern entrance is the **Casa-Museu Gaudí** (☎93 208 04 14; https://sagradafamilia.org; Park Güell, Carretera del Carmel 23a; adult/child €5.50/free; ⌚9am-8pm Apr-Sep, 10am-6pm Oct-Mar; 🚌V19, H6, D40, Bus Güell, Ⓜ Lesseps, Alfons X, Vallcarca), where Gaudí lived his last 20 years (1906–26). The Bus Güell shuttle (15 minutes; included in pre-bought tickets) zips visitors from Alfons X metro stop (*línia* 4) to the park's eastern entrance on Carretera del Carmel. One-hour guided tours cost €12 (plus park admission); pre-book online.

**★Casa Vicens** ARCHITECTURE

(☎93 547 59 80; www.casavicens.org; Carrer de les Carolines 20-26; adult/child €16/12, guided tour per person additional €4; ⌚10am-8pm Apr-Sep, 10am-3pm Mon, 10am-7pm Tue-Sun Oct-Mar, last admission 1hr 20min before closing; Ⓜ Fontana)

*continued on p272*

*continued from p267*

WORTH A TRIP

### BEACHES BEYOND BARCELONA

Many of Barcelona's most gorgeous beaches lie outside the centre, but are perfectly doable in a day trip, via *rodalies* trains R1 from Plaça de Catalunya or R2 from Passeig de Gràcia.

**Platja de Castelldefels** Beautiful long sweep of golden-blonde sand backed by dunes and beloved by kitesurfers, around 20km (35 minutes) southwest of Barcelona.

**Sitges** (p374) Spain's most famous LGBTIQ+ holiday town, 35km (40 minutes) southwest of Barcelona, has 17 fabulous beaches.

**Platja del Garraf** Tiny Garraf village, 30km (40 minutes) southwest of Barcelona, trickles down to a teal bay framed by old cottages and Soho House's Little Beach House (p278).

**Montgat** Around 20km (20 minutes) northeast of Barcelona, on the Costa del Maresme, Montgat is dotted with golden strands.

TOP SIGHT
# LA SAGRADA FAMÍLIA

**Gaudí's unparalleled, Unesco-listed La Sagrada Família inspires awe by its sheer verticality, and, in the manner of the medieval cathedrals it emulates, it's still under construction. Work began in 1882 and is hoped (perhaps optimistically) to be completed in 2026, a century after the architect's death (though the COVID-19 pandemic has inevitably delayed things). Unfinished it may be, but the cathedral attracts more than 4.5 million visitors a year and is Spain's most visited monument.**

## A Holy Mission

The Temple Expiatori de la Sagrada Família (Expiatory Temple of the Holy Family) was Antoni Gaudí's all-consuming obsession, and he saw its completion as his holy mission. In all, he spent 43 years on La Sagrada Família. Gaudí devised a temple 95m long and 60m wide, able to seat over 13,000 people, with a central tower 170m high above the transept (representing Christ) and another 17 of 100m or more. With his dislike for straight lines (there were none in nature, he said), Gaudí gave his towers swelling outlines inspired by the unusual peaks of the holy mountain Montserrat outside Barcelona, and encrusted them with a tangle of sculpture.

At Gaudí's death, only the crypt, the apse walls, one portal and one tower had been finished. In 1936 anarchists burned and smashed the interior, including original plans and models. Work began again in 1952, but controversy has always clouded progress. Opponents of the continuation of the project claim that the computer models based on what little of Gaudí's plans survived have led to the creation of a monster that has little to do with Gaudí's plans and style.

### DON'T MISS

- The apse, extraordinary pillars and stained glass
- Nativity Facade
- Passion Facade
- Schools of Gaudí & Museu Gaudí
- The crypt

### PRACTICALITIES

- ☎ 93 208 04 14
- www.sagradafamilia.org
- Carrer de la Marina
- adult/child €20/free
- ⏲ 9am-8pm Apr-Sep, to 7pm Mar & Oct, to 6pm Nov-Feb
- Ⓜ Sagrada Família

### The Interior & the Apse

The roof is held up by a forest of innovative, extraordinary angled pillars. As the pillars soar towards the ceiling, they sprout a web of supporting branches, creating the effect of a forest canopy. Everything was thought through, including the shape and placement of windows to create the mottled effect one would see with sunlight pouring through the branches of a thick forest. The pillars vary in colour and load-bearing strength, from the soft Montjuïc stone pillars along the lateral aisles through to granite, dark grey basalt and finally burgundy-tinged Iranian porphyry for the key columns at the intersection of the nave and transept. The stained glass, divided in shades of red, blue, green, yellow and ochre, creates a hypnotic, magical atmosphere when the sun hits the windows.

### Nativity Facade

The northeastern Nativity Facade (Façana del Naixement) is the artistic pinnacle of the building, mostly created under Gaudí's personal supervision. With prior booking you can climb high up inside some of the four towers by a combination of lifts and narrow spiral staircases – a vertiginous experience. Three sections of the portal represent, from left to right, Hope, Charity and Faith. Among the forest of sculpture on the Charity portal you can see, low down, the manger surrounded by an ox, an ass, the shepherds and kings, and angel musicians. At the top is a green cypress tree, a refuge for the white doves of peace. To the right of the facade is the Gothic-style Claustre del Roser.

### Passion Facade

The southwest Passion Facade (Façana de la Passió), on the theme of Christ's last days and death, was built between 1954 and 1978 based on surviving drawings by Gaudí – but was only officially completed in 2018. The late sculptor Josep Maria Subirachs (1927–2014) worked on its decoration from 1986 to 2006. He did not attempt to imitate Gaudí, instead producing angular, controversial images of his own.

### Glory Facade

The Glory Facade (Façana de la Glòria) will, like the others, be crowned by four towers – the total of 12 representing the Twelve Apostles. Inside will be the narthex, a kind of foyer made up of 16 'lanterns', a series of hyperboloid forms topped by cones. Further decoration will make the whole building a microcosmic symbol of the Christian church, with Christ represented by a massive 170m central tower above the transept, and the five remaining towers under construction symbolising the Virgin Mary and the four evangelists.

### A HIDDEN PORTRAIT

Careful observation of the Passion Facade will reveal a special tribute from sculptor Josep Maria Subirachs to Gaudí. The central sculptural group (below Christ crucified) shows, from right to left, Christ bearing his cross, Veronica displaying the cloth with Christ's bloody image, a pair of soldiers and, watching it all, a man called the evangelist. Subirachs used a rare photo of Gaudí, taken a couple of years before his death, as the model for the evangelist's face.

**Open at the same times as the church, the Museu Gaudí, below ground level next to the Passion Facade, meanders through interesting material on Gaudí's life and other works. A side hall towards the eastern end of the museum leads to a window above the simple neo-Gothic crypt in which the genius is buried.**

### SCHOOLS OF GAUDÍ

Immediately in front of the Passion Facade, the Schools of Gaudí (Escoles de Gaudí) make up one of the architect's simpler gems, built as a children's school in 1909.

# La Sagrada Família

## A TIMELINE

**1882** Construction begins on a neo-Gothic church designed by Francisco de Paula del Villar y Lozano.

**1883** Antoni Gaudí takes over as chief architect, completes the ❶ **crypt** and plans a far more ambitious church to hold 13,000.

**1909** The Escoles de Gaudí are completed.

**1926** Gaudí dies; work continues under Domènec Sugrañes i Gras. Much of the ❷ **apse** and ❸ **Nativity Facade** is complete.

**1930** ❹ **Bell towers** of the Nativity Facade completed.

**1936** Construction interrupted by Spanish Civil War; anarchists destroy Gaudí's plans.

**1939–40** Architect Francesc de Paula Quintana i Vidal restores the crypt and meticulously reassembles many of Gaudí's lost models, some of which can be seen in the ❺ **museum**.

**1976** ❻ **Passion Facade** steeples completed.

**1986–2006** Sculptor Josep Maria Subirachs adds sculptural details to the Passion Facade, amid much criticism for employing a style far removed from what was thought typical of Gaudí.

**2000** ❼ **Central nave vault** completed.

**2010** Pope Benedict XVI consecrates the church; work begins on a high-speed rail tunnel that will pass beneath the church's ❽ **Glory Facade**.

**2016-2019** Work continues on the five central towers; the Passion Facade is completed in 2018.

**2026** Projected completion date.

### TOP TIPS

➡ The best light through the stained-glass windows of the Passion Facade bursts into the heart of the church in the late afternoon.

➡ Visit at opening time on weekdays to avoid the worst of the crowds.

➡ Head up the Nativity Facade bell towers for the views.

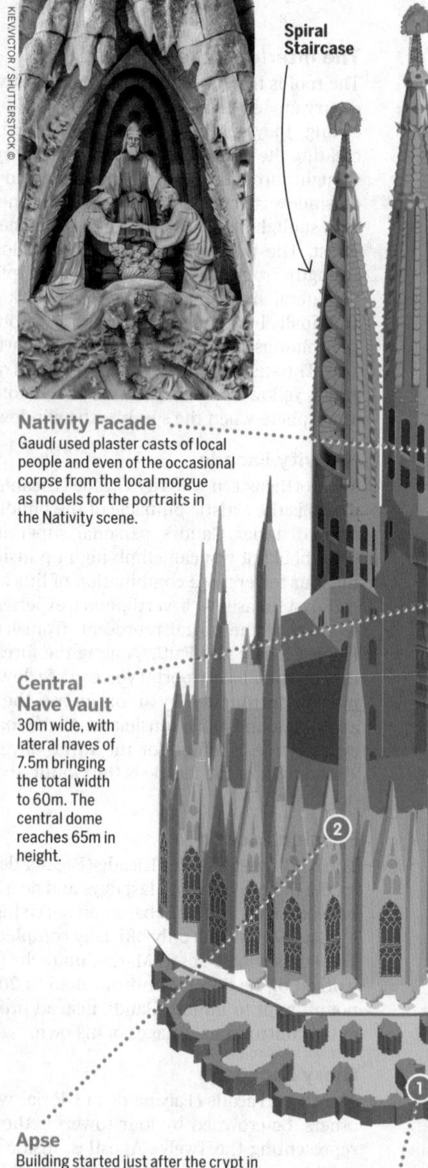


**Nativity Facade**
Gaudí used plaster casts of local people and even of the occasional corpse from the local morgue as models for the portraits in the Nativity scene.

**Central Nave Vault**
30m wide, with lateral naves of 7.5m bringing the total width to 60m. The central dome reaches 65m in height.

**Apse**
Building started just after the crypt in mostly neo-Gothic style. It is capped by pinnacles that show a hint of the genius that Gaudí would later deploy in the rest of the church.

**Crypt**
The first completed part of the church, the crypt is in largely neo-Gothic style and lies under the transept. Gaudí's burial place here can be glimpsed from the Museu Gaudí.

Bell Towers
The towers of the three facades will represent the Twelve Apostles. Eight are completed. Lifts whisk visitors up one tower of the Nativity and Passion Facades (the latter gets longer queues) for fine views.
NIKADA / GETTY IMAGES ©
Completed Church
Along with the Glory Facade, six other towers remain to be completed. They will represent the four evangelists, the Virgin Mary and, soaring above them all over the transept, a 170m colossus symbolising Christ.
Glory Facade
This will be the most fanciful facade of all, with a narthex boasting 16 hyperboloid lanterns topped by cones that will look something like an organ made of melting ice cream.
4
3
7
8
6
5
Escoles de Gaudí
Museu Gaudí
Jammed with old photos, drawings and restored plaster models that bring Gaudí's ambitions to life, the museum also houses an extraordinarily complex plumb-line device he used to calculate his constructions.
Passion Facade
See the story of Christ's last days from Last Supper to burial in an S-shaped sequence from bottom to top of the facade. Check out the cryptogram in which the numbers always add up to 33, Christ's age at his death.
LKONYA / GETTY IMAGES ©

## Gràcia

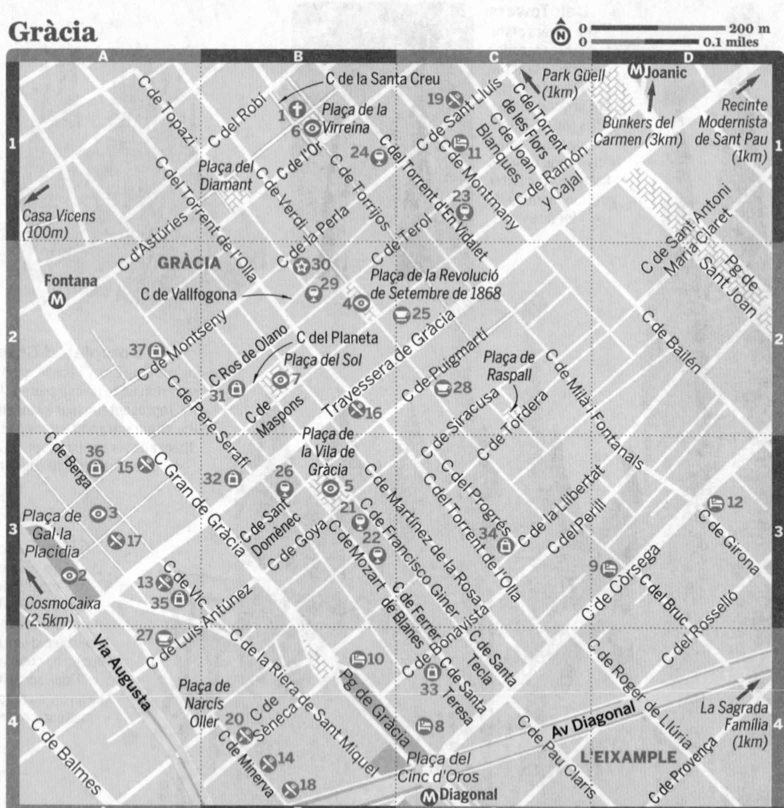


A Unesco-listed masterpiece, this angular, turreted 1885-completed private house was Gaudí's inaugural commission, when the architect was aged just 30, created for stock and currency broker Manuel Vicens i Montaner. Tucked away west of Gràcia's main drag, the richly detailed facade is awash with ceramic colour and shape, including distinctive marigold tiling, and opened to the public in 2017. You're free to wander but multilingual one-hour guided tours bring the building to life.

**Mercat de la Llibertat** MARKET
(Map p272; ☎93 217 09 95; www.facebook.com/elmercatdelallibertat; Plaça de la Llibertat 27; ⏰8.30am-8pm Mon-Fri, to 3pm Sat; Ⓜ Fontana, FGC Gràcia) Opened in 1888, the 'Market of Liberty' was covered in 1893 by Francesc Berenguer i Mestres (1866–1914), Gaudí's long-time assistant, in typically fizzy Modernista style, employing generous whirls of wrought iron. Despite a considerable facelift in 2009, it remains emblematic of Gràcia: full of life and fabulous fresh produce, and with tapas spots like **El Tast de Joan Noi** (Map p272; ☎635 706429; www.facebook.com/eltastdejoannoi; Plaça de la Llibertat 27, Mercat de la Llibertat; tapas €4-15; ⏰9am-5pm Tue-Fri, to 3pm Sat, closed Aug; Ⓜ Fontana, FGC Gràcia).

## Montjuïc, Poble Sec & Sant Antoni

**★ Museu Nacional d'Art de Catalunya** MUSEUM
(MNAC; Map p276; ☎93 622 03 60; www.museunacional.cat; Mirador del Palau Nacional, Parc de Montjuïc; adult/child €12/free, after 3pm Sat & 1st Sun of month free, audio guide €4, rooftop viewpoint only €2; ⏰10am-8pm Tue-Sat, to 3pm Sun May-Sep, 10am-6pm Tue-Sat, to 3pm Sun Oct-Apr; 55, Ⓜ Espanya) The spectacular neobaroque silhouette of the Palau Nacional can be seen on Montjuïc's slopes from across the city. Built for the 1929 World Exhibition and restored

## Gràcia



in 2005, it houses a vast collection of mostly Catalan art spanning the early Middle Ages to the early 20th century. The high point is the unique collection of extraordinary Romanesque frescoes.

Rescued from neglected country churches across northern Catalonia in the early 20th century, the Romanesque frescoes have been placed as they were when in situ, within re-created churches. Opposite is the museum's Gothic art gallery, with Catalan Gothic painting and works from other Spanish and Mediterranean regions. Next you pass into the Renaissance and Baroque gallery, including pieces by Velázquez, Zurbarán, Goya, Rubens, El Greco and Canaletto.

**★Fundació Joan Miró** GALLERY

(Map p276; ☎93 443 94 70; www.fmirobcn.org; Avinguda de Miramar; adult/child €13/free, multimedia guide €5; ⏱10am-8pm Tue-Sat, to 3pm Sun Apr-Oct, 10am-6pm Tue-Sat, to 3pm Sun Nov-Mar; 🚌55, 150, 🚡from Paral·lel) Joan Miró, the city's best-known 20th-century artistic progeny, bequeathed this art foundation to his home town in 1971. The light-filled buildings, designed by close friend and architect Josep Lluís Sert (who also built Miró's Mallorca studios), are crammed with seminal works, from Miró's earliest timid sketches to paintings from his last years.

Sert's shimmering white temple to one of Spain's artistic luminaries is considered one of the world's most outstanding museum buildings. The foundation holds the greatest single collection of Miró's work, including around 220 paintings, 180 sculptures, textiles and more than 8000 drawings.

**Castell de Montjuïc** FORTRESS

(Map p276; ☎93 256 44 40; https://ajuntament.barcelona.cat; Carretera de Montjuïc 66; adult/child €5/3, after 3pm Sun & 1st Sun of month free; ⏱10am-8pm Mar-Oct, to 6pm Nov-Feb; 🚌150, 🚡Telefèric de Montjuïc, Castell de Montjuïc) Enjoying commanding views over the Mediterranean, this forbidding fortress dominates the southeastern heights of Montjuïc. It dates, in its present form, from the late 17th and 18th centuries, though there's been a watchtower here since 1073. For most of its dark history, it has been used as a political prison and killing ground. Anarchists were executed here around the end of the 19th century, fascists during the civil war and Republicans after it – most notoriously Republican Catalan president Lluís Companys in 1940.

**Mercat de Sant Antoni** MARKET

(Map p276; ☎93 426 35 21; www.mercatdesantantoni.com; Carrer del Comte d'Urgell 1; ⏱8am-8.30pm Mon-Sat; Ⓜ Sant Antoni) Just beyond the western edge of El Raval, this glorious iron-and-brick market was originally completed in 1882, but reopened in 2018 with 250 stalls following a nine-year renovation job. It's a great place to stock up on seasonal produce or grab a bite in between browsing the fashion, textiles and homewares stalls. Also on display are the remains of a piece of the Roman Via Augusta and a 1st-century-CE mausoleum, as well as a ruined 17th-century defensive wall, all uncovered during restoration works.

**CaixaForum** GALLERY

(Map p276; ☎93 476 86 00; www.caixaforum.es; Avinguda de Francesc Ferrer i Guàrdia 6-8; adult/child €4/free, 1st Sun of month free; ⏲10am-8pm year-round, to 11pm Wed Jul & Aug; Ⓜ Espanya) The La Caixa building society prides itself on its involvement in (and ownership of) art, in particular all that is contemporary. The bank's premier expo space in Barcelona hosts part of its extensive global collection, as well as fascinating temporary international exhibitions, in the completely renovated former Casaramona factory, an outstanding brick Modernista creation by Josep Puig i Cadafalch. From 1940 to 1993, the building housed the First Squadron of the police cavalry unit.

**Font Màgica** FOUNTAIN

(Map p276; Avinguda de la Reina Maria Cristina; ⏲every 30min 9.30-10.30pm Wed-Sun Jun-Sep, 9-10pm Thu-Sat Apr, May & Oct, 8-9pm Thu-Sat Nov-Mar; Ⓜ Espanya) FREE Originally created for the 1929 World Exposition, this huge colour-lit fountain has again been a magnet since the 1992 Olympics, shimmering on the long sweep of Avinguda de la Reina Maria Cristina to the grand Palau Nacional. With a flourish, the 'Magic Fountain' erupts into a feast of musical, backlit aquatic life; it's a unique 15-minute night performance in which the water can look like seething fireworks or a mystical cauldron of colour.

**Museu d'Arqueologia de Catalunya** MUSEUM

(MAC; Map p276; ☎93 423 21 49; www.macbarcelona.cat; Passeig de Santa Madrona 39-41; adult/child €6/free; ⏲9.30am-7pm Tue-Sat, 10am-2.30pm Sun; 🚌55, Ⓜ Poble Sec) Occupying the 1929 World Exhibition's Graphic Arts Palace, this intriguing archaeology museum covers both Catalonia and cultures from across Spain. There's good material on the Balearic Islands (including 5th- to 3rd-century BCE statues of Phoenician goddess Tanit from Ibiza) and the Greek and Roman city of Empúries (Emporion), as well as the region's prehistoric inhabitants. Don't miss the 53,200-year-old human jaw found near Sitges, or the beautiful Roman mosaic depicting Les Tres Gràcies (The Three Graces), unearthed in the 18th century.

**Poble Espanyol** CULTURAL CENTRE

(Map p276; ☎93 508 63 00; www.poble-espanyol.com; Avinguda de Francesc Ferrer i Guàrdia 13; adult/child €14/7; ⏲9am-8pm Mon, to midnight Tue-Thu & Sun, to 3am Fri, to 4am Sat; 🚌13, 23, 150, Ⓜ Espanya) Welcome to Spain! All of it! This 'Spanish Village' is an intriguing scrapbook of Spanish architecture built for the local-crafts section of the 1929 World Exhibition. You can meander from Andalucía to Galicia in the space of a couple of hours, visiting surprisingly good to-scale copies of Spain's characteristic structures. The 117 buildings include restaurants, cafes, bars and clubs, and craft shops and workshops (for glass artists and other artisans), as well as souvenir stores.

**Museu Etnològic** MUSEUM

(Map p276; ☎93 256 34 84; www.barcelona.cat; Passeig de Santa Madrona 16; adult/child €5/free, from 3pm Sun & 1st Sun of month free; ⏲10am-7pm Tue-Sat, to 8pm Sun; 🚌55) Delving into Catalonia's rich heritage, Barcelona's ethnology museum presents an intriguing permanent display from its 70,000-object collection, with multilanguage panels. Exhibits cover origin myths, religious festivals, folklore, and the blending of sacred and secular.

WORTH A TRIP

## BUNKERS DEL CARMEL

For 360-degree Barcelona views, head to the El Carmel neighbourhood (under a kilometre east of Park Güell) and up the Turó de la Rovira hill to the **Bunkers del Carmel viewpoint** (Turó de la Rovira; ☎93 256 21 22; https://ajuntament.barcelona.cat; Carrer de Marià Labèrnia; ⏲museum 10am-2pm Wed, to 3pm Sat & Sun; 🚌V19, 22, 24) FREE. Above the weeds and dusty hillside, you'll find old concrete firing platforms where students and visitors gather, especially at sunset. The platforms were part of anti-aircraft battery during the Spanish Civil War; postwar, it was a shanty town until the early 1990s, then abandoned.

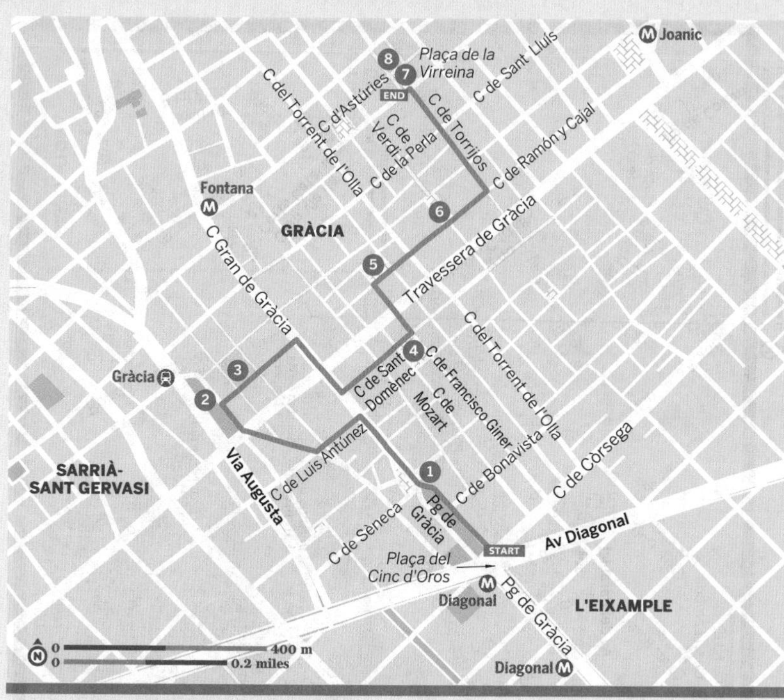


# City Walk
# Gràcia's Village Squares

**START** DIAGONAL METRO STATION
**END** PLAÇA DE LA VIRREINA
**LENGTH** 2KM; 50 MINUTES

From Diagonal metro station, head through Passeig de Gràcia and up Carrer Gran de Gràcia into Gràcia proper, where you'll find a grand Modernista edifice now turned hotel, 1 **Casa Fuster** (p289), designed by Domènech i Montaner.

A little northwest, the 2 **Plaça de Gal·la Placídia** (Map p272; FGC Gràcia) recalls the brief sojourn of the Roman empress-to-be Galla Placidia, captive and wife of the Visigothic chief Athaulf in the 5th century.

Just northeast, 3 **Plaça de la Llibertat** (Map p272; FGC Gràcia) is home to the bustling Modernista produce market of the same name, along with a couple of great little restaurants. The market was designed by Gaudí's protégé, Francesc Berenguer, who was busy in this part of town despite never having been awarded a diploma as an architect.

Heading east, you'll find the popular 4 **Plaça de la Vila de Gràcia** (Map p272; M Fontana, Diagonal, FGC Gràcia), which was until 2009 named after the mayor under whom Gràcia was absorbed by Barcelona, Francesc Rius i Taulet. It's fronted by the town hall, and at its heart stands the 1862 Torre del Rellotge (Clock Tower), long a symbol of Republican agitation. Just north lies the rowdiest of Gràcia's squares, 5 **Plaça del Sol** (Map p272; M Fontana), where bars and restaurants come to life on long summer nights. The square was the scene of summary executions after an uprising in 1870, and, during the civil war, an air-raid shelter was installed.

6 **Plaça de la Revolució de Setembre de 1868** (Map p272; M Fontana, Joanic) commemorates the toppling of Queen Isabel II, a cause of much celebration in this working-class stronghold. Pleasant terraces adorn the leafy, pedestrianised 7 **Plaça de la Virreina** (Map p272), presided over by the 19th-century 8 **Església de Sant Joan** (Map p272; Plaça de la Virreina; 8am-12.45pm & 4-8pm, hours vary; M Fontana, Joanic).

## Montjuïc, Poble Sec & Sant Antoni

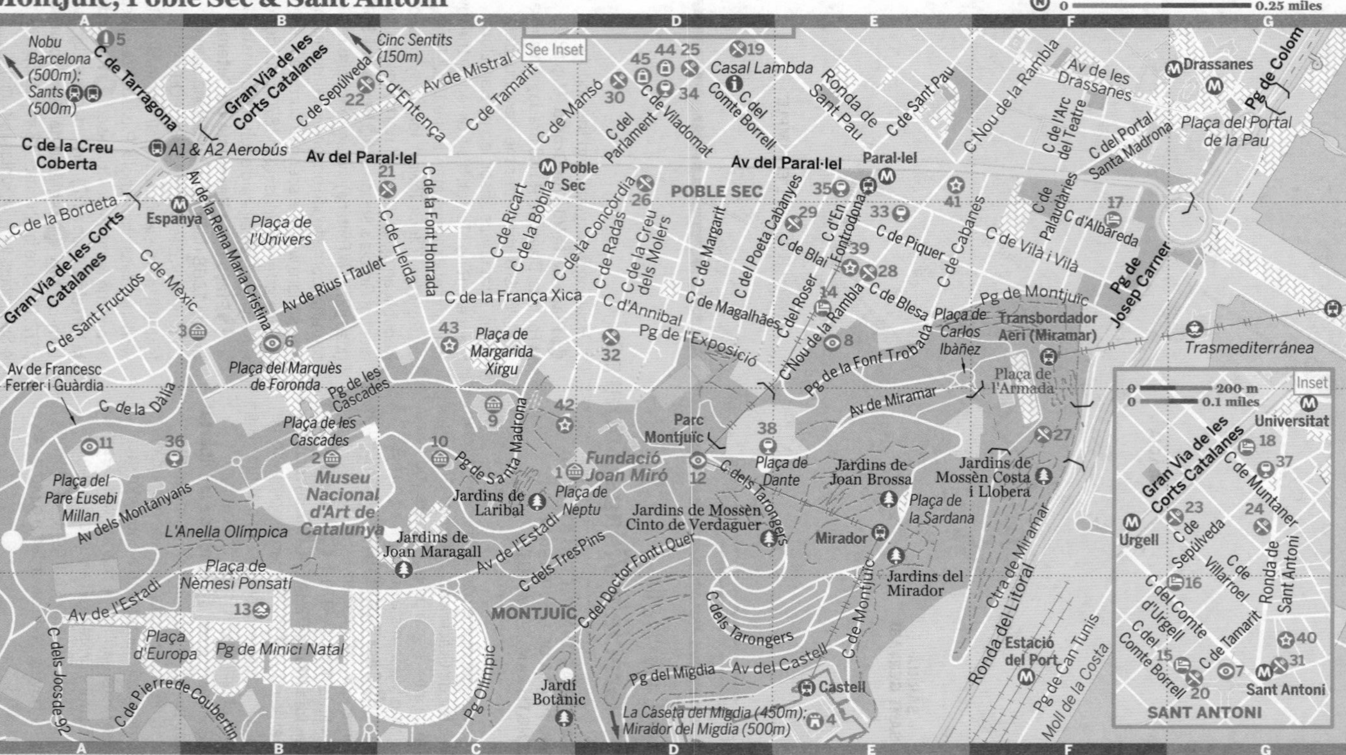

## Montjuïc, Poble Sec & Sant Antoni

**Top Sights**
1 Fundació Joan Miró ... C3
2 Museu Nacional d'Art de Catalunya ... B3

**Sights**
3 CaixaForum ... B2
4 Castell de Montjuïc ... E4
5 Dona i Ocell ... A1
6 Font Màgica ... B2
7 Mercat de Sant Antoni ... G4
8 MUHBA Refugi 307 ... E2
9 Museu d'Arqueologia de Catalunya ... C3
10 Museu Etnològic ... C3
11 Poble Espanyol ... A3
12 Telefèric de Montjuïc ... D3

**Activities, Courses & Tours**
13 Piscines Bernat Picornell ... B4

**Sleeping**
14 Hotel Brummell ... E2
15 Hotel Market ... G4
16 Pars Tailor's Hostel ... G4
17 Pars Teatro Hostel ... F2
18 TOC Hostel ... G3

**Eating**
19 Agust Gastrobar ... D1
Alkímia ... (see 24)
20 Bar Ramón ... G4
21 Casa de Tapas Cañota ... C1
22 Enigma ... B1
23 Escribà ... G3
24 Fàbrica Moritz ... G3
25 Federal ... D1
26 Mano Rota ... D1
27 Martínez ... F3
28 Palo Cortao ... E2
29 Quimet i Quimet ... E2
30 Sant Antoni Gloriós ... D1
31 Sésamo ... G4
32 Xemei ... D2

**Drinking & Nightlife**
33 Abirradero ... E2
34 Bar Calders ... D1
35 La Federica ... E1
36 La Terrrazza ... A3
37 Metro Disco ... G3
38 Salts Montjuïc ... D3

**Entertainment**
39 Gran Bodega Saltó ... E2
40 JazzSí Club ... G4
41 Sala Apolo ... E1
42 Teatre Grec ... C3
43 Teatre Mercat De Les Flors ... C2

**Shopping**
Brava ... (see 34)
44 Llibreria Calders ... D1
45 Popcorn Store ... D1

There are several *gegants* (massive Catalan papier-mâché figures), including depictions of King Jaume I and Queen Violant, and a dragon (you'll have to imagine the spewing burning embers it emits) and devil costumes used in *correfocs* (fire runs), which still figure prominently in Catalan festivals.

**MUHBA Refugi 307** HISTORIC SITE
(Map p276; ☎93 256 21 00; http://ajuntament.barcelona.cat; Carrer Nou de la Rambla 175; tour adult/child €3.50/free; ⊙tours 10.30am, 11.30am & 12.30pm Sun; Ⓜ Paral·lel) Barcelona was the city most heavily bombed by Franco's air forces during the Spanish Civil War, and as a result developed more than 1300 air-raid shelters. Now overseen by the Museu d'Història de Barcelona (MUHBA), the city's 307th refuge (one of its best preserved) was dug under a fold of northern Montjuïc by local citizens from 1937 to 1939. Compulsory tours (reservations essential) run on Sunday only: English at 10.30am, Spanish at 11.30am and Catalan at 12.30pm.

### Camp Nou, Pedralbes & La Zona Alta

**★Barça Stadium Tour & Museum** MUSEUM
(☎902 189900; www.fcbarcelona.com; Gate 9, Avinguda de Joan XXIII; adult/child 4-10 yr self-guided tour €29.50/23.50, guided tour €45/37; ⊙9.30am-7.30pm mid-Apr–mid-Oct, 10am-6.30pm Mon-Sat, to 2.30pm Sun mid-Oct–mid-Apr; Ⓜ Palau Reial) A pilgrimage site for football fans around the world, Camp Nou (p314) is a must for FC Barcelona fans. On this tour, which can be guided or self-guided, you'll get an in-depth look at the club, starting with a museum filled with multimedia exhibits, trophies and historical displays, followed by a tour of the stadium. Set aside at least 1½ hours.

**★Reial Monestir de Santa Maria de Pedralbes** MONASTERY
(☎93 256 34 34; http://monestirpedralbes.bcn.cat; Baixada del Monestir 9; adult/child €5/free, from

# Montjuïc

## A ONE-DAY ITINERARY

Montjuïc, perhaps once the site of pre-Roman settlements, is today a hilltop green lung looking over city and sea. Interspersed across varied gardens are major art collections, a fortress, an Olympic stadium and more. A solid one-day itinerary can take in the key spots.

Alight at Espanya metro stop and make for 1 **CaixaForum**, always host to three or four free top-class exhibitions. The nearby 2 **Pavelló Mies van der Rohe** is an intriguing study in 1920s futurist housing by one of the 20th century's greatest architects. Uphill, the Romanesque art collection in the 3 **Museu Nacional d'Art de Catalunya** is a must, and its restaurant is a pleasant lunch stop. Escalators lead further up the hill towards the 4 **Estadi Olímpic**, scene of the 1992 Olympic Games. The road leads east to the 5 **Fundació Joan Miró**, a shrine to the master surrealist's creativity. Contemplate ancient relics in the 6 **Museu d'Arqueologia de Catalunya**, then have a break in the peaceful 7 **Jardins de Mossèn Cinto Verdaguer**, the prettiest on the hill, before taking the cable car to the 8 **Castell de Montjuïc**. If you pick the right day, you can round off with the gorgeously kitsch 9 **La Font Màgica** sound and light show, followed by drinks and dancing in an open-air nightspot in 10 **Poble Espanyol**.

### TOP TIPS

➡ Ride the Transbordador Aeri from Barceloneta for a bird's eye approach to Montjuïc. Or take the Teleféric de Montjuïc cable car to the Castell for more aerial views.

➡ The Castell de Montjuïc features outdoor summer cinema and concerts (see http://salamontjuic.org).

➡ Bursting with colour and serenity, the Jardins de Mossèn Cinto Verdaguer are exquisitely laid out with bulbs, especially tulips, and aquatic flowers.

TONIFLAP/SHUTTERSTOCK ©

**CaixaForum**
This former factory and barracks designed by Josep Puig i Cadafalch is an outstanding work of Modernista architecture; like a Lego fantasy in brick.

**Poble Espanyol**
Amid the rich variety of traditional Spanish architecture created in replica for the 1929 Barcelona World Exhibition, browse the art on show in the Fundació Fran Daurel.

CATARINA BELOVA/SHUTTERSTOCK©

**Pavelló Mies van der Rohe**
Admire the inventiveness of the great German architect Ludwig Mies van der Rohe in this recreation of his avant garde German pavillion for the 1929 World Exhibition.

PIXEL SHOP/SHUTTERSTOCK ©

### La Font Màgica
Take a summer evening to behold the Magic Fountain come to life in a unique 15-minute sound and light performance, when the water glows like a cauldron of colour.

INU/SHUTTERSTOCK ©

### Museu Nacional d'Art de Catalunya
Make a beeline for the Romanesque art selection and the 12th-century polychrome image of Christ in majesty, which was recovered from the apse of a country chapel in northwest Catalonia.

### Museu d'Arqueologia de Catalunya
This archaeology museum, housed in what was the Graphic Arts palace during the 1929 World Exhibition, covers Catalonia and cultures from elsewhere in Spain. Items range from copies of pre-Neanderthal skulls to lovely Carthaginian necklaces and jewel-studded Visigothic crosses.

9

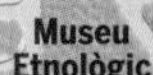

3

6

Museu Etnològic

Teatre Grec

5

7

Museu Olímpic i de l'Esport

4

Estadi Olímpic

Jardí Botànic

8

Jardins de Mossèn Cinto Verdaguer

### Castell de Montjuïc
Enjoy the sweeping views of the sea and city from atop this 17th-century fortress, once a political prison and long a symbol of oppression.

© JOAN MIRÓ COLLECTION

### Fundació Joan Miró
Take in some of Joan Miró's giant canvases, and discover little-known works from his early years in the Sala Joan Prats and Sala Pilar Juncosa.

SAILORR/SHUTTERSTOCK ©

WORTH A TRIP

## TIBIDABO

Framing the north end of the city, the pine-forested mountain of Tibidabo, which tops out at 512m, is the highest peak in Serra de Collserola. Much of its gorgeous green surrounding expanses are protected within the 80-sq-km Parc Natural de Collserola. Aside from the natural park's peaceful shaded paths and the superb views from the top of Tibidabo, highlights of a trip out here include an old-fashioned **amusement park** (☎93 211 79 42; www.tibidabo.cat; Plaça de Tibidabo 3-4; adult/child €28.50/10.30; ⊙Mar-Dec, hours vary; ⓘ; 🚌T2A, T2C); the 288m-high **Torre de Collserola** (☎93 406 93 54; www.torredecollserola.com; Carretera de Vallvidrera al Tibidabo; adult/child €5.60/3.30; ⊙noon-2pm Sat & Sun Mar-Dec, hours can vary; 🚌111, 🚡Funicular de Vallvidrera) telecommunications tower, designed by Sir Norman Foster; and the looming 20th-century **Basílica del Sagrat Cor de Jesús** (☎93 417 56 86; https://tibidabo.salesianos.edu; Plaça de Tibidabo; lift €4; ⊙11am-6pm; 🚌T2A, T2C).

At the time of writing, the long-running *tramvia blau* and the Tibidabo funicular railway – which combined linked the FGC Avinguda Tibidabo train station with the top of Tibidabo – were out of action for restoration works..

3pm Sun & 1st Sun of month free; ⊙10am-5pm Tue-Fri, to 7pm Sat, to 8pm Sun Apr-Sep, 10am-2pm Tue-Fri, to 5pm Sat & Sun Oct-Mar; 🚌H4, V5, 63, 68, 75, 78, 🚆FGC Reina Elisenda) Founded in 1327, this serene convent is now a museum of monastic life (the few remaining nuns have moved into more modern neighbouring buildings). It stands in a residential area that was countryside until the 20th century, and which remains a divinely quiet corner of Barcelona. The convent's architectural highlight is the large, elegant, three-storey cloister, a jewel of Catalan Gothic, built in the early 14th century. The sober church is another excellent example of Catalan Gothic.

**★CosmoCaixa** MUSEUM

(Museu de la Ciència; ☎93 212 60 50; www.cosmocaixa.com; Carrer d'Isaac Newton 26; adult/child €6/free, guided tours from €3, planetarium €4; ⊙10am-8pm; 🚌V15, V13, 196, 123, 🚆FGC Avinguda Tibidabo) One of the city's most popular family-friendly attractions, this science museum is a favourite with kids (and kids at heart). The single greatest highlight is the re-creation of more than 1 sq km of flooded **Amazon rainforest** (Bosc Inundat). More than 100 species of Amazon flora and fauna (including anacondas, colourful poisonous frogs, and capybaras) prosper in this unique, living diorama in which you can even experience a tropical downpour.

**Bellesguard** ARCHITECTURE

(☎93 250 40 93; www.bellesguardgaudi.com; Carrer del Bellesguard 20; adult/child 8-18 yr €9/7.20; ⊙10am-3pm Tue-Sun; 🚆FGC Avinguda Tibidabo) An entrancing work that combines Gothic and Modernista elements, this lesser-known Gaudí masterpiece was rescued from obscurity and opened to visitors in 2013. Built between 1900 and 1909, the private residence (still owned by the Guilera family) has a castle-like appearance with crenellated walls of stone and brick, narrow stained-glass windows, elaborate ironwork, gorgeous gardens and a soaring turret topped by a colourfully tiled Gaudían cross, along with spectacular city views. There's been a manor here since the 1400s.

**Parc Natural de Collserola** PARK

(☎93 280 35 52; www.parcnaturalcollserola.cat; Carretera de l'Església 92; ⊙Centre d'Informació 9.30am-3pm, Can Coll 9.30am-2.30pm Sun & holidays Sep–mid-Jun; 🚆FGC Baixador de Vallvidrera, 🚡Funicular de Vallvidrera) 🍃 *Barcelonins* needing an easy escape from the city seek out this protected pine-scented 80-sq-km park. It's a great place to hike, run and bike, and has a smattering of country chapels (some Romanesque), the ruined 14th-century Castellciuro castle in the west, various lookout points and, to the north, the grand 15th-century Can Coll farmhouse, now an environmental education centre. Pick up maps from park information centres such as the Carretera de l'Església 92 headquarters (near Baixador de Vallvidrera FGC station).

**Jardins del Palau de Pedralbes** PARK

(Avinguda Diagonal 686; ⊙10am-9pm Apr-Oct, to 7pm Nov-Mar; ⓂPalau Reial) FREE Sculptures, fountains, citrus trees, bamboo groves, fragrant eucalyptus, towering cypresses and bougainvillea-covered nooks lie scattered along the paths criss-crossing the small, enchanting gardens of the **Palau de Pedralbes** (closed to the public). Among the little-known treasures here are a vine-covered parabolic pergola and a gurgling fountain of Hercules (buried in thick vegetation before being rediscovered in 1984), both designed by Antoni Gaudí (the fountain's bust is a re-creation). At the park's northeast end stand the Gaudí-designed **Pavellons Güell** (☎93 317 76 52; Avinguda de Pedralbes 7; Ⓜ Palau Reial) gatehouses.

## Activities

**Molokai SUP Center** WATER SPORTS
(Map p258; ☎93 221 48 68; www.molokaisupcenter.com; Carrer de Meer 39; 2hr private SUP/surf lesson from €40/35, SUP/surf board rental per hour €15/12; ⏲10am-6pm Tue-Sat, to 3pm Sun; Ⓜ Barceloneta) This respected outfit will give you a crash course in surfing or stand-up paddleboarding (SUP). In addition to two-hour beginner's classes, Molokai can help you improve your technique (in intermediate and advanced lessons – all in two-hour blocks); gear and wetsuits are included. If you'd rather just hire a board, staff can quickly get you out to sea.

**Base Náutica Municipal** WATER SPORTS
(Map p258; ☎93 221 04 32; www.basenautica.org; Avinguda del Litoral, Platja de la Mar Bella; 2hr lessons from €40, equipment hire per hour from €15; ⏲9am-8pm; Ⓜ Poblenou) Just back from Platja de la Mar Bella, this established centre teaches the basics of kayaking, windsurfing, kitesurfing, catamaran sailing and stand-up paddleboarding. You can also hire equipment here. Prices for lessons are cheaper in groups of two or more. More in-depth multiday courses are also available.

**Piscines Bernat Picornell** SWIMMING
(Map p276; ☎93 423 40 41; www.picornell.cat; Avinguda de l'Estadi 30-38; adult/child €12.50/7.50, nudist hours €6.85/4.80; ⏲6.45am-midnight Mon-Fri, 7am-9pm Sat, 7.30am-4pm Sun; 🚌13, 150) Admission to Barcelona's official Olympic pool on Montjuïc also includes use of the complex's fitness room, sauna, Jacuzzi, steam bath and track. The outdoor pool, with incredible panoramic city views, has reduced hours outside summer and closes in December and January. Nudist-only swimming times are 9.15pm to 11pm Saturday and 4.15pm to 6pm Sunday October to May.

## Tours

**Barcelona Turisme** (Map p264; ☎93 285 38 32; www.barcelonaturisme.com; Plaça de Catalunya 17; Ⓜ Catalunya) runs guided walking tours (€18 to €25) themed around Modernisme, Picasso and the Barri Gòtic.

**Devour Barcelona** TOURS
(☎944 58 10 22; www.devourbarcelonafoodtours.com; tours €79-119) Knowledgeable guides lead terrific food tours around Gràcia, the Old City, Sant Antoni and La Barceloneta, mixing gastronomy with history. The various tastings and spots visited are especially focused on small, local producers and family-run joints, with vermouth, *cava* (sparkling wine) and local culinary specialities highlighted. Tours last three to four hours – and include enough for a full meal!

**Wanderbeak** FOOD & DRINK
(Map p252; ☎93 220 6 01; www.wanderbeak.com; Carrer del Comerç 29; group tour per person €79-99; ⏲9am-10pm; Ⓜ Jaume I, Barceloneta) Founded by a food-loving duo, Wanderbeak runs fun-filled, in-depth, small-group (maximum eight people) gastronomic experiences taking in Barcelona's history and foodie highlights; most dietary requirements are happily catered for on request, and there are cooking classes too. The signature Born to Eat tour leads you through El Born's buzzy lanes via three food stops and a relaxed wine-tasting session.

### MONTJUÏC CABLE CARS

The quickest and most scenic route from the beach to the mountain is via the **Telefèric del Port** (Map p258; www.telefericodebarcelona.com; Passeig de Joan de Borbó; one way/return €11/16.50; ⏲10.30am-8pm Jun-early Sep, shorter hours early Sep-May; 🚌V15, V19, Ⓜ Barceloneta) cable-car, which runs between the Torre de Sant Sebastiá in Barceloneta and the Miramar stop on Montjuïc. From the Parc Montjuïc cable car station on northern Montjuïc, the separate **Telefèric de Montjuïc** (Map p276; www.telefericdemontjuic.cat; Avinguda de Miramar 30; adult/child one way €8.40/6.60; ⏲10am-9pm Jun-Sep, to 7pm Mar-May & Oct, to 6pm Nov-Feb; 🚌55, 150) whizzes you up to the Castell de Montjuïc (p273) via the mirador (lookout point).

**Hidden City Tours** CULTURAL, WALKING
(www.hiddencitytours.com; tour per person €21.50) Around 20% of Spain's homeless population lives in Barcelona, and this British-founded social enterprise trains up guides who have been part of the city's homeless community. Sensitive, insightful two-hour tours of the Barri Gòtic and El Raval (English, Spanish, German) are interwoven with the guides' own stories, showing a side of Barcelona unseen by most visitors. Book ahead; minimum two people.

**Barcelona Architecture Walks** ARCHITECTURE
(Map p252; 682 497208; https://barcelonarchitecturewalks.com; Passatge de l'Hort de Velluters 5; 3hr tour €38; M Arc de Triomf) A keen multilingual team of Barcelona-based architects and architecture professors, which leads carefully curated small-group, design-based itineraries around town. The signature Barcelona & Gaudí tour provides a crash-course in all things Modernisme; Barcelona & The Market meanders through the Barri Gòtic's multilayered history and Enric Miralles' work; and Barcelona & The Future City tackles avant-garde architecture. Reservations essential.

**Bike Tours Barcelona** CYCLING
(Map p252; 93 268 21 05; www.biketoursbarcelona.com; Carrer de l'Esparteria 3; 3hr tour per person €25; 10am-7pm; M Jaume I) On the scene for 25 years, this efficient operator is one of the city's bike-tour originals, offering bike rental (from €5 per hour) and daily three-hour bicycle tours with multilingual guides around the Barri Gòtic, the waterfront, La Sagrada Família and other Gaudí landmarks (schedules online). There are also tours around the Penedès wineries (half-/full day €49/99), plus private itineraries.

**Runner Bean Tours** WALKING
(Map p244; 636 108776; www.runnerbeantours.com; by donation; tours 11am & 4.30pm Mar-Oct, 11am Nov-Feb; M Liceu) The brainchild of a Spanish-Irish couple, Runner Bean offers several daily thematic pay-what-you-wish tours with enthusiastic English-speaking local guides (it's best to book). The Gothic Quarter tour explores Barcelona's Roman and medieval history, visiting highlights of the Ciutat Vella (Old City); the Gaudí tour takes in the great works of Modernista Barcelona. All tours depart from Plaça Reial.

**Barcelona Street Style Tour** WALKING
(www.barcelonastreetstyletour.com; by donation) Highly entertaining, donation-based two-hour strolls around El Raval (10am, 4.45pm) and El Born/Barri Gòtic (2pm), delving into the history of Barcelona's street-art scene and its key artists. Tours are usually in English; book ahead online. Also does street-art workshops (from €26) and art-focused El Poblenou bike tours (€23 per person).

## Courses

**Barcelona Cooking** COOKING
(Map p244; 93 119 19 86; www.barcelonacooking.net; La Rambla 58, Principal 2; adult/child €65/32.50, under 5yr free, with market visit €78/39; M Liceu) Founded by three Galician friends, Barcelona Cooking hosts hands-on, four-hour culinary classes with bilingual chefs. Kick off with an expedition to the celebrated Mercat de la Boqueria, after which you'll be sizzling up a four-course meal (typically including paella), or try a wine-pairing class focused on traditional Catalan tapas. Thoughtful vegetarian, vegan and gluten-free adaptations on request. Book ahead.

OFF THE BEATEN TRACK

### A WANDER THROUGH OLD SARRIÀ

The old centre of elegant, affluent Sarrià is a largely pedestrianised haven of peace, with cosy squares, upmarket homes and slender streets. Founded in the 13th or 14th century and incorporated into Barcelona only in 1921, the neighbourhood unravels around sloping Carrer Major de Sarrià. At the street's top (north) end is **Plaça de Sarrià**, with its 18th-century **Església de Sant Vicenç de Sarrià**. Buses 68 and V7 pass by here.

Opposite the square is exclusive pastry shop **Foix de Sarrià** (93 203 04 73; www.foixdesarria.com; Plaça de Sarrià 12-13; pastries €2-5; 8am-9pm; FGC Reina Elisenda), where you can stop for coffee, before wandering south to leafy **Plaça del Consell de la Vila** and colourful **Plaça de Sant Vicenç de Sarrià**. Around 800m south you reach Gaudí's little-visited 1902 **Portal Miralles** on Passeig de Manuel Girona – an undulating wall and gateway adorned with (faded) white *trencadís* (ceramic fragments).

**Speakeasy** LANGUAGE
(Map p264; ☎93 342 71 97; www.speakeasybcn.com; Ronda de la Universitat 7; MUniversitat) A friendly Spanish-language school next to the university, popular for its small-group classes and social calendar (Sitges trips, street-art tours). Courses cater to all levels. An intensive 20-hour course, over four weeks, costs €129 per week.

## Festivals & Events

**Festes de Santa Eulàlia** CULTURAL
(http://lameva.barcelona.cat/santaeulalia; ⌚Feb) Around 12 February this big winter fest celebrates Barcelona's first patron saint with a week of cultural events, including parades of *gegants* (papier-mâché giants), theatre, *correfocs* (fire runs) and *castells* (human castles). It's held in conjunction with **Llum BCN** (http://lameva.barcelona.cat; ⌚mid-Feb), which takes place a few days later, during which light installations are set up.

**La Diada de Sant Jordi** CULTURAL
(⌚23 Apr) This is the day of Catalonia's patron saint (St George) and also World Book Day: lovers and friends give one another books and roses, publishers launch new titles. Rambla de Catalunya, Plaça de Sant Jaume and other central city streets and squares are filled with book and flower stalls.

**Festival de Flamenco de Ciutat Vella** DANCE
(www.ciutatflamenco.com; ⌚May) One of the best opportunities to see great flamenco in Barcelona, this festival happens over four days in May at the **Teatre Mercat de Les Flors** (Map p276; ☎93 256 26 00; www.mercatflors.cat; Carrer de Lleida 59; ⌚box office 2hr before show; 🚌55) and other venues such as BARTS (p314), Luz de Gas (p314) and JazzSí Club (p312).

**Primavera Sound** MUSIC
(www.primaverasound.com; ⌚May-Jun) For three days in late May/early June, the Parc del Fòrum is centre stage for a phenomenal range of international bands and DJs.

**Sónar** MUSIC
(www.sonar.es; ⌚mid-Jun) Usually held in mid-June, Sónar is Barcelona's massive celebration of electronic music, with DJs, exhibitions, sound labs, record fairs and urban art. The 2020 line-up included performers such as Carl Cox, Eric Prydz and Chemical Brothers. Locations change each year.

### BOAT TOURS

Several companies including **Las Golondrinas** (Map p244; ☎93 442 31 06; www.lasgolondrinas.com; Moll de les Drassanes; adult/child port tour €7.70/2.80; MDrassanes) and **Orsom** (Map p244; ☎630 619615; www.barcelona-orsom.com; Moll de les Drassanes; tours adult/child from €15.50/13.50; ⌚hours vary; MDrassanes) take passengers on short jaunts out on the water from Moll de les Drassanes near the southern end of La Rambla. Various outfitters can arrange private boat trips, including Wanderbeak (p281).

**Pride Barcelona** LGBT
(www.pridebarcelona.org; ⌚late Jun-early Jul) Barcelona's LGBTIQ+ Pride festival is a couple of weeks of celebrations held late June or early July, with a crammed program of culture and concerts, alongside the traditional Pride march on Saturday. It's also an opportunity to support social causes and raise awareness about issues affecting the LGBTIQ+ community.

**Festival del Grec** PERFORMING ARTS
(http://grec.bcn.cat; ⌚Jul) The major cultural event of the summer is a month-long performance fest in July, with dozens of theatre, dance and music shows held around town, including at the **Teatre Grec** (Map p276; www.barcelona.cat; Passeig de Santa Madrona; 🚌55, 150) amphitheatre on Montjuïc (from which the festival takes its name).

**Festa Major de Gràcia** CULTURAL
(www.festamajordegracia.org; ⌚Aug) Locals compete for the most elaborately decorated street in this popular week-long Gràcia festival held around 15 August. The fest also features free outdoor concerts, street fairs and other events such as *correfocs* and *castells*.

**Festes de la Mercè** CULTURAL
(www.barcelona.cat/merce; ⌚Sep) The city's biggest party involves four days of concerts, dancing and street theatre held at various locations across town. There are also *castells*, a fireworks display synchronised with the Montjuïc fountains, a parade of *gegants*, and *correfocs* – a show of fireworks-spitting monsters and demons who run with the crowd. Held around 24 September.

### ARTS & CRAFTS COURSES

**Alblanc Atelier** (Map p258; www.alblancatelier.com; Carrer de Badajoz 90; workshop from €65; 4.30-8pm Mon & Fri) Craft beautiful floral arrangements.

**Working in the Redwoods** (p317) Ceramics using all-natural materials.

**Amalia Vermell** (p318) Long-term jewellery-making workshops.

**Teranyina** (p316) Learn the ropes from a textiles master.

## Sleeping

### La Rambla & Barri Gòtic

**Itaca Hostel** HOSTEL €
(Map p244; 93 301 97 51; www.itacahostel.com; Carrer de Ripoll 21; dm €18-40, tr €88-130; ; M Jaume I) A cheerful, laid-back yet lively budget find near the cathedral, 1st-floor Itaca has spacious, fan-cooled mixed dorms (sleeping six, eight or 10) with spring colours, personal power outlets and lockers. Most rooms have balconies, and there's a well-equipped kitchen, cosy lounge and private triple. The friendly team organises pub crawls, sangria nights, walking tours and more, making it great for meeting people.

**Catalonia Portal de l'Àngel** HOTEL €€
(Map p244; 93 318 41 41; www.cataloniahotels.com; Avinguda Portal de l'Àngel 17; s €90-220, d €112-225; ; M Catalunya) A sensitively updated 19th-century palace in the thick of Barcelona, set around a handsome interior courtyard and marble staircase. Behind the restored neoclassical facade, rooms are smartly done in contemporary style with grey or beige velvet pillows, writing desks and tea/coffee kits. Those at the back have balconies, while a small pool, gardens and a glassed-in breakfast pagoda grace the quiet terrace.

★**Hotel Neri** BOUTIQUE HOTEL €€€
(Map p244; 93 304 06 55; www.hotelneri.com; Carrer de Sant Sever 5; r from €280; ; M Liceu) Occupying two chicly reimagined palaces from the 12th and 18th centuries, backing onto Plaça de Sant Felip Neri, this tranquil designer beauty wins everyone over. Sandstone walls lend a sense of history, while the 22 cream-toned, minimal-plastic rooms flaunt Molton Brown toiletries, pillow menus, world-roaming photos and jazzy carpets by the owners, and cutting-edge technology like infrared lights in the stone-clad bathrooms.

★**The Serras** BOUTIQUE HOTEL €€€
(Map p244; 93 169 18 68; www.hoteltheserrasbarcelona.com; Passeig de Colom 9; r €300-415, ste from €600; ; M Barceloneta) With terrific port views, this fresh five-star hotel offers every comfort – including a restaurant under Michelin-starred chef Marc Gascons and a rooftop bar and plunge pool – but never feels stuffy. The 28 chic white balconied rooms, with outsized tile-patterned headboards, have thoughtful extras like yoga mats, hair tongs, rain showers and luxurious mattresses; brighter front rooms have better views (some from the bathtub!).

**Soho House** BOUTIQUE HOTEL €€€
(Map p244; 93 220 46 00; www.sohohousebarcelona.com; Plaça del Duc de Medinaceli 4; r €230-400; ; M Drassanes) An elegant outpost of the famous London members' club, with luxuriously appointed rooms, an exclusive bar peopled with celebs, yoga classes, a 24-hour gym, a Cowshed spa and a rooftop pool with candy-striped loungers and incredible sea views. Vaulted brick ceilings, antique furniture and tiled floors highlight the building's 19th-century origins. Italian restaurant **Cecconi's** (Map p244; 93 220 46 40; www.cecconisbarcelona.com; Passeig de Colom 20, Soho House; mains €12-30; noon-1am Mon-Sat, to midnight Sun; ; M Drassanes, Barceloneta) is a draw in its own right.

**DO Reial** BOUTIQUE HOTEL €€€
(Map p244; 93 481 36 66; www.hoteldoreial.com; Plaça Reial 1; s €246-450, d €297-450; ; M Liceu) Overlooking the magnificent plaza for which it is named, this 18-room property has handsomely designed rooms with beamed ceilings, wooden floors, Molton Brown toiletries and all-important soundproofing. The service is excellent and the facilities extensive, with a roof terrace (bar in summer), dipping pool, solarium and spa. Its excellent market-to-table restaurants pull in visiting foodies.

**Hotel 1898** LUXURY HOTEL €€€
(Map p244; 93 552 95 52; www.hotel1898.com; La Rambla 109; r €135-500, ste from €410; ; M Catalunya, Liceu) The former Compañía de Tabacos Filipinas building has been resurrected as a handsome luxury hotel crowned by a sleek rooftop terrace and pool. Rooms

are smartly updated without losing their old-world elegance, with marble bathrooms, hardwood floors, tasteful furniture and rich red or navy walls; some are smallish, but deluxes and suites have terraces.

## El Raval

**Barceló Raval** DESIGN HOTEL €€
(Map p244; ☎93 320 14 90; www.barcelo.com; Rambla del Raval 17-21; d €100-260; ; Ⓜ Liceu) Part of the city's plans to pull El Raval up by the bootstraps, this cylindrical design tower makes a 21st-century splash. The rooftop terrace, plunge pool and 360° bar offer fabulous views, and the B-Lounge bar-restaurant is a lively tapas, brunch and cocktails spot. The fashion-forward rooms have slick aesthetics (white with lime-green or ruby-red splashes), coffee machines and rain showers.

**Chic&Basic Ramblas** DESIGN HOTEL €€
(Map p244; ☎93 302 71 11; www.chicandbasic.com; Passatge de Gutenberg 7; d €133-162, f €170-210; ; Ⓜ Drassanes) A couple of blocks into El Raval (despite the misleading name), this branch of the popular, excellent-value Chic&Basic chain is the most riotous to date, with quirky and colourful interiors that hit you from the second you see the vintage Seat 600 in the foyer. Stripped-back, neutral-toned rooms are inspired by 1960s Barcelona life, most with balconies and feature walls. Other branches include the stylish **Chic&Basic Born** (Map p252; ☎93 295 46 52; Carrer de la Princesa 50; s €110, d €123-132; ; Ⓜ Jaume I) in La Ribera.

**Hostal Grau** BOUTIQUE HOTEL €€
(Map p244; ☎93 301 81 35; www.hostalgrau.com; Carrer de les Ramelleres 27; d €104-180, apt from €160; ; Ⓜ Catalunya) A family *hostal* started in the 1860s, now thoughtfully reimagined, this 'small, urban, green' hideaway retains its original twirling tiled staircase but has chic, sparkling-white rooms with organic materials and other ecoconscious touches like timed lights. The design is calming and minimalist, with pops of colour and original decorative pieces. Some rooms have street-facing balconies; others overlook a vertical garden.

**Casa Camper** DESIGN HOTEL €€€
(Map p244; ☎93 342 62 80; www.casacamper.com; Carrer d'Elisabets 11; incl breakfast s €149-220, d €165-245; ; Ⓜ Catalunya) The massive foyer resembles a contemporary-art museum, but the rooms, boldly decorated in red, black and white, are the real surprise. Most have a sleeping and bathroom area, where you can contemplate hanging gardens outside, plus a separate lounge with balcony, TV and hammock across the corridor. Get to the rooftop for sweeping cityscapes, sunbeds and a cool-off shower.

## La Ribera & El Born

**★360 Hostel Arts & Culture** HOSTEL €
(Map p252; ☎93 530 56 77; https://360hostelarts.com; Ronda de Sant Pere 56; dm €27-55; ; Ⓜ Arc de Triomf) Loved for its lively social scene, 360 occupies the 1st floor of a lovely, bright, tile-floored old building near the Arc de Triomf. Comfortable, contemporary mixed dorms sleep six, eight or 16, with personal power outlets and lockers. Walls are adorned with art and there's a sunny terrace plus a well-equipped kitchen, daily walking tours and dinners, summer beach volleyball and more.

**Pensió 2000** PENSION €
(Map p252; ☎93 310 74 66; www.pensio2000.com; Carrer de Sant Pere més Alt 6; d €60-100; ; Ⓜ Urquinaona) Right opposite the anything-but-simple Palau de la Música Catalana, this family-run, good-value 1st-floor guesthouse (no lift) has seven spacious rooms with mosaic-tiled floors and large shuttered windows in a charmingly updated 18th-century building. Thoughtful extras from welcoming owners Orlando and Manuela include water refills, hairdryers, board games, complimentary tea and coffee and a quiet courtyard.

### APARTMENTS & OVERTOURISM

While private apartments might seem a convenient and cost-effective accommodation choice, it's important to know that Airbnb and other apartment rental agencies have been accused of contributing to Barcelona's overtourism problem and driving up prices (not to mention noise levels) for local residents. Barcelona's authorities stopped issuing new licences in 2014 and since 2016 have been firmly closing down unlicensed properties. Before booking your apartment, check whether it's licensed at www.fairtourism.barcelona.

**Hotel Banys Orientals** BOUTIQUE HOTEL €€
(Map p252; 93 268 84 60; www.hotelbanysorientals.com; Carrer de l'Argenteria 37; s/d €160/180; ; M Jaume I) Book well ahead for this magnetically popular, clean-lined designer haunt: a glammed-up 19th-century travellers' inn with a quiet, boutiquey charm, attached to a good Catalan restaurant. Soft pastels and sleek monochrome combine with dark-hued floors; rooms, though on the small side, look onto the street or back lanes and have queen-size beds and Rituals toiletries.

**Yurbban Passage** DESIGN HOTEL €€€
(Map p252; 93 882 89 77; www.yurbbanpassage.com; Carrer de Trafalgar 26; r €170-310; ; M Urquinaona) A soothing stripped-back designer look runs through this four-star boutique-feel newcomer, perched across the 1878 Passatge de les Manufactures in a reimagined textiles factory. The attractive, minimalist, good-value rooms have capsule-coffee kits, desks, kettles, rain showers, yoga mats and, for some, private terraces. A pale-turquoise pool and relaxed bar crown the rooftop terrace, while downstairs lies an adults-only vegan spa.

**Grand Hotel Central** LUXURY HOTEL €€€
(Map p252; 93 295 79 00; www.grandhotelcentral.com; Via Laietana 30; d €250-330, ste from €430; P ; M Jaume I) With super-soundproofed rooms, a warm professional welcome, an in-house spa and a fabulous rooftop infinity pool and all-day sky bar, this soothingly styled five-star is a standout along Via Laietana. Rooms are smartly decorated in whites, greys, blacks and beiges, with high ceilings, dark wooden floors and subtle lighting, in keeping with the building's art deco flair.

**Barcelona Edition** DESIGN HOTEL €€€
(Map p252; 93 626 33 30; www.editionhotels.com; Avinguda de Francesc Cambó 14; d €270-500; M Jaume I) Overlooking the Mercat de Santa Caterina, Ian Schrager's much-anticipated five-star Edition sees elegant, tech-forward rooms dressed in walnut wood, Spanish leather and natural tones, along with a superb rooftop bar and plunge pool with wraparound views. Enjoy gourmet Mediterranean cuisine at Bar Veraz, speciality cocktails at the speakeasy-inspired Punch Room, and wild dinner shows at clandestine Cabaret in the basement.

## Barceloneta, the Waterfront & El Poblenou

**Amistat Beach Hostel** HOSTEL €
(Map p258; 93 221 32 81; www.amistatbeachhostel.com; Carrer de l'Amistat 21-23; dm/d from €22/102; ; M Poblenou) A stylish Poblenou budget find, Amistat has sociable common areas including a beanbag-filled lounge with DJ set-up, low-lit TV room, terrace and guest kitchen. Dorms (including one women-only) sleep four to 12 and are clean but basic, aside from a splash of colour on the ceilings; the two doubles have private bathrooms. Upbeat staff organise club nights and other events.

**Poblenou Bed & Breakfast** GUESTHOUSE €€
(Map p258; 93 221 26 01; www.hostalpoblenou.com; Carrer del Taulat 30; s/d from €76/100; ; M Llacuna) A five-minute walk from Bogatell beach and steps from Rambla del Poblenou, this 1930s house, with original high ceilings and beautifully tiled floors, conceals six individually styled rooms named for Spanish artists. All have a fresh feel, light colours, potted plants, comfortable beds and beach towels in palm bags; some have tiny balconies. Breakfast (€10) is on the flower-filled terrace.

**Bed & Beach** GUESTHOUSE €€
(Map p258; 630 528156; www.bedandbeachbarcelona.com; Pasaje General Bassols 26; d €60-130; Easter-Oct; ; M Bogatell) Just 200m west of Platja de la Nova Icària on a quiet street, this warm guesthouse with a boho touch has eight cosy, spotless contemporary rooms in a refurbished 1902 building. Some lack natural light and/or share bathrooms, while others are bright and spacious, with in-room kitchens. There's also a communal kitchen, plus a rooftop terrace that's fabulous for a sunset drink.

★ **Hotel Arts Barcelona** LUXURY HOTEL €€€
(Map p258; 93 221 10 00; www.ritzcarlton.com; Carrer de la Marina 19-21; d/ste from €295/445; P ; M Ciutadella Vila Olímpica) A sky-high tower by Bruce Graham, looming above the Port Olímpic, the swish Arts is one of Barcelona's most fashionable hotels. Its 483 rooms are kitted out with high-end features, soaking tubs and unbeatable views; public spaces are graced by designer flowers and original artwork. Services range from the seductive top-floor **spa** (1hr treatment from €120; 9am-10pm) and infinity pool to six restaurants, including two-Michelin-star Enoteca.

**W Barcelona** DESIGN HOTEL €€€

(93 295 28 00; www.marriott.com; Plaça de la Rosa dels Vents 1; r/ste from €260/370; ; V15, V19, Barceloneta) Designed by Barcelona-born architect Ricardo Bofill in 2009, this glinting, spinnaker-shaped glass tower is a coastal landmark. Inside are 473 contemporary-chic, tech-forward rooms, most with coastal panoramas. Guests can flit between the gym, spa, infinity pool (with bar) and beach loungers, before sipping cocktails at the 26th-floor Eclipse bar and a seafood dinner at star chef Carles Abellán's La Barra (p297).

## La Sagrada Família & L'Eixample

**Rock Palace Hostel** HOSTEL €

(Map p264; 93 453 32 81; www.santjordihostels.com; Carrer de Balmes 75; dm/d from €25/35; ; Passeig de Gràcia) In a prime night-out-in-L'Eixample spot, this modern hostel is known for its sociable vibe, rooftop dip pool and buzzy club- and music-themed communal spaces. Well-kept mixed dorms with tiled floors, uncluttered white-and-green decor and personal lights, shelves, lockers and power outlets sleep three to 14; there are private doubles too. The Sant Jordi chain also has Sagrada Família and Gràcia branches.

★**Praktik Rambla** BOUTIQUE HOTEL €€

(Map p264; 93 343 66 90; www.hotelpraktikrambla.com; Rambla de Catalunya 27; s/d/tr from €122/135/169; ; Passeig de Gràcia) On a leafy boulevard, this early-19th-century gem of a mansion hides a gorgeous little boutique number designed by beloved local interior designer Lázaro Rosa-Violán. While high ceilings, patterned walls and original tiles have been maintained, the 43 rooms have bold ceramics, spot lighting and contemporary art. The relaxed library and back terrace are perfect for enjoying the complimentary coffee and croissants. Praktik has four other stylish boutique hotels in L'Eixample.

**Five Rooms** BOUTIQUE HOTEL €€

(Map p264; 93 342 78 80; www.thefiverooms.com; Carrer de Pau Claris 72; s/d/ste/apt incl breakfast from €129/150/160/200; ; Urquinaona) Thoughtfully expanded from its origins, the cosy-chic Five Rooms now hosts 12 rooms across a turn-of-the-century building on the southern edge of L'Eixample. Each minimal-design room is different (some with balconies), but all have open-brick walls, soothing tones, firm beds, restored tiles and stylish bathrooms. Breakfast is served in a book-lined lounge. Two kitchen-equipped, four-person apartments await just down the street.

**Casa Mathilda** BOUTIQUE HOTEL €€

(Map p264; 93 532 16 00; https://casamathilda.com; Carrer de Roger de Llúria 125-127; r €80-200; ; Diagonal) Named after welcoming owner Assumpta Baldó's mother, this stylishly homey 14-room boutique gem meanders across a beautiful 1920s building to an intimate terrace overlooking a classic L'Eixample courtyard. Each room is thoughtfully and individually styled in calming shades of purple, grey or green, with gorgeous tiling (some original, others custom-made), local artwork, in-room sinks and chic modern bathrooms with rain showers.

**Cami Bed & Gallery** BOUTIQUE HOTEL €€

(Map p264; 671 436822; www.camibedandgallery.com; Carrer de Casp 22; r without/with bathroom from €103/111; ; Catalunya) Just footsteps from the Plaça de Catalunya, this handsome and central Modernista building was reimagined by artist and designer Camila Vega and doubles as a gallery, staging exhibitions and cultural events. The seven airy and high-ceilinged, art-themed rooms are each slightly different in character and have oak or ceramic floors, coffee sets, hairdryers and bathrobes; some share bathrooms.

**Room Mate Pau** HOTEL €€

(Map p264; 93 343 63 00; www.room-matehotels.com; Carrer de Fontanella 7; r/ste from €157/218; ; Catalunya) Just off Plaça de Catalunya, the most central of fun, eco-conscious Room Mate's properties blends upscale hostel and boutique hotel. The 66 bright-white rooms are cleverly configured with designer furnishings, plump mattresses, colourful carpets, USB-connected TVs and tea/coffee kits. The two top-floor suites with terrace, bath and twin showers are popular, and there's a striking courtyard with a living wall.

**Retrome** BOUTIQUE HOTEL €€

(Map p264; 93 174 40 37; www.retrome.net; Carrer de Girona 81; r incl breakfast €125-160; ; Girona) Tucked into the quieter (eastern) side of La Dreta de L'Eixample, wonderfully original Retrome has a cosy, homey, retro-chic feel. The 15 stylishly antique-y rooms (king-sized beds, balconies, record players) are spread across two late 19th-century townhouses, with original features such as floor tiles offsetting vintage furnishings from the 1960s and 1970s. There's complimentary coffee plus a cafe-reception where staff dish out advice.

**★El Palace** HISTORIC HOTEL €€€
(Map p264; ☎93 510 11 30; www.hotelpalacebarcelona.com; Gran Via de les Corts Catalanes 668; d/ste from €260/380; P ❄ @ 📶 🏊; M Passeig de Gràcia) Launched in 1919 as the Ritz (with Paris, London and Madrid), Barcelona's dazzling luxury original continues to wow a century later. The 120 exquisitely updated rooms retain their historic charm; the six top-tier suites are styled for celebrity guests. It's all complemented by state-of-the-art facilities including a Mayan-inspired spa and Modernista-style rooftop gardens with pool, restaurant and bar basking in 360-degree views.

**★Casa Bonay** BOUTIQUE HOTEL €€€
(Map p264; ☎93 545 80 70; www.casabonay.com; Gran Via de les Corts Catalanes 700; d/f from €150/224; ❄ 📶; M Tetuan) 🍃 A beautifully revamped 1896 building laid with original tiles, Casa Bonay feels like a wonderfully chic friend's home. The minimalist-design rooms have been conceived working with local designers, from handmade throws to Santa & Cole lighting; some have glassed-in balconies, others terraces and outdoor showers. A summer *xiringuito* graces the rooftop terrace, which also hosts a herb garden and cool-off shower.

**Margot House** BOUTIQUE HOTEL €€€
(Map p264; ☎93 272 00 76; www.margothouse.es; Passeig de Gràcia 46; d/ste from €210/265; ❄ @ 📶; M Passeig de Gràcia) In the thick of L'Eixample, this elegant, intimate, supremely peaceful nine-room designer bolthole is styled in fresh minimalist whites and natural woods. Textiles, lamps and furniture come from Catalan designers, while Aesop toiletries grace the sleek bathrooms; the four light-bathed suites overlook Passeig de Gràcia, with freestanding tubs. The book-filled lounge has coffee and an honesty bar; there's a fabulous gourmet breakfast.

**Cotton House** LUXURY HOTEL €€€
(Map p264; ☎93 450 50 45; www.hotelcottonhouse.com; Gran Via de les Corts Catalanes 670; d/ste from €250/460; ❄ 📶 🏊; M Urquinaona) An exquisite 1879 building awash with wooden floors, carved ceilings and a rooftop pool, this splendid address occupies the former headquarters of the Cottonmakers' Guild, which you'll notice from the lobby's huge sprays of cotton bolls to the room names (Damask, Egyptian, Taffeta). All-white rooms are elegantly styled, with wide beds, rain showers and Ortigia toiletries; back rooms have balconies.

**Alma** DESIGN HOTEL €€€
(Map p264; ☎93 216 44 90; https://almahotels.com; Carrer de Mallorca 271; r from €300; ❄ 📶; M Diagonal) It's all about stripped-back, straight-lined luxury, sober-toned minimalism and spot-on service at this calming five-star beauty, with 72 tech-forward rooms in an early-20th-century building that marries original architecture with contemporary design. An all-white basement spa with pool, sauna and gym awaits, and the summer-only roof terrace gazes out on L'Eixample's sights, though the leafy hidden garden is the show-stealer.

**Sir Victor** DESIGN HOTEL €€€
(Map p264; ☎93 271 12 44; www.sirhotels.com; Carrer del Rosselló 265; r from €240; ❄ 📶 🏊; M Diagonal) Named for Catalan author Caterina Albert i Paradís, who published as Víctor Català, this rippling building has been plushly reincarnated by forward-thinking Amsterdam-born boutique chain Sir Hotels. Stylish rooms have coffee machines, balconies and works by emerging local artists. Other perks include excellent steak restaurant Mr Porter, a rooftop pool and bar, a luxe spa and a library spotlighting female writers.

## 🛏 Gràcia & Park Güell

**★Casa Gràcia** HOSTEL €
(Map p272; ☎93 174 05 28; www.casagraciabcn.com; Passeig de Gràcia 116; dm/s/d/tr/apt from €31/110/120/145/162; ❄ @ 📶; M Diagonal) Set across two reimagined historic buildings, Casa Gràcia raised the bar for Barcelona budget accommodation. Crisp white-design dorms sleeping four or six (with women-only options) have individual power outlets, lights and lockers. The best, brightest doubles face the street. Services include a leafy terrace, fully equipped kitchen and arty library lounge, a popular restaurant and DJ-fuelled bar, plus free yoga and walking tours.

**Yeah Hostel** HOSTEL €
(Map p272; ☎93 531 01 35; www.yeahhostels.com; Carrer de Girona 176; dm €30-45, d €120-130; ; Ⓜ Verdaguer) A lively, contemporary-design hostel with wood-and-white dorms for four or six (some women-only), a cosy communal lounge, a well-equipped kitchen and, best of all, a chilli-red pool on the roof. Dorm beds have curtains, lockers and power outlets, while the handful of private 'suites' sleeping two or four come with little balconies. Cheery staff arrange walking tours and group dinners.

**Generator Barcelona** HOSTEL €
(Map p272; ☎93 220 03 77; https://staygenerator.com; Carrer de Còrsega 373; dm/d/q/penthouse from €30/110/140/315; Ⓜ Diagonal) Part of the world-roaming, design-forward Generator brand, this stylish budget pick has much to recommend it, including a festival-inspired bar made from reclaimed lumber and recycled elevator parts, festooned with an explosion of paper lanterns. Fresh-white dorms are for six or eight people, with women-only rooms, and have personal shelves, lights, power outlets and under-bed lockers.

**Jam Hostel** HOSTEL €
(Map p272; ☎93 315 53 38; www.jamhostelbarcelona.com; Carrer de Montmany 38-42; dm €20-35, d €90; ; Ⓜ Joanic) This welcoming, original ecoconscious operation is a powerhouse of sustainable tourism, working with responsible local companies and using renewable energy, upcycled materials and fair-trade coffee. Minimalist dorms for four, eight or nine have personal power outlets, shelves and lockers; shared bathrooms are thoughtfully designed, with spacious showers and hairdryers. There are also private doubles, bike tours and yoga (€5).

★ **Hotel Casa Fuster** LUXURY HOTEL €€€
(Map p272; ☎93 255 30 00; www.hotelcasafuster.com; Passeig de Gràcia 132; d/ste from €250/350; P; Ⓜ Diagonal) Designed by Domènech i Montaner from 1908 to 1911, this sumptuous Modernista mansion is one of Barcelona's most luxurious addresses. Rooms are individual and plush (though standards are small), with chocolate-brown or soft-beige decor and marble bathrooms. Period features have been thoughtfully restored and complemented by hydromassage tubs and king-sized beds. The rooftop terrace (with pool and summer bar) offers spectacular views.

## Montjuïc, Poble Sec & Sant Antoni

★ **Pars Tailor's Hostel** HOSTEL €
(Map p276; ☎93 250 56 84; www.parshostels.com; Carrer de Sepúlveda 146; dm €25-32; ; Ⓜ Urgell) Decorated like a 1930s tailor's shop, this lively, friendly, budget-chic hostel is filled with old sewing machines, battered suitcases and other vintage pieces collected from around Barcelona. Fabric-themed dorms (including a women-only room) sleep six, eight or 12, with personal power outlets and lockers. You can relax in the comfy lounge or back terrace, cook in the well-equipped kitchen and join organised activities. The family team also runs **Pars Teatro Hostel** (Map p276; ☎93 443 94 66; Carrer d'Albareda 12; dm €25-44; ; Ⓜ Drassanes) in Poble Sec.

**TOC Hostel** HOSTEL €
(Map p276; ☎93 453 44 25; https://tochostels.com; Gran Via de les Corts Catalanes 580; dm/d from €36/140; ; Ⓜ Universitat) Inhabiting a graceful old building on the southern fringes of L'Eixample, TOC appeals with its sun-soaked back terrace and pool, stylish communal spaces (bar, kitchen, lounge), lively events and rotating art exhibitions. Bright, spacious dorms (including female-only), some overlooking Gran Via, for six or eight have personal plugs, lights, lockers and curtains. Private doubles have queen-size beds and, for some, terraces.

★ **Hotel Brummell** BOUTIQUE HOTEL €€
(Map p276; ☎93 125 86 22; www.hotelbrummell.com; Carrer Nou de la Rambla 174; r from €150; ; Ⓜ Paral·lel) With a creative soul, fun atmosphere and custom-designed furniture alongside European and Sri Lankan antiques, this thoughtfully styled Poble Sec boutique continues to turn heads. The 20 bright, bespoke rooms have minimalist design, rain showers and yoga mats; the best have terraces with views and outdoor tubs. Kind-hearted staff share tips, and there's a great restaurant/cafe plus a terrace with dip pool.

**Hotel Market** BOUTIQUE HOTEL €€
(Map p276; ☎93 325 12 05; www.hotelmarketbarcelona.com; Carrer del Comte Borrell 68; d/ste from €150/170; ; Ⓜ Sant Antoni) Attractively located in a renovated building just north of the Mercat de Sant Antoni, this chic boutique spot has 68 black-and-white

contemporary-design rooms with wide-plank floors, oversized armoires, bold art prints and carefully designed bathrooms (stone basins, rain showers). Some have tiny (two-seat) balconies; suites come with terraces. Downstairs are a smart Mediterranean restaurant and cocktail bar.

## Camp Nou, Pedralbes & La Zona Alta

**Pol & Grace** BOUTIQUE HOTEL €€

(93 415 40 00; www.polgracehotel.es; Carrer de Guillem Tell 49; s €100-180, d €140-200; ; FGC Molina, Sant Gervasi) At this stylish, ultracontemporary hotel, the 60 uniquely designed white-on-white rooms revolve around Barcelona themes (Gaudí, the Museu del Disseny, Catalan festivals and gastronomy) and are gradually being jazzed up with original artwork. All are decently sized and have ecofriendly toiletries; singles have small double beds. Neon-painted pillars, sunbeds, a shower and an organic garden dot the view-laden roof terrace.

**Anita's B&B** B&B €€

(670 064258; www.anitasbarcelona.com; Carrer d'August Font 24; r incl breakfast from €95; ; 124) Soul-stirring views of the city and the Mediterranean beyond sparkle from this sweet, family-owned hillside B&B on Tibidabo's lower slopes. The three fan-cooled rooms are generously sized, with sitting areas, tea/coffee kits, a cosy at-home feel and two share a terrace with sweeping panoramas. A 3.5km (one-hour) uphill hike leads to the top of Tibidabo.

★ **Gran Hotel La Florida** HISTORIC HOTEL €€€

(93 259 30 00; www.hotellaflorida.com; Carretera de Vallvidrera al Tibidabo 83-93; d/f/ste from €235/345/495; ; 111) Hemingway is among the former guests of this magnificent 1920s-built property atop Tibidabo, which had a designer makeover this century. Chilli-red sunbeds offset a metallic infinity pool with spectacular views across Barcelona, while other facilities include an indoor pool, a L'Occitane spa and three restaurants. The 70 elegant rooms are styled with soothing neutrals and Modernista touches.

# Eating

Barcelona has a celebrated food scene fuelled by a combination of world-class chefs, superb markets and magnificent ingredients fresh from farms and the sea. Catalan culinary masterminds like brothers Ferran and Albert Adrià, and Carles Abellán have become international icons, reinventing the world of haute cuisine, while classic old-world Catalan recipes and creative international flavours continue to earn accolades.

## La Rambla & Barri Gòtic

**Federal** CAFE €

(Map p244; 93 280 81 71; www.federalcafe.es; Passatge de la Pau 11; mains €7-10; 9am-11pm Mon-Sat, to 5pm Sun; ; Drassanes) Brick-walled industrial-chic design, a sea of open MacBooks, stacks of design mags – this welcoming, queue-out-the-door branch of the Sant Antoni Federal (p301) mothership delivers outrageously popular Australian-inspired brunches in a calming glassed-in space overlooking a quiet square. It's known for creative dishes such as baked eggs with spinach and gruyère, avocado toast with carrot hummus and French toast with berry compote.

**La Plata** TAPAS €

(Map p244; 93 315 10 09; www.barlaplata.com; Carrer de la Mercè 28; tapas €2.50-5; 10am-3.15pm & 6.15-11pm Mon-Sat; Jaume I) Tucked away in a narrow lane near the waterfront, tile-walled La Plata is a humble, well-loved bodega that has served just four simple, perfect plates since launching back in 1945: *pescadito frito* (fried fish), *butifarra* (sausage), anchovies and tomato salad. Throw in the drinkable, affordable wines and vermouth, and you have the makings of a fine, popular tapas spot.

**Milk** INTERNATIONAL €

(Map p244; 93 268 09 22; www.milkbarcelona.com; Carrer d'en Gignàs 21; mains €9-13; 9am-2am Thu-Mon, to 2.30am Fri & Sat; ; Jaume I) Also loved for its crafted cocktails, Irish-run Milk rescues Barcelona night owls with morning-after brunches (until 4.30pm!). Arrive early or join the wait list for lemon-dusted avocado toast, banana pancakes, egg-white omelettes stuffed with *piquillo* peppers and other deliciously rich hangover-beating dishes. It's all served in a cosy lounge with ornate wallpaper, framed prints and cushioned seating.

**Bar Celta** GALICIAN €

(Map p244; 93 315 00 06; www.barcelta.com; Carrer de Simó Oller 3; tapas €3-12; noon-midnight) Founded by a Galician couple in 1970, charmingly uncluttered Bar Celta shows off the northwestern region's famously seafood-tastic culinary riches with its house *pop a feira* (Galician-style octopus), now under the watch of the second and third family generation. Other traditional home-cooked goodies include salty *Padrón* peppers, *patatas bravas* and giant wedges of tortilla.

**★Cafè de l'Acadèmia** CATALAN €€

(Map p244; ☎93 319 82 53; cafedelaacademia@hotmail.com; Carrer dels Lledó 1; mains €10-20; ⏰1-4pm & 8-11pm Mon-Fri, closed Aug; 📶; Ⓜ Jaume I) Smartly executed traditional Catalan dishes with the odd creative twist and excellent regional wines make this wood-beamed, stone-walled spot a packed-out local favourite, with tables also on Plaça de Sant Just. City-hall workers pounce on the lunchtime *menú del día* (€16 – or €12 at the bar!), which might mean pear-and-parmesan salad, vegetable rice with Mahón cheese or grilled sole.

**★La Vinateria del Call** SPANISH €€

(Map p244; ☎93 302 60 92; www.lavinateriadelcall.com; Carrer Salomó Ben Adret 9; raciones €7-18; ⏰7.30pm-1am; 📶; Ⓜ Jaume I) In a magical, rambling setting in the former Jewish quarter, this tiny candlelit jewel-box of a wine bar serves up divine Iberian sharing plates dancing from Galician-style octopus and cider-cooked chorizo to perfect *truites* (omelettes) and Catalan *escalivada* (roasted peppers, aubergine and onions). Spot-on service, super-fresh local ingredients and a wonderful selection of wines and artisan cheeses from across Spain.

**★Bar Pinotxo** TAPAS €€

(Map p244; ☎93 317 17 31; www.pinotxobar.com; La Rambla 89, Mercat de la Boqueria; tapas €4-16; ⏰6.30am-4pm Mon-Sat; Ⓜ Liceu) Arguably La Boqueria's most brilliant tapas bar, standing strong since 1940. Ever-charming owner Juanito Bayén serves up superb Catalan classics: chickpeas with pine nuts and raisins, *cargols* (snails), smoky *escalivada* (grilled vegetables), soft baby squid with cannellini beans, or a quivering cube of caramel-sweet pork belly. Long-running and unpretentious, Pinotxo is also famous for its *forquilles* (traditional cooked breakfasts). Arrive early!

**★Belmonte** TAPAS €€

(Map p244; ☎93 310 76 84; Carrer de la Mercè 29; tapas €5-12; ⏰7pm-midnight Tue-Thu, 1-3.30pm & 7pm-midnight Fri & Sat; 📶; Ⓜ Jaume I) 🍃 Run by two welcoming sisters, this tiny, down-to-earth rust-walled bodega in the southern Barri Gòtic whips up beautifully prepared Tarragona-style small plates rooted in home-grown ingredients from the family garden. Try the excellent *truita* (omelette) beautifully rich *patatons* (salted new potatoes) with *romesco* or sliced chillies and courgette carpaccio topped with olive oil and goat's cheese, plus the house-made vermouth (€2.75).

**El Quim** TAPAS, CATALAN €€

(Map p244; ☎93 301 98 10; http://elquimdelaboqueria.com; La Rambla 89, Mercat de la Boqueria; tapas €3-5, mains €10-26; ⏰noon-4pm Mon & Wed, 8am-4pm Tue & Thu, 8am-5pm Fri & Sat; Ⓜ Liceu) This classic counter bar burrowed away in the Mercat de la Boqueria (p243) is ideal for traditional Catalan dishes such as fried eggs with baby squid (the house speciality) or *escalivada* (smoky grilled vegetables). Daily specials star market-fresh seasonal produce, and might include artichoke chips or port-sautéed wild mushrooms, as well as outstanding egg dishes from owner Quim Márquez. No bookings.

**Levante** MEDITERRANEAN €€

(Map p244; ☎93 858 26 79; www.bistrotlevante.com; Placeta de Manuel Ribé 1; mains €10-13; ⏰10am-midnight; 🌿; Ⓜ Jaume I) A snug, stylish and sunny space tucked into the old Call, Levante specialises in beautifully prepped sharing plates that delicately fuse Mediterranean and Middle Eastern flavours: spicy roast-carrot salad, coriander-infused shakshuka, zesty hummus with pomegranate, kumquats and pillowy pita. Polished-concrete floors and dangling plants grace the interior, and vegan and vegetarian options abound, as do natural wines and brunchy bites.

**Koy Shunka** JAPANESE €€€

(Map p244; ☎93 412 79 39; www.koyshunka.com; Carrer de Copons 7; tasting menus €93-137; ⏰1.30-2.30pm & 8.30-10.30pm Tue-Sat; Ⓜ Urquinaona) Down a narrow lane north of La Catedral, chef Hideki Matsuhisa's Michelin-starred Koy Shunka opens a portal to sensational dishes from the East – mouth-watering sushi, sashimi, seared Wagyu beef and richly flavoured seaweed salads are served alongside inventive fusion specialities. Don't miss the tender signature tuna belly.

LOCAL KNOWLEDGE

## EATING IN THE CIUTAT VELLA

First things first: skip La Rambla. Instead, venture into the Barri Gòtic: the northern half of the neighbourhood around Carrer de les Magdalenes and south between Plaça de Sant Jaume and the waterfront reveal old-time tapas bars as well as innovative newcomers. There are great restaurants around Placeta de Manuel Ribé and in the busy Mercat de la Boqueria (p243).

**Els Quatre Gats** CATALAN €€€
(Map p244; ☎93 302 41 40; www.4gats.com; Carrer de Montsió 3; mains €18-38; ⏲restaurant 1-4pm & 7pm-midnight, cafe 9am-1am; Ⓜ Urquinaona) Once the lair of Barcelona's Modernista artists, Els Quatre Gats is a stunning example of the movement, inside and out, with its colourful patterned tiles, geometric brickwork and wooden fittings designed by Josep Puig i Cadafalch. The local-focused cuisine (grilled meats, rice dishes, seafood tapas) isn't as thrilling as the setting, but you can just have coffee and a croissant.

## El Raval

★**Bar Central** CAFE €
(Map p244; Carrer d'Elisabets 6; snacks €2-7; ⏲10am-9pm; Ⓜ Catalunya) Launched in 2019 by the superstar foodie teams behind Barcelona hits Satan's Coffee (p304) and Xemei (p302), this fabulous tucked-away cafe-bar has taken over the palm-studded, ivy-wreathed courtyard and gardens and the priest's house of the 16th-century Casa de la Misericòrdia (a former orphanage). Classic coffees and vermouths accompany perfectly flaky croissants and delicate *entrepans* and salads. Find it via **La Central bookshop** (Map p244; ☎900 802109; www.lacentral.com; Carrer d'Elisabets 6; ⏲10am-9pm Mon-Sat; Ⓜ Catalunya).

★**El Pachuco** MEXICAN €
(Map p244; www.facebook.com/pachucobcn; Carrer de Sant Pau 110; dishes €6-11; ⏲1.30pm-2am Mon-Thu, to 2.30am Fri-Sun; Ⓜ Paral·lel) Get to El Pachuco early or jump on the wait list – this tiny, narrow and deservedly popular *mezcalería/taquería* gets completely packed with a low-key fashionable crowd. Exposed lightbulbs, dim lighting, bar stools and shelves cluttered with booze bottles and religious icons set the scene for first-rate tacos, quesadillas, guacamole and margaritas. There's a more spacious Barri Gòtic sister branch, **La Pachuca** (Map p244; www.facebook.com/LaPachucaBcn; Carrer d'en Carabassa 19; mains €7-9; ⏲1.30pm-2am Tue-Sun; Ⓜ Jaume I, Barceloneta).

**Caravelle** INTERNATIONAL €
(Map p244; ☎93 317 98 92; www.caravelle.es; Carrer del Pintor Fortuny 31; mains €7-15; ⏲9am-5pm Mon, to midnight Tue-Fri, 10am-midnight Sat, 10am-5pm Sun approx May-Sep, reduced hours Oct-Apr; 📶; Ⓜ Liceu) Beloved of El Raval's stylish crowd and anyone with a discerning palate, this soulful little cafe-restaurant dishes up seasonally changing tacos like you've never tasted (cod, lime aioli and radish, roast pumpkin with frijoles) and creative international-style brunches that see queues snaking out the door. Coffee comes from Nømad (p306), while craft beers are home-brewed.

**Sésamo** VEGETARIAN €
(Map p244; ☎ 93 441 64 11;Carrer de Sant Antoni Abat 52;tapas €4-7, mains €9-14;⏲7pm-midnight; Ⓜ Sant Antoni) Regularly lauded as one of the best veggie restaurants in the city, fun and cosy Sésamo transforms fresh, local ingredients into artful tapas: goat's-cheese salad, puff-pastry filled with feta and spinach, mushroom croquettes and more. Most people go for the seven-course tapas menu (vegetarian/vegan €25/30, wine included, minimum two people). Nice touches include the home-baked bread and cakes.

**Elisabets** CATALAN €
(Map p244; ☎93 317 58 26; Carrer de les Ramelleres 1; tapas €3-10, mains €8-10; ⏲7.30am-11.30pm Mon-Thu & Sat, to 1.30am Fri Sep-Jul, closed mid-Jul–mid-Aug; Ⓜ Catalunya) Now just around the corner from its original location, this brilliant old neighbourhood restaurant, its walls dotted with radio sets, is known for its unpretentious, good-value cooking. The popular *menú del dia* (€12) changes daily, but you might also try *ragú de jabalí* (wild-boar stew), *mel i mató* (dessert of cheese and honey) or tempting classic-Catalan tapas like *fuet* (thin pork sausage).

★**Cañete** TAPAS €€
(Map p244; ☎93 270 34 58; www.barcanete.com; Carrer de la Unió 17; tapas €2-15, sharing plates €7-22; ⏲1pm-midnight Mon-Sat; 📶; Ⓜ Liceu) Epitomising the ongoing trend in smartened-up

versions of traditional tapas bars, much-loved and always-busy Cañete centres on a bustling open kitchen with marble-topped bar. The long list of uberfresh tapas and *platillos* (sharing plates) packs in modern twists (such as wild-tuna tataki with seaweed) alongside traditional favourites, including gooey tortilla and Andalucian classics like *boquerones* (anchovies) and *tortillitas de camarones* (shrimp fritters).

**Suculent** CATALAN €€

(Map p244; 93 443 65 79; https://suculent.com; Rambla del Raval 45; mains €11-18, tasting menus €45-97; 1-4pm & 8-11.30pm Wed-Sun; ; M Liceu) Part of celebrity chef Carles Abellán's culinary empire, this old-style bistro showcases the best of contemporary Catalan cuisine courtesy of El Bulli–trained chef Toni Romero. From red-prawn ceviche with avocado to steak tartare over grilled bone marrow, only the finest ingredients make it into the smartly executed creations.

**Bar Muy Buenas** CATALAN €€

(Map p244; 93 807 28 57; http://muybuenas.cat; Carrer del Carme 63; mains €9-15; 1-3.30pm & 8-11pm Mon-Thu, 1-4pm & 8pm-midnight Fri, 1pm-midnight Sat, 1-11.30pm Sun; M Liceu) Modernista classic Muy Buenas has been a bar since 1928, and wears its past proudly with stunning and sinuous original woodwork, etched-glass windows, old tiles and a marble bar. Though the cocktails are impressive, these days it's more restaurant than bar, expertly turning out traditional Catalan dishes such as *esqueixada* (salad of shredded salted cod) and *fricandó* (pork-and-vegetable stew).

**Can Lluís** CATALAN €€

(Map p244; 93 441 11 87; www.restaurantcanlluis.cat; Carrer de la Cera 49; mains €10-22; 1-4pm & 8.30-11.30pm Mon-Sat; M Sant Antoni) Three generations have kept this spick-and-span old-time classic in business since 1929. Beneath olive-green beams in the back dining room you can see the spot where an anarchist's bomb went off in 1946, killing the then owner. Can Lluís is still going strong, however, with excellent seafood, succulent meats, a good *menú del dia* (€12) and almost exclusively Catalan wines.

**Casa Leopoldo** CATALAN €€

(Map p244; 93 441 30 14; www.casaleopoldo.es; Carrer de Sant Rafael 24; tapas €4-15, mains €12-19; 1-4pm & 8pm-late, closed Aug) Relaunched in 2017 by chefs Óscar Manresa and Romain Fornell, yet staying true to its classic roots, this charming El Raval old-timer has tile-patterned walls, bullfighting posters and smart white tablecloths. The kitchen showcases traditional Catalan favourites such as *cap i pota* (beef-and-chickpea stew) and oxtail in red wine, along with fried prawns, wild mushrooms and other deliciously uncomplicated tapas.

## La Ribera & El Born

**Bormuth** TAPAS €

(Map p252; 93 310 21 86; www.facebook.com/bormuthbarcelona; Carrer del Rec 31; tapas €5-10; 12.30pm-1.30am Sun-Thu, to 2am Fri & Sat; ; M Jaume I) Clad in bare brick and recycled wood, lively, split-level Bormuth specialises in homemade vermouth on tap, but also serves *cava*, artisan beers, Catalan wines and wonderful tapas. The kitchen whips up favourites from around Spain including tortilla, *pebrots del Padró* (fried green peppers), *espinacs a la catalana* (spinach with raisins and pine nuts) and *patates mojo picón* (potatoes in spicy red-pepper sauce).

**Casa Lolea** TAPAS €

(Map p252; 93 624 10 16; www.casalolea.com; Carrer de Sant Pere més Alt 49; tapas €4-14; 9am-1am; ) Dangling strings of tomatoes and garlic, red-and-black-spot decor and whitewashed brick walls lend an air of Andalucian charm to this cheerful tapas-and-vermouth tavern. It's popular for its lightly creative breakfast *entrepans* and classic-with-a-twist tapas like mushroom scrambles, just-cooked tortilla and platters of northern Spanish cheeses and cured ham. There are daily specials such as truffle risotto or octopus ceviche.

**Koku Kitchen Buns** ASIAN €

(Map p252; 93 269 65 36; www.kokukitchen.es; Carrer del Comerç 29; mains €9-11; 1-4pm & 7.30-11.30pm; ; M Barceloneta) A stylish brick-walled space with scattered plants and

**STREET-FOOD MARKETS**

Keep an eye out for hit pop-up food markets:

**Eat Street** (www.eatstreet.barcelona)

**All Those** (www.allthose.org)

**Van Van Market** (www.vanvanmarket.com)

communal tables, Koku serves delectable homemade bao stuffed with beef, pork or tofu, as well as dumplings, Vietnamese pho and fresh lemonade, sourcing most ingredients locally. The basement ramen-and-gyoza bar (closed lunch June to August) offers some of Barcelona's best steaming noodle bowls. On weekdays there's a great-value lunch *menú* (€13.50).

**Bar Joan** CATALAN €

(Map p252; ☎93 310 61 50; Avinguda de Francesc Cambó 16, Mercat de Santa Caterina; menú del dia €12.50, tapas €3-5; ⌚7.30am-3.30pm Mon, Wed & Sat, to 5pm Tue, Thu & Fri; 📶; Ⓜ Jaume I) A locally popular stop inside the Mercat de Santa Caterina (p253), old-school Bar Joan is known especially for its *arròs negre* (cuttlefish-ink rice) on Tuesdays and paella on Thursdays. It's a simple, friendly and good-value spot, serving only tapas, *entrepans* or the excellent-value *menú del dia*, with plenty of choice.

**Tantarantana** MEDITERRANEAN €

(Map p252; ☎93 268 24 10; www.gruposantelmo.com; Carrer d'en Tantarantana 24; tapas €5-10, mains €9-12; ⌚1pm-midnight; 📶; Ⓜ Jaume I) All patterned tiled floors, marble-top tables and wooden beams, shoebox-sized Tantarantana attracts a lively crowd who make the most of the terrace tables in warmer months. Well-prepared, market-driven Mediterranean dishes and tapas swing from wild-mushroom risotto and citrusy deep-fried aubergines to cod with ratatouille. The lemon-meringue cake is divine.

**Mosquito** ASIAN €

(Map p252; ☎93 268 75 69; www.mosquitotapas.com; Carrer dels Carders 46; dishes €3-6; ⌚7-11pm Mon, 1-5pm & 7-11pm Tue-Sun) Hang out in El Born for a few days and you'll inevitably end up at this pint-sized, always-busy, unadorned spot devoted to great-value 'Asian tapas'. Local Catalan ingredients are worked into fragrant Vietnamese pho, salted edamame, Chinese dim sum, Japanese gyoza and the like, accompanied by craft beers or teas from Barcelona emporium **Čaj Chai** (Map p244; ☎93 301 95 92; www.cajchai.com; Carrer de Salomó Ben Adret 12; ⌚10.30am-10pm Thu-Mon; Ⓜ Jaume I). No bookings.

**Casa Delfín** CATALAN €€

(Map p252; ☎93 319 50 88; www.casadelfinrestaurant.com; Passeig del Born 36; tapas €6-11, mains €12-20; ⌚noon-midnight Sun-Thu, to 1am Fri & Sat; 📶; Ⓜ Jaume I) One of El Born's culinary delights, Casa Delfín is everything you dream about Catalan-Mediterranean cooking in a traditional-style. Lined with wine bottles inside, the service is spot-on and creative presentation lends a contemporary touch. Menus change depending on market produce, but might offer salt-strewn *Padrón* peppers, plump anchovies from L'Escala, big seafood paellas or *suquet dels pescadors* (Catalan fish stew) for two.

**Euskal Etxea** PINTXOS €€

(Map p252; ☎93 310 21 85; www.gruposagardi.com; Placeta de Montcada 1-3; pintxos €2, mains €12-26; ⌚bar 10am-12.30am Sun-Thu, to 1am Fri & Sat, restaurant 1-4pm & 7pm-midnight; 📶; Ⓜ Jaume I) Barcelona has plenty of Basque-style *pintxo* bars, but this stone-walled, tile-floored Born favourite is the real deal. Tempting *pintxos* are stacked up on the bar – from prawns topped with peppers to deep-fried goat's cheese with quince jam – or, if hot, handed around on trays (try the mushroom croquettes!). Sip *txakoli* (Basque white wine) or just-poured cider, and keep the toothpicks for your bill.

**Can Cisa/Bar Brutal** SPANISH €€

(Map p252; ☎93 295 47 97, 93 319 98 81; www.cancisa.cat; Carrer de la Princesa 14; mains €11-20; ⌚7pm-1.30am Mon, 1-4pm & 7pm-2am Tue-Thu, 1pm-2am Fri & Sat Oct-Jun, 7pm-2am Mon-Thu, 1pm-2am Fri & Sat Jul-Sep; Ⓜ Jaume I) Can Cisa's elegant all-natural wines pair beautifully with Bar Brutal's innovative reimagining of fresh Catalan ingredients at this rowdy, fashionable wine-bar-restaurant venture from Barcelona culinary kings the Colombo brothers and team. Straight from the open kitchen, octopus with pak choi, watermelon-tomato salad and delicate artisan cheeses pull in a young, fun crowd until late. Wines are sourced from across Spain, Italy and France.

**Cal Pep** TAPAS €€

(Map p252; ☎93 310 79 61; www.calpep.com; Plaça de les Olles 8; mains €10-20; ⌚7.30-11.30pm Mon, 1-3.45pm & 7.30-11.30pm Tue-Sat, closed last 3 weeks Aug; Ⓜ Barceloneta) It's getting a foot in the door of this legendary tapas and seafood restaurant that's the problem – queues spread out into the square. Most people are happy elbowing their way to the bar for some of the tastiest seafood tapas in town. Pep recommends *cloïsses amb pernil* (clams and ham), the *trifàsic* (calamari, whitebait and prawns) or the supersmooth tortilla.

DON'T MISS

## VEGETARIAN & VEGAN RESTAURANTS

**Green Spot** (Map p258; ☎93 802 55 65; www.encompaniadelobos.com; Carrer de la Reina Cristina 12; mains €10-16; ⊙1pm-midnight Mon-Thu & Sun, to 2am Fri & Sat; ; MBarceloneta) Designer port dining room with dishes to match.

**Sésamo** (Map p276; ☎93 441 64 11; Carrer de Sant Antoni Abat 52; tapas €4-7, mains €9-14; ⊙7pm-midnight; ; MSant Antoni) Barcelona's finest veggie restaurant, tapas-style.

**Rasoterra** (Map p244; ☎93 318 69 26; www.rasoterra.cat; Carrer del Palau 5; small plates €8-14, tasting menu €32; ⊙7-11pm Tue-Fri, 1-4pm & 7-11pm Sat & Sun; ; MJaume I) Catalan-rooted vegetarian charmer in the Barri Gòtic.

**Veggie Garden** (Map p244; ☎93 180 23 34; https://veggiegardengroup.com; Carrer dels Àngels 3; mains €5-10; ⊙12.30-11.30pm; ; MLiceu) South Asian–influenced vegan cooking, in El Raval and L'Eixample.

**Flax & Kale** (Map p244; ☎93 317 56 64; www.teresacarles.com; Carrer dels Tallers 74b; mains €11-18; ⊙9am-11.30pm Mon-Fri, from 9.30am Sat & Sun; ; MUniversitat) A truly creative approach, in El Raval and La Ribera.

**Xavier Pellicer** (Map p264; ☎93 525 90 02; www.xavierpellicer.com; Carrer de Provença 310; mains €9-15; ⊙1-3.30pm & 8-10.30pm Tue-Sat; ; MDiagonal) Vegetables get the star-chef treatment in L'Eixample.

**Bar del Pla** TAPAS €€

(Map p252; ☎93 268 30 03; www.bardelpla.cat; Carrer de Montcada 2; tapas €4-11, mains €9-15; ⊙noon-11pm Mon-Thu, to midnight Fri & Sat; ; MJaume I) A bright and buzzy favourite, with glorious Catalan tiling, a vaulted ceiling and bottles of wine lining the walls. At first glance, the tapas at informal Bar del Pla are traditionally Spanish, but the riffs on a theme display an assured touch of creativity. Try the ham croquettes, wasabi mushrooms, T-bone steak or rice of the day.

**Nakashita** JAPANESE €€

(Map p252; ☎93 295 53 78; www.nakashitabcn.com; Carrer del Rec Comtal 15; mains €10-22; ⊙1-4pm & 8pm-midnight; ; MArc de Triomf) Brazil's particular immigration story means it has a tradition of superb Japanese food, and the Brazilian chef at Nakashita is no slouch, turning out excellent sashimi, maki rolls, softshell crab and *kakiage* (a mix of tempura). It's one of the top Japanese restaurants in Barcelona, with just a handful of tables – book if you can.

**Fismuler** MEDITERRANEAN €€€

(Map p252; ☎93 514 00 50; www.fismuler.com; Carrer del Rec Comtal 17; tapas €4-17, mains €20-25; ⊙1.30-4pm & 8-11pm Sun-Wed, to 11.30pm Thu-Sat; ; MArc de Triomf) The brainchild of three ex El Bulli chefs, the minimalist-design Barcelona outpost of this Madrid-born market-based sensation is one of the city's hottest tickets. Daily-changing menus throw seasonal local produce into expertly executed, unpretentious Spanish–Mediterranean dishes: Delta de l'Ebre oysters, cod omelette, truffle-and-burrata salad or slow-cooked fennel seabass, followed by gooey cheesecake and with Catalan wines to start.

## Barceloneta, the Waterfront & El Poblenou

★**Little Fern Café** CAFE €

(Map p258; ☎93 808 93 17; www.littleferncafe.com; Carrer de Pere IV; dishes €6-10; ⊙9am-5pm Mon, Thu & Fri, from 10am Sat & Sun; ; MPoblenou, Glòries) Worth a trip out to El Poblenou in itself, this beautiful Kiwi-Hungarian-owned cafe epitomises the area's new-found allure. White-brick walls, floor-to-ceiling windows and plants in terracotta pots form the backdrop to firmly original all-day-brunch bites fired by organic ingredients, such as fluffy corn fritters with smashed avocado and beetroot relish. There are also sunny mimosas, Edge Brewing craft beers, and coffee by London-based Ozone.

**Vaso de Oro** TAPAS €

(Map p258; ☎93 319 30 98; www.vasodeoro.com; Carrer de Balboa 6; tapas €3-10; ⊙11am-midnight, closed 3 weeks Sep; MBarceloneta) Always packed, this narrow old-school, tile-adorned bar gathers a high-spirited crowd, who come for fantastic tapas. Wisecracking, white-jacketed waiters serve plates of grilled *gambes* (prawns), *patates amanides* (Andalucian-style potato salad) or *solomillo* (sirloin) chunks. Want something a little different to drink? Ask for a *flauta cincuenta* – half lager and half dark beer.

**La Cova Fumada** TAPAS €

(Map p258; ☎93 221 40 61; Carrer del Baluard 56; tapas €3-12; ⏲9am-3.15pm Mon-Wed, 9am-3.15pm & 6-8.15pm Thu & Fri, 9am-1pm Sat; Ⓜ Barceloneta) The setting is decidedly frills-free, but this tiny, buzzing family-run tapas spot is something of a Barceloneta (and Barcelona) legend, with the queues to prove it. The secret? Mouth-watering *pop* (octopus), calamari, sardines, grilled *carxofes* (artichokes) and signature *bombes* (meat-and-potato croquettes with aioli) – all amazingly fresh and cooked in the open kitchen.

**Bodega La Peninsular** TAPAS €

(Map p258; ☎93 221 40 89; www.tabernaycafetin.es; Carrer del Mar 29; tapas €5-10; ⏲11.30am-midnight; Ⓜ Barceloneta) At this traditional-style bodega with marble-topped tables, over three dozen artfully presented tapas pair with Catalan vintages and house-made vermouth. Adhering to the Slow Food ethos, ingredients are organic, seasonal and locally sourced; try the *mojama* (salt-cured, air-dried tuna), the renowned spicy *bombes* (meat-and-potato croquettes) with tangy aioli, or a giant wedge of tortilla. It's standing room only most nights.

**El 58** TAPAS €

(Le cinquante huit; Map p258; ☎93 601 39 03; www.facebook.com/el58poblenou; Rambla del Poblenou 58; tapas €4-12; ⏲1.30-11pm Tue-Sat, to 4pm Sun; Ⓜ Poblenou) This French-Catalan fave serves imaginative, beautifully prepared seasonal tapas: braised tuna with romesco sauce and asparagus, fried aubergines with honey and rosemary, sausage-and-chickpea stew, and local cheeses. Solo diners can take a seat at the marble-topped front bar. The back dining room with its exposed-brick walls, industrial light fixtures and original artworks is a lively place to linger over a long meal.

**Bar Ángel** TAPAS €

(Map p258; ☎93 269 04 93; Carrer d'Ocata 2; tapas €7-10; ⏲1.30-6pm & 8.30-11pm Tue-Sat; Ⓜ Barceloneta) Hidden away just west of the Estació de França, this charming, slender brick-walled bodega wins over regulars with its thoughtfully prepared seasonal tapas, many of which star Iberian pork (as does the decor!). Grilled Tomino cheese with courgette carpaccio might accompany platters of *morcilla* (black pudding) from Extremadura, chorizo with chickpeas or scallops with pork jowl.

**Can Maño** SEAFOOD €

(Map p258; Carrer del Baluard 12; raciones €4-15; ⏲8-11pm Mon, 8.15-11am, noon-4pm & 8-11pm Tue-Fri, 8.15-11am & 12.15-4pm Sat; Ⓜ Barceloneta) It may look like a dive, but you'll need to wait before being squeezed in at a packed table for a raucous night of *raciones* (full-plate-size tapas servings) over a bottle of cloudy white *turbio* (Galician wine) at this family-run stalwart. The seafood is fresh and abundant, with first-rate squid, prawns and fish served at rock-bottom prices. Cash only.

**★ Minyam** SEAFOOD €€

(Map p258; ☎93 348 36 18; www.facebook.com/minyamcisco; Carrer de Pujades 187; tapas €2-10, mains €15-25; ⏲1-11pm Tue-Thu, to 11.30pm Fri & Sat, to 5pm Sun; Ⓜ Poblenou) Billowing with smoke beneath a tajine-like metal lid, smouldering herbs infuse the rice of Minyam's signature Vulcanus (smoked seafood paella with squid ink). Tapas dishes at this stylish, contemporary El Poblenou restaurant are equally inventive and include asparagus fritters, oysters with sea urchin and lemon, prawn omelettes and fondue with truffle oil. There's a popular €12.50 *menú del dia*.

**★ Can Recasens** CATALAN €€

(Map p258; ☎93 300 81 23; www.canrecasens.restaurant; Rambla del Poblenou 102; mains €8-21; ⏲restaurant 8pm-1am, delicatessen 8.15am-1.30pm & 5pm-1am Mon-Fri, 8.15am-1.30pm Sat; Ⓜ Poblenou) One of El Poblenou's most romantic settings, century-old Can Recasens conceals a warren of warmly lit rooms full of oil paintings, flickering candles, fairy lights and fruit baskets. The food is outstanding, with a mix of salads, smoked meats, fondues, and open sandwiches topped with delicacies like wild mushrooms and Brie, *escalivada* (grilled vegetables) and Gruyère, or *sobrasada* (spicy cured sausage) with rosemary honey.

**Red Fish** SEAFOOD €€

(Map p258; ☎93 171 68 94; www.redfishbcn.com; Moll de la Marina; tapas €2-12, mains €15-30; Ⓜ Ciutadella Vila Olímpica) Bamboo chairs, swaying straw lamps, niftily repurposed paddle-boat tables – this chic beachy seafooder sits on its own tucked-away patch of blonde sand at the northwest end of Platja de la Barceloneta. Utterly fabulous Barcelona panoramas unfold as you tuck into superb, fresh rice dishes (like creamy lobster rice), clams in sherry or grilled turbot, or kick back over mojitos, vermouth and sharing platters.

**Leka** INTERNATIONAL €€

(Map p258; ☎93 300 27 19; https://restauranteleka.com; Carrer de Badajoz 65; mains €7-16; ⏱1pm-late Thu-Sat, to 5pm Sun-Wed; ✎; Ⓜ Llacuna) Cooking up vegetables from its own garden, organic meats sourced from responsible Pyrenees producers and seafood fresh from Barceloneta's markets or the Delta de l'Ebre, Leka gets crammed for its generous weekday lunch *menú* (€12). Creative vegetarian-friendly delights might include sweet-potato noodles with tofu, portobello burgers or creamy mushroom pasta, while other options swing from grilled entrecôte to herb-infused mussels.

**★La Barra de Carles Abellán** SEAFOOD €€€

(☎93 295 26 36; www.carlesabellan.com; Plaça de la Rosa dels Vents 1, W Barcelona; tapas €5-25, mains €18-36; ⏱7-11am & 7-11.30pm Mon-Thu, 7-11am, 1.30-4pm & 7-11.30pm Fri & Sat, 7-11.30am & 1.30-4pm Sun; 🚌V15, V19, Ⓜ Barceloneta) Star Catalan chef Carles Abellán's stunning glass-encased, glossy-tiled restaurant (designed by favourite local interiorist Lázaro Rosa-Violán) celebrates seafood. Stellar tapas might include pickled octopus and *papas aliñás* (potato salad) with mackerel. Even more show-stopping are the mains: grilled razor clams with ponzu (citrus sauce), squid filled with spicy poached egg yolk, and hake *kokotxas* (jowls).

**★Can Solé** SEAFOOD €€€

(Map p258; ☎93 221 50 12; www.restaurantcansole.com; Carrer de Sant Carles 4; mains €15-40; ⏱1-4pm & 8-11pm Tue-Thu, 1-4pm & 8.30-11pm Fri & Sat, 1-4pm Sun; Ⓜ Barceloneta) Behind imposing wooden doors, this elegantly old-school restaurant with white-cloth tables, white-jacketed waiters and photos of celebrity customers has been serving terrific seafood since 1903. Freshly landed catch stars in traditional dishes such as *arròs caldòs* (rice broth with squid and langoustines) and 'grandmother'-style dishes like *zarzuela* (casserole with almonds, saffron, garlic, tomatoes, mussels, fish and white wine).

**★Oaxaca** MEXICAN €€€

(Map p258; ☎93 319 00 64; www.oaxacacuinamexicana.com; Pla de Palau 19; mains €14-28; ⏱restaurant 1-4pm & 8pm-midnight, bar 1pm-midnight; ✎; Ⓜ Barceloneta) Menorcan chef Joan Bagur trained in Mexico for a decade under traditional cooks and has his own garden of Mexican plants, which supplies ingredients for outstanding culinary creations like chargrilled octopus and *cochinita pibil* (slow-roasted pork tacos). Hefty tables are made from Mexican hardwoods, original Mexican art lines the walls and there's alfresco seating under the arches.

**★Xiringuito Escribà** SEAFOOD €€€

(Map p258; ☎93 221 07 29; www.xiringuitoescriba.com; Avinguda del Litoral 62; mains €18-26; ⏱noon-10.30pm; ✎; 🚌H16, V25, V27, Ⓜ Llacuna) The team behind Escribà (p309), which has been creating sweets since 1906, is also in charge of one of Barcelona's most popular waterfront seafood restaurants. A whirl of busy waiters and bubbling paellas, this is one of few places in town that does one-person paella or Catalan *fideuà*, as well as delicious vegetarian-friendly mushroom paella. Finish off with Escribà pastries. Reservations recommended.

**Restaurant 7 Portes** SEAFOOD €€€

(Map p258; ☎93 319 30 33; https://7portes.com; Passeig d'Isabel II 14; mains €18-32; ⏱1pm-1am; 📶; Ⓜ Barceloneta) Founded in 1836 as a cafe, then converted into a restaurant in 1929, 7 Portes has a grand setting beneath arches, and exudes an old-world atmosphere with its tiles, mirrors, beams and plaques naming luminaries – such as Orson Welles – who have passed through. Paella is the speciality (including one-person options), or try the *gran plat de marisc* ('big seafood plate').

**Els Pescadors** SEAFOOD €€€

(Map p258; ☎93 225 20 18; www.elspescadors.com; Plaça de Prim 1; mains €15-40; ⏱1-3.30pm & 7.45-11.30pm; 📶; Ⓜ Poblenou) On a picturesque square lined with low houses and long-established South American *bella ombre* trees, this quaint family restaurant continues to serve some of the city's best grilled fish and seafood-and-rice dishes. There are three dining areas inside: two are quite modern, while the main room preserves its old tavern flavour. On warm nights, try for a table outside.

**Blue Spot** MEDITERRANEAN €€€

(☎93 144 78 66; www.encompaniadelobos.com; Passeig Joan de Borbó 101, Edifici Ocean; mains €16-30; ⏱1-4pm & 8-11pm; ✎; 🚌V15, V19, Ⓜ Barceloneta) A subtle lobby unveils this exquisitely styled 8th-floor restaurant and cocktail bar, with leafy, fairy-lit indoor-outdoor design by renowned Brazilian architect Isay Weinfeld and unbeatable 360-degree views across Barcelona's seafront. Though really you're here for the setting, the creatively prepared, seasonal Mediterranean menu is good too: original pastas, seafood *arrossos* (rice dishes), locally sourced meats and fish.

**Can Ros** SEAFOOD €€€
(Map p258; 93 221 45 79; www.canros.cat; Carrer del Almirall Aixada 7; mains €15-27; 1-4pm & 7-11pm Tue-Sun; M Barceloneta) The fifth generation now leads this immutable seafood favourite, which first opened in 1908. In a restaurant where the decor is a reminder of simpler times, there's a straightforward guiding principle: juicy fresh fish cooked with a light touch, along with rich seafood rice dishes and *fideuà* with cuttlefish. Catalan wines, including organic options, accompany them.

## La Sagrada Família & L'Eixample

**★Tapas 24** TAPAS €
(Map p264; 93 488 09 77; www.carlesabellan.com; Carrer de la Diputació 269; tapas €4-12; 9am-midnight; ; M Passeig de Gràcia) Hotshot chef Carles Abellán runs this basement tapas haven known for its gourmet renditions of old faves, including the *bikini* (toasted ham-and-cheese sandwich, here with truffle and cured ham), freshly cooked tortilla and zesty lemon-infused *boquerones* (anchovies). You can't book, but it's worth the wait. For dessert, try the creamy *payoyo* cheese. Before 1pm, pop in for superb *entrepans* and omelettes.

**Granja Petitbo** MEDITERRANEAN €
(Map p264; 93 265 65 03; www.granjapetitbo.com; Passeig de Sant Joan 82; mains €5-11; 8.30am-11.30pm Mon-Fri, 10am-midnight Sat, 10am-11.30pm Sun; ; M Girona) High ceilings, battered leather armchairs, creative flower arrangements and soaring windows set the scene in this sunny little corner cafe, beloved of fashionable locals and young families. As well as an all-day parade of homemade cakes, freshly squeezed juices and terrific coffee, there are burgers, salads, pastas and Buddha bowls, along with a brunch menu, all made with local produce.

**Entrepanes Díaz** SANDWICHES, TAPAS €
(Map p264; 93 415 75 82; www.facebook.com/entrepanesdiaz; Carrer de Pau Claris 189; sandwiches €6-10, tapas €3-10; 1pm-midnight; M Diagonal) Gourmet sandwiches, from roast beef to suckling pig or the favourite crispy squid with squid-ink aioli, are the highlight at this sparkling old-style bar, along with sharing plates of Spanish specialities such as sea urchins, prawn fritters or blood-sausage croquettes. Service is especially charming; black-and-white photos of Barcelona line the walls.

**★Pepa** TAPAS €€
(Map p264; 93 611 18 85; www.pepapla.cat; Carrer d'Aribau 41; sharing plates €7-18; 5-11pm Sun-Thu, 1-11.30pm Fri & Sat, closed 2 weeks Aug; ; M Universitat) An old bookshop graced by original check-tiled floors and exposed-brick walls is the setting for this outstanding venture from the team behind El Born's beloved Bar del Pla (p295). Don't miss the mushroom carpaccio with strawberries and wasabi vinaigrette, or, in season, the fabulous eggs with truffle and chips. Desserts – like flambeed berries – are just as exquisite, while wines are natural, organic and/or biodynamic.

**★Auto Rosellon** INTERNATIONAL €€
(Map p264; 93 853 93 20; www.autorosellon.com; Carrer del Rosselló 182; breakfasts €4-9, mains €10-15; 8am-1am Mon-Wed, to 2am Thu & Fri, 9am-2am Sat, 9am-midnight Sun; ; M Diagonal, FGC Provença) With cornflower-blue paintwork and fresh produce on display, Auto Rosellon works mostly organic ingredients sourced from small producers and its own garden into creative dishes like avocado toast with feta, cauliflower doused in kale pesto, *gnudi* pasta with baked pumpkin, and slow-roasted pork tacos. Homemade juices, lemonade and cakes are exceptional, and there are natural wines, cocktails and craft beers.

**Hawker 45** ASIAN €€
(Map p264; 93 763 83 15; www.hawker45.com; Carrer de Casp 45; mains €10-16; 1-4pm & 8-11pm Mon-Sat; ; M Tetuan) Taking its cues from an Asian hawkers market, chef Laila Bazahm's aromatic restaurant sizzles up Asian–Latin American street-food dishes such as spicy Malaysian squid laksa, Indonesian lamb satay, Indian tandoori carrots and Thai green veg curry with avocado. Dine at the long, red bar overlooking the open kitchen or in the postindustrial dining space with bare beams and wall murals.

**Parking Pizza** PIZZA €€
(Map p264; ☎93 633 96 45; www.parkingpizza.com; Carrer de Londres 98; mains €11-15; ⏰1-4pm & 8-11pm Sun-Thu, to midnight Fri & Sat, closed 12-25 Aug; 👶; 🚇FGC Provença) In this garage-style space, you're likely to be sharing a long unvarnished wooden table, squeezed in on a cardboard-box stool, but that's half the fun. Wood-fired pizzas arrive loaded with toppings like creamy burrata stracciatella or earthy black truffle, while tempting starters include a superb red-quinoa salad with avocado and a poached egg. Also does pizza and pita in **eastern L'Eixample** (Map p264; ☎93 541 80 11; Passeig de Sant Joan 56; mains €11-15; ⏰1-4pm & 8-11pm Sun-Fri, to midnight Sat; 👶; Ⓜ Tetuan).

**Bicnic** INTERNATIONAL €€
(Map p264; ☎690 904614; www.bicnic.com; Carrer de Girona 68; sharing plates €9-19; ⏰1-4pm & 8-11pm; 👶; Ⓜ Girona) A fusion of sleek design and ambitious cooking, grown from a food-truck success story, this venture from chef Victor Ferrer puts a creative spin on local ingredients. Temptations include curried mussel croquettes, avocado fritters, truffled entrecôte, fried ray with lemon-and-butter emulsion or omelette made with organic eggs and Santa Pau beans.

**Gresca Bar** CATALAN €€
(Map p264; ☎93 451 6193; Carrer de Provença 230; sharing plates €7-16; ⏰1.30-4pm & 8.30-10.30pm; 👶; 🚇FGC Provença) 🌿 From the team behind smart restaurant Gresca (with which it shares an open-plan kitchen), this elegant gold-and-green wine and tapas bar is a whispered-about local hit. Chef Rafa Peña specialises in thoughtful, ambitious reinterpretations of quality seasonal produce, combined with exclusively natural wines. Try leeks sprinkled with burrata, veal sweetbreads or a *bikini* with mushrooms or pork loin and Comté cheese.

**Chichalimoná** MEDITERRANEAN €€
(Map p264; ☎93 277 64 03; www.chichalimona.com; Passeig de Sant Joan 80; mains €12-17; ⏰9.30am-1am Tue-Thu, to 2am Fri & Sat, to 5pm Sun; 📶; Ⓜ Girona) Bright, bustling Chichalimoná is a favourite along ever more fashionable Passeig de Sant Joan. Steak tartare with chipotle, spicy chicken tacos, basil-and-mascarpone ravioli or vegetable spring rolls dipped in coconut sauce might be among the original dishes, along with vermouth-hour bites like olives, hummus and squid. Weekend brunches star organic eggs. There's another branch at El Raval's **MACBA** (Map p244; ☎93 249 04 36; www.chichalimona.com; Plaça dels Àngels 1, MACBA; tapas €2-7, mains €7-11; ⏰8am-midnight Mon-Fri, from 9am Sat & Sun).

**La Cuina d'en Garriga** SPANISH €€
(Map p264; ☎93 250 37 00; https://lacuinadengarriga.com; Carrer d'Enric Granados 58; mains €9-20; ⏰1-11pm Wed-Sun; 📶👶; 🚇GFC Provença) 🌿 Tomatoes dangle above the open kitchen at this cheerful bistro-style spot with bright-red trim and checkered marble floors, popular with lunching *barcelonins*. Seasonal, organic farm-to-table menus highlight small, mostly local producers in creatively plated dishes like pea-and-mint hummus (served in a jar), grilled aubergine dressed with *romesco* sauce, fresh fish of the day or grilled *costella* (T-bone steak) for sharing.

**Taktika Berri** PINTXOS €€
(Map p264; ☎93 453 47 59; www.facebook.com/taktikaberri; Carrer de València 169; pintxos €4-15, mains €12-28; ⏰1-4pm & 8.30-11pm Mon-Fri, 1-4pm Sat, closed early-late Aug; Ⓜ Hospital Clínic) Reservations are essential at Taktika Berri, which teems with smartly dressed local diners who come for some of the best *pintxos* (Basque tapas) in town. Morsels like blood sausage, gooey tortilla or *bacallà* (salt cod) with potato gratin are snapped up as soon as they arrive fresh from the kitchen, so keep your eyes peeled.

**★Lasarte** MODERN EUROPEAN €€€
(Map p264; ☎93 445 32 42; www.restaurantlasarte.com; Carrer de Mallorca 259; mains €52-70; ⏰1.30-3pm & 8.30-10pm Tue-Sat; Ⓜ Diagonal) One of Barcelona's preeminent restaurants – and its first to gain three Michelin stars (in 2016) – Lasarte is overseen by lauded chef Martín Berasategui and headed up by Paolo Casagrande. From Duroc pig's trotters with Jerusalem artichoke to squid tartare with kaffir consommé, this is seriously sophisticated, seasonally inspired cookery, served in an ultra-contemporary dining room by staff who could put the most overawed diners at ease.

**★Disfrutar** MODERN EUROPEAN €€€
(Map p264; ☎93 348 68 96; www.disfrutarbarcelona.com; Carrer de Villarroel 163; tasting menus €155-195; ⏰1-2.15pm & 8-9.15pm Mon-Fri; 👶; Ⓜ Hospital Clínic) With two Michelin stars, Disfrutar ('Enjoy') is among the city's finest restaurants. Run by alumni of Ferran Adrià's game-changing El Bulli, nothing is as it seems, such as black and

green olives that are actually chocolate ganache with orange-blossom water. The Mediterranean-inspired decor is fabulously on point, with latticed brickwork and trademark geometric ceramics from Catalan design team Equipo Creativo.

**★Cinc Sentits** CATALAN €€€
(☎93 323 94 90; www.cincsentits.com; Carrer d'Entença 60; tasting menus €99-119; ⏲1.30-2.30pm & 8.30-9.30pm Tue-Sat; ; M Rocafort) Enter the realm of the 'Five Senses' to indulge in jaw-dropping eight- or 11-course tasting menus of small, experimental dishes concocted by chef Jordi Artal (no à la carte, although dishes can be tweaked on request). The use of fresh local produce, such as Costa Brava line-caught fish and top-quality Extremadura suckling pig, is key at this Michelin-star address.

**★Mont Bar** BISTRO €€€
(Map p264; ☎93 323 95 90; www.montbar.com; Carrer de la Diputació 220; tapas €4-10, mains €15-30; ⏲1-4pm & 7-11.30pm Wed-Mon; ; M Universitat) Named for the owner's Val d'Aran hometown, this stylish space with black-and-white floors, pine-green booths and bottle-lined walls offers next-level cooking fired by organic, seasonal ingredients, many of them home-grown. Exquisite tapas (like corn-and-jalapeño crisp-bread and oyster with mandarin tiger's milk) precede superb small-plate mains, such as celery risotto with truffle, and show-stopping desserts. Stunning wines (over 250) span all price points. Reservations recommended.

Next door **Mediamanga** (Map p264; ☎93 832 56 94; www.mediamanga.es; Carrer d'Aribau 13; sharing plates €10-30; ⏲1-4pm & 7-11.30pm; ; M Universitat), by the same team, delivers spectacular Catalan-inspired cuisine.

**La Dama** EUROPEAN €€€
(Map p264; ☎93 209 63 28; www.la-dama.com; Avinguda Diagonal 423-425; mains €22-30; M Diagonal, FGC Provença) Diagonal's 1917 Modernista Casa Sayrach has been reborn as a graceful multiroom gastro space filled with grand-yet-homey lounges, sparkling mirrors, floral-patterned wallpaper and rich velvet touches. Perfectly executed dishes wander around northern Spain, France and Italy, with a few other international hints: pork ribs with vegetable cream, squid-ink carbonara, sole meunière for two. There's also a fine cocktail bar.

## Gràcia & Park Güell

**Les Tres a la Cuina** MEDITERRANEAN €
(Map p272; ☎637 990078; www.lestresalacuina.com; Carrer de Sant Lluís 35; 2-/3-course menú €8.50/10; ⏲1-4pm Mon-Fri; ; M Joanic) Fresh local ingredients are thrown into creative, health-focused, home-cooked mixes at this eco-aware deli-restaurant, with compostable tableware and daily-changing menus that might mean delicately dressed fig-and-goat's-cheese salad, mango-and-cucumber soup or spiced chickpeas with fragrant rice. It's mostly takeaway.

**Bar Bodega Quimet** TAPAS €
(Map p272; ☎93 218 41 89; Carrer de Vic 23; tapas €3-12; ⏲10am-midnight Mon-Fri, noon-4pm & 6.30pm-late Sat & Sun; M Fontana) A relic from a bygone age, now lovingly managed by a pair of brothers, this is a delightfully atmospheric spot, with old bottles lining the walls, marble tables, tiled floors and a burnished wooden bar backed by house-vermouth barrels. The lengthy tapas list specialises in *conserves* (canned seafood), but also cheese platters and fresh anchovies and octopus.

**★La Pubilla** CATALAN €€
(Map p272; ☎93 218 29 94; www.lapubilla.cat; Plaça de la Llibertat 23; mains €10-18; ⏲8.30am-5pm Mon, to 11.30pm Tue-Sat; M Fontana) Hidden away behind a peachy-pink door by the Mercat de la Llibertat, La Pubilla specialises in hearty *'esmorzars de forquilla'* ('fork breakfasts') beloved by market workers and local residents. There's also an outrageously popular daily three-course *menú* (€16), which stars seasonal produce and Catalan dishes such as baked cod, or roast pork cheek with chickpeas; book ahead or arrive early.

Chef Alexis Peñalver also runs **Extra Bar** (Map p272; Carrer Torrent de l'Olla 79; raciones €5-13; ⏲6.30pm-midnight Tue-Thu, to 1am Fri, noon-3.30pm & 7.30pm-1am Sat; M), serving local-rooted *platillos*.

**Berbena** MEDITERRANEAN €€
(Map p272; ☎93 801 59 87; www.berbenabcn.com; Carrer de Minerva 6; set 4-dish menu €16.50; ⏲7.30-11pm Mon & Sat, 1-3.30pm & 7.30-11pm Tue-Fri; ; M Diagonal) Tucked away off busy Diagonal, Berbena specialises in ambitiously prepared, beautifully presented seasonal dishes from the open-plan kitchen. The daily-changing *menú* starts with home-baked bread, accompanied by a main such as zestily dressed burrata with pumpkin and

sides of tortilla or chilled green-vegetable soup. It's a tiny, minimalist-modern space, with seats in the window and coffee from neighbouring roaster SlowMov (p310).

**La Panxa del Bisbe** TAPAS €€

(☎93 313 70 49; Carrer del Torrent de les Flors 158; tapas €9-14, tasting menus €30-38; ⏲1.30-3.30pm & 8.30pm-midnight Tue-Sat; 📶🌶; Ⓜ Joanic) With its local buzz and artfully minimalist interior, the 'Bishop's Belly' is a pleasant surprise in upper Grácia, delivering creative tapas that earn high praise from both *barcelonins* and visitors. Feast on provolone-stuffed courgette flowers, grilled octopus with capers and celery, or Iberian ham with melon and mint. The wine list includes excellent picks from Catalonia and elsewhere in Spain.

**Lluritu** SEAFOOD €€

(☎93 855 38 66; www.lluritu.com; Carrer del Torrent de les Flors 71; dishes €5-15; ⏲1-4pm & 7.30-8.30pm Wed & Thu, to 12.30am Fri & Sat, noon-11.30pm Sun; Ⓜ Joanic) From salted sardines to king prawns and razor clams, perfectly grilled, unadorned bites fresh from the ocean are the order of the day at this self-styled *desenfadada* (casual) seafood restaurant, decorated with tile-patterned floors and a marble bar. Prized ingredients for the short, select menu are sourced from all along the Spanish coast but especially Catalonia.

**Les Filles** CAFE €€

(Map p272; ☎93 787 99 69; www.lesfillesbarcelona.com; Carrer de Minerva 2; mains €12-17; ⏲9am-11pm Mon-Fri, from 10am Sat & Sun; 🌶; Ⓜ Diagonal) 🍃 Both gorgeous design space and buzzing garden café-restaurant, Les Filles is adorned with pine-green booths, vases of fresh flowers and jazzy cushions and rugs. Rooted in fresh, seasonal flavours and organic ingredients, dishes take a health-focused turn, with options like wild-salmon pasta, quinoa bowls, creative breakfasts and cold-press juices from the owners' Loup & Filles line.

**Botafumeiro** SEAFOOD €€€

(Map p272; ☎93 218 42 30, Whatsapp 662 669337; www.botafumeiro.es; Carrer Gran de Gràcia 81; mains €22-55; ⏲noon-1am; Ⓜ Fontana) A wonderfully smart world of Galician seafood, Botafumeiro has long been a magnet for VIPs visiting Barcelona. It's a good place to try *percebes* (goose barnacles), often considered the ultimate fruit-of-the-sea delicacy. You can bring the price down by sharing a marine *mitges racion* (large tapas plates), followed by mains like baked spider crab, shellfish paella or charcoal-grilled wild hake.

**Roig Robí** CATALAN €€€

(Map p272; ☎93 218 92 22; www.roigrobi.com; Carrer de Sèneca 20; mains €21-36; ⏲1.30-4pm & 8.30-11.30pm Mon-Fri, 8.30-11.30pm Sat, closed 2 weeks Aug; Ⓜ Diagonal) 🍃 At this long-running altar to refined traditional cooking, the seasonally changing menu serves as a showcase for beautifully presented creations with local and organic ingredients. Dishes may include sautéed wild mushrooms to start, followed by outstanding seafood rice dishes, salt-baked market-fresh fish or slow-roasted Pyrenees lamb.

## Montjuïc, Poble Sec & Sant Antoni

**★Quimet i Quimet** TAPAS €

(Map p276; ☎93 442 31 42; www.quimetquimet.com; Carrer del Poeta Cabanyes 25; tapas €4-10, montaditos €3-4; ⏲noon-4pm & 8-10.30pm Mon-Fri, closed Aug; Ⓜ Paral·lel) Now led by its fourth generation, family-run Quimet i Quimet has been passed down since 1914. There's barely space to swing a *calamar* (squid) in this bottle-lined, standing-room-only place, but it's a treat for the palate. Try delectable made-to-order *montaditos* (tapas on bread), such as salmon with greek yoghurt or tuna belly with sea urchin, with a house wine or vermouth.

**Federal** CAFE €

(Map p276; ☎93 187 36 07; www.federalcafe.es; Carrer del Parlament 39; mains €7-12; ⏲8am-11.30pm Mon-Thu, to midnight Fri, 9am-midnight Sat, 9am-5.30pm Sun; 📶🌶; Ⓜ Sant Antoni) On Sant Antoni's main stretch, which now teems with cafes, Australian-founded Federal was the trailbazer, with its expertly crafted coffee (including flat whites) and superb creative brunches ranging from avocado toast with carrot hummus to baked eggs. Later in the day, try veggie burgers or grilled salmon with soba noodles. Head to the breezy roof terrace or grab a cushioned window seat.

**Bar Ramón** TAPAS €

(Map p276; ☎93 325 02 83; http://barramon.dudaone.com; Carrer del Comte Borrell 81; tapas €5-12; ⏲8.30-11.30pm Mon-Thu, 2-4pm & 8.30-11.30pm Fri & Sat; Ⓜ Sant Antoni) A much-loved Sant Antoni haunt, Bar Ramón is a lively blues-filled joint opposite the market. Old photos of American musical R&B legends (and a few guitars) line the walls – a fine backdrop for tapas like tender slices of cured ham, grilled prawns and house-speciality *jabuguitos* (chorizo cooked in cider with Cabrales-cheese sauce).

**Sant Antoni Gloriós** TAPAS €

(Map p276; ☎93 424 06 28; www.facebook.com/SantAntoniGlorioso; Carrer de Mansó 42; dishes €4-12; ⏱1-11pm Tue-Sat, 1-3pm Sun; Ⓜ Poble Sec) Launched by neighbourhood chef Fran Manduley, this smartly updated Sant Antoni bodega with oversized mirrors, wine-barrel tables and bottle-lined walls pulls in a local crowd. Tapas are unpretentious and expertly prepared, including vegetable-stuffed omelettes and charcuterie platters of truffled mortadella with Catalan cheeses. Vermouth-hour snacks include cod fritters and *patates braves*.

**★Agust Gastrobar** BISTRO €€

(Map p276; ☎93 162 67 33; www.agustbarcelona.com; Carrer del Parlament 54; mains €16-24; ⏱7pm-midnight Mon-Thu, 2-4pm & 7pm-midnight Fri-Sun; Ⓜ Poble Sec) Set up by two French chefs (one of whom trained under Gordon Ramsay), Agust occupies a fabulous mezzanine space with timber beams, exposed brick and textured metro tiles. Scallops gratinéed with asparagus and prawn-and-avocado stuffed cannelloni are savoury standouts, with housemade vermouth and inventive cocktails alongside. Desserts include the extraordinary 'el cactus' (chocolate-crumble soil, mojito mousse, lemon sorbet).

**Mano Rota** FUSION €€

(Map p276; ☎93 164 80 41; www.manorota.com; Carrer de la Creu dels Molers 4; mains €13-20; ⏱8-11.30pm Mon, 1-3.30pm & 8-11.30pm Tue-Sat; Ⓜ Poble Sec) Exposed brick, aluminium pipes, industrial lighting and recycled timbers set a pleasingly contemporary tone for inspired bistro cooking at Mano Rota ('broken hand', a Spanish idiom for consummate skill). Asian, South American and Mediterranean flavours meet in fusion temptations such as Thai-inspired coconut-laced *suquet* (Catalan fish stew), monkfish tagine or shiso-leaf quesadillas. The 12-course tasting menu is decent value at €65.

**Palo Cortao** TAPAS €€

(Map p276; ☎93 188 90 67; www.palocortao.es; Carrer Nou de la Rambla 146; medias raciones €7-10; ⏱8pm-1am Tue-Fri, 1-5pm & 8pm-1am Sat & Sun; Ⓜ Paral·lel) Chicly contemporary and welcoming Palo Cortao is renowned for its beautifully executed seafood and meat *raciones* with hints of Andalucía, accompanied by Jerez sherry and other elegant Spanish wines. Highlights include truffled-chicken cannelloni, fried aubergines with honey and miso, delicate cheese plates, and tuna tataki with *ajo blanco*. Dine at the long bar or seated in the intimate restaurant.

**Casa de Tapas Cañota** TAPAS €€

(Map p276; ☎93 325 91 71; www.casadetapas.com; Carrer de Lleida 7; tapas €5-15; ⏱1-4pm & 7.30pm-midnight Tue-Sat, 1-4pm Sun; Ⓜ Poble Sec) This friendly, unfussy old-timer serves affordable, nicely turned out tapas plates. Seafood is the speciality, with rich razor clams, garlic-fried prawns and tender octopus. Wash it down with a refreshing bottle of *albariño* (a Galician white). Book ahead for weekends. The Iglesias family also runs traditional seafood spot Rías de Galicia next door and Japanese-fusion Espai Kru, just upstairs.

**Xemei** VENETIAN €€

(Map p276; ☎93 553 51 40; www.xemei.es; Passeig de l'Exposició 85; mains €16-25; ⏱1.45-3.30pm & 8.45-11pm, closed 2 weeks Aug; Ⓜ Poble Sec) Everyone's favourite Italian, Xemei ('Twins' in Venetian) is a wonderful, authentically delicious slice of Venice in Barcelona, named for its twin Venetian owners Stefano and Max Colombo. To the accompaniment of gentle jazz and vintage-inspired design, you might try a light burrata salad or Venetian-fish platter, followed by *bigoli* pasta in anchovy-and-onion sauce, squid-ink spaghetti, grilled octopus or seasonal risotto.

**Fàbrica Moritz** GASTROPUB €€

(Map p276; ☎93 426 00 50; www.moritz.com; Ronda de Sant Antoni 41; tapas €4-10, mains €8-18; ⏱8.30am-1.30am Sun-Thu, to 2am Fri & Sat; Ⓜ Sant Antoni) In a building redesigned by architect Jean Nouvel, with a menu created by chef Jordi Vilà of Michelin-starred Alkímia (also on the premises), the popular Moritz brewery restaurant offers pan-European gastropub fare such as gourmet sandwiches, wood-oven-baked eggs, fish and chips, frankfurters with sauerkraut and *flammkuchen* (Alsatian-style pizza). The adjacent wine bar does tapas, vermouth and beer tastings.

**★Enigma** GASTRONOMY €€€

(Map p276; ☎616 696322; www.elbarri.com; Carrer de Sepúlveda 38-40; tasting menu €220; ⏱7-9.30pm Tue-Fri, 1-2.30pm & 7-9.30pm Sat;

Espanya) Resembling a 3D art installation, this conceptual Michelin-star creation from the famed Adrià brothers is a 40-course tour de force of cutting-edge gastronomy across six dining spaces. A meal takes 3½ hours and includes customised cocktail pairings (you can order additional drinks). Minimum of two diners; reserve months in advance (€100 nonrefundable deposit per guest).

**Alkímia** CATALAN €€€

(Map p276; 93 207 61 15; www.alkimia.cat; Ronda de Sant Antoni 41; mains €26-47, tasting menu €138; 1.30-3.30pm & 8-10.30pm Mon-Fri; Universitat) Inside the innovatively redesigned Fàbrica Moritz brewery, amid tile-patterned floors and shimmering white surfaces, culinary alchemist Jordi Vilà creates refined Catalan dishes with a twist that have earned him a Michelin star: potato-and-truffle soufflé, wild fish of the day in shellfish stew, mushrooms with caramelised cabbage and carrot toffee, and other seriously original visions.

**Martínez** SPANISH €€€

(Map p276; 93 106 60 52; www.martinezbarcelona.com; Carretera de Miramar 38; mains €20-35; 1-11pm; 150, Telefèric del Port, Miramar) With a fabulous panorama over the port, stylish Martínez is a standout among Montjuïc's lacklustre dining options. The terrace is ideal for warm-day lunches of the signature rice dishes. There are also oysters, calamari, fresh market fish and other seafood hits, plus cured ham and grilled meats. It's a fine spot for drinks too: the bar stays open until 1.30am or 2.30am.

## Camp Nou, Pedralbes & La Zona Alta

**Tapas 24** TAPAS €

(618 478461; www.carlesabellan.com; Carrer Arístides Maillol 12; tapas €4-12; 9am-9pm; Palau Reial) A culinary jewel just outside the FC Barcelona grounds, Michelin-starred chef Carles Abellán's Tapas 24 delivers all his beloved updated-Catalan signatures like the truffle-and-cured-ham *bikini*, roast-chicken croquettes, *ous estrellats* (fried eggs and chips) and lemon-drizzled anchovies. Branches in L'Eixample (p298) and on **Diagonal** (Map p264; 93 858 93 29; Avinguda Diagonal 520; tapas €4-12; 7.45am-midnight Mon-Fri, from 9am Sat & Sun; Diagonal).

LOCAL KNOWLEDGE

### CARRER DE BLAI

Carrer de Blai in Poble Sec is packed with busy tapas and *pintxos* (Basque tapas) bars, both classic and contemporary, where you can feast on bite-sized deliciousness at €1 to €2 a piece.

**Mitja Vida** TAPAS €

(www.morrofi.cat; Carrer de Brusi 39; tapas €4-8; 6-11.30pm Mon-Thu, noon-4pm & 6-11.30pm Fri & Sat, noon-4pm Sun, closed Aug; FGC Sant Gervasi) A young, fun, mostly local crowd gathers around the stainless-steel tapas bar of Sant Gervasi's tiny Mitja Vida. It's a jovial eating and drinking spot, with good-sized portions of anchovies, calamari, smoked herring, cheeses and *mojama* (salt-cured tuna).

**Vivanda** CATALAN €€

(93 203 19 18; www.vivanda.cat; Carrer Major de Sarrià 134; tapas €4-14, sharing plates €10-22; 1.30-3.30pm & 8.30-11pm Tue-Sat, 1.30-3.30pm Sun; ; FGC Reina Elisenda) Diners are in for a treat with the knockout menu conceived by acclaimed Catalan chef Jordi Vilà, who also runs Sant Antoni's Alkímia (p303). Delicate tapas and *platillos* (sharing plates) showcase the freshest seasonal fare, from artisan cheeses to vegetable ravioli. Hidden behind a reincarnated Sarrià home, the terrace has winter heat lamps, blankets and broths.

**Cerveceria San Fernández** SPANISH €€

(Casa Fernández; 93 201 93 08; www.drymartiniorg.com; Carrer de Santaló 46; tapas €4-12, mains €9-20; 1-5pm & 8pm-midnight Mon-Sat, noon-midnight Sun; FGC Gràcia) The family team behind gracefully old-school L'Eixample bar **Dry Martini** (Map p264; 93 217 50 72; Carrer d'Aribau 162-166; 1pm-2.30am Mon-Thu, 1pm-3am Fri, 6.30pm-3am Sat, 6.30pm-2.30am Sun; FGC Provença) is in charge at this smart, lively, long-running spot decorated with local artwork. With tables on the pavement or inside amid hot-red walls and jazzy murals, its ideal for elegantly yet unfussily prepared Catalan cuisine – Padrón peppers, L'Escala anchovies, *patatas braves*, fried eggs with home-cooked chips – and creative international bites. Next door, the team runs one of Barcelona's oldest cocktail bars, **Gimlet** (93 201 53 06; Carrer de Santaló 46; 6pm-1am Mon-Wed, to 2.30am Thu, to 3am Fri & Sat; T1, T2, T3 Francesc Macià, FGC Muntaner).

**La Molina** CATALAN €€
(☎93 417 11 24; www.restaurantemolina.net; Passeig de Sant Gervasi 65; mains €11-17; ⏰10am-11pm Tue-Thu, to midnight Fri, 11am-5pm Sat & Sun; FGC Avinguda Tibidabo) Charming La Molina looks like a typical fuss-free tapas hang-out at first glance – pavement tables, nondescript bar in front – but out the back you'll discover one of the neighbourhood's great unsung updated-Catalan restaurants. Menus change with the seasons, but might include creamy octopus rice, steamed white-wine mussels or stewed snails, all cooked with care and beautifully presented.

★**La Balsa** MEDITERRANEAN €€€
(☎93 211 50 48; www.labalsarestaurant.com; Carrer de la Infanta Isabel 4; mains €21-28; ⏰1.30-3.15pm & 8.30-10.30pm; 📶; FGC Avinguda Tibidabo) With its grand ceiling and scented gardens surrounding a main terrace dining area, La Balsa is one of the city's premier dining addresses, founded in 1979. The seasonally changing menu mixes traditional Catalan flavours and creative expression: suckling pig with apple and cardamom, scallops with cabbage and Iberian pork loin, for example. Lounge over a cocktail at the bar.

### BARRI GÒTIC CAFES

Some of Barcelona's most atmospheric cafes lie hidden in the Barri Gòtic.

**Caelum** An evocative coffee shop with medieval ruins.

**Salterio** (Map p244; ☎93 302 50 28; www.facebook.com/teteriasalterio; Carrer de Salomó Ben Adret 4; ⏰noon-midnight; 📶; M Jaume I) Fragrant mint teas and Turkish coffee in a candlelit teahouse.

**Satan's Coffee Corner** (Map p244; ☎666 222 599; www.satanscoffee.com; Carrer de l'Arc de Sant Ramón del Call 11; ⏰9am-6pm Mon-Fri, from 10am Sat & Sun; M Liceu, Jaume I) Punk-inspired Satan's is all about local roasters.

**Granja La Pallaresa** (Map p244; ☎93 302 20 36; Carrer del Petritxol 11; ⏰9am-1pm & 4-9pm Mon-Sat, 9am-1pm & 5-9pm Sun, closed Jul; 📶; M Liceu) Crispy churros with hot chocolate at a 1940s hangout.

# Drinking & Nightlife

## La Rambla & Barri Gòtic

★**Bar Zim** WINE BAR
(Map p244; www.formatgerialaseu.com; Carrer de la Dagueria 20; ⏰6-11pm Mon-Sat; 📶; M Jaume I) From the welcoming team behind the terrific Formatgeria La Seu (next door) comes this teensy, intimate, cavern-like bar where Catalan (Penedès, Empordà) and lesser-known Spanish wines (glass €3.60) take centre stage below beamed ceilings. Pair with one of the delicate platters of local cheeses or cold cuts with artisan jams – now this is why you came to Barcelona.

★**Caelum** CAFE
(Map p244; ☎93 302 69 93; www.facebook.com/CaelumBarcelona; Carrer de la Palla 8; ⏰10am-8.30pm Mon-Thu, to 9pm Fri-Sun; 📶; M Liceu) Centuries of heavenly Spanish gastronomic tradition collide at this exquisite medieval space in the heart of the city, which stocks sweets made by nuns across the country (including irresistible Toledo marzipan). The ground-floor cafe is a dainty setting for decadent cakes and pastries. In the stone-walled underground chamber, flickering candles cast a glow on the ruins of a medieval bathhouse.

**L'Ascensor** COCKTAIL BAR
(Map p244; ☎93 318 53 47; Carrer de la Bellafila 3; ⏰6pm-2.30am Sun-Thu, to 3am Fri & Sat; 📶; M Jaume I) Named after the lift (elevator) doors that serve as the front entrance, this clandestine drinking hideout – with its brick ceilings, vintage mirrors and marble-topped tables – gathers a faithful crowd for old-fashioned cocktails (from €7) and lively conversation against a soundtrack of up-tempo jazz and funk.

**Polaroid** BAR
(Map p244; ☎93 186 66 69; www.polaroidbar.es; Carrer dels Còdols 29; ⏰7.30pm-2.30am Sun-Thu, to 3am Fri & Sat; 📶; M Drassanes) For a dash of 1980s nostalgia, Polaroid is a blast from the past, with its wall-mounted VHS tapes, old film posters, comic-book-covered tables, action-figure displays and other kitschy decor. Not surprisingly, it draws a fun, unpretentious crowd who come for cheap *cañas* (draught beer), mojitos (from €6) and free popcorn.

**Bar Boadas** COCKTAIL BAR

(Map p244; ☎93 318 95 92; www.boadascocktails.com; Carrer dels Tallers 1; ⊙noon-2am Mon-Thu, to 3am Fri & Sat; Ⓜ Catalunya) One of Barcelona's oldest cocktail bars, Boadas is famed for its daiquiris. Amid old monochrome photos and a polished-wood bar, bow-tied waiters have been mixing unique, deliciously drinkable creations since Miguel Boadas opened it in 1933 – Miró and Hemingway both drank here. Miguel was born in Havana, where he was the first barman at the immortal El Floridita.

##  El Raval

Despite its vestigial edginess, this is a great place to go out. The lower end of El Raval has a history of insalubriousness and the area around Carrer de Sant Pau retains its seedy feel: drug dealers, pickpockets and prostitutes mingle with nocturnal hedonists. Keep your wits about you at night.

**★Two Schmucks** COCKTAIL BAR

(Map p244; ☎635 396 088; www.facebook.com/schmuckordie; Carrer de Joaquín Costa 52; ⊙5pm-2am Sun-Fri, to 2.30am Sat; Ⓜ Sant Antoni, Universitat) Originally a wandering pop-up bar, seriously edgy yet refreshingly unpretentious Swedish-run Two Schmucks has become one of Barcelona's (and Europe's) most talked-about cocktail bars, with ambitious owner-bartenders Moe and AJ sweeping multiple awards. Channelling a glammed-up dive-bar vibe, with recycled furniture and a fun friendly team, it mixes outstanding liquid concoctions like the signature Curry Colada (€9).

**★La Confiteria** BAR

(Map p244; ☎93 140 54 35; www.confiteria.cat; Carrer de Sant Pau 128; ⊙7pm-2am Mon-Thu, 6pm-3am Fri & Sat, 5pm-2am Sun; 📶; Ⓜ Paral·lel) This evocative tile-covered cocktail hang-out is a trip back to the 19th century. Until the 1980s it was a confectioner's shop, and though the original cabinets are now bursting with booze, the look barely changed with its conversion courtesy of one of Barcelona's foremost teams in nightlife wizardry. The scene these days is lively and creative.

**Casa Almirall** BAR

(Map p244; ☎93 318 99 17; www.casaalmirall.com; Carrer de Joaquín Costa 33; ⊙4.30pm-1.30am Mon, 4pm-2.30am Tue & Wed, noon-2.30am Thu, noon-3am Fri & Sat, noon-12.30am Sun; 📶; Ⓜ Universitat) In business since 1860, this unchanged corner bar is dark and intriguing, with Modernista decor and a mixed clientele. There are some great original pieces in here, such as the marble counter, and the cast-iron statue of the muse of the Universal Exposition, held in Barcelona in 1888. Absinthe and vermouth star on the menu.

### VERMOUTH REVIVAL

The classic Barcelona drink is a hardy vermouth – red or white wine infused with botanicals and fortified with brandy. Thought to have arrived in Catalonia in the mid-19th century, vermouth has experienced a dazzling revival over the last decade. Now, new vermouth bars are opening all over town and historical vermouth joints are more popular than ever. Join the *barcelonins* for *la hora del vermut* (the hour of vermouth), typically around noon and accompanied by tapas. The perfect vermouth is served over ice and with an olive, and, sometimes, a slice of orange.

**Bar Marsella** BAR

(Map p244; ☎93 442 72 63; Carrer de Sant Pau 65; ⊙6pm-2am Mon-Thu, 10pm-3am Fri, 6pm-2.30am Sat, 10pm-2.30am Sun; Ⓜ Liceu) Bar Marsella has been in business since 1820, and has served the likes of Dalí, Picasso, Gaudí and Hemingway. The latter was known to slump here over an *absenta* (absinthe) amid the tiled floors and glinting chandeliers. The bar still specialises in absinthe (€5), a drink to be treated with respect.

**Bar Pastís** BAR

(Map p244; ☎634 031 527; www.facebook.com/barpastisraval; Carrer de Santa Mònica 4; ⊙7.30pm-2am Tue-Sun; 📶; Ⓜ Drassanes) A French-cabaret theme (with lots of Piaf on the stereo) pervades this tiny, cluttered classic, which has been going, on and off, since the end of WWII, when it was founded by a French exile. You'll need to be in before 9pm to have any hope of sitting at or getting near the bar. Frequent live performances usually include French *chanson*.

**Granja M Viader** CAFE

(Map p244; ☎93 318 34 86; www.granjaviader.cat; Carrer d'en Xuclà 6; ⊙9am-1.15pm & 5-9pm Mon-Sat; Ⓜ Liceu) For over a century, people have been coming to this classically Catalan milk bar for hot chocolate ladled out with whipped cream (ask for a *suís*). The interior is delightfully old fashioned, with marble-top tables and floor tiling. It also sells cheeses, cakes and charcuterie. In 1931 the Viader clan invented Cacaolat, a bottled chocolate milk drink with iconic label design.

**La Monroe** BAR

(Map p244; 93 441 94 61; www.lamonroe.es; Plaça Salvador Seguí 1-9; noon-late; ; M Liceu) Peer through the glass walls of this lively LGBTQI-friendly hang-out inside the Filmoteca de Catalunya (p312), and you'll spot long wooden tables, rickety chairs, leafy plants, industrial touches and a cobbled floor that mimics the square outside. Great cocktails and vermouth, a €12 *menú del dia* and delectable tapas (€4 to €12) like grilled Huelva prawns and Catalan *fuet* (thin pork sausage).

**33 | 45** BAR

(Map p244; 93 187 41 38; www.facebook.com/3345bar; Carrer de Joaquín Costa 4; 5pm-2am Mon, 1pm-2am Tue-Thu, to 2.30am Fri & Sat, to 1.30am Sun; ; M Sant Antoni) A wonderfully low-key yet stylish bar on a street full of them, this busy industrial-chic place has excellent mojitos (€5 to €7), a fashionable crowd and a frequently changing exhibition of art on the walls. There are DJs most nights and sofas for kicking back over coffee.

**Moog** CLUB

(Map p244; 93 319 17 89; www.moogbarcelona.com; Carrer de l'Arc del Teatre 3; entry €5-10; midnight-5am Sun-Thu, to 5.30am Fri & Sat; M Drassanes) This fun and minuscule club is a standing favourite with the downtown crowd. In the main dance area, DJs dish out house, techno and electro, while upstairs you can groove to indie.

### PORT OLÍMPIC CLUB CLOSURES

The Port Olímpic's heaving clubs have become a growing source of conflict in recent years, with reports of robberies (often targeting tourists), disruptive drunken behaviour, serious fights and even several deaths. The city is expected to close down most clubs here (including legendary spots like Pacha, Opium, CDLC, Catwalk and Shôko), and refocus the area towards outdoor activities.

## La Ribera & El Born

**★ Dr Stravinsky** COCKTAIL BAR

(Map p252; 93 157 12 33; www.drstravinsky.cat; Carrer dels Mirallers 5; 6pm-2.30am; M Jaume I) At this alchemist-inspired temple to crafted-cocktail wizardry, named one of the World's 50 Best Bars in 2019, mixologist Antonio Naranjo and team prepare knockout signature drinks (€8 to €13) using house-made gin, their own essential oils and other home-grown ingredients. Behind chilli-red doors, the centuries-old building has been reborn in lab-like, vintage-loving style, with herb jars and flasks on walls.

**★ Paradiso/Pastrami Bar** COCKTAIL BAR

(Map p252; 639 310671; www.paradiso.cat; Carrer de Rera Palau 4; 7pm-1.15am Sun-Thu, to 2.15am Fri & Sat; ; M Barceloneta) A kind of Narnia-in-reverse, Paradiso is fronted by a snowy-white wardrobe-sized space, with pastrami sandwiches, pulled pork and other home-cured delights. But this is only the portal – step through the fridge door into a glam, sexy speakeasy guaranteed to raise the most world-weary of eyebrows, where highly creative, artfully prepared cocktails (€9 to €12) steal the show. Worth queueing for.

**★ Nømad Cøffee Lab & Shop** COFFEE

(Map p252; 628 566235; www.nomadcoffee.es; Passatge de Sert 12; 8.30am-5pm Mon-Fri; M Urquinaona) King of Barcelona's third-wave coffee scene, Nømad is known for its seasonally sourced, small-batch, Barcelona-roasted beans and experimental techniques. Owner and barista Jordi Mestre was inspired by his time in London and, at this snug, minimalist, lab-style cafe, it's all about coffee tastings and expertly poured espresso, flat whites, cold brews and Aeropress (€2 to €5).

Also branches in **El Raval** (Map p244; Carrer de Joaquín Costa 26; 8.30am-6.30pm Mon-Fri, 10am-7pm Sat & Sun; M Sant Antoni, Universitar) and **El Poblenou** (Map p258; Carrer de Pujades 95; 9am-5pm Mon-Fri; M Bogatell).

**Guzzo** COCKTAIL BAR

(Map p252; 93 667 00 36; www.guzzorestaurante.es; Plaça Comercial 10; 7-11.30pm Mon-Fri, 1-4pm & 7-11.30pm Sat & Sun; ; M Jaume I) With good vibes anytime of day, this old-school cocktail bar is run by much-loved Barcelona DJ Fred Guzzo, who is often at the decks spinning his delicious selection of funk, soul and rare groove. You'll also find frequent live-music acts.

**Mag by El Magnífico** COFFEE

(Map p252; 93 488 57 86; www.facebook.com/magbyelmagnifico; Carrer de Grunyí 10; 10am-6pm Fri-Sun; M Jaume I) One of Barcelona's best coffee roasters, El Magnífico (p316) now runs this stylish, Scandi-esque corner cafe breathing new life into a beautiful 19th-century building with wooden beams, Catalan arched ceilings, original stained glass and huge roasting machines.

**Bar Sauvage** COCKTAIL BAR

(Map p252; 93 832 51 84; https://barsauvage.com; Passeig del Born 13; 7pm-3am; M Jaume I) The ever-so-slightly more relaxed sister to party-hard **Creps al Born** (Map p252; 93 269 03 25; www.facebook.com/CrepsalBorn; Passeig del Born 12; 6pm-3am Mon-Fri, noon-4am Sat, noon-2am Sun; M Jaume I) across the road, this elegant good-time cocktail bar expertly knocks up original, fruity, herb-infused liquid mixes based on Latin spirits (€10 to €12), as well as Peruvian-Mexican street-food bites. Downstairs in the basement is a moody party lounge where DJs play.

**La Vinya del Senyor** WINE BAR

(Map p252; 93 310 33 79; www.facebook.com/vinyadelsenyor; Plaça de Santa Maria del Mar 5; noon-1am Sun-Thu, to 2am Fri & Sat; ; M Jaume I) Relax on the terrace in the shadow of the Basílica de Santa Maria del Mar or crowd into the tiny bottle-lined bar. From Priorat to Languedoc, the wine list is as long as *War and Peace*, with 20 drops by the glass. Cheese platters and cold meats keep you going. There's an even more intimate space up the twirling staircase.

**El Xampanyet** WINE BAR

(Map p252; 93 319 70 03; www.elxampanyet.es; Carrer de Montcada 22; noon-3.30pm & 7-11pm Tue-Sat, noon-3.30pm Sun; ; M Jaume I) Nothing has changed for decades at chaotic El Xampanyet, one of Barcelona's best-known *cava* (sparkling wine) bars. It's usually packed, but plant yourself at the bar or grab a table against the decoratively tiled walls for a glass or three of the house *cava* and delicious homemade tapas such as tangy *boquerones* (anchovies) in vinegar.

**El Diset** WINE BAR

(Map p252; 93 268 19 87; www.facebook.com/eldiset; Carrer Antic de Sant Joan 3; 7pm-2am Mon-Thu, to 3am Fri, 1pm-3am Sat, 1pm-2am Sun; M Barceloneta) Dealing almost exclusively in Catalan drops, El Disset is a sleek, candlelit wine, cocktail and tapas bar that also does tastings. Thin *torrades* (toasted bread) topped with, say, goat's cheese and stir-fried vegetables or tuna tataki and tapas of Catalan cheeses accompany glasses (€4 to €7) of Terra Alta, Montsant, Penedès, Priorat and more.

**La Catalista** WINE BAR

(Map p252; 93 212 87 75; www.lacatalista.com; Carrer dels Carders 11; 2pm-late Tue-Fri, 10am-late Sat, 10am-4pm Sun; ; M Jaume I) Draped greenery, a marble-topped bar and exposed-stone walls make a stylish setting for sampling Catalan wines (glass €4 to €6) sourced from artisan producers committed to local grapes, many of them organic, natural or biodynamic. Chef Laila Bazham, of Asian-fusion hit Hawker 45 (p298), is behind the creative pairing dishes, such as in-season mushrooms or grilled vegetables with labneh and black-garlic hummus.

**Bar de l'Antic Teatre** BAR

(Map p252; 93 315 23 54; www.anticteatre.com; Carrer Verdaguer i Callís 12; 10am-11.30pm Mon-Thu, to midnight Fri, 5pm-midnight Sat, 5-11.30pm Sun; ; M Urquinaona) There's often a queue for tables on the buzzy boho garden terrace at this relaxed community cafe-bar. It's set in the shade of a fig tree hidden away in a 17th-century building, down an alley opposite the Palau de la Música Catalana. Perfect for morning coffee, or beers and wine (€3) later on; proceeds go towards the Antic Teatre's cultural projects.

## Barceloneta, the Waterfront & El Poblenou

**★Perikete** WINE BAR

(Map p258; 93 024 22 29; www.gruporeini.com; Carrer de Llauder 6; noon-1am; M Barceloneta) Since opening in 2017, this fabulous wine spot has been jam-packed with *barcelonins* and visitors. Jabugo hams hang from the ceiling, vermouth barrels sit above the bar and wine bottles cram every available shelf space. There are over 200 varieties by the glass or bottle, accompanied by excellent tapas (€4 to €10) like made-to-order tortilla.

**Espai Joliu** CAFE

(Map p258; 93 023 24 92; www.facebook.com/espaijoliu; Carrer Badajoz 95; 9am-7pm Mon-Fri, 10am-3pm Sat; ; M Llacuna) Inspired by its owner's time in Berlin, this charmingly stylish former carpenters' workshop is Barcelona's original plants-and-coffee concept cafe (much-copied since). Potted plants, design mags and ceramics are sold up the front, while the peaceful cafe has recycled timber furniture, stone walls and exposed bulbs, and serves Barcelona-roasted Nømad coffee (€2 to €3) and organic cakes (try the gluten-free lemon-and-rosemary).

**Bodega Vidrios y Cristales** WINE BAR

(Map p258; ☎93 250 45 01; www.gruposagardi.com; Passeig d'Isabel II 6; ⊙noon-midnight; Ⓜ Barceloneta) In a history-steeped, stone-floored 1840 building, this atmospheric little jewel recreates an old-style neighbourhood bodega with tins of sardines, anchovies and other delicacies lining the shelves (and used in exquisite tapas, €3 to €15), house-made vermouth and a wonderful array of wines, including Andalucian *manzanilla* (sherry from Sanlúcar de Barrameda). A handful of upturned wine barrels let you rest your glass.

**Can Paixano** WINE BAR

(La Xampanyeria; Map p258; ☎93 310 08 39; www.canpaixano.com; Carrer de la Reina Cristina 7; ⊙9am-10.30pm Mon-Sat; Ⓜ Barceloneta) This lofty double-name *cava* bar has long been run on a winning formula: its own super-affordable bubbly rosé, served in elegant little glasses and combined with bite-sized *entrepans* and tapas (€2 to €4). It's usually packed, so elbowing your way to the bar can be a titanic struggle.

**Balius** COCKTAIL BAR

(Map p258; ☎93 315 86 50; www.baliusbar.com; Carrer de Pujades 196; ⊙5.30pm-1.30am Mon-Wed, to 2.30am Thu, 5pm-3am Fri & Sat, 5pm-1.30am Sun; Ⓜ Poblenou) There's an old-fashioned jauntiness to this vintage-style cocktail den in El Poblenou, marked by its original-period exterior with tiles and gin bottles in the window. Staff pour classic cocktails (€8 to €10) as well as vermouths, and there's a small tapas menu (€3 to €7) of nachos, cheeses, *patates braves* and so on. Stop by on Sunday for live jazz around 8pm.

**Madame George** COCKTAIL BAR

(Map p258; www.madamegeorgebar.com; Carrer de Pujades 179; ⊙6pm-2am Mon-Thu, to 3am Fri & Sat, to 12.30am Sun; Ⓜ Poblenou) A theatrical elegance marks the interior of this small, chandelier-lit lounge just off the Rambla del Poblenou. Deft bartenders stir well-balanced cocktails like a Lychee-tini (€9; vanilla-infused vodka, fresh lychees, homemade lychee liqueur and lime juice) in vintage glassware, while a DJ spins vinyl (mainly soul and funk) in the corner.

**BlackLab** MICROBREWERY

(Map p258; ☎93 221 83 60; www.blacklab.es; Plaça de Pau Vila 1; ⊙10.30am-2am daily Mar-Oct, 4-11pm Mon-Thu, 11.30am-1am Fri-Sun Nov-Feb; Ⓜ Barceloneta) Barcelona's first brewhouse opened in 2014 inside the 19th-century Palau de Mar (p257). Its taps feature 16 house-made brews, including saisons, double IPAs and dry stouts, and brewmaster Matt Boder is constantly experimenting. The kitchen sizzles up Asian-American bites (€4 to €10): burgers, dumplings, ramen. One-hour tours (€20; English/Spanish 5pm/6pm Sunday) take you behind the scenes, with a four-beer tasting.

**La Violeta** WINE BAR

(Map p258; ☎93 221 95 81; www.facebook.com/lavioletavinosnaturales; Carrer del Baluard 58; ⊙1-11pm; Ⓜ Barceloneta) A regularly changing line-up of natural wines (glass €3.50 to €5.50), both Spanish and international, wanders into the spotlight at this cosy bar with terrace tables and mismatched wooden furniture. There are plenty of exciting Catalan picks (try the Conca de Barberà *albariño* blend), as well as lovingly made slow-food tapas (€6 to €10) starring market-fresh fish and home-grown vegetables.

**Blue Wave** COCKTAIL BAR

(Map p258; ☎93 484 23 15; www.restaurantmarinaportvell.com; Moll de l'Escar 1; ⊙10am-2am; Ⓜ Barceloneta) Right on the water, this prize-winning, marine-inspired bar is designed like a tumbling wave, with shimmering blue tiling, earthy tones on the terrace, bobbing mega-yachts out front and exquisite sunsets. Catalan wines and well-prepared

DON'T MISS

### HIDDEN ALFRESCO BARS

Many Barcelona hotels house wonderful open-air bars. Some favourites:

Jardí del Alma, Alma (p288)

Batuar Terrace, Cotton House (p288)

Jardí Diana, El Palace (p288)

The Rooftop, Sir Victor (p288)

The Roof, Barcelona Edition (p286)

La Isabela, Hotel 1898 (p284)

cocktails (€15) shine, while elegant meals (mains €18 to €28) await in the restaurant. It's a glamorous place, so don't rock up straight from the beach.

## La Sagrada Família & L'Eixample

**Milano** COCKTAIL BAR

(Map p264; 93 112 71 50; www.camparimilano.com; Ronda de la Universitat 35; 1pm-4am, hours can vary; Catalunya) Subtly signed from street level, this gem of hidden Barcelona nightlife is a subterranean old-school cocktail bar with red-velvet banquettes and glass-fronted cabinets, presided over by white-jacketed waiters. Live music (Cuban, jazz, blues, flamenco, swing) plays nightly (schedules online); DJs take over after 11pm. Fantastic cocktails include the rum-infused Hemingway and seven different Bloody Marys (€10 to €15).

**Cosmo** CAFE

(Map p264; 93 105 79 92; www.galeriacosmo.com; Carrer d'Enric Granados 3; 10am-10pm; Universitat) Set on a pedestrian strip just behind the university, this cool cafe/cultural space has bicycles hanging from high, white walls and bright splashy murals, and even makes a feature of its fire hose. Along with fresh juices, hot chocolate, teas and pastries, it serves arty brunches and Nømad (p306) coffee, not to mention beer and wine.

**Garage Beer Co** CRAFT BEER

(Map p264; 93 528 59 89; www.garagebeer.co; Carrer del Consell de Cent 261; noon-midnight Sun-Thu, to 3am Fri & Sat; Universitat) One of the original craft-beer bars to pop up in Barcelona, Garage brews its own in a space at the bar and at its out-of-town brewery, and offers around 10 different styles at a time. The Ocata (a delicate session IPA) and Soup (a more robust IPA) are always on the board; other favourites include Circus Tears (an Imperial stout).

**Monkey Factory** COCKTAIL BAR

(Map p264; 93 270 31 16; www.facebook.com/monkeyfactorybcn; Carrer de Còrsega 234; 6.30pm-3am Tue-Sat; FGC Provença) DJs spin on weekends at this high-spirited venue but it's positively hopping from early on most nights, often hosting language-exchange sessions. Funky Monkey (triple sec, gin, lime and egg white), Chimpa Sour (cardamom-infused pisco sour) and Chita Tai (rum, lime, cacao, triple sec and almond syrup) are among the inventive cocktails mixed up behind the green-neon-lit bar.

### BEACH BARS

During summer, small bars known as *xiringuitos* (*chiringuitos* in Spanish) open up on the sand, many with party vibes and DJs. We love barefoot-chic **La Deliciosa** (Map p258; 93 309 12 91; www.panteabeach.com; Platja de Sant Miquel; 9am-midnight Mar-Nov; ; Barceloneta) and Polynesian-inspired **Vai Moana** (Map p258; 93 309 12 91; www.panteabeach.com; Avinguda del Litoral, Platja del Bogatell; 9am-late Mar-Nov; H16, V25, V27, Llacuna).

**El Viti** BAR

(Map p264; 93 633 83 36; www.elviti.com; Passeig de Sant Joan 62; noon-midnight Sun-Thu, to 1am Fri & Sat; ; Girona) Along fashionable Passeig de Sant Joan, modern-rustic El Viti ticks all the nouveau-tavern boxes – black subway tiles, soaring ceilings, open-brick walls, marble-top tables and a barrel of artisan vermouth on the bar. Inventive tapas (€4 to €11) take in smoked-aubergine croquettes, Castilian cheeses and squid.

**Hemingway** COCKTAIL BAR

(Map p264; 93 129 67 93; http://hemingwaybcn.com; Carrer de Muntaner 114; 4pm-2.30am Sun-Thu, to 3am Fri & Sat; Hospital Clínic) There's often a queue out the door for a table at this intimate, speakeasy-style basement cocktail den with a tiny front terrace. International whiskies, rare gins and lightly imaginative cocktails crafted with fresh-pressed citrus juices are owner-barista Luca Izzo's specialities; try the best-selling gin-based Montgomery (infused with ginger and Earl Grey tea; €12) or a classic G&T (€12).

## Gràcia & Park Güell

★**Bobby Gin** COCKTAIL BAR

(Map p272; 93 368 18 92; www.bobbygin.com; Carrer de Francisco Giner 47; 5pm-2am Sun-Thu, to 3am Fri & Sat; ; Diagonal) With over 80 varieties, this whitewashed stone-walled bar is a haven for gin lovers, and arguably Barcelona's top spot for a perfectly mixed, artfully garnished, goblet-sized G&T. Try an

## LGBTIQ+ BARCELONA

Barcelona has a vibrant LGBTIQ+ scene, with a lively array of bars, clubs, restaurants and even specialised bookshops in the 'Gaixample', an area of L'Eixample about five to six blocks southwest of Passeig de Gràcia around Carrer del Consell de Cent. Other LGBTQI-focused venues are dotted around Sant Antoni and Poble Sec.

**Metro Disco** (Map p276; ☎93 323 52 27; www.metrodiscobcn.com; Carrer de Sepúlveda 185; cover from €5; ⏰midnight-5am Sun-Thu, to 6.30am Fri & Sat; Ⓜ Universitat) The original gay club.

**Axel Hotel** (Map p264; ☎93 323 93 93; www.axelhotels.com; Carrer d'Aribau 33; r from €150; ❄📶🏊; Ⓜ Universitat) Stylish gay boutique hotel in the Gaixample.

**Arena Classic** (Map p264; ☎93 487 83 42; www.grupoarena.com; Carrer de la Diputació 233; cover incl drink Fri & Sat €6-12; ⏰11pm-3am Thu, to 6am Fri & Sat; Ⓜ Passeig de Gràcia) Hosts Barcelona's top lesbian club night, Aire.

**La Federica** (Map p276; ☎93 600 59 01; www.facebook.com/barlafederica; Carrer de Salvà 3; ⏰7pm-1am Tue, to 2am Wed & Thu, to 3am Fri & Sat; Ⓜ Paral·lel) Lively Poble Sec LGBTIQ+ bar.

**El Cangrejo** (Map p244; www.facebook.com/elcangrejodelraval; Carrer de Montserrat 9; entry incl drink €10; ⏰11pm-3am Fri & Sat; Ⓜ Drassanes) Popular bar duo; drag shows at the Raval branch.

**Arena Madre** (Map p264; ☎93 487 83 42; www.grupoarena.com; Carrer de Balmes 32; cover incl drink €10-12; ⏰12.30-5am Sun-Thu, to 6am Fri & Sat; Ⓜ Passeig de Gràcia) A top LGBTIQ+ club.

infusion-based concoction (€10 to €12), such as citrus-infused Nordés, or a cocktail like the L'Aperitiu Modernista, with cardamom bitters and thistle liqueur.

**El Ciclista** COCKTAIL BAR

(Map p272; ☎93 368 53 02; www.elciclistabar.com; Carrer de Mozart 18; ⏰7.30pm-2am Mon-Thu, to 3am Fri & Sat; Ⓜ Diagonal) As the name suggests, this elegant little cocktail bar is Barcelona's original cycle-themed boozy hang-out – expect bike-wheel chandeliers and tables, handlebar pieces, and bicycle frames on the walls. Among the list of classic cocktails is an excellent selection of gin and tonics, as well as plenty of flavoured mojitos.

**SlowMov** COFFEE

(Map p272; ☎93 667 27 15; www.slowmov.com; Carrer de Luis Antúnez 18; ⏰8.30am-3pm Tue-Fri, 10am-2pm Sat; 📶; Ⓜ Diagonal) 🍃 SlowMov founders Carmen and François work directly with coffee producers to responsibly source their seasonal, single-origin beans, which are roasted on-site at this light-flooded cafe with original floral-tiled floors, shared tables and local artwork. Laptop workers gather for flat whites (€2.50), coffee events are organised, and organic winesline shelves.

**Elephanta** COCKTAIL BAR

(Map p272; ☎93 237 69 06; www.elephanta.cat; Carrer del Torrent d'En Vidalet 37; ⏰6pm-1.30am Mon-Thu, to 3am Fri & Sat, to 12.30am Sun; 📶; Ⓜ Joanic) Off Gràcia's main drag, this petite cocktail bar has an old-fashioned feel, with plush green banquettes, art-lined walls and a five-seat bar with vintage stools. Gin (€8 to €12) is the drink of choice, with citrusy, botanical and classic dry options, including a selection of Catalan gins. Snacks include hummus, *empanades* and *torrades*.

**El Rabipelao** COCKTAIL BAR

(Map p272; ☎93 182 50 35; www.elrabipelao.com; Carrer del Torrent d'En Vidalet 22; ⏰7pm-1.30am Mon-Thu, to 3am Fri & Sat, 1-4.30pm & 7pm-1.30am Sun; Ⓜ Joanic) With DJs spinning salsa beats, occasional live music and a covered back patio, El Rabi is a celebratory space. Silent films play, red-washed walls are decorated with vintage photos, and there's a colourful mural above the bar. Gins and Caribbean rums and tropical cocktails (€6 to €10) like mojitos and caipirinhas pair with Venezuelan snacks such as *arepas* (filled cornbread patties).

**Viblioteca** WINE BAR

(Map p272; ☎93 284 42 02; www.viblioteca.com; Carrer de Vallfogona 12; ⏰7pm-midnight; Ⓜ Fontana) A glass cabinet piled high with ripe cheese (over 50 varieties), sourced from small-scale European producers, entices you into this small, white, cleverly designed contemporary space. The real speciality at Vibilioteca, however, is wine, and you can choose from 150 mostly local labels, many of them available by the glass.

**Syra Coffee** COFFEE
(Map p272; http://syra.coffee; Carrer de la Mare de Déu dels Desamparats 8; ⏲8am-7pm Mon-Fri, from 9am Sat, from 10am Sun; Ⓜ Joanic) A loyal crowd of regulars swings by teensy check-floored Syra for takeaway coffees (€2 to €3), accompanied by delicate Moroccan pastries, cookies and doughnuts. Its coffees are brewed with seasonal, single-origin, sustainably produced beans roasted at its shop just up the street. Syra also has a **Poblenou branch** (Map p258; Carrer de Pujades 100; ⏲9am-6pm Mon-Fri; Ⓜ Bogatell).

**La Vermu** BAR
(Map p272; ☎695 925012; www.facebook.com/lavermubcn; Carrer de Sant Domènec 15; ⏲6.30pm-midnight Mon-Thu, 12.30pm-12.30am Fri-Sun; FGC Gràcia) House-made *negre* (black) and *blanc* (white) vermouth (€2 to €3), served with a slice of orange and an olive, is the speciality of this stylish neighbourhood bar. The airy space with exposed timber beams, red trim and industrial lighting centres on a marble bar. Vermouth aside, it also has a small, stellar wine list and smartly presented tapas.

**La Nena** CAFE
(Map p272; ☎93 285 14 76; https://la-nena-chocolate-cafe.business.site; Carrer de Ramón y Cajal 36; ⏲8.30am-10.30pm Mon-Fri, from 9am Sat & from 9.30am Sun; ; Ⓜ Fontana) At this delightfully chaotic cafe, indulge in cups of *suïssos* (rich hot chocolate) served with heavy homemade whipped cream and *melindros* (spongy sweet biscuits), desserts, cakes and a few savoury dishes (including crêpes). The place is filled with old-fashioned photos, toys and board games.

## Montjuïc, Poble Sec & Sant Antoni

Poble Sec and neighbouring Sant Antoni host chic cafes, creative bars and busy clubs. Some of Barcelona's best LGBTIQ+ nightlife spots (p310) are here too.

**★La Caseta del Migdia** BAR
(☎617 956572; www.lacaseta.org; Mirador del Migdia; ⏲8pm-1am Wed-Fri, noon-1am Sat & Sun Apr-Sep, noon-sunset Sat & Sun Oct-Mar; 150) The effort of getting to what is, for all intents and purposes, a simple *xiringuito* (summer snack bar) perched atop Montjuïc's seaward slopes, is worth it. Gaze out on the Mediterranean over a beer or soft drink by day. As sunset approaches, the atmosphere changes, as reggae, samba and funk waft out over the hillside. Food is fired on outdoor grills.

The team also runs a view-washed tapas bar overlooking Montjuïc's municipal pools, **Salts Montjuïc** (Map p276; ☎616 893356; www.saltsmontjuic.com; Avinguda de Miramar 31; ⏲10am-midnight Sun-Wed & Thu, to 1am Fri & Sat; 55, 150).

**★Abirradero** MICROBREWERY
(Map p276; ☎93 461 94 46; www.abirradero.com; Carrer de Vilà i Vilà 77; ⏲noon-midnight Sun-Thu, to 2am Fri & Sat; ; Ⓜ Paral·lel) Barcelona is spoilt for choice with craft breweries, and this bright, buzzing space is one of the best. There are 40 of its own beers rotating on the taps, including IPAral·lel (a double IPA), Imperial Choco-Icecream-Cookies Stout, and Trigotopia. Tapas, sharing boards and burgers are standouts from the kitchen (dishes €5 to €14). You'll occasionally catch live jazz and blues here.

**Bar Calders** BAR
(Map p276; ☎93 329 93 49; Carrer del Parlament 25; ⏲5pm-2am Mon-Thu, to 2.30am Fri, 11am-2.30am Sat, 11am-12.30am Sun; Ⓜ Poble Sec) Neighbourhood fave Bar Calders bills itself as a wine bar, with a range of Catalan drops gracing its selection (glass €2 to €4). At weekends it's unbeatable as an all-day cafe, tapas and vermouth bar, and its outdoor tables on a tiny pedestrian lane have become the go-to meeting point for Sant Antoni's boho set.

**La Terrrazza** CLUB
(Map p276; ☎687 969825; http://laterrrazza.com; Avinguda de Francesc Ferrer i Guàrdia 13, Poble Espanyol; cover €10-15; ⏲midnight-6.30am Thu-Sat May-Sep; 13, 23, 150, Ⓜ Espanya) Come summer, this re-created Balearic-style mansion attracts squadrons of beautiful people, locals and visitors alike, for a full-on night of music (mainly house, techno and electronica), cocktails and vaguely Ibiza vibes. It's set partly under the stars, inside the Poble Espanyol (p274) complex.

## Camp Nou, Pedralbes & La Zona Alta

**El Maravillas** COCKTAIL BAR

(☎93 360 73 78; www.elmaravillas.cat; Plaça de la Concòrdia 15; ⊙noon-midnight Sun-Tue, to 1am Wed, to 2am Thu, to 3am Fri & Sat; M Les Corts, T1, T2, T3 Numància) Overlooking Les Corts' peaceful Plaça de la Concòrdia, El Maravillas is an escape from the crowded Ciutat Vella (Old City), filled with tiled floors, marble-top tables and mirrored walls. Andreu Estríngana, one of Spain's top mixologists, and team concoct creative cocktails (€7 to €12) named for celebrated sports players. Spanish wines and easy-drinking vermouths are other drinks of choice.

**Mirablau** BAR

(☎93 418 58 79; www.mirablaubcn.com; Plaça del Doctor Andreu; ⊙11am-3.30am Mon-Wed, to 4.30am Thu, 10am-5am Fri & Sat, 10am-2.30am Sun; 196, FGC Avinguda Tibidabo) Views over the entire city from this balcony bar, restaurant and club at the base of the Funicular del Tibidabo make up for sometimes patchy service. The bar is renowned for its impressive gin selection (€12 to €15). Wander downstairs to the tiny dance space, which opens at 11.30pm; in summer you can step out onto the even smaller terrace for a breather.

# Entertainment

## ☆ La Rambla & Barri Gòtic

**Gran Teatre del Liceu** THEATRE

(Map p244; ☎902 787397; www.liceubarcelona.cat; La Rambla 51-59; tickets €15-250; M Liceu) Barcelona's grand old opera house, skilfully restored after a fire in 1994, is one of the world's most technologically advanced theatres. Taking a seat in its grand auditorium, returned to all its 19th-century glory but with the very latest in acoustics, you'll time-travel to another age, or join a guided tour (p247) to explore its architectural beauty.

**El Paraigua** LIVE MUSIC

(Map p244; ☎93 317 14 79; www.elparaigua.com; Carrer del Pas de l'Ensenyança 2; ⊙noon-midnight Sun-Thu, to 3am Fri & Sat; M Liceu) FREE A tiny chocolate box of dark tinted Modernisme, the 'Umbrella' has been serving up drinks since the 1960s. But downstairs in the moody basement, travel from Modernisme to medieval amid 11th-century brick walls. Live bands – funk, soul, rock, blues, flamenco – regularly hold court on Friday and Saturday (check schedules online).

**Harlem Jazz Club** JAZZ

(Map p244; ☎93 310 07 55; www.harlemjazzclub.es; Carrer de la Comtessa de Sobradiel 8; tickets €8-12; ⊙8pm-3am Sun & Tue-Thu, to 5am Fri & Sat; M Jaume I) This narrow, old-city dive is one of the best spots in town for jazz, as well as funk, Latin, blues and gypsy jazz, and attracts a mixed crowd that maintains a respectful silence during performances. Most concerts start at 10.30pm or 11pm; get in early if you want a seat in front of the stage.

## ☆ El Raval

★ **Filmoteca de Catalunya** CINEMA

(Map p244; ☎93 567 10 70; www.filmoteca.cat; Plaça de Salvador Seguí 1-9; adult/concession €4/3; ⊙screenings 5-10pm, ticket office 10am-3pm Tue-Fri, plus 4-9.30pm Tue-Thu & Sun, to 10pm Fri & Sat; M Liceu) Relocated to El Raval in 2012 as part of plans to revive the neighbourhood's cultural offerings, Catalonia's national cinema occupies a modern 6000-sq-metre building in the midst of the most louche part of El Raval. The films shown are a superior mix of classics and more recent releases, with frequent themed cycles.

**23 Robadors** LIVE MUSIC

(Map p244; www.23robadors.wordpress.com; Carrer d'en Robador 23; entry €5; ⊙8pm-3am; M Liceu) On what remains a sleazy Raval street in spite of gentrification in the area, this narrow little bar has made a name for itself with its shows and live music. Jazz is the name of the game, but you'll also hear live poetry, flamenco and plenty more.

**JazzSí Club** LIVE MUSIC

(Map p276; ☎93 329 00 20; http://tallerdemusics.com; Carrer de Requesens 2; entry incl drink €6-12; ⊙8.30-11pm Mon & Thu, 7.45-11pm Tue & Wed, 8.45-11pm Fri & Sat, 6.30-10pm Sun; M Sant Antoni) A cramped little bar run by the Taller de Músics (Musicians' Workshop) school and foundation, staging a varied programme that ranges from jazz jams to some good flamenco (Friday and Saturday). Thursday is Cuban night, Tuesday and Sunday are rock, and the rest are devoted to jazz and/or blues sessions.

## ☆ La Ribera & El Born

**★Palau de la Música Catalana** CLASSICAL MUSIC

(Map p252; ☎93 295 72 00; www.palaumusica.cat; Carrer Palau de la Música 4-6; tickets from €15; ⌚box office 9.30am-9pm Mon-Sat, 10am-3pm Sun; Ⓜ Urquinaona) A feast for both the eyes and ears, this Modernista confection doubles as the city's most traditional venue for classical and choral music, though the wide-ranging programme also takes in flamenco, pop and – particularly – jazz. Just being here for a performance is an experience. Sip a pre-concert tipple in the foyer.

**Farola** LIVE MUSIC

(Map p252; ☎663 332643; www.farolabcn.com; Carrer del Rec 67; ⌚6pm-2.30am Sun-Thu, to 3.30am Fri & Sat) From soulful jazz to foot-stomping flamenco, live music meets expertly crafted cocktails and a world of carefully curated sherries at lively Farola, hidden off Passeig del Born. Performances are 9pm Thursday to Sunday (upcoming shows listed online). There's also a smart Italian-influenced tapas menu of homemade hummus, local-cheese boards, and focaccia topped with, say, gorgonzola or Italian ham.

## ☆ Barceloneta, the Waterfront & El Poblenou

**Razzmatazz** LIVE MUSIC

(Map p258; ☎93 320 82 00; www.salarazzmatazz.com; Carrer de Pamplona 88; tickets from €10; ⌚hours vary; Ⓜ Bogatell) Bands from far and wide occasionally create scenes of near hysteria at Razzmatazz, one of the city's classic live-music and clubbing venues. Bands appear throughout the week (check online), while on weekends live music gives way to club sounds. Five different rooms, with offerings varying from night to night, in one huge post-industrial space attract people of all dance persuasions and ages.

**Sala Monasterio** LIVE MUSIC

(Map p258; www.facebook.com/sala.monasterio; Moll de Mestral 30; tickets vary; ⌚10pm-5am Sun-Thu, to 6am Fri & Sat; Ⓜ Ciutadella Vila Olímpica) Overlooking the bobbing masts and slender palm trees of the Port Olímpic, this pocket-sized music spot stages an eclectic line-up of live bands, including jazz, *forró* (from Brazil), blues jams and rock.

**L'Auditori** CLASSICAL MUSIC

(Map p258; ☎93 247 93 00; www.auditori.cat; Carrer de Lepant 150; tickets vary; ⌚box office 5-9pm Tue-Fri, 10.30am-1pm & 5-9pm Sat; Ⓜ Marina) Barcelona's modern home for the Orquestra Simfònica de Barcelona i Nacional de Catalunya, L'Auditori stages performances of orchestral, chamber, religious and other music. Designed by Rafael Moneo and opened in 1999, the main auditorium can accommodate more than 2000 concertgoers. The **Museu de la Música** (Map p258; ☎93 256 36 50; www.museumusica.bcn.cat; Carrer de Lepant 150; adult/child €6/free, free 6-9pm Thu & 3-7pm Sun; ⌚10am-6pm Tue, Wed & Fri, to 9pm Thu, to 7pm Sat & Sun; Ⓜ Marina) is in the same building.

## ☆ La Sagrada Família & L'Eixample

**City Hall** LIVE MUSIC

(Map p264; ☎660 769865; www.cityhallbarcelona.com; Rambla de Catalunya 2-4; Ⓜ Catalunya) This former 19th-century theatre is the perfect size and shape for live music, holding a crowd of around 500 and with a varied line-up. The acoustics are great and the layout means everyone gets a good view of the stage. It's also home to a **nightclub** (cover incl drink from €10; ⌚midnight-5am Mon-Thu, to 6am Sat; Ⓜ Catalunya).

## ☆ Gràcia & Park Güell

**Soda Acústic** LIVE MUSIC

(Map p272; ☎93 016 55 90; www.soda.cat; Carrer de les Guilleries 6; tickets free-€5; ⌚8.30pm-2.30am Wed, Thu & Sun, 9pm-3am Fri & Sat; Ⓜ Fontana) One of Gràcia's most innovative performance spaces, this low-lit modern venue stages an eclectic line-up of bands, artists and jams: jazz, world music, Balkan swing, Latin rhythms and plenty of experimental, not-easily-classifiable musicians all receive their due.

## ☆ Montjuïc, Poble Sec & Sant Antoni

**Sala Apolo** LIVE MUSIC

(Map p276; ☎93 441 40 01; www.sala-apolo.com; Carrer Nou de la Rambla 113; club incl drink from €15; ⌚concerts from 8pm, club from midnight; Ⓜ Paral·lel) Red velvet dominates and you feel as though you're in a movie-set dancehall scene at this fine old theatre turned club and concert hall. 'Nasty Mondays' are aimed at a diehard, never-stop-dancing crowd. Earlier in the evening concerts take place here and in 'La 2', a smaller auditorium downstairs with everything from local bands and burlesque shows to big-name international acts.

**BARTS** LIVE PERFORMANCE
(Barcelona Arts on Stage; Map p244; ☎93 324 84 92; www.barts.cat; Avinguda del Paral·lel 62; Ⓜ Paral·lel) BARTS has a solid reputation for its innovative line-up of urban-dance troupes, electro swing, psychedelic pop, circus acrobatics and other eclectic shows. Its smart design combines a comfortable mid-sized auditorium with excellent acoustics. Hours and ticket prices vary; check online.

**Gran Bodega Saltó** LIVE MUSIC
(Map p276; ☎93 441 37 09; www.bodegasalto.net; Carrer de Blesa 36; ⏰6pm-1am Mon-Thu, noon-3am Fri & Sat, noon-midnight Sun; Ⓜ Paral·lel) The ranks of barrels and classic tapas menu give away this century-old bar's history as a traditional bodega. Now, after a little homemade psychedelic redecoration with mismatched lamps, figurines and old Chinese beer ads, it's a magnet for an eclectic barfly crowd and gets busy during live-music sessions (usually 8pm Thursday, 1pm and 8pm Friday to Sunday, but check online).

## ☆ Camp Nou, Pedralbes & La Zona Alta

**★Camp Nou** FOOTBALL
(☎902 189900; www.fcbarcelona.com; Carrer d'Arístides Maillol; Ⓜ Palau Reial) The massive stadium of Camp Nou ('New Field' in Catalan) is home to the legendary FC Barcelona. Attending a game amid the roar of the loyal crowds is an unforgettable experience; the season runs from August to May. Alternatively, get a taste of all the excitement at the interactive Barça Stadium Tour & Museum (p277). Tickets to FC Barcelona matches are available at Camp Nou and through FC Barcelona's website, the main Plaça de Catalunya tourist office (p319) and FC Botiga stores. Tickets can cost anything from €39 to upwards of €400. On match day the ticket windows are open at gate 9 and gate 14 from 9.15am until kick-off.

**Luz de Gas** LIVE MUSIC
(☎93 209 77 11; www.luzdegas.com; Carrer de Muntaner 246; entry from €15; ⏰midnight-6am Wed-Sat; Ⓜ Diagonal, Hospital Clínic, 🚊T1, T2, T3 Francesc Macià) Set in a grand former theatre, this club stages concerts ranging through rock and soul to salsa, jazz and pop several nights a week. From about 2am, the place turns into a club that attracts a well-dressed crowd with varying musical tastes.

# Shopping

## La Rambla & Barri Gòtic

**★Formatgeria La Seu** FOOD
(Map p244; ☎93 412 65 48; www.formatgeria laseu.com; Carrer de la Dagueria 16; ⏰10am-2pm & 5-8pm Tue-Sat; Ⓜ Jaume I) Dedicated to artisan cheeses from across Spain, this small shop is run by the oh-so-knowledgeable Katherine McLaughlin. The antithesis of mass production, it sells only the best from small-scale farmers and the stock changes regularly. Wine-and-cheese tastings (€9.50 to €32) in the cosy back room are fun.

**★L'Arca** CLOTHING
(Map p244; ☎93 302 15 98; www.larca.es; Carrer dels Banys Nous 20; ⏰11am-2pm & 4-8pm Mon-Sat; Ⓜ Liceu) Step inside this enchanting vintage boutique for beautifully crafted apparel from the past, mostly sourced from local homes: 18th-century embroidered silk vests, elaborate silk kimonos and 1920s shawls and wedding dresses, plus old-style earrings made by artisans in southern Spain. The incredible collection has provided fashion for films like *Titanic, Talk to Her* and *Perfume: The Story of a Murderer.*

**La Manual Alpargatera** SHOES
(Map p244; ☎93 301 01 72; www.lamanualalpar gatera.es; Carrer d'Avinyó 7; ⏰9.30am-8pm Mon-Fri, from 10am Sat; Ⓜ Liceu) Stars from Salvador Dalí to Penélope Cruz and Jean Paul Gaultier have ordered a pair of *espardenyes* (espadrilles; rope-soled canvas shoes) from this famous shoe specialist, founded just after the Spanish Civil War. The roots of the simple design date back hundreds of years and originated in the Catalan Pyrenees, though it incorporates contemporary trends.

**Escribà** FOOD
(Map p244; ☎93 301 60 27; www.escriba.es; La Rambla 83; ⏰9am-9pm; 📶; Ⓜ Liceu) Chocolates, dainty pastries and mouth-watering cakes can be nibbled behind the Modernista mosaic facade here or taken away for private, guilt-ridden consumption. This Barcelona favourite is owned by the Escribà family, a name synonymous with sinfully

good sweet things. More than that, it adds a touch of authenticity to La Rambla.

**Torrons Vicens** FOOD

(Map p244; www.vicens.com; Carrer del Petritxol 15; ⏱10am-9pm; Ⓜ Liceu) You can find a *turrón* (nougat) treat year-round at Torrons Vicens, which has been selling its signature sweets since 1775. As well as classic almond flavours, there are unusual options such as matcha tea, cheesecake, vermouth or white truffle, many created in collaboration with star chef Albert Adrià. There are several branches around the city.

**Herboristeria del Rei** COSMETICS

(Map p244; ☎93 318 05 12; www.herboristeriadelrei.com; Carrer del Vidre 1; ⏱3-8.30pm Tue-Thu, 11am-8.30pm Fri & Sat; Ⓜ Liceu) Once patronised by Queen Isabel II, this timeless corner store flogs all sorts of weird and wonderful herbs, spices and medicinal plants. It's been doing so since 1823 and the decor (with stained glass and watercolour landscapes) has barely changed since the 1860s – some of the products have, however, and nowadays you'll find everything from fragrant soaps to massage oils.

**Sabater Hermanos** COSMETICS

(Map p244; ☎93 301 98 32; Plaça de Sant Felip Neri 1; ⏱10.30am-9pm; Ⓜ Jaume I) Handcrafted soaps and soap petals in seductive flavours like olive oil and *tarongina* (orange blossom) are the draw at this fragrant little shop. Varieties such as fig, cinnamon, grapefruit and chocolate smell good enough to eat, while sandalwood, magnolia, mint, cedar and jasmine add spice to any bathtub.

**Joan La Llar del Pernil** FOOD

(Map p244; ☎93 317 95 29; www.joanlallardelpernil.com; Stalls 667-671, Mercat de la Boqueria; ⏱8am-3pm Tue-Thu, to 7pm Mon & Fri, 7.30am-4pm Sat; Ⓜ Liceu) This family-owned stall hidden away in the chaotic Mercat de la Boqueria (p243) sells some of the best *pernil* (cured Spanish-style ham; *jamón* in Castilian) and charcuterie in the city, much of which is sliced wafer-thin and presented in little cones as a snack by knowledgeable owner Joan. The specialty is *jamón ibérico de bellota*, sourced from free-roaming acorn-fed pigs.

**Cereria Subirà** HOMEWARES

(Map p244; ☎93 315 26 06; https://cereriasubira.cat; Baixada de la Llibreteria 7; ⏱10am-2pm & 4-8pm Mon-Sat Jun-Sep, 9.30am-1.30pm & 4-8pm Mon & Tue, 9.30am-8pm Wed-Sat Oct-May; Ⓜ Jaume I) Wafts of floral scents greet you at the oldest shop in Barcelona: its interior has a beautifully baroque quality with a sweeping *Gone With the Wind*-style staircase. Cereria Subirà has been churning out candles since 1761 and at this address (originally a textiles outlet) since the 19th century.

**La Colmena** FOOD

(Map p244; ☎93 315 13 56; www.pastisserialacolmena.com; Plaça de l'Angel 12; ⏱9am-9pm; Ⓜ Jaume I) One of Barcelona's most ancient pastry shops, 1868-opened La Colmena is still run by the same family who acquired it in 1927 and produces its treats according to the original recipes. The Roig family sells many delicacies, but is best known for its boiled sweets, pine-nut-encrusted *panellets* (almond cakes), meringues and *bolados* (18th-century powdered-sugar candy, flavoured with juice).

**Sombrerería Obach** HATS

(Map p244; ☎93 318 40 94; www.sombrereriaobach.es; Carrer del Call 2; ⏱10am-2pm & 4-8pm Mon-Fri, 10am-2pm & 4.30-8pm Sat Oct-Jul, 10am-2pm & 4-8pm Mon-Fri, 10am-2pm Sat Aug-Sep; Ⓜ Jaume I) Since 1924 this family-owned beauty has been purveying all manner of headgear: hipsterish short-brimmed hats, low-key fedoras, elegant straw sun hats, a full-colour spectrum of *barrets* (berets)…

## El Raval

**★Les Topettes** COSMETICS

(Map p244; ☎93 500 55 64; www.lestopettes.com; Carrer de Joaquín Costa 33; ⏱4-9pm Mon, 11am-2pm & 4-9pm Tue-Sat; Ⓜ Universitat) Globe-trotting products at this chic little temple to soap and perfume have been handpicked, by journalist Lucía and chef/interior designer Oriol, for their designs as much as for their qualities. You'll find gorgeously packaged scents, candles, soaps and creams from Diptyque, Cowshed and Hierbas de Ibiza, among others.

**★Grey Street** HOMEWARES

(Map p244; www.greystreetbarcelona.com; Carrer Peu de la Creu 25; ⏱11am-3pm & 4-9pm Mon-Sat; Ⓜ Sant Antoni) Named for the Canberra home of Australian owner Amy Cocker's grandparents, this stylishly reimagined former perfume shop is decked with tempting trinkets, many of them crafted by local or Spanish artists – handpainted ceramic mugs and plant pots, fair-trade incense, tarot cards,

### PRESERVING BARCELONA'S HISTORIC SHOPS

Barcelona's traditional, historical, specialist shops are just as key to the city's soul as Gaudí's Modernista creations. Over the last few years, however, some of the city's best-known shops have been forced to close, in part due to customers favouring bigger brands but also due to rising rents, and in some cases linked to growing numbers of tourist apartments pushing up prices.

But it's certainly not all lost: in 2015, 228 stores across Barcelona were given a special preservation status, which essentially means that their original facades and interiors can't be altered; 32 of these now can't be changed in any way at all. Visitors can show support by shopping (not just taking photos) at Barcelona icons such as Escribà bakery (p314), hat-maker Sombrerería Obach (p315) or dried-fruit specialist Casa Gispert. Several historical drinking dens have been given special preservation status too, most notably Els Quatre Gats (p292) near the cathedral, and Casa Almirall (p305) and La Confiteria (p305) in El Raval.

patterned wall prints, handmade swimwear, vegan skincare and more. There's another **branch** (Map p252; www.greystreetbarcelona.com; Carrer dels Agullers 12; 11am-8.30pm Mon-Sat; M Jaume I, Barceloneta) in El Born.

**Holala! Plaza** FASHION & ACCESSORIES

(Map p244; 93 302 05 93; www.holala-ibiza.com; Plaça de Castella 2; 11am-9pm Mon-Sat; M Universitat) Backing on to Carrer de Valldonzella, this Ibiza import is inspired by the Balearic island's long-established (and now somewhat commercialised) hippie tradition. Vintage clothes sourced from flea markets and reusable-fashion outlets across the globe are the name of the game, with lots of denim and vibrant colours on show, plus an eclectic exhibitions programme.

**Lantoki** FASHION & ACCESSORIES

(Map p244; www.lantoki.es; Carrer del Doctor Dou 15; 11am-8pm Mon-Fri, from noon Sat; M Catalunya, Liceu) Designers Urko Martinez and Sandra Liberal handcraft their own minimalist women's fashion in this bright, breezy El Raval studio-boutique, which also flaunts pieces by other local creatives. The emphasis is on original, slow-fashion artisan collections, and there are also design-your-own-clothes workshops (around €40 to €90).

**Teranyina** ARTS & CRAFTS

(Map p244; 93 317 94 36; www.textilteranyina.com; Carrer del Notariat 10; 11am-3pm & 5-8pm Mon-Fri; M Catalunya) Artist Teresa Rosa Aguayo runs this textile workshop in the heart of the artsy bit of El Raval. You can join workshops at the loom, admire some of the rugs and other pieces that Teresa has created and, of course, buy them.

**La Variété** HOMEWARES

(Map p244; 93 519 83 51; www.lavariete.net; Carrer d'Elisabets 7; 11am-3pm & 4-8.30pm Mon-Sat; M Catalunya, Liceu) Decorative pieces made from Chiang Mai wood, lampshades that reuse old bamboo lobster traps and handmade hanging terracotta plant pots are just a few of the tempting home-designed pieces at this calming interiors boutique.

## La Ribera & El Born

**★ Vila Viniteca** FOOD & DRINKS

(Map p252; www.vilaviniteca.es; Carrer dels Agullers 7; 8.30am-8.30pm Mon-Sat; M Jaume I) One of Barcelona's best wine stores (and there are a few…), Vila Viniteca has been hunting down the finest local and imported wines since 1932. There are year-round on-request tastings and a handful of bar tables, and on several November evenings it organises an almost riotous wine-tasting event at which cellars from across Spain present their young new wines.

**El Magnífico** COFFEE

(Map p252; www.cafeselmagnifico.com; Carrer de l'Argenteria 64; 10am-8pm Mon-Sat; M Jaume I) All sorts of coffee beans, sourced seasonally from around the world, have been roasted at much-loved third-generation family-owned El Magnífico (which you'll spot all over town) since the early 20th century – and the aromas hit as soon as you walk in. Sample a cup on-site or wander over to the sleek Mag cafe (p307) on nearby Carrer de Grunyí.

**Capsule** FASHION & ACCESSORIES

(Map p252; www.capsulebcn.com; Carrer dels Banys Vells 21; noon-8pm Tue-Sat; M Jaume I, Barceloneta) Elegantly understated fashion and homewares sourced from small, sustainable, independent Spanish and international brands grace this tucked-away boutique. Capsule occupies a reimagined brick-walled stable and spotlights female artisans working with traditional techniques and organic materials. The gorgeous own-brand babucha-style raffia shoes are handmade by a women's cooperative in Morocco.

**Working in the Redwoods** CERAMICS
(Map p252; ☎93 301 66 63; www.workingintheredwoods.com; Carrer de Lluís el Piadós 4; ⏰noon-8pm Mon-Sat; Ⓜ Arc de Triomf) Catalan designer Miriam Cernuda handcrafts beautiful, minimalist, earthy-toned bowls, mugs, vases and other ceramics from all-natural materials, inspired by the colours of the Costa Brava, at this soothing studio-workshop near the Arc de Triomf. There are also occasional ceramics classes (check online).

**Ozz Barcelona** FASHION & ACCESSORIES
(Map p252; ☎93 315 84 81; https://ozzbarcelona.com; Carrer dels Banys Vells 8; ⏰10.30am-9pm; Ⓜ Jaume I) Cutting-edge Barcelona designers take centre stage at slow-fashion-focused concept boutique and coworking space Ozz. Its handmade jewellery and bold clothing come courtesy of emerging, independent brands like Txell Miras, IKA, Ester Gueroa and Antonio Rodríguez.

**Casa Gispert** FOOD
(Map p252; ☎93 319 75 35; www.casagispert.com; Carrer dels Sombrerers 23; ⏰10am-8.30pm Mon-Sat; Ⓜ Jaume I) Wonderful, atmospheric, wood-fronted Casa Gispert has been toasting nuts and selling all manner of dried fruit since 1851. Pots and jars piled high on the shelves contain an unending variety of crunchy titbits: some roasted, some honeyed, all of them moreish. Your order is shouted over to the till, along with the price, in a display of old-world accounting.

**Hofmann Pastisseria** FOOD
(Map p252; ☎93 268 82 21; www.hofmann-bcn.com; Carrer dels Flassaders 44; ⏰9am-2pm & 3.30-8pm Mon-Sat, 9am-2pm Sun; Ⓜ Barceloneta, Jaume I) All painted wooden cabinets and tiffany-blue interiors, this bite-sized gourmet patisserie is linked to the prestigious Hofmann cooking school. Choose between jars of delicious jams, the prize-winning mascarpone-filled croissants (also in other flavours!) and more dangerous pastries, or an array of cakes and other sweet treats. Hofmann also has a **cafe** (Map p252; ☎93 295 65 09; Carrer dels Flassaders 40; ⏰10am-2pm Tue-Sun; Ⓜ Jaume I, Barceloneta) a few doors down.

## Barceloneta, the Waterfront & El Poblenou

**Palo Market Fest** MARKET
(Map p258; ☎93 159 66 70; https://palomarketfest.com; Carrer dels Pellaires 30; adult/child €4.50/free; ⏰11am-9pm 1st Sunday of month; Ⓜ Selva de Mar) One of the city's most loved events, festival-vibe Palo Market takes over an old Poblenou warehouse wreathed in flowers and greenery once a month. Local creatives – from up-and-coming fashion and jewellery designers to organic-cosmetics sellers and vintage experts – set up stalls alongside sizzling street-food trucks and lively vermouth bars, and there are also arty workshops.

**Mercat dels Encants** MARKET
(Fira de Bellcaire; Map p258; ☎93 245 22 99; www.facebook.com/EncantsBarcelona; Plaça de les Glòries Catalanes; ⏰9am-8pm Mon, Wed & Sat, 10am-5pm Fri & Sun; Ⓜ Glòries) In a gleaming open-sided complex near Plaça de les Glòries Catalanes, the 'Market of Charms' is Barcelona's biggest flea market, and one

DON'T MISS

### NEIGHBOURHOOD MARKETS

Barcelona's food markets are some of the best in Europe. Beyond the headlining Mercat de la Boqueria (p243) and La Ribera's Mercat de Santa Caterina (p253), every neighbourhood has its own central market.

**Mercat de Sant Antoni** (p273)

**Mercat de la Barceloneta** (Map p258; Plaça del Poeta Boscà 1-2; ⏰7am-2pm Mon-Thu, to 8pm Fri, to 3pm Sat; Ⓜ Barceloneta)

**Mercat del Poblenou** (Map p258; http://mercatpoblenou.com; Plaça de la Unió; ⏰8.30am-2pm Mon, 8.30am-2pm & 5-8.30pm Tue-Thu, 8.30am-8.30pm Fri, 8.30am-3pm Sat; Ⓜ Poblenou)

**Mercat de la Llibertat** (p272)

L'Eixample's **Mercat de la Concepció** (Map p264; ☎93 476 48 70; www.laconcepcio.cat; Carrer d'Aragó 313-317; ⏰8am-8pm Tue-Fri, to 3pm Mon & Sat early Sep–mid-Jul, 8am-3pm Mon-Sat mid-Jul–early Sep; Ⓜ Girona)

of Europe's oldest, with its roots in medieval times. More than 500 vendors ply their wares beneath massive mirror-like panels. It's all here, from antique furniture to secondhand clothes.

## La Sagrada Família & L'Eixample

**★Flores Navarro** FLOWERS

(Map p264; ☎93 457 40 99; www.floristeriasnavarro.com; Carrer de València 320; ⏰24hr; Ⓜ Girona) You never know when you might need flowers, and this vast, packed-to-the-rafters florist never closes. Established in 1960, it has two spaces on Carrer de València, and is worth a visit just for the bank of colour and wonderful fragrance, from sky-blue roses to tiny cacti.

**★Joan Múrria** FOOD & DRINKS

(Queviures Múrria; Map p264; ☎93 215 57 89; www.murria.cat; Carrer de Roger de Llúria 85; ⏰10am-2pm & 5-8pm Tue-Sat; Ⓜ Girona) Ramon Casas designed the 1898 Modernista shopfront advertisements at this culinary temple of speciality foods from around Catalonia and beyond. Artisan cheeses, Iberian hams, caviar, canned delicacies, olive oils, smoked fish, *cavas* and wines, coffee and loose-leaf teas are among the treats in store.

**Altaïr** BOOKS

(Map p264; ☎93 342 71 71; www.altair.es; Gran Via de les Corts Catalanes 616; ⏰10am-8.30pm Mon-Sat; 📶; Ⓜ Catalunya) Enter a travel wonderland at this extensive bookshop, founded in 1979, which has enough guidebooks, maps, travel literature and other works to induce a case of itchy feet. There's also a helpful travellers' noticeboardnd cafe.

**Avant** FASHION & ACCESSORIES

(Map p264; ☎93 300 76 73; www.theavant.com; Carrer d'Enric Granados 106; ⏰10.30am-8.30pm Mon-Fri, to 2.30pm Sat; Ⓜ Diagonal, 🚊 FGC Provença) Taking inspiration from the world of dance and cultures around the globe, *barcelonin* designer Silvia Garcia Presas creates her elegant women's dresses, shirts, shoes and other pieces working directly with local producers. The boutique setting is a chicly white, classically Modernista building.

**Bagués-Masriera** JEWELLERY

(Map p264; ☎93 216 01 74; www.bagues-masriera.com; Passeig de Gràcia 41; ⏰10am-8.30pm Mon-Fri, 11am-8pm Sat; Ⓜ Passeig de Gràcia) In thematic harmony with its location, inside the Modernista Casa Amatller (p261), this is more than just any old jewellery store. The team from Bagués-Masriera have been chipping away at precious stones and moulding metal since the 19th century. Many of the classic pieces here have a flighty, Modernista influence. Bagués backs it up with service that owes much to old-school courtesies.

## Gràcia & Park Güell

**★Colmillo de Morsa** FASHION & ACCESSORIES

(Map p272; www.colmillodemorsa.com; Carrer de Vic 15; ⏰11am-2.30pm & 4.30-7pm Mon-Fri, 11am-2.30pm Sat; 🚊 FGC Gràcia) Javier Blanco and Elisabet Vallecillo, who have made waves at Madrid's Cibeles Fashion Week, showcase their Barcelona-made women's designs at this flagship boutique-workshop filled with delicate dresses, jumpsuits and shirts in soothing tones.

**Casa Atlântica** CERAMICS

(Map p272; ☎93 382 18 88; www.casaatlantica.es; Carrer de la Llibertat 7; ⏰noon-8.30pm Mon-Sat; Ⓜ Diagonal) 🍃 The delicate basketry and beautiful custom-designed bowls, mugs, plant pots, vases and other ceramics dotting this charming studio-boutique are created by Galician artisans Belén and Lester, who collaborate with small-scale, family-owned village workshops across Galicia and Portugal to keep traditional crafts alive. Their work graces popular venues around town.

**Fromagerie Can Luc** CHEESE

(Map p272; ☎93 007 47 83; www.canluc.es; Carrer de Berga 4; ⏰5-9pm Mon, 10am-2.30pm & 5-8.30pm Tue-Sat; 🚊 FGC Gràcia) At any given time, this inviting shop stocks 150 different varieties of European cheese. Catalan favourites are the speciality, though you'll also spot a selection from France, Italy, the Netherlands, Switzerland and Britain. Wines, condiments, crackers and cheese knives, along with gourmet picnic hampers.

**Amalia Vermell** JEWELLERY

(Map p272; ☎655 754008; www.amaliavermell.com; Carrer del Planeta 11; ⏰5-9pm Mon-Thu, 10.30am-2.30pm & 5-9pm Fri & Sat, hours vary; Ⓜ Fontana) Striking geometric jewellery made from high-quality materials such as sterling silver is handcrafted right here in the atelier by designer-owner Pamela Masferrer, who also offers long-term jewellery-making workshops. Browse for pendants, necklaces, bracelets and rings, as well as vibrant homeware pieces and dresses by Barcelona brands.

**Bodega Bonavista** WINE
(Map p272; ☎93 218 81 99; www.facebook.com/bodegabonavistabcn; Carrer de Bonavista 10; ⏲10am-2.30pm & 5-9pm Mon-Fri, noon-3pm & 6-9pm Sat; Ⓜ Fontana) An excellent little neighbourhood bodega, Bonavista endeavours to seek out great wines at reasonable prices. The stock is mostly from Catalonia and elsewhere in Spain, but there's also a well-chosen French selection. The Bonavista also doubles as a deli, with some especially good cheeses.

**Hibernian** BOOKS
(Map p272; ☎93 217 47 96; www.hibernianbooks.com; Carrer de Montseny 17; ⏲4-8.30pm Mon, 10.30am-8.30pm Tue-Sat; Ⓜ Fontana) Barcelona's biggest secondhand English bookshop stocks thousands of titles covering all sorts of subjects, from cookery to children's classics. There's a smaller collection of new books in English, too.

**Amapola Vegan Shop** FASHION & ACCESSORIES
(Map p272; ☎93 010 62 73; www.amapolaveganshop.com; Travessera de Gràcia 129; ⏲5-8.30pm Mon, 10am-2pm & 5-8.30pm Tue-Sat; Ⓜ Fontana) A shop with a heart of gold, Amapola proves that you need not toss your ethics aside in the quest for stylish clothing and accessories. You'll find sleek leather alternatives for wallets, handbags, messenger bags, belts and boots by Matt & Nat, and elegant vegan scarves by Barts.

## Montjuïc, Poble Sec & Sant Antoni

**Popcorn Store** FASHION & ACCESSORIES
(Map p276; www.facebook.com/popcornstorebcn; Carrer Viladomat 30-32; ⏲11am-3pm & 4.30-8.30pm Mon-Sat) Cutting-edge Barcelona women's labels at this pink-patterned boutique mean asymmetrical tops, jackets and dresses, bold prints and delicate lace. Men will find stylish shirts, trousers and belts from Italian and other European designers.

**Llibreria Calders** BOOKS
(Map p276; ☎93 442 78 31; www.facebook.com/lacalders; Passatge de Pere Calders 9; ⏲10am-9pm Mon-Fri, 11am-9pm Sat, 11.30am-7pm Sun, closed Sun Aug; Ⓜ Poble Sec) Spread across what was once a button factory, this lively bookshop and literary hub stocks both secondhand and brand-new titles in a stylish concrete-covered space, and puts an emphasis on local authors.

**Brava** FASHION & ACCESSORIES
(Map p276; www.bravafabrics.com; Carrer del Parlament 25; ⏲11am-9pm Mon-Fri, 11am-3pm & 4-9pm Sat & Sun; Ⓜ Poble Sec) Inspired by travel and the arts, fair-trade Barcelona-born label Brava works exclusively with Catalan and other Spanish and Portuguese ateliers, and uses only sustainable materials to craft its stylishly minimalist men's and women's fashion. Finds include fun shirts and blouses in millennial-beloved prints such as avocados and bicycles.

## Camp Nou, Pedralbes & La Zona Alta

**Catalina House** HOMEWARES
(☎93 140 96 39; www.catalinahouse.net; Carrer d'Amigó 47; ⏲10.15am-2pm & 5-8pm Mon-Fri, 10.30am-2pm Sat; FGC Muntaner) After its decade-long success on the Balearic island of Formentera, Catalina House now has a second branch in Barcelona's Sant Gervasi. Sustainable materials such as linen, cotton, stone, glass, terracotta and oil-treated recycled timbers are used in stylish Mediterranean designs for the home including cushions, tableware, vases and furniture.

# Information

### ACCESSIBLE TRAVEL

All buses in Barcelona are wheelchair accessible, as are most street crossings and metro stations (check www.tmb.cat/en/barcelona/accessibility-mobility-reduced). Most hotels and public institutions have wheelchair access, and during summer months volunteers at several beaches provide amphibious chairs. Barcelona Turisme (p319) runs a wheelchair-accessible tour of the Barri Gòtic (€14). Adapted taxis include Taxi Amic (p321) and Greentaxi (p321).

### EMERGENCY & USEFUL NUMBERS

| | |
|---|---|
| **Ambulance** | ☎061 |
| **EU standard emergency number** | ☎112 |
| **Country code** | ☎34 |
| **International access code** | ☎00 |
| **Guàrdia Urbana** | ☎092 |

### TOURIST INFORMATION

**Plaça de Catalunya** (Map p264; ☎93 285 38 34; www.barcelonaturisme.com; Plaça de

### WARNING: WATCH YOUR BELONGINGS

- Petty crime (bag-snatching, pickpocketing) is a major problem, especially in the touristed centre.
- Avoid walking around El Raval and the southern end of La Rambla late at night.
- Take nothing of value to the beach and don't leave anything unattended.

Catalunya 17-S, underground; ⌚8.30am-9pm; Ⓜ Catalunya)

**Plaça Sant Jaume** (Map p244; ☎93 285 38 34; www.barcelonaturisme.com; Plaça de Sant Jaume; ⌚8.30am-8pm Mon-Fri, 9am-3pm Sat & Sun; Ⓜ Catalunya)

**Catedral** (Map p244; ☎93 368 97 00; www.barcelonaturisme.com; Plaça Nova, Col·legi d'Arquitectes; ⌚9am-7pm Mon-Sat, to 3pm Sun)

**Palau Moja (Barri Gòtic)** (Map p244; ☎93 285 38 34; www.barcelonaturisme.com; Carrer de la Portaferrisa 1; ⌚10am-9pm; Ⓜ Liceu)

**Aeroport del Prat** (☎93 285 38 32; www.barcelonaturisme.com; Aeroport de Barcelona–El Prat, Terminal 2; ⌚8.30am-8.30pm)

**Oficina de Turisme de Catalunya** (Regional Tourist Office; Map p264; ☎93 238 80 91; https://escasateva.catalunya.com; Passeig de Gràcia 107, Palau Robert; ⌚9am-8pm Mon-Sat, to 2.30pm Sun; Ⓜ Diagonal)

## Getting There & Away

### AIR

The **Aeroport de Barcelona–El Prat** (☎91 321 10 00; www.aena.es; 📶) lies 15km southwest of Plaça de Catalunya at El Prat de Llobregat. It has two terminals: T1 and older T2, itself divided into three areas (A, B and C). Some budget airlines use Girona–Costa Brava airport (p338) or Reus airport (p383).

### BOAT

Barcelona has ferry connections to the Balearic Islands with **Trasmediterránea** (Map p276; ☎902 454645; www.trasmediterranea.es; Moll de Barcelona; Ⓜ Drassanes), as well as links to/from Italy.

### BUS

Long-distance national buses operate from the **Estació d'Autobusos Barcelona Nord** (Estació del Nord; Map p258; ☎93 706 53 66; www.barcelonanord.cat; Carrer d'Alí Bei 80; Ⓜ Arc de Triomf) in El Fort Pienç, many under **Alsa** (☎902 422242; www.alsa.es). There are frequent services to Madrid (seven to eight hours), Valencia (four to 5½ hours) and Zaragoza (3½ hours), and several daily departures to distant destinations such as Seville.

**Eurolines** (www.eurolines.es) is the main international bus carrier, serving Europe and Morocco from the Estació del Nord and the **Estació d'Autobusos de Sants** (Carrer de Viriat; Ⓜ Sants Estació), 2.5km west of La Rambla. Much of the Pyrenees and the entire Costa Brava are served only by buses.

Most bus companies operating across Catalonia use the Estació del Nord, though **Hispano-Igualadina** (☎93 339 73 29; www.igualadina.com; Carrer de Viriat; Ⓜ Sants Estació) and **TEISA** (Map p264; ☎93 215 35 66; www.teisa-bus.com; Carrer de Pau Claris 117; Ⓜ Passeig de Gràcia) use the Estació de Sants and Carrer de Pau Claris in L'Eixample, respectively.

### TRAIN

Travelling by train is the most ecofriendly way of reaching Barcelona from other European cities and Spanish centres like Madrid. Long-distance trains arrive into Estació Sants (www.adif.es), 2.5km west of La Rambla.

A network of *rodalies/cercanías* (www.renfe.com) serves towns around Barcelona (and the airport).

Frequent high-speed Tren de Alta Velocidad Española (AVE) trains between Madrid and Barcelona run daily, several in under three hours. After the AVE come Euromed and other similarly modern trains; the most common long-distance trains are the slower Talgo.

## Getting Around

### TO/FROM THE AIRPORT

The **A1 Aerobús** (Map p276; ☎902 100104; www.aerobusbcn.com; Plaça d'Espanya; one way/return €5.90/10.20; ⌚5.05am-12.35am; Ⓜ Espanya) runs from T1 to Plaça de Catalunya (30 to 40 minutes depending on traffic) via Plaça d'Espanya, Gran Via de les Corts Catalanes (corner of Carrer del Comte d'Urgell) and Plaça de la Universitat every five to 10 minutes from 5.35am to 1.05am. Buses from Plaça de Catalunya to the airport run every five to 10 minutes from 5am to 12.30am, stopping at the corner of Carrer de Sepúlveda and Carrer del Comte d'Urgell, and at Plaça d'Espanya. The A2 Aerobús from T2 (stops outside areas A, B and C) to Plaça de Catalunya runs from 5.35am to 1am every 10 minutes, following the same route as the A1 Aerobús; in the reverse direction it's every 10 minutes 5am to 12.30am. Fares on both services are €5.90/10.20 single/return.

From 5.42am to 11.38pm, Renfe (www.renfe.com) runs the half-hourly R2 Nord train line from the airport to Barcelona's main train station, Estació Sants (20 minutes), and Passeig de

Gràcia (27 minutes) in central Barcelona. The first service for the airport from Passeig de Gràcia leaves at 5.08am and the last at 11.06pm; all pass through Estació Sants five minutes later. One-way tickets cost €4.20. The airport train station is a five-minute, 200m walk from T2. Free 24-hour shuttle buses (allow 10 to 20 minutes) link the train station and T2 with T1 every five to 15 minutes.

*Línia* 9 Sud (L9S) connects T1 and T2 with Zona Universitària (32 minutes) every seven minutes from 5am to midnight Sunday to Thursday, 5am to 2am on Friday and 24 hours on Sunday; change lines for Barcelona centre (€5.15).

Taxis between either terminal and the city centre (around 30 minutes) cost €25 to €35.

### BICYCLE

An extensive, ever-growing network of bike lanes has been laid out across Barcelona. You can transport your bicycle on the metro on weekdays, except between 7am and 9.30am or 5pm and 8.30pm. At weekends and during holidays and July and August, there are no restrictions. You can use FGC trains and Renfe's *rodalies* trains to carry your bike at any time. Bike-hire outlets (p282) charge from €5 per hour.

### CAR & MOTORCYCLE

With the convenience of public transport and the high price of parking, it's unwise to drive in Barcelona. However, if you're planning a road trip, a car is handy, and scooters are popular for zipping around town. Avis, Europcar, National/Atesa and Hertz have desks at El Prat airport, and most at the Estació Sants and Estació del Nord. Outlets in central Barcelona include **Enterprise** (☎ 93 323 07 01; www.enterprise.es; Carrer de Muntaner 45; ⌚ 8am-8pm Mon-Fri, 9am-1pm Sat; Ⓜ Universitat) and **Rent Electric** (☎ 902 474474; www.rentelectric.com; Carrer de Pepe Rubianes 1; electric bike hire per hour/day from €10/35; ⌚ 10am-7pm; Ⓜ Barceloneta).

### PUBLIC TRANSPORT

#### Bus

Barcelona's buses are the cleanest in Europe, with hybrids and natural-gas-powered vehicles. Transports Metropolitans de Barcelona (www.tmb.cat) buses run along most city routes every few minutes from 5am or 6.30am to around 10pm or 11pm. Nitbus (www.ambmobilitat.cat) runs 17 yellow night buses until 3am or 5am (including N17 to/from the airport); almost all *nitbus* routes pass through Plaça de Catalunya and most run every 30 to 45 minutes.

#### Metro & FGC

The **Transports Metropolitans de Barcelona** metro system (www.tmb.cat) has 11 numbered and colour-coded lines. It runs from 5am to midnight Sunday to Thursday and holidays, from 5am to 2am on Friday, and 24 hours on Saturday.

Suburban trains run by the **Ferrocarrils de la Generalitat de Catalunya** (FGC; www.fgc.net) include useful city lines. All lines heading north from Plaça de Catalunya stop at Carrer de Provença and Gràcia; L7 goes to near Tibidabo and L6 goes to Reina Elisenda, near the Monestir de Pedralbes. Other FGC lines head west from Plaça d'Espanya, including R5 towards Manresa which is handy for day-tripping to Montserrat (p370). FGC trains run from about 5am to 11pm or midnight Sunday to Thursday (to 1am Friday and Saturday).

#### Tickets & Passes

The metro, FGC trains, *rodalies/cercanías* (Renfe-run local trains) and buses come under a combined system; single-ride tickets within Zone 1 cost €2.40. *Targetes*, multitrip transport tickets, are sold at city-centre metro stations and may only be used by one person; children under four travel free. Prices here are for travel within Zone 1.

**Targeta T-Casual** (€11.35) – Ten rides (each valid for 1¼ hours) on the metro, buses, FGC trains and *rodalies*.

**T-Usual** (€40) – 30 days' unlimited use of all public transport.

**Targeta T-DIA** (€8.60) – unlimited travel on all transport for one day.

**Two-/three-/four-/five-day Hola Barcelona tickets** (€15.20/22.20/28.80/35.40) – Unlimited travel on all transport except the Aerobús.

**T-Jove** (€105) Unlimited travel for 90 days for those aged under 25.

### TAXIS

Taxis charge €2.25 flag fall plus meter charges of €1.18 per kilometre (€1.41 from 8pm to 8am and all day on weekends). A further €4.30 is added for all trips to/from the airport and €2.50/€4.30 for journeys starting from Estació Sants/the port. The call-out charge is €3.40 (€4.20 at night/weekends).

**Fonotaxi** (☎ 93 300 11 00; www.fonotaxi.net)

**Greentaxi** (☎ 900 827900; www.greentaxi.es) Wheelchair-accessible.

**Ràdio Taxi 033** (☎ 93 303 30 33; www.radiotaxi033.com)

**Taxi Amic** (☎ 93 420 80 88; www.taxi-amic-adaptat.com) For people with disabilities or requiring additional space.

**Taxi Ecològic** (☎ 93 278 30 00; http://taxiecologic.com) Electric or hybrid cars.

## AT A GLANCE

**POPULATION**
7.78 million

**CAPITAL**
Barcelona

**BEST ROCK PILLARS**
Montserrat (p370)

**BEST CAVA TASTING**
Codorníu (p380)

**BEST ROMANESQUE CHURCH**
Sant Climent de Taüll (p366)

**WHEN TO GO**

**May** The Costa Brava's beaches and trails are free from crowds (though the water is chilly).

**Sep** Perfect hiking in the Catalan Pyrenees, aflame in autumnal colours; quiet returns to the coast.

**Dec–Feb** Ski season in the winter-clothed Pyrenees.

Cala de Sa Tuna (p330)
HARRINGUER/SHUTTERSTOCK ©

# Catalonia & the Costa Brava

With its own language and unique local customs, Catalonia feels distinct from the rest of Spain, and, beyond Barcelona, its four provinces unveil an astounding wealth of natural splendour. Pyrenean peaks loom above meadows and glittering lakes, plains are pock-marked with ancient volcanic cones, rocky coves border sandy beaches and wind-blown capes give way to serene seaside paths and fertile vineyards.

The Costa Brava's shores are its biggest lure, though travellers will also uncover medieval architecture, Jewish history and culinary wizardry in Girona, and Dalí's gloriously surreal 'theatre-museum' in Figueres. South of Barcelona, Sitges fizzes with summer fun and Modernista mansions. North, where the Pyrenees rise to 3000m, hiking trails weave between hushed valleys and atmospheric Romanesque churches, while monasteries crown lonely villages. Spinning back in time, the Roman ruins of Tarragona and Empúries rank among Spain's most impressive, while entirely different landscapes await amid the Delta de l'Ebre's shimmering wetlands.

**INCLUDES**

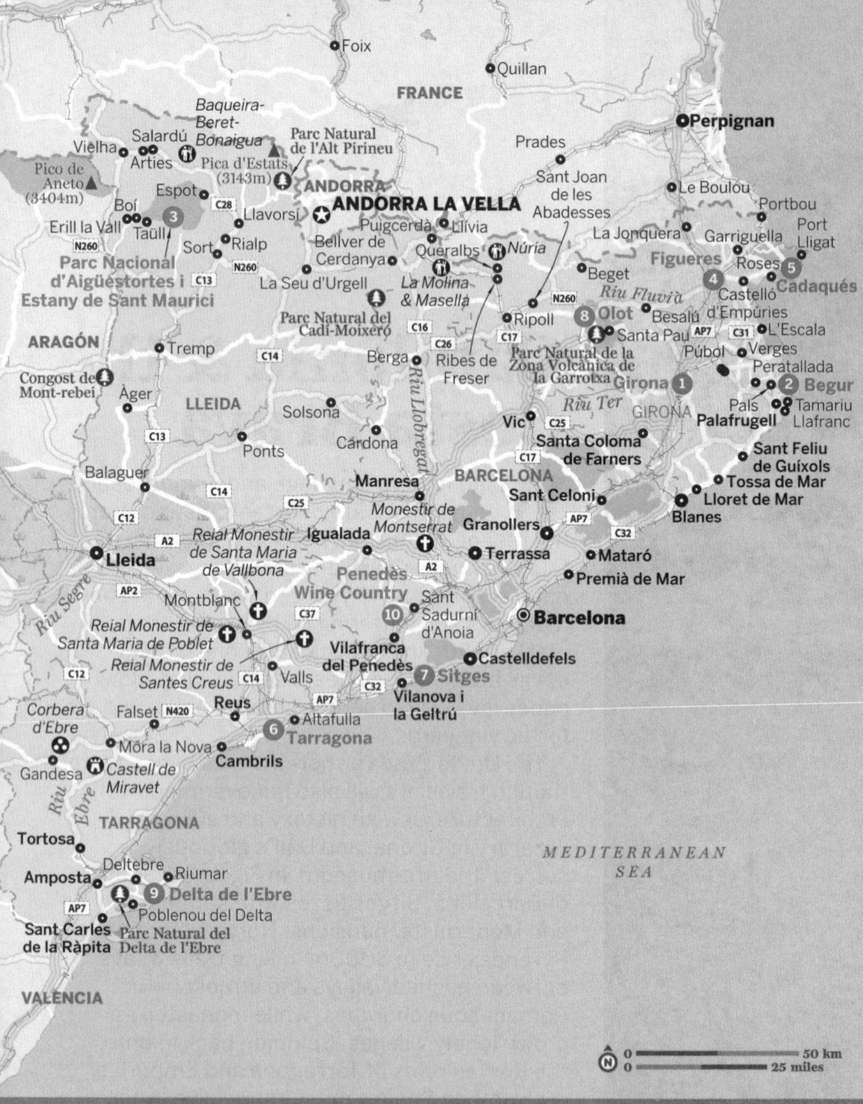


## Catalonia & Costa Brava Highlights

1 **Girona** (p331) Wandering the city's cobbled alleys and medieval Jewish quarter.

2 **Begur** (p330) Exploring the hidden beaches.

3 **Parc Nacional d'Aigüestortes i Estany de Sant Maurici** (p361) Conquering high-altitude lakeside trails.

4 **Teatre-Museu Dalí** (p347) Unravelling Salvador Dalí's theatre of the absurd in Figueres.

5 **Cadaqués** (p342) Wandering trails to Dalí's home and the wild Cap de Creus.

6 **Tarragona** (p378) Marvelling at Roman ruins in the heart of this lively city.

7 **Sitges** (p374) Partying hard in this beachside town.

8 **Olot** (p351) Dining on *cuina volcànica*.

9 **Delta de l'Ebre** (p384) Spotting flamingos in these biologically rich wetlands.

10 **Penedès Wine Country** (p377) Visiting celebrated vineyards and bodegas.

## COSTA BRAVA

Stretching north from Barcelona to the Spanish–French border, the Costa Brava (Rugged Coast) is undoubtedly the most beautiful of Spain's three main holiday coasts. Though there's plenty of tourism development, this wonderfully scenic region of Catalonia also unveils unspoiled coves, spectacular seascapes, wind-battered headlands, coast-hugging hiking paths, charming seaside towns with outstanding restaurants, and some of Spain's finest diving around the protected Illes Medes.

Delightful stone villages and the majestic Romanesque monastery of Sant Pere de Rodes nestle in the hilly backcountry, cloaked in the south in brilliant-green umbrella pine. Inland, wander northern Catalonia's biggest city, Girona, home to a moodily atmospheric, strikingly well-preserved medieval centre and one of the world's top restaurants. Neighbouring Figueres is famed for its bizarre Teatre-Museu Dalí, foremost of a series of sites associated with eccentric surrealist artist Salvador Dalí, who fell, like many others, for the wild natural beauty of seaside Cadaqués.

# Tossa de Mar

POP 5600

Tossa de Mar curves around a boat-speckled bay, guarded by a headland crowned with impressive defensive medieval walls and towers. Tourism has bolted a larger, modern extension onto this picturesque village of crooked, narrow streets, though its old town and clifftop views retain their beauty.

Tossa was one of the first places on the Costa Brava to attract foreign visitors: a small colony of artists and writers gravitated towards what Russian-French painter Marc Chagall dubbed 'Blue Paradise' in the 1930s. It was made famous by Ava Gardner in the 1951 film *Pandora and the Flying Dutchman*; a statue of the silver-screen queen lies on the path towards the lighthouse.

### Sights

The deep-ochre fairy-tale walls and towers on pine-dotted **Mont Guardí**, the headland at the southern end of Tossa's main beach, were built between the 12th and 14th centuries. They encircle the **Vila Vella** (old town), which reached peak splendour in the 15th century; it's now crammed with steep cobbled streets and whitewashed houses garlanded with flowers. A 1917 **lighthouse** crowns Mont Guardí.

### Sleeping & Eating

**Manà Manà** HOSTEL €

(972 34 25 49; www.manamanahostel.com; Carrer Sant Telm 9; dm €22-30, d €60-100; May-Sep; ) A colourful, sociable hostel just two minutes' walk from the beach, Manà Manà sleeps budgeteers in four- or six-bed dorms (including a female-only dorm) with individual lockers, shared bathrooms and lively decor.

**Cap d'Or** HOTEL €€

(972 34 00 81; www.hotelcapdor.com; Passeig del Mar 1; incl breakfast s/d/tr €92/142/180; Easter–early-Oct; ) Get wrapped up in Tossa's history at this family-run spot right below the old-town walls. The 10 rooms are simple but lovingly decorated with vintage-feel pictures and quaint marine miscellany; the best look straight onto the beach. There's a cheery all-day cafe-restaurant serving seafood, salads, omelettes and snacks.

**La Cuina de Can Simón** CATALAN €€€

(972 34 12 69; www.cuinacansimon.com; Carrer del Portal 24; mains €28-42, tasting menus €70-100; 1-3.30pm & 8-10.30pm, closed Mon Apr-Jul & Sep, closed Sun night, Mon & Tue Oct-Mar) This is the standout of a slew of restaurants hugging the old wall along Carrer del Portal. Within an 18th-century fisher's stone house, Michelin-starred La Cuina de Can Simón credits its innovative dishes to a dual heritage: the owners' grandparents were a fisherman and an artist. Flavoursome seasonal fusions include meunière sole with Iberian ham, or a seafood-packed bouillabaisse.

### Information

**Oficina de Turisme de Tossa de Mar** (972 34 01 08; www.infotossa.com; Avinguda del Pelegrí 25; 9am-9pm Mon-Sat, 10am-2pm & 5-8pm Sun Jun-Sep, 9.30am-2pm & 4-7pm Mon-Sat, 10am-2pm Sun Oct-May, closed Sun Nov-Mar) Next to Tossa's bus station.

### Getting There & Away

From Tossa's **bus station** (Plaça de les Nacions Sense Estat), Sarfa (www.sarfa.com) runs to/from Barcelona's Estació del Nord (€12.35, 1¼ hours, five to six daily) and airport (€14.50, 2¼ hours, two to five daily), plus Girona airport from mid-June to October (€10.10, 55 minutes, two daily).

# Palafrugell & Around

Halfway up the coast from Barcelona to the French border begins one of the most beautiful stretches of the Costa Brava. The town of Palafrugell, 4km inland, is the main access point for a cluster of enticing beach spots. Calella de Palafrugell, Llafranc and Tamariu, one-time fishing villages squeezed into gorgeous small bays, are three of the Costa Brava's most charming, low-key resorts.

Begur, 7km northeast of Palafrugell, is a handsomely conserved, castle-topped village with a cluster of less-developed beaches nearby. Inland, seek out tiny Pals and the fabulous cobbled village of Peratallada.

## Palafrugell

POP 22,900

Palafrugell, 4km west of the coast, is the main transport, shopping and services hub for the exquisite stretch of Costa Brava extending north from Calella de Palafrugell to Begur. But this inland town is more than just a way station en route to the beach. There are artistic and cultural treasures to uncover in Plaça Can Mario, plus the striking Gothic church of Sant Martí de Palafrugell.

### Information

**Oficina de Turisme Palafrugell** (☎972 30 02 28; www.visitpalafrugell.cat; Avinguda de la Generalitat 33; ⊙10am-8pm Mon-Sat Jul & Aug, 10am-1pm & 4-7pm Mon-Sat Easter-Jun & Sep–mid-Oct, 10am-5pm Mon-Fri, 10am-1pm & 4-7pm Sat mid-Oct–Easter, 9.30am-1.30pm Sun year-round) Just off the C31 on the southwest edge of town.

### Getting There & Away

From the **bus station** (Carrer de Lluís Companys), Sarfa (www.sarfa.com) connects Palafrugell with Barcelona (€18.85, 2¼ hours, six to seven daily) and Girona (€6.60, one to 1½ hours, 10 to 25 daily). Buses also run to Calella de Palafrugell, Llafranc and Tamariu (summer only) on the coast.

## Calella de Palafrugell

POP 740

The whitewashed buildings of Calella, the southernmost of Palafrugell's seaside crown jewels, cluster Aegean-style around a bay of rocky points and small, pretty beaches, with a few fishing boats hauled up on the sand. Though deservedly well known for its beauteous bay, Calella has resisted the temptation to sprawl, and maintains its agreeably tucked-away feel, despite being merrily packed with visitors in summer. Just outside of town, the lovely botanical gardens fill with song in July and August during the **Cap Roig Festival** (www.caproigfestival.com).

### Sights & Activities

From Calella, you can stroll along dreamy **coastal footpaths** – including the long-distance GR92 and Camí de Ronda (p346) – northeast to Llafranc (30 minutes, 1.5km), Tamariu (two to three hours, around 6km) and beyond, or south to Platja del Golfet, near Cap Roig (1.5km, 40 minutes).

**Jardins de Cap Roig** GARDENS

(☎972 61 45 82; http://fundacionlacaixa.org/ca/centros/jardines-de-cap-roig; Cap Roig; adult/senior & student/child €10/5/free; ⊙10am-8pm Apr-Sep, to 6pm Oct-Mar, weekends only Jan & Feb) Atop Cap Roig, 2km southwest of Calella, these beautiful botanical gardens contain approximately 1000 floral species, set around the early-20th-century castle-palace of Nikolai Voevodsky – a tsarist colonel with expensive tastes, who fell out of grace in his homeland after the Russian revolution.

From mid-July to late August, the gardens host open-air concerts (tickets from €30), featuring big-name performers like Sting, the Vamps and Julieta Venegas.

### Sleeping & Eating

**Hotel Mediterrani** HOTEL €€€

(☎972 61 45 00; www.hotelmediterrani.com; Carrer de Lladó 55; d incl breakfast €130-285; ⊙Apr-Oct; P❄📶) Fresh, boutique-ified rooms decked out with subdued murals over the beds, many with exquisite views of a sliver of sand and the aquamarine sea, make this long-standing family-run hotel at the southwest end of town very hard to beat.

★**La Blava** CATALAN €€

(☎972 61 40 60; www.lablava.com; Carrer de Miramar 3; mains €16-24; ⊙1-3.45pm & 8-10.45pm Jun-Oct, weekends only Apr & May) In a former fisher's house overlooking the beach, La Blava has earned a loyal following for its exquisite seafood, best enjoyed at outdoor tables overlooking the lapping waves. The small, well-curated menu ensures you can't go wrong, whether opting for the simple perfection of braised octopus with smoked paprika, or something richer like black rice with squid, cuttlefish and clams. Reservations essential.

# Costa Brava

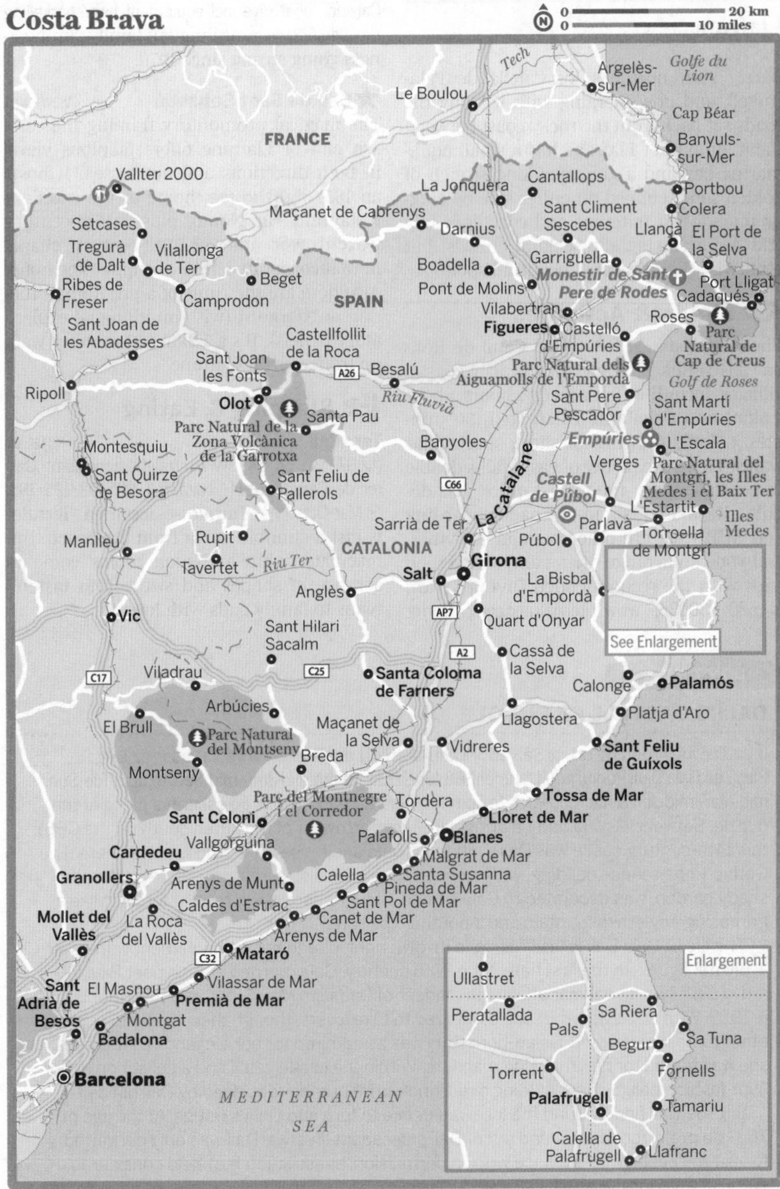


## Information

**Oficina de Turisme Calella de Palafrugell** (☎972 61 44 75; www.visitpalafrugell.cat; Carrer de les Voltes 4; ⊙10am-1pm & 5-8pm daily Jul & Aug, 10am-1pm & 4-7pm Mon-Sat, 10am-1pm Sun Jun & Sep, open weekends only Apr, May & early Oct) Seasonal info booth.

## Getting There & Away

**Sarfa/Moventis** (www.sarfa.com; www.moventis.es) buses link Calella with Palafrugell (€1.75, 15 minutes, three to 10 daily), plus Tamariu and Llafranc.

## Llafranc

POP 290

Barely 2km northeast of Calella de Palafrugell, and now merging with it along the roads set back from the rocky coast between them, upmarket Llafranc has a small aquamarine bay and a gorgeous long stretch of golden sand, cupped on either side by craggy pine-dotted outcrops and coastline. July and August bring sun-seeking crowds, but otherwise it's a peaceful, beautiful spot.

### Sights & Activities

The long-distance GR92 and Camí de Ronda (p346) link Llafranc with nearby coastal villages, including Tamariu (1½ hours, about 4.5km) and Calella de Palafrugell (30 minutes, 1.5km), allowing for short, spectacular walks. There are plenty of easy walks doable in beach sandals; the tourist office has details. Kayaking, stand-up paddleboarding and SUP yoga are other popular activities, and you can arrange diving and snorkelling trips with the recommended **Diving Triton** (☎620 530036; www.tritonllafranc.com; Carrer Carudo; boat dive incl equipment hire/snorkelling trip €46/22), a multilingual, family-run business going strong since 1979.

**★Cap de Sant Sebastià** VIEWPOINT

The magical promontory framing the eastern end of Llafranc offers fabulous views in both directions and out to sea. It hosts an 1857 **lighthouse**, home to the excellent restaurant Far Nomo, plus a 15th-century **watchtower** and an 18th-century chapel now incorporated into an upmarket hotel. Also here are the ruins of a pre-Roman Iberian **settlement** (with multilingual explanatory panels). It's a 1.2km (20-minute) walk up from central Llafranc.

### Sleeping & Eating

**Terralet** HOTEL €€

(☎972 30 64 54; www.terraletllafranc.com; Carrer de Carudo 12-14; tw/d/tr/f €85/98/125/195; ⏲Mar-Oct; 📶) Turquoise-accented Terralet is just a stumble north from the beach. Immaculate, white-and-aqua rooms come in a range of shapes and sizes, from tasteful twins to family pads with lounge.

DON'T MISS

### DALÍ'S CASTELL DE PÚBOL

If you're intrigued by artist Salvador Dalí, **Castell de Púbol** (www.salvador-dali.org; Plaça de Gala Dalí, Púbol; adult/student €8/6; ⏲10am-8pm mid-Jun–mid-Sep, to 6pm Tue-Sun mid-Mar–mid-Jun & mid-Sep–Oct, to 5pm Tue-Sun Nov-early Jan) is an essential piece of the puzzle. Between Girona and Palafrugell (22km northwest of the latter, south off the C66), this 14th-century castle was Dalí's gift to his wife and muse Gala, who is buried here. The Gothic-Renaissance building, with creeper-covered walls, spiral stone staircases and a shady garden, was decorated to Gala's taste, though there are surrealist touches like a grimacing anglerfish fountain and a pouting-lips sofa.

The life of Gala Dalí is fascinating in its own right, due to her entanglement with several pivotal figures in the first half of the 20th century. Gala married French poet Paul Éluard in 1917, had a two-year affair with pioneer of Dadaism Max Ernst, and then met Dalí in 1929. With Dalí's approval she continued to take lovers, though their loyalty to each other remained fierce. Russian-born Gala was as admired for her elegance as much as she was feared for her imposing manners. Within the castle you'll find a collection of her high-fashion ballgowns, including a red-brick-print number designed by Dalí himself.

In 1969 Dalí finally found the ideal residence to turn into Gala's refuge. At the age of 76, Gala preferred to flit in and out of Dalí's decadent lifestyle. Dalí was only permitted to visit the castle with advance written permission, a restriction that held considerable erotic charge for the artist.

Today the Castell de Púbol forms the southernmost point of Catalonia's 'Salvador Dalí triangle'. The sombre castle is almost an antithesis to the flamboyance of Figueres' Teatre-Museu Dalí (p347) and Dalí's seaside home (p342) in Port Lligat near Cadaqués. To get here, catch a bus to La Pera from Girona (€3.05, 40 minutes, six to nine daily) or Palafrugell (€3.15, 30 minutes, seven to 10 daily), and alight at the stop on the C66 then walk 2km south to the castle. Alternatively, take a train from Girona to Flaça (€3.30, 15 minutes, at least 15 daily), then taxi the last 5km.

**Hotel El Far** HOTEL €€€

(☎972 30 16 39; www.hotelelfar.com; Cap de Sant Sebastià; r incl breakfast €230-335; ⊙mid-Feb–mid-Jan; P❄📶) At romantic El Far – a happy marriage between secluded clifftop luxury and delectable local seafood – each plush, maritime-feel room has its own balcony, most affording superb sea vistas. The restaurant turns out fresh seafood and delectable rice dishes (mains €19 to €28), including good *fideuà*.

**Far Nomo** ASIAN €€

(☎972 30 15 21; www.gruponomo.com; Passeig de Pau Casals 64; sharing plates €8-18; ⊙1.30-4pm & 8-11.30pm Tue-Sun) Beneath the San Sebastià lighthouse, Far Nomo specialises in Asian-accented seafood served in a relaxed but stylish setting overlooking a pine-clad hillside and the Mediterranean beyond. Grab a table on the wisteria-fringed terrace and linger over tuna-belly tacos, sushi platters, perfectly crispy tempura and imaginative concoctions like the mouthwatering scallop brochette topped with foie gras.

**Casamar** CATALAN €€€

(☎972 300 104; www.hotelcasamar.net; Carrer del Nero 3; mains €21-28, set menus €55-84; ⊙1.30-3.30pm & 8.30-10.30pm Tue-Sat, 1.30-3.30pm Sun mid-Apr–Dec) Fabulously located on a headland overlooking Llafranc's bay, this top-notch Michelin-starred restaurant serves classy seafood and artful mains concocted with creatively selected ingredients, in a refreshingly friendly atmosphere.

## Information

**Oficina de Turisme de Llafranc** (☎972 30 50 08; www.visitpalafrugell.cat; Passeig de Cípsela; ⊙10am-1pm & 5-8pm Jul & Aug, 10am-1pm & 4-7pm Mon-Sat, 10am-1pm Sun Jun & Sep, weekends only Apr, May & early Sep) Seasonal kiosk at the western end of the beach.

## Getting There & Away

Sarfa/Moventis (www.sarfa.com; www.moventis.es) buses serve Llafranc from Palafrugell (€1.75, 20 minutes, three to 10 daily), as well as Tamariu and Calella de Palafrugell.

# Tamariu

POP 310

Just 4km north from Llafranc, tiny, quiet Tamariu fronts a fabulous, crescent-shaped cove infused with the scent of pine and fringed by pretty whitewashed houses. This beach has some of the most translucent waters on Spain's Mediterranean coast.

Lovely **coastal walks** start from Tamariu, mostly along the long-distance GR92 and Camí de Ronda (p346); the most popular walk is south to Llafranc via Cap de Sant Sebastià (1½ hours, about 4.5km). It's also easy to find kayaking and SUP outlets.

## Sleeping & Eating

**Hotel Tamariu** HOTEL €€

(☎972 62 00 31; www.tamariu.com; Passeig del Mar 2; incl breakfast s €85-110, d €115-185; ⊙late-Feb–early Nov; ❄📶) A former fisher's tavern, the jolly Hotel Tamariu has been family-run for four generations. It has spacious rooms with a clean, minimalist design, oversized windows and maritime-themed artwork on the walls. Some rooms have a balcony offering views of this little beach town. The owners also rent apartments nearby.

## Information

**Oficina de Turisme de Tamariu** (☎972 62 01 93; www.visitpalafrugell.cat; Carrer de la Riera; ⊙10am-1pm & 5-8pm Jul & Aug, 10am-1pm & 5-8pm Mon-Sat, 10am-1pm Sun Jun & Sep) Summer-only info booth.

## Getting There & Away

Sarfa/Moventis (www.sarfa.com; www.moventis.es) buses connect Tamariu with Palafrugell (€1.75, 15 minutes, three to eight daily) from mid-May to mid-October only.

# Begur & Around

POP 3930

Crowned by an 11th-century castle, with exquisite coast glistening in its surrounds, Begur is one of the most beautiful and sought-after spots along the Costa Brava. This fairy-tale town, 8km northeast of Palafrugell, has a tempting array of restaurants, beach-chic boutiques, soothing heritage and boutique hotels, and Modernista mansions that add splashes of colour among the stone streets of its medieval centre. And if that weren't enough, a series of scenic winding roads spiral down to dreamy little coves hemmed in by pines, like Aiguablava, Fornells, Sa Tuna, Sa Riera and Aiguafreda.

## Sights & Activities

There are some lovely **walking trails** around Begur, including to several attractive beaches and an 11.5km hike south to Tamariu (five

DON'T MISS

## TREASURED BEACHES AROUND BEGUR

With pocket-sized coves framed by pine trees and subtropical flowers, and lapped by crystalline water, the sublime coastline around Begur is home to some of Spain's most gorgeous beaches. Their small size and difficult access means many remain largely undeveloped, making them some of the Costa Brava's quieter spots to soak up some rays.

From mid-June to mid-September, Sarfa (www.sarfa.com) runs *bus platges* (€1) services to Sa Tuna, Sa Riera, Fornells and Aiguablava from Begur's Plaça de Forgas. Or you could follow one of several scenic walks to your beach of choice.

**Cala d'Aiguafreda** Around 4.5km northeast of Begur you'll find this tiny, divine rocky cove, where trails fringed by pine trees stretch around a headland. It's more a picturesque place for a stroll than a sunbathing spot.

**Platja Fonda** (Fornells) From just northeast of Fornells' car park (4km south of Begur), stone stairs lead down to signposted Platja Fonda, a slate-grey pebbly beach that lures sunbathers (though it can be choppy). A path signed 'Fornells' branches off just before the steps to reach a stunning stony outcrop with a natural pool.

**Cala de Sa Tuna** (Sa Tuna) The finely pebbled beach of Sa Tuna sits in a small cove 3km east of Begur, fringed by now-remodelled fishers' houses. There are restaurants and parking, though the water can be a little unsettled. This scenic stretch of coast is backed by an old stone watchtower. You can walk to Sa Tuna along a 2.3km path from Begur.

hours) along the GR92. Keep an eye out for Modernista and colonial-era buildings along Begur's old-town streets. The tourist office has leaflets for self-guided historical walking tours.

**Castell de Begur** VIEWPOINT

(Pujada al Castell; ⏲24hr) FREE There is little to explore aside from the ragged ruins of this medieval castle, still in much the same state as when it was wrecked by Spanish troops to impede the advance of Napoleon's army in 1810. A steep, signposted 1km walk leads from central Begur to the ramparts (25 minutes), with breathtaking views over hills rolling towards the Mediterranean.

## Sleeping & Eating

**Sa Barraca** B&B €€

(☎972 62 33 60; www.sabarraca.com; Carrer Begur–Aiguablava (GIV6532); r €72-118; P❄📶) This exceptionally welcoming, good-value B&B perches high on a pine-covered hillside, 3km south of Begur en route to Aiguablava beach, unveiling some of the finest coastal views around. It's expertly run by charming hosts who prepare fresh breakfasts (€8.50), and there are just seven homey, spacious rooms, all with wide-open terraces.

**★Cluc Hotel** BOUTIQUE HOTEL €€€

(☎972 62 48 59; www.cluc.cat; Carrer del Metge Pi 8; d incl breakfast €123-210; ❄📶) One of old-town Begur's chicest, yet friendliest, hotels unfolds across this ravishing, revamped 1800 *casa d'indians* (house built by a returned colonist). The 12 rooms are on the small side, but decorated in elegant vintage style with restored furniture and tile-covered floors. Expect an honesty bar, a library and homemade breakfasts on a charming terrace. No kids under 12.

**Sa Rascassa** HOSTAL €€€

(☎972 62 28 45; www.hostalsarascassa.com; Cala d'Aiguafreda; s/d incl breakfast €155/170; ⏲Mar-Oct; ❄📶🐾) It's a choice of five rooms at this glammed-up and efficiently operated *hostal* tucked away in pine-shaded Cala d'Aiguafreda, 4.5km northeast of Begur. Dove greys and cosy creams speckle the tasteful, unfussy rooms, all with garden views. There's ample outdoor lounging space, plus an honesty bar and a summer *xiringuito* (beach bar), and you can't beat the secluded location.

In the candlelit garden, the fantastic contemporary-Catalan **restaurant** (mains €14-24; ⏲1.30-3.30pm & 8.30-11pm Wed-Mon Mar-Oct; 📶) delights palates.

**Aiguaclara** HERITAGE HOTEL €€€

(☎972 62 29 05; www.hotelaiguaclara.com; Carrer Santa Teresa 3; r €176-230; ⏲mid-Feb–mid-Dec; P❄📶) Filled with both historical charm and boutique flavour, romantic Aiguaclara is set within a pink-washed mid 19th-century *casa d'indians*. Original soaring ceilings and antique tiles mingle with contemporary art, retro styling, pops of colour and gleaming modern bathrooms in the 10 airy, uncluttered rooms. Great breakfasts start the day, while a cocktail lounge and excellent **restaurant** (mains €15-22; ⏲ from 6pm Tue-Sat) occupy the garden.

## Information

**Oficina de Turisme de Begur** (☎ 972 62 45 20; www.visitbegur.com; Avinguda del Onze de Setembre 5; ⏲ 9am-8pm Mon-Fri, 10am-8pm Sat & Sun Jun-Sep, 9am-2.30pm Mon-Fri, 10am-2pm Sat Oct-May) Helpful office with information on Begur's sights, walks and beaches.

## Getting There & Away

Sarfa (www.sarfa.com) buses run to Barcelona's Estació del Nord (€19.85, two to 2½ hours, three daily), Palafrugell (€1.75, 15 minutes, four to 11 daily), and to Girona (€8.50, 1¼ hours, one daily weekdays).

# Pals

POP 2500

About 7km northwest of shimmering Begur, halfway to popular Peratallada, sits the gorgeous walled town of Pals. Although most of its historical buildings can only be admired from outside, simply wandering the uneven cobbled lanes and peeking into the many medieval corners makes a visit worthwhile.

The **tourist office** (☎ 972 63 73 80; www.visitpals.com; Plaça Major; ⏲ 10am-2.30pm & 5-8pm Apr-Sep, 10am-5pm Mon-Sat, to 2.30pm Sun Oct-Mar) provides detailed booklets (Catalan, Spanish and English) for self-guided walking tours of Pals' old town.

**Torre de les Hores** TOWER

(Clock Tower; Carrer de la Torre; €1; ⏲ 4-7pm Tue, 10.30am-2pm & 4-7pm Wed-Sun May-Sep, 10.30am-2pm & 4-7pm Sat & Sun Oct-Apr) Pals' main monument is the 15m-high Romanesque Torre de les Hores, originally part of a castle; its 16th-century bell still rings today. Climb to the top for a memorable view over fields and the distant seaside, with the Iles Medes visible on the horizon.

## Getting There & Away

Sarfa (www.sarfa.com) buses run from Pals to Barcelona's Estació del Nord (€20.40, 2¾ hours, three daily) and airport (€22.45, 3½ hours, two daily), plus Begur (€1.75, 10 to 20 minutes, three to nine daily), Palafrugell (€1.75, 25 minutes, three to nine daily) and Girona (€6.80, one hour, daily on weekdays).

# Peratallada

POP 460

As soon as you set foot in heart-stoppingly pretty Peratallada, 15km northwest of Begur, it's obvious why this fortified medieval town is beloved by Barcelona day trippers, French tourists and everyone else. Pale archways, cobbled squares and sandstone houses strung with ivy conjure an air of fairy-tale romance, though most of the historic buildings can only be gazed at from the outside. Peratallada's many visitors are well catered for by handicraft and clothing shops that beckon from laneways winding between crumbling walls and an 11th-century castle.

**El Cau del Papibou** HOTEL €€

(☎ 972 63 47 16; www.hotelelcaudelpapibou.com; Carrer Major 10; r €85-145; ⏲ Jan-Nov, closed Mon & Tue Oct-Mar; 📶) Stylish, colour-themed rooms with beamed ceilings, distressed-wood decor and rustic views fill this friendly, characterful hideaway in a 12th-century building in the heart of Peratallada. Downstairs, the restaurant serves an international menu of set lunches, pizzas and grilled dishes (mains €14 to €18) in an ivy-draped courtyard.

**El Borinot** CATALAN €€

(☎ 972 63 42 21; Carrer del Forn 15; mains €15-19; ⏲ noon-4pm Mon, 1-10.30pm Wed-Sun) Tucked along an ivy-clad medieval lane, El Borinot serves beautifully prepared seasonal cuisine with global accents, best enjoyed on the peaceful front terrace. Tuck into fish of the day with Asian-style veggies, fettuccini *amatriciana* (with bacon and tomato), Angus steak tacos, or refreshing salads of watermelon, bulgur and feta. Three-course lunch menus (€13.50) are excellent value.

## Getting There & Away

Weekday Sarfa (www.sarfa.com) buses serve Peratallada from Palafrugell (€3.45, 55 minutes, two weekdays), Begur (€2.25, 20 to 40 minutes, two weekdays) and Girona (€5.10, 55 minutes, one weekday).

# Girona

POP 100,500

Northern Catalonia's largest city, Girona is a jewellery box of museums, galleries and Gothic churches, strung around a web of cobbled lanes and medieval walls. Reflections of Modernista mansions shimmer in the Riu Onyar, which separates the walkable historic centre on its eastern bank from the gleaming commercial centre on the west.

## CATALONIA & SPAIN

Like many European nations, the kingdom of Spain was cobbled together by a series of conquests and dynastic alliances from what were once separate states. Though the last of these was over 500 years ago, people in the peninsula still tend to identify more strongly with their ancestral village or local region – the *patria chica* ('small fatherland') – than with the nation as a whole. There are separatist movements in parts of the peninsula, but especially in the Basque Country and Catalonia.

Away from Barcelona and the Costa Brava, Catalonia feels as if you've entered a separate country. Little Spanish is spoken and the red-and-yellow flag of the region flutters from balconies and town squares. The widespread feeling, as expressed by an often-encountered piece of graffiti, is that 'Catalonia is not Spain'.

The genesis of Catalonia began when the Franks, under Charlemagne, pushed back the Moors in the 8th and 9th centuries. The Catalan golden age came in the early 12th century when Ramon Berenguer III, who already controlled Catalonia and parts of southern France, launched the region's first seagoing fleet. In 1137 his successor, Ramon Berenguer IV, was betrothed to the one-year-old heiress to the Aragonese throne, thereby giving Catalonia sufficient power to expand its empire out into the Mediterranean but joining it to another crown. Modern Spain was effectively created when Fernando became king of Aragón in 1479, having already married Isabel, Queen of Castile.

Catalonia resented its new subordinate status but could do little to overturn it. After backing the losing side in the War of Spanish Succession (1702–14), Barcelona rose up against the Spanish crown, whose armies besieged the city from March 1713 until 11 September 1714. The victorious Felipe V abolished Catalan privileges, banned writing and teaching in Catalan, and farmed out Catalonia's colonies to other European powers.

Trade again flourished from Barcelona in the centuries that followed, and by the late 19th and early 20th centuries there were growing calls for greater self-governance. However, after the Spanish Civil War ended in 1939, pro-republic Catalonia was treated harshly by victorious General Franco. Reprisals and purges resulted in the shootings of at least 35,000 people. The use of Catalan in public was banned and all street and town names were changed into Spanish, which became the only permitted language in schools and the media. Self-government was returned after Franco's death in 1975, though the sense of grievance remains.

Recent decades have seen Catalan culture flourish, reflected in the reemergence of traditional festivals and dances, the prevalence of Catalan flags and the near-universal use of Catalan in public. For Catalans, their language is the key to their identity.

The issue of independence from Spain has been at the forefront of Catalan politics for years, and it took on greater importance and urgency following Spain's economic crisis be-

The Roman town of Gerunda lay on the Via Augusta from Gades (now Cádiz) to the Pyrenees. Taken from the Muslims by the Franks in the late 8th century, Girona became the capital of one of Catalonia's most important counties, falling under the sway of Barcelona in the late 9th century. Girona's wealth in medieval times produced many fine Romanesque and Gothic buildings that have survived repeated attacks, while a Jewish community flourished here until 1492.

## Sights

Girona's exquisitely preserved **Call** (Jewish Quarter) – a labyrinth of low-slung stone arches and slender cobbled streets – flourished around narrow Carrer de la Força for six centuries, until relentless Christian persecution forced the Jews (p336) out of Spain. For deeper insight into Girona, take a 90-minute walking tour (€12) offered daily (except Mondays) at noon by the Oficina de Turisme de Girona (p338).

### ★Catedral de Girona CATHEDRAL

(www.catedraldegirona.cat; Plaça de la Catedral; adult/concession incl Basílica de Sant Feliu €7/5; ⏲10am-7.30pm Jul & Aug, to 6.30pm Apr-Jun, Sep & Oct, to 5.30pm Nov-Mar) Towering over a flight of 86 steps rising from Plaça de la Catedral, Girona's imposing cathedral is far more ancient than its billowing baroque facade suggests. Built over an old Roman forum, parts of its foundations date from the 5th century. Today, 14th-century Gothic styling – added over an 11th-century Ro-

ginning in 2008. In September 2015, a pro-independence coalition led by Catalan President Carles Puigdemont promised to hold a referendum on Catalan independence.

The central Spanish government in Madrid, under Prime Minister Mariano Rajoy said that such a referendum would be illegal. The Catalan government went ahead and declared it was going to hold one on 1 October 2017. The Spanish government sent in the Policía Nacional (Spain's national police) to try to prevent the referendum taking place, resulting in some scenes of violence at polling stations, with, the Catalan government said, over 800 people injured. According to the Catalan government, of the 43% of potential voters who took part in the referendum, 90% voted for independence. Spain's constitutional court had declared the referendum illegal before it took place.

Large crowds, especially in Barcelona, protested against the Spanish police action and the Spanish government's attempt to stop the referendum. In the following days, however, a wave of support for Spanish national unity swept through much of the rest of the country and even Catalonia itself, including an anti-independence demonstration of 350,000 people in Barcelona. Before the referendum, some opinion polls had come up with the finding that only about 40% to 45% of the Catalan population supported independence.

On 27 October, the Catalan parliament voted for independence, and the national parliament in Madrid invoked Article 155 of the Spanish constitution (never used before), which allowed it to rescind the autonomy of regions in extreme circumstances, bringing them under direct rule from Madrid. Puigdemont and his cabinet were sacked, the Catalan parliament dismissed, and snap elections were called.

Not long after, Spain's attorney-general charged Puigdemont and 13 of his ministers with rebellion and sedition, which carry maximum sentences of 30 years and 15 years respectively. But by then Puigdemont and four ministers had disappeared to Brussels, and, as of 2021, remain there, adamant that they will not return to Spain unless they are guaranteed a fair trial. Meanwhile, nine separatist leaders who remained in Spain were thrown in jail. In late 2019, the Spanish supreme court sentenced the nine to prison terms ranging from nine to 13 years on charges of sedition, and a new arrest warrant was issued for Puigdemont. The ruling set off a wave of protests across Catalonia.

The overall situation remains uncertain, though the Catalan independence movement shows no signs of slowing down. Some Catalans feel their taxes subsidise the rest of the nation, and the tough economic times resulting from the 2008 economic crisis have exacerbated this feeling. But the very fact that Catalonia is such a valuable asset makes the central government unwilling to let it go. Catalans aren't universally in favour of independence. As of late 2019, regional polling indicated support for independence remains fairly evenly split.

manesque church – dominates, though a beautiful, double-columned Romanesque **cloister** dates from the 12th century. With the world's second-widest Gothic nave, it's a formidable sight to explore; audio guides are provided.

Highlights include the richly carved fantastical beasts and biblical scenes in the cloister's southern gallery, and a 14th-century silver altarpiece, studded with gemstones, portraying 16 scenes from the life of Christ. Also seek out the bishop's throne and the **museum**, which holds the masterly Romanesque *Tapís de la creació (Tapestry of the Creation)*; dating from the 11th or 12th century, the tapestry shows God surrounded by the creation of Adam, Eve, the animals, the sky, light and darkness.

**★Museu d'Història dels Jueus** MUSEUM
(www.girona.cat/call; Carrer de la Força 8; adult/child €4/free; ⏲10am-8pm Mon-Sat, to 2pm Sun Jul & Aug, 10am-6pm Tue-Sat, to 2pm Mon & Sun Sep-Jun) Until 1492, Girona was home to Catalonia's second-most important medieval Jewish community (p336), after Barcelona, and one of the country's finest Jewish quarters. This excellent museum takes pride in this heritage, without shying away from less salubrious aspects such as Inquisition persecution and forced conversions. You also see a rare 11th-century *miqvé* (ritual bath) and a 13th-century Jewish house.

**Museu d'Art de Girona** GALLERY
(www.museuart.com; Pujada de la Catedral 12; €6, incl Catedral and Basílica de Sant Feliu €10; ⏲10am-7pm Tue-Sat May-Sep, to 6pm Oct-Apr, to

## Girona

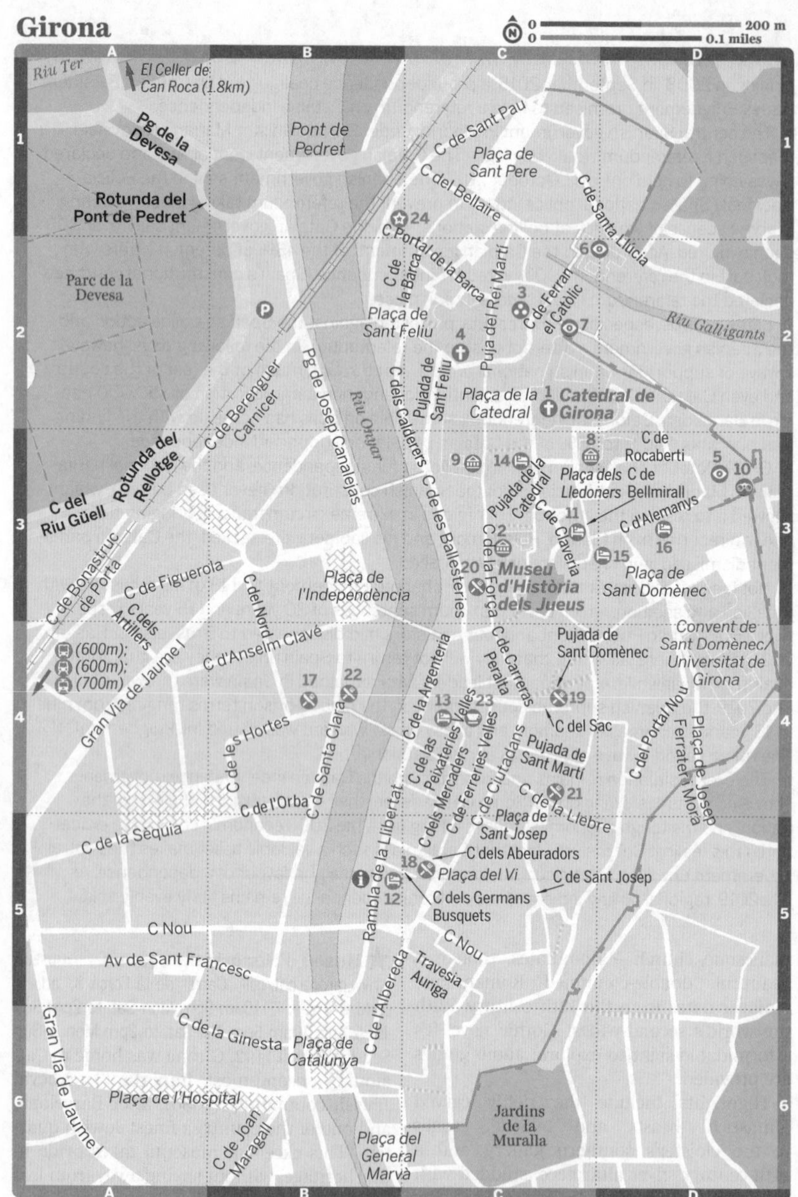


2pm Sun year-round) Next to the cathedral, in the 12th- to 16th-century Palau Episcopal, this art gallery impresses with the scale and variety of its collection. Around 8500 pieces of art, mostly from this region, fill its displays, which range from Romanesque woodcarvings and murals to paintings of the city by 20th-century Polish-French artist Mela Muter, early-20th-century sculptures by influential Catalan architect Rafael Masó i Valentí, and works by leading Modernista artist Santiago Rusiñol.

## Girona

### Top Sights
1 Catedral de Girona ........ C2
2 Museu d'Història dels Jueus ........ C3

### Sights
3 Banys Àrabs ........ C2
4 Basílica de Sant Feliu ........ C2
5 Jardins dels Alemanys ........ D3
6 Monestir de Sant Pere de Galligants ........ D2
7 Muralles de Girona ........ C2
8 Museu d'Art de Girona ........ C3
9 Museu d'Història de Girona ........ C3
10 Torre Gironella ........ D3

### Sleeping
11 Bellmiral ........ C3
12 Bells Oficis ........ B5
13 Bravissimo Girona ........ C4
14 Casa Cúndaro ........ C3
15 Hotel Històric ........ D3
16 Palau dels Alemanys ........ D3

### Eating
17 8de7 ........ B4
18 B12 ........ C5
19 Café Le Bistrot ........ C4
20 Federal ........ C3
21 La Fábrica ........ C4
22 Rocambolesc ........ B4

### Drinking & Nightlife
23 Espresso Mafia ........ C4

### Entertainment
24 Sunset Jazz Club ........ B1

**Basílica de Sant Feliu** BASILICA
(Plaça de Sant Feliu; adult/student incl Catedral €7/5; 10am-5.30pm Mon-Sat, 1-5.30pm Sun) Just downhill from the cathedral stands Girona's second great church, with its landmark truncated bell tower. The nave is majestic with Gothic ribbed vaulting, while St Narcissus, the city's patron, is venerated in an enormous marble-and-jasper, late-baroque side chapel. To the right of the chapel is the saint's Gothic, 1328 sepulchre (which previously held his remains), displaying his reclining form and scenes from his life including the conversion of women, martyrdom and expelling of an evil genie.

**Banys Àrabs** RUINS
(www.banysarabs.org; Carrer de Ferran el Catòlic; adult/child €2/1; 10am-7pm Mon-Sat Mar-Oct, to 6pm Mon-Sat Nov-Feb, to 2pm Sun year-round) Although modelled on earlier Islamic and Roman bathhouses, the Banys Àrabs are a finely preserved, 12th-century Christian affair in Romanesque style (restored in the 13th century). The baths contain an *apodyterium* (changing room), with a small octagonal pool framed by slender pillars, followed by a *frigidarium* and *tepidarium* (with respectively cold and warm water) and a *caldarium* (sauna) heated by a furnace.

**Muralles de Girona** WALLS
(Girona City Walls; Carrer de Ferran el Catòlic; dawn-dusk) FREE A walk along Girona's majestic medieval walls is a wonderful way to soak up the city landscape. There are several access points, including a lane east of the cathedral that leads into the thick greenery of the **Jardins dels Alemanys** (Carrer dels Alemanys). Nearby, you can clamber up a spiral staircase inside the **Torre Gironella** (Carrer dels Alemanys) for a fantastic lookout (and an excellent spot to watch the sunset). From there, you can continue along high above the rooftops to the Jardins de la Muralla where the wall ends.

**Monestir de Sant Pere de Galligants** MONASTERY
(www.mac.cat; Carrer de Santa Llúcia; adult/child incl Museu d'Arqueologia de Catalunya-Girona €6/4; 10am-6pm Tue-Sat Oct-Apr, to 7pm Tue-Sat May-Sep, to 2pm Sun year-round) This beautiful 11th- and 12th-century Romanesque Benedectine monastery has a sublime bell tower and a splendid cloister featuring otherworldly animals and mythical creatures on the 60 capitals of its double columns; there are some great architectural features in the church.

Spread across the monastery is the **Museu d'Arqueologia de Catalunya–Girona**, exhibiting artefacts dating from prehistoric to medieval times, including Roman mosaics, early-Christian sarcophagi and the 4th-century Roman marble *Sepulcre de les Estacions* (Sepulchre of the Seasons), unearthed from the ruins of Empúries (p340).

**Museu d'Història de Girona** MUSEUM
(www.girona.cat/museuhistoria; Carrer de la Força 27; adult/student/child €4/2/free; 10.30am-5.30pm Tue-Sat Oct-Apr, to 6.30pm Tue-Sat May-Sep, to 1.30pm Sun year-round) The 18th-century cloisters lend an appropriately antique feel to this journey from Roman Girona to medieval times to the present day. The museum's highlights include an exhibition illuminating the 3rd- to 4th-century Can

## GIRONA'S JEWS

The first records of a Jewish presence in Girona date to the 9th century and, by its 13th-century heyday, Girona's Jewish community was the second-largest in Catalonia (behind Barcelona). Jewish inhabitants lived, generally speaking, peacefully alongside their Christian neighbours, gaining in prosperity and contributing to fields as diverse as astronomy, mathematics and medicine.

Nevertheless, the Jewish communities came under Christian attack, especially in the 12th and 13th centuries. Girona's Call – a maze of slim alleys, surrounded by a stone wall – went from refuge to ghetto as Jews were gradually confined to their tiny corner of the town and banned from living beyond its western limits. Especially stomach-churning were the 'Disputes', rigged debates intended to ridicule pillars of the Jewish community against the supposedly superior logic of Christians. The spin of the day reported that these debates led to mass conversions, but it's likelier that Jews converted out of pressure and fear. Slander against Jews became increasingly grotesque, with tales of murdered Christian infants.

Things came to a head during a riot in 1391, when a mob broke into the Call, massacring 40 residents. Since the Jews were still under the king's protection, troops were sent in and the survivors confined to the Galligants Tower for 17 weeks (allegedly for their own safety), only to find their houses destroyed upon returning. Many converted to Christianity during the 15th century. In 1492 those who remained unconverted were expelled from Spain, ending a story that had been over 500 years in the making.

Pau Birol mosaic, which depicts a lively circus scene with charioteers, and an explanation of the 1808 to 1809 siege of Girona by Napoleonic troops. Many pieces on display are copies rather than originals. Spanish-, English- and French-language booklets help with the Catalan-only display labels.

## Sleeping

**★Bells Oficis** B&B €€

(☎972 22 81 70; www.bellsoficis.com; Carrer dels Germans Busquets 2; d incl breakfast €45-102; ❄📶) A lovingly restored 19th-century apartment towards the old town's southern end, Bells Oficis makes a stylish, ultra-welcoming base. It's the former home of Catalan artist Jaume Busquets i Mollera (a fresco he painted in 1921 adorns one room). Period details survive in the five very different rooms (one of which is a teeny two-bunk pad).

**Bravissimo Girona** APARTMENT €€

(☎608 480036; www.bravissimo-girona.com; Carrer Cort Reial 13; apt €120-325; ❄📶) This friendly, professional outfit rents out more than two-dozen attractive apartments around the old town. They range in size and features, from small modern studios to spacious three-bedrooms with old-world details that can sleep up to six. All are well-equipped (kitchens, reliable wi-fi, some with washing machines, others with river views).

**Casa Cúndaro** GUESTHOUSE €€

(☎972 22 35 83; www.casacundaro.com; Pujada de la Catedral 7; d €60-80, q & apt €110; ❄📶) The understated exterior of this medieval Jewish house hides five characterful rooms and four self-catering apartments (for two to five people), all mixing original open-stone walls and antique doors with modern comfort. It's right next to the cathedral – a boon or a bane, depending on whether you enjoy the sound of church bells.

The owners also run the upmarket **Hotel Històric** (☎972 22 35 83; www.hotelhistoric.com; Carrer de Bellmirall 4A; r €113-200; ❄📶) nearby, where 17 individually designed rooms blend historical flair (stone walls, beamed ceilings) and contemporary style in a medieval building with Roman-era foundations.

**Bellmiral** PENSION €€

(☎972 20 40 09; www.bellmirall.eu; Carrer de Bellmiral 3; incl breakfast s €50-68, d €90-100; 📶) An inviting rustic-feel guesthouse hidden up high in Girona's historic core, Bellmiral unravels across a centuries-old stone house artily decorated with paintings and bright accents of colour. The seven rooms, five of which have old-town views, are a tad more modern than you'd expect, with exposed-stone walls.

**★Palau dels Alemanys** HERITAGE HOTEL €€€

(☎618 536 852; www.facebook.com/palaudelsalemanys; Carrer dels Alemanys 10; r incl breakfast

€250; [P] [wifi]) A stay at this intimate historical beauty of an old-town hotel revolves around four exquisite 'suites' (mini-apartments with kitchenettes), under the watch of a keen young owner. Original architectural features, like Gothic arches and 18th-century stone walls, mingle with vintage furniture and chic contemporary styling. Breakfasts are brought to your door, and a chunk of Roman-era wall graces the courtyard.

## Eating

**★ La Fábrica** CAFE €

(www.lafabricagirona.com; Carrer de la Llebre 3; dishes €3-9; 9am-3pm; [wifi] [menu]) Girona's culinary talents morph into top-quality coffee and Catalan-inspired brunchy favourites starring local ingredients at this energetic German-Canadian–owned cycle-themed cafe. Pillowy artisan *torrades* (toasts) – perhaps topped with avocado, feta and peppers – arrive on wooden sliders, washed down with expertly poured brews made with beans sourced from eco-conscious suppliers.

**Federal** CAFE €

(872 26 45 15; www.federalcafe.es; Carrer de la Força 9; mains €7-14; 8.30am-8pm Mon-Thu, to 10pm Fri & Sat, 9am-7pm Sun; [wifi] [menu]) The same creative team behind the much-loved Barcelona cafe has opened a Federal in the heart of Girona's old town. Market-fresh organic ingredients star in a menu of brunch classics, delicious sandwiches and hearty salads. You'll also find decadent pastries and perfectly pulled espressos (plus a first-rate flat white).

**Rocambolesc** ICE CREAM €

(972 41 66 67; www.rocambolesc.com; Carrer de Santa Clara 50; ice cream €3-4.50; 11am-11pm Sun-Thu, to midnight Fri & Sat) Savour some of Spain's most lip-smackingly delicious ice cream at Rocambolesc, part of the world-famous El Celler de Can Roca culinary clan. Candy-striped decor sets the magical scene for creatively cool concoctions like baked-apple ice cream or mandarin sorbet sprinkled with passion-fruit flakes.

**B12** VEGETARIAN €€

(972 01 32 02; Plaça del Vi 11; 3-course set menu lunch/dinner €13.50/18; 11am-10pm Mon-Thu, to midnight Fri, 6-11pm Sat; [menu]) Poised under stone arches, low-key B12 throws organic vegan and vegetarian produce together into light, fresh and totally delicious plant-fuelled cooking. You might find yourself digging into cashew-cream pasta, veggie burgers, spicy Indonesian-style rice, or smoked tofu cakes with miso and mushrooms. There's also excellent craft beer on hand.

**Café Le Bistrot** CATALAN €€

(972 21 88 03; www.lebistrot.cat; Pujada de Sant Domènec 4; mains €8.50-18; 1-4pm & 7-11pm) Walls are draped in jasmine and tables spill out onto stairs climbing to a 17th-century church at this local favourite. The classic bistro-style menu twins French and Catalan cuisine, with crêpes, pastas, meaty mains, '*pagès*' pizzas and a huge array of *amanides* (salads) plus local cheeses.

**8de7** CATALAN €€

(972 10 44 30; Carrer de les Hortes 10; 3-course meal €18, tapas €4-9; 1-4pm & 9-11pm Tue-Sat) It's well worth venturing across the river to this low-key dining room serving up market-fresh daily specials like mouthwatering paella and grilled Iberian pork, as well as a fantastic tapas selection.

**★ El Celler de Can Roca** CATALAN €€€

(972 22 21 57; www.cellercanroca.com; Carrer Can Sunyer 48; degustation menus €190-220, with wine pairing €265-330; 8-9.30pm Tue, 12.30-2pm & 8-9.30pm Wed-Sat) Ever-changing avant-garde takes on Catalan dishes have catapulted El Celler de Can Roca to global fame. Holding three Michelin stars, it was named one of the best restaurants in the world numerous times by The World's 50 Best. Each year brings new innovations, from molecular gastronomy to multi-sensory food-art interplay, all with mama's home cooking as the core inspiration.

## Drinking & Nightlife

**Espresso Mafia** COFFEE

(www.espressomafia.cc; Carrer de la Cort Reial 5; 9am-7pm Mon-Thu, to 8pm Fri & Sat, 10am-4pm Sun; [wifi]) With stripped-back white-on-white decor and (nonsmoking) tables below moody stone arches, Espresso Mafia is your go-to caffeine-shot spot on Girona's growing coffee scene. From smooth espresso and art-adorned latte to good old *café amb llet* (coffee with milk), coffee creations here are based on sustainably sourced beans, and best enjoyed with a slab of homemade cake.

**Sunset Jazz Club** LIVE MUSIC

(872 08 01 45; www.sunsetjazz-club.com; Carrer Jaume Pons i Martí 12; 8pm-2.30am Thu-Tue) On the north end of the historic centre, this

WORTH A TRIP

### SLEEP UNDER THE STARS

Stargazers will adore **Mil Estrelles** (☎972 59 67 07; www.milestrelles.com; La Bastida, Borgonyà; d €143-293; P ❄ ☜), a unique, owner-designed country hideaway, 16km north of Girona. Fabulously combining old stone and modern plastic, it offers three lovably rustic rooms in a noble 18th-century farmhouse, as well as fun, stylish rooms (some with bathtubs) in clear plastic bubbles scattered around the garden, perfect for spotting constellations from the comfort of your double bed.

It's all designed for couples, with eco credentials in mind; there are no bathroom doors and facilities include a floatarium, sauna and hot tub, along with massages. Dinners are available, often delivered to your room. It's 1.5km northwest of Pont-Xetmar (which is on the C66) and well signposted. Book ahead, and leave the kids at home.

intimate, low-lit space makes a great setting for well-mixed cocktails and live jazz. There's live music most nights. Some concerts are free; others cost between €3 and €12.

## Information

**Oficina de Turisme de Girona** (☎972 01 00 01; www.girona.cat/turisme; Rambla de la Llibertat 1; ⏲9am-8pm Mon-Fri, 9am-2pm & 4-8pm Sat Apr-Oct, 9am-7pm Mon-Fri, 9am-2pm & 3-7pm Sat Nov-Mar, 9am-2pm Sun year-round) Helpful, multilingual office by the river.

## Getting There & Away

### AIR

The Aeroport de Girona–Costa Brava (www.aena.es), a Ryanair hub, is 13km southwest of central Girona.

### BUS

TEISA (www.teisa-bus.com) runs from Girona to Besalú (€4.15, 40 minutes to one hour, eight to 16 daily) and Olot (€7.60, one to 1½ hours, eight to 16 daily). Sarfa (www.sarfa.com) serves Cadaqués (€11, 1¾ hours, one weekdays, plus weekends in summer) and other coastal destinations. The **bus station** (☎972 21 23 19; Plaça d'Espanya) is next to the train station, 1km southwest of the old town.

### CAR & MOTORCYCLE

There's some free parking around Carrer Josep Morató i Grau, just south of the historic centre, plus free parking galore off the Carrer de Sant Gregori roundabout near El Celler de Can Roca, a 3km (30-minute) walk northwest of the centre.

### TRAIN

Girona is on the train line between Barcelona (€11.25 to €31.30, 40 minutes to 1¼ hours, at least half-hourly), Figueres (€4.10 to €6.90, 30 to 40 minutes, at least half-hourly) and Portbou, on the French border (€6.15 to €8.25, one hour, 11 to 15 daily). There are several through trains to France and beyond.

## Getting Around

### TO/FROM THE AIRPORT

**Sagalés** (www.sagales.com) connects the airport to Girona's bus/train station (€2.75, 20 to 30 minutes, hourly) and Barcelona's Estació del Nord (€16, 1¼ hours). Other direct bus services run to various Costa Brava destinations, including a Sarfa bus service to Tossa de Mar (€12, 55 minutes, two daily).

**Taxis** (☎972 22 23 23) to central Girona cost around €25 during the day and €35 at night.

# L'Estartit & the Illes Medes

L'Estartit, an 18km drive southeast of L'Escala and 6km east of Torroella de Montgrí, has a long, wide beach of fine sand and a cafe-dotted palm-lined promenade. But it's the fantastic diving that pulls travellers to this pretty stretch of Catalonia's coast. The protected Illes Medes, a spectacular group of rocky islets barely 1km offshore, are home to some of the most abundant marine life in coastal Spain.

## Sights & Activities

Kiosks by the harbour, at the northern end of L'Estartit beach, offer diving classes, snorkelling trips and glass-bottomed boat excursions (€22 for a 90-minute cruise) to the Illes Medes. You can also head out on 2½-hour kayaking trips with **MedAqua** (☎972 75 20 43; www.medaqua.com; Passeig Marítim 13, L'Estartit; kayak/sailing/snorkelling tour €27/27/20). Kayaks are available for hire on the beach (from €10 an hour) from late May to mid-September. A reliable, long-standing diving and snorkelling operator is **Les Illes** (☎972 75 12 39; www.hotellesilles.com; Carrer de les Illes 55, L'Estartit; dive incl equipment from €60; ⏲Apr-Oct).

**★Illes Medes** DIVE SITE, ISLAND

(☎972 75 17 01; www.gencat.cat/parcs/illes_medes) The allure of the Illes Medes, seven islets off L'Estartit beach, lies in their range of depths (down to 50m), kaleidoscopic marine life, and underwater cavities and tunnels. Since being gazetted as a *reserva natural submarina* in 1983, this archipelago has seen marine species thrive, making it Spain's most popular destination for snorkellers and divers. As of 2010, the islets form part of the protected 80-sq-km **Parc Natural del Montgrí, les Illes Medes i el Baix Ter**.

On and around rocks near the surface are colourful algae and sponges, as well as octopuses, crabs and various fish. Below 10m to 15m, cavities and caves harbour lobsters, scorpion fish and groupers. With luck, you'll spot some huge wrasse. If you get down to the sea floor, you may see thornback rays or marbled electric rays and dolphins.

## Sleeping

**★Les Medes** CAMPGROUND €

(☎972 75 18 05; www.campinglesmedes.com; Paratge Camp de l'Arbre, L'Estartit; sites €18-36, d bungalows €90-110); P ❄ 📶 🏊) Spread across leafy grounds 2km southwest of L'Estartit and 800m from the seaside, this friendly, year-round operation is one of Catalonia's best campgrounds. It has a sauna, two pools (one heated), bike rental, laundry facilities, a dive school and even massage service. There are also smart, modern bungalows.

**Hotel Les Illes** HOTEL €€

(☎972 75 12 39; www.hotellesilles.com; Carrer de les Illes 55, L'Estartit; incl breakfast s/d €85/140; ⏱mid-Mar–mid-Nov; ❄ 📶) With its excellent diving centre, this bright, white, family-friendly divers' hang-out just behind the harbour is a top pick if you want to venture beneath the waves. Rooms are functional though unremarkable; some have sea-view balconies.

## Information

**Oficina de Turisme de l'Estartit** (☎972 75 19 10; www.visitestartit.com; Passeig Marítim, L'Estartit; ⏱9am-9pm Jul & Aug, to 8pm Jun & Sep, to 6pm May & Oct, shorter hours Nov-Apr) At the northern end of Passeig Marítim; has info on diving and other activities.

## Getting There & Away

**Ampsa** (www.ampsa.org) buses link L'Estartit with Torroella de Montgrí (€1.75, 10 to 15 minutes, nine to 19 daily) and Girona (€7, 1¼ hours, six to 12 daily).

# L'Escala

POP 10,500

At the southern end of the 16km Golf de Roses, sprawling L'Escala is a resort town with a difference. Yes, summer brings sun-worshippers to amble along its seafront, lick ice cream on sandy beaches and clink glasses of wine. But merry L'Escala

### WHAT'S COOKING IN CATALONIA?

*Cuina Catalana* rivals Basque cuisine as Spain's best, drawing ingredients from *mar i muntanya* (sea and mountain). It has come a long way since medieval recipes for roast cat with garlic: its essence now lies in its quality local ingredients and sauces for meat and fish. There are five main sauces: *sofregit*, of fried onion, tomato and garlic; *samfaina*, *sofregit* plus red pepper and aubergine or courgette; *picada*, based on ground almonds, usually with garlic, parsley, pine nuts or hazelnuts, and sometimes breadcrumbs; *allioli*, garlic pounded with olive oil and egg yolk to make a mayonnaise; and *romesco*, an almond, tomato, olive oil, garlic and vinegar sauce, also used as a salad dressing.

Enjoy top-notch seafood all along the Costa Brava, served grilled or in *fideuà* (a noodle-based paella); some of the best is served up in casual restaurants in spots like Calella de Palafrugell or Cadaqués. Down south, don't miss duck with rice in the Delta de l'Ebre, the must-try dish of these gleaming wetlands.

Inland, cheeses, cured meats and root vegetables reign supreme. *Llonganissa* sausage, a speciality of Vic, is one must-try delicacy. *Calçots*, a type of long spring onion, are delicious as a starter with *romesco* sauce and in season in late winter/early spring. The La Garrotxa region around Olot is famous for its *cuina volcànica* (volcanic cuisine), flavoured with earthy ingredients like mushrooms, turnips, beans and walnut.

Catalans seem to live on *pa amb tomàquet*, bread slices rubbed with tomato, olive oil and garlic. There are few better regions for grabbing a hunk of bread and digging right in.

is also the access point to the magnificent Greco-Roman site Empúries, on the north edge of this bustling town behind a near-virgin beach facing the Mediterranean.

★**Empúries** ARCHAEOLOGICAL SITE
(☎972 77 02 08; www.mac.cat; Carrer Puig i Cadafalch; adult/child €6/free; ⏲10am-8pm Jun-Sep, to 6pm Oct–mid-Nov & mid-Feb–May, to 5pm & closed Mon mid-Nov–mid-Feb) The evocative seaside archaeological site of Empúries, 1.5km northwest of central L'Escala, immerses you in a strategic Greek, and later Roman, trading port. A lively audio guide commentary (included in the price) unravels the history of the **Greek town** in the lower part of the site, before leading up to the **Roman town**, with its reconstructed 1st-century-BCE forum. The **museum** exhibits the top finds, including a marble statue of Asclepius, Greek god of medicine, dating to the 2nd century BCE. Traders from Phocaea set up shop here in the 6th century BCE at what is now the charming village of Sant Martí d'Empúries, then an island. Soon afterwards they founded a mainland colony, Emporion (Market), which remained an important trading centre and conduit of Greek culture to the Iberians for centuries.

In 218 BCE Roman legions clanked ashore to cut off Hannibal's supply lines in the Second Punic War. Around 195 BCE they set up a military camp and by 100 BCE had added a town. A century later the Roman town had merged with the Greek one. Emporiae, as it was then known, was abandoned in the late 3rd century CE, after raids by Germanic tribes. Later, an early Christian basilica and cemetery were on the site of the Greek town, before the whole place disappeared under the sands for a millennium until its 20th-century excavation. Barely a quarter of the site has been excavated so far.

Points of interest in the Greek ruins include the thick southern **defensive walls**, the site of the **Asklepíeion** (shrine to the god of medicine) with a copy of his statue, and the **agora** (town square), with remnants of the early Christian **basilica** (4th to 7th centuries CE) and the Greek **stoa** (market complex) beside it. The larger Roman town includes palatial **Domus 1**, source of many of the finest mosaics (displayed April to October only, for conservation purposes), and excavated **Roman baths**. Outside the walls are the remains of an oval **amphitheatre**, dating to the 1st century BCE.

WORTH A TRIP

### SANT MARTÍ D'EMPÚRIES

Tiny walled Sant Martí d'Empúries, 1km north of L'Escala's ruins of Empúries , impresses with its glorious shores, gold-tinged lanes and medieval history. Until 1079 it was the seat of Empúries county before its vulnerability to pirate attacks prompted a power shift. These days it makes a wonderful excursion from L'Escala (4km south) or Castelló d'Empúries (p341), 16km north. Sandy beaches extend just beyond its historical centre. The main square, flanked by a broad 16th-century sandstone church, is packed with some excellent restaurants.

## Sleeping & Eating

**Hostal Spa Empúries** HOTEL €€€
(☎972 77 02 07; www.hostalempuries.com; Platja de Portitxol; r €155-335; P ❄ ☎) This stylish hotel next to the Greco-Roman ruins fronts a sandy splash of beach. Breezy neutral-toned rooms have mosaic bathrooms inspired by the ruins; some boast sea views. Those in the newer 'spa' wing, with rain showers and enormous beds, are particularly comfortable. The two restaurants (mains €18 to €30) specialise in creative Mediterranean and seafood dishes using local produce.

★**La Gruta** FUSION €€€
(☎972 77 62 11; www.restaurantlagruta.com; Carrer de la Casa Gran 1; mains €24-30, multi-course menu €30-50; ⏲12.30-3.30pm Mon, 12.30-3.30pm & 8-10.30pm Tue-Sat Apr-Oct, shorter hours Nov-Mar) A fusion of French and Spanish flavours, spiced with occasional Asian flair, impresses diners at this innovative restaurant overlooking a tiny beach in central L'Escala. Highlights include beef *tataki* with aubergine caviar, truffled *oeuf cocotte* (French-style baked egg), and courgette tossed with saffron, mussels and prawns, plus fine home-cooked desserts.

## Information

**Oficina de Turisme** (☎972 77 06 03; www.visitlescala.com; Plaça de les Escoles 1; ⏲9am-8.30pm Mon-Sat, 10am-1pm Sun Jun-Sep, 9am-1pm & 4-7pm Mon-Fri, 10am-1pm & 4-7pm Sat, 10am-1pm Sun Oct-May) Beside L'Escala's bus stop.

Praia As Catedrais (p566) **2.** Playa de la Concha (p448) **3.** Illas
s (p574) **4.** Bolonia (p675)

## CATALAN CULTURE

The fortunes of Catalonia have risen and fallen over the years, from its days as wealthy mercantile centre to a place of repression under the Franco regime, followed by a growing push for independence in recent years. Despite today's challenges, Catalan culture continues to flourish all across the region, with a staggering festival calendar and abundant pride in the Catalan language and its unusual traditions.

### Language

Throughout the region, born-and-bred locals proudly speak Catalan, a Romance language related to French, Spanish (Castilian) and Italian, and also spoken in Andorra, the Balearics and Valencia. It was only relatively recently, however, that Catalan was deemed 'legitimate'. After Catalonia was crushed in the War of the Spanish Succession in 1714, the use of Catalan was repeatedly banned or at least frowned upon. Franco was the last of Spain's rulers to clamp down on its public use. All that changed in 1980, when the first autonomous regional parliament was assembled and adopted new laws towards *normalització lingüística* (linguistic normalisation).

Today Catalonia's state school system uses Catalan as the language of instruction, though most Catalan speakers end up bilingual, particularly in urban areas. Across the region, Catalan is the lingua franca: advertising and road signs are in Catalan, while newspapers, magazines and other publications can be found in both Catalan and Spanish. There's also a mix of Catalan and Spanish programming on radio and TV stations.

### Folk Dancing

On weekends year-round, devotees of the folk dance *sardana* gather in town squares, while a small band puts everyone in motion. Catalans of all ages come out for the dance, which takes place in a circle with dancers holding hands. Together they move right, back and then left, hopping, raising their arms and generally building momentum as the tempo picks up. All are welcome to join in; watch a few rounds to get the hang of it.

### Festivals

Catalonia's best celebrations tend to revolve around religious holidays, and feature abundant merry making. You'll see plenty of *sardana*-dancing and *castell*-building, as well as *gegants* (huge papier-mâché giants: lords, princesses, sultans, fishers and historic and contemporary figures, often 'dancing' in pairs) and *capgrossos* (oversized heads worn by costumed actors).

Another feature of these Catalan festivals is the *correfoc* (fire running): horned devils brandishing firework-spouting pitchforks wreak mayhem in the streets, sometimes accompanied by firework-spouting dragons, or even wooden carts that are set alight. Full coverings (hats, gloves, goggles, long sleeves) are highly recommended for anyone who wants to get near. One of the big highlights of any traditional Catalan festival is the building of *castells* (human castles), a Catalan tradition (p382) born in the 18th century.

### Getting There & Away

Sarfa (www.sarfa.com) has daily buses to/from Barcelona's Estacó del Nord (€22.10, three hours, three daily), Girona (€6.55, one hour, two to five daily) and Figueres (€5, one hour, six daily). Arriving in L'Escala, buses stop on Plaça de les Escoles, outside the tourist office.

## Castelló d'Empúries

POP 3970

This handsome town once presided over Empúries, a medieval Catalan county that maintained a large degree of independence up to the 14th century. Modern Castelló d'Empúries retains the imperious aura and historical feel of a former capital, along with remnants of its once-thriving medieval Jewish community. Cobbled lanes fill with minstrel music, fire twirlers and swordplay during the medieval **Festival Terra de Trobadors** (www.terradetrobadors.com; Sep).

The town also makes a superb base for outdoors lovers. The nearby Parc Natural dels Aiguamolls de l'Empordà is popular for birdwatching and has a number of easy hikes and biking trails, while wind-blown (but peaceful) beaches lie just 6km east.

## Sights

Pick up a leaflet from the **tourist office** (☎972 15 62 33; www.castelloempuriabrava.com; Plaça dels Homes; ⏰10am-2pm & 4-8pm Jul & Aug, 10am-2pm & 4-6pm Mon-Sat, 10am-2pm Sun Sep, Oct & Apr-Jun, reduced hours Nov-Mar) for a self-guided tour of Castelló d'Empúries' Jewish quarter.

**Parc Natural dels Aiguamolls de l'Empordà** PARK
(☎972454222; www.gencat.cat/parcs/aiguamolls_emporda; GIV6216 Sant Pere Pescador-Castelló d'Empúries Km 4.2; parking motorbike or car €5, van €10; ⏰El Cortalet information centre 9am-6.30pm Easter-Sep, to 4pm Oct-Easter) The remnants of the mighty marshes that once covered the whole coastal plain here are preserved in this 47-sq-km natural park, complete with scenic walking trails and bird-watching observatories, just south of Castelló d'Empúries. The March to May and August to October migration seasons bring big numbers of wading birds. Keen twitchers may glimpse flamingos, purple herons, glossy ibis, spoonbills, rare black storks and more of the 329 species that pass through.

**Basílica de Santa María** BASILICA
(Plaça Mossèn Cinto Verdaguer; adult/child €2.50/free; ⏰9am-9pm Jul–mid-Sep, 10am-2pm & 4-6pm mid-Sep–Jun) This broad church seizes attention with its Romanesque tower, intricately carved portal, and a delicate sculpture on its tympanum (above the main entrance) of the Virgin Mary clasping Jesus while the three Magi look on admiringly. A church was first consecrated here in 1064, but today's imposing Catalan Gothic structure dates from the 13th to 15th centuries.

**Museu d'Historia Medieval de la Cúria-Presó** MUSEUM
(Plaça Jaume I; €2.50; ⏰10am-8pm Jul–mid-Sep, 10am-2pm & 4-6pm Tue-Sun mid-Sep–Jun) Set in the 14th-century Cúria (a centre of judicial power), this small museum provides a fascinating window into Castelló's medieval history. You'll find stone carvings from the old Jewish quarter, a model of the once-walled medieval village, and an interactive exhibition on the era's troubadours. The highlight is the collection of creepy prison cells.

## Sleeping & Eating

**Hostal Casa Clara** HOSTAL €€
(☎972 25 02 15; www.hostalcasaclara.com; Plaça de les Monges; d incl breakfast €90; ⏰Mar-Dec; P❄📶) Genial service and cosy rooms make this colourful *hostal* a splendid mid-range option in the heart of old-town Castelló d'Empúries. All eight spacious rooms feature natural light, comfortable beds and individual colour schemes. There's a pleasant lounge with books and board games.

**El Portal de la Gallarda** CATALAN €€
(☎972 25 01 52; Carrer Pere Estany 8; mains €15-25; ⏰12.30-2.30pm & 7-10.30pm Jun-Aug, 12.30-2.45pm Wed-Mon & 8-10.30pm Fri & Sat Sep-May) One of the village's top dining destinations also offers sweeping views over the countryside from its garden-like terrace just north-east of the cathedral. Locals pack the place on weekends for classic Catalan cooking, with standout dishes like black (cuttlefish) rice, anchovies from Roses, goat's-cheese salads, and lamb with rosemary.

## Getting There & Away

Sarfa (www.sarfa.com) runs buses to Figueres (€1.75, 15 minutes, eight to 18 daily), Cadaqués (€4.25, 45 minutes, six daily) and Barcelona's Estació del Nord (€21.10, two hours, one to two daily).

# Cadaqués

POP 2800

Cadaqués gleams above the cobalt-blue waters of a rocky bay on Catalonia's most easterly outcrop. This easy-going whitewashed village owes its allure in part to its windswept pebble beaches, meandering lanes, pretty harbour and the wilds of nearby Cap de Creus, but it's Salvador Dalí who truly gave Cadaqués its sparkle.

The surrealist artist spent family holidays here during his youth, and lived much of his later life at nearby Port Lligat, where the Dalís' other-worldly seaside home stands. Thanks to Dalí and other luminaries, such as his friend Federico García Lorca, Cadaqués pulled in a celebrity crowd, and still does.

Summer in Cadaqués is *very* busy, so advance bookings can make or break a trip.

## Sights & Activities

★**Casa Museu Dalí** HOUSE, MUSEUM
(☎972 25 10 15; www.salvador-dali.org; Port Lligat; adult/senior & student/child under 14yr €14/8/free; ⏰9.30am-9pm mid-Jun–mid-Sep, 10.30am-6pm mid-Sep–early Jan & mid-Feb–mid-Jun, closed early Jan–mid-Feb, plus Mon Nov–mid-Mar) Overlooking a peaceful cove in Port Lligat, a tiny fishing settlement 1km northeast of Cadaqués, this magnificent seaside complex was the residence and sanctuary of Salvador Dalí, who lived here with his wife Gala from 1930 to 1982. The splendid whitewashed structure is a mishmash of cottages and sunny terraces, linked by narrow labyrinthine corridors and containing an assortment of offbeat furnishings. Access is by semi-guided eight-person tour; book well ahead.





DON'T MISS

### MONESTIR DE SANT PERE DE RODES

Views of distant Pyrenean peaks and the deep-blue Mediterranean combine with a spectacular piece of Romanesque architecture at this hillside **monastery** (☎972 19 42 38; http://monuments.mhcat.cat/conjunt_monumental_de_sant_pere_de_rodes; GIP604 adult/child €6/free; ⏰10am-8pm Tue-Sun Jun-Sep, to 5pm Oct-May), 500m up in the hills 7km southwest of El Port de la Selva (which is 13km northwest of Cadaqués). Found the 9th century, it became the most powerful monastery in the county of Empúries. T great triple-naved, barrel-vaulted basilica is flanked by the square 12th-century Torre Sant Miquel bell tower and a two-level cloister dating from the 11th and 20th centurie

Also here is an **info centre** (☎972 19 31 91; http://parcsnaturals.gencat.cat/ca/cap-cr Palau de l'Abat, Monestir de Sant Pere de Rodes, GIP6041; ⏰10am-2pm & 3-6pm late Jun–mi Sep, 10am-3pm mid-Sep–late Jun) for the Cap de Creus natural park. Approaching from Port de la Selva, stop in the signposted car park, a 10-minute walk from the monaster

**Museu de Cadaqués** MUSEUM
(☎972 25 88 77; Carrer de Narcís Monturiol 15; €4; ⏰10am-1pm & 4-7pm approx Easter-Oct) Salvador Dalí often features strongly in the temporary exhibitions displayed here, as do his contemporaries also connected to Cadaqués, such as Picasso. Temporary exhibitions change several times a year, with closures between shows; stop in to see what's on.

**Kayaking Costa Brava** WATER SPORTS
(☎646 901588; www.kayakingcostabrava.com; off Av de Salvador Dalí, Port Lligat; kayak hire per hour/half-day from €12/31; ⏰10am-7pm Apr-Jul & Sep, 9am-8pm Aug) On the beach, a short stroll from the Casa Museu Dalí, this professional outfit hires kayaks for paddles along a sublime stretch of coastline. You can also sign up for guided tours (two-hour tour €25 per person). Call ahead for tours (and for kayak hire during the busy summer months).

**Beaches**

Cadaqués' main beach and others along the surrounding coast are small and pebbly, but their picturesqueness and beautiful blue waters more than make up for that. Overlooking **Platja del Llané**, south of the town centre, is Dalí's parents' holiday home. All the beaches here experience strong winds.

## Sleeping

★**Tramuntana Hotel** BOUTIQUE H
(☎972 25 92 70; www.hotel-tramuntana-cad com; Carrer de la Torre 9; r incl breakfast 140; ⏰Mar-Oct; P❄📶) A traditional v washed facade conceals 11 chic, soft-gre white rooms with balconies at this fab little boutique bolthole pocketed away i old town. It's expertly run and perso designed in minimalist contemporary by a knowledgeable local couple. Thoug touches include a pine-fringed terrace, minous lounge, an honesty bar, and lovi prepared breakfasts.

**Hostal Vehí** HOST
(☎972 258 470; www.hostalvehi.com; Carr l'Església 6; s/d €65/95; ⏰Mar-Oct; ❄📶) I heart of the old town, this warm family guesthouse has impeccably kept rooms homey touches such as floral duvets, v furnishings and natural light. Superior bles are vast, with views over Cada rooftops. Cars can't access this part of t but it's the best midrange deal around.

**L'Horta d'en Rahola** BOUTIQUE HOT
(☎972 25 10 49; www.hortacadaques.com; Sa Tarongeta 1; r €160-215; ⏰mid-Mar–mi P❄📶🏊) By the roundabout on the edge of Cadaqués, this characterful version of an 18th-century family-c farmhouse is adults-only and has a gor fruit-and-vegetable garden and tur pool. The nine contemporary rooms, a ferent, are light and bright with a ma feel. Personal service is excellent and made to feel very welcome.

WWW.CHRISTOPHEFAUGERE.COM/GETTY IMAGES ©

# Spain's Top Beaches

**Spaniards argue for hours about which is their district's finest beach, so picking favourites from 5000km of coastline is a controversial, albeit mighty pleasurable, task. The Mediterranean's gentle strands and pretty coves contrast with the rougher beauty of the Atlantic coasts.**

**Illas Cíes** (p574) A protected archipelago off Galicia, with beaches so stunning you'll gasp in disbelief.

**Aiguafreda & Platja Fonda** (p330) Serene Costa Brava coves near Begur, so divine that we couldn't choose between them.

**Playa de Mónsul** (p770) Among the prettiest of several wild and dramatic beaches fringing the semi-desert Cabo de Gata in Almería province.

**Platja des Coll Baix** (p785) Journey through the woods to reach this pristine island hideaway on Mallorca.

**Playa Oyambre** (p504) A soft-blonde sandy dream with frequently surfable waves, protected by Cantabria's Parque Natural Oyambre

**Playa de Torimbia** (p519) The walk down to this sheltered fingernail-shaped cove is an Asturian classic near Llanes. Clothing optional.

**Playa del Silencio** (p521) Backed by a natural rock amphitheatre, this Asturian jewel between Cudillero and Luarca is hard to beat.

**Playa de la Concha** (p448) A scallop-shaped stretch of sand in the heart of San Sebastián, and possibly Europe's finest city beach.

**Bolonia** (p675) A stretch of pristine sand, the finest of Andalucía's unspoiled Costa de la Luz. Nearby Zahara de los Atunes and Playa de los Lances are spectacular, too.

**Praia As Catedrais** (p566) The unearthly rock formations at this Galician strand near Ribadeo are such a drawcard that daily numbers are limited.

## THE CAMÍ DE RONDA

The 230km-long stretch of cliffs, coves, rocky promontories and pine groves that make up the signposted **Camí de Ronda** (also known as the Costa Brava Way) extends from Blanes in Catalonia to Collioure in France. Unsurprisingly, it offers some of the finest walks in Catalonia, from gentle rambles to high-octane scrambles. If you fancy tackling the whole thing, it's a demanding hike of around 10 days. The trail mostly follows the established GR92, but includes a number of coastal deviations. It became especially well known when used by military forces and the Guardia Civil on the lookout for smugglers in the 19th and 20th centuries.

Some of the most popular stretches link Calella de Palafrugell (p326), Llafranc (p328), Tamariu (p329) and the Begur area. Another choice route is central Cadaqués to the **Far Cap de Creus**, a relatively easy walk (8km; 2½ hours) that passes Port Lligat, before continuing along windswept, scrub-covered, rocky ground past several isolated beaches to reach the lighthouse.

## Eating & Drinking

**Lua** FUSION €€

(☎972 15 94 52; www.facebook.com/lua.cdqs; Carrer Santa Maria 1; dishes €9-20; ⊙1-4pm & 8pm-midnight May-Sep, closed Tue Oct-Apr, may close Jan-Mar; ☑) A mango-yellow door sets the jazzy tone for delicious, creative Mediterranean-Asian 'soul food' at this laid-back, Italian-run eatery with beer-barrel tables and benches on an old-town alley. It's perfect for vegetarians; try a Veggie Venus bowl of black rice, hummus and babaganoush, or cheese platters and original ceramic-bowl salads. Excellent seafood such as tuna tartare and salmon poke bowls.

**Enoteca MF** TAPAS €€

(Plaça des Poal 3; small sharing plates €6-13; ⊙noon-10pm Mon, Tue & Thu-Sat, to 4pm Sun) A short walk east of the main beach, this wine-centric gastrobar serves up outstanding tapas to tables on a small terrace facing the waterfront. Standouts include sea bass ceviche with thyme, tender razor clams, decadent foie with figs, and beef cheeks with truffle mashed potatoes.

**Compartir** FUSION €€€

(☎972 25 84 82; www.compartircadaques.com; Riera Sant Vicenç; mains €22-30; ⊙1-3.15pm & 8-10.15pm, closed Mon Jul & Aug, closed Mon & Tue Oct, Nov, Apr & May, closed Mon & Sun Nov-Mar) Headed up by a trio of El Bulli alumni, this terrace restaurant revolves around innovative, gourmet sharing plates (*'compartir'* means 'to share'), yet retains a (comparatively) laid-back feel. The always-evolving menu fuses traditional Catalan flavours into contemporary delights like Thai-style turbot or marinated sardines with raspberry, beetroot and pistachios.

**Mut** BAR

(www.facebook.com/Mutcadaques; Plaça Doctor Pont 12; ⊙9am-late Easter-Sep, weekends only Oct, hours vary) With its cluster of tables gazing out on Port Doguer, bohemian Mut is an excellent spot for vermouth and cocktails. There's also a chalkboard menu of creative small plates, from vegetable curry with basmati rice to lentil, duck and mango salad.

**Bar Boia** BAR, CAFE

(www.boianit.com; Passeig de Cadaqués 17; ⊙9am-3am Jun-Sep, to 10pm Oct-May; 📶) Frequented by arty types and intellectuals since 1946, this sand-side *xiringuito* has been voguishly reimagined as a fantastic high-profile cocktail bar. Expertly crafted liquid fusions (€10 to €13) – plankton-and-sea-fennel G&T, *cava*-loaded 'Gala Dalí' – come courtesy of award-winning, elBulli-trained mixologist Manel Vehí.

## Information

**Oficina de Turisme** (☎972 25 83 15; www.visitcadaques.org; Carrer del Cotxe 2; ⊙9am-9pm Mon-Sat, 10am-1pm & 5-8pm Sun Jul–mid-Sep, 9am-1pm & 3-6pm Mon-Sat, 10am-1pm Sun mid-Sep–Jun, closed Sun Oct-Mar)

**Oficina de Turisme** (www.visitcadaques.org; Port Lligat; ⊙10am-1pm & 4-7pm Tue-Sat, 10am-3pm Sun mid-Jul–mid-Sep) Summer booth next to the Casa Museu Dalí.

## Getting There & Away

Sarfa (www.sarfa.com) buses connect Cadaqués to Barcelona's Estació del Nord (€25, 2¾ hours, one to two daily) and airport (€27, 3½ hours, one to two daily), plus Figueres (€5.60, one hour, four daily) and Girona (€11, 1¾ hours, one weekdays, plus weekends in summer) via Castelló d'Empúries (€4.25, 45 minutes, six daily).

## Cap de Creus

Declared a nature reserve in 1998, Cap de Creus is the easternmost point of the Spanish mainland, and a place of sublime, rugged beauty, battered by the merciless *tramuntana* wind. With a steep, rocky coastline indented by coves of turquoise water, it's an especially magical spot to be at dawn or sunset.

The odd-shaped rocks, barren plateaux and deserted shorelines that fill Salvador Dalí's famous paintings were not just a product of his fertile imagination: this is the landscape that inspired the great surrealist artist.

The cape, crowned with a 19th-century lighthouse, is reached by a lonely, 8km-long road that winds its way northeast from Cadaqués through the moonscapes, or via a gorgeous 7km hike from Cadaqués (2½ hours each way).

The Cap de Creus peninsula is much loved for the walking trails along its craggy cliffs; pick up route maps at the information centre or Cadaqués' tourist office. **Itinerari 17**, from the Paratge de Tudela car park to Cala Culop (4km return), weaves past the huge Roca Cavallera, which morphed into the subject of Dalí's painting *The Great Masturbator*.

**Bar Restaurant Cap de Creus** CATALAN, INDIAN €€

(☎972 19 90 05; www.facebook.com/restaurante.capdecreus; Cap de Creus; mains €9-24; ⏲10am-7pm Mon-Thu, to midnight Fri-Sun Nov-Apr, 9am-midnight daily May-Oct, hours vary) Perched atop the cape, this all-day restaurant caters to exhausted hikers and beachgoers with an unexpected combination of Catalan and Indian food. The latter makes an agreeably aromatic change from Cadaqués' endless seafood grills; try a fragrant lamb curry or a veggie samosa. Coastal panoramas from the breezy terrace are exquisite and there's often live music.

### ℹ Information

**Espai Cap de Creus** (http://parcsnaturals.gencat.cat/ca/cap-creus; ⏲10am-2pm & 3-6pm late-Jun–mid-Sep, 10am-3pm May-late Jun & 2nd half Sep) The park's main information centre has walking route maps and displays about local fauna and flora, inside the cape's lighthouse.

## Figueres

POP 46,400

Fourteen kilometres inland from Catalonia's glistening Golf de Roses lies Figueres, birthplace of Salvador Dalí and now home to the artist's flamboyant theatre-museum. Although Dalí's career took him to Madrid, Barcelona, Paris and the USA, Figueres remained close to his heart. In the 1960s and '70s he created the extraordinary Teatre-Museu Dalí – a monument to surrealism and a legacy that outshines any other Spanish artist, in terms of both popularity and sheer flamboyance. Whatever your feelings about this complex, egocentric man, this museum is worth every euro and minute you can spare.

Beyond its star attraction, busy Figueres is a lively place with a couple of interesting museums, some good restaurants, pleasant shopping streets around Carrer de Peralada, and a grand 18th-century fortress. It's well worth staying to see the town breathe after Dalí daytrippers depart.

### Sights

**★Teatre-Museu Dalí** MUSEUM

(www.salvador-dali.org; Plaça de Gala i Salvador Dalí 5; adult/child under 9yr €15/free; ⏲9am-8pm Apr-Jul & Sep, 9am-8pm & 10pm-1am Aug, 9.30am-6pm Tue-Sun Oct & Mar, 10.30am-6pm Tue-Sun Nov-Feb) The first name that pops into your head when you lay eyes on this red castle-like building, topped with giant eggs and stylised Oscar-like statues and studded with plaster-covered croissants, is Salvador Dalí. An entirely appropriate final resting place for the master of surrealism, it has as-

#### ℹ VISITING THE TEATRE-MUSEU DALÍ

The Teatre-Museu Dalí is Spain's most visited museum outside Madrid (drawing over one million annual visitors), so it's worth double-checking opening hours (it's closed on Mondays from October to May) and reserving tickets online in advance. In August the museum opens at night from 10pm to 1am (admission €15, bookings essential). The biggest crowds arrive during weekends and on public holidays. Arrive early to avoid long queues.

sured his immortality. Exhibits range from enormous, impossible-to-miss installations – like *Taxi Plujós* (Rainy Taxi), an early Cadillac surmounted by statues – to the more discreet, including a tiny, mysterious room with a mirrored flamingo.

'Theatre-museum' is an apt label for this trip through the incredibly fertile imagination of one of the great showmen of the 20th century. Between 1961 and 1974, Dalí converted Figueres' former municipal theatre, destroyed by a fire in 1939 at the end of the civil war, into the Teatre-Museu Dalí. It's full of illusions, tricks and the utterly unexpected, and contains a substantial portion of Dalí's life's work, though you won't find his most famous pieces here (they're scattered around the world).

Even outside, the building aims to surprise, from its entrance watched over by medieval suits of armour balancing baguettes on their heads, to bizarre sculptures outside the entrance on Plaça de Gala i Salvador Dalí, to the pink walls along Pujada al Castell and Carrer Canigó. The **Torre Galatea**, added in 1983, is where Dalí spent his final years.

Opening the show is *Taxi Plujós*; put a coin in the slot and water washes all over the occupant of the car. The **Sala de Peixateries** (Fishmongers' Hall) holds a collection of Dalí oils, including the famous *Autoretrat Tou amb Tall de Bacon Fregit* (Soft Self-Portrait with Fried Bacon) and *Retrat de Picasso* (Portrait of Picasso). Beneath the former stage of the theatre is the crypt with Dalí's plain **tomb**, located at what Dalí modestly described as the spiritual centre of Europe.

After you've seen the more notorious pieces, such as climbing the stairs in the famous **Mae West Room**, see if you can track down a turtle with a gold coin balanced on its back, peepholes into a green-lit room where a mirrored flamingo stands amid fake plants, and Dalí's heavenly reimagining of the Sistine Chapel in the **Palau del Vent** (Palace of the Wind Room).

**Gala**, Dalí's wife and lifelong muse, is seen throughout – from the *Gala Nua Mirant el Mar Mediterrani* (Gala Nude Looking at the Mediterranean Sea) on the 2nd level, which also appears to be a portrait of Abraham Lincoln from afar (best seen from outside



## SALVADOR DALÍ

One of the 20th century's most recognisable icons, Salvador Dalí (1904–89) could have had the term 'larger-than-life' invented for him. He then would probably have decorated it with pink pineapples.

Born in Figueres, Dalí turned his hand to everything from film-making to painting to architecture to literature to jewellery-making. His surrealist trajectory through the often-serious landscape of 20th-century Spain brought him into contact and collaboration with figures such as Pablo Picasso, Luís Buñuel, Federico García Lorca and (controversially) Franco. A raft of foreign celebrities flocked to be seen in his extravagant company.

Self-consciously eccentric and a constant source of memorable soundbites, Dalí was nevertheless in some ways a conservative figure and devout Catholic. A 1929 visit to Cadaqués by French poet Paul Éluard and his Russian wife, Gala, caused an earthquake in Dalí's life: he ran off to Paris with Gala (who became his lifelong obsession and, later, his wife) and joined the surrealist movement. His long relationship with Gala provided the stable foundation that his whirligig life revolved around.

The celebrity, the extraordinarily prolific output and, let's face it, the comedy moustache tend to pull focus from the fact that Dalí was an artist of the highest calibre. In his paintings, Dalí's surrealism is often far more profound than it seems at first glance. The floppy clocks of his most famous work, *The Persistence of Memory*, are interpreted by some as a reference to the flexibility of time proposed by Einstein. His *Christ of St John of the Cross* combines expert composition, symbol-laden Renaissance-style imagery and a nostalgic, almost elegiac view of the Catalan coast that he so loved.

Northeastern Catalonia's so-called **Dalí Triangle** (which typically receives over 1.4 million visitors per year) encompasses the spectacularly out-of-this-world Teatre-Museu Dalí (p347) in Figueres, the artist's eclectic home at Port Lligat's Casa Museu Dalí (p342) near Cadaqués, and the conversely less flamboyant Castell de Púbol (p326), northeast of Girona.

the Mae West room), to the classic *Leda Atòmica* (Atomic Leda).

A separate entrance (same ticket and opening times) leads into **Dalí Joies**, a collection of 37 Dalí-designed jewels. Designed between 1941 and 1970, the jewellery was made by specialists in New York. Each piece, ranging from the disconcerting *Ull del Temps* (Eye of Time) to the *Elefant de l'Espai* (Space Elephant) and the *Cor Reial* (Royal Heart), is unique.

**Castell de Sant Ferran** FORT

(www.lesfortalesescatalanes.info; Pujada del Castell; adult/child €3.50/free; ⌚10am-8pm Jul–mid-Sep, 10.30am-6pm mid-Sep–Oct & Apr-Jun, to 3pm Tue-Sun Nov-Mar) Figueres' sturdy 18th-century fortress commands the surrounding plains from a low hill 1km northwest of the centre. The complex is a wonder of military engineering: it sprawls over 32 hectares, with the capacity for 6000 men to march within its walls and snooze in military barracks.

**Museu de l'Empordà** MUSEUM

(www.museuemporda.org; La Rambla 2; adult/child €4/free; ⌚11am-8pm Tue-Sat May-Oct, to 7pm Tue-Sat Nov-Apr, 11am-2pm Sun year-round) Extending over four floors, the local museum time travels from ancient amphorae to 7th-century sculptures to rotating installations of contemporary art. You'll find some exceptional early 20th-century works, including lush charcoal drawings by Juan Núñez Fernández, who was Dalí's drawing teacher. Other highlights include landscapes by the watercolour master Ramon Reig Corominas and portraits and still lifes by Marià Baig Minobis.

## Sleeping & Eating

**Hostel Figueres** HOSTEL €

(☎630 680575; www.hostelfigueres.com; Carrer dels Tints 22; dm/d €22/55; ❄📶) This energetic, fresh-faced hostel is exactly the backpacker hideaway Figueres needs. The four-, six- and eight-person dorms are modern, airy and spotless, with fans and lockers. The three air-con doubles share bathrooms, while the fully equipped three-bedroom apartment (from €65) suits groups. Staff fizz with recommendations, and the hostel provides a kitchen, terrace and lounge.

**Hotel Duran** HOTEL €€

(☎972 50 12 50; www.hotelduran.com; Carrer de Lasauca 5; r €65-100; P❄📶) For immersion in the Dalí legend, stay at this mid 19th-century hotel, where the artist and his wife often made appearances. There's a fitting blend of old-style elegance with contemporary design, surrealist touches, and photos of Dalí with the former hotel manager, whose descendants now proudly run the place. Rooms are bright and modern.

The art-filled **restaurant** (mains €17-28; ⌚12.45-4pm & 8-10.30pm) has smooth service, a three-course menu (€25) and lightly creative Catalan fare ranging from sole cooked in orange sauce to pineapple carpaccio.

★ **Integral** VEGETARIAN €€

(☎972 51 63 34; www.facebook.com/integral.figueres; Carrer de la Jonquera 30; mains €10-15; ⌚1-3.30pm Mon & Tue, 1-3.30pm & 8-10.30pm Wed-Sat; 🌿) A short stroll from the Teatre-Museu Dalí, cheery casual Integral prepares some of the best vegetarian dishes for miles around. Perch at the marble-topped bar to see the chefs in action while tucking into ginger-and-leek dumplings, zucchini carpaccio, shitake risotto, crunchy polenta balls and other delicacies – all made from high-quality regional organic ingredients.

**El Motel** CATALAN €€

(☎972 50 05 62; www.hotelemporda.com; Hotel Empordà, Avinguda Salvador Dalí 170; mains €15-29; ⌚12.45-3.30pm Sun & Mon, 12.45-3.30pm & 8.30-10.30pm Wed-Sat; P📶) Jaume Subirós, the chef and owner of this smart roadside hotel-restaurant 1km north of Figueres' centre, is a seminal figure of the transition from traditional Catalan home cooking to the polished, innovative affair it is today. Local, seasonal ingredients star on the menu, which may feature highlights like salted Roses shrimp, roasted rabbit, or a salad of figs, goat's cheese, mint and pistachio.

## Information

**Oficina de Turisme Figueres** (☎972 50 31 55; www.visitfigueres.cat; Plaça de l'Escorxador 2; ⌚9am-8pm Mon-Sat, 10am-3pm Sun Jul-Aug, 9.30am-6pm Mon-Fri, 10am-5pm Sat, to 2pm Sun Sep-Jun)

## Getting There & Away

Sarfa (www.sarfa.com) buses serve Cadaqués (€5.60, one hour, four daily) via Castelló d'Empúries (€1.75, 15 minutes, nine to 18 daily) from Figueres' **bus station** (Plaça de l'Estació 7).

Figueres train station, 800m southeast of the centre, has half-hourly trains to/from Girona (€4.10 to €6.90, 30 to 40 minutes) and Barcelona (€12 to €16, 1¾ to 2½ hours), plus hourly

WORTH A TRIP

## MUSEU MEMORIAL DE L'EXILI

Anyone familiar with Picasso's *Guernica* has an insight into the horror of civilian suffering during the Spanish Civil War. The thought-provoking **Museu Memorial de l'Exili** (☎972 55 65 33; www.museuexili.cat; Carrer Major 43-47, La Jonquera; adult/child €4/free; ⏰10am-7pm Tue-Sat Jun-Sep, to 6pm Tue-Sat Oct-May, to 2pm Sun year-round) traces the experiences of Catalonian people exiled and persecuted during this era. It's aptly located in La Jonquera, 20km north of Figueres, close to the Spain–France border where many Spaniards fled following the Republican defeat in 1939. It explains the build-up to and aftermath of the civil war through photographs, film footage, audioguides and haunting art installations.

trains to/from Portbou (€3.40, 30 minutes) on the French border. High-speed trains to Girona, Barcelona and into France depart from Figueres-Vilafant station, 1.5km west of central Figueres.

# Besalú

POP 2500

The delightfully well-preserved medieval town of Besalú looms into sight with its elegant, show-stopping 11th-century Pont Fortificat (Fortified Bridge) spanning the Riu Fluvià, and leading into the coiled maze of cobbled narrow streets that make up its historic core. Following a succession of Roman, Visigothic and Muslim rulers, during the 10th and 11th centuries Besalú was the capital of an independent county that stretched as far west as Cerdanya before it came under Barcelona's control in 1111. Today Besalú is a favourite day-trip destination from Girona (35km south) and the Olot area (20km west), with a steady stream of visitors roaming the ramparts and exploring its Jewish history.

## Sights & Activities

Guided walking tours of Besalú's old town are offered by the tourist office.

**★Pont Fortificat** BRIDGE

(Carrer del Pont) Besalú's fortified stone bridge is so old, it strains memory. The first records of the bridge date to 1075, though periodic modifications have bolstered its defensive structure. It was bombed in 1939 during the Spanish Civil War and repaired soon after. Today this exquisite pale sandstone bridge, with its two turreted gates and heavy portcullis, is an arresting vantage point for the loveliest views of medieval Besalú. From the bridge, there are trails along the river.

**Jewish Square** RUINS

(Baixada de Miqvé; guided tours €2.25-4.80) Besalú's thriving Jewish community fled the town in 1436 after relentless Christian persecution. It left behind a 12th-century riverside *miqvé* (ritual bath), a rare survivor of its kind in Spain, which was rediscovered in 1964. It sits inside a vaulted stone chamber, around which remnants of the 13th-century **synagogue** were unearthed in 2005. Access to the *miqvé* is by guided tour with the tourist office, but you can see the square and ruin exterior independently.

## Sleeping & Eating

**★Els Jardins de la Martana** HERITAGE HOTEL €€

(☎972 59 00 09; www.lamartana.com; Carrer del Pont Vell 2; s/d/tr €79/109/135; ❄📶) A charming, family-run hotel in a 1910 mansion at the out-of-town end of Besalú's grand medieval bridge. The 11 rooms have tiled floors, high ceilings and big windows (or balconies), and many offer views across the bridge to the town. Guests can relax in the lovely wood-panelled library, the terrace with its sweeping views, or the lounge.

**Casa Marcial** HOTEL €€

(☎608 029427; www.casa-marcial.com; Carrer del Comte Tallaferro 15; d/ste incl breakfast €115/142; ❄📶🏊) Partly set within a revamped turn-of-the-20th-century mansion, Casa Marcial makes an attractive old-town choice for its cordial service, small pool and 12 smart, uncluttered, contemporary rooms. Some rooms boast balconies and all have plenty of light; the five spacious 'suites', including a family-sized option, come with tea/coffee kits. A grassy garden wraps around a 12th-century church to reach the pool.

**Quina Llauna Besalú** TAPAS €

(☎972 59 19 71; Carrer d'Olot 1; tapas €2-14; ⏰1-4pm & 7pm-midnight) One of several well-placed eating and drinking spots on the scenic Plaça del Prat de Sant Pere, this vermouth-loving tapas joint has an excellent range of satisfying dishes. You can unwind on the terrace, over plates of tender octopus, zucchini carpaccio and glasses of Priorat red wine.

**Pont Vell** CATALAN €€
(☎972 59 10 27; www.restaurantpontvell.com; Carrer Pont Vell 24; mains €15-27; ⏰1-3.30pm Wed-Mon & 8.30-10.30pm Thu-Sat) The views to the old bridge (after which the restaurant is named) are enough to tempt you into this converted 18th-century building, even without considering the superb wide-ranging menu full of locally sourced delights, such as oxtail cooked in red wine, seafood paella or roast pigeon with prunes.

## Information

**Oficina de Turisme** (☎972 59 12 40; www.besalu.cat; Carrer del Pont 1; ⏰10am-2pm & 4-7pm) On the eastern side of the bridge, across from the centre; runs 30-minute to one-hour walking tours (€2.25 to €4.60).

## Getting There & Away

**Teisa** (www.teisa-bus.com) buses serve Barcelona (€15.70, two hours, four daily), Olot (€4, 40 minutes, 12 to 20 daily), Figueres (€4.10, 30 minutes, three daily) and Girona (€4.80, 40 minutes to one hour, eight to 12 daily).

# THE CATALAN PYRENEES

Catalonia's Pyrenees are much more than an all-season adventure playground, and, beyond the major resorts, conceal a raw natural beauty that invites discovery. Certainly, the Val d'Aran draws winter skiers and snowboarders (with resorts ranging from red-carpet to family-focused), while summer and autumn lure hikers to the jewel-like lakes and valleys of the Parc Nacional d'Aigüestortes i Estany de Sant Maurici, the low-lying countryside of Cerdanya, and the climbing terrain of the Serra del Cadí.

But there's also Catalan heritage to be uncovered amid the majestic scenery, plunging valleys and snow-dusted peaks. Thousand-year-old monasteries slumber in these mountains – including some of Spain's outstanding Romanesque architecture – meaning Pyrenean hikes are as likely to pass ruined churches as valley panoramas.

Meanwhile, taste buds yearning for more than hiking fodder will find full satisfaction in the rich volcanic gastronomy of Olot and the Parc Natural de la Zona Volcànica de la Garrotxa.

## Olot

POP 34,500 / ELEV 443M

If you perceive a rumbling sensation during your travels in Olot, it might be more than your appetite lusting after the rich local *cuina volcànica* (volcanic cuisine). This bustling town is the regional capital of La Garrotxa, a lush landscape of cone-shaped hills chiselled by more extreme geological activity up to 700,000 years ago, now protected as Catalonia's Parc Natural de la Zona Volcànica de la Garrotxa. The park completely surrounds Olot, making the town an excellent base for volcanic explorations.

Olot sprawls over a large area with broad, tree-lined boulevards, but the medieval centre is agreeably walkable, with a handful of museums, grand Modernista buildings, exceptional restaurants and a lively Monday market.

### Sights & Activities

Pick up a self-guided walking-tour leaflet of Olot's **Modernista architecture** (which includes Lluís Domènech i Montaner's 1916 floral-patterned Casa Solà Morales) at the tourist office (p352).

Four hills of volcanic origin stand sentry on the fringes of Olot. You can follow a 2km (45-minute) trail up the **Volcà del Montsacopa**, north of the centre.

**Museu dels Volcans** MUSEUM
(https://museus.olot.cat; Parc Nou, Avinguda de Santa Coloma; adult/child €3/free; ⏰10am-1pm & 3-6pm Tue-Fri, 10am-2pm & 3-6pm Sat, 10am-2pm Sun) In the middle of verdant Parc Nou (a botanical garden of Olot-area flora), this schoolroom-like museum has detailed displays on volcanoes, tremors, eruptions, Catalonia's volcanic history and La Garrotxa's geology. An audiovisual ends with a knee-trembling earthquake simulator.

### Sleeping & Eating

**Alberg Torre Malagrida** HOSTEL €
(☎972 26 42 00; www.xanascat.cat; Passeig de Barcelona 15; dm under/over 30yr €13/16; 📶) With tile-floored corridors and stone lions guarding the entrance to a marble-columned early-20th-century Modernista building, surrounded by gardens, it's hard to believe

that this is a youth hostel. The unadorned, locker-equipped dorms – for four, six, eight or 10 – are comfortable without living up to the grandeur of the exterior. Meals available.

**Can Blanc** CASA RURAL **€€**

(972 276 020; www.canblanc.es; Passatges de la Deu; s/d/tr incl breakfast €72/114/156; ) Surrounded by leafy parkland on the southeastern edge of Olot, this secluded dusty-pink country house is a charm. Colourful, simple, modern-rustic rooms come in a range of shapes and sizes. The gardens and small pool will put a smile on your face, as will the great breakfast.

**La Deu** CATALAN **€€**

(972 26 10 04; www.ladeu.es; Carretera La Deu; 3-course menú €15-23, mains €6-25; 1-4pm & 8-10.30pm Mon-Sat, 1-4pm Sun; ) Down a tree-lined road with a volcanic stone fountain bubbling away in its terrace dining area, family-run La Deu has been perfecting its filling *cuina volcànica* since 1885. Service is charmingly efficient, and there's huge culinary variety, including slow-cooked lamb, pork with sweet chestnuts, oven-baked hake, asparagus 'cake' lashed with basil oil, and the house spin on classic *patates d'Olot*.

★**Les Cols** CATALAN **€€€**

(972 26 92 09; www.lescols.com; Carretera de la Canya; degustation menu €125, incl wine €165; 1-3pm & 8.30-10pm Wed-Sat, 1-3.30pm Sun) Set in a converted 19th-century *masia* (farmhouse) 2km northeast of central Olot, Les Cols is the queen of La Garrotxa's fabulous restaurants. The interior has an avant-garde edge, with glass walls and glittery-gold decor. Two-Michelin-starred chef Fina Puigdevall's dishes are powered by local products and prepared with a silken touch.

LOCAL KNOWLEDGE

### VOLCANIC CUISINE

In Olot and around, since 1994, a dedicated group of chefs has been proudly carrying on the *cuina volcànica* tradition, which stems from the area's exceptionally fertile volcanic soil, responsible for a bounty of locally grown produce that forms the base of this hearty cuisine. Traditional ingredients include black radishes, wild mushrooms, Santa Pau beans, Montserrat tomatoes, *ratafia* (liquor with aromatic herbs, sometimes flavoured with walnut) and *piumoc* (dry pork sausage), though some of the final creations are deliciously contemporary. Find out more at www.cuinavolcanica.cat.

## Information

**Casal dels Volcans** (972 26 60 12; http://parcsnaturals.gencat.cat/ca/garrotxa; Parc Nou, Avinguda de Santa Coloma; 10am-2pm Tue-Sun) Official advice about the Parc Natural de la Zona Volcànica de la Garrotxa.

**Oficina de Turisme d'Olot** (972 26 01 41; www.turismeolot.cat; Carrer Doctor Fàbregas 6; 10am-2pm & 4-7pm Mon-Sat, to 2pm Sun) Slick, modern info office with multilingual staff, maps and park walking details.

## Getting There & Away

TEISA (www.teisa-bus.com) runs buses between Olot's **bus station** (Carrer del Bispe Lorenzana) and Girona (€7.60, one to 1½ hours, eight to 16 daily), some via Besalú (€3.50, 30 minutes, 12 to 25 daily), and to/from Barcelona (€14 to €19, 1½ to 2½ hours, nine to 11 daily).

# Parc Natural de la Zona Volcànica de la Garrotxa

The green-clad volcanic-origin hills surrounding Olot make up the 150-sq-km Parc Natural de la Zona Volcànica de la Garrotxa (http://parcsnaturals.gencat.cat/garrotxa). Volcanic eruptions began here about 350,000 years ago, but the last one was 11,500 years ago. As the African and Eurasian tectonic plates nudge ever closer (at a rate of 2cm per year), the occasional mild earthquake still sends a shiver across La Garrotxa, and more than 100 small earthquakes set Catalonia trembling each year (most are barely perceptible). La Garrotxa's volcanoes, however, have long snoozed under a blanket of meadows and oak forests.

The park has around 40 volcanic cones, up to 160m high and 1.5km wide. Together with the lush vegetation (resulting from fertile soils and a damp climate), these create a landscape of unique verdant beauty. The park's most interesting area lies between Olot and the pretty village of Santa Pau, 10km southeast.

## Sights

**Santa Pau** VILLAGE

(GI524) With its tangle of slender cobbled lanes leading past flower-filled corners and pottery workshops to the attractive colon-

## OUT & ABOUT IN CATALONIA'S PYRENEES

The Catalan Pyrenees provide magnificent walking. You can undertake strolls of a few hours, or embark on day walks that can be strung together into treks of several days. Nearly all can be done without camping gear, with nights spent in delightful villages or refugis (no-frills mountain shelters).

Most of the refugis are run by two mountain clubs, the Federació d'Entitats Excursionistes de Catalunya (FEEC; www.feec.cat) and the Centre Excursionista de Catalunya (CEC; www.cec.cat), which also provide info on trails. A night in a refugi costs €18 to €22 with breakfast. Moderately priced meals (around €16 to €22) are sometimes available in high season. It's worth booking ahead online or by phone to ensure your place (in summer, refugis fill up fast, and, in shoulder season, many are closed) and to ask if cooking facilities are available. La Central de Refugis (p363) (www.lacentralderefugis.com) is the handy booking portal.

The coast-to-coast GR11 long-distance trail traverses the entire Pyrenees from Cap de Creus on the Costa Brava to Hondarribia on the Bay of Biscay. Other hiking highlights include hardy trails between glittering high-altitude lakes in the Parc Nacional d'Aigüestortes i Estany de Sant Maurici (p359) and gentle rambles across the lush volcanic landscapes of the Parc Natural de la Zona Volcànica de la Garrotxa (p350).

The season for walking in the high Pyrenees is late June to early October, with quieter September providing some of the best all-round conditions. Always be prepared for fast-changing weather, no matter when you're visiting.

Local advice from tourist offices, park rangers, mountain refugis and other walkers is invaluable. Dedicated hiking maps are essential; Editorial Alpina (www.editorialalpina.com) produces some of the best.

There's boundless scope for climbing; Pedraforca in the Serra del Cadí (p356) offers some of the most exciting ascents. The ever-growing selection of other Pyrenees adventure activities includes whitewater rafting, kayaking, canyoning, vie ferrate, biking and more, for all of which the Pallars Sobirà (p358) region and the Val d'Aran (p362) are favourites. Skiing, of course, is the other speciality, with the richest pickings on the Val d'Aran's Baqueira-Beret-Bonaigua (p367) slopes.

naded Plaça Major, medieval Santa Pau is arguably La Garrotxa's most ravishing village. A 13th-century castle looms over the main square.

**Castellfollit de la Roca** VILLAGE

(GI522) Aside from the hills, one of La Garrotxa's most remarkable geological sights is the town of Castellfollit de la Roca (10km northeast of Olot), teetering on the edge of a blackened basalt cliff face made up of two superposed lava flows. The best views are from the road beneath town, near Hostal Mont-Rock.

**Sant Joan les Fonts** VILLAGE

Some 6km northeast of Olot, Sant Joan les Fonts has some lovely forest just beyond the village centre. From the Oficina de Turisme, you can pick up various paths that lead past waterfalls, impressive cliffs formed by volcanic lava flows and peaceful woodlands that follow a trickling stream. Paths go all the way to Olot (2½ hours) and Santa Pau (five hours) for serious walkers.

In the northern end of the village, the 12th-century **Monestir de Sant Joan les Fonts** (Sant Joan les Fonts; €2; ⏲ noon Sat & Sun) is a striking Romanesque riverside monastery. Visits are by 90-minute guided tour on weekends that also take in the Castell de Juvinyà and the Pont Medieval. These depart from the **Oficina de Turisme** (☎ 979 29 05 07; www.turismesantjoanlesfonts.com; Carrer de Sant Pere 2, Sant Joan les Fonts; ⏲ 10am-2pm Sun-Fri, 10am-2pm & 4-6pm Sat) in Sant Joan les Fonts. The village makes a pleasant stop between Olot and the dramatic cliffs of Castellfollit de la Roca.

## Activities

There are 28 hiking routes within the natural park, most clearly signposted.

A number of easy walking trails lead directly from the **car parks** near Olot and Santa Pau to the volcanic cones. The basalt lava flows near **Sant Joan les Fonts** are an especially stunning place to walk; routes are signposted from the town's tourist office.

One fine hike goes up and into the crater of **Volcà de Santa Margarida**, which hides a Romanesque chapel; the 2km trail begins from a signposted car park 3km west of Santa Pau on the GI524.

## Sleeping

**Camping Ecològic Lava** CAMPGROUND €
(☎972 68 03 58; www.campinglava.com; Carretera Olot-Santa Pau/GI524, Km 7; car & tent/adult/child €17/8/7, bungalow from €129; P 🛜 🏊) Wrapped in greenery 6km southeast of Olot, this animated year-round campground inside La Garrotxa's *parc natural* has solid amenities, including laundry facilities and hot showers, plus ample outdoor space, a pool (summer only), a restaurant and easy access to hiking trails and horse riding. There are also bungalows for four to 10 people.

**Cal Sastre** BOUTIQUE HOTEL €€
(☎972 68 00 95; www.calsastre.com; Plaça dels Balls, Santa Pau; d €125-160; ❄ 🛜) Inside two exquisitely revamped 15th-century houses, behind medieval arches, Cal Sastre's eight rooms have an air of updated old-world glamour, with gold-patterned bedheads and claw-foot baths set against sparkling modern bathrooms. It's just opposite the castle in the heart of pretty little Sant Pau, attached to the excellent family restaurant.

## Getting There & Away

TEISA (www.teisa-bus.com) runs buses from La Garrotxa's main hub Olot to Girona (€7.60, one to 1½ hours, eight to 16 daily), some via Besalú (€3.50, 30 minutes, 12 to 25 daily), and Barcelona (€14 to €19, 1½ to 2½ hours, nine to 11 daily).

## Getting Around

La Garrotxa is best explored by car or bicycle, as public transport around the region is light.

TEISA (www.teisa-bus.com) runs buses from Olot to Castellfollit de la Roca (€1.75, 15 minutes, six to 14 daily) via Sant Joan de les Fonts (€1.75, 10 minutes).

# Ripoll

POP 10,700 / ELEV 691M

With an especially impressive monastery at its heart, and another 10km northeast in tiny Sant Joan de les Abadesses, otherwise unremarkable Ripoll is a worthy stopover for admirers of Romanesque art.

Ripoll can claim, with some justice, to be the birthplace of Catalonia. In the 9th century it was the power base from which local strongman Guifré el Pilós (Wilfred the Hairy) succeeded in uniting several counties of the Frankish March along the southern side of the Pyrenees. Guifré later became the first in a line of hereditary counts of Barcelona. To encourage repopulation of the Pyrenean valleys, he founded (and now lies buried in) the Monestir de Santa Maria, medieval Catalonia's most powerful monastery.

Ripoll is well-positioned for rambling the vertiginous terrain of the Vall de Núria, extending from 13km north, or the dormant volcanoes of La Garrotxa, 30km east.

**★Monestir de Santa Maria** MONASTERY
(www.monestirderipoll.cat; Plaça de l'Abat Oliba; adult/child €6.80/5; ⏲10am-2pm & 4-7pm Apr-Sep, 10am-1.30pm & 3.30-6pm Mon-Sat, 10am-2pm Sun Oct-Mar) Consecrated in CE 888, Ripoll's monastery was Catalonia's spiritual and cultural heart from the mid-10th to mid-11th century. The five-naved **basilica** was adorned in about 1100 with a stone portal that ranks among Spain's most splendid Romanesque art; its well-restored interior contains admirable floor mosaics, a multi-language display on the Bibles of Ripoll (rare illustrated manuscripts created between 1008 and 1020), plus the **tomb of Guifré el Pilós**, who founded the monastery.

Two floors of **cloisters**, dating from the 12th to 16th centuries and whose columns are carved with fantastical beasts, overlook a gurgling fountain and neat gardens.

**La Trobada** HOTEL €€
(☎972 70 23 53; www.latrobadahotel.com; Passeig del Compositor Honorat Vilamanyà 4; s €48-100, d €70-152; P ❄ 🛜) Clean, simple and with polite, eager-to-please staff, La Trobada is Ripoll's most comfortable accommodation, on the east edge of town. Rooms are well maintained, many offering glimpses of the Monestir de Santa Maria; there are also five rather stylish junior suites added in 2019.

## Information

**Oficina de Turisme de Ripoll** (☎972 70 23 51; www.ripoll.cat/turisme; Plaça del Abat Oliba; ⏲10am-2pm & 4-7pm Mon-Sat Apr-Sep, 10am-1.30pm & 3.30-6pm Mon-Sat Oct-Mar, 10am-2pm Sun year-round) Next to the Monestir de Santa Maria, with an interpretation centre on the history of the town and monastery.

WORTH A TRIP

### SANT JOAN DE LES ABADESSES

Who gallops through the hills on stormy nights around Sant Joan de les Abadesses (10km northeast of Ripoll on the N260 towards Olot) on a horse engulfed in flames and accompanied by ravenous black dogs? If you believe the legends, it's the cursed Count Arnau, whose association with the Romanesque **Monestir de Sant Joan de les Abadesses** (www.monestirsantjoanabadesses.cat; Plaça de l'Abadia; adult/child €3/free; ⌚10am-7pm Jul & Aug, 10am-2pm & 4-7pm May, Jun & Sep, 10am-2pm & 4-6pm Oct, Mar & Apr, 10am-2pm Mon-Fri, 10am-2pm & 4-6pm Sat & Sun Nov-Feb) has bequeathed it a heritage of brooding fairy-tales alongside its centuries of spiritual activity. The monastery, founded in 887 CE by Guifré el Pilós, is notable for both its architectural treasures and the legend.

In the same building as Sant Joan's **tourist office** (☎972 72 05 99; www.santjoandelesabadesses.cat; Plaça de l'Abadia 9; ⌚10am-2pm & 4-7pm Mon-Sat, 10am-2pm Sun), the monastery's 14th-century **Palau de l'Abadia** houses a fascinating **audiovisual exhibition** (www.santjoandelesabadesses.cat; Plaça de l'Abadia 9; €2.50; ⌚10am-2pm & 4-7pm Mon-Sat, 10am-2pm Sun) tracing the source of the Count Arnau legend.

If you fancy stopping overnight in Sant Joan, **Hotelet de St Joan** (☎872 59 96 99; www.hoteletdestjoan.com; Carrer del Mestre Josep Maria Andreu 3; r €75-110; ❄📶) is a smartly minimalist, industrial-chic boutique find with good breakfasts (€8) and 10 rooms in calming greys. TEISA (www.teisa-bus.com) operates buses every one to two hours to/from Ripoll (€2.35, 20 minutes).

### Getting There & Away

Daily *rodalies* trains (line R3) run to/from Barcelona (€9.55, two hours, 11 to 17 daily) via Vic (€4.15, 40 minutes). North from Ripoll, trains reach Ribes de Freser (€2.50, 20 minutes, seven daily) and Puigcerdà (€5, one hour, six to seven daily).

## Vall de Núria & Ribes de Freser

A trio of little towns populates the Vall de Ribes and Vall de Núria, southeast of Cerdanya and north of Ripoll. Here, pine forests, plummeting dales and rugged hills huddle between the Serra Cavallera and Serra de Montgrony, rippling north to the Capçaleres del Ter i del Freser mountains.

Sheltered within the Vall de Ribes is small, well-equipped Ribes de Freser, 13km north of Ripoll. Six kilometres further north lies the charming stone village of **Queralbs** (1180m), home to a 10th-century church with a beautiful Romanesque portico. Beyond, accessible only by *cremallera* (rack railway), are **Núria** (1960m) and its lofty valley. Núria holds the revered Santuari de la Mare de Déu, though in winter it draws as many winter-sports devotees as pilgrims. A trip to Núria by *cremallera* is worth it for the views alone as the train rattles past lichen-wrapped rubble, miniature waterfalls, patches of forest, and gaping valleys.

### Sights & Activities

In winter, Núria transforms into a small-scale **ski resort** (☎972 73 20 20; www.valldenuria.cat/hivern; Núria; day pass incl train adult/child €31/23; ⌚Dec-Mar; 👪), while summer months lure energetic hikers, and rowboat and kayaks pop up on the lake.

The Vall de Núria has some lovely marked **hiking trails**; Nùria's tourist office (p356) provides maps. One of the best and most popular routes is the **Camí Vell**, which leads through the gorge from Núria to Queralbs (8km, two to three hours); allow double the time if making the ascent.

From Núria, you can also cap several 2700m to 2900m peaks on the main Pyrenees ridge in about 2½ to four hours' walking (around 4km to 9km each one way). The most popular is **Puigmal** (2909m).

**Santuari de la Mare de Déu** CHURCH
(www.valldenuria.cat; Núria; ⌚8am-6pm) FREE
The region's high point (literally and figuratively) is Núria's strangely austere 1911 sanctuary. A gold-and-pastel-painted passageway leads to its upper level, housing the Mare de Déu de Núria above the altar. Mary, looking regal in star-spangled robes, clasps a grown-up Jesus. The icon is in 12th-century Romanesque style, despite believers insisting that Sant Gil sculpted it in CE 700. The sanctuary's spartan feel initially underwhelms but the magnificent views and folklore make this a worthy trip.

## Sleeping & Eating

**Refugi de Coma de Vaca** CABIN €
(☎872 98 70 98; www.comadevaca.cat; dm incl breakfast €27, with half-board €47) Located in a spectacular valley (elevation 2000m) with grazing cows and a trickling stream nearby, this mountain refuge makes a memorable base for hikes in the area. Offers simple bunks and filling meals, and if you're just passing through, you can stop for a snack. It's about a 2½-hour walk from Núria, though you can also hike up from Queralbs.

**Alberg Pic de l'Àliga** HOSTEL €
(☎972 73 20 48; www.xanascat.cat; Núria; dm under/over 30yr incl breakfast €21.40/26.20; ⊙Dec-Oct; 📶) Fancy a cheap sleep 2122m above sea level? This youth hostel in a spacious lodge is perched at the top of the *telecabina* (cable car) whizzing up from Núria. Dorms sleep three to 18 people and it has a cafe, board games and a common room for mingling with other travellers.

★**Hotel Els Caçadors** HOTEL €€
(☎972 72 70 06; www.hotelsderibes.com; Carrer de Balandrau 24-26, Ribes de Freser; s €55-90, d €70-110, f €90-142; ⊙Dec-Oct; ❄📶) Family-run since 1920, this local institution has 37 spacious rooms in three grades. 'Bronze' is decked with warm beige tones and wood fittings, while 'silver' ramps up the comfort with skylights, balconies or hydromassage baths; romantic 'gold' rooms and suites are most luxurious. There's a top-floor lounge plus a terrace with a mountain-view hot tub.

The popular **restaurant** (mains €11-19; ⊙8-10.30am, 1-3.45pm & 8.30-10pm Mon-Sat, 8-10.30am & 1-3.45pm Sun Dec-Oct) dishes up excellent Catalan food, such as squid cannelloni or baked hake with prawns, and three-course weekday lunch menus (€18).

**Hostal les Roquetes** HOSTAL €€
(☎972 72 73 69; www.hostalroquetes.com; Carretera de Ribes 5; s/tw/d €38/68/78; P📶) This comforting stone guesthouse sits just above the train station in Queralbs, perfect for walking trips up to Núria via the *cremallera*.

## Information

**Oficina de Turisme de Núria** (☎972 73 20 20; www.valldenuria.cat; Núria; ⊙9am-5pm Mon-Fri, to 6pm Sat & Sun) Next to Núria's Santuari.

**Oficina de Turisme de Ribes de Freser** (☎972 72 77 28; www.vallderibes.cat; Carretera de Bruguera 2, Ribes de Freser; ⊙10am-2pm & 4-6pm Tue-Thu, 10am-2pm & 4-7.30pm Fri & Sat, 10am-2pm Sun)

## Getting There & Away

There are two train stations in Ribes de Freser, both on the *cremallera* line to Núria (which isn't reachable by car).

Ribes–Enllaç, at the south end of town, has *rodalies* trains to Barcelona (€10, two to 2½ hours, six daily) and Ripoll (€2.50, 20 minutes, six daily).

The central Ribes–Vila is a *cremallera* stop between Ribes–Enllaç and Queralbs. **Cremallera** (www.valldenuria.cat; Ribes de Freser–Núria return adult/child €26/16) trains run from Ribes de Freser to Núria (35 to 40 minutes) via Queralbs (15 to 20 minutes) six to 11 times daily. There are car parks at Ribes–Vila and Queralbs if you're day-tripping to Núria via *cremallera*; they're packed in high season, so go early.

# Cerdanya

Picturesque Cerdanya, along with French Cerdagne across the border, occupies a low-lying green basin between the higher reaches of the Pyrenees to its east and west. Although Cerdanya and Cerdagne, once a single Catalan county, were divided by the Treaty of the Pyrenees in 1659, Catalan is spoken on both sides of the border and Spain flows seamlessly into France. Hikers and mountain-bikers converge on Puigcerdà, the region's main town, and pretty nearby Llívia in summer, while winter sees skiers and snowboarders hit the slopes of La Molina and Masella. Cerdanya also makes an excellent jumping-off point to ramble and rock climb the Serra del Cadí (p358).

## Puigcerdà

POP 9000 / ELEV 1202M

Barely 2km south of France, Puigcerdà (puh-cher-*da*) dates back to the 12th century – not that you'd know it, since most of its historical buildings were obliterated during the civil war. Prior to that it was a favourite summer hangout for the Catalan bourgeoisie in the 19th century. Today, the town is essentially a way station, but it's a jolly one, with good shops and restaurants and a friendly buzz and a pretty lake, used as a base by skiers during the winter season and teeming with hikers in summer. A dozen Spanish, Andorran and French ski resorts lie within 45km.

**Església de Santa Maria** TOWER
(Plaça Santa Maria; tower adult/child €1.50/free; ⌚9.30am-1pm & 4-6.30pm Mon-Fri, 10am-1pm & 5-7.30pm Sat, 10am-1pm Sun) Though only the tower of the 17th-century Església de Santa Maria still stands, this stocky Romanesque structure dominates bustling Plaça Santa Maria. Climb up for fine views.

## Sleeping & Eating

**Mas Sant Marc** CASA RURAL €€
(☎972 88 00 07; www.santmarc.es; Camí de Sant Marc 34; d €95-117, ste €115-165; P 🛜 🏊) Sprawling grounds and plush beds greet you at this welcoming rural hideaway, 2km south of Puigcerdà's centre. Spacious wood-floored rooms are elegantly styled in soothing creams, and there's horse riding and bike riding plus a sauna, spa services, a lovely pool and plenty of outdoor space.

**Hotel Parada Puigcerdà** BOUTIQUE HOTEL €€
(☎972 14 03 00; www.hotelparadapuigcerda.com; Plaça de l'Estaciò; s/d €64/79; 🛜) Who knew railway stops could have so much style? Hidden within Puigcerdà's 20th-century train station, this boutique pick preserves the attractive original architecture, combining it with thoroughly up-to-date interiors. The 28 crisp, stripped-back rooms are washed in moody greys and cool whites; top-floor rooms have slanted wood-beamed ceilings.

**La Caixeta** INTERNATIONAL €
(☎619 202174; www.facebook.com/caixeta-bistro; Carrer Querol 22; sharing plates €5-15; ⌚7.30pm-2am Tue-Fri, noon-3.30pm & 7.30-11pm Sat & Sun; 🛜📝) All wood-block walls, mismatched furniture and arty decor, this buzzy cafe-bistro-bar criss-crosses the Spanish–French border with its beautifully presented creative tapas, from camembert, homemade guacamole and quiche of the day to salads, mini-burgers, *torrades* (topped toasts) and Catalan charcuterie.

## Information

**Oficina de Turisme de la Cerdanya** (☎972 14 06 65; www.cerdanya.org; N260; ⌚9am-1pm & 4-7pm Mon-Sat, 10am-1pm Sun) On the main road, 1km southwest of the centre.

**Oficina de Turisme de Puigcerdà** (☎972 88 05 42; www.puigcerda.cat; Plaça Santa Maria; ⌚9.30am-1.30pm & 4.30-7.30pm Mon-Fri, 10am-1.30pm & 5-8pm Sat, 10am-1.30pm Sun) Within a historical tower in central Puigcerdà.

LOCAL KNOWLEDGE

### CATALONIA ABLAZE

On **La Nit de Sant Joan** (23 June), Catalonia burns big bonfires at crossroads and town squares in a combined midsummer and St John's Eve celebration, and fireworks explode all night. Catalonia's supreme fire festival is **La Patum de Berga** (www.lapatum.cat), held 30km west of Ripoll in Berga. An evening of dancing and firework-spitting angels, devils, mulelike monsters, dwarfs, giants and men covered in grass culminates in a mass frenzy of fire and smoke on Corpus Christi (the Thursday 60 days after Easter Sunday).

## Getting There & Away

ALSA (www.alsa.es) buses run to/from Barcelona (€21, 3¼ hours, one or two daily) and La Seu d'Urgell (€7.05, one hour, four to six daily), stopping at Plaça de l'Estació, next to the train station just southwest of central Puigcerdà, as well as Plaça Barcelona.

*Rodalies* trains link Puigcerdà with Barcelona (€12, 3¼ hours, seven daily) via Ribes de Freser (53 minutes), Ripoll (1¼ hours) and Vic (1¾ hours). Five continue across the border to Latour-de-Carol (Catalan: La Tor de Querol), where you can connect to the French network.

From Barcelona, the C16 approaches Puigcerdà through the Túnel del Cadí (€12). Puigcerdà is also reachable via the picturesque N260 from Ribes de Freser, to the southeast. The main crossing into France is at Bourg-Madame, 1km east of central Puigcerdà.

# Llívia

POP 1430 / ELEV 1224M

Glance carefully at your map of the Spain–France border. Just 6km northeast of Puigcerdà, amid verdant meadows and little French villages, is Llívia, a tiny slate-roofed bastion of Catalonia beyond the main border between France and Spain. Under the 1659 Treaty of the Pyrenees, Spain ceded 33 villages to France, but Llívia was a *vila* (town), so, together with the 13 sq km of its municipality, it remained a Spanish possession. Much more than just a cartographical oddity, this small town has a gorgeous medieval centre, a couple of worthwhile hotels and more excellent restaurants than you'd expect for its size. Most visitors hike the hills during summer or access winter ski resorts in the Spanish and French Pyrenees.

## Sights

Llívia's few sights lie in its tiny medieval nucleus at the top (east end) of town.

**Castell de Llívia** CASTLE
(24hr) FREE Though little more than walls remain of Llívia's ruined hilltop castle, it's worth the hefty 15-minute climb for the fabulously beautiful wraparound views across the French countryside. Restoration works have unearthed parts of the fortress dating as far back as the 9th century.

**Església de Mare de Déu dels Àngels** CHURCH
(hours vary) Llívia's 16th-century, late-Gothic church is encircled by three defensive towers and contains a Romanesque baptismal font.

**Museu Municipal** MUSEUM
(Carrer dels Forns 10; adult/child €3.50/1; 3-6pm Tue, 9am-1.30pm & 3-6pm Wed-Sat, 10am-2pm Sun) Proudly occupying what's alleged to be Europe's oldest pharmacy (dating to 1415, it operated until 1926), this multi-language, multimedia museum explores the region's history from Paleolithic times to modern day.

## Sleeping & Eating

★**Set Terres** BOUTIQUE HOTEL €€
(972 89 64 99; www.setterres.com; Carrer Puigcerdà 8; r incl breakfast €90-150; ) A keen husband-and-wife team has transformed the stables of the 1772 family home into an exquisite boutique adult hideaway. There are just seven rooms, each different, designed with pared-back yet homey country-chic style, incorporating open-stone walls, crisp white decor and, for three top-floor rooms, sloping ceilings. Breakfast is a lovingly prepared local-produce buffet.

★**Can Ventura** CATALAN €€
(972 89 61 78; www.canventura.com; Plaça Major 1; mains €16-25; 1.30-3.30pm & 8-10.30pm, closed Sun dinner, Mon & Thu approx Sep-Jun) Skilfully updated Catalan cuisine pulls diners to this excellent modern-rustic restaurant set inside a 1791 building. Traditional Catalan flavours take pride of place, like scallops with black rice, slow-cooked lamb and smoky *trinxat* (potato and cabbage with a pork garnish), but you'll also find hints of Asian fusion and whispers of French flair.

## Information

**Oficina de Turisme** (972 89 63 13; www.llivia.org; Museu Municipal, Carrer dels Forns 10; 3-6pm Tue, 9am-1.30pm & 3-6pm Wed-Sat, 10am-2pm Sun) Has details on local hiking routes.

## Getting There & Away

ALSA (www.alsa.es) buses run from Puigcerdà to Llívia (€1.75, 20 minutes, four to eight daily).

# La Molina & Masella

The twin ski resorts of **La Molina and Masella** (www.lamolina.cat; day pass adult/child €48/38; mid-Nov–Apr) lie either side of

OFF THE BEATEN TRACK

### SERRA DEL CADÍ

The spectacular Serra del Cadí comprises a string of charming stone villages and rugged mountains that offer excellent walking for those suitably equipped and experienced. **Pedraforca** ('Stone Pitchfork'; 2506m) is the most legendary peak in the range, offering the most challenging rock climbing in Catalonia. The main Cadí range is part of the 410-sq-km **Parc Natural Cadí-Moixeró** (http://parcsnaturals.gencat.cat/ca/cadi) and hosts a number of staffed *refugis* (mountain refuges) in the park for serious multiday hikes.

The villages used as jumping-off points for exploring the area are strung along the picturesque B400 and C563, between the C16 to Puigcerdà and the C14 to La Seu d'Urgell. These include **Saldes** (a popular hiking base in the shadow of Pedraforca), **Gósol** (topped by a ruined 11th-century castle), **Josa de Cadí** and **Tuixent**. The best information points are Bagà's **Centre del Parc Natural del Cadí-Moixeró** (938 24 41 51; http://parcsnaturals.gencat.cat/cadi; Carrer de la Vinya 1, Bagà; 9am-1pm & 4-7pm Mon-Sat, 9am-1pm Sun) and Saldes' **tourist office** (938 25 80 05; www.saldes.cat; Saldes; 9am-2pm Tue, 9am-2pm & 4-7pm Mon & Wed-Fri), both on the eastern side of the Serra. The valley makes an exquisite drive: a longer, super-scenic route between Puigcerdà and La Seu d'Urgell.

**Tosa d'Alp** (2537m), 15km south of Puigcerdà, linked by the Alp 2500 lift. The site provides a combined total of 141km of runs of all grades, at altitudes of 1600m to over 2500m. Rental equipment and ski schools are available at both resorts, with La Molina a better choice for beginners. Lift passes cover the whole area.

La Molina is Spain's oldest ski resort, with its origins in the 1940s; in summer, it caters to activity lovers with its mountain-bike park, quad-biking, canyoning, open-air yoga and more.

**Hotel Adserà** HOTEL €€
(☎972 89 20 01; www.hoteladsera.com; Carrer Pere Adserà, La Molina; s/d/tr/q incl breakfast €75/115/155/180; ⏲Dec-Easter & Jul–mid-Sep; P 📶 🏊) Unlike many of the region's resorts, this homey hotel with comfy old-fashioned rooms offers a personal touch and a dash of historical charm. Just 2.5km below the slopes, it's an excellent choice for families with its rotating daily kids' activities, plus a games room, garden, pool and restaurant.

### ℹ Getting There & Away

In ski season, a special Skibus goes to the slopes from Barcelona (Plaça Catalunya) on Wednesdays and Fridays at 6.30am and returns at 4pm (€44, including lift pass). You can also buy a combo train-lift pass on the Skitren (€42 from Barcelona). There are also half-hourly or hourly buses between La Molina town and the slopes (€2), connecting with *rodalies* trains from Puigcerdà (20 minutes, six daily).

## La Seu d'Urgell

POP 12,100 / ELEV 691M

The lively valley town of La Seu d'Urgell (la *se*-u dur-*zhey*) is Spain's gateway to Andorra (p361), 10km north. La Seu has an attractive medieval centre full of arcaded stone streets, watched over by a beautiful Romanesque cathedral. When the Franks evicted the Muslims from this part of the Pyrenees in the early 9th century, they made La Seu a bishopric and capital of the counts of Urgell; it remains an important market and cathedral town.

### 👁 Sights & Activities

**★Catedral de Santa Maria & Museu Diocesà** CATHEDRAL
(Plaça dels Oms; adult/child €4/free; ⏲10am-1.30pm & 4-7pm Mon-Sat Jun-Sep, to 6pm Oct-May) Dominating La Seu d'Urgell's old town is the 12th-century, pale sandstone Santa Maria cathedral – one of Catalonia's outstanding Romanesque buildings. Its neat cloister, with three original galleries, is rich in characterful carved capitals depicting mythical beasts and grimacing gargoyles. The superb **museum** within exhibits a wealth of Romanesque frescoes from various churches, and one of just 25 famous **medieval illustrated Beatus manuscripts** still in existence.

Adjacent to the cloister is the 11th-century Romanesque **Església de Sant Miquel**, rougher-hewn and pleasantly unembellished; its 13th-century murals now live in Barcelona's Museu Nacional d'Art de Catalunya (p272).

**Rafting Parc** WATER SPORTS
(☎973 36 00 92; www.raftingparc.cat; off Carrer de Sota Palau; whitewater rafting/kayaking/hydrospeed €42/48/48, bike hire hour/half-day €10/22) Just a short stroll south of the old town, this aquatic centre with its white-water rapids offers adrenaline-fuelled adventures for solo or tandem kayakers, group rafting or the daredevil-esque hydrospeed (go headfirst along rushing waters manoeuvring a small floatboard). For something tamer, you can hire canoes (€15 per hour) for a paddle around the flat-water 800m channel.

### 🛏 Sleeping

**Groc Rooms** APARTMENT €€
(☎627 429908; www.grocrooms.com; Carrer Major 59; d €57-90; P 📶) Vintage mirrors, antique fireplaces and original-period tiled floors meet colourful, contemporary styling at these four 'boutique apartments' in a gorgeously revamped old-town house. The massive kitchen-equipped Loft apartment sleeps up to five, while others are more like cosy-chic rooms; the Suite features an in-room bathtub.

**Parador de La Seu d'Urgell** HERITAGE HOTEL €€
(☎973 35 20 00; www.parador.es; Carrer de Sant Domènec 6; r €105-120; P 📶 🏊) While not as palatial as some of Spain's other *paradores* (luxurious state-owned hotels), this pleasing hotel has plain, modern rooms surrounding an elegant Renaissance cloister, which hosts a cafe-bar between stone archways. Corridors are illuminated in colour at night, there's a good restaurant (mains €12 to €17) and indoor pool, and you're just up the street from La Seu d'Urgell's cathedral.

## Eating & Drinking

**Arbeletxe** CATALAN €€

(☎973 36 16 34; www.arbeletxe.com; Carrer de Sant Ermengol 22; mains €14-20; ⏰1-3pm Sun-Tue, 1-3pm & 9-11pm Thu-Sat; ✎) One of La Seu d'Urgell's best-loved dining destinations is this elegant but unpretentious, two-room restaurant just west of the Plaça Catalunya. Service is warm, and the price-quality ratio is excellent for plates of perfectly cooked *magret* (duck), *entrecot* (ribeye steak), *xipirons farcits* (stuffed squid) and a flavour-packed vegetable lasagna.

**PKtus** CATALAN €€

(☎973 35 32 59; Carrer de la Creu 14; sharing plates €6-12; ⏰1-4pm & 8.30-11pm Wed-Sat, 1-4pm Sun; 📶) Modern, minuscule and friendly, PKtus concentrates on a limited menu of delicious deli produce, with regional cheeses, creative salads, Iberian ham and outstanding croquettes (stuffed with oxtail, curry chicken, calamari and other delicacies), plus some excellent wines.

**Velo Cafe** COFFEE

(www.facebook.com/velocafelaseu; Carrer de Joaquim Viola 29; ⏰8am-4pm Mon, Tue, Thu & Fri, 9am-2pm Sat; 📶) This sun-drenched bicycle-themed spot northwest of the historic centre serves the best cappuccino in town. It's a favourite gathering spot for a post-ride espresso, or tasty snacks (cinnamon toast, carrot cake) and to pick up a Velo-branded jersey and other gear.

## Information

**Turisme La Seu** (☎973 35 15 11; www.turismeseu.com; Carrer Major 8; ⏰10am-2pm & 4-7pm Mon-Sat, 10am-1pm Sun, closed Sun approx Nov-Apr) Helpful office across the street from the cathedral offering maps for historical walks and displays on local history.

## Getting There & Away

The **bus station** (Carrer Mont) is on the northern edge of the old town. ALSA (www.alsa.es) runs buses to Barcelona (€29, three to 3½ hours, eight to 11 daily), Puigcerdà (€7.05, one hour, four to six daily) and Lleida (€20, 2¼ hours, three to seven daily).

# Pallars Sobirà

The Riu Noguera Pallaresa tumbles south from the heights of the Val d'Aran, with the pristine scenery of the Pallars Sobirà area extending from both sides. West of the river lies the majestic **Parc Nacional Aigüestortes i Estany de Sant Maurici**; to its east, the vast 698-sq-km **Parc Natural de l'Alt Pirineu** (http://parcsnaturals.gencat.cat/ca/alt-pirineu), sprinkled with lonely Romanesque churches among which weave hiking trails.

The river itself draws whitewater rafters and other adventure-sports enthusiasts to the small towns along its banks, principally (from north to south) **Llavorsí**, **Rialp** and **Sort**. Each of these towns is well-equipped with accommodation, cafes and restaurants, though outside the March-to-October season things are very quiet.

## Activities

Beyond white-water rafting, this valley packs in an astounding range of summer adventure activities, including kayaking, canyoning, SUP, horse riding, rock climbing, canoeing and guided hikes, plus wintertime skiing higher up. There are good independent hikes in the Parc Natural de l'Alt Pirineu; tourist offices in Llavorsí and Sort provide details.

The Riu Noguera Pallaresa's grade IV drops attract a constant stream of whitewater fans between mid-March and mid-October. Conditions are best in May and June, when the snow melts off the surrounding mountains.

The finest stretch is the 12km from Llavorsí to Rialp, on which standard two-hour raft outings cost around €45 per person. Longer rides to Sort and beyond cost more. Sort is the jumping-off point for the river's tougher grade IV rapids. There's usually a four-person minimum, but outfitters can combine smaller groups.

Llavorsí has several reliable rafting operators, including **Roc Roi** (☎973 62 20 35; www.rocroi.com; Plaça Biuse 8, Llavorsí; 2hr rafting from €45; ⏰mid-Mar–mid-Oct) and **Rafting Llavorsí** (☎973 62 21 58; www.raftingllavorsi.cat; Carrer Vilanova, Llavorsí; 2hr rafting €41; ⏰mid-Mar–mid-Oct); in Sort, **LA Rafting Company** (☎973 62 14 62; www.laraftingcompany.com; Plaça Caterina Albert 2, Sort; 2hr rafting €45-50, all-day €90; ⏰mid-Mar–mid-Oct) is a popular choice. For rafting, bring your own swimming costume and towel and a change of clothes.

## Sleeping & Eating

**Hostal Noguera** HOSTAL €€

(☎973 62 20 12; www.hostalnoguera.info; Carretera Vall d'Aran, Llavorsí; s/d incl breakfast €39/70; ⏰Apr-Nov; P 📶) This stone building

WORTH A TRIP

### ANDORRA

If you're on the lookout for outstanding hiking or skiing, fancy stocking up on duty-free booze, smokes, cosmetics or electronics, or just want to say you've been to another country, then the curious nation of Andorra (population 77,000), 10km north of La Seu d'Urgell, is worth a spin across the border. At only 468 sq km, it's one of Europe's smallest countries. Though it has its own democratic parliament, the nominal heads of state are two co-princes: the bishop of Urgell in Spain, and the French president. Catalan is the official language, though Spanish, French and, due to a large immigrant workforce, Portuguese are widely spoken. Beyond the duty-free shops, busy capital **Andorra la Vella** has a couple of intriguing sights, most notably the small, cobbled **Barri Antic** and its 16th-century **Casa de la Vall**, until 2011 home to the Consell General d'Andorra.

Hourly (less on Sunday) **Montmantell** (www.montmantell.com) buses link La Seu d'Urgell with Andorra la Vella (€3.50, 45 minutes). If driving, fuel up in Andorra; it's significantly cheaper. There's rarely any passport control, but you may be stopped by customs on the way back into Spain, so don't go over the duty-free limit. Although Andorra isn't part of the EU, it uses the euro.

on the southern edge of town has 15 pleasant rooms, nine with balconies overlooking the rushing river. The three wood-beamed top-floor rooms have a dash more charm, while the downstairs restaurant serves filling local specialities like grilled meats and fried eggs swimming in ratatouille.

**Hotel Pessets** SPA HOTEL **€€**
(☎973 62 00 00; www.hotelpessets.com; Avinguda de la Diputació 3, Sort; s/d incl breakfast from €70/90; ❄🛜🏊) At this wellness-focused hotel, lodgings range from unfussy neutral-toned doubles to smart suites with naturalist prints and wood-panelled ceilings. The highlights are the spa area with pool, a private outdoor lounge with mountain views, and a seasonal open-air pool.

## ℹ Information

**Oficina de Turisme del Pallars Sobirà** (☎973 62 10 02; http://turisme.pallarssobira.cat; Camí de la Cabanera, Sort; ⊙9am-3pm & 4-7pm Mon-Sat, 9am-3pm Sun late Jun–mid-Sep; 10am-2pm Mon-Thu & Sun, 10am-2pm & 4-7pm Fri & Sat mid-Sep–early Jun) The area's main tourist office, crammed with maps and walking info supplied by multilingual staff. Also has displays on local history and culture.

**Oficina de Turisme Llavorsí** (☎973 62 20 08; Carrer del Portal, Llavorsí; ⊙9am-2pm Mon-Fri, 9.30am-2.30pm & 3-5.30pm Sat) Small but helpful information desk.

## ℹ Getting There & Away

ALSA (www.alsa.es) runs buses to Llavorsí via Sort and Rialp from Barcelona (€36, one daily, five hours) and Lleida (€12, one to two daily, three hours). On-demand city-subsidised transport runs between La Seu d'Urgell and Sort (€5, one hour) with **Josep Colom** (☎689 495777); book a day ahead.

# Parc Nacional d'Aigüestortes i Estany de Sant Maurici & Around

Catalonia's only national park extends 20km east to west, and just 9km north to south. But the rugged mountain terrain within this small area sparkles with over 200 lakes and countless streams and waterfalls, combined with pine and fir forests, and open bush and grassland, decked with springtime wildflowers or fringed with scarlet autumn leaves. Created by glacial action over two million years, the park comprises two east–west valleys at 1600m to 2000m altitudes framed by jagged 2600m to 2900m peaks of granite and slate.

The national park lies at the core of a wider wilderness area. The outer limit, the *zona periférica*, includes some magnificent high country north and south. The main approaches are **Espot**, 4km east of the park and 8km from **Estany de Sant Maurici**, and the **Vall de Boí**, to the west. July to August is peak hiking season, but quieter September and October appeal more.

Private vehicles cannot enter the park. Wild camping is not allowed, nor is swimming in lakes and rivers.

The best park map is produced by Editorial Alpina (www.editorialalpina.com), for sale in Espot and Boí info offices (€12).

## Getting Around

The closest you can drive to the eastern side of the park is a car park 4km west of Espot; on the west side, it's a car park 3km north of Boí.

There are 4WD-taxi services between Espot and Estany de Sant Maurici (€5.25 each way) – with services available to some higher lakes and refuges – and between Boí and Aigüestortes (€5.25 each way), saving you, respectively, an 8km and 10km walk. Services run from outside the park information offices in Espot and Boí (9am to 6pm July to September, less frequent outside summer and in bad weather).

From late June to late September, ALSA (www.alsa.es) buses run twice daily (in each direction) between Espot and Taüll (€12.25, 2¾ hours), via Boí and Erill la Vall, enabling hikers to walk across the park and return by bus the same/next day.

# Espot

POP 350 / ELEV 1320M

Scenic little Espot is the main eastern gateway for the Parc Nacional d'Aigüestortes i Estany de Sant Maurici; the park begins 4km west of town. Espot makes an excellent, well-equipped base, with plenty of hotels, restaurants and charming stone buildings, while its mountain views will have you keen to lace up your hiking boots.

## Sleeping & Eating

**Camping Voraparc** CAMPGROUND €
(973 62 41 08; www.voraparc.com; Prat del Vedat; campsite €19, glamping tent €58-90, cabin €70-115; Easter–mid-Oct; ) This shady riverside campground, 1.5km northwest of town, is Espot's best. It has a cafe-bar, games room, play area, minimarket and pleasant swimming pool. If you don't have your own tent, there are some already set up, including three glamping ones.

★**Roca Blanca** HOTEL €€
(973 62 41 56; www.hotelrocablanca.com; Carrer Església; incl breakfast d €80-90, ste €120-125; ) From the 16 gleaming, impressively spacious rooms with modern bathrooms to the polished lounge with fireplace, this hotel is one of the region's most welcoming and inviting. Contemporary art adorns the walls, service is attentive and personal, and breakfast is a feast. Extra touches include a gym, sauna and gorgeous garden.

**Restaurant Juquim** CATALAN €€
(973 62 40 09; Plaça Sant Martí 1; mains €10-19; 1-4pm & 7.30-10.30pm; ) Spread over two levels, this popular place on Espot's main street focuses on filling country fare like grilled wild-boar leg, lamb ribs with fried potatoes and vegetarian-friendly mushroom cannelloni. Eat in the atmospheric stone-walled dining room downstairs or on the front terrace on sunny days.

## Information

**Casa del Parc d'Espot** (973 62 40 36; www.gencat.cat/parcs/aiguestortes; Carrer de Sant Maurici 5; 9am-2pm & 3.30-5.45pm, closed Sun afternoon Sep-Jun) Maps, hiking tips, transport advice, weather forecasts and more from Espot's national park office.

## Getting There & Away

ALSA (www.alsa.es) buses run from Barcelona (€39, five hours, daily) and Lleida (€13, 2½ hours, one to two daily) to Esterri d'Áneu stop at the Espot turn-off on the C13. From there, it's a 7km uphill walk west to Espot along the LV5004.

## Getting Around

Visit the Parc Nacional d'Aigüestortes i Estany de Sant Maurici with a little help from a fleet of **4WDs** (973 62 41 05; www.taxisespot.com; Carrer de Sant Maurici; 1-way Espot-Estany de Sant Maurici adult/child €5.25/3.25; 9am-7pm) offering fixed-rate trips to various drop-off points within the park. Usually you have to wait until there are at least four people, and operating hours depend on weather conditions.

# Boí

POP 220 / ELEV 1220M

The delightful valley location of petite Boí, 3km northwest of Taüll, draws hikers and winter-sports lovers, while its church bell tower is one of the jewels of the Vall de Boí's Catalan Romanesque architecture.

**Sant Joan de Boí** CHURCH
(www.centreromanic.com; Plaça del Treio; €2; 10am-2pm & 4-7pm Sep-Jun, to 8pm Jul & Aug) Boí's 11th-century church gives the village an air of romance with its angular five-storey stone bell tower, which was restored after a major 13th-century fire and can now be climbed (all 75 steps of it). The paintings that brighten the interior are copies of Romanesque originals, preserved in Barcelona's Museu Nacional d'Art de Catalunya.

**Santa Eulàlia d'Erill la Vall** CHURCH
(Erill la Vall; €2; 10am-2pm & 4-7pm Sep-Jun, to 8pm Jul & Aug) The slender six-storey,

## Parc Nacional d'Aigüestortes i Estany de Sant Maurici

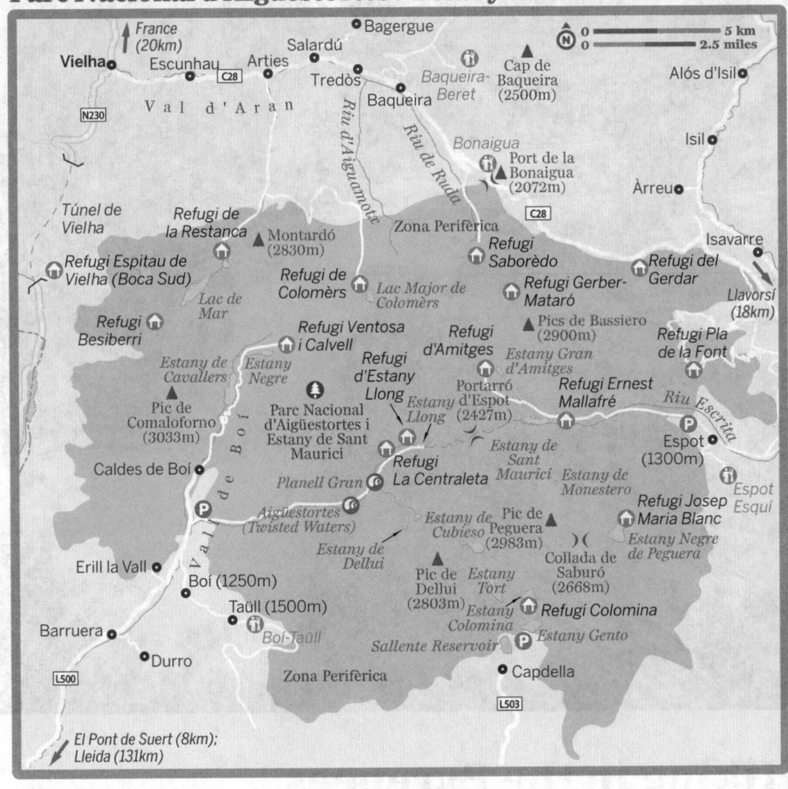


12th-century tower of Santa Eulàlia d'Erill la Vall, a 2.5km walk or drive west of Boí, once used for communications and valley surveillance, is thought to be the most elegant in the area. The church interior is decorated by copies of seven Romanesque poplar-wood sculptures depicting the Descent from the Cross; the originals are split between Barcelona's Museu Nacional d'Art de Catalunya and Vic's Museu Episcopal.

**Hotel-Hostal Pey** HOTEL, HOSTAL €€
(☎973 69 60 36; www.hotelpey.com; Plaça del Treio 3; incl breakfast d €75-95, tr/q €105/120; 📶) This mellow, popular two-part hotel in the heart of teeny Boí features comfy, home-style rooms and a decent restaurant (mains €10 to €16), plus ski storage, staff brimming with local advice and a lovely shop crammed with handmade Pyrenean soaps and Catalan wines. The smartest, most contemporary rooms live in the hotel half. Book ahead.

### ℹ Information

**Casa del Parc de Boí** (☎973 69 61 89; Carrer de les Graieres 2; ⏰9am-2pm & 3.30-5.45pm, closed Sun afternoon Sep-Jun) Pick up trekking and winter-sports information.

### ℹ Getting There & Away

ALSA (www.alsa) buses from Barcelona (€33, four to five hours, four to six daily) and Lleida (€18, two to 2¼ hours, six to 10 daily) to Vielha stop year-round at El Pont de Suert, 19km southwest of Boí. From here, there may be irregular services to Boí.

From late June to September, a twice-daily park bus connects Boí with Espot (€12.25, 2½ hours) via Erill la Vall and Vielha.

### ℹ Getting Around

Nine-person **taxis** (☎973 69 63 14; www.taxisvalldeboi.com; Plaça del Treio 3; one-way Boí-Estany de Sant Maurici adult/child €5.25/3.25; ⏰9am-7pm) spin between Boí and

# Hiking in the Pyrenees

**The Pyrenees aren't Europe's highest mountains, but they are certainly among its most formidable. The craggy behemoths stretch from the Bay of Biscay to the Mediterranean like a giant wall, with barely a low-level pass to break them. Spectacular for many reasons, not least the abundance of powerful waterfalls, they act like a siren's call for hikers.**

## The GR11

Anyone who hikes in the Spanish Pyrenees will get on to first-name terms with Gran Recorrido 11 (GR11), the long-distance footpath that runs the range's entire Spanish flank from Hondarribia on the Bay of Biscay to Cap de Creus on the Costa Brava. Approximately 820km long and with a cumulative elevation gain equivalent to five Mt Everests, it takes around 45 days without rest days. Most people just do a day walk or two – there are some fabulous short hops all along the trail. Well-frequented sections run along Aragón's Valle de Ordesa and past Catalonia's Estany de Sant Maurici.

## Hiking Bases

The Spanish Pyrenees also offer countless superb shorter walks, which can often be strung together into routes of several days with the aid of village accommodation, mountain *refugios* (refuges), or a tent. The two national parks, Ordesa y Monte Perdido (p411) in Aragón and Aigüestortes i Estany de Sant Maurici (p361) in Catalonia, have particularly high concentrations of spectacular trails. Wonderful full-day outings in Ordesa y Monte Perdido include the high-level Faja de Pelay path (to an exuberant waterfall) and the Balcón de

**1.** Parque Nacional de Ordesa y Monte Perdido (p411) **2.** *Refugio*, Parc Nacional d'Aigüestortes i Estany de Sant Maurici (p361) **3.** Hiker, GR11

ZEDSPIDER/SHUTTERSTOCK ©

PABLESKU/SHUTTERSTOCK ©

HENRIQUE FELICIANO PHOTOGRAPHY/GETTY IMAGES ©

Pineta route to a superb lookout. Fit walkers can cross the Aigüestortes park in one day along the Sant Maurici–Boí traverse, a 22km sequence of lakes, waterfalls, verdant valleys, rocky peaks and inspiring vistas. You'll need several days to complete the 55km Carros de Foc (www.carrosdefoc.com) circuit that links all nine of the park's *refugios*.

Other fine hiking bases with good accommodation and easy access to good trail networks include Hecho (p403) and Benasque (p416) in Aragón, and Olot (p351) in Catalonia, which has good, family-friendly walking terrain.

## Practicalities

June to October are generally the best months for hiking. There may be snow on passes and high valleys until mid-June or from October, and the weather is never predictable, so walkers should always be prepared for extreme conditions. However, since this is Europe (rather than Alaska), you're never too far from a mountain village with basic shops, bars and accommodation.

Up in the mountains are a variety of *refugios* (*refugis* in Catalan) – some staffed and serving meals, others providing shelter only. At holiday times staffed *refugios* often fill up, so book ahead. For *refugios* in Aragón, visit www.alberguesyrefugios.com (for booking) and www.fam.es. For *refugis* in Catalonia, see www.feec.cat and www.cec.cat.

Editorial Alpina (www.editorialalpina.com) and Prames (www.prames.com) produce excellent maps for walkers. The definitive English-language guide to the GR11 is the excellent *The GR11 Trail* by Brian Johnson (2018).

Aigüestortes (€5.25), 10km northeast in the Parc Nacional d'Aigüestortes i Estany de Sant Maurici; operating hours vary with the weather.

## Taüll

POP 270 / ELEV 1500M

Three kilometres southeast (uphill) from Boí, Taüll is by far the most picturesque place to stay on the west side of the Parc Nacional d'Aigüestortes i Estany de Sant Maurici. It's also home to two outstanding, Unesco-listed Catalan Romanesque churches.

### Sights

**★Sant Climent de Taüll** CHURCH
(www.centreromanic.com; €5; ⌚10am-2pm & 4-7pm Sep-Jun, to 8pm Jul & Aug) On Taüll's fringes, this 12th-century Romanesque church is a gem not only for its elegant, simple lines and slender six-storey bell tower (which you can climb), but also for the art that once graced its interior. The central apse contains a copy of a famous 1123 mural that now resides in Barcelona's Museu Nacional d'Art de Catalunya; at its centre is a Pantocrator, whose rich Mozarabic-influenced colours and expressive but superhuman features have become an emblem of Catalan Romanesque art. Time your visit for the outstanding audiovisual projection that casts the original art onto the church walls.

**Santa Maria de Taüll** CHURCH
(www.centreromanic.com; ⌚10am-7pm Sep-Jun, to 8pm Jul & Aug) Up in Taüll's old centre, at the northwestern end of town, the 12th-century Romanesque Santa Maria church is crowned by a five-storey tower. As with many churches in the Vall de Boí, its original artwork has been whisked away to Barcelona.

### Sleeping & Eating

**★Alberg Taüll** HOSTEL €
(☎645 750600; elalberguetaull@gmail.com; Avinguda Feixanes 5-7; dm/d/tr incl breakfast €38/49/100; P 📶) This is everything a hostel should be: stylish rooms for two to seven guests feature large beds with orthopaedic mattresses, the suite has a hot tub, there's underfloor heating for crisp mornings, and the lounge includes a large park map for planning hikes.

**Hotel Santa Maria Relax** BOUTIQUE HOTEL €€
(☎973 69 62 50; www.taull.com; Plaça Cap del Riu 3; r incl breakfast €110-130; P 📶 🐾) A grand stone archway leads into the hushed courtyard of this cosy country haven with a rose-draped balcony and friendly hosts. The four rooms and three apartments are tastefully furnished with antiques and a sprinkle of boutique style, while the ancient building is all stonework with a timber-and-slate roof.

### ℹ Getting There & Away

ALSA (www.alsa.es) buses run twice a day in each direction between Taüll and Espot (€12.25, 2½ hours), via Boí and Erill la Vall, from mid-June to September.

Year-round ALSA buses from Barcelona (€31, four to five hours, two to six daily) and Lleida (€11, two to 2¼ hours, six to 10 daily) stop at El Pont de Suert, from where irregular local buses reach Taüll.

# Val d'Aran

Catalonia's northernmost region, famous for its plunging valleys and snowy peaks huddled up against the French border, is an adventure playground for skiers and snowboarders. The Baqueira-Beret-Bonaigua pistes and Arties' luxe hotels lure the winter-sports jet set, while charming villages like Salardú enchant hikers with views of cloud-scraping mountains. Walkers can head over the mountains in any direction, notably southward to the Parc Nacional d'Aigüestortes i Estany de Sant Maurici.

The Val d'Aran was inaccessible until the 1948 completion of a 5km tunnel connecting its main town, Vielha, to the rest of Spain. A surge in tourism development followed, enabling the world to explore this spectacular region of tumbling valleys, stone-and-slate villages and notable Romanesque churches.

The Val d'Aran's native language is not Catalan but Aranese *(Aranés)*, a dialect of Occitan or the *langue d'oc*, the old Romance language of southern France.

## Vielha

POP 5500 / ELEV 974M

A charming sprawl of stone-and-slate houses, outdoor-gear shops and holiday apartments make up hectic Vielha, 'capital' of the Val d'Aran. The tiny town centre, anchored by the distinctive spire of the Gothic Sant Miquèu church, is packed with rustic restaurants, especially along the gushing Riu Garona. While Vielha doesn't have the charisma of the Val d'Aran's smaller towns, its shops, supermarkets, lively dining scene and varied accommodation make it a popular base for

## WALKING: PARC NACIONAL D'AIGÜESTORTES I ESTANY DE SANT MAURICI

The park is criss-crossed by walking paths, ranging from well marked to unmarked; hear expert advice and purchase good topographical maps at the **Casa del Parc** in either Espot (p362) or Boí.

### East–West Traverse

It's perfectly possible to walk right across the park in one day. The full **Espot–Boí** (or vice versa) walk is about 30km and takes about 9½ hours plus stops, but you can shorten this by using 4WD-taxis to/from Estany de Sant Maurici or Aigüestortes (4km southwest of Estany Llong) or both. **Espot** (1300m) to **Estany de Sant Maurici** (1950m) is 8km (two hours). A path then climbs to the **Portarró d'Espot pass** (2427m; around two hours), where there are spectacular views over both of the park's main valleys. From the pass you descend to **Estany Llong** (1985m; about 3½ hours from Estany de Sant Maurici) and **Aigüestortes** (1820m; 4½ hours from Estany de Sant Maurici). Then it's 3.5km to the park entrance, 4km to the L500 and 2.5km south to **Boí** (1250m) – a total of around three hours. It's best to walk the route east to west, and start with a 4WD-taxi (€5.25) from Espot to Estany de Sant Maurici to avoid the initial 8km uphill: this way you walk much more downhill than uphill, ending up 700m lower than you started. Make sure you have suitable clothing for a high-mountain trek.

### Carros de Foc

The Carros de Foc (www.carrosdefoc.com) – a circular 55km trek linking nine of the park's *refugis* – is a great walk, incorporating the best of the national park's glorious mountainscapes, at altitudes between 1885m and 2395m. It allows you to spend five to seven nights in the park, starting from whichever *refugi* you fancy.

### Shorter Walks

Numerous good walks of three to five hours return take you up into majestic side valleys from Estany de Sant Maurici or Aigüestortes.

From the eastern end of Estany de Sant Maurici, a path heads 2.5km south up the Monestero valley to **Estany de Monestero** (2171m; 1½ hours), passing the two peaks of **Els Encantats**. Another trail climbs 3km northwest via **Estany de Ratera** (2190m; 45 minutes) and Estany d'Obagues de Ratera to **Estany Gran d'Amitges** (2350m; 1¾ hours).

Espot's 4WD taxis (p362) run to several points further into the park than Estany de Sant Maurici, enabling walks beginning from Estany Gran d'Amitges, Estany de Ratera and Estany Negre (in the park's Peguera valley).

On the west side, from **Planell Gran** (1850m), 1km northeast up the Sant Nicolau valley from Aigüestortes, a path climbs 2.5km southeast to **Estany de Dellui** (2370m). You can descend to **Estany Llong** (1985m); it's about 5.5km, or four hours, total from Aigüestortes to Estany Llong.

### Mountain-Refuge Accommodation

Serious walkers are catered for by a network of a dozen *refugis* (mountain refuges) in and around the park. Most have large dorms with bunk beds (bring your own sleeping bag or sheet), and tend to be staffed over Easter and from early or mid-June to September, plus some weeks in the first half of the year for skiers. At other times, several leave a section open where you can stay overnight. Check prices, details and opening months and book ahead (crucial in summer) online through **La Central de Refugis** (☎973 64 16 81; www.lacentralderefugis.com). Most charge €20 to €25 per person (including breakfast), and provide lunches, dinners and picnics (sometimes also for passing day-hikers).

hiking, skiing and other adventures around the valley. It's best to have your own wheels: the Vall de Boí's hiking terrain is 20km south, while the Baqueira-Beret-Bonaigua ski pistes lie 15km east.

## Sleeping & Eating

★**Hotel El Ciervo** BOUTIQUE HOTEL €€
(☎973 64 01 65; www.hotelelciervo.net; Plaça de Sant Orenç 3; s/d incl breakfast €50/75;

(⊙mid-Dec–Easter & mid-Jun–mid-Oct; ) Central, family-owned and exceptionally welcoming, El Ciervo is a real departure from the mundane ski-town norm. With a facade covered in paintings of forest creatures and a delightfully cosy interior crammed with florals, pastels, check-prints and other decorative touches, it feels like a Pyrenean fairy tale.

**Parador de Vielha** HOTEL **€€**
(☎973 64 01 00; www.parador.es; Carretera del Túnel; r €95-165; ⊙early Dec–mid-Oct; ) Looming above town, Vielha's sprawling (roadside) *parador* makes a supremely comfortable place to lay your head after a hard day's hiking or skiing. Earthy creams and warm pastels dress the 118 smart rooms, scattered around a family-friendly complex that also features a pool, restaurant, garden and spa. Splash out on a 'superior' room, with balcony and valley or mountain views.

**Woolloomooloo** INTERNATIONAL **€**
(☎654 788327; rennyhut@hotmail.com; Carrèr Major 8; dishes €5-14; ⊙1-4pm & 7pm-1am Tue & Thu-Sat, 7pm-1am Sun & Mon) Quite the Vielha-centre surprise, this purple-walled, Australian-owned address whips up a globe-trotting rustic-modern menu of (mostly) Catalan, Italian and Aussie bites served at tree-trunk tables. From grilled prawns, *patatas bravas* (potatoes in spicy tomato sauce) and spinach-mushroom croquettes to Aussie-style patties and homemade-falafel salad coated in tzatziki, it's all brilliantly tasty. Finish with artisan ice cream or home-baked cakes.

**REFU Birreria** CRAFT BEER
(☎973 64 07 89; www.refubirreria.com; Carrer Major 18; ⊙6pm-midnight Tue-Sun) The ideal destination after a day of hiking or skiing is this congenial drinking den, with 14 taps of artisanal beer and a menu of global street food. Sample some of REFU's own brews (like refreshing Blonde Ale or the chocolatey-rich Imperial Oatmeal Stout) while munching on gourmet lamb or veggie burgers, goat's cheese-stuffed gyozas, tuna ceviche or beer-braised steak tacos.

## ℹ Information

**Oficina d'Informació Turística Val d'Aran**
(☎973 64 01 10; www.visitvaldaran.com; Carrèr de Sarriulèra 10; ⊙10am-1.30pm & 4.30-8pm Mon-Sat) Near Vielha's Sant Miquèu.

## ℹ Getting There & Away

From Vielha's **bus stop** (Carretera N230) on the northwest edge of town, ALSA (www.alsa.es) serves Barcelona (€37, five to six hours, five to seven daily) and Lleida (€15, 2¾ hours, eight to 10 daily), and runs east up the valley to Baqueira (€1.75, 10 to 15 times daily) via Arties (€1.20, 10 minutes) and Salardú (€1.75, 15 minutes).

Most travellers explore the Val d'Aran by car, though parking can be a problem. There's a massive free car park at the southeast end of town, a two-minute walk from the centre.

The N230 from Lleida and El Pont de Suert reaches the Val d'Aran through the 5km Túnel de Vielha. From the Pallars Sobirà region, the C28 tracks northwest across the Port de la Bonaigua pass (2072m) into the upper Aran valley, meeting the N230 at Vielha.

# Arties

POP 410 / ELEV 1143M

The fetching village of Arties sits astride the confluence of the Rius Garona and Valarties, 7km east of Vielha. Its proximity to the upmarket Baqueira-Beret-Bonaigua ski area (6km east) has allowed luxury hotels to flourish. Arties snoozes outside peak summer and winter seasons, but remains a pretty stop year-round, with geraniums overflowing from the balconies of its handsome houses.

DON'T MISS

### CATALAN ROMANESQUE CHURCHES IN THE VALL DE BOÍ

On the west side of the Parc Nacional d'Aigüestortes i Estany de Sant Maurici, the Vall de Boí is dotted with some of Catalonia's finest Romanesque churches – elegant, unadorned stone structures sitting in the crisp alpine air. Together, these 11th- to 14th-century constructions were declared a Unesco World Heritage site in 2000.

Some of the loveliest churches are in Boí (p362), Taüll (p366) and Erill la Vall (p362); other finds are **Sant Feliu** in Barruera and **La Nativitat** in Durro. Explore their history, book guided tours and pick up combined tickets (three churches €7) at Erill la Vall's **Centre del Romànic de la Vall de Boí** (☎973 69 67 15; www.centreromanic.com; Carrer del Batalló 5, Erill la Vall; €2; ⊙9am-2pm & 5-7pm).

**Banys d'Arties** THERMAL BATHS
(C28 Km 28; adult/child €3/free; ⏰10.30am-2.30pm & 4.30-8pm Tue-Sun Jul & Aug, 10am-5pm Tue-Sun Sep-Jun, hours vary) Soothe those all-hiked-out limbs with an open-air soak in these two small thermal pools (one adults-only). From the west end of Arties, follow a path west for 700m; if driving, take the 1.4km dirt track signposted off the C28 at Garòs, 2.5km west of Arties.

## Sleeping & Eating

**Hotel Besiberri** HOTEL €€
(☎973 64 08 29; www.hotelbesiberri.com; Carrer deth Fòrt 4; d incl breakfast from €95; 📶) In a great location in the centre of the village, the friendly, family-run Besiberri has attractive wood-floored rooms with ample natural light and vintage prints on the walls. The best rooms have small geranium-bedecked balconies overlooking the Río Valarties. A lounge with a roaring fire on cold days, and a good cooked breakfast add to the allure.

**Urtau** CATALAN, BASQUE €
(www.facebook.com/urtau; Plaça Urtau 12; tapas €2-11, mains €9-23; ⏰8am-midnight Tue-Sun) Overlooking Arties' main square, this self-styled mountain tavern is forever popular for its grilled meats, hearty breakfasts (bacon omelettes, ham-and-cheese scrambles) and Val d'Aran cheese platters. But the real culinary stars are the 70-odd varieties of *pintxos* that take over the bar from noon.

## Getting There & Away

ALSA (www.alsa.es) buses reach Arties from Vielha (€1.20, 10 minutes, 10 to 15 daily).

### Salardú

POP 590 / ELEV 1267M

Glamorous Arties lies 3km to its west, chic ski area Baqueira looms 3km east, yet pint-sized Salardú retains its own rugged, outdoorsy ambience, welcoming hikers with its decent budget and midrange digs. The even dinkier, flower-filled village of **Bagergue**, 2km northeast, is a tranquil spot for solitary treks and glorious mountain views.

**Església de Sant Andrèu** CHURCH
(Plaça Pica; ⏰10am-2pm & 4-7pm) FREE Within the remarkably colourful frescoed walls of this 12th- and 13th-century church, gaze upon the haunting Romanesque form of the Crist de Salardú. This gaunt wooden sculpture of Jesus on the cross dates to the 13th century, while the Renaissance frescoes lay hidden until the 20th century. Sant Andrèu's sturdy bell tower was a castle keep until 1649, though only the church and some ruined castle walls remain today.

## Sleeping

**Refugi Rosta** HOSTEL €
(☎973 64 53 08; www.refugirosta.com; Plaça Major 3; dm/d incl breakfast €29/76; P📶) Pyrenean mountain *refugis* are special, convivial places, and this creaky old building (going strong since 1858!) is one of the most characterful. There are no luxuries, but there's plenty of good cheer. Dormitories, with typical side-by-side sleeping, are comfortable enough. Bring a sleeping bag or hire sheets and towels.

**Hotel Seixes** HOTEL €€
(☎973 64 54 06; www.hotelseixes.com; Carretera Ta Bagergue 3; s/d/tr/q from €42/70/90/110; ⏰Dec-Mar & Jun-Oct; P📶) This efficiently run hikers' favourite, perched within tinkling distance of the pealing bell of Sant Feliu church in tiny Bagergue (2km northeast of Salardú), has simply furnished rooms, many with gorgeous valley views.

## Getting There & Away

**ALSA** (www.alsa.es) buses reach Salardú from Vielha (€1.75, 15 minutes, 10 to 15 daily).

# CENTRAL CATALONIA

## Vic

POP 45,100

This feisty Catalonian town, 70km north of Barcelona, en route to the Pyrenees, combines dreamy medieval architecture with youthful energy. Remarkably restored Roman ruins, jazzy Modernista houses and an 11th-century Romanesque bridge add to a spirited mix of architectural styles dotted across the old quarter's streets, which branch off smouldering Plaça Major and its ochre and brick-red mansions. Despite its resolutely Catalan political outlook, Vic is multicultural, with a large student population.

## Sights

★**Catedral de Sant Pere** CATHEDRAL
(Plaça de la Catedral; adult/child €2/free; ⏰9am-1pm & 4-7pm) Centuries of styles clash in Vic's exquisite cathedral. Most of the neoclassical exterior dates to the 18th century, but

the seven-storey Romanesque bell tower is one of few remnants from the 11th century. Within, the Stations of the Cross are animated in bold World War II–era frescoes by Josep Maria Sert, while Corinthian columns glow gold in the darkness. Entrance to the cathedral is free; admission (well worth it) applies to the 14th-century Gothic cloisters, 11th-century crypt and Pere Oller's impressive altarpiece.

**★Museu Episcopal** GALLERY
(www.museuepiscopalvic.com; Plaça Bisbe Oliba 3; adult/child €8/5; ⌚10am-7pm Tue-Sat Apr-Sep, 10am-1pm & 3-6pm Tue-Fri, 10am-7pm Sat Oct-Mar, 10am-2pm Sun year-round) This museum holds a marvellous collection of Romanesque and Gothic art, second only to Barcelona's Museu Nacional d'Art de Catalunya. The Romanesque collection contains strikingly gory images, including saints being beheaded or tortured, along with a fine 12th-century woodcarved Descent from the Cross group from the Pyrenees' Vall de Boí. The Gothic collection displays works by such key figures as Lluís Borrassà and Jaume Huguet, plus the beautiful original 1420s doors to Vic cathedral's altarpiece, designed by Pere Oller.

**Plaça Major** SQUARE
Vic's Plaça Major, the largest square in Catalonia, has a pleasing medley of medieval, baroque and Modernista architecture. A crop of cafes spills onto the square. It's also the site of the town's twice-weekly **market** (Tuesday and Saturday mornings), which sells local food and cheap clothing.

**Temple Romà** ROMAN SITE
(Plaça de la Pietat; ⌚11am-1pm & 6-8pm Tue-Sat, 6-8pm Sun) FREE This 1st-century Roman temple, painstakingly restored during the 19th and 20th centuries, is framed by the walls of an 11th-century castle.

## Sleeping & Eating

**Seminari Allotjaments** GUESTHOUSE €€
(☎938 86 15 55; www.seminarivic.cat; Ronda Francesc Camprodón 2; incl breakfast s/d/tr/q €55/76/95/130; P❄📶) Everything functions like clockwork at this pleasingly contemporary guesthouse within a former seminary, 600m north of Vic's Plaça Major. Spotless, minimalist rooms are decorated in bold primary colours and spread across a cavernous complex surrounding a grassy courtyard. It also houses university residences, so there's a student atmosphere, but expect helpful staff, on-site parking (€6), bike rental, 24-hour reception and a restaurant.

## Eating & Drinking

**Boira** CATALAN €€
(☎93 886 70 80; www.boiradevic.com; Carrer Sant Miquel dels Sants 3; menu weekday €15, weekend €27-37; ⌚1-3.30pm Wed, Thu & Sun, 1-3.30pm & 8-11pm Fri & Sat) Original tiling and stonework adorn Boira's elegant multiroom interior, where tables are sprinkled across an atmospheric old-town house. It's the perfect old-meets-new backdrop for a multi-course feast of Catalan ingredients and international flourishes: think grilled scallops with parmesan and mushrooms, lamb chops with mustard and mint, and black pasta with cuttlefish, prawns and romesco sauce.

**Clot dels Romans** BAR
(Plaça Montrodon 2; ⌚5pm-1am Mon-Fri, from noon Sat & Sun) Hidden off on a tiny lane near the Temple Romà, this stylish terrace bar makes a great spot for an afternoon or evening libation. Come for wines and vermouths, an excellent gin selection and delectable regional produce.

## Information

**Oficina de Turisme** (☎938 86 20 91; www.victurisme.cat; Plaça del Pes; ⌚10am-2pm & 4-8pm Mon-Fri, 10am-2pm & 4-7pm Sat, 10.30am-1.30pm Sun) Just off Plaça Major, within the town hall, this office has friendly, multilingual staff who provide audio guides (€2) and maps for exploring Vic, plus exhibits on Catalan culture. There's also a free iPhone and Android app (Vic) for exploring the town.

## Getting There & Away

Regular *rodalies* trains (line R3) run to/from Barcelona (€6.30, 1½ hours); the train station is 500m west of Plaça Major.

# Montserrat

ELEV 720M

Montserrat, 50km northwest of Barcelona, is at the heart of Catalan identity for its mountain, monastery and natural park weaving among distinctive rock formations. Montserrat mountain is instantly recognisable, sculpted over millennia by wind and frost. Its turrets of rock, a coarse conglomerate of limestone and eroded fragments, extend like gnarled fingers from its 1236m-high bulk. More than halfway up the mountain lies the

Benedictine Monestir de Montserrat, home to La Moreneta, one of Spain's most revered icons. Extending from this sacred spot is the **Parc Natural de la Muntanya de Montserrat**, superlative hiking terrain where brooks tumble into ravines and lookout points deliver panoramas of rocky pillars.

Montserrat (used interchangeably for the monastery and mountain) is a hugely popular day trip from Barcelona. The monastery throngs with day visitors, but serenity can still be found on the walking trails.

## Sights

**★Monestir de Montserrat** MONASTERY
(www.abadiamontserrat.net) Catalonia's most renowned monastery was established in 1025 to commemorate local shepherds' visions of the Virgin Mary, accompanied by celestial light and a chorus of holy music. Today, a community of 55 monks lives here. The monastery complex encompasses two blocks: on one side, the basilica and monastery buildings, and on the other, tourist and pilgrim facilities. Admirable monastery architecture lining the main **Plaça de Santa Maria** includes elegant 15th-century cloisters and a gleaming late-19th-century facade depicting St George and St Benedict.

**Cambril de la Mare de Déu** CHURCH
(⏲7-10.30am & noon-6.15pm) Signs to the right of the entrance to Montserrat's main basilica lead into the intimate Cambril de la Mare de Déu, where you can pay homage to the famous **La Moreneta** ('Little Brown One', or 'Black Virgin'), a revered 12th-century Romanesque wood-carved statue of the Virgin Mary with Jesus seated on her knee (and Catalonia's official patroness since 1881).

**Basílica** BASILICA
(www.abadiamontserrat.net; ⏲7am-8pm) With marbled floors and art nouveau–style frescoes visible between graceful archways, the open courtyard fronting Montserrat's basilica immediately sets an impressive tone. The basilica itself, consecrated in 1592, has a brick facade featuring carvings of Christ and the 12 Apostles, dating to the early 20th century. Beyond its heavy doors, the interior glitters with white marble and gold in Renaissance and Catalan Gothic styles.

**Museu de Montserrat** MUSEUM
(www.museudemontserrat.com; Plaça de Santa Maria; adult/child €8/4; ⏲10am-5.45pm, to 6.45pm late-Jun–mid-Sep, plus Sat & Sun Apr-Oct) This museum has excellent displays, ranging from an archaeological section with an Egyptian mummy to Gothic altarpieces to fine canvases by Caravaggio, El Greco, Picasso and several Impressionists (Monet, Degas), plus a collection of 20th-century Catalan art, and fantastic Orthodox icons.

> **WORTH A TRIP**
>
> ### TOP SKIING: BAQUEIRA-BERET-BONAIGUA
>
> Catalonia's premier **ski resort** (www.baqueira.es; day pass adult/child €55/36; ⏲late Nov-early Apr) is formed by Baqueira, 4km east of Salardú; Beret, 8km north of Baqueira; and Bonaigua, at the top of the 2072m pass of the same name (9km southeast of Baqueira). These gleaming slopes lure an upmarket crowd and lodgings tend to be luxe. Whether you're staying at the high-end resorts nearby or bussing in from further afield, there's plenty to enjoy on these peaks, which soar as high as 2510m. Most skiers have their own wheels or stay in winter-sports resorts. ALSA (www.alsa.es) buses reach Baqueira from Vielha (€1.75, 25 minutes, 10 to 15 daily), via Arties (€1.20, 15 minutes) and Salardú (€1.20, five minutes).

## Activities

Beyond the touristic hubbub surrounding Montserrat's monastery and basilica, there's tranquillity to be found in the web of walking trails across the mountain. The tourist office (p372) has basic maps.

Take the 10-minute **Funicular de Sant Joan** (www.cremallerademontserrat.cat; one-way/return €9.10/14; ⏲every 12min 10am-4.50pm Nov-Mar, to 5.50pm Apr-Jun & mid-Sep–Oct, to 6.50pm Jul–mid-Sep, closed 3 weeks Jan) for the first 250m uphill from the monastery; alternatively, it's a 45-minute walk along the road between the funicular's lower and upper stations. From the top, it's a 20-minute stroll (signposted) to the **Ermita de Sant Joan**, with fine westward views.

More exciting is the signposted 7.5km (2½-hour) loop walk from the Funicular de Sant Joan's upper station, northwest to Montserrat's highest peak, **Sant Jeroni** (1236m). The walk takes you across the upper part of the mountain, with a close-up experience of some of the rock pillars. Wear good walking boots, bring water, and, before setting out, check with the tourist office regarding weather and trail conditions.

## ☆ Entertainment

**Escolania de Montserrat** LIVE MUSIC

(www.escolania.cat; ⌚ performances 1pm & 6.45pm Mon-Thu, 1pm Fri, 11am & 6.45pm Sun) The clear voices of one of Europe's oldest boys' choirs have echoed through the basilica since the 14th century. The choir performs briefly on most days (except school holidays), singing *Virolai*, written by Catalonia's national poet Jacint Verdaguer, and *Salve Regina*, as well as at Sunday mass (at 11am). The 50 *escolanets*, aged between nine and 14, go to boarding school in Montserrat and must endure a two-year selection process to join the choir.

## ℹ Information

**Oficina de Turisme** (☎ 938 77 77 01; www.montserratvisita.com; ⌚ 9am-5.45pm Nov-Mar, to 6.45pm Apr-Jun, Sep & Oct, to 8pm Jul & Aug) At the entrance to the monastery complex, with information on walking trails.

## ℹ Getting There & Away

The R5 line trains operated by FGC (www.fgc.net) run half-hourly to hourly to/from Barcelona's Plaça d'Espanya station (one hour). Services start at 5.16am, but take the 8.36am train to connect with the first **AERI cable car** (☎ 938 35 00 05; www.aeridemontserrat.com; one-way/return €7.50/11.50; ⌚ every 15 min 9.40am-7pm Mar-Oct, to 5.15pm Nov-Feb, closed mid-late Jan) to the monastery from the Montserrat Aeri stop.

Alternatively, take the R5 to the next stop (Monistrol de Montserrat), from where **cremallera trains** (☎ 902 31 20 20; www.cremallerademontserrat.com; one-way/return €7.50/12.50; ⌚ every 20-40min 8.48am-6.15pm mid-Sep–Jun, to 8.15pm Easter & Jul–mid-Sep) run up to the monastery (15 minutes) every 20 to 40 minutes. There are various train/*cremallera* combo tickets available.

By car, take the C16 northwest from Barcelona, then the C58 northwest shortly beyond Terrassa, followed by the C55 south to Monistrol de Montserrat. You can leave your vehicle at the free car park and take the *cremallera* up to the top, or drive up and park (cars €7).

# Cardona

POP 4700

Long before arrival, you spy in the distance the outline of an impregnable 11th-century fortress towering above Cardona, 30km northwest of Manresa. Once ruled by the self-styled 'Lords of Salt', who brought Cardona wealth by mining the Muntanya de Sal (Mountain of Salt), today the castle lures tourists to admire its stocky watchtowers and Romanesque church. Aside from this standout attraction, Cardona is a sleepy place, best experienced as an atmospheric day trip or stopover between Barcelona and the Pyrenees – unless you're staying at the sumptuous *parador* that now inhabits the castle.

**★Castell de Cardona** CASTLE

(☎ 938 68 41 69; ⌚ 10am-1pm & 3-7pm Jun-Sep, 10am-1pm & 3-5pm Tue-Sun Oct-May) FREE Visible long before entering Cardona, this hilltop fortress broods above the modern town. From this strategic position, centuries of noblemen have kept a watchful eye over Cardona's Muntanya de Sal (Salt Mountain), the white gold that gave Cardona its wealth. The ramparts have panoramic views of the vast Lleida plain; the loftiest vantage point is the 11th-century **Torre de la Minyona**.

A fortress has stood on this spot since the 3rd century BCE, but the castle reached its zenith under the Lords of Cardona, who arrived in the 11th century and built the palace buildings and the elegant Romanesque **Canònica de Sant Vicenç** (€5; ⌚ tours 10.30am, 11.30am, 12.30pm, 3.30pm & 4.30pm), the only building with an admission charge. It has fine 12th- and 13th-century frescoes adorning its porticoed entrance, and a vaulted crypt, dedicated to St James, that's a stopping point for pilgrims plying the Camino de Santiago. The church played a starring role in Orson Welles' 1965 film *Chimes at Midnight*.

**★Parador de Cardona** HISTORIC HOTEL €€

(☎ 938 69 12 75; www.parador.es; Castell de Cardona; d €110-140; P ❄ 📶) Rooms occupy an adjoining modern building, but that doesn't dim the magic of sleeping like a lord at this *parador* within Cardona's medieval castle. Lodgings are spacious and comfortable, in old-world style, many with exceptional views. Common areas are resplendent with antique furnishings and displays of historical finery. The highlight is breakfast under Gothic arches in a monks' refectory.

**★La Volta del Rector** CATALAN €€

(☎ 938 69 16 37; www.lavoltadelrector.cat; Carrer de les Flors 4; mains €12-18; ⌚ 8am-5pm Tue-Thu & Sun, to midnight Fri & Sat; 🌶) The 12th-century stone walls mix with wild violet decor at La Volta del Rector, in the heart of medieval Cardona. The atmosphere is rustic, romantic and fashionable all at once, while dishes – from grills and wild game to the house special: mountain potatoes with free-range fried eggs and/or chorizo – are whipped up with flair.

## Information

**Oficina de Turisme** (☎938 69 27 98; www.cardonaturisme.cat; Avinguda del Rastrillo; ⏲10am-2pm daily, plus 4-7pm Fri & Sat) At the top of the old town, next to the path leading up to the castle.

## Getting There & Away

ALSA (www.alsa.es) buses reach Cardona from Barcelona (€13, 1¾ hours, two to four daily) and La Seu d'Urgell (€14, two hours, two daily). The bus stop is just north of the tourist office on Avinguda del Rastrillo.

# Lleida

POP 138,000

Lleida's battle-torn history has faded into memory, replaced by today's pacey, workaday city. During the 14th and 15th centuries, arid, inland Lleida was a centre of economic activity, fed in part by Jewish and Muslim communities. Culture and art flourished, thanks to surrounding monasteries, and a university was founded in 1300. Relics of the holy cloth and thorns made Lleida's cathedral a revered stopping point on the Camino de Santiago (the Camí de Sant Jaume in Catalonia) pilgrimage route towards Santiago de Compostela.

Battle lines were drawn here across Catalonia's history, with Lleida nearly always backing the losing side. The old town was destroyed during the War of the Spanish Succession, only for the conquerors' replacement settlement to be sacked by the French in 1812. The fortress-cathedral crowning the city evokes Lleida's former grandeur, while a smattering of museums and Modernista buildings offer other reasons to visit.

## Sights

The fortress-church at the top of the hill is Lleida's major attraction, but admirers of architecture will also want to seek out historical buildings in the old town. The elegant 15th-century **Antic Hospital de Santa Maria** and the 20th-century **Casa Magí Llorenç**, with its colourful Modernista ceiling frescoes, are worth a peep; grab a trail map of Lleida's prettiest buildings at the tourist office (p374).

**★La Seu Vella** CATHEDRAL

(www.turoseuvella.cat; adult/child incl Castell del Rei €6/5; ⏲10am-7.30pm Tue-Sat May-Sep, 10am-1.30pm & 3-5.30pm Tue-Fri, 10am-5.30pm Sat Oct-Apr, 10am-3pm Sun year-round) Lleida's 'old cathedral', enclosed within a later fortress complex, towers above the city from its commanding hilltop location. Work began on the cathedral in 1203, though today it is a masterpiece of bold Romanesque forms complemented by Gothic vaults and elaborate tracery. The octagonal 60m-high **bell tower**, crowned with Gothic flourishes, rises in the southwest corner of the beautiful 14th-century Gothic **cloister**, a forest of slender columns with expansive Lleida views. Climb the tower's 238 steps for the finest panoramas.

**Museu de Lleida** MUSEUM

(☎973 28 30 75; www.museudelleida.cat; Carrer del Sant Crist 1; adult/child €5/free; ⏲10am-2pm & 4-6pm Tue-Sat Oct-May, 10am-2pm & 5-7pm Tue-Sat Jun-Sep, 10am-2pm Sun year-round) This brilliant, expansive museum brings together artefacts reaching back to the Stone Age, through Roman remains, Visigothic relics and medieval art into the 19th century.

## Sleeping & Eating

**Parador de Lleida** HISTORIC HOTEL €€

(☎973 00 48 66; www.parador.es; Carrer del Cavallers 15; r €80-110; P ❄ 📶) Opened in 2017, Lleida's *parador* is an inspiring addition to the accommodation scene. Smartly contemporary rooms with oversized windows and warm wood details, rise up around the elegant, curtain-draped cloister of the converted 17th-century Convent del Roser.

**Bar Bodega Blasi** TAPAS €

(☎973 22 88 17; Carrer Sant Martí 2; tapas €4-12; ⏲10am-11.30pm Mon-Sat, noon-5pm Sun; 📶) With tables on a small plaza, the lively, long-running Bar Bodega Blasi is one of the best places to be on a warm evening. Join locals over vermouth and an extensive tapas selection including codfish tortilla, regional cheese platters, squid croquettes or fried artichokes in season.

**Macao** FUSION €€
(☎973 04 63 08; www.facebook.com/macaolleida; Carrer del Camp de Mart 27; mains €10-17; ⏲1-4pm & 8.30-11.30pm Tue-Sun; 📶) A triumphant marriage of Japanese, Catalan and Mediterranean flavours transforms into beautifully presented contemporary plates at this stylish, popular restaurant with an updated maritime feel, a 10-minute walk (750m) northwest of the old town's Carrer Major.

### Information

**Turisme de Lleida** (☎973 70 03 19; www.turismedelleida.cat; Carrer Major 31; ⏲10am-2pm & 4-7pm Mon-Sat, 10am-1.30pm Sun) On the main pedestrian street, providing maps and local tips.

### Getting There & Away

From Lleida's central **bus station** (Carrer de Saracibar, off Avinguda de Blondel), just southwest of the old town, ALSA (www.alsa.es) buses serve Zaragoza (€12, 1¾ to 2½ hours, two to three daily), Barcelona Nord (€23, 2½ hours, 10 to 14 daily), El Prat airport (€23, 2¾ to 3¼ hours, two to four daily), Vielha (€15, 2¾ hours, eight to 10 daily) and La Seu d'Urgell (€20, 2¼ hours, three to seven daily).

Regular trains reach Lleida from Barcelona (€20 to €43, 1¼ hours), some proceeding to Madrid (€47 to €75, 2¼ hours, 10 daily) via Zaragoza (€17 to €28, 41 minutes to 1¼ hours).

## COSTA DAURADA & AROUND

## Sitges

POP 29,100

Just 35km southwest of Barcelona, Sitges sizzles with beach life, late-night clubs and an enviable festival calendar. Sitges has been a resort town since the 19th century, and was a key location for the Modernisme movement, which paved the way for the likes of Picasso. These days it's Spain's most famous gay holiday destination. In July and August, Sitges cranks up the volume to become one big beach party, while Carnaval unbridles the town's hedonistic side. But despite the bacchanalian nightlife, Sitges remains a classy destination: its array of galleries and museums belie its small size, there's a good choice of upmarket restaurants in its historic centre (which is lined with chic boutiques), and though it's quieter during the off season, you can still get a feel for it.

### Sights

The most beautiful part of Sitges is the headland area, where noble Modernista palaces and mansions strike poses around the pretty **Església de Sant Bartomeu i Santa Tecla**, with the sparkling-blue Mediterranean as a backdrop.

★ **Museu del Cau Ferrat** MUSEUM
(www.museusdesitges.cat; Carrer de Fonollar; incl Museu de Maricel adult/child €10/free; ⏲10am-8pm Tue-Sun Jul-Sep, to 7pm Mar-Jun & Oct, to 5pm Nov-Feb) Built in the 1890s as a house-studio by Catalan artist Santiago Rusiñol, a pioneer of the Modernisme movement, this seaside mansion is crammed with his own art and that of his contemporaries (including his friend Picasso), as well as his extensive private collection of ancient relics and antiques. The visual feast is piled high, from Grecian urns and a 15th-century baptismal font to 18th-century tilework that glitters all the way to the floral-painted wood-beamed ceiling.

#### Beaches

Dotted with *xiringuitos*, Sitges' main beach is divided into nine sections (with different names) by a series of breakwaters and flanked by the attractive seafront Passeig Marítim. The most central beaches are lively **La Fragata**, just below Sant Bartomeu church, and **La Ribera**, immediately west. About 500m southwest of the centre, **L'Estanyol** has summer *xiringuitos* with sunbeds; 1.5km further southwest, **Les Anquines** and **Terramar** have paddleboat rental and deckchairs in summer. Northeast of the centre lie easy-access **Sant Sebastià**, sheltered **Balmins** (favoured by nudists; 1km northeast of town) and brown-sand **Aiguadolç** (500m further east). **Bassa Rodona**, immediately west of the centre, is Sitges' famous unofficial 'gay beach', though gay sunbathers are now spread out pretty evenly.

### Festivals & Events

The October **film festival** (Festival Internacional de Cinema Fantàstic de Catalunya; www.sitgesfilmfestival.com; ⏲Oct) draws culture fiends from miles around.

## Sitges

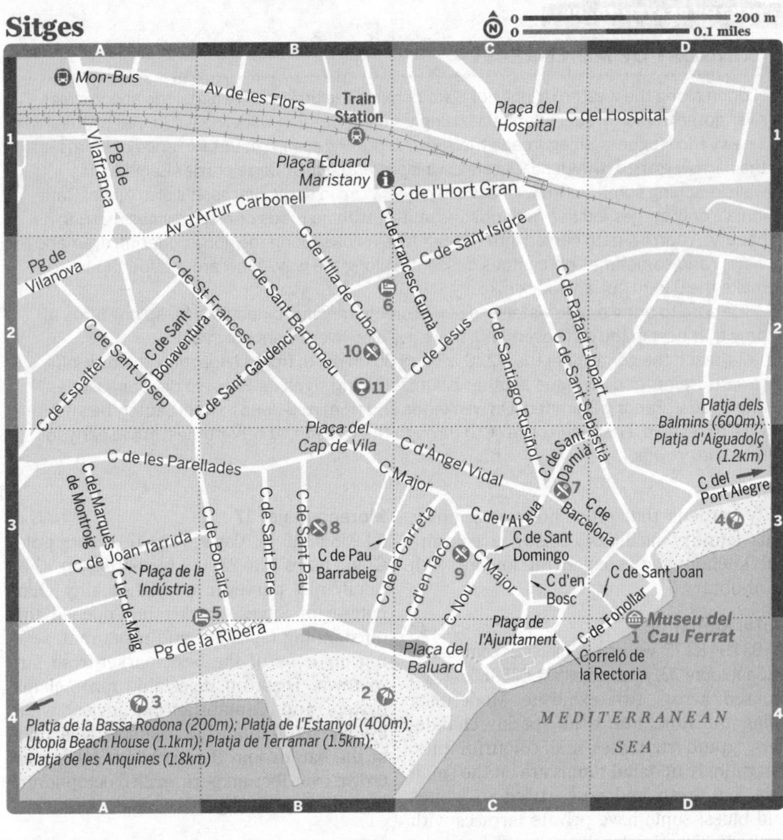


### Sitges

**Top Sights**
1 Museu del Cau Ferrat ........ D4

**Sights**
2 Platja de la Fragata ........ B4
3 Platja de la Ribera ........ A4
4 Platja de Sant Sebastià ........ D3

**Sleeping**
5 Hotel Platjador ........ B3
6 Hotel Romàntic ........ B2

**Eating**
7 El Cable ........ C3
8 Lady Green ........ B3
9 Moreno Major 17 ........ C3
10 Nem ........ B2

**Drinking & Nightlife**
11 La Sitgetana ........ B2

**Carnaval** CARNIVAL

(www.visitsitges.com; Feb/Mar) Carnaval in Sitges is a sparkly week-long booze-soaked riot, complete with masked balls and capped by extravagant gay parades held on the Sunday and Tuesday, featuring flamboyantly dressed drag queens, giant sound systems and a wild all-night party with bars open until dawn. Dates change yearly; check online.

## Sleeping

**Utopia Beach House** HOSTEL €

(938 11 11 36; www.utopiasitges.com; Carrer Socias 22; dm €22-40, d €60-110; ) A short walk from the beach, 1.5km west of central Sitges, this bubbly hostel has pastel-painted four-, six- or 10-person dorms (lockers and towels provided), and double rooms with private bathrooms and, for some, big balconies. There's a cheerful cafe-bar amid

OFF THE BEATEN TRACK

## CONGOST DE MONT-REBEI

Hidden along the western fringes of Catalonia, on the border of Aragón, the spectacular river gorge of Mont-rebei offers a dazzling vision of Catalan wilderness. Carved by the sinewy Rio Noguera Ribagorçana through the pre-Pyrenean mountain range of Montsec, the narrow **gorge** (www.fundaciocatalunya-lapedrera.com; off Carretera de Alsamora) has walls reaching some 500m with a width of just 20m in some places. It's also one of Catalonia's only gorges left in a near pristine state – with no roads or electric lines marring its beauty. A narrow path carved into the cliff face follows along the gorge, offering dramatic views (and sometimes precipitous descents) along the way. Allow around four hours to make the 9.2km out-and back hike.

Be sure to bring ample water and sun protection – plus binoculars for spying birds of prey that nest in the cliffs overhead; there are also river otters down below.

To reach the gorge, take the N230 around 85km north from Lleida, take the turn-off toward Tremp, and continue another 10km, following signs for Reserva del Congost de Mont-rebei. Parking is limited. On weekends and from mid-June to mid-September, it's wise to reserve a parking space (€5) through the website. At other times, arrive early to beat the crowds.

leafy gardens that often hosts live music, plus laundry facilities (€3.50), a communal kitchen and a colourful lounge with mini-library.

**Hotel Romàntic** HERITAGE HOTEL **€€**
(☎93 894 83 75; www.mediumhoteles.com; Carrer de Sant Isidre 33; r incl breakfast €85-160; ❄📶) Housed across two exquisite Modernista villas, the Romàntic is all sparkly chandeliers, grand staircases and colourful tiles. Charmingly updated rooms are on the small side, but fresh and cosy, styled in whites and blues; some have private terraces with sunbeds. There's a lovely garden cafe.

**Hotel Platjador** HOTEL **€€€**
(☎938 94 50 54; www.hotelsitges.com; Passeig de la Ribera 35; r €125-200; ❄📶🏊) This welcoming seafront hotel has fabulous colourful, modern rooms (many with balconies) featuring enormous plush beds and pillow menus. Enjoy the cool blue pool and rooftop bar overlooking the sea. It's superb value offseason, when rates drop by up to 50%.

## Eating

**★El Cable** TAPAS **€**
(☎938 94 87 61; www.facebook.com/elcablebarsitges; Carrer de Barcelona 1; tapas €2-8; ⏲7-11pm Mon-Fri, 12-3.30pm & 7-11pm Sat & Sun) Always packed, down-to-earth El Cable might just be Sitges' most loved tapas bar, rolling out classics like *patatas bravas* (often branded the best in town) alongside divine, inventive bite-sized creations.

**Moreno Major 17** TAPAS **€€**
(☎938 53 16 16; Carrer Major 17; sharing plates €7-16, mains €14-22; ⏲noon-midnight) The family-run purveyor of high-quality charcuterie in Sitges' market has opened this outstanding tapas bar and restaurant, serving up some of the best market-fresh fare in town. Feast on delectable razor clams, oysters and Cantabrian anchovies, while eyeing the tantalising seafood selections at the bar, or join the garrulous restaurant crowd over Iberian pork, grilled octopus and ingredient-packed goat's cheese salads.

**Nem** FUSION **€€**
(☎938 94 93 32; www.nemsitges.com; Carrer de l'Illa de Cuba 9; tapas €5-7; ⏲7.30-11pm Tue-Fri, 1.30-3.30pm & 7.30-11pm Sat; 📶) At this packed-out fusion tapas spot, Spanish and Asian flavours collide in short, often-changing menus of deliciously creative concoctions that might include sea-bream sashimi, roasted celery with gorgonzola and walnuts, and Thai curry roast beef. Dine in a semi-open space at cosy corner tables or at the bar.

**Lady Green** VEGETARIAN **€€**
(☎938 10 72 45; www.facebook.com/ladygreensitges; Carrer de Sant Pau 11; mains €13-20; ⏲7-10.30pm Mon, 1-3.30pm & 7-10.30pm Tue-Sun; 📶🌱) Indian-style pakoras with coconut curry, vegan cheeseburgers, shitake tempura with aioli, and delectable American-style vegan cheesecake: vegetarian Lady Green will satisfy even the most demanding taste buds with its imaginative meat-free and vegan dishes, bold flavours and tempting desserts.

## Drinking & Nightlife

Sitges' nightlife centres on one packed pedestrian strip just off the seafront: Carrer 1er de Maig (Calle del Pecado; Sin St), Plaça de la Indústria and Carrer del Marquès de Montroig.

**La Sitgetana** CRAFT BEER
(www.facebook.com/lasitgetanacraftbeer; Carrer de Sant Bartomeu 10; ⌚6.30-11.30pm Mon-Fri, noon-3pm & 6.30-11.30pm Sat & Sun; 📶) Spy the on-site brewery out the back at this ambitious, modern-minimalist craft-beer pub, with six taps devoted to artisan brews (pints around €5). Try a refreshing Weiss Subur (a Hefeweizen), the well-balanced Maricel (an American Pale Ale), or sip on Penedès wines by the glass.

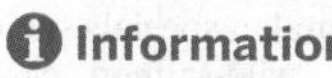

## Information

**Oficina de Turisme Sitges** (☎938 94 42 51; www.sitgestur.cat; Plaça Eduard Maristany 2; ⌚10am-2pm & 4-8pm Mon-Sat mid-Jun–mid-Oct, 10am-2pm & 4-6.30pm Mon-Sat mid-Oct–mid-Jun, 10am-2pm Sun year-round) By the train station.

## Getting There & Away

Mon-Bus (www.monbus.cat) runs to Barcelona (€4.10, 50 minutes, every 15 to 50 minutes) and Barcelona airport (€7.10, 30 minutes, half-hourly to hourly) from Passeig de Vilafranca, stopping along Passeig de Vilanova.

From 5am to 10pm, regular R2 *rodalies* trains run to Barcelona Passeig de Gràcia and Sants (€4.20, 40 minutes). For Barcelona airport (€4.20, 45 minutes), change at El Prat de Llobregat.

# Penedès Wine Country

Some of Spain's finest wines come from the Penedès plains west and southwest of Barcelona. Sant Sadurní d'Anoia, 35km west of Barcelona, is the capital of *cava*, a sparkling, Champagne-style wine popular worldwide and across Spain. The attractive historical town of Vilafranca del Penedès, 12km further southwest, is the heart of the Penedès Denominació d'Origen (DO; Denomination of Origin) region (www.dopenedes.cat), which produces noteworthy light whites and some very tasty reds.

## Sant Sadurní d'Anoia

POP 12,900

One hundred or so wineries around Sant Sadurní make it Spain's centre of *cava*, a sparkling wine made by the same method as French Champagne. Beyond the popping corks in Sant Sadurní's surrounds, the town is a sleepy place, though it has a pleasingly rich calendar of food and wine festivals.

DON'T MISS

### THE CISTERCIAN ROUTE

The **Cistercian Route** (Ruta del Cister; www.larutadelcister.info) weaves among the mountainous territory between Tarragona and Lleida, linking a trio of spectacular monasteries that feature some of Catalonia's most ancient and beautiful religious architecture: **Santa Maria de Poblet** (☎977 87 00 89; www.poblet.cat; Plaça Corona d'Aragó 11, Poblet; adult/student €12/8; ⌚10am-12.30pm & 3-5.25pm Mon-Sat, 10.30am-12.25pm & 3-5.25pm Sun), **Santes Creus** (☎977 63 83 29; www.larutadelcister.info; Plaça de Jaume el Just, Santes Creus; adult/senior & student €6/4; ⌚10am-7pm Jun-Sep, to 5.30pm Oct-May) and **Santa Maria de Vallbona** (☎973 33 02 66; www.monestirvallbona.cat; Carrer Major, Vallbona de les Monges; €5; ⌚visit by guided tour in Spanish 10.45am-5pm). Driving the route is a great way to explore the hilly scenery of inland Catalonia's Conca de Barberà wine-making region, while the long-distance GR175 walking trail links the three monasteries in a 104km loop.

Tackling all three monasteries is possible as a single-day drive from Lleida or, more conveniently, Tarragona, but it requires careful timing: two of the three monasteries only allow access by irregular guided tours. Start early, aiming to reach the first monastery by its 10am opening time. A combined ticket (€15; valid for a year) gives access to all three monasteries.

If returning to urban bustle feels like hard work, **Fèlix Hotel** (☎977 60 90 90; www.felixhotel.net; Carretera N240, Km 17, Valls; r €60-90; P ❄ 🏊) is a convenient, well-equipped roadside guesthouse just south of Valls, 17km north of Tarragona.

**Espai Xocolata Simón Coll** SHOWROOM
(☎938 91 10 95; www.simoncoll.com; Carrer de Sant Pere 37; adult/child €5.50/4; ⏰9am-7pm Mon-Fri, to 3pm Sat & Sun; 👪) Chocolate lovers shouldn't miss a visit to this family-run, bean-to-bar *fabricant de xocolata* (chocolate maker), which has been going strong since 1840 in Sant Sadurní. A tour (available in English, Spanish and Catalan) touches on the history and culture of chocolate making – with memorable tastings along the way. Afterwards, you can browse the beautifully packaged, high-quality chocolates in the store.

## ℹ Information

**Oficina de Turisme de Sant Sadurní d'Anoia** (☎938 91 31 88; www.turismesantsadurni.cat; Carrer de l'Hospital 23; ⏰9.15am-2.45pm & 4-6.30pm Tue-Fri, 10am-2pm & 4.30-7pm Sat, 10am-2pm Sun) Books winery tours, provides maps and houses Sant Sadurní's interactive *cava* interpretation centre.

## ℹ Getting There & Away

*Rodalies* trains run from Barcelona Sants to Sant Sadurní (€4.20, 42 minutes, half-hourly).

# Vilafranca del Penedès

POP 40,100

To experience Penedès wine country without attaching yourself to a long guided tour or having to drive (a burden for anyone sipping greedily), base yourself in Vilafranca. Livelier than nearby Sant Sadurní, the town sprawls, but its centre is dotted with uplifting medieval and Modernista architecture and enjoys a selection of truly excellent restaurants with equally impressive wine lists. Vineyard excursions are easy to organise from here.

Pick up pamphlets at the tourist office for a self-guided tour of Vilafranca's medieval and Modernista architecture.

**Vinseum** MUSEUM
(Museu de les Cultures del Vi de Catalunya; www.vinseum.cat; Plaça de Jaume I; adult/child €7/free; ⏰10am-7pm Tue-Sat May-Sep, 10am-2pm & 4-7pm Tue-Sat Oct-Apr, 10am-2pm Sun year round) School yourself on the history and cultural significance of wine in Penedès at this 17,000-item museum, housed in the medieval Palau Reial.

**Cal Figarot** CATALAN €€
(☎936 53 63 39; www.calblay.com; Carrer del General Prim 11; mains €10-15, lunch menu €13; ⏰noon-midnight Wed-Mon) Inside an impressive Modernista building, this casual eatery serves up satisfying Catalan cooking at excellent prices. Standouts include scrambled eggs with truffle and foie gras, various casseroles (like meatballs and cuttlefish), classic tapas, and cheese and meat boards.

The setting is a big draw as this is the headquarters of the Castellers de Vilafranca, and you can watch the group building human towers from the back terrace on Monday and Wednesday (8pm to 10pm) as well as Friday (9.30pm to midnight).

**El Convent** CATALAN €€
(☎931 69 43 84; www.facebook.com/elconvent1850; Carrer de la Fruita 12; mains €10-21; ⏰7pm-midnight Tue-Fri, 9am-4pm & 8pm-midnight Sat) This warren-like, modern-rustic tavern delivers well-executed Catalan specials such as Pyrenean entrecôte, wild-salmon carpaccio, goat's-cheese salad and fondues for two, along with oysters, steamed clams and tempting platters of cheese and charcuterie. It's friendly, low-key and very popular.

★**Cal Ton** CATALAN €€€
(☎938 90 37 41; www.restaurantcalton.com; Carrer Casal 8; mains €18-29, tasting menus €32-55; ⏰1-3.30pm Tue & Sun, 1-3.30pm & 8.30-10.30pm Wed-Sat; 📶) An evening of gastronomic wonder awaits at Cal Ton, going strong since 1982. From feather-light potato-and-prawn ravioli to oxtail in red wine with pears, meals at this crisp modern restaurant exhaust superlatives.

## ℹ Information

**Oficina de Turisme de Vilafranca del Penedès** (☎938 18 12 54; www.turismevilafranca.com; Carrer Hermenegild Clascar 2; ⏰3-6pm Mon, 9.30am-1.30pm & 3-6pm Tue-Sat, 10am-1pm Sun)

## ℹ Getting There & Away

*Rodalies* trains run frequently from Barcelona Sants to Vilafranca (€5, 52 minutes).

# Tarragona

POP 133,000

In this effervescent port city, Roman history collides with beaches, bars and a food scene that perfumes the air with freshly grilled seafood. The biggest lure is the wealth of ruins in Spain's second-most important Roman site, including a mosaic-packed museum and a seaside amphitheatre. A roll call of

## Tarragona

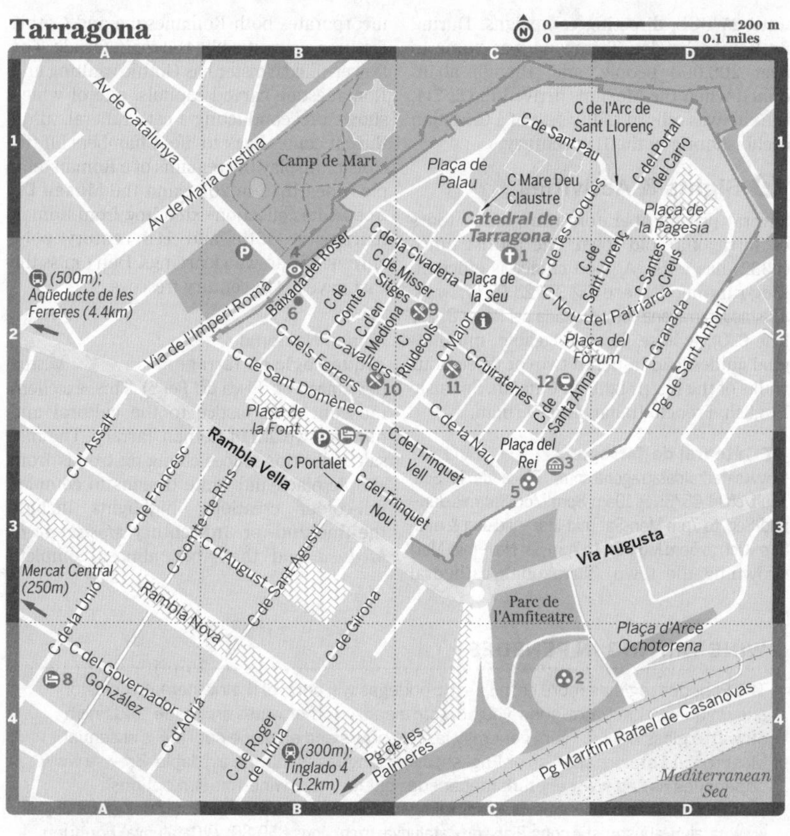


### Tarragona

**Top Sights**
1 Catedral de Tarragona ........ C2

**Sights**
2 Amfiteatre Romà ........ C4
3 Museu Nacional Arqueològic de Tarragona ........ C3
4 Passeig Arqueològic Muralles ........ B2
5 Pretori i Circ Romà ........ C3

**Activities, Courses & Tours**
6 Itinere ........ B2

**Sleeping**
7 Hotel Plaça de la Font ........ B3
8 Tarragona Hostel ........ A4

**Eating**
9 Arcs Restaurant ........ C2
10 Degvsta ........ B2
11 El Vergel ........ C2

**Drinking & Nightlife**
12 El Tamboret ........ C2

fantastic places to eat gives you good reason to linger in the knot of lanes in the attractive medieval centre, flanked by a towering cathedral with Romanesque and Gothic flourishes.

Tarragona is also a gateway to the Costa Daurada's sparkling beaches and the feast of Modernisme architecture in nearby Reus (p383).

## History

Tarragona was occupied by the Romans, who called it Tarraco, in 218 BCE; prior to that, the area was first settled by Iberians, followed by Carthaginians. In 27 BCE, Augustus made Tarraco the capital of his new Tarraconensis province (roughly three-quarters of modern Spain) and stayed until 25 BCE, directing campaigns. During its Roman heyday, Tarragona was home to over 200,000 people, and, though abandoned when the Muslims arrived in CE 714, the city was reborn as the seat of a Christian archbishopric in the 11th century.

## Sights & Activities

Several private operators run guided tours of Tarragona's old town; the tourist office (p382) has a list. A good choice is efficient, long-running **Itinere** (977 23 96 57; www.turismedetarragona.com; Baixada del Roser 8; 2hr tour €90), whose knowledgeable multilingual guides lead in-depth two- or three-hour walks of the main sights in Catalan, Spanish, English, French, Italian and German.

**★Catedral de Tarragona** CATHEDRAL
(www.catedraldetarragona.com; Plaça de la Seu; adult/child €5/3; 10am-8pm Mon-Sat mid-Jun–mid-Sep, to 7pm Mon-Sat mid-Mar–mid-Jun & mid-Sep–Oct, to 5pm Mon-Fri, to 7pm Sat Nov–mid-Mar) Crowning the town, Tarragona's cathedral incorporates both Romanesque and Gothic features, as typified by the main facade. The flower-filled cloister has Gothic vaulting and Romanesque carved capitals, one of which shows rats conducting a cat's funeral...until the cat comes back to life! Chambers off the cloister display the remains of a Roman temple (unearthed in 2015) and the **Museu Diocesà**, its collection extending from Roman hairpins to 13th- and 14th-century polychrome Virgin woodcarvings. Don't miss the east nave's 14th-century frescoes.

**Museu Nacional Arqueològic de Tarragona** MUSEUM
(www.mnat.cat; Plaça del Rei 5) This excellent museum does justice to the cultural and material wealth of Roman Tarraco. The mosaic collection traces changing trends from simple black-and-white designs to complex full-colour creations; highlights include the fine 2nd- or 3rd-century *Mosaic de la Medusa* and the large, almost complete

### WINE TASTING IN PENEDÈS

The Penedès region's more enthusiastic bodegas will unravel their winemaking history and unique architecture, show you how *cava* and/or other wines are made, and finish off with a glass or two. Tours generally last 1½ hours and advance booking is essential. Most run in Catalan, Spanish or English; other languages may be available. Browse www.dopenedes.es and www.enoturismepenedes.cat for more wine-tourism options.

If you're intent on serious wine sampling, **Catalunya Bus Turístic** (932 80 58 05; www.catalunyabusturistic.com; Plaça de Catalunya; excursions €50-80; M Catalunya) conducts day tours from Barcelona, with tastings at three different wineries in the Penedès (€75).

**Codorníu** (938 91 33 42; www.visitascodorniu.com; Avinguda de Jaume Codorníu, Sant Sadurní d'Anoia; adult/child €16/12; tours 10am-5pm Mon-Fri, to 1pm Sat & Sun) There is no more glorious spot to sip *cava* than the vaulted interior of Codorníu's palatial Modernista headquarters, designed by Catalan architect Josep Puig i Cadafalch, just beyond the northeast edge of Sant Sadurní d'Anoia. Codorníu's wine-making activities are documented back to the 16th century.

**Freixenet** (938 91 70 96; www.freixenet.es; Carrer de Joan Sala 2, Sant Sadurní d'Anoia; adult/child €15/10; tours 9am-4pm Mon-Sat, to 1pm Sun) The biggest *cava*-producing company, easily accessible right next to Sant Sadurní's train station. Book ahead for 1½-hour multilingual tours of its 1920s cellar, including a spin around the property on the tourist train and samples of Freixenet *cava*.

**Torres** (938 17 74 00; www.torres.es; Pacs del Penedès; tours from €15; 9am-6pm Mon-Sat, to noon Sun) Just 3km northwest of Vilafranca on the BP2121, this is the area's premier winemaker, with a family winemaking tradition dating from the 17th century and a strong emphasis on organic production and renewable energy.

**Jean León** (938 17 76 90; www.jeanleon.com; Châtêau Leon, Torrelavit; tours adult/child from €12/free; 9am-6pm Mon-Fri, to 3pm Sat & Sun) Since 1963, this winery has been using cabernet sauvignon and other French varietals to create high-quality wines. Ninety-minute visits (in Catalan, Spanish or English) to the wonderfully scenic vineyard, 12km north of Vilafranca, include a tasting of three wines and must be booked in advance.

3rd-century *Mosaic dels Peixos de la Pineda*, showing fish and sea creatures.

The museum is closed for renovations, and is slated to reopen in 2022. Until then, some of the most important pieces from the collection are on display in **Tinglado 4** (☎977 23 62 09; Moll de Costa, Port de Tarragona; adult/child incl audio guide €4/free; ⊙9.30am-8pm Tue-Sat Jun-Sep, to 6pm Tue-Sat Oct-May, 10am-2pm Sun year-round) in Tarragona's port; bus 22 takes you there from a stop near the Portal del Roser.

**Amfiteatre Romà** RUINS
(Parc de l'Amfiteatre; adult/child €3.30/free; ⊙9am-9pm Tue-Sat Easter-Sep, to 7pm Tue-Sat Oct-Easter, to 3pm Sun year round) Near the beach is Tarragona's well-preserved amphitheatre, dating from the 2nd century CE, where gladiators hacked away at each other or wild animals. In its arena are the remains of a 6th-century Visigothic church and a 12th-century Romanesque church, both built to commemorate Saint Fructuosus and two deacons, believed to have been burnt alive here in 259 CE. At the time of research, parts of the amphitheatre were undergoing restoration, though the upper viewing gallery was open (and admission free).

Much of the amphitheatre was picked to bits, the stone used to build the port and the two churches, so what you see now is a partial reconstruction.

**Aqüeducte de les Ferreres** BRIDGE
(Pont del Diable; ⊙24hr; P) FREE This magnificent aqueduct sits in a tangle of dusty pathways and glades 4km north of central Tarragona, just off the AP7 (near where it intersects with the N240). It is a fine stretch of two-tiered aqueduct (217m long and 27m high), which you can totter across. Buses 5 and 85 (€1.50, every 30 minutes) to Sant Salvador from Plaça Imperial de Tarraco stop nearby; you can walk 4.6km back to the city along the river (about 90 minutes).

If driving, park in one of the lay-bys signposted on the north side of the AP7 (just outside the freeway toll gates) or the east side of the N240.

**Pretori i Circ Romà** RUINS
(Plaça del Rei; adult/child €3.30/free; ⊙9am-9pm Tue-Sat, to 3pm Sun Apr-Sep, to 7pm Tue-Fri, 9.30am-6.30pm Sat, to 2.30pm Sun Oct-Mar) This sizeable complex with two separate entrances includes part of the vaults of Tarragona's well-preserved, late-1st-century **Roman circus**, where chariot races were once held, as well as the Plaça del Rei's **Pretori tower** (climb it for 360-degree city views) and part of the **provincial forum**, the political heart of Roman Tarraconensis province. The circus, over 300m long and accommodating 30,000 spectators, stretched from here to beyond Plaça de la Font to the west.

### MUSEU D'HISTÒRIA DE TARRAGONA

The **Museu d'Història de Tarragona** (MHT; www.tarragona.cat/patrimoni/museu-historia; adult per site/4 sites/all sites €3.30/7.40/11.05, child free) consists of various Unesco World Heritage Roman sites, as well as some other historic buildings around town. A combined ticket covers the Pretori i Circ Romans, Amfiteatre Romà, Passeig Arqueològic Muralles and Fòrum de la Colònia. Get exploring!

**Passeig Arqueològic Muralles** WALLS
(Avinguda de Catalunya; adult/child €3.30/free; ⊙9am-9pm Tue-Sat Apr-Sep, to 7pm Tue-Fri Oct-Mar, to 3pm Sun year-round) A peaceful walk takes you around the inland part of the old town's perimeter between two lines of city walls. The inner walls are mainly Roman and date back to the 3rd century BCE, while the outer ones were put up by the British in 1709 during the War of the Spanish Succession. The earliest stretches are a mighty 4m thick. There's a small but helpful interpretation centre (Catalan, Spanish and English).

## Sleeping

**Tarragona Hostel** HOSTEL €
(☎877 05 58 96; www.tarragonahostel.com; Carrer de la Unió 26; dm/tr €20/45; 🛜) All the backpacker essentials are well executed at this friendly central hostel with chirpy staff, a leafy patio, a comfy common room, a shared kitchen and laundry facilities. Choose from two eight-bed dorms and a more modern four-bed dorm (all with air-con and personal lockers), or a private fan-cooled triple room.

**Hotel Plaça de la Font** HOTEL €€
(☎977 24 61 34; www.hotelpdelafont.com; Plaça de la Font 26; s/d/tr €63/80/100; ❄🛜) Comfortable modern rooms, individually decorated with photos of local monuments, make this cheerful, convenient hotel one of Tarragona's most attractive options. Rooms at the front have tiny balconies and are well

soundproofed from the sociable murmur on bustling Plaça de la Font below. With tables right on the square, the hotel cafe is perfect for light breakfasts (€6).

**Gran Claustre** BOUTIQUE HOTEL €€€
(☎977 65 15 57; www.granclaustre.com; Carrer del Cup 2, Altafulla; s €115-170, d €120-225; P ❄ 📶 🏊) For an upmarket stay, seek out this soothing, floral-scented hideaway overlooking the 17th-century castle in Altafulla's attractive old town, 11km northeast of Tarragona. Minimalist style dominates the elegant rooms, but those with the most colour, character and historical feel occupy the original 18th-century building, where there's a pool between stone walls. Other perks: a spa, hot tub and smart restaurant.

## Eating & Drinking

For the quintessential Tarragona seafood experience, head to Serrallo, the town's fishing port. About a dozen bars and restaurants here sell the day's catch, and on summer weekends the place is packed. Elsewhere, there are excellent Catalan and fusion restaurants and tapas bars tucked away in the old town.

★**Mercat Central** MARKET €
(Plaza Corsini; ⏲8.30am-9pm Mon-Sat) In a striking Modernista building, this historic 1915 market is looking better than ever thanks to a €47-million renovation completed in 2017. Temptations abound, from delectable fruits to cheeses and bakery items, plus food counters doling out seafood, charcuterie, sushi and Catalan wines. There's also a supermarket hidden downstairs.

**LOCAL KNOWLEDGE**

**CATALONIA'S HUMAN CASTLES**

Among Catalonia's strangest spectacles are *castells*, or human 'castles'. This sport originated in the 18th century in Valls, 20km north of Tarragona, but has since spread to other parts of the region. Teams of *castellers* clamber onto each other's shoulders, then a daredevil child scrambles up the side of this human tower to perch at the top before the whole structure gracefully disassembles itself; towers up to nine levels high are built. For the most spectacular *castells*, swing by Tarragona's **Festival de Santa Tecla** (⏲mid-Sep).

**El Vergel** VEGAN €€
(☎877 06 48 50; www.elvergeltarragona.com; Carrer Major 13; 3-course set menu €12-18; ⏲1-11pm; 📶 ✍) 🌿 This fabulous, fashionable vegan spot turns out creative plant-based deliciousness in two- or three-course menus, between whitewashed walls offset by sage-green shutters, patterned tiles and original artwork.

**Degvsta** FUSION €€
(☎977 25 24 28; www.degvsta.com; Carrer Cavallers 6; mains €17-20; ⏲1.30-4pm & 9-11pm Tue-Sat) Beyond a stylish lounge/bar hides this rustic-chic restaurant styled in cool creams, adorned with a claw-foot bathtub (!) and specialising in deliciously inventive contemporary Catalan cuisine. Dishes delivered with flair might be avocado gazpacho, crispy prawns with romesco sauce, grilled tenderloin with shitake mushrooms, or goat's cheese salad with strawberry vinaigrette.

**Arcs Restaurant** CATALAN €€€
(☎977 21 80 40; www.restaurantarcs.com; Carrer de Misser Sitges 13; mains €18-24; ⏲1-4pm & 8.30-11pm Tue-Sat) Inside a medieval cavern decorated with bright contemporary art and original Gothic arches, dine on creative European cooking that follows the seasons. Sample fresh pasta stuffed with black truffle and mushrooms, lobster salad over squid-ink noodles, oxtail with Priorat wine reduction, or the always-excellent catch of the day.

**El Tamboret** WINE BAR
(Carrer de Santa Anna 10; ⏲7-11pm Tue, noon-3pm & 7-11pm Wed-Sat, noon-3pm Sun) Hidden along a narrow lane near the Plaça del Forum, this delightful jewel-box-sized wine bar serves up a well-curated selection of wines from across Catalonia. Try a luscious Artigas from Priorat country or a bubbly from *cava* luminaries like Miquel Pons. Selections change regularly, and the friendly French owner is happy to guide you toward something extraordinary.

## Information

**Tarragona Turisme** (☎977 25 07 95; www.tarragonaturisme.es; Carrer Major 37; ⏲10am-8pm late Jun–late Sep, 10am-2pm & 3-5pm Mon-Fri, 10am-2pm & 3-7pm Sat, 10am-2pm Sun late Sep-late Jun)

## Getting There & Away

**AIR**

Around 13km northwest of Tarragona, **Reus airport** (www.aena.es; off C14, Reus) has flights to London, Dublin, Manchester, Brussels, Eindhoven and Frankfurt–Hahn among others, mostly with Ryanair.

**BUS**

The **bus station** (Plaça Imperial Tarraco) is 1.5km west of the old town along Rambla Nova. ALSA (www.alsa.es) destinations include Barcelona Nord (€9.05, 1½ to two hours, seven daily) and Valencia (€23, three to 4½ hours, six daily). Hispano Igualadina (www.igualadina.com) serves Lleida (€7, 1¾ hours, one to five daily).

**CAR & MOTORCYCLE**

There's a central underground car park (€6 per day) just off Via de l'Imperi Romà, on the west edge of the old town. There's free parking on the outskirts, including along Carrer Ernest Lluch (parallel to Via Augusta), about a 10-minute walk southeast of the old town.

**TRAIN**

Tarragona has two train stations (www.renfe.com). The **local train station** (Tarragona) is a 10-minute walk south of the old town near the beach, with services to/from Barcelona (€8 to €21, one to 1½ hours, every 10 to 30 minutes) and Valencia (€18 to €32, two to four hours, 15 to 17 daily).

The second, out-of-town train station, Camp de Tarragona, lies 10km north of the centre (a 20-minute taxi ride). There are frequent high-speed trains to Barcelona (€16 to €32, 35 minutes) and Lleida (€15 to €26, 30 minutes). Make use of hotel transfers if arriving here late at night, as taxis can be erratic.

## Getting Around

**TO/FROM THE AIRPORT**

From Reus airport, Hispano Igualadina buses run to/from Tarragona bus station (p383) (20 minutes, €3.50, three to five daily) as well as to/from Barcelona (1¾ hours, €15.50, one daily).

WORTH A TRIP

### REUS' GAUDÍ CENTRE

Visionary Catalan architect Antoni Gaudí was born in Reus, 14km northwest of Tarragona, in 1852. Though there are no Gaudí buildings here, he was inspired by many of his home town's historical structures. The superb **Gaudí Centre** (www.gaudicentre.cat; Plaça del Mercadal 3, Reus; adult/child €9/5; 10am-8pm Mon-Sat mid-Jun–mid-Sep, 10am-2pm & 4-7pm Mon-Sat mid-Sep–mid-Jun, 10am-2pm Sun year-round) gives a thorough introduction to the man and his global influence through engaging multilingual and audiovisual displays. The inspiration Gaudí found in nature, along with his thoughtfulness, are portrayed alongside touchable scale models of his designs.

The museum doubles up as the tourist office; pick up a map to guide you around Reus' notable Modernista buildings. Regular trains connect Reus with Tarragona (€2.85, 20 minutes).

# Priorat & Montsant Wine Regions

Rambling across softly sloping vine-wrapped hills, 40km west of Tarragona, Catalonia's Priorat region famously produces some of Spain's most prestigious (and most expensive) wines under the Priorat Denominació d'Origen Qualificada (DOQ; www.doqpriorat.org). It's one of just two Spanish winemaking areas awarded this coveted categorisation (the other is Rioja), and specialises in robust reds, mostly from *cariñena* (carignan) and *garnatxa* (grenache) grapes. Priorat's wine country is almost completely encircled by the undulating vineyards of the Montsant Denominació d'Origen (www.domontsant.com) territory, also known for its full-bodied reds from the same grapes, as well as its unique kosher wines.

**Falset**, just north of the N420, is the region's main town, and its liveliest, best-equipped base. Alternatively, make for charming hilltop **Gratallops** (10km northwest of Falset), home to several of Priorat's most high-profile wineries.

**Clos Mogador** WINERY

(977 83 91 71; www.closmogador.com; Camí Manyetes, Gratallops; tours €35; hours vary) A five-minute walk southwest of Gratallops, Clos Mogador is one of Priorat's outstanding wineries, founded in 1979 by pioneering French winemaker René Barbier. It's the creator of two aromatic reds, mostly from *cariñena* and *garnatxa* grapes, plus a fine white (*garnatxa blanca* and *macabeu*). In-depth three-hour tours involve a vehicle jaunt across vineyards followed by a tasting of the three premier wines. Phone or email ahead for bookings and timings.

**Catedral del Vi** WINERY

(Cooperativa Falset-Marça; ☎977 83 01 05; www.etim.cat; Av de la Generalitat 16, Falset; tours €10; ⏲10am-1.30pm & 4.30-8pm Mon-Sat, 10am-2pm Sun, tours noon daily Apr-Dec) Combining Modernista and Noucentista styles, this majestic medieval-inspired winery with a dramatic vaulted interior dates from 1919 and was designed by Gaudí's architectural disciple Cèsar Martinell. It's still a working bodega, producing full-bodied Montsant reds and the odd white, rosé and vermouth. Visitors can pop in for free low-key tastings, or for theatrical weekend tours.

**Lotus Priorat** BOUTIQUE HOTEL €€

(☎977 83 10 45; www.lotuspriorat.com; Carrer de Baix 33, Falset; s/d/apt incl breakfast €75/85/105; ❄📶) Skillfully run by three brothers, this fabulous rustic-chic boutique find is tucked away in a stylishly revamped 18th-century townhouse in Falset's centre. The nine bold-coloured rooms are fun, cosy and contemporary, with open-stone walls, wood-beamed ceilings, tree-trunk bedside tables and antique doors as bedheads. Many have balconies, while some are apartment-style with kitchenettes.

The excellent on-site **bar-restaurant** (dishes €8-16; ⏲5-11pm Mon & Tue, 9am-3pm & 5pm-midnight Wed-Sun) serves homemade cakes, delicious breakfasts, Falset vermouth and imaginative Catalan-international bites infused with local ingredients, on a view-laden terrace.

WORTH A TRIP

### CASTELL DE MIRAVET

Southern Catalonia's finest **castle** (Miravet; adult/child €5/3; ⏲10am-7.30pm Tue-Sun Jun-Sep, to 5pm Mar-May & Oct–mid-Dec, to 3.30pm mid-Dec–Feb) castle. It was built in the 11th century by the Moors, conquered by the Christians in the 1150s before being given to the Templars, and later taken by Nationalist forces during the civil war. It's a formidable stronghold, with incredibly solid walls, towering above an impossibly pretty village that cascades down the banks of the Ebro. Miravet is 8km southwest of the N420, 70km west of Tarragona. A path meanders down from beside the castle entrance to the riverside at old Miravet, from where you get the best views.

**★ Brichs** CATALAN €€

(☎690 251206; www.brichsrestaurant.com; Carrer del Sindicat 10; mains €14-21; ⏲1.30-3.30pm Wed, Thu & Sun, 1.30-3.30pm & 9-11pm Fri & Sat) Brichs serves up beautifully prepared Catalan cuisine and regional wines amid an elegant dining room with floor-to-ceiling windows fronting a peaceful terrace. Start off with fig and smoked-eel salad or foie gras and truffle cannelloni before moving on to a rich rice and shrimp dish or lightly breaded lamb ribs. The three-course lunch menu offers outstanding value (€16 including a glass of wine).

## ℹ Information

**Oficina de Turisme del Priorat** (☎977 83 10 23; www.turismepriorat.org; Plaça de la Quartera 1, Falset; ⏲10am-2pm Tue-Sat, 11am-2pm Sun) Provides maps, advice and info on wineries in the Priorat and Montsant regions.

## ℹ Getting There & Away

Hispano Igualadina (www.igualadina.com) runs two daily buses Monday to Friday between Falset and Tarragona (50 minutes).

From Marçà-Falset station, 2.5km southwest of Falset, five to six daily trains run to/from Tarragona (€5.60, 50 minutes) and Barcelona Sants (€11.95, 2¼ hours). Buses run seven to eight times daily between the train station and Falset.

# Delta de l'Ebre

Laced by waterways that melt into the Balearic Sea, the Delta de l'Ebre, a 20km-long bulge of silt-formed land near Catalonia's southern border, comes as an unexpected highlight of the region. Flamingos and ibis strut in reed-fringed lagoons, dune-backed beaches are lashed by the wind, and marshes reflect sunsets like mirrors. This is the final flourish of Spain's most voluminous river, which meanders over 900km southeast from Fontibre in Cantabria. Exploring this remote rural landscape, with its whitewashed farmhouses marooned between electric-green rice paddies, lingers in the memory.

**Parc Natural del Delta de l'Ebre**, occupying 78 sq kms of this wild exposed place, is northern Spain's most important waterbird habitat, with 360 bird species. Migration season (October and November) sees bird populations peak, but birds are also numerous in winter and spring. The park's flat expanse of waterside trails is ideal for cyclists and ramblers, and watersports abound.

Scruffy, sprawling **Deltebre** sits at the centre of the delta, but smaller villages like **Riumar**, at the delta's easternmost point, or **Poblenou del Delta**, in the south of the delta area, are more appealing bases.

## Sights

**Ecomuseu** MUSEUM

(☎977 48 96 79; www.facebook.com/PNDeltaEbre; Carrer de Dr Martí Buera 22, Deltebre; €2.50; ⏲10am-1pm & 3-5pm Mon-Sat Sep, Oct & Mar-Jun, 10am-2pm & 4-7pm Mon-Sat Jul & Aug, 10am-1pm Mon-Sat Nov-Feb, 10am-1pm Sun year-round) This engaging open-air museum shines a light on the delta's ecosystems and traditional trades, especially fishing and rice cultivation. The garden's pathways and wooden boardwalks weave past local flora, birdlife, fishers' tools and even a *llagut*, an early 20th-century boat used to haul around 350 sacks of rice at once.

**MónNatura Delta** NATURE CENTRE

(☎977 05 38 01; www.monnaturadelta.com; Carretera del Poblenou a les Salines; adult/child €8/4 with guided tour €10/5; ⏲10am-8pm mid-Jul–mid-Sep, to 2pm Wed-Fri, to 6pm Sat & Sun mid-Sep–early Dec & mid-Feb–mid-Jun) In the former saltworks overlooking Tancada lagoon, this 41-hectare site provides an excellent overview of the delta's importance – delving into avian life as well as key industries like rice-farming and salt production. You can freely wander the site, checking out the salt pans, peering through binoculars at flamingos and other birds, and even trying your hand at punting aboard one of the shallow-hulled boats in the lagoon.

## Activities

### Birdwatching

Grab some binoculars and flock to **L'Encanyissada** and **La Tancada** lagoons and **Punta de la Banya**, all in the south of the delta. In 2019, nearly 3000 pairs of greater flamingos nesting at the lagoons and the Punta reared over 2200 chicks – one of the best years on record; the delta is one of only a few places in Europe where they reproduce.

L'Encanyissada has five free-access observation points and La Tancada two; others around the park are marked on maps provided by the Centre d'Informació (p386). Punta de la Banya, connected to the mainland by a narrow 5km sand spit with a dirt road, is mostly off-limits, but you can go as far as a lookout point on its east side.

Birdwatching is at its best during early mornings and dusk, when mosquitoes are also at their most active (bring repellent).

### Boat Trips

**Creuers Olmos** (☎645 927110; www.cruceros-deltadelebro.es; Passeig Reinosa, Deltebre; adult/child €12.50/8) and **Creuers Delta de l'Ebre** (☎977 48 01 28; www.creuersdeltaebre.com; Carretera Final Goles de l'Ebre, Riumar; adult/child €9/6.75) run boat trips (45 minutes to 1½ hours) to the mouths of the Ebro and the delta's tip. The frequency and timings of departures depend on the season, but each company usually offers at least two daily and up to seven or eight in high season.

### Cycling

Cycling is an excellent way to explore the delta, with recommended bike routes ranging from 7km to 43km; the Centre d'Informació (p386) provides maps and there are downloadable multilanguage route guides on http://parcsnaturals.gencat.cat. The 26km **Ruta de les Llacunes** (Itinerari 1) is particularly good for birdwatchers, taking in flamingo lagoons with hides. The gentle 7km **Desembocadura–Garxal–Riumar** loop (Itinerari 5) meanders past river viewpoints and Riumar's rice paddies. Bicycles can be rented at Deltebre, Riumar and Poblenou del Delta (€10 per day).

## Sleeping & Eating

**Mas del Tancat** CASA RURAL €

(☎656 901014; masdeltancat@gmail.com; Camí dels Panissos, Amposta; s/d €53/66; P❄📶🏊) A converted farmhouse poised between rice fields, Mas del Tancat is a friendly, tranquil escape with just five rooms sporting iron bedsteads and soothing colour schemes. Farm animals wander the grounds, a peaceful pool beckons, and breakfast (€7) and dinner are (€16) available. From Amposta, take the TV3405 3km east; then it's 1km south and signposted.

★**Masia Tinet** CASA RURAL €€

(☎977 48 93 89; www.masiatinet.com; Barrio Lepanto 13, Deltebre; d incl breakfast €80-100; P❄📶🏊) The six rooms at this cushy, family-run guesthouse are elegant but rustic, with wooden beams, high ceilings and bare-brick or cheery-coloured walls. There's a garden with deck chairs and a small pool,

OFF THE BEATEN TRACK

### MEMORIES OF THE CIVIL WAR

A once thriving medieval village, the hilltop settlement of Cordera de Ebre (www.poblevell.cat) stands as one of the most vivid reminders of the horrors of the Spanish Civil War. During the battle of Ebro in late 1938, when the village was at the vanguard of the divided Republican front, no building was left untouched over the course of a relentless Fascist bombing campaign and the fires that followed. Today, the eerie ruins of old homes still stand, and you can just make out a few lanes now covered in thick rubble. On one side of the hill, the pockmarked and partially restored church of Sant Pere still stands, though now roofless, and functions as a exhibition and cultural space. After the battle, the survivors rebuilt their town downhill from the *poble vell* (old village), but left the ruins as a permanent memorial to all those who were killed – both here and during the bloody 115-day-long Battle of Ebro.

Poble Vell de Cordera d'Ebre is located about 40km north of Tortosa, just off the N420.

so you can watch the sun set over marshlands speckled with birdlife. Breakfasts are a banquet of homemade preserves and fresh produce, and service has a personal touch.

**Hostal Cling 43** B&B €€
(☎659 335577; www.hostalcling43.com; Avinguda Colom 43, Deltebre; s/d/tr incl breakfast €50/70/90; ❄📶) Hidden away in a converted townhouse, this boutique-ified B&B is a fabulous find for its cosy-stylish rooms, warm welcome and brilliant local-produce breakfasts. Gorgeous hand-painted murals of local birds complement open-brick walls, wood-beamed ceilings and splashes of colour in the six all-different doubles. It's efficiently run by a charming duo who rent bikes and know the local area inside out.

★**Casa Nuri** SEAFOOD €€
(☎977 48 01 28; www.restaurantnuri.com; Carretera Final Goles de l'Ebre, Riumar; mains €14-26; ⏲10am-9pm, closed early Jan) Locals fill this bubbly riverfront restaurant, thanks to its long-standing reputation for superb local cuisine such as razor clams, rice glistening with squid ink, oven-baked sea bass, duck with orange sauce, and paella in all shapes and sizes (even vegetarian!). Book ahead for an outdoor table perched beside the river.

**Mas Prades** CATALAN €€
(☎977 05 90 84; www.masdeprades.cat; Carretera T340, Km 8, Deltebre; mains €16-24; ⏲1.30-4pm & 8.30-10.30pm, weekends only Nov-Mar; 📶) Gourmets travel all the way from Barcelona to this attractively revamped country house to sample its fantastic delta cuisine. The three-course €22 weekday lunch menu makes a lip-smacking introduction to local delicacies, while à la carte options range from baby squid, grilled sole and tender mussels roasted in garlic butter to the classic delta rice with wild duck.

## ℹ Information

**Casa de Fusta** (☎977 26 10 22; http://parcsnaturals.gencat.cat; Partida Cuixota, Poblenou del Delta; ⏲10am-1pm & 3-5pm Mon-Sat Sep, Oct & Mar-Jun, 10am-2pm & 4-7pm Mon-Sat Jul & Aug, 10am-1pm Mon-Sat Nov-Feb, 10am-1pm Sun year-round) Lagoonside park information centre.

**Centre d'Informació** (☎977 48 96 79; http://parcsnaturals.gencat.cat; Carrer de Dr Martí Buera 22, Deltebre; ⏲10am-1pm & 3-5pm Mon-Sat Sep, Oct & Mar-Jun, 10am-2pm & 4-7pm Mon-Sat Jul & Aug, 10am-1pm Mon-Sat Nov-Feb, 10am-1pm Sun year-round) In the same complex as Deltebre's Ecomuseu; pick up maps and cycle route brochures.

## ℹ Getting There & Around

Weekday Hife (www.hife.es) buses connect Tortosa with Deltebre (€4, 50 minutes, seven daily) and Poblenou del Delta (€5.25, one hour, one to two daily). Buses also head to delta towns Amposta and Sant Carles de la Ràpita from Tarragona (€12.20 to €14.25, 1¼ to 1½ hours, four to eight daily) and Tortosa (€2.30 to €2.80, 20 to 45 minutes, every 30 to 90 minutes).

If you don't reach the Delta de l'Ebre with your own wheels, consider renting a bike: the area has extremely limited public transport.

# Tortosa

POP 33,500

With a neck-straining castle, otherworldly sculpture garden and architectural gems spanning Gothic to Modernista styles, arid Tortosa is experiencing a quiet tourism renaissance. It's a sleepy, slightly scruffy town, 70km southwest of Tarragona, but one that's slowly becoming increasingly popular for cultural weekend breaks.

Tortosa was a battleground between medieval Christian and Moorish Spain. More recently, it was on the front line between Nationalists and Republicans during the civil war (suffering a staggering 86 air raids between 1937 and 1938) and the site of an epic battle, which destroyed much of its medieval centre and cost over 35,000 lives. Tortosa is also suffused with Jewish history that dates back to the 6th century.

The town is a convenient base for day trips such as to the Castell de Miravet or the Civil War-scarred ruins of Cordera de Ebre.

## Sights

Pick up a pamphlet from the tourist office to uncover Jewish Tortosa.

**Catedral de Santa Maria** CATHEDRAL

(Porta de Palau; adult/child €4.50/3.50; 10am-2pm & 4-7pm Tue-Sat, 11am-2pm Sun) Built between 1347 and the mid-18th century on the site of a Romanesque predecessor, this Gothic cathedral seizes attention with its many turrets, gargoyles jutting from every eave, and austere adjoining 13th-century cloister. Visits begin with an eerie underground wander through the cathedral's medieval tunnels, which were used as air-raid shelters during the civil war. Afterwards, you'll get an eyeful of Tortosa's ecclesiastical treasures, including a magnificent 15th-century altarpiece by Jaume Huguet.

**Museu de Tortosa** MUSEUM

(977 51 01 44; www.museudetortosa.cat; Rambla Felip Pedrell 3; adult/child €3/free; 10am-1.30pm & 5-7.30pm Tue-Sat May-Sep, 10am-1.30pm & 4-6.30pm Tue-Sat Oct-Apr, 11am-1.30pm Sun year-round) Within a splendid blue Modernista building, decorated with white checkerboard designs, lies Tortosa's modern, minimalist town museum. The 1908 building is worth ogling: formerly a city slaughterhouse, its design has delicate Moorish elements. Within, the museum does a great job of contextualising the area's history, from traces of early Iberian settlement to Roman rule, Moorish times and the devastation of the Spanish Civil War.

**Castell de la Suda** CASTLE

(Carrer del Castell de la Suda; 24hr) FREE Looming high above the old town, Tortosa's 10th-century fortress is a maze of unfinished stairways, trails to nowhere, and spectacular lofty views, now mostly occupied by the luxurious Parador de Tortosa. Next to the *parador* lies a small Islamic cemetery of the 10th to 12th centuries.

## Sleeping & Eating

**Parador de Tortosa** HISTORIC HOTEL €€

(977 44 44 50; www.parador.es; Castell de la Suda; r €95-130; ) Tortosa's formidable fortress encloses a *parador*, allowing you to repose in medieval surroundings overlooking vertiginous views of the town. Expect cosy old-world rooms, a smart restaurant, a hilltop pool, and a plush lounge bar with terrace.

**Mercat Central** MARKET €

(Plaça de Barcelona; dishes €4-9; 8am-2.30pm Tue & Wed, 8am-2.30pm & 5.30-8.30pm Thu & Fri, 8am-3pm Sat; ) In a Modernista building near the riverfront, Tortosa's capacious market is a culinary delight. You can pick up fresh fruits, breads, cheeses, cured meats, olives and other treats for picnic, or grab a bite at one of the *pintxos* counters in the front – some of which have outdoor tables on the plaza.

**Xampú Tortosa** TAPAS €€

(977 50 13 41; www.xampu.es; Rambla de Catalunya 41; sharing plates €5-17; 7-11pm Mon, 11.30am-4pm & 7-11pm Tue-Sat; ) This buzzing bar-restaurant on Tortosa's west bank serves up regional favourites alongside inventive tapas, allowing you to snack on ham, sheep-milk cheese and tomato-slathered bread just as easily as steamed Delta mussels and tuna tartare.

## Information

**Oficina de Turisme de les Terres de l'Ebre** (977 44 96 48; www.tortosaturisme.cat; Rambla Felip Pedrell 3; 10am-1.30pm & 4.30-7.30pm Mon-Sat May-Sep, 10am-1.30pm & 3.30-6.30pm Mon-Sat Oct-Apr, 9.30am-1.30pm Sun year-round) Attached to the Museu de Tortosa; also covers the Delta de l'Ebre area.

## Getting There & Away

Hife (www.hife.es) buses link Tortosa with Tarragona (€12.20, 1¼ hours, six to 14 daily), plus several towns in the Delta de l'Ebre area.

Trains reach Tortosa from Tarragona (€8.05, 1¼ hours, nine or 10 daily) and Valencia (€14 to €16, 2½ to three hours, three or four daily).

## AT A GLANCE

**POPULATION**
1.33 million

**CAPITAL**
Zaragoza

**BEST DAY HIKE**
Faja de Pelay (p411)

**BEST VILLAGE RESTAURANT**
Casa Pardina (p420)

**BEST GOYA COLLECTION**
Museo Goya (p393)

**WHEN TO GO**

**May–Jun & Sep–Oct** Best temperatures for enjoying Zaragoza and the rest of lowland Aragón.

**Jun–Oct** The best months for hiking in the spectacular Aragón Pyrenees.

**Oct** Zaragoza's Fiestas del Pilar combine the sacred with the city's famed love of revelry.

Parque Nacional de Ordesa y Monte Perdido (411)
1TOMM/SHUTTERSTOCK ©

# Aragón

Probably Spain's most underrated region, Aragón offers riches wherever you travel, from the crusader-like castles and Romanesque churches of the north to the outstanding Mudéjar architecture of Teruel in the south. The regional capital, Zaragoza, is a major Spanish city of ebullient nightlife and absorbing culture (not least the work of local artistic genius Francisco de Goya), while dozens of picturesque medieval villages dot the serrated landscape, from pink-hued Albarracín to stone-clothed Sos del Rey Católico. But what really sets Aragón apart is the majesty of the central Pyrenees along its northern fringe. This is the highest and, for many, most beautiful section of the mighty mountain range – a rare delight for the eyes and a massive natural adventure playground, with not only Spain's finest hiking and climbing but also much of its best skiing, canyoning, mountain-biking, rafting and paragliding.

**INCLUDES**

## History

Aragón came into existence as a tiny Christian bridgehead on the southern flank of the Pyrenees after the Muslim invasion of the Iberian Peninsula in the 8th century. Over the following centuries it grew into one of the strongest kingdoms on the peninsula as it expanded southward and then, in 1137, was united by royal betrothal with the neighbouring county of Barcelona (the combined kingdom-county is known as the Crown of Aragón). It was the marriage of the future Aragonese king Fernando II to his powerful Castilian counterpart Isabel in 1469 that effectively gave birth to modern Spain as we know it.

# ZARAGOZA

POP 638,000 / ELEV 200M

The ethereal image of the multi-domed Basílica del Pilar reflected in the Río Ebro is a potent symbol of Zaragoza, one of Spain's most underrated regional capitals. There's plenty more fine architecture here too, including a turreted castle with an interior like a mini-Alhambra, and some very creatively displayed underground Roman remains. But Zaragoza's appeal goes well beyond its monuments. Home to half of Aragón's 1.3 million population, it has one of the best tapas, bar and cafe scenes in the country and is well stocked with the epoch-defining art of local lad Francisco de Goya, the genius painter who was born a short horse ride away in 1746. The historic centre (between the Río Ebro, Calle del Coso and Avenida César Augusto) is refreshingly almost traffic-free, including the vast Plaza del Pilar alongside the famous basilica.

## History

Roman Caesaraugusta was founded in 14 BCE and prospered for almost three centuries with, at its peak, as many as 25,000 people concentrated in the city whose river traffic brought the known world to the banks of Río Ebro. In Islamic times, Zaragoza was capital of the Upper March, one of Al-Andalus' frontier territories. In 1118, it fell to Alfonso I, ruler of the expanding Christian kingdom of Aragón, and in the centuries that followed, Zaragoza grew into one of inland Spain's most important economic and cultural hubs. It's now Spain's fifth-largest city and, since the 2008 Expo, has greatly improved its modern infrastructure.

## Sights

**★Basílica de Nuestra Señora del Pilar** CHURCH

(www.basilicadelpilar.es; Plaza del Pilar; 6.45am-8.30pm Mon-Sat, to 9.30pm Sun) This great baroque cavern of Catholicism stands on the site where, the faithful believe, the Virgin Mary appeared to Santiago (St James the Apostle) atop a *pilar* (pillar) of jasper on 2 January 40 CE, leaving the pillar behind as testimony of her visit. A chapel was built around the pillar, followed by a series of ever more grandiose churches, culminating in the enormous basilica.

A **lift** (adult/child €3/free; 10am-2pm & 4-8pm mid-Apr–mid-Oct, to 6pm mid-Oct–mid-Mar) will whisk you most of the way up the basilica's northwest tower, leaving you to climb 109 steps to a superb viewpoint over the domes, river and city.

The basilica, originally designed in 1681 by local architect Felipe Sánchez y Herrera, was greatly modified in the 18th century by royal architect Ventura Rodríguez, who added the ultra-baroque **Santa Capilla** at the east end (housing the legendary pillar), and the flurry of 10 mini-domes around the main dome on the roof.

The famous **pillar** is topped by a small 15th-century Gothic sculpture of the Virgin and child, and is concealed inside an elaborate silver casing, which is itself usually three-quarters hidden by a long mantle (except on the 2nd, 12th and 20th of each month). A tiny oval-shaped portion of the pillar is exposed in the passage behind, and a steady stream of people lines up to brush lips with its polished and cracked cheek, which even popes have air-kissed. More than the architecture, these sacred symbols, and the devotion they inspire, are what make this church special.

Hung from the northeast column of the Santa Capilla are two wickedly slim bombs that were dropped on the basilica during the civil war. They failed to explode. A miracle, said the faithful; typical Czech munitions, said the more cynical.

The basilica's finest artwork is the 16th-century alabaster **retablo mayor** (main altarpiece) by Damián Forment, facing west in the basilica's middle. There are also two Goyas: *La adoración del nombre del Dios,* on the ceiling of the *coreto* (small choir) at the church's far east end, is an early classical piece from 1772; vastly different is *Regina Martirum* painted above the north

# Aragón Highlights

**1 Parque Nacional de Ordesa y Monte Perdido** (p411) Hiking the most spectacular mountainscapes of the Spanish Pyrenees.

**2 Albarracín** (p426) Exploring the pink-hued streets and unique medieval history of this charming village.

**3 Zaragoza** Delving into this city of fascinating monuments and superb tapas and bars.

**4 Valles de Hecho and Ansó** (p403) Meandering through remote Pyrenean valleys of verdant forests and ancient stone villages.

**5 Teruel** (p422) Discovering Spain's smallest provincial capital, with its superb Mudéjar architecture.

**6 Benasque** (p416) Getting outdoorsy around this pretty stone village, gateway to the Pyrenees' highest peaks.

**7 Jaca** (p408) Enjoying top tapas bars in a lively, historical Pyrenees gateway town.

## Zaragoza

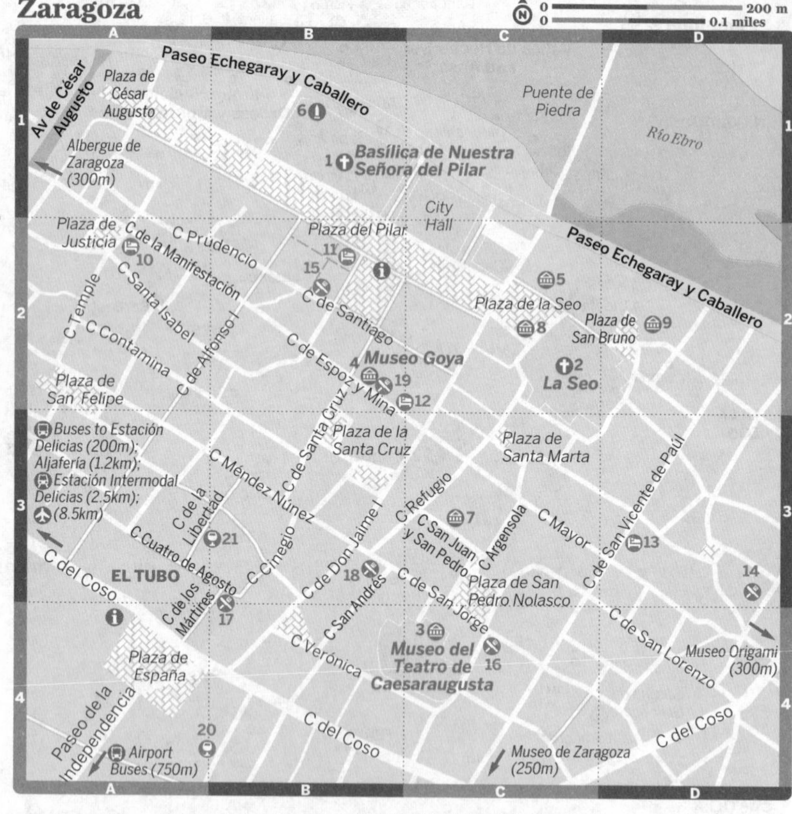


## Zaragoza

**Top Sights**
- 1 Basílica de Nuestra Señora del Pilar ........ B1
- 2 La Seo ........ C2
- 3 Museo del Teatro de Caesaraugusta ........ C4
- 4 Museo Goya ........ B2

**Sights**
- 5 Alma Mater Museum ........ C2
- 6 Basilica de Nuestra Señora del Pilar Tower ........ B1
- 7 Museo de las Termas Públicas ........ C3
- 8 Museo del Foro de Caesaraugusta ........ C2
- 9 Museo del Puerto Fluvial ........ D2

**Sleeping**
- 10 Catalonia El Pilar ........ A2
- 11 Hotel Pilar Plaza ........ B2
- 12 Hotel Sauce ........ C2
- Sabinas ........ (see 12)
- 13 The Bridge ........ D3

**Eating**
- 14 Birosta ........ D3
- 15 Café Botánico ........ B2
- 16 Café Nolasco ........ C4
- 17 Casa Lac ........ B3
- 18 La Clandestina Café ........ B3
- 19 Los Xarmientos ........ B2

**Drinking & Nightlife**
- 20 Cierzo ........ A4
- 21 Libertad 6.8 ........ B3

aisle in 1780 (in the third cupola from the east). With its blurry impressionistic figures, it was hugely controversial at the time.

**★La Seo** CATHEDRAL

(Catedral de San Salvador; ☎976 29 12 31; Plaza de la Seo; adult/child €4/free; ⏲10am-6.30pm & 7.45-9pm Mon-Thu, 10am-6.30pm Fri, 10am-12.30pm,

3-6.30pm & 7.45-9pm Sat, 10am-noon, 2-6.30pm & 7.45-9pm Sun mid-Jun–mid-Oct, 10am-2pm & 4-6.30pm Mon-Fri, 10am-noon & 4-6.30pm Sat & Sun mid-Oct–mid-Jun) Dominating the eastern end of Plaza del Pilar, La Seo is Zaragoza's finest work of Christian architecture, built between the 12th and 17th centuries and displaying a fabulous spread of styles from Romanesque to baroque. It stands on the site of Islamic Zaragoza's main mosque (which itself stood on the Roman forum's temple site).

La Seo's northeast external wall is a Mudéjar masterpiece, deploying classic brickwork and colourful ceramics in complex geometric patterns. Inside, beautiful fan vaulting adorns the ceiling while the numerous elaborate chapels, framed by encrusted stonework, ring the changes from the eerily solemn **Capilla de San Marcos** to the golden baroque baldachin of the **Capilla del Santo Cristo**. The exquisite 15th-century alabaster **high altarpiece** is well worth scrutiny too. The attached **Museo de Tapices** houses a collection of Flemish and French tapestries considered the best of its kind in the world.

**Alma Mater Museum** MUSEUM

(976 39 94 88; www.almamatermuseum.com; Plaza de la Seo 5; €3; 10am-8pm Tue-Sat, to 2pm Sun) Slick multimedia exhibits set an arty tone as you follow a skilfully laid-out trajectory through the older elements of the building (a former royal and episcopal palace), learning about Roman forums, the venerated Virgen del Pilar and Aragonese history (especially church history), before reaching the Renaissance feast of the top floor, with paintings by the two local Franciscos: Goya and Bayeu.

**★Museo Goya** MUSEUM

(976 39 73 87; http://museogoya.ibercaja.es; Calle de Espoz y Mina 23; adult/child €6/free, audio guide or tablet €2; 10am-8pm Mon-Sat, to 2pm Sun late Mar-Oct, 10am-2pm & 4-8pm Mon-Sat, 10am-2pm Sun Nov-late Mar) Apart from Madrid's Museo del Prado, this exceedingly well-laid-out museum contains arguably the best exposé of the work of one of Spain's greatest artists. Each of the three floors has a different focus, the 2nd floor being the one that exhibits Goya's own work. Four complete sets of his prints are on show, including the groundbreaking *Desastres de la guerra* (Disasters of War), a bitter attack on the cruelty of war.

Also here are Goya's first self-portrait (1775) and his well-known portraits of King Carlos IV and Queen María Luisa.

**★Aljafería** PALACE

(976 28 95 28; www.cortesaragon.es; Calle de los Diputados; adult/child €5/free, Sun free; 10am-2pm & 4.30-8pm Apr–mid-Oct, 10am-2pm & 4-6.30pm Mon-Sat, 10am-2pm Sun mid-Oct–Mar) The Aljafería is Spain's finest Islamic-era edifice outside Andalucía. Built as a fortified palace for Zaragoza's Islamic rulers in the 11th century, it passed into Christian hands in 1118. In the 1490s the Reyes Católicos (Catholic Monarchs), Fernando and Isabel, tacked on their own palace. Aragón's regional parliament has sat here since 1987.

Inside the main gate, cross an introductory courtyard into the **Patio de Santa Isabel**, which was the Islamic palace's central courtyard. Here you encounter the delicate interwoven arches typical of the geometric mastery of Islamic architecture. Behind the stunning northern portico is the **Salón de Oro**, the palace's throne room; opening off the portico is a small, octagonal **oratorio** (prayer room) whose finely chiselled floral motifs, inscriptions from the Quran and pleasingly simple cupola are fine examples of Islamic art.

Moving upstairs, you pass through rooms of the **Palacio Cristiano Medieval**, created by Aragonese monarchs in the 14th century, followed by the **Palacio de los Reyes Católicos** (Catholic Monarchs' Palace) which, as though in riposte to the Islamic finery beneath it, contains some exquisite Mudéjar coffered ceilings, especially in the lavish **Salón del Trono** (Throne Room).

Spanish-language tours take place several times a day, and there are two daily tours each in English and French in July and August. The palace is closed to visitors some Friday mornings and Thursdays when parliamentary sessions are on.

**Museo Origami** MUSEUM

(876 03 45 69; www.emoz.es; Centro de Historias, Plaza San Agustín 2; adult/student & senior €3/2; 10am-2pm & 5-9pm Tue-Sat, 10am-2.30pm Sun; ) Zaragoza's museum devoted to the art of folding paper has six galleries of exhibits of a staggeringly high standard. Even if you're not very familiar with origami, you will be amazed by what you see.

You can also take hour-long origami classes (€6); check the website for more information and to learn about Zaragoza's fascinating historical connection with origami (dating back to the 1940s).

**Museo de Zaragoza** MUSEUM

(www.museodezaragoza.es; Plaza de los Sitios 6; 10am-2pm & 5-8pm Tue-Sat, 10am-2pm Sun) FREE Exceptional Roman mosaics and 19 paintings by Goya are the highlights of the city museum, devoted to archaeology and fine arts. There's plenty more 18- to 20th-century art that's well worth looking at, too. It's 400m south of the Teatro Romano.

## Festivals & Events

**Fiestas del Pilar** RELIGIOUS

(Oct) This week of full-on celebrations (religious and otherwise) peaks on 12 October, the Día de Nuestra Señora del Pilar, when hundreds of thousands of devotees, many in colourful regional or national dress, pile a veritable mountain of flowers around the Virgin's image from the basilica, brought out onto Plaza del Pilar.

## Sleeping

**★Hotel Sauce** HOTEL €

(976 20 50 50; www.hotelsauce.com; Calle de Espoz y Mina 33; s €42-70, d €45-80; ) This stylish family-run hotel with a great central location provides fresh, cheerful, contemporary rooms with walk-in showers, tasteful watercolours, outstandingly friendly and helpful staff, and a pleasant 24-hour cafe serving excellent breakfasts, cakes and cocktails. Prices are very reasonable given everything the hotel provides.

The same family runs the 15 attractive apartments and 'deluxe rooms' of **Sabinas** (976 20 47 10; www.sabinas.es; Calle de Espoz y Mina 33; d/tr €60/75, apt for 2 €60-70, for 4 €90-100; ), all within a couple of minutes' walk of Hotel Sauce.

**The Bridge** HOSTAL €

(627 307932; www.facebook.com/zaragozathebridge; Calle de San Vicente de Paúl 30; s €35-45, d €40-60; ) The Bridge offers a friendly welcome and a hostel-ish atmosphere even though the dozen rooms are all private. They have practical but bright and stylish design, with tea/coffee makers, fridges and individual welcome messages. There's a well-equipped kitchen, and a blackboard listing music gigs.

**Albergue de Zaragoza** HOSTEL €

(976 28 20 43; www.behostels.com; Calle Predicadores 70; incl breakfast dm €16, d with shared bathroom €35; ) This large, popular hostel offers the choice of neat, clean, small private rooms or mixed dorms with metal bunks. All share clean bathrooms. The special feature is the brick-vaulted basement bar, La Bóveda, where varied live music happens most Thursday to Sunday nights.

**Hotel Pilar Plaza** HOTEL €€

(976 39 42 50; www.hotelpilarplaza.es; Plaza del Pilar 11; s €62-72, d €65-75, breakfast €9; ) The Goya museum might be round the corner, but this basilica-facing hotel prefers to exhibit more recent art by the likes of Banksy. The 50 rooms are comfy, shiny and almost boutique-ish in whites, blacks and greys, with a few more ornate touches such as chandeliers.

**Catalonia El Pilar** HOTEL €€

(976 20 58 58; www.cataloniahotels.com; Calle de la Manifestación 16; s/d €80/95, breakfast €14; ) Ten out of 10 for the facade, a handsome Modernista construction that has been artfully renovated to house this eminently comfortable hotel. Inside, rooms are spacious and decorated in restful, muted earth tones with elegant marble-clad bathrooms.

## Eating

Head to the quadrangle of lanes known as El Tubo, north of Plaza de España, for one of Spain's richest gatherings of tapas bars. This is a quintessential Zaragoza experience and a bubbling scene any night of the year. Just wander round, especially along Calles de la Libertad and Cuatro de Agosto, and see what takes your fancy.

### FOLLOW THE GOYA TRAIL

Francisco José de Goya y Lucientes, better known simply as Goya, was born in Aragón and his work can be seen all over his native region.

- Museo Goya (p393), Zaragoza
- Casa Natal de Goya (p397), Fuendetodos
- Museo del Grabado de Goya (p397), Fuendetodos
- Museo de Zaragoza, Zaragoza
- Museo de Huesca (p400), Huesca
- Basílica de Nuestra Señora del Pilar (p390), Zaragoza

## CAESARAUGUSTA – A CITY UNDERGROUND

Underneath modern Zaragoza's streets lies a parallel universe telling the story of Caesaraugusta, the Roman city founded in 14 BCE that flourished as one of Hispania's most important colonies.

Caesaraugusta lay buried and forgotten for more than 1500 years, until its crumbled remnants were resuscitated in the 1980s and '90s – and given new life in a brilliant quartet of subterranean museums: the **Museo del Foro de Caesaraugusta** (976 72 12 21; www.zaragozaturismo.es; Plaza de la Seo 2; adult/child €3/free; 10am-2pm & 5-9pm Tue-Sat, 10am-2.30pm Sun), in the excavated substructures of the Roman city's forum; the **Museo del Puerto Fluvial** (Plaza de San Bruno 8; adult/child €3/free; 10am-2pm & 5-9pm Tue-Sat, 10am-2.30pm Sun), erstwhile river port installations; the **Museo de las Termas Públicas** (Calle San Juan y San Pedro 3-7; adult/child €3/free; 10am-2pm & 5-9pm Tue-Sat, 10am-2.30pm Sun), public baths; and, best of all, the **Museo del Teatro de Caesaraugusta** (976 72 60 75; www.zaragozaturismo.es; Calle de San Jorge 12; adult/child €4/free; 10am-2pm & 5-9pm Tue-Sat, 10am-2.30pm Sun), showcasing a 6000-seat theatre that was one of the largest in Hispania. All are open from 10am to 2pm and 5pm to 9pm Tuesday to Saturday, and 10am to 2.30pm Sundays.

While the ruins might be, well, 'ruins' compared to better-preserved Roman sites in Mérida and Tarragona, the genius of Zaragoza's museums lies in their layout and creative extras. Well-curated exhibition chambers combine mock-ups of how things used to look with clever multimedia exhibits. The pièce de résistance is the Roman theatre, protected by a huge polycarbonate roof and perhaps best viewed through panoramic windows from its adjacent museum.

A joint ticket is available for all four museums (adult/child €7/free) and is a fantastic investment. Situated in close proximity to each other, the museums can easily all be visited in the same day.

**Café Nolasco** CAFE €

(www.facebook.com/cafenolasco; Calle San Jorge 18; breakfast items & cakes €2-4, mains €10-18, set menus €13-16; 8am-11pm or later Mon-Fri, 10am-11pm or later Sat & Sun; ) This stylish, clean-lined spot, overlooking a pretty old-town plaza, fulfils many roles – it's great for breakfasts, tasty lunches, evening drinks in a club/lounge atmosphere, plus coffee and wi-fi with tempting cakes any time of day!

**Birosta** VEGETARIAN €

(www.birosta.com; Calle Universidad 3; dishes €5-11; 11am-11pm Tue-Sat, to 5pm Sun Sep-Jul, from 7.30pm Mon-Sat Aug; ) Birosta is an excellent, cooperative-run, vegetarian restaurant-cafe-bar where lunch and dinner are served in a neat, pine-tabled dining room, or you can snack on tasty tapas in the front bar. The well-prepared and presented dishes range from inventive salads to pizza, moussaka, dolmades, lasagne or tofu offerings. Drinks include organic wines and Aragonese craft beers.

**Le Pastis** FUSION €

(Paseo de la Ribera; dishes €7-10; 6pm-1am or later Mon-Fri, from 11am Sat & Sun) The terrace under the trees here, at the top of a grassy riverbank beside the Puente del Pilar, is perfect for a drink and bite on a summer evening. The menu is short but sweet with the burger Le Pastis a good choice, or perhaps try a couscous salad.

**Café Botánico** CAFE €

(Calle de Santiago 5; cakes & snacks €2-5; 9am-8pm Sun-Thu, to 3am Fri & Sat; ) Greenery-decked Café Botánico, just off Plaza del Pilar, serves great coffee, teas, homemade lemonade, good *tostadas* (toast slices with various toppings) and some delicious cakes.

**La Clandestina Café** CAFE €€

(876 28 11 65; Calle San Andrés 9; brunch €15, light dishes €7-16; 10am-midnight or later Tue-Fri, from 11am Sat & Sun; ) There's an eye-catching huge pair of red lips painted on one white brick wall, but this place is as much about gastronomy as style, particularly in the brunch (11.30am to 3.30pm, including a glass of *cava*) and coffee-and-cake departments. The cold-pressed juices are divine on hot days, and the cheesecake with fruits of the forest may just be the best cheesecake you've ever tasted.

## WHAT'S COOKING IN ARAGÓN?

Aragonese tables are dominated by meat, which may come in old-fashioned grilled, roast or stewed form in more traditional restaurants, or in inventive combination with other ingredients in numerous gastro establishments.

The region's cold, harsh winds create the ideal conditions for curing *jamón* (ham), a top tapa here; some of the best comes from the Teruel area. Hearty *ternasco* (suckling lamb) is generally served roasted or as ribs with potatoes. Lamb (or chicken) may also be prepared *al chilindrón* – in a sauce of red peppers, tomatoes, garlic and ham. Vegetarians should seek out *pochas* (a much-favoured white bean), often found with assorted vegetables in the tasty broth *pochas viudas*.

Local cheeses, 130 varieties of them, should be tried wherever you go – those of Albarracín, Tronchón and Benasque are especially highly rated.

The Aragonese love their baked goods too: from Zaragoza northwards, look for *trenza de Almudévar*, a bread-like cake made with nuts and raisins, with its strands woven together like plaits *(trenzas)*. *Torrija*, the local version of French toast, is another favourite.

**Casa Lac** TAPAS €€

(☎976 39 61 96; www.restaurantecasalac.es; Calle de los Mártires 12; mains €16-27, tapas €3.50-6, raciones €14-19, set menus €40-43; ⏲1-4pm & 8pm-midnight Mon-Sat, 1-4pm Sun) The grande dame of Zaragoza dining, Casa Lac opened in 1825 and is reputedly Spain's oldest licensed restaurant. The cuisine today is tastily contemporary whether you go for 'gastro-tapas', a set menu (there's a vegetarian option) or à la carte. The ground-floor bar is smart but relatively casual; an elegant staircase leads to the slightly more formal upstairs dining room (reservations advised).

**Los Xarmientos** ARAGONESE €€

(☎976 29 90 48; www.facebook.com/xarmientos; Calle de Espoz y Mina 25; mains €12-16, set menus €15-35; ⏲1.30-4pm & 8.30-11pm Wed-Sat, 1.30-4pm Tue & Sun) Aragonese meat dishes are a speciality at this artfully designed restaurant. It styles itself as a *parrilla,* meaning dishes are cooked on a barbecue-style grill. It's a fine place to sample *ternasco asado*, Aragón's most emblematic dish, accompanied by a Somontano wine and perhaps preceded by a spinach and goat's-cheese salad...or even some snails?

## Drinking & Entertainment

After the tapas bars close around midnight, late-night and music bars come into their own. There's a good scattering of these in the historic centre. You can find live music somewhere almost any night except perhaps in quieter July and August. Pick up the free what's-on guide *Go!* (www.laguiago.com).

**Libertad 6.8** BAR

(www.facebook.com/libertad.terraza; Calle de la Libertad 6-8; ⏲8pm-1am Tue-Thu, 1pm-2am Fri & Sat, to 6pm Sun & Mon) A fashionable, half-open-air space in El Tubo serving 22 types of gin and plenty of cocktails. Does meals too.

**Cierzo** CRAFT BEER

(www.cierzobrewing.com; Calle Josefa Amar y Borbón 8; ⏲10am-midnight Sun-Wed, to 1am Thu-Sat) Zaragoza's large and lively first brewpub brews its own ales on the spot and serves up sharing plates to snack on with your beer.

## Information

**Municipal Tourist Office** (☎976 20 12 00; www.zaragoza.es/ciudad/turismo; Plaza del Pilar; ⏲10am-8pm; Wi-Fi) Has branch offices around town, including at the train station and airport.

**Oficina de Turismo de Aragón** (☎976 28 21 81; www.turismodearagon.com; Plaza de España 1; ⏲9.30am-2.30pm & 4.30-7.30pm) Helpful place with plenty of brochures covering all of Aragón.

## Getting There & Away

Trains and buses share the modern **Estación Intermodal Delicias** (Avenida de Navarra 80), 3km west of the city centre.

### AIR

**Zaragoza Airport** (☎976 71 23 00; www.zaragoza-airport.com), 10km west of the city, has direct Ryanair (www.ryanair.com) flights to/from London (Stansted), Brussels (Charleroi), Milan (Bergamo), Lisbon and Paris (Beauvais, March to October). Volotea (www.volotea.com) flies seasonally to Menorca, Munich and Venice.

### BUS

Dozens of bus lines fan out across Aragón and Spain from the **bus station** (☎976 70 05 99; www.estacion-zaragoza.es) in the Estación Intermodal Delicias.

**Alosa** (☎974 21 07 00; www.avanzabus.com) Runs 15 or more daily buses to Huesca (€8.30, 1¼ hours) and seven or more to Jaca (€17, 2½ hours).

**ALSA** (☎902 42 22 42; www.alsa.es) Buses to/from Madrid (from €17, 3½ to four hours, 27 or more daily) and Barcelona (from €16, 3½ to four hours, 21 or more daily).

**Autobuses Jiménez** (☎902 20 27 87; www.autobusesjimenez.com) Three or more daily buses to Teruel (€11, 2¼ hours).

**Conda** (www.conda.es) Eight or more daily buses to Pamplona (€16, two to 2¼ hours).

### TRAIN

**Renfe** (☎91 232 03 20; www.renfe.com) trains run all over Spain from the Estación Intermodal Delicias. Around 20 daily high-speed AVE services whizz to Madrid (€21 to €66, 1½ hours) and Barcelona (€23 to €60, 1¾ hours). Further direct AVE services head to Huesca (€7.85, 45 minutes, one or two daily) and to several Andalucian cities. Some slower, mostly cheaper trains also serve Barcelona, Madrid and Huesca. Two or three Huesca trains continue to Jaca (€15, 3¼ hours) and Canfranc-Estación (€17, four hours) in the Pyrenees. Four daily trains run to Teruel (€15 to €21, 2½ hours), and three to Valencia (€35, five hours).

## ℹ Getting Around

**Bus 501** (☎902 49 06 90) runs between Paseo María Agustín 7 and the airport (€1.85, 45 minutes) via Delicias station every half-hour (hourly on Sunday). **Bus 34** (€1.35) runs about every 10 minutes from the Estación Intermodal Delicias to Avenida César Augusto on the western fringe of the central area. To return to the station, catch it westbound on Calle Conde Aranda, 100m west of Avenida César Augusto.

### BICYCLE

Zaragoza is flat and has a good network of bike lanes and streets with speed limits of 30km/h. With a €50 deposit, you can rent bikes at the friendly cafe-bar **La Ciclería** (☎876 16 73 56; www.lacicleria.com; Calle Gavín 6; per 2/4/8/24/48hr €6/8/12/15/22; ⏲9am-2pm & 5-10pm Mon-Sat, 10am-2pm Sun, closed Sun Jul & Aug) and at **Bicicletas La Pomada** (☎876 03 62 69; www.lapomadabikestore.com; Calle Manifestación 17; per 2hr/half-day/day €5/6/12; ⏲10am-2pm & 4.30-8.30pm Mon-Fri, 10am-2pm Sat).

# CENTRAL ARAGÓN

Central Aragón is dominated by the flat valley of the Río Ebro, which meanders across the region west to east.

## Fuendetodos

POP 110

The tiny village of Fuendetodos, 45km south of Zaragoza and 25km east of Cariñena, is where Francisco José de Goya y Lucientes (Goya) was born in 1746.

**Casa Natal de Goya** MUSEUM

(www.fundacionfuendetodosgoya.org; Plaza de Goya; incl Museo del Grabado de Goya adult/child €3/free; ⏲11am-2pm & 4-7pm Tue-Sun) Goya's humble birthplace was owned by his family until the early 20th century. The great man himself spent just his first month here, his mother having returned to Fuendetodos for his birth in 1746 while the family house in Zaragoza was being rebuilt. The Fuendetodos house was wrecked during the civil war, but subsequently restored with furniture and exhibits relating to Goya's life and times.

**Museo del Grabado de Goya** MUSEUM

(www.fundacionfuendetodosgoya.org; Calle Zuloaga 3; incl Casa Natal de Goya adult/child €3/free; ⏲11am-2pm & 4-7pm Tue-Sun) This museum contains an important collection of Goya's engravings, and acts as the ticket office for the Casa Natal de Goya, 100m along the street. There are prints from three main series, all very dark and disturbing: *Los caprichos* (Caprices; 1797–99), *Desastres de la guerra* (Disasters of War; 1810–15) and *Disparates* (Nonsenses; 1815–19) – though you don't actually need to come here to see them, as they're also on display in Zaragoza's Museo Goya (p393).

## ℹ Getting There & Away

One or two buses daily head to Fuendetodos (€6.80, one hour) from Zaragoza.

## Tarazona

POP 10,260 / ELEV 480M

A pleasant stop between Zaragoza and the Basque Country or Castilla y León, Tarazona rewards the curious with an intriguing ochre-toned labyrinth of an old town, a large and fascinating Gothic and Mudéjar cathedral and, a few kilometres outside town, the beautiful Gothic Monasterio de Veruela.

## Sights

### ★Catedral Santa María de la Huerta
CATHEDRAL

(www.catedraldetarazona.es; Plaza de la Seo; adult/student & senior/child €4/3/free; ⏲10am-2pm & 4-7pm Tue-Sat, to 6pm Sun Apr-Oct, 11am-2pm Tue, 11am-2pm & 4-6pm Wed-Fri, 10am-2pm & 4-7pm Sat, 10am-2pm & 4-6pm Sun Nov-Mar) Tarazona's magnificent, multi-styled cathedral dates back to the 13th century. Its French-Gothic origins are evident in the vaulting and arches of the nave; Mudéjar influences permeate the intricate exterior masonry of the tower and dome; Renaissance artwork adorns the Capilla Mayor and the inside of the dome; and the baldachin over the main portal is a flight of baroque fancy.

An audio-guide is worth the €1.50 investment to understand the fascinating detail of the art and architecture, much of it revealed by restoration work since the 1980s.

### Ayuntamiento
ARCHITECTURE

(Town Hall; Plaza de España) The town hall's 16th-century facade is an astonishing storybook of sculpture. The larger carvings depict mythical beings (you'll spot Hercules on the left). Running along the facade's full 35m length is a frieze of hundreds of miniature mounted and walking figures, showing the parade for the papal coronation of Spanish King Carlos I as Holy Roman Emperor in Bologna in 1530.

### Palacio Episcopal
PALACE

(Bishop's Palace; Plaza Palacio; €1.50; ⏲1-2.30pm & 5.30-7.30pm Sat, 1-2.30pm & 4.30-6.30pm Sun year-round, noon-2pm & 5-7pm Tue-Fri Apr-Oct) On the site of a Muslim citadel and, subsequently, the residence of several Aragonese kings, the imposing Bishop's Palace was completed in the mid-16th century. Inside are a pretty Renaissance patio and, in the 15th-century Salón de Obispos, an outstanding series of episcopal portraits and a fine Mudéjar coffered ceiling.

### Judería
AREA

Tarazona has one of Spain's best-preserved medieval Jewish quarters, in a tight web of streets around Calle Judería, Rúa Alta de Bécquer and Rúa Baja de Bécquer. There are no actual monuments to visit, but you can take an informed stroll around the Judería with the aid of a map from the tourist office and/or explanatory boards (in Spanish, English and French) *in situ*.

### Monasterio de Veruela
MONASTERY

(☎976 64 90 25; Vera de Moncayo; adult/child €1.80/free; ⏲10.30am-8pm Tue-Sun Apr-Sep, to 6pm Tue-Sun Oct-Mar) The beautiful 12th-century Cistercian monastery of Veruela stands in a bucolic corner of the countryside 14km south of Tarazona, with the Sierra del Moncayo as an impressive backdrop. Highlights are the stately Gothic cloister with its tall fir trees and elegant *lavabo* (washing place), and the long, tall, austere monastery church. The complex also includes a wine museum explaining all about the local Campo de Borja wines, an up-and-coming DO (Denominación de Origen).

Winemaking here, as in much of Spain, owes a lot to the medieval monasteries.

## Festivals & Events

### Cipotegato
CULTURAL

(⏲27 Aug) In a country known for its bizarre festivals, Tarazona's Cipotegato takes the

> **WORTH A TRIP**
>
> **THE CIVIL WAR RUINS OF BELCHITE**
>
> The shattered buildings of the **Pueblo Viejo de Belchite** (Belchite Old Village; Belchite; tour €6), 45km southeast of Zaragoza, stand today as a haunting reminder of the horrors of the Spanish Civil War. The battle of Belchite in 1937 saw the Republicans drive out Nationalist forces from the village, with thousands killed and the buildings reduced to ruins. The Nationalists later retook Belchite (and won the war). They ordered that the village be left in its ruined state and had the new village built by Republican prisoners nearby. The ruins are now fenced off but guided tours (in Spanish, with English and French audio-guides available) are given two or three times daily by **Belchite tourist office** (☎976 83 07 71; www.belchite.es; Calle Becú, Pueblo Nuevo de Belchite; ⏲9.30am-1.30pm & 3-7pm, to 8pm Jul & Aug), situated next to the church in Belchite's new village. At any time you can view the ruins from outside the fence. They include four churches from the 18th century or earlier (one of them almost completely destroyed except for its Mudéjar clock tower).

weirdness to a new level. The star of the show is a hapless harlequin dressed in red, green and yellow, who emerges from Ayuntamiento at noon on 27 August and runs through the streets getting pelted with tomatoes by practically everyone in town.

## Sleeping & Eating

**Hostal Santa Águeda** HOSTAL €
(☎976 64 00 54; www.santaagueda.com; Calle Visconti 26; incl breakfast s €41-50, d €54-63; ) This 200-year-old home just off the central Plaza San Francisco has attractive old-style rooms with wooden beams, terracotta-tile floors and cheery decor. The little breakfast room and the lobby are a glorious shrine to local girl Raquel Meller, Aragón's queen of popular song in the early 20th century. You'll hear her crooning over your *tostadas*.

**Hotel Condes de Visconti** HOTEL €€
(☎976 64 49 08; www.condesdevisconti.com; Calle Visconti 15; r €56-72, ste €75-110; ) Beautiful rooms, mostly with colourful individual decor, plus a preserved Renaissance patio, make this 16th-century former palace a fine stopover. It also has a restaurant and good old-fashioned service. Breakfast is €6.60.

**Saboya 21** ARAGONESE €€€
(☎976 64 24 90; www.restaurantesaboya21.com; Calle Marrodán 34; mains €20-28, set menus €17-44; ⊙1-4pm Mon-Thu, 1-4pm & 9.30-11pm Fri, 1.30-4pm & 9.30-11pm Sat, 1.30-4pm Sun; ) Talented chef José Tazueco whips up a selection of culinary treats that zap traditional ingredients with a creative flair. Expect artistically presented dishes such as grilled turbot with caramelised spring onions or Iberian pork tenderloin with capsicum ragout. The lunch *menú*, including wine, is a good deal. The restaurant is upstairs from Cafetería Amadeo I. Reservations recommended.

## Information

**Tourist Office** (☎976 64 00 74; www.tarazona.es; Plaza San Francisco 1; tours €5-9; ⊙9.30am-2.30pm & 4-7pm Apr-Sep, 9.30am-2pm & 4-7pm Mon-Sat, 10am-6pm Sun Oct-Mar)

## Getting There & Away

Four or more **Therpasa** (☎976 64 11 00; www.therpasa.es; Avenida de Navarra) buses run daily to/from Zaragoza (€9.60, one to 1½ hours) and Soria (€7.40, one hour).

# THE ARAGÓN PYRENEES

As you leave behind central Aragón's parched flatlands, a hint of green tinges the landscape and there's a growing anticipation of very big mountains up ahead. The Aragonese Pyrenees reach well over the 3000m mark and, together with their counterparts on the French side, form the heart of the range, with much of its most magnificent scenery. Viewed from the south, their crenellated ridges fill the northern horizon wherever you look. The verdant river valleys are dotted with old stone-built villages, and the whole region forms a giant adventure playground to which Spaniards and in-the-know foreigners flock for wonderful walking and a host of other exciting activities.

## Huesca

POP 51,700 / ELEV 465M

The hard-working provincial capital of Huesca is a gateway to the northern mountains. It doesn't delay most travellers too long, but while here you can visit a multifarious museum juxtaposing Goya prints with a medieval palace, and take an eye-opening lesson in Gothic and Romanesque architecture courtesy of two outstanding churches.

### Sights

★**Catedral de Santa María** CATHEDRAL
(www.museo.diocesisdehuesca.org; Plaza de la Catedral; adult/child €4/free; ⊙10.30am-2pm & 4-6pm Mon-Fri, 10.30am-2pm Sat Mar-Jun & Sep-Oct, 10.30am-2pm & 4-7pm Mon-Sat Jul-Aug, 10.30am-2pm Mon-Sat Nov-Jan) This Gothic cathedral is one of Aragón's great surprises. The richly carved main portal dates from 1300, and the attached **Museo Diocesano** contains the cathedral's superbly carved 16th-century choir stalls, plus some extraordinary frescoes and painted altarpieces. The stately interior features a brilliant 16th-century alabaster altarpiece by Damián Forment showing scenes from Christ's crucifixion. Ascend the 180 steps of the **bell tower** for 360-degree views all the way to the Sierra de Guara.

★**Iglesia de San Pedro El Viejo** CHURCH
(www.sanpedroelviejo.com; Plaza de San Pedro; adult/child €2.50/1.50; ⊙11am-1pm & 5-6pm Mon, 10am-1.30pm & 3.30-7.30pm Tue-Fri, 10am-2pm & 3.30-7.30pm Sat, 11am-12.15pm & 1-2pm Sun Jun-Sep, 10am-1.30pm & 4.30-6pm Mon-Sat, 11am-12.15pm & 1-2pm Sun Oct-May) San Pedro

## ACTIVE ADVENTURES IN THE PYRENEES

With its wild and varied terrain, Aragón is Spain's natural adventure playground. The high point, literally, is the Aragonese Pyrenees, arguably the wildest and most stunning section of the Pyrenees either side of the Spanish–French border. There are plenty of chances to get up close and personal with the peaks and passes, with rock climbing (including a growing number of vie ferrate), mountain trails and snowy slopes providing year-round scope for adrenaline-charged outdoor activities.

Folk who prefer a gentler stroll can head for the foothills in places such as the awe-inspiring Parque Nacional de Ordesa y Monte Perdido with its waterfalls, crystal streams, cliffs and canyons. Aínsa and Benasque are burgeoning mountain-bike centres; water-sports fans can take the plunge with rafting, kayaking and canoeing on the Ríos Gállego and Ésera; canyon lovers can slide, jump and abseil down gorges around Alquézar and elsewhere; and paragliders can take to the air around Castejón de Sos. Montaña Segura (www.montanasegura.com) has a great deal of useful info about walks and climbs in Aragón's mountains, including walking route information in English and French in its 'Folletos' (Leaflets) section.

### Birdwatching

This is one of Europe's best regions for raptors, and birdwatchers flock here to spot red and black kites; Egyptian, griffon, and threatened lammergeier vultures; and, among the highest peaks, the majestic golden eagle. Even non-enthusiasts will be thrilled by vulture-viewing at the Miradores de Revilla (p413) or the cliffs at Riglos.

The regional tourism body has detailed information on 17 *rutas ornitológicas* spread all over Aragón (www.turismodearagon.com/aragon-listados/rutas-ornitologicas). Birders can also check www.birdingpirineos.com (for northwest Aragón) and www.birdingaragon.com.

is one of the oldest and most important Romanesque churches in Spain, dating from the early 12th century. Its open cloister is adorned with 38 beautifully carved Romanesque capitals, and its mausoleum contains the tombs of two Aragonese kings: the brothers Alfonso I (r 1104–34) and Ramiro II (r 1134–37).

**Museo de Huesca** MUSEUM
(Plaza Universidad 1; ⏲10am-2pm & 5-8pm Tue-Sat, 10am-2pm Sun) FREE The city museum, partly housed in a 12th-century Aragonese royal palace, contains well-displayed archaeology and early modern art collections, including several works by Goya. Note the 1880 canvas *La campana de Huesca* (The Bell of Huesca) by José Casado del Alisal, depicting a gruesome episode in which King Ramiro II had 13 uncooperative nobles decapitated. The event is believed to have occurred in the suitably gloomy Sala de la Campana, in the museum's palace section.

## Sleeping

**La Posada de la Luna** BOUTIQUE HOTEL €
(☎974 24 08 57; www.posadadelaluna.com; Calle Joaquín Costa 10; s €46-51, d €55-60; P❄📶) This attractive little eight-room hotel achieves a whimsical contemporary yet historical effect, juxtaposing century-old floor tiles and antique-style murals with designer bathrooms, in rooms themed on different celestial bodies. It's a comfortable place with a degree of charm, although some rooms are on the small side.

The Posada acts as reception for **Hostal Joaquín Costa** (Hostal Un Punto Chic; ☎974 24 17 74; www.hostaljoaquincosta.com; Calle Joaquín Costa 20; s €41-46, d €50-60; ❄📶) a few doors away, under the same management and also a convenient and comfy place to stay.

**Hotel Sancho Abarca** HOTEL €€
(☎974 22 06 50; www.hotelsanchoabarca.com; Coso Alto 52; s/d/ste incl breakfast €87/117/174; ❄📶) This stylish abode, close to all the old-city attractions, features parts of Huesca's Roman and medieval fortifications exposed to view within. Rooms are very comfy, with glass-walled bathrooms sporting big shower heads. There's a good Spanish-cuisine restaurant, and room rates include evening use of the top-floor spa.

## Eating

Tapas bars and lively outdoor tables are centred on Calle Padre Huesca, which runs south off Coso Bajo, just south of the old town.

**Tatau Bistro** TAPAS €€
(☎974 04 20 78; www.tatau.es; Calle Azara; dishes €6-24; ⏱1-3.30pm & 8.30-10.30pm Tue-Sat; 📶) This hugely popular gastro-bar has besuited staff, 1950s-inspired decor and seating at a few tables or along the bar. The changing menu of artistically presented offerings ranges from the relatively simple (meat croquettes) to the likes of trout tartare or succulent pressed duck. Servings are mostly small to medium-size, so be ready to order a few – and arrive early, or book ahead.

**El Origen** ARAGONESE €€€
(☎974 22 97 45; www.elorigenhuesca.com; Plaza del Justicia 4; mains €19-22, set menus €18-45; ⏱1.15-3.30pm & 9-11pm Mon, Tue & Thu-Sat, 1.15-3.30pm Sun, closed 1st half Sep) El Origen is an oasis of elegance and fine dining, with set menus that vary from traditional Aragonese to more innovative and seasonal. Organic produce is used as far as possible. Reservations recommended.

## Information

**Tourist Office** (☎974 29 21 70; www.huesca-turismo.com; Plaza López Allué 1; ⏱9am-2pm & 4-8pm) Excellent office providing information on all of Aragón.

## Getting There & Away

Buses and trains all start from the combined **Estación Intermodal** (Calle Gil Cávez 10).

**Avanza** (☎902 21 07 00; www.avanzabus.com) runs buses to/from Zaragoza (€8.30, one hour, 14 or more daily), Jaca (€8.05, 1¼ hours, six or more daily), Barbastro (€4.80, one hour, seven or more daily), Barcelona (€12, 3½ to four hours, six or more daily) and Benasque (€14, 2¾ hours, once on Sunday, twice other days).

Six to eight trains a day run to/from Zaragoza: one or two are high-speed AVE services (from €7.85, 40 minutes), continuing to/from Madrid (€22 to €58, 2¼ hours); the rest are regional trains (€7.40, one hour). Two or three regional trains run to/from Jaca (€8.55, two hours) and Canfranc-Estación (€11, 2¾ hours).

# Riglos & Around

POP (RIGLOS) 80 / ELEV (RIGLOS) 650M

Tiny Riglos, 43km northwest of Huesca, sits at the foot of the **Mallos de Riglos**, an awe-inspiring set of red rock towers that dwarf the village and wouldn't look out of place in the Grand Canyon. Los Mallos are a magnificent challenge for serious rock climbers – and popular too with large numbers of huge nesting griffon vultures.

For those who prefer to keep their feet on non-vertical terrain, a circular walk of about 2½ hours (plus stops), the **Camino del Cielo**, takes you around the top side of Los Mallos from Riglos.

**Murillo de Gállego** village on the A132, 2.5km southwest of Riglos across the Río Gállego (a 45-minute walk or 10km by road), is a busy centre for rafting and kayaking beneath the gaze of Los Mallos. Several companies offer half-day trips (per person from €40) from March to September.

There are several *casas rurales* (rural houses adapted for tourist accommodation) and *hostales* in both villages.

Riglos is on the Zaragoza–Canfranc railway, between Huesca (€3.80, one hour) and Jaca (€5.65, 1¼ hours), with two or three trains each way daily.

# Sos del Rey Católico

POP 490 / ELEV 625M

If King Fernando II of Aragón were reincarnated today, he'd probably still recognise his modest birthplace in Sos del Rey Católico. Take away the summer tourist crowds and outwardly not a huge amount has changed in this tightly packed hilltop village since 1452, when the future husband of Isabel of Castilla was born in the Sada palace. Legend has it that Fernando's mother travelled

WORTH A TRIP

### THE CASTILLO DE LOARRE

This much-visited, multi-towered, Reconquista-era **castle** (www.castillo-deloarre.es; Loarre; adult/child €5.50/4; ⏱10am-8pm mid-Jun–mid-Sep, to 7pm Mar–mid-Jun & mid-Sep–Oct, 11am-5.30pm Tue-Sun Nov-Feb; P 👪) looms dramatically on the hillside above Loarre village, 30km northwest of Huesca, and a 5km drive or 2km uphill walk from village to castle. The fortress, reminiscent of a crusader castle, was raised in the 11th century in what was then Christian/Muslim frontier territory by Sancho III of Navarra and expanded by Sancho Ramírez of Aragón. There's plenty to see, including a Romanesque chapel and crypt, and you can climb to the upper levels of the two main towers.

14km on horseback from Sangüesa in Navarra while already in labour, purely to ensure her son was born Aragonese. Royalty aside, Sos is a fine place to soak up the feel of an old Aragonese village, with its labyrinth of streets lined by stone houses.

## Sights

**Casa Palacio de Sada** HISTORIC BUILDING
(Plaza de la Hispanidad; adult/child €2.90/1.90; 10am-1pm & 4-7pm Mon-Fri, 10am-2pm & 4-7pm Sat & Sun, closed Mon Sep-Jun) Fernando II of Aragón was born in this building in 1452. It's an impressive mansion – more so now than back then, following a major expansion around 1600 and 20th-century restoration. The rooms contain Spanish-language information panels on Fernando's highly eventful and historically significant life, plus a model of Sos village in wood and a chapel where an audiovisual on Sos' history is shown.

**Iglesia de San Esteban** CHURCH
(Calle Salud; €1; 10am-1pm & 4-6pm Mon-Sat, 10am-12.30pm Sun) This Romanesque-Gothic church, with a weathered Romanesque portal, has a deliciously gloomy crypt decorated with medieval frescos.

**Castillo de la Peña Feliciano** CASTLE
The 12th-century keep and some of the walls are all that remain of the castle that once guarded the frontier between the two Christian kingdoms of Aragón and Navarra. Climb up for views over the village roofs.

## Sleeping

**Hostal Las Coronas** HOSTAL €
(948 88 84 08; www.hostallascoronas.com; Calle Pons Sorolla 2; s/d €43/59; ) Run by friendly Fernando, Las Coronas, on Sos' hauntingly hemmed-in plaza, has modest, rustic rooms. The ground-floor bar serves a good breakfast (€5), *bocadillos* (filled rolls), salads and greasy *platos combinados* (€12 to €19) to a refreshing classical soundtrack.

**Parador de Sos del Rey Católico** HOTEL €€
(948 88 80 11; www.parador.es; Calle Arquitecto Sainz de Vicuña 1; s/d incl breakfast from €92/109; mid-Feb–Dec; ) Though built in the 1970s, Sos' *parador* (luxurious state-owned hotel) is in harmony with the town's old architecture and provides all the expected services and comforts. You can sink sangrías on the restaurant terrace, or just lie back and enjoy your suitably regal bedroom. To ensure views, book a 'superior' room.

**Ruta del Tiempo** BOUTIQUE HOTEL €€
(948 88 82 95; www.rutadeltiempo.es; Plaza de la Villa; incl breakfast s €50, d €70-110; ) Evocatively located under the arches of the central plaza, this little family-run hotel has 1st-floor rooms themed around three Aragonese kings, while the four 2nd-floor rooms are dedicated to different continents. They all have charm, but spacious 'Asia' and 'Africa' are the best.

**El Peirón** BOUTIQUE HOTEL €€
(948 88 82 83; www.elpeiron.com; Calle Fernando el Católico 24; s from €75, d €85-140; Mar-Dec; ) Family-run El Peirón is an appealing mix of thick stone walls, wrought iron, period decor, contemporary art and ample bathrooms. It has 14 rooms, including two suites set in one of the old town gates, the Puerta de Zaragoza.

## Eating

**Landa Terraza** SPANISH €
(Calle Fernando el Católico 37; dishes €4-9, set menu €14; 9am-midnight; ) Straightforward food at very good prices, served with good humour, packs in the punters to this smallish bar and its bright open-air terrace. You could go for a *ración* or *media ración* of eggs and ham, or *longaniza* sausage with *setas* (wild mushrooms).

**La Cocina del Principal** ARAGONESE €€€
(948 88 83 48; www.lacocinadelprincipal.es; Calle Fernando el Católico 13; mains €19-26, set menu €28; 1.30-3.30pm & 8.30-10.30pm Tue-Sat Mar-Nov, by reservation Dec-Feb) This place wins plaudits for its roast *ternasco*, barbecued beef tenderloin and *pochas viudas*, a local beans-and-veggies stew. It's set down steps that seem to lead to a basement cellar but reveal a stone-walled dining room with a panoramic terrace.

## Information

**Tourist Office** (948 88 85 24; www.oficinaturismososdelreycatolico.com; Plaza Hispanidad; tours adult/child €4.40/1.90, incl Palacio de Sada €6.40/2.90; 10am-1pm & 4-7pm Mon-Fri, 10am-2pm & 4-7pm Sat & Sun, closed Mon Sep-Jun) Housed in the Palacio de Sada.

## Getting There & Away

**Autobuses Cinco Villas** (976 33 33 71; www.autobusescincovillas.com) runs a bus from Sos to Zaragoza (€13, 2¾ hours) at 7am Monday to Friday, returning at 5pm.

# Valles de Hecho & Ansó

These enchanting parallel river valleys, tucked away in Aragón's far northwest corner, run up through dense woodlands, punctuated by a few charming stone-built villages, between crags of increasing height and drama, to end at the main Pyrenean ridge along the French border. Little known to non-Spaniards, these valleys and mountains are a paradise for walkers, with everything from one-hour strolls to long-day peak ascents or multi-day hiking tours, on clear trails amid gorgeous scenery. There's plentiful accommodation.

Weather is never predictable, but June to October are generally the best months for hiking. The 1:25,000 map *Valles Occidentales Ansó-Echo,* published by Prames, is very useful. Local tourist offices have some printed route information, and there are route descriptions, maps and data in English at http://montanasegura.com/folletos-de-excursiones-por-valles.

## Getting There & Around

The good A176 road heads up to Hecho and Ansó villages (13km apart) from Puente la Reina on the N240. Lesser but adequate roads head up the valleys, fully paved as far as Selva da Oza from Hecho and Zuriza and the Refugio de Linza from Ansó.

Your own set of wheels is the best way to explore these remote valleys. **Autocares Escartín** (974 36 05 08; www.autocaresescartin.es) runs a daily (except Sundays) evening bus service from Jaca bus station to Hecho (€3.60, 1¼ hours), continuing to Siresa and Ansó. The return service starts back in the early morning.

## Hecho

POP 570 / ELEV 820M

There are few more pleasant spots from which to launch lung-stretching sorties into the Pyrenees than little Hecho (Echo), an attractive warren of stone houses with steep roofs, tall chimneys and flower-decked balconies.

**Val d'Echo Activa** ADVENTURE SPORTS

(974 37 54 21; www.valdechoactiva.com; Carretera de Oza 2; half-day per person €45-50; ) This professional firm offers a host of active adventures including exciting canyoning in the Boca del Infierno gorge and the Barranco del Hospital near Siresa, guided mountain hikes, and a via ferrata in the Selva de Oza.

**Casa Blasquico** HOSTAL €

(974 37 50 07; www.casablasquico.es; Plaza La Fuente 1; s/tr €50/75, d €55-60; Mar-Dec; ) The best place to stay in town, family-run Casa Blasquico has just seven rooms, so it's a good idea to book ahead. With its flower boxes, gables and woody decor, it might have been plucked out of the Swiss Alps. Great breakfasts available too.

It's also home to the excellent **Restaurante Gaby** (mains €13-20, set menu €25; 1.30-3.30pm & 8.30-10pm Mar-Dec; ), offering expertly prepared, uncomplicated mountain fare: the wild-mushroom crêpes, duck confit and *solomillo de ternera* (beef tenderloin) are all great, and there's an extensive wine list. Reservations advisable.

**Restaurante Canteré** SPANISH €€

(974 37 52 14; www.facebook.com/restaurante.cantere; Calle Aire 1; mains €15-25, set menu €24; 1.30-3.30pm & 8.30-10.30pm Jul-Sep, 1.30-1.30pm Thu-Tue Oct-Jun) Creative preparation of classic ingredients and welcoming service in a bright, contemporary-style dining room are the secrets of success here. The four-course *menú* is too tempting to overlook: options might include pumpkin pie with duck confit, beef entrecôte, or hake with mushrooms *au gratin* – and you can try every dessert on offer if you like!

## Information

**Tourist Office** (974 37 55 05, town hall 974 37 50 02; www.valledehecho.es; Carretera de Oza; 10am-1.30pm & 5.30-8pm Jul & Aug, 10am-1.30pm & 5.30-8pm Sat & Sun Jun & Sep)

## Siresa

POP 110 / ELEV 870M

Tiny Siresa, a couple of kilometres north of Hecho, is where medieval Christian Aragón got its start in life.

**Iglesia de San Pedro** CHURCH

(€2; 11am-1pm & 5-8pm Jul-Sep, 11am-1pm & 4-6pm Sat & Sun Oct-Jun) This imposing, thick-walled church was founded in the 9th century as part of a monastery that formed the hub of the nascent County of Aragón (a small Christian bridgehead on the south side of the Pyrenees following the Moorish conquests a century earlier). It was rebuilt in Romanesque style in the 11th century. Artworks inside include a wonderful Gothic crucifixion sculpture in polychromed wood, discovered during a 1990s restoration.

**Hotel Castillo d'Acher** HOTEL €

(☎974 37 53 13; www.castillodacher.com; Plaza Mayor; s/d/tr/q €45/55/75/80; ) This stone-built hotel has pleasant rooms, pine-furnished and relatively modern, and the spacious in-house restaurant does hearty *menús del día* (set menus) for €16 or €24.

**Hotel Usón** HOTEL €€

(☎974 37 53 58; www.hoteluson.com; Carretera Selva de Oza, Km 7; s €45-55, d €55-85; ⏰Apr-Oct; P) Cosy rooms in peaceful, wonderfully scenic surroundings are what you'll find here, 5km north of Siresa on the road to the Selva de Oza. A good base for walkers and birdwatchers, the Usón also serves decent home-style meals (breakfast/dinner €7/17), and the superb Pirineos Bier craft beer is brewed right here on the spot.

## Selva de Oza

The top end of the Valle de Hecho is particularly beautiful; the road runs parallel to the Río Aragón Subordán as it bubbles its way through thick woodlands. Around 7km beyond Siresa, the road squeezes into the **Boca del Infierno** (Hell's Mouth) gorge, emerging after 3km at the Puente de Oza bridge among the dense forests of the Selva de Oza. From here it continues another 3km, partly paved, to the junction of valleys and paths known as **La Mina** (A Mina).

The ascent of **Castillo d'Acher** (2384m) from the Puente de Oza is a magnificent if quite tough hike of three to four hours, and the same coming down, with 1300m of ascent and descent. Starting through shady woodlands, the trail gets steeper as you climb, especially on the approach to the rocky 'crown' ringing the mountain top.

Day hikes starting from La Mina include the trails up to **Puerto del Palo** pass on the French border, following the route of a Roman road across the Pyrenees (about five hours round trip; 750m ascent and descent); and to **Ibón d'Estanés** lake via **Aguas Tuertas** meadows. For this last you can drive 4.5km east (unpaved) from La Mina to shorten the walk to about 3½ hours each way (600m ascent and descent).

An easier, shorter hike of around 3½ hours (520m of ascent and descent) is the circuit round Boca del Infierno gorge from Puente de Santana bridge, which includes a stretch of the same Roman road.

**Camping Selva de Oza** CAMPGROUND €

(☎974 56 55 15; www.camping-selvadeoza.com; adult/tent/car €6/6/5.50, s/d/tr/q incl breakfast from €40/60/85/110; ⏰Easter-early Nov; ) This freshly maintained campground has a lovely riverside site among trees, a restaurant, a bar and seven decent pine-panelled rooms with well-sprung beds. You can rent tents for €25/40 single/double.

## Ansó

POP 430 / ELEV 840M

With a grid of narrow streets lined by neatly trimmed, slate-roofed, stone houses with flowery window boxes, Ansó is undoubtedly one of Spain's prettiest villages. It sits above the Río Veral, surrounded by beautiful mountain and forest vistas. The two focal points for your wanderings are the compact main square, Plaza Domingo Miral, home to the helpful **tourist office** (☎974 37 02 25; www.turismoanso.es; ⏰10am-1pm & 5-8pm Jul-mid-Sep, 5-8pm Fri, 10am-1pm & 5-8pm Sat, 10am-1pm Sun May & Jun), and the surprisingly large 16th-century Iglesia de San Pedro.

**★Posada Magoria** CASA RURAL €

(☎974 37 00 49; http://posadamagoria.com; Calle Milagros 32; d €50-63; ⏰closed Sun-Thu Nov-Easter; ) Just below the church, delightful Posada Magoria is crammed with vintage character and lovingly kept by a family with lots of local knowledge. The kitchen cooks up excellent vegan meals (dinner €10 to €16, breakfast €6), largely sourced from their own organic garden, and served at a long communal table. There's good organic wine to go with dinner too.

**Hostal Kimboa** HOSTAL €

(☎650 987837; www.hostalkimboa.com; Paseo Chapitel 24; s/d incl breakfast €45/60, incl half-board €50/85; ⏰Semana Santa-Oct; ) A welcoming family-owned *hostal* towards the top of the village, with pleasant pine-furnished rooms above a good restaurant specialising in traditional grilled meats (*menús* €15 to €35).

## Valle de Zuriza

Beyond the Foz Veral gorge, 11km north of Ansó, the valley widens into the Valle de Zuriza, a beautiful area of pastures, woodlands and rivers, where a few minor roads and some fine walking trails meet.

Eastward, it's a fine walk of about three hours each way up to the **Cuello Petrafi-cha** pass and back, with some 750m of ascent and descent. A bit more demanding is the ascent of **Achar d'Alano** (2078m; about seven hours round trip). You can cut half an hour each way off both these routes by driving the unpaved road as far as A Taxera.

A northward road heads 5km to the **Refugio de Linza**, a hikers' refuge with restaurant and bar, open all year. This is the starting point for **Mesa de los Tres Reyes** (2448m), at the meeting point of Aragón, Navarra and France, a round-trip hike of about eight hours with 1275m ascent and descent – and a slightly vertiginous stretch shortly before the summit.

**Camping Zuriza** CAMPGROUND €
(☎689 940022; www.campingzuriza.es; adult/tent/car €5.50/6.50/5.50, dm €15, d with/without bathroom €55/45, bungalow for 4-6 persons €85; P) Camping Zuriza offers a range of accommodation, a simple restaurant, a food shop and superb surroundings at the heart of the valley, though parts of the site are quite tightly packed.

## San Juan de la Peña

One of Spain's most fascinating old monastic complexes, San Juan de la Peña sits high on the rocky Sierra de la Peña above the pretty, stone-built village of **Santa Cruz de la Serós**, which is 17km west of Jaca (not served by public transport). Santa Cruz itself is spread around the 11th-century Romanesque Iglesia de Santa María, originally part of Aragón's earliest convent.

★**Monasterio de San Juan de la Peña** MONASTERY
(☎974 35 51 19; www.monasteriosanjuan.com; Monasterio Viejo/incl 1 Centro/incl 2 Centros adult €7/8.50/12, child €4.50/5/7; ⏲10am-2pm & 3.30-7pm mid-Mar–May, Sep & Oct, 10am-2pm & 3-8pm Jun-Aug, 10am-2pm Sun-Fri, 10am-5pm Sat Nov–mid-Mar; P) The road from Santa Cruz winds 7km up to the 10th-century **Monasterio Viejo**, tucked protectively under an overhanging lip of rock. A fire in 1675 led the monks to desert this original site and build the **Monasterio Nuevo** 1.5km further up the hill. Abandoned by the mid-19th century, these historic monasteries have since been rehabilitated and merit a visit by anyone interested in architecture, sculpture, history, scenery or wildlife.

LOCAL KNOWLEDGE

### VIEWPOINTS & VULTURES

From the **Balcón del Pirineo**, a 400m walk north of San Juan de la Peña's Monasterio Nuevo, you have superb vistas of the Pyrenees spread across the horizon and, with luck, some of the local vultures gliding the thermals in front of you.

To find out more about the area's natural attractions, visit the **Centro de Interpretación San Juan de la Peña y Monte Oroel** (☎974 36 14 76; ⏲10am-2pm & 3-7pm late Jun-early Sep, Sat & Sun only late Apr-late Jun, 9.30am-2pm & 2.30-5pm Sat & Sun early Sep-early Dec & late Feb-Mar) FREE, next to the Monasterio Nuevo.

The Monasterio Viejo, one of the most important monasteries of old Aragón, contains the tombs of Aragón's first three kings – Ramiro I (1036–64), Sancho Ramírez (1064–94) and Pedro I (1094–1104) – and two churches (the lower one Mozarabic, the upper one Romanesque). But its greatest highlight is the **Romanesque cloister**, with marvellous carved capitals depicting stories from Genesis and the life of Christ.

The Monasterio Nuevo is a larger, twin towered, brick complex, whose main church is now the **Centro de Interpretación del Reino de Aragón**, playing a 40-minute audiovisual about Aragónese history. Beside this, the **Centro de Interpretación del Monasterio** has been built over the archaeological remains of ruined parts of the monastery: it has Spanish-language panels on the monasteries' history and the kingdom of Aragón, plus a glass floor through which you look down on somewhat cheesy life-sized tableaux of monastic life.

Tickets for both monasteries are sold at the Monasterio Nuevo, and in peak periods (Semana Santa, July, August and a few holiday weekends) this is where you'll have to park. A free bus shuttles down to the Monasterio Viejo and back. Ticket prices depend on how many of the interpretation centres you wish to visit.

**Hostal Santa Cruz** HOSTAL €
(☎974 36 19 75; www.santacruzdelaseros.com; Calle Ordana, Santa Cruz de la Serós; s/d/tr €40/60/80; P 📶) Overlooking the church in Santa Cruz de la Serós, this is a beautiful

**1.** Aínsa (p415) **2.** Ansó (404) **3.** Alquézar (p419)
**4.** Albarracín (p426)

JESSICA LIM/GETTY IMAGES ©

# Villages of Aragón

**Aragón's small villages are, perhaps, the region's most surprising revelation, all of them unique but many sharing a similarly exotic time-stood-still atmosphere. Their settings – against a backdrop of Pyrenean peaks or hidden amid isolated southern canyons – are equally beguiling.**

## Albarracín

After several weeks of dissecting Aragón's prettiest rural settlements, quite a few travellers are happy to award the Oscar to Albarracín (p426). Something about its winding lanes of warped, pink-hued houses, agreeably ruined medieval watch-towers, lovingly resuscitated monuments and craggy backdrop just seems to click.

## Aínsa

Stick a perfect grey stone village on a rocky eminence with the snow-topped peaks of the Pyrenees lined up in the distance. Add arguably Spain's loveliest medieval plaza, an unadulterated Romanesque church and streets that haven't changed much since Christians and Moors crossed swords. Call it Aínsa (p415).

## Alquézar

Activity centres are rarely this historic. Beneath the adrenaline-hungry exterior of Spain's canyoning capital lies a tranquil sandy-hued village (p419) eerily redolent of a Tuscan hill town.

## Sos del Rey Católico

Uniformly cobbled streets, the whiff of erstwhile Aragonese kings and wonderfully preserved old stone mansions make Sos (p401) a memorable stop en route to or from the Pyrenees.

## Ansó

A warren of narrow streets lined by neatly trimmed stone houses, surrounded in all directions by beautiful mountain and forest vistas, Ansó (p404) is the perfect gateway to one of the most magical and remote Aragón Pyrenees valleys. Hecho, just a few kilometres away, is almost as quaint.

place with friendly service and eight charming rooms. It closes for a few weeks per year; check the website. Downstairs are a bar where you can get a *bocadillo*, and a restaurant serving steaks, venison and wild boar ragout, with good set menus (€14 to €18; closed Mondays except in August).

# Jaca

POP 11,800 / ELEV 820M

A gateway to the western Aragón Pyrenees, Jaca has a compact, attractive and mostly traffic-free old town, dotted with good bars and restaurants and remnants of its past as the 11th-century capital of the early Aragón kingdom. Summer tourism in July and August, and après-ski fun on winter weekends, keep a lively atmosphere into the night.

## Sights

**★Museo Diocesano** MUSEUM

(www.diocesisdejaca.org; Plaza de la Catedral; adult/child €6/3; 10am-2pm & 4-8.30pm Jul & Aug, 10am-1.30pm & 4-7pm Mon-Fri, 10am-1.30pm & 4-8pm Sat, 10am-1.30pm Sun Sep-Jun) The star turn of the excellent Diocesan Museum (accessed from inside the Catedral de San Pedro) is a collection of Romanesque and Gothic art rescued from Jaca diocese churches – most notably the recreation of the Bagüés village church whose 11th-century murals amount to one of the finest sets of European Romanesque painting.

The rest of the exhibits are by no means ballast. Check out the musical instruments, and the fine Gothic art upstairs.

**Catedral de San Pedro** CATHEDRAL

(Plaza de la Catedral; 11am-1.30pm & 4.15-8pm) Jaca's 11th-century cathedral is a formidable building, typical of the sturdy stone architecture of northern Aragón. It was once more gracefully French Romanesque in style, but Gothic and Renaissance alterations bequeathed a hybrid look. The interior retains some fine features, notably the northwest-corner chapel dedicated to Santa Orosia, Jaca's patron saint, whose martyrdom is depicted in mysterious murals.

**Ciudadela** FORTRESS

(Citadel; www.ciudadeladejaca.es; Avenida del Primer Viernes de Mayo; adult/senior & child €5/4, incl Museo de Miniaturas Militares €8/5; 10.30am-1.30pm & 4-8pm Apr-Jun & Sep–mid-Oct, 10.30am-1.30pm & 4.30-8.30pm Jul-Aug, 10.30am-1.30pm & 3.30-7.30pm mid-Oct–Mar) Jaca's large, star-shaped citadel, built in the 1590s to defend against possible French invasion, is surrounded by an equally star-shaped moat inhabited by a herd of deer. Inside, you can explore the bastions, casemates, powder magazines and chapel as well as the broad central Patio de Armas.

The citadel also hosts the surprisingly good **Museo de Miniaturas Militares** (www.museominiaturasjaca.es), a model soldier museum with detailed battle scenes providing a visual military history lesson from Hannibal's elephants to Franco's fascist tanks.

## Sleeping

**Hostal París** HOSTAL €

(974 36 10 20; www.hostalparisjaca.com; Plaza de San Pedro 5; with shared bathroom s €32-35, d €38-46; ) Close to the cathedral, the friendly París has high ceilings, creaky wooden floorboards, spotless, ample-sized rooms and smart shared bathrooms. Many rooms overlook the square.

**Jolio Jaca** HOTEL €

(974 36 13 67; www.joliojaca.com; Calle Carmen 23; s €40-45, d €48-80; ) The recently revamped Jolio offers 27 bright, all exterior, medium-size rooms, with light pine and blue or green trim giving a Nordic feel. There's a bright ground-floor cafe and a basement room for the €7 buffet breakfast.

**★Hotel Barosse** BOUTIQUE HOTEL €€€

(974 36 05 82; www.barosse.com; Calle Estiras 4, Barós; incl breakfast s €110-166, d €138-208; ) In a quiet hamlet 2km south of Jaca, Hotel Barosse has five individually styled rooms with lovely attention to detail, from exposed stone walls and splashes of colour to fine bathroom packages of goodies. A cosy sitting and reading room, pretty garden, spa, honesty bar and fine Pyrenees views all help make this a delightful, adults-only base.

Owners José and Gustavo are wonderful hosts, and prepare terrific dinners (€26 to €28) on request.

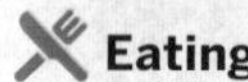

## Eating

**★La Tasca de Ana** TAPAS €

(Calle de Ramiro I 3; tapas €1.80-3.60, raciones €3-9; 12.30-3.30pm & 7.30pm-midnight Jul-Sep, 7-11.30pm Mon-Fri, 12.30-3.30pm & 7-11.30pm Sat & Sun Oct-Jun; ) One of Aragón's best tapas bars – hence the crowds – La Tasca has tempting options lined up along the bar, more choices cooked to order and a well-priced list of local wines. Check out its blackboard of *tapas mas solicitados* (most popular orders). Top contenders include the *tostada* topped with goat's cheese, *trigueros* (asparagus) and a hard-boiled egg.

**Baviera Jaca** SPANISH **€€**
(Calle Sancho Ramírez 6; dishes €12-22; ⏲8-10.30pm Tue-Wed, 1-3.30pm & 8-10.30pm Thu-Sun) Baviera has an old-style tavern appearance with a long (exceptionally well-stocked) wooden bar, tiled floor and walls, and a check-cloth dining area at one end. Delicious food offerings – some for sharing, some served as one-person plates – are prepared from market-fresh ingredients including seafood from Galicia and quality meats.

Star choices include the *huevos rotos de corral* (broken free-range eggs), served either with Iberian ham and potato slices or with boletus mushrooms, truffle and foie gras.

## Information

**Tourist Office** (☎974 36 00 98; www.jaca.es; Plaza de San Pedro 11-13; ⏲9am-9pm Mon-Sat, to 3pm Sun Jul & Aug, 9am-1.30pm & 4.30-7.30pm Mon-Sat Sep-Jun)

## Getting There & Away

From the central **bus station** (☎974 35 50 60; Plaza Biscós), seven or more Avanza (www.avanzabus.com) buses go daily to Huesca (€8.05, 1¼ hours) and Zaragoza (€17, 2¼ hours). La Burundesa (www.laburundesa.com) runs one or two daily services to Pamplona (€7.80, 1¾ hours).

Two or three daily trains go south to Huesca (€8.55, 2¼ hours) and Zaragoza (€15, 3¼ hours). Two head north to Canfranc-Estación (€2.90, 35 minutes).

# Valle del Aragón

From Jaca the N330 road runs north up the valley of the Río Aragón between impressive mountains, heading for 1640m-high Puerto de Somport pass on the French border. The river lent its name to the small Christian county born here and in the nearby Valles de Hecho and Ansó in the 8th century, and as the county grew into a powerful kingdom it carried the name with it. Today, apart from being a route to France's Vallée d'Aspe (with the 8.6km-long Somport tunnel now providing an alternative to the pass), the Valle del Aragón is home to the extraordinary Canfranc train station and the Astún and Candanchú ski resorts (p410).

There are beautiful summer day walks in side valleys including the Valle de Izás east has information.

Astún's **Telesilla a los Lagos chairlift** (www.astun.com; round-trip adult/child €11/7; ⏲9.30am-5pm Jul & Aug) operates in summer. From the top you can spend a half-day walking round seven mountain lakes either side of the French border.

**Estación Internacional de Canfranc** ARCHITECTURE
(Canfranc International Station; Canfranc-Estación; tour adult/child €4/1.50) The magnificent, 250m-long, Modernista structure of Canfranc station stands as a monument to a trans-Pyrenean railway that has lain idle for half a century – but, it's hoped, will be reopening again, with a project under way to rehabilitate the line and create a luxury hotel/residential complex at the station.

The station originally opened in 1928, housing customs and immigration on the then-new line between Zaragoza and Pau (France). The line and station closed in 1970, when a bridge collapsed on the French side.

Railway nuts and lovers of decaying grandeur will enjoy the 40-minute guided tours given by **Canfranc tourist office** (☎974 37 31 41; www.canfranc.es; Plaza del Ayuntamiento, Canfranc-Estación; ⏲9am-8pm Jul–mid-Sep, 9.30am-1.30pm & 4.30-8pm Tue-Sat, 9.30am-1.30pm Sun mid-Sep–Jun), which are the only way of visiting the now dilapidated grand edifice. The tours, in Spanish (with English and French audio-guides) go at various times daily; reservations are essential.

The station's short history is a fascinating one: during WWII it was a nest of pro-Allied spies who helped Jews and Allied aviators escape from Nazi-occupied France, as well as a conduit for Spanish tungsten (for armour-plating Nazi armaments) in exchange for gold stolen by the Nazis from Jews.

## Getting There & Away

Two daily trains run to Canfranc-Estación from Zaragoza (€17, 3¾ hours) via Huesca (€11, 2¾ hours) and Jaca (€2.90, 35 minutes), and back.

The Mancomunidad Alto Valle del Aragón (www.mavaragon.es) runs five daily buses from Jaca bus station to Astún (€2.95, 40 minutes) and back, calling at Canfranc-Estación (€2.05, 20 minutes), Candanchú and the Puerto de Somport.

## SKIING ARAGÓN

Aragón is one of Spain's premier skiing destinations, with the season in the Pyrenees running from late December to mid-April.

**Candanchú** (974 37 31 94; www.candanchu.com; ) About 30km north of Jaca, Candanchú offers 50km of varied pistes and a nice alpine village feel. A favourite with families as well as experts, it's one of Spain's less expensive ski stations.

**Astún** (974 37 30 88; www.astun.com) The Pyrenees' newest resort, purpose-built (and rather ugly) Astún is 3km from Candanchú, with which it shares ski passes and a free shuttle service. It has 40km of pistes, for a wide range of standards.

**Panticosa** (974 49 00 00; www.formigal-panticosa.com; ) An antidote to much bigger Formigal nearby, village-based Panticosa has mostly red and blue pistes.

**Formigal** (974 49 00 00; www.formigal-panticosa.com) High in the Valle de Tena, Formigal is Aragón's largest ski resort, with 141km of varied pistes in four different valleys. It has good modern facilities and a relatively lively après-ski scene.

**Cerler** (974 55 10 12; www.cerler.com) Well-equipped Cerler is closely connected with the town of Benasque and thus enjoys tonnes of eating, sleeping and après-ski options. Best for intermediate and beginner skiers, it has 77km of pistes.

French Nouvelle-Aquitaine regional buses (http://transports.nouvelle-aquitaine.fr) run at least four times daily from Canfranc-Estación to Bedous in the Vallée d'Aspe, France (€2, 40 minutes to one hour), and back, most connecting at Bedous with trains to/from Oloron Sainte Marie and Pau.

# Valle de Tena

The Valle de Tena, watered by the Río Gállego, runs north into the mountains from the town of Sabiñánigo, with the A136 road climbing to the Puerto del Portalet pass (1794m), gateway to France's Vallée d'Ossau.

The upper Valle de Tena is home to two ski resorts: Panticosa (small) and Formigal (large, with installations strung up the mountainsides for most of the 6km to the Portalet border). Between the two resorts stands the pretty, and much older, stone-built village of **Sallent de Gállego**, a good base for hikes with a range of decent accommodation. From Panticosa an 8km road winds up through the Garganta del Escalar gorge to the Baños de Panticosa hot-springs resort, set in a deep bowl surrounded by high peaks.

### Resort Balneario de Panticosa — SPA

(974 48 71 61; www.panticosa.com; Baños de Panticosa; 90min adult/child €32/12; 11am-9.30pm Jul-Aug, to 8.30pm Dec-Jun & Sep-Oct; ) The Balneario is a luxurious, recently remodelled spa resort, with two four-star hotels and several restaurants. You don't have to be staying here to enjoy the facilities, and all sorts of circuits and treatments are offered. The main *zona de aguas* (waters zone) includes four different pools, a sauna, Turkish bath, ice igloo, solarium and more.

### Respomuso Hike — WALKING

A fine day hike, avoiding ski installations, follows the well-named Río Aguas Limpias (Clean Waters River) up from Sallent de Gállego to the **Embalse de Respomuso**, a picturesque reservoir at 2200m, surrounded by high peaks. The walk is 12km up from Sallent (about 3½ hours, with 900m of ascent), and 12km back.

You can save about 3.5km and one hour in each direction by driving to Asador La Sarra restaurant above Sallent. There's popular dorm accommodation at the **Refugio de Respomuso** (974 33 75 56; www.alberguesyrefugios.com; Embalse de Respomuso; dm adult/child €17/9, breakfast €6.50, lunch or dinner €17; mid-Mar–mid-Dec) – book ahead if hiking in peak seasons.

### Pirineos Sur — MUSIC

(www.pirineos-sur.es; Jul) Sallent de Gállego and nearby Lanuza village host this terrific world-music festival, with 10 or more nights of concerts in the second half of July. Recent editions have featured the flamenco of Diego El Cigala and Duquende, west African stars Youssou N'Dour and Toumani Diabaté, and folk rockers the Waterboys.

## Sleeping

**La Casueña** DESIGN HOTEL €€

(974 48 85 38; www.lacasuena.com; Calle Troniecho 11, Lanuza; incl breakfast s €85, d €105-130; ) Tiny Lanuza village, 3km south of Sallent de Gállego, was abandoned in 1976 when the reservoir which it now so picturesquely overlooks was created. The waters never reached the village and its people have since gradually returned. One family decided to replace their cowshed with a small hotel and the result is this charming combination of highly original arts and crafts with cosy comfort.

The friendly owners serve good dinners (€15 to €25) if ordered earlier in the day, with vegetarian and coeliac dishes available.

★**Hotel Viñas de Lárrede** HOTEL €€€

(974 94 80 00; www.hotelvinasdelarrede.es; Calle San Juan de Busa 12, Lárrede; incl breakfast r €130-195, ste €250-360; P) Resembling an alpine chalet, Viñas de Lárrede makes a wonderfully comfortable and aesthetic rural base. The 17 rooms are all different but – like the very ample common spaces – all share a delightfully bright and spacious feel. Also here is one of the area's best restaurants, open to all for lunch and dinner daily (except lunch Monday to Thursday from September to June).

Outside, grassy gardens stretch to the pool area, and everything is surrounded by beautiful rural views. The restaurant serves up classic Spanish ingredients (mains €17 to €26) with a contemporary twist. It's 9km north of Sabiñánigo.

## Getting There & Away

From Jaca, one or two daily buses wind over to Panticosa village (€5.50, one hour), Sallent de Gállego (€6.45, 1¼ hours) and Formigal (€6.85, 1½ hours). There's also bus service to these villages from Huesca by Avanza (www.avanzabus.com).

# Parque Nacional de Ordesa y Monte Perdido

This is where the Spanish Pyrenees really take your breath away. The national park extends south from a dragon's back of limestone peaks along the French border and includes Monte Perdido (3355m), the third-highest summit in the Pyrenees. The wonderful scenery of plunging canyons, towering cliffs, thick forests, rivers, waterfalls, snow peaks, mountain lakes and high-level glaciers makes this *the* place to head for if you can manage only one destination in the Spanish Pyrenees. Chief among the valleys and canyons slicing down from the high ground are the Valle de Ordesa (west), Cañón de Añisclo (south), Valle de Escuaín (southeast) and Valle de Pineta (east). Main access towns are Torla for the Valle de Ordesa; Aínsa for Añisclo and Escuaín; and Bielsa for Pineta.

## Activities

The best weather and walking conditions are generally from mid-June to early September. Lower-level routes are practicable for longer, but once there's snow on the ground, easy paths become harder, and harder ones can become dangerous.

Carry a good map such as Editorial Alpina's *Parque Nacional de Ordesa y Monte Perdido* (1:25,000). Park information offices give out diagrams of the park's four sectors (Ordesa, Añisclo, Escuaín and Pineta) with walking route descriptions, and will provide further information verbally.

★**Cola de Caballo** WALKING

This very popular route heads 8km (with 500m ascent) along the Valle de Ordesa from Pradera de Ordesa, between soaring cliffs and passing numerous waterfalls, to the Circo de Soaso, a rock amphitheatre decorated by the Cola de Caballo (Horsetail) waterfall, where Monte Perdido towers far above. The 16km round trip takes about 5½ hours plus stops, but shorter segments are also well worth it.

★**Faja de Pelay** WALKING

An initially more demanding but more spectacular variation on the standard Cola de Caballo walk. From Pradera de Ordesa you zigzag up the Senda de los Cazadores (Hunters' Path), gaining 600m altitude in a remorseless 1½ hours. Then it's gently downhill almost the whole rest of the way, beginning with a spectacular high-level path leading to the Cola de Caballo waterfall.

From the waterfall, return to Pradera along the main valley path. Total time is about 6½ hours plus stops.

★**Balcón de Pineta** WALKING

This challenging but exhilarating hike (about seven hours round trip) begins at the car park near the west end of the Pineta valley and ascends 1300m to the Balcón – a barren, vaguely plateau-like area providing

## Parque Nacional de Ordesa y Monte Perdido

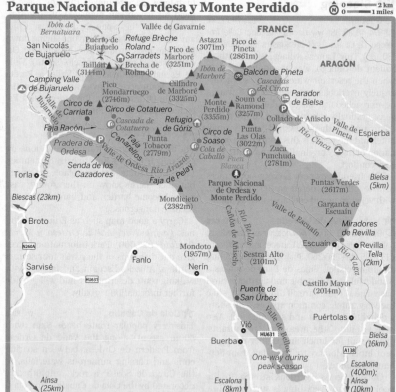


fantastic panoramas back down the valley and close-up views of the glacier-laden north side of Monte Perdido.

It takes about four hours to climb to the Balcón and three hours to return. Follow 'Camino Marboré' signs from the car park: after the signs give out, the way ahead is fairly obvious and marked by cairns. A short detour takes you to the impressive Cascadas del Cinca waterfalls. From the Balcón it's well worth continuing another half-hour to Ibón de Marboré lake, beneath the rocky ridge forming the French border.

### Refugio de Góriz & Monte Perdido WALKING

Fit walkers can climb the Circo de Soaso above the Cola de Caballo (p411) by a series of steep switchbacks to reach the Refugio de Góriz in 1½ to two hours. The refuge is a starting point for many high peaks, including Monte Perdido, and is one of the great crossroads of the Pyrenees.

Monte Perdido itself is a serious undertaking: most of the year the route is completely or partly snow-covered and requires mountaineering skills, crampons and ice axes. Even when snow-free (typically mid-July to some time in September), it's still very demanding, requiring fitness and mountain-hiking experience. You ascend from 2200m at Refugio de Góriz to 3355m, with a long, very steep section over loose stones – approximately four hours up and three hours down, and you should start early.

### Cañón de Añisclo WALKING

This gaping wound in the earth's fabric is 500m deep in parts. A trail up the canyon from Puente de San Úrbez bridge, beside the HU631 road, leads in about 2½ hours (450m ascent) to La Ripareta, where the Barranco de la Pardina joins the Río Bellós, and in a further two hours (300m more ascent) to another confluence below the powerful Fuen Blanca waterfall.

**Miradores de Revilla** BIRDWATCHING

Thanks to a feeding site established nearby by conservationists, there are high chances of seeing the rare lammergeier (bearded vulture), as well as Egyptian and griffon vultures and golden eagles, from the Miradores de Revilla observation points, reached by an easy 1.25km path from Revilla village. Revilla is 12km by a winding paved road off the A138 north of Aínsa.

## Sleeping

The only beds within the national park are in the Refugio de Góriz, but there is plenty of accommodation – campgrounds, walkers' refuges, hostels, *hostales*, holiday apartments, hotels – in the villages and countryside surrounding the park, including Torla, Broto, Aínsa, Escalona, Bielsa and the Valle de Bujaruelo. Reservations are essential everywhere during July and August. Some accommodation closes down from about November to March.

**Refugio de Góriz** HOSTEL €

(974 34 12 010; www.goriz.es; dm €18.10) One of the Spanish Pyrenees' star refuges sits at the crossroads of an enviable network of paths in the shadow of Monte Perdido, for which it acts as an unofficial base camp. The 80 bunks are normally fully occupied throughout July and August and on June and September weekends – reserve well ahead.

The quickest hike in (about four hours) is from Pradera de Ordesa via the Circo de Soaso. Staffed year-round, the refuge has an all-day bar, and offers picnic lunches as well as breakfast (€6.70) and dinner (€17.50).

## Information

The national park's main information offices (opening hours can vary):

**Centro de Visitantes de Torla** (974 48 64 72; Avenida Ordesa, Torla; 9am-2pm & 4.15-7pm late Mar-Oct, 9am-2pm & 3.15-6pm Nov-late Mar)

**Bielsa** (974 50 10 43; Casa Larraga, Plaza Mayor, Bielsa; 9am-2pm & 4.15-7pm Apr-Oct, 9am-2pm Mon-Fri, 9am-2pm & 3.15-6pm Sat & Sun Nov-Mar)

**Escalona** (974 50 51 31; Calle Mayor, Escalona; 9am-2pm & 4.15-7pm Apr-Oct, 9am-2pm Mon-Fri, 9am-2pm & 3.15-6pm Sat & Sun Nov-Mar)

**Escuaín** (9.30am-6.30pm Mar-Oct, 9am-6pm Sat & Sun Nov-Feb)

## Getting There & Around

The main jumping-off points for the national park are the village of Torla in the west; the small town of Aínsa, southeast of the park; and Bielsa village in the east, 34km north up the A138 from Aínsa. All three places can be reached by bus.

From Torla it's an 8km drive or walk to Pradera de Ordesa, starting point for walks in the Valle de Ordesa. Private vehicles may not go beyond Pradera de Ordesa at any time, and are banned from the Valle de Ordesa completely from Thursday to Sunday of Easter week and from late June to mid-September. During these periods a shuttle bus (one way/return adult €3/4.50, child free) runs between Torla's Centro de Visitantes and Pradera de Ordesa.

From Escalona, 11km north of Aínsa on the A138, a minor paved road, the HU631, crosses the park's southern tip, with a narrow section winding up the dramatic Valle de Bellos and giving access to walks in the spectacular Añisclo canyon (the upper reaches of the Bellos valley).

# Torla

POP 220 / ELEV 1040M

The pre-eminent gateway to the Parque Nacional de Ordesa y Monte Perdido, Torla is a lovely alpine-style village of slate-roofed stone houses clustered above Río Ara, with the national park's mountains forming an awe-inspiring backdrop. It gets extremely busy in July and August.

The village has a couple of ATMs, and shops selling outdoor gear, food and maps.

## Activities

**Vía Ferrata del Sorrosal** CLIMBING

(Broto) The Ordesa-Monte Perdido national park and surroundings are rich in adventure opportunities; one of the most exciting options is this via ferrata at Broto, 4km south of Torla. The spectacular two-hour route, practicable from about April to November, climbs up beside the 100m-high Cascada de Sorrosal waterfall and then continues up the Sorrosal canyon.

Numerous activity firms in the district offer guided climbs for around €45 per person, the only requirements being decent physical condition and a head for heights.

**Guías de Torla** ADVENTURE SPORTS

(974 48 64 22; www.guiasdetorlaordesa.com; Calle A Ruata; half-day canyoning per person from

€46; ) A well-established, professional company offering exhilarating canyoning routes down Pyrenees gorges (Easter to October) plus vie ferrate, rafting, peak ascents, guided hikes and climbing in the Aragón Pyrenees. It also sells and rents outdoor equipment and runs training courses.

**Ordesa Taxi** DRIVING
(630 418918; www.miradoresdeordesa.es; Calle A Ruata; adult/child €35/30; approximately May-Oct) You can admire some of the best of the national park scenery without walking more than a few minutes on twice-daily van tours to five lookout points along the southern rim of the Valle de Ordesa.

## Sleeping

**Edelweiss Hotel** HOTEL €
(974 48 61 73; www.edelweisshotelordesa.es; Avenida de Ordesa 1; incl breakfast s €40-62, d €55-62; Apr-Oct; P ) The rooms may lack decorative flair, but many have panoramic balconies, and staff are notably welcoming and helpful, prices are good, and the breakfast is ample. It's conveniently located beside the road to Ordesa, with a reasonable amount of (free) parking.

**Hotel Villa de Torla** HOTEL €€
(974 48 61 56; www.hotelvilladetorla.com; Plaza Aragón 1; s €40-50, d €50-80; @ ) Rooms here are tidy and stylish in whites and creams with patterned wallpaper. An undoubted highlight is the pool, from which there are lovely views. A generous buffet breakfast (€7.50) is available.

**Hotel Bujaruelo** HOTEL €€
(974 48 61 74; www.hotelbujarueloordesa.com; Avenida de Ordesa; s €50-60, d €60-80; Easter-Nov; P ) This well-run hotel is a solid midrange choice at the foot of the village beside the road to Ordesa, with parking for a dozen cars out front. Rooms are thoughtfully designed, providing comfort without being over-fussy. Those with mountain vistas are worth the few euros extra. The restaurant serves a good dinner menu (€18) and a generous breakfast buffet (€9).

## Eating

**La Brecha** ARAGONESE €
(974 48 62 21; www.lucienbriet.com; Calle A Ruata; set menu €17; 2-3.30pm & 8.30-10.30pm Easter-early Dec; ) Home-style local dishes like roast lamb, veal escalope and *longaniza* sausages are the speciality of this bustling upstairs restaurant. The *menú* includes wine but do give the homemade *pacharán* (sloe liqueur) a try too. Reservations advised.

**El Taillón** PIZZA €
(Calle A Ruata; pizza €7.50-15; 12.30-11.30pm) Tasty, light-crust, wood-oven pizzas, large salads, and a broad terrace that is an absolute blessing on summer evenings, are the recipe for success at this ever-popular eatery. In busy periods, go early in the evening to avoid a wait.

**Restaurante El Duende** ARAGONESE €€
(974 48 60 32; www.restauranteelduende.com; Calle de la Iglesia; mains €15-22, set menus €23-34; 1.30-3.30pm & 8-10.30pm Feb-Dec; ) Encased in a 19th-century building made from local stone, Duende (Elf) is the finest dining in town, serving top-class grilled meats, creative desserts and fine wines. Tables are in high demand; reserve ahead.

## Getting There & Away

**Avanza** (902 21 07 00; www.avanzabus.com) operates one or two daily buses to/from Sabiñánigo (€4.35, one hour), with bus and rail connections to/from Jaca and Zaragoza. There are one or two daily services to/from Aínsa (€4.45, one hour).

# Valle de Bujaruelo

A few kilometres north of Torla and just outside the western boundary of the Parque Nacional de Ordesa y Monte Perdido, the Bujaruelo valley has scenery rivalling parts of the national park, and is another excellent walking area.

Private vehicles can drive as far as San Nicolás de Bujaruelo, 10km from Torla, where a picturesque 13th-century stone bridge spans the Río Ara. There's a hikers' refuge, the **Refugio de Bujaruelo** (974 48 64 12; www.refugiodebujaruelo.com; San Nicolás de Bujaruelo; dm from €15.40, d €47.60, camping per adult/tent/car €5/5/5; mid-Mar–Oct; P), with dorms, private rooms and a camping area, here, and the well set-up **Camping Valle de Bujaruelo** (974 48 63 48; www.campingvalledebujaruelo.com; per adult/tent/car €5.20/5.20/5.20, dm/tr/q with shared bathroom €16/48/62, bungalow €81-106; Apr–mid-Oct; P ) 2.5km back down the road towards Torla. Both have restaurants open to all.

The grassy Ara riverbanks upstream from San Nicolás are idyllic for lying back with the limpid waters rippling past your feet.

There are easy walks into the **Valle de Otal** (west) and **Valle de Ordiso** (northwest) or a slightly harder circuit of about six hours combining the two. The beautiful mountain lake **Ibón de Bernatuara** is about 3½ hours' hike north from San Nicolás (with 975m ascent), and 2½ hours back down.

Eastward, it's a climb of 4.5km (about three hours, with 950m ascent) from San Nicolás to the **Puerto de Bujaruelo** on the French border, and 2½ hours back down. From this pass you could continue into France: either down to Gavarnie village (about three hours) or over to the **Refuge de la Brèche de Roland-Les Sarradets** (about 1½ hours) – and even, if snow conditions underfoot permit, about 45 minutes up from this refuge to the **Brecha de Rolando**, a truly spectacular gap in the mountain wall along the France–Spain frontier.

# Aínsa

POP 1620 / ELEV 560M

A masterpiece hewn from uneven stone, medieval Aínsa is one of Aragón's gems, albeit one that's half-swamped by tourism in high summer. From its perch, you'll have commanding panoramas of the mountains, particularly the great rock bastion of La Peña Montañesa. Modern Aínsa spreads out below the old town, around a busy crossroads and two rivers flowing down from the Pyrenees: the Ara and the Cinca.

## Sights

**★Plaza Mayor** SQUARE

Old Aínsa's broad, cobbled main plaza, lined by handsome stone arcades and houses, is one of Spain's loveliest. It was created as a marketplace and fairground back in the 12th and 13th centuries and the architecture has changed little since then – even if the buzz today comes not from market stalls but from the tables and sunshades of numerous restaurants.

**Castillo** CASTLE

FREE The castle precinct off Plaza Mayor mostly dates from the 16th and 17th centuries; there are good views from the walls. The two surviving towers house moderately interesting museums: the **Eco Museo** (974 50 05 97; www.quebrantahuesos.org; €4; 10.30am-2.30pm & 3.30-8pm Jul-Sep, 11am-7pm Oct-Jun) on Pyrenean birds of prey and other fauna, and the **Espacio del Geoparque de Sobrarbe** (www.geoparquepirineos.com; 9.30am-2pm & 4.30-7pm Wed-Sun Jul-Aug, hours vary Sep-Jun) FREE on the region's geology.

**Iglesia de Santa María** CHURCH

(tower €1; 10.30am-8pm) Aínsa's main church bears all the hallmarks of unadulterated Romanesque. Few embellishments mark its thick, bare walls, which date from the 11th century. Explore the beautiful little crypt and funny little trapezoid cloister, and you can climb the bell tower if you coincide with its variable opening hours.

## Sleeping

Several cute, olde-worlde lodgings are found around Plaza Mayor, but most accommodation is down in the newer part of town.

**Albergue Mora de Nuei** HOSTEL €

(676 415404; www.alberguemoradenuei.com; Calle del Portal de Abajo 2; dm/d €20/55; Feb-Dec; ) At the lower end of the old town, this is one of Aragón's best hostels. The colourful rooms and dorms all have their own bathrooms. The bar, with a pleasant terrace, has 30 beers and serves good light dishes in the evenings from about June to November.

**★Hotel Los Siete Reyes** BOUTIQUE HOTEL €€

(974 50 06 81; www.lossietereyes.com; Plaza Mayor; d €95-120; ) Tucked under an arcade on Aínsa's ancient main square and exhibiting a style best described as historical-boutique, the Siete Reyes offers six rooms fit for kings (and queens). Modern art hangs on old stone walls, mood lighting shines from ceilings crossed by wooden beams, and there's a wonderful subterranean bodega where you can take breakfast.

**Hotel Sánchez** HOTEL €€

(974 50 00 14; www.hotelsanchez.com; Avenida Sobrarbe 10; s €55-115, d €65-115, ste €95-170; P) This well-run place in the lower town offers tidy, medium-size, 'classic' rooms and a newer 'design zone', called Alojamientos Aínsa Sánchez (www.alojamientosainsasanchez.com), of spacious, comfortable, contemporary suites and apartments. Eating options are bright and excellent, too.

**Casa de San Martín** HISTORIC HOTEL €€€

(974 33 83 49; www.casadesanmartin.com; San Martín de la Solana; s/d incl breakfast from €130/150; Mar-Jan; P) A stunning rural retreat standing in splendid isolation overlooking a deserted valley, this tall, stone house has a history going back over 1000

## AÍNSA, ADVENTURE CAPITAL

With the Pyrenees and all their foothills on its doorstep, Aínsa is a natural centre for all kinds of adventure activities including mountain biking, canyoning, vie ferrate, rafting and kayaking, with several companies here offering trips.

Some 1000km of off-road tracks within reach make the area a mountain-biking paradise, and many of them are waymarked for bikers. The **Zona Zero project** (☎24hr 617 999585; www.zonazeropirineos.com; Municipal Tourist Office, Avenida Ordesa 5; ⌚4-7pm Tue-Fri, 10am-2pm Sat) provides masses of information for mountain bikers and brings together bike-friendly accommodation, repair shops, guides and bike-transport services. The free mobile app ZTrails provides up-to-the-minute information on trails and conditions. You can rent enduro mountain bikes (per half-/full day €40/60) at **T-T Aventura** (☎974 51 00 24; www.ttaventura.com; Avenida Pirenaica 10; ⌚office 9am-9pm Jul-Aug, 9am-2pm & 4-9pm Sep-Jun). **InterSport** (Avenida Sobrarbe 4; ⌚9am-9pm Mon-Sat, 9am-2pm & 4-9pm Sun) sells most things you could need for outdoor activities, from boots to backpacks, helmets to sleeping mats. It's good on maps, too.

years. It has been beautifully renovated with intriguing art and crafts, plenty of sitting areas, and spacious rooms featuring exposed stone and rustic wooden furnishings. Meals (dinner €25) are exceptional. Head 16km west from Aínsa on the N260, then 5km up an unpaved road from the 'San Martín de la Solana' sign.

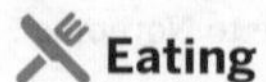

## Eating

**L'Alfil** TAPAS €

(Travesera de la Iglesia; raciones €6.50-10; ⌚10am-4pm & 7pm-midnight May-Oct, shorter hours Nov-Apr) This pretty little cafe-bar near the church, with floral accompaniment to its outside tables, serves *raciones* that are a little more creative than the norm, from casseroles of wild mushrooms, venison or snails to duck pâté or cured boar. It's also a good spot to try the locally celebrated sausage *longaniza de Graus*.

**Bodegón de Mallacán** ARAGONESE €€

(☎974 50 09 77; Plaza Mayor 6; mains €17-21, set menus €22; ⌚noon-4pm & 7-11pm) Meat-eaters won't want to wave *adiós* to Aragón without tasting *ternasco,* the slow-roasted local lamb, and this is a fine place to try it. Duck, boar, beef, partridge, frogs' legs and venison pâté are other classics you can enjoy here.

★**Restaurante Callizo** CONTEMPORARY SPANISH €€€

(☎974 50 03 85; www.restaurantecallizo.es; Plaza Mayor; set menus €60-80; ⌚1-2.30pm & 8.45-9.45pm Wed-Sun Apr-Oct) Callizo succeeds in marrying Aragonese tradition with modern gastronomic theatre and the result is not just a meal but a true eating experience. Dishes include Río Cinca trout, rack of lamb and veal tournedos, all in imaginative preparations – and with lovely views wherever you sit. It's essential to reserve (possible on the website) and to arrive on time!

## Information

**Municipal Tourist Office** (☎974 50 07 67; www.villadeainsa.com; Avenida Ordesa 5; ⌚10am-2pm & 4-7.30pm, closed Sun afternoon Sep-Jun) In the new town down the hill.

**Oficina Comarcal de Turismo** (District Tourist Office; ☎974 50 05 12; www.turismosobrarbe.com; Torre Nordeste, Plaza del Castillo 1; ⌚9.30am-2pm & 4-7pm) Inside the Castillo.

## Getting There & Away

Aínsa's bus stop is at the south end of the Río Ara bridge. **Avanza** (☎974 21 07 00; www.avanzabus.com) runs one or two daily buses to/from Barbastro (€5.85, one hour) and Torla (€4.35, one hour). For Huesca, Zaragoza or Barcelona, change at Barbastro. **Autocares Bergua** (☎974 50 06 01; www.autocaresbergua.com) heads to/from Bielsa (€5, one hour) once daily in July and August, and on Monday, Wednesday and Friday in other months.

The summer bus service **Tu Destino Pirineos** (☎974 50 06 01; www.tudestinopirineos.com; ⌚late-Jun–mid-Sep) connects Aínsa and nearby villages with various places of interest around the region, including Torla, the Valle de Bujaruelo and the Cañón de Añisclo. Timetables are designed so that you can take day trips, returning in the evening.

# Benasque

POP 1620 / ELEV 1150M

Aragón's northeastern corner is home to the Pyrenees' two highest peaks and many other high and shapely mountains, along with a few sadly receding glaciers. The likeable little town of Benasque, with its neat, alpine-style, stone-and-slate architecture, is a perfect gateway to the high valleys.

The region offers walkers almost limitless options, especially in the upper Benasque valley (p418) and its side valleys. The best season is from about May to October. Depending on snow cover, low-level routes may be practicable for longer, and higher-level ones for shorter periods.

As well as hiking, climbing, peak ascents and mountain-biking in the valleys and hills, there's good **skiing** at Cerler (p410), a few kilometres northeast of Benasque; some of Spain's best **paragliding** at **Castejón de Sos**, 14km south, with the year-round Liri take-off point at 2300m, and paragliding shops along the main street (tandem flights around €80); and one of the Pyrenees' major **rafting** centres (best from April to June) at **Campo** on the Río Ésera, 33km south. A good choice in Campo is **Sin Fronteras** (974 55 01 77; www.sinfronterasadventure.com; Carretera Benasque 1; half-day rafting €36-45; 10am-7pm Mar-Oct; ), which offers a slew of summer activities including canyoning in the nearby Aigüeta de Barbaruéns canyon, as well as rafting – all with child-friendly options. Several Benasque agencies can organise these activities for you.

**Compañía de Guías Valle de Benasque** ADVENTURE SPORTS
(974 55 16 90; www.guiasbenasque.com; Avenida de Francia, Edificio Els Ibons; office 10am-2pm & 4.30-8.30pm) This company has more than 20 years' experience and offers a vast range of activities and courses for both summer and winter. It also rents all the necessary kit.

**Puro Pirineo** MOUNTAIN BIKING
(www.bttpuropirineo.com) The hilly Benasque-Castejón de Sos region is endowed with over 20 waymarked mountain-bike trails, ranging from easy valley pedals to tough mountain routes with exciting downhills. The Puro Pirineo project groups bike-friendly accommodation, rental outfits, workshops, guides and bike-transport services, and provides maps (on its website or in paper form, sold locally for €2), and downloadable GPX and KMZ tracks.

Mountain-bike rental in Benasque costs around €18/24 per half/full day.

OFF THE BEATEN TRACK

## JÁNOVAS, A VILLAGE UNDER RECONSTRUCTION

An estimated 3000 deserted villages are dotted around Spain's countryside – ghostly places of crumbling streets, often with a church tower still poking forlornly above the trees growing through the roofs of derelict houses. Most of these '*despoblados*' are victims of isolation and the decline in rural employment since the mid-20th century.

Jánovas, on the poplar-lined banks of the Río Ara in the Valle de Solana, 15km west of Aínsa, has a different story. The village was expropriated in the 1960s for a hydroelectricity scheme – against the general will of its people. According to an information panel in the village today, Jánovas' school stayed open until an operative of the hydro company broke down its door and pulled the teacher out by her hair. The last villagers didn't leave till 1984. Some 15 other villages in the valley suffered the same fate.

But the hydro project never came to fruition and was finally abandoned in 2005. Jánovas' properties have started to be returned to their former owning families, who are piece by piece restoring the village.

A tiny 'Jánovas' sign on an S-bend of the N260, 15km west of Aínsa, points you south down an unpaved road. Park after 300m and walk across the bridge to the village. Signs announce that Jánovas is a 'Pueblo en Reconstrucción' and warn, for safety reasons, against entering any properties. In the village centre, the rebuilt Casa de Pueblo (Community House) stands proudly beside the shell of a still-derelict homestead. Funds are being raised to restore the Iglesia de San Miguel: the frescoes inside this church wear a surprisingly Eastern Orthodox look – they were painted in 2001 (when the village was empty) for the shooting of the film *Guerreros* (Warriors), set in Kosovo.

In June 2019 Jánovas staged the first of what's intended to be an annual music and theatre festival to raise funds for reconstruction, under the title Jánovas Insumergible (Jánovas Unsinkable).

## Sleeping

**★Sommos Hotel Aneto** HOTEL €€
(☎974 55 10 61; www.sommoshoteles.com; Avenida de Francia 4; incl breakfast s €60-170, d €70-215; ⏲closed May & Nov; P❄📶≋) Streamlined, modern Aneto is a cut above your average ski lodge with a wide selection of big, bright rooms in wood-dominated decor, from the snazzy to the positively luxurious. Bonuses include an indoor pool, a great lobby bar and filling breakfasts. Staff pull off that magic amalgamation of professionalism but thoroughly warm service.

**Hotel Vallibierna** HOTEL €€
(☎974 55 17 23; www.vallibiernahotel.com; Paseo Campalets; s/d incl breakfast €50/70; ⏲closed Nov; P📶) Away from the central hubbub, this former private home is a peaceful retreat with wood beams, parquet floors and a few hunting trophies, all redolent with the scent of tall pines from its garden. With good breakfasts and free parking, it's an excellent find. Rates rise in August.

**Hotel Aragüells** HOTEL €€
(☎974 55 16 19; www.hotelaraguells.com; Avenida de los Tilos; incl breakfast s €40-48, d €60-80; ⏲closed 1st half May & mid-Oct–Nov; P📶) One of a few broadly similar hotels along the main street of central Benasque, the Aragüells is marginally more expensive than the others but its medium-sized rooms have a slightly more modern and stylish touch. Like the others it's equipped with a restaurant, bar and streetside tables.

## Eating

**El Veedor de Viandas** SPANISH €
(www.elveedordeviandas.com; Avenida Los Tilos 6; tapas €2, mains €8-13; ⏲6-10.30pm Mon-Tue & Thu-Fri, noon-3.30pm & 6-11pm Sat & Sun; 📶) This welcoming informal space combines a gourmet deli, wine shop, tapas bar and restaurant. Tapas and *tostadas* have appetising toppings such as *solomillo* with caramelised onion and goat cheese, or roasted red pepper with cod and tuna. And there are salads, carpaccios, egg-based dishes and excellent cakes too.

**Mesón de Benás** ARAGONESE €€
(☎692 189 033; www.mesondebenas.es; Calle Mayor 47; mains €8-22, set menus €18-30; ⏲1-4pm & 8-11pm) Mesón d'Benás specialises in very good, home-style mountain fare with a strong emphasis on barbecued meats and good-value set menus. The three stone-walled rooms are adorned with interesting medieval-style paintings by a local priest.

## Shopping

**Barrabés** SPORTS & OUTDOORS
(www.barrabes.com; Avenida de Francia; ⏲10am-2pm & 5-9pm) This really is the one-stop sports store in town, selling equipment and sportswear for just about every activity you can think of. Good range of guides and maps.

## Information

**Tourist Office** (☎974 55 12 89; www.turismobenasque.com; Calle San Pedro; ⏲9.30am-1pm & 4.30-7.45pm, closed Sun & Mon Oct-Jun)

## Getting There & Away

Avanza (www.avanzabus.com) runs two buses daily (one on Sunday) to/from Huesca (€14, 2¾ hours) via Castejón de Sos, Campo and Barbastro.

# Upper Benasque Valley & the Maladeta Massif

Northeast of Benasque, the A139 continues up the valley of the Río Ésera (known as the Valle de Benasque) for 13km to dead-end 1.5km short of the mountain ridgeline along the French border. Just before the dead end, a 6km unpaved road forks east, following the upper Ésera past the Hospital de Benasque hotel to La Besurta, starting point of the walk to the Plan d'Aiguallut water meadows and other good routes. The Maladeta massif – a line of high, glacier-fringed peaks culminating in Aneto (3404m), the Pyrenees' highest summit – rises south of La Besurta.

Information on walking routes, including maps, is available at Benasque tourist office and at the starting point of the summer bus service at Vado del Hospital. Editorial Alpina's *Parque Natural Posets Maladeta* (1:25,000) is a good buy.

**Puerto de Benasque** WALKING
A fine route heading 4km (about two hours one-way; 700m ascent) from the Hospital de Benasque up to the Puerto de Benasque (Portillón de Benás) pass on the French border. The upper parts afford great panoramas of the Maladeta massif.

With a head for heights you can continue west along the ridgeline to the peak Tuca de Salvaguardia (1.5km and 300m more ascent), for further fantastic panoramas.

## PLAN D'AIGUALLUT WALKS

Surely one of the world's most perfect picnic spots, the Plan d'Aiguallut is a broad grassy meadow under the gaze of the Pyrenees' highest peak, Aneto, with half-a-dozen mountain streams meandering across it then uniting to tumble over its lip as the powerful Cascada d'Aiguallut. Fortunately, the 45-minute walk required to get here from La Besurta is sufficient to save it from getting overrun.

Numerous variations of the walk enable a great full day's outing. En route from La Besurta you can detour up to the **Refugio de la Renclusa** (☎974 34 46 46; www.alberguesyrefugios.com; dm €17, breakfast €6.50, lunch or dinner €17), then approach the Plan d'Aiguallut via the little Collado de Renclusa pass (1½ hours one-way from La Besurta to the Plan). From the Plan, it's 2.5km east (one hour one-way, with 200m ascent) up to **Ibón de Coll de Toro** lake; or you can head south-southeast up the lovely Barrancs valley to the lake **Ibón de Barrancs** (2km one-way, about 1½ hours, with 300m ascent) or even the **Collado de Salenques** pass (4km, about three hours, 750m ascent).

**Ibón d'Escarpinosa** WALKING

One of the best day hikes on the Valle de Benasque's west side: up the verdant Estós valley to two mountain lakes, the tiny Ibonet de Batisielles and the slightly bigger Ibón d'Escarpinosa, with a backdrop of jagged high peaks. It's 6km each way, with 750m ascent and descent (about five hours round-trip plus stops).

To start, head 3km up the A139 from Benasque then go left up the signposted Valle d'Estós road to a parking area after 700m.

**Hospital de Benasque** HOTEL €€

(☎0608 536 053; www.llanosdelhospital.com; Llanos del Hospital; incl breakfast s €65-90, d €95-130; ⏲closed May & Nov; P 📶) In the Ésera valley's beautiful upper reaches, 2km towards La Besurta off the A139, this 55-room mountain lodge borders on the luxurious. It has a spa, bar, museum and restaurant.

### ℹ Getting There & Away

From July to mid-September, private vehicles (unless going to the Hospital de Benasque) may not pass Vado del Hospital, 1.5km off the A139 along the La Besurta road. From here a shuttle bus (one way/return €2.90/5.20) runs to La Besurta and back. A few times a day the bus starts its run in Benasque (one way/return €8.20/13, 45 minutes). The rest of the year you can drive as far as La Besurta; there's no public transport.

## Alquézar

POP 200 / ELEV 610M

Like so many Aragonese villages, Alquézar takes you by surprise. You'll barely guess its charm until you're virtually inside its mazy web of cobbled streets lined by russet-red buildings, above the plunging cliffs of the Río Vero gorge. Beauty aside, Alquézar is Spain's capital of canyoning, with several companies offering to take you jumping, sliding and abseiling down the dramatic canyons carved into the surrounding Sierra de Guara in the Pyrenees foothills.

**Colegiata de Santa María** MONASTERY, CASTLE

(€3; ⏲11am-2pm & 4-7pm Sep-Jun, 10.30am-2pm & 4.30-7.30pm Jul-Aug) The Moorish *alcázar* (fortress) crowning Alquézar's highest point was replaced in 1099, after Christian conquest, by a fortified monastery. Some of the columns in its delicate cloister are topped by carved capitals depicting animals and flowers, as well as biblical scenes, and the cloister walls are covered with captivating murals. On the upper level is a museum of sacred art.

### Activities

The main season for easy and medium-level canyoning adventures is mid-June to mid-September. Prices are typically €45 to €50 per person, with around four hours' actual canyon descent. You need your own vehicle or a taxi for nearly all routes.

Recommended agencies, including **Guías Boira** (☎974 31 89 74; www.guiasboira.com; 👪) and **Vertientes** (☎974 31 83 54; www.vertientesaventura.como; 👪), line up along Paseo San Hipólito near the tourist office. Most also offer rock climbing, vie ferrate, and rafting (from Campo or Murillo de Gállego, both about 85km away).

**Ruta de las Pasarelas** WALKING

(☎974 56 49 39; www.pasarelasdealquezar.com; €4; ⏲8am-8pm) This 2km circular walk heads down along the Río Vero canyon below Alquézar, with some stretches along metal walkways attached to the canyon wall. Tickets (which include an obligatory helmet) are sold in the Ayuntamiento (Town Hall) on Calle Iglesia, near the start.

## Sleeping

**Hotel Maribel** BOUTIQUE HOTEL €€
(974 31 89 79; www.grupogervasio.com; Barrio Arrabal; d incl breakfast €98-150; closed Jan; P ❄ 🛜) This boutique hotel has plenty of charm and, while the decor juxtaposes tasteful contemporary with dashes of kitsch, the nine rooms are supremely comfortable (all with a hot tub, for example).

**Hotel Villa de Alquézar** HOTEL €€
(974 31 84 16; www.villadealquezar.com; Calle Pedro Arnal Cavero 12; incl breakfast s €68-86, d €76-125; closed late Dec-late Jan; P ❄ 🛜) This lovely larger hotel has plenty of style and period touches in its 34 airy rooms. The most expensive (top-floor) rooms are large with wonderful covered balconies – perfect for watching the sun set over town with a glass of Somontano wine. The 12m swimming pool is a notable plus.

**Casa Jabonero** INN €€
(974 31 89 08; Calle Pedro Arnal Cavero 14; d incl breakfast €60-80; closed Nov; P ❄ 🛜) Casa Jabonero has just six modest but well-kept rooms set above a bar and good restaurant specialising in grilled meats. There's handy free parking for guests with cars.

## Eating

**La Marmita de Guara** ARAGONESE €
(974 31 89 56; www.facebook.com/restaurantelamarmitadeguara; Paseo San Hipólito; set menu €14; 11am-midnight Wed-Sun) Choose between *pinchos* (snacks) in the bar or the more expansive *menú del día* on the panoramic terrace or in the air-conditioned upstairs dining room. Popular dishes include *caracoles* (snails), Pyrenees beef entrecôte, wild-mushroom lasagne or pink-tomato carpaccio.

★ **Casa Pardina** ARAGONESE €€
(660 399472; www.casapardina.com; Calle Medio; set menus €31-40; 1.30-3pm & 8.30-10.30pm Wed-Mon Easter-Oct, 1.30-3pm & 8-10pm Thu-Sat, 1.30-3pm Sun Nov-Easter) Casa Pardina is a very special restaurant where the food is based on traditional Aragonese home cooking yet also exudes contemporary creativity, and the setting is all soothing stonework and twinkling chandeliers. Among the many good choices are slow-roast lamb, stewed venison with dates and honey, and a salad of mango, orange and smoked cod. Reservations strongly recommended.

## Information

**Tourist Office** (974 31 89 40; www.alquezar.org; Paseo San Hipólito; 10am-2pm & 4.30-8pm Mon-Thu, 10am-8pm Fri-Sun Jul-Aug, 10am-2pm & 4.30-8pm five variable days per week Sep-Jun) Runs twice-daily village tours (€4, in Spanish, English or German) if eight people sign up.

## Getting There & Away

A bus to Barbastro (€2.50, 40 minutes) leaves Alquézar Monday to Friday at 7.30am during school terms and 9.25am in school holidays, starting back from Barbastro bus station at 2.30pm.

# Somontano Wine Region

The Somontano DO (Denominación de Origen), centred on the town of **Barbastro**, is Aragón's premier wine-growing region with more than 30 wineries producing reds, whites and rosés. Barbastro's older part around the late-Gothic cathedral and Paseo del Coso is pleasant enough, though Alquézar (p419), 26km northwest, is a more charming base for winery visits.

Barbastro's **tourist office** (974 30 83 50; www.barbastro.org/turismo-barbastro; Plaza Guisar 1-3, Barbastro; 9.30am-1.45pm & 4.15-7pm Tue-Sat Sep-Jun, 9.30am-1.30pm & 4.30-7.30-pm Tue-Sat Jul-Aug) and the websites Ruta del Vino Somontano (www.rutadelvinosomontano.com) and Vive! Somontano have plenty of information on wineries that can be visited for purchases, tours and/or tastings. For anything more than a call at a winery's shop, you should ring to arrange a time – the tourist office can help you do this. Three wineries offer free tastings in their shops: Viñas del Vero, its neighbour **Bodegas Pirineos**, and **Bodegas Otto Bestué**, 8km from Barbastro on the A138 towards Aínsa.

**Viñas del Vero** WINE
(974 30 22 16; www.vinasdelvero.es; Carretera Naval, Km 3.7; 1¾hr tour by reservation per person €10; 10am-2pm & 4-7pm Mon-Fri, 10am-2pm Sat) Aragón's best-known winery has hand-

OFF THE BEATEN TRACK

### LAGUNA DE GALLOCANTA

Spain's largest natural lake, the Laguna de Gallocanta, lies among low hills some 20km southwest of Daroca. When it's full, its waters cover about 15 sq km. It can almost dry up in summer, but in winter it provides a home or migration stopover for huge numbers of cranes, as well as many other species of waterfowl. The cranes start to arrive in mid-October and fly off back to their Scandinavian breeding grounds in late February or March. Numbers at the lake usually peak in December, at around 25,000 to 30,000 – though on 28 February 2013, an amazing 135,600 cranes were counted here.

The lake is circled by more than 30km of mostly unpaved roads, which pass a series of hides and observation points, and can be driven on in normal vehicles except after heavy rain. The **Centro de Interpretación Laguna de Gallocanta** (976 80 30 69; www.facebook.com/oficinaturismo.gallocanta; Gallocanta; adult/child €2/1; 9am-1.30pm & 3.30-6.30pm Oct-Mar, 10am-2pm & 4-7.30pm Wed-Sun Apr-Jun, 10am-2pm & 4.30-8pm Sat & Sun Jul–mid-Sep; P), at the lake's northeast corner, has binoculars and picture windows for lake viewing, plus cases of stuffed birds where you can press buttons to hear each bird's sound. There's also a boardwalk down to a lakeside hide.

some premises 3km out of Barbastro on the A1232 towards Alquézar, and offers free tastings in its spacious shop where you can inspect its full range of wines, priced from €5 to €68-plus for the top-of-the-line Blecua.

**Hotel San Ramón** BOUTIQUE HOTEL €€
(974 31 28 25; www.hotelsanramonsomontano.com; Calle Academia Cerbuna 2, Barbastro; incl breakfast s €75-95, d €90-125, ste from €144; P) Easily the best lodging in Barbastro, this hotel is set in a handsome Modernista building near the cathedral, transformed with 18 stylish, comfortable rooms all equipped with hydromassage showers or hot tubs – plus a spa, bar and restaurant.

**Trasiego** CONTEMPORARY SPANISH €€
(974 31 27 00; www.eltrasiego.com; Conjunto de San Julián, Avenida de la Merced 64, Barbastro; mains & raciones €6-20, set menu €19; noon-3.30pm & 8-10.30pm Tue-Sat, noon-4pm Sun) Trasiego and its adjoining gastrobar Trastienda offer delicious dishes in a setting – the Somontano DO's modern headquarters – that's as contemporary as the food. There are freshly made tapas and salads (try the prawns in spicy tempura), *raciones* to share, meat grills or roasts, and tempting desserts.

There's a big display of Somontano wine (€1.50 to €2.50 per glass) too.

### Getting There & Away

Barbastro's centrally located **bus station** (Plaza Aragón 2) has several daily services to/from Huesca (€4.80, 50 minutes), Zaragoza (€13, two hours) and Barcelona (€10, three hours), plus one or two to/from Aínsa (€6, one hour).

# SOUTHERN ARAGÓN

## Daroca

POP 2000 / ELEV 775M

The atmospheric old walled town of Daroca is the meeting point of two different Aragóns: the Romanesque north and the Mudéjar south. This cultural transition is etched into the town's buildings, which at times mix distinct Romanesque and Mudéjar elements, like sedimentary rock, on the same building.

Set in a narrow valley with a ring of evocatively crumbling medieval walls, Daroca once sported 114 towers, though only a handful remain. Since many of its old buildings are only viewable from the outside, it's best to enjoy Daroca as a kind of large alfresco museum.

### Sights

**Basílica de Santa María de los Sagrados Corporales** CHURCH
(Plaza de España; 5.30-7pm Mon, 11am-1pm & 5.30-7pm Tue-Sun mid-Sep–May, 6.30-8pm Mon, 11am-1pm & 6.30-8pm Tue-Sun Jun–mid-Sep) Pretty Plaza de España is dominated by this ornate Romanesque-Gothic-Mudéjar-Renaissance church, which boasts a stately interior with towering columns and elegant ceiling tracery.

**Castillo Mayor** CASTLE
FREE The hilltop castle on the north side of Daroca is not visible from the town below, but the hike up to it is well worthwhile for the evocatively ruined buildings and city

walls, and the town panoramas. Founded as a Muslim fort in the 8th century, the castle underwent numerous battles and rebuildings and was in use until the 19th-century Carlist Wars.



**Iglesia de San Miguel** CHURCH
(Plaza de San Miguel) Up in the northwest corner of town, 12th-century San Miguel is an austerely beautiful masterpiece of Romanesque architecture, but its greatest treasures are the colourful, 14th-century Gothic murals in the apse. You can go inside on guided tours run by the tourist office.

**Iglesia de San Juan** CHURCH
(Plaza de San Juan) Not generally open to the public, but no matter...what makes this church interesting is the delineation of its architecture. On the semicircular apse, you can clearly see the line where the builders in the mid-13th century switched from Romanesque grey stone to terracotta brick and finished the church in Mudéjar style – making this one of the earliest examples of Mudéjar architecture in Aragón.

## Tours

**Guided Walks** WALKING
(per person €5) The tourist office offers worthwhile guided walks. The special advantage of the 1¾-hour **Ruta Monumental** (11am, 4.30pm, 6pm, Tuesday to Sunday) is that it takes you into the otherwise closed Iglesia de San Miguel and the Puerta Baja city gate.

## Sleeping & Eating

**La Posada del Almudí** HERITAGE HOTEL €€
(976 80 06 06; www.posadadelalmudi.es; Calle Grajera 7; incl breakfast s €45, d €68-80; ) This lovely old place exudes charm. The rooms in the main building, a 16th-century palace, have been lovingly restored, while a separate building across the street houses more contemporary rooms with stylish black-and-white decor – all are ample-sized.

**Hotel Cien Balcones** HOTEL €€
(976 54 50 71; www.cienbalcones.com; Calle Mayor 88; incl breakfast s €56, d €72-90; P) Welcoming, family-run Cien Balcones has large, designer rooms, modern bathrooms and bold colour schemes throughout, plus free parking two minutes' walk away. The included breakfast is an ample buffet spread in the excellent restaurant (open for all meals). There's also a popular cafe.

## Information

**Tourist Office** (976 80 01 29; www.daroca.es/turismo; Calle Mayor 44; 10am-2pm & 4-8pm) Provides essential town maps marked with self-guided walking tours.

## Getting There & Away

Buses to Zaragoza (€7, two hours) leave at 8am and 4.30pm Monday to Friday, and 6pm Saturday and Sunday, from Mesón Félix bar (Calle Mayor 106), except from June to September when they go from the Puerta Baja gate, 70m down the street. For Teruel (€7, two hours), Autobuses Jiménez (www.autobusesjimenez.com) runs one to three daily buses from Hostal Legido at the east end of town.

# Teruel

POP 33,000 / ELEV 928M

The town of Teruel is synonymous with Mudéjar architecture. Nowhere else, except possibly Seville, is this glamorous amalgamation of Islamic craft and Christian taste in such evidence. Its hallmarks – patterns of terracotta bricks and glazed tiles, ornate wooden ceilings – are crafted skilfully into Teruel's towers and churches, four of which are Unesco-listed.

Teruel is Spain's smallest provincial capital, hidden in Aragón's isolated southern highlands, but it's a surprisingly bustling and lively place. Its Mudéjar architectural jewels were mostly erected in the 150 years after it was founded in 1171 by a conquering Christian king, Alfonso II. Teruel's most famous historical moment was also its most tragic: the battle of Teruel (1937–38) was one of the bloodiest in the Spanish Civil War, claiming an estimated 140,000 casualties.

## Sights

★**Fundación Amantes** MUSEUM
(www.amantesdeteruel.es; Calle Matías Abad 3; complete visit adult/senior/student €10/8.50/6; 10am-2pm & 4-8pm) Teruel's most popular attraction pulls out the stops on the city's famous legend of the tragic 13th-century lovers *(amantes)* Isabel and Juan Diego. The lovers' mausoleum sits in a side-chapel of the Mudéjar Iglesia de San Pedro and there are various ticket options for different parts of the complex, but the 50-minute complete visit to the mausoleum, church, cloister, tower and *ándito* (exterior walkway) is well worth it.

## Teruel

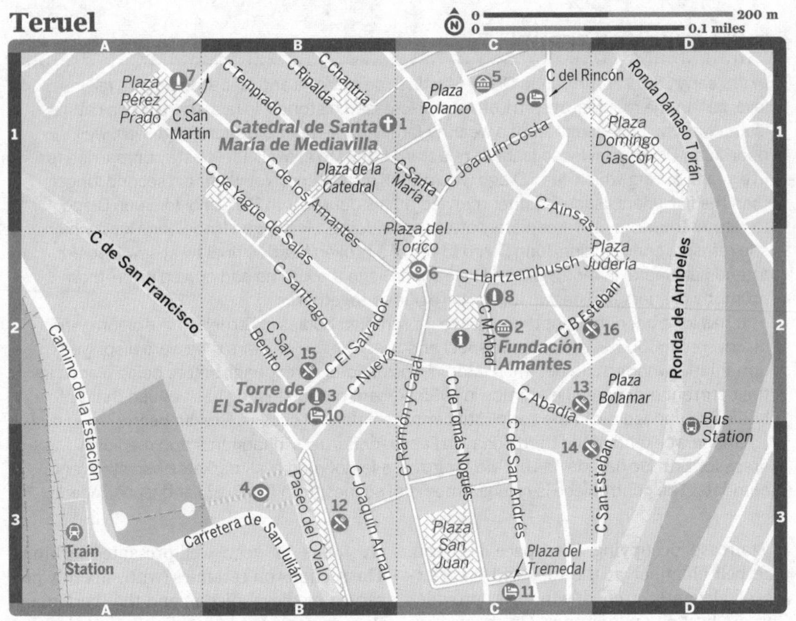


## Teruel

**Top Sights**
1 Catedral de Santa María de Mediavilla........B1
2 Fundación Amantes........C2
3 Torre de El Salvador........B2

**Sights**
Iglesia de San Pedro........(see 8)
4 La Escalinata........B3
5 Museo de Teruel........C1
6 Plaza del Torico........C2
7 Torre de San Martín........A1
8 Torre de San Pedro........C2

**Sleeping**
9 Fonda del Tozal........C1
10 Hotel El Mudayyan........B2
11 Hotel Teruel Plaza........C3

**Eating**
12 Bar Gregory........B3
13 La Barrica........C2
14 La Bella Neda........C3
15 La Torre del Salvador........B2
16 Locavore........D2

**Drinking & Nightlife**
Fonda del Tozal........(see 9)

The complete visits are guided in Spanish, but English and French audio-guides are available, and the only parts where you are obliged to follow the guide are the tower and *ándito*. In the Mausoleo de los Amantes itself, the lovers' remains are entombed beneath modern alabaster effigies, with their hands almost (but not quite) touching.

From the mausoleum you progress into the 14th-century **Iglesia de San Pedro** (Calle Matías Abad), which is Teruel's only Mudéjar church (as opposed to tower) – though the predominant impression is made by its colourful Modernista murals and gold-starred ceiling from around 1900. For a final flourish you are led up the 13th-century **Torre de San Pedro**, the oldest of Teruel's four surviving Mudéjar towers, and then round the *ándito* for panoramic views over Teruel.

**★Torre de El Salvador** TOWER
(www.teruelmudejar.com; Calle El Salvador 7; adult/child €2.50/2; ⌚11am-2pm Mon, 11am-2pm & 4.30-7.30pm Tue-Sun Feb-Jul & Sep-Oct, 10am-2pm Aug, 11am-2pm Mon, 11am-2pm & 4.30-6.30pm Tue-Sun Nov-Jan) The most impressive of Teruel's Mudéjar towers, 40m-tall El Salvador is an early-14th-century extravaganza of brick and ceramics built on the model of an Almohad minaret, with one tower inside another and

## THE LOVERS OF TERUEL

In the early 13th century, Juan Diego Martínez de Marcilla and Isabel de Segura fell in love, but, in the manner of some other star-crossed historical lovers, there was a catch: Isabel was the only daughter of a wealthy family, while poor old Juan Diego was, well, poor. Juan Diego convinced Isabel's reluctant father to allow Isabel to stay unmarried for five years, during which Juan Diego would seek his fortune. Not waiting a second longer than the five years, Isabel's father married off his daughter in 1217, only for Juan Diego to return, triumphant, immediately after the wedding. He begged Isabel for a kiss, which she refused, condemning Juan Diego to die of a broken heart. A final twist saw Isabel attend his funeral in mourning and give Juan Diego the kiss he had craved in life, then promptly die herself. The two lovers were buried together.

It has long been thought that the two mummified bodies in Teruel's mausoleum – first discovered in 1555 – are those of Isabel and Juan Diego. For years they were displayed upright in a wooden cabinet, then later in glass-lidded sarcophagi, before being placed in their current more dignified tombs in 1955. Recent carbon testing has verified that both bodies did indeed die in the early 13th century of natural causes. Broken hearts?

On the weekend of the third Friday in February, Teruel's inhabitants don medieval dress for **Las Bodas de Isabel de Segura**, a fair of medieval markets, food stalls and combats. The centrepiece is re-enactments of scenes from the Diego and Isabel legend.

a staircase occupying the space between. The bell chamber at the top, with two levels of elegantly arched windows, provides Teruel's best city panoramas. On the way up you'll find interesting exhibits on Mudéjar architecture and old Teruel.

**★Catedral de Santa María de Mediavilla** CATHEDRAL
(Plaza de la Catedral; incl Museo de Arte Sacro adult/child €5/3; ⏲11am-2pm & 4-8pm Apr-Oct, to 7pm Nov-Mar) The exterior of Teruel's cathedral is a rich example of the Mudéjar imagination at work with its kaleidoscopic brickwork and colourful ceramic tiles, notably on the superb 13th-century bell tower. Inside, the neck-craning Mudéjar ceiling *(techumbre)* is covered with paintings that add up to a full medieval cosmography – from musical instruments and hunting scenes to coats of arms and Christ's crucifixion.

**Plaza del Torico** SQUARE
(Plaza de Carlos Castel) Wandering around Teruel you're bound to arrive before long at this gently sloping, cafe-lined plaza that is the unquestioned centre of town. At its lower end the city's symbol, a tiny bronze bull called El Torico, just 35cm high and of unknown authorship, has stood on top of its tall stone column since 1865.

**Museo de Teruel** MUSEUM
(Plaza Polanco; ⏲10am-2pm & 4-7pm Tue-Fri, 10am-2pm Sat & Sun) FREE The provincial museum, in a 16th-century Renaissance palace, has six floors of very well-presented exhibits. The sections on ceramics (with superbly preserved medieval pieces) and the Iberian and Roman periods are highlights, and there's a huge Roman mosaic on the top floor.

**Torre de San Martín** TOWER
(Calle San Martín) The Torre de San Martín, the northwestern gate of the old city, is almost as beautiful as the Torre de El Salvador, though you can't climb it. Completed in 1316, it was incorporated into the city walls in the 16th century.

## Festivals & Events

**Fiestas del Ángel** FERIA
(www.vaquillas.es; ⏲Jul) For 11 days in early July (sometimes starting late June), Teruel parties in earnest for the Fiestas del Ángel, popularly known as La Vaquilla. Celebrations peak with La Puesta del Pañuelico (Placing of the Kerchief) on the second Saturday, when tumultuous crowds gather to witness a red cloth being placed round the neck of the tiny bronze bull atop its column in Plaza del Torico.

## Sleeping

**Fonda del Tozal** INN €
(☎649 103411; Calle del Rincón 5; s €25-27, d €38-45; 📶) Dating from the 16th century and one of the oldest inns in Spain, Tozal has a considerable variety of rooms, and all have a real sense of the past with beams, solid furniture and ancient floor tiles. While not de-

luxe, they're perfectly comfortable. In some, paintwork has been stripped back to reveal original faintly patterned plasterwork.

The cavernous wood-beamed **tavern** (Calle del Rincón 5; ⌚noon-midnight Sun & Tue-Thu, to 3am Fri & Sat) downstairs, in the inn's former stables, is classic old-school Spain, where the clack of dominoes and the click of pool balls compete with the thump of pop music, and all manner of ancient bric-a-brac hangs from the walls and ceiling.

**★Hotel El Mudayyan** BOUTIQUE HOTEL €€
(☎978 62 30 42; www.elmudayyan.com; Calle Nueva 18; s €40-95, d €45-120; ❄📶) The modern, clean, comfortable rooms and friendly, efficient staff are reason enough to stay here, but pushing the boat out further are fantastic buffet breakfasts, including bacon and eggs and homemade pastries (per person €5.90), and a secret 16th-century tunnel to the priest's house of the church next door (staff give free tours at 10am).

**Hotel Teruel Plaza** HOTEL €€
(☎978 60 88 17; www.hotelteruelplaza.com; Plaza del Tremedal 3; s €43-53, d €55-88; ❄📶) Vivid-coloured spot lighting and smart bathrooms enhance the contemporary feel of the 14 spacious, clean-lined doubles with sofas or armchairs and four narrow but still pleasant singles. Check out the amusing prints in the ground-floor cafe-restaurant.

## Eating

Landlocked Teruel promotes its local *jamón* and other *embutidos* (cured meats) with great enthusiasm. Available in almost every eatery is *delicias de Teruel* (slices of local ham with pieces of toast and a bowl of squished-up tomato).

Plaza del Torico is lined with cafes and restaurants open from breakfast until late-night drinks. Paseo del Óvalo has an attractive row of informal restaurants, among them the ever-reliable **Bar Gregory** (Paseo del Óvalo 6; mains €8-14; ⌚7am-midnight), with tables out on the broad pavement – great for summer evenings.

**★Locavore** CONTEMPORARY SPANISH €
(Calle Bartolomé Esteban 10; dishes €6-14; ⌚1-3.30pm & 8.30-11pm) A great little minimalist-design gastrobar with delicious, creatively concocted dishes and welcoming service. Try the *huevo Locavore* (a slow-cooked egg with creamy mashed potato and ham shavings – mix it all together!), or the melt-in-the-mouth *pluma de cerdo* (a cut of pork) with mustard-honey-soy sauce.

**La Barrica** TAPAS €
(Calle Abadía 5; tapas €2.30; ⌚9.30am-3.30pm & 8-11pm Mon-Fri, noon-3.30pm & 8-11pm Sat, noon-3.30pm Sun, closed Tue Sep-May, Sun Jun-Aug) Delicious tapas treats, composed from a variety of market-fresh ingredients, are displayed temptingly along the bar, Basque-style. Options might include eggs scrambled with ham, cod and potato, or goat's cheese with ham, raisins and tomato jam. It's a smallish space, so get there early if you want a seat.

**★La Bella Neda** GRILL €€
(☎978 60 59 17; www.labellaneda.com; Calle San Esteban 2; mains €14-27; ⌚1.30-3.30pm & 9-11pm Thu-Sat, 1.30-3.30pm Sun-Tue, closed Mon-Tue approx Sep-May) For a meaty feast head to this small, friendly, wood-beamed steakhouse with its open wood grill burning away in one corner. Choose between succulent entrecôte or tenderloin steaks, a *chuletón* (giant beef chop), or pork, lamb and seafood options. Nice wines too. Reservations advised.

**La Torre del Salvador** ARAGONESE €€
(☎978 60 52 63; Calle El Salvador; mains €11-20, menú €18; ⌚noon-4pm Tue, Wed & Sun, noon-4pm & 9-11pm Thu-Sat; 📶) This smart restaurant raises the stakes with subtle *nueva cocina aragonesa* dishes – the likes of duck in a sauce of red fruits and *pacharán*, or turbot cooked with vegetable tempura. It's very popular and not very big, so reserving or arriving early makes sense.

## ℹ Information

**City Tourist Office** (☎978 62 41 05; www.turismo.teruel.es; Plaza de los Amantes 6; ⌚10am-2pm & 4-8pm Sep-Jul, 10am-8pm Aug) A few steps from the Fundación Amantes.

## ℹ Getting There & Away

Destinations served from Teruel's **bus station** (☎978 61 07 89; www.estacionteruel.es; Ronda de Ambeles) include Barcelona (€32, six to seven hours, three buses daily), Cuenca (€12, 2½ hours, one daily), Daroca (€6.10, 1¾ hours, one to three daily), Madrid (€18, 4½ hours, two daily), Valencia (€8.50, 2¼ hours, four daily) and Zaragoza (€11, 2¼ to 3½ hours, six or more daily).

Teruel is on the railway between Zaragoza (€15 to €21, 2½ hours, four trains daily) and Valencia (€14 to €19, 2½ to three hours, three or four trains daily). The station is at the foot of the sweeping Escalinata.

### ARAGONESE MUDÉJAR – THE ULTIMATE IN CHRISTIAN-ISLAMIC FUSION

Many Spanish buildings are hybrids, but few cityscapes can equal the dynamic Christian-Islamic hybridisation of Teruel, Spain's capital of Mudéjar. This unique architectural style arose out of the peculiar history of the Reconquista, which saw towns and villages fall successively from Muslim back into Christian hands between the mid-8th century and 1492. Skilled Muslim architects and artisans living in the newly conquered lands were employed by the Christians to create their new buildings, applying Islamic building and decorative techniques to basic Christian models.

The style reached its apex between the 13th and 16th centuries in a rough triangle of land between Teruel, Zaragoza and Tarazona. The regional inspiration probably came from Zaragoza's Aljafería (p393).

Aragonese Mudéjar borrowed from both Romanesque and Gothic, but used terracotta brick rather than grey stone as its main building material. In Teruel a splendid quartet of bell-cum-lookout towers is adorned with graceful arches and decorated with glazed tiles in geometric patterns. The impression is not unlike the Almohad minarets of Morocco.

Mudéjar re-emerged briefly in Teruel in the early 20th century, reinvigorated by Gaudí-inspired Modernistas such as Pau Monguió. The decorative portico on the cathedral and the grand **Escalinata staircase** (Paseo del Óvalo) both date from this period.

## Albarracín

POP 1020 / ELEV 1150M

Many villages might claim to be Spain's prettiest, but few can rival Albarracín, with its ancient, pink-hued, half-timbered houses, wooden balconies overhanging twisting, narrow streets, and picturesque fortifications and churches on a high rocky promontory carved out by the Río Guadalaviar. Its unique medieval history as an independent mini-state, and the story of its resurrection from near-abandonment over the past 60 years, add to the fascination. The town is 38km west of Teruel and well worth a stay of a night or two.

The Banu Razin clan of Berbers ruled here as an independent dynasty from 1013 to 1104. The tiny statelet passed into Christian hands in 1170 but remained effectively independent until subsumed into Aragón in 1284. Christian Albarracín had its own bishop and cathedral, and prospered from livestock herding, but by the mid-20th century the town had declined into a state of semi-ruin. Restoration efforts since then have revived Albarracín as a living historical monument of fascinating authenticity.

### Sights

Many of Albarracín's sights are managed by the **Fundación Santa María de Albarracín** (978 70 40 35; www.fundacionsantamariadealbarracin.com; Calle Catedral; 10am-2pm & 4-8pm, closed Sun afternoon mid-Sep–Jun), and the cathedral and castle can only be entered on their Spanish-language guided visits. You can book these on the Fundación's website or at its info centre in the old bishop's stables.

**★Catedral del Salvador** CATHEDRAL
(Calle Catedral; tours €4; tours 10.30am, noon & 4.30pm, closed Sun afternoon mid-Sep–Jun) After two decades of painstaking restoration, Albarracín's 16th-century cathedral has been returned to its splendour of the 18th century, by which time baroque modifications had altered its original Gothic and Renaissance lines. You can visit on village tours with the Fundación Santa María de Albarracín.

**Museo Diocesano** MUSEUM
(Calle Catedral; €3; 10.30am-2pm & 4.30-8pm, closed Sun afternoon mid-Sep–Jun) The 18th-century Bishop's Palace, adjoining the cathedral, houses this rich collection of religious art, which is a cut well above your average church museum.

**★Muralla** WALLS
Albarracín's highest point, the **Torre del Andador** (Andador Tower) was built in the 10th century as a defensive outpost for the Muslim town huddled around the castle. The walls that climb so picturesquely up to the tower were added a century later as the town expanded. The reward for *your* climb up to it is a superb panorama over the town and the unique topography that made its location so strategic.

**Castle** CASTLE
(Castillo; tours €3) Albarracín's crag-top castle was founded in the 9th century. Apart from its perimeter wall and towers, everything you see, including the remains of the Banu Razin rulers' residence, has been excavated in recent years from what had become animal pasture.

**Museo de Albarracín** MUSEUM
(Calle San Juan; €3; ⏲10.30am-1pm & 4.30-7pm, closed Sun afternoon mid-Sep–Jun) This well-designed museum explains Albarracín's fascinating history in absorbing detail in Spanish. Displays include archaeological finds from the castle, which have contributed to the understanding of the town's history.

## Sleeping

For convenience and atmosphere, pick somewhere in the old town or on the main road just below it – not back along the road towards Teruel or in the newer eastern part of town called El Arrabal.

**Posada del Adarve** HERITAGE HOTEL €
(☎615 970769; www.posadadeladarve.com; Calle Portal de Molina 23; d €45-75; 📶) Set in a tower of the medieval walls, this prettily restored hotel has five beautifully decorated, if small, rooms, friendly service and a homey feel.

★**La Casa del Tío Americano** BOUTIQUE HOTEL €€
(☎978 71 01 25; www.lacasadeltioamericano.com; Calle Los Palacios 9; s/d incl breakfast €80/100; 📶) A wonderful small hotel, 'The House of the American Uncle' proffers brightly painted rooms and friendly, impeccable service. The village views from the breakfast terrace (and from galleried rooms 2 and 3) are magnificent. A welcoming bottle of bubbles is a lovely touch, and the generous breakfast features local cheeses, honey and ham.

**Casa de Santiago** HERITAGE HOTEL €€
(☎978 70 03 16; www.casadesantiago.es; Subida a las Torres 11; s €48-54, d €64-95; 📶) A beautiful place with prettily decorated rooms including exposed wood and tiled floors, and charming service to go with it, the Casa stands in the heart of the old town a few steps up from Plaza Mayor.

**La Casona del Ajimez** HERITAGE HOTEL €€
(☎978 71 03 21; www.casonadelajimez.com; Calle de San Juan 2; s/d €60/76; 📶) Like other lovingly restored Albarracín small hotels, this 18th-century house has warm and charming decor (with interesting botanical drawings), and fine views from some rooms – and nowhere else has a grassy, terraced garden right below the castle walls! Breakfast is €5.

## Eating

★**La Despensa** ARAGONESE €
(Calle del Chorro 18; dishes €3-12; ⏲12.30-4pm & 7.30pm-midnight Wed-Mon, closed lunch Mon-Fri Oct-Jun; 📶) It's a delight to find this tiny, friendly corner bar if you're seeking something tasty that's not a full sit-down meal. The specialities are local *embutidos* (cured meats and sausages) and cheeses, but there's also chicken curry, the ratatouille-like *pisto* with fried egg, and a great tomato-and-cheese salad.

★**Tiempo de Ensueño** CONTEMPORARY SPANISH €€
(☎978 70 60 70; www.tiempodeensuenyo.com; Calle Palacios 1B; mains €19-20, menú €42; ⏲1.30-3.30pm Mon & Wed, 1.30-3.30pm & 8.30-10.30pm Thu-Sun) This sleek, light-filled dining room comes with attentive but discreet service and changing menus of innovative food that you'll remember. The venison was the tenderest we've ever had, the *jamón* starter an enormous platter, and the dessert of caramelised *torrija* (French toast) with passion-fruit sorbet divine.

**Rincón del Chorro** ARAGONESE €€
(☎978 71 01 12; http://rincondelchorro.es; Calle del Chorro 15; mains €13-21, tasting menu €23; ⏲1-4pm & 8.15-11pm Aug-Dec, 1-4pm & 8.15-11pm Fri & Sat, 1-4pm Sun Jan-Jul) Traditional Albarracín dishes are the stars at this established favourite, including roast lamb, local kid *(cabrito),* and truffles and wild mushrooms at certain times of year. Save room for a dessert such as pumpkin pie or cheesecake with red fruits. There are good tapas and *raciones* in the ground-floor bar too, plus over 20 gins to tipple.

## Information

**Tourist Office** (☎978 71 02 62; www.turismosierradealbarracin.es; Calle San Antonio 2; ⏲10am-2pm & 4-8pm Mon-Sat, to 7pm Sun) Beside the main road just before you reach the old town coming from Teruel.

## Getting There & Away

A bus to Teruel (€4.50, 50 minutes) leaves Albarracín at 8.55am Monday to Saturday, starting back from Teruel bus station at 3.30pm.

## AT A GLANCE

**POPULATION**
3.2 million

**BIGGEST CITY**
Bilbao

**BEST OLD-SCHOOL PINTXO BAR**
Casa Victor Montes (p440)

**BEST SURF BREAK**
Mundaka (p445)

**BEST GAME OF THRONES LOCATION**
San Juan de Gaztelugatxe (p445)

**WHEN TO GO**

**May** Spring sees a bustling modern art scene in Bilbao's museums and galleries.

**Jul–Sep** Sunny San Sebastián is at its best with buzzing *pintxo* bars and superb surf.

**Sep** Harvest festivals bring revelry and free-flowing wine to La Rioja's villages.

San Sebastián (p448)

# Basque Country, Navarra & La Rioja

The two great Basque cities are Bilbao, an industrial hub reborn as a cultural powerhouse, and seaside San Sebastián, a belle-époque beauty with pumping surf. These are the capitals of the renowned Basque gastronomic scene, where you can indulge in everything from gourmet bite-sized *pintxos* (Basque tapas) to Michelin-starred feasts.

Linking the two cities is a picturesque shoreline of cliffs and coastal villages; inland rises the hilly Basque hinterland of jade-green forests and cider orchards. Here you'll find Gernika (Guernica), a symbol of Basque identity devastated during the civil war but reconstructed since, and Vitoria-Gasteiz, the Basque Country's busy administrative capital.

Further inland are La Rioja – Spain's premier wine region – and Navarra, stretching from the cool heights of the western Pyrenees via its capital Pamplona to hot southern plains dotted with turreted castles.

**INCLUDES**

# BASQUE COUNTRY

## History

No one quite knows where the Basque people came from (they have no migration myth in their oral history), but their presence here is believed to predate even the earliest known migrations. The Romans left the hilly Basque Country more or less to itself, but the expansionist Castilian crown gained sovereignty over Basque territories during the Middle Ages (1000–1450), although with considerable difficulty; Navarra constituted a separate kingdom until 1512. Even when they came within the Castilian orbit, Navarra and the three other Basque provinces (Guipúzcoa, Vizcaya and Álava) extracted broad autonomy arrangements, known as the *fueros* (the ancient laws of the Basques).

After the Second Carlist War in 1876, all provinces except Navarra were stripped of their coveted *fueros,* thereby fuelling nascent Basque nationalism. Yet, although the Partido Nacionalista Vasco (PNV; Basque Nationalist Party) was established in 1894, support was never uniform as all Basque provinces included a considerable Castilian contingent.

When the Republican government in Madrid proposed the possibility of home rule (self-government) to the Basques in 1936, both Guipúzcoa and Vizcaya took up the offer. When the Spanish Civil War erupted, conservative rural Navarra and Álava supported Franco, while Vizcaya and Guipúzcoa sided with the Republicans, a decision they paid a high price for in the four decades that followed.

It was during the Franco days that Euskadi Ta Askatasuna (ETA; Basque Homeland and Freedom) was first born. It was originally set up to fight against the Franco regime, which suppressed the Basques through banning the language and almost all forms of Basque culture. After Franco's death, ETA called for nothing less than total independence and continued its bloody fight against the Spanish government until, in October 2011, the group announced a 'definitive cessation of its armed activity'.

Today, while ETA is no longer active, there is still a peaceful but strong sense of nationalism, and you'll often see banners, posters and signs emblazoned with the words *Euskal Herriak Independentzia* (Basque Country Independence) throughout the region.

### BASQUE COUNTRY PLACE & STREET NAMES

The vast majority of places in the Basque Country have Basque-language names rather than Spanish (Castilian) ones (for example, Gernika rather than Guernica). A few places, however, retain Spanish as the primary spelling, the most notable being Bilbao (Basque: Bilbo) and San Sebastián (Basque: Donostia).

Street names in larger cities, towns and villages in the Basque Country use both Spanish and Basque. The street name is preceded by the Spanish, and followed by the Basque, for example 'Calle Correo Kalea' (*calle* is Spanish for 'street', while *kalea* is Basque for 'street'). In small villages, street names are sometimes only in Basque.

# Bilbao

POP 345,821

World-famous architecture, a venerable dining scene and stunning landscapes just outside the city centre: Bilbao is one of the great treasures of the Basque Country.

Surrounded for years by an environment of heavy industry and industrial wastelands, Bilbao's tough upbringing meant its riverfront landscapes and quirky buildings were hardly recognised or appreciated by travellers. Since the late 1990s, the city has undergone a metamorphosis, most prominently with the opening of the gleaming titanium Museo Guggenheim Bilbao, drawing the attention of art and architecture aficionados from around the world.

The *Botxo* (Hole), as it's fondly known to its inhabitants, has now matured into its role of a major European centre of art and culture. But at heart it remains a hard-working town with real character and a down-to-earth soul,

## Sights

**★Museo Guggenheim Bilbao** GALLERY

(☎944 359 080; www.guggenheim-bilbao.eus; Avenida Abandoibarra 2; adult/student & senior/child €15/7.50/free; ⏲10am-8pm, closed Mon Sep-Jun) Shimmering titanium Museo Guggenheim Bilbao is one of modern architecture's most iconic buildings. It played a

# Basque Country, Navarra & La Rioja Highlights

1. **San Sebastián** (p448) Savouring the celebrated cuisine, beaches and cobblestone lanes of this stylish seaside city.

2. **Bilbao** Finding artistic inspiration at the Guggenheim, one of Europe's great architectural treasures.

3. **Lekeitio** (p446) Strolling at low tide out to a scenic island just offshore of this picture-perfect village.

4. **La Rioja** (p481) Learning the secrets of a good drop in the vineyards and museums of La Rioja.

5. **Navarran Pyrenees** (p474) Exploring caves haunted by witches in this magnificent mountain region.

6. **Pamplona** (p469) Following in Hemingway's footsteps in this city famed for its Sanfermines.

7. **Olite** (p477) Stepping into a fairy tale amid the turrets and spires of Olite's old walled quarter.

## Bilbao

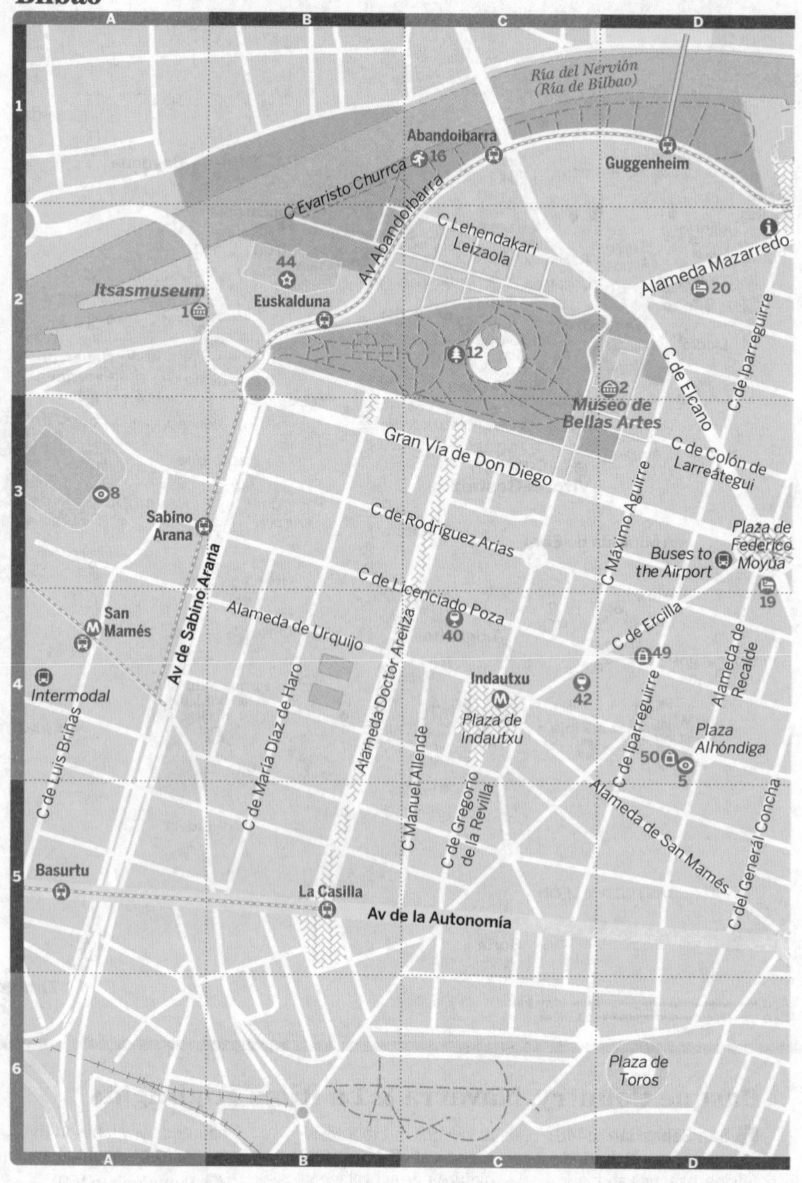


major role in helping to lift Bilbao out of its post-industrial depression and into the 21st century – and with sensation. It sparked the city's inspired regeneration, stimulated further development and placed Bilbao firmly in the international art and tourism spotlight.

Some might say that structure overwhelms function here and that the museum is more famous for its architecture than its content. But Canadian architect Frank Gehry's inspired use of flowing canopies, cliffs, promontories, ship shapes, towers and flying fins is irresistible.

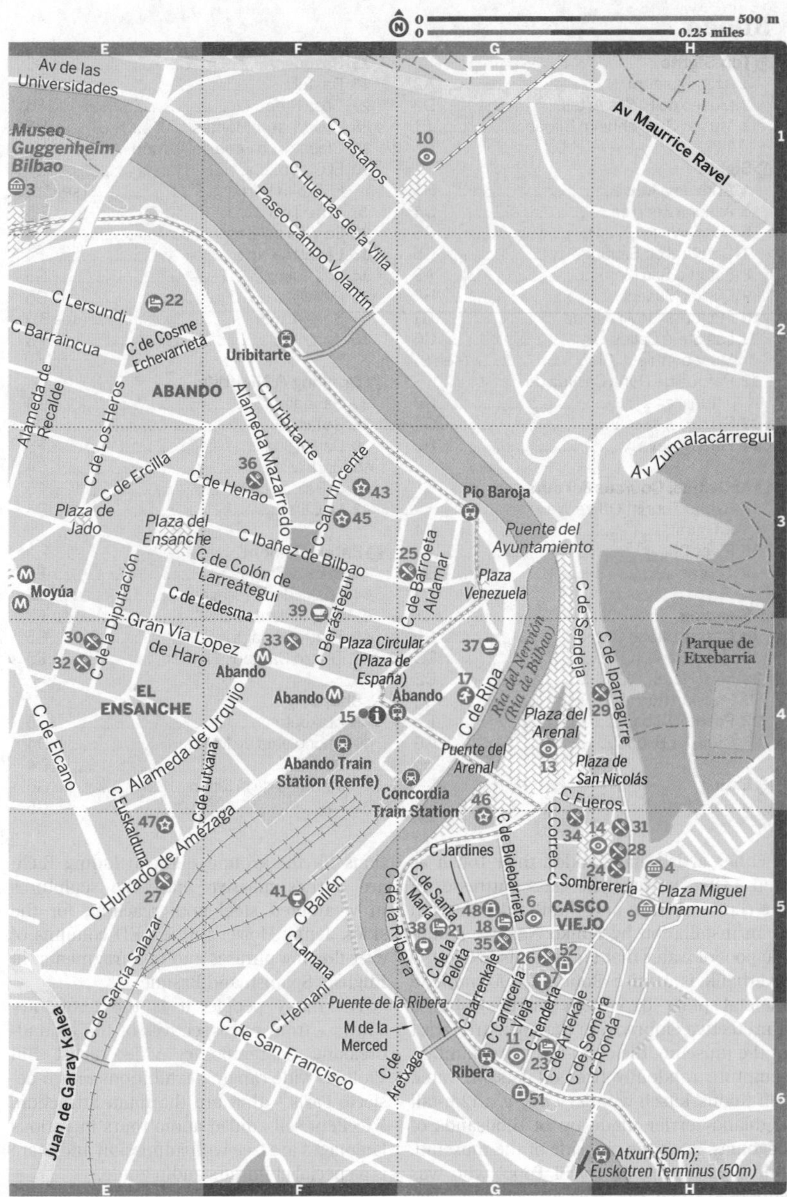


Gehry designed the museum with historical and geographical contexts in mind. The site was an industrial wasteland, part of Bilbao's wretched and decaying warehouse district on the banks of the Ría del Nervión. The city's historical industries of shipbuilding and fishing reflected Gehry's own interests, not least his engagement with industrial materials in previous works. The titanium tiles that sheathe most of the building like giant herring scales are said to have been inspired by the architect's childhood fascination with fish.

## Bilbao

**Top Sights**
1 Itsasmuseum........A2
2 Museo de Bellas Artes........D2
3 Museo Guggenheim Bilbao........E1

**Sights**
4 Arkeologi Museo........H5
5 Azkuna Zentroa........D4
6 Casco Viejo........G5
7 Catedral de Santiago........G5
8 Estadio San Mamés........A3
9 Euskal Museoa........H5
10 Funicular de Artxanda........G1
11 Las Siete Calles........G6
Museo Athletic Club........(see 8)
12 Parque de Doña Casilda de Iturrizar........C2
13 Plaza del Arenal........G4
14 Plaza Nueva........H5

**Activities, Courses & Tours**
15 Bilbao Tourist Office Walking Tours........F4
16 River Cheer........C1
17 Tourné........G4

**Sleeping**
18 Casual Bilbao Gurea........G5
19 Hotel Carlton........D3
20 Miró Hotel........D2
21 Pensión Iturrienea Ostatua........G5
22 Poshtel Bilbao........E2
23 Quartier Bilbao........G6

**Eating**
24 Bar Charly........H5
25 Basquery........G3
26 Baster........G5
27 Casa Rufo........E5
28 Casa Victor Montes........H5
29 Claudio: La Feria del Jamón........H4
30 El Globo........E4
El Txoko Berria........(see 18)
31 Gure Toki........H5
32 La Viña del Ensanche........E4
33 Ledesma No 5........F4
34 Los Fueros........G5
35 Rio-Oja........G5
Sorginzulo........(see 31)
36 Zortziko........F3

**Drinking & Nightlife**
37 Baobab........G4
38 Botanico........G5
39 Café Iruña........F3
40 Cork........C4
41 El Balcón de la Lola........F5
42 Le Club........C4

**Entertainment**
43 Back & Stage........F3
44 Euskalduna Palace........B2
45 Kafe Antzokia........F3
46 Teatro Arriaga........G5
47 Teatro Campos Elíseos........E5

**Shopping**
48 Ätakontu........G5
49 Chocolates de Mendaro........D4
50 DendAZ........D4
51 Mercado de la Ribera........G6
52 Rzik........G5

Other artists have added their touch as well. Lying between the glass buttresses of the central atrium and the Ría del Nervión is an installation by Fujiko Nakaya: a simple pool of water that emits a mist. Near the riverbank is Louise Bourgeois' *Maman*, a skeletal spider-like canopy said to symbolise a protective embrace. In the open area west of the museum, the child-favourite fountain sculpture randomly fires off jets of water. Jeff Koons' kitsch whimsy *Puppy*, a 12m-tall highland terrier made up of thousands of begonias, is on the city side of the museum. Bilbao has hung on to 'El Poop', who was supposed to be a passing attraction as part of a world tour. *Bilbaínos* will tell you that El Poop came first – and then they had to build a kennel behind it.

Heading inside, the interior is purposefully vast. The cathedral-like atrium is more than 45m high, with light pouring in through the glass cliffs. Permanent exhibitions fill the ground floor, including Richard Serra's massive maze-like sculptures in weathered steel and, reaching for the skies, Jenny Holzer's nine LED columns of ever-flowing phrases and text fragments (in English, Spanish and Basque).

For many people, it is the temporary shows – from retrospectives of the groundbreaking contemporary video artist Bill Viola to wide-ranging exhibitions on fin-de-siècle Paris – that are the main attraction. Excellent self-guided audio tours in various languages are free with admission and there is a special children's audio guide.

Free guided tours in Spanish take place at 5.45pm and 6.30pm; sign up half an hour before at the information desk. Tours can be conducted in other languages but you must ask at the information desk beforehand. Groups are limited to 20 (and there needs to be a minimum of eight), so get there early. It's also possible to organise private group tours in Spanish, English, French and German, among other languages, by prior arrangement.

The museum is equipped with specially adapted magnetic loop PDA video guides for those with hearing impairments, and is wheelchair accessible.

Entry queues can be horrendous, particularly on wet summer days and during holidays such as Easter; in busy times, you're best prebooking online with an allocated time slot.

**★Museo de Bellas Artes** GALLERY

(☎944 39 60 60; www.museobilbao.com; Plaza del Museo 2; adult/child €10/free, 6-8pm free; ⏰10am-8pm Wed-Mon) The Museo de Bellas Artes houses a compelling collection that includes everything from Gothic sculptures to 20th-century pop art. There are three main subcollections: classical art, with works by Murillo, Zurbarán, El Greco, Goya and Van Dyck; contemporary art, featuring works by Gauguin, Francis Bacon and Anthony Caro; and Basque art, with works of the great sculptors Jorge Oteiza and Eduardo Chillida, and strong paintings by the likes of Ignacio Zuloaga and Juan de Echevarría.

**★Itsasmuseum** MUSEUM

(☎946 08 55 00; www.itsasmuseum.eus; Muelle Ramón de la Sota 1; adult/child €6/free, free Tue Sep-Jun; ⏰10am-8pm Tue-Sun Apr-Oct, 10am-6pm Tue-Fri, 10am-8pm Sat & Sun Nov-Mar; 👪) On the waterfront, this interactive maritime museum brings the watery depths of Bilbao and Basque maritime history to life. Start with a 10-minute video for an overview of Bilbao history from the 1300s to the present before wandering through the two floors of displays, which show old shipbuilding techniques, harrowing shipwrecks (and innovative coastal rescue strategies), pirate threats and intricate models – including a full-scale recreation of the 1511 Consulate Barge. Outdoors, you can clamber about a range of boats.

**Casco Viejo** OLD TOWN

The compact Casco Viejo, Bilbao's atmospheric old quarter, is full of charming streets, boisterous bars and plenty of quirky and independent shops. At the heart of the Casco are Bilbao's original seven streets, **Las Siete Calles**, which date from the 1400s.

The 14th-century Gothic **Catedral de Santiago** (www.catedralbilbao.com; Plaza de Santiago; adult/child €5/free; ⏰10am-9pm Jul & Aug, to 8pm Sep-Jun) has a splendid Renaissance portico and pretty little cloister. Further north, the 19th-century arcaded **Plaza Nueva** (Plaza Barria) is a rewarding *pintxo* haunt. There's a small Sunday-morning **flea market** here, which is full of secondhand book and record stalls. Street performers and waiters with trays piled high weave in between, although the market is much more subdued in winter. A sweeter-smelling



## BILBAO CITY TOURS

There are a number of different city tours available. Some are general-interest tours, while others focus on specific aspects of the city such as architecture or food. The following are recommended.

**Bilbao Tourist Office Walking Tours** (☎944 79 57 60; www.bilbaoturismo.net; Plaza Circular 1; tour €4.50) Bilbao's main tourist office organises 1½-hour walking tours (€4.50) in English covering either Bilbao's old town (10am Saturday and Sunday) or architecture in the newer parts of town (noon Saturday and Sunday).

**Bilbao Greeters** (www.bilbaogreeters.com; by donation) A Bilbao local takes you on a tour (English available), showing you their favourite sights, places to hang out and, of course, *pintxo* bars. You need to reserve through the website at least a fortnight in advance.

**El Bote** (☎605 014365; www.elbotebilbao.com; Calle Manuel Calvo, Portugalete; 24hr ticket €8; ⏰Mon-Fri Apr-Sep, Sat & Sun year-round) Operates various cruises, including a circular hop-on, hop-off route from Portugalete, passing under the Puente Colgante transporter bridge, up to Santurtzi (on the Nervión's west bank), across to the Getxo marina and back. It sails four times per day, with the first departure at 11am.

**Tourné** (☎944 24 94 65; www.tournebilbao.com; Calle Villarias 1; bike hire per 2/4/8hr from €8/10/15, city bike tour €32; ⏰10am-9pm) Leads three-hour city bike tours (6km to 7km) departing at 10.30am daily, as well as various all-day and private tours, and also hires bikes.

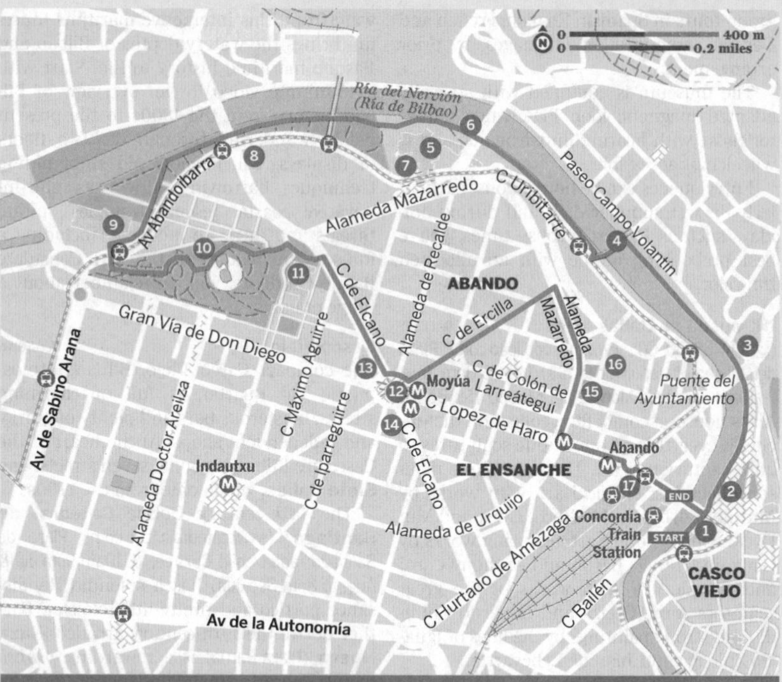


## City Walk
# Architecture and River Views

**START** TEATRO ARRIAGA
**END** TEATRO ARRIAGA
**LENGTH** 4KM; THREE HOURS

One of the pleasures of a visit to Bilbao is admiring its diverse architectural styles and the riverside walkways.

Start at the baroque 1 **Teatro Arriaga** (p441), on the edge of the Casco Viejo, which was built in 1890. Follow the river through the 2 **Plaza del Arenal** and pass by the grand 3 **ayuntamiento** (town hall), dating from the late 19th century. Continue upriver along the Paseo Campo Volantín. Cross over the 4 **Puente Zubizuri**; this wave-like bridge was designed by Santiago Calatrava and is the most striking bridge in the city.

Arriving on the other side of the river, turn right and carry on up the waterfront towards the city's most famous building, the 5 **Museo Guggenheim Bilbao** (p430). It's hard to unhinge your eyes from the museum, but do be sure to check out the spider-like 6 **Maman** and sweet-smelling 7 **Puppy**.

Continue walking along the river past numerous sculptures. On your left is the 8 **Iberdrola tower**, a 165m glass office block, the tallest building in the region. Eventually you arrive at the modern 9 **Euskalduna Palace** (p441). Turn left and enjoy the stroll through the whimsical 10 **Parque de Doña Casilda de Iturrizar**, pass by the 11 **Museo de Bellas Artes** (p435) and head down Calle de Elcano to 12 **Plaza de Federico Moyúa**, which marks the centre of the new town. This square is lined by impressive buildings including, on your right, the early-20th-century Flemish-style 13 **Palacio de Chávarri** and, opposite, the grand 14 **Hotel Carlton** (p438). Turn down Calle Ercilla, then right down Alameda Mazarredo until you come to the pretty 15 **Jardines Albia**, overlooked by the 16th-century church 16 **Iglesia San Vicente Mátir**. Cut down to Calle Lopez de Haro and, passing the art nouveau facade of the 17 **Concordia train station**, cross the Puente del Arenal to arrive back at the start of the walk.

**flower market** takes place on Sunday mornings in the nearby **Plaza del Arenal**.

**Euskal Museoa** MUSEUM

(Museo Vasco; ☎944 15 54 23; www.euskal-museoa.eus; Plaza Miguel Unamuno 4; adult/child €3/free, Thu free; ⏰10am-7pm Mon & Wed-Fri, 10am-1.30pm & 4-7pm Sat, 10am-2pm Sun) One of Spain's best museums devoted to Basque culture takes visitors on a journey from Palaeolithic days to the 21st century, giving an overview of life among the boat builders, mariners, shepherds and artists who have left their mark on modern Basque identity. Displays of clothing, looms, fishing nets, model boats, woodcutters' axes, sheep bells and navigational instruments illustrate everyday life, while iconic round funerary stones help segue into topics of Basque rituals and beliefs.

**Azkuna Zentroa** ARCHITECTURE

(Alhóndiga; ☎944 01 40 14; www.azkunazentroa.eus; Plaza Alhóndiga 4; ⏰7am-11pm Mon-Thu, 7am-midnight Fri, 8.30am-midnight Sat, 8.30am-11pm Sun) Take a neglected wine storage warehouse, convert it into a leisure and cultural centre, add a shot of Bilbao style and the result is the Azkuna Zentroa (Alhóndiga in Basque). Repurposed by renowned architect Philippe Starck, it now houses a cinema, art gallery, rooftop swimming pool with a glass bottom, a public media centre, cafes and restaurants. The ground floor is notable for its 43 tubby columns, each constructed with a unique design symbolising infinite cultures, architecture, wars and religion.

There's a Basque design shop, **DendAZ** (http://dendaz.azkunazentroa.eus; ⏰10am-9pm).

**Parque de Doña Casilda de Iturrizar** PARK

(Paseo de José Anselmo Clavé) Planted with maples, lindens, cedars, palms and 70 other species of trees, the Parque de Doña Casilda de Iturrizar was completed in 1920. The centrepiece of this elegant, English-style park is the small pond filled with ducks and swans.

**Arkeologi Museo** MUSEUM

(Plaza Miguel Unamuno; adult/child €3.50/free, Fri free; ⏰10am-2pm & 4-7.30pm Tue-Sat) This two-storey museum takes you deep into the past, beginning with 430,000-year-old fossils found in the Sierra de Atapuerca. On the 2nd floor, along the romp through the ages, you'll see models of early fortified villages, Celtiberian carvings, and statues and fragments from the Roman period; descend into the Visigothic times and the ensuing Middle Ages. Stones for catapults, a 10th-century trephined skull and jewellery from the 1200s are other curiosities.

**RIVER BOATING**

**River Cheer** (☎622 932042; www.rivercheer.com; Calle Evaristo Churruca 1; boat hire per 2/4 hr €70/120) puts you at the helm of a small four-person canopy-shaded aluminium boat, which you can pilot along the Nervión as far upstream as the old town, via the Guggenheim, with fantastic photo opportunities, and downstream to Getxo. No licence or experience is required; you're given a short tutorial before heading out. It's best to book in advance.

**Estadio San Mamés** STADIUM

(www.athletic-club.eus; Calle de Licenciado Poza) Bilbao's modern football stadium, home of local team Athletic Bilbao, overlooks the river to the west of the city centre. Opened in 2013, it has a capacity of 53,289 spectators – the largest in the Basque Country. It's within easy walking distance of the San Mamés metro station. There's a good cafe and *pintxo* bar on site.

Arrange stadium tours at the stadium's **museum** (☎944 66 11 00; btwn gates 19 & 20; museum adult/child €10/3, incl stadium tour €14/5; ⏰10am-8pm Tue-Sun Mar-Oct, to 7pm Tue-Sun Nov-Feb).

**Funicular de Artxanda** FUNICULAR

(Plaza Funicular; adult/child one-way €2/0.31; ⏰every 15min 7.15am-10pm Mon-Thu, to 11pm Fri & Sat, 8.15am-10pm Sun Jun-Sep, 7.15am-10pm Oct-May) Bilbao is a city hemmed in by hills and mountains, resting in a tight valley. For a breathtaking view over the city and the wild Basque mountains beyond, take a trip on the funicular railway that has creaked its way up the steep slope to the summit of Artxanda since 1915.

## Festivals & Events

**Aste Nagusia** CULTURAL

(⏰mid-Aug) Bilbao's grandest fiesta begins on the first Saturday after 15 August. It has a full program of cultural events over nine days and features music and dancing, Basque rural sports (like chopping wood and lifting heavy stones), parades of giants and nightly fireworks.

**Noche Blanca** CULTURAL

(Gau Zuria; ⌚Jun) For one night in June, the streets, bridges and plazas of Bilbao become a living art piece, with colourful light installations and audiovisual exhibitions. It usually happens on a Saturday night from about 8.30pm to 2am.

**Carnaval** CARNIVAL

(Aratusteak; ⌚Feb or Mar) Carnaval is celebrated with vigour in Bilbao, and features parades with floats and costumes, concerts, processions, dances and lots of hands-on children's activities. The revelry runs for six days, kicking off on the Thursday before Ash Wednesday and ending on Shrove Tuesday, with the ceremonial burning of the sardine. Casco Viejo is the place to be.

**Bilbao BBK Live** MUSIC

(www.bilbaobbklive.com; ⌚Jul) Bilbao's biggest musical event is Bilbao BBK Live, which draws top artists from around the globe – past performers have included Guns N' Roses, Ben Harper, The Chemical Brothers, Rammstein and Florence + the Machine. It takes place over three days (typically early to mid-July) in Parque Kobetamendi, a hillside park located 3km west of the centre.

## Sleeping

**Poshtel Bilbao** HOSTEL €

(☎944 25 65 86; www.poshtelbilbao.com; Calle de Los Heros 7; dm/d/f from €26/90/125, pilgrims' dorm from €22.50; ❄📶) Located just 300m southeast of the Museo Guggenheim Bilbao, this 'poshtel' lives up to its name, with an interior courtyard with a vertical garden, laundry facilities, and on-site restaurant, bar and sauna. All four- to eight-bed dorms and private rooms have en suite bathrooms, though not the 14-bed 'pilgrims' dorm'.

**Quartier Bilbao** HOSTEL €

(☎944 97 88 00; www.quartierbilbao.com; Calle de Artekale 15; dm/d with shared bathroom from €19/55; 📶) In a great location in the old town, this modern hostel has much to recommend it, including well-maintained facilities and helpful staff. It's spread over several floors of a six-storey building, and the bright common areas are good places to meet other travellers.

**Pensión Iturrienea Ostatua** PENSION €€

(☎944 16 15 00; www.iturrieneaostatua.com; Calle de Santa María 14; d/tr from €85/105; 📶) Located in a 1906 building on one of the charming pedestrian streets in the historic centre, nine-room Pensión Iturrienea Ostatua has an eclectic decor with vintage and antique furnishings. Street-facing rooms open to small wrought-iron balconies with tables and chairs.

**Casual Bilbao Gurea** PENSION €€

(☎944 16 32 99; www.casualhoteles.com; Calle de Bidebarrieta 14; d/tr from €85/125; 📶) The family-run Gurea has arty, modern rooms with wooden floors, good natural light and pretty blue-and-white murals stencilled on the walls. It's set on the 3rd and 4th floors of a building in the old town, with great dining options just steps from the entrance.

**Miró Hotel** DESIGN HOTEL €€€

(☎946 61 18 80; www.mirohotelbilbao.com; Alameda Mazarredo 77; d/ste from €168/283; ❄📶) This hip hotel facing the Museo Guggenheim Bilbao is the passion project of fashion designer Antonio Miró. It's filled with modern photography and art, quirky books, and minimalist decor – a perfect fit with art-minded Bilbao.

**Hotel Carlton** HISTORIC HOTEL €€€

(☎944 16 22 00; www.hotelcarlton.es; Plaza de Federico Moyúa 2; d/ste from €165/284; P❄📶) Style, class and sophistication: at Hotel Carlton, sitting proudly in a prominent position on Plaza de Federico Moyúa, it's old-fashioned glamour with a retro twist all the way. The grand building, constructed in French Empire style between 1919 and 1926, was the work of Bilbao architect Manuel María Smith.

## Eating

**★Basquery** INTERNATIONAL €

(☎944 07 27 12; www.basquery.com; Ibañez de Bilbao 8; mains €10-15; ⌚8.30am-10pm Mon-Thu, 9am-11pm Fri & Sat, 10am-4.30pm Sun) Equal parts cafe, bakery, microbrewery and dining destination, this post-industrial, multiroom space has a stunning line-up of daily dishes, from vegan burgers to sausages with beer-and-mustard sauce, plus charcuterie and appetisers (eg sweet potato–stuffed mushrooms) that pair perfectly with the in-house IPA, golden ale and session stout. Its deli, stocking tinned fish, preserved veggies and more, is next door.

**Casa Rufo** BASQUE €€

(☎944 43 21 72; www.casarufo.com; Hurtado de Amézaga 5; mains €16-20; ⌚1.30-4pm & 8.30-11pm Mon-Sat, 1.30-4pm Sun) Tucked in the back of a small deli and wine shop, Casa

## BEST PINTXO BARS IN BILBAO

Although Bilbao lacks San Sebastián's stellar reputation for *pintxos* (Basque tapas), prices are generally slightly lower here (all charge from around €2 per *pintxo*) and the quality is about the same. There are scores of *pintxo* bars throughout Bilbao, but the Plaza Nueva on the edge of the Casco Viejo offers especially rich pickings, as do Calle de Perro and Calle Jardines. Some of the city's standouts, in no particular order:

**Casa Victor Montes** (p440) As well known for its *pintxos* as for its full meals.

**La Viña del Ensanche** (944 15 56 15; www.lavinadelensanche.com; Calle de la Diputación 10; small plates €5-22.50, tasting menu €35; 8.30am-11pm Mon-Fri, noon-1am Sat) Hundreds of bottles of wine line the walls of this brilliant *pintxo* bar.

**Gure Toki** (www.guretoki.com; Plaza Nueva 12; pintxos €3-5.50; 9am-11.30pm Mon-Sat, 9.30am-4pm Sun) With a subtle but simple line in creative *pintxos*, including some made with ostrich.

**Baster** (www.facebook.com/BasterBilbao; Calle Correo 22; pintxos €2-4; 9.30am-10pm Tue-Thu, to 11pm Fri & Sat, to 4pm Sun; ) Outstanding *pintxos* include octopus skewers with potato, mini-quiches, house-made croquettes and delectable *jamón* (ham).

**Sorginzulo** (Plaza Nueva 12; pintxos €2-3.50; 7.30am-12.30am) A matchbox-sized bar with an exemplary spread of *pintxos*. The house special is calamari but it's only served on weekends.

**Claudio: La Feria del Jamón** (www.claudiojamones.com; Calle de Iparragirre 9-11; pintxos €2.80-5; 5.30-11pm Mon-Thu, 5.30-11.30pm Fri, 6-11.30pm Sat) A creaky old place full of ancient furnishings and dozens of legs of ham hanging from the ceiling.

**El Globo** (www.barelglobo.es; Calle de la Diputación 8; pintxos €2.50-4.50; 8am-11pm Mon-Thu, 8am-midnight Fri, 11am-midnight Sat) Favourites at this unassuming but popular bar include *txangurro gratinado* (spider crab).

**Bar Charly** (www.barcharly.com; Plaza Nueva 8; pintxos €2.50-6; 10am-10pm Sun-Thu, to 11.30pm Fri & Sat; ) Has at least three vegetarian *pintxos* per day, such as a roast courgette and mushroom *montadito* (mini baguette), or spinach and goat's-cheese croquettes.

**Ledesma No 5** (Calle de Ledesma 5; pintxos €3-5.50; 10am-11.30pm Mon-Wed, 10am-1am Thu, 10am-2.30am Fri, noon-2.30am Sat, noon-11pm Sun) An unmissable spot among the outdoor eateries on pedestrianised Ledesma.

Rufo feels like a hidden dining spot – albeit one that's terrible at keeping secrets (reserve ahead). Amid shelves packed with top-quality wines, diners tuck into delectable Navarran asparagus, house-smoked duck, baked cod with tomatoes and red peppers, and chargrilled steaks.

**El Txoko Berria** BASQUE €€
(944 79 42 98; www.eltxokoberria.com; Calle de Bidebarrieta 14; mains €8-16.50; 1-4pm & 7.30-11pm Sun-Thu, to midnight Fri & Sat) Set over two levels, with a beautifully tiled ground-floor dining room and a more contemporary space above, this welcoming restaurant excels at staples such as pork cheeks cooked in La Rioja red wine, cod *Bizkaina* style (with a sweet, slightly spicy pepper sauce) and risotto with mushrooms and smoked Idiazabal sheep's cheese.

**Los Fueros** BASQUE €€
(944 15 30 47; www.losfueros.com; Calle Fueros 6; pintxos €5-6.50, mains €12-24; 12.30-4pm & 8-11pm Mon & Wed-Sat, noon-3.30pm & 8-11pm Sun) Seafood stars at this backstreet bar-restaurant near Plaza Nueva, appearing in dishes such as cider-marinated sardines, chargrilled octopus, mussels steamed in *txakoli* (white wine) and dorado with salsa verde. Extending to a mezzanine, the rustic-contemporary setting is more stylish than many old town places, decked out in off-white and jade-green mosaic tiling and gleaming timber tables.

**Rio-Oja** BASQUE €€
(944 15 08 71; www.rio-oja.com; Calle del Perro 4; mains €16-26; 9am-11pm Tue-Sun) Going strong since 1959, Rio-Oja retains a rock-solid reputation for its traditional

Basque dishes. Its *cazuelitas* (stews served in the clay ramekins in which they're cooked) are ideal for sharing – varieties include *cordero guisado* (braised lamb) and *chipirones en sur tinta* (squid cooked in its own ink), as well as inland specialities such as snails, tripe and sheep brains.

★**Casa Victor Montes** BASQUE €€€
(☎944 15 70 67; www.victormontes.com; Plaza Nueva 8; mains €19.50-27.50, pintxos €2.80-6; ⊙1-4.45pm & 5-11pm) The 1849-built Victor Montes attracts numerous luminaries but locals also appreciate its exquisite gilding, marble and frescoes, 1000-strong wine list and superb food. *Pintxos* span foie gras with cider jelly to *lomo* (cured pork sausage) with prawns and rum-soaked raisins. If you're planning a full meal, book in advance and savour the house special, *txuleta* (seven-year-old dairy cow T-bone steak for two; €48).

★**Zortziko** GASTRONOMY €€€
(☎944 23 97 43; www.zortziko.es; Alameda Mazarredo 17; 7-/10-course menu €65/99; ⊙1-3.30pm & 8.30-11pm Tue-Sat) Black-truffle and cod soup with squid-ink ice cream; plankton ravioli with apple-pepper gel; smoked hake cheeks with turmeric and watermelon jelly; spiced rack of lamb with anchovy sponge cake; and a chocolate sphere with almond soil and rhubarb dust are just some of the highly technical creations on this elegant Michelin-starred restaurant's no-choice tasting menus. Book well ahead.

## Drinking & Nightlife

**Cork** WINE BAR
(Calle de Licenciado Poza 45; ⊙11am-4pm & 7-11pm Mon-Thu, to midnight Fri & Sat) Taste your way around some of Spain's finest small artisan vineyards at this cosy wine bar owned and run by Jonathan García, a former Basque sommelier champion. Its blackboard chalks up 25 whites and 40 reds available by the glass. Selections change every two months but always include lightly sparkling *txakoli* and rich reds from La Rioja.

**Le Club** ROOFTOP BAR
(www.hotelercilla.com; Calle de Ercilla 37-39, Hotel Ercilla; ⊙noon-midnight; 📶) Sweeping views over Bilbao's skyline extend from this 12th-floor, glass-walled rooftop bar at the top of the Hotel Ercilla. Especially at sunset and after dark, when its decking is flooded in neon-blue light, it's a spectacular spot for a craft beer, glass of wine or dry martini, accompanied by Basque cheeses and hams, *pintxos* and burgers.

### THE ART OF EATING PINTXOS

Just rolling the word *pintxo* ('peen-cho') around your tongue defines the essence of this cheerful, cheeky little slice of Basque cuisine. The perfect *pintxo* should have exquisite taste, texture and appearance, and should be savoured in two elegant bites. The Basque version of a tapa, the *pintxo* transcends the commonplace with its culinary panache.

Many *pintxos* are bedded on small pieces of bread or on tiny half-baguettes, upon which towering creations are constructed. Some bars specialise in seafood, with much use of marinated anchovies, prawns and strips of squid, all topped with anything from shredded crab to pâté. Others deal in pepper or mushroom delicacies, or simply offer a mix of everything. And the choice isn't normally limited to what's on the bar top in front of you: many of the best *pintxos* are the hot ones you need to order.

For many visitors, ordering *pintxos* can seem like one of the dark arts of local etiquette. Fear not: in many bars in Bilbao, San Sebastián and the Basque Country, it couldn't be easier. With so many *pintxo* varieties lined up along the bar, you either take a small plate and help yourself or point to the morsel you want. Otherwise, many places have a list of *pintxos*, either on a menu or posted up behind the bar. If you can't choose, ask for '*la especialidad de la casa*' (the house speciality) and it's hard to go wrong.

Another way of eating *pintxos* is to order *raciones* (literally 'rations'; large *pintxo* servings) or *medias raciones* (half-rations; bigger plates than tapas servings but smaller than standard *raciones*). These plates and half-plates of a particular dish are a good way to go if you particularly like something and want more than a mere *pintxo*. After a couple of *raciones*, however, most people are full. Locals often prefer to just have one or two *pintxos* in each bar before moving on to the next place. Bear in mind that *pintxos* are never free; the cost of a few mouthfuls can quickly add up.

**El Balcón de la Lola** CLUB
(Calle Bailén 10; ⌚11.45pm-6am Fri & Sat) Located under the railway lines, El Balcón de la Lola doesn't get going until late. One of Bilbao's most popular mixed gay/straight clubs, this is the place to end the night if you want to keep the weekend party rolling till daybreak. It has industrial decor and packs in dance lovers – the music is mostly house.

**Botanico** BAR
(www.botanicobilbao.com; Calle de la Ribera 16; ⌚11am-11pm Tue & Wed, to midnight Thu & Sun, to 2am Fri & Sat; 📶) Jungle-print wallpaper, lush plants hanging from the ceiling and adorning the walls, and a bar made from recycled timber create a tropical atmosphere at this bar. Opened in 2019, it has an extensive range of gins, rums and vermouth, including Bilbao-produced Anubis gin and Amatxu vermouth, and uses seasonal fruits and herbs in its changing selection of cocktails.

**Café Iruña** CAFE
(www.cafeirunabilbao.net; Calle de Colón de Larreátegui 13; ⌚7.30am-1am Mon-Thu, 7.30am-1.30am Fri, 10am-2am Sat, 10am-1am Sun) Moorish-style arches, exquisite tiling, polychrome wooden ceilings, frescoes and a marble bar are the defining characteristics of this grande dame dating from 1903. Still a wonderful place for people-watching, it works as well for afternoon coffee or an evening drink as it does for breakfast, lunch (don't miss the delicious *pinchos morunos*; spicy lamb kebabs) or dinner.

**Baobab** CAFE
(www.baobabteteria.com; Calle Príncipe 1; ⌚6-11.30pm Mon, 4-11.30pm Tue-Thu, 4pm-1am Fri, noon-1am Sat & Sun) 🍃 When the rains arrive, cosy Baobab is a fine place to retreat. This riverside cafe has an excellent array of teas, infusions, beer, wine, vermouth and snacks; everything is organic and Fair Trade. Works by local artists regularly cover the walls, and there's a regular line-up of acoustic jam sessions, poetry readings and more.

## ☆ Entertainment

**★ Kafe Antzokia** LIVE MUSIC
(☎944 24 46 25; www.kafeantzokia.eus; Calle San Vicente 2) Within a former cinema, this is the vibrant heart of contemporary Basque Bilbao, featuring international rock, blues and reggae, as well as the cream of Basque rock-pop. Weekend concerts run from 10pm to 1am, followed by DJs until 5am. During the day, it's a cafe, restaurant and cultural centre with Basque dancing classes (sign up online) all rolled into one.

### UNDERWATER WINERY

The world's first underwater winery, **Crusoe Treasure** (☎944 01 50 40; www.underwaterwine.com; Areatza Hiribidea, Plentzia; on-land tastings from €40, 3hr boat trip €262; ⌚by appointment) ages its vintages 20m below the surface on an artificial reef. Tastings of its whites and reds are available on land at its tasting room. For a truly immersive experience, take a scenic boat ride out to the reef, where barnacle-encrusted bottles are hauled up for you to taste. Swimming off the boat is possible; prices also include *pintxos*.

**Euskalduna Palace** LIVE MUSIC
(☎944 03 50 00; www.euskalduna.eus; Avenida Abandoibarra 4) Built on the riverside former shipyards in 1999, in a style that echoes the great shipbuilding works of the 19th century, this vast venue is home to the Bilbao Symphony Orchestra and the Basque Symphony Orchestra. With a 2164-capacity main hall and 18 smaller halls, it hosts a wide array of operas, concerts, musicals and films.

**Teatro Arriaga** THEATRE
(☎944 79 20 36; www.teatroarriaga.eus; Plaza Arriaga) The neobaroque facade of this 1200-seat venue commands the open spaces of El Arenal between the Casco Viejo and the river. It stages theatrical performances and classical music concerts. Guided behind-the-scenes tours lasting 50 minutes in English, Spanish and Basque (adult/child €5/free) take place hourly from 11am to 1pm on Saturdays and Sundays.

**Teatro Campos Elíseos** THEATRE
(☎944 43 86 10; www.teatrocampos.com; Calle de Bertendona 3) Restored to its art nouveau glory and modernised for contemporary productions in 2010, this showpiece was built in 1902. Today, the magnificent venue hosts plays, musicals, dance, concerts, comedy, puppet and magic shows, and occasional cinema screenings. Its multitiered main hall has a capacity of 805, while the more intimate, top-floor dome room accommodates 250 people.

### BARIK CARD

Save money by purchasing a Barik card for €3 at metro vending machines, topping it up with credit (from €5) and using it on Bilbao's metro, tram and bus lines. One card can be used for multiple people, and the card pays for itself after five uses. Single passes can also be purchased from metro machines.

**Back & Stage** LIVE MUSIC
(www.backandstage.com; Calle Uribitarte 8) This popular venue incorporates two separate spaces, Stage Live and the Back Room. Along with local and international bands, it hosts DJs and various parties; check the website to see what's on while you're here.

## Shopping

**Ätakontu** FASHION & ACCESSORIES
(www.atakontu.es; Calle Jardines 8; 11am-2.30pm & 5-8pm Mon-Sat) A pair of Bilbao textile artists created this small shop, which is making waves across the Basque Country. Graphic T-shirts are the speciality, featuring whimsical and art-naïf designs (the dinosaur head is an icon); all are manufactured locally, made with organic cotton and come in unisex sizes. And with limited production runs, you won't see these elsewhere.

**Mercado de la Ribera** MARKET
(www.mercadodelaribera.biz; Calle de la Ribera; 8am-2.30pm Mon & Sat, 8am-2.30pm & 5-8pm Tue-Fri) Overlooking the river, the Mercado de la Ribera is an expansive food market that draws many of the city's top chefs for their morning selection of fresh produce. If you're not planning a picnic, don't miss the *pintxo* counters upstairs (open till 10pm), which offer an excellent spread – plus seating indoors and out.

**Chocolates de Mendaro** CHOCOLATE
(www.chocolatesdemendaro.com; Calle de Licenciado Poza 16; 10am-2pm & 4.30-8pm Mon-Fri, 10am-2pm Sat) This old-time chocolate shop spills over with pralines, truffles and nougats in shapes including anchovies and oysters, and stocks its own hot chocolate mixes. It was founded in 1850 by the Saint-Gerons family, who installed a cocoa mill at their rural property, where chocolates are still made by hand today. Visits to the mill are possible by appointment.

**Rzik** FASHION & ACCESSORIES
(www.rzik.es; Calle Correo 25; 11am-2.30pm & 5-8.30pm Mon-Sat) Street fashion goes green at this hip little store, where everything is made from recycled materials. You'll find colourful messenger bags made from old advertising banners, sleek backpacks made of truck tyres, eye-catching belts made from former firefighter hoses, and bicycle inner tubes reconfigured into wallets. The designs are bright and bold – and make fine conversation pieces as well.

## Information

Bilbao's **main tourist office** (944 79 57 60; www.bilbaoturismo.net; Plaza Circular 1; 9am-8pm; ) has free wi-fi access, a bank of touch-screen information computers and helpful staff (take a number). There are also branches at the **airport** (944 03 14 44; www.bilbaoturismo.net; Bilbao Airport; 9am-9pm) and the **Museo Guggenheim Bilbao** (www.bilbaoturismo.net; Alameda Mazarredo 66; 10am-7pm Jul-Aug, to 3pm Sun Sep-Jun).

## Getting There & Away

### AIR

Bilbao's **airport** (BIO; 913 21 10 00; www.aena.es; Loiu; ) is in Loiu, near Sondika, 12km northeast of the city. A number of European carriers serve the city, including low-cost airlines.

### BUS

Bilbao's main bus station, **Intermodal** (944 39 50 77; www.bilbaointermodal.es; Gurtubay 1, San Mamés), is west of the centre. There are regular services to the following destinations:

| Destination | Fare (€) | Duration (hr) |
|---|---|---|
| Barcelona | 26-37 | 7-8½ |
| Biarritz (France) | 5-13 | 2½ |
| Logroño | 10-15 | 1¾ |
| Madrid | 20-55 | 4½-5½ |
| Oñati | 7-8.50 | 1¼ |
| Pamplona | 15-20 | 2-2½ |
| San Sebastián | 6-13.50 | 1¼ |
| Santander | 7-15.50 | 1¼ |
| Vitoria | 8-15 | 1½ |

Bizkaibus travels to destinations throughout the rural Basque Country, including coastal communities such as Mundaka (€2.55), Gernika (€2.55) and Lekeitio (€3.35).

If you're heading directly to San Sebastián, there's a direct service from Bilbao airport departing hourly from 6.45am to 11.45pm (€17.10, 1¼ hours).

### TRAIN

The **Abando train station** (☎902 432343; Plaza Circular 2) is just across the river from Plaza Arriaga and the Casco Viejo. There are frequent trains to the following destinations:

| Destination | Fare (€) | Duration (hr) |
|---|---|---|
| Barcelona | 33-39 | 6¾ |
| Burgos | 11.50-19 | 2¾ |
| Madrid | 25-48.50 | 5-6½ |
| Valladolid | 15.50-25 | 4 |

Nearby is the **Concordia train station** (Calle Bailén 2), with its handsome art nouveau facade of wrought iron and tiles. It is used by Renfe Feve (www.renfe.com), part of Spain's national Renfe line, which has trains running west into Cantabria. There are three slow daily trains to Santander (from €9, three hours) where you can change for stations in Asturias.

##  Getting Around

### TO/FROM THE AIRPORT

The **airport bus** (Bizkaibus A3247; one-way €3) departs from a stand on the extreme right as you leave arrivals. It runs through the northwestern section of the city, passing the Museo Guggenheim Bilbao, stopping at Plaza de Federico Moyúa and terminating at the Intermodal bus station. It runs from the airport every 15 minutes in summer and every 30 minutes in winter from 6.15am to midnight.

There is also a direct hourly bus from the airport to San Sebastián (€17.10, 1¼ hours), running from 7.45am to 11.45pm. Taxis from the airport to the Casco Viejo cost about €25 to €35 depending on traffic.

### METRO

There are metro stations at the city's main focal points, including the Casco Viejo. Tickets cost €1.60 to €1.90 (€0.91 to €1.19 with a Barik card), depending on distance travelled. The metro runs to the north coast from a number of stations on both sides of the river and makes it easy to get to the beaches closest to Bilbao.

### TRAM

Operated by Euskotren, Bilbao's tram line runs to and fro between Basurtu, in the southwest of the city, and the Atxuri train station. Stops include the Intermodal bus station, the Museo Guggenheim Bilbao and Teatro Arriaga by the Casco Viejo. Tickets cost €1.50 (€0.73 with a Barik card) and need to be validated in the machine next to the ticket dispenser before boarding.

# Around Bilbao

## Gernika

POP 16,972

A name synonymous with the brutality of the Spanish Civil War, Gernika (Guernica in Spanish) suffered a devastating bombing raid that levelled the city in 1937. That harrowing April day left a deep mark on the city's identity. Following the war, Gernika was quickly reconstructed, and although it lost its historic buildings, the narrow lanes of the centre are today brimming with life. You'll find some excellent museums that deal with the bombing as well as the indestructibility of Basque culture through the ages.

### Sights

**Museo de la Paz de Gernika** MUSEUM

(☎946 27 02 13; www.museodelapaz.org; Plaza Foru 1; adult/child €5/free, Sun free; ⏲10am-7pm Tue-Sat, 10am-2pm Sun Mar-Oct, 10am-2pm & 4-6pm Tue-Sat, 10am-2pm Sun Nov, Dec & Feb) Gernika's seminal experience is a visit to the Peace Museum, where audiovisual displays calmly reveal the horror of war, both in the Basque Country and around the world. Aside from creating a moving portrait of the events that transpired on 26 April 1937, the museum grapples with the topic of peace and reconciliation with illuminating insights by the Dalai Lama, Adolfo Pérez Esquivel and others.

WORTH A TRIP

**PUENTE COLGANTE**

Designed by Alberto Palacio, a disciple of Gustave Eiffel, the Unesco World Heritage–listed **Puente Colgante** (Vizcaya Bridge; www.puente-colgante.com; per person/car one-way €0.45/1.60, walkway €8, with audio guide €10; ⏲walkway 10am-7pm Nov-Mar, to 8pm Apr-Oct), also known as the Vizcaya or Bizkaia Bridge, was the world's first transporter bridge, opening in 1883. The bridge, which links Getxo and Portugalete, consists of a suspended platform that sends cars and passengers gliding silently over the Ría del Nervión. You can take a lift up to the superstructure at 46m and walk across for some great, though decidedly breezy, views.

**Museo de Euskal Herría** MUSEUM
(☎946 25 54 51; www.bizkaikoa.bizkaia.eus; Calle Allende Salazar 5; adult/child €3.50/2; ⏰10am-2pm & 4-7pm Tue-Sat, 10.30am-2.30pm Sun) Housed in the beautiful 18th-century Palacio de Montefuerte, this museum contains a comprehensive overview of Basque history, with old maps, engravings and a range of other documents and portraits. The top two floors are the most interesting and explore rich cultural traditions, with exhibits on dance, folklore, mythology and sports.

**Parque de los Pueblos de Europa** PARK
(Calle Allende Salazar) The Parque de los Pueblos de Europa contains a typically curvaceous **sculpture** by Henry Moore and a monumental work by renowned Basque sculptor Eduardo Chillida. The park leads to the attractive **Casa de Juntas**, where the provincial government has met since 1979. Nearby is the **Tree of Gernika**, under which the Basque parliament met from medieval times to 1876.

**Cuevas de Santimamiñe** CAVE
(☎944 65 16 57; www.santimamiñe.com; Basondo; adult/child €5/free; ⏰10am-5.30pm mid-Apr–mid-Oct, 10am-1pm Tue-Sun mid-Oct–mid-Apr) The walls of this cave system, 6.5km northeast of Gernika, are decorated with around 50 different Neolithic paintings depicting bison, horses, rhinos and the like. In order to protect these delicate artworks, only reproductions are on display. Tours take place on the hour and last 90 minutes. Call ahead to reserve an English-speaking guide.

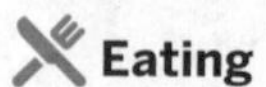

## Eating

Top-notch *pintxo* bars concentrate on and around Calle Pablo Picasso.

**Auzokoa** PINTXOS €
(www.facebook.com/AuzokoaTaberna; Calle Pablo Picasso 9; pintxos €2-3; ⏰8am-4pm & 7-11pm) Set on the restaurant-lined lane in the heart of Gernika, Auzokoa whips up some of the best *pintxos* in town. The highlights are scallop gratin served on the shell, and crab with anchovies and egg.

### THE BOMBING OF GERNIKA

The reasons Franco wished to destroy Gernika are pretty clear. The Spanish Civil War was raging and WWII was looming on the horizon. Franco's Nationalist troops were advancing across Spain, but the Basques, who had their own autonomous regional government consisting of supporters of the Left and Basque nationalists, stood opposed to Franco –and Gernika was the final town between the Nationalists and the capture of Bilbao. What's harder to understand is why Hitler got involved, but it's generally thought that the Nazis wanted to test the concept of 'terror bombing' on civilian targets. So when Franco asked Hitler for some help, he was only too happy to oblige.

On the morning of 26 April 1937, planes from Hitler's Condor Legion flew backwards and forwards over the town demonstrating their newfound concept of saturation bombing. In the space of a few hours, the town was destroyed and many people were left dead or injured. Exactly how many people were killed remains hard to quantify, with figures ranging from a couple of hundred to well over a thousand. The Museo de la Paz de Gernika (p443) claims that around 250 civilians were killed and several hundred injured. What makes the bombings even more shocking is that it wasn't the first time this had happened. Just days earlier, the nearby town of Durango suffered a similar fate, but that time the world had simply not believed what it was being told.

Aside from blocking the path to Bilbao, Gernika may also have been targeted by Franco because of its symbolic value to the Basques. It's the ancient seat of Basque democracy and the site at which the Basque parliament met beneath the branches of a sacred oak tree from medieval times until 1876. Today the original oak is nothing but a stump, but the Tree of Gernika lives on in the form of a young descendant oak tree.

The tragedy of Gernika gained international resonance with Picasso's iconic painting *Guernica*, which has come to symbolise the violence of the 20th century. A copy of the painting now hangs in the entrance hall of the UN headquarters in New York, while the original hangs in the Centro de Arte Reina Sofía in Madrid. In Gernika, you can find a full-size copy made in ceramic tiles on a wall on Calle Pedro Elejalde, near the Museo de la Paz de Gernika.

## Information

**Tourist Office** (☎946 25 58 92; www.gernika-lumo.org; Artekalea 8; ⏰10am-7pm Mon-Sat, to 2pm Sun Easter-Oct, 10am-6pm Mon-Fri, to 2pm Sat & Sun Nov-Mar) Friendly multilingual staff provide info on Gernika and nearby attractions.

## Getting There & Away

Gernika is an easy day trip from Bilbao by Euskotren train from Atxuri train station (€3.40, one hour). Trains run every half-hour; buses also make the journey.

# Central Basque Coast

The coastline between Bilbao and San Sebastián has spectacular seascapes, with cove after cove of sun-dappled waves and verdant fields suddenly ending where cliffs plunge into the sea. While some people stop for a day or two along the way, you could easily make a week of it, basking on lovely beaches, taking memorable walks along the craggy coastline and delving into the history of the place – everything from 110-million-year-old rock formations to a futuristic museum devoted to couture.

## Mundaka

POP 1835

Universally regarded as the home of the best left-hand wave in Europe, Mundaka is a name of legend for surfers across the world. The wave breaks on a perfectly tapering sandbar formed by the outflow of the Río Urdaibai and, on a good day, offers heavy, barrelling lefts that can reel off for hundreds of metres. Fantastic for experienced surfers, Mundaka is generally not a place for novices to take to the waves.

Despite all the focus being on the waves, Mundaka remains a resolutely Basque port with a pretty main square and harbour area.

**Playa de Laida** BEACH

Located just across the estuary, the lovely golden sands of Laida Beach make a fine setting for a fun day out. Where the water meets the shore, it's fairly shallow, making Laida a great place for children. Further out, you'll find good breaks for surfing. From Mundaka, it's a 23km drive, but a mere 200m-or-so paddle.

**Hotel Atalaya** HOTEL €€

(☎946 17 70 00; www.atalayahotel.es; Kalea Itxaropena 1; s/d from €110/140; P 📶) This grand hotel in a lovely 1911 building near the waterfront has light, spacious rooms, many with terraces facing the sea (there's also a communal sun terrace and a sauna open from October to July). The kind, English-speaking staff and great location make this a top choice (reserve well ahead).

**Restaurante Asador Portuondo** GRILL €€€

(☎946 87 60 50; www.restauranteportuondo.com; Portuondo Auzoa; mains €22-33; ⏰1.30-3.45pm & 8.30-11pm Jul & Aug, 1.30-3.45pm Wed, Thu & Sun, 1.30-3.45pm & 8.30-11pm Fri & Sat Feb-Jun & Sep-Nov) The pick of places to dine in the area is this sprawling traditional stone-walled, wooden-beamed place 2km south of Mundaka, which opens to an enormous terrace overlooking the estuary to Playa de Laida. Seafood, landed daily in Mundaka, is chargrilled alongside succulent steaks.

## Information

Pick up info on the area from the small **tourist office** (☎946 17 72 01; www.mundakaturismo.com; Calle Joseba Deunaren; ⏰10.30am-2pm & 4-7pm Jul & Aug, 10.30am-2.30pm Wed-Mon Sep-Jun) near the harbour.

## Getting There & Away

Buses and Euskotren trains between Bilbao and Bermeo (€3.40, 1½ hours) stop here. You can also catch a Bizkaibus bus from Bilbao (€2.55, one hour).

WORTH A TRIP

### SAN JUAN DE GAZTELUGATXE

One of the most photographed features of the Basque coast, 10km to Bermeo's northwest, is the small, rocky isle of **San Juan de Gaztelugatxe** (www.tiketa.eus/gaztelugatxe; island free, hermitage €1; ⏰island year-round, hermitage 11am-6pm Tue-Sat, to 3pm Sun Jul & Aug). Accessed from the mainland by climbing 241 steps via a stone footbridge, it's topped by a hermitage, Ermita de San Juan de Gaztelugatxe, which was built by the Knights Templar in the 10th century. Between Easter and September, island entry is only guaranteed by reserving an allocated time slot ahead of time online.

Local tradition holds that it was named after St John the Baptist, who allegedly visited the island. *Game of Thrones* fans will recognise the setting, as Dragonstone in season seven.

## Lekeitio

POP 7258

Bustling Lekeitio is gorgeous. The attractive old core is centred on the grand basilica and a busy harbour lined by multicoloured, half-timbered old buildings – some of which house fine seafood restaurants and *pintxo* bars. But for most visitors, it's the beaches that are the main draw.

### Sights

**Isla de San Nicolás** ISLAND

One of the great attractions of Lekeitio is the rocky island, known in Basque as Garraitz, sitting just offshore of the main beach (Playa Isuntza). When the tides are low, a paved path appears, allowing visitors to stroll straight out to the island, and take a 200m trail to the top for a fine view over the seaside. Be mindful of the tides, so you don't have to swim back! The tourist office posts tidal charts.

**Basílica de la Asunción de Santa María** BASILICA

(www.basilicadelekeitio.com; Calle Abaroa; ⌚8am-noon & 5-7.30pm Mon-Fri) Looming high over the old centre, this grand late-Gothic church, complete with flying buttresses topped with pinnacles, offers a vision of grandeur surprising for such a small town. In fact, Lekeitio's prolific whaling industry helped fund such extravagance. Highlights include the frieze-covered west facade, and a staggering Gothic-Flemish altarpiece, the third-largest in Spain after Seville and Toledo.

**Faro de Santa Catalina** LIGHTHOUSE

(☎946 84 40 17; www.faro-lekeitio.com; Santa Katalina Ibilpidea; adult/child €6/4.50; ⌚visits 11.30am, 1pm, 4.30pm & 6pm Wed-Sat, 11.30am & 1pm Sun Jul & Aug, weekends only Sep-Jun) On a clifftop 1.8km north of the centre, the working Santa Catalina lighthouse has an adjacent interpretation centre that gives a lively overview of coastal navigation and challenges for Basque fishermen on a one-hour immersive experience (English-language audio guide included). One room even features a simulator that puts you in a fishing boat during (mildly) rough weather, complete with breezes and misting rain, while another gives the perspective of a fisherman's wife labouring behind the scenes.

### Sleeping & Eating

**Hotel Zubieta** BOUTIQUE HOTEL €€

(☎946 84 30 30; www.hotelzubieta.com; Calle Atea; d from €90; P 📶 🏊) A 500m stroll south of the town centre, this romantic 23-room hotel occupies the 18th-century former stables of the Palacio de Zubieta (Zubieta Palace). It sits within beautiful flower-filled gardens and is surrounded by cherry trees that blossom in spring. There's a heated outdoor pool (open June to September) and an on-site restaurant serving traditional Basque cuisine.

**Hotel Metrokua** HOTEL €€

(☎946 84 49 80; www.metrokua.com; Playa de Karraspio; s/d from €96/120; P 📶) Beachfront Hotel Metrokua has nine small but light-filled rooms with wooden floors and mini-fridges. The best rooms open onto a shared terrace facing the shoreline below. If you're driving, ask about its limited parking, which is well worth snapping up in summer when spaces in the area are scarce.

**Taberna Bar Lumentza** PINTXOS €€

(Buenaventura Zapirain 3; pintxos €2-4, mains €12-16; ⌚11am-3.30pm & 8-10.30pm Tue-Sun) A big hit with the locals, this no-fuss place is tucked away in the side streets. Try *pintxos* including pickled anchovies with smoked salmon and quail egg, and Idiazabal cheese, ham and red peppers, or larger dishes such as octopus cooked on the plancha (grill) or garlic-laced cod *pil-pil*. All go well with a glass of wine or two.

★ **Mesón Arropain** SEAFOOD €€€

(☎946 24 31 83; Iñigo Artieta Etorbidea 5; mains €23-28; ⌚1-3.30pm & 8-11pm Jun-Aug, 1-3.30pm & 8-10.30pm Fri & Sat, 1-3.30pm Sun Sep-May) Situated 800m south of the centre, Mesón Arropain serves some of the best seafood for miles around. The chef lets the high-quality ingredients speak for themselves in simple but beautifully prepared dishes. Start off with its famous *arrain zopa* (fish soup) and move on to *zapo beltza* (anglerfish with fried Gernika peppers) or *legatzen kokotxak* (hake with prawns and clams).

### Information

**Tourist Office** (☎946 84 40 17; www.lekeitio.org; Plaza Independencia; ⌚10am-2pm & 4-8pm Jul & Aug, 10am-2pm Tue-Sun Sep-Jun) On the main square; stop by for info on self-guided tours of the old town.

## Getting There & Away

Bizkaibus bus A3512 leaves hourly from Bilbao's Intermodal bus station (€3.35, 1½ hours). Slower buses go via Gernika and Elantxobe (two hours). Buses also run four to five times daily from Lekeitio to San Sebastián (€7.25, 1½ hours).

# Getaria

POP 2,818

The medieval fishing settlement of Getaria is a world away from nearby cosmopolitan San Sebastián and is a wonderful place to get a feel for coastal Basque culture. The old village tilts gently downhill to a tiny harbour and a short but very pleasant beach, almost totally sheltered from all but the heaviest Atlantic swells.

At the end of the harbour is a forested former island known as El Ratón (the Mouse), which was attached via a breakwater in the 15th century during the harbour's construction. Perhaps it was this giant mouse that first encouraged the town's most famous son, the sailor Juan Sebastián Elcano, to take to the ocean. In the early 16th century, he became the first person to complete a circumnavigation of the globe, after the captain of his ship, Magellan, died halfway through the endeavour.

## Sights

**★Cristóbal Balenciaga Museoa** MUSEUM
(943 00 88 40; www.cristobalbalenciagamuseoa.com; Aldamar Parkea 6; adult/child €10/7; 10am-8pm Jul & Aug, 10am-7pm Tue-Sun Mar-Jun, Sep & Oct, 10am-3pm Tue-Sun Nov-Feb) Although Getaria is mainly about sun, sand and seafood, don't miss a visit to the Cristóbal Balenciaga Museoa. Local boy Cristóbal became a giant in the fashion world in the 1950s and '60s, and this impressive museum showcases some of his best works.

## Sleeping & Eating

**Hotel Itxas-Gain** HOTEL €€
(943 14 10 35; www.hotelitxasgain.com; Calle San Roque 1; s/d from €65/80; P) A short walk from two beaches, the Hotel Itxas-Gain is a great deal with a mixture of room types: some of its 16 rooms have little balconies and hydromassage baths that have views of the sea. Weather permitting, breakfast is served on the glass-framed terrace overlooking Playa de Gaztetape.

WORTH A TRIP

### SANTUARIO DE LOYOLA

The portentous **Santuario de Loyola** (www.loyola.global; Lugar Barrio Loyola, Azpeitia; basilica by donation, holy house adult/child €2/1; 10am-7.30pm Jul-Oct, 10am-1pm & 3.30-7pm Nov-Jun) is dedicated to St Ignatius, the founder of the Jesuit order. Its domed basilica, laden with grey marble and carved ornamentation, is decidedly imposing. Preserved in one of the two wings of the sanctuary is the house where the saint was born in 1490. Weekends are the most interesting times to come, as the sanctuary fills up with pilgrims. It's inland of Getaria, 24km to its southwest, off the GI631 just outside Azpeitia.

**★Hotel Iturregi** BOUTIQUE HOTEL €€€
(943 89 61 34; www.hoteliturregi.com; Askizu Auzoa; d/ste from €225/300; P@) Set among *txakoli* vineyards with views of Getaria's lighthouse and the sea beyond, this hideaway 4km west of Getaria has exquisite rooms and suites, most with balconies, decorated in contemporary shades of oyster-grey. There's a seasonal swimming pool, and free bike hire for guests. Gourmet breakfasts are served on the terrace.

**Txoko Getaria** SEAFOOD €€€
(943 14 05 39; www.txokogetaria.com; Calle Katrapona 5; mains €19-27; 12.30-4pm & 7.30-11.30pm) Overlooking the port, this breezy spot has earned many fans for its fresh sardines, sea bream and flounder – fired up on the grill out front. Fish aside, the seafood rices (particularly the aioli black rice with calamari) are outstanding. Call ahead to reserve an outdoor table.

**★Elkano** SEAFOOD €€€
(943 14 00 24; www.restauranteelkano.com; Calle Herrerieta 2; mains €26-39; 1-3.45pm & 8-11pm Wed-Sat, 1-3.45pm Sun & Mon) One of the world's most famous seafood restaurants, Elkano was founded in 1964 and embraces a 'fin-to-tail' ethos. Its speciality is seasonal fish prepared with disarming simplicity, such as its showstopping turbot, accompanied by vegetables from local farms.

## Getting There & Away

Buses run regularly to Getaria (€2.65, one hour) from San Sebastián's bus station. In Getaria, the buses stop on the main road, outside the **tourist office** (☎943 14 09 57; www.getariaturismo.eus; Plaza Gudarien Enparantza; ⏲9am-8pm Jul & Aug, 9am-1pm Tue-Fri, to 1.30pm Sat, to 7pm Sun Sep-Jun), on the edge of the historic quarter.

# San Sebastián

POP 186,665

Framed by golden beaches and forested mountains, San Sebastián has undeniable allure, from its grand architecture and packed cultural calendar to its venerable dining options, with Michelin stars galore and an unrivalled *pintxo* scene.

Just as good as the food is the summertime fun in the sun. For its setting, form and glamour, Playa de la Concha is the equal of any city beach in Europe, while Playa de la Zurriola is renowned for its surf.

San Sebastián's lively Parte Vieja (old quarter) lies across the neck of Monte Urgull, the bay's eastern headland, and is home to the city's most popular *pintxo* bars and least expensive guesthouses. South of the Parte Vieja is the new town's elegant commercial and shopping district, the Centro Romántica, its grid of late-19th-century buildings extending from behind Playa de la Concha to the banks of Río Urumea. On the east side of the river is the increasingly hip district of Gros.

## Sights

### ★Playa de la Concha — BEACH

(Paseo de la Concha) Fulfilling almost every idea of how a perfect city beach should be formed, Playa de la Concha (and its westerly extension, Playa de Ondarreta) is easily among the best city beaches in Europe. Tanned and toned bodies spread across the sand throughout the long summer months, when a fiesta atmosphere prevails. The swimming is almost always safe. At night, the view of the bay's twinkling lights and illuminated monuments is magical.

### ★Playa de la Zurriola — BEACH

Stretching 800m in front of Gros, from the Kursaal to Monte Ulía, 'Zurri', as it's known locally, has some excellent waves that draw surfers from near and far. It's a superb place to hang out and take in the local scene of volleyball, football and surf action; swimming here is at its best when there's no swell.

### ★Aquarium — AQUARIUM

(☎943 44 00 99; www.aquariumss.com; Plaza Carlos Blasco de Imaz 1; adult/child €13/6.50; ⏲10am-9pm Jul & Aug, 10am-8pm Mon-Fri, to 9pm Sat & Sun Easter-Jun & Sep, 10am-7pm Mon-Fri, to 8pm Sat & Sun Oct-Easter) Fear for your life as huge sharks bear down behind glass panes, or gaze at otherworldly jellyfish. The highlights of a visit to the city's excellent aquarium are the cinema-screen-sized deep-ocean and coral-reef exhibits and the long tunnel, around which swim creatures of the deep. The aquarium also contains a maritime museum section. Allow at least 1½ hours for a visit.

### San Telmo Museoa — MUSEUM

(☎943 48 15 80; www.santelmomuseoa.eus; Plaza de Zuloaga 1; adult/child €6/free, Tue free; ⏲10am-8pm Tue-Sun) One of the best museums in the Basque Country, the San Telmo Museoa has a thought-provoking collection that explores Basque history and culture in all its complexity. Exhibitions are spread between a restored convent dating back to the 16th century and a cutting-edge newer wing that blends into its plant-lined backdrop of Monte Urgull. The collection ranges from historical artefacts to bold fusions of contemporary art. San Telmo also stages some outstanding temporary exhibitions.

### Isla de Santa Clara — ISLAND

Lying 750m offshore from Playa de la Concha, this little island is accessible by **Motoras de la Isla** (☎943 00 04 50; www.motorasdelaisla.com; Lasta Plaza; return trip standard boat €4, glass-bottom boat €6.50; ⏲10am-8pm Jun-Sep) boats that run every half-hour from the fishing port in the summer. At low tide the island gains its own tiny beach and you can climb its forested paths to a small lighthouse. There are also picnic tables and a summertime kiosk.

### Monte Igueldo — VIEWPOINT

(www.monteigueldo.es; €2.30; ⏲10am-9pm Mon-Fri, to 10pm Sat & Sun Jul, 10am-10pm Aug, 10am-8pm Mon-Fri, to 9pm Sat & Sun Jun & Sep, shorter hours Oct-May) The views from the summit of Monte Igueldo (181m), just west of town, will make you feel like a circling hawk staring down over the vast panorama of the Bahía de la Concha and the surrounding coastline and mountains. The best way to get here is via the old-world **funicular railway** (Plaza del

Funicular; return adult/child €3.75/2.50; ⏲10am-10pm Jun-Aug, shorter hours Sep-May) to the **Parque de Atracciones** (☎943 21 35 25; Paseo de Igeldo; ⏲11am-11.30pm Aug, hours vary Feb-Jul & Sep-Dec), a small, old-fashioned funfair at the top of the hill. Opening hours vary throughout the year; check schedules online.

**Tabakalera** CULTURAL CENTRE
(International Centre for Contemporary Culture; ☎943 11 88 55; www.tabakalera.eu; Plaza Andre Zigarrogileak 1; ⏲9am-9pm Mon-Thu, 9am-10pm Fri & Sun, 10am-10pm Sat Sep-Jun, to 11pm Fri & Sat Jul & Aug) Sun-drenched cultural space Tabakalera occupies a beautifully reconfigured tobacco factory dating from 1913. It's a hub for the arts and design, as well as cultural enterprises such as the Basque Film Archive, the Kutxa Foundation and various galleries and innovative firms. For visitors, there's also an exhibition hall, a cinema and a regular line-up of seminars, workshops, discussions and other edifying fare. There's always something going on; check online or stop by for the latest.

**Peine del Viento** SCULPTURE
(Paseo de Eduardo Chillida) A symbol of the city, the *Peine del viento* (Wind Comb) sculpture, which lies at the far western end of the Bahía de la Concha, below Monte Igueldo, is the work of the famous Basque sculptor Eduardo Chillida and architect Luis Peña Ganchegui. Installed in 1977, the artwork is made of giant iron shapes anchored by pink granite and is spread across three nearby sites. Its powerful but mysterious forms look all the more striking against the wave-battered coastline.

**Monte Urgull** MOUNTAIN
You can walk to the summit of Monte Urgull (123m), topped by the low castle walls of the Castillo de la Mota and a grand statue of Christ, by taking a path from Plaza de Zuloaga or from behind the aquarium. The views are breathtaking and the shady parkland on the way up is a peaceful retreat from the city.

**Iglesia de San Vicente** CHURCH
(Calle de San Vicente 3; ⏲9am-1pm & 5-8pm) Lording it over the Parte Vieja, this striking church is thought to be the oldest building in San Sebastián. Its origins date to the 12th century, but it was rebuilt in its current Gothic form in the early 1500s. The towering facade gives onto an echoing vaulted interior, featuring an elaborate gold altarpiece and a 19th-century French organ. Also impressive are the stained-glass rose windows.

LOCAL KNOWLEDGE

### SAGÜÉS SUNSETS

San Sebastián's location ensures it has endless places from which to admire the setting sun, but for the best sunset of all head to the Sagüés neighbourhood at the far eastern end of Playa de la Zurriola. At the top of the steps leading from Calle de Zemoria up Monte Ulia is also another top sunset-viewing spot.

**Plaza de la Constitución** SQUARE
One of the Basque Country's most attractive city squares, the Plaza de la Constitución was built in 1813 at the heart of the old town on the site of an older square. It was once used as a bullring; the balconies of the fringing houses were rented to spectators.

**Basílica de Santa María del Coro** BASILICA
(Basilica of Our Lady of the Choir, Basilica de Nuestra Señora del Coro; Calle 31 de Agosto 46; €3; ⏲10.45am-1.15pm & 4.45-7.45pm) The Parte Vieja's most photogenic building is this baroque basilica, completed in 1774. Its ornate facade depicts St Sebastian and the altarpiece is dedicated to San Sebastián's other patron saint, Our Lady of the Choir.

**Parque de Cristina Enea** PARK
(Paseo Duque de Mandas; ⏲8am-9pm May-Sep, 9am-7pm Oct-Apr) Created by the Duke of Mandas in honour of his wife, the Parque de Cristina Enea is a favourite escape for locals. This formal park, the most attractive in the city, contains ornamental plants, ducks and peacocks, and open lawns. Its wooded paths make for a scenic stroll, past towering red sequoias and a magnificent Lebanese cedar.

## Activities & Tours

**Mimo San Sebastián** FOOD & DRINK
(☎943 00 80 70; www.mimofood.com; Paseo de la República Argentina 4) The highly recommended Mimo San Sebastián runs an array of *pintxo* tasting tours (from €75) and cookery courses (from €175) in and around the city, as well as wine tastings (from €60). Tours depart from the Hotel Maria Cristina (p453), where there's also a Mimo **shop** (⏲10am-

## San Sebastián

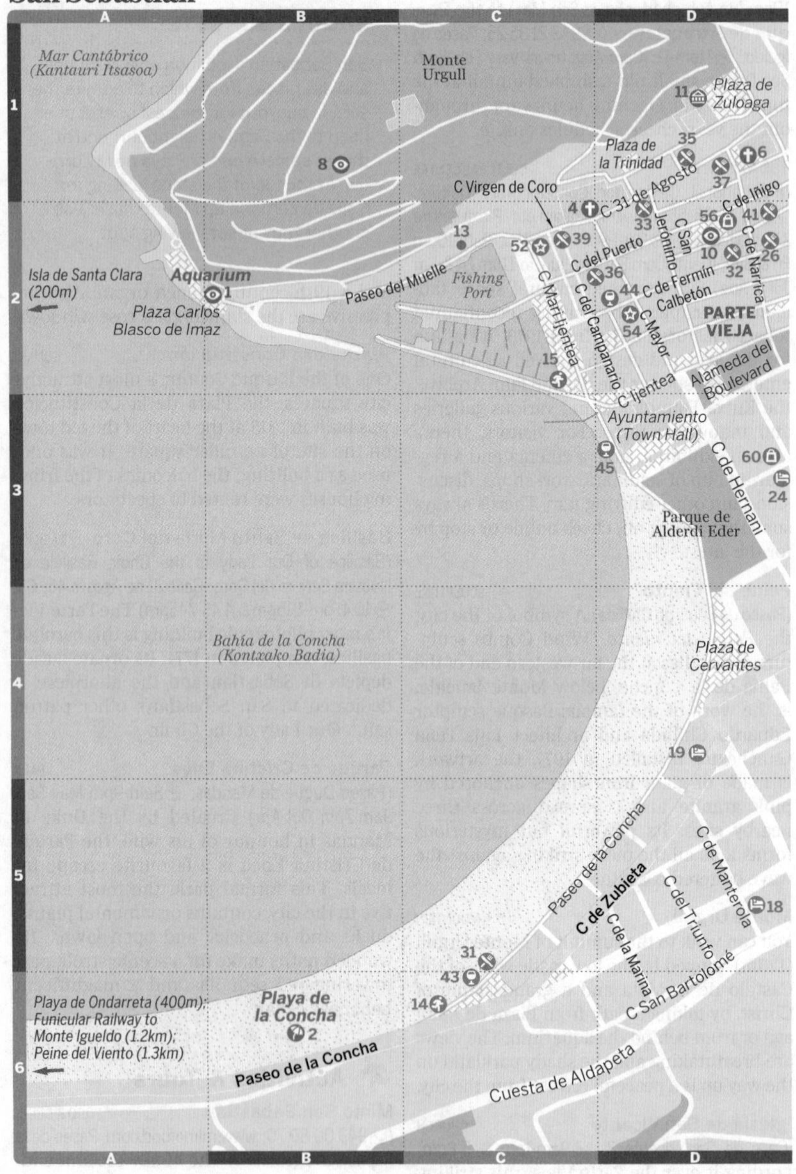




8pm Mon-Fri, 10am-7pm Sat & Sun) selling an array of high-quality local food and drink products.

**Pukas Surf Eskola** SURFING

(☎943 32 00 68; www.pukassurf.com; Zurriola Hiribidea 24; ⏰9am-2pm & 4-8pm Mon-Sat, 9am-2.30pm Sun) Aspiring surfers should drop by Pukas. Prices for classes vary depending on duration and group size, but start at €68 for a weekend course comprising a 1½-hour lesson each day. It also hires boards and wetsuits.

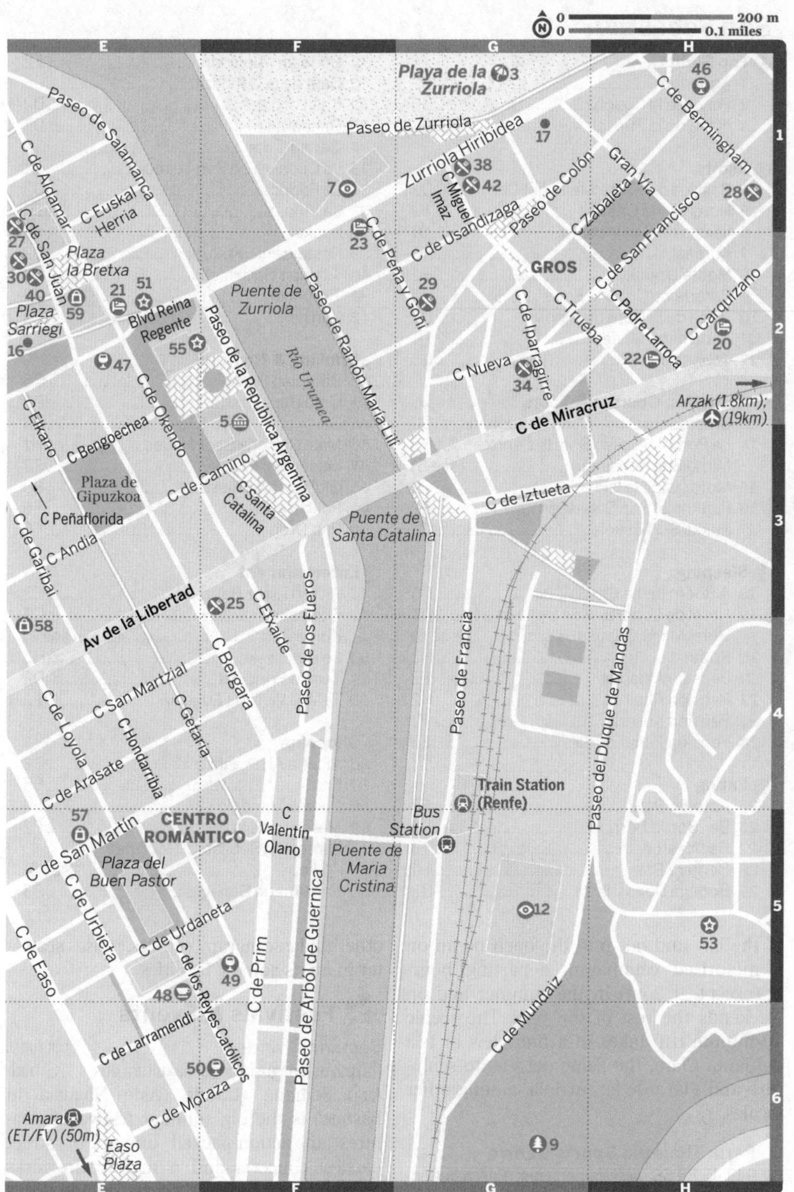


**Pintxos of San Sebastián** TOURS

(943 48 11 66; www.sansebastianturismo.eus; tours €65; noon & 7pm) The tourist office runs a two-hour tour in English of some of the city's *pintxo* haunts. Prices include four *pintxos* and four glasses of wine. The meeting point is outside the main tourist office (p460) on the edge of the old town.

**Catamarán Ciudad San Sebastián** CRUISE

(607 201155; www.ciudadsansebastian.com; Paseo del Muelle 14; adult/child €12/6; noon-8pm Jul-Aug, noon-7pm Sat & Sun Sep-Jun) Boat tours

## San Sebastián

**Top Sights**
1 Aquarium ... B2
2 Playa de la Concha ... B6
3 Playa de la Zurriola ... G1

**Sights**
4 Basílica de Santa María del Coro ... D2
5 Hotel Maria Cristina ... F2
6 Iglesia de San Vicente ... D1
7 Kursaal ... F1
8 Monte Urgull ... B1
9 Parque de Cristina Enea ... G6
10 Plaza de la Constitución ... D2
11 San Telmo Museoa ... D1
12 Tabakalera ... G5

**Activities, Courses & Tours**
13 Catamarán Ciudad San Sebastián ... C2
14 La Perla Thalasso Sports Centre ... C6
Mimo San Sebastián ... (see 5)
15 Motoras de la Isla ... C2
16 Pintxos of San Sebastián ... E2
17 Pukas Surf Eskola ... G1

**Sleeping**
18 A Room in the City ... D5
19 Hotel de Londres y de Inglaterra ... D4
Hotel Maria Cristina ... (see 5)
20 Koba ... H2
21 Pensión Aldamar ... E2
22 Pensión Altair ... H2
23 Pensión Kursaal ... F1
24 Pensión Peñaflorida ... E3

**Eating**
25 Antonio Bar ... F3
26 Bar Borda Berri ... D2
27 Bar Nestor ... E1
28 Bergara Bar ... H1
29 Bodega Donostiarra ... G2
30 Bodegón Alejandro ... E2
31 Café de la Concha ... C5
32 Casa Urola ... D2
33 Gandarias ... D2
34 Gerald's Bar ... G2
35 La Cuchara de San Telmo ... D1
36 La Fábrica ... D2
37 La Viña ... D1
38 Loaf ... G1
39 Restaurante Kokotxa ... C2
40 Txalupa Gastroleku ... E2
41 Txepetxa ... D2
42 Xarma ... G1

**Drinking & Nightlife**
43 Bataplan Disco ... C6
44 Côte Bar ... D2
45 Gu ... D3
46 Mala Gissona Beer House ... H1
47 Museo del Whisky ... E2
48 Old Town Coffee ... E5
49 Pokhara ... F5
50 Pub Drop ... F6

**Entertainment**
51 Altxerri Jazz Bar ... E2
52 Etxekalte ... C2
Kursaal ... (see 7)
53 Le Bukowski ... H5
54 Teatro Principal ... D2
55 Teatro Victoria Eugenia ... F2

**Shopping**
56 Alboka Artesanía ... D2
57 Erviti ... E5
58 Loreak Mendian ... E4
59 Mercado de la Bretxa ... E2
Mimo San Sebastián Gourmet Shop ... (see 5)
60 Perfumería Benegas ... D3

of the bay and out into the open ocean on a motorised catamaran, departing hourly (except at 3pm) in the summer and on weekends the rest of the year. The scenic 40-minute trip takes in a fine view of Isla de Santa Clara, the Peine del Viento sculpture and Playa de la Zurriola, among other locales.

**La Perla Thalasso Sports Centre** SPA
(943 45 88 56; www.la-perla.net; Paseo la Concha; 2/3hr session €29.50/33.50; 8am-10pm) Halfway along Playa de la Concha is the unmistakable white confection of La Perla Thalasso Sports Centre, a highly rated spa that offers a comprehensive set of treatments inside a grand 1912 building. There are various pools, a sauna, relaxation room, and a Jacuzzi with panoramic views. As with other thalassotherapy centres, it uses seawater in all its aquatic facilities.

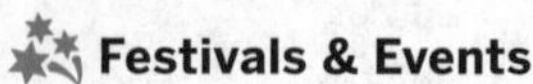

## Festivals & Events

**Semana Grande** CULTURAL
(http://astenagusia.donostiakultura.eus; mid-Aug) Semana Grande (Aste Nagusia in Basque) is the big summer festival. It features an action-packed line-up of street parties, concerts and a nightly fireworks competition, plus rural sports, an ambitious swim race (from Getaria to San Sebastián), children's activities and parades with giants and oversized heads.

**San Sebastián International Film Festival** FILM
(www.sansebastianfestival.com; Sep) Film buffs won't want to miss this world-renowned,

two-week film festival, which has been an annual fixture in the second half of September since the 1950s. It typically features an excellent line-up of films from Europe, the USA and Latin America, including a few big premieres. Screenings (around 200 to 250 in all) take place at venues citywide.

**Heineken Jazzaldia** MUSIC
(www.heinekenjazzaldia.eus; ⌚mid-Jul) This long-running, five-day music festival features world-class performers playing jazz and world music at over a dozen stages around town, including a huge outdoor one on Playa de la Zurriola, with many free shows.

**Día de San Sebastián** FIESTA
(⌚19-20 Jan) San Sebastián celebrates its patron saint with fervour. The big event is the Tamborrada, when thousands of drummers wearing 19th-century military dress and chefs' whites parade through the city. The fest runs for exactly 24 hours from midnight to midnight (late evening of the 19th to late evening of the 20th) and ends at the Plaza de la Constitución.

**Carnaval** CARNIVAL
(⌚Feb or Mar) Carnaval is a big event in San Sebastián, featuring parades with wild costumes and live music on the streets. It runs for six days, from the Thursday before Ash Wednesday to Shrove Tuesday (dates change), though the biggest events happen on the weekend.

## Sleeping

**Koba** HOSTEL €
(☎943 16 58 17; www.kobahostel.com; Calle Carquizano 5; dm/d/q from €25/80/120; 📶) A former garage in hip-and-happening Gros has been transformed into this stylish hostel. Dorms (sleeping six to eight people) and private rooms all have en suite bathrooms. Great socialising areas include an outdoor terrace; there's a kitchen, dining room, lounge and movie projector, and surfboard storage (you can also hire boards, wetsuits and bicycles on site). Rates include breakfast.

**A Room in the City** HOSTEL €
(☎943 42 95 89; www.aroominthecity.eu; Calle de Manterola 15; dm/tw/d from €35/100/120; 📶) Upstairs from a lively bar in a 1905-built former convent (aptly named 'Convent Garden'), and opening to its own roof terrace, this light, bright new-town hostel is a great place to get to know both locals and travellers. Dorms sleeping six to eight people have bunks with privacy curtains; higher-priced doubles come with en suite bathrooms.

**Pensión Altair** PENSION €€
(☎691 810403; www.pension-altair.com; Calle Padre Larroca 3; s/d from €85/115; 📶) This *pensión* occupies a beautifully restored Gros townhouse, with arched windows and modern, minimalist rooms that are a world away from the fusty decor of the old-town *pensiones*. Interior rooms lack the grandiose windows but are much larger. There's a minimum three-night stay at peak times.

**Pensión Aldamar** PENSION €€
(☎943 43 01 43; www.pensionaldamar.com; Calle de Aldamar 2; d from €140; ❄📶) A big step up in quality from many other San Sebastián *pensiones*, this friendly, professionally run place has sparkling modern rooms with white decor and stone walls, some with little balconies for watching the theatre of street life below. The same owners operate two other excellent old-town premises, Casa Nicolasa, next door, and Bule, around the corner.

**Pensión Kursaal** PENSION €€
(☎943 29 26 66; www.pensionkursaal.com; Calle de Peña y Goñi 2; d from €100; 📶) Some of the rooms at this *pensión* overlook the namesake Kursaal entertainment complex. Its charming wrought-iron lift, contemporary colour schemes, big windows and brilliant location, footsteps from Playa de la Zurriola, make this a top-value choice in Gros.

**Pensión Peñaflorida** PENSION €€
(☎943 43 53 31; www.pensionpenaflorida.es; Calle Peñaflorida 1; s/d from €115/125; 📶) In a great location near both Playa de la Concha and the old town, the Pensión Peñaflorida impresses with its contemporary design and welcoming staff. Named for local landmarks and towns, the nine rooms have style with their light timbers and pearl-grey hues. While some are rather small, the decorative balconies keep things from feeling too cramped.

**Hotel Maria Cristina** HISTORIC HOTEL €€€
(☎943 43 76 00; www.hotel-mariacristina.com; Paseo de la República Argentina 4; d/ste from €495/850; P❄@📶) Audrey Hepburn stayed here – as did Coco Chanel, Alfred Hitchcock and Mick Jagger, to name a few. The palatial Maria Cristina, opened in 1912, dominates the riverfront skyline. Glamorous

and impeccably maintained, with 136 luxurious rooms, it's still a favourite with royalty and Hollywood stars.

**Hotel de Londres y de Inglaterra** HISTORIC HOTEL €€€
(☎943 44 07 70; www.hlondres.com; Calle de Zubieta 2; d/ste from €295/485; P ❄ 📶) Queen Isabel II set the tone for the beachfront Hotel de Londres y de Inglaterra (Hotel of London and England) in the early 20th century, and it still exudes elegance. Many rooms have stunning views over Playa de la Concha, including some of the modern top-level rooms, which open to rooftop terraces. Staff are exceptionally helpful.

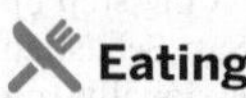

## Eating

With 15 Michelin stars in and around the city, San Sebastián is one of the culinary capitals of the planet. As if that alone weren't enough, the city is overflowing with bars – almost all of which have bar tops weighed down under a mountain of *pintxos* that are arguably the best in the country.

**Loaf** BAKERY €
(www.theloaf.eus; Zurriola Hiribidea 18; pastries €1-5.50, dishes €3.50-6.50; ⏰9am-8pm; 📶) Streetside viewing windows let you watch the Loaf baking breads, cakes (eg lemon drizzle), cookies and other treats, including rich, dense chocolate brownies. Beginning life as a shipping container pop-up, it now has a handful of branches around San Sebastián. This flagship Gros branch also incorporate a sit-down cafe serving salads, *tostas* (open-faced toasties) and sandwiches.

**La Fábrica** BASQUE €€
(☎943 43 21 10; www.restaurantelafabrica.es; Calle del Puerto 17; mains €17-25, tasting menu €40; ⏰1-3pm & 8.30-10.30pm Mon-Sat, 1-3pm Sun) The red-brick interior walls and white tablecloths lend an air of class to this restaurant, whose modern takes on Basque classics continue to make waves with San Sebastián locals. Multicourse tasting *menús* let you sample various delicacies, such as paprika-marinated octopus or king prawn flan with crab mayonnaise; there are cheaper weekday lunch menus. Advance reservations essential.

WORTH A TRIP

### MICHELIN-STARRED RESTAURANTS

The galaxy of Michelin stars surrounding San Sebastián includes the following once-in-a-lifetime experiences. Reserve well ahead.

**Arzak** (☎943 27 84 65; www.arzak.es; Avenida Alcalde Jose Elósegui 273; tasting menu €242; ⏰1.15-3.15pm & 8.45-10.30pm Tue-Sat) With three shining Michelin stars, acclaimed chef Juan Mari Arzak is king when it comes to Basque nouvelle cuisine and his restaurant, 3.5km east of San Sebastián, is considered one of the best in the world. Arzak is now assisted by his daughter Elena, and they never cease to innovate.

Boundary-pushing dishes such as cured sweetbreads with prawn-flavoured corn chips, or gingerbread topped with crab and sea grapes, are conceived in research and development kitchen, 'the lab', which draws on over 1000 ingredients to create ingenious creations. The unrivalled wine list runs over 46 pages.

**Martín Berasategui Restaurant** (☎943 36 64 71; www.martinberasategui.com; Calle Loidi 4, Lasarte-Oria; tasting menu €275; ⏰1-2.45pm & 8.30-10.15pm Wed-Sat, 1-2.45pm Sun) This superlative restaurant, 9km southwest of San Sebastián, is considered by gourmands to be among the world's finest dining addresses. The chef, Martín Berasategui, approaches cuisine as a science and the results are tastes you never knew existed, such as crystallised mullet with a squid-ink bonbon, and cod gel with pickled asparagus and caviar.

**Mugaritz** (☎943 52 24 55; www.mugaritz.com; Aldura Aldea 20, Errenteria; tasting menu €220; ⏰12.30-2pm & 8-9.30pm Tue-Sat Apr-Nov) Perched high up in the bucolic hills 10km southeast of San Sebastián, twin-Michelin-starred Mugaritz' calling card is chef Andoni Luis Aduriz' avant-garde cuisine incorporating produce foraged in the surrounding forest and gastronomic trickery, such as lemon-shaped oysters, edible river stones and even edible cutlery. The restaurant closes for four months per year, when the chef and his brigade come up with the new year's creations.

**Bar Nestor** BASQUE €€
(☎943 42 48 73; www.facebook.com/BarNestorSS; Calle de la Pescadería 11; tortilla €2.20, steak per kilo €44; ⊙1-3pm & 8-11pm Tue-Sat, 1-3pm Sun) Wonderfully eccentric Bar Nestor has a cult following for its tortillas made with green peppers (just one tortilla is cooked at lunch and at dinner; put your name on the list for a portion – in person only – an hour prior to service), and its steaks (advance reservations are possible by phone, otherwise arrive early as seating is limited).

**La Viña** BASQUE €€
(☎943 42 74 95; www.lavinarestaurante.com; Calle 31 de Agosto 3; pintxos €2-3.50, cheesecake €5; ⊙10.30am-5pm & 6.30pm-midnight Tue-Sun) The bar of this traditional spot displays a wonderful array of fishy *pintxos* and delectable snacks, but the real highlight is the creamy baked cheesecake. Prepared daily according to a special recipe and left to stand on shelves over the bar, it's ideal for a midmorning snack, afternoon dessert or really any time. One slice is large enough for two.

**★Xarma** BASQUE €€
(☎943 14 22 67; www.xarmacook.com; Calle Miguel Imaz 1; mains €16-26; ⊙1-3.30pm Tue & Sun, 1-3.30pm & 8.30-11.15pm Wed-Sat) A striking contemporary wood-lined dining room with bare-bulb downlighting is the backdrop for artistically presented dishes prepared in the open kitchen. A meal might start with watermelon gazpacho with melon-filled cucumber cannelloni, followed by smoked Basque trout with Ossau-Iraty sheep's cheese, fresh herbs and honey, or suckling pig's trotters with roast onion cream and caramelised figs.

**Antonio Bar** BASQUE €€
(☎943 42 98 15; www.antoniobar.com; Calle de Vergara 3; pintxos €2-4.50, mains €17-24; ⊙1-3.30pm & 7-11pm Mon-Sat) From the outside, Antonio Bar looks like the sort of cafe you'd get in a train station waiting room. Hidden downstairs, however, is its six-table basement dining room (reserve ahead), where house-speciality stews include *marmitako de bonito* (bonito, potato, red pepper and tomato) and *callos y morros* (beef tripe, blood sausage and chickpeas). *Pintxos* are served at the bar.

**Gerald's Bar** INTERNATIONAL €€
(☎943 08 30 01; www.geraldsbar.eu; Calle de Iparragirre 13; mains €12-20; ⊙1-4pm & 7-11pm Tue-Sun) Melbourne-based restaurateur Gerald Diffey fell so hard for San Sebastián that he decided to open a second Gerald's in the city – never mind that the first is 17,000km away. The menu changes daily but might feature steak-and-kidney pie, smoked duck breast with fig and red-onion chutney, or roast butternut squash with labneh (yogurt) and pistachio pesto.

**Café de la Concha** BASQUE €€
(☎943 47 36 00; www.cafedelaconcha.com; Paseo de la Concha 10; mains €13-20; ⊙9am-midnight; 📶) The Café de la Concha is inside a wonderful art deco building that recalls San Sebastián's aristocratic heyday. As regal as the history are the views – you're almost sitting among the sunbathers on the beach. Alongside beach cafe fare (breakfasts, salads, burgers...) are more gourmet mains such as truffle potato gratin, tuna tataki with tomato jam or 12-hour-cooked lamb confit.

**Restaurante Kokotxa** GASTRONOMY €€€
(☎943 42 19 04; www.restaurantekokotxa.com; Calle del Campanario 11; 9-/14-course menus €88/120; ⊙1.30-3pm & 8.30-10.30pm Tue-Sat, closed late Feb–mid-Mar, 1st week Jun & last 2 weeks Oct) Hidden in an overlooked Parte Vieja alley, this Michelin-starred restaurant rewards those who search. Most people opt for the *menú de mercado* and enjoy the flavours of the busy city market. Note that there are just 30 seats, making advance reservations essential, and that no-choice menus mean dietary restrictions can't be accommodated.

**Bodegón Alejandro** BASQUE €€€
(☎943 42 71 58; www.bodegonalejandro.com; Calle de Fermín Calbetón 4; mains €21-24; ⊙1-3.30pm & 8.30-10.30pm Jun–mid-Oct, 1-3.30pm Tue & Sun, 1-3.30pm & 8.30-10.30pm Wed-Sat mid-Oct–May) Tucked down the steps off a pedestrian-packed street, this handsome cellar restaurant is acclaimed for its Basque cooking. The small, changing menu has succulent treats such as local Idiazabal cheese soufflé, spider crab salad with fennel cream, crispy-skin hake with a zesty lemon vinaigrette, and roast quail with red wine jus.

## Drinking & Nightlife

**Bataplan Disco** CLUB
(☎943 47 36 01; www.bataplandisco.com; Paseo de la Concha 12; ⊙club 12.30am-6am Thu, 11.30pm-6.30am Fri & Sat year-round, terrace 2pm-2.30am Jun-Sep) San Sebastián's top club, a classic disco housed in a grand seafront complex, sets the stage for memorable beachside

# Basque Culture

**Covering 20,664 sq km (17,625 sq km on the Spanish side of the France–Spain border), this region has been the home of the Basque people for thousands of years, leading to deeply entrenched traditions.**

## Pelota

The national sport of the Basque country is *pelota vasca,* and every village in the region has its own court – normally backing up against the village church. Pelota can be played in several different ways: barehanded, with small wooden racquets, or with a long hand-basket called a *chistera,* with which the player can throw the ball at speeds of up to 300km/h. It's possible to see pelota matches throughout the region during summer.

## Traditional Basque Games

Basque sports aren't just limited to pelota: there's also log cutting, stone lifting, bale tossing and tug of war. Most stemmed from the day-to-day activities of the region's farmers and fisherfolk. Although technology has replaced the need to use most of these skills on a daily basis, the sports are kept alive at numerous fiestas.

## Lauburu

The most visible symbol of Basque culture is lauburu, the Basque cross. The meaning of this symbol is lost – some say it represents the four old regions of the Basque Country, others that it represents spirit, life, consciousness and form – but today many regard it as a symbol of

MMEEE/GETTY IMAGES ©

BRUCE YUANYUE BI/GETTY IMAGES ©

LAIOTZ/SHUTTERSTOCK ©

**1.** Sanfermines, Pamplona (p472) **2.** Pelota players **3.** Lauburu

prosperity, hence its appearance in modern jewellery and above house doors. It is also used to signify life and death, and is found on old headstones.

## Bulls & Fiestas

No other Basque festival is as famous as Sanfermines (p472), with its legendary *encierro* (running of the bulls) in Pamplona. The original purpose of the *encierro* was to transfer bulls from the corrals where they would have spent the night to the bullring where they would fight. Sometime in the 14th century, someone worked out that the quickest and 'easiest' way to do this was to chase the bulls out of the corrals and into the ring. It was only a small step from that to the full-blown carnage of Pamplona's Sanfermines.

## Traditional Dress

The daylight hours of most Basque festivals are a good time to see traditional Basque dress and dance. It's said that there are around 400 different Basque dances, many of which have their own special kind of dress.

## Basque Language

Victor Hugo described the Basque language as a 'country', and it would be a rare Basque who'd disagree with him. The language, known as Euskara, is the oldest in Europe and has no known connection to any Indo-European languages. Suppressed by Franco, Basque was subsequently recognised as one of Spain's official languages, and it has become the language of choice among a growing number of young Basques.

## BEST PINTXO BARS IN SAN SEBASTIÁN

Enter any bar in town, and the counter is sure to be groaning under a small mountain of tiny plates of culinary art. A few great places to begin the delectable culinary journey:

**La Cuchara de San Telmo** (943 44 16 55; Calle 31 de Agosto 28; pintxos €3-5; 7.30-11pm Tue, 12.30-5.30pm & 7.30-11.30pm Wed-Sun) This bustling, always packed bar offers miniature *nueva cocina vasca* (Basque nouvelle cuisine) from a supremely creative kitchen. Unlike many San Sebastián bars, this one doesn't have any *pintxos* laid out on the bar top; instead you must order from the blackboard menu behind the counter.

**Bar Borda Berri** (943 43 03 42; Calle de Fermín Calbetón 12; pintxos €2-4; 12.30-3.30pm & 7.30-11pm Wed-Sat, 12.30-3.30pm Sun Sep-Jun, also Mon & Tue Jul & Aug.) Perennially popular Bar Borda Berri is an old-school *pintxo* bar – with black-and-white chequerboard floors and mustard-coloured walls hung with old photos and strands of garlic – that really lives up to the hype. Hungry diners crowd in for house specials such as braised veal cheeks in wine, mushroom and Idiazabal sheep's cheese risotto, and beef-rib skewers.

**Gandarias** (943 42 63 62; www.restaurantegandarias.com; Calle 31 de Agosto 23; pintxos €2.50-4.75; 11am-3.30pm & 7pm-midnight) An obligatory destination for anyone interested in San Sebastián's foodie hotspots, Gandarias has a sterling reputation for its artfully prepared *pintxos*. You'll find all the classics on hand, with house specials such as seared foie gras with redcurrants, Joselito Iberian ham, scrumptious *solomillo* (tenderloin) sandwiches, stuffed mushrooms and delicious crab pie.

**Txepetxa** (943 42 22 27; www.facebook.com/bartxepetxa; Calle de la Pescadería 5; pintxos €2-3.50; 7-11pm Tue, noon-3pm & 7-11pm Wed-Sun) The humble *antxoa* (anchovy) is elevated to royal status at this old-fashioned, wood-panelled local favourite. You can order it in over a dozen different ways, topped with salmon roe or spider crab mayonnaise.

**Bodega Donostiarra** (943 01 13 80; www.bodegadonostiarra.com; Calle de Peña y Goñi 13; pintxos €2-4; 9.30am-4pm & 7-11pm Mon-Thu, to midnight Fri & Sat) The whitewashed stone walls, framed prints and black-and-white photos give this place a quirky charm, though the crowds can be so thick that you might not even notice during prime time. The draw? Some of the best *pintxos* this side of the Urumea: seared mackerel with salmon roe, black pudding with sweet red peppers, or grilled chorizo and octopus skewers.

**Txalupa Gastroleku** (www.txalupagastroleku.com; Calle de Fermín Calbetón 3; pintxos €2-5.50; noon-5pm & 7pm-midnight Mon, 7pm-midnight Wed, noon-5pm & 7pm-2am Thu & Fri, noon-3am Sat, noon-midnight Sun) A wooden bar shaped like a *txalupa* (traditional fishing boat), piled high with sublime *pintxos* prepared in the adjoining open kitchen, forms the centrepiece of this hotspot. Opened in 2019, its nautical theme extends to the ropes stretched across the ceiling and sea-green wall tiles.

**Casa Urola** (943 44 13 71; www.casaurolajatetxea.es; Calle de Fermín Calbetón 20; pintxos €2-4; noon-3pm & 7-11pm Wed-Mon) Founded in 1956, Casa Urola has hefty stone walls, hams hanging above the bar and a blackboard menu chalking up the day's *pintxos*. Join the lunch and evening crowds perfectly turned-out bites, such as grilled white asparagus, foie gras with pear compote, hake tacos, and mushroom and Idiazabal cheese tart.

**Bergara Bar** (www.pinchosbergara.es; General Artetxe 8; pintxos €2-4.50; 9.30am-11pm) The Bergara Bar is one of Gros' most highly regarded *pintxo* bars and has a mouth-watering array of delights piled on the bar counter, as well as others chalked on the board. You can't go wrong, whether you opt for its anchovy tortilla, *chupito* (spider crab mousse served in a shot glass) or rich foie gras with mango jam.

partying. The club action kicks in late, but in summer you can warm up with a drink or two on the street-level terrace. Note that door selection can be arbitrary and groups of men might have trouble getting in.

**Mala Gissona Beer House** CRAFT BEER
(www.malagissona.beer; Calle Zabaleta 53; 5-11.30pm Mon, 1-11.30pm Tue-Thu, to 1.30am Fri & Sat, noon-12.30am Sun; ) The long wooden bar, industrial fixtures and inviting front ter-

race make a suitable backdrop to the dozen quality brews on tap. Half are from its own brewery in nearby Oiartzun, such as Nao (pale ale) and Django (blanche), while the others are from other Basque and international brewers. Soak them up with bar food, including fantastic burgers.

**Old Town Coffee** COFFEE

(☎615 840753; Calle de los Reyes Católicos 6; ⊙9am-6pm Tue-Sat, to 1pm Sun) The name is a misnomer but this new-town place is spot-on for coffee. Set up by two Brazilian friends, it does small-batch roasting on-site, and uses boutique roasts such as Nomad (Barcelona) and Square Mile (London) in a variety of brewing techniques, including pour-overs, Aeropress and V20. Fresh-squeezed juices and all-day breakfasts (eg avocado toast) are also available.

**Côte Bar** COCKTAIL BAR

(www.facebook.com/cotebardonostia; Calle de Fermín Calbertón 48; ⊙5pm-3am Mon-Thu, 5pm-4.30am Fri & Sat, 4pm-3am Sun; 📶) Once the *pintxo* bars have battened down for the night, search out this low-key cocktail bar to see in the small hours. It's a stylish place, with a black granite bar and red, orange and yellow lighting, where you can sip on classic cocktails and superlative G&Ts.

**Gu** COCKTAIL BAR

(☎843 980 775; www.gusansebastian.com; Calle Mari Ijentea 9; ⊙5pm-2am Wed & Sun, to 5am Thu, to 6am Fri & Sat) Glorious beach views extend from this waterfront cocktail bar in the 1929-opened Real Club Náutico de San Sebastián building, designed to look like a boat. It's a stunning setting for a sundowner on the terrace and late-night cocktails. The DJ-fuelled club gets going at midnight.

**Pub Drop** CRAFT BEER

(☎943 35 98 57; Calle de los Reyes Católicos 18; ⊙4pm-midnight Mon-Thu, to 4am Fri, noon-4am Sat, noon-midnight Sun) One of a number of haunts on a popular drinking strip near the cathedral, Pub Drop is the place to get to grips with the local beer. There are up to 50 craft ales on offer, including 19 rotating on the taps. Try one of the brews from Basqueland Brewing Company, such as its Churros With Chocolate imperial stout.

**Museo del Whisky** BAR

(www.facebook.com/museodelwhisky; Alameda del Boulevard 5; ⊙3.30pm-3.30am Mon-Sat) Appropriately named, this atmospheric bar is full of bottles of Scotland's finest (3400 bottles to be exact, though only 200 varieties are served) as well as a museum's worth of whisky-related knick-knacks – old bottles, mugs and glasses – displayed in timber-framed glass cabinets.

**Pokhara** BAR

(☎943 45 50 23; Calle de Sànchez Toca 1; ⊙9am-2am Mon-Fri, from 3pm Sat & Sun) A hip favourite near the cathedral, Pokhara draws a wide cross-section of imbibers and party people to its weekend DJ sessions. During the week, it's a fine spot to relax with a well-made cocktail, especially at the alfresco tables in front. Try the house-speciality *carajillo,* a hot espresso served with flaming whisky.

## ☆ Entertainment

**Kursaal** LIVE PERFORMANCE

(☎943 00 30 00; www.kursaal.eus; Zurriola Hiribidea 1) An energetic and exciting array of performances are staged inside the **Kursaal** (☎943 00 30 00; www.kursaal.eus; Zurriola Hiribidea 1) centre, an architectural landmark dating to 1999. Everything from symphonic concerts and musicals to dance performances and rock shows features; check out the website for upcoming events.

**Altxerri Jazz Bar** LIVE MUSIC

(www.altxerri.com; Blvd Reina Regente 2; ⊙7pm-2.30am Sun-Thu, to 3.30am Fri & Sat) This jazz-and-blues temple has regular live gigs by local and international artists. Arrive early to get a seat and enjoy a cocktail while you wait; music generally starts around 8.30pm to 9pm. Jam sessions take over on nights with no gig; there's also an in-house art gallery that fosters the work of young contemporary artists.

**Etxekalte** JAZZ

(www.facebook.com/etxekaltejazzclub; Calle Mari 11; ⊙6pm-4am Tue-Thu & Sun, 6pm-5am Fri & Sat) Near the harbour, this late-night haunt set over two floors hosts live jazz and blues, plus other genres such as traditional Basque music, and often has DJs.

**Le Bukowski** LIVE MUSIC

(www.lebukowski.com; Calle Egia 18; ⊙10am-11pm Mon-Wed, to 2am Thu, to 4am Fri, 7pm-4am Sat, 7pm-midnight Sun; 📶) Live bands take the stage most nights at this nightspot, which also has DJs spinning a wide range of sounds – funk, hip-hop, soul, rock. It's located south of Gros near the mainline train station.

**Teatro Victoria Eugenia** THEATRE
(☎943 48 11 60; www.victoriaeugenia.eus; Paseo de la República Argentina 2; ⌚box office 11.30am-1pm & 5-8pm) Built in 1912 and refurbished between 2001 and 2007, the city's belle-époque theatre presents a varied collection of theatre and classical music. A frescoed dome crowns its main hall, which has a capacity of 910 people.

**Teatro Principal** THEATRE
(☎943 48 19 70; www.donostiakultura.eus; Calle Mayor 3) San Sebastián's oldest theatre dates back to 1843, although it has been reconstructed over the years. Today, the 576-seat hall hosts a packed calendar of theatre and dance performances.

## Shopping

**Alboka Artesanía** ARTS & CRAFTS
(Plaza de la Constitución; ⌚10.30am-1.30pm & 4-8pm Mon-Fri, 10.30am-8.30pm Sat, 11am-2.30pm Sun) Crafts and objects made in the Basque Country fill this shop on one of the old town's prettiest plazas. You'll find ceramics, tea towels, marionettes, picture frames, T-shirts, pelota balls and of course those iconic oversized berets.

**Loreak Mendian** CLOTHING
(www.loreakmendian.com; Calle de Hernani 27; ⌚10.30am-8pm Mon-Sat) Basque label Loreak Mendian specialises in affordable style for men and women – everything from T-shirts and hoodies to dresses and lightweight sweaters. This branch carries menswear, while its shop around the corner at Calle de Garibai 22 has women's fashions.

**Erviti** MUSICAL INSTRUMENTS
(www.erviti.com; Calle de San Martín 28; ⌚10am-1.30pm & 4-8pm Mon-Fri, 10am-1.30pm Sat) Erviti has published Basque musical scores since it was established in 1875. Now run by the fifth generation, it stocks traditional Basque musical instruments, including an *alboka* (single-reed woodwind instrument), *txistu* (three-holed wooden pipe), *ttun-ttun* (six-stringed instrument named for the sound it makes) and a *kirikoketa* and *txalaparta* (both wooden percussion instruments similar to xylophones). You can also buy violins, clarinets, saxophones and guitars here.

**Perfumería Benegas** PERFUME
(www.perfumeriabenegas.com; Calle de Garibai 12; ⌚10am-1.15pm & 4-8pm Mon-Sat) Founded in 1908, Benegas stocks leading international brands and in-house creations such as Ssirimiri, which uses San Sebastián as its inspiration – the rains, sunshine and sea breezes all packaged in one lovely box (featuring iconic imagery of the city). You'll also find make-up and gents' grooming products.

**Mercado de la Bretxa** MARKET
(Plaza la Bretxa; ⌚8am-9pm Mon-Sat) Dating to 1870, San Sebastián's Mercado de la Bretxa is now home to chain stores, but adjacent to it, accessed via escalators in a glass kiosk-like building, is the underground covered market where every chef in the old town comes to get the freshest produce. It's an ideal place to stock up on picnic supplies.

## Information

**Oficina de Turismo** (☎943 48 11 66; www.sansebastianturismo.com; Alameda del Boulevard 8; ⌚9am-8pm Mon-Sat, 10am-7pm Sun Jul-Sep, 9am-7pm Mon-Sat, 10am-2pm Sun Oct-May) This friendly office provides comprehensive information on the city and the Basque Country in general.

## Getting There & Away

### AIR

San Sebastián **airport** (EAS; ☎913 21 10 00; www.aena.es; Calle Gabarrari, Hondarribia) is 22km east of town, near Hondarribia. It has regular domestic services to Madrid and Barcelona.

Biarritz Airport (BIQ; www.biarritz.aeroport.fr), 48km northeast of San Sebastián in France, is a convenient arrival point for the region. Destinations served include the UK, Ireland and major continental European cities. Buses (€7, 45 minutes, up to eight daily) link the airport with San Sebastián's bus station.

### BUS

San Sebastián's **bus station** (Estación Donostia Geltokia; www.estaciondonostia.com; Paseo Federico García Lorca 1) is 1km southeast of the Parte Vieja, on the east side of the river, below the Renfe train station. All the bus companies have offices and ticket booths here.

There are daily bus services to the following:

| Destination | Fare (€) | Time (hr) |
|---|---|---|
| Biarritz (France) | 7-13 | 1¼ |
| Bilbao | 6.75-15 | 1¼ |
| Bilbao airport | 17.10 | 1¼ |
| Madrid | 16-53 | 5-6 |
| Pamplona | 8-20 | 1 |
| Vitoria | 12-20 | 1½ |

### TRAIN

The mainline **Renfe train station** (Paseo de Francia) is just across Río Urumea, on a line linking Paris to Madrid; trains linking Hendaye (France) with Lisbon also stop here. There are services to Madrid (€22 to €50, 5½ hours, several daily) and to Barcelona (€32 to €82, six hours, two daily).

For France you must first go to the French border town of Hendaye (€2.65, 35 minutes, every 30 minutes), served by Euskotren (www.euskotren.es), and change there. Trains depart every half-hour from **San Sebastián-Donostia Amara train station** (Easo Plaza 9), 1km south of the city centre, and also stop in Pasaia (€1.80, 14 minutes). Another line heads west to Bilbao via Zarautz, Zumaia and Durango, but it's painfully slow, so the bus is usually a better plan.

## Getting Around

DBus (www.dbus.eus) is the city's public bus network. The standard fare is €1.80 (€2.10 at night), payable to the bus driver.

Buses run roughly from 7.30am to 10.30pm. After that, more limited night bus services continue until about 4am.

One of the most useful routes is bus 16, which connects the city centre with Monte Igueldo.

# Around San Sebastián

## Pasaia

POP 16,128

Pasaia (Spanish: Pasajes), where the river Oiartzun meets the Atlantic, has multiple personalities. It is both a massive industrial port (the largest in the province of Guipúzcoa) and a sleepy village with quaint medieval houses hunkering over the waterfront. In fact, Pasaia is made up of four distinct districts, though it's Pasai Donibane and Pasai San Pedro that have all the charm. These two villages face each other on opposite sides of the river, and are sprinkled with sights that pay homage to the region's maritime history. Pasai Donibane on the east bank is the more appealing of the two, with several attractive squares and some notable seafood restaurants. A frequent passenger ferry connects the two towns. Dining aside, highlights include the spectacular entrance to the port, through a keyhole-like split in the cliff face – even more impressive when a huge container ship passes through it.

### SAN SEBASTIÁN TO PASAIA ON FOOT

A rewarding way of reaching Pasaia is to walk the coastal path from San Sebastián. This 7.7km trail, part of the Camino del Norte, takes about three hours and passes patches of forest and unusual cliff formations, offering lovely sea views. Halfway along, a hidden beach, Playa de Murgita, tempts when it's hot.

From San Sebastián, the route starts at the eastern end of Gros' Playa de la Zurriola, at the top of the steps leading from Calle de Zemoria up Monte Ulía. From Pasaia it climbs past the lighthouse on the western side of the port.

### Sights

**Albaola Foundation** MUSEUM

(943 39 24 26; www.albaola.com; Ondartxo Ibilbida 1, Pasai San Pedro; adult/child €7/5; 10am-2pm & 3-7pm Tue-Sun Easter–mid-Sep, to 6pm mid-Sep–Easter) This terrific museum charts the history of Pasaia's whaling industry. At the centre of the story is the *San Juan*, a galleon that sunk off the coast of Newfoundland in 1565. Models and explanatory panels describe the ship and illustrate how a team of Canadian underwater archaeologists discovered its wreck in 1978. The highlight, though, is the life-size replica of the ship being constructed using the same techniques and materials that were used to build the original.

**Casa Museo Victor Hugo** MUSEUM

(943 34 15 56; Calle Donibane 63, Pasai Donibane; 9am-2pm & 4-7pm Jul & Aug, 10am-2pm & 4-6pm Tue-Sat, 10am-2pm Sun Sep-Jun) FREE French author Victor Hugo spent the summer of 1843 in Pasaia, lodging at this typical 17th-century waterfront house and working on his travelogue *En voyage, Alpes et Pyrénées*. Sadly, his eldest daughter died in September, and he didn't write the book he intended. The 2nd floor retains a smattering of period furniture and various prints and first editions, plus audio commentary on Hugo's robust diet (peas, nectarines, oysters, cider and a glass of Malaga for breakfast).

**Faro de la Plata** LIGHTHOUSE

It's a 2.5km walk north from Pasai San Pedro, but the views from around the lighthouse

## CIDER

For the Basques, cider came before wine. The cool, rain-soaked hills of the Basque Country are ideal for growing apples, and where you find apples, you can bet you'll find cider as well. Basque cider is generally considered 'natural', in that it's not sparkling like most other European ciders. In order to add a little fizz, the cider is poured from wooden barrels into the glass from about arm's height.

A *sagardotegi* (*sidrería* in Spanish) is a cider house, one of the great institutions of Basque life. A *sagardotegi* isn't just about drinking cider, however, as they also serve food. Traditionally, a meal starts with a cod omelette, before moving onto charcoal-grilled steaks the size of a cow and finishing with dessert, which is invariably the local Idiazabal cheese with walnuts.

A night in a *sagardotegi* can be great fun. The average cost of a meal is around €25 to €30 per person, which includes all the cider you can drink. But you don't just go and get more cider as and when you please. Tradition states that each group of diners has someone who calls out '*txotx*' at regular intervals. This is your cue to get up from the table and head to the big barrels, where either a bartender or the leader of your group opens the tap and everyone takes turns filling up before heading back to the table and awaiting the next round.

Cider season is January to April, but year-round it's possible to visit a number of cider orchards, manufacturers and cider houses. Find locations online at www.sagardoa.eus or ask at the **Sagardoetxea** (☎943 55 05 75; www.sagardoarenlurraldea.eus; Kale Nagusia 48, Astigarraga; adult/child €4/2; ⏱11am-1.30pm & 4-7.30pm Mon-Sat, 11am-1.30pm Sun Jul & Aug, closed Mon Sep-Jun), a cider museum, where you can tour an orchard, taste a tipple of cider and learn all you ever wanted to know about the drink. It's located on the edge of the little town of Astigarraga, 6km south of San Sebastián. Buses A1 and A2 run here from San Sebastián-Donostia Amara station (€1.80, 25 minutes, every 15 minutes).

Surrounded by apple orchards, boutique hotel **Sagarlore** (☎843 93 10 00; www.sagarlore.eus; Petritegi Bidea 3, Astigarraga; d from €70; P 🛜 ❄) has been beautifully converted from a 16th-century former brick and tile factory. Its 16 rooms are named after local apple varieties, with apple-scented toiletries and its own cider, plus pressed apple juice and orchard-produced honey at breakfast (€9). It can also arrange tours of local cider producers.

(closed to the public) are worth the effort. It takes about 45 minutes one way.

## Eating

**Ziaboga Bistrot** SEAFOOD €€
(☎943 51 03 95; www.ziabogabistrot.com; Donibane Kalea 91, Pasai Donibane; mains €14-22, pintxos €1.80-4.50; ⏱9am-8pm Wed-Mon) Pasaia is full of excellent seafood restaurants, but Ziaboga Bistrot is one of the best. Take in the water views as you dine on delicacies such as crab-crusted hake fillet, chargrilled vivid-red Carabineros prawns, lobster *pil-pil* (in olive oil and garlic emulsion), or squid cooked in its own ink.

**Casa Cámara** SEAFOOD €€€
(☎943 52 36 99; www.casacamara.com; Calle San Juan 79, Pasai Donibane; mains €19-33; ⏱1.30-3.30pm Tue, Wed & Sun, 1.30-3.30pm & 8.30-10.30pm Thu-Sat) Managed by the same family since 1884, Casa Cámara is built half on stilts over the harbour. The majority of the menu is seafood based and the cooking is assured and traditional. The lobsters live in a cage lowered down through a hole in the middle of the dining area straight into the water.

## Information

In Pasai Donibane, within the same building as the Casa Museo Victor Hugo, the **tourist office** (☎943 34 15 56; www.oarsoaldeaturismoa.eus; Calle Donibane 63, Pasai Donibane; ⏱9am-2pm & 4-7pm Jul & Aug, 10am-2pm & 4-6pm Tue-Sat, 10am-2pm Sun Sep-Jun) has info on walks and other attractions in the area.

## Getting There & Away

Pasaia is practically a suburb of San Sebastián; numerous buses (€1.80, 30 minutes) ply the route between them. If you're driving, it's easier to park in Pasai San Pedro than in Pasai Donibane.

## Getting Around

Once in Pasaia, you'll want to use the tiny **ferry** (one-way €0.80; ⏱6.30am-11pm Mon-

Thu, 6.30am-midnight Fri, 7am-midnight Sat, 7.45am-11pm Sun) for the speedy crossing between Pasai San Pedro and Pasai Donibane.

## Hondarribia

POP 17,018

Picturesque Hondarribia (Spanish: Fuenterrabía), staring across the estuary at France, has a heavy Gallic accent, a charming Casco Antiguo and a buzzing beach scene.

### Sights

**Casco Histórico** OLD TOWN

Hondarribia's walled historic centre, much of which dates to the 15th and 16th centuries, is an atmospheric grid of graceful plazas, cobbled lanes, and buildings adorned with wood-carved eaves and wrought-iron balconies. The focal square is **Plaza de Armas**, where you'll find the local tourist office (p464), but prettier still is picture-perfect **Plaza de Gipuzkoa**.

**Monte Jaizkibel** MOUNTAIN

Monte Jaizkibel is a giant slab of rock sitting at 547m that acts as a defensive wall, protecting the inland towns and fields from the angry, invading ocean. A very strenuous walking trail (4km west of Hondarribia) and a car-taxing road wend their way up the mountain to a ruined fortress and spectacular views. From here you can walk all the way to Pasaia (another 12km).

**Castillo de Carlos V** CASTLE

(Plaza de Armas 14) Today it's a government-run hotel, but for over 1000 years this castle hosted knights and kings. Its position atop the old town hill gave it a commanding view over the strategic Bidasoa estuary, which has long marked the Spain–France border. Poke your head into the reception lobby to admire the medieval decor.

**Playa de Hondarribia** BEACH

Hondarribia's sheltered beach is lined with bars and restaurants, and offers calm swimming waters. When the swell is running, there's a long right-hand surf break off the breakwater. Located 2km north of the new town (La Marina), the beach is popular with locals, but foreign tourists are rare.

### Sleeping

**Hotel San Nikolás** HOTEL €€

(☎943 64 42 78; www.hotelsannikolas.es; Plaza de Armas 6; s/d from €78/95; 📶) Located inside a charming old building on the main plaza, in the heart of Hondarribia's historic centre, this small hotel has 16 individually decorated rooms. The best rooms have balconies overlooking the plaza to the sea beyond.

**Parador de Hondarribia** CASTLE €€€

(☎943 64 55 00; www.parador.es; Plaza de Armas 14; s/d/ste from €209/228/332; P ❄ @ 📶) It's not every day that the opportunity to sleep in a thousand-year-old fortress guarding the boundaries of Spain arises. This sumptuous offering from the Parador chain has modern guest rooms with hard-wood floors and stone walls, many with sea views. But the place to be at sunset is one of the castle's courtyards or terraces, glass of wine in hand.

### Eating

**Gran Sol** PINTXOS €

(☎943 64 27 01; www.bargransol.com; Calle San Pedro 65; pintxos €2-4.80; ⏰12.30-3.30pm & 8.30-10.30pm Tue-Sun) Wine barrels double as tables out the front of Gran Sol, one of Hondarribia's best-known addresses for *pintxos*. Standouts include mushrooms filled with cheese mousse, smoked cod with foie gras and peach jam, and pork three ways with beetroot mayonnaise. Along with *txakoli* and other local wines, it has a range of Basque craft beers.

★**Gastroteka Danontzat** BASQUE €€

(☎943 64 65 97; www.gastrotekadanontzat.com; Calle Denda 6; small plates €8-18; ⏰noon-4pm & 7.30pm-midnight Mon & Thu-Sun, 7.30pm-midnight Wed) Gastroteka Danontzat's fun, creative approach to dining combines beautifully prepared market-fresh fare with highly original presentation and props. Start off with smoked sardines, anchovies or crab croquettes, before moving on to tender tuna ceviche, squid cooked in its own ink or chargrilled entrecôte in red-pepper sauce. Small servings mean you can try a lot of flavours.

★**Laia Erretegia** GRILL €€€

(☎943 64 63 09; www.laiaerretegia.com; Arkolla Auzoa 33; mains €22-40; ⏰1-3pm Mon-Thu, 1-3pm & 8.30-10pm Fri, 1.30-3pm & 8.30-10pm Sat, 1.30-3pm Sun) Chef Jon Ayala and his maître d' sister Arantxa transformed these former stables into an open-plan dining space with glass cabinets where beef is aged for 30 to 60 days, wraparound shelves stocked with wine, and floor-to-ceiling windows overlooking the surrounding farmland and mountains. Steaks and daily caught seafood are grilled over charcoal.

**La Hermandad de Pescadores** SEAFOOD €€€
(☎943 64 27 38; www.hermandaddepescadores.com; Calle Zuloaga 12; mains €18-45; ⏲1-3.30pm & 8-10.30pm Tue-Sat, 1-3.30pm Sun) Housed in a traditional white-and-blue cottage, this institution dating to 1938 serves an array of seafood classics. It's best known for its *sopa de pescado* (fish soup), said by some to be the best in the area.

**Alameda** BASQUE €€€
(☎943 64 27 89; www.restaurantealameda.net; Calle Minasoroeta 1; tasting menus €78-115; ⏲noon-3.30pm Tue-Thu & Sun, noon-3.30pm & 7.30-11pm Fri & Sat) Michelin-starred Alameda helped pave the way to Hondarribia becoming the culinary hotspot it is today. What started life as a simple tavern is now a sophisticated fine-dining restaurant, complete with a garden and terrace, serving creative takes on traditional Basque cuisine, prepared with fresh, locally sourced ingredients.

## Drinking & Nightlife

**Vinoteka Ardoka** WINE BAR
(www.ardokavinoteka.com; Calle San Pedro 32; ⏲11.30am-3.30pm & 6-11.30pm Jul & Aug, closed Tue Sep-Jun) Behind its rustic stone facade, this contemporary wine bar has 50 wines by the glass, including locally produced *txakoli*, Tempranillo (full-bodied red wine) from Navarra, and reds and rosés from La Rioja, as well as over a dozen varieties of vermouth. Pair them with *pintxos* such as *txipiron* (squid-ink croquettes), *bacalao confitado* (confit cod) and *alcachofas fritas* (fried artichokes).

WORTH A TRIP

### HENDAYE, FRANCE

Just across the river from Hondarribia lies the pretty French town of Hendaye, linked by a regular passenger **ferry** (www.jolaski.com; Paseo Butron Ibilbidea; one-way €2; ⏲every 15min 10am-1am Jul–mid-Sep, 10.15am-7pm Mon-Fri, to 8pm Sat & Sun Apr-Jun & mid-Sep–late Sep, shorter hours Oct-Mar). Apart from nibbling on perfectly flaky croissants, Hendaye's main attraction is its 3km-long stretch of white-sand beach, a 250m stroll north of the ferry dock. It's protected by a headland that ensures calm waters for swimming.

**Amona Margarita** CAFE
(www.amonamargarita.com; Calle San Pedro 4; ⏲7.30am-9pm Mon-Fri, 8am-9pm Sat & Sun; 📶) With a light, airy interior, this cafe-bakery is a lovely place to rejuvenate with a freshly squeezed juice, coffee or home-baked cake.

## Information

On the main square in the walled old town, the **tourist office** (☎630 462948; www.hondarribiaturismo.com; Plaza de Armas 9; ⏲9.30am-7.30pm Jul–mid-Sep, 10am-6pm Mon-Sat & 10am-2pm Sun mid-Sep–Jun) has handy info on nearby attractions.

## Getting There & Away

Buses link Hondarribia's Calle Sabin Arana with San Sebastián's bus station (€2.65, 25 minutes, every 30 minutes).

# Oñati

POP 11,335

With magnificent architecture and a number of interesting sights scattered through the surrounding green hills, the small and resolutely Basque town of Oñati is a lovely place to get to know the rural Basque heartland. Many visitors pass through on their way to or from the nearby Santuario de Arantzazu.

## Sights & Activities

**Iglesia de San Miguel** CHURCH
(Avenida de Unibertsitate 1; ⏲hours vary) This late-Gothic confection has a cloister built over the river and a 17th-century crypt where the Counts of Guevara are buried. The church faces onto the main square, Foruen Enparantza, dominated by the eye-catching baroque *ayuntamiento* (town hall). Contact the tourist office for opening times and guided tours.

**Monastery of Bidaurreta** MONASTERY
(Calle Lazarraga; ⏲hours vary) Founded in 1510, this monastery contains a beautiful baroque altarpiece. As a still-functioning cloistered convent for the Poor Clares, it's rarely open to the public, but the tourist office sometimes arranges tours.

**Universidad de Sancti Spiritus** HISTORIC BUILDING
(Avenida de Universidad 8; ⏲hours vary) Oñati's most prominent building is the Renaissance treasure of the Universidad de Sancti Spiritus. Built in the 16th century, it was the first

university in the Basque Country and, until its closure in 1902, students were schooled in philosophy, law and medicine. Today it's been taken over as local council offices, but you can still enter the Mudéjar courtyard and admire its plateresque facade. Contact the tourist office to arrange a guided tour.

**Cuevas de Oñati-Arrikrutz** CAVE
(☎943 08 20 00; www.cuevasturisticas.es; Araotz Ibaia; 1hr tour adult/child €9/6; ⏰9.30am-2pm & 3.30-7pm Jul & Aug, shorter hours Mar-Jun & Sep-Dec) Located 5.5km southwest of Oñati, this cavern system has numerous slow-growing stalagmites and stalactites. Visits are by guided tour and take you through one 500m gallery of this vast 15km-long network, where skeletons of woolly rhinoceroses, Irish elks and cave hyenas have been discovered. Along the way, you'll see replicas of the now-extinct creatures that lived 35,000 years ago. Book tours through Oñati's tourist office before heading out.

**Menditxik** ADVENTURE
(☎616 858126; www.menditxik.com; Bizkai Etorbidea 1, Arrasate; 5-hr tours from €55; ⏰by appointment) Based 11km northeast of Oñati, Menditxik leads canyoning and mountaineering tours of the rugged Basque countryside.

## Sleeping

Oñati doesn't get a lot of tourists staying overnight. But the countryside around town is awash in *casas rurales* (rural homes) – ask at the tourist office for a list.

**Torre Zumeltzegi** HOTEL €€
(☎943 54 00 00; www.hoteltorrezumeltzegi.com; Calle Torre Zumeltzegi 11; s/d from €84/118; ❄📶) On a hillside adjacent to the town centre, Zumeltzegi occupies a restored fortified mansion dating from the 13th century. Its 12 unique rooms have beamed ceilings, stone walls and pretty views over town, and the peaceful terrace is a great spot to unwind. Also here is one of Oñati's best restaurants (mains €15 to €21), serving Basque and Spanish dishes.

## Information

**Tourist Office** (☎943 78 34 53; www.oñatiturismo.eus; Calle San Juan 14; ⏰9.30am-2pm & 3.30-7pm Jun-Sep, 10am-2pm & 4-6pm Tue-Sun Oct-Apr) Just west of Iglesia de San Miguel, by the river. It runs various guided tours of the town's attractions, though you'll need to contact them at least several days in advance for an English-speaking guide.

WORTH A TRIP

### SANTUARIO DE ARANTZAZU

Situated 10km south of Oñati, the **Santuario de Arantzazu** (☎943 780 951; www.arantzazu.org; Barrio de Arantzazu; ⏰9am-8pm) is a busy Christian pilgrimage site that's a fabulous conflation of piety and avant-garde art. The sanctuary stands where shepherd Rodrigo de Baltzategi reportedly discovered a statuette of the Virgin among thorn bushes in 1468. It owes its current austere but highly original look to a 1950s rebuilding by Basque architects. Controversies over the innovative style meant that the complex's sculpture and murals were not completed till the 1980s.

The overwhelming impression is one of mystery and abstract artistry. The facade of the main basilica is adorned with a line of 14 chiselled apostles and one cloakless Virgin standing over the prone figure of Christ – together comprising one monumental work created by the great Basque sculptor Jorge Oteiza. Descend into the crypt for a look at the powerful murals by Néstor Basterretxea.

## Getting There & Away

PESA buses serve Oñati from many destinations in the Basque Country, including Bilbao (€7.25, 60 to 75 minutes, three daily) and Vitoria-Gasteiz (€4.95, one hour, one daily).

# Vitoria-Gasteiz

POP 249,176 / ELEV 525M

Vitoria-Gasteiz – often shortened to simply Vitoria – has a habit of falling off the radar, yet it's actually the busy, residential administrative capital of not just the southern Basque province of Álava (Basque: Araba) but also the entire Basque Country. With an art gallery, a delightful old quarter, some great *pintxo* bars and restaurants and a large, lively student contingent, you have the makings of an enjoyable city.

## Vitoria-Gasteiz

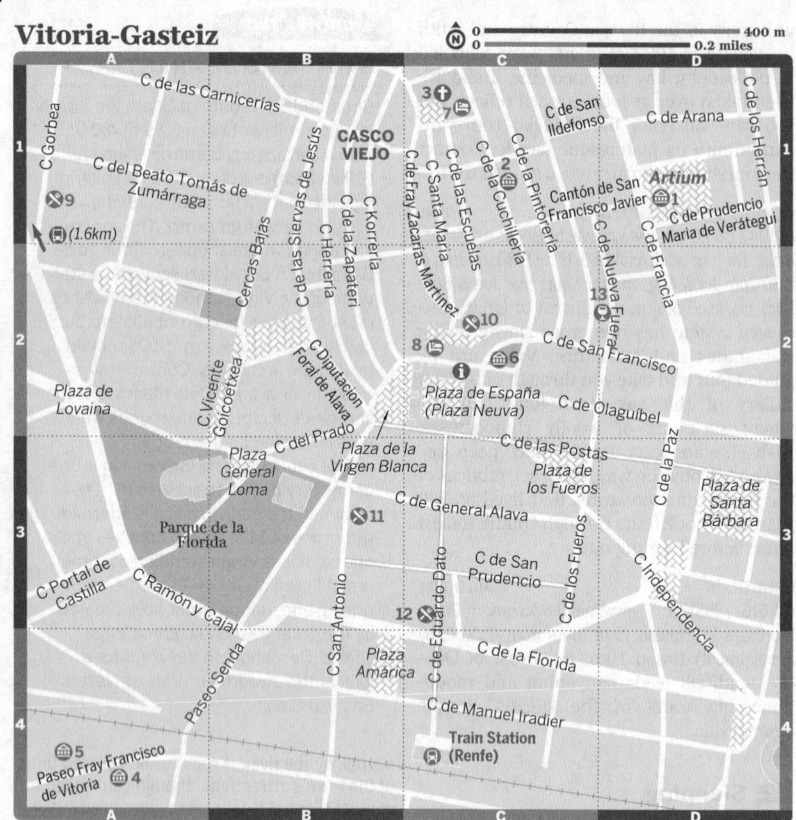




### Vitoria-Gasteiz

**Top Sights**
1 Artium....D1

**Sights**
2 Bibat....C1
3 Catedral de Santa María....C1
4 Museo de Armería....A4
5 Museo de Bellas Artes....A4
6 Paseo de los Arquillos....C2
8 La Casa de los Arquillos....C2

**Sleeping**
7 Albergue de la Catedral....C1

**Eating**
9 Andere....A1
10 Asador Matxete....C2
11 PerretxiCo....B3
12 Saburdi....C3

**Drinking & Nightlife**
13 La Cassette Vitoria....D2

## Sights

**★Artium** MUSEUM

(945 20 90 00; www.artium.eus; Calle de Francia 24; adult/child €5/free, by donation Wed & last weekend of month; 11am-2pm & 5-8pm Tue-Fri, 11am-8pm Sat & Sun; ) Art lovers shouldn't miss Vitoria's palace of modern art. The large subterranean galleries are filled with engrossing pieces by artists from the Basque Country (including Eduardo Chillida, Jorge Oteiza and Cristina Iglesias), Spain (Joan Miró, Salvador Dalí) and beyond (such as American Bill Viola and Argentine-Italian Fabian Marcaccio), complemented by thought-provoking temporary exhibitions. Multilingual audio guides are free. There

are hands-on activities for kids, periodic film screenings and concerts, and an in-house cafe.

**Catedral de Santa María** CATHEDRAL
(☎945 25 51 35; www.catedralvitoria.eus; Plaza Santa María; tours €8.50-10.50; ⏰10am-1pm & 4-7pm) At the summit of the old town and dominating its skyline is the Catedral de Santa María. Built between the 13th and 14th centuries in the Gothic style, this medieval masterpiece was declared a cathedral in 1861. Although restoration is ongoing, it is open for guided visits. English-language tours are offered at least once a day; call ahead or book a tour online. The recommended cathedral and tower tour includes underground chambers and the rooftop, with views over the city.

**Anillo Verde** PARK
Ringing the city is the Anillo Verde (Green Belt), a series of interconnecting parks, ponds and marshes linked to one another by 31km of cycling paths, which was established in 1994. Altogether, some 206 hectares of woodland, lakes and grassy expanse have been restored. It's an important ecological zone that attracts numerous waterfowl, as well as providing a refuge for the rare European mink and very tame herds of deer. Bird hides (blinds) are scattered around the lake shores.

**Bibat** MUSEUM
(☎945 20 37 00; www.araba.eus; Calle de la Cuchillería 54; ⏰10am-2pm & 4-6.30pm Tue-Sat, 11am-2pm Sun) FREE Bibat incorporates the Museo de Arqueología, whose 1500-piece archaeological collection covers the province of Álava, from prehistory to the Bronze Age (1st floor), the Iron Age to the birth of Christ (2nd floor) and the Romans to the Middle Ages (3rd floor). Also here is the Museo Fournier de Naipes, with an impressive collection of historic presses and playing cards, including some of the oldest European decks.

**Museo de Bellas Artes** GALLERY
(www.araba.eus; Paseo de Fray Francisco 8; ⏰10am-2pm & 4-6.30pm Tue-Sat, 11am-2pm Sun) FREE Housed in an exquisite neo-Renaissance building, with lovely stained-glass windows and a converted chapel that was part of the former Palacio de Augusti, the Museo de Bellas Artes has Basque paintings and sculpture from the 18th and 19th centuries, including the works of local son Fernando de Amaríca.

**Paseo de los Arquillos** HISTORIC BUILDING
Built between 1787 and 1802, this neoclassical covered arcade connects the old and new towns.

**Museo de Armería** MUSEUM
(www.araba.eus; Paseo de Fray Francisco 3; ⏰10am-2pm & 4-6.30pm Tue-Sat, 11am-2pm Sun) FREE On a peaceful, tree-lined boulevard, this low-lit armaments museum showcases weapons used over the centuries, from Bronze Age spearheads to 19th-century muskets.

## Festivals & Events

**Jazz Festival** MUSIC
(www.jazzvitoria.com; ⏰mid-Jul) This popular five-day music festival features some great bands from across the globe. Along with concerts held in venues such as the Teatro Principal, there are free outdoor shows around town.

**Fiestas de la Virgen Blanca** FIESTA
(⏰4-9 Aug) Fireworks, bullfights, concerts and street dancing are preceded by the symbolic descent of Celedón, a beret-wearing, umbrella-holding Basque effigy that flies down on strings from the Iglesia de San Miguel into the plaza below.

### THE PAINTED CITY

Vitoria-Gasteiz' old quarter is a kaleidoscopic open-air gallery. Beginning in 2007, artists Verónica and Christina Werckmeister transformed one of the city's blank walls into one massive fabric-like painting, *The Thread of Time*. They were joined by artists from around the globe, creating the Itinerario Muralístico Vitoria-Gasteiz (IMVG), a movement using the blank walls around town as canvases. Today there are over a dozen murals, many referencing Vitoria's history and Basque legends.

While you can explore the murals on your own, artists from **IMVG** (☎633 184457; www.muralismopublico.com; guided tour adult/child €8/6) lead fascinating 90-minute guided tours (English available). Confirm the departure point when you book.

## Sleeping

**Albergue de la Catedral** HOSTEL €
(945 27 59 55; http://alberguecatedral.com; Calle de la Cuchillería 87; dm/d from €22.50/50; ) Virtually built into the walls of the cathedral, this 17-room hostel has clean, unadorned rooms with exposed wooden roof beams. Dorms sleep four to eight; there are also several simple private rooms, including a couple of top-floor rooms under the roof.

**La Casa de los Arquillos** GUESTHOUSE €€
(945 15 12 59; www.lacasadelosarquillos.com; Paseo Los Arquillos 1; d from €120; ) Housed inside a beautiful 18th-century building in a prime location above the main square, this immaculate guesthouse has eight rooms set with light, high-end fabrics and facilities including a sofa bed, mini kitchens and a small breakfast nook. Some rooms have the original stone walls, five open to balconies, and the upstairs rooms have skylights.

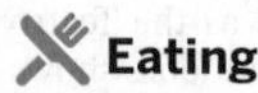

## Eating

**Saburdi** PINTXOS €
(www.saburdi.com; Calle de Eduardo Dato 32; pintxos €2-4; 8am-midnight Mon-Thu, 8am-1am Fri & Sat, 11am-midnight Sun) One of the best, if somewhat underrated, *pintxo* spots in town, Saburdi serves gourmet morsels of perfection in its stone-walled interior or sunny outdoor tables. Nibble on delicacies such as *txistorra* (Basque chorizo) with apple sauce, pickled anchovies with tomato jelly cubes and black-olive tapenade, or octopus and potato cakes.

**PerretxiCo** PINTXOS €
(945 13 72 21; www.perretxico.es; Calle San Antonio 3; pintxos €2.50-5, mains €8.50-15; 10am-midnight) This award-winning spot packs in the crowds with inspired bites such as octopus and sweet potato tacos, codfish tempura, and goat's-cheese, walnut and honey lollipops. For something more substantial, book a table in the back and linger over roasted whole turbot with mushrooms, or roast Navarran lamb with yellow-pepper relish. Until noon, it serves house-made churros and hot chocolate.

**Asador Matxete** GRILL €€
(945 13 18 21; www.matxete.com; Plaza de Matxete 4-5; mains €15-34; 1-3.45pm & 8.30-11pm Tue-Sat, noon-3.45pm Sun) There are two types of *asador* (restaurants specialising in barbecued meat): smoky old farmhouse-like places, and sleek new urban remakes. This one falls in the second category, firing up grilled steaks and whole fish served in a vaulted stone dining room and lovely summer terrace on a quiet old town plaza.

**Andere** SPANISH €€€
(945 21 49 30; www.restauranteandere.com; Calle Gorbea 8; mains €18-28.50; 1-3.45pm & 8.30-11pm Tue-Sun) This elegant restaurant rambles over several white-clothed dining spaces, including a glass-roofed terrace filled with greenery and flowers. Cutting-edge creations, such as roast wood pigeon with miso-braised quinoa, or hazelnut- and sage-stuffed lamb shoulder with thistle cream sauce, are served alongside such traditional dishes as *carrilleras al vino tinto* (beef cheeks in red wine sauce).

> **WORTH A TRIP**
>
> ### SALT VALLEY OF AÑANA
>
> For over 7000 years, 'white gold' has been produced at the **Valle Salado de Añana** (945 35 11 11; www.vallesalado.com; A2622, Gesaltza Añana; 1hr tour adult/child €8/free; 10am-6pm Apr-Oct, shorter hours Nov-Mar), where over 4km of wooden aqueducts transport high-saline spring water from 200-million-year-old underground salt deposits to a series of terraces where salt is collected after evaporation. Fascinating tours (English available) explain the history and process. From April to October, it also runs one-hour workshops (adult/child €8/5), where you can produce your own salt using traditional methods. It's 30km west of Vitoria-Gasteiz; you'll need your own transport.

## Drinking & Nightlife

The Casco Viejo's main action is at Calle de la Cuchillería/Aiztogile and neighbouring Cantón de San Francísco Javier, both of which are packed with busy bars. There's a heavy Basque nationalist atmosphere in some bars.

**La Cassette Vitoria** BAR
(www.facebook.com/lacassette.vitoria; Calle Nueva Fuera 7; 6-11pm Sun, Wed & Thu, to 4am Fri & Sat) Fun and festive, La Cassette draws all

ages for its outstanding mojitos and G&Ts. Things get lively on weekends, with DJs spinning highly danceable tunes from the '70s, '80s and '90s.

## Information

**Tourist Office** (☎945 16 15 98; www.vitoria-gasteiz.org/turismo; Plaza de España 1; ⏲10am-8pm Jul-Sep, 10am-7pm Mon-Sat, 11am-2pm Sun Oct-Jun) In the central square of the old town. Guided tours (English available) of the city, its murals and the extensive green spaces and birdwatching sites can be arranged by request.

## Getting There & Away

There are car parks by the train station, by the Artium, and just east of the cathedral.

Vitoria's **bus station** (www.vitoria-gasteiz.org; Plaza de Euskaltzaindia) is 2km northwest of the historic centre, reached by tram TG1 from the Parlamento stop near Parque de la Florida. Regular services include the following:

| Destination | Fare (€) | Duration (hr) |
|---|---|---|
| Barcelona | 29-35 | 7 |
| Bilbao | 8-15 | 1½ |
| Madrid | 25-44 | 4 |
| Pamplona | 9-13 | 1¾ |
| San Sebastián | 12-20 | 1½ |

The train station is located on Plaza Geltoki, 600m south of the historic centre. Trains go to the following:

| Destination | Fare (€) | Duration (hr) | Frequency (daily) |
|---|---|---|---|
| Barcelona | 32-65 | 5 | 4 |
| Madrid | 15-45 | 4-6 | up to 10 |
| Pamplona | 6.30-8 | 1 | 6 |
| San Sebastián | 8-17 | 1¾ | up to 10 |

## Getting Around

**Bicycle** Vitoria-Gasteiz is a bike-friendly city; to hire one, contact **Capital Bikes** (☎691 112292; www.capitalbikes.es; Casa de la Dehesa de Olárizu; bike per hr/day €3/14, electric bike per hr/day €12/22, 3-hr guided tour from €20; ⏲by appointment Mon-Wed, 10am-3pm Thu & Fri, 10am-2pm & 4.30-8pm Sat & Sun), which also runs guided bike tours around the Anillo Verde and the historic centre.

**Tram** The city's two tram lines are operated by Euskotren (www.euskotren.eus), tickets €1.45.

# NAVARRA

Several Spains intersect in Navarra (Nafarroa in Basque). The soft greens and bracing climate of the Navarran Pyrenees give way to stark plains, cereal crops and vineyards, sliced by high sierras with cockscombs of raw limestone, in the south. For centuries, pilgrims have used the pass at Roncesvalles to cross from France on their way to Santiago de Compostela (p542).

Navarra was historically the heartland of the Basques, but dynastic struggles and trimming due to reactionary politics, including Francoism, have left it a semi-autonomous province, with the north being Basque by nature and the south leaning towards Castilian Spain.

The Navarran capital, Pamplona, tends to grab the headlines with its world-famous running of the bulls, but the region's real charm lies in its spectacularly diverse landscapes and its picturesque small towns and villages.

## Pamplona

POP 199,066 / ELEV 456M

Senses are heightened in Pamplona (Basque: Iruña), capital of the fiercely independent Kingdom of Navarra and home to one of Spain's most famous and wildest festivals. Even when the bulls aren't thundering down the cobblestones through the centre of town, Pamplona is fascinating to explore. With its grand cathedral, archaeological treasures and 16th-century fortifications, there's much history hidden in these atmospheric medieval lanes. And with its lush parks and picturesque city centre full of vibrant eating and drinking spots, it's easy to see why so many visitors – Hemingway included – have fallen under Pamplona's spell. The city also sees its fair share of pilgrims arriving on foot along the Camino de Santiago.

### Sights

**★Museo de Navarra** MUSEUM

(☎848 42 64 93; www.navarra.es; Calle Cuesta de Santo Domingo 47; adult/child €2/free, free Sat afternoon & Sun; ⏲9.30am-2pm & 5-7pm Tue-Sat, 11am-2pm Sun) Housed in a former medieval hospital, this superb museum has an eclectic collection of archaeological finds (including a number of fantastic Roman mosaics unearthed mainly in southern Navarra) and art, including Goya's *Marqués*

## Pamplona

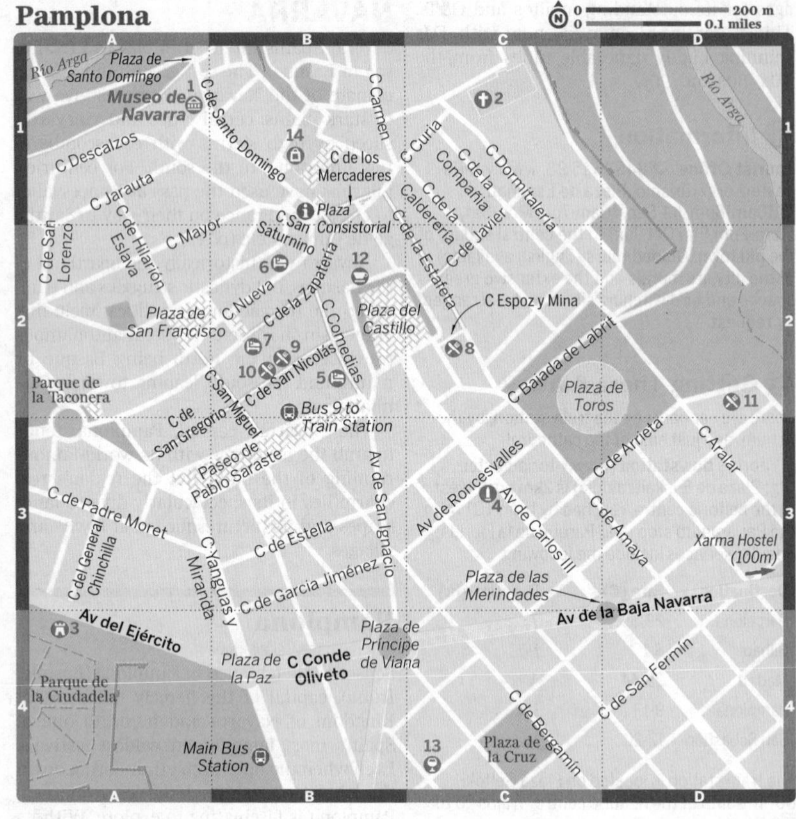


## Pamplona

**Top Sights**
1 Museo de Navarra ........ A1

**Sights**
2 Catedral de Santa María ........ C1
3 Ciudadela ........ A4
4 Monumento al Encierro ........ C3

**Sleeping**
5 Hostal Arriazu ........ B2
6 Hotel Maisonnave ........ B2
7 Palacio Guendulain ........ B2

**Eating**
8 Bar Gaucho ........ C2
9 Baserri Berri ........ B2
10 Katuzarra ........ B2
11 Restaurante Rodero ........ D2

**Drinking & Nightlife**
12 Café Iruña ........ B2
13 Vermuteria Darlalata ........ C4

**Shopping**
14 Mercado de Santo Domingo ........ B1

*de San Adrián*. Labelling is in Spanish only, but foreign translation leaflets are available.

**Catedral de Santa María** CATHEDRAL
(www.catedraldepamplona.com; Calle Dormitalería; adult/child €5/3; ⊙10.30am-7pm Mon-Sat Apr-Oct, to 5pm Nov-Mar, tower climb 11.15am) Pamplona's cathedral stands on a rise just inside the city ramparts amid a dark thicket of narrow streets. The cathedral is a late-medieval Gothic gem with an 18th-century neoclassical facade. Artefacts in the vast interior include a silver-plated Virgin and the splendid 15th-century tomb of Carlos III of Navarra and his wife Doña Leonor. The real joy is the Gothic cloister with delicate stonework. Admission includes a guided tour (English available with advance notice).

**Ciudadela** FORTRESS

(Avenida del Ejército; 8am-9.30pm Mon-Sat, from 9am Sun) FREE The walls and bulwarks of the grand fortified citadel, the star-shaped Ciudadela, were built between 1571 and 1645 under the direction of King Felipe II. They're considered one of the best examples of military architecture from the Spanish Renaissance. The former moats and bastions have become a setting for artists to display their works in the evenings from 6pm to 8.30pm Tuesday to Friday, noon to 2pm and 6pm to 8.30pm Saturday, and noon to 2pm Sunday.

**Monumento al Encierro** SCULPTURE

(Avenida de Roncesvalles) If you're not in town during the running of the bulls, you can get a dramatic sense of the action at this life-size bronze sculpture. Stretching 4m wide and 11m long, it vividly depicts nine bulls and 11 runners, several of whom have stumbled, with palpable fear on their faces. Designed by Bilbao artist Rafael Huerta, it was installed on this pedestrianised street in 2007.

## Sleeping

Outside of Sanfermines, you'll find a wide selection of enticing lodging options within the old centre. During the big festival, hotels raise their rates mercilessly – all quadruple their normal rack rates and many increase them fivefold – and it can be nearly impossible to get a room without reserving between six months and a year in advance.

**Xarma Hostel** HOSTEL €

(948 04 64 49; www.xarmahostel.com; Avenida de la Baja Navarra 23; dm/d from €18/40; ) Opening onto a large, sunny terrace with a barbecue area, this bright hostel has colourful rooms with wooden floors. Four- to six-bed dorms and private rooms (one of which can accommodate wheelchairs) share bathrooms. There's a communal kitchen; rates include breakfast.

**Hostal Arriazu** HOSTAL €

(948 21 02 02; www.hostalarriazu.com; Calle Comedias 14; d/tr from €62/80; ) Falling somewhere between a budget *pensión* and a midrange hotel, this good-value option is located in a former theatre, with a large guest lounge and pretty courtyard. The 14 rooms are small and old-fashioned, though the en suite bathrooms are perfectly modern, and it's centrally located just off the main square surrounded by bars and restaurants.

**Hotel Maisonnave** HOTEL €€

(948 22 26 00; www.hotelmaisonnave.es; Calle Nueva 20; d/ste from €120/180; ) In the centre of the old town, Hotel Maisonnave has spacious, contemporary rooms, and creature comforts including a small fitness centre, a sauna and a good restaurant. Book a superior room or a suite for views over the rooftops and church steeples of the historic quarter.

★**Palacio Guendulain** HISTORIC HOTEL €€€

(948 22 55 22; www.palacioguendulain.com; Calle de la Zapatería 53; d/ste from €205/485; P) Inside the converted 18th-century former home of the viceroy of New Granada, this sumptuous hotel is Pamplona's most atmospheric place to stay. On arrival, you're greeted by a museum-piece 17th-century carriage and grand staircases sweeping up to the 26 antique-filled rooms with *Princess and the Pea*–soft beds, enormous showers and regal armchairs. Its restaurant perfects Basque and Navarran cuisine.

## Eating

**Bar Gaucho** PINTXOS €

(948 22 50 73; Calle Espoz y Mina 7; pintxos €2-4.50; 8.30am-12.30am) This bustling bar's multi-award-winning *pintxos* are among the finest in the city. Highlights include smoked eel with tomato jelly, filo pastry-calf's tongue, a shot glass of truffled egg, mushroom crème and crispy ham, and sea urchin mousse served in the shell.

**Baserri Berri** BASQUE €€

(948 22 20 21; www.baserriberri.com; Calle de San Nicolás 32; 7-course tasting menu €28-35, pintxos €2-4; 1.30-3.30pm & 8.30-10.30pm Tue-Sat, 1.30-3.30pm Sun) On restaurant-lined Calle San Nicolás, Baserri Berri's artfully presented tasting menus incorporate intricate dishes such as smoked ostrich with Bloody Mary jelly, crab meringue with apple compote, and a 27-vegetable cube named Rubik's Cube. Equally inspired *pintxos* are served at the bar throughout the day and late into the evening.

**Restaurante Rodero** SPANISH €€€

(948 22 80 35; www.restauranterodero.com; Calle Emilio Arrieta 3; mains €23.50-32, tasting menus €67-87; 1.30-3.30pm Mon-Sat & 9-11pm Wed-Sat) For a memorable meal, book a table at this Michelin-starred, family-run restaurant just east of the bullring. Celebrated chef Koldo Rodero uses premium Navarran

## THE RUNNING OF THE BULLS

Liberated, obsessive or plain mad is how you might describe aficionados (and there are many) who regularly take part in Pamplona's Sanfermines (Fiesta de San Fermín), a nonstop cacophony of music, dance, fireworks and processions – and the small matter of running alongside a handful of agitated, horn-tossing *toros* (bulls) – that takes place from 6 to 14 July each year.

The bullrun is said to have originally developed way back in the 14th century as a way of herding bulls into market, with the seller running alongside the bulls to speed up their movement into the marketplace. In later times the same technique was used to transport bulls from the corrals to the bullring, and essentially that is still the case today. *El encierro*, the running of the bulls from their corrals to the bullring for the afternoon bullfight, takes place in Pamplona every morning during Sanfermines. Six bulls are let loose from the Coralillos de Santo Domingo to charge across the square of the same name. They continue up the street, veering onto Calle de los Mercaderes from Plaza Consistorial, then sweep right onto Calle de la Estafeta for the final charge to the ring. Devotees, known as *mozos* (the brave or foolish, depending on your point of view), race madly with the bulls, aiming to keep close – but not too close. The total course is some 825m long and lasts little more than three minutes.

Participants enter the course before 7.30am from Plaza de Santo Domingo. At 8am two rockets are fired: the first announces that the bulls have been released from the corrals; the second lets participants know they're all out and running. The first danger point is where Calle de los Mercaderes leads into Calle de la Estafeta. Here many of the bulls skid into the barriers because of their headlong speed on the turn. They can become isolated from the herd and are then always dangerous. A very treacherous stretch comes towards the end, where Calle de la Estafeta slopes down into the final turn to Plaza de Toros. A third rocket goes off when all the bulls have made it to the ring and a final one when they have been rounded up in the stalls.

Those who prefer to be spectators rather than action men (technically, women are forbidden from running, although an increasing number do anyway) bag their spot along the route early. A space doesn't mean an uninterrupted view because a second 'security' fence stands between the spectators and runners, blocking much of the view (only police, medical staff and other authorised people can enter the space between the two fences). Some people rent a space on one of the house balconies overlooking the course. Others watch the runners and bulls race out of the entrance tunnel and into the bullring by buying a ticket for a seat in the ring. Whatever the vantage point, it's all over in a few blurred seconds.

Each evening a traditional bullfight is held. Sanfermines winds up at midnight on 14 July with a candlelit procession, known as the Pobre de Mí (Poor Me), which starts from Plaza Consistorial.

Concern has grown about the high numbers of people taking part in recent *encierros*. Since records began in 1924, 16 people have died during Pamplona's bullrun. Many of those who run are full of bravado (and/or drink) and have little idea of what they're doing. The number of injuries differs from year to year, but serious injuries are common (usually due to goring, but also from pile-ups of participants). On top of the dangers to runners, the bulls themselves are all destined to die in the bullring and that aspect of the running, as well as the stress of the run itself and the possibility of the bulls slipping and injuring themselves in the stampede, have led to animal welfare groups condemning the spectacle as a cruel tradition.

ingredients to create dishes that dazzle the senses, such as *morcilla* (blood sausage) bonbons in langoustine and tomato consommé, cocoa-dusted lambs' hearts with smoked sweet potato, and hake with squid-ink powder and parsley foam.

**Katuzarra** GRILL **€€€**

(948 22 46 34; www.katuzarra.es; Calle San Nicolás 34; mains €17-32, pintxos €2.50-4.50; 1-3.30pm & 7-11pm) Contemporary *asador* Katuzarra uses Navarran oak to create the smoky charcoal used to cook its *Txuletón* (seven-

year-old dairy cow T-bone) alongside cuts of pork and lamb, as well as seafood dishes. Its timber-beamed stone dining room is behind the long *pintxo*-laden bar with hams hanging from the ceiling above.

## Drinking & Nightlife

**★Café Iruña** CAFE
(www.cafeiruna.com; Plaza del Castillo 44; 8am-midnight Mon-Thu, 9am-2am Fri-Sun) Opened on the eve of Sanfermines in 1888, Café Iruña's dominant position on the main square, powerful sense of history and belle-époque decor make this by far the most famous watering hole in the city. In addition to a long list of wine and spirits, it also has a superb range of *pintxos* and light meals.

Hemingway was a regular here – indeed, he helped immortalise the place in his novel *The Sun Also Rises*.

**Vermuteria Darlalata** BAR
(www.facebook.com/darlalatavermut; Calle Navarro Villoslada 14; noon-3.30pm & 7-11pm Tue-Fri & Sun, noon-3.30pm & 7pm-1.30am Sat) Just off the beaten path, this delightful little corner bar has obvious charm with its vintage decor and delicious spread of *pintxos*. The real draw though is the collection of vermouths, with more than 80 varieties on hand. It's a jovial but easy-going space that draws a fine cross-section of Pamplona society.

## Shopping

**Mercado de Santo Domingo** MARKET
(www.mercadosantodomingo.com; Calle del Mercado; 8am-2pm Mon-Thu & Sat, to 4.30pm Fri) Pamplona's oldest market dates from 1877. Inside are stalls selling local specialities including Basque, Navarran and other Spanish cheeses, cured hams, seafood, fruit, vegetables and cut flowers, as well as a couple of cafes and *pintxo* bars. Outside market hours, cultural events such as concerts sometimes take place here.

## Information

The well-organised **tourist office** (948 42 07 00; www.turismo.navarra.es; Calle San Saturnino 2; 9am-2pm & 3-8pm mid-Jun–mid-Sep, 10am-2pm & 3-7pm Mon-Sat, 10am-2pm Sun mid-Sep–mid-Jun) in the heart of the old town has plenty of information about the city and Navarra. There are a couple of summer-only tourist booths scattered throughout the city.

## Getting There & Away

### AIR

Pamplona's **airport** (PNA; 913 21 10 00; www.aena.es; Carretera del Aeropuerto; ), 7km south of the city, has regular flights to Madrid and Barcelona. Bus 16 travels between the bus station in the city and the suburb of Noáin (€3, 20 minutes, up to four per hour), from where it's a 950m walk southwest to the airport. A taxi costs €9 to €15.

### BUS

From the **main bus station** (948 20 35 66; www.estaciondeautobusesdepamplona.com; Calle Yanguas y Miranda 2), which is cleverly concealed underground near La Ciudadela, buses leave for most towns throughout Navarra. Service is restricted on Sunday.

Regular bus services travel to the following places:

| Destination | Fare (€) | Time (hr) |
|---|---|---|
| Bilbao | 15-18 | 2-2½ |
| Logroño | 10.85 | 2 |
| San Sebastián | 8-20 | 1 |
| Vitoria | 9-13 | 1¾ |

Regional destinations include the following:

| Destination | Fare (€) | Time (hr) | Frequency |
|---|---|---|---|
| Estella | 5.65 | 1 | up to 10 daily |
| Olite | 3.85 | ¾ | every 90min |

### TRAIN

Pamplona's train station, 2km northwest of the historic centre, is linked by **bus 9** (€1.35) from Paseo de Sarasate every 15 minutes; journey time is eight minutes.

Note that it's much quicker to take the bus to San Sebastián. Trains run to/from the following:

| Destination | Fare (€) | Time (hr) | Frequency |
|---|---|---|---|
| Madrid | 23-62 | 4 | up to 10 daily |
| San Sebastián | 13-20 | 1¾ | 2 daily |
| Tudela | 9-20 | 1 | up to 10 daily |
| Vitoria | 6.30-8 | 1 | 6 daily |

# Navarran Pyrenees

Cloaked in beech and oak forest, and often concealed in mists, the rolling hills, ribboned cliffs and snow-covered mountains that make up the Navarran Pyrenees on the border with France are a playground for outdoor enthusiasts and pilgrims on the Camino de Santiago. Firmly Basque in history, culture and outlook, the tiny towns and villages that hug these slopes add to the charm of exploring what are some of the most delightful and least exploited mountains in western Europe.

## Valle del Baztán

This is rural Basque Country at its most typical, a landscape of splotchy reds and greens. Minor roads take you in and out of charming little villages, such as **Arraioz**, known for the fortified Casa Jaureguizar, and **Ziga**, with its 16th-century church. Just beyond Irurita on the N121B is the valley's biggest town, **Elizondo**, a good base for exploring the area.

Beyond Elizondo, the NA2600 road meanders dreamily amid picturesque farms, villages and hills before climbing sharply to the French border pass of **Puerto de Izpegui**, where the world becomes a spectacular collision of crags, peaks and valleys. At the pass, you can stop for a short, sharp hike up to the top of **Mt Izpegui**.

The N121B continues northwards to the Puerto de Otxondo and the border crossing into France at Dantxarinea. Just before the border, a minor road veers west to the pretty village of **Zugarramurdi**.

### Sights & Activities

**La Cueva de Zugarramurdi** CAVE

(☎948 59 93 05; www.turismozugarramurdi.com; Calle Beitikokarrika 18, Zugarramurdi; adult/child €4.50/2.50; ⏰11am-7.30pm Jul-Sep, to 6pm Oct-Jun) According to the Inquisition, these caves (also known as Cuevas de Las Brujas, or Caves of the Witches) were once the scene of evil debauchery. True to form, inquisitors tortured and burned scores of alleged witches here. Pathways and boardwalks let you explore the caves, which are a level 500m walk west of Zugarramurdi's village centre.

**Museo de las Brujas** MUSEUM

(☎948 59 90 04; www.turismozugarramurdi.com; Calle Beitikokarrika 22, Zugarramurdi; adult/child €4.50/2; ⏰11am-7.30pm Tue-Sun mid-Jul–mid-Sep, to 6pm Wed-Sun mid-Sep–mid-Jul) Playing on the flying-broomstick theme of La Cueva de Zugarramurdi, this Zugarramurdi museum is a fascinating dip into the mysterious cauldron of witchcraft in the Pyrenees.

**Baztanabentura Park** ADVENTURE SPORTS

(☎948 59 23 22; www.navarraaventura.com; Barrio Beartzun, Elizondo; 1/3/4 activities from €17/53/62; ⏰10am-8pm Jun-Sep, shorter hours Oct-May) Outdoors enthusiasts will find plenty of adrenaline-pumping activities at this adventure park, from ziplining to canyoning, via ferrata (climbing route) and a dizzying pendulum swing (similar to a bungee jump). It also organises white-water rafting trips across the border in France. The park is 4km southeast of Elizondo on the NA2596.

### Sleeping

**Hostal Trinquete Antxitónea** HOSTAL €

(☎948 58 18 07; www.antxitonea.com; Braulío Iríarte 16, Elizondo; d/tr from €52/93; ❄📶) This well-run *hostal* has 23 plain rooms with flower-bedecked balconies, some with river views. The attached restaurant (open Monday to Saturday; mains €11 to €15) serves hearty Navarran cuisine.

### Getting There & Away

Zugarramurdi is located 76km north of Pamplona via the N121A. There's no public transport.

## Burguete

POP 242

A steady stream of pilgrims on the Camino de Santiago pass through this quaint 12th-century town. The main road runs tightly between neat, whitewashed houses with bare cornerstones at Burguete (Basque: Auritz). Despite lacking the Charlemagne associations, it actually makes a better night's halt than nearby Roncesvalles, 3km north.

### Sleeping

**Hostal Burguete** HOSTAL €

(☎948 76 00 05; www.hotelburguete.com; Calle de San Nicolás 71; s/d/tr from €35/51/71; 📶) On peaceful Burguete's main street , this pleasant inn has 20 simply furnished rooms. Hemingway fans should try to book room 23, where he allegedly worked on *The Sun Also Rises* during one of his many stays in the area, or, from April to early December, enjoy a sherry on the terrace just as Hemingway did.

## Camino Francés in Navarra & La Rioja

### THE CAMINO IN NAVARRA & LA RIOJA

At the gates of Spain, Navarra is the first Spanish leg of the journey to Santiago de Compostela for walkers on the Camino Francés pilgrimage route. The opening section, which crosses over the Pyrenees, is also one of the most spectacular parts of the entire Camino.

#### Roncesvalles to Pamplona

From the **Puerto de Ibañeta**, the Camino dramatically enters Spain and drops down to Roncesvalles (p476). Dominated by its great, imposing abbey, Roncesvalles admirably sets the tone for this extraordinary route. Inside the restored 13th-century Gothic church, you'll find the first statue of Santiago dressed as a pilgrim (with scallop shells and staff).

Pamplona (p469) became an official stop along the Camino in the 11th century, cementing its prosperity. Just inside the cathedral's bland neoclassical facade are the pure, soaring lines of the 14th-century Gothic interior.

#### Pamplona to Logroño & Beyond

Heading west out of Pamplona via Zariquiegui and the Sierra del Perdón, pilgrims reach Puente la Reina (p479), where the Camino Aragonés, coming from the east, joins up with the Camino Francés.

Estella (p480), the next stop, contains exceptional monumental Romanesque architecture: the outstanding portal of the Iglesia de San Miguel; the cloister of the Iglesia de San Pedro de la Rúa; and the Palacio de los Reyes de Navarra.

Outside Estella, evergreen oaks and vineyards fill undulating landscapes until a long, barren stretch leads through the sleepy towns of **Los Arcos**, **Sansol** and **Torres del Río**. In hillside Torres you'll find another remarkably intact eight-sided Romanesque chapel, the Iglesia del Santo Sepulcro.

The great Río Ebro marks the entrance to Logroño (p481) and explains its wealth and size. The dour Gothic Iglesia de Santiago houses a large Renaissance altarpiece depicting unusual scenes from the saint's life, including run-ins with the wicked necromancer Hermogenes.

**Nájera** literally grew out of the town's red cliff wall when King Ramiro discovered a miraculous statue of the Virgin in one of the cliff's caves in the 11th century.

Santo Domingo de la Calzada (p484) is one of the road's most captivating places. It is named for its energetic 11th-century founder, Santo Domingo, who cleared forests, built roadways, a bridge, a pilgrim's hospice and a church, and performed many wondrous miracles depicted masterfully in Hispano-Flemish paintings in the cathedral.

**Camping Urrobi** CAMPGROUND €
(948 76 02 00; www.campingurrobi.com; Carretera de Francia; campsite incl 1 adult & car from €33, 3-/5-/6-person bungalow from €110/130/150, dm from €13.50; Apr-Oct; ) Campers will be happy at this riverside campsite 2.3km south of town. It also has basic hostel accommodation and bungalows. There's an on-site restaurant; the swimming pool opens in July and August.

**Hotel Rural Loizu** HOTEL €€
(948 76 00 08; www.loizu.com; Calle de San Nicolás 13; s/d from €70/92; Apr-Dec; ) Comfortable 27-room Hotel Rural Loizu has upper rooms looking out over the village and countryside, and a good local restaurant (mains €12 to €19).

## Getting There & Away

Most visitors arrive by car or on foot, but there's also bus service from Pamplona (€5.50, two per day Monday to Saturday July to September, one Monday to Saturday October to June), continuing to Roncesvalles (€1.35, five minutes).

## Roncesvalles

POP 21

Legend has it that it was in Roncesvalles (Basque: Orreaga) that the armies of Charlemagne were defeated and Roland, commander of Charlemagne's rearguard, was killed by Basque tribes in 778. This event is celebrated in the epic 11th-century poem *Chanson de Roland* (Song of Roland).

Roncesvalles has long been a key point on the road to Santiago de Compostela, and today Camino pilgrims continue to give thanks at the famous monastery for a successful crossing of the Pyrenees, one of the hardest parts of the Camino de Santiago.

**Roncesvalles Monastery Complex** MONASTERY
(948 79 04 80; www.roncesvalles.es; Carretera de Francia; guided tours adult/child €5.20/2.50; 10am-2pm & 3.30-7pm Apr-Oct, 10am-2pm & 3-6pm Mar & Nov, 10.30am-2.30pm Thu-Tue Feb & Dec) Roncesvalles' monastery complex contains a number of different buildings of interest, including the 13th-century Gothic-style **Real Colegiata de Santa María** (9am-8.30pm) FREE and a cloister containing the tomb of King Sancho VII (El Fuerte) of Navarra. Reportedly 2.25m tall, he fought against the Muslims in the Battle of Las Navas de Tolosa in 1212. Guided tours lasting 90 minutes take in the library, museum and treasury.

**Casa de Beneficiados** HOTEL €€
(948 76 01 05; www.casadebeneficiados.com; Carretera de Francia; s/d/tr €80/90/115, apt €90-150; mid-Mar–Dec; ) In a former life this was an 18th-century monks' residence. Today it has modernised rooms, some overlooking the countryside, and the atmospheric common areas make fine places to unwind after a day's hike. You can also dine on local game, cheese and mountain trout at the good-value restaurant (mains €9 to €22), hire bicycles or arrange horse-riding trips.

## Getting There & Away

Many travellers arrive on foot or by car, but you can also get to Roncesvalles by bus from Pamplona (€5.50, one hour, two per day Monday to Saturday July to September, one Monday to Saturday October to June).

Buses also connect Roncesvalles with St-Jean-Pied-de-Port, France (€5, 45 minutes, three per day Monday to Saturday July to September, one Monday to Saturday October to June).

## Valle del Roncal

Navarra's most spectacular mountain area is around Roncal, and this easternmost valley, made up of seven small stone villages with simple accommodation and dining options (albeit limited shopping – plan ahead), is an alternative route for entering or leaving the Navarran Pyrenees. Isaba makes the best base.

### ISABA

POP 420

Lording it over the other villages in the valley, lofty Isaba, lying above the confluence of Ríos Belagua and Uztárroz, is a popular base for walkers and skiers. Heading north out of town towards the French border, the scenery becomes ever more spectacular. The road starts off confined between mountain peaks before suddenly opening out into high alpine pastures with a backdrop of the most majestic mountains in the western Pyrenees. Approaching the French border the road corkscrews up and up to the pass of Roncalia. Beyond is France and a large ski resort, Pierre St-Martin. There are signed walking trails on both sides of the border; a good one is to the Belabarze waterfall, 6km northeast of Isaba on the Spanish side.

**Onki Xin** GUESTHOUSE €
(☎618 317837; www.onkixin.com; Barrio Izarjentea 25; d €55, apt €110-140; 🛜) In a traditional house in the village centre, Onki Xin has nine wonderfully rustic rooms with beamed ceilings, antique furnishings and glorious views. For a bit more space, book one of its spacious two- or three-bedroom apartments around the corner. The kind English-speaking owners have a wealth of information on exploring the region.

**Hostal Lola** HOSTAL €€
(☎948 89 30 12; www.hostal-lola.com; Mendigatxa 17; d from €65; 🛜) This family-run place hidden down a narrow side alley offers great value for money and has 21 rooms with desks, sofas and big beds. There's a flower-hemmed terrace and a decent restaurant (*menú del día* €19.50) serving French and Navarran cuisine.

**Ezkaurre** BASQUE €€
(☎657 621467; www.hostalezkaurreisaba.com; Garagardoya 14; 2-/3-course menú del día €15/19.50; ⏲1-3.30pm & 7-9.30pm Mon-Sat) This humble-looking restaurant serves beautifully prepared recipes that feature market-fresh ingredients. Oven-baked Pyrenees trout, beef cheeks with truffled potatoes and risotto with wild mushrooms are highlights. Don't miss the *tarta de cuajada* (tart made from creamy Roncal sheep's cheese and sheep's milk curd) for dessert. It also has simple double rooms (from €60).

### Information

Stop by the **tourist office** (☎948 47 52 56; www.vallederoncal.es; Barrio Izarjentea 28; ⏲10am-5pm Mon-Thu, 10am-2pm & 4.30-7.30pm Sat, 10am-2pm Sun Jun-Sep, 10am-2pm Sun-Thu, 10am-2pm & 4.30-7pm Fri & Sat Oct-May) in the village centre for info on winter and summer activities including nearby walks.

### Getting There & Away

Most travellers arrive here in their own cars.

Buses to/from Pamplona serve Valle del Roncal villages, including Isaba (€10, two hours, two daily June to September, one daily October to May).

## Southern Navarra

In Southern Navarra, the deep greens of the region's north vanish, replaced with a lighter and more Mediterranean ochre. As the sunlight becomes more dazzling, the shark's-teeth hills flatten into tranquil lowland plains, while the lush forests become scorched vineyards and olive groves. Awaiting travellers in this region are storybook medieval villages and the desert-like landscape of the Bárdenas Reales.

## Olite

POP 3931 / ELEV 388M

The turrets and spires of Olite are filled with stories of kings and queens, brave knights and beautiful princesses. This quiet village was once the home of the royal families of Navarra, and the walled old quarter could be lifted from the pages of a fairy tale.

Founded by the Romans (parts of the town wall date back to Roman times), Olite first attracted the attention of royalty in 1276. However, it didn't really take off until it caught the fancy of King Carlos III (Carlos the Noble) in the 15th century, when he embarked on a series of daring building projects.

### Sights

★**Palacio Real** CASTLE
(Castillo de Olite; ☎948 74 12 73; www.guiartenavarra.com; Plaza Carlos III; adult/child €3.50/2; ⏲10am-8pm Jul-Aug, 10am-7pm Mon-Fri, 10am-8pm Sat & Sun May, Jun & Sep, shorter hours Oct-Apr) Carlos III is to thank for the exceptional Palacio Real, which towers over the village. Back in Carlos' day (early 15th century), the castle's inhabitants included not just royalty but lions and other exotic pets, as well as Babylon-inspired hanging gardens. Today, the restored castle makes a wonderfully atmospheric place to wander. To help bring the past to life, take a guided tour (in Spanish), or explore with a multilingual audio guide (€2). Prebook tickets at peak times to guarantee access.

You can clamber up scenic watchtowers, wander through once richly gilded halls, and stroll the ramparts, all while imagining the jousts, bullfights and even pelota games held back in medieval times. Integrated into the castle is the **Iglesia de Santa María la Real**, which has a superbly detailed Gothic portal.

**Laguna de Pitillas** LAKE
(☎619 463450; www.lagunadepitillas.org; ⏲visitor centre 10am-2pm & 4.30-7pm Wed-Sun mid-Jul–Sep, Sat & Sun only Oct–mid-Jul) FREE A protected Ramsar wetland site of international importance, the lakes and marshes

that make up the Laguna de Pitillas provide a home for around 160 permanent and migratory species, including marsh harriers, great bitterns and even ospreys. The visitor centre has free binoculars (deposit required) and trail maps. It's 11km southeast of Olite off the NA5330.

**Museo de la Viña y el Vino de Navarra** MUSEUM

(Navarra Vineyard and Wine Museum; ☎948 74 12 73; Plaza de los Teobaldos 10; adult/child €3.50/2; ⏱10am-2pm & 4-7pm Mon-Sat, 10am-2pm Sun Mar-Oct, shorter hours Nov-Feb) This comprehensive museum takes visitors on a fascinating journey through wine and wine culture. Over three floors, English signage and interactive displays reveal the grape in all its complexity, from the soils and grape varieties found in Navarra to old-fashioned harvesting techniques. There's also a case of scents (animal, spices, wood, etc) where you can breathe in elements found in many wines. Best of all is the glass of wine waiting for you at the end – free with admission.

## Sleeping & Eating

**★Parador de Olite** HISTORIC HOTEL €€

(☎948 74 00 00; www.parador.es; Plaza de los Teobaldos 2; s/d from €100/115; ❄📶) The most spectacular lodging option in town is set in a wing of Olite's restored medieval castle (though some rooms are in a newer extension). Part of the Parador chain and a national monument, this photogenic hotel has plenty of atmosphere with its heavy wood furniture, gilt-framed prints and, in some rooms, balconies with views over the countryside.

There's a superb regional restaurant (mains €13.50 to €24) open to guests and nonguests.

**Hotel el Juglar** BOUTIQUE HOTEL €€

(☎948 74 18 55; www.hoteljuglarolite.com; Rúa Romana 39; s/d/ste from €95/105/165; P❄📶🏊) In a stone-walled mansion 500m northwest of the village centre, Hotel El Juglar has nine elegantly furnished rooms, some with Jacuzzi baths, others with balconies. The sparkling pool is enticing on a hot summer day.

**Mesón el Sol de Olite** TAPAS €

(☎679 067727; www.mesonelsololite.es; Plaza Carlos III 3; tapas €2-3.50, mains €8-13.50; ⏱11am-3.30pm & 6pm-midnight; 📶) Decorated in colourful tiles, this stone-walled bar is cool in summer and cosy in winter, and opens to a busy terrace. It's a popular place for tapas dishes incorporating Navarran produce, such as olive croquettes, *chistorra* (pork sausage) with green peppers, or chargilled white asparagus.

## ℹ Information

Olite has a friendly and helpful **tourist office** (☎948 74 17 03; www.turismo.navarra.es; Plaza de los Teobaldos 4; ⏱10am-2pm & 4-7pm Mon-Sat, 10am-2pm Sun Mar-Oct, shorter hours Nov-Feb), in the same building as the wine museum.

## ℹ Getting There & Away

Up to 12 buses a day link Olite with Pamplona (€3.85, 45 minutes).

# Ujué

POP 177

Balancing atop a hill criss-crossed with terraced fields, the tiny village of Ujué, 18km east of Olite and overlooking the plains of southern Navarra, is a perfect example of a fortified medieval village. Today the almost immaculately preserved township is sleepy and pretty, with steep, narrow streets tumbling down the hillside.

The village plays host to a fascinating *romería* (pilgrimage) on the first Sunday after St Mark's Day (25 April), when hundreds of people walk through the night from Tudela to celebrate Mass in the village church.

**Iglesia-Fortaleza de Santa María de Ujué** CHURCH

(San Isidro 8; admission by donation; ⏱10am-6.30pm Apr-Oct, to 5.30pm Nov-Mar) Standing at the highest point in the village, this church of mixed Romanesque-Gothic style was completed in 1094. Aside from magnificent views over the valley from its outer walkways, the church contains the heart of Carlos II, and a rare statue of the Black Virgin, which is said to have been discovered by a shepherd who was led to the statue by a dove.

**Pastas Urrutia** CAFE €

(☎948 73 92 57; www.casaurrutia.net; San Isidro 41; dishes €8-16.50; ⏱cafe 1.30-3.30pm Thu-Tue, bakery & deli 10am-6pm Thu-Tue) At the village's northern entrance, Pastas Urrutia combines a bakery turning out aromatic loaves with a deli stocking local delicacies including chocolates, and a cafe with standout coffee and specialities such as *migas de Ujué* (a local shepherd's dish of bread croutons, garlic and mutton fat) and *codillo al horno* (roast pork knuckle).

### Getting There & Away

Ujué has no public transport, so you'll need your own.

## Parque Natural de las Bárdenas Reales

Navarra's badlands, the Bárdenas Reales, are a sunburnt desert, the dramatic landscape shaped by water, wind, and erosion.

There are hiking and cycling trails through the park, though many are only vaguely signposted. Given the heat, lack of shade and big distances involved, most people come to drive the park's 34km-long loop road.

**Parque Natural de las Bárdenas Reales** NATURE RESERVE
(948 83 03 08; www.bardenasreales.es; 8am-dusk) FREE Established as a natural park in 1999 and as a UN Biosphere Reserve in 2000, the Bárdenas Reales is a desiccated landscape of blank tabletop hills, open gravel plains and snakelike gorges covering over 410 sq km of southeastern Navarra. As well as spectacular scenery, the park plays host to numerous birds and animals, including the great bustard, golden eagles, Egyptian and griffon vultures, numerous reptiles, mountain cats and wild boar.

A **visitor centre** (948 83 03 08; www.bardenasreales.es; Carretera del Parque Natural Km 6, off Carretera NA8712; 9am-2pm & 4-7pm Apr-Aug, 9am-2pm & 3-5pm Sep-Mar) gives out information on park highlights.

**Cuevas Rurales Bardenas** APARTMENT €€€
(948 84 32 25; www.lasbardenas.com; Palomares 48, Valtierra; apt from €150; P ❄ 📶) In the small town of Valtierra, 12km west of the park, you can overnight inside a cave – albeit one with stylish contemporary furnishings and kitchenettes – carved into the hillside. The nine dwellings sleep from two to eight; most have terraces. Two- to four-night minimum stay required. Hiking and 4WD trips into the park can be arranged.

### Getting There & Away

There's no public transport to the park.

## Puente la Reina

POP 2843 / ELEV 344M

The chief calling card of Puente la Reina (Basque: Gares), 22km southwest of Pamplona on the A12, is the spectacular six-arched **medieval bridge** that dominates the western end of town. A key stop on the Camino de Santiago, the town's pretty streets throng with the ghosts of a multitude of pilgrims. Their first stop here was at the late-Romanesque **Iglesia del Crucifijo**, erected by the Knights Templar and still containing one of the finest Gothic crucifixes in existence.

**Santa María de Eunate** CHURCH
(www.santamariadeeunate.es; Carretera de Campanas; adult/child €1.50/1; 10.30am-1.30pm Tue-Fri, 11am-1.30pm & 4.30-6.30pm Sat & Sun Apr-Jun, Sep & Oct, 10.30am-1.30pm & 5-6.30pm Wed-Mon Jul & Aug) Surrounded by cornfields and brushed by wildflowers, the near-perfect octagonal Romanesque Santa María de Eunate, 5km east of Puente la Reina, is one of the most picturesque chapels along the whole Camino. Dating from the 12th century, its origins – and the reason why it's located in the middle of nowhere – are something of a mystery.

**Hotel Rural El Cerco** BOUTIQUE HOTEL €€
(948 34 12 69; www.hotelelcerco.es; Calle de Rodrigo Ximénez de Rada 36; s/d/tr from €50/75/105; 📶) At the eastern end of the old quarter, this is one of the most charming places to stay in town. Partially housed in a 13th-century defensive tower that was once part of the town walls, it has 10 stylish rooms with exposed stone walls and wooden roof beams.

**Casa Martija** CAFE €
(www.facebook.com/casamartija; Calle Mayor 104; dishes €2-7; 8am-2pm & 4.30-9pm) On a cobblestone lane, a short stroll from the bridge, Casa Martija serves coffees, wines and pastries, with tables out front. It's also a great spot for assembling picnic fare from the deli's cheeses, breads, olive oils and other gourmet goodies.

### Getting There & Away

Frequent buses run to/from Pamplona (€2.70, 45 minutes) via Puente la Reina en route to/from Estella (€2.05, 20 minutes).

## Estella

POP 13,673 / ELEV 483M

Estella (Basque: Lizarra) was known as 'La Bella' in medieval times because of the splendour of its monuments and buildings, and though the city has lost some of its beauty to modern suburbs, its historic centre is still thoroughly charming. During the 11th century, Estella became the main reception point for the growing flood of pilgrims along the Camino de Santiago. Today most visitors are continuing that tradition.

### Sights

**Iglesia de San Pedro de la Rúa** CHURCH
(Calle San Nicolás 10; 11am-1pm Mon-Fri, 10am-1.30pm & 6-7pm Sat & Sun) FREE This 12th-century church is the most important monument in Estella. Its cloisters are Navarra's finest Romanesque sculptural work.

**Museo Gustavo de Maeztu** MUSEUM
(948 54 60 37; www.museogustavodemaeztu.com; Calle San Nicolás 1; 9.30am-1.30pm Tue-Sat, 11am-2pm Sun) FREE A rare example of Romanesque civil construction, the Palacio de los Reyes houses a museum with an intriguing collection of paintings by Gustavo de Maeztu y Whitney (1887–1947), who was of Cuban-English parentage but emphatically Basque in upbringing and identity. Landscapes, portraits and full-bodied nudes reflect Maeztu's engaging sensual romanticism.

### Festivals & Events

**Semana Medieval** CULTURAL
(mid-Jul) For one week in mid-July, Estella hosts its exuberant medieval fair, complete with costumed performers, jousts, street theatre, falconry displays, markets and much merriment.

### Sleeping & Eating

**Hospedería Chapitel** HOTEL €€
(948 55 10 90; Chapitel 1; d/ste from €115/198; P) In a 17th-century building, Hospedería Chapitel has 14 comfortable rooms with wood floors and beamed ceilings that are peaceful despite the location right in Estella's historic centre.

**Casanellas Taller Gastronómico** CAFE €€
(948 98 26 11; Espoz y Mina 3; sandwiches €3.50-7, mains €16-22; 1.30-3.30pm Tue-Sat) Light, bright and contemporary, with a communal table at its centre, this is a great stop for a pastry, both sweet (such as cinnamon rolls) and savoury (lamb empanadas), a gourmet sandwich (eg truffled cream cheese with cucumber and semi-dried tomatoes), or a full meal (slow-roasted suckling pig, Navarran lamb with artichokes).

### Getting There & Away

Frequent buses link Estella with Pamplona (€4.40, 40 minutes) and Logroño (€4.40, one hour).

## Javier

POP 116 / ELEV 448M

Tiny Javier (Xavier), 54km southeast of Pamplona on the sun-baked plains, is utterly dominated by a castle so perfectly preserved you half expect the drawbridge to come crashing down and a knight in armour to gallop out on a white steed. It's the birthplace of the patron saint of Navarra, San Francisco Xavier.

**Castillo de Javier** CASTLE
(948 88 40 24; www.santuariojaviersj.org; Plaza del Santo; adult/child €3/1.50; 10am-6.30pm Mar-Oct, to 5pm Nov, to 4pm Dec-Feb) This 10th-century castle, strategically located on the border between the kingdoms of Navarra and Aragón, is Javier's main attraction. Inside, there's a small museum dedicated to the life of San Francisco Xavier, who was born here in 1506.

Xavier spent much of his life travelling, preaching, teaching and healing in Asia. Today his body lies in a miraculous state of preservation in a cathedral in Goa, India.

**Hotel Xabier** HOTEL €
(948 88 40 06; www.hotelxabier.com; Paseo de la Abadía 2; s/d/tr from €48/62/76; ) At the red-brick, ivy-clad Hotel Xabier, you can peer out of your window on a moonlit night and look for ghosts flitting around the castle keep. There's a good Navarran restaurant here (mains €14 to €24) and a bar serving Patxaran (local liqueur made from red sloebush berries, which grow wild throughout the region).

### Getting There & Away

Most travellers come here by car, but there's also a bus service to/from Pamplona (€5.40, 45 minutes, two daily July to September, one daily October to June).

WORTH A TRIP

### MONASTIC WANDERS

The countryside around Estella is littered with monasteries. One of the best is the **Monasterio de Irache** (off Carretera NA1110, Ayegui; ⌚10am-1.15pm & 4-6pm Wed-Sun mid-Jan–mid-Nov) FREE, 2.5km southwest of Estella, near Ayegui. This ancient Benedictine monastery has a lovely 16th-century plateresque cloister and its **Puerta Especiosa** is decorated with delicate sculptures. Opposite the monastery is the **Fuente de Vino** (Fountain of Wine). It's behind the **Bodegas Irache** (☎948 55 19 32; www.irache.com; Monasterio de Irache, off Carretera NA1110, Ayegui; ⌚shop 10am-2pm & 3-7pm Sat & Sun Jul-Sep, to 6pm Sat & Sun Oct-Jun), a well-known local wine producer (tours and tastings are available by reservation) and yes, it really is a free-flowing wine fountain, though you'll have to get here early since only 100L are released per day.

Situated 11km north of Estella, near Abárzuza, is the **Monasterio de Irantzu** (off Carretera NA7135, Abárzuza; €2.50; ⌚10am-2pm & 4-8pm Apr-Sep, to 6pm Oct-Mar). This grand Cistercian abbey was built between the 12th and 14th centuries, and has a beautiful setting amid the lush Yerri valley. The Gothic cloister, with its austere beauty and gurgling fountain, is a fine place to engage in a bit of quiet reflection.

# LA RIOJA

Get out the *copas* (glasses) for this region of ochre earth and vast blue skies, which produces some of Spain's best red wines. The bulk of the vineyards line Río Ebro around the town of Haro, but some also extend into neighbouring Navarra and the Basque province of Álava. This diverse region offers more than just the pleasures of the grape, though, from lively towns to quiet churches.

## Logroño

POP 151,113

Logroño is a stately wine-country service town with a heart of tree-studded squares, narrow streets and hidden corners. There are few monuments here, but perhaps more importantly to some, a great selection of bars serving tapas and Basque *pintxos*.

### Sights & Activities

**★Museo de la Rioja** MUSEUM

(☎941 29 12 59; www.museodelarioja.es; Plaza San Agustín 23; ⌚10am-2pm & 4-9pm Tue-Sat, 10am-2pm Sun) FREE Housed in a lovely 18th-century baroque building, this superb museum takes you on a wild romp through Riojan history and culture in both Spanish and English. Highlights include mystifying Celtiberian stone carvings from the 5th century BCE, beautiful jewellery and statuary displays from the Roman period and colourful medieval altarpieces, as well as lush portraits and landscape paintings from the 19th century.

**Catedral de Santa María de la Redonda** CATHEDRAL

(www.laredonda.org; Calle de Portales 14; ⌚8.30am-1pm & 6-8.45pm Mon-Sat, 8.30am-2pm Sun) The Catedral de Santa María de la Redonda sits on the site of a 12th-century oratory, and was built in varying styles between the 15th and 18th centuries. The eye-catching towers (known as the *gemelas* or twins) and splendid altarpiece are fine examples of the Rioja baroque manner. Don't miss the small exquisite painting depicting Christ on the Cross, attributed to Michelangelo. It's behind the main altar and can be illuminated by placing a coin in the box.

**Iglesia de San Bartolomé** CHURCH

(Calle San Bartolomé 2; ⌚11.30am-1.15pm) The impressive main entrance of Logroño's oldest church (built between the 12th and 13th centuries) has a splendid portico of deeply receding borders and an expressive collection of statuary. The interior is more austere, with unadorned pale stone columns, three naves and a semicircular apse.

**Rioja Trek** WINE

(☎941 58 73 54; www.riojatrek.com; Calle Francisco de Quevedo 12) Based 2.5km southeast of the centre, Rioja Trek offers a wide range of customisable winery tours (which can include visiting a traditional vineyard and bodega and even doing some winemaking yourself), along with wine tastings and hikes along some of La Rioja's fabulous mountain trails.

# Logroño

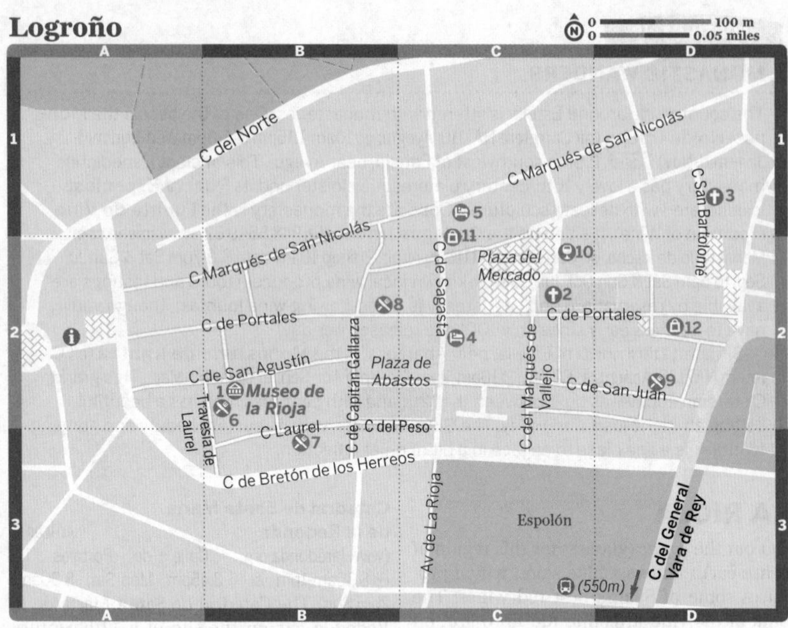


## Logroño

**Top Sights**
1 Museo de la Rioja ........ B2

**Sights**
2 Catedral de Santa María de la Redonda ........ C2
3 Iglesia de San Bartolomé ........ D1

**Sleeping**
4 Hostal La Numantina ........ C2
5 Hotel Calle Mayor ........ C1

**Eating**
6 Bar Soriano ........ B2
7 Bar Torrecilla ........ B3
8 La Cocina de Ramón ........ B2
9 Tastavin ........ D2

**Drinking & Nightlife**
10 Odeón Mercado Craft Beer ........ C2

**Shopping**
11 Félix Barbero Botas Rioja ........ C2
12 La Luci Delicatessen ........ D2

## Festivals & Events

**Fiestas de San Bernabé** FIESTA
(11 Jun) The Feast of San Bernabé commemorates the French siege of Logroño in 1521 with food and wine tasting, traditional concerts, fireworks and a re-enactment of the medieval battle.

**Fiesta de San Mateo** CULTURAL
(mid-Sep) Logroño's week-long Fiesta de San Mateo starts on the Saturday before 21 September and doubles as a harvest festival, during which all of La Rioja comes to town to watch grape-crushing ceremonies and drink copious quantities of wine.

## Sleeping

**Hostal La Numantina** HOSTAL €
(941 25 14 11; www.hostalnumantina.com; Calle de Sagasta 4; s/d/tr from €37/58/76; ) This budget-minded outfit has homey rooms, some with large bathtubs and tiny balconies with views over the street below. There's a communal space downstairs with comfy sofas and good maps of Logroño and the surrounding area.

**Hotel Calle Mayor** HOTEL €€
(941 23 23 68; www.hotelcallemayor.com; Calle Marqués de San Nicolás 71; s/d/ste from €95/125/235; P) Set within a restored 16th-century building, classy Hotel Calle Mayor has a dozen large, comfortable rooms

bathed in light, some with wooden beams and balconies, and modern neutral-toned bathrooms.

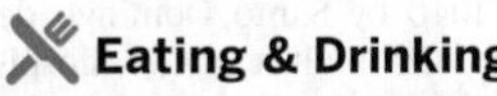

## Eating & Drinking

**Tastavin** PINTXOS €
(www.facebook.com/tastavinbardepinchos; Calle San Juan 25; pintxos €2.50-4; ⏲8-11pm Tue, 1-4pm & 8-11pm Wed-Sun; 📶) On *pintxo* bar–lined San Juan, stylish Tastavin whips up some of the tastiest morsels in town, including smoked trout and lemon cream cornets, fried artichokes, tuna tataki and braised oxtail. The wines are outstanding.

**Bar Torrecilla** PINTXOS €
(☎608 344694; Calle Laurel 15; pintxos €2-3.50; ⏲1-4pm & 8pm-12.30am Wed-Sun) The best *pintxos* in town? You be the judge. Go for the melt-in-your-mouth foie gras or the mini-burgers, or anything else that takes your fancy, at this modern bar on buzzing Calle Laurel.

**Bar Soriano** TAPAS €
(Travesía de Laurel 2; tapas €1.50; ⏲11.45am-3pm & 7-11.45pm Mon, Tue, Thu & Fri, 11am-3pm & 6-11pm Sat, 11am-10pm Sun) This venerable bar has been serving just one tapa, a mushroom stack topped with a prawn, since 1972.

**La Cocina de Ramón** SPANISH €€€
(☎941 28 98 08; www.lacocinaderamon.es; Calle de Portales 30; mains €18-27; ⏲1.30-4pm & 8.30-11pm Mon, Tue & Thu-Sat, 1.30-4pm Wed) It looks unassuming from the outside, but Ramón's high-quality, locally grown produce and tried-and-tested family recipes, such as chargrilled lamb cutlets or beef tenderloin cooked with wines from La Rioja, has earned him a lot of fans. The fine cooking is matched by the top service and white tablecloths; Ramón likes to come and explain the dishes to guests.

**Odeón Mercado Craft Beer** CRAFT BEER
(www.facebook.com/cerveceriaodeon.mercado; Plaza del Mercado 27; ⏲6.30pm-3am Wed, Thu & Sun, to 4am Fri & Sat) Brew lovers from far and wide descend on this laid-back bar on the plaza. You'll find 20 different craft beers on tap from the Basque Country, Catalonia and beyond. Live music often plays on weekends.

## Shopping

**La Luci Delicatessen** FOOD & DRINKS
(☎941 44 18 54; www.facebook.com/lalucideli; Calle de Portales 3; ⏲10.30am-2pm & 5.30-9pm Tue-Sun) Browse for wines, cheeses, olive oils, craft beers, vermouth and boxed biscuits in carousel tins at this tantalising little store.

**Félix Barbero Botas Rioja** ARTS & CRAFTS
(www.botasrioja.com; Calle de Sagasta 8; ⏲9am-1.30pm & 4-8pm Mon-Sat) Maintaining a dying art, fifth-generation artisan Félix Barbero handcrafts the classic Spanish animal-skin wine carriers, in which farmers carried their daily rations while working in the fields. Wine carriers can be embroidered.

## Information

**Tourist Office** (☎941 29 12 60; www.lariojaturismo.com; Calle de Portales 50; ⏲9am-2pm & 5-8pm Mon-Fri, from 10am Sat & Sun Jul-Sep, shorter hours Oct-Jun) At the historic centre's western edge; can provide lots of information on both the city and La Rioja in general.

## Getting There & Away

The **bus station** (Avenida de España 1) is 1km southeast of the historic centre.

Buses go to the following:

| Destination | Fare (€) | Time |
|---|---|---|
| Bilbao | 10-15 | 1¾hr |
| Haro | 5 | 40 min |
| Pamplona | 11 | 2hr |
| Santo Domingo de la Calzada | 2.50 | 40 min |

The train station is 300m southeast of the bus station. Regular services include the following:

| Destination | Fare (€) | Time |
|---|---|---|
| Bilbao | 9-11 | 2½hr |
| Burgos | 13-18.50 | 2hr |
| Madrid | 41-62 | 3½hr |
| Zaragoza | 12-23.50 | 2hr |

# San Millán de Cogolla

POP 222 / ELEV 728M

In a wooded valley 19km southeast of Santo Domingo de la Calzada, the hamlet of San Millán de Cogolla, has a long and fascinating Jewish history that dates back to the 10th century CE. But most people come here to see two remarkable monasteries that helped give birth to the Castilian language. On account of their linguistic heritage and artistic beauty, they have been recognised by Unesco as World Heritage Sites.

**Monasteria de Yuso** MONASTERY
(☎941 37 30 49; www.monasteriodesanmillan.com/yuso; Calle Convento; adult/child €7/3; ⏰10am-1.30pm & 4-6.30pm Tue-Sun Apr-Sep, also open Mon Aug, to 5.30pm Tue-Sun Oct-Mar) The 6th-century Monasterio de Yuso, sometimes called El Escorial de La Rioja, contains numerous treasures in its museum. You can only visit as part of a guided tour (in Spanish only; non-Spanish speakers will be given an information sheet in English and French). Tours last 50 minutes and run every half-hour or so. Maps detailing short walks in the region are available here.

**Monasterio de Suso** MONASTERY
(☎941 37 30 82; www.monasteriodesanmillan.com/suso; Calle de Suso; €4; ⏰9.30am-1.30pm & 3.30-6.30pm Tue-Sun Apr-Sep, to 5.30pm Oct-Mar) Built above the caves where San Millán once lived, the Monasterio de Suso was consecrated in the 10th century. It's believed that in the 13th century a monk, Gonzalo de Berceo, wrote some of the first Castilian words here. It can only be visited on a 40-minute guided tour. Tickets include a short bus ride up to the monastery from Monasterio de Yuso, whose reception area sells tickets; you can't arrive independently.

## Getting There & Away

San Millán de Cogolla is not served by pubic transport. It's a 44km drive southwest of Logroño.

# Santo Domingo de la Calzada

POP 6231 / ELEV 641M

Santo Domingo is small-town Spain at its best. A large number of the inhabitants continue to live in the partially walled old quarter, a labyrinth of medieval streets where the past is alive and the sense of community is strong. Santiago-bound pilgrims have long been a part of the fabric of this town, and that tradition continues to this day.

## Sights

**Catedral de Santo Domingo de la Calzada** CATHEDRAL
(☎941 34 00 33; www.catedralsantodomingo.com; Plaza del Santo 4; adult/child €7/2; ⏰10am-8pm Mon-Fri, to 7pm Sat, 10am-noon & 2-8pm Sun Apr-Oct, shorter hours Nov-Mar) The monumental cathedral and its attached museum glitter with the gold that attests to the great wealth the Camino has bestowed on otherwise backwater towns. An audio guide to the cathedral and its treasures is €1. Construction was begun in 1040 by Santo Domingo de la Calzada, who also built a bridge, hospital and pilgrims' hostel; he is buried in the cathedral.

The cathedral's most eccentric feature is the live white rooster and hen that forage in a glass-fronted cage opposite the entrance to the crypt (look up!), which have been changed every 15 days since 1350. Their presence celebrates a long-standing legend, the Miracle of the Rooster, which tells of a young man who was unfairly executed only to recover miraculously, while the broiled cock and hen on the plate of his judge suddenly leapt up and chickened off, fully fledged.

## Sleeping & Eating

**Hostal Rey Pedro I** HOSTAL €
(☎941 34 11 60; www.hostalpedroprimero.es; Calle San Roque 9; s/d/tr from €45/56/73; 📶) This carefully renovated townhouse, which has nine terracotta-coloured rooms with wooden roof beams and entirely modern bathrooms, is a terrific deal.

**Parador de Santo Domingo de la Calzada** HISTORIC HOTEL €€
(☎941 34 03 00; www.parador.es; Plaza del Santo 3; d from €100; P📶) Occupying the town's 12th-century former hospital opposite the cathedral, this palatial hotel has spacious rooms (some with canopied beds and small balconies) and magnificent public areas, including the in-house restaurant (mains €11 to €19).

**Parador Santo Domingo Bernardo de Fresneda** HOTEL €€
(☎941 34 11 50; www.parador.es; Plaza de San Francisco 1; d from €90; P📶) Just on the edge of the old town, the Parador Santo Domingo Bernado de Fresneda occupies a 16th-century convent and pilgrim hostel. With its 47 opulent rooms, some featuring four-poster beds, it's now a luxurious place to stay.

**Los Caballeros** SPANISH €€€
(☎941 34 27 89; www.restauranteloscaballeros.com; Calle Mayor 56; mains €18-32; ⏰1-3.30pm & 7.30-10.30pm Tue-Sat, 1-3.30pm Sun) Beside the cathedral in a classy dining room set with exposed brick, wood-beamed ceiling and stained-glass details, Los Caballeros serves

suckling pig and lamb, among other classic Navarran fare. Don't miss house speciality cinnamon and vanilla *nuestra tarta del abuelito* ('our grandfather's pudding') for dessert. Advance reservations are a must at busy times.

## Getting There & Away

Frequent buses run to Logroño (€5, one hour, six daily Monday to Saturday, four Sunday) from the bus stop on Plaza San Jerónimo Hermosilla, on the historic centre's southern edge.

# La Rioja Wine Region

Wine aficionados the world over know the famous wines of La Rioja, where vines have been cultivated since Roman times. Vineyards cover the hinterland of the Río Ebro; on the river's north bank, the region is part of the Basque Country and is known as La Rioja Alavesa.

## Haro

POP 11,776 / ELEV 479M

The capital of La Rioja's wine-producing region, Haro has a compact old quarter, leading off Plaza de la Paz, where intriguing alleyways shelter bars and wine shops.

There are plenty of bodegas in the vicinity of the town, some of which are open to visitors (almost always with advance reservation). The tourist office keeps a full list.

**Bodegas Muga** WINE

(941 31 18 25; www.bodegasmuga.com; Barrio de la Estación; 1hr winery tour €15, 2½hr hot-air balloon tour €170; by reservation Mon-Sat) Just after the railway bridge on the way out of town, this bodega is particularly receptive and gives daily guided tours (except Sunday) and tastings in Spanish and English. Hot-air balloon tours provide glorious views of the vineyard-ribboned countryside.

**Batalla del Vino** WINE

(Wine Battle; www.batalladelvino.com; 29 Jun) During the Batalla del Vino, Haro's otherwise mild-mannered citizens splash wine all over each other in the name of San Juan, San Felices and San Pedro. Plenty of it goes down the right way, too.

**Hotel Los Agustinos** HISTORIC HOTEL €€

(941 31 13 08; www.hotellosagustinos.com; San Agustín 2; d/tr from €99/121; P ❄ ☎) Occupying a 14th-century convent, Los Agustinos has 62 spacious rooms with wine-coloured carpets, and striped and floral fabrics The stunning covered courtyard is a wonderful place to linger over a glass or two. Regional dishes at the restaurant (mains €16 to €24) include slow-cooked lamb and chargrilled sirloin.

**El Rincón del Noble** SPANISH €€

(941 31 29 32; www.elrincondelnoble.net; Martinez Lacuesta 11; mains €13-20; 1-4pm Sun-Thu, 1-4pm & 9-11pm Fri & Sat) Simple but thoughtfully prepared classics at this easy-going spot include *huevos rotos* (fried potatoes topped with egg), *espinacas con garbanzos* (spiced chickpeas with spinach) and *caparrones* (bean and chorizo stew). Unsurprisingly, the wine list is superb.

### Information

**Tourist Office** (941 30 35 80; www.haroturismo.org; Plaza de la Paz 1; 10am-2pm Mon, 10am-2pm & 4-7pm Tue-Sun mid-Jun–Sep, 10am-2pm Tue-Thu & Sun, 10am-2pm & 4-7pm Fri & Sat Oct–mid-Jun) Just off the main plaza; provides useful info on the area's many wineries.

### Getting There & Away

Up to three trains per hour connect Haro with Logroño (€4.50 to €7.35, 40 minutes).

The **bus station** (Calle Castilla) is 400m southwest of the historic centre. Services include Bilbao (€6.65, one hour, up to seven daily), Laguardia (€7, 25 minutes, five daily) and Logroño (€5, one hour, up to four per hour).

## Briones

POP 766 / ELEV 501M

Perched on a hillside, the quaint, sunset-gold village of Briones has commanding views over the surrounding vine-carpeted plains. The chief draw is its excellent wine museum.

**Vivanco** MUSEUM

(Museo de la Cultura del Vino; 941 32 23 23; www.vivancoculturadevino.es; Carretera Nacional, Km 232; museum only adult/child €16.50/free, guided visit with wine tasting €45-97; 10am-6pm Tue-Fri & Sun, 10am-8pm Sat) A must for wine lovers, the high-tech Museum of the Culture of Wine delves into the history and culture of wine and the various processes that go into its production. The treasures on display include Picasso-designed wine jugs, Roman and Byzantine mosaics, and wine-inspired religious artefacts. Various guided tours take you behind the scenes of the winery and include tastings.

## EXPERIENCE THE WEALTH OF THE GRAPE

The humble grape has created great wealth for some of the villages around La Rioja. Proof of this are some of the extravagant bodegas and hotels that have sprung up in recent years in what otherwise appear to be backwater farming communities.

Before hitting the wine road, it's helpful to learn a few basics: wine categories in La Rioja are termed Young, Crianza, Reserva and Gran Reserva. Young wines are in their first or second year and are inevitably a touch 'fresh'. Crianzas must have matured into their third year and have spent at least one year in the cask, followed by a few months resting in the bottle. Reservas pay homage to the best vintages and must mature for at least three full years in cask and bottle, with at least one year in the cask. Gran Reservas depend on the very best vintages and are matured for at least two years in the cask followed by three years in the bottle. These are the 'velvet' wines.

When the owner of the Bodegas Marqués de Riscal, in the village of Elciego, decided he wanted to create something special, he didn't hold back. The result is the spectacular Frank Gehry–designed **Hotel Marqués de Riscal** (945 18 08 80; www.hotel-marquesderiscal.com; Calle Torrea 1, Elciego; d from €371; P ❄ wi-fi), opened in 2006. Costing around €85 million, the building is a flamboyant wave of multicoloured titanium sheets that stands in utter contrast to the village behind. Casual visitors are not, however, welcome at the hotel. If you want to see it, you have three options. The easiest is to join one of the bodega's **wine tours** (Vinos de los Herederos del Marqués de Riscal; 945 18 08 88; www.marquesderiscal.com; tours €12; tours 10.30am-1pm & 4-6pm) – there's at least one English-language tour a day, but it's best to book in advance. You won't get inside the building, but you will get to see its exterior from some distance.

A much closer look can be obtained by reserving a table at one of the two superb in-house restaurants: the Michelin-starred **Restaurante Marqués de Riscal** (www.restaurantemarquesderiscal.com; 14-/21-course menu €110/140; 8-10pm Tue, 1.30-3.30pm & 8-10pm Wed-Sun) or the **1860 Tradición** (mains €22-36; 1.30-3.30pm & 8-10pm). For the most intimate look at the building, you'll need to reserve a room for the night.

Located 2km north of Laguardia, the 2001-opened **Bodegas Ysios** (945 60 06 40; www.bodegasysios.com; Camino de la Hoya; 90min tour & tasting €25; tours 11am daily) was designed by Santiago Calatrava as a 'temple dedicated to wine'. It features an aluminium wave for a roof and a cedar exterior that blends into the mountainous backdrop and looks best at night, when pools of light flow out of it. Tours provide an insight into wine production; book ahead. There are several other, somewhat less confronting, wine cellars around Laguardia that can be visited, by reservation only – contact the tourist office ( in Laguardia for details.

**Bodegas Palacio** (945 60 00 57; www.bodegaspalacio.com; San Lazaro 1; 90min tour & tasting from €25), just 800m south of Laguardia, arranges tours and tastings by appointment. Check the website for details of its wine courses (from €35 for one hour).

Also on the edge of Laguardia, 700m to the southeast, is the **Centro Temático del Vino Villa Lucía** (945 60 00 32; www.villa-lucia.com; Carretera de Logroño; 90min tour €12; 9am-2pm & 4-8pm Tue-Sat, 9am-2pm Sun), a wine museum and shop selling high-quality wine from a variety of small, local producers. Museum visits are by guided tour only and finish with a 4D film and wine tasting.

**Los Calaos de Briones** HOTEL €€
(941 32 21 31; www.loscalaosdebriones.com; San Juan 13; d from €65) At this lovely hotel, some rooms have romantic four-poster beds; those facing east have beautiful views over the countryside. The attached restaurant (mains €11 to €17), in an old wine cellar, specialises in local lamb and seasonal vegetables.

### Getting There & Away

Frequent buses run from Logroño to Briones (€4, 50 minutes), continuing to Haro (€1.95, 15 minutes). In Briones, the bus stops on the edge of town, just off the highway at Plaza Ibarra.

## Laguardia

POP 1505 / ELEV 630M

The medieval fortress town of Laguardia, or the 'Guard of Navarra' as it was once appropriately known, sits proudly on its rocky hilltop. The walled old quarter, which makes up most of the town, is virtually traffic-free and is a joy to wander around. Laguardia is part of La Rioja Alavesa, the Basque Country's wine-producing region. Tours of the town's wineries depart regularly; the tourist office has a list.

### Sights

**Bodega El Fabulista** WINERY
(☎945 62 11 92; www.bodegaelfabulista.com; Plaza San Juan; 1hr tours from €8; ⊙tours by reservation 11.30am-1pm & 5.30-7pm) Tours of this traditional winery's medieval cellars, 7m below the Laguardia's historic heart, finish with a tasting of two of the bodega's wines. Reserve ahead for a one-hour English-language tour, or ask about tours incorporating local food pairings and tastings.

**Bodegas Casa Primicia** WINERY
(☎945 621 266; www.bodegascasaprimicia.com; Calle Páganos 78; 1¼hr tours €10; ⊙tours by reservation 11am, 1pm & 5.30pm Tue-Sun) Laguardia's oldest winery is 500m north of the historic centre. On a 75-minute tour through this atmospheric 16th-century building, knowledgeable guides will give you an overview of the winemaking process and the rich heritage of Rioja wines, with a tasting at the end. It's essential to reserve ahead.

**Torre Abacial** TOWER
(Calle Mayor 52; €3; ⊙10.30am-2.30pm & 3.30-7.30pm) For a splendid view over town and the vineyards beyond, climb the 100-plus steps of the 'Abbot's Tower' – so named as it was once part of a monastery. Parts of the structure date back to the 12th century.

**Iglesia de Santa María de los Reyes** CHURCH
(☎945 60 08 45; Travesía Mayor 1; tours €3; ⊙guided tours by reservation Jun-Sep) The impressive Iglesia de Santa María de los Reyes has a breathtaking late-14th-century Gothic doorway, adorned with beautiful sculptures of the disciples and other motifs. If the church doors are locked, stop by the tourist office, where you can get a key. Guided tours (English available) must be booked through the tourist office.

### Sleeping & Eating

**Posada Mayor de Migueloa** HISTORIC HOTEL €€
(☎945 60 01 87; www.mayordemigueloa.com; Calle Mayor 20; s/d incl breakfast from €83/106; ❄📶) This 17th-century mansion-hotel has seven atmospheric rooms that evoke a bygone age with old stone walls, low-beamed ceilings and polished antique furnishings. Be sure to pay a visit to the hotel's wine cellar. The on-site restaurant (mains €18 to €24.50) is also top-notch.

**Hospedería de los Parajes** HISTORIC HOTEL €€€
(☎945 62 11 30; www.hospederiadelosparajes.com; Calle Mayor 46-48; d/ste from €200/400; ❄📶) Blending old and new features, the 18 extraordinarily plush rooms at Hospedería de los Parajes have polished wood floors, artwork and original ceilings. Beds are comfortable, showers have rustic stone floors and the service is professional. In the basement is a small spa offering a range of treatments.

★**Restaurante Amelibia** SPANISH €€
(☎945 62 12 07; www.restauranteamelibia.com; Barbacana 14; mains €15-22; ⊙1-3.30pm Mon & Wed-Sun, 8.30-10.30pm Fri & Sat; 👪) Gaze out the windows at a view over the scorched plains and distant mountain ridges while dining on sublime traditional cuisine, such as oxtail and wild mushrooms in red wine sauce with seasonal vegetables, or pig's trotters in a sherry reduction. Half-portions are available for kids.

### Information

**Tourist Office** (☎945 60 08 45; www.laguardia-alava.com; Calle Mayor 52; ⊙10am-2pm & 4-7pm Mon-Sat, 10.45am-2pm Sun) On the main road in the heart of town; has a list of local bodegas that can be visited.

### Getting There & Away

Buses serve Bilbao (€8, 1½ hours, five daily) via Haro (€3.50, 25 minutes), and Logroño (€3, 20 minutes). Buses stop at the covered shelters on the main road that runs through town.

## AT A GLANCE

**POPULATION**
1.6 million

**BIGGEST CITY**
Gijón

**BEST GORGE WALK**
Ruta del Cares (p531)

**BEST CIDER STREET**
Calle de la Gascona (p511)

**BEST EASY CYCLING TRAIL**
Senda del Oso (p523)

**WHEN TO GO**

**May, Jun & Sep** The best times to visit: agreeable temperatures, reasonable prices, few crowds.

**Jul** Santander's Semana Grande kicks off the summer fun.

**Oct** Celebrate the apple harvest in Asturias' heavily laden orchards and bustling *sidrerías*.

Lago de la Ercina (p529), Covadonga
MARQUES/SHUTTERSTOCK ©

# Cantabria & Asturias

You can traverse either of these two regions from north to south in little more than an hour – but don't. Cantabria and Asturias reward those who linger. The stunning coastline is a sequence of sheer cliffs, beautiful beaches and small fishing ports. Behind it, gorgeously green river valleys dotted with stone-built villages rise to the 2000m-plus mountain wall of the Cordillera Cantábrica, which reaches majestic heights in the Picos de Europa. The beauty is endless.

Cantabria's and Asturias' fertile landscapes ensure that you'll eat and drink very well here: on offer are abundant local seafood, quality meat, local cheeses and Asturias' renowned cider. Meanwhile, travellers with a feel for history will be in their element: early humans painted some of the world's most magnificent prehistoric art at Altamira and elsewhere, and it was at Covadonga that the seed of the Spanish nation first sprouted 1300 years ago.

**INCLUDES**

# CANTABRIA

Verdant headlands and wild, cliff-backed beaches dominate Cantabria's 150km-long coastline, interspersed with colourful fishing ports and sandy beaches perfect for a summer day by the seaside (unreliable weather permitting). Inland rise Cantabria's strikingly green mountains, sliced by deep valleys connected by steep passes and culminating in the spectacular Picos de Europa. The verdant interior landscapes, sprinkled with villages of sturdy stone houses with red-tile roofs and flower-hung wooden balconies, prove a visual feast whether you're driving the country roads or walking the trails.

Lively capital Santander provides a slice of urban life, with buzzing beaches and bodegas. Santillana del Mar and Comillas entice with their medieval and Modernista trappings; and the prehistoric art of Altamira, El Castillo and Covalanas caves is some of the finest in the world. With so much variety, you could easily spend your entire vacation here.

## Santander

POP 172,000

The belle-époque elegance of El Sardinero aside, modern Santander is not the most beautiful of cities. A huge fire raged through the centre back in 1941, leaving little that's old or quaint. Still, Cantabria's capital is an engaging place, making the most of a superb setting along the northern side of the handsome Bahía de Santander. It's a lively spot to spend a night or two, with fine urban beaches, busy shopping streets, a heaving bar and restaurant scene, plenty of surf, and some intriguing cultural attractions. It's a popular summer holiday resort for Spaniards.

### Sights

**★Centro Botín** ARTS CENTRE

(942 04 71 47; www.centrobotin.org; Jardines de Pereda; galleries adult/child €8/free; 10am-9pm Tue-Sun Jun-Sep, to 8pm Oct-May) Santander's newest and splashiest landmark, this ambitious waterfront arts and cultural centre opened to great fanfare in 2017. The futuristic two-block building, designed by Italian Renzo Piano (architect of Paris' Centre Pompidou and London's Shard), is covered in 280,000 ceramic discs. It encompasses 2500 sq metres of gallery space for exhibitions of international contemporary art, along with open-air stairways, a rooftop viewing platform and a bright **cafe** (942 04 71 50; mains €11-15, lunch menús €13-18; 9.30am-midnight mid-Jul–Aug, 9.30am-8pm Tue-Thu, 9.30am-midnight Fri & Sat, 10am-8pm Sun Sep–mid-Jul) that's an excellent place to stop for a drink or bite.

**Jardines de Pereda** PARK

(Paseo de Pereda) The pretty, recently refurbished gardens around the Centro Botín are named after 19th-century Cantabrian writer José María de Pereda, whose bronze effigy tops a stone monument decked with scenes of Cantabrian life described in his works.

The bayside promenade continues east to Puerto Chico (Little Port), a marina, and is busy with strollers or joggers whenever the weather is half-decent.

**★Península de la Magdalena** PARK

(off Avenida Reina Victoria; 8am-10pm) At the eastern tip of the bay, this sprawling parkland is perfect for a stroll, and popular with picnickers. Kids will enjoy the resident seals, sea lions and penguins, and the train around the headland (adult/child €2.45/1.45).

**Palacio de la Magdalena** PALACE

(942 20 30 84; www.palaciomagdalena.com; tours €3; tours hourly 11am-1pm & 4-6pm Mon-Fri, 10am-noon Sat & Sun Oct–mid-Jun, 10am-noon Sat & Sun mid-Jun–Sep) The eclectically styled, English-inspired palace crowning the Península de la Magdalena was built between 1908 and 1912 as a gift from Santander to Spain's royal family, who used it every summer until 1930. Detailed 45-minute guided tours (in Spanish) show you oak floors, bronze chandeliers, surprisingly simple bedrooms, a carved chestnut-wood staircase and what was the king's study.

**Catedral de la Asunción** CATHEDRAL

(942 22 60 24; Plaza del Obispo José Eguino y Trecu; €1; 10am-1pm & 4.30-7pm Mon-Fri, 10am-1pm & 5-8pm Sat & Sun) Santander's serene cathedral comprises two Gothic churches, one above the other. The 14th-century **upper church**, extensively rebuilt after the 1941 fire, houses the tomb of Marcelino Menéndez Pelayo (1856–1912), a celebrated Santander-born intellectual. Its handome cloister dates from the 15th century. Below lies the 13th-century **Iglesia del Santísimo Cristo** (Iglesia Vieja; 942 21 15 63; Calle de Somorrostro; 8am-1pm & 4-8pm Jun-Sep, 8am-1pm & 5-8pm Oct-May, hours may vary), where you can view two silver heads containing the skulls of Santander's patron saints.

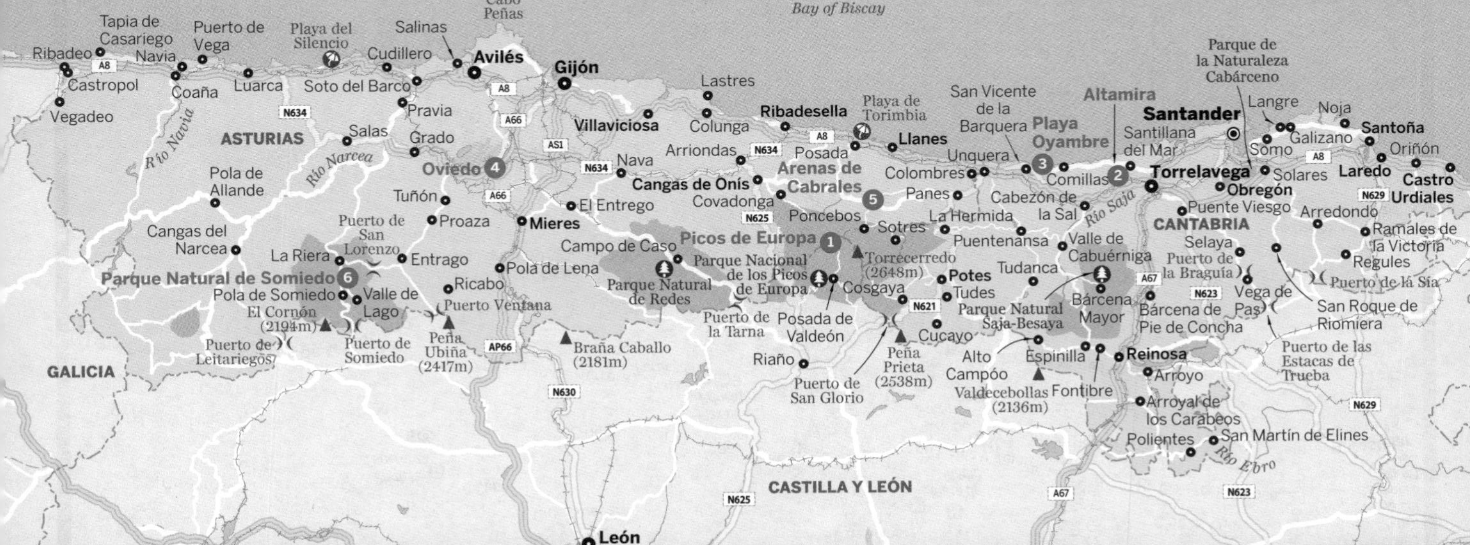


# Cantabria & Asturias Highlights

**1 Picos de Europa** (p526) Hiking the plunging gorges and soaring heights of these superb mountains.

**2 Cave art** (p501) Marvelling at the genius of the Stone Age artists of Altamira and other caverns.

**3 Beaches** (p504) Delighting in wild ocean strands like Oyambre and more secluded bays like golden Torimbia.

**4 Oviedo** (p507) Soaking up the cultural ambience of Asturias' capital and enjoying its fine food and cider scenes.

**5 Surf and turf** (p530) Revelling in the variety of fresh food from fish and crustaceans to free-range meat and tangy cave-matured cheese from Arenas de Cabrales.

**6 Inland valleys** (p524) Discovering green river vales, high passes, stone-built villages and rare wildlife like the bears of Parque Natural de Somiedo.

# Santander

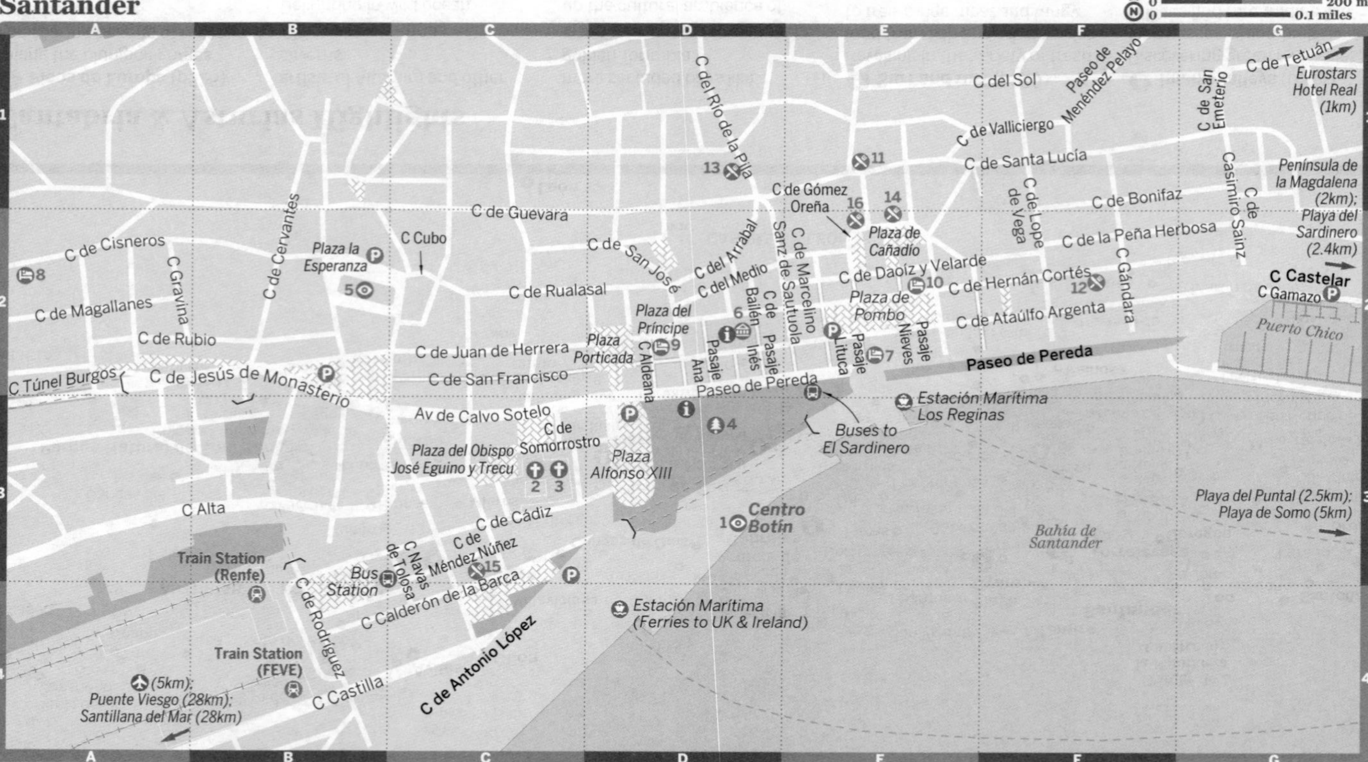
0 200 m
0 0.1 miles
C de Tetuán
Eurostars Hotel Real (1km)
C del Sol
Paseo de Menéndez Pelayo
C de San Emeterio
C de Valliciergo
C de Santa Lucía
C del Río de la Pila
C de Gómez Oreña
C de Bonifaz
C de Casimiro Sainz
Península de la Magdalena (2km); Playa del Sardinero (2.4km)
C de Guevara
C de Cisneros
C Gravina
C de Cervantes
Plaza la Esperanza
C Cubo
C de San José
C del Arrabal
C del Medio
C de Marcelino Sanz de Sautuola
Plaza de Cañadio
C de Lope de Vega
C de la Peña Herbosa
C de Daoíz y Velarde
C de Hernán Cortés
C Gándara
C Castelar
C Gamazo
C de Magallanes
C de Rualasal
Plaza del Príncipe
C de Bailén
Pasaje Inés
Plaza de Pombo
C de Ataúlfo Argenta
Puerto Chico
C de Rubio
C de Juan de Herrera
Plaza Porticada
C Aldeana
Pasaje Ana
Pasaje Lituca
Pasaje Nieves
Paseo de Pereda
C Túnel Burgos
C de Jesús de Monasterio
C de San Francisco
Av de Calvo Sotelo
Estación Marítima Los Reginas
Buses to El Sardinero
C de Somorrostro
Plaza del Obispo José Eguino y Trecu
Plaza Alfonso XIII
C Alta
Centro Botín
Bahía de Santander
Playa del Puntal (2.5km); Playa de Somo (5km)
Train Station (Renfe)
C de Cádiz
C de Méndez Núñez
C Navas de Tolosa
Bus Station
C Calderón de la Barca
C de Rodríguez
Estación Marítima (Ferries to UK & Ireland)
Train Station (FEVE)
C de Antonio López
C Castilla
(5km); Puente Viesgo (28km); Santillana del Mar (28km)

## Santander

**Top Sights**



**Museo de Prehistoria y Arqueología de Cantabria** MUSEUM

(MUPAC; ☎942 20 99 22; www.museosdecantabria.es; Calle de Bailén; adult/child €5/2, Sun from 5pm free; ⏲10am-2pm & 5-8pm Tue-Sun May-Sep, 10am-2pm & 5-7:30pm Tue-Sun Oct-Apr) The elegant prehistory and archaeology museum showcases Cantabria's archaeological wealth, with the help of interactive multimedia displays. Many exhibits focus on large numbers of small objects, but you'll also see prehistoric bear skeletons, giant stone discs carved by the ancient Cantabrians, a replica Roman patio, and sections on Stone Age cave art.

**Mercado La Esperanza** MARKET

(Plaza La Esperanza; ⏲8am-2pm & 5-7.30pm Mon-Fri, 8am-2pm Sat) Housed in a 19th-century cast-iron structure, the Esperanza market is a lively slice of Cantabrian life. Shoppers throng two floors of stalls laden with seafood, meat, cheese, fruit, vegetables, baked goods and *orujo* firewater from Liébana.

### Beaches

**Playa del Sardinero** BEACH

El Sardinero's 1.5km-long strand of gorgeous golden sand faces the open sea, north of the Península de la Magdalena. It's backed by some of Santander's most expensive real estate, including emblematic early-20th-century creations such as the **Gran Casino**. Surfers emerge in force when the waves are right, mainly in autumn and winter. Buses 1, 2, 4 and others (€1.30) run east to Sardinero from the Jardines de Pereda in the centre.

**Playa del Puntal** BEACH

A 2km-long finger of sand jutting across the bay towards Santander, Playa del Puntal is idyllic on calm days (but beware the currents). A couple of popular beach bars open up here over summer. Depending on the weather, passenger ferries (€2.90/4.20 one-way/return) sail over about every 30 minutes from 10.30am from the **Estación Marítima Los Reginas** (☎942 21 67 53; www.losreginas.com; Paseo Marítimo).

**Playa de Somo** BEACH

Across the bay from Santander, and just beyond Playa del Puntal, Playa de Somo is a beautiful, gold-tinged beach, often with pretty good surf. A year-round ferry (one way/return €2.90/5, 30 minutes) runs to Somo from the Estación Marítima Los Reginas every 30 or 60 minutes, 8.30am to 7.30pm.

## Activities

Surfing is one of Santander's favourite pastimes. You'll find several surf outfits in the Sardinero area and across the bay in Somo, all offering classes and equipment rentals. Most also offer increasingly popular stand-up paddleboarding (SUP) sessions.

**Escuela Cántabra de Surf** SURFING

(☎942 51 06 15, 609 482823; www.escuelacantabradesurf.com; Calle Isla de Mouro 12, Somo; 2hr group class per person €30, board & wetsuit hire per day €20) This well-established Somo-based school has been leading surf lovers into the waves since 1991, with classes run in English, Spanish or Italian and a range of surf camps and courses. It also does SUP classes (two-hour group/private per person €30/50) and excursions.

## Festivals & Events

**Semana Grande** FIESTA

(www.semanagrandesantander.com; ⏲Jul) Santander's big summer fiesta runs for 10 days of fun around 25 July.

## Sleeping

**Hostel Santander** HOSTEL €

(☎942 22 39 86; www.hostelsantander.es; Paseo de Pereda 15, 1st fl; dm incl breakfast €19-29; 📶) This good, central hostel is built into an old

WORTH A TRIP

## BEACHES AROUND SANTANDER

**Playas de Langre** (Langre; P) The two gorgeously wild golden beaches of Langre are backed by cliffs topped with rolling green fields, and often have surfable waves. Most beachgoers head for **Langre La Grande**, although the smaller, adjacent **Langre La Pequeña** is more protected. The beaches are 5km east of Somo and 500m northeast of Langre village – 8km east of Santander as the crow flies, but 30km round the bay if you're driving. **Playa de Valdearenas** (Playa de Liencres; Liencres; P) Protected by the pine-filled **Parque Natural de las Dunas de Liencres**, this 3km-long, gold-tinged beach has a delightful natural feel and is hugely popular with surfers and beach lovers alike. It's an 18km drive west of Santander: take the A67 west to Boo de Piélagos, then the CA231 and CA305 north.

townhouse facing the bay. The airy lounge provides TV, free tea, coffee and fruit, and sea views from its *galería* (glassed-in balcony). The three dorms – clean and fresh, with lockers and wood floors – sleep six to nine, mostly in three-tier bunks; the back one overlooks Plaza de Pombo.

**★Jardín Secreto** BOUTIQUE HOTEL €€
(942 07 07 14; www.jardinsecretosantander.com; Calle de Cisneros 37; r €60-95; ) Named for its little back garden, this is a charming, six-room world of its own, spread across a 200-year-old house near the city centre. It's run by a welcoming, on-the-ball brother-and-sister team, and designed by their mother in a stylish blend of silvers, greys and pastels with exposed stone, brick and wood. The complimentary morning coffee hits the spot.

**Los Balcones del Arte** APARTMENT €€
(942 03 65 47; www.losbalconesdelarte.com; Plaza del Príncipe 2, 5th fl; apt for 2 €85-190, for 4 €140-250; P) Four stunning contemporary-design apartments grace the top floors of a beautifully renovated, super-central building right beside Plaza Porticada. Each is impeccably designed in its own elegant character, with fun fabrics, splashes of bold detail and fully kitted-out kitchens.

**Le Petit Boutique Hotel** BOUTIQUE HOTEL €€
(942 07 57 68; www.lepetithotelsantander.com; Avenida de los Castros 10; d incl breakfast €65-150; ) The seven smart, individually styled rooms here make attractive (if slightly snug) lodgings near Playa del Sardinero. All have warm, tasteful decor inspired by different international locations, plus cushy beds, spotless bathrooms and jugs (not plastic bottles) of drinking water.

**Plaza Pombo B&B** B&B €€
(942 21 29 50; www.plazapombo.com; Calle de Hernán Cortés 25, 3rd fl; incl breakfast r €45-80, without bathroom €35-65; ) Fresh off a recent renovation, this long-established town-centre *pensión* (small private hotel) offers spacious common areas and nine bright, homey high-ceilinged rooms, with kettles and comfy beds; those at the front have balconies or galleries gazing out across Plaza de Pombo.

**★Eurostars Hotel Real** LUXURY HOTEL €€€
(942 27 25 50; www.eurostarshotelcompany.com; Paseo Pérez Galdós 28; incl breakfast r €84-539, ste €237-749; P) The Real was built, on a panoramic hilltop, in 1917 to house the royal family's guests. Following a full makeover it again offers a regal-style experience from the brilliantly white lounge, opening to a columned bay-view terrace, to the 123 updated classical-style rooms with rich chestnut furnishings and blue-and-gold trim. An additional draw is the thalassotherapy spa with its ample sea-water pool.

## Eating

**★Agua Salada** FUSION €€
(942 04 93 87; www.facebook.com/aguasaladasantander; Calle San Simón 2; lunch menú €14, mains €16-20; 1.30-4pm Mon, 1.30-4pm & 8-11pm Wed-Sun) A labour of love for owners Carlos García and Pilar Montiel, this intimate corner bistro serves top-notch, market-fresh cuisine that walks the line between traditional and innovative. Indulge in a superb tuna tartare with mustard ice cream, local beef entrecôte with roasted peppers and chips, or an endive salad with pears, Gorgonzola and hazelnut pesto. Half-portions are available for many dishes.

**★Bodega del Riojano** SPANISH **€€**
(☎942 21 67 50; www.bodegadelriojano.com; Calle Río de la Pila 5; mains €14-23; 🕐1.30-4pm & 8.30pm-midnight) The Riojano's high-ceilinged, wood-pillared dining room and bar, adorned with colourfully painted wine barrels, make an atmospheric setting for a fine range of northern Spanish favourites.

Whether you opt for a traditional stew of *cachón* (cuttlefish), *pochas* (Riojan green beans) with squid, or a more straightforward beef tenderloin, cod croquettes or Cantabrian cheese platter, it's all good, and the choice of wines is wide.

**Asubio Gastro** SPANISH **€€**
(☎942 03 52 38; Calle de Hernán Cortés 28; raciones €5-16; 🕐noon-4pm & 8pm-midnight Wed-Mon) This slick tapas bistro turns out all manner of tempting, well-executed delights, mostly cooked fresh to your order – from grilled octopus with sweet-potato puree or pork ribs with pineapple chutney, to a veggie burger or a gooey mushroom-and-cheese omelette. Choose between high stools in the bar area or tables in the restaurant section, both styled in brightly contemporary black, white and light wood.

**La Conveniente** TAPAS **€€**
(☎942 21 28 87; Calle de Gómez Oreña 9; raciones & tablas €5-22; 🕐7pm-midnight Mon-Sat) The cavernous Conveniente has soaring stone walls, wooden pillars and wine racks stacked up to the ceiling. Squeeze into the tram-like front enclosure, hope for a table in the main room or just snack at the bar. The food is straightforward – plates or *pinchos* (tapas-sized serves) of cheese, *embutidos* (sausages), ham, pâtés, anchovies – with generous servings.

**El Machi** SEAFOOD **€€€**
(El Machichaco; ☎942 21 87 22; www.elmachi.es; Calle de Calderón de la Barca 9; mains €16-30, raciones €9-24; 🕐9am-midnight Mon-Fri, to 1am Sat & Sun) A welcoming, good-value seafood spot convenient to all transport terminals and the city centre. Go for a plate of the Santander speciality *rabas de calamar* (deep-fried squid), or clams pan-fried with garlic, or heartier choices such as seafood *arroces* (rices) or battered hake in a spicy sauce with *patatas panaderas* (fried potato slices). Also good for light breakfasts.

**Cañadío** CANTABRIAN **€€€**
(☎942 31 41 49; www.restaurantecanadio.com; Calle de Gómez Oreña 15; raciones €10-17, mains €19-24; 🕐1-4pm & 9pm-midnight Mon-Sat; 📶) A tasteful spot with white-cloth tables, Cañadío offers top-notch creative cooking with local inspiration. Hake is prepared in a variety of styles, the escalopes are stuffed with Liébana cheese and ham, and you could start off with *pudin de cabracho* (scorpionfish pâté). Or join the crowds in the front bar for tempting *pinchos*.

## Drinking & Nightlife

Plaza de Cañadío and Calles de Daoíz y Velarde and Hernán Cortés have plenty of popular *bares de copas* (drinks bars) and tapas bars, where you can chat over beer, cocktails, spirits and wine. Calle de Santa Lucía, Calle del Sol and the upper half of Calle del Río de la Pila teem with more bohemian bars. Paseo de Pereda and its eastward continuation, Calle Castelar, are dotted with cafes.

## ℹ Information

**Oficina de Turismo de Cantabria** (☎942 31 07 08; www.turismodecantabria.com; Calle de Hernán Cortés 4; 🕐9am-9pm) Inside the Mercado del Este.

**Oficina de Turismo Municipal** (☎942 20 30 00; www.turismo.santander.es; Jardines de Pereda; 🕐9am-9pm mid-Jun–mid-Sep, to 7pm Mon-Fri, 10am-7pm Sat, to 2pm Sun mid-Sep–mid-Jun) A branch opens at El Sardinero from about mid-June to mid-September.

## ℹ Getting There & Away

### AIR

Santander's **Aeropuerto Seve Ballesteros** (☎91 321 10 00; www.aena.es; Carretera del Aeropuerto, Maliaño) is 7km south of the city centre. Buses run to the airport from Santander's bus station (€2.90, 10 minutes) at 6.30am, 6.50am and half-hourly from 7.15am to 10.45pm, starting back from the airport at 6.40am and half-hourly from 7am to 11pm.

Airlines and destinations:

**Iberia** (www.iberia.com) Madrid, Valencia.

**Ryanair** (www.ryanair.com) Barcelona, Berlin (Tegel), Bologna, Brussels (Charleroi), Budapest, Dublin, Edinburgh, London (Stansted), Málaga, Marrakesh, Milan (Bergamo), Rome (Ciampino), Valencia, Vienna.

**Volotea** (www.volotea.com) Seville.

**Vueling** (www.vueling.com) Barcelona.

**Wizz Air** (www.wizzair.com) Bucharest.

### BOAT

**Brittany Ferries** (www.brittany-ferries.co.uk) runs three car ferries each week, including one no-frills service, from Portsmouth, UK

(24 to 32 hours), and one from Plymouth, UK (20 hours), to the **Estación Marítima** (Calle de Antonio López) in downtown Santander. Fares vary considerably. A standard return trip for two adults and a car, with two-berth interior cabins, booked in January, can cost UK£1000 to UK£1200 for travel in July or August, or UK£900 in October, from either UK port. Taking the no-frills Portsmouth ferry, a similar deal costs approximately UK£800 to UK£900 for July/August and UK£600 for October.

### BUS

**ALSA** (☎902 422242; www.alsa.es) is the major company operating from Santander's **bus station** (☎942 21 19 95; Calle Navas de Tolosa).

| Destination | Fare (€) | Time (hr) | Frequency (daily) |
|---|---|---|---|
| Bilbao | 7-16 | 1¼-2 | 21 |
| Madrid | 29-41 | 6-8½ | 7 |
| Oviedo | 13-29 | 2¼-3¼ | 9 |
| San Sebastián | 14-31 | 2½-3¾ | 10 |

### TRAIN

There are two train stations, beside each other on Calle de Rodríguez: **Renfe** (☎91 232 03 20; www.renfe.com) runs to destinations to the south, while the narrow-gauge **FEVE** (☎91 232 03 20; www.renfe.com/viajeros/feve) serves destinations along Spain's northern coast.

**Bilbao** (€8.90, three hours, three FEVE trains daily)

**Madrid** (€16 to €52, four to 4½ hours, two to four Renfe trains daily) Via Palencia and Valladolid.

**Oviedo** (€16, five hours, two FEVE trains daily) Via San Vicente de la Barquera, Llanes, Ribadesella and Arriondas.

# Around Santander

Within easy reach of the city are some beautiful surf-mad beaches (p494), one of Spain's finest wildlife parks and, near sleepy little Puente Viesgo, some of the world's oldest cave art.

**Parque de la Naturaleza Cabárceno** ZOO

(☎902 210112; www.parquedecabarceno.com; Obregón; adult/child Apr-Sep €32/18, Oct-Mar €24/14, after 2pm Mon-Fri Oct-Mar €17/9; ⏲9.30am-6pm Mar-Oct, 10am-5pm Mon-Fri, 10am-6pm Sat & Sun Nov-Feb; Ⓟ) This open-air zoo 18km south of Santander is a curious but successful experiment: a free-range home on the site of former open-cut mines for everything from rhinos, wallabies, gorillas and lions to endangered Cantabrian brown bears. You'll need a car and about three hours to tour its 20km of roadways. Alternatively, enjoy 6km (50 minutes') worth of aerial perspectives from the park's two *telecabinas* (cable cars).

# Eastern Cantabria

The 95km stretch of coast between Santander and Bilbao (in the Basque Country) offers residents of both cities several seaside escapes. While the towns are less attractive than those on Cantabria's western coast, some of the beaches are excellent. You can quickly escape coastal crowds by driving inland up the wonderfully scenic, and much less visited, green valleys of the Pas, Asón and other pristine rivers that descend from the heights of the Cordillera Cantábrica on Cantabria's southeastern fringe.

## Santoña

POP 10,800

The engaging fishing port of Santoña, 42km east of Santander, is famed for its anchovies, which are caught, processed, and bottled or tinned here (with olive oil to preserve them), and sold all over town.

### Sights & Activities

**Playa de Berria** BEACH

Playa de Berria is a magnificent sweep of blonde sand and crashing surf on the open sea, 2.5km north of Santoña and linked to it by frequent buses (€1.55, five minutes).

**Monte Buciero** HIKING

Buciero is the hilly headland rising above the east side of Santoña. Explore by heading off on one of five hiking paths, the most complete of which is the scenic **Sendero de Faros y Acantilados**, which loops 12km through woodlands and past lighthouses, cliffs and fortifications, taking about four hours.

### Sleeping & Eating

**Hotel Juan de la Cosa** HOTEL €€

(☎942 66 12 38; www.hoteljuandelacosa.com; Playa de Berria 14; s €45-85, d €60-175; ⏲Apr-Oct; Ⓟ❄📶🏊) The Juan de la Cosa may be an unsympathetic-looking building, but about two-thirds of its spacious, blue-hued,

WORTH A TRIP

## CUEVAS DE MONTE CASTILLO

The four World Heritage–listed caves **Cuevas de Monte Castillo** (☎942 59 84 25; http://cuevas.culturadecantabria.com; Puente Viesgo; adult/child per cave €3/1.50; ⏰10am-2.30pm & 3.30-7pm Tue-Sat, 10am-3.30pm Sun mid-Jun–mid-Sep, reduced hours rest of year; 🅿) are 30km southwest of Santander. Two – **El Castillo** and **Las Monedas** – are open for 45-minute guided visits (in Spanish). Booking ahead online is highly recommended, especially for the more spectacular El Castillo. As you explore 300m into the cave, you'll see art almost as breathtaking as that of Cantabria's famous Cueva de Altamira (p501) – and unlike at Altamira, this is the genuine article, not a replica.

El Castillo's 275 paintings and engravings of deer, bison, horses, goats, aurochs, handprints, mysterious symbols and a mammoth (very rare) date from around 39,000 to 11,000 BCE. One red symbol, believed to be 40,800 years old, is Europe's oldest known cave art. El Castillo also has exquisite cathedral-like rock formations. Las Monedas contains less art (black animal outlines, from around 10,000 BCE), but has an astounding labyrinth of shimmering stalactites and stalagmites.

Five to seven daily buses run from Santander to Puente Viesgo (€2.45, 40 minutes), from where it's a 2km uphill walk or taxi ride to the cave.

maritime-inspired rooms have full-on beach views. It also offers a good restaurant with a seafood emphasis, and plain self-catering apartments designed for families.

**La Esquina de Tasca** CANTABRIAN €
(Calle Manzanedo 25; dishes €7-12; ⏰11am-4pm daily, plus 8pm-midnight Fri & Sat) Wander into the town centre for very good home-style cooking at this smallish corner bar. The €13.50 lunch *menú*, including grilled fish and meats, is an excellent deal. Varieties of sausage, fishcakes, *pudin de cabracho* (scorpionfish pâté) and salads are tempting too.

### ℹ Information

**Oficina de Turismo de Santoña** (☎942 66 00 66; www.turismosantona.es; Calle Santander 5; ⏰10am-2pm & 5-8pm mid-Jun–mid-Sep, 9am-4pm Mon-Fri, 10am-2pm Sat mid-Sep–mid-Jun)

### ℹ Getting There & Around

From March to November, **Excursiones Marítimas** (☎675 874742; www.excursionesmaritimas.com; Paseo Marítimo; ⏰9am-2.30pm Mon-Fri, to 6pm Sat & Sun Mar & Nov, 9am-6pm or later daily Apr-Oct) runs a shuttle passenger ferry from Santoña to the northwestern end of Laredo's long, sandy beach across the bay (one way/return €2/3.50, five minutes). The company also offers one-hour bay cruises.

ALSA and **Autobuses Palomera** (☎942 88 06 11; www.autobusespalomera.com) serve Santoña's **bus station** (Calle Marinos de Santoña). Seventeen buses run between Santoña and Santander (€4.40, one hour) Monday to Friday, with nine on Saturday and six on Sunday.

## Castro Urdiales & Around

POP 25,400

Just 31km west of Bilbao (Basque Country) and 69km east of Santander, Castro Urdiales is a lively, attractive seafront town with a dramatically Gothic church perched above its pretty harbour, and a tangle of narrow lanes dotted with seafood-focused taverns and tapas bars making up its historic core.

A few minutes' drive west of Castro Urdiales you'll find a contrasting pair of golden beaches that are well worth a stop if you have your own wheels.

The broad sandy strip of **Playa de Oriñón**, 1.5km off the A8 (signposted) 12km west of Castro, is set deep behind protective headlands, making the water calm and *comparatively* warm. The settlement here consists of ugly holiday flats and caravan parks.

The road continues 1km past Oriñón to the hamlet of Sonabia. Turn left 100m after the church to reach a parking area from which you can walk 200m down to **Playa de Sonabia**. This little, clothing-optional beach has a wild setting, tucked into a rock-lined inlet beneath high crags, above which huge griffon vultures circle the sky. There are a couple of seasonal bar-restaurants.

**Iglesia de Santa María de la Asunción** CHURCH
(⏰10am-noon & 4-6pm Mon-Fri, 10am-noon Sat) The haughty Gothic jumble that is the Iglesia de Santa María de la Asunción stands out spectacularly above Castro Urdiales'

OFF THE BEATEN TRACK

## CANTABRIA'S EASTERN VALLEYS

Rich in unspoilt rural splendour, the little-visited valleys and mountain passes of eastern Cantabria are ripe for exploration. The following route could be taken after visiting the Cuevas de Monte Castillo (p497) at Puente Viesgo, 30km southwest of Santander.

Turn east off the N623 3km south of Puente Viesgo and follow the CA270 and CA142 southeast to Selaya. Here turn right on the CA625 and follow signs 800m to the family-run **Quesería La Jarradilla** (942 59 03 42, 652 779660; www.quesoslajarradilla.com; Barcenilla 246, Tezanos de Villacarriedo; tours noon Sat, shop 11am-2pm & 6-8pm Mon-Sat Jul-Sep, 11am-2pm & 4.15-6.15pm Mon-Sat Oct-Jun), where you can taste, buy and find out all about the soft, young cheeses of the **Valles Pasiegos** (the Pas, Pisueña and Miera valleys), one of Cantabria's most traditional rural areas.

Continue south along the CA262 over the 720m **Puerto de la Braguía** pass (with stunning views) to **Vega de Pas**, the 'capital' of the Valles Pasiegos. Then climb southeast on the CA631 over the **Puerto de las Estacas de Trueba** pass (1154m) into Castilla y León, where the road becomes the BU570. Turn north after Las Machorras to follow the BU571 up over the 1200m **Puerto de la Sía** pass and down towards Arredondo, in Cantabria's southeastern **Alto Asón district** (www.altoason.com). The zigzag road takes you past the 50m cliff-face waterfall that constitutes the **Nacimiento (Source) del Río Asón**. Alternatively, fork right 9km down from the Puerto de la Sía to visit the **Centro de Interpretación Collados del Asón** (942 64 94 38, 619 892634; www.redcantabrarural.com/naturea-3; CA256, La Gándara; 10am-5pm Wed-Fri, to 7pm Sat & Sun Apr-Jun & Oct, to 7pm Jul-Sep, to 3.30pm Wed-Fri, to 6pm Sat & Sun Nov-Mar), which offers information on hiking routes in the area, and a viewpoint over the beautiful **Cascada La Gándara waterfall**.

Alto Asón claims more than half of Cantabria's 9000 known caves. You can go east from Arredondo or northeast from the interpretation centre to **Ramales de la Victoria**, a pleasant small valley town with a helpful **tourist office** (942 64 65 04; www.cantabriaorientalrural.es/turismo; Paseo Barón de Adzaneta 8; 9.30am-2pm & 4-7.30pm Jul-Sep, 9am-3.30pm Mon, 9.30am-2pm & 4-7pm Sat, 9.30am-2pm Sun Oct-Jun) and two outstanding visitable caves nearby. The **Cueva de Cullalvera** (942 59 84 25; http://cuevas.culturadecantabria.com/cullalvera-2; adult/child €3/1.50; 10am-2.30pm & 3.30-7pm Tue-Sat, 10am-3.30pm Sun mid-Jun–mid-Sep, reduced hours rest of year) is an impressively vast cavity but its prehistoric art is off-limits. The slim **Cueva de Covalanas** (942 59 84 25; http://cuevas.culturadecantabria.com/covalanas-2; adult/child €3/1.50; 10am-2.30pm & 3.30-7pm Tue-Sat, 10am-3.30pm Sun mid-Jun–mid-Sep, reduced hours rest of year), 2km up the N629 south from Ramales, then 650m up a footpath, is on the World Heritage list for its stunning depictions of deer and other animals, executed around 20,000 BCE in an unusual dot-painting technique. Visits to either cave are guided and last 45 minutes.

The Ramales area has some appealing lodgings. **Hotel Palacio Torre de Ruesga** (942 64 10 60; www.torrederuesga.com; Barrio de la Bárcena, Valle; incl breakfast d €79-129, ste €99-179, family bungalow €99-220; ), 6km west of Ramales, is a two-towered 1610 mansion remodelled into an atmospheric deluxe hotel. Sizeable, stylish rooms (many with large hot tubs) range from four-poster affairs in the main house to family bungalows in the extensive gardens, and the efficient management is a fount of local knowledge. Under the same talented ownership is **La Casa del Puente** (645 820418, 942 63 90 20; www.lacasadelpuente.es; Regules; r incl breakfast €79-199; ), 10km southwest of Ramales, a beautifully restored *casa de indianos* (mansion built by a returned emigrant).

harbour. It was built in the 13th century, but additions continued until the 19th. The church shares its little headland with the town's small medieval castle, now a lighthouse. A much-reworked, single-arched, medieval bridge leads across to Castro's 500m-long breakwater.

### Sleeping & Eating

**Ardigales 11** BOUTIQUE HOTEL €€
(942 78 16 16; www.pensionardigales11.com; Calle de Ardigales 11; s €42-56, d €58-88; ) Behind a solid stone exterior on the narrow main street of Castro's old town, this surprising hotel presents 11 slick modern rooms

decked out in tasteful blacks, whites and greys. Downstairs, soft neon lights brighten up the cosy lounge area, with its own bar.

★**Bar Javi** TAPAS €
(☎942 78 35 30; www.barjavi.com; Calle de Ardigales 42; pinchos €2.50-3; ⏱11.30am-4pm & 6.30pm-midnight) *¡Advertencia!* The warning on the napkins at this sweet local tapas bar says it all: 'We take no responsibility for addiction to our *pinchos*'. With daily specials ranging from delicately fried baby-squid croquettes to cod with braised mushrooms it's hard not to get hooked.

## Information

**Oficina de Turismo** (☎942 87 15 12; www.turismodecantabria.com; Parque Amestoy; ⏱9am-9pm Jul–mid-Sep, shorter hours mid-Sep–Jun) On the seafront.

## Getting There & Away

ALSA (p496) runs at least eight daily buses to Santander (€6.55, one to 1½ hours) from Castro's **bus station** (Calle Leonardo Rucabado 42).

**IRB Castro** (☎942 86 70 26; www.bilbao-castro.es) buses to Bilbao (€2.85, 45 minutes) run half-hourly, 6am to 10pm (from 8am Saturday, hourly from 7am Sunday), making various stops including at Calle La Ronda 52, half a block from the seafront.

# Western Cantabria

Three of Cantabria's most appealing small towns are strung like pearls across the green-cloaked coastal area west of Santander. First comes medieval beauty Santillana del Mar, with the prehistoric wonders of Altamira close by; then Comillas and its unexpected Modernista architecture; and, finally, the handsome port town of San Vicente de la Barquera.

Inland, a whole new world opens up in the off-the-beaten-track valleys of western Cantabria. Tucked in among lush green mountains, you'll find beautiful stone villages such as Bárcena Mayor and Tudanca, where you can get a feel for rural Cantabria's history and cultural traditions.

## Santillana del Mar

POP 950

This medieval jewel is in such a perfect state of preservation, with its bright cobbled streets, flower-filled balconies and huddle of tanned stone and brick buildings – it's a film set, surely? Well, no. People still live here, passing their grand, precious houses down from generation to generation. In summer, the streets fill up with curious visitors.

Strict town-planning rules were first introduced in 1575, and today they state that only residents or guests in hotels with garages may bring vehicles into the old heart of town. Other hotel guests may drive to unload luggage and then return to the car park at the town entrance. Santillana is a *bijou* in its own right, but also makes the obvious base for visiting nearby Altamira (p501).

**Colegiata de Santa Juliana** CHURCH
(Plaza del Abad Francisco Navarro; adult/child €3/free; ⏱10am-1.30pm & 4-7.15pm, to 6.15pm Nov-Mar, closed Mon Oct-Jun) A stroll along Santillana's cobbled main street, past solemn 15th- to 18th-century nobles' houses, leads to this beautiful 12th-century Romanesque ex-monastery. The big drawcard is the **cloister**, a formidable storehouse of Romanesque handiwork, with the capitals of its columns finely carved into a huge variety of figures. The monastery originally grew up around the relics of Santa Juliana (her name later modified to become Santillana), a 3rd-century Christian martyr from Turkey whose sepulchre stands in the centre of the church.

## Sleeping

There are dozens of appealing places to stay in and around Santillana, many of them in historic buildings beautifully converted for your comfort. Most hotels close (for varying periods) in winter.

★**Casa del Organista** HOTEL €€
(☎942 84 03 52; www.casadelorganista.com; Calle de Los Hornos 4; s €50-77, d €60-98; ⏱closed approximately 7-31 Jan; P 📶) The 14 rooms at this elegant 18th-century house, once home to the Colegiata's organist, are particularly attractive, with plush rugs, antique furniture, plenty of exposed oak beams and stonework, and up-to-date bathrooms. Some have balconies looking across fields to the Colegiata. Expect a warm welcome and excellent breakfasts (€6.90). Parking is free.

**Casa del Marqués** HISTORIC HOTEL €€
(☎942 81 88 88; www.hotelcasadelmarques.com; Calle del Cantón 24; r €79-209; ⏱early Mar-early Dec; P ❄ @ 📶) Feel like the lord or lady of the manor in this 15th-century mansion, once home to the Marqués de Santillana. Timber beams, thick stone walls and cool

LOCAL KNOWLEDGE

## WHAT'S COOKING IN CANTABRIA & ASTURIAS?

Classic Cantabrian and Asturian cooking is uncomplicated fare fuelled by the bounty of the mountains and sea. Sophisticated city eateries incorporate traditional ingredients into creative contemporary concoctions. It's a predominantly meat and seafood scene, with limited options for noncarnivores.

**Stews** Straightforward grilled meats are usually a fine choice for carnivores here, but filling stews combining meat or meat products with pulses and vegetables are a much-loved local staple. Asturias' *fabada* is a hearty bean stew jazzed up with meat, sausage and black pudding. Asturian *pote* is similar but contains potatoes and vegetables such as cabbage too – and Cantabria's rich, filling *cocido montañés* employs much the same ingredients. *Cocido lebaniego*, from Cantabria's Liébana valley, throws local chickpeas instead of beans, and often lamb or beef, into the pot. It's the *cocido lebaniego* at Posada de Cucayo (p533) that ranks as the best northern stew we've ever tasted!

**Cheese, glorious cheese** Ultra-tangy blue cheeses from the Picos de Europa, matured in mountain caves, are celebrated nationwide. King of Asturian cheeses is the powerful and surprisingly moreish *queso de Cabrales*, made from untreated cow's milk, or a cow/goat/sheep blend, in and around Arenas de Cabrales. On the Cantabrian side of the Picos, seek out piquant *queso Picón* (a cow/sheep/goat mix) from Tresviso and Bejes. But there's plenty more to the regions' cheeses and the soft, creamy youngsters of the Valles Pasiegos, south of Santander – for example from Quesería La Jarradilla (p498) – are a delightful contrast.

**Seafood** Fresh seafood abounds everywhere, courtesy of the Bay of Biscay, while inland rivers provide trout, salmon and eels. Fish is often best when grilled or baked and served simple. For a choice of traditional preparations or creative 'new proposals' head for the classy Real Balneario de Salinas (p520), near Avilés. Localised favourites range from *rabas de calamar* (deep-fried squid rings) in Santander to *llamparas* (barnacles) along the Asturian coast, while Santoña's anchovies are prized all over Spain.

**More favourites** The Valles Pasiegos are the home of two beloved Cantabrian treats: *quesada*, a dense dessert pudding made with cheese or yoghurt, and *sobao*, a rich sponge cake. Asturian *cachopo* is a carnivore's dream of breaded veal stuffed with ham, cheese and vegetables. Other oft-encountered Asturian favourites are *pitu* (free-range chicken) and *tortos* (maize pancakes), which can be topped with absolutely anything.

terracotta floors contribute to the atmosphere of the 15 sumptuous rooms (all different, some surprisingly modern). The owners are proud of their 700-year-old banister, made from a single tree. Buffet breakfast is €13.

**Parador de Santillana Gil Blas** HISTORIC HOTEL €€€
(☎942 02 80 28; www.parador.es; Plaza Ramón Pelayo 11; d incl breakfast €120-310; P ❄ ⓦ) Sleep in an exquisitely preserved, centuries-old nobles' home gazing out across Santillana's cobbled main plaza. The 28 rooms are comfy, stylish and well equipped, yet full of historical character, and there are oodles of tucked-away lounges to get lost in, complemented by an elegant walled garden where you can breakfast in summer.

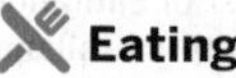

### Eating

**La Villa** CANTABRIAN €€
(☎942 81 83 64; www.lavillarestaurante.es; Calle La Gándara; menú €18, mains €17-20; ⊙1-3.30pm & 8-10.30pm, closed early Dec–mid-Mar, Tue & Wed mid-Mar–Jun & Oct–mid-Dec, Wed Sep) La Villa's three-course lunch menu, including a full bottle of wine, offers great value for touristy Santillana. Settle into the stone-walled garden courtyard and sample northern classics such as *cocido montañés* (Cantabrian stew with meat and beans) or veal entrecôte with Cabrales cheese.

**Restaurante Gran Duque** CANTABRIAN €€
(☎942 84 03 86; www.granduque.com; Calle del Escultor Jesús Otero 7; mains €12-20, menú €20; ⊙1-4pm & 8-11pm Dec-Oct, closed Sun dinner & Mon lunch Sep-Jun) Quality local fare is served in this stone house with noble trappings.

There's a good range of both surf and turf options, and a decent *menú del día* available.

## Information

**Oficina Regional de Turismo** (942 81 88 12; Calle del Escultor Jesús Otero 20; 9am-9pm Jul–mid-Sep, 9.30am-2pm & 3-6pm Mon-Sat, 9.30am-5pm Sun mid-Sep–Jun)

## Getting There & Away

**Autobuses La Cantábrica** (942 72 08 22; www.lacantabrica.net) runs three or more daily buses from Santander to Santillana (€2.70, 40 minutes), continuing to Comillas (€1.55, 30 minutes from Santillana) and San Vicente de la Barquera (€2.25, 50 minutes from Santillana). Buses stop by **Campo del Revolgo** (Calle Revolgo), just south of the main road.

# Altamira

Spain's finest prehistoric art, the wonderful paintings of bison, horses, deer and other animals in the **Cueva de Altamira**, 2.5km southwest of Santillana del Mar, was discovered in 1879 by Cantabrian historian and scientist Marcelino Sanz de Sautuola and his eight-year-old daughter María Justina. By 2002, Altamira had attracted so many visitors that the cave was closed to prevent deterioration of the art, but a replica cave in the museum here now enables everyone to appreciate the inspired, 13,000- to 35,000-year-old paintings. These magical carbon-and-ochre illustrations are particularly special for depicting completely coloured-in beasts, rather than animal outlines (as in other Cantabrian caves).

Since 2014 the Altamira authorities have allowed five lucky visitors, randomly selected by lottery, to enter the real Altamira cave each Friday morning. People entering the museum before 10.30am on Friday will be offered an application form if interested; the drawing takes place at 10.40am.

★**Museo de Altamira** MUSEUM
(942 81 80 05; www.culturaydeporte.gob.es/mnaltamira; Avenida Marcelino Sanz de Sautuola; adult/senior, student & child €3.50/free, Sun & from 2pm Sat free; 9.30am-8pm Tue-Sat, to 3pm Sun May-Oct, 9.30am-6pm Tue-Sat, to 3pm Sun Nov-Apr; P) The museum's highlight is the **Neocueva**, a dazzling, full-sized recreation of the real Cueva de Altamira's most interesting chamber, the **Sala de Polícromos** (Polychrome Hall), with its exquisite, 15,000-year-old ochre-and-black bison paintings created using the natural rock relief. The museum's interesting other displays cover prehistoric humanity and cave art worldwide, from Altamira to Australia.

## Getting There & Away

ALSA (p496) runs four daily buses from Santillana del Mar to Altamira (€1.55, five minutes); schedules change seasonally. Otherwise, from Santillana you can drive, walk (30 minutes on a paved path) or take a taxi (€5).

# Comillas & Around

POP 1700

Sixteen kilometres west of Santillana through verdant countryside, Comillas is set across hilltops crowned by some of the most original and beautiful buildings in Cantabria. For these, the town is indebted to the first Marqués de Comillas (1817–83), who was born here as plain Antonio López, made a fortune in Cuba as a tobacco planter, shipowner, banker and slave trader, then returned to commission leading Catalan Modernista architects to jazz up his home town. This, in turn, prompted the construction of other quirky mansions in Comillas. Adding to the town's charms are a lovely golden beach and a pleasant, cobbled old centre.

## Sights

★**Palacio de Sobrellano** HISTORIC BUILDING
(942 72 03 39; http://centros.culturadecantabria.com; Barrio de Sobrellano; adult/child €3/1.50, grounds free; 9.30am-6.30pm Tue-Sun Apr–mid-Jun & mid-Sep–Oct, 9.45am-7.30pm mid-Jun–mid-Sep, 9.30am-3.30pm Tue-Fri, to 5.30pm Sat & Sun Nov-Mar) With this marvellous 1888 building, the Marqués de Comillas' summer palace, Modernista architect Joan Martorell truly managed to out-Gothic real Gothic. The interior can only be seen on 30-minute guided tours (in Spanish), run five to eight times a day: you'll see the grand central hall with sweeping carved-stone staircases; a reception/billiard room featuring an ornate wood-carved fireplace with dragons by the young Gaudí; beautiful stained-glass windows; and vibrant murals detailing the marquis' story.

Martorell also designed the marquis' majestic family tomb next door, the **Capilla-Panteón de Sobrellano** (adult/child €3/1.50; 9.30am-6.30pm Tue-Sun Apr–mid-Jun & mid-Sep–Oct, 9.45am-7.30pm mid-Jun–mid-Sep, 9.30am-3.30pm Tue-Fri, to 5.30pm Sat & Sun Nov-Mar), open for 20-minute guided tours in Spanish, after the Palacio tours.

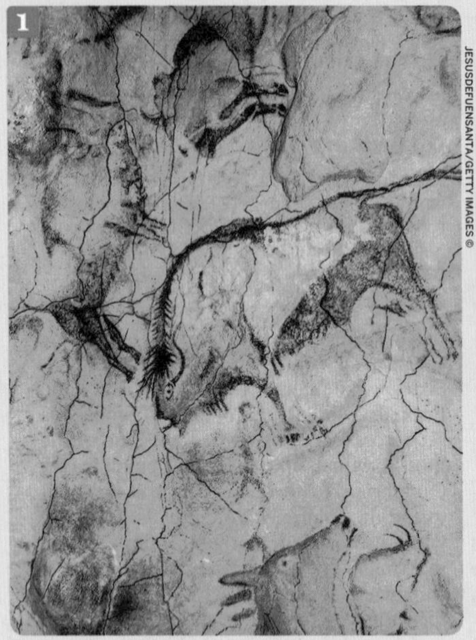

JESUSDEFUENSANTA/GETTY IMAGES ©

**1.** Cave art, Altamira (p501) **2.** Path to El Naranjo de Bulnes (p535), Picos de Europa (p526) **3.** Playa de Somo (p493), Santander **4.** *Sidrería*, Cudillero (p520)

IRMA SANCHEZ/GETTY IMAGES ©

# Surprises of the North

**The small northern regions of Cantabria and Asturias are a delightful discovery. Green valleys stretch down from snow-topped peaks to beautiful beaches. Locals drink cider and eat fantastic seafood and cheese, and the region's fascinating history begins with some of the world's most outstanding cave art.**

## Spectacular Peaks

Rising majestically only 15km inland, the Picos de Europa mark the greatest, most dramatic heights of the Cordillera Cantábrica, with enough awe-inspiring mountainscapes to make them arguably the finest hill-walking country in Spain. You can ramble past high-level lakes, peer over kilometre-high precipices or traverse the magnificent Garganta del Cares gorge (p531).

## Legendary Cider Bars

In a region that rolls out 80% of Spanish cider, Asturias' boisterous, fabulously fun *sidrerías* (cider bars) are a way of local life. There's no greater pleasure than knocking back a fizzing *culín* (cider shot), expertly poured from high above into a low-held glass (p514).

## Ancient Cave Art

Humanity's first accomplished art was painted, drawn and engraved on the walls of European caves by Stone Age hunter-gatherers between about 39,000 and 10,000 BCE, and reached some of its greatest artistic heights at the World Heritage–listed caves of Altamira (p501), Monte Castillo (p497) and Covalanas (p498) in Cantabria.

## Glorious Beaches

Wild, rugged and unspoilt, the hundreds of long sandy strands and mysterious secluded coves that line the 550km-long Cantabrian and Asturian coasts are some of Spain's most beautiful and breathtaking beaches – and when the waves are up, the region's surf scene comes alive.

★ **Capricho de Gaudí** ARCHITECTURE

(☎942 72 03 65; www.elcaprichodegaudi.com; Barrio de Sobrellano; adult/child €5/2.50; ⏲10.30am-8pm Mar-Jun & Oct, to 9pm Jul-Sep, to 5.30pm Nov-Feb) Antoni Gaudí left few reminders of his genius beyond Catalonia, but of them the 1885 Capricho is easily the most flamboyant. This brick building, one of Gaudí's earliest works and originally a summer playpad for the Marqués de Comillas' sister-in-law's brother, is striped all over the outside with ceramic bands of alternating sunflowers and green leaves. The elegant interior is comparatively restrained, with quirky touches including *artesonado* ceilings (interlaced beams with decorative insertions), stained-glass windows and slim spiral staircases.

**Cemetery** CEMETERY

(off Paseo de Garelly; ⏲hours vary) Comillas' cemetery, around the ruined medieval parish church, was remodelled by Catalan Modernista Lluís Domènech i Montaner in 1893. It's overlooked by a chilling white-marble statue of the exterminating angel, sword in hand, by Catalan sculptor Josep Llimona. The place has a distinctly spooky aura, especially when floodlit after dark.

**Antigua Universidad Pontificia** ARCHITECTURE

(☎630 256767; Paseo de Manuel Noriega; adult/child €3.50/free, car €2; ⏲tours hourly 10am-1pm, & 5-8pm Jun–mid-Sep, 4-7pm 2nd half Sep; Ⓟ) Several Modernistas had a hand in this imposing neo-Gothic former seminary, looming over the west end of town. Domènech i Montaner contributed its medieval flavour. It's now an international Spanish language and culture study centre, the **Centro Universitario CIESE-Comillas** (☎942 71 55 00; www.fundacioncomillas.es; group lessons per 1/2/3/4 weeks from €250/470/680/880). Thirty-minute visits to the elaborate interiors and patios are guided in Spanish (with leaflets in English available). Access to the grounds on foot is free.

★ **Playa Oyambre** BEACH

(Ⓟ) The 2km-long, soft-blonde Playa Oyambre, 5km west of Comillas, is a sandy dream protected by the Parque Natural Oyambre. It has frequently surfable waves, a couple of campgrounds and a dash of intriguing history as the emergency landing spot of the first-ever USA–Spain flight (1929). Waves and wind can be strong: swim only when the green flags fly.

## Sleeping & Eating

**Posada Los Trastolillos** INN €€

(☎942 72 22 12; www.lostrastolillos.com; Barrio Ceceño, El Tejo; d incl breakfast €70-170; ⏲closed early Dec-early Feb; Ⓟ📶) At this peaceful rural retreat between Comillas and Playa Oyambre, 13 bright rooms of varied sizes and colours, with tasteful, uncluttered decor, are complemented by a sunny breakfast room, a comfy *salón* with wood stove, and a library/reading room. Outside is a field of cows, with distant vistas of hills, rocky headlands and the ocean.

It's a fine base for surfing Oyambre and other nearby beaches.

**Hotel Marina de Campíos** BOUTIQUE HOTEL €€

(☎942 72 27 54, 607 441647; www.marinadecampios.com; Calle del General Piélagos 14; d €95-175; ⏲daily Jun–mid-Sep, Fri-Sun Easter-May & mid-Sep–Nov; ❄📶) This bright-red, 19th-century Comillas house has been revamped into a classy contemporary hotel with 19 boldly styled rooms, most sporting curtained beds, patterned walls and the names of famous operas. There's a lovely inner patio, with a piano bar and snack spot opening onto it. Breakfast costs €6.

**Restaurante Gurea** BASQUE €€

(☎942 72 24 46; Calle Ignacio Fernández de Castro 11; mains €9-17; ⏲1.15-4pm Tue, 1.15-4pm & 8.15-11pm Thu-Mon) A friendly, elegant restaurant and social bar, hidden a few blocks east of the town centre, Gurea dishes up Basque-Cantabrian fare with good meat, seafood and some vegetable dishes, and can throw together excellent salads. There's a lunchtime *menú* for €16.

## Information

**Oficina de Turismo** (☎942 72 25 91; www.comillas.es; Plaza de Joaquín del Piélago 1; ⏲9am-9pm Jul–mid-Sep, 10am-1pm & 4-6pm Mon-Sat, 9am-3pm Sun mid-Sep–Jun) Just off the main plaza.

## Getting There & Away

Autobuses La Cantábrica (p501) runs three or more daily buses each way between Santander and Comillas (€4.10, one to 1¼ hours) via Santillana del Mar, continuing to/from San Vicente de la Barquera. The main **bus stop** (Calle del Marqués de Comillas) is just west of the town centre.

## San Vicente de la Barquera & Around

POP 3150

The fishing port of San Vicente de la Barquera, the final town on the Cantabrian coast before you enter Asturias, sits handsomely on a point of land between two long inlets, backed by dramatic Picos de Europa mountainscapes. Together with Santander, Laredo and Castro Urdiales, it was one of the Cuatro Villas de la Costa, a grouping of four medieval ports and their hinterlands that became the province of Cantabria in 1778. The long sandy beaches east of town make San Vicente a busy summer spot, and it has plenty of seafood-focused restaurants.

### Sights & Activities

**Playas del Rosal & de Merón** BEACH

Along the coast east of town, these two beautiful beaches are basically one broad, 4km-long golden strand. Merón gets surf, while El Rosal (the western end) enjoys the prettiest San Vicente views. Heed the warning flags: red means don't swim, yellow means take care.

**Iglesia de Nuestra Señora de los Ángeles** CHURCH

(942 84 03 17; Calle Alta; adult/child €1.50/free; 10am-2pm & 4-9pm Jul–mid-Sep, 10am-1pm & 4-6pm Mon-Fri, 10am-2pm & 4-6pm Sat, 10am-12.45pm Sun mid-Sep–Jun) San Vicente's outstanding monument is the Iglesia de Nuestra Señora de los Ángeles, commissioned by Alfonso VIII in 1210. Though mostly Gothic, it sports a pair of impressive Romanesque doorways. Inside, the eerily lifelike statue of 16th-century Inquisitor Antonio del Corro (reclining on one elbow, reading) is deemed one of the best pieces of funerary art in Spain. Behind the church, there are lovely views along the Escudo estuary to the distant Picos de Europa.

**Castillo del Rey** CASTLE

(Calle Padre Antonio; adult/child €2/1; 10.30am-2pm & 4.30-8.30pm Jul–mid-Sep, 11am-2pm & 4-6.30pm Tue-Sun mid-Sep–Jun) San Vicente's 13th-century castle, one of Cantabria's best preserved, rises near the top of the old part of town. Sights inside are limited, and exhibits are Spanish-only, but on a clear day the views of the Picos de Europa, the Ría de San Vicente, the Bay of Biscay and the town itself are spectacular.

**Escuela de Surf Costa Norte** SURFING

(609 282963; www.escueladesurfcostanorte.com; Avenida Giner de los Ríos 46; surfboard & wetsuit hire per 2hr €18, 2hr group class per person €35) Based at Playa del Rosal, this popular surf school and shop offers group classes (board and wetsuit included) and three- to seven-day surf camps of varied levels, along with equipment rental and SUP (stand-up paddleboard) sessions (€30 to €35 per day).

### Sleeping & Eating

**Hotel Luzón** HOTEL €€

(942 71 00 50; www.hotelluzon.net; Avenida Miramar 1; s €35-45, d €60-80; closed Jan; ) The centrally positioned Luzón occupies a stately, century-old, stone mansion, still possessing an air of older times with its high ceilings, long corridors and ornate staircases. The 36 rooms are plain and simple.

**Boga-Boga** SEAFOOD €€€

(942 71 01 50; www.restaurantebogaboga.es; Plaza Mayor del Fuero 10; mains €12-29; 1-4pm & 8-11pm, closed Mon-Tue Oct-Jun) One of San Vicente's most reliably good seafood spots, Boga-Boga has a clean-lined, predominantly white design and friendly, efficient service by black-shirted waiters. Try *merluza al Boga-Boga* (line-caught hake cooked in a clay pot with prawns) or a grilled sole.

### Information

**Oficina Municipal de Turismo** (942 71 07 97; www.sanvicentedelabarquera.es; Avenida de los Soportales 20; 10am-2pm & 4-7pm Mon-Sat, 10.30am-2pm Sun Mar-Jun & Oct, 10am-2pm & 5-8pm Jul-Sep, 10am-4.30pm Mon-Sat, 10.30am-2pm Sun Nov-Feb)

### Getting There & Away

#### BUS

San Vicente's **bus station** (942 71 08 33; Avenida Miramar), next to the Puente de la Maza, is served by ALSA, Autobuses Palomera (p497) and Autobuses La Cantábrica (p501).

| Destination | Fare (€) | Time | Frequency |
|---|---|---|---|
| Llanes | 2.35 | 30min | 5-6 daily |
| Oviedo | 9.40 | 2hr | 5-6 daily* |
| Potes | 3.90 | 1-1¼hr | 2-3 daily |
| Santander | 4.90-5.30 | 1-1½hr | 8 or more daily** |

*some via Llanes, Ribadesella and Arriondas
**some via Comillas and Santillana del Mar

### NORTHERN WAYS: THE OTHER CAMINOS DE SANTIAGO

Around 55% of Camino de Santiago (p48) pilgrims reach the glorious cathedral of Santiago de Compostela (Galicia) via the classic Camino Francés, which marches across northern Spain through Navarra, the Basque Country and Castilla y León. Growing numbers of walkers looking for less-beaten paths today are setting their sights on even more northerly *caminos*, winding their way through green-cloaked landscapes unseen by the approximately 200,000 pilgrims a year who reach Santiago by the Camino Francés.

**Camino del Norte** The main northern route starts at Irún on the Spanish–French border and parallels Spain's north coast for over 600km to Ribadeo in Galicia, before heading inland to Santiago de Compostela. Some sections run alongside beautiful beaches and plunging cliffs, and other days you won't see the sea at all – but the inland scenery is gorgeous too. You pass through large cities – San Sebastián, Bilbao, Santander, Gijón – as well as pretty coastal towns like Comillas, Ribadesella and Luarca.

**Camino Primitivo** The 320km 'Original Way' follows the first recorded pilgrimage to what's believed to be the tomb of St James the Apostle (around which Santiago grew), made by Alfonso II of Asturias from Oviedo in the 820s. It's one of the most beautiful *caminos*, and relatively hard because it spends its first eight or nine days crossing the hills of western Asturias and eastern Galicia (sometimes impracticable in winter).

**Camino Lebaniego** Not actually a Camino de Santiago, the Lebaniego pilgrimage route travels from San Vicente de la Barquera on the Cantabrian coast to the Monasterio de Santo Toribio de Liébana (p533) in the Picos de Europa foothills – a 73km walk taking three or four days.

**Camino del Salvador** This 120km route doesn't reach Santiago de Compostela but crosses the Cordillera Cantábrica from León (Castilla y León) to the Asturian capital, Oviedo. Its origins lie with medieval pilgrims who diverted from the Camino Francés to visit Oviedo's Catedral de San Salvador (p508) and its holy relics..

#### TRAIN

San Vicente's train station is at La Acebosa, 2km south of town. Two FEVE (p496) trains in each direction stop here daily between Santander (€5.15, 1½ hours) and Oviedo (€11, 3½ hours).

## Southern Cantabria

Panoramas of high peaks and deep river valleys and warm stone villages flanked by patchwork quilts of green await travellers venturing into the Cantabrian interior. Spain's most voluminous river, the Ebro, begins its long journey to the Mediterranean here, and the area is dotted with fascinating historical relics.

### Reinosa & Around

POP 9100 / ELEV 851M

Southern Cantabria's main town, 70km south of Santander, has some handsome old stone architecture downtown but is an unexceptional place. There are plenty of curiosities nearby, however, including the remains of Cantabria's most important Roman settlement, some very impressive rock-cut and Romanesque churches, and the source of the mighty Río Ebro.

#### Sights

**Nacimiento del Río Ebro** SPRING

(Fontibre; P) The Río Ebro starts life at this tree-shaded spring 5km northwest of Reinosa. It's a stunningly serene spot, with deep-turquoise water, a tiny shrine and a few ducks splashing around. From here, the Ebro meanders 930km southeast via Logroño (La Rioja) and Zaragoza (Aragón) to meet the Mediterranean in Catalonia.

**Colegiata de San Pedro** CHURCH

(Cervatos; €2; hours vary) The elegantly proportioned 12th-century Romanesque church in Cervatos, 6km south of Reinosa, is most celebrated for the rare explicit sexual carvings on some of its corbels. But there's plenty of other absorbing sculptural detail to inspect, mainly on its exterior: animals, musicians, acrobats, and the beautiful multi-arched main entrance carved with six lions and an intricate interlaced-leaves pattern. If you're keen to go inside, call the villager's phone number posted on the door.

**Julióbriga** RUINS

(☎942 59 84 25; http://centros.culturadecantabria.com; Retortillo; adult/child €3/1.50; ⊙10am-2.30pm & 3.30-7pm Tue-Sat, 10am-3.30pm Sun mid-Jun–mid-Sep, shorter hours rest of year; P) The remains of Julióbriga, Cantabria's most significant Roman town, lie 4km east of Reinosa. Hourly guided visits (45 minutes, in Spanish) lead you through the **Museo Domus**, a full-scale recreation of one of Julióbriga's houses. You're free to explore the excavated parts of the town (about 10% of the total), with a 12th-century **Romanesque church** built over the Roman forum, independently.

## Sleeping & Eating

Reinosa offers half-a-dozen sleeping options. For a more peaceful and verdant village setting, head to Fontibre, 5km to the west.

**Posada Fontibre** INN €€

(☎942 77 96 55; www.posadafontibre.com; El Molino 23, Fontibre; s €50-65, d €62-92; ) A tranquil haven in little Fontibre village, this old stone *posada* offers six very well-kept rooms just steps from the source of the Río Ebro. Decor is comfortably rustic, with beamed ceilings, stone walls, colourful rugs, and interesting historical curios and photos dotted around. Breakfast is €5.50 and there are a couple of good dinner options in the village, including the enticing **Restaurante Fuentebro** (☎942 77 96 45; www.restaurantefuentebro.com; Fontibre; mains €14-22; ⊙1.30-4pm & 9-11pm, closed Sun, Tue, Wed & Thu lunchtime & all day Mon Sep–mid-Jun) overlooking the Nacimiento.

**La Cabaña** MEDITERRANEAN €€

(☎637 798731; www.braserialacabana.es; Calle de Juan José Ruano 4, Reinosa; mains €8-17; ⊙1.30-4pm Mon, 1.30-4pm & 9-11pm Wed-Sun; ) A Madrid-trained chef heads this brasserie specialising in fun, local- and internationally inspired concoctions that manage to be inventive without going over the top. Dishes, all cooked fresh to your order, focus on meat and seafood grills, huge salads, wok stir-fries and delicious homemade pasta (a rare find in these parts) and desserts. Reservations recommended.

## Information

**Oficina de Turismo** (☎942 75 52 15; www.surdecantabria.es; La Casona, Avenida del Puente de Carlos III 23; ⊙9.30am-2.30pm & 4-7pm Mon-Fri, 9.30am-2.30pm Sat) Has info on plentiful walking routes and other attractions throughout southern Cantabria.

## Getting There & Around

The best (and usually only) way to visit the main sights in the area is with your own vehicle. Six or more ALSA buses (€6.70, 1¾ hours) and four or five Renfe trains (€5.15 to €17, 1¼ hours) run daily between Reinosa and Santander. There are a few daily buses and trains south to Palencia, Valladolid and Madrid.

# ASTURIAS

*'Ser español es un orgullo'*, the saying goes, *'ser asturiano es un título'*. 'Being Spanish is a matter of pride, but to be Asturian is a mark of nobility.' Asturias, probably the sole patch of Spain never conquered by the Muslims, is – some claim – the real Spain: the rest is simply *tierra de reconquista* (reconquered land).

This gorgeously green region has both similarities with and differences from Cantabria, its smaller neighbour. The jagged coast is perhaps even more dramatic, strung with cliff-girt capes, colourful fishing ports and more than 200 beaches. Inland, the mountains (including much of the Picos de Europa) soar high, the valleys run deep and the villages are delightfully rustic. The wild Asturian hills are the main redoubt of Spain's surviving bear population. The verdant valleys grow, among other things, many millions of apples which make cider, uniquely in Spain, the favourite tipple here. For architecture lovers, Asturias is a land of quaint grain stores on wooden stilts, known as *hórreos*, and of the very early medieval style known as pre-Romanesque, most strikingly expressed in the World Heritage monuments in and around Oviedo.

## Oviedo

POP 186,000 / ELEV 232M

The characterful, historic *casco antiguo* (old town) of Asturias' civilised capital is agreeably offset by elegant parks and busy, modern shopping streets to its west and north. Oviedo is a fun, sophisticated city, with a stash of intriguing sights, some excellent restaurants and a lively student population. Out on the periphery, the hum and heave of factories is a reminder that Asturias has its gritty industrial side too. Oviedo is a major producer of textiles, weapons and food.

## Sights

**★Catedral de San Salvador** CATHEDRAL

(☎985 21 96 42; www.catedraldeoviedo.com; Plaza de Alfonso II; adult/child incl audio guide €7/free; ⊙10am-1pm & 4-6pm or 7pm Mar-Jun & Oct, 10am-7pm Jul-Aug, to 6pm Sep, 10am-1pm & 4-5pm Nov-Feb, closed Sun & from 5pm Sat year-round) Oviedo's stunning cathedral complex was built mainly in Gothic and baroque styles between the 13th and 18th centuries. But its origins and greatest interest lie in the World Heritage–listed **Cámara Santa**, a pre-Romanesque chapel begun in the 8th century by Alfonso II of Asturias to house important holy relics.

Visitors pass through the Gothic naves of the main church to reach the Cámara Santa with its collection of sacred relics and medieval treasures, including two jewel-encrusted gold crosses. These items are viewed from the **Sala Apostolar**, whose remarkable Romanesque sculptures of the 12 Apostles are in the style of Maestro Mateo, creator of Santiago de Compostela's Pórtico de la Gloria. Alfonso II presented the **Cruz de los Ángeles** (Cross of the Angels) to the cathedral in 808 CE, and it's still Oviedo's city emblem. A century later Alfonso III donated the **Cruz de la Victoria** (Cross of Victory), the emblem of Asturias, whose gold covering is said to encase King Pelayo's standard from the battle of Covadonga (p529).

The Cámara Santa also contains the **Santo Sudario**, a cloth said to have covered Christ's face after his death (the one on display is usually a replica). Turning to leave, you'll see the heads of the Virgin Mary, Christ and St John on Calvary remarkably sculpted from a single block of stone above the doorway; their bodies were originally painted on the wall below.

Upstairs, the **museum** displays an extensive collection of religious art and sculpture. From here you descend to the **cloister**, whose original ground-level framework of pure 14th-century Gothic arches – rare in Asturias – is overlaid with an 18th-century baroque upper storey.

**★Museo Arqueológico de Asturias** MUSEUM

(☎985 20 89 77; www.museoarqueologicodeasturias.com; Calle de San Vicente 3-5; ⊙9.30am-8pm Wed-Fri, 9.30am-2pm & 5-8pm Sat, 9.30am-3pm Sun) FREE Partly within a restored 16th-century monastery, Asturias' archaeology museum makes the most of the region's archaeological riches through video and informative artefact displays. Subject matter ranges from rhinoceros teeth and prehistoric cave art to *castro* culture (pre-Roman fortified villages, often considered Celtic), Roman times, the medieval Kingdom of Asturias and relics from Oviedo's unique pre-Romanesque buildings (p510).

**Museo de Bellas Artes de Asturias** MUSEUM

(☎985 21 30 61; www.museobbaa.com; Calle de Santa Ana 1; ⊙10.30am-2pm & 4-8pm Tue-Sat, 10.30am-2.30pm Sun Jul & Aug, 10.30am-2pm & 4.30-8.30pm Mon-Fri, 11.30am-2pm & 5-8pm Sat, 11.30am-2.30pm Sun Sep-Jun) FREE Oviedo's Fine Arts Museum, housed in two of the city's finest palaces, spans the centuries with its large and rewarding collection, featuring work by Spanish greats such as Goya, Zurbarán, El Greco, Ribera, Picasso, Miró, Dalí and Sorolla. Don't neglect some of the lesser known Spaniards from the 19th to 21st centuries, including impressive Asturians Ventura Álvarez Sala and Evaristo Valle and the seemingly Klimt-inspired Hermen Anglada-Camarasa.

## Sleeping

There's only a handful of places actually in the old town, but plenty more are scattered around its periphery and along the streets around the Campo de San Francisco. Prices are generally highest from July to September, spiking markedly in August.

**Hotel City Express Covadonga** HOTEL €

(☎985 20 32 32; www.hotelcityexpresscovadonga.es; Calle Covadonga 7; s €31-50, d €35-54; 📶) Small to medium-size rooms with comfy beds, up-to-date bathrooms and tasteful paintings make this central 44-room hotel a good bet in the budget bracket. .

**★Barceló Oviedo Cervantes** HOTEL €€

(☎985 25 50 00; www.barcelo.com; Calle de Cervantes 13; r €75-120; P❄@📶) Comprising a revamped century-old mansion and two modern smoked-glass wings, the Barceló is just two blocks northwest of the central Campo de San Francisco. Impeccably contemporary style runs throughout, from the cocktail-lounge-style lobby bar to the 72 spacious, luxurious rooms, with their chain curtains, multiple mirrors and glass-partitioned bathrooms. Service is simultaneously warm and professional.

## Oviedo

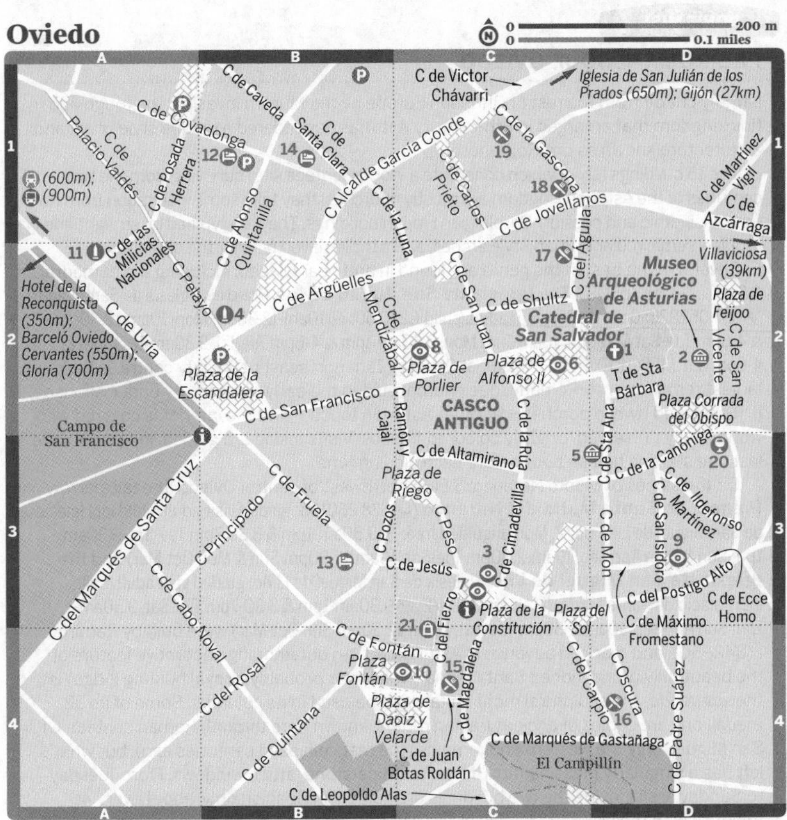


## Oviedo

**Top Sights**
1 Catedral de San Salvador ........ D2
2 Museo Arqueológico de Asturias........ D2

**Sights**
3 Ayuntamiento ........ C3
4 Culis Monumentalibus ........ B2
5 Museo de Bellas Artes de Asturias...... D3
6 Plaza de Alfonso II ........ C2
7 Plaza de la Constitución ........ C3
8 Plaza de Porlier ........ C2
9 Plaza del Paraguas ........ D3
10 Plaza Fontán ........ C4
11 Woody Allen Statue ........ A2

**Sleeping**
12 Hotel City Express Covadonga ........ B1
13 Hotel Fruela ........ B3
14 Hotel Vetusta ........ B1

**Eating**
15 Dos de Azúcar ........ C4
16 El Fartuquín ........ D4
17 Mar de Llanes ........ C2
18 Tierra Astur ........ C1
19 Tierra Astur Parrilla ........ C1

**Drinking & Nightlife**
20 Per Se ........ D3

**Shopping**
21 Mercado El Fontán ........ C4

**Hotel Fruela** HOTEL €€
(☎985 20 81 20; www.hotelfruela.com; Calle de Fruela 3; r €55-125; P ❄ ☎) With an attractive contemporary style, original art, professional yet friendly service and a cosy, almost intimate feel, the 28-room Fruela is easily the pick of lower-midrange options in central Oviedo. Behind its late-19th-century facade, business-oriented rooms are bright and

DON'T MISS

## PRE-ROMANESQUE OVIEDO

Largely cut off from the rest of Christian Europe by the Muslim invasion, the tough and tiny kingdom that emerged in 8th-century Asturias engendered a unique style of art and architecture known as pre-Romanesque.

The 15 buildings (six of which constitute a World Heritage site) surviving from the two centuries of the Asturian kingdom are mostly churches; they take some inspiration from Roman, Visigothic and possibly Carolingian French buildings. They are typified by straight-line profiles, semicircular Roman-style arches, and a triple-naved plan for the churches.

Several of the best of the genre are found in and near Oviedo, including the cathedral's Cámara Santa (p508). The **Iglesia de San Julián de los Prados** (Iglesia de Santuyano; ☎687 052826; Calle de Selgas 1; adult/child €2/0.50; ⏲10am-12.30pm Mon, 10am-12.30pm & 4-6pm Tue-Sat May-Jun, 10am-1pm Mon, 9.30am-1pm & 4-6pm Tue-Fri, 9.30am-12.30pm & 4-6pm Sat Jul-Sep, 10am-noon Mon-Sat Oct-Apr), 1km northeast of the city centre, is the largest remaining pre-Romanesque church, built in the early 9th century under Alfonso II. It's flanked by two porches – another Asturian touch – and the interior is covered with wonderfully preserved, brightly coloured frescos. Visits inside are guided, in Spanish, the last one starting half an hour before each closing time.

On the slopes of Monte Naranco, 3.5km northwest of central Oviedo, the tall, narrow **Palacio de Santa María del Naranco** (☎638 260163; guided visit adult/child incl Iglesia de San Miguel de Lillo €3/2, Mon unguided free; ⏲9.30am-1pm & 3.30-7pm Tue-Sat, 9.30am-1pm Sun & Mon Apr-Sep, 10am-2.30pm Tue-Sat, 10am-12.30pm Sun & Mon Oct-Mar) and the **Iglesia de San Miguel de Lillo** (Iglesia de San Miguel de Lliño; guided visit adult/child incl Palacio de Santa María del Naranco €3/2; ⏲9.30am-1pm & 3.30-7pm Tue-Sat, 9.30am-1pm Sun Apr-Sep, 10am-2.30pm Tue-Sat, 10am-12.30pm Sun Oct-Mar) were built by Ramiro I (842–50), and mark an advance in Asturian art. An outstanding decorative feature of the beautifully proportioned Santa María (which was probably a royal hunting lodge) is the *sogueado,* the sculptural motif imitating rope used in its columns. Some of its 32 medallions are copies of ancient Iranian motifs, known here through Roman contact. Of San Miguel, only the western end remains (the rest collapsed centuries ago), but what's left has a singularly pleasing form. Note its single-stone lattice windows. From Tuesday to Sunday, visits inside the two buildings are guided, in Spanish only, about every 40 minutes, with the last visit starting at the given closing times. There's no charge or restriction on admiring the buildings from outside.

About 100m below the Palacio de Santa María, the **Centro de Interpretación del Prerrománico** (☎985 18 58 60, 902 306600; www.prerromanicoasturiano.es; Monte Naranco; ⏲10am-2pm & 3.30-7pm Jul & Aug, 9.30am-1.30pm & 3.30-6pm Wed-Sun Mar-Jun, Sep & Oct, 9.30am-2.30pm Wed-Sun Nov, Dec & Feb; P) FREE has informative displays on the pre-Romanesque phenomenon in English, Spanish and French. You can reach Monte Naranco on bus A2 (€1.20), about hourly from 6.45am to 9.50pm, from the Uría Sur stop opposite the northeast side of Campo de San Francisco; bus A1 runs back down. By car, park 300m below Santa María and walk up.

From the Naranco monuments, you can drive or bike 4km on uphill (or walk 1.4km) to the **Monumento al Sagrado Corazón**, a 30m-high, 1981 stone sculpture of Christ that crowns Monte Naranco. The views are sensational.

welcoming, with desks, dangling lamps and plenty of electrical sockets.

**Hotel Vetusta** HOTEL €€
(☎985 22 22 29; www.hotelvetusta.com; Calle de Covadonga 2; s €45-100, d €50-150; ❄📶) Sixteen soundproofed, well-kept rooms with touches of crushed velvet, solid wooden furnishings, and in some cases glass galleries, make the Vetusta a sound midrange option. It has a convenient central location, friendly staff and a ground-floor cafe.

**Hotel de la Reconquista** HISTORIC HOTEL €€€
(☎985 24 11 00; www.eurostarshotels.com/eurostars-hotel-de-la-reconquista.html; Calle de Gil de Jaz 16; incl breakfast r €95-310, ste €185-680; P❄@📶) Oviedo's swishest lodgings, two blocks northwest of the Campo de San Francisco, began life in the 18th century as a hos-

pice. The 142 rooms frame a large patio and are perfectly balanced between old-fashioned elegance and comfort, with timber furniture and floor-to-ceiling windows.

## Eating

Oviedo's *sidrerías* (cider bars) deliver good food at reasonable prices. *El bulevar de la sidrerías*. The city hosts some of northern Spain's most sophisticated eateries.

**Dos de Azúcar** CAFE €
(☎985 22 68 15; www.dosdeazucarbakery.com; Calle del Fierro 19; cakes & pastries €2-5; ⏰9am-9pm; 📶) A sweet homey cafe near the market that's ideal for indulging in a range of coffees, big cups of tea, cakes (including vegan sponge cakes) and extra-thick hot chocolate. A good spot for breakfast too.

★**Tierra Astur** ASTURIAN €€
(☎985 20 25 02; www.tierra-astur.com; Calle de la Gascona 1; mains €9-25, set menus €15-25; ⏰1-4.30pm & 7.30pm-midnight; 📶) This particularly atmospheric *sidrería*-restaurant is famous for its prize-winning cider and good-value lunchtime *menús*. People queue for tables, settle for tapas at the bar or just buy traditional products for home. Try enormous salads, Asturian *cachopo*, giant grilled-veg platters or assorted seafood.

For longer hours and excellent grilled meats, head down the street to its sister restaurant, **Tierra Astur Parrilla** (☎984 84 66 24; Calle Gascona 9; mains €9-30; ⏰1pm-1am).

**El Fartuquín** ASTURIAN €€
(☎985 22 99 71; www.elfartuquin.es; Calle del Carpio 19; mains €10-23, set menus €10-17; ⏰noon-4pm & 7.30pm-midnight Mon-Fri, from 1pm Sat) Gluten-free Fartuquín's busy little dining room offers an excellent range of well-priced Asturian meat, fish and seafood, plus a great-value set menu (€10), including wine, available at lunchtime Monday to Friday (€17 on Saturdays). Locals pack the front bar for evening tapas and cider.

**Gloria** ASTURIAN €€
(☎984 83 42 43; www.estasengloria.com; Calle de Cervantes 24; tapas €3.50-8, raciones €14-19; ⏰1-4pm & 8pm-midnight Mon-Sat; 📶) Michelin-starred Asturian siblings Esther and Nacho Manzano bring their culinary talent to Oviedo with this stylish *casa de comidas* (eating house). Exquisitely prepared traditional-cum-contemporary dishes come as tapas, *medias raciones* or *raciones,* and there's a €20 weekday lunch *menú*. Bookings recommended.

**Mar de Llanes** SEAFOOD €€€
(☎984 29 22 84; www.mardellanes.es; Calle del Águila 11; mains €17-32; ⏰1.15-3.30pm & 8.15-11.45pm Tue-Sun) All the seafood at this friendly, family-run eatery is brought daily from the harbour at Llanes. Appetisers of *rabas* (fried squid) and main courses of perfectly grilled *merluza* (hake), *salmonete* (red mullet) and other seasonal fish come with sautéed vegetables, potatoes, crusty bread and superb olive oil in an unpretentious dining room with white linen tablecloths.

DON'T MISS

### PLAZAS & STATUES

One of Oviedo's greatest pleasures is exploring the old town's corners. **Plaza de Alfonso II**, home to the cathedral, and neighbouring **Plaza de Porlier** are fronted by elegant 17th- and 18th-century mansions. **Plaza de la Constitución** occupies a barely perceptible rise at the heart of old Oviedo, bordered by the 17th-century **ayuntamiento** (town hall) . Just south, past the colourful **Mercado El Fontán food market** (☎985 20 43 94; Plaza 19 de Octubre; ⏰8am-8pm Mon-Fri, to 3.30pm Sat), the streets round the arcaded **Plaza Fontán** fill with flower and clothes stalls during the Thursday, Saturday and Sunday morning *mercadillo* (street market). Not far away, **Plaza del Paraguas** got its name from its inverted-umbrella form; today a giant concrete umbrella *(paraguas)* protects people from the elements.

Wandering around central Oviedo, you'll run into an array of striking, modern, open-air sculptures, such as Eduardo Úrculo's **Culis Monumentalibus** (Calle Pelayo), a pair of legs topped by a pair of large buttocks; and a **statue of Woody Allen** (Calle de las Milicias Nacionales), who described Oviedo as 'a fairy tale' when shooting part of *Vicky Cristina Barcelona* here.

## Drinking & Nightlife

In the old city you'll pass a bar of some kind almost every few steps. Nothing much moves in the evenings before 8pm. For *sidrerías* head to Calle de la Gascona. On Friday and Saturday nights, the old town's narrow streets are packed with party-goers and bars stay open till 3am or later. The main post-midnight axis is Calle de Mon, with wall-to-wall bars, and its extension Calle Oscura. Calle del Carpio and Plaza del Sol get lively earlier in the evening. Other days are quieter and few bars stay open after 1am.

WORTH A TRIP

### TOURING THE EBRO'S ROCK-CUT CHURCHES

The Río Ebro, rising at Fontibre, scurries through Reinosa, fills the Embalse del Ebro reservoir, then meanders south and east into Castilla y León. Its course is strung with some fascinating, picturesque stops. You can follow it on the GR99 footpath (which runs the whole length of the river) or along the area's country roads.

From Reinosa, head east along the CA730, visiting Roman Julióbriga (p507) en route, if you fancy, then turn south at Arroyo along the CA735 and follow signs to the **Santuario de Montesclaros** (942 77 00 55, 942 77 05 59; Carretera CA741, Montesclaros; hours vary; P), a monastery with a fascinating early medieval crypt and a fine site overlooking the Ebro valley. From here, follow the CA741 southwest to Arroyal de los Carabeos, then the CA272 south to a roundabout where it meets the CA273. Nine kilometres west is the **Iglesia Rupestre de Santa María de Valverde** (Santa María de Valverde; 10am-2pm & 4-7pm Sat & Sun mid-Mar–Jun & Sep–mid-Dec, Tue-Sun Jul-Aug, Mass 1pm Sun year-round). This remarkable, multiarched church, hewn from solid rock, is the most impressive of several rock-cut churches in this area, dating from probably the 7th to 10th centuries. It can be visited in conjunction with the adjacent **Centro de Interpretación del Rupestre** (942 77 61 46; adult/child €1/free; 10am-2pm & 4-7pm Tue-Sun Jul & Aug, 10am-2pm & 4-7pm Sat & Sun mid-Mar–Jun & Sep–mid-Dec; P), detailing the rock-church phenomenon.

Head back east to La Puente del Valle, where you can cross the river, following small wooden signs, to the rock-cut tombs of the **Necrópolis de San Pantaleón**, then continue east to Campo de Ebro, where the tiny, rock-cut **Ermita de Santa Eulalia** is hidden behind a 17th-century church just off the main road. Three kilometres further east is **Polientes**, the area's biggest village, with a few places to eat and sleep, and the helpful **Oficina de Turismo de Valderredible** (942 77 61 46, 942 77 61 59; www.valderredible.es; Centro Cultural, CA272, Polientes; 10am-2pm & 4.30-8.30pm Tue-Sat, 10am-2pm Sun mid-Sep–Jun), 300m west of the central plaza. Contact this office in advance if you want to arrange visits inside any rock churches that are normally locked, such as Santa Eulalia and Arroyuelos. In summer the office moves to the Ayuntamiento (Town Hall) on the central plaza, opening 10am to 2pm daily.

A wonderful place to kick back is **Molino Tejada** (675 153340, 623 019059; www.molinotejada.com; Valdeperal 1, Polientes; incl breakfast ste for 2 €115-225, for 4-6 €195-275; closed Mon-Wed Oct-Feb; P), a stunningly renovated 16th-century watermill amid large riverside gardens, 1km east of Polientes. The nine large apartments and spacious common areas (including a mini-cinema) are endowed with soft furnishings, varied art and ethnic-flavoured artisanry, and a striking black-and-white colour scheme.

East of Polientes, along CA275, you'll find the dramatic two-level church at **Arroyuelos**. Across the Ebro here, **San Martín de Elines** is well worth a detour for its exquisite Romanesque church. Finally, the wonderfully sited little **El Tobazo** cave-church sits high up towards the top of the Ebro gorge east of Arroyuelos. Park just before the bridge into Villaescusa de Ebro, walk over the bridge and follow 'El Tobazo' signs up out of the village. It's about 1km gradually uphill to the top of a beautiful waterfall, where you'll find the cave-church (three small caves), some natural caves behind the falls and, above, the '*surgencia*' (spring) where the crystal-clear stream flows out of the rock before tumbling down the hillside – a magical spot where you can easily imagine a few *anjanas*, Cantabria's legendary water nymphs, skipping around the rocks. From Villaescusa, the CA275 continues along the Ebro gorge to pretty Orbaneja del Castillo in Castilla y León.

**Per Se** BAR

(Calle de la Canóniga 18; ⌚5pm-1am Mon-Wed, to 3.30am Thu, to 5.30am Fri, 4pm-5.30am Sat, to 1am Sun; 📶) A wonderfully comfy, cave-like cafe-bar crammed with fairy lights, chunky mirrors and sink-into seating. Kick back over a big choice of coffees and teas, home-made cakes, international beers, or cocktails served in artsy jars.

## ℹ Information

**Oficina de Turismo de Asturias** (☎984 49 35 60, 902 300202; www.turismoasturias.es; Plaza de la Constitución 4; ⌚9am-7pm Jun-Sep, to 6pm Mon-Fri, 10am-5.30pm Sat & Sun Oct-May) Covers all of Asturias.

**Oficina de Turismo El Escorialín** (☎985 22 75 86; www.oviedo.es/descubre; Calle del Marqués de Santa Cruz; ⌚9.45am-6.45pm) Municipal tourist office, at the Campo de San Francisco.

## ℹ Getting There & Away

### AIR

The **Aeropuerto de Asturias** (☎91 321 10 00; www.aena.es; Santiago del Monte) is 47km northwest of Oviedo and 40km west of Gijón. Direct buses leave Oviedo's bus station for the airport (€9, 45 minutes) hourly from 5am to 11pm, returning hourly from 6am to midnight.

Airlines and destinations include the following:

**Air Europa** (www.aireuropa.com) Madrid.

**Iberia** (www.iberia.com) Madrid, Valencia.

**Volotea** (www.volotea.com) Alicante, Palma de Mallorca, Seville, Valencia; plus seasonal flights to Ibiza, Menorca, Munich, Murcia, Venice.

**Vueling Airlines** (www.vueling.com) Alicante, Barcelona, London (Gatwick), Málaga, Seville.

### BUS

**ALSA** (☎902 422242; www.alsa.es) is the major company operating from Oviedo's **bus station** (☎985 96 96 96; www.estaciondeautobusesdeoviedo.com; Calle de Pepe Cosmen), 700m north of the central Campo de San Francisco.

| Destination | Fare (€) | Time | Frequency |
|---|---|---|---|
| Avilés | 2.65 | 30min-1hr | every 15-60min, 6.30am-11.30pm |
| Cangas de Onís | 7.25 | 1½hr | 7-13 daily |
| Gijón | 2.55 | 30min-1hr | every 10-30min, 6.30am-10.30pm |
| León | 9.10-13 | 1½-2¼hr | 11-14 daily |
| Llanes | 11.15 | 1¼-2¾hr | 10-11 daily |
| Madrid | 15-54 | 5-7hr | 12-14 daily |
| Ribadesella | 8.35 | 1¼-2hr | 6-8 daily |
| Santander | 9-39 | 2¼-3½hr | 9-12 daily |
| Santiago de Compostela | 31-44 | 4½-6¾hr | 2-3 daily |

### TRAIN

Oviedo's one **train station** (Avenida de Santander; 📶) serves both **Renfe** (☎91 232 03 20; www.renfe.com), for destinations to the south, and the narrow-gauge **FEVE** (☎91 232 03 20; www.renfe.com/viajeros/feve), on the upper floor, for destinations along Spain's north coast.

**Cudillero** (€3.30, 1½ hours, three direct FEVE trains daily; further services with a change at Pravia)

**Gijón** (€3.40, 20 to 30 minutes, half-hourly or hourly Renfe *cercanías* 7.15am to 10.45pm)

**León** (€8 to €20, two to three hours, four or five Renfe trains daily)

**Llanes** (€8.55, 2¾ hours, three to four FEVE trains daily) Via Arriondas and Ribadesella.

**Luarca** (€7.40, 2½ hours, two FEVE trains daily) Continuing (slowly) across Galicia.

**Madrid** (€16 to €71, 4½ to 7½ hours, four to six Renfe trains daily)

**Santander** (€16, five hours, two FEVE trains daily)

# Gijón

POP 257,500

Gijón (khi-*hon*), Asturias' largest city, lacks the history and cultural ambience of the regional capital Oviedo, but it has the sea, and a very good eating and drinking scene, and a warmly unpretentious population. It's surprising how quickly it can grow on you.

Gijón produces iron, steel and chemicals, and is the main loading terminal for Asturian coal, but a thorough 21st-century facelift has also given it pedestrianised streets, parks, seafront walks, cultural attractions, excellent restaurants and good shopping. It's a party and beach hotspot too, with endless summer entertainment.

The city's old core is concentrated on the headland called Cimavilla (Cimadevilla), the old fisherfolk quarter. The harmonious, porticoed Plaza Mayor marks the southern end of this promontory, leading into an enticing web of narrow lanes and small squares. To the west stretch the Puerto Deportivo (marina) and the broad golden Playa de Poniente. South lies the busy, 19th- and 20th-century city centre, bounded on its eastern side by Playa de San Lorenzo.

## Sights

**Parque del Cerro Santa Catalina** PARK

It's well worth wandering up through Cimavilla to this grassy, breezy, clifftop park with great views. It's home to Eduardo Chillida's 1990 sculpture **Elogio del Horizonte**, which has become something of a Gijón symbol, as well as some fortifications from the 18th to 20th centuries.

**Museo del Ferrocarril de Asturias** MUSEUM

(985 18 17 77; http://museos.gijon.es; Plaza de la Estación del Norte; adult/child €2.50/free, Sun free; 10am-7pm Tue-Fri, 10.30am-7pm Sat & Sun Apr-Sep, 9.30am-6.30pm Tue-Fri, 10am-6.30pm Sat & Sun Oct-Mar) Trains have played a big part in Asturias' story and Gijón's excellent railway museum, housed in a 19th-century former station, has a fascinating collection of 50 locomotives and carriages and all sorts of other weird and wonderful machinery, much of it once used in the region's ports, mines, foundries and power stations.

## Festivals & Events

**Fiesta de la Sidra Natural** FOOD & DRINK

(Natural Cider Festival; Aug) Gijón's week-long cider festival includes brewery tours, free tastings and cider-drinking music and song, and climaxes with a classic piece of Spanish multitudinous madness: the annual attempt to set a new world record for the number of people simultaneously pouring cider, on Playa de Poniente during the fourth weekend of August (9721 people in 2019).

**Semana Grande** SUMMER FESTIVAL

(Aug) Gijón's biggest fiesta spans a week in early August, with plenty of partying across the city's plazas, streets and beaches.

## Sleeping

Room prices peak in August, when finding a bed can be a challenge. Generally speaking Gijón's hotels aren't particularly good value for money.

**Hotel Central** HOTEL €€

(985 09 86 51; www.hotelcentralasturias.com; Plaza del Humedal 4; s €50-59, d €55-85; ) It's quite a surprise to find this welcoming, family-run, little hotel tucked inside an unlikely looking apartment block near the bus station, 900m south of Cimavilla. The Central is a fluffy-cushioned, parquet-floored world of its own with nine homey, soft-furnished rooms in a white-and-cream boutique style. Breakfast (€6) is served in the snug lounge.

**Parador de Gijón** HOTEL €€

(Parador Molino Viejo; 985 37 05 11; www.parador.es; Avenida Torcuato Fernández Miranda 15, Parque de Isabel la Católica; incl breakfast s

LOCAL KNOWLEDGE

### THE ART OF CIDER-DRINKING

Asturian cider is served *escanciada:* poured from a bottle held high overhead into a glass held low, which gives it some fizz. Don't worry, you don't have to do this yourself – bar staff will flaunt their own skills by not even looking at the glass or bottle as they pour, probably chatting to somebody else over their shoulder at the same time. A shot of cider, about one-fifth of a glass, is known as a *culete* or *culín;* the thing to do is to knock it back immediately in one go (leaving a tiny bit in the glass), before the fizz dissipates.

Every Asturian town has plenty of *sidrerías* (cider bars) but the epicentre of the scene is Oviedo's *Bulevar de la sidra* – Calle de la Gascona – lined with a dozen jam-packed *sidrerías*.

Asturias churns out 80% of Spanish cider: around 45 million litres a year, nearly all consumed in Asturias itself. Apples are reaped in autumn and crushed to a pulp (about three-quarters of which winds up as apple juice). The cider is fermented in *pipes* (barrels) kept in *lagares* (the places where the cider is made) over winter. It takes about 800kg of apples to fill a 450L *pipa,* which makes 600 bottles.

Since 2002, a Denominación de Origen Protegida (DOP) Sidra de Asturias has existed for Asturian ciders which meet particular technical and quality standards and make exclusive use of indigenous Asturian apple varieties. The DOP currently covers 31 producers.

The main cider-producing region is east of Oviedo, centred on Nava, Villaviciosa and Siero. Find out more at **Comarca de la Sidra** (www.lacomarcadelasidra.com).

€81-200, d €110-215; P ❄ 📶) Gijón's *parador* (state-owned luxury hotel) has a beautiful, tranquil setting inside a revamped watermill amid plenty of greenery, 2km southeast of Cimavilla. Rooms are classy and comfy, with floral curtains, varnished-wood floors and all the usual *parador* trimmings.

**Hotel Asturias** HOTEL €€
(☎985 35 06 00; www.hotelasturiasgijon.es; Plaza Mayor 11; r €59-154; ❄ 📶) The Asturias offers 87 plain but spacious and comfy rooms in a super-central location, overlooking Cimavilla's main square. 'Classic' rooms have a minimalist, old style; 'modern' rooms are bigger but have less character.

## Eating

The most atmospheric area to eat is Cimavilla, though the city centre has many options.

**La Galana** ASTURIAN €€
(☎985 17 24 29; www.restauranteasturianolagalana.es; Plaza Mayor 10; mains & raciones €8-26; ⏰noon-4pm & 7pm-midnight; 📶) The front bar is a boisterous *sidrería* for snacking on tapas (€6 to €9) or *raciones*, accompanied by free-flowing cider. For sit-down dining, head to the spacious back room with mural-covered ceilings. The food in both parts is wide-ranging and very good, with fish – like wild sea bass, or *pixín* (monkfish) in barnacle sauce – an especially strong suit.

**Gloria** ASTURIAN €€
(www.estasengloria.com; Plaza Florencio Rodríguez 3; mains & raciones €14-20, lunch set menu €20; ⏰noon-4pm & 8-11.30pm Tue-Sat, noon-4pm Sun) Shiny gastrobar Gloria's shortish but sweet menu includes the likes of blanched octopus in a garlicy sauce, or veal ribs with chimichurri, but also simpler ham croquettes or Asturian cheese platters. Many dishes are available as tapa, half-plate or full plate.

## Drinking & Nightlife

The *sidrerías* on Plaza Mayor and up the hill into Cimavilla are always a lively scene. Further up in Cimavilla a nocturnal student scene flourishes around Plaza Corrada. South of Cimavilla, both wine and beer bars – many with fine tapas too – congregate in *la ruta de los vinos* (the streets between Calles Merced and Buen Suceso). Popular bars also abound in the streets close to Playa de San Lorenzo and Playa de Poniente.

## Information

**Gijón Turismo** (☎985 34 17 71; www.gijon.info; Espigón Central de Fomento; ⏰10am-8pm May-Jul & Sep-Oct, to 9pm Aug, 10am-2.30pm & 4.30-7.30pm Nov-Apr) The main tourist office, on a Puerto Deportivo pier, is very helpful.

## Getting There & Away

### BUS

From the **bus station** (Calle de Magnus Blikstad), ALSA operates buses across Asturias and beyond.

| Destination | Fare (€) | Time | Frequency |
|---|---|---|---|
| Aeropuerto de Asturias | 9 | 45min | hourly 6am-11pm |
| Cudillero | 5.75 | 1¼hr | 4-8 daily |
| Oviedo | 2.55 | 30min-1hr | every 10-20min, 6.30am-10.30pm |
| Ribadesella | 7.10 | 1¾hr | 7-10 daily |
| Santander | 9-32 | 2¾-4¼hr | 9-12 daily |

### TRAIN

All Renfe and FEVE trains depart from the **Estación Sanz Crespo** (Calle Sanz Crespo), 1.5km west of the city centre. Destinations include Cudillero (€3.30, 1¾ hours, five to 10 direct FEVE trains daily) and Oviedo (€3.40, 30 minutes, two to three Renfe *cercanías* hourly 6am to 11.30pm).

Change at Pravia, El Berrón or Oviedo for most other FEVE destinations. Renfe also has several daily trains to León (€7 to €22, 2¾ hours) and Madrid (€17 to €73, five to eight hours).

# East Coast Asturias

Mostly Spanish holidaymakers seek out a summer spot among the beaches, coves and fishing towns along the Asturian coast east of Gijón, backed by the Picos de Europa, which rise only 15km inland.

## Villaviciosa & Around

POP 6340

At the inland end of the Ría de Villaviciosa estuary, about 27km east of Gijón, the agreeable town of Villaviciosa rivals Nava as Asturias' cider capital. Apart from the Romanesque **Iglesia de Santa María**, its pretty little town centre is mostly a child of the 18th century.

## Sights

**Playa de Rodiles** BEACH

(P) The beautiful, broad golden sands of 1km-long Playa de Rodiles, backed by eucalyptus trees, front the sea at the mouth of the Ría de Villaviciosa, 10km north of Villaviciosa.

**Iglesia de San Salvador de Valdediós** CHURCH

(670 242372; www.monasteriovaldedios.com; Valdediós; adult/child €5/1.50; 11am-1.30pm & 4.30-7pm Tue-Sun Apr-Sep, 11am-1.30pm Tue-Sun Oct-Mar) Don't miss this beautifully preserved, triple-naved, pre-Romanesque (p510) church, built in 893 CE as part of a palace complex for Asturian King Alfonso III. It's set in a beautiful, peaceful, green valley, 9km southwest of Villaviciosa. Visits inside the church are guided, half-hourly, and most include the handsome convent next door with its 13th-century Romanesque church and three-tier Renaissance cloister.

**El Gaitero** BREWERY

(985 89 01 00; www.sidraelgaitero.com; La Espuncia, Villaviciosa; tours every 30 or 45min 10am-12.45pm & 4-5.45pm Mon-Fri, 10am-12.45pm Sat mid-May–early Sep, 10am, 11.30am, 1pm, 4pm & 5.30pm Thu-Sun Oct-Dec & mid-Jan–mid-May; P) FREE You can immerse yourself in the world of cider at several bodegas around Villaviciosa. El Gaitero, 2km northeast, is one of the biggest and offers the most frequent visits. Set up in 1890, El Gaitero now produces up to 27 million bottles of cider a year. The one-hour tours (in Spanish) include a free tasting session and the detailed museum. Call ahead to book your slot.

## Sleeping & Eating

★ **La Casona de Amandi** HERITAGE HOTEL €€

(985 89 34 11; www.lacasonadeamandi.com; Calle de San Juan 6, Amandi; incl breakfast s €85-100, d €120-160; closed approximately Jan-Feb; P) This exquisite 19th-century country house in Amandi village, 1.5km south of Villaviciosa, oozes character. The wonderfully comfy rooms are endowed with antique furnishings, plenty of pillows, well-equipped bathrooms and original chestnut floors. Common areas are spacious and relaxing, especially the beautiful garden with centenarian wisteria and sequoia. There are weekly Pilates and yoga classes too.

Also here is the excellent restaurant **Pušáki** (622 017130; www.pusaki.es; menú €38 plus drinks; 2-4pm Thu-Sun), concocting highly original, internationally inspired creations from locally sourced, organic ingredients for its weekly six-course *menú*. They do dinner for hotel guests (€39 including drinks) Tuesday to Saturday, as well as lunches open to all.

**Lena** ASTURIAN €€€

(www.sidrerialena.com; Calle Cervantes 2, Villaviciosa; mains €14-25; 11.30am-4pm & 8-11.30pm Tue-Sat, 1.30-4pm Sun) Under the command of Michelin-starred Asturian chef Jaime Uz, this *'sidrería gastronómica'* delivers tip-top Asturian cooking with an original touch, plus a big variety of ciders, wines and cocktails. Standout dishes include superbly tender *solomillo de vaca* (beef tenderloin), the octopus-and-pigs'-trotters *guiso* (stew), and *cachopo*, made traditionally or with hake.

## Information

**Oficina de Turismo** (985 89 17 59; www.turismovillaviciosa.es; Calle Agua 29, Villaviciosa; 10am-2pm & 4-7pm Wed-Sun Apr-Jun & Sep, daily Jul-Aug, Tue-Sat Oct-Mar) Helpful place inside the 16th-century Casa de los Hevia.

## Getting There & Away

The **bus station** (Calle Ramón Rivero Solares, Villaviciosa) is a few blocks north of the centre. ALSA (p513) has seven or more buses daily to Oviedo (€4.45, one hour) and Ribadesella (€4, 35 minutes to one hour), three or four to Llanes (€6.65, 1¼ hours) and 13 or more to Gijón (€3.10, 35 minutes to 1¼ hours).

# Ribadesella

POP 2760

Straddling the Río Sella's estuary, Ribadesella is a low-key fishing town and lively beach resort. Its two halves are joined by the long, low Sella bridge. The western part (with most of the best hotels) has an expansive golden beach, **Playa de Santa Marina**, lined by handsome early-20th-century *casas de indianos* (houses built by emigrants returned from the Americas). The older part of town, with the fishing harbour and most of the bars and restaurants, is on the eastern side. The walk up to the **Ermita de la Guia** chapel here provides great views over the town and coast.

## Sights

★ **Cueva de Tito Bustillo** CAVE

(985 18 58 60, 902 306600; www.centrotitobustillo.com; Avenida de Tito Bustillo; adult/child

## WHERE THE RECONQUISTA BEGAN

Asturias occupies a key place in Spanish history as the starting point of the eight-centuries-long Christian reconquest of the Iberian Peninsula following the Muslim conquest of 711 CE. Rebels led by a surviving Visigothic chieftain, Pelayo, famously inflicted the first defeat on a Muslim force at the battle of Covadonga in the Asturian mountains in 722 CE, laying the foundations of the Kingdom of Asturias, from which modern Spain ultimately grew. The Asturian kingdom was headquartered at Cangas de Onís (c 722–774), then Pravia (c 774–791), then Oviedo (c 791–910), before the Reconquista's southward progress saw Asturias subsumed into the the Kingdom of León (capital: León) from 910. As a concession, Juan I of Castilla y León made Asturias a *principado* (principality) in 1388, and to this day the heir to the Spanish throne holds the title Príncipe or Princesa de Asturias (Prince or Princess of Asturias). The Premios Princesa de Asturias (Princess of Asturias Awards) handed out to personalities of distinction in Oviedo's Teatro Campoamor every October are Spain's equivalent of the Nobel prizes.

€4.14/2.12, Wed free; ⏲tours 10.15am-5pm Wed-Sun Mar-Oct; Ⓟ) Some of Spain's finest cave art, including superb horse paintings probably done around 15,000 to 10,000 BCE, is within this World Heritage–listed cave, 300m south of the western end of the Sella bridge. Daily visitor numbers are limited, so reservations (online or in person) are essential. If you miss the cave itself, the displays of the **Centro de Arte Rupestre Tito Bustillo** (☎985 18 58 60, 902 306600; www.centrotitobustillo.com; Avenida de Tito Bustillo; adult/child €5.45/3.29, Wed free; ⏲10am-6pm Wed-Fri, to 7pm Sat & Sun Mar-Jun & Sep-Oct, to 7pm Wed-Sun Jul & Aug, to 6pm Wed-Sun Nov-Dec & Feb; Ⓟ), 200m south, are well worth your time.

Of the cave's 12 clusters of paintings, only the **Panel Principal** (Main Panel; mostly deer, horses, goats and bison) can be visited. The one-hour visit (guided, in Spanish) includes some slippery stretches, and children under seven are not admitted.

**Playa de Vega** BEACH

The broad, 1.5km-long sands of Playa de Vega, 8km west of Ribadesella, are among the least known of northern Spain's finest beaches. There are three or four relaxed restaurant/bars (most closed in winter) at the east end, and it's a surfing beach, but it's big enough, and just hard enough to reach, never to feel crowded.

To find it turn off the N632 at Km 9.3 and continue 1.6km to the beach – or walk 7km from Ribadesella along part of the Camino del Norte (p506) in about two hours.

### Activities

Several agencies on the harbourfront Calle Marqués de Argüelles offer **canoe trips** of two to four hours down the Río Sella from Arriondas. They'll usually drive you to Arriondas and bring you back to Ribadesella afterwards, charging €20 to €25 per person.

**Surf schools** open up on Playa de Santa Marina and Playa de Vega in July and August.

### Festivals & Events

**Descenso Internacional del Sella** CANOEING

(www.descensodelsella.com; ⏲Aug) The Río Sella is at its busiest on the first Saturday after 2 August, when 1000-plus serious paddlers (followed by many more amateurs) race downriver to Ribadesella from Arriondas in this international canoeing event that's been making a splash since 1930. Both towns go mad for the weekend (and accommodation is near-impossible to find).

### Sleeping & Eating

The lively *sidrerías* (cider houses) along the waterfront and elsewhere in the eastern half of town are a good bet for seafood. Ribadesella also has some excellent top-end restaurants.

**Pensión Arbidel** HOSTAL €

(☎653 419349; www.arbidelpension.com; Calle Oscura 1; s €30-40, d €40-80; 📶) Clean, well-kept, homey rooms with comfy beds, framed art, ribboned curtains and cast-iron or wood furnishings make the Arbidel a perfect few-frills choice. It's amiably run, and has a couple of little patio areas where you can sit out.

**Villa Rosario** HISTORIC HOTEL €€€

(☎985 86 00 90; www.hotelvillarosario.com; Calle de Dionisio Ruisánchez 3-6; r incl breakfast €81-285; ⏲Mar–mid-Jan; Ⓟ❄@📶) Occupying a century-old *casa de indianos* (house built by an emigrant returned from the Americas), this luxurious, history-filled hotel overlooks Playa de Santa Marina. Interiors are pleasingly styled with wood floors, rich-toned carpets and an original cherry-wood staircase, while the 17 white-on-white rooms are tastefully contemporary. The buffet breakfast is excellent. The Villa Rosario 2 block out back is also comfortable, and cheaper, but lacks historical character.

**★ Arbidel** ASTURIAN €€€

(☎985 86 14 40; www.arbidel.com; Calle Oscura 1; mains €28-32, set menus €55-88 plus drinks; ⌚1.30-4pm & 8.30-11.30pm, closed Sun night & Mon Sep-Dec & Feb–mid-Jul, closed Sun night & Mon-Thu Jan) Michelin-starred Arbidel is famous for chef Jaime Uz's reinvention of classic Asturian flavours and ingredients with a distinctly modern flair. Exquisitely prepped, locally inspired delights might feature green-apple gazpacho, baked *pixín* with squid noodles and couscous, or Asturian beef tenderloin with local Casín cheese and veggies. The tasting menus are the best way to sample Arbidel's wide-ranging creativity.

## Getting There & Away

### BUS

ALSA buses depart from the **bus station** (Avenida del Palacio Valdés), 300m south of the Sella bridge, east of the river.

| Destination | Fare (€) | Time | Frequency (Daily) |
|---|---|---|---|
| Gijón | 7.10 | 1¾hr | 6-9 |
| Llanes | 2.85 | 30-45min | 7-9 |
| Oviedo | 8.35 | 1¼-1¾hr | 6-7 |
| Santander | 8.32 | 1½-2½hr | 2 |

### TRAIN

Three or four FEVE trains run daily to/from Oviedo (€6.65, 2¼ hours), Arriondas (€1.85, 30 minutes) and Llanes (€2.55, 35 minutes), and two to/from Santander (€9.65, 2¾ hours).

# Llanes & Around

POP 4400

Llanes was for a long time an independent town and whaling port with its own charter, awarded by Alfonso IX of León in 1206. Today, with a bustling harbour, a small medieval centre clustered around the bougainvillea-draped, Gothic Basílica de Santa María, some gorgeous beaches within easy reach, and the Picos de Europa not far away, it's one of northern Spain's more popular holiday destinations.

## Sights

**Bufones de Arenillas** LANDMARK

(Puertas de Vidiago) The Bufones de Arenillas are a dozen geyser-style jets of seawater, pumped up through rock cavities by the pressure of the tides – with heavy seas, some jets can spurt a spectacular 20m high (it's dangerous to get too close). When seas are calm, you'll just hear air and water whooshing eerily through the tunnels below.

From Puertas de Vidiago on the N634 9km east of Llanes, an unpaved road leads 2km down to the Bufones.

**Cueva del Pindal** CAVE

(☎608 175284; http://tematico.asturias.es/cultura/yacimientos/pindal.html; Pimiango; adult/child €3.15/1.60, Wed free; ⌚10am-4pm Wed-Mon) The World Heritage–listed Cueva del Pindal contains 31 Palaeolithic paintings and engravings of animals, mostly in ochre, including bison, horses and rare depictions of a mammoth and a fish. With its setting among wooded sea cliffs, close to a 16th-century chapel and ruined Romanesque monastery, it's an interesting visit.

Visits (45 minutes) must be booked by phone at least one day ahead; children under seven are not allowed. To find it, turn off the N634 opposite Hotel Casa Junco, 21km east of Llanes, then go 4km, through Pimiango village.

## Sleeping & Eating

Llanes and its surrounding area have plenty of accommodation catering to all budgets, but book ahead for June to mid-September. Some of Asturias' most outstanding hotels are in **La Pereda**, 4km south of Llanes.

The old town is liberally endowed with lively *marisquerías* (seafood eateries) and *sidrerías*.

**★ La Posada de Babel** DESIGN HOTEL €€

(☎985 40 25 25; www.laposadadebabel.com; La Pereda; s €55-93, d €88-130, ste €140-175; ⌚Easter–early Dec; P 📶) About 4km south of Llanes, this unique spot combines bold modern architecture and design and lots of original art with sprawling lawns and a relaxed, civilised vibe. The 12 different rooms occupy four contrasting buildings, including one in a typical Asturian *hórreo* on stone stilts. The kitchen puts an emphasis on market-fresh and organic food.

WORTH A TRIP

## BEACHES AROUND LLANES

More than 20 sandy stretches and concealed coves lie scattered along the dramatic coastline between Llanes and Ribadesella, 28km west.

**Playa de Torimbia** (Niembro) A beautiful, gold-blonde crescent bounded by rocky headlands and a bowl of green hills, 9km west of Llanes, Torimbia is truly spectacular. Turn off the AS263 at Posada to reach Niembro (2km), from where it's a further 2km (signposted) to the beach. Torimbia is clothing-optional and you have to walk the last kilometre or so, which keeps the crowds down.

**Playa de Toranda** (Niembro) About 8km west of Llanes, the 250m-long sands of Playa de Toranda are backed by green fields and a forested headland. Snorkellers should see a good variety of fish, especially at low tide. Head to Niembro as for Playa de Torimbia (p519); Toranda (signposted) is 500m beyond Niembro. In the busy summer months you may have to park at the entrance to Niembro then walk 1km.

There's a particularly good beach bar here, **Bar La Arena** (Playa de Toranda; dishes €4.50-16; ⏰mid-Jun–early Sep, hours variable), serving salads, *bocadillos* (baguette-style sandwiches), Galician-style octopus and juicy burgers in a grassy garden.

**Playa de Gulpiyuri** (Naves) This 50m-long strand framed by cliffs and greenery is 100m away from the sea! You can hear waves sloshing through tunnels to reach its gold-toned sands. It looks best at high tide. Gulpiyuri is a 400m walk from a parking area just off the A8 at the eastern end of Naves.

**Playa Ballota** (Andrín) A particularly attractive 350m-long beach 4.5km east of Llanes, hemmed in by green cliffs and with a rocky islet out front. It's signposted down a dirt track from the LLN2 Cué–Andrín road.

**Hotel Don Paco** HOTEL €€
(☎985 40 01 50; www.hoteldonpacollanes.com; Calle Colegio de la Encarnación 1; s €50-118, d €60-158; P Wi-Fi) Family-run Don Paco began life in the 17th century as a convent and exudes a strong sense of its role in Llanes' history, aided by the setting of its good restaurant in the old convent chapel. Facilities are far from historic and the 49 bright, all-exterior rooms, in pleasing blue-and-white, have up-to-date bathrooms and good fast wi-fi.

The restaurant (mains €14 to €30, set menus €22 to €40), with an appealing streetside terrace, does excellent original versions of traditional Asturian favourites.

**Cae a Claveles** DESIGN HOTEL €€
(☎658 110 774, 985 92 59 81; www.caeaclaveles.com; La Pereda; s €95-115, d €100-135; ⏰closed mid-Dec–mid-Jan; P Wi-Fi) Absolutely not what you'd expect in countryside Asturias, this exquisitely contemporary five-room design pad with a chic urban feel is built to resemble a miniature hill. The curvy, low-rise structure doubles as its warm artist-owner's home studio: her creations adorn the walls. Alluring, airy doubles are coolly minimalist, splashed with rich colours and flooded with light through floor-to-ceiling windows.

★ **El Bálamu** SEAFOOD €€€
(☎985 41 36 06; www.facebook.com/elbalamu; Puerto Pesquero; mains €14-30; ⏰1-3.30pm & 8-10.30pm, closed Wed Sep-Jun) Upstairs in the fish auction building (an outwardly anonymous harbourside block), El Bálamu is an amazingly bright, sleek space that is Llanes' best seafood eatery. You can't get closer to the source of fresh seafood than this. Snack on fried squid and *gambas al ajillo* (garlic shrimp) at the bar, or reserve ahead for a table overlooking the harbour and ocean.

## ℹ Information

**Oficina de Turismo** (☎985 40 01 64; www.llanes.es; Antigua Lonja, Calle Marqués de Canillejas 1; ⏰10am-2pm & 5-9pm mid-Jun–mid-Sep, 10am-2pm & 4-6.30pm Mon-Sat, 10am-2pm Sun mid-Sep–mid-Jun)

## ℹ Getting There & Away

### BUS

ALSA operates from the **bus station** (☎985 40 24 85; Calle Bolera).

Destination include:

| Destination | Fare (€) | Time | Frequency (daily) |
|---|---|---|---|
| Arriondas | 4.70 | 30-60min | 5-7 |
| Gijón | 9.03 | 1½-2¼hr | 4-5 |
| Oviedo | 11.15 | 1-2¼hr | 11-12 |
| Ribadesella | 2.85 | 20-40min | 6-8 |
| San Vicente de la Barquera | 2.34 | 30min | 4-7 |
| Santander | 6.17 | 1¼-2hr | 5-8 |

**TRAIN**

Three or four FEVE trains head daily to Ribadesella (€2.55, 35 minutes), Arriondas (€4, one hour) and Oviedo (€8.55, 2¾ hours), and two go to Santander (€7.80, 2¼ hours).

# West Coast Asturias

The cliffs of Cabo Peñas, 20km northwest of Gijón, mark the start of the western half of Asturias' coast. Gorgeous sandy stretches and towering cliffs dot this entire coastline. The industrial steel-producing town of Avilés is a world away from the colourful fishing ports of Cudillero and Luarca, to its west. Further west, you'll reach Galicia.

## Avilés

POP 73,700

Avilés, 34km north of Oviedo, is an old estuary port and steel-making town. Despite that unpromising introduction, its historic core's elegant colonnaded streets and its central Plaza de España make for a lovely stroll, and there are some good, authentic Asturian restaurants in and around town.

### Sights

**Centro Niemeyer** CULTURAL CENTRE

(☎984 83 50 31; www.niemeyercenter.org; Avenida del Zinc; tours adult/child €3/2; ⏲tours 12.30pm & 5pm Jul & Aug, 5pm Wed-Fri, 12.30pm & 5pm Sat & Sun Sep-Jun) This multifaceted international cultural centre, founded in 2011 on once-industrial land just across the river from the city centre, was designed by Brazilian architect Oscar Niemeyer as a cultural nexus between the Iberian Peninsula and Latin America. The bold-white complex hosts a range of avant-garde theatre, music, dance, cinema, literature and art shows.

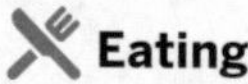

### Eating

**Casa Tataguyo** ASTURIAN €€

(☎985 56 48 15; www.tataguyo.com; Plaza del Carbayedo 6; mains €13-31, set menu €16-22; ⏲1-4pm & 8-11pm or later) On a corner of verdant Parque del Carbayedo, Tataguyo has being going strong since 1845. Feast on delectable classic meat- and fish-focused Asturian fare, including frills-free *guisos* and *lechazo al horno* (roast lamb), or keep it lighter with platters of cold meats and cheeses and piled-high salads. The high-quality, three-course lunchtime *menú* (including wine) is a good deal.

★ **Real Balneario de Salinas** SEAFOOD €€€

(☎985 51 86 13; www.realbalneario.com; Avenida de Juan Sitges 3, Salinas; mains €29-46, set menus €50-187 plus drinks; ⏲1-3.30pm & 8-11.30pm Tue-Sat, 1-3.30pm Sun, closed mid-Jan–mid-Feb) Serious food lovers: head to the beach at Salinas, 5.5km northwest of central Avilés. The beachside Real Balneario, opened as a bathing centre by King Alfonso XIII in 1916, is today a top seafood restaurant. Choose from traditional or creative 'new proposal' dishes, plus some very tempting desserts. The *bogavante* (giant crayfish/mini-lobster) *flambé* is a current favourite; the long-standing speciality is champagne sea bass.

### Information

**Oficina de Turismo** (☎985 54 43 25; www.avilescomarca.info; Calle de Ruiz Gómez 21; ⏲10am-8pm Jul–mid-Sep, 9.30am-3pm Mon-Fri, 10.30am-2.30pm Sat & Sun mid-Sep–Jun) Just off Plaza de España. Pick up a map to guide you round the sights.

### Getting There & Away

From the **bus station** (Avenida Telares), 800m north of Plaza de España, ALSA buses run at least 27 times daily to Oviedo (€2.65, 30 to 60 minutes) and Gijón (€2.50, 30 minutes).

From the **train station** (Avenida Telares), 700m north of Plaza de España, trains head to Gijón (€1.95, 40 minutes, at least 31 times daily), many with connections for Oviedo (€3.30, 1¼ to two hours).

## Cudillero

POP 1280

Cudillero, 60km northwest of Oviedo, is the most picturesque fishing village on the Asturian coast, with houses painted in a rainbow of pastels cascading down to a tiny

## CASAS DE INDIANOS

*Indiano* is the name given to Spanish migrants who made it rich in the Americas then returned home to splash their wealth on ostentatious mansions for themselves – and often schools, churches, roads, water systems or electricity for the communities they had sprung from.

It's estimated nearly five million Spaniards – many of them from the northern coastal regions – emigrated to Latin America or the Caribbean in search of a better life (or to avoid military service) between 1850 and 1930. Just a few eventually came home with big fortunes, but their mansions, known as *casas de indianos*, brighten up the scene all along Spain's north coast.

A typical *casa de indianos* is a florid, eye-catching edifice, often turreted, colourfully painted and with palm trees in ample gardens. Architectural styles may range from art nouveau and Modernista to neoclassical, neo-Gothic, neo-Mudéjar or some mélange of those.

The small eastern Asturias town of Colombres has a particularly fine concentration of *indiano* architecture. The most magnificent pile, La Quinta de Guadalupe, was built in 1906 for locally born, Mexico-enriched Íñigo Noriega Laso. It now houses the fascinating **Museo de la Emigración** (985 41 20 05; www.archivodeindianos.es; Plaza Manuel Ibáñez; adult/child €2.50/1; 10am-2pm & 4-7pm, to 8pm Jun-Sep), devoted to migration in the 19th and 20th centuries, with exhibits displayed in rooms around the mansion's superb three-storey atrium.

In Cantabria, Comillas (p501) has another exceptional collection of *indiano* buildings, the finest of them commissioned from top Catalan Modernista architects by local lad Antonio López, who amassed millions in Cuba and later gained the title Marqués de Comillas.

The Asturian fishing town Ribadesella boasts a string of *indiano* beachfront mansions. One of them is now a luxe hotel, Villa Rosario (p517). Other places with notable collections of *casas de indianos* include Llanes, Luarca and Somao village (near Cudillero) in Asturias, and Ribadeo (Galicia).

port on a narrow inlet. Despite its touristy feel in summer, Cudillero is reasonably relaxed and makes an appealing stop, even in mid-August when every room in town is taken. The surrounding coastline is a dramatic sequence of sheer cliffs and fine beaches.

### Sights

**Quinta de Selgas** MANSION

(985 59 01 20; www.selgas-fagalde.com; Carretera CU2, El Pito) This gorgeous 1880s mansion opens to visitors for about three months in some summers (recently, every one or two years). If you're here at the right time, go. Built by the wealthy local Selgas Albuerne brothers, it's sumptuously kitted out in Italian- and French-influenced styles, and contains a top-quality art collection including works by Goya, El Greco and Rubens. The gardens are a symphony of avenues, pavilions, pools, statuary, neatly clipped lawns and tall trees. It's up in El Pito village, 2km south of Cudillero's harbour area.

**Playa del Silencio** BEACH

(Castañeras) Silencio is one of Spain's most beautiful beaches: a long, silver-sandy cove backed by a natural rock amphitheatre. It isn't particularly good for swimming due to underwater rocks, but it's a stunning spot for a stroll and, weather permitting, some sun-soaking. It's 15km west of Cudillero: take exit 441 off the A8, then head 2.5km west on the N632 to Castañeras, where the beach is signposted. The last 500m is on foot.

### Sleeping & Eating

Accommodation in Cudillero itself is limited, especially during the low season, when many places shut down, but there are about 80 hotels, *pensiones*, holiday apartments and holiday houses within a few kilometres. Book ahead from June to August.

**La Casona de Pío** HOTEL €€

(985 59 15 12; www.lacasonadepio.com; Calle del Ríofrío 3; s €52-95, d €62-109; closed mid-Jan–mid-Feb; ) Pocketed away right behind the port is this charming, rustic-style hotel in a 200-year-old stone building, featuring 11 very comfortable, earth-toned rooms, some boasting timber terraces festooned with flowers. It serves a terrific breakfast (€8) full of homemade goodies.

**Hotel Casa Prendes** HOTEL €€

(☎985 59 15 00; www.hotelcasaprendes.com; Calle San José 4; d €58-118, 2-person apt €60-100, 4-person apt €78-135; ) A brilliantly maintained bright blue townhouse just back from Cudillero's harbour, Casa Prendes offers nine comfy, stone-walled rooms, attentive service and a small breakfast cafe that does, among other things, good bacon and eggs.

**El Faro** SEAFOOD €€

(☎985 59 15 32; Calle del Ríofrío 4; mains €14-30; ⊙noon-4pm & 8pm-midnight Thu-Tue, daily Aug, closed 2nd half Oct) El Faro's stone-and-timber surrounds and colourful artwork help create a welcoming atmosphere for digging into fish of the day, seafood salads, *parrilladas de marisco* (mixed grilled shellfish) or even an Asturian beef tenderloin with goat cheese. It's one street back from the port.

## Information

**Oficina de Turismo** (☎985 59 13 77; www.turismocudillero.com; Puerto del Oeste; ⊙10am-2pm & 4-7.30pm Jul & Aug, 11am-2pm & 4-6pm Jun & Sep, 10am-3pm Mon-Sat Oct-May) By the port.

## Getting There & Around

The only place to park is at the port, in front of or beyond the tourist office.

From the **bus stop** (Calle Juan Antonio Bravo), 800m uphill from the port, three or more daily ALSA buses go to Gijón (€5.75, 1¼ to 1½ hours) via Avilés (€3.30, 45 minutes), where you can connect for Oviedo.

The **train station** (Camin de la Estación) is 2km inland from the port: FEVE trains to Gijón (€3.30, 1¾ to two hours) run about hourly until 6pm (fewer on weekends); for Oviedo (€3.30, 1½ to 2½ hours) you usually change at Pravia. Two trains run west to Luarca (€3.60, 1¼ hours) and into Galicia.

# Luarca & Around

POP 3730

Marginally less scenic than its rival coastal town Cudillero, Luarca has a similar setting in a deep valley running down to an expansive harbour full of colourful fishing boats.

## Sights

**Atalaya** VIEWPOINT

(P) Find your way up to Luarca's Atalaya viewpoint, with its lighthouse, chapel, elaborate cemetery and dramatic coastal vistas, above the port's northern end.

**Playa de Barayo** BEACH

(Barayo; P) Part of a nature reserve, Playa de Barayo is a good sandy beach in a pretty bay with a river winding through wetlands and dunes, and caves at its east end. Leave the N634 11km west of Luarca onto the NV2 towards Puerto de Vega; after 800m turn right towards Vigo (1.5km) and follow signs. From the car park, you can walk to the beach in 30 minutes, or in 10 minutes by steps down to the beach's west end.

**Puerto de Vega** VILLAGE

The pretty fishing village of Puerto de Vega, 15km west of Luarca, is well worth a visit, with a colourful little harbour and scenic walks along the **Senda Costa Naviega** footpath to two beautiful, undeveloped, sandy beaches, Playa de Barayo, 5km east, and 750m-long, eucalyptus-backed **Playa de Frejulfe** (4km west). The pick of several restaurants is **Mesón El Centro** (Plaza de Cupido; mains €15-27, set menu €35; ⊙1.30-3.30pm & 8-11pm, closed Mon evening), preparing good fresh seafood with a touch of flair and without scrimping on the portions.

**Castro de Coaña** ARCHAEOLOGICAL SITE

(☎985 97 84 01; http://parquehistorico.org; Coaña; adult/child €3.15/1.60, Wed free; ⊙10.30am-5.30pm Wed-Sun Apr-late Sep, to 3.30pm late Sep-Mar; P) One of Spain's best-preserved *castros* (pre-Roman fortified villages, often considered to be Celtic), dating back to the 4th century BCE, lies 2km south of the small town of Coaña, 23km west of Luarca. From the visitors centre a footpath leads to a well-preserved collection of stone foundations, evocatively perched on a green hillside with sweeping views.

**Cabo Busto** CAPE

Wind-lashed Cabo Busto, 13km east of Luarca, is a fine example of the Asturian coast's wildness, with waves crashing onto its rocky cliffs below a 19th-century lighthouse. The views are fantastic and footpaths wend their way along the clifftops about half a kilometre in each direction.

**Ermita de la Regalina** CHAPEL, VIEWPOINT

(Cadavedo) Spectacularly positioned on a grassy headland fringed by jagged cliffs, sandy beaches and crashing seas, this delicate little blue-and-white chapel 16km east of Luarca is absolutely worth finding for the sensational views alone. A couple of typical stilted Asturian *hórreos* complete the panorama.

## Sleeping & Eating

**★3 Cabos** HOTEL €€

(☎985 92 42 52; www.hotelrural3cabos.com; Carretera de El Vallín, Km 4; d incl breakfast d €85-125; ⌚Feb-early Dec; P@📶) A beautiful conversion of a 120-year-old farmhouse, 3 Cabos enjoys fabulous panoramas from its elevated inland site. Six exquisitely designed rooms in the main house feature open-stone walls, comfy beds and spacious bathrooms, while a brand-new building at the side has three big, bright, sea-facing rooms opening into the grassy gardens.

The panoramic bar-restaurant (dinner mains €18 to €29) focuses on fresh local products. There are two cosy lounges with libraries, and your hosts have plenty of information on the area. Take the El Vallín turn-off from the N634, 4km southwest of central Luarca, and follow signs.

**★Hotel Torre de Villademoros** HOTEL €€

(☎985 64 52 64; www.torrevillademoros.com; Villademoros, Cadavedo; s €63-99, d €88-132, ste €286; ⌚Mar-Oct; P📶) The crowning glory of this gorgeous country retreat, 15km east of Luarca, is its medieval tower, now a luxurious three-level suite. Equally appealing are the 10 beautifully appointed rooms in the 18th-century main house and the spacious, relaxing common areas, all tastefully combining old stone walls, pale wood furnishings, kilims and contemporary art; the large garden; and the good in-house restaurant.

Out back, trails lead across the fields to beaches and dramatic coastal bluffs.

**Hotel Villa de Luarca** HOTEL €€

(☎985 47 07 03; www.hotelvilladeluarca.com; Calle Álvaro de Albornoz 6; d €50-106; 📶) Hotels in Luarca town are a moderate bunch but this 1906 *casa de indianos* has been renovated in very comfortable, diversely retro manner with real wood floors and furnishings. They do a good buffet breakfast for €7.70.

**El Barómetro** SEAFOOD €€

(☎985 47 06 62; Paseo del Muelle 5; mains €9-22; ⌚1-4pm & 8.30-11pm Wed-Mon) For the best seafood in town Luarca locals are likely to point you to this family-run portside eatery with its vintage barometer embedded in the outside wall. Specialities include *fabes con almejas* (clam-and-bean stew) and hake in sea-urchin sauce. The €14 lunchtime *menú* is especially popular. Book ahead.

## Information

**Oficina Municipal de Turismo** (☎985 64 00 83; www.valdes.es; Plaza Alfonso X; ⌚10.30am-1.45pm & 4-6.45pm Sep-Jun, to 7.15pm Jul-Aug)

## Getting There & Away

From Luarca's **bus stop** (Calle García Prieto), outside La Plaza supermarket, at least four daily ALSA buses run east to Oviedo (€10.30, 1¼ to 1¾ hours) and west to Ribadeo (€7.20, 1¾ hours) in Galicia.

The FEVE train station is 800m south of the town centre. Two trains run daily east to Cudillero (€3.60, 1¼ hours) and Oviedo (€7.40, 2¾ hours), and west to Ribadeo (€4.75, 1½ hours) and beyond.

# Inland Western Asturias

There's some gorgeous country in southwest Asturias. Even just driving through on scenic mountain roads into Castilla y León, such as the AS228 via the 1587m **Puerto Ventana** or the AS227 via the beautiful 1486m **Puerto de Somiedo**, can be rewarding. A very popular way of getting out into this countryside is the Senda del Oso cycling and hiking path, passing an enclosure where you'll probably be able to see two Cantabrian brown bears. The green valleys of the Parque Natural de Somiedo form one of the most beautiful parts of the Cordillera Cantábrica and are only just beginning to be discovered by non-Spaniards.

## Senda del Oso

The Senda del Oso (Path of the Bear) is a popular cycling and walking track along the course of a former mine railway southwest of Oviedo, running through spectacular valley scenery into deep, narrow canyons, with several bridges and more than 30 tunnels. It's easy to rent bikes here and the total rideable track is 45km, the most popular stretch being the 20km between Tuñón and Entrago villages. This is commonly ridden in the Entrago-to-Tuñón direction (south to north) because it's downhill that way, though gradients along the track are always easy. En route you'll probably see a couple of Cantabrian brown bears in large enclosures at the Cercados Oseros, and it's a fun outing with (or without) children.

## Sights

**Cercados Oseros** WILDLIFE RESERVE
(☎985 96 30 60; www.osodeasturias.es) About 5km south of Tuñón (or a 1km walk south from the Área Recreativa Buyera, where cars can park), the Senda del Oso reaches the Cercados Oseros, two compounds (one above the path, one below) housing two female Cantabrian brown bears considered unable to survive in the wild: Paca (born 1989) and Molina (born 2013). Of late both bears have been kept in the lower enclosure, where they're usually easily spotted from the Senda.

**Parque de la Prehistoria** MUSEUM
(☎985 18 58 60, 902 306600; www.parquedelaprehistoria.es; AS228, San Salvador de Alesga; adult/child €6.10/3.60; ⏲10.30am-8pm Jul & Aug, 10.30am-2.30pm & 4-6pm or 7pm Wed-Sun Feb-Jun & Sep-Dec; P) This park-museum 4km south of Entrago gives an excellent introduction to Spanish and European cave art. It includes replicas of Asturias' World Heritage–listed Tito Bustillo (p516) and Candamo caves and France's Niaux cave, along with a museum-gallery explaining all about Europe's Palaeolithic cave-art phenomenon.

Outside, you can observe peacefully grazing live specimens of animals that were depicted in prehistoric art.

**Casa del Oso** MUSEUM
(☎985 96 30 60; www.osodeasturias.es; Proaza; ⏲10am-2pm & 4-6pm) FREE The Casa del Oso at the north end of Proaza is the headquarters of the Fundación Oso de Asturias, which runs the Cercados Oseros bear conservation project, and has exhibits on Spanish brown bears. It doubles as the area's tourist office.

## Activities

Outfitters at Entrago, Proaza, the Área Recreativa Buyera and Tuñón rent out mountain or city bikes for riding the Senda del Oso. Day rental typically costs €12 to €20. A popular option for a few euros more is the 'Descenso de la Senda del Oso' on which you just ride downhill from Entrago to Proaza or Tuñón, with van transport to Entrago at the start or back to Entrago from your end point. The rental firms typically work daily from June to September, and on Saturdays and Sundays in April, May, October and November. Book a week or more ahead for July and August; at other times it's advisable to call the same day or the day before. Dependable options include **TeverAstur** (☎985 76 46 23; www.sendadelosoaventura.com; ⏲Mar-Dec) in Entrago and **Centro BTT Valles del Oso** (☎985 76 11 77, 659 209383; www.vallesdeloso.es; Tuñón; ⏲daily late Jun-late Sep, Sat & Sun mid-Mar–late Jun & late Sep-early Dec) in Tuñón.

## Sleeping & Eating

There are loads of *casas rurales* and village hotels in the Senda del Oso area, with **Proaza** being a convenient base.

**L'Esbardu** ASTURIAN €€
(☎985 76 11 52; www.lesbardu.es; Calle El Puente, Proaza; mains €8.50-20; ⏲2-4pm Wed-Sun, plus 8.30-11pm Fri & Sat) Take a short detour from the Senda del Oso to eat at this wonderfully rustic, stone-walled, wood-beamed restaurant at the south end of Proaza. Diners crowd in for skillets of potatoes, eggs, sausages, ham and peppers, bean stews, wild game specialities, including venison and wild boar, and a few vegetarian options.

## Getting There & Away

**Pullmans Llaneza** (☎985 46 58 78; www.pullmansllaneza.com) runs three or four daily buses from Oviedo bus station to Tuñón (€2.10, 30 minutes), Proaza (€2.10, 45 minutes) and Entrago (€2.60, one hour), continuing to San Martín ('Teverga' on timetables), 1km beyond Entrago and 3km before the Parque de la Prehistoria.

# Parque Natural de Somiedo

If you fancy exploring beautiful mountain country that few foreigners reach, head for this 291-sq-km, Unesco-listed biosphere reserve, with a network of mostly well-marked walking trails, on the northern flank of the Cordillera Cantábrica. With five verdant valleys descending from the Cordillera's 2000m-plus heights, the park combines thick woodlands, rocky mountains and green pastures dotted with *brañas* (groups of mostly abandoned herders' shelters). It's also a key stronghold of Spain's bear population.

The only town is plain **Pola de Somiedo** (70km southwest of Oviedo), which has a bank, ATM, two small supermarkets, a petrol station, the Oficina de Información del Parque Natural de Somiedo (p526), and the **Casa del Oso** (☎985 76 34 06, 942 23 49 00; www.fundacionosopardo.org; Calle Flórez Estrada; adult/child €3/1; ⏲11am-2pm & 5-8pm mid-Jun–mid-Sep, 11am-2pm & 4-7pm Sat & Sun mid-Apr–mid-Jun & mid-Sep–Oct), a good place to brush

## BEARS OF THE CORDILLERA CANTÁBRICA

Wild, mountainous southwest Asturias and northwestern Castilla y León, including the Parque Natural de Somiedo, form the main stronghold of Spain's biggest animal, the brown bear *(oso pardo)*. Bear numbers in the Cordillera Cantábrica have climbed to over 300, from as low as 70 in the mid-1990s, including around 50 in a separate easterly area around the convergence of Asturias, Cantabria and León and Palencia provinces. Killing bears has been illegal in Spain since 1973, but only since the 1990s have concerted plans for bear recovery been carried out.

The bears of the Cordillera Cantábrica are among the world's smallest brown bears, with males rarely exceeding 180kg or females 140kg. They can live 25 to 30 years, and have traditionally been disliked by farmers – despite being almost entirely vegetarian. Public support has played a big part in the bears' recent recovery, and owes a lot to the celebrated bears of Asturias' Senda del Oso. The bear population is not yet completely out of the woods – occasional shootings by hunters and illegal boar snares still pose threats, as do forest fires, new roads and ski stations. Experts warn that climate change may drastically reduce the numbers of oak trees (source of a favourite bear food, acorns) in mountain areas. You can see bears in large enclosures on the Senda del Oso and take guided bear-spotting hikes (p525) in the Parque Natural de Somiedo. Spain's major resource and advocate for brown bears is the **Fundación Oso Pardo** (www.fundacionosopardo.org).

up on bear facts. A wonderful road winds and climbs 8km east from Pola to **Valle de Lago** village, a good walking base at about 1300m elevation.

## Activities

The **Valle del Lago** stretching up from Valle de Lago village is one of Somiedo's best (and most popular) walking areas, with glacial lakes and high summer pastures. The **Ruta de Valle del Lago** trail heads 6km from the village (where you must leave vehicles) to Asturias' largest lake, the Lago del Valle (around two hours each way).

Other good walks include the one-way **La Peral-Villar de Vildas** route in the Valle del Pigüeña (13km, around five hours one way), which passes one of the largest and best-preserved *brañas,* La Pornacal (you'll need two vehicles or a taxi for this); and the walk from Alto de Farrapona to the **Lagos de Saliencia** (about 5km and 1½ hours each way). This last can be converted into a one-way walk continuing to Valle de Lago village (total 14km one-way, about five hours).

### Wildlife-Watching

Watching bears (normally from considerable distance through telescopes or binoculars provided by guiding firms) is most people's main priority, but chamois, deer, eagles and vultures are also commonly seen on guided trips here, and wolves are a possibility. The best times for bear sightings are May (if it's warm), June, late August and September.

**Somiedo Experience** WILDLIFE WATCHING
(☎617 060878, 687 222464; www.somiedoexperience.com; half/full day per person €40/70) Somiedo Experience has experienced local guides, who can speak English, and its outings combine wildlife-watching with hikes on which you'll learn plenty about Somiedo nature. Trips start from Pola de Somiedo.

**WildWatching Spain** WILDLIFE WATCHING
(☎987 74 08 05, 609 726444; www.wildwatchingspain.com; per day adult/child €90/50) The day includes two bear-watching outings of three or four hours each. Trips start from Pola de Somiedo.

## Sleeping & Eating

Pola de Somiedo has a dozen or so places to stay, some of them very characterful, and there are several more in Valle de Lago village.

**Hotel Rural Somiedo** HOTEL €
(☎985 76 39 35; www.hotelsomiedo.es; Valle de Lago; s/d/ste €35/50/65; ⊙closed late Dec-Jan; P📶) Half-a-dozen spotless, pine-furnished rooms, a bar where you can get breakfast, and friendly owners who are very helpful with walking information make this an excellent deal in Valle de Lago.

★**Palacio de Flórez-Estrada** HISTORIC HOTEL €€
(☎985 76 37 09, 616 170018; www.florezestrada.com; incl breakfast s €60-70, d €80-90, ste €95-

110, apt without breakfast €70-80; ⏱Easter-Oct, apt year-round; P📶🍴) Cosy rooms occupy a 15th-century tower and the 18th-century main house at this gorgeous, olde-worlde riverside mansion in sprawling gardens. Breakfast emphasises organic and fair-trade foods, and the owner hosts musical evenings, arts events, yoga courses and ornithology seminars.

**Casa Cobrana** ASTURIAN €€

(☎985 76 37 48; Valle de Lago; mains €8-18; ⏱8.30am-10.30pm Thu-Mon Jan, Mar–mid-Jun, 1st half Jul & Sep-Dec, daily mid-Jul–Aug) For traditional Asturian mountain cuisine, you can't beat this simple restaurant in Valle de Lago village. Classics such as *fabada asturiana* (bean, meat and sausage stew) and *cachopo de setas al Cabrales* (veal stuffed with wild mushrooms and Cabrales cheese) are served at sturdy tables. Order ahead for delicacies such as *cabrito guisado* (stewed kid goat).

## ℹ Information

**Oficina de Información del Parque Natural de Somiedo** (☎985 76 37 58; www.parquenaturalsomiedo.es; Calle Parque Natural de Somiedo, Pola de Somiedo; ⏱10am-2pm & 4-6pm, to 7pm Jun & Sep, to 8pm Jul-Aug, closed Sun afternoon & Mon Oct-May) Has displays and ample free information on the park and its walking trails.

## ℹ Getting There & Away

If you're coming from the Senda del Oso area with your own wheels, you can approach Somiedo by the spectacular AS265 west from San Martín to La Riera, via the Puerto de San Lorenzo pass (1347m, often snowed under in winter).

An ALSA bus departs Oviedo bus station for Pola de Somiedo (€9, two hours) at 5pm Monday to Friday and 10am Saturday and Sunday, returning from Pola at 6.45am Monday to Friday (you have to change buses at Grado) and at 5.30pm Saturday and Sunday (direct).

# PICOS DE EUROPA

The jagged, deeply fissured Picos de Europa straddle southeast Asturias, southwest Cantabria and northern Castilla y León with some of Spain's most spectacular mountain scenery and finest hiking.

The Picos comprise three majestic massifs: the western Macizo El Cornión, rising to 2596m; the eastern Macizo Ándara, with a highest point of 2444m; and the particularly rocky Macizo Central (or Macizo de los Urrieles), reaching 2648m. The 671-sq-km **Parque Nacional de los Picos de Europa** covers all three massifs. At the park's higher elevations, a wild landscape of imposing limestone peaks rises above sparkling lakes and open meadows filled with grazing cattle; down below, sheer rock faces plunge into a series of stunning river gorges.

Virtually deserted in winter, the area bursts with visitors in August. July is not far behind. June and September are quieter, a little cooler and just as likely to be as sunny as in August. The main Picos access towns (Cangas de Onís, Arenas de Cabrales, Potes, Posada de Valdeón) are packed with accommodation. Surrounding villages offer additional options. In the Picos themselves, *refugios* (mountain huts) provide bunks and often meals for hikers.

## ℹ Information

### MAPS

The best maps of the Picos, sold in shops for about €8 each, are published by Adrados Ediciones (www.infopicos.com): *Parque Nacional de los Picos de Europa* (1:50,000), *Picos de Europa Macizos Central y Oriental* (1:25,000) and *Picos de Europa Macizo Occidental* (1:25,000).

### TOURIST INFORMATION

The national park has three main information centres.

**Oficina de Información Casa Dago** (p528) In Cangas de Onís.

**Centro de Visitantes Sotama** (p534) Four kilometres north of Potes.

**Oficina de Información Posada de Valdeón** (☎987 74 05 49; El Ferial, Posada de Valdeón; ⏱8am-3pm Mon-Fri, 9am-2pm & 4-6.30pm Sat & Sun Jul-Sep, 8am-3pm Mon-Fri Oct-Jun) On the southern side of the Picos.

## ℹ Getting There & Around

Paved roads lead from Cangas de Onís southeast up to Covadonga and the Lagos de Covadonga; from Arenas de Cabrales south up to Poncebos then east up to Sotres and Tresviso; from Potes west to Fuente Dé; and from Posada de Valdeón north to Caín (this one's extremely narrow in parts). These four main access towns have fair to good bus connections with the outside world, but only a few bus services (mostly in summer) will get you into the hills from the access towns.

As well as regular taxis that stick to the better roads, 4WD taxi services can manage some of the mountain tracks. Several of these offer day trips in the Picos, typically for €45 or €50 per person.

## Picos de Europa

# Western Picos

Approaching the Picos from the Asturian (western) side, the Macizo Occidental (El Cornión) unfolds in a series of green-on-green pastures, gorgeous mountain lakes and bald-rock panoramas. Plain Cangas de Onís is the area's main base, while unassuming Arriondas, 8km to the northwest, is the starting point for canoe rides down the Río Sella. About 10km southeast of Cangas lies holy Covadonga, famous as the spot where in 722 CE Muslim forces suffered their first reverse after the Muslim conquest of the Iberian Peninsula in 711. From Covadonga, a mountain road straggles up to the beautiful (and incredibly popular) Lagos de Covadonga, where some fine hiking trails begin.

## Arriondas

POP 2370 / ELEV 85M

The ordinary little town of Arriondas, 8km northwest of Cangas de Onís, is the starting point for hugely popular and fun canoe trips down the tree-lined Río Sella to various end points between Toraño and Llovio (7km to 15km, 1½ to four hours).

Arriondas is mayhem on the first Saturday after 2 August, when tens of thousands of people converge for the Descenso Internacional del Sella (p517), an international canoeing event that sees 1000-plus serious paddlers racing off downriver to Ribadesella at noon, followed by more fun paddlers.

### Activities

Numerous agencies hire out canoes, paddles, life jackets and waterproof containers for the Río Sella trip, show you how to paddle and bring you back to Arriondas at the end. This stretch of the Sella has a few entertaining minor rapids, but it isn't a serious white-water affair. Anyone from about eight years old can enjoy the outing. The standard charge, including a picnic lunch, is €25/15 per adult/child. Starting time is normally between 11am and 1.30pm.

### Sleeping & Eating

**★Posada del Valle** HOTEL €€

(985 84 11 57; www.posadadelvalle.com; Collía; s €60-70, d €75-98; Apr-Oct; P) This remarkable, English-run spot, in a beautiful valley 3km north of Arriondas, is not only a charming 12-room rural retreat and a wonderful walking base, but also a working organic farm. Design and decor emphasise local art and artistry, and all rooms have valley views. Excellent breakfasts (€9) and four-course dinners (€28; nonguests by

reservation only) include vegetarian options. It's just past Collía village on the AS342.

★ **Casa Marcial** GASTRONOMY €€€
(☎985 84 09 91; www.casamarcial.com; AS342 Km 3, La Salgar; tasting menus €110-165 plus drinks; ⏱1-3pm Sun & Tue, 1-3pm & 9-11pm Wed-Sat) Hidden in gorgeous countryside 4.5km north of Arriondas is this double-Michelin-starred restaurant in chef Nacho Manzano's childhood home. Even the 'short' *menús* here are extravaganzas of a dozen or more dishes, showcasing creative preparations of local seafood and Manzano's trademark renderings of regional classics such as *fabada* and *pitu* (farmyard chicken).

**El Corral del Indianu** ASTURIAN €€€
(☎985 84 10 72; www.elcorraldelindianu.com; Avenida de Europa 14; mains €24-39; ⏱1.30-4pm & 8.30-11pm Mon, Tue, Fri & Sat, 1.30-4pm Wed & Sun) Putting a gourmet spin on Asturian cooking, Michelin-starred Corral is Arriondas' most original dining spot. If you don't fancy the extensive tasting menus (€75 or €95, plus drinks), you could choose traditional Asturian *fabada* (bean, meat and sausage stew), followed by baked red tuna or a beef chop.

## Getting There & Away

From Oviedo, ALSA (☎902 422242; www.alsa.es) runs at least seven buses daily to Arriondas (€6.45, 1¼ hours), continuing on to Cangas de Onís (€1.55, 15 minutes). There are also several daily ALSA buses from Llanes (€4.70, 30 minutes to one hour) and Ribadesella (€1.90, 25 minutes), on the coast.

Arriondas is on the FEVE railway between Oviedo, Ribadesella, Llanes and Santander, with two to four trains in each direction daily.

# Cangas de Onís

POP 3750 / ELEV 84M

The largely modern Asturian town of Cangas de Onís was (briefly, in the 8th century) the first capital of the medieval Kingdom of Asturias. Today it's the major launchpad for excursions into the western Picos. In August especially, Cangas bursts with hikers, campers and holidaymakers. It's a decent base, with loads of accommodation and places to eat and drink, and limitless opportunities for adventure activities nearby. There are plenty more places to stay in villages such as Soto de Cangas, Mestas de Con and Benia de Onís, along the AS114 towards Arenas de Cabrales.

**Puente Romano** BRIDGE
Arching like a cat in fright, the so-called 'Roman Bridge' spanning the Río Sella was actually built in the 13th century, but is no less beautiful for its mistaken identity. From it hangs a 1939 copy of the Cruz de la Victoria, the symbol of Asturias that resides in Oviedo's cathedral.

## Sleeping & Eating

**Hotel Nochendi** HOTEL €€
(☎985 84 95 13; www.elmolin.com/nochendi; Avenida Constantino González 4; r €60-120; ⏱early Feb-late Dec; 📶) Spread across one sparkling floor of an apartment block beside the Río Güeña, the Nochendi is a lovely surprise and an easy place to feel at home. Twelve spacious, spotless, bright rooms feature comfy beds, spot lighting, all-white decor and a touch of modern art, and most have river views.

**Parador de Cangas de Onís** HISTORIC HOTEL €€€
(☎985 84 94 02; www.parador.es; Villanueva de Cangas; r €90-234; ⏱Mar-early Jan; P❄@📶) Cangas' *parador* overlooks the Río Sella, 3km northwest of town. The main building, originally a monastery founded in the 12th century on the site of early Asturian King Favila's palace, houses 11 gorgeously characterful rooms (some former monks' cells).

**La Sifonería** ASTURIAN €€
(☎985 84 90 55; www.lasifoneria.net; Calle de San Pelayo 28; dishes €9-20; ⏱noon-4pm & 8pm-midnight Wed-Mon) Crammed with ancient cider-making siphons and photos of the friendly cider-pouring owners, this wonderfully down-to-earth tapas spot is perfect for tucking into uncomplicated Asturian cooking at good prices. Try Cabrales cheese croquettes, a variety of *revueltos* or heartier classics such as *cachopo* (stuffed veal).

★ **El Molín de la Pedrera** ASTURIAN €€€
(☎985 84 91 09; www.elmolin.com; Calle Río Güeña 2; mains €19-30; ⏱1-4.30pm & 8.30-11.30pm Thu-Tue early Feb-late Dec, closed last week Jun & Sun-Tue evenings approx Oct-May) This stone-and-brick-walled, family-run restaurant wins with both its traditional Asturian dishes – such as *fabada*, *tortos de maíz* (maize pancakes) and hearty meat grills.

## Information

**Oficina de Información Casa Dago** (☎985 84 86 14; Avenida de Covadonga 43; ⏱9am-2pm Mon-Fri, 10am-2pm & 4-8pm Sat & Sun)

**Oficina de Turismo** (☎985 84 80 05; www.cangasdeonis.es; Avenida de Covadonga 21; ⏲9am-9pm Jul–mid-Sep, 10am-2pm & 4-7pm Mon-Sat, 10am-2pm Sun mid-Sep–Jun)

## Getting There & Away

ALSA runs at least seven daily buses from Oviedo to Cangas (€7.25, 1½ hours) and back, stopping in Arriondas en route. Cangas' bus station is on the northern side of the Río Güeña, linked by a footbridge to the town centre.

**Taxitur** (☎985 84 87 97; Calle José González Soto 2) offers taxi service.

# Covadonga

POP 55 / ELEV 260M

Covadonga, 10km southeast of Cangas de Onís, is a scenic spot with a striking 19th-century basilica tucked between soaring mountains, but its importance lies more in what it represents than what it is. Somewhere hereabouts, in approximately 722 CE, the Muslims suffered their first defeat in Spain, at the hands of the Visigothic nobleman (and, later, Asturian king) Pelayo – an event considered to mark the beginning of the 800-year Reconquista.

**Santa Cueva** CAVE

(⏲9am-7pm) FREE This cave, now with a chapel installed, is where the Virgin supposedly appeared to Pelayo's warriors before their 722 CE victory over the Muslims. Weekends and summers see long queues of the faithful and curious lining up to enter. Of the cave's two tombs, one is claimed to contain the remains of Pelayo, his wife Gaudiosa and his sister; the other, Pelayo's daughter Ermesinda and her husband Alfonso I.

## Getting There & Away

Three or more ALSA (p528) buses run daily from Cangas de Onís to Covadonga (€1.55, 15 minutes). You can also use the Easter and summer shuttle bus (p530) from Cangas de Onís to reach Covadonga.

# Lagos de Covadonga

Don't let summer crowds deter you from continuing 12km uphill past Covadonga to these two beautiful little lakes, set against jaunty (often snow-topped) peaks. Most day trippers don't get past snapping selfies near the lakes, so walking here is as delightful as anywhere else in the Picos.

**Lago de Enol** is the first lake you'll reach, with the main car park and an info point just beyond it (downhill). It's linked to **Lago de la Ercina**, 1km away, by the paved road but also by a footpath (part of the PRPNPE2) via the **Centro de Visitantes Pedro Pidal** (☎985 84 86 14; ⏲10am-6pm Easter & Jun-Oct), which has displays on Picos flora and fauna.

> ### PICOS WEBSITES
>
> **Organismo Autónomo Parques Nacionales** (www.miteco.gob.es/es/red-parques-nacionales/nuestros-parques/picos-europa)National parks site.
>
> **El Anillo de Picos** (www.elanillodepicos.com) Challenging hiking circuits of the Picos, with useful info on *refugios*.
>
> **Incatur Picos de Europa** (www.picosdeeuropa.com) For the Asturian Picos.
>
> **Liébana y Picos de Europa** (www.liebanaypicosdeeuropa.com) For the eastern Picos.

## Activities

A marked loop walk, the **Ruta Lagos de Covadonga** (PRPNPE2; 5km, about 2½ hours), takes in the two lakes, the Centro de Visitantes Pedro Pidal and an old mine, the Minas de Buferrera. About 400m southwest of Lago de Enol, the route passes the **Refugio Vega de Enol** (Casa de Pastores; ☎630 451475; www.refugiovegadeenol.com; Lago de Enol; dm/half-board €15/35; ⏲year-round; 📶), whose 16 bunks are the nearest accommodation to the lakes. The refuge has a hot shower, serves good food (mains €9 to €12) and is reachable by vehicle.

Two other trails from the lakes will take you further afield. The PRPNPE4 leads 7.6km southeast from Lago de la Ercina, with an ascent of 610m, to the **Vega de Ario**, where the **Refugio Vega de Ario** (Refugio Marqués de Villaviciosa; ☎984 092 000, 656 843095; www.refugiovegadeario.es; dm/half-board €15/35; ⏲late May–mid-Oct) has 40 bunks and meal service. The reward for about three hours' effort in getting there is magnificent views across the Garganta del Cares to the Picos' Macizo Central.

The PRPNPE5 leads roughly south from Lago de Enol to the 59-bed **Refugio Vegarredonda** (☎985 922 952, 626 343366; www.refugiovegarredonda.com; dm/half-board €15/35; ⏲Mar-Nov) at 1410m, with meal service, and on to the **Mirador de Ordiales**, peering over a 1km sheer drop into the Valle de Angón. It's

### PICOS PRECAUTIONS

The best walking weather in the Picos de Europa is generally from May to September, although people hike at all times of year. In any season, it's essential to go properly equipped and prepared for sudden weather changes. Mist, rain, cold and snow are common problems – and can arrive suddenly without warning. When the summer sun shines, you need protection from that too. Higher up, trails may be less obvious and water sources are rare. Paying insufficient attention to these details has cost several lives over the years. For mountain weather forecasts see http://mountain-forecast.com (select 'Cantabrian Mountains'), or www.aemet.es/en/eltiempo/prediccion/montana. The emergency phone number is ☎112.

10km (about 3¼ hours' walking) each way – relatively easy along a mule track as far as the *refugio,* then a little more challenging on up to the *mirador.* Track conditions permitting, drivers can save about 30 minutes by driving as far as the Pandecarmen car park, 2km past Lago de Enol.

### Getting There & Away

To avoid traffic chaos for three weeks over Easter and from June to September, and on the early November and early December holiday weekends, private vehicles cannot continue past Covadonga on the road to the Lagos between 8.30am and 9pm. (They can, however, drive down at any time if they're already up there.)

During these periods a shuttle bus (day ticket adult/child €9/3.50) operates to the Lagos from four car parks (per vehicle €2) in Cangas de Onís (beside the bus station) and along the Cangas–Covadonga road. In the same periods Taxitur (p529) operates a half-hourly round-trip minibus service (per adult/child €12/5) between Cangas bus station and the lakes.

A regular taxi costs €30 one way from Cangas de Onís to the Lagos de Covadonga, or €48 round trip with one hour's waiting time at the lakes.

## Central Picos

The most famed attraction of the Picos' central massif is the gorge that divides it from the western Macizo El Cornión. The popular Garganta del Cares (Cares Gorge) trail running through it gets busy in summer, but the walk is always an exhilarating experience. This part of the Picos also has plenty of less heavily tramped paths and climbing challenges. Arenas de Cabrales, on the AS114 between Cangas de Onís and Panes, is a popular base, but Poncebos, Sotres, Bulnes and Caín also offer facilities.

## Arenas de Cabrales

POP 750 / ELEV 135M

Arenas de Cabrales (also Las Arenas), home of the tangy blue Cabrales cheese, lies at the confluence of the bubbling Ríos Cares and Casaño, 30km east of Cangas de Onís. The busy main road is lined with hotels, restaurants and bars, and just off it is a little tangle of quiet squares and back lanes, with several more local-style *sidrerías.* Arenas is a popular and engaging base for walking the spectacular Garganta del Cares gorge and other sorties into the central Picos.

### Sights & Activities

**Cueva del Queso de Cabrales** MUSEUM

(☎985 84 67 02; www.fundacioncabrales.com; Carretera AS264; adult/child €4.50/3; ⌚tours hourly 10.15am-1.15pm & 4.15-7.15pm) Learn all about and sample the fine smelly Cabrales cheese at Arenas' Cueva de Cabrales, a cheese-cave museum 500m south of the centre on the Poncebos road. Guided visits (45 minutes) are in Spanish; they'll lend you a tablet to read the commentary in English. Working hours may be shorter from November to Easter.

**Quesería Vega de Tordín** FOOD

(☎674 597738; www.vegadetordin.com; Barrio La Ería; tours incl tasting adult/child €4/3; ⌚45min tours about hourly 10am-2pm & 4-8pm Apr-Oct) For an eye-opener on contemporary Cabrales cheese-making, take a tour and tasting at this sixth-generation family-run dairy on the eastern edge of Arenas. Cows are milked by robot, and the cheese-making processes are all mechanised, following stringent hygiene regulations. The cheeses still have to mature for 60 days in caves (not included in the visit) to earn the name Cabrales.

### Sleeping & Eating

**Hotel Rural El Torrejón** HOTEL €

(☎985 84 64 28; www.hotelruraleltorrejon.es; Calle del Torrejón; r incl breakfast €50-71; ⌚mid-Feb–mid-Jan; P 📶) This friendly, family-run country house welcomes travellers with flower-filled balconies, gorgeous gardens and tastefully decorated rooms in a cosy rural style. The setting is idyllic, overlooking fields beside the Río Casaño.

**Apartamentos El Ardinal** APARTMENT €€
(☎653 940236, 985 84 64 34; www.apartamentoselardinal.com; Barriu del Riu; 1-bedroom apt €50-90; ⏲closed mid-Dec–mid-Jan; P ) In a tranquil elevated spot with mountain and village views, Ardinal offers four self-sufficient one- and two-bedroom apartments with plenty of wood, flowery prints and updated kitchens. Breakfasts are available for €5 or €6.

**Chigre L'Orbayu** SIDRERÍA €
(El Orbayu; Calle Pedro Niembro; raciones €4-12; ⏲noon-midnight) In the older, quieter part of Arenas off the main road, Orbayu is a relaxed, friendly place to enjoy drinks and plates of cheeses, cured meats, tuna-stuffed peppers, salads or the excellent *milhojas*, a mini-tower of cured pork, cheese, nuts and tomato.

### Getting There & Away

Two or more daily **ALSA** (☎902 422242; www.alsa.es) buses run from Cangas de Onís to Arenas (€3.05, 40 minutes) and back. There are also one or two daily buses to Panes (€2.25, 30 minutes to one hour).

## Garganta del Cares

The magnificent 1km-deep, 10km-long gorge of the Río Cares separates the Picos' western massif from its central sibling. This dramatic canyon extends between the hamlet of Poncebos, 6km south of Arenas de Cabrales in Asturias, and the marginally bigger hamlet of Caín in Castilla y León. People flock here year-round, but especially in summer, to walk the insanely popular Ruta del Cares connecting the two villages. The trail is carved high into and through the rugged walls of the gorge, with limestone peaks soaring far above.

There are two hotels in Poncebos and a handful in Caín, plus plenty more options in Arenas de Cabrales and in Cordiñanes and Posada de Valdeón villages south of Caín.

### Activities

**★Ruta del Cares** WALKING
(Garganta del Cares Walk; PRPNPE3) You can walk this trail, one of Spain's favourites, in either direction, but heading from north (Poncebos) to south (Caín) saves its finest stretches for last. The beginning involves a steady climb in the gorge's wide, mostly bare, early stages; you're over the highest point after about 3km.

As you approach the regional boundary with Castilla y León, the gorge becomes narrower and its walls thick with vegetation, creating greater contrast with the alpine heights high above. The southernmost stages of the walk are possibly the prettiest, and as you descend nearer the valley floor, you pass through a series of low, wet tunnels before emerging at the end of the gorge in Caín. If you're feeling fit, it's quite possible to walk the whole 10km and return in one day's outing; it takes six to seven hours plus stops. There are restaurants in Caín and Poncebos where you can lunch before heading back (though you can't be sure to find anything open from November to February). There's no drinkable water along the route, so bring your own.

### Getting There & Away

Agencies in Picos towns will transport you in 4WD vehicles to one end of the walk and pick you up at the other end. Service from Cangas de Onís to Caín and then back from Poncebos to Cangas typically costs €35 per person. Or you make your own way to Poncebos and walk the gorge to Caín, and they'll drive you from Caín back to Poncebos for €30 per person.

From about mid-July to early September ALSA operates several daily buses from Arenas de Cabrales to Poncebos (€3, 10 minutes) and back. In August ALSA also runs morning buses from Cangas de Onís to Caín (€8.30, two hours), and afternoon/early-evening buses from Poncebos to Cangas (€4.65, 45 minutes), enabling you to walk the Cares north from Caín to Poncebos, and return from Poncebos to Cangas the same day. Schedules vary from year to year.

## Bulnes & El Naranjo de Bulnes

POP 20 / ELEV 647M

The rust-roofed hamlet of Bulnes, inaccessible by road, sits high up a side valley off the Cares gorge. You can reach it by a 4km uphill walk (about 1½ hours; 400m ascent) from Poncebos on the PRPNPE19 trail – or aboard the Funicular de Bulnes, a tunnel railway that climbs steeply for more than 2km inside the mountain from its lower station just below Poncebos. At the top of this exciting ride, tiny Bulnes sits in a pretty, secluded valley surrounded by towering rocky peaks.

All amenities, including three or four seasonal cafe/bar/restaurants, are in the lower part of Bulnes, known as La Villa.

## Activities

Bulnes is a starting point for superb strenuous hikes up to the foot of the magnificent rock pillar **El Naranjo de Bulnes** (Pico Urriello, Picu Urriellu), which towers 500 very vertical metres from its base to its 2519m-high summit. El Naranjo is an emblem of the Picos de Europa and draws climbers from far and wide to the extremely challenging routes up its walls.

The easier (though not easy) route to El Naranjo from Bulnes is to follow the GR202 trail eastward up to the Collado de Pandébano pass (3.5km, 600m ascent, 1½ to two hours plus stops), then head 5km southwest up the PRPNPE21 to the Refugio de Urriellu, at the foot of El Naranjo, with 700m ascent (2½ to three hours plus stops).

The shorter (4.5km) but harder route is southward up the PRPNPE19 from Bulnes, reaching El Naranjo in about four hours plus stops, ascending 1300m over often stony slopes. Just a few minutes before the refuge there's a scramble up a near-vertical rock maybe 8m high.

You can also approach El Naranjo from Sotres, starting by walking 4km (one to 1½ hours plus stops, 400m ascent) on the PRPNPE21 to the Collado de Pandébano – or driving almost as far as the Collado de Pandébano up an unpaved road from the Invernales del Texu. Or you can just walk from Bulnes to Sotres via the Collado de Pandébano in around three hours.

## Sleeping & Eating

**La Casa del Chiflón** CASA RURAL €

(☎985 84 59 43; www.lacasadelchiflon.com; La Villa; s/d incl breakfast €45/60; ⊙Easter & Jun–mid-Oct; 📶) An attractive, stone-walled, wood-beamed house with six snug rooms, efficient management and a nearby riverside restaurant, La Casa del Puente.

**Refugio de Urriellu** HUT €

(☎638 278041, 650 780381, 984 090 981; www.refugiodeurriellu.com; Vega de Urriellu; dm adult/child €15/8, breakfast €5, lunch or dinner €15; ⊙mid-Mar–mid-Dec) The solidly stone-built Refugio de Urriellu provides 96 tightly squeezed bunks, and communal meals, for hikers and climbers at 1953m altitude at the foot of El Naranjo de Bulnes, enabling hikers to walk up there without having to hurry back down the same day, and explore the area at leisure. Reservations recommended in July and August.

## Getting There & Away

The **Funicular de Bulnes** (☎985 84 68 00; one way/return adult €18/22, child €4.30/6.70; ⊙10am-8pm Easter & Jun–early Oct, 10am-12.30pm & 2-6pm rest of year) makes its seven-minute trip between Poncebos and Bulnes every half-hour in both directions.

# Sotres

POP 110 / ELEV 1045M

A side road twists and turns 11km from Poncebos up to little Sotres, the highest village in the Picos. It has a handful of places to stay and is the starting point for a number of good walks.

## Activities

A popular walking route goes east to **Tresviso** village and on down to Urdón, on the Potes–Panes road. As far as Tresviso (11km) it's a paved road, but the final 6km is a dramatic walking trail, the **Ruta Urdón-Tresviso** (PRPNPE30), snaking 825m down to the Desfiladero de la Hermida gorge. Doing this in the upward direction, starting from Urdón, is also popular.

Many walkers head west along the PRPNPE21 trail from Sotres to the **Collado de Pandébano** pass (1212m) on the far side of the Duje valley, a 4km walk (one to 1½ hours). At Pandébano the massive rock pillar El Naranjo de Bulnes (p532) comes into view and you can continue up to its base in 2½ to three hours. Or you can descend 3.5km (about 1½ hours) west from Pandébano to Bulnes. You can also walk south from Sotres along 4WD tracks to the Hotel Áliva (p535) or Espinama in the southeast of the national park.

## Sleeping & Eating

**Hotel Peña Castil** HOTEL €

(☎985 94 50 49; www.hotelpenacastil.com; incl breakfast s €40, d €55-65; ⊙closed early Jan–early Feb; 📶) Friendly Hotel Peña Castil has 11 smallish but impeccably kept, homey rooms spread through a renovated stone house with, in some cases, little balconies – plus its own bar-restaurant serving typical Asturian fare (mains €11 to €17).

## Getting There & Away

The only ways to reach Sotres are to drive up from Poncebos, to walk, or to approach from the south (Hotel Áliva or Espinama) on a 4WD trip. A taxi from Arenas de Cabrales costs about €20.

## Eastern Picos

From the humdrum town of Panes, the N621 follows the Río Deva southward upstream through the impressive **Desfiladero de la Hermida** gorge to the town of **Potes**, the major base and activity hub for the eastern Picos. About 23km west of Potes lies **Fuente Dé**, where a dramatic cable car provides the main access to the high hills in this area.

## Potes & the Liébana Valley

POP 1350 / ELEV 291M

Potes is a hugely popular staging post on the southeastern edge of the Picos, with the Macizo Ándara rising close at hand. It's overrun in peak periods but still lively and delightful in its cobbled old town, and is the 'capital' of Liébana, a beautifully verdant and historic valley area lying between the Picos and the main spine of the Cordillera Cantábrica.

### Sights

The heart of Potes is a cluster of bridges, towers and charming backstreets restored in traditional slate, wood and red tile after considerable damage during the civil war. The bubbling Quiviesa and Deva rivers meet close to the heart of town.

**Monasterio de Santo Toribio de Liébana** MONASTERY
(942 73 05 50; www.santotoribiodeliebana.org; CA885; 10am-1pm & 4-7pm May-Sep, to 6pm Oct-Apr; P) Christian refugees, fleeing to Liébana from Muslim-occupied Spain in the 8th century, brought with them the **Lígnum Crucis**, purportedly the single biggest chunk of Christ's cross. Santo Toribio Monastery, 3km west of Potes, has housed this holy relic ever since, making it an important pilgrimage destination. Many pilgrims still arrive by walking the 73km Camino Lebaniego (p506) from San Vicente de la Barquera.

The monastery is also famous as the home of the 8th-century monk and theologian Beato de Liébana, celebrated across Europe for his *Commentary on the Apocalypse*. To learn more about Beato, visit Potes' **Torre del Infantado** (Calle Independencia, Potes; adult/child €3/1.50; 10am-2pm & 4-8pm Jun–mid-Sep, to 6pm mid-Sep–May) and/or the Centro de Visitantes Sotama (p534).

You can continue 500m past the monastery to the tiny 13th-century **Ermita de San Miguel**, a chapel with great valley and Picos views, or follow a dirt path 600m uphill to the **Ermita de Santa Catalina**, which has further fantastic panoramas.

**Iglesia de Santa María de Lebeña** CHURCH
(Lebeña; adult/child €2/free; 10am-1pm & 4-7.30pm Tue-Sat, 10am-1pm Sun Jun-Sep, to 6pm Oct-May; P) The fascinating Lebeña church, 9km northeast of Potes, dates back to the 9th or 10th century. The horseshoe arches are a telltale sign of its Mozarabic style, rare this far north in Spain. Its columns bear Visigothic floral motifs, and a Celtic engraved stone supports the 18th-century altarpiece, with its 15th-century image of the breastfeeding Virgen de la Buena Leche (Virgin of the Good Milk).

Outside the church stands the stump of a beloved, centuries-old yew tree destroyed by a storm in 2007. A sapling grown from a cutting from the tree was planted beside it in 2017.

### Activities

Potes is the main base for all eastern Picos activities, with several agencies offering a host of options, from mountain biking, horse riding and 4WD tours to climbing, canyoning and tandem paragliding. You can also take tours to see how cheese and *orujo* (a potent local liquor) are made.

**Quesería Alles** FOOD & DRINK
(942 73 35 13; www.quesopicon.es; Calle Mayor 6, Bejes; 9am-1pm & 4-8pm) FREE If you're keen on Cantabria's super-pungent blue Picón cheese, head 20km north of Potes up to tiny **Bejes** (signposted off the N621), where you can tour and taste at one of the region's most successful *queserías* (cheese makers). Detailed Spanish-language tours take in the cheese-making process and facilities, though not their cheese-maturing cave.

### Sleeping & Eating

★**Posada de Cucayo** HOTEL €
(942 73 62 46; www.laposadadecucayo.com; Cucayo; d incl breakfast €56-73; closed late Jan-Feb; P) Brilliant Posada de Cucayo sits at 950m altitude in a tiny red-roofed village on the slopes of the Cordillera Cantábrica. Eleven of the 12 spacious rooms enjoy sweeping views over the surrounding scarred mountain peaks and green fields. The excellent **restaurant** (mains €6-13; 2-3.30pm & 9-10.30pm Mar–late Jan; ) features produce from the owners' farm next door.

## POTES FIREWATER

The potent liquor *orujo*, made from leftover grape pressings, is drunk throughout northern Spain and is something of a Potes area speciality, with traditional copper stills in use. People here like to drink it as an after-dinner aperitif as part of a herbal tea called *té de roca* or *té de puerto*. Plenty of shops around town sell *orujo*, including varieties flavoured with honey, fruits, hazelnuts or herbs, and most will offer you tastings if buying.

Potes' fun-filled **Fiesta del Orujo** (www.facebook.com/fiestaorujo; ⌚Nov) happens on the second weekend in November, with practically every bar in town setting up a stall selling *orujo* shots for a few cents, the proceeds going to charity.

About 5km northwest of Potes, **El Coterón** (☎942 73 08 76; www.elcoteron.com; Argüébanes; ⌚8am-2pm & 3.30-6.30pm Mon-Fri, 9am-2pm & 4-7pm Sat & Sun) is a small family-run *orujo* distillery offering informative tours (sometimes in English) of its facilities and the chance to taste and purchase products at source. Bookings recommended.

**Casa Cayo** HOSTAL €
(☎942 73 01 19; www.casacayo.com; Calle Cántabra 6, Potes; s/d/tr €45/60/70; ⌚Apr–late Dec; 📶) Easily the best value in central Potes, friendly, well-run Casa Cayo has classically comfy, timber-beamed accommodation, with recently modernised bathrooms; several rooms look down on the burbling river below. You'll eat well in the **restaurant** (mains €9-19; ⌚1-4pm & 8-11pm Apr–late Dec), which is particularly strong on local meat dishes.

★**La Casa de las Chimeneas** APARTMENT €€
(☎648 531594, 942 73 63 00; www.lacasadelaschimeneas.es; Plaza Mayor, Tudes; 1-bedroom apt €66-116, 2-bedroom apt €99-170; P@📶🏊) In a pretty hillside hamlet 9km south of Potes stands this old farmstead converted into eight exquisitely comfy, well-equipped and characterful apartments, most on two or three levels. Each follows its own theme, detailed by beautifully intricate, medieval-inspired murals. Enjoy the curved infinity pool and fabulous Picos panoramas – and good food at the equally original **Taberna del Inglés** (☎942 73 61 19; mains €6-17; ⌚12.30pm-midnight Easter-Sep, 12.30pm-midnight Fri-Sun Oct-Dec) across the street.

**Posada San Pelayo** HOTEL €€
(☎942 73 32 10; www.posadasanpelayo.com; San Pelayo; s €50-60, d €70-90; ⌚Mar-Dec; P📶🏊) A welcoming, family-run rural hotel of recent construction in traditional country style, in a pretty hamlet 5km west of Potes. Spacious modern-rustic rooms are decorated in cheerful, earthy colours; there are plenty of cosy common areas, and a gorgeous garden and pool with exquisite mountain views. Breakfast (€8) is a good buffet.

**La Soldrería** INTERNATIONAL €€
(☎942 73 81 22; www.facebook.com/lasoldreria; Calle El Sol 13, Potes; mains €12-22; ⌚1-3.45pm & 8-11.30pm Wed-Mon) Lively, tavern-like La Soldrería is blessed with several diverse spaces: the back patio is a brilliant place to kick back on a sunny day, sipping local cider and sampling the half-Cantabrian, half-international menu. Specialities include veggie couscous, cider-simmered scallops, grilled mushrooms, teriyaki tenderloin and spinach-and-Picón-cheese croquettes.

### ℹ Information

**Centro de Visitantes Sotama** (☎942 73 05 55; Avenida Luis Cuevas 2A, Tama; ⌚9am-6pm) Has info on Picos de Europa hiking routes (including in English) and excellent displays on wildlife, history and geology. Beside the N621, 4km north of Potes.

**Oficina de Turismo** (☎942 73 81 26; www.ayuntamientodepotes.es; Calle Independencia, Potes; ⌚10am-2pm & 4-8pm Jun–mid-Sep, 10am-2pm & 4-6pm mid-Sep–May) In the deconsecrated 14th-century Iglesia de San Vicente.

### ℹ Getting There & Away

From Santander, **Autobuses Palomera** (☎942 88 06 11; www.autobusespalomera.com) travels via San Vicente de la Barquera, Panes and Lebeña to Potes (€8.50, 2½ hours), and back again, one to three times daily.

## Fuente Dé & Southeastern Picos

ELEV 1078M

A beautiful 23km trip following the Río Deva upstream from Potes, along the winding CA185, leads to tiny Fuente Dé village, set dramatically at the foot of the stark southern wall of the Picos' Macizo Central. The ridiculously popular Teleférico de Fuente Dé cable car whisks people to the top of the cliffs, where walkers and climbers can make their way deeper into the mountains.

## Sights

**★Teleférico de Fuente Dé** CABLE CAR
(☎942 73 66 10; www.cantur.com; Fuente Dé; adult/child return €18/7, one way €11/4; ⏱10am-6pm early Feb-Jun & mid-Sep–early Jan, 8am-7pm Jul–mid-Sep, hours may vary; P) In less than four minutes, this spine-tingling cable car whisks visitors up from the valley floor to the top of the 600m-high sheer southern wall of the Picos' central massif – an ascent of 753m in a horizontal distance of just 1.45km. Cable cars depart continually throughout the day, weather permitting. Book online at least 24 hours ahead to avoid queues.

**Mogrovejo** VILLAGE
One of Cantabria's most picturesque villages, tiny Mogrovejo (population 40) hugs a hillside 10km west of Potes. It's well worth a wander, especially in early morning or late afternoon, when its medieval watchtower, 16th-century houses and 17th-century church are vividly illuminated against a stunning Picos de Europa backdrop.

## Activities

There are some fantastic walks starting from the top of the Teleférico de Fuente Dé. Many hotels can organise 4WD trips into the mountains (around €100).

It's an easy 3.5km, one-hour walk from the top of the *teleférico* to the **Hotel Áliva** (☎942 73 09 99; www.cantur.com; s/d/tr €50/80/95; ⏱Jun–mid-Oct), where you'll find refreshments. From the hotel, two 4WD tracks descend into the valley that separates the central massif from its eastern sibling. One heads north to **Sotres** via Vegas de Sotres (about 9km); the other winds 7km south down to **Espinama** on the CA185. Both are two to 2½ hours' walking. The PRPNPE24 'Puertos de Áliva' trail, with contrasting landscapes of stark limestone peaks and lush alpine pastures, starts off along the Hotel Áliva–Espinama track, then branches off about halfway down to return to Fuente Dé (11km, about 3½ hours from the hotel).

A higher-elevation option from the top of the *teleférico* is the PRPNPE23, a route of 5km (one-way) northwest up to the **Collado de Horcados Rojos** pass, which opens up spectacular panoramas (including El Naranjo de Bulnes). Allow four to 4½ hours there and back; you'll ascend and descend about 500m, passing below the challenging climbers' peak Peña Vieja (2613m).

There are also some relatively gentle valley walking trails starting from valley villages such as **Brez** (5km north of Camaleño), Mogrovejo and Espinama.

## Sleeping & Eating

Loads of sleeping and eating options are strung along the valley between Potes and Fuente Dé, with particularly good options in Espinama and Cosgaya, 3.5km and 10km southeast of Fuente Dé, respectively. Fuente Dé itself has a campground and two hotels, including a sprawling *parador*.

**Hostal Remoña** HOSTAL €
(☎943 73 66 05, 652 874500; www.turismoruralremona.es; Espinama; s €45-59, d €55-70, 1-bedroom apt €60-80, 2-bedroom apt €110-130; P 📶) Family-run Remoña provides an on-the-ball welcome and 12 comfortable rooms in white and rich wood tones, with up-to-date bathrooms. Next door are seven roomy, fully equipped apartments. The owners are full of info on hikes and activities, the bar is lively, and the **restaurant** (Espinama; mains €14-23, menú €15; ⏱1.30-4pm & 8.30-10.30pm, closed Wed Oct-Jun) serves excellent home-style, locally sourced fare.

**★Hotel del Oso** HOTEL €€
(☎942 73 30 18; www.hoteldeloso.es; CA185, Cosgaya; s €61-73, d €73-92; ⏱mid-Mar–early Dec; P 📶 🏊) The ever-popular, flower-fringed Oso comprises majestic twin stone houses facing each other across the Río Deva and the road. Spacious, rustic-style rooms with timber floors and floral decor are very inviting, and there's a lovely big pool.

**Vicente Campo** CANTABRIAN €€
(☎942 73 66 58; Espinama; mains €9-21; ⏱1-4pm & 8.30-11pm) In business since 1959 in the heart of tiny Espinama, Vicente Campo prepares honest Cantabrian fare making ample use of the family's own livestock, in a bright new dining room. Dishes range from eggs scrambled with asparagus and prawns to grilled steaks with Tresviso cheese sauce.

## Getting There & Away

From July to mid-September Autobuses Palomera runs one to three buses daily between Potes and Fuente Dé (€2.10, 45 minutes). A taxi from Potes to Fuente Dé costs about €25.

# Wild Spain

Spain is one of Europe's best destinations for watching wildlife. Most of the excitement surrounds three species – the Iberian lynx, the Iberian wolf and the brown bear – but birdwatchers also rave about the twitching possibilities in Spain. Other opportunities include whale-watching off the south coast, especially from Tarifa, and Europe's only primate, the Barbary macaque, in Gibraltar.

## Iberian Lynx

The beautiful *lince ibérico* (Iberian lynx), one of the most endangered wild cat species on Earth, once inhabited large areas of the peninsula, but numbers fell below 100 at the beginning of the 21st century. A captive-breeding program and the reintroduction of captive-bred lynx into the wild have seen the wild population approach 700 individuals, with a further 150 in captivity.

Andalucía boasts the two largest wild lynx populations: in the Parque Nacional de Doñana (with nearly 100 lynxes); and the Sierra Morena (around 350) spread across the Guadalmellato (northeast of Córdoba), Guarrizas (northeast of Linares) and Andújar-Cardeña (north of Andújar) regions. Smaller numbers of lynxes can be found in the Sierra de Toledo, Extremadura and Portugal's Vale do Guadiana.

## Iberian Wolf

Spain's population of *lobo ibérico* (Iberian wolf) has been stable at between 2000 and 2500 for a few years now, up from a low of around 500 in 1970. Though officially protected, wolves are still considered an enemy by many country people and the hunting of wolves is permitted in some areas. The species is found in small populations across the north, including

**1.** Brown bear **2.** Iberian wolf **3.** Iberian lynx

the Picos de Europa. But Europe's densest and most easily accessible wild wolf population is in the Sierra de la Culebra, close to Zamora. Riaño, close to León, is another possibility.

## Brown Bear

The charismatic *oso pardo* (brown bear) inhabits the Cordillera Cantábrica (in Cantabria, Asturias and northern Castilla y León) with a further, tiny population in the Pyrenees – more than 300 bears survive, spread across the two populations. The last known native Pyrenean bear died in October 2010. The current population, which is on the rise thanks to intensive conservation measures, is entirely made up of introduced bears from Slovenia and their offspring.

The best place to see brown bears in the wild is the Parque Natural de Somiedo in southwestern Asturias. There is also a small chance of seeing bears in the Picos de Europa. A bear enclosure and breeding facility at Senda del Oso, also in Asturias, offers a good chance to get a little closer.

## Tour Operators

In addition to numerous local operators, the following outfits run recommended wildlife-watching tours:

**Iberian Wildlife** (www.iberianwildlife.com)

**Julian Sykes Wildlife Holidays** (www.juliansykeswildlife.com)

**Nature Trek** (www.naturetrek.co.uk)

**Wild Wolf Experience** (http://wildwolfexperience.com)

**Wildwatching Spain** (www.wildwatchingspain.com)

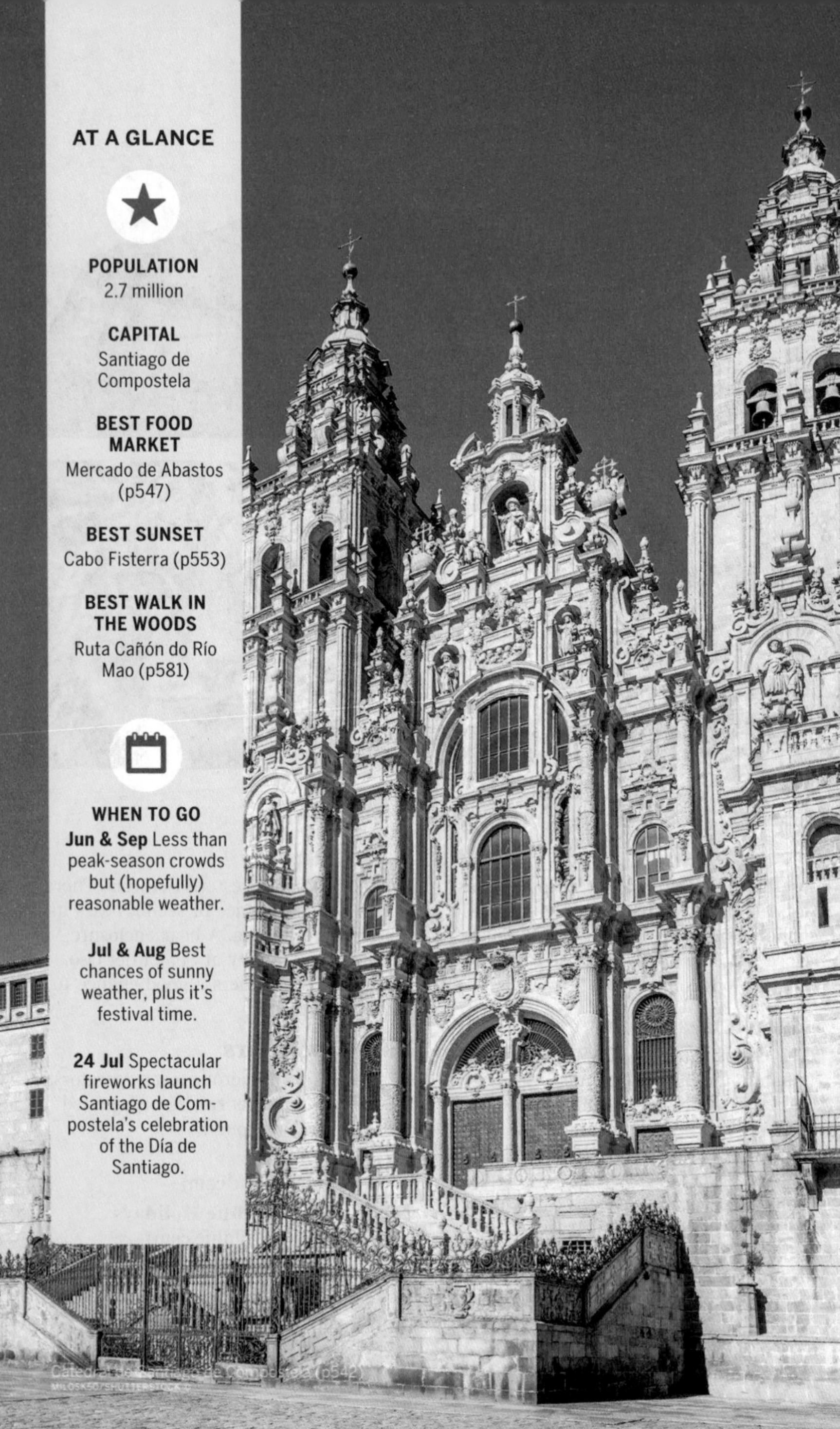

## AT A GLANCE

**POPULATION**
2.7 million

**CAPITAL**
Santiago de Compostela

**BEST FOOD MARKET**
Mercado de Abastos (p547)

**BEST SUNSET**
Cabo Fisterra (p553)

**BEST WALK IN THE WOODS**
Ruta Cañón do Río Mao (p581)

**WHEN TO GO**

**Jun & Sep** Less than peak-season crowds but (hopefully) reasonable weather.

**Jul & Aug** Best chances of sunny weather, plus it's festival time.

**24 Jul** Spectacular fireworks launch Santiago de Compostela's celebration of the Día de Santiago.

Catedral de Santiago de Compostela (p542)

MILOSK50/SHUTTERSTOCK ©

# Santiago de Compostela & Galicia

Galicia, a unique region with its own language and distinctive culture, is home to Santiago de Compostela, the destination of more than 350,000 souls who trek each year along the Camino de Santiago pilgrim trails. Santiago is one of Spain's most beautiful and magical cities, an exceptionally good reason for any traveller to make their way to Spain's northwestern corner.

But Galicia is much more than Santiago. The wild coastline is frayed up and down its 1200km length by majestic *rías* (coastal inlets), and strung with cliffs, beaches, islands and fishing ports. Inland is a labyrinth of deep-green valleys, speckled with stone villages, medieval monasteries and age-old vineyards. And as you travel you'll repeatedly run into reminders of Galicia's unique cultural identity: the sound of bagpipes, the wayside *cruceiros* (carved-stone crosses) and the *castro* fort-villages of Galicians' Celtic ancestors.

**INCLUDES**

## History

Early Galicians built numerous dolmens (megalithic tombs) and Iron Age *castros* (settlements of circular stone huts). Many of these monuments can be visited today. The *castro*-builders are widely reckoned to have been Celts. The Romans took control of the region in the 1st century BCE, founding cities including Lucus Augusti (Lugo).

A Germanic tribe, the Suevi, settled in Galicia in 409 CE, founding the Kingdom of Galicia, which endured, in name at least, until 1834. The supposed grave of Santiago Apóstol (St James the Apostle), discovered about 820 CE at what became Santiago de Compostela, grew into a potent rallying symbol for the Christian Reconquista of Spain. Pilgrims from all over Europe began trekking along the Caminos de Santiago, and the town grew into a key centre of Christendom. Medieval Galicia was absorbed into León and then Castilla, though it experienced independent spells in the 10th and 11th centuries, with northern Portugal closely tied to it in this period.

The two Irmandiño (Brotherhood) revolts of the 15th century, by Galician peasants, city dwellers and lesser nobility against the higher nobility, were among Europe's earliest 'social justice' revolts. The nobility's weakened grip made it easier for Spain's centralising Catholic Monarchs, Isabel and Fernando, to impose their will on Galicia at the end of the century.

In the 19th and 20th centuries, hundreds of thousands of impoverished Galicians departed on transatlantic ships in search of better lives in Latin America. The Rexurdimento, an awakening of Galician identity, surfaced late in the 19th century.

Galicia today is an important fishing, shipbuilding and agricultural region, with more ports than any other EU region. The Camino de Santiago, which had almost died out by the 19th century, has experienced a massive revival since the late 20th century, regaining its popularity of medieval times.

# SANTIAGO DE COMPOSTELA

POP 81,100

The final stop on the epic Camino de Santiago pilgrimage trail, Santiago is a unique city imbued with the aura of a millennium's worth of journeys. Long-gone centuries live on in its arcaded streets and magnificent stone architecture, of which the famous cathedral is the jewel in the crown.

Today over 350,000 Camino pilgrims and many thousands of others venture here each year, giving Santiago a greater international dimension than ever. Yet this is also the capital of the Spanish autonomous region of Galicia, with a strong local character – a place where the skirl of bagpipes wafts across plazas and countless restaurants and bars specialise in fine Galician seafood and local wines. It's hard not to be both wowed and charmed by this city. Even the precipitation has its upside: Santiago is, some feel, at its most beautiful when the stone streets are glistening in the rain.

The biggest numbers of people hit the city in July and August, but Santiago has a busy, festive atmosphere throughout the warmer half of the year.

## History

The faithful believe that Santiago Apóstol (St James the Apostle, one of Jesus' closest disciples) preached in Galicia and, after his execution in Palestine, was brought back by boat and buried here. The tomb was supposedly rediscovered in about 820 CE by a religious hermit, Pelayo, following a guiding star (hence, it's thought, the name Compostela – from Latin *campus stellae,* field of the star). Asturian King Alfonso II had a church erected above the holy remains, pilgrims began journeying to it, and Alfonso III replaced it with a bigger church in the 890s. This was destroyed by the Moorish raider from Córdoba Al-Mansur (Almanzor) in 997, but rapidly rebuilt, and by the 11th century the Camino de Santiago pilgrimage was a European phenomenon, flooding money into the city. The magnificent cathedral we see today was begun in 1075. Bishop Diego Xelmírez obtained archbishopric status for Santiago in 1100 and added numerous churches in the 12th century. The following centuries, however, were marked by squabbling between rival nobles, and the Camino de Santiago began a gradual decline in the 16th century.

The city has been revitalised since the 1980s as capital of the autonomous region of Galicia and a rediscovered tourist and pilgrimage destination.

## Sights

The magnificent cathedral and Praza do Obradoiro are the natural focus for exploring

# Santiago de Compostela & Galicia Highlights

1. **Santiago de Compostela** (p540) Soaking up the city's incomparable atmosphere, history and culture.
2. **Costa da Morte** (p553) Exploring the dramatic capes, lighthouses and beaches north from Cabo Fisterra.
3. **Seafood** (p560) Feasting on freshly caught fish, octopus or shellfish at ports like A Guarda.
4. **Illas Cíes** Sailing out to the pristine beaches and walking trails of these spectacular islands.
5. **Wine** (p567) Savouring fruity white albariño and visiting wineries near Cambados.
6. **Riás Altas** (p564) Gaping at the awe-inspiring coastlines of Spain's northwest tip at the Garita de Herbeira.
7. **Ribeira Sacra** (p581) Meandering around the wineries, monasteries and dramatic canyons of the 'Holy Riverbank'.

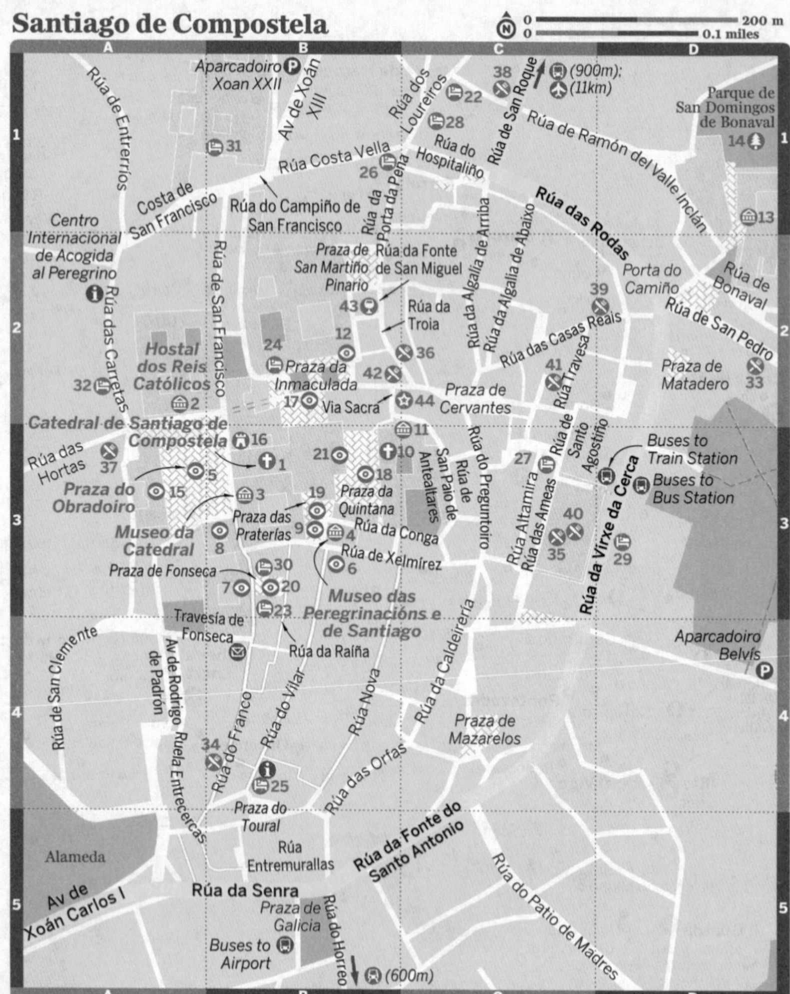




Santiago. The old town in which they sit – a roughly oval-shaped area bounded by the line of the medieval city walls – is where almost everything of interest is found. Its stone-paved streets are a delight to wander, with plenty of cafes, bars and restaurants to drop into as you go.

### ★Catedral de Santiago de Compostela CATHEDRAL

(www.catedraldesantiago.es; Praza do Obradoiro; Pórtico de la Gloria guided tour adult/concession/child €10/8/free; ⏲9am-8pm) The grand heart of Santiago, the cathedral soars above the city in a splendid jumble of spires and sculpture. Built piecemeal over several centuries, its beauty is a mix of an original Romanesque structure (constructed between 1075 and 1211) and later Gothic and baroque flourishes. The tomb of Santiago beneath the main altar is a magnet for all who come here. The cathedral's artistic high point is the Pórtico de la Gloria inside the west entrance, featuring 200 masterly Romanesque sculptures.

Over the centuries the cathedral has suffered considerable wear and tear from water seepage, settlement and humidity. A decade-long restoration programme, which saw parts of the building closed to visitors for

## Santiago de Compostela

**Top Sights**
1 Catedral de Santiago de Compostela ... B3
2 Hostal dos Reis Católicos ... A2
3 Museo da Catedral ... B3
4 Museo das Peregrinacións e de Santiago ... B3
5 Praza do Obradoiro ... A3

**Sights**
6 Casa do Deán ... B3
7 Colexio de Fonseca ... B3
8 Colexio de San Xerome ... B3
9 Fuente de los Caballos ... B3
10 Mosteiro de San Paio de Antealtares ... B3
11 Museo de Arte Sacro ... C3
12 Museo de San Martiño Pinario ... B2
13 Museo do Pobo Galego ... D1
14 Parque de San Domingos de Bonaval ... D1
15 Pazo de Raxoi ... A3
16 Pazo de Xelmírez ... B3
17 Praza da Inmaculada ... B2
18 Praza da Quintana ... B3
19 Praza das Praterías ... B3
20 Praza de Fonseca ... B3
21 Puerta Santa ... B3

**Sleeping**
22 Altaïr Hotel ... C1
23 Casa Celsa-Barbantes ... B3
24 Hospedería San Martín Pinario ... B2
25 Hostal Suso ... B4
26 Hotel Costa Vella ... B1
27 Hotel Pazo de Altamira ... C3
28 Moure Hotel ... C1
29 O Xardín de Julia ... D3
Parador Hostal dos Reis Católicos ... (see 2)
30 Pensión Libredón ... B3
31 San Francisco Hotel Monumento ... B1
32 Santiago Km. 0 ... A2

**Eating**
33 A Moa ... D2
34 A Noiesa ... B4
35 Abastos 2.0 ... C3
36 Bierzo Enxebre ... C2
Café de Altamira ... (see 27)
Café-Jardin Costa Vella ... (see 26)
37 Casa Marcelo ... A3
Cocina María ... (see 40)
38 La Bodeguilla de San Roque ... C1
39 La Flor ... D2
Mariscomanía ... (see 40)
40 Mercado de Abastos ... C3
Nave 5 Abastos ... (see 40)
41 O Curro da Parra ... C2
42 O Filandón ... B2

**Drinking & Nightlife**
43 Pub Atlántico ... B2

**Entertainment**
44 Casa das Crechas ... C2

years, was due to be completed by the end of 2020. The magnificent baroque western facade facing Praza do Obradoiro, and the Pórtico de la Gloria just inside it, are among sections that have been returned to their former glory. Before the restoration works, the main entrance to the cathedral was through this Obradoiro facade, erected in the 18th century to replace the weather-damaged Romanesque one. Today the main entrance is from Praza das Praterías by the southern facade – the only one that conserves its original Romanesque form.

Visits to the artistically unparalleled **Pórtico de la Gloria** (Galician: Porta da Gloria) are limited to 25 people at a time. **Guided visits** of 45 minutes are given several times daily, with tickets sold up to 90 days ahead through the cathedral website or on the same day (if available) at the **Pazo de Xelmírez** (Palacio de Gelmírez; Praza do Obradoiro), the 12th-century bishop's palace adjoining the cathedral, where the tour starts. Book as far ahead as possible. Tours are normally in Spanish but occasionally in English: you can ask at the Pazo on the day of your visit and change your tour time if necessary. Fifteen-minute **unguided visits** happen between 7pm and 8pm Monday to Saturday; 50 general-public tickets (free) for these are given out on a first-come-first-served basis between 7pm and 8pm the day before at the Fundación Catedral office in the **Casa do Deán** (Rúa do Vilar 3). For Monday visits go on Saturday. Take your ID document.

The Pórtico de la Gloria features 200 Romanesque sculptures by Maestro Mateo, who was placed in charge of the cathedral-building programme in the late 12th century. Now with much of their original colour restored, these detailed, inspired and remarkably lifelike sculptures in Galician granite add up to a comprehensive review of major figures and scenes from the Bible. The Old Testament and its prophets (including a famously smiling Daniel) are on the north side, the New Testament, Apostles and Last Judgement on the south, and glory and resurrection are depicted in the central archway.

The main figure in the central archway is a throned, resurrected Christ, surrounded by the four evangelists plus angels and symbols of Jesus' passion. Below Christ's feet is Santiago, and below him Hercules or Samson, holding open the mouths of two lions. Traditionally, visitors arriving in the cathedral said a brief prayer while placing their fingers in five holes above Hercules' head, created by the repetition of this very act by millions of faithful over centuries. On the central pillar's other side is a sculpture believed to represent Maestro Mateo himself. Another tradition called for visitors to bump heads with the maestro to acquire some of his genius. Countless knocks led to Mateo's notably flat nose; he and Hercules are now blocked off by metal barriers.

The three naves of the cathedral's main body are separated by majestic lines of Romanesque arches. Towards the east end of the building rises the fantastically elaborate, Churrigueresque **Altar Mayor** (High Altar). From the right side of the ambulatory (walkway) running round behind the Altar Mayor, a small staircase leads up to a statue of Santiago that has watched over the cathedral since its consecration in 1211. The faithful queue up here to kiss or embrace the statue. From the statue you emerge on the left side, then descend some steps into the **Cripta Apostólica**, where we are assured Santiago's remains lie, inside a large 19th-century silver casket. Behind the Altar Mayor is the **Puerta Santa** (Holy Door), which opens onto Praza da Quintana and is cracked open only in holy years – years when Santiago's feast day, 25 July, falls on a Sunday, and plenary indulgence (forgiveness of all sins) is granted to pilgrims – bringing even bigger numbers of people than usual flooding in Santiago. This happens in 2021 and 2027.

### GALEGO

Most Galicians speak both Spanish (Castilian) and the separate Galician language *(galego)*. Galician is close to Portuguese (which developed out of Galician in the late Middle Ages), and slightly less close to Castilian. We use the place names you're most likely to encounter during your travels. By and large, these are Galician.

A pilgrims' Mass is usually celebrated at the Altar Mayor at noon, and other Masses at least once daily. Check to see if the cathedral's **rooftop tours** resume after the restoration finishes. They offer fabulous views of the city, and of the cathedral's interior from its upper storeys.

**★Museo da Catedral** MUSEUM

(Colección Permanente; www.catedraldesantiago.es; Praza do Obradoiro; adult/concession/child €6/4/free; ⌚9am-8pm Apr-Oct, 10am-8pm Nov-Mar) The Cathedral Museum spreads over four floors and incorporates the cathedral's large 16th-century cloister. You'll see a sizeable section of Maestro Mateo's original carved-stone choir (destroyed in 1604 but pieced back together in 1999), an impressive collection of religious art (including the *botafumeiro*, the cathedral's famous giant censer, in the 2nd-floor library), the lavish 18th-century *sala capitular* (chapter house), a room of tapestries woven from designs by Goya, and the Panteón de Reyes, with tombs of kings of medieval León.

Museum tickets are sold at the entrance and on the cathedral website. Combined tickets with the Pórtico de la Gloria will save you a couple of euros.

**★Museo das Peregrinacións e de Santiago** MUSEUM

(http://museoperegrinacions.xunta.gal; Praza das Praterías; adult/pilgrim & student/senior & child €2.40/1.20/free, Sun & from 2.30pm Sat free; ⌚9.30am-8.30pm Tue-Fri, 11am-7.30pm Sat, 10.15am-2.45pm Sun) The brightly displayed Museum of Pilgrimages and Santiago gives fascinating insights into the phenomenon of Santiago (man, city and pilgrimage), with explanatory material in English as well as Spanish and Galician. Particularly absorbing sections are devoted to the changing image of Santiago the man down the centuries – from apostle and martyr to pilgrim to conquering knight – and to the sequence of buildings on the cathedral site, from Roman mausoleum to cathedral via three smaller medieval churches, with good models and illustrations.

**Museo de San Martiño Pinario** MONASTERY

(www.espacioculturalsmpinario.com; Praza da Inmaculada; adult/student, pilgrim & senior €4/3; ⌚10am-8pm Jun-Oct, 11am-7pm Nov-May) The enormous church of the huge baroque Benedictine monastery of San Martiño Pinario is open to visitors as part of a museum that's

## EXPLORING AROUND THE CATHEDRAL

The Catedral de Santiago de Compostela is surrounded by handsome plazas that invite you to wander through them.

### Praza do Obradoiro

The grand square in front of the cathedral's western facade earned its name (Workshop Sq) from the stonemasons' workshops set up here while the cathedral was being built. It's free of both traffic and cafes, and has a unique, magical atmosphere.

Stretching across the northern end of the plaza, the Renaissance-style **Hostal dos Reis Católicos** (981 58 22 00; www.parador.es; adult/child €3/free, Mon free; noon-2pm & 4-6pm Sun-Fri) was built in the early 16th century by order of the Catholic Monarchs, Isabel and Fernando, as a hostel for exhausted pilgrims. Today it's a *parador* (luxurious state-owned hotel) and shelters well-heeled travellers instead. Its four stately courtyards are open to visitors: the self-guided tour is well worthwhile.

Along the western side of the plaza stretches the elegant 18th-century **Pazo de Raxoi**, now Santiago's city hall. At the south end stands the 17th-century **Colegio de San Xerome** (Mon-Fri, hours vary), a former college for the poor that is now the rectorate of Santiago University. It has a 15th-century Romanesque/Gothic portal that was transferred from the college's earlier site.

### Praza de Fonseca

South of the cathedral, stop in cafe-lined Praza de Fonseca to look into the **Colexio de Fonseca** (Praza de Fonseca; cloister 9am-9pm Mon-Sat, exhibitions 11am-2pm & 5-8pm Mon-Sat) with its beautiful Renaissance courtyard; this was the original seat of Santiago's university (founded in 1495) and now houses the university library. Its Gothic chapel and Salón Artesonado, either side of the entrance, house assorted temporary exhibitions.

### Praza das Praterías

'Silversmiths' Square' is centred on an elegant 1825 fountain, the **Fuente de los Caballos** (Fountain of the Horses), a popular photo op, with the cathedral's Romanesque south portal at the top of the steps.

### Praza da Quintana

Broad Praza da Quintana opens up outside the cathedral's eastern end. The cathedral's Puerta Santa here is opened only in holy years: it's flanked by 24 Romanesque sculptures of biblical figures from the cathedral's original stone choir, created by Maestro Mateo and his team in the late 12th century.

The plaza's east side is lined by the long, stark wall of the **Mosteiro de San Paio de Antealtares** (Praza da Quintana), founded in the 9th century for the monks who looked after Santiago's relics (now a convent). Its **Museo de Arte Sacra** (Vía Sacra 5; €1.50; 10.30am-1.30pm & 4-7pm Mon-Sat, 4-7pm Sun), accessed through the convent church at the top of the plaza steps, contains the Ara (Altar) de Antealtares, a recycled Roman funerary plaque that was used as the original altar raised over those relics.

### Praza da Inmaculada

On the cathedral's north side, this is where most pilgrims arriving in Santiago first set eyes on the cathedral. Opposite looms the huge, austerely baroque **Mosteiro de San Martiño Pinario**, now a seminary.

well worth a visit. The church's centrepiece is its incredibly ornate main altarpiece, encrusted with carved saints, cherubim, flowers, horses and bishops. The walnut choir stalls behind this also merit close inspection.

Upstairs at the church's east end is the 17th-century Coro Lígneo, another set of choir stalls that originally sat in Santiago Cathedral. The monastery, founded in the 10th century, had its heyday in the 16th and 17th centuries, when it was the second biggest in Spain, after San Lorenzo de El Escorial.

**Museo do Pobo Galego** MUSEUM
(Museum of the Galician People; www.museodopobo.gal; Campo de San Domingos de Bonaval; adult/child €3/free, Sun free; 10.30am-2pm & 4-7.30pm Tue-Sat, 11am-2pm Sun) This museum in a former convent is a fascinating window into traditional Galician ways of life, which still persist in some rural areas. Displays range over music, agriculture, architecture, fishing and more, with fishing boats, bagpipes, costumes and antique printing presses. The upper floors are accessed by an extraordinary triple spiral staircase designed by Domingo de Andrade around 1700. Behind the museum, the **Parque de San Domingos de Bonaval** (8am-11pm Apr-Sep, 9am-8pm Oct-Mar) is a lovely, tranquil retreat.

## Festivals & Events

**Fiestas del Apóstol Santiago** RELIGIOUS
(Jul) Two weeks of music, parades and other festivities surround the Día de Santiago (Feast of St James; 25 July), which is simultaneously Galicia's 'national' day. Celebrations peak with a lasers-and-fireworks display, the Fuegos del Apóstol, on Praza do Obradoiro on the night of 24 July.

## Sleeping

From backpacker hostels to chic boutique lodgings and historic luxury hotels, Santiago has hundreds of places to stay at all price levels. Even so, the best-value and most central places can fill up weeks ahead in summer, especially July and August.

★ **Hostal Suso** HOSTAL €
(981 58 66 11; www.hostalsuso.com; Rúa do Vilar 65; r €40-80; @) Stacked above a convenient cafe (with excellent-value breakfasts), friendly, family-run Suso boasts immaculate, thoughtfully designed, bright rooms with up-to-date bathrooms, firm beds and thorough soundproofing.

**Santiago Km. 0** HOSTEL €
(604 029410; www.santiagokm0.es; Rúa das Carretas 11; dm €15-25; closed Dec-Feb) A well-designed, medium-size, centrally located hostel, new in 2018, with cotton sheets in capsule bunks, good clean bathrooms, a bright sitting area and pleasant little garden.

★ **Hotel Costa Vella** BOUTIQUE HOTEL €€
(981 56 95 30; www.costavella.com; Rúa da Porta da Pena 17; s €50-60, d €55-99; @) Tranquil, well-designed rooms (some with *galerías* – typically Galician glassed-in balconies), super-helpful staff and a lovely garden cafe (p548) make this family-run hotel a wonderful choice. It's just 400m from the cathedral; the €6 breakfast is substantial.

**Altaïr Hotel** BOUTIQUE HOTEL €€
(981 55 47 12; www.altairhotel.net; Rúa dos Loureiros 12; s €50-85, d €60-130; closed Jan) The Altaïr combines stone walls and solid oak floors with cosy comfort, attentive staff, soft furnishings and splashes of contemporary design. Breakfast is a gourmet affair.

**O Xardín de Julia** HOTEL €€
(626 004591; www.oxardindejulia.com; Rúa da Virxe da Cerca 20; r €45-90; closed Sun-Thu nights Jan & Feb) 'Julia's Garden' is a delightful little 10-room option on the edge of the old town. Everything is bright and clean-lined, with great mattresses, plenty of wood and stone, and no clutter. The icing on the cake is the lovely strip of garden.

**Moure Hotel** DESIGN HOTEL €€
(981 58 36 37; www.mourehotel.com; Rúa dos Loureiros 6; incl breakfast s €55-85, d €65-140; closed Jan; @) An award-winning conversion of a 19th-century building, the Moure will please anyone who likes a little contemporary design adventure. It's comfortable, friendly and practical, with spacious bathrooms and good beds, as well as being stylishly minimalist in whites, greys and splashes of bright lime green.

**Hotel Pazo de Altamira** BOUTIQUE HOTEL €€
(981 55 85 42; www.pazodealtamira.com; Rúa Altamira 18; r €60-140; closed Sun-Thu nights Jan & Feb; @) The Altamira, a sturdy stone house just steps from the bustling Mercado de Abastos, provides stylish, bright rooms with real wood floors, comfy beds and marble-lined bathrooms. Reception is helpful with Santiago tips, and also here is the good **Café de Altamira** (mains €10-23, lunch menú Mon-Fri €15; 1.30-3.45pm & 8.30-11.15pm, closed Sun night & Wed Nov-Mar), with inventive Galician cuisine.

**Pensión Libredón** HOSTAL €€
(981 57 65 20; www.libredon.com; Praza de Fonseca 5; s €45-65, d €60-85; closed 10 Nov–Mar;

## GALICIA'S TOP FIVE FOOD EXPERIENCES

**Mercado de Abastos** Santiago de Compostela's fascinating food market is piled high with the full bounty of Galicia's seas and countryside, and there are lively eateries and bars right on the spot.

**Albariño and seafood at Cambados** (p568) Galicia's best-known white wine is the perfect pairing to a plate of scallops, cockles, mussels or freshly caught fish in the taverns of albariño's 'capital', Cambados.

**Pulpo á feira** (p572) Galicia's iconic octopus dish: tender tentacle slices with olive oil and paprika, even better when accompanied by *cachelos* (sliced boiled potatoes). Perfect at Pontevedra's Casa Fidel and great almost everywhere.

**Tapas in Lugo** (p585) The tapas zones of A Coruña, Ourense and Pontevedra have legions of fans, but tapas-crawling in Lugo wins our accolade for the animated atmosphere and the fact that almost every door is a bar – and because they give you not just one but two tasty free tapas with every drink.

**Casa Fontequeiroso** (p555) Experience genuine home-cooked Galician local food at this lovable little Costa da Morte hotel, where owner Mari Carmen creates superb fresh dinners daily, preparing traditional Galician country meals from local, organic ingredients.

) Snug but thoughtfully designed rooms just steps from the cathedral.

**Hospedería San Martín Pinario** MONASTERY €€
(Seminario Mayor; 981 56 02 82; www.sanmartinpinario.eu; Praza da Inmaculada 3; s/d incl breakfast €50/70, 'pilgrim' rooms €25/40; ) This 127-room establishment offers the experience of staying inside part of a centuries-old monastery, now converted to a hotel. Rooms are small and spartan in decor but spotless, with comfy beds and glassed-in showers. The more basic 'pilgrim' rooms can only be reserved by email, telephone or in person.

**Casa Celsa-Barbantes** HOSTAL €€
(981 58 32 71; www.casacelsa.com; Rúa do Franco 3; s €36-62, d €42-94; Easter–mid-Dec; ) A well-run, well-kept, central *hostal* with cheerful art and tea/coffee-makers in rooms. The three superior corner rooms overlooking Praza de Fonseca are best.

**★San Francisco Hotel Monumento** HISTORIC HOTEL €€€
(981 58 16 34; www.sanfranciscohm.com; Campillo de San Francisco 3; incl breakfast s €105-138, d €154-334; ) The three cloister-courtyards and low-lit hallways recall the hotel's former life as a Franciscan monastery. But the rooms are large and all about contemporary comfort, and there's a great indoor pool as well as a huge grassy garden, cafe, and good restaurant.

**Parador Hostal dos Reis Católicos** HISTORIC HOTEL €€€
(981 58 22 00; www.parador.es; Praza do Obradoiro 1; incl breakfast s €145-251, d €167-272; ) Opened in 1509 as a pilgrims' hostel, with a claim to be the world's oldest hotel, this palatial *parador* is one of Santiago's major monuments. Even standard rooms are grand, with wooden floors, original art and good-sized bathrooms with big glass showers. Some have four-poster beds.

## Eating

Central Santiago is packed with eateries and there are good options for most palates and budgets, from cheap *menús del día* to gastronomic fusion. Busy Rúa do Franco is end-to-end restaurants and bars but the most appetising options are mainly scattered elsewhere. Don't leave without trying a *tarta de Santiago,* the city's famed almond cake.

**★Mercado de Abastos** MARKET €
(www.mercadodeabastosdesantiago.com; Rúa das Ameas 5-8; 8am-2pm Mon-Sat) Santiago's food market is a fascinating, always lively scene. It's very clean, with masses of fresh produce from the seas and countryside displayed at 300-odd stalls. Saturday is particularly festive, with Galician folk musicians sometimes playing in the surrounding bars. Stock up on *tetilla* cheese, cured meats, sausage, fruit, *empanada* (pastry pie) or the terrific homemade, take-away dishes of

**Cocina María** (www.cocinamaria.es; Nave 1, Posto C61; items €1.50-15; ⏲9.30am-3pm Mon-Sat) for a picnic.

Bars and restaurants line the street outside, but there are also good options within the market itself, especially **Nave 5 Abastos** (www.facebook.com/nave5abastos; Nave 5; dishes €4-16; ⏲11.30am-4.30pm Mon-Sat), where chefs in Aisle 5 cook up top-class fresh seafood and fish, *filloas* (Galician crêpes), Mexican tacos and more, and you sit at long tables or stools to enjoy it. Drinks too, at equally reasonable prices. Also in Nave 5, popular **Mariscomanía** (Nave 5, Posto 81; ⏲9am-3pm Tue-Sat) will, for €5 per person, cook up seafood or meat that you buy elsewhere in the market (though they don't do octopus or fish). Around the outside of the buildings you'll find stallholders selling the produce of their orchards or veggie gardens.

**★Café-Jardin Costa Vella** CAFE €

(www.costavella.com; Rúa da Porta da Pena 17; breakfast €2.90-6.15; ⏲8am-11pm; ) The garden cafe of Hotel Costa Vella (p546) is the most delightful spot for breakfast (or a drink later in the day), with its fountain, scattering of statuary and flowering fruit trees. If the weather takes a rainy turn, you can still enjoy it from the glass pavilion or the *galería*.

**La Flor** FUSION €

(Rúa das Casas Reais 25; dishes €8-11; ⏲10am-12.30am or later Mon-Sat, from noon Sun, kitchen 1.30-4pm & 8-11.45pm; ) La Flor is a buzzy bar for evening drinks (with free tapas), but also a place to enjoy an eclectic range of not-too-heavy dishes from Mexican *enchiladas* and homemade burgers to varied salads and vegetarian dishes – all amid a unique melange of art, *objets* and hanging lamps.

### BRING YOUR UMBRELLA

Swept by one rainy Atlantic front after another, Galicia has, overall, twice as much rain as the Spanish national average. Galicians have more than 100 words to describe different nuances of precipitation, from *babuxa* (a species of drizzle) to *xistra* (a type of shower) to *treboada* (a thunderstorm). Fortunately, you're never far from an umbrella shop in any Galician town: just ask for the nearest *paragüería* (par-ag-wer-ee-ah).

**O Filandón** TAPAS €

(Rúa Acibechería 6; medias raciones €10-12; ⏲1-4pm & 8pm-1am Mon-Sat) Squeeze past the cheese-shop counter into the thin, cellar-like bar area behind, where you'll receive exceedingly generous free *pinchos* (snacks) with drinks, and can order *empanadas* or plates of ham, cured meats or cheese. Thousands of words of wisdom scribbled by clients are pinned to the walls.

**★A Moa** GALICIAN €€

(☎981 07 18 18; www.amoa32.com; Rúa de San Pedro 32; mains €15-18, tapas €3-7, lunch menú Tue-Fri €10-15; ⏲1-4pm & 8pm-midnight Tue-Sat, 1-4pm Sun; ) A Moa produces a great mix of trad Galician and more international fare in its street-level wine bar and stone-walled downstairs restaurant opening onto a verdant garden area. Starters and tapas range over octopus croquettes, a great lemony ceviche, falafel and vegetarian salads. Main dishes are mostly a little more conventional: roast lamb, BBQ pork ribs, fish of the day.

It's all great, and enhanced by service which manages to be efficient, friendly and relaxed all at the same time.

**★Abastos 2.0** GALICIAN €€

(☎654 015937; www.abastoscompostela.com; Rúa das Ameas; dishes €7-15, menú from €30; ⏲noon-3.30pm & 8-11pm Mon-Sat) This incredibly popular marketside eatery offers delicious, mainly seafood-focused dishes concocted daily from the market's offerings. Inside is one 12-seat table (the 'Barra') with a daily-changing menu served in five sittings. Outside are streetside tables where they serve small to medium-size individual dishes. Opposite is the marginally more conventional dining room (open from 1.30pm), with a five-course *menú* for €30 plus drinks.

**O Curro da Parra** FUSION €€

(www.ocurrodaparra.com; Rúa do Curro da Parra 7; mains €17-23, starters & medias raciones €5-15; ⏲1.30-3.30pm & 8.30-11.30pm Tue-Sun; ) With a neat stone-walled dining room upstairs and a narrow food-and-wine bar below, Curro da Parra serves thoughtfully created, market-fresh fare, changing weekly. Everything is delicious; typical offerings might include seabream ceviche or beef tenderloin with wild mushrooms and sweet potato. The cheesecake is a favourite.

**La Bodeguilla de San Roque** SPANISH €€

(☎981 56 43 79; www.labodeguilla.gal; Rúa de San Roque 13; raciones & mains €5-18; ⏲9am-12.30am

### PIPERS & FIDDLERS

Galician folk music has much in common with Celtic traditions in Brittany, Ireland and Scotland, and the haunting sounds of the *gaita* (bagpipe), violin, *bombo* (a big drum), flutes and the extraordinary *zanfona* (a vaguely accordion-like combined wind and string instrument) provide the soundtrack to many moments here.

The most sure-fire spot for hearing a Galician piper is the passageway between Praza da Inmaculada and Praza do Obradoiro in Santiago de Compostela, a day-long haunt of local folk buskers. The best place to catch a live group on a regular basis is Santiago's Casa das Crechas. Several Celtic music festivals liven up the summer months. Biggest and best is the four-day **Festival Ortigueira** (www.festivaldeortigueira.com) at Ortigueira in the Rías Altas in mid-July, with bands and musicians from several countries and tens of thousands of music lovers. Also worth seeking out are the **Festival Intercéltico do Morrazo** (www.facebook.com/festivalintercelticomorrazo) at Moaña (Ría de Vigo) over a weekend in July or August, and the **Festa da Carballeira** (www.festadacarballeira.com), on the first weekend of August at Zas.

Leading *gaiteros* (bagpipers) and other folkies are popular heroes in Galicia. If you fancy tuning into this soulful, quintessentially Galician scene, look for gigs by piper and multi-instrumentalist Carlos Núñez, pipers Xosé Manuel Budiño or Susana Seivane, violinist Begoña Riobó, piper and singer Mercedes Peón, singer Uxía, harpist and *zanfona*-player Roi Casal, or groups Luar Na Lubre or Milladoiro.

Mon-Fri, 9am-4pm & 7pm-12.30am Sat & Sun) An amiable two-storey restaurant and wine bar on the edge of the old town, the Bodeguilla serves an eclectic range of appetising dishes, from sautéed octopus and prawns or Galician beef sirloin in port, to vegetarian salads or plates of cheeses, sausages or ham. The kitchen opens for dinner at 8.15pm.

**Bierzo Enxebre** SPANISH €€
(Rúa da Troia 10; raciones & mains €9-18; ⏲1-4pm & 8-11.30pm; 📶) This reliable spot focuses on hearty portions of good grilled and cured meats, fish, and *revueltos* (scrambled-egg dishes). There are salads, *parrilladas de verduras* (plates of grilled vegetables) and cheeses too.

**A Noiesa** GALICIAN €€
(☎881 30 72 38; Rúa do Franco 48; mains €10-23; ⏲7.30pm-midnight Wed, 12.30-5pm & 7.30pm-midnight Thu-Mon) Popular with locals and visitors alike, bright A Noiesa rises above the Rúa do Franco competition with excellent seafood, steaks and rice dishes, and helpful service even when staff are run off their feet. Try to get there early, or reserve.

**Casa Marcelo** FUSION €€€
(☎981 55 85 80; www.casamarcelo.net; Rúa das Hortas 1; dishes €10-22; ⏲1.30-3.45pm & 8.30-11.45pm Tue-Sat, closed half Feb and half Nov) Take an adventure into Galician-Japanese fusion at Michelin-starred Marcelo, where the thing is to order several small-to-medium-sized sharing dishes – the likes of tuna *temaki*, roast duck with *shimeji* mushrooms, steak tartare or fennel-and-cockles soup. Everything tastes (and looks) great but you'll need to spend a bit to satisfy a hungry appetite. Reservations advised.

## Drinking & Entertainment

On summer evenings every streetside nook in the old town is filled with people relaxing over tapas and drinks. Streets north, south and east of the cathedral have plenty of bars. Santiago's large student population comes out in full force around midnight, Thursday to Saturday.

**Pub Atlántico** BAR
(☎981 57 21 52; Rúa da Fonte de San Miguel 9; ⏲9pm-3am Tue-Thu & Sun, to 4.30am Fri & Sat) This buzzing bar pulls in an artsy crowd with excellent mojitos and gin-tonics, and a great soundtrack ranging from Cajun blues to Spanish indie.

★**Casa das Crechas** LIVE MUSIC
(www.facebook.com/casadascrechas; Vía Sacra 3; ⏲5.30pm-2.30am or later; 📶) There's no better place for Celtic and other live music. Head to the tightly packed downstairs bar at about 10.30pm most Wednesdays from September to May/June for terrific Galician folk sessions with the Banda das Crechas (entry €1.50). There's usually live jazz, folk or flamenco a few other nights each week.

# Camino de Santiago

Dozens of Camino de Santiago pilgrimage routes – long or short, busy or quiet – lead from all points of the Spanish compass, and beyond, to the magnificent cathedral of Santiago de Compostela in Galicia. On any of them, the subtly changing landscapes, the historic architecture, the release from everyday preoccupations and the fellowship of other pilgrims make walking the Camino an experience few travellers ever forget.

2

LUX BLUE/SHUTTERSTOCK ©

3

JUSTIN FOLKES/LONELY PLANET ©

**1. Galician countryside**
Inland Galicia is a labyrinth of deep-green valleys speckled with stone villages, monasteries and age-old vineyards.

**2. Catedral de Santa María, Lugo (p584)**
Lugo lies on the Camino Primitivo, which connects the Camino del Norte from Oviedo with the Camino Francés.

**3. Sarria (p582)**
Those walking just the last 100km of the Camino Francés, the minimum requirement for the official Compostela certificate, start at Sarria.

**4. Scallop shells**
These are the symbol of the Camino.

4

JUSTIN FOLKES/LONELY PLANET ©

## Information

**Centro Internacional de Acogida al Peregrino** (Pilgrim's Reception Office; ☎981 56 88 46; www.oficinadelperegrino.com; Rúa das Carretas 33; ⏰8am-8pm Easter-Oct, 10am-7pm Nov-Easter) People who have covered at least the last 100km of a Camino de Santiago on foot or horseback, or 200km by bicycle, for religious or spiritual reasons or with an 'attitude of search', can obtain their 'Compostella' certificate to prove it here. In busy seasons go early if you want your Compostella the same day; you can get a number then go back later. The website has a lot of useful info for pilgrims.

**Turismo de Santiago** (☎981 55 51 29; www.santiagoturismo.com; Rúa do Vilar 63; ⏰9am-8pm May-Oct, to 7pm Mon-Fri, 9am-2pm & 4-7pm Sat & Sun Nov-Apr) The very efficient city tourist office. Its website is a multilingual mine of information.

## Getting There & Away

### AIR

Santiago's busy **airport** (☎91 321 10 00; www.aena.es; Lavacolla) is 11km east of the city. Direct-flight destinations (some only during variable summer months) include the following:

**Aer Lingus** (www.aerlingus.com) Dublin.

**EasyJet** (www.easyjet.com) Basel-Mulhouse, Geneva, London (Gatwick).

**Iberia** (www.iberia.com) Bilbao, Madrid.

**Lufthansa** (www.lufthansa.com) Frankfurt.

**Ryanair** (www.ryanair.com) Alicante, Barcelona, London (Stansted), Madrid, Málaga, Malta, Milan (Bergamo), Palma de Mallorca, Seville, Valencia.

**Swiss** (www.swiss.com) Zurich.

**TAP Air Portugal** (www.flytap.com) Lisbon.

**Vueling Airlines** (www.vueling.com) Amsterdam, Barcelona, Brussels, Málaga, Palma de Mallorca, Paris (Charles de Gaulle), Zurich.

### BUS

The **bus station** (☎981 54 24 16; Praza de Camilo Díaz Baliño; 📶) is about a 20-minute walk northeast of the city centre. **Monbus** (☎982 29 29 00; www.monbus.es) runs to many places in Galicia; **Empresa Freire** (☎902 80 02 20; www.empresafreire.com) and **ALSA** (☎902 42 22 42; www.alsa.es) operate to Lugo; ALSA and Flixbus (www.flixbus.es) go to Porto (Portugal); ALSA also serves other destinations outside Galicia.

| Destination | Fare (€) | Time (hr) | Minimum Frequency (daily) |
|---|---|---|---|
| A Coruña | 5.05 | 1-1½ | 13 |
| Cambados | 4.35 | 1½ | 2 |
| Ferrol | 7.80 | 1½ | 5 |
| Fisterra | 9.85 | 2¼-3 | 4 |
| León | 31 | 6 | 1 |
| Lugo | 9.40-13 | 1½-2¾ | 11 |
| Madrid | 20-68 | 8¼-9¾ | 4 |
| Muxía | 8 | 1½ | 2 |
| Ourense | 7.60 | 1¾ | 4 |
| Oviedo | 31-44 | 4½-6¾ | 2 |
| Pontevedra | 5 | 1-1½ | 11 |
| Porto | 27-31 | 3½-4½ | 4 |

### TRAIN

The **train station** (www.renfe.com; Rúa do Hórreo) is about a 15-minute walk south from the old town. All trains are run by **Renfe** (☎91 232 03 20; www.renfe.com), which has a **ticket office** (Museo de San Martiño Pinario, Praza da Inmaculada; ⏰10am-2.30pm & 3.30-7.45pm Mon-Fri, 10am-2.45pm Sat) in the old town as well as at the station.

| Destination | Fare (€) | Time | Minimum Frequency (daily) |
|---|---|---|---|
| A Coruña | 6.30-16 | 30min | 20 |
| Madrid | 23-57 | 5¼hr | 2 |
| Ourense | 8.10-20 | 40min | 9 |
| Pontevedra | 6.30-7.60 | 35min-1hr | 15 |

## Getting Around

### TO/FROM THE AIRPORT

Empresa Freire (p552) runs buses to Santiago airport (€3, 45 minutes) from **Praza de Galicia** half-hourly from 6am to midnight, via the train and bus stations. Returning buses leave the airport every half-hour from 7am to 1am. Taxis charge around €21.

### TO/FROM THE TRAIN & BUS STATIONS

City bus 6 runs every 20 to 30 minutes from Rúa do Hórreo near the train station to Rúa da Virxe da Cerca, near the Mercado de Abastos. Going to the station, catch it on the west side of **Rúa da Virxe da Cerca**. Buses 5, P1 and P2 run frequently between the bus station, Rúa da Virxe da Cerca and Praza de Galicia. Going to the bus station, catch them on the **east side of Rúa da Virxe da Cerca**. Tickets cost €1.

### CAR

Private vehicles are barred from the old town. Underground car parks around its fringes mostly charge around €15 per 24 hours. Cheaper are **Aparcadoiro Xoan XXIII** (Avenida de Xoan XXIII;

per 24hr €11; ⏲24hr) and the open-air **Aparcadoiro Belvís** (Rúa das Trompas; per 24hr €7.50; ⏲24hr), both also offering seven-day deals for €30. Many old town lodgings offer small discounts on the underground car parks for guests.

# COSTA DA MORTE

Rocky headlands, winding inlets, small fishing towns, plunging cliffs, sweeping bays and many a remote, sandy beach – this is the eerily beautiful 'Coast of Death', the westernmost outpost of mainland Spain, where mysteries and legends abound. This thinly populated and, for the most part, unspoilt shore runs from Muros, at the mouth of the Ría de Muros y Noia, round to Caión, just before A Coruña. Inland, narrow lanes weave through woodlands between stone hamlets clustered around ancient churches in the folds of undulating hills. The treacherous coast has seen a lot of shipwrecks, and the idyllic landscape can undergo a rapid transformation when ocean mists blow in. Then it's time to settle into a local bar for fresh local seafood and good Galician wines.

## Fisterra & Around

POP 2750

The fishing port of Fisterra (Castilian: Finisterre) has a picturesque harbour, fine views across the Ría de Corcubión, and some beautiful beaches within a few kilometres, but the main reason throngs of people head here is to continue out to Cabo Fisterra. This beautiful, windswept cape has a magnetic appeal as the western edge of Spain (at least in popular imagination – the real westernmost point is Cabo Touriñán, 20km north) and the end point of a popular extension of the Camino de Santiago (86km from Santiago de Compostela).

### Sights & Activities

**★Cabo Fisterra** AREA

(Cabo Finisterre; Ⓟ) Panoramic Cabo Fisterra is a 3.5km drive or walk south of Fisterra town. It's crow cned by a lighthouse, the Faro de Fisterra. Camino de Santiago pilgrims ending their journeys here ritually burn smelly socks, T-shirts and the like on the rocks just past the lighthouse. Many people come for sunset but it's a magnificent spot at any time (unless shrouded in fog or rain). The former lighthouse-keepers' residence is now a comfortable modern hotel (p554), with a good cafe-bar and restaurant.

On the way out from Fisterra you pass the 12th-century **Igrexa de Santa María das Areas**. Some 600m past the church, a track signed 'Conxunto de San Guillermo' heads up the hill to the right, **Monte Facho**. This provides a longer (by 2km to 3km), but even more scenic alternative walking route to the cape, on which you can visit the mysterious **Ermida de San Guillerme** – a ruined medieval chapel and rock shelter which some believe may have been the location of a legendary *ara solis* (altar of the sun) that made Cabo Fisterra a place of pilgrimage long before Christianity arrived. It's also said that childless couples used to come here as recently as the 18th century to try to conceive.

**Praia do Mar de Fora** BEACH

Spectacular Praia do Mar de Fora, on the ocean (western) side of the Fisterra peninsula, is reachable via an 800m walk from the top of town. The scenery is glorious, but with strong winds and waves, the beach is not safe for swimming.

**Cruceros Fisterra** CRUISE

(☎607 198095; www.crucerosfisterra.com; Fisterra harbour; adult/child €12/6, sunset €15/10; ⏲mid-Mar–mid-Oct; 👪) For a view of Cabo Fisterra from the ocean and maybe some dolphin sightings, take a 1½-hour cruise from Fisterra harbour with Cruceros Fisterra. Weather permitting, there are three or more sailings per day.

### Sleeping

There are plenty of places to stay in Fisterra, including many hostels. Some places close for several months each winter.

**Albergue Cabo da Vila** HOSTEL €

(☎981 74 04 54; www.alberguecabodavila.com; Avenida Coruña 13; dm €12, s €30-35, d €40-60; ⏲mid-Mar–mid-Nov; @📶) Cabo da Vila is an especially welcoming hostel, with multilingual owners and 10 private rooms as well as the big 24-bunk dorm with its solid metal bunks partitioned into groups of two and four. Sheets and towel (included) are cotton, and the hostel has laundry facilities (€3/4 for washing/drying), an ample indoor sitting area and a small rear garden. Breakfast €4.

**★Hotel Mar da Ardora** DESIGN HOTEL €€

(☎667 641304; www.hotelmardaardora.com; Rúa Mar de Fora 17; incl breakfast s €75-110, d €85-110; ⏲closed mid-Dec–Jan; Ⓟ@📶🏊) 🍃 This delightful little family-run hotel sits at the top of town, with fantastic westward ocean views from the big windows and terraces of its six rooms. Everything is impeccably contemporary but comfortable, from the cubist architecture to the soothing colour schemes. Downstairs is a good spa and gym with solar-heated pool and Turkish bath.

**O Semáforo de Fisterra** BOUTIQUE HOTEL €€
(981 11 02 10; www.hotelsemaforodefisterra.com; Cabo Fisterra; r incl breakfast €99-290; closed Jan; ) Possibly Spain's most spectacularly located hotel, the former lighthouse-keepers' residence on Cabo Fisterra is a very comfortable seven-room lodging with bright, up-to-date rooms. The good **restaurant** (mains €15-23; 1-4pm & 8-11.30pm) and cafe prepare traditional Galician dishes from local fish and seafood. The views (when not obscured by rain or fog) are unbeatable.

**Hotel Costa da Morte** HOTEL €€
(981 19 25 43; www.hotelcostadamorte.net; Rúa Alcalde Fernández 73; incl breakfast r €59-119, ste €89-160; closed 2nd half Nov; ) This fresh hotel, which opened in 2019, has an airy, contemporary feel, with large, bright, wood-floored accommodation in pine, white and blue. Four of the 12 rooms and one of the two suites enjoy sea views; all have walk-in showers, coffee machines and smart TVs.

## Eating

**O Pirata** SEAFOOD €
(Paseo de Calafigueira; raciones €7-12; noon-5pm Tue-Sun) Overlooking the harbour with just half-a-dozen tables and a short but sweet menu, O Pirata dishes up the freshest of fish and seafood, in deliciously straightforward traditional preparations, at very good prices.

**O' Fragón** GALICIAN €€
(981 74 04 29; www.ofragon.es; San Martiño de Arriba 22; mains €14-22, tasting menus incl wine €40-50; 1.15-3.45pm & 8.15-10.45pm; P) More gastronomically refined than anywhere else in the district, O' Fragón serves beautifully prepared, market-based, mainly fish and seafood dishes in a stylish, picture-windowed dining room in a hillside hamlet 2km north of Fisterra. Service is expertly attentive and the vistas are fabulous. Look for its three-car parking area opposite house No 21 in San Martiño de Arriba.

## Information

**Oficina Municipal de Turismo** (627 239731; www.concellofisterra.com; Praza da Constitución 31; 10.30am-2pm & 3.30-6.30pm Jun-Sep, shorter hours Oct-May)

## Getting There & Away

Monbus (www.monbus.es) runs four to eight daily buses to/from Santiago de Compostela (€9.85, 2¼ to 3¼ hours) and can get you to Muxía with a transfer at Cée (Monday to Friday only). Arriva (www.arriva.gal) runs five daily buses (fewer Saturday and Sunday) to/from A Coruña (€15, 2¼ hours).

Taxis cost €30 to Muxía, €80 to Santiago de Compostela and €5 to Cabo Fisterra (one-way).

# Lires & Around

POP 150

Pretty Lires sits just inland from the coast, above the little Ría de Lires, amid typically green, wooded Costa da Morte countryside. By road it's 12km north of Fisterra and 19km south of Muxía. For walkers it's conveniently about halfway between Fisterra and Muxía on both the 28km Camino de Santiago route and the 51km Camiño dos Faros) route. With wonderful beaches nearby, it's a fine stop even if you're not following any *camino*.

**Praia de Nemiña** BEACH
This beautiful, 1.5km sandy curve, stretching north from the mouth of the Ría de Lires, attracts surfers in numbers from roughly April to November and has a couple of surf schools. The *ría* mouth can be crossed at low tide in summer, but otherwise it's a 2.5km walk (or a roundabout drive of 9km) from Lires village to the beach.

**Praia do Rostro** BEACH
(P) One of Galicia's most spectacular beaches, this broad 2km stretch of unbroken sand begins about 4km south of Lires and is a particularly magnificent sight from the headlands at either end, with the Atlantic surf pouring in. Unfortunately it's not good for swimming, but it's a wonderful walk.

**As Eiras** HOTEL, HOSTEL €
(981 74 81 80; www.ruralaseiras.com; Lires; dm €12, s €35-45, d €45-65; P) As Eiras has both a budget hostel (with solid bunks in four- to nine-person dorms) and a hotel section with well-sized, pastel-toned rooms sporting comfy beds and, in the best, sea-view terraces. It also has a decent, reasonably priced cafe-restaurant, where you can fuel up on varied breakfasts, salads or good seafood and meat dishes.

### CAMIÑO DOS FAROS

There's no better way to experience the essence of the Costa da Morte than to walk along its dramatic coastline. Thanks to what was originally a small local group of friends, who set out in 2012 to find a route as close to the shore as possible, there is now a 200km footpath, the Camiño dos Faros (Way of the Lighthouses; www.caminodosfaros.com), running from Malpica de Bergantiños, 40km west of A Coruña, to Cabo Fisterra in the southwest.

The route is a succession of spectacular vistas, as long sweeping beaches, plunging cliffs, high capes and picturesque fishing villages follow one after another. It's divided into eight one-day stages of between 18km and 32km. This is not a seaside stroll, but more like mountain hiking by the coast. There is a lot of up and down, the terrain is sometimes rough and the path narrow, and the route passes close to cliffs. Approach it with a sense of adventure, strong footwear with good grip, and appropriate caution where necessary. If you're not happy with where you're heading, retrace your steps.

The trail is marked only in the Malpica–Fisterra direction, with little green arrows and markers which are occasionally easy to miss. An upgrade to official GR long-distance footpath status is in the pipeline, which should mean improved trail quality and better route marking – in both directions. Until that's completed, don't try to walk it in the Fisterra–Malpica direction.

The website is a mine of helpful detailed information, including on places to stay and eat, but there isn't always an abundance of these at the end of each stage. Many people enjoy the Camiño dos Faros in day walks covering single stages. It's helpful to download the Wikiloc tracks to consult as you walk.

**★Casa Fontequeiroso** HOTEL €€
(☎617 490851; www.casafontequeiroso.com; Hotel Rural Fontequeiroso, Lugar de Queiroso; s/d incl breakfast Jul-Sep €65/80, Oct-Jun €55/70; P 📶) This restored, century-old stone house, 2km above Praia de Nemiña, is a welcoming and very well-run place to stay, with six thoughtfully designed rooms and a wonderfully tranquil rural situation. Owner Mari Carmen prepares superb dinners (from €20) based around traditional Galician country recipes with local, often organic ingredients.

**LiresCa** PENSION €€
(☎661 464345; www.liresca.com; Lires 31; s €40-90, d €50-90, q €90-130; ⏲Apr-Oct; 📶) Contemporary country-styled LiresCa combines eight bright, spacious, uncluttered rooms with a friendly welcome and an equally bright cafe/restaurant/gallery/terrace where you can enjoy homemade breakfasts (€3.50 to €10), light dishes and drinks and, in the busier seasons, lunch or dinner.

## Muxía & Around

POP 1470

The stone-built fishing village of Muxía, where legend says the Virgin Mary appeared to Santiago (St James), is one destination of the popular Camino de Muxía-Finisterre pilgrim route from Santiago de Compostela. The other is Cabo Fisterra: the branches separate just west of Hospital village, 60km from Santiago and about 25km from both Muxía and Cabo Fisterra. Completing the triangle, a 28km route through woodlands and countryside links Muxía with Fisterra.

A more demanding and adventurous trail from Muxía to Fisterra, the Camiño dos Faros, sticks close to the spectacular coast in a 51km route which visits dramatic capes such as Cabo Touriñán and spectacular beaches.

### Sights

**Santuario da Virxe da Barca** CHURCH
(⏲Mass 7pm Mon-Fri, noon & 7pm Sat & Sun; P) The 18th-century church on the rocky seashore at the north end of town marks the spot where (legend attests) the Virgin Mary arrived in a stone boat and appeared to Santiago (St James) while he was preaching here. A fire on Christmas Day 2013 gutted the church's interior; repairs continue.

Two of the rocks strewn on the foreshore, the **Pedra dos Cadris** and **Pedra d'Abalar**, are, supposedly, the boat's sail and keel.

**★Cabo Touriñán** NATURAL FEATURE
(P) Picturesque rocky, lighthouse-crowned Cabo Touriñán, 17km southwest of Muxía, is great for a breezy walk. The northwest

corner of the cape, Punta de Sualba, is the westernmost point of peninsular Spain (longitude 9°18').

## Sleeping & Eating

**Albergue Arribada** HOSTEL €
(☎981 74 25 16; www.arribadaalbergue.com; Rúa José María del Río 30; dm €15, s/d/tr €40/50/67; @ ) This well-designed, welcoming, modern hostel features two enormous private rooms, four 10-person dorms, and good bathroom, kitchen and laundry facilities. It even has a soothing saltwater foot bath.

**Bela Muxía** HOSTEL €
(☎687 798222; www.belamuxia.com; Rúa da Encarnación 30; dm €12, d €50-60; closed Jan-early Mar; @ ) Stylish Bela Muxía features bright, hotel-standard private rooms with bathroom, plus well-designed spacious dorms with good mattresses, and plenty of showers and toilets. Common areas, including the kitchen and dining area, are spacious, and there are great panoramas from the upper floors.

★**Casa de Trillo** HOTEL €€
(☎634 759557; www.casadetrillo.com; Santa Mariña; incl breakfast s €48-73, d €60-92, apt for 2 people €80-95; closed late Dec–Jan; P @ ) Deep in green Galician countryside about 8km south of Muxía (well signposted along the country lanes), this charming 16th-century manor house has history, cosy rooms, a nice bright dining room overlooking the lovely gardens, and home-grown food. It's a fine base for exploring the area or just relaxing, and the hospitable hosts can answer your every question.

**Lonxa d'Alvaro** GALICIAN €€
(☎981 74 25 01; www.alonxadalvaro.com; Rúa Marina 22; mains €12-21; 11am-4.30pm & 8-11.30pm Fri-Wed) Top-notch fish and shellfish *a la brasa* (chargrilled) and Galician steaks are favourites at this popular port-facing restaurant. Modern black-and-white decor (with a few dangling seagulls) and efficient staff in sailor-stripe shirts set the scene for excellent meals which could also include octopus done half-a-dozen ways, and tasty seafood-stuffed *filloas* (crêpes) to start.

## Getting There & Away

Hefe SL (www.grupoferrin.com) runs two daily buses to/from Santiago de Compostela (€8, 1½ hours). Monbus (www.monbus.es) has three buses to/from Camariñas (€2.15, 30 minutes) Monday to Friday only. Arriva (www.arriva.gal) operates to/from A Coruña (€14, two to three hours) via Camariñas daily (except Saturday in the Muxía–A Coruña direction). You can reach Fisterra with Arriva, Monday to Friday, changing at Cée.

# Camariñas to Camelle: The Ruta Litoral

POP 2500 (CAMARIÑAS)

Camariñas, wrapped around its colourful fishing harbour, is just 4km northeast of Muxía across the Ría de Camariñas, but 24km by road. Fortunately it's a pretty drive, via the inviting **Praia do Lago** and the *hórreo*-studded hamlet **Leis**.

The rugged coast between Camariñas and Camelle, to the northeast, is one of the most beautiful stretches of the Costa da Morte. You can drive or ride along and near it on 24km of partly paved, partly dirt/gravel roads, or walk the blue-signposted **Ruta Litoral de Camariñas** (Sendero Azul), which mostly coincides with the driving route. It's 5km northwest from Camariñas to **Cabo Vilán lighthouse** (with a cafe and an exhibition on shipwrecks and lighthouses) then a further 19km east to Camelle, winding past secluded beaches and weathered rock formations. **Praias da Pedrosa, da Balea and da Reira** are a picturesque set of short sandy strands a couple of kilometres past Cabo Vilán; then there's the **Cementerio dos Ingleses** (English Cemetery; Areal de Trece), the sad burial ground from an 1890 shipwreck that took the lives of 172 British naval cadets. For further information on Camariñas area walking routes, visit the **Oficina de Turismo** (☎981 73 72 04; www.turismocamarinas.net; Rúa Cantón Miguel Feijóo; 10am-2pm & 4-8pm Jul-Sep, 10am-2pm & 3.30-7pm Fri-Tue Oct-Dec) or its website.

Camelle village has no outstanding charm, but it does have two touching mementos of 'Man' (Manfred Gnädinger), a long-time German resident who died in 2002: the open-air **Museo Xardín de Man**, his quirky sculpture garden and hut by the pier, and the **Museo Man de Camelle** (☎981 71 02 24; www.mandecamelle.com; Rúa do Muelle 9, Camelle; adult/child €1/free; 11am-2pm & 5-8pm Tue-Sun mid-Jun–mid-Sep, 11am-2pm & 5-7pm Sat & Sun mid-Sep–mid-Jun; P), with some of his sketchbooks and *objets trouvés*. **Praia de Traba** is a lovely 4km walk east along the coast from Camelle.

### Sleeping & Eating

**Hotel Puerto Arnela** HOTEL €
(981 73 72 40; www.hotelpuertoarnela.com; Plaza del Carmen 20; incl breakfast s €35-45, d €40-60; Mar-Oct; ) A stone manor house facing Camariñas harbour with appealing country-style rooms and a **restaurant** (mains €7-13; 1-3.30pm & 8.45-11pm Mon-Sat, 1-3.30pm Sun Mar-Oct) serving good, uncomplicated shellfish, fish and meat dishes.

★**Lugar do Cotariño** CASA RURAL €€
(639 638634; www.docotarino.com; d incl breakfast €80-120; closed mid-Dec–early Jan; ) This beautifully reconstructed 400-year-old farmstead sits in verdant countryside 1km outside Camariñas. The seven rooms are homey and pretty in perfect country style, the two 'specials' in the main house being especially large and appealing.

### Getting There & Away

Arriva (www.arriva.gal) runs buses to A Coruña (€12 to €14, 1½ to 2¼ hours) at 6.30am Monday to Friday and 6.25pm on Sundays. From A Coruña to Camariñas, there are buses at 3pm Monday to Friday, 3.30pm Saturday, and 2.30pm and 5pm Sunday.

## Laxe & Around

POP 1750

A sweeping bay beach runs right along the waterfront of the fishing port of Laxe, and the 15th-century Gothic church of **Santa María da Atalaia** stands guard over the harbour. Laxe's **tourist office** (981 70 69 65; www.turismolaxe.gal; Avenida Cesáreo Pondal 26; 8am-2pm Mon-Fri) and **seasonal information point** (981 72 83 13; Paseo Marítimo; 10am-2pm & 4-8pm Jul–mid-Sep, 11am-2pm & 5-8pm Wed-Sun mid-Sep–Nov) have information on **walks** in the area, including a 4.6km round trip to the **lighthouse** at the tip of the Insua promontory, north of town (route PRG70), and the 8km (each way) coastal walk west to **Praia de Traba** via the surf beach Praia de Soesto.

Several inviting seafood eateries line up along the main beachfront road, Rúa Rosalía de Castro.

For a fascinating archaeological outing, drive 7km east to As Grelas, then 2.4km south on the AC430 to find the **Castro A Cidá de Borneiro**, a pre-Roman *castro* amid thick woodlands. One kilometre further along the AC430, turn right for 1km to the **Dolmen de Dombate** (9am-9pm Jul–mid-Sep, 9am-2pm & 3-8pm mid-Sep–Jun, free guided tours every 30min 11am-2pm & 4-8pm Jul–mid-Sep, 9am-1.30pm & 3-6pm Fri-Sun mid-Sep–Jun; ) FREE, a large prehistoric tomb dubbed the 'megalithic cathedral of Galicia' – now encased in a protective pavilion.

Laxe is linked to A Coruña by two or more daily direct Arriva (www.arriva.gal) buses (€9.40 to €11, 1½ to 2½ hours).

# RÍAS ALTAS

In few places do land and sea meet in such abrupt beauty. The untamed beaches, towering cliffs and powerful waves of the Rías Altas (Galicia's north coast from A Coruña eastward) are more dramatic, wilder, less touristed and less populated than the Rías Baixas, making an ideal destination for travellers yearning to get off the heavily beaten path. Add the allure of cultured, maritime A Coruña, several lively little fishing ports and the backdrop of a green, farmhouse-studded countryside, and you're in for a travel treat.

## A Coruña

POP 213,500

A Coruña (Castilian: La Coruña) is a port city and beachy hotspot; a busy commercial centre, yet historic and cultured; a proud modern metropolis with a fine food scene and buzzing nightlife – all in all, an intriguing place to discover if you're looking for a less touristic side of Galicia.

The city occupies a particularly contorted corner of the Galician coast. The centre sits on an isthmus straddled by the port on its southeast side and the main ocean beaches on the northwest. An irregularly shaped peninsula extends 2km north out to the World Heritage–listed Roman lighthouse, the Torre de Hércules.

### Sights

★**Torre de Hércules** LIGHTHOUSE
(www.torredeherculesacoruna.com; Avenida Doctor Vázquez Iglesias; adult/child €3/1.50, Mon year-round & Sat Oct-Jun free; 10am-9pm Jun-Sep, to 6pm Oct-May; ) It was actually the Romans who originally built this lighthouse at the windy northern tip of the city, in the 1st century CE – a beacon on the furthest edge of the 'civilised' world. The outer facing of the 59m-high tower was added in 1788–90, but

# A Coruña

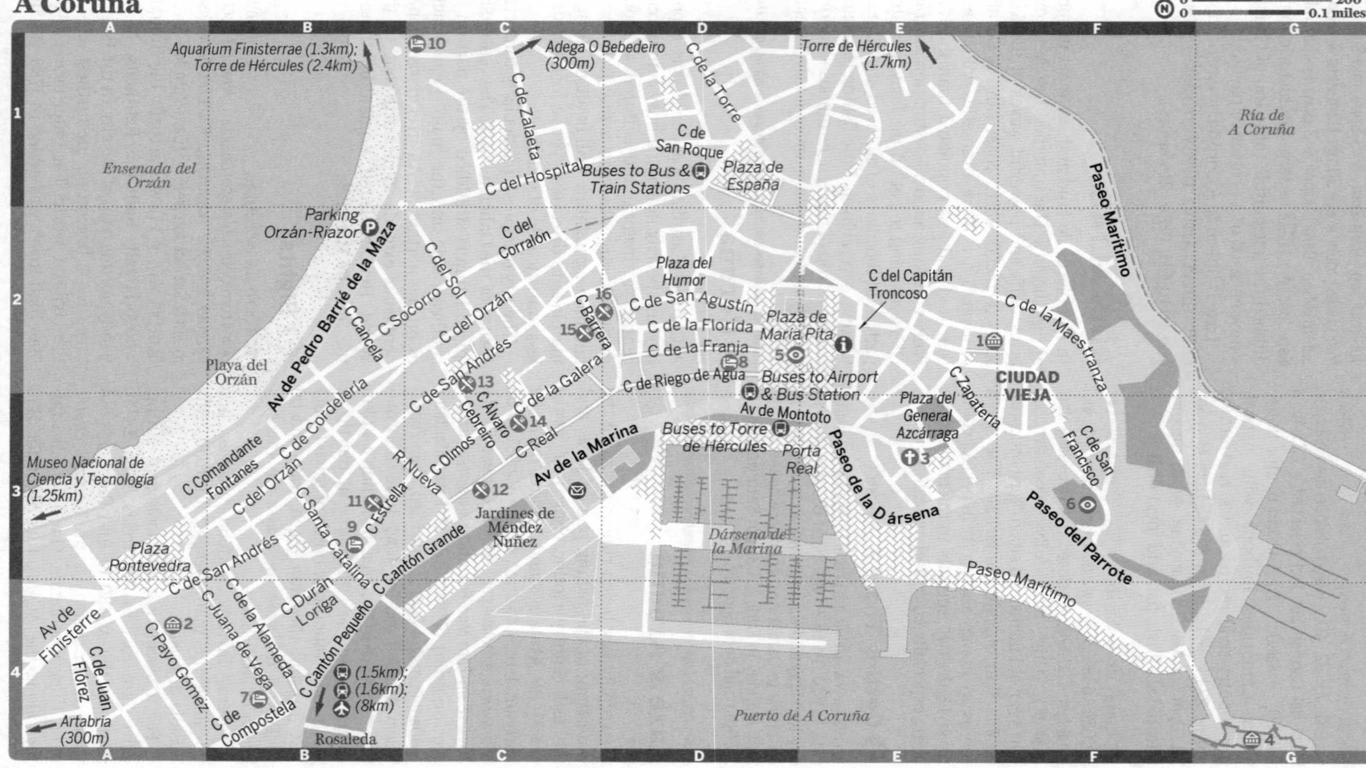

Aquarium Finisterrae (1.3km);
Torre de Hércules (2.4km)
10
Adega O Bebedeiro
(300m)
C de la Torre
Torre de Hércules
(1.7km)
Ría de
A Coruña
C de Zalaeta
C de
San Roque
Ensenada del
Orzán
C del Hospital
Buses to Bus &
Train Stations
Plaza de
España
Paseo Marítimo
Parking
Orzán-Riazor
Av de Pedro Barrié de la Maza
C del
Corralón
C del Sol
Plaza del
Humor
C del Capitán
Troncoso
C Socorro
C del Orzán
16
C Barrera
C de San Agustín
Plaza de
María Pita
C de la Maestranza
C Cancela
15
C de la Florida
C de la Franja
8
5
1
Playa del
Orzán
C de San Andrés
13
C de Riego de Agua
Buses to Airport
& Bus Station
C Zapatería
CIUDAD
VIEJA
C de Cordelería
C Álvaro
Cebreiro
C de la Galera
14
Av de Montoto
Plaza del
General
Azcárraga
C Comandante
Fontanes
C Olmos
C Real
Buses to Torre
de Hércules
Porta
Real
Paseo de la Dársena
3
C de San
Francisco
Museo Nacional de
Ciencia y Tecnología
(1.25km)
R Nueva
Av de la Marina
12
C del Orzán
11
C Estrella
C Santa Catalina
9
Jardines de
Méndez
Núñez
Dársena de
la Marina
6
Paseo del Parrote
Plaza
Pontevedra
C de San Andrés
C Cantón Grande
Paseo Marítimo
Av de
Finisterre
2
C Juana de Vega
C de la Alameda
C Durán
Loriga
C Payo Gómez
C Cantón Pequeño
C de Juan
Flórez
7
(1.5km);
(1.6km);
(8km)
C de
Compostela
Artabria
(300m)
Rosaleda
Puerto de A Coruña
4
200 m
0.1 miles

## A Coruña

**Sights**
1 Casa Museo María Pita ........................E2
2 Casa Museo Picasso ........................ A4
3 Iglesia de Santiago ............................E3
4 Museo Arqueológico e Histórico.......... G4
5 Plaza de María Pita............................ D2
6 Xardín de San Carlos...........................F3

**Sleeping**
7 Blue Coruña Hotel ............................. B4
8 Hostal Alborán................................... D2
9 Lois......................................................B3
10 Meliá María Pita ................................ C1

**Eating**
11 A Mundiña..........................................B3
12 A Mundiña..........................................C3
13 Abarrote..............................................C2
14 Jaleo ...................................................C3
15 O Tarabelo...........................................C2
16 Tasca A Troula.....................................D2

the inside is mostly original Roman. Climb the 200-plus steps for great panoramas over the headland and its outdoor sculpture park. Buses 3 and 5 run here from **Porta Real** near Plaza de María Pita.

**★Museo Nacional de Ciencia y Tecnología** MUSEUM
(www.muncyt.es; Plaza del Museo Nacional 1; ⏲11am-8pm Tue-Sat, to 3pm Sun Jul–mid-Sep, 10am-5pm Tue-Fri, 11am-7pm Sat, to 3pm Sun mid-Sep–Jun; ) FREE Not just for techies, the National Science and Technology Museum will engage everybody. You'll see the first computer used in Spain (a monstrous IBM 650 from 1959), and the entire front section of a Boeing 747. Perhaps most fascinating is the room displaying innovations from every year of the 20th century – a 1965 SEAT 600 (the tiny car that 'got Spain motoring'), a 1994 Sony PlayStation, a 1946 state-of-the-art pencil sharpener and much more.

**Aquarium Finisterrae** AQUARIUM
(981 18 98 42; www.coruna.gal/mc2/es/aquarium-finisterrae; Paseo Marítimo 34; adult/child €10/4; ⏲10am-8pm Jul & Aug, shorter hours rest of year; P) Kids love the seal colony and the underwater Nautilus room (surrounded by sharks and 50 other fish species) at this excellent aquarium on the city's northern headland. The focus is on the marine life of Galicia's coasts and the Atlantic.

**Casa Museo Picasso** MUSEUM
(Calle Payo Gómez 14, 2º; ⏲11am-1.30pm & 6-8pm Tue-Sat, noon-2pm Sun) FREE Pablo Picasso lived in this large apartment from the age of nine to 13 (1891–95), while his father taught art at a nearby school. The apartment is kitted out with period furniture and copies of the many paintings and drawings that Picasso did while here, testament to his precocious talent. Ring the bell to enter.

### Ciudad Vieja

Shady plazas, charming old churches, hilly cobbled lanes and a scattering of cafes and bars fill A Coruña's compact original nucleus, at the southern tip of the northern promontory. Start from stately **Plaza de María Pita** and make your way through the labyrinth to the 16th-century Castillo de San Antón guarding the entrance to the port, now housing the **Museo Arqueológico e Histórico** (981 18 98 50; Paseo Marítimo; adult/child €2/1, Sat free; ⏲10am-9pm Tue-Sat, to 3pm Sun Jul & Aug, to 7.30pm Tue-Sat, to 2.30pm Sun Sep-Jun), ranging over A Coruña's prehistory and history.

Interesting stops en route include the 12th-century **Iglesia de Santiago** (Calle de Santiago; ⏲11.30am-1.30pm & 6.30-7.30pm Mon-Fri, Mass 8pm daily); the **Casa Museo María Pita** (Calle Herrerías 28; ⏲11am-1.30pm & 6-8pm Tue-Sat, noon-2pm Sun) FREE, home of the city heroine who inspired the defeat of English invaders in 1589; and the **Xardín de San Carlos** (Calle de San Francisco; ⏲approx sunrise-sunset), where English general Sir John Moore, killed at the nearby battle of Elviña (1809), lies buried.

## Sleeping

**Hostal Alborán** HOSTAL €
(981 22 65 79; www.hostalalboran.es; Calle de Riego de Agua 14; s €33-50, d €49-75; ) Friendly, efficient Alborán offers 30 appealing, recently modernised rooms of varying sizes. They're well soundproofed with good, up-to-date bathrooms.

**Lois** HOTEL €€
(981 21 22 69; www.loisestrella.com; Calle Estrella 40; s €40-61, d €49-101; ) Little Lois provides comfy, stylish rooms in contemporary greys and whites, smart bathrooms, and its own stone-walled restaurant (breakfast €8).

LOCAL KNOWLEDGE

## GALICIA SHELLFISH TIPS

Galicia overflows with fresh seafood that may well be the best you have ever tasted. Shellfish fans will love the variety of *ameixas* (clams), *mexillons* (mussels), *vieiras* (scallops), *zamburiñas* (small scallops), *berberechos* (cockles) and *navajas* (razor clams). But Galicia's ultimate crustacean delicacy is the much-prized *percebes* (goose barnacles), which bear a disconcerting resemblance to fingernails or claws: you hold the 'claw' end, twist off the other end and eat the soft, succulent bit inside!

Other delicacies include the *bogavante* or *lubrigante*, a type of mini-lobster with two outsized claws, and various crabs, from little *nécoras* and *santiaguiños* to huge *centollos* (spider crabs) and the enormous *buey del mar* ('ox of the sea').

Shellfish in restaurants are often priced by weight: around 250g per person usually makes a fairly large serving. Simple steaming or hotplate-grilling *(a la plancha)* is almost always the best way to prepare shellfish, maybe with a dash of olive oil, garlic and herbs to enhance the natural flavour.

The few singles are a squeeze but the seven doubles are a good size, all with *galerías* (glassed-in balconies).

**Blue Coruña Hotel** BUSINESS HOTEL €€
(881 88 85 55; www.hotelbluecoruna.com; Calle Juana de Vega 7; s €70-130, d €75-175; ) Contemporary-style Blue has every room themed to a different world city. Everything is comfortable and convenient, with stylish bathrooms. Singles are on the small side, and interior rooms can be dingy, but superior doubles are bright and b-i-g.

**Meliá María Pita** HOTEL €€
(981 20 50 00; www.melia.com; Avenida Pedro Barrié de la Maza 3; incl breakfast s €89-171, d €109-208; ) This classy large hotel sports a big, glittery lobby, good eating options including an excellent buffet breakfast, plenty of parking (€20), and spacious rooms in grey, silver and white. Its biggest plus, though, is the glorious beach views from the upper floors.

## Eating

For tapas, *raciones* and wine, hit the streets west of Plaza de María Pita – Calles de la Franja, Barrera, Galera, Olmos and Estrella. Moving westward along these lanes the vibe mutates from old-style *mesones* (eating houses) to contemporary tapas bars. Try narrow **Tasca A Troula** (Calle Barrera 24; tapas from €1.50; 1-3.30pm & 8pm-midnight Mon-Sat), famed for its *cocodrilo* (crocodile), a slice of grilled beef and fried potatoes on a stick; the slightly cave-like **O Tarabelo** (Calle Barrera 15; tapas €1.50-3.50; 1-3.30pm & 8pm-midnight Mon-Sat), with assorted seafood, meat and cheese tapas; and the slightly more refined **Jaleo** (Calle de la Galera 43; tapas from €1.90, raciones & mains €6.50-19; noon-4pm & 7.30pm-midnight Wed-Mon) with tasty options like miniburgers with mustard, or anchovy-and-red-pepper toasts.

★ **Adega O Bebedeiro** GALICIAN €€
(981 21 06 09; www.adegaobebedeiro.com; Calle de Ángel Rebollo 34; mains €14-28; 1-4pm & 8pm-midnight Mon-Sat, 1-4pm Sun) It's on a humble street on the northern headland, but the interior is rustically neat with a conversation-inspiring assortment of Galician bric-a-brac. The cooking is classic home-style with some inventive touches, such as scallop-stuffed sea bass or Galician beef entrecôte with goat's cheese, all in generous quantities. Packed on weekends.

**Artabria** GALICIAN €€
(981 26 96 46; www.restauranteartabria.com; Calle Fernando Macías 28; mains €17-23; 1.30-4pm & 9-11.30pm Tue-Sat, 1.30-4pm Sun-Mon) Artabria marries an artistically bright interior with artistically presented dishes. Happily the tastes live up to the visuals in the inventive preparations of market-fresh Galician ingredients. Top dishes include octopus tempura, Galician beef tenderloin with Roquefort cheese, and the *cestilla de zamburiñas,* a crispy nest of scallops.

**Abarrote** CAFE €€
(www.abarrote.es; Calle San Andrés 53; mains €8-15; 8am-midnight Mon-Fri, 9am-midnight Sat; ) Bringing a global-cafe, blackboard-menu spin to A Coruña's eating scene, Abarrote serves up smoked-salmon focaccia, guacamole, chicken strips with jalapeño sauce,

vegetable-prawn woks, mango and goat's cheese salad, and carrot cake, all in a relaxed, blue-toned setting. Galician wines too.

**A Mundiña** GALICIAN €€€
(☎881 89 93 27; www.amundina.com; Calle Real 77; mains €18-24; ⏲1.30-3.30pm & 8.30-11.30pm Tue-Sat) Daily fresh local fish and shellfish are the top draw at this bright restaurant with arty wood panelling, but there's good Galician meat and a wide choice of wines and cheese too. Mundiña's separate, more casual **taberna** (Calle Estrella 10; raciones €10-20; ⏲1-4pm & 8.30pm-midnight Tue-Sat) is one of the best choices on Calle Estrella, a hub of popular indoor-outdoor bar-restaurants.

## Drinking & Nightlife

A Coruña buzzes with taverns, bars and clubs. Before midnight, head to Plaza de María Pita for low-key drinks or navigate the taverns and tapas bars to its west. From Thursday to Saturday, dozens of bars in the streets behind Playa del Orzán party on until 3am or 4am.

## Information

**Turismo de A Coruña** (☎981 92 30 93; www.turismocoruna.com; Plaza de María Pita; ⏲9am-8.30pm Mon-Fri, 10am-2pm & 4-8pm Sat, 10am-7pm Sun, to 7pm or 7.30pm Nov-Jan) Professional city tourist office, with information in several languages.

## Getting There & Away

### AIR

From **A Coruña airport** (Aeropuerto de Alvedro; ☎91 321 10 00; www.aena.es), 8km south of the city centre, Iberia (www.iberia.com) and Air Europa (www.aireuropa.com) both fly several times daily to Madrid. Vueling Airlines (www.vueling.com) flies daily to London (Heathrow) and Barcelona (three flights daily), and some days to Seville and Bilbao.

### BUS

From the **bus station** (☎981 18 43 35; www.coruna.gal/movilidad/es/medios-de-transporte/autobus/estacion-de-autobuses; Calle de Caballeros 21), 2km south of the city centre, Monbus (www.monbus.es) heads south to Santiago de Compostela (€5.05, one to 1½ hours, 12 or more daily) and beyond. Arriva (www.arriva.gal) serves the Costa da Morte, Ferrol, the Rías Altas, Lugo and Ourense; ALSA (www.alsa.es) heads to Madrid and destinations in Castilla y León, Asturias and beyond.

### TRAIN

The **train station** (Plaza de San Cristóbal) is 2km south of the city centre, from where Renfe (www.renfe.com) runs several direct services.

| Destination | Fare (€) | Time | Frequency (daily) |
|---|---|---|---|
| Ferrol | 6.30-16 | 1¼hr | 5-7 |
| Lugo | 11-22 | 1½-2hr | 3-5 |
| Madrid | 18-58 | 6-11hr | 3 |
| Santiago de Compostela | 6.30-16 | 30-40min | 20-26 |

Trains to the Rías Altas, Asturias, Cantabria and the Basque Country start from Ferrol and are operated by FEVE.

## Getting Around

Blue 'Aeropuerto' buses (€1.50, 30 minutes; www.autoscalpita.es) run to the airport from the central Porta Real, every half-hour from 7.15am to 10.45pm Monday to Friday, returning until 9.45pm. Weekend service is hourly.

City buses cost €1.20 per ride. Bus 5 runs from the train station to Porta Real, and back to the station from Plaza de España. Buses 1 and 1A run from the bus station to Porta Real; returning, take bus 4 from Plaza de España.

The least extortionately priced central car park is **Parking Orzán-Riazor** (Avenida de Pedro Barrié de la Maza; per 24hr €20; ⏲24hr), which stretches for 1.3km below the beachfront road Avenida de Pedro Barrié de la Maza, with several entrances. Hotels usually offer parking discounts of a few euros for guests.

# Betanzos

POP 10,200

Once a thriving estuary port rivalling A Coruña, Betanzos is renowned for its welcoming taverns and well-preserved medieval **old town** that harmoniously combines galleried houses, old-fashioned shops and monumental architecture. Take Rúa Castro up from central Praza Irmáns García Naveira to the handsome Praza da Constitución, flanked by a couple of appealing cafes plus the Romanesque/Gothic **Igrexa de Santiago**, whose main portico was inspired by Compostela's Pórtico de la Gloria. A short stroll northeast, two beautiful Gothic churches, **Santa María do Azougue** and **San Francisco** (Rúa San Francisco; adult/child €2/free; ⏲10-30am-1.30pm & 4.30-7pm Mar-Sep, to 6pm Oct-Feb), stand opposite the municipal market. San Francisco is full of particularly fine carved-stone tombs.

**Hotel Garelos** HOTEL €€

(☎981 77 59 30; www.hotelgarelos.com; Calle Alfonso IX 8; incl breakfast s €55-72, d €66-99; P ❄ 📶) Central Hotel Garelos has spick-and-span rooms with comfy beds, good bathrooms and original watercolours, and the buffet breakfast is good and generous.

**O Pote** GALICIAN €€

(www.mesonopote.com; Travesía do Progreso 9; mains €12-19; ⏲1.30-3.30pm & 8.30-11pm; 📶) One of several inviting taverns on two narrow streets descending from the central plaza, O Pote does a classic *tortilla de Betanzos* (the town's gooey version of the Spanish potato omelette), plus well-prepared octopus and other seafood options.

### ℹ Getting There & Away

Arriva (www.arriva.gal) buses head to/from A Coruña (€2.25, one hour) about half-hourly Monday to Friday and hourly at weekends. Four or more Arriva buses head to Pontedeume (€2.60, 25 minutes), and a few to Ferrol. All buses stop in Praza dos Irmáns García Naveira.

Betanzos Cidade station is northwest of town, across the Río Mendo. At least three trains go daily to/from A Coruña (€4.15, 40 minutes) and at least five to Pontedeume (€2.35, 15 minutes) and Ferrol (€4.15, 40 minutes).

## Pontedeume

POP 4400

Climbing a hillside above the Eume estuary, where fishing boats bob, Pontedeume's old town is an appealing combination of handsome galleried houses, cobbled lanes and occasional open plazas, liberally sprinkled with taverns and tapas bars. The stout, 18m-high **Torreón dos Andrade** (Avenida Torreón; interpretation centre adult/child €2/1, Mon free; ⏲11am-2pm & 4.30-8pm, from 11.30am mid-Sep–mid-Jun) was erected in the late 14th century, probably by Fernán Pérez de Andrade 'O Boo' (the Good), who was made lord of a sizeable chunk of northern Galicia by the Castilian king Enrique II. It contains a worthwhile interpretation centre on the Andrade family, who went on to dominate this area for two centuries, and also houses the local **tourist office** (☎981 43 02 70; www.pontedeume.gal; Torreón dos Andrade; ⏲11am-2pm & 4.30-8pm, from 11.30am mid-Sep–mid-Jun).

There are a few adequate *hostales* in town but the area's most enticing sleeping options are rural hotels, such as Casa do Castelo de Andrade.

## Parque Natural Fragas do Eume

East of Pontedeume, the valley of the Río Eume is home to Europe's best-preserved Atlantic coastal forest, with beautiful deciduous woodlands and rare relict ferns. The 91-sq-km Parque Natural Fragas do Eume (http://galicianaturaleunica.xunta.gal) has a helpful **Centro de Interpretación** (☎981 43 25 28; Carretera DP6902; ⏲9am-2pm & 4-8pm Jun-Sep, 9am-2pm Mon-Fri, 10am-2pm & 4-7pm Sat & Sun Oct-May), 6km from Pontedeume on the DP6902 Caaveiro road. From here the road leads along the thickly forested valley to the beautifully sited **Mosteiro de Caaveiro** FREE, dating back to the 9th century, 8km further east. Walkers can take an off-road path, the **Camiño dos Encomendeiros**, for the final 5km. You can look round the monastery any time; free guided tours are given in some seasons. Over Easter and from late June to early September, the last 6.5km of the road to Caaveiro is closed to cars, but is covered by a free bus service.

With time and a vehicle it's worth venturing to the park's further reaches. A particularly scenic walking route is the 6.5km **Camiño dos Cerqueiros** loop above the Encoro do Eume reservoir.

★**Casa do Castelo de Andrade** HOTEL €€

(☎981 43 38 39; www.casteloandrade.com; Lugar Castelo de Andrade; r €82-130; ⏲closed early Nov-Easter; P 📶) This enchanting rural hotel sits in the hills 7km southeast of Pontedeume, a short drive from the Parque Natural Fragas do Eume. It's a pretty stone farmhouse in enormous grounds, with spacious slate-floored common areas and 10 immaculate, olde-worlde-style, chestnut-floored rooms. The owner is a mine of helpful information about the area. Breakfast €11.

Nearby 14th-century Castillo de Andrade, oversees the area from its hilltop perch.

## Cedeira & Around

POP 4400

The coast north of the naval port of Ferrol is studded with small maritime towns and pretty beaches. Cedeira, a fishing port and low-key resort tucked into a sheltered *ría*, makes a very good base for exploring the Rías Altas. **Ferrol** itself is the western terminus of the FEVE railway along the coast from the Basque Country.

## Sights & Activities

Cedeira's cute, tiny old town sits on the west bank of the little Río Condomiñas, while **Praia da Madalena** fronts the modern, eastern side of town. Around the headland to the south (a 7km drive) is wilder **Praia de Vilarrube**, a long, sandy beach with shallow waters between two river mouths, in a protected area of dunes and wetlands.

**Praia de Pantín** SURFING, WALKING

(🚻) This beach 12km southwest of Cedeira has a great right-hander for surfers. Over a week in late August or early September, it hosts the **Pantín Classic** (⏲Aug/Sep), a qualifying event in the World Surf League (www.worldsurfleague.com). Several surf schools operate here from about late June to early September, charging around €30 per two-hour group class or €110 for five classes.

The schools rent boards and wetsuits (around €20/50 per two hours/day for both) and SUP boards (€20/45) too.

Part of the **Senda das Ondas** walking trail leads 6km southwest from Pantín to the beautiful 3km-long, lagoon-backed **Praia Frouxeira**, which also often has surfing waves – and great coastal views from Punta Frouxeira at its western end.

**Rutas Cedeira** BOATING

(☎722 615382; www.facebook.com/rutascedeira; Puerto de Cedeira; ⏲mid-Jun–mid-Sep) Weather permitting, you can take a scenic 'Ruta Acantilados' boat trip north past the spectacular Herbeira cliffs and Cabo Ortegal as far as Cariño and back (€30 per person, 1¾ hours, adults only) with Rutas Cedeira. The ride can be bumpy. Times vary and a minimum of six people is required.

It also does boat rides and guided kayak trips exploring the Ría de Cedeira, and rent skayaks, SUP boards and bicycles.

**Punta Sarridal Walk** WALKING

For a nice stroll of an hour or two, walk along Cedeira's waterfront to the fishing port, climb up to the 18th-century **Castelo da Concepción** FREE above it, and walk out to Punta Sarridal, overlooking the mouth of the *ría*.

## Sleeping

Cedeira town has a fair supply of *hostales* and small hotels, but two places in Cordobelas, off the main road 1km south, stand out.

**Casa Cordobelas** HOTEL €

(☎981 48 06 07; www.cordobelas.es; Cordobelas; s €44-55, d €55-72, 1-bedroom apt €61-83, 2-bedroom apt €83-110; ⏲closed mid-Dec–early Feb; P 📶) A charming stone-built property run by a friendly family, Casa Cordobelas comprises four century-old, village houses converted into one, with seven comfortable, spacious, rustic-style rooms, and a lovely garden. Breakfast €7.70.

★**Hotel Herbeira** DESIGN HOTEL €€

(☎981 49 21 67; www.hotelherbeira.com; Cordobelas; s €50-105, d €55-135; ⏲closed 20 Dec-12 Jan; P ❄ @ 📶 🏊) As sleek as Galicia gets, welcoming, family-run Herbeira offers 16 large, thoughtfully designed rooms with glassed-in galleries, well-equipped bathrooms and stunning views over the *ría* – a perfect combination of design, comfort and practicality. There's a beautiful pool at the front and a spacious cafe and sitting area for the good breakfasts (€4 to €9).

**Praia Madalena** HOTEL €€

(☎680 856643; info@praiamadalena.es; Rúa do Mariñeiro 6; incl breakfast s €50-105, d €55-130; ❄ 📶) This bright new small hotel is a good option in Cedeira. Most of the 10 medium rooms overlook the *ría* and beach, and bathrooms are smart and well designed.

## Eating

With its own small fishing fleet, Cedeira is a great place to enjoy fresh Galician seafood. Its *percebes* (goose barnacles) are a much-prized (and high-priced) delicacy.

**A Taberna do Jojó** SEAFOOD €€

(Rúa Ferrol 2; raciones €8-18; ⏲11am-4pm & 8-11pm Tue-Sun) For seafood as it should be done – top ingredients prepared with minimal fuss – head to this popular bar-restaurant and order some *berberechos/almejas/calamares a la plancha* (hotplate-grilled cockles/clams/squid), or *pulpo á feira* (octopus slices in olive oil and paprika) or *percebes*. Perfect with a glass of albariño.

## Information

**Tourist Office** (☎981 48 21 87; www.turismo.cedeira.gal; Avenida Castelao 18; ⏲9am-9pm Jun-Sep, shorter hours & closed Sun rest of year) On the main road in the new part of town.

**TOP SIX BREATHTAKING VIEWS**

- Garita de Herbeira (p564)
- Best Bank of the World (p565)
- Monte Faro (p574)
- Monte de Santa Trega (p576)
- Cabo Fisterra (p553)
- Cabo Ortegal (p564)

### Getting There & Away

From the south, you'll need to get to Ferrol, then take a Monbus bus from Praza de España to Cedeira (€1.50, 1¼ hours, eight daily Monday to Friday, three daily Saturday and Sunday). Cedeira's bus station is on Rúa Deportes in the new part of town.

## Cabo Ortegal & Around

The wild, rugged coastline for which the Rías Altas are famous begins in earnest above Cedeira. With your own transport, Galicia's northwestern corner is a spectacular place to explore, with vertigo-inducing cliffs, stunning oceanscapes, and horses roaming free over the hills.

### Sights & Activities

**San Andrés de Teixido** VILLAGE

Busloads of tourists and pilgrims descend on the holy hamlet of San Andrés de Teixido, renowned for its sanctuary of relics of St Andrew, in a fold of the coastal hills a 12km drive north from Cedeira. You can sample the area's famed *percebes* at several cafes (€15 to €20 per half-kilo), and take a scenic ramble along the clifftops from the Chao do Monte viewpoint, 4km up the road towards Cedeira (or a steep 1km walk).

**★ Garita de Herbeira** VIEWPOINT

(P) From San Andrés de Teixido, the DP2205 winds up and across the Serra da Capelada towards Cariño. Six kilometres from San Andrés is the must-see Garita de Herbeira, a naval lookout built in 1805, 615m above sea level and the best place to be awed by southern Europe's highest ocean cliffs.

**★ Cabo Ortegal** VIEWPOINT

(P) Four kilometres north of the workaday fishing town of Cariño looms the mother of Spanish capes, Cabo Ortegal, where the Atlantic Ocean meets the Bay of Biscay. Great stone shafts drop sheer into the ocean from such a height that the waves crashing on the rocks below seem pitifully benign. **Os Tres Aguillóns**, three jagged rocky islets, provide a home to hundreds of marine birds.

On the road from Cariño, you can stop at the Miradoiro Gabeira viewpoint to take the well-marked Senda de San Xiao path to the little **Ermida de San Xiao do Trebo** chapel (1.6km). The path traverses a forest, crosses the Río Soutullo and affords grand views. From the chapel you can rejoin the road and continue 1.5km to Cabo Ortegal.

### Sleeping & Eating

**A Miranda** HOTEL €€

(☎686 466814; www.hotelamiranda.com; Lugar do Barral; r incl breakfast €100-117; ⊙Mar-Oct; P) Five of the six comfortable rooms at this contemporary-style small hotel have balconies looking out over the Ría de Ortigueira. Breakfast is healthy and generous, there's a lounge, and lunch and dinner are available on request. It's 6.5km south of Cariño on the DP6121, then 200m up a side road.

**Muiño das Cañotas** HOTEL €€

(☎698 138588; www.muinodascanotas.es; A Ortigueira 10; r incl breakfast €48-95; P) Charming Muiño das Cañotas, in a pretty little valley just off the DP6121, 2km south of Cariño, has five country-style wood-and-stone rooms in a converted 14th-century watermill. Book ahead for the terrific home-cooked dinners (€13).

**Chiringuito de San Xiao** GALICIAN €€

(☎621 243651; www.facebook.com/sanxiaodotrevo; Lugar San Xiao do Trebo; raciones €6-18; ⊙noon-11.30pm Tue-Sun Easter-Sep, Fri-Sun mid-Oct–Easter) Fish and meat grilled over open coals, and *caldeiradas* (fish or seafood stews) are very good reasons to stop at this friendly little wood-beamed bar, with a dining room and terrace overlooking the ocean, beside the Cariño–Ortegal road, 1.5km before the cape.

### Getting There & Around

Your own wheels are the only practical way of getting around this area.

## Bares Peninsula

The Bares Peninsula is a marvellously scenic spur of land jutting north into the Bay of Biscay, with walking trails, beaches, cliffs and a few delightfully low-key spots to stay over. The road along the peninsula leaves the AC862 road at **O Barqueiro**, a classic fishing village of slate-roofed, white houses cascading down to the port. For an even quieter base, push north to tiny **Porto de Bares**, with a half-moon of sand lapped by the *ría's* waters.

From the lighthouse near the tip of the peninsula, a 400m path follows the spine of a rock outcrop to the **Punta da Estaca de Bares**, Spain's most northerly point, with awe-inspiring cliffs and fabulous panoramas. A few kilometres southwest, enjoy further fantastic vistas from the bench known as the 'Best Bank of the World', at the top of the dramatic **Acantilados de Loiba** cliffs. Little-known beaches such as **Praia do Picón** (P) are strung along the foot of these cliffs.

★ **Best Bank of the World** VIEWPOINT

(P) This bench 400m west of Praia do Picón affords magnificent panoramas along the jagged coast all the way from the Punta da Estaca de Bares to Cabo Ortegal. It has acquired celebrity status under the English name 'Best Bank of the World', thanks to a confusion about the Spanish word *banco*, meaning both bench and bank.

## Sleeping & Eating

**Hostal O Forno** HOSTAL €

(☎981 41 41 24; www.hostaloforno.com; Porto do Barqueiro, O Barqueiro; d €35-55; ⏲Easter-Oct; 📶) Overlooking O Barqueiro harbour, O Forno offers well-kept, medium-sized rooms in blue and white (about half with harbour views), and a restaurant for hotel guests only, serving good local fish and shellfish (mains €9 to €16).

**Semáforo de Bares** HOTEL €€

(☎981 417 147, 699 943 584; www.hotelsemaforodebares.com; Santa María de Bares; r €56-150, ste €220-250; P📶) For a treat, book a room in this maritime-signalling station turned five-room hotel, 3km above Porto de Bares village on a panoramic hilltop. The best rooms are quite indulgent. Breakfast (€10) and dinner (€50) are available for guests. Its cafe-bar opens to the public from July to mid-September, and on Saturday and Sunday in other periods.

**La Marina** SEAFOOD €€

(www.lamarinabares.es; Porto de Bares; mains €8-30; ⏲11-4pm & 8-11pm) With a panoramic dining room overlooking Porto de Bares' beach, La Marina does great seafood paellas plus a host of other maritime and terrestrial fare.

## Getting There & Away

A few daily FEVE trains and Arriva buses, on Ferrol–Viveiro routes, serve O Barqueiro. The trains also stop at Loiba station, 2km from Praia do Picón and the 'Best Bank'.

# Viveiro

POP 7500

Viveiro has a well-preserved historic quarter of stone buildings and stone-paved streets where outward appearances haven't changed very much since the town was rebuilt after a 1540 fire. A 500m-long, 15th-century bridge, the **Puente de la Misericordia**, still carries traffic across the *ría* in front of the old town.

Check out the Gothic **Igrexa de Santiago-San Francisco** (Rúa de Cervantes; ⏲11.30am-1.30pm & 6.30-8pm) and 12th-century Romanesque **Igrexa de Santa María do Campo** (Rúa de Felipe Prieto; ⏲7.30-8.30pm Mon-Sat, 11am-noon Sun), or make the 4km drive up to the **Mirador San Roque** for expansive panoramas.

**Playa de Area** is a fine, 1.2km-long stretch of sand with a semi-built-up backdrop, 5km northeast by the LU862. Five kilometres beyond – by the LUP2610 winding through woodlands or the Camino Natural de la Ruta del Cantábrico walking trail – is the lovely, less-frequented **Praia de Esteiro**, with good waves for beginner (and sometimes more experienced) surfers.

**Viveiro Urban Hotel** HOTEL €€

(☎982 56 21 01; www.urbanviveiro.es; Avenida Navia Castrillón 2; s €66-100, d €77-185; ❄📶) A class above Viveiro's other hotels, this black glass cube overlooking the *ría* boasts large, bright, super-comfortable rooms, with big mirrors, spot lighting and excellent bathrooms. Good catering options too.

**Hotel Ego** HOTEL €€

(☎982 56 09 87; www.hotelego.es; Playa de Area; s €88-110, d €110-165; P❄📶🏊) The classy, contemporary-style Hotel Ego is 5km north of Viveiro on the Ribadeo road, overlooking Playa de Area. Most of its 45 ample, bright rooms have sea views and balconies, and the spa with heated pool is free for guests. The adjacent **Restaurante Nito** (mains €20-40; ⏲1-4pm & 8pm-midnight) is one of the area's best eateries.

## Getting There & Away

From the bus station on the waterfront street Avenida Ramón Canosa, a few Arriva (www.arriva.gal) buses fan out daily to Lugo and Ribadeo and (Monday to Friday only) to A Coruña and Santiago de Compostela.

FEVE trains between Ferrol and Oviedo stop here.

# Ribadeo

POP 6800

This lively port town on the Ría de Ribadeo, which separates Galicia from Asturias, is a sun-seeker magnet in summer. The old town between the central Praza de España and the harbour is an attractive mix of handsome old galleried and stone houses. For a beach you'll have to head out of town, but Praia As Catedrais, 10km west, is one of Spain's most spectacular strands.

An excellent, well-marked walking and bike trail, the Camino Natural de la Ruta del Cantábrico, runs west for over 150km along the coast from Ribadeo. The first 3km, from Praza de España to the **Illa Pancha lighthouse**, make a nice *ría*-side leg stretch. From Illa Pancha, the route continues 17km along a beautiful length of coast to Praia As Catedrais, via more beaches and the fishing village of Rinlo, with good seafood eateries.

**WORTH A TRIP**

### CASTRO DE BAROÑA

The Ría de Muros y Noia, the most northerly of the four main Rías Baixas, is home to a couple of lively old towns, Muros and Noia, and some good beaches on the south shore, where you'll also find Galicia's most spectacularly sited prehistoric settlement, the **Castro de Baroña** (24hr; ) FREE. The *castro* sits poised majestically on a wind-blasted headland overlooking the Atlantic waves, 4km southwest of Porto do Son. Park near Cafe-Bar Castro and take the rocky 600m path down to the ruins. Clearly the exposed location was chosen for its defensive qualities: a moat and two stone walls protect its access across a small isthmus. Inside are the excavated bases of about 20 round stone buildings. The settlement was abandoned in the 1st century.

★ **Praia As Catedrais** BEACH

(Cathedrals Beach; www.ascatedrais.gal; ) This spectacular 1.5km sandy stretch is strung with awesome Gothic-looking rock towers, arches and chambers, sculpted by aeons of sea-water action. Avoid the hour or two either side of high tide when the beach is under water. Such is its popularity that during Semana Santa, July, August, September and some holiday weekends, permits (free from http://ascatedrais.xunta.gal) are required to go down on to the beach. Tickets or receipts from taxis, trains or buses to the beach are also valid for access.

## Sleeping & Eating

There's plenty of accommodation but it fills up fast in July and August.

**Pensión Linares** PENSION €

(982 12 96 33; www.pensionresidencialinares.es; Praza de España 9; incl breakfast s €30-40, d €40-55; ) One of four budget hotels lined up facing the central square, the Linares is endowed with a pleasant cafe and garden-patio and 19 smallish but spotless blue- or magenta-toned rooms.

**Hotel Rolle** HOTEL €€

(982 12 06 70; www.hotelrolle.com; Rúa de Ingeniero Schulz 6; r incl breakfast €60-98; ) The Rolle, two blocks from Praza de España, has spacious, attractive rooms in a rustically modern style, with up-to-date bathrooms. The helpful owner is keen to tell you about things to see and do locally.

**Texturas Galegas** GALICIAN €€

(982 10 74 58; www.texturasgalegas.es; Rúa Antonio Otero 7; mains €12-20; 1.30-4pm & 8.30-11pm Tue-Sat, 1.30-4pm Sun, closed Tue evening Nov-Mar) Enjoy original flavour combinations composed from classic Galician ingredients at this relaxed restaurant-bar in an old-town house. Dishes are nicely presented, and the courtyard is a boon on warm summer days.

## Information

**Tourist Office** (982 12 86 89; www.turismo.ribadeo.gal; Praza de España; 10am-2pm & 4-8pm Jul-Sep, 10am-2pm & 4-7pm Tue-Sat Oct-Jun)

## Getting There & Away

At least four daily buses head to Luarca and Oviedo in Asturias. For Viveiro eight buses run Monday to Friday, but only two on Saturday and Sunday. There's daily service to Lugo and

Santiago de Compostela. The bus station is on Avenida Rosalía de Castro, 500m north of Praza de España.

Multistop FEVE trains operate across Asturias to/from Oviedo (€12, four hours, two daily) and across Galicia to/from Ferrol (€11, three hours, four daily).

# RÍAS BAIXAS

Long, wide beaches and relatively calm (if chilly) waters have made Galicia's four longest *rías* (coastal inlets) – the Rías de Muros y Noia, de Arousa, de Pontevedra and de Vigo – into its most popular holiday destination. The Rías Baixas (Castilian: Rías Bajas) are much more built-up than most other stretches of the Galician coast, which obscures some of their natural beauty. Still, the mix of pretty villages, sandy beaches and wonderful seafood keeps most people happy. Throw in lovely old Pontevedra, the quaint albariño wine capital Cambados and offshore islands like the magnificent Illas Cíes, and you have a tempting travel cocktail.

There's a vast array of accommodation, but it's still a great idea to reserve ahead for the second half of July or August. At other times room prices often dip dramatically.

## Cambados & Around

POP 6800

Capital of albariño wine country, pretty *ría*-side Cambados makes an excellent base for touring the Rías Baixas. Its old streets are lined by stone architecture dotted with inviting taverns and eateries. Cambados is actually a fusion of three medieval villages – Fefiñáns at the north end of town (centred on beautiful Praza de Fefiñáns), Cambados proper in the middle, and the fishing quarter Santo Tomé in the south.

### Sights

You can visit and taste at more than 30 **wineries** in the Salnés zone (Cambados and the surrounding area within about 15km; www.rutadelvinoriasbaixas.com). The best-known wineries are in the countryside, but there are a couple of small, interesting ones in town. Cambados' **tourist office** (986 52 07 86; www.cambados.es; Edificio Exposalnés, Paseo da Calzada; 10am-2pm & 5-8pm Mon-Sat, 10.30am-2pm Sun Jun-Sep, 10am-1.30pm & 4-7pm Mon-Sat, 10.30am-1.30pm Sat Oct-May) has details on all visitable wineries – it's always advisable to reserve or call ahead.

## Rías Baixas

★ **Gil Armada** WINERY
(660 078252; www.bodegagilarmada.com; Praza de Fefiñáns; tours €7-12; tours noon, 12.30pm, 5.30pm, 6.30pm Mon-Sat, 12.30pm Sun Jun-Sep, noon, 12.30pm & 5.30pm Mon-Sat Oct-May) The handsome 17th-century Pazo de Fefiñáns steals the show on visits to the small, family-run winery that's housed in it. The basic one-hour tour (€7) covers the main rooms of the historic house (with some fascinating antiques and art), its distillery and its vast gardens with 150-year-old vines and an ancient woodland. You can add on a one-wine tasting for €3.

**Igrexa de Santa Mariña Dozo** CHURCH
(Rúa do Castro; 24hr) FREE This ruined 15th-century church is now roofless but still has its four semicircular roof arches intact, and is surrounded by a well-kept cemetery with elaborate graves – all very picturesque, and particularly atmospheric when floodlit. The five-minute walk up to the **Mirador de**

**A Pastora** is well worth it for expansive views over the Ría de Arousa.

**Martín Códax** WINERY
(☎986 52 60 40; www.martincodax.com; Rúa Burgáns 91, Vilariño; 3-wine tasting €5-15, tours incl tasting 2/3 wines €10/15; ⌚tours 11am, 11.30am, noon & 6.30pm Tue-Fri, 11am, 11.30am & noon Mon & Sat Jun-Sep, 11am, noon & 5pm Tue-Fri, 11am & noon Sat Oct-Dec & Mar-May; P) Galicia's best-known winery, a large, modern, cooperative operation 2.5km east of Cambados, offers tastings and a variety of tours. It's essential to call ahead or book by email. The 11am tours are in English only.

**Mar de Frades** WINERY
(☎986 68 09 11; www.mardefrades.es; Finca Valiñas, Arosa; tour incl 3-wine tasting €12; ⌚closed Mon & Tue Feb-Mar, Sun-Tue afternoons all year) A young, innovative winery, with eye-catching deep-blue bottles, Mar de Frades offers one-hour tours of its vineyard and modern installations 9km east of Cambados up to three times daily. Book via the website or by phone.

★**Pazo de Rubianes** GARDENS
(☎986 51 95 34; www.pazoderubianes.com; Rúa do Pazo 7, Rubiáns; gardens self-guided without/with wine tasting €7/10, gardens & house guided incl tasting €16; ⌚10am-5pm Mon-Fri, guided visits by reservation 11.30am daily, 5pm or 6pm Thu-Sat) This 18th-century country mansion, 13km northeast of Cambados, is surrounded by wonderful gardens containing 800 flower species, a large albariño vineyard and an amazing 4000 camellia trees. The camellias' gorgeous pink, red and white blooms appear from December to May; late February and early March is the perfect viewing period.

## Festivals & Events

**Festa do Albariño** WINE
(www.fiestadelalbarino.com; ⌚Aug) Concerts, fireworks, exhibitions and prizes for the year's best albariños accompany the consumption of huge quantities of wine and tapas during what's claimed to be Spain's biggest wine festival, on the first Sunday of August and the four preceding days.

## Sleeping

**Hotel O Lagar** HOTEL €
(☎986 52 08 07; www.hotelolagar.com; Rúa Pontevedra 14; incl breakfast s €40-50, d €50-65; P 📶) O Lagar has well-sized, spotless, recently modernised rooms, and a bar-cafe serving good-value *raciones* and *bocadillos*.

★**Quinta de San Amaro** BOUTIQUE HOTEL €€
(☎630 877590; www.quintadesanamaro.com; Rúa San Amaro 6, Meaño; incl breakfast s €95-130, d €110-190; P ❄ 📶 🏊 🐾) A dream base for enjoying the Rías Baixas, unique Quinta de San Amaro sits surrounded by vineyards 12km south of Cambados. With inspired traditional-meets-contemporary design, first-class service and a relaxed atmosphere, it unites 14 different rooms with diverse common spaces, including an inviting pool and lovely gardens.

An important part of the magic is the panoramic **restaurant** (mains €13-21; ⌚1.30-4pm & 8.30-11pm, closed Mon-Thu mid-Oct–Mar), serving delicious updates on traditional Galician cuisine (open to all; reservations recommended). Groups of four or more can do cooking classes (Galician, Mexican, Moroccan...) in a lovely big kitchen for €55 per person, including a full meal based on what you've prepared.

**Pazo A Capitana** HOTEL €€
(☎986 52 05 13; www.pazoacapitana.com; Rúa Sabugueiro 46; incl breakfast s €59-70, d €80-100; ⌚closed mid-Dec–Jan; P ❄ 📶) This 17th-century country house on the edge of Cambados is a lovely option, combining stately rooms, expansive gardens with vines and fruit trees, and a winery with century-old stone presses.

**Hotel Real Cambados** BOUTIQUE HOTEL €€
(☎986 52 44 04; www.hotelrealcambados.com; Rúa Real 8; s €55-90, d €75-125; ❄ 📶) A charmingly renovated central townhouse with eight pretty rooms featuring exposed stone and wallpaper, fresh white linen on soft beds, gleaming bathrooms and homey touches such as ribbon-wrapped towels.

## Eating

Seafood is top of the bill (scallops are a Cambados speciality) and there are endless varieties of albariño to complement it. Pedestrian-friendly Rúas Príncipe and Real have plenty of eateries mostly serving up decent food at decent prices.

**Taberna do Trasno** BRASSERIE €€
(www.atabernadotrasno.com; Rúa Príncipe 12; mains €16-22; ⌚1-3.45pm & 8.45-11.30pm Tue-Sun) The Trasno refreshes Cambados' dining scene with its soothing greenery, relaxed music, and mix of traditional Spanish *a la brasa* dishes with well-done contemporary

### GALICIAN WINES

There's no better partner to Galician food than Galician wines, which have a character all their own. Best known are the fruity whites from the albariño grape, produced in the Rías Baixas Denominación de Origen (DO), located in the Rías Baixas and along the lower Río Miño. Albariño's surge in popularity in recent decades has, to some palates, yielded wines that are *too* sweet and fruity. A good traditional albariño should have the aroma of a green apple and a slightly sour taste.

Inspired by albariño's success, vintners elsewhere in Galicia are expanding and innovating too. Many of the best reds come from the native mencía grape, and winemakers are reviving other native Galician grapes that almost disappeared in the 19th-century phylloxera plague – godello (whites), brancellao and merenzao (reds) and others. Galicians often order wine just by naming the grape: *'un mencía'* or *'un albariño'*...

Galicia's other DOs:

**Ribeira Sacra** In the southeast, yielding rich mencía and other reds, some of them grown on staggeringly steep hillsides above the Río Sil.

**Monterrei** In the warmest, driest part of the southeast, bordering Portugal. Look for Crego e Monaguillo's mencía reds and fruity godello whites.

**Ribeiro** Centred on Ribadavia, Ribeiro produces some good whites, mostly from treixadura grapes.

**Valdeorras** Southeastern region bordering Castilla y León, producing godello whites and mencía and brancellao reds.

and international creations. There's a good wine list – and yes, save room for the desserts.

**Restaurante Ribadomar** GALICIAN €€
(www.ribadomar.es; Rúa Valle Inclán 17; mains €13-25, menús €25-35; ⏰1.30-4pm & 9-11.30pm late Jul-Aug, 1.30-4pm Sun-Thu, 1.30-4pm & 8-11pm Fri & Sat Sep-Jan & mid-Feb–late Jul) For something more upscale than taverns, get a great Galician meal at the family-run Ribadomar, with dishes such as sole with scallops or a *chuletón de ternera* (giant beef chop), in a relatively formal setting with original art.

## ℹ Getting There & Away

The bus station is on Avenida de Galicia, 600m south of Praza de Fefiñáns. Monbus (www.monbus.es) runs to/from Santiago de Compostela (€4.35, 1½ hours) two or three times daily. Auto-cares Rías Baixas (www.autocaresriasbaixas.com) runs to/from Pontevedra (€3.20, one hour) up to nine times daily.

# Illa de Ons

POP 64

In summer you can escape urban civilisation by boating to vehicle-free Illa de Ons at the mouth of the Ría de Pontevedra. Part of the Parque Nacional de las Islas Atlánticas de Galicia, the wild, unspoiled island is 5.6km long with one tiny village, several sandy beaches, cliffs, a lighthouse, scenic viewpoints and four walking circuits of between 1km and 8km. You're unlikely to find it empty, though: up to 1800 visitors are allowed at one time. June and September are more tranquil than July and August.

**Camping Isla de Ons** TENTED CAMP €
(☎986 44 35 30; www.campingisladeons.com; Chan de Pólvora; tent site for 2/4 people €21/35, rentals standard tent for 2/4 €55/85, superior tent €85/130; ⏰Fri-Sun approx mid-Apr–May, daily Jul–mid-Sep; 📶) The well-appointed campground is at Chan de Pólvora, a 1km uphill walk from the boat jetty. It has tents and sleeping gear to rent, including a glamping option of 'superior' tents with beds, bedding, furniture and electric light.

**Casa Acuña** HOSTAL €€
(☎986 44 16 78; www.isladeons.net; r incl breakfast €90-95; ⏰Semana Santa & Jun-Sep; 📶) You can stay in bright, comfortable, pine-panelled rooms in Casa Acuña's several buildings in Ons village. Reservations strongly advised. The restaurant and cafeteria here, normally open daily from Easter to October, serve prize-winning *pulpo á feira*, Galicia's signature octopus dish (€19 per *ración*).

## ℹ Getting There & Away

Three companies, Cruceros Rías Baixas (www.crucerosriasbaixas.com), Naviera Mar de Ons (www.mardeons.com) and Nabia Naviera (www.piratasdenabia.com), sail to Ons from Sanxenxo and/or Portonovo on the north side of the Ría de Pontevedra, and Bueu on the south side of the *ría*. Typically there are several sailings a day from each port at Easter (Thursday to Sunday), on Saturdays and Sundays in June, and daily from late June to mid- or late September. The trip takes 30 to 60 minutes each way; return fares are €12 to €14 for adults, free or €7 for children. Tickets are available online; book ahead. For day visits between mid-March and mid-September, you need a national park authorisation, available free at www.autorizacionillasatlanticas.xunta.gal, before buying boat tickets.

# Combarro

POP 1820

Near Pontevedra on the Ría de Pontevedra's north shore, Combarro has a particularly quaint old quarter that's worth a meal stop. A jumble of *hórreos* (traditional stone grain stores on stilts) stands by the waterside, along with a smattering of restaurants and souvenir shops. Behind is a web of crooked lanes (some hewn directly from the rock bed) dotted with *cruceiros*. Combarro can, however, get extremely busy in high summer.

**Bodega O Bocoi** SEAFOOD €€

(☎986 77 11 42; Rúa do Mar 20; dishes €8-20; ⏲11am-11pm Wed-Mon) You won't beat Bocoi for perfectly prepared fresh seafood – the octopus, hotplate-grilled shellfish and fried fish are all delicious – and the bright dining room overlooks the *ría*.

# Pontevedra

POP 63,000

Pontevedra is an inviting, small riverside city that combines history, culture and style into a lively base for exploring the Rías Baixas. It's a pleasure to wander the narrow, traffic-free, stone-paved streets of the old town, linking more than a dozen plazas and abuzz with shops, markets, cafes, taverns and tapas bars. Back in the 16th century, Pontevedra was Galicia's biggest city and it's claimed that Columbus' flagship, the *Santa María*, was built here.

## Sights

**Museo de Pontevedra** MUSEUM

(☎986 80 41 00; www.museo.depo.gal) FREE Three of the six buildings of Pontevedra's eclectic museum are closed long-term for restoration, but the others are well worth your time. The **Edificio Sarmiento** (Rúa Sarmiento; ⏲10am-9pm Tue-Sat, 11am-2pm Sun), in a renovated 18th-century Jesuit college, houses a particularly absorbing collection encompassing Galician Sargadelos ceramics, modern art, two Romanesque sculptures of Biblical prophets that once stood on the exterior of Santiago de Compostela cathedral, and prehistoric Galician gold jewellery.

The adjoining, recently built **Sexto Edificio** (Rúa de Padre Amoedo; ⏲10am-9pm Tue-Sat, 11am-2pm Sun) has three floors of Galician and Spanish art from the 14th to 20th centuries – some interesting exhibits, though you won't find any really big names. The **Ruínas de San Domingos** (Gran Vía de Montero Ríos; ⏲10am-2pm & 4-7.30pm Tue-Sat, 11am-2pm Sun mid-Mar–Oct) comprise a ruined 14th-century church with an intriguing collection of heraldic shields, sepulchres and other medieval carvings.

**Basílica de Santa María a Maior** CHURCH

(Praza de Alonso de Fonseca; tower €1; ⏲9.30am-1.30pm & 5-9pm, except during Mass, tower closed Thu) Pontevedra's most impressive church is a beautiful, mainly late-Gothic affair, built by Pontevedra's sailors' guild in the 16th century. Busts of Columbus and Hernán Cortés flank the rosette window on the elaborate plateresque western facade.

**Praza da Ferrería** SQUARE

Praza da Ferrería has the best selection of cafes in town and is overlooked by the **Igrexa de San Francisco** (⏲8.30am-12.55pm & 5.15-8.15pm), said to have been founded in the 13th century by St Francis of Assisi. Just off the plaza, you can't miss the curved facade of the **Santuario da Virxe Peregrina** (Praza da Peregrina; ⏲9am-9pm), an 18th-century Portuguese-flavoured caprice with a ground plan in the shape of a scallop shell, symbol of the Camino de Santiago (whose Camino Portugués route passes through Pontevedra).

## Sleeping & Eating

The old town's plazas, and streets like Rúas Real and Princesa, are lined with restaurants and bars doing good-value lunches and evening tapas and *raciones*. **Praza da Leña** is a particularly quaint nook with no less than seven eating and drinking establishments.

## Pontevedra

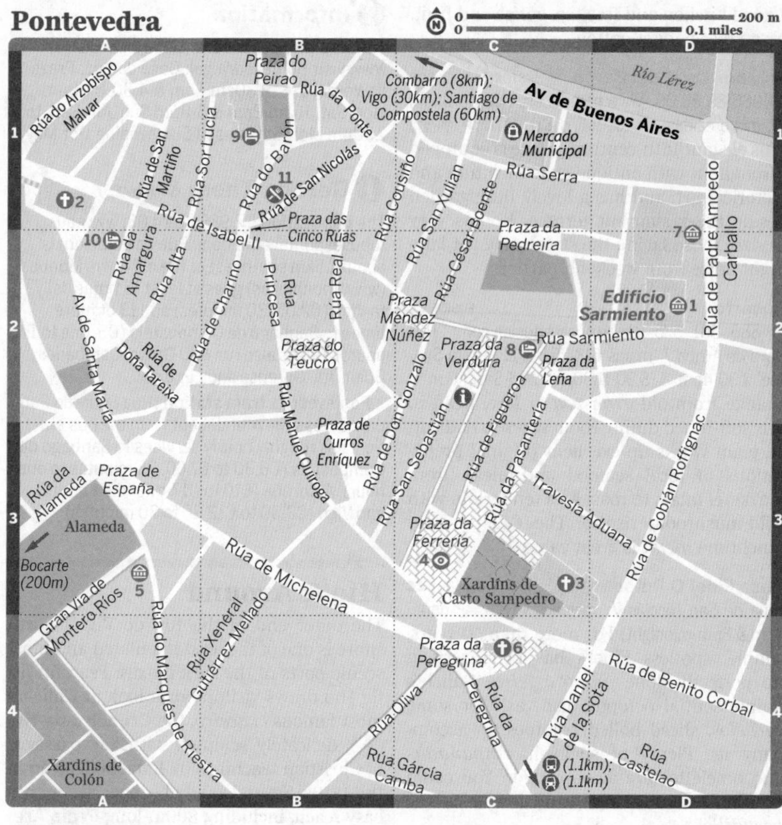


## Pontevedra

**Top Sights**
1 Edificio Sarmiento .......... D2

**Sights**
2 Basílica de Santa María a Maior .......... A1
3 Igrexa de San Francisco .......... C3
4 Praza da Ferrería .......... C3
5 Ruínas de San Domingos .......... A3
6 Santuario da Virxe Peregrina .......... C4
7 Sexto Edificio .......... D2

**Sleeping**
8 Hotel Rúas .......... C2
9 Parador Casa del Barón .......... B1
10 Slow City Hostel .......... A2

**Eating**
11 Casa Fidel O Pulpeiro .......... B1
Restaurante Rúas .......... (see 8)

**Hotel Rúas** HOTEL €
(☎986 84 64 16; www.hotelruas.net; Rúa de Figueroa 35; s €35-44, d €45-62; ❄@📶) The rooms are plain but pleasant, and some have nice plaza views – excellent value for this absolutely central old-town location. Reception is amiable and the hotel has both a good **restaurant** (mains €11-20; ⏰11am-4pm & 8pm-midnight), serving satisfying meat, fish, seafood, salads and egg dishes, and a cafe that is one of the town's most bustling breakfast spots.

**Slow City Hostel** HOSTEL €
(☎631 062896; www.slowcityhostelpontevedra.com; Rúa da Amargura 5; dm/d €18/40; ⏰closed Nov; 📶) Run by a welcoming, well-travelled local couple, Slow City has one spacious dorm with six solid and comfy bunks, and two spotless, all-white private doubles. With

a good kitchen and free tea, coffee and fruit, it's a great budget option.

**Parador Casa del Barón** HISTORIC HOTEL €€€
(☎986 85 58 00; www.parador.es; Rúa do Barón 19; incl breakfast s €101-156, d €117-207; P ❄ ☎) This elegant 16th-century palace is equipped throughout with antique-style furniture and historical art, and has a lovely little garden beside the restaurant terrace. Rooms vary in size; those facing the street may get late-night noise from weekend partiers.

**Bocarte** FUSION €€
(☎886 301 525; www.bocartefusion.com; Rúa Nova de Arriba 7; mains €13-25; ⏰1.30-4pm Sun-Tue, 1.30-4pm & 8.30-11.30pm Wed-Sat) For a change from old-town tavern fare, head to this soft-toned dining room where a dedicated team works up excellent original preparations of local seafood and meat, from mackerel tataki to roast beef tenderloin with wild-mushroom risotto. The €12 weekday lunchtime *menú* is great value.

**Casa Fidel O Pulpeiro** SEAFOOD €€
(Rúa de San Nicolás 7; raciones €6-16; ⏰noon-4pm & 8pm-midnight) For more than 50 years, simple, spotless Fidel's has been serving up perfectly done *pulpo á feira*, Galicia's quintessential octopus dish (ask for some *cachelos*, sliced boiled potatoes, to accompany it). Plenty of shellfish, *empanadas* and omelettes are also on offer. You could even go for an octopus and *tetilla* cheese *bocadillo*!

### PRAIA A LANZADA

The O Grove–Sanxenxo area, at the end of the peninsula separating the Rías de Arousa and Pontevedra, is Galicia's biggest magnet for Spanish summer beach tourism. The towns are not pretty, but there are some fine beaches. You'll find quieter, though in summer by no means deserted, beaches further south around Hío and Bueu. Dune-backed **Praia A Lanzada** sweeps a spectacular 2.3km along the isthmus leading to O Grove. It's Galicia's most splendid stretch of sand, and enticingly natural, but not exactly deserted, as the mammoth car parks attest.

## ℹ Information

**Turismo de Pontevedra** (☎986 09 08 90; www.visit-pontevedra.gal; Casa da Luz, Praza da Verdura; ⏰9.30am-2pm & 4.30-8.30pm Mon-Sat, 10am-2pm & 5-8pm Sun Jun-Sep, to 7.30pm Mon-Sat, closed Sun evening Oct-May)

## ℹ Getting There & Away

The **bus station** (☎986 85 24 08; www.autobusespontevedra.com; Rúa da Estación) is about 1.5km southeast of the old town. Monbus (www.monbus.es) goes at least 15 times daily to Vigo (€2.05, 30 minutes) and 13 or more times to Santiago de Compostela (€5, one to 1½ hours). Buses also run to O Grove, Cambados, Bueu, Tui, Ourense and Lugo.

Pontevedra's **train station** (Rúa Eduardo Pondal), across the roundabout from the bus station, has roughly hourly services to Santiago de Compostela (€6.30 to €7.60, 35 minutes to one hour), A Coruña (€10 to €17, one to 1¾ hours) and Vigo (€3.30 to €12, 15 to 30 minutes).

# Hío & Around

The outer end of the Ría de Vigo's north shore is one of the least populated and most scenic parts of the Rías Baixas. Peaceful little Hío draws visitors for a look at Galicia's most famous *cruceiro*, the **Cruceiro de Hío** (P), delicately sculpted with key passages of Christian teachings by Ignacio Cerviño in the 1870s. Several sandy beaches are within easy reach, including 800m-long **Praia Areabrava**, 3km north of Hío, and beautiful, woodland-backed **Praia da Barra** (clothing optional), stretching east from Cabo de Home.

**★Cabo de Home** AREA
(P) From the hamlet of Donón, 4km west of Hío, the windswept, rocky cape Cabo de Home stretches 2.5km south. It's strung with walking trails and a few driveable tracks, and has three lighthouses, a couple of beaches and great views of the Illas Cíes. The wonderfully panoramic Iron Age *castro* **Berobriga** sits atop Monte Facho nearby: reaching it involves an uphill walk of about 20 minutes, partly along a *castro*-era stone-paved track.

**Hotel Doade** HOTEL €€
(☎986 32 83 02; Rúa Baixada a Rioesteiro, Hío; d incl breakfast €55-120; ⏰closed Nov; P ❄ ☎) Friendly, sparkling clean Doade has eight cosy, spacious rooms with fresh white

linen and wood ceilings, and a top **restaurant** (mains €10-28, menú €10-20; ⏲1-4.30pm & 8.30-11.30pm Tue-Sun, closed Nov) focusing on super-fresh, very local seafood, with oven-baked fish a speciality.

# Vigo

POP 295,000

Depending where you point your lens, Vigo is a historic, cultured city or a gritty industrial port. Home to Europe's largest fishing fleet, this is an axis of commerce in northern Spain. Yet its central areas make for good strolling, and it's the main gateway to the beautiful Illas Cíes. Above all, Vigo is a place whose citizens really know how to enjoy life, especially after dark in the many buzzing tapas bars, restaurants and clubs.

The Casco Vello (Old Town) climbs uphill from the cruise-ship port; the heart of the modern city spreads east from here, with the parklike Praza de Compostela a welcome green space in its midst.

## Sights

At the heart of the intriguingly jumbled lanes of the **Casco Vello** is elegant, lively **Praza da Constitución**, good for a drink in one of its busy cafe-bars. Head down **Rúa dos Cesteiros**, with its quaint wicker shops, and you'll reach the old town's main church, the neoclassical **Concatedral de Santa María** (Colegiata; Praza da Igrexa; ⏲hours variable). Just below here is **Rúa Pescadería** (Rúa das Ostras; oysters per dozen €10-15), famed for its oyster shuckers who set up from 10.30am and 3.30pm: you can sit down to eat their oysters with a drink at one of the restaurants.

**Parque do Castro** PARK

(👪) Directly south (uphill) from the old town, this verdant park is a magnificent place to be when the sun is dropping into the ocean behind the Illas Cíes. You can look at the partly reconstructed **Castro de Vigo** (☎986 81 02 60; ⏲11am-1pm Tue-Fri, 5-7pm Sat Jul-Sep, 11am-1pm Tue, 11am-1pm & 4-6pm Fri, 4-6pm Sat Oct-Jun) FREE dating back to the 3rd century BCE, and poke around the hilltop **Castelo do Castro**, which formed part of Vigo's defences built in the 17th century.

★**Castelo de Soutomaior** CASTLE, GARDENS

(☎986 80 41 00; www.castelodesoutomaior.com; Rúa do Rial, Soutomaior; gardens free, castle adult/senior & child €5/2.50; ⏲10am-9pm May-Sep, 10am-7pm Tue-Sun Oct-Apr) The Soutomaior castle-palace, amid enormous and beautiful gardens, is well worth a 21km drive northeast from Vigo. Displays inside the castle, which dates back to the 12th century, detail its fascinating history in Spanish, Galician and English. Outside, you can happily stroll for at least an hour among huge sequoias and cedars, a large albariño vineyard, woodlands of oak and chestnut and over 200 camellias, which bloom brilliantly between November and April.

## Sleeping

**Hotel Compostela** HOTEL €

(☎986 22 82 27; www.hcompostela.com; Rúa García Olloqui 5; s €36-77, d €43-78; P 📶) Solidly comfy, spotlessly clean and reasonably spacious rooms make this efficient hotel near Praza de Compostela a sound choice. The cafe is handy for breakfast.

**Hotel América** HOTEL €€

(☎986 43 89 22; www.hotelamerica-vigo.com; Rúa de Pablo Morillo 6; incl breakfast s €65-91, d €81-141; P ❄ @ 📶) The América gets a big thumbs-up for its well-equipped, tasteful, spacious rooms; friendly, efficient staff; and quiet sidestreet location near the waterfront. Nearly all the 47 rooms are exterior-facing, and the breakfast is a large, excellent buffet.

**Gran Hotel Nagari** LUXURY HOTEL €€€

(☎986 21 11 11; www.granhotelnagari.com; Praza de Compostela 21; incl buffet breakfast s €110-235, d €136-273; P ❄ 📶 🏊) Luxurious Nagari has a welcome personal feel to its classy contemporary design and service. Beautiful rooms in silver, gold, white and grey boast remote-controlled colour lighting, giant-headed showers (also colour-changing) and hi-tech coffee makers, and there's a heated rooftop pool with fabulous views. Check for deals including the full-service spa.

## Eating

Good restaurants, tapas bars and cafes are scattered all over the central area, and beyond. The narrow lanes of the old town and the Praza de Compostela and Rúa de Rosalia de Castro areas all have plenty of options.

**Othilio Bar** GALICIAN €€

(☎986 19 00 17; Rúa Luis Taboada 9; mains €10-19, lunch menú Mon-Fri €14; ⏲1.30am-3.30pm & 9-11.30pm Tue-Sat) Friendly service by a busy team complements expertly prepared

WORTH A TRIP

## ILLAS CÍES

The Illas Cíes, three spectacularly beautiful islands that are home to some of Galicia's most splendid beaches, are a 45-minute (14km) ferry ride from Vigo. This small archipelago forms a 6km breakwater that protects the Ría de Vigo from the Atlantic's fury and is the main jewel of the **Parque Nacional de las Islas Atlánticas de Galicia** (Atlantic Islands of Galicia National Park; www.iatlanticas.es).

The Cíes are perfect for lolling on sandy beaches, such as the 1km-long, lagoon-backed crescent of **Praia das Rodas** (), or nudist **Praia das Figueiras**. They're also great for walking and exploring: trails such as the **Ruta Monte Faro** lead to some spectacular high lookouts. While the eastern coasts are relatively gentle, the western sides drop away dramatically in sheer cliffs.

The islands are vehicle-free and their nature pristine, but you won't be alone. Up to 3000 visitors are allowed at one time and this limit is often reached in July and August. Most people come on day trips. To stay overnight you must camp at **Camping Islas Cíes** (986 43 83 58; www.campingislascies.com; adult/child/tent €8.90/6.90/8.90, 2-person tent & bed rental per night €49-55, 4-person €79-85; Semana Santa, June–late Sep), which has a restaurant and supermarket, and a capacity of 800 people – often full in August. There's a two-night minimum stay if you're renting one of their tents. Reservations are required and can be made online or at the **camping office** (986 43 83 58; Estación Marítima de Ría, Vigo; 9am-1pm & 3-6.30pm Semana Santa, Jun & Sep, 8.30am-7pm Jul-Aug).

There are also two other restaurants besides the one at the campground.

### Getting There & Away

For day visits between mid-March and mid-September you need a free national park authorisation – available at www.autorizacionillasatlanticas.xunta.gal or through ferry companies' websites – before buying boat tickets.

Boats to the Cíes (round trip €16 to €19 for adults, free to €8 for children), operated by several different companies, sail from Vigo's **Estación Marítima de Ría** (Ferry Port; Rúa Cánovas del Castillo 3), from Cangas and from Baiona. Services from Vigo and Cangas normally go daily during Easter week and from June to mid-September, on Saturdays and Sundays in May and from mid-September to mid-October, and on variable weekends and holidays in winter: check with the boat companies. Baiona sailings normally happen in Semana Santa and from July to mid-September.

**Naviera Mar de Ons** (986 22 52 72; www.mardeons.es) and **Nabia Naviera** (986 32 00 48; www.piratasdenabia.com) usually offer the most sailings, between them up to 14 times a day from Vigo, 12 times from Cangas and seven times from Baiona. Book as far ahead as possible – online or by phone (with a credit card) or at the ports of departure.



fish, meat, shellfish and desserts here. It's contemporary Galician fare – steak tartare, lightly cooked marinated salmon – and very popular, so book ahead or get there in good time.

**Follas Novas** GALICIAN €€

(986 22 93 06; Rúa de Serafín Avendaño 10; mains €12-19; 1.15-3.45pm & 8.15-11.45pm Mon-Sat) It's well worth venturing about 400m east of Praza de Compostela to this small, unpretentious restaurant, where quality ingredients form the basis of top-class fare such as grilled shellfish, *saquitos rellenos* (mixed pork, leeks and mushrooms inside a pancake 'bag') and perfectly done fish or beef options. Attentive service seals the deal. Try to reserve as it fills up fast.

**Gamboa Vinte** SEAFOOD €€

(Rúa Gamboa 20; mains €15-20; 11am-5pm & 8pm-midnight Mon-Sat) Gamboa Vinte is a dependable, moderately priced option convenient to the Casco Vello for well-prepared fish and seafood – grilled, casseroled or in rice.

## Drinking & Entertainment

For early evening drinks, the bars around Praza da Constitución and Praza de Compostela are enticing. From around 11pm the action shifts east to the music bars and pubs along Rúa de Areal and Rúa de Rosalía de Castro. The Churruca district about 1km southeast of the old town is the epicentre of Vigo's alternative nightlife, kicking off around midnight. You'll find two of northern Spain's top small-scale clubs for live rock and indie: **La Iguana Club** (www.facebook.com/laiguanaclub; Rúa de Churruca 14; ⏲11.30pm-5am Thu-Sat, extra days & hours for some live gigs) and **La Fábrica de Chocolate Club** (www.fabricadechocolateclub.com; Rúa Rogelio Abalde 22; ⏲midnight-4.30am Thu-Sun, from 10pm for live gigs), with two or three gigs weekly.

## ℹ Information

**Oficina de Turismo de Vigo** (☎986 22 47 57; www.turismodevigo.org; Estación Marítima de Ría, Rúa Cánovas del Castillo 3; ⏲10am-5pm) Helpful tourist office in the ferry terminal.

## ℹ Getting There & Away

### AIR

Vigo's **Peinador airport** (☎91 321 10 00; www.aena.es), 9km east of the city centre, has direct flights to/from Madrid (Iberia and Air Europa), Barcelona (Vueling and Iberia), Bilbao (Iberia), and Valencia (Iberia).

### BUS

The **bus station** (☎986 37 34 11; Avenida de Madrid 57) is 2km southeast of the old town. Monbus (www.monbus.es) makes several trips daily to all main Galician cities, including Pontevedra (€2.05, 30 minutes to one hour), Santiago de Compostela (€6.80, 1½ to 2¼ hours) and Ourense (€8, 1½ hours). Autna (www.autna.com) heads at least three times daily to/from Porto (Portugal; €12, 2½ hours), with connections there for Lisbon.

### TRAIN

High-speed trains (nine or more daily) to/from Pontevedra (€3.80, 15 minutes), Santiago de Compostela (€12, 50 minutes to one hour) and A Coruña (€19, 1½ hours) go from **Vigo-Urzáiz station** (Praza da Estación), 1km southeast of the old town. **Vigo-Guixar station** (Rúa Areal), 1km east of the old town, has some slower, slightly cheaper trains to the same cities, plus trains to Ourense (€13 to €23, 1¼ to 2¾ hours, eight or more daily), Porto (Portugal; €15, 2½ hours, two daily) and other destinations including Ribadavia, Tui and Madrid.

## ℹ Getting Around

Bus L9A runs between the central Rúa Policarpo Sanz and the airport. The bus station and Vigo-Guixar train station are linked to Porta do Sol in the city centre by bus C2. Bus L4C runs between the bus station and Rúa Policarpo Sanz. Rides cost €1.35.

# SOUTHWEST GALICIA

Galicia's southwest corner is home to three towns that all make enjoyable stops on a circuit of the region or a journey to or from Portugal – the pretty fishing town A Guarda, the riverside cathedral town Tui, and the historic port and resort Baiona.

## Baiona

POP 2770

Baiona (Castilian: Bayona) is a popular resort whose moment in history came on 1 March 1493, when one of Columbus' small fleet, the *Pinta,* stopped in for supplies, bearing the remarkable news that the explorer had made it to the Indies (in fact, the West Indies). Baiona was later eclipsed as a trading port by Vigo, but there's still a hefty reminder of its old importance in the stout defensive walls and gun batteries of the pine-covered Monte Boi promontory jutting out from the waterfront.

A tangle of inviting old lanes, with plenty of taverns and restaurants, comprises Baiona's **casco histórico** (historic centre), behind the harbourfront road, Rúa Elduayen. Four kilometres east is the magnificent sweep of **Praia América** at Nigrán.

Get maps and more at the **tourist office** (☎986 68 70 67; www.turismodebaiona.com; Calle Arquitecto Jesús Valverde; ⏲9am-8pm Mon-Fri, 10am-2pm & 4-7.30pm Sat & Sun) at the entrance to the Monte Boi promontory.

**Fortaleza de Monterreal** FORTRESS

(pedestrian/car €1/5 approx Jun-Sep, rest of year free; ⏲10am-10pm; P) Dominating the **Monte Boi** promontory, this fortress was erected between the 11th and 17th centuries and its impregnable 3km circle of walls still stands, though there's not much old left inside it now. An enticing 40-minute walking trail loops round the rocky shoreline, broken up by a few small beaches. Within the precinct today is the luxurious, medieval-castle-style **Parador de Baiona** (☎986 35 50 00; www.parador.es; Monterreal; incl breakfast s €116-336, d €132-356; P❄📶🏊). Have a drink on its cafe terrace, with fabulous views across the bay.

## ℹ Getting There & Away

ATSA (www.automovilesdetuy.es) buses run to and from Vigo (€2.55, 45 minutes) every 30 or 60 minutes until at least 9pm. Just a couple a day go south to A Guarda (€3.25, 45 minutes). Catch buses in front of the Lonxa (fish-auction building) on Rúa Elduayen.

## A Guarda

POP 6050

A fishing port just north of where the Río Miño spills into the Atlantic, A Guarda (Castilian: La Guardia) is famed for its seafood, with a dozen eateries along Rúa do Porto facing the pretty harbour. There's also a cute little *casco antiguo* (old town) centred on Praza do Reló. But the prize attraction is Monte de Santa Trega, rising just outside town. A fine walking path also runs 3km south from the harbour to the heads of the Miño. All in all A Guarda is an enjoyable stopover, and the attractive Portuguese town of Caminha is just a short ferry ride away.

**★Monte de Santa Trega** HILL

(adult/child in vehicle Tue-Sun mid-Feb–Dec €1/0.50, Mon & Jan-mid-Feb free; P) The 341m summit of Monte de Santa Trega is a 4km drive or 2km walk (via the PRG122) from town. On the way up, stop to poke around the partly restored Iron Age **Castro de Santa Trega**. At the top, you'll find a 16th-century chapel, an interesting small **archaeological museum** (9am-9pm Jul & Aug, 10am-8pm Apr-Jun & Sep, to 7pm Mar & Oct, 11am-5pm 2nd half Feb, Nov & Dec; P) FREE on *castro* culture, a couple of cafes and souvenir stalls – and truly magnificent panoramas up the Miño, across to Portugal and out over the Atlantic.

**Castelo de Santa Cruz** FORT

(Avenida de Santo Domingo de Guzmán; 10am-9pm Apr-Sep, to 6pm Oct-Mar; P) FREE This fort with four arrowhead-shaped corner bastions makes an interesting short visit. It was built to defend A Guarda against the Portuguese in the 17th century.

**★Hotel Convento de San Benito** HISTORIC HOTEL €€

(986 61 11 66; www.hotelsanbenito.es; Rúa Concepción Arenal; s €42-61, d €54-99; closed mid-Dec–early Jan; P) A real treat, the San Benito is housed in a 16th-century former convent near the harbour. Its 33 rooms are elegant, individually decorated and very comfortable, and the whole place is like a mini-museum with fascinating antiques, paintings, sculptures and books at every turn. Great breakfast (€7.50) too.

**Casa Chupa Ovos** SEAFOOD €€

(986 61 10 15; Rúa A Roda 24; mains & raciones €8-26, lunch menú €10; 1.30-3.30pm Tue, 1.30-3.30pm & 8.30-11pm Thu-Mon, closed 3 weeks Oct/Nov) It's up a flight of steps from the harbourfront, and it doesn't have a sea view, but Chupa Ovos is a deserved favourite with locals and visitors alike for its perfectly prepared fresh seafood, friendly and prompt service, bright atmosphere and good wines.

### Getting There & Away

ATSA (www.automovilesdetuy.es) buses run to Vigo (€6.05, 80 minutes) every 30 or 60 minutes, 7am to 7pm (fewer on weekends). Most go via Tui, but a couple go via Baiona. Buses stop on the main street, Avenida de Galicia.

A **ferry** (986 61 15 26, Portugal 258 092 564; www.cm-caminha.pt; car/motorcycle/bicycle incl driver or rider €3.50/3/2, passenger & pedestrian €1.50) crosses the Miño several times daily from Camposancos, 2km south of A Guarda, to Caminha, Portugal. Exact timings depend on tides and seasonal variations. A Guarda's **tourist office** (986 61 45 46; www.turismoaguarda.es; Praza do Reló; 10am-2pm & 4.30-7.30pm Mon-Sat May-Sep, 10am-2pm & 4.30-6.30pm Mon-Fri, 10am-2pm Sat Oct-Apr) has current schedules on its website.

## Tui

POP 6070

Tui (Castilian: Tuy), sitting above the broad Río Miño 25km inland, is the main entry point into Spain of the Camino Portugués pilgrim route to Santiago de Compostela, with some 80,000 people a year passing through or starting their journeys here. It's well worth exploring the tightly packed medieval centre, with its magnificent cathedral and lively bar scene. At the southwest end of town the 19th-century **Puente Internacional** (International Bridge), with two levels (rail above, road below), crosses the Miño to Portugal's equally appealing Valença.

**★Catedral de Santa Maria** CATHEDRAL

(www.catedraldetui.com; Praza de San Fernando; incl audio-guide adult/senior/child €4/3.50/free; 10.45am-8pm Mon-Sat, 9am-12.45pm & 4-8pm Sun Apr-Sep, to 7pm Oct-Mar, closed 2-4pm Mon-Sat Oct-Jun) The highlight of the old town is the fortress-like Catedral de Santa Maria. Begun in the 12th century, it reflects a stoic Romanesque style in most of its construction, though the ornate main portal is reckoned the earliest work of Gothic sculpture on the Iberian Peninsula. Admission covers the lovely Gothic cloister and its viewpoints, plus the main nave and chapels.

**Ideas Peregrinas** HOSTEL €

(☎986 07 63 30; www.ideas-peregrinas.com; Porta da Pía 1; dm €13-15, r €35-55; @ 📶) Spotless and friendly, this family-run old-town hostel with lemon-and-white colour schemes is a boon for Camino Portugués travellers and anyone else. There's a choice between private rooms (some with private bathroom) or four-person dorms, all with real cotton sheets – plus three spacious lounges, a meditation room, washing machines and a kitchen.

The same people also run a very good **cafe** (items €4-12; ⏰7am-10pm Mon-Sat; 📶 🖉) downstairs, with healthy fare such as hummus, salads, avocado toast, combo juices, breakfasts and tapas.

**La Sigrina** HOSTAL €€

(☎647 534155; www.lasigrina.es; Rúa do Foxo 8; r incl breakfast €60-75; ❄ 📶) Two multilingual brothers have converted their family home into this stylish, welcoming and spacious lodging. The eight uncluttered, tasteful rooms come in white with flashes of colour, smart TVs and wood-look ceramic floors. Inviting common areas include a large terrace and a citrus-tree-shaded courtyard. Breakfasts are substantial.

**O Novo Cabalo Furado** GALICIAN €€

(Praza do Concello; mains €11-24, menú del día €14; ⏰1.15-3.30pm & 8.15-11pm, closed Sun Jul-Aug) A couple of doors from the cathedral, this popular restaurant is great for fish, shellfish and heaping plates of lamb chops.

## Information

**Oficina Municipal de Turismo** (☎677 418405; www.concellotui.org; Praza de San Fernando; ⏰10am-2pm & 4-8pm, closed Sun-Mon Oct-Apr) In front of the cathedral.

## Getting There & Away

**ATSA** (www.automovilesdetuy.es) buses run to Vigo (€3.30, 40 minutes) and A Guarda (€3.25, 40 minutes), both every 30 or 60 minutes until 7.30pm or later (fewer services on weekends), stopping on Paseo de Calvo Sotelo in front of Pensión La Corredera. There are also two daily trains each to Vigo (€4.15, 45 minutes) and Valença (Portugal; €2.20, 10 minutes) from Tui station, 1km north of the centre.

# EASTERN GALICIA

Though often overshadowed by Galicia's glorious coastline and the better-known attractions of Santiago de Compostela, eastern Galicia is a treasure trove of enticing provincial cities, lovely landscapes, wine-growing regions and old-fashioned rural enclaves – perfect territory for travellers who like digging out their own gems.

## Ourense

POP 98,700

Galicia's unsung but beguiling third-largest city, Ourense (Castilian: Orense) has an appealingly labyrinthine historic quarter, a lively tapas scene and delightful riverside thermal baths. The broad Río Miño runs east–west across the city, crossed by several bridges, including the elegant, part-Roman Ponte Vella (Old Bridge) and the soaring concrete-and-metal Ponte do Milenio (Millennium Bridge). The central area, including the old town, rises south of the river.

### Sights

The old town unfolds around the 12th-century Catedral de San Martiño, in a maze of narrow streets and small plazas that are a pleasure to wander. Among the stone-flagged streets, stone-faced buildings and stone arcades, with almost no traffic, you may have to remind yourself you're in the 21st century. The largest square is sloping **Praza Maior**, with cafes under the arcades and the classical-facaded **Casa do Concello** at its foot.

**Catedral de San Martiño** CATHEDRAL

(www.catedralourense.com; Praza do Trigo; incl audio-guide adult/pilgrim/child €5/3.50/free; ⏰10.30am-7.30pm Mon-Sat, 1-7pm Sun Mar-Oct, 10.30am-3pm & 4-6.30pm Mon-Thu, 10.30am-6.30pm Fri & Sat, 12.30-6.30pm Sun Nov-Feb) The artistic highlight of Ourense's Romanesque-Gothic cathedral, built mainly in the 12th and 13th centuries, is the elaborately gilded Santo Cristo chapel, inside the northern entrance. At the west end is the colourfully painted, Gothic Pórtico do Paraíso, based on Santiago de Compostela's Pórtico de la Gloria.

### Sleeping

**Hotel Novo Cándido** HOTEL €

(☎988 98 91 25; www.hotelnovocandido.com; Rúa San Miguel 14; s/d €40/55; ❄ 📶) A step up from other similarly priced options, the very central Novo Cándido has 14 bright, spick-and-span rooms with discreet lighting, wood-look floors and panelling and

## OURENSE'S THERMAL POOLS

Ourense's original *raison d'être*, back in Roman days, was its hot springs, and today the city's attractively modernised thermal pools (www.turismodeourense.gal/termalismo) enable everyone to take a soothing, reviving and therapeutic warm open-air dip, even in winter. Along a prettily landscaped 4km stretch of the north bank of the Miño are four sets of free, beautifully maintained open-air pools (with changing rooms and lockers) and one larger, privately run set of indoor and outdoor pools, the Termas Outariz.

You can walk to any of the pools, but another option is the mini train **Tren das Termas** (www.urbanosdeourense.es; one way €0.85; ⌚hourly 10am-1pm & 4-8pm, reduced frequency approx Nov-Apr), which runs to all the riverbank pools from Praza Maior. You'll need swimming gear, a towel and flip-flops (thongs), and remember that the waters are hot (around 40°C) and mineral-laden, so don't bathe longer than about 10 minutes without a break. The pools are not recommended for children under seven years.

**Termas Outariz** (☎988 36 46 50; www.termasoutariz.com; Outariz; 2hr session €5.70; ⌚10am-11pm or later Wed-Mon) A delightful experience, the attractively designed Outariz baths comprise 10 hot/warm and three cold pools of varied sizes – some indoors, some out, some equipped with waterfalls or underwater jets – in a verdant riverbank setting. There's a cafe too, and you can rent a swimming outfit, towel and flip-flops if you need to. The baths are a 6km walk northwest of the old town, and served by the Tren das Termas (40 minutes from Praza Maior). The Outariz parking area across the river is a 1km walk away via a footbridge: you can reach it by car along the OU402 or by city bus 5 from the central Parque San Lázaro (€0.85, 10 minutes, every 40 minutes Monday to Friday, every 80 minutes Saturday and Sunday).

**Zona Termal Muiño da Vega** (Quintela; ⌚10am-7pm) These four relatively large (up to 15m long) pools are the most enticing of Ourense's free open-air thermal pools, sitting in a pleasantly green spot beside the Miño about 5km northwest of the old town.

**Termas A Chavasqueira** (Campo da Feira; ⌚10am-7pm) The three small open-air pools of A Chavasqueira, right on the riverbank, are the closest to the city centre of Ourense's riverside thermal pools. You can walk there in 20 to 30 minutes from the old town.

big mirrors. Some bathrooms are equipped with walk-in showers; others have bathtubs. There's a handy ground-floor cafe-bar.

**NH Ourense** HOTEL €€
(☎988 60 11 11; www.nh-hotels.com; Rúa Celso Emilio Ferreiro 24; incl breakfast s €65-110, d €90-130; ❄📶) Ourense's best hotels are provided by upscale Spanish chains and the NH has the choicest combination of style, location, comfort and service. Decor is contemporary with cheerful reds and purples, silver-framed mirrors and pleasing landscape photos. The buffet breakfast is a good spread.

## Eating

*Ir de tapeo* (going for tapas) is a way of life in Ourense, and streets near the cathedral including Fornos, Paz, Lepanto, Viriato, San Miguel and Praza do Ferro brim with taverns where having to push your way to the bar is a sign of quality. Tapas start at €1.50 and are ideally washed down with a glass of Galician wine. Top spots include tiny **Bar Fuentefría** (Rúa Viriato 6; tapas €1.50-3.50; ⌚8pm-12.30am), with a speciality in *afumadas* (smoked fish on toast slices) but also pretty tasty bread rolls filled with *solombo con piquillo* (tenderloin with red pepper); the cellar-like **Arco da Vella** (Rúa dos Fornos 9; tapas €2-4, raciones €4-12; ⌚7.30pm-12.30am or later), celebrated for its gooey *tortilla de patatas* (potato omelette); and **Casa do Pulpo** (Rúa de Juan de Austria; raciones €5-12; ⌚1-4pm & 8pm-midnight; 📶), serving up perfect octopus and combination bites like *solomillo* (tenderloin) with cheese, bacon and red pepper.

**Sybaris 2.0** SPANISH €€
(Rúa Santo Domingo 15, entrance Rúa Cardenal Quiroga 22; dishes €9-19, 4-course lunch menú Mon-Fri €12.50, tasting menú €25-34; ⌚restaurant 1.30-4pm Mon-Wed, 1.30-4pm & 8.30-11.30pm Thu-Sat, shop 11am-8pm Mon-Fri, noon-5pm Sat) Sybaris is not just a restaurant with a tastily original twist on Spanish fare, but also a well-stocked wine shop and Galicia-specialist deli (cheeses and hams, of course, but also lampreys in oil, crab pâté and sea-urchin caviar). The

oft-changing menus might include dishes like veal in mencía wine, turbot in a crab marinade, or smoked-pigeon salad.

## Entertainment

**Café Latino** JAZZ
(www.cafelatino.es; Praza Santa Eufemia 7; 7.30am-3am Mon-Sat, 8.30am-2am Sun; ) Classy, wood-lined Café Latino has a fabulous corner stage that hosts live jazz at 11pm on Thursdays from about October to April, and a jazz festival in April and May. It's been serving up jazz for three decades and is also a good spot for breakfast or any kind of drink at any time of day.

## Information

**Oficina Municipal de Turismo** (988 36 60 64; www.turismodeourense.gal; Calle Isabel La Católica 2; 9am-2pm & 4-8pm Mon-Fri, 11am-2pm Sat & Sun) Helpful place beneath the Xardins Padre Feijóo park.

## Getting There & Away

### BUS

From Ourense's **bus station** (988 21 60 27; Carretera de Vigo 1), 2km northwest of the centre, Monbus (www.monbus.es) runs to Santiago (€7.60, 1¾ hours, four or more daily), Vigo (€8, 1½ hours, four or more daily), Pontevedra (€7.10, 1¾ hours, one or more daily except Saturday) and Lugo (€6.40, 1¾ hours, two or more daily). Avanza (www.avanzabus.com) journeys to Madrid (€35 to €41, six to seven hours, four daily). ALSA (www.alsa.es) operates daily services to cities in Castilla y León, Asturias, Extremadura and Andalucía.

### TRAIN

The **train station** (Avenida de Marín) is 500m north of the Río Miño. Renfe (www.renfe.com) runs to Santiago (€6 to €20, 40 minutes to 1¾ hours, eight or more daily), Lugo (€12 to €20, 1¾ hours, three or four daily), Vigo (€6 to €20, 1½ to two hours, eight or more daily), León (€10 to €35, 3¾ to 4½ hours, four daily), Madrid (€14 to €48, 4¾ to 9½ hours, five or more daily) and elsewhere. High-speed trains, possibly starting in 2021, should halve trip times to Madrid.

## Getting Around

Local buses 1, 3, 6A and others (€0.85) run between the train station and the central Parque de San Lázaro. Buses 6A, 6B and 12 connect the bus station with Parque San Lázaro.

# Ribadavia & the Ribeiro Wine Region

POP 3150

Ribadavia, the headquarters of the Ribeiro wine Denominación de Origen (DO), sits beside the Río Avia 30km west of Ourense, among green, rolling hills strewn with vineyards and old stone villages. The Avia valley north of town is particularly charming. Ribadavia's little historic centre is an enticing maze of narrow, stone-paved streets lined with stone arcades and broken up by diminutive plazas; within this, in medieval times, was Galicia's largest Jewish quarter, centred on Rúa Merelles Caulla.

## Sights & Activities

The Ribeiro DO produces some of Galicia's best white wines, principally from the treixadura grape, and more than 20 wineries in the area are visitable, though this is not a highly developed activity here. Apart from **Viña Costeira** (988 47 72 10; www.costeira.es; Valdepereira; 45min tour incl 1-wine tasting €3, longer tours €5-10; 45min tours 11am, noon, 1pm & 5pm Mon-Fri, noon Sat, longer tours by reservation; P), Ribeiro's biggest winery, 3km northeast of Ribadavia, wineries don't have regular visiting times and require a phone call in advance. The best plan is to ask at the **tourist office** (988 47 12 75; www.turismoribadavia.com; Praza Maior 7; 10am-2pm & 4-8pm Mon-Sat, 10.30am-2.30pm Sun Jun-late Aug, 9.30-3pm Mon-Fri, 10am-2pm & 4-7pm Sat, 10.30am-2.30pm Sun Sep-May) on Ribadavia's main plaza, where staff know their wineries and can help arrange visits. For further information, check www.rutadelvinoribeiro.com and www.ribeiro.wine.

**Museo Sefardí** MUSEUM
(Centro de Información Xudía de Galicia; Praza Maior 7; adult/child incl Castelo dos Sarmento & audio guide €3.50/free; 10am-2pm & 4-8pm Mon-Sat, 10.30am-2.30pm Sun Jun-Sep, 9.30-3pm Mon-Fri, 10am-2pm & 4-7pm Sat, 10.30am-2.30pm Sun Oct-May) Above the tourist office on the lovely main square, this centre has exhibits on the Jews of Galicia before and after their expulsion from Spain in 1492.

**Castelo dos Sarmento** CASTLE
(Castelo dos Condes; Rúa Progreso; adult/child incl Museo Sefardí & audio guide €3.50/free; 10am-2pm & 4-8pm Mon-Sat, 10.30am-2.30pm Sun Jun-Sep, 9.30-3pm Mon-Fri, 10am-2pm & 4-7pm Sat, 10.30am-2.30pm Sun Oct-May) The large,

### THE ULTIMATE OCTOPUS FEAST

Most Galicians agree that the best *pulpo á feira* (Galicia's signature octopus dish) is cooked far from the sea in the modest inland town of O Carballiño, 30km northwest of Ourense and 20km north of Ribadavia. Cooks here invented the recipe in the Middle Ages, when the local monastery received copious supplies of the cephalopod from its coastal properties. Today, tens of thousands of people pile into O Carballiño on the second Sunday of August for the **Festa do Pulpo de O Carballiño** (www.facebook.com/festadopulpodocarballino; 2nd Sun in Aug). Happily, several restaurants in town also cook up octopus year-round. A fine choice is bright and lively **Pulpería Carral** (988 60 39 95; Rúa Marcelino Parrondo 16; mains €8-15; 1-4pm & 9pm-midnight Tue-Sat, 1-4pm Sun). While here take a look at the the extraordinary **Templo da Veracruz** (Rúa de Evaristo Vaamonde, O Carballiño; 10am-1pm & 5-7pm), rising like some Disneyesque fantasy amid the grey apartment blocks. It resembles a great Gothic cathedral but was actually built in the 1940s and '50s.

chiefly 15th-century castle of the Counts of Ribadavia is one of Galicia's biggest castles and contains a medieval necropolis within its bare stone precinct, which is brought alive by the audio guide. Tickets are sold at the tourist office.

**Paseo Fluvial** WALKING

Relax with a stroll along this riverside path beside the Ríos Avia and Miño. You can access it by steps down from Praza Buxán, next to Praza Madalena in Ribadavia's Judería (old Jewish quarter): it's 600m to the Avia's confluence with the much bigger Miño, then 1.8km along the Miño to the path's end.

## Festivals & Events

**Feira do Viño do Ribeiro** WINE

(www.feiravinoribeiro.com; May) Ribadavia parties on the first weekend in May with this big wine festival.

## Sleeping & Eating

Lodgings in town are modest but there are some excellent rural hotels in the area, especially in the beautiful Avia valley, full of vineyards, woodlands and quaint little villages, to the north.

Ribadavia's central Praza Maior is ringed by cafes and restaurants.

★ **Casal de Armán** HOTEL €€

(699 060464; www.casaldearman.net; O Cotiño, San Andrés; r incl breakfast €75-90; P) You can kill several birds with one stone at this dignified country house set among vineyards and lovely Avia valley countryside, 6km northeast of Ribadavia. The six cosy rooms feature plenty of exposed stone, and toiletries made from grape extract! Also here is a top Ribeiro **winery** (638 043335; incl 2-wine tasting €8; visits by reservation, Tue-Sun Nov-Aug; P) and the fine restaurant **Sábrego** (988 49 18 09; www.sabregorestaurante.com; mains €17-21, 7-course menú €43; 1.15-3.45pm & 8.45-11.15pm Tue-Sun mid-Jun–mid-Sep, 1.15-3.45pm Tue-Sun & 8.45-11.15pm Fri & Sat mid-Sep–mid-Jun; P), serving a seasonal array of delicious, chiefly Galician fare with some creative twists.

Standout dishes might include the lamb shoulder with *cachelos* (boiled potatoes), or the San Martiño fish (John Dory) with cockles and cream of celeriac. Reservations essential for weekends. When the restaurant isn't open, you'll have to go out to Ribadavia or O Carballiño to eat.

**Pazo de Esposende** HOTEL €€

(696 378670; www.pazoesposende.es; Carretera OU211, Esposende; r incl breakfast €60-100; P) This 16th-century mansion in the Avia valley, a few kilometres north of Ribadavia, boasts appealingly comfortable, up-to-date rooms with subtle lighting and full-wall murals of local scenes, but retains its thick stone walls, handsome pillared courtyard and charming views over the village and countryside. The welcome is friendly, the flowers brilliantly colourful, and the breakfast good and filling.

## Getting There & Away

At least two buses and two trains run daily to Ourense and Vigo from stations in the east of town, just across the Río Avia.

## Ribeira Sacra

Northeast of Ourense, along the plunging valleys of the Ríos Sil and Miño, unfold the natural beauty and unique cultural heritage of the Ribeira Sacra (Sacred Riverbank) – so called for the many medieval monasteries founded here after early Christian hermits and monks were drawn to this remote area. Amid the beautiful, sometimes severe scenery – particularly dramatic along the Cañón do Sil (Sil Canyon) – you can walk and cycle beautiful trails, take river boat trips, and visit wineries of the Ribeira Sacra DO, producing some fine vintages on often spectacularly steep slopes, which have earned the label *viticultura heroica* (heroic viticulture) for the activity of winemaking here.

The area is poorly served by public transport, but makes for a marvellous driving trip. A good route is to head from Ourense to Monforte de Lemos via the Mosteiro de San Pedro de Rocas, Mosteiro de Santo Estevo, Parada de Sil and Castro Caldelas. Allow two days to make the most of the area.

The multilingual website Ribeira Sacra (www.ribeirasacra.org) is a very useful resource with, among other things, detailed information on the area's wineries and 20 walking routes (with maps). There are tourist information offices in Parada de Sil (www.paradadesil.es) and Castro Caldelas (www.castrocaldelas.es) and the **Centro do Viño da Ribeira Sacra** (☎982 10 53 03; www.centrovino-ribeirasacra.com; Rúa Comercio 6; tour incl glass of wine €2.50; ⏲10am-2pm & 5-9pm Tue-Sun Jul-Sep, 10am-2pm & 4.30-8pm Tue-Sun Oct-Jun) in Monforte de Lemos is good for information on the whole area.

★**Mosteiro de San Pedro de Rocas** MONASTERY

(☎661 508243; www.centrointerpretacionribeirasacra.com; ⏲10.30am-1.45pm & 4-7.45pm daily Apr-Sep, 10.30am-1.45pm & 4-6pm Tue-Sun Oct-Mar; P) FREE This enchanting mini-monastery, founded in 573 CE, stands hidden among dense woodlands 11km south of Luintra. It contains three cave chapels, originally carved out of the rock as retreats for early hermits, and a number of rock-cut graves from the 10th century onwards. The adjacent interpretation centre has informative displays on the Ribeira Sacra. From here the Camiño Real (PRG4) footpath follows a lovely 9km circuit of about 2½ hours through picturesque countryside.

To drive direct from Ourense, take the OU536 east as far as Tarreirigo. Here, 500m past the Km 15 post, turn left on to the OU0509 and follow signs 4km along minor roads to the monastery. Afterwards you can continue north to Luintra on the OU0509.

★**Mosteiro de Santo Estevo** MONASTERY

(Monasterio de San Esteban; ⏲closed Jan–late Feb; P) FREE The enormous Mosteiro de Santo Estevo, in the steep, thickly wooded Sil valley, dates from the 12th century and has three magnificent cloisters (one Romanesque-Gothic, two Renaissance), a Romanesque-Gothic church and an 18th-century baroque facade. It's now a **parador hotel** (☎988 01 01 10; www.parador.es; s/d incl breakfast from €113/131; ⏲closed Jan–mid-Feb; P❄☎) and one of the Ribeira Sacra's most luxurious places to stay, but everyone is free to wander round the main monumental sections and eat in the cafe or restaurant. Santo Estevo is 5km east from Luintra along the OU0508, then 1km north.

### Parada de Sil & Around

POP 185 / ELEV 660M

The village of Parada de Sil sits high above the Cañón do Sil, 21km east of Luintra. Coming from Luintra, turn off after 14km into Vilouxe village, park and then walk about 15 minutes (following signs) to the **Miradoiros de Vilouxe**, probably the two most breathtaking of all lookout points over the Sil Canyon. Take care – there are no guard rails!

From Parada de Sil village, separate roads lead 1km to the **Balcóns de Madrid** viewpoint and 4km down to the lovely little **Mosteiro de Santa Cristina de Ribas de Sil** (www.paradadesil.es; €1; ⏲church 11am-2pm & 4-6pm mid-Jun-Oct, 11am-4pm Wed-Sun Nov & Mar-mid-Jun, hrs may vary, exterior 24hr; P), with its 12th-century Romanesque church, hidden among trees above the canyon. Part of the PRG98 walking trail heads down to the monastery and back up to the viewpoint in a 10km loop from the village.

★**Ruta Cañón do Río Mao** WALKING

(PRG177) This excellent hike starts at the Albergue A Fábrica da Luz (p583), 11km east of Parada de Sil. The full circuit is 16km but you can shorten it to an enjoyable 5km loop (about 2½ hours) by descending the pretty Mao canyon (initially on an 850m boardwalk) to Barxacova village, then climbing

## CAMINO FRANCÉS IN GALICIA

All of the Camino de Santiago (p48) routes converge in Galicia, their shared goal. Growing numbers of pilgrims today reach Santiago de Compostela by routes such as the Camino Portugués (entering Galicia from Portugal at Tui or A Guarda), Camino del Norte (along the coast from the Basque Country to Ribadeo then inland across Galicia), Camino Primitivo (from Oviedo via Lugo) or Camino Inglés (from Ferrol or A Coruña). But the classic route remains the Camino Francés, which starts in the Pyrenees and enters Galicia from Castilla y León at **O Cebreiro**, 1300m high at the top of its longest, hardest climb. About half of O Cebreiro's buildings are bar-restaurants, *pensiones* or hostels: among them are several *pallozas* (circular, thatched dwellings known in rural Galicia since pre-Roman times). The nicest accommodation is the five wood-beamed rooms in the main building of **Hotel Cebreiro** (982 36 71 82; www.hotelcebreiro.com; s/d €40/50; ), which is also a good food stop; room reservations advised.

From O Cebreiro, 154km remain across welcome green countryside to Santiago de Compostela. In Triacastela, 19km downhill from O Cebreiro, the *camino* divides (both paths reunite later in Sarria). The longer (25km) route passes through **Samos**, a village built around the very fine **Mosteiro de Samos** (982 54 60 46; www.abadiadesamos.com; tours €5; tours hourly 9.30am-12.30pm & 4.30-6.30pm Mon-Sat, 12.45pm & hourly 4.30-6.30pm Sun May-Oct, hourly 10am-noon, 4.30pm & 5.30pm Mon & Wed-Sat, 12.45pm, 4.30pm, 5.30pm Sun Nov-Apr; P). This Benedictine monastery has two beautiful big cloisters – one Gothic, with distinctly unmonastic Greek nymphs adorning its fountain; the other neoclassical and filled with roses. Samos has plenty of inexpensive lodgings, but a good option is **Casa de Díaz** (982 54 70 70; www.hotelcasadediaz.com; Vilachá; r €42-68, breakfast €4-8; Apr-Oct; P @), a welcoming 18th-century farmhouse turned rural hotel 3.5km west. It has 12 comfy rooms in olde-worlde style and lovely, big gardens.

People undertaking just the last 100km of the *camino* (the minimum requirement for the 'Compostella' certificate) start 12km west of Samos at **Sarria**, with oodles of accommodation. From here the *camino* winds through villages, forests and fields, then descends steeply to Portomarín, above the Río Miño. After a tough 25km stretch to Palas de Rei, the next 15km to Melide (where the Camino Primitivo joins the Francés) follow some lovely rural lanes. From Melide 53km remain through villages, countryside and, finally, city streets. From Praza da Inmaculada on the northern side of Catedral de Santiago de Compostela, take a few more steps down through an archway to emerge on magnificent Praza do Obradoiro, before the cathedral's famous western facade.

If you're touring Galicia rather than *camino*-ing it, the 30km from O Cebreiro to Samos make a marvellous drive, winding down through green countryside with great long-distance views, and frequently criss-crossing the *camino*.

## Camino Francés in Galicia

1.5km past vineyards to San Lourenzo village, then descending back to A Fábrica.

At San Lourenzo there's an interesting 500m (each way) detour to the medieval necropolis of San Vítor.

The full, relatively demanding circuit takes about seven hours with a total ascent of nearly 1000m. From San Lourenzo it continues south to the upland villages of A Miranda and Forcas and a medieval bridge at Conceliños, before heading back down the Mao valley to San Lourenzo and A Fábrica da Luz.

**A Casa da Eira** CASA RURAL €

(☎696 749493; www.acasadaeira.com; Lugar Alberguería 31, Cerreda; r €60-63, apt for up to 4 €100-144; P 📶) Five cosy rooms and two self-catering apartments are set in an appealingly renovated, 130-year-old granite-and-timber farmhouse in the hamlet of Alberguería, just off the OU0508 10km west of Parada de Sil. The hosts are full of helpful information on numerous walks and other things to do, and serve up big breakfasts (€5.50) with homemade jams.

A pretty little garden, long wooden verandah, comfy sitting areas, tasteful art and plenty of books add to the appeal.

**Reitoral de Chandrexa** CASA RURAL €

(☎605 867622, 988 20 80 99; www.chandrexa.com; Chandrexa; d €48-56; ⏲closed mid-Dec–Jan; P 📶) 🍃 The former curate's house next to Chandrexa church, 4.5km east of Parada de Sil, has three comfy, stone-walled, wood-ceilinged rooms with good bathrooms. Downstairs is a cosy farmhouse-style dining-cum-sitting room where the owners serve up excellent organic breakfasts (€6) and dinners (€12 to €16), with many ingredients from their garden.

**Albergue A Fábrica da Luz** HOSTEL €

(☎679 060509; www.afabricadaluz.com; Carretera OU0605, Km 5.7; dm/d incl breakfast €18/36; ⏲Jun-Sep; P 📶) This well-run hostel and activities hub occupies a converted small hydroelectric station in the leafy canyon of the Río Mao (a Sil tributary), 11km east of Parada de Sil. The Ruta Cañón do Río Mao (p581) starts right here. The two 14-bunk dorms and two double rooms (sharing bathrooms) are clean and well kept, and good, inexpensive food is available. You might like to try the 'treetents' – off-ground tents strung between trees, costing €40 to €50 for two or three people with sleeping bags included.

The hostel functions as the Centro BTT Ribeira Sacra (Ribeira Sacra Mountain Bike Centre), with bikes to rent (guests/nonguests €13/18 per day including helmet). There are kayaks (guests/nonguests €14/20 per half-day), too, at the foot of the canyon.

## Castro Caldelas & Around

POP 610 / ELEV 780M

The hilltop village of Castro Caldelas, 52km east of Ourense, with its cobbled streets and old stone houses with Galician *galerías* and well-tended flower boxes, is a good spot to spend the night. Explore the old quarter at the top of the village, crowned by a panoramic 14th-century **castle** (adult/child €2/free; ⏲10am-2pm & 4-8pm, to 7pm Nov-Mar; P), also housing the local tourist office, which can inform you about local day-hikes.

From Castro Caldelas, the OU903 winds 10km north down to the Cañón do Sil, crosses the river on the Ponte do Sil bridge, then becomes the LU903 as it climbs across almost vertical vineyards towards Monforte de Lemos. Interesting smaller wineries to visit on this route include Ponte da Boga (p583) and **Adega Vella** (☎660 047602; www.adegavella.com; OU903, Abeleda; tour incl 9-wine tasting €5, free with wine purchases; ⏲11.30am-2.30pm & 4.30-8.30pm; P) on the way down to the Sil, and **Adega Algueira** (☎982 41 02 99; www.adegaalgueira.com; Doade; tour incl 3-wine tasting €10; ⏲1hr tours in English noon, Spanish 1pm; P) at Doade, a few kilometres up on the other side. It's worth calling ahead to ensure that visits are available.

From the Ponte do Sil, you can take scenic river cruises on the 12-passenger **Brandán** (☎982 41 02 99; www.adegaalgueira.com; Embarcadero Abeleda, Carretera OU903; adult incl wine tasting €15, child €7; ⏲1hr cruises 4-6 times a day Thu-Tue approx Mar-Nov) or larger boats operated by the **Diputación de Lugo** (☎982 26 01 96; http://reservas.rutasembalses.es; Embarcadoiro Doade, Carretera LU903; adult/senior & child €9/5; ⏲2hr cruises 11.30am & 4 or 4.30pm Wed-Sun mid-Apr–May & Oct, daily Jun-Sep, Fri-Sun Nov-early Dec, also 7pm daily Jun–mid-Sep). Schedules may vary. You can combine a *Brandán* trip with visiting Adega Algueira (same owners).

**Ponte da Boga** WINERY

(☎988 20 33 06; www.pontedaboga.es; Carretera OU903, Km 21.8, O Couto, San Paio; 45min tour incl 7-wine tasting €6; ⏲10am-10pm Easter-Oct, 10am-2pm & 3-7pm Nov-Easter; P) Ponte da Boga dates back to 1898 and is one of several wineries that are reviving autochthonous Galician grape varieties. Some of its wines are among Ribeira Sacra's best; you get to taste seven of them on the standard tour.

**Hotel Casa de Caldelas** HOTEL €
(☎638 234067; www.hotelcasadecaldelas.com; Praza do Prado 5, Castro Caldelas; incl breakfast s €35-40, d €45-55; ⏲closed Nov; 📶) Snug, up-to-date rooms and bathrooms set in a handsome 18th-century stone house on the village's main square make this small, welcoming hotel a great choice.

**Merenzao** GALICIAN €€
(☎674 225854; www.merenzao.es; Doade; mains €15-22; ⏲1.30-4pm Thu-Mon Mar-Jun, Thu-Tue Jul, Sep & Oct, daily Aug, Fri-Sun Nov-Dec, dinner from 9pm Fri & Sat Aug; Ⓟ) For a lunch treat make your way to this minimalist dining room in Doade. Galician meat and seafood are prepared with delicious contemporary flair, the atmosphere is comfortable, and fine local wines and rural views through the picture windows add to your contentment.

## Monforte de Lemos

POP 16,100 / ELEV 300M

This crossroads town is neither as compact nor as pristine as other stops in the region, but it has a historic heart and a few good restaurants, and it's well worth making your way north of the centre up the **Monte de San Vicente**. Here the 17th-century Monasterio de San Vicente is occupied by a *parador* hotel whose elegant neoclassical courtyard, cafe and restaurant are open to all, and you can visit the **Torre da Homenaxe** (€1.50; ⏲11am-2pm & 4-7pm Tue-Sun approx Jun-Sep, Sat & Sun rest of year; Ⓟ), the last vestige of the Counts of Lemos' medieval castle. You can drive up the hill, but it's interesting to walk up past medieval walls and houses from Praza de España in the town centre. Follow Rúas Zapaterías, Pescaderías and Falagueira then head up the 'Castillo' path a few metres inside the Porta Nova gate.

# Lugo

POP 90,000

The grand Roman walls encircling old Lugo are considered the best preserved of their kind in the world and are the number-one reason visitors land here. Within the fortress is a beautifully preserved web of streets and squares, most of them pedestrian-only, with plenty of interesting (and many free) things to see and a terrific tapas-bar scene. Lucus Augusti was a major town of Roman Gallaecia, and Lugo today is a quiet but beguiling city.

## Sights

**★Roman Walls** WALLS
(⏲24hr; 👪) FREE The path running right round the top of the World Heritage–listed Roman walls is to Lugo what a maritime promenade is to a seaside resort: a place to jog, take an evening stroll, see and be seen. The walls, erected in the 3rd century CE, make a 2.2km loop around the old town, rise 15m high and are studded with 85 stout towers. They failed, however, to save Lugo from being taken by the Suevi in 460 and the Muslims three centuries later.

The **Centro de Interpretación de la Muralla** (Praza do Campo 11; ⏲10am-2pm & 4-8pm Jun–mid-Oct, to 6pm mid-Oct–May) FREE, sharing premises with the helpful **Oficina Municipal de Turismo** (☎982 25 16 58; www.lugo.gal; ⏲10am-8pm Jun–mid-Oct, to 6pm mid-Oct–May) a block north of Lugo's cathedral, gives interesting background on the Roman walls, with videos and audio guides, all available in English.

**Catedral de Santa María** CATHEDRAL
(☎608 505531; www.catedraldelugo.es; Praza Pio XII; adult/pilgrim incl audio guide €5/3; ⏲11am-7pm Mon-Sat, 2-6pm Sun Apr-Oct, 11am-6pm Mon-Sat Nov-Mar) Lugo's serene cathedral, inspired by Santiago de Compostela's, was begun in 1129, though work continued for centuries, yielding a stylistic melange ranging from Romanesque transepts to the neoclassical west facade. The ultra-baroque high altar is surrounded by colourful stained-glass windows. Behind it sits the beautiful Gothic image of Nosa Señora dos Ollos Grandes (Our Lady of the Big Eyes). Spanish-language guided visits (€5 per person; minimum five people) at noon and 1pm climb to the towers and visit the 18th-century cloister.

**Museo Provincial** MUSEUM
(www.redemuseisticalugo.org; Praza da Soidade; ⏲9am-9pm Mon-Fri, 10.30am-2pm & 4.30-8pm Sat, 11am-2pm Sun) FREE Lugo's main museum includes parts of the Gothic Convento de San Francisco and is one of Galicia's best and biggest museums. Well-displayed exhibits include ancient gold jewellery, Roman mosaics, Sargadelos ceramics and plentiful 19th- and 20th-century Galician art.

**Casa dos Mosaicos** ARCHAEOLOGICAL SITE
(Rúa de Doutor Castro 20-22; ⏲10am-2pm & 4.30-8.30pm Jun–mid-Oct, 10am-1.30pm & 4.30-7.30pm Tue-Sun mid-Oct–May) FREE These remains of a Roman mansion sit beneath an old town street, with some wonderfully preserved mosaics and murals.

## Festivals & Events

**Arde Lucus** FIESTA
(www.ardelucus.com; ⏲Jun; ) Around half a million people pack into Lugo over three or four days in June (sometimes running into July), as the city celebrates its Roman roots with chariot races, gladiator fights and much more.

## Sleeping

**Hostel Cross** HOSTEL €
(☎604 026605; www.hostelcross.com; Rúa da Cruz 14; dm from €15; ) In the heart of the old town, shiny, modern Hostel Cross is a favourite with Camino Primitivo travellers but makes a good tight-budget lodging for anyone. You sleep in well-arranged capsule bunks, and there are washing machines and an adequate number of bathrooms.

**Hotel Méndez Núñez** HOTEL €€
(☎982 23 07 11; www.hotelmendeznunez.com; Rúa da Raíña 1; r €50-135; @) The 70-room Méndez Núñez offers bright, spacious quarters with good beds and gleaming bathrooms. With a great old-town location, and parking nearby for €6, it's a good deal when rates are towards the lower end of their range. The panoramic 6th-floor terrace is great for breakfast, drinks or snacks.

**Orbán e Sangro** BOUTIQUE HOTEL €€€
(Hotel Pazo de Orbán; ☎982 24 02 17; www.pazodeorban.es; Travesía do Miño 6; d €88-220, incl breakfast €110-253; P) The rooms of this welcoming hotel, in an 18th-century mansion, are regal, with rich linen, antique furnishings, designer bathrooms and (in most) huge 2.15m beds. The great 'ecological' breakfast focuses on local produce, and the hotel is full of intriguing antiques and art.

## Eating

The old town, especially Rúa da Cruz, Rúa Nova and Praza do Campo, north of the cathedral, is riddled with inviting bar-restaurants serving both tapas and main dishes. Many offer two free tapas with each drink, one of which you have to select from a list recited verbally (usually at high speed!) by bar staff.

**A Nosa Terra** GALICIAN €€
(www.currunchoanosaterra.com; Rúa Nova 8; mains €14-33; ⏲1-3.30pm & 8-11.30pm Thu-Tue, closed Nov) An inviting Rúa Nova classic. Stand in the narrow bar for tapas and drinks, or sit down in the back for pork *solomillo* (tenderloin) in Arzúa cheese sauce, or cod with prawns and clams.

**Restaurante Paprica** GALICIAN €€€
(www.paprica.es; Rúa das Nóreas 10; mains €19-29, menús €29-37; ⏲1.30-3.45pm & 8.30-10.45pm Apr-Jun, closed Mon night & Sun mid-Jun–Sep, Sun night & Mon Oct–mid-Jun) The talented team here creates satisfying original dishes based on locally sourced, organic ingredients of fresh seafood and vegetables, cheeses and quality meat. You can eat light in the bar or sit down to full meals. Everything is delicious, including the desserts!

**Mesón de Alberto** GALICIAN €€€
(☎982 22 83 10; www.mesondealberto.com; Rúa da Cruz 4; mains €13-30; ⏲1-3.30pm Sun & Mon, 1-3.30pm & 8-11.30pm Wed-Sat) The classiest place in the tapas zone, Alberto's serves traditionally prepared meat, fish and shellfish with a few inventive touches – meals upstairs, tapas on the ground floor.

## Getting There & Away

From the **bus station** (☎982 22 39 85; Praza da Constitución), just outside the southern walls, Empresa Freire (www.empresafreire.com) runs to Santiago de Compostela (€9.75, 1½ to 2¼ hours, six or more daily); Arriva (www.arriva.gal) heads to A Coruña (€9.45, 1¼ to 2¼ hours, five or more daily). Other services head to Ourense, Pontevedra, Ribadeo, León, Madrid, Asturias and beyond. The bus station may move to the train station (set for a revamp), 400m east of the walled city, in 2021 or later.

Renfe (www.renfe.com) trains head three or more times daily to A Coruña (€11 to €19, 1½ to two hours) and Ourense (€10 to €20, 1¾ hours), and at least once to Madrid (€17 to €56, 6¾ to 9½ hours).

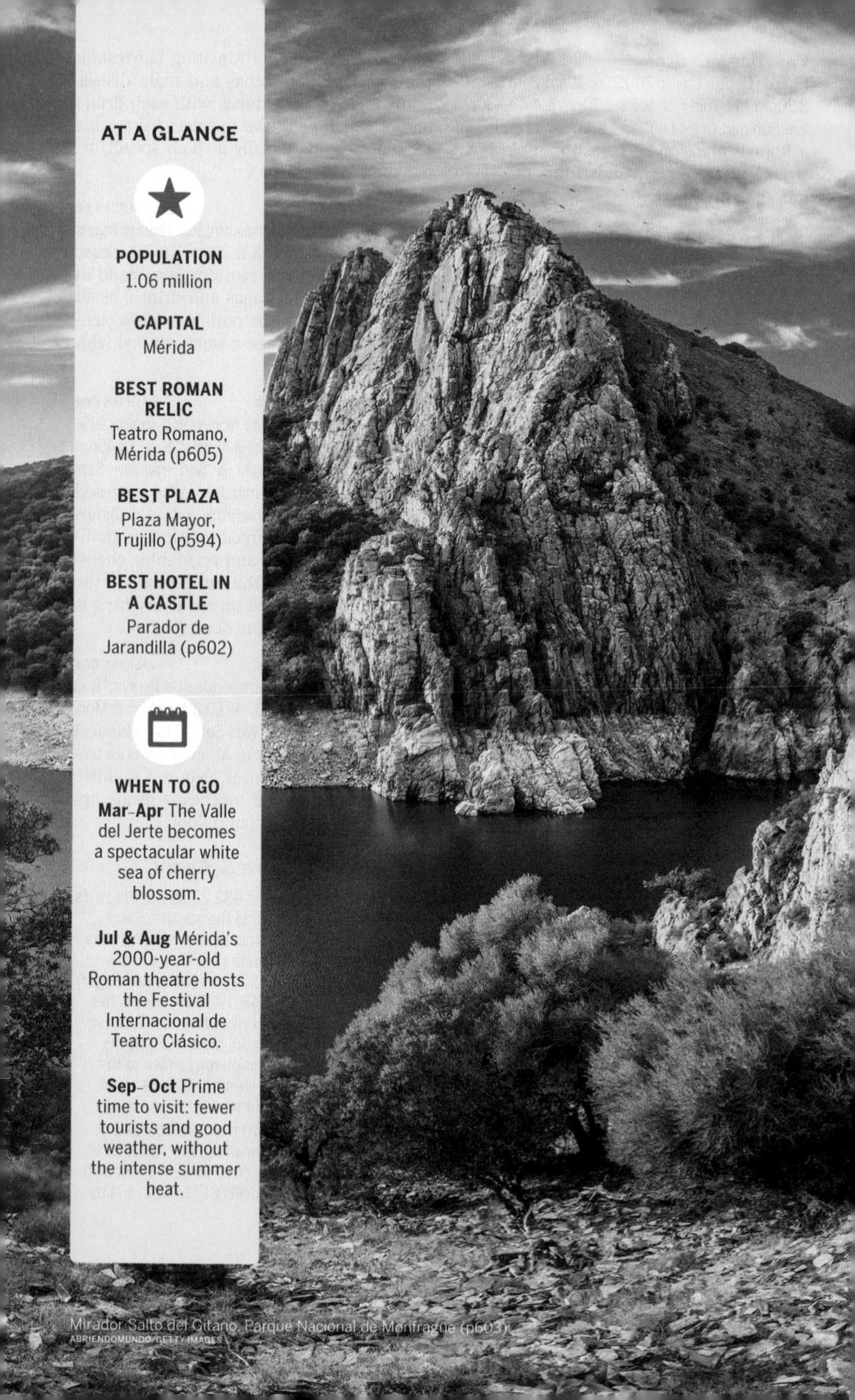

## AT A GLANCE

**POPULATION**
1.06 million

**CAPITAL**
Mérida

**BEST ROMAN RELIC**
Teatro Romano, Mérida (p605)

**BEST PLAZA**
Plaza Mayor, Trujillo (p594)

**BEST HOTEL IN A CASTLE**
Parador de Jarandilla (p602)

**WHEN TO GO**

**Mar–Apr** The Valle del Jerte becomes a spectacular white sea of cherry blossom.

**Jul & Aug** Mérida's 2000-year-old Roman theatre hosts the Festival Internacional de Teatro Clásico.

**Sep– Oct** Prime time to visit: fewer tourists and good weather, without the intense summer heat.

Mirador Salto del Gitano, Parque Nacional de Monfragüe (p603)
ABRIENDOMUNDO/GETTY IMAGES

# Extremadura

Exploring Extremadura is a journey into the heart of old Spain, from the country's finest Roman ruins to mysterious medieval cities and time-worn villages. Mérida, Cáceres and Trujillo rank among Spain's most beautifully preserved historical settlements. *Extremeño* hamlets have a timeless charm, from the remote northern hills to sacred eastern Guadalupe and seductive Zafra on the cusp of Andalucía in the south.

Few foreign travellers make it this far. Spaniards, however, know Extremadura as a place to sample some of inland Spain's best food: roasted meats, the pungent, creamy Torta del Casar cheese and the finest Monesterio *jamón* (ham).

This is a region of broad blue skies and vast swathes of sparsely populated land with isolated farmhouses and crumbling hilltop castles. Wooded sierras rise along the northern, eastern and southern fringes, while the raptor-rich Parque Nacional de Monfragüe is Extremadura's most dramatic corner.

**INCLUDES**

## Extremadura Highlights

1 **Cáceres** Wandering the Ciudad Monumental's magical cobbled streets and packed-out tapas bars.

2 **Mérida** (p605) Clambering over Spain's finest Roman ruins.

3 **Trujillo** (p594) Travelling to the medieval hometown of infamous conquistadors.

4 **Zafra** (p608) Feasting on tapas beneath the Plaza Grande's palms, then sleeping in a castle.

5 **Parque Nacional de Monfragüe** (p602) Spotting majestic birds of prey high above the Tajo.

6 **Guadalupe** (p598) Admiring the fabulous art and architecture at Guadalupe's extraordinary monastery.

7 **Alcántara** (p593) Checking out the mighty Roman bridge over the Tajo.

8 **La Vera** (p601) Exploring half-timbered villages and rushing rivers, then marvelling at the cherry blossom of the adjacent Valle del Jerte.

9 **Granadilla** (p604) Pacing the quiet lanes of this restored historic museum village.

10 **Monesterio** (p611) Learning all about Spain's favourite food, *jamón* (ham), at the Museo del Jamón, and then tasting it.

## Cáceres

POP 96,070

Visiting the Unesco World Heritage–listed old city of Cáceres is like stepping back into the Middle Ages. Narrow cobbled streets twist and climb among ancient stone walls lined with palaces, mansions, arches and churches, while the skyline is decorated with turrets, spires, gargoyles and enormous storks' nests. Protected by defensive walls, it has survived almost intact from its 16th-century period of splendour. It's a magical place, one that rewards as much time as you can devote to exploring it.

### Sights

#### Plaza de Santa María & Around

Most visitors approach the stunning Ciudad Monumental – Cáceres' incredibly well-preserved medieval core – from the Plaza Mayor, passing under the 18th-century **Arco de la Estrella** (Calle Arco de la Estrella) onto the **Plaza de Santa María**. Notable facades on the Plaza de Santa María include the **Palacio Episcopal** (Bishop's Palace), the **Palacio de Mayoralgo** (Plaza de Santa María) and the **Palacio de Ovando** (Plaza de Santa María), all in 16th-century Renaissance style, as well as the Renaissance-style **Palacio de la Diputación** (Plaza de Santa María), a little further to the southeast.

**★Torre de Bujaco** TOWER
(☎927 24 67 89; Plaza Mayor; adult/child €2.50/free; ⏲10am-2pm & 5.30-8.30pm Tue-Sun May-Sep, 10am-2pm & 4.30-7.30pm Tue-Sun Oct-Apr) As you head up the steps to the Ciudad Monumental from the Plaza Mayor, turn left to climb the 25m-high, 12th-century Torre de Bujaco, home to an interpretative display on Cáceres' history. From the rooftop there's a fabulous stork's-eye view over the Plaza Mayor. From here, you can also walk across the top of the 18th-century Arco de la Estrella.

**Concatedral de Santa María** CATHEDRAL
(Plaza de Santa María; adult/child €4/free; ⏲10am-9pm Mon-Sat, 10am-6.30pm Sun May-Sep, hours vary Oct-Apr) This 15th-century Gothic cathedral creates an impressive opening scene for the Ciudad Monumental. Inside, you'll find a magnificent carved 16th-century cedar **altarpiece**, fine noble tombs and chapels, and a small ecclesiastical **museum**. Beautiful colourful murals (including dragons) adorn the vaulted ceiling above the altarpiece. Climb the **bell tower** for old-town views.

**Palacio de Carvajal** HISTORIC BUILDING
(☎927 25 55 97; Calle Amargura 1; ⏲8am-8.45pm Mon-Fri, 10am-1.45pm & 5-7.45pm Sat, 10am-1.45pm Sun) FREE Just off the northeastern corner of the main Plaza de Santa María stands this late 15th-century mansion. The building was abandoned after fires tore through in the 19th century. Now restored, it houses a modern display on the province's attractions and the helpful regional tourist office (p592).

**Palacio Toledo-Moctezuma** HISTORIC BUILDING
(Plaza del Conde Canilleros) Just north of the Plaza de Santa María lies the domed 16th-century Palacio Toledo-Moctezuma, once home to Isabel Moctezuma, daughter of the Aztec emperor Moctezuma II, who was brought to Cáceres as a conquistador's bride. The palace now contains the municipal archives and hosts temporary exhibitions.

**Iglesia de San Francisco Javier** CHURCH
(Iglesia de la Preciosa Sangre; Plaza de San Jorge; adult/child €1.50/free; ⏲10am-2pm & 5-8pm Apr-Sep, 10am-2pm & 4.30-7.30pm Oct-Mar) This 18th-century Jesuit church, with a baroque facade that rises above the Plaza de San Jorge, has towers that you can climb for glorious old-town views (obscured a little by netting).

#### Plaza de San Mateo & Around

**★Palacio de los Golfines de Abajo** HISTORIC BUILDING
(☎927 21 80 51; www.palaciogolfinesdeabajo.com; Plaza de los Golfines; tours adult/child €2.50/free; ⏲tours hourly 10am-1pm & 5-7pm Tue-Sat, 10am-1pm Sun May-Sep, 10am-1pm & 4-6.30pm Tue-Sat, 10am-1pm Sun Oct-Apr) The sumptuous home of Cáceres' prominent Golfín family has been beautifully restored. Built piecemeal between the 14th and 20th centuries, it's crammed with historical treasures: original 17th-century tapestries and armoury murals, a 19th-century bust of Alfonso XII, and a signed 1485 troops request from the

## Cáceres

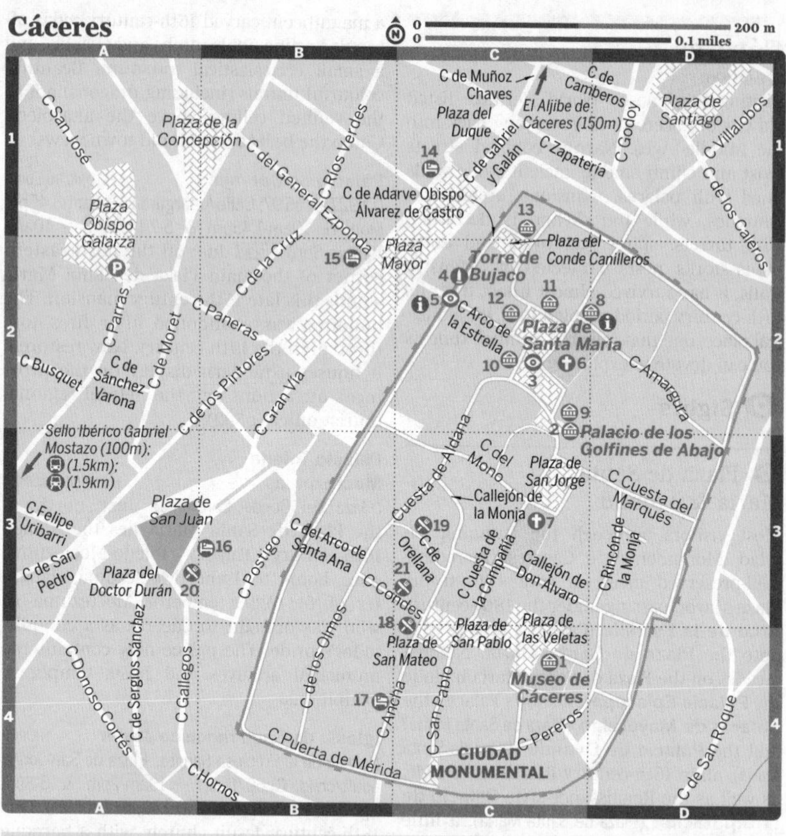


## Cáceres

**Top Sights**

1 Museo de Cáceres .......... C4
2 Palacio de los Golfines de Abajo .......... C2
3 Plaza de Santa María .......... C2
4 Torre de Bujaco .......... C2

**Sights**

5 Arco de la Estrella .......... C2
6 Concatedral de Santa María .......... C2
7 Iglesia de San Francisco Javier .......... C3
8 Palacio de Carvajal .......... D2
9 Palacio de la Diputación .......... C2
10 Palacio de Mayoralgo .......... C2
11 Palacio de Ovando .......... C2
12 Palacio Episcopal .......... C2
13 Palacio Toledo-Moctezuma .......... C1

**Sleeping**

14 Hotel La Boheme .......... C1
15 Hotel Soho Boutique Casa Don Fernando .......... B2
16 NH Collection Palacio de Oquendo .......... B3
17 Parador de Cáceres .......... B4

**Eating**

18 Atrio .......... C4
19 La Cacharrería .......... C3
20 Tapería Yuste .......... A3
21 Torre de Sande .......... C3

Reyes Católicos (Catholic Monarchs) to their Golfín stewards. But it's the detailed, theatrical tours (Spanish, English, French or Portuguese), through four richly decorated lounges, an extravagant chapel and fascinating documents room, that stand out.

★ **Museo de Cáceres** MUSEUM

(☎927 01 08 77; http://museodecaceres.juntaex.es; Plaza de las Veletas; adult/child €1.20, EU citizens free, Sun free; ⏲9.30am-2.30pm & 4-8pm Tue-Sat, 10am-3pm Sun) The excellent Museo de Cáceres, spread across 12 buildings in a

16th-century mansion built over an evocative 12th-century *aljibe* (cistern), is the only surviving element of Cáceres' Moorish castle. The impressive archaeological section includes an elegant stone boar dated to the 4th to 2nd centuries BCE, while the equally appealing fine-arts display (behind the main museum; open only in the mornings) showcases works by such greats as Picasso, Miró, Tàpies and El Greco. It's one of Spain's most underrated collections.

## Activities

**El Aljibe de Cáceres** HAMMAM
(927 22 32 56; www.elaljibedecaceres.com; Calle de Peña 5; bath with aromatherapy/massage €23/30; 10am-2pm & 6-10pm Tue-Sun) This luxurious recreation of the Moorish-style bath experience combines soothing architecture and a range of treatments. The basic thermal bath pass includes aromatherapy and herbal tea, but you can also throw in a range of massages.

## Tours

Numerous guide associations vie for your business along the eastern side of the Plaza Mayor. Most run similar 1½- to two-hour Spanish-language tours taking in the highlights of the Ciudad Monumental; standard walking tours cost €6 per person.

**★Cuentatrovas de Cordel** WALKING
(667 776205, 666 836332; www.cuentatrovas.com; adult/child from €5/free; hours vary) Guides and other actors dress up in period costume and take you on a tour with a difference through the Ciudad Monumental. It's fun, informative (for Spanish speakers) and very much recommended. Times vary, with after-dark tours the speciality, departing from the Arco de la Estrella.

## Festivals & Events

**Fiesta de San Jorge** FIESTA
(22-23 Apr) Cáceres celebrates the Fiesta de San Jorge, in honour of its patron saint, with shows, fireworks, competitions, a recreation of a Christian-Moorish battle and a giant dragon on the Plaza Mayor.

**Womad** MUSIC
(World of Music, Arts & Dance; www.womadespana.com; May) For three fiesta-fuelled days in mid-May, Cáceres stages a long-running edition of Womad, with international bands playing in the old city's squares.

## Sleeping

**Hotel La Boheme** HOTEL €
(927 21 73 51; www.hotellaboheme.com; Plaza Mayor; d/ste from €50/60; ) At the lower, northern end of the Plaza Mayor, La Boheme has large rooms with a wonderfully whimsical air to them – plenty of colour and character but never overdone. The terrace suite is particularly good. Rooms overlooking the plaza have plenty of light but can also be noisy.

**★Hotel Soho Boutique Casa Don Fernando** BOUTIQUE HOTEL €€
(927 62 71 76; www.sohohoteles.com; Plaza Mayor 30; s/d from €55/70; P) Cáceres' smartest midrange choice sits on the Plaza Mayor right opposite the Arco de la Estrella. Boutique-style rooms, spread over four floors, are tastefully modern, with gleaming bathrooms through glass doors. Pricier 'superiors' enjoy the best plaza views (though weekend nights can be noisy), and attic-style top-floor rooms are good for families. Service hits that perfect professional-yet-friendly note.

**NH Collection Palacio de Oquendo** HISTORIC HOTEL €€
(927 21 58 00; www.nh-collection.com; Plaza de San Juan 11; r from €90; ) Classy, spacious cream-coated rooms, complete with coffee kits, chunky mattresses, soothing lighting and stylish modern bathrooms, await within this beautifully revamped 16th-century palace. Best are the balcony rooms with views across the Plaza de San Juan. Step into on-site **Tapería Yuste** (tapas €5, raciones €10-19, set menus from €26.40; 1-4pm & 8pm-midnight) for deliciously inventive tapas.

**★Parador de Cáceres** HISTORIC HOTEL €€€
(927 21 17 59; www.parador.es; Calle Ancha 6; r €90-195; P@) This old-town conglomeration of 14th-century Gothic palaces has swish, modern interiors, with bedrooms and bathrooms filled with style and comfort. Superior rooms are standouts: one sporting original arched red-brick ceilings, another fantastic Ciudad Monumental views. Specify if you'd like a double bed (most rooms are twins).

WORTH A TRIP

## CASAR DE CÁCERES

Extremadura may be well known for its *jamón*, but its Torta del Casar cheese is equally celebrated in Spanish culinary circles. Casar de Cáceres (population 4610), 12km north of Cáceres and well signposted off the N630 to/from Plasencia, is where this regional treasure was born and is still produced – it's an easy excursion from Cáceres.

Apart from picking up a wheel of the cheese from any one of the shops lining the main street, visit the **Museo del Queso** (☎927 290 081; Calle Barrionuevo Bajo 7; ⏲10am-2pm & 4-6pm Tue-Sat, 10am-2pm Sun) FREE, dedicated to this pungent, creamy cheese that's aged for 40 days and eaten most often as a spread on *tostas* (topped toast).

Eight buses run daily Monday to Friday (two on Saturday) between Casar de Cáceres and Cáceres bus station (€2.30, 20 minutes).

## Eating

From the Plaza Mayor restaurants you can watch swallows and storks glide among the turrets of the old town, however, there's a better quality tapas and dining scene around the old town and nearby Plaza de San Juan.

**★La Cacharrería** TAPAS €€
(☎927 10 16 79; lacacharreria@live.com; Calle de Orellana 1; tapas €4.50, raciones €10-19; ⏲restaurant 12.30-4pm & 8.30pm-midnight Thu-Mon; ✎) Local flavours and ingredients combine in exquisite, international-inspired concoctions at this packed-out, minimalist-design tapas bar tucked into an old-town house. *Solomillo* (tenderloin) in Torta del Casar cheese arrives in martini glasses. Delicious guacamole, hummus, falafel and 'salsiki' are a godsend for vegetarians. No advance reservations: get here when the doors open.

**★Atrio** CONTEMPORARY SPANISH €€€
(☎927 24 29 28; www.restauranteatrio.com; Plaza de San Mateo 1; menús from €145; ⏲2-4pm & 8.30-11.30pm; ✎) With a stunning location in the heart of old-town Cáceres, this is Extremadura's top restaurant. Chic contemporary design and service that's both formal and friendly back up the wonderful, inventive culinary creations. The focus is on local produce of the highest quality, via a 12- to 13-course degustation menu. Vegetarian and gluten-free menus available with advance notice. Bookings essential.

**Torre de Sande** SPANISH €€€
(☎927 21 11 47; www.torredesande.com; Calle Condes 3; mains €19-26, set menus from €35; ⏲1.30-4pm & 8.30pm-midnight Wed-Sun; ✎) Sit in the pretty courtyard and dine on roast suckling pig or kid, or on ambitious seasonal dishes such as seafood-filled *merluza* (hake) or tomato and basil soup with goat's cheese and figs at this elegant gourmet restaurant in the heart of the Ciudad Monumental. For something more modest, stop for drinks and tapas at the busy interconnecting *tapería*.

## Shopping

**Sello Ibérico Gabriel Mostazo** FOOD & DRINKS
(☎927 24 28 81; www.mostazo.es; Calle de San Antón 6; ⏲9.30am-2pm & 5-8.30pm Mon-Sat, 10am-2pm Sun) One of the best delis in town, with plenty of cheeses, *jamón*, wines and fresh and tinned local products.

## Information

**Oficina de Turismo** (☎674 301332, 927 11 12 22; www.turismoextremadura.com; Plaza Mayor; ⏲10am-2pm & 5.30-8.30pm Jun-Sep, 10am-2pm & 4.30-7.30pm Oct-May) On the Plaza Mayor, focusing on the city and wider Extremadura attractions.

**Oficina de Turismo** (☎927 25 55 97; www.turismocaceres.org; Palacio de Carvajal, Calle Amargura 1; ⏲8am-8.45pm Mon-Fri, 10am-1.45pm & 5-7.45pm Sat, 10am-1.45pm Sun) Inside the Palacio de Carvajal.

## Getting There & Away

### BUS

The **bus station** (☎927 23 25 50; www.estacionautobuses.es; Calle Túnez 1; ⏲6.30am-10.30pm) is 2km southwest of the old town.

| Destination | Fare (€) | Time | Frequency (daily) |
|---|---|---|---|
| Badajoz | 6.75 | 1¼hr | 3-6 |
| Madrid (normal/express) | 24/33 | 4½/3¾hr | 5/2 |
| Mérida | 5.70 | 1hr | 2-3 |
| Plasencia | 6 | 50min | 1-4 |
| Trujillo | 3.80 | 45min | 5-6 |

### TRAIN

From the train station, 2.5km southwest of the old town, trains run to/from Madrid (€20 to €34, 3¼ hours to 4¼ hours, five daily), Mérida (€6.30 to €9.40, one hour, up to seven daily) and Plasencia (from €5.40, one hour, four daily).

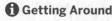

## Getting Around

Bus L8 from outside the bus station (400m east of the train station) runs to/from the central Plaza Obispo Galarza.

# Alcántara

POP 1480

Alcántara is Arabic for 'the Bridge', and sure enough, below this remote Extremaduran town, a spectacular Roman bridge extends across the Río Tajo. The town itself retains old walls, a ruined castle of Moorish origin, several imposing mansions and churches, and the enormous Renaissance Conventual de San Benito. It all adds up to one of Extremadura's most rewarding (and least-known) detours.

## Sights

Alcántara's *barrio judío* (Jewish quarter) lies southeast of the **Plaza de España** and is bordered by the pretty **Plaza Corredera**. For a partial view of the Puente Romano from above, walk 100m west from the Iglesia de Santa María de Almocóvar down Calle de Carnicería, then continue along the pedestrian-only stone path that leads downhill for around 250m to a **mirador**.

There's an even better **mirador** that takes in both the town and Puente Romano in one sweep. To get there, drive across the Puente Romano northwest of town in the direction of Portugal. After just over a kilometre, take the turn-off signposted 'Embalse' and the (now closed) campsite; the lookout is 400m along this road on your right.

**Puente Romano** BRIDGE

On the northwest side of Alcántara, a magnificent 2nd-century Roman bridge – 204m long, 61m high, with six arches and much reinforced over the centuries – spans the Río Tajo below a huge dam retaining the Embalse de Alcántara. The restorations may have dulled the bridge's obvious antiquity but it's still a stirring sight. From the bridge, a beautiful 20km walking circuit follows the river then loops up into the hills via a village and a prehistoric menhir (standing stone).

**Conventual de San Benito** CONVENT

(☎927 39 00 81; Calle Regimiento de Argel; ⏲tours hourly 10.15am-1.15pm & 5-7pm Mon-Fri, 11.15am-1.15pm & 5-7pm Sat, 11.15am-1.15pm Sun Apr-Oct, hours vary Nov-Mar) FREE What a surprise this is out in Extremadura's backblocks! Built in the 16th century to house the Orden de Alcántara, an order of Reconquista knights – part monks, part soldiers – who ruled much of western Extremadura as a kind of private fiefdom, this grand Renaissance convent was abandoned in the 19th century. The highlights of the restored monastery include the Gothic cloister and the perfectly proportioned three-tier loggia. Admission is by free guided visit (ring the bell if the door is shut).

## Sleeping

**Hospedería Conventual de Alcántara** HISTORIC HOTEL €€

(☎927 390 638; www.hospederiasdeextremadura.es; Carretera del Poblado Iberdrola; r incl breakfast

### WHAT'S COOKING IN EXTREMADURA?

Famous among Spaniards for its high-quality ingredients, Extremaduran cooking is overwhelmingly meaty. Typical treats include *cochinillo asado* (roast suckling pig), *caldereta de cabrito* (stewed kid), first-rate *jamón*, creamy Torta del Casar cheese from Casar de Cáceres, *pimentón* (paprika) from La Vera and, in season, ripe cherries from the Valle del Jerte.

➡ *Migas extremeñas* (breadcrumbs fried with garlic, peppers and pork) at Mesón La Troya (p597) or with honey at Tábula Calda (p608).

➡ *Caldereta de cabrito* (stewed kid) at Villa Xarahiz (p602).

➡ Torta del Casar (a strong, creamy cheese served on toast), at many places, including Casa Juan (p601).

➡ *Jamón ibérico* (Iberian ham), anywhere, but especially the bars of Monesterio (p611); the mountain hamlet of Montánchez is also known for its first-rate *jamón*.

OFF THE BEATEN TRACK

## GARROVILLAS DE ALCONÉTAR

If you're driving between Alcántara and Cáceres or Plasencia, make time for a stop in little Garrovillas de Alconétar. This otherwise unremarkable town is distinguished by a truly remarkable **Plaza Mayor** (Plaza de la Constitución), surrounded by arched porticoes and two-storey buildings dating back as far as the 15th century – it's one of the most beautiful in Extremadura.

Right on the main square, the four-star **Hospederia Puente de Alconétar** (927 30 94 25; www.hospederiasdeextremadura.es; Plaza de la Constitución 18; s/d €67/75; ) inhabits a restored 15th-century palace. Rooms are modern and attractively clean-lined, though some in the older wing have lovely feature walls in stone or brick that add a real sense of character. The restaurant (mains €13 to €21) is similarly excellent.

Garrovillas de Alconétar lies along the EX302, 10km west of the N630. It's a 40km drive east from Alcántara or 47km north from Cáceres. Public transport amounts to the occasional bus from Cáceres.

from €75; P) On the eastern edge of town, this comfortable and stylish modern hotel enjoys a marvellous setting in a 15th-century monastery turned flour factory. It offers bright, lime-green rooms bursting with colour. The restaurant serves up Extremaduran specialities such as pheasant and all manner of dishes that include wild mushrooms and the pungent creamy Torta del Casar cheese.

## Shopping

**Artesanía Pepi** FOOD

(605 929657; www.facebook.com/dulceriaartesaniapepi; Calle Arco de la Concepción 3; 10am-2pm & 5-8pm) This wonderful old pastry shop sells the much-loved local pastry, known as *mormentera*, which is filled with honey and almonds and has strong links to Arab and Sephardic recipes from the region's past. Opening hours vary - ask at the tourist office if you find it closed.

## Information

**Oficina de Turismo de Alcántara** (927 39 08 63; www.alcantara.es; Avenida de Mérida 21; 10am-2pm & 4.30-6.30pm Mon-Fri, 10.30am-2.30pm Sat & Sun)

## Getting There & Away

**Mirat** (927 23 33 54; www.mirat-transportes.es) runs four buses Monday to Friday to/from Cáceres (€7.60, 1½ hours), but none on weekends.

# Trujillo

POP 9195

Trujillo can feel enchanted. Crowned by a castle and composed almost entirely of stone buildings, grand and medieval, with terracotta roofs, the town is a labyrinth of mansions, leafy courtyards, fruit gardens, quiet plazas, churches and convents enclosed within 900m of walls circling the upper town. It all dates to the 16th century, when Trujillo's favourite sons returned home from the Americas as wealthy conquistadors, and what they bequeathed to their home town lives on in a most beautiful way.

## Sights

Don't miss the less-visited western end of the upper old town, with its cobbles, palaces and flower-filled plazas. A small section of the **muralla** (city wall) can be climbed near the **Puerta del Triunfo** (Plaza del Cementerio); it was through this gate that conquering Christian troops marched in 1232 when they wrested the city from the Muslims.

**★Plaza Mayor** SQUARE

Trujillo's main square is one of Spain's most spectacular plazas, surrounded by baroque and Renaissance stone buildings sporting intricately carved facades, topped with a skyline of towers, turrets, cupolas, crenellations and nesting storks.

A large, bronze equestrian **statue** (Plaza Mayor) of the conquistador Francisco Pizarro by American sculptor Charles Rumsey dominates the plaza. But all is not as it seems. Apparently Rumsey originally sculpted it as a statue of Hernán Cortés to present to Mexico, but Mexico, which takes a dim view of Cortés, declined it, so it was given to Trujillo as Pizarro instead.

On the south side of the plaza, carved images of Pizarro and his lover Inés Yupanqui (sister of the Inca emperor Atahualpa) adorn the corner of the 16th-century **Palacio de la Conquista**. To the right is their daughter Francisca Pizarro Yupanqui with her husband (and uncle), Hernando Pizarro. The mansion was built in the 1560s for Hernando and Francisca after Hernando (the only Pizarro brother not to die a bloody death in Peru) emerged from 20 years in jail for murder. Higher up, a bas-relief carving shows the Pizarro family shield (two bears and a pine tree), the walls of Cuzco (in present-day Peru) and Pizarro's ships.

Off the plaza's northeastern corner lies the 16th-century **Palacio de los Duques de San Carlos** (Palacio de los Carvajal Vargas), with its sober classical patio, grand granite staircase and distinctive brick chimneys built in Mudéjar style (though some say they represent New World cultures conquered by Spain). Nowadays it's a convent for the Jerónimo order.

Also looming over the plaza is the 16th-century **Iglesia de San Martín** (dult/child €1.50/free; ⏲10am-2pm & 5-8pm Apr-Sep, 10am-2pm & 4-7pm Oct-Mar), with delicate Gothic ceiling tracery in its single nave, striking stained-glass windows, a 1724 altarpiece and a grand 18th-century organ. Climb up to the choir loft for the best view.

**★Castillo de Trujillo** CASTLE

(adult/child €1.50/free; ⏲10am-2pm & 5-8pm Apr-Sep, 10am-2pm & 4-7pm Oct-Mar) Atop the town's 600m-high summit, Trujillo's castle is of 10th-century Islamic origin (note the horseshoe arch just inside the entrance) and was later strengthened by the Christians. Patrol the battlements for magnificent views (sunsets are exquisite), visit the derelict *aljibe* (cistern) and climb to the hermitage of Our Lady of the Victory, Trujillo's patron. A 50-*céntimo* coin makes her spin around in her alcove; you can also spot her above the entrance gate as you approach.

**Iglesia de Santa María la Mayor** CHURCH

(Plaza de Santa María; adult/child €2/free; ⏲10.30am-2pm & 4.30-7.30pm) This 13th-century church is a stunner. It has a mainly Gothic nave and two towers that you can climb for fabulous views across Trujillo, the castle and the sprawling countryside. The church's magnificent altarpiece includes 25 brilliantly coloured 15th-century paintings by Spanish artist Fernando Gallego in the Hispano-Flemish style, depicting scenes from the lives of Mary and Christ. The 124-step Torre Julia is a Romanesque stunner, while the 106-step Torre Nueva has some interesting architectural notes.

**Centro de Visitantes Los Descubridores** MUSEUM

(Cuesta de la Sangre; adult/child €1.50/free; ⏲10am-2pm & 5-8pm Apr-Sep, 10am-2pm & 4-7pm Oct-Mar) This museum inhabits the 17th-century Iglesia de la Preciosa Sangre de Cristo with a high-tech display on Spain's conquest of the Americas and the larger-than-life Trujillo heroes who very often led the way. Displays include the role of religion, a timeline of conquest and Trujillos around the world. Surprisingly, the Americas' indig-

WORTH A TRIP

## MALPARTIDA DE CÁCERES & LOS BARRUECOS

The pretty whitewashed town of Malpartida de Cáceres (www.malpartida-decaceres.es), southwest of Cáceres, is reason enough to detour off the N521 on your way to/from Mérida or Valencia de Alcántara. From May to September in particular, the Plaza de los Paraguas is given shade cover by more than a thousand brightly coloured raised umbrellas. But arguably the region's greatest attraction is the **Monumento Natural Los Barruecos**, a stirring world of beautiful boulders piled high along the shores of pretty natural lakes and with important (and picturesque) breeding colonies for white storks. The cinematic beauty of the landscapes here also caught the eye of producers of *Game of Thrones* – the epic battle scenes in episodes 4 and 5 of season 7 were filmed here.

enous population is barely mentioned, save for a wooden bust of Atahualpa – it's as if they didn't exist.

**Casa-Museo de Pizarro** MUSEUM
(Calle del Convento de las Jerónimas; adult/child €1.50/free; 10am-2pm & 5-8pm Apr-Sep, 10am-2pm & 4-7pm Oct-Mar) High in the upper old town (and signposted from the Puerta de Santiago), this small museum occupies a 15th-century home believed to have belonged to the Pizarro family. It includes period furniture, various knick-knacks from the Pizarro boys' conquests, a handy Pizarro family tree and, upstairs, historical displays (in Spanish and, in parts, English) detailing Spanish conquests in the Americas.

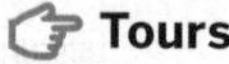

## Tours

Informative, fast-paced two-hour guided tours of Trujillo (in Spanish) leave from the tourist office daily at 11am and 5.30pm (4.30pm from October to March). Tickets cost €7.50 (kids free) and take in the Castillo de Trujillo, Iglesia de Santa María la Mayor, Casa-Museo de Pizarro, Iglesia de Santiago, Aljibe Hispano-Musulmán (otherwise off limits) and Plaza Mayor. Tickets also entitle you to free entry into a handful of other sights.

Private company **Turismo Trujillo** (☎927 32 05 10; www.turismotrujillo.es; Plaza Mayor; tours adult/child €10/5; tours 11am year-round, also 5.30pm & 8pm May–mid-Oct) offers guided Spanish- and English-language walking tours around Trujillo, with sunset itineraries (May to October) and wine, oil and cheese tastings thrown into the mix. It also has an additional sunset tour at 8pm from May to mid-October.

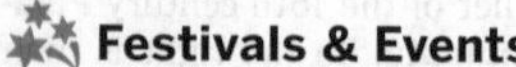

## Festivals & Events

**Feria del Queso** FOOD & DRINK
(www.feriadelquesotrujillo.es; late Apr–early May) Cheesemakers from all over Spain (and beyond) converge on the Plaza Mayor for Trujillo's pungent cheese fair.

## Sleeping

**El Mirador de las Monjas** HOTEL €
(☎927 65 92 23; www.elmiradordelasmonjas.com; Plaza de Santiago 4; r with/without breakfast €65/55; ❄) High in the old town, this super-friendly six-room *hostería* (small hotel) has bright, spotless, modern rooms decorated in a minimalist-chic style with lots of creams and whites and gorgeous, gleaming bathrooms. Upstairs rooms with sloping ceilings and pretty vistas are slightly better than

### EXTREMADURA'S TOP FOOD & WINE EXPERIENCES

For the liveliest tapas scenes, head to Cáceres, Mérida, Plasencia or smaller towns such as Zafra.

- Tracking down one of Spain's most celebrated cheeses, the Torta del Casar, in Casar de Cáceres' Museo del Queso (p592).
- Visiting the Museo del Jamón (p611) and sampling the region's best *jamón* in Monesterio.
- Learning everything there is to know about Spain's famous paprika at the **Museo del Pimentón** (☎927 46 08 10; Plaza Mayor 7; 10am-2pm & 5-7pm Tue-Sat, 9.30am-2.30pm Sun May-Sep, 10am-2pm & 4-6pm Tue-Sat, 9.30am-2.30pm Sun Oct-Apr) FREE in Jaraíz de la Vera.
- Glamming up for one of Spain's most sought-after fine-dining experiences at Atrio (p592) in Cáceres.
- Going food shopping for an Extremaduran picnic in Zafra at Iberllota (p610) and La Cava del Queso (p610).
- Sampling the robust reds of the Ribera del Guadiana wine-producing region, at Bodegas Medina (p609), and Bodegas Ruíz Torres (p598).
- Enjoying the best in Spanish cheeses at Trujillo's late-April Feria del Queso, or year-round at Zafra's Quesería La Bendita (p610).
- Eating until you can eat no more at Trujillo's Mesón La Troya.
- Trying a tapa of *pestorejo* (nape of a pig's neck) at Mérida's Mesón El Pestorejo (p608).
- Tasting Alcántara's local pastry, known as *mormentera*, at Artesanía Pepi (p594).

those below, but all are outrageously good value, plus there's a restaurant attached.

**Posada Dos Orillas** HISTORIC HOTEL €
(☎927 65 90 79; www.dosorillas.com; Calle de Cambrones 6; d €50-70; ) In a fantastic old-town corner, this tastefully renovated 15th-century mansion is full of character. The 13 comfy rooms replicate Spanish colonial taste and are named for countries containing towns called Trujillo. Twin-room 'Extremadura' has glimpses of Santa María church from its bathroom. Nights are deliciously quiet, while personal service from the welcoming owners couldn't be better. Rooms cost €10 more on weekends.

**★Eurostars Palacio de Santa Marta** HOTEL €€
(☎927 65 91 90; www.eurostarshotels.com; Calle de los Ballesteros 6; d standard/premium from €60/90; ) Above the Plaza Mayor, the refurbished 16th-century Santa Marta Palace combines slick, wood-floored chambers with original features such as exposed stone walls and high ceilings. There's a summer-only pool. For prime vistas over the square, book a superior or premium room. Spacious room 208, with its little pillared balcony, is stunning, as is two-balconied 206. Outstanding breakfasts, too.

**Parador de Trujillo** HISTORIC HOTEL €€
(☎927 32 13 50; www.parador.es; Calle Santa Beatriz de Silva 1; r €75-175; ) Given Trujillo's delightful overdose of hotels in historic buildings, it's no surprise that this *parador* (luxurious state-owned hotel) occupies a former 16th-century convent. Large terracotta-tiled rooms with understated historical touches branch off two evocative orange-and-olive-tree-dotted cloisters. Breakfast is served in a restored chapel and there's a summer pool. It's in the old town's winding backstreets, 350m east of the Plaza Mayor.

## Eating

**★Mesón La Troya** SPANISH €
(☎927 32 13 64; www.mesonlatroya.es; Plaza Mayor 10; mains €7-22, set menus €16-25; ⊙1-4pm & 8-11pm; ) Famous across Spain for its copious servings of no-frills *comida casera* (home-style cooking), Troya enjoys a prime location on Trujillo's main square. The food is decent, but it's more about quantity. At lunchtime, you'll be directed to one of several dining areas, where plates of tortilla and lettuce-and-tomato salad materialise before you've even ordered your three-course *menú*. Weekend queues stretch out the door.

**El 7 de Sillerías** SPANISH €€
(☎927 32 18 56; www.el7desillerias.es; Calle Sillerías 7; raciones €9-22, mains €12-24; ⊙noon-late Wed-Mon; ) With a friendly local buzz, snug wood-beamed interior and elegantly presented traditional fare, this cafe-bar-restaurant just southeast off the Plaza Mayor is one of Trujillo's better eateries. Tasty menu choices include Extremaduran *jamón*/cheese boards, plenty of Iberian pork and huge *parrilladas de verduras* (grilled vegetable platters). The cafe-bar area dishes out *raciones* (large plate servings), *bocadillos* (filled rolls) and *tostas* (topped toast).

**Restaurante Corral del Rey** SPANISH €€
(☎927 32 30 71; www.corraldelreytrujillo.com; Plazuela Corral del Rey 2; mains €12-28, set menus €25-36; ⊙1.30-4pm & 9-11.30pm Mon-Sat Apr-Sep, 1.30-4pm & 8.30-11pm Oct-Apr, closed Wed & Sun night Oct-Apr) Pocketed into a Plaza Mayor corner, this classically smart restaurant has four intimate dining rooms – choose the subterranean vaulted brick dining room for atmosphere. Excellent set menus are the way to go, or choose from a tempting range of grills, roasts, fish and soups. One speciality is *bacalao Corral del Rey* (grilled cod in courgette and roasted garlic sauce).

## Shopping

**★Pastelería Basilio** FOOD
(☎927 32 01 63; www.facebook.com/pasteleriabasilio; Calle de los Herreros 1; ⊙10am-2pm & 4.30-8.30pm Mon-Fri, 10am-9pm Sat & Sun) Just down the hill south of the Plaza Mayor, this old-school pastry shop has been around since 1939 and is still run by the same family. It serves up traditional Spanish pastries in all their glory, as well as regional delicacies like *pimentón de La Vera*. One real local speciality is *perrunillas*, delicate cookies made with lard, lemon and cinnamon.

## Information

**Oficina de Turismo** (☎927 32 26 77; www.turismotrujillo.com; Plaza Mayor; ⊙10am-1.30pm & 5-8pm Apr-Sep, 10am-1.30pm & 4-7pm Oct-Mar) Right on the Plaza Mayor.

## Getting There & Away

**BUS**

The **bus station** (☎927 32 12 02; Avenida de Extremadura) is 1km south of the Plaza Mayor.

| Destination | Fare (€) | Time | Frequency |
|---|---|---|---|
| Badajoz (normal/ express) | 12.80/22 | 2/1¾hr | 4/4 daily |
| Cáceres | 3.80 | 45min | 5-6 daily |
| Madrid (normal/ express) | 20/32 | 3½/2¾hr | 10/3 daily |
| Lisbon (normal/ express) | 31.60/36 | 4¼/4hr | 2/1 daily |

## Getting Around

Note that parking is (in theory) only allowed in the parking spots of the Plaza Mayor for 30 minutes between 10am and 8pm from Monday to Friday. For unlimited street parking, head north of the Plaza Mayor along Calle de García de Paredes and Avenida de la Coronación.

# Guadalupe

POP 1885

Revered by pilgrims and rising from forests of chestnut, oak and cork deep within the Sierra de Villuercas, Guadalupe is a glorious apparition. Stories of history, architecture and faith swirl around the tight tangle of medieval buildings, while the gilded, whitewashed monastery at the village's heart is a soaring monument to religious devotion. More prosaic attractions, like vineyards, hiking trails and good local food, add to the appeal.

## Sights

**★Real Monasterio de Santa María de Guadalupe** MONASTERY, CHURCH

(☎927 36 70 00; www.monasterioguadalupe.com; Plaza de Santa María de Guadalupe; church free, monastery by guided tour adult/child €5/2.50; ⏲church 9am-7.30pm, monastery 9.30am-1pm & 3.30-6pm) Guadalupe's renowned, Unesco World Heritage–listed monastery is located, according to legend, on the spot where, in the early 14th century, a shepherd received a vision of the Virgin Mary. A sumptuous church-monastery was built on the site, drawing pilgrims from across the world ever since. Now cared for by nine Franciscan monks, it remains one of Spain's most important pilgrimage sites, especially for South American and Filipino Catholics. The building is an architectural delight, crammed with historical riches.

**Bodegas Ruíz Torres** WINERY

(☎927 36 90 27; www.ruiztorres.com; Carretera EX116, Km 33; ⏲by appointment 10am-2pm Tue-Sat) Around 6km south of Guadalupe, close to the Puerta Llano, this well-regarded winery produces whites, reds and *cavas* (sparkling wine), and occupies a lovely perch overlooking the hills. It offers a comprehensive hour-long tour of its operations and the winemaking process, with a chance to taste and buy at the end. It's just south of the pass, along the road to/from Navalvillar de Pela.

## Activities

There are some excellent walks in the Guadalupe area. The tourist office hands out hiking maps with detailed instructions describing easy-to-medium circular walking routes of three to five hours, plus limited information on some more challenging hikes. For more information on routes, check out the Spanish-only www.geoparquevilluercas.es/rutas. You could also contact **NatRural** (☎654 376803; www.rutasgeoparquevilluercas.com), which offers hiking excursions into the hills, and walking tours of the town (€5).

## Festivals & Events

**Fiesta de la Virgen de Guadalupe** RELIGIOUS

(⏲6-8 Sep) Guadalupe honours its beloved Virgen de Guadalupe with an intricate ceremony that sees the Virgin's image removed from its usual *camarín* (chamber), dressed in special jewels and temporarily displayed to the public. A statue is paraded around on the evening of the 6th and again on the 8th (which also happens to be Extremadura's regional feast day).

## Sleeping & Eating

**★Hospedería del Real Monasterio** HISTORIC HOTEL €€

(☎927 36 70 00; www.hotelhospederiamonasterioguadalupe.com; Plaza de Juan Carlos I; s €55-62, d/tr €75/103; ⏲closed mid-Jan–mid-Feb; P❄🛜) Centred on the Real Monasterio's beautiful Gothic cloister (now housing a bar and cafe), this old-fashioned hotel lets you live it

### OUR LADY OF GUADALUPE

Few shrines in Spain incite quite so much fervour as Our Lady of Guadalupe (Virgen de Guadalupe). The story begins back in the 8th century CE, when priests fleeing the Muslim assault on Seville in 712 buried a statue of the Virgin Mary high in the mountains above the Río Guadalupe. Devotees claim that the statue was carved by Luke the Evangelist. Six centuries after it was buried, in the 14th century, the Virgin appeared to a local shepherd named Gil Cordero who was looking for a lost animal. According to Cordero, the Virgin told him to bring priests to the exact site where he had seen the vision and for them to dig. Upon doing so, the priests found the statue lost centuries before. A shrine was built over the site, and it grew into the lavish monastery you see today over the centuries that followed.

The first pilgrims began arriving in 1326, and 14 years later King Alfonso XI built a Hieronymite monastery on the site after claiming that the Virgin's intercession was responsible for his victory over the Muslim armies at the Battle of Río Salado. In 1492, the Reyes Católicos, Isabel and Fernando, signed the official documents authorising the first voyage of Christopher Columbus (Cristobal Colón) to the Americas, and Columbus came here to give thanks after his successful journey. On 12 October 1928, Pope Pius XI carried out what is known as a canonical coronation using the diamond-and-sapphire-encrusted crown that can be seen on the guided tour of the monastery.

up in a national monument without paying *parador*-style prices. High-ceilinged rooms are darkish and venerable but comfortable and full of character. There's a sumptuous flower-filled patio just off the lobby.

Dine grandly at the **restaurant** (raciones €6.50-21, mains €13-25; 1-3pm & 9-10.30pm, closed mid-Jan–mid-Feb; P) under the arches of the magnificent Gothic cloister or in the lavish dining hall, rich with 17th-century timber furnishings and antique ceramics

**Parador de Guadalupe** HISTORIC HOTEL **€€**
(927 36 70 75; www.parador.es; Calle Marqués de la Romana 12; r €85-155; P) Guadalupe's *parador* occupies a converted 15th-century hospital and 16th-century religious school opposite the monastery. Spacious rooms are tastefully decorated and the cobbled courtyard is delightful, with its central fountain, lemon and orange trees and surrounding cloister-like colonnade with arches. There's a gorgeous summer-only pool, along with a smart (if slightly overpriced) **restaurant** (927 36 70 75; www.parador.es; Calle Marqués de la Romana 12; mains €16-29, set menu €25-38; 1.30-4pm & 8.30-11pm) serving Extremaduran specialities.

## Information

**Oficina de Turismo de Guadalupe** (927 15 41 28; www.guadalupeturismoblog.wordpress.com; Plaza de Santa María de Guadalupe; 10am-2pm & 4-6pm) On the main square, opposite the monastery.

## Getting There & Away

Buses stop on Avenida Conde de Barcelona, near the town hall, 200m south of the Plaza de Santa María de Guadalupe. **Mirat** (927 23 33 54; www.mirat-transportes.es) runs two services Monday to Friday (one on Sunday) to/from Cáceres (€14, 2½ hours) via Trujillo. **Samar** (917 23 05 06; www.samar.es) has one to two daily buses to/from Madrid (€19, four hours).

# Plasencia

POP 40,140

Medieval walls surround the attractive provincial town of Plasencia, enclosing an attractive old quarter of narrow streets, Romanesque churches and stately stone palaces that together rise above a bend of the Río Jerte. A buzzing tapas scene keeps things lively, and the town also makes a good base for forays into the nearby La Vera, Jerte and Ambroz valleys.

## Sights

**Catedral de Plasencia** CATHEDRAL
(927 42 44 06; www.catedraldeplasencia.org; Plaza de la Catedral; adult/child €4/free; 11am-2pm & 5-8pm Apr-Sep, 11am-2pm & 4-7pm Tue-Sun Oct-Mar) Plasencia's magnificent cathedral is two-in-one. The 16th-century **Catedral Nueva** is a Gothic-Renaissance blend with a handsome plateresque facade, a soaring 17th-century *retablo* (altarpiece) and intricate walnut-carved choir stalls featuring seats dedicated to the Reyes Católicos

## EXTREMADURA & THE AMERICAS

The *extremeños* jumped at the opportunities presented by Christopher Columbus' 1492 discovery of the Americas – hardly surprising given that Extremadura was one of Spain's poorest regions.

In 1501, Fray Nicolás de Ovando from Cáceres was named governor of all the Indies. Among the 2500 followers who joined him in his Caribbean capital of Santo Domingo, many were from Extremadura, including Francisco Pizarro, illegitimate son of a minor noble family from Trujillo. In 1504, Hernán Cortés, from a similar family in Medellín, arrived in Santo Domingo.

Both young men prospered. Cortés took part in the conquest of Cuba in 1511 and settled there. Pizarro, in 1513, accompanied Vasco Núñez de Balboa (from Jerez de los Caballeros) to Darién (Panama), where they 'discovered' the Pacific Ocean. In 1519, Cortés led a small expedition to what's now Mexico, rumoured to be full of gold and silver. By 1524, with combined fortitude, cunning, luck and ruthlessness, Cortés and his band had subdued the Aztec empire.

Pizarro returned to Spain and, before returning to the New World, visited Trujillo, where he received a hero's welcome and collected his four half-brothers, as well as other relatives and friends. Their expedition set off from present-day Panama in 1531, with just 180 men and 37 horses, and managed to capture the Inca emperor Atahualpa, despite the 30,000-strong Inca army. Pizarro demanded an enormous ransom, which was paid, but Trujillo's finest went ahead and executed Atahualpa anyway. The Inca empire, with its capital in Cuzco and extending from present-day Colombia to Chile, soon fell to a combination of casual brutality, broken alliances, cynical realpolitik and civil war between Pizarro and his longtime ally, Diego de Almagro. Pizarro was eventually assassinated in 1541 by the executed Almagro's son and is buried in the cathedral of Lima, Peru. Of the Pizarro brothers, only Hernando returned to Spain alive.

About 600 people of Trujillo made their way to the Americas in the 16th century, so it's no surprise that there are more than 20 other Trujillo towns in Central and South America. Conquistadors and colonists from all over Spain also took with them the cult of the Virgen de Guadalupe (p599) in eastern Extremadura, which remains widespread throughout Latin America.

(Catholic Monarchs). Within the Romanesque **Catedral Vieja** are 13th-century cloisters surrounding a fountain and lemon trees. The octagonal **Capilla de San Pablo** has a dramatic 1569 Caravaggio painting of John the Baptist, a religious museum and an arched Romanesque doorway.

**Plaza Mayor** SQUARE

Plasencia life flows through the lively, arcaded Plaza Mayor: meeting place of 10 streets, home to plenty of bar-restaurants and scene of a Tuesday farmers market since the 12th century. The jaunty figure striking the hour atop the Gothic **town hall** is El Abuelo Mayorga, a 1970s replica of the 13th-century original and the unofficial symbol of the town. The town hall also sports a Carlos I coat of arms.

## Sleeping

**Palacio Carvajal Girón** HISTORIC HOTEL €€

(☎927 42 63 26; www.palaciocarvajalgiron.com; Plaza Ansano 1; r €83-164; P❄📶🏊) An impressive conversion job has transformed this formerly ruined palace in the heart of the old town into a chic address. Rooms have modern fittings and fresh white decor, plus original features, including fireplaces. The top-floor attic-style standard rooms have sloping ceilings and in-room concrete baths or showers, while the swish 1st-floor suite has an XXL bathroom with original tilework.

★ **Parador de Plasencia** HISTORIC HOTEL €€€

(☎927 42 58 70; www.parador.es; Plaza de San Vicente Ferrer; r €100-180; P❄📶🏊) One of Extremadura's finest, Plasencia's *parador* is a classic – oozing the atmosphere and austerity of its 15th-century convent roots, with massive stone columns, soaring ceilings and a traditional Renaissance cloister. The 66 rooms are far from monastic, luxuriously furnished with rugs, rich fabrics, wood-carved bedheads, red-velvet curtains and varnished terracotta floors. The on-site bar occupies an old bodega.

## Eating

**Succo** CONTEMPORARY SPANISH €€
(☎927 41 29 32; www.restaurantesucco.es; Calle Vidrieras 7; mains €11-21; ⊙9am-11.30pm; ) In the heart of Plasencia's eating area, just off the Plaza Mayor, this urban-chic tapas bar plates up delectable inventive tapas and *raciones*, delicately presented at tall white tables or in the bamboo-dotted dining room. The *huevos rotos* (smashed eggs) with *jamón* and *patatas panaderas* (potatoes with tomato and onion) gets a big thumbs up, as does the friendly service.

**Casa Juan** EXTREMADURAN €€
(☎927 42 40 42, 655 585146; www.restaurantecasajuan.com; Calle de las Arenillas 2; mains €14-19; ⊙1.30-4pm & 8.30-11pm, closed Jan; ) Tucked down a quiet old-town lane, welcoming Casa Juan does well-prepared Extremaduran meat dishes (such as roast suckling pig) plus some tasty vegetarian and gluten-free bites. Start with locally made olive oil and bread, then try the homemade Torta del Casar gratin or the expertly hung local *retinto* beef. Fairly priced wines from around Spain seal an excellent deal.

## Information

**Oficina de Turismo** (☎927 42 38 43; www.plasencia.es; Calle de Santa Clara 4; ⊙9am-2pm & 4-7pm Mon-Sat, 10am-2pm & 4-7pm Sun) Information on Plasencia and northern Extremadura.

## Getting There & Away

### BUS

The **bus station** (☎927 41 45 50; Calle de Tornavacas 2) is 1km east of the Plaza Mayor. Destinations include Cáceres (€6, 50 minutes, one to four daily), Madrid (from €15, 3½ hours, two to three daily) and Salamanca (€7.30, 1½ to 2¼ hours, seven to eight daily). Buses also serve smaller destinations around northern Extremadura.

### TRAIN

The train station is off Avenida de España (the Cáceres road), 1km southwest of town. Trains depart up to four times daily from Plasencia for Madrid (from €25, 2¾ hours), Cáceres (from €5.40, 1¼ hours) and Mérida (from €13, two hours).

# La Vera

Surrounded by mountains sometimes still capped with snow as late as May, Extremadura's fertile La Vera region is famous throughout Spain for its *pimentón* (paprika), sold in charming old-fashioned tins and with a distinctive smoky flavour. Typical, too, are half-timbered houses leaning at odd angles, their overhanging upper storeys supported by timber or stone pillars. The area makes for a terrific excursion in Extremadura's north.

## Sights

**★Monasterio de Yuste** MONASTERY
(☎902 044 454; www.patrimonionacional.es; Carretera de Yuste, Cuacos de Yuste; adult/concession €7/4, guide €4, admission free for EU & Latin American citizens & residents Wed & last 3hr Sun; ⊙10am-8pm Tue-Sun Apr-Sep, to 6pm Oct-Mar; P) In a lovely shady setting 1.5km northwest of Cuacos de Yuste, this monastery is where Carlos I of Spain (Charles I; also known as Carlos V of Austria) came in 1557 to prepare for death after abdicating his emperorship over much of Western and Central Europe. It's a soulful, evocative place amid the forested hills, and a tranquil counterpoint to the grandeur of so many formerly royal buildings elsewhere in Spain.

## Festivals & Events

**Los Empalaos** RELIGIOUS
(Valverde de la Vera; ⊙Easter) At midnight on Good Friday eve, Valverde hosts one of Spain's more impassioned religious festivities, Los Empalaos ('the Impaled'). Penitent locals strap their arms to a beam, their near-naked bodies wrapped tight with 60m-long cords from waist to fingertips. Barefoot, veiled, with two swords strapped to their backs and wearing crowns of thorns, these 'walking crucifixes' follow a painful Way of the Cross.

DON'T MISS

### EXTREMADURA'S PRETTIEST VILLAGES


- Guadalupe (p598)
- Garrovillas (p594)
- Alcántara (p593)
- Jerez de los Caballeros (p610)
- Olivenza (p612)
- Trujillo (p594)

WORTH A TRIP

### EL MEANDRO DEL MELERO

One of Extremadura's most beautiful geographical features, El Meandro del Melero is where the Río Alagon does an extraordinary loop, forming a near-perfect oxbow formation around a forested, teardrop-shaped island. It's at its best when the river is at full capacity, but even during a recent drought with little water it was still spectacular. The best views are from the Mirador de La Antigua.

To get here, take the EX204 (known as the SA225 on the Castilla y León side) to Riomalo de Abajo. On the Extremadura side of the bridge, take the road (Calle Escuelas) that runs south along the river. The road twists up into the hills for 1.5km, where the paved road ends. To continue, you'll either need to drive the rough dirt track – it's OK for 2WD vehicles if you drive carefully, but it's treacherous after rains – or, better, walk the remaining 1.6km to the lookout. The Meandro itself lies within Castilla y León, but the lookout is in Extremadura.

## Sleeping & Eating

★**Parador de Jarandilla** HISTORIC HOTEL **€€**
(☎927 56 01 17; www.parador.es; Avenida de García Prieto 1, Jarandilla de la Vera; d €90-210; P❄📶🏊) Be king or queen of the castle at this 15th-century castle-turned-hotel with a warm, welcoming feel. Carlos I stayed here for a few months while waiting for his monastery digs to be completed. Within the stout walls and turrets lie period-furnished rooms that are wonderfully comfy without being ostentatiously grand, plus a classic courtyard where you can dine royally from the **restaurant** (mains €12-26; ⏰1.30-4pm & 8.30-11pm; P📶✍) menu.

**La Vera de Yuste** CASA RURAL **€€**
(☎927 17 22 89; Calle Teodoro Perianes 17, Cuacos de Yuste; s/d incl breakfast €55/75; ❄) This beauty is set in two typical 18th-century village houses near Cuacos de Yuste's Plaza Mayor. The wood-beamed rooms have chunky rustic furniture and the garden is a delight, surrounded by rose bushes with a small courtyard and vegetable patch.

★**Villa Xarahiz** SPANISH **€€**
(☎927 66 51 50; www.villaxarahiz.com; Carretera EX203, Km 32.8, Jaraíz de la Vera; mains €10-23; ⏰1.30-3.45pm & 9-10.45pm Tue-Sat, 1.30-3.45pm Sun; 📶👪) Offering spectacular sierra views from the terrace and the upmarket wood-beamed dining room, this hotel-restaurant 1km north of Jaraíz is one of La Vera's best bets for Spanish wines and smart regional pan-Spanish food, featuring local peppers, Torta del Casar cheese, Extremaduran *jamón* and stewed kid, among other quality Extremaduran produce. The €12 weekday lunch *menú* is a hit.

## Information

**Oficina de Turismo de Jarandilla de la Vera** (☎927 56 04 60; www.jarandilla.com; Avenida Soledad Vega Ortiz, Jarandilla de la Vera; ⏰10am-2pm & 4.30-7.30pm Tue-Sat, 10am-2pm Sun) The most useful of a number of tourist offices dotted around La Vera.

**Oficina de Turismo de Villanueva de la Vera** (☎639 068544; www.facebook.com/turismo.villanuevadelavera/; Avenida de la Vera, Villanueva de la Vera; ⏰9am-3pm Wed & Thu, to 5pm Fri & Sun) On the main road through Villanueva de la Vera.

## Getting There & Away

**Mirat** (☎927 23 33 54; www.mirat-transportes.es) runs three buses Monday to Friday from Plasencia to Jarandilla (€6.60, one hour) via Jaraíz (€4.40, 50 minutes) and lower La Vera villages, and one on Sunday. Some continue further up the valley. There's also one daily bus Monday to Friday and Sunday between Cáceres and Jarandilla (€17.80, 2¼ hours).

# Parque Nacional de Monfragüe

Spain's 14th national park is a dramatic, hilly 180-sq-km paradise for birdwatchers (and other nature lovers). Straddling the Tajo valley, it's home to spectacular colonies of raptors and more than 75% of Spain's protected species. Among some 175 feathered varieties are around 300 pairs of black vultures (the largest concentration of Europe's biggest bird of prey) and populations of two other rare large birds: the Spanish imperial eagle (around a dozen pairs) and the black stork (close to 30 pairs). Deer, otters, genets, badgers, rabbits, foxes and wild boar are other inhabitants.

The best time to visit is between March and October, since many bird species winter in Africa.

The pretty hamlet of **Villareal de San Carlos**, from where most hiking trails leave, is the most convenient base. There are also amenities in **Torrejón el Rubio**, on the south side of the park.

## Sights

**★Mirador Salto del Gitano** VIEWPOINT
(P) Arguably the most spectacular spot in the national park is the Mirador Salto del Gitano. From this lookout point, 5km south of Villareal along the EX208, there are stunning views across the Río Tajo gorge to the Peña Falcón crag, home to a colony of circling griffon vultures. The 8km 'Ruta Roja' (Red Route) walk between Villareal de San Carlos and the Castillo de Monfragüe passes through here.

**★Castillo de Monfragüe** CASTLE
The hilltop Castillo de Monfragüe, a ruined 9th-century Islamic fort, has sweeping 360-degree views across the park, with birds swooshing by above and below. It's signposted up a steep winding road off the EX208, 8km south of Villareal. The castle can also be reached via an attractive 8km, 1½-hour walk from Villareal, along the Ruta Roja.

## Tours

**Monfragüe Vivo** OUTDOORS
(☎620 941778, 927 45 94 75; www.monfraguevivo.com) Monfragüe Vivo offers birdwatching tours and a variety of park activities, including walking, kayaking and jeep trips, with local guides.

**Iberian Nature** BIRDWATCHING
(☎676 784221; www.iberian-nature.com) Local birdwatching experts offering guided hikes (from €35 per person) and courses.

**Birding Extremadura** BIRDWATCHING
(☎927 31 93 49; www.birdingextremadura.com; Casa Rural El Recuerdo, Calle Aguaperal 8, Pago de San Clemente) Birdwatching trips run by British ornithologist Martin Kelsey.

## Sleeping & Eating

**★Casa Rural El Recuerdo** CASA RURAL €€
(☎609 684719, 927 31 93 49; www.casaruralelrecuerdo.com; Calle Aguaperal 8, Pago de San Clemente; s/d incl breakfast €59/70; P 🛜 🏊) Birdwatchers won't want to miss this love-

OFF THE BEATEN TRACK

### LAS HURDES

North of Plasencia, Las Hurdes is one of Extremadura's most remote corners, although quiet mountain roads connect the region with the Sierra de Francia in Castilla y León.

A worthwhile loop could begin in **Las Mestas**, home to the handsome 17th-century stone **Iglesia de Nuestra Señora del Carmen**, and the **Hospedería Hurdes Reales** (☎927 434 139; www.hospederiasdeextremadura.es; Calle Factoría; s/d incl breakfast from €75/90; P ❄ 🛜), an excellent base for exploring Las Hurdes. From here a pretty, serpentine road climbs up through the **Valle de Las Batuecas** to La Alberca (20km) in Castilla y León. If you stay in Extremadura, continue on to picturesque **Ladrillar**, which tumbles down a steep ridge, then on to tiny **Riomalo de Arriba**, home to Las Hurdes' best collection of original stone-and-slate homes; just three inhabitants lived here at last count. The road then climbs steeply to the **Mirador de las Carrascas**, with vast views down the two main valleys of Las Hurdes. Continue on to **Casares de Las Hurdes**, with its tangle of narrow thoroughfares and its church which, unusually, has a free-standing clocktower separate from the main building. Continue your descent to lively **Nuñomoral**, then take the quiet 9km detour to **El Gasco**, home to some traditional Las Hurdes houses and **Restaurante La Meancera** (☎674 189792, 927 03 53 68; mains €14-18, set menus €20-30; ⏰1-4pm & 8-11pm), one of Extremadura's best restaurants with classy, intimate decor, warm service and fabulous seasonal food, mostly sourced from its own gardens and neighbouring farms. Around 1km before reaching El Gasco (or on the return journey as you'll need to return to Nuñomoral), stop at the **Mirador de El Gasco**, for fine views down into the river valley with a striking double oxbow defining the stream's path through it.

DON'T MISS

## GRANADILLA & YACIMIENTO ROMANO DE CÁPARRA

In Extremadura's far north, in the Valle de Ambroz, are two of Extremadura's most intriguing historical attractions – evocative, abandoned Granadilla and the Roman ruins of Cáparra.

About 25km west of Hervás, the ghost village of **Granadilla** (927 01 49 75; Carretera CC168; 10am-1.30pm & 4-8pm Tue-Sun Apr-Oct, 10am-1.30pm & 4-6pm Tue-Sun Nov-Mar; P) is a beguiling reminder of how Extremadura's villages must have looked before modernisation. Founded by the Moors in the 9th century and abandoned in the 1960s when the nearby dam was built, Granadilla's traditional architecture has been painstakingly restored since the 1980s as part of a government educational project. Enter through the narrow **Puerta de Villa**, overlooked by the sturdy 15th-century **castle**, which you can climb for brilliant panoramas.

From the Puerta de Villa, the cobblestone Calle Mayor climbs up to the delightfully rustic **Plaza Mayor**, surrounded by vibrant buildings. On the right stands the beautiful **Casa de las Conchas**, its peach-coloured exterior studded with white ceramic shells. Some buildings function as craft workshops or exhibition centres in summer. Don't miss a stroll along the top of the 1km-long Almohad walls, with evocative views of village, lake, eucalyptuses and pinewoods.

**Yacimiento Romano de Cáparra** (927 19 94 85; Carretera CC13.3; 10am-2pm & 5-8pm Tue-Sat, 10am-2pm Sun Jun-Sep, 10am-2pm & 4-7pm Tue-Sat, 10am-2pm Sun Oct-May; P), unearthed in 1929, is a fascinating, substantial remains of the once-splendid Roman city of Cáparra dating to around the 1st century. Initially favoured for its strategic location on the Vía de la Plata, the city fell into decay in the 4th century and was eventually deserted. Wander the 14-hectare site to spot its crumbled walls, gates, forum, thermal baths and amphitheatre. Most impressive of all is the wonderfully preserved, late 1st-century **Arco de Cáparra**, a four-arch granite gateway.

To get here, take exit 455 off the A66 (24km southwest of Hervás or 16km northeast of Plasencia) and drive 5.5km west.

ly six-room *casa rural* just 12km southeast of Trujillo. It's run by expert birdwatchers, Martin and Claudia, who also run Birding Extremadura. Each room is different, but they're nicely turned out and inhabit a former winery, with olive groves in abundance. There's also a dinner-only restaurant (€20) in the wine cellar.

**Hospedería Parque de Monfragüe** HOTEL €€
(927 45 52 78; www.hospederiasdeextremadura.es; Carretera EX208, Km 39, Torrejón el Rubio; d incl breakfast €75-125; P) This tranquil four-star hotel, 1km north of Torrejón el Rubio, looks out across the plains to the national park and is partly run on solar power and bioenergy. Freshly revamped dark-turquoise and varnished-wood rooms come with desks, squeaky floors and tile-covered bathrooms. Duplexes are good for families, and there's a decent **restaurant** (mains €14-23, set menu €15-35; 1.30-4pm & 8.30-11pm) that dishes up good Extremaduran dishes.

## Information

**Centro de Visitantes** (927 19 91 34; Villareal de San Carlos; 10am-7.30pm daily Jul-Sep, 9.30am-6pm Mon-Fri, 9am-6pm Sat & Sun Oct-Jun) The park's main information centre advises on hikes and birdwatching spots, and has displays on local history, fauna and flora.

**Monfragüe Bird Center** (927 19 95 79; www.centrosurmonfrague.com; Monfragüe Centro de Visitantes Sur, Torrejón el Rubio; 10am-2pm Tue-Sat, 4-6pm Wed & Thu, 4-7pm Fri & Sat, hours vary) Maps and advice on birdwatching spots, plus Spanish-language displays on local birds, migration patterns and, next door, Monfragüe's prehistoric cave art.

**Oficina de Turismo de Torrejón el Rubio** (927 45 52 92; www.torrejonelrubio.com; Calle Madroño 1, Torrejón el Rubio; 10am-2pm & 4-6pm Tue & Wed, 10am-2pm & 4-7pm Thu-Sun) Helpful for hiking, birdwatching and other park activities.

## Getting There & Away

Public transport through the park is limited. **Emiz** (927 24 72 21; www.emiz.es) runs one bus daily Monday to Friday in each direction between Plasencia and Torrejón el Rubio (€4.60,

45 minutes), stopping in Villareal de San Carlos. There's also one bus on Monday and Friday between Torrejón el Rubio and Trujillo (€4.60, 45 minutes).

# Mérida

POP 59,350

Home to Spain's most extensive Roman ruins, Mérida is a must-see in Extremadura's south. Once the capital of the Roman province of Lusitania, Mérida's ruins lie sprinkled around town, often appearing in the most unlikely corners. One can only wonder what still lies buried beneath what is now a lively, modern city.

## History

The Roman city of Emerita Augusta, centred on the site of modern Mérida, was founded by Emperor Augustus in 25 BCE as a colony for veterans of Rome's campaigns in Cantabria; the Roman name translates roughly as 'bachelors' or 'discharged soldiers' from the army of Augustus. The city's location also served the strategic purpose of protecting a nearby pass and the bridge over the Río Guadiana. The city prospered and became the capital of the Roman province of Lusitania and one of the empire's most important cultural and political centres, with a population of 40,000 in its heyday. After the fall of the Western Roman Empire, the city became the Visigoth capital of Hispania in the 6th century and its monuments remained largely intact. The city later passed into Muslim hands in the 8th century and has been Christian since 1230. During Napoleon's 19th-century invasion of Spain, many of Mérida's monuments were destroyed.

## Sights

**★Teatro Romano** RUINS

(Paseo Álvarez Sáez de Buruaga; adult/child incl Anfiteatro €12/6, combined 6-site ticket adult/concession/child €15/7.50/free; 9am-9pm Apr-Sep, 9.30am-6.30pm Oct-Mar) Mérida's most spectacular Roman monument, and the only one to once again fulfil its original function – by hosting performances during the Festival Internacional de Teatro Clásico (p607) in summer – the Teatro Romano is the city's indisputable highlight. It was built around 15 BCE to seat 6000 spectators. The adjoining (slightly less dazzling) **Anfiteatro** (adult/child incl Teatro Romano €12/6, combined 6-site ticket adult/concession/child €15/7.50/free; 9am-9pm Apr-Sep, to 6.30pm Oct-Mar) opened in 8 BCE for gladiatorial contests and held 14,000; the gladiator-versus-lion fresco in the Museo Nacional de Arte Romano was taken from here.

**★Puente Romano** BRIDGE

Don't miss the extraordinarily powerful spectacle of the Puente Romano spanning the Río Guadiana. At 792m in length with 60 granite arches, it's one of the longest bridges built by the Romans. It was constructed in 25 BCE when Emerita Augusta (modern-day Mérida) was founded, and then partly restored in the 17th century. The 20th-century **Puente Lusitania**, a sleek suspension bridge designed by Santiago Calatrava, mirrors it to the northwest. The best Roman bridge views are from the Alcazaba's southwestern ramparts.

**★Museo Nacional de Arte Romano** MUSEUM

(924 31 16 90; www.culturaydeporte.gob.es/mnromano; Calle de José Ramón Mélida; adult/child €3/free, after 2pm Sat & all day Sun free; 9.30am-8pm Tue-Sat, 10am-3pm Sun Apr-Sep, 9.30am-6.30pm Tue-Sat, 10am-3pm Sun Oct-Mar) Even if you visit only a handful of Mérida's sights, make sure one of them is this fabulous museum, which has a superb three-floor collection of statues, busts, mosaics, frescoes, coins, pottery and other Roman artefacts, all beautifully displayed alongside information panels in Spanish and English. Designed by Navarran architect Rafael Moneo, the soaring arched brick structure makes a stunning home for the collection, its walls hung with some of the largest, most beautiful mosaics.

### COMBINED TICKET

Admission to most of Mérida's Roman sites is via a combined ticket (€15 for adults, €7.50 for students and pensioners, free for children under 12). It covers admission to the Teatro Romano and Anfiteatro, Los Columbarios, Casa del Mitreo, Alcazaba, Circo Romano, Cripta de Santa Eulalia and the Zona Arqueológica de Morería. The Museo Nacional de Arte Romano is not included. The ticket allows you one entry to each sight, has no time limit and can be bought at any of the sights except the Zona Arqueológica de Morería.

# Mérida

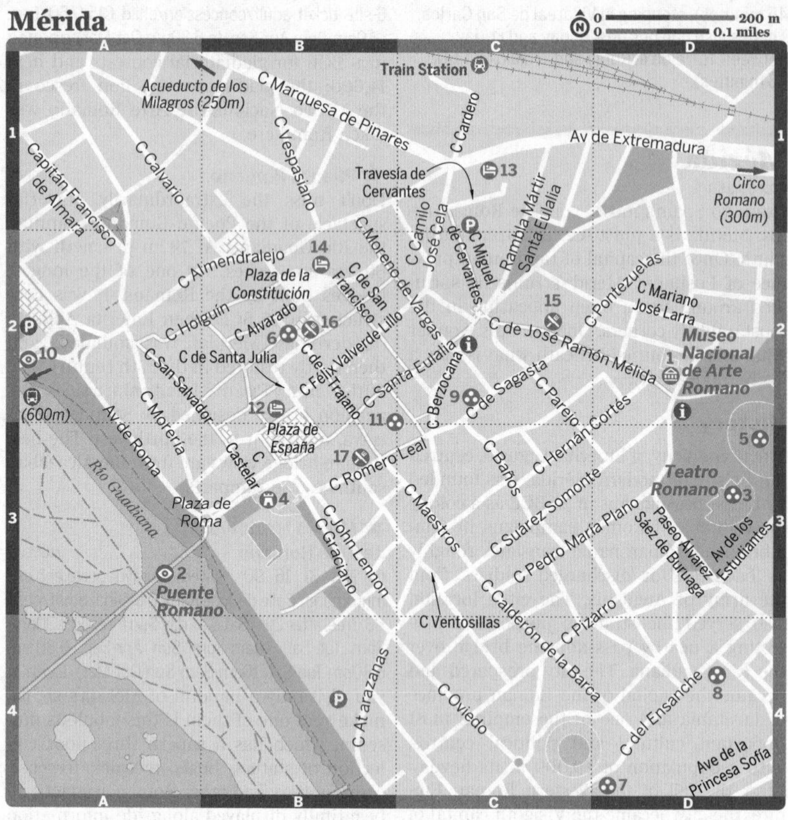


## Mérida

**Top Sights**
1 Museo Nacional de Arte Romano........D2
2 Puente Romano.................A3
3 Teatro Romano.................D3

**Sights**
4 Alcazaba.................B3
5 Anfiteatro.................D3
6 Arco de Trajano.................B2
7 Casa del Mitreo.................D4
8 Los Columbarios.................D4
9 Pórtico del Foro.................C2
10 Puente Lusitania.................A2
11 Templo de Diana.................B2

**Sleeping**
12 Hotel Ilunion Mérida Palace.................B2
13 La Flor de Al-Andalus.................C1
14 Parador de Mérida.................B2

**Eating**
15 Mesón El Pestorejo.................C2
16 Sybarit.................B2
17 Tábula Calda.................B3

**Alcazaba** FORTRESS

(Calle Graciano; adult/child €6/3, combined 6-site ticket adult/concession/child €15/7.50/free; 9am-9pm Apr-Sep, to 6.30pm Oct-Mar) This large Islamic fort was built in the mid-9th century on a site already occupied by the Romans and Visigoths, probably becoming the first ever *alcazaba* in Al-Andalus. In the middle of the complex, its pretty goldfish-populated *aljibe* (cistern) reuses Visigothic marble, flower motifs and stone slabs, while the ramparts look out over the Puente Romano and the Río Guadiana. The 15th-century monastery in the northeast corner now serves as government offices.

**Circo Romano** RUINS
(Avenida Juan Carlos I; adult/child €6/3, combined 6-site ticket adult/concession/child €15/7.50/free; ⊙9am-9pm Apr-Sep, to 6.30pm Oct-Mar) The 1st-century Circo Romano could accommodate 30,000 spectators. Discovered in the 16th century, its remains represent the only surviving hippodrome of its kind in Spain. In the attached interpretive centre you can read all about Diocles, a champion *auriga* (horse and chariot racer) who served his apprenticeship in Mérida before going on to the big league in Rome.

**Acueducto de los Milagros** RUINS
(Calle Marquesa de Pinares) Built between the 1st century BCE and the 3rd century, the 830m-long Acueducto de los Milagros once supplied Roman Mérida with water from the dam at Lago Proserpina, 6km north of town. It's now favoured by nesting storks.

**Casa del Mitreo** RUINS
(Calle de Oviedo; adult/child €6/3; ⊙9am-9pm Apr-Sep, to 6.30pm Oct-Mar) Beside Mérida's Plaza de Toros, the Casa del Mitreo is a late-1st- or 2nd-century Roman house with a well-preserved fresco and several intricate mosaics. Among the mosaics you'll find the partial but beautiful remains of the 3rd-century *mosaico cosmológico* (with its bright colours and allegories about the creation of the world), which was damaged by a fire. The Casa del Mitreo is connected by footpath to the adjacent **Los Columbarios** (Calle del Ensanche; adult/child €6/3; ⊙9am-9pm Apr-Sep, to 6.30pm Oct-Mar) Roman funeral site.

**Templo de Diana** RUINS
The soaring columns here are one of Mérida's most dramatic, incongruous sights, surrounded as they are by the buildings of a modern Spanish city. Inaccurately named, for it's now known to have been dedicated to the Imperial cult, this 1st-century-BCE temple stood in the municipal forum, where the city government was based. Parts of the temple were later incorporated into a 16th-century mansion built within it; there's a small **interpretation centre** (free entry, but with variable hours) in the mansion.

The forum's restored **Pórtico del Foro** is 100m northeast up Calle de Sagasta.

**Arco de Trajano** RUINS
(Calle de Trajano) This imposing 15m-high granite archway isn't known to have anything to do with Roman emperor Trajan, but it was situated on one of Mérida's main Roman streets and, in its original marble-covered form, may have served as an entrance to a sacred area.

## Festivals & Events

**Festival Internacional de Teatro Clásico** THEATRE
(www.festivaldemerida.es; €15-45; ⊙Jul-Aug) This prestigious summer festival, held at Mérida's Roman theatre and amphitheatre, features Greek and more recent drama classics, plus music, photography and dance. It starts at 10.45pm most nights.

## Sleeping

★ **La Flor de Al-Andalus** HOSTAL €
(☎924 31 33 56; www.hostallaflordeal-andalus.com; Avenida de Extremadura 6; s €33-50, d €45-90; ❄📶) If only all *hostales* were such good value. A self-appointed 'boutique *hostal*', La Flor de Al-Andalus has 18 comfy, colourful rooms beautifully decorated in Andalucian style (with elegant tiles, elaborate mirrors and hanging lanterns), plus friendly service and a convenient location within walking distance of Mérida's main sights. Try to avoid ground-floor rooms by reception.

**Hotel Ilunion Mérida Palace** HISTORIC HOTEL €€
(☎924 38 38 00; www.ilunionmeridapalace.com; Plaza de España 19; r €80-210; P❄📶🏊) Set across two linked 18th- and 19th-century buildings flanking the palm-dotted Plaza de España, five-star Mérida Palace is smart, efficient and wonderfully characterful. Swish pastel-painted rooms sport Roman-themed touches such as mosaic-print bedheads, black-and-white ancient-Mérida drawings and decorative Roman coins. Enter through the beautiful arched, blue-toned atrium and, in summer, enjoy the rooftop pool overlooking the plaza's palms and fountain.

**Parador de Mérida** HISTORIC HOTEL €€€
(Parador Vía de la Plata; ☎924 31 38 00; www.parador.es; Plaza de la Constitución 3; r €85-225; P❄📶🏊) You'll be sleeping on the site of a Roman temple in what was once an 18th-century convent, though this isn't Extremadura's finest *parador*. The lounge is a former chapel, which then served as both hospital and prison. The gardens' assembled hunks of Roman, Visigothic and Mudéjar artefacts whizz you through Mérida's architectural history.

## Eating

**★ Restaurante Milanesa** SPANISH €€
(☎924 37 11 23; www.facebook.com/lamilanesa merida; Avenida de la Libertad 51; mains €11-20; ⏲1-4pm & 8.30-11.30pm) Despite the less-than-promising location (across the bridge from the old town and next to the bus station), this is one of Mérida's top tables. Everything's good, but it's most famous for its rice dishes. You'll need two to make up an order, but half of Mérida will happily be your friend if you ask them to eat here.

The same owners run **Sybarit** (☎924 30 81 81; www.facebook.com/sybaritgastroshop; Calle de Trajano 6A; tapas from €4, mains €12-17; ⏲noon-midnight Tue-Sun, 8.30pm-midnight Mon), which is great for tapas, especially outside near the Arco de Trajano on a warm, summer's evening.

**Tábula Calda** SPANISH €€
(☎924 30 49 50; www.tabulacalda.es; Calle Romero Leal 11; mains €13-22, set menu €13-25; ⏲1-4.30pm & 8.30pm-midnight) This inviting yellow-washed space, filled with tilework and greenery, serves well-priced, quality meals encompassing Spain's favourite staples. Everything either comes from its garden or is sourced from within 100km of the kitchen. Before your food arrives, you'll enjoy a complimentary tapa, house salad (orange, sugar and olive oil, reflecting the family's Jewish roots) and olives. Manuel is a welcoming host.

## Information

**Oficina de Turismo** (☎924 38 01 91; www.turismomerida.org; Calle Santa Eulalia 64; ⏲9am-8pm Mon-Wed, 10am-2pm & 5-8pm Thu-Sun) At the top (northeastern) end of the main shopping street.

**Oficina de Turismo (Teatro Romano)** (☎924 33 07 22; www.turismomerida.org; Paseo Álvarez Sáez de Buruaga; ⏲9am-7.30pm Apr-Sep, to 6.30pm Oct-Mar) Next to the Roman theatre.

DON'T MISS

### LOCAL SPECIALITY: PESTOREJO

You don't find it in many places these days, but *pestorejo* (a fleshy cut of pork from the nape of the pig's neck) is an old Mérida favourite which you can savour at **Mesón El Pestorejo** (☎924 30 94 58; Calle de José Ramón Mélida; tapas from €5; ⏲noon-11.30pm) . The taste is all pork, the texture a little fatty, so it's best tried in small doses. Just as well, then, that you get a tapa of *pestorejo* free here when you order a drink. There's another outlet down the southern end of the Plaza de España.

## Getting There & Away

### BUS

Buses depart from the **bus station** (☎924 37 14 04; Avenida de la Libertad), across the river via the Puente Lusitania.

| Destination | Fare (€) | Time | Frequency |
|---|---|---|---|
| Badajoz | 4.95 | 50min | 3-6 daily |
| Cáceres | 5.70 | 1hr | 2-3 daily |
| Lisbon (normal/express) | 25/31 | 4/3hr | 1/1 daily |
| Madrid (normal/express) | 30/41 | 5/4hr | 4/4 daily |
| Seville | 15 | 2¾hr | 5 daily |
| Zafra | 5.15 | 1¼hr | 5-10 daily |

### TRAIN

From the station, just off Avenida de Extremadura, trains run to Madrid (€31 to €47, 4½ to 7½ hours, six or seven daily), Cáceres (€6.40 to €7.80, one hour, four to five daily), Seville (€23, 3¾ hours, one daily) and Zafra (€6.30, 45 minutes, three daily).

# Zafra

POP 16,775

Looking for all the world like an Andalucian *pueblo blanco* (white village), gleaming-white Zafra is a serene, attractive stop along the A66 between Seville and Mérida. Affectionately labelled *'Sevilla la chica'* ('the little Seville'), Zafra was originally a Muslim settlement. Its narrow streets are lined with baroque churches, old-fashioned shops, glassed-in balconies and traditional houses decorated with overflowing bougainvillea and splashes of geraniums. The newer part of town isn't all that enthralling, but Zafra's historic core is a beauty.

## Sights

Zafra's 15th-century **castle**, a blend of Gothic, Mudéjar and Renaissance architecture, is now the luxurious Parador de Zafra, which dominates the town. The **Plaza Grande**

WORTH A TRIP

## MEDELLÍN

Around 40km northeast of Mérida and signposted east off the A5, Medellín is one of Extremadura's best-kept secrets. Rising above the plains and reached via a pretty bridge over the Río Guadiana, Medellín was an important town in Roman times, before it was eclipsed by Mérida (Emerita Augusta). In the 15th century, one of Spain's most famous conquistadors, Hernán Cortés, was born here; the name Medellín was used throughout South America by local conquistadors eager to honour their home town.

**Teatro Romano de Medellín** (adult/child €3/free; ⊙3.30-6pm Tue, 10.30am-2pm & 3.30-6pm Wed-Sun, guided tours 4pm & 5pm Tue, 11am, noon, 4pm & 5pm Wed-Sun) Carved into the hillside above Medellín, this Roman theatre is one of Spain's most beautiful, as much for the views as the steep-walled theatre. The museum at the entrance has archaeological finds from the site, and there's a Spanish-language video (around 15 minutes) that explains Medellín's position in the Ancient Roman world. Spanish-language guided tours run on the hour when there are enough people.

**Castillo de Medellín** (adult/child €2/free; ⊙3.30-6pm Tue, 10.30am-2pm & 3.30-6pm Wed-Sun) Few castles can command such extensive views as this one. Wonderfully restored walls remain of this 12th-century castle built by the Muslim Almohads, although it fell into Christian hands in 1234 and was later much modified. The views from the ramparts down to the Roman theatre and beyond are superb.

and the adjoining **Plaza Chica** are both beautifully arcaded and ideal for soaking up Zafra life. The southwestern end of the Plaza Grande, with its palm trees and centuries-old homes, is one of Extremadura's prettiest. Guarding the western entry point to the old town is the **Puerta de Jerez**, part of Zafra's 15th-century wall.

**Bodegas Medina** WINERY
(☎924 57 50 60; www.bodegasmedina.net; Carretera de Córdoba/N432; tours with/without tasting €6/12; ⊙by appointment 8.30am-2pm & 4-7pm Mon-Fri, 10am-1pm Sat) Extremadura's only wine DO (Denominación de Origen) is Ribera del Guadiana. Just east of town, you can tour and taste on 45- to 90-minute visits at one of the DO's most prominent southern wineries, Bodegas Medina, which produces reds, whites, rosés and *cava* (sparkling wine). Bookings required.

**Convento de Santa Clara** CONVENT
(☎924 55 14 87; www.museozafra.es; Calle Sevilla 30; ⊙10am-2pm Tue-Sun mid-Jun–mid-Oct, 11am-2pm & 5-7pm Tue-Sat, 11am-2pm Sun mid-Oct–mid-Jun) FREE Off Zafra's main shopping street, this imposing 15th-century Mudéjar convent is a working convent with cloistered nuns. Visitors can, however, explore the on-site museum covering the sisters' lives and Zafra's history. Visits include the gilded chapel, where Jane Dormer, lady-in-waiting to Mary I of England, is buried. The sisters also sell pastries in the **shop** (⊙10am-2pm & 5-7pm Mon-Fri, 10.30am-2pm & 5-7pm Sun).

## Sleeping

★**Hotel Plaza Grande** HOTEL €
(☎924 56 31 63; www.hotelplazagrande.es; Calle Pasteleros 2; incl breakfast s €32-42, d €55; P❄📶) Right on the Plaza Grande, this friendly, sparkling gem of a hotel is an excellent deal. Modern-rustic decor accentuates terracotta with cream paintwork, exposed brick, floral prints and soft pastels. Go for room 108, with its corner balconies overlooking the plaza; room 208 is the same but with windows instead of balconies. The lively downstairs **cafe-restaurant** (tapas €4.50-7, raciones €9-19, mains €14-21; ⊙12.30pm-midnight; 📶🌱) is reliably good.

**Hotel Huerta Honda** HOTEL €€
(☎924 55 41 00; www.hotelhuertahonda.com; Calle de López Asme 30; s/d/superior/ste €55/65/85/120; P❄📶🏊) Whichever room type you go for, the rich-orange-and-yellow Huerta Honda is a classy choice. Standard rooms are comfy, contemporary and tastefully styled in muted tones. 'Gran Clase' rooms are sumptuous suites with neo-Moorish decor, woodcarved ceilings, four-poster beds, tiled bathrooms and antiques. Ask for a room overlooking the bougainvillea-draped courtyard and Zafra's castle.

**Parador de Zafra** HISTORIC HOTEL €€
(☎924 55 45 40; www.parador.es; Plaza Corazón de María 7; r €80-125, ste €120-195; P ❄ 📶 🏊) Beyond the exquisite marble-pillared Renaissance patio in this gorgeously restored 15th-century fortress, airy rooms come richly decorated with burgundy-coloured fabrics and antiques. Ivy and turrets surround the secluded pool, and the **restaurant** (mains €13-21, set menu €25-40; ⊙1.30-4pm & 8.30-11pm mid-Dec–Oct) is excellent. Guests can climb up to the battlements for Zafra's finest views.

## Eating

★ **La Rebotica** SPANISH €€
(☎924 55 42 89; www.lareboticazafra.com; Calle Boticas 12; mains €15-23; ⊙1.30-4pm & 8.30pm-midnight Tue-Sat, 1.30-4pm Sun; 📶) This refined restaurant in the heart of Zafra's old town delivers with its traditional meaty menu (note the innovative twists) and subtly sophisticated setting among wall mirrors and leather chairs. Dine on elegantly prepared *rabo de toro* (oxtail stew) and different pork dishes, plus a few seafood or veggie options; finish with outstanding desserts. Reservations recommended.

**Quesería La Bendita** CHEESE €€
(☎615 266265; Plaza Chica 14; tapa/ración from €4/11; ⊙12.30-3.30pm & 7.30pm-midnight Tue-Sat, 12.30-4pm Sun) One of the more original choices for tapas in Zafra, La Bendita specialises in cheeses from around Spain and Portugal, as well as some international choices. Order a tapa to get a taste or go for a full *ración*. Either way, it's an idea we wish other tapas bars around Spain would emulate.

DON'T MISS

### EXTREMADURA'S CASTLES

- Alcazaba, Badajoz
- Castillo de Trujillo (p595)
- Castillo de Medellín (p609)
- Castillo de Olivenza (p613)
- Castillo de Monfragüe (p603)
- Burguillos del Cerro
- Castillo Templario, Fregenal de la Sierra
- Castillo de Jerez de los Caballeros
- Castillo de Feria

## Shopping

**La Cava del Queso** CHEESE
(☎637861336; www.facebook.com/lacavadelquesozafra; Calle de Huelva 32; ⊙10am-2pm & 6.30-9pm Wed, 11am-1.30pm & 8-10.30pm Thu, 10am-2pm & 8-10.30pm Fri, 10am-3pm Sat & Sun) This enticing cheese shop is like a one-stop introduction to Extremadura's and Spain's cheeses, with a focus on little-known local cheeses. There are plenty of opportunities to try before you buy.

**Iberllota** FOOD
(☎924 55 59 95; www.iberllota.com; Calle de López Asme 36; ⊙10am-2pm & 5-8pm Mon-Sat, 10am-2pm Sun) Specialising in the finest cured meats, cheeses and some Extremudran wines, Iberllota is perfect for picnic treats and local-flavour gifts.

## Information

**Oficina de Turismo** (Turismo Zafra; ☎924 55 10 36; www.visitazafra.com; Plaza de España 8; ⊙10am-2pm & 5.30-7.30pm Mon-Fri, 10am-2pm Sat & Sun) In the Plaza de España off the southern edge of the old town.

## Getting There & Away

### BUS

Zafra's **bus station** (☎924 55 39 07; Carretera Badajoz-Granada 4) is 1km northeast of the old town. Destinations include Badajoz (€6.50, 1¼ hours, five to seven daily), Cáceres (€11, 1¾ to 2¼ hours, six daily), Mérida (€5.15, 1¼ hours, five to 10 daily) and Seville (€13, 1¾ hours, four to six daily).

### TRAIN

Destinations from Zafra by train include Mérida (from €6.30, 45 minutes, three daily), Cáceres (from €9.50, two hours, four daily) and Seville (€16, 2¾ hours, one daily).

# Around Zafra

From Zafra, roads head southwest into northern Huelva province (Andalucía) through the rolling Sierra de Aracena and southeast into the Parque Natural Sierra Norte de Sevilla (Andalucía).

Quiet **Burguillos del Cerro**, 19km southwest of Zafra, is overlooked by a 15th-century **castle** atop a grassy hill. **Fregenal de la Sierra**, 40km southwest of Zafra, appeals with its churches, noble homes, bullring and 13th-century **Castillo Templario** (Calle El Rollo 1; ⊙10am-2.45pm & 6-8pm Jul & Aug,

WORTH A TRIP

### MONESTERIO

Since the completion of the A66 motorway, many bypassed towns have disappeared into quiet obscurity, but not Monesterio: this is one of Spain's (and certainly Extremadura's) most celebrated sources of *jamón* (ham), reason enough to take the motorway exit. **Los Templarios** (☎924 51 61 88; www.lostempIariosmonesterio.com; Calle de los Templarios 20; mains €13-18; ⏲10am-midnight) has been around since 1980 and the *jamón* and other pork or steak dishes are first-rate.

**Museo del Jamón** (☎924 51 67 37; www.museodeljamondemonesterio.com; Paseo de Extremadura 314; ⏲9.30am-2pm & 4.30-7pm Mon-Sat, 10am-2pm Sun; P) Occupying pride of place at the southern end of Monesterio, the excellent Museo del Jamón is arguably the best of its kind in Spain. Displays, interactive exhibits and videos starring local ham producers (all in Spanish) take visitors through the process of *jamón* production, from types of Iberian pigs and their ideal habitats to the *matanza* (killing of the pigs) and the curing process. English-language audio guides provided.

10am-2.45pm & 5-7pm Sep-Jun) FREE; from 8am to 2pm Tuesday and Friday, there's a lively market within the castle's grounds. The (much reworked) 13th-century **Iglesia de Santa María** (Plaza de la Constitución) FREE is attached to the castle. It's mainly intriguing for its 18th-century baroque altarpieces.

Walled, hilly and handsome **Jerez de los Caballeros**, 42km southwest of Zafra, was a cradle of conquistadors. Attractions here include the 13th-century **Templars' castle** (Plaza del Ayuntamiento, Jerez de los Caballeros; ⏲8am-10pm) FREE, plus several stunning churches, three with towers emulating Seville's Giralda. The 15th-century **Iglesia de San Miguel** (Plaza del Padre Ruíz; ⏲12.15-2.30pm) FREE dominates the main plaza.

About 19km northwest of Zafra, little **Feria** rose to fame in the 14th century as home of the formidable local Feria dynasty. With its sensational hilltop perch, the refurbished 15th-century **castle** (☎685 147292; adult/child €5/2.50; ⏲11.30am-1.30pm & 5.30-8.30pm mid-Mar–mid-Sep, 11am-2pm & 4-6pm mid-Sep–mid-Mar) is a regional highlight.

## Information

**Oficina de Turismo de Frenegal de la Sierra** (☎924 70 00 00, ext 81663; www.frenegaldelasierra.es; Calle El Rollo, Frenegal de la Sierra; ⏲10am-2.45pm & 6-8pm Jul & Aug, 10am-2.45pm & 5-7pm Sep-Jun)

**Oficina de Turismo de Jerez de los Caballeros** (☎924 73 03 72; www.jerezcaballeros.es; Plaza de San Agustín 1, Jerez de los Caballeros; ⏲10am-2pm & 4.30-6.30pm Mon-Sat, 10am-2pm Sun)

## Getting There & Away

From Zafra, buses run once daily Monday to Friday to/from Fregenal de la Sierra (€3.55, 50 minutes) and Jerez de los Caballeros (€3.90, 45 minutes to one hour), via Burguillos (€2.20, 20 minutes). For Feria, it's your own wheels or nothing.

# Badajoz

POP 150,530

Close to the Portuguese border, Badajoz wouldn't win a beauty contest. But persist past the scruffy, sprawling and industrial outskirts, and you'll find an intriguing old town with an expansive castle and fine museums. It's worth a few hours if you're in the area.

## Sights & Activities

**★Alcazaba** FORTRESS

(⏲24hr; P) FREE Badajoz' majestic eight-hectare, 12th-century Alcazaba, the largest in Spain, lords over the city above the Plaza Alta. Guarding all is the **Torre de Espantaperros** (Scare-Dogs Tower), symbol of Badajoz, constructed by the Moors and topped by a 16th-century Mudéjar bell tower wrapped around an older original.

**Baraka** HAMMAM

(☎924 25 08 26; www.barakalasoledad.com; Calle Virgen de la Soledad 14; 90min session per person €23-70; ⏲sessions noon, 6pm & 8pm Wed & Thu, noon, 6pm, 8pm & 10pm Fri & Sat, noon & 6pm Sun) A beautiful take on the hot-warm-and-cold

DON'T MISS

## EXTREMADURA'S PARADORES

**Parador de Jarandilla** (p602) Feel like a king in this 15th-century castle.

**Parador de Cáceres** (p591) Refurbished luxury in the heart of Cáceres' old town.

**Parador de Trujillo** (p597) Noble mansion in medieval town of many.

**Parador de Guadalupe** (p599) Whitewashed comfort in Extremadura's most sacred town.

**Parador de Zafra** (p610) Another formidable castle with luxurious rooms.

**Parador de Plasencia** (p600) A former convent turned into a dreamy and atmospheric stay.

**Parador de Mérida** (p607) Sleep on the site of a Roman temple that became an 18th-century convent.

Moorish-style baths with dazzling architecture, soothing beats, mint tea and a range of massages (hot stone, anti-stress) and beauty treatments (facials, scrubs). Book ahead.

## Festivals & Events

**Carnaval** CARNIVAL

(www.carnavalbadajoz.es; Feb) Badajoz' colour-bursting Carnaval celebrations and street parties have been kicking on since (at least) the 19th century and are among Spain's most elaborate and popular.

## Sleeping & Eating

**Hotel San Marcos** HOTEL €

(924 22 95 18; www.hotelsanmarcos.es; Calle Meléndez Valdés 53; s €35-60, d €40-66; P ❄ ☎) Polished service and excellent facilities make this superfriendly, vanilla-scented central hotel top value. Rooms are a good size, with plenty of light, plus fridges, safes and, for some, balconies. Bathrooms are sleek and modern and many feature hydromassage showers.

**NH Gran Hotel Casino Extremadura** HOTEL €€

(924 28 44 02; www.nh-hotels.com; Avenida Adolfo Díaz Ambrona 11; r €65-135; P ❄ ☎) Several of Badajoz' classiest hotel picks are just across the Río Guadiana, a short walk west of the old town. This swish, sprawling complex sports modern, elegant, business-style rooms decked out in smart dark woods, with desks and in-room espresso machines. It offers an on-site spa and gym, plus a friendly yet professional welcome.

**Papabuey** GRILL €€

(924 18 15 93; www.papabuey.com; Calle Vicente Barrantes 5; mains €9-17; 1.30-4.15pm Tue-Thu, 1.30-4.15pm & 8.30-11.30pm Fri & Sat, 1.30-4.30pm Sun) Succulent meats grilled to perfection are the key to astounding success at this busy little *asador* (restaurant specialising in roasted meats), just off the Plaza de España. Carnivores will drool over the meat-packed menu, featuring specialities such as *chuletón de buey* (giant beef chop) and classic *extremeño cochinillo asado* (roast suckling pig). The three-course weekday lunchtime *menú* (€15) gets you started.

## Information

**Oficina Municipal de Turismo** (924 22 49 81; www.turismobadajoz.es; Paseo de San Juan; 10am-2pm & 5.30-8pm Mon-Sat, 10am-2pm Sun Jul-Sep, 10am-2pm & 5-7.30pm daily Oct-Jun) Just off the central Plaza de España.

## Getting There & Away

Buses leave from the **bus station** (924 25 86 61; Calle José Rebollo López), 1.5km south of the main Plaza de España. Destinations include Cáceres (€10, 1¼ hr) and Lisbon (normal/express €20/28, 2½/2 hours).

# Olivenza

POP 11,985

Pretty, intriguing Olivenza, 27km southwest of Badajoz, clings to its Portuguese heritage – it has only been Spanish since 1801. The town's cobbled ancient core is distinctive for its whitewashed houses, impressive churches and castle, typical turreted defensive walls and taste for beautiful blue-and-white ceramic tilework.

## Sights

The most impressive section of Olivenza's original defensive **walls** is around the 18th-century Puerta del Calvario, on the western side of the old town.

**Castillo de Olivenza** CASTLE
(☎924 49 02 22; Plaza Santa María del Castillo; adult/child €2.50/free; ⏱10.30am-2pm & 5-8pm Tue-Fri, 10am-2.15pm Sun May-Sep, hours vary Oct-Apr) Smack-bang in the old-town centre stands Olivenza's majestic 14th-century castle, dominated by the 36m-high **Torre del Homenaje**. Make your way to the roof for exquisite panoramas over the town and surrounding countryside. Tickets also include the detailed **Museo Etnográfico Extremeño** (adult/child €2.50/free; ⏱10.30am-2pm & 5-8pm Tue-Sat, 10am-2.15pm Sun May-Sep, 10.30am-2pm & 4-7pm Tue-Sat, 11am-2.15pm Sun Oct-Apr).

## Sleeping & Eating

**Hotel Heredero** HOTEL €
(☎924 49 08 35; www.hotelheredero.net; Carretera de Badajoz, Km 23.7; s/d incl breakfast €40/70; P ❄ ☎) The charmless modern exterior of this place just north of the old town means that the handsome, old-style rooms come as something of a surprise. The wood furnishings give it a touch of old-world style, although the effect is muted rather than over-the-top.

**Casa Maila** EXTREMADURAN €€
(☎924 49 15 05; Calle Colón 3; tapas €4-6, mains €12-19; ⏱noon-midnight Tue-Sun, to 4pm Mon) Refreshingly down to earth, friendly Casa Maila is excellent for both tapas and *raciones* and more elaborate, mostly meaty, mains, on the edge of bubbly Plaza de España.

## Information

**Oficina de Turismo** (☎924 49 01 51; Plaza de San Juan de Diós; ⏱9.30am-2pm & 5-7pm Tue-Sat, 10am-2pm Sun May-Sep, 9.30am-2pm & 4-6pm Tue-Sat, 10am-2pm Sun Oct-Apr) In the Convento San Juan de Dios.

## Getting There & Away

From the **bus station** (☎924 49 05 31; Calle Avelino Palma Brioa), there are buses to/from Badajoz (€2.40, 25 minutes) almost hourly Monday to Friday and twice on Saturday.

## AT A GLANCE

**POPULATION**
4.5 million

**BIGGEST CITY**
Seville

**BEST TAPAS**
Bar-Restaurante Eslava (p636)

**BEST BEACH**
Punta Paloma (p677)

**BEST BOUTIQUE HOTEL**
La Casa del Califa (p672)

**WHEN TO GO**

**Mar–Apr** Sombre Semana Santa processions are followed by exuberant spring fairs.

**May–Jun** Warm, sunny weather, excellent hiking, and yet more colourful festivals.

**Sep–Oct** Ideal period for hiking and beach going without the crowds.

Plaza de España, Parque de María Luisa (p631)
MARQUES/SHUTTERSTOCK ©

# Seville & Andalucía's Hill Towns

With its Moorish-inspired architecture, *pueblos blancos* (white towns) and flamenco traditions, western Andalucía encapsulates much of the spirit and beauty of Spain's sun-baked south. Its charismatic capital, Seville, is one of Spain's most seductive cities, while to the south Cádiz charms with its sea-bound old town and Jerez de Frontera promises world-famous sherry. Sparsely populated hinterland is home to a string of white towns that once marked the border between Christian Spain and Moorish Al-Andalus. Andalucía's Moorish history has had an enduring impact on the region and everywhere you go you'll find remnants of its Islamic past, most spectacularly in the form of Córdoba's Mezquita. Nature lovers are also well served in these parts with everything from bird-rich wetlands in the Parque Nacional de Doñana to windswept beaches at Tarifa and the tracts of unspoiled wilderness crisscrossed by walking trails.

**INCLUDES**

# Seville & Andalucía's Hill Towns Highlights

**1 Seville** (p618) Exploring Andalucía's beguiling capital with its architectural treasures, brilliant tapas and fiery passions.

**2 Jerez de la Frontera** (p657) Unravelling a fashionable world of flamenco, horses, sherry, and bodegas.

**3 Córdoba** (p684) Marvelling at the mesmerising Mezquita in the heart of this historic yet buzzing contemporary city.

**4 Zuheros** (p694) Basing yourself in this charming white village to explore the canyons, caves and castles of the Parque Natural Sierras Subbéticas.

**5 Cádiz** (p650) Travelling through 3000 years of history as you wander Cádiz' salty old town.

**6 Tarifa** (p675) Soaking up the beach scene, kitesurfing and windsurfing with Morocco looming on the horizon.

**7 Parque Nacional de Doñana** (p644) Watching wildlife in the ethereal wetlands of this hauntingly beautiful national park.

**8 Vejer de la Frontera** (p671) Wandering the tangled streets of this magical white hilltop town.

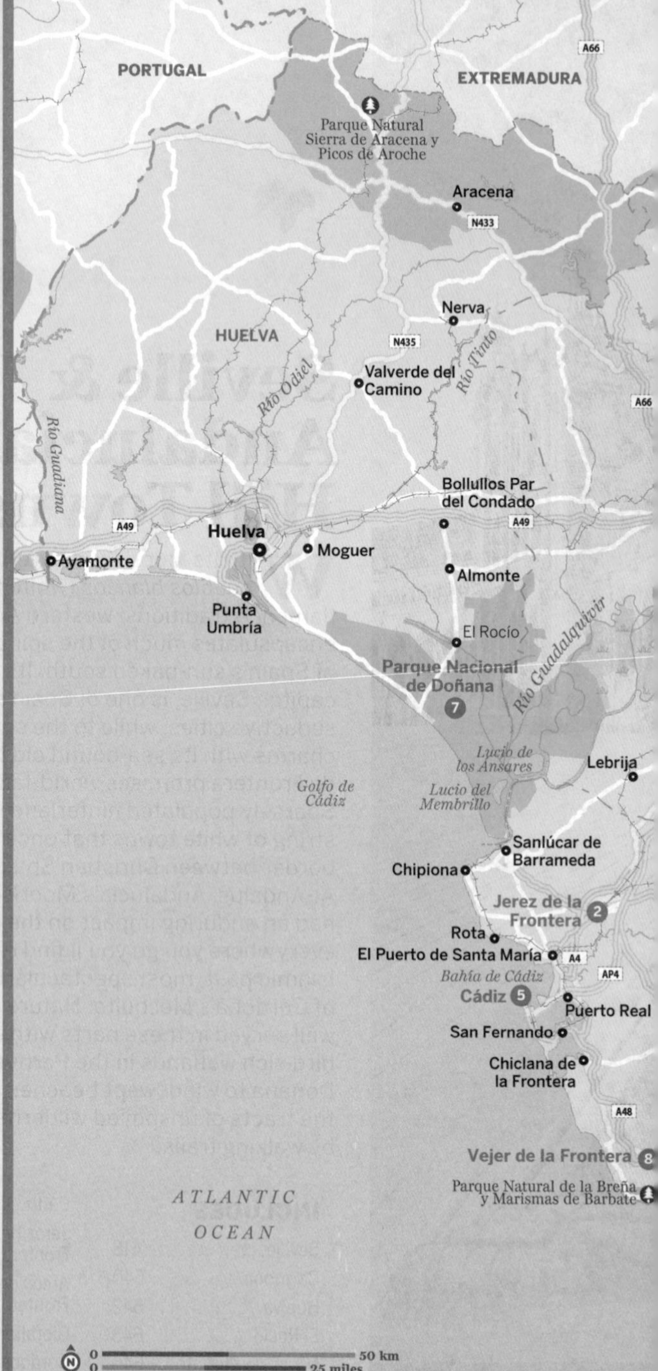

Peñarroya-Pueblonuevo
N432
N502
CÓRDOBA
Río Guadiato
N432
N420
Montoro
Cazalla de la Sierra
Parque Natural Sierra Norte
Parque Natural Sierra de Hornachuelos
Medina Azahara
Córdoba
3
A4
Constantina
Río Huéznar
A431
JAÉN
SEVILLA
A45
Palma del Río
Lora del Río
N432
Baena
Pradollano
Río Corbones
Écija
A4
Montilla
Carmona
A4
Aguilar de la Frontera
Zuheros
4
Seville
1
A45
Priego de Córdoba
Parque Natural Sierras Subbéticas
Alcalá de Guadaira
Puente Genil
Lucena
La Tiñosa (1570m)
Dos Hermanas
A92
Marchena
Arahal
Río Guadaira
Osuna
A92
Utrera
Los Palacios y Villafranca
Morón de la Frontera
A45
A92
AP4
GRANADA
Antequera
A384
Olvera
Embalse del Conde del Guadalhorce
Villamartín
A384
Zahara de la Sierra
MÁLAGA
Setenil de las Bodegas
Arcos de la Frontera
Embalse de Bornos
El Torreón (1648m)
Álora
A382
Parque Natural Sierra de Grazalema
Grazalema
Ronda
Torrecilla (1918m)
Vélez Málaga
Cártama
Ubrique
Málaga
Torre del Mar
Coín
Parque Natural Sierra de las Nieves
CÁDIZ
Río Guadiaro
Mijas
Río Genal
Marbella
Fuengirola
Medina Sidonia
A381
AP7
San Pedro de Alcántara
Playa La Luna
Jimena de la Frontera
Estepona
Embalse de Barbate
Parque Natural Los Alcornocales
Costa del Sol
Barbate
A7
La Línea de la Concepción
N340
MEDITERRANEAN SEA
Algeciras
Gibraltar
Bahía de Algeciras
6
Tarifa
Strait of Gibraltar
MOROCCO
Ceuta (Spain)

# SEVILLE

POP 688,710

Drenched in sunshine for much of the year, Seville is one of Spain's hottest and most seductive cities. Its historic centre, lorded over by a colossal Gothic cathedral, is an intoxicating mix of sumptuous Mudéjar palaces, baroque churches and romantic, orange-scented patios. Cramped flamenco clubs keep the intensity of this centuries-old tradition alive, while aristocratic mansions recall the city's past as a showcase Moorish capital and, later, a cosmopolitan metropolis rich on the back of New World trade.

But while history reverberates all around, Seville is as much about the here and now as the past. It's about eating tapas in a crowded bar or seeing out the day over a drink on a buzzing plaza. *Sevillanos* have long since mastered the art of celebrating and the city's Semana Santa and Feria de Abril festivities are among Spain's most heartfelt.

## History

Seville started life as an Iberian settlement before growing to become an important Roman port (Hispalis). But it was under a succession of Islamic rulers that the city really came into its own. It enjoyed a heyday in the late 11th century as a major cultural centre under the Abbadid dynasty, and then again in the 12th century when the Almohads took control. Almohad power dwindled after a disastrous defeat in 1212, and in 1248, the city fell to Castilla's Catholic king Fernando III (El Santo; the Saint).

Some 240-odd years later, the discovery of the Americas paved the way for another golden era. In 1503, the city was awarded an official monopoly on Spanish trade with the new-found continent. The riches poured in and Seville blossomed into one of the world's largest, richest and most cosmopolitan cities.

But it was not to last. A plague in 1649 killed half the city's population and in 1717 the Casa de la Contratación (Contracting House), the government office controlling commerce with the Americas, was transferred to Cádiz. The city went into decline.

More recently, the city was made capital of the autonomous Andalucía region in 1982, and in 1992 it hosted the Expo world fair.

### CATHEDRAL TICKETS TIP

To avoid queueing for tickets at the cathedral, you can either book through the cathedral's website or buy tickets at the Iglesia Colegial del Divino Salvador (p629). There are rarely queues at this church, which sells combined tickets covering admission to the church, the cathedral and Giralda. Note also that entry to the cathedral is free on Monday afternoons between 4.30pm and 6pm. Numbers are limited, though, so you'll need to reserve a slot on the website.

## Sights

### Catedral & Barrio de Santa Cruz

Once Seville's medieval *judería* (Jewish quarter), Santa Cruz is a tightly-packed warren of cobbled alleyways, white buildings and lovely plant-decked plazas. Seville's immense Gothic cathedral dominates the skyline and the Real Alcázar stuns with its Arabesque interiors and fabulous gardens.

**★Catedral & Giralda** CATHEDRAL
(Map p626; 902 09 96 92; www.catedraldesevilla.es; Plaza del Triunfo; adult/child incl Iglesia Colegial del Divino Salvador €10/free, incl rooftop guided tours €16, 4.30-6pm Mon free; 11am-3.30pm Mon, to 5pm Tue-Sat, 2.30-6pm Sun Sep-Jun, 10.30am-4pm Mon, to 6pm Tue-Sat, 2-7pm Sun Jul & Aug) Seville's showpiece church is awe-inspiring in its scale and majesty. The world's largest Gothic cathedral, it was built between 1434 and 1517 over the remains of what had previously been the city's main mosque. Highlights include the Giralda, the mighty bell tower, which incorporates the mosque's original minaret; the monumental tomb of Christopher Columbus and the Capilla Mayor with an astonishing gold altarpiece.

Audio guides cost €3. Note also that children under nine are not permitted on rooftop tours. You can also tour the cathedral's stained glass windows – see the website for details and booking.

The history of the cathedral goes back to the 15th century but the history of Christian worship on the site dates to the mid-13th century. In 1248, the Castilian king Fernando III captured Seville from its Almohad rulers and transformed their great 12th-century mosque into a church. Some 153 years later, in 1401, the city's ecclesiastical authorities decided to replace the former mosque, which had been damaged by an earthquake in 1356, with a spectacular new cathedral: 'Let's construct a church so large future generations will think we were mad', they quipped (or so legend has it).

The result is the staggering cathedral you see today, officially known as the Catedral de Santa María de la Sede. It's one of the world's largest churches and a veritable treasure trove of art, with notable works by Zurbarán, Murillo, Goya and others.

**➡ Exterior**

With its immense flying buttresses and Gothic embellishments, the cathedral's exterior provides a suitably dramatic shell for the treasures within. Pause to look at the **Puerta del Perdón** (now the cathedral's exit) on Calle Alemanes, which is one of the few remaining elements of the original mosque.

**➡ Sala del Pabellón**

Selected treasures from the cathedral's art collection are exhibited in this room, the first after the ticket office. Much of what's displayed here, as elsewhere in the cathedral, is the work of masters from Seville's 17th-century Golden Age.

**➡ Tomb of Christopher Columbus**

Once inside the cathedral proper, head right until you come to the tomb of Christopher Columbus (the Sepulcro de Cristóbal Colón) in front of the **Puerta del Príncipe** (Door of the Prince). The monument supposedly contains the remains of the great explorer, but debate continues as to whether the bones are actually his.

Columbus' remains were moved many times after his death (in 1506 in Valladolid, northern Spain), and there are those who claim his real bones lie in Santo Domingo. Certainly his bones spent time in the Dominican Republic after they were shipped to Spanish-controlled Hispaniola from their original resting place, the Monasterio de la Cartuja (p631), in 1537. However, they were later sent to Havana and returned to Seville in 1898. DNA testing in 2006 proved a match between the bones supposed to be Columbus' and bones known to be from his brother Diego. And while that didn't conclusively solve the mystery, it strongly suggested that the great man really is interred in the tomb that bears his name.

**➡ Sacristía de los Cálices**

To the right of Columbus' tomb are a series of rooms containing some of the cathedral's greatest masterpieces. First up is the Sacristy of the Chalices, behind the Capilla de los Dolores, where Francisco de Goya's painting of the Sevillan martyrs, *Santas Justa y Rufina* (1817), hangs above the altar.

**➡ Sacristía Mayor**

Next along is this large room with a finely carved stone cupola, created between 1528 and 1547. Pedro de Campaña's 1547 *El descendimiento* (Descent from the Cross), above the central altar at the southern end, and Francisco de Zurbarán's *Santa Teresa*, to its right, are two of the cathedral's most precious paintings. Also look out for the *Custodia de Juan de Arfe*, a huge 475kg silver monstrance made in the 1580s by Renaissance metalsmith Juan de Arfe.

**➡ Sala Capitular**

The circular chapter house, also called the Cabildo, features a stunning carved dome and a Murillo masterpiece, *La inmaculada*, set high above the archbishop's throne. The room, whose design was inspired by Michelangelo's Piazza del Campidoglio in Rome, was built between 1558 and 1592 as a venue for meetings of the cathedral hierarchy. Also impressive is the Antecabildo with its decorated vaulted ceiling.

**➡ Capilla Mayor**

Even in a church as spectacular as this, the Capilla Mayor (Main Chapel) stands out with its astonishing Gothic retable, reckoned to be the world's largest altarpiece. Begun by Flemish sculptor Pieter Dancart in 1482 and finished by others in 1564, this sea of gilt and polychromed wood holds more than 1000 carved biblical figures. At the centre of the lowest level is a tiny 13th-century silver-plated cedar image of the Virgen de la sede (Virgin of the See), patron of the cathedral.

**➡ Coro**

West of the Capilla Mayor and dominating the central nave is the 16th-century Coro (Choir). This giant box-like structure incorporates 114 elaborately wooden seats in Gothic-Mudéjar style and a vast organ.

**➡ Capilla de San Antonio**

The chapels along the sides of the cathedral hold yet more artistic treasures. Of particular note is the Capilla de San Antonio, at the western end of the northern aisle, housing Murillo's gigantic 1656 depiction of the *Visión de San Antonio de Padua* (Vision of St Anthony of Padua). The painting was victim of a daring art heist in 1874.

# Seville

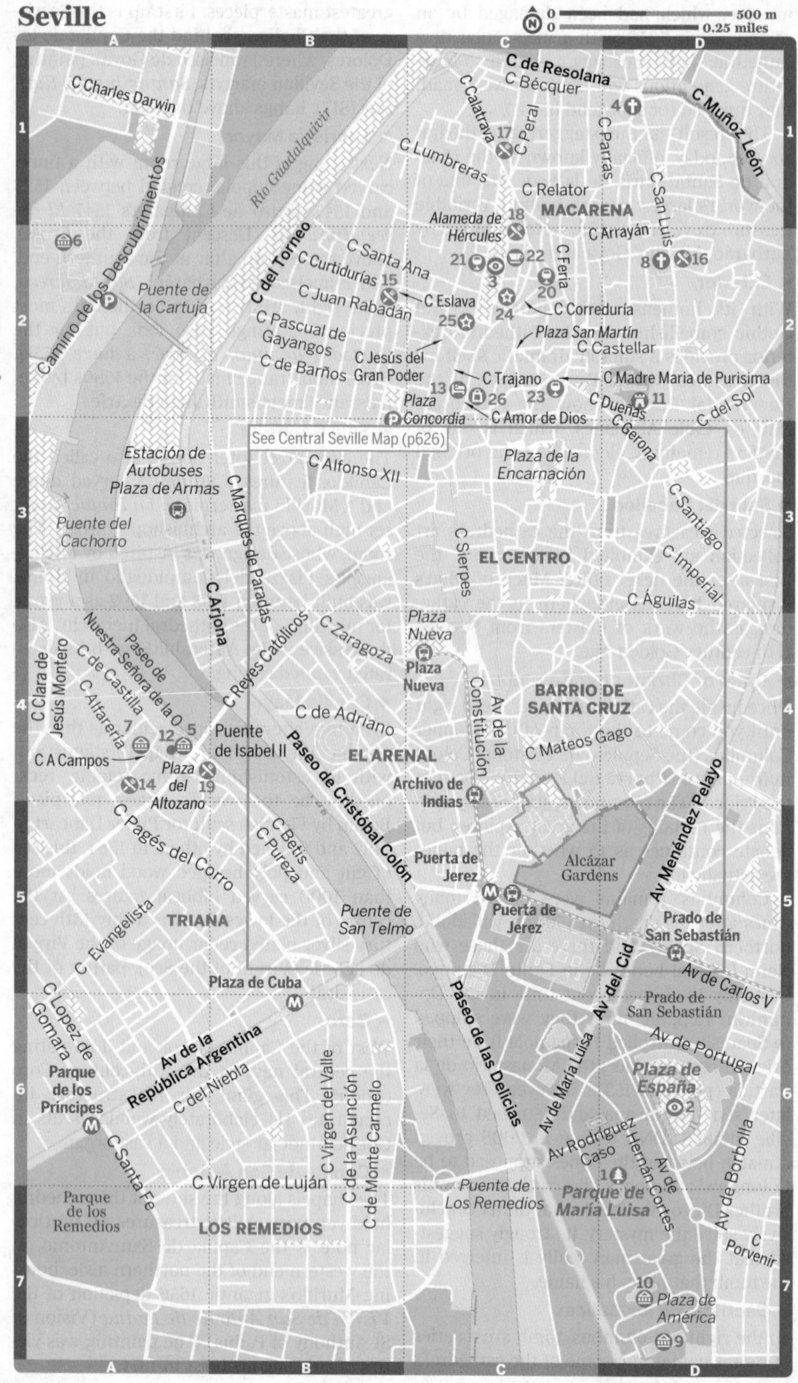
0 500 m
0 0.25 miles
A
B
C
D
1
2
3
4
5
6
7
C de Resolana
C Bécquer
C Muñoz León
C Charles Darwin
C Calatrava
C Peral
C Parras
C Lumbreras
Río Guadalquivir
C Relator
C San Luis
MACARENA
Alameda de Hércules
C Arrayán
Camino de los Descubrimientos
C del Torneo
C Santa Ana
C Curtidurías
C Feria
Puente de la Cartuja
C Juan Rabadán
C Eslava
C Correduría
C Pascual de Gayangos
Plaza San Martín
C Castellar
C Jesús del Gran Poder
C de Barños
C Trajano
C Madre Maria de Purisima
Plaza Concordia
C Amor de Dios
C Dueñas
C del Sol
C Gerona
See Central Seville Map (p626)
Estación de Autobuses Plaza de Armas
C Alfonso XII
Plaza de la Encarnación
C Marqués de Paradas
Puente del Cachorro
C Santiago
C Sierpes
EL CENTRO
C Imperial
C Arjona
C Águilas
Plaza Nueva
C Reyes Católicos
C Zaragoza
C Clara de Jesús Montero
Paseo de Nuestra Señora de la O
C de Castilla
C Alfarería
Plaza Nueva
Constitución
Av de la
BARRIO DE SANTA CRUZ
C de Adriano
Puente de Isabel II
Paseo de Cristóbal Colón
C A Campos
Plaza del Altozano
EL ARENAL
C Mateos Gago
Archivo de Indias
Av Menéndez Pelayo
C Pagés del Corro
C Betis
C Pureza
Puerta de Jerez
Alcázar Gardens
Puerta de Jerez
Puente de San Telmo
TRIANA
C Evangelista
Prado de San Sebastián
Av de Carlos V
Plaza de Cuba
Av del Cid
Prado de San Sebastián
C Lopez de Gomara
Paseo de las Delicias
Av de Portugal
Av de la República Argentina
Parque de los Príncipes
C del Niebla
Av de María Luisa
Plaza de España
C Virgen del Valle
C de la Asunción
C de Monte Carmelo
Av Rodríguez Caso
Hernán Cortes
Av de
Av de Borbolla
C Santa Fe
C Virgen de Luján
Puente de Los Remedios
Parque de María Luisa
Parque de los Remedios
LOS REMEDIOS
C Porvenir
Plaza de América
1
2
3
4
5
6
7
8
9
10
11
12
13
14
15
16
17
18
19
20
21
22
23
24
25
26

## Seville

**Top Sights**



**Sights**



**Activities, Courses & Tours**



**Sleeping**



**Eating**



**Drinking & Nightlife**



**Entertainment**



**Shopping**



### ➡ Giralda

In the northeastern corner of the cathedral you'll find the entrance to the Giralda. The climb to the top involves walking up 35 ramps, built so that the guards could ride up on horseback, and a small flight of stairs at the top. Your reward is sensational rooftop views.

The decorative brick tower, which tops out at 104m, was the minaret of the mosque, constructed between 1184 and 1198 at the height of Almohad power. Its proportions, delicate brick-pattern decoration, and colour, which changes with the light, make it perhaps Spain's most perfect Islamic building. The topmost parts – from bell level up – were added in the 16th century, when Spanish Christians were busy 'improving on' surviving Islamic buildings. At the very top is El Giraldillo, a 16th-century bronze weather vane representing 'faith', that has become a symbol of Seville.

### ➡ Patio de los Naranjos

Outside the cathedral's northern flank, this patio was originally the mosque's main courtyard. It's planted with 66 *naranjos* (orange trees), and has a small Visigothic fountain in the centre. Look out for a stuffed crocodile hanging over the courtyard's doorway – it's a replica of a gift the Sultan of Egypt gave Alfonso X in around 1260.

### ★ Real Alcázar — PALACE

(Map p626; ☎954 50 23 24; www.alcazarsevilla.org; Plaza del Triunfo; adult/student/child €11.50/3/free, 6-7pm Mon Apr-Sep free, 4-5pm Mon Oct-Mar free; ⏲9.30am-7pm Apr-Sep, to 5pm Oct-Mar) A magnificent marriage of Christian and Mudéjar architecture, Seville's royal palace complex is a breathtaking spectacle. The site, which was originally developed as a fort in 913, has been revamped many times over the 11 centuries of its existence, most spectacularly in the 14th century when King Pedro added the sumptuous Palacio de Don Pedro, still today the Alcázar's crowning glory. More recently, the Alcázar featured as a location for the *Game of Thrones* TV series.

Note that long entry queues are the norm here. To cut waiting time, it pays to pre-purchase tickets at www.alcazarsevilla.org.

The Alcázar started life in the 10th century as a fort for the Cordoban governors of Seville but it was in the 11th century that it got its first major rebuild. Under the city's Abbadid rulers, the original fort was enlarged and a palace known as Al-Muwarak (the Blessed) was built in what's now the western part of the complex. Subsequently, the 12th-century Almohad rulers added another palace east of this, around what's now the Patio del Crucero. The Christian king Fernando III moved into the Alcázar when he captured Seville in 1248, and several later monarchs used it as their main residence.

# Seville Cathedral

## THE HIGHLIGHTS TOUR

In 1402 the inspired architects of Seville set out on one of the most grandiose building projects in medieval history. Their aim was to shock and amaze future generations with the size and magnificence of the building. It took until 1506 to complete the project, but 500 years later Seville Cathedral is still the largest Gothic cathedral in the world.

To avoid getting lost, orient yourself by the main highlights. To the right of the visitor entrance is the grand ❶ **Tomb of Columbus**. Continue into the southeastern corner to uncover some major art treasures: a Goya in the Sacristía de los Cálices, a Zurbarán in the ❷ **Sacristía Mayor**, and Murillo's shining *La inmaculada* in the Sala Capitular. Skirt the cathedral's eastern wall past the often-closed ❸ **Capilla Real**, home to some important royal tombs. By now it's impossible to avoid the lure of the ❹ **Capilla Mayor** with its fantastical altarpiece. Hidden over in the northwest corner is the ❺ **Capilla de San Antonio** with a legendary Murillo. That huge doorway nearby is the rarely opened ❻ **Puerta de la Asunción**. Make for the ❼ **Giralda** next, stealing admiring looks at the high, vaulted ceiling on the way. After looking down on the cathedral's immense footprint, descend and depart via the ❽ **Patio de los Naranjos**.

### TOP TIPS

➡ Don't try to visit the Alcázar and cathedral on the same day. There is far too much to take in.

➡ Take time to admire the cathedral from the outside. It's particularly stunning at night from the Plaza de la Virgen de los Reyes, and from across the river in Triana.

➡ Skip the line by booking tickets online or buying them at the Iglesia Colegial del Divino Salvador on Plaza del Salvador.

**Capilla de San Antonio**
One of 80 interior chapels, you'll need to hunt down this little gem notable for housing Murillo's 1656 painting, *Vision of St Anthony of Padua*. The work was pillaged by thieves in 1874 but later restored.

**Patio de los Naranjos**
Inhale the perfume of 60 Sevillan orange trees in a cool patio bordered by fortress-like walls – a surviving remnant of the original 12th-century mosque. Exit is gained via the horseshoe-shaped Puerta del Perdón.

**Puerta del Perdón**

8

5

6

**Iglesia del Sagrario**

**Puerta del Bautismo**

**Puerta de la Asunción**
Located on the western side of the cathedral and also known as the Puerta Mayor, these huge, rarely opened doors are pushed back during Semana Santa to allow solemn processions of Catholic *hermandades* (brotherhoods) to pass through.

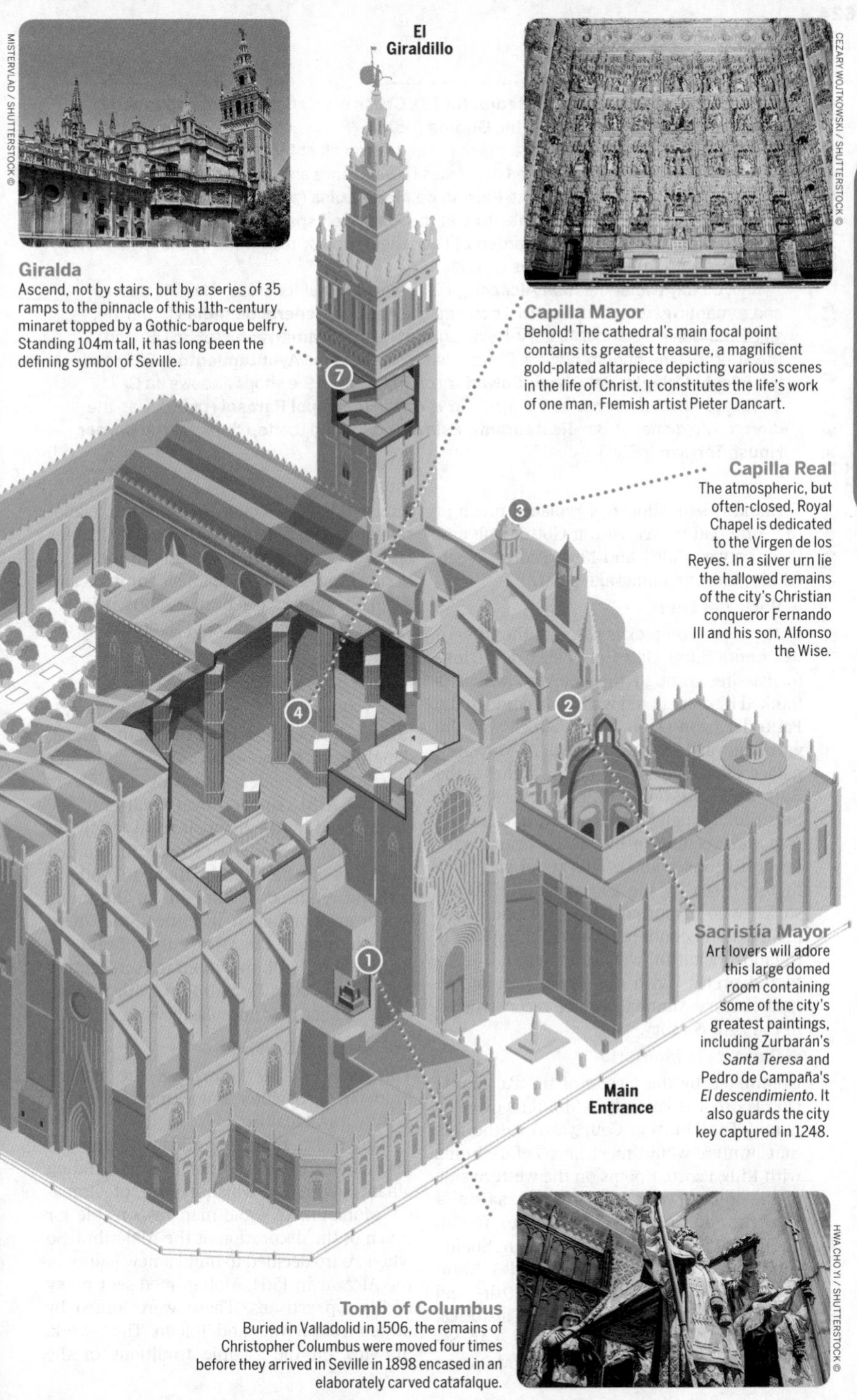


**Giralda**
Ascend, not by stairs, but by a series of 35 ramps to the pinnacle of this 11th-century minaret topped by a Gothic-baroque belfry. Standing 104m tall, it has long been the defining symbol of Seville.

**Capilla Mayor**
Behold! The cathedral's main focal point contains its greatest treasure, a magnificent gold-plated altarpiece depicting various scenes in the life of Christ. It constitutes the life's work of one man, Flemish artist Pieter Dancart.

**Capilla Real**
The atmospheric, but often-closed, Royal Chapel is dedicated to the Virgen de los Reyes. In a silver urn lie the hallowed remains of the city's Christian conqueror Fernando III and his son, Alfonso the Wise.

**Sacristía Mayor**
Art lovers will adore this large domed room containing some of the city's greatest paintings, including Zurbarán's *Santa Teresa* and Pedro de Campaña's *El descendimiento*. It also guards the city key captured in 1248.

**Tomb of Columbus**
Buried in Valladolid in 1506, the remains of Christopher Columbus were moved four times before they arrived in Seville in 1898 encased in an elaborately carved catafalque.

## SEVILLE IN TWO DAYS

Start at Seville's vast **Gothic Catedral** (p618). Check out Christoper Columbus' tomb and scale the famous bell tower, the **Giralda** (p618). When you're done, delve into the labyrinthine Barrio de Santa Cruz, making sure to stop off at the **Hospital de los Venerables Sacerdotes** for some masterpieces by Velázquez and pals. After lunch at **La Azotea** (p634), strike south to the **Parque de María Luisa** (p631), Seville's elegant central park. Feast on fairy-tale architecture at the **Plaza de España** (p631) before strolling through the park's landscaped gardens. Finish the day back in Santa Cruz with a flamenco show at the **Tablao Los Gallos** (p637).

Kick off day two at the **Real Alcázar** (p621), marvelling at its Arabian Nights decor and romantic gardens. Afterwards, pop into the **Archivo General de Indias** for an insight into Spain's colonial history. Next, lunch at nearby **Mamarracha** (p635). Spend the afternoon reconnoitering the Centro district. Take in the **Ayuntamiento** (p629) and the **Iglesia Colegial del Divino Salvador** (p629), browse the shop windows on Calle Sierpes, and catch memorable sunset views on the **Metropol Parasol** (p630). Cap the day off with dinner at **Bar-Restaurante Eslava** (p636) and rooftop drinks at the **Corner House Terraza** (p636).

Fernando's son Alfonso X replaced much of the Almohad palace with a Gothic one and then, between 1364 and 1366, Pedro I created his stunning namesake palace.

### ➡ Patio del León

Entry to the complex is through the **Puerta del León** (Lion Gate) on Plaza del Triunfo. Passing through the gateway, which is flanked by crenellated walls, you come to the Patio del León (Lion Patio), which was the garrison yard of the original Al-Muwarak palace. Off to the left before the arches is the **Sala de la Justicia** (Hall of Justice), with beautiful Mudéjar plasterwork and an *artesonado* (ceiling of interlaced beams with decorative insertions). This room was built in the 1340s by the Christian king Alfonso XI, who disported here with one of his mistresses, Leonor de Guzmán, reputedly the most beautiful woman in Spain. It leads to the pretty **Patio del Yeso**, part of the 12th-century Almohad palace reconstructed in the 19th century.

### ➡ Patio de la Montería

Dominated by the facade of the Palacio de Don Pedro, the Patio de la Montería owes its name (The Hunting Courtyard) to the fact that hunters would meet here before hunts with King Pedro. Rooms on the western side of the square were part of the **Casa de la Contratación** (Contracting House), founded in 1503 to control trade with Spain's American colonies. The **Salón del Almirante** (Admiral's Hall) houses 19th- and 20th-century paintings showing historical events and personages associated with Seville. The room off its northern end has an international collection of beautiful, elaborate fans. The **Sala de Audiencias** (Chapter House) is hung with tapestry representations of the shields of Spanish admirals and Alejo Fernández' celebrated 1530s painting *Virgen de los mareantes* (Madonna of the Seafarers).

### ➡ Cuarto Real Alto

The Alcázar is still a royal palace. In 1995 it hosted the wedding feast of Infanta Elena, daughter of King Juan Carlos I, after her marriage in Seville's cathedral. The **Cuarto Real Alto** (Upper Royal Quarters), the rooms used by the Spanish royal family on their visits to Seville, are open for guided tours (€4.50; half-hourly 10am to 1.30pm; booking required). Highlights of the tours, which are conducted in either Spanish or English, include the 14th-century **Salón de Audiencias**, still the monarch's reception room, and Pedro I's bedroom, with marvellous Mudéjar tiles and plasterwork.

### ➡ Palacio de Don Pedro

This palace, also known as the Palacio Mudéjar, is Seville's single most stunning architectural feature.

King Pedro, though at odds with many of his fellow Christians, had a long-standing alliance with the Muslim emir of Granada, Mohammed V, the man responsible for much of the decoration at the Alhambra. So when Pedro decided to build a new palace in the Alcázar in 1364, Mohammed sent many of his top artisans. These were joined by others from Seville and Toledo. Their work, drawing on the Islamic traditions of the

Almohads and caliphal Córdoba, is a unique synthesis of Iberian Islamic art.

Inscriptions on the palace's facade encapsulate the collaborative nature of the enterprise. While one, in Spanish, announces that the building's creator was the 'highest, noblest and most powerful conqueror Don Pedro, by God's grace King of Castilla and León', another proclaims repeatedly in Arabic that 'there is no conqueror but Allah'.

At the heart of the palace is the sublime **Patio de las Doncellas** (Patio of the Maidens), surrounded by beautiful arches, plasterwork and tiling. The sunken garden in the centre was uncovered by archaeologists in 2004 from beneath a 16th-century marble covering.

To the north of the patio, the **Alcoba Real** (Royal Quarters) feature stunningly beautiful ceilings and wonderful plaster and tile work. Its rear room was probably the monarch's summer bedroom.

Continuing on brings you to the covered **Patio de las Muñecas** (Patio of the Dolls), the heart of the palace's private quarters, featuring delicate Granada-style decoration; indeed, plasterwork was actually brought here from the Alhambra in the 19th century, when the mezzanine and top gallery were added for Queen Isabel II. The **Cuarto del Príncipe** (Prince's Suite), to its north, has an elaborate gold ceiling intended to recreate a starlit night sky.

The most spectacular room in the Palacio, and indeed the whole Alcázar, is the **Salón de Embajadores** (Hall of Ambassadors), south of the Patio de las Muñecas. This was originally Pedro I's throne room, although the fabulous wooden dome of multiple star patterns, symbolising the universe, was added later in 1427. The dome's shape gives the room its alternative name, Sala de la Media Naranja (Hall of the Half Orange).

On the western side of the Salón, the beautiful **Arco de Pavones**, named after its peacock motifs, leads onto the **Salón del Techo de Felipe II**, with a Renaissance ceiling (1589–91), and beyond, to the **Jardín del Príncipe** (Prince's Garden).

#### ➡ Palacio Gótico (Salones de Carlo V)

Reached via a staircase at the southeastern corner of the Patio de las Doncellas is Alfonso X's much remodelled 13th-century Gothic palace. The echoing halls here were designed for the 16th-century Spanish king Carlos I and are now known as the **Salones de Carlos V** (after his second title as Holy Roman Emperor Charles V). Of the rooms, the most striking is the **Salone de los Tapices**, a vaulted hall with a series of vast tapestries.

#### ➡ Patio del Crucero

Beyond the Salone de los Tapices, the Patio del Crucero was originally the upper storey of a patio from the 12th-century Almohad palace. Initially it consisted only of raised walkways along its four sides and two cross-walkways that met in the middle. Below grew orange trees, whose fruit could be plucked at hand height by the lucky folk strolling along the walkways. The patio's lower level was built over in the 18th century after it suffered earthquake damage.

#### ➡ Gardens

On the other side of the Salone de los Tapices are the Alcázar's gardens. Formal gardens with pools and fountains sit closest to the palace. From one, the **Jardín de la Danza** (Garden of the Dance), a passage runs beneath the Salones de Carlos V to the photogenic **Baños de Doña María de Padilla** (María de Padilla Baths). These are the vaults beneath the Patio del Crucero – originally the patio's lower level – with a grotto that replaced the patio's original pool.

One of the gardens' most arresting feature is the **Galeria de Grutesco**, a raised gallery with porticoes fashioned in the 16th century out of an old Islamic-era wall. There is also a fun hedge maze, which will delight children. The gardens to the east, beyond a long wall, are 20th-century creations

### Archivo General de Indias — ARCHIVES

(Map p626; ☎954 50 05 28; Avenida de la Constitución; ⏲9.30am-5pm Tue-Sat, 10am-2pm Sun) FREE Occupying a former merchant's exchange on the western side of Plaza del Triunfo, the Archivo General de Indias provides fascinating insight into Spain's colonial history. The archive, established in 1785 to house documents and maps relating to Spain's American empire, is vast, boasting 7km of shelves, 43,000 documents, and 80 million pages dating from 1492 to the end of the empire in the 19th century. Most documents are filed away, but you can examine fascinating letters and hand-drawn maps.

### ★Hospital de los Venerables Sacerdotes — MUSEUM

(Map p626; ☎954 56 26 96; www.hospitaldelosvenerables.es; Plaza de los Venerables 8; adult/student/child €10/8/free; ⏲10am-8pm Mar-Jun

## Central Seville

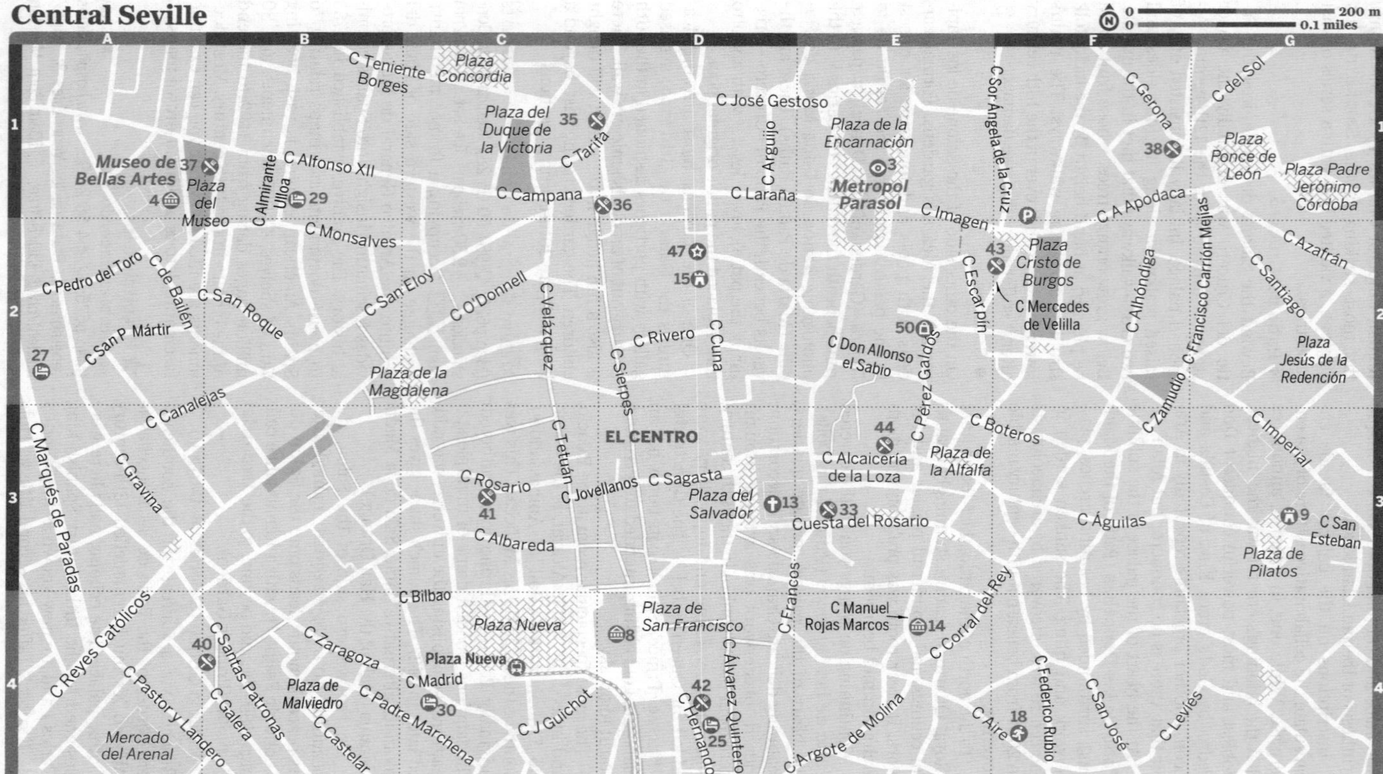

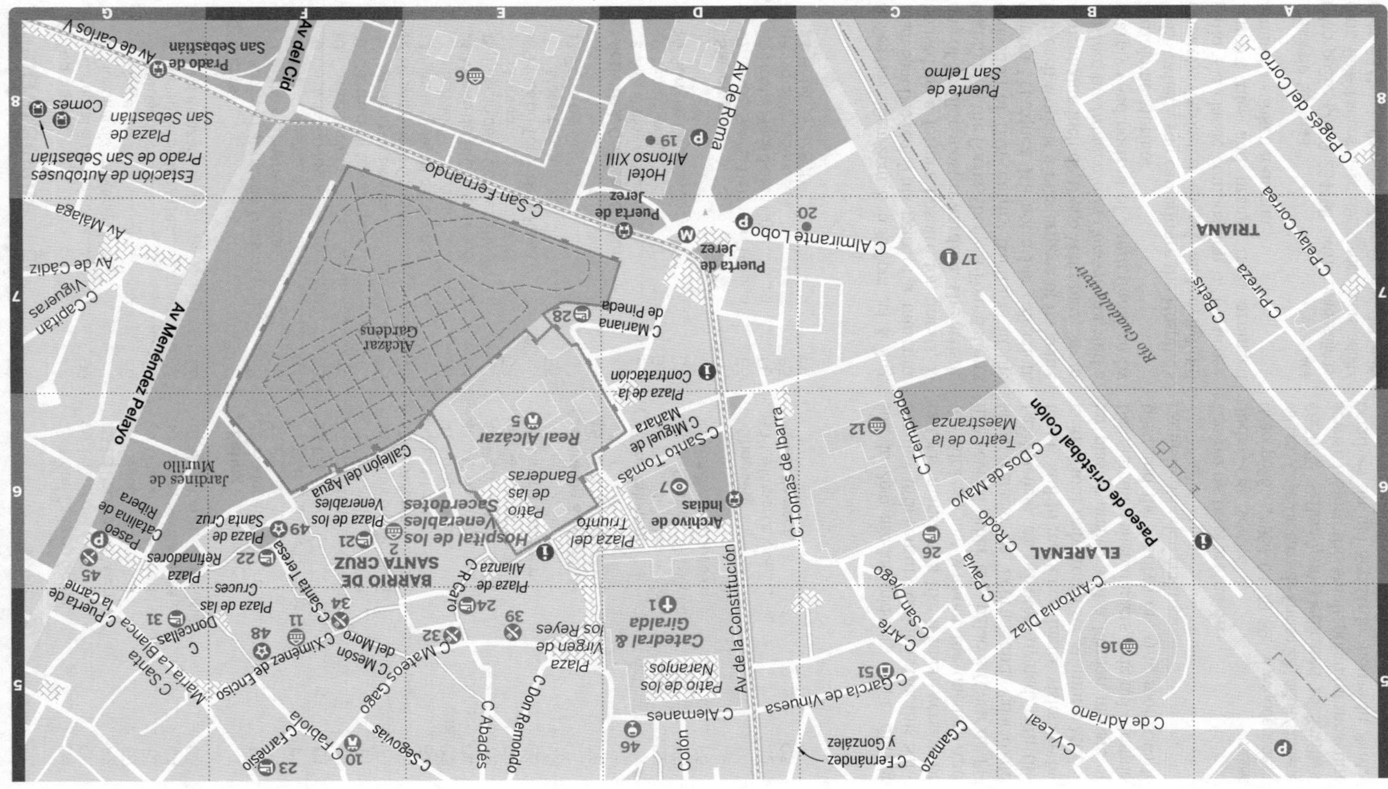
Av Menéndez Pelayo
Av del Cid
Av de Carlos V
Prado de San Sebastián
Estación de Autobuses Prado de San Sebastián
Plaza de San Sebastián
Comes
Av Málaga
Av de Cádiz
C Capitán Vigueras
C Puerta de la Carne
Paseo Catalina de Ribera
Jardines de Murillo
C Santa María La Blanca
C Doncellas
Plaza Refinadores
Plaza de Santa Cruz
Plaza de las Cruces
C Ximénez de Enciso
C Farnesio
C Fabiola
C Santa Teresa
C Mesón del Moro
BARRIO DE SANTA CRUZ
Plaza de los Venerables
Callejón del Agua
Alcázar Gardens
C Segovias
C Mateos Gago
Hospital de los Venerables Sacerdotes
C R Caro
Plaza de Alianza
C Abadés
C Don Remondo
Patio de las Banderas
Real Alcázar
C San Fernando
Plaza Virgen de los Reyes
Plaza del Triunfo
C Mariana de Pineda
Puerta de Jerez
Hotel Alfonso XIII
Catedral & Giralda
Patio de los Naranjos
Colón
C Alemanes
Archivo de Indias
C Santo Tomás
C Miguel de Mañara
Plaza de la Contratación
Av de la Constitución
Av de Roma
C Tomas de Ibarra
C Almirante Lobo
C Fernández y González
C García de Vinuesa
C Arfe
C San Diego
C Temprado
C Gamazo
C Pavía
C Rodo
C Dos de Mayo
Teatro de la Maestranza
Puente de San Telmo
C V Leal
C Antonia Díaz
EL ARENAL
Paseo de Cristóbal Colón
C de Adriano
Río Guadalquivir
C Betis
TRIANA
C Pureza
C Pelay Correa
C Pagés del Corro
A
B
C
D
E
F
G
5
6
7
8
1
2
5
6
7
10
11
12
16
17
19
20
21
22
23
24
26
28
31
32
34
39
45
46
48
49
51

## Central Seville

**Top Sights**
1 Catedral & Giralda ... D5
2 Hospital de los Venerables Sacerdotes ... F6
3 Metropol Parasol ... E1
4 Museo de Bellas Artes ... A1
5 Real Alcázar ... E6

**Sights**
6 Antigua Fábrica de Tabacos ... E8
7 Archivo General de Indias ... D6
8 Ayuntamiento ... D4
9 Casa de Pilatos ... G3
10 Casa de Salinas ... F5
11 Centro de Interpretación Judería de Sevilla ... F5
12 Hospital de la Caridad ... C6
13 Iglesia Colegial del Divino Salvador ... D3
14 Museo del Baile Flamenco ... E4
15 Palacio de la Condesa de Lebrija ... D2
16 Plaza de Toros de la Real Maestranza ... B5
17 Torre del Oro ... C7

**Activities, Courses & Tours**
18 Aire Baños Árabes ... F4
19 Mimo Sevilla ... D8
20 Surf the City ... C7

**Sleeping**
21 Casual Sevilla Don Juan Tenorio ... F6
22 Hostal Plaza Santa Cruz ... F6
23 Hotel Amadeus ... F5
24 Hotel Casa 1800 ... E5
25 Hotel Casa de Colón ... D4
26 La Banda ... C6
27 La Parada del Marqués ... A2
28 Legado Alcázar ... E7
29 Oasis Palace Hostel ... B1
30 Suites Sevilla Plaza ... C4
31 Un Patio en Santa Cruz ... G5

**Eating**
32 Bodega Santa Cruz ... E5
33 Bolas ... E3
34 Café Bar Las Teresas ... F5
35 Cocome ... C1
36 Confitería La Campana ... D1
37 Créeme ... B1
38 El Rinconcillo ... F1
39 La Azotea ... E5
40 La Brunilda ... B4
41 Lobo López ... C3
42 Mamarracha ... D4
43 Palo Cortao ... F2
44 Sal Gorda ... E3
45 Vinería San Telmo ... G6

**Drinking & Nightlife**
46 La Terraza del Eme ... D5

**Entertainment**
47 Casa de la Memoria ... D2
48 La Casa del Flamenco ... F5
49 Tablao Los Gallos ... F6

**Shopping**
50 La Importadora ... E2
51 La Oleoteca ... C5

& Sep-Nov, 10am-2pm & 5.30-9pm Jul & Aug, 10am-6pm Dec-Feb) This gem of a museum, housed in a former hospice for priests, is one of Seville's most rewarding. The artistic highlight is the Focus-Abengoa Foundation's collection of 17th-century paintings in the Centro Velázquez. It's not a big collection, but each work is a masterpiece of its genre – highlights include Diego Velázquez' *Santa Rufina*, his *Inmaculada Concepción*, and a sharply vivid portrait of *Santa Catalina* by Bartolomé Murillo.

Elsewhere, you can admire the Hospital's ornately decorated chapel and delightful patio – a classic composition of porticoes, ceramic tiles and orange trees arranged around a sunken fountain.

### Casa de Salinas — PALACE

(Map p626; ☎619 254498; www.casadesalinas.com; Calle Mateos Gago 39; guided tours adult/child €8/4; ⏰10am-6pm Mon-Fri mid-Oct–mid-Jun, to 2pm mid-Jun–mid-Oct) Built during Seville's 16th-century Golden Age, this Santa Cruz mansion is like a micro-version of the Alcázar, just without the queues. And like several other city palaces (Casa de Pilatos, Palacio de Lebrija and Palacio de Las Dueñas), it's privately owned, with the family still in residence, hence visits are by guided tour only. You'll see stunning Mudéjar plaster arches and a Roman mosaic of Bacchanalian shenanigans, original ceramic tiles, and the family's drawing rooms with exquisite wooden ceilings.

### Centro de Interpretación Judería de Sevilla — MUSEUM

(Map p626; ☎954 04 70 89; www.juderiadesevilla.es; Calle Ximénez de Enciso 22; adult/student €6.50/5; ⏰11am-7pm) Dedicated to Seville's Jewish history, this small, poignant museum occupies an old Sephardic house in Santa

Cruz, the one-time Jewish neighbourhood that never recovered from a brutal massacre in 1391. The massacre and other historical happenings are catalogued inside, along with a few surviving mementos including documents, costumes and books.

## El Centro & El Arenal

### ★Museo de Bellas Artes MUSEUM

(Fine Arts Museum; Map p626; ☎955 54 29 42; www.museodebellasartesdesevilla.es; Plaza del Museo 9; EU/non-EU citizens free/€1.50; ⏰9am-9pm Tue-Sat, to 3pm Sun) Housed in a grand Mannerist palace, the former Convento de la Merced, the Museo de Bellas Artes is one of Spain's premier art museums. Its collection of Spanish and Sevillan paintings and sculptures comprises works from the 15th to 20th centuries, but the focus is very much on brooding religious paintings from the city's 17th-century Siglo de Oro (Golden Age).

### Iglesia Colegial del Divino Salvador CHURCH

(Map p626; ☎954 21 16 79; www.iglesiadelsalvador.es; Plaza del Salvador; adult/child €5/free, incl Catedral & Giralda €10/free; ⏰11am-5.30pm Mon-Sat, 3-7pm Sun Sep-Jun, 10am-5.30pm Mon-Sat, 3-7pm Sun Jul & Aug) Overlooking Plaza del Salvador, this baroque church was built between 1674 and 1712 on the site of Muslim Ishbiliya's main mosque. Its Mannerist red-brick facade masks a cavernous, light-filled interior crowned by a soaring dome and filled with extravagant gold altarpieces. Particularly breathtaking is the retablo behind the main altar, a 21m-high composition crafted by the Portuguese artist Cayetano de Acosta between 1770 and 1779. A second, and earlier, Acosta altarpiece graces the Capilla Sacramental.

### Museo del Baile Flamenco MUSEUM

(Map p626; ☎954 34 03 11; www.museoflamenco.com; Calle Manuel Rojas Marcos 3; adult/child €10/6, incl show €26/15; ⏰10am-7pm) The brainchild of *sevillana* flamenco dancer Cristina Hoyos, this museum illustrates the dance with interactive displays, paintings, displays of period dresses, and photos of revered erstwhile (and contemporary) performers. Even better are the fantastic nightly performances (at 5pm, 7pm and 8.45pm; €22) staged both in the courtyard and the more intimate basement space (€37 including a drink). Combined museum and show tickets are a good option.

### Casa de Pilatos PALACE

(Map p626; ☎954 22 52 98; www.fundacionmedinaceli.org; Plaza de Pilatos; ground fl €10, whole palace €12; ⏰9am-7pm Apr-Oct, to 6pm Nov-Mar) The haunting Casa de Pilatos, which is still occupied by the ducal Medinaceli family, is one of the city's most glorious mansions. Originally dating to the late 15th century, it incorporates a wonderful mix of Mudéjar, Gothic and Renaissance decor, with some beautiful tilework and *artesonados* (ceilings of interlaced beams with decorative insertions). The effect is like a mini-Alcázar. Note there is free admission for EU citizens (take ID) on Monday (3pm to 7pm).

### Palacio de la Condesa de Lebrija PALACE

(Map p626; ☎954 22 78 02; www.palaciodelebrija.com; Calle Cuna 8; adult/child incl guided tour €12/6, ground fl 6pm & 7pm Mon free; ⏰10.30am-7.30pm) This aristocratic 16th-century mansion, set around a beautiful Renaissance-Mudéjar courtyard, boasts an eclectic look that blends a range of decorative elements, including Roman mosaics, Mudéjar plasterwork and Renaissance masonry. Its former owner, the late Countess of Lebrija, was an archaeologist; she remodelled the house in 1914, filling many of the rooms with treasures from her travels.

Visits to the top floor are by guided tour only (in English or Spanish), though this is included in the ticket price.

### Ayuntamiento HISTORIC BUILDING

(Casa Consistorial; Map p626; https://casaconsistorialsevilla.sacatuentrada.es; Plaza de San Francisco; tours Mon-Thu €4, Sat free; ⏰tours 7pm Mon-Thu, 10am Sat) Sandwiched between Plaza de San Francisco and Plaza Nueva is Seville's striking city hall, the Ayuntamiento. In its original form, the building dates to the 16th century, but a major 19th-century makeover saw the addition of an imposing neoclassical facade on the Plaza Nueva side. On its eastern walls you can see some ornate Renaissance carvings.

Visits, by 50-minute guided tour only, take in its richly furnished staterooms.

### Plaza de Toros de la Real Maestranza MUSEUM

(Map p626; ☎954 21 03 15; www.realmaestranza.com; Paseo de Cristóbal Colón 12; tours adult/child €8/3, 3-7pm Mon free; ⏰9.30am-9pm Apr-Oct, to 7pm Nov-Mar, to 3pm bullfight days) In the world of bullfighting, Seville's white and yellow-trimmed bullring is the equivalent of football's Old Trafford or Camp Nou – if you're selected to fight here, you've made it. In addition to having almost religious significance to fans, it's also the oldest ring in Spain – construction started in 1761 and continued on and off until 1881 – and one of the biggest, with a capacity of up to 14,000. A visit enables you to learn about bullfighting's deep-rooted traditions without witnessing a fight.

**Hospital de la Caridad** MUSEUM

(Map p626; ☎954 22 32 32; www.santa-caridad.es; Calle Temprado 3; adult/child 7-17yrs €8/€2.50, 3.30-7.30pm Mon free; ⏲10.30am-7.30pm Mon-Sat, 10.30am-12.30pm & 2-7.30pm Sun) The Hospital de la Caridad, a sturdy building one block east of the river, was established in the late 17th century as a hospice for the poor and elderly. It was founded by Miguel de Mañara, by legend a notorious libertine who supposedly changed his ways after seeing a vision of his own funeral procession. The hospital's showpiece attraction is its gilded chapel, decorated with works by several Golden Age painters and sculptors, most notably Murillo, Valdés Leal and Roldán.

**Torre del Oro** TOWER

(Map p626; ☎954 22 24 19; Paseo de Cristóbal Colón; adult/child €3/1.50, Mon free; ⏲9.30am-6.45pm Mon-Fri, 10.30am-6.45pm Sat & Sun) This distinctive tower, one of Seville's signature landmarks, has been guarding the Río Guadalquivir since the 13th century. The original dodecagonal structure, built to bolster the city's fortified walls, was subsequently heightened, first in the 14th century and then again in the late 1700s. Over the centuries, the tower has served as a chapel, prison and naval office; nowadays it houses a small maritime museum and a rooftop viewing platform.

## La Macarena & Alameda de Hércules

**★Metropol Parasol** LANDMARK

(Map p626; ☎606 635214; www.setasdesevilla.com; Plaza de la Encarnación; €3; ⏲9.30am-10.30pm Sun-Thu, to 11pm Fri & Sat) The Metropol Parasol, known locally as Las Setas (The Mushrooms), is one of Seville's iconic modern landmarks. Built in 2011 to a design by German architect Jürgen Mayer H, the colossal sunshade is a hypnotic sight with its undulating honeycombed canopy – said to be the world's largest wooden-framed structure – and massive support trunks. Lifts run up from the basement, where you can enjoy killer views from a winding walkway.

**Palacio de Las Dueñas** PALACE

(Map p620; ☎954 21 48 28; www.lasduenas.es; Calle Dueñas 5; adult/child €10/€8; ⏲10am-8pm Apr-Oct, to 6pm Nov-Mar) This gorgeous 15th-century palace was the favourite home of the late Duchess de Alba, one of Spain's most prominent aristocrats. Renaissance in design, it boasts beautiful gardens and a lovely arcaded courtyard. Inside, you can admire paintings and tapestries, as well as the Duchess' collection of Semana Santa, bullfighting and football memorabilia (she was a Betis fan). A plaque commemorates famous Spanish poet Antonio Machado, who was born here in 1875.

**Iglesia de San Luis de los Franceses** CHURCH

(Map p620; ☎954 55 02 07; Calle San Luis 37; €4, 4-8pm Sun free; ⏲10am-2pm & 4-8pm Tue-Sun) The finest example of baroque architecture in Seville, this imposing (and deconsecrated) 18th-century church is a former Jesuit novitiate dedicated to King Louis IX of France. Designed by Leonardo de Figueroa, its unusual circular interior harbours four extravagantly carved and gilded altarpieces inset with paintings (Louis' image is topped by a huge crown), and a central cupola. You can also visit the chapel decorated with macabre reliquaries (saints' bones) in glass boxes, and the crypt.

**Basílica de La Macarena** BASILICA

(Map p620; ☎954 90 18 00; Calle Bécquer 1; basilica/museum free/€5; ⏲9am-2pm & 6-9.30pm Mon-Sat, 9.30am-2pm & 6-9.30pm Sun Jun–mid-Sep, 9am-2pm & 5-9pm Mon-Sat, 9.30am-2pm & 5-9pm Sun mid-Sep–May) This 20th-century neo-baroque basilica is home to Seville's most revered religious treasure, the *Virgen de la Esperanza Macarena* (Macarena Virgin of Hope), known popularly as the Macarena. This magnificent 17th-century statue, a star of the city's fervent Semana Santa (Holy Week) celebrations, stands in splendour behind the main altarpiece, adorned with a golden crown, lavish vestments and five flower-shaped diamond and emerald brooches donated by the famous matador Joselito El Gallo in 1912.

**Alameda de Hércules** PLAZA

(Map p620) Flanked by bars, cafes and restaurants, this tree-lined plaza is a hugely popular hangout, frequented by families, tourists and students. It's also the historic hub of Seville's gay scene. The square was originally laid out in the late 16th century and became a fashionable promenade during the city's 17th-century Golden Age.

The two Roman columns at its southern end are 2000-year-old originals, topped by statues of Hercules and Julius Caesar.

## Parque de María Luisa & South of Centre

**★Parque de María Luisa** PARK

(Map p620; 8am-10pm Sep-Jun, to midnight Jul & Aug; ) A glorious oasis of green, the 34-hectare Parque de María Luisa is the perfect place to escape the noise and heat of the city, with duck ponds, landscaped gardens and paths shaded by soaring trees. The land, formerly the estate of the Palacio de San Telmo, was donated to the city in the late 19th century and developed in the run-up to the 1929 Exposición Iberoamericana.

Amid the lush gardens, the park contains several notable drawcards. Chief among them is **Plaza de España** (Map p620; Avenida de Portugal), the most flamboyant of the building projects completed for the 1929 Expo. A vast brick-and-tile confection, it features fountains, mini-canals, and a series of gaudy tile pictures depicting historical scenes from each Spanish province. You can hire row boats to pootle around the plaza's canals for €6 (for 35 minutes).

In the south of the park, the **Museo Arqueológico** (Map p620; 955 12 06 32; www.museosdeandalucia.es/web/museoarqueologicodesevilla; Plaza de América; EU/non-EU citizens free/€1.50; 9am-9pm Tue-Sat, to 3pm Sun Sep-Jun, 9am-3pm Tue-Sun Jul & Aug) has some wonderful Roman sculptures, mosaics and statues – many gathered from the archaeological site of Itálica just outside Seville.

Opposite is the **Museo de Artes y Costumbres Populares** (Map p620; 955 54 29 51; www.museosdeandalucia.es/web/museodeartesycostumbrespopularesdesevilla; Plaza de América 3; EU/non-EU citizens free/€1.50; 9am-9pm Tue-Sat, to 3pm Sun Sep-Jun, 9am-3pm Tue-Sun Jul & Aug), dedicated to local customs, costumes and traditions.

The park is a great place for children to let off steam and families to bond over a bike ride – four-person quad bikes are available to hire for €14 per half-hour.

**Antigua Fábrica de Tabacos** HISTORIC BUILDING

(Map p626; 954 55 10 00; Calle San Fernando; 8am-9pm Mon-Fri, to 2.30pm Sat) FREE Now home to the University of Seville, this massive former tobacco factory – workplace of Bizet's fictional heroine, Carmen – was built in the 18th century and is said to be the second-largest building in Spain after the El Escorial monastery northwest of Madrid.

You can wander in at will or pick up an audio guide at the porter's office in the main entrance hall – it's free but you'll need to leave photo ID as a deposit.

## Triana

Triana, on the west bank of the Río Guadalquivir, has long had a reputation as an 'outsider' neighbourhood and was once home to Seville's Roma community, as well as the city's historic ceramics industry. Nowadays, it's a colourful district of churches, ceramic shops and waterfront bars.

**Castillo de San Jorge** MUSEUM

(Map p620; 955 47 02 55; Plaza del Altozano; 11am-5.30pm Tue-Sat, 10am-2.30pm Sun) FREE Adjacent to the Puente de Isabel II, the Castillo de San Jorge is steeped in notoriety: it was here that the infamous Spanish Inquisition had its headquarters from 1481 to 1785. When the Inquisition fires were finally doused in the early 19th century, the castle was demolished and a market built over its ruins. These remains were subsequently rediscovered in 1990, and they now house a museum illustrating the Inquisition's activities and life in the *castillo*.

**Centro Cerámica Triana** MUSEUM

(Map p620; 954 34 15 82; Calle Antillano Campos 14; adult/child €2.10/free; 11am-5.30pm Tue-Sat, 10am-2.30pm Sun) Housed in a former tile factory, this small museum provides a fascinating introduction to Triana and its industrial past. Exhibits, which include brick-lined kilns and a comprehensive collection of tiles, chart the methodology and history of ceramic production, cleverly tying it in with the wider history of the neighbourhood and its residents.

## Isla de la Cartuja

**Centro Andaluz de Arte Contemporáneo** MUSEUM

(Map p620; 955 03 70 70; www.caac.es; Avenida Américo Vespucio 2; admission €3, 7-9pm Tue-Fri &

all day Sat free; ⏲11am-9pm Tue-Sat, 10am-3.30pm Sun) Contemporary art goes hand in hand with 15th-century architecture at the Centro Andaluz de Arte Contemporáneo. The centre, sensitively housed in the Monasterio de Santa María delas Cuevas, hosts temporary exhibitions by Andalucian and international artists alongside some truly bizarre permanent pieces. Look out for *Alicia* by Cristina Lucas, a massive head and arm poking through two windows that was supposedly inspired by *Alice in Wonderland*. Elsewhere, several brick kilns testify to the monastery's past as a 19th-century ceramics factory.

## Activities

**Aire Baños Árabes** HAMMAM

(Map p626; ☎955 01 00 24; www.beaire.com; Calle Aire 15; bath/bath with massage from €37/56; ⏲10am-10pm Sun-Tue, to 11pm Wed & Thu, to midnight Fri & Sat) These smart, Arabic-style baths win prizes for tranquil atmosphere, historic setting (in a centuries-old Mudéjar townhouse) and Moroccan riad-style decor. Various bath and massage packages are available – see the website for details. It's always best to book a day or so in advance.

## Courses

**LaCasa Sevilla** LANGUAGE

(☎666 882981; www.lacasasevilla.com; 2hr from €28) Fun and dynamic Spanish classes take students out and about in the city. Join Cristina, who hails from Cádiz and has lived in both the UK and US, to learn how to buy fruit and vegetables in a local market, or explore some of Seville's most beautiful and historic monuments while learning the language.

**Taller Andaluz de Cocina** COOKING

(Map p620; ☎955 31 25 74; www.tallerandaluzdecocina.com; Mercado de Triana, Plaza del Altozano; courses €44-60) Located in Triana Market, this cooking school offers a range of hands-on courses covering classic Spanish cuisine and tapas, as well as sherry tastings and market tours. Lessons and guided tours are all available in English – check the website for details.

## Tours

**Pancho Tours** TOURS

(☎664 642904; www.panchotours.com) FREE Runs excellent free tours, although you're welcome to tip the hard-working guide who'll furnish you with an encyclopedia's worth of anecdotes, stories, myths and theories about Seville's fascinating past. The 2½-hour tours kick off daily at 11am – check the website for details. Pancho also offers bike tours (€25), skip-the-line cathedral (€21) and Alcázar visits (€18), and nightlife tours (from €17).

**Mimo Sevilla** FOOD & DRINK

(Map p626; ☎854 55 68 00; www.mimofood.com/en/location/sevilla; Calle San Fernando 2; tastings/tours/classes from €45/115/125) Based at its foodie shop in the lobby of the Hotel Alfonso XIII, Mimo runs wine tastings, cooking classes, tapas tours and day trips, including one to the sherry city of Jerez. Bank on €115 for a three-hour tapas tour, €45 for two hours of wine tasting.

## Festivals & Events

**Semana Santa** RELIGIOUS

(www.semana-santa.org; ⏲Mar/Apr) Every day from Palm Sunday to Easter Sunday, elaborate, life-size *pasos* (floats carrying revered statues of Christ or the Virgin Mary) are paraded across town from their home churches to the cathedral. For the best views, park yourself near the cathedral in the early evening.

**Feria de Abril** FERIA

(https://feriadesevilla.andalunet.com; El Real de la Feria; ⏲Apr) Seville's celebrated spring fair is held two weeks after Easter on the Real de la Feria fairground in the Los Remedios area west of the Río Guadalquivir. For six days and nights, *sevillanos* dress up in elaborate finery, parade around in horse-drawn carriages (the *paseo de caballos*), eat, drink and dance the *sevillana* (a popular style of fiesta dance).

**Bienal de Flamenco** FLAMENCO

(www.labienal.com; ⏲Sep) The big names of the flamenco world descend on Seville for this major flamenco festival. Held in September in even-numbered years, it features a comprehensive program of performances, exhibitions and workshops in venues across town.

There's a good selection of hotels, hostels and *pensiones* in the three most atmospheric areas: Barrio de Santa Cruz, El Arenal and El Centro. The Alamada de Hércules area offers a trendy, grungier alternative.

Expect high season rates March to June and in September and October. Rates also skyrocket during Semana Santa and the Feria de Abril, for which you'll have to book well in advance.

## Catedral & Barrio de Santa Cruz

**★Legado Alcázar** BOUTIQUE HOTEL €€
(Map p626; ☎954 09 18 18; www.legadoalcazarhotel.com; Calle Mariana de Pineda 18; d €124-150; ❄@📶) Formerly part of the Alcázar royal palace, this stylish art-clad hotel looks onto the palace gardens, whose peacocks used to roost in one of the suites. Rooms range from bijou, with archaeological remains under the floor, to majestic, with wood-beamed ceilings, contemporary furniture, garden views and an outdoor balcony shower. Set-menu breakfasts (€15) are served in a pretty cafe-style room.

**★Hotel Amadeus** BOUTIQUE HOTEL €€
(Map p626; ☎954 50 14 43; www.hotelamadeussevilla.com; Calle Farnesio 6; d €92-195, tr €121-335, q €180-365; P❄📶) A soothing oasis of calm in the heart of the old *judería* (Jewish quarter), this delightful hotel charms with its ceramic-tiled lobby, period furniture and collection of musical instruments (which guests are free to play). Rooms, named after composers, are equally stylish, and there's a small rooftop terrace offering views over to the Giralda.

**Un Patio en Santa Cruz** HOTEL €€
(Map p626; ☎954 53 94 13; www.patiosantacruz.com; Calle Doncellas 15; s €55-210, d €65-220; ❄📶) This immaculate two-star has stark white walls hung with bright artworks and cascading plants. The sunny, light-filled rooms, complete with parquet, chandeliers and dashes of lilac, are good looking and comfortable, staff are friendly, and there's a cool rooftop terrace with Moroccan-mosaic tables.

**Casual Sevilla Don Juan Tenorio** HOTEL €€
(Map p626; ☎955 54 44 16; www.casualhoteles.com; Plaza de los Venerables 5; r €45-155; ❄📶) Atmospherically located off a Santa Cruz plaza, this bright hotel offers slick modern rooms, each themed after a character from *Don Juan Tenorio*, with quirky lights, stencils and stone-effect wall coverings. It has excellent wi-fi and hydromassage showers, and loans out useful mobile-phone packs with routers, chargers and selfie sticks (free if registered on the website, otherwise €2).

**Hostal Plaza Santa Cruz** HOTEL €€
(Map p626; ☎954 22 88 08; https://santacruz.alojamientosconencantosevilla.com; Calle Santa Teresa 15; d €40-120; ❄@📶) Offering a lovely location in the Barrio de Santa Cruz, this welcoming outfit has rooms spread over three buildings. Those in the main hotel, just off Plaza Santa Cruz, are fairly featureless with laminated parquet or marble floors and the occasional blast of colourful wallpaper, while the apartments are slightly more colourful with tiles, artworks and fully equipped kitchens.

**★Hotel Casa 1800** LUXURY HOTEL €€€
(Map p626; ☎954 56 18 00; www.hotelcasa1800sevilla.com; Calle Rodrigo Caro 6; d €170-750, ste €360-1050; ❄@📶🏊) A short hop from the cathedral and Alcázar, this stately *casa* (house) is positively regal. Setting the tone is the elegant, period decor – wooden ceilings, chandeliers, parquet floors and plenty of gilt – but everything about the place charms, from the helpful staff to the panoramic rooftop pool and complimentary afternoon tea.

## El Centro & El Arenal

**★La Banda** HOSTEL €
(Map p626; ☎621 012891, 955 22 81 18; www.labandahostel.com; Calle Dos de Mayo 16; dm €18-38; ❄📶) Run by a young, sociable crew, this Arenal hostel ticks all the boxes. It's within easy walking distance of the big sights, the mixed dorms are clean and tidily furnished, and it has a great rooftop bar. Evening meals (€8, or €10 for Saturday paella and sangria) are available and a weekly program of events means there's always something going on.

**Oasis Palace Hostel** HOSTEL €
(Map p626; ☎955 26 26 96; www.oasissevilla.com; Calle Almirante Ulloa 1; dm €18-30, d €70-140; ❄@📶🏊) A veritable oasis in the busy city-centre district, this buzzing hostel occupies a palatial 19th-century mansion. There are various sleeping options ranging from mixed 14-person dorms to doubles with en suite bathrooms, and excellent facilities, including a cafe-bar, fully equipped kitchen and rooftop deck with a small pool. Breakfast, not included in most rates, is available for €3.50.

**★Hotel Casa de Colón** BOUTIQUE HOTEL €€
(Map p626; ☎955 11 78 28; www.hotelcasadecolon.com; Calle Hernando Colón 3; d €70-220; ) A superb location, warm service, and quirky decorative features combine to winning effect at this charming, family-run hotel. Look out for white cast-iron pillars, bedsteads made from old doors and cobalt blue stained glass in the neo-Mudéjar windows. Some rooms have exposed-brick walls and side views of the cathedral, while top-floor *aticos* have private terraces. Continental breakfast is available for €9.

**La Parada del Marqués** BOUTIQUE HOTEL €€
(Map p626; ☎954 44 83 70; www.laparadadelmarques.com; Calle Marqués de Paradas 45; d €100-150; ) Clean, contemporary styling, helpful staff and reasonable rates make this small hotel close to the Plaza de Armas bus station an excellent midrange option. Eco touches include energy-saving keys and insulated windows (for keeping road noise out), while antique furniture, exposed brick walls and original tiled floors feature in the high-ceilinged white rooms.

**Suites Sevilla Plaza** APARTMENT €€
(Map p626; ☎955 03 85 33; www.suitessevillaplaza.com; Calle Zaragoza 52; 1-bedroom €80-240, 2-bedroom €140-450; ) With eight self-catering apartments and a central location handy for just about everywhere, Suites Sevilla Plaza is ideal for families, groups or longer stays. Apartments, which sleep from two to six, are spacious and tastefully attired in an unfussy modern style. Added bonuses include a laundry, bike hire (€10), and a rooftop space with views of the Giralda.

## La Macarena & Alameda de Hércules

**Corner House** HOTEL €€
(Map p620; ☎954 91 32 62; www.thecornerhousesevilla.com; Alameda de Hércules 11; d €45-120; ) This self-styled 'urban' hotel sits well with the buzzing bars and cafes on the Alameda de Hércules. Modern in look and upbeat in vibe, it offers sun-filled rooms with minimal white decor, hanging lamps and the occasional blast of designer colour. There's a ground-floor restaurant, El Disparate, and a great rooftop bar (p636).

**Hotel Boutique Doña Lola** BOUTIQUE HOTEL €€
(Map p620; ☎954 91 52 75; www.donalolasevilla.com; Calle Amor de Dios 19; s €40-110, d €45-110, apt €75-190; ) A short hop from the bar action on the Alameda de Hércules, gay-friendly Doña Lola is well positioned for sorties pretty much everywhere. From the lobby, complete with a coloured chequered floor, stairs lead to rooms which, although small, are modern and minimally furnished. There are also mini-apartments over the road, and an al fresco hot-tub.

# Eating

The city is brimming with bars, cafes, restaurants and markets. Hotspots include the Barrio de Santa Cruz, the streets around Plaza de la Alfalfa and the Alameda de Hércules. Note that some restaurants close for part of August.

## Catedral & Barrio de Santa Cruz

**Bodega Santa Cruz** TAPAS €
(Map p626; ☎954 21 86 18; Calle Rodrigo Caro 1; tapas €2.50; ⏰8am-midnight) This is as old-school as it gets, a perennially busy bar staffed by gruff waiters and frequented by Sevillans and visitors alike. Traditional tapas such as *montaditos de pringá* (bread rolls stuffed with slow-cooked pork and sausage) are best enjoyed al fresco with a cold beer as you watch the armies of tourists traipse past.

**★La Azotea** ANDALUCIAN €€
(Map p626; ☎954 21 58 78; www.laazoteasevilla.com; Calle Mateos Gago 8; tapas €3.50-6.50, mains €12-22; ⏰9am-midnight) The best of the bars and restaurants in the cathedral area, this is one of several Azotea branches around town. It takes a contemporary approach to dining, offering sleek, modern design, energetic service, and creative Andalucian cuisine. Particularly outstanding are its seafood dishes, such as grilled *calamar* (squid) and sea bass curry.

**Vinería San Telmo** TAPAS €€
(Map p626; ☎954 41 06 00; www.vineriasantelmo.com; Paseo Catalina de Ribera 4; tapas €3.50-6.50, medias raciones €6.90-15; ⏰1-4.30pm & 8pm-midnight) San Telmo's innovative tapas continue to wow diners, and its tables, either outside or in the brick tiled interior, are a prized commodity. Bag one, for which you'll either have to wait or book, and sit down to the likes of pan-fried octopus with red onions and grilled foie gras with apple compote.

### ICE CREAM

In a city where summer temperatures regularly top 40°C, a cooling ice cream is always a good idea. One of the city's best *heladerias* (ice-cream parlours) is **Créeme** (Map p626; ☎954 91 08 32; www.facebook.com/creemehelado; Plaza del Museo 2; cones & tubs €3-5; ⏰12.30pm-1am), a modern outfit near the Museo de Bellas Artes, which serves exquisite flavours such as *caramelo de mantequilla salada* (caramel with salted butter).

Other top choices include **Bolas** (Map p626; ☎954 22 74 11; Cuesta del Rosario 1; cones €2.20-4, tubs €2.80-5; ⏰2pm-midnight Mon-Thu, to 12.30am Fri & Sat, to 11.30pm Sun), where you can enjoy exotic combos like its Medina sorbet of orange, ginger and cinnamon, and **Freskura** (Map p620; Calle Vulcano 4; cones & tubs €3-4.80; ⏰noon-1am), an Alameda outpost which specialises in smooth, Italian-style gelato.

**Café Bar Las Teresas** TAPAS €€
(Map p626; ☎954 21 30 69; www.lasteresas.es; Calle Santa Teresa 2; tapas €2.50-4.50, mains €8-24; ⏰10am-1am) The hanging hams look as ancient as the bar itself, a sinuous wrap-around affair with a cheerfully cluttered interior. Locals congregate at the bar while tourists take to the wonky streetside tables for traditional tapas like *espinacas con garbanzos* (spinach with chickpeas) and hearty *salchichón ibérico* (sausage).

## El Centro & El Arenal

**Sal Gorda** ANDALUCIAN €
(Map p626; ☎955 38 59 72; Calle Alcaicería de la Loza 23; tapas €3.20-8.50; ⏰1-4.30pm & 8-11.30pm Wed-Mon) Incongruously located in an old shoe shop, this tiny, low-key place serves innovative takes on Andalucian dishes – try *ajo blanco* (white gazpacho soup) with *mojama* (salt-cured tuna), and a first-class version of the ubiquitous tuna tartare. Mushroom risotto with langoustines is a firm favourite, and the wine list features good local whites such as El Mirlo Blanco from Constantina. Reservations recommended.

**Palo Cortao** SPANISH €
(Map p626; ☎649 446120; www.palo-cortao.com; Calle Mercedes de Velilla 4; tapas €3.50-7, mains €6-12; ⏰1-4.30pm Tue-Sun, 8.30-11.30pm Tue-Sat) This excellent sherry bar, tucked away in a side street near the Metropol Parasol, offers excellent, knowledgeable service (Ana) and imaginative cooking (Angel). Choose from more than 30 sherries by the glass (*palo cortao* is a less common type), accompanied by premium *chacinas* (cold meat) and cheeses, plus tapas such as cuttlefish balls in red shrimp sauce.

**Confitería La Campana** PASTRIES €
(Map p626; ☎954 22 35 70; www.confiterialacampana.com; Calle Sierpes 1-3; pastries from €2.50; ⏰8am-10pm) A landmark art deco patisserie and cafe, La Campana has been catering to Seville's sweet toothed since 1885. Join the mixed crowd in its elegant interior for a *yema* (soft, crumbly biscuit cake wrapped like a toffee), or a coffee and *torta de aceite* (flat, crumbly biscuit made with olive oil).

★**La Brunilda** TAPAS €€
(Map p626; ☎954 22 04 81; Calle Galera 5; tapas €4-7.50, mains €6.50-15; ⏰1-4pm & 8.30-11.30pm Tue-Sat, 1-4pm Sun) Hidden away in an anonymous Arenal backstreet, this tapas hotspot is a guarantee of good times. The look is modern casual with big blue doors, brick arches and plain wooden tables, and the food is imaginative and brilliantly executed. Arrive promptly or expect long queues.

★**Mamarracha** TAPAS €€
(Map p626; ☎955 12 39 11; www.mamarracha.es; Calle Hernando Colón 1-3; tapas €2.50-12, mains €5.50-14; ⏰1-4.30pm & 8.30pm-midnight) Sharp decor, young staff in black T-shirts, cool tunes and an international menu, this is a fine example of the modern tapas bars that Seville so excels at. Its interior sports distressed cement, exposed vents and a vertical garden wall, while its menu reveals some slick combos, including a terrific focaccia with marinated Iberian pork.

**Lobo López** MEDITERRANEAN €€
(Map p626; ☎854 70 58 34; Calle Rosario 15; tapas €3-8, mains €10-19; ⏰8am-11.30pm Mon-Sat, from 12.30pm Sun; 📶🌶) From the hip-yet-historic decor (concrete-cast art, vertical garden, exposed brick arches) to the cheeky waiters, this place rocks a cool vibe. The food doesn't disappoint, with a short but well-chosen menu, including some tasty international

interpretations – Hawaiian tuna poke, Vietnamese pulled pork rolls. Unusually, it's open all day, so it's also an ideal mid-afternoon cake-and-smoothie stop.

## La Macarena & Alameda de Hércules

**Cocome** CAFE €

(Map p626; ☎955 11 15 66; www.cocomefresco.com; Calle Tarifa 4; breakfasts €3.50-5.50; ⏰9am-noon & 1-5pm Mon-Sat; 🔌) Get your day off to a sunny start with breakfast at this cheery cafe near Plaza del Duque. Staff are delightful and there's an impressive selection of toast, fruit bowls, granola, yoghurts, cereals and smoothies. For lunch, there's soup, or make-your-own salads, wraps and sandwiches. Sit at the front window bar for street views, or the tables at the back.

**Duo Tapas** TAPAS €

(Map p620; ☎955 23 85 72; Calle Calatrava 10; tapas €3-5, medias raciones €8-12; ⏰12.30-4.30pm & 8.30pm-midnight) Exciting tapas go hand in hand with a casual, bustling vibe at this 'new-school' bar just off the Alameda de Hércules. Squeeze yourself into a table and eat your way through a menu that ranges from excellent pork cheeks in wine to fusion fare with an Asian twist, such as tempura veggies and shrimp spring rolls.

★**Bar-Restaurante Eslava** TAPAS €€

(Map p620; ☎954 90 65 68; www.espacioeslava.com; Calle Eslava 3; tapas €2.90-4.50, restaurant mains €13.50-26; ⏰bar 12.30pm-midnight Tue-Sat, restaurant 1.30-4pm & 8.30pm-midnight Tue-Sat) You'll almost certainly have to wait for a table at the bar, but it's so worth it, especially if you use the time to start on the excellent wine list. The tapas are superb: contemporary, creative, brilliantly executed and incredible value for money. Standouts include slow-cooked egg served on mushroom puree, and a filo pastry cigar stuffed with cuttlefish and algae.

★**conTenedor** ANDALUCIAN €€

(Map p620; ☎954 91 63 33; www.restaurantecontenedor.com; Calle San Luis 50; mains €9-22; ⏰1.30-4.30pm & 8-11.30pm Mon-Thu, 1.30-4.30pm & 8.30pm-midnight Fri & Sat, 1.30-4.30pm & 8.30-11.30pm Sun) The atmosphere at this slow-food restaurant in boho Macarena is arty and relaxed, with an open kitchen, mismatched furniture and colourful paintings by co-owner Ricardo on the walls. The food is equally appealing with dishes composed to show off locally sourced organic produce. Try the duck rice, the house speciality, or keep it green with a creative salad.

## Triana

★**Manu Jara Dulcería** PASTRIES €

(Map p620; ☎675 873674; Calle Pureza 5; pastries €2-3.50; ⏰9.30am-2.30pm & 4.30-9pm Mon-Thu, 9.30am-9pm Fri & Sat, 10am-8.30pm Sun) No day in Triana would be complete without a stop at this exquisite patisserie. With its traditional wood and tiled interior, it sets the perfect backdrop for an array of artfully crafted cakes and pastries, including a sensational *milohajas* (mille feuille or vanilla slice). There's another branch in Nervión by the Sevilla FC stadium, and in the nearby Triana Market.

**Alfarería 21** ANDALUCIAN €€

(Map p620; ☎955 83 48 75; www.facebook.com/alfarera21Triana; Calle Alfarería 21; tapas €2.80-4.50, mains €7-15; ⏰12.30-4pm & 8pm-midnight) This bar occupies an old Triana ceramic factory: Montalván's original brick-and-tile facade and *azulejo* wall tiles maintain the traditional feel, while the short menu veers towards the modern with updated twists on traditional Sevillan fare. Downstairs there's a casual vibe, with stools and low or high tables, while upstairs is more formal.

# Drinking & Nightlife

Popular drinking areas include Calle Betis in Triana, Plaza de Salvador, the Barrio de Santa Cruz, and the Alameda de Hércules, host to a lively bar scene and the city's gay nightlife. In summer, dozens of *terrazas de verano* (open-air bars) pop up on the river's banks.

★**Corner House Terraza** ROOFTOP BAR

(Map p620; ☎954 91 32 62; www.thecornerhousesevilla.com; Corner House, Alameda de Hércules 11; ⏰5-11pm Wed-Sun Nov-Feb, 4pm-midnight daily Mar-Oct) With its wooden decking, handmade tables and grandstand views over the vibrant, tree-lined plaza below, the rooftop terrace at the Corner House is a top spot to kick back and enjoy a cool evening cocktail. The mojitos (€8) are particularly fine, sharply flavoured and packing a formidable punch.

★**Bier Kraft** CRAFT BEER
(Map p620; ☎955 12 41 80; Calle Correduría 35; ⏰6pm-2am Tue-Thu, 1pm-3am Fri & Sat, 1pm-2am Sun) Sporting high ceilings and a retro-industrial look, Bier Kraft has been flying the flag for craft beer since 2017. Its collection of national and international beers is one of the city's best, providing fuel for many happy hours of elbow-raising experimentation. For an easy start, try the hoppy blonde Río Azul.

**El Viajero Sedentario** CAFE
(Map p620; www.facebook.com/viajerosedentario; Alameda de Hércules 77; ⏰9.30am-1am Tue-Sat, 10.30am-11pm Sun) This inviting Alameda cafe is a lovely place to hang out with its bright murals, shady courtyard and tiny book-stacked interior. Early evening is a good time for a relaxed pre-dinner beer, and it's not uncommon to find people dancing to low-key jazz tunes on sultry summer nights.

**Gallo Rojo** CRAFT BEER
(Map p620; www.facebook.com/gallorojofactoria decreacion; Calle Madre Maria de Purisima 9; ⏰5pm-midnight Tue-Thu, to 2am Fri & Sat, to 10pm Sun) Housed in a former factory, arty Rojo is a lively yet laid-back spot that regularly hosts concerts, readings and flamenco performances. It's also a cool place to drink, with mismatched vintage furniture, huge plate glass windows and excellent craft beer – try the house Zurda golden ale or choose from the selection of guest Sevillan and European brews.

**La Terraza del Eme** ROOFTOP BAR
(Map p626; www.emecatedralmercer.com; Calle de los Alemanes 27; ⏰2pm-2am Sun-Thu, to 2am Fri & Sat) Enjoy spectacular cathedral close-ups and classic cocktails at the chic roof terrace bar of the five-star EME Catedral Hotel. Drinks are on the pricey side at around €16 for a G&T, but DJs create a lively lounge vibe and the Catedral views really are special.

## ☆ Entertainment

★**Casa de la Memoria** FLAMENCO
(Map p626; ☎954 56 06 70; www.casadelamemoria.es; Calle Cuna 6; adult/student/child €18/15/10; ⏰11am-6pm, shows 7.30pm & 9pm) Occupying the old stables of the 16th-century Palacio de la Condesa de Lebrija, this cultural centre stages authentic, highly charged flamenco shows, as well as housing a small exhibition of flamenco memorabilia. The nightly shows are perennially popular, and as space is limited, you'll need to reserve tickets a day or so in advance by calling or visiting the venue.

**LOCAL KNOWLEDGE**

**SEVILLE'S OLDEST BAR**

The blueprint for centuries' worth of imitators, **El Rinconcillo** (Map p626; ☎954 22 31 83; www.elrinconcillo.es; Calle Gerona 40; tapas €2.50-3.50, raciones €7.50-20; ⏰1pm-1.30am) is the oldest bar in Seville – and some say, Spain – dating to 1670. Over the centuries, it's become pretty touristy, but it's managed to retain a gnarled sense of authenticity. With its hanging hams, ceramic tiles and dark wood ceilings, it sets a memorable stage for classic tapas.

**Tablao Los Gallos** FLAMENCO
(Map p626; ☎954 21 69 81; www.tablaolosgallos.com; Plaza de Santa Cruz 11; adult/child €35/20; ⏰shows 8pm & 10pm) Located on a pretty Santa Cruz plaza, this is Seville's oldest *tablao* (choreographed flamenco show), dating from 1966. Its two-nightly shows feature a wider range of performers (all top-notch) than most set-ups, with four dancers, three singers and three guitarists – hence its above-average admission price.

**Naima Café Jazz** JAZZ
(Map p620; ☎653 753976; Calle Trajano 47; ⏰8pm-2am Mon-Wed, 4pm-2am Thu & Sun, 4pm-3am Fri & Sat) This mellow bar is an evergreen favourite for jazz and blues, staged most nights. Drinks are reasonably priced and its tiny interior – you could easily find yourself squeezed in next to the drummer with a hi-hat crashing inches from your nose – ensures a humming vibe. Gigs are free if you buy a drink, otherwise there's a €3 'donation'.

**La Casa del Flamenco** FLAMENCO
(Map p626; ☎955 02 99 99; www.lacasadelflamencosevilla.com; Calle Ximénez de Enciso 28; adult/student/child €20/15/10; ⏰shows 7pm winter & autumn, 7pm & 8.30pm spring, 8.30pm summer) A beautiful patio in an old Sephardic Jewish mansion in Santa Cruz is home to La Casa del Flamenco. Shows, performed on a stage hemmed in by seating on three sides, are mesmerising.

**Fun Club** LIVE MUSIC
(Map p620; ☎636 669023; Alameda de Hércules 86; €6-12; ⏰9.30pm-7am Thu-Sat) The iconic

Fun Club has been entertaining the nocturnal Alameda de Hércules crowd since the late 1980s. It still packs them in, drawing a young, energetic crowd to its club nights and regular gigs – indie, rock and hip-hop.

## Shopping

**★La Oleoteca** FOOD

(Map p626; ☎954 86 91 85; www.oleotecasevilla.com; Calle García de Vinuesa 39; ⌚10.30am-2pm & 5-8pm Mon-Sat, 10.30am-2pm Sun) If you're looking to take some Spanish olive oil home, super-enthusiastic Andrés García is the person to help you. At his well-stocked shop, he'll talk you through the finer points of his collection and steer you to the blends that best suite your tastes and budget. Reckon on around €5 for a half-bottle, €7 to €20 for a full-sized one.

**La Importadora** CLOTHING

(Map p626; ☎954 56 18 29; www.laimportadora.es; Calle Pérez Galdós 2; ⌚10.30am-2pm & 5-8.30pm Mon-Fri, 11am-2.30pm & 5.30-8.30pm Sat) Part-boutique, part-gallery, La Importadora captures the hip Alfalfa vibe with its exposed white-brick walls, contemporary (and original) artworks, pot plants and racks of shabby-chic vintage clothes. You'll find everything from seasonal fashions, often by local designers, to bijou jewellery and cool shoes.

**Tarico** FOOD & DRINKS

(Map p620; ☎954 02 68 03; Calle Amor de Dios 14; ⌚10am-2.30pm & 5.30-10pm mid-Jul–mid-Oct, shorter hours mid-Oct–mid-Jul) From award-winning extra-virgin olive oil from Jaén to goat's milk cheese from Huelva, this airy food store showcases quality produce from small regional producers. Items have been personally selected by the owner, who's happy to guide you through his stock of craft beers, wines, cheeses, cured meats, pâtés, honeys and chocolates.

**Cerámica Triana** CERAMICS

(Map p620; ☎954 33 21 79; www.ceramicatriana.com; Calle Callao 14; ⌚10am-9pm Mon-Fri, to 8pm Sat) Seville specialises in distinctive *azulejos* (ceramic tiles) and they are best bought in Triana, the historic hub of the city's ceramic industry. Cerámica Triana has been around for more than 50 years and its tiled shopfront is something of a local landmark. Inside, you'll find every inch of space crammed with decorative crockery, tiles, signs, crucifixes and figurines.

## Information

Tourist information is readily available at official tourist offices throughout the city.

**Airport Tourist Office** (☎954 78 20 35; www.andalucia.org; Seville Airport; ⌚9am-7.30pm Mon-Fri, 9.30am-3pm Sat & Sun)

**Central Tourist Office** (Map p626; ☎954 21 00 05; www.turismosevilla.org; Plaza del Triunfo 1; ⌚9am-7.30pm Mon-Fri, 9.30am-7.30pm Sat & Sun; 📶)

**Municipal Tourist Office** (Map p626; ☎955 47 12 32; www.visitasevilla.es; Paseo Marqués de Contadero; ⌚9am-2.30pm Mon-Fri)

**Train Station Tourist Office** (☎954 78 20 02; www.andalucia.org; Estación Santa Justa; ⌚9am-7.30pm Mon-Fri, 9.30am-3pm Sat & Sun)

There are also private City Expert offices providing information and booking services. There is a useful office in the **centre** (Map p626; ☎900 920 092; www.cityexpert.travel; Avenida de la Constitución 23B; ⌚9.30am-9pm). Tourist staff generally speak English.

## Getting There & Away

### AIR

**Seville Airport** (Aeropuerto de Sevilla; ☎913 21 10 00; www.aena.es; A4, Km 532), 7km northeast of the city, has flights to/from Spanish cities and destinations across Europe including London, Paris, Amsterdam, Dublin, Frankfurt and Rome. It's served by international airlines such as Ryanair, EasyJet and Vueling.

### BUS

**Estación de Autobuses Plaza de Armas** (Map p620; ☎955 03 86 65; www.autobusesplazadearmas.es; Avenida del Cristo de la Expiración) is Seville's main bus station. From here, **ALSA** (☎902 42 22 42; www.alsa.es) buses serve Málaga (€19 to €24, 2¾ to three hours, six to seven daily), Granada (€23 to €30, three hours, 11 to 12 daily), Córdoba (€13, 1¾ to two hours, seven daily) and Almería (€38 to €47, 5¼ to 8¾ hours, four daily). **Damas** (☎959 25 69 00; www.damas-sa.es) runs buses to Huelva province and **Flixbus** (☎919 01 06 32; www.flixbus.es) has international services to cities in Portugal including Faro, Lisbon and Porto.

**Estación de Autobuses Prado de San Sebastián** (Map p626; Plaza San Sebastián) has services to many smaller towns in Andalucía. Damas operates buses to Ronda and Marbella, while **Comes** (Map p626; ☎902 19 92 08; www.tgcomes.es) runs to Cádiz, Jerez de la Frontera and some of the harder-to-reach *pueblos blancos* (white towns) in Cádiz province.

WORTH A TRIP

### ITÁLICA

Some 9km northwest of Seville, the white village of Santiponce is home to Andalucía's most thrilling Roman site.

The evocative ruins of ancient **Itálica** (☎600 141767; www.museosdeandalucia.es; Avenida de Extremadura 2; EU/non-EU citizens free/€1.50; ⊙9am-9pm Tue-Sat, to 3pm Sun Apr–mid-Jun, shorter hours mid-Jun-Mar; P) are impressive and wonderfully maintained. Broad paved streets lead to the remains of houses set around beautiful mosaic-laid patios and, best of all, a stunning 25,000-seat **amphitheatre**, one of the largest ever built.

Itálica, founded in 206 BCE and later the birthplace of emperors Trajan and Hadrian, enjoyed a golden age in the 2nd century CE, when many of its finest buildings were constructed. To get to the site, bus M170 (A or B) runs from Seville's Plaza de Armas station to Santiponce (€1.60, 25 minutes, at least half-hourly), making its final stop near the site's entrance.

#### TRAIN

Seville's principal train station, **Estación Santa Justa** (Avenida Kansas City), is 1.5km northeast of the centre.

High-speed AVE trains go to/from Madrid (€50 to €88, 2½ to 3¼ hours, hourly) and Córdoba (€14 to €32, 45 minutes to 1¼ hours, up to 35 daily). Slower trains head to Cádiz (€17 to €24, 1¾ hours, 16 daily), Huelva (€13, 1½ hours, four daily), Granada (€31 to €61, 2½ to 4¼ hours, nine daily) and Málaga (€25 to €47, two to 3½ hours, 12 daily). Note that the cheapest services to Granada and Málaga involve travelling part of the way by bus.

## Getting Around

Central Seville is relatively compact and is best explored on foot. Getting around by bike is also an option – the city is flat and bike lanes are ubiquitous. Driving is not recommended in the city centre.

Public transport comprises buses, trams and a metro. Buses are the most useful for getting around the main visitor areas.

#### TO/FROM THE AIRPORT

The **EA Bus** (☎955 010010; www.tussam.es; one way/return €4/6) connects the airport to the city centre, running to/from the Plaza de Armas bus station via Santa Justa train station and Prado de San Sebastián.

Departures from the airport are every 15 to 30 minutes between 5.20am and 1am; from Plaza Armas between 4.30am and 12.10am. Services are reduced very early in the morning and late at night.

Taxis charge set fares: €23 (daytime Monday to Friday); €25 (weekends, nighttime Monday to Friday, daytime Easter and the Feria de Abril); €32 (nighttime Easter and the Feria de Abril). Note that these rates apply only to the journey to/from the airport. If you phone for a taxi, you'll also be charged for the drive to your pick-up point.

#### BUS

Buses run from around 6am to midnight. Useful routes include:

**C1 and C2** External circular route around the centre.

**C3 and C4** Internal circular route around the centre.

**C5** Runs through the centre.

Tickets can be bought on buses, at stations or at kiosks next to stops. A standard ticket is €1.40 but a range of passes are also available, including one-/three-day travel cards for €5/10.

#### BICYCLE

**Sevici** (☎900 900722; www.sevici.es), Seville's excellent bike-share scheme, provides 2500 bikes and 250 docking stations.

Visitors can use bikes by getting a seven-day subscription directly at a docking station. This costs €15 (plus a €150 returnable deposit). Once you've saddled up, the first 30 minutes of usage are free. Beyond that, it's €1.03 for the first hour and €2.04 every hour thereafter.

Bike hire and tours are available with **Surf the City** (Map p626; ☎693 261910; www.surfthecity.es; Calle Almirante Lobo 2, Edificio Cristina Local 15; kickscooter tours €20-50, bike tours €25; ⊙10am-8pm; 👪).

#### CAR & MOTORCYCLE

Driving in Seville is generally not worth the hassle. Traffic restrictions are in force and the narrow streets of the historic centre are not car-friendly. Parking is no fun either.

For car hire, there's **Avis** (☎902 11 02 83; www.avis.com; Estación Santa Justa; ⊙8am-11pm) or **Enterprise** (☎954 41 26 40; www.enterprise.es; ⊙7.30am-10pm Mon-Fri, to 9pm Sat & Sun) at Santa Justa train station, and all the normal firms at the airport.

### TRAM

Operated by **Tussam** (☎ 955 010 010; www.tussam.es), Seville's tram service has a single line. T1 runs between Plaza Nueva and San Bernardo via Avenida de la Constitución, Puerta de Jerez and Prado de San Sebastián.

The standard ticket is €1.40 but a range of passes is available if you're likely to use it a lot.

Buy tickets from the ticketing machines at the tram stops.

# SEVILLA PROVINCE

Just outside Seville, the ruins of ancient Itálica comprise one of southern Spain's most remarkable Roman sites. To the east, the vast, shimmering plains of La Campiña are punctuated by a string of handsome towns, most notably Carmona, Écija and Osuna.

## Carmona

POP 28,620

Rising above a sea of golden, sun-baked plains 35km east of Seville, Carmona is a delight. Its hilltop centre is packed with noble palaces, majestic Mudéjar churches and two Moorish forts; nearby, a haunting Roman necropolis tells of the town's ancient origins.

### Sights

**★ Necrópolis Romana** ROMAN SITE

(Roman cemetery; ☎ 600 143632; www.museosdeandalucia.es; Avenida de Jorge Bonsor 9; EU/non-EU citizens free/€1.50; ⌚ 9am-9pm Tue-Sat, to 3pm Sun Apr–mid-Jun, 9am-3pm Tue-Sun mid-Jun–mid-Sep, 9am-6pm Tue-Sat, to 3pm Sun mid-Sep–Mar) This ancient Roman necropolis is one of the most important of its kind in Andalucía. The site, which is slightly let down by a lack of signage, contains hundreds of tombs, some elaborate and many-chambered, hewn into the rock in the 1st and 2nd centuries. Most of the inhabitants were cremated: in the tombs are wall niches for the box-like stone urns. You can enter the huge **Tumba de Servilia** and climb down into several others.

**Alcázar de la Puerta de Sevilla** FORTRESS

(☎ 954 19 09 55; Plaza de Blas Infante; adult/child €2/1, Mon free; ⌚ 10am-6pm Mon-Sat, to 3pm Sun Sep-Jun, 9am-3pm Mon-Fri, 10am-3pm Sat & Sun Jul & Aug) Carmona's signature fortress is a formidable sight. Set atop the Puerta de Sevilla, the imposing main gate of the old town, it had already been standing for five centuries when the Romans reinforced it and built a temple on top. The Muslim Almohads added an *aljibe* (cistern) to the upper patio, which remains a hawk-like perch from which to admire the typically Andalucian tableau of white cubes and soaring spires. Buy tickets at the tourist office.

**Prioral de Santa María de la Asunción** CHURCH

(☎ 954 19 14 82; www.santamariacarmona.org; Plaza Marqués de las Torres; adult/child €3/1.80; ⌚ 9.30am-2pm & 5-7pm Tue-Fri, 9.30am-2pm Sat) This splendid church was built mainly in the 15th and 16th centuries on the site of Carmona's former mosque. The Patio de los Naranjos, through which you enter, has a Visigothic calendar carved into one of its pillars. The interior, crowned by high Gothic vaults, is centred on a towering altarpiece detailed to a mind-boggling degree with 20 panels of biblical scenes framed by gilt-scrolled columns.

### Sleeping

**Hostal Comercio** HOSTAL €

(☎ 954 14 00 18; hostalcomercio@hotmail.com; Calle Torre del Oro 56; s €35, d €45-50, tr €70, q €94; ❄ 📶) A warm welcome awaits at this traditional family-run *hostal*. It's a modest outfit but its location, just inside the Puerta de Sevilla, is ideal and its 14 simply furnished rooms, set around a plant-filled patio with Mudéjar-style arches, are good for the money with their brick-flagged floors and solid wood furniture.

**★ El Rincón de las Descalzas** BOUTIQUE HOTEL €€

(☎ 954 19 11 72; www.elrincondelasdescalzas.com; Calle de las Descalzas 1; s €46-66, d €50-116, ste €121-178; ❄ 📶) Discreetly sited in a revamped 18th-century townhouse, this delightfully sprawling hotel offers 13 colourful rooms and a picturesque, orange-hued patio. Each room is different, and some are better than others, but all sport a refined heritage look with carved-wood beds, exposed brick and sandstone, timber arches and fireplaces.

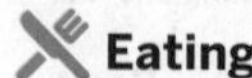

### Eating

**Molino de la Romera** ANDALUCIAN €€

(☎ 954 14 20 00; www.molinodelaromera.es; Calle Sor Ángela de la Cruz 8; tapas €3.50-6, mains €12-19; ⌚ 1-4pm & 8.30-11.30pm Mon-Sat) Housed in a cosy, 15th-century olive-oil mill

WORTH A TRIP

### OSUNA

Set in an otherwise empty landscape of vast, billowing plains, Osuna boasts a series of grand baroque mansions and an attractive white centre crowned by a mighty Renaissance church, the **Colegiata de Santa María de la Asunción** (954 81 04 44; Plaza de la Encarnación; guided tours €5; tours 9.30am & hourly 10.15am-1.15pm Tue-Sun, plus 7pm & 8pm Thu mid-Jun–mid-Sep, hourly 10.15am-1.15pm plus 4pm & 5pm Tue-Sun mid-Sep–mid-Jun). Most of the town's notable buildings were commissioned by the fabulously wealthy dukes of Osuna and built between the 16th and 18th centuries.

Local information is available from the helpful **tourist office** (954 81 57 32; www.osuna.es; Calle Sevilla 37; 9.30am-2.30pm Tue-Sun & 7-9pm Thu mid-Jun–mid-Sep, 10am-2pm & 5-8pm Tue-Sun mid-Sep–mid-Jun), housed in the **Museo de Osuna** (954 81 57 32; Calle Sevilla 37; €2.50, Wed free; 9.30am-2.30pm Tue-Sun & 7-9pm Thu mid-Jun–mid-Sep, 10am-2pm & 5-8pm Tue-Sun mid-Sep–mid-Jun). This small museum displays an eclectic mix of local relics, as well as exhibits and cast photos from the *Game of Thrones*, whose fifth season was partly filmed in town.

For an excellent tapas lunch, join the townsfolk at **Taberna Jicales** (954 81 04 23; www.tabernajicales.es; Calle Esparteros 11; tapas €2-3.50, raciones €7.50-16; 8am-5.30pm Thu-Tue).

Osuna is 91km southeast of Seville, off the Granada–Seville A92. **Monbus** (www.monbus.es) runs eight daily buses (six on Sunday) to/from Seville (€8, 1½ hours).

complete with panoramic terrace, a lovely courtyard and coolly rustic interior, this popular restaurant serves hearty, well-prepped meals with a splash of contemporary flair. Particularly good are its chargrilled meat dishes, including juicy cuts of tender Galician beef.

**Cervecería San Fernando** ANDALUCIAN €€
(661 654960; Plaza de San Fernando 18; tapas €2.50, mains €9-17; noon-5pm & 8pm-midnight Tue-Sun) With ringside seating on Carmona's vibrant central square, enthusiastic service and flavoursome food, Cervecería San Fernando promises memorable dining. Get things rolling with a cold beer and plate of artichokes capped by lavish slices of *jamón* before moving onto a steak or perhaps some scrambled eggs with sausage.

## Information

**Tourist Office** (954 19 09 55; www.turismo.carmona.org; Alcázar de la Puerta de Sevilla; 10am-6pm Mon-Sat, to 3pm Sun Sep-Jun, 9am-3pm Mon-Fri, 10am-3pm Sat & Sun Jul & Aug)

## Getting There & Away

**Casal** (954 99 92 90; www.autocarescasal.com) runs buses to Seville (€2.85, 1¼ hours, at least seven daily) from a stop on Paseo del Estatuto.

**ALSA** (902 42 22 42; www.alsa.es) has three daily buses to Córdoba (€9.83, 1½ hours) via Écija (€4.85, 35 minutes) leaving from a stop on the other side of Paseo del Estatuto.

# Écija

POP 39,880

Écija, the least known of the Campiña towns, often slips under the radar. Many travellers overlook it, perhaps put off by its reputation as *la sartén de Andalucía* (the frying pan of Andalucía) – in July and August temperatures can reach a suffocating 45°C. But avoid high summer and you'll find it's a quietly confident town rich in architectural and historic interest.

## Sights

★**Museo Histórico Municipal** MUSEUM
(954 83 04 31; http://museo.ecija.es; Plaza de la Constitución 1; €3; 10am-1.30pm & 4.30-6.30pm Tue-Fri, 10am-2pm & 5.30-8pm Sat, 10am-3pm Sun mid-Sep–May, 10am-2.30pm Tue-Fri, 10am-2pm & 8-10pm Sat, 10am-3pm Sun Jun–mid-Sep) FREE Écija's history museum, housed in the 18th-century Palacio de Benamejí, is an authentic gem. It has rooms dedicated to the area's prehistory and protohistory, but its chief drawcard is its fabulous collection of local Roman finds. These include a graceful sculpture of a wounded Amazon (a legendary female warrior) and a series of stunningly preserved mosaics, mostly unearthed in and around the town. A high-

light is the *Don del Vino* mosaic depicting scenes related to the mythical 'birth' of wine.

**Palacio de Peñaflor** PALACE

(Calle Emilio Castelar 26; €2; ⊙10am-1.30pm & 4.30-6.30pm, 10am-2pm & 5.30-8pm Sat, 10am-3pm Sun) The huge, 18th-century 'Palace of the Long Balconies' is Écija's most iconic image. Its curved facade is a florid example of baroque exuberance with its ornate, columned portal, wrought-iron balconies and traces of flamboyant frescoes. Inside, much of the palace is off limits but you can take in the vaulted ground-floor stables, an impressive double staircase and the old marquis' office. Up yet more stairs, a *mirador* (viewing terrace) offers fine rooftop views.

## Sleeping & Eating

**★Hotel Palacio de los Granados** HISTORIC HOTEL €€

(☎955 90 53 44; www.palaciogranados.com; Calle Emilio Castelar 42; d €60-70, ste €125-200; ) This charming palace hotel, sections of which date to the 15th century, is a delight. Its interiors have been lovingly restored and its rooms, all of which are slightly different, reveal a stately look with wood-beamed ceilings, Mudéjar arches, 18th-century brick floors and even the occasional fireplace. Adding to the romance is a tiny courtyard where pomegranate trees grow over a tiny plunge pool.

**Hispania** SPANISH €€

(☎954 83 26 05; www.hispaniacafe.com; Pasaje Virgen de Soterraño 3; mains €10-18; ⊙12.30-3.30pm & 8-10.30pm Tue-Sun) Stylish and perennially packed, this slick side-street operation ensures a full house with its contemporary approach to Spanish cooking. In line with the modern decor, dishes are creative and forward-looking, with everything from red tuna tataki to burritos of Iberian ham and wok-fried rice combos. Book ahead Thursday to Saturday.

## Information

**Tourist Office** (☎955 90 29 33; www.turismoecija.com; Calle Elvira 1; ⊙10am-2pm & 4.30-6.30pm Mon-Sat, 10am-2pm Sun)

## Getting There & Away

Écija is 53km east of Carmona on the A4 between Córdoba and Seville.

From the **bus station** (Avenida del Genil), ALSA buses connect with Carmona (€4.85, 35 minutes, three daily), Córdoba (€5.15, one hour, six daily) and Seville (€7.53, 1¼ hours, three daily).

# HUELVA PROVINCE

Huelva province, Andalucía's most westerly, end-of-the-line destination, packs in a mix of historical intrigue, natural beauty and sun worship, but still remains largely off the beaten track for foreign visitors. Here you'll find sleepy mountain villages, relics from Columbus' voyages of discovery, endless stretches of untainted coastline and Spain's most beloved national park. Foodies will enjoy the province's prized pork products while festival goers can join the pilgrims at the boisterous Romería del Rocío festival.

## Huelva

POP 143,660

The capital of Huelva province is a modern, unpretentious industrial port set between the Odiel and Tinto estuaries. Despite its unpromising outskirts, Huelva boasts an appealingly lively pedestrianised centre, and the city's people – called *choqueros* because of their supposed preference for the locally abundant *chocos* (cuttlefish) – are noted for their warmth.

### Sights

**Muelle-Embarcadero de Mineral de Río Tinto** HISTORIC SITE

An odd legacy of the area's mining history, this impressive iron pier curves out into the Odiel estuary 500m south of the port. It was designed for the Rio Tinto company in the 1870s by British engineer George Barclay Bruce. Equipped with boardwalks on upper and lower levels, it makes for a delightful stroll or jog to admire the harbour and ships. It's 1km southwest of Plaza de las Monjas.

**Museo de Huelva** MUSEUM

(☎959 65 04 24; www.museosdeandalucia.es; Alameda Sundheim 13; EU/non-EU citizens free/€1.50; ⊙9am-9pm Tue-Sat, to 3pm Sun) This wide-ranging museum is stuffed with history and art. The permanent ground-floor exhibition concentrates on Huelva province's impressive archaeological pedigree, with interesting items culled from its Roman and mining history; upstairs houses a collection of Spanish painting spanning seven centuries. Don't miss the stunning ancient

Roman *noria* (waterwheel), the best preserved of its kind anywhere in the world.

## Festivals & Events

**Fiestas Colombinas** CULTURAL
(late Jul/early Aug) Huelva celebrates Columbus' departure for the Americas (3 August 1492) with this six-day festival of music, dance, cultural events and bullfighting.

## Sleeping & Eating

**Senator Huelva Hotel** BUSINESS HOTEL €
(959 28 55 00; www.senatorhuelvahotel.com; Avenida Pablo Rada 10; r from €59; ) Catering to the business set, this impeccably maintained hotel is definitely your best bet in Huelva. Bright red banisters draped in greenery liven up the lobby, and staff are charmingly efficient. All 162 rooms are smartly outfitted with dark-wood desks and crisp white sheets.

★ **Azabache** TAPAS €€
(959 25 75 28; www.restauranteazabache.com; Calle Vázquez López 22; raciones €13-22; 8.30am-midnight Mon-Fri, to 4pm Sat) Join the sophisticated local crowd squeezing into this narrow tiled tapas bar in the heart of Huelva's pedestrianised downtown. Busy, helpful waiters are quick to deliver cheese and *jamón* (ham) platters, scrambled *gurumelos* (local wild mushrooms), fried *chocos* (cuttlefish) and fresh fish specials. Beyond the front bar is a more formal restaurant.

★ **Acánthum** GASTRONOMY €€€
(959 24 51 35; www.acanthum.com; Calle San Salvador 17; 11-/18-course tasting menu €65/85; 1.30-3.30pm Tue-Sun, 9-11.30pm Thu-Sat) Celebrating the flavours of his native Huelva, Chef Xanty Elias's exuberant multicourse menus have earned him Michelin star status since 2015. Reserve ahead for a table in the sleek stone-walled dining room, and settle in for a feast that draws equally from Huelva's coast and mountains, prominently featuring the region's famous *gambas blancas* (white shrimp), *chocos* and DOC Iberian pork.

## Information

**Municipal Tourist Office** (959 54 18 17; http://turismo.huelva.es; Plaza del Punto; 10am-2pm daily, plus 5-8pm Mon-Sat)

**Regional Tourist Office** (959 25 74 67; www.turismohuelva.org; Calle Fernando el Católico 14; 9am-2pm Mon-Fri) Helpful for the whole province.

## Getting There & Away

Most buses from the bus station are operated by **Damas** (959 25 69 00; www.damas-sa.es; Avenida Doctor Rubio). Destinations include Almonte (for El Rocío, €4, 1¼ hours), Aracena (€11, 2½ to three hours), Isla Cristina (€4, one to 1¼ hours), Moguer (€1.75, 45 minutes), Matalascañas (€4, 1¼ hours), Palos de la Frontera (€1.75, 30 minutes) and Seville (€8.95, 1¼ to two hours). Frequency is reduced on Saturday, Sunday and public holidays.

From Huelva's **train station** (Avenida de Italia), Renfe runs three daily services to Seville (€13, 1½ hours) and one direct high-speed ALVIA train to Córdoba (€39, 1¾ hours) and Madrid (€58, 3¾ hours).

# Lugares Colombinos

The 'Columbian Sites' are the three townships of La Rábida, Palos de la Frontera and Moguer, along the eastern bank of the Tinto estuary. All three played a key role in Columbus' preparation for his journey of discovery and can be visited as an easy day trip from Huelva, Doñana or Huelva's eastern coast. As the countless greenhouses suggest, this is Spain's main strawberry-growing region (Huelva province produces 90% of Spain's crop).

In La Rábida, directly across the Río Tinto from Huelva, a waterfront museum and hilltop monastery pay homage to Columbus' memory. Some 4km northeast, the port of Palos de la Frontera is where Columbus and his compatriots set sail into the unknown. The town provided the explorer with two of his ships, two captains (brothers Martín Alonso Pinzón and Vicente Yáñez Pinzón) and more than half his crew. Another 8km northeast, the sleepy whitewashed town of Moguer is where Columbus' ship, the *Niña*, was built. It also has a historical claim to fame as the home town of Nobel Prize–winning poet Juan Ramón Jiménez.

## Sights

### La Rábida

**Monasterio de la Rábida** MONASTERY
(959 35 04 11; www.monasteriodelarabida.com; Paraje de la Rábida; adult/student €3.50/3; 10am-6pm Tue-Sun; P) In the pretty, peaceful village of La Rábida, don't miss this palm-fringed, hilltop Franciscan monastery, visited several times by Columbus before his great voyage of discovery. Highlights include

a chapel with a 13th-century alabaster Virgin before which Columbus prayed, and a fresco-lined Mudéjar cloister, one of the few parts of the original structure to survive the 1755 earthquake.

**Muelle de las Carabelas** HISTORIC SITE
(Wharf of the Caravels; adult/reduced €3.60/1.50; 10am-9pm Tue-Sun mid-Jun–mid-Sep, 9.30am-7.30pm Tue-Sun mid-Sep–mid-Jun; P) On the waterfront below the Monasterio de la Rábida is this pseudo 15th-century quayside, where you can board life-size replicas of the *Niña,* the *Pinta* and the *Santa María* – the three ships used by Columbus in his initial trans-Atlantic expedition. A single ticket grants access to all three ships and the attached museum, which features excellent bilingual (English-Spanish) displays tracing the history of Columbus' voyages. Here you can see instruments of navigation and get a glimpse of the indigenous experience at the time of the Spaniards' arrival.

## Palos de la Frontera

**Casa Museo Martín Alonso Pinzón** MUSEUM
(959 10 00 41; Calle Colón 24; adult/concession €1/0.50; 10am-2pm & 5-8.30pm Mon-Fri) The former home of the Pinzón brothers (captains of the *Niña* and the *Pinta*) now houses a permanent exhibition on Palos' crucial contribution to Columbus' famous first expedition.

**Iglesia de San Jorge** CHURCH
(Calle Fray Juan Pérez; hours vary) Towards the northern end of Calle Colón is this 15th-century Gothic-Mudéjar church, where Columbus and his sailors took Communion before embarking on their great expedition. Water for their ships came from La Fontanilla well nearby.

## Moguer

**Monasterio de Santa Clara** MONASTERY
(959 37 01 07; www.monasteriodesantaclara.com; Plaza de las Monjas; guided tours adult/reduced €3.50/2.50, free Sun; tours 10.30am, 11.30am, 12.30pm, 5.30pm & 6.30pm Tue-Sat, 10.30am & 11.30am Sun) Columbus spent a night of vigil and prayer at this grand 14th-century monastery upon returning from his first voyage in March 1493. Highlights of the 45-minute guided visit include a lovely Mudéjar cloister, a 14th-century kitchen, the whitewashed Claustro de las Madres, illuminated manuscripts and a one-of-a-kind 14th-century Nasrid choir stall bearing images of Alhambra-inspired lions, columns and Arabic capitals.

**Casa Museo Zenobia y Juan Ramón Jiménez** HISTORIC BUILDING
(959 37 21 48; www.casamuseozjrj.com; Calle Juan Ramón Jiménez 10; adult/concession €3.50/2.50; 10am-2pm & 4-8pm Tue-Fri, 10am-2.30pm Sat & Sun mid-Jun–mid-Sep, reduced hours rest of year) The lovingly maintained former home of renowned poet Juan Ramón Jiménez and his writer wife, Zenobia Camprubí Aymar, is open for both guided and independent visits, encompassing the poet's private library and several upstairs rooms filled with original period furniture. All exhibits are in Spanish.

### Information

**Tourist Office** (959 37 18 98; Teatro Municipal Felipe Godínez, Calle Andalucía 17; 10am-2pm & 5-7pm Tue-Sat) Moguer's excellent tourist office is inside the Teatro Municipal.

### Getting There & Around

At least 11 daily buses leave Huelva for La Rábida (€1.75, 25 minutes) and Palos de la Frontera (€1.40, 30 minutes); half continue to Moguer (€1.75, 45 minutes). The same buses allow easy transport connections between the three towns.

# Parque Nacional de Doñana

The World Heritage–listed Parque Nacional de Doñana is a place of haunting natural beauty and exotic horizons, where flocks of flamingos tinge the evening skies pink above one of Europe's most extensive wetlands (the Guadalquivir delta), huge herds of deer and boar flit through *coto* (woodlands), and the elusive Iberian lynx battles for survival. Here, in the largest roadless region in Western Europe, and Spain's most celebrated national park, you can experience nature at her most raw and powerful.

The 601-sq-km national park extends 30km along or close to the Atlantic coast and up to 25km inland. Much of the perimeter is bordered by the separate **Parque Natural de Doñana**, under less strict protection, which forms a 682-sq-km buffer for the national park.

To visit the park's interior, you'll need to sign up for a **private tour**, although anyone

### NATIONAL PARK TOURS

To enter Parque Nacional de Doñana from the western side you'll need to join a guided jeep tour. These generally last about four hours (€30 per person) and involve rides in eight- to 30-passenger all-terrain vehicles. Bookings can be made directly with various accredited agencies, including **Doñana Nature** (630 978216, 959 44 21 60; www.donana-nature.com; Calle Moguer 10), **Cooperativa Marismas del Rocío** (959 43 04 32; www.donanavisitas.es; Centro de Visitantes El Acebuche) and **Doñana Reservas** (959 44 24 74, 629 060545; www.donanareservas.com; Avenida de la Canaliega; tours per person €30). Especially in the larger vehicles, the experience can feel a bit theme-park-like, but guides have plenty of in-depth information to share.

During spring, summer and holidays, book as far ahead as possible, but otherwise a week or less is usually sufficient notice. Bring binoculars (if you like), drinking water and mosquito repellent (except in winter). English-, German- and French-speaking guides are normally available if you ask in advance.

can walk or cycle along the 28km Atlantic beach between Matalascañas and the mouth of the Río Guadalquivir (which can be crossed by boat from Sanlúcar de Barrameda in Cádiz province), as long as they do not stray inland.

## Information

The park has seven information points. The most important four for visitors accessing the park from Huelva province are:

**Centro de Visitantes La Rocina** (959 43 95 69; A483; 9am-3pm & 4-7pm Feb-Oct, to 6pm Nov-Jan) Beside the A483, 1km south of El Rocío.

**Centro de Visitantes El Acebrón** (600 144625; 9am-3pm & 4-7pm Feb-Oct, to 6pm Nov-Jan) Located 6km along a minor paved road west from the Centro de Visitantes La Rocina.

**Centro de Visitantes El Acebuche** (959 43 96 29; 8am-3pm & 4-9pm May–mid-Sep, to 7pm mid-Sep–Mar, to 8pm Apr) Twelve kilometres south of El Rocío on the A483, then 1.6km west, El Acebuche is the national park's main visitor centre.

**Centro de Visitantes José Antonio Valverde** (671 564145; 10am-8pm Apr-Sep, to 7pm Mar & Oct, to 6pm Nov-Feb) On the eastern edge of the park. The easiest way to reach it is by authorised tour from El Rocío; the alternative is to drive yourself on rough roads from Villamanrique de la Condesa or La Puebla del Río to the northeast.

## Getting There & Away

You cannot enter the national park in your own vehicle, though you can drive to the four main visitor centres. **Damas** (www.damas-sa.es) runs eight to 10 buses daily between El Rocío and Matalascañas (€1.40, 25 minutes), which stop at the turn-off to El Acebuche on the A483 on request. Some tour companies will pick you up from Matalascañas with advance notice.

# El Rocío

POP 1370

El Rocío, the most significant town in the vicinity of the Parque Nacional de Doñana, surprises first-timers. Its sand-covered streets are lined with colourful single-storey houses with sweeping verandahs, left empty half the time. But this is no ghost town: these are the well-tended properties of 115 *hermandades* (brotherhoods), whose pilgrims converge on the town every Pentecost (Whitsunday) weekend for the Romería del Rocío, Spain's largest religious festival.

Beyond its uniquely exotic ambience, El Rocío impresses with its striking setting in front of luminous Doñana *marismas* (wetlands), where herds of deer drink at dawn and, at certain times of year, flocks of flamingos gather in massive numbers.

Whether it's the play of light on the marshes, an old woman praying to the Virgin at the Ermita, a rider prancing through the streets on horseback or someone passing by in a flamenco dress, there's always something to catch the eye on El Rocío's dusky, sand-blown streets.

## Sights

**Ermita del Rocío** CHURCH

(Calle Ermita; 8am-9pm Apr-Sep, to 7pm Oct-Mar) A striking splash of white at the heart of the town, the Ermita del Rocío was built in its present form in 1964. This is the permanent home of the celebrated Nuestra Señora del Rocío (Our Lady of El Rocío), a small wooden image of the Virgin dressed in long, jewelled robes, which normally stands above the main altar.

## Activities

The marshlands in front of El Rocío, which have water most of the year, offer some of the best bird- and beast-watching in the entire Doñana region. Deer and horses graze in the shallows and you may be lucky enough to spot a big pink cloud of flamingos wheeling through the sky. Pack a pair of binoculars and stroll the waterfront promenade.

**Francisco Bernis Birdwatching Centre** BIRDWATCHING
(☎959 44 23 72; www.facebook.com/centrofranciscobernis; Paseo Marismeño; ⏲9am-2pm & 4-6pm Tue-Sun) FREE Run by national bird conservation group SEO Birdlife (www.seo.org), this birdwatching facility backs on to the marshes about 700m east of the Ermita. Flamingos, glossy ibises, spoonbills and more can be spied through the rear windows or from the observation deck with high-power binoculars (free). Experts offer help identifying species and information about migratory birds and where to see them.

**Doñana Horse Adventure** HORSEBACK RIDING
(☎626 784628; www.donanahorseadventure.com) Lovely French owner Sandrine offers a wide range of equestrian experiences, from two-hour private beginner's lessons (€45, in Spanish or English) to three-day horseback excursions through the Parque Nacional de Doñana (€350).

## Sleeping & Eating

**Hotel Toruño** HOTEL €€
(☎959 44 23 23; www.toruno.es; Plaza Acebuchal 22; s €35-59, d €50-80, all incl breakfast; P❄📶) This brilliantly white villa 350m east of the Ermita directly abuts the wetlands, where you can spot flamingos going through their morning beauty routine. Inside, tile murals continue the wildlife theme. Interior rooms are uninspiring, especially on the ground floor; request one overlooking the marshes if available. Across the plaza, the hotel's Restaurante Toruño is among El Rocío's best.

★**Hotel La Malvasía** HOTEL €€€
(☎959 44 27 13; www.hotellamalvasia.com; Calle Sanlúcar 38; s €100-110, d €120-170, ste €185-205; ❄📶) This idyllic hotel occupies a grand *casa señorial* (manor house) overlooking the marshes at the eastern end of town. Rooms have character: rustic tiled floors, vintage El Rocío photos and floral-patterned iron bedsteads. The top-floor sun terrace makes a spectacular bird-viewing perch, as does the suite, with its front-facing views of the lagoon.

**Aires de Doñana** ANDALUCIAN €€
(La Choza; ☎959 44 22 89; www.airesdedonana.com; Avenida de la Canaliega 1; mains €15-22; ⏲1.30-4pm Tue-Sun, 8.30-11pm Tue-Sat) Affectionately nicknamed La Choza (the Hut), this thatched-roofed, whitewashed local institution has one big thing going for it: knockout views of the Ermita framed by horse pastures and bird-thronged wetlands. The menu includes everything from local Mostrenca beef to seafood; either way, you can't go wrong sipping drinks on the terrace at sunset.

## Information

**Tourist Office** (☎959 44 23 50; www.almonte.es; Avenida de la Canaliega; ⏲9.30am-2pm) Relocated from the town hall to El Rocío's shoreline in 2020.

## Getting There & Away

**Damas** (www.damas-sa.es) buses run from Seville's Plaza de Armas to El Rocío (€6.55, 1½ hours, two to three daily), continuing to Matalascañas (€1.40, 25 minutes). From Huelva, take a Damas bus to Almonte (€4, 1¼ hours, one to four daily), then another to El Rocío (€1.40, 20 minutes, eight to 10 daily).

# Minas de Riotinto

POP 3850 / ELEV 420M

Tucked away on the southern fringe of Huelva's Sierra Morena is one of the world's oldest mining districts; King Solomon of Jerusalem is said to have mined gold here for his famous temple, and the Romans were digging up silver by the 4th century BCE. In the 1870s, the British Rio Tinto company made this one of the world's key copper-mining centres. Nowadays it's a fascinating place to explore, with a superb museum, and opportunities to visit the old mines and ride the mine railway.

## Sights & Activities

**Museo Minero** MUSEUM
(☎959 59 00 25; www.parquemineroderiotinto.es; Plaza Ernest Lluch; adult/reduced €5/4; ⏲10.30am-3pm & 4-8pm mid-Jul–mid-Sep, to 7pm

rest of year; P) Riotinto's mining museum offers a sweeping overview of the area's unique history and geology, from the megalithic tombs of the 3rd millennium BCE to the British colonial era, and from impressively colourful locally quarried gemstones to ruddy rust-tinged Roman statues discovered on site. Two of the most memorable displays are an elaborate 200m-long recreation of a Roman mine, and the Vagón del Maharajah, a luxurious train carriage built in 1892 for a tour of India by Britain's Queen Victoria.

**Peña de Hierro** MINE

(959 59 00 25; www.parquemineroderiotinto.es; adult/reduced €8/7; hours vary) These are old copper and sulphur mines 3km north of Nerva (6km east of Minas de Riotinto). Here you see the source of the Río Tinto and a 65m-deep opencast mine, and are taken into a 200m-long underground mine gallery. There are three guaranteed daily visits but schedules vary, so it's essential to book ahead through the Museo Minero (by phone or online).

**Ferrocarril Turístico-Minero** RAIL

(959 59 00 25; www.parquemineroderiotinto.es; adult/reduced €11/10; 1.30pm & 5.30pm daily mid-Jul–mid-Sep, 1pm Mon-Fri, 1.30pm Sat & Sun mid-Feb–mid-Jul & mid-Sep–mid-Nov, 1.30pm Sat & Sun mid-Nov–mid-Feb) A fun way to see the area – especially with children – is to ride this historic railway through Riotinto's surreal landscape in restored early 20th-century carriages. The entire train journey (22km return) parallels the rust-red river, so you can appreciate its constantly shifting hues. Advance booking is required, either at the mining museum or the railway station 4km east of town.

## Getting There & Away

**Damas** (www.damas-sa.es) runs three to five daily buses between Minas de Riotinto and Huelva (€7.10, 1¾ hours).

DON'T MISS

### SPAIN'S GREATEST RELIGIOUS PILGRIMAGE: ROMERÍA DEL ROCÍO

Every Pentecost (Whitsunday) weekend, seven weeks after Easter, El Rocío transforms from a quiet backwater into an explosive mess of noise, colour and passion. This is the culmination of Spain's biggest religious pilgrimage, the Romería del Rocío, which draws up to a million joyous pilgrims.

The focus of all this revelry is the tiny image of Nuestra Señora del Rocío (Our Lady of El Rocío), which was found in a marshland tree by a hunter from Almonte village back in the 13th century. When he stopped for a rest on the way home, the Virgin magically returned to the tree. Before long, a chapel was built on the site of the tree (El Rocío) and pilgrims started arriving.

Solemn is the last word you'd apply to this quintessentially Andalucian event. Participants dress in their finest Andalucian costume and sing, drink, dance, laugh and romance their way to El Rocío. Most belong to the 115 *hermandades* (brotherhoods) who arrive from towns all across southern Spain on foot, horseback and in colourfully decorated covered wagons.

The weekend reaches an ecstatic climax in the very early hours of Monday. Members of the Almonte *hermandad*, which claims the Virgin as its own, barge into the church and bear her out on a float. Violent struggles ensue as others battle for the honour of carrying La Paloma Blanca (the White Dove). The crush and chaos are immense, but somehow the Virgin is carried round to each of the *hermandad* buildings before finally being returned to the church in the afternoon. Upcoming dates are 24 May 2021, 6 June 2022 and 29 May 2023.

In recent years, Spaniards' rising concern for animal rights, spearheaded by animal-welfare political party PACMA (www.pacma.es), has drawn attention to mistreatment and neglect of animals, particularly horses and mules, during the Romería del Rocío festivities, and, despite the presence of voluntary veterinary services, seven horses died during the 2019 *romería*.

# Aracena & the Sierra de Aracena

POP 8110 / ELEV 673M

Sparkling white in its mountain bowl, the thriving old market town of Aracena is an appealingly lively place that's wrapped like a ribbon around a medieval church and ruined castle.

West of town lies the Sierra de Aracena, dotted with old stone villages and oak-fringed pastures where the region's famed black pigs forage for acorns. The area is threaded by an extensive network of well-maintained walking trails. Picturesque villages such as Alájar, Linares de la Sierra and Almonaster la Real make perfect bases for exploring the area.

## Sights

### Aracena

**★Gruta de las Maravillas** CAVE

(Cave of Marvels; ☎663 937876; www.aracena.es; Calle Pozo de la Nieve; tours adult/child €10/7; ⏰10am-1.30pm & 3-6pm) Beneath Aracena's castle hill is a web of caves and tunnels carved from the karstic topography. An extraordinary 1.2km, 50-minute loop takes you through 12 chambers and past six underground lakes, all beautifully illuminated and filled with weird and wonderful rock formations, which provided a backdrop for the film *Journey to the Center of the Earth*.

**Museo del Jamón** MUSEUM

(☎663 937870; www.aracena.es; Gran Vía; adult/child €3.50/2.50; ⏰11am-2.30pm & 4-7.30pm) The *jamón* for which the sierra is famed gets due recognition in this modern museum. You'll learn why the acorn-fed Iberian pig gives such succulent meat, about the importance of the native pastures in which they are reared, and about traditional and contemporary methods of slaughter and curing. Displays are in Spanish, with free audio guides available in four other languages. Afterwards, the museum shop invites visitors to 'pig' out with a free tasting of local *bellota* ham.

**Castillo** CASTLE

(Cerro del Castillo; guided tour adult/child €2.50/1; ⏰tours 11.30am, 12.30pm, 1.30pm, 6pm, 7pm & 8pm Apr-Oct, 11.45am, 12.45pm, 1.45pm, 4pm, 5pm & 5.45pm Nov-Mar) Dramatically dominating the town are the tumbling, hilltop ruins of the *castillo*, built by the kingdoms of Portugal and Castilla in the 12th century atop the ruins of an earlier Islamic settlement. Directly adjacent is the Gothic-Mudéjar **Iglesia Prioral de Nuestra Señora del Mayor Dolor** (Plazoleta Virgen del Mayor Dolor; ⏰10am-5pm Sep-Jun, to 7.30pm Jul & Aug). Both are reached via a steep lane from Plaza Alta; guided tours grant access to the castle's interior, though it's honestly more impressive from the outside.

### Almonaster la Real

**★Mezquita** HISTORIC BUILDING

(Mosque; Calle Castillo 10; ⏰9am-dusk) FREE Dating to the 9th and 10th centuries, this rare jewel of a *mezquita* (mosque) perches a five-minute walk above Almonaster's main square. The almost perfectly preserved structure is like a miniature version of Córdoba's great mosque. Despite being Christianised in the 13th century, it retains nearly all its original Islamic features: the horseshoe arches, the semicircular *mihrab* (prayer niche; reputedly the Iberian peninsula's oldest), an ablutions fountain and various Arabic inscriptions. Even older are the Roman and Visigothic columns nearest the *mihrab*.

## Sleeping

### Aracena & Around

**★Finca Buenvino** INN €€

(☎959 12 40 34; www.fincabuenvino.com; Los Marines; s/d incl breakfast €90/140, 4-person cottage per week €600-850; 📶🏊) For four decades, the Chesterton family has been welcoming guests to their spectacularly sited salmon-pink farmhouse on a hilltop 10 minutes west of Aracena. Six rooms in varying configurations (including a couple of family-friendly suites) all have high ceilings, charming decor and lovely views over the surrounding countryside. There's a grand living room and a sun porch with wraparound windows.

**★Hotel Convento Aracena** HISTORIC HOTEL €€€

(☎959 12 68 99; www.hotelconventoaracena.es; Calle Jesús y María 19; d €95-163, ste €195-243; P❄📶🏊) Glossy, modern rooms contrast with flourishes of original Andalucian baroque architecture at this thoughtfully converted 17th-century convent, Aracena town's finest lodging. Enjoy the on-site spa, sierra cuisine and year-round saltwater pool, with gorgeous village views and summer bar. Room 9 is fabulously set in the church dome (though be forewarned that it's windowless, save for the skylight in the cupola).

## Alájar

★**Finca La Fronda** HOTEL €€

(☎959 50 12 47, 659 963510; www.fincalafronda.com; Carretera Cortegana-Aracena, Km 22; r incl breakfast €89-140; P❄📶🏊) Tucked away amid cork/chestnut forest, La Fronda makes the perfect hillside hideaway. Modern-rustic charm abounds in the bright lounge, Mudéjar-inspired patio and huge, flowery rooms with splashes of British character. Spectacular vistas of Alájar and the Peña de Arias Montano unfold from the rose-fringed pool, and the Saturday evening dinner concerts in the *finca's* dining room are not to be missed.

★**Posada de San Marcos** INN €€

(☎667 906132, 959 12 57 12; www.sanmarcosalajar.com; Calle Colón 12; s/d incl breakfast €68/95; P❄@📶🏊) Andalucía's first European Eco-Label hotel, this brilliantly restored 200-year-old house bordering a stream in the heart of Alájar runs on geothermal energy, rain harvesting and natural-cork insulation. The six comfortably rustic, airy rooms have big terraces, breakfast is homemade, and welcoming Spanish-English hosts Ángel and Lucy are experts on local hiking. The pool looks across the village to the *peña*.

# Eating

## Aracena

**Rincón de Juan** TAPAS €

(Avenida de Portugal 3; tapas €2-3, raciones €10-14; ⏰7.30am-4pm Mon-Sat, 6.30pm-midnight Wed-Sat) It's standing room only at this wood-beamed, stone-walled corner bar, indisputably Aracena's favourite local hangout for traditional tapas. Iberian ham is the star attraction and forms the basis for a variety of *montaditos* (small stuffed rolls) and *rebanadas* (sliced loaves for several people). The local goat's cheese is always a good bet.

★**Experience by Fuster** FUSION €€

(☎634 682988; www.facebook.com/experiencebyfuster; Gran Vía 21; tapas €2.50-4, raciones €9-18; ⏰9am-midnight Mon, Tue, Thu & Fri, from 10am Sat & Sun) Aracena's home-grown celebrity chef Javier Fuster created an instant sensation when he opened this casual downtown restaurant in 2019. Sourcing ingredients largely from Huelva province, Fuster gives traditional Andalucian flavours a gourmet international twist in dishes like tempura battered pork tenderloin with cream of porcini mushrooms or seafood risotto with wakame seaweed.

## Linares de la Sierra

★**Restaurante Arrieros** ANDALUCIAN €€€

(☎959 46 37 17; www.arrieros.net; Calle Arrieros 2; mains €15-21, tasting menus from €35; ⏰1-4pm Thu-Tue, closed mid-Jun–mid-Jul) The art of slow food is taken to the extreme here with meals normally spinning out over several lazy hours. The innovative approach to local pork products and wild mushrooms, such as the mushroom-and-apple stuffed *solomillo* (pork sirloin) and *carrilleras* (pig cheeks) in red wine, makes this one of the sierra's top places to eat.

# Information

**Centro de Visitantes Cabildo Viejo** (☎959 12 95 53; Plaza Alta; ⏰generally 9.30am-2pm year-round, plus 4-7pm Fri & Sat Mar-May & Oct-Dec) Gives out hiking information and maps, and has an exhibit on the Parque Natural Sierra de Aracena y Picos de Aroche. Hours vary by month.

**Tourist Office** (☎663 937877; www.aracena.es; Calle Pozo de la Nieve; ⏰10am-2pm & 4-6pm) Opposite the Gruta de las Maravillas; sells a good walking map.

# Getting There & Away

The **bus station** (Calle José Andrés Vázquez) is 700m southeast of Plaza del Marqués de Aracena. **Damas** (www.damas-sa.es) runs two to three daily buses from Seville (€7.70, 1¼ hours), continuing to Cortegana via Alájar or Jabugo. From Huelva, there are two afternoon departures Monday to Friday, and one on weekends (€11.25, 2½ to 2¾ hours). There's also a local service between Aracena and Cortegana via Linares de la Sierra, Alájar and Almonaster la Real.

# CÁDIZ PROVINCE

If you had to pick just one region to explain Andalucía in its full, complex beauty, it'd be Cádiz. Lying in wait across mainland Spain's southernmost province are oceans of olive trees, craggy mountains, thrillingly sited *pueblos blancos* (white towns), glorious sherry, flamenco in its purest incarnation, the font of Andalucian horse culture, and a dreamy blonde-sand coastline, the uncommercial Costa de la Luz, sprinkled with kitesurf-cool towns like Tarifa.

North of cheerful provincial capital Cádiz, the three corners of Spain's famous 'sherry triangle' are marked by Jerez de la Frontera, Sanlúcar de Barrameda and El Puerto de Santa María, while in the province's northeastern reaches lie a string of classic white towns (Arcos, Zahara, Grazalema). Packed in among all this condensed culture are two expansive natural parks, covering an unbroken tract of land from Olvera in the north to Algeciras in the south. The same line once marked the ever-changing frontier between Christian Spain and Moorish Granada, and many of the castle-topped, whitewashed towns that still dot this ancient border flaunt a 'de la Frontera' suffix that testifies to their volatile history.



# Cádiz

POP 116,030

You could write several weighty tomes about Cádiz and still fall short of nailing its essence. Cádiz is generally considered to be the oldest continuously inhabited settlement in Europe, founded as Gadir by the Phoenicians in about 1100 BCE. Now well into its fourth millennium, the ancient centre, surrounded almost entirely by water (and originally an island), is a romantic, wind-swept jumble of sinuous streets where Atlantic waves crash against eroded sea walls, cheerful taverns sizzle up fresh fish and salty beaches teem with sun-worshippers. Spain's first liberal constitution (La Pepa) was signed here in 1812, while the city's urban model provided an identikit for fortified Spanish colonial cities in the Americas. Enamoured return visitors talk fondly of Cádiz' seafood, sands, university buzz and intriguing monuments. More importantly, they gush happily about the *gaditanos*, an upfront, sociable bunch whose upbeat *alegrías* (flamenco songs) warm your heart.

## Sights

To understand Cádiz, first you need to befriend its *barrios* (districts). The old city is split into classic quarters: the cobbled Barrio del Pópulo, home of the cathedral, nexus of the once prosperous medieval settlement, and the oldest part of town; the Barrio de Santa María, the old Roma and flamenco quarter; the newer Barrio de la Viña, a former vineyard that became the city's main fishing quarter and Carnaval epicentre; and the Barrio del Mentidero, centred on Plaza de San Antonio in the northwest.

### ★Catedral de Cádiz — CATHEDRAL

(956 28 61 54; www.catedraldecadiz.com; Plaza de la Catedral; incl Museo Catedralicio & Torre del Reloj adult/child €6/free; 10am-9pm Mon-Sat, 1.30-9pm Sun Jul & Aug, 10am-2pm Mon-Sat, 1.30-8pm Sun Apr-Jun, Sep & Oct, 10am-7pm Mon-Sat, 1.30-7pm Sun Nov-Mar) Cádiz' beautiful yellow-domed cathedral is an impressively proportioned baroque-neoclassical construction, best appreciated from seafront Campo del Sur in the evening sun. Though commissioned in 1716, the project wasn't finished until 1838, by which time neoclassical elements (the dome, towers and main facade) had diluted architect Vicente Acero's original baroque plan. Highlights within are the intricate wood-carved choir (one of Andalucía's finest) and, in the crypt, the stone tomb of renowned 20th-century *gaditano* composer Manuel de Falla (1876–1946).

Tickets include audio guides and a climb up the **Torre del Reloj** (Torre de Levante; incl Catedral de Cádiz & Museo Catedralicio adult/child €6/free; 10am-9pm Jul & Aug, to 8pm Apr-Jun, Sep & Oct, to 7pm Nov-Mar).

### ★Museo de Cádiz — MUSEUM

(856 105023; www.museosdeandalucia.es; Plaza de Mina; EU/non-EU citizen free/€1.50; 9am-9pm Tue-Sat, to 3pm Sun) Set in a dusty-pink 19th-century neoclassical building, this is the province's top museum. Stars of the ground-floor archaeology section are two Phoenician marble sarcophagi carved in human likeness (uncovered a century apart in 1887 and 1980), along with lots of headless Roman statues and a giant marble 2nd-century Emperor Trajan (with head) from Bolonia's Baelo Claudia. Upstairs, the excellent fine-art collection (closed for renovation at research time) displays Spanish art from the 18th to early 20th centuries, including 18 superb 17th-century canvases by Zurbarán.

### Iglesia de Santa Cruz — CHURCH

(Catedral Antigua; Plaza de Fray Félix; 5.30-7.30pm Mon, 9.45am-12.45pm & 5.30-7pm Tue-Sat, 10.30am-12.30pm & 5.30-6.30pm Sun) Cádiz' most ancient church and original cathedral was a Gothic-Mudéjar creation commissioned by Alfonso X El Sabio in 1263, on the site of a former mosque. After suffering serious damage during the 1596 Dutch-British sacking of the city, it was rebuilt in the 18th century. Beyond the restrained facade, its moody interior has a gilded 17th-century baroque main altarpiece, above which rise beautiful vaulted ceilings and arches.

**Teatro Romano** ARCHAEOLOGICAL SITE

(677 982945; Calle Mesón 11-13; EU/non-EU citizen free/€1.50; 11am-5pm Mon-Sat, 10am-2pm Sun Apr-Sep, 10am-4.30pm Mon-Sat, to 2pm Sun Oct-Mar, closed 1st Mon of month) On the seaward edge of the Barrio del Pópulo, Cádiz' Roman theatre dates from the late 1st century BCE and, originally, had space for 10,000 spectators. A Moorish castle was later erected here, then rebuilt by Alfonso X El Sabio. You can access the excavated theatre via its modern interpretation centre, which has English- and Spanish-language displays detailing the site's history.

**Plaza de Topete** SQUARE

About 250m northwest of the cathedral, this triangular plaza is one of Cádiz' most intimate. Bright with flowers, it's usually talked about as Plaza de las Flores (Square of the Flowers). Beside is the revamped 1838 **Mercado Central de Abastos** (Plaza de la Libertad; 9am-3pm), the oldest covered market in Spain (note the original pillars), now also a buzzing gastromarket (p655).

**Oratorio de la Santa Cueva** CHURCH

(956 22 22 62; Calle Rosario 10; adult/child €5/2, Sun free; 10.30am-2pm & 5.30-8.30pm Tue-Fri Jun-Sep, 10.30am-2pm & 4.30-8pm Tue-Fri Oct-May, 10.30am-2pm Sat, 10am-1pm Sun year-round) Behind an unassuming door, the Santa Cueva conceals quite the surprise. Of its two superposed neoclassical 18th-century chapels (built on trade wealth from the Americas), the bare, pillared subterranean **Capilla de la Pasión** is washed in white. Above is the richly adorned, oval-shaped **Capilla del Santísimo Sacramento**, its altar graced by six Corinthian columns, and with five religious canvases strung between its pillars – three of them important works by Goya.

**Museo de las Cortes de Cádiz** MUSEUM

(956 22 17 88; Calle Santa Inés 9; 9am-6pm Tue-Fri, to 2pm Sat & Sun) FREE A fairly dry collection of portraits and maps focusing especially on the revolutionary Cádiz Parliament of 1812, which took place in the baroque **Oratorio de San Felipe Neri** (662 642233; Plaza de San Felipe Neri; adult/child €4/2; 10.30am-2pm & 4.30-8pm Tue-Fri, 10.30am-2pm Sat & 10am-1pm Sun) next door, and the Napoleonic siege which the city was suffering at that time. The highlight is the 1770s model of 18th-century Cádiz, made in mahogany, silver and ivory by Alfonso Ximénez.

**Playa de la Caleta** BEACH

Hugging the western side of the Barrio de la Viña, this small, popular golden city beach catches the eye with its mock-Moorish *balneario* (bathhouse). It's flanked by two forts: the **Castillo de San Sebastián** (Paseo Fernando Quiñones) FREE, for centuries a military installation (and closed to the public at research time), and the star-shaped **Castillo de Santa Catalina** (956 22 63 33; Calle Antonio Burgos; 11am-8.30pm Mar-Oct, to 7.30pm Nov-Feb) FREE, built after the 1596 Anglo-Dutch sacking of the city and with a 1683 chapel.

**Playa de la Victoria** BEACH

An enjoyable walk/jog along the promenade from the Barrio de Santa María, this fine, wide strip of Atlantic sand, with summer beach bars, starts 1km south of the Puerta de Tierra and stretches 4km back along the peninsula.

## Courses

**K2 Internacional** LANGUAGE

(956 21 26 46; www.k2internacional.com; Plaza Mentidero 19) Based in a renovated 19th-century Barrio del Mentidero building, this old-city school offers special courses for long-term students and people over 50 years old, as well as regular classes. An intensive one-week course costs €175. It also organises tours, accommodation, and flamenco, cooking and even surf courses.

## Tours

**Cadizfornia Tours** WALKING

(692 205412; www.cadizforniatours.com) Cadizfornia has terrific twice-daily pay-what-you-like tours (English or Spanish) of Cádiz' old town, plus wine-and-tapas and bike tours (both €25) and day trips out into the province. Also in Jerez and El Puerto de Santa María.

**Las Bicis Naranjas** CYCLING

(956 90 76 71; www.lasbicisnaranjas.com; Calle Sagasta 9; bike hire per hr/day €4/15, 3hr tours

## Cádiz

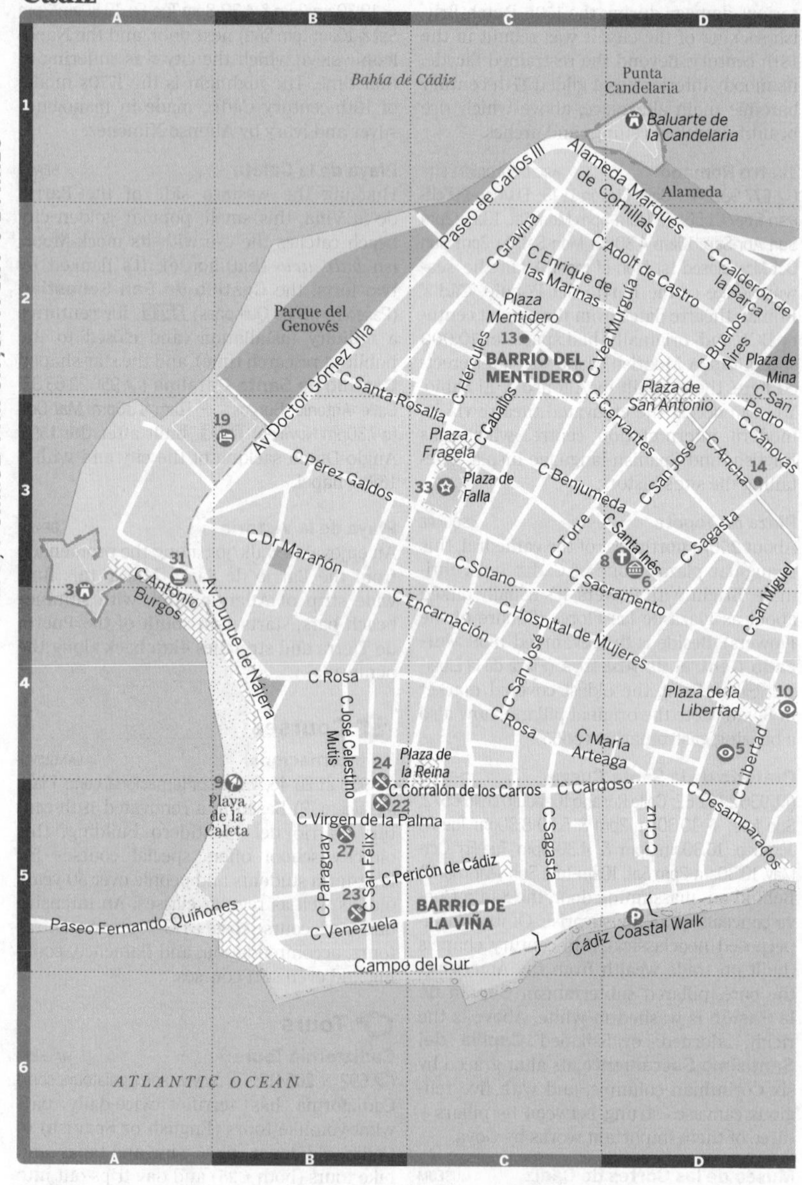


€29; ⏲10am-9pm) Bike hire and a range of multi-language bike trips around Cádiz, from basic three-hour city jaunts (€29) to four-hour bike-and-tapas trails (€45) and half-day bike-and-surf combos (€35).

## Sleeping

**★Casa Caracol** HOSTEL **€**

(☎956 26 11 66; www.casacaracolcadiz.com; Calle Suárez de Salazar 4; incl breakfast dm from €17, d from €48, d without bathroom €37; 📶) 🌿 Mellow, solar-powered Casa Caracol is Cádiz'

original old-town backpacker. Cheery as only Cádiz can be, it has colourful, contemporary dorms for four, six or seven (including one female-only), with handmade bunks and individual lights, plugs and lockers, along with three private doubles (one duplex-style). Other perks include a social kitchen, a roof terrace/bar with hammocks, yoga, and bike and surfboard rental. The on-the-ball team also has five boutiquey rooms at nearby **Casa Piratas** (956 26 11 66; www.casacaracolcadiz.com; Callejón de los Piratas; d/studio from €44/55; ).

## Cádiz

**Top Sights**
1 Catedral de Cádiz ... E5
2 Museo de Cádiz ... E2

**Sights**
3 Castillo de Santa Catalina ... A4
4 Iglesia de Santa Cruz ... E5
5 Mercado Central de Abastos ... D4
6 Museo de las Cortes de Cádiz ... D3
7 Oratorio de la Santa Cueva ... E3
8 Oratorio de San Felipe Neri ... D3
9 Playa de la Caleta ... B5
10 Plaza de Topete ... D4
11 Teatro Romano ... F5
12 Torre del Reloj ... E5

**Activities, Courses & Tours**
13 K2 Internacional ... C2
14 Las Bicis Naranjas ... D3

**Sleeping**
15 Casa Caracol ... F5
16 Casa de las Cuatro Torres ... E2
17 Casa Piratas ... E5
18 Hotel Argantonio ... E3
19 Parador de Cádiz ... B3

**Eating**
20 Almanaque ... E2
21 Café Royalty ... E4
22 Casa Manteca ... B5
23 El Faro de Cádiz ... B5
24 Freidor Casa Manteca ... B5
25 La Candela ... E4
26 La Cepa Gallega ... F5
27 La Tabernita ... B5
28 La Tapería de Columela ... E4
Rincón Gastronómico ... (see 5)
29 Taberna La Sorpresa ... E5

**Drinking & Nightlife**
30 La Clandestina ... E4
31 Quilla ... A3
32 Taberna La Manzanilla ... E4

**Entertainment**
33 Gran Teatro Falla ... C3
34 Peña Flamenca La Perla ... G6

**Hotel Argantonio** HOTEL €€
(☎956 21 16 40; www.hotelargantonio.com; Calle Argantonio 3; incl breakfast s €80-150, d €100-180; ) Rambling across an 18th-century home, this stylishly charming hotel in Cádiz' old quarter sparkles with its hand-painted, wood-carved doors, colourfully tiled floors adorning bedrooms, bathrooms and corridors, and intricate Moorish-style arch and fountain in the lobby. The 1st floor is Mudéjar-inspired, the 2nd 'colonial romantic', the 3rd a mix. There's a tucked-away roof-terrace lounge, plus a cafe and good breakfasts.

**Casa de las Cuatro Torres** BOUTIQUE HOTEL €€€
(☎956 90 31 33; www.casadelascuatrotorres.com; Plaza de Argüelles 3; d €135-185, apt €195-265; ) Inhabiting part of a listed early-18th-century neoclassical *palacete* (mansion), in the northeastern old city, the historical-chic Cuatro Torres is a design delight of original sky-reaching ceilings, wooden doors, beams, vaults, skylights and exposed-stone walls, all skilfully reimagined with boutique flair. From the pillared marble patio with a library lounge, you can head up to the rooftop terrace, bar and tower.

**Parador de Cádiz** LUXURY HOTEL €€€
(☎956 22 69 05; www.parador.es; Avenida Duque de Nájera 9; incl breakfast d €156-310, ste €254-330; ) Bold, beautiful and right beside Playa de la Caleta, the so-called Parador Atlántico contrasts with Andalucía's other *paradores* (luxurious state-owned hotels) in that it's ubermodern and built from scratch. Sultry reds, ocean blues and bright turquoises throw character into the sleek, contemporary rooms with balcony and floor-to-ceiling windows. Soak in four sea-view swimming pools, or seek out the spa.

## Eating

Calle Virgen de la Palma, in the Barrio de la Viña, is the city's go-to fresh-seafood street. Calles Plocia and Sopranis, off Plaza de San Juan de Dios, are upmarket eat streets, and there are good options off Plaza de Mina in the Barrio del Mentidero.

★**Casa Manteca** TAPAS €
(☎956 21 36 06; www.facebook.com/tabernamanteca; Calle Corralón de los Carros 66; tapas €2.50, medias raciones €4-10; noon-4pm & 8.30pm-12.30am, may close Sun & Mon evenings Nov-Mar) The hub of the Barrio de la Viña fun, with every inch of its walls covered in flamenco, bullfighting and Carnaval paraphernalia, always-busy Casa Manteca is full of old tapas favourites. Ask the chatty waiters for mussels, *chicharrones* (pressed pork with a squeeze of lemon) or *payoyo* cheese with asparagus marmalade, and it'll fly across the bar on waxed paper.

Opposite is a terrific fried fish specialist, **Manteca Freidor** (☎956 21 36 03; www.face

book.com/freidorcasamanteca; Calle Corralón 59; raciones €7-10; ⏲12.30-4pm & 8.30-11pm).

**La Tapería de Columela** TAPAS €
(☎956 07 42 97; www.facebook.com/lataperiadecolumela; Calle Columela 4; tapas €3-8; ⏲1-4pm & 8-11pm Mon-Sat; ) There's always a queue trailing out the door at wonderful, packed-out Columela, where diners both local and international feast on delicately prepped tradition-meets-innovation tapas of local tuna, perhaps as tartare with mustard dressing. Squeeze in at the marble-top bar for respected local chef Agustín Campos' creations, which also include deep-fried aubergine drizzled with cane honey and slivers of *payoyo* cheese.

**Taberna La Sorpresa** TAPAS €
(☎956 22 12 32; www.tabernalasorpresa.com; Calle Arbolí 4; tapas €2.50-5.50; ⏲11.30am-4.30pm & 8.30-11.30pm Tue-Sat, 11.30am-4.30pm Sun) Barrels of Pedro Ximénez, *manzanilla* (chamomile-coloured sherry) and *oloroso* (sweet, dark sherry) stack up behind the bar at this down-to-earth 1956 tavern, thoughtfully revamped keeping Cádiz' old-school scene alive. Tapas focus on *almadraba* tuna, but there are plenty of other tasty bites, such as mussels, *chicharrones* and Iberian *bellota* ham, along with Cádiz-province wines and vermouth on tap.

**Rincón Gastronómico** TAPAS €
(Mercado Central de Abastos, Plaza de la Libertad; tapas €2-8; ⏲9am-4pm Mon, 9am-3.30pm & 7pm-midnight Tue-Fri, 9am-4pm & 8pm-1am Sat; ) Cádiz' neoclassical 1838 Mercado Central de Abastos is the setting for this ultra-buzzy globe-roaming gastromarket. Sample gloriously simple local specialities like *patatas aliñadas*, *payoyo* cheese and *ibérico* ham; pick your fresh fish and have it grilled before your eyes; venture into a plant-based world of vegan tortilla (convincingly delicious!); or hit the sherry stands.

**La Cepa Gallega** TAPAS €
(☎956 28 60 29; Calle Plocia 9; tapas €2-5; ⏲10.30am-4pm & 8pm-late Mon-Sat, 10.30am-4pm Sun) Founded in 1920, this venerable old *ultramarinos* (grocer) under keen new ownership does delectable wax-paper tapas of Cádiz cheeses, buttered anchovies, *ibérico* ham and tinned seafood to pair with its wide-roaming collection of Spanish wines and sherries. It's rustic-style, with wine-barrel tables and bottles lining the walls.

**La Tabernita** TAPAS €
(www.facebook.com/rafatabernita; Calle Virgen de la Palma 32; tapas €2.50; ⏲8.30-11.30pm Thu & Fri, 1.30-4pm & 8.30-11.30pm Sat & Sun; ) Despite its limited opening times, La Tabernita gets immediately rammed for its superb homemade, family-style tapas. *Cazón al coñac* (dogfish in brandy), cuttlefish-in-ink 'meatballs' and *tortillitas de camarones* (shrimp fritters) are favourites to sample on the Barrio de la Viña's liveliest street.

**Almanaque** ANDALUCIAN €€
(☎956 80 86 63; Plaza de España 5; raciones €12-18; ⏲1-4pm Mon & Sun, 1-4pm & 8.30-11pm Wed-Sat) A rustic-chic modern-day *casa de comidas* with open stone, tiled floors and bright-white walls creates an intriguing setting for sampling traditional, often-forgotten *gaditano* family recipes unlikely to be found elsewhere. Short, smartly prepared seasonal menus might star *carabinero* prawns with fried eggs, *tagarninas* (thistles) with tuna belly, or pork, chickpea and turnip rice.

**La Candela** TAPAS €€
(☎956 22 18 22; www.facebook.com/lacandelatapasbar; Calle Feduchy 3; tapas €4-8, mains €8-12; ⏲1.30-4pm & 8.30-11.30pm; ) Like an arty cafe meets colourful tapas bar, La Candela surprises with its floral-stamped windows, rustic-industrial decor and brilliantly original Andalucian-Asian tapas and mains. From the busy little open kitchen at the back come bold creations with local inspiration – prawn and sea-bream ceviche, honeyed goat's-cheese salad, strawberry *salmorejo* (thick cilled soup) with tuna tartare, fried *boquerones* (anchovies) topped with wasabi mayonnaise.

DON'T MISS

## CÁDIZ CARNAVAL

No other Spanish city celebrates **Carnaval** (⏲Feb) with as much spirit, dedication and humour as Cádiz. Here it becomes a 10-day singing, dancing and drinking fancy-dress street party spanning two alcohol-fuelled weekends. The 300-odd officially recognised *murgas* (costumed group performers) are judged by a panel in the **Gran Teatro Falla** (☎956 22 08 34; www.facebook.com/teatrofalla; Plaza de Falla); tickets are near-impossible to come by.

**★El Faro de Cádiz** TAPAS €€€
(☎956 21 10 68; www.elfarodecadiz.com; Calle San Félix 15; tapas €2.50-4; ⏲1-4pm & 8.30-11.30pm) Ask any *gaditano* for their favourite Cádiz tapas bar and there's a strong chance they'll choose El Faro. Seafood, particularly the *tortillitas de camarones* (shrimp fritters) and superb *boquerones*, is why people come here, though the *rabo de toro* (oxtail stew) and vegetarian-friendly *patatas aliñadas* have their devotees. El Faro's upmarket restaurant (mains €17 to €24) gets mixed reviews.

**Café Royalty** CAFE €€€
(☎956 07 80 65; www.caferoyalty.com; Plaza Candelaria; tapas €4.50-10, mains €23-30; ⏲cafe 9.30am-11pm, restaurant 12.30-4pm & 8pm-midnight; 🗷) Originally opened in 1912 on the centenary of the 1812 constitution, the restored Royalty was once a discussion corner for the intellectuals of the day, including beloved *gaditano* composer Manuel de Falla. The frescoed, mirrored, intricately carved interior is – no exaggeration – breathtaking. It's fantastic for breakfast, tapas, cocktails, cakes and elegant updated-Andalucian meals: *almadraba* red-tuna sashimi, Sanlúcar king prawns, a two-person *chuletón* (steak).

## Drinking & Entertainment

The Plaza de Mina–Plaza San Francisco–Plaza de España triangle is the centre of the old city's late-night bar scene, especially Calle Beato Diego. More bars are scattered around the Barrio del Pópulo, east of the cathedral, and in summer, down along Playa de la Victoria, on and around Calle Muñoz Arenillas.

**Quilla** CAFE
(www.quilla.es; Playa de la Caleta; ⏲11am-midnight Sun-Thu, to 2am Fri & Sat; 📶) A bookish cafe-bar encased in what appears to be the rusty hulk of an old ship overlooking Playa de la Caleta, with coffee, pastries, tapas, wine, art exhibitions, gratis sunsets and lightly modernised Andalucian dishes (burgers, salads, *tostas*, grilled fish; €8 to €13).

**La Clandestina** CAFE
(www.la-clandestina.com; Calle José del Toro 23; ⏲9.30am-2pm & 5.30-9pm Mon-Fri, 10am-2pm Sat; 📶) A cosy, boho bookshop-cafe and cultural space where you can flick through the day's papers over coffee, homemade cakes, fresh orange juice, and breakfast *tostadas* (€2 to €3) with artisan jams and olive oils served on pretty ceramic plates.

**Taberna La Manzanilla** WINE BAR
(www.lamanzanilladecadiz.com; Calle Feduchy 19; ⏲11am-3.30pm & 7-10.30pm Mon-Fri, 11am-3.30pm Sat & Sun; 📶) Family-run since the 1930s, La Manzanilla is a gloriously time-warped sherry tavern bedecked with bull-fighting posters, on a spot once occupied by a pharmacy. The speciality, of course, is *manzanilla* from the giant oak barrel. Keep an eye out for tastings and other events.

**★Peña Flamenca La Perla** FLAMENCO
(☎956 25 91 01; www.laperladecadiz.es; Calle Carlos Ollero; €7) Paint-peeled, sea-splashed La Perla, set romantically next to the crashing Atlantic surf in the Barrio de Santa María, hosts flamenco at 9.30pm most Fridays, more often in spring and summer, for an audience full of aficionados. An unforgettable experience.

## Information

**Centro de Recepción de Turistas** (☎956 24 10 01; www.turismo.cadiz.es; Paseo de Canalejas; ⏲9am-7pm Mon-Fri, to 5pm Sat & Sun Jun-Sep, 8.30am-6.30pm Mon-Fri, 9am-5pm Sat & Sun Oct-May)

**Oficina de Turismo Regional** (☎956 20 31 91; www.andalucia.org; Avenida Ramón de Carranza; ⏲9am-7.15pm Mon-Fri, 10am-2.45pm Sat & Sun)

## Getting There & Around

### BOAT

From Cádiz' **Terminal Marítima Metropolitana** (Muelle Reina Victoria), **Consorcio de Transportes Bahía de Cádiz** (CMTBC; ☎955 03 86 65; www.cmtbc.es) catamarans run to/from El Puerto de Santa María (€2.80, 30 minutes) at least 16 times daily Monday to Friday, and at least eight times daily at weekends.

Urban buses (€1.10) fan out from Plaza de España. Useful routes include 1 and 7 for Playa de la Victoria; bus 7 also goes to Playa de la Caleta.

### BUS

All out-of-town buses leave from Cádiz' **bus station** (Avenida de Astilleros), on the eastern side of the train station (at the southeastern end of the old city). Most are operated by **Comes** (☎956 80 70 59; www.tgcomes.es), **Damas** (☎959 25 69 00; www.damas-sa.es), ALSA or the CMTBC, which serves Jerez airport (p662).

| Destination | Cost (€) | Time | Frequency |
|---|---|---|---|
| Arcos de la Frontera | 6-7.50 | 1-1½hr | 3-8 daily |
| El Puerto de Santa María | 2.80 | 45min | every 30-60min |
| Jerez de la Frontera | 3.90 | 50min | 2-7 daily |
| Málaga | 29 | 4½hr | 4 daily |
| Ronda | 16 | 3¼hr | 1-2 daily |
| Sanlúcar de Barrameda | 5.10 | 1hr | 5-13 daily |
| Seville | 13 | 1¾hr | 9-10 daily |
| Tarifa | 10 | 1¼-1¾hr | 6 daily |
| La Barca de Vejer | 6 | 1-1½hr | 5-6 daily |

**TRAIN**

Frequent trains go to El Puerto de Santa María (€3.40 to €5.25, 35 minutes) and Jerez de la Frontera (€3.90 to €6.25, 45 minutes), as well as Seville (€17 to €24, 1¾ hours, 11 to 15 daily). Three daily high-speed Alvia trains go to Madrid (€47 to €65, 4¼ hours).

# Jerez de la Frontera

POP 191,790

Stand down, all other claimants. Jerez, as most savvy Hispanophiles know, *is* Andalucía. It just doesn't broadcast it in the way that Seville and Granada do. Jerez is the capital of Andalucian horse culture, stop one on the famed Sherry Triangle and – cue protestations from Cádiz, Seville and Granada – the cradle of Spanish flamenco. The *bulería*, Jerez' jokey, tongue-in-cheek antidote to Seville's tragic *soleá,* was first concocted in the legendary Roma *barrios* of Santiago and San Miguel. But Jerez is also a vibrant modern Andalucian city, where fashion brands live in old palaces and stylishly outfitted businesspeople sit down to distinctly contemporary, perhaps Michelin-star cuisine before moving on to bubbly *tabancos* (simple taverns serving sherry).

## Sights & Activities

Jerez (the word even means 'sherry') has around 20 sherry bodegas. Most require bookings for visits, but a few offer tours where you can just turn up. The tourist office (p662) has details.

**★Bodegas Tradición** WINERY

(☎956 16 86 18; www.bodegastradicion.com; Plaza Cordobeses 3; tours €35) An intriguing, evocative bodega, not only for its extra-aged sherries (at least 20, mostly 30 years old) but also because it houses the **Colección Joaquín Rivero**, a private 14th- to 19th-century Spanish art collection that includes important works by Goya, Velázquez, El Greco and Zurbarán. Tours (1½ hours; in English, Spanish or German) require bookings and include a tasting session, and are well worth splashing out on.

**Alcázar** FORTRESS

(☎956 14 99 55; Alameda Vieja; Alcázar €5, incl camera obscura €7; ⊙9.30am-5.30pm Mon-Fri, 9.30am-2.30pm Sat & Sun Jul–mid-Sep, 9.30am-2.30pm daily mid-Sep–Jun) Jerez' muscular yet elegant 11th- or 12th-century fortress is one of Andalucía's best-preserved Almohad-era relics. It's notable for its octagonal tower, typical of Almohad defensive forts, reached through Islamic-style **gardens**, past a 12th-century **mosque-turned-chapel**, the sprawling **Patio de Armas** and the 17th- and 18th-century baroque **Palacio Villavicencio**, which unveils city views through its camera obscura.

**Catedral de San Salvador** CATHEDRAL

(☎956 16 90 59; www.catedraldejerez.es; Plaza de la Encarnación; incl Iglesia de San Miguel adult/child €6/free; ⊙10am-6.30pm Mon, to 8pm Tue-Sat, 1-7pm Sun Apr-Sep, 10am-6.30pm Mon-Sat, 1-6.30pm Sun Oct-Mar) Echoes of Seville colour Jerez' dramatic cathedral, a surprisingly harmonious mix of baroque, neoclassical and Gothic styles. Standout features are its broad flying buttresses and intricately carved stone ceilings. Behind the main altar, a series of rooms and chapels shows off the cathedral's collection of silverware, religious garments and art, including Zurbarán *Virgen niña meditando* (Virgin Mary as a Child, Asleep). Across the square, the bell tower is 15th-century Gothic-Mudéjar on its lower half and 17th century at the top.

**Bodegas González–Byass** WINERY

(Bodegas Tío Pepe; ☎956 35 70 16; www.bodegastiopepe.com; Calle Manuel María González 12; tours from €16) Home to the famous Tío Pepe brand, 1835-founded González–Byass is one of Jerez' biggest sherry houses, just west of the Alcázar. There are several daily tours in Spanish, English and German; check schedules and book online (not essential). Basic

# Jerez de la Frontera

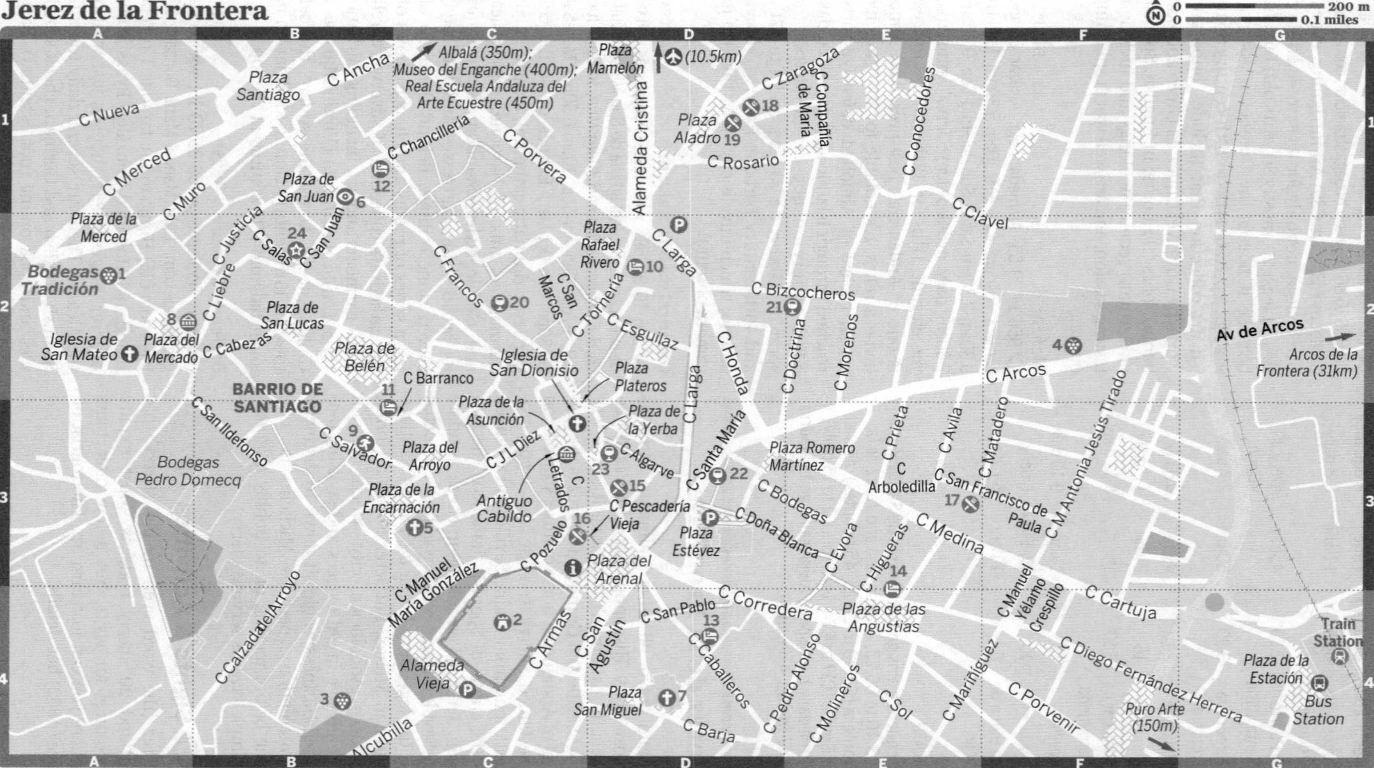

## Jerez de la Frontera



visits include the Gustav Eiffel–designed La Concha bodega, and a sampling of two wines in the glossy designer tasting room; others add tapas and extra sherries. A luxe, on-site González-Byass hotel was in the works at research time.

**Bodegas Lustau** WINERY
(956 34 15 97; www.lustau.es; Calle Arcos 53; tours 11.30am & 1.30pm Mon & Sat, 10am, 11.30am, 1pm & 3pm Tue-Fri) Book ahead for the excellent-value, English- or Spanish-language tours of the handsome, vine-shaded Lustau bodega, founded in 1896. 'Standard' visits (€18) include five wines and a vermouth, while 'complete tastings' (€28) take in seven wines and two vermouths.

**Museo Arqueológico** MUSEUM
(956 14 95 60; Plaza del Mercado; adult/child €5/free; 9am-2.30pm Tue-Sun mid-Jun–mid-Sep, 10am-2pm & 4-7pm Mon-Fri, 9am-2.30pm Sat & Sun mid-Sep–mid-Jun) In the Santiago quarter, Jerez' modern archaeology museum houses fascinating local relics dating from Paleolithic to 20th-century times. Grab a detailed audio guide and look especially for the 7th-century-BCE Greek bronze helmet found in the Río Guadalete, two cylindrical marble Copper Age idols from the 2nd or 3rd century BC, and a fragment of a rare 15th-century Gothic-Mudéjar mural.

**Iglesia de San Miguel** CHURCH
(956 34 33 47; www.catedraldejerez.es; Plaza de San Miguel; incl Catedral de San Salvador adult/child €6/free; 10am-7pm Mon-Sat Apr-Sep, to 6pm Oct-Mar) Built between the 15th and 18th centuries, this richly adorned church blends Gothic, Renaissance and baroque architecture, and was modelled on Seville cathedral (with whom it possibly shares an architect). Its three-tiered, elaborately carved baroque bell tower is topped by a tile-patterned roof, while part of the main hall is graced by intricately sculpted, Portuguese-influenced late-Gothic pillars. Audio guides provide detail.

**Hammam Andalusí** HAMMAM
(956 34 90 66; www.hammamandalusi.com; Calle Salvador 6; baths €29, incl 15/30min massage €39/60; 10am-10pm) The magical Hammam Andalusí evokes Jerez' Moorish past. Incense, essential oils, fresh mint tea and the soothing sound of trickling water welcome you through the door, then you enjoy three turquoise pools (tepid, hot and cold) and, if you like, a massage. Book ahead.

### Festivals & Events

**Feria del Caballo** FAIR
(late Apr-early May) Jerez' week-long horse fair is one of Andalucía's grandest festivals, with music, dance, and equestrian competitions and parades. Bullfighting, which visitors may wish to avoid, also features – but there is growing opposition from animal rights activists.

## Sleeping

**Life Astuto Boutique** HOSTEL €
(956 08 56 54; www.lifeapartments.es; Calle Chancillería 21; dm €12-14, d €40-70; ) Set in a stylishly converted historical building, this great little hostel has crisp, contemporary shared-bathroom dorms (mixed or women-only) for four or six, with personal lockers, lamps, plugs and shelves, as well as private doubles in low-key boutique design. A plunge pool graces the inner courtyard and garden, while a roof terrace unveils views across Jerez' rooftops.

**Nuevo Hotel** HOTEL €
(956 33 16 00; www.nuevohotel.com; Calle Caballeros 23; s €25-32, d €36-43; ) The Nuevo is a sweet 19th-century noble home filled with comfortable, simple, good-value rooms. The star is spectacular room 208, replete with Moorish-style stucco work and blue-and-white tiling creeping up the walls; you'll wake thinking you've taken up residence in Granada's Alhambra. Other rooms are plain, with antique furnishings. Cold breakfast (€5) available.

**La Fonda Barranco** BOUTIQUE HOTEL €€
(956 33 21 41; www.lafondabarranco.com; Calle Barranco 12; d €62-86; ) Dating back to at least 1865, this peaceful family-owned former merchant's house blends historical Moorish-inspired character with contemporary touches. You arrive into a cool patio (a glass of sherry is rustled up!), off which twisting staircases lead to a roof terrace and 10 charming, pristinely kept rooms with open-stone walls, wooden beams, carved doors, brick arches, pastel tones and decorative ceramic bowls.

**YIT Casa Grande** HOTEL €€
(956 34 50 70; www.hotelcasagrandejerez.com; Plaza de las Angustias 3; d €66-115; ) A beautifully restored 1920s mansion hosts 15 smartly classic rooms (marble floors, vintage furniture) over three floors surrounding a light-flooded, palm-dotted patio and a plush library lounge. Local-produce breakfasts are served in the courtyard, or beside the fantastic roof terrace with views across Jerez.

**Casa Palacio María Luisa** LUXURY HOTEL €€€
(956 92 62 63; www.casapalaciomarialuisa.com; Calle Tornería 22; r €250-310, ste €320-600; ) A five-star revamp of a dazzling 19th-century mansion has breathed fresh energy into Jerez' accommodation scene. The 21 luxe rooms are set around a chequered marble patio fragrant with flowers; vertical gardens adorn interior courtyards; and there's a smart restaurant plus a tranquil open-air bar. Each room has its own soothing boutique style, incorporating historical charm alongside bold wallpaper, velvet textures and original artwork.

## Eating & Drinking

Some of Jerez' most authentic eating and drinking spots are its tabancos.

**Bar Juanito** ANDALUCIAN €
(956 33 48 38; www.bar-juanito.com; Calle Pescadería Vieja 8-10; medias raciones €5-10; 12.30-4pm & 8-11pm Mon-Sat, 12.30-4pm Sun) With its outdoor tables, rustic red chairs and check-print tablecloths, Juanito is like a slice of village Andalucía in the heart of the city, rustling up scrumptiously simple tapas since the 1940s. Its *alcachofas* (artichokes) are a past winner of the National Tapa Competition, but there's plenty more, all served with Cádiz wines. Live flamenco often happens on Saturday afternoon.

★ **La Carboná** ANDALUCIAN €€
(956 34 74 75; www.lacarbona.com; Calle San Francisco de Paula 2; mains €15-21; 1.30-4pm & 8-11pm Wed-Mon, closed Jul; ) This cavernous, imaginative restaurant occupies an exquisite old bodega set around a suspended fireplace. Delicately presented market-based specialities include grilled meats, fresh fish, boletus rice jazzed up with razor clams or *almadraba* tuna tartare with egg-yolk-and-*amontillado* (dry sherry) emulsion, plus outstanding local wines. Or go all-in with sherry-pairing menus (€45).

**Albalá** ANDALUCIAN, FUSION €€
(956 34 64 88; www.restaurantealbala.com; cnr Calle Divina Pastora & Avenida Duque de Abrantes; tapas €2-4, mains €9-20; noon-4pm & 8.30pm-midnight; ) Slide into blonde-wood booths amid minimalist decor for *jerezano* chef Israel Ramos' beautifully creative contemporary dishes fuelled by typical Andalucian ingredients. House specials include *rabo de toro* (oxtail) croquettes, fried eggs with truffle, *almadraba* red-tuna tartare with guacamole, and deliciously crispy asparagus tempura dipped in soy aioli. It's 1km north of Plaza del Arenal.

Ramos is also behind highly innovative, Cádiz-rooted Michelin-starred restaurant

**Mantúa** (☎856 65 27 39; www.restaurantemantua.com; Plaza Aladro 7; tasting menus €75-90, incl wines €110-140; ⊙1.30-3.15pm & 8.30-10.30pm Tue-Sat, 1.30-3.15pm Sun) 🌿.

**Albores** ANDALUCIAN **€€**
(☎956 32 02 66; www.restaurantealbores.com; Calle Consistorio 12; tapas €2-5, mains €8-19; ⊙8am-midnight) Pitching itself among age-old city-centre favourites, Albores brings a contemporary edge to local flavours and traditional recipes with its original, seasonally inspired tapas and plates. Chef Julián Olivares' show-stealing seafood includes clams in sherry-vinegar sauce and, in season, *almadraba* tuna specials, while other delectable bites range from goat's-cheese *tosta* to *papas aliñás*. One of Jerez' top breakfast spots.

**LÚ, Cocina y Alma** GASTRONOMY **€€€**
(☎695 408481; www.universolu.com; Calle Zaragoza 2; tasting menus €90-150, incl wine €140-220; ⊙1-3pm & 8.30-10pm Tue-Sat, 1-3pm Sun) 🌿 Hotshot local chef Juan Luis Fernández, who trained at El Puerto's celebrated Aponiente, was awarded Jerez' first Michelin star in 2018 for his astonishing, wildly creative cookery, which reinvents superb Cádiz produce with effortlessly elegant French technique. The few tables overlook an open kitchen, chef's-table style, and there are three experimental, seasonal tasting menus, paired with Spanish and French wines.

## ☆ Entertainment

**Real Escuela Andaluza del Arte Ecuestre** LIVE PERFORMANCE
(☎956 31 80 08; www.realescuela.org; Avenida Duque de Abrantes; training sessions adult/child €11/6.50, shows adult €21-27, child €13-17; ⊙training sessions 10am-2pm Mon-Wed & Fri, shows noon Tue & Thu) Jerez' renowned Royal Andalucian School of Equestrian Art trains horses and riders. On 'thematic visits', you can watch them going through their paces in training sessions and visit the **Museo del Arte Ecuestre** and nearby **Museo del Enganche** (www.realescuela.org; Calle Pizarro; adult/child €4.50/2.50; ⊙10am-2pm Mon-Fri). The big highlight is the official *exhibición* (show), in which the beautiful horses show off their tricks to classical music. Book tickets online; schedules can vary.

Note that some animal rights advocates consider the training techniques for dressage and other similar horse performances to be cruel.

DON'T MISS

### JEREZ' TABANCO REVIVAL

Sprinkled across the city centre, Jerez' famous old *tabancos* are, essentially, simple taverns serving sherry from the barrel. Most date from the early 20th century and, although *tabanco* comes from the fusion of *tabaco* (tobacco) and *estanco* (tobacco shop), the focus is indisputably the local sherry. In danger of dying out just a few years ago, Jerez' *tabancos* have sprung back to life as fashionable modern-day hang-outs, reinvigorated by keen new ownership. Several host regular flamenco (though you're just as likely to catch an impromptu performance) and sherry tastings. The tourist office (p662) has information on the official **Ruta de los Tabancos de Jerez** (www.facebook.com/rutadelostabancosdejerez), though there are plenty of others, too.

**Tabanco Plateros** (☎956 10 44 58; www.facebook.com/tabanco.plateros; Calle Algarve 35; ⊙noon-4pm & 8pm-midnight Mon-Sat, 8pm-midnight Sun) Join the crowds spilling out from this lively *despacho de vinos* for a glass of *fino* alongside ingeniously simple tapas (€2 to €3). Plateros kickstarted the *tabanco* comeback, and sometimes does sherry tastings.

**Tabanco El Pasaje** (☎956 33 33 59; www.tabancoelpasaje.com; Calle Santa María 8; ⊙11am-3.30pm & 7pm-midnight Sun-Fri, 11am-4pm & 8pm-midnight Sat; 📶) Born in 1925, Jerez' oldest *tabanco* serves up its excellent sherry selection and pleasantly uncomplicated tapas (€2.50) with suitably raw twice-daily flamenco sessions (2pm and 9pm or 10pm).

**Tabanco El Guitarrón de San Pedro** (☎649 656918; www.facebook.com/guitarrondesanpedro; Calle Bizcocheros 16; ⊙noon-4pm & 8pm-midnight Mon-Sat) Revitalised by sherry-loving owners (who offer pairings and tastings), El Guitarrón hosts regular flamenco dancing and singing, plus simple tapas (€2 to €4).

### JEREZ' FLAMENCO SCENE

Jerez' moniker as the 'cradle of flamenco' is regularly challenged by aficionados in Cádiz, Seville and Granada, but the claim has merit. This comparatively untouristed city harbours two Roma quarters, Santiago and San Miguel, which have produced numerous renowned artists, including Roma singers Manuel Torre and Antonio Chacón. Like its rival cities, Jerez has its own flamenco *palo* (musical form), the intensely popular *bulería*, a fast, rythmic musical style with the same *compás* (accented beat) as Seville's *soleá*.

At the architecturally intriguing **Centro Andaluz de Flamenco** (956 90 21 34; www.centroandaluzdeflamenco.es; Plaza de San Juan 1; 9am-2pm Mon-Fri) FREE, you can pick up information on performances, *peñas* and flamenco dance, song and guitar lessons. In the Santiago quarter, you'll find dozens of *peñas* known for their accessibility and intimacy; entry is normally free if you buy a drink. The *peña* scene is particularly lively during the flamenco-focused **Festival de Jerez** (www.facebook.com/FestivalDeJerez; late Feb-early Mar). Jerez' revitalised *tabancos* (taverns that serve sherry from the barrel) are also fantastic for flamenco.

**Centro Cultural Flamenco Don Antonio Chacón** (956 34 74 72; www.facebook.com/DAChaconFlamencoJerez; Calle Salas 2) One of the best *peñas* in town (and hence Andalucía), the Chacón often sees top-notch flamenco performers grace its stage.

**Puro Arte** (647 743832; www.puroarteflamencojerez.com; Calle Madre de Dios 10; €30, incl tapas/dinner €45/49) Jerez' main *tablao* (choreographed flamenco show) stages popular local-artist performances two or three times daily.

**Damajuana** (www.facebook.com/damajuanajerez; Calle Francos 18; 8pm-3.30am Tue-Thu, 4pm-3.30am Fri-Sun) One of two historic bars on Calle Francos, with live music, tapas (€2 to €5.50) and a fun *movida flamenca* (flamenco scene) in a 16th-century mansion.

## Information

**Oficina de Turismo** (956 33 88 74; www.turismojerez.com; Plaza del Arenal; 8.30am-2pm & 4.30-6pm Mon-Fri, 8.30am-2.30pm Sat & Sun)

## Getting There & Away

### AIR

The **Aeropuerto de Jerez** (956 15 00 00; www.aena.es; Carretera A4), the only one serving Cádiz province, is 10km northeast of town.

### BUS

The **bus station** (956 14 99 90; Plaza de la Estación) is 1.3km southeast of the centre, served by CMTBC, Comes, Damas and **Monbus** (982 29 29 00; www.monbus.es).

| Destination | Cost (€) | Time | Frequency |
|---|---|---|---|
| Arcos de la Frontera | 3.10 | 40min | 10-20 daily |
| Cádiz | 3.90 | 45min | 2-8 daily |
| El Puerto de Santa María | 1.70 | 15-20min | 2-7 daily |
| Ronda | 13 | 2¾hr | 1-2 daily |
| Sanlúcar de Barrameda | 2 | 40min | 7-13 daily |
| Seville | 9 | 1¼hr | 3-4 daily |

### TRAIN

Jerez' train station is beside the bus station.

| Destination | Cost (€) | Time | Frequency |
|---|---|---|---|
| Cádiz | 3-15 | 35-45min | at least 20 daily |
| Córdoba | 25-35 | 2-3hr | 7-14 daily |
| El Puerto de Santa María | 2.80-12 | 8min | at least 20 daily |
| Seville | 12-20 | 1¼hr | 11-15 daily |

## Getting Around

### TO/FROM THE AIRPORT

Eight to 10 daily trains run between the airport and Jerez (€1.10 to €2.55, seven to 11 minutes), El Puerto de Santa María (€1.70 to €3.80, 15 minutes) and Cádiz (€3.90 to €6.25, 45 minutes). Taxis to/from the airport cost €15.

# El Puerto de Santa María

POP 43,100

When you're surrounded by such cultural luminaries as Cádiz, Jerez de la Frontera and Seville, it's easy to overlook the small print; such is the fate of El Puerto de Santa María, despite its collection of well-known icons, just across the bay from Cádiz. With its abundance of sandy blonde beaches, half a dozen sherry wineries (including renowned Osborne), seafood restaurants and a smattering of architectural heirlooms, El Puerto can seem like southern Andalucía in microcosm. It's an easy day trip from Cádiz or Jerez.

## Sights

**★Bodegas Osborne** WINERY

(☎956 86 91 00; www.osborne.es; Calle los Moros 7; tours from €15, tastings €10-55) Creator of the legendary black-bull logo still exhibited on life-size billboards all over Spain (now without the name), Osborne is El Puerto's best-known sherry winery. Set up by an Englishman, Thomas Osborne Mann, in 1772, it remains one of Spain's oldest companies run continuously by the same family.

The bodega offers tours with tastings at 10am (English), 11am (German) and noon (Spanish; plus 7.30pm in summer); book ahead. Some visits include sampling Huelva's much-lauded Cinco Jotas *jamón*.

On-site **Toro Tapas** (☎956 90 50 20; www.torotapaselpuerto.com; tapas €4-9, raciones & mains €7-18; ⏲8.30am-4.30pm & 8.30-11.30pm) is excellent.

**Bodegas Gutiérrez Colosía** WINERY

(☎607 450066, 956 85 28 52; www.gutierrezcolosia.com; Avenida de la Bajamar 40; tours €10) An intimate, family-run, 1838-founded sherry bodega, right beside the catamaran dock. Tours (1½ hours) end with a six-wine tasting, which can include tapas and flamenco on request, and run at 11.15am in English and 12.30pm in Spanish Monday to Friday, and at 1pm in both languages on Saturday; evening tours may happen July to September.

The Gutiérrez Colosía family also has a great nearby rustic-chic sherry and tapas bar, **Bespoke** (☎956 10 64 12; www.bespokepuerto.com; Avenida de la Bajamar 40; raciones €4-12; ⏲12.30-4pm & 8.30pm-late; ).

**Castillo de San Marcos** CASTLE

(☎627 569335; www.caballero.es; Plaza Alfonso X El Sabio; adult/child €10/5; ⏲tours 10am, 11.30am & 1pm daily, plus 6pm & 7.30pm Mon-Sat, reduced hours Oct-May) Heavily restored in the 20th century and now owned by Bodegas Caballero, El Puerto's castle was constructed over an Islamic mosque by Alfonso X El Sabio after he took the town in 1260. The original mosque inside, now converted into a church, is the highlight. Visits, in English or Spanish, last 1½ hours and end with a five-sherry tasting; book ahead.

## Sleeping

**El Baobab Hostel** HOSTEL €

(☎956 85 89 64; www.baobabhostel.com; Calle Pagador 37; per person €15-40; ⏲Apr-Oct; ) In a converted 18th-century building near the bullring, this sunny 10-room hostel is El Puerto's budget pick, with a homey, friendly feel, simple interiors, and a communal kitchen and courtyard. Stripped-back private rooms sleep two to eight.

**Palacio San Bartolomé** BOUTIQUE HOTEL €€€

(☎956 85 09 46; www.palaciosanbartolome.com; Calle San Bartolomé 21; r €68-170, ste €198-250; ) Fancy a room with its own plunge pool, sauna, hot tub and deckchairs? It's all yours with the Spa Suite at the deftly designed, welcoming San Bartolomé, set in a sensitively converted 18th-century palace. Rambling off a light-flooded patio, the 10 other rooms are equally enticing: four-poster beds, oversized showers, tile-carpeted floors, bright styling and contemporary elegance.

## Eating & Drinking

El Puerto is famous for its outstanding seafood and tapas bars. Look along central Calles Luna and Misericordia, Calle Ribera del Marisco to the north, Avenidas de la Bajamar and Aramburu de Mora to the south, and Calle La Placilla near Plaza de España.

**★Aponiente** SEAFOOD €€€

(☎956 85 18 70; www.aponiente.com; Molino de Mareas El Caño, Calle Francisco Cossi Ochoa; 21-course menu €215, incl wine €315; ⏲1-4.30pm & 8-11.30pm Tue-Sat mid-Mar–Jun & Sep-early Dec, 1-4.30pm & 8-11.30pm Mon-Sat Jul & Aug) Audacious is the word for the bold experimentation of leading Spanish chef Angel León, whose seafood-biased *nueva cocina* has won a cavalcade of awards, transforming Aponiente into Andalucía's first triple-Michelin-starred restaurant. Occupying a design-led 19th-century tide mill, Aponiente splits opinion in traditional El Puerto: some snort at its pretension, others salivate at the thought of its uber-imaginative 21-course tasting menus.

For a tapas-sized taster, dine at León's creative sister venture, **La Taberna del Chef del Mar** (☎956 11 20 93; www.latabernadelchefdelmar.com; Calle Puerto Escondido 6; tapas

& raciones €6-22; ⏲1-4pm & 8.30-11.30pm Mon-Sat, 1-4pm Sun Apr-Oct) 🍃.

**El Faro del Puerto** ANDALUCIAN €€€

(📞956 87 09 52; www.elfarodelpuerto.com; Avenida de Fuentebravía, Km 0.5; tapas €4-15, mains €18-27; ⏲1.30-4.30pm & 8.30-11pm Mon-Sat, 1.30-4.30pm Sun; 📝) Upmarket El Faro gets busy for its traditional-with-a-hint-of-innovation take on local seafood, excellent Spanish wine list, and classically smart, multiroom setting inside an old *casa señorial* (manor house). Menus change with the seasons; the *almadraba* tuna tartare is a highlight. The bar/tapas menu has some exciting vegetarian and gluten-free choices. It's at the northwestern end of Calle Valdés.

**Bodega Obregón** BAR

(📞956 85 63 29; Calle Zarza 51; ⏲9am-2pm & 6-9pm Mon-Fri, 9am-late Sat, 10am-2pm Sun) At this wood-beamed, family-run, spit-and-sawdust-style bar, the house sweet stuff is siphoned from woody barrels, and the home-cooked Saturday-lunch *guisos* (stews) are a firm local favourite.

## Information

**Oficina de Turismo** (📞956 48 37 15; www.turismoelpuerto.com; Plaza de Alfonso X El Sabio 9; ⏲10am-8pm Jul & Aug, 10am-2pm & 5-7pm Mon-Sat, 10am-4pm Sun May, Jun, Sep & Oct, reduced hours Nov-Mar)

## Getting There & Away

### BOAT

**Catamarans** (www.cmtbc.es; ⏲7.10am-7.50pm Mon-Fri, 9.30am-9.15pm Sat, 9.30am-6.30pm Sun) run to/from Cádiz (€2.80, 30 minutes) at least 16 times daily Monday to Friday, and at least eight times daily on weekends.

### BUS

El Puerto has two bus stops. CMTBC buses to Cádiz (€2.80, 45 minutes, every 30 to 60 minutes), Jerez de la Frontera (€1.70, 20 minutes, two to eight daily) and Sanlúcar de Barrameda (€2.05, 30 minutes, six to 14 daily) go from the **bus stop** (Plaza Elías Ahuja) outside the bullring. Comes buses to Seville (€11, 1½ to two hours, one to two daily) go from outside the train station.

### TRAIN

From the train station at the northeastern end of town, frequent trains go to/from Jerez de la Frontera (€1.80, 10 minutes), Cádiz (€3.40 to €5.25, 35 minutes) and Seville (€14, 1¼ hours).

# Sanlúcar de Barrameda

POP 46,880

Sanlúcar is one of those lesser-known Andalucian towns that delight and enamour. Firstly, there's the gastronomy: Sanlúcar cooks up some of the region's best seafood on the hallowed waterside strip Bajo de Guía. Secondly, Sanlúcar's unique Atlantic-facing location at the northern tip of the esteemed Sherry Triangle enables its earthy bodegas, nestled in the somnolent, monument-strewn old town, to produce the much-admired one-of-a-kind *manzanilla*. Thirdly, sitting at the mouth of the Río Guadalquivir estuary, Sanlúcar provides a quieter, less touristed entry point into the ethereal Parque Nacional de Doñana than the more popular western access points in Huelva province.

## Sights

**★Bodegas Hidalgo–La Gitana** WINERY

(📞669 663008; www.lagitana.es; Calle Banda de la Playa; tours €14; ⏲tours 1pm Mon-Sat, in English 11am Mon-Sat) Now run by the eighth generation, family-owned 1792-founded Bodegas Hidalgo still produces the famed La Gitana *manzanillas* that made its name, along with VORS sherries such as a small-scale *amontillado*. Detailed two-hour introductory tours are outstanding, while specialised visits include sunset tastings among the vines (€40) and summer night tours (€35).

**Bodegas Barbadillo** WINERY

(📞956 38 55 21; www.barbadillo.com; Calle Sevilla 6; tours €10; ⏲tours noon & 1pm Tue-Sun, in English 11am Tue-Sun) With its Barrio Alto 1821-founded bodega, Barbadillo was the first family to bottle Sanlúcar's famous *manzanilla* and also produces one of Spain's most popular *vinos*. Guided one-hour tours end with a four-wine tasting. This evocative 19th-century building also houses the **Museo de la Manzanilla** (📞956 38 55 21; http://barbadillo.com; Calle Sevilla 6; ⏲10am-3pm) FREE.

**Palacio de los Guzmán** PALACE

(📞956 36 01 61; www.fcmedinasidonia.com; Plaza Condes de Niebla 1; tours €5; ⏲tours noon Thu, 11.30am & noon Sun) Just off the old town's Calle Caballeros, this rambling palace was the home of the Duques de Medina Sidonia, the aristocratic family that once owned more of Spain than anyone else. The mostly 17th-century house, of 12th-century origin, bursts with antiques, and paintings by Goya,

Zurbarán and other Spanish greats. Stop for coffee and cakes in its old-world **cafe** (☎956 36 01 61; www.fcmedinasidonia.com; Plaza Condes de Niebla 1; ⏲9am-9pm), with tables amid palm- and hibiscus-sprinkled gardens.

**Iglesia de Nuestra Señora de la O** CHURCH
(Plaza de la Paz; €4; ⏲10.30am-2pm & 4.30-6.30pm) Fronting Calle Caballeros, this medieval church stands out among Sanlúcar's many others for its elaborate 1360s Gothic-Mudéjar portal and its rich interior embellishment, particularly the Mudéjar *artesonado* (ceiling of interlaced beams), one of the region's best preserved. The bell tower was built reusing a tower from the Moorish *alcázar* (fortress) that once stood here.

## Tours

Trips into the Parque Nacional de Doñana (p644) are run by the licensed **Visitas Doñana** (☎956 36 38 13; www.visitasdonana.com; Centro de Visitantes Fábrica de Hielo, Bajo de Guía; ⏲9am-8pm Apr-Sep, to 7pm Feb-Mar & Oct–mid-Dec, to 6pm mid-Dec–Jan). The best option is a 2½-hour boat/jeep combination (€35), which goes 30km through the park's dunes, marshlands and pine forests in 21-person 4WD vehicles, operated in conjunction with the Cooperativa Marismas del Rocío (p645), based in El Rocío, Huelva province; there are four trips a day. Book online or through the Centro de Visitantes Fábrica de Hielo, as far ahead as possible.

**Viajes Doñana** (☎956 36 25 40; www.viajesdonana.es; Calle San Juan 20; ⏲9am-2pm & 5-8.30pm Mon-Fri, 10.30am-2pm Sat) agency books 3½-hour tours (€40 per person) with the Cooperativa Marismas del Rocío in 21- or 29-person 4WDs, going 70km into the park, and private on-demand jeep tours for up to six people (€270 per jeep).

**Sanlúcar Smile** WALKING
(☎669 663008; www.sanlucarsmile.com) A knowledgeable, engaging *sanluqueño* duo runs excellent three-hour walking tours of Sanlúcar (adult/child €25/5), typically including a *manzanilla* stop, as well as sherry bodega visits, tapas-and-wine tours, kayaking trips on the Guadalquivir, adventures into Doñana, and more.

## Festivals & Events

**Romería del Rocío** RELIGIOUS
(⏲7th weekend after Easter) Many pilgrims and covered wagons set out from Sanlúcar bound for El Rocío in Huelva province on Spain's largest religious pilgrimage, the Romería del Rocío (p647).

**Feria de la Manzanilla** WINE
(⏲late May/early Jun) A big *manzanilla*-fuelled fair kicks off Sanlúcar's summer.

## Sleeping

★**La Alcoba del Agua** BOUTIQUE HOTEL €€
(☎956 38 31 09; www.laalcobadelagua.com; Calle Alcoba 26; s €50-130, d €59-159; P❄📶🏊) The laid-back, highly original, skillfully put together 14-room Alcoba feels like something architect Frank Lloyd Wright might have conceived. Rooms styled with vintage pieces, rain showers and feature walls rise around a statement courtyard complete with loungers, hammock and lap pool. It's wonderfully homey, functional and central (just off Calle Ancha). Breakfast (€7) is a good buffet.

★**La Casa** BOUTIQUE HOTEL €€
(☎617 575913; www.lacasasanlucar.com; Calle Ancha 84; d €50-85, q €100-120; ❄📶) A friendly team manages this gorgeously fresh, outstanding-value boutique guesthouse. Custom-designed in blues, pinks and turquoises, the eight rooms are inspired by Doñana national park, blending traditional charm (19th-century shutters, marble floors) with contemporary style (see-through showers, geometric lamps, rectangular sinks), and have thoughtful touches including coffee kits.

## Eating

Strung out along **Bajo de Guía**, 1km northeast of the centre, is one of southern Spain's most famous eating strips, once a fishing village and now a haven of high-quality seafood restaurants that revel in their simplicity. Plaza del Cabildo is also a culinary hot spot.

★**Casa Balbino** TAPAS €
(☎956 36 05 13; www.casabalbino.es; Plaza del Cabildo 14; tapas €2-3; ⏲noon-5pm & 8pm-midnight) No matter when you arrive, Casa Balbino is always overflowing with people drawn in by its unbeatable seafood tapas. You'll have to elbow your way through and shout your order to a waiter. The options are endless, but the *tortillitas de camarones* (shrimp fritters), fried-egg-topped *tagarninas* (thistles) and *langostinos a la plancha* (grilled king prawns) are the stuff of Andalucian dreams.

★ **Casa Bigote** SEAFOOD €€
(☎956 36 26 96; www.restaurantecasabigote.com; Bajo de Guía 10; mains €12-20; ⏰1.30-4pm & 8pm-midnight Mon-Sat, closed Nov) A touch more elegant than its neighbours, long-established Casa Bigote is seafood-tastic Bajo de Guía's most renowned restaurant. House specials include *almadraba* tuna tataki with *salmorejo* sauce, cod in sour-citrus sauce and grilled squid with wild-mushroom rice, or fish of the day baked, grilled or salted. Waiters flit across to permanently packed **Barra Bigote** (tapas €5 to €18).

**El Espejo** FUSION €€
(☎651 141650; www.elespejo-sanlucar.es; Calle Caballeros 11; mains €12-18, tasting menus €35-42; ⏰12.30-3.45pm & 8.30-11.30pm Wed-Sun Apr-Jun & Sep-Dec, 12.30-3.45pm & 8.30-11.30pm Thu-Sun, 8.30-11.30pm Mon-Wed Jul & Aug, reduced hours Jan-Mar) Flavours from Cádiz collide with international flair in imaginative, market-fuelled concoctions at this romantic patio restaurant up in the old town. Tables huddled between palms and geranium pots set the tone for elegantly prepped dishes such as delicate Sanlúcar-grown vegetables, *almadraba* red-tuna tartare, or rice with boletus, truffle and *payoyo* cheese.

## Information

**Centro de Visitantes Fábrica de Hielo** (☎956 38 65 77; www.juntadeandalucia.es; Bajo de Guía; ⏰9am-8pm Apr-Sep, to 7pm Feb-Mar & Oct–mid-Dec, to 6pm mid-Dec–Jan)

**Oficina de Información Turística** (☎956 36 61 10; www.sanlucarturismo.com; Avenida Calzada Duquesa Isabel; ⏰10am-2pm & 5-7pm Mon-Sat, 10am-2pm Sun)

## Getting There & Away

From Sanlúcar's **bus station** (Avenida de la Estación), Damas goes to/from El Puerto de Santa María (€2.15, 30 to 45 minutes, six to 14 daily), Cádiz (€5.10, one hour, five to 13 daily) and Seville (€8.77, 1¼ to two hours, 10 to 12 daily). Monbus has seven to 13 daily buses to/from Jerez (€2, 40 minutes).

# Arcos de la Frontera

POP 21,980

Everything you've ever dreamed a *pueblo blanco* (white town) could be miraculously materialises in Arcos de la Frontera (33km east of Jerez): a thrilling strategic clifftop location, a volatile frontier history, a low-key flamenco scene and a soporific old town full of mystery, with whitewashed arches soaring above slender, twisting alleys, grand old mansions and Roman-era pillars.

For a brief period during the 11th century, Arcos was an independent Berber-ruled *taifa* (small kingdom). In 1255 it was claimed by Christian king Alfonso X El Sabio for Seville and it remained literally *de la frontera* (on the frontier) until the fall of Granada in 1492.

## Sights

Highly rated, multilingual **Infotur Arcos** (☎654 921792; www.visitasguiadasarcos.es; tours per person €5) runs guided tours.

**Plaza del Cabildo** SQUARE
Lined with fine ancient buildings, Plaza del Cabildo is the heart of Arcos' old town, its vertiginous **mirador** affording exquisite panoramas over the Río Guadalete. The Moorish-origin **Castillo de los Duques**, rebuilt in the 14th and 15th centuries, is closed to the public, but its outer walls frame classic Arcos views. On the square's eastern side, the Parador de Arcos de la Frontera is a reconstruction of a grand 16th-century magistrate's house; pop in for a drink.

**Basílica Menor de Santa María de la Asunción** BASILICA
(Plaza del Cabildo; €2; ⏰10am-12.45pm & 4-6.30pm Mon-Fri, 10am-1.30pm Sat Mar–mid-Dec) This Gothic-baroque creation is one of Andalucía's more beautiful, intriguing churches, built over several centuries on the site of a mosque. Check out the ornate gold-leaf altarpiece (a miniature of that in Seville's cathedral) carved between 1580 and 1608, the striking painting of San Cristóbal (St Christopher), the restored 14th-century Gothic-Mudéjar mural, the woodcarved 18th-century choir and the Isabelline ceiling tracery. The original bell tower was toppled by the 1755 Lisbon earthquake; its neoclassical replacement remains incomplete.

**Iglesia de San Pedro** CHURCH
(Calle San Pedro 4; €2; ⏰10am-12.45pm & 4-6.45pm Mon-Fri, 10am-1.30pm Sat) Containing a 16th-century main altarpiece said to be the oldest in Cádiz province, this Gothic-baroque confection contains one of Andalucía's most magnificent small-church interiors, behind an 18th-century facade, and may have been constructed atop an Almohad-era fortress.

## Festivals & Events

**Semana Santa** RELIGIOUS
(Mar/Apr) Dramatic Semana Santa processions see hooded penitents inching through Arcos' narrow streets.

## Sleeping

★ **La Casa Grande** HERITAGE HOTEL €€
(956 70 39 30; www.lacasagrande.net; Calle Maldonado 10; r €74-105, ste €110-125; closed 6-31 Jan; ) This gorgeous, rambling, cliffside mansion dating to 1729 once belonged to the great flamenco dancer Antonio Ruiz Soler, and still feels more arty home than hotel, with original tiling and arches. The seven rooms are individually styled with modern-rustic design and most have divine valley views. Great breakfasts (€10), a well-stocked library, a rooftop terrace, and on-demand massage and yoga complete a tempting package.

★ **Cortijo Bablou** AGROTURISMO €€
(691 016576, 620 759698; www.cortijobablou.com; Carretera Arcos-Algar, Km 4; r/yurt/caravan incl breakfast €115/85/135; Apr–mid-Oct; ) In flower-filled, lavender-scented grounds, 6km southeast of Arcos, French-owned adults-only Bablou comprises a creatively converted, four-room 19th-century farmhouse done with boho-chic style and decorative pieces collected from Morocco, as well as three glamping yurts (with bathroom) and a Romanian caravan. Breakfasts are a homemade treat, hammocks sway under the trees, the pool overlooks rolling countryside, and open-air massages are arranged.

**Casa Campana** GUESTHOUSE €€
(600 284928; www.casacampana.com; Calle Núñez de Prado 4; d €70-95, apt €95-130; ) One of several charming guesthouses in old Arcos, Casa Campana has two cosy doubles, a four-person room and a five-person apartment, all filled with character, in a house dating back at least 600 years. The patio is dotted with loungers and flowers, and the rooftop terrace is flooded with views. It's expertly run by knowledgeable owners who supply excellent walking-tour leaflets.

**Parador de Arcos de la Frontera** HERITAGE HOTEL €€
(956 70 05 00; www.parador.es; Plaza del Cabildo; r €120-150; ) A rebuilt 16th-century magistrate's residence that combines classic *parador* luxury with a splendid setting and the best views in town. Eight of the 24 traditional-style rooms have balconies opening onto sweeping clifftop panoramas; most others look out on Plaza del Cabildo. The elegant **cafe-restaurant** (mains €12-21; 8-11am, 1-4pm & 8-10.30pm; ), with its sunny terrace, offers a smart menu rooted in local specialities.

## Eating

★ **Taberna Jóvenes Flamencos** TAPAS €
(657 133552; www.facebook.com/pg/taberna.jovenesflamencos; Calle Deán Espinosa 11; tapas €2-4; noon-midnight Thu-Tue; ) Along with oh-so-Andalucía flamenco/bullfighting decor, tiled floors and hand-painted tables, cheerful and popular Jóvenes Flamencos has an enticing menu of meat, seafood and vegetarian tapas and *raciones,* including chunky tortilla, goat's cheese drizzled with local honey and soul-warming onion soup topped with *payoyo* cheese. All ingredients and wines are from Cádiz province; service is impeccable; and music and dance break out regularly.

The team also runs nearby **Aljibe** (622 83 65 27; Calle Cuesta de Belén; mains €10-19; 12.30-4pm & 7.30-11.30pm Wed-Mon; ), where Andalucian produce is laced with the influences of Moorish cuisine.

**El Sombrero de Tres Picos** SPANISH €€
(956 70 03 18; Avenida El Sombrero de Tres Picos 3; tapas €2.50-4, mains €8-14; noon-late Tue-Sun; ) Perched by the lake, 3.5km northeast of Arcos, this well-known restaurant has been revitalised by keen new owners, plating up traditional meats, stews and tapas prepared with creative flair and international influences, as well as classic Valencia-style paellas. Grab a table on the waterside terrace or in the wood-beamed dining room for garlicky wild-mushroom tempura, grilled octopus and *retinto* entrêcote.

## Information

**Oficina de Turismo** (956 70 22 64; www.turismoarcos.com; Calle Cuesta de Belén 5; 9.30am-2pm & 3-7.30pm Mon-Sat, 10am-2pm Sun)

## Getting There & Away

Buses from Arcos' **bus station** (Calle Los Alcaldes) are operated by Comes, Damas and/or the Consorcio de Transportes Bahía de Cádiz (p656).

| Destination | Cost (€) | Time | Frequency |
|---|---|---|---|
| Cádiz | 5.73-7.30 | 1hr | up to 11 daily |
| Jerez de la Frontera | 2.05-3.10 | 30-40min | at least 20 daily |
| Ronda | 10 | 2hr | 2 daily Mon-Fri, daily Sat & Sun |
| Seville | 8.90 | 2hr | 2 daily |

## Parque Natural Sierra de Grazalema & Around

The rugged, pillar-like peaks of the Parque Natural Sierra de Grazalema rise abruptly from the plains northeast of Cádiz, revealing sheer gorges, rare firs, wild orchids and the province's highest summits, against a beautifully green backdrop at altitudes of 260m to 1648m. This is the wettest part of Spain – stand aside, Galicia and Cantabria, Grazalema village logs an average 2200mm annually. It's gorgeous walking country (best months: May, June, September and October), and, for the more intrepid, adventure activities abound. The 534-sq-km park, named Spain's first Unesco Biosphere Reserve in 1977, extends into northwestern Málaga province.

### Activities

Hiking (p670), caving, canyoning, kayaking, rock climbing, cycling, birdwatching, horse riding, paragliding, vie ferrate – this beautiful protected area crams it all in. For the more technical stuff, go with a guide; Grazalema's **Horizon** (956 13 23 63, 655 934565; www.horizonaventura.com; Calle Las Piedras 1; 10am-2pm & 5-8pm, reduced hours Oct-Apr) is a respected adventure-activity outfit. Horse riding (hour/day €30/120) can be arranged through Tambor del Llano.

### Grazalema

POP 1550 / ELEV 825M

Few white towns are as generically perfect as Grazalema, with its spotless whitewashed houses of rust-tiled roofs sprinkled on the steep, rocky slopes of its eponymous mountain range. Hikes fan out in all directions, making Grazalema the most popular base for adventures into the Parque Natural Sierra de Grazalema. The village is also an age-old producer of blankets, honey, stews and cheese.

**La Mejorana** GUESTHOUSE €
(956 13 25 27; www.lamejorana.net; Calle Santa Clara 6; d incl breakfast €62; ) An exceptionally welcoming house towards the upper end of Grazalema, La Mejorana has nine comfy rooms in colourful, updated rustic style. Some have private lounges and sky-blue Moroccan-style arches; others balconies, terraces, huge mirrors or wrought-iron bedsteads. A lounge, library and breakfast terrace, with gorgeous village views, overlook the leafy hammock-strung garden and twinkling pool.

★**Tambor del Llano** HOTEL €€
(674 484885; www.tambordelllano.es; Cañada Grande–Los Alamillos; r incl breakfast €87-111; P) Named for a Lorca poem, this wonderful rural hideaway hosts 10 cosily contemporary rooms in a thoughtfully converted stable on a 32-hectare, middle-of-nowhere oak-forest estate 6km southeast of Grazalema. Sample organic homegrown produce and olive-oil power meals, and the team runs yoga, Spanish-language and creative retreats, plus horse-riding excursions (including multi-night trips). A pool was on the way at research time.

**La Maroma** TAPAS €€
(956 13 22 79; www.facebook.com/gastrobarlamaroma; Calle Santa Clara; tapas €2-6, mains €6-16; noon-5pm & 7.30-11pm Tue-Sun; ) The cooking is more fun and inventive than the rustic check-cloth, beamed-ceiling, bull-festival-inspired decor suggests at this cosy gastrobar, run by a young family team. Creative local-inspired tapas and *raciones* throw mountain ingredients into tasty bites like mushrooms in honey-and-thyme sauce, wafer-thin chips, *huevos rotos* (fried eggs with potatoes), or *payoyo*-cheese salad with Grazalema-honey dressing. There's a dedicated vegan/vegetarian menu.

**Oficina de Turismo** (956 13 20 52; www.grazalema.es; Plaza de los Asomaderos; 9am-3pm Tue-Sun Jun-Sep, 10am-2pm & 3-5.30pm Tue-Sun Oct-May) Excellent Parque Natural Sierra de Grazalema walking information, plus last-minute hiking permits.

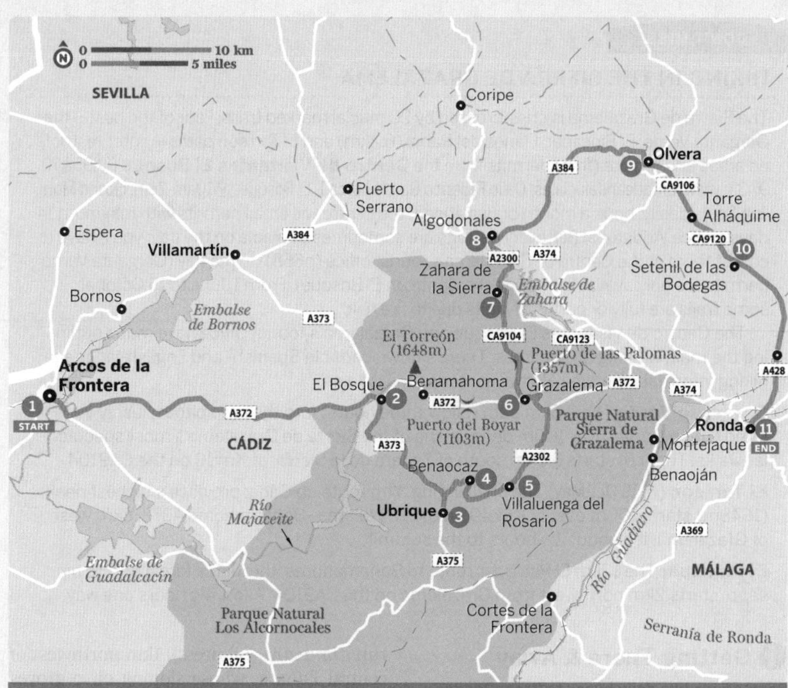


# Driving Tour White Towns

**START** ARCOS DE LA FRONTERA
**END** RONDA
**LENGTH** 147KM; TWO DAYS

Rev up in dramatic 1 **Arcos de la Frontera** (p666), a Roman-turned-Moorish-turned-Christian citadel perched atop a sheer-sided sandstone ridge. Head 31km east along the A372 to 2 **El Bosque**, the western gateway to Cádiz province's Parque Natural Sierra de Grazalema. The A373 takes you 13km south round to leather-making 3 **Ubrique**, close to the borders of the Grazalema and Alcornocales natural parks. Mountains rise quickly as you drive 7km up the A2302 to tiny 4 **Benaocaz**, where several Grazalema park hikes start/finish, then another 7km on to equally diminutive 5 **Villaluenga del Rosario** with its artisanal-cheese museum. Taking the A372 west brings you to 6 **Grazalema** (p668), a red-roofed park-activity nexus also famous for its blanket making and honey. Count the switchbacks on the steep CA9104 as you climb to 1357m Puerto de las Palomas and its lookout. Another 11km north is quintessential white town 7 **Zahara de la Sierra** (p670), with its huddle of houses spread around the skirts of a castle-topped crag; nearby is the famous Garganta Verde hiking trail. The A2300 threads 10km north to 8 **Algodonales**, a white town on the edge of the natural park known for its guitar-making workshop and hang-gliding/paragliding obsession. Take the A384 19km northeast from here past the Peñón de Zaframagón (an important refuge for griffon vultures) to reach 9 **Olvera** (p671), visible for miles around thanks to its Moorish castle but also known for its olive oil and *vía verde* cycling/hiking path. Following the CA9106 southeast, you'll pass the little-known white town of Torre Alháquime. From here, the CA9120 winds 11km southeast towards the border with Málaga province and **Setenil de las Bodegas** (p672), a recently revitalised village instantly recognisable for its cave-houses. From Setenil, head 17km south and wrap up in beautiful gorge-top **Ronda** (p744) in Málaga province.

DON'T MISS

### HIKING IN THE SIERRA DE GRAZALEMA

The Sierra de Grazalema is criss-crossed by 20 official marked trails. Four of the best – the Garganta Verde, El Pinsapar, Llanos del Rabel (6.2km) and El Torreón paths – enter restricted areas and require (free) permits from the **Centro de Visitantes El Bosque** (956 70 97 33; www.juntadeandalucia.es; Calle Federico García Lorca 1, El Bosque; 10am-2pm, closed Mon Jun-Sep). Ideally, book a month or two ahead; the centre will email permits with minimum 14 days' notice. Additional (leftover) permits are sometimes available on the day; you'll have to collect them at the Centro or Grazalema's tourist office (p668) on the day (Garganta Verde permits are only available through the Centro in El Bosque). From 1 June to 15 October, some trails are fully or partly off limits due to fire risk.

The Centro de Visitantes El Bosque and Grazalema's tourist office have maps outlining the main walking possibilities. There's downloadable Spanish- and English-language hiking information online at www.juntadeandalucia.es.

**Garganta Verde** The 2.5km path (allow three hours) into the precipitous, lushly vegetated Green Gorge, over 100m deep, is one of the Sierra de Grazalema's most spectacular walks. The trail starts 3.5km south of Zahara de la Sierra, at Km 10 on the CA9104.

**El Torreón** (16 Oct-May) The challenging 3km route up Cádiz province's highest peak (1648m) starts 100m east of Km 40 on the Grazalema–Benamahoma A372, 8km west of Grazalema. It's about 2½ hours to the summit.

**El Pinsapar** The 12km El Pinsapar route to Benamahoma, through a forest of rare *pinsapo*, starts 2km northwest from Grazalema on the CA9104. Allow 4½ hours one way.

## Getting There & Away

Damas runs two daily buses to/from Ronda (€3, 1½ hours); two to three daily to/from Ubrique (€2.32, 40 to 60 minutes), two of them via Benaocaz (€1.61, 10 to 30 minutes); and one daily Monday to Friday to/from El Bosque (€1.44, 40 minutes), where you can change for Arcos de la Frontera.

## Zahara de la Sierra

POP 1200 / ELEV 550M

Strung around a vertiginous crag at the foot of the Grazalema mountains, overlooking the glittering turquoise Embalse de Zahara (Zahara Reservoir), rugged Zahara hums with Moorish mystery. For over 150 years in the 14th and 15th centuries, it stood on the old medieval frontier facing off against Christian Olvera, visible in the distance. These days Zahara ticks all the classic white-town boxes, its streets framed by hot-pink bougainvillea, with a 12th-century **castle** (24hr) FREE high above. It's also a great base for hiking the Garganta Verde, so it's popular. During the afternoon siesta, however, you could hear a pin drop.

**Oleum Viride** AGRICULTURAL CENTRE
(www.oleumviride.com; Finca Haza Las Lajas; tours €12) Learn all about inland Cádiz' age-old olive oil production at this enthusiastically run *almazara* (oil press), 1km northwest of central Zahara, whose sloping olive groves are still tended to by hand. The 1½-hour tour includes a four-oil tasting, or book in for local-produce tapas accompanied by the estate's own organic red wine (€25); minimum two people.

**Al Lago** BOUTIQUE HOTEL €€
(956 12 30 32; www.al-lago.es; Calle Félix Rodríguez de la Fuente; incl breakfast d €85-117, f €98-110, apt €82-92; Mar-Oct; ) Understated rustic-chic elegance runs through the six colourfully contemporary, individually styled rooms and two kitchen-equipped apartments created by designer-owner Mona at this gorgeous British-American-run boutique hotel looking out on Zahara's reservoir. All rooms feature tea/coffee makers and private balconies with lake views; the two superiors have bath tubs; and there's a little terrace alcove for lounging.

Chef Stefan crafts seasonal local produce into superb contemporary-Andalucian menus in the excellent **restaurant** (mains €8-20; 12.30-4.30pm & 8-10.30pm Thu-Tue Mar-Oct; ) .

## Getting There & Away

Comes runs two daily weekday buses to/from Ronda (€4.60, 45 to 75 minutes).

## Olvera

POP 7930 / ELEV 643M

Dramatically topped by a Moorish-era castle, Olvera (27km northeast of Zahara de la Sierra) beckons from miles away across olive-tree-covered country. Reconquered by Alfonso XI in 1327, this relatively untouristed town was a bandit refuge until the mid-19th century. People (mostly Spaniards) come to Olvera to walk or cycle the Vía Verde de la Sierra, but, as a white town par excellence, it's also renowned for its olive oil (you may be able to visit local producers), two striking churches and roller-coaster history, which probably started with the Romans.

**Castillo Árabe** CASTLE

(Plaza de la Iglesia; incl La Cilla €2; ⌚10.30am-2pm & 4-8pm Tue-Sun Jun–mid-Sep, 10.30am-2pm & 4-6pm Tue-Sun mid-Sep–May) Perched on a crag at 623m high above town is Olvera's late 12th-century castle, which later formed part of Nasrid-era Granada's defensive systems. Clamber up to the tower, with ever-more-exquisite town and country views opening up as you go. The surrounding web of narrow streets, the Barrio de la Villa, was once the Moorish medina.

**★Vía Verde de la Sierra** CYCLING

(www.viasverdes.com) This 36km relatively flat route between Olvera and Puerto Serrano via Coripe is regularly labelled the finest of Spain's *vías verdes* (greenways; railway lines transformed into traffic-free thoroughfares for bikers, hikers and horse riders). It's one of 23 such routes in Andalucía that together total 500km. Four spectacular viaducts, 30 tunnels and three stations turned hotel-restaurants await amid rugged mountain terrain.

**Sesca** (☎657 987432, 687 676462; www.sesca.es; Calle Pasadera 4; regular/electric bike hire per day €10/20; ⌚9am-2pm & 4-6pm Oct-May, reduced hours Jun-Sep; 👪) hires bikes at the route's eastern start point, 1km north of Olvera.

**No 31** B&B €€

(☎856 09 21 83; www.no31olvera.com; Calle Maestro Amado 31; r incl breakfast €70-75; ❄📶) A charming boutique conversion of a 19th-century townhouse, Canadian-owned adults-only No 31 has three intimate rooms with original tiling, wooden beams and whitewashed walls. It's just downhill from Olvera's castle (which you'll spy from the roof terrace) and breakfasts are a delight.

### ℹ Information

Oficina de Turismo (p662)

### ℹ Getting There & Away

Damas runs one daily bus to/from Jerez de la Frontera (€9.12, 2½ hours) and Ronda (€5.55, 1¼ hours), and only daily weekday buses to/from Málaga (€12, 2¼ hours). Comes has one daily bus Monday to Friday to/from Cádiz (€15, 3¼ hours).

# Cádiz' Costa de la Luz

Bereft of tacky resorts and unplanned development, the Costa de la Luz is a world of flat-capped farmers, spinning wind turbines and glugs of dry sherry. Throw in beautiful blonde, windswept beaches and a string of spectacularly located white towns, and you're unequivocally in Andalucía. A buzzing surfing/kitesurfing scene and some of southern Spain's most thrilling hotels add to the appeal. Spaniards, well aware of this, flock to places like Tarifa, Zahara de los Atunes and Los Caños de Meca in July and August, while a little upmarket flair is creeping in around Vejer de la Frontera. The Costa de la Luz continues west into neighbouring Huelva province, up to the Portugal border.

## Vejer de la Frontera

POP 9090

Vejer – the jaw drops, the eyes blink, the eloquent adjectives dry up. Looming moodily atop a rocky hill above the busy N340, 50km south of Cádiz, this serene, compact white town is something special. Yes, there's a labyrinth of twisting old-town streets encircled by imposing 15th-century walls, some serendipitous viewpoints, a ruined castle, a booming culinary scene, a smattering of dreamy hotels and a tangible Moorish influence. But Vejer has something else: an air of magic and mystery, an imperceptible touch of *duende* (spirit).

### 👁 Sights & Activities

**Plaza de España** SQUARE

With its elaborate 20th-century, Seville-tiled fountain and perfectly white town hall, Vejer's palm-studded, cafe-filled Plaza de España is a favourite hang-out. There's a small lookout above its western side (via Calle de Sancho IV el Bravo).

WORTH A TRIP

## SETENIL DE LAS BODEGAS

While most white towns sought protection atop lofty crags, the people of Setenil de las Bodegas (14km southeast of Olvera) burrowed into the dark caves beneath the steep cliffs of the Río Trejo. It took the Christian armies a 15-day siege to dislodge the Moors from their well-defended positions in 1484. Setenil (pop 2150) has long been known for its olive, honey and cured meats, but over the last few years the town has been smartened up, with rapidly growing tourism bringing new energy (and income) to its ancient streets. Many original cave-houses remain, some now recast as hotels and restaurants.

The **tourist office** (☎659 546626; www.setenil.com; Calle Villa 2; ⊙10.30am-2pm Tue-Sun) is near the top of the town in the 16th-century **Casa Consistorial** (with a rare wooden Mudéjar ceiling) and runs guided tours. Above is the 12th-century **castle** (Calle Villa; €1; ⊙11am-6pm). Setenil has some great tapas bars. Start with the cave bar-restaurants built into the rock along Calles Cuevas del Sol and Cuevas de la Sombra, and work your way up to Plaza de Andalucía and long-running **Restaurante Casa Palmero** (☎956 13 43 60; Plaza de Andalucía 4; mains €8-19; ⊙1pm-late Fri-Wed; 📶), loved for its village recipes.

**Castillo** CASTLE
(Calle del Castillo; ⊙10am-2pm & 5-9pm approx May-Sep, 10am-2pm & 4-8pm approx Oct-Apr) FREE Vejer's much-reworked castle, once home of the Duques de Medina Sidonia, dates from the 10th or 11th century. You can wander through the Moorish entrance arch, past the original rainwater *aljibe* (cistern), and climb the hibiscus-fringed ramparts for fantastic views across town to the white-sand coastline.

**Estatua de la Cobijada** STATUE
(Calle Trafalgar) Just below the castle is a lookout guarded by this statue of a woman dressed in Vejer's cloak-like, all-black traditional dress, the *cobijada*, which covers the entire body except the right eye. Despite its similarities to Islamic clothing, the *cobijada* is believed to be of 16th- or 17th-century Christian origin; it was banned in the 1930s and, after the civil war, few women had managed to hang on to their full outfits. Today it appears only for local festivities.

**Iglesia del Divino Salvador** CHURCH
(Plaza Padre Ángel; ⊙mass 8.30pm Mon-Wed & Fri, 9pm Sat & Sun) Built atop an earlier mosque, this unusual church is 14th-century Mudéjar at the altar end and 16th-century Gothic at the other. In the late afternoon the sun shines surreally through its stained-glass windows, projecting multicoloured light above the altar.

**Museo de Vejer** MUSEUM
(☎956 55 33 99; Calle Marqués de Tamarón 10; adult/child €2.50/free; ⊙10am-2pm & 6-10pm Mon-Sat May-Sep, 10am-2pm & 4-6pm Oct-Apr) Housed in a 17th- to 18th-century mansion, Vejer's museum has a small, impressive history and archaeology collection, running from the area's early Paleolithic inhabitants to Roman and Moorish times to the civil war. Highlights include a Visigothic sarcophagus from the 6th or 7th century CE and a hand-painted Iberian urn dating to between the 4th and 2nd centuries BCE.

★**Annie B's Spanish Kitchen** COOKING
(☎620 560649; www.anniebspain.com; Calle Viñas 11; 1-day course €155) Master the art of Andalucian cooking with sherry educator and local-cuisine expert Annie Mansion, whose popular day classes (Andalucian, Moroccan, seafood) end with lunch by the pool or on the roof terrace at her gorgeous old-town house. Annie also runs multi-day cooking courses, Morocco day trips, and tapas, food and sherry tours of Vejer, Cádiz and Jerez.

## Sleeping

★**La Casa del Califa** BOUTIQUE HOTEL €€
(☎956 44 77 30; www.califavejer.com; Plaza de España 16; incl breakfast r €100-165, ste €170-250; P ❄ 📶) Rambling over several floors of labyrinthine corridors, this gorgeous hotel is Vejer's original hideaway, inhabiting a 16th-century building with its roots in the 10th century. The 20 calming rooms take inspiration from North Africa: antique furniture, original arches, terracotta-tiled floors. Special 'emir' service (€46) brings flowers, pastries and *cava* (sparkling wine) Breakfast is a local-focussed feast in the fabulous Moroccan–Middle Eastern restaurant. A Califa-team hammam is due in 2021.

★**Casa Shelly** BOUTIQUE HOTEL €€
(☎639 118831; www.casashelly.com; Calle Eduardo Shelly 6; r €85-140; ⊙Mar-Oct; ❄📶) All quiet, understated Scandi-Andalucian style, adults-only Casa Shelly feels as though it's wandered out of an interior-design magazine and into the thick of Vejer's old town. Beyond a peaceful lounge and fountain-bathed patio, the gorgeously converted mid-18th-century townhouse has seven design-led rooms with original wooden doors, antique-inspired tiles, wood-beamed ceilings, vintage Swedish furniture and queen-size beds, in dusty pinks, blues and greys. Coffee, tea and snacks included.

★**La Fonda Antigua** BOUTIQUE HOTEL €€
(☎625 372616; www.chicsleepinvejer.com; Calle San Filmo 14; r incl breakfast €85-150; ❄📶) A *jerezano* couple with an eye for interiors runs this adults-only boutique bolthole on the fringes of Vejer's old town. In the 11 all-different rooms, antique doors morph into bedheads, mismatched vintage tiles dot polished-concrete floors, and cheeky features include glass-walled showers and, for several, free-standing baths. The rooftop terrace, where Vejer-produce breakfasts are served, opens up sprawling old-town panoramas.

★**Plaza 18** BOUTIQUE HOTEL €€€
(☎956 44 77 30; www.califavejer.com; Plaza de España 18; r incl breakfast €187-300; P❄📶) 🍃 This 2019-opened boutique beauty is a luxe, six-room conversion of an 1896 merchant's house built atop a 13th-century home. The soothing entrance patio, with original check-print tiles and light well, sets the tone for boldly, individually styled rooms with beamed ceilings, colour-feature walls, luxury furnishings, rain showers, international art and Vejer-scented toiletries. Breakfast next-door at La Casa del Califa.

**V...** BOUTIQUE HOTEL €€€
(☎956 45 17 57; www.hotelv-vejer.com; Calle Rosario 11-13; r €153-329; ❄📶) V... (for Vejer) is an exquisite creation: a beautifully restored 17th-century mansion set around a leafy patio, high above which a view-laden rooftop with sunbeds and hot tub awaits. Creative contemporary design (open-plan bathrooms, chic tubs, oversized mirrors) mixes with antiques in the 12 neutral-toned rooms, and breakfast (€10) arrives on enormous trays. The ancient *aljibe* (cistern) is now a massage room.

## Eating

Vejer has quietly morphed into a gastronomic highlight of Andalucía, where you can just as happily tuck into traditional, age-old recipes as Moroccan-fusion dishes.

**Mercado de Abastos** ANDALUCIAN €
(Calle San Francisco; dishes €2-8; ⊙noon-4pm & 8pm-midnight) Now glammed up gastro-bar-style, Vejer's early 20th-century Mercado de San Francisco has become a buzzy foodie hotspot full of world-wandering stalls. Grab a *vino* and choose between Andalucian classics and contemporary twists: Iberian ham *raciones, tortilla de patatas*, fried fish in paper cups and popular sushi.

★**El Jardín del Califa** MOROCCAN €€
(☎956 45 17 06; www.califavejer.com; Plaza de España 16; mains €12-18; ⊙1-4pm & 8-11.30pm; 🖉) 🍃 Sizzling atmosphere and flawless cooking combine at this beautiful restaurant hidden within a cavernous 16th-century, Moorish-origin house where even finding the bathroom is a full-on adventure; it's also a fabulous hotel and *tetería* (teahouse). The seasonal, local produce Moroccan–Middle Eastern menu – tagines, couscous, hummus, falafel – is crammed with Maghreb flavours (saffron, figs, almonds). Book ahead, for the palm-sprinkled garden or the moody interior.

★**Corredera 55** ANDALUCIAN €€
(☎956 45 18 48; www.califavejer.com; Calle de la Corredera 55; mains €11-22; ⊙noon-11.30pm; 🖉) 🍃 Exquisitely styled with boho-chic Vejer flair, Corredera 55 delivers elegant, inventive seasonal cuisine packed with local, organic ingredients and Cádiz-meets-international flavours. Andalucian wines pair perfectly with creations such as mushroom-garlic risotto, cauliflower fritters with honey-yoghurt dressing, or *cava*-baked prawn-stuffed fish of the day. Perch at street-side tables (winter blankets provided!) or eat in the cosy dining room amid Vejer paintings.

## Information

**Oficina Municipal de Turismo** (☎956 45 17 36; www.turismovejer.es; Avenida Los Remedios 2; ⊙10am-2.30pm & 4.30-9pm Mon-Sat, 10am-2pm Sun, reduced hours Oct-Apr)

## Getting There & Away

From Avenida Los Remedios, Comes runs buses to Cádiz, Zahara de los Atunes, Jerez and Seville.

All other buses stop at La Barca de Vejer on the N340 (a €6 taxi from town).

| Destination | Cost (€) | Time | Frequency |
|---|---|---|---|
| Cádiz | 5.96 | 1¼hr | 5 daily |
| Jerez de la Frontera | 8.01 | 1½hr | daily Mon-Fri |
| La Línea (for Gibraltar) | 9.11 | 1¾hr | up to 6 daily |
| Seville | 18 | 2¼hr | 4 daily |
| Seville (from Avenida Los Remedios) | 17 | 3hr | daily |
| Tarifa | 4.55 | 40min | 8 daily |
| Zahara de los Atunes | 2.57 | 25min | at least 1 daily |

## Los Caños de Meca & El Palmar

POP 820

Laid-back Los Caños de Meca, 16km southwest of Vejer, straggles along a series of spectacular white-sand beaches. Once a hippie haven, Caños still attracts beach lovers of all kinds and nations – especially in summer – with its alternative, hedonistic scene and clothing-optional beaches, as well as kitesurfing, windsurfing and board-surfing opportunities. Immediately northwest is the beach resort of **Zahora** and, northwest again, El Palmar, which has Andalucía's best board-surfing waves from October to May and whose salt-white sands get busy in summer with surf schools, beach bars and yoga.

**DON'T MISS**

**SANTA LUCÍA DINING**

A 5km drive north of Vejer, the leafy hamlet of Santa Lucía hosts two of the area's top restaurants. With a lovely shaded terrace and thatched interior, 1945-founded **Venta El Toro** (☎956 45 14 07; www.facebook.com/ventaeltoro; Santa Lucía; tapas €2-3, mains €6-10; ⏲9.30am-9pm Wed-Mon) is loved for its fried farm-fresh eggs with hand-cut chips and other typically *vejeriego* goodies, including delicious breakfasts made with bread from Conil. Across the road at **Restaurante Castillería** (☎956 45 14 97; www.restaurantecastilleria.com; Santa Lucía; ⏲1.30-4pm Mar-Nov), courtesy of Juan and Ana Valdés, you can feast on succulent, expertly wood-fired meats sourced from responsible small-scale farms across Spain.

### Sights & Activities

**★Parque Natural de la Breña y Marismas del Barbate** NATURE RESERVE
(www.juntadeandalucia.es) This 50-sq-km coastal park protects important marshes, cliffs and pine forest from Costa del Sol–type development. Its main entry point is a 7.2km (two-hour) walking trail, the **Sendero del Acantilado**, between Los Caños de Meca and Barbate, along clifftops that rival Cabo de Gata in their beauty.

**Cabo de Trafalgar** LIGHTHOUSE
At the western end of Los Caños de Meca, a side road (often half-covered in sand) leads out to an 1860 **lighthouse** on a low spit of land. This is the famous Cabo de Trafalgar, off which Spanish naval power was swiftly terminated by a British fleet under Admiral Nelson in 1805.

**Escuela de Surf 9 Pies** SURFING, YOGA
(☎620 104241; www.escueladesurf9pies.com; Paseo Marítimo; board & wetsuit rental per 2/4hr €12/18, 2hr group class €28) A professional surf school offering board hire and surf classes for all levels, plus yoga sessions (€10) and SUP rental (€15 for two hours), towards the northern end of El Palmar beach.

### Sleeping & Eating

**Hotel Madreselva** HOTEL €€
(☎956 43 72 55; www.califavejer.com; Avenida de Trafalgar 102; d €75-135; ⏲Apr–mid-Oct; P ☜ ≋) Strung around a leafy courtyard, this mellow, peachy-orange hacienda-style hideaway has 18 charmingly rustic rooms with surfy vibes, vintage furniture and private terraces. There's a summer-only Spanish restaurant, all just a minute's walk from Caños' beach.

**Las Dunas** CAFE €
(☎956 43 72 03; www.barlasdunas.es; Carretera del Cabo de Trafalgar; dishes €4-12; ⏲9am-midnight Sep-Jun, to 3am Jul & Aug; ☜) The ultimate relaxation spot, where kitesurfers kick back between sessions on the beach beside the Cabo de Trafalgar. There is Bob Marley on the speakers, great *bocadillos* (filled rolls), fresh juices, *platos combinados* and a laid-back, beach-shack feel, plus occasional concerts.

### Getting There & Away

Comes has at least two daily weekday buses from Los Caños de Meca to Cádiz (€6, 1½ hours) via El Palmar (€2, 15 minutes).

## Zahara de los Atunes

POP 1060

About 20km southeast of Los Caños de Meca, Zahara de los Atunes fronts a fantastic 12km-long, west-facing sweep of white-gold sand. For years a traditional fishing village famous for its Atlantic bluefin *almadraba* tuna, today Zahara is a popular, easygoing summer beach hang-out that's forging its way into the local culinary scene. Zahara's tiny old core centres on the ruined 15th-century **Castillo de las Almadrabas** (Avenida Hermanos Doctores Sánchez Rodríguez), where the tuna catch was once processed. Southeast of Zahara is the more developed resort of **Atlanterra**.

**Restaurante Antonio** SEAFOOD €€€

(☎956 43 95 42; www.restauranteantoniozahara.com; Bahía de la Plata, Km 1, Atlanterra; mains €15-30; ⏲1.30-4pm & 8-11pm Feb–mid-Dec) Prize-winning Antonio, 1km south of Zahara, is widely recommended for its top-quality seafood, delivered by attentive staff in a sparkling modern-design sea-view setting. *Almadraba* bluefin tuna, of course, is the star, dished up in a million incarnations from *atún encebollado* (tuna-onion stew) to sashimi. The tuna tartare is a speciality.

It's also a hotel with a beach-facing pool and uncluttered rooms (€100 to €212).

## Bolonia

POP 90

Tiny Bolonia village, off the N340 15km northwest of Tarifa, overlooks a gloriously white beach framed by a large dune, rolling pine-dotted or field-covered hills, and the impressive Roman remains of Baelo Claudia. From a small parking area 3km west of Baelo Claudia, along the CA8202, a 1.5km dirt track leads down to the Faro Camarinal, from where you can access quiet, nudist-friendly **Playa El Cañuelo**. In July and August, three weekday **Horizonte Sur** (☎699 427644; www.horizontesur.es) buses run between Bolonia and Tarifa (€2.50, 30 to 40 minutes).

**★Baelo Claudia** ARCHAEOLOGICAL SITE

(☎956 10 67 97; www.museosdeandalucia.es; EU/non-EU citizens free/€1.50; ⏲9am-9pm Tue-Sat Apr–mid-Jun, 9am-3pm & 6-9pm Tue-Sat mid-Jun–Jul, 9am-3pm Tue-Sat Aug–mid-Sep, 9am-6pm Tue-Sat mid-Sep-Mar, 9am-3pm Sun year-round) The ruined town of Baelo Claudia is one of Andalucía's most important Roman archaeological sites. These majestic beachside ruins – with views across to Morocco – include the substantial remains of a theatre, a paved forum, thermal baths, a market and the columns of a basilica, and the workshops that turned out the products that made Baelo Claudia famous in the Roman world: salted fish and *garum* (spicy seasoning made from leftover fish parts). There's a good museum.

**Las Rejas** SEAFOOD €€

(☎685 010274, 956 68 85 46; www.lasrejasrestaurante.com; El Lentiscal; raciones €8-20; ⏲12.30-5.30pm & 8.30-11.30pm Wed-Sun May–mid-Oct, 12.30-5.30pm & 8.30-11.30pm Sat & Sun mid-Oct–Apr) A well-established, smartish spot just back from Bolonia's beach, specialising in super-fresh fish, salty paellas and superb Cádiz seafood *raciones* like grilled prawns or *tortillitas de camarones*.

## Tarifa

POP 13,640

Tarifa's southern-tip-of-Spain location, where the Mediterranean and the Atlantic meet, gives it a different climate and character to the rest of Andalucía. Atlantic winds draw surfers, windsurfers and kitesurfers

### THE GREAT ALMADRABA

One of the joys of Cádiz cuisine is the fresh Atlantic bluefin tuna caught using the ancient *almadraba* method, introduced by the Phoenicians. The *almadraba* is considered one of the world's most sustainable fishing methods, with nets tied to the seabed and raised only once a day during wild-tuna migration season (May/June). **El Campero** (☎650 42 07 92; www.restauranteelcampero.es; Avenida de la Constitución 5C; raciones & mains €11-25; ⏲12.30-5pm & 8pm-midnight Tue-Sun) in Barbate (9km southeast of Vejer) is known as 'the temple of tuna' for its superb contemporary-twist *almadraba* dishes such as tuna-back ceviche and *jamón marino* (salted tuna belly). Many Costa de la Luz towns, including Zahara de los Atunes, host tuna festivals in May or June.

who, in turn, lend this ancient yet deceptively small settlement a refreshing, laid-back international vibe. With its winding whitewashed streets and tangible North African feel, Tarifa's walled windswept old town could easily pass for Morocco's Chefchaouen or Essaouira. It's no secret, however, and, in August especially, Tarifa gets packed (that's half the fun).

Tarifa may be as old as Phoenician Cádiz and was definitely a Roman settlement. It takes its name from Tarif ibn Malik, who led a Muslim raid in 710 CE, the year before the main Islamic arrival on the peninsula.

## Sights

Tarifa's narrow old-town streets, mostly of Moorish origin, hint at Morocco. Wander through the fortified Moorish **Puerta de Jerez**, embellished after the Reconquista, then pop into the lively neo-Mudéjar **Mercado de Abastos** (Calle Colón; ⏲8.30am-2pm Tue-Sat) before winding your way to the mainly 16th-century **Iglesia de San Mateo** (Calle Sancho IV El Bravo; ⏲8.45am-1pm & 6-8.30pm May-Sep, 8.45am-1pm & 5.30-8pm Oct-Apr). The **Miramar** (☎607 984871; Calle Amargura; ⏲10am-4pm), atop part of the castle walls, has spectacular views across to Africa.

**Castillo de Guzmán el Bueno** CASTLE
(Calle Guzmán el Bueno; adult/child €4/free; ⏲10am-4pm) Though built in 960 on the orders of Cordoban caliph Abd ar-Rahman III, this restored fortress is named after Reconquista hero Guzmán el Bueno. In 1294, when threatened with the death of his captured son unless he surrendered the castle to Merenid attackers from Morocco, El Bueno threw down his own dagger for his son's execution. Guzmán's descendants later became the Duques de Medina Sidonia, one of Spain's most powerful families. Above the interior entrance, note the 10th-century castle-foundation inscription.

> ### ALGECIRAS: GATEWAY TO MOROCCO
>
> The major port linking Spain with Africa is an ugly industrial fishing town famous for producing the greatest flamenco guitarist of the modern era, Paco de Lucía, who was born here in 1947 and died in 2014 in Playa del Carmen, Mexico. Ferries from Algeciras to Tangier drop you in Tangier Med, 40km east of Tangier itself, and are operated by **FRS** (☎956 68 18 30; www.frs.es) and **Trasmediterránea** (☎902 45 46 45; www.trasmediterranea.es).

## Activities

### Kitesurfing & Windsurfing

Tarifa's legendary winds have turned the town into one of Europe's premier windsurfing and kitesurfing destinations. The most popular strip is along the coast between Tarifa and Punta Paloma, 10km northwest. Dozens of schools offer equipment hire and classes, from beginner to expert level. The best months are May, June and September.

**ION Club Hurricane** WINDSURFING, KITESURFING
(☎956 68 90 98; www.ion-club.net; Carretera N340, Km 78, Hurricane Hotel; 6hr group kitesurfing or windsurfing beginner course €250; ⏲10.30am-8.30pm Jul & Aug, to 7pm Jun & Sep, to 6.30pm Mar-May & Oct-Dec) Recommended group/private windsurfing and kitesurfing classes (beginner, intermediate or advanced level), equipment rental (€90 per day) and paddle-boarding (two-hour trip €40), 7km northwest of Tarifa. Spanish, English, French, Italian and German spoken. Also at **Valdevaqueros** (☎619 340913; Carretera N340, Km 76, Playa de Valdevaqueros), 10km northwest of town.

**Spin Out** WATER SPORTS
(☎956 23 63 52; www.tarifaspinout.com; Carretera N340, Km 75.5, Playa de Valdevaqueros; 90min windsurfing class per person €59, board & sail rental per hr €30; ⏲10.30am-7pm Apr-Oct) Daily windsurfing classes and five-day courses (€349) for beginners, kids and experts, from a switched-on, multilingual team, 11km northwest of town. There's also a kitesurfing school, plus SUP gear rental.

### Horse Riding

One-hour beach rides along Playa de los Lances cost €30 to €45 and two-hour beach-and-mountain rides cost €80. Excellent **Aventura Ecuestre** (☎626 480019, 956 23 66 32; www.aventuraecuestre.com; Carretera N340, Km 79.5, Hotel Dos Mares), 5km northwest of Tarifa, has multilingual guides and four-hour rides (€140) across the Parque Natural Los Alcornocales or the Punta Paloma dunes. **Molino El Mastral** (☎679 193503; www.mastral.com; Carretera Santuario Virgen de la Luz; per hr €30), 5km north of Tarifa, is also reliable.

DON'T MISS

## TARIFA BEACH BLISS

Jazzed up by the colourful kites and sails of kitesurfers and windsurfers whizzing across turquoise waves, with Morocco looming behind, the exquisite bleach-blonde beaches that stretch northwest from Tarifa along the N340 are some of Andalucía's (and Spain's) most beautiful. In summer they fill up with sun-kissed beach lovers and chill-out *chiringuitos* (beach bars).

**Playa de los Lances** This broad snow-white sandy beach stretches for 7km northwest from Tarifa. The low dunes behind it are a *paraje natural* (protected natural area).

**Playa de Valdevaqueros** Sprawling between 7km and 10km northwest of Tarifa, to the great white dune at Punta Paloma, Valdevaqueros is one of Tarifa's most popular kitesurfing beaches, blessed with dusty alabaster-hued sand, aqua waters and a few summer beach bars.

**Punta Paloma** One of Andalucía's most fabulous beaches, Punta Paloma, 10km northwest of Tarifa, is famous for its huge blonde sand dune. At its far western end, you can lather yourself up in a natural mud bath.

### Whale Watching

The waters off Tarifa are one of the best places in Europe to see whales and dolphins as they swim between the Atlantic and the Mediterranean from April to October. Sperm whales swim the Strait of Gibraltar from April to August; the best months for orcas are July and August. You might also spot striped and bottlenose dolphins, long-finned pilot whales, and endangered fin whales and common dolphins.

**FIRMM** WHALE WATCHING
(956 62 70 08; www.firmm.org; Calle Pedro Cortés 4; 2hr tours adult/child €30/20; Apr-Oct) Among Tarifa's dozens of whale-watching outfits, not-for-profit FIRMM is a good option. Its primary purpose is to study the whales and record data, which gives rise to environmentally sensitive two- or three-hour tours and week-long whale-watching courses. Book two to three days ahead.

### Yoga

**OmShala** (722 147636; www.omshalatarifa.com; Avenida de Andalucía 13; single class €15) and **Mandalablue Yoga** (644 772377; www.mandalablueyoga.es; single class €15) offer drop-in sessions, workshops and retreats.

## Sleeping

**★Hostal África** HOSTAL €
(956 68 02 20; www.hostalafrica.com; Calle María Antonia Toledo 12; s €40-75, d €60-95, tr €90-120; Mar-Nov; ) This mellow, revamped 19th-century house within Tarifa's old town is one of Cádiz province's best *hostales* (budget hotels). Full of potted plants and sky-blue-and-white arches, it's run by hospitable, on-the-ball owners, and the 13 unfussy, all-different rooms (including one triple) sparkle with bright colours. Enjoy the lovely roof terrace, with its loungey cabana and Africa views.

**La Cocotera** HOSTEL €
(956 68 22 19; www.lacocotera.com; Calle San Rosendo 12; dm €18-36, d €36-100, q €51-140; ) At this popular hostel and coworking space full of digital nomads, the fruity-named, white-styled four-bunk dorms are crisp and spotless, with personal plugs and lights. Facilities include a well-equipped kitchen, two laptop-working spaces and a rooftop terrace with Morocco views.

**Aristoy Tarifa** BOUTIQUE HOTEL €€
(956 68 31 72; www.aristoytarifa.com; Calle Calderón de la Barca 3; r €90-225; ) From the team behind several top Tarifa foodie ventures, the old-town Aristoy occupies a creatively revamped 18th-century building crowned by a terrace and plunge pool. Design combines the original beams and patio with polished concrete, bamboo touches and crisp white-on-white styling. A few rooms have terraces and/or sloping attic-style ceilings.

**Posada La Sacristía** BOUTIQUE HOTEL €€
(956 68 17 59; www.lasacristia.net; Calle San Donato 8; r incl breakfast €131-181; ) A beautifully renovated 17th-century townhouse (once a Moorish stable) hosts this elegant historical-boutique find in the heart of town. Attention to detail is impeccable, with 10 stylishly updated rooms (four-poster beds,

beamed ceilings, antique furniture) over two floors around a courtyard. Massages can be arranged, and, downstairs, there's a plush lounge for drinks and fuss-free tapas.

**Arte Vida** HOTEL €€

(☎956 68 52 46; www.hotelartevidatarifa.com; Carretera N340, Km 79.3; r incl breakfast €95-170; P ❄ 📶) In a dreamy beachfront spot, 6km northwest of Tarifa, the Arte Vida has a deliciously laid-back feel and a handful of stripped-back, contemporary-design rooms with arty touches and cerulean walls. There's also a kitesurf and windsurf school, plus a good Mediterranean restaurant, a seasonal *chiringuito* (beach bar), a lounge area and summer DJ sessions.

★**Riad** BOUTIQUE HOTEL €€€

(☎856 92 98 80; www.theriadtarifa.com; Calle Comendador 10; d €99-210) A seductively converted 17th-century townhouse, the Riad opens through a polished-concrete lobby adorned by an ornamental fountain/pool, fresh lilies and flickering candles. It's dressed with original architecture: exposed-stone walls, antique doors, red-brick arches, a frescoed facade. Off the patio are a hammam, a rooftop lounge and nine intimate rooms styled with *tadelakt* (waterproof plaster) walls, Morocco-made tiles and soothing Andalucía-meets-Morocco design.

**Hotel Dos Mares** HOTEL €€€

(☎956 68 40 35; www.dosmareshotel.com; Carretera N340, Km 79.5; r incl breakfast €95-250; P ❄ 📶 🏊) Opening onto blinding-white sands 5km northwest of town, Morocco-flavoured Dos Mares has bright, tile-floored rooms and bungalows washed in yellow, blue and burnt orange, some with sea-facing balconies. Other perks include a cafe, a gym, a pool, a kitesurfing school, a *chiringuito* and an excellent horse-riding school (p676).

## Eating

Tarifa is full of good food with a strong international flavour and wonderful vegetarian/vegan meals.

★**Café Azul** CAFE €

(www.cafeazul-tarifa.com; Calle Batalla del Salado 8; dishes €2-9; ⏱9am-3pm; 📶 📋) 🌿 This long-established Italian-run cafe with eye-catching blue-and-white Morocco-inspired decor whips up some of the best breakfasts in Andalucía. You'll want to eat everything. The fruit salad with muesli, yoghurt and coconut, and the fruit-and-yoghurt-stuffed crêpe are works of art. It also serves Italian coffee, honey-sweetened teas, fresh smoothies and juices, *bocadillos* and cooked breakfasts, with delicious gluten-free and vegan options.

★**Surla** CAFE €

(☎956 68 51 75; www.facebook.com/surlatarifa; Calle Pintor Pérez Villalta 64; dishes €4-8; ⏱9am-5pm Mon-Fri, to 7pm Sat & Sun; 📋) 🌿 Decorative surf boards, wall-mounted chairs and Balinese umbrellas fill the leafy, tropical-feel interior of this wonderful laid-back cafe, where the focus is on organic local, seasonal ingredients: *jamón* from Huelva's mountains, Granada olive oil, Cádiz' own free-range eggs, salt and *payoyo* cheese.

★**Tangana** INTERNATIONAL €

(☎606 415028; www.tanganatarifa.com; Carretera N340, Km 75.5, Playa de Valdevaqueros; dishes €6-12; ⏱10am-9pm Apr-Oct; 📶 📋) Set around a boho-chic boutique and a series of chill-out lounges and self-catering bungalows, 11km northwest of Tarifa, this mellow bar-restaurant rustles up some of the best beachy bites in the Tarifa area. Turquoise-washed bench-style tables set a lazy-life scene for sipping mojitos and caipirinhas, or enjoying rustic *bocadillos*, creative salads, tuna tacos, seasonal paella and dreamy home-cooked breakfasts.

**El Francés** TAPAS €

(Calle Sancho IV el Bravo 21; raciones €7-13; ⏱12.30pm-midnight Fri-Tue Mar-Dec; 📋) Squeeze into the standing-room-only bar or battle for your terrace table at El Francés, which gives Andalucian classics a subtle twist. Tarifa's favourite tapas bar is a buzzing place, serving *patatas bravas* and *tortillitas de camarones* (shrimp fritters) alongside mini chicken-veg couscous or cheese-stuffed mushrooms. No reservations; pop in on the day to secure a table (dinner from 6.30pm only).

**Café 10** CAFE €

(☎956 62 76 86; www.facebook.com/cafe10tarifa; Calle Nuestra Señora de la Luz 10; dishes €2-6; ⏱9am-2am, closed Jan; 📶 📋) Old-town favourite Café 10 delivers the breakfast/snack goods in a snug, neo-rustic lounge with wall art and pink-cushioned chairs spilling out onto the sloping street. Tuck into home-made cakes, great coffee, fresh juices, sweet and salty crêpes, and *revueltos* (scrambles) and *molletes* (small toasted rolls). Later on, the G&Ts and mojitos come out.

**Chilimosa** VEGETARIAN €
(☎956 68 50 92; www.facebook.com/chilimosa; Calle Peso 6; mains €5-10; ⏲7pm-midnight Mon-Thu, 1-4.30pm & 7pm-midnight Fri-Sun, closed Jan-early Mar; ) A cosy, casual vegetarian restaurant at the top of the old town, with just a handful of tables, Chilimosa is Tarifa at its low-key best. The unpretentious home-cooked Middle Eastern menu is fired by ingredients from the owners' garden, turning out such meat-free delights as vegetable samosas, falafel-hummus wraps, meze platters and tofu burgers. Takeaway, too.

**El Lola** TAPAS €€
(☎956 62 73 07; www.facebook.com/ElLolaTarifa; Calle Guzmán El Bueno 5; tapas €2-5, raciones €5-15; ⏲1-4pm & 7pm-midnight Apr-Oct; ) With whitewashed walls and bright geraniums, busy El Lola is known for its delectable, lightly creative tapas and *raciones* of Atlantic bluefin *almadraba* tuna, from smooth tataki to a full degustation. Other Cádiz-flavoured temptations include just-cooked tortilla, grilled king prawns and croquettes stuffed with *ibérico* ham or spinach.

**La Oca da Sergio** ITALIAN €€
(☎615 686571; Calle General Copons 6; mains €8-19; ⏲1-4pm & 8pm-midnight daily Jun-Oct & Dec, reduced hours Jan-May) Amiable Sergio roams the tables Italian style, armed with loaded plates and amusing stories, and presides over genuine home-country cooking at this forever popular restaurant tucked behind the Iglesia de San Mateo. Look forward to *caprese* salads, homemade pasta (try the truffle pappardelle), wood-oven thin-crust pizzas and after-dinner *limoncello*.

## Drinking & Nightlife

Tarifa's busy bar scene centres on the old town's narrow Calles Cervantes, San Francisco and Santísima Trinidad.

**Tumbao** LOUNGE
(www.facebook.com/tumbaotarifa; Carretera N340, Km 76, Playa de Valdevaqueros; ⏲10am-midnight Easter-Sep) The ultimate Tarifa-cool beach hang-out, Tumbao serves up cocktails, *tinto de verano*, and loungey sunset beats on a grassy, beanbag-strewn patch overlooking the kitesurfing action on Playa de Valdevaqueros, 10km northwest of town. The kitchen delivers burgers, salads, nachos and other tasty bites.

**Waikiki** LOUNGE
(☎956 79 90 15; https://waikikitarifa.com; Playa de los Lances; ⏲noon-late) Live music, DJ sets and sunny cocktails keep things busy at boho-cool beachfront lounge spot Waikiki, on the west side of the old town. Mojitos, daiquiris and other updated classics fill the menu, which also has excellent local-inspired dishes (€7 to €20) such as red-tuna tartare and goat's-cheese salad.

## Information

**Oficina de Turismo** (☎956 68 09 93; www.turismodetarifa.com; Paseo de la Alameda; ⏲10am-1.30pm & 4-6pm Mon-Fri, 10am-1.30pm Sat & Sun)

## Getting There & Away

### BOAT

**FRS** (☎956 68 18 30; www.frs.es; Avenida de Andalucía 16; adult/child/car/motorcycle one way €45/15/125/33) runs six daily one-hour ferries between Tarifa and Tangier (Morocco). All passengers need a passport.

### BUS

Comes operates from the **bus station** (☎956 68 40 38; Calle Batalla del Salado) at the northwest end of town.

| Destination | Cost (€) | Time | Frequency |
|---|---|---|---|
| Algeciras | 2.45 | 30-60min | 11-18 daily |
| Cádiz | 11 | 1½hr | 6 daily |
| Jerez de la Frontera | 13 | 2½hr | 2 daily |
| La Línea (for Gibraltar) | 4.51 | 1hr | 6 daily |
| Málaga | 17-18 | 2½-3hr | 3-4 daily |
| Seville | 21 | 3-4hr | 4 daily |

# GIBRALTAR

POP 32,700

Red pillar boxes, fish-and-chip shops, creaky 1970s seaside hotels: Gibraltar – as British writer Laurie Lee once commented – is a piece of Portsmouth sliced off and towed 500 miles south. 'The Rock' overstates its Britishness, a bonus for pub-grub and afternoon-tea lovers, but a confusing double-take for modern-day British folk who thought the days of Lord Nelson memorabilia were long gone. Poised strategically at the jaws of Europe and Africa, Gibraltar, with its Palladian architecture, camera-hogging Barbary macaques, swashbuckling local history and

## Gibraltar

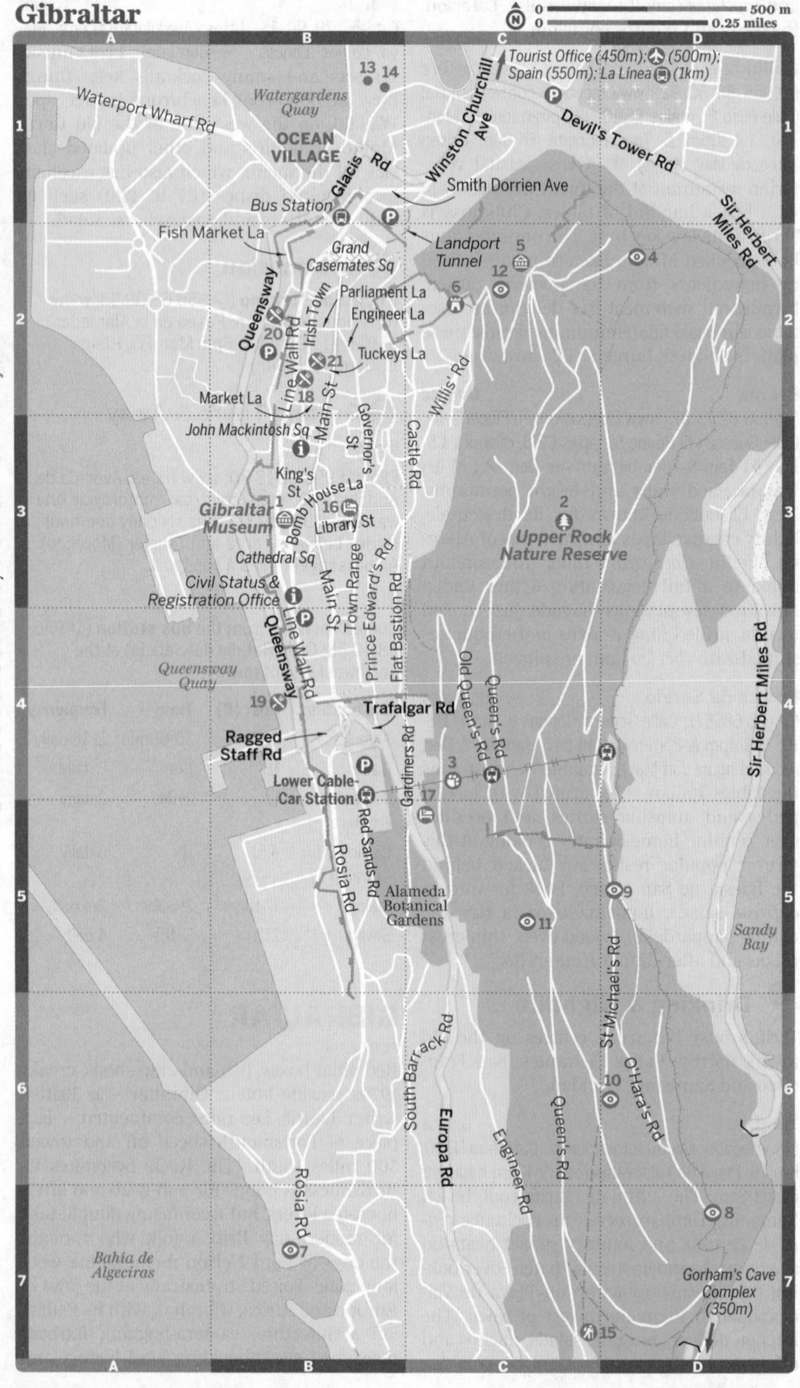
0 500 m
0 0.25 miles
Tourist Office (450m); (500m); Spain (550m); La Línea (1km)
Waterport Wharf Rd
Watergardens Quay
OCEAN VILLAGE
Glacis Rd
Winston Churchill Ave
Devil's Tower Rd
Smith Dorrien Ave
Bus Station
Fish Market La
Grand Casemates Sq
Landport Tunnel
Sir Herbert Miles Rd
Queensway
Irish Town
Parliament La
Engineer La
Tuckeys La
Line Wall Rd
Market La
Main St
Governor's St
Castle Rd
Willis' Rd
John Mackintosh Sq
King's St
Bomb House La
Library St
Gibraltar Museum
Cathedral Sq
Upper Rock Nature Reserve
Civil Status & Registration Office
Town Range
Prince Edward's Rd
Flat Bastion Rd
Queensway Quay
Old Queen's Rd
Queen's Rd
Trafalgar Rd
Ragged Staff Rd
Gardiners Rd
Lower Cable-Car Station
Red Sands Rd
Rosia Rd
Alameda Botanical Gardens
Sandy Bay
South Barrack Rd
St Michael's Rd
O'Hara's Rd
Europa Rd
Engineer Rd
Bahia de Algeciras
Gorham's Cave Complex (350m)

## Gibraltar

**Top Sights**
1 Gibraltar Museum ........ B3
2 Upper Rock Nature Reserve ........ C3

**Sights**
3 Apes' Den ........ C4
4 Great Siege Tunnels ........ D2
5 Military Heritage Centre ........ C2
6 Moorish Castle ........ C2
7 Nelson's Anchorage ........ B7
8 O'Hara's Battery ........ D7
9 Skywalk ........ D5
10 St Michael's Cave ........ D6
11 Windsor Suspension Bridge ........ C5
12 WWII Tunnels ........ C2

**Activities, Courses & Tours**
13 Dolphin Adventure ........ B1
14 Dolphin Safari ........ B1
15 Mediterranean Steps ........ C7

**Sleeping**
16 Eliott ........ B3
17 Rock Hotel ........ C5

**Eating**
18 Clipper ........ B2
19 Lounge ........ B4
20 My Wines ........ B2
21 Sacarello's ........ B2

spectacular natural setting, makes an interesting change to bordering Cádiz province.

The towering 5km-long limestone ridge rises to 426m, with cliffs on its northern and eastern sides. Gibraltarians speak English, Spanish and a curiously accented, sing-song mix of the two, often swapping mid-sentence. Signs are in English.

## History

Both the Phoenicians and the ancient Greeks left traces here, but Gibraltar really entered the history books in 711 CE when Tariq ibn Ziyad, the Muslim governor of Tangier, made it the initial bridgehead for the Islamic invasion of the Iberian Peninsula, landing with an army of 10,000 men. The name Gibraltar derives from Jebel Tariq (Tariq's Mountain).

In 1704, an Anglo-Dutch fleet captured Gibraltar during the War of the Spanish Succession. Spain ceded the Rock to Britain by the 1713 Treaty of Utrecht, but it didn't give up military attempts to regain it until the failure of the Great Siege of 1779–83; Spain has wanted it back ever since.

In 1969, Francisco Franco (infuriated by a referendum in which Gibraltarians voted by 12,138 to 44 to remain under British sovereignty) closed the Spain–Gibraltar border. The same year a new constitution committed Britain to respecting Gibraltarians' wishes over sovereignty, and gave Gibraltar domestic self-government and its own parliament, the House of Assembly (now the Gibraltar Parliament). In 1985, just before Spain joined the European Community (now the EU), the border was reopened after 16 long years.

Gibraltarians believe in their right to self-determination and, in a 2002 vote, resoundingly rejected the idea of joint British-Spanish sovereignty. The thorny issue of the Rock's long-term future continues to hit headlines, with debates sparked by conflict over who controls its surrounding waters and, most recently, the still-unclear effects of the UK's decision to leave the EU.

In the UK's 2016 EU-membership referendum, Gibraltarians voted by 96% against Brexit (a higher pro-Remain percentage than anywhere else in Britain), but Gibraltar officially left the EU along with the rest of the UK in January 2020. While at the time of writing there are few visible changes on the ground, there are concerns (among other issues) that potential delays to crossings at a non-EU Spain–Gibraltar border would seriously complicate matters for the 15,000 Spain-based workers who cross into Gibraltar each day.

## Sights & Activities

Most Gibraltar sojourns start in Grand Casemates Sq, accessible through Landport Tunnel (at one time the only land entry through Gibraltar's walls), then continue along Main St, a slice of the British high street under the Mediterranean sun.

### ★ Upper Rock Nature Reserve — NATURE RESERVE

(incl attractions adult/child £13/8, excl attractions pedestrian £5, combined ticket incl cable car adult/child £22/14; 9.30am-6.45pm Apr-Sep, 9am-5.45pm Oct-Mar) The Rock is one of the most dramatic landforms in southern Europe. Most of its upper sections fall within the Upper Rock Nature Reserve. Tickets include admission to **O'Hara's Battery** (9.2 Gun; O'Hara's Rd) on the Rock's summit, **St Michael's Cave** (St Michael's Rd), full of stalagmites and stalactites, the **Apes' Den**, the **Great Siege Tunnels** hewn out of the Rock during the siege of 1779–83, the 1333 **Moorish Castle** (Tower of Homage; Willis' Rd), the **Military Heritage Centre** (cnr Willis' & Queen's Rds), Nelson's Anchorage and the spine-tingling **Windsor Suspension Bridge** and glass-floor, 340m-high **Skywalk** (St Michael's Rd).

The **WWII tunnels** (☎20071649; Willis' Rd, Hay's Level; tours adult/child £8/4; ⏱9am-6.15pm), where the Allied invasion of North Africa was planned, can also be visited, but you'll need to book ahead. You must have a nature-reserve ticket to access the tunnels, but they aren't actually included in that ticket.

**★Gibraltar Museum** MUSEUM

(☎200 74289; www.gibmuseum.gi; 18-20 Bomb House Lane; adult/child £5/2.50; ⏱10am-6pm Mon-Fri, to 2pm Sat) Gibraltar's swashbuckling history unfolds in this fine museum, which comprises a labyrinth of rooms and exhibits ranging from prehistoric and Phoenician Gibraltar to the infamous Great Siege (1779–83). Don't miss the well-preserved 14th-century Islamic baths, and a 7th-century-BC Egyptian mummy found in the bay in the 1800s.

**Nelson's Anchorage** LANDMARK

(100-Tonne Gun; Rosia Rd; incl Upper Rock Nature Reserve adult/child £13/8; ⏱9.30am-6.15pm Apr-Sep, 9am-5.45pm Oct-Mar) At the southwestern end of town, Nelson's Anchorage pinpoints the site where Nelson's body was brought ashore from the HMS *Victory* after the Battle of Trafalgar – preserved in a rum barrel, so legend says. A 100-tonne, British-made Victorian supergun commemorates the spot.

**Gorham's Cave Complex** CAVE

(www.gibmuseum.gi; viewing platform adult/child £5/2.50; ⏱viewing platform 10am-2pm Mon-Fri) Inscribed on Unesco's World Heritage list in 2016, these four archaeologically rich cliffside caves on Gibraltar's southeastern coast were inhabited by Neanderthals from around 127,000 to 32,000 years ago. Though the caves themselves are off limits, you can see them from the nearby viewing platform.

**★Mediterranean Steps** HIKING

Not the most well-known attraction in Gibraltar, but surely the most spectacular, this narrow, ancient path with steep steps – many hewn into the limestone – starts at the nature reserve's southern entrance at Jews' Gate and traverses the southern end of Gibraltar before steeply climbing the crag on the eastern escarpment to emerge on the ridge near O'Hara's Battery.

The views along the way are stupendous, though the 1.5km trail is mildly exposed; allow 45 minutes to an hour.

## Sleeping

**Rock Hotel** HOTEL €€€

(☎20073000; www.rockhotelgibraltar.com; 3 Europa Rd; incl breakfast r £105-170, ste £195-340; P ❄ 📶 🏊) As famous as the local monkeys, Gibraltar's grand old dame overlooks the botanical gardens and has 86 elegant yet cosy, creamy, wood-floored rooms with fresh flowers, tea/coffee kits, sea views and, for some, private balconies. Tick off gym, pool, welcome drink, writing desks, bathrobes, a sparkling terrace cafe-bar (open to all), winter Sunday roasts and summer barbecues.

**Eliott** HOTEL €€€

(☎20070500; www.eliotthotel.com; 2 Governor's Pde; r £124-215, ste £250-315; ❄ 📶 🏊) This super-central, four-star establishment has chicly updated, smartly contemporary rooms styled in warm blues, yellows and greys, some with capsule-coffee kits and/or balconies. Bonuses include a pool on the rooftop, where there's also a view-laden bar and an international restaurant.

## Eating & Drinking

Goodbye tapas, hello fish and chips. Gibraltarian cuisine is unashamedly British – and pretty pricey compared to Andalucía, just across the border. The staples are pub grub, beer, sandwiches, chips and stodgy desserts, though a few international flavours can be found at Queensway Quay, Marina Bay and Ocean Village (this last has lots of global chains). There's a cluster of good tapas bars and restaurants on Fish Market Lane, just outside Grand Casemates Sq.

**My Wines** TAPAS €

(☎20069463; www.mywinesgibraltar.com; 11-12 The Strip, Chatham Counterguard; tapas £3-11; ⏱7.30am-11pm Mon-Thu, to 2am Fri, 10am-3.30pm & 6pm-2am Sat; 🖉) One of several buzzy Chatham spots, this wine boutique rustles up drops from 23 countries, served alongside a seasonally changing menu of lightly inventive Spanish-inspired tapas like mushroom croquettes, spicy *patatas bravas*, *huevos rotos* with ham or *pil pil*, or deep-fried goat's cheese. Live music, occasional wine pairings and a busy after-work scene.

**Clipper** PUB FOOD €
(☎20079791; www.theclipper.gi; 78B Irish Town; mains £7-9; ⏰9am-11pm Mon-Fri, 9am-4pm Sat, 10am-11pm Sun; 📶) Ask five…10…20 people in Gibraltar for their favourite pub and, chances are, they'll choose the packed-out Clipper. Looking sparklingly modern nowadays, the Clipper does real pub grub in traditionally large portions. British faves include jacket potatoes, chicken tikka masala, Sunday roasts and that essential all-day breakfast.

**Sacarello's** INTERNATIONAL €€
(☎20070625; www.sacarellosgibraltar.com; 57 Irish Town; mains £8-15; ⏰9am-7.30pm Mon-Fri, to 4pm Sat; 📶🌿) Founded in the 1980s, Sacarello's offers a great range of Spanish-international vegetarian food (pastas, quiches, soups) alongside pub-style dishes in an old multilevel coffee warehouse full of history. There's good house coffee, plus home-baked cakes, a salad bar and daily specials. From 3.30pm to 7.30pm, linger over cream tea.

**Lounge** INTERNATIONAL €€€
(☎20061118; www.facebook.com/TheLoungeGastro; 17A & B Ragged Staff Wharf, Queensway Quay; mains £10-20; ⏰10am-4pm & 6-10pm Fri-Mon & Wed, 10am-11pm Tue & Thu; 🌿) This popular, stylish waterside gastrobar and lounge, just south of the centre, serves a globetrotting, fresh-produce menu of salads, pastas, risottos, seafood, sandwiches and steaks, along with creative seasonal specials, all overlooking Queensway Quay's mega-yachts.

## ℹ Information

### TOURIST INFORMATION

**Tourist Office** (☎20045000; www.visitgibraltar.gi; Heritage Bldg, 13 John Mackintosh Sq; ⏰9am-4.30pm Mon-Fri, 9.30am-3.30pm Sat, 10am-1pm Sun)

### VISAS & PASSPORTS

To enter Gibraltar, you need a passport or EU national identity card. American, Canadian, Australian, New Zealand and EU passport holders are among those who do not need visas for Gibraltar. For further information, contact Gibraltar's **Civil Status & Registration Office** (☎20 076948; www.gibraltar.gov.gi; 2-8 Secretary's Lane). Requirements for EU citizens may change once final Brexit deals have been agreed on (or not) by the British and EU governments.

### ℹ CABLE CAR

The best way to explore the Rock is to whizz up on the **cable car** (Lower Cable-Car Station; Red Sands Rd; adult one way/return £16/14, child one way/return £7/7; ⏰9.30am-7.45pm Apr-Oct, to 5.15pm Nov-Mar) to the **top cable-car station**, then stop off at all the Upper Rock Nature Reserve sights on your way down. Note that the lower cable-car station stops selling tickets about two hours before the reserve closes. For the Apes' Den, hop out at the **middle station** (⏰closed Apr-Oct). Combined dolphin-watching and cable-car tickets (adult/child £41/19) are also available through dolphin-watching companies.

## ℹ Getting There & Away

### AIR

Gibraltar's well-connected **airport** (☎20 012345; www.gibraltarairport.gi) is at the northern end of the Rock, next to the Spanish border.

**British Airways** (www.britishairways.com) London (Heathrow).

**EasyJet** (www.easyjet.com) London (Gatwick/Luton), Bristol, Edinburgh, Manchester.

**Royal Air Maroc** (www.royalairmaroc.com) Casablanca, Tangier.

### BUS

No buses go directly to Gibraltar, but the **bus station** (Avenida de Europa) in La Línea de la Concepción (Spain) is only 400m north of the border. From here, regular buses go to/from Algeciras, Cádiz, Málaga, Seville, Tarifa and beyond.

### CAR & MOTORCYCLE

Long vehicle queues at the border and congested streets in Gibraltar make it far less time-consuming to park in La Línea and walk south across the frontier (1.5km to Casemates Sq). To take a car into Gibraltar (free), you need an insurance certificate, a registration document, a nationality plate and a driving licence. Gibraltar drives on the right.

In Gibraltar, there are car parks on Line Wall Rd, Reclamation Rd and Devil's Tower Rd (£1.30 per hour). La Línea has some street parking, but it's easier and safer to use the underground car parks (from €11 per 24 hours) just north of Avenida Príncipe de Asturias.

## ℹ Getting Around

Bus 5 runs between town and the border every 10 to 20 minutes. Bus 2 serves Europa Point,

### DOLPHIN WATCHING

The Bahía de Algeciras has a sizeable year-round population of dolphins (striped, bottlenose and short-beaked common) and a Gibraltar highlight is spotting them. Responsible operators **Dolphin Adventure** (☎20050650; www.dolphin.gi; 9 The Square, Marina Bay; adult/child £25/13), led by marine biologists, and **Dolphin Safari** (Blue Boat; ☎20071914; www.dolphinsafari.gi; 6 The Square, Marina Bay; adult/child £25/15) run dolphin-watching trips of one to 1½ hours. Most of the year both usually run two to three daily excursions. Dolphin Adventure also does summer whale-watching trips in the Strait of Gibraltar (adult/child £40/30). Advance bookings essential. September to November are the best months.

and bus 3 the southern town; buses 4 and 8 go to Catalan Bay. All these buses (www.gibraltarbuscompany.gi; Market Pl) stop at Market Pl, immediately northwest of Grand Casemates Sq. Tickets cost £1.80, or £2.50 for a day pass.

# CÓRDOBA PROVINCE

Once the dazzling beacon of Al-Andalus, historic Córdoba is the main magnet of Andalucía's northernmost province. But there's plenty of less-trampled territory to explore outside the provincial capital. To the south of the city, olive trees and grapevines cloak the rippling landscape, yielding some of Spain's best olive oils and the unique, sherry-like Montilla-Moriles wines. There's also fine walking to be enjoyed in the verdant, unspoiled hills of the Parque Natural Sierras Subbéticas.

## Córdoba

POP 325, 710 / ELEV 110M

One building alone is reason enough to set your sights on Córdoba. The astounding, multi-arched Mezquita is one of the world's greatest Islamic buildings, an enduring symbol of Córdoba's golden age as capital of Islamic Spain and western Europe's largest and most cultured city. Of course, there's more to the city than its star attraction and it merits far more than the fleeting visit many travellers give it. Its medieval centre is a charming pocket of winding lanes, white buildings, and flower-bedecked patios, while nearby, bars and restaurants line its lively riverside. A short walk to the north, the vibrant modern town offers a more local vibe and yet more excellent eating and drinking options.

### History

Córdoba's origins date back to the late Bronze Age when a settlement was set up on the Río Guadalquivir in the 8th or 9th century BCE. However, the city proper was founded in the 2nd century BCE. In about 25 BCE, Emperor Augustus made it capital of Baetica, one of the three Roman provinces on the Iberian Peninsula, heralding an era of prosperity and cultural ascendancy that saw it produce the famous writers Seneca and Lucan. But by the 3rd century, the Roman city was in decline, and in 711 CE it fell to Islamic invaders.

Over the next few centuries, Córdoba grew to become the greatest city in Islamic Spain. In 756, Abd ar-Rahman I set himself up here as the emir of Al-Andalus (the Muslim-controlled parts of the Iberian Peninsula), founding the Umayyad dynasty and building the Mezquita. However, it was under Abd ar-Rahman III (r 912–61) that the city, and Al-Andalus, enjoyed its greatest period. In 929, Abd ar-Rahman declared himself caliph, ushering in the Córdoba caliphate.

Córdoba was by now the largest city in western Europe with a population of around 250,000 and a flourishing economy. But its glory days were to be short-lived – in 1031 the Umayyad caliphate collapsed after a violent power struggle, and then, in 1069, the city was incorporated into the Seville *taifa* (small kingdom). It has been overshadowed by Seville ever since.

### ◉ Sights

#### ◉ Mezquita & Around

**★Mezquita** MOSQUE

(Mosque; ☎957 47 05 12; www.mezquita-catedraldecordoba.es; Calle Cardenal Herrero 1; adult/child €10/5, 8.30-9.30am Mon-Sat free; ⏲10am-7pm Mon-Sat, 8.30-11.30am & 3-7pm Sun Mar-Oct, to 6pm Nov-Feb) A medieval mosque with a Christian cathedral set inside it, Córdoba's Mezquita is one of the world's greatest works of Islamic architecture. It was originally built in the 8th century but enlargements over the next couple of centuries saw it become one of the largest and most architecturally sophisticated mosques of its age. Some five centuries on and it remains an astonishing sight with its serene columned interior, lustrous decoration and extraordinary *mihrab*.

The history of worship on the site actually pre-dates the Mezquita, going back to the mid-6th century when a small Visigoth church, the Basilica of San Vincente, stood here. Arab chronicles recount how Abd ar-Rahman I purchased half of the church for the Muslim community's Friday prayers, and then, in 784 CE, bought the other half as a site for a new mosque. His original structure, built between 786 and 788, subsequently underwent three extensions, increasing its size fivefold and bringing it to the form you see today – with one major alteration: a Christian cathedral was added to the middle of the mosque in the 16th century (hence the often-used description 'Mezquita-Catedral').

**➡ Patio de los Naranjos**

This lovely courtyard, with its orange, palm and cypress trees and fountains, was the site of ritual ablutions before prayers in the mosque. There are several entrances (it's free to go in and have a look around), the most impressive of which is the **Puerta del Perdón**, a 14th-century Mudéjar archway next to the bell tower. The Mezquita's ticket offices are just inside here.

**➡ Bell Tower (Torre Campanario)**

You can climb the 54m-high bell tower for fine panoramas and an interesting bird's-eye angle on the main Mezquita building. Originally built in 951–52 as the Mezquita's minaret, the *torre* was encased in a strengthened outer shell and heightened by the Christians in the 16th and 17th centuries. You can still see some caliphal vaults and arches inside. The original minaret, which would have looked very similar to Seville's Giralda, influenced all minarets subsequently built in the western Islamic world.

Up to 20 people are allowed up the tower every half hour between 9.30am and 6.30pm from March to October (to 5.30pm November to February, to 2.30pm July and August). Note, however, that there are no admissions at 11.30am and 1pm on Sundays. Tickets (€2) are sold at the ticket offices near the tower: they often sell out well ahead of visit times, so it's worth buying early in the day.

**➡ The Interior**

Though stunning from the outside, it's only by stepping into the Mezquita's mind-blowing interior that you get the full measure of its beauty. To help you navigate, there are free leaflets available just inside the visitor entrance.

The Mezquita's architectural importance lies in the fact that, structurally speaking, it was a revolutionary building for its time. Earlier Islamic buildings such as the Dome of the Rock in Jerusalem and the Great Mosque in Damascus placed an emphasis on verticality, but the Mezquita was intended as a simple, democratically horizontal space, where the spirit could roam freely and communicate with God – a kind of glorious refinement of the original Islamic prayer space (usually the open yard of a desert home).

Men prayed side by side on the *argamasa*, a floor made of compact, reddish slaked lime and sand. The flat roof, decorated with gold and multicoloured motifs, was supported by striped arches suggestive of a forest of date palms. The arches rested on, eventually, 1293 columns (of which 856 remain today).

Abd ar-Rahman I's initial prayer hall – the area immediately inside the entrance – was divided into 11 'naves' by lines of arches striped in red brick and white stone. The columns of these arches were a mishmash of material collected from the earlier church on the site, Córdoba's Roman buildings and places as far away as Constantinople. To raise the ceiling high enough to create a sense of openness, inventive builders came up with the idea of a two-tier construction, using taller columns as a base and planting shorter ones on top.

Later enlargements, southward by Abd ar-Rahman II in the 9th century and Al-Hakim II in the 960s, and eastward by Al-Mansur in the 970s, extended the mosque to an area of nearly 14,400 sq metres, making it one of the largest mosques in the world.

The final Mezquita had 19 doors along its north side, filling it with light and creating a sense of openness. Most of these doorways have since been closed off, dampening the vibrant effect of the red-and-white double arches. Christian additions to the building, such as the cathedral and the many chapels around the fringes, further enclose the airy space.

**➡ Mihrab & Maksura**

In the southern wall, opposite the visitor entrance, the *mihrab* and *maksura* (royal

# Mezquita

## TIMELINE

**6th century AD** Foundation of a Christian church, the Basilica of San Vicente, on the site of the present Mezquita.

**786-87** Salvaging Visigothic and Roman ruins, Emir Abd ar-Rahman I replaces the church with a *mezquita* (mosque).

**833-48** Mosque enlarged by Abd ar-Rahman II.

**951-2** A new minaret is built by Abd ar-Rahman III.

**962-71** Mosque enlarged, and superb new 1 **mihrab** added, by Al-Hakim II.

**991-4** Mosque enlarged for the last time by Al-Mansur, who also enlarged the courtyard (now the 2 **Patio de los Naranjos**), bringing the whole complex to its current dimensions.

**1236** Mosque converted into a Christian church after Córdoba is recaptured by Fernando III of Castilla.

**1271** Instead of destroying the mosque, the Christians modify it, creating the 3 **Capilla de Villaviciosa** and 4 **Capilla Real**.

**1523** Work on a Gothic/Renaissance-style cathedral inside the Mezquita begins, with permission of Carlos I. Legend has it that on seeing the result the king lamented that something unique in the world had been destroyed.

**1593-1664** The 10th-century minaret is reinforced and rebuilt as a Renaissance-baroque 5 **belltower**.

**2004** Spanish Muslims petition to be able to worship in the Mezquita again. The Vatican doesn't consent.

### TOP TIPS

➡ The Patio de los Naranjos can be enjoyed free of charge at any time.

➡ Entry to the main Mezquita building is offered free every morning, except Sunday, between 8.30am and 9.30am.

➡ Group visits are prohibited before 10am, meaning the building is quieter and more atmospheric in the early morning.

**The Mihrab**
Everything leads to the mosque's greatest treasure – the beautiful prayer niche, in the wall facing Mecca, that was added in the 10th century. Cast your eyes over the gold mosaic cubes crafted by sculptors imported from Byzantium.

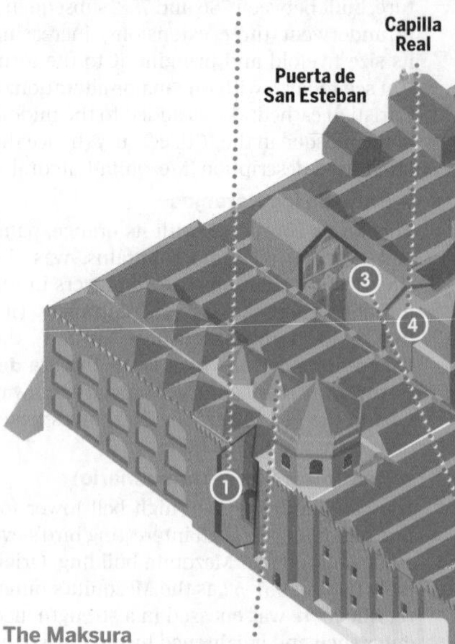


**The Maksura**
Guiding you towards the mihrab, the *maksura* was the former royal enclosure where the caliphs and their retinues prayed. Its lavish, elaborate arches were designed to draw the eye of worshippers towards the mihrab and Mecca.

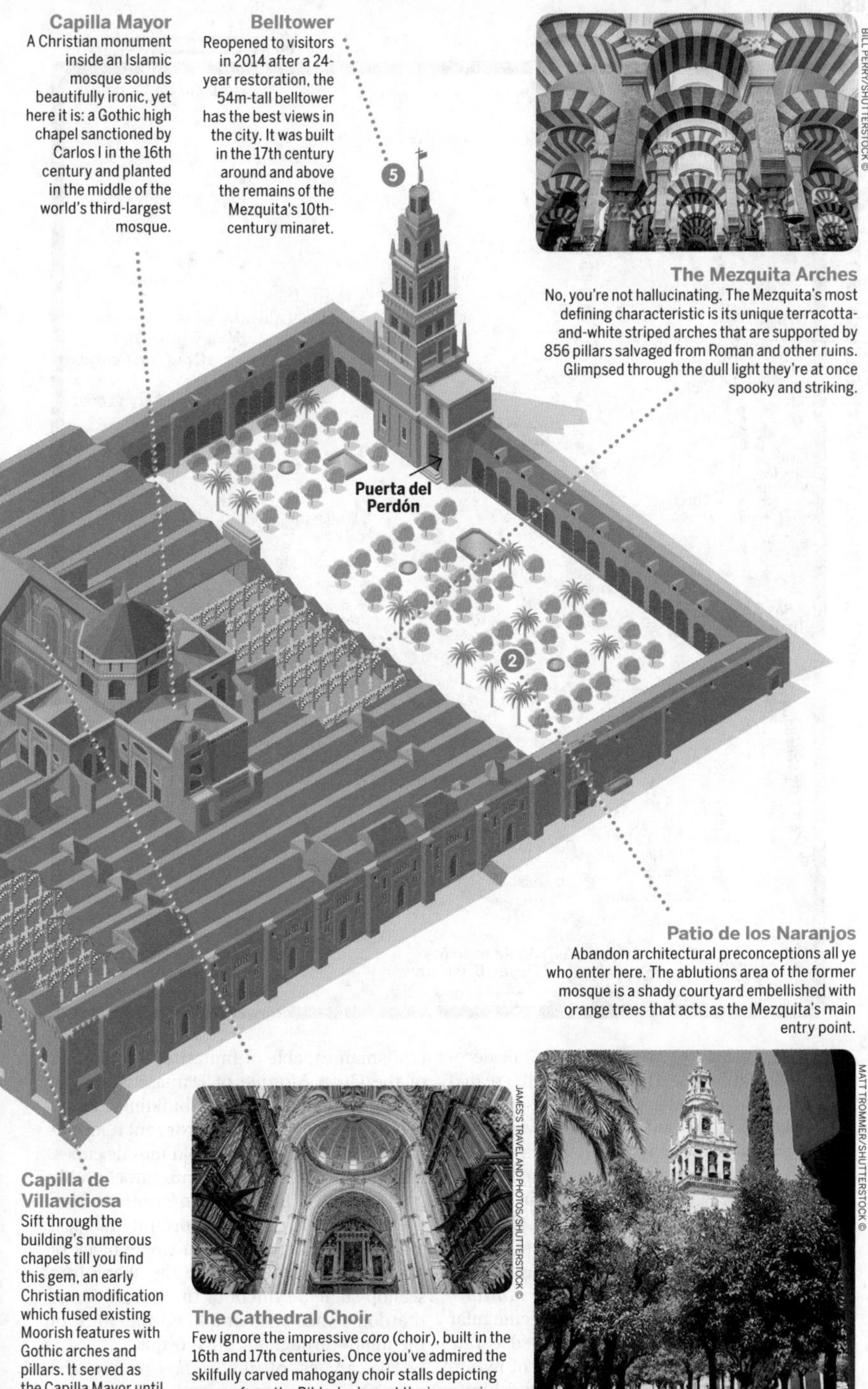


**Capilla Mayor**

A Christian monument inside an Islamic mosque sounds beautifully ironic, yet here it is: a Gothic high chapel sanctioned by Carlos I in the 16th century and planted in the middle of the world's third-largest mosque.

**Belltower**

Reopened to visitors in 2014 after a 24-year restoration, the 54m-tall belltower has the best views in the city. It was built in the 17th century around and above the remains of the Mezquita's 10th-century minaret.

**The Mezquita Arches**

No, you're not hallucinating. The Mezquita's most defining characteristic is its unique terracotta-and-white striped arches that are supported by 856 pillars salvaged from Roman and other ruins. Glimpsed through the dull light they're at once spooky and striking.

**Patio de los Naranjos**

Abandon architectural preconceptions all ye who enter here. The ablutions area of the former mosque is a shady courtyard embellished with orange trees that acts as the Mezquita's main entry point.

**Capilla de Villaviciosa**

Sift through the building's numerous chapels till you find this gem, an early Christian modification which fused existing Moorish features with Gothic arches and pillars. It served as the Capilla Mayor until 1607.

**The Cathedral Choir**

Few ignore the impressive *coro* (choir), built in the 16th and 17th centuries. Once you've admired the skilfully carved mahogany choir stalls depicting scenes from the Bible, look up at the impressive baroque ceiling.

# Córdoba

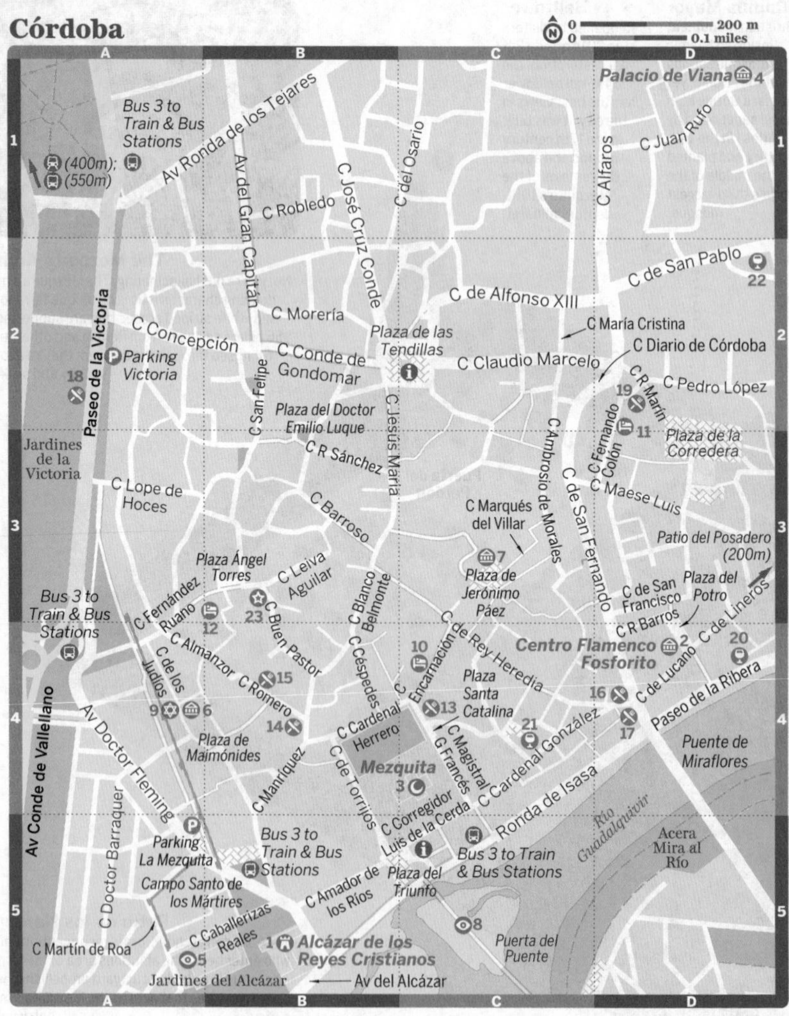


prayer enclosure) are the Mezquita's decorative highlights. They were both created as part of an extension commissioned by Al-Hakim II in the 960s. The naves of the prayer hall were lengthened and a new *qiblah* wall (indicating the direction of Mecca) and *mihrab* were added. The bay in front of the *mihrab* and the bays to each side of it form the *maksura*, the area where the caliphs and courtiers would have prayed.

Particularly spectacular is the *mihrab's* **portal** – a crescent arch with a rectangular surround known as an *alfiz*. To decorate this, Al-Hakim asked the emperor of Byzantium, Nicephoras II Phocas, to send him a craftsman capable of imitating the mosaics of the Great Mosque of Damascus, one of the great Syrian Umayyad buildings. In response, the Christian emperor sent a mosaicist along with 1600kg of gold mosaic cubes. And it's this gold, shaped into unbelievably intricate flower motifs and inscriptions from the Quran, that gives the portal its magical glitter. Inside the *mihrab*, a single block of white marble sculpted into the shape of a scallop shell, a symbol of the Quran, forms the dome that once amplified the voice of the imam throughout the mosque.

The arches of the *maksura* are the mosque's most intricate and sophisticated,

## Córdoba



forming a forest of interwoven horseshoe shapes. Above them the sky-lit domes are a spellbinding sight, with their star-patterned stone vaulting. Each **dome** is held up by four interlocking pairs of parallel ribs, a highly advanced technique for 10th-century Europe.

**➡ Cathedral**

Following the Christian conquest of Córdoba in 1236, the Mezquita was used as a cathedral but remained largely unaltered for nearly three centuries. However, in the 16th century King Carlos I gave the cathedral authorities permission to construct a new Capilla Mayor (main altar area) and *coro* (choir) in the centre of the Mezquita.

Legend has it that when the king saw the results of the work he was horrified, exclaiming that the builders had destroyed something unique in the world. The church, which is still today Córdoba's official cathedral, took nearly 250 years to complete (1523–1766) and exhibits a range of architectural styles, from Gothic and plateresque to late Renaissance and Spanish baroque. Among its standout features are the Capilla Mayor's rich 17th-century jasper and red-marble **retable** (altar screen), and the fine mahogany stalls in the **choir**, carved in the 18th century by Pedro Duque Cornejo. Capping everything is a towering 16th-century **dome**.

**➡ Night Visits**

A one-hour sound-and-light show ('El Alma de Córdoba'), in nine languages via audio guides, is presented in the Mezquita twice nightly except Sundays from March to October, and on Fridays and Saturdays between November and February. Tickets are €18 (senior or student €9). Further details are available on the website.

**★ Alcázar de los Reyes Cristianos** FORTRESS

(Fortress of the Christian Monarchs; ☎957 42 01 51; https://cultura.cordoba.es; Calle Caballerizas Reales; adult/student/child €5/2.50/free; ⊙8.30am-2.30pm Tue-Sun mid-Jun–mid-Sep, 8.15am-8pm Tue-Fri, 9.30am-6pm Sat, 8.15am-2.45pm Sun mid-Sep–mid-Jun) This formidable fort-palace dates to the 14th century when it was commissioned by King Alfonso XI and built over an earlier Moorish palace. It was Córdoba's main royal residence and it was here that Fernando and Isabel met Christopher Columbus in 1486. Inside, the highlight is a series of Roman mosaics, discovered under Plaza de la Corredera in the 1950s, while outside, the exquisite Moorish-style gardens are a joy to explore.

**Puente Romano** BRIDGE

Spanning the Río Guadalquivir just below the Mezquita, this handsome 16-arch bridge originally formed part of Via Augusta, the ancient Roman road that connected Girona in Catalonia with Cádiz. It has been rebuilt several times since the 1st century CE and now makes for a lovely traffic-free stroll.

Cross the bridge look back to the Mezquita dominating the skyline.

**Caballerizas Reales** STABLES

(Royal Stables; ☎671 949514; www.cordobaecuestre.com; Calle Caballerizas Reales 1; adult/child training €5/1, show €16.50/11.50; ⊙10am-1.30pm daily plus 4-7pm Tue, 4-6.30pm Wed-Sat, show 9pm Wed-Sat mid-Apr–mid-Sep, 7.30pm mid-Sep–mid-Apr) These elegant stables were built on the orders of King Felipe II in 1570 as a centre for developing the tall Spanish thoroughbred warhorse *(caballo andaluz)*. The centre still breeds these fine horses as well as running riding courses. You can watch training from 11am in the morning, or attend the 70-minute show that sets equestrian manoeuvres to flamenco music and dance.

## East & North of the Mezquita

**Museo Arqueológico** MUSEUM
(957 35 55 17; www.museosdeandalucia.es; Plaza de Jerónimo Páez 7; EU/non-EU citizen free/€1.50; 9am-9pm Tue-Sat, to 3pm Sun Sep-Jun, 9am-3pm Tue-Sun Jul & Aug) Córdoba's excellent archaeological museum traces the city's many changes in size, appearance and lifestyle from pre-Roman to early Reconquista times. Its collection, one of Spain's largest, includes some fine sculpture, an impressive coin collection, and an array of finds relating to domestic life and religion; explanations are provided in English and Spanish. In the basement, you can walk through the excavated remains of the city's Roman theatre.

★**Centro Flamenco Fosforito** MUSEUM
(Posada del Potro; 957 47 68 29; www.centroflamencofosforito.cordoba.es; Plaza del Potro; 8.45am-3.15pm Tue-Sun mid-Jun–mid-Sep, 8.15am-8pm Tue-Fri, 9.30am-6pm Sat, 8.15am-2.45pm Sun mid-Sep–mid-Jun) FREE Charmingly housed in a historic inn, this passionately curated museum is a must for anyone with even a passing interest in flamenco. Exhibits, which include photos, film footage, recordings and instruments, are combined with information panels in English and Spanish to chart the history of the art form and its great exponents.

Free concerts and flamenco performances are occasionally held here – check the website for upcoming events.

★**Palacio de Viana** MUSEUM
(957 49 67 41; www.palaciodeviana.com; Plaza de Don Gome 2; whole house/patios €8/5, 2-5pm Wed free; 10am-7pm Tue-Sat, to 3pm Sun Sep-Jun, 9am-3pm Tue-Sun Jul & Aug) A noble Renaissance palace, the Palacio de Viana is a particular delight in spring when its 12 plant-filled patios are awash with colour. The much-modified 14th-century mansion was home to the aristocratic Marqueses de Viana until 1980, and its stately rooms are crammed with art and antiques. Visits to the palace are by guided tour only, but you're free to explore the pretty courtyards on your own.

## Festivals & Events

**Fiesta de los Patios de Córdoba** FIESTA
(http://patios.cordoba.es; May) This 'best patio' competition sees 50 or more of Córdoba's private courtyards open for free public viewing for two weeks in early May. Some of the best are on and around Calle San Basilio and in the Alcázar Viejo area 400m southwest of the Mezquita. Flamenco and concerts are staged in patios and plazas across town.

★**Noche Blanca del Flamenco** MUSIC
(http://nocheblancadelflamenco.cordoba.es; mid-Jun) This all-night fest of top-notch flamenco features free performances by leading artists in picturesque venues such as Plaza del Potro and the Mezquita's Patio de los Naranjos.

**Festival de la Guitarra de Córdoba** MUSIC
(www.guitarracordoba.es; early Jul) A 10-day celebration of the guitar. Theatres across town stage concerts of classical, flamenco, rock, blues, and more by top Spanish and international names.

## Sleeping

**Hospedería Alma Andalusí** HOTEL €
(957 20 04 25; www.almaandalusi.com; Calle Fernández Ruano 5; s €38-65, d €76-128; ) This cosy hotel in a quiet section of the Judería makes a great base. Rooms are small but attractive, with thoughtfully chosen furnishings, large photos of Córdoba's sights, and polished-wood or traditional-tile floors. The room rates we quote are fully refundable but there are also cheaper, non-refundable rates.

★**Patio del Posadero** BOUTIQUE HOTEL €€
(957 94 17 33; www.patiodelposadero.com; Calle Mucho Trigo 21; r incl breakfast €95-155; ) It's not the easiest to find – down a side alley 1km east of the Mezquita – but this refined hideaway is well worth the search. Housed in a converted 15th-century building, it marries contemporary design with traditional Córdoba-Moorish touches. From its brick-arched patio, stairs lead up to a salon and terrace with a small plunge pool, and six handsome, individually styled rooms.

DON'T MISS

## JUDERÍA

The Judería, Córdoba's old Jewish quarter, forms the heart of the city's historic centre. Narrow, cobbled streets weave through the area, which extends west and northwest of the Mezquita, leading past whitewashed buildings and wrought-iron gates allowing glimpses of plant-filled patios. Some streets are choked with gaudy souvenir shops and touristy restaurants, but others remain quiet and unblemished.

In the heart of the district, and once connected by tunnel to the synagogue, the **Casa de Sefarad** (957 42 14 04; www.casadesefarad.es; cnr Calles de los Judíos & Averroes; adult/child €4/3; 11am-6pm Mon-Sat, to 2pm Sun) is an interesting museum devoted to the Sephardic (Iberian Peninsula Jewish) tradition. Close by is a small, probably private, **Sinagoga** (957 74 90 15; Calle de los Judíos 20; EU/non-EU citizen free/€0.30; 9am-9pm Tue-Sat, to 3pm Sun). Constructed in 1315, this is one of the few surviving testaments to the Jewish presence in medieval Andalucía. Its light-filled main hall is decorated with extravagant stucco work that includes Hebrew inscriptions and intricate Mudéjar star and plant motifs.

**Casa de los Azulejos** HOTEL €€
(957 47 00 00; www.casadelosazulejos.com; Calle Fernando Colón 5; incl breakfast s €59-90, d €67-151; ) With its Andalucian-Mexican look, sunny, plant-filled patio, and basement microbrewery, there's a lot to like about this stylish nine-room hotel. Its attractive rooms (named after Mexican plants) feature lilacs, lemons and sky blues, and jazzy bathroom tiles that complement the traditional Spanish floor *azulejos* (tiles) that give the place its name.

★ **Balcón de Córdoba** BOUTIQUE HOTEL €€€
(957 49 84 78; www.balcondecordoba.com; Calle Encarnación 8; d incl breakfast €142-427; ) Offering top-end boutique luxury a stone's throw from the Mezquita, the Balcón is a magazine spread waiting to happen. Its effortlessly cool decor blends a muted contemporary approach with historic touches, such as heavy wooden shutters, brick-arched patios and ancient stone relics. Service doesn't miss a beat and there are memorable Mezquita views from the rooftop terrace.

## Eating

Córdoba's signature dish is *salmorejo*, a thick, chilled soup, sprinkled with hard-boiled egg and strips of ham. Along with *rabo de toro* (oxtail stew), it appears on every menu. Another city speciality is *flamenquín*, a roll of breaded pork wrapped around slices of ham. Don't miss the sweet local Montilla-Moriles wine.

★ **La Bicicleta** CAFE €
(666 544690; Calle Cardenal González 1; dishes €5-16; noon-1am Mon & Fri, 10am-1am Tue-Thu & Sun, 9am-1am Sat; ) Locals and visitors enjoy the shabby-chic Bicicleta, an inviting, laid-back cafe where you can sip on fruit juices and cocktails, dig into delish cakes or sit down to avocado-and-ham toasties or light meals such as hummus with salad.

**Mercado Victoria** FOOD HALL €
(www.mercadovictoria.com; Paseo de la Victoria; items €2-19; 11am-1am Sun-Thu, to 2am Fri & Sat mid-Jun–mid-Sep, 10am-midnight Sun-Thu, to 2am Fri & Sat mid-Sep–mid-Jun) If you fancy a tasty fill-up without the formality of a restaurant meal, this buzzing food hall is ideal. Occupying a 19th-century pavilion in the Victoria gardens just west of the old city, its stalls cook up everything from Argentine empanadas and Mexican burritos to sushi, pizzas and classic Spanish seafood.

**Taberna Salinas** ANDALUCIAN €
(957 48 29 50; www.tabernasalinas.com; Calle Tundidores 3; mains €7.75-11; 12.30-3.30pm & 8-11pm Mon-Sat, closed Aug) A historic bar-restaurant (since 1879) with a patio and several rooms, Salinas is adorned in classic Córdoba fashion with tiles, wine barrels, art and photos of bullfighter Manolete. It's popular with tourists, but it retains a traditional atmosphere and its classic regional food is reliably good (and served in huge helpings).

**Bar Santos** TAPAS €
(Calle Magistral González Francés 3; tapas €2.30-5; 10am-midnight Mon-Fri, from 11am Sat & Sun) For one of Córdoba's signature eating ex-

periences, join the queues at this legendary bar and order a *tortilla de patata* (potato omelette). You'll be handed a paper plate weighed down by a thick wedge of the stuff, deftly cut from a giant yellow ball. Balancing this and your plastic cutlery, cross the street and eat under the Mezquita's walls.

★**Casa Pepe de la Judería** ANDALUCIAN €€
(☎957 20 07 44; www.restaurantecasapepedelajuderia.com; Calle Romero 1; tapas €3.60-14, mains €12-39; ⏲1-4pm & 7.30-11pm; 📶) Expertly prepared Andalucian fare, on a sunny roof terrace or in rooms adorned with Cordoban art, keeps Pepe's high in the popularity charts. Whether you go for tapas or the more expensive restaurant menu, quality is high, culminating in some fabulous meat dishes – try the sensational *presa ibérica* (steak of Iberian pork). Service remains attentive and friendly, even when it's packed.

**Garum 2.1** TAPAS €€
(☎957 48 76 73; Calle de San Fernando 122; tapas €4-8, mains €10-17; ⏲1-4pm & 8-11pm) Blending a bistro-style approach with gourmet tapas, Garum 2.1 touts itself as a bistronomic tapas bar. This sounds faintly ridiculous but there's nothing off-putting about its tapas which are creatively presented and often quite inspired. A case in point are its churros, here filled with oxtail and chocolate, and the award-wining octopus served with smoked pig's ears. Excellent wine too.

**El Churrasco** GRILL €€€
(☎957 29 08 19; www.elchurrasco.com; Calle Romero 16; tapas €2-6.15, mains €12-34; ⏲1-4pm & 8-11.30pm Sun-Thu, to midnight Fri & Sat) Renowned for its chargrilled meats, including its signature *churrasco cordobés* (pork tenderloin grilled over oak charcoal, with Arabic sauces), this busy bar-restaurant stands out in the touristy Mezquita area. Service can be a bit gruff at the bar, but the expert grillers know their stuff and the food is consistently good – mainly steaks and traditional meat dishes but also some fish options.

> **WORTH A TRIP**
>
> **CASA OLEA**
>
> Set amidst olive groves in an unspoiled river valley 12km north of Priego de Córdoba, **Casa Olea** (☎696 748209; www.casaolea.com; Carretera CO7204, near El Cañuelo; s/d incl breakfast €121/132; P ❄ 📶 🏊) 🍃 is a rustic farmhouse set-up with a beautifully spacious and relaxed feel. It makes a delightful base for exploring the Sierras Subbéticas, with six simply attired rooms, easy access to walks and mountain bikes to rent (€15 per day). There's a lovely pool, and excellent dinners (two/three courses €21/26) are available five nights a week.

## Drinking & Entertainment

The bars and cafes on and around Plaza de las Tendillas are a favourite evening hangout. Another popular area is the riverfront Pasero de la Ribera.

★**Jugo** WINE BAR
(www.facebook.com/quierojugovivo; Plaza San Andres 5; ⏲noon-1.45pm & 6-10pm Mon-Thu, noon-1.45pm & 6-11pm Fri, noon-3.30pm & 7-11pm Sat, noon-3pm Sun) A bit of a hike from the main tourist haunts, Jugo is a real find, a natural wine shop doubling as a bar. Run with welcoming cheer by English-speaking Javi and Gaby, it's a great place to escape the hordes and enjoy a tranquil glass or two, either in the rustic interior or on the plaza outside.

**El Barón** BAR
(Plaza de Abades 4; ⏲12.30pm-midnight) Set on a charming old town plaza, the outside tables at this unassuming bar are a lovely place for a relaxed drink. It has Montilla wines and *cava*, craft beers, and a choice of sweet and savoury snacks (€2.50 to €9), including a rich house pâté and lush chocolate cake.

**Amapola** BAR
(www.facebook.com/amapolabarcordoba; Paseo de la Ribera 9; ⏲4pm-2.30am, from noon Fri-Sun) With Elvis Costello providing the soundtrack, beer served in pints, and a retro feel about the sparsely furnished interior, everything is in place to make this riverside bar your go-to drinking hang-out. There's a terrace looking down to the river and cool music, either spun by DJs or live most Friday and/or Saturday nights.

**Tablao Cardenal** FLAMENCO
(☎691 217922; www.tablaocardenal.es; Calle Buen Pastor 2; shows incl 1 drink €23; ⏲shows 8.15pm Mon-Thu, 9pm Fri & Sat) A 17th-century aristocratic house in the Judería provides the atmospheric setting for professional, passionate flamenco shows featuring song, music and dance.

## Information

Information on Córdoba and its province is available at www.cordobaturismo.es. There are currently two tourist offices in town:

**Centro de Visitantes** (Visitors Centre; 902 20 17 74; www.turismodecordoba.org; Plaza del Triunfo; 9am-7pm Mon-Fri, 9.30am-2.30pm Sat & Sun) The main tourist office near the Mezquita; can provide maps and printed material in English and Spanish.

**Municipal Tourist Information Kiosk** (www.turismodecordoba.org; Plaza de las Tendillas; 9am-1.30pm & 5-7.15pm daily).

## Getting There & Away

### TRAIN

Córdoba's modern **train station** (902 320 320; Plaza de las Tres Culturas), 1.2km northwest of Plaza de las Tendillas, is served by fast AVE services and slower regional trains.

| Destination | Cost (€) | Time | Frequency (daily) |
|---|---|---|---|
| Andújar | 910 | 50min | 4 |
| Antequera (Santa Ana) | 17-34 | 30-40min | 17-18 |
| Granada | 25-49 | 1½-2¼hr | 6 |
| Jaén | 15 | 1¾hr | 4 |
| Madrid | 39-63 | 1¾-2¼hr | 33-34 |
| Málaga | 21-42 | 1hr | 16-17 |
| Seville | 14-32 | 45-75min | 29-35 |

## Getting Around

### BUS

**Bus 3** (957 76 46 76; www.aucorsa.es) runs every 14 to 20 minutes (€1.30) from Avenida Vía Augusta (the street between the train and bus stations) down Calle de San Fernando to the riverside Paseo de la Ribera, east of the Mezquita. For the return trip, catch it on Ronda de Isasa (Ronda de Isasa) near the main tourist office, or from Campo Santo de los Mártires, Glorieta Cruz Roja or Avenida de Cervantes.

### CAR

Driving in Córdoba is no picnic – the one-way system is nightmarish and cars are banned from most of the historic centre unless unloading or parking at a hotel.

There is free, unmetered parking south of the river across the Puente de Miraflores, and a mixture of free and metered parking on Paseo de la Victoria. Expect to pay around €0.85 per hour in a metered zone (marked with blue lines), though you can generally stop for free between 2pm and 5pm, overnight from 9pm to 9am, and from 2pm Saturday to 9am Monday. Convenient car parks include **Parking Victoria** (Paseo de la Victoria; per 24hr €13; 24hr) and **Parking La Mezquita** (Avenida Doctor Fleming; per 24hr €15; 24hr).

# Parque Natural Sierras Subbéticas

Some 70km southeast of Córdoba, the Parque Natural Sierras Subbéticas encompasses some 320 sq km of craggy, emerald-green hills pocked with caves, springs and streams.

### BUSES FROM CÓRDOBA

The **bus station** (957 40 40 40; www.estacionautobusescordoba.es; Avenida de la Libertad) is located behind the train station, 1.3km northwest of Plaza de las Tendillas.

**ALSA** (902 42 22 42; www.alsa.es)

**Autocares Carrera** (957 50 16 32; www.autocarescarrera.es)

**Autocares San Sebastián** (957 42 90 30; www.autocaressansebastian.es)

**Cambus** (679 730134; www.cambusautocares.com)

**Socibus** (902 22 92 92; www.socibus.es)

| DESTINATION | BUS COMPANY | COST (€) | TIME (HR) | FREQUENCY (DAILY) |
|---|---|---|---|---|
| Baeza | Alsa | 12 | 2¼ | 2 |
| Granada | Alsa | 15 | 2¾-4 | 9-11 |
| Jaén | Cambus | 11 | 2 | 4-7 |
| Madrid | Socibus | 18-25 | 4¼-5 | 7-8 |
| Málaga | Alsa | 12 | 2½-3 | 3-4 |
| Seville | Alsa | 13 | 1¾-2 | 7 |
| Úbeda | Alsa | 13 | 1¾-2½ | 4-5 |

WORTH A TRIP

## MEDINA AZAHARA

Some 8km west of Córdoba stand the ruins of **Medina Azahara** (Madinat al-Zahra; ☎957 10 49 33; www.museosdeandalucia.es; Carretera Palma del Río, Km 5.5; EU/non-EU citizen free/€1.50, shuttle bus adult/child €2.50/1.50; ⏰9am-9pm Tue-Sat Apr–mid-Jun, to 3pm mid-Jun–mid-Sep, to 6pm mid-Sep–Mar, 9am-3pm Sun year-round; P), the 10th-century palace-city built by Caliph Abd ar-Rahman III. Only about a tenth of the original city has been excavated and visits, which start in a modern museum some 2km below the hillside ruins, are limited to the central section of the Alcázar, the quarter that comprised the caliph's palace and attendant offices and residential blocks.

Get your entrance tickets at the **museum** by the car park. Here you can also watch an introductory film and browse informative displays illustrating Medina's planning and construction, its inhabitants and its rapid downfall.

From the car park, a shuttle bus ferries you up to the ruins, which you enter through the city's original northern gate. Highlights include the arched **Edificio Basilical Superior**, which housed the main state admin offices, a row of **red-striped arches** from the Grand Portico, and the **Casa de Yafar**, believed to have been residence of the caliph's prime minister.

To get to Medina Azahara by car from Córdoba, head west on the A431, exiting after about 6km. Alternatively, a bus runs to the site from Glorieta Cruz Roja at 10.15am, 11am and 11.45am Tuesdays to Sundays, plus 2.40pm on Saturdays – check these times as seasonal variations apply. Buy tickets (adult/child €9/5 return including the shuttle bus to/from the ruins) on the bus or at Córdoba's tourist office – buying in advance is sensible for weekends and public holidays. The bus then starts back from Medina 3¼ hours after it leaves Córdoba.

There's wonderful hiking in its valleys, canyons and peaks (including the highest, the 1570m La Tiñosa), ideally in April, May, September or October.

Park information is available at the **Centro de Visitantes Santa Rita** (☎957 50 69 86; Carretera A339, Km 11.2; ⏰9am-2pm Wed-Sun, 6-8pm Sat & Sun May-Aug, 9am-2pm Wed-Sun Sep, 9am-2pm Wed-Sun Sep, 9am-2pm Wed-Sun, 4-6pm Sat & Sun Oct-Apr), 15km west of Priego de Córdoba on the road to Cabra.

# Zuheros

POP 640 / ELEV 660M

Tiny Zuheros is the most picturesque of the villages in the Parque Natural Sierras Subbéticas. A jumble of white, red-roofed houses capped by a crag-top castle, it crouches in the lee of towering hills surrounded by olive groves stretching as far as the eye can see. Approached by twisting roads up from the A318, it has a delightfully relaxed atmosphere.

## Sights

**Castillo de Zuheros** CASTLE
(☎957 69 45 45; Plaza de la Paz; adult/child incl Museo Arqueológico €2/1.25; ⏰10am-2pm & 5-7pm Tue-Fri, tours 11am, 12.30pm, 2pm, 5pm & 6.30pm Sat & Sun Apr-Sep, 10am-2pm & 4-6pm Tue-Fri, tours 11am, 12.30pm, 2pm, 4pm & 5.30pm Sat & Sun Oct-Mar) Grafted onto a rocky pinnacle, Zuheros' castle is of 9th-century Moorish origin, but most of what survives is a Christian construction from the 13th and 14th centuries, with remains of a 16th-century Renaissance palace attached. It's small but panoramic, with fine views from the top. Visits on weekends and holidays are guided; other days, you're free to visit on your own. Tickets are sold at the small **Museo Arqueológico**, just across the square, which also doubles as Zuheros' tourist office.

**Cueva de los Murciélagos** CAVE
(Cave of the Bats; ☎957 69 45 45; adult/child €7.50/6; ⏰12.30-5.30pm Tue-Fri, tours 11am, 12.30pm, 2pm, 5pm & 6.30pm Sat & Sun Apr-Sep, 12.30-4.30pm Tue-Fri, tours 11am, 12.30pm, 2pm, 4pm & 5.30pm Sat & Sun Oct-Mar; P) Carved out of the limestone massif 4km above Zuheros is this extraordinary cave. From the vast hall at the start of the tour, it's a 415m loop walk (with 700 steps) through a series of corridors filled with fantastic rock formations and traces of Neolithic rock paintings showing abstract figures of goats. Visits are by guided

tour only: reserve by phoning between 10am and 1.30pm Tuesday to Friday or by emailing turismo@zuheros.es.

## Activities

Zuheros offers excellent walking with several trails leading through the surrounding slopes. Hotel Zuhayra can provide good hiking information.

**Vía Verde del Aceite** CYCLING
(Vía Verde de la Subbética; www.viasverdes.com; ) The area's easiest and best marked trail is the *vía verde* (greenway; a disused railway converted to a cycling and walking track). Running for 58km through the western and northern fringes of the Parque Natural Sierras Subbéticas, this local stretch of the 128km-long *vìa* – which, in its entirety, traverses Córdoba and Jaén provinces – is ideal for a relaxed, easy-going workout.

**Centro Cicloturista Subbética** CYCLING
(672 605088, 691 843532; www.subbeticabikesfriends.com; per half-/full day bikes €12/18, electric bikes €12/25; 10am-12.30pm Sat & Sun mid-Jun–mid-Sep, 10am-2pm Mon-Fri, to 7pm Sat & Sun mid-Sep–mid-Jun; ) The nearest bike-rental spot to Zuheros is the Centro Cicloturista Subbética at Doña Mencía station, 4km downhill from the village. It has a range of different bikes, including children's and electric bikes, and can provide local tourist information as well as showers and other services for cyclists.

## Sleeping & Eating

**★Hotel Zuhayra** HOTEL €
(957 69 46 93; www.zercahoteles.com; Calle Mirador 10; incl breakfast s €43-55, d €53-70; ) An arrow's shot from Zuheros' castle, this sunny hotel has breathtaking views of the countryside from each of its white, tile-floored rooms. You can hire bikes here (€10 for four hours, €15 for longer) and the welcoming proprietors, the Ábalos brothers (who speak English), are a mine of local information. There is also a first-class **restaurant** (mains & raciones €7-19; 1-3.30pm & 8-10.30pm) on the first floor.

**Mesón Atalaya** ANDALUCIAN €€
(957 69 47 65; Calle Santo 58; mains €6-19; 1-4pm & 9-11pm Tue-Sun) One of the first buildings you come to when entering Zuheros from the east, this rustic, family-run establishment does a fine line in filling country fare – no-nonsense meat dishes and *cazuelas* (types of stew), local cheeses and homemade desserts. There are two plant-filled patios and a small sunny terrace out front.

## Information

**Tourist Office** (957 69 45 45; www.zuheros.es/turismo; Plaza de la Paz 1; 10am-2pm & 5-7pm Tue-Fri, 11am-2pm Sat & Sun Apr-Sep, 10am-2pm & 4-6pm Tue-Fri, 11am-2pm Sat & Sun Oct-Mar) Zuheros' helpful tourist office shares premises with the archaeological museum. Come here for tickets or guided visits to the castle.

## Getting There & Away

Buses depart from Mesón Atalaya.

Autocares Carrera has two to four daily buses to/from Córdoba (€6.65, 1¾ hours). **Monbus** (982 29 29 00; www.monbus.es) has three or more buses to/from Seville (€17.37, 3¾ hours).

## AT A GLANCE

**POPULATION**
3.97 million

**BIGGEST CITY**
Málaga

**BEST WHITE VILLAGES**
Barranco del Poqueira (p724)

**BEST BOUTIQUE HOTEL**
Aire de Ronda (p745)

**BEST COUNTRY TOWN**
Cazorla (p760)

**WHEN TO GO**

**Mar & Apr** Festivals and Easter processions (plus crowds and high-season prices).

**May, Jun, Sep & Oct** Sunny months ideal for hiking, touring and exploring.

**Nov–Feb** Winter means fewer tourists, bargain prices and skiing in the Sierra Nevada.

Granada (p700)
CGE2010/SHUTTERSTOCK

# Granada & South Coast Andalucía

From lively beachside towns to sparkling-white mountain villages seemingly forgotten by time, Andalucía's eastern half and southern coastline combine a compelling package of sunny Mediterranean fun, rich and intriguing culture, and outstanding natural beauty.

Gorgeous Granada thrills with its Moorish influence and magical Alhambra palace, while to the south, vibrant Málaga continues to reinvent itself as an arty hub of contemporary culture. Summer holidaymakers flock to the brazen beach resorts of the Costa del Sol and the spectacular hill town of Ronda.

Away from the cities and coast is a quieter side. The sky-reaching Sierra Nevada awaits with rustic villages, soul-stirring panoramas and superb hiking trails. To the north, the handsome Renaissance towns of Jaén province beckon. In the far southeast, Almería's refreshingly undeveloped Cabo de Gata is a world of haunting semi-desert terrain and exquisite beaches.

**INCLUDES**

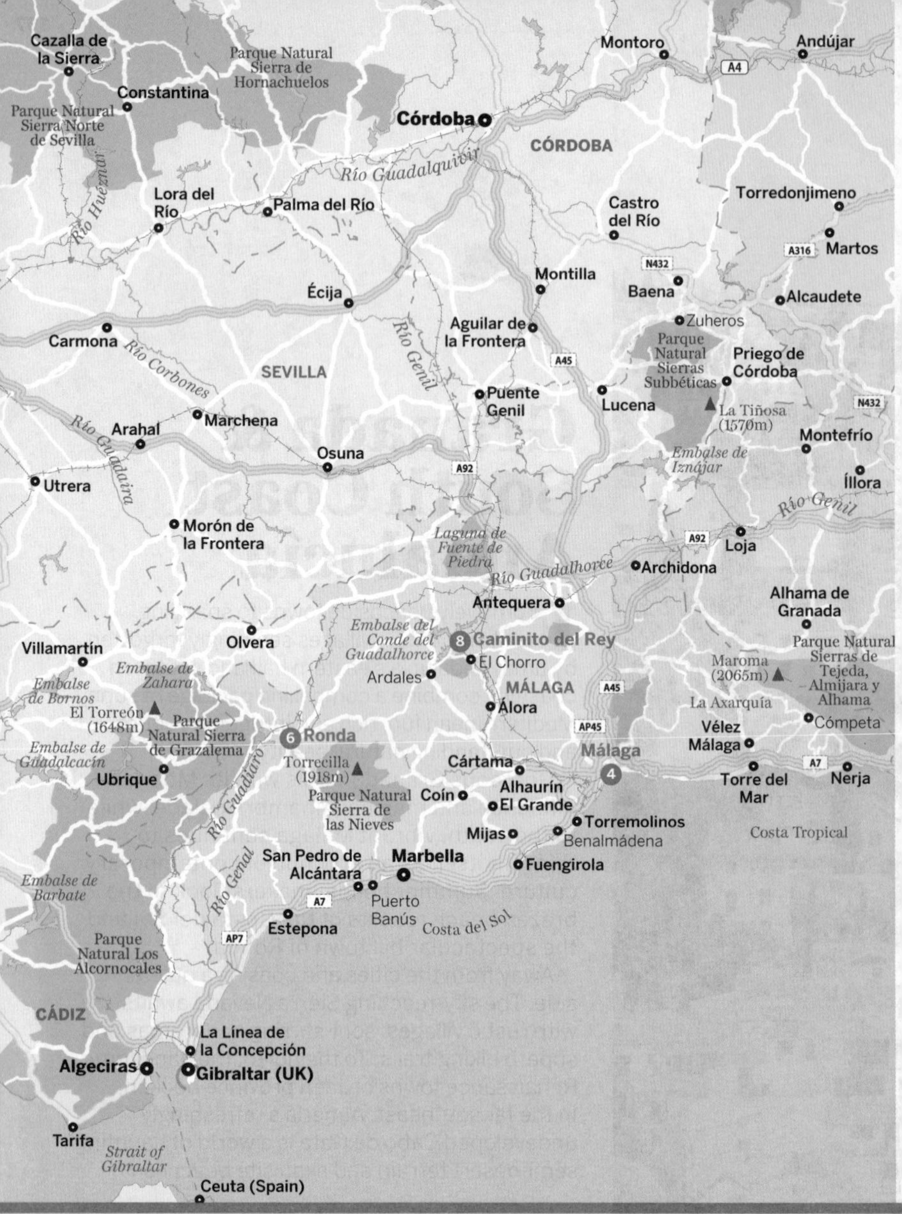


## Granada & South Coast Andalucía Highlights

1. **Granada** (p700) Admiring the Alhambra, a masterpiece of Moorish architecture, then tapas-hopping around the history-rich city.

2. **Parque Natural de Cabo de Gata-Níjar** (p767) Lazing on the Almerian beaches of Andalucía's coastline.

3. **Las Alpujarras** (p723) Hiking through the white villages and vertiginous canyons of the Sierra Nevada's southern slopes.

4. **Málaga** (p730) Taking a trip from Picasso to modern street art to culinary wizardry.

5. **Parque Natural Sierras**

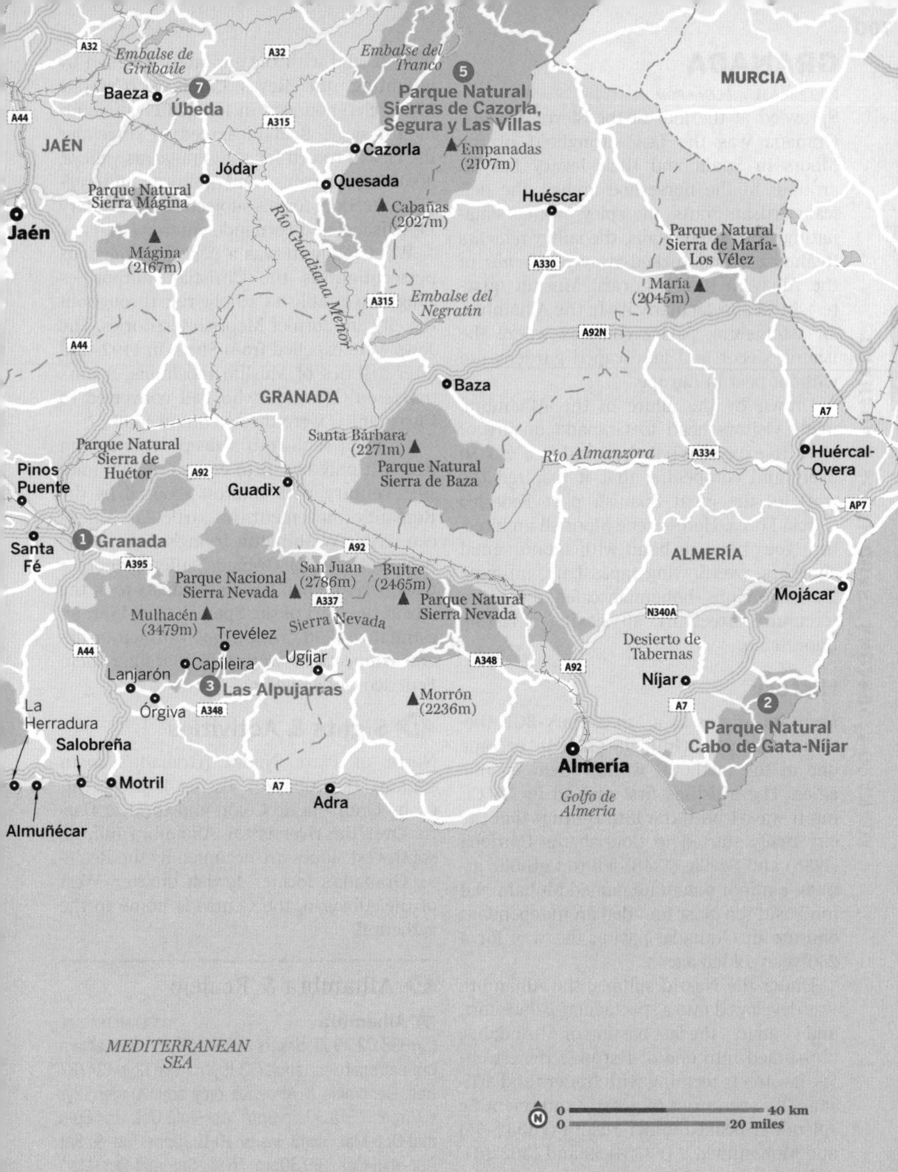


**de Cazorla, Segura y Las Villas** (p761) Roaming craggy mountains and scenic villages, eyes peeled for wildlife.

6 **Ronda** (p744) Strolling this picturesque gorge-hugging *malagueño* town.

7 **Úbeda** (p756) Indulging the senses with inspired architecture and cuisine.

8 **Caminito del Rey** (p748) Following a narrow, spine-tingling elevated path through El Chorro gorge.

# GRANADA

POP 227,631 / ELEV 680M

Sprawled at the foot of the Sierra Nevada, Granada was the last stronghold of the Moors in Spain and their legacy lies all around: in the horseshoe arches, the delicate artisan crafts, the spicy aromas emanating from street stalls, the sultry *teterías* (teahouses) and tucked-away *cármenes* of the Albayzín (the historical Muslim quarter). Most spectacularly it's in the Alhambra, an astonishing palace complex where the Islamic decor and landscaped gardens are without peer in Europe.

Drawn by the allure of the Alhambra, many visitors head to Granada unsure of what to expect. What they find is a city so lively and compelling that it inspired the work of the great Spanish poet Federico García Lorca. Here serene Moorish architecture goes hand in hand with monumental churches, overflowing tapas bars, intimate flamenco clubs, bohemian cafes and counterculture street art, all leaving a lasting impression.

## History

From its origins as a 5th-century-BCE Iberian settlement, Granada grew to become one of the medieval world's great Islamic cities. The Muslims first arrived in 711 CE but it wasn't until the 13th century that the city really started to flourish. As Córdoba (1236) and Seville (1248) fell to Catholic armies, a minor potentate named Mohammed ibn Yusuf ibn Nasr founded an independent emirate in Granada, paving the way for a 250-year golden age.

Under the Nasrid sultans, the Alhambra was developed into a spectacular palace-fort, and Granada, the last bastion of Al-Andalus, blossomed into one of Europe's richest cities, its streets teeming with traders and artisans. Two centuries of artistic and scientific splendour peaked under Yusuf I (r 1333–54) and Mohammed V (r 1354–59 and 1362–91).

In the late 15th century, the economy stagnated and court politics turned violent as rival factions argued over the throne. One faction supported the emir Abu al-Hasan and his Christian concubine, Zoraya, while another backed Boabdil (Abu Abdullah), Abu al-Hasan's son by his wife Aixa – even though Boabdil was still just a child. In 1482 civil war broke out and, following Abu al-Hasan's death in 1485, Boabdil won control of the city. It proved a pyrrhic victory, though, and with the emirate weakened by infighting, the Reyes Católicos (Catholic Monarchs) pounced in 1491. After an eight-month siege, Boabdil agreed to surrender the city in return for the Alpujarras valleys, 30,000 gold coins, and political and religious freedom for his subjects. On 2 January 1492, Isabel and Fernando entered Granada.

What followed was a period of religious persecution as the Christian authorities sought to establish Catholic rule throughout the city and former Moorish territories. The Jews were expelled from Spain in 1492, and after a series of Muslim rebellions, Spain's *moriscos* (Muslims who had converted to Christianity) were thrown out in 1609.

Granada sank into a deep decline from which it only began to emerge in the mid-19th century, with interest aroused by the Romantic movement, in particular American writer Washington Irving's *Tales of the Alhambra* (1832). Granada suffered another dark period when the Nationalists took the city at the start of the Spanish Civil War: an estimated 4000 *granadinos* with left or liberal connections were killed, among them Federico García Lorca.

## Sights & Activities

North of Plaza Nueva (Granada's main square), the Albayzín district is demarcated by Gran Vía de Colón and the Río Darro. Over the river is the Alhambra hill; its southwest slopes are occupied by the Realejo, Granada's former Jewish quarter. West of the Albayzín, the Centro is home to the cathedral.

### Alhambra & Realejo

**★Alhambra** ISLAMIC PALACE

(958 02 79 71, tickets 858 95 36 16; www.alhambra-patronato.es; adult/12-15yr/under 12yr €14/8/free, Generalife & Alcazaba only adult/under 12yr €7/free; 8.30am-8pm Apr–mid-Oct, to 6pm mid-Oct–Mar, night visits 10-11.30pm Tue & Sat Apr–mid-Oct, 8-9.30pm Fri & Sat mid-Oct–Mar) The Alhambra is Granada's – and Europe's – love letter to Moorish culture. Set against the brooding Sierra Nevada peaks, this fortified palace started life as a walled citadel before becoming the opulent seat of Granada's Nasrid emirs. Their showpiece palaces, the 14th-century Palacios Nazaríes, are among the finest Islamic buildings in Europe and, together with the Generalife gardens, form the Alhambra's great headline act. Tickets

## ALHAMBRA PRACTICALITIES

The Alhambra is Spain's second most visited tourist attraction (after Barcelona's Sagrada Família), drawing almost 2.5 million visitors a year. You'll need to book as far ahead as possible, even during low season, and choose a time to enter the Palacios Nazaríes.

### Tickets

Some parts of the Alhambra can be visited free of charge, but for the main areas you'll need a ticket.

**General** (€14) All areas.

**Gardens, Generalife & Alcazaba** (€7) Excludes the Palacios Nazaríes.

**Night Visit Palacios Nazaríes** (€8) Year-round.

**Night Visit Gardens & Generalife** (€5) April, May, September, October and, possibly, early November.

**Dobla de Oro** (€19.65) Covers the Alhambra and five sights in the Albayzín.

### How to Buy a Ticket

You can buy tickets from two hours to three months in advance: online, by phone or at the Alhambra ticket office (some foreign cards might not work online). A few 'leftover' tickets *may* be available at the ticket office on the day, but this is rare.

➡ You can show your ticket on your phone, print it yourself or pick it up from the ticket machines at the Alhambra Entrance Pavilion ticket office, the information point (p720) next to the Palacio de Carlos V, or the Corral del Carbón (p711) in central Granada.

➡ All children's tickets must be collected at the Alhambra ticket office as you'll need to prove your kids' ages (take IDs).

### Tours

Many local agencies offer private guided Alhambra tours, with tickets included, and guides can be invaluable. Note, however, that there have been complaints of tickets booked through some tour operators falling through at the very last minute – it's always best to book your own ticket through the official portal. Audio guides cost €6.

### For Families

Strollers and prams are not permitted in the Palacios Nazaríes or the Generalife; you can leave them at the main ticket office or at the services pavilion next to the Puerta del Vino (which also lends baby carriers).

### Getting There

By foot, walk 800m up Cuesta de Gomérez from Plaza Nueva through the woods to the Puerta de la Justicia; enter here if you already have your ticket or are able to collect it at the information point, otherwise continue to the main (southeastern) ticket office. Bus C30 runs to the ticket office from just off **Plaza Isabel la Católica** (Plaza Isabel La Católica).

sell out, so book ahead; you'll have to choose a time to enter the Palacios Nazaríes.

The origins of the Alhambra, the name of which derives from the Arabic *al-qala'a al-hamra* (the Red Castle), are mired in mystery. The first references to construction in the area appear in the 9th century but it's thought that buildings may already have been standing since Roman times. In its current form, it largely dates to the 13th and 14th centuries when Granada's Nasrid rulers transformed it into a fortified palace complex. Following the 1492 Reconquista (Christian reconquest), its mosque was replaced by a church and the Habsburg emperor Charles V had a wing of palaces demolished to make space for the huge Renaissance building that still bears his name. In the early 19th century, French Napoleonic forces destroyed part of the palace and attempted to blow up the entire site. Restoration work began in the mid-1800s and continues to this day.

# Alhambra

## A TIMELINE

**900 CE** The first reference to *al-qala'a al-hamra* (the Red Castle) atop the Sabika hill.

**1237** Mohammed I, founder of the Nasrid dynasty, moves his court to Granada. Threatened by belligerent Christian armies he builds a new defensive fort, the ❶ **Alcazaba**.

**1302–09** Designed as a summer palace and country estate for Granada's rulers, the bucolic ❷ **Generalife** is begun by Mohammed III.

**1333–54** Yusuf I initiates the construction of the ❸ **Palacios Nazaríes**, still considered the highpoint of Islamic culture in Europe.

**1350–60** Up goes the ❹ **Palacio de Comares**, taking Nasrid lavishness to a whole new level.

**1362–91** The second coming of Mohammed V ushers in even greater architectural brilliance, exemplified by the construction of the ❺ **Patio de los Leones**.

**1527** The Christians add the ❻ **Palacio de Carlos V**. Inspired Renaissance palace or incongruous crime against Moorish art? You decide.

**1829** The languishing, half-forgotten Alhambra is 'rediscovered' by American writer Washington Irving during a protracted sleepover.

**1954** The Generalife gardens are extended southwards to accommodate an outdoor theatre.

### TOP TIPS

- Booking tickets as far ahead as possible is essential; by phone or online.
- You can visit the general areas of the palace free of charge any time by entering through the Puerta de la Justicia.
- Within the Alhambra grounds, the lavish Parador de Granada is a fabulous (and pricey) place to stay, or just pop in for a drink or meal.

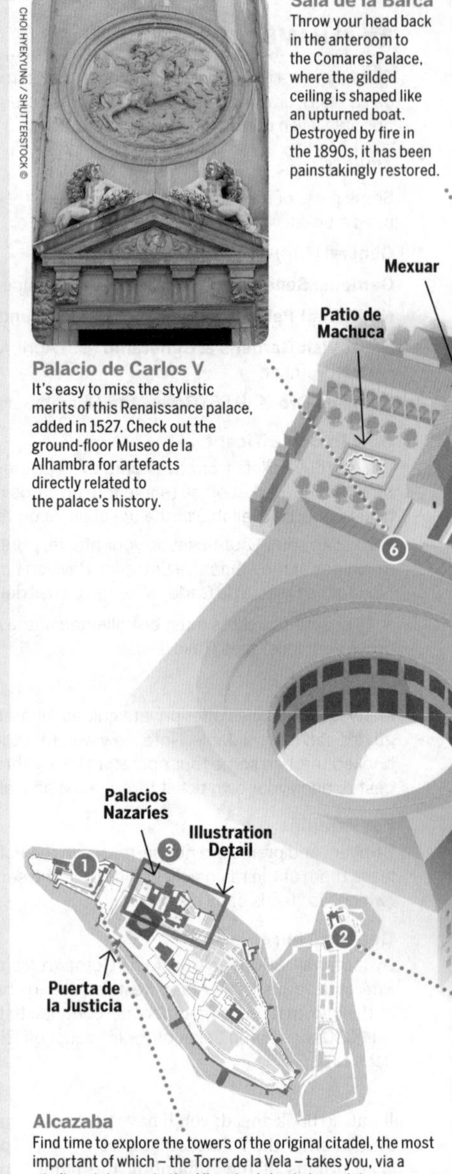


**Sala de la Barca**
Throw your head back in the anteroom to the Comares Palace, where the gilded ceiling is shaped like an upturned boat. Destroyed by fire in the 1890s, it has been painstakingly restored.

**Palacio de Carlos V**
It's easy to miss the stylistic merits of this Renaissance palace, added in 1527. Check out the ground-floor Museo de la Alhambra for artefacts directly related to the palace's history.

**Alcazaba**
Find time to explore the towers of the original citadel, the most important of which – the Torre de la Vela – takes you, via a winding staircase, to the Alhambra's best viewpoint.

EMPEROROSCOSAR / SHUTTERSTOCK ©

TAKASHI IMAGES / SHUTTERSTOCK ©

### Patio de los Arrayanes

If only you could linger longer beside the rows of *arrayanes* (myrtle bushes) that border this calming rectangular pool. Shaded porticos with seven harmonious arches invite further contemplation.

### Palacio de Comares

The largest room in the Palacio de Comares, renowned for its rich geometric ceiling, is the Salón de los Embajadores – a negotiating room for the emirs and a masterpiece of Moorish design.

JOSE IGNACIO SOTO / SHUTTERSTOCK ©

**Salón de los Embajadores**

4

**Baños Reales**

**Washington Irving Apartments**

**Patio de los Arrayanes**

**Patio de la Lindaraja**

5

**Sala de los Reyes**

**Sala de los Abencerrajes**

**Jardines del Partal**

**Palacio del Partal**

### Sala de Dos Hermanas

Focus on the *dos hermanas* – two marble slabs either side of the fountain – before enjoying the intricate cupola embellished with 5000 tiny moulded stalactites. Poetic calligraphy decorates the walls.

### Generalife

A coda to most people's visits, the 'architect's garden' is no afterthought. While Nasrid in origin, the horticulture is relatively new: the pools and arcades were added in the early 20th century.

SKANDARAMANA / SHUTTERSTOCK ©

### Patio de los Leones

Count the 12 lions sculpted from marble, holding up a gurgling fountain. Then pan back and take in the delicate columns and arches built to signify an Islamic vision of paradise.

FOTOGRAFIECOR.NL / SHUTTERSTOCK©

# Granada

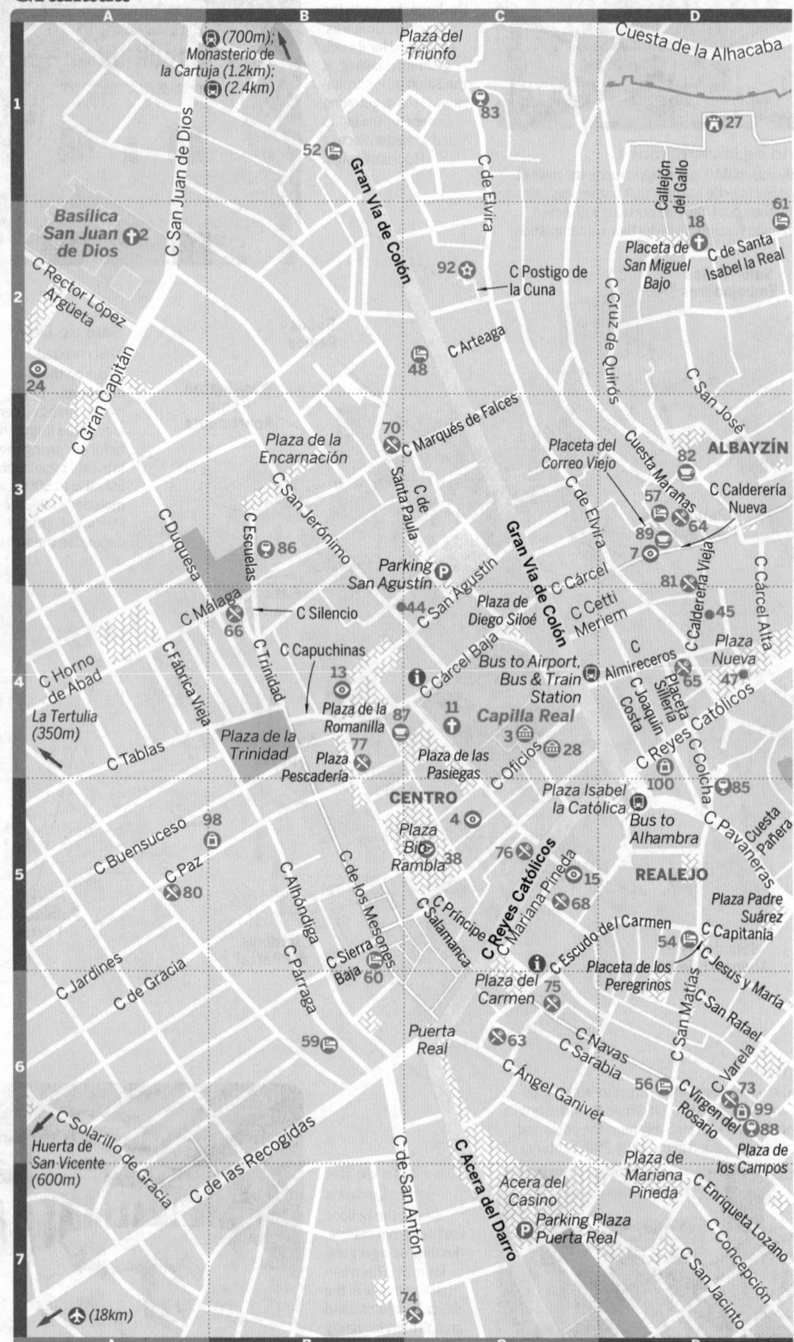

Cuesta de la Alhacaba
Plaza del Triunfo
(700m); Monasterio de la Cartuja (1.2km); (2.4km)
C San Juan de Dios
Gran Vía de Colón
C de Elvira
Callejón del Gallo
Basílica San Juan de Dios
Placeta de San Miguel Bajo
C de Santa Isabel la Real
C Postigo de la Cuna
C Rector López Argüeta
C Cruz de Quirós
C Arteaga
C Gran Capitán
C San José
C Marqués de Falces
Plaza de la Encarnación
Placeta del Correo Viejo
Cuesta Marañas
ALBAYZÍN
C San Jerónimo
C de Santa Paula
C Caldería Nueva
C Duquesa
C Escuelas
Parking San Agustín
C Calderería Vieja
C Cárcel Alta
C Málaga
C Silencio
C San Agustín
Plaza de Diego Siloé
C Cárcel
C Cetti Meriem
C Capuchinas
C Trinidad
C Cárcel Baja
Bus to Airport, Bus & Train Station
C Almireceros
Plaza Nueva
C Horno de Abad
C Fábrica Vieja
Placeta Sillería
C Joaquín Costa
C Reyes Católicos
La Tertulia (350m)
Plaza de la Romanilla
Capilla Real
Plaza de la Trinidad
C Tablas
Plaza Pescadería
Plaza de las Pasiegas
C Oficios
C Colcha
CENTRO
Plaza Isabel la Católica
Bus to Alhambra
C Pavaneras
Cuesta Pañera
C Buensuceso
C Paz
Plaza Bib-Rambla
REALEJO
C Alhóndiga
C de los Mesones
C Príncipe
C Salamanca
C Mariana Pineda
Plaza Padre Suárez
C Escudo del Carmen
C Capitanía
C Sierra Baja
C Párraga
Placeta de los Peregrinos
C Jesus y María
C Jardines
C de Gracia
Plaza del Carmen
C San Matías
C San Rafael
Puerta Real
C Navas
C Sarabia
C Varela
C Ángel Ganivet
C Virgen del Rosario
C Solarillo de Gracia
Huerta de San Vicente (600m)
C de las Recogidas
C de San Antón
C Acera del Darro
Plaza de los Campos
Plaza de Mariana Pineda
C Enriqueta Lozano
Acera del Casino
Parking Plaza Puerta Real
C Concepción
C San Jacinto
(18km)

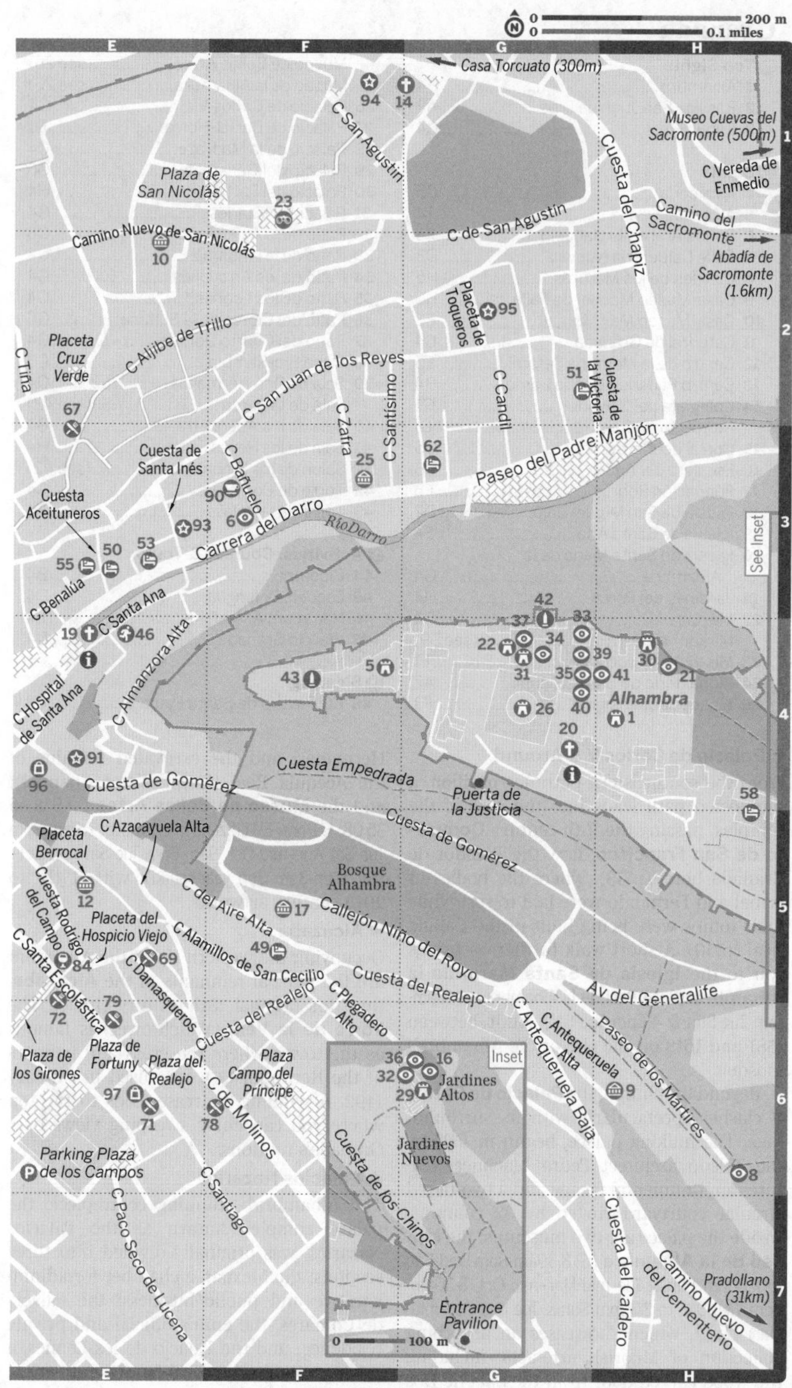

Casa Torcuato (300m)
Museo Cuevas del Sacromonte (500m)
C Vereda de Enmedio
Camino del Sacromonte
Abadía de Sacromonte (1.6km)
Plaza de San Nicolás
C San Agustín
C de San Agustín
Cuesta del Chapiz
Camino Nuevo de San Nicolás
Placeta de Toqueros
C Aljibe de Trillo
Placeta Cruz Verde
C Tiña
C San Juan de los Reyes
C Zafra
C Santísimo
C Candil
Cuesta de la Victoria
Paseo del Padre Manjón
Cuesta de Santa Inés
C Bañuelo
Cuesta Aceituneros
Carrera del Darro
Río Darro
C Benalúa
C Santa Ana
C Almanzora Alta
C Hospital de Santa Ana
Alhambra
Cuesta Empedrada
Puerta de la Justicia
Cuesta de Gomérez
Placeta Berrocal
C Azacayuela Alta
Bosque Alhambra
Cuesta Rodrigo del Campo
Placeta del Hospicio Viejo
C del Aire Alta
Callejón Niño del Royo
C Alamillos de San Cecilio
C Damasqueros
C Santa Escolástica
Cuesta del Realejo
C Plegadero Alto
Av del Generalife
C Antequeruela Alta
C Antequeruela Baja
Paseo de los Mártires
Plaza de los Girones
Plaza de Fortuny
Plaza del Realejo
Plaza Campo del Príncipe
C de Molinos
Inset
Jardines Altos
Jardines Nuevos
Cuesta de los Chinos
Entrance Pavilion
Parking Plaza de los Campos
C Santiago
C Paco Seco de Lucena
Cuesta del Caidero
Camino Nuevo del Cementerio
Pradollano (31km)
See Inset
200 m
0.1 miles
100 m

## Granada

**Top Sights**
1 Alhambra ..... H4
2 Basílica San Juan de Dios ..... A2
3 Capilla Real ..... C4

**Sights**
4 Alcaicería ..... C5
5 Alcazaba ..... F4
6 Baños Árabes El Bañuelo ..... F3
7 Calle Caldereria Nueva ..... D3
8 Carmen de los Mártires ..... H6
9 Casa-Museo Manuel de Falla ..... H6
10 Casa-Museo Max Moreau ..... E2
11 Catedral de Granada ..... C4
12 Centro de la Memoria Sefardí ..... E5
13 Centro Federico García Lorca ..... B4
14 Colegiata del Salvador ..... G1
Convento de San Francisco ..... (see 58)
15 Corral del Carbón ..... C5
16 Escalera del Agua ..... G6
17 Fundación Rodríguez-Acosta ..... F5
18 Iglesia de San Miguel Bajo ..... D2
19 Iglesia de Santa Ana ..... E4
20 Iglesia de Santa María de la Alhambra ..... G4
21 Jardines del Partal ..... H4
22 Mexuar ..... G4
Mirador de Daraxa ..... (see 39)
23 Mirador San Nicolás ..... F1
24 Monasterio de San Jerónimo ..... A2
25 Museo Arqueológico ..... F3
Museo de Bellas Artes ..... (see 26)
Museo de la Alhambra ..... (see 26)
26 Palacio de Carlos V ..... G4
27 Palacio de Dar-al-Horra ..... D1
28 Palacio de la Madraza ..... C4
29 Palacio del Generalife ..... G6
30 Palacio del Partal ..... H4
31 Palacios Nazaríes ..... G4
32 Patio de la Acequia ..... G6
33 Patio de la Lindaraja ..... G4
34 Patio de los Arrayanes ..... G4
35 Patio de los Leones ..... G4
36 Patio del Ciprés de la Sultana ..... G6
37 Patio del Cuarto Dorado ..... G4
38 Plaza Bib-Rambla ..... C5
39 Sala de Dos Hermanas ..... G4
Sala de la Barca ..... (see 42)
40 Sala de los Abencerrajes ..... G4
41 Sala de los Reyes ..... H4
Salón de los Embajadores ..... (see 42)
42 Torre de Comares ..... G4
43 Torre de la Vela ..... F4

**Activities, Courses & Tours**
44 Cicerone ..... B4
45 Escuela Delengua ..... D4
46 Hammam Al Ándalus ..... E4
47 Walk in Granada ..... D4

**Sleeping**
48 AC Palacio de Santa Paula ..... C2

### ➡ Palacio de Carlos V & Around

From the southeastern entrance pavilion, a signposted path leads into the core of the complex, passing the 15th-century **Convento de San Francisco**, now the Parador de Granada hotel (p713), where the bodies of Isabel and Fernando were laid to rest while their tombs were being built in the Capilla Real (p710). A short walk further on brings you to the **Iglesia de Santa María de la Alhambra** (Calle Real de la Alhambra; ⏲10am-1pm Tue-Sun & 4-6pm Tue-Sat), built between 1581 and 1618 on the site of the Alhambra's mosque.

Beyond the church, the **Palacio de Carlos V** clashes spectacularly with its surroundings. The hulking palace, begun in 1527 by the Toledo architect Pedro Machuca, features a monumental facade and a two-tiered circular courtyard ringed by 32 columns. Inside the palace are two museums: the **Museo de la Alhambra** (⏲8.30am-8pm Wed-Sat, to 2.30pm Sun & Tue mid-Mar–mid-Oct, 8.30am-6pm Wed-Sat, to 2.30pm Sun & Tue mid-Oct–mid-Mar) FREE, which showcases an absorbing collection of Moorish artefacts, including the wood-carved door from the Sala de Dos Hermanas, and the excavated remains of the Acequia Real (Royal Water Channel); and the **Museo de Bellas Artes** (☎958 56 35 08; EU/non-EU citizens free/€1.50; ⏲9am-8pm Tue-Sat Apr–mid-Oct, 9am-6pm Tue-Sat mid-Oct–Mar, 9am-3pm Sun year-round), with 15th- to 20th-century artworks.

### ➡ Alcazaba

Occupying the western tip of the Alhambra are the martial remnants of the **Alcazaba**, the site's original 13th-century citadel. The **Torre de la Vela** (Watchtower) is famous as the tower where the cross and banners of the Reconquista were raised in January 1492. A winding staircase leads to the top where you can enjoy sweeping views over Granada's rooftops.

### ➡ Palacios Nazaríes

The Alhambra's stunning centrepiece, the palace complex known as the Palacios Nazaríes, was originally divided into three sections: the Mexuar, a chamber for administrative and public business; the Palacio de Comares, the emir's official and private residence; and the Palacio de los Leones, a private area for the royal family and harem.

49 Carmen de la Alcubilla del Caracol....... F5
50 Casa del Capitel Nazarí....................... E3
51 Casa Morisca........................................ G2
52 Eco Hostel............................................. B1
53 El Ladrón del Agua ............................... E3
54 Gar-Anat ............................................... D5
55 Hotel Casa 1800 Granada.................... E3
56 Hotel Palacio de Los Navas.................. D6
57 Oasis Backpackers Hostel ..................... D3
58 Parador de Granada.............................. H5
59 Párragasiete ......................................... B6
60 Room Mate Leo ..................................... B5
61 Santa Isabel la Real .............................. D2
62 White Nest............................................ G3

**Eating**
63 Alameda................................................ C6
64 Arrayanes .............................................. D3
65 Bodegas Castañeda............................... D4
66 Botánico ................................................ B4
67 Café 4 Gatos.......................................... E3
68 Cisco y Tierra......................................... C5
69 Damasqueros......................................... E5
70 El Bar de Fede........................................ B3
71 El Piano .................................................. E6
72 Hicuri Art Restaurant ........................... E5
73 La Botillería........................................... D6
74 La Fábula Restaurante .......................... C7
75 Los Diamantes....................................... C6
76 Más Que Vinos....................................... C5
77 Oliver...................................................... B4
78 Papaupa ................................................ F6
Parador de Granada ....................(see 58)
79 Picoteca 3Maneras ............................... E6
80 Poë ......................................................... A5
81 Samarkanda.......................................... D3

**Drinking & Nightlife**
82 Abaco Té............................................... D3
83 Al Sur de Granada.................................. C1
84 Candela ................................................. E5
85 Casa de Vinos La Brujidera ................... D5
86 El Bar de Eric.......................................... B3
87 La Finca.................................................. B4
88 Taberna La Tana .................................... D6
89 Tetería Dar Ziryab ................................. D3
90 Tetería El Bañuelo.................................. F3

**Entertainment**
91 Casa del Arte Flamenco......................... E4
92 Eshavira ................................................. C2
93 Flamenco Los Olvidados ....................... E3
94 Jardines de Zoraya ................................ F1
95 Peña La Platería..................................... G2

**Shopping**
96 Artesanías González............................... E4
97 Gil de Avalle........................................... E6
98 La Cata Con Botas .................................. B5
99 La Oliva................................................... D6
100 Tienda Librería de la Alhambra ............ D4

Access is limited to 300 people every half hour. Entrance is through the **Mexuar**, a 14th-century hall where the council of ministers would sit and the emir would adjudicate citizens' appeals. Two centuries later, it was converted into a chapel, with a prayer room at the far end. Look up here and elsewhere to appreciate the geometrically carved wood ceilings and elegant tiling.

From the Mexuar, you pass into the **Patio del Cuarto Dorado**, a courtyard where the emirs gave audiences, with the **Cuarto Dorado** (Golden Room) on the left, looking out on the Albayzín. Opposite the Cuarto Dorado is the entrance to the **Palacio de Comares** through a beautiful facade of glazed tiles, stucco and carved wood. A dog-leg corridor (a common strategy in Islamic architecture to keep interior rooms private) leads through to the **Patio de los Arrayanes** (Courtyard of the Myrtles). This elegant patio, named after the myrtle hedges around its rectangular pool, is the central space of the palace built in the mid-14th century as Emir Yusuf I's official residence.

The southern end of the patio is overshadowed by the walls of the Palacio de Carlos V. To the north, in the 45m-high **Torre de Comares** (Comares Tower), the **Sala de la Barca** (Hall of the Boat), with its sculpted ceilings, leads into the **Salón de los Embajadores** (Chamber of the Ambassadors; also the Salón de Comares), where the emirs would have conducted negotiations with Christian emissaries. The room's domed marquetry ceiling contains more than 8000 cedar pieces in an intricate star pattern representing the seven heavens of Islam.

The Patio de los Arrayanes leads into the **Palacio de los Leones** (Palace of the Lions), built in the second half of the 14th century under Muhammad V. The palace rooms branch off the **Patio de los Leones** (Lion Courtyard), centred on an 11th-century fountain channelling water through the mouths of 12 marble lions. The courtyard layout, using the proportions of the golden ratio, demonstrates the complexity of Moorish geometric design – the 124 slender columns that support the ornamented pavilions are placed in such a way that they are symmetrical on numerous axes.

Of the four halls around the patio, the **Sala de los Abencerrajes**, on the south side, is the most impressive. Boasting a

**GRANADA CARD**

The five-day Granada Card (adult €36 to €40, child €11; www.granadatur.com; 858 88 09 90) covers admission to 10 city monuments, including the Alhambra, and nine free trips on city buses.

mesmerising octagonal stalactite ceiling, this is the legendary site of the murders of the noble Abencerraj family, whose leader, the story goes, dared to dally with Zoraya, Abu al-Hasan's favourite concubine.

At the eastern end of the patio is the **Sala de los Reyes** (Hall of the Kings), which has three leather-lined ceiling alcoves painted by 14th-century Christian artists. The central alcove is thought to depict 10 Nasrid emirs.

On the patio's northern side is the richly decorated **Sala de Dos Hermanas** (Hall of Two Sisters), probably named after the slabs of white marble flanking its fountain. It features a dizzying *muqarnas* (honeycomb-vaulted) dome with a central star and 5000 tiny cells, reminiscent of the constellations. The carved wood screens in the upper level enabled women (and perhaps others involved in palace intrigue) to peer down from hallways above without being seen. At its far end, the tile-trimmed **Mirador de Daraxa** (Daraxa Lookout) was a lovely place for palace denizens to look on the garden.

From the Sala de Dos Hermanas, a passageway leads through the **Estancias del Emperador** (Emperor's Chambers), built for Carlos V in the 1520s, and later used by the American author Washington Irving. From here descend to the **Patio de la Reja** (Patio of the Grille) and the **Patio de la Lindaraja**, where, in the southwest corner you can peer into the **Baño Real de Comares** bathhouse, lit by star-shaped skylights.

You eventually emerge into the **Jardines del Partal**, an area of terraced gardens laid out at the beginning of the 20th century. Here a reflecting pool stands in front of the **Palacio del Partal**, a small porticoed building with its own tower (the Torre de las Damas) dating to the early 14th century.

**➡ Generalife**

The Generalife, the sultans' gorgeous summer estate, dates to the 14th century. A soothing ensemble of pathways, patios, pools, fountains, trees and, in season, flowers of every imaginable hue, it takes its name from the Arabic *jinan al-'arif,* meaning 'the overseer's gardens'.

A string of elegant rectangular plots with tinkling water features, the **Jardines Nuevos**, leads up to the whitewashed **Palacio del Generalife**, the emirs' summer palace. The courtyards here are particularly graceful: the first, the **Patio de la Acequia**, has gorgeous gardens and distant views of the Palacios Nazaríes, while in the second one, the **Patio de la Sultana**, the trunk of a 700-year-old cypress tree suggests the delicate shade that would once have graced the area. Beyond this courtyard, the **Escalera del Agua** is a delightful work of landscape engineering with water channels running down a shaded staircase.

**Carmen de los Mártires** GARDENS

(958 84 91 03; Paseo de los Mártires; 10am-2pm & 6-8pm Mon-Fri, 10am-8pm Sat & Sun Apr-Oct, 10am-2pm & 4-6pm Mon-Fri, 10am-6pm Sat & Sun Nov-Mar) FREE A peaceful oasis on the hillside south of the Alhambra, these romantically dishevelled gardens sprawl around a restored 19th-century mansion, with uplifting views of the city and surrounding mountains. Over the years the site has hosted a prison, a chapel, a convent and more; today it's a great spot to escape the crowds.

**Casa-Museo Manuel de Falla** MUSEUM

(958 22 21 88; www.museomanueldefalla.com; Calle Antequeruela Alta; adult/reduced €3/1; 10am-5pm Tue-Sat, to 3pm Sun Oct-May, 9am-2.30pm Tue-Sun Jun & Sep, 9am-2.30pm Wed-Sun Jul & Aug) Arguably Spain's greatest classical composer and an artistic friend of Lorca, Manuel de Falla (1876–1946) was born in Cádiz, but spent his key years in Granada until the civil war forced him into exile. Learn all about the man at the attractive Carmen del Ave María where he lived and composed; the sky-blue shutters were inspired by the Cádiz sea. Ring the bell to get in; visits are guided (Spanish, English, French).

**Fundación Rodríguez-Acosta** MUSEUM

(958 22 74 97; www.fundacionrodriguezacosta.com; Callejón Niño del Royo 8; tour adult/child €5/3, 2-5pm Sun free; 10am-6.30pm Apr–mid-Oct, to 4.30pm mid-Oct–Mar) On the Realejo hill, the Carmen Blanco houses the Rodríguez-Acosta foundation in a building created in 1914 by Granada-born modernist artist José María Rodríguez-Acosta (1878–1941). It's a whimsical place that borrows from several architectural genres including art deco, Nasrid, Greek and baroque. One-hour guided

tours take you through the house's subterranean tunnels and a well-curated museum containing works by Francisco Pacheco, Alonso Cano and Francisco de Zurbarán.

**Centro de la Memoria Sefardí** MUSEUM
(☎610 060255; museosefardidegranada@gmail.com; Placeta Berrocal 5; tour €5; ⏲10am-2pm & 5-8pm Sun & Tue-Thu, 10am-2pm Fri Apr-Oct, 10am-2pm & 4-8pm Sun & Tue-Thu, 10am-2pm Fri Nov-Mar) Since being expelled en masse in 1492, there are very few Sephardic Jews left living in Granada. But this didn't stop one enterprising couple from opening a museum to their memory in 2013, the year the Spanish government began offering Spanish citizenship to any Sephardic Jew who could prove their Iberian ancestry. The owners also do Realejo tours on advance request.

## Plaza Nueva & Around

**Iglesia de Santa Ana** CHURCH
(Plaza Santa Ana; ⏲mass 7pm Tue-Sat, 12.30pm & 7pm Sun Jun-Sep, 6pm Tue-Sat, 12.30pm & 6pm Sun Oct-May) Off the eastern corner of Plaza Nueva, Plaza Santa Ana is dominated by this 16th-century Mudéjar church where the bell tower incorporates the minaret of the mosque over which it stands; it was designed by Diego de Siloé. It's only open during Mass.

**Hammam Al Ándalus** HAMMAM
(☎958 22 99 78; www.granada.hammamalandalus.com; Calle Santa Ana 16; baths €38, with massage from €50; ⏲10am-midnight) With three pools of different temperatures, plus a steam room and the option of skin-scrubbing massages, this is the best of Granada's Moorish-style baths. Its dim, tiled rooms are suitably sybaritic and relaxing. Reservations required.

## Albayzín

The Albayzín, Granada's old Muslim quarter, is sprawled over a hill facing the Alhambra. It's a fascinating, history-rich district of steep cobblestone streets, whitewashed *cármenes* and Alhambra views – you'll almost certainly get lost at some point. Bus C31 loops through the Albayzín in a circular route to/from Plaza Nueva, every eight to 15 minutes from 7am to 11pm (to 1am Friday and Saturday).

**Mirador San Nicolás** VIEWPOINT
(Plaza de San Nicolás) For classic sunset shots of the Alhambra sprawled along a wooded hilltop with the Sierra Nevada mountains looming in the background, wander up through the Albayzín to this well-known lookout (reached via Callejón de San Cecilio). Expect pastel-hued sunsets and crowds of camera-toting tourists, students and buskers; it's also a haunt of pickpockets and bag-snatchers, so keep your wits about you. Other fab viewpoints pop up across the surrounding streets.

**Colegiata del Salvador** CHURCH
(☎958 27 86 44; Plaza del Salvador; ⏲mass 8pm Mon-Fri, 11.30am Sun Apr-Oct, 7pm Mon-Fri, noon Sat & Sun Nov-Mar) Dominating the Plaza del Salvador near the top of the Albayzín, the 16th-century Colegiata del Salvador rests on the site of the Albayzín's former mosque, the patio of which still survives (with its original *aljibe* and horseshoe arches). It's only open during Mass.

**Museo Arqueológico** MUSEUM
(☎600 143141; www.museosdeandalucia.es; Carrera del Darro 43; EU/non-EU citizen free/€1.50; ⏲9am-8.45pm Tue-Sat, to 3pm Sun) Relaunched in 2018 after an eight-year restoration, Granada's archaeology museum is spread across the 16th-century Casa de Castril, with its elaborate Renaissance facade. The small, thoughtfully presented collection (in Spanish and English) shows off 120 pieces unearthed in Granada province, from the Paleolithic to late-Moorish times. The star

### GRANADA'S CÁRMENES

Granada's *cármenes* (from the Arabic *karm* for 'vine') are quiet, private houses, many of them adapted from Moorish homes post-Reconquista, with high walls that conceal beautiful terraced gardens of fruit trees, vines, fountains and scented flowers. The Albayzín, with its awe-inspiring Alhambra views, has the richest concentration of *cármenes*.

Most remain true to their original concept – private and hidden – though a few are open to visitors, including the gardens of the Carmen de los Mártires (p708) opposite the Alhambra. A handful have been converted into museums, such as the Fundación Rodríguez-Acosta (p708), while others, such as the Realejo's Carmen de la Alcubilla del Caracol (p713), have been reborn as intimate hotels.

**HIDDEN SPACES**

Each month the Alhambra authorities open a different, otherwise off-limits section of the monument to visitors, usually included in tickets. Ask for the Espacio del Mes (Space of the Month).

is the 1.4-million-year-old Orce tooth – Europe's most ancient human remain. Other finds include a 4th-century-BCE alabaster urn from Almuñécar, a 15th-century marquetry casket and a 1481 Granada-made Moorish astrolabe.

**Baños Árabes El Bañuelo** ARCHITECTURE
(Carrera del Darro 31; €5, Sun free; 9.30am-2.30pm & 5-8.30pm May–mid-Sep, 10am-5pm mid-Sep–Apr) Sitting by the Río Darro, this well-preserved Moorish bathhouse dates to the 11th or 12th century. Light beams into its vaulted brick rooms through octagonal star-shaped shafts, illuminating columns, capitals and marble-tiled floors. The ticket includes entrance to the Palacio de Dar-al-Horra.

**Casa-Museo Max Moreau** MUSEUM
(Carmen de los Geranios; 958 29 33 10; Camino Nuevo de San Nicolás 12; 10.30am-1.30pm & 6-8pm Tue-Sat) FREE Get a rare (and free) glimpse of one of Granada's secret *cármenes* (p709) at the former home of 20th-century Belgian portrait painter and composer Max Léon Moreau. His attractive house, dotted with terraces and gardens, has been converted into a museum displaying his former living quarters and study, along with a gallery showcasing his finest portraits.

**Palacio de Dar-al-Horra** PALACE
(671 563553; Callejón de las Monjas; €5, Sun free; 9.30am-2.30pm & 5-8.30pm May–mid-Sep, 10am-5pm mid-Sep–Apr) Up high in the Albayzín – down a lane off Placeta de San Miguel Bajo and Callejón del Gallo – this 15th-century Nasrid palace was the home of sultana Aixa, the mother of Boabdil, Granada's last Muslim ruler. It's surprisingly intimate, with rooms set around a central courtyard and fabulous views across the surrounding neighbourhood and over to the Alhambra. After the Reconquista, it was incorporated into the adjacent Monasterio de Santa Isabel la Real. Admission includes entry to the El Bañuelo Moorish baths.

**Iglesia de San Miguel Bajo** CHURCH
(Placeta de San Miguel Bajo; hours vary) One of the Albayzín's loveliest churches, overlooking a snug cafe-dotted plaza, the whitewashed Mudéjar San Miguel Bajo church was built atop an old mosque, and still retains its original brick *aljibe*.

## Centro

**★Capilla Real** HISTORIC BUILDING
(958 22 78 48; www.capillarealgranada.com; Calle Oficios; adult/child €5/free; 10.15am-6.30pm Mon-Sat, 11am-6pm Sun) The Royal Chapel is the last resting place of Spain's Reyes Católicos (Catholic Monarchs), Isabel I de Castilla (1451–1504) and Fernando II de Aragón (1452–1516), who commissioned the elaborate Isabelline-Gothic-style mausoleum that was to house them. Commenced in 1505, it wasn't completed until 1517, hence the royals' interment in the Alhambra's Convento de San Francisco (p700) until 1521. Their monumental marble tombs (and those of their heirs) lie behind a 1520 gilded wrought-iron screen by Bartolomé de Jaén.

The tombs are just for show, however, as the monarchs actually lie in simple lead coffins in the crypt beneath the chancel. Also here are the coffins of Isabel and Fernando's unfortunate daughter, Juana la Loca (Juana the Mad); her husband Felipe el Hermoso (Philip the Handsome); and Miguel, Prince of Asturias, who died as a boy.

The sacristy contains a small but impressive museum, with Fernando's sword and Isabel's silver sceptre, silver crown and personal art collection, which is mainly Flemish but also includes Botticelli's *Prayer in the Garden*. Felipe Vigarny's two early-16th-century wood-carved statues of the Catholic Monarchs at prayer are also here. Audio-guides are included.

**Catedral de Granada** CATHEDRAL
(958 22 29 59; www.catedraldegranada.com; Plaza de las Pasiegas; adult/child €5/free; 10am-6.30pm Mon-Sat, 3-5.45pm Sun) From street level, it's difficult to appreciate the immensity of Granada's cavernous, boxed-in cathedral. But it's nonetheless a monumental work of architecture, and one of Spain's largest cathedrals. Built atop Granada's former mosque, it was originally intended to be Gothic, but over the two centuries of its construction (1523–1704) it underwent major modifications. Most notably, architect Diego de Siloé changed its layout to a Renaissance

style, and Alonso Cano added a magnificent 17th-century baroque facade.

Cano was also responsible for two wooden busts of Adam and Eve in the Capilla Mayor (main chapel), which sit above small praying statues of the Reyes Católicos, who rest in the adjacent Capilla Real. The cathedral's interior is vast with 20 huge white piers rising from a black-and-white tiled floor to a ceiling capped by a 30m-high dome.

**Palacio de la Madraza** HISTORIC BUILDING

(☎676 385600; Calle Oficios; tour €2; ⏲10.30am-7.45pm) Easily recognisable by the trompe l'oeil on its facade, La Madraza was founded in 1349 by Yusuf I as a school and university – and still belongs to Granada University. Since extensive renovations in the early 2010s, you can wander in to view its interesting, and sometimes contradictory, mix of Moorish, Mudéjar and baroque architecture. Highlights include an elaborate *mihrab* (prayer niche), a baroque dome and some coloured stucco. Student guides lead 15-minute tours in multiple languages.

**Alcaicería** STREET

(off Calle Oficios) This skinny street lined with gaudy souvenir shops is all that's left of what was once Granada's great bazaar (the Alcaicería), a claustrophobic warren of alleyways packed with stalls selling silks, spices and much more. The original bazaar was destroyed by fire in the 19th century and rebuilt in a much reduced form.

**Corral del Carbón** COURTYARD

(Calle Mariana Pineda; ⏲9am-8pm) FREE Just east of Calle Reyes Católicos, an elaborate horseshoe arch leads through to the 14th-century Corral del Carbón, a cobbled, much-restored courtyard with a well and surrounded by two storeys of brick galleries. Initially, this was a Nasrid-era corn exchange, but in subsequent centuries it was used as an inn for coal dealers (hence its name, Coal Yard) and later as a theatre.

## Outside the Centre

**★Basílica San Juan de Dios** BASILICA

(☎958 27 57 00; www.basilicasanjuandedios.es; Calle San Juan de Dios 19; adult/child €5/free; ⏲10am-8pm Mon-Sat, 2-8pm Sun Jun-Sep, to 7pm Oct-May) Built between 1737 and 1759, this spectacular basilica unveils a blinding display of opulent baroque decor. Barely an inch of its interior lacks embellishment, most of it in gleaming gold and silver. Frescos by Diego Sánchez Sarabia and Italian artists Corrado Giaquinto and Tomás Ferrer adorn the ceilings and side chapels, while up above the basilica's dome soars to 50m. The highlight, however, is the extraordinary gold altarpiece in the Capilla Mayor (main chapel). Audio guides bring the details to life.

**Monasterio de San Jerónimo** MONASTERY

(☎958 27 93 37; Calle Rector López Argüeta 9; €4; ⏲10am-1.30pm & 4-7.30pm Apr-Oct, 10am-1.30pm & 3-6.30pm Nov-Mar) With Gothic cloisters,



LOCAL KNOWLEDGE

### SACROMONTE

The Sacromonte, Granada's historical Roma neighbourhood, sits northeast of the neighbouring Albayzín (p709). Renowned for its flamenco traditions and cave-houses, it draws tourists to late-night shows and aficionados to music schools, yet still feels like the fringes of the city. Some of the caves dug out of its hillside date back to the 14th century, but many were devastated by floods in the early 1960s, after which some of the Sacromonte's Roma community was forced to relocate. The caves were then forgotten until the 1980s, when an international hippie crowd began to trickle in. Today around 500 people live here, including immigrants and Roma dancers and musicians.

Centred on the Camino del Sacromonte, the area unveils some of Granada's best views, particularly from the Vereda de Enmedio lookout and the San Miguel Alto chapel, which both overlook the Alhambra and Albayzín. At the **Museo Cuevas del Sacromonte** (☎958 21 51 20; www.sacromontegranada.com; Barranco de los Negros; €5; ⏲10am-8pm mid-Mar–mid-Oct, to 6pm mid-Oct–mid-Mar) you can see what a traditional cave-home once looked like, while at the hillside **Abadía del Sacromonte** (☎958 22 14 45; www.sacromonteabbey.com; Abadía del Sacromonte; adult/child €5/free; ⏲10.30am-5.30pm), towards the *barrio's* eastern end, you can explore catacombs and underground cave-chapels. Several local companies run guided walks of the Sacromonte, such as the sensitive tours with Walk in Granada (p712).

DON'T MISS

### GRANADA STREET ART: EL NIÑO DE LAS PINTURAS

While the UK has Banksy, Granada has El Niño de las Pinturas (real name Raúl Ruíz), a street artist whose creative graffiti has become a defining symbol of the city. Larger-than-life, lucid and thought-provoking, El Niño's murals, many of which are dotted around the Realejo, often juxtapose vivid close-ups of human faces with short poetic stanzas in highly stylised lettering. Over the last two decades, El Niño has become a famous underground personality in Granada. Although he risks criticism and occasional fines for his work, most *granadinos* agree that his art brings creative colour and a contemporary edge to the streets of their ancient city. Seek out El Niño's work at vegan restaurant Hicuri (p715) and bar Candela (p718) opposite; at his old home at Calle de Molinos 44; on the wall beside the Hotel Molinos; and, as of early 2020, on the facade of Federico García Lorca's birthplace in Fuente Vaqueros (p714), 17km northwest of Granada.

fragrant orange trees and a lavishly decorated interior, this 16th-century monastery is one of Granada's most stunning Catholic buildings. Behind a plateresque entrance by Diego de Siloeé, the church mixes late-Gothic and Renaissance styling, and reveals a profusion of painted sculptures and vivid colours, most spectacularly on the apse's immense eight-level gilt retable.

Gonzalo Fernández de Córdoba, the Reyes Católicos' military man known as El Gran Capitán, is entombed in the church.

## Courses

**Escuela Delengua** LANGUAGE
(☎958 20 45 35; www.delengua.es; Calle Caldería Vieja 20; single private class €31, 2-week course from €275) This Spanish-language school in the heart of the Albayzín runs a range of courses, individual lessons and extracurricular activities, including guided tours, tapas nights and visits to traditional craftworkers. It's also actively involved in the local community and supports young non-Spanish-speaking immigrants in Granada.

## Tours

**Spain Food Sherpas** FOOD
(☎644 329806; www.spainfoodsherpas.com; tour/cooking class €69/71) Join a local gastronomy expert for a fabulous small-group wander off the usual trail. The spotlight is on Granada's glorious produce, speciality dishes and intriguing backstory: you might taste mango-infused *salmorejo* (cold tomato-based soup), zesty *remojón* (cod, orange and olive salad) or *jamón* croquettes, with Alpujarras wines. Also does wine tastings, paella classes and more.

**Granada Tapas Tours** FOOD
(☎619 444984; www.granadatapastours.com; tours per person €40) Engaging guides lead small-group food tours (in Spanish, English, French, Italian or German) delving into Granada's gastronomic history and specialities, with plenty of extra recommendations, as well as walks through the Albayzín and craft-beer jaunts.

**Walk in Granada** WALKING
(☎630 070893; www.walkingranada.com; Plaza Nueva) This energetic operation runs three pay-what-you-like tours: the central-Granada sights walk at 11am daily, and thoughtful afternoon walks around the Sacromonte or the Albayzín. Other fixed-price options include Lorca-themed walks and adapted itineraries for wheelchair users.

**Cicerone** CULTURAL
(☎607 691676, 958 56 18 10; www.ciceronegranada.com; Calle San Jerónimo 10; group tours from €23) Offers a range of private and small-group walking tours, as well as thematic itineraries and guided Alhambra visits.

## Festivals & Events

**Semana Santa** RELIGIOUS
(Mar/Apr) The two most striking events in Granada's Holy Week are Los Gitanos (Wednesday), when members of the *fraternidad* (brotherhood) parade to the Abadía del Sacromonte (p711), and El Silencio (Thursday), when the street lights are turned off for a silent candlelit march.

**Feria del Corpus Christi** RELIGIOUS
(May/Jun) The most spectacular of Andalucía's Corpus Christi celebrations, this is Granada's big annual party. Held approximately 60 days after Easter, it involves a

week of dancing (including flamenco), parades and processions. Bullfighting, which visitors may wish to avoid, is also part of it – but there is growing opposition from animal rights activists.

**Festival Internacional de Música y Danza** PERFORMING ARTS
(www.granadafestival.org; ⏲ Jun & Jul) For three weeks in June and July, first-class classical and modern performances are staged at the Alhambra and other historical sites.

## Sleeping

Granada's accommodation scene is a delight, with everything from excellent hostels to centuries-old mansions to flashy five-stars. Some of the prettiest lodgings are in the sloping Albayzín, though many aren't accessible by vehicle; the Realejo has some characterful picks too. The few hotels near the Alhambra are scenic but a hassle for sightseeing elsewhere.

### Alhambra & Realejo

**Gar-Anat** BOUTIQUE HOTEL €€
(☎958 22 55 28; www.hotelgaranat.com; Placeta de los Peregrinos 1; d €88-190; ❄📶) Gleaming, literary-themed boutique style runs through this sharply repurposed 16th-century house (later a pilgrims' hostel), set around a courtyard where a metallic wishing tree awaits. The 15 contemporary-design rooms (some with hot tubs) are inspired by greats in music and literature; there's even one with Alhambra glimpses.

**Hotel Palacio de Los Navas** HERITAGE HOTEL €€
(☎958 21 57 60; www.hotelpalaciodelosnavas.com; Calle Navas 1; incl breakfast s €72-150, d €85-195; ❄📶) A glassed-in atrium, terracotta-tiled floors and smooth cream styling set the tone at this gorgeously revamped 16th-century building, strung around a classic columned patio just off a busy tapas street. The 19 rooms have wrought-iron bedheads and an instantly soothing feel; those on the top floor are attic-style with sloping wood-beamed ceilings. Staff are charmingly helpful and there's complimentary *merienda* (afternoon tea).

**★Carmen de la Alcubilla del Caracol** B&B €€€
(☎958 21 55 51; www.alcubilladelcaracol.com; Calle Aire Alta 12; r €149-185; ⏲closed mid-Jul–Aug; P❄📶) A painstakingly restored traditional 1880s *cármene* (p709), this much-sought-after, utterly charming hideaway sits on the Alhambra's southern slopes, in the upper Realejo. Homey decor, antiques and seven quietly refined rooms washed in pale pastels are complemented by the warm welcome from knowledgeable host Manuel. Outside, bask in fabulous views from the spectacular terraced gardens of palms, bougainvillea and citrus trees.

**Parador de Granada** HERITAGE HOTEL €€€
(☎958 22 14 40; www.parador.es; Calle Real de la Alhambra; r €225-420; P❄📶) Few Andalucian moments rival waking up in within the walls of the dazzling Alhambra (p700). Granada's luxurious *parador* (state-run-hotel) is housed in a 15th-century convent (also a former Moorish palace), in which you can still see 14th-century tilework and the Reyes Católicos' original tombs. Rooms are smartly updated in creams, greys or silvers. It's popular, as is the modern-Andalucian **restaurant** (mains €15-25; ⏲1-4pm & 8-11pm).

### Albayzín

**Oasis Backpackers Hostel** HOSTEL €
(☎958 21 58 48; www.oasisbackpackershostels.com; Placeta Correo Viejo 3; dm €16-23, d €70; ❄@📶) Bohemian Oasis is one of Granada's original, most successful hostels (now also in Seville and Málaga), occupying a historical building with tiled floors and a central patio, just off Calle de Elvira. Dorms (mixed or women-only) sleep four to 10, with individual plugs, lights and lockers; some have balconies. Perks include a well-equipped kitchen, group excursions and a roof terrace.

**White Nest** HOSTEL €
(☎958 99 47 14; www.nesthostelsgranada.com; Calle Santísimo 4; dm €11-20, d €80; ❄📶) A beautiful old building graced by a pillared patio, marble floors, wood-carved doors and dangling textiles has been reimagined as a colourfully contemporary budget bolthole at the foot of the Albayzín. Dorms (including one women-only) have personal lights, lockers and plugs. It's a welcoming, popular place, and the lively social scene runs from free Sacromonte tours to mojito nights.

**El Ladrón del Agua** BOUTIQUE HOTEL €€
(☎958 21 50 40; www.ladrondeagua.com; Carrera del Darro 13; r €111-200; ❄📶) A sensitively restored 16th-century mansion overlooking the Río Darro, in the lower Albayzín, family-run El Ladrón centres on a marble-clad

## LORCA'S LEGACY

Spain's greatest poet and playwright, Federico García Lorca (1898–1936), epitomised many of Andalucía's potent hallmarks – passion, ambiguity, exuberance and innovation. Born in Fuente Vaqueros, 17km northwest of Granada, he won international acclaim in 1928 with *El romancero gitano* (Gypsy Ballads), a collection of verses on Roma themes, full of startling metaphors yet crafted with the simplicity of a flamenco song. Between 1933 and 1936 he wrote the three tragic plays for which he's best known: *Bodas de sangre* (Blood Wedding), *Yerma* (Barren) and *La casa de Bernarda Alba* (The House of Bernarda Alba) – brooding, dramatic works dealing with themes of entrapment and liberation. In 1922, Lorca helped organise Granada's flamenco-reviving Concurso de Cante Jondo as part of the local El Rinconcillo group of poets, writers and musicians.

Lorca was killed at the start of the civil war in August 1936. It's generally held that he was executed by military authorities loyal to Franco for his perceived left-wing political views and his homosexuality. Despite ongoing searches, his remains have never been found.

Near the cathedral, the **Centro Federico García Lorca** (958 27 40 62; www.centrofedericogarcialorca.es; Plaza de la Romanilla; 10am-2pm & 5-9pm Tue-Sat mid-Mar–mid-Sep, 10am-2pm & 4-8pm Tue-Sat mid-Sep–mid-Mar, 11am-2pm Sun year-round) FREE houses the Lorca foundation, with exhibitions and cultural events. Lorca's early 20th-century summer house, the **Huerta de San Vicente** (958 84 91 12; www.huertadesanvicente.com; Calle Virgen Blanca; adult/child €3/1, Tue free; 9am-3pm Tue-Sun Jun–mid-Sep, 9.30am-5pm Tue-Sun mid-Sep–May), sits amid the modern Parque Federico García Lorca, 1.5km west of the centre; visits are by 30-minute guided tour, in Spanish or English.

In Fuente Vaqueros, the **Museo Casa Natal Federico García Lorca** (958 51 64 53; www.patronatogarcialorca.org; Calle Poeta Federico García Lorca 4; adult/child €3/1.50, Wed free; tours hourly 10am-1pm Tue-Sat year-round, 4-5pm Oct-Mar, 5-6pm Apr-Jun) displays photos, posters and costumes for the writer's plays; visits are by guided tour in Spanish. Famous Granada street artist El Niño de las Pinturas (p712) adorned its facade with a vibrant mural in early 2020. **Ureña** (953 22 01 71; www.urena.es) has buses to Fuente Vaqueros (€2, 25 minutes, hourly to two-hourly) from Avenida de Andalucía, 1.5km southwest of Granada bus station.

patio with a fountain and original pillars. A creative theme fills the 15 tastefully updated rooms, which are named for poems by Juan Ramón Jiménez and decorated with lovely tiling and antique desks. Breakfasts are served in the arched *aljibe*.

**Casa del Capitel Nazarí** HERITAGE HOTEL €€
(958 21 52 60; www.hotelcasacapitel.com; Cuesta Aceituneros 6; s €71-90, d €89-161; ) Another slice of Albayzín magic in a 1503 Renaissance palace that's as much architectural history lesson as three-star hotel. The sound of trickling water follows you through columned courtyards to 18 traditional, low-ceilinged rooms clad in tiles, bricks, beams, murals and *artesonado*, and there's free tea, coffee and cakes mid-afternoon. Just off Plaza Nueva at the foot of the Albayzín.

**★Casa Morisca** HERITAGE HOTEL €€€
(958 22 11 00; www.hotelcasamorisca.com; Cuesta de la Victoria 9; d €131-231; ) Live like a Nasrid emir at Granada's original boutique hotel, an exquisite late 15th-century mansion in the lower Albayzín lovingly restored by architect owners. Atmosphere and history are laid on thick in the form of timber-beamed ceilings, brick columns, original stuccowork and an enchanting turquoise-tiled courtyard. Of the 14 intimate, attractive and individually decorated rooms, the best have Alhambra views.

**★Hotel Casa 1800 Granada** BOUTIQUE HOTEL €€€
(958 21 07 00; www.hotelcasa1800.com; Calle Benalúa 11; r €148-210, ste €229-350; ) Hidden in a venerable 16th-century building, the Casa de los Migueletes, this elegant 25-room boutique property charms with its delightful old-world-inspired decor: beds with gilded headboards, coffered ceilings, exposed-stone walls, original *artesonado*, a lovely courtyard overlooked by wood-balustraded balconies. Service is warm and efficient, and complimentary *merienda* appears each afternoon.

**Santa Isabel la Real** HERITAGE HOTEL €€€
(☎958 29 46 58; www.hotelsantaisabellareal.com; Calle de Santa Isabel la Real 19; r €115-210; ❄📶) Up in the Albayzín, this welcoming small hotel occupies a whitewashed 16th-century home that was once a *casa de vecinos* (house lived in by different families). Many original architectural features endure, from marble columns to flagstone floors to the fountain-studded patio. Each of the 11 rooms is adorned with embroidered pictures and hand-woven rugs.

## Centro

**Eco Hostel** HOSTEL €
(☎958 29 29 24; www.ecohostel.es; Gran Vía de Colón 53; dm/d from €17/50; 📶) 🍃 Inhabiting a gracefully restored 1920s Gran Vía building, this minimal-chic hostel is a maze of tiled floors, open-brick walls, bright murals and upcycled furnishings, with a vegan cafe, a shared kitchen and no single-use plastics. Dorms of four or six (including a women-only room) have personal lockers, lights and plugs; family rooms sleep up to four. The helpful team organises free walking tours, yoga, paella dinners and more.

**Párragasiete** BOUTIQUE HOTEL €€
(☎958 26 42 27; www.hotelparragasiete.com; Calle Párraga 7; s €45-65, d €70-115; ❄📶) With its blond-wood floors, smart furniture and clean modern lines, this warmly styled hotel feels more Scandinavia than southern Spain. But Granada pops up in wall sketches of local monuments, a glassed-in interior patio, and a sleek downstairs bar-restaurant, Vitola – popular with *granadinos* and ideal for breakfast or tapas.

**Room Mate Leo** HOTEL €€
(☎958 53 55 79; www.room-matehotels.com; Calle de los Mesones 15; r €71-145; ❄📶) 🍃 Granada's outpost of the popular, youthful and eco-sensitive Room Mate chain opens through a jazzy lobby filled with crimson sofas and splashes of sparkle. Stylish yet unfussy rooms (some with terraces) channel a fun, colourful design, with lots of gold, black and antique-inspired flourishes. Great value in a super-central shopping area, just steps from Plaza Bib-Rambla.

**AC Palacio de Santa Paula** HERITAGE HOTEL €€€
(☎958 80 57 40; www.marriott.co.uk; Gran Vía de Colón 31; s €140-200, d €193-300; P❄📶) The modern frontage of this super-central five-star gives no hint of what lies behind. A cobbled cloister (where you can sip a Granada *vino*) forms the elegant centrepiece of what was once a 16th-century convent but is now a luxe, glossy hotel with subtly stylish rooms, a contemporary-Andalucian restaurant, a gym, a sauna and a Turkish bath.

# Eating

Eating out in Granada is all about the joys of tapas, traditional Andalucian fare and, increasingly, contemporary creativity, with fresh ingredients from across the province starring on most menus. Moroccan cuisine is another speciality, particularly in the Albayzín. Granada is also one of Spain's most vegetarian- and vegan-friendly cities.

## Alhambra & Realejo

**Hicuri Art Restaurant** VEGAN €
(☎858 98 74 73; www.restaurantehicuriartvegan.com; Plaza de los Girones 3; mains €7.50-10, menú del día €14; ⏰noon-11pm Mon-Sat; 🌿) 🍃 Granada's leading street artist, El Niño de las Pinturas (p712), has been let loose inside Hicuri, creating a psychedelic backdrop to the wonderful vegan food and organic wines served at this easy-going, hugely popular restaurant. Zingy salads, creative veggie burgers and curried seitan sit alongside plant-based renditions of Andalucian faves, such as shiitake croquettes or *pisto* (ratatouille) with *patatas a lo pobre*.

**Papaupa** TAPAS €
(☎958 99 18 44; www.facebook.com/papaupa retrofusionfood; Calle de los Molinos 16; raciones €7-12, 3-course menú del día €9.95; ⏰1-4pm & 8pm-midnight Mon, 12.30-4pm & 8pm-midnight

WORTH A TRIP

### CORTIJO DEL MARQUÉS

Hidden in a sea of olive groves, this gorgeous farmstead, **Cortijo del Marqués** (☎958 34 00 77; www.cortijodelmarques.com; Albolote; r incl breakfast €129-189; ⏰mid-Mar–early Nov; P❄📶🏊), dating to the 16th century has been beautifully restored by welcoming Dutch-Austrian owners and makes for a fabulous escape. The main building is strung around a cobbled patio, the pool gazes out on rolling hills, and the 15 individually styled rooms blend country elegance with original features. It's 25km north of Granada (4km off the A44).

## FREE TAPAS

Granada is one of the last bastions of the highly civilised practice of serving a free tapa with every drink. Place your drink order at the bar and a plate will magically appear with a generous portion of something delicious-looking on it. The process is repeated with every round you buy, and many places now let you pick your tapa and even do vegetarian options if you ask. Packed shoulder-to-shoulder with tapas institutions, Calle de Elvira and Calle Navas are popular central strips, but are heavily touristed. You'll find many excellent spots sprinkled around west and south of the cathedral, in the Realejo and the Albayzín, and in outer *barrios*.



Wed, 12.30pm-midnight Thu-Sun; ) With brick arches, a marble-top bar and a subtle bohemian edge, this Realejo hideaway specialises in self-styled 'retro-fusion food'. Inventive dishes marry Spanish, Latin American and Asian flavours – yuca croquettes, tuna tacos, *arepas* (corn-based round bread) – and pair well with a glass of vermouth or *manzanilla* (sherry from Sanlúcar de Barrameda).

**El Piano** VEGAN €
(☎858 81 56 40; www.facebook.com/elpiano.granada; Calle Santiago 2; 4-dish plate €11.95; ⌚noon-11.30pm; ) Punchy world-wandering dishes such as coconut dahl accompany plant-based twists on Andalucian classics such as tortilla, *arroces* (rice dishes) and *albóndigas* (meatballs) at this cheery, good-value vegan and gluten-free deli-restaurant. Mango-yellow walls, Mexican placemats and ceramic plates add colour. Also hosts yoga classes.

★**Picoteca 3Maneras** ANDALUCIAN €€
(☎958 22 68 18; www.facebook.com/picoteca3maneras; Calle Santa Escolástica 19; mains €12-17; ⌚1-4.30pm & 8pm-midnight Tue-Sat, 1-4.30pm Sun; ) Glorious fresh produce, spot-on service, chic whitewashed decor, excellent Spanish wines and a deliciously creative approach to local cuisine make Picoteca a Realejo gem. South American and various Asian flavours infuse ambitiously reimagined dishes such as pork-and-wild-mushroom risotto, pear-and-pancetta gnocchi, and tuna in orange sauce.

**La Botillería** SPANISH €€
(☎958 22 49 28; www.labotilleriagranada.es; Calle Varela 10; mains €10-20; ⌚12.30pm-midnight) La Botillería continues to get rave local reviews thanks to its imaginatively presented food, thoughtful wine list and smart-casual modern design. Dine on starters of Cantabrian anchovies and Trevélez ham, followed by original mains such as *milhoja de presa ibérica* (millefeuille with pork and avocado).

**Cisco y Tierra** TAPAS €€
(☎694 504906; www.facebook.com/ciscoytierra1920; Calle Lepanto 3; raciones €8-18, mains €12-19; ⌚1pm-midnight Thu-Tue, 1-4pm & 8pm-midnight Wed) Beamed ceilings, a marble bar and barrels of homemade vermouth grace the spruced-up 1920s interior of this tiny tapas bar. Seasonal produce fuels the menu, which marries traditional recipes with contemporary creativity in elegantly prepped plates such as octopus parmentier and Iberian-pork *pluma* in mushroom sauce, but also stars classic cheese and meat boards.

**Los Diamantes** TAPAS €€
(☎958 227 070; www.barlosdiamantes.com; Calle Navas 26; raciones €10-14; ⌚12.15-5.30pm & 7.15pm-midnight) A Granada institution, going strong since 1942, this scruffy, always-busy joint is one of the best tapas hangouts on bar-packed Calle Navas. It's standing room only, but the seafood – fried squid, grilled prawns, *boquerones* (anchovies) – is excellent and there's a sociable scene. Branches around town, including on Plaza Nueva.

**Damasqueros** ANDALUCIAN €€€
(☎958 21 05 50; www.damasqueros.com; Calle Damasqueros 3; tasting menu €40, with wine €59-89; ⌚1-3.30pm & 8.30-10.30pm Mon-Sat, 1-3.30pm Sun; ) *Granadina* chef Lola Marín, who trained at some of Spain's top restaurants, unveils her gourmet, market-based cuisine in a tucked-away, white-tableclothed corner of the Realejo. Granada-rooted tasting menus change weekly, with seasonal ingredients taking centre stage, paired with wines from across the province and beyond.

### Plaza Nueva & Around

**Bodegas Castañeda** TAPAS €
(☎958 21 54 64; www.facebook.com/BodegasCastaNeda; Calle Almireceros 1; tapas €2-6; ⌚11.30am-1am Mon-Thu, to 2am Fri-Sat) At this traditional, forever-popular tapas bar, crowds of hun-

gry punters jostle for food under hanging hams. Don't expect any experimental nonsense here: just classic tapas and *raciones* of paella, tortilla, bean stew, *ibérico* ham, Andalucian cheeses and more, all served lightning-fast, with vermouth, sherries and wines poured from big wall-mounted casks.

## Albayzín

**Café 4 Gatos** CAFE €
(☎958 22 48 57; www.cafe4gatos.com; Placeta Cruz Verde 6; breakfasts €2-7; ⊙8.30am-4pm Mon, Tue & Thu, to 8pm Wed & Fri, 9am-8pm Sat, 9am-4pm Sun, closed Aug) A buzzy box-sized cafe, with terrace tables and old black-and-white Granada photos, 4 Gatos has a friendly neighbourhood vibe and terrific Granada-style breakfasts. Gracing the menu are artisan jams, homemade cakes, and enormous organic *tostadas* topped with Manchego cheese, *escalivada* (smoky grilled vegetables) or other goodies, as well as local wines and craft beers.

**Casa Torcuato** ANDALUCIAN €
(☎958 28 81 48; www.casatorcuato.com; Calle Pagés 31; raciones €4-15; ⊙noon-10.30pm Mon, to 6pm Tue, to midnight Sat, to 5pm Sun, 9am-10.30pm Thu, to midnight Fri) Crowds spill out into a pretty plaza from a blue-and-white-tiled interior at long-running, fourth-generation Casa Torcuato in the upper Albayzín. Delectable, smartly traditional tapas swing from fresh gazpacho and aubergines with honey to succulent seafood including grilled prawns, squid and *boquerones*. The *arroz* tapa is famous.

**Arrayanes** MOROCCAN €€
(☎619 076862, 958 22 84 01; www.rest-arrayanes.com; Cuesta Marañas 7; mains €10-17; ⊙1.30-4.30pm & 7.30-11.30pm Wed-Sun, closed mid-Jan–mid-Feb; ✍) Granada hosts some excellent Moroccan kitchens, especially in the Albayzín, and long-established Arrayanes is one of its best. Tinkling fountains, ceramic tiles and ornate arches set the stage for superb North African staples, from *bisara* split-pea soup to steaming tagines and flaky *pastelas* (savoury pies). No alcohol, but the mint lemonade is perfect.

**Samarkanda** LEBANESE €€
(☎958 21 00 04; www.facebook.com/RestauranteLibanesSamarkanda; Calle Calderería Vieja 3; mains €8-16; ⊙1-4.30pm & 7.30-11.30pm Thu-Tue; ✍) Despite the rather tired decor, this friendly family-run Lebanese restaurant cooks up a tempting menu of traditional mainstays in the backstreets of the Albayzín. Kick off with hummus, *labneh* and falafel before digging into a bowl of *kafta* (ground beef baked and served with potatoes and a sesame sauce), steaming couscous, or rice with almonds and raisins.

## Centro

**Poë** TAPAS €
(☎985 43 67 81; www.barpoe.com; Calle Verónica de la Magdalena 40; tapas €1.50, raciones €5; ⊙8pm-12.30am; ✍) It might not look much from the outside, but 'El Poë' is a whole different world once you walk through the door. Students, *granadinos* and visitors mingle over globe-trotting tapas such as Brazilian *feijoada* (black bean and pork stew), chickpea salad, Portuguese-style cod and spicy-hot Thai chicken, courtesy of well-travelled owners Ana and Matt.

★ **El Bar de Fede** ANDALUCIAN €€
(☎958 28 88 14; www.facebook.com/ElbardeFede1; Calle Marqués de Falces 1; raciones €9-15; ⊙9am-2am Mon-Thu, to 3am Fri & Sat, 11am-2am Sun) 'Fede' refers to hometown poet Federico García Lorca, whose free, creative spirit seems to hang over this chicly styled, gay-friendly bar. Patterned wallpaper, stone arches and high tables set around a ceramic-tiled island create a casual feel, and the food is a joy. Standouts include aubergines drizzled with honey, chicken in orange sauce and perfect garlic-parsley squid.

**Más Que Vinos** TAPAS €€
(☎958 56 09 86; www.restaurantemasquevinos.es; Calle Tundidores 10; raciones €9-19; ⊙noon-5pm & 8pm-midnight Sun-Fri, noon-1am Sat; ✍) Down an alley just off Plaza Bib-Rambla, the rustic-modern tavern Más Que Vinos puts the spotlight on Granada province's wonderful produce and up-and-coming wines. Fried aubergines are drizzled with Motril honey, chunky tortilla is filled with local potatoes, and other delights include garlic-fried squid, *payoyo* cheese from Cádiz and croquettes stuffed with cured ham.

**Alameda** ANDALUCIAN €€
(☎958 22 15 07; www.alameda.com.es; Calle Rector Morata 3; mains €12-25; ⊙noon-1am; ✍) A glassed-in, split-level gastrobar and strong wines set the contemporary-cuisine tone at elegant Alameda, where traditional, seasonal Andalucian and Spanish flavours and ingredients are given a creative twist.

Croquettes arrive stuffed with oxtail or wild mushroom, cod cheeks are cooked in *pil pil* sauce, and steaming *arroz* is laced with *pluma ibérica* (a fine pork loin cut).

**Botánico** MEDITERRANEAN €€

(☎958 27 15 98; www.botanicocafe.es; Calle Málaga 3; mains €11-19; ⊙1pm-1am Mon-Thu, to 2am Fri & Sat, to 6pm Sun; ☑) Casual restaurant at lunch, cafe at *merienda* time, and buzzing bar come evening, Botánico wears plenty of hats. Amid sleek orange-on-white decor, the fusion kitchen plates up Mediterranean dishes with hints of Asia and Latin America (lamb tagine, pumpkin tagliatelle, seitan or chicken fajitas), and does a market-fired weekday *menú del día* (€13).

**Oliver** SEAFOOD €€

(☎958 26 22 00; www.restauranteoliver.com; Plaza Pescadería 12; raciones €6-15, mains €11-22; ⊙9am-4pm & 8pm-midnight Mon-Sat) One of the best of the seafood bar-restaurants that throng central Granada's Plaza Pescadería. Everyone from lunching professionals to curious visitors packs in to devour *raciones* of garlicky shrimps, grilled mushrooms, Galician-style octopus and fried seafood treats at the mobbed bar or terrace tables.

**★La Fábula Restaurante** GASTRONOMY €€€

(☎958 25 01 50; www.restaurantelafabula.com; Calle de San Antón 28, Hotel Villa Oniria; mains €23-30, tasting menus €80-125; ⊙2-3.30pm & 8.30-10.30pm) A formal fine-dining restaurant set in a stylishly restored 1909 *palacete* (now the Hotel Villa Oniria), La Fábula is the domain of star chef Ismael Delgado López, whose artfully composed plates of contemporary-Spanish cuisine with strong, seasonal Granada flavours impress: fresh fish from Motril, *ibérico* pork cheeks, Riofrío caviar, smoked-cheese ravioli with garlic and honey. The terrace garden is lovely for a drink.

## Drinking & Nightlife

Scruffy Calle de Elvira, Carrera del Darro at the base of the Albayzín, touristed Calle Navas, the area just off northern Gran Vía, and the streets of the Realejo are hotspots, but you'll find drinking dens all over the place.

**Taberna La Tana** WINE BAR

(☎958 22 52 48; www.facebook.com/TabernaLaTana; Placeta del Agua 3; ⊙12.30-4pm & 8.30pm-midnight, closed Sat & Sun Jul & Aug) With bottles stacked to the rafters, hanging strings of garlic and a small wood-and-brick interior, friendly La Tana is one of Granada's greatest wine bars. It specialises in Spanish labels (over 400 of them!), backed up with some beautifully paired tapas.

**La Finca** COFFEE

(☎658 852573; www.facebook.com/lafincacoffee; Calle Colegio Catalino 3; ⊙9am-8pm Mon-Fri, from 10am Sat & Sun; 📶) Bringing third-wave, Granada-roasted coffee to the city with astounding success, this small rustic-chic cafe sources its fair-trade speciality beans directly from growers. The expertly poured espresso goes perfectly with the fresh cakes, cookies and pastries, amid open-stone walls and dangling fairy lights.

**Al Sur de Granada** WINE BAR

(☎958 27 02 45; www.facebook.com/alsurdegranadagram; Calle de Elvira 150; ⊙9.30am-11.30pm Mon-Sat, from 10am Sun) Shelves laden with fragrant olive oils, coffee from roaster La Finca organic produce and other Andalucian goodies tempt you through the door. Al Sur specialises in local natural wines, best enjoyed with a platter of artisanal cheese or *jamón* cured in the Sierra Nevada, or a tapa from the seasonal, daily changing menu. Wine-and-tapas pairing sessions at 7pm.

**El Bar de Eric** BAR

(☎958 27 63 01; www.facebook.com/elbardeeric; Calle Escuelas 8; ⊙8pm-2am Mon-Thu, 1pm-3am Fri-Sun) Strewn with old posters and framed photos of musical heroes, from Debbie Harry to Jim Morrison, this laid-back bar is the creation of Spanish drummer Eric Jiménez of indie rock band Los Planetas. Get into the swing with some fusion tapas, and check online for upcoming gigs, tastings and theatre.

**Casa de Vinos La Brujidera** WINE BAR

(☎958 22 25 95; www.facebook.com/casadevinoslabrujidera; Calle Monjas del Carmen 2; ⊙1-4pm & 8.30pm-1am Sun-Thu, 1-5pm & 8.30pm-2am Fri & Sat) A cosy wood-panelled bar with hams in the window and an astonishing collection of wines (per glass €3 to €4) from all over Spain – everything from organic Granada reds and Jerez sherries to Galician *albariño* and Catalan Penedès chardonnay.

**Candela** BAR

(☎958 22 70 10; www.facebook.com/barelcandela; Calle Santa Escolástica 9; ⊙1-4pm & 8.30pm-1am) Murals by local street artist El Niño de las Pinturas (p712) adorn the walls and shutters at this lively, well-established neighbourhood bar in the lower Realejo, with low-key

## GRANADA'S TEAHOUSES

Granada's *teterías* (teahouses) have proliferated in recent years, but there's still something inviting about their dimly lit interiors, stuffed with lace veils, stucco and low cushioned seats. Most serve a long list of aromatic teas and infusions and Arabic sweets, and many still offer *cachimbas* (hookah pipes). Souk-like **Calle Caldereria Nueva** in the Albayzín is Granada's famous '*tetería* street'.

**Abaco Té** (www.abacote.com; Calle Álamo de Marqués 5; ⌚3-9.30pm; 📶) Hidden up in the Albayzín, outrageously popular Abaco puts an arty contemporary spin on the traditional *tetería* (no hookahs), with infusions (€2.50 to €4), fresh juices, excellent cakes, vegetarian snacks and an irresistible roof terrace.

**Tetería Dar Ziryab** (☎655 446775; Calle Caldereria Nueva 11; ⌚1pm-1am) One of Granada's original tearooms: tiling, cushioned benches, Moorish latticework arches, herbal teas (€2.50 to €4), *cachimbas*. Occasionally hosts cultural events.

**Tetería El Bañuelo** (Calle Bañuelo 5; ⌚11am-11pm) This minimalist *tetería* is loved for its vine-shaded roof terrace looking out on the Alhambra. Rustle up a fresh mint tea (€3 to €4), with Moroccan sweets.

ambient beats and a steady supply of beer and tapas.

## ☆ Entertainment

★**Peña La Platería** FLAMENCO
(☎603 473228, 958 21 06 50; www.laplateria.org.es; Placeta de Toqueros 7) Founded in 1949, La Platería claims to be Spain's oldest flamenco club. Unlike some of Andalucía's more private clubs, it regularly opens its doors to nonmembers for soulful, foot-stomping performances on Thursday nights at 10pm, as well as on other sporadic occasions. Tapas and drinks are available. Book ahead!

**Jardines de Zoraya** FLAMENCO
(☎958 20 62 66; www.jardinesdezoraya.com; Calle Panaderos 32; show €20, with dinner from €49; ⌚shows 8pm & 10.30pm; 👪) Up in the Albayzín, this carmen-turned-restaurant appears, on first impression, to be a tourist-focused *tablao* (choreographed flamenco show). But reasonable entry prices, talented performers and a highly atmospheric patio, where Mediterranean meals are served (kids' menus available), make it a worthwhile stop for any aficionado.

**Flamenco Los Olvidados** FLAMENCO
(☎958 19 71 22; www.flamencolosolvidados.com; Cuesta de Santa Inés 6; adult/child €18/12; ⌚shows 8.15pm & 9.30pm) As the sun sets, the Albayzín's 16th-century Palacio de los Olvidados (also, inexplicably, a museum of Spanish Inquisition torture instruments) morphs into an intimate flamenco space, with quality performers stomping their stuff in the courtyard.

**Casa del Arte Flamenco** FLAMENCO
(www.casadelarteflamenco.com; Cuesta de Gomérez 11; shows €20; ⌚shows 7.30pm & 9pm) A small flamenco venue that is neither a *tablao* nor a *peña* (private club), but something in between. The performers are invariably top-notch, managing to conjure a highly charged mood in the intimate space.

**Eshavira** JAZZ, FLAMENCO
(☎958 29 08 29; https://eshaviraclub.wordpress.com; Calle Póstigo de la Cuna 2; €6-18; ⌚10pm-6am) Just off Calle Azacayas, this is one of Granada's historical jazz and flamenco haunts, staging a regular program of gigs, jam sessions and flamenco performances.

**La Tertulia** LIVE PERFORMANCE
(☎674 037595; www.tertuliagranada.com; Calle Pintor López Mezquita 3; ⌚8pm-2am Tue & Thu, to 1am Wed, 7pm-2am Fri & Sat, to 11pm Sun) A *tertulia* is an artistic gathering, and that's what you generally get at this bohemian bar where the emphasis is on the stage – film screenings, poetry jams, book presentations and, every Tuesday, free tango sessions.

## 🛍 Shopping

Many shops in Granada play on the city's Moorish heritage: bags of spices, curly-toed slippers and handmade leather bags. A local craft speciality to look out for is *taracea* (marquetry), with shell, silver or mother-of-pearl inlay, applied to boxes, tables and more; just a few specialist workshops continue this intricate art that has flourished in Granada since around the 14th century.

**★La Oliva** FOOD & DRINKS

(☎650 182358, 958 22 57 54; www.laoliva.eu; Calle Virgen de Rosario 9; ⏲11am-2.30pm & 7-10pm Mon-Fri, 11am-2.30pm Sat) By day, La Oliva sells fine Spanish wines, high-end olive oils and other gourmet treats. By night, the tables come out and multilingual owner Francisco welcomes a handful of guests to dine on his €38.50 tasting menu (bookings essential; cash only).

**La Cata Con Botas** WINE

(☎958 37 27 37; www.lacataconbotas.com; Calle Paz 4; ⏲11am-2.15pm & 5-9pm Mon-Fri, 11am-2.15pm Sat Sep-Jul, 10.30am-2.30pm Mon-Fri Aug) Perfectly pairing with its clever name (a *vino*-themed pun on Puss in Boots), this bright wine specialist stocks almost exclusively drops from Granada province. Renowned local labels such as **Anchurón** (☎958 27 77 64; www.anchuron.es; Darro; tour €12), Pago de Almaraes and **Cuatro Vientos** (☎616 407250; www.bodegacuatrovientos.es; Murtas; tours €12; ⏲10am-6pm Sat & Sun) grace the shelves.

**Tienda Librería de la Alhambra** BOOKS

(☎958 22 78 46; www.alhambratienda.es; Calle Reyes Católicos 40; ⏲9.30am-8.30pm) A fabulous shop for Alhambra aficionados, with a great collection of books dedicated to the monument, its art and its history. You'll find everything from simple guidebooks to glossy coffee-table tomes on Islamic art, plus quality gifts including hand-painted fans, stylish stationery, Alhambra-scented candles and stunning photographic prints.

**Artesanías González** ARTS & CRAFTS

(Cuesta de Gomérez 12; ⏲11am-8pm) Specialising in the ancient art of *taracea* since 1920, this artisan shop is a great place to pick up a small piece of Granada: handcrafted inlaid boxes, coasters, chess sets and beautiful backgammon boards.

**Gil de Avalle** MUSIC

(☎625 619201; www.gildeavalle.com; Plaza del Realejo 15; ⏲10am-1.30pm & 5-8pm Mon-Fri, 10.30am-1.30pm Sat) The workshop of master guitar-maker Daniel Gil de Avalle is a paradise for aficionados, with a range of exquisite handmade flamenco and classical guitars, as well as castanets and sheet music. It also offers guitar lessons (from €30).

## ℹ Information

**Oficina de Información Turística (Alhambra)** (☎958 02 79 71; www.granadatur.com; Calle Real de la Alhambra; ⏲7.30am-8.30pm May-Oct, to 6.30pm Nov-Apr)

**Oficina de Turismo Municipal** (☎958 24 82 80; www.granadatur.com; Plaza del Carmen 9; ⏲9am-6pm Mon-Sat, to 2pm Sun) City information.

**Oficina de Turismo Provincial** (☎958 24 71 28; www.turgranada.es; Calle Cárcel Baja 3; ⏲9am-8pm Mon-Fri Mar-Oct, to 7pm Nov-Feb, 10am-7pm Sat, 10am-3pm Sun year-round) For Granada province.

**Oficina de Turismo Regional** (☎958 57 52 02; www.andalucia.org; Calle Santa Ana 2; ⏲9am-7.30pm Mon-Fri, 9.30am-3pm Sat & Sun) Covers the whole of Andalucía.

## ℹ Getting There & Away

### AIR

The **Aeropuerto Federico García Lorca Granada-Jaén** (☎913 211000; www.aena.es) is 17km west of Granada, just south of the A92. Flights connect with airports across Spain (including Madrid, Barcelona, Tenerife and Mallorca), as well as Berlin, Bordeaux, Milan, Naples, London Gatwick and Manchester. Airlines include easyJet, Vueling and Iberia.

### BUS

Granada's **bus station** (Avenida Juan Pablo II) is 3km northwest of the city centre. ALSA runs buses across the region, including to/from Las Alpujarras (p724), and has one to two daily direct connections to Madrid's Barajas airport (€47, 4¾ hours).

| Destination | Cost (€) | Time (hr) | Frequency (daily) |
|---|---|---|---|
| Almuñécar | 8.58 | 1¼–1¾ | 8–9 |
| Córdoba | 12–18 | 2¾–3¾ | 12–13 |
| Guadix | 5.65 | 45min | 10–15 |
| Jaén | 9.13 | 1–1¼ | 15 |
| Málaga | 11–14 | 1½–1¾ | 24–25 |
| Seville | 23–30 | 3–4½ | 9 |

### TRAIN

The train station is 1.5km northwest of the centre. A new high-speed line between Granada and Antequera was inaugurated in 2019, linking with the high-speed Madrid–Cordoba–Málaga AVE line.

| Destination | Cost (€) | Time (hr) | Frequency (daily) |
|---|---|---|---|
| Algeciras | 32 | 4¼–5 | 3 |
| Almería | 21 | 2½–3 | 4 |
| Barcelona | 36–75 | 6¼–7½ | 3 |
| Córdoba | 15–49 | 1¼–2 | 7–9 |

| Madrid | 37–81 | 3¼ | 3 |
|---|---|---|---|
| Seville | 29–62 | 2¼–4 | 9 |

## Getting Around

### TO/FROM THE AIRPORT

ALSA buses runs from the airport to the city centre (€3, 20 to 40 minutes) at 6am and then roughly hourly between 9.20am and 10pm. They stop at various points, including **Gran Vía de Colón** (Gran Vía de Colón) near the cathedral. Returns are roughly timed with flights. Taxis to/from Granada cost around €25 to €30.

### BICYCLE

**Rent-a-Bici** (www.rent-a-bici.com; 1- or 2-day hire €50)

### BUS

One-way tickets (€1.40; €1.50 at night) can be bought on buses (cash only). Useful lines:

**C30** Plaza Isabel II–Alhambra (via Realejo)
**C31** Plaza Nueva–Albayzín
**C34** Plaza Nueva–Sacromonte
**4** Gran Vía–Train station
**33** Gran Vía–Bus station

### CAR & MOTORCYCLE

Driving in central Granada is frustrating and best avoided; central car parks cost €20 to €25 per night. Arrive by bus or train, or park on the outskirts and hop in by public transport.

### TAXI

**Taxis** (☎958 28 00 00; www.granadataxi.com) congregate in Plaza Nueva and at the train and bus stations.

# GRANADA PROVINCE

The mighty peaks of the Sierra Nevada provide Granada's magnificent backdrop and outdoor playground. Hiking possibilities range from summiting mainland Spain's highest mountain to hiking through the bucolic gorges, olive groves and white villages of Las Alpujarras on the range's southern reaches, while skiers can enjoy Europe's southernmost ski resort. To the south, you can soak up the sun on the silver-pebble beaches of the Costa Tropical.

## Sierra Nevada

The wild snowcapped peaks of the Sierra Nevada range are home to the highest point in mainland Spain (Mulhacén, 3479m) and Europe's most southerly ski resort at Pradollano. The Sierra Nevada extends about 75km from west to east, with 15 peaks over 3000m. The lower southern reaches, peppered with bucolic white villages, are collectively known as Las Alpujarras.

Some 862 sq km are encompassed by the Parque Nacional Sierra Nevada, Spain's largest national park, designated in 1999. This vast protected area is home to 2100 of Spain's 7000 plant species, including unique types of crocus, narcissus, thistle, clover and poppy, as well as Andalucía's largest ibex population (around 15,000). Bordering the national park at lower altitudes is the 864-sq-km Parque Natural Sierra Nevada.

From July to early September, the higher mountains offer wonderful multiday trekking and day hikes. Outside of this period, there's a risk of inclement weather, but the lower Alpujarras are always welcoming, and the ski scene swings into action from around November to April.

## Information

**Centro de Visitantes El Dornajo** (☎958 34 06 25; www.juntadeandalucia.es; A395, Km 23; ⌚8am-3pm Wed-Sun mid-Jun–mid-Sep, 9am-3pm Wed-Fri, 10am-5pm Sat & Sun mid-Sep–mid-Jun) Information centre for the Sierra Nevada, including Mulhacén and Veleta (p726); on the A395 to/from Pradollano, about 23km from Granada.

### Pradollano

POP 233 / ELEV 2100M

The modern village of Pradollano is the gateway to Europe's most southerly ski resort. In summer, skiing gives way to mountain biking in the **Sierra Nevada Bike Park** (www.sierranevadabikepark.com; day pass €22; ⌚lifts 9.30am-6pm late Jun–early Sep), with 18.5km over four routes. It's about 30km southeast of Granada, along the A395.

From December to April, **Autocares Tocina** (☎958 46 50 22; www.autotransportetocina.es) has buses to Pradollano from Granada's bus station (€5, one hour) at 8am, 10am and 5pm (plus 3pm on weekends), returning at 9am, 4.30pm and 6.30pm (plus 1pm on weekends). Outside ski season there's one daily bus (9am from Granada, returning at 5pm). Taxis to/from Granada cost €60.

**Sierra Nevada Ski** SKIING
(☎958 70 80 90; www.sierranevada.es; ski pass adult €47-52, child €31-34; ⌚Nov-Apr) The resort is popular with day-trippers from Granada and beyond and gets supremely busy

# Western Sierra Nevada & Las Alpujarras

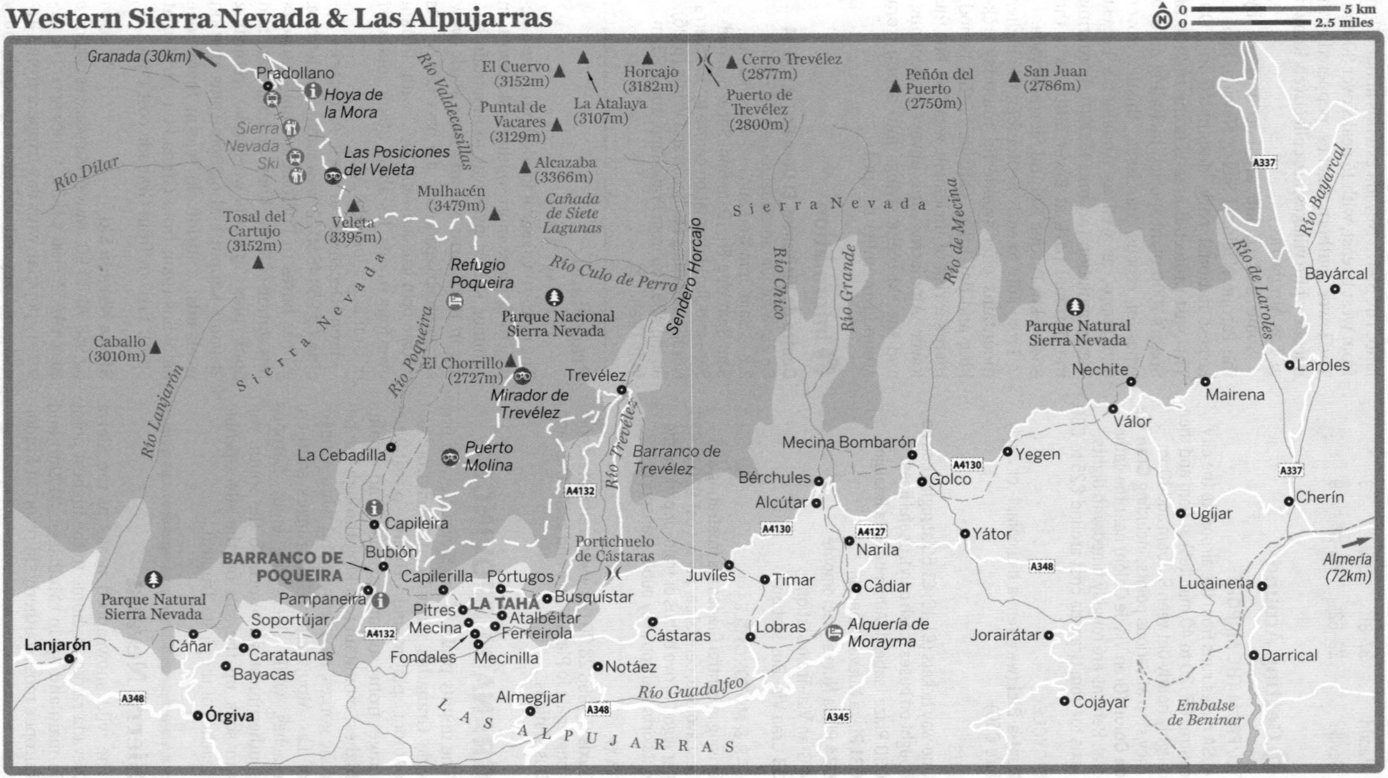

0 5 km
0 2.5 miles

Granada (30km)
Pradollano
Hoya de la Mora
Sierra Nevada Ski
Las Posiciones del Veleta
Río Dílar
Tosal del Cartujo (3152m)
Veleta (3395m)
Mulhacén (3479m)
Río Valdecasillas
El Cuervo (3152m)
Puntal de Vacares (3129m)
Alcazaba (3366m)
La Atalaya (3107m)
Horcajo (3182m)
Cañada de Siete Lagunas
Cerro Trevélez (2877m)
Puerto de Trevélez (2800m)
Peñón del Puerto (2750m)
San Juan (2786m)
Sierra Nevada
Río Culo de Perro
Refugio Poqueira
Parque Nacional Sierra Nevada
Sendero Horcajo
Río Chico
Río Grande
Río de Mecina
Río de Laroles
Río Bayarcal
A337
Bayárcal
Parque Natural Sierra Nevada
Laroles
Nechite
Mairena
Válor
Caballo (3010m)
Río Lanjarón
Río Poqueira
El Chorrillo (2727m)
Mirador de Trevélez
Trevélez
Río Trevélez
Barranco de Trevélez
La Cebadilla
Puerto Molina
Mecina Bombarón
Yegen
A4130
Golco
Bérchules
Alcútar
A4132
Capileira
Ugíjar
Cherín
Yátor
A4127
Narila
Portichuelo de Cástaras
Bubión
BARRANCO DE POQUEIRA
Capilerilla
Pórtugos
Busquístar
Juvíles
Timar
Cádiar
A348
Almería (72km)
Lucainena
Parque Natural Sierra Nevada
Pampaneira
LA TAHÁ
Pitres
Atalbéitar
Mecina
Ferreirola
Fondales
Mecinilla
Soportújar
Cástaras
Lobras
Alquería de Morayma
Jorairátar
Lanjarón
Cáñar
Carataunas
Bayacas
Notáez
Darrical
Río Guadalfeo
Almegíjar
Órgiva
A345
Cojáyar
Embalse de Beninar
LAS ALPUJARRAS

on winter weekends. It caters to all levels with 110km of pistes ranging from tough black descents to mild green runs, plus cross-country trails, many on the flanks of the mighty Veleta (3395m). Gear rental is available for around €25 per day.

## Las Alpujarras

A 70km stretch of valleys and deep gorges extending across the southern flank of the Sierra Nevada, Las Alpujarras is famed for its picturesque white villages, which cling to the steep hillsides, their Berber-style flat-roofed houses recalling the region's past as a refuge for Moors escaping the Christian conquest of Granada. The Moorish influence lingers today in the local architecture, crafts and cuisine. Between the villages, terraced farmlands made fertile by snow-fed mountain waters sit amid woodlands and rocky, arid slopes, with well-trodden footpaths criss-crossing the hills for superlative hiking. Local wineries are blossoming. These days, many villages host a mixed population of *alpujarreños* and expats.

### ℹ Getting There & Away

Bus services are operated by ALSA.

### Lanjarón

POP 3218 / ELEV 659M

The main gateway to the western Alpujarras, Lanjarón is an attractive, leafy mountain town best known for its therapeutic spa waters, which have long been a major source of income and still draw coach-loads of visitors. It also profits from its pure spring water, bottled and sold across Spain, and its air-cured *jamón serrano* (ham). It's 45km south of Granada, along the A44 and A348.

**Caballo Blanco** HORSE RIDING

(☎627 794891; www.caballoblancotrekking.com; 2/4hr rides €40/70, full day incl picnic €95) This well-established outfit offers horse-riding lessons and treks into the surrounding hills and mountains, including multi-day trips; book ahead. English, Spanish, German and a little French are spoken. It's about 5km east of Lanjarón.

**Arca de Noé** SPANISH €€

(☎958 77 00 27; www.facebook.com/arcadenoegustavorubio; Avenida de la Alpujarra 38; raciones €6-18; ⏲10am-3.30pm & 6.30-10.30pm Mon-Sat, 10am-3pm Sun) The orderly rows of hanging hams and shelves laden with wine bottles, conserves and marinated goodies give the game away. This deli-eatery is the place to sample the celebrated local *jamón*, as well as a smorgasbord of regional delicacies: spicy sausages, goat's cheese and tomato salads.

**SIERRA NEVADA MAPS**

The best maps for the Sierra Nevada and Las Alpujarras are Editorial Alpina's *Sierra Nevada, La Alpujarra* (1:40,000) and Editorial Penibética's *Sierra Nevada* (1:40,000). Both come with booklets describing walking, cycling and skiing routes, and are available at the Centro de Visitantes El Dornajo (p721) near Pradollano. *Walking and Trekking in the Sierra Nevada* (Cicerone; 2017) by Richard Hartley is a great resource, as is the Discovery Walking Guides map/booklet.

#### ℹ Getting There & Away

Lanjarón has ALSA buses to/from Granada (€4.40, one to 1½ hours, six to nine daily), Málaga (€13, 4½ hours, one daily Monday to Saturday), and Motril (€4.13, 1¼ hours, two daily Monday to Friday, one Saturday).

### Órgiva

POP 3589 / ELEV 450M

Surrounded by citrus and olive trees, Órgiva, the main town of the western Alpujarras, is a bit scruffier and considerably larger than neighbouring villages, with 68 different nationalities living here and a fertile hippie scene. The alternative lifestyle community of Beneficio sits in the woodlands north of town and its inhabitants regularly pop in to sell their wares at the Thursday market. British visitors might recognise Órgiva from Chris Stewart's best-selling book *Driving Over Lemons*.

**Casa Rural Jazmín** CASA RURAL €€

(☎621 223140; www.casaruraljazmin.com; Calle Ladera de la Ermita; d incl breakfast €53-70; P❄📶🏊) A warm welcome awaits at this peaceful sanctuary hidden behind a swirl of bougainvillea in the upper part of town. It's a cosy set-up with four colourful, homey rooms, each decorated in a different style and some larger than others. Outside, there's a tucked-away flower-filled garden where breakfast is served in summer and you can splash around in the pool.

**Tetería Baraka** INTERNATIONAL €€

(☎958 78 58 94; www.teteria-baraka.com; Calle Estación 12; snacks €2-8, mains €5-14; ⏰10am-11pm; 📶🅥) A laid-back local haunt, especially on market days, Baraka whips up zingy hummus, falafel wraps, tofu burgers, Moroccan tagines, tortilla omelettes and other delights, amid tiled tables and cosy corners. Teas are sweetened with Alpujarras honey and most ingredients are local and organic, including Órgiva olive oil. Home-baked treats spin from vegan brownies to Moroccan sweets.

## ℹ Information

**Oficina de Turismo de Órgiva** (☎958 78 42 66; www.orgivaturismo.wordpress.com; Plaza de la Alpujarra; ⏰10am-2pm & 5-8pm Mon-Fri, 10am-2pm & 5-9pm Sat, 10am-2pm Sun)

**Sierra Nevada Outdoor** (☎958 78 41 11; www.sierranevadaoutdoor.es; Avenida González Robles 14D; ⏰10am-2pm & 5-8pm Mon-Fri, 10am-2pm Sat) Helpful outdoor shop with maps, books and advie on hikes.

## Barranco del Poqueira

The Barranco del Poqueira (Poqueira Gorge) is home to three of Las Alpujarras' most celebrated (and most visited) villages: Pampaneira, Bubión and Capileira, respectively 14km, 18km and 20km northeast of Órgiva along the A4132 and A4129. Seen from a distance they resemble flecks of white paint flicked Jackson Pollock–style on the vertiginous green landscape above the Río Poqueira. Up close, they're textbook models of the charming, steeply stacked white villages for which the Alpujarras are so famous, with their arches, irrigation channels and *tinaos* (passageways beneath houses).

The valley is also known for its handicrafts and you'll find shops selling leather goods, woven rugs and tilework, as well as locally produced ham, jam, cheese, honey and more. Paths fan out from all three villages, with many routes doable in a day. The 9km Sendero Pueblos de Poqueira runs up the gorge from Pampaneira to Capileira (around four hours) via Bubión. Capileira's **Servicio de Interpretación de Altas Cumbres** (SIAC, High Summits Interpretation Service; ☎671 564406; www.reservatuvisita.es; Carretera de Sierra Nevada, Capileira; ⏰10am-2pm & 5-8pm approx Easter-early Dec) has invaluable hiking information, as do Pampaneira's terrific outdoors experts **Nevadensis** (☎659 109662, 958 76 31 27; www.nevadensis.com; Plaza de la Libertad; ⏰10am-2pm Mar, Jul, Aug & Nov, 10am-2pm & 4-6pm Apr-Jun, Sep & Oct, 10am-2pm Fri-Sun Dec-Feb), who also offer a huge range of activities, from mountaineering courses to guided hikes.

### PAMPANEIRA

POP 275 / ELEV 1060M

The lowest of the Barranco del Poqueira's three villages, Pampaneira is also one of the Alpujarras' most obviously tourist-driven, set around the Plaza de la Libertad and its 16th-century Mudéjar **church** (Plaza de la Libertad; ⏰10.30-11.30am). The GR7 hiking route passes through town.

**Estrella de las Nieves** HOTEL €€

(☎958 76 39 81; www.estrelladelasnieves.com; Calle Huertos 21; s/d/ste €50/75/100; 🅿📶🏊) At the top of town, this dazzling-white complex offers elegant, understated modern rooms with local artwork, hydromassage showers or baths, and terraces overlooking the mountains and pleasant gardens.

### LAS ALPUJARRAS BUSES TO/FROM GRANADA

| DESTINATION | COST (€) | TIME (HR) | FREQUENCY (DAILY) |
|---|---|---|---|
| Bubión | 6.26 | 2–2½ | 3 |
| Cádiar | 9 | 2¾ | 3 |
| Capileira | 6.30 | 2–3 | 3 |
| Lanjarón | 4.40 | 1–1½ | 6–9 |
| Órgiva | 5.26 | 1½–1¾ | 6–9 |
| Pampaneira | 6.22 | 1¾–2¼ | 3 |
| Pitres | 7 | 2¾–3¼ | 2 |
| Trevélez | 8.21 | 2¾–3¾ | 3 |
| Válor | 11 | 3½ | 2 |
| Yegen | 10 | 3½ | 2 |

DON'T MISS

## WALKING IN LAS ALPUJARRAS

The alternating ridges and valleys of Las Alpujarras are criss-crossed by a network of mule paths, irrigation ditches and hiking routes, providing a near-infinite number of walks between villages or into the wild – all amounting to some of Andalucía's (and Spain's) most outstanding hiking. The best months are April to mid-June and mid-September to early November, when temperatures are just right and the flora is at its most colourful.

The three villages in the Barranco del Poqueira (p724) – Pampaneira, Bubión and Capileira – are the most popular starting points, but even here, you'll pass few other hikers on the trail. Colour-coded routes, ranging from 4km to 23km (two to eight hours), run up and down the gorge, and you can also summit Mulhacén (p726) from Capileira as well as from Trevélez further east. Get maps and advice at long-running Nevadensis (p724) in Pampaneira or Sierra Nevada Outdoor (p724) in Órgiva; many local hotels provide their own maps with walk descriptions. Otherwise, handy maps (p723) showing most of the trails include those by Editorial Alpina and Discovery Walking Guides. Nevadensis also organises guided hikes, as do reputable **Spanish Highs** (www.spanishhighs.co.uk; guided day hike from €45 per person) and many Alpujarras hotels.

Of the long-distance footpaths that traverse Las Alpujarras, the GR7 (well signposted by red-and-white markers) follows the most scenic route – you can walk it from Lanjarón to Válor (80km) in around five days. Buses serve all these villages, allowing you to split it into shorter walks, such as the steep Bubión–Pitres section (4.5km, 1½ hours).

The 300km, relatively well-signposted GR240 (known as the Sulayr) circuits the Sierra Nevada at a higher altitude than the GR7; it takes 15 to 19 days to walk in its entirety.

**Bodega El Lagar** ANDALUCIAN €
(☎673 636394; Calle Silencio; raciones €10; ⏰11am-5pm & 8pm-midnight) Hidden behind Plaza de la Libertad, this tiny bodega is one of Pampaneira's best spots to eat: huge helpings of reassuring farmhouse food, including chargrilled steaks, almond soups and the *plato alpujarreño*, plus a €10 set lunch.

### BUBIÓN

POP 279 / ELEV 1350M

The smallest and quietest of the Barranco del Poqueira villages, Bubión is an impossibly picturesque spot with Moorish backstreets, whitewashed arches, flat-roofed houses, and a 16th-century Mudéjar **church** (Plaza Doctor Pérez Ramón; ⏰noon-1pm) built on the site of an old mosque. The GR7 cross-continental footpath bisects the village.

**Hilacar ArtesAna** WORKSHOP
(☎658 106576; www.jarapahilacar.com; Calle Carretera 29; ⏰11am-7pm Thu-Tue, hours vary) FREE At the top of town, this is the Alpujarras' only remaining artisan workshop of *jarapas*, those colourful rugs you'll spot all over the Poqueira villages. You can see the 200-year-old loom in action, buy handmade *jarapas* (from €45) or even make your own in a two-hour workshop (enquire ahead).

**Teide** ANDALUCIAN €
(☎958 76 30 37; www.restauranteteide.com; Calle Carretera 1; mains €6-17; ⏰1-4pm & 7.30-10.30pm Wed-Mon, closed 2 weeks Feb) With shaded outdoor tables and a large wood-beamed dining hall, long-running roadside Teide serves up generous, home-cooked *alpujarreño* dishes, such as goat with garlic and almonds, roast leg of lamb, trout with *patatas a lo pobre* (poor man's potatoes), and local *jamón*.

### CAPILEIRA

POP 550 / ELEV 1436M

Overlooked by a lily-white 18th-century church, Capileira is the highest, largest and prettiest village in the Barranco del Poqueira (and Las Alpujarras' most touristed). It's also the departure point for high-altitude hikes up and around Mulhacén.

★**Hotel Real de Poqueira** HOTEL €€
(☎958 76 39 02; www.hotelespoqueira.es; Plaza Panteón Viejo; s €50, d €55-95; ⏰mid-Feb–mid-Jan; ❄📶🏊) Occupying a typical old house opposite Capileira's church, this terrific three-star is the pick of several village accommodations run by the same welcoming family. Rooms are elegantly minimalist and modern, with smart bathrooms and shimmery bedding, and there's a small pool, garden bar and a restaurant.

DON'T MISS

## MULHACÉN & VELETA

Tempting thrill-seekers across Spain, the Sierra Nevada's two highest peaks – Veleta (3395m) and Mulhacén which, at 3479m, is the tallest mountain in mainland Spain – stand on the western end of the range. Both can be summitted from a national park post at **Hoya de la Mora** (2512m) on the mountains' northern flank, accessible by road from Granada and the Pradollano ski resort (which is 3km away).

The Hoya de la Mora post sits by the entrance to a mountain pass that runs over to the Alpujarras village of Capileira on the southern side. However, the top road is closed to private vehicles and the mountains' upper reaches can only be accessed by a national park shuttle bus that's operational between late June and October (snow permitting). It's always best to check availability and schedules for the shuttle buses ahead. Weather permitting, bicycles can use the top road freely.

To climb Mulhacén or Veleta from the north, the easiest approach is to take the **shuttle bus** (☎671 564407; www.reservatuvisita.es; one way/return €6/10; ⊙8am-6pm Jun-Oct) from the Albergue Universitario at Hoya de la Mora. This drops you at the Posiciones del Veleta (3100m), from where it's a 4km trek (1½ hours) to the top of Veleta or 14km (four to five hours) to the summit of Mulhacén.

To tackle Mulhacén from the south side, base yourself in Capileira (p725). From the village's Servicio de Interpretación de Altas Cumbres office (p724) you can catch a summer shuttle bus (one way/return €13/9) to the **Mirador de Trevélez** (2710m; also called El Chorrillo), from where it's around a three-hour hike to the summit (5.1km, 800m ascent). To make the trip into an overnight excursion, you can bunk down at the **Refugio Poqueira** (☎958 34 33 49; www.refugiopoqueira.com; adult/child €18/7), which has bunks and home-cooked meals at 2500m (cash only; book ahead by phone). From the Mirador de Trevélez, it's 3.3km to the *refugio*, then 4.4km to the top of Mulhacén (six to seven hours total). You can also summit Mulhacén on a demanding hike from the Alpujarras village of Trevélez(24km, 10 to 12 hours return).

The routes described here are suitable for walkers of good to moderate fitness. However, in winter they should only be attempted by experienced mountaineers or with a guide. Always check on weather forecasts beforehand and be prepared for changing conditions and possible high winds. Good sources of information include Sierra Nevada Guides (www.sierranevadaguides.co.uk), Nevadensis (p724) and Spanish Highs (p725), all of which also run guided hikes.

**El Corral del Castaño** ANDALUCIAN €€
(☎958 763 414; Plaza del Calvario 16; mains €8-23; ⊙1-4pm & 8-10pm Thu-Tue; ) Enjoy a lovely plaza setting and excellent Andalucian cooking with creative, international influences at this welcoming village restaurant. The menu roams from traditional Alpujarras classics such as the meaty *plato alpujarreño* to inventive numbers such as Moroccan-style veg-stuffed *pastela* or pork cheeks in red wine, plus home-baked pizzas and desserts.

## La Tahá

In La Tahá, the beautiful valley immediately east of the Barranco del Poqueira, life slows and the number of tourists drops noticeably. The area, still known by the Arabic term *taha* for the administrative districts into which the Nasrid emirate of Granada divided the Alpujarras, consists of Pitres (6.5km east of Pampaneira on the A4132) and its outlying villages – Mecina, Capilerilla, Mecinilla, Ferreirola, Fondales and Atalbéitar.

Ancient paths (usually labelled 'Sendero Local Pitres–Ferreirola') link the hamlets, wending their way through woods and orchards, while the tinkle of running water provides the soundtrack. About 1.5km below Mecina Fondales (a 20-minute walk), a Moorish-era bridge spans the deep gorge of the Río Trevélez. The GR142 runs through the bottom of the valley, and there's a clutch of lovely places to stay and eat.

★**Casa Ana** B&B €€
(☎678 298497; www.casa-ana.com; Calle Artesa 7-9, Ferreirola; incl breakfast s €55-70, d €95; ⊙Mar-Dec; ) A beautifully restored 400-year-old house in tiny Ferreirola, 4km

southeast of Pitres, Casa Ana has just 10 rustic-chic rooms (handmade tiles, chestnut beams, rain showers) set around gardens of lavender and wisteria. Writing, painting, yoga and other creative retreats are the speciality. British owner Anne organises walking holidays with author Chris Stewart.

**Hotel Fuente Capilerilla** HOTEL €€
(686 888076; www.fuentecapilerilla.com; Calle Fuente Escarda 5, Capilerilla; r €63-140; Feb–mid-Dec; ) Total tranquillity, mountain views and 12 smartly rustic rooms (some with terraces) await at this Spanish-Belgian–owned hideaway in Capilerilla, La Tahá's highest hamlet at 1350m. Massages, steam baths, a sparkling pool, guided hikes and wellness retreats add to the appeal. Breakfast (€5 to €12), tapas and dinners are available. It's 1.5km up a steep road from Pitres.

**L'Atelier** VEGETARIAN €€
(958 85 75 01; www.facebook.com/latelierveg restaurant; Calle Alberca 21, Mecina; mains €11-14; 1-4pm & 7.30-10pm; ) Set in a traditional 350-year-old house in the hamlet of Mecina Fondales, 4km south of Pitres, this long-established, candlelit restaurant is worth the trip, unveiling a feast of globe-trotting vegetarian and plant-based dishes including spiced couscous, hummus shawarma, coconut tofu curry, wild-mushroom risotto. Book ahead, particularly outside summer.

## Trevélez

POP 724

Trevélez is celebrated for its *jamón serrano*, one of Spain's finest cured hams, which matures perfectly in the crisp, rarefied mountain air. To hikers it's a spaghetti junction of hiking paths and the gateway to high mountain trails, including one of the main routes up Mulhacén, mainland Spain's highest peak. To statisticians it's the second-highest village in Spain after Valdelinares in Aragón. It's 10km north of Busquístar on the almost treeless slopes of the Barranco del Trevélez.

**Hotel La Fragua II** HOTEL €€
(958 85 86 26; www.hotellafragua.com; Calle Posadas; d/tr/q €76/95/125; Mar-Dec; ) With a smart alpine look, a white-and-stone exterior, potted flowers, and 10 spacious, sun-filled rooms (with kettles and balconies), La Fragua II makes a cosy upper-Trevélez base. Outside, you can revel in mountain views by the pool. It's something of a mini-chain, along with a snug attached *alpujarreño* **restaurant** (958 85 85 73; Calle San Antonio; mains €9-14; 12.30-4pm & 8-10.30pm Mar-Dec; ) and the more modest **Hotel La Fragua I** (Calle San Antonio 4; s/d €38/55; Mar-Dec; ).

**Jamones Cano González** FOOD
(958 85 86 32; www.jamonescanogonzalez.com; Calle Pista del Barrio Medio 18; 10am-2pm & 5-7pm Mon-Fri, 11am-2pm & 4-8pm Sat, 11am-2pm Sun) Load up on Trevélez *jamón* at this shop bursting with cured meats, local cheeses, organic olive oil and Alpujarras wines.

# Costa Tropical

There's a hint of Italy's Amalfi Coast about the Costa Tropical, Granada province's 80km coastline. Named for its subtropical microclimate (which produces mangoes, bananas, avocados, custard apples and more), it's far less developed than Málaga's Costa del Sol to the west, and often dramatically beautiful, with dun-brown mountains cascading into the sea and whitewashed villages huddled into bays. The main resorts of Almuñécar and Salobreña are popular summer destinations with long pebble beaches, hilltop castles and handsome historical centres, while La Herradura is a water-sports hub.

### GRANADA WINES

Though wine has been produced across Granada for centuries, it was, until fairly recently, typically for personal consumption. With the establishment of the Vinos de Granada Denominación de Origen Protegida (DOP; Denomination of Origin; www.dopvinosdegranada.es) in 2018, Granada wines are having something of a renaissance. The two main wine-growing areas are Guadix and El Altiplano, where vines sit at up to 1500m and produce deliciously rich reds, and the Contraviesa–Alpujarras area (between the Mediterranean and the Sierra Nevada), where the high-altitude grapes yield reds, whites and rosés. Many bodegas now welcome visitors.

OFF THE BEATEN TRACK

## EASTERN ALPUJARRAS

The eastern reaches of Granada's Alpujarras reveal a harsher, barer, more open landscape. The small villages here – Bérchules, Cádiar, Mecina Bombarón, Yegen, Válor, Mairena – provide oases of greenery, but for the most part this is tough, isolated mountain country, with Ugíjar its main town. Significantly fewer visitors make it this far, and those who do are often on long, solitary hiking expeditions – the long-distance GR7 path traverses the area.

**Espacio Brenan** (Carretera A4130) FREE The old Fonda de Manuel Juliana is where British author Gerald Brenan stayed upon first arriving in Yegen in the 1920s. It's now a small, fascinating museum filled with photos of 20th-century village life. No official opening hours; if next-door bar El Tinao is open, pop in for a coffee and ask for the key.

**Las Chimeneas** (659 137461, 958 76 00 89; www.laschimeneas.com; Calle Amargura 6; d incl breakfast €90; closed Christmas & Jan) A solar-powered 800-year-old village house, this rustic-chic bolthole makes a dreamy walking base, 7km east of Válor in tiny Mairena. The nine rooms exude character with antiques, timber beams, grey-blue shutters and some of the Alpujarras' best views, while the outstanding **restaurant** (3-course dinner €25; 7.30-11pm) serves Andalucian specialities made with organic homegrown vegetables and local produce and wines.

**Alquería de Morayma** (958 34 32 21, 605 051841; www.alqueriamorayma.com; Carretera A348, Km 50; s €52, d €70-78, 4-person apt €120) On a 40-hectare estate of organic vineyards, fruit trees and woodland, this comfortable farmstead is a gorgeous rural retreat. Wood-beamed ceilings, stone-flagged floors and colour-painted arches adorn the rooms and apartments. Own-label wines and olive oil feature in the wonderful season-inspired **restaurant** (raciones €8-12, mains €11-16; 8.30-11am, 1.30-4.30pm & 7.30-11pm) It's 2km south of Cádiar.

## Almuñécar & La Herradura

POP 17,900 (ALMUÑÉCAR), 4215 (LA HERRADURA)

The Costa Tropical's main resort town, Almuñécar heaves in summer as crowds of Spanish holidaymakers and northern European sun-seekers flock to its palm-fringed esplanade and two pebble beaches. It's not an obviously attractive place back from the seafront, but beyond the dreary high-rises you'll uncover a picturesque *casco antiguo* (old town) filled with narrow lanes, whitewashed homes and bar-flanked plazas, and topped by a striking Moorish castle.

About 7km west of Almuñécar, less touristed La Herradura caters to a lively crowd of windsurfers, divers, kayakers and other water-sports fans. Its shimmering horseshoe-shaped bay has a subtle castaway vibe, a lengthy pebble beach and plenty of holiday apartments and seafront *chiringuitos* (snack bars).

### Sights & Activities

**Castillo de San Miguel** CASTLE

(650 027584; Explanada del Castillo; combined ticket Museo Arqueológico adult/child €2.35/1.60, free 10am-1pm Fri; 10am-1.30pm & 6.30-9pm Tue-Sat, 10am-1pm Sun Jul–mid-Sep, shorter hours mid-Sep–Jun) Almuñécar's impressive hilltop castle was built over Islamic, Roman and Phoenician fortifications by the conquering Christians in the 16th century, was severely damaged during the Napoleonic Wars, and later became the town's cemetery until the 1980s. Tickets include Almuñécar's small **archaeology museum** (958 83 86 23; Calle San Joaquín; 10am-1.30pm & 6.30-9pm Tue-Sat, 10am-1pm Sun Jul–mid-Sep, shorter hours mid-Sep–Jun), set in a series of 1st-century vaulted underground cellars.

**Windsurf La Herradura** WATER SPORTS

(958 64 01 43; www.windsurflaherradura.com; Paseo Marítimo 34; windsurf/paddleboard/kayak hire from €20/10/7; beach stand 10.30am-8pm Easter-Oct, shop 10.30am-2pm & 5.30-8.30pm year-round) An established La Herradura all-rounder renting windsurfing gear, kayaks and paddleboards, and offering classes (one-hour windsurf class €40), courses, SUP yoga sessions (€12; June to August), and guided kayaking and paddleboarding excursions to sea caves (two hours €20).

**Buceo La Herradura** DIVING
(☎958 82 70 83; www.buceolaherradura.com; Puerto Deportivo Marina del Este; single dive incl equipment €48; ⏰9am-2pm & 4-7pm daily year-round, to 8.30pm Mon-Fri Jun-Sep) This long-established outfit runs dives, 'baptisms' (€70) and PADI courses.

## Sleeping & Eating

**Hotel Casablanca** HOTEL €€
(☎958 63 55 75; www.hotelcasablancaalmunecar.com; Plaza de San Cristóbal 4; s €48-90, d €57-124; ❄📶) Convenient for both the beach and Almuñécar's lively centre, this welcoming family-run hotel is dressed in neo-Moorish style, with smartly contemporary rooms in calming pastel tones.

★**Los Geráneos** ANDALUCIAN €€
(☎958 63 40 20; www.facebook.com/losgeraneos; Plaza de la Rosa 4; menú del día €15; ⏰1-5pm & 7.30-11pm Tue-Sat, 1-5pm Sun; 🖉) 🌿 With tables on a cobbled plaza beneath sky-blue windows or amid wood beams and dangling onions in the charmingly rustic interior, Los Geráneos is a packed Almuñécar favourite. The excellent-value home-style *menú* is a delight of zingy salads, superb fresh grilled fish and meats, and homemade desserts.

## Information

**Oficina de Turismo Palacete de La Najarra**
(☎958 63 11 25; www.turismoalmunecar.es; Avenida de Europa; ⏰9.30am-1.30pm & 4.30-7pm) In the 19th-century neo-Moorish Palacete de la Najarra.

## Getting There & Away

Almuñécar's **bus station** (Avenida Juan Carlos I 1) is 600m north of the town centre. ALSA runs to/from Granada (€8.60, 1½ to two hours, nine daily), Málaga (€7.65, 1½ to two hours, eight or nine daily), Almería (€12.20, two to 3½ hours, five daily), Órgiva (€4.82, 1¼ hours, daily Monday to Saturday) and Nerja (€3, 25 to 45 minutes, 13 to 15 daily). **Fajardo** (☎958 88 27 62; www.grupofajardo.es) goes to/from La Herradura (15 minutes, five to 10 daily).

# MÁLAGA PROVINCE

After decades of being pointedly ignored, particularly by tourists to the coastal resorts, revitalised Málaga is now the Andalucian city everyone is talking about. Its 30-odd

WORTH A TRIP

### GUADIX

A lively provincial town, Guadix (gwah-deeks) is best known for its cave dwellings, many of which are still lived in by local townsfolk. Guadix is also graced by a handsome historical core and has some excellent tapas bars, while the surrounding 4722-sq-km Unesco Geoparque de Granada is a Mars-like semi-desert landscape. If you're overnighting, the **YIT Abentofail** (☎958 66 92 81; www.hotelabentofail.com; Calle Abentofail; s €41-57, d €49-97; 🅿❄📶) is a comfortable boutiquey base, and no-frills **La Bodeguilla** (Calle Doctor Pulido 4; tapas €1-4; ⏰9am-3.30pm & 6.30pm-late) does terrific tapas.

The town is 50km northeast of Granada near the northern foothills of the Sierra Nevada. ALSA buses run to/from Granada (€5.65, one hour, seven to 11 daily), Almería (€9.65, 1½ to two hours, two to three daily) and Málaga (€19, three to 3½ hours, three daily). There are four trains daily to Granada (€9.85, one hour) and six to Almería (€11 to €13, 1½ to two hours).

**Guadix' old quarter** The handsome sandstone-covered old town is graced by the 11th-century **Alcazaba** (Calle Barradas 3), the late-16th-century Renaissance **Plaza de la Constitución** and the flamboyant **Catedral de Guadix** (☎958 66 51 08; www.catedraldeguadix.es; Paseo de la Catedral; adult/child €6/4.50; ⏰10.30am-2pm & 5-7.30pm Jun-Sep, hours vary rest of year), built between the 16th and 18th centuries on the site of the former main mosque and mixing Gothic, Renaissance and baroque styles.

**Barrio de las Cuevas** Around 2000 dwellings are burrowed into the rocky terrain of Guadix' main cave district – a weird, otherworldly place where stumpy chimneys, antennae, white walls and doors emerge from undulating yellow-brown hillocks.

**Castillo de La Calahorra** (☎667 038523, 958 67 70 98; www.lacalahorra.es; La Calahorra; ⏰10am-1pm & 4-6pm Wed) FREE Built between 1509 and 1512, on the ruins of a Moorish fortress, this forbidding castle conceals a magnificent Renaissance interior; visits are by 30-minute guided tour (in Spanish and English). It's 16km southeast of Guadix.

museums and edgy urban art scene are well matched by contemporary-chic dining choices, a stash of new boutique hotels and a shopping street voted one of the most stylish in Spain. Málaga is at its most vibrant during the annual August feria, when the party atmosphere is infused with flamenco, *fino* (dry, straw-coloured sherry) and carafe-loads of fiesta spirit.

Each region of the province has equally fascinating diversity, from the mythical mountains of La Axarquía to the tourist-driven razzle-dazzle of the Costa del Sol. Inland are the *pueblos blancos* (white towns) and the under-appreciated, elegant old town of Antequera, with its nearby archaeological site and fabulous *porra antequera* (a thick, garlicky, tomato soup).

# Málaga

POP 574,654

If you think the Costa del Sol is soulless, you clearly haven't been to Málaga. Loaded with history and brimming with a youthful vigour that proudly acknowledges its multi-layered past, the city that gave the world Picasso has transformed itself in spectacular fashion, with art galleries, a radically rethought port area and a nascent art district called Soho. Not that Málaga was ever lacking in energy: the Spanish-to-the-core bar scene could put bags under the eyes of an insomniac *madrileño*, while the food culture encompasses both Michelin stars and tastefully tatty fish shacks.

Come here for tapas washed down with sweet local wine, and stay in a creative boutique hotel sandwiched between a Roman theatre, a Moorish fortress and the polychromatic Pompidou Centre, while you reflect on how eloquently Málaga has reinvented itself for the 21st century. Look out, Seville.

> **WORTH A TRIP**
>
> **PLAYA DE CANTARRIJÁN**
>
> Hemmed in by rocky cliffs and the glittering Mediterranean, gorgeous grey-pebble Playa de Cantarriján is one of Andalucía's original and favourite clothing-optional beaches. It's 7km west of La Herradura and 1.4km off the N340; from mid-June to mid-September park at the top and catch a shuttle bus (€1). Year-round beachfront *chiringuito* **La Barraca**) cooks up super-fresh fish and delicious paellas (including vegetarian).

## Sights

### ★Museo Picasso Málaga — MUSEUM

(☎952 12 76 00; www.museopicassomalaga.org; Calle San Agustín 8; €9, incl temporary exhibition €12, free last 2hr before closing Sun; ⏲10am-8pm Jul & Aug, to 7pm Mar-Jun, Sep & Oct, to 6pm Nov-Feb) This unmissable museum in the city of Picasso's birth provides a solid overview of the great master and his work, although, surprisingly, it only came to fruition in 2003 after more than 50 years of planning. The 200-plus works in the collection were donated and loaned to the museum by Christine Ruiz-Picasso (wife of Paul, Picasso's eldest son) and Bernard Ruiz-Picasso (Picasso's grandson) and catalogue the artist's sparkling career with a few notable gaps (the 'blue' and 'pink' periods are largely missing).

Nonetheless, numerous gems adorn the gallery's lily-white walls. Highlights include a painting of Picasso's sister Lola undertaken when the artist was only 13; sculptures made from clay, plaster and sheet metal; numerous sketches; a quick journey through cubism; and some interesting late works when Picasso developed an obsession with musketeers. The museum, which is housed in the 16th-century Buenavista Palace, has an excellent cafe and holds revolving temporary exhibitions.

### ★Catedral de Málaga — CATHEDRAL

(☎952 22 03 45; www.malagacatedral.com; Calle Molina Lario; cathedral & Ars Málaga €6, incl roof €10; ⏲10am-6pm Sat, 2-6pm Sun year-round, 10am-8pm Mon-Fri Apr-Jun & Oct, to 9pm Jul-Sep, to 6.30pm Nov-Mar) Málaga's elaborate cathedral was started in the 16th century on the site of the former mosque. Of the mosque, only the **Patio de los Naranjos** survives, a small courtyard of fragrant orange trees. Inside, the fabulous domed ceiling soars 40m into the air, while the vast colonnaded nave houses an enormous cedar-wood choir. Aisles give access to 15 chapels with gorgeous 18th-century retables and religious art. It's worth taking the guided tour up to the *cubiertas* (roof) to enjoy panoramic city views.

Building the cathedral was an epic project that took some 200 years. Such was the project's cost that by 1782 it was decided that work would stop. One of the two bell towers was left incomplete, hence the ca-

## ARTISTIC REVIVAL

Befitting Picasso's birthplace, Málaga has an art collection to rival those of Seville and Granada, particularly in the field of modern art, where galleries and workshops continue to push the envelope. It wasn't always thus.

Little more than 15 years ago, Málaga's art scene was patchy and understated. The first big coup came in 2003, when, after 50 years of on-off discussion, the city finally got around to honouring its most famous son with the opening of the Museo Picasso Málaga (p730). More galleries followed, some focusing on notable *malagueños* such as Jorge Rando and Félix Revello de Toro, while others – such as the Museo Carmen Thyssen (p732), which shines a light on *costumbrismo* (Spanish folk art) – take in a broader sweep of Spanish painting. Then, in 2015, Málaga earned the right to be called a truly international art city when it opened offshoot galleries of St Petersburg's prestigious Russian State Museum and Paris' Pompidou Centre. The finishing touches to this colourful canvas were added in 2016: after 20 years in the dark, Málaga's 2000-piece-strong fine-arts collection was reinstated in the city's beautifully restored old customs house (p731) down by the port.

Málaga's vibrant artistic spirit is especially evident in in the Soho neighbourhood, where street artists have launched **MAUS** (Málaga Arte Urbano en el Soho; www.mausmalaga.com), an edgy urban-renewal project that fosters a free creative space for street and graffiti artists.

thedral's well-worn nickname, La Manquita (The One-Armed Lady). The ticket price includes use of an audio guide as well as entry to the **Ars Málaga** (www.arsmalaga.es; Plaza del Obispo; €4, incl cathedral €6; ⌚10am-9pm Mon-Fri, to 6.30pm Sat, 2-6.30pm Sun Apr-Oct, closes 6.30pm daily Nov-Mar) museum of religious art and African artefacts in the Bishop's House opposite.

### ★Alcazaba — CASTLE

(☎952 22 72 30; http://alcazabaygibralfaro.malaga.eu; Calle Alcazabilla 2; €3.50, incl Castillo de Gibralfaro €5.50; ⌚9am-8pm Apr-Oct, to 6pm Nov-Mar) No time to visit Granada's Alhambra? Then Málaga's Alcazaba can provide a taster. The entrance is beside the Roman theatre (p731), from where a meandering path climbs amid lush greenery: crimson bougainvillea, lofty palms, fragrant jasmine bushes and rows of orange trees. Extensively restored, this palace-fortress dates from the 11th-century Moorish period; the caliphal horseshoe arches, courtyards and bubbling fountains are evocative of this influential period in Málaga's history. The dreamy **Patio de la Alberca** is especially redolent of the Alhambra.

### Castillo de Gibralfaro — CASTLE

(☎952 22 72 30; http://alcazabaygibralfaro.malaga.eu; Camino de Gibralfaro; €3.50, incl Alcazaba €5.50; ⌚9am-8pm Apr-Sep, to 6pm Oct-Mar) One remnant of Málaga's Islamic past is the craggy ramparts of the Castillo de Gibralfaro, spectacularly located high on the hill overlooking the city. Built by 8th-century Córdoban emir Abd ar-Rahman I, and later rebuilt in the 14th century when Málaga was the main port for the emirate of Granada, the castle originally acted as a lighthouse and military barracks. Nothing much is original in the castle's interior, but the protective walkway around the ramparts affords superb views over Málaga.

### Teatro Romano — LANDMARK

(Roman Theatre; ☎951 50 11 15; Calle Alcazabilla 8; ⌚10am-6pm Tue-Sat, to 4pm Sun) FREE The story of the unearthing of Málaga's Roman theatre is almost as interesting as the theatre itself. Dating from the time of Augustus (1st century AD), it was rediscovered in 1951 by workers building the foundations for a new Casa de Cultura. Today the theatre sits fully exposed beneath the walls of the Alcazaba (p731). A small interpretive centre next door outlines its history and displays a few artefacts shovelled from its crusty foundations.

### Museo de Málaga — MUSEUM

(☎951 91 19 04; www.museosdeandalucia.es/museodemalaga; Plaza de la Aduana; EU member/non-member free/€1.50; ⌚9am-9pm Tue-Sat, to 3pm Sun) Spread out over two floors in Málaga's neoclassical Palacio de Aduana, this vast, newly renovated museum houses art and archaeological collections. The 1st-floor fine-arts collection consists primarily of 19th-century Andalucian landscape and

## Málaga

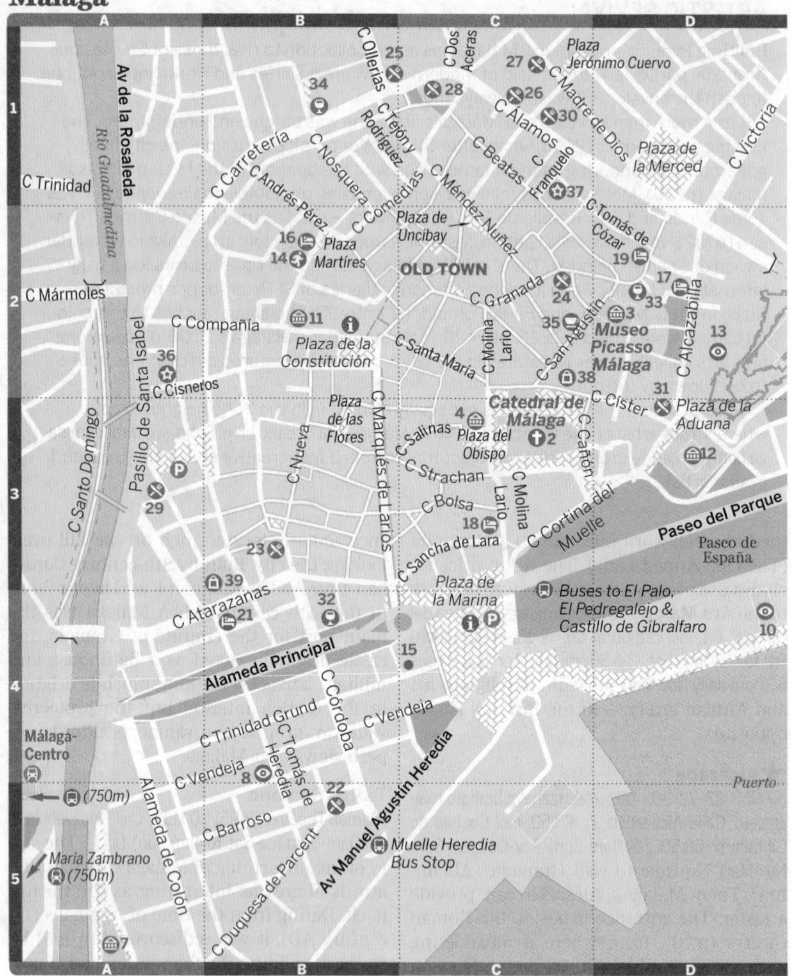


genre paintings, with additional rooms devoted to more modern work. The extensive archaeological collection, bequeathed to the city by the noble Loring-Heredia family, ranges from Neolithic shards uncovered in the nearby Cueva de Nerja (p750) to a headless statue of a Roman noblewoman.

**Centre Pompidou Málaga** MUSEUM

(☎951 92 62 00; www.centrepompidou.es; Pasaje Doctor Carrillo Casaux, Muelle Uno; €7, incl temporary exhibition €9; ⊙9.30am-8pm Wed-Mon) Down by Málaga's port, this offshoot of Paris' Pompidou Centre is housed in a low-slung modern building crowned by artist Daniel Buren's playful multicoloured cube. Thought-provoking, well-curated main exhibits rotate through on an annual or biannual basis, drawing on the museum's vast collection of contemporary art. There are also audiovisual installations, talking 'heads' and temporary exhibitions.

**Museo Carmen Thyssen** MUSEUM

(www.carmenthyssenmalaga.org; Calle Compañía 10; €10, afternoons 2.30-4pm €6; ⊙10am-8pm Tue-Sun) Located in an aesthetically renovated 16th-century palace in the heart of the city's former Moorish quarter, this extensive collection concentrates on 19th-century

Spanish and Andalucian art by painters such as Joaquín Sorolla y Bastida and Ignacio Zuloaga. It's particularly interesting for its almost cartoonish costumbrismo paintings that perpetuated a sentimental myth of 19th-century Spain as a place of banditry, flamenco, fiestas, bar-room brawls and bullfighting (and little else). There are also regular temporary exhibitions and a lovely patio cafe.

**Museo de Arte Flamenco** MUSEUM
(☎952 22 13 80; Calle Franquelo 4; €2; ⏱10am-2pm Mon-Sat) Laid out over two floors in the HQ of Málaga's oldest and most prestigious *peña* (flamenco club), this collection of photos, posters, costumes, fans, guitars and other paraphernalia is testament to the city's illustrious flamenco scene.

**Centro de Arte Contemporáneo** MUSEUM
(Contemporary Art Museum; ☎952 20 85 00; www.cacmalaga.org; Calle Alemania; ⏱9am-9.30pm Tue-Sun) FREE The contemporary-art museum is housed in a skilfully converted 1930s wholesale market on the river estuary. The bizarre triangular floor plan of the building has been retained, with its cubist lines and shapes brilliantly showcasing the modern art on display. Painted entirely white, windows and all, the museum hosts temporary shows featuring the work of well-known contemporary artists and has an obvious Spanish bias. It's usually filled with plenty of spectacularly weird exhibits.

**Muelle Uno** PORT
The city's long-beleaguered port area underwent a radical rethink in 2013 and was redesigned to cater to the increase in cruise-ship passengers. Wide quayside walkways now embellish Muelle 1 and Muelle 2, which are lined by palm trees and backed by shops, restaurants, bars and a small kid-focused aquarium, the **Museo Aula del Mar** (☎951 60 01 08; www.auladelmar.info; Palmeral de las Sopresas, Muelle 2; adult/child/family €7/5/20; ⏱11am-2pm & 5-8pm Jul–early Sep, 10.30am-2pm & 4.30-6.30pm early Sep–Jun).

## Activities

**Hammam Al-Andalus** HAMMAM
(☎952 21 50 18; www.hammamalandalus.com; Plaza de los Mártires 5; baths €34; ⏱10am-midnight) These Moorish-style baths provide *malagueños* with a luxurious marble-clad setting in which to enjoy the same relaxation benefits as those offered by similar facilities in Granada and Córdoba. Massages are also available.

## Tours

★**Málaga Bike Tours** CYCLING
(☎606 978513; www.malagabiketours.eu; Calle Trinidad Grund 5a; tours €25; ⏱10am-8pm Apr-Sep, to 7pm Oct-Mar; 👪) One of the best tours in town and certainly the best on two wheels. Málaga Bike Tours was a pioneer in city cycling when it was set up a decade ago. Its perennially popular excursions, including the classic **City Bike Tour**, are available

## Málaga

**Top Sights**
1 Alcazaba ... E2
2 Catedral de Málaga ... C3
3 Museo Picasso Málaga ... D2

**Sights**
4 Ars Málaga ... C3
5 Castillo de Gibralfaro ... F1
6 Centre Pompidou Málaga ... F3
7 Centro de Arte Contemporáneo ... A5
8 MAUS ... B4
9 Muelle Uno ... E4
10 Museo Aula del Mar ... D4
11 Museo Carmen Thyssen ... B2
Museo de Arte Flamenco ... (see 37)
12 Museo de Málaga ... D3
13 Teatro Romano ... D2

**Activities, Courses & Tours**
14 Hammam Al-Andalus ... B2
15 Málaga Bike Tours ... C4

**Sleeping**
16 Dulces Dreams ... B2
17 Hotel Boutique Teatro Romano ... D2
18 Molina Lario ... C3
19 Palacio Solecio ... D2
20 Parador Málaga Gibralfaro ... F1
21 The Lights Hostel ... B4

**Eating**
22 Al Yamal ... B5
23 Casa Aranda ... B3
24 Casa Lola ... C2
25 Colmado 93 ... B1
Dulces Dreams Cafeteria ... (see 16)
26 El Mesón de Cervantes ... C1
27 La Peregrina Centro ... C1
28 La Tranca ... C1
Óleo ... (see 7)
29 Recyclo Bike Café ... A3
30 Tapeo de Cervantes ... C1
31 Uvedoble Taberna ... D3

**Drinking & Nightlife**
32 Antigua Casa de Guardia ... B4
33 Bodegas El Pimpi ... D2
34 La Madriguera Craft Beer ... B1
35 La Tetería ... C2

**Entertainment**
36 Kelipe ... A2
37 Peña Juan Breva ... C1

**Shopping**
38 Alfajar ... C2
39 Mercado Atarazanas ... B3

in at least five languages, with kids' seats on offer if you're bringing the family.

Daily tours leave from outside the municipal tourist office in Plaza de la Marina at 10am. Reservations are required. Book at least 24 hours ahead. Alternatively, you can rent your own bike from €5 for four hours.

## Festivals & Events

**Semana Santa** RELIGIOUS

Each night from Palm Sunday to Good Friday, six or seven *cofradías* (brotherhoods) bear holy images for several hours through the city, watched by large crowds.

**Feria de Málaga** FAIR

(www.feria.malaga.eu; mid-Aug) Málaga's nine-day feria, launched by a huge fireworks display, is the most ebullient of Andalucía's summer fairs. It resembles an exuberant Rio-style street party, with plenty of flamenco and *fino*; head for the city centre to be in the thick of it. At night, festivities switch to large fairgrounds and nightly rock and flamenco shows at Cortijo de Torres, 3km southwest of the city centre; special buses run from all over the city.

## Sleeping

Hotels have been another beneficiary of Málaga's 21st-century renaissance. Boutique apartments, rooftop swimming pools, funky hostels and throwback Moorish guesthouses are here in abundance.

★**Dulces Dreams** GUESTHOUSE €

(951 35 78 69; www.dulcesdreamshostel.com; Plaza de los Mártires 6; d with shared/private bathroom from €60/74; ) Managed by an enthusiastic young team and delightfully situated in a pedestrianised plaza overlooking a red-brick church, Dulces (sweet) Dreams is a great budget option. The bright, high-ceilinged and whimsically decorated rooms are, appropriately, named after desserts: Cupcake is one of the best. Note that there's no lift, and street noise can be an issue for light sleepers.

**The Lights Hostel** HOSTEL €

(951 25 35 25; www.thelights.es; Calle Torregorda 3; dm €19-38; ) Never mind this hostel's rather bleak exterior. Ride the elevator up to reception and things brighten considerably, with a great roof terrace, a nice guest kitchen and air-conditioned four- to 10-bed

dorms with thick mattresses and ample bedside conveniences (power outlets, reading lights, privacy curtains). Friendly staff organise frequent activities, from dinners to bar crawls to beach and cultural outings.

**Hotel Boutique Teatro Romano** BOUTIQUE HOTEL €€
(952 20 44 38; www.facebook.com/hotelteatroromano; Calle Zegrí 2; r €122-177; ) Reasonably priced for its ultra-central location, this boutiquey two-star overlooks the Roman theatre (p731), with eight family-friendly apartments and 13 sparkling white rooms so clean they look as if they've never been used. The whole place is modern, well managed, and studded with interesting design accents. The healthy breakfasts in the bright on-site cafe are a bonus.

**★Palacio Solecio** BOUTIQUE HOTEL €€€
(952 22 20 00; www.palaciosolecio.com; Calle Granada 61; d €165-305, ste €320-415; ) Málaga's splashiest new boutique hotel opened in late 2019 in a sumptuously renovated 18th-century edifice, paces from the Museo Picasso in the heart of the pedestrian zone. Original architectural details are beautifully enhanced by modern designer touches in the luxurious rooms and suites. There's a colonnaded courtyard bar and an on site restaurant presided over by Michelin-starred chef José Carlos García.

**★Molina Lario** HOTEL €€€
(952 06 20 02; www.hotelmolinalario.com; Calle Molina Lario 20; d €198-325; ) Situated within confessional distance of the cathedral, this four-star hotel has gracious service and a sophisticated, contemporary feel. The spacious, recently remodeled rooms are decorated in subdued tones of beige and white, with natural wood, crisp white linens and marshmallow-soft pillows. Topping it all off is a fabulous rooftop terrace and pool with views to the sea and the cathedral.

**Parador Málaga Gibralfaro** HISTORIC HOTEL €€€
(952 22 19 02; www.parador.es; Castillo de Gibralfaro; r incl breakfast €180-225; ) Perched next to Málaga's Moorish castle (p731) on the pine-forested Gibralfaro, the city's stone-built *parador* (luxurious state-owned hotel) hums with a sultan-like essence. Like most Spanish *paradores*, the kick is more in the setting and facilities than in the modern, businesslike rooms – though most have spectacular views from their terraces.

## Eating

Málaga has a staggering number of tapas bars and restaurants (more than 400 at last count), particularly around the historic centre.

**★La Peregrina Centro** SEAFOOD €
(952 60 66 76; Calle Madre de Dios 17; tapas €2.50, raciones €5-12; 1-4.30pm & 8.15-11.45pm Tue-Sat, 1-4pm Sun) A seafood lover's dream, this white-tiled shoebox of a tapas bar is a fantastic place to indulge your 'try-everything-on-the-menu' fantasies, with tapas-sized portions of every seafood item imaginable, from squid to shrimp to sardines. It's especially fun on a Sunday afternoon, when local families are out in force.

**★Casa Aranda** CAFE €
(www.casa-aranda.net; Calle Herrería del Rey 3; churro €0.50, chocolate €1.95; 8am-12.30pm & 5-9pm) Casa Aranda is in a narrow alleyway next to the market and, since 1932, has been *the* place in town to enjoy chocolate and churros (tubular-shaped doughnuts). The cafe has taken over the whole street, with several outlets overseen by an army of mainly elderly, white-shirted waiters who welcome everyone like an old friend (and most are).

**Recyclo Bike Café** CAFE €
(www.recyclobike.com; Plaza Enrique García Herrera 16; breakfast/lunch from €3/6; 9am-midnight Mon-Thu, to 2am Fri & Sat, 10am-midnight Sun; ) Trendy cafe with affiliated bike shop where you can enjoy a 'Wiggins' salad or exceedingly cheap cakes, coffee and breakfasts. Old bikes adorn the walls and ceiling.

**★El Mesón de Cervantes** TAPAS €€
(952 21 62 74; www.elmesondecervantes.com; Calle Álamos 11; medias raciones €4-10, raciones €8-18; 7pm-midnight Wed-Mon) Cervantes started as a humble tapas bar run by expat Argentine Gabriel Spatz, but has now expanded into four bar-restaurants (each with a slightly different bent), all within a block of each other. This one is the HQ, where pretty much everything on the menu is a show-stopper – lamb stew with couscous; pumpkin and mushroom risotto; and, boy, the grilled octopus!

**★Óleo** FUSION €€
(952 21 90 62; www.oleorestaurante.es; Edificio CAC, Calle Alemania; mains €14-22; 1.30-4pm & 8.30pm-midnight Tue-Sat; ) Located at the

LOCAL KNOWLEDGE

### TAPAS TRAIL

The pleasures of Málaga are essentially undemanding, easy to arrange and cheap. One of the best is a slow crawl around the city's numerous tapas bars and old bodegas (cellars).

**La Tranca** (www.latranca.es; Calle Carretería 92; tapas €1.60-3.90; ⌚12.30pm-2am Mon-Sat, to 4pm Sun) Drinking in this always busy bar is a physical contact sport, with small tapas plates passed over people's heads.

**Colmado 93** (www.facebook.com/colmado93; Calle Carretería 93; tapas €1-3.50; ⌚noon-midnight Mon-Sat) The floor-to-ceiling shelves in this vintage ex-grocery create an atmospheric backdrop for sampling small plates of *mojama* (salt-cured tuna), sheep and goat's cheese, and *malagueña* sausage.

**Casa Lola** (www.tabernacasalola.com; Calle Granada 46; tapas €2.10-3.50; ⌚11am-4pm & 7pm-midnight) Fronted by traditional blue-and-white tiles, this ever-bustling spot serves a luscious range of *pinchos* (Basque-style tapas), accompanied by free-flowing vermouth on tap.

**Tapeo de Cervantes** (☎952 60 94 58; www.eltapeodecervantes.com; Calle Cárcer 8; media raciones €4.50-8, raciones €8.50-14; ⌚1-3.30pm & 7.30-11.30pm Tue-Sun) This original Cervantes bar-restaurant (there are now four) is a bit more boisterous and intimate than the Mesón (p735) around the corner, yet the tapas lineup is virtually identical – ie, among the best in the city.

**Uvedoble Taberna** (www.uvedobletaberna.com; Calle Císter 15; tapas €2.40-3.90; ⌚12.30-4pm & 8pm-midnight Mon-Sat; 📶) If you're seeking something a little more contemporary, head to this popular spot with its innovative take on traditional tapas.

city's Centro de Arte Contemporáneo (p733) with white-on-white minimalist decor, Óleo provides diners with the unusual choice of Mediterranean or Asian food, with some subtle combinations such as duck breast with a side of seaweed with hoisin, as well as gourmet palate-ticklers such as candied roasted piglet.

**Al Yamal** MOROCCAN €€

(☎952 21 20 46; www.facebook.com/restaurante.alyamal; Calle Blasco de Garay 7; mains €14-20; ⌚noon-4.30pm & 7-11.30pm Mon-Sat) Moroccan restaurants are less common in Málaga than in Granada, but Al Yamal, family-run for four decades in the heart of the Soho district, serves the authentic stuff, including tagines, couscous and *kefta* (meatballs). The street profile looks unpromising, but the tiny dining room has six cosy booths decorated with vivid Moroccan fabrics and a trickling fountain.

**El Balneario de los Baños del Carmen** SEAFOOD €€

(☎951 90 55 78; www.elbalneariomalaga.com; Calle Bolivia 40, La Malagueta; mains €12-22; ⌚8.30am-1am Sun-Thu, to 2.30am Fri & Sat; 🅿📶) Enjoying front-row views of the beach at La Malagueta, El Balneario is a wonderful place to sit outside on a balmy evening and share a plate of prawns or grilled sardines, along with some long, cold beverages. Built in 1918 to cater to Málaga's bourgeoisie, it's rekindling its past as one of the city's most celebrated venues for socialising.

## Drinking & Nightlife

The international brigade has yet to cotton on to the fact that Málaga has one of the raciest nightlife scenes in Spain (and that's saying something). The city might not be as big as Madrid, but it's just as fun. The pedestrianised old town is the main hive, especially around Plaza de la Constitución and Plaza de la Merced.

**★La Tetería** TEAHOUSE

(www.la-teteria.com; Calle San Agustín 9; speciality teas €2.70; ⌚9am-10pm Tue & Wed, to 11pm Thu & Sun, to 1am Fri, 3pm-1.30am Sat, 3-10pm Mon) There are numerous *teterías* in Málaga, but only one *La* Tetería. While it's less Moorish than some of its more atmospheric brethren, it still sells a wide selection of fruity teas, backed by a range of rich cakes. Along with the cafe's location next to the Museo Picasso Málaga (p730), this ensures that the place is usually close to full.

**★Bodegas El Pimpi** BAR

(www.elpimpi.com; Calle Granada 62; noon-2am; ) This rambling bar is an institution. The interior encompasses a warren of rooms, and there's a courtyard and open terrace overlooking the Teatro Romano (p731). Walls are decorated with historical feria posters and photos of visitors past, while the enormous barrels are signed by more well-known passers-by, including Tony Blair and Antonio Banderas. Tapas and meals are also available.

**Antigua Casa de Guardia** BAR

(www.antiguacasadeguardia.com; Alameda Principal 18; 10am-10pm Mon-Thu, to 10.45pm Fri & Sat, 11am-3pm Sun) This atmospheric tavern dates to 1840 and is the oldest bar in Málaga. The peeling custard-coloured paintwork and black-and-white photographs of local boy Picasso look fittingly antique. Try the dark brown, sherry-like *seco* (dry), the romantically named *lágrima trasañejo* (very old teardrop), or any of the dozen other Málaga wines served from giant barrels running the length of the bar.

**La Madriguera Craft Beer** CRAFT BEER

(663 523577; www.facebook.com/lamadrigueracraftbeer; Calle Carretería 73; 5pm-1am Wed & Thu, 5pm-3am Fri, noon-3am Sat, noon-5pm Sun) The 'Rabbit Hole', as its name translates, keeps the punters happy with daily listings of a dozen ever-changing craft beers and an equal number of more permanent light bites to soak them up.

## Entertainment

**★Peña Juan Breva** FLAMENCO

(Calle Juan Franquelo 4; shows €15) You'll feel like a gatecrasher at this private *peña*, but persevere: the flamenco is *muy puro*. Watch guitarists who play as though they've got 24 fingers and listen to singers who bellow forth as if their heart was broken the previous night. There's no set schedule. Ask about dates at the on-site Museo de Arte Flamenco

**Kelipe** FLAMENCO

(665 097359; www.kelipe.net; Muro de Puerta Nueva 10; shows €25; shows 9pm Thu-Sun) There are many flamenco clubs springing up all over Andalucía, but few are as soul-stirring as Kelipe. Not only are the musicianship and dancing of the highest calibre, but the talented performers create an intimate feel and a genuine connection with the audience.

## Shopping

The chic, marble-clad Calle Marqués de Larios is home to designer stores and boutiques. In the surrounding streets are family-owned small shops in handsomely restored old buildings, selling everything from flamenco dresses to local sweet Málaga wine. Don't miss the fabulous **Mercado Atarazanas** (Calle Atarazanas; market 8am-3pm Mon-Sat).

**Alfajar** ARTS & CRAFTS

(www.alfajar.es; Calle Císter 1; 10am-9pm) Perfect for handcrafted Andalucian ceramics produced by local artisans. You can find traditional designs and glazes, as well as more modern, arty and individualistic pieces.

## Information

**Municipal Tourist Office** (951 92 60 20; www.malagaturismo.com; Plaza de la Marina; 9am-8pm Apr-Oct, to 6pm Nov-Mar) Offers a range of city maps and booklets. It also operates information kiosks at the Alcazaba entrance (Calle Alcazabilla), at the main train station (Explanada de la Estación), on Plaza de la Merced and on the eastern beaches (El Palo and La Malagueta).

**Regional Tourist Office** (951 30 89 11; Plaza de la Constitución 7; 9am-7.30pm Mon-Fri, 9.30am-3pm Sat & Sun) Located in a noble 18th-century former Jesuit college with year-round art exhibitions, this small tourist office carries a range of information on all of Málaga province, including maps of the regional cities.

## Getting There & Away

### AIR

**Málaga airport** (AGP; 952 04 84 84; www.aena.es), the main international gateway to Andalucía, is 9km southwest of the city centre. It is a major hub in southern Spain, serving top global carriers as well as budget airlines

### BUS

The **bus station** (952 35 00 61; http://estabus.malaga.eu; Paseo de los Tilos) is 1km southwest of the city centre and has links to all major cities in Spain. The main bus line is **ALSA** (952 52 15 04; www.ALSA.es). **Interbus** (www.interbus.es) runs to the Madrid airport.

Buses to the Costa del Sol (east and west) also usually stop at the more central **Muelle Heredia bus stop**.

Destinations include the following; note that the prices listed are the minimum quoted for the route.

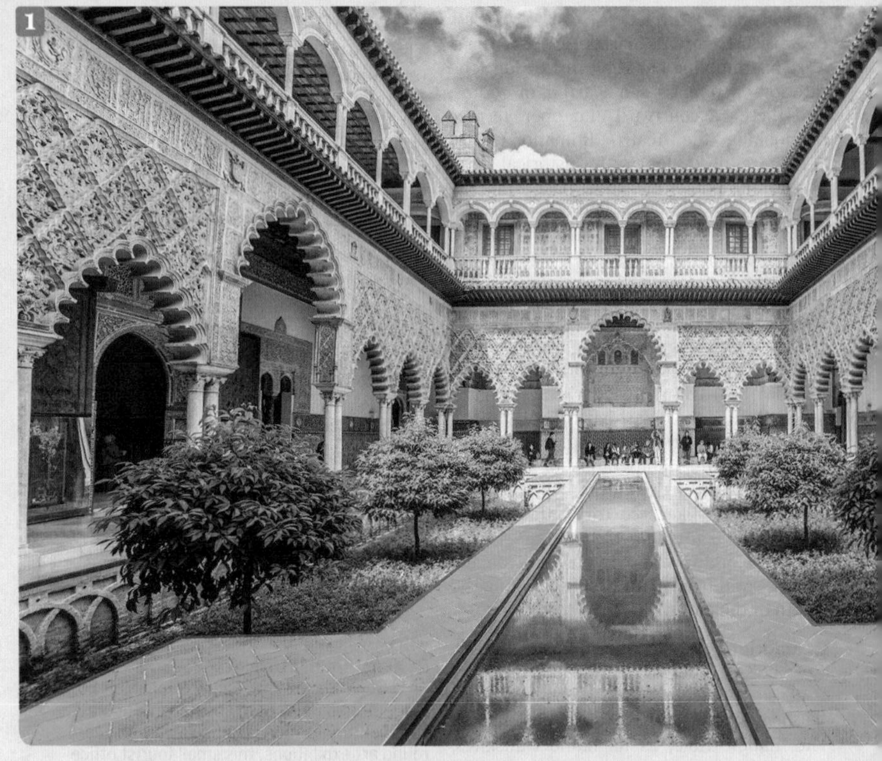

# Legacy of the Moors

**Between 711 and 1492, Andalucía spent nearly eight centuries under North African influence and reminders flicker on every street, from the palatial Alhambra to the tearooms and bathhouses of Córdoba and Málaga.**

## Teterías

Moorish-style *teterías* (tearooms), carrying a touch of Fez or even Cairo in their ornate interiors, have been revived in Andalucía. Calle Caldería Nueva in Granada's Albayzín kicked off the trend some years back; now even Torremolinos has a couple! Look for dimly lit, cushion-filled, fit-for-a-sultan cafes where pots of sugary fresh-mint tea arrive on a silver salver with light Arabic sweets.

## Hammams & Arab Baths

Sitting somewhere between a Western spa and a Moroccan *hammam*, Andalucía's modern bathhouses possess enough old-fashioned elegance to satisfy a latter-day emir with a penchant for Moorish-era opulence. You'll be reclining in candlelit bliss sipping mint tea and experiencing the same kind of bathing ritual – successive immersions in cold, tepid and hot bathwater – that the Moors did, often followed by a massage. Seville, Granada, Almería, Córdoba and Málaga all have excellent Arab-style bathhouses.

## Architecture

Granada's Alhambra and Córdoba's Mezquita were undoubtedly the pinnacles of Moorish architecture in Andalucía, but there are many other buildings that draw inspiration from the rulers of Al-Andalus.

1. Real Alcázar (p621), Seville 2. *Tetería*

Mudéjar constructions, such as the Palacio de Don Pedro in Seville's Real Alcázar, were the work of Muslim artisans for Christian overlords after the Reconquista, while neo-Moorish revivalist styles popped up in later centuries. Hundreds of Andalucian towns and villages still preserve their original Moorish labyrinthine street plans, and many of the region's churches are converted mosques.

## Cuisine

Spain's cuisine, particularly in Andalucía, draws heavily upon the food of North Africa, where sweet spicy meat is melded with Mediterranean ingredients. The Moors introduced many key ingredients into Spanish cooking: saffron, used in paella; almonds, used in Spanish desserts; aubergines and apricots, the former present in the popular tapa *berenjenas con miel de caña* (aubergines with molasses); and numerous spices. The irrigated terrace systems created by the Moors to grow crops and vegetables remain a key source of the same foods today.

### MOORISH HIGHLIGHTS

**Granada** Alhambra (p700), Albayzín (p709)

**Córdoba** Mezquita (p684), Medina Azahara (p694)

**Seville** Real Alcázar (p621), Giralda (p620), Torre del Oro (p630)

**Málaga** Alcazaba (p731), Castillo de Gibralfaro (p731)

**Almería** Alcazaba (p763)

**Las Alpujarras** Berber-style houses in villages such as Capileira (p725)

| Destination | Cost (€) | Time (hr) | Frequency (daily) |
|---|---|---|---|
| Almería | 20 | 2½–5 | 8 |
| Córdoba | 13 | 2¼–4 | 4 |
| Granada | 12 | 1½–2 | 23 |
| Jaén | 21 | 2¾–4¾ | 5 |
| Madrid airport | 17 | 6½ | 1 |
| Seville | 19 | 2¾ | 8 |

### TRAIN

Málaga is the southern terminus of the Madrid–Málaga high-speed train line.

**Málaga María Zambrano Train Station** (☎902 43 23 43; www.renfe.com; Explanada de la Estación) is near the bus station, a 15-minute walk from the city centre. Destinations include Córdoba (€30 to €42, 45 minutes to one hour, 19 daily), Seville (€25 to €47, two to 3½ hours, 11 daily) and Madrid (€82, 2¾ hours, 14 daily).

## Getting Around

### TO/FROM THE AIRPORT

Bus Line A to the city centre (€3, 20 minutes) leaves from outside the arrivals hall every 20 to 25 minutes between 7am and midnight. The bus to the airport leaves from the eastern end of Paseo del Parque, and from outside the bus and train stations, with roughly the same frequency starting at 6.25am daily.

Suburban train C1 (€2.30) runs from airport terminal T3 to María Zambrano station (eight minutes) and Málaga-Centro station beside the Río Guadalmedina (11 minutes) every 20 minutes between 6.44am and 12.54am. Departures from the city to the airport are every 20 minutes from 5.20am to 11.30pm.

A taxi to the city centre costs €22 to €25.

### BUS

EMT (Empresa Malagueña de Transportes) runs several useful buses around town (€1.30 for all trips around the centre), including buses 3 and 7 to the **Museo Ruso de Málaga**, bus 34 to **El Pedregalejo and El Palo**, and bus 35 to Castillo de Gibralfaro, all departing from points along Paseo del Parque and the Alameda Principal near Plaza Marina.

# Costa del Sol

Regularly derided but perennially popular, Spain's famous 'sun coast' is a chameleonic agglomeration of end-to-end resort towns that were once (hard to believe) mere fishing villages. Development in the last 60 years has been far-reaching and not always subtle, throwing up a disjointed muddle of *urbanizaciones*, each with its own niche. Torremolinos is a popular gay resort, Benalmádena plugs theme parks and aquariums, Marbella is loudly rich and partial to big yachts and golf, while Estepona maintains a semblance of its former Spanish self. Take your pick.

## Torremolinos & Benalmádena

POP 136,789

Once a small coastal village dotted with *torres* (towers) and *molinos* (watermills), 'Terrible Torre' became a byword for tacky package holidays in the 1970s, when it welcomed tourism on an industrial scale and morphed into a magnet for lager-swilling Brits whose command of Spanish rarely got beyond the words '*dos cervezas, por favor*'. But the times, they are a-changing. Torre has grown up and widened its reach. These days the town attracts a far wider cross-section of people, including trendy clubbers, beach-loving families, gay visitors and, yes, even some Spanish tourists. Waiting for them is an insomniac nightlife, 7km of unsullied sand and a huge array of hotels, most of which subscribe to an architectural style best described as 'disastrous'.

Benalmádena, Torre's western twin, is more of the same with a couple of added quirks: a large marina designed as a kind of homage to Gaudí and a giant Buddhist stupa.

### Sights

**Casa de los Navajas** HISTORIC BUILDING
(Calle del Bajondillo, Torremolinos; ⏱11am-2pm & 6-8pm) FREE Impossible to miss in the concrete jungle of Torremolinos is this neo-Mudéjar beauty, a mini palace that formerly belonged to a local sugar baron, António Navajas. Originally constructed in 1925 in a style not dissimilar to that of Seville's Plaza de España, the house was renovated in 2014 and subsequently opened to the public. While there's no specific museum here, the terraced gardens, detailed architecture and sweeping views from the upstairs balconies are all impressive.

**La Carihuela** BEACH
(Torremolinos) Torremolinos' westernmost beach, stretching from a small rocky outcrop (La Punta) to Benalmádena, La Carihuela is a former fishing district and one of the few parts of town that hasn't suffered rampant overdevelopment. The beachside promenade is lined with low-rise shops, bars and

restaurants, and is one of the most popular destinations for *malagueños* to enjoy fresh seafood at weekends.

**Buddhist Stupa** MUSEUM, MONUMENT

(www.stupabenalmadena.org; Benalmádena Pueblo; 10am-2pm & 4-6.30pm Tue-Sun; P) FREE The largest Buddhist stupa in Europe is in Benalmádena Pueblo. It rises up, majestically out of place, on the outskirts of the village, surrounded by new housing and with sweeping coastal views. The lofty interior is lined with exquisitely executed devotional paintings.

## Sleeping & Eating

**★Hostal Guadalupe** HOSTAL €€

(952 38 19 37; www.hostalguadalupe.com; Calle del Peligro 15, Torremolinos; s €46-90, d €48-139, d/tr/q apt from €71/86/105; ) At the bottom of the staircases that lead down to Torre's main beach is this nugget of old Spain that sits like a wonderful anachronism amid the concrete jungle. Enter through a delightful tiled tavern and ascend to plain but comfortable rooms, several with terraces overlooking the sea. There's also a couple of apartments with kitchen facilities for longer stays.

**★El Gato Lounge** FUSION €€

(676 452504; www.elgatolounge.com; Paseo Marítimo 1K; mains €5-10, tapas box menus €16-22; noon-late Feb-Oct) Don't expect the default sardines at this trendsetting fusion favourite across from Playamar beach's western end. Asian flavours abound in offerings such as Sri Lankan curry, chicken satay, tuna tataki and Thai shrimp cakes – but the real showstopper is El Gato's 'tapas experience', featuring a flamboyant assortment of 12 Mediterranean-Asian tapas finished off with apple pie and cinnamon ice cream.

The relaxing beach-facing interior has a luxuriant allure, and the cocktails and highly attentive staff mean most people linger. The restaurant and the beach in front have long been favourite hangouts for Torre's gay community.

**Casa Juan** SEAFOOD €€

(952 37 35 12; www.losmellizos.net; Calle San Ginés 20, La Carihuela; mains €14-22; 1-4.30pm & 8pm-midnight Tue-Sat, 1-4.30pm Sun) The business dates back to the 1950s, but the fish is fresh daily at La Carihuela's most famous seafood restaurant, attracting shoals of *malagueños* on Sundays. It's been expanded into four dining spaces, so you can't go wrong provided you order carefully – some fish is sold by weight, so the bill can add up.

## Information

The main **tourist office** (951 95 43 79; www.turismotorremolinos.es; Plaza de Andalucía, Torremolinos; 9.30am-6pm) is in the town centre. There are additional tourist kiosks at **Playa Bajondillo** (Playa Bajondillo; 10am-2pm) and **La Carihuela** (Playa Carihuela; 10am-2pm).

## Getting There & Away

### BUS

**Avanzabus/Portillo** (955 03 86 65; http://malaga.avanzagrupo.com) runs services to Málaga (€1.50, 20 minutes, 21 daily), Marbella (€3.40, 30 minutes, 13 daily) and Ronda (€11.15, 2½ hours, six daily).

### TRAIN

Trains from Málaga (€2.55, 18 minutes) run on the Renfe *cercanías* line to **Torremolinos** (Avenida Palma de Mallorca 53) and **Arroyo de la Miel-Benalmádena** (Avenida de la Estación 3) every 20 minutes from 5.20am to 11.30pm.

# Marbella

POP 143,386

The Costa del Sol's bastion of bling is, like most towns along this stretch of coast, a two-sided coin. Standing centre stage in the tourist showroom is the 'Golden Mile', a conspicuously extravagant collection of star-studded clubs, shiny restaurants and expensive hotels stretching as far as Puerto Banús, the flashiest marina on the coast, where black-tinted Mercs slide along a quay populated by luxury yachts.

But Marbella has other, less ostentatious attractions. Its natural setting is magnificent, sheltered by the beautiful Sierra Blanca mountains, while its surprisingly attractive *casco antiguo* (old town) is replete with narrow lanes and well-tended flower boxes.

Long before Marbella starting luring golfers, zillionaires and retired Latin American dictators, it was home to Phoenicians, Visigoths, Romans and Moors. One of the joys of a visit to the modern city is trying to root out their legacy.

## Sights

**Plaza de los Naranjos** SQUARE

At the heart of Marbella's *casco antiguo* is the extremely pretty Plaza de los Naranjos, dating back to 1485, with tropical plants, palms, orange trees and, inevitably, overpriced bars.

**Museo Ralli** MUSEUM
(www.museoralli.es; Urbanización Coral Beach; ⏲10am-3pm Tue-Sat) FREE This superb private art museum exhibits works by primarily Latin American and European artists in bright, well-lit galleries. Part of a nonprofit foundation with four other museums (in Chile, Uruguay and Israel), its wide-ranging, regularly rotating exhibitions include sculptures by Salvador Dalí, vibrant contemporary paintings by Argentinian surrealist Alicia Carletti and Peruvian artist Herman Braun-Vega, and works by heavyweights such as Joan Miró, Henry Moore and Giorgio de Chirico. It's 6km west of central Marbella near Puerto Banús.

## Sleeping & Eating

**Hostal El Gallo** HOSTAL €
(☎952 82 79 98; www.hostalelgallo.com; Calle Lobatas 46; s/d from €40/55; 📶) In expensive Marbella, El Gallo – a traditional Spanish bar with a few rooms upstairs – is what you might call a rough in the diamond. Run by a welcoming family, it inhabits a narrow whitewashed street with flower boxes and throwback charm, and has all you need for a comfortable but economical stay.

★**Claude** BOUTIQUE HOTEL €€€
(☎952 90 08 40; www.hotelclaudemarbella.com; Calle San Francisco 5; r €257-410; ❄📶) The former summer home of Napoleon III's wife has updated its regal decor to create a hotel fit for a 21st-century empress. Situated in the quieter upper part of town, the Claude's arched courtyards and shapely pillars successfully marry contemporary flourishes with the mansion's original architecture, while claw-foot bath tubs and crystal chandeliers add to the classic historical feel.

**Garum** INTERNATIONAL €€
(☎952 85 88 58; www.garummarbella.com; Paseo Marítimo; mains €12-23; ⏲noon-11.30pm; 📶) Finnish-owned and set in a dreamy location right on the 'Golden Mile' across from the beach, Garum has a menu that will please those seeking a little gourmet variety. Expect dishes ranging from smoked-cheese soup to Moroccan chicken samosas and red-lentil falafel.

★**The Farm** SPANISH €€€
(☎952 82 25 57; www.thefarm-marbella.com; Plaza Altamirano 2; mains €14-23; ⏲noon-11pm; 🖉👪) It's not a farm, but instead an exceptionally pretty restaurant in Marbella's old town, consisting of a patio, a terrace and a dining room furnished with modern 'chill-out' flourishes. The food's all farm fresh though, and there's a brilliant selection of set menus showcasing organic ingredients, including vegetarian and kids' options. Check the website calendar for occasional flamenco shows.

## Drinking & Nightlife

For the most spirited bars and nightlife, head to Puerto Banús, 7km west of Marbella. In town, the best area is around the small Puerto Deportivo. There are also some beach clubs open only in summer.

## Information

**Tourist Office** (☎952 76 87 07; www.turismo.marbella.es; Plaza de los Naranjos; ⏲8am-8.30pm Mon-Fri, 10am-5pm Sat & Sun, to 9pm Jul & Aug) Has plenty of leaflets and a good town map.

## Getting There & Away

The **bus station** (☎952 82 34 09; Avenida del Trapiche) is 1.5km north of the old town just off the A7 *autovía*.

Avanzabus/Portillo (p741) runs buses to Estepona (€3.35 to €4.50, 30 to 40 minutes, hourly), Málaga (€6.50 to €8.85, 45 minutes to 1½ hours, half-hourly) and Ronda (€6.85, 1½ hours, nine daily).

# Estepona

POP 68,286

Estepona was one of the first resorts to attract foreign residents and tourists almost 50 years ago and, despite the surrounding development, the centre of the town still has a cosy, old-fashioned feel. There's good reason for that: Estepona's roots date back to the 4th century. Centuries later, during the Moorish era, the town was an important and prosperous centre due to its strategic proximity to the Strait of Gibraltar.

Estepona is steadily extending its promenade to Marbella; at its heart is the pleasant Playa de la Rada beach. The Puerto Deportivo is the focal point of the town's nightlife, especially at weekends, and is also excellent for water sports.

## Sleeping & Eating

**Hotel Boutique Casa Veracruz** BOUTIQUE HOTEL €€

(☎951 46 64 70; www.hotelboutiquecasaveracruz.com; Calle Veracruz 22; d €79-115; ❄☎) The 'boutique' label barely does this place justice. With its diminutive courtyard, trickling fountain, stately paintings and stylish antique furniture, it's like a little slice of historic Seville dispatched to the Costa del Sol – and all yours for a very economical sum. Extra touches include Nespresso machines, ample continental breakfasts, and complimentary tea, coffee and sweets available all day.

★ **La Escollera** SEAFOOD €

(☎952 80 63 54; Puerto Pesquero; mains €8-14; ⏱1-4.30pm & 8-11.30pm Tue-Sat, 1-4.30pm Sun) Locals in the know – from dock workers swigging beers to families celebrating a first communion – flock to this port-side eatery to dine on arguably the freshest and best seafood in town. The atmosphere is agreeably bustling and no-frills basic, with plastic tables and paper cloths. But when the fish tastes this good and the beer is this cold, who cares?

**Venta García** EUROPEAN €€

(☎952 89 41 91; Carretera de Casares, Km 7; mains €12-20; ⏱12.30-4pm & 7.30-10.30pm Tue-Sat, 12.30-4.30pm Sun; P) Venta Garcia specialises in superbly conceived dishes using local produce, complemented by sublime countryside views. There's an emphasis on meat such as venison (served with a red fruit sauce) and pork: the Montes de Málaga dish executes a local take on pork served with peppers, fried egg and chips. It's on the road to Casares, 7km from Estepona. Reserve at weekends.

## Information

**Tourist Office** (☎952 80 80 81; www.estepona.es; Plaza de las Flores; ⏱9am-3pm Mon-Fri, 10am-2pm Sat) Located on a historical square, this office has brochures and a decent map of town.

## Getting There & Away

Avanzabus/Portillo (p741) buses run over a dozen times a day to Marbella (€3.35 to €4.50, 30 to 45 minutes) and Málaga (from €9.25, 1¼ to two hours).

# Mijas

POP 82,742 / ELEV 428M

The story of Mijas encapsulates the story of the Costa del Sol. Originally a humble village, it's now the richest town in the province. Since finding favour with discerning bohemian artists and writers in the 1950s and '60s, Mijas has sprawled across the surrounding hills and down to the coast, yet it's managed to retain the throwback charm of the original *pueblo* (village).

## Sights

**Virgen de la Peña** HISTORIC SITE

(Avenida Virgen de la Peña; ⏱9.30am-6pm) If you walk past the *ayuntamiento* (town hall), you will reach this grotto where the Virgin is said to have appeared to two children who were led here by a dove in 1586. Within the clifftop cave is a flower-adorned altar in front of an image of the Virgin, plus some religious vestments and silverwork in glass cases. It's a poignant spot despite the barrage of visitors.

**Centro de Arte Contemporáneo de Mijas** MUSEUM

(CAC; www.cacmijas.info; Calle Málaga 28; adult/child €3/free; ⏱10am-6pm Mon-Sat) Notwithstanding its diminutive size, this museum houses the world's second-largest collection of Picasso ceramics, along with bronze figurines, glassware, bas-reliefs, engravings and lithographs by Salvador Dalí, and a room dedicated to temporary exhibitions.

## Sleeping & Eating

**Casa Tejón** APARTMENT €

(☎661 669469; www.casatejon.com; Calle Málaga 15; 2-person apt per day/week €50/325; ☎) The small apartments here are cosily kitted out with a happy mishmash of furniture and textiles, and set around a small courtyard decorated with pots of scarlet geraniums. It's bang in the centre of the village, and the owners run a handy bar and restaurant next door.

**Tomillo Limón** TAPAS €

(☎951 43 72 98; www.facebook.com/tomillolimonmijas; Avenida Virgen de la Peña 11; tapas €3.50-5; ⏱noon-11pm Tue-Sat, to 5pm Sun) Great for a glass of wine and a tapa or three, the 'Thyme and Lemon' is one of the better options in Mijas' array of mainly tourist-oriented eating stops. It's modern with a country-kitchen-meets-hip-bistro feel, and everything from the prawns *pil-pil* to the mini-burgers is presented creatively on dishes, newspaper, tins or slates.

## Getting There & Away

The M112 bus runs four times daily to/from Málaga (€2.35, one to 1¼ hours). If you're driving, Mijas' centrally located 10-level car park is a bargain at €1 per day.

# The Interior

The mountainous interior of Málaga province is an area of raw beauty and romantic white villages sprinkled across craggy landscapes. Beyond the mountains, the verdant countryside opens out into a wide chequerboard of floodplains. It's a far cry from the tourist-clogged coast.

## Ronda

POP 33,877 / ELEV 744M

Built astride a huge gash in the mountains carved out by the Río Guadalevín, Ronda is a brawny town with a dramatic history littered with outlaws, bandits, guerrilla warriors and rebels. Its spectacular location atop El Tajo gorge and its status as the largest of Andalucía's white towns have made it hugely popular with tourists – particularly notable when you consider its relatively modest size. Modern bullfighting was practically invented here in the late 18th century, and the town's fame was spread further by its close association with American Europhiles Ernest Hemingway (a lover of bullfighting) and Orson Welles (whose ashes are buried in the town).

South of the gorge, Ronda's old town largely dates from Islamic times, when it was an important cultural centre filled with mosques and palaces. Further north, the grid-shaped 'new' town is perched atop steep cliffs, with parks and promenades looking regally over the surrounding mountains.

### Sights

La Ciudad, the historical old town on the southern side of El Tajo gorge, is an atmospheric area for a stroll, with its evocative, still-tangible history, Renaissance mansions and wealth of museums. The newer town, where you'll be deposited if you arrive by bus or train, harbours the emblematic bullring and the leafy Alameda del Tajo gardens. Three bridges crossing the gorge connect the old town with the new.

**Plaza de Toros** NOTABLE BUILDING

(Calle Virgen de la Paz; €8, incl audio guide €9.50; ⌚10am-8pm Apr-Sep, to 7pm Mar & Oct, to 6pm Nov-Feb) In existence for more than 200 years, this is one of Spain's oldest bullrings and the site of some of the most important events in bullfighting history. A visit is a way of learning about this deep-rooted Spanish tradition without actually attending a bullfight. The on-site Museo Taurino is crammed with memorabilia such as blood-spattered costumes worn by 1990s star Jesulín de Ubrique. It also includes artwork by Picasso and photos of famous fans such as Orson Welles and Ernest Hemingway.

**Casa del Rey Moro** GARDENS

(House of the Moorish King; ☎617 610808; www.casadelreymoro.org; Calle Cuesta de Santo Domingo 9; adult/reduced €6/3; ⌚10am-9.30pm May-Sep, to 8pm Oct-Apr) Several landscaped terraces give access to La Mina, an Islamic stairway of nearly two hundred steps cut into the rock all the way down to the river at the bottom of the gorge. These steps enabled Ronda to maintain water supplies when it was under attack. It was also the point where Christian troops forced entry in 1485. The steps are dark, steep and wet in places. Take care.

**Museo Joaquín Peinado** MUSEUM

(☎952 87 15 85; www.museojoaquinpeinado.com; Plaza del Gigante; adult/reduced €4/2; ⌚10am-5pm Mon-Fri, to 3pm Sat) Native Ronda artist Joaquín Peinado was an amigo and contemporary of Picasso's, a fact reflected in his work, with its strong abstract lines, flirtations with cubism and seeming obsession with female nudes. Nearly two hundred of his pieces are displayed in the 18th-century Palacio Marqueses de Moctezuma, a typically Andalucian space that's been fitted with a plush minimalist interior.

**Iglesia de Santa María La Mayor** CHURCH

(Calle José M Holgado; adult/child €4.50/2; ⌚10am-8pm Apr-Sep, to 7pm Mar & Oct, to 6pm Nov-Feb, closed 12.30-2pm Sun) The city's original mosque metamorphosed into this elegant church. Just inside the entrance is an arch covered with Arabic inscriptions that was part of the mosque's *mihrab*. The church has been declared a national monument, and its interior is a riot of decorative styles and ornamentation. A huge central cedar choir stall divides the church into two sections: aristocrats to the front, everyone else at the back.

**Baños Árabes** HISTORIC SITE
(Arab Baths; Calle San Miguel; €3.50, Tue free; ⊙10am-3pm Sat & Sun year-round, to 7pm Mon-Fri Apr-Sep, to 6pm Mon-Fri Oct-Mar) Backing onto Ronda's river, these 13th-century Arab baths are among the best-preserved in all of Andalucía, with horseshoe arches, columns and clearly designated divisions between the hot and cold thermal areas. An excellent 10-minute video (in Spanish and English) helps you visualise the baths in their heyday. Enjoy the pleasant walk down here from the centre of town.

**Puerta de Almocábar** GATE
The old town is surrounded by massive fortress walls pierced by two ancient gates: the Islamic Puerta de Almocábar, which in the 13th century was the main gateway to the castle, and the 16th-century **Puerta de Carlos V**. Inside, the Islamic layout remains intact, but the maze of narrow streets now takes its character from the Renaissance mansions of powerful families whose predecessors accompanied Fernando el Católico in the taking of the city in 1485.

## Sleeping

**Hotel Ronda** BOUTIQUE HOTEL €€
(☎952 87 22 32; www.hotelronda.net; Ruedo Doña Elvira 12; s/d €53/70; ❄📶) With its geranium-filled window boxes and whitewashed *pueblo* exterior, Hotel Ronda offers relatively simple (for Ronda) contemporary rooms painted in vivid colours and accentuated by punchy original abstracts. Several rooms overlook the beautiful Mina gardens across the way. It's a bargain for the price. Just up the street, its brand-new sister **Hotel Ronda Nuevo** (Ruedo Doña Elvira 6; r €100-160; ❄📶) offers three spacious modern rooms.

★ **Aire de Ronda** BOUTIQUE HOTEL €€
(☎952 87 59 82; www.airederonda.com; Calle Real 25; r €125-170; P📶) Located in a particularly tranquil part of town, this hotel is one of those old-on-the-outside, super-modern-on-the-inside places that Spain does so well. Smart minimalist rooms come in punchy black and white, and fabulous bathrooms have shimmering silver- or gold-coloured mosaic tiles and walk-in showers.

★ **Hotel Soho Boutique Palacio San Gabriel** HOTEL €€
(☎952 19 03 92; www.sohohoteles.com; Calle Marqués de Moctezuma 19; d incl breakfast from €90; ❄📶) Despite new chain-hotel management, this heavyweight historical edifice retains its age-old charm, filled with antiques and faded photographs that offer an insight into Ronda's history – bullfighting, celebrities and all. Ferns hang down the huge mahogany staircase, and there's a billiard room, a cosy living room stacked with books, and a DVD-screening room with 10 velvet-covered seats rescued from Ronda's theatre.

**Parador de Ronda** HOTEL €€€
(☎952 87 75 00; www.parador.es; Plaza de España; r €143-326; P❄@📶≋) Acres of shining marble and deep-cushioned furniture give this modern *parador* a certain appeal, but really it's all about the views. The terrace is a wonderful place to drink in the sight of the gaping gorge with your coffee or wine, especially at night.

## Eating

Typical Ronda food is hearty mountain fare, with an emphasis on stews (called *cocido*, *estofado* or *cazuela*), *trucha* (trout), *rabo de toro* (oxtail stew) and game such as *conejo* (rabbit), *perdiz* (partridge) and *codorniz* (quail).

**Tragatá** TAPAS €€
(☎952 87 72 09; www.tragata.com; Calle Nueva 4; mains €12-25; ⊙1.15-3.45pm & 8-11pm; 📶) A small outpost for Ronda's gourmet guru, Benito Gómez, who runs the nearby Bardal, Tragatá allows you to sample some of the same *cocina alta* (haute cuisine) at a fraction of the price. The eruption of flavours ranges from tomato salad with mint and basil to Japanese tatakis to pig's trotter and pig's snout stew.

**Tropicana** ANDALUCIAN €€
(☎952 87 89 85; www.facebook.com/tropicanaronda; cnr Avenida Málaga & Calle Acinipo; mains €12-20; ⊙12.30-3.30pm & 7.30-10pm Wed-Sun) A little off the trail in Ronda's new town, the Tropicana has nonetheless garnered a strong reputation for its certified-organic food, served in a small but handsome restaurant with the feel of a modern bistro.

★ **Almocábar** ANDALUCIAN €€
(☎952 87 59 77; Calle Ruedo Alameda 5; tapas €2, mains €15-25; ⊙12.30-4.30pm & 8-11pm Wed-Mon) Tapas here include *montaditos* (small pieces of bread) topped with delicacies such as duck breast and chorizo. Mains are available in the elegant dining room, where meat dominates – rabbit, partridge, lamb and beef

# Ronda

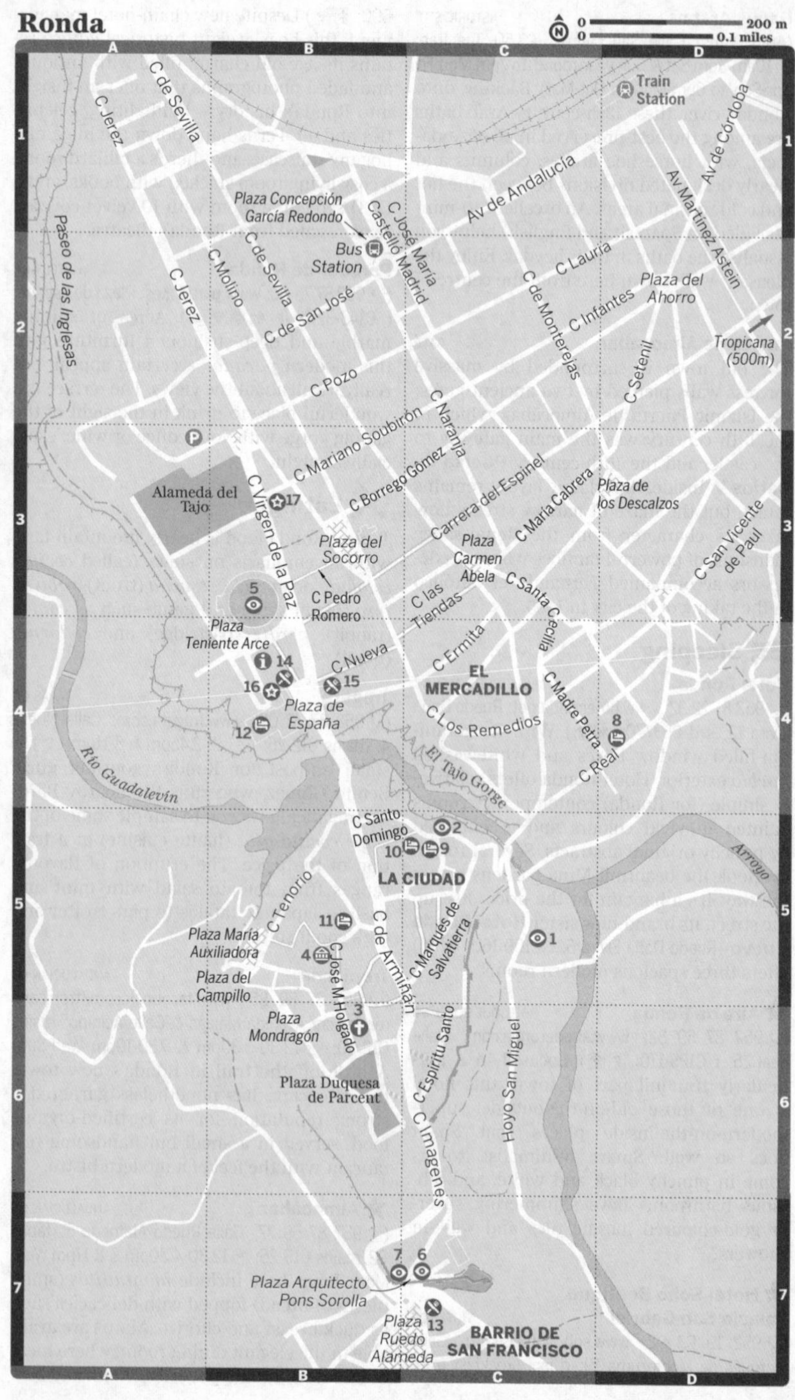
0 200 m
0 0.1 miles
Train Station
C de Sevilla
C Jerez
Av de Córdoba
Av de Andalucía
Av Martínez Astein
Plaza Concepción García Redondo
C José María Castello Madrid
Bus Station
C Lauria
Paseo de las Inglesas
C Molino
C de Sevilla
C Jerez
C de Monterejas
Plaza del Ahorro
C Infántes
C de San José
Tropicana (500m)
C Setenil
C Pozo
C Naranja
C Mariano Soubirón
C Borrego Gómez
Carrera del Espinel
Alameda del Tajo
C Virgen de la Paz
17
Plaza de los Descalzos
C María Cabrera
Plaza del Socorro
Plaza Carmen Abela
C San Vicente de Paul
C Pedro Romero
C las Tiendas
C Santa Cecilia
5
Plaza Teniente Arce
14
C Nueva
C Ermita
EL MERCADILLO
16
15
Plaza de España
C Madre Petra
12
C Los Remedios
8
C Real
Río Guadalevín
El Tajo Gorge
C Santo Domingo
2
10
9
Arroyo
LA CIUDAD
C Tenorio
11
C Marqués de Salvatierra
1
Plaza María Auxiliadora
4
C José M Holgado
C de Armiñán
Plaza del Campillo
3
C Espíritu Santo
Plaza Mondragón
Hoyo San Miguel
Plaza Duquesa de Parcent
C Imagenes
7
6
Plaza Arquitecto Pons Sorolla
Plaza Ruedo Alameda
13
BARRIO DE SAN FRANCISCO

## Ronda

**Sights**

1 Baños Árabes .......... C5
2 Casa del Rey Moro .......... C5
3 Iglesia de Santa María La Mayor .......... B6
4 Museo Joaquín Peinado .......... B5
5 Plaza de Toros .......... B3
6 Puerta de Almocábar .......... C7
7 Puerta de Carlos V .......... B7

**Sleeping**

8 Aire de Ronda .......... D4
9 Hotel Ronda .......... C5
10 Hotel Ronda Nuevo .......... C5
11 Hotel Soho Boutique Palacio San Gabriel .......... B5
12 Parador de Ronda .......... B4

**Eating**

13 Almocábar .......... C7
14 Bardal .......... B4
15 Tragatá .......... B4

**Entertainment**

16 El Quinqué .......... B4
17 Ronda Guitar House .......... B3

cooked on a hot stone at your table. There's a bodega upstairs, and wine tastings and dinner can be arranged for a minimum of eight people (approximately €50 per person).

**Bardal** GASTRONOMY **€€€**
(☎951 48 98 28; www.restaurantebardal.com; Calle José Aparicio 1; 15-course/19-course tasting menu €115/140; ⏲noon-4.30pm & 8-11.30pm Tue-Sat) You'll need to reserve ahead in order to enjoy a meal at Bardal, the flagship restaurant of celebrity chef Benito Gómez. The astounding 15- to 19-course menu is a whistle-stop tour through oyster stew, yellow-tomato gazpacho, frozen apple water, monkfish foie gras and other such uncommon dishes. Hold onto your hat – and fork.

### Entertainment

**Ronda Guitar House** CONCERT VENUE
(☎951 91 68 43; www.rondaguitarhouse.com; Calle Mariano Soubirón 4; tickets €15; ⏲concerts 7pm) A little different to the standard flamenco venues, this small performance space offers guitar recitals rather than full-blown shows. Virtuoso performer Paco Seco covers a multitude of acoustic genres: classical, flamenco, jazz or a fusion of all three. The same venue hosts the **Ronda Guitar Festival** (www.rondaguitarfestival.com; ⏲Jun) every summer.

**El Quinqué** LIVE PERFORMANCE
(☎633 778181; Paseo de Blas Infante; tickets €12-21; ⏲shows 2pm & 8.30pm Tue-Sun) For a traditional flamenco show employing a three-pronged attack of voice, guitar and dance, come to El Quinqué. Entry prices are very reasonable for the 45-minute lunchtime shows. Evening shows are double the length.

### Information

**Tourist Office** (☎952 18 71 19; www.turismoderonda.es; Paseo de Blas Infante; ⏲9.30am-6pm Mon-Fri, to 5pm Sat, to 2.30pm Sun) Opposite the Plaza de Toros; provides information on the town and region.

### Getting There & Away

**BUS**

From the town's **bus station** (Plaza Concepción García Redondo 2), **Comes** (☎956 80 70 59; www.tgcomes.es) runs to Cádiz (€18, 3½ hours). **Damas** (☎959 25 69 00; www.damas-sa.es) goes to Seville (€13, 1¾ to 2¾ hours) via Algodonales (€3.60, 40 minutes) and Grazalema (€3, 50 minutes). **Avanzabus/Portillo** (☎912 72 28 32; www.avanzabus.com) has four daily buses to Málaga (€130, 2¾ to three hours) and eight to Marbella (€6.85, 1¼ hours).

**TRAIN**

Ronda's **train station** (☎952 87 16 73; www.renfe.com; Avenida de Andalucía) is on the line between Bobadilla and Algeciras. Trains run to Algeciras (€12 to €20, 1½ to two hours, five daily) via Gaucín and Jimena de la Frontera. This train ride is one of Spain's finest and worth taking just for the views. Other trains depart for Málaga (€12, two to 2¾ hours, one daily), Madrid (€56, four hours, three daily) and Granada (€17, 2½ to three hours, three daily). For Seville, change at Bobadilla or Antequera-Santa Ana. It's less than 1km from the train station to most accommodation. A taxi will cost around €7.

## Ardales & El Chorro

Fifty kilometres northwest of Málaga, the Río Guadalhorce carves its way through the awesome **Garganta del Chorro** (El Chorro gorge). Also called the Desfiladero de los Gaitanes, the gorge is about 4km long, as much as 400m deep and sometimes just 10m wide. Its sheer walls, and other rock faces nearby, are a magnet for rock climbers, with hundreds of bolted climbs snaking their way up the limestone cliffs.

While Ardales (population 2700) is the main town in the area, most people use the hamlet of El Chorro, with its train station, hiking trails and decent hotel, as a base. Lying 6km west is the serene **Embalse del Conde del Guadalhorce**, a huge reservoir that dominates the landscape and is noted for its carp fishing. This is also the starting point for the legendary and recently revitalised Caminito del Rey path. The whole area is protected in a natural park.

## Activities

**★El Caminito del Rey** HIKING

(www.caminitodelrey.info; self-guided/guided visit €10/18; ⏲9.30am-5pm Tue-Sun Apr-Oct, to 3pm Nov-Mar) The Caminito del Rey (King's Path) – so named because Alfonso XIII walked along it when he opened the Guadalhorce hydroelectric dam in 1921 – consists of a 2.9km boardwalk that hangs 100m above the Río Guadalhorce and snakes around the cliffs, affording breathtaking views at every turn. Required walks to/from the northern and southern access points make the total hiking distance 7.7km.

The *caminito* had fallen into severe disrepair by the late 1990s, and it became known as the most dangerous pathway in the world; it officially closed in 2000 (though some daredevils still attempted it). Following an extensive €5.5-million restoration, it reopened in 2015; it is now safe and manageable for anyone with a reasonable head for heights, and has become one of Andalucía's top tourist attractions.

The boardwalk is constructed with wooden slats; in some sections the old crumbling path can be spied just below. The walk can only be done in one direction (north–south), and it's highly advisable to book a time slot online; tickets often sell out days or even weeks in advance.

Buses run half-hourly from El Chorro train station to the starting point, where there are a couple of restaurants. From here you must walk 2.7km to the northern access point of the *caminito*, where you'll show your ticket and be given a mandatory helmet to wear. At the end of the *caminito* there's another 2.1km to walk from the southern access point back to El Chorro. Allow three to four hours total for the walk and connecting bus ride, as the views are made for savouring.

The most convenient public transport to the area is the twice-daily train from Málaga to El Chorro station. If you're driving, you can park at either end of the gorge and use the bus to make your connection.

## Getting There & Away

Trains run twice daily from Málaga to El Chorro (€6.25, 40 minutes), continuing north from El Chorro to Seville (€20.80, 2¾ hours).

A half-hourly shuttle bus (€1.55, 20 minutes) runs between the train station and the starting point of the Caminito del Rey.

# Antequera

POP 41,239 / ELEV 577M

Known as the crossroads of Andalucía, Antequera sees plenty of travellers pass through but few lingering visitors. But those who choose not to stop are missing out. The town's foundations are substantial: two Bronze Age burial mounds guard its northern approach and Moorish fables haunt its grand Alcazaba. The undoubted highlight here, though, is the opulent Spanish-baroque style that gives the town its character and that the civic authorities have worked hard to restore and maintain. There's also an astonishing number of churches – more than 30, many with ornate interiors.

## Sights

**★Antequera Dolmens Site** ARCHAEOLOGICAL SITE

(⏲9am-3pm & 8-10pm Tue-Sat, 9am-3pm Sun Jul–mid-Sep, hours vary rest of year) FREE Antequera's two earth-covered burial mounds – the **Dolmen de Menga** and the **Dolmen de Viera** – were built out of megalithic stones by Bronze Age people around 2500 BCE. When they were rediscovered in 1903, they were found to be harbouring the remains of several hundred bodies. Considered to be some of the finest Neolithic monuments in Europe, they were named a Unesco World Heritage site in 2016.

**Alcazaba** FORTRESS

(adult/child €4/2, incl Colegiata de Santa María la Mayor €6/3; ⏲10am-6pm) Favoured by the Granada emirs of Islamic times, Antequera's hilltop Moorish fortress has a fascinating history and covers a massive 62,000 sq metres. The main approach to the hilltop is from Plaza de San Sebastián, up the stepped Cuesta de San Judas and then through an impressive archway, the **Arco de los Gigantes**, built in 1585 and formerly bearing huge sculptures of Hercules. All that's left today are the Roman inscriptions on the stones.

**Colegiata de Santa María la Mayor** CHURCH

(Plaza Santa María; adult/child €3/1.50, incl Alcazaba €6/3; ⏲10am-6pm) Just below the Alcazaba is the large 16th-century Colegiata de Santa María la Mayor. This church-college played an important part in Andalucía's 16th-century humanist movement, and flaunts a beautiful Renaissance facade, lovely fluted stone columns inside and a Mudéjar *artesonado*. It also plays host to some excellent musical events and exhibitions. Just outside the church entrance, don't miss the ruins of Roman baths dating from the 3rd century AD.

**Dolmen del Romeral** ARCHAEOLOGICAL SITE

(Cerro Romeral; ⏲9am-3.30pm Tue-Sun mid-Jun–mid-Sep, hours vary rest of year) FREE This megalithic burial site was constructed around 1800 BCE and features much use of small stones for its walls. To get here, continue 2.5km past the town's other two, more ancient dolmens through an industrial estate, then turn left following 'Córdoba, Seville' signs. After 500m, turn left at a roundabout and follow 'Dolmen del Romeral' signs for 200m.

**Museo de la Ciudad de Antequera** MUSEUM

(Museo Municipal; Plaza del Coso Viejo; ⏲10am-2pm & 4.30-6.30pm Tue-Fri, from 9.30am Sat, 9.30am-2pm Sun) FREE Antequera's town-centre municipal museum displays an impressive collection of Roman artefacts from the surrounding area, including glassware, jewellery, stone carvings and fragmentary mosaics. Its pride and joy is an elegant and athletic 1.4m bronze statue of a boy, *Efebo*. Discovered on a local farm in the 1950s, it's possibly the finest example of Roman sculpture found in Spain.

**Museo Conventual de las Descalzas** MUSEUM

(Plaza de las Descalzas; €3.30; ⏲10am-1.30pm & 5-7pm Tue-Fri, 9am-noon & 5-6.30pm Sat, 9am-noon Sun) This museum, in the 17th-century convent of the Carmelitas Descalzas (barefoot Carmelites), approximately 150m east of the town's Museo de la Ciudad de Antequera, displays highlights of Antequera's rich religious-art heritage. Outstanding works include a painting by Lucas Giordano of St Teresa of Ávila (the 16th-century founder of the Carmelitas Descalzas), a bust of the Dolorosa by Pedro de Mena and a *Virgen de Belén* sculpture by La Roldana.

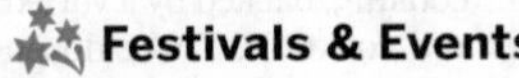

## Festivals & Events

**Semana Santa** RELIGIOUS

(Holy Week; ⏲Mar or Apr) One of the most traditional celebrations in Andalucía; items from the town's treasure trove are used in the religious processions.

## Sleeping

**Hotel Coso Viejo** HOTEL €

(☎952 70 50 45; www.hotelcosoviejo.es; Calle Encarnación 9; d incl breakfast €43-56; P❄📶) This converted 17th-century neoclassical palace is right in the heart of Antequera, opposite Plaza Coso Viejo and the town museum. The simply furnished rooms are set around a handsome patio with a fountain, and the excellent Mesón Las Hazuelas tapas bar and restaurant is just next door.

**Parador de Antequera** HISTORIC HOTEL €€

(☎952 84 02 61; www.parador.es; Paseo García del Olmo 2; d €95-160; P❄📶🏊) This *parador* is in a quiet area of parkland north of the bullring and near the bus station. It's comfortably furnished and set in pleasant gardens with wonderful views, especially at sunset.

## Eating

Welcome to a bastion of traditional cooking. Antequera specialities include *porra antequerana* (a thick and delicious garlicky soup that's similar to gazpacho), *bienmesabe* (literally 'tastes good to me'; a sponge dessert) and *angelorum* (a dessert incorporating meringue, sponge and egg yolk). Antequera also does a fine breakfast *mollete* (soft bread roll), served with a choice of fillings.

★**Arte de Cozina** ANDALUCIAN €€

(☎952 84 00 14; www.artedecozina.com; Calle Calzada 27; tapas €2.80-3.50, mains €15-24; ⏲1-11pm; 📶) It's hard not to notice the surrounding agricultural lands as you approach Antequera, and this fascinating little hotel-restaurant combo is where you get to taste what they produce. Slavishly true to traditional dishes, it plugs little-known Antequeran specialities such as gazpacho made with green asparagus or *porra* (a cold, thick tomato soup) with oranges, plus meat dishes that include *lomo de orza* (preserved pork loin).

**Recuerdos Tapas Bodega** TAPAS €€
(☎951 35 63 65; Calle Laguna 5; tapas €1.85-3.90, raciones €8-16; ⏰12.30-5pm & 8pm-midnight) Classy, casual Recuerdos stands out for its innovative home cooking, backed by a varied lineup of wines and cocktails. Three dozen flavourful offerings – Iberian pork loin with pineapple, homemade partridge pâté with rosemary oil and Seville orange marmalade, shrimp fritters with avocado aioli – all come as tapas, *medias raciones* and *raciones*. It's a 10-minute walk north of the tourist office.

## Information

**Municipal Tourist Office** (☎952 70 25 05; http://turismo.antequera.es; Calle Encarnación 4; ⏰9.30am-7pm Mon-Sat, 10am-2pm Sun) A helpful tourist office with information about the town and region.

## Getting There & Away

### BUS

The **bus station** (Paseo García del Olmo) is 1km north of the centre. ALSA (p737) runs buses to Seville (€14, 2½ hours, five daily), Granada (€9, 1½ hours, five daily), Córdoba (€11, two hours 40 minutes, one daily), Almería (€23, six hours, one daily) and Málaga (€6, one hour, five daily).

Buses run between Antequera and Fuente de Piedra village (€2.50, 30 minutes, two daily).

### TRAIN

Antequera has two train stations. Closest to town is the **Antequera-Ciudad train station** (Avenida de la Estación), 1.5km north of the centre. At research time, work was still underway on a new high-speed train tine that will eventually connect Antequera-Ciudad with Granada. In the meantime, Antequera-bound train passengers must disembark at **Antequera-Santa Ana station**, 18km northwest of the town, and catch a free Renfe bus transfer into town.

High-speed AVE trains travel from Antequera Santa Ana to Málaga (€27, 25 minutes, eight daily), Córdoba (€34, 35 minutes, 13 daily) and Madrid (€76, 2½ hours, 10 daily).

At the time of research, train service from Antequera Santa Ana to Granada and Almería was disrupted due to track work on the new high-speed line, with Renfe providing alternate bus service.

# East of Málaga

The coast east of Málaga, sometimes described as the Costa del Sol Oriental, is less developed than the coast to the west. The suburban sprawl of Málaga extends through a series of unmemorable and unremarkable seaside towns that pass in a concrete highrise blur before culminating in more attractive Nerja.

The area's main redeeming feature is the rugged region of La Axarquía, which is just as stunning as Granada's Las Alpujarras, yet less well known. For non-Spanish speakers it can be difficult to pronounce – think of taking a chopper to one of those Scandinavian flatpack stores: 'axe-ikea'). It's full of great walks.

## Nerja

POP 21,091

Backed by the Sierra Almijara, the seaside town of Nerja has succeeded in rebuffing developers, allowing its centre to retain a lowrise village charm despite the proliferation of souvenir shops and the large number of visitors it sees. At its heart is the perennially beautiful Balcón de Europa, a palm-lined promontory built on the foundations of an old fort that offers panoramic views of the cobalt-blue sea flanked by honey-coloured coves.

The town is increasingly popular with package holidaymakers and 'residential tourists', which has pushed it far beyond its old confines. There's significant urbanisation, especially to the east. The holiday atmosphere, and seawater contamination, can be overwhelming from July to September, but the place is more *tranquilo* the rest of the year. It's 56km east of Málaga.

### Sights

**★Cueva de Nerja** CAVE
(www.cuevadenerja.es; adult/child €14/12; ⏰10am-4.30pm Sep-Jun, to 7pm Jul & Aug) It's hard to imagine the surreal world that lies beneath the mountain foothills 4km east of Nerja, and it's even harder to believe that these vast caverns weren't discovered until five local *chicos* (young men) who had gone out looking for bats stumbled across an opening in 1959. Hollowed out by water around five million years ago and once inhabited by Stone Age hunters, this theatrical wonderland of extraordinary rock formations, subtle shifting colours, and stalactites and stalagmites is evocative of a submerged cathedral.

**Balcón de Europa** VIEWPOINT
Located in the heart of town, the fabulous *balcón* juts out like a natural pier, forming a

beautiful palm-lined terrace with panoramic views of the sea. The only downside is that it's perennially crowded.

**Playa Burriana** BEACH

This is Nerja's longest and best beach, with plenty of towel space on the sand. From Balcón de Europa, walk east down bleached-white Calle Carabeo and continue about 15 minutes to the beach. Burriana is backed by a line of *merenderos* (open-sided restaurants). You can rent kayaks or paddleboards here for €6 per hour.

## Sleeping

**★Hotel Carabeo** HOTEL €€

(952 52 54 44; www.hotelcarabeo.com; Calle Carabeo 34; d/ste incl breakfast from €100/210; mid-Mar–mid-Nov; ) Full of stylish antiques and wonderful paintings, this small, family-run seafront hotel is set above manicured terraced gardens. There's a pool on a terrace overlooking the sea, and the on-site Restaurante 34 (p751) is excellent. The building is an old schoolhouse and is located on one of the prettiest pedestrian streets in town, festooned with pink bougainvillea.

**Hotel Balcón de Europa** HOTEL €€

(952 52 08 00; www.hotelbalconeuropa.com; Paseo Balcón de Europa 1; d with breakfast/half board from €144/180; ) This terraced hotel sticks out on a small promontory like a boat departing for Africa. Outside it's usually mayhem (this is Nerja's popular tourist playground), but inside the mood is surprisingly tranquil, with private room balconies overlooking a snug section of beach lapped by the translucent Mediterranean. A pool, sauna, piano bar and restaurant with a view all add value.

## Eating

**★Chiringuito de Ayo** SEAFOOD €

(www.ayonerja.com; Playa Burriana; all-you-can-eat paella €8; 8am-7pm; P) The menu is listed in nine languages, but the only word you need to understand at beachside Ayo is 'paella'. They cook the rice dish every day in a huge pan atop an open wood-burning fire. A plateful is yours for €8; better yet, you can walk on up for a free refill as many times as you like.

**Restaurante 34** EUROPEAN €€€

(952 52 54 44; www.hotelcarabeo.com; Hotel Carabeo, Calle Carabeo 34; mains €17-27.50; 1-3pm & 7-11pm Tue-Sun Mar-Nov; ) There's a truly gorgeous setting here, both indoors and outside in the garden, which is gently stepped to its furthest section overlooking the sea. Delicious and exotic food combinations are served – roast suckling pig with apple compote is a favourite – and there's an adjacent tapas bar for smaller appetites. Live music Wednesday and Sunday evening.

**Pápalo** FUSION €€€

(951 50 52 39; Calle Almirante Ferrándiz 53; mains €17-24; 1-3.30pm & 7-10.30pm) On a busy corner in the heart of the pedestrian zone, Pápalo is the newest venture of one of Nerja's long-standing star chefs. Artistic presentation and international flavours are the



WORTH A TRIP

### PARAJE NATURAL TORCAL DE ANTEQUERA

South of Antequera are the weird and wonderful rock formations of the Paraje Natural Torcal de Antequera. This 12-sq-km area of gnarled, serrated and pillared limestone formed as a sea bed 150 million years ago and now rises to 1336m (El Torcal). This other-worldly landscape fanned by fresh mountain breezes was declared a Unesco World Heritage site, along with Antequera's dolmens (p748), in 2016.

There are three marked walking trails that you can do unguided. The 1.5km **Ruta Verde** (Green Route) and the 3km **Ruta Amarilla** (Yellow Route) both start and end at the **Centro de Visitantes** (952 24 33 24; www.torcaldeantequera.com; 10am-7pm Apr-Oct, to 5pm Nov-Mar) and take in the full sweep of rocky surrealism. Be prepared for plenty of rock-hopping. The 3.7km **Ruta Naranja** (Orange Route) runs between the upper and lower car parks, tracking below the road. Gentler options are the miradors (lookouts) near the Centro de Visitantes, about 500m down the road.

There's no public transport to El Torcal. If you're travelling by car, leave central Antequera along Calle Picadero, which soon joins the Zalea road. After 1km or so you'll see signs on the left to Villanueva de la Concepción. Take this road and, after 12km (before entering Villanueva), turn right and head 3.75km uphill to the information centre.

constants in a menu that ranges from tagliatelle with prawns, octopus, white wine and chives to duck breast with sweet potatoes in a molasses and lemongrass reduction.

### Information

**Tourist Office** (☎952 52 15 31; http://turismo.nerja.es; Calle Carmen 1; ⊙10am-2pm & 4.30-8pm Mon-Fri, 10am-1.30pm Sat & Sun) Has plenty of useful leaflets.

### Getting There & Away

ALSA runs regular buses to/from Málaga (€4.65, 1¼ to 1½ hours, 23 daily), Antequera (€9.30, 2½ hours, three daily), Almería (€14.65, 2½ to four hours, five daily) and Granada (€11.10, 2¼ hours, six daily).

There's no bus station, just a ticket office and **bus stop** on the main roundabout on Carretera N340.

## La Axarquía

The Axarquía region is riven by deep valleys lined with terraces and irrigation channels that date to Islamic times – nearly all the villages dotted around the olive-, almond- and vine-planted hillsides were founded in this era. The wild inaccessible landscapes, especially around the Sierra de Tejeda, made it a stronghold of *bandoleros* who roamed the mountains without fear or favour. Nowadays, its chief attractions include fantastic scenery; pretty white villages; strong, sweet wine made from sun-dried grapes; and good walking in spring and autumn.

The 'capital' of La Axarquía, **Vélez Málaga**, 4km north of Torre del Mar, is a busy but unspectacular town, although its restored hilltop castle is worth a look. Some of the most dramatic La Axarquía scenery is up around the highest villages of **Alfarnate** (925m) and **Alfarnatejo** (858m), with towering, rugged crags such as Tajo de Gomer and Tajo de Doña Ana rising to their south.

### Information

You can pick up information on La Axarquía at the tourist offices in Málaga (p737), Nerja, Torre del Mar or **Cómpeta** (☎952 55 36 85; Avenida de la Constitución; ⊙10am-2.30pm Mon-Sat, to 2pm Sun). Prospective walkers should ask for the leaflet on walks in the Parque Natural Sierras de Tejeda, Almijara y Alhama. Good maps for walkers are *Mapa topográfico de Sierra Tejeda* and *Mapa topográfico de Sierra Almijara* by Miguel Ángel Torres Delgado, both at 1:25,000. You can also follow the links at www.axarquia.es for walks in the region.

## Cómpeta

POP 3922

This instantly attractive whitewashed village, with its panoramic views, steep, winding streets and central bar-lined plaza overlooking a 16th-century church, has long attracted a large foreign population. This has contributed to an active cultural scene, and Cómpeta is home to one or two above-*pueblo*-average restaurants serving contemporary cuisine. The village also has a couple of charity shops (rare in Spain) and a big following among organised walking groups. Not surprisingly, Cómpeta is a base for hiking and adrenalin-fuelled activities.

### Getting There & Away

Loymer runs three daily buses from Málaga to Cómpeta (€4.50, 1½ hours), stopping in Torre del Mar.

# JAÉN PROVINCE

For anyone who loves culture, nature, history and good food, this relatively little-visited province turns out to be one magical combination. Endless lines of pale-green olive trees – producing one-fourth of all the world's olive oil – carpet much of the landscape. Castle-crowned hills are a reminder that this was once a frontier zone between Christians and Muslims, while the gorgeous Renaissance architecture of Unesco World Heritage towns Úbeda and Baeza showcases the wealth amassed by the Reconquista nobility.

Beyond the towns and olive groves, Jaén has wonderful mountain country. The Parque Natural Sierras de Cazorla, Segura y Las Villas, Spain's biggest protected area, is a highlight of Andalucía for nature lovers, with rugged mountains, deep green valleys, prolific wildlife and dramatically perched villages – plus good lodgings, roads and trails to help you make the most of it.

## Jaén

POP 112,999 / ELEV 575M

Set amid vast olive groves, upon which its precarious economy depends, Jaén is somewhat overshadowed by the beauty of nearby Úbeda and Baeza, and is often passed over by visitors to the province. But once you make it into town you will discover a charming, if mildly dilapidated, historical centre with hidden neighbourhoods, excellent tapas bars and a grandiose cathedral.

Muslim Yayyan was a significant city before its conquest by Castilla in 1246. For almost 250 years Christian Jaén remained important thanks to its strategic location near the border with Nasrid Granada – until the Muslims were finally driven out of Granada in 1492. Jaén then sank into a decline with many of its people emigrating to the Spanish colonies – hence the existence of other Jaéns in Peru and the Philippines.

## Sights

**★Catedral de la Asunción** CATHEDRAL

(www.catedraldejaen.org; Plaza de Santa María; adult incl audio guide €5, child/senior €1.50/2; ⏲10am-2pm & 4-7pm Mon-Fri, to 5.30pm Sat, 10-11.30am & 4-5.30pm Sun) Jaén's massive cathedral still dwarfs the rest of the city, especially when seen from the hilltop eyrie of Cerro de Santa Catalina. Its construction lasted from 1540 to 1724, replacing a crumbling Gothic cathedral which itself stood on the site of a mosque. Its perceived perfection of design – by Andrés de Vandelvira, the master architect of Úbeda and Baeza, and his father Pedro – made Jaén Cathedral a model for many of the great churches of Latin America.

**★Castillo de Santa Catalina** CASTLE

(Cerro de Santa Catalina; adult/reduced €3.50/1.50, 3-6pm Wed free; ⏲10am-6pm Mon-Sat, to 3pm Sun; P) High above the city, atop cliff-girt Cerro de Santa Catalina, this fortress' near-impregnable position is what made Jaén important during the Muslim and early Reconquista centuries. At the end of the ridge stands a large cross, on the spot where Fernando III had a cross planted after Jaén finally surrendered to him in 1246; the views are magnificent.

**Palacio de Villardompardo** MUSEUM

(Centro Cultural Baños Árabes; www.bañosarabesjaen.es; Plaza de Santa Luisa de Marillac; ⏲9am-10pm Tue-Sat, to 3pm Sun) FREE This Renaissance palace houses one of the most intriguing collections of historical, archaeological and artistic exhibits found under one roof in Andalucía: the beautiful 11th-century **Baños Árabes**, one of the largest surviving Islamic-era bathhouses in Spain; the **Museo de Artes y Costumbres Populares**, with extensive, diverse exhibits showcasing the life of pre-industrial Jaén province; and the **Museo Internacional de Arte Naïf** with a large collection of colourful and witty Naïve art.

**Museo Íbero** MUSEUM

(☎953 00 16 96; www.museosdeandalucia.es/museoibero; Paseo de la Estación 41; EU citizens/non-citizens free/€1.50; ⏲9am-9pm Tue-Sat, to 3pm Sun Sep-Jun, to 3pm Tue-Sun Jul & Aug) Opened in 2017, Jaén's newest museum has a permanent exhibit focused on the importance of four archetypal figures in pre-Roman Iberian culture: the prince, the princess, the hero and the goddess. Each is illustrated by archaeological artefacts discovered around Jaén province, including arresting statues of a hero battling a wolf, a warrior in full double armor and the *Diosa del los Carneros*, a goddess holding a pair of rams in her arms. Rotating temporary exhibits fill the adjoining rooms.

## Sleeping

**Hotel Xauen** HOTEL €

(☎953 24 07 89; www.hotelxauenjaen.com; Plaza del Deán Mazas 3; incl breakfast s €46-66, d €56-82; ) The Xauen has a superb location in the centre of town. Communal areas are decorated with large colourful photos on a random range of themes, while the rooms are a study in brown and are moderately sized, but comfy and well cared for. The rooftop sun terrace has stunning cathedral views. Parking nearby is €14.

**★Parador Castillo de Santa Catalina** LUXURY HOTEL €€

(☎953 23 00 00; www.parador.es/parador-de-jaen; Castillo de Santa Catalina; d €120-183; P ) Next to the castle high on the Cerro de Santa Catalina, Jaén's *parador* reopened in spring 2020 after an exhaustive renovation. Beyond the allure of its incomparable setting, it dazzles with theatrically vaulted halls and luxuriously dignified rooms with plush furnishings, some with four-poster beds. There is also an excellent restaurant and a bar with panoramic terrace seating.

## Eating

There aren't many fancy restaurants in Jaén, but one of Andalucía's best tapas zones is here, north of the cathedral, along and between Calles Maestra and Cerón. There are plenty of bars to choose from, but in the wafer-thin alleys that run between the two

WORTH A TRIP

## COMARES

Comares sits like a snowdrift atop its lofty hill. The adventure really is in getting there: you see it for kilometre after kilometre, before a final twist in an endlessly winding road lands you below the hanging garden of its cliff. From a little car park you can climb steep steps to the village. Look for ceramic footprints underfoot and simply follow them through a web of narrow, twisting lanes past the **Iglesia de la Encarnación** and eventually to the ruins of Comares' **castle** and a remarkable summit **cemetery**.

The village has a history of rebellion, having been a stronghold of Omar ibn Hafsun, but today there is a tangible sense of contented isolation, enjoyed by locals and many newcomers. Visitors are often of the adventurous variety. The village has established itself as a nexus for climbing and hiking excursions and has what is reputedly Andalucía's longest **zip line** (1/2 rides €15/20).

Bus M-360 leaves Málaga bus station (p737) for Comares at 6pm and starts back at 7am the next morning (one way €3.20, 1½ hours). There's no service on Sunday.



streets, you'll find a couple of particularly cherished establishments that have been going strong for well over a century.

**Taberna La Manchega** ANDALUCIAN €
(Calle Bernardo López 8; bocadillos €2-3, platos combinados & raciones €6-12; ⏲10am-4pm & 8pm-midnight Wed-Mon) La Manchega has been in action since 1886; apart from enjoying the *bocadillos* (long bread rolls with fillings including five types of *tortilla*) and *raciones* (full servings of tapas items) such as *chorizo de ciervo* (venison chorizo), *conejo al ajillo* (rabbit in garlic) and *solomillo* (pork tenderloin), you can drink wine and practise your Spanish with the old-time bartenders.

★**Panaceite** SPANISH €€
(☎953 24 06 30; Calle de Bernabé Soriano 1; tapas €3-6, raciones €6.50-23.50; ⏲7am-2am) Always packed, this corner bar near the cathedral has a semicircle of outside tables. It serves some seriously good tapas and *raciones*, such as pork tenderloin with a choice of four sauces or aubergines in sugar-cane syrup, as well as salads, *bocadillos* and wines by the glass.

**Casa Antonio** SPANISH €€€
(☎953 27 02 62; www.casantonio.es; Calle Fermín Palma 3; mains €19-24; ⏲1-4pm & 8.30-11.30pm Tue-Sat, 1-4pm Sun, closed Aug) This elegant little restaurant, in an unpromising street off Parque de la Victoria, prepares top-class Spanish fare rooted in local favourites, such as partridge in *escabeche* (an oil-vinegar-wine marinade), lamb chops or roast shoulder of goat kid. There's also excellent seafood. Nothing complicated, just top ingredients expertly prepared. Service is polished and attentive.

## ℹ Information

**Oficina de Turismo** (☎953 19 04 55; www.turjaen.org; Calle Maestra 8; ⏲9am-7.30pm Mon-Fri, 10am-3pm & 5-7pm Sat, 10am-3pm Sun) Combined city and regional tourist office with helpful multilingual staff.

## ℹ Getting There & Away

Jaén's **train station** (www.renfe.com; Plaza Jaén por la Paz) has four trains a day to Cádiz (€39, five hours), via Córdoba (€15, 1¾ hours) and Seville (€29, three hours), and four to Madrid (€37, 3¾ hours). For Málaga (€37, three hours), make connections in Córdoba.

# Baeza

POP 15,841 / ELEV 760M

With its beautiful historical centre enshrined as a Unesco World Heritage site, Baeza (ba-*eh*-thah) is easily visited on a day trip from its larger sister city Úbeda – though it has some good restaurants and accommodation of its own that may just tempt you to stick around. Here, a handful of wealthy, fractious families, rich from grain-growing and cloth and leather production, left a marvellous catalogue of perfectly preserved Renaissance churches and civic buildings.

Baeza was one of the first Andalucian towns to fall to the Christians (in 1227), and little is left today of the Muslim town of Bayyasa after so many centuries of Castilian influence.

## Sights

Baeza's main sights mostly cluster in the narrow streets south of the central Plaza de España and the broad Paseo de la Constitución (once Baeza's marketplace and bullring).

**★Oleícola San Francisco** WORKSHOP
(☎953 76 34 15; www.oleoturismojaen.com; Calle Pedro Pérez, Begíjar; tours in Spanish €7.50, in English or French €8.50; ⏲tours in Spanish 11am & 5pm, in English or French 12.30pm & 4.30pm) These fascinating tours of a working oil mill near Baeza will teach you all you could want to know about the process of turning olives into oil, how the best oil is made and what distinguishes extra virgin from the rest. At the end you get to taste a few varieties, and you'll probably emerge laden with a bottle or two of San Francisco's high-quality product. Reserve ahead and specify your preferred language.

**★Catedral de Baeza** CATHEDRAL
(Plaza de Santa María; adult/child €4/1.50, free 9.30-11am Mon; ⏲9.30am-2pm & 4-7pm Mon, 10am-2pm & 4-7pm Tue-Fri, 10am-7pm Sat, 10am-6pm Sun) As was the case in much of Andalucía, the Reconquista destroyed Baeza's mosque and in its place built a cathedral. It's a stylistic melange, though the predominant style is 16th-century Renaissance, visible in the facade on Plaza de Santa María and in the basic design of the three-nave interior (by Andrés de Vandelvira).

**★Palacio de Jabalquinto** PALACE
(Plaza de Santa Cruz; ⏲10.30am-1pm & 4-6pm) FREE Baeza's most flamboyant palace was probably built in the late 15th century for a member of the noble Benavides clan. Its chief glory is the spectacular facade in decorative Isabelline Gothic style, with a strange array of naked humans clambering along the moulding over the doorway; above is a line of shields topped by helmets with mythical birds and beasts. The patio has a two-tier Renaissance arcade with marble columns, an elegant fountain, and a magnificent carved baroque stairway.

**Plaza del Pópulo** SQUARE
(Plaza de los Leones) This handsome square is surrounded by elegant 16th-century buildings. The central **Fuente de los Leones** (Fountain of the Lions) is made of carvings from the Ibero-Roman village of Cástulo and is topped by a statue reputed to represent Imilce, a local princess who became one of the wives of the famous Carthaginian general Hannibal.

## Festivals & Events

**Semana Santa** RELIGIOUS
(⏲Mar/Apr) Baeza's Easter processions – numbering 19 between Palm Sunday and Easter Sunday – are solemn, grand and rooted very deep in the town's traditions.

**Feria** FERIA
(⏲mid-Aug) The summer fair starts with a big Carnaval-style procession of *gigantones* (papier-mâché giants) and other colourful figures, and continues with five days of fireworks, a huge funfair, concerts and bullfights.

## Sleeping

**Hostal Aznaitín** HOSTAL €€
(☎953 74 07 88; www.hostalaznaitin.com; Calle Cabreros 2; incl breakfast s €50-75, d €60-85; ) Welcoming, bright Aznaitín is a far cry from the dreary *hostales* of old. Rooms are stylish and well sized, with good mattresses and large, appealing photos of Baeza sights. The recently opened in-house restaurant serves three-course dinners at bargain prices (€9.50 including a drink).

**Hotel Puerta de la Luna** HERITAGE HOTEL €€
(☎953 74 70 19; www.hotelpuertadelaluna.com; Calle Canónigo Melgares Raya 7; d €87-175; P) If they were to return today, Baeza's Renaissance-era nobility would doubtless stay at this luxurious hotel in a 17th-century mansion. Orange trees and a pool grace its elegant patio, complemented by beautifully furnished salons with welcoming fireplaces. The spacious rooms are enhanced by classical furnishings, artwork and large bathrooms. Buffet breakfast costs €15, and **Bar Pacos** (Calle de Santa Catalina; tapas & medias raciones €5-10; ⏲1.30-4pm & 8.30pm-midnight) downstairs serves good tapas.

## Eating & Drinking

Paseo de la Constitución and Plaza de España are lined with bar-cafe-restaurants that are great for watching local life, but most of the best finds are tucked away in the narrow old-town streets. As throughout the province, you'll get a free tapa with your drink in almost every bar.

## BUSES TO/FROM JAÉN

ALSA (p759), **Cambus** (☎679 730134; www.cambusautocares.com) and **Autocares Samar** (☎902 25 70 25; www.samar.es) run services from the **bus station** (☎953 23 23 00; www.epassa.es/autobus; Plaza de la Libertad).

| DESTINATION | COMPANY | COST (€) | TIME (HR) | FREQUENCY (DAILY) |
|---|---|---|---|---|
| Baeza | ALSA | 4.60 | 1 | 10–16 |
| Cazorla | ALSA | 9.50 | 2–2½ | 3 |
| Córdoba | Cambus | 11 | 2 | 6–9 |
| Granada | ALSA | 9.15 | 1¼ | 11–14 |
| Madrid | Samar | 27 | 4–5 | 3–4 |
| Málaga | ALSA | 21 | 2¾–4¾ | 4 |
| Úbeda | ALSA | 5.55 | 1–1¾ | 10–17 |

**★El Arcediano** TAPAS €

(Calle Barbacana 4; montaditos €3-7, raciones €7-15; ⏰8.30pm-midnight Thu, 1-4pm & 8.30pm-midnight Fri-Sun) Always buzzing with locals, this welcoming spot with dangling chandeliers, grapevines painted on the ceiling and tables on the narrow pedestrian lane out front serves up excellent large *montaditos* (slices of toasted bread with toppings). Scrumptious standouts such as thin-sliced Barbate tuna and smoked cod complement more standard offerings such as pork, anchovies, assorted cheeses, or mashed tomato and olive oil.

**★Palacio de Gallego** SPANISH €€€

(☎667 760184; www.palaciodegallego.com; Calle de Santa Catalina 5; mains €15-32; ⏰8-11pm Wed, 1.30-3.30pm & 8-11pm Thu-Mon) In the atmospheric setting of a 16th-century house, with tables on the delightful patio as well as in an old wood-beamed dining room, the Gallego serves up superb meat and fish dishes, barbecued and otherwise. There's a list of well over 100 Spanish wines, and you won't come across many starters better than their goat's cheese, orange and walnut salad.

**★Café Teatro Central** BAR

(☎953 74 43 55; www.facebook.com/cafeteatrocentral; Calle Barreras 19; ⏰4pm-3am Sun-Thu, to 4am Fri & Sat; 📶) The most original and consistent nightspot in the province, with fascinatingly eclectic decor and determined support for live music, the Central fills up around midnight Thursday to Saturday with an arty-indie crowd. Live acts play to enthusiastic revellers amid the Buddha statues, historical instruments and coloured lighting. Their Facebook page lists upcoming shows.

## ℹ Information

**Tourist Office** (☎953 77 99 82; www.andalucia.org; Plaza del Pópulo; ⏰9am-7.30pm Mon-Fri, 9.30am-3pm Sat & Sun) Housed in the 16th-century Casa del Pópulo.

## ℹ Getting There & Away

### BUS

ALSA (p759) runs services from the **bus station** (☎953 74 04 68; Avenida Alcalde Puche Pardo), 900m northeast of Plaza de España.

| Destination | Cost (€) | Time (hr) | Frequency (daily) |
|---|---|---|---|
| Cazorla | 5 | 1¼–1½hr | 3 |
| Córdoba | 12 | 2½hr | 2 |
| Granada | 13 | 2–2½hr | 7–9 |
| Jaén | 4.60 | 45min–1¼hr | 7–14 |
| Úbeda | 1.20 | 15min | 13–18 |

### TRAIN

The nearest station is Linares–Baeza (www.renfe.com), 13km northwest of town, with a few daily trains to Almería, Córdoba, Jaén, Madrid and Seville. ALSA runs limited bus service to the station from Úbeda (€2.20, 30 to 50 minutes) and Baeza (€2.80, one hour). A taxi costs around €25.

# Úbeda

POP 34,345 / ELEV 760M

Beautiful Renaissance buildings grace almost every street and plaza in the *casco antiguo* (old quarter) of World Heritage–listed Úbeda (*oo*-be-dah). Charming hotels in several historic mansions, and some top-class restaurants and tapas bars, make a stay here an all-round delight.

Úbeda's aristocratic lions jockeyed successfully for influence at the Habsburg court in the 16th century. Francisco de los Cobos y Molina became state secretary to King Carlos I, and his nephew Juan Vázquez de Molina succeeded him in the job and kept it under Felipe II.

High office exposed these men to the Renaissance aesthetic just then reaching Spain from Italy. Much of the wealth that they and a flourishing agriculture generated was invested in some of Spain's purest examples of Renaissance architecture. As a result, Úbeda (like its little sister Baeza) is one of the few places in Andalucía boasting stunning architecture that was *not* built by the Moors.

## Sights

**Plaza Vázquez de Molina** SQUARE

The lovely Plaza Vázquez de Molina is the monumental heart of Úbeda's old town and the perfect place to start exploring. An early case of Andalucian urban redevelopment, the plaza took on its present aspect in the 16th century when Úbeda's nobility decided to demolish existing buildings to make way for an assemblage of grand Renaissance buildings befitting their wealth and importance.

**★Sacra Capilla del Salvador** CHAPEL

(Sacred Chapel of the Saviour; www.fundacionmedinaceli.org; Plaza Vázquez de Molina; adult/child incl audio guide €5/2.50; ⌚9.30am-2.30pm & 4.30-7.30pm Mon-Sat, 11.30am-3pm & 4.30-7.30pm Sun Apr-Sep, to 6pm Mon-Sat, to 7pm Sun Oct-Mar) This famous chapel, built between 1536 and 1559, is the flagship of Úbeda Renaissance architecture. Commissioned by Francisco de los Cobos y Molina as his family's funerary chapel, it presents a marked contrast between the relatively sober proportions of the interior (by Diego de Siloé, architect of Granada's cathedral) and the more decorative western facade. The facade, a pre-eminent example of plateresque style, was designed by Andrés de Vandelvira, one of Siloé's stonemasons, who took over the project in 1540.

**★Sinagoga del Agua** HISTORIC BUILDING

(☎953 75 81 50; www.sinagogadelagua.com; Calle Roque Rojas 2; tours adult/child €4.50/3.50; ⌚tours every 45min 10.30am-1.30pm & 4.45-7pm Sep-Jun, 10.30am-1.30pm & 5.45-8pm Jul & Aug) The medieval Sinagoga del Agua was discovered in 2006 by a refreshingly ethical property developer who intended to build apartments here, only to discover that every swing of the pickaxe revealed some tantalising piece of an archaeological puzzle. The result is this sensitive recreation of a centuries-old synagogue and rabbi's house, using original masonry whenever possible. Features include the women's gallery, a bodega with giant storage vessels, and a *miqvé* (ritual bath).

**★Palacio de Vázquez de Molina** HISTORIC BUILDING

(Plaza Vázquez de Molina; ⌚8am-8pm Mon-Fri, 10am-2pm & 5-7.30pm Sat & Sun) FREE Úbeda's *ayuntamiento* (town hall) is undoubtedly one of the most beautiful – if not *the* most beautiful – in Spain. It was built by Vandelvira in about 1562 as a mansion for Juan Vázquez de Molina, whose coat of arms surmounts the doorway. The perfectly proportioned, deeply Italian-influenced facade is divided into three tiers by slender cornices, with the sculpted caryatids on the top level continuing the lines of the Corinthian and Ionic pilasters on the lower tiers.

**Casa Museo Andalusí** MUSEUM

(☎659 508766; www.vandelviraturismo.com; Calle Narváez 11; €4; ⌚tours 11.30am or by arrangement) Úbeda's fascinating Casa Museo Andalusí comprises a 16th-century private home that was inhabited by *conversos* (Jews who converted to Christianity) and a huge, diverse collection of antiques assembled by owner Paco Castro. Informal guided tours of the house, led by his art historian daughter

WORTH A TRIP

### FORTALEZA DE LA MOTA

From a distance the **Fortaleza de la Mota** (www.tuhistoria.org; Alcalá la Real; adult/child €6/3; ⌚10.30am-7.30pm Apr–mid-Oct, 10am-6pm mid-Oct–Mar; P) looks more like a city than a mere fort, with its high church tower and doughty keep rising above the surrounding walls. And in a sense that's what it was, for back in the Middle Ages this fortified hill now looming over the town of Alcalá la Real *was* Alcalá la Real. It's a marvellous stop if you're heading along the Granada–Córdoba road across southwestern Jaén province, and well worth a detour even if you're not.

WORTH A TRIP

## PARQUE NATURAL SIERRA DE ANDÚJAR

This large (748 sq km) natural park north of Andújar town has the biggest expanses of natural vegetation in the Sierra Morena as well as plenty of bull-breeding ranches. It's an exciting destination for wildlife-spotters, with numerous large mammals and birds found here including five emblematic endangered species: the Iberian lynx, wolf, black vulture, black stork and Spanish imperial eagle. The Iberian lynx population is the largest in the world, with around 200 lynxes here and in the neighbouring Parque Natural Sierra de Cardeña y Montoro (Córdoba province). There are also 25 breeding pairs of Spanish imperial eagle in the Andújar park (one-tenth of the total population of this mighty bird, found only in the Iberian Peninsula).

Staff at the park visitors centre, the **Centro de Visitantes Viñas de Peñallana** (953 53 96 28; Carretera A6177, Km 13; 10am-2pm Thu-Sun plus 3-6pm Fri-Sun, closed afternoons mid-Jun–mid-Sep, closed Thu Jul & Aug), 13km north of Andújar town, can tell you the best areas for wildlife sightings, though you also need luck on your side. The best months for spotting lynxes are December and January, the mating season. Local guiding outfits can take you onto private land where sighting prospects are often higher: they include **Birds & Lynx Ecotourism** (659 936566; www.birdslynxecotourism.com; Centro de Visitantes Viñas de Peñallana, Carretera A6177, Km 13; 1-/2-/3-/4-person tour per person €150/100/80/70), **IberianLynxLand** (636 984515, English 626 700525; www.iberianlynx-land.com; 2-/3-/4-person tour per person €80/65/55) and **Turismo Verde** (628 916731; www.lasierradeandujar.com; tour per person €75).

On a hilltop in the heart of the park stands the **Santuario de la Virgen de la Cabeza** (Carretera A6177, Km 31, Cerro del Cabezo; P), a chapel that is the focus of one of Spain's biggest and most emotive religious events, the **Romería de la Virgen de la Cabeza**, on the last weekend in April.

A great base for wildlife watchers, hotel **La Caracola** (640 758273; www.lacaracolahotelrural.com; Carretera A6177, Km 13.8; s/d incl breakfast €42.50/70; P) sits among woodlands and offers bright, contemporary rooms, comfortable common areas and good meals (lunch or dinner €15). They'll serve breakfast as early as you like, or make you a picnic. It's 1.4km off the A6177: the signed turn-off is 800m north of the park visitors centre.

Andújar town is served by several daily trains and buses from Jaén and Córdoba, and by buses from Baeza and Úbeda. There are buses to the sanctuary on Saturday and Sunday.

Eva Castro Martos, make it all come alive. The first hint that this is somewhere special is the original 16th-century heavy carved door. Ring the bell if it's closed, or schedule visits in advance via WhatsApp.

Eva Castro's agency, Vandelvira Turismo, also leads tours of two other nearby mansions – Casa Solar de los Granadas Venegas and Casa Sinagoga de Salomón – equally laden with aesthetic treasures; a visit to all three costs €12 and comes complete with fascinating historical commentary about Úbeda.

**Centro de Interpretación Olivar y Aceite** VISITOR CENTRE
(953 75 58 89; www.centrodeolivaryaceite.com; Corredera de San Fernando 32; €2.80; 10am-2pm Tue-Sun year-round, plus 6-8.30pm Tue-Sat Jun-Sep, 5-7.30pm Tue-Sat Oct-May) Úbeda's olive-oil interpretation centre explains all about the area's olive-oil history, and how the oil gets from the tree to your table, with the help of models, mill equipment and videos in English and Spanish. You get the chance to taste different oils, and to buy from a broad selection.

## Sleeping

**★Las Casas del Cónsul** HERITAGE HOTEL €€
(953 79 54 30; www.lascasasdelconsul.es; Plaza del Carmen 1; d Sun-Thu €65-70, Fri & Sat €80-90; ) An attractive Renaissance mansion conversion, the welcoming 'Consul's Houses' has elegant, predominantly white rooms with old-time touches, and spacious common areas centred on a two-storey pillared patio – but what really sets it apart is the fabulous panoramic terrace (with pool).

**★Afán de Rivera** HERITAGE HOTEL €€
(953 79 19 87; www.hotelafanderivera.com; Calle Afán de Rivera 4; s/d/tr incl breakfast Sun-Thu €50/70/90, Fri & Sat €56/110/120; )

This superb five-room hotel lies inside one of Úbeda's oldest buildings, predating the Renaissance. Expertly run by the amiable Jorge, it has beautiful historical common areas, and comfortable rooms that offer far more than is usual at these prices: shaving kits, fancy shampoos and tastefully eclectic decor combining the traditional and the contemporary.

**Hotel Ordóñez Sandoval** HOTEL €€
(☎679 803942; www.hotelordonezsandoval.es; Calle Antonio Medina 1; r incl breakfast midweek/weekend €60/90; ) Housed in a dusky pink neoclassical mansion, this small hotel offers a peaceful and elegant refuge in the heart of Úbeda. Rooms are bright and incredibly spacious, with high ceilings, original antique furniture and private baths. Affable owner Pepe lovingly maintains the place and regales guests with fresh-squeezed orange juice at breakfast.

**Parador de Úbeda** HISTORIC HOTEL €€€
(Parador Condestable Dávalos; ☎953 75 03 45; www.parador.es; Plaza Vázquez de Molina; r €100-220; ) One of Spain's original *paradors* (opened in 1930), this plush hotel occupies a historical monument, the **Palacio del Deán Ortega**, on the wonderful Plaza Vázquez de Molina. It has been comfortably modernised in period style and the rooms and common areas are appropriately luxurious. The best rooms have their own little garden patios. Breakfast costs €17.

## Eating & Drinking

Úbeda is the culinary hotspot of Jaén province; its talented *andaluz*-fusion chefs are one reason why Spaniards flock here.

★**Cantina La Estación** ANDALUCIAN €€
(☎687 777230; www.cantinalaestacion.com; Cuesta Rodadera 1; mains €15-24; 1-3pm & 8pm-midnight Thu-Mon, 1-3pm Tue; ) The charming originality here starts with the design – three rooms with railway themes (the main dining room being the deluxe carriage). Seasonally inspired fusion dishes, such as wild boar in red-wine sauce, or octopus with garlic chips and paprika, share the menu with traditional Úbeda recipes such as *andrajos* (a stew of meat and/or fish with tomatoes, peppers and spices).

★**Misa de 12** ANDALUCIAN €€
(☎953 82 81 97; www.facebook.com/MisaDe12Ubeda; Plaza 1º de Mayo 7; raciones €10-24; noon-4pm & 8.30pm-midnight Wed-Sun) Grab a table overlooking the plaza or hunker down in the cosy interior to sample a succession of truly succulent platters – from perfectly grilled slices of *presa ibérica* (a tender cut of Iberian pork) to *revuelto de pulpo y gambas* (eggs scrambled with octopus and shrimp). Despite the place's wild popularity, staff are unfailingly attentive and efficient.

**Llámame Lola** ANDALUCIAN €€
(☎953 04 16 55; Calle Baja del Salvador 5; tapas €7-12, mains €12-20; noon-midnight; ) With an inviting location under the trees near the Sacra Capilla del Salvador, Lola serves up good, creative *andaluz* fare with less fanfare than some other places. The *solomillo ibérico* (pork tenderloin), the octopus and the *revueltos* are all very tasty, as are the miniature fried shrimp from Cadiz.

**La Bodega de Úbeda** BAR
(☎667 565469; Calle Real 19; noon-1am Sun-Thu, to 2am Fri & Sat) Among the many bars and restaurants lining Úbeda's main pedestrian street, La Bodega stands out for its distinctive cellar, where low-lit vaulted stone walls shelter a treasure trove of century-old ceramic urns once used to store oil and wine. It's an atmospheric spot to savour the proud Jaén tradition of free tapas with every round of drinks.

## Shopping

Calles Real and Juan Montilla in the old town are dotted with shops selling local crafts and products such as oils, wines, olives and honey. The main high-street-style shopping streets are Calles Mesones and Obispo Cobos, between Plaza de Andalucía and the Hospital de Santiago.

## Information

**Oficina de Turismo** (☎953 77 92 04; www.turismodeubeda.com; Plaza de Andalucía 5; 9am-7.30pm Mon-Fri, 9.30am-3pm & 5-7.30pm Sat, 9.30am-3pm Sun) Helpful place on the northwestern edge of the old town.

## Getting There & Away

### BUS

**ALSA** (☎902 42 22 42; www.ALSA.es) runs services from the **bus station** (☎953 79 51 88; Calle San José 6), which is in the new part of town, 700m west of Plaza de Andalucía.

| Destination | Cost (€) | Time | Frequency (daily) |
|---|---|---|---|
| Baeza | 1.20 | 15min | 13–18 |
| Cazorla | 4.35 | 1hr | 3–5 |
| Córdoba | 13 | 2½hr | 4–5 |
| Granada | 13 | 2–2¾hr | 7–12 |
| Jaén | 5.55 | 1–1¼hr | 9–15 |

### TRAIN

The nearest station is **Linares–Baeza** (www.renfe.com), 21km northwest, which you can reach on four daily buses (€2.20, 30 to 50 minutes).

| Destination | Cost (€) | Time | Frequency (daily) |
|---|---|---|---|
| Almería | 27 | 3¾hr | 3 |
| Córdoba | 20 | 1½hr | 1 |
| Jaén | 6.25 | 45min | 3–4 |
| Madrid | 24–33 | 3–4hr | 6–7 |
| Seville | 18–21 | 3¼hr | 1 |

# Cazorla

POP 7441 / ELEV 826M

This picturesque, bustling white town sits beneath towering crags just where the Sierra de Cazorla rises up from a rolling sea of olive trees, 45km east of Úbeda. It makes the perfect launching pad for exploring the beautiful Parque Natural Sierras de Cazorla, Segura y Las Villas, which begins dramatically among the cliffs of Peña de los Halcones (Falcon Crag) directly above the town.

## Sights

The heart of town is **Plaza de la Corredera**, with busy bars and the elegant *ayuntamiento* and clock tower looking down from the southeast corner. Canyonlike streets lead south to the **Balcón de Zabaleta**. This little mirador is like a sudden window in a blank wall, with stunning views up to the Castillo de la Yedra and beyond. From here another narrow street leads down to Cazorla's most picturesque square, **Plaza de Santa María**.

**★Castillo de la Yedra** CASTLE

(Museo del Alto Guadalquivir; EU/non-EU citizen free/€1.50; ⏲tours 10.30am, noon, 1.30pm, 4pm, 5.30pm & 7pm Tue-Sat, 10.30am, noon & 1.30pm Sun) Cazorla's dramatic Castle of the Ivy, a 700m walk above Plaza de Santa María, offers superb views and houses the interesting Museum of the Upper Guadalquivir, with diverse collections that include traditional agricultural and kitchen utensils, religious art, models of an old olive mill, and a small chapel featuring a life-size Romanesque-Byzantine crucifixion sculpture. Interior visits are by guided tour only. The castle is of Muslim origin, comprehensively rebuilt in the 14th century after the Reconquista.

## Activities & Tours

There are some great walks straight out of Cazorla town – all uphill to start with, but your reward is beautiful forest paths and fabulous panoramas of cliffs, crags and circling vultures. Agencies here offer a host of other activities locally, including canyoning in the *parque natural* and an exciting via ferrata for climbers at the neighbouring village of La Iruela.

**Via Ferrata La Mocha** CLIMBING

(La Iruela) This high-adrenaline challenge is a set of steel ladders, steps, cables and chains fixed into the precipitous rocky cone, La Mocha, above La Iruela village just outside Cazorla. It ascends 130m and includes a 'Tibetan bridge' – a set of horizontal cables strung across a precipice. **Tierraventura** (☎953 71 00 73; www.aventuracazorla.com; Carretera A319, Km 16.5, La Iruela; ⏲10am-2pm & 5-8pm Mon-Sat) offers guided climbs (€35 per person, about three hours).

**Turisnat** WILDLIFE WATCHING

(☎953 72 13 51; www.turisnat.es; Calle José Martínez Falero 11; tours per person €30-49; ⏲office 10am-2pm & 5-8pm Mon-Sat, to 2pm Sun) This highly experienced agency is a good option for 4WD trips along the forest tracks of the *parque natural*, with an emphasis on wildlife-spotting. English- or French-speaking guides are available at no extra cost.

## Sleeping & Eating

**Casa Rural Plaza de Santa María** CASA RURAL €

(☎953 72 20 87; www.plazadesantamaria.com; Callejón Plaza Santa María 5; s/d/ste incl breakfast €40/50/60, extra bed per person €13; ) At this multilevel house in the heart of town, nine cheerily decorated rooms come complemented by a lovely garden-patio and a rooftop terrace with superb views over the plaza, the castle and the mountains beyond. It's well worth paying €10 extra for one of the three superior rooms with perks such as large windows, sitting rooms and views.

**La Yedra** ANDALUCIAN €

(☎953 71 02 92; Calle Cruz de Orea 51; mains €9-14; ⊙noon-midnight Mon-Sat) Rub elbows with the locals at this down-to-earth spot near Cazorla's market, where the lunchtime *menú del día* (including appetiser, main course, dessert and drink) goes for €11. Expect traditional country fare such as *sopa de ajo* (garlic soup) followed by filling mains such as stewed pork with tomatoes, peppers and potatoes.

**Mesón Leandro** SPANISH €€

(☎953 72 06 32; www.mesonleandro.com; Calle Hoz 3; mains €10-28; ⊙1.30-4pm & 8.30-11pm Wed-Mon) Leandro is a step up in class from most other Cazorla eateries – professional but still friendly service in a bright dining room with lazy music, and only one set of antlers on the wall. The broad menu of nicely presented dishes ranges from partridge-and-pheasant pâté to *fettuccine a la marinera* and a terrific *solomillo de ciervo* (venison tenderloin).

## Information

**Oficina Municipal de Turismo** (☎953 71 01 02; www.cazorla.es/turismo; Plaza de Santa María; ⊙10am-1pm & 4-8pm Tue-Sun Apr-Oct, to 7pm Nov-Mar) Inside the remains of Santa María church, with some information on the natural park as well as the town.

**Punto de Información Cazorla** (☎670 943880; Calle Martínez Falero 11; ⊙10am-2pm & 5.30-8.30pm Mon-Sat, 10am-2pm Sun Jul–mid-Sep, hours vary rest of year) Good for information on the *parque natural* as well as the town and surrounds.

## Getting There & Away

ALSA (www.alsa.es) runs three to five daily buses to Úbeda (€4.35, one hour), Baeza (€5, 1¼ hours), Jaén (€9.50, two to 2½ hours) and Granada (€18.20, 3½ to four hours). The **bus station** (Calle de Hilario Marco) is 500m north of Plaza de la Corredera via Plaza de la Constitución.

# Parque Natural Sierras de Cazorla, Segura y Las Villas

One of the biggest drawcards in Jaén province – and, for nature lovers, in all of Andalucía – is the mountainous, lushly wooded Parque Natural Sierras de Cazorla, Segura y Las Villas. This is the largest protected area in Spain: 2099 sq km of craggy mountain ranges, deep, green river valleys, canyons, waterfalls, remote hilltop castles and abundant wildlife, threaded by well-marked walking trails and forest roads, with a snaking, 20km-long reservoir, the Embalse del Tranco, in its midst. The abrupt geography, with altitudes varying from 460m up to 2107m at the summit of Cerro Empanadas, makes for dramatic changes in the landscape. The Río Guadalquivir, Andalucía's longest river, rises in the south of the park, and flows northwards into the Embalse del Tranco, before heading west across Andalucía to the Atlantic Ocean. The best times to visit the park are spring and autumn, when the vegetation is at its most colourful and temperatures are pleasant. The park is hugely popular with Spanish tourists and attracts several hundred thousand visitors each year. Peak periods are Semana Santa, July, August, and weekends from April to October.

## Getting There & Away

Cazorla is the only park gateway with dependable bus service. To conveniently explore the park, you'll need your own wheels.

## Getting Around

Exploring the park is far easier if you have a vehicle. The network of paved and unpaved roads and footpaths reaches some remote areas and offers plenty of scope for panoramic day walks or drives. If you don't have a vehicle, you have the option of guided walks, 4WD excursions and wildlife-spotting trips with agencies based in Cazorla (p760) and elsewhere. Bus services are effectively nonexistent.

## Segura de la Sierra

POP 1790 / ELEV 1145M

One of Andalucía's most picturesque and strategically placed historical villages, Segura de la Sierra perches on a steep hill crowned by a Reconquista castle. The village takes some of its character from its five Moorish centuries before the Knights of Santiago captured it in 1214, after which it became part of the Christian front line against the Almohads and then the Granada emirate.

As you drive up into the village, the **Puerta Nueva**, one of four gates of Islamic Saqura, marks the entrance to the old part of Segura. Signs to the Castillo lead you round to a junction on the northern side by the little walled bullring. Turn left here for the castle itself.

DON'T MISS

## RÍO BOROSA WALK

The most popular walk in the Cazorla natural park follows the crystal-clear Río Borosa upstream to its source through scenery that progresses from the pretty to the majestic, via a gorge, two tunnels and a mountain lake. The walk is about 11km each way, with an ascent of about 600m, and takes six to seven hours there and back.

To reach the start, turn east off the A319 at the 'Sendero Río Borosa' sign opposite the **Centro de Visitantes Torre del Vinagre** (953 71 30 17; Ctra A319, Km 48; 10am-2pm & 5-8pm Jul–mid-Sep, hours vary rest of year), and go 1.7km. The first section of the walk criss-crosses the tumbling, beautiful Río Borosa on a couple of bridges. After just over 3km, where the main track starts climbing to the left, take a path forking right, clearly signposted for 'Cerrada de Elías.' This leads through a lovely 1.5km section where the valley narrows to a gorge, the **Cerrada de Elías**, and the path becomes a wooden walkway cantilevered out over the river. You re-emerge on the dirt road and continue 4km to the **Central Eléctric**a, a small hydroelectric station.

Beyond the power station, the path crosses a footbridge, after which a 'Nacimiento Aguas Negras, Laguna Valdeazores' sign directs you onward and upward. The path winds its way up the valley, getting gradually steeper as it climbs through increasingly dramatic scenery past a series of waterfalls. After about an hour, you enter the first of two tunnels cut through the rock for water flowing to the power station. It takes about five minutes to walk the narrow path through the first tunnel (the path is separated from the watercourse by a metal handrail), then there's a short section in the open air before a second tunnel, which takes about one minute to get through. You emerge just below the dam of the **Embalse de los Órganos** (Laguna de Aguas Negras), a small reservoir surrounded by forested hills. From the top of the dam, follow the trail along the reservoir's left bank and in five minutes you reach the **Nacimiento de Aguas Negras**, where the Río Borosa begins life welling out from under a rock. Enjoy your picnic beneath the spreading boughs of a large tree here, then head back down the way you came.

Due to its popularity, it's preferable to do this walk on a weekday. Do carry a water bottle: all the trackside springs are good and drinkable but the last is at the Central Eléctrica. A torch (headlamp) is comforting, if not absolutely essential, for the tunnels.

## Sights

**★Castillo de Segura** CASTLE

(627 877919; adult/child €4.50/3.50; 10.30am-2pm & 5-8.45pm mid-Jul–Aug, shorter hours rest of year) This lofty castle dates from Moorish times but was rebuilt after the Christian conquest in the 13th century. Abandoned in the 17th century, it was restored in the 1960s and has now become a 'frontier territory' interpretation centre. The ticket office is also Segura's main tourist information point.

## Eating

**La Mesa Segureña** ANDALUCIAN €€

(953 48 21 01; Calle Postigo 2; mains €12-18; 10am-10pm Mon-Sat, to 5pm Sun) Hidden down a small lane between th castle and the Arabic baths, La Mesa Segureña makes for a festive lunch break. Meaty mountain specialties – from pork chops to venison stew – are the star attractions, served by bustling black-clad waitresses in a dining room with cheerful orange-and-green walls.

## Getting There & Away

Several country roads meet here: the main approach is from the A317 between Cortijos Nuevos and La Puerta de Segura.

# ALMERÍA PROVINCE

Silent mountain valleys, sublime beaches and vast tracts of semidesert scrubland – Almería province is an area of haunting natural beauty. Despite this, and despite enjoying 3000 hours of annual sunshine, it remains relatively unknown outside of Spain. Its obvious drawcard is its glorious coastline, most notably the thrilling beaches of the Parque Natural de Cabo de Gata-Níjar, and the lively, good-time resort of Mojácar. But venture inland, and you'll discover plenty to explore in its sparsely populated and often other-worldly hinterland. Tour the spaghetti-western badlands of the Desierto de Tabernas and discover underground treasures in the Sorbas caves. Further north, the wooded peaks of Los Vélez provide a majestic backdrop for mountain walking. After so much nature, the port city of Almería offers a welcome blast of urban energy with its impressive monuments, handsome centre and buzzing tapas bars.

## Almería

POP 198,533

An energetic port city with an illustrious past, Almería is one of Andalucía's emerging destinations. Until fairly recently the city was generally overlooked by travellers, but ongoing efforts to spruce it up continue to pay dividends. It has a handsome centre, punctuated by palm-fringed plazas and old churches, several interesting museums and a plethora of fantastic tapas bars. Best of all – and reason alone for a visit – is its spectacular Moorish Alcazaba (fortress).

### Sights

Almería's top sights are the Alcazaba and the cathedral, both of which can be explored in a morning, but there are plenty of interesting additional distractions in the city's meandering streets. Orientate yourself from Paseo de Almería, the city's main drag, which runs north–south through the historic centre.

**★Alcazaba** FORTRESS

(950 80 10 08; Calle Almanzor; 9am-3pm & 7-10pm Tue-Sat mid-Jun–mid-Sep, 9am-8pm Tue-Sat Apr–mid-Jun, 9am-6pm Tue-Sat mid-Sep–Mar, 9am-3pm Sun year-round) FREE A looming fortification with great curtain-like walls rising from the cliffs, Almería's Alcazaba was founded in the mid-10th century and went on to become one of the most powerful Moorish fortresses in Spain. It's survived in good shape and while it lacks the intricate decoration of Granada's Alhambra, it's still a magnificent sight. Allow about 1½ hours to explore everything. Pick up a guide leaflet at the kiosk inside the four-arch entrance gate.

The Alcazaba is divided into three distinct *recintos* (compounds). The lowest, the **Primer Recinto**, was residential, with houses, streets, wells, baths and other necessities – now replaced by lush gardens and water channels. From the battlements, you can look over the city's huddled rooftops and down to the **Muralla de Jayrán**, a fortified wall built in the 11th century to defend the outlying northern and eastern parts of the city.

Further up in the **Segundo Recinto** you'll find the ruins of the Muslim rulers' palace, built by the *taifa* ruler Almotacín (r 1051–91), under whom medieval Almería reached its peak, as well as a chapel, the **Ermita de San Juan**, which was originally a mosque. The highest section, the **Tercer Recinto**, is a castle added by the Catholic Monarchs.

**★Catedral de la Encarnación** CATHEDRAL

(605 396483; www.catedralalmeria.com; Plaza de la Catedral 8, entrance Calle Velázquez; €5; 10am-7pm Mon-Fri, 10am-2.30pm & 3.30-7pm Sat, 1.30-7pm Sun Apr-Sep, to 6.30pm Oct-Mar) Almería's formidable, six-towered cathedral, begun in 1525, was conceived both as a place of worship and a refuge for the population from frequent pirate raids from North Africa. It was originally Gothic-Renaissance in style, but baroque and neoclassical features were added in the 18th century. The Gothic interior, entered through a fine neoclassical cloister, is an impressive spectacle with its sinuous, ribbed ceiling, 16th-century walnut choir stalls and monumental Capilla Mayor (Chancel).

**Museo de la Guitarra** MUSEUM

(950 27 43 58; Ronda del Beato Diego Ventaja; adult/reduced €3/2; 10.30am-1.30pm Tue-Sun year-round, plus 6-9pm Tue-Sat Jun-Sep, 5-8pm Tue-Sat Oct-May) It's worth establishing two important facts before you enter this absorbing museum. First: the word 'guitar' is derived from the Andalucian-Arabic word *qitara,* hinting at its Spanish roots. Second: all modern acoustic guitars owe a huge debt to Almerian guitar-maker Antonio de Torres (1817–92), to whom this museum is dedicated. The museum itself details the history of the guitar and pays homage to Torres' part in it.

**Museo de Almería** MUSEUM

(Museo Arqueológico; 950 01 62 56; www.museosdeandalucia.es/museodealmeria; Calle Hermanos Pinzón 91; 9am-9pm Tue-Sat, to 3pm Sun) FREE Almería's excellent archaeology museum focuses on two local prehistoric cultures – Los Millares (3200–2250 BCE), probably the Iberian Peninsula's first metalworking culture, and El Argar (2250–1550 BCE), which ushered in the Bronze Age.

Artefacts are well displayed and accompanied by Spanish and English explanatory panels. The third floor features finds relating to the area's Roman and Islamic past.

**Refugios de la Guerra Civil** HISTORIC SITE
(Civil War Shelters; ☎950 26 86 96; Plaza de Manuel Pérez García; adult/reduced €3/2; ⏱tours 10.30am & noon Tue-Sun year-round, plus 6pm & 7.30pm Tue-Sat Jun-Sep, 5pm & 6.30pm Tue-Sat Oct-May) During the civil war, Almería was the Republicans' last holdout in Andalucía, and was repeatedly and mercilessly bombed. The attacks prompted a group of engineers to design and build the Refugios, a 4.5km-long network of concrete shelters under the city. Visits – by 1¼-hour guided tour, in Spanish – take you through 1km of the tunnels, including the recreated operating theatre and storerooms. An engaging 10-minute film (in Spanish with English subtitles) features local survivors recounting their personal experiences in the shelters.

## Sleeping

**Hotel Nuevo Torreluz** HOTEL €
(☎950 23 43 99; www.torreluz.com; Plaza de las Flores 10; s/d from €45/58; P ❄ 📶) A polished four-star enjoying a superb location on a small square in the historical centre. Carpeted corridors lead to smallish but comfortable rooms sporting parquet floors and modern pearl-grey tones. Unlimited fresh-squeezed orange juice is a highlight of the optional breakfast (€7). The hotel also runs a trio of cafes and restaurants around the square. Parking is available for €11.90.

★ **Aire Hotel & Ancient Baths** BOUTIQUE HOTEL €€
(☎950 28 20 96; www.airehotelalmeria.com; Plaza de la Constitución 4; d €99-159, ste €149-179; ❄ 📶) Attached to the plush **Hammam Aire de Almería** (☎950 28 20 95; www.beaire.com; Plaza de la Constitución 5; 1½hr session €29 Mon-Thu, €35 Fri-Sun; ⏱9am-10.30pm), this elegant hideaway is perfectly situated on beautiful Plaza de la Constitución, just steps from some of the city's top tapas bars. Its slick, contemporarily attired rooms come with high ceilings, polished wood floors and vast photo-walls of local sights such as Cabo de Gata.

**Hotel Catedral** BOUTIQUE HOTEL €€€
(☎950 27 81 78; www.hotelcatedral.net; Plaza de la Catedral 8; r €120-190; ❄ 📶) In a prime location overlooking the cathedral, this debonair four-star occupies a handsome 1850s building. Inside, the decor slickly marries the old and the new, combining clean contemporary lines with Gothic arches and an *artesonado* ceiling in the restaurant. Rooms are large and high-ceilinged, and the roof terrace offers heady cathedral views.

## Eating

Fresh off its 2019 stint as Spain's official culinary capital (Capital Española de la Gastronomía), Almería is a fabulous place to eat. The city is awash with restaurants and tapas bars, ranging from old-school bodegas to trendy modern hangouts.

★ **Tetería Almedina** MOROCCAN €€
(☎629 277827; Calle Paz 2, off Calle de la Almedina; mains €10-15, fixed-price menús €17-30; ⏱noon-11pm Tue-Sun; 🌶) For a break from tapas, this welcoming little tearoom-restaurant is the answer. Hidden in a backstreet below the Alcazaba, it serves a reassuring menu of homestyle Moroccan staples – tagines, tabbouli, couscous and lightly spiced legume soups, with many vegetarian options in the mix. To drink, a herbed tea or infusion is the way to go. The restaurant is run by a local group dedicated to revitalising the old town, with its many Moroccan immigrants, and reviving the culture of Al-Andalus.

OFF THE BEATEN TRACK

### ALMERÍA'S GARGANTUAN GEODE

In 2019 the world's second-largest geode, **La Geoda de Pulpí** (☎950 96 27 27; www.geodapulpi.es; Calle Sierra de los Filabres, Los Jurados, Pulpí; adult/child €22/10; ⏱9am-2pm & 4-9pm), opened to the public in northeastern Almería's Sierra del Aguilón. Measuring an astounding 8m long by 2m tall, this rare geological marvel was discovered by Madrid-based mineralogists in the abandoned Mina Rica, where iron, lead and silver were mined until the Spanish Civil War. Guided tours lead visitors 60m underground down corridors and metal steps, culminating with a chance to clamber inside the geode and view its dazzling collection of translucent gypsum crystals. Tours leave half-hourly throughout the day and must be booked in advance via the website.

LOCAL KNOWLEDGE

## TAPAS TOUR

The area between Paseo de Almería and Plaza de la Constitución is packed with busy and atmospheric tapas bars, frequented as much by locals as by out-of-towners. Many maintain the civilised tradition of serving a free tapa with your drink. As a rule, portions are generous, and for the hungry – or to share – almost everywhere offers *raciones* and *medias raciones* (full- and half-sized plates of tapas items). Two perennial favourites are Casa Puga (p765) and Jovellanos 16 (p765), but there are plenty more to choose from.

**Nuestra Tierra** (www.tabernanuestratierra.com; cnr Calles Jovellanos & Marín; tapas €2-6, raciones €14-25; ⌚7.30am-noon Mon, to midnight Tue-Thu, to 1am Fri, 8.30am-1.30am Sat, noon-midnight Sun) Head to this good-looking modern eatery on bar-heavy Calle Jovellanos for creative tapas made with seasonal Andalucian ingredients. Showstoppers include IGP Sierra de los Filabres lamb with caramelised peppers, and octopus grilled to buttery softness.

**El Quinto Toro** (☎950 23 91 35; www.facebook.com/elquintotoroalmeria; Calle Juan Leal 6; tapas from €1.50, raciones €7-18; ⌚noon-5pm Mon-Sat & 8pm-midnight Mon-Fri) Keep it traditional at this old-school bar near the central market. Don't expect culinary fireworks, just tried-and-tested staples such as *chorizo ibérico* (spicy sausage) and *albóndigas* (meatballs) in wine sauce.

**Tortillería La Mala** (☎619 350816; www.facebook.com/tortillerialamala; Calle Real 69; tapas €1.20-5, tortillas €9-12, raciones €8-18; ⌚noon-4pm Tue, noon-4pm & 8pm-1am Wed-Sun) This buzzing corner bar fills quickly on weekend evenings. With its boho decor and young crowd, it's a great spot to try a genuine Spanish tortilla (omelette), here prepared with everything from tuna to prawns and chilli.

**Cervecería Las Tiendas** (☎640 684947; Calle de las Tiendas; tapas €1.20-5, raciones €8-18; ⌚10am-4pm Mon-Wed, to midnight Thu-Sat) Every seafood tapa imaginable is yours for a song at this streetside venue. Patrons sip beers throughout the evening as waiters sling plates of steamed mussels, grilled tuna, fried squid, sardines, octopus and more.

**★Casa Puga** TAPAS €€
(☎950 23 15 30; www.barcasapuga.es; Calle Jovellanos 7; tapas from €1.70, raciones €7-18; ⌚noon-4pm & 8pm-midnight Mon-Sat) For an authentic tapas experience, make a beeline for this long-standing favourite, on the go since 1870. Shelves of ancient wine bottles and walls plastered with lottery tickets and ancient maps set the scene while well-practised waiters work the bar, dishing out classical tapas prepared at the tiny cooking station. Arrive early or expect crowds.

**★Jovellanos 16** TAPAS €€
(☎660 547354; www.facebook.com/jovellanos16; Calle Jovellanos 16; tapas €1.80, raciones €10-18; ⌚12.30-4.30pm & 8pm-midnight Tue-Sat, 12.30-4.30pm Sun) Wtth friendly service and a prime people-watching location opposite Plaza Constitución, Jovellanos 16 is a rising star on Almería's 'tapas row'. Don't miss their *hamburguesa Jovellanos* (a scrumptious mini-burger with bacon, cheese and tomato on a crunchy roll) or the *secreto ibérico con ajo verde* (pork with garlicky green sauce), both served with crispy, perfectly salted fried potatoes.

**Casa Joaquín** SEAFOOD €€€
(☎950 26 43 59; Calle Real 111; raciones €12-30; ⌚noon-3.30pm & 9-11pm Mon-Fri, noon-3.30pm Sat) Fresh seafood is the draw at this historical Almería bodega, classically attired with hanging hams and rustic clutter. What's on offer depends on the day's catch but regular crowd-pleasers include juicy *gambas rojas* (red prawns) cooked *a la plancha* (grilled on a hotplate), and fried *calamares* (squid).

## Drinking & Entertainment

**La Cueva** PUB
(☎950 08 25 21; www.lacueva-almeria.com; Calle Canónigo Molina Alonso 23; ⌚4pm-4am) Craft beer goes hand-in-hand with jam sessions and live music at this laid-back pub. The subdued lighting and walls plastered with posters and concert flyers create an intimate vibe for everything from blues and rock to punk, rap and heavy metal. Gigs typically cost between €3 and €7.

LOCAL KNOWLEDGE

## THE OLD MEDINA

Sprawled at the foot of the Alcazaba (p763), the maze-like Almedina is one of Almería's most atmospheric neighbourhoods. This was the area occupied by the original Almería – a walled medina (city), bounded by the Alcazaba to the north, the sea to the south, and what are now Calle de la Reina and Avenida del Mar to the east and west. At its heart was the city's main mosque – whose *mihrab* (a prayer niche indicating the direction of Mecca) survives inside the **Iglesia de San Juan** (Calle General Luque; ⊙open for Mass 8pm Apr-Sep, 7pm Oct-Mar, closed Tue & Fri) FREE – with the commercial area of markets and warehouses spread around it. Calle de la Almedina still traces the line of the old main street running diagonally across the medina.

An excellent place for refreshment is Tetería Almedina (p764), a friendly teahouse-restaurant. Also worth seeking out is the **Plaza de Pavía market** (Plaza de Pavía; ⊙9am-2pm Mon-Sat), at its liveliest on Saturdays, with stalls selling everything from cheap shoes to churros.

**Clasijazz** JAZZ
(☎640 581457; www.clasijazz.com; Calle Maestro Serrano 9; shows €3-35) Located in a bland shopping centre, Clasijazz is a thriving music club that stages four or five weekly gigs – ranging from jam sessions to jazz, flamenco, big band and classical concerts – in a clean, contemporary space. Check the website for upcoming events.

**MadChester** LIVE MUSIC
(☎661 696930; www.facebook.com/madchester club; Parque Nicolás Salmerón 9; cover €8-16; ⊙11pm-late Thu-Sat, 6-11pm Sun) This club venue hosts Spanish and international DJs and regular gigs by bands playing indie, rock and electronica.

## ℹ Information

**Oficina Municipal de Turismo** (☎950 21 05 38; www.turismodealmeria.org; Paseo de Almería 12; ⊙9am-2pm & 4-7pm Mon-Fri, 10am-2pm & 4-7pm Sat, 10am-2pm Sun Sep-Jun, 10am-2pm & 5-8pm Jul & Aug) Helpful English-speaking staff can provide maps and city information.

## ℹ Getting There & Around

### AIR

Almería's small **airport** (☎913 21 10 00; www.aena.es) is 9km east of the city centre. **EasyJet** (☎902 59 99 00; www.easyjet.com) and **Ryanair** (www.ryanair.com) fly direct to/from various English airports; Ryanair also flies from Dublin, Milan and Brussels. **Iberia** (☎901 11 15 00; www.iberia.com) and **Vueling** (☎902 80 80 05; www.vueling.com) serve Spanish destinations.

**Surbus** (☎950 17 00 50; www.surbusalmeria.es) city bus 30 (€1.05, 35 minutes) runs from the airport to the city centre every 25 to 35 minutes (less frequently on Sunday), stopping at the main Estación Intermodal, among other places. Services run between 7.15am and 11pm daily.

### BOAT

**Trasmediterránea** (☎902 45 46 45; www.trasmediterranea.es) sails from Almería's **passenger port** (☎950 23 68 20; www.apalmeria.com) to the North African ports of Melilla (from €38, 5½ to eight hours) and Nador, Morocco (from €45, seven hours) at least once daily, and to the Algerian cities of Ghazaouet (€90, eight hours) and Orán (€90, nine hours) at least once weekly.

### BUS

Buses and trains share the **Estación Intermodal** (☎950 17 36 02; Plaza de la Estación), just east of the centre. **Bus Bam** (☎902 22 72 72; www.busbam.com) runs eight daily buses to/from Madrid (€30, 6¼ to 7¼ hours). Most other intercity services are operated by ALSA (p769).

| Destination | Cost (€) | Time (hr) | Frequency (daily) |
|---|---|---|---|
| Córdoba | 30 | 5 | 1 |
| Granada | 15–18 | 2–4¾ | 9 |
| Guadix | 10 | 1½–2 | 3 |
| Jaén | 20–24 | 3–5¼ | 6 |
| Málaga | 19–23 | 2½–5½ | 8 |
| Murcia | 14 | 2¾–4 | 8 |
| Seville | 38–47 | 5½–8½ | 5 |

### TRAIN

From the Estación Intermodal, there are trains to Granada (€21, three hours, four daily), Seville (€43, seven hours, four daily) and Madrid (€25 to €85, 6¾ to 7¾ hours, three daily). Note that at the time of research, Renfe was providing train passengers with alternate bus transport on the segments between Almería and Huércal-Viator and between Granada and Osuna due to ongoing track improvement work.

## Desierto de Tabernas

Travel 30km north of Almería and you enter another world. The Desierto de Tabernas (Tabernas desert) is a strange and haunting place, a vast, sun-baked scrubland of shimmering, dun-coloured hills scattered with tufts of tussocky brush. In the 1960s the area was used as a film location for Sergio Leone's famous spaghetti westerns (*A Fistful of Dollars; For a Few Dollars More; The Good, the Bad and the Ugly;* and *Once Upon a Time in the West*), and still today film-makers come to shoot within its rugged badlands. Many of its 'Western' sets have now been incorporated into Wild West theme parks, which make for a fun family day out. The main town in the area is Tabernas, on the N340A road.

### Sights & Activities

**Fort Bravo** AMUSEMENT PARK

(Texas Hollywood; ☎902 07 08 14; www.fortbravo.org; Carretera N340A, Km 468; adult/child €19.40/9.90; ⏲9am-7.30pm Mar-Sep, to 6pm Oct-Feb; 🅿) Situated in the desert outside Tabernas, this popular Wild West theme park has a certain dusty charm with its movie sets – which are still used for filming – and daily cowboy and can-can shows. There's a pool (in summer only), buggy rides and horse treks; plus you can stay overnight in a log cabin. The park is 1km off the N340A, signposted 31km from Almería.

**Oasys Mini Hollywood** AMUSEMENT PARK

(☎950 36 52 36; www.oasysparquetematico.com; Carretera N340A, Km 464; adult/child €22.90/13.60; ⏲10am-7.30pm Jun & Sep, to 9pm Jul & Aug, to 6pm Oct-May, closed Mon-Fri Nov-mid-Apr; 🅿) Tabernas' best known and most expensive Wild West park provides good family entertainment. The set itself is in decent condition, and the well-kept zoo has some 800 animals, including lions, giraffes, tigers and hippos. Children usually enjoy the 20-minute shoot-outs, while adults may prefer the clichéd can-can show (or at least the beer) in the saloon. There are also two summer pools, restaurants and cafes. Take sunscreen and a hat: there's little shade.

**Malcaminos** TOURS

(☎652 022582; www.malcaminos.com; Avenida de las Angustias, Tabernas) Malcaminos' enthusiastic local guides offer tours of Tabernas' cinematic landscape – not just its filmic geography but also its history and geology. Packages include a two-hour 4WD tour (€30) of the area's movie locations. Groups meet at the Bar Portichuelo, across from Tabernas' tourist office.

## Parque Natural de Cabo de Gata-Níjar

Extending southeast of Almería, the Parque Natural de Cabo de Gata-Níjar has some of Spain's most flawless and least crowded beaches. The park, which stretches from Retamar in the west up to Agua Amarga in the east, encompasses 340 sq km of dramatic cliff-bound coastline and stark semidesert terrain punctuated by remote white villages and isolated farmsteads. Adding to the often eerie atmosphere are the abandoned mines and bizarre rock formations that litter the landscape.

There is plenty to do in the area besides enjoying the beaches and walking: diving, snorkelling, kayaking, sailing, cycling, horse riding, and 4WD and boat tours are all popular. A host of operators offers these activities from the coastal villages during Easter and from July to September; a few carry on year-round. The park's main hub is **San José**, a popular resort on the east coast.

### Sights

**Faro de Cabo de Gata** LIGHTHOUSE

Marking the southwest point of the promontory, this photogenic lighthouse commands stirring views of a jagged volcanic reef known as the **Arrecife de las Sirenas** (Reef of the Mermaids), after the monk seals that used to lounge here. From the site, a side road runs 3km up to the **Torre Vigía Vela Blanca**, an 18th-century watchtower boasting even more coastal vistas.

**Mirador de la Amatista** VIEWPOINT

(🅿) On the main road between La Isleta del Moro and Rodalquilar, this high viewpoint commands breathtaking views of the vertiginous, unspoilt coastline. From here the road snakes down into the basin of the Rodalquilar valley.

## Cabo de Gata

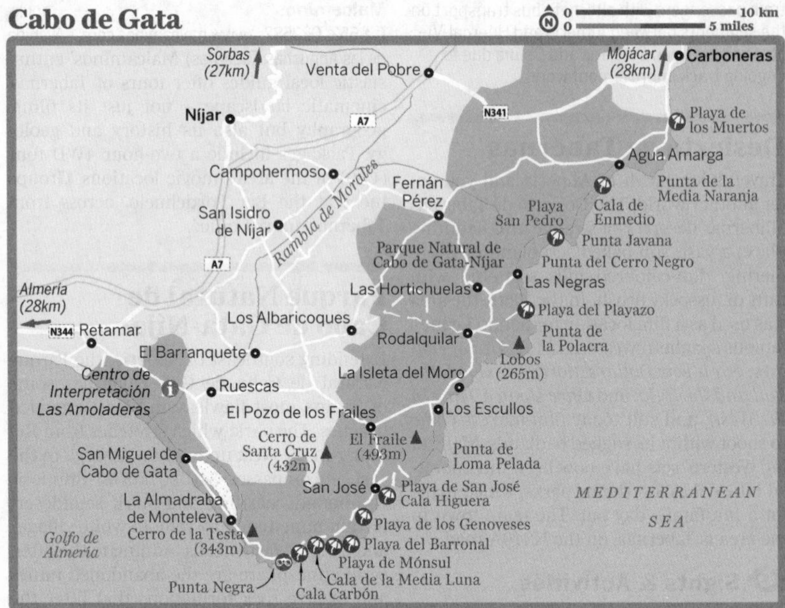


**Gold Mines** RUINS

(P) Set amid the Martian red-rock terrain at the top of the village, the skeletal remains of Rodalquilar's gold mines are an eerie sight. The complex, which was fully operational as recently as the mid-20th century, lies abandoned – and you're free to explore its former crushing towers and decantation tanks.

**Jardín Botánico El Albardinal** GARDENS

(☎671 561226; Calle Fundición; ⏰10am-1pm & 6-8.30pm Tue-Sun Jun-Aug, 9am-2pm Tue-Fri, 10am-2pm & 4-6pm Sat & Sun Sep-May; P) FREE Rodalquilar's extensive botanical gardens showcase the vegetation of Andalucía's arid southeast. It's well planned, with every plant, tree and shrub identified. There's also a charming *huerta* (vegetable garden), complete with jam recipes and a scarecrow.

### Tours

**El Cabo a Fondo** BOATING

(☎637 449170; www.elcaboafondo.es; 1½hr tour adult/child €25/20) Some of the most spectacular views of the Cabo de Gata coast are from the sea – a perspective you'll get on Cabo a Fondo's outings, which start from La Isleta del Moro, Las Negras or La Fabriquilla. Tours run up to seven times daily and are offered year-round, weather permitting (minimum numbers may be needed in low season). Reservations required.

### Sleeping

**El Jardín de los Sueños** CASA RURAL €€

(☎950 38 98 43, 669 184118; www.eljardindelossuenos.es; Calle Los Gorriones; incl breakfast s €65-85, d €80-118, ste €110-150; P❄📶🏊) Just outside Rodalquilar, signposted off the main road, this year-round retreat is ideal for getting away from it all. The main farmhouse is surrounded by a beautiful garden of dry-climate plants and fruit trees, some of which contribute to the substantial breakfasts.

★**Oro y Luz** RESORT €€

(☎722 789973; www.oroyluz.com; Paraje Los Albacetes; ste €89-177; 📶) Backed by olive trees, palms and Cabo de Gato's rugged coastal landscape, this whitewashed villa near the turnoff for beautiful Playa del Playazo offers seven stand-alone suites with private entrances and terraces. The welcoming new Italian owners have added a dose of designer flair, and the on-site restaurant is one of the province's best.

**Hostal El Dorado** HOSTAL €€

(☎950 38 01 18; www.hostaleldorado.es; Camino del Aguamarina; d €55-95; ❄📶🏊) Perched on a hillside about 500m inland from San José's waterfront, El Dorado offers an appealing combination of affordable rates and fine sea views. There's nothing fancy about the 27 rooms, but most face the Mediterranean, and all come with balconies or terraces. A rooftop swimming pool sweetens the deal.

★**MiKasa** BOUTIQUE HOTEL €€€
(☎950 13 80 73; www.mikasasuites.com; Carretera Carboneras 20; d incl breakfast €160-300; P ❄ ☎ ≋) In the heart of Agua Amarga village, MiKasa is an enchanting romantic retreat. A few blocks back from the beach (but still within easy walking distance), it's a lovely villa set up with charming, individually styled rooms, two pools, a jacuzzi, a spa, a well-stocked honesty bar and a variety of comfy common areas. Room rates drop considerably outside August.

## Eating

★**Oro y Luz** ANDALUCIAN €€
(☎950 80 88 19; www.oroyluz.com; Paraje Los Albacetes; mains €14-24; ⊙1.30-4pm Mon, 1.30-4pm & 8-10.30pm Wed-Sun) This smart restaurant impresses with its modern regional cuisine. and terrace views over the olive trees. Seafood, such as marinated squid and lightly seared tuna *tataki* seasoned with vinegar and ginger, stars on the menu, complemented by a series of rich meaty mains. Expect artistic presentation – smoked sardine appetisers dangling from a miniature clothesline – along with friendly service and exquisite flavours.

**Casa Miguel** SPANISH €€
(☎950 38 03 29; www.casamiguelentierradecine.es; Avenida de San José 43; mains €9-26; ⊙1-4.30pm & 7.30-11.30pm Tue-Sun) Service and food are reliably good at this long-standing San José favourite, one of several places with outdoor seating on the main drag. There's plenty to choose from on the extensive menu but you'll rarely go wrong ordering the grilled fish of the day.

★**4 Nudos** SEAFOOD €€€
(☎620 938160; www.4nudosrestaurante.com; Club Náutico, Puerto Deportivo; mains €16-25; ⊙1.30-4pm & 8-11pm Tue-Sun Mar-Oct, 1.30-4pm Tue-Sun Nov-Feb) Of San José's various seafood restaurants, the 'Four Knots' is the star performer. Aptly housed in the Club Náutico at the marina, it serves classic Spanish dishes – paella included – alongside more innovative creations such as baby-prawn ceviche and tuna marinated in soy sauce, ginger and rosemary.

★**La Gallineta** FUSION €€€
(☎950 38 05 01; Carretera Nijar-San José, El Pozo de los Frailes; mains €15-30; ⊙1.30-3.30pm & 9-11pm) An elegant restaurant in El Pozo do los Frailes village, 4km north of San José, La Gallineta is a hit with city escapees who make the drive out for its innovative, outward-looking cuisine. Menu highlights include tuna with Cambodian spices and carpaccio of red prawns with citrus and mango.

## Information

**Centro de Información** (☎950 38 02 99; www.cabodegata-nijar.com; Avenida San José 27; ⊙10am-2pm & 6-9pm Apr-Oct, 10am-2pm & 4.30-6pm Nov-Mar) Park information centre in San José.

**Centro de Interpretación Las Amoladeras** (☎950 16 04 35; Carretera Retamar-Pujaire, Km 7; ⊙10am-2pm daily Jul-Sep, hours vary rest of year) The park's main visitor centre, 2km west of Ruescas on the main road from Almería.

## Getting There & Away

**ALSA** (☎902 42 22 42; www.ALSA.es) runs one daily bus from Almería's Estación Intermodal to Las Negras (€2.95, 1¼ hours) and Rodalquilar (€2.95, 1½ hours).

**Autocares Bernardo** (☎950 25 04 22; www.autocaresbernardo.com) operates buses from Almería to San José (€2.95, 1¼ hours, two to four daily).

WORTH A TRIP

### CUEVAS DE SORBAS

The rare and spectacular **Cuevas de Sorbas** (☎950 36 47 04; www.cuevasdesorbas.com; basic tour adult/child €15/10.50; ⊙tours 11am, 1pm & 4pm Oct-May, 10am-8pm Jun-Sep; P) are part of a vast network of underground galleries and tunnels. Guided visits lead through the labyrinthine underworld, revealing glittering gypsum crystals, tranquil ponds, stalactites, stalagmites and dark, mysterious tunnels. The basic tour, suitable for everyone from children to seniors, lasts about 1½ hours. Tours need to be reserved at least one day ahead; English- and German-speaking guides are available. The caves are 2km east of Sorbas.

DON'T MISS

## CABO DE GATA BEACHES

Cabo de Gata's best beaches are strung along the south and east coasts. Some of the most beautiful lie southwest of San José, reached by a dirt road signposted 'Playas' and/or 'Genoveses/Mónsul'. Note that from mid-June to mid-September, the road is closed to cars once the beach car parks (€5) fill up, typically by about 10am, but a bus (€1 one way) runs from town every half hour from 9am to 9pm.

The first beach outside of San José is **Playa de los Genoveses** (P), a 1km stretch of sand where the Genoese navy landed in 1147 to help the Christian attack on Almería. A further 2.5km on, pristine **Playa de Mónsul** (P) is another glorious spot – you may recognise the large free-standing rock on the sand from the film *Indiana Jones and the Last Crusade*. Tracks behind the large dune at Mónsul's east end lead down to nudist **Playa del Barronal**, 600m from the road. If you bear left just before Barronal and work your way over a little pass just left of the highest hillock, you'll come to **El Lance del Perro**. This beach, with striking basalt rock formations, is the first of four gorgeous, isolated beaches called the **Calas del Barronal**. Tides permitting, you can walk round the foot of the cliffs from one to the next. A little west of Playa de Mónsul, paths lead from the road to two other less-frequented beaches, **Cala de la Media Luna** and **Cala Carbón**.

San José has a busy sandy beach of its own, and to the northeast there are reasonable beaches at **Los Escullos** and **La Isleta del Moro**. Much finer is **Playa del Playazo** (P), a broad, sandy strip between two headlands 3.5km east of Rodalquilar (the last 2km along a drivable track from the main road) or 2.5km south of Las Negras via a coastal footpath. With its own part-sandy, part-stony beach, **Las Negras** is also a gateway to the fabulous **Playa San Pedro**, 3km to the northeast. Set between dramatic headlands and home to a small New Age settlement, this fabled beach can be reached only on foot or by boat (€12 return) from Las Negras.

Further up the coast, the small resort of **Agua Amarga** is fronted by a popular sandy beach. A short but steep 1.5km trek to the southwest leads to **Cala de Enmedio**, a pretty, secluded beach enclosed between eroded rocks.

# Mojácar

POP 6403

Both a massively popular beach resort and a charming hill town, Mojácar is divided into two quite separate parts. Mojácar Pueblo is the attractive historical centre, a picturesque jumble of white-cube houses daubed down an inland hilltop. Some 3km away on the coast, Mojácar Playa is its young offspring, a modern low-rise resort fronting a 7km-long sandy beach.

As recently as the 1960s, Mojácar was decaying and almost abandoned. But a savvy mayor managed to resurrect its fortunes by luring artists and travellers to the area with offers of free land – which brought a distinct bohemian air that endures to this day.

## Sights

The main sight is Mojácar's hilltop *pueblo,* with its whitewashed houses, charming plazas, bars and cafes centred on the fortress-like Iglesia de Santa María. Beach lovers should head down to Mojácar Playa, which boasts 7km of mainly sandy beach. To reach the *pueblo* from the *playa* turn inland at the roundabout by the Parque Comercial, a large shopping centre towards the north end of the beach. Regular buses also connect the two.

**Mirador del Castillo** VIEWPOINT

(Plaza Mirador del Castillo, Mojácar Pueblo) Perched on the highest point in town – originally the site of a castle – this hilltop *mirador* (viewpoint) looks down to the sea and over a hazy brown-green landscape studded with white buildings and stark volcanic cones just like the one Mojácar occupies.

**Casa La Canana** HOUSE

(950 16 44 20; Calle Esteve 6, Mojácar Pueblo; adult/child €2.50/1; 10.30am-2.30pm daily, plus 5-8pm Tue, Wed, Fri & Sat) Beautifully maintained and thoughtfully interpreted by the owners (who live upstairs), this house-museum re-creates a well-to-do villager's dwelling from the first half of the 20th century. Much

of the interior decor – including furniture, tiles, bedspreads, fireplaces and everyday household items – is original to the house, while bilingual information panels, photos, tools and model animals illustrate the lifestyle of the time.

**Fuente Pública** FOUNTAIN
(Public Fountain; Calle La Fuente, Mojácar Pueblo) Hidden near the foot of the hilltop *pueblo*, this historical fountain is a village landmark. Locals and visitors come to fill containers with the water that pours out of 13 spouts into marble troughs and tinkles along a courtyard below colourful plants. A plaque states that in 1488 this was where the envoy of the Reyes Católicos (the Catholic Monarchs Fernando and Isabel) met Mojácar's last Moorish mayor, Alavez, to negotiate the village's surrender.

## Sleeping & Eating

★**Hostal El Olivar** HOSTAL €
(950 47 20 02; www.hostalelolivar.es; Calle Estación Nueva 11, Mojácar Pueblo; d incl breakfast €53-70; ) Friendly owners Alberto and Michaela have completely revamped this stylish boutiquey *hostal*, with new paint, curtains, bedspreads, mini-fridges, handmade furniture and a massage room. Three rooms have balconies, and there's a delightful sun terrace for lounging or lingering over breakfast.

★**Hostal Arco Plaza** HOSTAL €
(647 846275, 950 47 27 77; www.hostalarcoplaza.es; Calle Aire 1, Mojácar Pueblo; s €30, d €39-45, tr €45-50; ) Right in the heart of the action, this friendly, excellent-value *hostal* has attractive sky-blue rooms with wrought-iron beds and terracotta-tiled floors. The best have private balconies overlooking Plaza Nueva, though you can enjoy the same views from the communal rooftop terrace.

**Tito's Cantina** MEXICAN €
(950 47 88 41; www.facebook.com/lacantina.mojacar; Paseo del Mediterráneo, Mojácar Playa; mains €8-14; 7pm-midnight Apr-Oct; ) Founder and local legend Tito has passed away, but his legacy lives on at this festive cane-canopied cantina under the palms along Mojácar's beachfront. Expect all the old favourites – enchiladas, quesadillas, fajitas, tacos and guacamole – plus enough tequila and Mexican beer to ensure a grand old time.

**Viento Norte** BASQUE €€
(www.vientonorte.es; Plaza Frontón 2; mains €10-18; noon-4pm & 8pm-midnight Jul & Aug, shorter hours rest of year; ) Bringing a touch of Spain's Basque Country to the Andalucian coast, the 'North Wind' entices with red-and-white checked tablecloths and a blackboard menu that runs the gamut from grilled octopus to *txistorra* (garlicky Basque sausage).

**La Taberna** ANDALUCIAN €€
(950 61 51 06; Plaza del Caño, Mojácar Pueblo; raciones €7-16; noon-4pm & 6pm-midnight, closed Wed Sep-Jun) A Mojácar mainstay since 1982, this traditional tapas bar sits smack in the heart of the whitewashed centre. Its cosy warren of rooms, decked out with tiles, wood panelling and beamed ceilings, is often full of chattering diners enjoying its extensive selection of tapas and *raciones*.

## Information

**Oficina Municipal de Turismo** (950 61 50 25; www.mojacar.es; Plaza Frontón, Mojácar Pueblo; 9.30am-2pm & 4.30-7pm Mon-Fri, 10am-2pm & 4.30-7pm Sat, 10am-2pm Sun) Up in Mojàcar's hilltop *pueblo*.

**Tourist Information Point** (www.mojacar.es; Playa Villazar, Mojácar Playa; 10am-2pm daily & 4.30-7pm Mon-Sat) Down on the beach in front of the Parque Comercial (shopping centre).

## Getting There & Away

Intercity buses stop at various spots around the Parque Comercial roundabout in Mojácar Playa and on Avenida de Andalucía in Mojácar Pueblo. ALSA runs buses to/from Almería (€7.90, 1¼ to 1¾ hours, two to four daily) and Murcia (€9.25, 2½ to three hours, two daily). Buy tickets at **Mojácar Tour** (950 47 57 57; www.viajesmojacar.grupoairmet.com; Centro Comercial Montemar, Avenida de Andalucía, Mojácar Playa; 10am-1.30pm & 5.30-8pm), a travel agency at the Parque Comercial in Mojácar Playa.

A local bus (€1.20) runs a circuit from **Mojácar Pueblo** along the full length of the beach and back again, roughly every half-hour from 9.15am to 11.35pm June to September, and until 9.15pm from October to May.

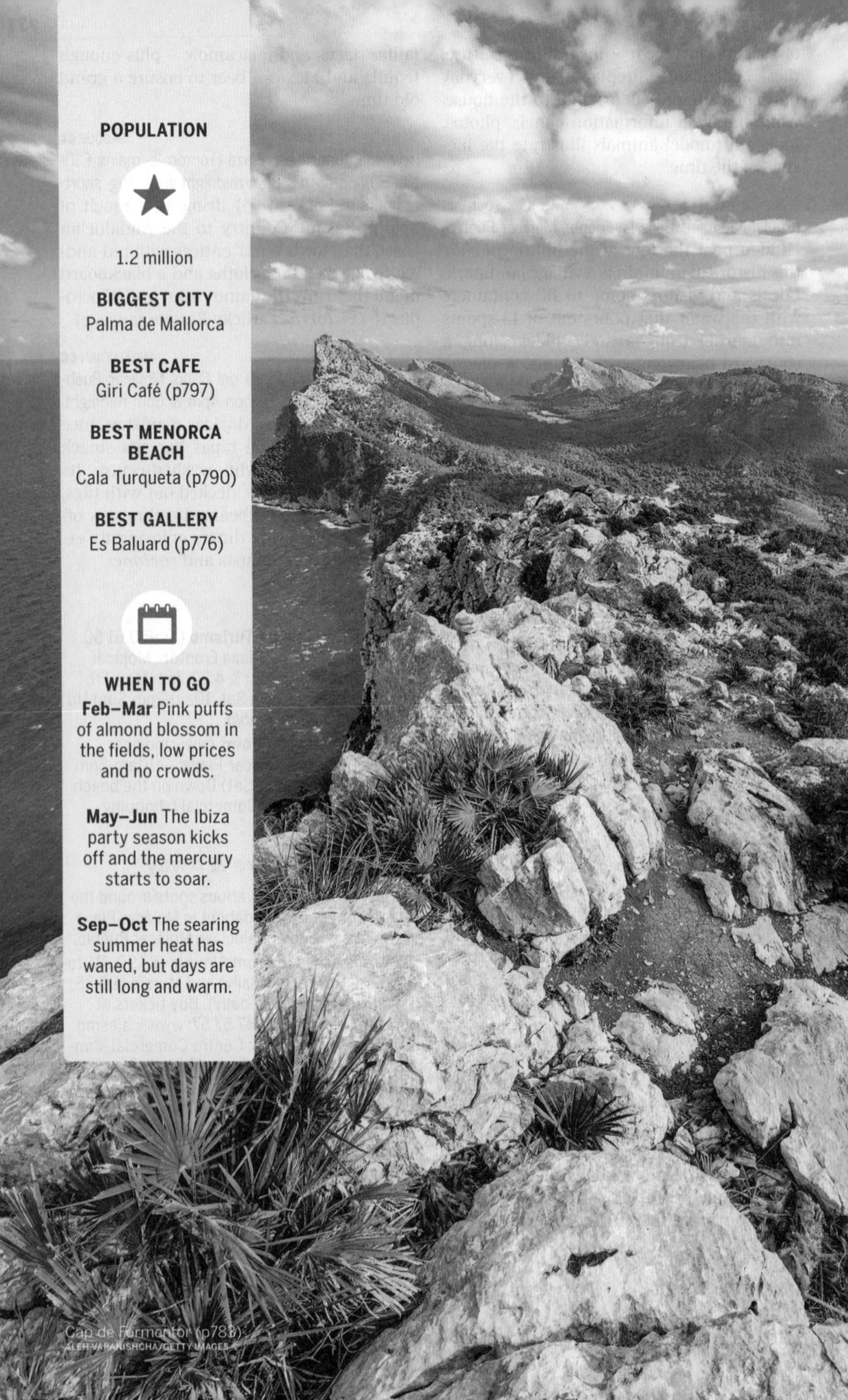

**POPULATION**

1.2 million

**BIGGEST CITY**
Palma de Mallorca

**BEST CAFE**
Giri Café (p797)

**BEST MENORCA BEACH**
Cala Turqueta (p790)

**BEST GALLERY**
Es Baluard (p776)

**WHEN TO GO**

**Feb–Mar** Pink puffs of almond blossom in the fields, low prices and no crowds.

**May–Jun** The Ibiza party season kicks off and the mercury starts to soar.

**Sep–Oct** The searing summer heat has waned, but days are still long and warm.

Cap de Formentor (p783)
ALEH VARANISHCHA/GETTY IMAGES ©

# Balearic Islands

Etymologists may wrangle over the origins of their name, but there's no disputing the seductive magic of the Balearic Islands, clustered in the west Mediterranean. Sharing a deep Catalan identity, each of the four principal islands – Mallorca, Menorca, Ibiza and Formentera – has a shoreline strewn with soft-sand beaches and hidden coves, overlooking some of the most azure waters on the planet. From corkscrewing, precipitous mountain roads to somnolent, sun-baked villages in the valleys and shimmering plains, glorious travel opportunities await the visitor. There's plenty for you here whether you're packing hiking boots, dancing shoes or both. Ibiza's party-hard spirit draws masses of exuberant young people in summer, while a glut of hiking trails wind through the islands' woods of holm oak and Aleppo pine, gnarled olive and almond, and past valleys of citrus fruit, dry stone walls, and the soft tinkling of goat-bells. And the night skies must be seen to be believed.

## INCLUDES

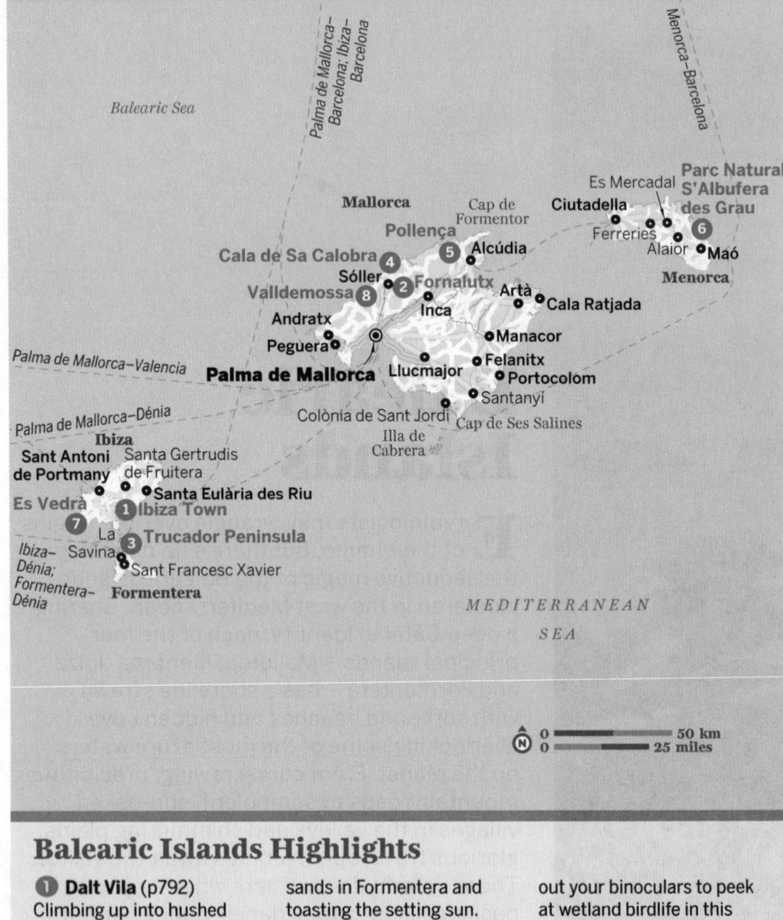


## Balearic Islands Highlights

1 **Dalt Vila** (p792) Climbing up into hushed and delightful lanes and immersing yourself in historical charm in Ibiza Town.

2 **Fornalutx** (p782)Delving into the tidy stone alleyways and nooks of this supremely picturesque Mallorca mountain village.

3 **Trucador Peninsula** (p798) Lounging on silky sands in Formentera and toasting the setting sun.

4 **Cala de Sa Calobra** (p783) Twisting your way down the hairpin bends to Sa Calobra and Cala Tuent.

5 **Pollença** (p785) Exploring the medieval streets of this ancient pilgrimage town in Mallorca.

6 **Parc Natural S'Albufera des Grau** (p788) Fishing out your binoculars to peek at wetland birdlife in this Menorca biosphere reserve.

7 **Es Vedrà** (p795) Gazing out to the sublime form of this islet poking sharply off the Ibiza coast.

8 **Valldemossa** (p780) Wandering through the cobblestone streets of this gorgeous town in Mallorca's Serra de Tramuntana.

## History

The Balearic Islands were first settled around 5000 BCE. The Phoenicians were quick to occupy the archipelago, but after the fall of Carthage, the islands were invaded by the Romans in 123 BCE, followed by the Vandals who overran the Balearics in the 5th century. Growing Moorish control of the islands was completed in 902, leaving a profound mark on their character and heritage. Moorish control ended with the Reconquista, led by King James I of Aragón (Jaume el

Conqueridor), who took Palma de Mallorca in 1229, then invaded Ibiza and Menorca, establishing Catalan supremacy over the islands.

Short-lived prosperity was followed by decline as the Balearics endured pirate raids. Mallorca and Ibiza were occupied by the Bourbon Monarchy in 1715, while Menorca (along with Gibraltar) was handed over to the British in 1713 under the provisions of the Treaty of Utrecht; British rule of Menorca ended in 1802.

The economies of all the islands today are heavily based on tourism, which has been a mixed blessing: bringing great wealth, but at the cost of over-tourism and the rampant development of resorts along the coastline.

WORTH A TRIP

### CALA PI

Located 45km from Palma on the southeast coast and accessed via a steep staircase (follow the signs along Cami de la Cala Pi), this beach is only 50m wide but is a beauty, stretching more than 100m inland and flanked on either side by craggy cliffs that ensure startlingly turquoise water in the inlet as still as bath water. There are no facilities at beach level – just rows of boathouses – so bring any provisions you're likely to need. Bus 525 links Cala Pi and Palma once in the morning and once in the evening (€5.75, 70 minutes).

# MALLORCA

POP 896,000

For Miró it was the pure Mediterranean light. For hikers and cyclists it is the Serra de Tramuntana's formidable limestone spires. For others, it is as fleeting as the almond blossom snowing on meadows in spring, the interior's vineyards in their autumn mantle of gold or the embarrassment of idyllic beaches. Wherever your journey takes you, Mallorca never fails to seduce. Cars conga along the coast in single file for views so enticing the resort postcards resemble cheap knock-offs. Even among the tourist swarms of mid-August you can find pockets of tranquillity – trek to hilltop monasteries, pedal through honey-stone villages, sit under a night sky and engrave Mallorca's lyrical landscapes onto your memory.

## Information

The **provincial tourist office** (☎971 17 39 90; www.infomallorca.net; Plaça de la Reina 2, Palma de Mallorca; ⏰8.30am-8pm Mon-Fri, to 3pm Sat; 📶) can help with information about the island, as well as provide maps. The **Airport Tourist Office** (☎971 78 95 56; www.visitpalma.com; Aeroport de Palma; ⏰8am-8pm Mon-Sat, to 2pm Sun) has a lot of useful information about the city.

## Getting There & Away

Most visitors to Mallorca fly into Palma's international airport, though it's possible to arrive by ferry from points along the Spanish coast (Barcelona, Dénia and Valencia). The neighbouring islands of Ibiza and Menorca are also linked to Mallorca by air and ferry.

### AIR

Palma de Mallorca Airport (p779) is 8km east of Palma de Mallorca. In summer especially, masses of charter and regular flights form an air bridge to Palma from around Europe, among them many low-cost airlines. Departure tax is included in the price of a ticket.

### SEA

Ferry services connect Mallorca to the Spanish mainland and to Menorca, Ibiza and Formentera. Most services operate only from Easter to late October, and those that continue into the winter reduce their departure times. Most ferry companies allow you to transport vehicles on longer routes and have car holds (advance bookings are essential). Check routes and compare prices at Direct Ferries (www.directferries.com).

Ferry companies that operate to and from Mallorca include the following:

**Trasmediterránea** (☎902 454 645; www.trasmediterranea.es)

**Baleària** (☎902 160180; www.balearia.com)

## Getting Around

**Bus** The island's buses cover major towns and many villages. You'll be limited to a handful of services in the low season, while some services (for instance those to beaches) stop entirely.

**Car** Great for exploring the island's more remote beaches, hill towns and mountains. Cars can be hired in every town or resort.

**Train** Modestly priced and fairly frequent. There's one heritage line to Sóller in the west, and three passing through the centre to Sa Pobla, Inca and Manacor.

### BUS ROUTES

The island is roughly divided into five bus zones radiating from Palma. Bus line numbers in the

100s cover the southwest, the 200s the west (as far as Sóller), the 300s the north and much of the centre, the 400s a wedge of the centre and east coast and the 500s the south. These services are run by a phalanx of small bus companies, but you can get route and timetable information for all by contacting **Transport de les Illes Balears** (TIB; ☎971 17 77 77; www.tib.org).

## Palma de Mallorca

Palma is a stunner. Rising in honey-coloured stone from the broad waters of the Badia de Palma, this enduring city's history encompasses the 13th-century Christian reconquest of the island, and the Moors, Romans and Talayotic people before that. A richly studded diadem of historical sites, Palma also shelters a seemingly endless array of galleries, restaurants, craft studios and bars.

### Sights

**★Catedral de Mallorca** CATHEDRAL
(La Seu; www.catedraldemallorca.org; Plaça del Almoina; €8, incl roof terraces €12; ⏲10am-6.15pm Mon-Fri Jun-Sep, to 5.15pm Apr, May & Oct, to 3.15pm Nov-Mar, 10am-2.15pm Sat year-round, terraces 10am, 11am, noon, 4pm, 5pm & 6pm) Palma's vast cathedral ('La Seu' in Catalan) is the city's major architectural landmark. Aside from its sheer scale, treasures and undoubted beauty, its stunning interior features, designed by Antoni Gaudí and renowned contemporary artist Miquel Barceló, make this unlike any cathedral elsewhere in the world. The awesome structure is predominantly Gothic, apart from the main facade, which is startling, quite beautiful and completely mongrel. The stunning rose window is the largest in Europe, see it up close by visiting the roof terraces.

**★Es Baluard** GALLERY
(Museu d'Art Modern i Contemporani; ☎971 90 82 00; www.esbaluard.org; Plaça de Porta de Santa Catalina 10; adult/child €6/free; ⏲10am-8pm Tue-Sat, to 3pm Sun) Built with flair and innovation into the shell of the Renaissance-era seaward walls, this contemporary art gallery is one of the finest on the island. Its temporary exhibitions are worth viewing, but the permanent collection – works by Miró, Barceló and Picasso – gives the gallery its cachet. Anyone on a bike is charged just €2.

**★Museu Fundación Juan March** GALLERY
(☎97 171 35 15; www.march.es; Carrer de Sant Miquel 11; ⏲10am-6.30pm Mon-Fri, 10.30am-2pm Sat) FREE The 17th-century Can Gallard del Canya, a 17th-century mansion overlaid with minor Modernist touches, now houses a small but significant collection of paintings and sculptures. The permanent exhibits – some 80 pieces held by the Fundación Juan March – constitute a veritable who's who of contemporary Spanish art, including Miró, Picasso, Juan Gris, Dalí, and the sculptors Eduardo Chillida and Julio González.

**★Palau de l'Almudaina** PALACE
(https://entradas.patrimonionacional.es; Carrer del Mirador; adult/child €7/4, audio guide €3, tour €4, Wed afternoon free; ⏲10am-8pm Tue-Sun Apr-Sep, to 6pm Oct-Mar) Originally an Islamic fort, this mighty construction opposite the cathedral was converted into a residence for the Mallorcan monarchs at the end of the 13th century. The King of Spain resides here still, at least symbolically. The royal family is rarely in residence, except for the occasional ceremony, as they prefer to spend summer in the Palau Marivent (in Cala Major). At other times you can wander through a series of cavernous stone-walled rooms that have been lavishly decorated.

### Sleeping

**Hostal Pons** GUESTHOUSE €€
(☎971 72 26 58; www.hostalpons.com; Carrer del Vi 8; s/d from €45/75; 📶) Bang in the heart of old Palma, this sweet, family-run guesthouse offers 21 rooms with solid timber furniture and clean white walls. Downstairs a cat slumbers in a plant-filled patio and upstairs you'll find a book-lined lounge and a roof terrace for unwinding. Cheaper rooms share communal bathrooms.

DON'T MISS

**SÓLLER TO PORT DE SÓLLER TRAM**

A real blast from the past, Sóller's old-world, open-sided (and expensive) tooting **trams** (Tranvías; one way €7; ⏲every 30 or 60min 8am-8.30pm) trundle 2km down to Port de Sóller on the coast. They depart from outside the train station in Sóller but also stop at the northwest corner of Plaça de la Constitució on the way to the Port; pick up a timetable from the tourist office. The train journey (p779) from Palma to Sóller is also a highlight.

## Palma de Mallorca

## Palma de Mallorca

**Top Sights**
1 Catedral de Mallorca ........ C3
2 Es Baluard ........ A2
3 Museu Fundación Juan March ........ D1
4 Palau de l'Almudaina ........ C3

**Sights**
5 Església de Santa Eulàlia ........ D2
6 Jardí del Bisbe ........ C3

**Activities, Courses & Tours**
7 Palma on Bike ........ B3

**Sleeping**
8 Hostal Pons ........ B2
9 Hotel Tres ........ B2

**Eating**
10 Ca'n Joan de S'Aigo ........ D2
11 El Camino ........ C1
12 Fornet de la Soca ........ D1

**Drinking & Nightlife**
13 Atlantico Café ........ B2
14 Lórien ........ C1

★**Hotel Tres** BOUTIQUE HOTEL €€€
(☎971 71 73 33; www.hoteltres.com; Carrer dels Apuntadors 3; s €252, d €280-315, ste €345; ) Hotel Tres swings joyously between 16th-century town palace and fresh-faced Scandinavian design. Centred on a courtyard with a single palm, the rooms are cool and minimalist, with cowhide benches, anatomy-inspired prints, and nice details such as rollaway desks and Durance aromatherapy cosmetics. Head up to the roof terrace at sunset for a steam and dip as the cathedral begins to twinkle. If you want a terrace, request room 101, 201 or 206. Young, friendly staff amp up the feel-good factor.

## Eating

★**Fornet de la Soca** BAKERY €
(Forn des Teatre; ☎673 499446; www.fornetdelasoca.com; Plaça de Weyler 9; pastries from €1.50; ⏲9am-8pm Mon-Sat) Tomeu Arbona is the master baker here. He is also the author of *Traditional Cooking in Mallorca* and is something of a culinary legend in town. Arbona describes himself as a gastronomic archaeologist, seeking out age-old recipes and reinventing them. The mouthwatering selection of cakes, pastries and savoury pies here, including vegetarian, is testimony to his dedication.

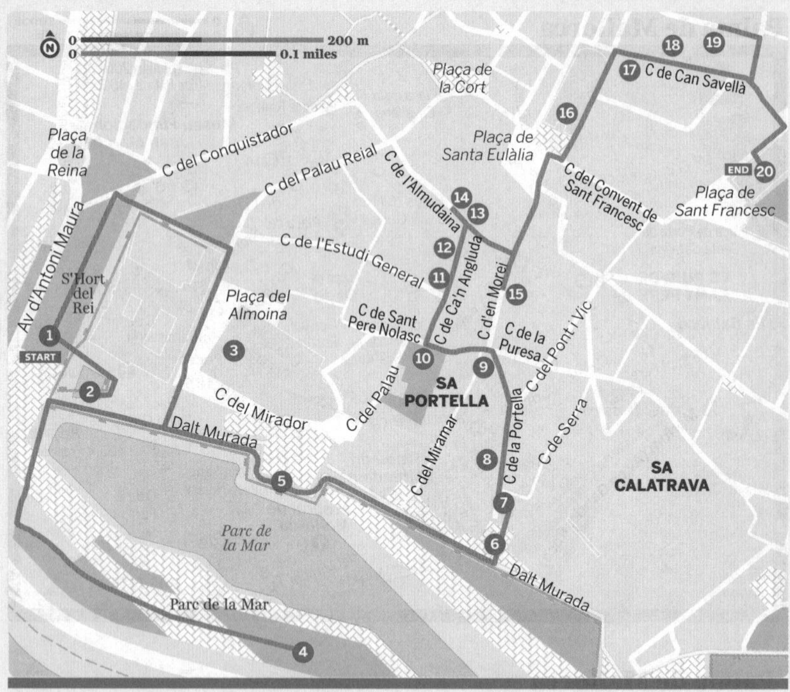


# City Walk
# Historical Palma & Hidden Patios

**START** S'HORT DEL REI
**END** BASÍLICA DE SANT FRANCESC
**LENGTH** 2.5KM; TWO TO THREE HOURS

Begin in ❶ **S'Hort del Rei** (King's Garden), where ❷ **Arc de sa Drassana** arches above a pond. Amble north to Miró's bronze sculpture ('the egg'). Climb the steps past Palau March to the immense Gothic ❸ **Catedral** (p776). Head down to ❹ **Parc de la Mar**, with its fountain-draped lake.

Soak up views along the Renaissance sea-wall, the ❺ **Dalt Murada**. Turn left at medieval gateway ❻ **Sa Portella**, noting its keystone and coat of arms. Carrer de la Portella hides many historical courtyards: 17th-century ❼ **Cal Marquès de la Torre** and 19th-century ❽ **Can Espanya-Serra**, with a neo-Gothic staircase. Swing left onto Carrer de la Puresa, pausing at ❾ **Can Salas**, one of Palma's oldest *patis* (patios), with carved pillars, a beautiful loggia and 13th-century coat of arms.

Pause in tiny ❿ **Jardí del Bisbe** (Carrer de Sant Pere Nolasc 6; ⏲7am-1.30pm Mon-Sun) FREE or continue north up Carrer de Ca'n Angluda to ⓫ **Cal Poeta Colom**, named for its one-time resident poet. Its baroque patio features fine wrought-iron and tapered columns. Further along is grand medieval manor ⓬ **Can Marquès**.

On Carrer de l'Almudaina, the medieval gateway ⓭ **Porta de l'Almudaina** was originally part of the Roman walls. Close by is ⓮ **Can Oms**, with its impressive Gothic portal. Nearby, on Carrer d'en Morei, ⓯ **Can Oleza** is a baroque patio with loggia, Ionic columns, low arches and a wrought-iron balustrade. Pass spired ⓰ **Església de Santa Eulàlia** (☎971 71 46 25; Plaça de Santa Eulàlia 2; church free, belfry vist €5; ⏲10am-6pm Mon-Sat) – climb to the rooftop if time permits – and Carrer de Can Savellà, home to Corinthian column-lined ⓱ **Can Vivot** and ⓲ **Can Catlar del Llorer**, one of Palma's oldest Gothic *patis*. Detour a street north for hot chocolate at old-school ⓳ **Ca'n Joan de S'Aigo** (☎971 71 07 59; www.canjoandesaigo.com; Carrer de Can Sanç 10; pastries €1.30-3; ⏲8am-9pm) before ending at venerable ⓴ **Basílica de Sant Francesc**.

**★Toque** INTERNATIONAL €€

(☎971 28 70 68; www.restaurante-toque.com; Carrer Federico García Lorca 6; mains €17-19, 3-course lunch menú €16.50; ⏲1-4pm & 7-11pm Tue-Sat; 👪) A father-and-son team run this individual little place with real pride and warmth. The food is Belgian-meets-Mallorcan (steak tartare with fries and salad, or suckling pig on a sweet potato puree) and has generated a loyal following among *palmeros*. Wines are well chosen and modestly priced; the three-course €16.50 lunch *menú* is a bargain.

**★El Camino** MODERN SPANISH €€

(www.elcaminopalma.es; Carrer de San Brondo 4; tapas €7-10; ⏲1-4pm & 6-10.45pm Mon-Sat; 📶) Worthy of all the hype, this new concept tapas bar is super stylish with coffered ceilings, oak panelling, mosaic tiles and a long marble bar from where you can watch your tasty bites being prepared. The dishes are classic, the execution superb: slices of moist tortilla, garlicky fried squid, blistered Padrón peppers, crispy melt-in-your-mouth croquettes. No reservations.

## Drinking & Nightlife

**★Atlantico Café** BAR

(☎971 72 62 85; www.cafeatlantico.es; Carrer de Sant Feliu 12; ⏲7pm-2.30am Mon-Thu, to 3am Fri-Sun) Spangled with an upended cornucopia of bric-a-brac, blessed with welcoming, laid-back staff and capable of cranking the merriment up to 11, this is one of Palma's most charismatic bars. Ever-expanding swaths of graffiti testify to the numberless nights of bonhomie and cocktails downed since the place opened in 1997.

**★Lórien** CRAFT BEER

(☎971 72 32 02; www.sauep.com; Carrer de les Caputxines 5; ⏲5pm-1am Tue-Fri; 📶) The helpful owner can guide you through the vast choice of craft ales on offer here, be they local, Spanish or international. It's a friendly, cosy and informal pub where recent taps have included a highly touted brown ale from Mallorca's Sa Cerviseria brewery.

## Getting There & Away

### AIR

**Palma de Mallorca Airport** (PMI; ☎902 404704; www.aena-aeropuertos.es) lies 8km east of the city and receives an impressive level of traffic. Sometimes referred to as Son Sant Joan Airport, it's Spain's third largest, with direct services to 105 European and North African cities.

### BOAT

Palma is the island's main port. There are numerous boat services to/from Mallorca from mainland Spain and the other islands of the Balearics. Palma is also becoming increasingly (and somewhat controversially) popular as a cruise liner destination.

### BUS

All island buses to/from Palma depart from (or near) the **Estació Intermodal de Palma** (☎971 17 77 77; www.tib.org; Plaça d'Espanya) . Services head in all directions, including Valldemossa (€1.90, 30 minutes, up to 17 daily), Sóller (€2.45 to €3.90, 45 minutes, regular daily), Pollença (€5.50, 45 to 60 minutes, up to 14 daily) and Alcúdia (€5.45, one hour, up to 18 daily).

### TRAIN

The **Ferrocarril de Sóller** (Sóller Railway; ☎971 75 20 51; www.trendesoller.com; Carrer Eusebio Estada 1; single/return €25/50; ⏲10.10am-

### FERRY SERVICES

| TO | FROM | COMPANY | PRICE (SEAT) | FREQUENCY | TIME (HR) | SLEEPER BERTH |
|---|---|---|---|---|---|---|
| Palma | Barcelona | Trasmediterránea, Baleària | from €49 | 1-2 daily | 7½ | yes |
| Palma | Denia | Baleària | from €66 | 2 daily | 8 | yes |
| Palma | Ibiza (Ibiza City) | Baleària | from €46 | 2 daily | 4 | yes |
| Palma | Mahon (Menorca) | Trasmediterránea | from €34 | Sun | 3½ | no |
| Palma | Valencia | Trasmediterránea, Baleària | from €47 | 1 daily | 8 | yes |
| Port d'Alcúdia | Barcelona | Baleària | from €48 | 2 daily | 6 | yes |
| Port d'Alcúdia | Ciutatdella (Menorca) | Trasmediterránea, Baleària | from €48 | 2 daily | 1-2 | no |

DON'T MISS

**CALA FIGUERA**

A twisting fissure in the coastal slab of southern Mallorca forms the impossibly picturesque harbour town of Cala Figuera, 57km southeast of Palma. Steep scrubby escarpments rise up on all sides from the glassy water, leaving little space for the few houses, bars and restaurants to cling to. Despite its great charm, and proximity to some of Mallorca's busiest resorts, it remains the fishing village it has always been. While a few yachts line up beside the smaller working boats, local fishermen still make their way down the winding inlet before dawn, returning in the evening to mend their nets. Many of their houses have no street access, only private slipways for their launches.

Bus 503 connects Cala Figuera with Palma (€7.30, 1½ hours, four daily Monday to Saturday, with transfer at Santanyí) and Santanyí (€1.50, 20 minutes).

7.40pm Apr-Oct, 10.30am-6pm Nov-Mar; ) is a popular heritage railway running from the old station (next to Palma's Estació Intermodal de Palma) to the northwestern town of Sóller, stopping en route at Bunyola. The Estació Intermodal (p779) itself is the terminus for Mallorca's three regular lines: the T1 (to Inca; €3.15, 25 to 40 minutes), the T2 (Sa Pobla; €3.75, one hour) and the T3 (Manacor; €3.44, 55 minutes).

## Getting Around

### TO/FROM THE AIRPORT

Bus 1 runs around every nine minutes from the airport to Plaça d'Espanya/Estació Intermodal de Palma in central Palma (€5, 20 minutes) and on to the entrance of the ferry terminal. Buy tickets from the driver.

Taxis are generally clean, honest and abundant (when not striking), and the ride from the airport to central Palma will cost around €19 to €22.

### BICYCLE

Bicycle is a great way to explore Palma and Badia de Palma. There are also plenty of operators who rent out city and mountain bikes, including **Palma on Bike** (971 71 80 62; www.palmaonbike.com; Avinguda d'Antoni Maura 10; city/mountain/e-bike per day €12/36/28; 9.30am-1pm & 3-7pm).

### BUS

There are 29 local bus services around Palma and its bay suburbs run by **EMT** (971 21 44 44; www.emtpalma.es). These include line 1 between the airport and port (€5), and line 23 serving Palma–S'Arenal–Cala Blava via Aqualand. Single-trip tickets on lines other than those to the airport and port cost €2 or you can buy a 10-trip card for €15.

### TO/FROM THE BUS STATION

Bus 1 (the airport bus) runs every 15 minutes from the Estació Marítima (Ferry Port) across town (via Plaça d'Espanya/Estació Intermodal de Palma) and on to the airport. A taxi from/to the city centre will cost around €10 to €12.

# Western Mallorca

The Serra de Tramuntana range ripples all along the west coast, surveying the Mediterranean from above. Skirted by olive groves and pine forest, its razorback limestone mountains plunge 1000m down to the sea like the ramparts of some epic island fortress. Some of the island's loveliest towns and villages perch high on hilltops and deep in verdant valleys, with grandstand mountains and sea views.

## Valldemossa

Crowned by the spire of its Carthusian monastery, which slowly lifts the gaze to the Tramuntana's wooded slopes, Valldemossa is one of the island's most eye-catching sights. Set on a gentle rise, the village insists on aimless wandering and chance discoveries along pinched lanes, as breathtaking vistas onto the surrounding valley and hills, and pockets of almost indescribable charm, await.

**★ Real Cartuja de Valldemossa** MONASTERY

(www.cartujadevalldemossa.com; Plaça Cartoixa; adult/child €10/6.50; 10am-4.30pm Mon-Sat Feb-Oct) This grand old monastery and former royal residence has a chequered history. It was once home to kings, monks and a pair of 19th-century celebrities: composer Frédéric Chopin and writer George Sand. A series of cells shows how the monks lived, bound by an oath of silence they could only break for half an hour per week in the library. Various items related to the time Sand and Chopin spent here, including Chopin's pianos, are also displayed.

## Mallorca

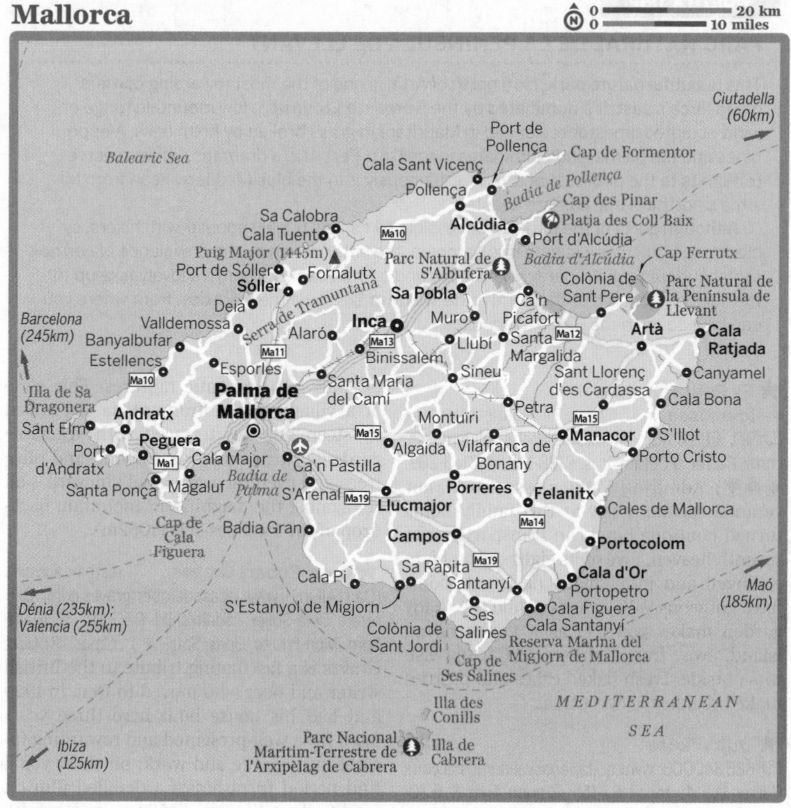


**Sa Foradada** LANDMARK

Visit **Son Marroig** (www.sonmarroig.com; Carretera de Valldemossa-Deià; adult/child €4/free; ⊙9.30am-6pm Mon-Sat May-Oct, shorter hours Nov-Apr), the delightful, rambling former residence of Habsburg Archduke Ludwig Salvator, and ask permission to wander down to this strange hole-in-the-wall rock formation by the water, which resembles an elephant from afar. It's a stunning 3km walk (one way) through olive groves tinkling with sheep bells and along paths flanked by pine trees and caves. A soothing swim in the lee of the odd formation is the reward. Avoid the midday heat as there is little shade.

### PARC NACIONAL MARÍTIM-TERRESTRE DE L'ARXIPÈLAG DE CABRERA

Nineteen uninhabited islands and islets make up this **national park** (☎971 72 50 10; ⊙Easter-Oct), unique in the Balearic Islands. The archipelago comprises dry, hilly islands known for their birdlife, rich marine environment and healthy populations of 10 different kinds of lizard. Lying 16km from Colònia de Sant Jordi, many of the islands are reserved for wildlife research, and only the largest, Illa de Cabrera, can be visited. Access is limited to 200 to 300 people per day, and hiking, birdwatching and swimming are the main draws. It is possible, with prior permission from the **park authority** (☎971 17 76 45; http://en.balearsnatura.com; Carrer Gremí de Corredors 10, Palma de Mallorca; ⊙11am-3pm Mon-Fri), to visit the park in your own boat but it's best go with a tour operator such as **Excursions a Cabrera** (☎971 64 90 34; www.excursionsacabrera.es; Carrer Dofi 11; adult/child boat €45/26, speedboat €49/30; ⊙8am-10pm high season, to 4pm low season, closed Nov-Feb; 👪).

WORTH A TRIP

### PARC NATURAL DE LA PENÍNSULA DE LLEVANT

This beautiful nature park, 5km north of Artà, is one of the most rewarding corners of Mallorca's east. It's dominated by the **Serra de Llevant**, a low mountain range of wind-sculpted limestone, cloaked in Mauritanian grass broken by holm oaks, Aleppo pines and fan palms, and culminates in the **Cap Ferrutx**, a dramatic nature reserve (off-limits to the public) that drops vertiginously into the blue Mediterranean from Mallorca's northern and eastern coasts.

Although parts of the park are accessible by car, it's hugely popular with hikers, cyclists and binocular-wielding birdwatchers; the latter drawn by the prevalence of cormorants, Audouin's gulls, peregrine falcons and booted eagles. There's a lovely hike up to the secluded church of the **Ermita de Betlem** FREE via the **mirador**, from where you can hike down to the Badia d'Alcúdia.

**★Es Petit Hotel de Valldemossa** BOUTIQUE HOTEL €€
(☎971 61 24 79; www.espetithotel-valldemossa.com; Carrer d'Uetam 1; s €128-188, d €143-209; ❄@📶) Admiring Valldemossa from your veranda rocking chair at this family home turned boutique hotel can transport you to seventh heaven. Five of its eight sunny, high-ceilinged and individually designed rooms have gorgeous valley views, while the shady garden makes you feel as if you're on an island, away from the flow of Cartuja visitors outside. Fresh-baked cakes and pastries make breakfast a sweet treat.

**★QuitaPenas** TAPAS €
(☎626 840006; www.quitapenasvalldemossa.com; Carrer Vell 4; tapas €3-15; ⏲noon-4pm & 6.30-9.30pm) Spread over three stone-clad rooms in a former simple village house, this unpretentious tapas bar serves highly appertising takes on *pa amb oli* (bread with olive oil and vine-ripened tomatoes) or tangy *sobrassada* (cured pork sausage flavoured with paprika and spices) with caramelised fig. Couple with chilled Mallorcan wine or one of the local craft brews.

### ℹ Getting There & Away

The 210 bus from Palma to Valldemossa (€1.90, 30 minutes) runs four to nine times a day. Three to four of these continue to Port de Sóller (€2.65, one hour) via Deià.

## Deià

When the late afternoon sun warms Deià's honey-coloured houses, which clamber steeply up a conical hillside, and the sea deepens to darkest blue on the horizon, it's enough to send even the most prosaic of souls into romantic raptures. This eyrie of a village in the Tramuntana is flanked by steep hillsides terraced with vegetable gardens, citrus orchards, almond and olive trees and even the occasional vineyard – all set against the magnificent mountain backdrop of the Puig des Teix (1062m).

**★Casa Robert Graves** HISTORIC BUILDING
(Ca N'Alluny; www.lacasaderobertgraves.com; Carretera Deià-Sóller; adult/child €7/3.50; ⏲10am-5pm Mon-Fri, to 3pm Sat; 🅿) Casa Robert Graves is a fascinating tribute to the British writer and poet who moved to Deià in 1929 and had his house built here three years later. It's a well-presented and rewarding insight into his life and work; on show you'll find period furnishings, a detailed film on his life, love life and writings, and sundry books, pictures and everyday objects that belonged to Graves himself.

### ℹ Getting There & Away

Deià is 15 minutes up the winding road from Valldemossa on the 210 bus route between Palma (€2.95, 45 to 60 minutes) and Port de Sóller (€1.65, 30 to 40 minutes). As Deià is popular with visitors, parking can be tricky. But you may be able to find a spot to park alongside the Ma10 roadside just east of town.

## Fornalutx

Fornalutx (the name means 'oven light') is one of Mallorca's most enchanting stone-built villages. Ascending its steps, you'll find the village is postcard pretty, the effect heightened by green shuttered windows, flower boxes, well-kept gardens and all-embracing mountain views.

**Plaça d'Espanya** SQUARE

The communal heart of the village, this gorgeous square is flanked on one side by the magnificent steps up to the church, the side wall of which occupies another flank; the steps continue on up to the top of the village and beyond, forming a delightful clamber for visitors. On a further side of the square, a cafe occupies pole position, alongside a small supermarket. Opposite here stands the principal village fountain, supplying fresh, potable water.

### Getting There & Away

A local service connects Fornalutx with Sóller (€1.50, 15 minutes, two to four daily), via Biniaraix.

## Cala de Sa Calobra & Cala Tuent

The hairpin-riddled 12km helter-skelter of a road down to Sa Calobra and Cala Tuent is one of Mallorca's top experiences. Whether you're swooning over the giddy ravine views or gulping as a coach squeezes through an impossibly narrow cleft in the rock, this spectacularly serpentine road, which branches north off the Ma10, is pure drama.

**Cala de Sa Calobra** BEACH

Past the turning to Cala Tuent, the road winds down to this small and undeniably attractive white-pebble cove, but it's a coach-fest during the summer crush, when carloads of visitors also descend. There is parking at the end of the road, but you will need to pay. A short trail and walkway leads around the coast to a rocky river gorge, the **Torrent de Pareis**, the dramatic conclusion to the torrent's descent from Escorca.

**Cala Tuent** BEACH

To skip the Sa Calobra crowds, follow a turn-off west, some 2km before Sa Calobra, to reach Cala Tuent, a tranquil emerald-green inlet in the shadow of Puig Major, with a single tall pine tree right by the beach. The broad pebble and shingle beach is backed by a couple of houses and a great, green bowl of vegetation that climbs up the mountain flanks. Cars park alongside the road near the beach, but things can get tight.

### Getting There & Away

One bus a day (bus 355, Monday to Saturday, May to October) comes from Ca'n Picafort (9.30am) via Alcúdia, Cala Sant Vicenç, Pollença and the Monestir de Lluc. It returns at 3pm. The whole trip takes just under four hours to Sa Calobra (with a one-hour stop at the Monestir de Lluc) and 2½ hours on the return leg. From Ca'n Picafort, you pay €9.05 one way. Boats make excursions to Sa Calobra and Cala Tuent from Port de Sóller. The best advice by far is to get behind the wheel.

## Southern Mallorca

The forbidding geography of the coast between the Badia de Palma (Bay of Palma) and Colònia de Sant Jordi has preserved this area as one of Mallorca's least developed. Beyond the cliffs are intimate coves, long swathes of fine sand and some of Mallorca's best beaches.

★**Cap de Ses Salines** LIGHTHOUSE

(Carretera de Cap de Ses Salines) Follow the Ma6110 highway 12km south of Ses Salines to reach the Cap de Ses Salines, a beautiful bluff on Mallorca's southernmost tip with a **lighthouse** (Far des Cap de ses Salines; closed to the public) dating back to 1863. There's not much here, but stretching out along either side are wonderfully unspoilt beaches protected by the Reserva Marina del Migjorn de Mallorca.

## Interior Mallorca

Mallorca's serene interior is the alter ego to the island's coastal buzz. Although the beaches are rarely more than an hour's drive, the interior feels light years away, with its vineyards, hilltop monasteries and

**WORTH A TRIP**

**CAP DE FORMENTOR**

The most dramatic stretch of Mallorca's coast, Cap de Formentor is an otherworldly domain of razor-edge cliffs and wind-buckled limestone peaks jutting far out to sea; from a distance, it looks like an epic line of waves about to break.

The 25km stretch to the northeast from Pollença (via the Ma2200 and Ma2210) is best done with your own vehicle, bicycle or feet; by public transport from Pollença, take bus 340 (€1.50, 20 minutes, regular) to Port de Pollença and change for 353 to Platja de Formentor (€1.55, 20 minutes, four daily Monday to Saturday; summer months only).

WORTH A TRIP

**PARC NATURAL DE S'ALBUFERA**

The 688-hectare **Parc Natural de S'Albufera** (☎971 892 250; www.mallorcaweb.net/salbufera; ⊙visitor centre 9am-6pm Apr-Sep, to 5pm Oct-Mar) FREE, west of the Ma12 between Port d'Alcúdia and Ca'n Picafort, is prime birdwatching territory, with 303 recorded species (more than 80% of recorded Balearic species), 64 of which breed within the park's boundaries. More than 10,000 birds overwinter here, among them both residents and migrants. Entrance to the park is free, but permits must be obtained from the visitor centre, which is a 1km walk from the entrance gates on the main road.



meadows stippled with olive, almond and carob trees.

## Felanitx

Felanitx is an important regional centre with a reputation for ceramics, white wine and capers (of the culinary variety). A handsome if unspectacular town, it's perhaps most visited as the gateway to the Santuari de Sant Salvador.

★**Santuari de Sant Salvador** MONASTERY
(www.santsalvadorhotel.com; ⊙church 8am-11pm) One of inland Mallorca's most spectacular viewpoints, the hermitage Santuari de Sant Salvador crowns a hilltop 5km southeast of Felanitx and 509m above sea level. Built in 1348, the year of the Black Death, it's plausible that the hermits were safe here. The church, added to over the years, is a strange mix, with gaudy columns and an elaborate cave nativity scene offset by an unadorned barrel-vaulted ceiling and a delicately carved stone altarpiece.

### ℹ Getting There & Away

From Palma buses 490 (and 491 express) connect with Felanitx (€5.40, one hour, up to 12 daily).

# Eastern Mallorca

There's a reason tourists arrive in Eastern Mallorca in their hundreds of thousands on their annual sun pilgrimage: this is one of prettiest coasts on an island of many. Cala Ratjada is the main resort, but it's not all development along the east coast – you can discover perfectly formed caves, coves and inlets, some only reachable on foot, while to the north you'll find wild stretches of natural park and stunning medieval towns such as Artà.

## Artà

The antithesis of Cala Ratjada's buzzing resort culture just a few kilometres away, the quiet inland town of Artà beckons with its maze of narrow streets, appealing cafes and medieval architecture, which culminates in an impressive 14th-century hilltop fortress that dominates the town centre.

★**Santuari de Sant Salvador** CASTLE
(Carrer del Castellet; ⊙8am-8pm Apr-Oct, shorter hours Nov-Mar) FREE Rising high and mighty above Artà, this walled fortress was built atop an earlier Moorish enclave and encloses a small church. The 4000-sq-metre complex, extensively restored in the 1960s, reveals all the hallmarks of a medieval bastion, down to the stone turrets ringing the top and the metre-thick walls. The views from here sweep over the rooftops of the medina-like old town and beyond to the bald, bumpy peaks of the Serra de Llevant.

★**Ses Païsses** ARCHAEOLOGICAL SITE
(off Carretera Artà-Capdepera; adult/child €2/free; ⊙10am-5pm Mon-Fri, to 2pm Sat) Just beyond Artà proper lies the remains of a 3000-year-old Bronze Age settlement, the largest and most important Talayotic site on the island's eastern flank. The site's looming stone gateway, composed of rough, 8-tonne slabs, is an impressive transition into the mystery-shrouded world of prehistoric Mallorca. You can traverse the tree-shaded site in under 30 minutes, but may appreciate a longer visit. From the large roundabout east of Artà's tourist office, follow the signs towards Ses Païsses.

★**Forn Nou** MEDITERRANEAN €€
(☎971 82 92 46; www.fornnou-arta.com; Carrer del Centre 7; 3-course dinner €30, mains from €21; ⊙6.30-11pm; 📶) Forn Nou's terrace perches high above Artà's medieval maze and peers across the rooftops to the church and fortress. The season-driven menu changes twice monthly, but you can expect clean, bright Mediterranean flavours, along the lines of

Atlantic anchovies with roasted peppers and paprika, or lobster risotto. The wine cellar is visible through the lobby's glass floor.

### Getting There & Away

Bus services to/from Artà's Avinguda de Costa i Llobera include bus 411 to Palma (€9.90, 90 minutes, four to five daily) via Manacor (€2.95, 25 minutes), and bus 446 to Port d'Alcúdia (€5.45, one hour, three daily Monday to Saturday) and Port de Pollença (€6.85, 70 minutes).

## Northern Mallorca

Northern Mallorca is the island's heart and soul, bundling coastal drama, cultured towns with spirited fiestas, a pair of white-sand bays and an exciting portfolio of adventure sports into one enticing package.

The Serra de Tramuntana is at its most fabulous where the range culminates on the Cap de Formentor, flicking out into the Med like a dragon's tail.

### Pollença

Pollença is quite beautiful. On a late-summer afternoon, when its stone houses glow in the fading light, cicadas strike up their tentative drone and the burble of chatter floats from cafe terraces lining the Plaça Major, the town is like the Mallorca you always hoped you would discover. Saunter through its gallery- and boutique-lined backstreets or pull up a ringside chair on the square at sundown to watch the world go by and you too will be smitten.

**★Calvari** CHRISTIAN SITE

(Carrer del Calvari) They don't call it Calvari (Calvary) for nothing. Some pilgrims do it on their knees, but even just walking up the 365 cypress-lined steps from the town centre to the lovely 18th-century hilltop chapel, the **Església del Calvari**, with its simple, spartan and serene interior, is penance enough. This may not be a stairway to heaven, but there are soul-stirring views to savour back over the town's mosaic of terracotta rooftops and church spires to the Tramuntana beyond.

**★Santuari de la Mare de Déu des Puig** MONASTERY

(Puig de Maria; 9am-6pm Oct-Mar, 8.30am-8.30pm Apr-Sep) FREE South of Pollença, off the Ma2200, one of Mallorca's most tortuous roads bucks and weaves up 1.5km of gasp-out-loud hairpin bends to this 14th-century former nunnery, which sits atop 333m **Puig de Maria**. If you come pilgrim style (the best way), the stiff hike through woods of holm oak, pine and olive will take you around an hour – Pollença shrinks to toytown scale as you near the summit. Be sure to avoid the midday heat and pack some water.

### Getting There & Away

From Palma, bus 340 heads nonstop for Pollença (€5.50, 45 minutes, up to 12 daily). It then continues on to Port de Pollença (€1.50, 20 minutes, up to 30 daily). Bus 345 runs from Pollença to Cala Sant Vicenç (€1.50, 20 minutes, frequent).

### Alcúdia

Just a few kilometres inland from the coast, Alcúdia is a town of quiet charm and character, ringed by mighty medieval walls that enclose a maze of narrow lanes, historic mansions, cafe-rimmed plazas and warm-stone houses. On the fringes of town are the captivating remains of Pol·lèntia, once the island's prime Roman settlement.

**★Medieval Walls** LANDMARK

Although largely rebuilt, Alcúdia's fine city walls are impressive. Those on the north side are largely the medieval originals while near the **Porta Roja** (Red Gate) are

WORTH A TRIP

#### PLATJA DES COLL BAIX

It's a fantastic ramble to Platja des Coll Baix – and what a bay! Snug below sheer, wooded cliffs, this shimmering crescent of pale pebbles and translucent water is soul-stirring stuff. The catch: it's only accessible on foot or by boat. Come in the early morning or evening to see it at its peaceful best. From Alcúdia, it's about 8km to an open spot in the woods where you can park. Follow the purple road signs for the Fundación Yannick y Ben Jakober and keep on for another 2km.

From this spot, you could climb the south trail to Talaia d'Alcúdia, then follow the signs to Coll Baix, a fairly easy half-hour descent. The main trail will lead you to the rocks south of the beach, from where you have to scramble back around to reach Platja des Coll Baix.

## TRANQUIL COVES AROUND CALA RATJADA

Heading north from Cala Ratjada, you'll find a wonderfully undeveloped stretch of coastline flecked with beaches. Long-time favourites of nudists, these out-of-the-way coves are no secret, but their lack of development has kept them calm and pristine.

Broad, family-friendly **Cala Mesquida**, surrounded by sand dunes and a small housing development, is the most accessible, with free parking, a few beach bars in season and a regular bus service (bus 471) from Cala Ratjada (€1.90, 25 minutes, up to eight daily).

It requires more determination to access the undeveloped coves due west. Often-windy **Cala Torta**, tiny, sheltered **Cala Mitjana** and the beachless **Cala Estreta** are all found at the end of a narrow road that ventures through the hills from Artà, yet a more interesting way to arrive is via the one-hour walking path from Cala Mesquida.

Further west, and following a 20-minute trek along the coast from Cala Estreta, **Cala Matzoc** comes into view. Often empty, the spacious sandy beach backs onto a hill where you'll find the ruins of a prehistoric *talayot* (watchtower).

remnants of an 18th-century bridge. From the bridge, you can climb up and walk around 250m atop the walls, as far as Carrer del Progres, with fine views over town and towards the distant hills. Beyond the bridge to the northeast, the Plaça de Toros (bullring) has been built into a Renaissance-era fortified bastion.

**★Pol·lèntia** ARCHAEOLOGICAL SITE

(www.pollentia.net; Avinguda dels Prínceps d'Espanya; adult/child incl Museu Monogràfic €4/2.50; ⌚9.30am-9pm Mon-Sat, 9am-1pm Sun May-Oct, shorter hours Nov-Apr) Ranging over a sizeable (but walkable) area, the fascinating ruins of the Roman town of Pol·lèntia lie just outside Alcúdia's walls. Founded around 70 BCE, it was Rome's principal city in Mallorca and is the most important archaeological site on the island. Pol·lèntia reached its apogee in the 1st and 2nd centuries CE and covered up to 20 hectares. To the north, the one-room **Museu Monogràfic** (www.pollentia.net; Carrer de Sant Jaume 30; adult/child incl Pol·lèntia €4/2.50; ⌚9.30am-8.30pm Tue-Sat, 10am-2pm Sun May-Sep, shorter hours Oct-Apr) has a fascinating but limited collection on Pol·lèntia.

**★S'Arc** INTERNATIONAL **€€**

(☎971 54 87 18; www.restaurantsarc.com; Carrer d'en Serra 22; mains €15-25, menú €13.90; ⌚noon-3.30pm & 6.30-11.30pm; 👪) Part of the Petit Hotel Ca'n Simó, this old-town charmer has a lovable inner courtyard, exposed-stone walls and Mediterranean cuisine pepped up with some inventive twists, such as Iberian pork with lemon couscous and tuna tataki with mango vinaigrette. World flavours also shine here, from Peruvian ceviche to Thai red curry.

### ℹ Getting There & Away

The 351 bus from Palma to Platja de Muro calls at Alcúdia (€5.45, 45 minutes, up to 16 daily). Bus 352 connects Ca'n Picafort (€1.85, 45 minutes) with Alcúdia as often as every 15 minutes from May to October. Local service 356A connects Alcúdia with Port d'Alcúdia and Platja d'Alcúdia (€1.55, 15 minutes, every 15 minutes from May to October).

# MENORCA

POP 93,397

Arrive on the sun-bleached shores of Menorca after a spell on Mallorca or Ibiza and notice the drop in volume – here it's more birdsong than Pete Tong. Its twinset of sea-splashed cities, eastern Anglo-Spanish Maó and western maze-like Ciutadella, are delightfully low-key and distinctive, and the white- and golden-sand bays that stud its 216km coastline are among the loveliest in the Mediterranean.

In 1993, Unesco declared Menorca a Biosphere Reserve, aiming to preserve environmental areas, such as the Parc Natural S'Albufera des Grau (p788) wetlands, and its liberal sprinkling of mysterious Bronze Age sites.

### ℹ Information

The **Oficina d'Informació Turística Aeroport** (☎971 15 71 15; www.menorca.es; Aeroport de Menorca; ⌚7.30am-9pm Thu-Mon, 8am-3.30pm Tue & Wed) is in the arrivals hall at the airport. The main **tourist office** (☎971 36 37 90; www.menorca.es; Plaça de la Constitució 22; ⌚9.30am-4.15pm Mon & Sat, to 8.30pm Tue-Fri) is in Maó's town centre.

## Menorca

### Getting There & Away

**AIR**

The **Aeroport de Menorca** (☎902 40 47 04; www.aena.es; Me14) is 5km southwest of Maó, and has direct flights to destinations across Spain and Europe.

**SEA**

**Trasmediterránea** (☎902 454645; www.trasmediterranea.es; Estació Marítima) operates once- to twice-weekly ferries between Maó and Palma de Mallorca (from €39, 5½ hours). **Baleària** (☎865 60 84 23; www.balearia.com) has twice-daily ferries between Port d'Alcúdia in Mallorca (€25 to €55, 1½ to two hours) and Son Oleo, just south of Ciutadella.

### Getting Around

**BUS**

You can reach most destinations from Maó's **bus station** (Carrer de Vassallo), with **TMSA** (☎971 36 04 75; www.tmsa.es), **Autos Fornells** (☎971 15 43 90; www.autosfornells.com) or **Autocares Torres** (☎902 075066; www.bus.e-torres.net). Ciutadella is served by TMSA and Autocares Torres. There are high-season buses to some beaches and coastal resorts, but services elsewhere on the island are generally patchy.

**CAR & MOTORCYCLE**

With your own wheels, you'll reach some of Menorca's most beautiful spots. Daily hire costs start from around €35 for the lowest-category cars.

## Maó

Sitting pretty on the world's second-largest natural harbour (5km long), Maó (Mahón) has an unusual blend of Anglo and Spanish characteristics. It has been Menorca's capital since the British moved it here from Ciutadella in 1713, and the influence of their almost-100-year presence (the island reverted to Spanish rule in 1802) is still evident in the city's distinctive architecture, traditions and culture. The closest decent beaches are **Sa Mesquida**, 7km northeast, **Es Grau**, 10km north, and Platja de **Punta Prima**, 9km south. All have bus links to to Maó during summer months.

★**Ca n'Oliver** MUSEUM

(☎971 35 65 23; http://canoliver.menorca.es; Carrer d'Anuncivay 2; adult/child/under 10 €5/2.50/free, Nov-Apr free; ⏲10am-1.30pm & 6-8pm Tue-Sat, 10am-1.30pm Sun May-Oct, 10am-1.30pm & 6-8pm Thu-Sat, 10am-1.30pm Tue, Wed & Sun Nov-Apr) Built in the early 1800s for the prominent bourgeois Oliver family (who lived here until 1920), this magnificent mansion has been exquisitely restored into an engaging multimedia museum. Its elegant interiors display Maó's **Col·lecció Hernández Sanz–Hernández Mora**, devoted to Menorcan themes, illustrated by artworks, maps and decorative items dating back to the 18th century. The mansion's distinctive painted-canvas ceilings and grand imperial staircase, with its wrought-iron banisters and mythological-inspired mural, are the work of two 19th-century Sicilian artists.

**Plaça d'Espanya** SQUARE

Just above the port, the central Plaça d'Espanya is flanked by colourful houses and the neoclassical 18th-century **Església del Carme**. On the square itself, explore the pungent fish market Mercat de Peix.

**★Casa Albertí** HERITAGE HOTEL €€€

(☎971 35 42 10; www.casalberti.com; Carrer d'Isabel II 9; d incl breakfast €140-240, ste €160-258; ⊙closed Jan; ❄📶) Within this elegant 1700s TV-free mansion, each of the six high-ceilinged, stylishly historical rooms is decorated with statement colours and modern-vintage flair. Relax in the chandelier-lit salon or climb the marble staircase with wrought-iron banisters to the rooftop terrace. Breakfast emphasises local organic produce, with squeeze-your-own juice, Menorcan cheeses, freshly baked bread and pastries and more.

**Mercat de Peix** MARKET €

(Plaça d'Espanya; tapas €2-5; ⊙market 8am-1pm Tue-Sat, tapas bars 12.30-10pm May-Sep, 12.30-4pm Fri & Sat Oct-Apr) Housed in a purpose-built, olive-green 1927 building, Maó's colourful fish market is now also a lively tapas hangout, where you can feast on bite-sized seafood delights, Menorcan cheeses, local wines, artisan island beers, *montaditos* (mini open sandwiches) and more.

**Café Mirador** BAR

(☎971 35 21 07; Plaça d'Espanya 2; ⊙noon-11pm Mon-Sat) Seize a ringside seat outside for tapas, mojitos, local wines or G&Ts starring Menorcan Xoriguer gin. The Mirador is a perennial favourite thanks to its glorious port views, reasonable prices and occasional live music, and rustles up light bites (€5 to €12) of burgers, scrambles, Iberian ham and *patatas bravas* (potatoes in a spicy tomato sauce). Find it on a short cul-de-sac behind the fish market.

### Getting There & Away

See the Menorca Getting There & Away section for details on reaching Maó by air and sea.

Autocares Torres bus 10 runs between the airport (€2.65, 10 minutes) and Maó's bus station, 700m southwest of the old town's centre, every 30 to 60 minutes. Taxis cost around €15 to/from Maó.

TMSA operates regular buses to Ciutadella (€5.10, one hour) and other destinations. Autos Fornells links Maó to north-coast destinations including Es Grau (€1.65, 20 minutes, four to five daily mid-June to mid-September) and Fornells (€3.25, 50 minutes, two to four daily).

## North Coast Menorca

Menorca's north coast is rugged and rocky, perforated with small, scenic coves. It's less developed (and less accessible) than the south, but with your own transport and some footwork, you'll discover some of the Balearics' best off-the-beaten-track beaches. Towards the northeastern end, the bird-rich Parc Natural S'Albufera des Grau makes up the core of Menorca's protected Unesco Biosphere Reserve. Further north and west along the coast, the inviting, whitewashed northern fishing village of Fornells sits on a long slim bay, with sheltered, unruffled waters ideal for novice windsurfers.

### Sights & Activities

**★Parc Natural S'Albufera des Grau** NATURE RESERVE

(☎971 17 77 05; https://balearsnatura.com; ⊙9am-5pm Tue-Thu, to 3pm Fri-Mon) This freshwater lagoon and its shores form the 'nucleus zone' of Menorca's protected Unesco Biosphere Reserve. It's a haven for wetland birdlife (including coots and fish eagles) and species such as Lilford's wall lizards and Hermann's tortoises. The park's **reception centre** (☎609 601249; ⊙9am-3pm) is 1km north of the Me5 (Maó–Es Grau) road, signposted 2.5km southwest of Es Grau. From here, follow two easy, signed trails of 800m (30 minutes) and 1.4km (45 minutes); a third 1.7km path begins in Es Grau.

**Cala d'Algaiarens** BEACH

(La Vall) Tucked between Cala Morell and Cala Carbó on the island's northwest coast, this crescent of powder-soft white sand is fringed by dunes, pines and azure waters. It's 13km northeast of Ciutadella: take the road to Cala Morell then follow signs east to Algaiarens. There are two car parks, around 500m and 1km south of the beach.

**Punta Nati** NATURAL FEATURE

At Punta Nati, 7km north of Ciutadella on Menorca's distant northwestern corner, the landscapes morph into an arid, rust-hued world of stone walls, rocky expanses and Mallorca looming in the distance. The promontory's **lighthouse** dates to 1913; it's closed to the public, but you can clamber around outside soaking up the sensational coastal panoramas.

**Menorca en Kayak** KAYAKING

(☎669 097977; www.menorcaenkayak.com; Carrer S'Arribada 8, Es Grau; ⏲Easter-Oct) Explore the Parc Natural S'Albufera des Grau from the sea by hiring a kayak (per hour €9) or SUP board (per hour €10) from these long-established Es Grau–based watersports professionals. There's also kayaking and SUP tours (from €35 for two hours) and sea-kayak courses.

**Wind Fornells** WATER SPORTS

(☎664 335801; www.windfornells.com; Carretera Es Mercadal-Fornells, Fornells; ⏲mid-Apr–Oct) Ramon and co at reliable Wind Fornells offer windsurfing and dinghy sailing courses (1½-hour sessions from €42), plus two-hour SUP trips with snorkelling (€45). They also rent out stand-up paddleboards (two hours €24) and windsurfing kits (two hours €37).

## Sleeping

**Hostal La Palma** HOSTAL €€

(☎971 37 66 34; www.hostallapalma.com; Plaça s'Algaret 3, Fornells; s incl breakfast €45-71, d €65-95; ⏲Easter-Oct; ❄☎≋) Behind a busy tapas and seafood bar-restaurant in the heart of Fornells, La Palma's rooms are fresh and stylishly contemporary, with balconies. They're styled in smart greys and whites; the best have views across the pool and gardens to the surrounding countryside.

## Getting There & Away

Autos Fornells links Fornells with Maó and Es Mercadal, and Es Grau with Maó, while Autocares Torres serves Cala Morell and Cala d'Algairens from Ciutadella. Generally speaking, you'll need your own wheels (and then probably a bit of walking) to reach most of Menorca's most exciting northern destinations.

# Ciutadella

Known as Vella i Bella ('Old and Beautiful'), Menorca's second city is an attractive, distinctly Spanish west-coast settlement with a picturesque port and an engaging, evocative old quarter lined by grand gold-tinged buildings. Ciutadella's character is entirely different to that of Maó, and its historic centre (almost completely traffic free) is arguably more appealing.

**Catedral de Menorca** CATHEDRAL

(www.bisbatdemenorca.com; Plaça de la Catedral; adult/child €5/free; ⏲10am-4pm Mon-Sat May-Oct) Ciutadella's 14th-century, single-nave cathedral was built in Catalan Gothic style on the site of Medina Minurqa's central mosque (the belltower visibly reuses part of the original minaret), though its baroque facade with Corinthian columns wasn't added until the early 19th century. The cathedral was badly damaged during both the 1558 Turkish attack and the Spanish Civil War, leading to extensive 20th-century restorations.

**Plaça des Born** SQUARE

Ciutadella's main square is a gracious affair, framed by handsome 19th-century buildings such as the neoclassical **Palau Torre-Saura** and fortress-like **Ajuntament**. The **obelisk** at its centre was raised to commemorate the townsfolk who died trying to ward off the Turks on 9 July 1558. For the finest view of the port and the town's remaining bastions and bulwarks, sneak behind the *ajuntament* (town hall) and up to the 14th-century **Bastió d'Es Governador** (⏲9am-7pm Mon-Sat) FREE.

**Palau Salort** HISTORIC BUILDING

(Palau Martorell; Carrer Major des Born; adult/child €3/1.80; ⏲10am-2pm Mon-Sat May-Oct) A couple of Ciutadella's magnificent noble homes are open to the public seasonally, including the splendid 1813 Palau Salort, which unfolds behind a neoclassical facade. On the ceiling of the entrance hall you'll spot the Salort family crest, before climbing to the dance hall, British-inspired library, kitchen (allegedly Menorca's largest) and glimmering 'Room of Mirrors', where the walls are adorned with 12 Louis XVI mirrors.

★**Mon** SPANISH €€€

(☎971 38 17 18; www.monrestaurantfonda.com; Passeig de Sant Nicolau 4; 3-/7-course tasting menu €28/45; ⏲7-11pm Mon-Sat) With Michelin-starred, Ciutadella-born chef Felip Llufriu (who trained under Catalonia's celebrated Roca brothers) at the helm, Mon offers just two tasting menus. Your three or seven deliciously inventive courses highlight locally sourced fish, meat and produce, featuring, perhaps, crayfish-stuffed avocado cannelloni or fresh fish of the day with orange-and-olive sauce. Choose between the sleek white-on-white interior or the back patio.

## Getting There & Away

### BOAT

Baleària runs twice-daily ferries between Port d'Alcúdia in Mallorca (€25 to €55, 1½ to two hours) and Son Oleo, just south of Ciutadella.

### BUS

Autocares Torres buses serve the coast south of Ciutadella, departing from the **bus stop** (Plaça dels Pins) on Plaça dels Pins. Half-hourly to hourly TMSA buses to Maó (€5.10, one hour) stop in Ferreries (€2.05, 15 minutes) and Es Mercadal (€2.85, 25 minutes) and leave from the **bus stop** (Avinguda Josep Mascaró Passarius) on Avinguda Josep Mascaró Passarius, 600m east of the old quarter.



# South Coast Menorca

Menorca's southern flank is home to some of the island's finest beaches (and the greater concentration of development). The jagged southern coastline is occasionally interrupted by a small inlet with a sandy white beach and aqua-tinted waters, backed by a cluster of sparkling-white villas, largely small-scale and in Moroccan-Mediterranean style. Some of the top beaches are sprinkled along the southwest coast. Menorca's leading winery – Bodegas Binifadet – is just outside the inland town of Sant Lluís, 5km due south of Maó.

**★Bodegas Binifadet** WINERY

(☎971 15 07 15; www.binifadet.com; Camí de Ses Barraques, Sant Lluís; tours adult/child €10/free; ⏱11am-midnight May, Jun, Sep & Oct, to 2am Jul & Aug, closed Mon May & Oct) At Menorca's top winery, 500m northeast of Sant Lluís, you can amble around vineyards at your own pace, or book in a one-hour guided tour that concludes with a tasting of three house wines with tangy Menorcan goat's cheese. Tours run at 11.30am, 3pm and 6pm in English, and 1pm, 4.30pm and 7.30pm in Spanish (no afternoon tours September and October). Alternatively, pop in to sample the grapes at the stylish all-day wine bar or dine in the fine **restaurant** (mains €15-19; ⏱noon-4pm & 7-11pm May-Oct, closed Mon May & Oct; 🖉).

**Binibèquer Vell** VILLAGE

(Binibeca) Gleaming white and something of a tourist beehive, Binibèquer's core looks like a charming age-old fishing village, but, in fact, it was modelled on one in the early 1970s. Its sugar-cube houses and tight alleys are appealing, whatever their genesis, and there are a few restaurants and cafes dotted around. Villas sprawl across the immediate surrounds and, 1km southeast of the 'old' village centre, you'll reach a sandy cove with transparent water.

**★Cala Turqueta** BEACH

One of Menorca's most beautiful and sought-after coves, salt-white Cala en Turqueta gets its name from the turquoise-hued waters that tumble onto its south-coast sands. It's 11km southeast of Ciutadella, about a 1km walk from its car park.

**Cala Mitjana** BEACH

Ah, bliss! Pine-brushed cliffs enshroud this silky sugar-white cove, set deep into a headland 7km southwest of Ferreries. Park in the free car park just before the entrance to the resort of **Cala Galdana**, then walk around 1.5km (20 minutes) to reach it.

**★Biniarroca** HOTEL €€€

(☎971 15 00 59; www.biniarroca.com; Camí Vell 57, Sant Lluís; r incl breakfast from €220; ⏱Easter-mid-Oct; P❄📶🏊) Crank up the romance at this rambling, whitewashed, adults-only retreat, 1.5km northeast of Sant Lluís. Draped in bougainvillea, the 18th-century farmhouse is expertly run by a British artist-designer and charming team. Two jade-green pools lie in a beautiful garden planted with tamarisk and almond trees. Rooms are stylishly rustic-modern, while the gourmet **restaurant** (mains €17 to €28) is open to all.

**★Cova d'en Xoroi** BAR

(www.covadenxoroi.com; Carrer de sa Cova, Cala en Porter; adult/child incl drink day €9/5, sunset €13/13, night adult €30; ⏱noon-6am May-Sep) For a night on the rocks, head to Menorca's most famous bar-club, perched like an eyrie in a vertiginous cliffside cave. Sunset is primetime, with chillout beats, cocktails and seriously spectacular sea views. DJs play everything from house to hippie grooves as the night wears on in one the Balearics' most magical clubs, full of troglodyte nooks and crannies.

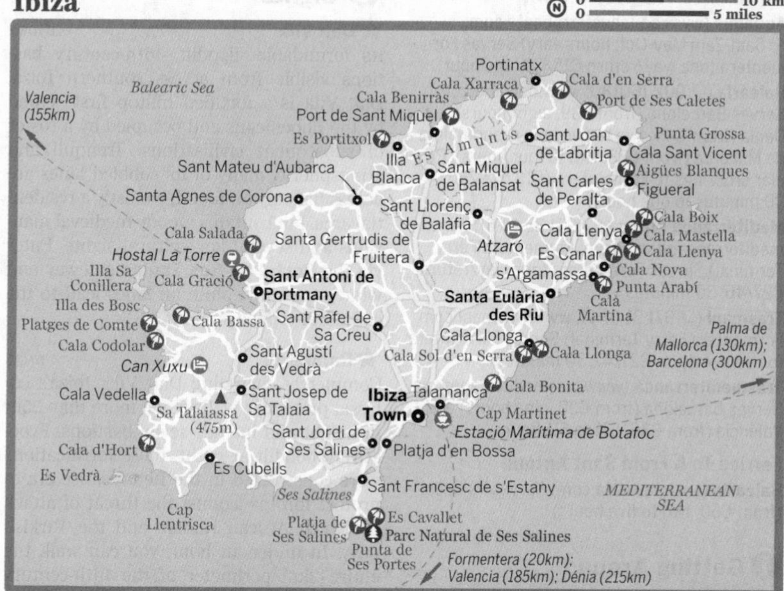


## Getting There & Away

TMSA buses serve southeast destinations, plus the Cala Galdana area, while Autocares Torres run to destinations on Menorca's southwest coast; many are summer services that run only from around May to October. A car gives you the most freedom.

# IBIZA

POP 148,000

All-night raver, boho-cool hippy, blissed-out beach lover – Ibiza is all this and more to the many, many fans who have a soft spot for the Balearics' party-hard sister. In summer the cream of the world's DJs (David Guetta, Sven Väth, Armin van Buuren et al) descend on the island, making it the ultimate destination for clubbers. Ibiza's modest population is swallowed whole by the seven-million-odd tourists that arrive en masse each year, and nowhere does sunset chilling or boho-glam style quite like the White Isle.

But there's more to this sun-kissed, beach-bejewelled, pine-clad island than meets the bleary eye. Step off the beaten track for a spell in a rural hotel, a hidden hamlet, a hushed church or on a secluded north-coast cove to discover Ibiza's surprisingly peaceful side. Or roam the ramparts of Ibiza Town's World Heritage–listed Dalt Vila to immerse yourself in the island's rich history and heritage. Even better, turn up in the low season and find the island deserted.

## Information

**Turismo de Ibiza** (☎971 30 19 00; http://ibiza.travel; Avinguda de Santa Eulària; ⏲9am-8pm Mon-Sat, to 3pm Sun, reduced hours mid-Oct–Apr) In Ibiza Town.

## Getting There & Away

### AIR

Ibiza's airport is 7km southwest of Ibiza Town. Airlines serving Ibiza include Iberia, Air Europa, British Airways, Ryanair and Vueling. The majority of flights operate seasonally. Departure tax is included in the price of a ticket.

### SEA

Most long-distance ferries arriving/departing Ibiza use the **Estació Marítima de Botafoc** (Ferry Terminal; Botafoc Peninsula), across the harbour from central Ibiza Town and its old Estación Marítima. Ferries linking Ibiza Town with Formentera have their own **terminal** (off Avinguda de Santa Eulària), 400m north of central Ibiza Town. There are also a few ferries between the mainland and Sant Antoni.

### Ferries To & From Ibiza Town

**Aquabus** (www.aquabusferryboats.com; 6am-2am May-Oct, hours vary) Serves Formentera (one way/return €15/29, one hour).

**Baleària** (902 160180; www.balearia.com) Serves Barcelona (from €39, eight hours), Dénia (from €49, two to five hours) and Palma de Mallorca (from €28, two to four hours). Regular crossings to Formentera (€18 to €25.50, 30 minutes to one hour).

**Mediterránea Pitiusa** (971 31 44 61; www.mediterraneapitiusa.com; Formentera Ferry Terminal) Serves Formentera (one way/return €27/46, 30 minutes).

**Trasmapi** (971 31 07 11; www.trasmapi.com; Formentera Ferry Terminal) Serves Formentera (one way/return €27/47, 30 minutes).

**Trasmediterránea** (www.trasmediterranea.es) Serves Barcelona (from €39, nine hours) and Valencia (from €36, 5¾ to 6½ hours).

### Ferries To & From Sant Antoni

**Baleària** (www.balearia.com) Serves Valencia (from €50, two to five hours).

## Getting Around

Ibiza is small and easy to get around, with good, sensibly priced public transport. If hiring a car or motorbike, remember Spain drives on the right.

**Bicycle** Ibiza has decent cycle paths.

**Boat** Seasonal ferries link most of Ibiza with Ibiza Town.

**Bus** Much cheaper (and slower) than car hire. Services link most major destinations, though many run May to September only. Check schedules through Ibiza Bus (http://ibizabus.com).

**Car** The best way to explore: flexibility, independence and the chance to reach remote destinations.

**Motorbike/Moped** Particularly convenient for easy parking at busy beaches in high season.

**Taxi** A good alternative, though journeys add up.

**Walking** Ibiza has some lovely hikes, and the major towns are all walkable.

# Ibiza Town

The heart and soul of the island, Ibiza Town (Eivissa) is a vivacious, stylish and elegant capital with a magical, fortified World Heritage–listed old quarter topped by a castle and cathedral, set against a spectacular natural harbour. It's also a shopaholic's dream, a hedonist's paradise and a world-famous party destination.

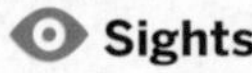

## Sights

### ★Dalt Vila — OLD TOWN

Its formidable, floodlit, 16th-century bastions visible from across southern Ibiza, Dalt Vila is a fortified hilltop first settled by the Phoenicans and occupied by a roster of subsequent civilisations. Tranquil and atmospheric, many of its cobbled lanes are accessible only on foot. It's mostly a residential area, but contains moody medieval mansions and several key cultural sights. Enter via the **Portal de Ses Taules** gateway and wind your way uphill: all lanes lead to the cathedral-topped summit.

### ★Ramparts — WALLS

Completely encircling Dalt Vila, Ibiza's colossal protective walls reach more than 25m in height and include seven bastions. Evocatively floodlit at night, these fortifications were constructed in the Renaissance era to protect Ibizans against the threat of attack by North African raiders and the Turkish navy. In under an hour, you can walk the entire 2km perimeter of the 16th-century ramparts, which were designed to withstand heavy artillery. Along the way, enjoy great views over the port and south across the water to Formentera.

### Passeig Marítim — STREET

Ibiza Town's elegant harbour promenade showcases the city's magnificent waterfront. It's a delight to explore, lined with cafes, bars, shops and restaurants. Yachts bob about on the marina on the north bank, while whitewashed old fishermen's homes fill its south side, in the shadow of sparkling superyachts.

### S'Estanyol — BEACH

Something of a secret beach, S'Estanyol is a tiny, gorgeous pebbly cove, only accessible by a dirt road (rough in parts). A few fishing huts dot the seaweed-filled shoreline and offshore you'll find excellent snorkelling. It's 3km northeast of Talamanca, signposted from the northeast end of the bay; the last 1.5km is a dirt track.

## Sleeping & Eating

### Vara de Rey — GUESTHOUSE €€

(971 30 13 76; http://hibiza.com; Passeig de Vara de Rey 7; s €65-75, d €85-165, ste €170-210; ) Tucked into a restored 20th-century mansion overlooking tree-dotted Vara de Rey, this boho-flavoured guesthouse blends

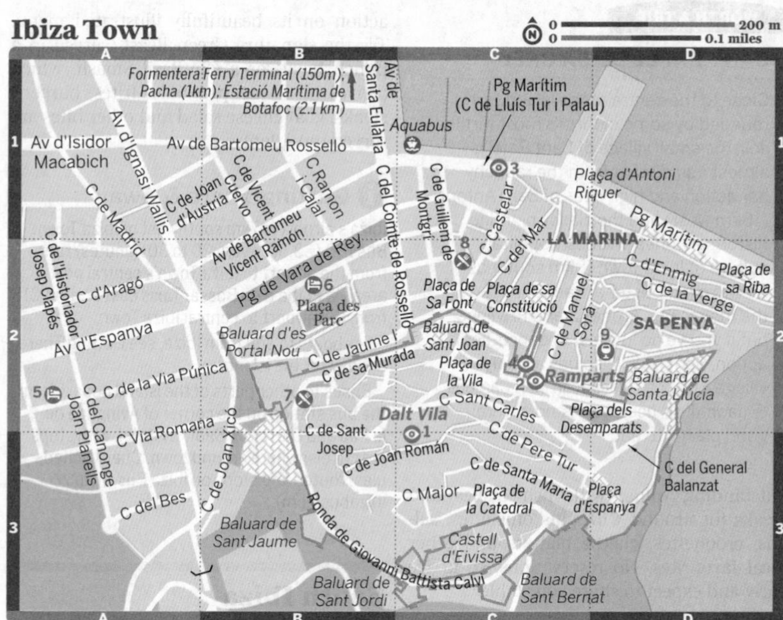


## Ibiza Town

**Top Sights**
1 Dalt Vila ........ C3
2 Ramparts ........ C2

**Sights**
3 Passeig Marítim ........ C1
4 Portal de Ses Taules ........ C2

**Sleeping**
5 Urban Spaces ........ A2
6 Vara de Rey ........ B2

**Eating**
7 S'Escalinata ........ B2
8 Comidas Bar San Juan ........ C2

**Drinking & Nightlife**
9 Bar 1805 ........ D2

patterned tiled floors, wood-beamed ceilings and vintage furniture with elegant styling and lively colour schemes. Apart from one double and the suite, rooms share bathrooms (but have their own sinks). There's a small library with a tea/coffee stand. It's three floors up, without a lift.

**★Urban Spaces** DESIGN HOTEL €€€
(☎601 199302; info@urbanspacesibiza.com; Carrer de la Via Púnica 32; r €240-295; ⌚Apr-early Jan; ❄@📶) Some of the world's most prolific street artists (N4T4, Inkie, Jerom) have pooled their creativity in this design hotel with an alternative edge. The roomy, mural-splashed suites sport clever backlighting, proper workstations and balconies with terrific views. Extras such as summer rooftop yoga and clubber-friendly breakfasts until 1pm are sure-fire people pleasers. Rates drop considerably in April, May, September and October.

**★S'Escalinata** MEDITERRANEAN €
(☎653 371356; Carrer des Portal Nou 10; dishes €7-13; ⌚10am-3am Apr-Oct; 📶) With its low-slung tables and colourful cushions cascading down a steep stone staircase, this boho-chic cafe-bar-restaurant enjoys a magical location inside Dalt Vila. On the tempting menu are healthy breakfasts, tapas, *bocadillos* (filled rolls) and delicious light dinners of hummus, tortilla or goat's-cheese salads. It's open late into the night, mixing up freshly squeezed juices, G&Ts and fruity cocktails.

**★Comidas Bar San Juan** SPANISH €
(☎971 31 16 03; Carrer de Guillem de Montgrí 8; mains €7-11; ⌚1-3.30pm & 8.30-11pm Mon-Sat) More traditional than trendy, this popular family-run operation, with two small dining rooms, harks back to the days before Ibiza became a byword for glam. It offers

WORTH A TRIP

### SANT RAFEL DE SA CREU

Close to the centre of the island, surrounded by some of Ibiza's most fertile soil, the small village of Sant Rafel is almost equidistant from the raunchy bar action and high rises of Sant Antoni (10km west) and the classy nightlife, historical riches and cosmopolitan culture of Ibiza Town (8km southeast). Its two blockbuster attractions are the megaclubs Amnesia and Privilege, but if you've no interest in dance-floor action, Sant Rafel also has a lovely village **church** (Plaça Joan Marí Cardona; ⌚dawn-dusk, hours vary) and several good places to eat.



outstanding value, with fish dishes and steaks for around €10, plus omelettes, salads, croquettes, cheese platters and other local favourites. No reservations, so arrive early and expect to share your table.

**Cala Bonita** SEAFOOD **€€**
(☎605 450592, 971 94 86 21; http://calabonitaibiza.com; S'Estanyol; mains €14-25; ⌚1-9pm Mar-Jan) Hidden away on a secluded cove, 3km northeast of Talamanca bay, this sophisticated Australian/South African-owned *chiringuito* (beach bar) turns out fresh seafood, polished paellas and a modern-Mediterranean menu, including inventive salads such as quinoa with burrata. It doubles as a smart tapas and cocktail bar, and hosts DJ sessions plus sunbeds on the sand. Opening hours vary outside summer.

## Drinking

**★Pacha** CLUB
(www.pachaibiza.com; Avinguda 8 d'Agost; from €15; ⌚midnight-7am May-Sep) Going strong since 1973, Pacha is Ibiza's original megaclub and the islanders' party venue of choice. It's built around the shell of a farmhouse, boasting a multilevel main dance floor, a Funky Room (for soul and disco beats), a huge VIP section and myriad other places to dance or lounge.

**Bar 1805** COCKTAIL BAR
(☎651 625972; www.bar1805ibiza.com; Carrer Baluard de Santa Llúcia 7; ⌚8pm-4am mid-Apr-Oct; 📶) Tucked away on a Sa Penya backstreet, this boho bar mixes some of the best cocktails in town, with lots of absinthe action on its beautifully illustrated menu. Try the signature Green Beast (served in a punch bowl) or a Gin-Basil Smash, which arrives in a teacup. Moules-frites, burgers, steaks, goat cheese salad and other bites are served until 2am.

## ℹ Getting There & Away

Ibiza's airport is 7km southwest of Ibiza Town. Bus L10 (€3.50, every 20 to 30 minutes) runs from the airport to Ibiza Town's central port area via Platja d'en Bossa. Taxis cost around €18 from the airport to central Ibiza Town.

For boats to and from Ibiza, see Getting There & Away for the island.

Buses to other parts of the island depart from the bus station on the corner of Avinguda de la Pau and Carrer de Sant Cristòfol, with stops dotted elsewhere around town. Check schedules, routes and stops on Ibiza Bus (http://ibizabus.com).

# South Ibiza

The island's spectacular southern reaches include Ibiza's highest peak (Sa Talaiassa; 475m), its most beautiful snow-white-sand beaches and the enigmatic, enticing southwest islet of Es Vedrà.

## Sights

**★Platja de Ses Salines** BEACH
Arguably Ibiza's best beach, Platja de Ses Salines is a gorgeous sweep of white sand with glass-clear sea, backed by rolling sand dunes, patches of sabina pine woodland and buzzy *chiringuitos*. Sunseekers of all kinds flock here to work the bronzed, blissed-out Ibiza look. The scene varies from northwest (family-friendly) to southeast (with a more boho vibe and some nudism); things can get busy in summer. There's a huge, quick-to-fill car park (€6); buses L11 and L11B run here from Ibiza Town.

**★Parc Natural de Ses Salines** NATURE RESERVE
(☎971 17 76 88; www.balearsnatura.com) Encompassing southeastern Ibiza and stretching south across the water to northern Formentera, this 168-sq-km World Heritage-listed nature reserve comprises marshes, sparkling salt pans, sandy cream-coloured beaches and pine-cloaked coastal cliffs. It's a safe haven for 210 species of birds, such as

the Audouin's gull, the Balearic shearwater and hot-pink flocks of migrating flamingos.

**★ Es Vedrà** ISLAND

Off Ibiza's southwest tip, the exquisite, vertiginous island of Es Vedrà is one of the most startling sights in the Balearics, emerging abruptly from the glittering Mediterranean like an offshore volcano. Dramatically reaching a height of 382m, the island is associated with numerous local myths and legends, from sirens to UFOs to the Virgin Mary. Since Ibiza's southern-coast road is surrounded by high mountains, the effect is spellbinding when Es Vedrà unexpectedly pops into view.

**★ Es Cavallet** BEACH

On the eastern side of a slender peninsula, the wonderful, wild-feel, salt-white beach of Es Cavallet is one of the island's most perfect strips of sand. It was designated Ibiza's first naturist beach in 1978; today it's the island's main gay beach. The northern section is more family-geared, while the southern half is almost exclusively gay.

## Sleeping

**★ Can Xuxu** AGROTURISMO €€€

(☎971 80 15 84; www.canxuxu.com; Carretera Sant Josep-Cala Tarida Km 4; r incl breakfast €230-690, ste €350-810; ⏱Apr-Oct; P❄📶🏊) Owner Alex and his staff really make this luxe rural hotel, doting on guests, preparing homemade food and keeping things creatively stylish. It's set in a 150-year-old *finca* (estate), 4.5km northwest of Sant Josep and decked out with Asian inspiration, and there's a lovely, secluded pool area. For an utterly memorable stay, book one of the converted 19th-century Javanese teak houses.

## Drinking & Nightlife

**★ Amnesia** CLUB

(☎971 19 80 41; www.amnesia.es; Carretera Eivissa-Sant Antoni Km 5, Sant Rafel de Sa Creu; €40-70; ⏱midnight-6am late May-Oct) Amnesia is arguably Ibiza's most influential and legendary club, its decks having welcomed such DJ royalty as Sven Väth, Paul Van Dyk, Paul Oakenfold, Tiësto and Avicii. There's a warehouse-like main room and a terrace topped by a graceful atrium. Big nights include techno-fests Cocoon and Music On, trance-mad Cream and foam-filled Espuma, which always draws a big local crowd.

**★ Hï Ibiza** CLUB

(www.hiibiza.com; Carretera de Platja d'en Bossa; €45-60; ⏱midnight-6am Jun-early Oct) A glitzy newcomer to Ibiza's superclub scene, Hï is part of the ever-growing Ushuaïa empire. Refreshing the site originally occupied by Ibizan clubbing institution Space, it has cocktail menus, two main rooms, nightly changing light shows, a bathroom DJ and a chic, tepee-dotted open-air garden. DJs Martin Garrix, Eric Prydz and Armin Van Buuren have had residencies here.

**★ Ushuaïa** CLUB

(☎971 92 81 93; Platja d'en Bossa 10; €40-100; ⏱3 or 5pm-midnight May-Oct; 📶) Queen of daytime clubbing, ice-cool Ushuaïa is an open-air megaclub, packed with designer-clad hedonistas and waterside fun. The party starts early, with superstar DJs such as David Guetta, Martin Garrix, Luciano and Robin Schulz, and poolside lounging on Bali-style beds. Check out the Sky Lounge for sparkling sea views, or stay the night in the minimalist-chic **hotel** (www.ushuaiabeachhotel.com; r €330-992, ste €720-1550; ⏱May-Oct; P❄📶🏊).

**★ Privilege** CLUB

(www.privilegeibiza.com; Carretera Eivissa-Sant Antoni, Sant Rafel de Sa Creu; €35-60; ⏱midnight-6am May-Sep) The world's biggest club, Privilege is a mind-blowing space that regularly hosts 10,000 clubbers. The venue was originally an open-air affair called Ku: stars including Freddie Mercury and James Brown headlined. Privilege's best times were undoubtedly during Manumission's infamous residency (1994–2006), with groundbreaking theatrics (including live sex shows). DJs Tiësto and Armin Van Buuren have also enjoyed seasons here.

## Getting There & Away

With your own wheels you'll have the most freedom to explore hidden parts of the south, though summer parking can be a nightmare.

Buses link Ibiza Town and Sant Antoni with many southern beaches. Most are May-to-October services only; check Ibiza Bus (http://ibizabus.com).

# East Coast Ibiza

The 'capital' of Ibiza's east coast and the island's third-largest town, Santa Eulària des Riu is a pretty coastal resort with an easygoing vibe, a large marina, a fine seaside

WORTH A TRIP

## SANT CARLES DE PERALTA

A quiet, unhurried village, 6km northeast of Santa Eulària des Riu, pretty Sant Carles de Peralta has been pulling in bohemian travellers since the 1960s hippy era. Lead was mined in the region from Roman times until the early 20th century, but today it's tourism that fires the local economy. The town's major draw is the massive, world-famous Saturday hippy market, **Las Dalias** (www.lasdalias.es; Carretera Santa Eulària-Sant Carles Km 12; ⌚10am-8pm Sat year-round, plus 7pm-1am Mon & Tue Jun-Sep & Sun Aug), but it's also surrounded by rolling countryside, has an elegant 18th-century **church** (Plaça de l'Església; ⌚hours vary), a fine example of an Ibizan **casament** (⌚Mar-Oct, hours vary), or farmhouse, which is signposted just beyond the southern edge of town, and stands close to some wonderful north-eastern beaches.

promenade, good down-to-earth eateries and a small but beautiful historical quarter centred on its Puig de Missa hilltop. Dotting the surrounding countryside are a string of lovely (and lively) beaches: family-friendly **Cala Llonga** sits just south of Santa Eulària, while gorgeous coves such as **Cala Martina**, **Cala Nova**, **Cala Llenya**, **Cala Boix** and particularly charming **Cala Mastella** extend along the coast northeast of town.

**★Puig de Missa** HISTORIC SITE

The hillock looming at the southwest end of Santa Eulària was a perfect retreat for the town's citizens during the centuries when Ibiza was plagued by pirate attacks. Crowning its 52m summit is a remarkable **fortress-church** (⌚10am-6pm, Mass 11am Sun), with its very own defence tower. There are a couple of interesting museums here, too. The most scenic route up is on the steep stairs from Carrer de Sant Jaume.

**★Cala Mastella** BEACH

This little sandy cove is tucked into a deep inlet where pine trees reach down and almost kiss the emerald-green water, 9km northeast of Santa Eulària. Outside high season, you might have it entirely to yourself. A seasonal kiosk serves mojitos and *bocadillos*. Scramble around the rocks at the beach's northeastern end to reach renowned seafood restaurant **El Bigotes** (☎650 797633; meals €25; ⌚noon-4pm Easter-Oct).

**★Amante** MEDITERRANEAN €€€

(☎971 19 61 76; www.amanteibiza.com; Cala Sol d'en Serra; mains €16-30; ⌚restaurant 11am-midnight mid-Apr–mid-Oct; 📶) Gazing out over the Mediterranean from cliffs above a hidden cove, 1km southwest of Cala Llonga, Amante is one of Ibiza's most fashionable and romantic restaurants. During daylight it's a glitzy beach club (with €30 sun loungers), but from sunset it becomes an exquisitely beautiful place to dine, with a creative, delicious (if expensive) Spanish-Italian menu infused with home-grown ingredients.

### ℹ Getting There & Away

Santa Eulària is well linked to Ibiza Town, Sant Antoni and the northern beaches by frequent bus services, some of which also stop at various east-coast beaches. For up-to-date schedules, see Ibiza Bus (http://ibizabus.com). Some buses are summer-only.

## North & Interior Ibiza

The least-populated and most rustic part of the island, northern Ibiza has a boho, off-grid vibe thanks to its strong hippy heritage and spectacular, remote landscapes, which appeal to cyclists, walkers and wanderers alike.

Portinatx is the north's busiest resort, while Sant Joan de Labritja offers a slice of low-key Ibizan life and Sant Carles de Peralta gets lively with its hippy market. A little further south, gorgeous interior villages such as Sant Llorenç de Balàfia and Santa Gertrudis de Fruitera await discovery.

**Benirràs** BEACH

Reached by two spectacular serpentine roads, the distant, silvery northern bay of Benirràs has high, forested cliffs, a trio of bar-restaurants and sun loungers with jade-hued umbrellas to rent. It's a dreamy location for sunset, one that Ibiza's boho tribe has favoured for decades. On Sundays, there's always an assembly of drummers banging out a salutation to the sinking sun.

**Aigües Blanques** BEACH

This exposed, east-facing, gold-sand beach gets its name ('White Waters') from the surf, which whips up here in strong winds. Most of the year it's actually very tranquil, and the scenery is stunning, with several sandy bays divided by crumbling cliffs. This is an official nudist beach, very popular with northern Ibiza's hippy community. It's also the perfect spot to witness a sunrise over the Mediterranean. It's 4km northeast of Sant Carles; park and walk 10 (steep) minutes down.

**Cala d'en Serra** BEACH

This sheltered bay, 2.5km east of Portinatx, is one of the island's prettiest, reached by a scenic road offering a succession of vistas over the azure water below (the road is in terrible condition; walk down in 10 minutes). A collection of fishers' shacks dots the small sandy beach, sadly somewhat disfigured by the concrete carcass of a long-abandoned hotel just above.

**★Atzaró** SPA HOTEL €€€

(☎971 33 88 38; www.atzaro.com; Carretera Santa Eulària-Sant Joan Km 15; r €495-545, ste €630-1190; P❄📶🏊) Atzaró is the ultimate in rural-Ibiza luxury. Most rooms have private terraces or gardens and are served up with iPads, smart TVs and plush robes; some also come with fireplaces or private pools and all-teak, four-poster beds. Besides a well-regarded restaurant (set menu €30), there's a divine **spa** (☎971 33 88 38; www.atzaro.com; Carretera Santa Eulària-Sant Joan Km 15; day pass €45; ⏲10am-8pm) within fragrant orange groves. Atzaró is 2.5km east of Sant Llorenç.

**★Giri Café** SPANISH €€

(☎971 33 34 74; https://cafe.thegiri.com; Plaça d'Espanya 5, Sant Joan de Labritja; mains €11-25; ⏲10am-midnight Apr-Oct; 📶) This stunning cafe-restaurant, with an exquisitely stylish rustic-chic interior and a blissful garden, ticks all the right progressive foodie boxes: seasonal, locally sourced, sustainably produced and (mainly) organic ingredients. But does raved-about Giri deliver? It certainly does. From Iberian ham platters and rosemary-sprinkled chips to falafel burgers and salmon tartare with avocado, parsley-coriander mayo and yuzu, imaginative dishes are beautifully presented.

## ℹ Getting There & Away

Public transport is more limited in the north than elsewhere on the island. There are some bus services, many of which only operate from May to October; see Ibiza Bus (http://ibizabus.com).

# West Ibiza

Ibiza's western coastline conceals some beautiful sandy coves, while just inland lie sprawling vineyards and charming white-washed villages. Infamous Sant Antoni ('San An') certainly lives up to its reputation as a Brits-abroad booze-up destination, but there's also a more chilled-out scene to be found in the west, such as along the town's Sunset Strip, the beaches to the town's north and southwest, or just north at mellow seaside hang-out Hostal La Torre.

**★Platges de Comte** BEACH

Occupying a low-lying headland, this dreamy cluster of three blonde-sand coves enjoys shallow, fabulously clear aquamarine waters. The beaches face directly west, making this a ridiculously popular late-afternoon spot, when hundreds gather to watch the sun sink into the Mediterranean, often from ultra-boho-cool bar-restaurant **Sunset Ashram** (☎661 347222; www.sunsetashram.com; Platges de Comte; ⏲10am-8pm Apr & May, to 2am Jun-Oct).

**★Hostal La Torre** BAR

(☎971 34 22 71; www.latorreibiza.com; Cap Negret; ⏲8am-1am) Big international names such as DJ Harvey join resident DJs for daily in-season sessions at this clifftop, sea-view, in-the-know terrace bar-restaurant renowned for its laid-back, uncommercial, old-Ibiza vibe. It's a magical sunset spot, with tables across the hillside and light bouncing off the glassy Mediterranean. Try a Balearic Spritz (gin, vermouth, passionfruit and *cava*) or any other fabulously creative cocktail.

### SANT ANTONI'S COASTAL SURROUNDS

There are some wonderful beaches near Sant Antoni. The town borders a natural harbour and reasonable beach, but there are finer options further afield. Swooping southwest, **Cala Bassa** is a beautiful (busy) cove with sheltered azure waters. Beyond, **Platges de Comte** have top sunsets and some of Ibiza's clearest seas. To the north, **Calas Salada** and **Gració** are white-sand delights.

## Getting There & Away

Bus L8 runs between Sant Antoni's bus station and Ibiza Town (€2, 25 minutes, every 15 to 30 minutes).

West-coast buses run from Sant Antoni's **bus station** (Carrer Londres).

# FORMENTERA

POP 12,216

Dangling off the south coast of Ibiza, a mere half-hour away by fast ferry, the 20km-long island of Formentera is a beautifully pure, get-away-from-it-all escape. Formentera's pace of life is blissfully languid, designed for lazy days spent lounging on some of Europe's (dare we say the world's?) most exquisite beaches, where frost-white slithers of sand are smoothed by water in unbelievable shades of azure, turquoise and lapis lazuli. Tourism is tightly tied to environmental ethics, with hotel numbers restricted, construction controlled and most visitors exploring on two wheels.

## Sights

With sugar-white sands and perfectly turquoise water, the astonishingly beautiful, pencil-slim Trucador Peninsula rivals the world's finest beaches. Dreamy Platja Illetes slinks along the west side of this narrow sliver of land; on its east coast (just a few steps away) is the equally gorgeous Platja Llevant. In high season, these back-to-back twin beaches get very busy, but they're still an essential Formentera experience.

Since it's mostly flat, Formentera has some lovely, relatively easy walking and cycling routes, ranging from short coastal rambles to a 9km, 2¾-hour countryside hike from Sant Francesc to Cap de Barbària. Tourist offices provide maps outlining 32 signposted routes totalling 100km.

**★Platja Illetes** BEACH

Forming the western section of the slender Trucador Peninsula, stunning Platja Illetes is as close a vision of the Caribbean (minus the coconut trees) as you could imagine in Europe, with bleach-blonde sand and trans-

### FORMENTERA IN A DAY

Breeze into your Formentera stay with a lazy breakfast at **Ca Na Pepa** (608 576060; www.canapepa.com; Plaça de Sa Constituciò 5; breakfasts €2-10, mains €9-17; 8.30am-11pm Apr-Oct; ), in the pretty island capital Sant Francesc Xavier. Check out the 18th-century **fortress-church** (Plaça de Sa Constitució; hours vary) and wander the village's boutiques, including uber-tasteful **Muy** (971 32 16 22; Carrer Sant Joan 55; 10am-2pm & 7-10pm May–mid-Oct), espadrille sensation **Alma Gemela** (946 11 26 60; http://almagemelaformentera.com; Carrer d'Isidor Macabich 9; 10am-2pm & 6pm-midnight May-Sep) and bikini-bliss **Janne Ibiza** (971 32 89 63; www.janneibiza.es; Carrer d'Isidor Macabich 11; 11.30am-2pm & 6.30-10.30pm).

You can't beat the impossibly beautiful bleach-blonde sands of the idyllic Trucador Peninsula; take your pick from Platja Illetes or Platja Llevant and gaze out on mirage-like turquoise waters. If you're hungry, lunch in a stylishly converted mill at **Es Molí de Sal** (971 18 74 91; https://esmolidesal.es/en; Calle Afores; mains €20-45; 1-11pm Apr–mid-Oct) or, for a slightly more budget menu, at beachside **Restaurante Tanga** (971 18 79 05; www.restaurantetanga.com; Platja Llevant; mains €15-28; 8.30am-8pm May-Oct).

Post-beach, head to the island's southeastern coast and La Mola peninsula to marvel at the famous 19th-century Far de Sa Mola (p800) and swing by gorgeous cafe Codice Luna (p800). Then it's an easy backtrack to Platja de Migjorn for sundowners at Chiringuito Bartolo (p800), Piratabus (p800), **10.7** (660 985248; www.10punto7.com; mains €22-28; 1-5pm & 8-11pm late May-Sep; ) or glitzy Gecko Beach Club (p800), followed by a beachside seafood dinner at **Sa Platgeta** (971 18 76 14, 622 005913; Es Ca Marí; mains €10-25; 1-11pm mid-Apr–mid-Oct). Alternatively head to Sant Ferran for local cuisine and perhaps some live music at old hippy hangout **Fonda Pepe** (Carrer Major 55, Sant Ferran de Ses Roques; 8pm-1am Apr-Oct). If you fancy, after midnight, hit Formentera's one and only club: **Tipic** (676 885452; www.clubtipic.com; Avinguda Miramar 164; €30-45; 11pm-6am May–mid-Oct), in Es Pujols.

## Formentera

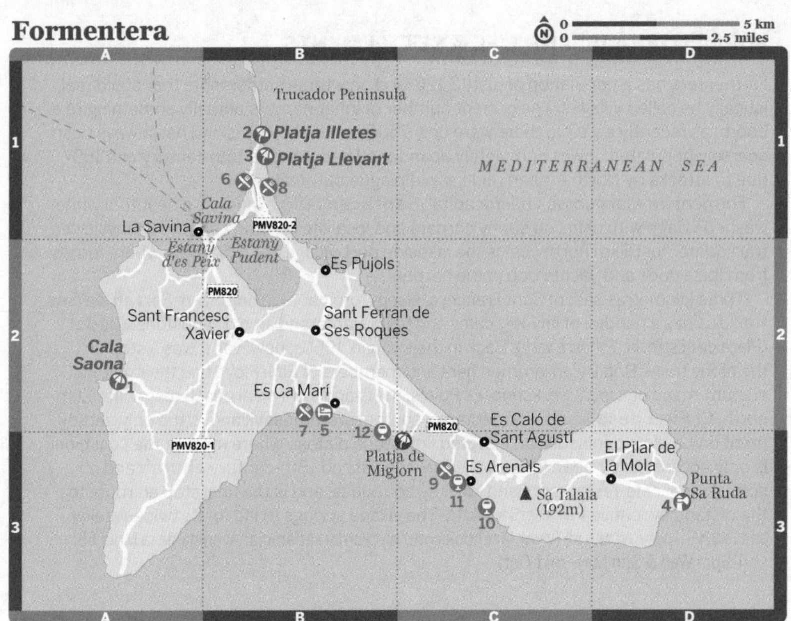


### Formentera

**Top Sights**
1 Cala Saona ........ A2
2 Platja Illetes ........ B1
3 Platja Llevant ........ B1

**Sights**
4 Far de Sa Mola ........ D3

**Sleeping**
5 Gecko Beach Club ........ B2

**Eating**
Codice Luna ........ (see 4)
6 Es Molí de Sal ........ B1
7 Sa Platgeta ........ B2
8 Restaurante Tanga ........ B1
9 10.7 ........ C3

**Drinking & Nightlife**
10 Chiringuito Bartolo ........ C3
11 Piratabus ........ C3
12 Blue Bar ........ B3

lucent turquoise waters. You may never want to leave. Just offshore are the two small *illetes* (islets), Pouet and Rodona, that give the beach its name. In high season, expect lots of day trippers from Ibiza.

**★Platja Llevant** BEACH

Through the steep sand dunes on the eastern side of the Trucador Peninsula, Platja Llevant is a divine, undeveloped beach. The powdery sand is so white it dazzles your eyes, and the aquamarine water is fantastically clear. It's also very shallow, so safe for children, and the sea warms to bathtub temperatures on summer days. There can be strong winds here, so do heed the warning flags.

**★Cala Saona** BEACH

Delectable Cala Saona is a fabulous west-coast beach where the water glows a startling shade of luminous turquoise and the powder-soft sand is salt white. Though popular, it isn't too developed, bar a couple of laid-back, good-vibe summer beach shacks, a kayak/SUP-rental stand and a hotel at the back of the bay. It's 3km west of the Sant Francesc–Cap de Barbària road and signposted 2km southwest of Sant Francesc.

## Sleeping

With just over 50 *hostals* and hotels on Formentera, beds are like gold dust in summer and often booked out in a flash. Make reservations well ahead, though generally

## FORMENTERA ISLAND LIFE & SETTLEMENTS

Formentera has a population of just 12,126, and only three settlements that could realistically be called villages. The current number of inhabitants is actually something of a boom: as recently as 2005 there were only 7500 residents. The island has always been sparsely populated; it was completely abandoned between the 15th century and 1697, due to attacks by North African raiders and plague outbreaks.

Formentera's languorous microcapital, **Sant Francesc Xavier**, is a beautiful whitewashed village with cafes on sunny corners and local life revolving around its idyllic central square. Just 3km northwest is the lakeside port-village of **La Savina**, where ferries from Ibiza dock and yachts bob in the harbour.

Three kilometres east of Sant Francesc, sleepy, ordinary-looking **Sant Ferran de Ses Roques** has a handful of low-key cafes and restaurants, and an old sandstone **chapel** (Plaça de l'Església; ⏰hours vary). Back in the swingin' 1960s, however, it was a stop on the hippy trail – Bob Dylan jammed here and members of Pink Floyd had their guitars custom-made at a local workshop. Es Pujols, the island's only real beach resort, lies 2km north. **El Pilar de la Mola**, Formentera's southeasternmost village, is the only settlement on La Mola peninsula, an elevated limestone plateau where most of the coastline is only accessible by boat. It has a pretty whitewashed 18th-century **church** and a sprinkling of cafe-restaurants and low-key boutiques, and is the final stop en route to the distant, evocative **Far de Sa Mola**. The village springs to life for its twice-weekly **artisan-hippy market** (www.facebook.com/hippiemarketlamola; Avenida de la Mola 65; ⏰4-9pm Wed & Sun May–mid-Oct).

speaking, prices are quite steep. Rental apartments are a better deal, especially for stays of a week or more.

**★Gecko Beach Club** HOTEL €€€
(☎971 32 80 24; www.geckobeachclub.com; Es Ca Marí; r incl breakfast from €500; P ❄ 📶 🏊) Formentera slips into the glam shoes of Ibiza at this gorgeous beachside beauty of a hotel, recently sleekly remodelled. It occupies what was originally an old *casa payesa* (farmhouse), pairing minimalist-modern rooms (some featuring private plunge pools) with a laid-back vibe and A-list credentials – think poolside yoga (including retreats), cabana beds, signature cocktails and hammocks strung between palms.

## Eating

**Codice Luna** CAFE €
(www.codiceluna.com; Far de Sa Mola; dishes €3.50-15; ⏰10.30am-9pm Apr-Oct) Right beside the La Mola lighthouse, Codice Luna is a beautifully designed cafe-restaurant, all whitewashed wood with an exquisite terrace opening up soul-stirring views of the Mediterranean. A small tapas-style menu includes tasty breakfast *tostadas* with local cheese, homemade cakes and platters of Iberian ham. A DJ party celebrates every full moon in summer.

**Ca Na Joana** MEDITERRANEAN €€€
(☎971 32 31 60; http://canajoanaformentera.es; Carrer Berenguer Renart 2, Sant Francesc Xavier; mains €18-30; ⏰8pm-1am May-Oct) The magically seductive setting is half the appeal at this exquisitely restored 17th-century house (one of Formentera's most ancient): all blanched walls, exposed stone and candlelit tables on a bougainvillea-shaded terrace. Service is slick and efficient, and modern-Mediterranean dishes are elegantly prepared, from chilled carrot soup to squid-ink pasta, seafood specials and Iberian ham carved in the garden.

## Drinking & Nightlife

**Chiringuito Bartolo** BAR
(Platja de Migjorn; ⏰10am-sunset May-Oct) Colourful Chiringuito Bartolo, at the far southeastern end of Platja de Migjorn, must be the world's tiniest beach bar, and is much loved by islanders. Sitting cheerfully on stilts, it hosts just a smattering of tables, and serves up drinks and snacks (€7 to €10) such as burgers and sandwiches to wander away with if there's nowhere to sit.

**Piratabus** BAR
(Platja de Migjorn; ⏰10am-sunset May-Oct) A sun-bleached little beach shack that's something of a low-key Formentera legend, Piratabus is perfect for sipping a mojito (€10) and

demolishing a few tapas (tortilla, nachos, potato salad; €5) or a *bocadillo* while drinking in the sensational coastal panoramas.

**Blue Bar** BAR

(☎666 758190; www.bluebarformentera.com; Platja de Migjorn; ⊙1pm-4am Apr-Oct; 📶) This psychedelic, sea-splashed bar is prime sunset stuff. Back in the '60s, word has it, it even played host to Bob Marley, Pink Floyd and King Crimson. Everything is blue – seats, sunshades, tables, toilets, walls. There's even a blue curaçao-based cocktail! Follow the signposted dirt track from Km 7.8 on the PM820.

## Information

Formentera's main **tourist office** (☎971 32 20 57; www.formentera.es; Carrer de Calpe, La Savina; ⊙10am-7pm Mon-Fri, 10am-2pm & 5-7pm Sat & Sun May-Oct, 10am-2pm & 5-7pm Nov-Apr) is beside the ferry landing point in La Savina.

## Getting There & Away

Formentera has no airport. The only point of entry is the ferry port of La Savina, on the north side of the island, with excellent facilities, including a tourist office and bike and scooter rental.

Regular passenger ferries run between Ibiza Town and La Savina, with departures every 20 to 30 minutes May to October and reduced services November to April. Day-trip boats run from most Ibiza resorts and the Ibizan towns of Sant Antoni and Santa Eulària. Services include:

**Aquabus** (p792) One way/return €15/20; one hour

**Baleària** (p792) One way €18 to €25.50, return €25 to €44; 30 minutes to one hour

**Mediterránea Pitiusa** (p792) One way/return €27/46; 30 minutes

**Trasmapi** (p792) One way/return €27/47; 30 minutes

## Getting Around

Formentera has a decent bus network run by Autocares Paya (http://busformentera.com). Schedules vary considerably according to the time of year; some services operate only mid-April to mid-October. Regular bus tickets cost €1.80 to €2.55. Routes include:

- L1 La Savina–Sant Francesc–Sant Ferran–Es Pujols–La Savina
- L2 La Savina–Sant Francesc–Sant Ferran–Platja de Migjorn–Far de Sa Mola
- L7 La Savina–Platja Illetes–Es Pujols–Sant Ferran–Platja de Migjorn–Far de Sa Mola

Flat Formentera is perfectly set up for cyclists. Island tourist offices provide maps of 28 dedicated cycle paths around the island.

Bicycles (€8 to €10 per day), motorbikes (€30 to €40 per day) and cars (from €40) are available from rental outlets in La Savina (where you'll find many rental outlets right by the ferry terminal) and Es Pujols.

Taxis are fairly expensive on Formentera. From La Savina, expect to pay €12 to Es Pujols and around €15 to Platja de Migjorn.

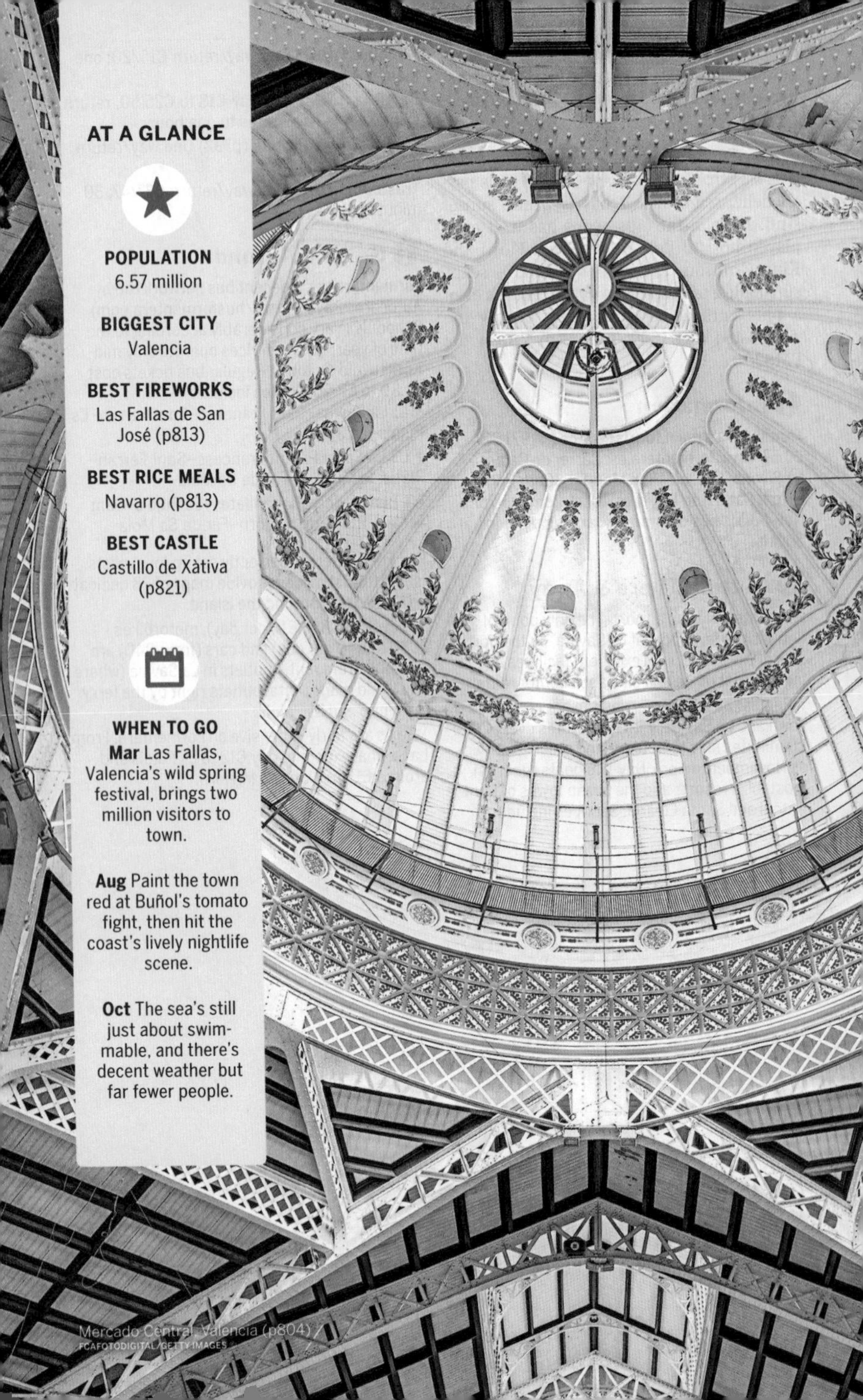

## AT A GLANCE

**POPULATION**
6.57 million

**BIGGEST CITY**
Valencia

**BEST FIREWORKS**
Las Fallas de San José (p813)

**BEST RICE MEALS**
Navarro (p813)

**BEST CASTLE**
Castillo de Xàtiva (p821)

**WHEN TO GO**

**Mar** Las Fallas, Valencia's wild spring festival, brings two million visitors to town.

**Aug** Paint the town red at Buñol's tomato fight, then hit the coast's lively nightlife scene.

**Oct** The sea's still just about swimmable, and there's decent weather but far fewer people.

Mercado Central, Valencia (p804)
FCAFOTODIGITAL/GETTY IMAGES

# Valencia & Murcia

The home of one of Spain's most famous exports, paella, is a marvellous stretch of coast offering fine beaches, truly wonderful eating and fabulous festivals. Valencia city's sophisticated cultural scene and stunning architecture make it one of Spain's most addictive metropolises.

Throughout this sunbathed coastal pleasure ground, a wealth of festivals awaits, whether you fancy top-notch rock music at Benicàssim, dynamic processions and friendly rivalry at Lorca's Semana Santa, re-enactments of Reconquista battles in the Moros y Cristianos festivals or one of the world's biggest food fights at La Tomatina.

While some coastal resorts are notoriously overdeveloped, there are plenty that aren't, with towns such as Dénia and Xàbia managing to conserve great charm. The ancient port of Cartagena has a magnificent array of Roman and Carthaginian ruins, while Murcia is a buzzy regional capital with pleasant parks and a cracking eating scene.

**INCLUDES**

# VALENCIA

POP 791,400

Spain's third-largest city is a magnificent place, content for Madrid and Barcelona to grab the headlines while it gets on with being a wonderfully liveable spot with thriving cultural, dining and nightlife scenes. Never afraid to innovate, Valencia diverted its flood-prone river to the outskirts and converted the former riverbed into a glorious green ribbon of park winding right through the city. On it are the strikingly futuristic buildings of the Ciudad de las Artes y las Ciencias, designed by local boy Santiago Calatrava. Other brilliant contemporary buildings grace the city, which also has a fistful of fabulous Modernista buildings, great museums, a long stretch of beach and a large, characterful old quarter.

## Sights

### North Ciutat Vella

**★Catedral de Valencia** CATHEDRAL
(Map p810; ☎963 91 81 27; http://museocatedralvalencia.com; Plaza de la Reina; adult/child/family €8/5.50/18; ⊙10.30am-6.30pm Mon-Fri, 10.30am-5.30pm Sat, 2-5.30pm Sun Mar–mid-Jul & mid-Sep–Oct, 10.30am-6.30pm Mon-Sat, 2-6.30pm Sun mid-Jul–mid-Sep, 10.30am-5.30pm Mon-Sat, 2-5.30pm Sun Nov, 10.30am-5.30pm Mon-Sat Dec-Feb) Valencia's cathedral was built over a mosque after the 1238 reconquest. Its low, wide, brick-vaulted triple nave is mostly Gothic, with neoclassical side chapels. Highlights are its museum, rich Italianate frescoes above the altarpiece, a pair of Goyas in the **Capilla de San Francisco de Borja**, and, in the flamboyant Gothic **Capilla del Santo Cáliz**, what's claimed to be the **Holy Grail** from which Christ sipped during the Last Supper. Admission includes an audio guide.

**Museo Catedralicio Diocesano** MUSEUM
(Map p810; ☎963 91 81 27; http://museocatedralvalencia.com; Catedral de Valencia; incl in cathedral entry, €3 when cathedral visits closed; ⊙10am-6.30pm Mon-Sat year-round, 2-6.30pm Sun Jun-Sep, 10am-2pm Sun Mar-May & Oct, closed Sun Nov-Feb) The cathedral museum is a good-looking blend of the modern and venerable. There are some excellent religious paintings here; it's intriguing to see the huge evolution in style in just one generation between the Renaissance paintings of Vicente Macip and those of his son, the great Juan de Juanes. The highlights, though, are the wonderful 14th-century carved apostles, precursors of those that flank the cathedral's main door. In the basement you can view Roman and medieval remains.

**★Mercado Central** MARKET
(Map p810; ☎963 82 91 00; www.mercadocentralvalencia.es; Plaza del Mercado; ⊙7.30am-3pm Mon-Sat) Valencia's vast Modernista covered market, constructed in 1928, is a swirl of smells, movement and colour. Spectacular seafood counters display cephalopods and crustaceans galore and numerous fish species; meat stalls groan under the weight of sausages and giant steaks; and the fruit and vegetables, many produced locally in Valencia's *huerta* (area of market gardens), are of special quality. A classy tapas bar here lets you sip a wine and enjoy the atmosphere.

**★La Lonja** HISTORIC BUILDING
(Map p810; ☎962 08 41 53; www.valencia.es; Calle de la Lonja; adult/child €2/1, Sun free; ⊙10am-7pm Mon-Sat, to 2pm Sun) This splendid building, a Unesco World Heritage site, was originally Valencia's silk and commodity exchange, built in the late 15th century when the city was booming. It's one of Spain's finest examples of a civil Gothic building. Two main structures flank a citrus-studded courtyard: the magnificent Sala de Contratación, a cathedral of commerce with soaring twisted pillars, and the Consulado del Mar, where a maritime tribunal sat. The Consulado's top floor has a stunning coffered ceiling brought here from another building.

**★Iglesia de San Nicolás** CHURCH
(Map p810; ☎963 91 33 17; www.sannicolasvalencia.com; Calle de Caballeros 35; adult/child incl Museo de la Seda €7/free; ⊙10.30am-7.30pm Tue-Fri, 10.30am-6.30pm Sat, 1-8pm Sun Oct-Jun, 10.30am-9pm Tue-Fri, 10.30am-7.30pm Sat, 11.30am-9pm Sun Jul-Sep) Recently reopened to the public after a magnificent restoration, this single-naved church down a passageway is a striking sight. Over the original Gothic vaulting, the ceiling is a painted baroque riot, with enough cherubs for a documentary on childhood obesity. The altarpiece is in similar style, with corkscrew (Solomonic) columns framing the twin saints who share the church: San Nicolás saving boys from the pickling tub, and San Pedro Mártir with a cutlass in his head.

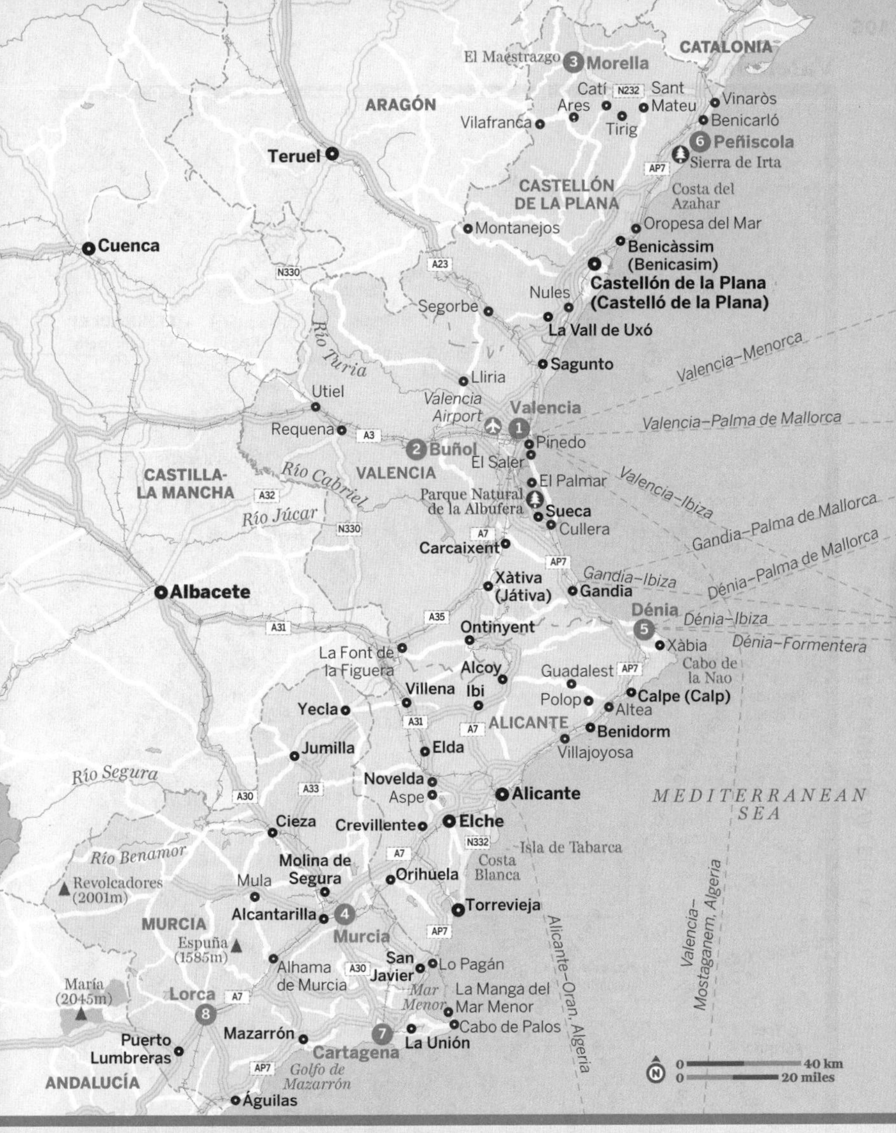


# Valencia & Murcia Highlights

1 **Valencia** (p804) Marvelling at city architecture and superb eating scene.

2 **La Tomatina** (p820) Painting the town red at this famous tomato fight in Buñol.

3 **Morella** (p825) Savouring your first glimpse of this stunning medieval fortress town from afar.

4 **Murcia** (p839) Strolling the pretty centre of this underrated city and exploring the tapas culture.

5 **Dénia** (p830) Exploring the most characterful of the Costa Blanca towns.

6 **Peñíscola** (p823) Savouring the stunning sea views from the old town.

7 **Cartagena** (p842) Discovering the fascinating Roman and Carthaginian sites of this intriguing port city.

8 **Lorca** (p846) Enjoying the noble beauty of the old town and its castle, as well as Spain's most lively Semana Santa celebrations.

# Valencia

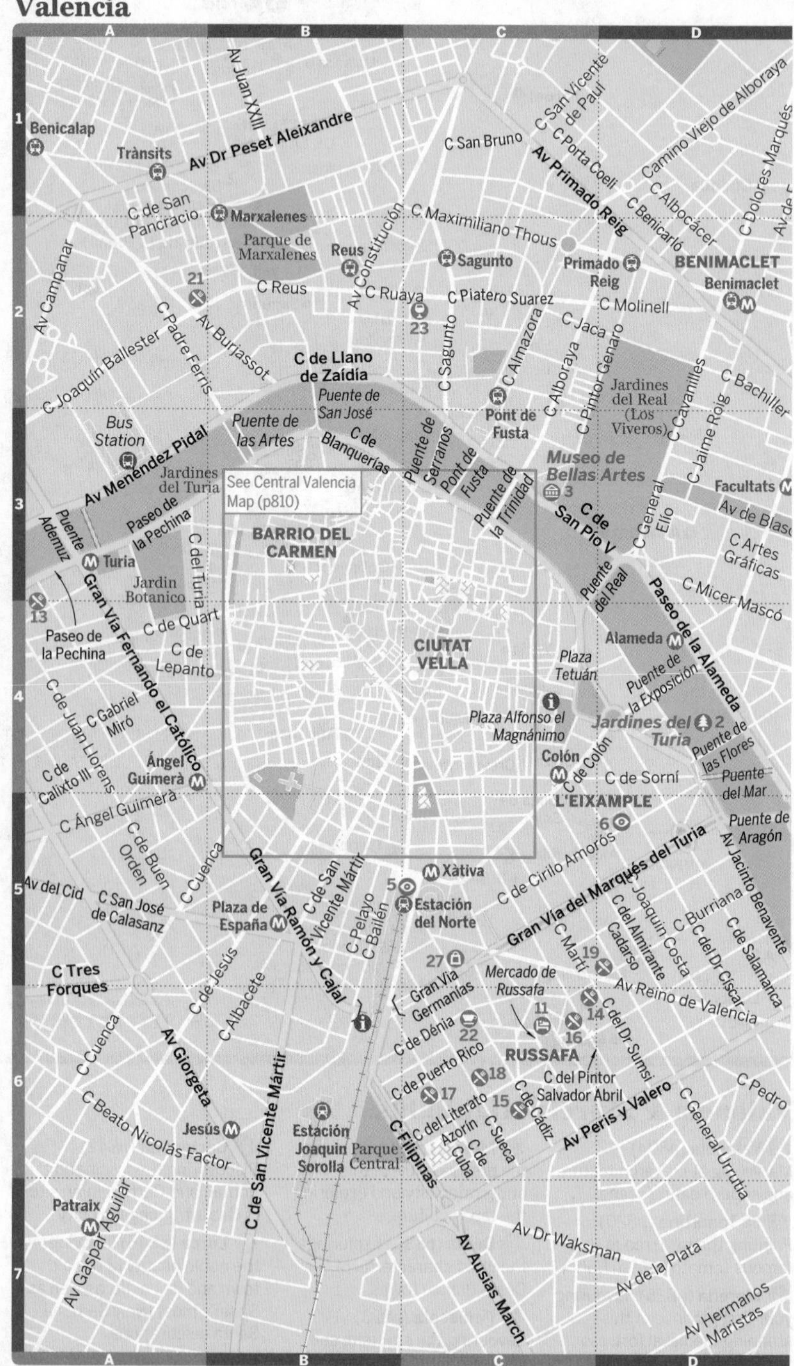

Benicalap
Trànsits
Av Dr Peset Aleixandre
Av Juan XXIII
C de San Pancracio
Marxalenes
Parque de Marxalenes
Reus
Av Constitución
C Maximiliano Thous
Sagunto
C San Bruno
C San Vicente de Paul
C Porta Coeli
Av Primado Reig
Camino Viejo de Alboraya
C Albocàcer
C Benicarló
C Dolores Marqués
Primado Reig
BENIMACLET
Benimaclet
Av Campanar
C Reus
C Ruaya
C Piatero Suarez
C Molinell
C Jaca
C Padre Ferris
Av Burjassot
C Joaquín Ballester
C de Llano de Zaídía
C Sagunto
C Almazora
C Alboraya
C Pintor Genaro
Jardines del Real (Los Viveros)
C Cavanilles
C Jaime Roig
C Bachiller
Puente de San José
Pont de Fusta
Bus Station
Puente de las Artes
C de Blanquerías
Puente de Serranos
Pont de Fusta
Puente de la Trinidad
Museo de Bellas Artes
Av Menéndez Pidal
Jardines del Turia
See Central Valencia Map (p810)
C de San Pío V
C General Elío
Facultats
Av de Blasco
Puente Ademuz
Paseo de la Pechina
BARRIO DEL CARMEN
C del Turia
C Artes Gráficas
Turia
Jardin Botanico
Puente del Real
Paseo de la Alameda
C Micer Mascó
Paseo de la Pechina
C de Quart
Gran Vía Fernando el Católico
C de Lepanto
CIUTAT VELLA
Alameda
Plaza Tetuán
Puente de la Exposición
C de Juan Llorens
C Gabriel Miró
Plaza Alfonso el Magnánimo
Jardines del Turia
Puente de las Flores
C de Calixto III
Ángel Guimerà
Colón
C de Colón
C de Sorní
Puente del Mar
C Ángel Guimerà
L'EIXAMPLE
Puente de Aragón
C de Buen Orden
C Cuenca
Gran Vía Ramón y Cajal
C de San Vicente Mártir
Xàtiva
C de Cirilo Amorós
Gran Vía del Marqués del Turia
Av Jacinto Benavente
Av del Cid
C San José de Calasanz
Plaza de España
C Pelayo
C Bailén
Estación del Norte
C Joaquín Costa
C del Almirante Cadarso
C Martí
C Burriana
C del Dr Císcar
C de Salamanca
C Tres Forques
C de Jesús
C Albacete
Gran Vía Germanías
Mercado de Russafa
Av Reino de Valencia
C de Dénia
C del Dr Sumsi
C Cuenca
Av Giorgeta
C de Puerto Rico
RUSSAFA
C del Pintor Salvador Abril
C Pedro
C del Literato Azorín
C de Cádiz
Av Peris y Valero
C General Urrutia
C Beato Nicolás Factor
Jesús
Estación Joaquín Sorolla
Parque Central
C Filipinas
C Sueca
C de Cuba
Patraix
Av Gaspar Aguilar
Av Dr Waksman
Av Ausias March
Av de la Plata
Av Hermanos Maristas

## Valencia

**Top Sights**

1 Ciudad de las Artes y las Ciencias ........ F7
2 Jardines del Turia ........ D4
3 Museo de Bellas Artes ........ C3
4 Museo de las Ciencias Príncipe Felipe ........ F7

**Sights**

5 Estación del Norte ........ C5
6 Mercado de Colón ........ D5
7 Museo Fallero ........ E6
8 Oceanogràfic ........ F7
9 Palau de les Arts Reina Sofía ........ E6

**Activities, Courses & Tours**

10 Gulliver ........ E6

**Sleeping**

11 Russafa Youth Hostel ........ C6

**Eating**

12 Balansiya ........ F3
13 Bar Ricardo ........ A4
14 Canalla Bistro ........ C6
15 Casa Viva ........ C6
16 Dos Estaciones ........ C6
17 Dulce de Leche ........ C6
18 El Rodamón de Russafa ........ C6
19 Goya ........ D5
20 Gran Azul ........ E5
21 Ricard Camarena ........ A2

**Drinking & Nightlife**

22 Cafe Berlin ........ C6
23 Deseo 54 ........ C2
Mercado de Colón ........ (see 6)

**Entertainment**

24 Hemisfèric ........ F7
25 Valencia Club de Fútbol ........ E4
26 Wah Wah ........ F4

**Shopping**

27 Abanicos Carbonell ........ C5

## South Ciutat Vella

**★Museo del Patriarca** GALLERY, CHURCH

(Colegio de San Juan; Map p810; ☎692 491769; www.patriarcavalencia.es; Calle de la Nave 1; admission €3; ⏲11am-1.30pm, also often 5-7pm Mon-Fri)
This seminary was founded in the late 16th century by Juan de Ribera, a towering Counter Reformation figure who wielded enormous spiritual and temporal power in Spain and beyond. With an impressive if austere Renaissance courtyard-cloister, its main attraction is a small but excellent religious-art museum. El Greco and locals José de Ribera,

DON'T MISS

## CIUDAD DE LAS ARTES Y LAS CIENCIAS

**Ciudad de las Artes y las Ciencias** (City of Arts & Sciences; Map p806; ☎961 97 46 86; www.cac.es; Avenida del Professor López Piñero; 👪) is a stunning complex occupying a massive 350,000-sq-metre swath of the old Turia riverbed. It's occupied by a series of spectacular buildings that are mostly the work of world-famous, locally born architect Santiago Calatrava. The principal buildings are a majestic opera house, a science museum, a 3D cinema and an aquarium. Calatrava is a controversial figure for many Valencians, who complain about the complex's expense and various design flaws. Nevertheless, if your taxes weren't involved, it's awe-inspiring and pleasingly family-oriented.

**Palau de les Arts Reina Sofía** (Map p806; ☎tours 672 062523; www.lesarts.com; Avenida del Professor López Piñero 1; guided visit adult/child €11/8.80; ⊙guided visits 11am, 12.15pm, 1.30pm, 3.45pm & 5pm) Brooding over the riverbed like a giant beetle, its shell shimmering with translucent mosaic tiles, this ultramodern arts complex grafted onto the Ciudad de las Artes y las Ciencias has four auditoriums and enticing levels of plants poking out from under the ceramic exoskeleton. Outside of performance times, you can't enter except by guided visits. These run five times daily in Spanish and English. Book via the website.

**Museo de las Ciencias Príncipe Felipe** (Map p806; ☎961 97 47 86; www.cac.es; adult/child €8/6.20, with Hemisfèric €12/9.30; ⊙10am-6pm or 7pm mid-Sep–Jun, 10am-9pm Jul–mid-Sep; 👪) This brilliant science museum, stretching like a giant whale skeleton within the Ciudad de las Artes y las Ciencias, has a huge range of interactive material covering everything from outer space to brain biology. It's loads of fun for all ages and goes into good detail on its themes, incorporating issues such as the environment and nailing that elusive concept of learning for fun. All info is available in English.

**Oceanogràfic** (Map p806; ☎960 47 06 47; www.oceanografic.org; Camino de las Moreras; adult/child €30.70/22.90, audio guide €3.70, combined ticket with Hemisfèric & Museo de las Ciencias Príncipe Felipe €38.20/28.60; ⊙10am-6pm Sun-Fri, to 8pm Sat mid-Sep–mid-Jun, 10am-8pm mid-Jun–mid-Jul & early Sep, 10am-midnight mid-Jul–Aug; 👪) Spain's most famous aquarium is the southernmost building of the Ciudad de las Artes y las Ciencias. It's an impressive display, divided into a series of climate zones, reached overground or underground from the central hub building. The sharks, complete with tunnel, are an obvious favourite, while a series of beautiful tanks present species from temperate, Mediterranean, Red Sea and tropical waters. Less happily, the aquarium also keeps captive dolphins and belugas – research suggests this is detrimental to their welfare.

**Hemisfèric** (Map p806; ☎961 97 46 86; www.cac.es; Ciudad de las Artes y las Ciencias; sessions adult/child €8/6.20, incl Museo de las Ciencias Príncipe Felipe €12/9.30; ⊙from 10am) The unblinking, heavy-lidded eye of the Hemisfèric is at once planetarium, IMAX cinema and laser show. Sessions are roughly hourly, with a break at lunchtime, and multilingual soundtracks are available. It's definitely worth booking ahead in summer, as it has limited capacity and often fills up.



Juan de Juanes and Pedro Orrente are represented; there are also paintings from Caravaggio's workshop. Most surprising is the manuscript Thomas More was writing while awaiting execution in the Tower of London.

★**Museo Nacional de Cerámica** MUSEUM
(Map p810; ☎963 08 54 29; www.culturaydeporte.gob.es/mnescultura; Calle del Poeta Querol 2; adult/child €3/free, Sat afternoon & Sun free; ⊙10am-2pm & 4-8pm Tue-Sat, 10am-2pm Sun) Inside a striking palace, this ceramics museum celebrates an important local industry. Downstairs, as well as seeing a decadent hand-painted 1753 carriage, you can learn about the history of ceramics from baroque to modern, with great information (albeit sometimes a little difficult to relate to the pottery on display). Upstairs, historical ceramics are cleverly dotted with modern works, but the sumptuous, over-the-top interiors, ornate stucco, chinoiserie, damask panels and elaborate upholstery pull

plenty of focus. It's an outrageous rococo extravaganza.

**Estación del Norte** NOTABLE BUILDING
(Map p806; Calle de Xàtiva; ⏲5.30am-midnight) Trains first chugged into this richly adorned Modernista terminal in 1917. Its main foyer is decorated with ceramic mosaics and murals – and mosaic 'bon voyage' wishes in major European languages. There's a riot of oranges and greenery outside and the wooden ticket booths inside are especially lovely. Don't miss the ceramic paintings by Gregorio Muñoz Dueñas in a room to your right.

## Barrio del Carmen

The northwest corner of the old town is Valencia's oldest quarter, offering bohemian local character and several good museums. El Carme, as it is known in Valenciano, is fertile ground for eating and drinking, with a profusion of little bars and restaurants to track down in its narrow, confusing medieval street plan.

★**Torres de Quart** GATE
(Map p810; ☎618 803907; www.valencia.es; Calle de Guillem de Castro; adult/child €2/1, Sun free; ⏲10am-7pm Tue-Sat, to 2pm Sun) Spain's most magnificent city gate is quite a sight from the new town. You can clamber to the top of the 15th-century structure, which faces towards Madrid and the setting sun. Up high, notice the pockmarks caused by French cannonballs during the 19th-century Napoleonic invasion.

**Torres de Serranos** GATE
(Map p810; ☎963 91 90 70; www.valencia.es; Plaza de los Fueros; adult/child €2/1, Sun free; ⏲10am-7pm Mon-Sat, to 2pm Sun) Once the main exit to Barcelona and the north, the imposing 14th-century Torres de Serranos overlooks the former bed of the Río Turia. Together with the Torres de Quart, it is all that remains of Valencia's old city walls. Climb to the top for a great overview of the Barrio del Carmen and riverbed.

**Institut Valencià d'Art Modern** GALLERY
(IVAM; Map p810; ☎963 17 66 00; www.ivam.es; Calle de Guillem de Castro 118; adult/child €6/3, Sun free; ⏲11am-7.30pm Tue-Thu, Sat & Sun, to 9pm Fri) This impressive gallery hosts excellent temporary exhibitions and owns a small but impressive collection of 20th-century Spanish art. The most reliably permanent exhibition on display is the Julio González collection. This Catalan sculptor (1876–1942) lived in Paris and produced exquisite work with iron that influenced later artists such as David Smith and Eduardo Chillida.

## L'Eixample & Southern Valencia

**Mercado de Colón** MARKET
(Map p806; ☎963 37 11 01; www.mercadocolon.es; Calle de Cirilo Amorós; ⏲7.30am-2am Sun-Thu, to 3am Fri & Sat) This magnificent building, now colonised by cafes and boutique food outlets, was formerly a market, built in 1916 to serve the rising bourgeoisie of the new L'Eixample suburb. Its handsome metal skeleton is garnished with Modernista flourishes to create a stunning ensemble. It's a good place to try *horchata* (a sugary drink made from tiger nuts) and a fine refuge for families, as kids can run around and there's all-day food available.

## Northern & Eastern Valencia

★**Jardines del Turia** PARK
(Map p806; 👪) Stretching the length of the Río Turia's former course, this 9km-long lung of green is a fabulous mix of playing fields, cycling, jogging and walking paths, lawns and playgrounds. As it curves around the eastern part of the city, it's also a pleasant way of getting around. See Lilliputian kids scrambling over a magnificent, ever-patient **Gulliver** (⏲10am-8pm Sep-Jun, 10am-2pm & 5-9pm Jul & Aug; 👪; 🚌19, 95) south of the Palau de la Música concert hall.

★**Museo de Bellas Artes** GALLERY
(San Pío V; Map p806; ☎963 87 03 00; www.museobellasartesvalencia.gva.es; Calle de San Pío V 9; ⏲10am-8pm Tue-Sun) FREE Bright and spacious, this gallery ranks among Spain's best. Highlights include magnificent late-medieval altarpieces, and works by several Spanish masters, including some great Goya portraits, a haunting Velázquez self-portrait, an El Greco *John the Baptist* and works by Murillo, Ribera and the Ribaltas, father and son. In a dedicated wing, an excellent series of rooms focuses on the great, versatile Valencian painter Joaquín Sorolla (1863–1923), who, at his best, seemed to capture the spirit of an age through sensitive portraiture.

## Central Valencia

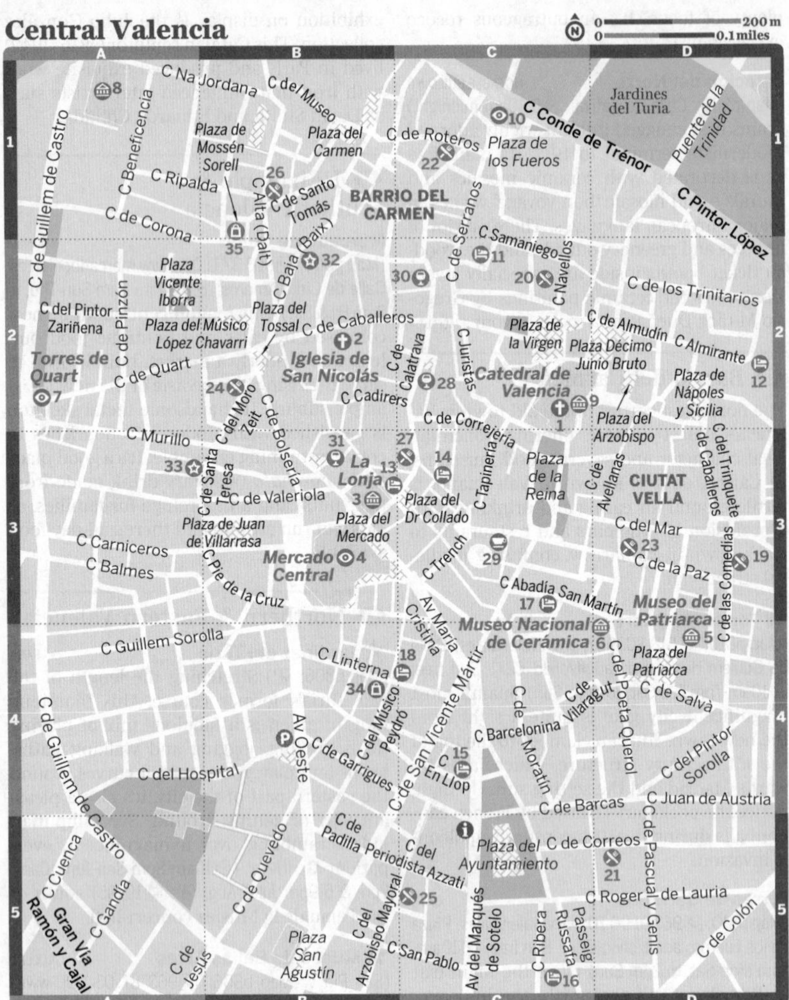


## Valencia's Beaches

Valencia's town beaches are 3km from the centre. Playa de las Arenas runs north into Playa de la Malvarrosa and Playa de la Patacona, forming a wide strip of sand some 4km long. It's bordered by the Paseo Marítimo promenade and a string of restaurants and cafes. The marina and port area is south of here, backed by the intriguing and increasingly trendy fishing district of El Cabanyal, which makes for excellent exploration.

## Activities & Courses

There's plenty to do outdoors in Valencia, and walking, running or cycling the green strip of the former riverbed, the Jardines del Turia (p809), is an excellent starting point. There are numerous walking tours of the city and the excellent new system of bike lanes means that cycling is very in, with hire outlets and tours all over town. Cultural activities can be sought out in a variety of arts centres, while the beach and marina zone offers scope for watery activities.

## Central Valencia



## Sleeping

### North Ciutat Vella

**Home Youth Hostel** HOSTEL €

(Map p810; ☎963 91 62 29; www.homehostelsvalencia.com; Calle de la Lonja 4; dm €25-40, d €60-80; ❄@📶) Offering location, facilities and plenty more, this hostel sits right opposite the Lonja, a few steps from the central market. The rooms have happy retro decor, proper beds with decent sheets, coin-deposit lockers and not too many roommates. Kitchen, film library and cheery staff make this a top budget spot. Dorm prices vary substantially according to demand.

★**Hostal Antigua Morellana** HOSTAL €€

(Map p810; ☎963 91 57 73; www.hostalam.com; Calle En Bou 2; s/d €55/70; ❄@📶) This friendly, family-run, 18-room spot occupies a renovated 18th-century *posada* (where wealthier merchants bringing produce to market would spend the night) and has cosy, good-sized rooms, many with balconies. It's kept shipshape by the house-proud owners and there are lots of great features, including memory-foam mattresses, handsome fabrics and a lounge with coffee. Higher floors have more natural light. Great value.

**Ad Hoc Carmen** HOTEL €€

(Map p810; ☎960 45 45 45; www.adhochoteles.com; Calle Samaniego 20; s/d/q €69/89/149; ❄📶) Strategically placed for sorties to the centre's historical buildings or the bars and restaurants of Barrio del Carmen, this hotel offers a variety of handsome modern rooms with clean lines and whitewashed wood. Many rooms are duplexes, offering good sleeping solutions for families, groups or squabbling couples. No breakfast or parking available. Good value.

★**Caro Hotel** HOTEL €€€

(Map p810; ☎963 05 90 00; www.carohotel.com; Calle Almirante 14; d €170-350; P❄📶) Housed in a sumptuous 19th-century mansion, this hotel sits atop two millennia of Valencian history, with restoration revealing a hefty hunk of the Arab wall, Roman column bases and Gothic arches. Each room is furnished in soothing dark shades, with a great king-size bed and varnished concrete floors. Bathrooms are tops. For special occasions, reserve the Marqués suite, once the ballroom.

### South Ciutat Vella

★**Hotel Sorolla Centro** HOTEL €€

(Map p810; ☎963 52 33 92; www.hotelsorollacentro.com; Calle Convento Santa Clara 5; d €80-120;

DON'T MISS

**RUSSAFA**

The new town's most captivating corner, the district of Russafa may be comparatively compact but it packs a weighty punch. A downmarket *barrio* turned trendy, its collection of quirky galleries and vintage shops keeps people entertained by day, while by night it becomes the city's best zone for eating and cafe-bar nightlife – a buzzing hub of quality tapas, modish vermouth bars, literary cafes and innovative cultural offerings. It's a district with its own very distinctive feel and an essential Valencian evening experience, particularly at weekends.

) Neat and contemporary but without any flashy design gimmicks, this hotel offers very solid value for comfortable, well-thought-out modern rooms with powerful showers and plenty of facilities. Staff are extremely helpful and the location, on a pedestrian street close to the main square, is fab.

**Hostal Venecia** HOSTAL €€
(Map p810; 963 52 42 67; www.hotelvenecia.com; Plaza del Ayuntamiento 3; r €97-159; ) Right on Valencia's main square, this sumptuous building's functional interior doesn't give many hints of the noble exterior, but it offers compact modern rooms, many with small balcony. Rates vary substantially; it's a good deal if you pay around €80. Despite the *hostal* name, facilities are those of a midrange hotel. Strong points are friendly service and its prime location.

★ **One Shot Mercat 09** BOUTIQUE HOTEL €€€
(Map p810; 963 11 00 11; www.hoteloneshotmercat09.com; Calle del Músico Peydró 9; r €120-220; ) Opened in 2017, this handsome hotel occupies a strategic corner in an area of quiet lanes near the market. With just 22 rooms, it's a personal, intimate place with art exhibitions in the lobby and a lovely rooftop pool. The four room types vary by size and outlook; the executive- and junior-suite categories face the street. There's an excellent restaurant.

**Marqués House** HOTEL €€€
(Map p810; 960 66 05 06; www.marqueshouse.com; Calle Abadía de San Martín 10; r €120-220; ) This hotel brings a touch of modern style to this part of central Valencia while remaining faithful to the historical architecture. Rooms are well designed, with lots of natural light, great extras and powerful showers. The superiors are quite a bit larger and worth the upgrade. The downstairs bar-restaurant is a very stylish spot and a romantic roof terrace opens at weekends.

### L'Eixample & Russafa

★ **Russafa Youth Hostel** HOSTEL €
(Map p806; 963 31 31 40; www.russafayouthhostel.com; Carrer del Padre Perera 5; dm €20-27, s with shared bathroom €35-55, d with shared bathroom €50-70; ) You'll feel instantly at home in this super-welcoming, cute hostel set over various floors of a venerable building in the heart of vibrant Russafa. It's all beds, rather than bunks, and with a maximum of three to a room, there's no crowding. Sweet rooms and spotless bathrooms make for a mighty easy stay.

## Eating

Valencia is surrounded by its *huerta,* a fertile coastal agricultural plain that supplies it with excellent fruit and vegetables. You're seriously spoiled for choice when it comes to the numerous restaurants. Less tapas-hopping is done in Valencia than in the rest of Spain; locals tend to sit down at bar or table to eat a meal of various tapas portions. Many restaurants close in August.

### North Ciutat Vella

**Tasca Ángel** TAPAS €
(Map p810; 963 91 78 35; Calle de la Purísima 1; sardines €4; 10.30am-3pm & 7-11pm Mon-Sat) This no-frills place has been in business for 75 years and is famous for its fishy tapas, but in particular grilled sardines, which are fresh and delicious, with a great hit of garlic and salt. Order them with a cold beer or white wine and find inner peace.

**La Pilareta** TAPAS €
(Bar Pilar; Map p810; 963 91 04 97; www.barlapilareta.es; Calle del Moro Zeit 13; mussels €7.10; noon-midnight) Earthy, century-old and barely changed, La Pilareta is great for hearty tapas and *clóchinas* (small, juicy local mussels), available between May and August. For the rest of the year it serves *mejillones* (mussels), altogether fatter if less tasty. A platterful comes in a spicy broth that you scoop up with a spare shell. It's got atmosphere in spades.

**★Delicat** TAPAS €€

(Map p810; ☎963 92 33 57; Calle Conde Almodóvar 4; dishes €8-18; ⏲1.45-3.30pm & 8.45-11.30pm Tue-Sat, 1.45-3.30pm Sun; 📶) At this particularly friendly, intimate option, the open kitchen offers an unbeatable-value set menu of samplers for lunch (€14.50) and delicious tapas choices for dinner. The decor isn't lavish but the food is memorable, with a range of influences at play. It's best to book ahead as the small space fills fast.

**★Cinnamon** FUSION €€

(Map p810; ☎963 15 48 90; Calle de las Comedias 5; dishes €8-14; ⏲1.30-4pm Mon, 1.30-4pm & 8.30-11pm Tue-Sat; 📶✔) This intimate space is so tiny, you wonder how it prepares anything more elaborate than a fried egg. But wonders emerge from the open kitchen, in dishes bursting with taste and freshness. Creative plates include the crunchy house salad, a fab daily special and good options for vegetarians. A very worthwhile dining experience, if there's room.

**★Entrevins** SPANISH €€€

(Map p810; ☎963 33 35 23; www.entrevins.es; Calle de la Paz 7; mains €20-27; ⏲1.30-3.30pm & 8.30-11pm Tue-Sat) With a quiet, restrained elegance, this upstairs restaurant makes a lovely lunchtime retreat from the bustle of the street and is handy for several nearby sights. Grab a window table to watch the passers-by below and enjoy the seriously tasty food. The lunchtime set menu (€22, weekdays only) is top value for this quality and includes two shared starters.

## South Ciutat Vella

**★Navarro** VALENCIAN €€

(Map p810; ☎963 52 96 23; www.restaurantenavarro.com; Calle del Arzobispo Mayoral 5; rice dishes €15-18; ⏲1-4pm Mon-Sat; 📶) Known in the city for decades for its quality rice dishes, Navarro is run by the grandkids of the original founders. It offers plenty of choice, outdoor seating and helpful service.

**★El Poblet** GASTRONOMY €€€

(Map p810; ☎961 11 11 06; www.elpobletrestaurante.com; Calle de Correos 8; degustation menus €85-125; ⏲1.30-2.30pm & 8.30-10pm Mon & Wed-Fri, 8.30-10pm Sat; 📶) This upstairs restaurant, overseen by famed Quique Dacosta and with Luis Valls as chef, offers elegance and fine gastronomic dining at prices that are very competitive for this quality. Modern French and Spanish influences combine to create sumptuous degustation menus. Some of the imaginative presentation has to be seen to be believed, and staff are genuinely welcoming and helpful.

## Barrio del Carmen

**★L'Ostrería del Carme** SEAFOOD €

(Map p810; ☎629 145026; www.laostreriadelcarmen.com; Plaza de Mossén Sorell; oysters €3-4; ⏲11am-3pm Mon-Sat & 5-8.30pm Thu & Fri) This



### LAS FALLAS

The exuberant, anarchic swirl of **Las Fallas de San José** (www.fallas.com) – fireworks, music, festive bonfires and all-night partying – is a must if you're visiting Spain in mid-March. The *fallas* themselves are huge sculptures of papier mâché on wood, built by teams of local artists.

Each neighbourhood sponsors its own *falla*, and when the town wakes after the *plantà* (overnight construction of the *fallas*) on the morning of 16 March, more than 350 have sprung up. Reaching up to 15m in height, with the most expensive costing hundreds of thousands of euros, these grotesque, colourful effigies satirise celebrities, current affairs and local customs. They range from comical to moving. It's a custom that grew through the 19th and 20th centuries.

Around-the-clock festivities include street parties, paella-cooking competitions, parades, open-air concerts, bullfights and free fireworks displays. Valencia considers itself the pyrotechnic capital of the world and each day at 2pm from 1 to 19 March, a *mascletà* (more than five minutes of deafening thumps and explosions) shakes the window panes of Plaza del Ayuntamiento.

After midnight on the final day, each *falla* goes up in flames – backed by yet more fireworks. A popular vote spares the most-cherished *ninot* (figure), which gets housed for posterity in the **Museo Fallero** (Map p806; ☎962 08 46 25; www.valencia.es; Plaza Monteolivete 4; adult/child €2/free, Sun free; ⏲10am-7pm Mon-Sat, to 2pm Sun).

LOCAL KNOWLEDGE

## RICE DISHES OF VALENCIA

There's something life-affirming about a proper paella, cheerily coloured and bursting with intriguing morsels. But there's more to this most Valencian of dishes than meets the eye.

### Types of Rice Dish

There's a whole world of rices in Valencia. Paella has all the liquid evaporated, *meloso* rices are wet, and *caldoso* rices come with broth. Rices reflect the seasons, with winter and summer ingredients making their way into the dish depending on the month. Almost any ingredient can be used, including all types of vegetables, fish, seafood and meat.

Paellas are typical of the Valencian coast. Meat paellas normally have chicken and rabbit, with green beans and other vegetables in summer, or perhaps fava beans and artichokes in winter. Fish rices tend to be served more liquid, with calamari or cuttlefish supplying the flavour and prawns or langoustines for decoration. If you add prawns to a meat paella, it's a *paella mixta*. *Arroz negro* (black rice) is another typical coastal rice that's made with squid ink and fish stock. *Fideuà* is similar, but made with fine pasta; fresh rockfish are used to make the stock. Popular seafood-based winter rices include a cauliflower and salt-cod paella. In the interior, rices tend to be heavier. In Alcoy and Xàtiva, rices are baked in the oven and might have pork, sausage, beans and black pudding. In Alicante's interior one typical rice has snails, rabbit and chickpeas, while around Orihuela *arroz con costra* (crusty rice) is made in the oven with a crust of beaten egg on top.

### Secrets of the Rice

The base always includes short-grain rice, garlic, olive oil and saffron. The best rice is *bomba*, which opens accordion-like when cooked, allowing for maximum liquid absorption while remaining firm. Paella should be cooked in a large shallow pan to enable maximum contact with flavour. And for the final touch of authenticity, the grains on the bottom (and only those) should form a crunchy, savoury crust known as the *socarrat*.

### Tips on Ordering

For Valencians, rice is exclusively a lunchtime dish, though a few places do prepare it at dinnertime for the tourist trade. Restaurants should take 20 minutes or more to prepare a rice dish – beware if they don't – so expect to wait. You'll need two people or more to order a rice dish à la carte.

little stall inside the **Mossén Sorell market** (Map p810; Plaza de Mossén Sorell; ⌚7.30am-3pm Mon-Sat, plus 5-8.30pm Thu & Fri Sep-Jul) is a cordial spot and a fabulous snack stop. It has oysters of excellent quality from Valencia and elsewhere; sit down with a glass of white wine and let them shuck you a few.

**★El Tap** VALENCIAN €€

(Map p810; ☎963 91 26 27; www.facebook.com/restauranteeltapvalencia; Calle de Roteros 9; mains €10-18; ⌚7.30-11.30pm Mon-Fri, 1.30-3.30pm & 7.30-11.30pm Sat; 📶) The Tap is one of Barrio del Carmen's rich selection of small, characterful restaurants and is genuinely welcoming. The food is market-based and originally and delightfully prepared. Dishes with local tomatoes are a standout, and there's a carefully chosen list of both wines and boutique beers. Excellent value.

**★Refugio** FUSION €€

(Map p810; ☎690 617018; www.refugiorestaurante.com; Calle Alta 42; mains €14-23, set menu €15-18; ⌚2-4pm & 9-11.30pm; 📶) Named for the civil-war hideout opposite and simply decorated in whitewashed brick, Refugio preserves some of the Carmen *barrio's* former revolutionary spirit. Excellent Med-fusion cuisine is presented in lunchtime menus of surprising quality: there are some stellar plates on show, though the veggie options aren't always quite as flavoursome. Evening dining is high quality and innovative. Warm and welcoming.

## Russafa

Russafa is Valencia's best place for an evening meal, with a staggering variety of options in a small area. Most lean towards modern, fusion cuisine or international specialities. It gets very busy at weekends, when the buzz is intoxicating.

**Casa Viva** VEGAN €

(Map p806; ☎963 03 47 13; Calle de Cádiz 76; mains €6-13; ⏰1-3.45pm & 8.30-11pm Wed-Mon; 🌱) The Valencia branch of a rural restaurant makes an enticing stop for its effusively cordial welcome and inventive, colourful vegetarian and vegan dishes presented with élan. Decor is cute, with low seats and plenty of greenery.

**Dulce de Leche** CAFE €

(Map p806; ☎963 03 59 49; www.facebook.com/DulceDeLecheRuzafa; Calle del Pintor Gisbert 2; brunch €8; ⏰9am-9pm; 📶) Delicious sweet and savoury snacks with an Argentine twist are the stock-in-trade of this delicately decorated corner cafe. The coffee is organic, the juices hit the spot and the service is quality. It looks posh but prices are reasonable. Weekend brunch is well priced and tasty, but you might have to bring out your Mr Hyde to bag a street table. There are a few branches around town.

★**El Rodamón de Russafa** FUSION, TAPAS €€

(Map p806; ☎963 21 80 14; www.elrodamon.com; Calle Sueca 47; tapas €7-13; ⏰2-4pm & 8.30-11.30pm Wed-Mon, evenings only Jul–mid-Sep; 📶) The deal here is that they've picked their favourite dishes encountered around the world and made a Valencian tapas plate from them, so you can pick from a whole range of eclectic morsels from several nations, including Spain. It's modern and buzzy, with excellent staff, and the quality is very high. There are several dozen wines available by the glass.

**Canalla Bistro** FUSION €€

(Map p806; ☎963 74 05 09; www.canallabistro.com; Calle del Maestro José Serrano 5; mains €10-17; ⏰1.30-3.30pm & 8-11pm; 📶) Chic but commodious, with an interior featuring packing crates, cartoon chickens and other decorative quirks, this is where top Valencian chef **Ricard Camarena** (Map p806; ☎963 35 54 18; www.ricardcamarenarestaurant.com; Avenida de Burjassot 54; degustation menu €125-155; ⏰1.30-3pm & 8-10pm Wed-Sat; 📶) can be a little more lighthearted. Sensationally presented dishes draw their inspiration from street food from around the world. Creative, fun and delicious.

★**Dos Estaciones** SPANISH €€€

(Map p806; ☎963 03 46 70; www.restaurante2estaciones.com; Calle del Pintor Salvador Abril 28; mains €19-23, degustation menus €35-50; ⏰1.30-3.45pm Tue & Thu-Sat, 8.30-11pm Tue-Sat) Two talented chefs oversee this small restaurant, where an open kitchen and welcoming folk provide a personal gourmet experience. Some extraordinary creations are produced here at a very reasonable price; freshness and innovation are guaranteed, and they'll easily tailor things to your dietary needs and mood. There's also pleasant outdoor seating.

## L'Eixample & Southern Valencia

**Goya** VALENCIAN €€

(Map p806; ☎963 04 18 35; www.goyagalleryrestaurant.com; Calle Burriana 3; mains €13-25; ⏰food 1-4pm & 8.15-11.15pm Tue-Sat, 1-4pm Sun) Decorated with style and featuring real dedication to guests' comfort and pleasure, this busy local classic is outstanding. The menu takes in Valencian favourites such as delicious seafood rices and typical tapas, and includes some more avant-garde foodie bravura. It's all strong on presentation and great on taste. Its blend of traditional values and modern cooking makes it stand out.

## Northern & Eastern Valencia

**Balansiya** MOROCCAN €

(Map p806; ☎963 89 08 24; www.balansiya.com; Paseo de las Facultades 3; mains €8-13; ⏰1.30-4.30pm & 8.30pm-midnight) This restaurant in a student neighbourhood near the university is worth seeking out. Elegantly decorated in Moroccan style, it's a warmly welcoming spot serving a wide range of dishes, including excellent sweets. The aromas will have you instantly slavering. No alcohol served, though there's an unusually long list of non-alcoholic wines such as homemade hibiscus.

★**Gran Azul** VALENCIAN €€€

(Map p806; ☎961 47 45 23; www.granazulrestaurante.com; Avenida de Aragón 12; mains €17-24; ⏰1.30-4pm & 8.30-11.30pm Mon-Sat; 📶) Spacious and stylish, this main-road spot is a temple to excellent dining. The focus is on rice dishes and the grill, with premium quality steaks from mature cows as well as superb fresh fish simply done and garnished with flair. For a starter, try the *molletes* – mini burgers with fillings such as steak tartare or bull's tail.

### HORCHATA

A summer delight across Spain, *horchata (orxata)*, a Valencian speciality, is a vegan, opaque sugary drink made from pressed *chufas* (tiger nuts: despite the name, it's a small tuber), into which you dip a large finger-shaped bun called – no sniggering – a *fartón*. A traditional place to sample *horchata* in the heart of town is **Horchatería de Santa Catalina** (Map p810; ☎963 91 23 79; www.horchateriasantacatalina.com; Plaza de Santa Catalina 6; ⏰8.15am-9.30pm; 📶), while the **Mercado de Colón** (Map p806; www.mercadocolon.es; Calle de Cirilo Amorós; ⏰7.30am-2am Sun-Thu, to 3am Fri & Sat; 📶) has several choices. Head out on a tour with **Horta Viva** (☎691 093721; www.hortaviva.net) if you want to understand more about *chufas* and the *horchata*-making process.

## Western Valencia

★**Bar Ricardo** TAPAS €€
(Map p806; ☎963 22 69 49; www.barricardo.es; Calle de Doctor Zamenhof 16; mains €10-18; ⏰8am-midnight Tue-Sat Sep-Jul) Ice-cold beer and a fabulous array of tapas and other dishes characterise this gloriously traditional place, with its old-style mezzanine, pleasant terrace and top-notch service. Snails, top-quality seafood, one of Valencia's best *cañas* (small draught beers) and many other delights await you. The kitchen is open all day, so it's a good spot for eating outside of normal Spanish hours.

## Valencia's Beaches

**Bar La Paca** TAPAS €
(☎637 860528; Calle del Rosario 30; tapas €3-8; ⏰1pm-1am) Cosy and buzzing, this bar has an eclectic crowd and an uplifting atmosphere. Visually striking with its chessboard tiles and deep reds, it does simple, tasty tapas (including vegetarian options) and craft beers at fair prices. It's the sort of place where you wish you lived upstairs.

★**Bodega Casa Montaña** TAPAS €€
(☎963 67 23 14; www.emilianobodega.com; Calle de José Benlliure 69; tapas €4-14; ⏰1-4pm & 7.30-11.30pm Mon-Sat, 12.30-4pm Sun) One of Valencia's most characterful spots, with venerable barrels and the atmosphere of a bygone era, this place has been around since 1836. There's a superb, changing selection of wines and a long list of exquisite tapas, including many seafood conserves. We fell in love with the smoked eel, but it's all great.

★**Bar Cabanyal** SEAFOOD €€
(☎961 33 53 77; www.facebook.com/barcabanyal; Calle de Martí Grajales 5; dishes €6-15; ⏰8-11pm Tue, 1-4pm & 8-11pm Wed-Sat, 1-4pm Sun) Opposite the market in the traditional fishing district, you'd expect a bit of a marine flavour, and indeed the young and enthusiastic team does an excellent line in quality seafood at very reasonable prices. Everything is delicious and it's an upbeat, optimistic spot. Opening hours are extended in summer.

## Drinking & Nightlife

★**Café Negrito** BAR
(Map p810; ☎963 91 42 33; www.facebook.com/CafeNegritoValencia; Plaza del Negrito; ⏰4pm-4am; 📶) Something of a local legend, this cafe-bar on a little old-town square has an intellectual, socially aware, left-wing clientele and art exhibitions often focused on sustainable development or NGOs. The large terrace is a top spot to while away an evening.

**Tyris on Tap** MICROBREWERY
(Map p810; ☎961 13 28 73; www.cervezatyris.com; Calle Taula de Canvis 6; ⏰6.30pm-1am Tue-Sun; 📶) This outlet for a local microbrewery has 10 taps issuing some pretty tasty craft beers by the pint and half-pint. There's one of our favourite central terraces out front to enjoy it, and some simple bar food such as nachos to soak it up. You can book a Saturday tour of the brewery via the website or on ☎961 06 40 50.

**L'Ermità** BAR
(Map p810; ☎963 91 67 59; www.facebook.com/lermitacafe; Calle Obispo Don Jerónimo 4; ⏰7pm-1.30am Mon-Fri, noon-1.30am Sat & Sun) On a very central backstreet, this is a top option for a drink, with decent music, regular cultural events, a friendly crowd of regulars and cordial staff. The quirky interior is comfortably cosy but can overheat: the streetside tables are prime territory on a warm night.

**Deseo 54** GAY & LESBIAN
(Map p806; ☎697 699166; www.deseo54.com; Calle de la Pepita 13; ⏰1.30am-7.30am Fri & Sat night; 📶) It's mostly the young and beautiful at this upmarket and famous *discoteca*,

which plays quality electronic music to a largely, but by no means exclusively, LGBT crowd. Admission prices vary depending on night and DJ, but you can buy cheaper advance tickets on the website.

**Cafe Berlin** CAFE

(Map p806; ☎640 781372; www.facebook.com/cafeberlinvalencia; Calle de Cádiz 22; ⏰6pm-1am Mon-Wed, 6pm-2.30am Thu & Fri, 4.30pm-2.30am Sat, 4.30pm-1am Sun; 📶) Russafa does bohemian so well, and this is one of many quality cafe-bars of this type, offering a lounge-like ambience with books, art exhibitions and decent drinks, including well-made cocktails. Loads of atmosphere. It does language-exchange sessions, which can be a good way to meet locals.

**★La Fábrica de Hielo** CAFE

(☎963 68 26 19; www.lafabricadehielo.net; Calle de Pavia 37; ⏰5pm-midnight Mon, 5pm-1am Tue-Thu, to 1.30am Fri, 11am-1.30am Sat, 11am-midnight Sun) It's difficult to classify this former ice factory, converted with great charm into a sizeable multi-purpose space that does cultural events, drinks and tapas just back from the beach. Just drop by and see what's going down – Sundays are loads of fun, with paella and dancing, but there's always a great atmosphere.

**Marina Beach Club** BAR

(☎961 15 00 07; http://marinabeachclub.com; Marina Real Juan Carlos I; ⏰11am-3.30am) A super-popular bar and club with two restaurants at an enviable location overlooking the sand between Valencia's marina and Playa de las Arenas. The open-air space features palm trees, an infinity pool and stunning beach views. A hit with locals and visitors, it gets particularly crowded in the height of summer.

## ☆ Entertainment

**★Jimmy Glass** LIVE MUSIC

(Map p810; www.jimmyglassjazz.net; Calle Baja 28; ⏰8pm-2.30am Mon-Thu, 9pm-3.30am Fri & Sat; 📶) Atmospheric Jimmy Glass is just what a jazz bar should be, with dim lighting and high-octane cocktails. It has four live performances a week, many of them free, and runs an annual jazz festival in October/November that attracts some top musicians. At other times it plays tracks from the owner's vast CD collection. Tapas are available Thursday to Saturday.

**★Radio City** LIVE PERFORMANCE

(Map p810; ☎963 91 41 51; www.radiocityvalencia.es; Calle de Santa Teresa 19; ⏰10.30pm-4am, opens earlier for some events) Almost as much a mini cultural centre as a club, Radio City, which fills up from around 1am, pulls in the punters with activities such as language exchange, and DJs or live music every night. There's everything from flamenco (Tuesday) to reggae and funk, and the crowd is eclectic and engaged. Check the website to see what's on.

**★Valencia Club de Fútbol** FOOTBALL

(Estadio de Mestalla; Map p806; ☎963 37 26 26; www.valenciacf.com; Avenida de Aragón) The city's principal team, and a major player in Spanish football, with famously demanding fans. A move to a new ground in the city's northwest has been stalled for several years, so for now it's still at Mestalla, an atmospheric, steeply tiered ground close to the centre. You can buy tickets a few weeks in advance through the website.

**Wah Wah** LIVE MUSIC

(Map p806; www.facebook.com/salawahwah; Calle de Ramón Campoamor 52; ⏰10.30pm-3am Thu-Sat Sep-Jun; 📶) For many, Wah Wah remains Valencia's hottest venue for live music, especially for underground and international indie, though classic Spanish garage and rock also get a good airing. Check the website; tickets are sometimes cheaper if purchased in advance.

## 🛍 Shopping

**★Cestería El Globo** ARTS & CRAFTS

(Map p810; ☎963 52 64 15; www.facebook.com/cesteriaelglobo; Calle del Músico Peydró 16; ⏰9.45am-1.30pm & 4.30-8pm Mon-Fri, 10am-2pm & 5-8.15pm Sat) In business since 1856, this charming shop features piles of traditional wickerwork – how about a basket for your bicycle? – plus rocking horses and other solid wooden toys.

**★Abanicos Carbonell** ARTS & CRAFTS

(Map p806; ☎963 41 53 95; www.abanicoscarbonell.com; Calle de Castellón 21; ⏰9.30am-1.30pm & 4-8pm Mon-Fri) This historic fan-maker, in business since 1810, offers hand-painted manual cooling units ranging from a very reasonable €10 for the basic but pretty ones, to works by famous fan painters that run to thousands of euros. It's been run by the same family for five generations.

### BIKING VALENCIA

Cycling is a great way to get around: the riverbed park gives you easy access to most of the city and there's an excellent network of bike lanes. There are numerous hire places, and most accommodation can organise a hire bike. **Valenbisi** (www.valenbisi.es) is the city-bike scheme – sign up for a week-long contract (€13.30) at machines at the bike racks or online.

## Information

The city's tourism website is www.visitvalencia.com. There is a tourist office at the airport and a few around the city, including a mobile van that parks up at busy areas.

**Ayuntamiento Tourist Office** (Map p810; 963 52 49 08; www.visitvalencia.com; Plaza del Ayuntamiento 1; 9am-6.50pm Mon-Sat, 10am-1.50pm Sun) In the town hall.

**Joaquín Sorolla Station Tourist Office** (Map p806; 963 80 36 23; www.visitvalencia.com; Estación Valencia Joaquín Sorolla; 10am-5.50pm Mon-Fri, to 2.50pm Sat & Sun) At the fast train station.

**Paz Tourist Office** (Map p806; 963 98 64 22; www.visitvalencia.com; Calle de la Paz 48; 9am-6.50pm Mon-Sat, 10am-1.50pm Sun)

## Getting There & Away

### AIR

Valencia's **airport** (VLC; 902 404 704; www.aena.es) is 10km west of the city centre along the A3, towards Madrid. Flights, including many budget routes, serve major European destinations, including London, Paris and Berlin. The airport is a 20-minute Metro journey from central Valencia.

### BOAT

Trasmediterránea (p820) and **Baleària** (865 608 423; www.balearia.com) operate car and passenger ferries to Ibiza and Mallorca. Less frequent ferries go to Menorca and Algeria.

### BUS

Valencia's **bus station** (Map p806; 963 46 62 66; Avenida Menéndez Pidal) is located beside the riverbed park. **Avanza** (www.avanzabus.com) operates regular bus services to/from Madrid (€28 to €36, 4¼ hours). ALSA (www.alsa.es) has services to/from Barcelona (€29 to €38, four to six hours, up to 10 daily) and Alicante (€21 to €25, 2½ to 5½ hours, more than 10 daily), most via Benidorm.

### TRAIN

All fast trains now use the **Valencia Joaquín Sorolla station** (www.adif.es; Calle San Vicente Mártir 171), 800m south of the old town. It's meant to be temporary, but looks like sticking around for a long time. It's linked with nearby Estación del Norte (p809), 500m away, by free shuttle bus. Estación del Norte has slow trains to Gandia, Alicante, Barcelona and Madrid, as well as local *cercanía* lines. Most *cercanía* lines to the west leave from **Valencia San Isidro/Sant Isidre** in the west of the city.

Major destinations include the following:

| Destination | Cost (€) | Time (hr) | Frequency (daily) |
|---|---|---|---|
| Alicante | 16-21 | 1½-2 | 11 |
| Barcelona | 27-46 | 3¼-3½ | 15 |
| Madrid | 28-73 | 1¾-7¾ | 21 |

## Getting Around

Most buses run until about 10.30pm, with various night services continuing until around 1.30am (3am at weekends). Buy a **Bonobús** (€8.50 for 10 journeys) at metro stations, most tobacconists and some newspaper kiosks, or pay as you get on (€1.50). One-/two-/three-day travel cards valid for the bus, metro and tram cost €4/6.70/9.70.

The tram is a pleasant way to get to the beach and port. Pick it up at Pont de Fusta or where it intersects with the metro at Benimaclet.

Metro (www.metrovalencia.es) lines cross town and serve the outer suburbs. The closest stations to the city centre are Ángel Guimerá, Xàtiva, Colón and Pont de Fusta.

# VALENCIA PROVINCE

## La Albufera

About 15km south of Valencia, La Albufera is a huge freshwater lagoon separated from the sea by a narrow strip of pine-forested sand dunes. Legendary for the rice that is grown here, it's also an important dune and wetland ecosystem, with much of the area covered by the **Parque Natural de la Albufera** (www.parquesnaturales.gva.es) FREE. The zone is great for birdwatching. The most interesting Albufera communities are **El Palmar**, right on the lagoon, and **El Saler**, which has a beach backed by piney dunes and a lagoon side. It's worth exploring beyond El Palmar with a bike or car, following the narrow roads, barely above the water at times, that divide the paddies. Make your way to Sollana, from where you can head north to Valencia again.

Sunsets can be spectacular in La Albufera, with the **Mirador El Pujol** (CV500, Km 9.5) a particularly popular viewpoint. You can take a boat trip from El Palmar or El Saler out on the lagoon, joining the local fisherfolk, who use flat-bottomed boats and nets to harvest fish and eels from the shallow waters. *All i pebre* is a classic local eel dish offered everywhere.

Bus 25 runs from central Valencia to El Saler every 20 minutes or so, with some continuing to El Palmar (others go to a different village). Buses 14 and 15 serve Pinedo. These services are all part of the urban Valencia system. Cycle lanes run from Valencia right down to El Saler, making bike a great way to explore the area.

## Sagunto

POP 65,700

The port town of Sagunto (Valenciano: Sagunt), 25km north of Valencia, primarily offers spectacular panoramas of the coast, Balearics and a sea of orange groves from its vast but ruinous hilltop castle complex. It's an easy half-day excursion from Valencia.

**★Castillo de Sagunto** CASTLE

(☎962 61 71 67; www.aytosagunto.es; ⏲10am-6pm or 8pm Tue-Sat, 10am-2pm Sun) FREE Sagunto's castle is majestically located, with stone walls girdling twin hilltops for almost 1km. Its seven rambling, mostly ruinous sections each speak of a different period in Sagunto's history. The fortress could do with a bit of care and is currently best for a stroll among the ruins, appreciating the magnificent vistas along the coast, rather than gaining a detailed understanding of its long, long history. Don't expect interpretative panels or an audio guide.

### Information

**Tourist Office** (☎962 65 58 59; http://turismo.sagunto.es; Plaza Cronista Chabret; ⏲9.30am-2.30pm & 4-6.30pm Mon-Fri, 9am-2pm Sat & Sun Sep-Jun, 9am-2pm & 4.30-7.30pm Mon-Sat, 10am-2pm Sun Jul & Aug) A 15-minute walk from the train station. In summer there's an office by the beach.

### Getting There & Away

The best option from Valencia to Sagunto is taking the *cercanía* train on lines C5 and C6 (one way €3.70, 30 minutes, regular departures).

## Gandia

POP 73,800

The pleasant, spacious town of Gandia (Spanish: Gandía), once home to a branch of the Borja dynasty (more familiar as the infamous Borgias), is a prosperous commercial centre with a lively atmosphere. The other side of the coin is the fun-in-the-sun beach town, 6km away. The adjacent port area has a ferry connection to the Balearics.

**★Palacio Ducal dels Borja** PALACE

(☎962 87 14 65; www.palauducal.com; Calle Duc Alfons el Vell 1; adult/child €6/4, audio guide €2; ⏲10am-1.30pm & 3-6.30pm Mon-Sat, 10am-1.30pm Sun Nov-Mar, 10am-1.30pm & 4-7.30pm Mon-Sat, 10am-1.30pm Sun Apr-Oct) Gandia's magnificent palace was built in the early 1300s and was for centuries the home of the Borja dukes of Gandia, who included the Jesuit saint Francis Borgia. Though much remodelled in the 19th century, the building preserves some original detail. The fine Salón de las Coronas is one of several sumptuous spaces, while the highlight is the Galería Dorada, a suite of decorated rooms culminating in a tiled floor depicting the world composed of the four elements.

**★Telero** VALENCIAN €€

(☎962 86 73 18; www.telero.es; Calle Sant Ponç 7; mains €13-22; ⏲1.30-3.30pm & 8.30-11.30pm Mon-Fri, 1.30-3.30pm Sat) Tucked away but worth seeking out, this intimate restaurant focuses on quality ingredients. Admire the cosy, exposed-brick dining area in the traditional house, then listen to what is available off-menu and choose a meal based on top-quality vegetables and fish sourced locally.

### Information

**Town Tourist Office** (☎962 87 77 88; www.visitgandia.com; Avenida Marqués de Campo; ⏲9.30am-1.30pm & 3.30-7.30pm or 4-8pm Mon-Fri, 9.30am-1.30pm Sat) Opposite the bus and train station. There are also two kiosks on the beach.

### Getting There & Around

*Cercanía* trains run between Gandia and Valencia (€5.80, one hour) every 30 minutes (hourly on weekends). The combined bus and train station is opposite the town tourist office; there's also a stop near the beach.

ALSA runs regular buses to Dénia (€3.75, one hour) and other coastal towns. Stopping beside

DON'T MISS

### LA TOMATINA

The last Wednesday in August marks Spain's messiest festival. **La Tomatina** (www.latomatina.info; tickets €12) is a tomato-throwing orgy attracting more than 20,000 visitors to Buñol, a town of just 9000 inhabitants. At 11am, more than 100 tonnes of squishy tomatoes are tipped from trucks to the waiting crowd. For one hour, everyone joins in a cheerful, anarchic tomato battle. After being pounded with pulp, expect to be sluiced down with hoses by the local fire brigade.

Participation costs €12 through the official website, though there are numerous tour operators offering tickets and packages from Valencia (40km east), Alicante and elsewhere. There are cloakroom facilities on-site, as you aren't allowed to take bags or cameras into the festival area. Bring a set of fresh clothes to change into afterwards. In the Tomatina itself, some people choose a pair of goggles to protect their eyes. Flip-flops don't work very well; you're better off with shoes, but don't expect them to be clean again.

If you're buying a package, try to opt out of the 'paella and sangría' add-ons, as these are readily available for less on the street in Buñol. While most visitors just come in from Valencia for the event, it can be worthwhile staying over the night before and after. La Tomatina is one element of the locals' main fiesta and there's plenty of atmosphere, as well as concerts, across a whole week. On the Saturday before the Tomatina, there's a children's version, which is free to enter for four- to 14-year-olds.



the town tourist office, La Marina Gandiense buses run to Playa de Gandia every 20 minutes. **Trasmediterránea** (☎902 454 645; www.trasmediterranea.es) runs fast ferries to Ibiza Sant Antoni (two hours, one or more daily) and Palma de Mallorca (5½ hours, daily).

## Requena

Requena, 65km west of Valencia, grew rich from silk, though today it's primarily wine and livestock country, producing robust reds (try the local bobal grape), *cavas* (sparkling wines), rich sausages and spicy meats. From its heart rears La Villa, the medieval nucleus, with its twisting streets, network of underground cellars and blind alleys. It's great to explore – atmospheric without being dolled up for tourism. Check out the 15th-century guard tower at its entrance, the lovely Gothic facades, small museums and the narrow lanes of the one-time Jewish quarter.

There are several small museums around the old town, with joint tickets available from the tourist office. Opening hours of sights in Requena are very restricted and changeable, as they struggle to find staff to cover them. In the old town, be sure to admire the wonderful late-Gothic facade of the Iglesia de Santa María and the handsome restored baroque interior of the Iglesia San Nicolás. On the square, which has various accommodations and restaurants, **Cuevas de la Villa** (www.turismorequena.es; Plaza de Albornoz 6; adult/child €4/free; ⏲10.30am-2pm & 5-7pm Tue-Sun) is a fascinating network of interlinked cellars dating back to Moorish times.

Venues for wine lovers include **Bodega Murviedro** (☎962 95 59 98; www.murviedro.es; Plaza de Albornoz 10; visit/premium visit €7/15; ⏲10am-2pm Sun-Wed, 10am-2pm & 4-7pm Thu-Sat), a winery on the old-town square, **Museo del Vino** (☎962 30 32 81; Carrer Somera 13; adult/child €2/free; ⏲noon-1.30pm Wed-Sun), a wine museum within the handsome 15th-century Palacio del Cid, and **Ferevin** (☎962 30 57 06; www.ferevin.org; Cuesta de las Carnicerías; ⏲11am-2pm & 4-7pm Mon-Sat, 11am-2.30pm Sun), a showroom for local wine producers. There's a wine festival in late August. A useful website is www.rutavino.com.

An excellent lunch stop in the old town is **El Yantar** (☎962 34 91 21; www.restauranteelyantar.com; Calle Fortaleza 24; mains €12-18; ⏲1-4pm & 8.30pm-midnight Wed-Sun), which has romantic cellar seating and creative dishes including seafood carpaccios and delicious salads.

The helpful **tourist office** (☎962 30 38 51; www.turismorequena.es; Calle García Montés 1; ⏲10am-2pm Tue-Fri & Sun, 10am-2pm & 4-7pm or 5-8pm Sat) is at the base of the old town. There are regular buses (€5.78, one hour) and *cercanías* (€5.80, 1½ hours) to/from Valencia. Pricier fast trains use a different station, 6km from town.

## Xàtiva

POP 29,000

Xàtiva (Spanish: Játiva) makes an easy and rewarding day trip from Valencia, or a stop on the way north or south. It has an intriguing historical quarter and a mighty castle strung along the crest of the Serra Vernissa, with the town snuggled at its base.

### Sights

The old town lies south and uphill from the main avenue through town. Ask at the tourist office for its English brochure, *Xàtiva: Monumental Town*. There are several noble buildings in the town, which merit an extended stroll. Look out for the handsome facade of the Renaissance hospital opposite the main church and the historic pharmacy nearby at Calle Noguera 10.

**★Castillo de Xàtiva** CASTLE
(962 274 274; www.xativaturismo.com; adult/child €2.40/1.20; 10am-6pm Tue-Sun Nov-Mar, to 7pm Apr-Oct) Xàtiva's castle, which clasps the summit of a double-peaked hill overlooking the old town, is one of the most evocative and interesting in the Valencia region. Behind its crumbling battlements you'll find flower gardens (bring a picnic), tumbledown turrets, towers and other buildings (some used in the 20th century and hence much changed), such as dungeons and a pretty Gothic chapel. The walk up to the castle is a long one (2km following the road), but the views are sensational.

If you think it's big today, imagine what it must have looked like 300 years ago at full size. Sadly, it was badly damaged by an earthquake in 1748 and never really recovered.

Before the current incarnation, the castle hill was always a fortified vantage point thanks to its crucial strategic position. It was important in the wars between Rome and Carthage, as well as in the Roman strife of the 1st century BCE.

On the way up, the 18th-century **Ermita de Sant Josep** is on your left, and to the right is the mid-13th-century **Iglesia de Sant Feliu**, a lovely Romanesque structure that's Xàtiva's oldest church. You'll also pass by the very battered remains of part of the old **Muslim town**. A tourist train zips up the hill a couple of times a day from the tourist office (€4.20).

### Sleeping & Eating

**★Montsant** HOTEL €€
(962 275 081; www.mont-sant.com; Subida al Castillo; incl breakfast s €108-144, d €120-168; Feb-Dec; P) Enthusiastic management makes for a wonderful stay at this enchanting place between the old town and the castle. Set amid city walls, convent ruins and palm and citrus gardens, it feels way out in the countryside rather than just a few minutes' walk from town. Stay in the beautifully adapted main building or in a more modern wood-faced cabin. All rooms have balconies or terraces; one suite has a private pool. The restaurant is fairly upmarket. Don't leave without seeing the amazing medieval cistern.

**La Picaeta de Carmeta** VALENCIAN €€
(619 511971; Plaça de Mercat 19; mains €13-19; 1.30-4pm Tue-Thu & Sun, 1.30-4pm & 8.30pm-midnight Fri & Sat) At one end of an attractive old-town square (a promising destination for drinks and tapas), this is a fine restaurant, with a cool, sober decor of exposed brick and well-selected art. There's a selection of meaty rices, as well as simply cooked fish and tastily creative salads. It's all delicious, and there are some fine wines to accompany your meal.

### Information

**Tourist Office** (962 27 33 46; www.xativaturismo.com; Avenida Selgas 2; 10am-5pm Tue-Thu, to 6pm Fri, 10am-2pm Sat & Sun) On Xàtiva's shady main avenue. Download their free app Xàtiva Turismo.

### Getting There & Away

Frequent *cercanía* trains on line C2 connect Xàtiva with Valencia (€4.35, 45 minutes, half-hourly), and most Valencia–Madrid trains also stop here, though these are more expensive. You can also reach Alicante by train (€13 to €23, one to 1½ hours, seven daily) from here.

# CASTELLÓN PROVINCE

## Castellón

POP 171,700

Castellón de la Plana (Valenciano: Castelló) is a provincial capital that's off the tourist radar. Though not over-endowed with sights, it's a pleasant place with good-value accommodation and a lively eating scene in its centre. Some 4km from the centre, the Grao district is centred on the fishing port, and just north of here are the city's beaches.

**Tryp Castellón Center** BUSINESS HOTEL €€
(☎965 34 27 77; www.melia.com; Ronda del Millars; r €59-80; P ❄ ☰) As Castellón sees relatively few tourists, its hotel offerings are reduced to chain business establishments dotted around the edge of the central district. This is the best of them, with very spacious rooms, gleaming new parquet and a bit of an effort to make it feel more personal. Prices for this standard are great.

**Bodega La Guindilla** TAPAS €€
(☎964 22 88 94; www.grupolaguindilla.com; Calle Asarau 2; mains €13-17; ⊙8.30am-5pm & 7pm-midnight Mon-Thu, 8.30am-midnight Fri, noon-1am Sat) Sit around barrels, grab an outdoor table or head downstairs to the dining room at this bright corner spot, an expansion of its crowded Calle Barracas tapas bar. There's a seafood focus, but everything is delicious and superbly presented. Expect cuttlefish on slates, creamy cod balls and succulent daily specials.

## ℹ Information

**Tourist Office** (☎965 35 86 88; www.castellonturismo.com; Plaza de la Hierba; ⊙10am-6pm Mon-Fri, to 2pm Sat) In the centre of things, by the cathedral. There's another office in the port area.

## ℹ Getting There & Away

### AIR

A famous white elephant of the Spanish building boom – one year there were more landings on Mars than here – Castellón's **airport** (☎964 23 90 18; www.aeroportcastello.com; Carretera CV13, Benlloch), 33km north of town, now has a handful of European budget flights. There are bus services to Castellón (€12, one hour) and other coastal destinations run by Autos Mediterráneo (p825) that must be pre-booked online.

### BUS & TRAIN

Castellón is a regional bus hub, with services throughout the province. Buses run five or more times a day to Valencia (€6.85, 1¼ hours). It's also the northern terminus of the C6 *cercanías* local train line to Valencia (€5.80, one to 1½ hours, half-hourly). Very frequent faster trains (€6 to €29, 45 minutes to one hour) run to Valencia on the standard train network. There are also regular services to Barcelona (€25 to €47, two to four hours) via Tarragona.

# Benicàssim

POP 18,100

Likeable Benicàssim stretches for 6km along the coast. It has been a popular resort since the 19th century, when wealthy Valencian families built summer residences here. It's still a place more characterised by local than foreign tourism, with plenty of Valenciano spoken on the streets. It's also famous for its huge summer music festival.

**Desierto de les Palmes** NATURE RESERVE
The twisting, climbing CV147 leads, after about 6km, to this occasionally misty inland range – cooler than the coast – with a Carmelite monastery and **restaurant** (☎964 30 09 47; CV147, Km 9; mains €13-22; ⊙hours vary, roughly 10am-7pm Wed-Mon Mar-May & early Sep-Dec, to midnight Jun-early Sep) with a view at its heart. Far from being a desert (for the monks that meant a place for mystic withdrawal), the reserve is a green area perfect for outdoor activities. From **Monte Bartolo** (728m), its highest point, there are staggering views. The tourist office hands out an excellent booklet listing a range of different hill walks.

**★Festival Internacional de Benicàssim** MUSIC
(FIB; www.fiberfib.com; ⊙mid-Jul) Fans gather by the tens of thousands for this annual four-day bash, one of Europe's major outdoor music festivals. Top acts in recent years have included some classic names, but the majority are up-to-the-minute acts popular with the predominantly 20-something crowd. Late-afternoon starts mean you can spend the day on the beach.

**★Hotel Voramar** HOTEL €€
(☎964 30 01 50; www.voramar.net; Paseo Pilar Coloma 1; s/d incl breakfast €110/135, with sea view €150/175; P ❄ ☰) Venerable (same family for four generations) and bloodied in battle (it was a hospital in the Spanish Civil War), this place has character and is spectacularly located at the beach's northeastern end. The rooms with balconies (and hammock) have utterly magnificent sea views and sounds. The first-class restaurant also has great perspectives. It hires bikes and kayaks (free for guests).

**El Charquito** TAPAS €€
(☎674 230999; Calle Santo Tomás 3; mains €9-16; ⊙6pm-1.30am Mon-Sat) Draw a Spanish

bar from muscle memory and this is what you get: hanging hams, strings of garlic and peppers, orderly family frenzy behind the counter, seafood gleaming on ice and a cosy, noisy conviviality. The food is tasty, the people are sound and the price is right. A Benicàssim classic.

## Information

**Tourist Office** (☎964 30 01 02; http://turismo.benicassim.es; Calle Santo Tomás 74; ⏲9am-2pm & 4-7pm Mon-Fri, 10.30am-1.30pm & 4-7pm Sat, 10.30am-1.30pm Sun Oct-May, 9am-2pm & 5-8pm Mon-Fri, 10.30am-1.30pm & 5-8pm Sat & Sun Jun-Sep) Inland, in the centre of town. There's an additional summer office on the beach.

## Getting There & Away

There are nine daily trains from Benicàssim to Valencia (€5.90 to €15.10, one to 1½ hours), and services north to Tarragona and Barcelona. Buses run every 15 minutes to nearby Castellón (€1.85), from where there are more connections.

# Peñíscola

POP 7600

Peñíscola's spectacular old town, all cobbled streets and whitewashed houses, huddles within stone fortress walls that protect this rocky promontory jutting into the sea. It's an unforgettable setting that gets pretty busy in summer, with ranks of souvenir shops and restaurants competing for trade. Below the old town, the seafront promenade makes for pleasant walking, and the beach, which extends as far as neighbouring Benicarló, is superb, sandy and more than 5km in length. Peñíscola is quiet in low season, but there's enough on to ensure it's not spooky – and you'll have the old town to yourself.

**Castillo de Peñíscola** CASTLE

(☎964 48 00 21; http://castillodepeniscola.dipcas.es; Calle Castillo; adult/9-16yr €5/3.50; ⏲10.30am-5.30pm mid-Oct–Easter, 9.30am-9.30pm Easter–mid-Oct) This austere and atmospheric castle was built by the Knights Templar in the early 14th century on Arab foundations and later became home to Pedro de Luna ('Papa Luna', the deposed Pope Benedict XIII). There are various exhibits and videos on Templar history, and utterly magnificent sea views. Entry includes a visit to a nearby former cannon outpost converted into a garden.

## Sleeping & Eating

**Pensión Chiki** PENSION €

(☎605 280295; www.pensionrestaurantechiki.es; Calle Mayor 3-5; d €55-85; 📶) Right in the old town, this place has eight cheerily coloured, spotless rooms with tiny balconies and some views. The nearby church chimes tinnily from 8am. It's homey, cosy and the price is right. From March to October it has an attractive restaurant with a great-value three-course *menú*.

★**Olvido 22** BOUTIQUE HOTEL €€€

(☎692 207141; www.hostalboutiqueolvido22.com; Calle Olvido 22; r €150-175; ❄📶) The five exquisite maritime-themed rooms here all have brilliant outlooks over the old-town ramparts to the sea. It's a romantic spot that's particularly good value in low season, but wonderful at any time. Alicia offers a great welcome and puts on brilliant breakfasts featuring freshly made Spanish omelette and delicious juice from their own orange trees. No children.

**Hotel La Mar** BOUTIQUE HOTEL €€€

(☎964 48 00 57; www.hotelboutiquelamar.com; Calle Porteta 16; r €192-267; ⏲Jun–mid-Oct & weekends Mar-May; P❄📶) With a lovely old-town waterside location, looking down the sweep of beach and bay, this refined, modern hotel offers excellent comfort, a fine restaurant and a warm welcome. Rooms are sleek and modern, with some looking up to the old town, others over the sea. The sublime roof terrace has wraparound vistas. Prices plunge outside high summer. No children.

**La Taverneta de Sant Roc** SPANISH €€

(☎964 48 21 70; Calle San Roque 15; mains €11-18; ⏲11am-4pm & 7pm-midnight, reduced hours low season) In the touristy heart of Peñíscola, you fear the worst from the throng of places with photos of food out on the street. But this is a real exception: a generous, kindly spot intent on its customers leaving full and happy. There's an excellent range of fare, from croquettes to seafood and decent steaks.

**La Mar Salá** VALENCIAN €€

(☎964 48 21 87; www.lamarsala.net; Plaza Antonelli; mains €13-18; ⏲8.30am-midnight Wed-Mon) Just below the old town, La Mar Salá offers a range of excellent-value set meals, which include tasty chargrilled seafood and meat. It's one of the few reliable year-round choices, and the glass-walled dining room is an attractive dinner spot.

## Information

**Main Tourist Office** (☎964 48 02 08; www.peniscola.es; Paseo Marítimo; ⊙10am-8pm mid-Jun–mid-Sep, 10am-7pm Apr–mid-Jun & mid-Sep–mid-Oct, 9.30am-5.30pm Mon-Sat, 10am-2pm Sun mid-Oct–Mar) At the southern end of Paseo Marítimo. You can also get town information from the website.

## Getting There & Away

Buses run at least half-hourly between Peñíscola, Benicarló and Vinaròs, from where you can connect to Valencia or Castellón. In the high summer season there is usually also a service to Peñíscola/Benicarló train station, 7km from town.

# El Maestrazgo

Straddling northwestern Valencia and southeastern Aragón, El Maestrazgo (Valenciano: El Maestrat) is a mountainous land, a world away from the coastal strip. Its spectacular ancient *pueblos* (villages) huddle on rocky outcrops and ridges. The Maestrazgo is great, wild, on-your-own trekking territory.

Blazing your own trails across the Maestrazgo on foot, bike or by car is an appealing adventure. There are numerous lonely landscapes, amazingly old olive trees and lovely villages to discover.

## Sant Mateu

POP 2000

Not as picturesque from a distance as the hilltop villages further into the region, Sant Mateu, once capital of the Maestrazgo, has a lovely town centre nonetheless, framed around a pretty plaza. The solid mansions and elaborate facades recall the town's more illustrious past and former wool-based wealth.

### LOCAL WALKS

Radiating from the village of Sant Mateu are signed circular walking trails of between 2½ and five hours that lead through the surrounding hills. Ask for the free tourist-office pamphlet *Senderos de Sant Mateu* (in Spanish). The website (http://turismosantmateu.es) also has details.

## Sights

**Ermita de la Mare de Déu dels Àngels** CHURCH
(☎605 382935; ⊙11am-6pm Tue-Sun) Follow signs from the Plaza Mayor to this loveable chapel perched on a rocky hillside, a 2.5km drive, or somewhat shorter walk, away. It was a monastery until the Spanish Civil War and preserves a baroque chapel with a typical regional tiled floor and a cherub-infested altarpiece. The views are great, and there's an excellent restaurant. Midweek opening is unreliable; you can phone to check or arrange a visit.

**Iglesia Arciprestal** CHURCH
(☎964 41 66 58; http://turismosantmateu.es/iglesia-arciprestal; Calle Santo Domingo 6; adult/youth/child €1.50/1.20/free; ⊙10am-2pm & 4-7pm Jun-Sep, guided visits only Oct-May) Just off the plaza, this Gothic village church has a Romanesque portal and a fine interior. The frescoed neoclassical side chapel has a macabre reliquary with a skeleton apparently dressed for a local Moorish and Christian fiesta. Guided tours, optional in summer and the only way to enter at other times, include the sacristy and a small museum with jewellery, processional crosses and two pieces of the true cross. The church interior is visible through a glass screen any time.

**Museo de Valltorta** MUSEUM
(☎964 33 60 10; www.museudelavalltorta.gva.es; Pla de l'Om, Tirig; ⊙10am-2pm & 4-6pm or 5-8pm Tue-Sun) FREE This informative museum, 2km from Tirig (10km southwest of Sant Mateu), presents a detailed overview of prehistoric art and El Maestrazgo's World Heritage ensemble of rock paintings. There's a reproduction of the most interesting piece – a hunting scene – and info in various languages available. From here, free guided walks to the painting sites leave a couple of times daily.

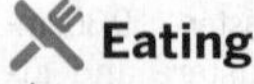

## Eating

★**Farga** VALENCIAN €€
(☎663 909586; www.facebook.com/FargaRestaurant; Ermita de la Mare de Déu dels Àngels; set menus €25-35; ⊙8-11pm Fri, noon-11pm Sat, noon-6pm Sun, extended hrs summer) This quality restaurant at a former monastery perched on a hill 2.5km from town offers sublime views of the surrounding plain from its terrace, and a characterful vaulted interior space. It's run by a friendly young couple who offer

delicious, sophisticated cuisine. Opening hours vary widely by season; call ahead.

**La Perdi** SPANISH €€
(☎964 41 60 82; www.laperdi.es; Calle de Historiador Betí 9; mains €8-15; ⏰1-4pm & 7.30-11pm, closed Sun-Wed evenings Nov-Mar) Our favourite place for a traditional meal in the centre of Sant Mateu, the Perdi has been run for generations by the same family. A couple of set menus and solid à la carte options showcase warming regional cuisine in a pleasantly rustic ambience. Try the local dish *olleta,* a filling stew of chickpeas, rice, vegetables, lamb and black pudding.

They've also got five plain but good-value budget rooms upstairs.

## Information

**Tourist Office** (☎964 41 66 58; http://turismosantmateu.es; Calle de Historiador Betí 13; ⏰10am-2pm & 4-6pm Tue-Sat, 10am-2pm Sun) Very helpful. Just off the main square in a sturdy palace. Sometimes opens daily in summer.

## Getting There & Away

**Autos Mediterráneo buses** (☎964 22 00 54; www.autosmediterraneo.com) link Sant Mateu with Castellón (€6.45, 1½ hours, three Monday to Friday, one Saturday), Morella (€4.25, 45 minutes, two Monday to Friday, one Saturday) and Vinaròs (€3, one hour, four Monday to Friday).

# Morella

POP 2400 / ELEV 984M

Bitingly cold in winter and refreshingly cool in summer, striking Morella is the Valencian Maestrazgo's principal settlement. This outstanding example of a medieval fortress town, breathtaking at first glimpse, is perched on a hilltop, crowned by a castle and girdled by an intact rampart wall more than 1.5km long and studded with imposing towers and gates. It's the ancient capital of Els Ports, the 'Mountain Passes', a rugged region offering some outstanding scenic drives and strenuous cycling excursions, plus excellent possibilities for walkers.

## Sights

**Castillo de Morella** CASTLE
(adult/child €3.50/2.50; ⏰11am-5pm Oct-Apr, to 7pm May-Sep) Though badly knocked about, Morella's castle well merits the long wiggly ascent to savour breathtaking views of the town and surrounding countryside. Built by the Moors, it was regularly remodelled and saw action in the Napoleonic and Carlist Wars of the 19th century. Carlists took it in 1838 by climbing up through the long-drop toilet. At its base is the bare church and cloister of the **Convento de San Francisco**, by which you enter.

**Basílica de Santa María la Mayor** CHURCH
(☎964 16 03 79; Plaza Arciprestal; adult/child €2.50/1; ⏰10am-2pm & 3-6pm or 7pm Mon-Sat, 10-11.30am & 12.15-3pm Sun) This imposing and beautiful Gothic basilica has two elaborately sculpted doorways on its southern facade, one preserving a significant amount of colour. A richly sculpted and coloured staircase leads to the unusual overhead choir with its characterful Gothic frieze of the Last Judgement. The organ and gilt altarpiece are later baroque additions, with cherubs clambering and peeking all over them. There's a small three-level museum that houses the church's treasures and some religious art.

**Torres de San Miguel** GATE
(Plaza San Miguel; adult/child €1.50/free; ⏰10am-1pm & 4-6pm Tue, Thu & Sat) The twin towers of this imposing city gateway are a good place to begin your exploration of the town. With a solid octagonal form, they were first built in the 14th century. The interior holds

OFF THE BEATEN TRACK

### EXPLORING THE MAESTRAZGO

If you have time, it's worth exploring away from the major villages and seek out some smaller ones. **Ares**, 30km south of Morella, is one of the most spectacular, hanging over a cliff, its ruined castle perched on a picturesque rocky outcrop. Around 13km from here, **Vilafranca** (del Cid) has a museum – the excellent **Museo de la Pedra en Sec** (☎964 44 14 32; www.turismevilafranca.es; Calle de la Iglesia, Villafranca del Cid; adult/child €2/1.50; ⏰10am-1.30pm & 4-7pm Fri & Sat, 10.30am-1.30pm Sun) – that explores its dry-stone-wall tradition. If there's no one there, ask in the tourist office opposite. And don't miss some stunning spots just over the border in Teruel province; Cantavieja and Mirambel are two of the prettiest villages.

a collection of traditional children's games as well as art objects. The highlight is the access to a picturesque stretch of city wall. Views are great.

## Sleeping

Though the project was shelved for years, the proposal to turn part of the Convento de Santo Domingo into a *parador* (luxurious state-run hotel) seems to be going ahead, though it will likely take a few years.

**Hotel Cardenal Ram** HOTEL €€
(☎964 16 00 46; www.hotelcardenalram.com; Cuesta Suñer 1; s €65, d €85-110; P ❄ ☜) Bang in the heart of old Morella, this noble Renaissance palace is now a comfortable hotel. Half the rooms have splendid views (and cost a little more); those without are generally very spacious. It all feels a little on the slide, but it's still the town's best lodging.

## Eating & Drinking

Morella has an excellent eating scene, with quality restaurants and lots of shops selling high-quality local deli produce. Look out for truffle season in the early months of the year, when restaurants put on special menus featuring the delicacy.

**★Daluan** SPANISH €€
(☎964 16 00 71; http://daluan.es; Carreró de la Presó 6; mains €12-21, set menus €18.50-33.50; ⏲1-3.30pm Thu-Tue & 9-10.30pm Fri & Sat, closed Jan) Daluan is run by Avelino Ramón, a cookery teacher by trade, and his wife Jovita: a very friendly team! Its small upstairs interior is satisfyingly contemporary and its terrace, filling a quiet alley, is equally relaxing. Expect amiable service and a hugely creative menu that changes regularly with the seasons. A backstreet gem and very well priced for this standard.

**Mesón del Pastor** SPANISH €€
(☎964 16 02 49; www.mesondelpastor.com; Cuesta Jovaní 5; mains €9-15, set menus €20-31; ⏲1-4.30pm Thu-Tue & 9-11pm Fri & Sat) Within the sizeable dining room, bedecked with the restaurant's trophies and diplomas, this traditional family-run place is all about robust mountain cuisine with modern touches: thick stews in winter, rabbit, juicy sausages, partridge, wild boar and goat. It's located a short walk from the hotel of the same name. In August, it opens for dinner every day bar Wednesday.

**Canyero's Bar** BAR
(☎653 078703; Calle Blasco de Alagón 29; ⏲noon-3pm & 7-10pm) Small enough that you could almost fit it on a postcard – perhaps one of the several offbeat cards behind the counter – this bar has real soul and great local information. Grab a table under the columned arcade or shoulder up at the bar for a pre-lunch or -dinner apéritif. The excellent artisanal vermouth comes from a nearby village.

## Information

**Tourist Office** (☎964 17 30 32; www.morellaturistica.com; Plaza San Miguel 3; ⏲10am-2pm & 4-7pm Mon-Sat, 10am-2pm Sun Apr–mid-Oct, 10am-2pm & 4-6pm Tue-Sat, 10am-2pm Sun mid-Oct–Mar) Just inside the imposing San Miguel towers and upper main entrance gate to the old town.

## Getting There & Away

Two daily weekday buses (€10.60, 2¼ hours) and one Saturday service with Autos Mediterráneo (p825) run to/from Castellón's train station. There are also weekday buses to Vinaròs on the coast and twice-weekly services to Alcañiz in Teruel province.

If coming by car, the easiest way is to ignore the first town entrance to Puerta San Mateo, and continue on the main road to the top of town and the Puerta San Miguel entrance, where there's a council car park just outside the gates.

# ALICANTE PROVINCE

## Alicante

POP 334,900

Of all Spain's mainland provincial capitals, Alicante (Valenciano: Alacant) is one of the most influenced by tourism, thanks to the nearby airport and resorts. Nevertheless, it is a dynamic, attractive Spanish city with a castle, old quarter and long waterfront. The eating scene is exciting and the nightlife is absolutely legendary, whether you're chugging pints with the stag parties at 7pm or twirling on the dance floor with the locals seven hours later. On a weekend night it's impossibly busy and buzzy year-round.

## Sights & Activities

**★Museo de Arte Contemporáneo de Alicante** GALLERY
(MACA; ☎965 21 31 56; www.maca-alicante.es; Plaza Santa María 3; ⏲10am-8pm Tue-Sat,

# Alicante

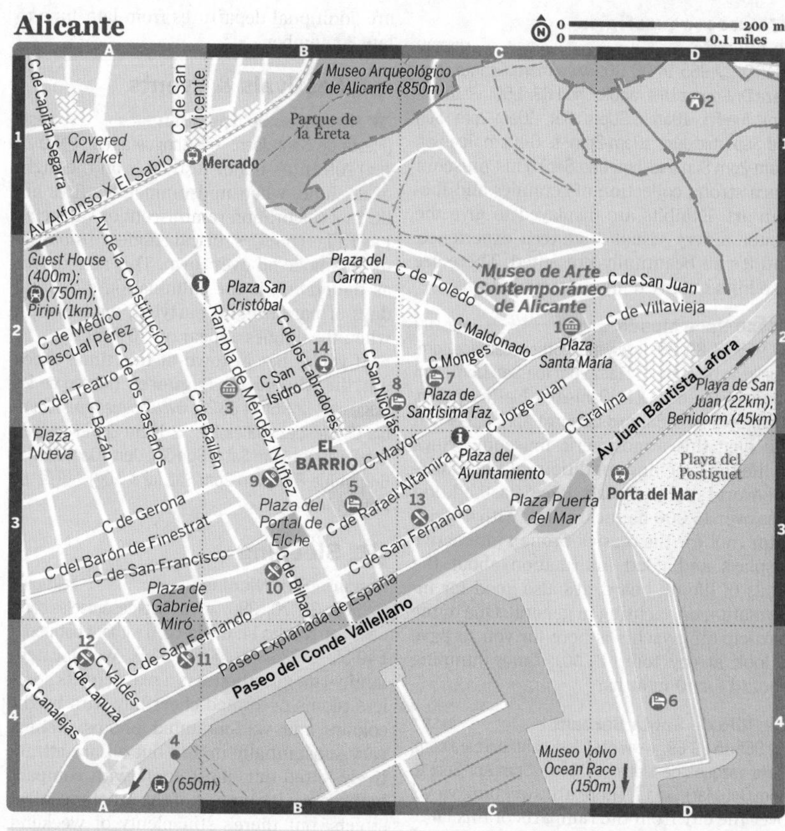


## Alicante

**Top Sights**
1 Museo de Arte Contemporáneo de Alicante .......... C2

**Sights**
2 Castillo de Santa Bárbara .......... D1
Museo de la Ciudad de Alicante .......... (see 2)
3 Museu de Fogueres .......... B2

**Activities, Courses & Tours**
4 Kon Tiki .......... A4

**Sleeping**
5 Hotel Hospes Amérigo .......... B3
6 Hotel Spa Porta Maris .......... D4
7 Les Monges Palace .......... C2
8 Pensión San Nicolás .......... B2

**Eating**
9 Cervecería Sento .......... B3
10 El Portal .......... B3
11 La Barra de César Anca .......... A4
12 OneOne .......... A4
13 Taberna del Gourmet .......... C3

**Drinking & Nightlife**
14 El Coscorrón .......... B2

from 11am summer, 10am-2pm Sun) FREE This beautiful gallery, a modern space inside the 17th-century Casa de la Asegurada, has an excellent collection of 20th-century Spanish art, including works by Dalí, Miró, Chillida, Gargallo, Tàpies and Picasso. The pieces on display rotate regularly, as the collection is a sizeable one. The foundation of the collection was a donation by noted geometric abstract artist Eusebio Sempere (1923–85), an Alicante native who has a section to himself. His shimmering steel creations are best viewed in motion: ask an attendant to oblige.

★**Museo Arqueológico de Alicante** MUSEUM
(MARQ; ☎965 14 90 00; www.marqalicante.com; Plaza Dr Gómez Ulla; adult/child €3/1.50; ⏰10am-7pm Tue-Fri, 10am-8.30pm Sat, 10am-2pm Sun mid-Sep–mid-Jun, 10am-2pm & 6-10pm Tue-Sat, 10am-2pm Sun mid-Jun–mid-Sep) This museum has a strong collection of ceramics and Iberian art. Exhibits are displayed to give the visitor a very visual, high-tech experience, and it's all beautifully presented. There are also high-quality temporary exhibitions.

**Ocean Race Museo** MUSEUM
(☎965 13 80 80; www.museotheoceanrace.com; Muelle de Levante; ⏰11am-9pm Tue-Sat, 11am-3pm Sun mid-Apr–mid-Oct, 10am-2pm Tue-Thu & Sun, 10am-6pm Fri & Sat mid-Oct–mid-Apr) FREE On the pier, this atmospheric museum brings to life the gruelling conditions of the round-the-world Volvo Ocean Race (last edition was over 45,000 nautical miles) with a simulator (not for the seasick-prone), interactive displays and good information about the trials of life on board. It's also good for information on yachting in general. One of the participating yachts is here for you to have a look at (by tour; €1.50): fancy jumping aboard for 10 months?

**Castillo de Santa Bárbara** CASTLE
(☎965 15 29 69; www.castillodesantabarbara.com; Calle Vázquez de Mella; ⏰10am-10pm Apr-Sep, to 8pm Oct-Mar) FREE There are sweeping views over the city from the ramparts of this large 16th-century castle, which houses a **museum** (MUSA; Castilo de Santa Bárbara; ⏰10am-2.30pm & 4-8pm) FREE recounting the history of Alicante and a couple of chambers with temporary exhibitions. It's a sweaty walk up the hill to the castle, but there's a **lift** (up/down €2.70/free; ⏰10am-7.30pm) that rises through the bowels of the mountain to the summit. To return, it's a pleasant stroll down through Parque de la Ereta.

**Playa de San Juan** BEACH
Northeast of the town, Playa de San Juan, easily reached by the tram (Londres or Costa Blanca stops), is very long and usually less crowded than the city beach.

**Kon Tiki** BOATING
(☎686 994538; www.cruceroskontiki.com; Puerto Deportivo; return €20; ⏰Tue, Thu, Sat & Sun Mar-Dec) Makes the 45-minute boat trip to the popular island of Tabarca, giving you about 4½ hours there. It leaves Alicante at 11pm, departing from the island at 4.30pm. There are additional departures from late June to late September.

## Festivals & Events

★**Hogueras de San Juan** FIESTA
(Fiesta de Sant Joan; www.hogueras.es; ⏰20-24 Jun) Alicante's major festival is on the night of 24 June, when midsummer bonfires are lit. In a celebration reminiscent of Valencia's Las Fallas (p813), satirical effigies *(ninots)* go up in smoke all over town. This act, known as the *cremà,* is the culmination of several days of parades and partying, which begin when the effigies appear on 20 June.

If you're not in town at this time, check out the **Museu de Fogueres** (Museo de las Hogueras; ☎965 14 68 28; www.hogueras.es; Rambla de Méndez Núñez 29; ⏰10am-2pm & 5-8pm Tue-Fri, 10am-2pm Sat & Sun Sep-Jun, 10am-2pm & 6-9pm Tue-Fri, 10am-2pm Sat Jul & Aug) FREE to get an idea.

## Sleeping

**Pensión San Nicolás** PENSION €
(☎965 21 70 39; www.alicantesanicolas.com; Calle San Nicolás 14; d €45-63, d without bathroom €40-55, s €25-35; ❄📶) This well-located, family-run guesthouse is a real gem, its spotless rooms decorated cheerfully with bright colours and wall-mounted photos. Rooms vary substantially in size but all are attractively kitted out; most come with compact bathrooms. It's on one of the quieter central streets, but there's still plenty of weekend noise and it's a great partying base. Substantially cheaper if you pay in advance.

**Guest House** HOSTAL €
(☎650 718353; www.guesthousealicante.com; Calle Segura 20; s/d/apt €40/60/90; P❄📶) At this well-maintained budget choice, each of the eight large, tastefully decorated rooms differs. Some have exposed stone walls and others are painted in pale green, daffodil yellow or deep-sea blue. All come with a safe, full-sized fridge and Nespresso machine. There are also a couple of well-equipped apartments. Ring ahead as it's not always staffed.

**Les Monges Palace** BOUTIQUE HOTEL €€
(☎965 21 50 46; www.lesmonges.es; Calle San Agustín 4; s incl breakfast €56-75, d incl breakfast €75-90; P❄@📶) This agreeably quirky place in the nightlife zone is a treasure with winding corridors, tiles, mosaics and antique furniture. Each room is individually decorated – some are considerably more

spacious than others – with plenty of character; some are in a more modern wing. To really pamper yourself, choose one of the two spa rooms (€120). The rooftop terrace bar is great.

**Hotel Hospes Amérigo** HOTEL €€€
(965 14 65 70; www.hospes.es; Calle de Rafael Altamira 7; r €180-320; ) Within an old Dominican convent, this commodious five-star choice harmoniously blends the traditional and ultramodern. Enjoy the views from the small rooftop pool and spa, or build up a sweat in the fitness area…if you can tear yourself away from the comfort of your smartly designed room. There are very few parking spaces, so make sure you prebook one.

**Hotel Spa Porta Maris** HOTEL €€€
(965 14 70 21; www.hotelspaportamaris.com; Plaza Puerta del Mar 3; r €180-260; ) The better of the hotels on the pier, this is a short walk from the centre but quiet. It offers magnificent views over the beach from the rooms facing that way, and from the luminous breakfast area. Rooms are spacious, with comfortable mattresses, pillow menu and plenty of facilities.

## Eating

Where's the tapas zone? Virtually the whole centre: wherever it seems all the action is, you can be sure there's even more going on in another node a couple of streets further on. Unusually for Spain, lots of restaurants and tapas bars have all-day opening.

★**Cervecería Sento** TAPAS €
(www.somossento.es; Calle Teniente Coronel Chápuli 1; tapas €2-10; 9am-midnight Sun-Thu, to 1am Fri & Sat) Top-notch *montaditos* (little rolls) and inventive grilled tapas (try the turrón and pork 'Chupa Chups') are the reason to squeeze into this brilliant little bar. Watching the cheeky, nonstop staff in action is quite an experience too: they make every visit intriguing. It has bigger branches nearby, but this one has the atmosphere.

**OneOne** BISTRO €€
(965 20 63 99; Calle Valdés 9; mains €12-20; 2-3.30pm & 9-11pm Tue-Sat, closed mid-Aug–mid-Sep) It's easier if you speak a little Spanish at this wonderfully eccentric place with its faithful following of regulars, but your ebullient host will make sure you get the best anyway. It's a true bistro, with the walls scarcely visible for Parisian-style photos and posters, and there's no menu. Just listen carefully as Bartolomé intones. Characterful and memorable.

**Taberna del Gourmet** SPANISH €€
(965 20 42 33; www.latabernadelgourmet.com; Calle de San Fernando 10; dishes €10-30; 12.30pm-midnight) This side project of the chef in charge of one of Alicante's most famed restaurants offers brilliant produce in an upbeat atmosphere, with excellent service a key. The cramped bar tables are lively, but numerous tables out back offer a quieter experience. Go with the flow and check out the specials such as *erizos* (sea urchins) or *berberechos* (cockles) are great.

**La Barra de César Anca** SPANISH €€
(965 12 43 62; www.grupocesaranca.com; Calle Ojeda 1; dishes €7-22; 8am-4pm & 8pm-midnight Tue-Fri, noon-4pm & 8pm-midnight Sat, noon-4pm Sun; ) Upmarket and buzzy, this is a fun place to sit at the bar and try some high-class gastro creations featuring plenty of excellent fish and showcasing fine presentation. There's sit-down restaurant seating too, but the bar is more fun. It's also a popular spot for a mid-morning coffee and bite.

**El Portal** SPANISH €€€
(965 14 44 44; www.elportaltaberna.com; Calle Bilbao 2; mains €18-30; 1pm-2am; ) This plush corner spot sports deliberately OTT decor that changes biannually. Squeeze up at the bar (better service here) to enjoy plump Dénia prawns, excellent tuna, fresh fish or mouthwatering ham. The atmosphere is smart but relaxed, with a DJ responding to the mood as plates of seafood make way for G&Ts in the mid-afternoon and at night.

**Piripi** VALENCIAN €€€
(965 61 64 25; www.grupogastronou.com; Avenida Oscar Esplá 30; mains €12-30; 1-4pm & 8.15-11.30pm Mon-Sat, 1-4pm Sun; ) This quality restaurant is strong on rice, seafood and fish, which arrives fresh daily from the wholesale markets of Dénia and Santa Pola. There's a huge variety of tapas and a *valenciano* speciality that changes daily. It's a short walk west of the centre or downhill from the train station. The upstairs restaurant is fairly formal; the downstairs bar is buzzier.

## Drinking & Nightlife

Alicante's nightlife is an impressive thing to behold. Wet your night-time whistle in the wall-to-wall weekend bars of the old quarter (known as El Barrio) around Catedral de San Nicolás. Alternatively, head for the sea. Paseo del Puerto, tranquil by day, is a double-decker line of casino, restaurants, bars and nightclubs. Calle de los Castaños is worth a wander for a quieter, all-week scene.

★ **El Coscorrón** BAR
(☎965 21 27 27; Calle Tarifa 5; ⏲8.30pm-3am Wed-Sat) Mind your head – actually, it's more like bend double – as you enter this intriguing cellar bar, presciently named 'bump on the head'. Once inside, enjoy the cosy atmosphere with the mellow soundtrack, friendly regulars and walls plastered with graffiti and notes. The mojitos (€4) are served out of a mint-filled teapot on the bar and are great.

## Information

**Main Tourist Office** (☎965 20 00 00; www.alicanteturismo.com; Rambla de Méndez Núñez 41; ⏲10am-6pm Mon-Fri, to 2pm Sat) There are also branches at the **town hall** (☎965 14 92 19; www.alicanteturismo.com; Plaza del Ayuntamiento 1; ⏲10am-2pm & 5-8pm mid-Mar–mid-Oct, 10am-2pm & 4-7pm Mon-Sat, 10am-2pm Sun mid-Oct–mid-Mar) and at the **train station** (☎965 12 56 33; www.alicanteturismo.com; Avenida de Salamanca; ⏲10am-2pm & 5-8pm mid-Mar–mid-Oct, 10am-2pm & 4-7pm Mon-Sat, 10am-2pm Sun mid-Oct–mid-Mar), beach and airport.

## Getting There & Away

### AIR

Alicante's **airport** (☎913 211 000; www.aena.es; L'Altet), gateway to the Costa Blanca, is around 12km southwest of the city centre. It's served by budget airlines, charters and scheduled flights from all over Europe.

Bus C-6 (www.aerobusalicante.es) runs between Plaza Puerta del Mar and the airport (€3.85, 30 minutes, every 20 minutes), passing by the north side of the bus station and the train station.

### BUS

From the **bus station** (Avenida de Loring), destinations include Murcia (€6.35, one to two hours, 11 to 17 daily) and Valencia (€21 to €25, 2½ to 5½ hours, more than 10 daily).

### TRAIN

Mainline destinations from the principal train station include the following. For Murcia, there are also regular *cercanía* trains (€5.75, 1¼ hours) via Elche and Orihuela.

| Destination | Cost (€) | Time (hr) | Frequency (daily) |
|---|---|---|---|
| Barcelona | 52-64 | 4½-5½ | 8 |
| Madrid | 52-70 | 2¼-2¾ | 10 |
| Murcia | 10-19 | 1¼ | 5 |
| Valencia | 16-21 | 1½-2 | 11 |

### TRAM

The coastal tram/light-rail service is a handy option; see the TRAM (www.tramalicante.es) website. Scenic Line 1 heads to Benidorm with a connection to Dénia. Catch it from beside the covered market.

# Dénia

POP 41,700

A major passenger port for the Balearic Islands, Dénia (Spanish: Denia) is a cheery place that lives for more than just tourism. The old town snuggles up against a small hill surmounted by a tumbledown castle, and the streets buzz with life and top foodie choices. The beaches of La Marina, to its northwest, are good and sandy, while southeastwards the fretted coastline of Les Rotes and beyond offers less-frequented rocky coves. With its excellent selection of hotels and restaurants, and mix of local and tourist life, Dénia is perhaps the Costa Blanca's most appealing base.

## Sights & Activities

As well as the numerous options for getting out on the water, climbing Montgó (p832) is a popular activity. **My Denia Rent** (☎673 673771; www.mydeniarent.com; Calle Sandunga 60; bike hire 4hr/day €8/12; ⏲10am-6.30pm Mon-Sat) hires out bikes, paddleboards and inflatable kayaks.

**Castillo de Dénia** CASTLE
(☎966 42 06 56; www.denia.net/castillo-de-denia; Calle San Francisco; adult/child €3/1; ⏲10am-6pm or later Sep-Jun, to 12.30am Jul & Aug) From Plaza de la Constitución steps lead up to the ruins of Dénia's castle, from where there's a great overview of the town and coast. The castle grounds contain the **Museo Arqueològic de Dénia**, a collection of potsherds illustrating the town's long history. The closing time changes according to the time of year; check the website for exact times.

**Museo de la Mar** MUSEUM
(www.denia.es; Esplanada de Cervantes 2; ⏲10am-1pm & 4-8pm Oct-Apr, 10am-1pm & 5-9pm May-

Sep) FREE On the waterfront, the former fish market now holds an exhibition on Dénia's maritime history, with a series of photos, models and objects retrieved from the deeps on display.

## Sleeping

**★Hotel Chamarel** BOUTIQUE HOTEL €€
(☎966 43 50 07; www.hotelchamarel.com; Calle Cavallers 13; d/ste incl breakfast €90/150; P ❄ 📶) This delightful hotel, tastefully furnished in period style, occupies a lovably attractive 19th-century bourgeois mansion. Rooms surround a tranquil patio and are all different, with space, lots of character and bathrooms that artfully combine modern fittings with venerable floor tiles. The internal salon with marble-topped bar is equally relaxing. The whole place is a capacious gallery for the artist-owner's paintings.

**Hotel Nou Romá** BOUTIQUE HOTEL €€
(☎966 43 28 43; www.hotelnouroma.com; Calle Nou 28; d incl breakfast €90-144; P ❄ 📶) Perfectly located for excursions to the Calle Loreto eating strip, this hotel is on a quietish backstreet but very central. Staff are really excellent, and the spacious rooms with their bright-tiled bathrooms are a delight. The on-site restaurant is worthwhile and the overall package very impressive. Lots of thoughtful details add that extra something to your stay.

**Hostal L'Anfora** HOSTAL €€
(☎966 43 01 01; www.hostallanfora.com; Esplanada de Cervantes 8; s/d €49/69; ❄ 📶) The genial boss here is rightly proud of this top *hostal* on the waterfront strip. Rooms are compact but new in feel, with colourful bedcovers, faultless bathrooms and not a speck of dust or dirt. Outside of high summer, prices are very fair: it's an affordable gem. Rooms with a sea view cost a few euros more.

**Posada del Mar** HOTEL €€€
(☎966 43 29 66; www.laposadadelmar.com; Plaza Drassanes 2; s/d incl breakfast €178/198, ste €221-314; P ❄ @ 📶) Sensitively renovated, this hotel occupies a 13th-century building that last functioned as Dénia's customs house. Each of its 25 rooms is individually decorated with a nautical theme, and light streams through large windows overlooking the harbour. The junior suites, with a double outlook, are particularly luminous. It can be a bargain in the low season.

## Eating

Dénia has a superb, vibrant eating scene – it's one of this coast's top gastronomic locales – and is famous for its pricey but undeniably delicious striped prawns *(gambas rayadas)*. The smaller *gambetas* are a bit more wallet-friendly. Restaurants run along the waterfront, while pedestrianised Calle Loreto, a 10-minute stroll back from the beach, is another main tapas and dining zone and a fun spot to eat. Don't miss a morning wine and tapa in one of the bars inside the food market on Calle Magallanes. An evening glass of wine is good in the **Els Magazinos complex** (www.elsmagazinos.com; Calle Puente 19; ⊙9am-1.30am Tue-Sun), though you're probably better dining elsewhere.

**Bar Bus** SEAFOOD €
(☎965 78 11 37; Plaza del Archiduque Carlos 4; mains €9-13; ⊙8am-4pm & 8-11.45pm; 📶) Though the name remains, this now has a pleasant outdoor terrace where the bus station used to be. It's a place to try simple, quality seafood selected daily from the market. Oysters, cuttlefish and other delights are reliably excellent, though service is patchy.

**★El Baret de Miquel Ruiz** TAPAS €€
(☎WhatsApp only 673 740 595; www.miquelruizcuiner.com; Carrer Historiador Palau 1; large plates €14-24; ⊙1.30-3.30pm & 8.30-10pm Tue-Sat Sep-Jul) This is a real find for gastronomes. The chef had a Michelin-starred restaurant but chose to reject that world in favour of a more normal existence. Deliciously inventive, traditionally influenced sharing dishes using market produce are taste sensations, amid the simple, retro-casual vibe of the front room of an old house. Book well ahead, though you may be lucky with cancellations.

**Aitana** SEAFOOD €€
(☎965 78 60 69; Calle de Sandunga 53; seafood meal around €30; ⊙1.30-4pm Tue-Sat & 8.30-11pm Fri) Perhaps the best place in Dénia to try the deservedly famous local prawns, this unusual backstreet bar gets thronged, so try to book a table or get there early and wait for a spot at the bar. Just let the boss, gruff but kind, start feeding you seafood and go with the flow. Tender mussels, delicious cuttlefish, tiny clams...it's all marvellous.

**Els Tomassets** TAPAS €€
(☎966 43 25 60; www.facebook.com/elstomassets.denia; Calle Loreto 35; mains €8-18; ⊙9am-midnight; 📶) Informal and vibrant, with an

open kitchen, this spot turns out delicious fare. In winter, chargrilled artichokes *(alcachofas a la brasa)* are a delight, while the acquired, rich taste of sea urchins will tempt those who like their food spiky. Seafood is a forte, but meat dishes are also above average for this coast.

**★Quique Dacosta** SPANISH €€€
(965 78 41 79; www.quiquedacosta.es; Calle Rascassa 1, El Poblet; degustation menu €210, wine flight €110; 1.30-3pm & 8.30-10.30pm Jul & Aug, Wed-Sun Feb-Jun & Sep-Nov) In sleek, white, minimalist premises near the beach 3km west of Dénia, this coolly handsome place is one of the peninsula's temples to modern gastronomy. The eponymous chef employs molecular and other contemporary techniques to create a constantly surprising cornucopia of flavours and textures.

## Information

**Main Tourist Office** (966 42 23 67; www.denia.net; Plaza Oculista Buigues 9; 10am-2pm & 3-6pm Mon-Sat, 10am-2pm Sun Nov-Feb, 9.30am-1.30pm & 4.30-7.30pm Mon-Sat, 9.30am-1.30pm Sun Mar–mid-Jun & mid-Sep–Oct, 9.30am-8pm Mon-Fri, 9.30am-1.30pm & 3-8pm Sat & Sun mid-Jun–mid-Sep) Near the waterfront and ferry and also close to the tram/light-rail station.

**Consell Tourist Office** (966 52 34 20; www.denia.net; Plaza del Consell; 9.30am-1.30pm mid-Jun–mid-Sep, 9.30am-1.30pm & 4.30-7.30pm Mon-Fri, 9.30am-1.30pm Sat Mar–mid-Jun & mid-Sep–Oct, 10am-2pm & 3-6pm Mon-Fri Nov-Feb) In the heart of town near the castle and Calle Loreto eating strip.

## Getting There & Away

**Baleària** (865 608 423; www.balearia.com; Moll de la Pansa) runs ferries year-round to/from Mallorca (passenger €70 to €100, car €100 to €150, five to seven hours, daily) and Ibiza (passenger €70 to €105, car €120 to €160, two to 3½ hours, daily), and from May to September directly to Formentera (passenger €70 to €100, car €80 to €110, 2½ hours, five weekly).

ALSA (www.alsa.es) buses run around a dozen times daily to Valencia (€11.50, 1½ to two hours) and Alicante (€11.80, 1½ to three hours). There are also services to Benidorm and other Costa Blanca towns.

Hourly light-rail services (replaced by bus services as far as Calp until late 2021) follow the scenic route southwards via Calp and Altea to Benidorm, connecting with the tram for Alicante.

# Xàbia

POP 27,200

With a large expat resident population, Xàbia (Spanish: Jávea) is a gentle, family-oriented place that has largely resisted the high-rise tourist developments that blight so much of the Costa Blanca. Pleasant, relaxed and picturesque, it comes in three flavours: the small old town, 2km inland; El Puerto (the port), directly east of the old town; and the beach zone of El Arenal, a couple of kilometres south. Inviting headlands and coves reward further exploration of this section of coast.

## Activities

Various operators offer diving, kayaking and all manner of other watery pursuits. The tourist office has a map of various diving routes, which you will need a boat to access.

You can rent a cycle at **Xàbia's Bike** (966 46 11 50; www.xabiasbike.com; Avenida Lepanto 5; per day/week from €13/56; 9.30am-1.30pm & 4.30-8.30pm Mon-Fri, 10am-2pm Sat) in the port area (among several other operators). It also does weekend rides and can organise guided bike tours. The tourist office has a booklet of cycling excursions.

**Montgó** HIKING
A popular walk is ascending Montgó, the craggy mountain looming over the town. It's a climb best started in the morning or late afternoon, as it's fairly exposed to the sun. It's a stony and arduous but not difficult path to the top. Access the trail from the road between Xàbia and Dénia; it's about 8km return from the car park.

## Sleeping

**Hotel Triskel** BOUTIQUE HOTEL €€
(966 46 21 91; www.hotel-triskel.com; Calle Sor María Gallart 3; d €130; P ❄ 🛜 🐾) By the old-town market, this cordially run place is a standout. The five lovely rooms are subtly and beautifully decorated according to themes, with thoughtful details, objets d'art and pleasing handmade wooden furniture. Everything is done with a warm personal touch and the cosy bar downstairs does a cracking G&T. Pets welcome and prices nearly halve in low season.

**Hotel Jávea** HOTEL €€
(965 79 54 61; www.hotel-javea.com; Calle Pio X 5; d €80, with sea view €125; ❄ 🛜) This

extra-friendly small hotel is in the heart of the port district, with bars and restaurants on the doorstep. Offbeat decor and smart modern rooms make it a top spot. The sea view costs a fair bit extra, but it's a lovely perspective over the whole sweep of the bay. The top-floor restaurant makes the most of the vistas, too.

## Eating & Drinking

**Sotavent** SPANISH €
(☎660 341226; www.facebook.com/Sotaventportjavea; Calle Cristo del Mar 8; dishes €6-15; ⏰10am-4pm & 7pm-midnight Thu-Tue) This friendly spot near the waterfront in the port area gets everything right, with sizeable, delicious portions of seafood, rices, liver and more at extremely reasonable prices. There's a patio space that is the place to sit on balmy Xàbia evenings.

**Taverna Octopus** PUB
(Paseo del Tenista David Ferrer; ⏰11am-3am; 📶) In business for several decades now, this grungy spot keeps things likeably simple, with ice-cold beer in miniature tankards and a rocking soundtrack. Grab an outdoor table and watch the world walk by along the beachfront promenade. It's easily the Arenal's best bar.

## Information

There are tourist offices at **El Arenal** (☎966 46 06 05; www.xabia.org; Paseo del Tenista David Ferrer; ⏰9.30am-2pm & 5-9pm Easter-Sep), the **old town** (☎965 79 43 56; www.xabia.org; Plaza de la Iglesia; ⏰9.30am-5pm Mon-Fri, 10am-1pm Sat) and the **port** (☎965 79 07 36; www.xabia.org; Plaza Presidente Adolfo Suárez 11; ⏰9.30am-5pm Mon-Fri, 10am-1pm Sat & Sun).

## Getting There & Around

ALSA (www.alsa.es) runs at least six buses daily to Valencia (€12.45, two to three hours) and Alicante (€10.55, two to three hours). There are also services to Dénia (€2, 30 minutes), Madrid, Benidorm, Gandia and Calp, as well as direct buses to the Valencia and Alicante airports.

Buses (€1.50, hourly with a siesta) link the different zones of Xàbia.

# Calp

POP 21,600

The striking Gibraltaresque Peñon de Ifach, a giant limestone molar protruding from the sea, rears up from the seaside resort of Calp. Two large bays sprawl either side of the Peñon: Playa Arenal on the western side is backed by the central part of town, while Playa Levante (La Fossa) to the north is a glorious beach backed by tourist apartments.

## Sights & Activities

Head down to the fishing port, in the shadow of the mighty Peñón, to watch the day's catch get auctioned off in the **lonja fish market** (Puerto Pesquero; €1 donation; ⏰around 5pm Mon-Sat).

**Peñon de Ifach** WALKING
(www.parquesnaturales.gva.es; ⏰visitor centre 8.30am-2.30pm Mon-Fri, 9am-2pm Sat & Sun) From the Peñon's Aula de Naturaleza (Nature Centre), a fairly strenuous walking trail – allow two hours for the round trip – heads through a tunnel and then climbs towards the 332m-high summit, offering magnificent views from the top. There's a limit of 150 people on the mountain at any one time, so in July and August you may have a short wait. You'll need walking shoes once you traverse the tunnel onto the rocky massif. A side trail leads to a spectacular viewpoint over the sea.

## Sleeping & Eating

**Hotel Maravillas del Mundo** HOTEL €€
(☎635 200213; www.hotelmaravillas.es; Calle Huelva 4; r €90-120; ❄📶) A short stroll from the beach, this small hotel is impeccably clean and features comfortable beds, blindingly white fittings and a picture of one of the wonders of the world in each room. The top-floor terrace is a sweet spot. Prices halve in the low season.

**Hostal Terra de Mar** BOUTIQUE HOTEL €€
(☎629 665124; www.grupoterrademar.com; Calle Justicia 31; r €80-170; ❄📶🐾) At this artistic and highly original hotel, a range of influences combine to exquisite effect. Each floor has its own style (via the stairs you can travel from Japan to Morocco to Paris). There are numerous appealing details, such as intricately folded towels and a personal tea box, and some rooms have mini-balconies looking over the old-town street.

★**El Bodegón** SPANISH €€
(☎965 83 01 64; www.bodegoncalpe.es; Calle Delfín 8; mains €8-16; ⏰1-4pm & 7-11pm Mon-Sat) Tried and true, this traditional Spanish restaurant hasn't changed in decades and is all the better for it. Reliably good classic meals

such as rabbit, seafood and hearty steaks make this a favourite for locals and visitors alike.

## Information

**Beach Tourist Office** (965 83 69 20; www.calpe.es; Avenida Ejércitos Españoles 44; 9am-9pm Mon-Fri, 9am-2.30pm Sat Jul & Aug, 9am-4pm Mon-Fri, 10am-2.30pm Sat Sep-Jun) Near the lagoon.

**Old Town Tourist Office** (965 83 85 32; www.calpe.es; Plaza del Mosquit; 8am-3pm Mon-Fri)

## Getting There & Away

Buses connect Calp with Alicante (€7.50, 1½ hours, six to 10 daily) and Valencia (€14.50, 2¾ to 3¾ hours, six or seven daily). There are also regular services to other nearby coastal destinations.

Trams travel daily northwards to Dénia (€2.50, 40 minutes, buses replacing trams until late 2021) and south to Benidorm (€2.50, 30 minutes), connecting with trams for Alicante.



# Benidorm

POP 67,600

Benidorm's appealing side is its old town, set on a hill between the two beaches. From the platform where once a castle stood, the evening light and sunsets can be incredible. The place is packed in summer, with happy throngs of sun seekers and party animals, including a sizeable LGBT scene. The area is also popular with families for its excellent theme parks.

Benidorm is infamous for mass tourism along its two wide sandy beaches and the high-rise development that backs them. Bingo, karaoke, fish 'n' chips, all-day fry-ups... it's all here, while the profusion of expat bars, where not a word of Spanish is spoken, give it an atmosphere of its own.

## Activities

**Terra Mítica** AMUSEMENT PARK
(902 020 220; www.terramiticapark.com; adult/4-12yr €39/28; 10.30am-7pm, 9pm or 10.30pm Jul & Aug, Tue-Sun Jun & early Sep, Fri-Sun May, Sat & Sun Apr & mid-Sep–Oct; ) This theme park is not what it used to be but is still a fun day out, especially if you're with children. It's Mediterranean (well, kind of) in theme, with plenty of scary rides, street entertainment and areas devoted to ancient Egypt, Greece, Rome, Iberia and the islands. Opening days are complex, so check its website outside high season. Terra Mítica has its own tram stop.

**Aqualandia** WATER PARK
(965 86 01 00; www.aqualandia.net; adult/child €39/29; 10am-7pm, 8pm or 9pm mid-May–Sep; ) Aqualandia is one of Europe's largest water parks and can easily entertain for a full day. It's quite a bit cheaper if you book online, and there's discounted combined entry with other attractions in the area.

## Sleeping

**Hostal Irati** HOSTAL €€
(965 84 96 07; www.hotelirati.com; Calle Condestable Zaragoza 5; r incl breakfast €60-85; ) In the old town, this place has comfortable, neat rooms with pleasing tiled bathrooms above a friendly bar. It's an excellent deal and there's a stairway down to the beach right opposite. Parking available.

★**Villa Venecia** BOUTIQUE HOTEL €€€
(965 85 54 66; www.hotelvillavenecia.com; Plaza San Jaime 1; s €210-330, d €320-560; ) Up high opposite the old town's church and lording it over the seething beach crowds below, this plush five-star hotel has it all. Rooms have sweeping sea views and ultramodern bathrooms. As you lounge beside its diminutive rooftop pool after a spa session, you could be nautical miles from Benidorm. Its bar and excellent restaurant are open to all comers.

## Eating & Drinking

★**La Cofradía** VALENCIAN €€
(622 300670; www.facebook.com/Lacofra; Calle Gardenias 7; mains €12-20; 11am-4pm & 8-11pm) Off the tourist beat in an unremarkable backstreet, this looks like a standard *barrio* (neighbourhood) bar but shines out for the brilliant quality of its produce. The speciality is seafood, so be guided by what's recommended that day, but the slow-cooked meat is also fabulous. Look out for delicious *zamburiñas* (queen scallops). *Fideuá* and rice dishes are also very tasty.

**La Cava Aragonesa** TAPAS €€
(966 80 12 06; www.lacavaaragonesa.es; Plaza de la Constitución; mains €10-18; noon-midnight Sep-Jun, to 1.30am Jun-Sep) Once a tiny bar this has grown into a sprawling, dizzying spread of tapas, fat canapés and plates of cold cuts, all arrayed before you at the bar with music pumping. The sit-down restaurant offers

wooden platters of mixed foods and a huge wine list. This zone is replete with tapas options so make a satisfying crawl of it.

**D-vora** COCKTAIL BAR
(☎965 27 08 74; www.d-vora.com; Plaza Sant Jaume 5; ⏱8am-midnight Sun-Thu, to 1am Fri & Sat) Drop by this hotel bar for a cocktail with a magnificent view over sea and beach from an old-town perch right over the water. In summer they open a roof terrace. The modern Spanish food here (mains €15 to €24) is pretty good as well.

## Information

**Old Town Tourist Office** (☎965 85 13 11, WhatsApp 672 110188; www.visitbenidorm.es; Plaza de Canalejas; ⏱9am-9pm Mon-Fri, 10am-5.30pm Sat & Sun) In the old town at the end of the eastern beach, this is the principal of several Benidorm tourist offices. It will also answer WhatsApp queries.

## Getting There & Away

From Benidorm's bus station (served by local buses 41 and 47), ALSA (www.alsa.es) runs to **Alicante** (€4.80 to €6.10, 45 minutes to one hour, frequent); **Alicante Airport** (€9.80, 40 to 50 minutes, hourly); and **Valencia** (€17.15 to €21, 1¾ to 3¾ hours, frequent). Some services also leave from the more central Avenida Europa 8 stop, a couple of blocks back from the beach.

The tram/light-rail runs to Alicante (€3.75, 1¼ hours, every 30 minutes) and in the other direction to Altea, Calp and Dénia (buses replace trams in the last section until late 2021).

# Elche

POP 230,600

Thanks to Moorish irrigation, Elche (Valenciano: Elx) is an important fruit producer and a Unesco World Heritage site twice over: for the *Misteri d'Elx*, its annual medieval play, and for its marvellous, extensive palm groves, which are Europe's largest and were originally planted by the Phoenicians. The palms, the mosque-like churches and the historical buildings in desert-coloured stone give the city, 23km southwest of Alicante, a North African feel in parts.

## Sights

Around 200,000 palm trees, each with a lifespan of some 250 years, make the heart of this busy industrial town a veritable oasis. A signed 2.5km **walking trail** (ask at the tourist office for the leaflet) leads from the **Museu del Palmerar** (☎965 42 22 40; Porta de la Morera 12; adult/child €1/0.50, Sun free; ⏱10am-2pm & 3-6pm Tue-Sat, 10am-2pm Sun) through the groves.

WORTH A TRIP

### ALTEA

Separated from Benidorm only by the thick wedge of the Sierra Helada, Altea is an altogether quieter place, with a fishing harbour and beaches composed mostly of pebbles. The modern part is a pleasant enough, fairly standard low-rise coastal resort. By contrast, the whitewashed **old town**, perched on a hilltop overlooking the sea, is a delightfully pretty *pueblo*.

**★Huerto del Cura** GARDENS
(☎965 45 19 36; http://jardin.huertodelcura.com; Porta de la Morera 49; adult/child €5.50/2.75, audio guide €2; ⏱10am-sunset Mon-Sat, 10am-3pm or 6pm Sun) In the Islamic world, a garden is considered an earthly representation of Paradise. Elche's past and culture couldn't therefore be any more obvious than in these privately owned gardens, where humanity and nature have joined forces to produce something that truly approaches that ideal. The highlights are the water features and the cactus gardens.

**Parque Municipal** PARK
(Paseo Estación; ⏱7am-9pm Nov-Mar, to 11pm Apr-Jul, Sep & Oct, to 11.45pm Aug) This lovely park on the northern side of central Elche is one of several appealing places to stroll among the rustling palm trees. A small visitor centre within (open 10am to 3pm Monday to Saturday, to 2pm Sunday, plus 4pm to 6pm Friday and Saturday) has a multimedia presentation.

**Museo Arqueológico y de Historia de Elche** MUSEUM
(MAHE; ☎966 65 82 03; www.elche.es/museos/mahe; Calle Diagonal del Palau 7; adult/child €3/1, Sun free; ⏱10am-6pm Mon-Sat, to 3pm Sun) This museum is a superb introduction to the town's long and eventful history. Everything is particularly well displayed and labelled, and it occupies both a purpose-built building and the town's castle. Starting with archaeological finds from the Neolithic period, you progress into the history of the Muslim

occupation and Reconquest. In the castle's keep, a replica of the famous *Dama de Elche* statue holds pride of place; locals live in hope that the original will return from Madrid one day.

## Festivals & Events

**★Misteri d'Elx** THEATRE

(www.misteridelx.com; 14-15 Aug, & 1 Nov in even years) A lyric drama dating from the Middle Ages, this is performed annually in the baroque **Basílica de Santa María**. The mystery's two acts, *La Vespra* (the eve of the Virgin Mary's death) and *La Festa* (the celebration of her Assumption), are performed in Valenciano by the people of Elche on 14 and 15 August respectively (with public rehearsals on the three previous days).

In even-numbered years, there's a single-day performance on 1 November, with two rehearsals in the days before.

One distant day, according to legend, a casket washed up on Elche's Mediterranean shore. Inside were a statue of the Virgin and the *Consueta*, the music and libretto of a mystery play describing Our Lady's death, assumption into heaven and coronation. The story tells how the Virgin, realising that death is near, asks God to allow her to see the Apostles one last time. They arrive one by one from distant lands and, in their company, she dies at peace. Once received into Paradise, she is crowned Queen of Heaven and Earth to swelling music, the ringing of bells, cheers all round and spectacular fireworks.

You can see a multimedia presentation and learn more about the Misteri in the **Museu de la Festa** (965 45 34 64; Carrer Major de la Vila 25; adult/child €3/1, Sun free; 10am-2pm & 3-6pm Tue-Sat, 10am-2pm Sun).

## Sleeping & Eating

**★Hotel Huerto del Cura** BOUTIQUE HOTEL €€

(966 61 00 11; www.hotelhuertodelcura.com; Porta de la Morera 14; r €90-165; ) A lovely hotel with stylish white rooms and antique wooden furnishings, offering accommodation in trim bungalows within lush, palm-shaded gardens. It's a family-friendly place with a playground, large pool and babysitting service. Complete the cosseting at Elche's oldest luxury hotel by dining in its renowned Els Capellans restaurant. If you aren't too mobile, request a room close to reception.

**★El Granaino** SPANISH €€

(966 66 40 80; www.mesongranaino.com; Carrer Josep María Buck 40; mains €14-24; 10am-4pm & 8pm-midnight Mon-Sat; ) Across the river from the centre, El Granaino, with its bar lined with quiet, well-dressed people scarfing down a quick, quality lunch, is worth the 10-minute walk. Top seafood, delicious stews and a fine range of tapas showcase classic, quintessentially Spanish cuisine. Fuller meals can be enjoyed outside or in the adjacent dining room. Excellent service.

**La Musa de Velarde** FUSION €€

(965 45 08 57; www.lamusadevelarde.com; Calle Velarde 17; dishes €7-15; 1.30-3.30pm Tue, Wed & Sun, 1.30-3.30pm & 8.30-11.30pm Thu-Sat; ) Offering a warmly decorated interior and a welcoming young team in a location near both palm groves and the centre, this makes a tempting lunch stop. They've drawn on influences from all around the world for the short menu, but give them their own touch. Delicious dumplings, whole fried tomatoes and mushroom waffles are all tasty, as are the creations with slow-cooked pork.

## Information

**Tourist Office** (966 65 81 96; www.visitelche.com; Plaza Parque 3; 9am-6pm Mon-Fri, 10am-6pm Sat, 10am-2pm Sun Nov-Mar, to 7pm Apr-Oct) By the palm grove that is the Parque Municipal.

## Getting There & Away

Elche is on the Alicante–Murcia *cercanía* train line. About 20 trains rattle through daily, bound for Alicante (€2.70) or Murcia (€3.70) via Orihuela (€2.70). Train and bus stations are beside each other on Avenida de la Libertad (Avenida del Ferrocarril).

From the bus station, destinations served at least hourly include Alicante (€2.30, 30 minutes), Murcia (€4.67, 45 minutes to two hours) and Valencia (€13.69, 2½ to four hours). Buses also run to Alicante Airport. See www.aerobusalicante.es for details.

# Villena

POP 34,000

Pleasant Villena, between Alicante and Albacete, is the most attractive of the towns along the corridor of the Val de Vinalopó. Plaza de Santiago is at the heart of its old quarter, which is topped by a castle. It feels a long way from the Costa Blanca here, with a more Castilian atmosphere.

WORTH A TRIP

## GUADALEST

The little village of (El Castell de) Guadalest, reached by a natural tunnel, is marvellously picturesque, with stunning views down the valley to the sea and over a turquoise reservoir below. You'll be far from the first to discover it – coaches, heading up from the Costa Blanca resorts, disgorge millions of visitors yearly. But get here early, or stay around after the last bus has pulled out, and the place will be almost your own.

The ruined **castle** (965 88 53 93; adult/child €4/2; 10am-6pm, 7pm or 8pm) offers the best vistas of the area, though there's not much else to see. To reach it you pass through Casa Orduña, a beautiful village house with its original 18th-century furnishings. On Thursday and Sunday, it shuts for an hour for lunch at 2pm. There are half a dozen or so novelty museums; make sure you call by the **Museo de Saleros y Pimenteros** (965 88 50 06; Avenida de Alicante 2; adult/child €3/1; 10.30am-6pm, to 8.30pm in summer) for its sheer quirkiness. Its cabinets cascade with more than 20,000 salt and pepper pots of every imaginable shape and theme; it's an extraordinary collection.

**Cases Noves** (965 88 53 09; www.facebook.com/casesnoves; Calle Achova 1; r incl breakfast standard €95-105, superior €125-165; ) makes an exceptional place to stay. Run by the brilliant Sofia and Toni, this is B&B taken to a whole new level and worth travelling a long way for. The five thoughtfully designed bedrooms come with numerous excellent details, while the gorgeous terrace offers views of the floodlit village and distant sea. There's a fireplace in winter and year-round great advice on local sights and the splendid opportunities for hill walking and cycling (they'll fit you out with a hiking kit and a packed lunch for €7.50). Three-course evening meals (€24.50) are fantastic, but the 10-course Saturday-evening affair (€33, not in summer) is absolutely fabulous. Book ahead.

Avanza Bus line 16 runs from Benidorm to Guadalest (€3.90, one hour) on weekday mornings and returns early afternoon, with a day trip possible. In July and August they also run on Saturday and Sunday. If you drive you'll be charged €2 to park.

Lovely though Guadalest is, it's very touristy. But the parallel valleys to the north of the town are much less visited. Head on past Guadalest and follow your nose into the Vall del Pop or the Vall de Ebo. There's some wild country, picturesque villages and solid game-based mountain food to be had.

## Sights

**Castillo de la Atalaya** CASTLE

(www.turismovillena.com; Calle Libertad; adult/child €3/1.50; guided tours 11am, noon, 1pm, 4pm & 5pm Tue-Sat, 11am, noon & 1pm Sun) Perched above the old town, this 12th-century castle has been handsomely restored and is splendidly lit at night. Entrance is by guided visit, in Spanish with English asides. Tickets can be bought at the town's tourist office or at the visitor centre near the castle's base. A double wall encloses the central *patio de armas* courtyard, overlooked by a high square keep. The highlights are the superbly detailed graffiti etched by former prisoners, and the views from the top.

## Sleeping & Eating

**La Casa de los Aromas** B&B €

(666 475612; www.hotelcasadelosaromas.com; Calle Arco 1; s/d €35/55; ) In the heart of the old centre, this place offers a genuine welcome and five sweet rooms, all with an individual aroma. It's got lots of charm, and staff can arrange winery visits and other activities. You get access to a fridge and microwave as well as an appealing common room with a vinyl collection to play.

Breakfast is an extra €4 per person. Two of the rooms are great for families.

**La Despensa** VALENCIAN €€

(965 80 83 37; www.mesonladespensa.com; Calle Cervantes 27; mains €12-20; 9.30am-4pm & 8-11pm Mon & Wed-Sat, 9.30am-4pm Tue, 1-5pm Sun; ) Near the station, La Despensa offers handsome traditional decor and excellent cuisine. It does some great rices, including a very tasty one with rabbit and snails, as well as some impressive slabs of meat on the grill. For tapas, try the house special with ham, quail's egg and *sobrasada* (Mallorcan pork and paprika spread).

## Information

**Tourist Office** (966 15 02 36; www.turismovillena.com; Plaza de Santiago 5; 9am-2pm Mon-Fri, 11am-2pm Sat & Sun) Villena's tourist office is on the main square opposite the town hall.

**Visitor Centre** (965 80 38 93; www.turismovillena.com; Calle de General Prim 2; 10am-2pm & 4-6pm Tue-Sat, 10am-2pm Sun) Near the castle.

## Getting There & Away

Nine trains run daily between Alicante and Villena (€4.40 to €16.50, 35 to 50 minutes), as well as buses; there are also train services to Valencia. Note that the Villena AV station, served by fast trains, is 10km southwest of town.

# Orihuela

POP 34,000

Beside the Río Segura and flush with the base of a barren mountain of rock, the historical heart of Orihuela, with superb Gothic, Renaissance and, especially, baroque buildings, well merits a detour. Once the second city of the Kingdom of Valencia, the old town is strung out between the river and a mountain topped by a ruined castle. The main sights are dotted along the district, more or less in a line, and are well signposted throughout. Orihuela has a vibrant **Moros y Cristianos** (http://morosycristianosorihuela.es; mid-Jul) festival, and reprises the atmosphere with an enormous medieval market at the end of January.

## Sights

**★Catedral de San Salvador** CATHEDRAL
(965 30 48 28; Calle Doctor Sarget; adult/child €2/free; 10.30am-2pm & 4-6.30pm Mon-Fri, 10.30am-2pm Sat) Low slung but achieving an understated majesty nonetheless, this cathedral is built of light-coloured stone and features three finely carved portals. Unusually, the altar is enclosed at the front by an ornate Renaissance *reja* (filigree screen); another closes off the choir, while an earlier Gothic one, alive with vegetal motifs, screens a rear chapel that was originally the altar. The highlight, though, is the tiny, exquisite two-level Renaissance cloister on the street behind, brought here from a nearby convent in the 1940s.

**Colegio de Santo Domingo** MONASTERY
(965 30 02 40; http://colegio.cdsantodomingo.com; Calle Adolfo Clavarana; adult/child €2/1; 9.30am-1.30pm or 2pm & 4-7pm or 5-8pm Tue-Fri, from 10am Sat, 10am-2pm Sun) A 16th-century monastery and university with two fine Renaissance cloisters and a refectory clad in 18th-century tile work, Santo Domingo was built on a monumental scale and still houses a school; a small museum room relates the history. The stern but noble lines of the building stretch towards one of the city gates. It's quite a contrast moving from the cloister into the baroque riot of the church, full of colour and bristling with cherubs.

## Eating

**Bodega La Venganza** TAPAS €
(665 455938; www.facebook.com/bodegalavenganzaorihuela; Calle Togores 3; tapas €4-15;

DON'T MISS

### MOROS Y CRISTIANOS

More than 80 towns and villages in the south of the Valencia region hold their own Fiesta de Moros y Cristianos (festival of Moors and Christians) to celebrate the Reconquista, the region's liberation from Muslim rule.

The biggest and best known is in the town of **Alcoy** (22-24 Apr), where hundreds of locals dress up in elaborate traditional costumes representing different 'factions' – Muslim and Christian soldiers, slaves, guild groups, town criers, heralds, bands – and march through the streets in colourful processions with mock battles. Processions converge upon Alcoy's main square and its huge, temporary wooden fortress. It's an exhilarating spectacle of sights and sounds.

Each town has its own variation on the format, steeped in traditions that allude to the events of the Reconquista. So, for example, Villena's **festival** (www.turismovillena.com; 5-9 Sep) features night-time parades, while La Vila Joiosa's festival (24 to 31 July), near Benidorm, re-enacts the landing of Muslim ships on the beaches. Some are as early as February, so you've a good chance of finding one whenever it is that you visit the region.

⊙12.30-4.30pm & 7.30-11pm or later Wed-Sun) It's impossible not to love this tiny, sassy tapas joint, which expands out to tree-shaded tables on a pretty plaza behind the Iglesia de las Santas Justa y Rufina.

**Bar Manolo** TAPAS €
(☎965 30 20 93; www.barmanoloorihuela.com; Calle del Río 36; raciones €9-14; ⊙8am-11pm Mon-Thu, to midnight Fri, 11.30am-midnight Sat; 📶) Though it doesn't look much from outside (or inside, come to think of it), Bar Manolo has outdoor seating next to the river. But it's the warm, personal service and cheap but scrumptious food that make this a fine tapas or meal stop. Half-portions and set menus available.

## Information

**Tourist Office** (☎965 30 46 45; www.orihuelaturistica.es; Plaza de la Soledad; ⊙8am-2pm Mon, 8am-2pm & 4-7pm or 5-8pm Tue-Fri, 10am-2pm & 4-7pm or 5-8pm Sat, 10am-2pm Sun) Helpful, switched on and well furnished with information about what to see around town. Guided tours of the town available.

## Getting There & Away

Orihuela is on *cercanía* train line C1 between Murcia (€2, 20 minutes) and Alicante (€4.20, one hour, hourly). The train and bus stations are 1km south of the old centre.

# MURCIA PROVINCE

## Murcia

POP 447,200

Officially twinned with Miami, Murcia is the antithesis of the city of vice; it's a sizeable but laid-back provincial capital with a handful of interesting sights and a pleasant, strollable centre. Like Valencia, it is famous for its *huerta*, a surrounding zone of market gardens dating back to Moorish times, which supply the city's restaurants with excellent fresh produce and drive a thriving tapas scene. It makes a top spot to visit for a couple of days.

## Sights

★**Real Casino de Murcia** HISTORIC BUILDING
(☎968 21 53 99; www.realcasinomurcia.com; Calle de la Trapería 18; adult/child €5/3; ⊙10.30am-7pm Sep-Jul, to 2.30pm Mon-Sat Aug) Murcia's resplendent casino first opened as a gentlemen's club in 1847. Painstakingly restored to its original glory, the building is a fabulous combination of historical design and opulence, providing an evocative glimpse of bygone aristocratic grandeur. Beyond the decorative facade are a dazzling Moorish-style patio; a classic English-style library with 20,000 books; a magnificent ballroom with glittering chandeliers; and a compelling *tocador* (ladies' powder room) with a ceiling fresco of cherubs, angels and an alarming winged woman in flames.

**Catedral de Santa María** CATHEDRAL
(☎968 21 63 44; www.catedralmurcia.com; Plaza del Cardenal Belluga; adult/child €5/3; ⊙10am-5pm Tue-Sat & services at other times) Murcia's beautiful cathedral was built in 1394 on the site of a mosque. The Gothic building was given a playful baroque facelift in 1748, with a stunning facade facing the plaza. The interior has two extraordinary chapels: **Capilla de los Vélez**, with Flamboyant Gothic flutes and curls; and the **Capilla de Gil Rodríguez de Junterón** with its fan-like Renaissance cupola. Beautiful Gothic grilles encase the altar and choir. The **cathedral museum** has several fine works by Salzillo (including a superb San Jerónimo).

**Museo Salzillo** MUSEUM
(☎968 29 18 93; www.museosalzillo.es; Plaza de San Agustín 3; adult/child €5/free; ⊙10am-2pm Mon-Fri mid-Jun–mid-Sep, 10am-5pm Mon-Sat, 11am-2pm Sun mid-Sep–mid-Jun) Located in the baroque chapel of Ermita de Jesús, this well-laid-out space is devoted to Murcian sculptor Francisco Salzillo (1707–83). Highlights are his exquisite *pasos* (figures carried in Semana Santa processions) and nativity figurines.

**Museo Arqueológico** MUSEUM
(☎968 23 46 02; www.museosregiondemurcia.es; Avenida Alfonso X El Sabio 7; ⊙10am-2pm Tue-Fri, 11am-2pm Sat & Sun Jul & Aug, 10am-2pm & 5-8pm Tue-Fri, 11am-2pm & 5-8pm Sat, 11am-2pm Sun Sep-Jun) FREE The Museo Arqueológico has well-documented and well-laid-out exhibits spread over two floors. The main focus is on two periods: the 2nd-millennium BCE Argar culture and, upstairs, the intriguing Iberian period (500–200 BCE). Ask for the English summary at the front desk. The trendy cafe with pleasant outdoor seating is a popular spot.

## Murcia

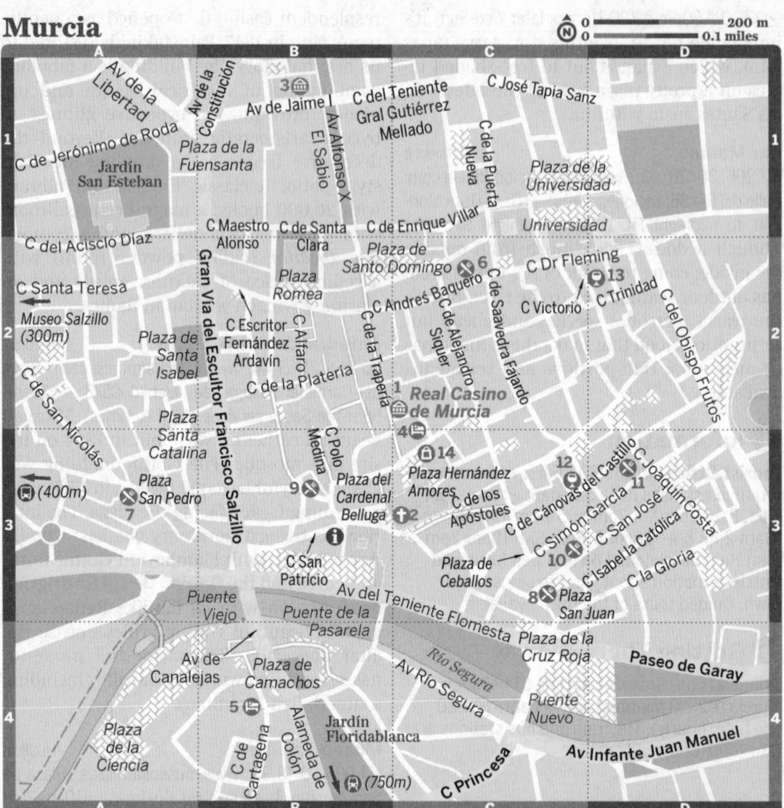


## Murcia

**Top Sights**
1 Real Casino de Murcia........................ C2

**Sights**
2 Catedral de Santa María ..................... C3
3 Museo Arqueológico............................ B1

**Sleeping**
4 Hotel Cetina........................................ C3
5 Pensión Segura ................................... B4

**Eating**
6 Alborada.............................................. C2
7 El Pasaje de Zabalburu........................ A3
8 La Pequeña Taberna............................ C3
9 Los Zagales.......................................... B3
10 Pura Cepa .......................................... C3
11 Salzillo................................................ D3

**Drinking & Nightlife**
12 La Ronería y La Gintonería ................. C3
13 Sala Revolver ..................................... D2

**Shopping**
14 Salmentum .......................................... C3

## Festivals & Events

**Semana Santa** RELIGIOUS
(Mar/Apr) The city's Easter processions are of the traditional kind and are considered some of Spain's best, due especially to their excellent sculptural ensembles. Several notable baroque artists worked on them, and they are full of life and emotion.

**Bando de la Huerta** FIESTA
(Mar/Apr) Two days after Easter Sunday, the mood changes from sombre to joyful as the city celebrates this annual spring festival with parades, food stalls, folklore and carafe-fulls of fiesta spirit.

## Sleeping

**Pensión Segura** HOSTAL €

(968 21 12 81; www.pensionsegura.es; Plaza de Camachos 14; d €40-50; ) Just across a bridge from the heart of town, Segura makes a fine budget base. Staff go the extra mile to make you feel welcome, and the rooms are decent and shining clean, though bathrooms are generally tiny.

**Hotel Cetina** HOTEL €€

(968 10 08 00; www.hotelcetina.com; Calle Radio Murcia 3; r €55-80; ) This upbeat hotel offers decent value for its spacious, stylish, commodious rooms in the heart of town. Showers are good and staff are helpful; the only issue is that it's quite a walk to their associated car park.

## Eating

**★El Pasaje de Zabalburu** TAPAS €

(622 622167; www.facebook.com/elpasajedezabalburu; Plaza San Pedro 3; tapas €4-14; noon-5pm & 8pm-midnight; ) It's difficult to imagine tastier tapas than the inventive, exquisite creations at this bar on the west side of the centre. Grab a pew at the long bar (or a table out back) and enjoy fabulous fare presented with flair. Seafood is especially good, with stellar grilled calamari, delicious sturgeon and oysters shucked to order.

**Los Zagales** SPANISH €

(968 21 55 79; www.facebook.com/barloszagales.murcia; Calle Polo de Medina 4; dishes €3-12; 9.30am-4pm & 7pm-midnight Mon-Sat) Handy to stop by after a cathedral visit, the old-style, traditional Los Zagales, run by the same family for nearly 100 years, dishes up superb, inexpensive tapas, *raciones, platos combinados* (mixed platters), homemade desserts...and homemade chips. It's popular locally so you may have to wait for a table, or just graze at the bar.

**La Pequeña Taberna** SPANISH €€

(968 21 98 40; www.lapequenataberna.com; Plaza San Juan 7; mains €10-21; 1.30-5pm & 8.30pm-midnight Mon-Sat, 1.30-5pm Sun) Look for the cascade of market vegetables outside the door when locating this quality restaurant, which isn't quite as small as it claims. Excellent service furnishes its tables, divided by boxes of tomatoes, melons and the like, with dishes such as fish carpaccio, *huevas de mújol* (preserved fish eggs), *codillo* (pork knuckle), and quality salad and vegetable platters. The wines are delicious, too.

**Pura Cepa** TAPAS €€

(968 21 73 97; www.puracepamurcia.com; Plaza Cristo del Rescate 8; dishes €6-18; 1-4pm & 8pm-midnight Tue-Sat, 1-4pm Sun; ) There's an innovative kick to the dishes here, which shine out for their quality. Artichokes, octopus and other local, delicious morsels appear in everything from stir-fries to salads to exquisite one-bite appetisers (it's worth trying plenty of these). Eat outside on the heated terrace, at high tables in the bar area, or in the smart dining room. Really excellent wines are available too.

**Alborada** SPANISH €€

(968 23 23 23; www.alboradarestaurante.com; Calle Andrés Baquero 15; mains €15-24; 10am-5pm & 8pm-midnight Tue-Sat, 10am-5pm Sun) This high-ceilinged, minimalist dining space offers reliably excellent cuisine using carefully selected natural products. Presentation is modern without being avant-garde, and the flavour combinations are all pleasing. The bar area has a different scene, lively with good-value tapas portions (€3 to €6) and a bargain weekday lunch for €12.

**Salzillo** SPANISH €€€

(968 22 01 94; www.restaurantesalzillo.com; Calle de Cánovas del Castillo 28; mains €20-26; 1-4.30pm & 9-11.30pm Mon-Sat, 1-4.30pm Sun

DON'T MISS

### TAPAS IN MURCIA

Surrounded by a *huerta* (area of market gardens), Murcia has great fresh produce and is excellent for tapas, with plenty of variety, generous portions and a considerable vegetarian choice. Many of the city's restaurants are fronted by tapas bars or serve *raciones* (large/full-plate tapas servings), which are great for sharing. Overall, *murciano* tapas are more inventive than the norm and reflect the province's comprehensive agriculture with their use of fresh seasonal ingredients. A local classic is the *marinera,* a scoop of Russian salad served on a loop of breadstick and topped by an anchovy. Delicious.

The network of streets on and northeast of Plaza San Juan are particularly fertile ground, and there's a lively scene around Plaza Santa Catalina and Plaza de las Flores, a short distance west of the old town.

Sep-Jun, closed weekends Jul, closed Aug) Favoured by well-heeled conservative Murcians, this elegant but comfortable spot has a lively bar and truly excellent dining in its split-level restaurant area. Starters run to elaborate creations with local artichokes, and the quality of the meaty mains is sky-high: order *a la brasa* for the flavoursome barbecue aromas.

##  Drinking & Nightlife

**La Ronería y La Gintonería** BAR

(☎968 90 00 05; www.la-roneria-y-la-gintoneria.com; Calle de Cánovas del Castillo 17; ⏱3pm-3am Tue-Sat, 3pm-2am Mon & Sun) A quite incredible selection of rums – a Guinness world record – greets you on entering this pleasantly cosy bar. There are well over 1000 available; ask staff for advice. Once you've tried them all, stagger up the stairs and start on the G&Ts – there are 800 gins and dozens of tonics.

**Sala Revolver** BAR

(☎868 12 49 17; www.facebook.com/salarevolver.murcia; Calle Victorio 36; ⏱3.30pm-3.30am or 4am; 📶) This bar in the heart of the university-driven nightlife zone is a rock 'n' roll classic with red-vinyl booth seating, curios and photos on the walls and regular live music. It's very atmospheric, with real rock-bar cred.

##  Shopping

**Salmentum** FOOD

(☎968 21 86 08; www.facebook.com/salmentum; Plaza Hernández Amores 4; ⏱10am-3pm & 5-9pm Mon-Wed, 10am-9pm Thu-Sat, 11am-3pm Sun) Near the cathedral, Salmentum has a great selection of salted-fish products. Sit down and try the delicious *mojama* (dried tuna) or *huevas de mújol* (dried fish roe) with a glass of wine (tapas €2 to €6).

## ℹ Information

**Tourist Office** (☎968 35 87 49; www.murciaturistica.es; Plaza del Cardenal Belluga; ⏱10am-7pm Mon-Sat, 10am-2pm Sun; 📶) On the cathedral square.

## ℹ Getting There & Away

Opened in 2019, the **Aeropuerto Internacional Región de Murcia** (Aeropuerto de Corvera; www.aena.es; Avenida de España, Lo Jurado) is 27km south of the city off the A30. It is served by several international and domestic budget airlines. Interbus (www.interbus.es) run services here (€5, 30 minutes, one to five daily) from the bus station.

At least 10 buses run daily from Murcia's bus station, 1km west of the centre, to both Cartagena (€4.75, 45 minutes to 1¼ hours) and Lorca (€5.95, 1½ hours).

Up to six trains travel daily to/from Madrid (€57, three to four hours). *Cercanía* trains run to Alicante (€5.75, 1¼ hours) and Lorca (€5.75, 50 minutes).

## ℹ Getting Around

Buses 26 and 28, among others, connect the bus station to the centre. From the centre, board at Avenida del Teniente Flomesta near the corner of Gran Vía. From the train station, hop aboard bus R17.

Murcia has a tram line, but it's not of much use for visitors, mainly serving to bring people into town from the extensive northern suburbs.

# Cartagena

POP 213,900

Cartagena's fabulous natural harbour has been used for thousands of years. Stand on the battlements of the castle that overlook this city and you can literally see layer upon layer of history spread below you: the wharf where Phoenician traders docked their ships; the street where Roman legionaries marched; the plaza that once housed a mosque where Islamic Spain prayed to Allah; the hills over which came the armies of the Christian Reconquista; the factories of the industrial age; the Modernista buildings; and the contemporary warships of what is still an important naval base. The city is finally starting to get the recognition it deserves as one of Spain's most historically fascinating places. Its extensive network of pedestrian streets and lovely waterfront make it eminently strollable.

## History

In 223 BCE, the Carthaginian general Hasdrubal marched his invading army into what had been the Iberian settlement of Mastia, refounding it as Qart Hadasht. The town prospered as Carthago Nova during Roman occupation, had a brief period of Byzantine administration and, under Muslim rule, became the independent emirate of Cartajana, finally reconquered by the Christians in 1242. Though badly bombed in the civil war – it was the principal Republican naval harbour – industry and the population flourished during the 1950s and '60s.

## Sights

**Museo del Teatro Romano** MUSEUM, RUIN

(www.teatroromanocartagena.org; Plaza del Ayuntamiento 9; adult/child €6/5; 10am-8pm Tue-Sat, 10am-2pm Sun May-Sep, 10am-6pm Tue-Sat, 10am-2pm Sun Oct-Apr) This impressive complex was designed by top Spanish architect Rafael Moneo. The tour transports visitors from the initial museum on Plaza del Ayuntamiento, via escalators and an underground passage beneath the ruined cathedral, to the restored Roman theatre dating from the 1st century BCE. The layout of the museum is minimalist, taking you back through Cartagena's fascinating layers of urban history with a careful selection of statuary, pottery and other artefacts.

**Barrio del Foro Romano** RUINS

(www.cartagenapuertodeculturas.com; Calle Honda; adult/child €5/4; 10am-8pm Jul–mid-Sep, to 7pm Tue-Sun mid-Mar–Jun & mid-Sep–Oct, to 5.30pm Tue-Sun Nov–mid-Mar) Set alongside the Molinete hill are the evocative remains of a whole town block and street linking the port with the forum, dating from the 1st century BCE and including an arcade and thermal baths. One of the houses preserves a courtyard and important fragments of wall paintings.

**Casa de la Fortuna** RUINS

(www.cartagenapuertodeculturas.com; Plaza Risueño; adult/child €2.50/2; 10.30am-3.30pm Tue-Sun mid-Mar–Dec, Sat & Sun only Jan–mid-Mar) The Casa de la Fortuna consists of the fascinating remains of an aristocratic Roman villa dating back to the 1st century BCE, complete with some well-preserved murals and mosaics, and part of an excavated road.

★**Museo Nacional de Arqueología Subacuática** MUSEUM

(ARQUA; 968 12 11 66; http://museoarqua.mcu.es; Paseo de Alfonso XII 22; adult/child €3/free, Sat afternoon & Sun free; 10am-8pm or 9pm Tue-Sat, 10am-3pm Sun) This excellent, attractive space dives into the fascinating world of underwater archaeology. It starts off by explaining the work of those divers in the deep and then sails on into the maritime history and culture of the Mediterranean. There's a particular focus on a wrecked Phoenician vessel found at Mazarrón.

### DISCOUNT PASSES

Visiting all the different archaeological sites and museums in Cartagena can work out to be quite expensive (it's slightly cheaper online at www.cartagenapuertodeculturas.com). Fortunately help is at hand in the form of a variety of passes that provide cheaper admission (entry to four/five/six museums adult €12/15/18, child €9/11.25/13.50). A pass to all of them costs €22/18. Valid for 15 days, passes are available from the tourist office or the sites themselves. The Museo del Teatro Romano counts as two museum entries. Other options include a tourist boat and/or bus trip.

**Museo Refugio de la Guerra Civil** MUSEUM

(www.cartagenapuertodeculturas.com; Calle de Gisbert; adult/child €3.50/2.50; 10am-8pm Jul–mid-Sep, 10am-7pm Tue-Sun mid-Mar–Jun & mid-Sep–Oct, 10am-5.30pm Tue-Sun Nov–mid-Mar) Cartagena, as base of the Republican fleet and with an important arms industry, was the target of heavy bombing during the Spanish Civil War. This atmospheric air-raid shelter dug into the castle hill, one of many that protected the city's citizens, brings back those days with personal testimonies, posters, good Spanish-English information and a Charlie Chaplin clip.

**Castillo de la Concepción** CASTLE, MUSEUM

(www.cartagenapuertodeculturas.com; adult/child €3.75/2.75; 10am-8pm Jul–mid-Sep, 10am-7pm Tue-Sun mid-Mar–Jun & mid-Sep–Oct, 10am-5.30pm Tue-Sun Nov–mid-Mar) For a sweeping panoramic view, stride up to Castillo de la Concepción through the peacocked gardens, or hop on the **lift** (Calle de Gisbert; adult/child €2/1, with Castillo de la Concepción €4.25/3.75; 10am-8pm Jul–mid-Sep, 10am-7pm Tue-Sun Apr-Jun & mid-Sep–Oct, 10am-5.30pm Tue-Sun Nov-Mar). The first part of the visit is all about the city vistas, before you pass through a worthwhile display on Cartagena's tumultuous history; there are several interesting audiovisuals with English subtitles.

From the pedestrian area, the castle is most easily reached via Calle Doctor Tapia Martínez.

## Festivals & Events

**Carthagineses y Romanos** FIESTA
(Cartagineses y Romanos; www.cartaginesesy romanos.es; Sep) For 10 days during September, locals play war games in a colourful fiesta that re-enacts the battles between rival Carthaginian and Roman occupiers during the Second Punic War.

## Sleeping

**LoopINN** HOSTEL €
(868 45 17 60; www.loopinnhostels.com; Calle San Crispín 34; dm €22-26, d €48-63; ) On a backstreet near the train and bus stations, this modern hostel is a cheery place with a variety of comfortable dorms and rooms, including family options. White walls, wood and the odd quirky feature give it a summery feel, while a gym, kitchen and sundeck are among the facilities. Don't miss the slide between floors!

**Pensión Balcones Azules** HOSTAL €
(968 50 00 42; www.pensionbalconesazules.com; Calle Balcones Azules 12; s €36-42, d economy/superior €52/65; ) On a quiet central street overlooking the ruins of the forum, this modern option offers plenty of quality for the price. The superior rooms have bigger bathrooms, but there are some spacious 'economy' choices, too.

**NH Cartagena** HOTEL €€
(968 12 09 08; www.nh-hotels.com; Calle Real 2; r €90-140; ) The location of this business hotel can't be bettered, steps from the waterfront and the Roman theatre and just behind the town hall.

## Eating

**La Fuente** TAPAS €
(868 04 73 22; www.facebook.com/bodega lafuenteCT; Calle Jara 17; drink & tapa €1.90; 10am-5pm & 7.30pm-midnight Mon-Fri, 11am-5pm & 7.30pm-midnight Sat & Sun; ) Bright and busy, this place, which lives up to its name by indeed featuring a fountain, makes a top stop for a quick drink and a tapa. The speciality is anchovies, long and tasty, from the Bay of Biscay. A knot of similar bars here also offer a cheap drink-and-snack deal.

**La Marquesita** SPANISH €€
(968 50 77 47; www.lamarquesita.net; Plaza Alcolea 6; mains €13-24; 1-4.30pm Tue, Wed & Sun, 1-4.30pm & 8-11.30pm Thu-Sat; ) On a tucked-away plaza just off the pedestrian main drag, this place is easily spotted by its riot of pot plants. Sit in or out to enjoy quality fish dishes in particular, with other traditional plates on offer. The €22.50 weekday set lunch is excellent.

**El Barrio de San Roque** SPANISH €€
(968 50 06 00; www.elbarriodesanroque.com; Calle Jabonerías 30; mains €14-26; 1.30-4pm & 8.30-11pm Mon-Fri, 1.30-4pm Sat) Done with Roman ruins and it's time for a decent central meal? Much of the pedestrian area is taken up with fairly mediocre restaurants pulling in cruise-ship visitors with frozen paellas, but this discreet, elegant place offers real quality. The €23 lunchtime *menú* is excellent, and the exposed brick, sizeable tables and polite service make this a pleasant haven.

★ **Magoga** SPANISH €€€
(968 50 96 78; www.restaurantemagoga.com; Plaza Doctor Vicente García Marcos 5; mains €19-35, degustation menu €85; 1.30-3.30pm & 8.30-10.30pm Wed-Sat, 1.30-3.30pm Tue & Sun; ) On a nondescript pedestrian boulevard off Calle Carlos III is one of southeastern Spain's best restaurants. The gastronomic enthusiasm of the young owners shines through in the food, which gives market-driven ingredients and traditional dishes a modern twist to great effect. Good-value rices and stews take their place alongside superbly prepared and presented fish and meat mains.

## Shopping

**Centro para la Artesanía** ARTS & CRAFTS
(968 52 46 31; www.murciaartesana.es; Calle Honda 10; 10am-2pm & 5-8.30pm Mon-Fri, 11am-1.30pm Sat) This sizeable government-funded shop displays the work of local artisans, with an excellent range of everything from paintings to honey. It's a great spot to browse.

## Information

Most of the Roman sites can furnish you with a city map and information; handy if you arrive outside tourist-office hours.

**Ayuntamiento Tourist Office** (968 12 89 55; www.cartagenaturismo.es; Plaza del Ayuntamiento 1; 10am-1.30pm & 5-7pm Mon-Sat May-Sep, 10am-1.30pm & 4-6pm Mon-Sat Oct-Apr, 10.30am-1.30pm Sun year-round) Near the waterfront in the heart of town.

**Puertas de San José Tourist Office** (968 12 89 55; https://turismo.cartagena.es; Plaza Basterreche; 10am-2pm & 4-6pm Mon-Fri,

10am-1.30pm Sat Mar, Apr & Oct, 10am-2pm & 5-7pm Mon-Fri, 10am-1.30pm Sat May-Sep, 10am-4pm Mon-Fri, 10am-1.30pm Sat Nov-Feb) Plenty of excellent information near the bus station. If it's shut, go to the desk in the **Muralla Púnica** (www.cartagenapuertodeculturas.com; Calle San Diego 25; adult/child €3.50/2.50; ⌚10am-8pm Jul–mid-Sep, 10am-7pm Tue-Sun mid-Mar–Jun & mid-Sep–Oct, 10am-5.30pm Tue-Sun Nov–mid-Mar) opposite.

### Getting There & Away

Buses run seven times daily to Alicante (€9.45, 2¾ hours) via Alicante airport, and roughly hourly to Murcia (€4.75, 45 minutes to 1¼ hours) from the **bus station** (Avenida Trovero Marín). There are also buses to Almería and to several northern Spanish cities.

For Renfe train destinations, you'll mostly have to change in Murcia (from €5.65, 50 minutes, eight to 11 daily), though there are some through trains. There are buses to Murcia airport (€5, 35 minutes, one to three daily); a taxi costs approximately €50 (30 minutes).

# Costa Cálida

Stretching westwards to the border with Andalucía, the Costa Cálida (Warm Coast) is aptly named. It offers a hot, dry climate with more than 300 days of annual sunshine. While the sprawling resort of La Manga is unappealing, quieter seaside towns offer a more engrossing experience.

## The Mar Menor

The Mar Menor is a 170-sq-km saltwater lagoon where the warm waters are excellent for water sports, including jet-skiing, kitesurfing, kayaking and water-skiing. From the southern side juts **La Manga**, a narrow 22km peninsula stretched between lagoon and sea, overdeveloped with close-packed high-rise holiday accommodation.

**Cabo de Palos**, at the peninsula's southern limit, is more appealing, with a picturesque small harbour surrounded by low-rise restaurants and holiday apartments. The waters around the tiny, protected **Islas Hormigas** are great for diving; the harbour is lined with dive shops.

At the lagoon's northern end, **Lo Pagán** is a mellow, low-rise resort with a long promenade, pleasant beach, and plenty of bars and restaurants.

## Águilas

POP 35,000

Nearing the border with Andalucía, and 30km south along the coast from Mazarrón, you'll reach low-key Águilas, with a slowish vibe and pleasant centre. The waterfront in town is beautiful, and still shelters a small fishing fleet; back from here is lovely Plaza de España, with its dignified trees. Town beaches are divided from each other by a low headland topped by an 18th-century **fortress**. The really charming beaches, though, are the **Cuatro Calas** a few kilometres south of town. These four coves are largely unmolested by tourist development (though they get very busy in summer) and have shimmering waters that merge into desert rock: about as perfect as you'll find on the Spanish Med coast.

Águilas' **Carnaval** (www.carnavaldeaguilas.org; ⌚Feb/Mar) celebrations are some of Spain's most interesting.

### Sleeping

**Pensión Rodríguez** PENSION €

(☎649 540380, 968 41 06 15; http://aguilaspensionrodriguez.blogspot.com; Calle Ramón y Cajal 7; with shared/private bathroom s €24/28, d €39/44; 📶) In a relatively central part of town and a short stroll to the beach, Pensión Rodríguez offers spotless rooms for a low price. Matilde the boss is very helpful and kind. A good deal.

★**Hotel Mayarì** HOTEL €€

(☎964 41 97 48; www.hotel-mayari.com; Calle Río de Janeiro 14, Calabardina; s/d incl breakfast €65/98; ⌚Mar-Nov; P ❄ 📶) In the seaside settlement of Calabardina, 7km from Águilas, this airy villa offers exceptional hospitality among dry, handsome hillscapes. Rooms are simple, comfortable and all different, with cool, fresh decor. Some have sea views, and brilliant home-cooked dinners are available by request, as well as helpful hill-walking advice and bikes to explore the area.

### Eating

**El Pimiento** SPANISH €

(Calle Joaquín Tendero 1; tapas €1-12; ⌚7pm-1am Wed-Mon) Cheerfully super-Spanish decor of horse paraphernalia, tiles and hanging hams makes this an upbeat place from the get-go. The colourful tables inside and sprawling down the steps outside are always packed, adding plenty of atmosphere. The tapas are simple – think big, generous chunks of meat, bread, potatoes, tomato – very tasty and extremely well priced. An enjoyable spot.

**★El Poli** SEAFOOD €€

(968 41 34 21; www.facebook.com/elpolirest; Calle Floridablanca 23; dishes €5-15; 1.30-4pm & 8.30-11pm Wed-Sat, 1.30-4pm Sun) With a traditional varnished wood interior, albeit with a shipboard feel, this looks like another *barrio* cafe until you realise that the menu is all locally caught fish and shellfish. Don't spend too much time browsing it though, as only what was available in the fish market is offered. It's cooked simply and is delicious, served by brilliant staff at generous prices.

This is a great spot to try fish that rarely appear on restaurant menus.

## Information

**Tourist Office** (660 474477, 968 49 32 85; www.aguilas.es; Plaza Antonio Cortijos; 10am-2pm & 5-7pm Mon-Sat, 10am-2pm Sun mid-Sep–Apr, to 8pm May & Jun, 9.30am-2pm & 5-9pm Mon-Fri, 10am-2pm & 5-9pm Sat, 10am-2pm Sun Jul–mid-Sep) Near the water in the heart of town.

## Getting There & Away

Buses go to Lorca (€3, 30 minutes to one hour, three to seven daily), Murcia (€8.90, 1½ hours, two to five daily), Cartagena (€7.23, 1¾ hours, two to three daily) and Almería (€9.62, 2¼ hours, two to three daily).

*Cercanía* trains on the C2 line run from Murcia (€7.95, 2 hours) via Lorca three times daily.

# Lorca

POP 93,100

The market town of Lorca has long been known for its pretty old town crowned by a 13th-century castle and for hosting Spain's most flamboyant Semana Santa (Holy Week) celebrations. In 2011 an earthquake struck here, leaving nine people dead, and many injured and homeless. It caused significant material damage, with the old town affected particularly badly. Lorca has bounced back now and is a great place to visit.

## Sights

**Colegiata de San Patricio** CHURCH

(968 46 99 66; Plaza de España; adult/child €3/free; 11am-1pm & 5-6pm Mon-Fri, to 7pm Sat, 11am-noon Sun) This stately and beautiful gem of a church presides in golden-stone majesty over Lorca's lovely central square. The sober and handsome triple-tiered baroque facade conceals a lofty, bare triple-naved Renaissance interior with some fine altar paintings. It was heavily damaged in the civil war and 2011 earthquake; the latter disaster's silver lining was the discovery of previously unknown wall paintings and crypts. Buy tickets in the adjacent tourist office (p848); last visit is 30 minutes before closing.

**Museo de Bordados del Paso Azul** MUSEUM

(MASS; 968 47 20 77; www.museoazul.com; Calle Cuesta de San Francisco; adult/child €3/1.50; 10am-2pm & 5-7.30pm Mon-Sat, 10.30am-2pm Sun Oct-Mar, 10am-2pm & 5.30-8pm Mon-Sat, 10.30am-2pm Sun Apr-Sep, mornings only Aug) Attached to the San Francisco monastery, this is the modern museum of the Azul (Blue) Holy Week brotherhood, and gives an excellent idea of what Semana Santa means to the locals. As well as stirring videos and background information, the marvellous costumes are on display. If you go on a weekday, you may find people at work on them in the embroidery workshop upstairs – a great chance to see the process up close.

Some cloaks are up to 5m in length and all are elaborately hand-embroidered in silk, depicting colourful religious and historical scenes.

One of the museum sections takes you into the galleries of the church, an interesting outlook. To visit the church from ground level, it's an extra €1.

**Museo de Bordados del Paso Blanco** MUSEUM

(muBBla; 968 46 18 13; www.mubbla.org; Calle Santo Domingo 8; adult/child €2.50/free; 10.30am-2pm & 5-8pm Mon-Sat, 10.30am-2pm Sun) Attached to the church of Santo Domingo, this is the museum of the Blanco (White) Semana Santa brotherhood. Here you can see a collection of the beautifully elaborate hand-stitched robes worn by them during the passionately supported Holy Week processions. They are well displayed and extraordinary, depicting scenes from the Bible and antiquity, with video footage of the robes in use. Don't miss the room with the most historic pieces up the back. If language coincides, the guided tour (included) is recommended.

You might be advised to put sunglasses on for the shiny baroque gold of the adjacent chapel of the Virgen del Rosario.

**★Castillo de Lorca** CASTLE

(968 95 96 46; www.lorcatallerdeltiempo.com; Carretera de la Parroquia; adult/child €6/5; 10.30am-dusk; ) Lorca's castle, high over town, is an impressive place, a huge medieval complex characterised by two towers. The basic entry includes an audio guide and access to the **Torre del Espolón**, reconstructed after the earthquake, as well as various cisterns, ramparts and exhibition spaces. The handsome **Torre Alfonsina** and the reconstructed synagogue plus **ruins of the Jewish quarter** can be visited twice or more daily by recommended guided tour (€4 each). A combined €10 entrance fee includes both tours.

## Festivals & Events

**★Semana Santa** RELIGIOUS

(http://semanasantalorca.com; Mar/Apr) If you're from Lorca, you're probably passionately Blanco (White) or Azul (Blue), the colours of the two major brotherhoods that have competed since 1855 to see who can stage the most lavish Semana Santa display. Lorca's Easter parades are very distinctive; while still deeply reverential, they're full of colour and vitality, mixing figures from antiquity and Old Testament tales with the Passion story.

Both major brotherhoods have a statue of the Virgin, a banner and a spectacular museum – Museo de Bordados del Paso Azul and Museo de Bordados del Paso Blanco. The result of this intense and mostly genial year-round rivalry is just about the most dramatic Semana Santa you'll see anywhere in Spain. Processions feature horses, theatrical set pieces, colourful characters – gods, emperors and heroes – stirring music and plenty of emotion.

## Sleeping

**★Parador de Lorca** HOTEL €€

(968 40 60 47; www.parador.es; Castillo de Lorca; r €90-185; ) Memorably situated in the castle complex way above town, this hotel is a modern mirror of the fortress. Facilities and public areas are very handsome; rooms are simpler but comfortable with red marble bathrooms. There's an indoor pool and spa and the views are just stunning. Various archaeological fragments are integrated into the hotel, including a reconstructed synagogue next to the car park.

DON'T MISS

### A RURAL RETREAT

For luxurious relaxation, you can't beat **Bajo el Cejo** (968 66 80 32; www.bajoelcejo.com; Calle El Paso; s incl breakfast €81, d €105-140; ), delicious countryside hideaway in El Berro. It's located inside a converted watermill under a bluff and is an away-from-it-all heaven. Rooms are spacious and superb, but it's the terrace, pool and delightful setting overlooking citrus groves and valley that are utterly memorable. There's an exceptional personal welcome and brilliant organic food, much of it produced here.

The restaurant is excellent. Rates are normally around the €90 mark, but tend to be much higher on Saturdays.

**Jardines de Lorca** HOTEL €€

(968 47 05 99; www.hoteljardinesdelorca.com; Alameda de Rafael Méndez; r €60-79; ) A short stroll from the centre, and handy for bus and train stations, this large complex has something of a resort feel. Its spacious rooms are comfortable, marble-tiled and come with a balcony, but there's some echoing noise from passageways. Facilities are excellent, including free parking, a spa, summer-only pool, gym and tennis courts. Prices are variable but very reasonable.

## Eating

**Albedrío** TAPAS €

(660 409702; www.albedrio.es; Plaza Calderón de la Barca 2; tapas €1-7; 11am-12.30am Tue-Sun, kitchen closed 4.30-8pm; ) This bright and buzzy spot keeps Lorca's tapas scene humming. A mural of Bogart and Hepburn overlooks chunky wooden tables, where you can order from a wide range of locally inflected tapas. It's extraordinarily good value, with homemade croquettes, juicy battered prawns and open toasted sandwiches among the delights.

**Casa Roberto** SPANISH €€

(968 44 25 58; Calle Corredera 21; mains €14-18; 1-4pm & 8-11pm Mon-Sat, 1-4pm Sun) In an attractive pink house on the principal pedestrian street, this is a sound bet. There's a series of rooms converted into intimate dining areas, as well as a pleasant courtyard.

Dishes such as roast turbot and *zarangollo* (eggs scrambled with garden vegetables) cover a good range of traditional and contemporary Spanish ingredients.

## Shopping

★ **Centro para la Artesanía** ARTS & CRAFTS (☎968 46 39 12; www.carm.es; Calle Lope Gisbert; ⏲10am-2pm & 5-8.30pm Mon-Fri, 11am-1.30pm Sat) It's quite a surprise to go through the door here, and gradually descend into an enormous concrete structure replete with all kinds of handicrafts, from colourful rugs to wine and marvellous ceramics. A government initiative, it's great to browse and buy.

## Information

**Centro de Visitantes** (☎968 47 90 03; www.lorcatallerdeltiempo.es; Puerto de San Ginés; ⏲10am-2pm) On the edge of the old town, this visitor centre has tourist information, sells visitor tickets and is a handy place to park.

**Tourist Office** (☎968 44 19 14; www.lorcaturismo.es; Plaza de España 7; ⏲10am-2pm & 4-6.30pm Mon-Sat, 10am-2pm Sun, extended opening Jul & Aug) In the heart of the old town.

## Getting There & Around

Hourly buses (€5.95, 1½ hours) and C2-line *cercanía* trains (€5.75, 50 minutes) run between Lorca and Murcia. Various bus services run into Almería province and beyond.

Bus 5 runs up to the castle a few times a day (€1.30), stopping at Plaza de España and the Centro de Visitantes.

# Parque Regional de Sierra Espuña

The Sierra Espuña, a 40-minute drive southwest of Murcia towards Lorca, is an island of pine and holm-oak forest rising high into the sky above an ocean of heat and dust. Sitting just north of the N340, the natural park that protects this fragile and beautiful environment has more than 250 sq km of unspoilt highlands covered with trails and is popular with walkers, climbers, cyclists and mountain bikers. Limestone formations tower above the sprawling forests. In the northwest of the park are many *pozos de la nieve* (ice houses) where, until the arrival of industrial refrigeration, snow was compressed into ice, then taken to nearby towns in summer.

Access to the park is best via **Alhama de Murcia**. The informative **Centro de Visitantes Ricardo Codorniu** (☎968 43 14 30; www.murcianatural.carm.es; ⏲9am-2pm & 3-5.30pm Tue-Sat, 9am-3pm Sun mid-Sep–mid-Jun, 9am-3pm Tue-Thu & Sun, 9am-3pm & 4-7.30pm Fri & Sat mid-Jun–mid-Sep) is located in the heart of the park. A few walking trails leave from this visitor centre, and it can provide good maps for these and several other picturesque hikes. There's a nature exhibition here too (Spanish only).

Mountain bikers should check out www.espubike.com, which details a four-stage 146km route around the park, starting at El Berro. It's been designed to be accessible for all abilities.

The village of **El Berro**, 9km past the visitor centre, makes a great base for the sierra. It has trailheads for a couple of good circular walks, restaurants, friendly **Camping Sierra Espuña** (☎968 66 80 38; www.campingsierraespuna.com; Calle de Juan Bautista; site per person €5, tent €5, car €5, bungalows €55-106; P 📶 🏊) and the standout Bajo el Cejo (p847).

Another base for the sierra, and for northern Murcia in general, is the town of **Mula**. The town is a web of old streets squashed up against a pinnacle of dry rock topped by the very battered remnants of a **castle**. From a distance, Mula actually looks like it's dropped straight out of a Middle Eastern fairy tale. Great-value rural accommodation is available at **El Molino de Felipe** (☎968 66 20 13; www.hotelruralmula.com; Carretera Ribera de los Molinos 321, El Niño de Mula; d €45, apt for 2/4/6 €70/106/142; P ❄ 📶 🏊), about 4km from town.

## Getting There & Away

The park is best accessed by car. The town of Alhama de Murcia is easily reached by *cercanía* train from Murcia (€2.70, 30 minutes), but it's 12km from here to the visitor centre in the heart of the park. Mula is also accessible by bus from Murcia (€3.30, 45 minutes).

# Understand Spain

# History

**Spain's story is one of Europe's grand epics. It embraces the great struggles between Muslims and Christians of the Middle Ages, one of the world's biggest-ever empires, and, in the 20th century, civil war, dictatorship and a stunning return to democracy. As you travel around the country, it's delightfully easy to get in touch with Spain's fascinating past through its countless well-preserved monuments and historical sites, and excellent museums.**

## Spain & the Ancient Civilisations

Spain can make a convincing claim to be the cradle of humanity in Western Europe: in 2007, Western Europe's oldest confirmed remains – 1.2 million years old – of the genus *Homo* were discovered at Atapuerca, near the northern city of Burgos. But it was not until around 3000 years ago that Spain entered history's mainstream.

### Phoenicians, Celts & Greeks

Madrid's Museo Arqueológico Nacional (National Archaeology Museum) is a great place to get a feel for the depth of Spanish history, with collections running through the Iberians, Romans and Visigoths right up to the Middle Ages.

The Phoenicians were the first of the major civilisations of the ancient world to set their sights on Spain. From their base along what is now the southern Lebanese coast, the Phoenicians may have been the world's first rulers of the sea. They were essentially traders rather than conquerors, and it was commerce that first brought them to Spain around 1000 BCE (BC). They arrived on Spanish shores bearing perfumes, ivory, jewellery, oil, wine and textiles, which they exchanged for Spanish silver and bronze.

Conquest may not have been the Phoenicians' aim, but as their reach expanded, so too did their need for safe ports around the Mediterranean rim. One of these was Carthage in modern-day Tunisia, founded in 814 BCE; in Iberia they established coastal trading colonies at Cádiz (which they called Gadir), Almuñécar (Ex or Sex), Huelva (Onuba) and Málaga (Malaka). Cádiz, that breezy and thoroughly Andalucian city in Spain's deep south, can as a result make a pretty strong claim to be the oldest continuously inhabited settlement in Europe.

After the Phoenicians, Greek traders began to arrive further north along the coast. In the 7th century BCE, the Greeks founded a series

**TIMELINE**

**c 39,000–10,000 BCE**

Palaeolithic (Old Stone Age) hunters paint beautiful, sophisticated animal images in caves at Altamira and other sites along Spain's northern coastal strip.

**6th century BCE**

Carthage, a former Phoenician colony in North Africa, supplants the Phoenicians and Greeks as the major trading power in the western Mediterranean.

**218 BCE**

Roman legions arrive in Spain during the Second Punic War against Carthage, initiating the 600-year Roman occupation of the Iberian Peninsula; it takes two centuries to subdue all local resistance.

of trading settlements mainly along the Mediterranean coast. The most important gifts of the Phoenicians and Greeks to Spain were not cities, only fragments of which remain today, but rather what they brought with them. The technology of working iron and several things now considered quintessentially Spanish – the olive tree, the grapevine and the donkey – arrived with the Phoenicians and Greeks, along with other useful skills and items such as writing, coins, the potter's wheel and poultry.

Around the same time as the Phoenicians brought iron technology to the south, Celts, originally from Central Europe, brought that knowledge – and beer making – to the north. Celts in the northwest typically lived in hill fort-villages known as *castros*, many of which can be visited today in Galicia and northern Portugal. On the *meseta* (the high tableland of central Spain) Celts merged with Iberians (the general name given to most inhabitants of the Iberian Peninsula at this time) to become what are known as Celtiberians.

## The Romans

From about the 6th century BCE, the Phoenicians and Greeks were pushed out of the western Mediterranean by newly independent Carthage, a former Phoenician colony that established a flourishing settlement on Ibiza. The next new Mediterranean power to arise was Rome, which defeated Carthage in the First and Second Punic Wars, and fought for control over the Mediterranean in the 3rd century BCE. Between the two wars, Carthage conquered southern Spain. The Second Punic War (218–201 BCE) saw Carthaginian general Hannibal march his elephants on from here and over the Alps to threaten Rome, but Rome's victory at Ilipa, near Seville, in 206 BCE ultimately gave it control over the Iberian Peninsula. The first Roman town in Spain, Itálica, was founded near the battlefield soon afterwards.

The Romans held sway on the Iberian Peninsula for 600 years. It took them 200 years to subdue the fiercest of the local tribes, but by 50 CE (AD) most of Hispania (as the Romans called the peninsula) had adopted the Roman way of life.

Rome's legacy to Spain was incalculable, giving Hispania a road system, aqueducts, temples, theatres, amphitheatres and bathhouses, along with the religion that still predominates today – Christianity – and a Jewish population that was to play a big part in Spanish life for more than 1000 years. The languages now most widely spoken on the Iberian Peninsula – Castilian Spanish, Catalan, Galician and Portuguese – are all versions of the colloquial Latin spoken by Roman legionaries and colonists, filtered through 2000 years of linguistic mutation; the Basques, though defeated, were never romanised like the rest and hence their language never came within the Latin orbit.

### Top Prehistoric Sites

*Cueva de Altamira*

*Atapuerca (near Burgos)*

*Cueva de Tito Bustillo (Ribadesella)*

*Dolmens (Antequera)*

*Cueva de la Pileta (near Ronda)*

*Siega Verde (near Ciudad Rodrigo)*



**1st to 3rd centuries CE**

Pax Romana (Roman Peace), a period of stability and prosperity. The Iberian Peninsula is divided into three provinces: Baetica (capital: Córdoba), Lusitania (Mérida) and Tarraconensis (Tarragona).

**4th to 7th centuries CE**

Germanic tribes enter the Iberian Peninsula, ending the Pax Romana. Starting in the 6th century, 200 years of Visigoth rule bring relative stability in which Hispano-Roman culture survives.

**711**

Muslims invade Iberia from North Africa, overrunning it within a few years, and becoming the dominant force on the peninsula for nearly four centuries and then a potent one for four centuries more.

**718**

Christian nobleman Pelayo establishes the Kingdom of Asturias in northern Spain. With his victory over a Muslim force at the Battle of Covadonga around 722, the Reconquista begins.

It was also the Romans who first began to cut (for timber, fuel and weapons) the extensive forests that in their time covered half the Spanish *meseta*. In return, Hispania gave Rome gold, silver, grain, wine, fish, soldiers, emperors (Trajan, Hadrian, Theodosius) and the literature of Seneca, Martial, Quintilian and Lucan.

The Roman centuries were something of a golden age for Spain, but the Pax Romana (Roman Peace; the long, prosperous period of stability under the Romans) in Spain started crumbling in the 3rd and 4th centuries CE when Germanic tribes began to sweep down across the Pyrenees. The Visigoths, another Germanic people, sacked Rome itself in 410 but later became allies. Pushed out of Gaul in the 6th century by the Germanic Franks, the Visigoths ultimately settled in the Iberian Peninsula, making Toledo their capital.

Throughout their rule, the roughly 200,000 Visigoths maintained a precarious hold over the millions of more sophisticated Hispano-Romans, to the extent that the Visigoths tended to ape Roman ways. Nonetheless, the Roman era had come to an end.

## Moorish Spain & La Reconquista

A recurring theme in early Spanish history is Spain's susceptibility to foreign invasion – to empires that rose and fell on Spanish soil but invariably came from elsewhere. In time, that pattern would transform into a struggle for the soul of Spain.

**Top Roman Remains**

- *Mérida*
- *Segovia*
- *Itálica (Santiponce, near Seville)*
- *Tarragona*
- *Baelo Claudia (Bolonia, near Tarifa)*
- *Lugo*
- *Villa Romana La Olmeda (Montaña Palentina)*
- *Villa Romana La Dehesa (near Soria)*

### The Muslim Arrival

The death of the Prophet Mohammed in far-off Arabia in 632 sent shock waves far and wide, and Spain, too, would soon feel the effects. Under Mohammed's successors, known as caliphs (from the Arabic word for 'follower'), the new religion spread with extraordinary speed. Much of the Middle East was theirs by 656, and by 682 Islam had reached the shores of the Atlantic in Morocco. Spain, and with it Europe, now lay within sight.

The Muslims had chosen a good moment to arrive: with the disintegration of the Visigothic kingdom through famine, disease and strife among the aristocracy, the Iberian Peninsula was in disarray and ripe for invasion.

For all its significance, there is an element of farce to what happened next. If you believe the myth, the Muslims were ushered into Spain by the sexual misadventures of the last Visigoth king, Roderic, who reputedly seduced Florinda, the daughter of the governor of Ceuta on the Moroccan coast. The governor, Julian, sought revenge by approaching the Muslims with a plan to invade Spain, and in 711 Tariq ibn Ziyad, the Muslim

**756**

Abd ar-Rahman I establishes himself in Córdoba as the emir of Al-Andalus (the Islamic areas of the peninsula) and launches nearly three centuries of Cordoban supremacy.

**929**

Abd ar-Rahman III inaugurates the Córdoba caliphate, under which Al-Andalus reaches its zenith and Córdoba, with up to half a million people, becomes Europe's biggest and most cultured city.

**1031**

The Córdoba caliphate disintegrates into dozens of *taifas* (small kingdoms) after a devastating civil war. The most powerful *taifas* include Seville, Granada, Toledo and Zaragoza.

**1035**

Castilla, a county of the northern Christian kingdom of León (successor to the kingdom of Asturias), becomes an independent kingdom and goes on to become the leading force of the Reconquista.

## THE MOORISH LEGACY

Muslim rule left an indelible imprint upon Spain. Great architectural monuments such as the Alhambra in Granada and the Mezquita in Córdoba are the stars of the Moorish legacy, but thousands of other buildings large and small are Moorish in origin (including the many churches that began life as mosques). The tangled, narrow street plans of many a Spanish town and village, especially in the south, date back to Moorish times, and the Muslims also developed the Hispano-Roman agricultural base by improving irrigation and introducing new fruits and crops, many of which are still widely grown today. The Spanish language contains many common words of Arabic origin, including the names of some of those new crops – *naranja* (orange), *azúcar* (sugar) and *arroz* (rice). Flamenco, though brought to its modern form by Roma people in post-Moorish times, has clear Moorish roots. It was also through Al-Andalus that much of the learning of ancient Greece and Rome – picked up by the Arabs in the eastern Mediterranean – was transmitted to Christian Europe, where it would exert a profound influence on the Renaissance.

governor of Tangier, landed at Gibraltar with around 10,000 men, mostly Berbers (indigenous North Africans).

Roderic's army was decimated, probably near Río Guadalete or Río Barbate in western Andalucía, and he is thought to have drowned while fleeing the scene. Visigothic survivors fled north and within a few years the Muslims had conquered the whole Iberian Peninsula, except for small areas behind the mountains of the Cordillera Cantábrica in the north. Their advance into Europe was only checked by the Franks at the Battle of Poitiers in 732.

### Al-Andalus: The Early Years

The enlightened Islamic civilisation that would rule much of the Iberian Peninsula for centuries would be called Al-Andalus.

Initially Al-Andalus was part of the caliphate of Damascus, which ruled the Islamic world. Once again, as it had been in ancient times, Spain had become a distant outpost of someone else's empire. In 750, however, the Umayyads were overthrown in Damascus by a rival clan, the Abbasids, who shifted the caliphate to Baghdad. One aristocratic Umayyad survivor made his way to Spain and established himself in Córdoba in 756 as the independent emir of Al-Andalus, Abd ar-Rahman I. It was he who began construction of Córdoba's Mezquita, one of the world's greatest Islamic buildings. Just as importantly, Córdoba was the capital of an empire that relied on no foreign powers. For almost the first time, Spain (in this case, Al-Andalus) was both powerful and answerable only to itself.

Richard Fletcher's *Moorish Spain* is an excellent short history of Al-Andalus (the Muslim-ruled areas of the peninsula) and assumes little prior knowledge of the subject. Other titles include *Homage to al-Andalus* by Michael B Barry and *The Ornament of the World* by María Rosa Menocal.



**1085**

Castilla captures the major Muslim city of Toledo in central Spain after infighting among the *taifas* leaves them vulnerable to attack.

**1091**

North African Muslim Almoravids invade the peninsula, unifying Al-Andalus, ruling it from Marrakesh and halting Christian expansion. Almoravid rule crumbles in the 1140s; Al-Andalus splits again into *taifas*.

**1160–73**

The Almohads, another strict Muslim sect from North Africa, conquer Al-Andalus. They make Seville their capital and revive arts and learning.

**1195**

The Almohads inflict a devastating defeat on Alfonso VIII of Castilla at the Battle of Alarcos, near Ciudad Real – the last major Christian reverse of the Reconquista.

## Córdoba's Golden Age

From the middle of the 8th century to the mid-11th century, the frontier between Muslim and Christian territory lay across the north of the peninsula, roughly from southern Catalonia to northern Portugal, with a protrusion up towards the central Pyrenees. South of this line, Islamic cities such as Córdoba, Seville and Granada developed with beautiful palaces, mosques and gardens, universities, public baths and bustling *zocos* (markets). Al-Andalus' rulers allowed freedom of worship to Jews and Christians (known as Mozarabs) under their rule. Jews mostly flourished, but Christians had to pay a special tax, so most either converted to Islam or left for the Christian north. The Muslim settlers themselves were not a homogeneous group: beneath the Arab ruling class was a larger number of North African Berbers, and Berber rebellions weren't infrequent.

**Best Moorish Sites**

- *Alhambra (Granada)*
- *Mezquita (Córdoba)*
- *Albayzín (Granada)*
- *Alcázar (Seville)*
- *Giralda (Seville)*
- *Aljafería (Zaragoza)*
- *Alcazaba (Málaga)*

In 929, the ruler Abd ar-Rahman III gave himself the title caliph, launching the caliphate of Córdoba (929–1031), during which Al-Andalus reached its peak of power and lustre. Córdoba in this period was the biggest and most dazzling city in Western Europe. Astronomy, medicine, mathematics and botany flourished and one of the great Muslim libraries was established in the city.

Later in the 10th century, the fearsome Cordoban general Al-Mansur (or Almanzor) terrorised the Christian north with 50-odd forays in 20 years. He destroyed the cathedral at Santiago de Compostela in northwestern Spain in 997 and forced Christian slaves to carry its doors and bells to Córdoba, where they were incorporated into the great mosque. There was, it seemed, no limit to Córdoba's powers.

## Al-Andalus: The Later Years

Just when it seemed that Córdoba's golden age would last forever, Al-Andalus turned the corner into a long, slow decline.

After Al-Mansur's death the caliphate collapsed into a devastating civil war, ending Umayyad rule, and in 1031 it finally broke up into dozens of *taifas* (small kingdoms).

Political unity was restored to Al-Andalus by the invasion of a strict Muslim Berber sect from North Africa, the Almoravids, in 1091. The Almoravids had conquered North Africa and were initially invited to the Iberian Peninsula to support Seville, one of the strongest *taifas*, against the growing Christian threat from the north. Seventy years later a second Berber sect, the Almohads, invaded the peninsula after overthrowing the Almoravids in Morocco. Both sects roundly defeated the Christian armies they encountered in Spain, and maintained the Muslim hold over the southern half of the peninsula.

**1212**

Combined armies of northern Christian kingdoms defeat the Almohads at Las Navas de Tolosa in Andalucía, and the momentum of the Christian–Muslim struggle swings decisively in favour of the Christians.

**1218**

The University of Salamanca is founded by Alfonso IX, King of León, making it the oldest – and still the most prestigious – university in the country.

**1229–38**

King Jaume (Jaime) I of the Crown of Aragón, which includes Catalonia, takes the Balearic Islands and Valencia from the Muslims, making his kingdom the western Mediterranean's major power.

**1248**

Having captured Córdoba 12 years earlier, Castilla's Fernando III takes Seville after a two-year siege, leaving the Nasrid emirate of Granada as the last surviving Muslim state on the peninsula.

Almohad power eventually disintegrated in the early 13th century due to infighting and continuing Christian military pressure from the north. Seville fell to the Christians in 1248, leaving the emirate of Granada (about half of modern Andalucía) as the last Muslim territory on the Iberian Peninsula. Ruled from the lavish Alhambra palace by the Nasrid dynasty, Granada saw Islamic Spain's final cultural flowering as the Christian armies of the Reconquista were closing in.

## La Reconquista

The Christian reconquest of the Iberian Peninsula began in about 722 at Covadonga, Asturias, and ended with the fall of Granada in 1492. Between these two dates lay almost eight centuries of misadventures, stirring victories and missed opportunities, during which different Christian kingdoms were almost as often at war with each other as with Muslims.

An essential ingredient in the Reconquista was the cult of Santiago (St James), one of the 12 Apostles. In about the 820s, the saint's supposed tomb was discovered in Galicia. The city of Santiago de Compostela grew around the site, becoming the third-most-popular medieval Christian pilgrimage goal, after Rome and Jerusalem. Christian generals experienced visions of Santiago before forays against the Muslims, and Santiago became the inspiration and special protector of soldiers in the Reconquista, earning the sobriquet Matamoros (Moor-slayer). Today he is the patron saint of Spain.

**Medieval Jewish Sites**

- *Judería (Toledo)*
- *The Call (Girona)*
- *Ribadavia (Galicia)*
- *Judería (Córdoba)*
- *Hervás (Extremadura)*
- *Centro Didáctico de la Judería (Segovia)*

### Castilla Rises

Covadonga lies in the Picos de Europa mountains in Asturias, where some Visigothic nobles took refuge after the Muslim conquest. Christian versions of the 722 battle there tell of a small band of fighters under their leader, Pelayo, defeating an enormous force of Muslims; Muslim accounts make it a less important skirmish. Whatever the facts of Covadonga, by 757 Christians had clawed back nearly a quarter of the Iberian Peninsula.

The Asturian kingdom eventually moved its capital south to León and became the kingdom of León, which spearheaded the Reconquista until the Christians were set on the defensive by Al-Mansur in the 10th century. Castilla, initially a small principality within León, developed into the dominant Reconquista force as hardy adventurers set up towns in the no man's land of the Duero basin. It was the capture of Toledo in 1085, by Alfonso VI of Castilla, that led the Seville Muslims to call in the Almoravids from North Africa.

In 1212 the combined armies of the Christian kingdoms routed a large Almohad force at Las Navas de Tolosa in Andalucía (near the modern town of Santa Elena). This was the beginning of the end for Al-Andalus: León took key towns in Extremadura in 1229 and 1230; Aragón took

**1469**

Isabel, the 18-year-old heir to Castilla, marries Fernando, heir to Aragón and one year her junior, uniting Spain's two most powerful Christian states.

**1478**

Isabel and Fernando, the Reyes Católicos (Catholic Monarchs), stir up religious bigotry and establish the Spanish Inquisition that will see thousands killed between now and its abolition in 1834.

**January 1492**

Isabel and Fernando capture Granada, completing the Reconquista. Boabdil, the last Muslim ruler, is scorned (legend has it) by his mother for weeping like a woman over the loss.

**April 1492**

Isabel and Fernando expel 200,000 Jews who refuse Christian baptism. Spain's economy suffers from the loss of their skills and knowledge.

Valencia in the 1230s; Castilla's Fernando III El Santo (Ferdinand the Saint) took Córdoba in 1236 and Seville in 1248; and the Muslims were expelled from Portugal in 1249. The sole surviving Muslim state on the peninsula was now the emirate of Granada.

## Granada Falls

In 1476 Emir Abu al-Hasan of Granada refused to pay any more tribute to Castilla, spurring the Reyes Católicos (Catholic Monarchs) – Isabel, queen of Castilla, and her husband, Fernando, king of Aragón – to launch the Reconquista's final crusade, against Granada. With an army largely funded by Jewish loans and the Catholic Church, the Christians took full advantage of a civil war within the Granada emirate, and on 2 January 1492 Isabel and Fernando entered the city of Granada at the beginning of what turned out to be the most momentous year in Spanish history.

The surrender terms were fairly generous to Boabdil, the last emir, who got the Alpujarras valleys south of Granada and 30,000 gold coins. History has been less kind. Whether true or not, it is often recounted how Boabdil turned for one last tearful look at his beloved Granada as he headed into exile, whereupon his mother scolded him by saying: 'Do not weep like a woman for what you could not defend like a man!' The remaining Muslims were promised respect for their religion, culture and property, but eight centuries after it began, Al-Andalus was no more.

### THE CATHOLIC MONARCHS

Few individuals in any time or place have had such an impact on their country's history as Spain's Reyes Católicos (Catholic Monarchs), Isabel of Castilla and Fernando of Aragón. Indeed, Spain owes its very existence to their marriage in 1469 (which effectively united the Iberian Peninsula's two biggest Christian kingdoms) and to their conquest of Granada (1492) and annexation of Navarra (1512).

Isabel, by all accounts, was pious, honest, virtuous and very determined, while Fernando was an astute political operator – a formidable team. Isabel resisted her family's efforts to marry her off to half a dozen other European royals before her semi-clandestine wedding to Fernando at Valladolid – the first time the pair had set eyes on each other. They were second cousins; she was 18 and he 17. Isabel succeeded to the Castilian throne in 1474, and Fernando to Aragón's in 1479. By the time Isabel died in 1504, the pair had: set up the Spanish Inquisition (1478); completed the Reconquista by conquering Granada (1492); expelled all Jews (1492) and Muslims (1500) who refused to convert to Christianity; helped to fund Columbus' voyage to the Americas (1492), opening the door to a vast overseas empire for Spain; and crushed the power of Castilla's rebellious nobility.

Today Isabel and Fernando lie side by side in the beautiful Gothic church they commissioned as their own mausoleum, Granada's Capilla Real.

**October 1492**

Christopher Columbus, funded by Isabel and Fernando, lands in the Bahamas, opening up the Americas to Spanish colonisation and tilting the balance of Spanish sea trade from Mediterranean to Atlantic ports.

**1494**

The Treaty of Tordesillas (near Valladolid) divides recently discovered lands west of Europe between Spain and Portugal, giving the Spanish the right to claim vast territories in the Americas.

**1512**

Fernando, ruling as regent after Isabel's death in 1504, annexes Navarra, bringing all of Spain under one rule for the first time since Roman days.

**1517–56**

Reign of Carlos I, Spain's first Habsburg monarch, who comes to rule more of Europe than anyone since the 9th century, plus rapidly expanding areas of South and Central America.

## Spain's Empires

Having secured the Iberian Peninsula as their own, the Catholic Monarchs turned their attention elsewhere. The conquest of Granada coincided neatly with the opening up of a whole new world of opportunity for a confident Christian Spain. Columbus' voyage to the Americas, in the very same year as Granada fell, presented an entire new continent in which the militaristic and crusading elements of Spanish society could continue their efforts.

### Conquering a New World

In April 1492 the Catholic Monarchs granted the Genoese sailor Christopher Columbus (Cristóbal Colón in Spanish) funds for his voyage across the Atlantic in search of a new trade route to the Orient.

Columbus sailed from the Andalucian port of Palos de la Frontera on 3 August 1492, with three small ships and 120 men. After a near mutiny as the crew despaired of sighting land, they finally arrived on the island of Guanahaní, in the Bahamas, and went on to find Cuba and Hispaniola. Columbus returned to a hero's reception from the Catholic Monarchs in Barcelona, eight months after his departure. Columbus made three more voyages, founding the city of Santo Domingo on Hispaniola, finding Jamaica, Trinidad and other Caribbean islands, and reaching the mouth of the Orinoco and the coast of Central America. But he died impoverished in Valladolid in 1506, still believing he had reached Asia.

Brilliant but ruthless conquistadors such as Hernán Cortés and Francisco Pizarro followed Columbus' trail, seizing vast tracts of the American mainland for Spain. By 1600 Spain controlled nearly all of present-day Mexico and Central America, a large strip of South America, all the biggest Caribbean islands, and Florida. The new colonies sent huge cargoes of silver, gold and other riches back to Spain, where the crown was entitled to one-fifth of the bullion (the *quinto real*, or royal fifth). Seville enjoyed a monopoly on this trade and grew into one of Europe's richest cities.

### Entangled in the Old World

It wasn't just the Americas that the Catholic Monarchs thought should be theirs. Isabel and Fernando embroiled Spain in European affairs by marrying their five children into the royal families of Portugal, the Holy Roman Empire and England. After Isabel's death in 1504 and Fernando's in 1516, their thrones passed to their grandson Carlos I (Charles I), who arrived in Spain from Flanders in 1517, aged 17. In 1519 Carlos also succeeded to the Habsburg lands in Austria and was elected Holy Roman Emperor (as Charles V) – meaning he now ruled all of Spain, the Low Countries, Austria, several Italian states, parts of France and Germany, and the expanding Spanish colonies in the Americas.

**Echoes of the Middle Ages**

- *Sos del Rey Católico (Aragón)*
- *Albarracín (Aragón)*
- *Santiago de Compostela*
- *Morella (Valencia)*
- *La Tahá (Las Alpujarras)*
- *Santo Domingo de la Calzada (La Rioja)*
- *Ávila*
- *Albayzín (Granada)*

The Crown of Aragón was one of the most powerful kingdoms in medieval Spain, created in 1137 when Ramón Berenguer IV, count of Barcelona, was betrothed to Petronilla, heiress to the kingdom of Aragón, creating a formidable new Christian power block in the northeast, with Barcelona as its centre.

**1521**

Hernán Cortés, from Medellín, Extremadura, conquers the Aztec empire, in present-day Mexico and Guatemala, with a small band of conquistadors, in the name of the Spanish crown.

**1533**

Francisco Pizarro, from Trujillo, Extremadura, conquers the Inca empire in South America with a small band of conquistadors, in the name of the Spanish crown.

**1556–98**

Reign of Felipe II, the zenith of Spanish power. The American territories reach from Florida to Chile, and enormous wealth arriving from the colonies is used for grandiose architectural projects.

**1561**

The king makes the minor country town of Madrid the capital of his empire. Despite many new noble residences, the overwhelming impression of the new capital is one of squalor.

For all Spain's apparent power, European conflicts soaked up the bulk of the monarchy's new American wealth, and a war-weary Carlos abdicated shortly before his death in 1556, retiring to the Monasterio de Yuste in Extremadura and dividing his many territories between his son Felipe II (Philip II; r 1556–98) and his brother Fernando.

Felipe got the lion's share, including Spain, the Low Countries and the American possessions, and presided over the zenith of Spanish power, though his reign is a study in contradictions. He enlarged the American empire and claimed Portugal on its king's death in 1580, but he lost Holland after a long, drawn-out rebellion. His navy defeated the Ottoman Turks at Lepanto in 1571, but the Spanish Armada of 1588 was routed by England. He was a fanatical Catholic who spurred the Inquisition to new persecutions, yet he readily allied with Protestant England against Catholic France. He received greater flows of silver than ever from the Americas but went bankrupt.

Like his father, Felipe died in a monastery – the immense one at San Lorenzo de El Escorial, which he himself had commissioned, and which stands as a sombre monument to his reign and to the contradictions of Spain's colonial era.

**Echoes of Spain's American Colonies**

- *Trujillo (Extremadura)*
- *Lugares Colombinos (near Huelva)*
- *Casa-Museo de Colón (Valladolid)*
- *Columbus' Tomb (Seville Cathedral)*
- *Tordesillas (near Valladolid)*
- *Palacio de Sobrellano (Comillas)*
- *Museo de América (Madrid)*

## Riches to Rags

In Spain's finest hour, at a time when it ruled large swaths of the world, the country's rulers sowed the seeds of its disintegration. So much of the fabulous wealth that accrued from Spain's American and other colonies was squandered on lavish royal lifestyles and on indulgences that did little to better the lives of ordinary Spaniards. The result was a deeply divided country that would for centuries face repeated battles of royal succession and its fair share of external wars.

### Out of Step with Europe

At one level, a flourishing arts scene in 17th-century Spain created the illusion of a modern European nation. Spain was being immortalised in paint by great artists such as Velázquez, El Greco, Zurbarán and Murillo, and in words by the likes of Miguel de Cervantes (author of *Don Quijote*) and the prolific playwright Lope de Vega.

And yet weak, backward-looking monarchs, a highly conservative Church and an idle nobility allowed the economy to stagnate, leading to food shortages and gross inequalities between the haves and the have-nots. Spain lost Portugal and faced revolts in Catalonia, Sicily and Naples. Silver shipments from the Americas shrank disastrously. And the sickly Carlos II (Charles II; r 1665–1700), known as El Hechizado (the Bewitched), failed to produce children, a situation that led to the War of the Spanish Succession (1702–13). Felipe V (Philip V; r 1700–46), to whom Carlos II had bequeathed the Spanish throne, managed to hold on to it,

**1571**

The Holy League fleet, led by Spain and Venice and commanded by Felipe II's half-brother Don Juan de Austria, defeats the Ottoman Turkish fleet at Lepanto, ending Ottoman expansion into Europe.

**c 1580–1660**

Spain enjoys a cultural golden age, with the literature of Cervantes and the paintings of Velázquez, Zurbarán and El Greco scaling new heights of artistic excellence as the empire declines.

**1609–14**

The *moriscos* (converted Muslims) are expelled from Spain in a final purge of non-Christians that undermines an already faltering economy.

**1676**

The devastation caused by the third great plague to hit Spain in a century is compounded by poor harvests. In all, more than 1.25 million Spaniards die through plague and starvation during the 17th century.

## THE SPANISH INQUISITION

Spain's new Catholic rulers made it clear from the beginning that any enlightened policies of religious coexistence were a thing of the past.

Not content with territorial conquest, the Catholic Monarchs' zeal led to the founding of the Spanish Inquisition to root out those believed to be threatening the Catholic Church. The Inquisition's leading figure was Grand Inquisitor Tomás de Torquemada, who was appointed Queen Isabel's personal confessor in 1479. He was, centuries later, immortalised by Dostoevsky as the articulate Grand Inquisitor who puts Jesus himself on trial in *The Brothers Karamazov,* and satirised in *Monty Python's Flying Circus*.

The Inquisition focused first on *conversos* (Jews converted to Christianity), accusing many of continuing to practise Judaism in secret; in an interesting footnote to history, Torquemada was himself born to *converso* parents. During the Inquisition, the 'lucky' sinners had their property confiscated (this served as a convenient fundraiser for the wars against Granada). The condemned were then paraded through towns wearing the *sambenito,* a yellow shirt emblazoned with crosses that was short enough to expose their genitals, marched to the local church and flogged.

If you were unlucky, you underwent unimaginable tortures before going through an *auto-da-fé,* a public burning at the stake. Those who recanted and kissed the cross were garrotted before the fire was set, while those who just recanted were burnt quickly with dry wood. If you stayed firm, the wood used was green and slow-burning.

In the 15 years that Torquemada was Inquisitor General of the Castilian Inquisition, he ran some 100,000 trials and sent about 2000 people to burn at the stake. On 31 March 1492, Fernando and Isabel, on Torquemada's insistence, issued their Edict of Expulsion, as a result of which all Jews who refused Christian baptism were forced to leave Spain within two months on pain of death. Up to 100,000 converted, but some 200,000 – the first Sephardic Jews – left Spain for other Mediterranean destinations. The bankrupt monarchy seized all unsold Jewish property. A talented middle class was gone.

Cardinal Cisneros, Torquemada's successor as overseer of the Inquisition, tried to eradicate Muslim culture, too. In the former Granada emirate he carried out forced mass baptisms, burnt Islamic books and banned the Arabic language. After a revolt in Andalucía in 1500, Muslims were ordered to convert to Christianity or leave. Most (around 300,000) underwent baptism and stayed, becoming known as *moriscos* (converted Muslims), but their conversion was barely skin deep and they never assimilated. The *moriscos* were finally expelled between 1609 and 1614.

but during the war Spain lost its last possessions in the Low Countries to Austria, and Gibraltar and Menorca to Britain. Felipe V was the first of the Bourbon dynasty, still in place today. This was Europe's Age of Enlightenment, but Spain's powerful Church and Inquisition were at odds with the rationalism that trickled in from France. Two thirds of the land was in the hands of the nobility and Church, and inequality and unrest were rife.

**1700**

Felipe V, first of the Bourbon dynasty, takes the throne after the Habsburg line dies out with Carlos II. Felipe is second in line to the French throne, causing concern across Europe.

**1702–13**

Rival European powers support Charles of Austria against Felipe V in the War of the Spanish Succession: Felipe survives as king, but Spain loses Gibraltar and the Low Countries.

**1793**

Spain declares war on France after Louis XVI is beheaded, but within a couple of years the country is supporting the French in their struggles against the British.

**1805**

A combined Spanish-French fleet is defeated by British ships under Nelson at the Battle of Trafalgar. Spanish sea power is effectively destroyed; discontent about King Carlos IV's pro-French policies grows.

## France Invades

When France's Louis XVI, cousin to Spain's Carlos IV (Charles IV; r 1788–1808), was guillotined in 1793 in the aftermath of the French Revolution, Spain declared war on France, only to make peace with the French Republic two years later. In 1805 a combined Spanish-French navy was beaten by the British fleet, under Admiral Nelson, off Andalucía's Cabo de Trafalgar, putting an end to Spanish sea power.

In 1807, French forces poured into Spain, supposedly on the way to Portugal, but by 1808 this had become a French occupation of Spain, and Carlos IV was forced to abdicate in favour of Napoleon's brother Joseph Bonaparte (José I).

In Madrid crowds revolted, as immortalised by Goya in his paintings *El dos de mayo* and *El tres de mayo*, which now hang in Madrid's Museo del Prado. Across the country Spaniards took up arms guerrilla-style, reinforced by British and Portuguese forces led by the Duke of Wellington. A national Cortes (parliament) meeting at Cádiz in 1812 drew up a new liberal constitution, incorporating many of the principles of the American and French prototypes. The French were finally driven out after their defeat at Vitoria in 1813.

The village of Belchite in central Aragón, reduced to shattered ruins by a fierce civil-war battle in 1937, was preserved in its devastated state after the war. The haunting ruins, including what's left of four churches, can be visited on daily tours with the local tourist office.

## Spain's Decline

Although momentarily united to see off the French, Spain was deeply divided, not to mention increasingly backward and insular. For much of the 19th century, internal conflicts raged between liberals (who wanted vaguely democratic reforms) and conservatives (the Church, the nobility and others who preferred the earlier status quo).

Uncertainties over royal succession resulted in the First Carlist War (1833–39). During the war, violent anticlericalism emerged, religious orders were closed and, in the Disentailment of 1836, church property and lands were seized and auctioned off by the government. It was the army alone that emerged victorious from the fighting. Another Carlist War (1872–76) followed, this time between the supporters of not just two but three claimants to the throne.

In 1873 the liberal-dominated Cortes proclaimed the country a federal republic. But this First Republic could not control the regions, and the army put Queen Isabel II's son Alfonso on the throne as Alfonso XII (r 1874–85), in a coalition with the Church and landowners.

Barely able to hold itself together, Spain had little chance of maintaining its few remaining colonies. In 1898, Spain lost Cuba, the Philippines, Guam and Puerto Rico after being defeated in the Spanish-American War by the USA. For a country that had ruled one of the greatest empires of the age, this sealed an ignominious fall from grace.

**1808–13**

French forces occupy Spain; Carlos IV abdicates in favour of Napoleon's brother, José I. The ensuing Peninsular War sees British forces helping the Spanish defeat the French.

**1809–24**

Most of Spain's colonies win independence as Spain is beset by problems at home. By 1824 only Cuba, Puerto Rico, Guam and the Philippines are under Spanish rule.

**1814**

Fernando VII becomes king and revokes the 1812 Cádiz Constitution (an attempt by Spanish liberals to introduce constitutional reforms) just weeks after agreeing to uphold its principles.

**1833–39**

The First Carlist War, triggered by disputes over the succession between backers of Fernando VII's infant daughter, Isabel, and his brother, Don Carlos. Isabel eventually becomes queen in 1843.

# The Spanish Civil War

The Spanish Civil War (1936–39) was a long time coming. In many ways, the seeds of division were sown centuries before in the profound inequalities that flowed from Spain's colonial riches, and in the equally profound social divisions that began to surface in the 19th century.

## Seeds of War

By the early years of the 20th century, Spain was locked in an unending power struggle between left-wing and conservative forces, with neither able to maintain the upper hand for long.

For a time, the left seemed ascendant. Anarchism and socialism both gained large followings and founded powerful unions. In the 1890s and the 1900s, anarchists bombed Barcelona's Liceu opera house, assassinated two prime ministers and killed 24 people with a bomb at King Alfonso XIII's wedding to Victoria Eugenie of Battenberg in May 1906. Parallel to the rise of the left came the growth of Basque and Catalan separatism. In Catalonia this was led by business interests who wanted to pursue policies independent of Madrid; in the Basque Country, nationalism emerged in the 1890s in response to a flood of Castilian workers into Basque industries: some Basques considered these migrants a threat to their identity. In 1909 a contingent of Spanish troops was wiped out by Berbers in Spanish Morocco. The government's decision to call up Catalan reservists sparked the so-called Semana Trágica (Tragic Week) in Barcelona, which began with a general strike and turned into a frenzy of violence. The government responded by executing many workers.

Spain stayed neutral during WWI but remained a deeply troubled nation. In 1921, 10,000 Spanish soldiers were killed by Berbers at Anual in Morocco, and two years later General Miguel Primo de Rivera, an eccentric Andalucian aristocrat, led an army uprising and established a mild dictatorship, resigning in 1930 in the midst of an economic downturn following the Wall Street Crash. King Alfonso XIII departed for exile in 1931 and Spain's Second Republic was launched.

National elections in 1931 brought in a government composed of socialists, republicans and centrists. A new constitution gave women the vote, granted autonomy-minded Catalonia its own parliament, legalised divorce, stripped Catholicism of its status as the official religion, and banned priests from teaching. But Spain lurched back to the right in elections in 1933. One new force on the right was the fascist Falange, led by José Antonio Primo de Rivera, son of the 1920s dictator.

By 1934, violence was spiralling out of control. Catalonia declared itself independent (within a putative federal Spanish republic), and workers' committees took over the northern mining region of Asturias. A violent campaign against the Asturian workers by the Spanish Legion

### Civil War Reads

*For Whom the Bell Tolls* by Ernest Hemingway

*Homage to Catalonia* by George Orwell

*The Spanish Civil War* by Hugh Thomas

*Spain in Our Hearts* by Adam Hochschild

**1872–76**

The Second Carlist War, between three monarchist factions, brings Isabel II's son, Alfonso XII, to the throne after the brief, chaotic First Republic of 1873.

**1898**

Spain loses Cuba, Puerto Rico, Guam and the Philippines, its last remaining colonies, after being defeated in the Spanish-American War by the US, which declared war in support of Cuban independence.

**1923–30**

General Miguel Primo de Rivera launches an army rising in support of King Alfonso XIII and then establishes himself as dictator. He retires and dies in 1930.

**1931**

Alfonso XIII goes into exile after Republicans score sweeping gains in local elections. Spain's Second Republic is launched, left-wing parties win a national election, and a new constitution enfranchises women.

(set up to fight Moroccan tribes in the 1920s), led by generals Francisco Franco and José Millán Astray, split the country firmly into left and right.

In the February 1936 elections, the right-wing National Front was narrowly defeated by the left-wing Popular Front, with communists at the fore. Something had to give.

## The Civil War Begins

On 17 July 1936, the Spanish army garrison in Melilla, North Africa, rose up against the left-wing Popular Front government, followed the next day by garrisons on the mainland. The leaders of the plot were five generals, among them Francisco Franco. The civil war had begun.

Giles Tremlett's *Catherine of Aragón: The Spanish Queen of Henry VIII* brings to life all the scheming and intrigue of royal Europe in the 16th century through the story of Isabel and Fernando's daughter.

The war would split communities, families and friends, kill an estimated 350,000 Spaniards (some writers say 500,000), and cause untold damage and misery. Both sides committed atrocious massacres and reprisals. The rebels, who called themselves Nationalists because they believed they were fighting for Spain, shot or hanged tens of thousands of supporters of the Republic. Republicans did likewise to Nationalist sympathisers, including some 7000 priests, monks and nuns.

At the start of the war many of the military and the Guardia Civil police force went over to the Nationalists, whose campaign quickly took on overtones of a crusade against the enemies of God. In Republican areas, anarchists, communists or socialists ended up running many towns and cities, and social revolution followed.

## Nationalist Advance

Most cities with military garrisons fell immediately into Nationalist hands – this included almost everywhere north of Madrid except Catalonia and the north coast, plus parts of Andalucía. Franco's force of legionnaires and Moroccan mercenaries was airlifted to Seville by German war planes in August. Essential to the success of the revolt, the force moved north through Extremadura towards Madrid, wiping out fierce resistance in some cities. At Salamanca in October, Franco pulled all the Nationalists into line behind him.

Madrid, reinforced by the first battalions of the International Brigades (armed foreign idealists and adventurers organised by the communists), repulsed Franco's first assault in November and then endured, under communist inspiration, over two years' siege. But the International Brigades never numbered more than 20,000 and couldn't turn the tide against the better-armed and -organised Nationalist forces.

Nazi Germany and Fascist Italy supported the Nationalists with planes, weapons and men (75,000 from Italy, 17,000 from Germany), turning the war into a testing ground for WWII. The Republicans had some Soviet planes, tanksand advisers, but other countries refused to become involved (some 25,000 French fought on the Republican side).

**1933–35**

Right-wing parties win a new election, political violence spirals and a ruthless army operation against workers in Asturias irrevocably polarises Spain into left- and right-wing camps.

**1936**

The left-wing Popular Front wins a national election. Right-wing 'Nationalist' rebels led by General Francisco Franco rise up against it, starting the Spanish Civil War.

**1936–39**

The Spanish Civil War: the Nationalist rebels, under Franco, supported by Nazi Germany and Fascist Italy, defeat the USSR-supported Republicans. About 350,000 people die in fighting and atrocities.

**1939–50**

Franco establishes a right-wing dictatorship, imprisoning hundreds of thousands. Spain stays out of WWII but is later excluded from NATO and the UN and suffers an international trade boycott.

### Republican Quarrels

With Madrid besieged, the Republican government moved to Valencia in late 1936 to preside over the quarrelsome factions on its side, which encompassed anarchists, communists, moderate democrats and regional separatists.

In April 1937 German planes bombed the Basque town of Gernika (Guernica), causing terrible casualties; this became the subject of Picasso's famous pacifist painting, which now hangs in Madrid's Centro de Arte Reina Sofía. All the north coast fell to the Nationalists that year, while Republican counter-attacks near Madrid and in Aragón failed. Meanwhile, divisions among the Republicans erupted into fierce street fighting in Barcelona, with the Soviet-influenced communists completely crushing the anarchists and Trotskyites, who had run the city for almost a year. The Republican government moved to Barcelona in autumn 1937.

### Nationalist Victory

In early 1938, Franco repulsed a Republican offensive at Teruel in Aragón, then swept eastward with 100,000 troops, 1000 planes and 150 tanks, isolating Barcelona from Valencia. In July the Republicans launched a last offensive in the Ebro Valley. This bloody encounter, won by the Nationalists, cost 20,000 lives. The USSR withdrew from the war in September 1938, and in January 1939 the Nationalists took Barcelona unopposed. The Republican government and hundreds of thousands of supporters fled to France. The Republicans still held Valencia and Madrid, and had 500,000 people under arms, but in the end their army simply evaporated. The Nationalists entered Madrid on 28 March 1939 and Franco declared the war over on 1 April.

## Franco's Dictatorship

Bloodied and battered Spain may have been after the Civil War, but there was no peace dividend: Spain's new ruler, General Francisco Franco, began as he meant to continue.

### The Early Franco Years

An estimated 100,000 people were killed or died in prison in the years immediately following the war. The hundreds of thousands imprisoned included many intellectuals and teachers; others fled abroad, depriving Spain of a generation of scientists, artists, writers, educators and more.

Though Franco promised Hitler an alliance, Spain remained on the sidelines of WWII. In 1944 Spanish leftists launched an attack on Franco's Spain from France; this attack failed. Small leftist guerrilla units continued a hopeless struggle in parts of the north, Extremadura and Andalucía until the 1950s. After WWII Franco's Spain was excluded

**Bourbon Baubles**

- *Palacio Real (Madrid)*
- *Palacio Real (Aranjuez)*
- *La Granja de San Ildefonso (near Segovia)*

**Pre-Civil War Books**

- *As I Walked out One Midsummer Morning by Laurie Lee*
- *South from Granada by Gerald Brenan*
- *The Spanish Labyrinth by Gerald Brenan*
- *Sketches of Spain by Federico García Lorca*

**1955–65**

Spain is admitted to the UN after agreeing to host US bases. The economy is boosted by US aid and mass tourism on the Costa Brava and Costa del Sol.

**1959**

Euskadi Ta Askatasuna (ETA; Basque Homeland and Freedom) is founded to fight for Basque independence. The terrorist group will murder more than 800 people before ending armed activity in 2011.

**1960s**

After two decades of extreme economic hardship, the decade becomes known as the *años de desarrollo* (years of development), with investment and rural immigrants flooding into Madrid and other cities.

**1975**

Franco dies and is succeeded by King Juan Carlos I. The monarch had been schooled by Franco to continue his policies but soon demonstrates his desire for change.

from the UN and NATO, and suffered a UN-sponsored trade boycott that helped turn the late 1940s into Spain's *años de hambre* (years of hunger). But with the onset of the Cold War, the US wanted bases in Spain, and Franco agreed to the establishment of four, in return for large sums of aid. In 1955 Spain was admitted to the UN.

## Franco's Spain

Franco ruled absolutely, never allowing any one powerful lobby – the Church, the army, the Movimiento Nacional (the only legal political party) or the bankers – to dominate. Regional autonomy aspirations were not tolerated, and minority languages such as Catalan were suppressed. The army provided many government ministers and enjoyed a most generous budget. And Catholic supremacy was fully restored.

In 1959 a new breed of technocrats in government, linked to the Catholic group Opus Dei, engineered a Stabilisation Plan, which brought an economic upswing. Spanish industry was modernised, transport was updated, and new dams provided irrigation and hydropower.

The recovery was funded in part by US aid and remittances from more than a million Spaniards who had gone to work abroad, but above all it was funded by tourism, which was developed initially along Andalucía's Costa del Sol and Catalonia's Costa Brava. By 1965 the number of tourists arriving in Spain was 14 million a year. These were the so-called *años de desarrollo* (years of development). Industry took off, foreign investment poured in, and the services and banking sectors blossomed. In 1960 fewer than 70,000 cars were on the road in Madrid. Ten years later, more than half a million clogged the capital's streets.

Spaniards' standard of living was improving, but the jails were full of political prisoners and large garrisons were still maintained outside every major city. From 1965 opposition to Franco's regime became steadily more vocal. The universities were scenes of repeated confrontation, and clandestine trade unions began to make themselves heard. In the Basque Country the terrorist group Euskadi Ta Askatasuna (ETA; Basque Homeland and Freedom) began to fight for Basque independence. Its first significant action outside the Basque Country was the 1973 assassination in Madrid of Admiral Carrero Blanco, Franco's prime minister and designated successor.

In what seemed like a safe bet, Franco then chose as his successor Prince Juan Carlos, the Spanish-educated grandson of Alfonso XIII. In 1969 Juan Carlos swore loyalty to Franco and the Movimiento Nacional. Cautious reforms by Franco's last prime minister, Carlos Arias Navarro, provoked violent opposition from right-wing extremists, and Spain seemed to be sinking into chaos when Franco died on 20 November 1975.

### Echoes of the Napoleonic Wars

- *Cabo de Trafalgar (Los Caños de Meca)*
- *Trafalgar Cemetery (Gibraltar)*
- *Museo de las Cortes de Cádiz (Cádiz)*
- *Xardín de San Carlos (A Coruña)*
- *Cementerio de la Florida (Madrid)*

**1976**

The king appoints Adolfo Suárez as prime minister. Suárez engineers a return to democracy. Left-wing parties are legalised, despite military opposition, and the country holds free elections in 1977.

**1978**

A new constitution, overwhelmingly approved by referendum, establishes Spain as a parliamentary democracy with no official religion and the monarch as official head of state.

**1981**

On 23 February a group of armed Guardia Civil led by Antonio Tejero attempts a coup by occupying the parliament building. The king denounces them on national TV; the coup collapses.

**1982–96**

Spain is governed by the centre-left PSOE, led by Felipe González. The country experiences an economic boom, but the government becomes increasingly associated with scandals and corruption.

## Democratic Spain

Spain's way forward was hard to discern on Franco's death. The country remained as divided as ever and at its helm was an untested Franco protégé. But again in Spanish history, not all was as it seemed.

### The Transition

Juan Carlos I, aged 37, took the throne on 22 November 1975, two days after Franco's death. The new king's links with the dictator inspired little confidence in a Spain now clamouring for democracy, but Juan Carlos had kept his cards close to his chest. In July 1976 he appointed Adolfo Suárez, a 43-year-old former Franco apparatchik with film-star looks, as prime minister. To general surprise, Suárez got the Cortes (parliament) to approve a new, two-chamber parliamentary system, and in 1977 political parties, trade unions and strikes were all legalised. Franco's Movimiento Nacional was abolished.

Suárez' centrist party, the Unión de Centro Democrático (UCD; Central Democratic Union), won nearly half the seats in the new Cortes in 1977. A new constitution in 1978 made Spain a parliamentary monarchy with no official religion. In response to a fever for local autonomy, principally in Catalonia, the Basque Country and Galicia, by 1983 the country was divided into 17 'autonomous communities' with their own regional governments controlling a range of policy areas. Personal and social life enjoyed a rapid liberation after Franco. Contraceptives, homosexuality and divorce were legalised, and the Madrid party and arts scene known as *la movida madrileña* formed the epicentre of a newly unleashed hedonism that still reverberates through Spanish life.

The Suárez government granted a general amnesty for deeds committed in the civil war and under the Franco dictatorship. There were no truth commissions or trials for the perpetrators of atrocities. For the next three decades, Spain cast barely a backward glance.

During the First Republic some Spanish cities declared themselves independent states, and some, such as Seville and nearby Utrera, even declared war on each other.

### A Maturing Democracy

The main left-of-centre party, the Partido Socialista Obrero Español (PSOE; Spanish Socialist Workers' Party), led by a charismatic young lawyer from Seville, Felipe González, came second in the 1977 election and then won power with a big majority in 1982. González was to be prime minister for 14 years. The PSOE's young and educated leadership came from the generation that had opened the cracks in the Franco regime in the late 1960s and early 1970s. Unemployment rose from 16% to 22% by 1986, but that same year, Spain joined the European Community (now the EU), bringing on a five-year economic boom. The middle class grew ever bigger, the PSOE established a national health system and improved public education, and women streamed into higher education and jobs.

Paul Preston's searing *The Spanish Holocaust: Inquisition and Extermination in Twentieth-Century Spain* lays bare the brutality of Spain's civil war (neither side comes out well) and the oppression by victorious Franco forces after the war.

**1986**

Spain joins the European Community (now the EU). Along with its membership of NATO since 1982, this is a turning point in the country's post-Franco international acceptance.

**1992**

Barcelona holds the Olympic Games, putting Spain in the international spotlight and highlighting the country's progress since 1975. Madrid is European Capital of Culture and Seville hosts a world expo.

**1996**

Disaffection with PSOE sleaze gives the centre-right Partido Popular (PP), led by José María Aznar, a general-election victory at the start of a decade of sustained economic growth.

**2004**

A terrorist bombing kills 191 people on 10 Madrid commuter trains. Three days later, the PSOE led by José Luis Rodríguez Zapatero sweeps to power and ushers in 7½ years of Socialist rule.

In 1992 – the 500th anniversary of the fall of Granada and Columbus' first voyage to the Americas – Spain celebrated its arrival in the modern world by staging the Barcelona Olympics and the Expo 92 world fair in Seville. The economy, however, was in a slump and the PSOE was mired in scandals. It came as no surprise when the PSOE lost the 1996 election.

The party that won the 1996 election was the centre-right Partido Popular (PP; People's Party), led by José María Aznar, a former tax inspector from Castilla y León. Aznar promised to make politics dull, and he did, but he presided over eight years of solid economic progress, winning the 2000 election as well. The PP cut public investment and sold off state enterprises, and liberalised sectors such as telecommunications; during the Aznar years Spain's economy grew a lot faster than the EU average, while unemployment fell dramatically.

## Turbulent Times

On 11 March 2004, Madrid was rocked by 10 bombs on four rush-hour commuter trains heading into the capital's Atocha station. When the

### LA MOVIDA

After the long, dark years of dictatorship and conservative Catholicism, Spaniards, especially those in Madrid, emerged onto the streets with all the zeal of ex-boarding-school teenagers as Spain returned to democracy in the late 1970s. Nothing was taboo in the phenomenon known as *la movida* (the scene) or *la movida madrileña* (the Madrid scene), as young Spaniards discovered the '60s, '70s and early '80s all at once. All-night partying was the norm, drug taking in public was not a criminal offence and Madrid in particular howled. Summer terraces roared to the chattering, drinking, carousing crowds, and young people from all over Europe flocked to join the revelry.

What was remarkable about *la movida* in Madrid is that it was presided over by Enrique Tierno Galván, an ageing former university professor who had been a leading opposition figure under Franco and was affectionately known throughout Spain as 'the old teacher'. A socialist, he became mayor in 1979 and, for many, launched *la movida* by telling a public gathering '*a colocarse y ponerse al loro*', which loosely translates as 'get stoned and do what's cool'. Unsurprisingly, he was Madrid's most popular mayor ever and when he died in 1986, a million *madrileños* turned out for his funeral.

*La movida* was also an explosion of creativity among the country's musicians, designers and film-makers. The most famous of these was director Pedro Almodóvar, whose riotously colourful films featured larger-than-life characters who pushed the limits of sex and drugs. Although his later films became internationally renowned, his first films, *Pepi, Luci, Bom y otras chicas del montón* (Pepi, Luci, Bom and the Other Girls; 1980) and *Laberinto de pasiones* (Labyrinth of Passion; 1982) are where the spirit of the movement really comes alive..

**2008**

Spain's unemployment rate soars from less than 6% to 12.3% in a single month. The finance minister admits that Spain has entered 'its deepest recession in half a century'.

**2010**

After decades of underachievement, Spain's national football team wins the World Cup for the first time, two years after its first European Championship trophy.

**2011**

The conservative Partido Popular, led by Mariano Rajoy, sweeps to power in national elections, announcing austerity measures to combat Spain's economic crisis.

**2014**

After a series of scandals that envelop the Spanish royal family, King Juan Carlos, who had reigned since 1975, abdicates and his son begins his reign as Felipe VI.

dust cleared, 191 people had died and 1755 were wounded, many of them seriously. Perpetrated by an Islamic group with links to Al-Qaeda, this was the biggest such terror attack in the nation's history.

Three days after the attack, in a stunning reversal of pre-poll predictions, the PP, which insisted that the ETA was responsible despite overwhelming evidence to the contrary, was defeated by the PSOE in elections. José Luis Rodríguez Zapatero's new socialist government gave Spain a makeover by introducing a raft of liberalising social reforms. Gay marriage was legalised, Spain's arcane divorce laws were overhauled, almost a million illegal immigrants were granted residence, and a law seeking to apportion blame for the crimes of the Spanish Civil War and Franco dictatorship entered the statute books. Although Spain's powerful Catholic Church cried foul, the changes played well with most Spaniards. Spain's economy was booming – the envy of Europe.

And then it all fell apart. Spain's economy went into free fall in late 2008 with the global credit crunch, the bursting of the country's property bubble, and the international slump. In an economy heavily dependent on tourism and construction, two exceptionally vulnerable industries during economic downturns, unemployment rose above 27% (six million people) by 2013, and catastrophic youth-unemployment rates nudged 60%. Young professionals fled the country in unprecedented numbers. A wave of anger at corruption and the political and financial elite spread across Spain, spearheaded by a protest movement known as *los indignados* ('the indignant ones'), who camped out in central Madrid for months.

In the elections of November 2011, Zapatero's PSOE was replaced by a PP government led by Mariano Rajoy that launched a deep austerity drive, cutting into the generous welfare state on which Spaniards had come to depend. Spanish banks were bailed out by the EU to the tune of €100 billion. The conservative government also turned back the liberalising reforms of the socialists, introducing some of Europe's strictest anti-abortion laws and restoring the role of the Catholic Church in education. In 2015 and 2016, a groundswell of popular anger from the years of economic crisis roiled Spanish politics, with two new anti-corruption parties – the radical, anti-austerity Podemos ('We Can') and the centrist, pro-business Ciudadanos (Citizens) – winning scores of seats in general elections. The PP eventually managed to form a minority government, but this came to a dramatic end in June 2018, when it was unseated by a parliamentary vote of no confidence. The vote followed the so-called Gürtel case, one of numerous long-running corruption cases that have embroiled Spanish political circles in recent years.

New prime minister Pedro Sánchez of the PSOE gave early signals of stability, but it turned out to be just the beginning of another turbulent period in Spanish politics. The next two years saw increased fragmentation

In the 12th century Córdoba, despite being past its caliphate golden age, produced the two most celebrated scholars of Al-Andalus: the Muslim Averroës (1126–98) and the Jewish Maimonides (1135–1204), multitalented men best known for their efforts to reconcile religious faith with Aristotelian reason.



### Films Set in Franco's Spain

*Pan's Labyrinth* (2006)

*The Spirit of the Beehive* (1973)

*¡Bienvenido, Mr Marshall!* (Welcome, Mr Marshall!; 1953)

*Las 13 rosas* (The 13 Roses; 2007)

**2015**

A political earthquake sweeps the country as new parties Podemos (left-wing) and Ciudadanos (centrist) make strong gains in the general election, leaving no single party or group of parties able to form a government.

**2016**

A new general election again fails to produce a clear winner; in October the PSOE abstains in a parliamentary confidence vote, allowing the Partido Popular to form a minority government.

**2017**

Catalonia declares independence from Spain following an October referendum deemed unconstitutional by Madrid. Spain's national government suspends Catalonia's regional autonomy.

**2018**

The Partido Popular is unseated by a parliamentary no-confidence vote following sentencing in the Gürtel corruption case. The PSOE forms a new minority government, with Pedro Sánchez as prime minister.

and polarisation, with two new national elections held in 2019. As 2020 began, the far-right Vox party had surged to hold 52 seats in the Congress of Deputies, while Pedro Sánchez's PSOE presided over a fragile coalition government with left-leaning Unidas Podemos.

## Constitutional Crisis in Catalonia

In 2015 an alliance of pro-independence parties, led by Carles Puigdemont, came to power in Catalonia, promising to hold a binding referendum on independence. Despite uncompromising opposition to such a referendum from the PP government in Madrid, and a judgement by Spain's constitutional court that it would be illegal, the referendum was held on 1 October 2017. Madrid sent in national police to try to prevent voting at some polling stations, resulting in some violent scenes. According to the Catalan government, 43% of the Catalonia electorate voted in the referendum, and 90% of those voted for independence.

In reaction to the referendum, a wave of support for Spanish national unity swept through much of Spain. Huge demonstrations, both for and against independence, took place in Barcelona (by most estimates slightly more than half the population of Catalonia opposed independence). On 27 October the Catalan parliament went ahead and declared Catalonia independent, prompting the national parliament in Madrid to invoke Article 155 of the Spanish Constitution, suspending Catalonia's regional autonomy and the Catalan parliament with it.

New Catalan elections in December 2017 saw separatist parties win a narrow majority in the regional parliament, though the Spanish government continued its direct rule over Catalonia for another seven months, finally restoring regional autonomy in June 2018.

Relations between Madrid and Barcelona hit another flashpoint in October 2019, when Spain's Supreme Court unanimously convicted nine former Catalan government officials – including former vice president Oriol Junqueras – of sedition and misappropriation of public funds for their role in the 2017 independence referendum. Sentences ranged from nine to 13 years, provoking massive protests, with hundreds of thousands taking to the streets of Barcelona. Despite calls from the Catalan president, Quim Torra, for talks with the Spanish government, Prime Minister Pedro Sánchez made it clear that he rejected any further discussion of Catalonian independence.

A new election in Catalonia in February 2021 saw separatist parties slightly increase their majority in the regional parliament and their leaders calling for another referendum. But with the national government opposed to this, and Catalonia's population still split on the independence issue, there was no obvious way out of the crisis. Meanwhile, Catalonia's ex-president Carles Puigdemont, who still faced Spanish charges of sedition, remained in self-imposed exile in Belgium, where he had fled in 2017.

**Modern Spain Reading**

*Ghosts of Spain* by Giles Tremlett

*The Nekingw Spaniards* by John Hooper

*Juan Carlos* by Paul Preston

*Roads to Santiago* by Cees Nooteboom

*Driving Over Lemons* by Chris Stewart

**2019**

Spain's Supreme Court sentences nine former Catalonian leaders to prison terms of nine to 13 years, charging them with sedition and misappropriation of funds for their role in Catalonia's independence movement.

**2019**

The Spanish government stirs controversy by exhuming Francisco Franco's remains, transferring them from the public basilica where he had laid buried since 1975 to a private crypt.

**2019**

Fledgling right-wing party Vox assumes a prominent minority role in Spain's government, finishing third in the November general election and claiming 52 seats in the country's Congress of Deputies.

**2020-21**

Spain confirms its first COVID-19 case on 31 January 2020. A year later the number of confirmed cases reaches 3 million, over 60,000 have died, and the country undergoes its third series of lockdowns.

# Art & Architecture

**Spain's artistic and architectural landscapes are among the richest in Europe. A star-studded lineage of painters – El Greco, Velázquez, Goya, Picasso, Miró, Dalí – is one of the country's cultural hallmarks, while Spain's architecture narrates the full sweep of its history, from glorious Moorish creations in Andalucía to soaring cathedrals to the singular imagination of Gaudí to wacky contemporary creativity.**

## Architecture

You can almost see centurions marching beneath the great Roman aqueduct in Segovia, while the Alhambra conjures up vivid images of Spain's Islamic era. Elsewhere, castles dot the countryside from Catalonia to Extremadura, the Middle Ages come alive amid Santo Domingo de Silos' Romanesque cloisters, and great Gothic cathedrals adorn Burgos, Palma de Mallorca and Toledo. And who in Barcelona isn't carried away by Gaudí's Modernista fantasies? Welcome to Spain, one of Europe's most intriguing architectural stories.

### The Introduction of Islam

By 784 CE, Córdoba was well established as the new capital of the Umayyads, who in 750 had been deposed as caliphs (supreme rulers) in Damascus by the Abbasids. Syrian architects set to work on the grand Mezquita, conjuring up their homeland with details that echoed the Umayyad Mosque in Damascus, such as delicate horseshoe arches and exquisite decorative tiles with floral motifs. But the building's most distinctive feature – more than 500 columns that crowd the mosque's interior – was repurposed from Roman and Visigothic ruins.

In the centuries that followed, Moorish architecture incorporated trends from all over the Islamic world. The technique of intricately carved stucco detailing was developed in 9th-century Iraq, while *muqarnas* (honeycomb) vaulting arrived via Egypt in the 10th century. Square minarets, such as the Giralda in Seville (now a cathedral tower), came with the Almohad invasion from Morocco in the 12th century.

The finest remnants of the Islamic era are in Andalucía, although the Aljafería in Zaragoza is a beautiful exception. Perhaps the most magnificent creation is the core of Granada's Alhambra, the Palacios Nazaríes (Nasrid Palaces). From the 13th to the 15th centuries, architects and artisans achieved new heights of elegance, creating a study in balance between inside and outside, light and shade, spareness and intricacy. Eschewing innovation, the Alhambra refined well-tried forms, as if in an attempt to freeze time and halt the collapse of Moorish power, which had already been pushed back to an area smaller than today's Andalucía.

**Roman Relics**

- *Segovia aqueduct*
- *Teatro Romano (Mérida)*
- *City walls (Lugo, Galicia)*
- *Museu d'Història de Tarragona (Catalonia)*
- *Itálica (Santiponce, near Seville)*
- *Baelo Claudia (Bolonia, Andalucía)*

### Hybrid Styles: Mozarabic & Mudéjar

By the 10th century, Moorish rule had produced a class of people called Mozarabs – practising Christians who lived in Islamic territory and spoke Arabic. When Mozarab artisans moved or travelled north into Christian Spain, they took elements of classic Islamic construction with them.

For example, the Monasterio de San Miguel de Escalada, east of León, imitates the Mezquita, with horseshoe arches atop leafy Corinthian capitals reused from Roman buildings. Many arches are boxed in by an *alfiz* (rectangular decorative frame) around the upper portion of the arch. This became a signature detail in Mozarabic architecture.

Only a few small parts of northern Spain were never conquered by the Muslims. In one of these, Asturias, a unique building style (known as pre-Romanesque) emerged during the 9th century, exaggerating Visigothic styles. Oviedo's Palacio de Santa María del Naranco, for instance, has dramatically elongated proportions, delicate relief carvings and tall, thin arches.

Later, as the Reconquista started to gain ground, another border-crossing class emerged: Mudéjars (Muslims who stayed on in now-Catholic parts of Spain). Mudéjar artisans, largely disenfranchised, offered cheap labour and great talent. The Mudéjar style, in evidence from the 12th century on, is notable first for the use of relatively inexpensive materials – gone were the days of lavish government commissions, and the Roman stones had all been used up. Instead, brick, tile and plaster were worked with incredible skill to conjure opulence. Teruel in Aragón in particular is dotted with intricate brick towers, trimmed in glazed tiles.

Another telltale Mudéjar feature is extravagantly decorated timber ceilings done in a style called *artesonado*. They can be barrel vaults, but the most typical style is a flat wood ceiling made of interlocking beams that are inset with multicoloured wood panels in geometric patterns.

## Romanesque & Gothic

In Spain, the Romanesque style moved with the Reconquista, taking root in part because it was the aesthetic opposite of Islamic fashions. Catalan architect and art historian Josep Puig i Cadafalch posited that each Romanesque detail was a systematic riposte to an Islamic one. These buildings were spare, angular and heavy, inspired by classical proportions.

Romanesque structures had perfectly semicircular arches. In churches, this was expressed in a semicylindrical apse (or, in many cases, triple apse), a shape previously found in Byzantine churches. The round arch also graced doorways, windows, cloisters and naves. Entrances supported stacks of concentric arches – the more eye-catching because they were often the only really decorative detail. The pilgrimage cathedral of Santiago de Compostela is arguably Spain's greatest Romanesque building; other examples include the Iglesia de San Martín in Frómista, and Taüll's Sant Climent de Taüll.

During the 12th century, Spanish architects began edging towards the Gothic style, as they added pointed arches and ribbed vaults. The cathedrals in Ávila, Sigüenza and Tarragona all display transitional elements. The trend elsewhere in Europe towards towering cathedrals made possible by the newfangled flying buttresses caught on in Spain by the 13th century, when the cathedrals at Burgos, León and Toledo were begun. Gothic is scattered liberally across Andalucía, where the Reconquista arrived just when the style was coming into fashion. The massive, mainly 15th-century, Gothic cathedral of Seville is one of the largest churches in the world. Most of the innumerable castles scattered across the country also went up in Gothic times – an extraordinary example is the sumptuous castle at Coca, not far from Segovia.

The Camino de Santiago was one of the chief avenues by which Romanesque architecture entered Spain, bringing such beauties as the Abadía de Santo Domingo de Silos, the smaller cloister in the Monasterio de las Huelgas in Burgos, and the cathedral itself in Santiago de Compostela.

The Isabelline Gothic look (inspired by the queen's fondness for Islamic exotica and heraldic imagery) is on display in Toledo's San Juan de los Reyes and the Capilla Real in Granada, where Isabel and her husband, Fernando, are buried. The Gothic fascination lasted into the 16th century, when there was a revival of pure Gothic, best exemplified in the new cathedral in Salamanca. The Segovia cathedral was the last, and possibly most pure, Gothic structure raised in Spain.

## Renaissance to Baroque

Arising from the pan-European Renaissance, the uniquely Spanish vision of plateresque drew partly on Italian styles and was also an outgrowth of Isabelline Gothic. It is so named because facade decoration was so ornate that it appeared wrought by *plateros* (silversmiths). To visit Salamanca, where the Spanish Renaissance first took root, is to receive a concentrated dose of the most splendid work in the genre.

A more purist Renaissance style, reflecting classical proportions and styles already established in Italy and France, prevailed in Andalucía, as seen in the Palacio de Carlos V in Granada's Alhambra. The Renaissance wild card was Juan de Herrera, whose work bears almost no resemblance to anything else of the period because it is so austere. His masterpiece is the palace-monastery complex of San Lorenzo de El Escorial.

Aside from the late-18th-century Cádiz cathedral, there are few from-scratch baroque buildings in Spain. But exuberant baroque decoration is so eye-catching that it easily overtakes the more sober earlier buildings to which it's usually attached. The leading exponents of this often overblown style were the Churriguera brothers, sons of a respected sculptor who specialised in *retablos*, enormous carved-wood altar backdrops.

The hallmark of Churrigueresque is the so-called Solomonic (or Salomonic) column, a delightful twisting pillar that, especially when covered in gold leaf or vines, seems to wiggle its way to the heavens. Later practitioners took the Churrigueras' innovations and ran with them. Leading examples of the Churrigueresque style are found in the Palacio de los Cepeda in Osuna; the Iglesia del Carmen in Antequera; Madrid's Antiguo Cuartel del Conde Duque; the Catedral Nueva, Plaza Mayor and Convento de San Esteban, all in Salamanca; the Església de Puig de Missa in Santa Eulària des Riu; the Catedral de Santiago de Compostela; and Toledo's Catedral.

**Best Baroque**

- *Monasterio de la Cartuja (Granada)*
- *Plaza Mayor (Salamanca)*
- *Santiago de Compostela cathedral west facade*
- *Catedral de Santa María (Murcia)*
- *Real Academia de Bellas Artes (Madrid)*

## Modernisme & Art Deco

At the end of the 19th century, Barcelona's prosperity unleashed one of the most imaginative periods in Spanish architecture. The architects at work here, who drew on prevailing art-nouveau trends as well as earlier Spanish styles, came to be called the Modernistas. Chief among them, Antoni Gaudí sprinkled Barcelona with jewels of his singular imagination. They range from his immense Sagrada Família (which is still being built) to the simply weird Casa Batlló and the only slightly more sober La Pedrera. Gaudí's structural approach owed much to the austere era of Catalan Gothic, which inspired his own inventive work with parabolic arches. The works of two other Catalan architects, Lluís Domènech i Montaner and Josep Puig i Cadafalch, are also Barcelona landmarks.

While Barcelona went all wavy, Madrid embraced the rigid glamour of art deco. This global style arrived in Spain just as Madrid's Gran Vía was laid out in the 1920s. One of the more overwhelming caprices from that era is the Palacio de Comunicaciones on Plaza de la Cibeles. The 1936–39 civil war and more than three decades of dictatorship brought such frivolities to an abrupt end.

Robert Hughes' *Barcelona* is a thorough, erudite history of the city, with an emphasis on architecture. The Gaudí chapters provide special insight into the designer's surprisingly conservative outlook.

## Contemporary Innovation

After Franco, Spain has made up for lost time and, particularly since the 1990s, the unifying theme appears to be that anything goes.

Local heroes include Santiago Calatrava, who built his reputation with swooping, bone-white bridges. In 1996 he designed Valencia's futuristic Ciudad de las Artes y las Ciencias complex, followed in 2000 by Bilbao's Sondika Airport, which has been nicknamed La Paloma (the Dove) for the winglike arc of its aluminium skin. Catalan Enric Miralles had a short career, but his Mercat de Santa Caterina in Barcelona shows brilliant colour and inventive use of arches. His Gas Natural building, also in Barcelona, is a poetic skyscraper that juts both vertically and horizontally. In 1996 Rafael Moneo won the Pritzker Prize, the greatest international honour for living architects, largely for his long-term contributions to Madrid's cityscape, such as the revamping of the Atocha railway station.

In the years since, Spain has become something of a Pritzker playground. It's perhaps this openness – even hunger – for outside creativity that marks the country's built environment today. Norman Foster designed the Bilbao metro system, completed in 1995; the transparent, wormlike staircase shelters have come to be called *fosteritos*. But it was Frank Gehry's 1998 Museo Guggenheim Bilbao that really sparked the quirky-building fever. Now the list of contemporary landmarks includes Jean Nouvel's spangly, gherkin-shaped Torre Glòries in Barcelona; Richard Rogers' dreamy, wavy Terminal 4 at Madrid's Barajas airport; and Jürgen Mayer's Metropol Parasol in Seville.

Though he predated the golden-age peak, the Cretan Doménikos Theotokópoulos, known as El Greco (The Greek; 1541–1614), ranks among Spain's great artists for his inspired, unconventional, colourful canvases populated by gaunt figures. See his highly recognisable work in the Museo del Prado and around Toledo, where he made his career.

# Art

Spain has an artistic legacy rivalling that of any country in Europe. In centuries past, this impressive portfolio (dominated by Goya and Velázquez, in particular) owed much to the patronage of Spanish kings, who lavished money upon the great painters of the day. In the 20th century, however, the true masters were relentlessly creative artists such as Pablo Picasso, Salvador Dalí and Joan Miró, all of whom thumbed their noses at the establishment and artistic convention.

## The Golden Century: Velázquez & Friends

The star of the 17th-century art scene, which became known as Spain's artistic golden age, was the genius court painter Diego Rodríguez de Silva Velázquez (1599–1660). Born in Seville, Velázquez later moved to Madrid as court painter and composed scenes (landscapes, royal portraits, religious subjects, snapshots of everyday life) that owe their vitality not only to his photographic eye for light, contrast and the details of royal finery, but also to a compulsive interest in the humanity of his subjects, who seem to breathe on the canvas. With Velázquez, any trace of the idealised stiffness that characterised the previous century's spiritless mannerism fell by the wayside. His masterpieces include *Las meninas* (Maids of Honour) and *La rendición de Breda* (Surrender of Breda), both in Madrid's Museo del Prado.

The mystically inclined Francisco de Zurbarán (1598–1664), a friend and contemporary of Velázquez, is best remembered for the startling clarity and light in his portraits of monks, a series of which hangs in Madrid's Real Academia de Bellas Artes de San Fernando, with other works in the Museo del Prado. Other masters of the era whose works hang in the Prado include José (Jusepe) de Ribera (1591–1652), who was influenced by Caravaggio and produced fine chiaroscuro works, and the Sevillan Bartolomé Esteban Murillo (1618–82), whose soft-focus beggar images and baroque Immaculate Conceptions struck a popular chord.

### Where to See Goya

- *Museo del Prado, Madrid*
- *Real Academia de Bellas Arts de San Fernando, Madrid*
- *Ermita de San Antonio de la Florida, Madrid*
- *Museo Goya, Zaragoza*
- *Museo del Grabado de Goya, Fuendetodos*
- *Basilica de Nuestra Señora del Pilar, Zaragoza*
- *Museo de Huesca, Huesca*

## Goya & the 19th Century

There was nothing in the provincial upbringing of Francisco José de Goya y Lucientes (1746–1828), who was born in a tiny village in Aragón, to suggest that he would become one of the towering figures of European art. Goya began his career as a cartoonist in the Real Fábrica de Tapices (Royal Tapestry Workshop) in Madrid. Illness in 1792 left him deaf; many critics speculate that his condition was largely responsible for his wild, often merciless style that would become increasingly unshackled from convention. By 1799 Goya was appointed Carlos IV's court painter.

Several distinct series and individual paintings mark his progress. In the last years of the 18th century he painted enigmatic masterpieces, such as *La maja vestida* (The Young Lady Dressed) and *La maja desnuda* (The Young Lady Undressed), identical portraits but for the lack of clothes in the latter. The Inquisition was not amused by the artworks, which it covered up. Nowadays all is bared in Madrid's Museo del Prado.

The arrival of the French and the war in 1808 profoundly impacted Goya. Unforgiving portrayals of the brutality of war include *El dos de mayo* (The Second of May) and, more dramatically, *El tres de mayo* (The Third of May). The latter depicts the execution of Madrid rebels by French troops.

Goya saved his most confronting paintings for the end. After he retired to the Quinta del Sordo (Deaf Man's House) in Madrid, he created the nightmarish *Pinturas negras* (Black Paintings), which now hang in Madrid's Museo del Prado. *Saturno devorando a su hijo* (Saturn Devouring His Son) captures the essence of Goya's genius, while *La romería de San Isidro* (The Pilgrimage to San Isidro) and *El akelarre* (*El gran cabrón;* The Great He-Goat) are profoundly unsettling, dominated as they are by the compelling individual faces of the condemned souls of Goya's creation.



## Picasso, Dalí & Miró

In the early years of the 20th century, the genius of the mischievous *malagueño* (Málaga native) Pablo Ruiz Picasso (1881–1973) came like a thunderclap. A teenager when he moved with his family to Barcelona, Picasso was formed in an atmosphere laden with the avant-garde freedom of Modernisme.

Picasso's work underwent repeated revolutions as he passed from one creative phase to another. From his gloomy Blue Period through the brighter Pink Period and on to cubism – in which he was accompanied by Madrid's Juan Gris (1887–1927) – Picasso was nothing if not surprising. Cubism, his best-known form, was inspired by his fascination with primitivism, primarily African masks and early Iberian sculpture. This highly complex form reached its peak in Picasso's *Guernica* (1937), but he continued cranking out paintings, sculptures, ceramics and etchings until the day he died. A good selection of his early work can be viewed in Barcelona's Museu Picasso, while the Museo Picasso Málaga has more than 200 Picasso works.

Every February, the Madrid exhibition centre IFEMA (www.ifema.es) hosts one of the world's major contemporary art fairs, named ARCOmadrid, with around 200 Spanish and international galleries participating.

Separated from Picasso by barely a generation, two other artists reinforced the Catalan contingent in the vanguard of 20th-century art: Dalí and Miró. Although he started off dabbling in cubism, Salvador Dalí (1904–89) became more readily identified with the surrealists. This complex character's 'hand-painted dream photographs', as he called them, are virtuoso executions brimming with fine detail and nightmare images dragged up from a feverish and Freud-fed imagination. Preoccupied with Picasso's fame, Dalí built himself a reputation as an outrageous showman and shameless self-promoter. The single best display of his work can be seen at the Teatre-Museu Dalí in Figueres, but you'll also find important works in Madrid's Centro de Arte Reina Sofía, and often in exhibitions at the Museu de Cadaqués, while the Casa Museu Dalí at nearby Port Lligat gives fascinating insight into the man's eccentric private life.

Slower to find his feet, Barcelona-born Joan Miró (1893–1983) developed a joyous and almost childlike style that earned him the epithet 'the most surrealist of us all' from the French writer André Breton. His later period is his best known, characterised by the simple use of bright colours and forms in combinations of symbols that represent women, birds (the link between earth and the heavens) and stars (the unattainable heavenly world, source of imagination). Barcelona's Fundació Joan Miró and the Fundació Pilar i Joan Miró in Palma de Mallorca are the pick of the places to see his work, with some further examples in Madrid's Centro de Arte Reina Sofía.

# People & Culture

**Spain's iconic forms of entertainment and public cultural expression capture the powerful passions of a nation. Flamenco is one of the world's most recognisable musical styles, an uplifting combination of sorrow and joy, while the controversial and quintessentially Spanish realm of bullfighting may leave you angry or spellbound but never indifferent. And then there's football, that obsession of a large proportion of the country's people. Put them all together and you'll find yourself looking through a window into the Spanish soul.**

## Flamenco

Flamenco's passion is clear to anyone who has heard its melancholic strains in the background of a crowded Spanish bar or during an uplifting live performance. At times flamenco can seem like an impenetrable world, but if you're lucky, you'll experience that uplifting moment when flamenco's raw passion and rhythm suddenly transport you to another place (known as *duende*), where joy and sorrow threaten to overwhelm you. If you do, you'll quickly become one of flamenco's lifelong devotees.

The traditional flamenco costumes – shawl, fan and long, frilly *bata de cola* (tail gown) for women, and flat Cordoban hat and tight black trousers for men – date from Andalucian fashions in the late 19th century.

### The Essential Elements

A flamenco singer is known as a *cantaor* (male) or *cantaora* (female); a dancer is a *bailaor* or *bailaora*. Most of the songs and dances are performed to a blood-rush of guitar from the *tocaor* or *tocaora* (male or female flamenco guitarist). Percussion is provided by tapping feet, clapping hands, the *cajón* (a box beaten with the hands) and sometimes castanets.

Flamenco *coplas* (songs) come in many types, from the anguished *soleá* or the intensely despairing *siguiriya* to the livelier *alegría* or the upbeat *bulería*. The first flamenco was *cante jondo* (deep song), an anguished instrument of expression for a group on the margins of society. *Jondura* (depth) is still the essence of pure flamenco.

### Birth of Flamenco

Flamenco's origins have been lost to time, but most musical historians agree that it probably dates back to a fusion of songs brought to Spain by the Roma people, with music and verses from North Africa crossing into medieval Muslim Andalucía.

Flamenco as we now know it first took recognisable form in the 18th and early 19th centuries among Roma people in the lower Guadalquivir valley in western Andalucía. The Seville, Jerez de la Frontera and Cádiz axis is still considered flamenco's heartland and it's here, purists say, that you'll encounter the most authentic flamenco experience.

For an entertaining journey into the modern legacy of Moorish Spain, read Jason Webster's *Andalus: Unlocking the Secrets of Moorish Spain*.

### Flamenco Legends

The great singers of the 19th and early 20th centuries were Silverio Franconetti and La Niña de los Peines, from Seville, and Antonio Chacón and Manuel Torre, from Jerez de la Frontera. Torre's singing, legend has it, could drive people to rip their shirts open and upturn tables.

After a trough in the mid-20th century, when it seemed that the *tablaos* (touristy flamenco shows emphasising the sexy and the jolly) were in danger of taking over, *flamenco puro* got a new lease of life in the 1970s through singers such as Terremoto, La Paquera, Enrique Morente, Chano Lobato and, above all, Camarón de la Isla (real name: José Monge Cruz), from San Fernando near Cádiz.

Paco de Lucía (1947–2014), from Algeciras, was the doyen of flamenco guitarists. In 1968 he began flamenco's most exciting partnership, with his friend Camarón de la Isla; together they recorded nine classic albums. De Lucía would go on to transform the flamenco guitar into an instrument of solo expression with new techniques, scales, melodies and harmonies that have gone far beyond traditional limits.

### Top Flamenco Festivals

*Festival de Jerez, Jerez de la Frontera*

*Suma Flamenca, Madrid*

*Noche Blanca del Flamenco, Córdoba*

*Bienal de Flamenco, Seville*

## Flamenco Today

Rarely can flamenco have been as popular as it is today, and never so innovative.

Singer José Mercé (b 1955) from Jerez is universally acclaimed. Estrella Morente from Granada (Enrique Morente's daughter and internationally best known for being the 'voice' behind the 2006 film *Volver*) and Miguel Poveda from Barcelona (b 1973) are younger singers who have already carved out niches in the first rank of performers. Grammy Award–winning singer Rosalía (b 1993) is another rising star, who has regularly woven flamenco influences into her pop repertoire.

Dance, often the readiest of flamenco arts to cross boundaries, has reached its most adventurous horizons in the person of Joaquin Cortés, born in Córdoba in 1969. Seemingly indefatigable, Cortés fuses flamenco with contemporary dance, ballet and jazz in spectacular shows all over the world, with music at rock-concert amplification. Top-rank, more purist dancers include Sara Baras, who performs internationally with her own company, and Antonio Canales.

Among guitarists, listen out for Manolo Sanlúcar from Cádiz, as well as Vicente Amigo from Córdoba and Moraíto Chico from Jerez, who both accompany today's top singers, and rising star from Málaga Daniel (Dani) Casares (b 1980).

### Flamenco Playlist

*Camarón de la Isla, La leyenda del tiempo (1979)*

*Pata Negra, Blues de la frontera (1987)*

*Paco de Lucía, Antología (1995)*

*Chambao, Flamenco chill (2002)*

*Diego El Cigala & Bebo Valdés, Lágrimas negras (2003)*

*Paco de Lucía, Cositas buenas (2004)*

*Enrique Morente, Sueña la Alhambra (2005)*

*Diego El Cigala, Indestructible (2016)*

*Rosalía, Los Angeles (2017)*

## Seeing Flamenco

The intensity and spontaneity of flamenco have never translated well onto CDs or studio recordings. Instead, to raise the goosebumps and inspire the powerful emotional spirit known to aficionados as *duende,* you have to be there.

Flamenco is easiest to catch in Seville, Jerez de la Frontera, Granada and Madrid. The best places for live performances are generally *peñas* (clubs where flamenco fans band together). The atmosphere in such places is authentic and at times very intimate, proof that flamenco feeds off an audience that knows its stuff. Most Andalucian towns have several *peñas,* and many tourist offices – especially those in Seville, Jerez de la Frontera and Cádiz – have lists of those that are open to visitors.

More easily accessible but pricier are the *tablaos* (restaurants where flamenco is performed); expect to pay €20 to €35 just to see the show. The admission price usually includes a drink, but you pay extra for further drinks or meals that aren't always worth the money. For that reason, it's recommended that you eat elsewhere and simply pay for the show (having bought tickets in advance). The other important thing to remember is that most of these shows are geared towards tourists. That's not to say that the quality isn't often top-notch – on the contrary, often it's magnificent, spine-tingling stuff – it's just that the shows sometimes lack the genuine, raw emotion of spontaneous flamenco.

Local bars are your best bet to see flamenco on the cheap, although the music and dancing in these places is sometimes more akin to mad jamming sessions than authentic *cante jondo*. Entry is usually free as long as you buy a drink. Well-known flamenco neighbourhoods, such as Triana in Seville and Santiago in Jerez, have a multitude of bars and are known as places where dancers and musicians come together to talk, drink and, if you're lucky, perform.

Flama (www.guiaflama.com) is a good resource for upcoming live flamenco concerts, festivals and background information.

Festivals are another place to see fabulous live flamenco, with flamenco festivals attracting the finest artists in the genre.

## Football

Watching *fútbol* seems to be many a Spaniard's main hobby. Hundreds of thousands of fans attend the games in the *primera división* (first division) of La Liga (the League) every weekend from September to May, with millions more following the games on TV.

Spain's La Liga is one of the world's best football leagues, and almost any match is worth attending, if only to experience the Spanish crowd. Unlike in the UK and elsewhere, Spanish football stadiums are extraordinarily one-sided places, with very few travelling fans, but the atmosphere can be electric.

Matches between eternal rivals Real Madrid and FC Barcelona – this fixture is known as El Clásico – stir even greater passions, not just because they are Spain's two biggest clubs but also because of the political relationship between Catalonia and Spain's central government. These two clubs have something approaching a duopoly on the silverware: between them they had carried off the league title 59 times by 2019 – Real Madrid 33 times, Barcelona 26. Barça, inspired by Argentine superstar and six-time Ballon d'Or winner Lionel Messi, has enjoyed a dream run since the mid-2000s, winning La Liga in 10 out of the 15 years from 2005 to 2019. And its domination spread beyond Spain's borders: in 2009 FC Barcelona became the first team ever to win all six major football titles open to it (La Liga, Copa del Rey, Supercopa de España, Champions League, UEFA Super Cup and the FIFA Club World Cup).

Real Madrid has been giving Barça more of a run for its money of late, and it remains the most successful club in European history, having won the UEFA Champions League and its predecessor the European Cup a record 13 times, including in 2014, 2016, 2017 and 2018. Barcelona has won this title five times.

While other clubs struggle to keep pace, Atlético de Madrid, Madrid's second team and Spain's third most successful club, has enjoyed something of a revival in recent years. In 2018 it won the UEFA Europa League title and went on to claim the UEFA Super Cup by defeating cross-city rival Real Madrid. Its La Liga title in 2014 was its 10th, and in 2014 and 2016 it reached the UEFA Champions League final, only to lose to Real Madrid on both occasions – in 2016 in a penalty shootout.

Other leading football clubs include Valencia (which last won the league in 2004), Athletic Bilbao (1984 – but with 23 victories in the Copa del Rey, the Spanish Cup, it ranks second to Barcelona), Real Sociedad of San Sebastián (1982) and Sevilla (1946). Although winning few domestic trophies, Sevilla has won UEFA's secondary competition, the Europa League, a record five times, including in 2014, 2015, 2016 and 2020.

## Bullfighting

An epic drama of blood and heroism or a cruel form of torture that has no place in modern Europe? The only thing certain is that bullfighting remains one of Spain's most enduring and controversial traditions.

## LAND OF MANY LANGUAGES

Many of Spain's quintessential cultural expressions – from flamenco to the Spanish language itself – are rooted in the central sweep of territory between the country's Castilian heartland and the sunny Andalucian south. But explore around the edges and you'll discover millions of people who speak one of Spain's three other official languages – Catalan, Gallego and Basque – each with its own associated culture, history and identity.

### Catalan

Inhabiting an area much vaster than their namesake region of Catalonia, Spain's Catalan speakers number more than nine million – with historical, geographical and linguistic ties to southern France as much as to the Iberian Peninsula. A Romance language whose origins date back more than 1000 years, Catalan (together with its main variant, Valenciano) is closely related to Provençal French. It's spoken throughout northeastern Spain, from the Pyrenees and the French border 500km down the coast to Valencia, and across the Mediterranean to the Balearic Islands and Sardinia (Italy).

Catalan speakers have a variety of unique cultural traditions. Among the quirkiest are the human pyramids known as *castells,* seen at festivals from Barcelona to Valencia to the Balearic Islands and formed by people standing on each other's shoulders to create towers reaching up to 10 levels high. Equally memorable is Barcelona's Diada de Sant Jordi (23 April), a springtime tradition that fills Barcelona's streets with flower vendors, book stalls and couples regaling each other with books and roses. Two months later, the Fogueres de Sant Joan celebrates the summer solstice with fireworks and the ancient tradition of jumping over bonfires. Come Christmastime, keep your eyes open for the lovable *caganer* (pooper), a peculiar figurine that can be found...yes, taking a poop! – somewhere in the corner of every Catalonian nativity scene.

### Gallego

Up in Spain's far northwestern corner, the verdant coastline of Galicia is rich in Celtic cultural influences, from ancient *pallozas* (round stone huts) to pagan-derived festivals to music played on the *gaita* (bagpipes). Gazing north towards Ireland and Wales, Galicia is more reminiscent of Gaelic lands than of the sun-drenched landscapes you'd expect in Spain – and the language here reflects this, with 100 different words for gradations of drizzle and rain. The lingua franca of Galicia's three million people is *gallego,* a Romance language closely related to Portuguese, with a kooky writing system that transforms the Spanish 'j' into 'x' (as in Xurxo, the *gallego* equivalent of Jorge or George). For a full immersion in Galicia's uncommon culture, set off on the pilgrimage route to Santiago de Compostela or attend one of the region's Celtic music festivals (p554).

### Basque

Straddling the Pyrenees and the Atlantic coast near Spain's border with southwestern France, the Basque Country is home to one of Europe's most ancient peoples. Spain's 700,000 native Basques speak a language unrelated to anything else on the continent – or the planet, for that matter. The Basques' unusual name for their language – Euskera – and its unique system of orthography reflect its status as a linguistic isolate without Indo-European roots. Basque customs (p444), like the language, go way back, and a strong but peaceful sense of nationalism prevails here. You'll often see banners, posters and signs emblazoned with the words 'Euskal Herriak Independentzia' (Basque Country Independence).

## The Basics

As a rule, in a professional *corrida* (bullfight) three different matadors will fight two bulls each. Each fight takes about 20 minutes. The *matador* (literally, 'killer') – more often called the *torero* (bullfighter) in Spanish – is the leader of the team, adorned in a glittering *traje de luces* (suit of lights). A complex series of events takes place in each clash. *Peones* (the matador's 'footmen') dart about with grand capes in front of the bull to test its strength; horseback picadors drive lances into the bull's withers; and *banderilleros* (flagmen) charge headlong at the bull in an attempt to stab its neck. Finally, when the bull seems tired out, the matador, facing the animal head-on, aims to sink a sword cleanly into its neck for an instant kill – the *estocada*. A skilful, daring performance followed by a clean kill will have the crowd on its feet, perhaps waving handkerchiefs in an appeal to the fight president to award the matador an ear of the animal.

Bullfights are bloody spectacles, involving considerable pain and distress for the animals involved. The bull's back and neck are repeatedly pierced by lances and harpoon-like prods, and the bull gradually becomes weakened through blood loss before the matador delivers the final sword thrust. If this is done with precision, the bull dies instantly – but if the coup de grâce is not delivered accurately, the animal sometimes dies an excruciatingly slow death.

## The Bullfighting Debate

While bullfighting remains strong in some parts of Spain, notably Andalucía, Madrid and the two Castillas, it has never been such a strong part of local culture in northern areas such as Galicia, Asturias and Catalonia. Bullfighting has even been banned in the Canary Islands, Catalonia and the Balearic Islands – though courts in the latter two regions later lifted the prohibition.

A recent national opinion poll found that only 19% of Spaniards aged between 16 and 65 supported bullfighting, while 58% opposed it. Among 16- to 24-year-olds, the level of support was just 7%. The number of bullfights in Spanish bullrings has fallen dramatically, from 3651 in 2007 to 1521 in 2018, according to government figures. There has, however, been a rise in the number of cheaper-to-organise *festejos populares* – other events involving varying degrees of bull torment, such as Pamplona-style bullrunning through the streets, *toros ensogados* (pulling bulls around by ropes tied to their horns) and *toros embolados* (setting fire to bunches of inflammable material attached to bulls' horns). Nearly 18,000 such events took place in 2018.

The anti-bullfighting movement in Spain has grown steadily during the 21st century, but the pro-bullfighting lobby is also strong, and politicians and public figures, including King Felipe VI, continue to glorify bullfighting as a centrepiece of Spain's cultural heritage. Large anti-bullfighting demonstrations happen regularly in Madrid, but there have also been pro-bullfighting demonstrations.

That there is a debate at all about the morality of bullfighting owes much to Spain's growing integration with the rest of Europe. Much of the anti-bullfighting impetus has come from groups beyond Spanish shores, among them PETA (www.peta.org.uk) and World Animal Protection (www.worldanimalprotection.org.uk). But homegrown Spanish anti-bullfighting, pro-animal-rights organisations are increasingly active, including a political party, PACMA (www.pacma.es), which won 328,000 votes in the 2019 general elections; the parliamentary grouping APDDA (www.apdda.es); the vets-against-bullfighting association AVATMA (http://avatma.org); and the animal-rights NGO ADDA (www.addaong.org).

# Survival Guide

# Directory A–Z

## Accessible Travel

Spain is not overly accommodating for travellers with disabilities, but things are slowly changing. For example, disabled access to some museums, official buildings and hotels represents a change in local thinking. In major cities, more is slowly being done to facilitate disabled access to public transport and taxis; in some cities, wheelchair-adapted taxis are called 'Eurotaxis'. Newly constructed hotels in most areas of Spain are required to have wheelchair-adapted rooms. With older places, you need to be a little wary of hotels that advertise themselves as being disabled-friendly, as this can mean as little as wide doors to rooms and bathrooms, or other token efforts.

Some tourist offices – notably those in Madrid and Barcelona – offer guided tours of the city for travellers with disabilities.

**Inout Hostel** (☎93 280 09 85; www.inouthostel.com; Major del Rectoret 2; dm €22-33; @ 📶 🏊; 🚆FGC Baixador de Vallvidrera) 🌿 Worthy of a special mention is Barcelona's Inout Hostel, which is completely accessible for those with disabilities, and nearly all the staff who work there have disabilities of one kind or another. The facilities and service are first class.

**Museo Tifológico** (Museum for the Blind; ☎91 589 42 19; http://museo.once.es; Calle de la Coruña 18; ⏰10am-3pm & 4-7pm Tue-Fri, 10am-2pm Sat, closed 2nd part of Aug; Ⓜ Estrecho) FREE This attraction is specifically for people who are visually impaired. Run by the Organización Nacional de Ciegos Españoles (National Organisation for the Blind, ONCE), its exhibits (all of which may be touched) include paintings, sculptures and tapestries, as well as more than 40 scale models of world monuments, including Madrid's Palacio Real and Cibeles fountain, as well as La Alhambra in Granada and the aqueduct in Segovia. It also provides leaflets in Braille and audio guides to the museum.

### PRACTICALITIES

**Weights & Measures** The metric system is used.

**Smoking** Banned in all enclosed public spaces.

**Newspapers** The three main newspapers are the centre-left *El País* (www.elpais.com), centre-right *El Mundo* (www.elmundo.es) and right-wing *ABC* (www.abc.es); the widely available *International New York Times* includes an eight-page supplement of articles from *El País* translated into English, or check out www.elpais.com/elpais/inenglish.html.

**Radio** Radio Nacional de España (RNE; www.rtve.es/radio) has Radio 1, with general interest and current-affairs programs; Radio 5, with sport and entertainment; and Radio 3, with a varied mix of music. Stations covering current affairs include the left-leaning Cadena Ser (www.cadenaser.com) and the right-wing COPE (www.cope.es). The most popular commercial pop and rock stations are Los 40 (www.los40.com), Kiss FM (www.kissfm.es), Cadena 100 (www.cadena100.es) and Onda Cero (www.ondacero.es).

**TV** National channels are the state-run Televisión Española (TVE1 and La 2) and the independent Antena 3, Tele 5, Cuatro and La Sexta. Regional governments run local stations, such as Madrid's Telemadrid, Catalonia's TV-3 and Canal 33 (both in Catalan), Galicia's TVG, the Basque Country's ETB-1 and ETB-2 and Andalucía's Canal Sur.

## Organisations

**Madrid Accesible** (Accessible Madrid; www.esmadrid.com/madrid-accesible) Your first stop for information on accessibility for travellers in Madrid should be this tourism-focused website, where you can download a PDF of the excellent *Guía Madrid Accesible* in English or Spanish. It has an exhaustive list of the city's attractions and transport and a detailed assessment of their accessibility, as well as a list of accessible restaurants. Most tourist offices in Madrid have a *mapa turístico accesible* in Spanish, English and French.

**Barcelona Turisme Accesible** (www.barcelona-access.cat) Website devoted to making Barcelona accessible for visitors with a disability. Offers information on barrier-free hotels, museums and beaches adapted to disabled visitors, wheelchair-accessible and sign language tours, and more.

**COCEMFE** (www.cocemfe.es) Spanish NGO offering a wide range of services and support to people with physical disabilities, from accessible tourism to education, training, employment and legal assistance.

**ONCE** (Organización Nacional de Ciegos Españoles; ☎91 577 37 56, 91 532 50 00; www.once.es; Calle de Prim 3; Ⓜ Chueca, Colón) The Spanish association for those who are blind. You may be able to get hold of guides in Braille to Madrid, although they're not published every year.

**Accessible Spain Travel** (www.accessiblespaintravel.com; Pujades 152, 3-1, Barcelona) Organises accessible tours, transport and accommodation throughout Spain for travellers with limited mobility.

**Society for Accessible Travel & Hospitality** (www.sath.org) A good resource, which gives advice on how to travel with a wheelchair, kidney disease, sight impairment or deafness.

## Transport

Madrid and Barcelona's metro systems have both taken great strides in recent years to improve accessibility. Stations built or upgraded since the late 1990s generally have elevators and other facilities for wheelchair users, though the older lines can still be ill-equipped. For full details, see www.metromadrid.es/en/accessibility and www.tmb.cat/en/barcelona/accessibility-mobility-reduced.

The single-deck *piso bajo* (low floor) buses are now commonplace in most Spanish cities. They have no steps inside and in some cases have ramps that can be used by people in wheelchairs.

If you call any taxi company and ask for a 'Eurotaxi' you should be sent one adapted for wheelchair users.

### ACCESSIBLE TRAVEL ONLINE RESOURCES

Download Lonely Planet's free *Accessible Travel* guides from http://shop.lonelyplanet.com/categories/accessible-travel.com.

# Accommodation

## Seasons

What constitutes low or high season depends on where and when you're looking. Most of the year is high season in Barcelona and Madrid, especially during trade fairs that you're unlikely to know about. August can be dead in the cities, but high season along the coast. Winter is peak season in the ski resorts of the Pyrenees and low season along the coast (indeed, many coastal towns largely shut down between November and Easter).

Weekends are high season for boutique hotels and *casas rurales* (rural homes), but low season for business hotels (which often offer generous specials) in Madrid and Barcelona.

## Reservations

Reserving a room is always recommended in the high season. Finding a place to stay without booking ahead in July and August along the coast can be difficult and many places require a minimum stay of at least two nights during high season. Always check out hotel websites for discounts.

Although there's usually no need to book ahead for a room in the low or shoulder season (Barcelona is a notable exception), booking ahead is usually a good idea, if for no other reason than to avoid a wearisome search for a room. Most places will ask for a credit-card number or will hold the room for you until 6pm, unless you have provided credit-card details as security or you have let them know that you'll be arriving later.

Online booking services such as Airbnb (www.airbnb.com) offer a range of accommodation types, from apartments and houses to private rooms in somebody's house.

## Prices

Accommodation in Spain can be outrageously good value by European standards. All deals are off, however, during

### BOOK YOUR STAY ONLINE

For more accommodation reviews by Lonely Planet authors, check out www.lonelyplanet.com/spain/hotels. You'll find independent reviews, as well as recommendations on the best places to stay. Best of all, you can book online.

big festivals, when prices skyrocket – sometimes quadrupling (or more) during major events such as Pamplona's Sanfermines (San Fermín) festival.

At the lower end of the budget category, there are dorm beds (from around €15 per person) in hostels or private rooms with shared bathrooms in the corridor. If you're willing to pay a few euros more, there are many budget places, usually *hostales* (family-run, small-scale budget hotels), with good, comfortable rooms and private bathrooms. In relatively untouristed or rural areas, the prices of some boutique or other hotels can sometimes drop into the budget category, especially during low season.

Spain's midrange hotels are generally excellent; you should always have your own private bathroom, and breakfast is sometimes included in the room price. Boutique hotels, including many that occupy artistically converted historical buildings, largely fall into this category and are almost always excellent choices.

Top-end hotels range from stunning, character-filled temples of good taste to reliably luxurious international chains.

And a final word about terminology. An *habitación doble* (double room) is frequently just that: a room with two beds (which you can often shove together). If you want to be sure of a double bed *(cama matrimonial)*, ask for it!

## Accommodation Types

### HOTELS

Spain's *hoteles* run the gamut of quality, from straightforward roadside places, bland but clean, through to charming boutique gems and on to super-luxurious hotels. Even in the cheapest hotels, rooms are likely to have an attached bathroom and there will probably be a restaurant or, at the very least, a breakfast room.

Among the more tempting hotels for those with a little fiscal room to manoeuvre are the 90 or so *paradores*, a state-funded chain of hotels in often stunning locations, including towering castles and former medieval convents. Similarly, you can find beautiful hotels in restored country homes and old city mansions, and these are not always particularly expensive.

A raft of cutting-edge, hip design hotels with cool staff and a New York feel can be found in the big cities and major resort areas. At the top end you may pay more for a room with a view – especially sea views or with a *balcón* (balcony) – and you will often have the option of a suite.

Many places have rooms for three, four or more people where the per-person cost is lower than in a single or double, which is good news for families.

Many of the agencies listed under Apartments, Villas & Casas Rurales (p883) also have a full portfolio of hotels.

### CAMAS, FONDAS & HOSPEDAJES

At the budget end of the market, the most basic – and increasingly rare – accommodations are places advertising *camas* (beds), *fondas* (simple, traditional inns) and *casas de huéspedes* or *hospedajes* (guesthouses). These bare-bones lodgings generally have shared bathrooms, although if you're lucky you may get an in-room *lavabo* (washbasin). In winter you may need to ask for extra blankets.

### PENSIONES

A *pensión* is usually a small step up from the *camas, fondas* and *hospedajes* in standard and price. While amenities are simple, many *pensiones* are charming, family-run places with clean rooms and willing service.

### HOSTALES

*Hostales* are a step up from *pensiones* and operate as simple, small hotels. You'll find them everywhere across the country, and the better ones can be bright and spotless, with rooms boasting full en-suite bathrooms – *baño privado*, most often with a *ducha* (shower) rather than a bathtub – and usually a TV, air-conditioning and/or heating.

### HOSTELS

Spain has more than 350 hostels. These are often the cheapest places for lone travellers, but two people can usually get a better double room elsewhere for a similar price.

The hostel experience in Spain varies widely. Some

**SLEEPING PRICE RANGES**

The following price ranges refer to a double room with private bathroom in high season:

**€** less than €65

**€€** €65–€140

**€€€** more than €140

The price ranges for Madrid, Barcelona, Ibiza and Mallorca are inevitably higher:

**€** less than €75

**€€** €75–€200

**€€€** more than €200

older, more institutional hostels are only moderate value, lacking in privacy, often heavily booked by school groups, and with no cooking facilities (though some may have a cafeteria). Others, however, are conveniently located, open 24 hours and composed mainly of small dorms, sometimes with a private bathroom. An increasing number have rooms adapted for people with disabilities. Some even occupy fine historic buildings.

Prices at most hostels depend on the season, and vary from about €15 to €30. In some hostels the price includes breakfast. A few hostels require you to rent sheets (around €2 to €5 for your stay) if you don't have your own or a sleeping bag.

Spain's largest and oldest hostel network, the **Red Española de Albergues Juveniles** (www.reaj.com), is geared towards the country's youth market. REAJ hostels generally require you to have a HI card or a membership card from your home country's hostel association; you can obtain a HI card on the spot at most Spanish hostels.

Generally more appealing for foreign travellers are hostel-style places not connected with HI or REAJ. These have individual rooms as well as the more typical dormitory options. A good resource for seeking out hostels, affiliated or otherwise, is **Hostelworld** (www.hostelworld.com).

Yet another category of budget accommodation are the hundreds of independent *albergues* (hostels) catering to walkers and cyclists along the various branches of the Camino de Santiago (p48). These generally offer basic dormitory accommodation for around €6 to €12; many now have more expensive private rooms as well. As a general rule, *albergues* run by municipal or regional governments are cheaper and more basic than privately run establishments.

## HISTORIC LUXURY: STAYING IN SPAIN'S PARADORES

Sleeping like a king has never been easier than in Spain's *paradores* – a chain of several dozen state-run hotels founded by King Alfonso XIII in the 1920s. Often palatial and always supremely comfortable, **paradores** (☎91 374 25 00; www.parador.es) are scattered across the country, with many housed in former castles, palaces, monasteries and convents. Ranking among Europe's most atmospheric sleeping experiences, many are sited on prime real estate – like inside the grounds of Granada's Alhambra (p713) – and prices are more reasonable than you might imagine, especially if you book online and far in advance. It's a wonderful way to experience the country's lavish past without the five-star price tag.

### REFUGIOS

*Refugios* (hostels) for walkers and climbers are liberally scattered around most of the popular mountain areas (especially the Pyrenees), except in Andalucía, which has only a handful. They're mostly run by mountaineering and walking organisations. Accommodation, usually bunks squeezed into a dorm, is sometimes on a first-come, first-served basis, although for most *refugios* you can now book ahead. During busy seasons, *refugios* fill up quickly; you may need to book several months in advance to be sure of a place during July, August, Semana Santa (Holy Week) and *puentes* (long holiday weekends). Prices per person range from nothing to €15 or more a night. Many *refugios* have a bar and offer meals (dinner typically costs €10 to €16), as well as a cooking area (but no cooking equipment). Blankets are usually provided, but you'll have to bring your own bedding (sheets or sleeping bag) or rent it at the *refugio*. Bring a torch too.

The Pyrenees are particularly well served with *refugios;* check out the following:

**Albergues & Refugios de Aragón** Information and reservations for Aragon's *refugios* and *albergues*.

**Catalan Pyrenees** For info and bookings at *refugios* in the Pyrenees of Catalonia, check out the Federació d'Entitats Excursionistes da Catalunya (FEEC; www.feec.cat), the Centre Excursionista de Catalunya (CEC; www.cec.cat) and La Central de Refugis (www.lacentralderefugis.com).

### APARTMENTS, VILLAS & CASAS RURALES

Throughout Spain you can rent self-catering apartments and houses from one night upwards. Villas and houses are widely available on the main holiday coasts and in popular country areas.

A simple one-bedroom apartment in a coastal resort for two or three people might cost as little as €40 per night, although more often you'll be looking at nearly twice that much, and prices jump even further in high season. More luxurious options with a swimming pool might come in at anything between €200 and €400 for four people.

Rural tourism has become immensely popular, with accommodation available in many new and often charming *casas rurales*. These are usually comfortably renovated village houses or farmhouses with a handful of rooms – check whether you're renting a room or the whole house (which is more common). They often go by other names, such as *cases de pagès* in Catalonia, *agroturismos* in the Basque Country and the Balearics, *casas de aldea* in Asturias, *posadas* and *casonas* in Cantabria and so on. Some just provide rooms, while others offer meals or self-catering accommodation. Lower-end prices typically hover around €30/50 for a single/double per night, but classy boutique establishments can easily charge €100 or more for a double. Many are rented out by the week. Agencies include the following:

**Associació Agroturisme Balear** (www.rusticbooking.com)

**Casas Cantabricas** (www.casas.co.uk)

**Cases Rurals a Catalunya** (www.casesrurals.com)

**Escapada Rural** (www.escapadarural.com)

**Fincas 4 You** (http://en.fincas4you.com)

**HomeAway** (www.homeaway.co.uk)

**James Villa Holidays** (www.jamesvillas.co.uk)

**Ruralka** (www.ruralka.com)

**Rustic Rent** (www.rusticrent.com)

**Rusticae** (www.rusticae.es)

**Secret Places** (www.secretplaces.com)

**Top Rural** (www.toprural.com)

**Traum Ferienwohnungen** (www.traum-ferienwohnungen.de)

**Vintage** (www.vintagetravel.co.uk)

## CAMPING & CARAVAN PARKS

Spain has around 1000 officially graded *campings* (camping grounds). Some of these are well located in woodland or near beaches or rivers, but others are on the outskirts of towns or along highways. Few of them are near city centres, and camping isn't particularly convenient if you're relying on public transport. Tourist offices can always direct you to the nearest camping ground. Campsites are officially rated as 1st class (1ªC), 2nd class (2ªC) or 3rd class (3ªC). There are also some that are not officially graded, usually equivalent to 3rd class. Facilities generally range from reasonable to very good, although any campground can be crowded and noisy at busy times (especially July and August). Even a 3rd-class camping ground is likely to have hot showers, electrical hook-ups and a cafe. The best ones have heated swimming pools, supermarkets, restaurants, laundry service, children's playgrounds and tennis courts.

Campsites usually charge per person, per tent and per vehicle – typically €5 to €10 for each. Children usually pay less than adults. Many camping grounds close from around October to Easter. You occasionally come across a *zona de acampada* or *área de acampada*, a country campground with minimal facilities (maybe just tap water or a couple of barbecues), little or no supervision and little or no charge. If it's in an environmentally protected area, you may need to obtain permission from the local environmental authority to camp there. With certain exceptions – such as many beaches and environmentally protected areas and a few municipalities that ban it – it is legal to camp outside camping grounds (but not within 1km of official ones). Signs usually indicate where wild camping is not allowed. If in doubt, you can always check with tourist offices. You'll need permission to camp on private land.

Useful websites:

**Campings Online** (www.campingsonline.com/espana) Booking service.

**Campinguía** (www.campinguia.com) Comments (mostly in Spanish) and links.

**Guía Camping** (www.guiacampingfecc.com) Online version of the annual *Guía Camping* (€16) published by the Federación Española de Clubes Campistas (FECC; Federation of Spanish Camping Grounds), available in bookshops around the country.

## MONASTERIES

An offbeat possibility is staying in a monastery. In spite of the expropriations of the 19th century and a sometimes rough run in the 20th, numerous monastic orders have survived across the country. Some offer rooms to outsiders – often fairly austere monks' or nuns' cells.

Monastery accommodation is generally a single-sex arrangement, and the idea in quite a few is to seek refuge from the outside world and indulge in quiet contemplation and meditation. On occasion, where the religious order continues ancient tradition by working on farmland, orchards and/or vineyards, you may have the opportunity (or there may be the expectation) to work, too.

### EATING PRICE RANGES

The following price ranges refer to a standard main dish:

**€** less than €12

**€€** €12–€20

**€€€** more than €20

# Climate

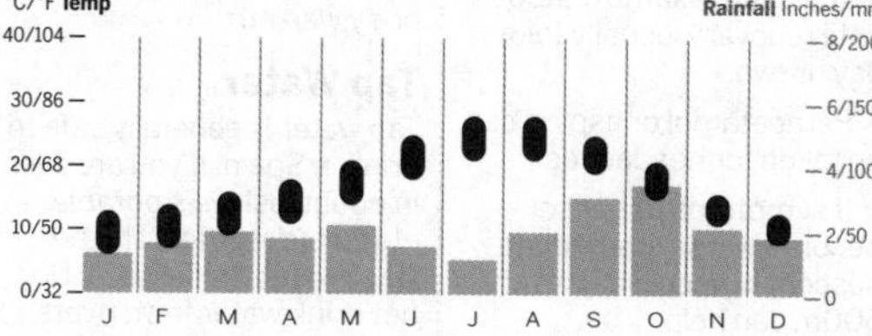


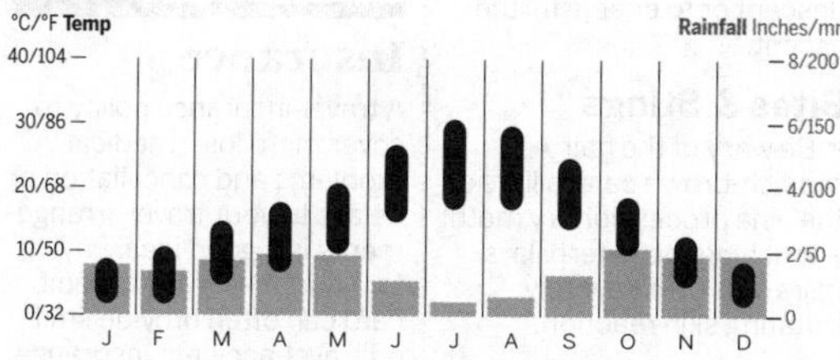


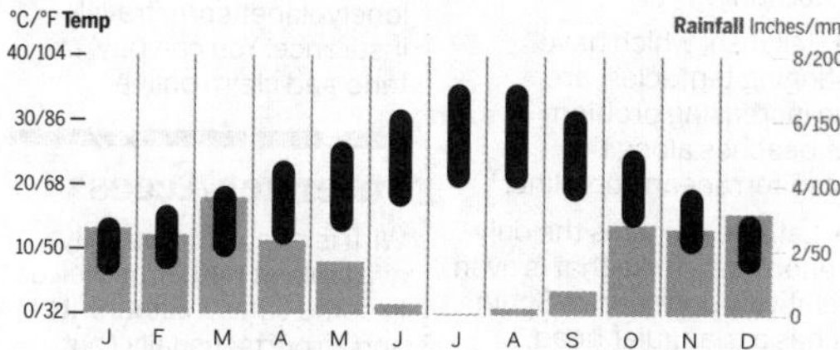


# Customs Regulations

Duty-free allowances for travellers entering Spain from outside the EU include 2L of wine (or 1L of wine and 1L of spirits), and 200 cigarettes or 50 cigars or 250g of tobacco. There are no restrictions on the import of duty-paid items into Spain from other EU countries for personal use. You *can* buy VAT-free articles at airport shops when travelling between EU countries.

# Discount Cards

Many museums and other attractions offer discounts for students, youth, children, families and/or seniors.

**Seniors** Reduced prices for people over 60 or 65 (depending on the place) at various museums and attractions (sometimes restricted to EU citizens) and occasionally on transport. Proof of age (passport or other official ID) is generally sufficient.

**Student cards** Discounts on museums, transport and more for students. You will need some kind of identification (eg an International Student Identity Card; www.isic.org) to prove student status.

**Youth cards** Travel, sights and accommodation discounts available to young people 30 and under with the European Youth Card (www.eyca.org) – known as Carné Joven in Spain – and the International Youth Travel Card (IYTC) issued by ISIC (www.isic.org) and sold at outlets such as STA Travel (www.statravel.com).

# Electricity

Spain uses the two-pin continental plugs typical throughout mainland Europe. In Gibraltar, both these and the three-square-pin plugs from the UK are used, though the latter is more common.

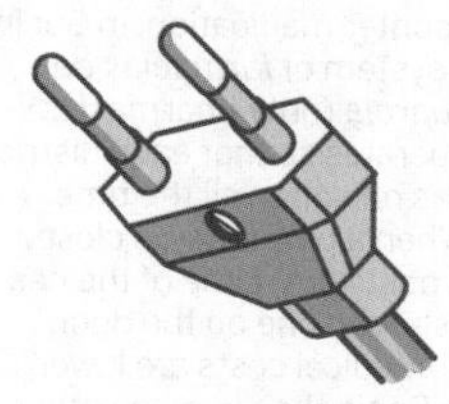

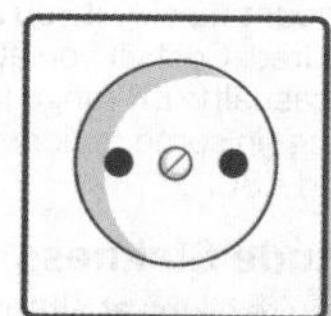

Type C
230V/50Hz

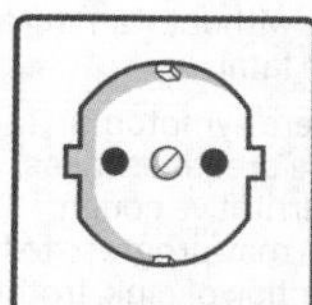

Type F
230V/50Hz

# Health

Spain has an excellent healthcare system.

### Availability & Cost of Healthcare

If you need an ambulance, call ☎061 or the general emergency number ☎112. For emergency treatment, go straight to the *urgencias* (casualty/ER) section of the nearest hospital.

*Farmacias* offer valuable advice and sell over-the-counter medication. In Spain, a system of *farmacias de guardia* (duty pharmacies) operates so that each district has one open all the time. When a pharmacy is closed, it posts the name of the nearest open one on the door.

Medical costs are lower in Spain than in many other European countries, but can still mount quickly if you are uninsured. Costs if you attend casualty/ER range from nothing (in some regions) to around €80.

### Altitude Sickness

➡ If you're hiking at altitude, altitude sickness may be a risk. Lack of oxygen at high altitudes (over 2500m) affects most people to some extent.

➡ Symptoms of Acute Mountain Sickness (AMS) usually develop during the first 24 hours at altitude, but may be delayed by up to three weeks.

➡ Mild symptoms include headache, lethargy, dizziness, difficulty sleeping and loss of appetite.

➡ AMS may become more severe without warning and can be fatal.

➡ Severe symptoms include breathlessness, a dry, irritative cough (which may progress to the production of pink, frothy sputum), severe headache, lack of coordination and balance, confusion, irrational behaviour, vomiting, drowsiness and unconsciousness.

➡ Treat mild symptoms by resting at the same altitude until recovery, usually for a day or two.

➡ Paracetamol or aspirin can be taken for headaches.

➡ If symptoms persist or become worse, immediate descent is necessary; even 500m can help.

➡ Drug treatments should never be used to avoid descent or to enable further ascent.

### Bites & Stings

➡ Be wary of the hairy reddish-brown caterpillars of the pine processionary moth – touching the caterpillars' hairs sets off a severely irritating skin reaction.

➡ Some Spanish centipedes have a very nasty but non-fatal sting.

➡ Jellyfish, which have stinging tentacles, are an increasing problem at beaches along the Mediterranean coastline.

➡ Lataste's viper is the only venomous snake that is even relatively common in Spain. It has a triangular head, grows up to 75cm long, and is grey with a zigzag pattern. It lives in dry, rocky areas, away from humans. Its bite can be fatal and needs to be treated with a serum, which state clinics in major towns keep in stock.

### Hypothermia

➡ The weather in Spain's mountains can be extremely changeable at any time of year.

➡ Proper preparation will reduce the risks of getting hypothermia: always carry waterproof garments and warm layers, and inform others of your route.

➡ Hypothermia starts with shivering, loss of judgement and clumsiness; unless warming occurs, the sufferer deteriorates into apathy, confusion and coma.

➡ Prevent further heat loss by seeking shelter, wearing warm dry clothing, drinking hot sweet drinks and sharing body warmth.

### Tap Water

Tap water is generally safe to drink in Spain. If you are ever in doubt, ask, *¿Es potable el agua (del grifo)?* (Is the (tap) water drinkable?). Do not drink water from rivers or lakes, as it may contain bacteria or viruses.

# Insurance

A travel-insurance policy to cover theft, loss, medical problems and cancellation or delays to your travel arrangements is a good idea. Paying for your ticket with a credit card can often provide limited travel-accident insurance.

Worldwide travel insurance is available at www.lonelyplanet.com/travel-insurance. You can buy, extend and claim online.

# Internet Access

Wi-fi is almost universally available at hotels, as well as in some cafes, restaurants and airports; usually (but not always) it's free. Connection speed often varies from room to room in hotels (and coverage is sometimes restricted to the hotel lobby), so if you need a good connection, always ask when you check in or make your reservation. Some tourist offices can provide a list of wi-fi hot spots in their area.

A convenient and more universally reliable alternative to wi-fi – especially if you're travelling outside the cities – is to purchase a Spanish SIM card for your phone. Many local prepaid plans include generous data allowances at low rates.

# Language Courses

Among the more popular places to learn Spanish are Barcelona, Granada, Madrid,

Salamanca and Seville. In these places and elsewhere, Spanish universities offer good-value language courses. The **Escuela Oficial de Idiomas** is a nationwide language institution where you can learn Spanish and other local languages. Classes can be large and busy but are generally fairly cheap. There are branches in many major cities.

Private language schools as well as universities cater for a wide range of levels, course lengths, times of year, intensity and special requirements. Many courses have a cultural component as well as language. University courses often last a semester, although some are as short as two weeks or as long as a year. Private language schools can be more flexible. One with a good reputation is **donQuijote** (www.donquijote.org), with branches in 11 Spanish cities.

It's also worth finding out whether your course will lead to any formal certificate of competence. The Diplomas de Español como Lengua Extranjera (DELE) are recognised by Spain's Ministry of Education.

## Legal Matters

If you're arrested, you will be allotted the free services of an *abogado de oficio* (duty solicitor or court-appointed lawyer), who may speak only Spanish. You're also entitled to make a phone call. If you use this to contact your embassy or consulate, the staff will probably be able to do no more than refer you to a lawyer who speaks your language. If you end up in court, the authorities are obliged to provide a translator.

In theory, you are supposed to have your national ID card or passport with you at all times. If asked for it by the police, you are supposed to be able to produce it on the spot. In practice it is rarely an issue and many people choose to leave passports in hotel safes. One option is to carry a photocopy.

The Policía Local or Policía Municipal operates at a local level and deals with such issues as traffic infringements and minor crime. The Policía Nacional (091) is the state police force, dealing with major crime and operating primarily in the cities. The military-linked Guardia Civil (created in the 19th century to deal with banditry) is largely responsible for highway patrols, borders, security, major crime and terrorism. Several regions have their own police forces, such as the Mossos d'Esquadra in Catalonia and the Ertzaintza in the Basque Country.

Cannabis has been decriminalised in Spain, but only for personal use and in small quantities. Note that public consumption, sale or purchase of any illicit drug – including cannabis – is illegal. Travellers entering Spain from Morocco should be prepared for drug searches, especially if you have a vehicle.

## LGBTIQ+ Travellers

Spain has become perhaps the most gay-friendly country in southern Europe. Homosexuality is legal, and same-sex marriages were legalised in 2005 – the latter move was extremely popular but met with opposition from the country's powerful Catholic Church.

Lesbians and gay men generally keep a fairly low profile in rural areas, but are quite open in the cities. Madrid, Barcelona, Sitges, Torremolinos and Ibiza have particularly lively scenes. Sitges is a major destination on the international gay-party circuit; gays take a leading role in the wild **Carnaval** (www.visitsitges.com; ⌚Feb/Mar) there. There are also gay parades, marches and events in several cities on and around the last Saturday in June, including Madrid's **Día del Orgullo LGTBI** (www.orgullolgtb.org; ⌚Jun) and Seville's **Orgullo de Andalucía** (www.orgullolgtbiandalucia.es).

Madrid also hosts the annual **Les Gai Cine Mad** (☎91 593 05 40; www.lesgaicinemad.com; ⌚late Oct/early Nov) festival, a celebration of lesbian, gay and transsexual films.

### Resources

In addition to the following resources, check out Madrid Turismo's LGBT Madrid page (www.esmadrid.com/en/madrid-lgbt), the Barcelona LGTBI-friendly page at Barcelona Turisme (www.barcelonaturisme.com) and Seville's Spanish-language LGBT guide, *Municipios Orgullosos de la Provincia de Sevilla* (downloadable from www.turismosevilla.org).

**Chueca** (www.chueca.com) Useful gay portal with extensive links.

**Gay Madrid 4 U** (www.gaymadrid4u.com) A good overview of Madrid's gay bars and nightclubs. There are similar 'Gay 4 U' pages for Barcelona, Seville and Torremolinos.

**NightTours.com** (www.nighttours.com) A reasonably good guide to gay nightlife and other attractions in Madrid, Barcelona and several other Spanish locations.

**Patroc** (www.patroc.com) Gay guides to Barcelona, Bilbao, Madrid, Seville, Sitges, Torremolinos and Valencia.

**Shangay** (www.shangay.com) For news, upcoming events, reviews and contacts. Shangay also publishes *Shanguide* – a Madrid-centric biweekly magazine jammed with listings (including saunas and hard-core clubs) and contact ads – along with other magazines such as *Shangay Fashion & Lifestyle* and the travel-focused *Shangay Voyager*. They're available in gay bookshops, and gay and gay-friendly bars, or you can browse back issues at www.shangay.com/hemeroteca.

## Organisations

**Casal Lambda** (Map p276; ☎93 319 55 50, WhatsApp 679 205204; www.lambda.cat; Carrer del Comte Borrell 22; ⊙5-9pm Mon-Sat; Ⓜ Barceloneta) A gay and lesbian social, cultural and information centre in Barcelona.

**Colectivo LGTB+ de Madrid** (Cogam; Map p102; ☎91 523 00 70; www.cogam.es; Calle de la Puebla 9; ⊙5-9pm Mon-Thu, 6-9pm Fri, to 8pm Sat; Ⓜ Callao, Gran Vía) Offers activities and has an information office and social centre.

**Federación Estatal de Lesbianas, Gays, Trans & Bisexuales** (Map p102; ☎91 360 46 05; www.felgtb.org; Calle de las Infantas 40, 4th fl; ⊙8am-3.30pm Mon-Fri; Ⓜ Gran Vía) A national advocacy group, based in Madrid, that played a leading role in lobbying for the legalisation of gay marriage.

**Fundación Triángulo** (☎91 593 05 40; www.fundaciontriangulo.org; Calle de Meléndez Valdés 52, 1st fl; ⊙10am-2pm & 4-8pm Mon-Fri; Ⓜ Argüelles) One of several sources of information on gay issues in Madrid.

# Maps

Spain has some excellent maps if you're driving around the country – many are available from petrol stations. Topographical and hiking maps are available from specialist stores.

## Small-Scale Maps

Some of the best maps for travellers are by Michelin, which produces the 1:1,000,000 *Spain Portugal* map and six 1:400,000 regional maps covering the whole country. These are all pretty accurate and are updated regularly, even down to the state of minor country roads. Also good are the **GeoCenter maps** published by Germany's RV Verlag.

Probably the best physical map of Spain is *Península Ibérica, Baleares y Canarias* published by the **Centro Nacional de Información Geográfica** (CNIG), the publishing arm of the Instituto Geográfico Nacional (www.ign.es). Ask for it in good bookshops.

## Walking Maps

Useful for hiking and exploring some areas (particularly in the Pyrenees) are the Alpina 25 and Alpina 50 series published by **Editorial Alpina** (www.editorialalpina.com). These combine information booklets in Spanish (and sometimes Catalan) with detailed maps at scales ranging from 1:25,000 to 1:50,000. They are an indispensable tool for hikers (and some come in English and German), though they have their inaccuracies.

The **Institut Cartogràfic i Geològic de Catalunya** (http://ebotiga.icgc.cat) puts out some 1:25,000 maps for the Catalan Pyrenees that are often more useful for hiking than their Editorial Alpina counterparts. To explore the ICGC catalog, click on 'Mapes topogràfics', then 'Espais Naturals 1:25.000'.

**Prames** (www.libreriaprames.com) publishes another good series of 1:25,000 maps for Spain's national parks and nature reserves (search its website for 'Mapa TOP 25') – as does the **CNIG** (www.cnig.es).

You can often pick up these maps at bookshops near trekking areas, and at specialist bookshops such as the following:

**Altaïr** (Map p264; ☎93 342 71 71; www.altair.es; Gran Via de les Corts Catalanes 616; ⊙10am-8.30pm Mon-Sat; 📶; Ⓜ Catalunya) In Barcelona.

**De Viaje** (Map p98; ☎91 577 98 99; www.deviaje.com; Calle de Serrano 41; ⊙10am-8.30pm Mon-Fri, 10.30am-2.30pm & 5.30-8.30pm Sat; Ⓜ Serrano) In Madrid.

**La Tienda Verde** (☎91 534 33 13; www.facebook.com/latiendaverde; Calle de Maudes 23; ⊙10am-2pm Mon-Fri; Ⓜ Cuatro Caminos) In Madrid.

**Librería Desnivel** (Map p84; ☎91 429 12 81; www.libreriadesnivel.com; Plaza de Matute 6; ⊙10am-8.30pm Mon-Fri, 11am-8pm Sat; Ⓜ Antón Martín) In Madrid.

# Money

The most convenient way to bring your money is in the form of a debit or credit card, with some extra cash in case of an emergency.

Many credit and debit cards can be used for withdrawing money from *cajeros automáticos* (ATMs) that display the relevant symbols such as Visa, MasterCard, Cirrus etc. Some Spanish banks such as Unicaja and Liberbank may offer ATM cash withdrawals free of charge, while others charge rather exorbitant fees (€5 to €7 per transaction); it pays to shop around. Note that your home bank may also impose a fee over and above whatever the Spanish bank charges.

## Cash

Most banks will exchange major foreign currencies and offer better rates than exchange offices at the airport. Ask about commissions – these can vary from bank to bank – and take your passport.

## Credit & Debit Cards

These can be used to pay for most purchases. You'll often be asked to show your passport or some other form of identification. Among the most widely accepted are Visa, MasterCard, American Express (Amex), Cirrus, Maestro, Plus and JCB. Diners Club is less widely accepted. If your card is lost, stolen or swallowed by an ATM, you can call the card issuer's free-call telephone number to have an immediate stop put on its use.

## Moneychangers

You can exchange both cash and travellers cheques at *cambio* (exchange) offices. Generally they offer longer opening hours and quicker service than banks, but worse exchange rates and higher commissions.

## Taxes

➡ In Spain, value-added tax (VAT) is known as IVA (ee-ba; *impuesto sobre el valor añadido*).

➡ Hotel rooms and restaurant meals attract an additional 10% (usually included in the quoted price, but always ask); most other items have 21% added.

### REFUNDS

Visitors are entitled to a refund of the 21% IVA on purchases costing more than €90.15 from any shop, if they are taking them out of the EU within three months.

Spain has an electronic tax refund system known as DIVA. Ask the shop for an official DIVA refund form showing the price and IVA paid for each item, and identifying the vendor and purchaser. Upon arrival at your departure airport, get your refund forms electronically stamped by scanning them at a DIVA kiosk, or have them manually stamped by a customs agent. You can then present the stamped forms at tax-free kiosks in the boarding area to get your refund.

## Tipping

Tipping is almost always optional.

**Bars** It's rare to leave a tip in bars (even when the bartender gives you your change on a small dish).

**Restaurants** Many Spaniards leave small change, others up to 5%, which is considered generous.

**Taxis** Optional, but locals sometimes round up to the nearest euro.

# Post

**Correos** (www.correos.es), the Spanish postal system, is generally reliable, if a little slow at times.

Delivery times are erratic, but ordinary mail to other Western European countries can take up to a week (although often as little as three days); to North America up to 10 days; and to Australia or New Zealand between 10 days and three weeks.

➡ *Sellos* (stamps) are sold at most *estancos* (tobacconists; look for 'Tabacos' in yellow letters on a maroon background), as well as at post offices.

➡ A postcard or letter weighing up to 20g costs €1.45 from Spain to other European countries, and €1.55 to the rest of the world.

➡ For a full list of prices for *certificado* (certified) and *urgente* (express) post, go to www.correos.es and click on 'Tarifas Correos'.

# Public Holidays

The two main periods when Spaniards go on holiday are Semana Santa (the week leading up to Easter Sunday) and July and August. At these times accommodation in resorts can be scarce and transport heavily booked, but other places are often half-empty.

There are at least 14 official holidays a year – some observed nationwide, some locally. When a holiday falls close to a weekend, Spaniards like to make a *puente* (bridge), meaning they take the intervening day off too. Occasionally when two holidays fall within the same week, they make an *acueducto* (aqueduct)! Here are the national holidays:

**Año Nuevo** (New Year's Day) 1 January

**Viernes Santo** (Good Friday) March/April

**Fiesta del Trabajo** (Labour Day) 1 May

**La Asunción** (Feast of the Assumption) 15 August

**Fiesta Nacional de España** (National Day) 12 October

**La Inmaculada Concepción** (Feast of the Immaculate Conception) 8 December

**Navidad** (Christmas) 25 December

Regional governments set five holidays and local councils two more. Common dates include:

**Epifanía** (Epiphany) or **Día de los Reyes Magos** (Three Kings' Day) 6 January

**Jueves Santo** (Maundy Thursday) March/April; not observed in Catalonia and Valencia.

**Corpus Christi** June; the Thursday after the eighth Sunday after Easter Sunday.

**Día de Santiago Apóstol** (Feast of St James the Apostle) 25 July

**Día de Todos los Santos** (All Saints' Day) 1 November

**Día de la Constitución** (Constitution Day) 6 December

# Safe Travel

Most visitors to Spain never feel remotely threatened, but enough have unpleasant experiences to warrant some care. The main thing to be wary of is petty theft.

➡ In cities, especially Madrid and Barcelona, stick to areas with plenty of people around and avoid deserted streets.

➡ Keep valuables concealed or locked away in your hotel room.

➡ Try not to look like a tourist (eg don't consult maps in crowded tourist areas).

➡ Be wary of pickpockets in areas heavily frequented by tourists, such as the Madrid metro or Seville's crowded streets and squares during Semana Santa parades.

## Scams

There must be 50 ways to lose your wallet. As a rule, talented petty thieves work in groups and capitalise on distraction. Tricks usually involve a team of two or more (sometimes one of them an attractive woman to distract male victims). While one attracts your attention, the other empties your pockets. More imaginative strikes include someone dropping a milk mixture onto the victim from a balcony. Immediately a concerned citizen comes up to help you brush off what you assume to be pigeon poo, and thus suitably occupied, you don't notice the contents of your pockets slipping away.

Beware: not all thieves look like thieves. Watch out for an old classic: the ladies offering flowers for good luck. We don't know how they do it, but if you get too involved in a friendly chat, your pockets sometimes wind up empty.

On some highways, especially the AP7 from the French border to Barcelona, bands of thieves occasionally operate. Beware of men trying to distract you in rest areas, and don't stop along the highway if people driving alongside indicate you have a problem with the car. While one inspects the rear of the car with you, his pals will empty your vehicle. Another gag has them puncturing tyres of cars stopped in rest areas, then following and 'helping' the victim when they stop to change the wheel. Hire cars with the company's stickers and those with foreign plates are especially targeted. When you do call in at highway rest stops, try to park close to the buildings and leave nothing of value in view. If you do stop to change a tyre and find yourself getting unsolicited aid, make sure doors are all locked and don't allow yourself to be distracted.

Even parking your car can be fraught. In some towns, fairly dodgy self-appointed parking attendants operate in central areas where you may want to park. They will direct you frantically to a spot. If possible, ignore them and find your own. If unavoidable, you may well want to pay them some token not to scratch or otherwise damage your vehicle after you've walked away. You definitely don't want to leave anything visible in the car (or open the boot – trunk – if you intend to leave luggage or anything else in it) under these circumstances.

## Theft

Theft is mostly a risk in tourist resorts, big cities and when you first arrive in a new destination and may be off your guard. You are at your most vulnerable when dragging around luggage to or from your hotel. Barcelona, Madrid and Seville have the worst reputations for theft and, on very rare occasions, muggings.

Anything left lying on the beach can disappear in a flash when your back is turned. At night, avoid dingy, empty city alleys and backstreets, or anywhere that just doesn't feel 100% safe.

Report thefts to the national police – visit www.policia.es for a full list of *comisarías* (police stations) around the country; click 'Comisaría Virtual', then 'Dependencias'. You are unlikely to recover your goods, but you need to make a formal *denuncia* for insurance purposes. To avoid endless queues at the *comisaría*, you can make the report by phone (902 102 112) in various languages or online at www.policia.es (click on 'Denuncias por internet'); instructions are in Spanish, English, French and German. The following day you go to the station of your choice to pick up and sign the report, without queuing.

# Telephone

Phones from anywhere within the EU can be used in Spain without roaming charges. If you're bringing an unlocked phone from outside the EU, you'll often save money by purchasing a local SIM card. Other economical options include calling from your computer using an internet-based service such as Skype or from your mobile phone using WhatsApp.

## Mobile Phones

Prepaid Spanish SIM cards can be used in any unlocked European or Australian phone, and in most newer phones brought from elsewhere (Spain uses GSM 900/1800). The leading Spanish mobile-phone companies (**MoviStar**, **Orange**, **Vodafone** and **Yoigo**) all offer *prepagado* (prepaid) accounts for mobiles. A SIM card costs from €10, and promotional packages including start-up amounts of calls, texts and data are widely available. You can top up your account as needed at phone company shops or outlets such as *estancos* (tobacconists) and newspaper kiosks. Smaller providers such as **Pepephone** (www.pepephone.com) are another option.

If you're from the EU, there is EU-wide roaming so that call and data plans for mobile phones from any EU country should be valid in Spain without any extra roaming charges. If you're from elsewhere and want to use your home country phone plan in Spain, check with your mobile provider for information on roaming charges.

## Phone Codes

Mobile (cell) phone numbers start with 6. Numbers starting with 800 and 900 are national toll-free numbers, while those starting with 901 to 906 come with varying costs. A common one is 902, which is a national standard rate number, but which can only be dialled from within Spain. In a similar category are numbers starting with 803, 806 and 807. There are no local area codes.

**International access code** ☎00

**Spain country code** ☎34

## Time

**Time zone** Same as most of Western Europe (GMT/UTC plus one hour during winter and GMT/UTC plus two hours during the daylight-saving period).

**Daylight saving** From the last Sunday in March to the last Sunday in October. Note that the European Parliament has voted to scrap daylight saving time effective in 2021, with EU member states choosing to stay on either permanent summer or winter time. Spain's decision is pending – stay tuned!

**12- and 24-hour clock** Although the 24-hour clock is used in most official contexts (train timetables, for example), you'll find people generally use the 12-hour clock in everyday conversation.

## Toilets

Public toilets are rare to nonexistent in Spain, and it's not really the done thing to go into a bar or cafe solely to use the toilet; ordering a quick coffee is a small price to pay for relieving the problem. Otherwise you can usually get away with it in larger, crowded places, where they can't really keep track of who's coming and going. Another option in some larger cities is to visit the department stores of El Corte Inglés.

## Tourist Information

All cities and many smaller towns have an *oficina de turismo* or *oficina de información turística*. In the country's provincial capitals you will sometimes find more than one tourist office – one specialising in information on the city alone, the other carrying mostly provincial or regional information. National and natural parks also often have their own visitor centres offering useful information.

**Turespaña** (www.spain.info) is the country's national tourism body, and it operates branches around the world. Check the website for office locations.

## Visas

Spain is one of 26 member countries of the Schengen Agreement, under which 22 EU countries (all but Bulgaria, Cyprus, Croatia, Ireland and Romania) plus Iceland, Norway, Liechtenstein and Switzerland have abolished checks at common borders.

The visa situation for entering Spain is as follows:

**Citizens or residents of EU and Schengen countries** No visa required for stays of up to 90 days.

**Citizens or residents of the UK, Australia, Canada, Israel, Japan, New Zealand, the USA and most Latin American countries** No visa required for tourist visits of up to 90 days. However, effective 1 January 2021, nationals of the above countries will require prior authorisation to enter Spain under the new European Travel Information and Authorisation System (ETIAS; www.etias.com). Travellers can apply online; the cost is €7 for a three-year, multi-entry authorisation.

**Other countries** Check with a Spanish embassy or consulate for current visa requirements.

**To work or study in Spain** A special visa may be require.

### Extensions & Residence

Schengen visas – 90-day visas that allow free travel within the 26 countries of Europe's Schengen zone, including Spain – cannot

### GOVERNMENT TRAVEL ADVICE

The following government websites offer travel advisory services and information for travellers:

**Australian Department of Foreign Affairs and Trade** (www.smartraveller.gov.au)

**Global Affairs Canada** (www.travel.gc.ca)

**Ministère de l'Europe et des Affaires Étrangères** (www.diplomatie.gouv.fr/fr/conseils-aux-voyageurs)

**Auswärtiges Amt, Länder und Reiseinformationen** (www.auswaertiges-amt.de)

**Italian Ministero degli Affari Esteri e della Cooperazione Internazionale** (www.viaggiaresicuri.mae.aci.it)

**Japanese Ministry of Foreign Affairs** (www.anzen.mofa.go.jp)

**Ministerie van Buitenlandse Zaken** (www.rijksoverheid.nl/ministeries)

**New Zealand Ministry of Foreign Affairs and Trade** (www.safetravel.govt.nz)

**UK Foreign & Commonwealth Office** (www.gov.uk/foreign-travel-advice)

**US Department of State** (www.travel.state.gov)

be extended. These are the most common visas for short stays in Spain, typically granted to foreign nationals who do not qualify for a visa exemption.

You can apply for no more than two visas in any 12-month period and they are not renewable once you are in Spain.

Nationals of EU countries, Iceland, Norway, Liechtenstein and Switzerland can enter and leave Spain at will and don't need to apply for a *tarjeta de residencia* (residence card) unless they wish to remain in Spain for more than 90 days.

UK nationals with established residence in Spain prior to 31 December 2020 are entitled to maintain their resident status post-Brexit, along with immediate family members. Rules for UK nationals wishing to move to Spain beyond 1 January 2021 were still being negotiated as of mid 2020. For the latest info, see www.gov.uk/guidance/living-in-spain.

People of other nationalities who want to stay in Spain longer than 90 days have to get a residence card, and for them it can be a drawn-out process.

# Volunteering

Volunteering possibilities in Spain:

**Earthwatch Institute** (www.earthwatch.org) Occasionally organises Spanish conservation projects.

**Go Abroad** (www.goabroad.com) Dozens of different volunteering opportunities in Spain.

**Sunseed Desert Technology** (☎950 52 57 70; www.sunseed.org.uk) This UK-run project, developing sustainable ways to live in semi-arid environments, is based in the hamlet of Los Molinos del Río Aguas in Almería.

**Transitions Abroad** (www.transitionsabroad.com) A good website to start your research.

# Women Travellers

Travelling in Spain as a woman is as easy as travelling anywhere in the Western world. That said, foreign women *can* attract unwanted male attention, especially when travelling solo and in small, remote places.

Be choosy about your accommodation. Bottom-end fleapits with all-male staff can be insalubrious locations to bed down for the night. Lone women should also take care in city streets at night – stick with the crowds, and inquire locally about any no-go zones (areas that are sketchy at night or even in the day during quiet siesta hours). Hitching for solo women travellers is never recommended.

Spanish men under about 40, who've grown up in the liberated post-Franco era, conform far less to old-fashioned sexual stereotypes, although you might notice that sexual stereotyping becomes a little more pronounced as you move from north to south in Spain, and from city to country.

# Work

Nationals of EU countries, Switzerland, Liechtenstein, Norway and Iceland may freely work in Spain. If you are offered a contract, your employer will normally steer you through any bureaucracy. Effective 1 January 2021, most UK citizens will no longer be eligible to work freely in Spain as they did before Brexit. However, British citizens who were resident in Spain prior to the end of 2020 can continue working in Spain in 2021 and beyond, provided they remain resident in Spain.

Virtually everyone else is supposed to obtain a work permit from a Spanish consulate in their country of residence, and if they plan to stay more than 90 days, a residence visa. These procedures are well-nigh impossible unless you have a job contract lined up before you begin them. You could look for casual work in fruit picking, harvesting or construction, but this is generally done with imported labour from Morocco and Eastern Europe, with pay and conditions that are often poor.

## Language Teaching

Language-teaching qualifications are a big help when trying to find work as a teacher, and the more reputable places will require TEFL certification. Sources of information on possible teaching work – in a school or as a private tutor – include foreign cultural centres such as the British Council and Alliance Française, foreign-language bookshops, universities and language schools.

## Tourist Resorts

Summer work on the Mediterranean coasts is a possibility, especially if you arrive early in the season and are prepared to stay a while. Check any local press in foreign languages, such as the Costa del Sol's *Sur in English* (www.surinenglish.com), which lists ads for waiters, nannies, chefs, babysitters, housekeepers and the like.

## Yacht Crewing

It is possible to stumble upon work as crew on yachts and cruisers. The best ports at which to look include (in descending order) Palma de Mallorca, Gibraltar and Puerto Banús. In summer the voyages tend to be restricted to the Mediterranean, but from about November to January, many boats head for the Caribbean. Such work is usually unpaid; the best way to find out is to ask around on the docks.

# Transport

## GETTING THERE & AWAY

Spain is one of Europe's top holiday destinations and is well linked to other European countries by air, rail and road. Regular car ferries and hydrofoils run to and from Morocco, and there are ferry links to the UK, Italy, the Canary Islands and Algeria.

Flights, cars and tours can be booked online at www.lonelyplanet.com/bookings.

### Entering Spain

Immigration and customs checks (which usually only take place if you're arriving from outside the EU) normally involve a minimum of fuss, although there are exceptions.

Your vehicle could be searched on arrival from Andorra. The tiny principality of Andorra is not in the European Union (EU), so border controls remain in place. Spanish customs look out for contraband duty-free products destined for illegal resale in Spain. Similarly, travellers arriving from Morocco or the Spanish North African enclaves of Ceuta and Melilla may be searched for controlled substances. Expect long delays at these borders, especially in summer.

#### Passports

Citizens of EU member states, as well as those from Norway, Iceland, Liechtenstein and Switzerland, can travel to Spain with their national identity card alone. All other nationalities must carry a valid passport.

In the aftermath of the UK's departure from the EU, British citizens, like citizens of the US and elsewhere, are allowed to enter Spain visa-free (p891) for stays of up to 90 days only. Check with your local Spanish embassy or consulate for the latest rules.

By law you are supposed to carry your passport (p886) or ID card with you in Spain at all times.

### Air

There are direct flights to Spain from most European countries, as well as from North America, South America, Africa, the Middle East and Asia. Those coming from Australasia will usually have to make at least one change of flight.

High season in Spain generally means Christmas, New Year, Easter and roughly June to September. The applicability of seasonal fares varies depending on the specific destination. You may find reasonably priced flights to Madrid from elsewhere in Europe in August, for example, because it is stinking hot and everyone else has fled to the mountains or the sea. As a general rule, November to March (aside from Christmas and New Year) is when airfares to Spain are likely to be at their lowest, and the intervening months can be considered shoulder periods.

#### Airports & Airlines

All of Spain's airports share the user-friendly website and flight information telephone number of **Aena** (☎91 321 10 00; www.aena.es), the national airports authority. To find more information on each airport, choose 'English' and click 'Airports'. Each airport's page has practical information, including parking and public transport, and a full list of (and links to) airlines using that airport. It also has current flight information.

Spain's national carrier is **Iberia** (www.iberia.com), with an extensive international network of flights and a good safety record.

Madrid's **Adolfo Suárez Madrid-Barajas Airport** (☎902 404704; www.aena.es; Ⓜ Aeropuerto T1, T2 & T3, Aeropuerto T4) was Spain's busiest (and Europe's sixth-busiest) airport in 2019, followed closely by Barcelona's **El Prat Airport** (☎91 321 10 00; www.aena.es; wifi) – second-busiest in Spain, seventh in Europe. Other major airports include Málaga, Palma de Mallorca, Alicante, Girona, Valencia, Seville, Vigo and Bilbao.

## Land

Spain shares land borders with France, Portugal and Andorra.

Apart from shorter cross-border services, **FlixBus/Eurolines** (www.flixbus.com) is the main operator of international bus services to Spain from most of Western Europe.

For information on trains connecting Spain with France and Portugal, and onward services between France and other countries, visit the Viajes Internacionales (International Journeys) section of www.renfe.com, the website of the Spanish national railway company, Renfe.

### Andorra

Regular buses (including winter ski buses) connect Andorra with Barcelona and other destinations in Spain (including Madrid) and France. **Directbus** (www.andorradirectbus.es) offers the most frequent service between Andorra and Barcelona's Estació d'Autobusos de Sants (€31, three hours) or El Prat Airport (€34, 3½ to 3¾ hours).

### France

#### BUS

**FlixBus/Eurolines** (www.flixbus.com) heads to Spain from Paris and more than 20 other French cities and towns. It connects with Madrid (from €45, 15½ to 17¾ hours), Barcelona (from €35, 13¾ to 15¾ hours) and many other destinations. There's at least one departure per day for main destinations.

#### CAR & MOTORCYCLE

The main road crossing into Spain from France is the A9 *autoroute* that links up with Spain's AP7 tollway, which runs down to Barcelona and follows the Spanish coast south (with a branch, the AP2, going to Madrid via Zaragoza). A series of links cuts across the Pyrenees from France and Andorra into Spain, and there's a coastal route that runs from Biarritz in France into the Spanish Basque Country.

#### TRAIN

The principal rail crossings into Spain pierce the Franco-Spanish frontier along the Mediterranean coast and via the Basque Country. Another minor rail route runs inland across the Pyrenees from Latour-de-Carol to Barcelona. For English-language information on French rail services, check out the **OuiSNCF** (http://en.oui.sncf) website.

There are plans for a high-speed rail link between Madrid and Paris. In the meantime, high-speed international services travel via Barcelona, where you can make connections with the Spanish AVE train to Madrid. The fastest cross-border services are as follows:

**Paris to Barcelona** Two direct high-speed trains (advance-purchase promo fares from €34, standard 2nd-class fares from €89, 6¾ hours) run daily via Valence, Nîmes, Montpellier, Beziers, Narbonne, Perpignan, Figueres and Girona.

**Lyon to Barcelona** One high-speed train daily (promo/standard fares from €29/62, five hours).

**Marseilles to Barcelona** One high-speed train daily (promo/standard fares from €29/52, five hours).

Slower options from Paris to Madrid involve an additional change of train in Montpellier, Toulouse and/or Perpignan.

In addition to the trains listed above, two or three TGVs (high-speed trains) leave from Paris-Montparnasse for Hendaye (from €39, 4¾ hours), where you can catch the half-hourly light-rail service operated by Euskotren (www.euskotren.es) across the border to San Sebastián-Donostia Amara station (€2.65, 35 minutes).

### Portugal

#### BUS

**Avanza** (☎91 272 28 32; www.avanzabus.com) runs daily buses between Lisbon and Madrid (€42 to €47, seven hours, two to three daily).

Other bus services run north via Porto to Tui, Santiago de Compostela and A Coruña in Galicia, while local buses cross the border from towns such as Huelva in Andalucía, Badajoz in Extremadura and Ourense in Galicia.

#### CLIMATE CHANGE & TRAVEL

Every form of transport that relies on carbon-based fuel generates $CO_2$, the main cause of human-induced climate change. Modern travel is dependent on aeroplanes, which might use less fuel per kilometre per person than most cars but travel much greater distances. The altitude at which aircraft emit gases (including $CO_2$) and particles also contributes to their climate change impact. Many websites offer 'carbon calculators' that allow people to estimate the carbon emissions generated by their journey and, for those who wish to do so, to offset the impact of the greenhouse gases emitted with contributions to portfolios of climate-friendly initiatives throughout the world. Lonely Planet offsets the carbon footprint of all staff and author travel.

#### CAR & MOTORCYCLE

The A5 freeway linking Madrid with Badajoz crosses the Portuguese frontier and continues on to Lisbon. For Porto and other northern Portuguese destinations, the most convenient border crossing is at Fuentes de Oñoro/Vilar Formoso. There are many other road connections up and down the length of the Spain–Portugal border.

#### TRAIN

From Portugal, the main line runs from Lisbon across Extremadura to Madrid.

**Lisbon to Irún-Hendaye** Chair/sleeper class from €43/77, 13¼ hours, one daily.

**Lisbon to Madrid** Chair/sleeper class from €38/69, 10 hours, one daily.

**Porto to Vigo** €15, 2½ hours, two daily).

## Sea

A useful website for comparing routes and finding links to the relevant ferry companies is www.ferrylines.com.

### Algeria

**Algérie Ferries** (www.algerieferries.dz) Operates year-round services from Alicante to Oran (one to three weekly) as well as summer services from Alicante to Algiers and Barcelona to Oran.

**Trasmediterránea** (☎902 454 645; www.trasmediterranea.es) Runs year-round ferries from Almería to the Algerian ports of Ghazaouet and Oran (at least once weekly).

**Baleària** (☎865 608 423; www.balearia.com) Operates a ferry service at least once weekly from Valencia to Mostaganem.

### Italy

Most Italian routes are operated by **Grimaldi Lines** (www.grimaldi-lines.com) or **Grandi Navi Veloci** (www.gnv.it).

**Civitavecchia (near Rome) to Barcelona** 20 hours, six weekly.

**Genoa to Barcelona** 19 hours, two to three weekly.

**Porto Torres (Sardinia) to Barcelona** 12 hours, at least two weekly.

**Savona (near Genoa) to Barcelona** 20 hours, weekly in summer.

### Morocco

Ferries run to Morocco from mainland Spain. Most services are run by the Spanish national ferry company, **Trasmediterránea** (☎902 454 645; www.trasmediterranea.es). You can take vehicles on most routes. Other companies that connect Spain with Morocco:

**Baleària** (www.balearia.com)

**FRS Iberia** (www.frs.es)

**Grandi Navi Veloci** (www.gnv.it)

**Grimaldi Lines** (www.grimaldi-lines.com)

**Naviera Armas** (www.navieraarmas.com)

#### ROUTES

Services between Spain and Morocco include the following:

**Al-Hoceima to Motril** Five hours, two weekly.

**Nador to Almería** Four to seven hours, daily.

**Nador to Barcelona** 27 hours, weekly.

**Nador to Motril** Five to 7½ hours, two weekly.

**Tangier to Algeciras** One to two hours, up to 12 daily. Buses from several Moroccan cities converge on Tangier to make the ferry crossing to Algeciras, then fan out to the main Spanish centres.

**Tangier to Barcelona** 27 to 35 hours, one to two weekly.

**Tangier to Motril** Eight hours, daily.

**Tangier to Tarifa** One hour, up to 15 daily.

### UK & Ireland

**Brittany Ferries** (☎in the UK 0330 159 7000; www.brittany-ferries.co.uk) runs the following services:

**Plymouth to Santander** 19 hours, weekly. Mid-March to October only.

**Portsmouth to Bilbao** 24 to 32 hours, two weekly.

**Portsmouth to Santander** 24 to 32 hours, three weekly.

**Rosslare to Bilbao** 27 to 31½ hours, two weekly.

# GETTING AROUND

Spain's network of train and bus services is one of the best in Europe and there aren't many places that can't be reached using one or the other. The tentacles of Spain's high-speed train network are expanding rapidly, while domestic air services are plentiful over longer distances and on routes that are more complicated by land.

## Air

Spain has an extensive network of internal flights. These are operated by both Spanish airlines and a handful of low-cost international airlines. Carriers include the following:

**Air Europa** (www.aireuropa.com) Madrid to A Coruña, Alicante, Barcelona, Bilbao, Málaga, Oviedo, Seville, Vigo, the Canaries and the Balearics, as well as other routes between Spanish cities.

**Iberia** (www.iberia.com) Spain's national airline, together with its subsidiaries Iberia Express and Iberia Regional-Air Nostrum, has an extensive domestic network.

**Ryanair** (www.ryanair.com) Some domestic Spanish routes.

**Volotea** (www.volotea.com) Budget airline that flies domestically and internationally. Domestic routes take in Alicante, Bilbao, Málaga, Murcia, Oviedo, Santander, Seville, Tenerife, Valencia, Zaragoza and the Balearics (but not Madrid or Barcelona).

**Vueling** (www.vueling.com) Spanish low-cost company with lots of domestic flights within Spain, especially from Barcelona.

# Bicycle

Years of highway improvement programs across the country have made cycling a much easier prospect than it once was, although there are few designated bike lanes. Cycling on *autopistas* (tollways) is forbidden. Driver attitudes on open roads are generally good; less so in the cities, where cycling is not for the faint-hearted.

If you get tired of pedalling, it is often possible to take your bike on the train. All regional trains have space for bikes – usually marked by a bicycle logo on the carriage, where you can simply load the bike. Bikes are also permitted on most *cercanías* (local-area trains around big cities such as Madrid and Barcelona). Bike transport is free for journeys under 100km; for longer trips you'll need to pay a €3 surcharge.

On long-distance and high-speed trains such as the AVE, there are more restrictions. As a rule, bikes on these trains must be folded or disassembled and enclosed in a box or carrier.

It's often possible to take your bike on a bus – usually you'll just be asked to remove the front wheel.

## Hire & Bike-Sharing Schemes

Bicycle hire is not as widespread as in some European countries, though it's becoming more so, especially in the case of *bicis todo terreno* (mountain bikes) and in Andalucía, Barcelona and popular coastal towns. Costs vary considerably, but expect to pay around €8 to €10 per hour, €15 to €25 per day, or €60 to €75 per week.

A number of cities have introduced public bicycle systems with dozens of automated pick-up and drop-off points. These schemes involve paying a small subscription fee, which then allows you to pick up a bicycle at one location and drop it off at another.

**BiciMAD** (☎91 529 82 10, 010; www.bicimad.com; 1/2hr €2/4; ⏲24hr) Madrid

**Sevici** (☎900 900722; www.sevici.es) Seville

# Boat

Ferries and hydrofoils link the mainland (La Península) – or more specifically, Barcelona, Valencia, Denia and Gandia – with Palma de Mallorca, Menorca, Ibiza and/or Formentera. There are also services from various Andalucian ports to Gran Canaria and Tenerife in the Canary Islands, and to Spain's North African enclaves of Ceuta and Melilla.

**Baleària** (www.balearia.com) Runs multiple routes between the mainland and the Balearic Islands. On overnight services, you can opt for seating or sleeping accommodation in a cabin.

**Trasmediterránea** (☎902 454 645; www.trasmediterranea.es) The main national ferry company runs a combination of slower car ferries and modern, high-speed, passenger-only fast ferries and hydrofoils.

# Bus

There are few places in Spain where buses don't go. Numerous companies provide bus links, from local routes between villages to fast intercity connections. It is often cheaper to travel by bus than by train, particularly on long-haul runs, but also less comfortable.

Local services can get you just about anywhere, but most buses connecting villages and provincial towns are not geared to tourist needs. Frequent weekday services reduce to a trickle, if they operate at all, on Saturday and Sunday. Often just one bus runs daily between smaller places during the week, and none operate on Sunday. It's usually unnecessary to make reservations; just arrive early enough to get a seat.

On many regular runs – say, from Madrid to Toledo – the ticket you buy is for the next bus due to leave and *cannot* be used on a later bus. Advance purchase in such cases is generally not possible. For longer trips (such as Madrid to Seville or to the coast), and certainly in peak holiday season, you can (and should) buy your ticket in advance. On some routes you have the choice between express and stopping-all-stations services.

### BUS PASSES

Travellers planning broader European tours that include Spain could find one of the following options useful.

**Busabout** (☎in Canada 844-888-0216; www.busabout.com) A Canada-based hop-on, hop-off bus service aimed at younger travellers. Its network includes more than three dozen destinations in 14 countries. While it's mainly of interest to those travelling a lot beyond Spain, it does offer a 15-day Ultimate Iberian Adventure (from €1389 per person including accommodation).

**FlixBus** (www.flixbus.com) Offers the InterFlix ticket, allowing five one-way trips anywhere in its European network for €99. Pay up front via the website and receive five voucher codes, which must be activated for travel within three months.

In most larger towns and cities, buses leave from a single *estación de autobuses* (bus station). In smaller places, buses tend to operate from a set street or plaza, often unmarked. Locals will know where to go and where to buy tickets.

Bus travel within Spain is not overly costly, but there's a vast range of prices. The trip from Madrid to Barcelona starts from around €22 one way but can cost more than double that. Tickets from Barcelona to Seville – one of Spain's longest domestic journeys (15 to 17 hours) – can cost as much as €91 one way.

People under 26 should inquire about discounts on long-distance trips.

Among the hundreds of bus companies operating in Spain, the following have the largest range of services:

**ALSA** (☎902 42 22 42; www.alsa.es) The biggest player, this company has routes all over the country in association with various other companies. Check online for discounts for advance ticket purchases.

**Avanza** (☎91 272 28 32; www.avanzabus.com) Operates buses from Madrid to Extremadura, western Castilla y León and Valencia via eastern Castilla-La Mancha (eg Cuenca), often in association with other companies.

**Socibus** (☎902 22 92 92; www.socibus.es) Operates services between Madrid, western Andalucía and the Basque Country.

## Car & Motorcycle

Every vehicle should display a nationality plate of its country of registration and you must always carry proof of ownership of a private vehicle. Third-party motor insurance is required throughout Europe. A warning triangle and a reflective jacket (to be used in case of breakdown) are compulsory.

### BEATING PARKING FINES

If you've parked in a street parking spot and return to find that a parking inspector has left you a ticket, don't despair. If you arrive back within a reasonable time after the ticket was issued (what constitutes a reasonable time varies from place to place, but it is rarely more than a couple of hours), don't go looking for the inspector, but instead head for the nearest parking machine. Most machines in most cities allow you to pay a small penalty (usually around €5) to cancel the fine (keep both pieces of paper just in case). If you're unable to work out what to do, ask a local for help.

It's also worth noting that metered street-parking zones (*zonas azules*, indicated by blue lines on the road or roadside) are generally free of charge at the following times, although always check the signs:

- from about 2pm to 4pm or 5pm
- through the night from about 8pm to 9am or 10am
- on Saturday afternoons and evenings
- all day on Sundays and public holidays

### Driving Licences

All EU member states' driving licences are fully recognised throughout Europe. Those with a non-EU licence are technically required to obtain a 12-month International Driving Permit (IDP) to accompany their national licence, which your national automobile association can issue. In practice, however, car-hire companies and police rarely ask for one. If you have held residency in Spain for one year or more, you should apply for a Spanish driving licence or check whether your home licence entitles you to a Spanish licence under reciprocal agreements between countries.

### Fuel

- *Gasolina* (petrol) is pricey in Spain, but generally slightly cheaper than in its major European neighbours (including France, Germany, Italy and the UK); *gasóleo* is diesel fuel.
- Petrol is about 10% cheaper in Gibraltar than in Spain and 15% cheaper in Andorra.
- You can pay with major credit cards at most service stations.

### Hire

To rent a car in Spain, you have to have a licence, be aged 21 or over and, for the major companies at least, have a credit card; note that some car-hire companies don't accept debit cards. Smaller firms in areas where car hire is particularly common sometimes waive this last requirement. Those with a non-EU licence should officially also carry an IDP, though you will find that national licences from countries such as Australia, Canada, New Zealand and the US are usually accepted without question.

Rates vary by season. In winter you can find deals as low as €5 per day, while summer rates are significantly higher. You'll almost always save money by booking ahead. With some of the low-cost companies, beware of 'extras' that aren't quoted in initial prices.

**Avis** (☎902 180 854; www.avis.es)

**Enterprise Rent-a-Car** (902 100 101; www.enterprise.es)

**Europcar** (91 150 50 00; www.europcar.es)

**Firefly** (91 305 43 29; www.fireflycarrental.com)

**Hertz** (91 749 90 69; www.hertz.es)

**Pepecar** (902 996 666; www.pepecar.com)

**Sixt** (871 18 01 92; www.sixt.es)

Other possibilities:

**Auto Europe** (www.autoeurope.com) US-based clearing house for deals with major car-rental agencies.

**BlaBlaCar** (www.blablacar.com) Car-sharing site that can be really useful for outlying towns, and if your Spanish is up to it, you get to meet people too.

**Holiday Autos** (902 848304; www.holidayautos.com) A clearing house for major international companies.

**Ideamerge** (www.ideamerge.com) Car-leasing plans, motorhome hire and much more.

## Insurance

Third-party motor insurance is a minimum requirement in Spain and throughout Europe. Ask your insurer for a European Accident Statement form, which can simplify matters in the event of an accident. A European breakdown-assistance policy such as those provided by AA (www.theaa.com) or RAC (www.rac.co.uk) is a good investment.

Car-hire companies also provide this minimum insurance, but be careful to understand what your liabilities and excess are, and what waivers you are entitled to in case of accident or damage to the hire vehicle.

## Road Rules

**Blood-alcohol limit** The limit is 0.05%. Breath tests are common, and if found to be over the limit, you can be judged, condemned, fined and deprived of your licence within 24 hours. Fines range up to around €600 for serious offences. Nonresident foreigners may be required to pay up on the spot (at 30% off the full fine). Pleading linguistic ignorance will not help – the police officer will produce a list of infringements and fines in as many languages as you like.

**Mobile phones** Use of handheld mobile phones and similar devices while driving is strictly prohibited and punishable by a €200 fine.

**Legal driving age** Minimum age is 18 years for cars, 16 years for motorcycles and scooters. A licence is required.

**Motorcyclists** Must use headlights at all times and wear a helmet if riding a bike of 125cc or more.

**Overtaking** Spanish truck drivers often take the courtesy to turn on their right indicator to show that the way ahead of them is clear for overtaking (and the left one if it is not and you are attempting this manoeuvre). Make sure, however, that they're not just turning right!

**Roundabouts (traffic circles)** Vehicles already in the circle have right of way.

**Side of the road** Drive on the right.

**Speed limits** In built-up areas, 50km/h (and in some cases, such as inner-city Barcelona, 30km/h), which increases to 100km/h on major roads and up to 120km/h on *autovías* and *autopistas* (toll-free and tolled dual-lane highways, respectively). Cars towing caravans are restricted to a maximum speed of 80km/h.

# Local Transport

Most of the major cities have excellent local transport. Madrid and Barcelona have extensive bus and metro systems, and other major cities also benefit from generally efficient public transport. By European standards, prices are relatively cheap.

## Bus

Cities and provincial capitals all have reasonable bus networks. You can buy single tickets (usually between €1 and €2) on the buses or at *estancos* (tobacconists), but in cities such as Madrid and Barcelona, you are better off buying combined 10-trip tickets that allow the use of a combination of bus and metro, and which work out cheaper per ride. These can be purchased in any metro station and from some tobacconists and newspaper kiosks.

Regular buses run from about 6am to shortly before midnight and, in some cases, as late as 2am. In the big cities, a night bus service generally kicks in on a limited number of lines in the wee hours. In Madrid they are known as *búhos* (owls), while Barcelona has the more prosaically named NitBus (night bus).

## Metro

Madrid and Barcelona have the country's most extensive metro networks. Valencia, Bilbao, Granada, Seville and Palma de Mallorca have limited but nonetheless useful metro (or light rail) systems.

- Tickets must be bought in metro stations (from counters or vending machines), or sometimes from *estancos* (tobacconists) or newspaper kiosks.
- Single tickets generally cost the same as for buses.
- Visitors wanting to move around the major cities over a few days are best off getting 10-trip tickets, known in Madrid as Metrobús and in Barcelona as T-10.
- Monthly and seasonal passes are also available.

## Taxis & Ride-Sharing

You can find taxi ranks at train and bus stations, or you can telephone for radio taxis. In larger cities, taxi ranks are also scattered about the centre, and taxis will stop if you hail them in the street – look for the green light and/or the *libre* sign on the passenger side of the windscreen. The bigger cities are well populated with taxis, although you might have to wait a bit longer on a Friday or Saturday night. No more than four people are allowed in a taxi.

➡ Daytime minimum charge (generally to 10pm) is, for example, €2.40 in Madrid, and up to €2.90 after 9pm to 7am, and on weekends and holidays. You then pay €1.05 to €1.20 per kilometre depending on the time of day.

➡ There are airport and (sometimes) luggage surcharges.

➡ A cross-town ride in a major city will cost about €10 – absurdly cheap by European standards – while a taxi between the city centre and airport in either Madrid or Barcelona will cost €30 with luggage.

Ride-sharing and e-hailing companies such as Cabify (www.cabify.com) and Uber (www.uber.com) exist in Spain, but their presence is subject to local political whims. Some cities, such as Barcelona and Valencia, have banned Uber outright at times, while others require that regular taxis be included in any ride-hailing app. Your best bet is to check the situation on the ground when you arrive.

## Tram

Trams were stripped out of Spanish cities decades ago, but they're making a minor comeback in some. Barcelona has a couple of new suburban tram services in addition to its tourist Tramvia Blau run to Tibidabo. Valencia has some useful trams to the beach, while various limited lines also run in Seville, Bilbao, Murcia and Zaragoza.

# Train

**Renfe** (☎91 232 03 20; www.renfe.com) is the excellent national train system that runs most of the services in Spain. A handful of small private railway lines also operate.

You'll find *consignas* (left-luggage facilities) at all main train stations. They are usually open from about 7am to 10pm and charge between €3.10 and €5.20 per day per piece of luggage.

## RAIL PASSES

### Interrail

Interrail (www.interrail.eu) passes are available to legal residents of any European country, regardless of citizenship. They can be bought at most major stations, student travel outlets and online.

Youth passes are for people aged 12 to 27, adult passes for ages 26 to 59, and senior passes for ages 60 and older. Children aged 11 and under travel for free if travelling on a family pass.

**Global Pass** Encompasses 33 countries and comes in 10 versions, ranging from four days' travel in one month to a full three months of unlimited travel. Check out the website for a full list of prices.

**One Country Pass** Can be used for three, four, five, six or eight days within one month in Spain. For the eight-day pass you pay €374/281/243 for adult 1st class/adult 2nd class/youth 2nd class.

### Eurail

Eurail (www.eurail.com) passes are for non-European residents. They are supposed to be bought outside Europe, either online or from leading travel agencies.

Be sure you will be covering a lot of ground to make your Eurail pass worthwhile. To be certain, check the Renfe (www.renfe.com) website for sample prices in euros for the places where you intend to travel.

The following passes are available in 1st and 2nd class versions, regardless of age. Each adult pass includes free travel for up to two children aged between four and 11. The Eurail website has a full list of prices, including special family rates and other discounts.

**Eurail Global Pass** Good for travel in 33 European countries; forget it if you intend to travel mainly in Spain. There are 10 different passes, from four days within one month to three months' continuous travel.

**Spain Pass** With the one-country Spain Pass you can choose from three to eight days' train travel in a one-month period. The eight-day Spain Pass costs €423/318/275 for adult 1st class/adult 2nd class/youth 2nd class.

Spain has several types of trains, and *largo recorrido* or Grandes Líneas (long-distance trains) in particular have a variety of names.

**Alaris, Altaria, Alvia, Avlo & Avant** Long-distance intermediate-speed services.

**Cercanías** (*rodalies* in Catalonia) For short hops and services to outlying suburbs and satellite towns in Madrid, Barcelona and 11 other cities.

**Euromed** Similar to the Tren de Alta Velocidad Española (AVE) trains, they connect Barcelona with Valencia and Alicante.

**FEVE (Ferrocarriles de Vía Estrecha)** Narrow-gauge network along Spain's north coast between Bilbao and Ferrol (Galicia), with a branch down to León.

**Regionales** Trains operating within one region, usually stopping at all stations.

**Talgo & intercity** Slower long-distance trains.

**Tren de Alta Velocidad Española (AVE)** High-speed trains that link Madrid with Albacete, Alicante, Barcelona, Córdoba, Cuenca, Granada, Huesca, León, Lleida, Málaga, Palencia, Seville, Valencia, Valladolid and Zaragoza. There are also Barcelona–Seville, Barcelona-Granada, Barcelona–Málaga and Valencia–Seville services. Additional AVE routes under construction include Madrid–Bilbao and Madrid–Badajoz.

**Trenhotel** Overnight trains with sleeper berths.

## Classes & Costs

All long-distance trains have 2nd and 1st classes, respectively known as *turista* and *preferente*. The latter is 20% to 40% more expensive.

Fares vary enormously depending on the service (faster trains cost considerably more) and, in the case of some high-speed services such as the AVE, on the time and day of travel. Tickets for AVE trains are by far the most expensive. A one-way trip in 2nd class from Madrid to Barcelona (a route served almost exclusively by AVE trains) can cost as much as €129, or less than half that amount if you book well in advance or choose to travel at off-peak times.

Children aged between four and 13 years are entitled to a 40% discount. Those aged under four travel for free if sharing a seat with an adult; on high-speed trains, a free child ticket *(billete*

## Train Routes

## MEMORABLE TRAIN JOURNEYS

The romantically inclined could opt for an opulent and slow-moving, old-time rail adventure with numerous options across mainland Spain.

**Al-Andalus** (☎91 255 59 12; www.renfe.com/trenesturisticos) This luxurious train journey loops through Andalucía, taking the slow route between Seville, Ronda, Granada and Córdoba among other stops. Prices for the seven-day/six-night itinerary start at €3700 per person in high season; the single supplement costs €1850.

**Transcantábrico** (☎91 255 59 12; www.renfe.com/trenesturisticos) A journey on a picturesque narrow-gauge rail route, from Santiago de Compostela (by bus as far as Ferrol) via Oviedo, Santander and Bilbao along the coast, and then a long inland stretch to finish in León. The eight-day trip costs from €5500 per person in high season; there's a €2500 single supplement. The trip can also be done in reverse or in smaller chunks. There are 14 departures annually, between late April and October. The itinerary includes various visits along the way, such as the Museo Guggenheim Bilbao, the Museo de Altamira near Santillana del Mar, and the Covadonga lakes in the Picos de Europa. The food is exceptional, with some meals served in the train's elegant dining car and others in restaurants en route.

The trains don't travel at night, making sleeping aboard easy and providing the opportunity to stay out at night.

*gratuito de niño)* is required for children under four. Buying a return ticket often gives you a 10% to 20% discount on the return trip. Students and people up to 30 years of age with a European Youth Card (Carné Joven in Spain) are entitled to 20% off most ticket prices.

If you're travelling as a family, ask for a group of four seats with a table when making your reservation.

Certain overnight routes are served by special sleeping cars known as *trenhoteles*. It's worth paying extra for a *litera* (couchette; a sleeping berth in a six- or four-bed compartment) or, if available, single or double cabins in *preferente* or *gran clase* class. The cost depends on the class of accommodation, type of train and length of journey. The lines covered are Madrid–A Coruña–Pontevedra, Madrid–Ferrol, Barcelona–A Coruña–Vigo and Madrid–Lisbon, as well as international services from Lisbon to France via San Sebastián and Hendaye.

## Reservations

Reservations are recommended for long-distance trips; you can make them in train stations, **Renfe** (☎91 232 03 20; www.renfe.com) offices and travel agencies, as well as online. In a growing number of stations, you can pick up pre-booked tickets from machines scattered about the station concourse.

# Language

Spanish *(español)* – or Castilian *(castellano)*, as it is also called – is spoken throughout Spain, but there are also three co-official, regional languages: Catalan *(català)*, spoken in Catalonia, the Balearic Islands and Valencia; Galician *(galego)*, spoken in Galicia; and Basque *(euskara)*, which is spoken in the Basque Country and Navarra.

The pronunciation of most Spanish sounds is very similar to that of their English counterparts. If you read our coloured pronunciation guides as if they were English, you'll be understood. Note that kh is a throaty sound (like the 'ch' in the Scottish *loch*), r is strongly rolled, ly is pronounced as the 'lli' in 'million' and ny as the 'ni' in 'onion'. You may also notice that the 'lisped' th sound is pronounced as s in Andalucía. In our pronunciation guides, the stressed syllables are in italics.

Where necessary in this chapter, masculine and feminine forms are marked with 'm/f', while polite and informal options are indicated by the abbreviations 'pol' and 'inf'.

## BASICS

| | | |
|---|---|---|
| **Hello.** | *Hola.* | o·la |
| **Goodbye.** | *Adiós.* | a·*dyos* |
| **Yes./No.** | *Sí./No.* | see/no |
| **Excuse me.** | *Perdón.* | per·*don* |
| **Sorry.** | *Lo siento.* | lo *syen*·to |
| **Please.** | *Por favor.* | por fa·*vor* |

### WANT MORE?

For in-depth language information and handy phrases, check out Lonely Planet's *Spanish Phrasebook*. You'll find it at **shop.lonelyplanet.com**, or you can buy Lonely Planet's iPhone phrasebooks at the Apple App Store.

### QUESTION WORDS

| | | |
|---|---|---|
| **How?** | *¿Cómo?* | *ko*·mo |
| **What?** | *¿Qué?* | ke |
| **When?** | *¿Cuándo?* | *kwan*·do |
| **Where?** | *¿Dónde?* | *don*·de |
| **Who?** | *¿Quién?* | kyen |
| **Why?** | *¿Por qué?* | por ke |

| | | |
|---|---|---|
| **Thank you.** | *Gracias.* | *gra*·thyas |
| **You're welcome.** | *De nada.* | de *na*·da |
| **How are you?** | *¿Qué tal?* | ke tal |
| **Fine, thanks.** | *Bien, gracias.* | byen *gra*·thyas |

**What's your name?**
*¿Cómo se llama Usted?* — *ko*·mo se *lya*·ma oo·*ste* (pol)
*¿Cómo te llamas?* — *ko*·mo te *lya*·mas (inf)

**My name is ...**
*Me llamo ...* — me *lya*·mo ...

**Do you speak English?**
*¿Habla inglés?* — a·bla een·*gles* (pol)
*¿Hablas inglés?* — a·blas een·*gles* (inf)

**I don't understand.**
*No entiendo.* — no en·*tyen*·do

## ACCOMMODATION

| | | |
|---|---|---|
| **hotel** | *hotel* | o·*tel* |
| **guesthouse** | *pensión* | pen·*syon* |
| **youth hostel** | *albergue juvenil* | al·*ber*·ge khoo·ve·*neel* |
| **I'd like a ... room.** | *Quisiera una habitación ...* | kee·*sye*·ra *oo*·na a·bee·ta·*thyon* ... |
| **single** | *individual* | een·dee·vee·*dwal* |
| **double** | *doble* | *do*·ble |
| **air-con** | *aire acondicionado* | *ai*·re a·kon·dee·thyo·*na*·do |

| | | |
|---|---|---|
| **bathroom** | *baño* | *ba*·nyo |
| **window** | *ventana* | ven·*ta*·na |

**How much is it per night/person?**
*¿Cuánto cuesta por noche/persona?* — *kwan*·to *kwes*·ta por *no*·che/per·*so*·na

**Does it include breakfast?**
*¿Incluye el desayuno?* — een·*kloo*·ye el de·sa·*yoo*·no

# DIRECTIONS

**Where's ...?**
*¿Dónde está ...?* — *don*·de es·*ta* ...

**What's the address?**
*¿Cuál es la dirección?* — kwal es la dee·rek·*thyon*

**Can you please write it down?**
*¿Puede escribirlo, por favor?* — *pwe*·de es·kree·*beer*·lo por fa·*vor*

**Can you show me (on the map)?**
*¿Me lo puede indicar (en el mapa)?* — me lo *pwe*·de een·dee·*kar* (en el *ma*·pa)

| | | |
|---|---|---|
| **at the corner** | *en la esquina* | en la es·*kee*·na |
| **at the traffic lights** | *en el semáforo* | en el se·*ma*·fo·ro |
| **behind ...** | *detrás de ...* | de·*tras* de ... |
| **in front of ...** | *enfrente de ...* | en·*fren*·te de ... |
| **left** | *izquierda* | eeth·*kyer*·da |
| **next to ...** | *al lado de ...* | al *la*·do de ... |
| **opposite ...** | *frente a ...* | *fren*·te a ... |
| **right** | *derecha* | de·*re*·cha |
| **straight ahead** | *todo recto* | *to*·do *rek*·to |

# EATING & DRINKING

**What would you recommend?**
*¿Qué recomienda?* — ke re·ko·*myen*·da

**What's in that dish?**
*¿Que lleva ese plato?* — ke *lye*·va e·se *pla*·to

**I don't eat ...**
*No como ...* — no *ko*·mo ...

**Cheers!**
*¡Salud!* — sa·*loo*

**That was delicious!**
*¡Estaba buenísimo!* — es·*ta*·ba bwe·*nee*·see·mo

**Please bring us the bill.**
*Por favor, nos trae la cuenta.* — por fa·*vor* nos *tra*·e la *kwen*·ta

| | | |
|---|---|---|
| **I'd like to book a table for ...** | *Quisiera reservar una mesa para ...* | kee·*sye*·ra re·ser·*var oo*·na *me*·sa *pa*·ra ... |
| **(eight) o'clock** | *las (ocho)* | las (*o*·cho) |
| **(two) people** | *(dos) personas* | (dos) per·*so*·nas |

## NUMBERS

| | | |
|---|---|---|
| **1** | *uno* | *oo*·no |
| **2** | *dos* | dos |
| **3** | *tres* | tres |
| **4** | *cuatro* | *kwa*·tro |
| **5** | *cinco* | *theen*·ko |
| **6** | *seis* | seys |
| **7** | *siete* | *sye*·te |
| **8** | *ocho* | *o*·cho |
| **9** | *nueve* | *nwe*·ve |
| **10** | *diez* | dyeth |
| **20** | *veinte* | *veyn*·te |
| **30** | *treinta* | *treyn*·ta |
| **40** | *cuarenta* | kwa·*ren*·ta |
| **50** | *cincuenta* | theen·*kwen*·ta |
| **60** | *sesenta* | se·*sen*·ta |
| **70** | *setenta* | se·*ten*·ta |
| **80** | *ochenta* | o·*chen*·ta |
| **90** | *noventa* | no·*ven*·ta |
| **100** | *cien* | thyen |
| **1000** | *mil* | meel |

## Key Words

| | | |
|---|---|---|
| **bottle** | *botella* | bo·*te*·lya |
| **breakfast** | *desayuno* | de·sa·*yoo*·no |
| **(too) cold** | *(muy) frío* | (mooy) *free*·o |
| **dinner** | *cena* | *the*·na |
| **food** | *comida* | ko·*mee*·da |
| **fork** | *tenedor* | te·ne·*dor* |
| **glass** | *vaso* | *va*·so |
| **highchair** | *trona* | *tro*·na |
| **hot (warm)** | *caliente* | ka·*lyen*·te |
| **knife** | *cuchillo* | koo·*chee*·lyo |
| **lunch** | *comida* | ko·*mee*·da |
| **market** | *mercado* | mer·*ka*·do |
| **(children's) menu** | *menú (infantil)* | me·*noo* (een·fan·*teel*) |
| **plate** | *plato* | *pla*·to |
| **restaurant** | *restaurante* | res·tow·*ran*·te |
| **spoon** | *cuchara* | koo·*cha*·ra |
| **vegetarian food** | *comida vegetariana* | ko·*mee*·da ve·khe·ta·*rya*·na |

## CATALAN

The recognition of Catalan as an official language in Spain is the end result of a regional government campaign that began when the province gained autonomy at the end of the 1970s. Until the Battle of Muret in 1213, Catalan territory extended across southern France, taking in Roussillon and reaching into the Provence. Catalan was spoken, or at least understood, throughout these territories and in what is now Catalonia and Andorra. In the couple of hundred years that followed, the Catalans spread their language south into Valencia, west into Aragón and east to the Balearic Islands. It also reached Sicily and Naples, and the Sardinian town of Alghero is still a partly Catalan-speaking outpost today. Catalan is spoken by up to 10 million people in Spain.

In Barcelona you'll hear as much Spanish as Catalan. Your chances of coming across English speakers are also good. Elsewhere in the province, don't be surprised if you get replies in Catalan to your questions in Spanish. However, you'll find that most Catalans will happily speak to you in Spanish, especially once they realise you're a foreigner. This said, the following Catalan phrases might win you a few smiles and perhaps help you make some new friends.

| | |
|---|---|
| **Hello.** | *Hola.* |
| **Goodbye.** | *Adéu.* |
| **Yes.** | *Sí.* |
| **No.** | *No.* |
| **Please.** | *Sisplau./Si us plau.* |
| **Thank you (very much).** | *(Moltes) gràcies.* |
| **You're welcome.** | *De res.* |
| **Excuse me.** | *Perdoni.* |
| **May I?/Do you mind?** | *Puc?/Em permet?* |
| **I'm sorry.** | *Ho sento./Perdoni.* |
| **What's your name?** | *Com et dius?* (inf) |
| | *Com es diu?* (pol) |
| **My name is ...** | *Em dic ...* |
| **Where are you from?** | *D'on ets?* |
| **Do you speak English?** | *Parla anglès?* |
| **I understand.** | *Ho entenc.* |
| **I don't understand.** | *No ho entenc.* |
| **Could you speak in Castilian, please?** | *Pot parlar castellà sisplau?* |
| **How do you say ... in Catalan?** | *Com es diu ... en català?* |
| **I'm looking for ...** | *Estic buscant ...* |
| **How do I get to ...?** | *Com puc arribar a ...?* |
| **Turn left.** | *Giri a mà esquerra.* |
| **Turn right.** | *Giri a mà dreta.* |
| **near** | *a prop de* |
| **far** | *a lluny de* |

| | |
|---|---|
| **Monday** | *dilluns* |
| **Tuesday** | *dimarts* |
| **Wednesday** | *dimecres* |
| **Thursday** | *dijous* |
| **Friday** | *divendres* |
| **Saturday** | *dissabte* |
| **Sunday** | *diumenge* |

| | |
|---|---|
| **1** | *un/una* (m/f) |
| **2** | *dos/dues* (m/f) |
| **3** | *tres* |
| **4** | *quatre* |
| **5** | *cinc* |
| **6** | *sis* |
| **7** | *set* |
| **8** | *vuit* |
| **9** | *nou* |
| **10** | *deu* |
| **11** | *onze* |
| **12** | *dotze* |
| **13** | *tretze* |
| **14** | *catorze* |
| **15** | *quinze* |
| **16** | *setze* |
| **17** | *disset* |
| **18** | *divuit* |
| **19** | *dinou* |
| **20** | *vint* |
| **100** | *cent* |

## Meat & Fish

| | | |
|---|---|---|
| **beef** | *carne de vaca* | kar·ne de va·ka |
| **chicken** | *pollo* | po·lyo |
| **duck** | *pato* | pa·to |
| **lamb** | *cordero* | kor·de·ro |
| **lobster** | *langosta* | lan·gos·ta |
| **pork** | *cerdo* | ther·do |
| **prawns** | *camarones* | ka·ma·ro·nes |
| **tuna** | *atún* | a·toon |
| **turkey** | *pavo* | pa·vo |
| **veal** | *ternera* | ter·ne·ra |

## Fruit & Vegetables

| | | |
|---|---|---|
| **apple** | *manzana* | man·tha·na |
| **apricot** | *albaricoque* | al·ba·ree·ko·ke |
| **banana** | *plátano* | pla·ta·no |
| **beans** | *judías* | khoo·dee·as |
| **cabbage** | *col* | kol |
| **capsicum** | *pimiento* | pee·myen·to |
| **carrot** | *zanahoria* | tha·na·o·rya |
| **cherry** | *cereza* | the·re·tha |
| **corn** | *maíz* | ma·eeth |
| **cucumber** | *pepino* | pe·pee·no |
| **fruit** | *fruta* | froo·ta |
| **grape** | *uvas* | oo·vas |
| **lemon** | *limón* | lee·mon |
| **lettuce** | *lechuga* | le·choo·ga |
| **mushroom** | *champiñón* | cham·pee·nyon |
| **nuts** | *nueces* | nwe·thes |
| **onion** | *cebolla* | the·bo·lya |
| **orange** | *naranja* | na·ran·kha |
| **peach** | *melocotón* | me·lo·ko·ton |
| **peas** | *guisantes* | gee·san·tes |
| **pineapple** | *piña* | pee·nya |
| **plum** | *ciruela* | theer·we·la |
| **potato** | *patata* | pa·ta·ta |
| **spinach** | *espinacas* | es·pee·na·kas |
| **strawberry** | *fresa* | fre·sa |
| **tomato** | *tomate* | to·ma·te |
| **vegetable** | *verdura* | ver·doo·ra |
| **watermelon** | *sandía* | san·dee·a |

## Other

| | | |
|---|---|---|
| **bread** | *pan* | pan |
| **cheese** | *queso* | ke·so |
| **egg** | *huevo* | we·vo |
| **honey** | *miel* | myel |
| **jam** | *mermelada* | mer·me·la·da |
| **rice** | *arroz* | a·roth |
| **salt** | *sal* | sal |
| **sugar** | *azúcar* | a·thoo·kar |

### GALICIAN

Galician is the official language of the Autonomous Community of Galicia and is also widely understood in the neighbouring regions of Asturias and Castilla y Léon. It's very similar to Portuguese. Galicians are likely to revert to Spanish when addressing a stranger, especially a foreigner, but making a small effort to communicate in Galician will always be welcomed.

| | |
|---|---|
| **Hello.** | *Ola.* |
| **Good day.** | *Bon dia.* |
| **Goodbye.** | *Adeus./Até logo.* |
| **Many thanks.** | *Moitas grácias.* |
| **Do you speak English?** | *Fala inglés?* |
| **I don't understand.** | *Non entendo.* |
| **Could you speak in Castilian, please?** | *Pode falar en español, por favor?* |
| **What's this called in Galician?** | *Como se chama iso en galego?* |

## Drinks

| | | |
|---|---|---|
| **beer** | *cerveza* | ther·ve·tha |
| **coffee** | *café* | ka·fe |
| **(orange) juice** | *zumo (de naranja)* | thoo·mo (de na·ran·kha) |
| **milk** | *leche* | le·che |
| **red wine** | *vino tinto* | vee·no teen·to |
| **tea** | *té* | te |
| **(mineral) water** | *agua (mineral)* | a·gwa (mee·ne·ral) |
| **white wine** | *vino blanco* | vee·no blan·ko |

# EMERGENCIES

| | | |
|---|---|---|
| **Help!** | *¡Socorro!* | so·ko·ro |
| **Go away!** | *¡Vete!* | ve·te |
| **Call ...!** | *¡Llame a ...!* | lya·me a ... |
| **a doctor** | *un médico* | oon me·dee·ko |
| **the police** | *la policía* | la po·lee·thee·a |

**I'm lost.**
*Estoy perdido/a.* es·*toy* per·*dee*·do/a (m/f)

**I'm ill.**
*Estoy enfermo/a.* es·*toy* en·*fer*·mo/a (m/f)

**It hurts here.**
*Me duele aquí.* me *dwe*·le a·*kee*

**I'm allergic to (antibiotics).**
*Soy alérgico/a a (los antibióticos).* soy a·*ler*·khee·ko/a a (los an·tee·*byo*·tee·kos) (m/f)

**Where are the toilets?**
*¿Dónde están los servicios?* *don*·de es·*tan* los ser·*vee*·thyos

## SHOPPING & SERVICES

**I'd like to buy ...**
*Quisiera comprar ...* kee·*sye*·ra kom·*prar* ...

**I'm just looking.**
*Sólo estoy mirando.* *so*·lo es·*toy* mee·*ran*·do

**Can I look at it?**
*¿Puedo verlo?* *pwe*·do *ver*·lo

**I don't like it.**
*No me gusta.* no me *goos*·ta

**How much is it?**
*¿Cuánto cuesta?* *kwan*·to *kwes*·ta

**That's too expensive.**
*Es muy caro.* es mooy *ka*·ro

**Can you lower the price?**
*¿Podría bajar un poco el precio?* po·*dree*·a ba·*khar* oon *po*·ko el *pre*·thyo

**There's a mistake in the bill.**
*Hay un error en la cuenta.* ai oon e·*ror* en la *kwen*·ta

| | | |
|---|---|---|
| **ATM** | *cajero automático* | ka·*khe*·ro ow·to·*ma*·tee·ko |
| **internet cafe** | *cibercafé* | thee·ber·ka·*fe* |
| **post office** | *correos* | ko·*re*·os |
| **tourist office** | *oficina de turismo* | o·fee·*thee*·na de too·*rees*·mo |

## TIME & DATES

| | | |
|---|---|---|
| **What time is it?** | *¿Qué hora es?* | ke o·ra es |
| **It's (10) o'clock.** | *Son (las diez).* | son (las dyeth) |
| **Half past (one).** | *Es (la una) y media.* | es (la *oo*·na) ee *me*·dya |
| **At what time?** | *¿A qué hora?* | a ke o·ra |
| **At ...** | *A la(s) ...* | a la(s) ... |

| | | |
|---|---|---|
| **morning** | *mañana* | ma·*nya*·na |
| **afternoon** | *tarde* | *tar*·de |
| **evening** | *noche* | *no*·che |

| | | |
|---|---|---|
| **yesterday** | *ayer* | a·*yer* |
| **today** | *hoy* | oy |
| **tomorrow** | *mañana* | ma·*nya*·na |
| **Monday** | *lunes* | *loo*·nes |
| **Tuesday** | *martes* | *mar*·tes |
| **Wednesday** | *miércoles* | *myer*·ko·les |
| **Thursday** | *jueves* | *khwe*·bes |
| **Friday** | *viernes* | *vyer*·nes |
| **Saturday** | *sábado* | *sa*·ba·do |
| **Sunday** | *domingo* | do·*meen*·go |

## TRANSPORT

### Public Transport

| | | |
|---|---|---|
| **boat** | *barco* | *bar*·ko |
| **bus** | *autobús* | ow·to·*boos* |
| **plane** | *avión* | a·*vyon* |
| **train** | *tren* | tren |

| | | |
|---|---|---|
| **first** | *primer* | pree·*mer* |
| **last** | *último* | *ool*·tee·mo |
| **next** | *próximo* | *prok*·see·mo |

**BASQUE**

Basque is spoken at the western end of the Pyrenees and along the Bay of Biscay – from Bayonne in France to Bilbao in Spain, and inland, almost to Pamplona. No one quite knows its origin, but the most likely theory is that Basque is the lone survivor of a language family that once extended across Europe, and was wiped out by the languages of the Celts, Germanic tribes and Romans.

| | |
|---|---|
| **Hello.** | *Kaixo.* |
| **Goodbye.** | *Agur.* |
| **How are you?** | *Zer moduz?* |
| **Fine, thank you.** | *Ongi, eskerrik asko.* |
| **Excuse me.** | *Barkatu.* |
| **Please.** | *Mesedez.* |
| **Thank you.** | *Eskerrik asko.* |
| **You're welcome.** | *Ez horregatik.* |
| **Do you speak English?** | *Ingelesez ba al dakizu?* |
| **I don't understand.** | *Ez dut ulertzen.* |

| | | |
|---|---|---|
| **a ... ticket** | *un billete de ...* | oon bee·*lye*·te de ... |
| **1st-class** | *primera clase* | pree·*me*·ra *kla*·se |
| **2nd-class** | *segunda clase* | se·*goon*·da *kla*·se |
| **one-way** | *ida* | *ee*·da |
| **return** | *ida y vuelta* | ee·da ee *vwel*·ta |

| | | |
|---|---|---|
| **aisle seat** | *asiento de pasillo* | a·*syen*·to de pa·*see*·lyo |
| **station** | *estación* | es·ta·*thyon* |
| **ticket office** | *taquilla* | ta·*kee*·lya |
| **timetable** | *horario* | o·*ra*·ryo |
| **window seat** | *asiento junto a la ventana* | a·*syen*·to *khoon*·to a la ven·*ta*·na |

**I want to go to ...**
*Quisiera ir a ...* kee·*sye*·ra eer a ...

**At what time does it arrive/leave?**
*¿A qué hora llega/sale?* a ke o·ra *lye*·ga/*sa*·le

**Does it stop at (Madrid)?**
*¿Para en (Madrid)?* *pa*·ra en (ma·*dree*)

**Which stop is this?**
*¿Cuál es esta parada?* kwal es *es*·ta pa·*ra*·da

**Please tell me when we get to (Seville).**
*¿Puede avisarme cuando lleguemos a (Sevilla)?* *pwe*·de a·vee·*sar*·me *kwan*·do lye·*ge*·mos a (se·*vee*·lya)

**I want to get off here.**
*Quiero bajarme aquí.* *kye*·ro ba·*khar*·me a·*kee*

## Driving and Cycling

| | | |
|---|---|---|
| **I'd like to hire a ...** | *Quisiera alquilar ...* | kee·*sye*·ra al·kee·*lar* ... |
| **4WD** | *un todo-terreno* | oon *to*·do·te·*re*·no |
| **bicycle** | *una bicicleta* | *oo*·na bee·thee·*kle*·ta |
| **car** | *un coche* | oon *ko*·che |
| **motorcycle** | *una moto* | *oo*·na *mo*·to |
| **child seat** | *asiento de seguridad para niños* | a·*syen*·to de se·goo·ree·*da* *pa*·ra *nee*·nyos |
| **helmet** | *casco* | *kas*·ko |
| **mechanic** | *mecánico* | me·*ka*·nee·ko |
| **petrol** | *gasolina* | ga·so·*lee*·na |
| **service station** | *gasolinera* | ga·so·lee·*ne*·ra |

**How much is it per day/hour?**
*¿Cuánto cuesta por día/hora?* *kwan*·to *kwes*·ta por *dee*·a/*o*·ra

### SIGNS

| | |
|---|---|
| **Abierto** | Open |
| **Cerrado** | Closed |
| **Entrada** | Entrance |
| **Hombres** | Men |
| **Mujeres** | Women |
| **Prohibido** | Prohibited |
| **Salida** | Exit |
| **Servicios/Aseos** | Toilets |

### BASQUE SIGNS

In many towns in the Basque region street names and signs are changing from Spanish to Basque. Not everyone uses these new names though, and many maps remain in Spanish, which can make navigating a little tricky for travellers. In this book we've provided the most commonly used version or have included both Spanish and Basque. Here are some Basque words commonly used in signs, followed by their Spanish counterpart and English translation:

| | |
|---|---|
| **aireportua** | *aeropuerto* (airport) |
| **erdialdea** | *centro* (city centre) |
| **jatetxea** | *restaurante* (restaurant) |
| **kalea** | *calle* (street) |
| **kale nagusia** | *calle mayor* (main street) |
| **komunak** | *servicios* (toilets) |
| **kontuz** | *atención* (caution/beware) |
| **nekazal turismoak** | *casas rurales* (village/farmstead accommodation) |
| **ongi etorri** | *bienvenido* (welcome) |
| **turismo bulegoa** | *oficina de turismo* (tourist office) |

**Is this the road to (Barcelona)?**
*¿Se va a (Barcelona) por esta carretera?* se va a (bar·the·*lo*·na) por *es*·ta ka·re·*te*·ra

**(How long) Can I park here?**
*¿(Por cuánto tiempo) Puedo aparcar aquí?* (por *kwan*·to *tyem*·po) *pwe*·do a·par·*kar* a·*kee*

**The car has broken down (at Valencia).**
*El coche se ha averiado (en Valencia).* el *ko*·che se a a·ve·*rya*·do (en va·*len*·thya)

**I have a flat tyre.**
*Tengo un pinchazo.* *ten*·go oon peen·*cha*·tho

**I've run out of petrol.**
*Me he quedado sin gasolina.* me e ke·*da*·do seen ga·so·*lee*·na

# GLOSSARY

Unless otherwise indicated, the following terms are from Castilian Spanish. The masculine and feminine forms are indicated with the abbreviations 'm/f'.

**ajuntament** – Catalan for *ayuntamiento*

**alameda** – tree-lined avenue

**albergue** – refuge

**albergue juvenil** – youth hostel

**alcázar** – Muslim-era fortress

**aljibe** – cistern

**artesonado** – wooden Mudéjar ceiling with interlaced beams leaving a pattern of spaces for decoration

**autopista** – tollway

**autovía** – toll-free highway

**AVE** – Tren de Alta Velocidad Española; high-speed train

**ayuntamiento** – city or town hall

**bailaor/bailaora** – m/f flamenco dancer

**baile** – dance in a flamenco context

**balneario** – spa

**barrio** – district/quarter (of a town or city)

**biblioteca** – library

**bici todo terreno (BTT)** – mountain bike

**bodega** – cellar (especially wine cellar); also a winery or a traditional wine bar likely to serve wine from the barrel

**búhos** – night-bus routes

**cabrito** – kid

**cala** – cove

**calle** – street

**callejón** – lane

**cama** – bed

**cambio** – change; also currency exchange

**caña** – small glass of beer

**cantaor/cantaora** – m/f flamenco singer

**capilla** – chapel

**capilla mayor** – chapel containing the high altar of a church

**carmen** – walled villa with gardens, in Granada

**Carnaval** – traditional festive period that precedes the start of Lent; carnival

**carretera** – highway

**carta** – menu

**casa de huéspedes** – guesthouse; see also *hospedaje*

**casa de pagès** – *casa rural* in Catalonia

**casa rural** – village, country house or farmstead with rooms to let

**casco** – literally 'helmet'; often used to refer to the old part of a city; more correctly, *casco antiguo/histórico/viejo*

**castellano/a (m/f)** – Castilian; used in preference to *español* to describe the national language

**castellers** – Catalan human-castle builders

**castillo** – castle

**castro** – Celtic fortified village

**català** – Catalan language; a native of Catalonia

**catedral** – cathedral

**cercanías** – local train network

**cervecería** – beer bar

**churrigueresco** – ornate style of baroque architecture named after the brothers Alberto and José Churriguera

**ciudad** – city

**claustro** – cloister

**CNIG** – Centro Nacional de Información Geográfica; producers of good-quality maps

**cofradía** – see *hermandad*

**colegiata** – collegiate church

**coll** – Catalan for *collado*

**collado** – mountain pass

**comarca** – district; grouping of *municipios*

**comedor** – dining room

**comunidad** – fixed charge for maintenance of rental accommodation (sometimes included in rent); community

**conquistador** – conqueror

**copa** – drink; literally 'glass'

**cordillera** – mountain range

**coro** – choir: part of a church, usually the middle

**correos** – post office

**Cortes** – national parliament

**costa** – coast

**cruceiro** – standing crucifix found at many crossroads in Galicia

**cuesta** – lane, usually on a hill

**custodia** – monstrance

**dolmen** – prehistoric megalithic tomb

**embalse** – reservoir

**encierro** – running of the bulls Pamplona-style; also happens in many other places around Spain

**entrada** – entrance

**ermita** – hermitage or chapel

**església** – Catalan for *iglesia*

**estació** – Catalan for *estación*

**estación** – station

**estación de autobuses** – bus station

**estación de esquí** – ski station or resort

**estación marítima** – ferry terminal

**estany** – Catalan for *lago*

**Euskadi Ta Askatasuna (ETA)** – the name stands for Basque Homeland & Freedom

**extremeño/a (m/f)** – Extremaduran; a native of Extremadura

**fallas** – huge sculptures of papier mâché (or nowadays more often polystyrene) on wood used in Las Fallas festival of Valencia

**farmacia** – pharmacy

**faro** – lighthouse

**feria** – fair; can refer to trade fairs as well as to city, town or village fairs that are basically several days of merrymaking; can also mean a bullfight or festival stretching over days or weeks

**ferrocarril** – railway

**festa** – Catalan for *fiesta*

**FEVE** – Ferrocarriles de Vía Estrecha; a private train company in northern Spain

**fiesta** – festival, public holiday or party

**fútbol** – football (soccer)

**gaditano/a (m/f)** – person from Cádiz
**gaita** – Galician version of the bagpipes
**gallego/a (m/f)** – Galician; a native of Galicia
**gitanos** – Roma people
**glorieta** – big roundabout (traffic circle)
**Gran Vía** – main thoroughfare
**GRs** – *(senderos de) Gran Recorrido;* long-distance hiking paths
**guardia civil** – military police

**hermandad** – brotherhood (including men and women), in particular one that takes part in religious processions
**hórreo** – Galician or Asturian grain store
**hospedaje** – guesthouse
**hostal** – cheap hotel
**huerta** – market garden; orchard

**iglesia** – church
**infanta/infante** – princess/prince
**IVA** – *impuesto sobre el valor añadido,* or value-added tax

**jamón** – cured ham
**jardín** – garden
**judería** – Jewish *barrio* in medieval Spain

**lago** – lake
**librería** – bookshop
**lidia** – the art of bullfighting
**locutorio** – private telephone centre

**madrileño/a (m/f)** – person from Madrid
**malagueño/a (m/f)** – person from Málaga
**manchego/a (m/f)** – La Manchan; a person from La Mancha
**marcha** – action, life, 'the scene'
**marismas** – wetlands
**marisquería** – seafood eatery
**medina** – narrow, maze-like old section of an Arab or North African town
**mercado** – market
**mercat** – Catalan for *mercado*
**meseta** – plateau; the high tableland of central Spain
**mihrab** – prayer niche in a mosque indicating the direction of Mecca
**mirador** – lookout point
**Modernista** – an exponent of Modernisme, the architectural and artistic style influenced by art nouveau and sometimes known as Catalan Modernism, whose leading practitioner was Antoni Gaudí
**monasterio** – monastery
**morería** – former Islamic quarter in a town
**movida** – similar to *marcha; zona de movida* is an area of a town where lively bars and discos are clustered
**mozárabe** – Mozarab (Christian living under Muslim rule in early medieval Spain)
**Mozarabic** – style of architecture developed by Mozarabs, adopting elements of classic Islamic construction to Christian architecture
**Mudéjar** – Muslims who remained behind in territory reconquered by Christians; also refers to a decorative style of architecture using elements of Islamic building style applied to buildings constructed in Christian Spain
**muelle** – wharf or pier
**municipio** – municipality, Spain's basic local administrative unit
**muralla** – city wall
**murgas** – costumed groups
**museo** – museum
**museu** – Catalan for *museo*

**nitbus** – Catalan for 'night bus'

**oficina de turismo** – tourist office; also *oficina de información turística*

**parador** – luxurious state-owned hotels, many of them in historic buildings
**parque nacional** – national park; strictly controlled protected area
**parque natural** – natural park; protected environmental area
**paseo** – promenade or boulevard; to stroll
**paso** – mountain pass
**pasos** – figures carried in *Semana Santa* parades
**pelota vasca** – Basque form of handball, also known simply as *pelota,* or *jai-alai* in Basque
**peña** – a club, usually of flamenco aficionados or Real Madrid or Barcelona football fans; sometimes a dining club
**pensión** – small private hotel
**pinchos** – tapas
**pintxos** – Basque tapas
**piscina** – swimming pool
**plaça** – Catalan for *plaza*
**plateresque** – early phase of Renaissance architecture noted for its intricately decorated facades
**platja** – Catalan for *playa*
**playa** – beach
**plaza** – square
**plaza de toros** – bullring
**port** – Catalan for *puerto*
**PP** – Partido Popular (People's Party)
**PRs** – *(senderos de) Pequeño Recorrido;* short-distance hiking paths
**PSOE** – Partido Socialista Obrero Español (Spanish Socialist Workers Party)
**pueblo** – village
**puente** – bridge; also means the extra day or two off that many people take when a holiday falls close to a weekend
**puerta** – gate or door
**puerto** – port or mountain pass
**punta** – point or promontory

**ración/raciones** – large/full-plate-size tapas serving; literally 'rations'
**rambla** – avenue or riverbed

**rastro** – flea market; car-boot sale

**REAJ** – Red Española de Albergues Juveniles; the Spanish HI youth hostel network

**real** – royal

**Reconquista** – Christian reconquest of the Iberian Peninsula from the Muslims (8th to 15th centuries)

**refugi** – Catalan for *refugio*

**refugio** – mountain shelter, hut or refuge

**Renfe** – Red Nacional de los Ferrocarriles Españoles; the national rail network

**retablo** – altarpiece

**Reyes Católicos** – Catholic monarchs; Isabel and Fernando

**ría** – estuary

**río** – river

**riu** – Catalan for *río*

**rodalies** – Catalan for *cercanías*

**romería** – festive pilgrimage or procession

**ronda** – ring road

**sacristía** – sacristy; the part of a church in which vestments, sacred objects and other valuables are kept

**sagrario** – sanctuary

**sala capitular** – chapter house

**salinas** – salt-extraction lagoons

**santuario** – shrine or sanctuary

**Semana Santa** – Holy Week; the week leading up to Easter Sunday

**Sephardic Jews** – Jews of Spanish origin

**seu** – cathedral (Catalan)

**sidra** – cider

**sidrería** – cider bar

**sierra** – mountain range

**tablao** – tourist-oriented flamenco performances

**taifa** – small Muslim kingdom in medieval Spain

**tasca** – tapas bar

**techumbre** – roof

**teleférico** – cable car; also called *funicular aéreo*

**terraza** – terrace; pavement cafe

**terrazas de verano** – open-air late-night bars

**tetería** – teahouse, usually in Middle Eastern style, with low seats around low tables

**torero** – bullfighter

**torre** – tower

**trascoro** – screen behind the *coro*

**turismo** – means both tourism and saloon car; *el turismo* can also mean 'tourist office'

**urgencia** – emergency

**vall** – Catalan for *valle*

**valle** – valley

**villa** – small town

**VO** – abbreviation of *versión original;* a foreign-language film subtitled in Spanish

**zarzuela** – Spanish mix of theatre, music and dance

# Behind the Scenes

## SEND US YOUR FEEDBACK

We love to hear from travellers – your comments keep us on our toes and help make our books better. Our well-travelled team reads every word on what you loved or loathed about this book. Although we cannot reply individually to your submissions, we always guarantee that your feedback goes straight to the appropriate authors, in time for the next edition. Each person who sends us information is thanked in the next edition – the most useful submissions are rewarded with a selection of digital PDF chapters.

Visit **lonelyplanet.com/contact** to submit your updates and suggestions or to ask for help. Our award-winning website also features inspirational travel stories, news and discussions.

Note: We may edit, reproduce and incorporate your comments in Lonely Planet products such as guidebooks, websites and digital products, so let us know if you don't want your comments reproduced or your name acknowledged. For a copy of our privacy policy visit lonelyplanet.com/privacy.

## WRITER THANKS

### Gregor Clark

*Muchísimas gracias* to all of the many Andalucians and fellow travellers who shared their recommendations, expertise and enthusiasm for Spain's sunny south – especially Ramón, Laura, José Manuel, Michaela, Eva, Daniel, Alfredo, Alberto, John and Isabella. Across the Atlantic, *un gran abrazo* to Gaen, who makes every day a voyage of discovery, and coming home always the best part of the trip.

### Duncan Garwood

I owe a lot of thanks, starting with Rachel, Steve, Robert and Nick whose company in Seville was much enjoyed. Thanks also to fellow writers Isabella Noble and Gregor Clark, and, at Lonely Planet, Tom Stainer, Darren O'Connell and Sandie Kestell. In Spain, *gracias* to Cristina Diaz, Félix, Paula Alcayada García, Salomé Rodríguez García, José Fabra Garrido, Ana Jimenez, José Peláez, María José Álvarez Rodríguez, Virginia Rivera, Miriam Toro and Tim. As always, a big hug to Lidia, Ben and Nick.

### Anthony Ham

Madrid is home and it is impossible to thank everyone who has contributed to this guide. Special thanks to Javi and Sandra for so many key suggestions, and to Marina and Alberto for their ongoing kindness and hospitality. Many thanks also to so many skilled and dedicated people with whom I have worked with at Lonely Planet down through the years.

### Damian Harper

Many thanks to everyone who helped with tips along the way in this forever-charming island, especially Robert Landreth, Daniel Hands, Emmanuelle Arbona, Biel and Yunli, Dave in Pollença, Norma Gray, Isabel, Francesco Bellini, Cristina, Steffi, Luisa Martínez, Francoise, Jaime, Miguel, Tomeu, Timothy, Emma and Daisy.

### Catherine Le Nevez

*Eskerrik asko/muchas gracias* to Julian, and to all of the locals and fellow travellers in the Basque Country, Navarra and La Rioja who provided insights, information and great times. Huge thanks too to Sandie Kestell, Genna Patterson, Darren O'Connell, Tom Stainer and everyone at Lonely Planet. As ever, *merci surtout* to my family.

### Isabella Noble

In Barcelona, *gràcies* to Sally Davies, Esme Fox, Marwa El-Hennawey Preston, Tom Stainer, the Devour team, Clementina Milà, Joan Pau Aragón, María del Río, Vera de Frutos, Suzy Taher, Isabelle Kliger, Nigel Haywood, Alex Pérez, Lorna Turnbull, José Fabra, Pau Gavaldà and David Doyes. In Andalucía, thanks to Molly Piccavey, June Windon, Anne Hunt, Nancy Laforest, Lorrane Dean, Emma and David Illsley, Silvia Roth-Bruggers, James Stuart, Annie Manson, Barbara Seine and Víctor Vidal. *Gracias* to my hard-working cowriters, and my loyal assistants Jack Noble, John Noble and Andrew Brannan.

### John Noble

Extra special thanks to Carmen and Luis, Eneida and Nacho, Lucía, Rafa, Bruno and Mari Carmen; to Camino and camping companions Rick, Sue, Katie, Bertie, Ted, María, Kaje (officially Sarkaaj), Jean Marie and Margarete, who contributed much to my prior research and enthusiasm for the green north; and to Isabella, the ideal colleague.

### Josephine Quintero

Many thanks to my many friends in Mallorca, including Isabel Carmona, Felipe Diaz and my wonderful Airbnb hostess, Nicole in Palma, as well as other countless people who shared their enthusiasm and love of all things Mallorcan. Thanks too to my ever-supportive family and, not forgetting, the ever-conscientious editorial team at Lonely Planet.

### Regis St Louis

I'm indebted to countless locals, expats and fellow travellers who shared tips and cultural insight along the way. Special thanks to co-authors Gregor Clark and John Noble. I'm also grateful to Lara Yuste in Toledo, Isabel Fernández in El Toboso, Saray García in Cuenca, Ramon and Amparo in Villanueva de los Infantes and Álvaro Jimenez in Oropesa. *Besos* to Cassandra, Magdalena and Genevieve for the warm homecoming.

### Andy Symington

My excellent friends in Valencia always help enthusiastically with research and provide brilliant hospitality. I'm grateful to all, but especially to Rosa Martínez Sala, Delfina Soria Bonet, Enrique Lapuente Ojeda and Dolors Roca Ferrerfabrega, who went out of their way to assist me. Huge thanks also to Richard Prowse and José Vicente Revilla García for bringing a bit of León to Valencia. Most of all, I would like to thank my father, who loved Spain and who will be deeply missed.

## ACKNOWLEDGEMENTS

Climate map data adapted from Peel MC, Finlayson BL & McMahon TA (2007) 'Updated World Map of the Köppen-Geiger Climate Classification', *Hydrology and Earth System Sciences*, 11, 1633–44.

Illustrations p94-5, p270-1, p278-9, p622-3, p686-7 and p702-3 by Javier Zarracina.

Cover photograph: Catedral, Salamanca, Shaun Egan/AWL Images ©

## THIS BOOK

This 13th edition of Lonely Planet's *Spain* guidebook was researched and written by Gregor Clark, Duncan Garwood, Anthony Ham, Damian Harper, Catherine Le Nevez, Isabella Noble, John Noble, Josephine Quintero, Regis St Louis and Andy Symington. The previous edition was written by Gregor, Duncan, Anthony, Catherine, Isabella, John, Josephine, Regis, Andy, Sally Davies and Brendan Sainsbury. This guidebook was produced by the following:

**Senior Product Editors**
Dan Bolger, Sandie Kestell

**Senior Cartographer**
Anthony Phelan

**Product Editors**
Paul Harding, James Appleton, Will Allen

**Book Designer**
Ania Bartoszek

**Assisting Editors**
James Bainbridge, Nigel Chin, Andrea Dobbin, Carly Hall, Anne Mulvaney, Rosie Nicholson, Charlotte Orr, Monique Perrin, Christopher Pitts, Tamara Sheward, Gabrielle Stefanos, Brana Vladisavljevic

**Cover Researcher**
Naomi Parker

**Thanks to**
Ronan Abayawickrema, Vanessa Cyriacopoulos, Grace Dobell, Gordon Dow, Karen Henderson, Amy Lynch, Rudy Mumm, Darren O'Connell, Genna Patterson, Jess Ryan, Saralinda Turner

# Index

## A



Map Pages **000**
Photo Pages **000**

Map Pages **000**
Photo Pages **000**

## C

## D



## E



## F

## G



## H



Map Pages **000**
Photo Pages **000**

## I



## J



## K



## L

Map Pages **000**
Photo Pages **000**

Map Pages **000**
Photo Pages **000**

# Map Legend

## Sights

- Beach
- Bird Sanctuary
- Buddhist
- Castle/Palace
- Christian
- Confucian
- Hindu
- Islamic
- Jain
- Jewish
- Monument
- Museum/Gallery/Historic Building
- Ruin
- Shinto
- Sikh
- Taoist
- Winery/Vineyard
- Zoo/Wildlife Sanctuary
- Other Sight

## Activities, Courses & Tours

- Bodysurfing
- Diving
- Canoeing/Kayaking
- Course/Tour
- Sento Hot Baths/Onsen
- Skiing
- Snorkelling
- Surfing
- Swimming/Pool
- Walking
- Windsurfing
- Other Activity

## Sleeping

- Sleeping
- Camping
- Hut/Shelter

## Eating

- Eating

## Drinking & Nightlife

- Drinking & Nightlife
- Cafe

## Entertainment

- Entertainment

## Shopping

- Shopping

## Information

- Bank
- Embassy/Consulate
- Hospital/Medical
- Internet
- Police
- Post Office
- Telephone
- Toilet
- Tourist Information
- Other Information

## Geographic

- Beach
- Gate
- Hut/Shelter
- Lighthouse
- Lookout
- Mountain/Volcano
- Oasis
- Park
- Pass
- Picnic Area
- Waterfall

## Population

- Capital (National)
- Capital (State/Province)
- City/Large Town
- Town/Village

## Transport

- Airport
- Border crossing
- Bus
- Cable car/Funicular
- Cycling
- Ferry
- Metro station
- Monorail
- Parking
- Petrol station
- S-Bahn/Subway station
- Taxi
- T-bane/Tunnelbana station
- Train station/Railway
- Tram
- U-Bahn/Underground station
- Other Transport

## Routes

- Tollway
- Freeway
- Primary
- Secondary
- Tertiary
- Lane
- Unsealed road
- Road under construction
- Plaza/Mall
- Steps
- Tunnel
- Pedestrian overpass
- Walking Tour
- Walking Tour detour
- Path/Walking Trail

## Boundaries

- International
- State/Province
- Disputed
- Regional/Suburb
- Marine Park
- Cliff
- Wall

## Hydrography

- River, Creek
- Intermittent River
- Canal
- Water
- Dry/Salt/Intermittent Lake
- Reef

## Areas

- Airport/Runway
- Beach/Desert
- Cemetery (Christian)
- Cemetery (Other)
- Glacier
- Mudflat
- Park/Forest
- Sight (Building)
- Sportsground
- Swamp/Mangrove

*Note: Not all symbols displayed above appear on the maps in this book*